The Catalogue of Printed Music in the British Library to 1980

The Catalogue
of Printed Music
in the British Library
to 1980

35

LEHAR - LITTE

1984

K·G·Saur

London · München · New York · Paris

Managing editor
Laureen Baillie B.A., Dip. Lib.

Editor
Robert Balchin M.A.

Assistant editor
Michael D. Chapman B.Mus., A.R.C.M.

Editorial assistants
Helen Dwyer B.A.
Robert L. Greenhill G.R.N.C.M.
Elizabeth Robinson M.Mus., B.A., A.R.C.M.
Maurice Rogers B.Mus., A.K.C.
Garance Worters A.L.A., L.T.C.L., Cert. Ed.

British Library Cataloguing in Publication Data

British Library
   The catalogue of printed music
   in the British Library to 1980
   Vol 35: Lehar – Litte
   1. British Library. Department of Printed
   Books — Catalogs
   I. Title   II. Baillie, Laureen

ISBN 0-86291-332-2
ISBN 0-86291-300-4 Set of 62 vols

Copyright © 1984 British Library

Computerised typesetting by Satz-Rechen-Zentrum, Hartmann & Heenemann,
Lützowstrasse 105—106, 1000 Berlin 30.

Printed and bound in the Federal Republic of Germany

GUIDE TO THE ARRANGEMENT OF ENTRIES

1. Entry points

In principle each work in the Catalogue has one main entry, which is made under the name of the person or body with the primary intellectual responsibility for the work. In practice the main entry for a work may appear: under the name of the composer, if it appears in the publication; under the name of a compiler, e.g. of a songbook; under the name of a corporate author, e.g. a society; or under a heading derived from the title, if anonymous. The Catalogue also contains cross references of various kinds. These are explained in greater detail below.

2. Choice of main heading

Composers

If the composer or compiler is known, an entry will be found under his or her name. Most publications involving two composers are entered under the joint heading. A publication consisting of contributions by three or more authors will generally be entered: under the first named, with cross references from the other names; under the name of the editor or compiler, if there is one; or under a word derived from the title according to the rules for anonymous works.

Pseudonymous works

Works in which the composer is identified by initials or by a pseudonym are entered under those forms. Works in which the composer is identified by a descriptive *word* are entered under that word, but if a descriptive *phrase* is used the work is entered according to the rules for anonymous works. Thus, *Six Songs, by a Lady* is entered under LADY; but *Six Songs, by an Irish Lady* is entered under SONGS.

Anonymous works

Anonymous works are generally entered under the first word of the title* with the following exceptions:

> *Single songs.* Because the titles of anonymous songs often vary, while the words generally remain constant, anonymous single songs have their main entry under the first word of the text. A cross reference is made from the first word of the title.

> *Preferential headings.* Certain commonly occurring words (mainly denoting musical forms) are used as preferential headings. If such a word occurs in the title proper of an anonymous work, the work is entered under that word, not under the first word of the title. But if two or more preferential terms occur in the title proper, then the work is treated like other anonyma, and entered under the first word of the title. Thus, *A collection of French songs* is entered under SONGS; but *A collection of French songs and duets* is entered under COLLECTION ("songs" and "duets" are both preferential terms). Examples of preferential headings are: Airs, Anthems, Chansons, Concertos, Country Dances, Dances, Duets, Glees, Instructions, Madrigals, Marches, Masses, Minuets, Motets, Quadrilles, Sonatas, Songs, Tutors, Waltzes. Four preferential headings are treated somewhat differently: Hymns, Psalms, Chants [Anglican], Christmas Carols.

Here and throughout, this means the first word of the title other than the article.

These contain in addition cross references to collections of relevant material entered elsewhere in the Catalogue; they are arranged in chronological order, while HYMNS and PSALMS are also subdivided according to the language of the text.

An anonymous edition of a work whose composer is known is treated as an anonymous work. A cross reference is made from the name of the composer to the appropriate anonymous heading where the main entry will be found.

Editions of collective manuscripts without compiler are entered under the library where the manuscript is deposited, e.g. editions of the Fitzwilliam Virginal Book are entered under CAMBRIDGE. – University of Cambridge. – *Fitzwilliam Museum*.

Periodicals

Periodicals published by societies or other corporate authors are entered under the heading for the society; others are entered under the heading PERIODICAL PUBLICATIONS, followed by the name of the town where publication took place. In both cases a cross reference is made from the first word of the title of the periodical.

3. Cross references

Cross references are made from various alternative entry points. The more important of these are:

from the names of editors, arrangers, etc. Note that cross references are not made from the names of the authors of the words of vocal works;

from the first word of the title of a vocal work, provided that the title is distinctive, e.g. *Songs of Travel* (song cycle) and not merely conventional, e.g. *Six Songs* Op.45. Note that cross references are not made for any titles of instrumental works, or vocal anthologies, e.g. *Songs for Hikers*;

from the first word of the name of a corporate body to the place where the body is entered, e.g. SOCIETY. Society for Promoting Christian Knowledge. *See* ENGLAND. – *Church of England*;

from one composition to other compositions based on it, e.g. from Donizetti to Liszt for his "Réminiscences de Lucia di Lammermoor".

4. Arrangement of headings

Headings are arranged in alphabetical order, in accordance with the following list:

B.	Single initial representing a personal name.
B., M.K.	Two or more initials, ditto. The last initial in the book is normally taken to represent the family name and appears first in the Catalogue.
BBC	Other combinations of initials, or initials and words, and acronyms.
ROSE	Common noun, e.g. a flower or tool.
ROSE	Place names.
ROSE	Author.
ROSE AMELIA, *Queen*	Compounds in two or more words, irrespective of meaning. (Not compound surnames.)
ROSE AND COMPANY	
ROSE (J.)	Surnames.
ROSE (John)	
ROSE (John Daniel)	

ROSEBUD   Compounds, read as one word.
ROSE-JONES (J.)
ROSE Y HER-
    NÁNDEZ (C.)

5. Arrangement of entries within each heading

Under the names of composers entries are generally arranged as follows:

Thematic catalogues.

Collected editions of the composer's works, arranged in chronological order by date of publication. In the case of some large headings these may be further subdivided.

Composite works, e.g. BORODIN (A.P.) [*Composite Works.*] Kismet... Based on themes of A. Borodin.

General alphabetical sequence of single works and of collections of works which, if published separately, would all file in the same place, e.g. collections of quartets, sonatas, symphonies, etc. Note that this does not apply to collections of, e.g., overtures, since the individual overtures if published separately would be filed in the alphabetical place appropriate to their title.

Doubtful and supposititious works.

Appendix of cross references.

These sub-divisions may or may not be marked by printed sub-headings, depending on the extent of the composer's entries.

Within the general alphabetical sequence certain filing principles are tacitly observed even though they apparently contradict the alphabetical order:

certain types of composition are grouped together regardless of the title of any specific edition, e.g. Concerto, Concert, Konzert, Klavierkonzert, Violinkonzert, etc., are all grouped together under "C" for "Concerto".

certain adjectives which may vary from edition to edition are usually ignored, e.g. grand, famous, favourite, celebrated, admired, brilliant.

numbers which have an enumerative function only are ignored, e.g. *Three Songs* is filed under *Songs*. But numbers which are an integral part of the title are used as alphabetical filing elements, e.g. *Three fishers went sailing* will be under *Three*.

Within the general alphabetical sequence all editions of a work or parts of a work are grouped together under the title of the first edition, or the composer's own title (in the original language). They are arranged on the general principles that complete versions come before selections, original versions before adaptations, and scores before sets of parts. In addition to these general principles, special arrangements are used for major vocal works (operas, oratorios, etc.) and for major instrumental works (quartets, sonatas, symphonies, etc.). These are in outline as follows:

Vocal works
Complete work
   Scores
   Parts
   Vocal scores
   Instrumental arrangements
Selections
   Vocal

Instrumental

Individual items
  Overture
  Arias and other individual excerpts, e.g. marches, arranged alphabetically
    Original version
    Adaptations
    Cross references to works based on the excerpt, e.g. sets of variations
Appendix of cross references to works based on more than one part of the opera, e.g. "Fantasia on themes from. . ."
Note that the language of editions of vocal works is not a filing factor.

Instrumental works

Complete collections (of sonatas, etc.)

Incomplete and miscellaneous collections

Selections

Single works (usually in numerical order)
  Complete work
  Selections
  Individual movements (alphabetically by tempo designation, not in numerical order)
  Cross references, e.g. to a set of variations on a theme from the work

In the case of a particularly large group of entries these sub-divisions may be further subdivided, e.g. the miscellaneous instrumental selections from an opera may be subdivided into: orchestral, military band, chamber ensemble, piano, piano duet, other instruments. After all sub-divisions have been made, the arrangement within each is chronological.

6. Content of individual entries

Because the Catalogue has grown over a period of many years, the items of information in any individual entry and their form of presentation have changed in various ways. Some of the more important of these are:

Works in series. Where a whole series is placed at one shelfmark, the modern practice is to catalogue the individual works, giving the title of the series in an italic footnote. The older practice was to give the title of the series at the end of the entry, preceded by the word *See*, e.g. CAUSTON (Thomas) Evening Service for unequal voices in four parts. 1912. *See* SHORE (S.R.) The Cathedral Series. No. 4. [1912, *etc.*] Such entries are in effect main entries, and should not be confused with cross references.

Imprint and pagination. The name of the publisher is given only in entries made after 1889, the pagination (or number of parts) only in those made after 1946.

Dating. The date given in each entry is the date of issue of the particular copy being catalogued, so far as can be ascertained. The following conventions are used:

1852	Date of publication printed in the work.
[1852]	Firm date supplied from other source of information, whether internal or external.
[WM 1802]	Date appears in the watermark.
[1852?]	Probable date – actual date may be the year before or after.
[c. 1845] or [c. 1850]	Date approximate or conjectural. In older catalogue entries the form [1845?] or [1850?] was used.

LEHÁR (Franz)

COLLECTIONS

— 12 Compositions. 1. Polonaise Royale. 2. Valse Américaine. 3. Mazurka. 4. Printemps d'Amour. Valse. 4. Danse Exotique. 6. Sons d'Ischl. Valse. 7. Ländler. 8. Humeurs d'Automne. Valse. 9. Plaisanterie-Polonaise. 10. Valse des Fleurs. 11. Menuet. 12. Caprice-Valse. (Arranged by F. Saddler.) [P. F.] *C. K. Harris: New York, Chicago,* 1909. 4°.　**g. 232. n. (8.)**

— Viennese Memories of Lehar. [Arranged by] Henry Hall. [Orchestrial parts.] 20 pt. *Chappell & Co.: London,* [1933.] 4°. [*Chappell & Co.'s Operatic and popular Selections for Orchestra by various Composers. no. 274.*] *The first violin part is in duplicate.*　**f. 424.**

— Viennese Memories of Lehár ... [Arranged by] Henry Hall. ⟨Arranged for military band by Dan Godfrey. Conductor [and parts].⟩ 31 pt. *Chappell & Co.: London,* [1933.] fol. [*Chappell's Army Journal. no. 604.*]　**h. 1562.**

— Five famous Waltzes. ⟨[1.] Gold and Silver. [2.] The Merry Widow. [3.] Wild Roses. [4.] Where the Lark sings. [5.] Paradise Waltz.⟩ Piano solo. pp. 19. *Glocken Verlag: London,* [1958.] 4°.　**f. 770. (5.)**

— Lehár Melodies ... Selected and arranged by Roger Barsotti. ⟨Conductor [and military band parts].⟩ 22 pt. *Glocken Verlag: London,* [1959.] fol.　**h. 3210. i. (540.)**

— Lehár Melodies ... Selected and arranged by Roger Barsotti. ⟨Solo B♭ cornet (conductor) [and brass band parts].⟩ 24 pt. *Glocken Verlag: London,* [1959.] 4°. *Various parts are in duplicate.*　**h. 3210. i. (541.)**

— Fifty golden Melodies of Franz Lehár. Favourite tunes arranged for the descant or treble recorder by Harry Dexter, *etc.* pp. 22. *Glocken Verlag: London,* [1965.] obl. 8°.　**a. 40. aa. (10.)**

— Twenty-five golden Melodies of Franz Lehár. Arranged as duets for descant & treble recorder by Harry Dexter, *etc.* [Score.] pp. 20. *Glocken Verlag: London,* [1965.] obl. 8°.　**a. 40. aa. (11.)**

— Fifteen favourite Melodies, *etc.* ⟨For C and G chord organs.⟩ pp. 16. *Glocken Verlag: London,* [1969.] 4°.　**g. 1378. kk. (6.)**

— Twelve Melodies for Organ. Twelve favourite Lehár melodies arranged for Hammond and all tab organs by Bryan Rodwell. pp. 35. *Glocken Verlag: London,* [1978.] 4°.　**f. 337. l. (13.)**

COMPOSITE WORKS

— Rose de noël. Opérette en 2 actes et 18 tableaux. Livret et lyrics de Raymond Vincy. D'après une idée de Karl Kristof ... Adaptation musicale du Professeur Rekaï, *etc.* 2 rec. *Royalty éditions musicales: Paris,* [1958.] fol.　**H. 3616. f. (1.)**

— [Rose de noël.] Mon petit papa ... Duo, *etc.* pp. 3. *Glocken Verlag: Londres, Vienne; Paris* [printed, 1958.] fol.　**H. 3616. f. (2.)**

— Adria Waltz ... Arranged Isy Geiger. ⟨Piano-conductor [and orchestral parts].⟩ 24 pt. *Glocken Verlag: London,* [1961.] 4°.　**h. 3210. i. (678.)**

— Amaranthe. *See infra:* [Mitislaw der Moderne.]

— [Aus eiserner Zeit.] Ich hab' ein Hüglein im Polenland ... Ein Frauenlied. Text von Karl Dankwart Zwerger. pp. 3. *Ludwig Krenn: Wien,* [1915.] fol. *The title page bears a MS dedication in the composer's autograph. With alternative words by Beda added throughout by the composer.*　**H. 2134. m. (35.)**

LEHÁR (Franz)

Die blaue Mazur

— Die blaue Mazur. Operette in zwei Akten und einem Zwischenspiel von Leo Stein und Béla Jenbach ... Klavierauszug mit Text, *etc.* pp. 111. *W. Karczag: Leipzig, Wien,* [1920.] 4°.　**G. 1344. i.**

— Songs from The Blue Mazurka ... Original book and lyrics by Leo Stein und Bela Jenbach. English lyrics by Harry Graham. *Eng. & Ger.* pp. 35. *Glocken Verlag: London,* [1980.] 4°.　**F. 1424. h. (2.)**

— The Blue Mazurka. Selection. Selected and arranged by H. M. Higgs. Orchestra by Arthur Wood. [Orchestral parts.] 19 pt. *Chappell & Co.: London,* [1927.] 4°. [*Chappell & Co.'s Operatic and popular Selections for Orchestra by various Composers. no. 188.*] *The part for "Drums, etc." is in duplicate.*　**f. 424.**

— The Blue Mazurka. Selection. Arranged for military band by Dan Godfrey, *etc.* ⟨Conductor [and parts].⟩ 28 pt. *Chappell & Co.: London,* [1927.] fol. [*Chappell's Army Journal. no. 544.*]　**h. 1562.**

— [Was sich ein Mädchen erträumt.] Shine bright Moon. Valse song. ⟨Arranged for military band by Dan Godfrey. Solo clarinet in B♭. (Conductor) [and parts].⟩ 28 pt. *In:* Gensler (Lewis E.) and Hanley (J. F.) [Queen High.] Cross your Heart, *etc.* [1927.] fol. [*Chappell's Army Journal. no. 543.*]　**h. 1562.**

— A Carnival for Life. *See infra:* [Der Graf von Luxemburg.—Tonight we'll have a special boom.]

— La Chanson du bonheur. *See infra:* [Schön ist die Welt.]

— Cloclo. Operette in 3 Akten von Bela Jenbach. [Vocal score.] pp. 129. *Drei Masken-Verlag: Berlin, etc.,* [1924.] 4°.　**G. 1344. dd.**

— Cloclo. Operette in 3 Akten von Bela Jenbach. ⟨Klavierauszug zu zwei Händen. Arrangement von Gustav Volk.⟩ pp. 72. *Drei Masken-Verlag: Berlin, etc.,* [1924.] 4°.　**G. 1344. x. (2.)**

— Concertino in B minor for Violin and Orchestra ... Reduction for violin & piano, *etc.* [Score and part.] 2 pt. *Glocken Verlag: London,* [1978.] 4°.　**g. 422. m. (13.)**

— The Count of Luxembourg. *See infra:* [Der Graf von Luxemburg.]

— Cousins of the Czar. *See infra:* [Der Graf von Luxemburg.—You will be à Royal Highness.]

— Czarevitch. *See infra:* [Der Zarewitsch.]

— Das is a einfache Rechnung. *See infra:* [Der Rastelbinder.]

— Dorela valse. [P. F.] pp. 5. *Herman Darewski: London,* [1920.] fol.　**h. 3577. b. (1.)**

— Dorela. (Vocal Valse.) Words by B. Lawrence. *H. Darewski Music Publishing Co.: London,* 1921. fol.　**H. 1846. x. (45.)**

— Elfentanz. Valse de concert. 1ˢᵗ violin (conductor) [and orchestral parts]. 18 pt. *Hawkes & Son: London,* [1907.] 8°. *The 1ˢᵗ clarinet part is in duplicate.*　**f. 800. (808.)**

— Elfentanz Valse, *etc.* [Military band parts.] *See* Filipovsky (F.) Chant du Rossignol ... and Elfentanz Valse, *etc.* 1909. fol.　**h. 3211. a. (77.)**

— Endlich allein. Operette in drei Akten von Dr. A. M. Bodanzky ... Klavierauszug mit Text, *etc.* pp. 167. *W. Karczag: Leipzig, etc.,* [1914.] 4°.　**G. 1344. j.**

— English Lasses. *See infra:* [Wiener Frauen.—Ein hohes und frohes vergeistertes Lied.]

LEHÁR (FRANZ)

Eva

— Eva ... Klavierauszug zu zwei Händen mit unterlegtem Text.—(Arrangement von) G. Blasser. *L. Doblinger: Leipzig*, (1911.) 4°.
g. 361. d. (1.)

— Eva. A Comic Opera in three Acts. English book and lyrics by G. Macdonough ... American Arrangement by A. Heindl. Vocal Score. *G. Schirmer: New York*, 1912. 4°.
H. 3616. a. (1.)

— Eva. Operette in drei Akten von Dr. A. M. Willner, Robert Bodansky ... Klavierauszug mit Text (Klavierpartitur), *etc.* pp. 155. *Ludwig Doblinger: Wien*, [c. 1950.] 4°. **G. 1344. m.**

— Eva. Operette in drei Akten (Texte von) Dr. A. M. Willner, (und) R. Bodanzky, *etc.* [Nineteen detached vocal no.] *L. Doblinger: Leipzig*, (1911.) fol. **H. 3616. (19.)**

— Eva, *etc.* [Seven detached no.] *G. Schirmer: New York*, 1911. fol. **H. 3616. b. (4.)**

— Vorspiel ... für Klavier zu zwei Händen. *L. Doblinger: Leipzig, Wien*, (1911.) fol. **h. 3577. (26.)**

— Vorspiel ... Für Klavier zu zwei Händen, erleichtert. (Arrangement von G. Blasser.) *L. Doblinger: Leipzig, Wien*, (1911.) fol. **h. 3577. (27.)**

— Pariser-Pflaster. Marsch ... für Klavier zu zwei Händen. *L. Doblinger: Leipzig, Wien*, (1911.) fol. **h. 3577. (25.)**

— [Wär' es auch nichts als ein Traum.] One Hour of Love ... Waltz Song, English words by A. Grein. [Two editions.] *Schott & Co.: London*, 1914. fol. **H. 3616. b. (6.)**

— Walzer-Szene ... für Klavier zu zwei Händen. Original. (Erleichtert.) 2 no. *L. Doblinger: Leipzig, Wien*, (1911.) fol.
h. 3577. (28.)

— Eva-Walzer nach Motiven der gleichnamigen Operette ... für Klavier zu zwei Händen. *L. Doblinger: Leipzig, Wien*, (1911.) fol. **h. 3577. (23.)**

— Eva-Valse. On melodies from the operetta: Eva ... Piano solo. ⟨New edition.⟩ pp. 11. *Schott & Co.: London*, [1912.] fol.
h. 1226. c. (15.)

— Eva Waltz. Arranged by Ronald Hammer. Piano conductor [and orchestral parts]. 23 pt. *Glocken Verlag: London*, [1959.] 4°. **h. 3210. i. (538.)**

— Frasquita. Operette in drei Akten von Dr. A. M. Willner und Heinz Reichert ... Vollständiger Klavierauszug mit Text. pp. 153. *Josef Weinberger: Leipzig*, [1922.] 4°.
G. 1344. x. (1.)

— [Frasquita.—Hab' ein blaues Himmelbett.] Serenade ... Arranged as a two-part song by Purcell J. Mansfield. Words by Reginald Arkell. [Staff and tonic sol-fa notation.] pp. 7. *Ascherberg, Hopwood & Crew: London*, [1964.] 8°.
[*Ascherberg Series of Part-songs. no.* 607.] **F. 1659. a.**

— Frederica. *See* infra: [Friederike.]

Friederike

— Friederike. Singspiel in drei Akten von Ludwig Herzer und Fritz Löhner ... Klavierauszug mit Text, *etc.* pp. 103. *Crescendo Theaterverlag: Berlin*, [1928.] 4°. **G. 1344. v. (1.)**

— [Friederike. Vocal score. Five sets of proof sheets, with MS corrections, partly by the composer.]
  1. [Sheets stamped with various dates from 6 Feb. to 2 March 1928.] ff. 6, 7, 12–17, 15–59, 84–93.
  2. [Sheets stamped with the date 8 Sept. 1928.] ff. 3–72, 76–94, 98–124.
  3. [Undated sheets of Sept. or Oct. 1928.] ff. 9, 10, 77–90.

LEHÁR (FRANZ)

  4. [Sheets stamped with the date 31 Oct. 1928.] ff. 3–90, 92–103.
  5. [Sheets stamped with the date 6 Nov. 1928.] ff. 52–53, 68, 98, 103.
[*Crescendo Theaterverlag: Berlin*, 1928.] fol.
With a publicity pamphlet of 31 *pp. entitled "Franz Lehár, Friederike ... im Lichte der Kritik", printed in* 1929.
H. 3616. g.

— Frederica. A Musical Play in three acts by L. Herzer & F. Löhner, English version by A. Ross, lyrics by H. S. Pepper. Vocal Score. *Chappell & Co.: London, etc.*, 1930. 4°.
F. 690. ww. (3.)

— Frederica. Operetta in three acts ... Adapted and arranged by Ronald Hanmer. Original book by Ludwig Herzer and Fritz Löhner. New book by Bernard Dunn. Original English lyrics by Harry S. Pepper. Additional lyrics by Bernard Dunn. Vocal score. pp. 196. *Glocken Verlag: London*, [1976.] 4°. **G. 1344. w. (3.)**

— Frederica. Selection. Arranged by Guy Jones. [Orchestral parts.] 11 pt. *Chappell & Co.: London*, [1930.] 4°.
[*Chappell & Co.'s Operatic and popular Selections for Orchestra by various Composers. no.* 236.] **f. 424.**

— Frederica. Selection. Arranged [for military band] by Dan Godfrey, *etc.* ⟨Conductor [and parts].⟩ 31 pt. *Chappell & Co.: London*, [1930.] fol.
[*Chappell's Army Journal. no* ⌐⌐3.] **h. 1562.**

— Frühling. Operette in einem Akt (drei Bildern) von Rudolf Eger ... Klavierauszug mit Text, *etc.* pp. 66. *Drei Masken-Verlag: Berlin, München*, [1922.] fol. **G. 1344. t.**

— Frühling. Operette in einem Akt (drei Bildern) von Rudolf Eger ... Klavierauszug mit Text (mit Singstimme). Originalausgabe des Komponisten. pp. 60. *Glocken-Verlag: Wien*, [1940.] 4°. **G. 1344. z. (2.)**

— Das Fürstenkind. Operette in einem Vorspiel und zwei Akten (teilweise nach einer Erzählung About's) von Victor Léon ... Klavierauszug mit Text, *etc.* pp. 110. *Ludwig Doblinger: Leipzig*, [1909.] 4°. **G. 1344.**

— [Das Fürstenkind.] Maids of Athens. An Operetta in three acts by V. Léon, book and lyrics by C. Wells. [Six detached no.] *Chappell & Co.: London*, 1914. fol. **H. 3616. b. (3.)**

— [Das Fürstenkind.] Maids of Athens ... Selection. [P. F.] (Arranged by C. Lucas.) *Chappell & Co.: New York, etc.*, 1914. fol. **h. 3577. (31.)**

— [Das Fürstenkind.] Maids of Athens. (Waltz.) On melodies from the operetta. [P. F.] *Chappell & Co.: New York, etc.*, 1914. fol. **h. 3577. (32.)**

— Die gelbe Jacke. Operette in 3 Akten von Victor Léon ... Klavierauszug mit Text, *etc.* pp. 124. *W. Karczag: Leipzig, Wien*, [1923.] 4°. **G. 1344. k.**

— Gipsy Love. *See* infra: [Zigeunerliebe.]

— Girls were made to love and kiss. *See* infra: [Paganini.—Gern hab' ich die Frau'n geküsst.]

— Giuditta. Musikalische Komödie in 5 Bildern. Buch von Paul Knepler und Fritz Löhner. Orchesterpartitur, *etc.* 3 vol. pp. 388. *Verlag W. Karczag: Leipzig, etc.; Wien* [printed, c. 1935.] fol. **H. 3616. c.**

— Giuditta ... Klavierauszug mit Text. Originalausgabe des Komponisten, *etc.* pp. 165. *Glocken-Verlag: Wien*, [1933.] 4°.
G. 1344. u.

— [Giuditta.—Du bist meine Sonne.] Stay with me for ever. Song from the Musical Play Giuditta, words by D. Carter from the German of P. Knepler and F. Löhner. *Chappell & Co.: London, etc.*, 1935. 4°. **G. 1270. ll. (37.)**

LEHÁR (FRANZ)

— [Giudetta.—Meine Lippen, sie küssen so heiss.] On my Lips every Kiss is like Wine ... [Song.] Words by Geoffrey Dunn from the German of Paul Knepler and Fritz Löhner. pp. 4. *Chappell & Co.: London,* [1964.] 4°. **G. 1276. bb. (22.)**

— Der Göttergatte. Operette in einem Vorspiel und 2 Acten von Victor Léon u. Leo Stein ... Clavierauszug mit Text, *etc.* pp. 117. *Ludwig Doblinger: Wien,* [1904.] 4°. **G. 1344. y.**

Gold und Silber

— Gold and Silver ... L'Or et l'Argent. Valse. [P. F.] *Hawkes & Son: London,* 1903. fol. **h. 3286. dd. (58.)**

— Gold und Silber ... Waltz ... and La Voix des Cloches, Rêverie, by A. Luigini. (Arranged for Military Band by G. Miller.) [Parts.] *Hawkes & Son: London,* 1905. fol. *Part of "Hawkes & Son's Military Band Edition".* **h. 3211. a. (23.)**

— Gold & Silver. Waltz. Arranged for piano duet by Malcolm Williamson. pp. 7. *Boosey & Hawkes: London,* [1957.] 4°. **g. 1123. f. (11.)**

— Gold and Silver. Waltz ... Arranged for orchestra by Ronald Hanmer. Piano conductor [and parts]. 24 pt. *Glocken Verlag: London,* [1958.] 4°. **h. 3210. i. (539.)**

— Gold and Silver. Waltz, *etc.* ⟨Arranged for piano solo by Tony Lowry.⟩ pp. 8. *Glocken Verlag: London,* [1958.] 4°. **f. 770. (7.)**

— Gold and Silver ... Arranged as a part-song for S. A. T. B. by Ronald Hanmer with lyrics by Phil Park. [Staff and tonic sol-fa notation.] pp. 24. *Glocken Verlag: London,* [1959.] 8°. **F. 1744. aa. (2.)**

— Gold and Silver. (Vocal edition.) Waltz ... Lyric by Phil Park. pp. 11. *Glocken-Verlag: London,* [1960.] 4°. **G. 1344. s. (7.)**

— Ein Herz, das dich liebt ... Die gesungene Fassung des berühmten Walzers ... Text: Werner Raschek. Ausgabe für Gesang und Klavier/Akkordeon. Bearbeitung: Charly Dieter. *Bosworth & Co.: Köln, etc.,* [1968.] 4°. **G. 1271. ll. (5.)**

— Golden Star. *See infra:* [Der Graf von Luxemburg.—Lieber Freund, man greift nicht nach den Sternen.]

Der Graf von Luxemburg

— Der Graf von Luxemburg. Operette in drei Akten von A. M. Willner und Rob. Bodansky ... Klavierauszug mit Text. pp. 142. *W. Karczag: Wien,* [1909.] 4°. **F. 1424. b.**

— The Count of Luxembourg ... Musical Play in Two Acts by A. M. Willner and R. Bodanzky. Adapted for the English stage by B. Hood, lyrics by B. Hood and A. Ross. Vocal Score. *Chappell & Co.: London, etc.,* 1911. 4°. **F. 1424. a. (1.)**

— Der Graf von Luxemburg. Operette in drei Akten von A. M. Willner und Rob. Bodanzky ... Klavierauszug mit Text, *etc.* ⟨Neufassung.⟩ pp. 163. *Glocken-Verlag: Wien,* [1937.] 4°. *The titlepage bears a MS dedication in the composer's autograph.* **G. 1344. o. (2.)**

— The Count of Luxembourg. (Operetta in 3 acts.) Original book and lyrics by A. M. Willner and R. Bodanzky ... Translated and adapted by Eric Maschwitz. Music arranged and adapted by Bernard Grun. Vocal score, *etc.* pp. 173. *Glocken-Verlag: London,* [1965.] 4°. **G. 1344. w. (1.)**

— The Count of Luxembourg ... Pianoforte Solo. Arranged by H. M. Higgs. *Chappell & Co.: London, etc.,* 1911. 4°. **f. 540. cc. (1.)**

LEHÁR (FRANZ)

— Songs from The Count of Luxembourg ... Original book and lyrics by A. M. Willner and R. Bodanzky. English by Eric Maschwitz, *etc.* Eng. & Ger. pp. 29. *Glocken Verlag: London,* [1976.] 4°. **F. 1198. r. (2.)**

— The Count of Luxembourg. Selection. Selected and arranged by H. M. Higgs. ⟨Full orchestra.—Small orchestra.⟩ [Parts.] 2 no. *Chappell & Co.: London,* [1911.] 4°. *[Chappell & Co.'s Operatic and popular Selections for Orchestra by various Composers. no. 99.]* **f. 424.**

— Waltzes from The Count of Luxembourg ... Arranged by Ronald Hanmer. Piano-conductor. pp. 6. *Glocken-Verlag: London,* [1963.] 4°. **g. 352. b. (33.)**

— Waltzes from The Count of Luxembourg ... Arranged by James Howe. Solo B♭ cornet (Conductor) [and brass band parts]. 25 pt. *Glocken Verlag: London,* [1968.] 8°. *With several copies of various parts.* **h. 3210. j. (216.)**

— Der Graf von Luxemburg. Melodienfolge. Gekürzte Fassung ... Blasmusik. Neues Arrangement: Allred Hofbauer. ⟨Neue Ausgabe. Direktion in B [and parts].⟩ 52 pt. *Glocken-Verlag: Chur; printed in Austria,* [1978.] 8°. *Various parts are in duplicate.* **h. 3210. j. (982.)**

— Luxemburg-Walzer, *etc.* ⟨Für Klavier.⟩ pp. 11. *W. Karczag & C. Wallner: Wien, Leipzig,* [1909.] fol. **h. 61. rr. (13.)**

— [Luxemburg-Walzer.] Luxemburg Valse, on melodies from the operetta "The Count of Luxemburg". ⟨Piano solo. New edition.⟩ pp. 11. *Chappell & Co.: London,* [1910.] fol. **h. 725. m. (11.)**

— [Act II. Opening scene and dance.] Valse-Intermezzo ... Piano Solo. *Chappell & Co.: London, etc.,* 1911. fol. **h. 3577. (22.)**

— [Are you going to dance?] The Staircase Dance ... Piano Solo. *Chappell & Co.: London, etc.,* 1911. fol. **h. 3577. (21.)**

— Kukuška. Russian Peasant Dance ... Arranged for Military Band by F. Winterbottom. [Parts.] *Hawkes & Son: London,* 1905. fol. *Part of "Hawkes & Son's Military Band Edition".* **h. 3211. a. (27.)**

— Russian dance, "Kukuska" ... Piano Solo. *Chappell & Co.: London, etc.,* 1911. fol. **h. 3577. (20.)**

— [Lieber Freund, man greift nicht nach den Sternen.] Golden Star. Song, *etc. Chappell & Co.: London, etc.,* 1911. fol. **H. 3616. (15.)**

— [Pièrre, der schreibt an klein Fleurette.] Pierrette and Pierrot. Song, *etc. Chappell & Co.: London, etc.,* 1911. fol. **H. 3616. (16.)**

— [Say not love is a dream.] Valse-Song. *etc. Chappell & Co.: London, etc.,* 1911. fol. **H. 3616. (18.)**

— [Since first I burst upon the scene.] Rootsie-Pootsie. Song, *etc. Chappell & Co.: London, etc.,* 1911. fol. **H. 3616. (17.)**

— [Tonight we'll have a special boom.] A Carnival for Life. Duet. *Chappell & Co.: London, etc.,* 1911. fol. **H. 3616. b. (2.)**

— [Tonight we'll have a special boom.] Luxembourg March ... Piano Solo. *Chappell & Co.: London, etc.,* 1911. fol. **h. 3577. (17.)**

— [You will be a Royal Highness.] Cousins of the Czar. Duet, *etc. Chappell & Co.: London, etc.,* 1911. fol. **H. 3616. (14.)**

— *See* HIGGS (H. M.) Rootsie-Pootsie. Two-Step on Melodies from ... The Count of Luxembourg, *etc.* 1911. fol. **h. 3577. (19.)**

LEHÁR (FRANZ)

— [Grossfürstin Alexandra.—Du und ich sind füreinander bestimmt.] You, only you. Waltz Song, words by C. Lucas. *Ascherberg, Hopwood & Crew: London*, 1934. 4°.
    G. 1270. jj. (36.)

— Gypsy Love. *See* infra: [Zigeunerliebe.]

— Ein Herz, das dich liebt. *See* supra: [Gold und Silber.]

— Home. *See* infra: [Die lustige Witwe.—Ja, was—ein trautes Zimmerlein.]

— I love you so. *See* infra: [Die lustige Witwe.—Lippen schweigen.]

— I'm off to chez Maxime. *See* infra: [Die lustige Witwe.—O Vaterland.]

— Ich bin ein Wiener Kind. *See* infra: [Der Rastelbinder.]

— Ich hab' ein Hüglein im Polenland. *See* supra: [Aus eiserner Zeit.]

— Die ideale Gattin. Operette in drei Akten von Julius Brammer und Alfred Grünwald и Евгенія Сперо ... Klavierauszug mit Text vom Komponisten, *etc*. pp. 168. *Ludwig Doblinger: Leipzig*, [1913.] 4°.
    G. 1344. a.

— [Die ideale Gattin.] Ideal Wife. Waltzes. [P. F.] *J. W. Stern & Co.: New York, etc.*, (1913.) fol.
    h. 3577. (24.)

— Die Juxheirat. Operette in drei Acten von Julius Bauer ... Vollständiger Clavier-Auszug mit Text, *etc*. pp. 133. *Joseph Weinberger: Leipzig*, [1904?] 4°.
The cover bears a MS. dedication in the composer's autograph.
    G. 1344. l.

— Kukuška. *See* supra: [Der Graf von Luxemburg.]

Das Land des Lächelns

— Das Land des Lächelns. Romantische Operette in drei Akten nach Viktor Léon von Ludwig Herzer und Fritz Löhner. [Vocal score.] pp. 94. *W. Karczag: Leipzig, etc; Wien* [printed, 1929.] 4°.
Imperfect; wanting the titlepage. The title is taken from the head of p. 3.
    G. 1344. p. (2.)

— The Land of Smiles ... A musical play in three acts by Ludwig Herzer and Fritz Löhner. English version by Harry Graham ... Vocal score. *Chappell & Co.: London*, [1949.] 4°.
    F. 943. v. (2.)

— The Land of Smiles ... English version by Harry Graham. New book and additional lyrics by Conrad Carter and Fred S. Tysh. Music adapted by Hans May ... Vocal score. ⟨Revision edition.⟩ pp. 227. *Chappell & Co.: London*, [1953.] 4°.
    F. 1424. f.

— Vocal Gems ... in The Land of Smiles ... A Musical Play by L. Herzer & F. Löhner from the original by V. Leon. English version by H. Graham, *etc*. *Chappell & Co.: London, etc.*, 1931. 4°.
    G. 1270. cc. (3.)

— Libellentanz. Operette in drei Akten von Carlo Lombardo und Dr. A. M. Willner ... Klavierauszug mit Text. pp. 93. *W. Karczag: Leipzig, Wien*, [1923.] 4°.
    G. 1344. v. (2.)

— [Libellentanz.] The Three Graces. A musical play. Revised book and lyrics by Ben Travers. (From the German by Carlo Lombardo and Dr. A. M. Willner.) ⟨Vocal score.⟩ pp. 133. *B. Feldman & Co.: London*, [1952.] 4°.
    G. 1344. g.

— Liebesmelodie. Zwei Lieder. 1. Die ganze Welt dreht sich um Liebe. 2. Schau mich an sei mir gut. Walzerlied. Worte von H. Rameau. *Ascherberg, Hopwood & Crew: London*, [1936.] 4°.
    G. 1270. ll. (36.)

— Love live forever and rule my Heart. *See* infra: [Paganini. —Liebe, du Himmel auf Erden.]

LEHÁR (FRANZ)

— "The Love Theme" from Viennese Ladies. *See* infra: [Wiener Frauen.—Endlich allein mit Dir Allein.]

— A Lullaby-Song. *See* infra: [Der Mann mit den drei Frauen.—Bienchen, summt nicht mehr.]

Die lustige Witwe

— Die lustige Witwe. Operette in drei Akten (teilweise nach einer fremden Grundidee) von Victor Léon u. Leo Stein ... Klavierauszug mit Text, *etc*. pp. 142. *Ludwig Doblinger: Leipzig, Wien*, [1906.] 4°.
    G. 1344. h.

— The Merry Widow. New Musical Play, adapted from the German of V. Leon and L. Stein. Lyrics by A. Ross ... Arranged for the Piano by H. M. Higgs. Vocal Score. *Chappell & Co.: London, etc.*, 1907. 4°.
    F. 1424.

— The Merry Widow. Original book and lyrics by Victor Léon and Leo Stein ... New book and lyrics by Phil Park. Music adapted and arranged by Ronald Hanmer. ⟨Vocal score.⟩ pp. 195. *Glocken Verlag: London*, [1958.] 4°.
    G. 1344. q.

— The Merry Widow ... Original book and lyrics by Victor Léon & Leo Stein. English version by Christopher Hassall. Vocal score. pp. 142. *Glocken Verlag: London*, [1959.] 4°.
    G. 1344. s. (1.)

— The Merry Widow. Original book and lyrics by Victor Leon and Leo Stein. English lyrics by Sheldon Harnick. Vocal score. *Eng*. pp. 142. *Chappell & Co.:* [New York, 1980?] 4°.
    G. 1344. bb. (1.)

— The Merry Widow ... An Ernst Lubitsch Merry Musical Romance, based on book & lyrics by V. Leon & L. Stein ... New lyrics by L. Hart, *etc*. [Four detached vocal no.] *Robbins Music Corporation: New York*, 1934. 4°.
    G. 1275. pp. (8.)

— Album of Songs from ... The Merry Widow ... English version by Christopher Hassall. pp. 18. *Glocken Verlag: London*, [1959.] 4°.
    G. 1344. s. (6.)

— Songs from The Merry Widow ... Original book and lyrics by Victor Leon and Leo Stein. English lyrics by Sheldon Harnick, *etc*. *Eng. & Ger*. pp. 25. *Glocken Verlag: London*, [1979.] 4°.
    F. 1424. h. (1.)

— The Merry Widow. Selection ... Orchestra by Barter Johns. ⟨Full orchestra.—Small orchestra.⟩ [Parts.] 2 no. *Chappell & Co.: London*, [1907.] 4°.
[Chappell & Co.'s Operatic and popular Selections for Orchestra by various Composers. no. 83.]
    f. 424.

— Gems from "The Merry Widow" ... Orchestration by Ronald Hanmer. ⟨Piano-conductor [and parts].⟩ 22 pt. *Glocken Verlag: London*, [1958.] 4°.
    h. 3210. i. (542.)

— The Merry Widow. Selection. Arranged for military band by Dan Godfrey. ⟨Conductor [and parts].⟩ 32 pt. *Chappell & Cº: London*, [c. 1970.] fol.
[Chappell's Army Journal. no. 331.]
    h. 1562.

— The Merry Widow ... Arranged for the Piano by H. M. Higgs. Pianoforte Solo. *Chappell & Co.: London, etc.*, 1907. 4°.
    f. 540. y. (2.)

— Selection from ... The Merry Widow ... arranged for the Pianoforte by H. M. Higgs. *Chappell & Co.: London, etc.*, 1907. fol.
    h. 3577. (1.)

— [Another edition.] Selection ... arranged for the Pianoforte by H. M. Higgs. *Chappell & Co.: London, etc.*, 1907. fol.
    h. 3577. (2.)

— Merry Widow Gems. Piano selection ... Selected and arranged by Tony Lowry. pp. 15. *Glocken Verlag: London*, [1959.] 4°.
    f. 770. (6.)

LEHÁR (FRANZ)

— Die lustige Witwe. Ouverture … Partitur für grosses
Orchester. pp. 52. *Glocken-Verlag: Wien*, [1940.] fol.
*The titlepage bears a MS. dedication in the composer's
autograph.*   **h. 3577. a.**

— Overture to "The Merry Widow" … Arranged by Robert
Stolz. Piano-conductor [and orchestral parts]. 24 pt. *Glocken
Verlag: London*, [1959.] 4°.   **h. 3210. i. (543.)**

— [Butterflies.] The Merry Widow. Two-Step … Arranged for
the Pianoforte by H. M. Higgs. *Chappell & Co.: London, etc.*,
1907. fol.   **h. 3577. (4.)**

— [Another edition. Butterflies.] The Merry Widow. Two-Step
… Arranged for the Pianoforte by H. M. Higgs. *Chappell &
Co.: London, etc.*, 1907. fol.   **h. 3577. (5.)**

Die lustige Witwe.—Es lebt eine Vilja

— Vilia. Song … Arranged for the Piano by H. M. Higgs, *etc.*
3 no. [In E flat, F and G.] *Chappell & Co.: London, etc.*,
1907. fol.   **H. 3616. (9.)**

— Vilia. Song … in G. *Chappell & Co.: London, etc.*, (1908.)
fol.   **H. 3616. (10.)**

— Vilia … English version by Christopher Hassall. [For voice
and P. F.] pp. 4. *Glocken Verlag: London*, [1958.] 4°.
                                           G. 1344. s. (5.)

— Vilia … Four part mixed chorus (S. A. T. B.). Arranged by
William Stickles, *etc.* [Staff and tonic sol-fa notation.] pp. 7.
Chappell & Co.: London, [1958.] 8°.
[*Vocal Library. no.* 325.]   **G. 440.**

— Vilia … Three-part chorus (or trio). (S. S. A.) Arranged by
William Stickles, *etc.* [Staff and tonic sol-fa notation.] pp. 7.
Chappell & Co.: London, [1958.] 8°.
[*Vocal Library. no.* 326.]   **G. 440.**

— Vilia … Arranged for mixed choir (S. A. T. B. and piano).
English version by Christopher Hassall. [Staff and tonic
sol-fa notation.] pp. 7. *Glocken Verlag: London*, [1959.] 8°.
                                           F. 1744. aa. (3.)

— Vilia … Arranged for women's choir (S. S. A. A. and piano).
English version by Christopher Hassall. [Staff and tonic
sol-fa notation.] pp. 4. *Glocken Verlag: London*, [1959.] 8°.
                                           F. 217. p. (31.)

— Vilia … Arranged for orchestra by Harry Dexter.
⟨Piano-conductor [and parts].⟩ 21 pt. *Glocken Verlag:
London*, [1958.] 4°.   **h. 3210. i. (544.)**

— Vilia-Song … Transcribed for the Pianoforte by H. M. Higgs.
Chappell & Co.: London, etc., 1907. fol.   **h. 3577. (6.)**

— [Another edition.] Vilia Song … Transcribed for the
Pianoforte by H. M. Higgs. *Chappell & Co.: London, etc.*,
1907. fol.   **h. 3577. (7.)**

— Vilia. Intermezzo … Arranged by H. M. Higgs. [P. F.]
Chappell & Co.: London, etc., 1907. fol.   **h. 3577. (8.)**

Die lustige Witwe—Other numbers

— [I was born, by cruel fate, in a little Balkan State.] Quite
Parisian. Song … Arranged for the Piano by H. M. Higgs,
etc. Chappell & Co.: London, etc., 1907. fol.   **H. 3616. (7.)**

— [I was born, by cruel fate, in a little Balkan State.] Quite
Parisian. Song, *etc. Chappell & Co.: London, etc.*, (1908.) fol.
                                           H. 3616. (8.)

Die lustige Witwe.—Ja, was—ein trautes Zimmerlein

— Home. Song … Arranged for the Piano by H. M. Higgs, *etc.
Chappell & Co.: London, etc.*, 1907. fol.   **H. 3616. (1.)**

— Home. Song, *etc. Chappell & Co.: London, etc.*, (1908.) fol.
                                           H. 3616. (2.)

LEHÁR (FRANZ)

Die lustige Witwe.—Lippen schweigen

— I love you so. Valse Song … Arranged for the Piano by
H. M. Higgs, *etc.* 3 no. [In E flat, F and G.] *Chappell & Co.:
London, etc.*, 1907. fol.   **H. 3616. (3.)**

— When your Lips pressed mine … [Song.] English setting by
A. Dallas … Arr. by W. Lange. *Woodward & Teschner: New
York*, (1907.) fol.   **H. 3616. (13.)**

— I love you so. Valse Song … in G. *Chappell & Co.: London,
etc.*, (1908.) fol.   **H. 3616. (4.)**

— Merry Widow Waltz. (Love unspoken.) [Song.] Original
words by Viktor Leon & Leo Stein. English lyric by
Christopher Hassall. pp. 4. *Glocken Verlag: London*, [1958.]
4°.   **G. 1344. s. (3.)**

— I love you so … Arranged for three-part female chorus
(S. S. A.) by Felton Rapley, *etc.* pp. 4. *Chappell & Co.:
London*, [1952.] 8°.
[*Chappell's vocal Library. no.* 244.]   **G. 440.**

— The Merry Widow Waltz. (Love unspoken.) Arranged for
mixed choir S. A. T. B. ⟨male voices T. T. B. B.⟩, *etc.* [Staff and
tonic sol-fa notation.] 2 no. *Glocken Verlag: London*, [1959.]
8°.   **F. 1196. l. (3.)**

— The Merry Widow Waltz … Orchestration by Harry Dexter.
⟨Piano conductor [and parts].⟩ 20 pt. *Glocken Verlag:
London*, [1958.] 4°.   **h. 3210. i. (465.)**

— The Merry Widow. Valse … Arranged by L. Williams. Edited
by H. M. Higgs. [P. F.] *Chappell & Co.: London, etc.*, 1907.
fol.   **h. 3577. (13.)**

— The Merry Widow.—Ballsirenen.—Valse … Arranged by
L. Williams. [P. F.] *Chappell & Co.: London, etc.*, 1907. fol.
                                           h. 3577. (12.)

— The Merry Widow. Valse … Arranged for Violin and Piano
by H. M. Higgs. *Chappell & Co.: London, etc.*, 1907. fol.
                                           h. 3577. (9.)

Die lustige Witwe.—Other numbers

— [O Vaterland.] Maxim's. Song … Arranged for the Piano by
H. M. Higgs, *etc. Chappell & Co.: London, etc.*, 1907. fol.
                                           H. 3616. (5.)

— [O Vaterland.] Maxim's. Song, *etc. Chappell & Co.: London,
etc.*, (1908.) fol.   **H. 3616. (6.)**

— [O Vaterland.] I'm off to chez Maxime … English version by
Christopher Hassall. [For voice and P. F.] pp. 7. *Glocken
Verlag: London*, [1958.] 4°.   **G. 1344. s. (2.)**

— To-night will teach me to forget. [Song.] From
Metro-Goldwyn-Mayer's Production The Merry Widow, lyric
by G. Kahn. [Voice part only.] *Chappell & Co.: London, etc.*,
1934. *s. sh.* 8°.   **F. 636. yy. (2.)**

— [Wie eine Rosenknospe.] Red as the Rose of Maytime …
English version by Christopher Hassall. [For voice and P. F.]
pp. 7. *Glocken Verlag: London*, [1958.] 4°.   **G. 1344. s. (4.)**

Die lustige Witwe.—Appendix

— The Merry Widow March … Arranged for the Pianoforte by
H. M. Higgs. *Chappell & Co.: London, etc.*, 1907. fol.
                                           h. 3577. (3.)

— See FREY (Hugo) A Farsovian Review. Composed by H. Frey
on melodies of the "Merry Widow", *etc.* [1908.] fol.
                                           h. 4120. u. (15.)

— See KIEFERT (C.) The Merry Widow. Lancers on Melodies by
F. Lehar, *etc.*, 1907. fol.   **h. 3286. ll. (6.)**

LEHÁR (Franz)

— Luxembourg March. *See* supra: [Der Graf von Luxemburg.— Tonight we'll have a special boom.]

— Luxemburg Valse. *See* supra: [Der Graf von Luxemburg.— Luxemburg-Walzer.]

— Maids of Athens. *See* supra: [Das Fürstenkind.]

— The Man with three Wives. *See* infra: [Der Mann mit den drei Frauen.]

Der Mann mit den drei Frauen

— Der Mann mit den drei Frauen. Operette in 3 Akten von Julius Bauer. ⟨Klavierauszug mit Text.⟩ pp. 156. *Ludwig Doblinger: Wien, Leipzig,* [1907.] 4°.　　**G. 1344. b.**

— The Man with three Wives. [Musical play.] Lyrics by P. Potter, *etc.* [Four detached vocal no.] *Chappell & Co.: New York, etc.,* 1910. fol.　　**H. 3616. (24.)**

— The Man with three Wives, *etc.* [Seven detached no.] *Chappell Co.: New York,* 1913. fol.　　**H. 3616. b. (1.)**

— The Man with three Wives. Selection ... arranged by C. Lucas. [P. F.] *Chappell & Co.: New York, etc.,* 1910. fol.　　**h. 3577. (15.)**

— [Ach, Rosen ohne Zahl.] Red Roses. Song, *etc.* 3 no. [In F, G and A.] *Chappell & Co.: New York, etc.,* 1910. fol.　　**H. 3616. (23.)**

— [Bienchen, summt nicht mehr.] A Lullaby Song, *etc. Chappell & Co.: New York, etc.,* 1910. fol.　　**H. 3616. (22.)**

— Der Mann mit den drei Frauen. (The Man with the three Wives.) Valse ... Piano solo. ⟨Arranged by H. M. Higgs.⟩ pp. 7. *Chappell & Cⁱᵉ: London,* [1908.] fol.　　**h. 1203. v. (2.)**

— Red Roses.—Rote Rosen.—Valse on Melodies from the Operetta "Der Mann mit den drei Frauen". [P. F.] *Chappell & Co.: London,* 1908. fol.　　**h. 3577. (11.)**

— Maxim's Song. *See* supra: [Die lustige Witwe.—O Vaterland.]

— Mazurka ... Op. 68. Arr.: Bruno Hartmann ... Orchester. [Parts.] 30 pt. *Bosworth & Co.: Köln, Wien,* [1963.] 8°.　　**h. 3210. i. (885.)**

— The Merry Widow. *See* supra: [Die lustige Witwe.]

— The Merry Widow Waltz. *See* supra: [Die lustige Witwe.— Lippen schweigen.]

— Mitislaw der Moderne. Operette in 1 Akt von F. Grünbaum u. R. Bodanzky ... Klavierauszug mit Text, *etc.* pp. 55. *Theater an der Wien: Wien,* [1905.] 8°.　　**F. 1424. e.**

— [Mitislaw der Moderne.] "Amaranthe". Valse on Melodies from the ... Operetta "Mitislaw". [P. F.] *Ascherberg, Hopwood & Crew: London,* 1910. fol.　　**h. 3577. (14.)**

— [Mitislaw der Moderne.] "Amaranthe". ⟨Valse.⟩ Franz Lehar. ⟨Arr. by M. Retford.⟩ ... "Gnats". ⟨Two-step.⟩ Roger Eckersley. ⟨Arr. by M. Retford.⟩ ... "Hello!" ⟨Two-step.⟩ Lawrence Vale. Arr. by A. H. Behrend. [Military band parts.] 33 pt. *Boosey & Co.: London,* 1911. fol. [*Boosey & Co.'s new supplemental Journal for military Bands. no.* 87.]　　**h. 1544. a.**

— Mon petit papa. *See* supra: [*Composite Works.*] [Rose de noël.]

— Napolitana. *See* infra: [Der Zarewitsch.]

— On my Lips every Kiss is like Wine. *See* supra: [Giuditta.—Meine Lippen, sie küssen so heiss.]

LEHÁR (Franz)

— One Hour of Love. *See* supra: [Eva.—Wär' es auch nichts als ein Traum.]

Paganini

— Paganini. Operette in drei Akten von Paul Knepler und Bela Jenbach ... Klavierauszug mit Text, *etc.* pp. 107. *Crescendo Theaterverlag: Berlin; Wien* [printed, 1925.] 4°.　　**G. 1344. o. (1.)**

— Paganini. Operette in drei Akten von Paul Knepler und Bela Jenbach ... Klavierauszug mit Text, *etc.* pp. 111. *Glocken-Verlag: Wien,* [1936.] 4°.　　**G. 1344. z. (1.)**

— Paganini. An Operette in 3 acts by Paul Knepler und Bela Jenbach, adapted by A. P. Herbert and Reginald Arkell. [Vocal score.] *Francis, Day & Hunter: London,* [1937.] 4°.　　**F. 943. n. (1.)**

— Franz Lehar's Paganini. A light opera in 3 acts by Paul Knepler and Bela Jenbach. The story and lyrics newly adapted and written by A. P. Herbert. Musical adaption [*sic*] by Harry Dexter. [Vocal score.] pp. 139. *Francis, Day & Hunter: London,* [1963.] 4°.　　**G. 1268. i. (2.)**

— Selection ... New orchestral edition by Ronald Hanmer, *etc.* [P. F. conductor and parts.] 34 pt. *Franz Lehár's Glocken Verlag: New York;* [*London* printed, 1955.] 4°. *The first violin A and percussion parts are in duplicate.*　　**h. 3210. i. (270.)**

— [Gern hab' ich die Frau'n geküsst.] Girls were made to love and kiss ... Arranged for mixed voices and pianoforte by John Clements. pp. 8. *Francis, Day & Hunter: London,* [1949.] 8°. [*F. D. H. choral Library. no.* 6.]　　**F. 672. l.**

— [Gern hab' ich die Frau'n geküsst.] Girls were made to love and kiss ... Orchestral arrangement by Len Stevens, *etc.* [P. F. conductor and parts.] 34 pt. *Franz Lehár's Glocken Verlag: New York;* [*Vienna* printed, 1955.] 4°. *The first violin A part is in duplicate.*　　**h. 3210. i. (271.)**

— [Liebe, du Himmel auf Erden.] Love live forever and rule my Heart ... Orchestration by Len Stevens, *etc.* [P. F. conductor and parts.] 35 pt. *Franz Lehár's Glocken Verlag: New York;* [*London* printed, 1955.] 4°. *The violins A and percussion parts are in duplicate.*　　**h. 3210. i. (272.)**

— Paradise Waltz. *See* infra: [Wiener Frauen.—Aber nur nicht verzagen.]

— Pariser-Pflaster. Marsch. *See* supra: [Eva.]

— Peter und Paul im Schlaraffenland. Operette für Kinder in einem Vorspiel und fünf Bildern von Robert Bodanzky und Fritz Grünbaum. [Vocal score.] pp. 59. *W. Karczag & C. Wallner: Wien,* [1907.] 4°.　　**G. 1344. c.**

— Pierrette and Pierrot. *See* supra: [Der Graf von Luxemburg.—Pièrre, der schreibt an klein Fleurette.]

— [Pikanterien-Walzer.] Piquant. Waltz. [P. F.] *J. W. Stern & Co.: New York, etc.,* (1911.) fol.　　**h. 3577. (18.)**

— [Pikanterien-Walzer.] Valse piquante ... Arranged by Ronald Hanmer. ⟨Piano-conductor [and orchestral parts].⟩ 24 pt. *Glocken Verlag: London,* [1959.] 4°.　　**h. 3210. i. (567.)**

— Piquant. *See* supra: [Pikanterien-Walzer.]

— Quite Parisian. *See* supra: [Die lustige Witwe.—I was born, by cruel fate, in a little Balkan State.]

Der Rastelbinder

— Der Rastelbinder. Operette in einem Vorspiel und zwei Acten, *etc.* ⟨Conducteur.⟩ [Vocal score.] pp. 232. *Josef Weinberger: Leipzig,* [1903.] fol.　　**H. 3616. e.**

LEHÁR (FRANZ)

— Der Rastelbinder. Operette in einem Vorspiel und zwei Acten von V. Léon ... Clavier-Auszug mit Text. *J. Weinberger: Leipzig*, [1903.] 4°.　　　　**G. 782. c. (1.)**

— Das is a einfache Rechnung.—That's a simple Example.— (Song.) English version by M. H. Rosenfeld ... Arr. by A. C. Ely. *J. W. Stern & Co.: New York, etc.*, (1909.) fol.　　**H. 3616. (11.)**

— Ich bin ein Wiener Kind. I am a Viennese. [Song.] English version by B. S. Simon ... Arr. by A. C. Ely. *J. W. Stern & Co.: New York, etc.*, [1909.] fol.　　**H. 3616. (21.)**

— Wenn zwei sich lieben.—When two love dearly.—(Song.) English version by M. H. Rosenfeld ... Arr. by A. C. Ely. *J. W. Stern & Co.: New York, etc.*, (1909.) fol.　　**H. 3616. (12.)**

— Red as the Rose of Maytime. *See* supra: [Die lustige Witwe.—Wie eine Rosenknospe.]

— Red Roses. *See* supra: [Der Mann mit den drei Frauen.— Ach, Rosen ohne Zahl.]

— Rootsie-Pootsie. *See* supra: [Der Graf von Luxemburg.— Since first I burst upon the scene.]

— Schön ist die Welt! Operette in 3 Akten von Ludwig Herzer und Fritz Löhner ... Klavierauszug mit Text. pp. 101. *W. Karczag: Leipzig, Wien*, [1930.] 8°.　　**G. 1344. d.**

— [Schön ist die Welt.] La Chanson du bonheur. Opérette en 3 actes et 8 tableaux. Livret français de André Mauprey ... Traduction de H. Geiringer ... Partition piano et chant, *etc.* pp. 131. *Éditions Salabert: Paris*, [1935.] fol.　　**H. 3616. f. (3.)**

— Serenade. *See* supra: [Frasquita.—Hab' ein blaues Himmelbett.]

— Serenade (A-dur) für Violine und Klavier. [Parts.] 2 pt. *Glocken-Verlag: Wien*, [1941.] fol.　　**h. 1613. h. (8.)**

— Shine bright Moon. *See* supra: [Die blaue Mazur.—Was sich ein Mädchen erträumt.]

— The Staircase Dance. *See* supra: [Der Graf von Luxemburg.—Are you going to Dance?]

— The Stargazer. *See* infra: [Der Sterngucker.]

— Stay with me for ever. *See* supra: [Giuditta.—Du bist meine Sonne.]

— Der Sterngucker. Operette in 3 Akten von Dr. Fritz Löhner und Dr. A. M. Willner ... Klavierauszug mit Text, *etc.* pp. 91. *W. Karczag: Leipzig, Wien*, [1916.] 4°.　**G. 1344. p. (1.)**

— Der Sterngucker ... Potpourri. Ausgabe für Klavier zu zwei Händen mit beigefügtem Text. pp. 15. *W. Karczag: Leipzig, etc.*, [1916.] fol.　　**H. 1653. nn. (3.)**

— [Der Sterngucker.] The Stargazer. Operetta in 3 acts ... book by C. Hamilton, lyrics by M. Woodward, *etc.* [Nine detached no.] *Karczag Publishing Co.: New York*, 1917. fol.　　**H. 3616. b. (7.)**

— Die Tangokönigin. Operette in drei Akten von Julius Brammer und Alfred Grünwald ... Klavierauszug mit Text, *etc.* pp. 127. *Ludwig Doblinger: Leipzig, Wien*, [1921.] 4°.　　**G. 1344. n.**

— Tatjana. Oper in 3 Acten (4 Bildern). Text von Felix Falzari u. Max Kalbeck ... Klavierauszug mit Text. pp. 183. *Emil Berté & cie: Wien*, [1909.] 8°.　　**G. 1344. e.**

— The Three Graces. *See* supra: [Libellentanz.]

— To-night will teach me to forget. *See* supra: [Die lustige Witwe.]

LEHÁR (FRANZ)

— Valse piquante. *See* supra: [Pikanterien-Walzer.]

— Valse-Song. *See* supra: [Der Graf von Luxemburg.—Say not love is a dream.]

— Viennese Ladies. *See* infra: [Wiener Frauen.]

— Vilia. *See* supra: [Die lustige Witwe.—Es lebt eine Vilja.]

— Eine Vision. (Meine Jugend.) Ouverture ... Für grosses Orchester. Partitur, *etc.* pp. 42. *Ludwig Doblinger: Leipzig, Wien*, [1907.] fol.　　**h. 1564. k. (1.)**

— Walzer (aus der Komödie "Walzer" von Georg Ruttkay). [P. F.] pp. 7. *Ludwig Krenn: Wien*, [1917.] fol.　　**h. 3577. c. (1.)**

— Wenn zwei sich lieben. *See* supra: [Der Rastelbinder.]

— When your Lips pressed mine. *See* supra: [Die lustige Witwe.—Lippen schweigen.]

— Where the Lark sings. *See* infra: [Wo die Lerche singt.]

Wiener Frauen

— Wiener Frauen. Operette in 3 Akte von Ottokar Tann-Bergler und Emil Norini ... Klavier-Auszug 2/ms mit Text. pp. 119. *Emil Berté & cie: Wien*, [1904.] 8°. P. 119 *is followed by the words only of no.* 1–4, 10a–16.　　**G. 1344. f.**

— Wiener Frauen. Operette in 3 Akten von Ottokar Tann-Bergler und Emil Norini ... Klavierauszug mit Text. pp. 110. *W. Karczag: Leipzig, etc.*, [c. 1915.] 4°.　　**G. 1344. aa. (1.)**

— Ouvertüre ... Salonorchester-Arrangement von Viktor Hruby nach der Original-Partitur des Komponisten. ⟨Klavier-Kondukteur.⟩ pp. 15. *W. Karczag: Leipzig, etc.*, [1928.] 8°.　　**e. 670. c. (6.)**

— Overture from ... Viennese Ladies ... Orchestration by Harry Dexter, *etc.* [P. F. conductor and parts]. 35 pt. *Franz Lehár's Glocken Verlag: New York;* [*London* printed, 1955.] 4°. *The percussion part is in duplicate.*　　**h. 3210. i. (273.)**

— Overture from ... Viennese Ladies ... Arranged for military band by Roger Barsotti. [Conductor and parts.] 22 pt. *Glocken Verlag: London*, [1957.] 4°. *Various parts are in duplicate.*　　**h. 3210. i. (388.)**

— Overture to the Operetta Viennese Ladies ... Arranged for brass band by Roger Barsotti. [Solo B flat cornet conductor and parts.] 25 pt. *Glocken Verlag: London*, [1957.] fol. *With several copies of various parts.*　　**h. 3210. i. (387.)**

— [Aber nur nicht verzagen.] Paradise Waltz from ... "Viennese Ladies". Arranged and orchestrated by Harry Dexter. Piano conductor [and parts]. 15 pt. *Franz Lehár's Glocken Verlag: New York, London;* [*London* printed, 1955.] 4°.　　**h. 3210. i. (274.)**

— [Aber nur nicht verzagen.] The Paradise Waltz ... Arranged for brass band by Roger Barsotti. ⟨Solo B♭ cornet conductor [and parts].⟩ 14 pt. *Glocken Verlag: London*, [1958.] 4°. *With several copies of various parts.*　　**h. 3210. i. (482.)**

— [Endlich allein mit Dir allein.] The Love Theme from Viennese Ladies ... Arranged for orchestra by Harry Dexter, *etc.* [P. F. conductor and parts.] 34 pt. *Franz Lehár's Glocken Verlag: New York;* [*Vienna* printed, 1955.] 4°. *The first violin A part is in duplicate.*　　**h. 3210. i. (275.)**

— [Ein hohes und frohes vergeistertes Lied.] English Lasses. Song, words by A. Ross. *Chappell & Co.: London and Melbourne*, 1905. fol.　　**H. 1794. l. (2.)**

— [Nechledil Marsch.] Viennese Ladies. March ... Orchestrated by R. Hanmer. ⟨Piano conductor [and orchestral parts].⟩ 18 pt. *Glocken Verlag: London*, [1959.] 4°.　　**h. 3210. i. (568.)**

LEHÁR (Franz)

— [Nechledil Marsch.] Viennese Ladies ... March. Arranged by Allan Street. ⟨Conductor B♭ [and brass band parts].⟩ 24 pt. *Glocken Verlag: London*, [1963.] 8°.
Various parts are in duplicate.   **h. 3210. i. (886.)**

— Wiener Frauen. Valse. [P. F.] *Chappell & Co.: London*, 1906. fol.   **h. 3577. (10.)**

— Wilde Rosen. Walzer ... für Klavier 2/ms. pp. 5. *Glocken-Verlag: Wien*, [1943.] fol.   **h. 3577. c. (2.)**

— Wo die Lerche singt ... Operette in drei Akten (nach einem Entwurf des Dr. Franz Martos) von Dr. A. M. Willner und Heinz Reichert ... Klavierauszug mit Text, *etc.* pp. 115. *W. Karczag: Leipzig, Wien*, [1918.] 4°.   **F. 1424. c.**

— Wo die Lerche singt ... Operette in vier Bildern (nach einem Entwurf des Dr. Franz Martos) von A. M. Willner und Heinz Reichert ... Klavierauszug mit Text. pp. 108. *Glocken-Verlag: Wien*, [1937.] 4°.   **G. 1344. v. (3.)**

— [Wo die Lerche singt.] Selection ... from ... "Where the Lark sings" ... Orchestration by Ronald Hanmer, *etc.* [P. F. conductor and parts.] 27 pt. *Franz Lehár's Glocken Verlag: New York; [London* printed, 1955.] 4°.
The violin A part is in duplicate.   **h. 3210. i. (276.)**

— [Wo die Lerche singt.] Where the Lark sings ... ⟨Selection of waltz melodies from "Where the Lark sings".⟩ Orchestration by Len Stevens. Piano conductor [and parts]. 12 pt. *Franz Lehár's Glocken Verlag: New York, London; [London* printed, 1955.] 4°.   **h. 3210. i. (277.)**

— You, only you. *See supra:* [Grossfürstin Alexandra.—Du und ich sind füreinander bestimmt.]

Der Zarewitsch

— Der Zarewitsch. Operette in 3 Akten von Bela Jenbach und Heinz Reichert. (Frei nach Zapolska-Scharlitt) ... Vollständiger Klavierauszug mit Text, *etc.* pp. 114. *Drei Masken-Verlag: Berlin*, [1927.] 4°.   **F. 1424. d.**

— Der Zarewitsch. Operette in drei Akten. (Frei nach Zapolska-Scharlitt) ... Vollständiger Klavierauszug mit Text. Original-Ausgabe des Komponisten. (Neue Fassung.) pp. 107. *Glocken-Verlag: Wien*, [1937.] 4°.   **G. 1344. z. (3.)**

— The Czarevitch. Operetta in three acts ... Original book and lyrics by Heinz Reichert & Bela Jenbach (adapted from Zapolska-Scharlitt). English version by Adam Carstairs. Vocal score of the revised version by the composer. pp. 107. *Glocken-Verlag: London*, [1980.] 4°.   **G. 1344. bb. (2.)**

— Songs from the Czarevitch. Original book and lyrics by Heinz Reichert and Bela Jenbach. English by Adam Carstairs. pp. 26. *Glocken Verlag: London*, [1973.] 4°.   **G. 1344. w. (2.)**

— Selection of Music from F. Lehár's Operetta "Czarevitch" ... Book and lyrics by Bela Jenbach and Heinz Reichert. Orchestration by Ronald Hanmer, *etc.* [P. F. conductor and orchestral parts.] 33 pt. *Franz Lehár's Glocken Verlag: New York; [London* printed, 1955.] 4°.
The first violin A part is in duplicate.   **h. 3210. i. (268.)**

— Napolitana ... Arranged by Len Stevens. Piano conductor [and orchestral parts.] 16 pt. *Franz Lehár's Glocken Verlag: New York, London; [London* printed, 1955.] 4°.   **h. 3210. i. (269.)**

Zigeunerliebe

— Zigeunerliebe. Romantische Operette in 3 Bildern. Text von A. M. Willner und Rob. Bodanzky, *etc.* [Score.] pp. 452. 43. *W. Karczag & K. Wallner: Wien, Leipzig*, [1910.] fol.   **H. 3616. d.**

LEHÁR (Franz)

— Zigeunerliebe. Romantische Operette ... Klavierauszug mit Text, *etc.* pp. 165. *W. Karczag & C. Wallner: Wien*, [1909.] 4°.   **G. 1344. r.**

— Gypsy love. A Romantic Comic Opera in Three Acts, book by H. B. Smith, lyrics by H. B. and R. B. Smith, from the German by A. M. Willner and R. Bodanzky. Vocal Score. pp. 157. *Chappell & Co.: New York, etc.*, 1911. 4°.   **F. 1424. a. (2.)**

— Gipsy Love. New musical play in three acts. Book by A. M. Willner and Robert Bodanzky. English libretto by Basil Hood. Lyrics by Adrian Ross ... Vocal score. *etc.* pp. 216. *Chappell & Co.: London*, [1912.] 4°.   **F. 1424. g.**

— Zigeunerliebe. Romantische Operette in 3 Akten von A. M. Willner und Robert Bodanzky ... Klavierauszug mit Text, *etc.* pp. 162. *Glocken-Verlag: Wien*, [1938.] 4°.   **G. 1344. cc.**

— Gipsy Love. Operetta ... New book and lyrics by Phil Park ... Music adapted and arranged by Ronald Hanmer. Vocal score, *etc.* pp. 183. *Glocken Verlag: London*, [1964.] 4°.   **G. 1344. s. (8.)**

— Gipsy Love ... Pianoforte Solo, arranged by H. M. Higgs. *Chappell & Co.: London, etc.*, 1912. 4°.   **f. 540. dd. (2.)**

— Gipsy Love, *etc.* [Ten detached vocal no.] *Chappell & Co.: New York, etc.*, 1911. fol.   **H. 3616. (20.)**

— Gipsy Love. [Eight detached no.] *Chappell & Co.: London*, 1912. fol.   **H. 3616. b. (5.)**

— Songs from Gipsy Love ... Original book and lyrics by A. M. Willner and R. Bodanzky. English by Adam Carstairs. *Eng. & Ger.* pp. 24. *Glocken Verlag: London*, [1976.] 4°.   **F. 1198. r. (3.)**

— Gipsy Love. Selection. Selected and arranged by H. M. Higgs. [Parts for full and small orchestra.] 2 no. *Chappell & Co.: London*, [1912.] 4°.
[*Chappell & Co.'s Operatic and popular Selections for Orchestra by various Composers. no.* 106.]   **f. 424.**

— Zigeunerliebe. Melodienfolge. Gekürzte Fassung ... Blasmusik. Neues Arrangement: Alfred Hofbauer. ⟨Neue Ausgabe. Direktion in B [and parts].⟩ 52 pt. *Glocken-Verlag: Chur; printed in Austria*, [1978.] 8°.
Various parts are in duplicate.   **h. 3210. j. (983.)**

— Zigeunerliebe ... Selection. (Arranged by C. Lucas.) [P. F.] *Chappell & Co.: New York, etc.*, (1911.) fol.   **h. 3577. (29.)**

— Selection ... Arranged for the Pianoforte by H. M. Higgs. *Chappell & Co.: London, etc.*, 1912. fol.   **h. 3577. (16.)**

— Gipsy Love Lancers. On melodies from the musical play ... Arranged by H. M. Higgs. Piano solo, *etc.* pp. 9. *Chappell & Co.: London*, [1912.] fol.   **h. 61. p. (26.)**

— Gipsy Love ... Valse on Melodies from the Operetta ... Piano Solo. *Chappell & Co.: London, etc.*, 1911. fol.   **h. 3577. (30.)**

— Waltzes from Gipsy Love ... Arranged by Ronald Hanmer. [Orchestra.] ⟨Piano-conductor.⟩ pp. 8. *Glocken Verlag: London*, [1963.] 4°.   **g. 1780. r. (4.)**

— *See* BROWN (Albert W.) and LEHÁR (F.) Hello! hello! ... [Song.] Music by A. W. Brown and F. Lehar, [or rather, the music apparently by Brown alone, sung in the operetta "Der Mann mit den drei Frauen" by Lehár]. [1913.] fol.   **H. 3989. qq. (27.)**

— *See* GRUN (Bernard) Rhapsody on Lehár Melodies ... Adapted and arranged by B. Grun, *etc.* [1959.] 4°.   **h. 3210. i. (570.)**

LÉHÉMAN

— Léhéman, ou la Tour de Neustadt. Opéra. *See* DALAYRAC (N.)

LEHEY (JACK)

— *See* MACK (Johnny) How'd you like to be Mary? ... ⟨The barn-dance song.⟩ Arrangement by J. Lahey. [1908.] fol.
H. 3985. ii. (46.)

LEHFELDT (MARIA)

— Fairest of all. Waltz. [P. F.] *Weekes & Co.: London*, [1888.] fol.
h. 975. v. (7.)

— Up! quit thy bow'r. Song, words by J. Baillie. *London*, [1881.] fol.
H. 1787. j. (27.)

LEHMAN (EVANGELINE)

— Bois de Boulogne. A set of six Songs for Medium Voice ... Words and music by E. Lehman. *G. Schirmer: New York*, 1935. 4°.
G. 1275. pp. (9.)

LEHMAN (ROSALIND)

— In the Valley by the Stream. [Song.] Words by Allen J. Wiener and Edna C. Ullman. pp. 3–5. *Plunkett & Co.: [New York, 1906.] fol.*
H. 3985. q. (26.)

LEHMAN (SAMUEL)

— Danny Tucker. (An American intermezzo.) Two-step. [P. F.] *Plunkett & Co.: [New York, 1906.] fol.*
h. 4120. oo. (6.)

— Everybody works but Father. ⟨Song.⟩ Words by Chas. W. McClintock. pp. 5. *Jos. W. Stern & Co.: New York*, [1905.] fol.
H. 3985. q. (27.)

— He is a Piker. [Song.] Written by Edward Laska. pp. 5. *Edward Laska & Samuel Lehman: New York*, [1905.] fol.
H. 3985. q. (28.)

— Hoot Mon. [Song.] Lyric by Edward Laska. pp. 2–5. *Plunkett & Co.: New York*, [1906.] fol.
H. 3985. q. (29.)

— It's a very pleasant Day. [Song.] Lyric by Edw. Laska. pp. 2–5. *Plunkett & Co.: New York*, [1906.] fol.
H. 3985. q. (30.)

— [Little Indian Maid.] My little Indian Maid. [Song.] Words by Maurice Stonehill. pp. 5. *T. B. Harms & Co.: [New York*, 1904.] fol.
H. 3985. q. (31.)

— Little Indian Maid. March intermezzo. [P. F.] pp. 5. *T. B. Harms & Co.: New York*, [1904.] fol.
h. 4120. oo. (7.)

— My California Belle. [Song.] Lyrics by Edward Laska. pp. 3–5. *Plunkett & Co.: New York*, [1906.] fol.
H. 3985. q. (32.)

— My little Indian Maid. *See* supra: [Little Indian Maid.]

— My Little Seaside Girl. [Song.] Words by Robert A. Ullman. *Wolf & Co.: Philadelphia*, [1907.] fol.
H. 3985. q. (33.)

— Since my poor Joe's gone ... Negro lullaby. pp. 5. *Plunkett & Co.: New York*, [1906.] fol.
H. 3985. q. (34.)

— "Texas." An American intermezzo. [P. F.] pp. 2–5. *Franklin-Barrett Co.: New York*, [1907.] fol.
h. 4120. oo. (8.)

— When Cupid comes a-tapping. [Song.] Lyric by Lloyd Barret. pp. 2–5. *Franklin-Barret Co.: New York*, [1906.] fol.
H. 3985. q. (35.)

— When two Hearts beat as one. [Song.] Lyric by David Kemp. pp. 3–5. *Plunkett & Co.: New York*, [1906.] fol.
H. 3985. q. (36.)

LEHMAN (SAMUEL)

— Won't you come down little Moonbeam. [Song.] Lyric by David Kemp. pp. 2–5. *Plumkett [sic] & Co.: New York*, [1906.] fol.
H. 3985. q. (37.)

— Wow wow wow ... [Song.] Words by W. Murdoch Lind. pp. 5. *Plunkett & Co.: New York*, [1905.] fol.
H. 3985. q. (38.)

LEHMAN (SAMUEL) and JOHNSON (ROSAMOND)

— Everybody works but Father ... Two step ... Arr. by Wm. M. Redfield. [Orchestral parts.] 12 pt. *Jos. W. Stern & Co.: [New York*, 1905.] 8°.
f. 800. (809.)

LEHMAN (WILLIAM)

— Des Moines City waltz. [P. F.] *Chicago*, 1864. fol.
h. 1459. g. (10.)

LEHMAN (ADOLPH VON) *Baron*

— *See* LEHMANN (F. A. von)

LEHMANN (AMELIA)

— *See* L., A.

LEHMANN (CARL)

— Gavotte for the pianoforte. Op. 5. *Novello, Ewer & Co.: London & New York*, [1891.] fol.
g. 605. f. (15.)

LEHMANN (CH. E.)

— Le Calme du Soir, mélodie-rêverie pour Piano. *Paris*, [1867.] fol.
h. 1462. r. (35.)

— Haÿda. 2e. mazurka pour le Piano. *Paris*, [1868.] fol.
h. 1462. r. (36.)

— Valse brillante pour le Piano. *Paris*, [1868.] fol.
h. 1462. r. (37.)

LEHMANN (EMILE)

— Testament d'un Volontaire Pontifical, mourant dans la Chapelle de Lorette. [Solo and chorus, begins: "Sa blessure est mortale".] Paroles du R. P. J. Perrollaz. *Paris*, [1869.] fol.
H. 1774. e. (23.)

LEHMANN (ERNEST)

— Heraclitus. *See* infra: Two Songs. No. 1.

— Two Songs. 1. Heraclitus. 2. Remember. Words by W. J. Cory. *Augener: London*, [1910.] fol.
G. 807. yy. (30.)

— [Another edition.] Two Songs. 1. Heraclitus, *etc. Augener: London*, [1910.] fol.
G. 807. yy. (31.)

LEHMANN (ERWIN)

— 3 Morceaux pour piano. [No. 1.] Op. 26. In the moonlight. [No. 2.] Op. 27. Golden blossoms. [No. 3.] Op. 28. Marjolaine. 3 no. *Schott & Co.: London*, 1915. fol.
g. 606. bb. (27.)

LEHMANN (FRIEDRICH ADOLPH VON) *Baron*

— Sieben Englische Lieder mit Deutscher Uebersetzung und Begleitung des Fortepianos, *etc. Berlin*, [1820?] obl. fol.
F. 636. t. (1.)

— [Sieben Englische Lieder. No. 3.] Mary's Dream. *Eng. & Ger.* [1803.] 4°. [*Beilage zur Allgemeinen musikalischen Zeitung. Jahrg. 6. no. 2.*] *See* MARY.

LEHMANN (FRIEDRICH ADOLPH VON) *Baron*

— The Grand Leipzig March and Troop, or Waltz, for the piano forte or harp, *etc. C. Wheatstone: London*, [WM 1811.] fol. **H. 1648. n. (6.)**

LEHMANN (FRITZ)

— 20 der bekanntesten ... Choräle, zur Benutzung neben jeder Klavierschule ... harmonisirt und herausgegeben von F. Lehmann. Op. 2. *A. Fürstner: Berlin*, [1883.] *obl.* 4°. **d. 210. b. (2.)**

LEHMANN (GUSTAV)

— Happy Thoughts. Educational Pieces for the Piano. 1. Thoughts of Fairyland. 2. The Garden enchanted. 3. Chasing Butterflies. 4. Woodland Nymphs. 5. Fairy Haunt. 6. Whims and Fancies. 6 no. *Beal, Stuttard & Co.: London*, 1912. fol. **h. 3284. g. (6.)**

LEHMANN (HANS ULRICH)

— Episoden für Bläserquintett ... Spielpartitur. *Ars Viva Verlag: Mainz*, [1965.] fol.
Consisting of preliminaries and Blatt 1–16. **h. 2784. jj. (2.)**

— Instants pour piano. (1968.) pp. 5. *Ars viva Verlag: Mainz*, [1971.] fol. **h. 1568. kk. (4.)**

— Monodie für ein Blasinstrument (1970). pp. 5. *Ars viva Verlag: Mainz*, [1973.] 4°. **g. 1796. (1.)**

— Régions III. Für Klarinette, Posaune und Violoncello ... (1970). Studien-Partitur. pp. 15. *Ars viva Verlag: Mainz*, [1972.] 4°. **g. 1780. vv. (2.)**

LEHMANN (HENRY)

— The Rose of Yesterday ... Valse-Idyll ... Piano Solo. *Keith, Prowse & Co.: London*, 1912. fol. **h. 3284. g. (7.)**

LEHMANN (J. G.)

— Choralbuch, enthaltend eine Auswahl von 272 ... Kirchengesänge in vierstimmiger Bearbeitung ... Nebst einem Anhange, bestehend aus 69 von J. S. Bach ... herausgegeben von J. G. Lehmann. Op. 15. Dritte Auflage. *Breitkopf & Härtel: Leipzig*, [1873.] *obl.* 4°. **d. 191.**

— Liederalbum. 60 Gesänge verschiedener Componisten für eine Singstimme mit Begleitung des Pianoforte ... ausgewählt von J. G. Lehmann. *Leipzig*, [1875.] 8°. **F. 418.**

— Theoretisch-praktische Elementar-Violinschule herausgegeben von J. G. Lehmann. Op. 20. *Breitkopf & Härtel: Leipzig*, [1878.] fol. **g. 617.**

LEHMANN (JENNIFER)

— *See* HOLBORNE (Antony) [Pauans, Galiards, Almains and other short Æirs. No. 3, 32, 4, 56.] Dances, grave and light. For recorder quintet ... Edited by D. Dana and J. Lehmann. [1967.] 4°. **g. 109. bb. (5.)**

LEHMANN (KAREN MARIA)

— *See* WEBER (R.) Bilder und Träume. Lieder aus alter und neuer Zeit für Singstimme und Klavier. ⟨Herausgegeben von R. Weber unter Mitarbeit von K.-M. Lehmann.⟩ [1969.] 4°. **G. 809. s. (7.)**

LEHMANN, afterwards **BEDFORD** (LIZA)

— [The Daisy Chain. More Daisies.] Selection from the two Cycles ... arranged for the Pianoforte by A. Schmid. *Boosey & Co.: London*, 1903. fol. **h. 3282. kk. (27.)**

LEHMANN, afterwards **BEDFORD** (LIZA)

— Liza Lehmann Album. [Songs.] Low (High). 2 no. *Chappell & Co.: London, etc.*, [1909.] 4°.
Part of "The Portrait Series". **G. 1121. (5.)**

— Nine Favourite Soprano Songs. *Boosey & Co.: London and New York*, [1911.] 4°. **G. 425. g. (2.)**

— Abou Ben Adhem and the Angel. Song, words by L. Hunt, *etc. Chappell & Co.: London, etc.*, 1910. fol. **H. 3601. c. (1.)**

— Ah! gather Roses. *See* infra: [The Twin Sister.]

— Ah, Moon of my Delight. *See* infra: [In a Persian Garden.]

— "The Air of Courts may be sweet." *See* infra: [The Vicar of Wakefield.]

— Alabaster. *See* infra: [The Golden Threshold.]

— Alas! that Spring should vanish with the Rose. *See* infra: [In a Persian Garden.]

— Album of nine English Songs. [Words of no. 2, 4 and 9 by Shakespeare, of no. 3 and 7 by Shelley, no. 5 by Coleridge, and no. 6 by Moore.] *Boosey & Co.: London and New York*, 1895. 4°. **G. 385. j. (7.)**

— Album of German Songs, with English translations. *S. Lucas, Weber & Co.: London*, [1889.] 4°. **F. 636. j. (7.)**

— Album of twelve German Songs with English Translations. *J. Williams: London*, [1902.] 4°.
No. 216 of J. Williams's Albums. **F. 1619.**

— Album of ten pianoforte sketches. *Chappell & Co.: London*, [1892.] 4°. **f. 133. f. (11.)**

— Album of five Tenor Songs. *Chappell & Co.: London, etc.*, 1913. fol. **H. 3601. d. (13.)**

— "Amoroso." [Song.] Three Epigrams by W. Watson, *etc. Boosey & Co.: London and New York*, 1908. fol. **H. 3601. b. (25.)**

— As Bess one Day. *See* infra: [The Vicar of Wakefield.]

— At Love's Beginning. Duet for Soprano and Baritone, the words by T. Campbell. *Boosey & Co.: London and New York*, 1903. fol. **H. 3601. a. (10.)**

— At Sunset — A Slumber Song — The Words by E. O. Cooke. *Boosey & Co.: London and New York*, 1901. fol. **H. 3601. a. (1.)**

— At the Gate. Song, the poem by Lord Tennyson, *etc. Boosey & Co.: London & New York*, 1912. fol. **H. 3601. d. (1.)**

— Aunt Eliza. Song, the words by A. L. Harris. 2 no. [In C and E flat.] *Ascherberg, Hopwood & Crew.: London*, 1912. fol. **H. 3601. c. (2.)**

— The Beautiful Lady. Song, words by W. De la Mare. *Elkin & Co.: London*, 1912. fol. **H. 3601. d. (2.)**

— The Beautiful Land of Nod. Song, the words by E. W. Wilcox, *etc. Boosey & Co.: London and New York*, 1908. fol. **H. 3601. b. (26.)**

— Beautiful Maiden. Song, the words ... from the Polish of Brodzinski by J. Bowring. *Metzler & Co.: London*, 1895. fol. **H. 3601. (8.)**

— The Bee. See infra: [The Life of a Rose.]

— Behind the Nightlight. Hibbertoo and other Animals invented by Joan Maude ... recorded by her mother — N. Price, with Incidental Music ... by L. Lehmann. [P. F.] *Boosey & Co.: London and New York*, 1913. 4°. **g. 232. x. (8.)**

LEHMANN, afterwards BEDFORD (LIZA)

— Two Biblical Songs. No. 1. By the Rivers of Babylon ...
No. 2. Recit: Surely there is a Mine for Silver ... Arioso,
Happy is the Man who findeth Wisdom, *etc. Metzler & Co.:
London*, 1913. 4°.   **G. 390. i. (8.)**

— A Bird in the Sky. Song, words by W. M. Anderson, *etc.
Metzler & Co.: London*, 1926. 4°.   **G. 1270. t. (29.)**

— Bird Songs. [No. 1.] The Woodpigeon. [No. 2.] The
Yellowhammer. [No. 3.] The Starling. [No. 4.] The Wren.
[No. 5.] The Owl. The words by A. S. [For soprano.] *Boosey
& Co.: London and New York*, 1907. 4°.   **G. 383. r. (5.)**

— Bird Songs. The woodpigeon. The yellowhammer. The
starling. The wren. The owl. The words by A. S. ⟨For
mezzo-soprano.⟩ pp. 25. *Boosey & Co.: London*, [c. 1910.] 4°.
                                            G. 383. ii. (1.)

— [Bird Songs. No. 3.] The Starling, *etc. Boosey & Co.: London
and New York*, 1907. fol.   **H. 3601. b. (36.)**

— The Birth of the Flowers. Quartet for female voices, words by
M. L. Ryley. *Chappell & Co.: London, etc.*, 1916. 8°.
[*Chappell's Vocal Library of Part-Songs. New Series. No. 178.*]
                                                      G. 440.

— Bleak Weather. Song, the words by E. W. Wilcox, *etc.
Boosey & Co.: London and New York*, 1908. fol.
                                            H. 3601. b. (27.)

— [Bleak Weather.] Love in a Mist. Song, the words by E. W.
Wilcox, *etc. Boosey & Co.: London and New York*, 1908. fol.
                                            H. 3601. b. (28.)

— Blind Cupid. Song, the words by Shakespeare. *Boosey &
Co.: London and New York*, 1895. fol.   **H. 3601. (9.)**

— The Bobbie's Beano. *See infra*: [Sergeant Brue.]

— Bonnie wee Thing. Song, the words by R. Burns, *etc. Boosey
& Co.: London & New York*, 1912. fol.   **H. 3601. d. (3.)**

— Breton Folk-songs. The lyrics written ... by Frances
M. Gostling. Set to music (for soprano, contralto, tenor and
bass) by Liza Lehmann. pp. 74. *Chappell & Co.: London*,
[1909.] 4°.   **G. 935. (4.)**

— By the Lake. Song, poem by E. Clifford, *etc. Daily
Telegraph: London*, 1914. 4°.
Pp. 110 and 111 of "King Albert's Book".   **K. T. C. 104. b. 3.**

— Cameos. Five Greek Love-Songs. The poems translated from
Rufinus, Meleager, Paul the Silentiary, and anon., by J. M.
Sedgwick. *Enoch & Sons: London*, 1901. 4°.
                                              G. 424. k. (11.)

— [Cameos. No. 4.] Greek Love-Song, *etc. Enoch & Sons:
London*, [1903.] fol.   **H. 3601. a. (18.)**

— The Castilian Maid. Song, the words by T. Moore. *Boosey &
Co.: London*, [1890.] fol.   **H. 3601. (1.)**

— Four Cautionary Tales and a Moral. Set for two voices, solos
and duets (contralto or mezzo-soprano and baritone, bass or
tenor). The verses by Hilaire Belloc. pp. 43. *Chappell & Co.:
London, etc.*, [c. 1925.] 4°.   **G. 1276. nn. (21.)**

— A Child's Prayer. *See infra*: [More Daisies. no. 11.]

— Six Celebrated Classic Songs—Series III.—Edited by
L. Lehmann. English adaptations by R. H. Elkin, *etc. Elkin
& Co.: London*, 1920. 4°.
*Series I. and II. edited by A. Randegger are catalogued
separately.*   **G. 390. y. (32.)**

— Clementina's Song.—A Maiden sat at her Casement wide.—
[Song.] Words adapted from a Polish Folk Song, *etc.* 3 no. [In
F minor, G minor and A minor.] *Chappell & Co.: London,
etc.*, 1910. fol.   **H. 3601. c. (3.)**

LEHMANN, afterwards BEDFORD (LIZA)

— Cobweb Castle. Arranged for orchestra by H. M. Higgs.
[Orchestral parts.] 17 pt. *Chappell & Co.: London*, [1919.] 4°.
[*Chappell & Co.'s Operatic and popular Selections for
Orchestra by various Composers. no. 133.*]   **f. 424.**

— Le Colibri. *See infra*: Five French Songs. [No. 3.]

— Come, dance the Romaika. Song, the words ... by T. Moore.
Boosey & Co.: London, 1891. fol.   **H. 3601. (2.)**

— Country Courtship. *See infra*: [Hips and Haws. No. 2.]

— Cowboy Ballads. I. The Rancher's Daughter. II. Night-herding
Song. III. The Skew-ball Black. The words taken from
"Cowboy Songs and other Frontier Ballads," collected by
J. A. Lomax, *etc. Chappell & Co.: London, etc.*, 1912. 4°.
                                              G. 385. ss. (6.)

— Cruikston Castle.—Es tost um Cruikston.—Old Gaelic Song,
English words by Tannahill, German translation by
B. Marchesi. Arranged by L. Lehmann. *J. Williams: London*,
(1904.) fol.   **H. 3601. b. (1.)**

— The Cuckoo. *See infra*: [More Daisies. No. 7.]

— Cupid and the Rose. Song, the words by A. Perceval. *Boosey
& Co.: London and New York*, 1902. fol.   **H. 3601. a. (12.)**

— Daddy's Sweetheart. Song, words by C. Hardin-Burnley. 3 no.
[In F, G and B flat.] *Chappell & Co.: London, etc.*, 1911. fol.
                                            H. 3601. c. (4.)

— Daddy's Sweetheart. Duet, or Two-part Song. Arranged by
C. Lucas, *etc. Chappell-Harms: New York*, 1928. 8°.
                                            E. 263. h. (13.)

— Daddy's Sweetheart. Arranged for Female Trio ... by
C. Lucas, *etc. Chappell-Harms: London*, 1928. 8°.
                                            F. 217. d. (3.)

— The Daisy Chain ... Song, the words by A. P. Graves.
Boosey & Co.: London and New York, 1893. fol.
                                              H. 3601. (10.)

— The Daisy-Chain. Twelve Songs of Childhood to be sung by
four Solo Voices ... with Pianoforte Accompaniment. The
Words by L. Alma Tadema, R. L. Stevenson, N. Gale, W. B.
Rands and Anon. *Boosey & Co.: London & New York*, 1900.
4°.   **G. 424. h. (3.)**

— [The Daisy Chain. No. 5.] Stars. Song, *etc. Boosey & Co.:
London and New York*, [1903.] fol.   **H. 3601. a. (33.)**

— [The Daisy-Chain. No. 8.] The Swing. Song, *etc. Boosey &
Co.: London and New York*, 1900. fol.   **H. 3601. a. (7.)**

— The Daisy's Wedding. Two-part Song, words by T. Hood.
1918. *See* DUNHILL (T. F.) Singing Class Music, *etc.* No. 127.
1918. *etc.* 8°.   **E. 802.**

— Dear little Heart. *See infra*: [Sergeant Brue.]

— The Dewdrop. Song, the words by R. B. Birnbaum. *Boosey
& Co.: London and New York*, 1905. fol.   **H. 3601. b. (2.)**

— Didn't you know? Song, words by G. Gould, *etc.* 2 no. [In C
and E flat.] *Chappell & Co.: London, etc.* 1914. fol.
                                            H. 3601. c. (19.)

— Dream-Birds.—O Light-of-Heart.—Song, the words by W. L.
Randell. *Boosey & Co.: London and New York*, 1907. fol.
                                            H. 3601. b. (30.)

— [Dream-Birds.] O Light-of-Heart. Song, *etc. Boosey & Co.:
London and New York*, 1907. fol.   **H. 3601. b. (31.)**

— Dusk in the Valley. *See infra*: Three Songs, *etc.* [No. 2.]

— The Dustman. Song, words by M. E. Lowndes. 3 no. [In E
flat, F and G.] *Chappell & Co.: London, etc.*, 1912. fol.
                                            H. 3601. c. (20.)

LEHMANN, afterwards **BEDFORD** (Liza)

— Echoes. Song, words by J. T. White. 3 no. [In B flat, C and E flat.] *Chappell & Co.: London, etc.,* 1914. fol.
H. 3601. c. (21.)

— Endymion. [Scena.] For Soprano. [Words by] Longfellow. *J. Church & Co.: [Cincinnati,]* 1899. fol. **H. 3601. (27.)**

— Endymion ... Arranged for four-part chorus of women's voices. *J. Church & Co.: Cincinnati, etc.* 1917. 8°.
F. 943. d. (2.)

— The Eternal Feminine. A Musical Monologue, by L. Eldée. *Chappell & Co.: London,* 1902. 4°. **G. 782. (3.)**

— [The Eternal Feminine.] The Letter Song ... Written by L. Eldée. *Chappell & Co.: London,* 1902. fol.
H. 3601. a. (4.)

— [The Eternal Feminine.] To a careless Lover. Song ... Written by L. Eldée. *Chappell & Co.: London,* 1902. fol.
H. 3601. a. (8.)

— Eulalie. Song, the words by S. M. Peck. *Boosey & Co.: London and New York,* 1892. fol. **H. 3601. (3.)**

— Evensong. Fold your white wings, dear angels. [Song.] Words by C. Morgan. *Chappell & Co.: London, etc.,* 1916. fol.
H. 3601. d. (14.)

— [Another edition.] Evensong, *etc. Chappell & Co.: London, etc.,* [1917.] fol. **H. 3601. d. (15.)**

— Everybody's Secret. Song, words by L. Rand, *etc.* 3 no. [In E flat, F and G.] *Chappell & Co.: London, etc.,* 1910. fol.
H. 3601. c. (5.)

— Evolution. Song, words by M. L. Ryley, *etc. Chappell & Co.: London, etc.,* 1909. fol. **H. 3601. c. (6.)**

— The Exile. Song, the words by Lady Lindsay. 2 no. [In B flat and C.] *Boosey & Co.: London and New York,* 1893. fol.
H. 3601. (11.)

— Fair, kind, and true ... Sonnet by Shakespeare. 3 no. [In C, E flat and F.] *Chappell & Co.: London,* 1898. fol.
H. 3601. (28.)

— A Farewell. Song, the words by C. Kingsley. *Boosey & Co.: London and New York,* 1902. fol. **H. 3601. a. (13.)**

— Fidelity.—Come, rest in this Bosom.—Song, the words by T. Moore. *Boosey & Co.: London and New York,* 1908. fol.
H. 3601. b. (32.)

— The First Rose. Song, words by F. Ward. 3 no. [In A flat, B flat and C.] *Chappell & Co.: London, etc.,* 1913. fol.
H. 3601. c. (22.)

— A Flower Fancy.—Love lies bleeding.—Song, the words by E. Collett. *Enoch & Sons: London,* 1902. fol.
H. 3601. a. (14.)

— Fly away, pretty Moth. Old Song, arranged by L. Lehmann. *Chappell & Co.: London, etc.,* 1916. fol. **H. 3601. d. (16.)**

— The Fountains mingle with the River. Song, the poem by P. B. Shelley. *Boosey & Co.: London and New York,* 1895. fol.
H. 3601. (12.)

— The Four Sunbeams. Duet for Soprano and Contralto. *Boosey & Co.: London and New York,* 1904. fol.
H. 3601. a. (15.)

— Five French Songs ... [No. 1.] Paix du soir.—Peace of Night.—[No. 2.] La Rose ... [No. 3.] Le Colibri.—The Humming Bird.—[No. 4.] L'Oiseleur.—The Fowler.—[No. 5.] La Race.— A Child of Brittany, am I.—(Words by G. Boutelleau [and F. Plessis], English words by J. Ahrem.) 4 no. *J. Church Co.: Cincinnati, etc.* 1901. fol.
Wanting no. 4. **H. 3601. a. (16.)**

LEHMANN, afterwards **BEDFORD** (Liza)

— From the Chase on the Mountain.—Von der Jagd in den Bergen.—Old Gaelic Song, English words by Maclaren, German translation by B. Marchesi. Arranged by L. Lehmann. *J. Williams: London,* (1904.) fol.
H. 3601. b. (3.)

— Eight German Songs. *Chappell & Co.: London,* [1888.] 4°.
F. 636. i. (5.)

— Gipsy Love-Song. Romance. The poem by R. L. Stevenson. *Boosey & Co.: London and New York,* 1901. fol.
H. 3601. a. (2.)

— Go, Fortune! *See* infra: [The Vicar of Wakefield.]

The Golden Threshold

— The Golden Threshold. An Indian Song-Garland for four solo voices—Soprano, Contralto, Tenor and Baritone—, Chorus and Orchestra ... The poems by Sarojini Naidu, *etc.* [Vocal score.] *Boosey & Co.: London and New York,* 1906. 8°. **F. 1425. a. (1.)**

— The Golden Threshold ... New edition. *Boosey & Co.: London and New York,* 1907. 8°. **F. 1425. a. (2.)**

— Selection ... for four Solo voices—S. A. T. B.—, Chorus and Orchestra, *etc. Boosey & Co.: London and New York,* [1910.] 8°. **F. 637. hh. (9.)**

— The Golden Threshold ... Choruses only. *Boosey & Co.: London and New York,* [1929.] 8°. **F. 1267. d. (3.)**

— Alabaster. Song, *etc. Boosey & Co.: London and New York,* 1907. fol. **H. 3601. b. (23.)**

— Indian Love Song.—"You flaunt your Beauty in the Rose," *etc. Boosey & Co.: London and New York,* 1907. fol.
H. 3601. b. (24.)

— Good Morning, Brother Sunshine. Song, words by J. W. Foley. *Chappell & Co.: London, etc.,* 1916. fol.
H. 3601. d. (17.)

— Good Morning, Brother Sunshine! Arranged as Duet or Two-part Song by C. Lucas, *etc. Chappell-Harms: New York,* 1926. 8°. **F. 217. a. (28.)**

— Good Morning, Brother Sunshine! Two-part Song ... Arranged by C. Lucas. *Chappell & Co.: London, etc.,* [1935.] 8°. **E. 263. j. (37.)**

— Good Night and Good Morning. *See* infra: [More Daisies. No. 4.]

— Good-Night, Babette! A Musical Idyll for Soprano and Baritone ... with accompaniments for pianoforte, violin and violoncello, the poem ... by Austin Dobson. *Boosey & Co.: London and New York,* 1898. 4°. **G. 770. b. (4.)**

— [Good Night, Babette.] Babette's Song—Once at the Angelus— ... With Pianoforte accompaniment only. *Boosey & Co.: London & New York,* 1900. fol. **H. 3601. (26.)**

— Greek Love-Song. *See* supra: [Cameos. No. 4.]

— The Guardian Angel. Song ... Words by E. Nesbit. pp. 7. *E. Ascherberg & Cᵒ: London,* [1898.] fol. **H. 1654. uu. (2.)**

— The Guardian Angel. Song ... Words by E. Nesbit. pp. 7. *Ascherberg, Hopwood & Crew: London,* [1925?] 4°.
G. 1270. zz. (1.)

— The Guardian Angel. Arranged as a two-part song (S. A.) by Purcell J. Mansfield, *etc.* pp. 8. *Ascherberg, Hopwood & Crew: London,* [1951.] 8°.
[*Ascherberg's Series of Part Songs. no. 287.*] **F. 1659. a.**

LEHMANN, afterwards **BEDFORD** (Liza)

— The Happy Prince. A Story by Oscar Wilde, with incidental music. [P. F.] *Chappell & Co.: London, etc.*, 1908. fol.
h. 3283. jj. (43.)

— Haste not to end, oh Day, so soon. *See* infra: [The Vicar of Wakefield.]

— Hey! ho! *See* infra: [Sergeant Brue.]

— The High Tide.—On the Coast of Lincolnshire, 1571.—A Poem by J. Ingelow with incidental music by L. Lehmann. [P. F.] *Elkin & Co.: London*, 1912. fol. **H. 3601. c. (7.)**

— Hips and Haws. Five Country Songs. For a Baritone voice. I. I be thinkin'. II. Country Courtship. III. Jealousy. IV. Bells across the Meadows. V. Tramping. Words by M. Radcliffe-Hall. *Chappell & Co.: London, etc.* 1913. 4°.
G. 390. h. (4.)

— [Hips and Haws. No. 2.] Country Courtship ... Song, *etc.* *Chappell & Co.: London, etc.*, 1914. fol. **H. 3601. d. (4.)**

— How sweet the Moonlight sleeps upon this Bank. Duet for Mezzo-Soprano and Baritone ... the words by Shakespeare, *etc. Boosey & Co.: London and New York*, 1912. fol.
H. 3601. c. (8.)

— The Hundred Pipers. Scotch Song, written by Caroline Baronesse Nairne, arranged by L. Lehmann. *Chappell & Co.: London*, 1903. fol. **H. 3601. a. (19.)**

— I have a Garden of my own. Song, the words by T. Moore. *E. Ascherberg & Co.: London*, 1901. fol. **H. 3601. a. (21.)**

— I'm just a young Man in a Shop. *See* infra: [Sergeant Brue.]

— I praise the tender Flower. Song, the words by R. Bridges. *J. Williams: London*, 1895. fol. **H. 3601. (15.)**

— I send you my Heart. Song, words and music by L. Lehmann. 3 no. [In C, E flat and F.] *Chappell & Co.: London, etc.*, 1913. fol. **H. 3601. c. (23.)**

— If I built a World for you. Song, the words by H. Fordwych. *Boosey & Co.: London and New York*, 1904. fol.
H. 3601. b. (4.)

— If I built a World for you. Song. [In E flat.] The words by Herbert Fordwych. [c. 1905.] fol.
A pirated edition. **H. 1848. b. (18.)**

— If I built a World for you. [Orchestral parts.] 12 pt. *Boosey & Co.: [New York*, 1906.] 8°. **f. 800. (810.)**

— Song, "If I built a World for you". ⟨Arranged [for military band] by M. Retford. Solo clarinet in B♭ (conductor) [and parts].⟩ 35 pt. *In:* GERMAN (*Sir* Edward) Abendlied, *etc.* 1907. fol. [*Boosey's military Journal. ser.* 122. *no.* 4.] **h. 1549.**

— If I had but two little Wings. Song, words by S. T. Coleridge. *J. B. Cramer & Co.: London*, 1921. 4°. **G. 1270. f. (13.)**

— If I only knew! Song, words by M. Pond. *G. Ricordi & Co.: London*, 1904. fol. **H. 3601. a. (20.)**

— If thou wilt be the falling Dew. Folk Song of Provence, translated by the Countess E. Martinengo Cesaresco. *Chappell & Co.: London*, [1888.] fol. **H. 1788. v. (18.)**

In a Persian Garden

— In a Persian Garden. A Song-Cycle for four solo voices ... with Pianoforte Accomp¹. The words selected from the Rubaiyát of Omar Khayyám (Fitzgerald's Translation), *etc.* *Metzler & Co.: London*, 1896. 4°. **G. 385. m. (7.)**

— In a Persian Garden. Selection from the song cycle ... Transcribed for orchestra by John Crook. [Orchestral parts.] 15 pt. *Hawkes & Son: London; Leipzig* [printed, 1903.] 4°.
g. 1800. (202.)

LEHMANN, afterwards **BEDFORD** (Liza)

— Selection ... Arranged for the Pianoforte ... by H. E. Geehl. *Metzler & Co.: London*, 1912. fol. **h. 3284. g. (9.)**

— Selection ... Arranged for organ solo by H. F. Ellingford. *Metzler & Co.: London*, 1924. fol. **h. 2731. t. (21*.)**

— In a Persian Garden. Suite ... Selected and orchestrated by A. Schmid. [Piano conductor and parts.] *G. Schirmer: [New York,]* 1929. 4°. **h. 3210. h. (303.)**

— Ah, Moon of my Delight, *etc.* [Song.] *Metzler & Co.: London*, 1896. fol. **H. 3601. (13.)**

— Recit. and Air. Ah! Moon of my Delight, transcribed for Violin and Pianoforte Accompaniment. *Metzler & Co.: London*, 1896. fol. **h. 1612. h. (3.)**

— Alas! that Spring should vanish with the Rose, *etc. Metzler & Co.: London*, 1896. fol. **H. 3601. (29.)**

— Myself when Young, *etc.* [Song.] *Metzler & Co.: London*, 1896. fol. **H. 3601. (14.)**

— Myself when young, *etc.* [Song.] [c. 1900.] fol.
A pirated edition. Imperfect; wanting all after p. 1.
H. 1848. b. (19.)

— In Lotos Land.—The Land of Fair Dreams.—Song, the words by T. Heffernan. *Boosey & Co.: London and New York*, 1905. fol. **H. 3601. b. (5.)**

— In Memoriam. A Song-Cycle for a Solo Voice ... with pianoforte accompt. The words selected from the poem by Lord Tennyson. *J. Church Co.: Cincinnati, etc.*, 1899. fol.
H. 3601. (30.)

— In Sherwood Forest. A Vocal Intermezzo for Female Voices, words by B. Hood, *etc. Chappell & Co.: London*, 1910. 4°.
G. 425. e. (6.)

— In some sublimer Star. Song, a triolet by C. Emra. *T. Presser Co.: Philadelphia*, 1921. 4°. **G. 1275. i. (12.)**

— In the Tassel-Time of Spring. Song, words by R. U. Johnson. 3 no. [In D flat, E flat and F.] *Chappell & Co.: London*, 1903. fol. **H. 3601. a. (22.)**

— In the Watches of the Night. Song, words by E. Young. *Chappell & Co.: London, etc.*, 1921. 4°. **G. 1270. f. (14.)**

— Incident of the French Camp. Song, the poem by R. Browning, *etc. Chappell & Co.: London, etc.*, 1910. fol.
H. 3601. c. (9.)

— Indian Love Song. *See* supra: [The Golden Threshold.]

— Irish Love-Song ... The words by Sir S. Ferguson. *Boosey & Co.: London and New York*, 1894. fol. **H. 3601. (16.)**

— It's dowie in the Hint o' Hairst.—Gar traurig tönt der Schnitter Lied.—Old Gaelic Song, English words by H. Ainslie, German translation by B. Marchesi. Arranged by L. Lehmann. *J. Williams: London*, (1904.) fol.
H. 3601. b. (6.)

— It was a Lover and his Lass. *See* infra: [The Vicar of Wakefield.]

— Je pense à toi. Romance. [P. F.] *Chappell & Co.: New York, etc.*, 1912. fol. **h. 3284. g. (8.)**

— Kathleen O'More. Song, the words old Irish. *Boosey & Co.: London and New York*, 1898. fol. **H. 3601. (31.)**

— King Henry to Fair Rosamund. Song, the words by M. Drayton. *Enoch & Sons: London*, 1897. fol.
H. 3601. (17.)

LEHMANN, afterwards **BEDFORD** (LIZA)

—— A Lake and a fairy Boat. Duet—for Sopr. and Baritone or Bass—words by T. Hood. *E. Ascherberg & Co.: London,* 1902. fol. **H. 3601. a. (23.)**

—— The Lake Isle of Innisfree. Song, the poem by W. B. Yeats, *etc. Boosey & Co.: London and New York,* 1911. fol. **H. 3601. c. (10.)**

—— Lead, kindly Light. Hymn for Soprano Solo and Chorus or Quintet of solo voices ... with Organ or Pianoforte Accompaniment ... Words ... by Cardinal Newman. 2 no. [In E minor and D minor.] *Novello & Co.: London,* 1901, 1902. fol. **H. 3601. a. (3.)**

—— The Letter Song. *See* supra: [The Eternal Feminine.]

—— The Life of a Rose. A Group of seven short Songs, the words and music by L. Lehmann. *Boosey & Co.: London and New York,* 1905. 4°. **G. 424. r. (3.)**

—— The Life of a Rose. A group of seven short songs. The words and music by L. Lehmann. ⟨New edition. For medium voice.⟩ pp. 30. *Boosey & Co.: London,* [1906.] 4°. **G. 295. jj. (7.)**

—— [The Life of a Rose.] The Bee. Song, *etc. Boosey & Co.: London and New York,* 1905. fol. **H. 3601. b. (7.)**

—— [The Life of a Rose.] Lovers in the Lane. Song, *etc. Boosey & Co.: London and New York,* 1905. fol. **H. 3601. b. (8.)**

—— Lilies of the Valley. A medley of old English Songs arranged for girls' voices. *Chappell & Co.: London,* 1917. 4°. **G. 425. v. (15.)**

—— Lilies of the Valley ... Choruses only. *Chappell & Co.: London, etc.,* 1917. 8°. **F. 1623. e. (21.)**

—— [Lilies of the Valley. No. 2.] I've been roaming ... Arranged by L. Lehmann, *etc. See* HORN (C. E.) I've been roaming, *etc.* 1917. fol. **H. 1846. t. (44.)**

—— [Lilies of the Valley. No. 5.] Cherry ripe ... Arranged by L. Lehmann, *etc. See* HORN (C. E.) Cherry ripe, *etc.* 1917. fol. **H. 1846. t. (43.)**

—— Lillian's Fair. Song, the words by S. M. Peck. *Boosey & Co.: London and New York,* 1895. fol. **H. 3601. (18.)**

—— The Little Blush Rose. A Netherland Love Song, the words and music by L. Lehmann. *Boosey & Co.: London and New York,* 1907. fol. **H. 3601. b. (33.)**

—— [Another edition.] The Little Blush Rose, *etc. Boosey & Co.: London and New York,* 1907. fol. **H. 3601. b. (34.)**

—— Little brown Brother. Baby Seed Song ... words by E. Nesbit. *Chappell & Co.: London, etc.,* 1918. fol. **H. 3601. d. (18.)**

—— Five Little Love Songs. The words by Cora Fabbri, *etc.* (No. 1. There's a Bird beneath your Window. No. 2. Along the sunny Lane. No. 3. Just a Multitude of Curls. No. 4. If I were a Bird, I would sing all Day. No. 5. Clasp mine closer, little dear white Hand.) 2 no. [Medium and high.] *Chappell & Co.: London, etc.,* 1910. 4°. **G. 385. nn. (3.)**

—— [Five Little Love Songs. No. 1, 4.] There's a Bird beneath your Window, and If I were a Bird, I would sing all Day, *etc.* 2 no. [Medium and high.] *Chappell & Co.: London, etc.,* 1911. fol. **H. 3601. c. (16.)**

—— Little Moccasins. *See* infra: [Prairie Pictures.]

—— Little Star of the Forest. Song, the words by F. E. Weatherley. *Boosey & Co.: London & New York,* 1912. fol. **H. 3601. d. (5.)**

—— Little white Rose. Song, words by A. Perceval. 2 no. [In C and E flat.] *Chappell & Co.: London, etc.,* 1908. fol. **H. 3601. b. (35.)**

LEHMANN, afterwards **BEDFORD** (LIZA)

—— Long ago in Egypt. Song, words by E. Clifford. *Chappell & Co.: London,* 1903. fol. **H. 3601. a. (24.)**

—— Love enthroned. *See* infra: [Songs of Love and Spring.]

—— Love, if you knew the Light. *See* infra: Three Songs, *etc.* [No. 3.]

—— Love in a Mist. *See* supra: [Bleak Weather.]

—— Lovers in the Lane. *See* supra: [The Life of a Rose.]

—— Lullaby of an Infant Chieftain. Song, words by Sir W. Scott. *Chappell & Co.: London,* [1888.] fol. **H. 1788. v. (19.)**

—— The Mad Dog. *See* infra: [The Vicar of Wakefield.]

—— Das Mädchen spricht ... Song, words by R. Prutz. *S. Lucas, Weber & Co.: London,* [1888.] fol. **H. 1788. v. (20.)**

—— [Das Mädchen spricht.] The Maiden speaks. Oh, dearest Moon. Song, *etc. J. Williams: London,* [1924.] fol. **H. 1846. ll. (18.)**

—— Magdalen at Michael's Gate. Song, words by H. Kingsley, *etc.* 3 no. [In F sharp minor, A minor and B minor.] *Chappell & Co.: London, etc.,* 1913. fol. **H. 3601. c. (24.)**

—— The Maiden speaks. *See* supra: [Das Mädchen spricht.]

—— Mairè, my Girl. Song, the words by J. K. Casey. *Boosey & Co.: London and New York,* 1892. fol. **H. 3601. (4.)**

—— The Minuet ... Song, Words Anon, *etc.* 2 no. [In C and (with flute or violin obligato) in D.] *Boosey & Co.: London and New York,* 1898. fol. **H. 3601. (32.)**

—— Mirage. Song, the words by H. Malesh. *Enoch & Sons: London,* 1894. fol. **H. 3601. (19.)**

—— Molly Murray. *See* infra: [Sergeant Brue.]

—— Molly's Spinning Song.—Marianchen's Spinnerlied.—The English Words by A. P. Graves, from the German of A. Wall. *Boosey & Co.: London and New York,* 1902. fol. **H. 3601. a. (26.)**

More Daisies

—— More Daisies. New Songs of Childhood, for four solo voices ... with Pianoforte Accompaniment, *etc.* (More Daisies. Encore Songs for the 'Daisy Chain'.) *Boosey & Co.: London and New York,* 1902. 4°. **G. 383. b. (5.)**

—— "Every Night my Prayers I say," and "The Captain". Two Songs of Childhood, *etc. Boosey & Co.: London and New York,* [1906.] fol. **H. 3601. b. (20.)**

—— [No. 4.] Good Night and Good Morning. Song ... the words by Lord Houghton. *Boosey & Co.: London and New York,* 1902. fol. **H. 3601. a. (16.)**

—— [No. 7.] The Cuckoo. Song ... the words by W. B. Rands. *Boosey & Co.: London and New York,* 1902. fol. **H. 3601. a. (11.)**

—— [No. 7.] The Cuckoo. For Ladies Voices, S. S. A., Sop. and Contr. Solo ... Arr. by W. Howorth. *Boosey Hawkes Belwin, Inc.: New York,* 1940. 8°. **F. 217. j. (5.)**

—— [No. 7.] The Cuckoo. S. A. T. B. ... Arr. by the Krones, Beatrice & Max. *Boosey Hawkes Belwin, Inc.: New York,* 1941. 8°. **F. 1744. d. (16.)**

—— [No. 9.] My Shadow. Song, *etc. Boosey & Co.: London and New York, etc.,* [1911.] fol. **H. 3601. c. (12.)**

—— [No. 11.] A Child's Prayer, *etc.* [Song.] *Boosey & Co.: London and New York,* 1907. fol. **H. 3601. b. (29.)**

LEHMANN, afterwards **BEDFORD** (Liza)

— Morning. Song, words by W. Akerman. 3 no. [In B flat, D flat and E flat.] *Chappell & Co.: London, etc.,* 1912. fol.
H. 3601. c. (25.)

— Mother Sleep. Song, written by H. D. Lowry. *Metzler & Co.: London,* 1901. fol.
H. 3601. a. (5.)

— Mr Coggs and other Songs for Children. The words by E. V. Lucas. pp. 25. *Chappell & Co.: London, etc.,* [1908.] 4°.
G. 1487. q. (1.)

— My Heart can wait. Song, words by M. Pond. *Willis Music Co.: London,* 1904. fol.
H. 3601. a. (27.)

— My Lady Busy. *See infra:* [Sergeant Brue.]

— My lovely Child.—Mutter-Tändelei.—Song. The Poem by Bürger, the English adaptation by M. F. Heaton. *Boosey & Co.: London and New York,* 1899. fol.
H. 3601. (33.)

— My Secret. *See infra:* [Songs of Love and Spring.]

— My Shadow. *See supra:* [More Daisies. No. 9.]

— My true Love hath my Heart. Song, words by Sir Philip Sidney. *Metzler & Co.: London,* [1888.] fol.
H. 1788. v. (21.)

— Myself when Young. *See supra:* [In a Persian Garden.]

— Die Nachtigall, als ich sie fragte ... Song, words from Mirza-Schaffy,—Bodenstedt. *S. Lucas, Weber & Co.: London,* [1889.] fol.
H. 1788. v. (22.)

— [Die Nachtigall, als ich sie fragte.] O tell me, Nightingale ... (Song.) Words from Mirza-Schaffy ... (New and revised edition.) 2 no. [In D minor and C minor.] *J. Williams: London,* (1910.) fol.
H. 3601. c. (13.)

— Never mind the Weather. *See infra:* [Sergeant Brue.]

— The Nightingale's Mistake. Song, *etc. Boosey & Co.: London,* [1890.] fol.
H. 3601. (5.)

— No Candle was there and no Fire. Arranged as Quartet, or Anthem (Three Female Voices. Two-part Anthem) ... by W. Stickles. Words by F. M. Gostling. 3 no. *Chappell-Harms: New York,* 1929–31. 8°.
E. 335. e. (29.)

— No Candle was there and no Fire. Mixed Voices. Arranged by W. Stickles, *etc. Chappell & Co.: New York,* 1938. 8°.
F. 585. zz. (29.)

— No, no, no! Song, the words from Weelkes' Madrigals—1604—with a 2nd verse added. *Chappell & Co.: London,* 1895. fol.
H. 3601. (20.)

— Nonsense Songs.—The Songs that came out wrong—from Alice in Wonderland. A Song-Cycle for Soprano, Contalto, Tenor and Bass, the lyrics by Lewis Carroll. pp. 57. *Chappell Co.: London, etc.,* 1908. 4°.
G. 424. v. (4.)

— Nonsense Songs. (The Songs that came out wrong.) From Alice in Wonderland. A song-cycle for soprano, contralto, tenor and bass. The lyrics by Lewis Carroll. pp. 62. *Chappell & Co.: London, etc.,* [1908.] 4°.
G. 1271. yy. (2.)

— A Nook of Paradise. Song, the poem by W. E. Henley. *Novello and Co.: London,* 1904. fol.
H. 3601. b. (9.)

— Oh! bother, sang the Thrush. Song, words by M. Radclyffe-Hall. 3 no. [In B flat, C and D.] *Chappell & Co.: London, etc.,* 1913. fol.
H. 3601. c. (26.)

— O Light-of-Heart. *See supra:* [Dream-Birds.]

— Oh! Mistress mine. The Clown's Song ... from Shakespeare's "Twelfth Night". *Metzler & Co.: London,* [1897.] fol.
H. 3601. (25.)

— 1055tell me, Nightingale. *See supra:* [Die Nachtigall, als ich sie fragte.]

LEHMANN, afterwards **BEDFORD** (Liza)

— On the Day I get to Heaven. Song, words by S. Levey. 3 no. [In C, B flat and F.] *Chappell & Co.: London, etc.,* 1912. fol.
H. 3601. d. (6.)

— Once at the Angelus. *See supra:* [Good Night, Babette.]

— Once upon a Time. A Fairy Cantata. The Ancient Story of The Sleeping Beauty, retold and lyrically arranged by G. H. Jessop. ⟨New edition.⟩ pp. 112. *Boosey & Co.: London and New York,* 1903. 8°.
F. 158. h. (5.)

— [Once upon a Time.] Princess Mayblossom's Waltz. Song, *etc. Boosey & Co.: London and New York,* 1903. fol.
H. 3601. a. (29.)

— [Once upon a Time.] "Princess Mayblossom's Waltz Song" ... Arranged by M. Retford. ⟨Conductor [and military band parts].⟩ 31 pt. *In:* JULLIEN (Louis A.) The Original Napolitaine, *etc.* 1903. fol. [*Boosey's supplemental military Journal.* no. 442.]
h. 1544.

— Paix du soir. *See supra:* Five French Songs. [No. 1.]

— Parody Pie. A Song Cycle for four voices ... with Pianoforte accompaniment, the lyrics by A. S. Walker, N. Pain, W. Rose, *etc. Chappell & Co.: London, etc.,* 1914. 4°.
G. 390. k. (11.)

— Pas Seul. *See infra:* [The Twin Sister.]

— "The Passion Flower" and "Speedwell". Two short Songs, the words by T. Heffernan and A. Kirkland. *Boosey & Co.: London and New York,* 1905. fol.
H. 3601. b. (19.)

— Pearl and Song.—There was a Star.—Song, words by C. Fabbri, *etc.* 3 no. [In B flat, D flat and E flat.] *Chappell & Co.: London, etc.,* 1910. fol.
H. 3601. c. (14.)

— Philomela. [Song.] Words by Sir Philip Sidney. 1896. *See* GALE (J. R. C.) and SPEER (C. T.) An English Series of ... Songs, *etc.* No. 14. 1896, *etc.* fol.
G. 1005.

— The Poet and the Nightingale. Song, words by J. T. White, *etc.* 2 no. [In E flat and F.] *Chappell & Co.: London, etc.,* 1914. fol.
H. 3601. d. (7.)

— Practical Hints for Students of Singing. *Enoch & Sons: London, etc.,* 1913. 4°.
G. 844. j. (2.)

— Prairie Pictures. North American Indian ... Song Cycle for four voices ... with Pianoforte accompaniment, words and music by L. Lehmann. *Chappell & Co.: London, etc.,* 1911. 4°.
G. 385. ww. (6.)

— [Prairie Pictures.] Little Moccasins. Song, *etc.* 2 no. [In D minor and E minor.] *Chappell & Co.: London, etc.,* 1911. fol.
H. 3601. c. (11.)

— [Prairie Pictures.] Trysting Song, *etc. Chappell & Co.: London, etc.,* 1913. fol.
H. 3601. d. (9.)

— Prince Charming. *See infra:* [The Vicar of Wakefield.]

— Princess Mayblossom's Waltz. *See supra:* [Once upon a Time.]

— Printemps d'Avril. An April Song, the words by T. de Banville. 2 no. [In E flat and F.] *Chappell & Co.: London,* [1891.] fol.
H. 3601. (6.)

— Prospice. *See infra:* Three Songs, *etc.* [No. 1.]

— La Race. *See supra:* Five French Songs. [No. 5.]

— Romance for the pianoforte, *etc. Chappell & Co.: London,* 1892. fol.
h. 1489. s. (31.)

— Romance for Violin with Pianoforte accompaniment. *Chappell & Co.: London,* 1892. fol.
h. 1608. x. (37.)

LEHMANN, afterwards BEDFORD (LIZA)

— Romantic Suite for Violin and Pianoforte ... No. 1. First Meeting. No. 2. Jealousy and Lover's Quarrel. No. 3. Love lies bleeding. No. 4. Reconcilation. No. 5. Promise. No. 6. Happy Ending. *Keith, Prowse & Co.: London*, 1903. 4°.
g. 223. l. (9.)

— La Rose. *See* supra: Five French Songs. [No. 2.]

— Rose and Lily. *See* infra: [The Vicar of Wakefield.]

— Rose Song. [Song.] Words from the Persian by F. A. Steel. *Chappell & Co.: London*, 1903. fol. **H. 3601. a. (31.)**

— Roses after Rain. Song, written by F. S. Stanton. *Metzler & Co.: London*, 1903. fol. **H. 3601. a. (30.)**

— Run away and play. *See* infra: [Sergeant Brue.]

— Run, run, little Page ... Song, the words by C. Scollard. *Boosey & Co.: London and New York*, 1895. fol.
H. 3601. (22.)

— The Sapphire. *See* infra: Songs of Love and Spring.

— Two Seal Songs. "The Mother Seal's Lullaby" and "You must'nt swim till you're six weeks old". From "The Jungle Book" by R. Kipling, *etc.* 4 no. [Contralto, mezzo-soprano, soprano and high soprano.] *Chappell & Co.: London, etc.*, 1908. 4°. **G. 383. v. (8.)**

— The Secrets of the Heart. A Musical Dualogue for Soprano & Contralto ... with pianoforte accompaniment. The words from Austin Dobson's "Proverbs in Porcelain". *J. Williams: London*, [1895.] 4°. **F. 689. c. (3.)**

Sergeant Brue

— Sergeant Brue. A Musical Farce, book by O. Hall, lyrics by J. H. Wood. Vocal Score. *Hopwood & Crew: London*, 1904. 4°. **F. 690. n. (4.)**

— Sergeant Brue ... Arranged for the Pianoforte by A. E. Godfrey. *Hopwood & Crew: London*, 1904. 4°.
f. 540. o. (2.)

— Selection ... [Arranged by] A. E. Godfrey. Arr. [for military band] by M. Retford. [Parts.] 29 pt. *Boosey & Co.: London*, 1905. fol.
[*Boosey & Co.'s new supplemental Journal for military Bands. no. 16.*] **h. 1544. a.**

— Selection ... Arranged for the Pianoforte by A. E. Godfrey. *Hopwood & Crew: London*, 1904. fol. **h. 3282. ww. (37.)**

— The Bobbies' Beano. Song, *etc. Hopwood & Crew: London*, 1904. fol. **H. 3601. b. (11.)**

— Dear little Heart. Song ... words by M. Pond. *Hopwood & Crew: London*, 1904. fol. **H. 3601. b. (12.)**

— Hey! ho! Song, *etc. Hopwood & Crew: London*, 1904. fol.
H. 3601. b. (13.)

— I'm just a young Man in a Shop. Song, *etc. Hopwood & Crew: London*, 1904. fol. **H. 3601. b. (14.)**

— Molly Murray. Song, *etc. Hopwood & Crew: London*, 1904. fol. **H. 3601. b. (15.)**

— My Lady Busy. Song, *etc. Hopwood & Crew: London*, 1904. fol. **H. 3601. b. (16.)**

— Never mind the Weather. Song ... words by T. Heffernan. *Hopwood & Crew: London*, 1905. fol. **H. 3601. b. (17.)**

— Run away and play. Song, *etc. Hopwood & Crew: London*, 1904. fol. **H. 3601. b. (18.)**

— *See* GODFREY (A. E.) Sergeant Brue. Lancers (Waltz) on Airs from L. Lehmann's Musical Farce, *etc.* 1904. fol.
h. 2930. (31.)

LEHMANN, afterwards BEDFORD (LIZA)

— Four Shakesperian Part-Songs for S. A. T. B., unaccompanied. 1. I know a Bank. 2. When Icicles hang by the Wall. 3. Tell me, where is Fancy bred. 4. Under the Greenwood Tree, *etc. Novello and Co.: London*, 1911. 8°. **F. 321. z. (28.)**

— The Silver Rose. Song, the words by M. R. Hall. *J. Church Co.: Cincinnati, etc.*, 1911. fol. **H. 3601. c. (15.)**

— Sleep, little ruffly, fluffly Bird. [Song.] Words by K. H. M. Jackson. *J. Church Co.: Cincinnati, etc.*, (1904.) fol.
H. 3601. b. (10.)

— Three Snow Songs. I. Snowflakes. II. Robin Redbreast. III. Christmas Eve. Words & music by L. Lehmann. 2 no. [Mezzo-soprano and soprano.] *Chappell & Co.: London, etc.*, 1914. 4°.
With ad libitum parts to no. 3 for organ, bells and female chorus. **G. 805. yy. (10.)**

— Snowdrops. Two little Duets. The Poems by A. Matheson. *Boosey & Co.: London and New York*, 1901. fol.
H. 3601. a. (6.)

— Two Songs. April cometh, and Love's Caution. The words by E. Sweetman. *Boosey & Co.: London and New York*, 1900. fol. **H. 3601. (34.)**

— Three Songs for low voice. [No. 1.] Prospice. (R. Browning.) [No. 2.] Dusk in the valley. (G. Meredith.) [No. 3.] Love, if you knew the light. (R. Browning.) 3 no. *G. Schirmer: New York*, 1922. 4°. **G. 1275. i. (11.)**

— Songs of a "Flapper". Words and music by L. Lehmann. (I. In the Garden. II. This beautiful World. III. My Sister Nell. IV. The Ball. V. Good-night, little Stars.) *Chappell & Co.: London, etc.*, 1911. 4°. **G. 425. h. (4.)**

— Songs of Good Luck. (Superstitions.) The words by Helen Taylor ... 1. The Falling Star. 2. If I drink from Your Glass. 3. The New Moon. 4. Cuckoo Counts. 5. The Black Cat, *etc.* ⟨High voices.⟩ pp. 23. *Enoch & Sons: London*, [1913.] 4°.
G. 425. o. (9.)

— Songs of good Luck. (Superstitions.) The words by Helen Taylor ... 1. The Falling Star. 2. If I drink from your Glass. 3. The New Moon. 4. Cuckoo Counts. 5. The Black Cat, *etc.* ⟨Low voice.⟩ *Enoch & Sons: London*, [1913.] 4°.
G. 383. mm. (1.)

— Songs of Love and Spring; a Song-Cycle for two voices with Pianoforte accompaniment, the Poems translated from the German of E. Geibel by A. P. Graves. (Supplement to Songs of Love and Spring. The Sapphire.—Contralto.—The words by A. P. Graves.) 2 no. *Boosey & Co.: London and New York*, 1903. 4°. **G. 383. e. (3.)**

— [Songs of Love and Spring.] Love enthroned. Duet, *etc. Boosey & Co.: London and New York*, 1904. fol.
H. 3601. a. (25.)

— [Songs of Love and Spring.] My Secret Song, *etc. Boosey & Co.: London and New York*, 1904. fol. **H. 3601. a. (28.)**

— Five Songs of Olden Times. Arranged by L. Lehmann, *etc. Ascherberg, Hopwood & Crew: London*, 1924. 4°.
G. 1270. m. (3.)

— Soul's Blossom. Song, words by R. U. Johnson. 3 no. [In E flat, E and G.] *Chappell & Co.: London*, 1903. fol.
H. 3601. a. (32.)

— Star-Children. [Song.] Words by F. G. Bowles. *J. Church Co.: Cincinnati, etc.*, (1904.) fol. **H. 3601. b. (21.)**

— The Starling. *See* supra: [Bird Songs. No. 3.]

— Stars. *See* supra: [The Daisy Chain. No. 5.]

LEHMANN, afterwards BEDFORD (Liza)

— Studies in Recitative ... for all voices ... Compiled and
edited by L. Lehmann. *Chappell & Co.: London*, 1915, *etc.*,
4°.
Vol. 1, 2 *only.* **G. 1118. a.**

— The Swing. *See* supra: [The Daisy-Chain. No. 8.]

— Tell me! Song, words by F. D. Sherman. *Chappell & Co.:
London and Melbourne*, 1905. fol. **H. 3601. b. (22.)**

— There are Birds in the Valley. *See* infra: [The Vicar of
Wakefield.]

— There are Fairies at the Bottom of our Garden. Song, words
by R. Fyleman. *Chappell & Co.: London, etc.*, 1917. fol.
H. 3601. d. (19.)

— There are Fairies at the Bottom of our Garden. Arranged for
Female Trio ... by C. Lucas, *etc. Chappell-Harms: New
York*, 1929. 8°. **F. 217. d. (4.)**

— There, little Girl, don't cry! Song, words by J. W. Riley.
Chappell & Co.: London, etc., 1916. fol. **H. 3601. d. (20.)**

— Thoughts have Wings. Song, words by F. M. Gostling, *etc.*
3 no. [In D flat, E flat and F.] *Chappell & Co.: London, etc.*,
1909. fol. **H. 3601. b. (37.)**

— 'Tis the Hour of Farewell. A Modern Folk-Song, words by
O. H., *etc.* 3 no. [In G, A flat and B flat.] *Chappell & Co.:
London, etc.*, 1914. fol. **H. 3601. d. (8.)**

— Titania's Cradle ... Song, the words from Shakespeare's
"Midsummer Night's Dream". *Boosey & Co.: London and
New York*, 1892. fol. **H. 3601. (7.)**

— Titania's Cradle. I know a Bank. Part Song for Female
Voices ... Arr. by H. L. Vibbard. *Boosey & Co.: New York*,
1932. 8°. **F. 217. f. (9.)**

— To a careless Lover. *See* supra: [The Eternal Feminine.]

— To a little red Spider.—Araignée du soir,—espoir!—Song, the
words by L. A. Cunnington. *Boosey & Co.: London and New
York*, 1903. fol. **H. 3601. a. (34.)**

— To all you Ladies. Old English Ditty, the words by the Earl
of Dorset ... Arranged by L. Lehmann. 2 no. [In A and D.]
Chappell & Co.: London, etc., 1908. fol. **H. 3601. b. (38.)**

— To Dianeme ... Song, words by Herrick. *Keith, Prowse &
Co.: London*, 1897. fol. **H. 3601. (23.)**

— To her black satin Shoe. Song, the words by O. Grey. 2 no.
[In E flat and F.] *Chappell & Co.: London*, 1900. fol.
H. 3601. (35.)

— To my Beloved. Song, written by A. Procter. *Metzler & Co.:
London*, 1895. fol. **H. 3601. (24.)**

— Trysting Song. *See* supra: [Prairie Pictures.]

— A Tuscan Serenade. *See* infra: [The Twin Sister.]

— Twilight. It is the Hour when from the Boughs. Duet for
Soprano and Baritone or Contralto, the poem by Lord
Byron. *Boosey & Co.: London & New York*, 1912. fol.
H. 3601. d. (10.)

— [The Twin Sister.] Ah! gather Roses. Pietro's Song from the
incidental music to "The Twin Sister". *Boosey & Co.:
London and New York*, 1902. fol. **H. 3601. a. (9.)**

— [The Twin Sister.] Pas Seul. Angiolina's Dance, *etc.* [P. F.]
Boosey & Co.: London and New York, 1902. fol.
h. 3282. kk. (28.)

— [The Twin Sister.] A Tuscan Serenade [song], *etc. Boosey &
Co.: London and New York*, 1902. fol. **H. 3601. a. (35.)**

LEHMANN, afterwards BEDFORD (Liza)

— [The Twin Sister.] A Tuscan Serenade ... New Edition.
Boosey & Co.: London and New York, 1902. fol.
H. 3601. a. (36.)

— Under the greenwood Tree. Duet for Mezzo-Soprano &
Baritone or Bass, the words by Shakespeare, *etc. Boosey &
Co.: London & New York*, 1912. fol. **H. 3601. d. (11.)**

— Useful teaching Songs for all voices. Compiled and edited by
L. Lehmann. 5 vol. *Chappell & Co.: London, etc.*, 1914, 15.
4°. **G. 1118.**

— Useful Teaching Songs for all Voices. Compiled & edited by
L. Lehmann. 10 no. *Chappell & Co.: London, etc.*, [1934.] 4°.
A series of selected no. **G. 1118. b.**

— A Valentine. Song, the words by A. B. Pain. *J. Church Co.:
Cincinnati, etc.*, 1911. fol. **H. 3601. c. (17.)**

— Trois Valses de Sentiment for the pianoforte, *etc. Chappell &
Co.: London*, 1892. fol. **h. 1489. s. (32.)**

The Vicar of Wakefield

— The Vicar of Wakefield. A Romantic Light Opera in Three
Acts, founded on Oliver Goldsmith's Novel. The lyrics by
L. Housman, additional lyrics by O. Goldsmith, Shakespeare,
Ben Jonson, *etc. Boosey & Co.: London and New York*, 1907.
4°. **F. 1425.**

— Sophia's Song—"The Air of Courts may be sweet", *etc.
Boosey & Co.: London and New York*, 1908. fol.
H. 3601. b. (39.)

— As Bess one Day.—Tomorrow.—Song, *etc. Boosey & Co.:
London and New York*, 1907. fol. **H. 3601. b. (40.)**

— Go, Fortune! Duet or Solo, *etc. Boosey & Co.: London and
New York*, 1907. fol. **H. 3601. b. (41.)**

— Haste not to end, oh Day, so soon. Quintette, *etc. Boosey &
Co.: London and New York*, 1907. fol. **H. 3601. b. (42.)**

— It was a Lover and his Lass. Song, *etc. Boosey & Co.:
London and New York*, 1907. fol. **H. 3601. b. (43.)**

— The Mad Dog. Song, *etc. Boosey & Co.: London and New
York*, 1907. fol. **H. 3601. b. (44.)**

— Prince Charming. Song, *etc. Boosey & Co.: London and New
York*, 1907. fol. **H. 3601. b. (45.)**

— Rose and Lily. Duet, *etc. Boosey & Co.: London and New
York*, 1908. fol. **H. 3601. b. (46.)**

— There are Birds in the Valley. Song, *etc. Boosey & Co.:
London and New York*, 1907. fol. **H. 3601. b. (47.)**

— With my Bible and my Staff. Recit. and Air, *etc. Boosey &
Co.: London and New York*, 1907. fol. **H. 3601. b. (48.)**

———

— The Waters of Lethe.—The Waters of Oblivion.—Song,
words by H. Hammond-Spencer, *etc.* 2 no. [In C minor and
D minor.] *Chappell & Co.: London, etc.*, 1908. fol.
H. 3601. b. (49.)

— The Weathercock. Song, the words by Longfellow, *etc.
Boosey & Co.: London & New York*, 1913. fol.
H. 3601. d. (12.)

— The Well of Sorrow. Three Songs for a Contralto voice, the
words from "The Bard of Dimbovitza," Roumanian
Folk-Songs collected by H. Vacaresco, translated by Carmen
Sylva and A. Strettell. (I. Forsaken. II. The Broken Spindle. III.
Beside the Maize-Field.) *Boosey & Co.: London and New
York*, 1912. 4°. **G. 365. ss. (7.)**

— Wenn ich an Dich gedenke.—Deutsche Volksweise.—Song,
German words by E. Geibel. *S. Lucas, Weber & Co.:
London*, [1889.] fol. **H. 1788. v. (23.)**

LEHMANN, afterwards BEDFORD (LIZA)

— Were I a Butterfly. Song, words by Lady Strachey. *Chappell & Co.: London, etc.*, 1921. 4°. **G. 1270. f. (15.)**

— What shall we play? A Child's Song, the words by Mrs. Aria. *Boosey & Co.: London and New York*, 1902. fol. **H. 3601. a. (37.)**

— When I am dead my Dearest. Song, the words by C. Rossetti, *etc. Boosey & Co.: London, etc.*, 1919. fol. **H. 3601. d. (21.)**

— When the green Leaves come again. [Song.] Words by H. Bailey. *Boosey & Co.: London and New York*, 1911. fol. **H. 3601. c. (18.)**

— When the Shadows fall To-night. Song, words by W. M. Anderson, *etc. Metzler & Co.: London*, 1926. 4°. **G. 1270. t. (30.)**

— Whene'er a Snowflake leaves the Sky. Song, *etc. J. B. Cramer & Co.: London*, 1918. 4°. **G. 426. d. (48.)**

— Who is Sylvia? Song, the poem by Shakespeare. *Boosey & Co.: London and New York*, 1908. fol. **H. 3601. b. (50.)**

— With a Woodland Nosegay. Song, the words and music by L. Lehmann. *Boosey & Co.: London and New York*, 1907. fol. **H. 3601. b. (51.)**

— With my Bible and my Staff. *See* supra: [The Vicar of Wakefield.]

— Wynken, Blynken and Nod. A Dutch Lullaby for Three-Part Female Chorus with Pianoforte accompaniment and Violin—ad lib.—, the words by E. Field, *etc. Boosey & Co.: London and New York*, 1912. 4°. **G. 425. i. (4.)**

— Wynken, Blynken and Nod ... For three-part Female Chorus with Pianoforte accompaniment and Violin, ad lib., *etc. Boosey & Co.: London and New York*, [1929.] 8°. [*Boosey's Modern Festival Series, No.* 212.] **F. 160. f.**

— You and I.—Cradle Song.—The words from "Poems of Childhood", *etc. Boosey & Co.: London and New York*, 1897. fol. **H. 3601. (21.)**

— Young Lochinvar. Ballad for baritone solo and chorus. The poem by Sir Walter Scott. pp. 31. *Boosey & Cº.: London, New York*, [1898.] 8°. **E. 1766. aa. (8.)**

— Young Lochinvar. Ballad for Baritone Solo and Chorus, the poem by Sir Walter Scott. Revised edition. pp. 31. *Boosey & Co.: London and New York*, [1899.] 8°. **F. 1274. q. (3.)**

— Young Lochinvar. Ballad, *etc.* [String parts.] *Boosey & Co.: London and New York*, 1899. fol. **h. 1508. e. (14.)**

— *See* ARNE (T. A.) Polly Willis. Song ... arranged ... by L. Lehmann. [1890.] fol. **H. 1797. b. (36.)**

— *See* BALFE (M. W.) Killarney ... Arranged by L. Lehmann, *etc.* 1929. 4°. **G. 1270. z. (2.)**

— *See* BIANCHI (F.) [Vien qua, Dorina bella.] Vieni, Dorina bella ... The accompaniment arranged by L. Lehmann. [1893.] fol. **H. 1798. c. (8.)**

— *See* HOOK (J.) When first the East begins to dawn. Song ... accompaniment arranged by L. Lehmann. [1891.] fol. **H. 1797. m. (4.)**

— *See* L., A. Twelve Old Scotch Songs, *etc.* (Edited by L. Lehmann.) 1912. 4°. **G. 425. l. (5.)**

LEHMANN (LOUIS)

— In Georgia. [Song.] Words by Arthur Gillespie. *M. Witmark & Sons:* [*New York*, 1903.] fol. **H. 3985. q. (39.)**

LEHMANN (MARKUS)

— *See* FORTNER (W.) In seinem Garten liebt Don Perlimplín Belisa. Vier Bilder eines erotischen Bilderbogens in der Art eines Kammerspieles ... Klavierauszug von M. Lehmann. [1962.] 4°. **G. 1269. f. (4.)**

— *See* HARTMANN (K. A.) Gesangsszene für Bariton und Orchester ... Klavierauszug von M. Lehmann, *etc.* [1964.] 4°. **G. 1268. qq. (4.)**

— *See* HENZE (H. W.) Elegy for young Lovers. Opera ... Piano score by M. Lehmann. [1961.] 4°. **G. 1349. c.**

— *See* ZIMMERMANN (B. A.) Die Soldaten. Oper ... Klavierauszug von M. Lehmann. [1966.] 4°. **H. 231. cc.**

LEHMANN (R. FRANK)

— Lift up your Heads.—Anthem.—[Staff and tonic sol-fa notation.] *Bayley & Ferguson: London, Glasgow*, [1908.] *s. sh.* 8°. *Anniversary Hymns, No.* 21. **F. 272. c.**

— 'Neath the Banner of God's Love. [Hymn, words by] L. E. Brauff. [Staff and tonic sol-fa notation.] *Bayley & Ferguson: London, Glasgow*, [1908.] *s. sh.* 8°. *Anniversary Hymns, No.* 18. **F. 272. c.**

— Soldiers of the King. [Hymn, words by] B. Bell. [Staff and tonic sol-fa notation.] *Bayley & Ferguson: London, Glasgow*, [1908.] *s. sh.* 8°. *Anniversary Hymns, No.* 13. **F. 272. c.**

LEHMANN (ROBERT)

— Elegie in C moll. [Violoncello and P. F.] Op. 29. *Berlin*, [1882.] fol. *No.* 10 *of "Im Concert und im Salon".* **h. 1847. f. (30.)**

— Nocturno in A dur ... für Violoncello und Orgel oder Harmonium mit Harfe—oder Clavier—ad libit ... Op. 25. *C. Simon: Berlin*, [1878.] fol. **h. 2851. c. (9.)**

— Seerosen Walzer. Op. 34. [Orchestral parts.] *Hannover*, [1885.] fol. **h. 3210. c. (13.)**

— Serenade für Violoncell oder Violine mit Pianoforte oder Harfe. Op. 28. *C. Simon: Berlin*, [1882.] fol. **h. 1608. q. (40.)**

— Wiegenlied für Violine oder Violoncell mit Pianoforte. Op. 27. *C. Simon: Berlin*, [1882.] fol. **h. 1608. q. (39.)**

— *See* WILLIAM II., *German Emperor*. Sang an Aegir ... (eingerichtet von R. Lehmann), *etc.* 1894. fol. 8°. **H. 1380.**

LEHMANN (Mrs RUDOLF)

— *See* L., A.

LEHMANN (URSULA)

— *See* HOLZBAUER (I.) Instrumentale Kammermusik. Herausgegeben von U. Lehmann. 1953 [1954]. fol. [*Das Erbe deutscher Musik. Bd.* 24.] **H. 995. b.**

LEHMANN (WILLIBALD)

— Beloved come. (Geliebter komm.) Song. *J. Church Co.: Cincinnati, etc.*, (1907.) fol. **H. 1794. vv. (31.)**

LEHMANN (WILLY)

— A Souvenir, for Violoncello Solo—or Violin—and Pianoforte, *etc. W. H. Priestley & Sons: Birmingham*, 1910. fol. **h. 1851. f. (2.)**

LEHMANN (WILLY)

— A Souvenir, for Violoncello Solo—or Violin—and
Pianoforte, *etc. City Music Publishing Co.: Lichfield*, 1910.
fol.   **h. 1851. f. (3.)**

— They say that Love is blind. Four-Part Song the words by
A. B. Talbot. *Novello and Co.: London*, [1913.] 8°.
                                                        F. 321. z. (29.)

LEHMEYER (SIGISMOND)

— Le Couronnement, suite de valses brillantes á la Hongroise
pour Piano. *London*, [1861.] fol.   **h. 1460. v. (12.)**

— Près du lac, Idylle pour le piano. *London*, [1854.] fol.
                                                        h. 723. m. (1.)

LEHN (FRANZ)

— *See* ROHR (H.) and LEHN (F.) Flötenbüchlein für die Schule,
etc. [1939.] *obl.* 8°.   **A. 1117.**

— *See* ROHR (H.) and LEHN (F.) Treble Recorder Pieces. [1953.]
8°.   **a. 40. h. (8.)**

— *See* ROHR (H.) and LEHN (F.) Vortragsbüchlein für die Schule
zum Flötenbüchlein, *etc.* [1969.] *obl.* 8°.   **b. 411. h. (8.)**

— *See* ROHR (H.) and LEHN (F.) Vortragsbüchlein zur
Altblockflötenschule für den Anfang. Alte und neue Stücke
für 1–3 Altblockflöten, Schlagwerk ad lib ... [Edited by]
H. Rohr and F. Lehn. [1970.] *obl.* 8°.   **a. 40. u. (8.)**

— *See* ROHR (H.) and LEHN (F.) Vortragsbüchlein für das
Zusammenspiel, Sopran- und Altblockflöten, Schlagwerk ad
lib. [1971.] *obl.* 8°.   **a. 40. gg. (1.)**

LEHNE

— Lehn' deine Wang' an meine Wang'. [Song.] *See* GEISLER (P.)
Gesänge. Erste Folge. No. 8.

— Lehn' deine Wang' an meine Wang'. [Song.] *See*
GRUENBERGER (L.)

— Lehn' deine Wang' an meine Wang! [Song.] *See* NEVIN
(E. W.) [Sketch Book. Op. 2. No. 6.]

— Lehn' deine Wang' an meine Wang'. [Song.] *See* SCHAEFFER
(H.) Drei Lieder. No. 2.

— Lehn' deine Wang'. [Song.] *See* WARBURG (F. S.)

LEHNER (FRANZ XAVER)

— Sonatine für Posaune und Klavier. [Score and part.] 2 pt.
Bosse Edition: Regensburg, [1964.] 4°.   **f. 760. s. (2.)**

LEHNER (J. L.)

— Hundert geistliche Lieder aus dem XVI. und XVII. Jahrhundert
... herausgegeben von J. L. Lehner. *Leipzig*, 1847. *obl.* 4°.
                                                        D. 723.

LEHNERT (JULIUS)

— Guter Rath. Gedicht von R. Baumbach [begins: "Dass dir die
Lieb' versagt dein Schatz"], für vierstimmigen Männerchor.
Breslau, [1883.] 8°.   **E. 308. n. (27.)**

LEHNHARDT (GUSTAV)

— [Goldene Träume.] La Balletense Quadrille, Edelslein
Galopp, Waldmeisterblüthen Polka, Milliarden-Galopp über
Themen aus dem Zaubermärchen, *etc.* [P. F.] 4 no. *Berlin &
Posen*, [1874.] fol.   **h. 1487. p. (33.)**

— Kaiser Wilhelm's Lieblings-Melodien ... Für Militair-Musik.
Stimmen. *C. Paez: Berlin*, [1886.] fol.   **h. 1508. b. (6.)**

LEHNHARDT (GUSTAV)

— Kaiser Wilhelm's Lieblings-Melodien. Tongemälde in Form
eines Potpourri's ... Für Pianoforte. *C. Paez: Berlin*, [1886.]
fol.   **h. 3281. l. (16.)**

— Eine Komödie. Schwank mit Gesang in einem Akt von K. T.
Gaedertz ... mit zwei Musikbeilagen. *Berlin*, [1886.] 8°.
                                                     11746. ee. 14. (3.)

— Une Perle de Danse, polka gracieuse über Themen aus dem
Zaubermärchen "Die Sieben Raben". [P. F.] *Berlin & Posen*,
[1875.] fol.   **h. 1487. p. (34.)**

LEHNHARDT (JULIUS)

— An die Gewehre! Marsch für Pianoforte. Op. 18. *C. Paez:
Berlin*, [1887.] fol.   **h. 3281. l. (19.)**

— An die Gewehre! ... Op. 18. [Band parts.] *C. Paez: Berlin*,
[1887.] fol.   **h. 1508. b. (8.)**

— Mit Gott für Kaiser und Reich! Marsch für Pianoforte.
Op. 16. *C. Paez: Berlin*, [1886.] fol.   **h. 3281. l. (17.)**

— Mit Gott für Kaiser und Reich ... Op. 16. [Band parts.]
C. Paez: Berlin, [1886.] fol.   **h. 1508. b. (7.)**

— Ordre de Bataille. Marsch für Pianoforte. Opus 20. *C. Paez:
Berlin*, [1887.] fol.   **h. 3281. l. (20.)**

— Ordre de Bataille ... Op. 20. [Band parts.] *C. Paez: Berlin*,
[1887.] fol.   **h. 1508. b. (8*.)**

— Der Regimentskamerad. Marsch für Pianoforte. Op. 24.
C. Paez: Berlin, [1887.] fol.   **h. 3281. l. (21.)**

— Der Regimentskamerad ... Op. 24. [Band parts.] *C. Paez:
Berlin*, [1887.] fol.   **h. 1508. b. (9.)**

— Sanct Hubertus. Marsch für Pianoforte. Opus 26. *C. Paez:
Berlin*, [1887.] fol.   **h. 3281. l. (22.)**

— Sanct Hubertus ... Op. 26. [Band parts.] *C. Paez: Berlin*,
[1887.] fol.   **h. 1508. b. (9*.)**

— Schneidige Truppe! Marsch für Pianoforte. Op. 17. *C. Paez:
Berlin*, [1886.] fol.   **h. 3281. l. (18.)**

— Schneidige Truppe ... Op. 17. [Band parts.] *C. Paez: Berlin*,
[1886.] fol.   **h. 1508. b. (7*.)**

LEHNSMANN

— Lehnsmann's Abschied. [Song.] *See* NAUMANN (E.)
Loschwitzer Liederbuch. No. 6.

LE HOUITEL (E.)

— *See* KOCZALSKI (R. A. G.) Rymond. Oper ... Vollständiger
Klavierauszug mit Text bearbeitet von ... E. le Houitel.
[1902.] 8°.   **F. 1256. (3.)**

LEHR (MICHAEL)

— Mass of Saints & Sinners. [For voice, solo guitar and organ.]
pp. 24. *Josef Weinberger: London*, [1966.] 8°.
                                                     F. 1183. b. (1.)

LEHRE

— Lehre. [Song.] *See* FRANZ (R.) Sechs Gesänge, *etc.* Op. 41.
No. 5.

— Die Lehre. [Song.] *See* GOLDSCHMIDT (A. von)

— Die Lehre. [Duet.] *See* ZENGER (M.) Fünf Duette, *etc.* No. 3.

LEHRER (OSCAR J.)

— Ensemble Method for the violin for class instruction.
T. Presser Co.: Philadelphia, 1922. 4°.   **g. 498. z. (9.)**

— Lelkem. Sweetheart. Hungarian song and czárdás for violin and piano. *T. Presser Co.: Philadelphia*, 1916. fol.
h. 1612. hh. (9.)

— First Mazurka, for violin and piano. *T. Presser Co.: Philadelphia*, 1919. 4°.   **g. 500. b. (12.)**

— The Pennant. A Comic Operetta in two Acts ... lyrics by F. M. Colville. *T. Presser Co.: Philadelphia*, (1912.) 8°.
F. 688. q. (2.)

— Polyphonic Studies for Violin Classes, *etc. T. Presser Co.: Philadelphia*, 1924. 4°.   **g. 498. bb. (11.)**

LEHRER (TOM)

— The Tom Lehrer Song Book ... Introduction by Al Capp. Illustrated by Grisha Dotzenko. ⟨Words and music by T. Lehrer.⟩ pp. 63. *Elek Books: London*, [1958.] 8°.
E. 1501. r.

LEHRSTUECK

— Lehrstück. *See* HINDEMITH (P.)

LEHRSTUNDE

— Die Lehrstunde ... für zwei Sopran-Stimmen. *See* ROMBERG (A.)

LEHTONEN (ALEKSI)

— *See* MAASALO (A.) Koraalikirja, *etc.* [By A. Maasalo, T. Kuusisto and A. Lehtonen.] 1952. *obl.* 4°.   **C. 550. r.**

LE HURAY (PETER)

— Anthems for Men's Voices. Edited by P. Le Huray, Nicholas Temperley, Peter Tranchell, David Willcocks. Volume I. Altos, tenors and basses. ⟨Volume II. Tenors and basses.⟩ 2 vol. *Oxford University Press: London*, [1965.] 8°.
F. 1176. uu. (5.)

— *See* AMNER (John) [Sacred Hymns.] O ye little Flock ... Edited by P. le Huray. [1964.] 8°. [*Church Music Society Reprints. no.* 47.]   **E. 1617.**

— *See* BATESON (Thomas) First Set of Madrigals (1604). ⟨Edited by E. H. Fellowes. Revised by Thurston Dart [and P. le Huray].⟩ [1958.] 8°. [*English Madrigalists.* 21.]   **F. 1709. g.**

— *See* CHILD (William) Turn Thou us, O good Lord. Anthem ... Edited by P. le Huray. [1964.] 8°. [*Oxford Anthems. A* 208.]
F. 1776.

— *See* DANIEL (Ralph T.) and LE HURAY (P.) The Sources of English Church Music 1549–1660. Compiled by R. T. Daniel and P. Le Huray. 1972. 8°. [*Early English Church Music. Supplementary vol.* 1.]   **E. 461.**

— *See* EAST (Michael) [Fourth Set of Bookes. No. 20.] When David heard, *etc.* ⟨Edited with keyboard reduction by P. Le Huray.⟩ [1963.] 8°.   **E. 442. gg. (3.)**

— *See* HOOPER (Edmund) Behold it is Christ, *etc.* ⟨Anthem. Edited by P. le Huray.⟩ [1961.] 8°.   **E. 442. bb. (8.)**

— *See* HOOPER (Edmund) Evening Service for Verses ... Edited by P. le Huray. [1963.] 8°.   **F. 1158. p. (18.)**

— *See* HOOPER (Edmund) The 'Short' Evening Service. Edited by P. Le Huray. [1964.] 8°. [*Oxford Church Services. S* 560.]
F. 1777. c.

LE HURAY (PETER)

— *See* KNIGHT (Gerald H.) and REED (W. L.) The Treasury of English Church Music. ⟨Volume two. 1545–1650. Edited by P. LeHuray.⟩ [1965.] 4°.   **F. 1171. ww.**

— *See* LOCKE (Matthew) [*Collections.*] Anthems and Motets. Transcribed and edited by P. le Huray. 1976. fol. [*Musica Britannica.* 38.]   **N. 10.**

— *See* STANLEY (John) [Six Concertos. Op. 10. No. 4.] Concerto in C minor ... [Organ.] Edited by P. Le Huray. [1967.] 4°.
g. 1378. x. (13.)

— *See* STANLEY (John) [Six Concertos. Op. 10. No. 5.] Concerto in A major ... Edited by P. Le Huray. [Organ.] [1968.] 4°.
g. 1378. ii. (10.)

— *See* STANLEY (John) [Six Concertos. Op. 10. No. 6.] Concerto in C major ... Edited by P. le Huray. [Organ.] [1974.] 4°.
g. 1378. tt. (11.)

— *See* TALLIS (Thomas) If ye love me. ⟨S. A. T. B.⟩ Transcribed and edited by P. le Huray, *etc.* [1972.] 8°. [*Tudor Church Music.* 69.]   **F. 1140. j.**

— *See* TERRY (*Sir* Richard R.) Tudor Church Music ... Edited by R. R. Terry, [E. H. Fellowes and others] *etc.* [Revised editions by P. Le Huray, D. Willcocks.] [1963, *etc.*] 8°.
F. 1140. j.

— *See* TYE (Christopher) Deliver us, good Lord. ⟨S. A. T. B. unacc.⟩ Edited by P. Le Huray. [1968.] 8°. [*Oxford Anthems. A* 252.]   **F. 1776.**

— *See* WEELKES (Thomas) Collected Anthems. Transcribed and edited by D. Brown ... and P. Le Huray. 1966. fol. [*Musica Britannica.* 23.]   **N. 10.**

— *See* WEELKES (Thomas) Evening Service. 'For trebles' ... Newly edited by P. Le Huray. [1962.] 8°. [*Church Services. no.* 327.]   **F. 1137.**

— *See* WHITE (Matthew) O praise God in his Holiness. Ps. 150. Matthew White. [Also attributed to Robert White.] Edited by P. le Huray. [1966.] 8°. [*Oxford Anthems. A* 237.]   **F. 1776.**

— *See* WHITE (William) *Chorister of Westminster Abbey.* O praise God in his Holiness ... Edited by P. le Huray. ⟨S. S. A. A. T. T. B. B.⟩ [1966.] 8°. [*Oxford Anthems. A* 237*.]
F. 1776.

LEI

— Lei perduta. Aria. *See* DONIZETTI (D. G. M.) [Pia de' Tolomei.]

— Lei Sold. [Song.] *See* MARIANI (A.) La Rose Felsinea. No. 8.

LEI (YÜ-SHENG)

— Ch'un-t'ien lai-le. [The Fu-chien folk song "Ts'aich'a-teng," adapted for kao-hu and two ku-cheng, by Lei Yü-sheng. Score.] pp. 17. *Yin-yüeh Ch'u-pan-she: Peking*, 1958. 8°.
G. 1363. l. (7.)

LEIBER

— *See* LIEBER.

LEIBL (CARL)

— Fest Cantate aufgeführt bei der Feier der Grundsteinlegung für den Fortbau des Cölner Domes ... Partitur. pp. 39. *Bei Eck & Comp.: Cöln*, [1844?] *obl.* fol.   **E. 601. kk. (1.)**

— Festkantate zur Feier der Grundsteinlegung für den Fortbau des Kölner Doms 1842. Herausgegeben von Paul Mies. pp. 40. *Musikverlag Schwann: Düsseldorf*, 1955. 4°. [*Denkmäler rheinischer Musik. Bd.* 5.]   **G. 1391.**

LEIBLING ( )

— Galopp-Waltzer, composed for the piano-forte. *In:* The Harmonicon. vol. 6, pt. 2. pp. 36, 37. 1828. 4°. **P. P. 1947.**

LEIBNER (RAYMOND)

— Agitato pour Piano et Violoncelle. *Paris,* [1877.] fol. **h. 1847. a. (13.)**

LEIBOLD (C.)

— "Hocher Peter" March ... Arranged [for military band] by Fred Godfrey. [Parts.] 25 pt. *S. A. Chappell: London,* [1872.] *obl.* 8°.
[*Army Journal. no.* 86.] *Printed on one side of the leaf only.* **h. 1562.**

LEIBOWITZ (RENÉ)

— A se stesso. (An sich selbst.) For double chorus (SATB) a cappella. [Words by] Giacomo Leopardi. German translation by Albrecht Betz and Luce Lombardi ... Op. 37, No. 3. ⟨Italian-German.⟩ pp. 25. *Boelke-Bomart: Hillsdale, N.Y.,* [1976.] 8°.
Part of "20th Century choral Music Series". **F. 1874. b. (18.)**

— Empedokles. For mixed chorus (SATB) a cappella. [Words by] Friedrich Hölderlin. Frend version by J. L. Monod ... Op. 13. ⟨German-French.⟩ pp. 13. *Boelke-Bomart: Hillsdale, N.Y.,* [1976.] 8°.
Part of "20th Century choral Music Series". **F. 1874. b. (19.)**

— Epigramma (Epigramm). For mixed chorus (S. M-s. A. T. Bar. B.) a cappella. [Words by] Torquato Tasso. German translation by Albrecht Betz and Luca Lombardi ... Op. 37, No. 2. ⟨Italian-German.⟩ pp. 11. *Boelke-Bomart: Hillsdale, N.Y.,* [1976.] 8°.
Part of "20th Century choral Music Series". **F. 1874. b. (20.)**

— Explanation of Metaphors. For two pianos, harp, percussion and narrator. ⟨Op. 15. [Words by] Raymond Quenéau. English version by R. L.⟩ [Score.] *Eng. & Fr.* pp. 27. *Bomart Music Publications: New York,* [1950.] 4°. **G. 814. f. (2.)**

— La Notte (Die Nacht). For mixed chorus (S. A. T. B.) a cappella. [Words by] Angelo Poliziano ... Op. 37, No. 1. ⟨German translation by Albrecht Betz and Luca Lombardi. Italian-German.⟩ pp. 9. *Boelke-Bomart: Hillside, N. Y.,* [1976.] 8°.
Part of "20th Century chorus Music Series". **F. 1874. b. (21.)**

— Quatre pièces pour piano. Vier Klavierstücke. Op. 8. pp. 28. *Universal-Edition: Wien,* [1947.] 4°. **g. 1128. p. (8.)**

— Three Poems of Pierre Reverdy, from "Les Ardoises du toit" for vocal quartet (or chamber choir) and piano. Spanish translations by Sylvia and Carlos Tuxen-Bang ... Op. 92. I. Son de cloche. ⟨II. Air. III. Solei.⟩ *Fr. & Span.* pp. 14. *Boelke-Bomart: Hillsdale, N. Y.,* [1976.] 8°.
Part of "20th Century choral Music Series". **F. 1874. b. (22.)**

— Two Settings after Poems by William Blake. For mixed chorus (SATB) a cappella. ⟨Op. 71. No. 1. The Sick Rose. No. 2. Never seek to tell thy Love. French version by J. L. Monod.⟩ English-French. pp. 10. *Boelke-Bomart: Hillsdale, N. Y.,* [1976.] 8°.
Parts of "20th Century choral Music Series". **F. 1874. b. (23.)**

— Suite for 9 Instruments. Op. 81. [Score.] ⟨Printed from the original manuscript.⟩ pp. 39. *Jobert: Paris,* [1975.] fol.
"Imprimé en Belgique". **h. 1564. ss. (3.)**

— Variations pour quatuor de saxophones. Op. 84. [Score.] pp. 24. *Éditions Jobert: Paris,* [1975.] 4°.
"Imprimé en Belgique". **h. 2270. e. (4.)**

— *See* LASSO (O. di) [Moduli sex, septem et duodecim vocum.] Laudate Dominum ... Transcription pour 12 instruments et étude de R. Leibowitz. [1949.] 4°. **G. 519. u. (16.)**

LEIBOWITZ (RENÉ)

— *See* SCHNABEL (A.) Duodecimet. ⟨Op. posth.⟩ Instrumentation by R. Leibowitz, *etc.* [1963.] 8°. **b. 276. b. (1.)**

LEIBROCK (J. A.)

— Transcriptionen classicher Lieder und Gesänge für Violoncello oder Violine mit Begleitung des Pianoforte von J. A. Leibrock. No. 1–12. *Braunschweig,* [1854, *etc.*] fol. **h. 1912.**

— *See* BERLIOZ (Louis H.) [Ouverture du Roi Lear. Op. 4.] Grande ouverture du Roi Léar ... Op. 4. Arrangée pour le piano à quatre mains par J. A. Leibrock. [1843?] fol. **g. 701. e. (1.)**

— *See* BERLIOZ (Louis H.) [Ouverture du Roi Lear. Op. 4.] Grande ouverture du Roi Lear ... arrangée pour le pianoforte ... par J. A. Leibrock. [1854.] fol. **h. 723. m. (2.)**

— *See* S., E. D. de [Santa Chiara.] Melodies favorites de l'opéra Sainte Claire (Santa Chiara) d'E. D. de S. pour le Pianoforte par J. A. Leibrock. [1857.] fol. **h. 725. f. (26.)**

LEICESTER

— Leicester. Opéra comique. *See* AUBER (D. F. E.)

LEICESTER, *County of.— County Council*

—— County of Leicester. Prayers & Hymns for use in Schools. The Hymn-book being an abridged edition of "Songs of Praise" together with a few additional hymns. *Oxford University Press, for the Leicestershire County Council: London,* [1928.] 8°. **3433. ee. 22.**

LEICESTER (EDWARD)

— A Love Story. Duet, the story by P. J. O'Reilly. *Ascherberg, Hopwood & Crew: London,* 1911. fol. **H. 1792. s. (1.)**

— Sacred Gems, arranged for the Piano or American Organ by E. Leicester, *etc. G. Newnes: London,* [1914.] fol.
No. 101 *of "The Music-Lovers' Library".* **H. 3928.**

LEICESTERSHIRE

— The Leicestershire Harmony. [Sacred music.] *See* ARNOLD (J.)

LEICHENBEGAENGNISS

— Leichenbegängniss. [Part-song.] *See* LACHNER (Franz) Vier Gesänge, *etc.* Op. 186. No. 1.

LEICHT

— Leicht Gepäck. [Song.] *See* NAUMANN (T. W.) [3 Lieder. Op. 2. No. 3.]

— Leicht' Gepäck. [Part-song.] *See* WALLAS (H.)

— Leicht im Herzen. [Song.] *See* LACHNER (Franz) Sechs Lieder, *etc.* Op. 152. No. 6.

LEICHTE

— Leichte Cavallerie. Komische Oper. *See* SUPPÉ (F. von)

— Leichte Klavierstücke russischer und sowjetischer Komponisten. Easy piano pieces by Russian and Soviet composers, *etc.* pp. 24. *Edition Peters: Leipzig,* [1968.] 4°. **g. 1138. t. (3.)**

— Leichte und singbare Melodien ... von J. F. G. [Variously attributed to Johann Friedrich Gräfe and Johann Friedrich Gräser.] 1780. 8°. *See* G., J. F. **K. 5. b. 21.**

LEICHTE

— Leichte zeitgenössische Stücke. Easy contemporary Pieces.
Violoncello & Piano. [By Bernhard Krol, Helmut Degen,
Dietrich Manicke and others. Score and part.] 2 pt.
D. Rahter: Hamburg, London, [1967.] 4°.
The cover bears the title "Violoncello + Piano".

g. 511. n. (11.)

LEICHTENTRITT (HUGO)

— Ausgewählte Werke von A. Hammerschmidt. Herausgegeben
von H. Leichtentritt. 1910. *See* DENKMAELER. Denkmäler
deutscher Tonkunst. Erste Folge, *etc.* Band XL. 1892, *etc.* fol.

H. 993.

— Ausgewählte Werke von H. Praetorius, herausgegeben von
H. Leichtentritt. 1905. *See* DENKMAELER. Denkmäler
Deutscher Tonkunst. Erste Folge, *etc.* Band XXIII. 1892, *etc.*
fol.

H. 993.

— Deutsche Hausmusik aus vier Jahrhunderten. Ausgewählt
und zum Vortrag eingerichtet, nebst erläuterndem Text von
H. Leichtentritt. (Die Musik herausgegeben von R. Strauss.)
Bard, Marquardt & Co.: Berlin, 1907. 4°.   **F. 1724. a.**

— Deutsche Hausmusik aus vier Jahrhunderten. Ausgewählt
und zum Vortrag eingerichtet, nebst erläuterndem Text von
H. Leichtentritt. [The music edited by Richard Strauss.]
pp. 110. *In Max Hesses Verlag: Berlin,* [1910?] 4°.

Hirsch M. 939.

— Mehrstimmige Lieder alter deutscher Meister für den Vortrag
bearbeitet von H. Leichtentritt. Sängerpartitur. (Heft I.
H. Isaak, H. Finck, A. von Bruck. Heft II. L. Senfl. Heft III. ...
IV. H. L. Hassler. Heft V. Leonard de Langenau, L. Lemlin,
T. Stoltzer, M. Eckel, J. Eccard und unbekannte Tonsetzer.)
5 Hft. *Breitkopf & Härtel: Leipzig, etc.,* [1906–08.] 8°.
*Part of "Meisterwerke Deutscher Tonkunst. Erlesene
Meisterwerke ... bezeichnet auf Grund der Denkmäler
deutscher Tonkunst", etc.*   **F. 1724.**

— Scherzi Musicali per la Viola da Gamba ... door Johan
Schenk. Op nieuw uitgegeven door Dr. H. Leichtentritt. 1907.
fol. *See* AMSTERDAM.— *Vereeniging voor Noord-Nederlands
Muziekgeschiedenis. Uitgave van oudere
Noord-nederlandsche Meesterwerken.* No. XXVIII. 1869, *etc.*
8° & fol.   **G. 12. a.**

— *See* HASSE (J. A.) Miserere. Psalm LI. ... Edited by
H. Leichtentritt. 1937. 8°.   **E. 602. vv. (21.)**

— *See* MONTEVERDI (C.) 12 fünfstimmige Madrigale ...
bearbeitet von H. Leichtentritt, *etc.* [1909.] 8°.   **G. 58. a. (1.)**

— *See* MONTEVERDI (C.) [Il quinto libro de madrigali a cinque
voci.—Era l'anima mia.] Madrigal Nr. XI. ... Bearbeitet von
H. Leichtentritt. [1963?] 8°.   **F. 8. d. (4.)**

— *See* TRAETTA (T.) Ausgewählte Werke. (Klavierauszug von
H. Leichtentritt und A. Beer-Walbrunn.) 1914. fol. [*Denkmäler
deutscher Tonkunst. Zweite Folge. Denkmäler der Tonkunst in
Bayern. Jahrg. XIV. Bd. I. Jahrg. XVII.*]   **H. 993. a.**

LEICHTER

— Leichter Sinn. [Song.] *See* GUMBERT (F.)

— Leichter Sinn. [Song.] *See* HILLER (F.)

— Leichter Sinn. [Trio.] *See* RAFF (J. J.)

— Leichter Verlust. [Song.] *See* MEYER-HELMUND (E.) Neues
Singen ... Op. 5. No. 1.

LEICHTSINN

— Leichtsinn. [Part-song.] *See* LACHNER (F.) Vier Gesänge, *etc.*
Op. 185. No. 3.

LEID

— Leid. [Song.] *See* KARG-ELERT (S.) Impressionen und
Gedichte ... Op. 63 ... Heft II. No. 7.

— Leid und Freud. [Song.] *See* ABT (F. W.) 5 Lieder. Op. 333.
No. 3.

— Leid und Lust. [Song.] *See* WALLNOEFER (A.) 4 Gesänge.
Op. 4. No. 4.

LEIDEN

— Leiden eines Choristen. [Musical sketch.] *See* BOSSET (C.)

— Das Leiden und die Auferstehung Jesu Christi. Passionspiel
mit Gesang und lebenden Bildern von einem Priester des
Bisthums Mainz. *F. Kirchheim: Mainz,* 1884. 8°.

11746. f. 15. (2.)

LEIDERITZ (FRANZ)

— Angioletta. Morceau de Salon for piano. *J. Williams:
London,* [1892.] fol.   **h. 1489. s. (33.)**

— Butterfly. Valsette for piano. *J. Williams: London,* [1892.] fol.

h. 1489. s. (34.)

— Chant d'Amour. [Flute and P. F.] *Rudall, Carte & Co.:
London,* [1889.] fol.
Part of "The Flute Player's Journal. First Series".

h. 232. a. (14.)

— Evening on the Solent, for the pianoforte. *C. Jefferys:
London,* [1888.] fol.   **h. 1484. s. (36.)**

— Flirtation. Morceau de Salon pour piano. *E. Ashdown:
London, etc.,* [1894.] fol.   **g. 605. f. (16.)**

— Flowers from Home. [Song.] Words by Oonagh. *H. Klein:
London,* [1886.] fol.   **H. 1788. v. (24.)**

— Friendship. Valses ... Arranged by F. Leideritz. [Orchestral
parts.] *J. Williams: London,* [1888.] 8°.   **e. 79. h. (1.)**

— From Happy Childhood. Four short ... pieces for the
Pianoforte. Op. 15. No. 1. Cradle Song. No. 2. Mother's
Prayer. No. 3. Sweet Dream. No. 4. Sunny Morning, *etc.*
F. Leideritz: London, [1885?] fol.   **h. 721. c. (2.)**

— Gypsy Gabriel. Lancers (Waltz) on subjects from the opera
... by F. Pascal. [P. F.] 2 no. *J. Williams: London,* [1892.] fol.

h. 3285. q. (24.)

— Gypsy Gabriel. Lancers. On airs from the Comic Opera ...
by F. Pascal. Arr. by F. Leideritz. [Orchestral parts.]
J. Williams: London, [1888.] 8°.   **e. 79. g. (17.)**

— Gypsy Gabriel. Waltz. On airs from the Comic Opera ... by
F. Pascal. Arr. by F. Leideritz. [Orchestral parts.] *J. Williams:
London,* [1883.] 8°.   **e. 79. h. (2.)**

— Hans und Liesel. Fantasia. [Flute and P. F.] *Rudall, Carte &
Co.: London,* [1889.] fol.
Part of "The Flute Player's Journal. Second Series".

h. 232. b. (12.)

— Ländler für das Pianoforte. (Op. 22.) *H. Klein: London,*
[1886.] fol.   **h. 1484. s. (35.)**

— Ländler für das Pianoforte. Op. 22. *E. Ashdown: London,*
1896. fol.   **g. 605. x. (9.)**

— The Land of Song. Song, words by H. A. Salmoné. *H. Klein:
London,* [1886.] fol.   **H. 1788. v. (25.)**

— La Libelle. Tarantelle ... for the piano. *J. William: London,*
[1892.] fol.   **h. 1489. s. (35.)**

— Maybreeze. (s'Mailüfterl.) Paraphrase on a popular German
air. [Orchestral parts.] 17 pt. *Lafleur & Sons: London; Paris*
[printed, 1892.] fol. & 8°.   **f. 800. (811.)**

LEIDERITZ (Franz)

— May Breeze ... Paraphrase on a German Popular Air for the Flute [and P. F.]. *Lafleur & Son: London*, [1892.] fol.
h. 2140. m. (8.)

— Quatre Morceaux pour violon et piano. 1. Polonaise. 2. Bolero. 3. Valsette. 4. Élégie. 4 no. *E. Donajowski: London*, [1891.] fol.
h. 1608. x. (38.)

— Quatre Morceaux de Salon. [No. 1.] Romance. [No. 2.] Nocturne. [No. 3.] Seladon Waltz. [No. 4.] Slavonski Mazurka. (Edited by A. de Lorgné.) [Violin and P. F.] 3 no. *F. W. Chanot & Sons: London*, (1903.) fol.
No. 4 was announced but has not been published.
h. 1681. n. (11.)

— My Soul is weary. [Song.] Words by H. A. Salmoné. *H. Klein: London*, [1887.] fol.
H. 1788. v. (26.)

— Nocturne for pianoforte. Op. 8. *S. Lucas, Weber & Co.: London*, [1884.] fol.
h. 1484. s. (34.)

— Polonaise in C für das Pianoforte. (Op. 24.) *H. Klein: London*, [1886.] fol.
h. 1484. s. (37.)

— Polonaise in C for the Pianoforte. Op. 24. *E. Ashdown: London*, 1896. fol.
g. 605. x. (10.)

— Skizzen. Kleine Phantasiebilder für das Pianoforte. *Leipzig*, [1882.] fol.
h. 3276. g. (14.)

— Song of the Waves. [Flute and P. F.] *Rudall, Carte & Co.: London*, [1892.] fol.
Part of "The Flute Player's Journal. First Series".
h. 232. a. (15.)

— The Spinning-Wheel, for the pianoforte. *E. Donajowski: London*, [1898.] fol.
h. 3282. f. (24.)

— Tosca. Morceau de salon pour piano. *E. Ashdown: London*, [1887.] fol.
g. 543. j. (25.)

— Trust me. Song, words written by Oonagh, *etc. H. Klein: London*, [1886.] fol.
H. 1788. v. (27.)

— Vanished. Song, words by H. W. Reinhard. *H. Klein: London*, [1884.] fol.
H. 1788. v. (28.)

— Zariphah. Mélodie pour piano. *E. Ashdown: London*, [1887.] fol.
g. 543. j. (26.)

— *See* HEMMING (Hall) The Oatlands Park Waltz ... Arranged for the orchestra by F. Leideritz. [1888.] 8°.
f. 800. (617.)

— *See* KLEIN (Henry) "Submission" ... Arranged for the orchestra by F. Leideritz. [1888.] 8°.
f. 800. (718.)

LEIDESDORF (J. M.)

— *See* LEIDESDORF (Max J.)

LEIDESDORF (Max Joseph)

— Carnival Waltz ... for the piano-forte. *In:* The Harmonicon. vol. 4, pt. 2. p. 64. 1826. 4°.
P. P. 1947.

— Fantasia and variations on airs from [D. G. M. Donizetti's opera] Lucrezia Borgia, for the Piano Forte. *Z. T. Purday: London*, [1844.] fol.
h. 702. (39.)

— Fantasie for the Piano Forte on Airs from Rossini's Opera Semiramide. ⟨New & superior edition.⟩ pp. 11. *Metzler & Son, for the Proprietors: London*, [c. 1830.] fol.
h. 1226. f. (7.)

— Fantasia on airs from Rossini's ... opera of Semiramide. [P. F.] *London*, [1835?] fol.
g. 272. p. (4.)

— Fantaisie pour le Piano-Forte ... sur des Motifs de la Semiramis. [By G. A. Rossini.] *[Paris? 1835?]* fol.
La Grande Bibliothèque musicale pour le Piano-Forte, No. 69.
g. 232. d. (21.)

LEIDESDORF (Max Joseph)

— Die heilige Cäcilia. [Cantata.] Gedicht von Theodor Körner ... 87tes Werk. Vollständige Partitur nebst beigefügtem — vom Verfasser eingerichteten — Klavierauszug. pp. 110. *Bei S. A. Steiner und Comp.: Wien*, [1818.] fol.
With Italian words added in MS throughout and alternative versions in MS to passages on pp. 43, 44 and 78. **H. 230. zz.**

— La Perseverance. Sonate pour le pianoforte ... Oeuvre 132. pp. 28. *Chez S. A. Steiner et comp.: Vienne*, [1822.] obl. fol.
e. 282. ii. (2.)

— Polonaise brillante ... Pour le piano, *etc*. pp. 11. *Au magasin de musique de Henry Lemoine: Paris*, [c. 1820.] fol.
h. 721. z. (14.)

— Premier quatuor pour deux violons, alto & violoncelle ... Oeuvre 144. [Parts.] 4 pt. *Sauer & Leidesdorf: Vienne*, [1823?] 4°.
g. 410. b. (6.)

— Rondo brillant pour le pianoforte ... Oeuv. 163. pp. 12. *M. J. Leidesdorf: Vienne*, [1827?] fol.
h. 3870. r. (18.)

— Rondo elegant on [L. van Beethoven's] melodies (Heart, my heart, *etc*.) arr: by L. V. Hammas. *See* RUDOLPHUS (C.) Les Aimables, duets for piano & violin, *etc*. No. 11. [1846, *etc*.] fol.
h. 1720.

— Rondeau pour le Piano Forte ... sur des Motifs de la Donna del Lago. [By G. A. Rossini.] *[Paris? 1835?]* fol.
La Grande Bibliothèque musicale pour le Piano-Forte, No. 55.
g. 232. d. (22.)

— Rondeau pour le Piano Forte ... sur des Motifs de Maometto II. [By G. A. Rossini.] *[Paris? 1835?]* fol.
La Grande Bibliothèque musicale pour le Piano-Forte, No. 49.
g. 232. d. (23.)

— Sonate brillante pour le piano-forte seul ... Op. 30. pp. 15. *Chez Pierre Mechetti: Vienne*, [1815.] obl. fol. **f. 770. v. (4.)**

— Grand trio pour pianoforte, flûte et alto ... Op. 14. *Au bureau des arts et d'industrie: Vienne*, [1807.] obl. fol.
A slip bearing the imprint "Chez Breitkopf & Härtel: Leipsic" has been pasted below the original imprint. Imperfect; wanting the flute and viola parts. **E. 1050. z. (10.)**

— Six valses caractéristiques pour le Piano Forte. *London*, [1833.] fol.
h. 117. (16.)

— Huit Variations pour le Piano Forte sur le Rondo favori de Rossini. Non più mesta. *[Paris? 1835?]* fol.
La Grande Bibliothèque musicale pour le Piano-Forte, No. 74.
g. 232. d. (24.)

— *See* GALLENBERG (W. R. von) La Tombe d'Ismaan. Ballet ... arrangé pour le Pianoforté par M. J. Leidesdorf. [1820?] *obl.* fol.
f. 271. (1.)

— *See* MERCADANTE (S.) [L'Apoteose d'Ercole.] Overtura ... ridotta per pianoforte a 4 mani da J. M. Leidesdorf. [1825?] *obl.* fol.
e. 379. (7.)

— *See* MOZART (W. A.) [Don Giovanni.] Don Juan ... Für das Piano-Forte eingerichtet von M. J. Leidesdorf. [1821?] *obl.* fol.
Hirsch IV. 1211.

— *See* MOZART (W. A.) Die Entführung aus dem Serail ... Vollständiger Auszug für das Piano-Forte allein, *etc*. [Arranged by M. J. Leidesdorf.] [1819.] *obl.* fol.
e. 490. r.

— *See* MOZART (W. A.) Die Entführung ... Für das Piano-Forte eingerichet von M. J. Leidesdorf. [1819.] *obl.* fol.
Hirsch IV. 1192. a.

— *See* MOZART (W. A.) Die Entführung aus dem Serail ... Für das Piano-Forte allein ... eingerichtet von M. J. Leidesdorf. [c. 1820.] *obl.* fol.
Hirsch IV. 1191.

— *See* MOZART (W. A.) Die Entführung ... Für das Piano-Forte eingerichtet von M. J. Leidesdorf. [1820?] *obl.* fol.
Hirsch IV. 1192.

LEIDESDORF (MAX JOSEPH)

— *See* MOZART (W. A.) [Le Nozze di Figaro.] Figaro's Hochzeit ... Für das Pianoforte allein ... eingerichtet von M. J. Leidesdorf. [1821?] *obl.* fol.   **Hirsch IV. 1201.**

— *See* MOZART (W. A.) [Le Nozze di Figaro.] Die Hochzeit des Figaro ... Für das Pianoforte allein ... eingerichtet von M. J. Leidesdorf. [1830.] *obl.* fol.   **Hirsch IV. 1200.**

— *See* ROSSINI (G. A.) Adelaide di Borgogna ... ridotto per il cembalo solo da M. I. Leidesdorf. [1824.] *obl.* fol.   **Hirsch IV. 1248.**

— *See* ROSSINI (G. A.) Armida ... ridotta per il cembalo solo da M. I. Leidesdorf. [1823.] *obl.* fol.   **Hirsch IV. 1249.**

— *See* ROSSINI (G. A.) Armida ... Ridotta per il cembalo solo da M. I. Leidesdorf. [1823.] *obl.* fol.   **Hirsch M. 480.**

— *See* ROSSINI (G. A.) Aureliano in Palmira ... ridotto per il cembalo solo da M. I. Leidesdorf. [1825?] *obl.* fol.   **Hirsch IV. 1250.**

— *See* ROSSINI (G. A.) Der Barbier von Sevilla ... Für das Pianoforte ... eingerichtet von M. J. Leidesdorf. [1820?] *obl.* fol.   **Hirsch IV. 1251.**

— *See* ROSSINI (G. A.) [La Cambiale di matrimonio.] Il Matrimonio per cambiale. Farsa in un atto ... Ridotta per il cembalo sola da M. I. Leidesdorf. [1826.] *obl.* fol.   **e. 279. p.**

— *See* ROSSINI (G. A.) [La Cenerentola.] Aschenbrödel ... für das Piano allein ... von M. J. Leidesdorf. [1820?] *obl.* fol.   **E. 187. qq.**

— *See* ROSSINI (G. A.) Demetrio e Polibio ... ridotta per il cembalo solo da M. I. Leidesdorf. [1825?] *obl.* fol.   **Hirsch IV. 1254.**

— *See* ROSSINI (G. A.) La Donna del Lago ... ridotto per il cembalo solo da M. I. Leidesdorf. [1828?] *obl.* fol.   **Hirsch IV. 1255.**

— *See* ROSSINI (G. A.) Edoardo e Cristina ... ridotto per il cembalo solo da M. I. Leidesdorf. [1828?] *obl.* fol.   **Hirsch IV. 1256.**

— *See* ROSSINI (G. A.) La Gazza ladra ... Für das Piano-Forte eingerichtet von M. J. Leidesdorf. [1820?] *obl.* fol.   **e. 279. l.**

— *See* ROSSINI (G. A.) Inganno felice. Opera buffa ... ridotto per cembalo solo da M. I. Leidesdorf. [1824?] *obl.* fol.   **e. 279. n.**

— *See* ROSSINI (G. A.) Matilde di Chabran ... ridotto per il cembalo solo da M. I. Leidesdorf. [1824?] *obl.* fol.   **Hirsch IV. 1262.**

— *See* ROSSINI (G. A.) [Matilda di Chabran.] Corradino, dramma in due atti ... per il canto e piano-forte, ridotto da J. M. Leidesdorf. [1822.] fol.   **F. 69. v.**

— *See* ROSSINI (G. A.) Mosé in Egitto ... ridotto per il cembalo solo da M. I. Leidesdorf. [1823.] *obl.* fol.   **e. 279. h.**

— *See* ROSSINI (G. A.) La Pietra del Paragone ... ridotto per il cembalo solo da M. I. Leidesdorf. [1825.] *obl.* fol.   **Hirsch IV. 1267.**

— *See* ROSSINI (G. A.) Ricciardo e Zoraide. Opera seria ... ridotto per il cembalo solo da M. I. Leidesdorf. [1824.] *obl.* fol.   **Hirsch M. 487.**

— *See* ROSSINI (G. A.) La Scala di seta. Farsa ... ridotta per il cembalo solo da M. I. Leidesdorf. [1824.] *obl.* fol.   **e. 279. f.**

— *See* ROSSINI (G. A.) [Il Signor Bruschino.] Il Bruschino ... ridotto per il cembalo solo da M. I. Leidesdorf. [1824.] *obl.* 4°.   **e. 279. g. (3.)**

LEIDESDORF (MAX JOSEPH)

— *See* ROSSINI (G. A.) Il Turco in Italia ... ridotto per il cembalo solo da M. I. Leidesdorf. [1823.] *obl.* fol.   **Hirsch IV. 1272.**

— *See* ROSSINI (G. A.) Zelmira ... ridotta per il piano forte da M. J. Leidesdorf, *etc.* [1821.] *obl.* fol.   **Hirsch IV. 1274.**

— *See* SCHOBERLECHNER (F.) Valse Martellini. Variations sur une Valse ... de M. J. Leidesdorf, *etc.* [1835?] fol.   **R. M. 25. k. 7. (9.)**

— *See* UMLAUF (M.) and GYROWETZ (A.) Lodoiska ... Vollständiger Clavierauszug eingerichtet von M. J. Leidesdorf. [1825?] *obl.* fol.   **e. 1003.**

— *See* WEBER (C. M. F. E. von) [Euryanthe. – Die Thale dampfen.] Jäger Chorus ... arranged for the piano-forte by Leidesdorf. 1825. 4°. [*Harmonicon. vol. 3, pt. 2. pp.* 38, 39.]   **P. P. 1947.**

— *See* WEBER (C. M. F. E. von) Der Freyschütze ... Ausgabe mit Hinweglassung der Worte für das Piano-Forte von M. J. Leidesdorf. [1822?] *obl.* fol.   **R. M. 10. e. 11.**

— *See* WEBER (C. M. F. E. von) First Grand Quatuor. Edited by M. J. Leidesdorf. [1845?] fol.   **h. 2785. k. (5.)**

— *See* WEBER (C. M. F. E. von) Fourth Grand ... Sonata, Op. 70 ... Edited by M. J. Leidesdorf. [1848?] fol.   **h. 1336. e. (5.)**

LEIDGEBEL (A. L.)

— Capriccio für zwei Pianos. *Berlin,* [1874.] fol.   **h. 1487. p. (35.)**

— Sonate für das Pianoforte. *Berlin,* [1874.] fol.   **h. 1487. p. (36.)**

LEIDIG (VERNON)

— *See* NIEHAUS (Lennie) and LEIDIG (V.) A la mañana (Based on Latin rhythms) ... Arranged by L. Niehaus and V. Leidig, *etc.* [Orchestra.] [1961.] 4°.   **h. 3210. i. (745.)**

— *See* NIEHAUS (Lennie) and LEIDIG (V.) Indian Chant and Dance (Based on American Indian themes) ... Arranged by L. Niehaus and V. Leidig, *etc.* [Orchestra.] [1961.] 4°.   **h. 3210. i. (744.)**

— *See* NIEHAUS (Lennie) and LEIDIG (V.) Pastorale and Hymn (Based on traditional melodies) ... Arranged by L. Niehaus and V. Leidig, *etc.* [Orchestra.] [1961.] 4°.   **h. 3210. i. (746.)**

— *See* VERDI (F. G. F.) [La Traviata. – Libiamo nei lieti calici.] Waltz from "La Traviata" ... Arranged by L. Niehaus and V. Leidig, *etc.* [Orchestra.] [1961.] 4°.   **h. 3210. i. (747.)**

LEIDING (GEORG DIETRICH)

— 2 Praeludien. [In E flat and C.] (Herausgegeben von Max Seiffert.) [Organ.] *See* SEIFFERT (M.) Organum, *etc.* Reihe 4. Hft. 7. c. [1924–30?] fol.   **Hirsch M. 1204.**

— Praeludium in B. Herausgegeben von Friedrich Wilhelm Riedel. [Organ.] pp. 16. *Kistner & Siegel & Co: Lippstadt,* [1961.] *obl.* 4°. [*Die Orgel. Reihe 2. no. 15.*]   **e. 1093. ss.**

LEIDZÉN (ERIK W. G.)

— Debonnaire. Overture. Full Score. *C. Fischer: New York, etc.,* 1937. 4°.   **g. 727. j. (11.)**

— Dixie Rhapsody. Symphonic Band. Full Score. *Ernest Williams School of Music: Brooklyn,* 1941. 4°.   **g. 727. m. (11.)**

— Holiday. Overture. Full Score. *C. Fischer: New York, etc.,* 1937. 4°.   **g. 727. j. (12.)**

LEIDZÉN (Erik W. G.)

— Scottish Rhapsody. Symphonic Band. Full Score. *Ernest Williams School of Music: Brooklyn*, 1941. 4°.

g. 727. m. (12.)

— Sinfonietta. For brass Band, *etc.* ⟨Full score.⟩ pp. 47. *R. Smith & Co.: London*, [1955.] *obl.* 8°. **e. 503. l. (11.)**

— Triofolium. Trio (Duet) (Solo) for B♭ Cornets (Trumpets) with Piano accompaniment. 3 no. *Carl Fischer: New York, etc.*, 1941. 4°. **g. 1105. a. (11.)**

— The Trumpeters. Cornet or Trumpet Quartet with Piano accompaniment. [Parts.] *Chappell & Co.: London*, [1942.] 4°. **g. 1105. a. (12.)**

— *See* BACH (J. S.) [Geistliche Lieder aus Schemelli's Gesangbuch und dem Notenbuch der Anna Magdalena Bach. No. 42.] Komm, süsser Tod. Come, sweet Death ... Transcribed ... by E. W. G. Leidzén. 1936. 8°. **h. 3210. h. (534.)**

— *See* BACH (J. S.) [Herz und Mund und That und Leben.—Wohl mir, dass ich Jesum habe.—Instrumental.] Jesu, Joy of Man's Desiring ... Transcribed ... by E. W. G. Leidzén. 1936. 4°. **h. 3210. h. (535.)**

— *See* BACH (J. S.) [3 Sonaten für Klavier und Flöte. B. G. Jahrg. 9. No. 2.] Siciliano ... Transcribed ... by E. W. G. Leidzén. 1936. 8°. **h. 3210. h. (538.)**

— *See* BACH (J. S.) [Das wohltemperirte Clavier. Tl. 1. No. 22.] Prelude and Fugue ... Arranged by E. W. G. Leidzén, *etc.* 1937. 4°. **h. 3210. h. (596.)**

— *See* BACH (J. S.) [Das wohltemperirte Clavier. Tl. 1. Prelude 22.] Prelude on Psalms. For full chorus of mixed voices a cappella ... Arranged by E. Leidzen. [1962.] 8°. **F. 956. hh. (7.)**

— *See* BEETHOVEN (L. van) Ecossaises ... [K.-H. 83.] Transcribed ... by E. W. G. Leidzén. [1935.] 4°. **h. 3210. h. (489.)**

— *See* BERLIOZ (L. H.) [Episode de la vie d'un artiste. Op. 14. Marche au supplice.] March to the Scaffold ... Transcribed ... by E. W. G. Leidzén. 1937. 4°. **h. 3210. h. (542.)**

— *See* BERLIOZ (L. H.) [Les Troyens. 2ᵐᵉ Partie.—Les Troyens à Carthage.] Marche Troyenne ... Arranged ... by E. W. G. Leidzén. 1939. 4°. **h. 3210. h. (680.)**

— *See* BORODIN (A. R.) [Symphony No. 2.] First Movement from the Second Symphony ... Arranged ... by E. W. G. Leidzén. 1940. 4°. **g. 727. l. (5.)**

— *See* BORODIN (A. P.) [Symphony No. 2.] First Movement from the Second Symphony ... Arranged ... by E. W. G. Leidzén. 1940. 12°. **h. 3210. h. (762.)**

— *See* BUCK (D.) Triumphal March ... (Op. 26), *etc.* (Arranged by E. W. G. Leidzén.) 1938. 4°. **h. 3210. h. (604.)**

— *See* DVOŘAK (A.) [Symphonies. No. 9.] Finale from the New World Symphony. Transcribed ... by E. W. G. Leidzén, *etc.* 1936. 4°. **h. 3210. h. (499.)**

— *See* GLIER (R. M.) [Красный мак.—Танец советских матросов.—Яблочко.] Russian Sailors' Dance ... Transcribed ... by E. W. G. Leidzén. 1937. 4°. **h. 3210. h. (613.)**

— *See* GLINKA (M. I.) [Жизнь за Царя.] Finale from the Opera A Life for the Czar ... Transcribed ... by E. W. G. Leidzén. 1937. 4°. **h. 3210. h. (559.)**

— *See* GOLDMAN (Edwin F.) Introduction and Tarantella. Cornet solo with piano accompaniment, *etc.* ⟨Arr. by E. Leidzén.⟩ [1950.] 4°. **g. 1105. e. (14.)**

— *See* HOLST (G. T. von) [Two Songs without Words. Op. 22. No. 2.] Marching Song ... Arranged ... by E. W. G. Leidzén. 1940. 4°. **h. 3210. h. (770.)**

LEIDZÉN (Erik W. G.)

— *See* KREBS (J. L.) Burlesca ... [Band.] Transcribed by E. Leidzén. [1945.] 8°. **h. 3210. i. (34.)**

— *See* KREISLER (F.) Caprice viennois ... Transcribed for string quartet (or string orchestra) by E. Leidzén. [1948.] 4°. **h. 1694. c. (19.)**

— *See* KREISLER (F.) [Klassische Manuskripte. No. 10.] Liebesfreud ... Arranged by E. Leidzen. 1945. 4°. **h. 1694. c. (6.)**

— *See* KREISLER (F.) [Klassische Manuskripte. No. 10.] Liebesfreud ... Transcribed for string quartet (or string orchestra) by E. Leidzén. [1948.] 4°. **h. 1694. c. (20.)**

— *See* KREISLER (F.) [Klassische Manuskripte. No. 11.] Liebesleid ... Arranged for Horn in F and Piano by E. Leidzén. 1945. 4°. **h. 1694. c. (8.)**

— *See* KREISLER (F.) [Klassische Manuskripte. No. 11.] Liebesleid ... Arranged for Trombone ... and Piano by E. Leidzén. 1945. 4°. **h. 1694. c. (9.)**

— *See* KREISLER (F.) [Klassische Manuskripte. No. 11.] Liebesleid ... Arranged for Solo B♭ Trumpet ... ⟨and Piano⟩ by E. Leidzén. 1945. 4°. **h. 1694. c. (10.)**

— *See* KREISLER (F.) [Klassische Manuskripte. No. 11.] Liebesleid ... Transcribed for string quartet ⟨or string orchestra⟩ by E. Leidzén. [1948.] 4°. **h. 1694. d. (1.)**

— *See* KREISLER (F.) [Klassische Manuskripte. No. 12.] Schön Rosmarin ... Arranged ... by E. Leidzén. 1945. 4°. **h. 1694. c. (11.)**

— *See* KREISLER (F.) [Klassische Manuskripte. No. 12.] Schön Rosmarin ... Transcribed for string quartet ⟨or string orchestra⟩ by E. Leidzén. [1948.] 4°. **h. 1694. d. (3.)**

— *See* KREISLER (F.) [Marche miniature viennoise.] Miniature Viennese March ... Adapted for clarinet by E. Leidzén. [1948.] 4°. **h. 1694. d. (9.)**

— *See* KREISLER (F.) [Marche miniature viennoise.] Miniature Viennese March ... Adapted for E♭ alto saxophone by E. Leidzén. [1949.] 4°. **h. 1694. d. (8.)**

— *See* KREISLER (F.) [Marche miniature viennoise.] Miniature Viennese March ... Adapted for ⟨cornet or⟩ trumpet by E. Leidzén. [1949.] 4°. **h. 1694. d. (10.)**

— *See* KREISLER (F.) [Marche miniature viennoise.] Miniature Viennese March ... Transcribed for string quartet ⟨or string orchestra⟩ by E. Leidzén. [1949.] 4°. **h. 1694. d. (2.)**

— *See* KREISLER (F.) Rondino on a Theme of Beethoven ... Arranged for 1 or 2 Horns in F and Piano by E. Leidzén. 1945. 4°. **h. 1694. c. (15.)**

— *See* KREISLER (F.) Rondino on a Theme of Beethoven ... Arranged for Trombone ⟨and Piano⟩ ... by E. Leidzén. 1945. 4°. **h. 1694. c. (16.)**

— *See* KREISLER (F.) Rondino on a Theme of Beethoven ... Arranged for 1 or 2 B♭ Trumpets ... and Piano by E. Leidzén. 1945. 4°. **h. 1694. c. (17.)**

— *See* KREISLER (F.) Rondino on a Theme of Beethoven ... Arranged for 1, 2, or 3 clarinets and piano by E. Leidzén. [1949.] 4°. **h. 1694. d. (11.)**

— *See* KREISLER (F.) Tambourin chinois ... Adapted for clarinet by E. Leidzén. [1948.] 4°. **h. 1694. d. (14.)**

— *See* KREISLER (F.) Tambourin chinois ... Transcribed for string quartet ⟨or string orchestra⟩ by E. Leidzén. [1949.] 4°. **h. 1694. d. (4.)**

— *See* MONIUSZKO (S.) Halka. Overture ... Transcribed ... by E. W. G. Leidzén. 1938. 4°. **h. 3210. h. (635.)**

LEIDZÉN (Erik W. G.)

— See Musorgsky (M. P.) [Boris Godounov.] Coronation Scene ... Transcribed ... by E. W. G. Leidzén. 1936. 4°.

h. 3210. h. (571.)

— See Musorgsky (M. P.) [Tableaux d'une Exposition.] Pictures at an Exhibition ... Part 1 ... Transcribed ... by E. W. G. Leidzén. 1941. 4°.

h. 3210. h. (779.)

— See Musorgsky (M. P.) [Tableaux d'une Exposition.] Pictures at an Exhibition ... Part 3 ... Transcribed ... by E. W. G. Leidzén. 1938. 4°.

h. 3210. h. (636.)

— See Prokof'ev (S. S.) [Musique d'enfants. Op. 65. No. 6, 5, 10.] Summer Day Suite ... Scored for band by E. Leidzen. [1948.] 4°.

h. 3210. i. (43.)

— See Rakhmaninov (S. V.) [Rapsodie sur un thème de Paganini. Op. 43.] Eighteenth Variation from Rapsodie on a Theme of Paganini, etc. ⟨Piano part edited by E. Leidzen.⟩ [1954.] 4°.

h. 3984. h. (10.)

— See Respighi (O.) [Pini di Roma.—I Pini della Via Appia.] Pines of the Appian Way ... Edited for American bands by E. Leidzen, etc. [1949.] 4°.

g. 1228. (2.)

— See Rimsky-Korsakov (N. A.) [Mlada.—Marche des Princes.] Procession of Nobles ... Arranged ... by E. W. G. Leidzén. 1938. 4°.

h. 3210. h. (645.)

— See Rossini (G. A.) [Guillaume Tell.] William Tell. Overture ... Arranged by E. W. G. Leidzén. 1938. 4°.

h. 3210. h. (722.)

— See Speaks (O.) [Two Songs. No. 2.] Sylvia ... Arranged by E. Leidzen, etc. 1946. 4°.

g. 1112. a. (14.)

LEIERING (Volckman)

— I know that my Redeemer lives. (Based on O Filii et Filae by V. Leiering) for 3 part and 4 part mixed choruses a capella (or 3 solo voices and 4 part mixed chorus). ⟨[Words by] Samuel Medley (1775). Arranged by George Lynn.⟩ pp. 8. *Mercury Music Corporation: New York*, [1953.] 8°. **F. 1776. s. (20.)**

LEIERKASTENMANN

— Leierkastenmann. [Song.] See Pfitzner (H.) Vier Lieder ... Op. 15. No. 1.

LEIFER (Fred)

— The Li'l Abner official Square Dance Handbook. Easy-to-learn steps, calls, games, profit-making ideas, music and illustrations by F. Leifer. Musical arrangements for piano by Manny Blanc. pp. 127. *A. S. Barnes and Co.: New York*, [1953.] 8°. **7922. ee. 11.**

LEIFS (Jón)

— Ættjarðarlög. ⟨Op. 27. Karlakór.⟩ pp. 6. *Landsútgáfan:* [*Reykjavík*, c. 1950.] fol. **G. 1448. (3.)**

— Alþýðusöngvar. ⟨Op. 32.⟩ [S. A. T. B.] *Landsútgáfan: Reykjavík*, [1950.] fol. **I. 525. (7.)**

— Island-uverture. ⟨Op. 9.⟩ pp. 63. *Islandia Edition: Reykjavík;* [*Stockholm* printed,] 1950. 8°. **d. 134. vv.**

— Íslenzk þjóðlög ... Fyrir tvær hendur ... I. Icel., Norw. & Ger. pp. 18. *Georg Kallmeyer Verlag: Wolfenbüttel, Berlin*, 1929. 8°. **E. 1885. t. (1.)**

— Kirkjulög. Kirkesange. Kirchenlieder. Three Hymns. ⟨Op. 12a.⟩ [Words by Hallgrímr Pétursson.] Icel., Dan., Ger. & Eng. pp. 5. *Islandia Edition: Reykjavík*, [1950.] fol. **G. 1448. (1.)**

LEIFS (Jón)

— Fjögur lög fyrir pianoforte ... Four pieces for the piano. Op. 2. pp. 7. *Verlag für neuzeitliche Kunst Max Thomas: Magdeburg*, [1923.] fol. **h. 62. e. (8.)**

— Ný rímnadanzlög. Neue Island-Tänze. Op. 14 b. Piano. *Islandia Edition: Reykjavík*, [1950.] fol. **g. 230. r. (13.)**

— Ouvertüre zu "Loftr". Forleikr að "Galdra-Lofti" ... Op. 10. Partitur. pp. 51. *Fr. Kistner & C. F. W. Siegel: Leipzig*, [1933.] fol.
With a catalogue of works by Leifs published by Kistner and Siegel inserted. **h. 1564. yy. (2.)**

— Preludiae organo. pp. 7. *Islandia Edition: Reykjavík*, 1951. fol. **g. 1380. ff. (9.)**

— Requiem. Úr íslenzkum þjóðvísum och efter Jonas Hallgrímsson. ⟨Op. 33b.⟩ [Part-song.] Icel. & Swed. pp. 4. *Islandia Edition: Reykjavík*, [1949.] 8°. **E. 460. h. (9.)**

— Rímnadanslög. Karlakór. ⟨Op. 11.⟩ 4 no. *Landsútgáfan: Reykjavík*, [1950.] 8°. **F. 1771. ll. (3.)**

— Rímnadanslög. Icelandic dances. ⟨Op. 11.⟩ pp. 7. *Islandia Edition: Reykjavík*, [1950.] fol. **g. 230. r. (14.)**

— Söngvar. ⟨Op. 14a.⟩ [Words by Jóhann Jónsson.] Icel., Ger., Dan. & Eng. pp. 5. *Islandia Edition: Reykjavík*, [1950.] 8°.

G. 1448. (4.)

— Þjóðhvöt. Cantata nazionale Op. 13. Kvæði eftir Davið Stefánsson. Deutsch von Wolfgang Mohr. [Score.] Icel. & Ger. pp. 81. *Kistner & Siegel: Leipzig*, [1934.] 4°.
No. 73 of an edition of 100 copies. **G. 190. m. (1.)**

— Þjóðlög. Karlakór. *Islandia Edition: Reykjavík*, [1950.] 8°.

F. 1771. ll. (2.)

— Þrjú íslenzk sálmalög til kirkjusöngs. Chorales islandici. ⟨Op. 17b.⟩ *Islandia Edition: Reykjavík*, [1950.] obl. 8°.

B. 418. h.

— Tilbrigði við tema eftir Beethoven. Variazioni pastorali. Op. 8. [Score.] pp. 44. *Kistner & Siegel: Leipzig*, [1933.] 4°.
No. 87 of an edition of 100 copies. **g. 270. ff. (1.)**

LEIGH.— Leigh Choral Union

— The Service Book for the fourth annual Festival ... held ... on ... 10th August, 1881. Edited by Rev. Jackson Smith. pp. 31. *Printed by Novello, Ewer & Cᵒ: London*, [1881.] 8°.

B. 512. ss. (1.)

LEIGH (Allan)

— Come and whisper. Song. Written by G. W. Southey. *Arthur & Co.: Birmingham*, [1899.] fol. **H. 1799. h. (27.)**

LEIGH (Arthur George)

— The Chorley Tune Book. A Manual of 166 Hymn Tunes, 217 ... Chants, 53 Kyrie Eleisons, and a Setting of "The Story of the Cross," edited by A. G. Leigh. *C. Vincent: London*, [1899.] 8°. **F. 1171. z. (4.)**

— L'Eau de Nil (The Water of the Nile) polka. [P. F.] *London*, [1876.] fol. **h. 1482. z. (24.)**

— The Fairies' Revel, sketch for the Pianoforte. *London*, [1873.] fol. **h. 1482. z. (23.)**

— Sacred Music, consisting of 33 hymn tunes, 10 responses to the Commandments, and 33 single and double chants. pp. 36. [1882.] 8°.
The imprint has been obliterated. **C. 20. rr. (1.)**

— The Snowdrop and the Violet, deux morceaux faciles ... pour le Piano. 2 no. *London*, [1876.] fol. **h. 1482. z. (25.)**

LEIGH (ARTHUR GEORGE)

— The Storm Waltzes. [P. F.] *London*, [1878.] fol.
h. 1494. q. (16.)

— *See* KYRIES. The Cathedral Collection of Kyries ... by ...
A. G. Leigh, *etc*. [1893.] *obl.* 4°. **B. 512. c. (2.)**

LEIGH (ASHTON)

— Playtime. Sketch for pianoforte. *J. H. Larway: London*,
[1893.] fol. **g. 605. f. (17.)**

LEIGH (CLINTON)

— Danse Moresque. [P. F.] *S. Brainards Sons Co.: New York,
Chicago*, 1899. fol. **h. 3282. w. (39.)**

LEIGH (EGERTON)

— Ballads & Legends of Cheshire. [With musical settings of
some poems.] pp. xviii. 314. *Longmans & Co.: London*, 1867.
4°. **11602. h. 1.**

LEIGH (ERIC)

— The Buckle. Unison song. Words by Walter de la Mare. [Staff
and tonic sol-fa notation.] pp. 4. *J. B. Cramer & Co.:
London*, [1962.] 8°.
[*Cramer's Library of Unison and Part-songs. no.* 297.]
E. 1678. a.

— Two Carols. [1.] Puer natus. ⟨[2.] Dormi Jesu.⟩ [S. A. T. B.]
B. Feldman & Co.: London, [1970.] 8°. **F. 260. rr. (13.)**

— The Cupboard. Words by Walter de la Mare. [Unison song.
Staff and tonic sol-fa notation.] pp. 3. *Novello & Co.:
London*, [1960.] 8°.
[*School Songs.* 2047.] **F. 280. d.**

— Two Hymn Preludes. For organ ... Dundee. Song 67. pp. 5.
B. Feldman & Co.: London, [1971.] 4°. **f. 337. d. (5.)**

— Leisure. A two-part canon for equal voices. Words by W. H.
Davies. pp. 4. *Novello & Co.: London*, [1960.] 8°.
[*Two-part Songs.* 368.] **F. 280. e.**

— The Linnet. Unison Song. Words by Walter de la Mare. [Staff
and tonic sol-fa notation.] pp. 4. *J. B. Cramer & Co.:
London*, [1962.] 8°.
[*Cramer's Library of unison and Part-songs. no.* 293.]
E. 1678. a.

— Mary ... ⟨Song for unison voices.⟩ Words by Walter de la
Mare. pp. 4. *Chappell & Co.: London*, [1962.] 8°.
E. 812. b. (47.)

— Tillie. Words by Walter de la Mare. [Unison song. Staff and
tonic sol-fa notation.] pp. 3. *Novello & Co.: London*, [1960.]
8°.
[*School Songs.* 2046.] **F. 280. d.**

LEIGH (ERNEST)

— The Princess of Wales galop. [P. F.] *London*, [1880.] fol.
h. 1494. q. (17.)

LEIGH (ERNEST E.)

— The Mayflower. Patriotic Song. [*The Composer: Halifax,
N. S.,*] 1899. fol. **H. 1799. h. (28.)**

LEIGH (FELIX)

— You tell Dinah that. [Song, begins: "Grandmother's uncle
died of the pip".] *London*, [1876.] fol. **H. 1778. y. (4.)**

LEIGH (FRED W.)

— Belinda the barber-ous. [Song.] Written and composed by
F. W. Leigh, *etc*. pp. 5. *Howard & Co.: London*, [1895.] fol.
H. 3980. qq. (5.)

— Bridget. ⟨Song.⟩ Written and composed by F. W. Leigh. [Staff
and tonic sol-fa notation. Voice part.] *Francis, Day &
Hunter: London*, [1906.] *s. sh.* fol. **H. 3985. q. (40.)**

— Bridget. Song, *etc*. [With separate voice part.] 2 pt. *Francis,
Day & Hunter: London*, [1906.] fol. **H. 3985. q. (41.)**

— "Dear Mr. Admiral!" ... ⟨Song.⟩ Written and composed by
F. W. Leigh. [Staff and tonic sol-fa notation. Voice part.]
Francis, Day & Hunter: London, [1908.] *s. sh.* fol.
H. 3985. q. (42.)

— "Dear Mr. Admiral!" *etc*. ⟨Song.⟩ [With separate voice part.]
2 pt. *Francis, Day & Hunter: London*, [1908.] fol.
H. 3985. q. (43.)

— Does it hurt you very much? ⟨Song.⟩ Written and composed
by F. W. Leigh, *etc*. [Staff and tonic sol-fa notation. Voice
part.] *Francis, Day & Hunter: London*, [1901.] *s. sh.* fol.
H. 3985. q. (44.)

— Does it hurt you very much? *etc*. ⟨Song.⟩ [With separate voice
part.] 2 pt. *Francis, Day & Hunter: London*, [1901.] fol.
H. 3985. q. (45.)

— 'E's takin' a mean Advantage. ⟨Song.⟩ Written and composed
by F. W. Leigh, *etc*. [Staff and tonic sol-fa notation. Voice
part.] *Francis, Day & Hunter: London*, [1901.] *s. sh.* fol.
H. 3985. q. (52.)

— 'E's takin' a mean Advantage, *etc*. ⟨Song.⟩ [With separate
voice part.] 2 pt. *Francis, Day & Hunter: London*, [1901.] fol.
H. 3985. q. (53.)

— Father's Phonograph. ⟨Song.⟩ Written and composed by
F. W. Leigh, *etc*. [Staff and tonic sol-fa notation. Voice part.]
Francis, Day & Hunter: London, [1903.] *s. sh.* fol.
H. 3985. q. (46.)

— Father's Phonograph. Humorous song, *etc*. [With separate
voice part.] 2 pt. *Francis, Day & Hunter: London*, [1903.] fol.
H. 3985. q. (47.)

— Fifteen of 'em on the Parlour Floor. Written and composed
by F. Leigh. Arranged by John S. Baker, *etc*. [Song. Staff and
tonic sol-fa notation. Voice part.] *Francis, Day & Hunter:
London*, [1897.] *s. sh.* fol. **H. 3980. qq. (6.)**

— Go 'way, good Massa Bee. ⟨Song.⟩ Written and composed by
F. W. Leigh. [Staff and tonic sol-fa notation. Voice part.]
Francis, Day & Hunter: London, [1901.] *s. sh.* fol.
H. 3985. q. (48.)

— Go 'way, good Massa Bee, *etc*. ⟨Song.⟩ pp. 5. *Francis, Day &
Hunter: London*, [1901.] fol. **H. 3985. q. (49.)**

— Good—for nothing! ... ⟨Song.⟩ Written and composed by
F. W. Leigh. [Staff and tonic sol-fa notation. Voice part.]
Francis, Day & Hunter: London, [1907.] *s. sh.* fol.
H. 3985. q. (50.)

— Good—for nothing! *etc*. ⟨Song.⟩ [With separate voice part.]
2 pt. *Francis, Day & Hunter: London*, [1907.] fol.
H. 3985. q. (51.)

— The Horse the Missis dries the Clothes on. ⟨Song.⟩ Written
and composed by F. W. Leigh, *etc*. [Staff and tonic sol-fa
notation. Voice part.] *Francis, Day & Hunter: London*,
[1901.] *s. sh.* fol. **H. 3985. q. (54.)**

— The Horse the Missis dries the Clothes on, *etc*. ⟨Song.⟩ [With
separate voice part.] 2 pt. *Francis, Day & Hunter: London*,
[1901.] fol. **H. 3985. q. (55.)**

LEIGH (Fred W.)

— I ain't nobody in perticuler. ⟨Song.⟩ Written by Scott MacKenzie, etc. [Staff and tonic sol-fa notation. Voice part.] *Francis, Day & Hunter: London*, [1907.] *s. sh.* fol.

H. 3985. r. (1.)

— I ain't nobody in perticuler, etc. ⟨Song.⟩ [With separate voice part.] 2 pt. *Francis, Day & Hunter: London*, [1907.] fol.

H. 3985. r. (2.)

— I don't know what I'm to do. ⟨Song.⟩ Written by Edgar Bateman, etc. [Staff and tonic sol-fa notation. Voice part.] *Francis, Day & Hunter: London*, [1902.] *s. sh.* fol.

H. 3985. r. (3.)

— I don't know what I'm to do, etc. ⟨Song. Arranged by Orlando Powell.⟩ [With separate voice part.] 2 pt. *Francis, Day & Hunter: London*, [1902.] fol. **H. 3985. r. (4.)**

— I don't want to go any farther. ⟨Song.⟩ Written and composed by F. W. Leigh, etc. [Staff and tonic sol-fa notation. Voice part.] *Francis, Day & Hunter: London*, [1901.] *s. sh.* fol.

H. 3985. r. (5.)

— I don't want to go any farther, etc. ⟨Song.⟩ [With separate voice part.] 2 pt. *Francis, Day & Hunter: London*, [1901.] fol.

H. 3985. r. (6.)

— "I'm a little bit deaf to-day." ⟨Song.⟩ Written by Edgar Bateman, etc. [Staff and tonic sol-fa notation. Voice part.] *Francis, Day & Hunter: London*, [1907.] *s. sh.* fol.

H. 3985. r. (7.)

— "I'm a little bit deaf to-day," etc. ⟨Song.⟩ [With separate voice part.] 2 pt. *Francis, Day & Hunter: London*, [1907.] fol.

H. 3985. r. (8.)

— I never work upon a Monday. ⟨Song.⟩ Written by George Arthurs, etc. [Staff and tonic sol-fa notation. Voice part.] *Francis, Day & Hunter: London, New York*, [1906.] *s. sh.* fol. **H. 3985. r. (9.)**

— I never work upon a Monday, etc. ⟨Song.⟩ [With separate voice part.] 2 pt. *Francis, Day & Hunter: London*, [1906.] fol.

H. 3985. r. (10.)

— I want to go home again. ⟨Song.⟩ Written and composed by F. W. Leigh, etc. [Staff and tonic sol-fa notation. Voice part.] *Francis, Day & Hunter: London*, [1902.] *s. sh.* fol.

H. 3985. r. (11.)

— I want to go home again, etc. ⟨Song.⟩ [With separate voice part.] 2 pt. *Francis, Day & Hunter: London*, [1902.] fol.

H. 3985. r. (12.)

— I was the only Gentleman there. ⟨Song.⟩ Written and composed by F. W. Leigh, etc. [Staff and tonic sol-fa notation. Voice part.] *Francis, Day & Hunter: London*, [1908.] *s. sh.* fol.

H. 3985. r. (13.)

— I was the only Gentleman there, etc. ⟨Song.⟩ [With separate voice part.] 2 pt. *Francis, Day & Hunter: London*, [1908.] fol.

H. 3985. r. (14.)

— Jack of all Trades. ⟨Song.⟩ Written by Edgar Bateman, etc. [Staff and tonic sol-fa notation. Voice part.] *Francis, Day & Hunter: London*, [1907.] *s. sh.* fol. **H. 3985. r. (15.)**

— Jack of all Trades, etc. ⟨Song.⟩ [With separate voice part.] 2 pt. *Francis, Day & Hunter: London*, [1907.] fol.

H. 3985. r. (16.)

— The Jilted Shoeblack ... ⟨Song.⟩ Written by Hal Wright and Edgar Bateman, etc. [Staff and tonic sol-fa notation. Voice part.] *Francis, Day & Hunter: London*, [1903.] *s. sh.* fol.

H. 3985. r. (17.)

— The Jilted Shoeblack, etc. ⟨Song. Arranged by T. W. Thurban.⟩ [With separate voice part.] 2 pt. *Francis, Day & Hunter: London*, [1903.] fol. **H. 3985. r. (18.)**

LEIGH (Fred W.)

— Johnny Macintyre. ⟨Song.⟩ Written and composed by F. W. Leigh. [Staff and tonic sol-fa notation. Voice part.] *Francis, Day & Hunter: London*, [1908.] *s. sh.* fol. **H. 3985. r. (19.)**

— Johnny Macintyre, etc. ⟨Song.⟩ [With separate voice part.] 2 pt. *Francis, Day & Hunter: London*, [1908.] fol.

H. 3985. r. (20.)

— Let go, Eliza! ⟨Song.⟩ Written and composed by F. W. Leigh, etc. [Staff and tonic sol-fa notation. Voice part.] *Francis, Day & Hunter: London*, [1902.] *s. sh.* fol. **H. 3985. r. (21.)**

— Let go, Eliza! etc. ⟨Song.⟩ [With separate voice part.] 2 pt. *Francis, Day & Hunter: London*, [1902.] fol.

H. 3985. r. (22.)

— Little Tommy Tit-bit ... [Song.] Written and composed by F. Leigh, etc. ⟨Arranged by Henry E. Pether.⟩ pp. 5. *Reeder & Walsh: London*, [1898.] fol. **H. 3980. qq. (7.)**

— Look at the Kiltie-boys—hooch aye! ⟨Song.⟩ Written and composed by F. W. Leigh, etc. [Staff and tonic sol-fa notation. Voice part.] *Francis, Day & Hunter: London*, [1909.] *s. sh.* fol.

H. 3985. r. (23.)

— Look at the Kiltie-boys—hooch aye! etc. ⟨Song.⟩ [With separate voice part.] 2 pt. *Francis, Day & Hunter: London*, [1909.] fol. **H. 3985. r. (24.)**

— The Medical Man ... ⟨Song.⟩ Written and composed by F. W. Leigh, etc. [With separate voice part.] 2 pt. *Hopwood & Crew: London*, [1902.] fol. **H. 3985. r. (25.)**

— Molly, the jolly little Lady. ⟨Song.⟩ Written and composed by F. W. Leigh. [Staff and tonic sol-fa notation. Voice part.] *Francis, Day & Hunter: London*, [1905.] *s. sh.* fol.

H. 3985. r. (26.)

— Molly, the jolly little Lady, etc. ⟨Song.⟩ [With separate voice part.] 2 pt. *Francis, Day & Hunter: London*, [1905.] fol.

H. 3985. r. (27.)

— Molly, the jolly little Lady, etc. [Song.] [1905?] fol. *A pirated edition.* **H. 1848. b. (20.)**

— More Work for the Undertaker. Written and composed by F. W. Leigh, etc. [Song. Staff and tonic sol-fa notation. Voice part.] *Francis, Day & Hunter: London*, [1895.] *s. sh.* fol.

H. 3980. qq. (8.)

— Obadiah Binks ... Written and composed by F. W. Leigh, etc. [Song. Staff and tonic sol-fa notation. Voice part.] *Francis, Day & Hunter: London*, [1896.] *s. sh.* fol. **H. 3980. qq. (9.)**

— Oh, what an Exhibition! ⟨Song.⟩ Written and composed by F. W. Leigh, etc. [Staff and tonic sol-fa notation. Voice part.] *Francis, Day & Hunter: London*, [1908.] *s. sh.* fol.

H. 3985. r. (28.)

— Oh, what an Exhibition! etc. ⟨Song.⟩ [With separate voice part.] 2 pt. *Francis, Day & Hunter: London*, [1908.] fol. **H. 3985. r. (29.)**

— On Top! Written and composed by F. W. Leigh, etc. [Song. Staff and tonic sol-fa notation. Voice part.] *Francis, Day & Hunter: London*, [1899.] *s. sh.* fol. **H. 3980. qq. (10.)**

— ... "Philosophy." ⟨Song.⟩ Written by Charles Wilmott. [Staff and tonic sol-fa notation. Voice part.] *Francis, Day & Hunter: London*, [1900.] *s. sh.* fol. **H. 3985. r. (30.)**

— Ringing the Changes. [Song.] Written and composed by F. Leigh, etc. ⟨Arranged by Henry E. Pether.⟩ pp. 5. *Reeder & Walsh: London*, [1897.] fol. **H. 3980. qq. (11.)**

— Rosie Gray ... Written and composed by F. W. Leigh, etc. [Song. Staff and tonic sol-fa notation. Voice part.] *Francis, Day & Hunter: London*, [1896.] *s. sh.* fol. **H. 3980. qq. (12.)**

LEIGH (FRED W.)

— Send for a P'liceman! ⟨Song.⟩ Written and composed by F. W. Leigh, *etc.* [Staff and tonic sol-fa notation. Voice part.] *Francis, Day & Hunter: London*, [1909.] *s. sh.* fol.
H. 3985. r. (31.)

— Send for a P'liceman! *etc.* ⟨Song.⟩ [With separate voice part.] 2 pt. *Francis, Day & Hunter: London*, [1909.] fol.
H. 3985. r. (32.)

— Snuggle. ⟨Song.⟩ Written and composed by F. W. Leigh. [Staff and tonic sol-fa notation. Voice part.] *Francis, Day & Hunter: London*, [1909.] *s. sh.* fol.
H. 3985. r. (33.)

— Snuggle, *etc.* ⟨Song.⟩ [With separate voice part.] 2 pt. *Francis, Day & Hunter: London*, [1909.] fol.
H. 3985. r. (34.)

— There ain't a Bit o' Pride about me. ⟨Song.⟩ Written and composed by F. W. Leigh, *etc.* [Staff and tonic sol-fa notation. Voice part.] *Francis, Day & Hunter: London*, [1900.] *s. sh.* fol.
H. 3985. r. (35.)

— There's another Fellow just like me. [Song.] pp. 5. *T. B. Harms; Francis, Day & Hunter: New York*, [1909.] fol.
H. 3985. r. (36.)

— They won't know Oi coom from the Coontry … ⟨Song.⟩ Written and composed by F. W. Leigh. [Staff and tonic sol-fa notation. Voice part.] *Francis, Day & Hunter: London*, [1909.] *s. sh.* fol.
H. 3985. r. (37.)

— They won't know Oi coom from the Coontry, *etc.* ⟨Song.⟩ [With separate voice part.] 2 pt. *Francis, Day & Hunter: London*, [1909.] fol.
H. 3985. r. (38.)

— Too, too, too, too strong, Written by Frank W. Carter & F. W. Leigh, *etc.* [Song. Staff and tonic sol-fa notation. Voice part.] *Francis, Day & Hunter: London*, [1897.] *s. sh.* fol.
H. 3980. qq. (13.)

— Well caught! ⟨Song.⟩ Written and composed by F. W. Leigh, *etc.* [Staff and tonic sol-fa notation. Voice part.] *Francis, Day & Hunter: London*, [1901.] *s. sh.* fol.
H. 3985. r. (39.)

— Well caught!, *etc.* ⟨Song.⟩ [With separate voice part.] 2 pt. *Francis, Day & Hunter: London*, [1901.] fol.
H. 3985. r. (40.)

— What I say I do do, I do do! ⟨Song.⟩ Written and composed by F. W. Leigh, *etc.* [Staff and tonic sol-fa notation. Voice part.] *Francis, Day & Hunter: London*, [1904.] *s. sh.* fol.
H. 3985. r. (41.)

— What I say I do do, I do do! *etc.* ⟨Song.⟩ [With separate voice part.] 2 pt. *Francis, Day & Hunter: London*, [1904.] fol.
H. 3985. r. (42.)

— What the—what the—what the—shall we do? Written and composed by F. W. Leigh, *etc.* [Song. Staff and tonic sol-fa notation. Voice part.] *Francis, Day & Hunter: London*, [1898.] *s. sh.* fol.
H. 3980. qq. (14.)

— When Juggins was twenty-one. ⟨Song.⟩ Written by Edgar Bateman, *etc.* [Staff and tonic sol-fa notation. Voice part.] *Francis, Day & Hunter: London*, [1903.] *s. sh.* fol.
H. 3985. r. (43.)

— When Juggins was twenty-one, *etc.* ⟨Song.⟩ [With separate voice part.] 2 pt. *Francis, Day & Hunter: London*, [1903.] fol.
H. 3985. r. (44.)

— Why do the Girls love Charlie? … ⟨Song.⟩ Written and composed by F. W. Leigh. [Staff and tonic sol-fa notation. Voice part.] *Francis, Day & Hunter: London*, [1906.] *s. sh.* fol.
H. 3985. r. (45.)

— Why do the Girls love Charlie? *etc.* ⟨Song.⟩ [With separate voice part.] 2 pt. *Francis, Day & Hunter: London*, [1906.] fol.
H. 3985. r. (46.)

LEIGH (FRED W.)

— W-o-m-a-n … ⟨Song.⟩ Written and composed by F. W. Leigh, *etc.* [Staff and tonic sol-fa notation. Voice part.] *Francis, Day & Hunter: London*, [1902.] *s. sh.* fol.
H. 3985. r. (47.)

— W-o-m-a-n, *etc.* ⟨Song.⟩ [With separate voice part.] 2 pt. *Francis, Day & Hunter: London*, [1902.] fol.
H. 3985. r. (48.)

— You can't do this, and you can't do that … ⟨Song.⟩ Written by Edgar Bateman, *etc.* [Staff and tonic sol-fa notation. Voice part.] *Francis, Day & Hunter: London*, [1902.] *s. sh.* fol.
H. 3985. r. (49.)

— You can't do this, and you can't do that, *etc.* ⟨Song.⟩ [With separate voice part.] 2 pt. *Francis, Day & Hunter: London*, [1902.] fol.
H. 3985. r. (50.)

— *See* ARNOLD (Malcolm) and LEIGH (F. W.) I'm proud of the Corps I belong to. ⟨Song.⟩ Written & composed by M. Arnold and F. W. Leigh. [1915.] fol.
H. 3988. uu. (13.)

— *See* ARNOLD (Malcolm) and LEIGH (F. W.) Only a little Box of Soldiers. ⟨Song.⟩ Written and composed by M. Arnold and F. Leigh, *etc.* [1901.] fol.
H. 3982. e. (24.)

— *See* ARTHURS (George) and LEIGH (F. W.) I forgot the Number of my House. ⟨Song.⟩ Written and composed by G. Arthurs and F. W. Leigh, *etc.* [1911.] *s. sh.* fol.
H. 3988. uu. (60.)

— *See* ARTHURS (George) and LEIGH (F. W.) What's the Good of sighing? ⟨Song.⟩ Written and composed by G. Arthurs and F. W. Leigh, *etc.* [1909.] *s. sh.* fol.
H. 3982. e. (55.)

— *See* ARTHURS (George) and LEIGH (F. W.) "What's the Good of sighing," *etc.* ⟨Song.⟩ [1909.] fol.
H. 3982. e. (56.)

— *See* ARTHURS (George) and LEIGH (F. W.) "You mustn't keep your damp Boots on, John!" ⟨Song.⟩ Written and composed by G. Arthurs and F. W. Leigh. [1912.] fol.
H. 3988. uu. (61.)

— *See* BATEMAN (Edgar) and LEIGH (F. W.) We should like a Girl. ⟨Song.⟩ Written and composed by E. Bateman and F. W. Leigh, *etc.* [1911.] fol.
H. 3989. g. (53.)

— *See* CASTLING (Harry) and LEIGH (F. W.) All I want … ⟨Song.⟩ Written and composed by H. Castling & F. W. Leigh. [1905.] *s. sh.* fol.
H. 3982. rr. (33.)

— *See* CASTLING (Harry) and LEIGH (F. W.) All I want, *etc.* ⟨Song.⟩ [1905.] fol.
H. 3982. rr. (34.)

— *See* CASTLING (Harry) and LEIGH (F. W.) The Bullfighter. ⟨Song.⟩ Written and composed by H. Castling and F. W. Leigh, *etc.* [1918.] fol.
H. 3990. k. (53.)

— *See* CASTLING (Harry) and LEIGH (F. W.) Don't we like to hear of Victory! *etc.* ⟨Song.⟩ [1900.] *s. sh.* fol.
H. 3982. rr. (35.)

— *See* CASTLING (Harry) and LEIGH (F. W.) I'm going back, back, back to Alabam. [Song.] Written and composed by H. Castling and F. W. Leigh. [1918.] fol. **H. 3990. k. (54.)**

— *See* CASTLING (Harry) and LEIGH (F. W.) 'Is old Man's 'at won't fit 'im … [Song.] Written and composed by Castling and Leigh, *etc.* [1899.] *s. sh.* fol. **H. 3980. h. (69.)**

— *See* CASTLING (Harry) and LEIGH (F. W.) Out of Work. ⟨Song.⟩ Written and composed by H. Castling and F. W. Leigh, *etc.* [1901.] *s. sh.* fol.
H. 3982. rr. (36.)

— *See* CASTLING (Harry) and LEIGH (F. W.) Out of Work, *etc.* ⟨Song.⟩ [1901.] fol.
H. 3982. rr. (37.)

— *See* CASTLING (Harry) and LEIGH (F. W.) They're all like Life … [Song.] Written and composed by Castling and Leigh, *etc.* [1898.] *s. sh.* fol.
H. 3980. h. (70.)

LEIGH (FRED W.)

— *See* CASTLING (Harry) and LEIGH (F. W.) Where's Old Bill? [Song.] Written and composed by H. Castling and F. W. Leigh. pp. 4. [1918.] fol. **H. 3990. k. (55.)**

— *See* COLLINS (Charles) and LEIGH (F. W.) Better than all the Toys. ⟨Song.⟩ Written and composed by C. Collins and F. W. Leigh. [1902.] *s. sh.* fol. **H. 3983. f. (39.)**

— *See* COLLINS (Charles) and LEIGH (F. W.) Better than all the Toys, *etc.* ⟨Song.⟩ [1902.] fol. **H. 3983. f. (40.)**

— *See* COLLINS (Charles) and LEIGH (F. W.) Don't dilly dally on the Way. (The "cock linnet" song.) ... Written and composed by C. Collins and F. W. Leigh. [1919.] fol. **H. 3990. y. (15.)**

— *See* COLLINS (Charles) and LEIGH (F. W.) Now you've got yer Khaki on. ⟨Song.⟩ Written and composed by C. Collins and F. W. Leigh, *etc.* [1916.] fol. **H. 3990. y. (16.)**

— *See* COSTELLO (Thomas) On Monday I met him. ⟨Song.⟩ By T. Costello, F. W. Leigh, *etc.* [1909.] *s. sh.* fol. **H. 3983. m. (15.)**

— *See* COSTELLO (Thomas) On Monday I met him. ⟨Song.⟩ By T. Costello, F. W. Leigh, *etc.* [1909.] fol. **H. 3990. gg. (3.)**

— *See* COSTELLO (Thomas) and LEIGH (F. W.) Comrades in the Trenches. ⟨Song.⟩ Written and composed by T. Costello and F. W. Leigh. [1916.] fol. **H. 3990. gg. (5.)**

— *See* COSTELLO (Thomas) and LEIGH (F. W.) Mary Devine. [Song.] Written and composed by T. Costello and F. W. Leigh. [1915.] fol. **H. 3990. gg. (6.)**

— *See* COSTELLO (Thomas) and LEIGH (F. W.) Nellie Brown. [Song.] Written and composed by T. Costello and F. W. Leigh. [1919.] fol. **H. 3990. gg. (7.)**

— *See* DEANE (Charles) and LEIGH (F.) All in a Row. [Song.] Written & composed by C. Deane and F. Leigh, *etc.* [1894.] fol. **H. 3980. o. (22.)**

— *See* HARRINGTON (John P.) The Charge of the 21st. [Song.] By J. B. Harrington, F. Murray and F. Leigh, *etc.* [1898.] *s. sh.* fol. **H. 3980. dd. (7.)**

— *See* KEEN (Walter P.) and LEIGH (F. W.) I like my Glass of foaming Beer. [Song.] Written and composed by Keen and Leigh, *etc.* [1899.] *s. sh.* fol. **H. 3980. mm. (25.)**

— *See* KEEN (Walter P.) and LEIGH (F. W.) They were very, very good to me. [Song.] Written and composed by W. P. Keen & F. Leigh, *etc.* [1899.] *s. sh.* fol. **H. 3980. mm. (26.)**

— *See* KRONE (Percy) and LEIGH (F. W.) Because you are tender and true. ⟨Song.⟩ Written and composed by P. Krone and F. W. Leigh. [1901.] *s. sh.* fol. **H. 3985. e. (31.)**

— *See* KRONE (Percy) and LEIGH (F. W.) Because you are tender and true, *etc.* ⟨Song.⟩ [1901.] fol. **H. 3985. e. (32.)**

— *See* MURRAY (Fred) What a Kid 'e is. ⟨Song.⟩ Written and composed by Murray, Leigh, *etc.* [1902.] *s. sh.* fol. **H. 3986. l. (26.)**

— *See* MURRAY (Fred) What a Kid 'e is. ⟨Song.⟩ Written and composed by Murray, Leigh, *etc.* [1902.] fol. **H. 3986. l. (27.)**

— [For editions and arrangements of songs written and composed by F. W. Leigh in sole collaboration with Fred Murray:] *See* MURRAY (Fred) and LEIGH (F. W.)

— *See* WATKINS (Harry) and LEIGH (F. W.) When are you going to stop? ⟨Song.⟩ Written and composed by H. Watkins and F. W. Leigh. [1899.] *s. sh.* fol. **H. 3981. oo. (27.)**

— *See* WESTON (Robert P.) and LEIGH (F. W.) The Order of dear old Pals. ⟨Song.⟩ Written and composed by R. P. Weston and F. W. Leigh, *etc.* [1899.] *s. sh.* fol. **H. 3981. rr. (14.)**

LEIGH (FRED W.) and ARNOLD (MALCOLM)

— Dotty-otty, *etc.* [Song. Staff and tonic sol-fa notation. Voice part.] *Francis, Day & Hunter: London*, [1898.] *s. sh.* fol. **H. 3980. qq. (15.)**

LEIGH (FRED W.) and BASTOW (GEORGE)

— She's proud and she's beau-tie-ful, *etc.* ⟨Song.⟩ [Staff and tonic sol-fa notation. Voice part.] *Francis, Day & Hunter: London*, [1906.] *s. sh.* fol. **H. 3985. r. (51.)**

— She's proud and she's beau-tie-ful, *etc.* ⟨Song.⟩ [With separate voice part.] 2 pt. *Francis, Day & Hunter: London*, [1906.] fol. **H. 3985. r. (52.)**

LEIGH (FRED W.) and GODWIN (WILL J.)

— Wire in, my Lads! *etc.* ⟨Song.⟩ [Staff and tonic sol-fa notation. Voice part.] *Francis, Day & Hunter: London*, [1906.] *s. sh.* fol. **H. 3985. r. (53.)**

— Wire in, my Lads! *etc.* ⟨Song.⟩ [With separate voice part.] 2 pt. *Francis, Day & Hunter: London*, [1906.] fol. **H. 3985. r. (54.)**

LEIGH (FRED W.) and KEEN (WALTER P.)

— All through the Rain. Written and composed by F. W. Leigh and W. P. Keen, *etc.* [Song. Staff and tonic sol-fa notation. Voice part.] *Francis, Day & Hunter: London*, [1897.] *s. sh.* fol. **H. 3980. qq. (16.)**

— Like a good little Wife should do! ... ⟨Song.⟩ Written and composed by Leigh and Keen, *etc.* [With separate voice part.] 2 pt. *Hopwood & Crew: London*, [1901.] fol. **H. 3985. r. (55.)**

LEIGH (G. A. BOUGHTON)

— The Rose Melody. Song, words & music by G. A. Boughton-Leigh. *West & Co.: London*, 1914. fol. **H. 1793. t. (1.)**

LEIGH (GWENDOLINE)

— By and by. Song, words by E. R. Boyer, *etc.* 2 no. [In E flat and G.] *J. Williams: London*, [1913.] fol. **H. 1793. t. (2.)**

LEIGH (HARRINGTON) *pseud.* [i. e. CHARLES ARTHUR RAWLINGS.]

— Asleep 'neath the dark blue Wave. Descriptive Song, words by C. Bingham. *J. H. Larway: London*, 1908. fol. **H. 1794. vv. (32.)**

— In the Depths of the Choral Caves. Song, words: E. Teschemacher. *J. H. Larway: London*, 1909. fol. **H. 1794. vv. (33.)**

— Mary's Choice. [Song.] Words by E. Teschemacher. *J. H. Larway: London*, 1907. fol. **H. 1794. vv. (34.)**

— Poor old Maids! Song, words: E. W. *J. H. Larway: London*, 1908. fol. **H. 1794. vv. (35.)**

— *See* RUBINSTEIN (A. G.) [Melody in F. Op. 3. No. 1.] The Melody of Life ... Arranged by H. Leigh. 1906. fol. **H. 1794. r. (39.)**

LEIGH (HELENA)

— Petite Marche. Duo for the Pianoforte. *Lyon & Hall: Brighton and Hove*, 1908. fol. **h. 3290. r. (14.)**

LEIGH (HENRY S.)

— Cod Liver Oil, a drinking song for invalids [begins: "On the bleak shores"]. *London*, [1870.] fol. **H. 2618. (5.)**

— First Impressions, or Memories of the Cradle. A comic ditty. *London*, [1881.] fol. **H. 1787. j. (29.)**

LEIGH (Henry S.)

— Julius Caesar, a comic history. [Song, begins: "All Europe".] *London*, [1866.] fol.   **H. 2618. (2.)**

— Over the Water. Humorous song, written & composed by Henry S. Leigh. pp. 4. *W. J. Willcocks & Cᵒ: London*, [1885?] fol.   **H. 1660. a. (14.)**

— Say Mama ... Song [begins: "Pray Mama"]. ⟨In B flat.⟩ *Liverpool*, [1869.] fol.   **H. 2618. (3.)**

— Say Mama. ⟨In C.⟩ *Liverpool*, [1870.] fol.   **H. 2618. (4.)**

— Say Mama, if he pops shall I send him to you. Song. *Leeds*, [1874.] fol.   **H. 2618. (7.)**

— The Twin Brothers, a song of mystery [begins: "In form and feature"]. *London*, [1865.] fol.   **H. 2618. (1.)**

— Uncle John, the lay of the hopeful nephew. [Song, begins: "I've never reared".] *London*, [1870.] fol.   **H. 2618. (6.)**

LEIGH (Leyland)

— Leaf by leaf. Song. *London*, [1862.] fol.   **H. 1775. u. (14.)**

— Nelly. Ballad [begins: "Oh! the sorrow's come at last"]. *London*, [1862.] fol.   **H. 1775. u. (15.)**

— So che operare Amante. Arietta da Camera. *London*, [1860.] fol.   **H. 1775. u. (11.)**

— Tornate sereni. Arietta da Camera. *London*, [1860.] fol.   **H. 1775. u. (12.)**

— When o'er the World condemned to roam. Ballad. *London*, [1860.] fol.   **H. 1775. u. (13.)**

LEIGH (Mitch)

— [Man of La Mancha.] Vocal Selections from Man of La Mancha ... Lyrics by Joe Darion. pp. 23. *Sam Fox Publishing Co.: New York*, [1973?] 4°.   **G. 1282. gg. (2.)**

— Man of La Mancha. Piano selection ... Arranged by Denes Agay. pp. 16. *Sam Fox Publishing Co.; KPM Music Group: London*, [1973.] 4°.   **g. 352. gg. (5.)**

LEIGH (Norman)

— An Irish Love Song. [Song, words by] D. J. Shea. *T. Presser Co.: Philadelphia*, (1912.) fol.   **H. 1792. s. (2.)**

— Mimi. Danse des Grisettes ... Arr. (for Mandolin Orchestra) by R. E. Hildreth. 1st Mandolin or Violin. *W. Jacobs: Boston, Mass.*, (1914.) 4°.
Wanting the other parts.   **g. 1102. e. (16.)**

LEIGH (P.)

— Fleurs-de-Lys. Valse-lente. [P. F.] *Phillips & Page: London*, [1904.] fol.   **h. 3286. dd. (59.)**

— Forty Winks. Valse. [P. F.] *Phillips & Page: London*, [1904.] fol.   **h. 3286. dd. (60.)**

— Two Songs. [No. 1.] Why the Blush Rose blushes ... [No. 2.] You! Words by K. Balberine. *Leonard & Co.: London*, 1907. fol.   **G. 805. mm. (29.)**

LEIGH (Percival)

— When I was one-and-twenty. From "A Shropshire Lad" by A. E. Housman, set ... as a Song. *Boston Music Co.: Boston, Mass.*, (1908.) fol.   **G. 805. mm. (30.)**

LEIGH (Percy L.)

— The Boy Scout. [Song.] Words by H. Begbie, *etc. Year Book Press: London*, 1909. fol.   **H. 1792. s. (3.)**

— I wonder why. Song, written and composed by P. L. Leigh. *West & Co.: London*, 1914. fol.   **H. 1793. t. (3.)**

LEIGH (Sir Samuel Egerton)

— The Genius of England's Invocation to Britannia, [song on the restoration to health of George III.,] as sung by Mr. Incledon ... at Vauxhall Gardens, *etc. G. Goulding: London*, [1789.] fol.   **G. 360. (31*.)**

— The Genius of England's Invocation to Britannia. [Song.] As sung by Mʳ Incledon ... at Vauxhall Gardens ... On His Majesty's recovery. pp. 3. *Longman & Broderip, for the benefit of a distress'd family: London*, [c. 1790.] fol.
A different setting from the preceding.   **H. 1654. kk. (13.)**

— The Grove. A favorite Song and Duett ... properly adapted for the Voice, Harp, Harpsichord, Flute & Guitar. *London*, [1794.] fol.   **G. 354. (22.)**

— It's Henry I love. A Favorite Song, *etc. A. Bland: London*, [1790?] fol.   **G. 808. e. (31.)**

— The New Hours of Love, containing Morning, Noon, Evening and Night; [songs,] written by a Young Lady ... set to Music ... for the Piano Forte, Violin, Gerⁿ Flute & Guittar. *Fentum: London*, 1789. obl. fol.   **D. 392. (8.)**

LEIGH (Summer)

— The Beating of my own heart. (I wandered by the brookside.) ... Song, words by R. M. Milnes. *Leeds*, [1872.] fol.   **H. 1775. u. (16.)**

LEIGH (Sydney)

— Falling Shadows. Song, the words by Clarice. *Enoch & Sons: London*, [1884.] fol.   **H. 1788. v. (29.)**

LEIGH (Walter) *B. A.*

— Paradise, Lost and Regained, or The Fall and Redemption. An Oratorio. [Words partly by Milton.] *Novello, Ewer & Co.: London*, [1868?] fol.   **H. 1040.**

LEIGH (Walter) *Composer of "The Pride of the Regiment"*

— By the Dark Lagoon. Island Serenade. [Song.] Words by V. C. Clinton Baddeley. *Keith Prowse & Co.: London*, 1935. 4°.   **G. 1270. jj. (37.)**

— The Children's Voices guileless sing. *See infra:* The Pride of the Regiment.

— Concertino für Cembalo oder Klavier und Streichorchester. Partitur zugleich Cembalostimme, *etc.* pp. 19. *Chr. Friedrich Vieweg: Berlin*, [1936.] fol.   **g. 727. gg. (3.)**

— Concertino for Harpsichord or Piano and String Orchestra ... Score, *etc.* pp. 19. *Oxford University Press: London*, [1949.] 4°.   **g. 727. n. (9.)**

— Daisy goes out with Bert. *See infra:* [Little Revue.]

— Eclogue, *etc.* (Piano.) *Oxford University Press: London*, 1940. 4°.
Part of "The Oxford Home Music Series".   **g. 1570. (2.)**

— The Frogs of Aristophanes ... For the performance of the Play by Members of Cambridge University in 1936, with an English version of the words of the Choruses by Winton Dean. (Vocal Score.) *Oxford University Press: London*, 1937. 4°.   **G. 770. t. (1.)**

— Jolly Roger; or, The Admiral's Daughter. A Comic Opera in three acts, book by S. Mackenzie and V. C. Clinton-Baddeley, lyrics by V. C. Clinton-Baddeley. Vocal Score. *Boosey & Co.: London*, 1933. 4°.   **F. 943. h. (2.)**

— [Jolly Roger.] Vocal Gems from the Musical Burlesque Jolly Roger, or the Admiral's Daughter. Book by S. Mackenzie & V. C. Clinton-Baddeley. Lyrics by V. C. Clinton-Baddeley, *etc.* (Arr. by S. Baynes.) *Boosey & Co.: London*, 1933. 4°.   **G. 1275. ll. (3.)**

— [Little Revue.] Selection with words from Herbert Farjeon's "Little Revue" ... Book and lyrics by Herbert Farjeon. pp. 11. *Ascherberg, Hopwood & Crew: London*, [1939.] 4°.   **G. 1270. ww. (47.)**

LEIGH (WALTER) *Composer of "The Pride of the Regiment"*

— [Little Revue.] "Two Cameos." [No. 1.] Winter in Torquay. [No. 2.] A very nice Paper. [Songs.] From Herbert Farjeon's "Little Revue," *etc.* pp. 8. *Ascherberg, Hopwood & Crew: London*, [1940.] 4°.　　**G. 1270. ww. (48.)**

— [Little Revue.] Daisy goes out with Bert ... [Song] from Herbert Farjeon's "Little Revue," *etc.* pp. 7. *Ascherberg, Hopwood & Crew: London*, [1939.] 4°.　　**G. 1270. ww. (49.)**

— Love calls as no one supposes. *See infra*: The Pride of the Regiment.

— Musik für Streichorchester ⟨I–III⟩ ... Partitur. ⟨Musik für Streichorchester IV.⟩ 2 no. *Wilhelm Hansen: København*, [1949, 32.] 4°.　　**g. 727. ff. (9.)**

— The Pride of the Regiment, or, Cashiered for his Country. A Comic Opera, the book by V. C. Clinton-Baddeley and S. Mackenzie, the lyrics by V. C. Clinton-Baddeley. Vocal Score. *Boosey & Co.: London*, 1932. 4°.　　**F. 943. g. (2.)**

— The Pride of the Regiment; or Cashiered for his country ... The children's voices guileless sing. Love calls as no one supposes. [Songs.] 2 no. *Boosey & Co.: London*, [1932.] 4°.　　**G. 1276. d. (16.)**

— Drei Sätze für Streichquartett. Three Movements for String Quartet. [Score and parts.] 5 pt. *Wilhelm Hansen: København*, [1931.] 4°. *Das Hauskonzert. no. 3.*　　**g. 417. rr. (2.)**

— Sonatina for Treble Recorder or Flute & Piano. *Schott & Co.: London*, 1944. 4°. *Part of "Contemporary Music for Recorder or Flute".*　　**g. 109. (14.)**

— Drei Stücke für Liebhaberorchester. (Für vierstimmiges Streichorchester oder auch mit Hinzuziehung von andern Melodie-Instrumenten (Bläser) ad lib.) [Score.] pp. 3. *Gebrüder Hug & Co.: Zürich, Leipzig*, [1934.] 8°. *Laien-Musik. Blatt-Ausgabe. nr. 2.*　　**d. 85. f. (6.)**

— Suite für kleines Orchester zu Shakespeares Sommernachtstraum. Streichquartett einfach oder chorisch besetzt sowie nach Belieben mit Kontrabass, Flöte, Klarinette und Trompete in B, Schlagzeug und begleitendes Cembalo oder Klavier. Spieleinrichtung, Vorwort und Spielanweisung von Hilmar Höckner. Partitur zugleich Cembalostimme, *etc.* pp. 35. *Chr. Friedrich Vieweg: Berlin*, [1937.] 4°. *With a "Spielanweisung" of four pages inserted.*　　**g. 727. gg. (4.)**

— Trio. For flute, oboe and piano. [Score and parts.] 3 pt. *Oxford University Press: London*, [1960.] 4°.　　**g. 409. mm. (7.)**

— Violets. Song, words by V. C. Clinton-Baddeley. *Ascherberg, Hopwood & Crew: London*, 1943. 4°.　　**G. 1270. tt. (35.)**

LEIGH (WILLIAM)

— The Pembroke Skating Song [begins: "Autumn golden dyes"]. *Rochester* [*N. Y.*], 1864. fol.　　**H. 1780. f. (14.)**

LEIGH (WILLIAM AUSTEN)

— Stone Walls do not a Prison make. A Madrigal for S. S. A. T. B., the words by Lovelace. *Novello, Ewer and Co.: London & New York*, [1895.] 8°.　　**F. 321. j. (26.)**

— *See* SCHOLEFIELD (C. C.) A Wedding Hymn ... [2 versions.] Set to music [respectively] by C. C. Scholefield and W. Austen Leigh. [1889.] 8°.　　**F. 1171. f. (47.)**

LEIGH (ZOE)

— The gossip polka. [P. F.] *Salisbury*, [1857.] fol.　　**h. 977. f. (30.)**

LEIGH-SHARPE (W. HAROLD)

— *See* SHARPE.

LEIGHTER (HENRY CLOUGH)

— Adoration. Christmas Processional [for S. A. T. B., words] translated from the German by J. M. Neale. *O. Ditson Co.: [Boston,]* 1906. 8°.　　**F. 1529. e. (19.)**

— After. Song with Pianoforte accompaniment, words by F. E. Coates. *A. P. Schmidt: Boston, etc.*, 1914. fol.　　**G. 806. mm. (7.)**

— Ah, dear one. *See infra*: Seven Songs. Opus 57. No. 7.

— Amen, amen! Easter Processional. [Words by] J. Julian. *O. Ditson Co.: [Boston,]* 1905. 8°.　　**F. 1529. d. (22.)**

— An April Heart. Song Cycle. Six lyrics by C. H. Towne. Op. 24. *Boston Music Co.: Boston, Mass.*, (1902.) 4°.　　**F. 637. q. (3.)**

— April Rapture. *See infra*: 5 Songs ... Op. 54. No. 1.

— Arise, shine, for thy Light is come. Christmas Anthem ... Op. 25. No. 1. *O. Ditson Co.: [Boston,]* 1902. 8°.　　**F. 231. r. (19.)**

— Ave, Astra! *See infra*: Three Songs ... Op. 38. No. 2.

— Behold your God. Christmas Anthem for Chorus of mixed voices with Organ accompaniment. (Op. 50. No. 5.) *G. Schirmer: New York*, (1911.) 8°.　　**F. 281. bb. (20.)**

— The Bells of Youth. *See infra*: [Youth and Spring. Op. 45. No. 1.]

— Break forth into Joy. Introit Anthem for Easter ... Op. 37. No. 2. *O. Diston Co.: [Boston,]* 1906. 8°.　　**F. 281. c. (14.)**

— The Butterfly Chase. Trio Capriccio for women's voices. [Words by] A. Coll ... Op. 39. No. 1. *O. Ditson Co.: [Boston,]* 1906. 8°.　　**F. 328. d. (23.)**

— The Christ-Child. Christmas Carol with Organ accompaniment. [Words by C. F. Alexander.] *G. Schirmer: New York*, (1905.) 8°. *G. Schirmer's ... Octavo Church Music, No.* 4598.　　**F. 1529. e. (16.)**

— "Christ is born." Christmas Carol for Two-Part Chorus, text translated from the German [of P. Gerhardt, by C. Winkworth]. *G. Schirmer: New York*, (1905.) 8°. *G. Schirmer's ... Part-Songs ... for women's voices, No.* 4599.　　**F. 1529. e. (15.)**

— The Christ of the Andes. Symphonic ode for chorus ... with ... accompaniment of two pianos, the poem by C. Ryan. Vocal Score. *Boston Music Co.: Boston*, 1916. 8°.　　**F. 1269. w. (3.)**

— Christ shall give thee Light. Easter Anthem for Chorus ... with Tenor and Baritone Solos and Organ accompaniment, *etc.* (Op. 56. No. 9.) *G. Schirmer: New York*, (1913.) 8°.　　**F. 281. gg. (49.)**

— Christ the Lord is risen to-day. Easter Processional [for S. A. T. B., words by] T. Scott and T. Gibbons. *O. Ditson Co.: [Boston,]* 1906. 8°.　　**F. 1529. e. (21.)**

— Christ Triumphant. A Cantata for Easter-Tide, for Soli, Chorus and Organ. Compiled from the Scriptures. Op. 35. *O. Ditson Co.: Boston*, 1905. 8°.　　**F. 1274. dd. (1.)**

— Short Communion Service in D, for Chorus of mixed voices, with Organ accompaniment. (Op. 50. No. 4.) *G. Schirmer: New York*, (1911.) 8°.　　**F. 1169. q. (19.)**

— Short Communion Service in E minor, for Chorus of mixed voices with Organ accompaniment. (Op. 50. No. 6.) *G. Schirmer: New York*, (1912.) 8°.　　**F. 1169. s. (12.)**

— Short Communion Service in C minor ... Op. 56. No. 4. *Boston Music Co.: Boston, Mass.*, (1913.) 8°.　　**E. 597. v. (10.)**

— Day-Dreams. *See infra*: 5 Songs ... Op. 54. No. 3.

— Dreamy Sleep. *See infra*: Songs. Op. 3. No. 1.

LEIGHTER (Henry Clough)

— Two Easter Processionals, for Chorus of mixed voices, with Organ accompaniment. [No. 1.] "Welcome happy Morning." [Words by V. Fortunatus, translated by J. Ellerton.] [No. 2.] Victory. (Translated from the Latin by ... F. Pott.) *G. Schirmer: New York*, (1906.) 8°. *G. Schirmer's ... Octavo Church Music, No.* 4679.
F. 1529. e. (17.)

— Two Easter Processionals for Chorus with Organ accompaniment. No. 1. "The Risen King." [Words by J. Allen.] No. 2. "Christ victorious." *G. Schirmer: New York*, (1907.) 8°. *G. Schirmer's ... Octavo Church Music, No.* 4872.
F. 281. e. (28.)

— The Faery Folk of Edom. Terzetto for women's voices, with Piano accompaniment. Words by I. L. McDavitt. (Op. 55. No. 3.) *G. Schirmer: New York*, (1914.) 8°. **F. 328. v. (25.)**

— Fair Daffodils. Terzetto for women's voices. [Words by] R. Herrick. Op. 55. No. 1, *etc. Boston Music Co.: Boston, Mass.*, (1912.) 8°. **F. 328. p. (23.)**

— For marching Men. [Song, words by] T. V. Beard. (Op. 65. No. 2.) *Boston Music Co.: Boston*, 1919. 4°. **G. 390. u. (3.)**

— Gift o' God. *See* infra: Five Songs. Op. 43. No. 1.

— Gladness of Spring. *See* infra: Five Songs. Op. 43. No. 5.

— Hark! ten Thousand Voices sounding. Easter Processional [for S. A. T. B., words by] T. Kelly. *O. Ditson Co.:* [*Boston,*] 1906. 8°. **F. 1529. e. (22.)**

— Hark! the Herald Angels sing. Christmas Processional [for S. A. T. B., words by] C. Wesley. *Boston Music Co.: Boston, Mass.*, (1908.) 8°. **F. 281. m. (27.)**

— Her Songs, my Tears. *See* infra: Two Rossetti Lyrics. Op. 60. No. 1.

— Heralds of Spring. *See* infra: 5 Songs ... Op. 54. No. 2.

— Hills o' Skye. *See* infra: Five Songs. Op. 43. No. 4.

— I drink the Fragrance of the Rose. [Song.] Words by C. H. Towne. (Op. 19. No. 1.) *O. Ditson Co.: Boston*, 1902. fol.
H. 1799. cc. (55.)

— I tell you over and over. *See* infra: Seven Songs. Opus 57. No. 4.

— I wonder, little Girl. *See* infra: Songs. Op. 3. No. 2.

— The Immortal Cup. Drinking Song for Bass voice, words by M. V. Freese. Op. 12. No. 2. *O. Ditson Co.: Boston*, (1906.) fol. **H. 1794. l. (3.)**

— In Cadiz. [P. F.] *Boston Music Co.: Boston*, 1919. 4°.
g. 1129. k. (14.)

— It was a Lover and his Lass. [Song, words by] W. Shakspere, *etc. O. Ditson Co.: Boston*, (1906.) fol. **H. 1794. l. (4.)**

— Jesus came, the Heavens adoring. Christmas Processional [for S. A. T. B., words by] G. Thring. *O. Ditson Co.:* [*Boston,*] 1906. 8°. **F. 1529. e. (18.)**

— Lasca. A Frontier Ballad for Tenor voice with Orchestra or Pianoforte accompaniment, poem by F. Desprez. Op. 47, *etc. Boston Music Co.: Boston, Mass.*, (1909.) fol.
H. 1792. s. (5.)

— Life eternal.—Vita æterna.—Easter Processional. [Words by] W. J. Irons. *O. Ditson Co.:* [*Boston,*] 1905. 8°.
F. 1529. d. (20.)

— Five little Piano Studies in Rhythm, Phrasing and Expression. [No. 1.] April Fancies. [No. 2.] Elfin Dance. [No. 3.] Goblin Fun. [No. 4.] You follow me. [No. 5.] Where Poppies grow. 5 no. *O. Ditson Co.: Boston*, (1904.) fol.
h. 3282. ww. (38.)

— Longing. *See* infra: Three Songs ... Op. 40. No. 2.

LEIGHTER (Henry Clough)

— A Love-Garden. Song Cycle. Six Lyrics by C. H. Towne. Op. 22. *Boston Music Co.: Boston, Mass.*, 1902. 4°.
F. 637. q. (4.)

— Love-Life. [Song-cycle.] Opus 46 ... 1. The Mystery. C. E. Thomas. 2. Absence. O. Meredith. 3. The Thought of you. C. M. Robinson. *Boston Music Co.: Boston*, (1909.) 4°.
G. 385. hh. (7.)

— Love-Sorrow. A Song-Cycle for a high voice, with Violin and Violoncello obbligato and Piano accompaniment ... Opus 44. 1. "Dearest, when I am dead" ... Words ... by C. [or rather W.] E. Henley. 2. "And if he come again" ... Words by M. Maeterlinck. 3. "The Day she died" ... Words by C. H. Towne. *G. Schirmer: New York*, 1908. 4°. **G. 383. t. (9.)**

— Love's Magnificat. *See* infra: Seven Songs. Opus 57. No. 1.

— Two Lyrics, after the French of Victor Hugo, by A. Lang, for a high voice with Piano accompaniment. Op. 53. 1. One Rose. 2. Butterflies. *G. Schirmer: New York*, (1912.) 4°.
G. 425. j. (7.)

— [Magnificat and Nunc dimittis. Op. 25. No. 2.] Magnificat in C ... Op. 25. No. 2a. *O. Ditson Co.:* [*Boston,*] 1903. 8°.
E. 597. q. (13.)

— [Magnificat and Nunc dimittis. Op. 25. No. 2.] Nunc dimittis in C ... Op. 25. No. 2b. *O. Ditson Co.:* [*Boston,*] 1903. 8°.
E. 597. q. (14.)

— [Magnificat and Nunc dimittis. Op. 25. No. 3.] Magnificat in F ... Op. 25. No. 3a. *O. Ditson Co.:* [*Boston,*] 1904. 8°.
E. 597. q. (15.)

— [Magnificat and Nunc dimittis. Op. 25. No. 3.] Nunc dimittis in F ... Op. 25. No. 3b. *O. Ditson Co.:* [*Boston,*] 1904. 8°.
E. 597. q. (16.)

— Magnificat and Nunc dimittis in F, for Chorus of mixed voices, with Organ accompaniment. (Op. 50.) *G. Schirmer: New York*, (1910.) 8°. **F. 1169. o. (20.)**

— Magnificat and Nunc dimittis in C for Four-Part Chorus ... with Organ accompaniment, *etc.* (Op. 51. No. 3, 4.) *G. Schirmer: New York*, (1913.) 8°. **E. 597. v. (12.)**

— Magnificat for Chorus ... with Organ accompaniment. Op. 56. No. 1, *etc. G. Schirmer: New York*, (1914.) 8°.
F. 1169. v. (16.)

— Magnificat (Nunc dimittis) in D, for Chorus ... Op. 56. No. 5 (No. 6), *etc. Boston Music Co.: Boston, Mass.*, (1913.) 8°.
E. 597. v. (11.)

— Magnificat (Nunc dimittis) in G, for Chorus ... Op. 56. No. 10 (No. 11). *Boston Music Co.: Boston, Mass.*, (1913.) 8°. **F. 1169. v. (17.)**

— Magnificat and Nunc dimittis, in B flat, *etc.* (Op. 58.) *O. Ditson Co.: Boston*, (1914.) 8°. **F. 1169. v. (18.)**

— Memories. *See* infra: Three Songs ... Op. 40. No. 1.

— Mid-rapture. Song ... with Pianoforte accompaniment set to the xxvith sonnet of D. G. Rossetti. Op. 62. No. 1. *Boston Music Co.: Boston, Mass.*, (1915.) fol. **G. 806. mm. (11.)**

— My Wish. *See* infra: 5 Songs ... Op. 54. No. 5.

— Nova Vita.—Easter Processional for mixed voices.— (Translated from the Greek by J. M. Neale.) *O. Ditson Co.: Boston*, (1912.) 8°. **F. 281. ee. (59.)**

— "Now is Christ risen." Introit Anthem for Easter, for Chorus with Tenor Solo and Organ accompaniment. (Op. 41. No. 2.) *G. Schirmer: New York*, (1907.) 8°. *G. Schirmer's ... Octavo Church Music, No.* 4871.
E. 335. b. (17.)

— Nunc Dimittis. *See* supra: Magnificat.

— O Heart of mine. [Part-song for S. S. A. A., words by] L. Heald. Op. 34. No. 4. *A. P. Schmidt: Boston, etc.*, (1909.) 8°. **F. 328. j. (27.)**

LEIGHTER (Henry Clough)

— O Heart of mine. [Part-song for male voices, words by] L. Heald. Op. 34. No. 4. *A. P. Schmidt: Boston, etc.*, (1909.) 8°. **F. 163. k. (23.)**

— O Heart of mine! Song with Pianoforte accompaniment ... Op. 34. No. 4. *Schott & Co.: London*, [1914.] fol. **G. 806. mm. (8.)**

— Oh, what comes over the Sea. *See* infra: Seven Songs. Opus 57. No. 5.

— O would I were the cool Wind. *See* infra: Five Songs. Op. 43. No. 3.

— On Christmas Day. Carol (for mixed voices). [Words by] Rev. J. McG. Foster. *Boston Music Co.: Boston*, (1906.) 8°. **F. 281. e. (29.)**

— Five Piano Studies in Expression, for the young student. 1. Little Caprice.—Capriccietto.— 2. Pensive Monody.— Cantilena.— 3. Elfinesque.—Scherzino.— 4. In the still Woodland.—Pastorale.— 5. Told in the Firelight.— Legend. *Boston Music Co.: Boston, Mass.*, [1908.] 4°. **g. 337. n. (6.)**

— Possession. *See* infra: Three Songs ... Op. 38. No. 1.

— Processional and Recessional for the Easter festival. a. Christ the Lord is risen. [Words by C. F. Alexander.] b. Jesus, our risen King. [Words by J. Allen.] *Boston Music Co.: Boston, Mass.*, (1908.) 8°. **F. 281. k. (22.)**

— Recessional. A Victorian Ode by R. Kipling ... for ... Chorus ... with Piano or Orchestra accompaniment. Opus 61. Vocal Score. *Boston Music Co.: Boston, Mass.*, (1915.) 8°. **F. 1269. p. (2.)**

— Rejoice in the Day. Anthem, *etc. White-Smith Music Publishing Co.: Boston, etc.*, (1915.) 8°. **F. 281. tt. (29.)**

— Rejoice! rejoice! Christmas Processional [for S. A. T. B., words by] W. C. Dix. *O. Ditson Co.: [Boston,]* 1905. 8°. **F. 1529. e. (23.)**

— Rejoice, ye Righteous. Christmas Anthem ... Op. 37. No. 1. *O. Ditson Co.: [Boston,]* 1905. 8°. **F. 281. c. (15.)**

— Requiescat. *See* infra: Seven Songs. Opus 57. No. 6.

— Ring the Bells. Christmas Carol. *O. Ditson Co.: [Boston,]* 1902. 8°. **F. 1529. d. (21.)**

— The Risen Christ. Easter Anthem for mixed voices. Op. 63. No. 2. *Boston Music Co.: Boston*, 1921. 8°. **F. 538. h. (18.)**

— Roseen-dhu. *See* infra: Five Songs. Op. 43. No. 2.

— Roses for the Flush of Youth. *See* infra: Seven Songs. Opus 57. No. 2.

— Two Rossetti Lyrics. [Songs.] (Op. 60. No. 1.) Her Songs, my Tears. C. Rossetti. (No. 2.) Shadowed in your Hand. D. G. Rossetti. 2 no. *G. Ricordi & Co.: New York, etc.*, 1914. fol. **G. 806. mm. (9.)**

— Saw you never in the Twilight. Christmas Carol. *O. Ditson Co.: [Boston,]* 1902. 8°. **F. 1529. d. (19.)**

— Sea-Gypsy. [Song, words by] R. Hovey. Op. 65. No. 1. *Boston Music Co.: Boston*, 1919. 4°. **G. 390. u. (2.)**

— The Secret. *See* infra: Seven Songs. Opus 57. No. 3.

— Shadowed in your Hand. *See* supra: Two Rossetti Lyrics. Op. 60. No. 2.

— Shadows, Laddie. *See* infra: Songs. Op. 3. No. 3.

— Sleep, little Treasure. Trio for women's voices. Lithuanian Folk-Song. Arr. by H. C. Leighter. *Boston Music Co.: Boston, Mass.*, (1908.) 8°. **F. 328. g. (28.)**

— Songs. Op. 3. No. 1. Dreamy Sleep ... No. 2. I wonder, little Girl ... No. 3. Shadows, Laddie, *etc.* [Words by M. V. Freese.] 3 no. *O. Ditson Co.: Boston*, 1902-3. fol. **H. 1799. vv. (36.)**

LEIGHTER (Henry Clough)

— Three Songs, with Piano accompaniment. Op. 38. No. 1. Possession.—K. K. Gusling.— ... No. 2. Ave, Astra!— A. S. Riggs.— ... [No. 3.] "Who knows?"—G. Rogers.—, *etc.* 3 no. *G. Schirmer: New York*, (1906.) fol. **G. 807. kk. (2.)**

— Three Songs, with Piano accompaniment. Op. 40. No. 1. Memories ... Words by C. E. Thomas. No. 2. Longing ... Words by G. Rogers. No. 3. To-morrow ... Words by T. Garrison. 3 no. *G. Schirmer: New York*, (1906.) fol. **G. 807. kk. (3.)**

— Five Songs. No. 43. No. 1. Gift o' God. Words by L. K. Smith. No. 2. Roseen-dhu. Words by Fiona Macleod. No. 3. O would I were the cool Wind. Words by Fiona Macleod. No. 4. Hills o' Skye. Words by W. McLennan. No. 5. Gladness of Spring. Words by C. H. Towne. 5 no. *Boston Music Co.: Boston, Mass.*, (1907.) fol. **G. 805. mm. (31.)**

— 5 Songs with Pianoforte accompaniment. Op. 54. No. 1. April Rapture ... (C. H. Towne.) No. 2. Heralds of Spring ... (C. H. Towne.) No. 3. Day-Dreams ... No. 4. Sympathy ... (L. Simmons.) No. 5. My Wish, *etc.* (C. G. Rossetti.) 5 no. *A. P. Schmidt: Boston, etc.*, 1911. fol. **H. 1792. s. (6.)**

— Seven Songs. Opus 57. 1. Love's Magnificat. A. Symons. 2. Roses for the Flush of Youth. C. G. Rossetti. 3. The Secret. F. L. Knowles. 4. I tell you over and over. C. H. Towne. 5. Oh, what comes over the Sea. C. G. Rossetti. 6. Requiescat. O. Wilde. 7. Ah, dear one. D. G. Rossetti. 7 no. *Boston Music Co.: Boston, Mass.*, (1914.) fol. **G. 806. mm. (10.)**

— Summer Night.—Sommernacht.—[Song, words by] J. Ambrosius, translated by J. Remington. Op. 19. No. 2. *O. Ditson Co.: Boston*, 1902. fol. **H. 1799. vv. (37.)**

— Sympathy. *See* supra: 5 Songs ... Op. 54. No. 4.

— Festival Te Deum in B major ... Op. 9. No. 1. *O. Ditson Co.: [Boston, etc.,]* 1897. 8°. **F. 1529. b. (35.)**

— Te Deum laudamus in G major ... Op. 10. No. 1. *G. Schirmer: New York*, 1898. 8°. **F. 1173. (24.)**

— Te Deum laudamus in C. Op. 25. No. 2c. *O. Ditson Co.: [Boston,]* 1903. 8°. **E. 597. q. (12.)**

— Thy Light is come. Christmas Introit Anthem for Chorus of mixed voices, with Organ accompaniment. (Op. 50. No. 1.) *G. Schirmer: New York*, (1910.) 8°. **F. 281. w. (28.)**

— 'Tis here. [Song, words by] J. L. French. Op. 65. No. 3. *Boston Music Co.: Boston*, 1920. 4°. **G. 426. n. (27.)**

— 'Tis Love! *See* infra: [Tofana.]

— To the Name of our Salvation. Christmas Recessional [for S. A. T. B., words by] J. M. Neale. *Boston Music Co.: Boston, Mass.*, (1908.) 8°. **F. 281. m. (28.)**

— [Tofana.] 'Tis Love! [Song.] From the Opera "Tofana". [Words by] M. V. Freese. Op. 18. No. 5. 2 no. [In C and A.] *H. B. Stevens Co.: Boston*, (1902.) fol. **H. 1794. l. (5.)**

— To-morrow. *See* supra: Three Songs ... Op. 40. No. 3.

— Triumphant Bells. Easter Carol, [words by] M. V. Freese. *O. Ditson Co.: [Boston,]* 1906. 8°. **F. 1529. e. (20.)**

— The Unknown Wind. Terzetto for women's voices. [Words by] F. Macleod. Op. 55. No. 5, *etc. Boston Music Co.: Boston, Mass.*, (1915.) 8°. **F. 328. v. (26.)**

— The Victory through Christ. Easter Anthem for Chorus of mixed voices, with Tenor solo and Organ accompaniment. [Op. 42. No. 1.] *G. Schirmer: New York*, (1908.) 8°. **F. 281. k. (23.)**

LEIGHTON (   ) and LEIGHTON (   )

— Every Dollar carries Trouble of its own. [Song.] *Helf & Hager: New York*, [1905.] fol. **H. 3985. s. (1.)**

— Susie Jane. [Song.] pp. 5. *Helf & Hager: New York*, [1905.] fol. **H. 3985. s. (2.)**

LEIGHTON (CECIL)

— A Wish. Song, words by E. Saxe. *J. Williams: London,* (1912.) fol.   H. 1792. s. (7.)

LEIGHTON (DOUGLAS M.)

— Life's Lucky Bag. Song, words by H. Simpson. *Lublin & Co.: London,* 1907. fol.   H. 1794. vv. (36.)

LEIGHTON (G. A.)

— Juvenile Lessons. Popular and national melodies, arranged & fingered for the use of beginners on the piano forte, by G. A. Leighton. no. 1–7, 10. *Jos^h Blackman: London,* [c. 1850.] fol. *Imperfect; wanting the other no.*   **h. 1203. qq.**

— The Juvenile Pianists Library, a selection of the most admired national & operatic melodies, arranged ... for young performers on the piano forte by G. A. Leighton, *etc.* no. 6, 11. *Jos^h Blackman: London,* [c. 1850.] fol. *Imperfect; wanting the other no.*   **h. 1203. n.**

— A new and improved Preceptor for the Pianoforte. *London,* [1845?] fol.   **h. 1485. s. (42.)**

LEIGHTON (GEORGE A.)

— Forty Miniatures in Étude-Form for Piano. Cuarenta miniaturas ... Traducido por M. P. Gainsborg. *G. Schirmer: New York,* 1924. 4°.   **g. 338. a. (12.)**

LEIGHTON (HARRY)

— Everything is beautiful in the Garden. Written and composed by H. Leighton, *etc.* [Song. Staff and tonic sol-fa notation. Voice part.] *Francis, Day & Hunter: London,* [1897.] *s. sh.* fol.
                                                    H. 3980. qq. (17.)

— I have. ⟨Song.⟩ Written by Harry Wincott, *etc.* pp. 5. *Hopwood & Crew: London,* [1899.] fol.   **H. 3985. s. (3.)**

— I never let it upset me. ⟨Song.⟩ Written and composed by H. Leighton, *etc.* [Staff and tonic sol-fa notation. Voice part.] *Francis, Day & Hunter: London,* [1901.] *s. sh.* fol.
                                                    H. 3985. s. (4.)

— I never let it upset me, *etc.* ⟨Song.⟩ [With separate voice part.] 2 pt. *Francis, Day & Hunter: London,* [1901.] fol.
                                                    H. 3985. s. (5.)

— I've got something to be thankful for. ⟨Song.⟩ Written by H. Leighton and W. Barnes, jun^r, *etc.* [Staff and tonic sol-fa notation. Voice part.] *Francis, Day & Hunter: London,* [1901.] *s. sh.* fol.   **H. 3985. s. (6.)**

— I've got something to be thankful for, *etc.* ⟨Song.⟩ [With separate voice part.] 2 pt. *Francis, Day & Hunter: London,* [1901.] fol.   **H. 3985. s. (7.)**

— It isn't the first Time. Written and composed by H. Leighton, *etc.* [Song. With separate voice part.] ⟨Arranged by John S. Baker.⟩ 2 pt. *Howard & Co.: London,* [1898.] fol.
                                                    H. 3980. qq. (18.)

— Kempton Park. Written and composed by H. Leighton, *etc.* [Song. Staff and tonic sol-fa notation. Voice part.] *Francis, Day & Hunter: London,* [1898.] *s. sh.* fol.   **H. 3980. qq. (19.)**

— My last Shilling. ⟨Song.⟩ Written and composed by H. Leighton, *etc.* [Staff and tonic sol-fa notation. Voice part.] *Francis, Day & Hunter: London,* [1901.] *s. sh.* fol.
                                                    H. 3985. s. (8.)

— My last Shilling, *etc.* ⟨Song.⟩ [With separate voice part.] 2 pt. *Francis, Day & Hunter: London,* [1901.] fol.   **H. 3985. s. (9.)**

— Now, here's an important Case. ⟨Song.⟩ Written and composed by H. Leighton, *etc.* [Staff and tonic sol-fa notation. Voice part.] *Francis, Day & Hunter: London,* [1903.] *s. sh.* fol.   **H. 3985. s. (10.)**

— Now, here's an important Case, *etc.* ⟨Song.⟩ [With separate voice part.] 2 pt. *Francis, Day & Hunter: London,* [1903.] fol.
                                                    H. 3985. s. (11.)

LEIGHTON (HARRY)

— Oh, oh, oh oh oh! ⟨Song.⟩ Written & composed by H. Leighton. pp. 4. *B. Feldman & Co.: London,* [1903.] fol.
                                                    H. 3985. s. (12.)

— Opinions differ; or, Art Criticism ... ⟨Song.⟩ Written and composed by Harry Leighton, *etc.* pp. 4. *Charles Sheard & Co.: London,* [1901.] fol.   **H. 1654. rr. (31.)**

— To-morrow's Men ... ⟨Song.⟩ Written and composed by H. Leighton, *etc.* [Staff and tonic sol-fa notation. Voice part.] *Francis, Day & Hunter: London,* [1903.] *s. sh.* fol.
                                                    H. 3985. s. (13.)

— To-morrow's Men, *etc.* ⟨Song.⟩ [With separate voice part.] 2 pt. *Francis, Day & Hunter: London,* [1903.] fol.
                                                    H. 3985. s. (14.)

— *See* DAVID (Worton) Prisoner at the Bar. ⟨Song.⟩ Written & composed by W. David, H. Leighton, *etc.* [1910.] fol.
                                                    H. 3990. yy. (22.)

— *See* HOWARD (Carl) and LEIGHTON (H.) Oh! what a wicked World we live in! [Song.] Written and composed by C. Howard and H. Leighton, *etc.* [1899.] *s. sh.* fol.
                                                    H. 3980. ii. (26.)

— *See* HOWARD (Carl) and LEIGHTON (H.) The Usual Morning Performance. [Song.] Written and composed by C. Howard and H. Leighton, *etc.* [1895.] *s. sh.* fol.   **H. 3980. ii. (27.)**

— *See* MURRAY (Fred) "All alone in old Cologne." ⟨Song.⟩ Written and composed by Murray, Leighton, *etc.* [1907.] *s. sh.* fol.   **H. 3986. l. (2.)**

— *See* MURRAY (Fred) "All alone in old Cologne." ⟨Song.⟩ Written and composed by Murray, Leighton, *etc.* [1907.] fol.
                                                    H. 3986. l. (3.)

— *See* MURRAY (Fred) And the Lovers lingered longer. [A cycle song.] Written and composed by F. Murray, H. Leighton, *etc.* [1907.] *s. sh.* fol.   **H. 3986. l. (6.)**

— *See* MURRAY (Fred) And the Lovers lingered longer. (A cycle song.) Written and composed by F. Murray, H. Leighton, *etc.* [1907.] fol.   **H. 3986. l. (7.)**

— *See* MURRAY (Fred) Comrades, here's Health to you! ... ⟨Song.⟩ Written and composed by Murray, Leighton, *etc.* [1907.] *s. sh.* fol.   **H. 3986. l. (8.)**

— *See* MURRAY (Fred) Comrades, here's Health to you! ... ⟨Song.⟩ Written and composed by Murray, Leighton, *etc.* [1907.] fol.   **H. 3986. l. (9.)**

— *See* MURRAY (Fred) In my Aeroplane. Written and composed by F. Murray, H. Leighton, *etc.* [Song.] [1907.] fol.
                                                    H. 3986. l. (12.)

— *See* MURRAY (Fred) There's a Maid in Germany. Song. Words & music by F. Murray, H. Leighton, *etc.* [1907.] fol.
                                                    H. 3986. l. (23.)

— *See* MURRAY (Fred) Whit Cunliffe's Book of popular Songs. ⟨Songs.⟩ Written and composed by Murray, Leighton, *etc.* [1907.] *s. sh.* fol.   **H. 3986. l. (28.)**

— *See* MURRAY (Fred) Whit Cunliffe's Book of popular Songs. ⟨Song.⟩ Written and composed by Murray, Leighton, *etc.* [1907.] fol.   **H. 3986. l. (29.)**

— *See* WELLS (Gilbert) Lusitania Lucy. ⟨Song.⟩ Written and composed by G. Wells, H. Leighton, *etc.* [1908.] *s. sh.* fol.
                                                    H. 3988. s. (6.)

— *See* WELLS (Gilbert) Lusitania Lucy. ⟨Song.⟩ Written and composed by G. Wells, H. Leighton, *etc.* [1908.] fol.
                                                    H. 3988. s. (7.)

— *See* WELLS (Gilbert) and LEIGHTON (H.) "The Sun is always shining" ... ⟨Song.⟩ Written and composed by G. Wells and H. Leighton. [1908.] *s. sh.* fol.   **H. 3988. s. (15.)**

— *See* WELLS (Gilbert) and LEIGHTON (H.) "The Sun is always shining," *etc.* ⟨Song.⟩ [1908.] fol.   **H. 3988. s. (16.)**

LEIGHTON (HARRY)

— *See* WINCOTT (Harry) "I'm going home to my Mother!" ⟨Song.⟩ Written and composed by H. Wincott, H. Leighton, *etc.* [1904.] *s. sh.* fol.   **H. 3988. bb. (9.)**

— *See* WINCOTT (Harry) I'm going home to my Mother! ⟨Song.⟩ Written and composed by H. Wincott, H. Leighton, *etc.* [1904.] fol.   **H. 3988. bb. (10.)**

— *See* WINCOTT (Harry) Pom tiddly om pom! ... ⟨Song.⟩ Written and composed by H. Wincott, H. Leighton, *etc.* [1903.] fol.   **H. 3988. bb. (18.)**

— *See* WINCOTT (Harry) "Pom tiddly om pom!" ... ⟨Song.⟩ Written and composed by H. Wincott, H. Leighton, *etc.* [1903.] *s. sh.* fol.   **H. 3988. bb. (17.)**

— [For editions and arrangements of songs written and composed by H. Leighton in sole collaboration with Harry Wincott:] *See* WINCOTT (Harry) and LEIGHTON (H.)

LEIGHTON (HARRY) and EVERARD (GEORGE)

— All Girls to me are fair. ⟨Song.⟩ Written and composed by H. Leighton & G. Everard. pp. 4. *Shapiro, von Tilzer Music Co.: London*, [1906.] 4°.   **H. 3985. s. (15.)**

— Don't say it like that, please ... ⟨Song.⟩ Written and composed by H. Leighton and G. Everard, *etc.* [With separate voice part.] 2 pt. *Hopwood & Crew: London*, [1900.] fol.   **H. 3985. s. (16.)**

— Fly away! ... ⟨Song.⟩ Written and composed by H. Leighton and G. Everard. [Staff and tonic sol-fa notation. Voice part.] *Francis, Day & Hunter: London*, [1906.] *s. sh.* fol.   **H. 3985. s. (17.)**

— Fly away! *etc.* ⟨Song.⟩ [With separate voice part.] 2 pt. *Francis, Day & Hunter: London*, [1906.] fol.   **H. 3985. s. (18.)**

— It suited her just as well! ⟨Song.⟩ Written and composed by H. Leighton and G. Everard, *etc.* [Staff and tonic sol-fa notation. Voice part.] *Francis, Day & Hunter: London*, [1902.] *s. sh.* fol.   **H. 3985. s. (19.)**

— It suited her just as well! *etc.* ⟨Song.⟩ [With separate voice part.] 2 pt. *Francis, Day & Hunter: London*, [1902.] fol.   **H. 3985. s. (20.)**

— Molly, now don't be teasing! ⟨Song.⟩ Written and composed by H. Leighton & G. Everard, *etc.* [Staff and tonic sol-fa notation. Voice part.] *Francis, Day & Hunter: London*, [1905.] *s. sh.* fol.   **H. 3985. s. (21.)**

— What did Patsy do? ⟨Song.⟩ Written and composed by H. Leighton and G. Everard, *etc.* [Staff and tonic sol-fa notation. Voice part.] *Francis, Day & Hunter: London*, [1901.] *s. sh.* fol.   **H. 3985. s. (22.)**

— What did Patsy do? *etc.* ⟨Song.⟩ [With separate voice part.] 2 pt. *Francis, Day & Hunter: London*, [1901.] fol.   **H. 3985. s. (23.)**

— Why should my Color make a Difference? ⟨Song.⟩ Written and composed by H. Leighton & G. Everard. pp. 4. *Shapiro, von Tilzer Music Co.: London*, [1906.] fol.   **H. 3985. s. (24.)**

LEIGHTON (HARRY) and HILBURY (CHARLES E.)

— Lady! Lady! (The fortune teller song.) Written and composed by H. Leighton and C. Hilbury. *Jos. W. Stern & Co.: New York*, [1908.] fol.   **H. 3985. s. (25.)**

— Up to one of your Tricks again. ⟨Song.⟩ Written and composed by H. Leighton and C. Hilbury, *etc.* pp. 6. *Empire Music Publishing Co.: London*, [1907.] fol.   **H. 3985. s. (26.)**

LEIGHTON (HARRY) and HILBURY (CHARLES E.)

— "What is it makes all the Girls love you?" ⟨Song.⟩ Written and composed by H. Leighton and C. Hilbury. [Staff and tonic sol-fa notation. Voice part.] *Francis, Day & Hunter: London*, [1907.] *s. sh.* fol.   **H. 3985. s. (27.)**

— "What is it makes all the Girls love you?" *etc.* ⟨Song.⟩ [With separate voice part.] 2 pt. *Francis, Day & Hunter: London*, [1907.] fol.   **H. 3985. s. (28.)**

LEIGHTON (HARRY) and NOBLE (GORDON)

— "I'm a bit too young and tender," *etc.* [Song. Staff and tonic sol-fa notation. Voice part.] *Francis, Day & Hunter: London*, [1899.] *s. sh.* fol.   **H. 3980. qq. (20.)**

LEIGHTON (HARRY) and POWELL (ORLANDO)

— The Willow Tree. (Ballad.) Written and composed by H. Leighton and O. Powell, *etc.* [Staff and tonic sol-fa notation. Voice part.] *Francis, Day & Hunter: London*, [1904.] *s. sh.* fol.   **H. 3985. s. (29.)**

— The Willow Tree. Ballad, *etc.* [With separate voice part.] 2 pt. *Francis, Day & Hunter: London*, [1904.] fol.   **H. 3985. s. (30.)**

LEIGHTON (HARRY) and WELLS (GILBERT)

— "I'll never love another Girl like you." ⟨Song.⟩ Written and composed by H. Leighton and G. Wells, *etc.* [Staff and tonic sol-fa notation. Voice part.] *Francis, Day & Hunter: London*, [1909.] *s. sh.* fol.   **H. 3985. s. (31.)**

— "I'll never love another Girl like you," *etc.* ⟨Song.⟩ [With separate voice part.] 2 pt. *Francis, Day & Hunter: London*, [1909.] fol.   **H. 3985. s. (32.)**

LEIGHTON (HARRY) *of Leeds*

— When silver locks replace the gold ... Song & chorus, Words by S. N. Mitchell. *Leeds*, [1876.] fol.   **H. 1778. y. (5.)**

LEIGHTON (J. A.)

— Hellow, my Creole Belle, hello. [Song.] Words and music by J. A. Leighton. pp. 5. *Wizard Music Co.: Esterwood, La.*, [1909.] fol.   **H. 3985. s. (33.)**

LEIGHTON (KENNETH)

— Adventante Deo. (Lift up your Heads, Gates of my Heart.) ⟨Words by John Addington Symonds, 1840–1893. Anthem for SATB and organ.⟩ pp. 20. *Novello & Co.: [Borough Green, London, 1972.]* 8°.
[*Novello Church Music.* 36.]   **E. 618. f.**

— Alleluia, Amen. Festival anthem for baritone solo. SATB and organ. ⟨Revelation 19, vv. 1, 4.⟩ pp. 21. *Novello & Co.: London*, [1962.] 8°.
[*Anthems.* 1416.]   **E. 618. a.**

— The Birds. Suite for soprano (or tenor) solo, chorus, strings and piano. [Vocal score.] pp. 77. *Novello & Co.: London*, [1957.] 8°.   **E. 270. m. (1.)**

— Burlesque for Orchestra. Opus 19. Full score. pp. 64. *Novello & Co.: London*, [1961.] 4°.   **g. 1620. y. (7.)**

— Three Carols. For soprano solo and S. A. T. B. (unaccompanied) ... Opus 25. [No.] 1. The Star-song. Words by Robert Herrick. pp. 12. *Novello & Co.: London*, [1956.] 8°.
[*Carols.* 604.]   **C. 754.**

— Three Carols. For soprano solo and S. A. T. B. (unaccompanied) ... Opus 25. [No.] 2. Lully, lulla, thou little tiny Child. Words from the Pageant of the Shearmen and

LEIGHTON (KENNETH)

Tailors, Coventry, 15th century. pp. 7. *Novello & Co.: London*, [1956.] 8°.
[*Musical Times. no.* 1363.] **P. P. 1945. aa.**

— Three Carols. For soprano solo and S. A. T. B. (unaccompanied) ... Opus 25. [No.] 3. An Ode on the Birth of our Saviour. Words by Robert Herrick. pp. 8. *Novello & Co.: London*, [1956.] 8°.
[*Carols*. 605.] **C. 754.**

— A Christmas Caroll. Baritone solo and S. A. T. B. Words by Robert Herrick ... Opus 21. pp. 16. *Novello & Co.: London*, [1954.] 8°.
[*Carols*. 579.] **C. 754.**

— Communion Service in D. For unison voices, S. A. T. B. (optional) and organ ... Opus 45, *etc.* [Score.] ⟨Congregational part⟩. 2 pt. *Oxford University Press, for the Church Music Soc.: London*, [1965.] 8°.
[*Church Music Society Publications.* O. 1.] **E. 1618.**

— Concerto for String Orchestra. ⟨Opus 39.⟩ Score. pp. 46. *Novello & Co.: London*, [1964.] 4°. **e. 668. jj. (15.)**

— Concerto for String Orchestra ... Opus 39. [Parts.] 5 pt. *Novello & Co.: London*, [1962.] 4°. **h. 3210. i. (787.)**

— Concerto for Violin and small Orchestra. Arranged by the composer for violin and piano. ⟨Opus 12.⟩ [Score and part.] 2 pt. *Novello and Co.: London*, [1956.] 4°. **g. 500. dd. (12.)**

— Concerto for Violoncello and Orchestra. ⟨Opus 31.⟩ Arranged by the composer for violoncello and piano. [Score and part.] 2 pt. *Novello & Co.: London*, [1963.] 4°. **g. 510. p. (3.)**

— Conflicts. Fantasy on two themes. For piano. Opus 51. pp. 34. *Novello & Co.: Borough Green, London*, [1971.] 4°. **g. 1138. z. (12.)**

— Crucifixus pro nobis. ⟨Opus 38.⟩ Cantata for tenor (or soprano) solo, S. A. T. B. and organ ... Words by Patrick Carey and Phineas Fletcher. pp. 35. *Novello & Co.: London*, [1961.] 8°. **F. 1195. dd. (1.)**

— [Crucifixus pro nobis.—4. Hymn.] Drop, drop, slow Tears ... Anthem for S. A. T. B. unaccompanied. Words by Phineas Fletcher. pp. 4. *Novello & Co.: London*, [1963.] 8°.
[*Short Anthems.* 340.] **F. 280. f.**

— Dance Suite in D ... Opus 53 ... Full score. [A facsimile of the composer's autograph.] pp. 88. *Novello & Co.: Borough Green, London*, [1969.] 4°.
Part of "Novello orchestral Series". **f. 641. i. (3.)**

— Dance Suite No. 2 [for orchestra] ... Opus 59 ... Full score. pp. 80. *Novello: Borough Green*, [1977.] 4°.
Part of "Novello orchestral Series". **f. 641. ss. (3.)**

— Drop, drop, slow Tears. *See* supra: [Crucifixus pro nobis.—4. Hymn.]

— An Easter Sequence, *etc.* ⟨For boys' or female voices and organ with optional trumpet. Opus 55.⟩ [Score.] pp. 24. *Oxford University Press: London*, [1970.] 8°. **E. 270. ww. (2.)**

— An Easter Sequence, *etc.* ⟨Trumpet in B♭.⟩ *Oxford University Press: London*, [1970.] 4°. **g. 1105. o. (2.)**

— Elegy for Violoncello & Piano. [Score and part.] 2 pt. *Alfred Lengnick & Co.: London*, [1953.] 4°. **g. 510. m. (14.)**

— Et resurrexit. Theme, fantasy and fugue for organ. Opus 49. [With a portrait.] pp. 28. *Novello & Co.: Borough Green, London*, [1968.] 4°.
[*International Series of contemporary Organ Music.* no. 32.] **g. 1023. g.**

— Fantasia contrappuntistica. (Homage to Bach.) Per pianoforte, *etc.* ⟨Op. 24.⟩ pp. 21. *G. Ricordi & c.: Milano*, [1958.] 4°. **g. 1126. s. (9.)**

LEIGHTON (KENNETH)

— Fantasia on the name Bach. For viola and piano. ⟨Opus 29.⟩ [Score and part.] 2 pt. *Novello & Co.: London*, [1957.] 4°. **g. 762. m. (16.)**

— Fantasy on an American Hymn-tune. ⟨Words and melody by Robert Lowry, 1865.⟩ Clarinet, cello & piano. Opus 70. [Score and parts.] 3 pt. *Novello: Borough Green*, [1980.] 4°. **g. 1635. a. (7.)**

— Festive Overture. Score. pp. 55. *Novello & Co.: London*, [1964.] 4°.
[*Music for Today. no.* 7.] **g. 214.**

— Give me the Wings of Faith. Anthem for soprano and baritone soli, SATB and organ. Words by Isaac Watts, *etc.* pp. 11. *Novello & Co.: London*, [1962.] 8°.
[*Anthems.* 1422.] **E. 618. a.**

— God's Grandeur. Motet for S. A. T. B. (unaccompanied). Words by Gerard Manley Hopkins. pp. 10. *Novello & Co.: London*, [1959.] 8°.
[*Part-song Book.* 1584.] **F. 280. b.**

— A Hymn of the Nativity. Carol for soprano solo and S. A. T. B. (unaccompanied). Words by Richard Crashaw. pp. 15. *Novello & Co.: London*, [1960.] 8°.
[*Carols.* no. 633.] **C. 754.**

— Improvisation. In memoriam Maurice de Sausmarez. [Organ.] pp. 7. *Novello & Co.: Borough Green, London*, [1972.] obl. 4°.
[*Novello Modern Organ Repertory. no.* 7.] **e. 1096. bb.**

— Jack-in-the-box, *etc.* [P. F.] pp. 3. *G. Ricordi & Co.: London*, [1960.] 4°. **g. 1128. mm. (4.)**

— Let all the World in every Corner sing. Anthem for SATB and organ. Words by George Herbert. pp. 12. *Novello & Co.: London*, [1965.] 8°.
[*Octavo Anthems.* 1458.] **E. 618. a.**

— Lift up your Heads, O ye Gates. Anthem for SATB (unaccompanied). Psalm 24, vv. 9, 10. pp. 15. *Novello & Co.: London*, [1966.] 8°.
[*Octavo Anthems.* 1463.] **E. 618. a.**

— The Light invisible. Sinfonia sacra for tenor solo, chorus and orchestra. ⟨Opus 16.⟩ [Vocal score.] pp. 78. *Novello & Co.: London*, [1958.] 8°. **F. 1195. g. (6.)**

— Magnificat and Nunc dimittis. Collegium Magdalenae Oxoniense. [S. A. T. B.] pp. 24. *Novello & Co.: London*, [1960.] 8°.
[*Parish Choir Book.* 1383.] **E. 618.**

— Marcia capricciosa. [Flute and P. F.] *In:* MODERN. Modern Flute Music, *etc.* bk. 1. no. 1. [1971.] 4°. **h. 250. y. (1.)**

— Mass. (Opus 44.) ⟨For double mixed chorus and organ.⟩ Latin text, *etc.* pp. 82. *Oxford University Press: London*, [1966.] 8°. **F. 1183. e. (4.)**

— Metamorphoses. For violin and piano. Opus 48, *etc.* [Score and part.] 2 pt. *Novello & Co.: Borough Green, London*, [1970.] 4°. **g. 500. vv. (1.)**

— Missa brevis. For SATB (unaccompanied) ... Opus 50. pp. 28. *Novello & Co.: London*, [1968.] 8°.
[*Novello Church Music.* 2.] **E. 618. f.**

— Missa sancti Thomae. 1162–1962. SATB chorus & organ. Opus 40. pp. 51. *Novello & Co.: London*, [1965.] 8°. **F. 274. cc. (6.)**

— Morning Canticles. For unison voices, SATB and organ ... Venite. ⟨Te Deum laudamus—Jubilate Deo.⟩ 3 no. *Novello & Co.: London*, [1968.] 8°.
[*Novello Church Music.* 5–7.] **E. 618. f.**

— Morning Canticles, *etc.* ⟨Unison part.⟩ 3 pt. *Novello & Co.: London*, [1968.] 8°.
[*Novello Church Music.* 5A–7A.] **E. 618. f.**

LEIGHTON (KENNETH)

— Nocturne. For violin and piano. [Score and part.] 2 pt. *Novello & Co.: London*, [1962.] 4°. **g. 500. mm. (6.)**

— O be joyful in the Lord. (Jubilate Deo.) Psalm 100. 〈S. A. T. B.〉 pp. 12. *Oxford University Press: London*, [1967.] 8°. [*Oxford Anthems. A* 240.] **F. 1776.**

— O God, enfold me in the Sun. 〈S. A. T. B.〉 Words by Jacqueline Froom. pp. 10. *Oxford University Press: London*, [1968.] 8°. [*Oxford Anthems. A* 246.] **F. 1776.**

— Of a Rose is all my Song. (A Christmas carol.) 15th c. anonymous words. 〈S. A. T. B. (unacc.)〉 pp. 11. *Oxford University Press: London*, [1970.] 8°. [*Oxford choral Songs. X* 203.] **F. 1777. m.**

— Paean. [Organ.] *In:* WILLCOCKS (*Sir* David V.) Modern Organ Music. Book 2, *etc.* pp. 3–8. [1967.] 4°. **g. 1378. bb. (1.)**

— Partita. For violoncello and piano. Opus 35. [Score and part.] 2 pt. *Novello & Co.: London*, [1963.] 4°. **g. 510. p. (2.)**

— Passacaglia, Chorale and Fugue. For orchestra. 〈Opus 18.〉 [Score.] pp. 96. *Novello & Co.: London*, [1961.] 4°. **g. 1620. y. (1.)**

— Pieces for Angela. For piano. Opus 47. pp. 17. *Novello & Co.: Borough Green*, [1967.] 4°. **g. 1138. s. (3.)**

— Preces and Responses. For SATB unaccompanied ... (1964). pp. 8. *Novello & Co.: London*, [1965.] 8°. [*Parish Choir Book.* 1415.] **E. 618.**

— Prelude, Scherzo and Passacaglia. For organ. 〈Opus 41.〉 pp. 26. *Novello & Co.: London*, [1964.] 4°. [*International Series of contemporary Organ Music. no.* 17.] **g. 1023. g.**

— Three Psalms For TT Bar. BB unaccompanied ... Opus 54 ... 1. Like as the Hart. 〈2. The Lord is my Shepherd. 3. O sing unto the Lord a new Song.〉 pp. 38. *Novello & Co.:* [*Borough Green*, 1974.] 8°. [*Novello Church Music.* 34.] **E. 618. f.**

— Quam dilecta! Motet for soprano solo and SATB chorus (unaccompanied) ... Psalm 84 vv. 1–9, 12, 13. pp. 19. *Novello & Co.: London*, [1968.] 8°. [*Octavo Anthems.* 1471.] **E. 618. a.**

— String Quartet No. 1. Score. pp. 35. *Alfred Lengnick & Co.: London*, [1958.] 8°. **e. 668. y. (4.)**

— String Quartet No. 2. 〈Op. 33.〉 Score. pp. 37. *Alfred Lengnick & Co.: London*, [1960.] 8°. **d. 85. aa. (8.)**

— Quartet in one Movement. Contrasts and Variants. For violin, viola, cello & piano. Opus 63. 〈Score-Parts.〉 4 pt. *Novello: Borough Green*, [1978.] 4°. **g. 410. jj. (6.)**

— Quintet. For piano and string quartet. Opus 34. [Score and parts.] 5 pt. *Novello & Co.: London*, [1962.] 4°. **g. 420. oo. (1.)**

— Scherzo. For two pianos. pp. 19. *Alfred Lengnick & Co.: London*, [1953.] 4°. *Two copies.* **g. 1122. n. (13.)**

— Sequence for All Saints. For SATB choir, baritone solo and organ. [Partly based on Song 67 by O. Gibbons.] Words from English Hymnal 731 [and by I. Watts] ... Opus 75, *etc.* pp. 43. *Roberton Publications: Wendover*, [1978.] 8°. **E. 1857. a. (15.)**

— The Second Service. (Magnificat and Nunc dimittis.) S. A. T. B. ... Opus 62. pp. 24. *Oxford University Press: London*, [1972.] 8°. [*Church Music Society Publications. O.* 4.] **E. 1618.**

LEIGHTON (KENNETH)

— Solus ad victimam. Words by Peter Abelard. Translated by Helen Waddell. 〈S. A. T. B.〉 pp. 5. *Oxford University Press: London*, [1973.] 8°. [*Oxford Anthems. A* 309.] **F. 1776.**

— Sonata for Pianoforte. pp. 35. *Alfred Lengnick & Co.: London*, [1950.] 4°. **g. 1128. i. (5.)**

— Sonata No. 2 for Pianoforte. 〈Op. 17.〉 pp. 31. *Alfred Lengnick & Co.: London*, [1954.] 4°. **g. 1128. t. (1.)**

— Sonata for Violin & Piano. [Score and part.] 2 pt. *Alfred Lengnick & Co.: London*, [1951.] 4°. **g. 505. ww. (5.)**

— Sonata No. 2 for Violin & Piano. 〈Op. 20.〉 [Score and part.] 2 pt. *Alfred Lengnick & Co.: London*, [1956.] 4°. **g. 505. yy. (6.)**

— Sonata for Cello solo. Opus 52. pp. 17. *Novello & Co.: Borough Green, London*, [1971.] 4°. **g. 512. m. (1.)**

— Sonatina No. 1 for Pianoforte. pp. 16. *Alfred Lengnick & Co.: London*, [1949.] 4°. **G. 1128. i. (6.)**

— Sonatina No. 2 for Pianoforte. pp. 16. *Alfred Lengnick & Co.: London*, [1949.] 4°. **g. 1128. i. (7.)**

— Five Studies for Piano. 〈Opus 22.〉 pp. 30. *Novello & Co.:* [*London*, 1956.] 4°. **g. 1126. h. (12.)**

— Six Studies. Study-variations. For piano. Opus 56. pp. 37. *Novello & Co.: Borough Green, London*, [1972.] 4°. **f. 770. ff. (7.)**

— Symphony. Opus 42. For orchestra. [Score. A facsimile of the composer's autograph.] pp. 149. *Novello & Co.: London*, [1966.] 8°. **e. 669. dd. (1.)**

— Te Deum laudamus. For S Bar soli, SATB and organ. pp. 20. *Novello & Co.: London*, [1964.] 8°. [*Parish Choir Book. no.* 1417.] **E. 618.**

— Trio. For violin, cello & piano. Opus 46. [Score and parts.] 3 pt. *Novello & Co.: Borough Green, London*, [1968.] 4°. **g. 409. xx. (9.)**

— Nine Variations ... Opus 36. [With a portrait. P. F.] pp. 21. *Novello & Co.: London*, [1970.] 4°. [*Virtuoso. no.* 5.] **g. 1138. m.**

— Seven Variations for string Quartet. Opus 43. Score, *etc.* pp. 33. *Novello & Co.: London*, [1966.] 8°. **c. 160. l. (4.)**

— Veris gratia. Suite for oboe, cello & strings. Opus 9. Study score. pp. 67. *Novello & Co.: Borough Green, London*, [1972.] 4°. **f. 390. ll. (1.)**

— *See* HALSEY (Louis) and RAMSEY (B.) Sing Nowell. 51 carols, *etc.* [With contributions by K. Leighton.] [1963.] 8°. **F. 260. ff.**

LEIGHTON (*Sir* WILLIAM)

— The Teares or Lamentacions of a Sorrowfull Soule: Composed with Musicall Ayres and Songs, both for Voyces and diuers Instruments. Set foorth by Sir William Leighton Knight ... And all Psalmes that consist of so many feete as the fiftieth Psalme, will goe to the foure parts for Consort. *William Stansby: London*, 1614. fol. *Bound in white vellum, stamped in gold with the arms of Charles I., when Prince of Wales, to whom the book is dedicated. The composers are: Sir W. Leighton, J. Dowland, J. Milton, R. Johnson, T. Ford, E. Hooper, R. Kindersley, N. Gyles, J. Cuperario, J. Bull, W. Byrde, F. Pilkington, T. Lupo, R. Jones, M. Peerson, O. Gibbons, T. Weelkes, J. Warde, A. Ferrabosco, J. Wilbye, and T. Thopull.* **K. 1. i. 9.**

LEIGHTON (Sir WILLIAM)

— The Tears or Lamentations of a sorrowful Soul. Transcribed and edited by Cecil Hill. pp. xxi. 218. *Stainer & Bell: London*, [1970.] 8°.
[*Early English Church Music.* 11.]   E. 461.

— [The Teares or Lamentations of a Sorrowfull Soule.] Sacred Motets or Anthems for four and five voices by W. Byrde and his contemporaries. Edited by Sir F. Bridge, *etc.* [1922.] 8°.
See BRIDGE (*Sir* J. F.)   F. 560. h. (4.)

LEIGHTON-VANCOURT (ELLEN)

— *See* VANCOURT.

LEIKER (MARGIT)

— Gebed bij de bevrijding. [Song.] Text: F. Schurer ... Amsterdam, 10 Mei 1945. *D. A. V. I. D.: [Amsterdam, 1945.]* fol.   I. 600. g. (47.)

— Gebed voor ons nieuwe leger. [Song. Words by Jan Hendrik. Music by M. Leiker.] [1944.] fol. *See* ALS. Als wij weer vrij zijn, Heer.   H. 1860. y. (21.)

— Gevangenislied, *etc.* [By M. Leiker.] ⟨Tekst van Titus Brandsma. Voor sopraan met guitaarbegeleiding.⟩ 1945. 8°.
See O. O Jezus, als ik U aanschouw.   I. 600. g. (41.)

— Lied op den verrader Frans Vergonet. Tweestemmig met guitaar begeleiding. [Words by Fedde Schurer, music by M. Leiker.] 1944. *s. sh.* fol. *See* HOORT. Hoort het lied van een verrader.   P. 1504. (2.)

— Een nieuw Welkomstlied. Tweestemmig met Guitaarbegeleiding. [Words by Halbo Christiaan Kool, music by M. Leiker.] [1944.] *s. sh.* fol. *See* DAAR. Daar zijn ze die Wilhelmus blazen.   P. 1504. (1.)

— Nieuw Welkomstlied. [Two-part song. Words by Halbo Christiaan Kool. Music by M. Leiker.] [1944.] *s. sh.* fol. *See* DAT. Dat zijn ze die Wilhelmus blazen.   P. 1504. (5.)

LEILA

— Leila. Ballad. *See* HAIGH (T.) *of Manchester.*

— Leïla. Opérette. *See* INGHELBRECHT (D. E.)

— Leila. Duetto. *See* LINLEY (G.)

— Leila. [Song.] *See* ROGER (J.)

— Leila. Song. *See* RUBENS (P. A.) [Great Caesar.]

— Leila. Serenade. *See* SALAMAN (C. K.)

— Leila. Song. *See* THOMPSON (R. G.)

— Leila. Song. *See* WHITE (F. H.) The Songs of Felix White. [No. 1.]

— Leila to her Rose Tree. [Song.] *See* SMART (H.) Three Ariettes. No. 2.

— Leila when I gaze on thee ... Glee for three voices. *London*, [1810?] fol.   H. 2831. a. (13.)

— Leila's Song. *See* SUPPÉ (F. von)

LEILA

— Soft Eyes of Blue. [Song, begins: "Sweet eyes".] The poetry by W. Bennett. The music ... by Leila. *London*, [1865.] fol.   H. 1772. r. (30.)

— Sweetness of Night. Song [begins: "How beautiful"] written & composed by Leila. *London*, [1867.] fol.   H. 1772. r. (31.)

LEIMERT (VOLKMAR)

— Fünf Orchesterlieder. Text: Franz Fühmann. Bariton und Orchester. Klavierauszug. pp. 52. *Verlag Neue Music: Berlin*, [1979?] 4°.   G. 1443. w. (3.)

LEIMONTINUS (ISRAEL OLAI)

— *See* PSALMS. [*Swedish.*] Koralbok, skriven af I. O. Leimontinus ... år 1675, *etc.* 1956. 8°.   W. P. 16306/6.

— *See* SPOHR (L.) Konzert für Klarinette und Orchester ... Op. 26. Herausgegeben von ... F. Leinert. [1957.] 8°.   b. 121. oo. (1.)

— *See* SPOHR (L.) Sechs Lieder ... Op. 25. Herausgegeben von F. O. Leinert. [1949.] fol.   H. 680. g. (1.)

— *See* SPOHR (L.) Sechs deutsche Lieder ... Op. 103. Herausgegeben von F. O. Leinert. [1949.] fol.   H. 680. g. (2.)

— *See* SPOHR (L.) Sechs deutsche Lieder für eine Singstimme, Klarinette und Klavier ... Op. 103. Herausgegeben von ... F. Leinert. [1971.] 4°.   H. 680. k. (1.)

— *See* SPOHR (L.) Streichquartette Op. 15. Nr. 1: Es-dur. Nr. 2: D-dur. Herausgegeben von F. O. Leinert. [1955.] 8°.   c. 140. kk. (9.)

— *See* SPOHR (L.) Streichquartette. Op. 29. Nr. 1: Es-dur. Herausgegeben von F. O. Leinert. [1955.] 8°.   c. 140. qq. (4.)

— *See* SPOHR (L.) Trio IV B-dur ... Op. 133. Herausgegeben von ... F. Leinert. [1958.] fol.   h. 1099. aa. (5.)

— *See* SPOHR (L.) Trio in B für Klavier, Violine und Violoncello ... Op. 133. Herausgegeben von ... O. Leinert. [1969.] 4°.   g. 653. l. (1.)

LEIP (HANS)

— Frühe Lieder. Mit Singweisen und Holzschnitten vom Verfasser. pp. 61. *Hamburgische Bücherei: Hamburg*, 1948. 8°.   B. 5.

LEIPOLD (J.)

— Anima Christi. Solo ... with an Accompaniment for the organ and violin. *R. Butler: London*, [1885.] fol.   H. 879. e. (13.)

— Caro mea, for four voices. *R. Butler: London*, [1885.] fol.   H. 879. e. (14.)

— Jesus dulcis memoria, solo for Mezzo Soprano or Baritone. *London*, [1881.] fol.   H. 1028. i. (35.)

— O Salutaris & Tantum ergo. [Solo.] *London*, [1881.] *s. sh.* fol.   H. 1028. i. (36.)

— Salve Regina, solo for Mezzo Soprano or Baritone. *London*, [1881.] fol.   H. 1028. i. (37.)

LEIPOLD (J. HENRY)

— Feathery Spray. Morceau de Salon for the pianoforte. *E. Donajowski: London*, [1890.] fol.   h. 1489. s. (38.)

— Good Night, Jeannette. Song, words by J. English. *C. Woolhouse: London*, [1898.] fol.   H. 1798. u. (40.)

— How shall I love thee? [Song.] Words by W. Layton. *J. & J. Hopkinson: London*, [1886.] fol.   H. 1788. v. (30.)

— Midnight Forest. Scenes for the pianoforte. *C. Woolhouse: London*, [1898.] 4°.   g. 603. b. (10.)

— The Poet's Guerdon. Song, the words by M. Ambient. *Boosey & Co.: London and New York*, 1895. fol.   H. 1798. u. (41.)

LEIPOLD (J. Henry)

— The Prince of Love. Song. Words by W. Blake, *etc.* 2 no. [In B flat and D flat.] *J. B. Cramer & Co.: London*, 1898. fol.
H. 1799. h. (29.)

— The Sleeping Beauty. Song. Words by S. Roger. 2 no. [In E flat and G flat.] *J. B. Cramer & Co.: London*, 1898. fol.
H. 1799. h. (30.)

LEIPSIC

— *See* Leipzig.

LEIPZIG

— The Leipzig Album. A Collection of two-part songs ... containing W. Taubert. Op. 140. H. Lichner. Op. 70. R. Thoma. Op. 37. E. Köllner. Op. 32. B. Ramann. Op. 57. 2 pt. Staff notation edition. *J. Curwen & Sons: London*, [1887.] 8°.
E. 847.

— The Leipzig Album ... Tonic sol-fa notation. 2 pt. *J. Curwen & Sons: London*, [1887.] 8°.
C. 738. b. (4.)

LEIPZIG

Bach-Gesellschaft

— Johann Sebastian Bach's Werke. [With "Supplementbd." Jahrg. 47, and a revised edition of Jahrg. 4.] Jahrg. 1–47. [1851–1935.] fol. *See* Bach (J. S.) [*Collected Works.—a.*]
H. 910.

Deutsche Händelgesellschaft

— *See infra: Händel-Gesellschaft.*

Gesellschaft zur Herausgabe von Denkmälern der Tonkunst in Bayern

— Denkmäler deutscher Tonkunst. Zweite Folge. Denkmäler der Tonkunst in Bayern, *etc.* ⟨Veröffentlicht ... unter Leitung von Adolf Sandberger.⟩ 30 Jahrg. *Breitkopf & Härtel: Leipzig*, 1900–31. fol.
Jahrg. 21–30 bear the imprint "Dr. Benno Filser Verlag, Augsburg". Jahrg. 31–36 were issued as part of "Das Erbe deutscher Musik. Reihe 2. Landschaftsdenkmale. Bayern".
H. 993. a.

— [Another copy.] **Hirsch IV. 958.**

Gluckgesellschaft

— Chr. Will. von Gluck ... Sämtliche Werke. Bd. 1. Die Pilger von Mekka. *Verlag der "Gluckgesellschaft": [Leipsic,* 1910.] fol. *No more published.*
H. 526.

— [Another copy.] **Hirsch II. 288.**

— Gluck-Jahrbuch ... 1913 [*etc.*] ... herausgegeben von H. Albert. *Breitkopf & Härtel: Leipzig*, 1913, *etc.* 8°.
Ac. 5142.

— [Another copy.] **F. 16. a.**

— Veröffentlichungen der Gluckgesellschaft. 4 no.
  [no. 1.] 1ᵉʳ Acte de l'opéra Demofoonte (1742). Airs et marche transcrits ... par Julien Tiersot. pp. 56. 1914.
  [no. 2.] Orpheus und Eurydike. Klavierauszug mit Text ... bearbeitet von Hans Kleemann. pp. iv. 139. 1916.
  [no. 3.] Klopstocks Oden für eine Singstimme und Klavier ... herausgegeben von Dr. Gustav Beckmann. pp. 13. 1917.
  [no. 4.] Sonaten Nr. 1–3 für 2 Violinen, Violoncell (Bass)

LEIPZIG

und Pianoforte ... herausgegeben von Dr. Gustav Beckmann. [Score and parts.] 3 pt. [1919?] *Breitkopf & Härtel: Leipzig*, 1914–[1919?]. 8° & fol.
Hirsch M. 940.

— [Another copy of no. 1.] **F. 16.**

Händel-Gesellschaft

— Georg Friedrich Händel's Werke. Ausgabe der Deutschen Händelgesellschaft, *etc.* [1859–1902.] fol. *See* Haendel (G. F.) [*Collected Works.—a.*]
H. 990.

— [G. F. Händel's Werke. Ausgabe der Deutschen Händelgesellschaft.] Supplemente enthaltend Quellen zu Händel's Werken. 1888–1902. 8°. *See* Haendel (G. F.) [*Collected Works.—a.*]
G. 517.

— Veröffentlichungen der Händel-Gesellschaft. no. 1–9. *Breitkopf & Härtel: Leipzig*, [1928–33.] 8°.
F. 249. t.

— Veröffentlichungen der Händel-Gesellschaft. no. 2–10. *Breitkopf & Härtel: Leipzig*, [1928–34.] 8° & 4°. *No. 2–9 are duplicates of the corresponding parts of the preceding.*
Hirsch M. 176. a.

Leipziger Bibliophilen-Abend

— Sperontes. Singende Muse an der Pleisse. 1736, *etc.* [Edited by Georg Witkowski.] [*Leipzig,*] 1905. 8°. *No. 9 of an edition of twenty-seven copies on Japanese paper, with the bookplates of the "Leipziger Bibliophilen Abend" and of Hans F. Helmolt.*
Hirsch M. 217.

Max Reger-Gesellschaft

— Veröffentlichungen der Max Reger-Gesellschaft. No. 1. Lief. 1–4. *Breitkopf & Härtel: Leipzig*, [1933–36.] 8°. *Imperfect; wanting Lief 5–8.*
F. 1753. d.

— [Another copy of Lfg. 1–4.] **Hirsch 192.**

— [Another copy of Lfg. 1–3.] **Hirsch 193.**

Musikgeschichtliche Kommission

— Denkmäler deutscher Tonkunst. Erste Folge. Herausgegeben ⟨Bd. 4–42⟩ ... unter Leitung des ... Freiherrn von Liliencron. ⟨Bd. 43–59. Unter Leitung des ... Professor Dr. Hermann Kretzschmar. Bd. 60, 63–65. Unter Leitung von ... Arnold Schering. Bd. 61, 62. Unter Leitung von ... Hermann Abert.⟩ 65 Bd. *Breitkopf & Härtel: Leipzig*, 1892–1931. fol.
H. 993.

— [Another copy.] **Hirsch IV. 957.**

Neue Bachgesellschaft

— Veröffentlichungen der Neuen Bachgesellschaft. Joh. Seb. Bachs Werke. Nach der Ausgabe der Bachgesellschaft. Jahrg. 1–36. 1901–36. *See* Bach (J. S.) [*Collected Works.—a.*]
G. 562.

Thomaskirche

— Das Graduale der St. Thomaskirche zu Leipzig. *See* Wagner (P.)

LEIPZIGER (Mark)

— Love's Souvenir. [Song.] Words by L. Feist. *J. W. Stern & Co.: New York*, 1895. fol.
H. 1798. u. (42.)

— Marcella. Waltzes. [P. F.] *M. Witmark & Sons: New York & Chicago*, 1898. fol.
h. 3286. g. (28.)

LEIPZIGER (P.)

— Queen of Gems. March and Two-Step. [P. F.] *Feist & Frankenthaler: New York*, 1897. fol.
h. 3286. g. (29.)

LEISCHNER (Charles)

— At the little rustic Bridge down by the Stream. [Song.] Words by Henry Howard Ohlsen. pp. 5. *Willis Woodward & Co.: New York*, [1906.] fol.   **H. 3985. s. (37.)**

LEISE

— Leis' bewegt hat sich der Vorhang. Romanze. *See* Davidoff (C.) Drei Romanzen. Op. 26. No. 3.

— Leise flehen meine Lieder. [Song.] *See* Schubert (F. P.) Schwanengesang. No. 4.

— Leise Lieder. [Song.] *See* Reger (M.) Sieben Lieder ... Op. 48. No. 2.

— Leise Lieder. [Song.] *See* Strauss (R. G.)

— Leise rudern hier, mein Gondolier. [Song.] *See* Jensen (A.) 7 Lieder, *etc.* Op. 50. No. 4.

— Leise sinkt auf Berg und Thal. [Song.] *See* Abt (F. W.) Vier Lieder, *etc.* Op. 400. No. 2.

— Leise sinkt auf Berg und Thal. [Four-part song.] *See* Engel (D. H.) Fünf Lieder, *etc.* Op. 53. No. 2.

— Leise zieht durch mein Gemüth. [Duet.] *See* Angelina.

— Leise zieht durch mein Gemüth. [Song.] *See* Franz (R.) Sechs Gesänge, *etc.* Op. 41. No. 1.

— Leise zieht durch mein Gemüth. [Duet.] *See* Siebmann (F.) Sechs zweistimmige Lieder. Op. 54. No. 1.

— Leise zieht durch mein Gemüth. [Song.] *See* Spicker (M.)

LEISENTRIT (Johann)

— Catholicum Hymnologium Germanicum Orthodoxæ verequè Apostolicæ Ecclesiæ ... iam denuò reuisum auctum & elaboratum. (Das Ander Theil. Christlicher Catholischer Gesengen von der allerheiligsten Jungfrawen Maria ... auffs new ubersehen gemehret vnd gebessert, *etc.*) 2 pt. *Michael Wolrab: Budissin*, 1584. 8°.   **1221. d. 36, 37.**

— Geistliche Lieder vnd Psalmen, der alten Apostolischer recht und warglaubiger Christlicher Kirchen ... Auffs fleissigste und Christlichste zusamen bracht. Durch Johann: Leisentrit, *etc.* (Das ander Theil Geistlicher lieder von der allerheiligsten Jungfrawen Maria, *etc.*) 2 pt. *Hans Wolrab: Budissin*, 1567. 8°.   **A. 255.**

— [Another copy.]   **3433. bbbb. 35.**

— Geistliche Lieder und Psalmen, *etc.* ⟨Das ander Theil Geistlicher lieder. Gesangbuch von 1567. Faksimileausgabe mit einem Nachwort von Walther Lipphardt.⟩ *Bärenreiter-Verlag: Kassel, etc.*, 1966. 8°.   **B. 740. bb.**

— Geistliche lieder vnd Psalmen ... zusamen bracht, gemehret vnd gebessert ... Durch ... J. Leisentrit, *etc.* (Das Ander Theil Geistlicher lieder von der allerheiligsten Jungfrawen Maria, *etc.*) 2 pt. *Michael Wolrab: Budissin*, 1573. 8°.   **1221. b. 56.**

— Kurtzer Aufzug: Der Christlichen vnd Catholischen Gesäng, des ... Herrn Joannis Leisentritij ... Auss Beuelch des ... Herrn Veiten, Bischoffen zu Bamberg ... für derselbigen ... Stifft also auss zuziehen vnd zusingen verordnet. *Gedruckt ... durch Sebaldum Mayer: Dilingern*, 1575. 8°.   **3425. e. 12.**

LEISER (Herbert)

— Canadian Girl. March-two step. [P. F.] pp. 5. *Herbert Leiser: Victoria, B. C.*, [1905.] fol.
Printed on one side of the leaf only.   **h. 4120. oo. (9.)**

— Castle Courteous. A waltz. [P. F.] pp. 7. *Pacific Music Co.: Victoria, B. C.*, [1906.] fol.   **h. 4120. oo. (10.)**

LEISER (Herbert)

— Johnny Canuck. March song. Words and music by H. Leiser. pp. 3–5. *H. Leiser:* [*Victoria, B. C.*, 1907.] 4°.   **H. 3985. s. (34.)**

— Mánono. A Maori love song. Words and music by H. Leiser. pp. 3–5. *H. Leiser:* [*Victoria, B. C.*, 1907.] 4°.   **H. 3985. s. (35.)**

— Vi ... [Song. Words by] G. M. Grant. pp. 3–5. *H. Leiser:* [*Victoria, B. C.*, 1907.] 4°.   **H. 3985. s. (36.)**

LEISES

— Leises Lied. [Song.] *See* Strauss (R. G.) Fünf Lieder ... Op. 41. No. 5.

LEISRING (Volckmar)

— Let all the Nations praise the Lord. *See* infra: [O filii et filiae.]

— Lift up your Heads, ye mighty Gates. Motet ... a cappella. [Words by] G. Weissel ... Tr. Cath. Winkworth ... Edited by Dr. M. N. Lundquist. *Willis Music Co.: Cincinnati*, 1938. 8°.   **E. 335. i. (45.)**

— O Filii. *See* Nouvelle. Nouvelle Bibliothèque chorale. No. 2. [1866.] 8°.   **E. 600. h. (4.)**

— O Filii et Filiae. For double Chorus, edited by F. Damrosch. *G. Schirmer: New York*, 1899. 8°.   **F. 1179. (21.)**

— [O filii et filiae.] Let all the Nations praise the Lord ... Arranged by Lara Hoggard. ⟨For mixed chorus.⟩ pp. 7. *Shawnee Press: New York*, [1948.] 8°.   **E. 335. o. (32.)**

— [O filii et filiae.] Ye Sons and Daughters of the King. SATB. English text by K. K. D. .... Arranged and edited by Katherine K. Davis. pp. 4. *Warner Bros. Music: New York*, [1970.] 8°.   **F. 1106. e. (24.)**

— Ye Sons and Daughters of the King. *See* supra: [O filii et filiae.]

LEIST (Robert L.)

— Christmas Triptych. For concert band. Arranged by R. L. Leist. I. Welcome Yule! Full band. 15th century. (Gritton.) II. Mary at the Crib, Woodwinds and horns. César Franck (Lethbridge). III. Hodie Christus natus est. Full band with optional chorus. Gordon Young, *etc.* ⟨Condensed score [and parts].⟩ 49 pt. *Galaxy Music Corp.: New York; Galliard: London*, [1967.] 4°.
With several copies of various parts.   **h. 3210. j. (138.)**

— *See* Bach (J. S.) [Fantasie G dur. B. G. 38. No. 10.— Gravement.] Fantasia in G major ... Transcribed by Richard Franko Goldman and R. L. Leist, *etc.* [1960.] 4°.   **h. 3210. i. (598.)**

— *See* Bush (Geoffrey) [The Blind Beggar's Daughter.] Old London Suite. For concert band ... Arranged by R. Leist, *etc.* [1967.] 8°.   **f. 246. o. (2.)**

— *See* Foster (Stephen C.) Santa Ana's Retreat from Buena Vista (1848) ... Arranged by R. L. Leist. Full band, *etc.* [1962.] 4°.   **h. 3210. i. (778.)**

— *See* Scott (Cyril M.) [Pastoral Suite. No. 5.] Passacaglia, *etc.* ⟨Arranged for band by R. Leist.⟩ [1958.] 4°.   **h. 3210. i. (554.)**

— *See* Ward (Robert) Jubilation. An overture ... Arranged by R. Leist ... Condensed score. [1958.] 4°.   **h. 3210. i. (492.)**

LEISTER (François)

— *See* Leister (J. F.)

LEISTER (Joachim Friedrich)

— Fantaisie pour la flûte ... Oeuvre 7. pp. 5. *Chez Artaria & Comp.: Vienne*, [1808.] fol.   **g. 71. (10.)**

— LX variations pour la flûte sur l'air des Tyroliens (Wann i in der Früh aufsteh ai ei ei a), tirées [*sic*] de la pièces [*sic*] Der Lügner. pp. 3. *Chez Artaria et comp.: Vienne*, [c. 1820.] fol.   **h. 2050. o. (4.)**

LEISURE

— Leisure. Unison-Song. *See* Greenhill (Harold W.)

— Leisure. Two-part Song. *See* Johnson (R.)

— Leisure. Two-part canon. *See* Leigh (Eric)

— Leisure. [Two-part song.] *See* Milford (R. H.) [Rain, Wind and Sunshine.]

— Leisure Hours. Piano Duets. *See* Mussestunden.

— Leisure Hours. Ballad. *See* Phillips (H.)

LEISY (James F.)

— Folk Song Fest. Songs and ideas for performance artistry ... Folk songs/ballads/blues and blue grass. pp. 68. *Sam Fox Publishing Co.: New York*, [1965.] 8°.   **F. 1771. hh. (19.)**

— Scrooge. A musical play in two acts based on Charles Dickens' "A Christmas Carol". Book, lyrics and music by James Leisy. Arranged for s. a. b. voices and piano by James Lambert ... Vocal score with dialogue. pp. 93. *Josef Weinberger: London*, [1980.] 4°.   **F. 1208. (1.)**

— Songs for Pickin' and Singin' ... Edited by James F. Leisy. ⟨Third printing.⟩ [Melodies only.] pp. 208. *Fawcett Publications: Greenwich, Conn.*, 1964. 8°. *Gold Medal Books. no. d* 1356.   **C. 738. cc.**

LEITCH (Donovan)

— [The Pied Piper.] Sailing homeward. ⟨The theme from the film "The Pied Piper".⟩ People call me the Pied Piper (Pied Piper's song) & the Piper's Theme. ⟨Words and music by D. Leitch.⟩ pp. 12. *Donovan (Music): London*, [1973.] 4°.   **F. 1198. i. (3.)**

— [Poor Cow.] Piano Album of the Music from 'Poor Cow,' *etc.* pp. 7. *Donovan (Music): London*, [1967.] 4°.   **g. 1128. zz. (11.)**

LEITCH (J. Roger)

— Our Heroes' Requiem. Song, the words by L. Pinkerton. *Novello and Co.: London*, 1919. 4°.   **G. 390. x. (18.)**

LEITCH (S. W.)

— Cronan nan Tonn ... The Croon of the Sea. By Duncan Johnston, *etc.* [Music arranged by S. W. Leitch.] ⟨Part one.⟩ *A. Sinclair: Glasgow*, 1938. 8°. *No more published.*   **F. 1837.**

LEITE (Antonio da Silva)

— *See* Silva Leite.

LEITE (Ernestine)

— Alice, grande valse brillante pour Piano. *Paris*, [1881.] fol.   **h. 3272. j. (20.)**

— Habanera-Berceuse [begins: "Sommeille doucement"], paroles de F. Mousset. Op. 39. *Paris*, [1886.] fol.   **H. 2836. h. (42.)**

LEITE (Ernestine)

— Paris-Grelot. Polka pour piano. Op. 38. *Brandus & Cie.: Paris*, [1886.] fol.   **h. 3281. l. (23.)**

— Les Premières Fleurs. Légende [begins: "Ève s'éveillait à peine"], paroles de F. Mousset. (Op. 37.) *Paris*, [1885.] fol.   **H. 2836. h. (41.)**

— Tristesse d'Amour. Havanaise [begins: "J'aime une enfant"]. Paroles de G. Mainiel. *Paris*, [1880.] fol.   **H. 1786. e. (35.)**

— Valse des Hirondelles pour Chant & Piano [begins: "Dans le bousquet".—"Nell'orticel"]. Paroles françaises de F. Mousset. Trad. italiana di C. da Prato. *Paris*, [1881.] fol.   **H. 1786. e. (34.)**

— *See* Meyerbeer (G.) [Le Pardon de Ploermel.] Ouverture ... arrangée ... par E. Leite. [1877.] fol.   **h. 1493. q. (1.)**

LEITENANT

— Лейтенант Шмидт. Опера. *See* Kravchenko (Boris P.)

LEITERMAYER (A.)

— Quadrille nach Motiven der Operette "Die schönen Weiber von Georgien," von J. Offenbach für Pianoforte. *C. A. Spina: Wien*, [1865?] fol.   **g. 442. e. (22.)**

LEITERT (Georg)

— Blätter der Liebe. Drei Stücke für Pianoforte. 3 no. *Leipzig*, [1876.] fol.   **h. 1487. p. (42.)**

— [Daheim.] *See* Devrient (F.) Dans ses Foyers ... Polka-Mazurka pour piano, d'après G. Leitert. [1887.] fol.   **h. 3281. e. (31.)**

— 6 Danses pour le Piano. *Mayence*, [1878.] fol.   **h. 1493. o. (13.)**

— [Frühlingsboten.] *See* Devrient (F.) Messagers du Printemps ... Polka pour piano, d'après G. Leitert. [1887.] fol.   **h. 3281. e. (36.)**

— Frühlingsnächte. Spring Nights. Drei Fantasiestücke für Pianoforte. *Dresden*, [1876.] fol.   **h. 1487. p. (40.)**

— Frühlingsnahen. (L'Approche du Printemps.) Fantasiestück für Pianoforte. *Leipzig*, [1876.] fol.   **h. 1487. p. (43.)**

— In Dämmerstunde ... 2 Improvisationen für Pianoforte. *Mainz*, [1878.] fol.   **h. 1493. o. (14.)**

— [Lenzblüthen.] *See* Devrient (F.) Fleurs Printanières ... Polka pour piano, d'après G. Leitert. [1887.] fol.   **h. 3281. e. (33.)**

— 4 Lieder für eine Singstimme mit Begleitung des Pianoforte. Op. 4. 4 no. *Mainz*, [1877.] fol.   **H. 1781. i. (13.)**

— Drei Lieder für eine Singstimme mit Pianofortebegleitung. Op. 8. 3 no. *Dresden*, [1877.] fol.   **H. 1781. i. (14.)**

— Lose Blätter. Drei Stücke für Pianoforte. *Leipzig*, [1876.] fol.   **h. 1487. p. (41.)**

— [Maiblumen.] *See* Devrient (F.) Muguets ... Polka pour piano d'après G. Leitert. [1887.] fol.   **h. 3281. e. (38.)**

— Maiensonnen. (Soleils de Mai.) Fünf Stimmungs-Blätter für Pianoforte. 5 no. *Leipzig*, [1876.] fol.   **h. 1487. p. (39.)**

— Minnelied. (Chant d'Amour.) Für Pianoforte. *Leipzig*, [1876.] fol.   **h. 1487. p. (44.)**

— Romance pour Piano. *Leipzig*, [1878.] fol.   **h. 1493. o. (16.)**

— Sinnen und Winnen. Drei Stimmungsbilder für Pianoforte. 3 no. *Dresden*, [1877.] fol.   **h. 1493. o. (12.)**

LEITERT (GEORG)

— Strahlen und Schatten. (Rayons et Ombres.) Vier Clavierstücke. 4 no. *Dresden*, [1875.] fol. **h. 1487. p. (37.)**

— Unter Wachen und Träumen ... Improvisation für Pianoforte. *Leipzig*, [1877.] fol. **h. 1493. o. (11.)**

— Valse-Caprice pour Piano. *Leipzig*, [1878.] fol. **h. 1493. o. (15.)**

— 7 Walzer für Pianoforte zu vier Händen. *Leipzig*, [1875.] fol. **h. 1487. p. (38.)**

LEITH (ALEXANDER)

— Sing me the Song I love. Song, words by M. Q. *Elkin & Co.: London*, 1909. fol. **H. 1794. vv. (37.)**

LEITH (CHRISTINA MORLOCK)

— Father of Love give Peace. Quartette, words and music by C. M. Leith. *Hawkes & Harris Music Co.: [Toronto,]* 1915. *s. sh.* 8°. **E. 602. ee. (15.)**

— When the Boys of Canada are marching Home. Song, words and music by C. M. Leith. *Hawkes & Harris Music Co.: Toronto*, (1915.) fol. **H. 1793. t. (5.)**

LEITH (J. WELSH)

— Tendresse. Waltz. [P. F.] *C. Herzog & Co.: London*, [1883.] fol. **h. 975. v. (8.)**

LEITH (LEONORE)

— Arcadia. [Song.] Text by L. L. Op. 77. No. 1. *T. Presser Co.: Philadelphia*, 1920. 4°. **G. 426. l. (27.)**

— Love is a Song. [Song.] Text by L. L. Op. 78. No. 1. *T. Presser Co.: Philadelphia*, 1920. 4°. **G. 426. l. (28.)**

LEITZ (DARWIN)

— Magnificat and Nunc dimittis. For mixed voices in ... E minor, *etc.* pp. 11. *H. W. Gray Co.: New York*, [1953.] 8°. **F. 1158. n. (4.)**

LEJAY (   )

— La Volupté. Cantatille à voix seule avec simphonie ... Gravée par Chambon. [Score.] pp. 12. *Chez l'auteur, etc.: Paris*, [c. 1755.] fol. **H. 346. d. (1.)**

LEJEAL (ALOIS F.)

— Asperges me, in G, for mixed voices. Op. 63. *O. Ditson Co.: Boston*, 1915. 8°. **F. 274. r. (6.)**

— Concentrated Technic for the Pianoforte. *T. Presser Co.: Philadelphia*, (1913.) fol. **h. 3820. y. (4.)**

— O Salutaris, in E♭, for mixed voices. Op. 67. *O. Ditson Co.: Boston*, 1916. 8°. **F. 274. q. (11.)**

— Tantum ergo, in D, for mixed voices. Op. 64. *O. Ditson Co.: Boston*, 1916. 8°. **F. 274. q. (12.)**

— Veni Creator, in G. Mixed voices. (Op. 66.) *O. Ditson Co.: Boston*, 1916. 8°. **F. 274. r. (7.)**

LEJEUNE (   )

— D'une fleur à peine éclose. [Song.] Paroles de M. D. G. D., *etc.* [*Paris*,] 1769. *s. sh.* 8°. *Mercure de France, July*, 1769. **297. e. 25.**

LE JEUNE (ANTHONY) *the Elder*

— The Home of Happiness; ballad [begins: "I've roam'd"], the words by E. B. Smithis. *London*, [1844.] fol. **H. 1695. (10.)**

— Messe [for 4 voices and organ]. *London*, [1835?] *obl.* fol. **E. 1422.**

— *See* ANGIOLI (A. de) Tantum ergo ... the organ accompaniment by A. Lejeune. [1839.] fol. **H. 1660. (16.)**

LE JEUNE (ANTHONY) *the Younger*

— Sacred Music for the Offertory and Benediction. 6 no. *London*, [1865.] fol. **H. 1772. r. (32.)**

LE JEUNE (ARTHUR)

— Air de Ballet ... pour le piano. (Op. 24.) *R. Cocks & Co.: London*, [1884.] fol. **h. 1484. s. (38.)**

— La Belle Paysanne. Danse rustique pour piano. *J. Williams: London*, [1884.] fol. **h. 1484. s. (39.)**

— Cascade ... for the pianoforte. (Op. 22.) *R. Cocks & Co.: London*, [1884.] fol. **h. 1484. s. (40.)**

— Cavatina in G, for the Violin with Pianoforte accompaniment. *E. Ascherberg & Co.: London*, [1888.] fol. **h. 210. e. (23.)**

— Clementina. Mazurka de Salon for the pianoforte. *C. Jefferys: London*, [1882.] fol. **h. 1484. s. (41.)**

— Coronation March, for the Pianoforte. *Augener & Co.: London*, 1902. fol. **g. 605. ee. (33.)**

— [Another edition.] Coronation March. Pianoforte Solo. *Augener & Co.: London*, 1902. fol. **g. 605. ee. (34.)**

— Coronation March ... Pianoforte Duet. *Augener & Co.: London*, 1902. fol. **h. 3290. p. (13.)**

— Coronation March for the Organ. *Augener & Co.: London*, 1902. *obl.* fol. **f. 314. k. (14.)**

— [Another edition.] Coronation March, *etc.* [Organ.] *Augener & Co.: London*, 1902. *obl.* fol. **f. 314. k. (15.)**

— Coronation March ... Violin and Pianoforte. *Augener & Co.: London*, 1902. fol. **g. 505. s. (20.)**

— [Coronation March.] King, high and glorious. Coronation Song for solo or unison voices. Words by M. Byron, *etc. Augener & Co.: London*, 1902. fol. **G. 807. t. (22.)**

— Duos for the Violin and Pianoforte. Canzone, and Ye olde English Fayre Dance. *C. Jefferys: London*, [1883.] fol. **h. 210. e. (24.)**

— Élégie, pour Violon and Piano. *E. Ascherberg & Co.: London*, 1901. fol. **h. 1612. i. (47.)**

— Evening song, Morceau de Salon for the Violin, with an Accompaniment for the Pianoforte. *D. Davison & Co.: London*, [1884.] fol. **h. 210. e. (25.)**

— Florence. Morceau de Salon pour piano. *J. Williams: London*, [1884.] fol. **h. 1484. s. (42.)**

— Gavotte Royale pour Piano. *London*, [1879.] fol. **h. 1494. q. (12.)**

— Gwynnie. Gavotte for the pianoforte. *R. Cocks & Co.: London*, 1893. fol. **h. 1489. s. (36.)**

— Gwynnie. Gavotte for the pianoforte. Duet. *R. Cocks & Co.: London*, 1893. fol. **h. 3290. l. (28.)**

— Gwynnie. Gavotte. Arranged for Mandoline with Pianoforte Accompt[s] by P. Dabiero. *R. Cocks & Co.: London*, 1896. fol. **h. 188. e. (30.)**

LE JEUNE (ARTHUR)

— Gwynnie. Gavotte for violin & piano. *R. Cocks & Co.: London*, 1893. fol.   **g. 505. m. (12.)**

— Harlequinade, pour Violon and Piano. *E. Ascherberg & Co.: London*, 1901. fol.   **h. 1612. i. (48.)**

— Heiterkeit ... Clavierstück. Op. 47. *E. Ascherberg & Co.: London*, [1886.] fol.   **h. 1484. s. (43.)**

— Ines. Air de Ballet pour piano. *J. Williams: London*, [1884.] fol.   **h. 1484. s. (44.)**

— King, high and glorious. *See* supra: [Coronation March.]

— Liebeslied, for Violin and Pianoforte. *D. Davison & Co.: London*, [1884.] fol.   **h. 210. e. (26.)**

— Second Liebeslied for violin or violoncello with pianoforte accompaniment. *Beal & Co.: London*, [1892.] fol.   **h. 1608. x. (39.)**

— Life in Love. Song [begins: "The green vales are buried"]. The words by W. B. *London*, [1882.] fol.   **H. 1787. j. (28.)**

— Love's Return. Song, words by C. M. Lacy. 3 no. [In C, D and E flat.] *Beal & Co.: London*, [1890.] fol.   **G. 807. h. (11.)**

— Marche Héroïque ... for the piano. *H. Beresford: London and Birmingham*, [1895.] fol.   **h. 1489. s. (37.)**

— Marche héroïque, *etc.* [P. F. duet.] *H. Beresford: London*, [1897.] fol.   **h. 3290. n. (27.)**

— Melody in F, for the Pianoforte. *E. Ascherberg & Co.: London*, 1897. fol.   **h. 3282. w. (38.)**

— Melody in G for the Violin with Pianoforte accompaniment. *E. Ascherberg & Co.: London*, [1888.] fol.   **h. 210. e. (27.)**

— Ye olde English Fayre. Dance. [P. F.] *Moutrie & Son: London*, [1882.] fol.   **h. 1484. s. (46.)**

— Rêverie, pour Piano. *Lincoln & Co.: London*, 1904. 4°.   **g. 603. p. (4.)**

— Rippling Waters. Morceau de Salon for the pianoforte. *Willey & Co.: London*, [1886.] fol.   **h. 1484. s. (45.)**

— Romance pour Piano. *London*, [1879.] fol.   **h. 1494. q. (13, 14.)**

— Romance en fa pour violon avec accompagnement de piano. *F. W. Chanot: London*, (1897.) fol.   **h. 1681. o. (13.)**

— Sketches for Violin and Piano. 10 no. *E. Donajowski: London*, [1889–94.] fol.   **h. 1608. x. (40.)**

— Sketches. No. 1, 4, 7, 2, 3, 5. [Clarinet and P. F.] *See* TROUSSELLE (J.) Twelve Sketches, *etc.* No. 6–11. [1892.] fol.   **h. 3221. (6.)**

— Spring Breezes, morceau de salon. [P. F.] *London*, [1879.] fol.   **h. 1494. q. (28*.)**

— Sur le Lac. Intermezzo pour Piano. *Agate & Co.: London*, [1901.] fol.   **g. 605. x. (11.)**

— Tarentelle in F minor for the Piano. *London*, [1879.] fol.   **h. 1494. q. (15.)**

— Venezia—Serenata-Barcarola—per Violino e Pianoforte. *Lincoln & Co.: London*, 1904. 4°.   **g. 603. p. (5.)**

— *See* CALKIN (J. B.) [Lieder ohne Worte. Op. 6. No. 1.] Song without Words ... Arranged ... by A. Le Jeune. [1902.] fol.   **g. 505. s. (8.)**

— *See* SMITH (E. S.) Barcarolle ... Arranged ... by A. Le Jeune. [1902.] fol.   **h. 3024. l. (19.)**

— *See* SMITH (E. S.) Berceuse ... Arranged ... by A. Le Jeune. [1901.] fol.   **h. 3024. l. (6.)**

LE JEUNE (ARTHUR)

— *See* SMITH (E. S.) Cantilena ... Arranged ... by A. Le Jeune. [1902.] fol.   **h. 3024. l. (20.)**

— *See* SMITH (E. S.) Eloquence ... Arranged ... by A. Le Jeune. [1903.] fol.   **h. 3024. l. (23.)**

— *See* SMITH (E. S.) Rêverie ... Arranged ... by A. Le Jeune. [1901.] fol.   **h. 3024. l. (15.)**

LE JEUNE (CÉCILE)

— *See* LE JEUNE (Claude) Airs à III., IIII., V. et VI. Parties. [With a dedication by Cécile Le Jeune.] 1608. *obl.* 8°.   **A. 143.**

— *See* LE JEUNE (Claude) Octonaires de la Vanité, et Inconstance du Monde, *etc.* [With a dedication by Cécile Le Jeune.] 1606. *obl.* 4°.   **B. 283. c.**

— *See* LE JEUNE (Claude) Premier Liure, Contenant Cinquante Pseaumes de Dauid, *etc.* [With a dedication by Cécile le Jeune.] 1602. *obl.* 4°.   **B. 283. a.**

— *See* LE JEUNE (Claude) Second Liure, Contenant Cinquante Pseaumes de Dauid, *etc.* [With a dedication by Cécile Le Jeune.] 1608. *obl.* 4°.   **B. 283. f.**

— *See* LE JEUNE (Claude) Les Pseaumes de Dauid, mis en Musique a quatre & cinq parties. [With a dedication by Cécile Le Jeune.] 1627. 4°.   **K. 3. i. 1.**

— *See* LE JEUNE (Claude) Les Cent Cinquante Pseaumes de Dauid, mis en Musique à quatre parties, *etc.* [With a dedication by Cécile Le Jeune.] 1650. *obl.* 8°.   **A. 143. a.**

— *See* LE JEUNE (Claude) Pseaumes en vers mezurez, *etc.* [With a dedication by Cécile Le Jeune.] 1606. *obl.* 4°.   **R. M. 15. b. 1. (1.)**

LE JEUNE (CHARLES ALEXANDER)

— Like as the Hart. Quemadmodum desiderat. Motett for four voices. *C. A. Le Jeune: London*, [1914.] 8°.   **E. 442. q. (20.)**

LE JEUNE (CLAUDE)

— Octonaires de la vanité et inconstance du Monde, IX–XII. Pseaumes des Meslanges de 1612. Dialogue à sept parties, 1564. *Éditions Maurice Senart: Paris*, 1928. 4°. [*Monuments de la Musique française au temps de la Renaissance. Liv.* 8.]   **G. 59. a.**

— [Quatre Chansons de Claude Le Jeune.] Las! où vas-tu sans moy. Je pleure, je me deux. Comment pensés-vous que je vive. Nostre vicaire, un jour de feste. [Part-songs. Score. Edited by H. Expert. With a portrait.] pp. 24. *A la cité des livres: Paris*, 1929. 8°. [*Florilège du concert vocal de la renaissance. no.* 6.]   **Hirsch IV. 961.**

— Airs à III. IIII. V. et VI. Parties. [With a dedication by Cécile Le Jeune.] (Second Livre des Airs, *etc.*) Cinquiesme. *Pierre Ballard: Paris*, 1608. *obl.* 8°.   **A. 143.**

— Airs (1608). Edited by D. P. Walker. In four volumes ... Introduction by François Lesure and D. P. Walker, *etc.* 4 vol. *American Institute of Musicology: Rome*, 1951, 59. fol. *Publications of the American institute of Musicology. Miscellanea.* 1.   **H. 21.**

— Beneath the lattic'd Vine in May. *See* infra: [Meslanges.—Debat la noste trill' en May.]

— Debat la noste trill'en May. *See* infra: [Meslanges.]

— Dodecacorde selon les douze Modes, à II. III. IIII. V. VI. et VII. Voix ... Sous lesquels ont esté Mises des paroles Morales. ⟨Dessus.—Haute-contre.—Taille.—Basse-contre.— Cinquiesme.—Sixiesme.⟩ 6 pt. *Par Pierre Ballard: Paris*, 1618. *obl.* 4°.

LE JEUNE (Claude)

In the taille part, sig. A i–iii only are of the 1618 edition, the remainder of an earlier edition with the original words.
B. 283. j.

— Dodecachorde, contenant douze Pseaumes de David, *etc.* 1ᵉʳ Fascicule. 1900. *See* Expert (H.) Les Maîtres Musiciens de la Renaissance Française, *etc.* 11ᵉ Livraison. 1894, *etc.* 8°.
G. 59.

— Hélas! mon Dieu. *See* infra: [Meslanges. Liv. 2.]

— How can my Love. *See* infra: [Meslanges. Liv. 2.—S'ébahit-on si je vous aime.]

— Ihre Augen. *See* infra: [Meslanges.—O occhi manza mia.]

Meslanges

— Livre de melanges … Contratenor. *De l'imprimerie de Christofle Plantin: Anvers*, 1585. 4°. *Imperfect; wanting the other parts.*
D. 17.

— Meslanges de la Musique … A 4. 5. 6. 8. & 10. parties. (Superius.) (Haute-Contre.) (Tenor.) (Bassus.) (Quinta Pars.) (Sexta Pars.) 6 pt. *Adrian le Roy, & Robert Ballard: Paris*, 1586. *obl.* 4°. *The title-page and fol. Aii of the Superius are mutilated.*
B. 283.

— Meslanges de la Musique de Clau. Le Ieune. A 4. 5. 6. 8. & 10. parties. Haute-Contre. (Taille.) (Basse-Contre.) 3 pt. *Pierre Ballard: Paris*, 1607. *obl.* 4°. *The Haute-Contre part wants fol. 2–8, which are supplied in MS.*
B. 283. d.

— Mélanges. Premier Fascicule. 1903. *See* Expert (H.) Les Maîtres Musiciens de la Renaissance Française, *etc.* 16ᵉ livr. 1894, *etc.* 8°.
G. 59.

— "Debat la noste trill' en May."—"Beneath the lattic'd Vine in May."— Villageoise de Gascogne [for S. A. T. B.] … Edited by L. Benson. The English words by A. C. Curtis. [1909.] *See* Oriana. The Oriana, *etc.* No. 54. [1905, *etc.*] 8°.
F. 1685.

— [Debat la noste trill' en May.] Within our Arbour green in May … Villageoise de Gascogne. English translation by Harold Heiberg … Piano score arr. by Herbert Zipper. *Eng. & Fr.* pp. 11. *Edward B. Marks Music Corporation: New York*, [c. 1960.] 8°.
[*Arthur Jordan Choral Series. no.* 20.]
F. 1864.

— O occhi manza mia.—Ihre Augen.—Vierstimmiges Lied … Deutscher Text von T. Rehbaum, *etc.* [1902.] *See* Squire (W. B.) Ausgewählte Madrigale, *etc.* No. 18. [b.] [1895, *etc.*] 8°.
F. 1604.

— O Vilanella. Vierstimmiges Lied, *etc.* [1897.] *See* Squire (W. B.) Ausgewählte Madrigale, *etc.* No. 9. [b.] [1895, *etc.*] 8°.
F. 1604.

— Tu ne l'enten pas, la la la. You don't understand, la la la. Mixed chorus a cappella. ⟨SATB.⟩ Edited with an English translation by Gerald Kechley. *Fr. & Eng.* pp. 16. *Galliard: London; Galaxy Music Corp.: New York; printed in U. S. A.*, [1969.] 8°.
F. 1874. k. (4.)

Meslanges. Liv. 2

— Second Liure des Meslanges de Cl. Le Ieune, *etc.* [With a dedication by Judith Mardo.] Haute-Contre. (Taille.) (Basse-Contre.) 3 pt. *Pierre Ballard: Paris*, 1612. *obl.* 4°.
B. 283. i.

— Trois fantaisies instrumentales, *etc.* ⟨Restitution et registration: Jean Bonfils.⟩ [Score and parts for trumpet and trombone.] 3 pt. *Éditions musicales de la Schola Cantorum et de la Procure générale de musique: Paris*, [1956.] 4°. *Orgue et Liturgie.* 39.
h. 2785. cc. (4.)

LE JEUNE (Claude)

— Hélas! mon Dieu … ⟨S. A. A. T. B. (unacc.)⟩ [Words.] 'Souspir d'un malade.' (1573) … Edited, with English text, by John Eliot Gardiner. *Fr. & Eng.* pp. 14. *Oxford University Press: London*, [1971.] 8°.
[*Oxford choral Songs. X* 202.]
F. 1777. m.

— [S'ébahit-on si je vous aime.] How can my Love. Chanson for SATB … Edited by John A. Parkinson. English translation by Stephen R. Parkinson. *Eng. & Fr.* pp. 4. *J. A. Parkinson: S. Croydon*, [1973.] 8°.
F. 321. dd. (19.)

— Missa ad Placitum … cum v. & vi. vocibus. *Ex Officina Petri Ballard: Lutetiæ*, 1607. fol.
K. 10. b. 3.

— Missa Ad placitum. À 5 ou 6 voix. Édition par Michel Sanvoisin. pp. 46. *Heugel & cⁱᵉ: Paris*, [1967.] 4°.
[*Le Pupitre.* 2.]
G. 51.

— O occhi manza mia. *See* supra: [Meslanges.]

— O Vilanella. *See* supra: [Meslanges.]

— Octonaires de la Vanité, et Inconstance du Monde. Mis en musique à 3. & à 4. parties, *etc.* [With a dedication by Cécile Le Jeune.] Dessus. (Haute-Contre.) (Taille.) (Basse-Contre.) 4 pt. *Pierre Ballard: Paris*, 1606. *obl.* 4°.
B. 283. c.

— [Another copy.]
R. M. 15. b. 1. (3.)

— Octonaires de la Vanité et Inconstance du Monde, mis en Musique à 3. & à 4. parties, *etc.* [Dessus.] (Haute-Contre.) (Taille.) (Basse-Contre.) 4 pt. *Robert Ballard: Paris*, 1641. *obl.* 4°. *Imperfect; wanting the Dessus part, which is supplied in MS.*
B. 283. k.

— Octonaires de la vanité et inconstance du monde. I–VIII. *Éditions Maurice Senart: Paris*, 1924. 4°. [*Monuments de la musique française au temps de la Renaissance. Vol. I.*]
G. 59. a.

— Le Printemps … A deux. 3. 4. 5. 6. 7. et 8. parties. Dessus. (Taille.) (Haute-Contre.) (Basse-Contre.) (Cinquiesme.) (Sixiesme.) 6 pt. *La Veufue R. Ballard & son Fils Pierre Ballard: Paris*, 1603. *obl.* fol.
R. M. 15. b. 1. (2.)

— Le Printemps … à deux 3. 4. 5. 6. 7. et 8. Parties. 3 fasc. 1900, 01. *See* Expert (H.) Les Maîtres Musiciens de la Renaissance Française, *etc.* 12ᵉ (–14ᵉ) Livraison. 1894, *etc.* 8°.
G. 59.

— [Le Printemps.—Revecy venir du printans] See, oh see the Spring … Chanson for S. A. T. B. (unaccompanied) … translated and edited by Neil Saunders. pp. 7. *Novello & Co.: London*, [1959.] 8°.
[*The Oriana.* 120.]
F. 1685.

— Premier Liure, Contenant Cinquante Pseaumes de Dauid, Mis en Musique a III. parties, *etc.* [With a dedication by Cécile Le Jeune.] Moienne. (Basse.) 2 pt. *Par la Veufue R. Ballard, & son Fils Pierre Ballard: Paris*, 1602. *obl.* 4°.
B. 283. a.

— Second Liure, Contenant Cinquante Pseaumes de Dauid, Mis en Musique à III. Parties. [With a dedication by Cécile Le Jeune.] Haute. (Moyenne.) (Basse.) 3 pt. *Pierre Ballard: Paris*, 1608. *obl.* 4°.
B. 283. f.

— [Another copy.]
The Haute part is imperfect, wanting the last four leaves.
B. 283. e.

— Troisiesme Liure des Pseaumes de Dauid, Mis en Musique à III. Parties, *etc.* [With a dedication by Judith Mardo.] Haute. (Moyenne.) (Basse.) 3 pt. *Pierre Ballard: Paris*, 1610. *obl.* 4°.
B. 283. g.

— [Another copy. Moyenne.]
B. 283. h.

LE JEUNE (CLAUDE)

— Les [Cent cinquante] Pseaumes de Dauid, mis en Musique a quatre & cinq parties. [With a dedication by Cécile Le Jeune.] Superius. (Hautecontre.) (Tenor.) (Bassecontre.) (Cinquiesme partie.) 5 pt. *François le Febure: Genève*, 1627. 4°.
The Cinquiesme partie bears the imprint 'A Genève, pour Iean de Tournes'. **K. 3. i. 1.**

— Les Cent cinquante pseaumes de Dauid, mis en musique à quatre parties, *etc.* [With a dedication by Cécile Le Jeune.] ⟨Haute-contre.—Basse-contre.⟩ *Par Robert Ballard: Paris*, 1650. *obl.* 8°.
Imperfect; wanting the Dessus, Taille and Cinquiesme parts, and sig. A i-iii of the Haute-contre part. **A. 143. a.**

— [Les Cent cinquante pseaumes de Dauid.] The First Twelve Psalms in Four Parts ... adapted to the English Versions by a Professor of Music. *Longman, Lukey & Co.: London*, [1775?] fol. **G. 807. a. (8.)**

— Pseaumes en vers mezurez mis en musique a 2. 3. 4. 5. 6. 7. & 8. parties, *etc.* [With a dedication by Cécile Le Jeune.] Dessus. (Haute-Contre.) (Basse-Contre.) (Taille.) (Cinquiesme.) (Sixiesme.) 6 pt. *Pierre Ballard: Paris*, 1606. *obl.* 4°. **R. M. 15. b. 1. (1.)**

— [Another copy of the Haute-Contre, Taille and Basse-Contre parts.]
Imperfect; wanting the other parts. **B. 283. b.**

— Pseaumes en Vers mezurez. Fascicule. 1905 (06). *See* EXPERT (H.) Les Maîtres Musiciens de la Renaissance Française, *etc.* 20ᵉ(–22ᵉ) livr. 1894, *etc.* 8°. **G. 59.**

— See, oh see the Spring. [Part-song.] *See* supra: [Le Printemps.—Revecy venir du printans.]

— Tu ne l'enten pas, la la la. *See* supra: [Meslanges.]

— Within our Arbour green in May. *See* supra: [Meslanges.—Debat la noste trill' en May.]

— You don't understand, la la la. *See* supra: [Meslanges.—Tu ne l'enten pas, la la la.]

— *See* DOUEN (E. O.) Clément Marot et le Psautier Huguenot ... contenant ... des spécimens d'harmonie de ... C. Le Jeune, *etc.* 1878–9. 8°. **3089. gg. 2.**

LEJEUNE (ELIZABETH)

— The Fairies' Dance. Song [begins: "This is the hour"]. (Written by J. S., Esq.) *London*, [1840?] fol. **H. 2852. i. (53.)**

LE JEUNE (GEORGE)

— Age's anger and repentance; [song, begins: "The old man leant,"] written by G. Soane. *London*, [1842.] fol. **H. 1345. (2.)**

— "Brighter than day dreams;" air. *London*, [1842.] fol. **H. 1345. (1.)**

— "Grazie grazie volate." Solo and quartett. *London*, [1842.] fol. **H. 1345. (6.)**

— The Naiad's song [begins: " 'Tis sweet"], written by G. Soane. *London*, [1842.] fol. **H. 1345. (3.)**

— The Old Man and the Child. Ballad. *London*, [1873.] fol. **H. 1778. y. (3.)**

— Pickwick melodies, written by G. Soane. No. 1–6. *London*, [1842.] fol. **H. 1345. (7.)**

— Su ridiam, cari amici. Duettino, written by F. Pistrucci. *London*, [1842.] fol. **H. 1345. (5.)**

— "Vieni all'ombra." Aria ... written by F. Pistrucci. *London*, [1842.] fol. **H. 1345. (4.)**

LE JEUNE (GEORGE F.)

— Communion Service in C ... for four voices, soli and chorus, with ... Organ. *Novello and Co.: London*, 1903. 8°. **E. 597. p. (20.)**

— [Communion Service in C.] First Mass in C ... for four voices, soli and chorus with ... Organ. *Novello and Co.: London*, 1903. 8°. **F. 274. e. (5.)**

— Grand Coronation March, *etc.* [P. F.] *Novello and Co.: London*, 1902. fol. **g. 605. ee. (35.)**

— Twelve hymns with original tunes. *London*, [1883.] 8°. **E. 605. k. (42.)**

— Light of Light. Choral Processional March. (Words by J. Julian and G. Rorison.) *Novello, Ewer and Co.: London & New York*, 1895. 8°. **E. 442. n. (42.)**

— First Mass in C. *See* supra: [Communion Service in C.]

— Mon Devoir. Song, words by Van Tassel Sutphen. *E. Ashdown: New York*, 1895. fol. **G. 805. aa. (5.)**

— To God our never failing strength. Full anthem for four voices. *London*, [1884.] 8°. **E. 442. i. (26.)**

— Where is true Love? Song, words by W. Younge. *E. Ashdown: New York*, 1895. fol. **G. 805. aa. (6.)**

LE JEUNE (HENRI)

— Fantasia a cinque. ⟨In 'Harmonie universelle' by Marin Mersenne. 1636.⟩ [Edited by Arnold Dolmetsch and others. Score and parts.] 6 pt. *Chappell: [London;] Dolmetsch: Haselemere*, [1978.] 4°.
Part of "The Dolmetsch Library". **g. 109. cc. (4.)**

LEJLA

— Lejla. Opera. *See* BENDL (K.)

LEJOS

— Lejos de ti. [Song.] *See* PONCE (M. M.)

LE JOUBIOUX (   )

— Doué ha mem Bro. Dieu et mon Pays, poésies bretonnes, avec la traduction ... et quelques mélodies nationales, *etc.* [Melodies and words only.] *Bas.-Bret. & Fr. J.-M. Galles: Vannes*, 1844. 8°. **11595. h. 10.**

LEJSEK (FRANTIŠEK KVĚTOSLAV)

— Moravsko-slezské písně. ⟨Písně rušného rázu (pochodevého) ve tvrdých i měkkých toninách. Písně mírného tempa ve tvrdých i měkkých toninách.⟩ pp. 76. *Nákladem Aloise Šaška: Velké Meziříčí*, 1930. 8°. **A. 959. e. (1.)**

LEKBERG (SVEN)

— Blessed is the Man. *See* infra: A Litany of Psalms. 2.

— Bow my Head, O Lord. For full chorus of mixed voices a cappella. [Words by] S. L. pp. 6. *G. Schirmer: New York*, [1967.] 8°. **E. 335. ff. (14.)**

— Four Carols for a holy Night. For four-part chorus of mixed voices a cappella. [Words by] S. L. 1. Sing Noel. ⟨2. Earth so lovely. 3. The Little Boy Jesus. 4. These are the Blossoms.⟩ pp. 14. *G. Schirmer: New York*, [1969.] 8°. **F. 260. ll. (5.)**

— Come hither, Child, and rest. For unaccompanied mixed choir. [Words by] Ernest Dowson. pp. 6. *Galaxy Music Corporation: New York*, [1963.] 8°. **F. 1744. nn. (24.)**

— Come o'er the eastern Hills. For four-part chorus of mixed voices a cappella. [Words by] William Blake. pp. 8. *G. Schirmer: [New York*, 1971.] 8°. **F. 1874. p. (5.)**

LEKBERG (SVEN)

— Counterpoint. *See* infra: Three Peávinations. [3.]

— Far away across the Mountain. For four-part chorus of mixed voices a cappella. Text by S. L. pp. 8. *G. Schirmer: New York, London*, [1972.] 8°.　　**F. 1874. v. (16.)**

— For as the Rain cometh down. For four-part chorus of mixed voices a cappella. Isaiah 55; v. 10–13. pp. 12. *G. Schirmer: New York*, [1967.] 8°.　　**E. 335. ff. (55.)**

— Give Ear to my Prayer, O God. *See* infra: A Litany of Psalms. 5.

— Gloria and Alleluia. For four-part chorus of mixed voices a cappella. pp. 8. *G. Schirmer: [New York, London*, 1973.] 8°.　　**F. 1174. h. (3.)**

— Glory be to the Father. For four-part chorus of mixed voices a cappella. [Words] from "The Liturgy". pp. 8. *G. Schirmer: New York*, [1968.] 8°.　　**E. 335. ff. (54.)**

— God with me lying down. For four-part chorus of mixed voices a cappella. [Words] from the Celtic. Translation by A. Carmichael. pp. 4. *G. Schirmer: [New York*, 1966.] 8°.　　**E. 335. zz. (12.)**

— Hail the Day that sees him rise. [Words by] Charles Wesley. 〈S. A. T. B.〉 pp. 11. *Galaxy Music Corp.: New York*, [1968.] 8°.　　**E. 335. uu. (11.)**

— Have Mercy upon us. For four-part chorus of mixed voices a cappella. Psalm 51. pp. 8. *G. Schirmer: [New York*, 1968.] 8°.　　**E. 335. ff. (56.)**

— He is risen. (We will rejoice.) 〈For mixed voices a cappella.〉 [Words] from Luke 24, Psalm 139 and Psalm 118. pp. 11. *Galaxy Music Corp.: New York; Galliard: London*, [1969.] 8°.　　**F. 1106. b. (41.)**

— How long wilt Thou forget me, O Lord? *See* infra: A Litany of Psalms. 7.

— I will lift up mine Eyes. *See* infra: A Litany of Psalms. 6.

— In the Beauty of Holiness. For unaccompanied mixed chorus. S. A. T. B. Psalm 29. pp. 10. *Galaxy Music Corp.: New York*, [1966.] 8°.
Part of "Music for the new Church".　　**E. 335. zz. (5.)**

— It is a good Thing to give Thanks. For four-part chorus of mixed voices a cappella. [Words] from Psalm 92. pp. 8. *G. Schirmer: [New York*, 1968.] 8°.　　**E. 335. ff. (58.)**

— It lies not on the sunlit Hill. For mixed voices a cappella. [Words by] Fiona Macleod. pp. 10. *Clayton F. Summy Co.: [Chicago*, 1956.] 8°.　　**F. 1744. s. (11.)**

— Lament. For unaccompanied mixed choir with soprano solo. [Words] from the Amerindian. pp. 6. *Galaxy Music Corporation: New York*, [1960.] 8°.　　**F. 1744. ff. (31.)**

— A Lamp unto my Feet. For unaccompanied mixed chorus S. A. T. B. [Words] from Psalm 119. pp. 12. *Galaxy Music Corp.: New York; printed in England*, [1966.] 8°.　　**E. 335. zz. (6.)**

— Let all the World in every Corner sing. For four-part chorus of mixed voices a cappella. [Words by] George Herbert, *etc.* pp. 8. *G. Schirmer: New York*, [1969.] 8°.　　**F. 1106. (14.)**

— Let all the World in every Corner sing. For four-part chorus of women's voices a cappella, *etc.* pp. 8. *G. Schirmer: New York*, [1971.] 8°.　　**F. 1874. v. (17.)**

— A Litany of Psalms ... Mixed chorus. [1.] Praise ye ... 〈Psalm 113.〉 [2.] Blessed is the Man ... 〈Psalm 1.〉 [3.] With my whole Heart have I sought Thee ... 〈Psalm 119.〉 [4.] The Lord is my Shepherd ... 〈Psalm 23.〉 [5.] Give Ear to my Prayer, O God ... 〈Psalm 55.〉 [6.] I will lift up mine Eyes ... 〈Psalm 121.〉

LEKBERG (SVEN)

[7.] How long wilt Thou forget me, O Lord? ... 〈Psalm 13.〉 [8.] Praise ye the Lord ... 〈Psalm 150.〉 8 no. *Galaxy Music Corporation: New York*, [1963.] 8°.　　**E. 335. dd. (43.)**

— Little Sorrows sit and weep. For four-part chorus of mixed voices a cappella. [Words by] William Blake. pp. 4. *G. Schirmer: New York*, [1971.] 8°.　　**F. 1874. p. (4.)**

— The Lord is my Shepherd. *See* supra: A Litany of Psalms. 4.

— Lord of the Earth and Sky. A cantata ... 〈Words and music by S. Lekberg.〉 For four-part chorus of mixed voices with soprano and bariton (or alto) soli with piano accompaniment. pp. 51. *G. Schirmer: New York*, [1970.] 8°.　　**F. 1257. d. (5.)**

— May the Blessing of Light be on you. For four-part chorus of mixed voices a cappella. Old Irish blessing. pp. 6. *G. Schirmer: New York*, [1969.] 8°.　　**F. 1874. j. (35.)**

— Moment musical. *See* infra: Three Peávinations. [2.]

— Now from the Altar of my Heart. [Words by] John Mason (1683). 〈S. A. T. B.〉 pp. 8. *Galaxy Music Corp.: New York*, [1968.] 8°.　　**F. 1106. a. (14.)**

— O come, let us sing unto the Lord. For medium voice with organ accompaniment. Psalm 95: 1–7. pp. 7. *Galaxy Music Corporation: New York*, [1963.] 4°.　　**G. 519. bb. (15.)**

— O, Lord, thou hast searched me. For voice and piano ... Text/Psalm 139: 1, 4, 8. pp. 5. *G. Schirmer: New York, London*, [1972.] 4°.　　**G. 517. rr. (1.)**

— O Wonder of this Christmas Night. For four-part chorus of mixed voices a cappella. Words and music by S. Lekberg. pp. 7. *G. Schirmer: New York*, [1964.] 8°.　　**E. 335. rr. (4.)**

— Pavane. *See* infra: Three Peávinations. [1.]

— Three Peávinations. [Words] by Leigh McBradd. For mixed chorus ... [1.] Pavane ... [2.] Moment musical ... [3.] Counterpoint, *etc.* 3 no. *G. Schirmer: New York*, [1970.] 8°.　　**F. 1874. m. (17.)**

— Praise ye. *See* supra: A Litany of Psalms. 1.

— Praise ye the Lord. *See* supra: A Litany of Psalms. 8.

— She walks in Beauty. For three-part chorus of mixed voices a cappella. [Words by] Lord Byron. pp. 7. *G. Schirmer: New York, London*, [1972.] 8°.　　**F. 1874. v. (18.)**

— So wondrous sweet and fair. For four-part chorus of mixed voices a cappella. [Words by] Edmund Waller (1606–1687). pp. 8. *G. Schirmer: New York*, [1967.] 8°.　　**F. 1874. f. (2.)**

— Softly along the Road of Evening. [Words by] Walter de la Mare. For four-part chorus of mixed voices a cappella. pp. 7. *G. Schirmer: New York*, [1964.] 8°.　　**F. 1744. qq. (3.)**

— The Spring and the Fall ... Poem by Edna St. Vincent Millay. For voice and piano. pp. 7. *G. Schirmer: New York*, [1971.] 4°.　　**G. 295. vv. (5.)**

— The Trees stand silent. For five-part chorus of mixed voices. S. S. A. T. B. a cappella. [Words by] Thomas Keohler. pp. 8. *G. Schirmer: New York, London*, [1972.] 8°.　　**F. 1874. v. (19.)**

— The Truth of the Lord endureth forever. For four-part chorus of mixed voices a cappella. Psalm 117. pp. 8. *G. Schirmer: New York*, [1971.] 8°.　　**F. 321. ff. (18.)**

— A Villanelle. For unaccompanied mixed choir. [Words by] Ernest Dowson. pp. 8. *Galaxy Music Corporation: New York*, [1963.] 8°.　　**F. 1744. nn. (31.)**

— Walk in the Light. For four-part chorus of mixed voices a cappella. [Words by] Bernard Barton (1784–1849). pp. 7. *G. Schirmer: New York*, [1968.] 8°.　　**E. 335. ff. (57.)**

LEKBERG (SVEN)

— We are the Music-Makers. For four-part chorus of mixed voices with descant a cappella. [Words by] Arthur O'Shaughnessy (1844–1881). pp. 8. *G. Schirmer:* [*New York,* 1972.] 8°. **F. 1874. v. (20.)**

— Weep you no more, sad Fountains. For four-part chorus of mixed voices a cappella. [Words] anonymous. pp. 8. *G. Schirmer: New York, London,* [1972.] 8°. **F. 1874. v. (21.)**

— When the green Woods laugh. For four-part chorus of mixed voices. [Words by] William Blake, *etc.* pp. 7. *G. Schirmer: New York,* [1968.] 8°. **F. 1874. f. (41.)**

— With my whole Heart have I sought Thee. *See* supra: A Litany of Psalms. 3.

— *See* BELLMAN (C. M.) Five Songs. Harmonized and set for chorus of mixed voices, a cappella, and with English versions by S. Lekberg, *etc.* [1952.] 8°. **F. 1744. k. (16.)**

LEKERT (OTTO)

— Victoria. 1897. Grand March for the pianoforte. *E. Ashdown: London,* [1897.] fol. **g. 605. p. (23.)**

— Victoria. 1897. Grand March. Arranged for the Organ by J. Wodehouse. *E. Ashdown: London,* [1897.] fol. **g. 575. d. (13.)**

LEKEU (GUILLAUME)

— *See* LEKEU (J. J. N. G.)

LEKEU (JEAN JOSEPH NICOLAS GUILLAUME)

— Adagio pour quatuor d'orchestre ... Op. 3. Partition d'orchestre, *etc.* pp. 13. *Rouart, Lerolle & cⁱᵉ: Paris,* [1937?] fol. **h. 1507. t. (3.)**

— Andromède. Poème lyrique et symphonique pour soli, chœurs et orchestre. Texte de Jules Sauvenière. Réduction pour piano et chant, *etc.* pp. 66. *Veuve Léopold Muraile: Liége; Leipzig* [printed, 1892?] 8°.
An additional vocal line has been added in MS. on pp. 54–57.
  F. 1196. o. (2.)

— Chanson de mai. Paroles de Jean Lekeu. pp. 7. *Rouart, Lerolle & cⁱᵉ: Paris,* [1909.] fol. **H. 1846. rr. (6.)**

— Fantaisie pour orchestre sur deux airs populaires angevins. Partition, *etc.* pp. 51. *Rouart, Lerolle & Cie.: Paris,* [1909.] fol. **h. 1508. l. (11.)**

— Fantaisie contrapuntique sur un cramignon liégeois (1890). Partition d'orchestre, *etc.* pp. 12. *Rouart, Lerolle & cⁱᵉ: Paris,* [1925.] fol. **h. 1507. t. (4.)**

— Les Pavots. [Song.] Poésie de A. de Lamartine. pp. 7. *Rouart, Lerolle & cⁱᵉ: Paris,* [1909.] fol. **H. 1846. rr. (8.)**

— Trois pièces pour piano. Chansonnette sans paroles. Valse oubliée. Danse joyeuse. pp. 11. *Veuve Léopold Muraille: Liége, Leipzig* printed, [1891.] fol. **h. 1203. t. (17.)**

— Trois poèmes ([Words by] G. Lekeu.) [Song.] ... n° 1. Sur une tombe ... n° 2. Ronde ... n° 3. Nocturne, *etc.* no. 1. *Rouart, Lerolle & cⁱᵉ: Paris,* [1909.] fol.
Imperfect; wanting no. 2, 3. **H. 1846. rr. (7.)**

— Poèmes. Chant et piano. Sur une tombe—Ronde—Nocturne, *etc.* pp. 21. *Rouart, Lerolle & cⁱᵉ: Paris,* [c. 1915.] 8°. **F. 1196. d. (8.)**

— Quatuor (inachevé) pour piano, violon, alto et violoncelle. [The second movement completed by Vincent d'Indy. Score and parts.] 4 pt. *E. Baudoux & cⁱᵉ: Paris,* [c. 1895.] fol.
Imperfect; wanting the titlepage. **h. 4090. n. (6.)**

LEKEU (JEAN JOSEPH NICOLAS GUILLAUME)

— [A reissue.] Quatuor (inachevé) pour piano, violon, alto & violoncelle. [Score and parts.] 4 pt. *Rouart, Lerolle & Cⁱᵉ: Paris,* [1935?] fol. **h. 2784. m. (7.)**

— Sonate pour piano. pp. 19. *E. Baudoux & cⁱᵉ: Paris,* [c. 1900.] fol. **h. 62. e. (9.)**

— Sonate pour piano. pp. 19. *Rouart, Lerolle & cⁱᵉ: Paris,* [1920?] fol. **h. 3865. n. (1.)**

— Sonate pour Piano et Violon, *etc.* *Rouart, Lerolle & Cie: Paris,* [1907.] fol. **h. 1612. aa. (14.)**

— Sonate en sol pour piano et violon. Nouvelle édition revue et doigtée par Mathieu Crickboom, *etc.* [Score and part.] 2 pt. *Rouart, Lerolle & cⁱᵉ: Paris,* [1934.] fol. **h. 1613. h. (13.)**

— Sonate en fa pour piano et violoncelle. Revue et terminée par Vincent d'Indy. 2 pt. *Rouart, Lerolle & Cⁱᵉ: Paris,* 1923. fol. **h. 1851. m. (12.)**

— Sur une tombe. *See* supra: Trois poèmes. No. 1.

— Trio pour Piano, Violon & Violoncelle. *Rouart, Lerolle & Cie: Paris,* 1908. fol. **h. 2850. t. (6.)**

LE KEUX (LOUIS)

— Remembrance. [Song.] Words by E. Oxenford. *T. Holloway: London,* [1899.] fol. **H. 1799. h. (31.)**

— The Word is said. Song, written by E. Oxenford. *T. Holloway: London,* [1900.] fol. **G. 807. o. (42.)**

LEKSTUGAN

— Lekstugan. Old Swedish Folk Dances. The collection adopted by the Society of Lovers of Swedish Folk Dance ... Translated by E. Lindelöf. [With plates.] pp. viii. 72. *J. Curwen & Sons: London; Curwen: Philadelphia,* [1926?] 4°. **g. 822. z.**

LELAND (ARTHUR)

— Almost persuaded. [Hymn.] Words [and music] by P. P. Bliss. Arr. [for male voices] by A. Leland. *Anglo-Canadian Music Publishers' Association: Toronto,* [1914.] 8°. **E. 602. dd. (24.)**

— Beyond the Smiling. [Sacred solo, with humming accompaniment.] *Whaley, Royce & Co.:* [*Toronto,*] 1913. 8°. **F. 538. f. (48.)**

— He wipes the Tear from every Eye. [Anthem.] Arr. by A. Leland [from the song by G. A. Lee]. *Whaley, Royce & Co.:* [*Toronto,*] 1913. 8°. **F. 538. f. (38.)**

— Jesus, Lover of my Soul. [Anthem.] Arr. by A. Leland. *Whaley, Royce & Co.:* [*Toronto,*] 1913. 8°. **F. 538. f. (40.)**

— Lead, kindly Light. Tune, Sandon [by C. H. Purday]. Arr. [for male voices] by A. Leland. *Anglo-Canadian Music Publishers' Association: Toronto,* [1914.] 8°. **E. 602. dd. (22.)**

— The Sands of Time. [Hymn.] Arr. [for male voices] by A. Leland. *Anglo-Canadian Music Publishers' Association: Toronto,* [1914.] 8°. **E. 602. dd. (23.)**

— Soldiers of Christ, arise. [Anthem.] *Whaley, Royce & Co.:* [*Toronto,*] 1913. 8°. **F. 538. f. (47.)**

— *See* JORDAN (   ) Guide us! Guard us ... [arranged by A.] Leland. 1913. 8°. **F. 538. f. (49.)**

LELAND (FRED)

— Can Mother see me now? ⟨Song, *etc.*⟩ [The music attributed on the cover to Geo. Devene, on p. 2. to Fred Leland.] Written by Fred Leland. pp. 3. [1910.] fol. *See* DEVENE (George) **H. 3991. h. (6.)**

LELAND (FRED)

— *See* FAGAN (Frank) and LELAND (F.) "Mind the red Light, Mary!" ... ⟨Song.⟩ Written and composed by F. Fagan and F. Leland, *etc.* [1902.] *s. sh.* fol.   **H. 3983. mm. (13.)**

— *See* FAGAN (Frank) and LELAND (F.) Mind the red Light, Mary! *etc.* ⟨Song.⟩ [1902.] fol.   **H. 3983. mm. (14.)**

— *See* FAGAN (Frank) and LELAND (F.) The Old Brass Ring. [Song.] [1898.] *s. sh.* fol.   **H. 3980. s. (70.)**

LELAND (HARRY G.)

— God so loved the World. Sacred Song. *O. Ditson Co.: Boston, etc.*, 1897. fol.   **H. 1187. u. (7.)**

— Lift thine Eyes. Sacred Song. *O. Ditson Co.: Boston, etc.*, 1895. fol.   **H. 1187. u. (8.)**

LELAND (HENRY)

— Christ our Saviour is born. For mixed chorus (SATB) a cappella. Edited and arranged by Edward H. Hastings. Words and music by H. Leland. pp. 10. *Mercury Music Corporation: New York*, [1958.] 8°.   **F. 260. m. (22.)**

LELAND (HERBERT S.)

— The Morning is dawning. Song & Chorus for the times [begins: "The gloom of the night is melting away"], words & music by H. S. Leland. *New York*, 1863. fol.   **H. 1780. p. (34.)**

LELAWALA

— Lelawala. Operetta. *See* CADMAN (C. W.)

LELE

— Леле Яно. [Song.] *See* ZLATEV-CHERKIN (G.)

LELEI ( )

— *See* LOEHLEIN (Georg S.)

LÊLET-AL-NUKTAR

— Lêlet-al-Nuktar. [Song.] *See* GREENE (G.) Four Songs, *etc.* [No. 3.]

LELEU (JEANNE)

— Quatuor pour violon, alto, violoncelle et piano. [Score and parts.] 4 pt. *Heugel: Paris*, [1926.] fol.   **h. 2801. bb. (4.)**

— Suite symphonique pour instruments à vent et piano. 1. Prélude. 2. L'Arbre plein de chants. 3. Mouvements de foule. 4. Bois sacré. 5. Joie populaire. Partition d'orchestre, *etc.* pp. 62. *Alphonse Leduc: Paris*, [1926.] fol.   **h. 1508. bb. (7.)**

LELIA

— Lelia, my Quadroon Maid. Song. *See* ROBSON (T. F.) and EDGAR (P.)

LELIÈVRE-LEE (AMELIA W.)

— *See* LEE.

LELIO

— Lelio, ou le Retour à la vie. Monodrame lyrique. *See* BERLIOZ (L. H.)

LELIWA (T.)

— *See* ALYAB'EV (A. A.) [Соловей.] Słowik. Zapisany przez T. Leliwę w Neapolu w 1905 r. jak spiewała A. Patti ... Układ A. Oppel, uzupełniony przez T. Leliwę. [c. 1930.] fol.   **H. 1847. f. (2.)**

LELLAN (T. C. MAC)

— *See* MACLELLAN.

LELLI

— Lelli dear, remember. Song. *See* BIRCH (W. H.)

LELOIR (EDMOND)

— *See* BEETHOVEN (L. van) [Sonatas. P. F. and horn. Op. 17.] Sonata F-dur, *etc.* ⟨Rev.: E. Leloir.⟩ [1965.] 4°.   **g. 250. l. (9.)**

— *See* BRAHMS (J.) Gesänge für Frauenchor ... mit Begleitung von 2 Hörnern und Harfe, *etc.* ⟨Op. 17. Rev. E. Leloir.⟩ [1967.] 4°.   **G. 473. i. (5.)**

— *See* BRAHMS (J.) [*Doubtful and Supposititious Works.*] [12 Etudes for Trumpet. No. 1, 3, 5–12.] 10 Etüden für Waldhorn. (Nachgelassenes Werk.) ... Révision E. Leloir. [1964.] 4°.   **g. 609. ff. (1.)**

— *See* GALLAY (J. F.) 30 études pour cor ⟨Op. 13⟩ ... Revision d'E. Leloir. [1965.] 4°.   **g. 1094. k. (6.)**

— *See* GALLAY (J. F.) 18 études mélodiques pour cor ... ⟨Op. 53.⟩ Revision d'E. Leloir. [1961.] 4°.   **g. 1094. g. (5.)**

— *See* GALLAY (J. F.) [22 fantaisies mélodiques. Op. 58.] 22 études-fantaisies mélodiques pour cor ... Revision d'E. Leloir. [1962.] 4°.   **g. 1094. i. (8.)**

— *See* HAYDN (F. J.) Concerto in mi ♭ maggiore per due corni e orchestra ... ⟨Hob. VII^d: 5. Arranged by E. Leloir.⟩ Horns & piano, *etc.* [1966.] 4°.   **h. 655. a. (8.)**

— *See* HOFFMEISTER (F. A.) Quintett Es-dur ... Horn, 2 Violinen & Violoncello, *etc.* ⟨Rev.: E. Leloir.⟩ [1964.] 4°.   **g. 1067. e. (4.)**

— *See* MERCADANTE (Saverio) Concerto per corno e orchestra da camera. Riduzione e revisione per corno e pianoforte di E. Leloir. [1977.] 4°.   **h. 2785. y. (9.)**

— *See* MOZART (J. G. L.) Concerto for two Horns in E fl, *etc.* ⟨Arrangement for orchestra reconstituted by E. Leloir.⟩ [1971.] 4°.   **g. 1094. n. (6.)**

— *See* PURCELL (Henry) [King Arthur.] Concerto pour cor et orchestre à cordes. Reconstitution, revision et arrangement par ... E. Leloir. Cor et piano, *etc.* [1980.] 4°.   **g. 25. o. (9.)**

— *See* REICHA (A. J.) [Trios. Op. 82.] 8 Trios für 3 Hörner in E. ⟨Rev.: E. Leloir.⟩ [1964.] 4°.   **g. 1094. k. (8.)**

— *See* ROSETTI (F. A.) Concerto N° 2 in mi♭ maggiore per corno e orchestra, *etc.* ⟨Reconstitution and cadenzas by E. Leloir.⟩ [1966.] 4°.   **g. 1094. n. (8.)**

— *See* ROSETTI (F. A.) Horn Concerto No. 5 in E maj. Reconstitution: E. Leloir. [1976.] 4°.   **g. 1067. rr. (7.)**

— *See* ROSSINI (G. A.) 5 Duos für 2 Hörner in Es, *etc.* ⟨Rev.: E. Leloir.⟩ [1961.] 4°.   **g. 637. c. (4.)**

— *See* ROSSINI (G. A.) Introduction, Andante, Allegro. Fantaisie pour cor et piano. Révision et arrangement de E. Leloir. [1970.] 4°.   **g. 637. h. (1.)**

— *See* ROSSINI (G. A.) Le Rendez-vous de chasse. Fantaisie für 4 Hörner in D, *etc.* ⟨Rev.: E. Leloir.⟩ [1963.] 4°.   **g. 637. c. (5.)**

— *See* SCHUBERT (F. P.) 5 Duos für 2 Hörner in Es, *etc.* [D. 199, 202–5.] ⟨Rev.: E. Leloir.⟩ [1962.] 4°.   **g. 567. z. (6.)**

LELOIR (Edmond)

— See TELEMANN (G. P.) Concerto D-Dur ... für Horn und Orchester ... herausgegeben von E. Leloir, *etc.* [1964.] 4°.
g. 401. k. (6.)

LE LONG (Colum)

— The Good red Wine. Song. Words by S. O. Jenkins. *Jefferys: London*, 1900. fol. **H. 1799. h. (32.)**

LELOUP ( ) *Maître de flûte*

— 2^e(—huitiéme) recueil des récréations de Polimnie, ou Choix d'ariettes, et airs tendres et légers, avec accompagnement de violon, flute, hautbois, pardessus-de-viole &c. ... Recueillis et mis en ordre par Mr Leloup ... Éditeur de ces recueils. Gravées par Mlle Petitot [recueil 2–6], *etc. Chez l'éditeur: Paris*, [c. 1765–c. 1770.] *obl.* fol.
Recueil 4–7 bear the imprint "Chez l'éditeur ... chez Mr Debrie"; recueil 8 bears the imprint "chez l'éditeur ... chez Mr Henaut". An earlier collection entitled "Récréations de Polymnie," without an editor's name, is entered under RÉCRÉATIONS. **E. 1717. h. (2.)**

LÉLU ( )

— Les Adieux de Belamour ... Romance de garnison [begins: "Z'adieu donc"]. *Paris*, [1825?] fol. **G. 547. (16.)**

— Blanche portera ma couronne. [Song.] Paroles de Mr de Rougemont ... avec accompagnement de piano. pp. 3. *Chez Lélu: Paris*, [1818?] fol. **G. 561. c. (23.)**

— C'est dans cette fête civique. *Hymne* chanté par le Peuple dans le Panthéon devant les mânes de Barra et Viala. Parolles et Musique de Lélu, *etc. Chez Imbault:* [*Paris*, 1794.] 8°. **B. 362. d. (50.)**

— C'est en vain que le nord enfante. *Chant Républicain* sur la Battaille de Fleurus, par Lebrun. *Chez Imbault:* [*Paris*, 1794.] 8°. **E. 1717. b. (47.)**

— Les Chevaliers Rose-croix. Romance avec accompagnement de piano-forte, *etc.* pp. 3. *Chez l'auteur: Paris*, [c. 1810.] fol. **G. 561. c. (24.)**

— Idylles et Romances, extraites de l'ouvrage intitulé "Les Fleurs," par Mr. Constant Dubos. [Set to music by Mr. Lélu and Mr. Guichard.] *Paris*, 1808. 8°. **1065. l. 30.**

— O fille de l'Être suprême. *Hymne à l'Égalité.* Paroles du C^{en} Malingre, *etc. Chez Imbault: Paris*, [1794?] 8°. **B. 362. d. (42.)**

— O toi dont la sagesse a rempli. *Hymne à l'Éternel* ... Paroles du C^{en} Huard, *etc. Chez Imbault: Paris*, [1793?] 8°. **B. 362. d. (40.)**

— Vesper. Romance [begins: "Déjà dans le sein"]. *Paris*, [1810?] fol. **G. 547. (4.)**

— *See* MEISSONNIER (A.) Oui, je vous fuis ... Accompt. de Piano ... par Lélu. [1810?] fol. **G. 554. (47.)**

LEMACHER (Heinrich)

— Trifolium. Drei Klavierstücke. Op. 10. *Henry Litolff's Verlag: Braunschweig*, 1937. 4°.
Collection Litolff, No. 2855. **g. 1127. xx. (1.)**

— *See* BRUCKNER (A.) Quadrille ... Erstmalig herausgegeben von H. Lemacher. [1944.] *obl.* 4°. **e. 282. i. (1.)**

— *See* HAYDN (F. J.) [Divertimenti. Hob. II/11.] Mann und Weib, oder Der Geburtstag ... Herausgegeben von H. Lemacher, *etc.* [1932.] 4°. **g. 455. e. (12.)**

— *See* HAYDN (F. J.) Ouvertüre [Hob. Ia/4] in D-dur ... Herausgegeben von ... H. Lemacher, *etc.* 1931. 4°.
g. 455. e. (13.)

LE MACK (Thomas)

— Everybody has their Day. Song and refrain. Words and music by T. Le Mack. pp. 5. *Oliver Ditson Co.: Boston*, [1896.] fol. **H. 3980. qq. (21.)**

— A Growler on a String. [Song.] Words & music by T. Le Mack. pp. 5. *Howley, Haviland & Co.: New York*, [1900.] fol. **H. 3985. s. (38.)**

— My black Baby mine! [Song.] Words and music by T. Le Mack. pp. 5. *M. Witmark & Sons: New York*, [1896.] fol. **H. 3980. qq. (22.)**

— Our Girls. [Song.] Words & music by T. Le Mack. pp. 5. *T. B. Harms & Co.:* [*New York*, 1894.] fol. **H. 3980. qq. (23.)**

— Seek and you may find, my Lad. Song and chorus, *etc.* ⟨Words and music by T. Le Mack.⟩ pp. 5. *Howley, Haviland & Co.: New York*, [1897.] fol. **H. 3980. qq. (24.)**

LEMAIGRE (Edmond)

— Air de ballet pour piano. *Paris*, [1884.] fol.
h. 3280. k. (41.)

— Contemplation. *See infra:* Fragments Symphoniques. No. 1.

— Danse Mauresque p. Orchestre. Partition. *Paris*, [1884.] 8°.
No. 3 of Fragments Symphoniques. **e. 666. h. (8.)**

— Danse Mauresque pour piano. *Paris*, [1884.] fol.
h. 3280. k. (42.)

— Echo du Petit Trianon, gavotte Louis XV. pour Piano. *Paris*, [1881.] fol. **h. 3272. j. (21.)**

— Fragments Symphoniques pour orchestre. No. 1. Contemplation ... No. 2. Marcietta des Archers. Partition. 2 no. *Paris*, [1883.] 8°. **e. 666. g. (18.)**

— Fragments Symphoniques pour orchestre. Parties séparées. no. 5, 6. *Richault et Cie.: Paris*, [1887.] fol.
Imperfect; wanting no. 1–4. **h. 3210. f. (6.)**

— Marcietta des Archers. *See supra:* Fragments Symphoniques. No. 2.

— Orientale pour le piano. *Paris*, [1884.] fol. **h. 3280. k. (43.)**

— Douze Pièces pour orgue ou piano à pédale. 1er volume. *Paris*, [1883.] 8°.
No. 60 *of the Bibliothèque-Leduc. Imperfect; wanting vol.* 2.
f. 314. b. (1.)

— Douze Pièces nouvelles pour orgue ... Divisées en 6 cahiers. *Richault et Cie.: Paris*, [1886.] fol.
Imperfect; wanting cah. 4–6. **h. 2732. d. (13.)**

— Royat-Valse pour piano. *Paris*, [1883.] fol. **h. 3285. b. (59.)**

— Scherzo-Valse pour piano. *Paris*, [1884.] fol.
h. 3280. k. (44.)

— Séduction-Valse pour piano. *Paris*, [1884.] fol.
h. 3285. b. (58.)

LEMAIRE (A.)

— Airs populaires Persans pour Piano. *Paris*, [1882.] fol.
h. 3276. g. (15.)

— Avâz^e Mâhoûr. Mélodie persane transcrite pour Piano et Chant par A. Lemaire ... Traduction française de Gantin. [*Paris*,] 1900. 8°.
Supplement to "L'Illustration," No. 2996. **P. P. 4283. m. (3.)**

— Hymne national persan. Transcription pour Piano. [*Paris*,] 1900. 8°.
Supplement to "L'Illustration," No. 2996. **P. P. 4283. m. (3.)**

— Quadrille Persan composé sur des airs populaires. [P. F.] *Paris*, [1882.] fol. **h. 3276. g. (16.)**

LEMAIRE (Auguste)

— Le Réveil de la Nature. Chœur à trois voix avec accompagnement de piano ... Paroles et musique de A. Lemaire. Partition. *E. Lauweryns Fils: Bruxelles*, [1889.] fol. **H. 1795. e. (3.)**

LEMAIRE (Edwin H.)

— *See* LEMARE.

LEMAIRE (Gaston)

— Bergerette-Watteau, pour Piano. *Schott & Co.: London*, 1907. fol. **g. 605. vv. (35.)**

— En dansant la Gavotte. Pantomime-Mélodie ... poésie de A. Dreville. [*Paris*,] 1897. 8°.
Supplement to "L'Illustration," No. 2840. **P. P. 4283. m. (3.)**

— L'Intermezzo de H. Heine. Visions lyriques en dix-neuf scènes ... Scènes au bord de la mer, Barcarolle. [P. F.] [*Paris*,] 1901. 8°.
Supplement to "L'Illustration," No. 3032. **P. P. 4283. m. (3.)**

— Promenade à Richmond, pour Piano. *Schott & Co.: London*, 1907. fol. **g. 605. vv. (36.)**

— Rêve d'Amour.—Loving Dream.— Valse lente pour Piano. *Schott & Co.: London*, 1907. fol. **h. 3286. ll. (25.)**

— La Tabatière. [Song.] Poésie de G. Visés, English words by E. Teschemacher. *B. Schott's Söhne: Mayence*, 1907. fol. **G. 805. mm. (32.)**

LE MAIRE (Jean)

— Premier livre de sonates pour le violon avec la basse continüe. ⟨Gravé par Mlle Michelon.⟩ pp. 35. *Chez l'autheur, etc.: Paris*, 1739. fol. **h. 1728. j.**

LEMAIRE (Jules)

— Helen's Babies galop. [P. F.] *London*, [1877.] fol. **h. 1482. z. (26.)**

— The Marseillaise [by C. J. Rouget de Lisle] arranged as a Pianoforte duet. *London*, [1872.] fol. **h. 1485. s. (45.)**

— The Maypole, transcription of the ... Old English ballad "Come Lasses and Lads," for the Pianoforte. *London*, [1864.] fol. **h. 1460. v. (15.)**

— Prenez garde. Polka. [P. F.] *Ransford & Son: London*, [1883.] fol. **h. 975. v. (9.)**

— Rosy Morn, transcription of Shield's ... trio "When the Rosy Morn appearing," for the Pianoforte. *London*, [1864.] fol. **h. 1460. v. (16.)**

— Le Ruisseau. Morceau de Salon pour le piano. *Ransford & Son: London*, [1883.] fol. **h. 1484. s. (47.)**

— The Sea-Nymph, transcription of the ... Ethiopian melody "Beautiful Sea" for the Pianoforte. *London*, [1863.] fol. **h. 1460. v. (13.)**

— Souvenir de la Jeunesse, transcription of Bellini's ... ballad "Remembrance of the Past" for the Pianoforte. *London*, [1864.] fol. **h. 1460. v. (18.)**

— Sunny Days, transcription of H. Russell's song "Sunny days will come again," for the Pianoforte. *London*, [1864.] fol. **h. 1460. v. (17.)**

— The Thorn, brilliant transcription of Shield's ... ballad ... for the Pianoforte. *London*, [1863.] fol. **h. 1460. v. (14.)**

LEMAIRE (L.)

— Forty-two Progressive Pieces for the Piano Forte. Selected, fingered ... for the use of new beginners by L. Lemaire, *etc.* pp. 14. *C. Bradlee:* [*Boston*, 1835.] fol. **h. 1500. (36.)**

LEMAIRE (Louis)

— Après avoir tant bû. *Air à Boire, etc.* [*Paris*,] 1737. *s. sh.* 4°.
Mercure de France, March, 1737. **297. b. 18.**

— Ariane. Cantatille Nouvelle, avec Accompagnement de Flûttes, Violons et Hautbois ... Gravée par Dumont. *Chez l'Auteur, etc.: Paris*, 1732. obl. fol. **C. 124. (3.)**

— L'Aurore, Cantatille Nouvelle, Avec Accompagnement de Flûtes, Violons & Haut-bois, *etc.* *J. B. C. Ballard: Paris*, [1734.] obl. fol. **C. 124. (4.)**

— La Bergère Impatiente. Cantatille Nouvelle. Avec Accompagnement de Flûtes, Violons & Haut-bois, *etc.* *J. B. C. Ballard: Paris*, [1734.] obl. fol. **C. 124. (5.)**

— Climène et Tircis. 5eme musette. Cantatille nouvelle pour un dessus, avec accompagnement de flûttes, violons, et musette ... Gravée par Melle Bertin. ⟨Quarante neuviême cantatille.⟩ [Score.] pp. 601–612. *Chez l'Auteur, etc.: Paris*, 1744. obl. 4°. **C. 124. a. (8.)**

— La Constance. Cantatille Nouvelle ... avec Accompagnement de Flûtes, Violons et Hautbois ... Gravée par Melle Louise Roussel. *Chez l'Auteur, etc.: Paris*, [1730?] obl. fol. **C. 124. (2.)**

— Le Dépit amoureux. Cantatille nouvelle, pour une basse taille, avec accompagnement de violons et flûtes ... Gravée par Melle Bertin. ⟨Cinquantieme cantatille.—Les paroles sont de M^r d'Ormoy.⟩ pp. 613–622. *Chez l'Auteur, etc.: Paris*, 1744. obl. 4°. **C. 124. a. (9.)**

— Diane vangée et punie. Tirée des Albanes ive et dernier tableau. Cantatille nouvelle, pour un dessus, avec accompagnement de violons et flûtes ... Gravée par Melle Bertin. ⟨Quarante huitiéme cantatille.⟩ [Score.] pp. 589–599. *Chez l'Auteur, etc.: Paris*, 1744. obl. 4°. **C. 124. a. (7.)**

— Les Effets de l'Absence. Cantatilles Nouvelle, Avec Accompagnem^t de Flûtes, Violons et Hautbois ... Gravée par L. Hue. (Les Paroles sont de Mr. B.***.) *Chés L'Auteur, etc.: Paris*, 1735. obl. fol. **C. 124. (7.)**

— Epithalame. Cantatille Nouvelle. Avec Accompagnem^t de Flûtes, Violons et Hautbois, *etc.* *Chez l'Auteur, etc.: Paris*, 1738. obl. fol. **C. 124. (9.)**

— La Fête de Nanette. 4me musette. Cantatille nouvelle, avec accompagnem^t de violons, flutes et musette. ⟨Labassée sculpsit.—Trente huitieme cantatille.⟩ [Score.] pp. 253–264. *Chez l'Auteur: Paris*, 1741. obl. 4°. **C. 641. b. (1.)**

— Les Forges de l'amour. Tirée des Albanes IIe tableau. Cantatille nouvelle, pour un dessus, avec accompagnement de violons et flûtes ... Gravée par Melle Bertin. ⟨Quarante sixième cantatille.⟩ [Score.] pp. 563–576. *Chez l'Auteur, etc.: Paris*, 1744. obl. 4°. **C. 124. a. (5.)**

— Les Francs Maçons. Cantatille nouvelle, pour une basse-taille. ⟨Cinquante et uniéme cantatille.⟩ [Score.] pp. 623–636. [*The author: Paris*, 1744.] obl. 4°.
Without titlepage. **C. 124. a. (10.)**

— Hebé. Cantatille Nouvelle [words by Laffichard], Avec Accompagnement de Flûtes, Violons & Haut-bois, *etc.* *J. B. C. Ballard: Paris*, [1734.] obl. fol.
Pp. 57–78 of the 2nd vol. of Cantatilles. **C. 641. a.**

— L'Hyver des ans a blanchi mes cheveux. *Air à Boire, etc.* [Words by] L'Affichard. [*Paris*,] 1740. *s. sh.* 4°.
Mercure de France, Oct., 1740. **298. b. 7.**

— Il n'est point volage. *Air badin, etc.* [*Paris*,] 1733. *s. sh.* 4°.
Mercure de France, Dec., 1733. **297. b. 1.**

LEMAIRE (Louis)

—— Il n'est point volage. Air, *etc.* [*Paris,*] 1748. *s. sh.* 4°.
Mercure de France, May, 1748.   **297. c. 16.**

—— L'Inconstance. Cantatille Nouvelle, Sans Accompagnement, *etc. Chez l'Auteur, etc.: Paris,* 1738. *obl.* fol.   **C. 124. (10.)**

—— L'Indifférence. Cantatille Nouvelle, Sans accompagnement, *etc. Chez l'Auteur, etc.: Paris,* 1741. *obl.* fol.   **C. 124. (13.)**

—— Je vois sortir du Ciel. *Chanson, etc.* [*Paris,*] 1733. *s. sh.* 4°.
Mercure de France, August, 1733.   **298. a. 30.**

—— Le Jour. Cantatille Nouvelle, Avec accompagnement de Violons et Flûtes, *etc. Chez l'Auteur, etc.: Paris,* 1743. *obl.* fol.   **C. 124. (15.)**

—— Mercure et Pan. Cantatille nouvelle, pour un dessus, avec accompagnement de violons et flûtes ... Gravée par Melle Bertin. ⟨Quarante quatrieme cantatille.⟩ [Score.] pp. 537–547. *Chez l'Auteur, etc.: Paris,* 1743 [1744]. *obl.* 4°.   **C. 124. a. (3.)**

—— Le Musette. ⟨Iere musette. Dix-septieme cantatille. Les paroles sont de Mr B.***.⟩ Cantatille nouvelle avec accompag^t de musette, vieille, hautbois et violons ... Gravée par L. Huë. pp. 207–219. *Chez l'auteur, etc.: Paris,* 1735 [1748?]. *obl.* 4°.   **C. 738. dd.**

—— Nous nous plaignons que la Parque. *Chanson, etc.* [*Paris,*] 1736. *s. sh.* 4°.
Mercure de France, May, 1736.   **297. b. 13.**

—— Orphée. Cantatille ... Pour un Dessus, Avec accompagnement de Violons et Flûtes ... Gravée par Melle Bertin. *Chez l'Auteur, etc.: Paris,* 1743. *obl.* fol.   **C. 124. (16.)**

—— [A reissue.] Orphée. Cantatille, *etc.* pp. 523–536. *Paris,* 1743 [1744]. *obl.* 4°.   **C. 124. a. (2.)**

—— Père du jour, quitte le sein de l'Onde. *Air de Basse, etc.* [*Paris,*] 1731. *s. sh.* 4°.
Mercure de France, May, 1731.   **298. a. 17.**

—— Les Plaisirs Champêtres. 2me Musette. Cantatille Nouvelle. Avec Accompagnement de Musette, Vieille, Flûtes, Violons, *etc. Chez L'Auteur, etc.: Paris,* 1738. *obl.* fol.   **C. 124. (8.)**

—— Psiché. Cantatille Nouvelle, Avec accompagnem^t de Violons et Flûtes, *etc. Chez l'Auteur, etc.: Paris,* 1741. *obl.* fol.   **C. 124. (12.)**

—— Qu' ai-je donc fait aux Dieux! *Air, etc.* [*Paris,*] 1748. *s. sh.* 4°.
Mercure de France, May, 1748.   **297. c. 16.**

—— Que t'ay-je fait, cruel Amour? *Air sérieux, etc.* [*Paris,*] 1731. *s. sh.* 4°.
Mercure de France, May, 1731.   **298. a. 17.**

—— Quel bruit affreux. *Recit de Basse, etc.* [*Paris,*] 1748. *s. sh.* 4°.
Mercure de France, April, 1748.   **297. c. 16.**

—— Quoi! toujours des Chansons à boire! *Chanson à Manger.* [*Paris,*] 1735. *s. sh.* 4°.
Mercure de France, March, 1735.   **297. b. 8.**

—— La Reconnoissance. Cantatille nouvelle, pour un dessus, avec accompagnement de violons, et fluttes ... Gravé par Melle Bertin. ⟨Cinquante troisième cantatille.⟩ [Score.] pp. 659–669. *Chez l'Auteur, etc.: Paris,* 1745. *obl.* 4°.   **C. 124. a. (12.)**

—— Recueil d'Airs Serieux et à Boire, Mêlez de Vaudeville, Ronde de Table, Duo, Recit de Basse, Airs tendres, et chansons à danser. *Chez l'Auteur: Paris,* 1738. *obl.* fol.   **C. 641.**

—— Le Rendez-vous Pastoral. Cantatille Nouvelle, Sans Accompagnem^t, *etc. Chez l'Auteur, etc.: Paris,* 1738. *obl.* fol.   **C. 124. (11.)**

LEMAIRE (Louis)

—— Reviens, cher objet que j'adore. *Air Sérieux, etc.* [*Paris,*] 1741. *s. sh.* 4°.
Mercure de France, August, 1741.   **298. b. 12.**

—— Le Sacrifice d'Amour. Cantatille Nouvelle ... Gravez par Melle Louise Roussel. *Chez l'Auteur, etc.: Paris,* [1728.] *obl.* fol.   **C. 124. (1.)**

—— Sapho. Cantatille ... Avec accompagnem^t de Violons et Flûtes, *etc. Chez l'Auteur, etc.: Paris,* 1741. *obl.* fol.   **C. 124. (14.)**

—— Le Sommeil de Climène. Cantatille Nouvelle, Avec Accompagnement de Flûtes, Violons & Haut-bois, *etc.* (Les Paroles sont de Monsieur Laffichard.) *J. B. C. Ballard: Paris,* [1734.] *obl.* fol.   **C. 124. (6.)**

—— La Toilette de Vénus. Tirée des Albanes Ier tableau. Cantatille nouvelle, pour un dessus, avec accompagnement de violons et flûtes ... Gravée par Melle Bertin. ⟨Quarante cinquième cantatille.⟩ [Score.] pp. 549–561. *Chez l'Auteur, etc.: Paris,* 1744. *obl.* 4°.   **C. 124. a. (4.)**

—— Vénus et Adonis. Tirée des Albanes IIIe tableau. Cantatille nouvelle, pour un dessus, avec accompagnement de violons et flûtes ... Gravée par Melle Bertin. ⟨Quarante septième cantatille.⟩ [Score.] pp. 577–588. *Chez l'Auteur, etc: Paris,* 1744. *obl.* 4°.   **C. 124. a. (6.)**

—— La Victoire. Cantatille nouvelle, en duo, pour un dessus, et une basse-taille. Avec accompagnement de violons, flutes et hautbois, et bassons ... Gravé par Melle Bertin. ⟨Cinquante deuxieme cantatille.⟩ [Score.] pp. 637–658. *Chez l'Auteur, etc.: Paris,* 1745. *obl.* 4°.   **C. 124. a. (11.)**

—— La Voix de Climène. Cantatille nouvelle, pour un dessus, avec accompagnement de violons et flûtes ... Gravée par Melle Bertin. ⟨Quarante deuxieme cantatille.⟩ [Score.] pp. 511–522. *Chez l'Auteur, etc.: Paris,* 1743 [1744]. *obl.* 4°.   **C. 124. a. (1.)**

—— Vôtre gaité me désespere. *Brunette, etc.* [*Paris,*] 1748. *s. sh.* 4°.
Mercure de France, Sept., 1748.   **297. c. 18.**

LEMAIRE (Nicolas)

—— Six New Cottillons and Six Country Dances with three favorite Minuets, *etc. Printed for R. Wornum: London,* [1773?] *obl.* 4°.   **a. 9. e. (7.)**

LEMAIRE (Richard)

—— Nearer my God to Thee and Sun of my Soul. As sung at the Guards' Chapel, Wellington Barracks. [Hymn.] *C. Vincent: London,* 1899. 8°.   **F. 1771. bb. (40.)**

—— Sun of my Soul. *See supra:* Nearer my God to Thee.

LEMAIRE (Théophile) and LAVOIX (Henri Marie)

—— Le Chant, ses principes et son histoire, par T. Lemaire et H. Lavoix. *Paris,* 1881. 8°.   **7896. ff. 14.**

LE MAISTRE (Matthæus)

—— Catechesis Numeris Musicis Inclusa, et ad Puerorum Captum Accomodata, tribus uocibus composita ... Pars infima. *In Officina Ioannis Montani, & Ulrici Neuberi: Noribergæ,* 1559. *obl.* 16°.   **K. 8. i. 4. (18.)**

—— [Geistliche vnd weltliche teutsche Gesng mit vier und fünf Stimmen.] Bassus. *Johan Schwertel: Wittembergk,* 1566. *obl.* 4°.
The full title is printed in the tenor part only.   **A. 130.**

LE MAISTRE (MATTHÆUS)

— Missa Regnum mundi. Motette Regnum mundi [anonymous]. Herausgegeben von Gernot Gruber. pp. x. 44. *Akademische Druck- u. Verlagsanstalt: Graz*, 1965. 4°. [*Musik alter Meister. Hft.* 14.] **G. 920.**

— *See* EPITHALAMIA. Epithalamia … Composita per … Matthæum le Maistre, *etc.* 1568. obl. 4°. **A. 18.**

— *See* KADE (L. O.) Mattheus le Maistre … ein Beitrag zur Musikgeschichte des 16. Jahrhunderts … mitt Musikbeilagen versehen, *etc.* 1862. 8°. **10759. k. 18.**

LE MAITRE ( )

— Dans nos hameaux tout nous engage. *Chanson en Musette.* [*Paris*,] 1726. *s. sh.* 4°. *Mercure de France, Nov.*, 1726. **297. a. 24.**

— Une maîtresse trop austere. *Chanson, etc.* [*Paris*,] 1727. *s. sh.* 4°. *Mercure de France, Oct.*, 1727. **297. a. 29.**

— Que j'ayme à voir Iris. *Air gracieux, etc.* [*Paris*,] 1729. *s. sh.* 4°. *Mercure de France, Dec.*, 1729. **298. a. 8.**

— Quels affreux Tourbillons! *Air, etc.* [*Paris*,] 1730. *s. sh.* 4°. *Mercure de France, Aug.*, 1730. **298. a. 12.**

LE MAÎTRE (ADÈLE)

— Grande Marche Militaire pour piano. *Whaley, Royce & Co.: Toronto*, 1896. fol. **g. 605. p. (24.)**

— Let British Might uphold the Right … Song … words by J. F. Le Maître. *Whaley, Royce & Co.: Toronto*, 1896. fol. **G. 805. aa. (7.)**

— Litany of the Blessed Virgin in C for five voices; duet, solo and chorus with organ accompaniment. *Whaley, Royce & Co.: Toronto*, 1896. fol. **H. 879. l. (3.)**

— O Salutaris. [Song.] … Avec Accompagnement d'Orgue. [*Toronto*,] 1896. fol. **G. 517. j. (18.)**

LEMAÎTRE (PAUL)

— *See* VIOTTI (G. B.) 22ᵉ concerto de violon avec accompagnement de piano. Révision par P. Lemaître. [1921.] 4°. **g. 618. b. (9.)**

LEMALTE (E. F.)

— *See* MEURANT (E.) Sérénade. Transcription pour la Flute arr. par E. F. Lemalte. [1903.] fol. **h. 2050. d. (14.)**

LEMAN (ALEXIS)

— Una Memoria, for the Violoncello—or Violin—with Pianoforte accompaniment. *Orchestral Publishing Co.: London*, (1910.) fol. **h. 1851. f. (4.)**

LEMAN (JAMES)

— A New Method of Learning Psalm-Tunes, with an Instrument of Musick call'd the Psalterer. *G. Smith, for the Author: London*, 1729. 4°. *This work contains psalm tunes by J. Church, J. W. [John Weldon?], Mr. Hart, J. Clark and W. Croft.* **7897. bb. 59.**

LEMARCHAND ( )

— *See* GLUCK (C. W. von) Alma sedes. *Motet* … Mis au Jour par Mʳ Lemarchand, *etc.* [1785?] fol. **H. 1187. f. (8.)**

LE MARCHAND (ANDRÉ)

— La Ballade de Fougères, *etc.* [Song.] (Paroles attribuées à A. Chartier.) *Fougères*, [1923.] 8°. **E. 1830. b. (13.)**

LEMARE (CHARLOTTE)

— Dream Song … Transcribed for the organ by E. H. Lemare. *H. W. Gray Co.: New York*, 1921. 4°. **g. 1380. h. (4.)**

LEMARE (EDWIN HENRY)

— Above the Clouds. A reverie for the organ. Opus 143. *Forster Music Publisher: Chicago*, 1925. 4°. **g. 587. d. (22.)**

— Air with Variations on a Diatonic Scale. Op. 97. (Organ.) *Schott & Co.: London*, 1920. fol. **h. 2710. b. (9.)**

— Album of Organ Pieces. *W. Paxton & Co.: London*, [1930.] obl. 4°. **e. 1093. r. (36.)**

— Allegretto in B minor. [Organ.] 1896. *See infra*: The "Recital Series" of original Organ compositions. No. 11.

— Allegro pomposo. Op. 86, *etc.* (Organ.) *Schott & Co.: London, etc.*, (1912.) fol. **h. 2710. a. (20.)**

— Alpine Dance, for the Organ. Opus 147. *Forster Music Publisher: Chicago*, 1925. 4°. **g. 587. d. (23.)**

— And God shall wipe away all Tears. Anthem, *etc. Stainer & Bell: London*, (1911.) 8°. *Stainer & Bell's Church Choir Library, No.* 99. **F. 1137. b.**

— Andante Cantabile for the Organ. (Op. 37.) *Novello and Co.: London*, 1900. 4°. **g. 587. b. (3.)**

— Andante grazioso, for the Organ. Opus 146. *Forster Music Publisher: Chicago*, 1925. 4°. **g. 589. d. (24.)**

Andantino in D flat

— Andantino in D flat for the organ. *R. Cocks & Co.: London*, 1892. obl. fol. **e. 174. x. (8.)**

— Andantino in D flat, for the Organ. *Novello and Co.: London*, [1899.] 4°. **g. 587. b. (1.)**

— Andantino. Pianoforte conductor. *Novello & Co.: London*, 1916. 8°. **h. 3210. h. (155.)**

— Andantino … Arranged for Small Orchestra by G. von Holst. [Parts.] *Novello & Co.: London*, [1909.] fol. **h. 3210. h. (82.)**

— Andantino in D flat … Arranged for Military Band by C. Hoby. [Parts.] *Novello & Co.: London*, (1911.) fol. **h. 2710. b. (4.)**

— Andantino in D flat—transposed to D— … Arranged as a Quintet … by G. von Holst. 1909. *See* NOVELLO AND CO. Novello, Ewer & Co.'s Albums for Pianoforte and Stringed Instruments. No. 29. [1893, *etc.*] 4°. **g. 1023.**

— Andantino … Organ Solo transcribed for the Pianoforte by A. E. Godfrey. *R. Cocks & Co.: London*, 1892. fol. **h. 3282. f. (25.)**

— Andantino in D flat—transposed to D— … Arranged for Violin and Pianoforte by C. Monk. *Novello & Co.: London*, 1907. 4°. **g. 223. p. (9.)**

— Andantino … Arranged (for Violin and Piano) by W. F. Ambrosio. *C. Fischer: New York, etc.*, 1936. 4°. **g. 500. q. (37.)**

— Andantino arranged for two Violins & Piano by A. Hickling. *R. Cocks & Co.: London*, 1894. fol. **h. 2850. m. (5.)**

— Andantino. (Song of the Soul) … arranged for violoncello and pianoforte by W. H. Squire. *Novello & Co.: London*, 1918. 4°. **g. 510. f. (8.)**

LEMARE (Edwin Henry)

— Valse Andantino ... Arranged by the composer as a waltz, *etc.* [P. F.] *Harms: New York,* 1924. 4°.　　**g. 587. d. (21.)**

— Nocturne ... [Three-part song.] S. A. B. [Words by] J. L. Vandevere ... Arr. by G. Pitcher. *C. C. Birchard & Co.: Boston,* 1928. 8°.　　**F. 585. rr. (25.)**

— Andantino. Starlight and Sunshine. [Song.] Lyric by H. Johnson. (Transcription by H. Frey.) *Robbins Music Corporation: New York,* 1933. 4°.　　**G. 1275. nn. (18.)**

— Moonlight and Roses (bring Mem'ries of you). S. A. T. B. Adapted ... by Ben Black and Neil Morèt. [Staff and tonic sol-fa notation.] pp. 7. *Francis, Day & Hunter: London,* [1958.] 8°.
[*New Century choral Edition. no. 23.*]　　**F. 672. m.**

— Second Andantino in D flat. 1902. *See infra:* The "Recital Series" of original Organ Compositions. No. 25.

— The Angelus. Opus 179. (Organ.) *White-Smith Music Publishing Co.: Boston, New York,* 1930. 4°.　　**g. 575. ii. (26.)**

— The Apostles' Creed, the Lord's Prayer and the Nicene Creed, for voices in monotone with simple Organ accompaniment. *Stainer & Bell: London,* (1912.) 8°.
　　F. 1169. t. (10.)

— Arcadian Idyll—Serenade, Musette, Solitude—for the Organ. (Op. 52.) *Novello & Co.: London,* 1907. 4°.
Original Compositions, etc., No. 22.　　**g. 587. b. (16.)**

— At Close of Day. [Song.] *H. W. Gray Co.: New York,* 1923. 4°.　　**G. 1275. i. (13.)**

— Aubade. Organ. Op. 145. *A. P. Schmidt Co.: Boston, New York,* 1926. 4°.　　**g. 587. d. (25.)**

— Barcarolle for the organ. *R. Cocks & Co.: London,* 1896. *obl. fol.*　　**e. 1093. (6.)**

— Barcarolle, for Violin and Piano. *Stainer & Bell: London,* (1912.) fol.
A different work from the preceding.　　**h. 2710. b. (2.)**

— Barcarolle ... Transcribed [from the version for violin and P. F.] for the Organ by B. Johnson. (1912.) *See* JOHNSON (B.) The Organ Recitalist, *etc.* New Series. No. 25. (1912, *etc.*) 4°.
　　f. 342. a.

— Behold how good and joyful. Anthem ... Op. 195. *C. Fischer: New York, etc.,* 1935. 8°.　　**E. 335. h. (14.)**

— Bell Scherzo. Op. 89, *etc.* (Organ.) *Schott & Co.: London,* (1912.) fol.　　**h. 2710. a. (22.)**

— The Bells of Rheims. Song, the word by H. de Vere Stacpoole. *Boosey & Co.: London, etc.,* 1915. fol.
　　H. 1793. t. (6.)

— Benedicite, omnia opera. *R. Cocks & Co.: London,* 1893. 8°.
No. 1 *of the "Burlington Series of Modern Church Music".*
　　F. 1172. (1.)

— Benedicite, omnia Opera. No. 1. in B♭. 1893. *See* NOVELLO AND CO. Novello's Parish Choir Book, *etc.* No. 429. [1866, *etc.*] 8°.　　**E. 618.**

— Bénédiction nuptiale. Op. 85, *etc. Schott & Co.: London, etc.,* (1911.) fol.　　**h. 2710. a. (19.)**

— Benedictus ... in the key of F. *See infra:* [Festival Service in F.]

— Berceuse in D, for the Organ. *Novello & Co.: London,* [1901.] 4°.　　**g. 587. b. (7.)**

— A Birthday in November. Song for Mezzo-Soprano or Baritone. Words by F. Bourdillon. *G. Schirmer: New York,* 1901. fol.　　**G. 807. t. (23.)**

LEMARE (Edwin Henry)

— Cantique d'Amour for the Organ. (Op. 47.) *Novello & Co.: London,* 1903. 4°.
Original Compositions, etc. No. 17.　　**g. 587. b. (11.)**

— Canzonetta. Op. 70. *See infra:* Two Compositions for Organ. [No. 2.]

— Caprice orientale for the Organ. (Op. 46.) *Novello & Co.: London,* 1903. 4°.
Original Compositions, etc. No. 16.　　**g. 587. b. (10.)**

— Carillon, for the Organ. Op. 74. *Novello & Co.: London,* 1911. 4°.
Original Compositions, etc., No. 33.　　**g. 587. c. (7.)**

— Cathedral Shadows. "Fare thee well." A reminiscence. Op. 129. (Organ.) *T. Presser Co.: Philadelphia,* 1923. 4°.
　　g. 587. d. (12.)

— Cecilia. A Series of Transcriptions for the Organ. 19 no. *Augener & Co.: London,* [1900, 02.] *obl. fol.*　　**e. 1152. a.**

— Chanson Caprice, for the Organ. Opus 150. *Forster Music Publisher: Chicago,* 1925. 4°.　　**g. 587. d. (26.)**

— Chanson d'été, for the Organ. *Novello & Co.: London,* 1902. 4°.　　**g. 587. b. (9.)**

— Chant de Bonheur. Op. 62. *See infra:* Deux Pièces d'Orgue. [No. 1.]

— Chant sans Paroles. [Organ.] 1901. *See infra:* The "Recital Series" of original Organ Compositions. No. 22.

— Chant sans paroles. Violin conductor. *Novello & Co.: London,* 1916. *s. sh.* 8°.　　**h. 3210. h. (156.)**

— Chant sans Paroles. Arranged for small orchestra by W. H. Bell. [Orchestral parts.] *Novello & Co.: London,* 1901. fol.
　　h. 1508. i. (3.)

— Chant sans Paroles ... Arrangement for Pianoforte Solo. *Novello & Co.: London,* 1909. 4°.　　**g. 543. oo. (12.)**

— Chant sans Paroles ... Arrangement for Violin and Pianoforte by E. F. R. *Novello & Co.: London,* 1901. 4°.
　　g. 223. l. (8.)

— Chant Séraphique, for the Organ. Op. 75. *Novello & Co.: London,* 1911. 4°.
Original Compositions, etc., No. 34.　　**g. 587. c. (8.)**

— Cheer up. [Song, words by] R. L. Casson. *H. W. Gray Co.: New York,* (1911.) 4°.　　**G. 383. y. (6.)**

— Christmas Bells. Op. 118. [Organ.] *H. W. Gray Co.: New York,* 1921. 4°.　　**g. 1380. l. (31.)**

— Christmas Hymns and Carols [words] by Mrs. Gaskell. pp. 14. *Weekes & Co.: London,* [1879.] 8°.　　**D. 620. k. (15.)**

— Christmas Hymns and Carols. Words by Anne Gaskell. pp. 22. *Weekes & Co.: London,* [c. 1880.] 8°.
A different work from the preceding.　　**C. 20. oo. (5.)**

— Christmas Song. Op. 82, *etc.* (Organ.) *Schott & Co.: London, etc.,* (1911.) fol.　　**h. 2710. a. (15.)**

— Church Series for Organ. (Opus 156.) I. Adoration. II. Solemn processional. III. Evening blessing. IV. Vesper-tide. V. Offertory. VI. Recessional. *Forster Music Publisher: Chicago,* 1926. 4°.　　**g. 587. d. (33.)**

— Clair de Lune. Op. 104. *See infra:* Two Compositions. [No. 1.]

— Cloches sonores.—Basso ostinato.— Symphonic Sketch. (Op. 63.) *See infra:* Deux Pièces d'Orgue. [No. 2.]

— Communion. Peace. For the Organ. (Op. 68.) *Novello & Co.: London,* 1911. 4°.
Original Compositions, etc., No. 35.　　**g. 587. c. (9.)**

LEMARE (Edwin Henry)

— Communion Service in F for solo voices, chorus, orchestra or organ. Op. 22. *R. Cocks & Co.: London*, 1895. 8°.
No. 17 of the "Burlington Series of Modern Church Music".
F. 1172. (19.)

— Two Compositions for Organ. [No. 1.] Sunset. A Song without Words. Op. 69. [No. 2.] Canzonetta. Op. 70. 2 no. *G. Schirmer: New York*, (1910.) fol. **h. 2710. a. (2.)**

— Two Compositions. [No. 1.] Clair de lune. Op. 104. [No. 2.] Morning serenade. Op. 105, *etc.* 2 no. *G. Schirmer: New York, Boston*, 1917. 4°. **g. 1380. d. (24.)**

— Concert Fantasia on the Tune "Hanover" for the organ. Op. 4. *Novello & Co.: London*, 1892. 4°. **g. 587. b. (1*.)**

— Concert Fantasia on the tune "Hanover," for the organ. *R. Cocks & Co.: London*, 1892. fol. **g. 575. b. (25.)**

— Concert Fantasia. Improvisation No. 1, upon The Sailor's Hornpipe, British Grenadiers, Rule Britannia. Op. 91, *etc.* (Organ.) *Schott & Co.: London*, (1912.) fol. **h. 2710. a. (24.)**

— Concert Gavotte. Op. 121. [Organ.] *H. W. Gray Co.: New York*, 1922. 4°. **g. 587. d. (2.)**

— Concertstück written in the form of a Polonaise. Op. 80, *etc.* (Organ.) *Schott & Co.: London, etc.*, (1911.) fol. **h. 2710. a. (13.)**

— Concertstück, No. 2. (In the South.) In the form of a Tarantella. Op. 90, *etc.* (Organ.) *Schott & Co.: London*, (1913.) fol. **h. 2710. a. (23.)**

— Consolation. Op. 79. No. 2, *etc.* (Organ.) *Schott & Co.: London, etc.*, (1911.) fol. **h. 2710. a. (12.)**

— Contemplation for the Organ. Op. 42. *Novello & Co.: London*, 1901. 4°. **g. 587. b. (6.)**

— The Dawn of Love. Song. [Words by R. L. Casson.] *T. Presser Co.: Philadelphia*, 1919. 4°. **G. 426. f. (14.)**

— Seven Descriptive Pieces for the Organ. Op. 126, *etc.* *H. W. Gray Co.: New York*, 1923. 4°. **g. 587. d. (4.)**

— Dream Frolic. Op. 115. [Organ.] *H. W. Gray Co.: New York*, 1921. 4°. **g. 587. d. (3.)**

— Easter Morn. [Organ.] *H. W. Gray Co.: New York*, 1921. 4°. **g. 587. d. (1.)**

— Elegy for the organ. *R. Cocks & Co.: London*, 1895. *obl.* fol. **e. 1093. (5.)**

— The Encore Series of Organ Transcriptions by E. H. Lemare, *etc.* *H. W. Gray Co.: New York*, 1920, *etc.* 4°. **g. 587. d. (11.)**

— Evening Pastorale. "The Curfew." Op. 128. (Organ.) *T. Presser Co.: Philadelphia*, 1923. 4°. **g. 587. d. (13.)**

— Evening Service. *See* infra: [Magnificat and Nunc dimittis.]

— Eventide. Vesper Hymn. *H. W. Gray Co.: New York*, 1907. 8°. **F. 538. d. (23.)**

— Fairest of all. Song, words by R. Howitt. 2 no. [In C and D.] *R. Cocks & Co.: London*, 1892. fol. **H. 1797. o. (35.)**

— Faith in His Love. [Anthem.] Words by E. H. L. Opus 161. *A. P. Schmidt Co.: Boston, New York*, 1927. 8°. **E. 335. d. (20.)**

— Famous Melodies old and new, transcribed for the organ by E. H. Lemare. 12 no. *T. Presser Co.: Philadelphia*, 1923. 4°. **g. 587. d. (14.)**

— Fantasia and Fugue. Op. 99. (Organ.) *Schott & Co.: London*, 1920. fol. **h. 2710. b. (10.)**

LEMARE (Edwin Henry)

— Fantaisie Dorienne—en forme de variations—for organ. (Op. 101.) *E. Ashdown: London, etc.*, 1915. fol. **h. 2710. b. (5.)**

— Fantaisie Fugue for the Organ. (Op. 48.) *Novello & Co.: London*, 1903. 4°.
Original Compositions, etc. No. 18. **g. 587. b. (12.)**

Festival Service in F

— Festival Service in F. Benedictus. *R. Cocks & Co.: London*, 1893. 8°.
No. 4 c of the "Burlington Series of Modern Church Music". **F. 1172. (5.)**

— Benedictus ... in the key of F. [1899.] *See* NOVELLO AND CO. Novello's Parish Choir Book. No. 432. [1866, *etc.*] 8°. **E. 618.**

— Festival Service in F. Magnificat. *R. Cocks & Co.: London*, 1893. 8°.
No. 4e of the "Burlington Series of Modern Church Music". **F. 1172. (6.)**

— Magnificat and Nunc dimittis ... in F. [1899.] *See* NOVELLO AND CO. Novello's Parish Choir Book. No. 433. [1866, *etc.*] 8°. **E. 618.**

— Festival Service in F. Te Deum. *R. Cocks & Co.: London*, 1893. 8°.
No. 4a of the "Burlington Series of Modern Church Music". **F. 1172. (4.)**

— Te Deum laudamus ... in ... F. [1899.] *See* NOVELLO AND CO. Novello's Parish Choir Book. No. 447. [1866, *etc.*] 8°. **E. 618.**

— Festival-Suite. Op. 100. (Organ.) *Schott & Co.: London*, 1920. fol. **h. 2710. b. (11.)**

— Final Amen, for men's voices. [1899.] *See* NOVELLO AND CO. Novello's Services, Anthems, *etc.* No. 46. [1899, *etc.*] 8°. **F. 280. g.**

— Folk Song. Opus 113. (Organ.) *H. W. Gray Co.: New York*, 1921. 4°. **g. 587. d. (10.)**

— Freedom's Day. Song, words by F. L. Myrtle. *T. Presser Co.: Philadelphia*, 1919. 4°. **G. 426. f. (15.)**

— From the West. Symphonic Poem for the Organ. Op. 60. I. In Missouri. II. In North Dakota, *etc.* *G. Schirmer: New York*, (1909.) fol. **h. 2710. a. (1.)**

— Gavotte à la Cour. Op. 84, *etc.* (Organ.) *Schott & Co.: London, etc.*, (1911.) fol. **h. 2710. a. (18.)**

— Gavotte moderne for the piano. *R. Cocks & Co.: London*, 1892. fol. **h. 1489. s. (39.)**

— Gavotte moderne for the organ. *R. Cocks & Co.: London*, 1893. *obl.* fol. **e. 1093. (4.)**

— Grand Cortège—Finale—for the Organ, *etc.* (Op. 67.) *Novello & Co.: London*, 1910. 4°.
Original Compositions, etc. No. 30. **g. 587. c. (4.)**

— Heyday. Song, the words by M. L. Campbell. 3 no. [In C, D and E.] *R. Cocks & Co.: London*, [1883.] fol. **H. 1788. v. (31.)**

— Humoresque, for the Organ. Opus 151. *Forster Music Publisher: Chicago*, 1925. 4°. **g. 587. d. (27.)**

— A Hymn on the Jubilee of Her Most Gracious Majesty the Queen. 1887. Words by Mrs S. Roberts, jun. [Sheffield, 1887.] *In:* COLLECTION. [A collection of hymnal broadsheets, *etc.* vol. 4. p. 97.] [1794–1917.] 8°. **3442. c. 18.**

LEMARE (Edwin Henry)

— I will lift up mine Eyes, *etc.* [Sacred song.] *O. Ditson Co.: Boston*, (1910.) fol. **H. 1187. rr. (9.)**

— Idyll in E flat for the organ. *R. Cocks & Co.: London*, 1894. fol. **e. 1093. (3.)**

— Impromptu in A, for the Organ. *Novello & Co.: London*, 1906. 4°. *Original Compositions, etc., No.* 20. **g. 587. b. (14.)**

— In the South. *See* supra: Concertstück, No. 2.

— Inspiration, for violin and pianoforte. *H. W. Gray Co.: New York*, 1921. 4°. **g. 500. h. (4.)**

— Inspiration. Transcribed for the organ by the Composer. *H. W. Gray Co.: New York*, 1921. 4°. **g. 587. d. (5.)**

— Intermezzo in B flat for the Organ. (Op. 39.) *Novello & Co.: London*, 1900. 4°. **g. 587. b. (2.)**

— Intermezzo. Moonlight, *etc.* (Op. 83. [No. 2.] Transcribed for the Organ by the Composer.) *Schott & Co.: London, etc.*, (1911.) fol. **h. 2710. a. (17.)**

— Intermezzo pour Piano. (Moonlight.) Op. 83. No. 2. Transcription par M. Laistner. *Schott & Co.: London, etc.*, (1911.) fol. **h. 2710. b. (3.)**

— Intermezzo. Moonlight ... Violin & Piano. (Arr. by A. Kaiser.) *Schott & Co.: London, etc.*, (1911.) fol. **h. 2710. b. (1.)**

— Six Kyries. *R. Cocks & Co.: London*, 1894. 8°. *No.* 9 *of the "Burlington Series of Modern Church Music".* **F. 1172. (11.)**

— Six Kyries. [1899.] *See* NOVELLO AND CO. Novello's Parish Choir Book. No. 453. [1866, *etc.*] 8°. **E. 618.**

— Second Set of Kyries and Final Amen for men's voices. *R. Cocks & Co.: London*, 1895. 8°. *No.* 16 *of the "Burlington Series of Modern Church Music".* **F. 1172. (18.)**

— Five Kyries. [1899.] *See* NOVELLO AND CO. Novello's Parish Choir Book. No. 454. [1866, *etc.*] 8°. **E. 618.**

— The Lament. Op. 79. No. 1, *etc.* (Organ.) *Schott & Co.: London, etc.*, (1911.) fol. **h. 2710. a. (11.)**

— Liebestraum, for the Organ.—Op. 55. *Novello & Co.: London*, 1908. 4°. *Original Compositions, etc., No.* 25. **g. 587. b. (19.)**

— Life's short Tale. Song, the words by R. L. Casson. *Boosey & Co.: London and New York*, 1908. fol. **H. 1794. vv. (38.)**

— The Lord is my shepherd. Anthem. *London*, [1881.] 8°. **E. 442. d. (25.)**

— Love divine. Anthem for mixed voices. [Words by] C. Wesley. *O. Ditson Co.: Boston*, (1910.) 8°. **F. 281. u. (25.)**

— Lullaby. Op. 81, *etc.* (Organ.) *Schott & Co.: London, etc.*, (1911.) fol. **h. 2710. a. (14.)**

— Madrigal for the Organ. *Novello & Co.: London*, 1904. 4°. *Original Compositions, etc. No.* 19. **g. 587. b. (13.)**

— [Magnificat and Nunc dimittis.] Evening Service in A major. *R. Cocks & Co.: London*, 1897. 8°. **F. 1171. w. (24.)**

— Magnificat and Nunc dimittis ... in the Key of A. [1899.] *See* NOVELLO AND CO. Novello's Parish Choir Book. No. 434. [1866, *etc.*] 8°. **E. 618.**

— Magnificat and Nunc dimittis ... in ... B flat ... —Op. 40.— 1900. *See* NOVELLO AND CO. Novello's Parish Choir Book, *etc.* No. 525. [1866, *etc.*] 8°. **E. 618.**

LEMARE (Edwin Henry)

— Magnificat and Nunc dimittis ... in ... E. Op. 36. 1900. *See* NOVELLO AND CO. Novello's Parish Choir Book. No. 489. [1866, *etc.*] 8°. **E. 618.**

— Evening Service. Magnificat and Nunc Dimittis ... in ... F. *C. Vincent: London*, [1898.] 8°. **F. 1171. w. (28.)**

— Magnificat and Nunc dimittis ... in ... F. 1900. *See* NOVELLO AND CO. Novello's Parish Choir Book. No. 490. [1866, *etc.*] 8°. **E. 618.**

— Marche Héroïque. Op. 74. *See* infra: The "Recital Series" of original Organ compositions, *etc.* No. 39.

— Marche moderne ... for the organ. *Weekes & Co.: London*, [1885.] fol. **h. 2732. i. (47.)**

— Marche solennelle. [Organ.] 1896. *See* infra: The "Recital Series" of original Organ compositions. No. 12.

— May-time, for the Organ. Opus 153. *Forster Music Publisher: Chicago*, 1925. 4°. **g. 587. d. (28.)**

— Meditation in D flat for the Organ. Op. 38. *Novello & Co.: London*, 1900. 4°. **g. 587. b. (4.)**

— Melodic Sketches for the Organ. Opus 140, *etc.* *Sam Fox Pub. Co.: Cleveland and New York*, 1925. obl. 4°. **e. 1093. n. (8.)**

— Minuet nuptiale for the organ. Op. 103. *Novello & Co.: London*, 1915. 4°. *Original Compositions, etc. No.* 36. **g. 587. c. (10.)**

— Minuet nuptiale. Op. 103. [Orchestral parts.] *Novello & Co.: London*, 1916. fol. **h. 3210. h. (157.)**

— Moonlight and Roses. *See* supra: [Andantino in D flat.]

— Morning-Day. Op. 94, *etc.* (Organ.) *Schott & Co.: London*, 1912. fol. **h. 2710. a. (25.)**

— Morning Serenade. Op. 105. *See* supra: Two Compositions. [No. 2.]

— My God, I thank thee. Anthem for Weddings or General Use. The Words ... by A. A. Procter. 1899. *See* NOVELLO AND CO. Novello's Collection of Anthems. No. 617. [1876, *etc.*] 8°. **E. 618. a.**

— Nocturne. *See* supra: [Andantino in D flat.]

— Nocturne in B minor for the Organ. Op. 41. *Novello & Co.: London*, 1901. 4°. **g. 587. b. (5.)**

— Nocturne, "Vox séraphique," for the Organ. Opus 154. *Forster Music Publisher: Chicago*, 1925. 4°. **g. 587. d. (29.)**

— O Lord, Thy Word endureth, *etc.* [Anthem.] *A. P. Schmidt Co.: Boston, New York*, 1926. 8°. **E. 335. c. (24.)**

— October Serenade. "Greetings to Portland, Me." Opus 120. [Organ.] *H. W. Gray Co.: New York*, 1922. 4°. **g. 587. d. (6.)**

— Oft in the stilly Night. [Part-song for T. T. B. B.] Words by T. Moore. *H. W. Gray Co.: New York*, 1923. 8°. **F. 163. u. (44.)**

— Overture in F minor. "The Schenley." Op. 49. [Organ.] *Novello & Co.: London*, 1908. 4°. *Original Compositions, etc., No.* 23. **g. 587. b. (17.)**

— Pastoral Poem, for the Organ.—Op. 54. *Novello & Co.: London*, 1908. 4°. *Original Compositions, etc., No.* 24. **g. 587. b. (18.)**

— Pastorale in E for the organ. *R. Cocks & Co.: London*, 1892. obl. fol. **e. 174. x. (9.)**

— Pastorale in E ... Pianoforte Transcription by A. Hollier. *Novello & Co.: London*, 1903. 4°. **g. 603. o. (5.)**

LEMARE (Edwin Henry)

— Pastorale No. 2, in C. [Organ.] *R. Cocks & Co.: London,*
1897. obl. fol.   **e. 1093. b. (4.)**

— Pater Noster ... for the Celebration of the Holy Communion,
etc. R. Cocks & Co.: London, 1892. 8°.
No. 6 of the "Burlington Series of Modern Church Music".
                                                    F. 1172. (8.)

— Pater noster [in E flat], *etc.* 1892. *See* Novello and Co.
Novello's Parish Choir Book, *etc.* No. 548. [1866, *etc.*] 8°.
                                                    E. 618.

— Pater Noster and Final Amen. *R. Cocks & Co.: London,*
1894. 8°.
No. 12 of the "Burlington Series of Modern Church Music".
                                                    F. 1172. (14.)

— Pater noster. No. 2 & Final Amen in G♭. [1899.] *See* Novello
and Co. Novello's Parish Choir Book. No. 435. [1866, *etc.*] 8°.
                                                    E. 618.

— Pater Noster No. 3. *R. Cocks & Co.: London,* 1897. 8°.
                                                    F. 1171. w. (25.)

— Pater noster [in G]. No. 3. 1897. *See* Novello and Co.
Novello's Parish Choir Book, *etc.* No. 547. [1866, *etc.*] 8°.
                                                    E. 618.

— Six Picture Scenes for the Organ. Opus 134, *etc. White-Smith*
Music Publishing Co.: Boston, etc., 1924. 4°.   **g. 587. d. (15.)**

— Deux Pièces d'Orgue. [No. 1.] Chant de Bonheur. (Op. 62.)
[No. 2.] Cloches sonores.—Basso ostinato.—Symphonic
Sketch. (Op. 63.) 2 no. *G. Schirmer: New York,* (1909.) fol.
                                                    h. 2710. a. (3.)

— The Quest, for the Organ. Op. 71. *Novello & Co.: London,*
1911. 4°.
Original Compositions, etc., No. 31.   **g. 587. c. (5.)**

— The Recital Series of original Compositions for the Organ.
See infra: The "Recital Series" of original Organ
compositions.

— The "Recital Series" of original Organ compositions. (The
Recital Series of original Compositions for the Organ.)
Collected and edited by E. H. Lemare. *R. Cocks & Co.*
[*Novello & Co.*]: *London,* 1893, *etc.* obl. fol. & 4°.   **e. 1152.**
                                                    & g. 587. a.

— The Recital Series of Transcriptions for the Organ. *Novello*
& Co.: London, 1899, *etc.* 4°.   **g. 587.**

— Rêverie for the organ. (Op. 20.) *R. Cocks & Co.: London,*
1875. obl. fol.   **e. 1093. (2.)**

— Rhapsody in C minor, for the Organ. *Novello & Co.:*
London, 1902. 4°.   **g. 587. b. (8.)**

— Romance in D♭. *See* supra: The "Recital Series" of original
Organ compositions. No. 4.

— Second Romance in D flat. Opus 112. [Organ.] *H. W. Gray*
Co.: New York, 1920. 4°.   **g. 587. d. (7.)**

— Romance triste. Marche funèbre. Opus 119. [Organ.]
H. W. Gray Co.: New York, 1922. 4°.   **g. 587. d. (8.)**

— Rondo capriccio—A Study in Accents—for the Organ.—
Op. 64—, *etc. Novello & Co.: London,* 1910. 4°. *Original*
Compositions, etc. No. 29.   **g. 587. c. (3.)**

— Rustic Scene, for the Organ. Op. 72. *Novello & Co.: London,*
1911. 4°.
Original Compositions, etc., No. 32.   **g. 587. c. (6.)**

— Salut d'Amour. Op. 127. (Organ.) *T. Presser Co.:*
Philadelphia, 1923. 4°.   **g. 587. d. (16.)**

LEMARE (Edwin Henry)

— Scherzo Fugue ... Op. 102. 1915. *See* supra: The Recital
Series of ... Compositions for the Organ, *etc.* No. 47. 1893,
etc. 4°.   **g. 587. a.**

— The Search.—A Melody.—Op. 92. (Organ.) *Schott & Co.:*
London, 1915. fol.   **h. 2710. b. (6.)**

— Twelve Short Improvisations for the organ. (Op. 124.) 2 bk.
H. W. Gray Co.: New York, 1922. 4°.   **g. 587. d. (9.)**

— Lemares Five Sketches for Organ, *etc.* (Op. 153.) *Forster*
Music Publisher: Chicago, 1925. 4°.   **g. 587. d. (30.)**

— Slumber Song for the Organ. (Opus 139.) *Sam Fox Pub. Co.:*
Cleveland and New York, 1925. obl. 4°.   **e. 1093. n. (9.)**

— Sonata No. 1 in F, for the organ. Op. 95. *Schott & Co.:*
London, 1914. fol.   **h. 2710. b. (7.)**

— A Song of Songs. A short Cantata from "The Song of
Solomon" and Psalm CXXI., for solo voices, chorus and
orchestra.—Opus 51. *Boosey & Co.: London and New York,*
1906. 8°.   **F. 1274. jj. (2.)**

— Soutenir—A Study on one note—for the Organ.—Op. 58, *etc.*
Novello & Co.: London, 1909. 4°.*
Original Compositions, etc. No. 27.   **g. 587. c. (1.)**

— Souvenir joyeux. Op. 87, *etc.* (Organ.) *Schott & Co.: London,*
etc., (1911.) fol.   **h. 2710. a. (21.)**

— Spanish Serenade, for the Organ. Opus 149. *Forster Music*
Publisher: Chicago, 1925. 4°.   **g. 587. d. (31.)**

— The Spirit of the Lord ... Motet for Chorus of mixed voices
with Baritone Solo and Organ accompaniment. Op. 53.
G. Schirmer: New York, (1908.) 8°.   **F. 1269. b. (4.)**

— Spring Song—"From the South"—for the Organ.—Op. 56.
Novello & Co.: London, 1908. 4°.*
Original Compositions, etc., No. 26.   **g. 587. b. (20.)**

— Summer Sketches. Op. 73. *See* supra: The "Recital Series" of
original Organ compositions, *etc.* No. 40.

— Sun of my Soul. [Anthem.] *A. P. Schmidt Co.: Boston, New*
York, 1924. 8°.   **F. 281. zz. (29.)**

— Sunset. A Song without Words. Op. 69. *See* supra: Two
Compositions for Organ. [No. 1.]

— Sunshine, *etc.* (Melody. Organ.) Op. 83. [No. 1.] *Schott &*
Co.: London, etc., (1911.) fol.   **h. 2710. a. (16.)**

— Symphony in G minor for the organ. Op. 35. *Novello & Co.:*
London, 1899. 4°.   **g. 575. e. (2.)**

— Symphony in D minor, for the Organ.—Op. 50. *Novello &*
Co.: London, 1906. 4°.*
Original Compositions, etc., No. 21.   **g. 587. b. (15.)**

— Te Deum & Jubilate in A. *Weekes & Co.: London,* [1889.] 4°.
                                                    F. 334. (25.)

— Te Deum laudamus, set to music in the key of C. *London,*
[1880.] 8°.   **F. 1170. a. (24.)**

— Te Deum in E♭. Op. 27. *R. Cocks & Co.: London,* 1897. 8°.
                                                    F. 1171. w. (26.)

— Te Deum laudamus. Composed for the ... Thanksgiving
Service of the House of Commons ... June 20, 1897 ...
Op. 27. [1899.] *See* Novello and Co. Novello's Parish Choir
Book. No. 449. [1866, *etc.*] 8°.   **E. 618.**

— "Tears" and "Smiles". Opus 133. (Organ.) *J. Fischer & Bro.:*
New York, Birmingham, 1924. obl. 4°.   **e. 1093. o. (30.)**

— Thankfulness. Hymn. Words by A. A. Procter. *R. Cocks &*
Co.: London, 1898. 8°.   **F. 1171. x. (28.)**

LEMARE (EDWIN HENRY)

— Thanksgiving March ... for the organ. *T. Presser Co.: Philadelphia*, 1919. 4°.   **g. 1380. c. (30.)**

— This is the Day. Anthem for Easter. 1899. *See* NOVELLO AND Co. Novello's Collection of Anthems, *etc.* No. 621. [1876, *etc.*] 8°.   **E. 618. a.**

— This is the Day. Anthem, *etc.* 1899. *See* NOVELLO AND Co. Novello's Tonic Sol-fa Series. No. 1085. [1876, *etc.*] 4°.   **B. 885.**

— Threefold Amen. [In G.] 1894. *See* NOVELLO AND Co. Novello's Parish Choir Book. No. 574. [1866, *etc.*] 8°.   **E. 618.**

— 'Tis the Spring of Souls today. Cantata for Easter ... for Soli, Chorus, Orchestra, and Organ. Op. 30. *Novello and Co.: London*, 1898. 8°.   **E. 541. j. (6.)**

— 'Tis the Spring of Souls today. Anthem. Op. 30. *R. Cocks & Co.: London*, 1898. 8°.   **F. 1171. w. (27.)**

— Toccata and Fugue. Op. 98 ... Organ. *Schott & Co.: London*, 1915. fol.   **h. 2710. b. (8.)**

— [Another edition.] Toccata and Fugue. Op. 98. [Organ.] *Schott & Co.: London*, 1920. fol.   **h. 2710. b. (12.)**

— Toccata di Concerto.—Op. 59.— *See* infra: The "Recital Series" of original Organ Compositions. No. 35.

— Transcriptions for the Organ. *Schott & Co.: London*, 1899–1914. fol.
No. 6 (published by R. Cocks & Co., oblong folio) is catalogued separately; no. 33. was not published.   **h. 2710.**

— 5 Transcriptions [for the Organ. No. 1]. Gurlitt, Andantino. [No. 2.] Goltermann, Berceuse. [No. 3.] Moszkowski, Russia. [No. 4.] Nicodé, Chanson d'Amour & [No. 5.] La Pénitence. [1909.] *See* CECILIA. Cecilia. Series II., *etc.* bk I. [1909–10.] *obl.* fol.   **e. 1106. a.**

— 3 Transcriptions [for the Organ. No. 1]. Nicodé, Canzonetta. [No. 2.] Moszkowski, Menuet ... [No. 3.] Strelezki, Notturno in A. [1909.] *See* CECILIA. Cecilia. Series II., *etc.* bk. IV. [1909–10.] *obl.* fol.   **e. 1106. a.**

— Transcriptions for the Organ, *etc. Laudy & Co.: London*, 1912, *etc.* fol.   **h. 2710. a. (26.)**

— Traumlied, for the Organ.—Op. 61—, *etc. Novello & Co.: London*, 1909. 4°.
Original Compositions, etc. No. 28.   **g. 587. c. (2.)**

— Twilight Sketches for Organ. Op. 138, *etc. A. P. Schmidt Co.: Boston, New York*, 1925. 4°.   **g. 587. d. (17.)**

— Twilight Sketches. Organ ... Op. 138. *W. Paxton & Co.: London*, 1927. 4°.   **g. 575. hh. (9.)**

— Unda Maris, for the Organ. Opus 144. *Forster Music Publisher: Chicago*, 1925. 4°.   **g. 587. d. (32.)**

— Valse Andantino. *See* supra: [Andantino in D flat.]

— Variations sérieuses. Op. 96. (Organ.) *Schott & Co.: London*, 1920. fol.   **h. 2710. b. (13.)**

— Vesper Chimes. Opus 157. (Organ.) *Forster Music Publisher: Chicago*, 1926. 4°.   **g. 587. d. (34.)**

— Victory March. Opus 109. (Organ.) *H. W. Gray Co.: New York*, 1919. 4°.
No. 131 of the "St. Cecilia Series," etc.   **g. 1380. e. (40.)**

— Voices are calling. Song, the words by R. L. Casson. *Boosey & Co.: London and New York*, 1909. fol.   **H. 1794. vv. (39.)**

— The Waif. Song, words by M. L. Campbell. 2 no. [In C and G.] *R. Cocks & Co.: London*, [1884.] fol.   **H. 1788. v. (32.)**

LEMARE (EDWIN HENRY)

— What sudden Blaze of Song. [Anthem, words by] Dr. J. Keble. Op. 141. *A. P. Schmidt Co.: Boston, New York*, 1924. 8°.   **F. 281. zz. (30.)**

— Woodland Reverie. Andantino in C, for organ. Op. 135. *A. P. Schmidt Co.: Boston, New York*, 1924. 4°.   **g. 587. d. (18.)**

— Woodland Reverie. Organ. (Op. 135.) *W. Paxton & Co.: London*, 1927. 4°.   **g. 575. hh. (10.)**

— Your lovely Eyes. Song for a medium voice, words by R. L. Casson. *O. Ditson Co.: Boston*, (1910.) fol.   **H. 1792. s. (8.)**

— *See* BACH (J. S.) [*Collected Works.—f.*] Selected Organ Works. Edited by E. H. Lemare. 1911. fol.   **h. 3007. d. (15.)**

— *See* BOCCHERINI (L.) [*Quintet. Op. 13. No. 5.*] Minuet ... Transcribed by E. H. Lemare. (1909.) fol.   **h. 2710. a. (4.)**

— *See* BRAHMS (J.) Tragische Ouverture ... Op. 81. Transcribed [for the organ] ... by E. H. Lemare. 1912. 4°.   **g. 575. w. (4.)**

— *See* CAPUA (E. di) O sole mio ... Transcribed for the organ by E. H. Lemare. 1924. 4°.   **g. 1380. k. (4.)**

— *See* CAREY (Henry) [*Doubtful and Supposititous Works.*] Sally in our Alley ... Transcribed by E. H. Lemare. 1946. 4°.   **g. 1380. v. (8.)**

— *See* CHAIKOVSKY (P. I.) [*Collected Works.—c.*] Organ Album, *etc.* [Arranged by ... E. H. Lemare, *etc.*] 1910. 4°.   **g. 575. o. (4.)**

— *See* CHAIKOVSKY (P. I.) Roméo et Juliette. Ouverture-Fantaisie ... Transcribed ... by E. H. Lemare. (1909.) fol.   **h. 2710. a. (9.)**

— *See* CHOPIN (F. F.) Nocturne. Op. 9. No. 2, arranged ... by E. H. Lemare. [1894.] *obl.* fol.   **e. 1093. (7.)**

— *See* COLBY (F. H.) Old Dance ... Edited by E. H. Lemare. 1919. 4°.   **g. 1380. c. (9.)**

— *See* ELGAR (*Sir* E. W.) *Bart.* Idylle ... Arranged by E. H. Lemare. (1910.) fol.   **h. 3930. g. (14.)**

— *See* ELGAR (*Sir* E. W.) *Bart.* Pomp and Circumstance ... —Op. 39.—No. 1 in D ... Arranged as an Organ Solo by E. H. Lemare. 1902. fol.   **h. 3930. c. (8.)**

— *See* EYTON (Robert) and LEMARE (E. H.) Chants as used in Holy Trinity Church, Chelsea. Arranged by ... R. Eyton ... and E. H. Lemare. [1894?] 4°.   **E. 556. hh.**

— *See* GOUNOD (C. F.) [*Faust.—Selections, instrumental.*] Faust ... Transcribed ... for the organ by E. H. Lemare. 1921. 4°.   **g. 1380. g. (18.)**

— *See* GRIEG (E. H.) [*Lyrische Stücke. Op. 43. No. 6.*] An den Frühling ... Transcr. ... by E. H. Lemare. (1909.) fol.   **h. 2710. a. (5.)**

— *See* GRIEG (E. H.) Peer Gynt Suite I. (Op. 46.)—Movements I–III ... Transcribed ... by E. H. Lemare. (1909.) fol.   **h. 2710. a. (6.)**

— *See* GRIEG (E. H.) [*Sörgemarsch over Rikard Nordraak.*] Funeral March ... Arranged ... by E. H. Lemare. 1893. *obl.* fol.   **e. 1093. (8.)**

— *See* GUILMANT (F. A.) Selected Popular Compositions ... Nouvelle édition revue par ... E. H. Lemare. [1914, *etc.*] fol.   **h. 2697. j.**

— *See* HAENDEL (G. F.) [*Serse.—Ombra mai fù.*] Largo ... Transcribed ... by E. H. Lemare. (1909.) fol.   **h. 2710. a. (7.)**

— *See* JOHNSON (B.) Pavane in A ... Arrangement for Pianoforte Solo by E. H. Lemare. (1912.) 4°.   **g. 232. t. (8.)**

LEMARE (Edwin Henry)

—— *See* KELLIE (L.) The City of Night ... Song arranged for the organ by E. H. Lemare. 1892. *obl.* fol.   **e. 174. x. (7.)**

—— *See* KELLIE (L.) Crossing the Bar. Anthem ... Arranged ... by E. H. Lemare. 1893. 8°.   **F. 1172. (7.)**

—— *See* LEMARE (C.) Dream Song ... Transcribed for the organ by E. H. Lemare. 1921. 4°.   **g. 1380. h. (4.)**

—— *See* MASCHERONI (A.) Ave Maria ... Arranged ... by E. H. Lemare. 1893. *obl.* fol.   **e. 1093. (9.)**

—— *See* MENDELSSOHN-BARTHOLDY (J. L. F.) [*Collected Works.—k.*] Compositions for the Organ ... Edited by E. H. Lemare. 1910. 4°.   **g. 575. r. (2.)**

—— *See* RAMEAU (J. P.) [Le Temple de la Gloire.] Gavotte ... Transcribed ... by E. H. Lemare. (1909.) fol.   **h. 2710. a. (8.)**

—— *See* READING (J.) Adeste fideles ... Transcribed for the organ by E. H. Lemare. 1923. 4°.   **g. 587. d. (19.)**

—— *See* RHEINBERGER (J. G.) Pastoral Sonata ⟨Op. 88⟩ ... For the organ. Revised and edited by E. H. Lemare. [1951.] 4°.   **g. 1230. b. (4.)**

—— *See* RHEINBERGER (J. G.) Sonata in A minor. For the organ, *etc.* ⟨Op. 98. Revised and edited by E. H. Lemare.⟩ [1951.] 4°.   **g. 1230. b. (3.)**

—— *See* RHEINBERGER (J. G.) Sonata No. 12 ... Op. 154. Revised and edited for the modern organ by E. H. Lemare. [1950.] 4°.   **g. 1230. b. (2.)**

—— *See* SABIN (W. A.) Bouree in D ... Edited by E. H. Lemare. 1919. 4°.   **g. 1380. c. (47.)**

—— *See* SCHUBERT (F. P.) [Schwanengesang.] Schubert's Sérénade arranged ... by E. H. Lemare. [1895.] *obl.* fol.   **e. 1093. (10.)**

—— *See* SMART (H.) [Organ Book.] Twelve Pieces for the Organ ... Edited ... by E. H. Lemare. 1912. 4°.   **g. 575. u. (8.)**

—— *See* SULLIVAN (*Sir* A. S.) [Cox and Box.—Hush'd is the Bacon.] Lullaby ... Arranged for the Organ by E. H. Lemare. 1912. fol.   **h. 2731. u. (29.)**

—— *See* SUPPÉ (F. von) [Dichter und Bauer.] Poet and Peasant. Overture ... Transcribed (for the organ) by E. H. Lemare. 1924. 4°.   **g. 587. d. (20.)**

—— *See* WAGNER (W. R.) [*Collected Works.—d.*] Album for the Organ, *etc.* [Containing arrangements by E. H. Lemare.] [1906.] fol.   **h. 356. m. (17.)**

—— *See* WAGNER (W. R.) [Tristan und Isolde.] Vorspiel und Isoldens Liebestod ... Transcribed ... by E. H. Lemare. (1909.) fol.   **h. 2710. a. (10.)**

LEMARE (Frederick)

—— Chanting, a companion to the Prayer Book, *etc. Godalming,* [1850?] 24°.   **3476. a. 1.**

—— Home; rondo for the Piano Forte. *London,* [1834.] fol.   **h. 117. (17.)**

—— Home, rondo for the Pianoforte. [*London,* 1845?] fol.   **g. 272. w. (14.)**

—— The Last Day. A descriptive hymn [begins: "Mourn, mourn"]. *London,* [1835?] fol.   **H. 2832. n. (4.)**

—— A mother's grief, [a song, begins: "To mark the sufferings,"] the words by the Rev^d. Mr. Dale. *London,* [1826.] fol.   **H. 1675. (22.)**

—— Select Harmony of psalm & hymn tunes and cathedral chants, arranged ... by F. Lemare. *Guildford,* [1845.] 8°.   **B. 659.**

LEMARE (Frederick)

—— Souvenir divertimento for the Piano Forte. *London,* [1834.] fol.   **h. 117. (18.)**

LEMARE (William)

—— The Lay of Albert Graeme. Song, words by Sir W. Scott. *C. Herzog & Co.: London,* [1883.] fol.   **H. 1788. v. (33.)**

—— Magnificat and Nunc Dimittis set to music in the key of F. *London,* [1883.] 8°.   **E. 597. e. (16.)**

LEMARIÉ (A.)

—— Esmeralda, polka-mazurka pour Piano. *London,* [1868.] fol.   **h. 1485. s. (43.)**

—— Phoebus polka-mazurka. [P. F.] *London,* [1868.] fol.   **h. 1485. s. (44.)**

—— *See* GUHR (C. W. F.) [Ueber Paganini's Kunst die Violine zu spielen.] L'Art de jouer du violon de Paganini ... Édition augmentée de 12 études ... par A. Lemarié. [c. 1860.] fol.   **h. 1597.**

LE MARREC (J.)

—— Cantiques bretons du diocèse de Quimper et de Léon. Livre d'accompagnements. [Organ.] pp. 91. *En dépôt aux librairies Guivarc'h, etc.: Quimper,* [1942.] 4°. *With a list of corrigenda.*   **E. 1717. u. (8.)**

LE MASSENA (Clarence E.)

—— How beautiful are the Days of Spring. Song for a high voice with Piano accompaniment, words by L. W. Allen. *G. Schirmer: New York,* (1911.) fol.   **H. 1792. s. (9.)**

—— Pandora. An Operetta in three acts ... founded on Hawthorne's story "The Paradise of Children". *T. Presser Co.: Philadelphia,* 1915. 8°.   **F. 943. c. (3.)**

LEMB (Renate)

—— Reime, Reigen, Lieder für die Kleine. 36 alte Kinderreime, fröhliche Tanz- und Spiellieder und religiöse Lieder für Kindergarten und Familie. Melodieausgabe mit Gitarre bezifferung, *etc.* pp. 53. *B. Schott's Söhne: Mainz,* [1970.] 8°.   **C. 374. i. (5.)**

LEMBA (Artur)

—— Kaksteistkümmend karakterpala klaverile. pp. 27. *RK "Ilukirjandus ja kunst": Tallinn,* 1947. fol.   **h. 140. tt. (1.)**

—— Oktett vaskpillidele ja klaverile. ⟨Октет для двух труб, двух валторн, трех тромбонов и фортепиано.⟩ Partituur [and parts]. 8 pt. *Eesti riiklik Kirjastus: Tallinn,* 1960. 4°.   **g. 897. b. (4.)**

LEMBCKE (G. A.)

—— Udvalgte Sange med Piano. 1901. *See* COPENHAGEN.— *Samfundet til Udgivelse af dansk Musik.* Bilag 1901. 1872, *etc.* fol.   **G. 728.**

LEMBLIN (Laurentius)

—— *See* LEMLIN (Lorenz)

LEMCKE (Heinrich)

—— Aux élèves assidus. *See infra:* [Rondos. Op. 16.]

—— The death warning, and the broken ring; two songs, the poetry imitated from the German by T. Oliphant. *London,* [1841.] fol.   **H. 1691. (6.)**

LEMCKE (Heinrich)

— Kinderlieder mit Begleitung des Pianoforte ... Op. 11.
2 Lieferungen. *N. Simrock: Bonn*, [1850?] *obl. fol.*
F. 607. y. (10.)

— Ein- und zweistimmige Kinderlieder mit Pianoforte
Begleitung. Op. 19. 3tes. Heft der Kinderlieder. *N. Simrock:
Bonn*, [1855?] *obl. fol.*
F. 607. y. (11.)

— Deux morceaux élégants pour le Forte Piano. *London*,
[1840.] fol.
h. 700. (40.)

— Deux notturnes pour le Piano Forte. Op. 14. *London*, [1841.]
fol.
h. 700. (41.)

— Rondeau brillant pour le Forte Piano. Op. 15. *London*,
[1841.] fol.
h. 700. (42.)

— Deux rondeaux pour le Forte Piano. Op. 16. *London*, [1841.]
fol.
h. 700. (43.)

— [Rondos. Op. 16.] Aux élèves assidus. Deux petits rondeaux,
doigtés pour le forte piano, par H. Lemke ... Op. 16. ⟨N° 2.⟩
R. Cocks & C⁰: London, [1841.] fol.
Imperfect; wanting no. 1.
h. 3865. pp. (24.)

— Variations brillantes sur une marche de Bellini, I Puritani
pour le Forte Piano. Op. 20. *London*, [1841.] fol.
h. 700. (44.)

LEMENU DE SAINT PHILBERT (Christophe)

— Premier Livre de Cantatilles. Six Cantatilles en Simphonie.
Engraved by Labassée.] *Chez L'Auteur, etc.: Paris*, [1742?]
fol.
*Each Cantatille has a separate titlepage (Ariane, La Viele,
Hypomène et Atalante, L'Impatience, L'Étincelle, L'Himen),
but the pagination is continuous. There is no general titlepage,
but the volume is advertised in the composer's Motets as
'Premier Livre de Cantatilles'.*
H. 1034. (2.)

— Motets sur les principales fêtes de l'Année. À une et deux
Voix, avec et sans Simphonie ... Gravés par Labassée.
Seconde Édition augmentée. *Chés l'Auteur: Paris*, [1740?]
fol.
H. 1034. (1.)

— Principes de Musique, courts et faciles. *Chez l'Auteur: Paris*,
[1740?] *obl. fol.*
D. 644.

— II^[e] recueil d'airs, serieux et à boire, melé de vaudeville, ronde
de table, duo, recit de basse ... Gravé par Labassée. pp. 28.
Chez l'auteur: Paris, [1740?] *obl. fol.*
Hirsch III. 892.

LE MERCIER (Amy)

— Napier Pianoforte School. Elementary Scales and Arpeggios.
Arranged by A. Le Mercier. *Reynolds & Co.: London*, [1905.]
fol.
h. 3820. t. (7.)

— Napier Pianoforte School. Preliminary Theory Exercises.
Arranged by A. Le Mercier. *Reynolds & Co.: London*, [1905.]
obl. 4°.
b. 400. f. (2.)

LEMERCIER (Eugène)

— *See* CHANSONNIERS. Les Chansonniers de Montmartre. [Music
by E. Lemercier.] [1906–09.] fol.
H. 2275.

LE MERCIER (T.)

— A set of new quadrilles. [P. F.] *London*, [1816?] fol.
h. 117. (19.)

LE MERCIER D'ERM (Camille)

— Les Hymnes nationaux des peuples celtiques, Irlande,
Écosse, Galles, Bretagne. Textes gaëliques, gallois, bretons,
anglo-écossais et anglais, publiés avec traduction française,
notices documentaires et musique. *Plihon et Hommay:
Rennes*, 1919. 8°.
11595. de. 39.

LEMEUNIER (Raphael)

— The Psalms for Wartime, adapted to choral chanting ...
words by C. Engel, after the French of M. Maningue, *etc.*
Boston Music Co.: Boston, 1918. 8°.
F. 538. g. (36.)

LE MIERE (F. A.)

— *See* LEMIÈRE DE CORVEY (J. F. A.)

LEMIÈRE DE CORVEY (Jean Frédéric Auguste)

— La Bataille d'Jena gagnée sur les Prussiens le 14 d'octobre
1806. Par les troupes françaises ... Pour le piano-forte ...
Oeuvre 36, *etc.* pp. 19. *Chez Mr Meysel: Leipzig; chez M^rs
Gail et Hedler: Francfort*, [1806?] *obl. fol.*
e. 282. m. (6.)

— Duo concertant pour harpe et forte piano ... 23e œuvre.
⟨Forte piano.⟩ *Chez Naderman: Paris*, [1805?] fol.
Imperfect; wanting the harp part.
Hirsch M. 1280. (5.)

— [Another issue.] Duo concertant pour harpe et forte piano.
23e. œuvre. 2 pt. *Paris*, [1810?] fol.
h. 173. b. (8.)

— [Duo concertant. Op. 24.] A favorite Duet, for the harp and
piano forte ... Op. 24. [Parts.] 2 pt. *R^l. Birchall: London*,
[^WM 1800.] fol.
g. 1123. p. (7.)

— Deuxième duo concertant pour harpe et piano ... Œuvre 24.
⟨Forte piano.⟩ *Chez Naderman: Paris*, [1805?] fol.
Imperfect; wanting the harp part.
Hirsch M. 1280. (6.)

— Troisième duo concertant pour harpe et piano ... Œuvre 28.
⟨Forte piano.⟩ pp. 23. *Chez Naderman: Paris*, [1805?] fol.
Imperfect; wanting the harp part.
Hirsch M. 1280. (7.)

— La Plus Jolie. Romance ... Paroles de Mr. H. de Pas ...
London, [1810?] fol.
G. 809. b. (15.)

— Le Porte-Feuille du Troubadour. Recueil de Romances,
parmi lesquelles il y en a vingt notées avec une basse qui
peut être exécutée ... sur le Piano ou la Harpe. [Edited by
J. F. A. Lemière de Corvey.] *Chez Rosa: Paris*, 1821. *obl. 12°.*
11475. a. 26.

— La Reprise de Toulon. [For songs, etc., published
anonymously:] *See* REPRISE.

— La Révolution du 10 aoust 1792. Pot-pourri national
composé pour le forte-piano ... Œuvre XIe. pp. 5. *Chez
Imbault: Paris*, [1792?] *obl. fol.*
f. 133. yy. (9.)

— La Révolution du 10 aoust, pot pourri national ... Arrangée
pour deux violons par J. B. Cartier. [Parts.] 2 pt. *Chez Frère:
Paris*, [1793?] fol.
Hirsch IV. 1592.

— Les Rivaux de village ou La Cruche cassée. Air ⟨N° 1–9⟩ ...
arrangé pour piano par l'auteur. 9 no. *Au magasin de
musique et d'instruments de Ph. Petit: Paris*, [1819?] fol.
H. 233. s. (2.)

— [Les Rivaux de village.] Ouverture des Rivaux de village ou
La Cruche cassée ... Arrangée pour piano ou harpe avec
accompagnement de violon ou flûte ad libitum par l'auteur.
[Parts.] 2 pt. *Au magasin de musique et d'instruments de
Ph. Petit: Paris*, [1819?] fol.
H. 233. s. (1.)

— *See* ROSSINI (G. A.) [La Donna del Lago.] La Dame du Lac.
Opéra ... Arrangée pour la scène française par M^r. Le Mière
de Corvey, *etc.* [1825?] fol.
H. 385. k.

— *See* ROSSINI (G. A.) [La Donna del Lago.] La Dame du lac ...
Arrangée pour la scène française par M^r le Mière de Corvey,
etc. [1825?] fol.
Hirsch II. 806.

LEMIÈRE DE CORVEY (Jean Frédéric Auguste)

— *See* Rossini (G. A.) [Tancredi.] Tancrède. Opéra ... Arrangé pour la scène française ... par M. Le Mière de Corvey, *etc.* [1827.] fol.   **H. 385. h.**

LEMIERRE (J. F. A.)

— *See* Lemière de Corvey (J. F. A.)

LEMIEUX (Anton) *pseud.* [i. e. Frederic Mullen.]

— Benares. Valse indienne. [P. F.] pp. 5. *Swan & Co.: London,* [1914.] fol.   **h. 3866. i. (23.)**

— Idylls of the Woodland. Miniature suite for pianoforte. 1. A woodland lament. 2. A shepherd roundelay. 3. Zephyr. 4. By a sunlit stream. *Swan & Co.: London,* 1920. 4°.
Magnus Albums, No. 54.   **g. 1129. r. (28.)**

— Mecca. Valse arabesque. [P. F.] pp. 4. *Watson, Wilcock & C⁰.: London,* [1912.] fol.   **h. 3866. i. (24.)**

— Phantasmion. Five impressions for pianoforte on reading the book ... by Sara Coleridge, *etc.* *Swan & Co.: London,* 1916. 4°.
Magnus Albums, No. 17.   **g. 1129. d. (5.)**

— Romance. Suite for pianoforte. *Swan & Co.: London,* 1918. 4°.   **g. 603. xx. (8.)**

— Très chic. Valse. [P. F.] pp. 7. *Swan & Co.: London,* [1917.] fol.   **h. 3866. i. (25.)**

LEMIEUX (E. C.)

— The Klondyke-Waltz. [P. F.] *E. M. Allum & Co.: Eganville, Ont.,* 1898. fol.   **h. 3286. g. (30.)**

LEMIRE (Desiré)

— Qui t'a vue doit t'aimer. Chansonnette [begins: "Adèlie si jolie"] ... Paroles de C. Catelin. *Paris,* [1815?] fol.   **G. 546. (48.)**

LEMKE (Henri)

— *See* Lemcke (Heinrich)

LEMLIN (Lorenz)

— Der Kuckuck: "Der Kuckuck auf dem Zaune sass". Sopran-Solo und vierstimmigen Chor. [1902.] *See* Thiel (C.) Auswahl hervorragender Meisterwerke, *etc.* Band III. No. 5. [1898, *etc.*] 8°.   **F. 1767.**

— [Der Kuckuck.] Cuckoo Song. Der Gutzgauch. For Four-part Chorus of Mixed Voices with Cuckoo-Calls for Sopranos a cappella. English version by M. Bernstein ... Edited by C. Deis. *G. Schirmer: New York,* 1934. 8°.   **F. 585. vv. (23.)**

— *See* Leichtentritt (H.) Mehrstimmige Lieder alter deutscher Meister, *etc.* (Heft v. ... L. Lemlin, *etc.*) [1906–08.] 8°.   **F. 1724.**

LEMMEL (Helen Howarth)

— One-and-Twenty Choruses. [Hymns.] *Marshall Bros.: London and Edinburgh,* [1925.] 8°.   **C. 507. (9.)**

— Glad Songs ... Words and music by H. H. Lemmel, with foreword by C. Bonner. *National Sunday School Union: London,* 1922. 8°.   **D. 622. a. (3.)**

— Honey mine. A Song. (Lyric & music by H. H. Lemmel.) *H. Flammer: New York,* 1918. 4°.   **G. 390. r. (3.)**

— Li'l black Lamb. Song ... (Lyric and music) by H. H. Lemmel. *H. Flammer: New York City,* 1919. 4°.   **G. 426. f. (16.)**

LEMMENS (Jacques Nicolas)

— Œuvres inédites, *etc.* 4 tom. *Breitkopf & Härtel: Leipzig et Bruxelles,* 1883–7. *obl.* fol.   **e. 169. b.**

— 4 Favourite Pieces for Organ. 1. Marche Triomphale. 2. Fanfare. 3. Andante with Variations. 4. Finale. Edited by Dr. J. Warriner. *A. Hammond & Co.: London,* [1911.] 4°.
The Academic Edition, No. 487.   **g. 1130. z. (4.)**

— Selected Compositions for Organ ... Selected & edited by O. A. Mansfield. *W. Paxton & Co.: London,* 1935. 4°.
                    g. 575. ll. (23.)

— Adoration.—Theme from Lemmens.— ... Adapted to the modern Organ by M. C. Baldwin. *M. C. Baldwin: Middletown, Conn.,* (1911.) *obl.* fol.
No. 11 *of "Compositions and Arrangements for Organ by M. C. Baldwin".*   **e. 1093. f. (3.)**

— Berceuse for Harmonium. *London,* [1865.] fol.
                    h. 2552. (2.)

— Cantabile. *See infra:* [École d'Orgue.]

— The Corn Field. A Four-part Song, poetry by W. Duthie. *See* Novello and Co. Novello's Part-Song Book. Second Series. Vol. v. No. 167. [1869, *etc.*] 8°.   **F. 280. b.**

— Drops of Rain. A Four-part Song. Poetry by W. Duthie. *See* Novello and Co. Novello's Part-Song Book. Second Series. Vol. v. No. 162. [1869, *etc.*] 8°.   **F. 280. b.**

— Drops of Rain. A four-part Song. Words by W. Duthie. [1886.] *See* Novello and Co. Novello's Tonic Sol-fa Series. No. 407. [1876, *etc.*] 4°.   **B. 885.**

École d'Orgue

— École d'Orgue basée sur le Plain-chant. Romain. *Paris,* [1862.] fol.   **h. 2715.**

— Organ-School ... New edition. The English translation, fingering, and the adaptation to English organs ... by W. T. Best. *London, etc.,* [1884.] fol.   **h. 2715. a. (1.)**

— Collection of pieces in various styles for church and concert purposes selected from the Organ school ... New edition, adapted to English organs by W. T. Best. 18 no. *Mayence,* [1884.] fol.   **h. 2715. a. (2.)**

— Cantabile. (Edited by J. E. West.) [Organ.] *Novello & Co.: London,* [1913.] 4°.
Original Compositions for the Organ. New Series, No. 11.
                    g. 1270.

— Cantabile. *See* Weber (C.) Morceaux favoris transcrits pour violon avec acc. de piano. No. 7. [1887.] fol.
                    h. 1608. r. (43.)

— Fanfare. (Edited by J. E. West.) [Organ.] *Novello & Co.: London,* [1913.] 4°.
Original Compositions for the Organ. New Series. No. 10.
                    g. 1270.

— Finale. (Edited by J. E. West.) [Organ.] *Novello & Co.: London,* [1913.] 4°.
Original Compositions for the Organ. New Series, No. 12.
                    g. 1270.

— Ite missa est. (Edited by J. E. West.) [Organ.] *Novello & Co.: London,* [1913.] 4°.
Original Compositions for the Organ. New Series. No. 8.
                    g. 1270.

— Triumphal March. (Edited by J. E. West.) [Organ.] *Novello & Co.: London,* [1913.] 4°.
Original Compositions for the Organ. New Series, No. 9.
                    g. 1270.

LEMMENS (Jacques Nicolas)

— The Fairy Ring. A Four-part Song, poetry by W. Duthie. *See* Novello and Co. Novello's Part-Song Book. Second Series. Vol. v. No. 163. [1869, *etc.*] 8°.   **F. 280. b.**

— Fanfare. *See* supra: [École d'Orgue.]

— Finale. *See* supra: [École d'Orgue.]

— Six Four-part Songs. The poetry by W. Duthie. *London*, [1869.] 8°.
Bk. 21 *of* "*Novello's Part-song Book. Second series*".
          F. 280. b. (21.)

— Grand Fantasia in E minor. Known as "The Storm" ... for the organ ... Edited by C. W. Councell. *Schott & Co.: London*, [1922.] *obl.* fol.
The Castle Series of Music Books, No. 576.   **f. 314. ee. (24.)**

— Grand Fantasia in E minor. "The Storm." [Organ.]
W. Paxton & Co.: London, 1927. *obl.* 4°.
Part of the "*Anthology of Organ Music*".   **e. 1093. r. (13.)**

— Four Harmonium pieces for the drawing room. *London*, [1864.] fol.   **h. 2552. (1.)**

— Harmonium pieces. no. 1. *London*, [1866.] fol.
          h. 3213. h. (14.)

— Hosannah! Grand Chœur pour orgue. [1857.] *See* Niedermeyer (L.) La Maîtrise, *etc.* 1ʳᵉ Année. No. 7. [1857–61.] fol.   **H. 1237.**

— 10 improvisations pour orgue dans le style sévère et chantant avec ou sans pédale, *etc.* pp. 11. *B. Schott's Söhne: Mayence*, [c. 1880.] *obl.* 4°.   **e. 1096. gg. (8.)**

— Ite missa est. *See* supra: [École d'Orgue.]

— The Light of Life. A Four-part Song. Poetry by W. Duthie. *See* Novello and Co. Novello's Part-Song Book. Second Series. Vol. v. No. 164. [1869, *etc.*] 8°.   **F. 280. b.**

— Marche des Volontaires. [Transcription for harmonium by A. Guilmant.] *B. Schott's Söhne: Mainz, Leipzig*, [1924.] fol.   **h. 2697. l. (7.)**

— Mine, song [begins: "O how my heart is beating"]. Words by the author of John Halifax Gentleman [i. e. D. M. Mulock, afterwards Craik]. *London*, [1871.] fol.   **H. 1775. u. (17.)**

— Morceaux pour Orgue-Mélodium. *Mayence*, [1884.] 8°.
          f. 78. b. (4.)

— Oh, welcome him. A Four-part Song, poetry by W. Duthie. *See* Novello and Co. Novello's Part-Song Book. Second Series. Vol. v. No. 165. [1869, *etc.*] 8°.   **F. 280. b.**

— Four Organ Pieces, in the free style. *London*, [1866.] *obl.* fol.   **e. 169.**

— Organ-School. *See* supra: École d'Orgue.

— Rêverie for Harmonium. *London*, [1865.] fol.   **h. 2552. (3.)**

— Romance sans paroles, for Harmonium. *London*, [1865.] fol.
          h. 2552. (4.)

— Trois Sonates ... pour Orgue. *Paris*, [1876.] *obl.* fol.
          e. 169. a.

— Songs without Words, for the Harmonium. bk. 1. Twenty-four Irish melodies. *London*, [1871.] fol.   **h. 2552. (6.)**

— Sunshine through the Clouds. A Four-part Song, poetry by W. Duthie. *See* Novello and Co. Novello's Part-Song Book. Second Series. Vol. v. No. 166. [1869, *etc.*] 8°.   **F. 280. b.**

— Sunshine through the Clouds. A four-part Song. Poetry by W. Duthie. [1885.] *See* Novello and Co. Novello's Tonic Sol-fa Series. No. 278. [1876, *etc.*] 4°.   **B. 885.**

— Triumphal March. *See* supra: [École d'Orgue.]

LEMMENS (Jacques Nicolas)

— Six Voluntaries for the Harmonium. *London*, [1869.] fol.
          h. 2552. (5.)

— Volunteers' march for the Harmonium, *etc. London*, [1872.] fol.   **h. 2552. (7.)**

— *See* Gheyn (M. van den) Morceaux fugués ... publiés avec la collaboration de J. N. Lemmens, *etc.* [1865.] fol.
          h. 1493. i. (17.)

— *See* Purcell (A.) Great Masters ... arranged for Pianoforte ... Selections from ... Lemmens ... bk. 12, *etc.* [1907, *etc.*] 4°.
          g. 1330.

— *See* Rossini (G. A.) Stabat Mater ... The accompaniments arranged ... by J. Lemmens. [1879.] 4°.   **g. 637.**

LEMMENS SHERRINGTON (H.) *Madame*

— *See* Sherrington, afterwards Lemmens.

LEMMER (P. J.)

— Ons eie. Kinderliedjies. [Composed and arranged by P. J. Lemmer. Staff and tonic sol-fa notation.] pp. 15. *Athena: Kaapstad*, [1962.] 4°.   **G. 1276. z. (16.)**

LEMMON (Alfred E.)

— *See* Portogallo (Marco A.) *pseud.* Sonata y variaciones ... Revisión: A. E. Lemmon. 1976. 4°.   **g. 1129. aa. (21.)**

LEMMONÉ (John)

— Aria, for flute solo with accompaniment for pianoforte.
W. H. Paling & Co.: Sydney, etc., 1915. fol.   **h. 2140. o. (5.)**

— Danse Romantique. Flute solo with pianoforte accompaniment. *W. H. Paling & Co.: Sydney, etc.*, 1924. 4°.
Paling's Flute Series, No. 19.   **g. 70. g. (12.)**

— Fantasie Caprice, for flute solo with accompaniment for pianoforte. *W. H. Paling & Co.: Sydney, etc.*, 1915. fol.
          h. 2140. o. (6.)

— Nocturne. A mountain idyl. Flute solo with pianoforte accompaniment. *W. H. Paling & Co.: London*, 1923. 4°.
Paling's Flute Series, No. 1.   **g. 70. g. (13.)**

LEMOGNE (Karl)

— *See* Wickins and Co. Wickins' Orchestral Half-Hours ... Arranged [by ... K. Lemogne], *etc.* [1894, *etc.*] fol.   **h. 2832.**

LEMOINE (A.)

— Royal Holyrood quadrille on Scotch airs. [P. F.] *London*, [1863.] fol.   **h. 1460. v. (19.)**

LEMOINE (A. Henry) *the Elder*

— *See* Lemoine (Henry)

LEMOINE (A. Henry) *the Younger* and **MOHR** (D.)

— Fantaisie sur des motifs de Mathilde de Sabran, de Rossini, pour Piano et Violoncelle. *Paris*, [1870.] fol.   **h. 1849. (20.)**

LEMOINE (Achille Philibert)

— Air de Ballet pour deux pianos (arrangé ... par C. Lentz). *Paris*, 1885. fol.   **h. 3291. (11.)**

— *See* Boccherini (L.) [Quintets. Op. 13. No. 5.] Menuet ... arrangé pour piano et violon par A. Lemoine. 1875. 4°.
          g. 505. g. (1.)

LEMOINE (ACHILLE PHILIBERT)

— *See* DONIZETTI (Domenico G. M.) [La Fille du régiment.] Airs favoris de l'opéra La Fille du régiment ... arrangés en quatuor pour clarinette, violon, cornet et violoncelle, par A. Lemoine, *etc.* [1840?] fol.   **g. 155. a. (4.)**

— *See* DONIZETTI (Domenico G. M.) [La Fille du régiment.] Ouverture de La Fille du régiment, arrangée en quatuor pour clarinette, violon, cornet et violoncelle, par A. Lemoine. [1840?] fol.   **g. 155. a. (3.)**

LEMOINE (ALEXANDRE)

— Cours complet de Musique Vocale. (Théorie et pratique.) 1ère Partie. Cours élémentaire. *Paris*, 1867. 8°.   **F. 445.**

LEMOINE (ANTOINE)

— Turner's Cornet Journal, No. 1 (No. 2), containing Solos for Cornet with Pianoforte accompaniment and a separate Cornet part. (Compiled and arranged by A. Lemoine.) 2 no. *J. A. Turner: London*, [1897.] 4°.   **e. 325. b. (3.)**

— *See* KOTTAUN (C.) The Cornet Treasury ... arranged ... by C. Kottaun (A. Lemoine). [1902, *etc.*] 4°.   **f. 422.**

LEMOINE (ANTOINE MARCEL)

— La Comparaison. Chansonnette, Avec Accompagnement de Guitare, par le Citoyen Lemoine. *Chez Imbault: Paris*, [1795?] 8°.   **B. 362. c. (24.)**

— [Another copy.]   **B. 362. g. (67.)**

— Nouvelle méthode de lyre ou guitarre à six cordes, *etc.* pp. 85. *Chez l'auteur: Paris*, [c. 1810.] fol.   **h. 259. v.**

— *See* BOIELDIEU (F. A.) [Beniowski.] De l'amitié daigne entendre la voix. *Air* ... Accomp¹ de Guitare par Lemoine. [1800.] 8°.   **E. 1717. (59.)**

— *See* BOIELDIEU (F. A.) [Le Calife de Bagdad.—Pour obtenir celle qu'il aime.] Chanson de table ... Avec accompagnement de guitarre par Lemoine. [1820?] 8°.   **E. 1717. c. (37.)**

— *See* CHAUVET (C. R.) [Premier recueil de trois romances. no. 2.] Le Voile ... Accompagnement de lyre ou guitare par Lemoine. [c. 1810.] 8°.   **E. 1717. p. (15.)**

— *See* DALAYRAC (N.) [Ambroise.—Sans être belle on est aimable.] Air d'Ambroise ou Voilà ma journée ... Accompagnement de guitare par Lemoine. [c. 1810.] 8°.   **E. 1717. o. (16.)**

— *See* DALAYRAC (N.) [Gulistan.—Ils vont venir.] Duo ... Accomp¹ de lyre ou guitare, par Lemoine. [1810?] 8°.   **Hirsch M. 660. (12.)**

— *See* DALAYRAC (N.) [La Maison à vendre.—Chère Lise, dis moi je t'aime.] Duo ... Avec accompagnement de guitare par Lemoine. [1810?] 8°.   **E. 1717. c. (35.)**

— *See* DALAYRAC (N.) [La Maison à vendre.—Depuis longtems j'ai le desir.] Duo ... Avec accompagnement de guitare par Lemoine. [1820?] 8°.   **E. 1717. c. (36.)**

— *See* DALAYRAC (N.) [Nina.] Quand le bien aimé reviendra ... Accp¹ de Guitarre par Mʳ Le Moine, *etc.* [1786.] 8°.   **B. 362. f. (41.)**

— *See* DALAYRAC (N.) [Roméo et Juliette.—Avant d'avoir vu ce mortel.] Romance ... Arrangée avec accompagnem¹ de guitarre par Lemoine. [1801?] 8°.   **E. 1717. p. (20.)**

— *See* DALAYRAC (N.) [La Tour de Neustadt.—Un voyageur s'est égaré.] Romance ... Avec accompagnem¹ de guitare par Lemoine. [1801?] 8°.   **E. 1717. p. (21.)**

— *See* DALVIMARE (M. P.) Complainte de Nérie sur la mort d'Enna ... Accompagnement de lyre ou guitare par Lemoine. [c. 1800.] 8°.   **E. 1717. p. (22.)**

LEMOINE (ANTOINE MARCEL)

— *See* DALVIMARE (M. P.) O vous que Mars rend invincible ... Accompagnement de lyre ou guitare par Lemoine. [1805?] 8°.   **E. 1717. g. (3.)**

— *See* DEVIENNE (F.) L'Innocence Reconnue ... Accomp¹ de Guittare par le Cᵉⁿ Lemoine. [1795?] 8°.   **B. 362. a. (112.)**

— *See* DOMNICH (H.) Charmant ruisseau ... Accompagnement de lyre ou guitare par Lemoine. [1805?] 8°.   **E. 1717. g. (12.)**

— *See* FERRARI (G. G.) L'Amant malheureux et constant ... Accomp¹ de Guittare par M. Le Moine, *etc.* [1790?] 8°.   **B. 362. b. (197.)**

— *See* GARAT (P. J.) Le Départ d'un jeune guerrier pour l'armée ... Accomp¹ de lyre ou guitare par A. M. Lemoine, *etc.* [1802?] 8°.   **E. 1717. o. (33.)**

— *See* GARAT (P. J.) Il était là. Romance ... Accomp¹ de lyre ou guitare par Lemoine. [1805?] 8°.   **E. 1717. e. (5.)**

— *See* GATAYES (G. P. A.) Objet charmant. Romance ... Accompagnement de lyre ou guitare par Lemoine. [1815?] 8°.   **E. 1717. c. (20.)**

— *See* GAVEAUX (P.) [L'Amour filial.] Jeunes amants, cueillés des fleurs ... Accompagnement de Guitare par M. Le Moine. [1792.] 8°.   **B. 362. a. (50.)**

— *See* GAVEAUX (P.) [Sophie et Moncars.—Quand la beauté.] Romance ... Avec accomp¹ de guitare par Lemoine. [c. 1805.] 8°.   **E. 1717. p. (44.)**

— *See* GOSSEC (F. J.) [Le Camp de Grand-Pré.] Vous aimables fillettes ... Accompagnement de Guitarre du C. Lemoine. [1793.] 8°.   **B. 362. a. (43.)**

— *See* GOSSEC (F. J.) [Rosine.] Aujourd'hui cesse la fête. *Vaudeville* ... Accompagnement de Guitarre, par M. Lemoine, *etc.* [1786.] 8°.   **B. 362. h. (9.)**

— *See* GOULÉ (J. N.) Amour et folie ... Accompagnement de lyre ou guitare par A. M. Lemoine. [1822?] 8°.   **E. 1717. o. (46.)**

— *See* LAMBERT (G. J. L.) La Violette ... Accomp¹ de lyre ou guitarre par Lemoine. [c. 1815.] 8°.   **E. 1717. p. (45.)**

— *See* MARTINI (G.) *il Tedesco, pseud.* Plaisir d'amour. *Romance du Chevrier dans Célestine* ... Accompagnement de lyre ou guitare par Lemoine. [1808?] 8°.   **E. 1717. o. (56.)**

— *See* MOZART (W. A.) [Die Zauberflöte.—Der Vogelfänger bin ich ja.] Air des Mystères d'Isis ... Accompagnement de guittare par Lemoine. [1810?] 8°.   **E. 1717. c. (34.)**

— *See* PAER (F.) Chanson à toi ... Accompagnement de lyre ou guitarre par Lemoine. [1805?] 8°.   **Hirsch M. 660. (2.)**

— *See* PAER (F.) Tu le veux donc. *Romance* ... Accompagnement de lyre ou guitare par Lemoine. [1805?] 8°.   **Hirsch M. 660. (4.)**

— *See* PAISIELLO (G.) [Nina.—Il mio ben quando verrà.] Cavatina ... avec accompagne¹ de lyre ou guitarre par Mʳ Lemoine. [1805?] 8°.   **Hirsch M. 660. (15.)**

— *See* PAISIELLO (G.) [Proserpine.—Ah! quelle injustice cruelle.] Air ... Accompagnement de lyre ou guitare par Lemoine. [1805?] 8°.   **E. 1717. g. (8.)**

— *See* PAISIELLO (G.) [Proserpine.—Les beaux jours et la paix.] Duo et chœur ... Accompagnement de lyre ou de guitare par Lemoine. [1805?] 8°.   **E. 1717. g. (9.)**

— *See* PAISIELLO (G.) [Proserpine.—Rendez moi donc le bien.] Duo ... Accompagnement de lyre ou guitare par Lemoine. [1805?] 8°.   **E. 1717. g. (10.)**

LEMOINE (Antoine Marcel)

— *See* PLANTADE (C. H.) Bocage que l'aurore embellit. Romance ... Avec accompagnement de lyre ou guitarre, par Lemoine. [1825?] 8°.   **E. 1717. c. (14.)**

— *See* PLANTADE (C. H.) Stances à l'amitié. [Song] ... Avec accomp.^t de guitarre ou lyre par Mr Lemoine. [1805?] 8°.   **E. 1717. g. (21.)**

— *See* PLEYEL (I. J.) Loin de nous le vain délire. *Hymne à la Liberté* ... Accomp.^t de Guittare par M. Le Moine. [1791.] 8°.   **B. 362. d. (23.)**

— *See* QUAISAIN (A.) [La Vendange.] Ah! comme l'amour vous tracasse ... Accompagnement de Piano par le C. Lemoine. [1798.] fol.   **G. 554. a. (41.)**

— *See* ROMAGNESI (A.) Le Tombeau de Rolland. [Song] ... Accompagnement de lyre ou guitarre par Lemoine. [1810?] 8°.   **Hirsch M. 660. (10.)**

— *See* ROZE (L.) Vivat in æternum ... Accompag.^t de guittare ou lyre par Mr Lemoine musicien. [c. 1810.] 8°.   **E. 1717. o. (69.)**

— *See* SOLIÉ (J. P.) [Chapitre second.—Dans tous les romans de la vie.] Vaudeville du Chapitre second ... Avec accomp.^t de guitarre par Lemoine. [c. 1800.] 8°.   **E. 1717. p. (65.)**

— *See* SOLIÉ (J. P.) [Chapitre second.—Non je ne veux.] Air ... Avec accomp.^t de guitarre par Mr Lemoine. [1800?] 8°.   **E. 1717. g. (11.)**

— *See* SOLIÉ (J. P.) [Le Secret.—Je te perds fugitive espérance.] Romance du Secret ... Accompagnement de guitare par Lemoine. [c. 1800.] 8°.   **E. 1717. p. (66.)**

— *See* SOLIÉ (J. P.) [Le Secret.—Qu'on soit jaloux.] Air du Secret ... Accompagnement de guitare par Lemoine. [c. 1800.] 8°.   **E. 1717. p. (67.)**

— *See* SPONTINI (G. L. P.) *Count of St. Andrea.* [Julie.—Il a donc fallu pour la gloire.] Romance ... Accompagnement de lyre ou guitare par Le Moine. [c. 1805.] 8°.   **E. 1717. n. (23.)**

— *See* SPONTINI (G. L. P.) *Count of St. Andrea.* [Milton.—J'aurai le sort.] Romance ... Accomp.^t de lyre ou guitare, par le Moine. [1810?] 8°.   **E. 1717. e. (4.)**

— *See* SPONTINI (G. L. P.) *Count of St. Andrea.* [La Vestale. —Licinius je vais donc te revoir.] Air de La Vestale. Avec récitatif et marche triomphale ... Accomp.^t de lyre ou guitarre par Lemoine. [1807?] 8°.   **E. 1717. l. (49.)**

— *See* VACHER (P. J.) Mon dernier mot. Romance ... Avec accomp.^t de guitare par Lemoine. [1810?] 8°.   **Hirsch M. 660. (9.)**

— *See* WOETS (J. B.) Le Conscription de Cythère ... Accompagnement de lyre ou guitare par Lemoine. [c. 1810.] 8°.   **E. 1717. n. (25.)**

LEMOINE (Ernest)

— The King can do no wrong. Song ... written by C. J. Rowe. *London*, [1878.] fol.   **H. 1783. o. (43.)**

— The Ship Boy's Prayer. [Song, begins: "Cold blew the wind".] Words by C. J. Rowe. *London*, [1879.] fol.   **H. 1783. o. (45.)**

— The Soldier's Rose. [Song, begins: "With trembling lip".] Words by F. E. Weatherly. *London*, [1879.] fol.   **H. 1783. o. (44.)**

LEMOINE (Felix) *pseud.* [i. e. ALFRED WILLIAM RAWLINGS.]

— The Court Menuet Suite of stately Dances for the Pianoforte. *C. Sheard & Co.: London*, (1913.) 4°.   **g. 232. z. (9.)**

— Dreams of Venice. Moonlight idyll. [P. F.] *C. Sheard & Co.: London*, 1917. fol.   **h. 3284. nn. (42.)**

LEMOINE (Felix) *pseud.* [i. e. ALFRED WILLIAM RAWLINGS.]

— Gavotte Album, *etc.* [P. F.] *C. Sheard & Co.: London*, (1914.) 4°.   **g. 1129. (11.)**

LEMOINE (Frederic) *pseud.* [i. e. GEORGE FREDERICK WEST.]

— Une Cascade des Fleurs, bagatelle de salon ... pour Piano. *London*, [1871.] fol.   **h. 1485. s. (47.)**

— Une Cascade de Fleurs. Bagatelle ... arranged as a pianoforte duet. *R. Cocks & Co.: London*, [1883.] fol.   **h. 3290. f. (38.)**

— Le Chant du Soldat (La Dame Blanche, Boieldieu) transcrit pour Piano. *London*, [1874.] fol.   **h. 1482. z. (28.)**

— Classics for Young Pianists. 6 no. *R. Cocks & Co.: London*, [1882.] fol.   **h. 1484. s. (48.)**

— Clementia, bagatelle d'amour pour le Piano. *London*, [1873.] fol.   **h. 1482. z. (27.)**

— Columbine. Mazurka. [P. F.] *See* WEST (G. F.) Easy Lessons, *etc.* No. 11. [1886.] fol.   **h. 1395. f. (12.)**

— Don't forget me, melody by C. Pinsuti, transcribed for the Pianoforte. *London*, [1880.] fol.   **h. 1494. q. (23.)**

— Eglantine, bagatelle de salon ... pour le Piano. *London*, [1875.] fol.   **h. 1482. z. (29.)**

— Far Away (Miss Lindsay) transcribed for the Pianoforte. *London*, [1877.] fol.   **h. 1482. z. (33.)**

— La fleur des champs, polka. [P. F.] *London*, [1852.] fol.   **h. 964. (30.)**

— The Highland Home quadrille. [P. F.] *London*, [1868.] fol.   **h. 1485. s. (46.)**

— L'Hyacinthe, bagatelle pour Pianoforte. *London*, [1876.] fol.   **h. 1482. z. (32.)**

— I love the merry sunshine, melody by S. Glover, transcribed for the Pianoforte. *London*, [1878.] fol.   **h. 1494. q. (21.)**

— Lascia ch' io pianga, aria from Handel's Rinaldo, transcribed for the Pianoforte. *London*, [1881.] fol.   **h. 3275. j. (32.)**

— March founded on a popular Venetian melody of the 17th century. [In fact, based on "Pur dicesti" by A. Lotti. P. F.] *London*, [1878.] fol.   **h. 1494. q. (18.)**

— [March founded on a popular Venetian melody.] The Venetian March ... arranged for the Organ by Dr. Westbrook. *London*, [1883.] *obl.* fol.   **e. 174. n. (27.)**

— May Day (Müller) arranged for the Pianoforte. *London*, [1878.] fol.   **h. 1494. q. (19.)**

— [Mein gläubiges Herz.] J. S. Bach's melody known as My Heart ever faithful (Mein gläubiges Herz) arranged for Pianoforte. *London*, [1876.] fol.   **h. 1482. z. (30.)**

— Mélodie Bohémienne variée pour le Piano. *London*, [1876.] fol.   **h. 1482. z. (31.)**

— My old friend John ... (E. Land) transcribed for the Pianoforte. *London*, [1880.] fol.   **h. 1494. q. (26.)**

— Les petits amusements de Jenny Lind. Rondos on Favorite Melodies, from La Figlia del Reggimento [by D. G. M. Donizetti] arranged for the Piano Forte by F. Lemoine. 4 no. *London*, [1847.] fol.   **h. 715. (32.)**

— Six Rondos on favorite melodies, as sung by the Ethiopian Serenaders. *London*, [1847.] fol.   **h. 715. (31.)**

— La Rose d'Angleterre, polka élégante, pour piano, *etc.* *London*, [1858.] fol.   **h. 977. f. (31.)**

— The Sea is England's glory, melody by S. Glover, transcribed for the Pianoforte. *London*, [1878.] fol.   **h. 1494. q. (20.)**

LEMOINE (Frederic) *pseud.* [i. e. George Frederick West.]

— Sérénade (C. Gounod) transcribed for the Pianoforte.
London, [1881.] fol.   **h. 3275. j. (29.)**

— Soft Star of the West, melody by C. Pinsuti, transcribed for
the Pianoforte. *London*, [1879.] fol.   **h. 1494. q. (22.)**

— Steering, melody by F. H. Cowen, transcribed for the
Pianoforte. *London*, [1880.] fol.   **h. 1494. q. (25.)**

— Thy Voice is near (melody by W. T. Wrighton) arranged for
the Pianoforte. *London*, [1877.] fol.   **h. 1482. z. (34.)**

— The Venetian March. *See* supra: [March founded on a
popular Venetian melody.]

— Verdi prati e selve amene, aria from Handel's Alcina,
arranged for the Pianoforte. *London*, [1881.] fol.
                                           h. 3275. j. (31.)

— The Vicar of Bray, old English melody ... arranged for the
Pianoforte. *London*, [1881.] fol.   **h. 3275. j. (30.)**

— What shall I sing to thee? Melody by C. Pinsuti, arranged for
the Pianoforte. *London*, [1880.] fol.   **h. 1494. q. (24.)**

— *See* HAENDEL (G. F.) [Serse.—Ombra mai fù.] Handel's Largo,
transcribed ... by F. Lemoine. [1880.] fol.   **h. 435. b. (19.)**

— *See* KETTERER (E.) Caprice Hongrois ... arranged ... by
F. Lemoine. [1881.] fol.   **h. 3275. i. (34.)**

— *See* KETTERER (E.) Caprice hongrois ... Arranged as a
pianoforte duet by F. Lemoine. [1881.] fol.   **h. 61. cc. (22.)**

— *See* LEFÉBURE-WÉLY (L. J. F.) Processional march ... adapted
... by F. Lemoine. [1880.] fol.   **h. 1494. q. (8.)**

— *See* MEYERBEER (G.) [Le Prophète.—Marche du sacre.] The
Coronation march ... transcribed ... by F. Lemoine. [1880.]
fol.   **h. 1494. u. (14.)**

LEMOINE (G.)
— The Fairy Polka & Waltzes ... Composed & arranged for the
piano forte by G. Lemoine. pp. 2. *Duncombe & Moon:
London*, [c. 1850.] fol.   **h. 3821. r. (7.)**

LEMOINE (*Madame* Gustave)
— *See* PUGET, afterwards LEMOINE (L.)

LEMOINE (Henry)
— Amusement de société, contredanses brillantes ... à quatre
mains pour le piano forte. no. 1, 2. *R. Cocks & Cᵒ.: London*,
[1833.] fol.
Imperfect; wanting no. 3.   **h. 580. (4.)**
                                          & h. 580. a.

— Trois bagatelles pour le Piano Forte, arrangées par
H. Lemoine. *London*, [1832.] fol.   **h. 580. (20.)**

— [Bagatelles. No. 5, 12.] Isaure et Les Clercs ... pour le piano
forte. Le premier [*sic*] livraison formant: le [*sic*] 5ᵐᵉ bagatelle
sur un air catalan d'Isaure, d'Adam. Le [*sic*] seconde livraison
formant: le [*sic*] 12ᵐᵉ bagatelle sur la Ronde du Pré aux
clercs, d'Hérold, *etc.* 2 no. *Wessel & Cᵒ: London*, [1835.] fol.
                                          h. 723. bb. (26.)

— [Bagatelles. No. 21, 22.] Deux petits souvenirs de Paris. 21ᵉ et
22ᵉ Bagatelle sur des motifs de Halévy et Beauplan, pour le
Piano Forte. *London*, [1837.] fol.   **h. 580. (11.)**

— Bagatelle sur des motifs du ballet "Le Diable amoureux,"
pour Piano. *London*, [1841.] fol.   **h. 580. (23.)**

— Bagatelle pour le Piano sur les motifs de F. Burgmüller,
intercalés dans le Ballet de Giselle. *London*, [1841.] fol.
                                          h. 580. (24.)

LEMOINE (Henry)
— Bagatelle for the Piano Forte on the Palmer's Ballad in
Meyerbeer's Opera of Robert le Diable, *etc. S. Chappell:
London*, [1835.] fol.   **R. M. 25. k. 1. (24.)**

— Bagatelle ou morceau facile pour le Forte Piano sur les
motifs favoris de [C. M. F. E. von Weber's opera] Robin des
Bois. *Paris*, [1830?] fol.   **h. 726. b. (2.)**

— Ninth bagatelle on a chansonette by C. Plantade, for the
Piano Forte, with Violin or flute accompaniment ad libitum.
London, [1833.] fol.   **h. 580. (6.)**

— Seizième bagatelle pour le Piano Forte sur la valse favorite
du Duc de Reichstadt [by J. Strauss the Elder]. *London*,
[1834.] fol.   **h. 580. (7.)**

— Dix huitième bagatelle pour le Piano Forte, sur une
Chansonette de F. Bérat. *London*, [1835.] fol.   **h. 580. (8.)**

— Dix-neuvième bagatelle pour le Piano Forte, sur l'air
militaire de "La sentinelle perdue" de V. Rifaut. *London*,
[1835.] fol.   **h. 580. (9.)**

— Vingtième bagatelle sur l'Opéra de Monpou "Les deux
Reines" ... pour le Pianoforte. *London*, [1836.] fol.
                                          h. 580. (10.)

— [Bagatelles. No. 24.] "La Duvernay." 24ᵐᵉ Bagatelle sur le
"Cachucha" ... pour le Pianoforte. *London*, [1837.] fol.
                                          h. 580. (12.)

— 30ᵗʰ Bagatelle from Auber's Opera "The Crown Diamonds,"
for the Piano Forte. *London*, [1845.] fol.   **h. 99. (4.)**

— 50ᵉ Bagatelle pour le Piano, sur un motif de l'opéra 31 de
H. Rosellen. *London*, [1849.] fol.   **h. 715. (34.)**

— "Les belles fleurs," pour le Piano Forte. no. 1–4. *London*,
[1832.] fol.   **h. 580. (13.)**

— [Le Bijou.] Quadrille facile et brillante intitulée Le Bijou,
composée pour le Piano à quatre mains. *London*, [1830?] fol.
No. 11 of "Les Soirées de Londres".   **g. 270. i. (33.)**

— Le Bijou quadrille pour le Piano Forte, avec violon où flute
ad libitum. *London*, [1835.] fol.   **h. 580. (27.)**

— La Brigantine. Ballade. Paroles de Mʳ Casimir Delavigne,
mises en musique avec accompagnement de piano, *etc. Chez
Henry Lemoine: Paris*, [c. 1830.] fol.   **G. 559. a. (4.)**

— Caprice composé pour le Piano sur deux thêmes
d'A. Panseron, *etc. Paris*, [1835?] fol. **g. 272. p. (5.)**

— La Catarina Cellarius valse. *See* infra: The Masaniello
quadrille, *etc.*

— La Chatte metamorphosée en Femme, musique de
A. Montfort. Premier quadrille sur de motifs du ballet ...
pour Piano avec acct. de Violon, Flûte, Flageolet, Basse et
Piston, ad lib. *Paris*, [1837.] obl. fol.   **e. 272. (11.)**

— Contredanses nouvelles pour le piano forte, *etc.* 3 cah. *Chez
Lemoine: Paris*, [c. 1810.] obl. fol.   **f. 133. ww. (2.)**

— Divertimento on celebrated dances, arranged for the Piano
Forte. *London*, [1832.] fol.   **h. 580. (22.)**

— Divertimento for the Piano Forte, on subjects from Carafa's
"l'Orgie". *London*, [1832.] fol.   **h. 580. (21.)**

— Divertimento for the Piano Forte, on airs from Hérold's
Opera "Zampa". *London*, [1844.] fol.   **h. 700. (48.)**

— La Duvernay. *See* supra: [Bagatelles. No. 24.]

— "Les élégantes," pour le Piano Forte. *London*, [1853.] fol.
                                          h. 580. (17.)

— L'enfantin quadrille, suivi de deux valses et un galop pour le
Piano Forte, avec violon ad libitum. *London*, [1835.] fol.
                                          h. 580. (26.)

LEMOINE (HENRY)

—— [Études Enfantines. Op. 37.] Fifty infantile studies for the Piano Forte. bk. 1, 2. *London*, [1841.] fol. **h. 580. (5.)**

—— [Études Enfantines. Op. 37.] 50 Melodious Studies for the Piano Forte ... for small hands ... bk. 1. *R. Cocks & Co.: London*, [1870?] fol.
Wanting bk. 2. **h. 3820. s. (15.)**

—— [Études Enfantines. Op. 37.] 50 Studies ... for the Pianoforte. *Augener & Co.: London*, [1898.] 4°. **g. 337. e. (3.)**

—— Études enfantines for the Piano. (Op. 37.) Revised and edited by William Scharfenberg. pp. 49. *G. Schirmer: New York; Chappell & Co.: London;* [*London* printed, 1950.] 4°. *Schirmer's Library of musical Classics. vol.* 175. **g. 338. o. (4.)**

—— "Le favori," Quadrille pour le Piano. *London*, [1833.] fol. **h. 580. (33.)**

—— Le favori; brilliant quadrilles for two Performers on one Piano Forte. *London*, [1833.] fol. **h. 580. (34.)**

—— A favorite Italian air, arranged, with variations for the Piano Forte, by H. Lemoine. *London*, [1833.] fol. **h. 580. (19.)**

—— La fête Alsacienne. Rondoletto pour le Piano. Op. 42. *London*, [1842.] fol. **h. 700. (46.)**

—— Les Fleurettes de St Denis. Sept petits morceaux d'amusemens ... pour le piano forte, *etc.* no. 2. *Wessel & Cº: London*, [1849?] fol.
Imperfect; wanting no. 1, 3–7. **g. 1529. n.**

—— The four sisters, for the Piano Forte. no. 1–4. *London*, [1841.] fol. **h. 580. (2.)**

—— Grande Methodo theorico e practico de Piano. *See* infra: [Méthode pratique et théorique pour le Piano.]

—— Impromptu pour le piano forte, sur des motifs de Matilde di Sabran, musique de Rossini, *etc.* pp. 13. *R. Cocks & Cº: London*, [1836.] fol. **h. 722. xx. (29.)**

—— Maria et Clara. 2 Enfantillages pour le Piano. Op. 50. *London*, [1850.] fol. **h. 723. m. (3.)**

—— The Masaniello quadrille ... and La Catarina Cellarius valse. [P. F.] *London*, [1855.] fol.
No. 232 of the "Musical Bouquet". **H. 2345.**

—— A practical and theoretical method for the Piano Forte. Méthode pratique et théorique pour le Piano. Fourth edition. *London*, [1843.] fol. **h. 1051.**

—— [Méthode pratique et théorique pour le Piano.] Grande Methodo theorico e practico de Piano. *Paris*, [1881.] fol. **h. 1051. a.**

—— Le Mignon. Second quadrille de Tivoli, for the Pianoforte, *etc. London*, [1830?] fol. **g. 270. i. (32.)**

—— Le Mignon, seconde quadrille de Tivoli, for the piano forte, with violin ad lib., *etc.* pp. 5. *Wessel & Cº: London*, [1839?] fol.
The P. F. part only. **h. 1203. l. (6.)**

—— Deux morceaux choisis pour le Piano Forte. *London*, [1833.] fol. **h. 580. (15.)**

—— Quatre petits morceaux brillants pour le Piano Forte. *London*, [1833.] fol. **h. 580. (16.)**

—— Deux petits souvenirs de Paris. *See* supra: [Bagatelles. No. 21, 22.]

—— A practical and theoretical method for the Piano Forte. *See* supra: Méthode pratique et théorique pour le piano.

LEMOINE (HENRY)

—— A Set of Quadrilles from Auber's Opera, Le Cheval de Bronze. Arranged for two performers on the Piano Forte. no. 1. *D'Almaine & Co.: London*, [1836.] fol. **R. M. 25. i. 7. (11.)**

—— Quadrilles, the subjects from the Opera of "Gustavus the third" by Auber, arranged for two performers on the Piano Forte by H. Lemoine. *London*, [1834.] fol. **h. 580. (3.)**

—— Quadrilles, from the favorite ballet de L'Orgie [by M. E. F. V. A. P. Carafa di Colobrano]. Arranged as duets for the piano forte by Henry Lemoine. pp. 11. [*Edinburgh*, c. 1833.] fol. **h. 61. tt. (5.)**

—— Quadrille de Contredanses pour le Piano, arrangé sur des motifs de "Il Pirata" de Bellini. *London*, [1832.] fol. **h. 580. (14.)**

—— Quadrilles de Bellini, selected from his celebrated opera Il Pirata, arranged for the piano forte, with an accompaniment (ad lib.) for the flute or violin, by Henry Lemoine. [Parts.] 2 pt. *T. Welsh: London*, [c. 1835.] fol.
The parts for flute and violin are printed in score. **h. 61. s. (9.)**

—— Favorite Quadrilles from La Somnambule [by Vincenzo Bellini], composed and arranged for the piano forte, with an accompaniment for the flute (ad lib.) by Henry Lemoine. *Metzler & Cº, for the Proprietors: London*, [1843?] fol.
Imperfect; set 1 *only, without the accompaniment.* **h. 61. tt. (6.)**

—— Trois Recréations de la Jeunesse pour le Piano. 3 no. *London*, [1862.] fol. **h. 1460. v. (21.)**

—— Les Riens. 2 très petits rondos pour le Piano. *London*, [1842.] fol. **h. 700. (45.)**

—— Le Roitelet. Quadrille facile pour le Piano. *London*, [1843.] fol. **h. 700. (47.)**

—— Rondino, sur la [*sic*] galop de la Tentation [opera by J. F. F. E. Halévy with ballet music by C. Gide], pour le piano forte. pp. 5. *G. Walker & Son: London*, [c. 1845.] fol. **h. 61. oo. (6.)**

—— Rondoletto brillant pour le Piano Forte, sur un motif de l'Opéra d'Adam "Une bonne fortune". Op. 27. *London*, [1834.] fol. **h. 580. (29.)**

—— Sans l'oublier. Romance. Paroles de Mme. Desbordes Valmore. *Paris*, [1835?] fol. **H. 2831. f. (14.)**

—— Les Soirées de Londres ... Première et seconde Quadrilles sur les motifs favoris de Hérold, de l'Opéra Zampa ... à quatre mains pour le Piano Forte, *etc.* 2 no. *Wessel and Co.: London*, [1833?] fol. **R. M. 25. i. 5. (4.)**

—— [Les Soirées de Londres.] Deux Quadrilles de Contredanses, the subjects from Hérold's opera of Zampa, arranged for two performers on the Pianoforte. set 1. *London*, [c. 1850.] fol.
Imperfect; wanting set 2. **h. 1481. c. (12.)**

—— Six Solos, Morceaux de Concours pour Piano. Op. 47. *London*, [1847.] fol. **h. 715. (33.)**

—— Souvenirs de Vienne. Trois petites pièces en forme de Rondos pour le Piano Forte. Op. 32. *London*, [1835.] fol. **h. 580. (25.)**

—— [Traité d'harmonie pratique.] Treatise on practical harmony. Translated ... by W. Aspull. *London*, 1835. fol. **H. 2872.**

—— La valse et le galop; divertissement pour le Piano Forte à quatre mains. Op. 30. *London*, [1835.] fol. **h. 580. (28.)**

—— Valse et Galop, Divertissement ... Op. 30. arrangé pour piano à six mains par L. Lemoine. *See* ORCHESTRE. L'Orchestre au Salon, *etc.* No. 43. [1874, *etc.*] fol. **h. 1427.**

LEMOINE (Henry)

— The Zampa quadrilles. [P. F.] *London*, [1855.] fol.
No. 107 *of the "Musical Bouquet".*   **H. 2345.**

— *See* Adam (A. C.) Giselle ... pour le Piano Forte par
H. Lemoine. [1841.] fol.   **h. 580. (35.)**

— *See* Adam (A. C.) [La Jolie fille de Gand.] The Waltz and
Galop in ... The Beauty of Ghent ... arranged for the piano
forte by H. Lemoine. [1843.] fol.   **h. 1460. v. (20.)**

— *See* Bertini (Henri J.) [Etüden. Op. 29, 100.] R. Cocks & Cᵒ's
improved Edition of Bertini's celebrated Studies ... A new
edition revised and corrected by H. Lemoine. [1840.] fol.
    h. 552. c.

— *See* Carulli (G.) and Lemoine (H.) Solfège des Solfèges ...
(Les 4ᵉ, 6ᵉ, 7ᵉ, 8ᵉ, 9ᵉ, et 10ᵉ volumes par H. Lemoine, *etc.*)
[1876–]1886. 4°.   **G. 487.**

— *See* Chaulieu (C.) Contredanses ... arrangées par
H. Lemoine. [1832.] fol.   **h. 580. (18.)**

— *See* École. École de la vélocité. Choix d'études ... pour
piano extraites des œuvres de ... H. Lemoine, *etc.* [1881.] fol.
    h. 3820. e. (2.)

— *See* Gomis (J. M.) [Revenant.] La Piquante ... arrangée par
H. Lemoine. [1834.] fol.   **h. 580. (32.)**

— *See* Hammers (J. E.) J. Clinton's and Lemoine's Bagatelles for
the Clarionet and Piano Forte, *etc.* [1845.] fol.   **h. 3212. (3.)**

— *See* Hérold (L. J. F.) Au clair de la lune ... Op. 19. 3ᵉ édition
... Revue et doigtée par H. Lemoine. [c. 1890.] fol.
    g. 981. b. (11.)

— *See* Jullien (L. A.) Le Parisien quadrille et une valse ...
arrangés ... par H. Lemoine. [1840?] *obl.* fol.   **e. 272. (5.)**

— *See* Jullien (L. A.) Quadrille et walse sur des motifs du ballet
du Diable boiteux, musique de Casimir Gide ... Arrangées
pour le piano ... par H. Lemoine. [1840?] *obl.* fol.
    Hirsch M. 1290. (3.)

— *See* Jullien (L. A.) Quadrille de contredanses sur ... "La
Sentinelle perdue" ... arranged par H. Lemoine. [1835.] fol.
    h. 580. (30.)

— *See* Jullien (L. A.) Le Rataplan quadrille ... arrangé ... par
H. Lemoine. [1840?] *obl.* fol.   **e. 272. (3.)**

— *See* Jullien (L. A.) La Sᵗ. Hubert, ou la chasse royale. Grand
quadrille ... Arrangé pour piano à quatre mains, par
H. Lemoine et Julien. [In fact, composed by L. A. Jullien and
arranged by H. Lemoine.] [1837?] fol. [*Les Soirées de Londres.
no.* 19.]   **h. 1385.**

— *See* Jullien (L. A.) Les Sérénades Italiennes arrangé par
H. Lemoine. 1835. fol.   **h. 580. (31.)**

— *See* Marcailhou (G.) The Indiana valse, arranged by
H. Lemoine. [1848.] fol.   **h. 987. (5.)**

— *See* Musard (P.) Les Puritains. Quadrille ... et Polonaise ...
arrangés ... par H. Lemoine. [1836.] fol.   **R. M. 25. i. 7. (12.)**

— *See* Tolbecque (J. B. J.) Quadrilles ... sur les motifs de La
Tentation ... arranged for two performers on the Pianoforte
by H. Lemoine. [1833?] fol.   **R. M. 25. i. 4. (1.)**

LEMOINE (Henry) and **LOUIS** (Nicolas)

— Fantaisie pour Piano et Flute ou violon avec accompᵗ. de
Basse sur le Ballet de l'Orgie, musique de Carafa. *London*,
[1833.] fol.   **h. 580. (36.)**

— Les inseparables. No. 1. Divertissement pour Piano et violon
et violoncello ad libitum, sur les motifs de l'opéra de
V. Rifaut "La sentinelle perdue". *London*, [1835.] fol.
    h. 580. (1.)

LEMOINE (Henry) and **SOR** (Ferdinand)

— Ecole de la Mesure et de la Ponctuation musicale. Cent
pièces pour Piano à quatre mains par H. Lemoine et F. Sor,
etc. 4 pt. *Paris*, [1877.] 4°.   **g. 744.**

LEMOINE (Léon)

— Allegretto Scherzando de la 8ᵉ. Symphonie ... de Beethoven;
arrangé à 6 mains par L. Lemoine. [P. F.] *See* Orchestre.
L'Orchestre au Salon ... no. 37. [1874, *etc.*] fol.   **h. 1427.**

— L'Attente. Mélodie [by] F. Schubert. Transcription de
L. Lemoine. *See* Album. Album Lyrique ... no. 17. [1881.] fol.
    h. 1481. p. (1.)

— Le Barbier de Seville. Introduction. Transcription de
L. Lemoine. *See* Album. Album Lyrique ... no. 4. [1881.] fol.
    h. 1481. p. (1.)

— La Belle de Seville. Valse sur le Divertissement Espagnol de
F. Thomé. 2 no. [P. F. solo and duet.] *Lemoine et Fils: Paris*,
[1886.] *obl.* fol.   **e. 272. o. (7.)**

— Le Chalet. Couplets ... Transcription de L. Lemoine. *See*
Album. Album Lyrique ... no. 33. [1883.] fol.
    h. 1481. p. (1.)

— Le Chant du Départ. E. H. Méhul. Transcription de
L. Lemoine. *See* Album. Album Lyrique ... no. 24. [1883.] fol.
    h. 1481. p. (1.)

— Dernière pensée de Weber. Transcription de L. Lemoine. *See*
Album. Album Lyrique ... no. 9. [1881.] fol.   **h. 1481. p. (1.)**

— Divertissement d'Orphée [by] Gluck ... Transcription pour
piano à 6 mains par L. Lemoine. *See* Orchestre. L'Orchestre
au Salon ... no. 49. [1874, *etc.*] fol.   **h. 1427.**

— Don Juan. Air ... Transcription de L. Lemoine. *See* Album.
Album Lyrique ... no. 16. [1881.] fol.   **h. 1481. p. (1.)**

— La Fille du Régiment, polka-mazurka pour Piano [on
D. G. M. Donizetti's opera], *etc.* *H. Lemoine: Paris*, [1880.]
fol.   **h. 3272. j. (22.)**

— La Flûte Enchantée. Duetto. Transcription de L. Lemoine.
See Album. Album Lyrique ... no. 10. [1881.] fol.
    h. 1481. p. (1.)

— La Juive. Finale du 1ᵉʳ Acte. Transcription de L. Lemoine.
See Album. Album Lyrique ... no. 30. [1883.] fol.
    h. 1481. p. (1.)

— Marche Funèbre d'une Marionnette de C. Gounod, transcrite
pour piano à 6 mains par L. Lemoine. *See* Orchestre.
L'Orchestre au Salon ... no. 30. [1874, *etc.*] fol.   **h. 1427.**

— Marche Hongroise de Rakoczy, arrangée pour piano par
L. Lemoine. No. 1, à 2 mains. No. 2, à 4 mains. 2 no.
H. Lemoine: Paris, [1879.] 4°.
Part of the "Panthéon des Pianistes".   **g. 545. b. (4.)**

— Marche Hongroise de Rakoczy, arrangée à 6 mains par
L. Lemoine. [P. F.] *See* Orchestre. L'Orchestre au Salon ...
no. 32. [1874, *etc.*] fol.   **h. 1427.**

— Marche Turque extraite de la Sonate de La majeur de
Mozart, arrangée à 6 mains par L. Lemoine. [P. F.] *See*
Orchestre. L'Orchestre au Salon ... no. 22. [1874, *etc.*] fol.
    h. 1427.

— La Marseillaise. Transcription de L. Lemoine. *See* Album.
Album Lyrique ... no. 23. [1883.] fol.   **h. 1481. p. (1.)**

— Mazurk des Traineaux de J. Ascher, arrangée à 6 mains par
L. Lemoine. [P. F.] *See* Orchestre. L'Orchestre au Salon ...
no. 31. [1874, *etc.*] fol.   **h. 1427.**

— Menuet du 11ᵉ Quintette de Boccherini, arrangé à six mains
par L. Lemoine. [P. F.] *See* Orchestre. L'Orchestre au Salon
... no. 35. [1874, *etc.*] fol.   **h. 1427.**

LEMOINE (Léon)

— Ouverture de la Flûte Enchantée [by] W. A. Mozart, arrangée pour piano à six mains par L. Lemoine. *See* ORCHESTRE. L'Orchestre au Salon ... no. 44. [1874, *etc.*] fol.   **h. 1427.**

— Polka Nationale. Transcription de L. Lemoine. *See* ALBUM. Album Lyrique ... no. 31. [1883.] fol.   **h. 1481. p. (1.)**

— Refrains de l'Ecolier. Recueil de petits chants à une voix choisis et accompagnés par L. Lemoine. 2 cah. Edition avec acc^t de piano. *Paris*, [1881–4.] 4°.   **B. 880. f. (9.)**

— Les Refrains de la Jeunesse. Recueil illustré de petits chants à une, deux et troix voix. Paroles de J. Ruelle. Choisis et accompagnés par L. Lemoine. 3 cah. Sans accompagnement. *Paris*, [1881–4.] 8°.   **C. 738. (7.)**

— Les Refrains de la Jeunesse. Recueil illustré de petits chants ... Paroles de J. Ruelle. Choisis et accompagnés par L. Lemoine. 3 cah. *Paris*, [1883–4.] 8°.   **F. 1565.**

— Romance de la Symphonie: La Reine de Haydn. Arrangée à 6 mains par L. Lemoine. [P. F.] *See* ORCHESTRE. L'Orchestre au Salon ... no. 27. [1874, *etc.*] fol.   **h. 1427.**

— Symphonie de la Reine. Romance. Transcription de L. Lemoine. *See* ALBUM. Album Lyrique ... no. 12. [1881.] fol.   **h. 1481. p. (1.)**

— Tarentelle [by] T. Lack. Arrangée à 6 mains par L. Lemoine. [P. F.] *See* ORCHESTRE. L'Orchestre au Salon ... no. 46. [1874, *etc.*] fol.   **h. 1427.**

— Valse et Galop, Divertissement. [By] H. Lemoine. Op. 30. Arrangé pour piano à six mains par L. Lemoine. *See* ORCHESTRE. L'Orchestre au Salon ... no. 43. [1874, *etc.*] fol.   **h. 1427.**

— Six Valses de Beethoven. Arrangées à 6 mains par L. Lemoine. *See* ORCHESTRE. L'Orchestre au Salon ... no. 33. [1874, *etc.*] fol.   **h. 1427.**

— 6 Valses et une Marche funèbre, pour Piano. (Arrangement à 4 mains par L. Lemoine.) [1882.] fol. *See* BEETHOVEN (L. van) [*Doubtful and Supposititious Works*.] [Waltzes. K.-H. Anhang 14.]   **h. 400. i. (6.)**

— [Another edition.] 6 Valses, *etc.* (Arrangement ... par L. Lemoine.) [1882.] 4°. *See* BEETHOVEN (L. van) [*Doubtful and Supposititious Works*.] [Waltzes. K.-H. Anhang 14.]   **g. 545. b. (1.)**

— 3e Valse, Beethoven ... Transcription de L. Lemoine. *See* ALBUM. Album lyrique ... no. 3. [1881.] fol.   **h. 1481. p. (1.)**

— *See* ADAM (A. C.) Le Chalet ... Partition réduite pour piano par L. Lemoine. [1882.] 4°.   **g. 361. (1.)**

— *See* ADAM (A. C.) [Le Chalet.] Ouverture ... arrangée pour piano par L. Lemoine. [1880.] 4°.   **g. 362. (3.)**

— *See* AUBER (D. F. E.) [Le Maçon.] Ouverture ... arrangée pour piano par L. Lemoine. [1880.] 4°.   **g. 362. (1.)**

— *See* BACHMANN (G.) L'Angelus. Pièce Pittoresque ... Transcrit pour piano par L. Lemoine. [1887.] fol.   **h. 3330. c. (4.)**

— *See* BACHMANN (G.) Le Guet. Petite Marche ... transcrite pour piano par L. Lemoine. [1887.] fol.   **h. 3330. c. (10.)**

— *See* BAZIN (F. E. J.) Maître Pathelin. Opéra Comique ... partition réduite pour piano par L. Lemoine. [1886.] 8°.   **g. 361. (2.)**

— *See* BAZIN (F. E. J.) [Le Voyage en Chine.] Ouverture ... [P. F.] Arrangée à 6 mains par L. Lemoine. [c. 1885.] fol. [*ORCHESTRE. L'Orchestre au Salon, etc. no.* 29.]   **h. 1427.**

— *See* BAZIN (F. E. J.) Le Voyage en Chine ... Ouverture arrangée pour piano et flûte (par L. Lemoine). 1885. fol.   **h. 2050. a. (11.)**

LEMOINE (Léon)

— *See* BAZIN (F. E. J.) [Le Voyage en Chine.] Ouverture ... arrangée pour piano et violon. 1885. fol.   **h. 1609. s. (8.)**

— *See* BROUTIN (C.) Ouverture triomphale ... Op. 13. Arrangée pour piano à 4 mains par L. Lemoine. 1885. fol.   **h. 3290. g. (8.)**

— *See* BROUTIN (C.) Ouverture triomphale ... Transcrite pour 2 pianos par L. Lemoine. 1885. fol.   **h. 3291. a. (2.)**

— *See* CROISEZ (A.) Petite Caprice sur ... La Fille du Régiment, *etc.* (Arrangé à 4 mains par L. Lemoine.) [1881.] fol.   **h. 1259. b. (9.)**

— *See* DONIZETTI (D. G. M.) La Fille du Régiment ... partition réduite pour piano par L. Lemoine. [1885.] 4°.   **g. 361. (3.)**

— *See* DONIZETTI (D. G. M.) [La Fille du Régiment.] Ouverture ... arrangée pour piano par L. Lemoine. [1882.] 4°.   **g. 362. (5.)**

— *See* DONIZETTI (D. G. M.) La Fille du Régiment. Entr'acte. Transcription de L. Lemoine. [P. F.] [1881.] fol. [*Album Lyrique. No.* 19.]   **h. 1481. p. (1.)**

— *See* GIRARD (N.) [Les Deux Voleurs.] Sarabande ... transcrite ... par L. Lemoine. [1878.] fol.   **h. 3272. f. (18.)**

— *See* GOUNOD (C. F.) Fête de Jupiter ... arrangée par L. Lemoine. [1877.] fol.   **h. 2575. h. (5.)**

— *See* GOUNOD (C. F.) Jésus sur le Lac de Thibériade ... Partition Piano et Chant réduite par L. Lemoine. [1878.] 4°.   **G. 517. e. (2.)**

— *See* GOUNOD (C. F.) [Maid of Athens.] Vièrge d'Athènes, mélodie transcrite pour piano par L. Lemoine. [1887.] fol.   **h. 80. e. (11.)**

— *See* GOUNOD (C. F.) Messe du Sacré Cœur de Jésus ... arrangée ... par L. Lemoine. [1878.] 4°.   **g. 272. y. (5.)**

— *See* GOUNOD (C. F.) Petite Étude-Scherzo ... Transcription pour piano par L. Lemoine. [1888.] fol.   **h. 80. e. (1.)**

— *See* GOUNOD (C. F.) [Polyeucte.] Airs de ballet, réduits pour le Piano ... par L. Lemoine. [1879.] fol.   **h. 80. c. (14.)**

— *See* GOUNOD (C. F.) [Polyeucte.] Bacchanale ... réduite pour Piano par L. Lemoine. [1879.] fol.   **h. 80. c. (15.)**

— *See* GOUNOD (C. F.) Vision de Jeanne d'Arc ... Transcription ... par L. Lemoine. [1887.] fol.   **h. 80. e. (10.)**

— *See* KETTEN (H.) Air de Ballet ... (Arrangé pour piano à 4 mains par L. Lemoine.) 1886. fol.   **h. 3290. h. (9.)**

— *See* LAVIGNAC (A.) Galop-Marche ... arrangé ... par L. Lemoine. [1875.] fol.   **h. 1487. p. (10.)**

— *See* LEROY (É.) Galop de Chasse ... (Arrangement à 4 mains par L. Lemoine.) [1886.] fol.   **h. 3290. h. (21.)**

— *See* MENDELSSOHN-BARTHOLDY (J. L. F.) [Overture. Op. 26. Die Hebriden.] Ouverture ... Arrangée pour piano par L. Lemoine. [1881.] 4°.   **g. 362. (4.)**

— *See* MENDELSSOHN-BARTHOLDY (J. L. F.) [Overture. Op. 95. Ruy Blas.] Ouverture ... Arrangée pour piano par L. Lemoine. [1881.] 4°.   **g. 362. (6.)**

— *See* MENDELSSOHN-BARTHOLDY (J. L. F.) [Ein Sommernachtstraum.] Scherzo du Songe d'une nuit d'été ... transcrit pour piano par L. Lemoine. [1883.] fol.   **h. 575. n. (9.)**

— *See* MICHEL (A.) and LEMOINE (L.) Pique-Nique quadrille, *etc.* [1883.] *obl.* fol.   **e. 272. m. (34.)**

— *See* MOZART (W. A.) [Le Nozze di Figaro.] Ouverture ... arrangée pour piano et violon par L. Lemoine et A. Blanc. [1880.] 4°.   **g. 362. (8.)**

LEMOINE (Léon)

— *See* MOZART (W. A.) [Symphony in G Minor. K. 550.] Menuet ... transcrit pour piano, *etc.* [1884.] fol.   **h. 321. g. (4.)**

— *See* SIVORI (E. C.) Deux Romances ... transcrites ... par L. Lemoine. [1887.] fol.   **g. 543. p. (20*.)**

— *See* STREABBOG (L.) *pseud.* Charles VI. Petite fantaisie pour piano ... [Duet] (arrangement ... par L. Lemoine). [1884.] fol.   **h. 3197. c. (18.)**

— *See* STREABBOG (L.) *pseud.* L'Éclair ... fantaisie pour piano. (Arrangement à 4 mains par L. Lemoine.) [1882.] fol.   **h. 3197. c. (5.)**

— *See* STREABBOG (L.) *pseud.* La Juive. Fantaisie pour piano ... à 4 mains (arrangement par L. Lemoine). [1882.] fol.   **h. 3197. c. (8.)**

— *See* STREABBOG (L.) *pseud.* Les Mousquetaires de la Reine ... fantaisie pour piano (arrangement à 4 mains par L. Lemoine). [1885.] fol.   **h. 3197. c. (6.)**

— *See* STREABBOG (L.) *pseud.* La Reine de Chypre ... Fantaisie pour piano ... [Duet] (arrangement ... par L. Lemoine). [1884.] fol.   **h. 3197. c. (20.)**

— *See* STREABBOG (L.) *pseud.* Le Val d'Andorre ... Fantaisie pour piano ... [Duet] (arrangement par L. Lemoine). [1884.] fol.   **h. 3197. c. (19.)**

— *See* STREABBOG (L.) Le Voyage en Chine ... fantaisie pour piano ... [Duet] (arrangement de L. Lemoine). [1883.] fol.   **h. 3197. c. (15.)**

— *See* THOMÉ (F. L. J.) Arlequin et Colombine. Air de Ballet arrangé pour piano à 4 mains par L. Lemoine. [1887.] fol.   **h. 3227. a. (7.)**

— *See* THOMÉ (F. L. J.) Gavotte et musette ... Op. 109. Transcription pour piano à 4 mains par L. Lemoine. [c. 1900.] fol.   **h. 1226. i. (8.)**

— *See* THOMÉ (F. L. J.) Marche Croate ... arrangée pour piano à 4 mains par L. Lemoine. [1887.] fol.   **h. 3227. a. (3.)**

— *See* THOMÉ (F. L. J.) [Les Noces d'Arlequin.] Sérénade d'Arlequin arrangée pour piano à 4 mains par L. Lemoine. Op. 56. 1886. fol.   **h. 3227. a. (2.)**

— *See* VERDI (F. G. F.) [Nabucodonosor.] Ouverture ... arrangée pour piano par L. Lemoine. [1881.] 4°.   **g. 362. (2.)**

— *See* WEBER (C. M. F. E. von) [12 Allemandes. Op. 4. No. 1–9.] Neuf Valses ... Arrangées à 4 mains par L. Lemoine. [1880.] 4°.   **g. 545. b. (7.)**

LEMOINE (Louise) *Mrs*

— *See* PUGET, afterwards LEMOINE.

LEMOINIER (Tom)

— *See* LEMONIER.

LEMON

— The Lemon Girl. [Tonadilla.] *See* ARANAZ (P.) [La Maja limonera.]

— A Lemon in the Garden of Love. [Song.] *See* CARLE (Richard F.)

— The Lemon Tree. [Song.] *See* MADDEN (Edward)

LEMON (Audrey Heath)

— Lute-book Lullaby. [Sacred song.] Words XVII century. *Novello & Co.: London,* [1938.] 8°.   **F. 1176. l. (35.)**

LEMON (Ella)

— Two Songs. —a— Spring-Time. —b— Dawn. Words and music by E. Lemon. *Arthur & Co.: London,* (1908.) fol.   **H. 1794. vv. (40.)**

LEMON (H. E.)

— Anna Held. Waltzes. [P. F.] *National Music Co.: Chicago & New York,* 1897. fol.   **h. 3286. g. (31.)**

LEMON (Laura G.)

— Acushla Machree. Song, words by S. S. Stitt. *J. Williams: London,* (1908.) fol.   **H. 3619. (1.)**

— As once I saw thee. Song, the words adapted from the German. *Boosey & Co.: London and New York,* 1896. fol.   **H. 1798. u. (43.)**

— Auld Scotland. Song set to an old Gaelic Air, the words by A. Grant. The music arranged by L. G. Lemon, *etc. Boosey & Co.: London and New York,* 1907. fol.   **H. 3619. (2.)**

— Back in dear old Blighty. Marching Song, words by A. Fleming, *etc. Weekes & Co.: London,* 1916. fol.   **H. 3619. (31.)**

— Canada. March. [P. F.] *Boosey & Co.: London and New York,* 1908. fol.   **h. 3283. p. (19.)**

— Canada ever! Patriotic Song, the words by W. Mills, *etc. Boosey & Co.: London and New York,* 1907. fol.   **H. 3619. (3.)**

— Canadian Song Cycle, the words by A. Fleming, *etc.* ([No. 1.] A Song of the Prairie. [No. 2.] The Chipmunk. [No. 3.] In old Quebec. [No. 4.] Sleep, my little Papoose.) *Boosey & Co.: London and New York,* 1911. 4°.   **G. 383. z. (10.)**

— Cassandra. Waltz. [P. F.] *Ascherberg, Hopwood & Crew: London,* 1910. fol.   **h. 3286. uu. (45.)**

— Chant sans Paroles ... for the Violin with Pianoforte accompaniment. *Boosey & Co.: London and New York,* (1910.) fol.
No. 3 of "Four Solos for the Violin," etc.   **h. 1612. v. (4.)**

— Columbia. Minuet for the Pianoforte. *E. Ashdown: London,* [1903.] fol.   **g. 605. ll. (17.)**

— Comfort one another. Song, the words by M. E. Sangster, *etc. Boosey & Co.: London and New York,* 1907. fol.   **H. 3619. (4.)**

— Coronach.—Lament.— [Song, words] By Sir W. Scott. *Boosey & Co.: London and New York,* 1908. fol.   **H. 3619. (5.)**

— A Cottage Song. [Song.] The words by A. Fleming, *etc. Boosey & Co.: London and New York,* 1908. fol.   **H. 3619. (6.)**

— Culloden Muir. Scotch Song, the words by W. Mills. *Boosey & Co.: London and New York,* 1910. fol.   **H. 3619. (16.)**

— Dear little one. Song, the words by A. Fleming. *Boosey & Co.: London and New York,* 1912. fol.   **H. 3619. (17.)**

— Don't go! Teddy Bear, don't go! Children's Song, the words by A. Fleming, *etc. Novello and Co.: London,* 1912. fol.   **H. 3619. (18.)**

— Down the blue Niagara. Canadian Love Song, the words by A. Fleming. *Novello and Co.: London,* 1912. fol.   **H. 3619. (19.)**

— Glad is the World. Song. Words by A. Fleming. *Chappell & Co.: London,* 1899. fol.   **H. 1799. h. (33.)**

— The Grand Match. Irish Song, the words by M. O'Neill, *etc. Boosey & Co.: London and New York,* 1907. fol.   **H. 3619. (7.)**

LEMON (Laura G.)

— Hey nonny no! Old English Lyric. *Boosey & Co.: London and New York*, 1897. fol. **H. 1798. u. (44.)**

— The Home Country. Song, the words by E. Teschemacher. *Boosey & Co.: London and New York*, 1910. fol. **H. 3619. (20.)**

— Hush, ma Bairnie! Scotch Cradle Song, the words by A. Grant. *Boosey & Co.: London and New York*, 1908. fol. **H. 3619. (8.)**

— I envy the Bird that sings. Song, the words by C. M. Hammill. *Boosey & Co.: London and New York*, 1897. fol. **H. 1798. u. (45.)**

— In alien Lands. Song, the words by G. Hubi-Newcombe. *Boosey & Co.: London & New York*, 1914. fol. **H. 3619. (25.)**

— [In alien Lands.] In distant Lands. Song, *etc. Boosey & Co.: New York, etc.*, 1915. fol. **H. 3619. (26.)**

— In distant Lands. *See* supra: [In alien Lands.]

— In Spring. Song. Words by A. Fleming. *Chappell & Co.: London*, 1899. fol. **H. 1799. h. (34.)**

— In the Apple Tree. Song, the words by H. Lulham. *Boosey & Co.: London, etc.*, 1920. fol. **H. 3619. (33.)**

— Land of the lonely Pines. Song, words by E. Newman. 2 no. [In E flat and F.] *Ascherberg, Hopwood & Crew: London*, 1912. fol. **H. 3619. (27.)**

— Liebeslied ... for the Violin with Pianoforte accompaniment. *Boosey & Co.: London and New York*, (1910.) fol. *No. 4 of "Four Solos for the Violin," etc.* **h. 1612. v. (5.)**

— Six Little Songs. *J. Williams: London*, 1900. 4°. **F. 637. j. (5.)**

— [Six Little Songs. No. 5.] My ain Love and my Dearie. Scotch Songs, words by I. MacDonald. *J. Williams: London*, (1900.) fol. **H. 1794. l. (8.)**

— Little Teddy Bear, good night! A Children's Song, words and music by L. G. Lemon, *etc. Boosey & Co.: London and New York*, 1908. fol. **H. 3619. (9.)**

— Love is a Butterfly. Song, the words by W. Mills. *Boosey & Co.: London and New York*, 1909. fol. **H. 3619. (10.)**

— Love's Necklet. Song, words by L. C. Shadwell. 2 no. [In F and G.] *Ascherberg, Hopwood & Crew: London*, 1913. fol. **H. 3619. (28.)**

— March on, O mighty Empire! [Song.] Words by E. Teschemacher. *Novello and Co.: London*, [1914.] 8°. **F. 636. hh. (13.)**

— Mighty Dominion.—Hymn of the Dominion.— [Sacred song.] Words by W. Mills. *Boosey & Co.: London and New York*, 1910. 8°. **F. 260. a. (9.)**

— Molly ochone. Irish Song, words by B. O'Malley. *Elkin & Co.: London*, 1905. fol. **H. 1794. l. (6.)**

— Three Moravian Dances for Violin and Piano. No. 1. Mazurka in G. No. 2. Mazurka in E minor. No. 3. Mazurka in G, *etc.* 3 no. *Weekes & Co.: London*, 1910. fol. **h. 1612. v. (3.)**

— My ain Folk. A ballad of home, *etc.* ⟨N° 1 in D♭.⟩ pp. 7. *Boosey & Co.: London, New York*, [1904.] fol. **G. 1276. hh. (15.)**

— My ain Folk. A Ballad of Home, the words by W. Mills. ⟨No. 2 in E♭.⟩ pp. 7. *Boosey & Co.: London and New York*, 1904. fol. **H. 1794. l. (7.)**

— My ain Folk. S. S. A. ... Arr. by G. Shackley. *Boosey Hawkes Belwin, Inc.: New York*, 1942. 8°. **F. 217. j. (32.)**

LEMON (Laura G.)

— My ain Folk. Arranged for Men's Voices by D. Arnold, *etc. Boosey & Co.: London*, 1943. 8°. [*Boosey's Choral Miscellany. no.* 215.] **F. 160. e.**

— My ain Folk. Arranged for female voices (S. S. A.) by Ronald Curtis, *etc.* pp. 12. *Boosey & Hawkes: London*, [1953.] 8°. [*Boosey's choral Miscellany. no.* 281.] **F. 160. e.**

— My ain Love and my Dearie. *See* supra: [Six Little Songs. No. 5.]

— My Hieland Hame. Scotch Song, words by A. Grant, *etc. E. Donajowski: London*, [1907.] fol. **H. 3619. (11.)**

— My Hieland Hame. Scotch Song, *etc. Boosey & Co.: London and New York*, 1907. fol. **H. 3619. (12.)**

— My Laddie o'er the Sea. Song, words by W. Mills. *Keith, Prowse & Co.: London*, 1920. fol. **H. 3619. (34.)**

— My Lady Daffodil. Song, the words by M. Hope. *Novello and Co.: London*, 1912. fol. **H. 3619. (29.)**

— The Neddy Lover. Song, the words by N. W. Byng. *Boosey & Co.: London, etc.*, 1920. fol. **H. 3619. (35.)**

— The Nightingale on Oakwood Spray. Song, the words by M. Byron. *Boosey & Co.: London and New York*, 1909. fol. **H. 3619. (21.)**

— Nobody knows. Song, the words by A. Fleming. *Boosey & Co.: London and New York*, 1896. fol. **H. 1798. u. (46.)**

— O fragrant Mignonette.—An old sweet Memory.— Song, the words by G. Hubi Newcombe. *Boosey & Co.: London and New York*, 1907. fol. **H. 3619. (13.)**

— O fragrant Mignonette. Male Quartette ... Arr. by G. O'Hara. *Boosey & Co.: New York and London*, (1911.) 8°. *No. 6 of "Boosey & Co.'s Series of famous Songs ... arranged for Male Voices".* **F. 163. m. (33.)**

— Oh! her Face is so fair. Song, the words by F. E. Gilder. *Boosey & Co.: London and New York*, 1910. fol. **H. 3619. (22.)**

— Three Old English Dances. [P. F.] *Bosworth & Co.: London*, 1918. 4°. **g. 603. tt. (7.)**

— Pas de Quatre pour Piano. *E. Ashdown: London*, [1904.] fol. **g. 605. ll. (18.)**

— Romance, for Violin with Pianoforte accompaniment. *Boosey & Co.: London and New York*, 1908. fol. **h. 1612. p. (25.)**

— The Rose Garden. Song, words by A. Fleming. 3 no. [In D flat, E flat, and F.] *Chappell & Co.: London*, [1896–7.] fol. **H. 1798. u. (47.)**

— Rouse, Caledonians. A Scottish National Song, the words by A. Grant, *etc. Boosey & Co.: London and New York*, 1908. fol. **H. 3619. (14.)**

— A Shielin' on the Brae. Scottish Song, the words by T. McRorie. *Paterson & Sons: Edinburgh, etc.*, 1917. fol. **H. 3619. (32.)**

— Slumber Song. The words by A. Fleming. *Chappell & Co.: London*, [1895.] fol. **H. 1798. u. (48.)**

— Two Songs. (a.) Tell me true.—Words by A. Fleming.—(b.) The World may change.—Old English Lyric. *J. B. Cramer & Co.: London*, 1896. fol. **H. 1798. u. (49.)**

— Spanish Dance, for Violin with Pianoforte accompaniment. *Boosey & Co.: London and New York*, 1908. fol. **h. 1612. p. (26.)**

— The Summer's quickly passing. Song, the words by A. Fleming. *Boosey & Co.: London and New York*, 1910. fol. **H. 3619. (23.)**

LEMON (Laura G.)

— Sweet Ann Page.—Old English Dance.— For the Piano.
J. Williams: London, (1907.) fol.   **h. 3283. p. (20.)**

— There are Pearls. Song for a high or low voice, words by
A. Fleming, *etc. Leonard & Co.: London*, 1909. fol.
          H. 3619. (24.)

— There is no Star that shineth. Song, the words by A. Fleming.
Boosey & Co.: London and New York, 1896. fol.
          H. 1798. u. (51.)

— 'Tis now! Song, the words by A. Fleming. *Chappell & Co.:
London*, [1896.] fol.   **H. 1798. u. (50.)**

— A Wee Bit o' Heather. Song, the words by A. Grant, *etc.
Boosey & Co.: London and New York*, 1907. fol.
          H. 3619. (15.)

— Where are the Boys who'll fight for dear old England?
Marching Song. [Words by] A. Fleming. *Novello and Co.:
London*, [1915.] fol.   **H. 3619. (30.)**

— Youth and Age. Song. Words by Lord Byron. *Chappell &
Co.: London*, 1899. fol.   **H. 1799. h. (35.)**

LEMON (Lucylle)

— Send down your Blessings. [Anthem.] Words and music by
L. Lemon. pp. 3. *Elma & Carl's Music Publishers: Detroit*,
[1962.] 8°.   **E. 335. rr. (5.)**

LEMON (M. K.)

— My Boyish Love. Song [begins: "Out of the vista"]. *London*,
[1876.] fol.   **H. 1783. o. (46.)**

LEMON (Mary Mark)

— Fidelis. Song, written [and] composed ... by M. M. Lemon.
Enoch & Sons: London, [1883.] fol.   **H. 1788. v. (34.)**

LE MON (Melvin)

— The Miner Sings. A Collection of Folk Songs and Ballads of
the Anthracite Miner. Transcriptions and musical
arrangements by M. Le Mon ... Introduction and editorial
notes by G. Korson. *J. Fischer & Bro.: New York*, 1936. 8°.
          F. 1771. f. (16.)

— *See* Korson (G.) Minstrels of the Mine Patch. Songs and
Stories of the Anthracite Industry. [With words and melodies
transcribed by M. Le Mon.] 1938. 8°.   **12299. b. 4.**

LEMON (W. G.)

— Helter-skelter. Xylophone solo. ⟨Conductor [and military
band parts].⟩ 32 pt. *In:* Steck (Arnold) Morning Canter, *etc.*
[1954.] fol. [*Chappell's Army Journal.* no. 784.]   **h. 1562.**

— The Joyful Skeleton. (Xylophone solo), *etc.* ⟨Arranged for
military band by W. J. Duthoit. Conductor [and parts].⟩ 34 pt.
In: Rycoth (Denis) Red Square Review, *etc.* [1961.] 4°. [*Army
Journal.* no. 830.]   **h. 1562.**

— The Territorial Army. (Golden Jubilee March), *etc.*
[Conductor and military band parts.] 44 pt. *Hawkes & Son:
London*, [1960.] 8° & *obl.* 8°.   **h. 3210. i. (584.)**

— Xylophonics. (Xylophone solo.) Arranged for military band
by W. J. Duthoit. ⟨Conductor [and parts].⟩ 33 pt. *In:* Williams
(Charles) *Composer of film music. A Quiet Stroll, etc.* [1960.]
fol. [*Chappell's Army Journal.* no. 824.]   **h. 1562.**

LEMON (William J.)

— The Moon rose o'er the battle plain ... Ballad. *London*,
[1867.] fol.   **H. 1772. r. (33.)**

LEMON (William J.)

— Soldiers funeral march ... for the piano. *Philadelphia*, 1854.
fol.   **h. 1459. p. (6.)**

LEMONADE

— Lemonade and Sherry. Song. *See* Coote (R.)

LEMONIER (Thomas)

— All wise Chickens follow me. [Song.] Words by Henry
S. Creamer. pp. 5. *Archer & Lemonier: New York*, [1906.] fol.
          H. 3985. s. (39.)

— Billy Weeper the Chimney Sweeper. ⟨Coon song.⟩ Words by
Hen. Wise. pp. 5. *Harmony Music Co.: New York*, [1906.] fol.
          H. 3985. s. (40.)

— Dinah, come kiss your Baby. [Song.] Words by Henry
S. Creamer. *Archer & Lemonier:* [*New York*, 1906.] 4°.
          H. 3985. s. (41.)

— "Good Afternoon, Mr. Jenkins." [Song.] Words by R. C.
McPherson. pp. 5. *Jos. W. Stern & Co.: New York*, [1901.] fol.
          H. 3985. s. (42.)

— I'd like to be a real Lady ... [Song.] Words by Alex. Rogers.
pp. 5. *Shapiro, Bernstein & Co.: Chicago, etc.*, [1902.] fol.
          H. 3985. s. (43.)

— I'll be your Dewdrop Rosey ... Song & refrain. Words by
Richard H. Gerard. pp. 5. *M. Witmark & Sons: New York,
etc.*, [1904.] fol.   **H. 3985. s. (44.)**

— I wonder how the old Folks are at Home. [Song.] Lyric by
Henry S. Creamer. pp. 5. *Archer & Lemonier: New York*,
[1906.] fol.   **H. 3985. s. (45.)**

— I wonder what makes it snow. [Song.] Words by Tom Brown.
Howley, Dresser Co.: New York, [1904.] fol.   **H. 3985. s. (46.)**

— If ma Babe could see me now. [Song.] Words by Frank
B. Williams & Harry Brown. pp. 5. *Chas. F. Lietz & Co.:
New York*, [1905.] fol.
*The name of the publisher "Nathan Bivins" has been erased
from p. 2 of the music and "Chas. F. Lietz" substituted with a
stamp.*   **H. 3985. s. (47.)**

— It's the same old "Suwanee". [Song.] Words by Richard
H. Gerard. pp. 5. *M. Witmark & Sons: New York, etc.*, [1904.]
fol.   **H. 3985. s. (48.)**

— "Junie." [Song.] Words by R. G. McPherson. pp. 5. *Jos.
W. Stern & Co.: New York*, [1901.] fol.   **H. 3985. s. (49.)**

— Just one Word of Consolation. [Song.] Words by Frank
B. Williams. pp. 5. *Chas. K. Harris: New York*, [1905.] fol.
          H. 3985. s. (50.)

— "The Leader of the Ball." [Song.] Words by A. C. McPherson.
pp. 5. *Jos. W. Stern & Co.: New York*, [1901.] fol.
          H. 3985. s. (51.)

— "Lets play a Game of Soldier." [Song.] Words by James
T. Quirk. pp. 3–5. [*Gotham Music Pub. Co.: New York*, 1905.]
4°.
The publisher's name has been impressed on p. 3 with a stamp.
          H. 3985. s. (52.)

— The Lily, Rose and Vine. [Song.] Words by Leigh
R. Whipper. pp. 5. [1905.] fol.   **H. 3985. s. (53.)**

— Little Kickapoo. [Song.] Words by Alfred Bryan, *etc.* pp. 5.
Howley, Dresser Co.: New York, [1904.] fol.   **H. 3985. s. (54.)**

— Love me all the Time. [Song.] Words and music by
T. Lemonier. pp. 5. *Nathan Bivins: New York*, [1906.] fol.
          H. 3985. s. (55.)

— Mary Ellen. [Song.] Words by Alfred Bryan. pp. 5. *Howley,
Haviland & Dresser: New York*, [1903.] fol.   **H. 3985. s. (56.)**

LEMONIER (Thomas)

— "Miss Hannah from Savannah." [Song.] Words by A. C. McPherson. pp. 5. *Jos. W. Stern & Co.: New York,* [1901.] fol. **H. 3985. s. (57.)**

— My Cabin Door. [Song.] Words by Grant Stewart. pp. 3–6. *T. B. Harms Co.:* [*New York,* 1905.] fol. **H. 3985. s. (58.)**

— My dear Luzon. [Song.] Words by J. A. Shipp. *F. A. Mills: New York,* [1904.] fol. **H. 3985. s. (59.)**

— My little Dinah Lee. [Song.] Words by James J. Burris. pp. 3. *Howley, Haviland & Dresser: New York,* [1903.] fol. **H. 3985. s. (60.)**

— My tantalizin' little Susie Ann. [Song.] Words by Elmer Bowman. pp. 5. *F. A. Mills: New York,* [1903.] 4°. **H. 3985. s. (61.)**

— Prove it to me. [Song.] Words by R. C. McPherson. pp. 5. *M. Witmark & Sons: New York, etc.,* [1904.] fol. **H. 3985. s. (62.)**

— When the Grand Army's out on Parade. [Song.] Words by Frank B. Williams. pp. 5. *Nathan Bivins Music Pub. Co.: New York,* [1905.] fol. **H. 3985. s. (63.)**

— *See* BROWN (Harry) *Singing comedian,* and LEMONIER (T.) I'm just barely living, dat's all. [Song.] Words and music by H. Brown and T. Lemonier. [1903.] fol. **H. 3982. bb. (4.)**

— *See* ENGEL (S. C.) and LEMONIER (T.) Fazie, *etc.* [Song.] [1905.] fol. **H. 3983. jj. (5.)**

— *See* HOGAN (Ernest) and LEMONIER (T.) Is everybody happy? *etc.* [Song.] [1905.] fol. **H. 3984. bb. (19.)**

— *See* HOGAN (Ernest) and LEMONIER (T.) Mobile Mandy, *etc.* [Song.] [1905.] fol. **H. 3984. bb. (20.)**

— *See* INGRAM (Henry B.) and LEMONIER (T.) Where a Baby runs to meet you, and kiss you, that is Home, *etc.* [Song.] [1906.] fol. **H. 3984. nn. (41.)**

— *See* VAUGHN (Jim) and LEMONIER (T.) The Coon with the Panama, *etc.* [Song.] [1902.] 4°. **H. 3988. j. (23.)**

— *See* VAUGHN (Jim) and LEMONIER (T.) When Sousa comes to Coon-town, *etc.* [Song.] [1902.] 4°. **H. 3988. j. (24.)**

LEMONIER (Thomas) and LARKINS (John)

— De Sun am shinin' why don't you go? [Song.] Words by Madison Reid. ⟨Arr. by Herman Carle.⟩ pp. 5. *Archer & Lemonier:* [*New York,* 1906.] fol. **H. 3985. s. (64.)**

LEMONT (Cedric Wilmot)

— Barnyard Denizens. 6 half-minute fancies for ... young piano players. *C. Fischer: New York, etc.,* 1916. 4°. **g. 442. w. (5.)**

— Children at Play. Six Pieces for the Piano, *etc.* (Op. 2.) *Gamble Hinged Music Co.: Chicago,* [1913.] 4°. **g. 603. z. (7.)**

— Cinderella. A fairy tale for piano. *Gamble Hinged Music Co.: Chicago,* 1913. fol. **h. 3578. (10.)**

— Compositions for Piano. 1. Sylvan Dance ... 2. Hush-a-bye Lady ... 3. On tiptoe ... 4. A Moorish Dance ... 5. Over the Hills to Faerie ... 6. Twinkling Stars ... 7. A Stately Dance ... 8. Tag ... 9. The Boy Scouts ... 10. The Graceful Dancer ... 11. Petit Ballet ... 12. Dancing Shadows, *etc.* 12 no. *Gamble Hinged Music Co.: Chicago,* (1912.) fol. **g. 606. n. (38.)**

— Creole Sketches for the piano. Op. 15. *O. Ditson Co.: Boston,* 1916. 4°. **g. 112. c. (7.)**

— The Dancers. *See* infra: [Dream Pictures. Op. 6. No. 2.]

LEMONT (Cedric Wilmot)

— Dear Lord and Father. Hymn-Anthem ... [Words by] J. G. Whittier, adapted. *White-Smith Music Publishing Co.: Boston, etc.,* 1927. 8°. **E. 335. d. (58.)**

— Dream Pictures, for the Piano. Opus 6. *O. Ditson Co.: Boston,* (1914.) 4°. **g. 603. bb. (4.)**

— [Dream Pictures. Op. 6. No. 2.] The Dancers. Transcribed (for violin and piano) by K. Rissland. *O. Ditson Co.: Boston,* 1914. fol. **h. 3578. (9.)**

— Fairyland. A Set of instructive Pieces for the Piano. 1. The Fairy Guard. 2. The Goblin. 3. The Water Nymph. 4. The Sprite. 5. Elves. 6. The Last of the Fairies. 7. Lament for the Fairies. 7 no. *C. F. Summy Co.: Chicago,* (1912.) fol. **h. 3284. g. (12.)**

— Three Fantasie Pieces. Op. 18. 1. Pastel. 2. Tendresse. 3. Valse serenade. 3 no. [P. F.] *O. Ditson Co.: Boston,* 1917. fol. **h. 3578. (6.)**

— For the Piano. Op. 3. No. 1. A Merry Prank. No. 2. Coquetry. No. 3. Dancing the Minuet. Op. 4. No. 1. The Calisthenic Drill. No. 2. Chasing Butterflies. No. 3. The Polish Dancer. 6 no. *O. Ditson Co.: Boston,* (1913.) fol. **h. 3284. g. (10.)**

— From an old Garden. Four characteristic pieces for the pianoforte, *etc.* 4 no. *T. Presser Co.: Philadelphia,* 1924. 4°. **g. 1127. w. (2.)**

— Glory to God on High. (Song.) Words by Dr. A. D. Watson. *Methodist Book and Publishing House: Toronto,* 1920. fol. **H. 3161.**

— God hath sent His Angels. Easter Hymn-Anthem ... [Words by] H. Brooks. *White-Smith Music Publishing Co.: Boston, etc.,* 1927. 8°. **E. 335. d. (21.)**

— Golden Harps are sounding. Easter Hymn-Anthem ... [Words by] F. R. Havergal. *White-Smith Music Publishing Co.: Boston, etc.,* 1928. 8°. **E. 335. d. (59.)**

— Hark! what mean those holy Voices. Christmas Hymn-Anthem ... [Words by] J. Cawood. *White-Smith Music Publishing Co.: Boston, etc.,* 1927. 8°. **E. 335. d. (60.)**

— In a Gondola. (Piano.) *Gamble Hinged Music Co.: Chicago,* 1914. fol. **h. 3578. (11.)**

— In Springtime. (Piano.) *Gamble Hinged Music Co.: Chicago,* 1914. fol. **h. 3578. (12.)**

— Katrina. Waltz Intermezzo. (Piano.) *C. F. Summy Co.: Chicago,* (1912.) fol. **h. 3284. g. (14.)**

— Kiddies. Six short and easy descriptive pieces for piano, *etc.* 6 no. *G. Schirmer: New York,* 1922. 4°. **g. 1127. h. (1.)**

— The Kiss. [Song, words by] S. Teasdale. *O. Ditson Co.: Boston,* 1917. fol. **H. 1846. x. (46.)**

— The Merrymakers. Six Melodious Practice Pieces for the Piano. Op. 5. 1. The Merrymakers. 2. Playing Soldier. 3. The Dancing Girl. 4. The Flower Girl. 5. Before the Mirror. 6. Sunshine and Shadow. 6 no. *O. Ditson Co.: Boston,* (1913.) fol. **h. 3284. g. (11.)**

— Military Sketches ... for the piano. Op. 19. 1. The Old Guard. 2. The Artillery Corps. 3. Infantry. 4. Cavalry. 4 no. *O. Ditson Co.: Boston,* 1917. fol. **h. 3578. (7.)**

— Four Musical Fancies for piano, *etc.* *C. F. Summy Co.: Chicago,* 1915. 4°. **g. 603. ii. (9.)**

— On the Bayou. (Piano.) *Gamble Hinged Music Co.: Chicago,* 1922. 4°. **g. 1125. k. (13.)**

— Three Pictures of medium difficulty, for the piano. [No. 1.] Just a-dreaming. [No. 2.] By-gone days. [No. 3.] Serenade. 3 no. *G. Schirmer: New York,* 1922. 4°. **g. 1127. h. (2.)**

LEMONT (Cedric Wilmot)

— Picturettes for the piano. Op. 20. 1. At the window. 2. In a Troika. 3. The Spanish girl. 4. Whimsies. 5. Summer breezes. *O. Ditson Co.: Boston*, 1918. fol.
Wanting no. 2–5.   **h. 3578. (8.)**

— Three Pieces for violin and piano. [No. 1.] Cantilena amorosa. [No. 2.] Punchinello. [No. 3.] Le tambourin, *etc.* 3 no. *O. Ditson Co.: Boston*, 1917. fol.   **h. 3578. (13.)**

— Playtime Fancies for the piano. Op. 16. 1. After school. 2. Down the line. 3. Dance of the flowers. 4. In grandmother's time. 5. Will-o'-the-wisp. 5 no. *O. Ditson Co.: Boston*, 1915. fol.   **h. 3578. (4.)**

— Pleasant Memories ... for the piano. Opus 9. 1. At the carnival. 2. The Bird-clock. 3. In the park. 4. March of the clowns. 5. A Storiette. 5 no. *O. Ditson Co.: Boston*, 1914. fol.   **h. 3578. (3.)**

— Two Poems by A. Symons. [No. 1.] Memory. [No. 2.] In Fountain Court. 2 no. *G. Schirmer: New York*, 1922. 4°.   **G. 1275. i. (14.)**

— Rippling Brooklet. [P. F.] *C. F. Summy Co.: Chicago*, 1919. 4°.   **g. 1129. l. (28.)**

— The Shepherd's Pipe. (Piano.) *C. F. Summy Co.: Chicago*, 1912. fol.   **h. 3284. g. (13.)**

— Shule, shule, shule agrah! [Song, words by] F. Macleod. *O. Ditson Co.: Boston*, 1917. fol.   **H. 1846. x. (47.)**

— Silhouettes. Four short pieces for piano, *etc.* 4 no. *C. F. Summy Co.: Chicago*, 1925. 4°.   **g. 1127. w. (3.)**

— Two Songs for high voice, words by A. Symons. [No. 1.] At seventeen. [No. 2.] After love. 2 no. *G. Schirmer: New York*, 1923. 4°.   **G. 1275. i. (15.)**

— Two Songs ... [No. 1.] O lady, leave thy silken thread. (T. Hood.) [No. 2.] I wish I knew. (H. E. Mason.) 2 no. *G. Schirmer: New York*, 1925. 4°.   **G. 1275. s. (1.)**

— Springtime Sketches ... for the piano. Opus 8. 1. An April shower. 2. Clotilde. 3. Care-free. 4. La Débutante. 5. Nocturnette. 6. A roundelay. 7. Shadow pictures. 8. The wood-nymph. 8 no. *O. Ditson Co.: Boston*, 1914. fol.   **h. 3578. (2.)**

— Nine Storiettes for the piano. *O. Ditson Co.: Boston*, 1916. 4°.   **g. 603. hh. (8.)**

— Story Book Folk ... For the piano. Op. 7, *etc. O. Ditson Co.: Boston*, 1914. fol.   **h. 3578. (1.)**

— Sylvan Sketches ... for the piano. Op. 17. 1. On the green. 2. Nodding flowerets. 3. In summertime ... 4. Tripping along. 5. The fawn. 6. Danza. 6 no. *O. Ditson Co.: Boston*, 1917. fol.   **h. 3578. (5.)**

— When Twilight falls, for the pianoforte. *T. Presser Co.: Philadelphia*, 1922. 4°.   **g. 1127. h. (3.)**

LEMONT (Wilmot)

— *See* Lemont (Cedric Wilmot)

LEMORE (Harry)

— Little Gussie. Written by J. W. Nubley, *etc.* [Song. Staff and tonic sol-fa notation. Voice part.] *Francis, Day & Hunter: London*, [1896.] *s. sh.* fol.   **H. 3980. qq. (25.)**

LEMOS (Iberê)

— *See* Iberê de Lemos (A.)

LEMOYNE (Gabriel)

— La Noce au Village. 2ᵉ Fantaisie pour le pianoforte ... Opera 17. *Paris*, [1800?] fol.   **g. 492.**

LE MOYNE (Jean Baptiste)

— Electre. Tragédie, en Trois Actes ... Gravée par Dupré. [Score.] *Chez l'Auteur: Paris*, [1782.] fol.   **G. 641. a.**

— [Another copy.]   **Hirsch II. 508.**

— [Louis IX. en Égypte.] Du Français asservi j'ai sçu briser les chaines. *Air de Louis* IX. [by J. B. Le Moyne], *etc.* [1790.] 8°. *See* Louis.   **B. 362. h. (35.)**

— [Miltiade à Marathon.] Mon fils vole aux champs de l'honneur. *Air, etc.* [By J. B. Le Moyne.] [1793.] 8°. *See* Miltiade.   **B. 362. d. (7.)**

— Nephté, tragédie en trois actes ... Gravée par Huguet. [Score.] pp. 361. *Chez l'auteur: Paris*, [1789?] fol. *With a leaf bearing a dedication, following the titlepage.*   **Hirsch II. 509.**

— Nephté. Tragédie en Troix Actes [written by F. B. Hoffmann] ... Gravée par Huguet, *etc.* [Score.] *Chez l'Auteur: Paris*, [1795?] fol. *Without the leaf bearing the dedication.*   **G. 641. c.**

— Phêdre. [For songs, etc., published anonymously:] *See* Phêdre.

— Phêdre. Tragédie en Trois Actes ... Gravée par Huguet, *etc. Chez Le Duc: Paris*, [1786.] fol.   **G. 641.**

— Phêdre. Tragédie en trois actes ... Gravée par Huguet. [Score.] pp. 339. *Chez Le Duc: Paris*, [1790?] fol. *Plate number* 824.   **Hirsch II. 510.**

— Les Pommiers et le Moulin. [For songs, etc., published anonymously:] *See* Pommiers.

— Les Pommiers et le moulin. Comédie lyrique ... Gravée par Huguet. [Score.] pp. 167. *Chez l'auteur: Paris*, [1790?] fol.   **Hirsch II. 511.**

— Les Prétendus. [For songs, etc., published anonymously:] *See* Prétendus.

— Les Prétendus. Comédie Lirique ... Gravée par Huguet, *etc.* [Score.] *Chez l'Auteur: Paris*, [1789.] fol.   **G. 641. b.**

— [Another copy.]   **Hirsch II. 512.**

— [Les Prétendus.] Ouverture des Prétendus [by J. B. Le Moyne], Arrangée ... par Mʳ Mezger. [1789.] fol. *See* Mezger (F.)   **g. 272. r.**

LEMPRIERE (H. A.)

— "The God of Love;" a ballad [begins: "To guard the virgin heart"], written by T. Lempriere. *London*, [1817.] fol.   **H. 1675. (24.)**

— Innocence; a song [begins: "O ye, with pure"]. *London*, [1815?] fol.   **H. 1675. (23.)**

LÉMUNE (Gaston) *pseud.* [i. e. Frederic Mullen.]

— Au Forêt. A Woodland Idyll. [P. F.] *E. Ashdown: London, etc.*, [1909.] fol.   **h. 3283. jj. (44.)**

— L'Automne. Mélodie pour Piano. *E. Ashdown: London, etc.*, [1908.] fol.   **h. 3283. p. (21.)**

— L'Automne ... Violin and Piano. *E. Ashdown: London, etc.*, [1909.] fol.   **g. 505. bb. (27.)**

— Chant du Printemps, pour Piano. *E. Ashdown: London, etc.*, 1912. fol.   **g. 606. n. (39.)**

LÉMUNE (GASTON) *pseud.* [i. e. FREDERIC MULLEN.]

— Dance Fancies. Four pieces for the pianoforte. [No. 1.] Valse légère. [No. 2.] Gavotte d'amour. [No. 3.] Menuet tendre. [No. 4.] Danse neige. *E. Ashdown: London*, 1919. 4°.
g. 1129. r. (16.)

— Marche scandinavienne, pour Piano. *E. Ashdown: London, etc.*, [1910.] fol.
g. 606. f. (22.)

— Marche scandinavienne pour Piano ... Duet. *E. Ashdown: London, etc.*, [1911.] fol.
h. 3290. v. (28.)

— Pensée lyrique. [P. F.] *E. Ashdown: London, etc.*, [1910.] fol.
g. 606. f. (23.)

— Polichinelle. Morceau Humoristique. [P. F.] *E. Ashdown: London, etc.*, [1911.] fol.
h. 3284. g. (15.)

— Romance, pour Piano. *E. Ashdown: London, etc.*, 1911. fol.
h. 3284. g. (16.)

— Songe d'Été. Mélodie. Pianoforte Solo. *E. Ashdown: London, etc.*, 1910. fol.
h. 3284. g. (17.)

— Valse française, pour Piano. *E. Ashdown: London, etc.*, [1910.] fol.
g. 606. f. (24.)

— Venise. Barcarolle. Pour Piano. *E. Ashdown: London, etc.*, 1912. fol.
g. 606. n. (40.)

LENA

— Lena. [Song.] *See* NICHOLS (George A.)

— Lena. Melodia. *See* WINTER (G. C.)

— Lena de l'Orme. [Song.] *See* WHITING (A. B.) Three Heart Dreamings. No. 1.

— Lena Schmitt. [Song.] *See* PETRIE (Henry W.)

LEÑADOR

— Leñador, no tales el pino. [Part-song.] *See* BAL Y GAY (J.)

LENAERTS (PIETER)

— Een Nieu liedt-boeck, genaemt den Druyuen-tros der amoureusheyt ... 1602. Met een inleiding en aanteekeningen uitgegeven door P. J. Meertens. pp. xi. 192. *W. Landstra: Utrecht*, 1929. 8°.
[*Liederen van Groot-Nederland. vol.* 1.] **F. 1663. a.**

LENAERTS (RENÉ BERNARD)

— Fünfzehn flämische Lieder der Renaissance zu 2 bis 5 Stimmen. Herausgegeben von R. B. Lenaerts. *Flem. & Ger.* pp. iv. 44. *Möseler Verlag: Wolfenbüttel*, [1964.] 8°.
[*Das Chorwerk. no.* 92.] **E. 1317.**

— Die Kunst der Niederländer. pp. 117. *Arno Volk Verlag: Köln*, [1962.] fol.
[*Das Musikwerk. Hft.* 22.] **G. 16.**

— [Die Kunst der Niederländer.] The Art of the Netherlands. ⟨Translation by Robert Kolben.⟩ pp. 117. *Arno Volk Verlag: Köln*, [1964.] 4°.
[*Anthology of Music. no.* 22.] **G. 16. a.**

— Het Nederlands polifonies Lied in de zestiende eeuw. *Mechelen, Amsterdam*, 1933. 8°. **7894. tt. 3.**

— Nederlandse polyfonie uit spaanse bronnen. 1. Noe Bauldewijn. Missa En douleur et tristesse. 2. Matheus Gascongne. Missa Es hat ein sin. 3. Theo Verelst. Missa quatuor vocum ... Edidit R. B. Lenaerts. pp. xi. 77. *Vereniging voor Muziekgeschiedenis: Antwerpen*, 1963. fol. [*Monumenta musicae belgicae.* 9.] *With a sheet of addenda to the sources on p. vi and p. xi inserted.* **H. 15.**

LENAERTS (RENÉ BERNARD)

— *See* LA RUE (P. de) Drie missen. ⟨Ediderunt R. B. Lenaerts et Jozef Robijns.⟩ 1960. fol. [*Monumenta musicä belgicae.* 8.]
H. 15.

— *See* MONTE (F. di) Philippi de Monte opera ... New complete edition ... General editor R. B. Lenaerts. 1975, *etc.* fol.
H. 307.

LEND

— Lend a Hand. [Song.] *See* SPAULDING (G. L.)

— Lend a helping Hand. Song. *See* COMBEN (A.)

— Lend a helping hand. Song. *See* SCHLEYER (C. F.)

— Lend an Ear, Lady fair. [Part-song.] *See* ABT (F. W.)

— Lend me Thine Eyes. [Sacred song.] *See* JEWITT (J. M.)

— Lend me thy Fillet, Love. Song. *See* BROCKWAY (H.)

— Lend me thy Fillet, Love. Song. *See* HAMMER (M. von)

— Lend me thy Voice. Song. *See* COHNREICH (L.)

— Lend me your Aid. Recit and Air. *See* GOUNOD (C. F.) [La Reine de Saba.—Inspirez-moi, race divine!]

— Lend me your fairy Wand. Song. *See* ELLERTON (Alfred) *the Elder.*

— Lend me your Wings, little Bird. Song. *See* AUCKLAND (Arthur)

— Lend unto time thy wings, O Love! Song. *See* RODWELL (G. H.) [The seven maids of Munich.]

— Lend your aid now my muse. *Taste Alamode.* A New Song. [*London*, 1765.] 8°.
Royal Magazine, Vol. XII., p. 269. **P. P. 5441.**

— Lend your Ear, pretty Maid. [Part-song.] *See* MACLELLAN (H.)

LENDEMAIN

— Le Lendemain du Bal. Romance. *See* CLARKE (A.)

LENDERS (MARIE)

— The Dawn of Love. Song, words by B. Landor. *Bach & Co.: London*, (1912.) fol. **G. 806. mm. (12.)**

— Lovelight. Valse chantante, words by B. Landor, *etc. Bach & Co.: London*, (1913.) fol. **G. 806. mm. (13.)**

LENDLE (WOLFGANG)

— *See* GIULIANI (M.) Divertimenti für Gitarre. Opus 37 ⟨40⟩. Herausgegeben von F. Nagel, *etc.* ⟨Gitarreneinrichtung von W. Lendle.⟩ [1970.] 4°. **g. 660. ss. (8.)**

LENDORFF (MATTHIAS CASIMIR)

— Fundamenta Practica et Solida des General-Basses ... mit Beyspielen erläutert ... und aufgesetzet von Matthia Casimiro Lendorff, *etc. Gedruckt ... im Fürstlichen Gotteshause: St. Gallen*, 1776. *obl.* fol. **d. 173.**

LENDVAI (ERWIN)

— Monumenta Gradualis. Collectio carminium sacrorum ad 3–16 voces æquales et inæquales. Opus 37, *etc.* Lib. I ⟨II⟩. *B. Schott's Soehne: Mainz*, 1926. fol. **H. 1186. e. (27.)**

— Wahlspruch der Menschheit, für achtstimmigen Doppelchor ohne Begleitung. Partitur. *B. Schott's Söhne: Mainz*, 1926. 8°. **F. 585. nn. (19.)**

LENDVAY (Kamilló)

— String Quartet. Score ⟨parts⟩. 5 pt. *Boosey & Hawkes: London, etc.; Editio musica: Budapest; printed in Hungary,* 1971. 4°.   **g. 834. w. (3.)**

LENECKE (Max)

— Auf Wanderschaft (On a Journey). *See* infra: Nippsachen ... Op. 21. No. 4.

— Bright Summer Morning (Ein Morgen im Sommer). *See* infra: Six Recreations ... Op. 20. No. 3.

— Frisch gewagt (The Acrobats). *See* infra: Nippsachen ... Op. 21. No. 8.

— Fröhlicher Augenblick (Joyous Moments). *See* infra: 5 leichte Salonstücke für Pianoforte ... Op. 19. No. 3.

— Frühling, komm' wieder! (Return of Spring.) *See* infra: Nippsachen ... Op. 21. No. 7.

— Frühlingsreigen (Springtime Dance). *See* infra: 5 leichte Salonstücke für Pianoforte ... Op. 19. No. 4.

— Frühlingszauber (Spring's Charm). *See* infra: Sechs leichte Tänze ... Op. 18. 1.

— Graceful Floweret (Blümlein wunderhold). *See* infra: Six Recreations ... Op. 20. No. 4.

— Hans und Grete (The young Comrades). *See* infra: Sechs leichte Tänze ... Op. 18. 4.

— Heckenrose—Wild Rose. *See* infra: Rosenblätter ... Op. 17. 2.

— Heitere Nachenfahrt (Jolly Boat Ride). *See* infra: Nippsachen ... Op. 21. No. 3.

— Im Sonnenschein (In Sunshine). *See* infra: 5 leichte Salonstücke für Pianoforte ... Op. 19. No. 1.

— Kleine Spinnerin (The Little Spinner). *See* infra: Nippsachen ... Op. 21. No. 5.

— Kleiner Schelm (Little Rogue). *See* infra: Sechs leichte Tänze ... Op. 18. 3.

— Kleiner Schmeichler (Little Flatterer). *See* infra: Sechs leichte Tänze ... Op. 18. 5.

— 5 leichte Salonstücke für Pianoforte ... Op. 19. No. 1. Im Sonnenschein (In Sunshine). No. 2. Maienlust (Happy Maytime). No. 3. Fröhlicher Augenblick (Joyous Moments). No. 4. Frühlingsreigen (Springtime Dance). No. 5. Lustige Kameraden (Happy Comrades). 5 no. *B. F. Wood Music Co.: Boston, etc.; Leipzig* [printed, 1907.] fol.   **h. 4120. oo. (11.)**

— Sechs leichte Tänze zu vier Händen. Six easy Dances for four hands ... Op. 18. 1. Frühlingszauber (Spring's charm). 2. Mit frischem Mut (With fresh Courage). 3. Kleiner Schelm (Little Rogue). 4. Hans und Grete (The Young Comrades). 5. Kleiner Schmeichler (Little Flatterer). 6. Die Lotusblume (Lotus Flower). 6 no. *B. F. Music Co.: Boston, etc.; Leipzig* [printed, 1906.] fol.   **h. 4120. oo. (12.)**

— Die Lotusblume (Lotus Flower). *See* supra: Sechs leichte Tänze ... Op. 18. 6.

— Lustige Kameraden (Happy Comrades). *See* supra: 5 leichte Salonstücke für Pianoforte ... Op. 19. No. 5.

— Maienlust (Happy Maytime). *See* supra: 5 leichte Salonstücke für Pianoforte ... Op. 19. No. 2.

— Mit frischem Mut (With fresh Courage). *See* supra: Sechs leichte Tänze ... Op. 18. 2.

— Moosrose—Moss Rose. *See* infra: Rosenblätter ... Op. 17. 1.

— Neuer Frühling (Springtime). *See* infra: Nippsachen ... Op. 21. No. 2.

LENECKE (Max)

— Nippsachen (Bric-a-brac). 8 Unterhaltungsstücke (Recreations) zu vier Händen (for four hands) für Pianoforte ... Op. 21. No. 1. Vögleins Sehnsucht (The Little Bird's Longing). No. 2. Neuer Frühling (Springtime). No. 3. Heitere Nachenfahrt (Jolly Boat Ride). No. 4. Auf Wanderschaft (On a Journey). No. 5. Kleine Spinnerin (The Little Spinner). No. 6. Zwischen Licht und Dunkel (At Twilight). No. 7. Frühling, komm' wieder! (Return of Spring.) No. 8. Frisch gewagt (The Acrobats). 8 no. *B. F. Wood Music Co.: Boston, etc.,* [1909.] fol.   **h. 4120. oo. (13.)**

— Playing Soldiers (Wir spielen Soldat). *See* infra: Six Recreations ... Op. 20. No. 6.

— Six Recreations. For piano four hands ... Op. 20. No. 1. Spring Blossoms (Frühlingsblumen). No. 2. When the Elder blooms (Wenn der Flieder blüht). No. 3. Bright Summer Morning (Ein Morgen im Sommer). No. 4. Graceful Floweret (Blümlein wunderhold). No. 5. The Violet by the Brook (Veilchen am Bache). No. 6. Playing soldiers (Wir spielen Soldat). 6 no. *B. F. Wood Music Co.: Boston, etc.,* [1908.] fol.   **h. 4120. oo. (14.)**

— Rosenblätter. Sechs sehr leichte Stücke für Klavier ... Rose Leaves. Six very easy pieces for pianoforte ... Op. 17. 1. Moosrose (Moss Rose). 2. Heckenrose (Wild Rose). 3. Zwergrose (Dwarf Rose). 4. Weisserose (White Rose). 5. Roterose (Red Rose). 6. Teerose (Tea Rose). 6 no. *B. F. Wood Music Co.: Boston, etc.; Leipzig* [printed, 1906.] fol.   **h. 4120. oo. (15.)**

— Roterose—Red Rose. *See* supra: Rosenblätter ... Op. 17. 5.

— Spring Blossoms (Frühlingsblumen). *See* supra: Six Recreations ... Op. 20. No. 1.

— Teerose—Tea Rose. *See* supra: Rosenblätter ... Op. 17. 6.

— The Violet by the Brook (Veilchen am Bache). *See* supra: Six Recreations ... Op. 20. No. 5.

— Vögleins Sehnsucht (The Little Bird's Longing). *See* supra: Nippsachen ... Op. 21. No. 1.

— Weisserose—White Rose. *See* supra: Rosenblätter ... Op. 17. 4.

— When the Elder blooms (Wenn der Flieder blüht). *See* supra: Six Recreations ... Op. 20. No. 2.

— Zwergrose—Dwarf Rose. *See* supra: Rosenblätter ... Op. 17. 3.

— Zwischen Licht und Dunkel (At Twilight). Melodie. *See* supra: Nippsachen ... Op. 21. No. 6.

LENEL (Ludwig)

— *See* ANTES (John) [Twelve Moravian Chorales. No. 4.] What splendid Rays ... ⟨S. A.⟩ ... Setting by L. Lenel. [1965.] 8°.   **F. 1176. ss. (11.)**

LENEPVEU (Charles Ferdinand)

— A me finor della selva le fronde. *See* infra: [Velléda.]

— Adieu. Mélodie. Poésie de A. de Musset. *Paris,* [1875.] fol.   **H. 1777. h. (44.)**

— Aubade [begins: "L'étoile d'or a déserté les cieux"]. Poésie de E. Guinand. *Paris,* [1882.] fol.   **H. 1793. d. (8.)**

— Aujourd'hui. [Song, begins: "Au temps où notre âme commence".] Poésie de E. Blau. *Paris,* [1876.] fol.   **H. 1777. h. (45.)**

— Ave Maria pour Soprano solo. *Paris,* [1880.] fol.   **H. 1028. j. (11.)**

— Ballade pour Piano. *Paris,* [1870.] fol.   **h. 1462. r. (40.)**

LENEPVEU (CHARLES FERDINAND)

— Barcarolle pour Piano. *Paris*, [1870.] fol. **h. 1462. r. (38.)**

— Berceuse pour Piano. *Paris*, [1870.] fol. **h. 1462. r. (39.)**

— Caprice pour Piano. *Paris*, [1870.] fol. **h. 1462. r. (41.)**

— La Caravane. Scène chorale pour voix d'hommes [begins: "Le désert, le désert sans bornes"]. Poésie de A. Vautier. [*Paris*, 1875.] 8°. **E. 308. b. (15.)**

— Chanson [begins: "Nous venions de voir"]. Poésie de A. de Musset. *Paris*, [1870.] fol. **H. 1774. e. (25.)**

— Chanson. Poésie de A. de Musset. *Paris*, [1882.] fol. **H. 1793. d. (9.)**

— Chant du Crépuscule. [Song, begins: "Hier la nuit d'été".] Poésie de V. Hugo. *Paris*, [1873.] fol. **H. 1777. h. (42.)**

— Contemplation. [Song, begins: "Étoile qui descends".] Poésie de A. de Musset. *Paris*, [1881.] fol. **H. 1786. e. (42.)**

— Contemplation [Song, begins: "Pâle étoile du soir"], poésie de A. de Musset. *Paris*, [1886.] fol. **H. 2836. h. (44.)**

— Dal terreno ambri fallace. *See* infra: [Velléda.]

— Dormeuse. [Song, begins: "Dormez, dormez".] Poésie de E. Guinand. *Paris*, [1873.] fol. **H. 1777. h. (41.)**

— Dormeuse. [Song.] Poésie de Guinand. *Paris*, [1881.] fol. **H. 1786. e. (39.)**

— [Dormeuse.] Romance sans paroles, transcription de la Dormeuse pour Violoncelle ou Violon et Piano. *Paris*, [1880.] fol. **h. 1849. k. (16.)**

— Le Florentin, opéra comique en trois actes de M. de Saint-Georges ... Partition Piano et Chant réduite par L. Soumis. *Paris*, [1874.] 4°. **G. 652.**

— Gallia, ahime! *See* infra: [Velléda.]

— Idylle, imitée de l'ode d'Horace. Duo pour Mezzo-Soprano et Baryton [begins: "Du temps où tu m'aimais"], poésie de P. Fuchs. *Paris*, [1886.] fol. **H. 2836. h. (43.)**

— Iphigénie. Scène lyrique. Poésie de E. Guinand. Pour soli, chœurs & orchestre. Réduction de piano par l'auteur. *Paris*, [1887.] 8°. **F. 1452.**

— Jeanne d'Arc. Drame Lyrique en trois parties. Poème de P. Allard. Réduction de piano par l'auteur. *Paris*, [1887.] 8°. **F. 1171. a. (4.)**

— La Jeune Captive. Scene [begins: "L'épi naissant"]. Poésie de A. Chénier. *Paris*, [1870.] fol. **H. 1774. e. (24.)**

— La Jeune Captive. [Song.] Poésie de A. Chenier. *Paris*, [1881.] fol. **H. 1786. e. (38.)**

— Lamento. Mélodie [begins: "Ma belle amie est morte"]. Poésie de T. Gautier. *London*, [1881.] fol. **H. 1786. e. (40.)**

— Laudate Dominum in sono tubæ. Motet pour basse, solo & chœur ... Partition d'orchestre. *Lemoine et Fils: Paris, Bruxelles*, [1887.] fol. **H. 1187. k. (19.)**

— Laudate Dominum in sono tubæ. Motet pour basse, solo & choeur avec accompagnement de grand orgue et de contrebasse. *Paris*, [1884.] fol. **H. 1187. i. (27.)**

— Méditation sur des vers de P. Corneille. Tirés de sa Traduction de l'Imitation de Jesus-Christ, pour Soli, Chœurs & Orchestre. Réduction de piano par l'auteur. *Paris*, [1886.] 8°. **F. 1274. (2.)**

— Nocturne. Scène [begins: "Dona Sol"] tirée d'Hernani (5me. acte). Poésie de V. Hugo. *Paris*, [1875.] fol. **H. 1777. h. (43.)**

LENEPVEU (CHARLES FERDINAND)

— Nocturne. Scène tirée du 5e. acte de Hernani [begins: "Tout à l'heure"]. Poésie de V. Hugo. *Paris*, [1881.] fol. **H. 1786. e. (37.)**

— O Doux Printemps. Idylle pour deux voix. Poésie de E. Guinand. *Paris*, [1870.] fol. **H. 1774. e. (27.)**

— O doux printemps. Idylle pour 2 voix de femmes. Poésie de E. Guinand. *Paris*, [1882.] fol. **H. 1793. d. (10.)**

— Oh rest. *See* infra: [Velléda.—Dors, o prêtresse.]

— O Salutaris Hostia pour chant avec accompagnement d'orgue et de Violoncelle obligé. *Paris*, [1882.] fol. **H. 1187. e. (17.)**

— O Salutaris pour Orgue ou Piano. *Paris*, [1878.] fol. **H. 1028. h. (25.)**

— Le Poète Mourant. Scène. Poésie de Millevoye. *Paris*, [1870.] fol. **H. 1774. e. (26.)**

— [Le Retour de Jeanne.] Chœur des servantes. *See* RÉCRÉATIONS. Récréations Musicales. Chœurs ... Extraits d'opéras-comiques ... par ... C. Lenepveu, *etc.* 1888. 4°. **C. 457.**

— Rêverie. [Song, begins: "L'astre qui brille".] Poésie de E. Guinand. *Paris*, [1873.] fol. **H. 1777. h. (40.)**

— Rêverie. [Song.] Poésie de E. Guinand. *Paris*, [1882.] fol. **H. 1793. d. (11.)**

— Romance sans paroles. *See* supra: [Dormeuse.]

— Scène et Duo [begins: "Voici l'heure"] ... de Renaud dans les Jardins d'Armide. Poésie de C. Du Locle. *Paris*, [1881.] fol. **H. 1786. e. (36.)**

— Souvenir. [Song, begins: "Puisque j'ai mis ma lèvre".] Poésie de V. Hugo. *Paris*, [1881.] fol. **H. 1786. e. (41.)**

— Væ Victis! *See* infra: [Velléda.]

Velléda

— Velléda. Opéra en quatre actes. Paroles de A. Challamel & J. Chantepie. Partition Piano & Chant. *Paris*, [1883.] 8°. **G. 652. a.**

— Divertissement extrait de l'Opéra Velléda ... pour piano. [Solo and duet.] 2 no. *Paris*, [1884.] fol. **h. 3280. k. (45.)**

— Introduction & Cantabile. Transcription pour violoncelle avec accompagnement de piano, sur des motifs de Velléda. *Lemoine & Fils: Paris, Bruxelles*, 1886. fol. **h. 1847. (40.)**

— A me finor della selva le fronde ... Cavatina, *etc. Chappell & Co.: London*, [1882.] fol. **H. 1788. v. (35.)**

— Dal terreno ambri fallace ... Duo, *etc. Chappell & Co.: London*, [1882.] fol. **H. 1788. v. (37.)**

— [Dors, o prêtresse.] Oh rest ... [Chorus.] *See* CHAPPELL AND Co. Chappell's vocal library of part songs ... No. 88. [1882.] 8°. **G. 440.**

— Gallia, ahimè! Ballata, *etc. Chappell & Co.: London*, [1882.] fol. **H. 1788. v. (36.)**

— Væ Victis! Canzone, *etc. Chappell & Co.: London*, [1882.] fol. **H. 1788. v. (38.)**

— Vien, vien, m'è noto asil si caro ... Cavatina, *etc. Chappell & Co.: London*, [1882.] fol. **H. 1788. v. (39.)**

— Vien, vien, m'è noto asil si caro. *See* supra: [Velléda.]

— Vision. Mélodie. Poésie de P. Gérard. *A. O'Kelly: Paris*, [1886.] fol. **H. 2836. v. (25.)**

LENEPVEU (Charles Ferdinand)

— *See* Contes. Contes Mystiques ... Musique de ...
C. Lenepveu, *etc.* 1890. 8°.   **F. 970.**

LÉNER (Jenö)

— The Technique of String Quartet Playing ... Die Technik des
Streich Quartett-Spiels. Score and Parts. *J. & W. Chester:
London*, 1935. 4°.   **g. 417. v. (2.)**

— [Another copy.]   **Hirsch M. 941.**

LENETS (A. V.)

— *See* Chopin (F. F.) [Waltz. Op. 64. No. 1.] Вальсъ ... Op. 64.
no. 1. (Для балалайки съ фортепiано.) Арр. А. Ленецъ. [1900?]
fol.   **g. 664. (3.)**

— *See* Oginski (M. C.) *Count.* "Прощай отчизна ... " (Для
балалайки съ фортепiано.) Арр. А. В. Ленецъ. [1900?] fol.
    g. 664. (4.)

LE NEVE NUNES (Gertrude)

— *See* Nunes.

L'ENFANT (   )

— *See* Boucher (H.) called L'Enfant.

L'ENFANT (Édouard)

— Pierrot et Colombine, pour le Piano. *J. Williams: London*,
(1908.) fol.   **h. 3283. p. (22.)**

L'ENFANT (Jean)

— Tick-a-tack galop. [P. F.] *London*, [1879.] fol.
    h. 1494. q. (27.)

LENG (Alfonso)

— Poema. [P. F.] pp. 4. *Ediciones de la Rivista Aulos:* [*Santiago,*]
1932. 4°.   **g. 352. j. (4.)**

— Preludio No. 7. [P. F.] *In:* Boletín latino-americano de música.
tom. 4. Suplemento musical. pp. 83, 84. 1938. 4°.
    Ac. 2694. hb.

— Sonata para piano, *etc.* pp. 17. *Pan American Union:
Washington, D. C.*, [1959.] 4°.   **g. 1129. dd. (14.)**

LENG (George)

— *See* Leveaux (E.) The Scarborough Promenade ... arranged
by G. Leng. [1842.] fol.   **h. 932. (33.)**

LENG (Robert)

— Original sacred melodies ... for four voices, with an
accompaniment for the organ or pianoforte. *Leeds*, 1847. 4°.
    B. 880. g. (11.)

LENGARD (I. A.)

— [Чдача от неудачи, или Приключение в жидовской корчме.]
Ouverture und Gesænge aus dem komischen Liederspiel: Das
Abentheuer in der pohlnischen Schenke. Aus dem Russischen
frei übertragen von Louis Angely. Vollständiger
Clavierauszug von C. W. Henning. [An edition of "Чдача от
неудачи," music compiled and arranged by I. A. Lengard,
words by P. N. Semenov.] pp. 32. [1826?] *obl.* fol. *See*
Henning (Carl W.) [Abentheuer in der pohlnischen Schenke.]
    E. 724. k. (15.)

LENGNICK AND CO

— Lengnick's Pianoforte Tutor ... Newly revised and enlarged
edition. [1909.] fol. *See* Laubach (A.)   **h. 3820. v. (3.)**

LENGNICK (Wilson)

— The Land of the Midnight Sun. 4 pianoforte pieces.
A. Lengnick & Co.: London, 1916. 4°.   **g. 272. ii. (3.)**

LENGTH

— The Length of Day. [Song.] *See* Tyler (A. R.)

LENGTHENING

— Lengthening Day. [Song.] *See* Bellingham (G.)

— Length'ning Shadows. Aria. *See* Bach (J. S.) [Mer hahn en
neue Oberkeet.—Klein-Zschocher müsse so zart und süsse.]

LENGYEL (Endre)

— *See* Pejtsik (A.) and Lengyel (E.) Violoncello Music.
(Intermediate.) ... Edited by A. Pejtsik, E. Lengyel. [1973.] 4°.
    g. 511. r. (11.)

LENGYEL (Endre) and **PEJTSIK** (Árpád)

— Violoncello Music for Beginners. Edited by E. Lengyel,
A. Pejtsik. [Violoncello and P. F. Score and part.] 2 pt.
*Boosey & Hawkes: London, etc.; Editio musica: Budapest;
printed in Hungary*, 1970. 4°.   **g. 511. l. (2.)**

LENIN

— Lenin. Orchestermusik mit Schlusschor. *See* Dessau (Paul)

— Ленин. Драматическая симфония. *See* Shebalin (V. Ya.)

— Lenin in Siberia. [Part-song.] *See* Muradeli (V. I.)

— Lenin-Lied. [Song.] *See* Dessau (P.)

— Lenin Lieder für Gesang und Klavier von Komponisten der
Deutschen Demokratischen Republik. pp. 30. *Edition Peters:
Leipzig*, [1970.] 4°.   **F. 1196. uu. (4.)**

— Ленин с нами. Кантата. *See* Eshpai (Andrei Ya.)

— Ленин в сердце народном. Оратория. *See* Shchedrin (R. K.)

LENINGRAD

— Ленинград. Оратория. *See* Dzerzhinsky (I. I.)

LENINGRAD.—*Академия Наук СССР.—Институт
Литературы*

— Белорусские народные песни. (Сборник составлен
З. В. Эвальд ... Тексты на белорусском языке под редакцией
М. Я. Гринблата. Перевод для пения М. А. Фромана.)
Москва, Ленинград, 1941. 4°.
Part of the series "Песни народов СССР".   **F. 1594. c.**

    *Академия Наук СССР.—Институт Русской
    Литературы (Пушкинский Дом)*

— Русские народные песни о крестьянских войнах и восстаниях.
(Составители: Б. М. Добровольский и А. Д. Соймонов. Общая
редакция и вступительная статья А. Н. Лозановой.
Музыкальный редактор Ф. В. Соколов.) pp. 206. *Москва,
Ленинград*, 1956. 4°.   **E. 878. a.**

LENINGRAD.—*Ленинградская Ордена Ленина Государственная Консерватория имени Н. А. Римского-Корсакова*

— Хрестоматия по истории фортепианной музыки в России, конец XVIII и первая половина XIX веков. Составили Л. А. Баренбойм и В. И. Музалевский, *etc.* pp. 323. *Москва; Ленинград*, 1949. 4°.　　　　　　　**g. 1590. c.**

LENINGRADSKAYA

— Ленинградская Ордена Ленина Государственная Консерватория имени Н. А. Римского-Корсакова. *See* LENINGRAD.

LENINTSUI

— Ленинцы. Кантата. *See* KABALEVSKY (D. B.).

LENKEI (GABRIELLA)

— Music for Violin. (Intermediate.) Edited by Gabriella Lenkei. [Violin and P. F. Score and part.] 2 pt. *Boosey & Hawkes: London, etc.; Editio Musica: Budapest; printed in Hungary*, [1973.] 4°.　　　　　　　**g. 422. p. (6.)**

— Violin Music for Beginners. Edited by G. Lenkei. [Violin and P. F. Score and part.] 2 pt. *Boosey & Hawkes: London, etc.; Editio musica: Budapest; printed in Hungary*, 1970. 4°.　　　　　　　**g. 422. o. (4.)**

LENN (JAY)

— A Morning Prayer. Words and music by J. Lenn. [S. A. T. B. Staff and tonic sol-fa notation.] *Fred Benson: London*, [1961.] 8°.　　　　　　　**E. 460. g. (3.)**

LENNARD (ARTHUR)

— Occupations. [Song.] Written, composed ... by A. Lennard. ⟨Arranged by F. W. Venton.⟩ pp. 4. *R. Maynard: London*, [1893.] fol.　　　　　　　**H. 3980. qq. (26.)**

— The Phonograph. Written, composed ... by A. Lennard. [Song. Staff and tonic sol-fa notation. Voice part.] *Francis, Day & Hunter: London*, [1894.] s. sh. fol.　　**H. 3980. qq. (27.)**

— Sister 'Ria. Words by A. J. Mills, *etc.* [Song. Staff and tonic sol-fa notation. Voice part.] *Francis, Day & Hunter: London*, [1895.] s. sh. fol.　　　**H. 3980. qq. (28.)**

— That's what I'm weeping for! Written by Albert Hall, *etc.* [Song. Staff and tonic sol-fa notation. Voice part.] *Francis, Day & Hunter: London*, [1895.] s. sh. fol.　　**H. 3980. qq. (29.)**

— There's an old-fashioned Cottage ... Written by Steve Leggett and A. Lennard, *etc.* [Song. Staff and tonic sol-fa notation. Voice part.] *Francis, Day & Hunter: London*, [1896.] s. sh. fol.　　　　　　　**H. 3980. qq. (30.)**

LENNARD (CARRIE)

— Jeannette. Waltz. [P. F.] *Weekes & Co.: London*, [1894.] fol.　　　　　　　**h. 3285. q. (25.)**

LENNARD (EMMA BARRETT) *Lady*

— Selection from the Songs composed by Lady Barrett-Lennard, arranged for Pianoforte and String Quartet—ad lib. [Separate parts.] *Novello, Ewer & Co.: London & New York*, [1895.] fol.　　　　　　　**h. 2784. d. (5.)**

— At Maestricht. Song, the word by F. Tayler, *etc. Novello and Co.: London*, (1915.) fol.　　　　**G. 806. mm. (14.)**

— Bright Days will come again. Song, the words written by C. Hamilton. *Novello and Co.: London*, 1907. fol.　　　　　　　**G. 805. nn. (1.)**

LENNARD (EMMA BARRETT) *Lady*

— Britannia. Song, the words by H. De Vere Stacpoole. *Novello and Co.: London*, (1915.) fol.　　**G. 806. mm. (15.)**

— The Canadian Guns. Song, the words by R. F. W. Rees, *etc. Novello and Co.: London*, [1915.] fol.　　**G. 806. mm. (16.)**

— Cavaliers, come away. Song, the words by F. Taylor. *Novello and Co.: London*, (1914.) fol.　　**G. 806. mm. (17.)**

— Christmas Clouds. Song ... Words ... by A. C. Steele. *Novello & Co.: London*, 1901. fol.　　**G. 517. m. (28.)**

— Christmas Dawn. Song, the words ... by G. W. *Novello and Co.: London*, 1900. fol.　　**G. 517. k. (23.)**

— The Christmas Eucharist. Sacred Song, the words by G. W. *Novello and Co.: London*, 1904. fol.　　**G. 517. p. (2.)**

— Courage, poor Heart of Stone. [Song.] Lines ... by Alfred, Lord Tennyson. *Novello and Co.: London*, 1904. fol.　　　　　　　**G. 807. z. (33.)**

— Crossing the Bar. Words by Alfred, Lord Tennyson. *Lyon & Hall: Brighton*, [1893.] fol.　　**H. 1187. r. (1.)**

— The Daisy's Wooing. Song, the words ... by T. B. Hennell. *Novello and Co.: London*, 1906. fol.　　**G. 807. kk. (4.)**

— Diantha's Song ... written by A. C. Steele. *Novello, Ewer & Co.: London & New York*, [1894.] fol.　　**G. 805. aa. (8.)**

— Down the cool Hills of Coolree. Song, the words by A. Hancock. *Novello and Co.: London*, 1909. fol.　　　　　　　**G. 805. nn. (2.)**

— Down the Hill. Song, the words by E. Oxenford. *Novello and Co.: London*, 1909. fol.　　**G. 807. yy. (32.)**

— Dreams of Love. Song [begins: "Sadly yet calmly"]. *Brighton*, [1866.] fol.　　**H. 1772. r. (34.)**

— Echoes from the Downs. Song, the words ... by W. E. Vaughan. *Novello, Ewer & Co.: London & New York*, [1895.] fol.　　　　　　　**G. 805. aa. (9.)**

— An English Gipsy Song. Song, the words by L. S. Bethell. *Novello and Co.: London*, (1913.) fol.　　**G. 806. mm. (18.)**

— A Fairy Wood. Song, the words by C. E. M. E. Bradhurst, *etc. Novello and Co.: London*, 1909. fol.　　**G. 805. nn. (3.)**

— The Fall of the Year. Song, the words ... by L. Gordon. *Novello, Ewer & Co.: London & New York*, [1895.] fol.　　　　　　　**G. 805. aa. (10.)**

— The Find. Song, the words ... by C. Kingsley. *Novello, Ewer & Co.: London & New York*, [1894.] fol.　　**G. 805. aa. (11.)**

— Gallant Gentlemen all. Song, the words by T. B. Hennell. *Novello and Co.: London*, (1913.) fol.　　**G. 806. mm. (19.)**

— Good old England. Song, the words by E. Oxenford. *Novello and Co.: London*, 1908. fol.　　**G. 805. nn. (4.)**

— The Harrow Stage. [Song.] The words ... by E. M. White. *Novello and Co.: London*, [1904.] fol.　　**G. 807. z. (34.)**

— Haunted. Song, the words ... by A. C. Steele. *Novello and Co.: London, etc.*, 1900. fol.　　**G. 807. o. (43.)**

— Heart's Delight. Song, words by A. C. Steele. *B. Hollis & Co.: London*, 1895. fol.　　**G. 805. aa. (19.)**

— Here's a Health to every Sportsman. Song, the words written by L. Gordon. *Novello, Ewer & Co.: London & New York*, [1896.] fol.　　**G. 805. aa. (12.)**

— King o' the Sea. Song, the words by E. Oxenford. *Novello and Co.: London*, 1908. fol.　　**G. 805. nn. (5.)**

— The Larch Wood. Song, the words by A. Hancock, *etc. Novello and Co.: London*, 1909. fol.　　**G. 805. nn. (6.)**

LENNARD (Emma Barrett) *Lady*

— The Lords of the restless Sea. Song, the words ... by T. B. Hennell. *Novello and Co.: London*, 1906. fol.
G. 807. kk. (5.)

— Love's River. Song, the words by E. Oxenford. *Novello and Co.: London*, 1908. fol.
G. 805. nn. (7.)

— Marsh Fires. Valse for the Pianoforte. *Novello and Co.: London*, 1910. fol.
h. 3286. uu. (46.)

— La Memzie valse, composed and arranged from her own songs by Lady B. Lennard. [P. F.] *Brighton*, [1866.] fol.
h. 1460. v. (22.)

— Plymouth Hoe ... Song, the words ... by H. Newbolt. *Novello & Co.: London*, 1901. fol.
G. 807. t. (24.)

— Retrospection. Song, the words ... by O. Meredith. *Novello, Ewer & Co.: London & New York*, [1895.] fol.
G. 805. aa. (13.)

— The Reveillé. Song, the words by B. Harte. *Novello and Co.: London*, (1914.) fol.
G. 806. mm. (20.)

— The Ring. Song, words by W. Oakes. *Novello and Co.: London*, 1901. fol.
G. 807. yy. (33.)

— The Rose of Ballysheely. Song, the words by A. Hancock. *Novello and Co.: London*, 1911. fol.
G. 807. yy. (34.)

— Sacred Melodies, the words selected chiefly from the hymns of ... Heber. Bk. 1. *J. Duff and Co.: London*, [1850?] fol.
H. 1778. y. (6.)

— [Another copy.]
Bound (by Hayday) in purple morocco, white watered silk doublures stamped with royal arms.
R. M. 14. e. 9.

— Serenade. Song, the words ... by A. C. Steele. *Novello & Co.: London*, 1901. fol.
G. 807. t. (25.)

— Slumber little one. Song, the words by Mrs. M. Davies. *Novello and Co.: London*, 1908. fol.
G. 805. nn. (8.)

— Snows are rife. Song, the words ... by L. Gordon. *Novello, Ewer & Co.: London & New York*, [1895.] fol.
G. 805. aa. (14.)

— Through devious Paths. Song, the words ... by Emma Carolina, Lady Wood. *Novello & Co.: London*, 1901. fol.
G. 517. m. (29.)

— A Toast. Song, the words ... by A. C. Steele. *Novello & Co.: London*, 1901. fol.
G. 807. t. (26.)

— Told in the Twilight. Song, the words by E. Oxenford. *Novello and Co.: London*, 1908. fol.
G. 805. nn. (9.)

— Tristram's Song ... Written by Alfred, Lord Tennyson. *Novello, Ewer & Co.: London & New York*, [1894.] fol.
G. 805. aa. (15.)

— Up Hill. Song, the words ... by C. G. Rossetti. *Novello, Ewer & Co.: London & New York*, [1894.] fol.
G. 805. aa. (16.)

— Up the airy Mountain. Song, the words ... by W. Allingham. *Novello and Co.: London*, [1904.] fol.
G. 807. z. (35.)

— Wee Rose on the Highway. Song, the words translated from Goethe, by C. E. M. E. Bradhurst, *etc. Novello and Co.: London*, 1909. fol.
G. 805. nn. (10.)

— The Welcome. Song, the words ... by T. Davis. *Novello, Ewer & Co.: London & New York*, [1894.] fol.
G. 805. aa. (17.)

— When. Song the words ... by A. C. Steele. *Novello, Ewer & Co.: London & New York*, [1895.] fol.
G. 805. aa. (18.)

— Who'll buy my Lavender? Song, the words by A. Hancock. *Novello and Co.: London*, 1911. fol.
G. 807. yy. (35.)

LENNARD (Emma Barrett) *Lady*

— You. Song, the words by A. C. Steele. *Novello and Co.: London*, 1909. fol.
G. 807. yy. (36.)

LENNARD (George)

— Sons of Britain ... Marching Song, words by H. Gordon, *etc. C. Sheard & Co.: London*, (1914.) fol.
H. 1793. t. (7.)

LENNARD (Herbert Fendick)

— Gallant Heroes back from War. [Hymn.] Words and music by H. F. Lennard. *Weekes & Co.: London*, 1919. 8°.
C. 799. w. (29.)

— This Christmas brings us Victory. [Christmas carol.] Words and music by H. F. Lennard. *H. F. Lennard: London*, [1919.] 4°.
Lithographed.
E. 602. hh. (5.)

LENNARD (Martin)

— The Billy 'Possums' Frolic ... Two-Step. [P. F.] *Phillips & Page: London*, 1909. fol.
h. 3286. uu. (47.)

LENNARD (Mary Barrett) *Mrs*

— Addio mio vita. Romanza per Voce di Basso, *etc. Pittarelli: Roma*, [1855?] fol.
Lithographed throughout.
H. 345. b. (19.)

LENNARD (Roy)

— Can't yer try an' love me? (A nigger serenade.) Written and composed by R. Lennard. [Song. Staff and tonic sol-fa notation. Voice part.] *Francis, Day & Hunter: London*, [1901.] *s. sh.* fol.
H. 3985. t. (1.)

— Can't yer try an' love me? A nigger serenade, *etc.* [Song.] pp. 6. *Francis, Day & Hunter: London*, [1901.] fol.
H. 3985. t. (2.)

LENNAVAN-MO

— Lennavan-Mo. Song. *See* WHITEHEAD (P. A.)

LENNEP (H. Martyn van)

— The Bal Masqué. Waltz-Song, words by H. G. Sims. *A. H. Stockwell: London*, [1928.] 4°.
G. 1270. x. (31.)

— Bessie. Song, *etc. Weekes & Co.: London*, 1892. fol.
H. 1568. (20.)

— Can I forget? *See infra*: [Head or Heart.]

— The Child asleep. Cradle Song. Quartette for mixed voices, *etc. Weekes & Co.: London*, [1885.] 4°.
E. 308. p. (8.)

— Come back. A Song, words by Mrs. Coke. *Weekes & Co.: London*, [1886.] fol.
H. 1568. (1.)

— Come unto Me. Sacred Song. *Weekes & Co.: London*, [1889.] fol.
H. 879. e. (15.)

— Could I recall! Song, words and music by H. M. van Lennep. *J. & J. Hopkinson: London*, [1886.] fol.
H. 1568. (2.)

— L'Egyptienne. Valse pour piano. *Weekes & Co.: London*, [1887.] fol.
h. 975. v. (10.)

— Enchantingly the Bird-Song floats. Song, words by L. Thompson. *Novello and Co.: London*, 1928. 4°.
G. 1270. x. (32.)

— Flitting Shadows, a fireside reverie, for the pianoforte, *etc. Weekes & Co.: London*, [1886.] fol.
h. 1484. s. (49.)

LENNEP (H. Martyn van)

— [Head or Heart.] Can I forget? Song ... words by
A. Chapman. 3 no. [In C, E flat and F.] *Stanley Lucas,
Weber & Co.: London*, 1892–3. fol.   **H. 1568. (16.)**

— Hush! ... Song, words & music by H. M. van Lennep. 3ʳᵈ
edition, revised. *Weekes & Co.: London*, [1885.] fol.
H. 1568. (3.)

— In Seville's Groves. Spanish Bolero Song. Words by R. S.
Hichens. 2 no. [In D and F.] (In Seville's Groves ... arranged
for voice & guitar by N. Levy.) *R. Cocks & Co.: London*,
1890. fol.   **H. 1568. (17.)**

— In the Firelight. Song, words by G. C. Bingham. *Weekes &
Co.: London*, [1885.] fol.   **H. 1568. (4.)**

— The King's Mere. Song, words by F. E. Weatherly. 3 no. [In
C, E flat and G.] *R. Cocks & Co.: London*, 1891. fol.
H. 1568. (18.)

— Little Sweetheart. Valse, *etc.* [P. F.] *Stanley Lucas & Co.:
London*, 1889. fol.   **h. 3285. q. (26.)**

— Love's Prisoner. A Song, words from the Novellette "My
Prisoner" by S. Hallett. *Weekes & Co.: London*, [1886.] fol.
H. 1568. (5.)

— Moorish Dance for the pianoforte. *Weekes & Co.: London*,
[1887.] fol.   **h. 1484. s. (50.)**

— Moorish Dance for the pianoforte. Duet. *Weekes & Co.:
London*, [1895.] fol.   **h. 3290. l. (29.)**

— My little Sweetheart true! Song, words by G. H. Newcombe.
3 no. [In D, F, and A flat.] *S. Lucas, Weber & Co.: London*,
[1889.] fol.   **H. 1568. (6.)**

— Oh! Fräulein. A humorous Song. *Weekes & Co.: London*,
[1889.] fol.   **H. 1568. (15.)**

— Our World. Song, words ... by G. C. Bingham. 4 no. [In C,
E flat, F, and E flat, simplified edition.] *S. Lucas, Weber &
Co.: London*, [1889.] fol.   **H. 1568. (7.)**

— The Reason Why. Song, words by A. Chapman. *B. Mocatta
& Co.: London*, [1889.] fol.   **H. 1568. (14.)**

— Return with the May. Song, words by M. Marras. 3 no. [In
B flat, C and D.] *R. Cocks & Co.: London*, 1890. fol.
H. 1568. (19.)

— Ring, Blue-Bells, ring! ... Song, words by P. C. 3ʳᵈ edition,
revised. *Weekes & Co.: London*, [1886.] fol.   **H. 1568. (8.)**

— Romance in A flat for the pianoforte. *Weekes & Co.:
London*, [1890.] fol.   **h. 1489. s. (40.)**

— So do I love thee. Song, words by C. Lorraine. *E. Ascherberg
& Co.: London*, [1888.] fol.   **H. 1568. (9.)**

— The Stars are with the Mariner. Vocal Trio for
Mezzo-Soprano, Contralto, and Baritone; words by T. Hood.
S. Lucas, Weber & Co.: London, [1887.] fol.   **H. 1568. (10.)**

— Sunshine through the Mist. Song, the words by A. Chapman.
3 no. [In E flat, G, and A.] *R. Cocks & Co.: London*, [1889.]
fol.   **H. 1568. (11.)**

— Thirza. Song, words by H. Aherne. *Phillips & Page: London*,
[1915.] fol.   **H. 1793. t. (8.)**

— Visions. Song, words by Mrs. G. Jackson. *E. Ascherberg &
Co.: London*, [1888.] fol.   **H. 1568. (12.)**

— The Voice of the Sea. [Song.] Words by H. Newte.
J. B. Cramer & Co.: London, 1893. fol.   **H. 1568. (21.)**

— Whither?—Que me veux-tu?—A Song, from the French of
A. de Musset, composed and arranged to English words by
H. M. van Lennep. *Weekes & Co.: London*, [1885.] fol.
H. 1568. (13.)

LENNEP (H. Martyn van)

— *See* Dotto (P.) Barcarola ... Edited by M. van Lennep. 1892.
fol.   **G. 807. f. (26.)**

— *See* Kjerulf (H.) [Hvile i Skoven.] Afar in the Wood ... With
an ad lib. accompaniment for the Violin or Violoncello by
H. M. van Lennep. [1889–90.] fol.   **H. 3584. (1.)**

— *See* Mascheroni (A.) For all Eternity, *etc.* (Arranged by
M. van Lennep.) 1891. fol.   **H. 3634. (4.)**

— *See* Walker (M. L.) Papillons noirs, *etc.* (Edited by
H. Martyn van Lennep.) [1926.] 4°.   **g. 1125. r. (20.)**

LENNON (John)

— [For songs by J. Lennon contributed to the Beatles' Souvenir
Song Albums and to the "Golden Beatles Series":] *See*
Beatles.

— Songs of John Lennon. [With portraits.] pp. 80. *Wise
Publications: London, New York*, [1971.] 4°.   **F. 1875. (18.)**

— Imagine. ⟨Words and music by J. Lennon.⟩ [Songs, with
portraits.] pp. 43. *Wise Publications: London, New York*,
[1971.] 4°.   **F. 1199. rr. (3.)**

— Jealous Guy. [Song.] Words and music by John Lennon.
pp. 3. *Northern Songs; Music Sales: London*, [c. 1980.] 4°.
G. 296. t. (8.)

LENNON (John) and MACCARTNEY (Paul)

— 50 Hit Songs, *etc.* pp. 132. *Northern Songs: London*, [1965.]
4°.   **G. 1276. ii. (3.)**

— The Second Book of 50 Hit Songs, *etc.* [With portraits.]
pp. 141. *Northern Songs: London*, [1967.] 4°.
G. 809. ee. (1.)

— The Third Book of 50 Hit Songs, *etc.* [With portraits.] pp. 151.
Northern Songs: London, [1970.] 4°.   **F. 1199. z. (1.)**

— 50 great Songs. ⟨All organs.—C & G chord organs.⟩ 2 no.
Music Scales: London, [1971.] 4°.   **G. 295. ww. (1.)**

— Eine kleine Beatlemusik. String quartet with optional double
bass. Original music by J. Lennon and P. McCartney. Devised
by Fritz Spiegl. Arranged by Harry Wild. Transcribed by Jeff
Muston, *etc.* [Score.] pp. 18. *Northern Songs: London*, [1965.]
8°.   **b. 204. p. (2.)**

— Eine kleine Beatlemusik. Piano solo. Original music by
J. Lennon and P. McCartney. Devised by Fritz Spiegl.
Arranged by Harry Wild. Transcribed by Jeff Muston, *etc.*
pp. 10. *Northern Songs: London*, [1965.] 4°.
g. 1129. ee. (19.)

— All my Loving. By John Lennon and Paul McCartney.
Arranged by Jerry Nowak. [Concert band. Score and parts.]
ATV Music Publications: Los Angeles, [1980.] 4°.
*Part of "Cherry Lane Young Band Series". With several copies
of various parts.*   **h. 3210. j. (680.)**

— All together now ... [Originally performed by the Beatles.]
Arranged by Dan Fox. [Concert band. Score and parts.] 53 pt.
ATV Music Publications: Los Angeles, [1980.] 4°.
*Part of "Cherry Lane young Band Series". With several copies
of various parts.*   **h. 3210. j. (681.)**

— Eight Days a Week. ⟨Beatles song. SSCB (with piano and
optional guitar/bass/drums).⟩ Words and music by John
Lennon & Paul McCartney. Arranged by Dave Riley and
Dana Wilson. [Score.] pp. 12. *ATV Music Publications: Los
Angeles*, [1980?] 8°.
Part of "Joy of Singing Series".   **E. 1501. vv. (22.)**

— Let it be. Souvenir song album. 8 songs by J. Lennon &
P. McCartney as featured in the film "Let it be," *etc.* pp. 24.
Northern Songs: London, [1970.] 4°.   **G. 295. ww. (3.)**

LENNON (JOHN) and **MACCARTNEY** (PAUL)

— Yellow Submarine ... Arranged by Michael Burnett for school ensemble, *etc.* [Score and parts.] 5 pt. *Chappell: [London,* 1977.] 4°.
Part of "Pop into School". **h. 3210. j. (942.)**

LENNOX (ARTHUR)

— Venetian Twilight-Song. Serenata. Words by A. H. Hyatt. *St. Cecilia Music Co.: London,* 1898. fol. **H. 1799. h. (36.)**

LENNOX (CECIL)

— The Cecil Lennox Song & Dance Album, *etc.* *C. Lennox: London,* [1931.] 4°. **F. 607. rr. (6.)**

LENNOX (ELLEN GEORGINA)

— The Brownlow Quadrille. [P. F.] *London,* 1850. fol. **h. 947. (45.)**

— The Lindsay galop. [P. F.] *London,* [1865.] fol. **h. 1460. v. (23.)**

— The Rosenburg Polka, *etc.* [P. F.] pp. 5. *R. Addison & C°: London,* [1850?] fol. **h. 61. oo. (7.)**

LENNOX (EVA M.)

— The Coming of the King. A Cantata for solo voices and chorus, *etc.* *J. Curwen & Sons: London,* 1895. 8°. **E. 541. d. (4.)**

— The Coming of the King ... Tonic Sol-fa Edition. 1895. *See* CURWEN (J.) The Tonic Sol-fa Library, *etc.* No. 50. [1881, *etc.*] 4°. **A. 858. b.**

LENNOX (LINDSAY)

— Abiding Love. Song, written and composed by L. Lennox. *Moore, Smith & Co.: London,* [1892.] fol. **H. 3603. (1.)**

— Across the Desert. Arabian Love Song. Written and Composed by L. Lennox. *D. Wilcock: London,* [1893.] fol. **H. 3603. (18.)**

— The Angel of the Dawn. Song. The words by S. Gray. 2 no. [In F and G.] *W. Morley & Co.: London,* 1896. fol. **H. 3603. (19.)**

— The Beautiful Prayer. [Song.] Words by S. Gray. *T. Holloway: London,* [1898.] fol. **H. 3603. (34.)**

— The Beautiful Promise. Song. Words by S. Gray. 2 no. [In F and D.] *E. Ashdown: London,* 1897. fol. **H. 3603. (20, 35.)**

— Beneath the Wayside Cross. Song, words and music by L. Lennox. *Agate & Co.: London,* 1890. fol. **H. 3603. (2.)**

— Blow, jolly Breeze. [Song.] Words and music by L. Lennox. *W. Paxton: London,* 1892. fol. **H. 3603. (3.)**

— By the Fireside. Song, words ... and ... music ... by L. Lennox. *Marshalls: London,* [1890.] fol. **H. 3603. (4.)**

— [By the Fireside.] *See* SAINT QUENTIN (E.) By the Fireside. Waltz, on L. Lennox's ... Song. [1890.] fol. **h. 1397. (6.)**

— Castagnetta. Spanish Love Song, written and composed by L. Lennox. *Evans & Co.: London,* [1890.] fol. **H. 3603. (5.)**

— Cycling Song. Words by S. Gray. *T. Holloway: London,* [1898.] fol. **H. 3603. (36.)**

— Dona nobis pacem ... Song ... words ... & ... music ... by L. Lennox. *H. Beresford: Birmingham,* [1890.] fol. **H. 3603. (6.)**

LENNOX (LINDSAY)

— A Dream at Twilight. Song, written and composed by L. Lennox. *Bowerman & Co.: London,* [1891.] fol. **H. 3603. (7.)**

— The Dream I dreamt. [Song.] Written and Composed by L. Lennox. *Francis, Day, & Hunter: London,* 1895. fol. **H. 3603. (21.)**

— Farewell, dear old Dad. [Song.] Words and music by L. Lennox. *H. Gembici & Co.: London,* [1900.] fol. **H. 3603. (37.)**

— For the sake of the Motherland. Good-bye, Daddy. Song, written and composed by L. Lennox, *etc.* *H. Scott: Birmingham,* [1914.] fol. **H. 1793. t. (9.)**

— For thy dear Sake, new waltz refrain song, written & composed by the composer of Love's golden Dream. pp. 7. *C. Sheard & C°: London,* [c. 1895.] fol. **H. 1654. tt. (7.)**

— Forget-me-not ... Song, words and music by L. Lennox. *J. Burdon: Stockton-on-Tees,* 1901. fol. **H. 1799. cc. (56.)**

— The Friar's Dream. Song, words and music by L. Lennox. *Ransford & Son: London,* [1892.] fol. **H. 3603. (8.)**

— The Friar's Dream ... Duet for violoncello and pianoforte, arranged by F. Jacoby. *Ransford & Son: London,* 1892. fol. **h. 1851. c. (23.)**

— Gipsy Jack. Song, written and composed by L. Lennox. *H. Beresford: London,* [1890.] fol. **H. 3603. (9.)**

— Good-bye, dear Heart. [Song.] Words & Music by L. Lennox. *T. Holloway: London,* [1898.] fol. **H. 3603. (38.)**

— The Green little Shamrock. [Song.] Words and Music by L. Lennox. *Francis, Day, & Hunter: London,* 1893. fol. **H. 3603. (22.)**

— Honey dear I do love you ... Song. Words and Music by L. Lennox. *W. H. Broome: London,* [1896.] fol. **H. 3603. (23.)**

— I lub a yaller Gal. Plantation Song. Words & Music by L. Lennox. *T. Holloway: London,* [1898.] fol. **H. 3603. (39.)**

— In a Gondola. Song ... words ... and ... music ... by L. Lennox. *Enoch & Sons: London,* [1890.] fol. **H. 3603. (10.)**

— The Ingle Nook. Song, written and composed by L. Lennox. *F. McGlennon: London,* 1902. fol. **H. 1799. vv. (38.)**

— Just as of old. Song. Words ... and music ... by L. Lennox. *Arthur & Co.: Birmingham,* [1899.] fol. **H. 3603. (40.)**

— Life's Dreams, or What the Cuckoo said, song, words written by Auguste Hancock. pp. 7. *C. Sheard & C°: London,* [c. 1895.] fol. **H. 1654. tt. (8.)**

— Little Lays for Lads and Lasses, words and music by L. Lennox. *Agate & Co.: London,* [1890.] 4°. **F. 636. l. (7.)**

— Longings. Song. Words by S. Gray. *Keith, Prowse, & Co.: London,* 1895. fol. **H. 3603. (24.)**

— Love me again. Song ... words ... and ... music ... by L. Lennox. *Ransford & Son: London,* [1892.] fol. **H. 3603. (11.)**

— Love me for ever. Song, words by S. Gray. *J. Purcell: Rawtenstall,* [1900.] fol. **H. 3603. (41.)**

— Love's golden Dream. Song written and composed by L. Lennox. pp. 7. *London Music Publishing C°: London; Leipzig printed,* [c. 1895.] fol. **H. 1653. ff. (19.)**

— [Love's golden Dream.] *See* BONHEUR (T.) *pseud.* Love's golden Dream. Waltz on L. Lennox's ... song, *etc.* ⟨30ᵗʰ edition.⟩ [c. 1890.] fol. **h. 722. v. (7.)**

LENNOX (LINDSAY)

— Love's Message. [Song.] Words by S. Gray. *T. Holloway: London*, [1898.] fol. **H. 3603. (42.)**

— Love's sweet Chime. Song ... words ... and ... music ... by L. Lennox. *B. Williams: London*, 1891. fol. **H. 3603. (12.)**

— May-Fair. Old English Dance. [P. F.] *London Music Publishing Stores: London*, [1905.] fol. **h. 3282. ww. (39.)**

— Merry Rhymes for merry Times. A Set of Songs for children. No. 1. Little Fairies. No. 2. Playing at Soldiers. No. 3. Speak kindly. No. 4. Merry Playmates. Words and music by L. Lennox. *T. Holloway: London*, [1902.] fol. **H. 1799. cc. (57.)**

— The Message of the Angelus. [Song.] Words by S. Gray. *Keith, Prowse, & Co.: London*, 1894. fol. **H. 3603. (25.)**

— A Minster Dream. Song. Words by S. Gray. 2 no. [In D and E flat.] *E. Ashdown: London, etc.*, 1897. fol. **H. 3603. (26.)**

— Mother's Songs of long ago. [Song.] Words and music by L. Lennox. *F. Dean & Co.: London*, 1901. fol. **H. 1799. cc. (58.)**

— Mother's Songs of long ago, *etc. W. Paxton: London*, [1907.] fol. **H. 1794. vv. (41.)**

— Never forgotten. Song. Written and Composed by L. Lennox. *Willis & Hall: London*, [1897.] fol. **H. 3603. (27.)**

— The Old Gavotte. [Song.] Words and music by L. Lennox. *B. Williams: London*, [1889.] fol. **H. 1788. uu. (37.)**

— The Old Gavotte. Song ... arranged for the pianoforte by Seymour Smith. *B. Williams: London*, [1889.] fol. **h. 1489. s. (41.)**

— The Old Grenadier. Military Song. Words by S. Gray. *F. Dean & Co.: London*, 1896. fol. **H. 3603. (28.)**

— The Old Waltz. Song. Words by S. Gray. 2 no. [In G and B flat.] *W. H. Broome: London*, [1894.] fol. **H. 3603. (29.)**

— On the Cliffs by the Sea. Song, written and composed by L. Lennox. *Ransford & Son: London*, 1892. fol. **H. 3603. (14.)**

— Only for you. Song, words & music by L. Lennox. 2 no. [In G and B flat.] *Ransford & Son: London*, 1891. fol. **H. 3603. (13.)**

— Only thine for aye! Song. Words by S. Gray. *Keith, Prowse & Co.: London*, 1894. fol. **H. 3603. (30.)**

— Peacefully sleep. Song, words and music by L. Lennox. *Ransford & Son: London*, [1892.] fol. **H. 3603. (15.)**

— Remembered yet. Ballad, written and composed by L. Lennox, *etc. Howard & Co.: London*, [1899.] fol. **H. 3603. (43.)**

— Roun' de Cabin Door. [Song.] Words & Music by L. Lennox. *T. Holloway: London*, [1898.] fol. **H. 3603. (44.)**

— The Song I love. [Song.] Written and composed by L. Lennox. *T. Holloway: London*, [1896.] fol. **H. 3603. (31.)**

— The Song I love. Written & composed by L. Lennox. *T. Holloway: London*, [1898.] fol. **H. 3603. (45.)**

— Songs and Jokes for Little Folks ... Twelve ... songs for children. Words and music by L. Lennox. *Ransford & Son: London*, 1892. 4°. **F. 636. q. (7.)**

— [Thine, only thine.] Song, written and composed by L. Lennox. *H. Beresford: Birmingham*, [1889.] fol. **H. 1788. uu. (38.)**

— Thine, only thine. *See* BYARS (G.) Thine, only thine. Waltz on L. Lennox's ... Song. [1889.] fol. **h. 3285. h. (67.)**

LENNOX (LINDSAY)

— Trust me once more. Song. Words by S. Gray. *F. Dean & Co.: London*, 1895. fol. **H. 3603. (32.)**

— The Turning of the Tide. Song, words & music by L. Lennox. *C. Jefferys: London*, [1890.] fol. **H. 3603. (16.)**

— The Twilight Shore. Song, words and music by L. Lennox. *Hopwood & Crew: London*, 1893. fol. **H. 3603. (17.)**

— A Venetian Love Dream. Song, words by S. Gray. *W. H. Broome: London*, 1898. fol. **H. 3603. (46.)**

— A Vesper Story. Song. Words by S. Gray. *E. Ashdown: London, etc.*, 1895. fol. **H. 3603. (33.)**

— Victoria's noble Reign. [Song.] Written & composed by L. Lennox. *T. Holloway: London*, [1898.] fol. **H. 3603. (47.)**

— Welcome, Victors! Song, words & music by L. Lennox. *T. Holloway: London*, [1901.] fol. **H. 3603. (48.)**

LENNOX (MARIA JANE) *Lady William Lennox*

— The Appeal. Ballad [begins: "Oh! who is your real love"]. *London*, [1867.] fol. **H. 1775. u. (18.)**

— Joy-Bells in the Air. Song, the words and music by Lady William Lennox. *Boosey & Co.: London*, [1884.] fol. **H. 1788. v. (41.)**

— The 9th Royal Lancers March. [P. F.] *London*, [1866.] fol. **h. 1460. v. (24.)**

— Song of the River [begins: "Clear and cool"] written by ... C. Kingsley. *London*, [1868.] fol. **H. 1775. u. (19.)**

— Waltz. [P. F.] *In:* The Harmonicon. vol. 8, pt. 1. p. 32. 1830. 4°. **P.P. 1947.**

— The Admired Waltzes, for the piano forte, *etc.* pp. 4. *Mori & Lavenu: London*, [1830.] fol. **h. 61. oo. (8.)**

LENNOX (WALTER)

— The First Rose of the Year. Primrose Song, words by E. Ringwood. *S. Lucas, Weber & Co.: London*, [1886.] fol. **H. 1788. v. (40.)**

LENOIR (JEAN)

— [Parlez-moi d'amour.] Speak to me of Love ... Waltz song, words by Bruce Sievier. ⟨French words and music by J. Lenoir.⟩ pp. 3. *Ascherberg, Hopwood & Crew: London*, [1931.] 4°.
The verso of p. 3 bears a voice part with the French words. **G. 1271. b. (25.)**

— [Parlez-moi d'amour.] Speak to me of Love ... Arranged for mixed voices (S.A.T.B.) by Purcell J. Mansfield, *etc.* [Staff and tonic sol-fa notation.] pp. 4. *Ascherberg, Hopwood & Crew: London*, [1945.] 8°.
[Ascherberg's Series of Part-Songs. no. 385.] **F. 1659. a.**

— Speak to me of Love. *See supra:* [Parlez-moi d'amour.]

LENOIR (PIERRE)

— Fantasie over Troubadouren. Af G. Verdi. [P. F.] pp. 7. *Chr. E. Hornemans Forlag: Kjøbenhavn*, [1865.] fol.
Fantasier og Salonstykker for Pianoforte. Aarg. 1. no. 2. **h. 61. n. (18.)**

LENOIR DE LA FAGE (JUSTE ADRIEN)

— Alma redemptoris, à 3 voix. *See* RÉPERTOIRE. Répertoire de Musique d'église, *etc.* No. 16. [1860?] fol. **H. 3341.**

LENOIR DE LA FAGE (Juste Adrien)

—— Ave Regina, à 3 voix. *See* Répertoire. Répertoire de Musique d'église, *etc.* No. 15. [1860?] fol.　**H. 3341.**

—— Ave Regina pour deux Tenors et Basse avec Accompagnement d'Orgue. *See* Periodical Publications.— *Paris*. L'Illustration Musicale, *etc.* No. 4[b]. 1863. 8°.　**P.P. 1948. t.**

—— Ave Regina. *See* Dessoff (G.) Geistliche Chöre, *etc.* No. 7. [1904, *etc.*] 8°.　**F. 993.**

—— Cours complet de Plain-Chant, *etc.* (Appendice.) *Paris,* 1855, 56. 8°.　**Hirsch 906.**

—— [Another copy of the Appendix.]　**7897. c. 38.**

—— Essais de diphthérographie musicale, ou notices, descriptions, analyses, extraits, et reproductions de manuscrits relatifs à la pratique, à la théorie et à l'histoire de la musique. (Exemples de musique.) *Paris,* 1864. 8°.　**7896. dd. 5.**

—— [Another copy.] *The "Exemples de musique only".*　**Hirsch M. 218.**

—— Histoire générale de la musique et de la danse. 2 tom. *Paris,* 1844. 8°.　**785. h. 21.**

——— [Plates.] *Paris,* 1844. 4°.　**785. m. 25.**

—— Manuel de l'organiste. Plain-Chant Romain harmonisé ... Édition colligée par A. de la Fage. *Paris,* [1884.] 4°.　**f. 314. (6.)**

—— O salutaris Hostia. Motet d'Élévation pour quatre voix d'Hommes et Orgue—ad libitum. *See* Periodical Publicatons.— *Paris*. L'Illustration Musicale, *etc.* No. 4[a]. 1863. 8°.　**P.P. 1948. t.**

—— Recueil de dix-neuf Cantiques, disposés a quatre Parties d'après de très anciennes Mélodies Italiennes, pour le Mois de Marie par A. de La Fage. *E. Repos: Paris,* [1860?] 8°.　**F. 1171. cc. (16.)**

—— Recueil de Motets en Plain-Chant à une et à plusieurs voix, tirés des Meilleurs Auteurs ... revus et mis en ordre par J. A. de La Fage ... Deuxième édition. *Delloye: Paris,* 1838. obl. 4°.　**A. 568.**

—— Routine pour accompagner le Plain-Chant. *Paris,* 1858. 8°.　**E. 739.**

—— *See* Frelon (L. F. A.) L'Orgue, journal des dimanches et des fêtes, publié sous la direction de L. F. A. Frelon, avec le concours de MM. A. de la Fage, *etc.* 1858. fol.　**h. 1004.**

—— *See* Palestrina (G. P. da) Vingt Motets ... édition revue ... par A. de Lafage. [1850?] 8°.　**F. 23. d.**

LENOM (Clément)

—— Rhythm by Solfeggio. A practical method for the development of the sense of time and of rhythm, *etc. The New England Conservatory of Music: Boston,* 1927. 8°.　**F. 1781.**

LENONCOURT (A. Sublet de)

—— *See* Sublet de Lenoncourt.

LENORE

—— Lenore. [Song.] *See* Ah. Ah, broken is the golden Bowl, *etc.* [1891.] fol.　**H. 1797. z. (35.)**

—— Lenore. [Song.] *See* André (J.)

—— Lenore. [Song.] *See* Cadman (C. W.)

—— Lénore. [Song.] *See* Donizetti (D. G. M.)

—— Lenore. Liederspiel. *See* Eberwein (C.)

LENORE

—— Lenore. [Recitation with music.] *See* Hawley (S.) Recitation-Music Series. No. 14.

—— Lenore. [Song.] *See* Hemberger (T.)

—— Lenore. [Song.] *See* Henderson (V.) Two Songs, *etc.* [No. 1.]

—— Lenore. Ballad. *See* Ingram (Henry B.)

—— Lenore. Ballade. *See* Kuegele (R.)

—— Lenore. [Melodrama.] *See* Liszt (F.)

—— G. A. Bürgers Lenore. [Cantata.] *See* Paradis (M. T.)

—— Lenore. [Song.] *See* Robyn (Alfred G.)

—— Lenore. Ballade. *See* Tomašek (V. J.)

—— Lenore. [Song.] *See* Zumsteeg (J. R.)

—— Lenore and the Wonder House. Musical play. *See* Dale (Ralph A.)

—— Lenore, my own Lenore. [Song.] *See* Solman (Alfred)

LENORMAND (Léonce)

—— Trop tard! Romance ... Paroles de M^r Et. Bourlet Delavallée. *Chez Janet & Cotelle: Paris,* [1835?]　**Hirsch M. 1298. (16.)**

LENORMAND (René)

—— Pièces pour Piano. Op. 59, 60 et 61. *J. Williams: London,* (1902.) 4°. *No. 275 of J. Williams' Albums.*　**G. 785.**

—— Darby O'Dun. Mélodie irlandaise, tirée du Manuscrit Petrie par R. Lenormand. [Violin and P. F.] *J. Williams: London,* (1906.) fol.　**h. 1612. p. (27.)**

—— Départ. *See* infra: Deux mélodies ... Op. 20. No. 1.

—— Il Dolce Far Niente. Chœur pour voix de femmes avec accompagnement de piano à 4 mains [begins: "Reposer mollement"], paroles de G. de Larenaudière. Op. 17. *Paris,* [1885.] fol.　**H. 1795. a. (8.)**

—— Trois Marches pour le Piano à quatre mains. 3 no. *Hamburg,* [1874.] fol.　**h. 1487. p. (46.)**

—— Deux Mélodies pour une voix avec accompagnement de piano. Op. 20. No. 1. Départ [begins: "Vous partez, et mon cœur"] (fragment de poésie de G. de Larenaudière). No. 2. Sérenade. *Paris,* [1885.] fol. *Imperfect; wanting no. 2.*　**H. 2836. h. (46.)**

—— Sept Mélodies pour Chant et Piano, avec paroles Françaises, Anglaises et Allemandes. [Op. 62.] *J. Williams: London,* (1903.) 4°. *No. 277 of J. Williams' Albums.*　**F. 1619.**

—— [Sept Mélodies. Op. 62. No. 2. Le Rossignol.] The Nightingale ... Poem by A. Ceris, *etc. J. Williams: London,* [1921.] fol.　**H. 1846. jj. (6.)**

—— Mélodies irlandaises. Violon et Piano. [Arranged by] R. Lenormand. *J. Williams: London,* (1906.) 4°. *No. 344 of J. Williams' Albums.*　**G. 785.**

—— The Nightingale. *See* supra: [Sept Mélodies. Op. 62. No. 2. Le Rossignol.]

—— [Petite Suite. Op. 61. No. 3.] Presto-Agitato ... Arranged by C. M. Campbell. [Orchestral parts.] *J. Williams: London,* 1924. 4°. *The Joseph Williams Cinema Edition, Series 2, No. 2.*　**h. 3210. h. (210.)**

—— Petites Pièces pour le Piano à quatre mains. Op. 5. 2 no. *Hamburg,* [1875.] fol.　**h. 1487. p. (47.)**

LENORMAND (René)

— Quatre pièces pour le Piano. Op. 2. *Hamburg*, [1874.] fol.
h. 1487. p. (45.)

— Presto-Agitato. *See* supra: [Petite Suite. Op. 61. No. 3.]

— Sais-tu?—Im Lenz! [begins: "Sais-tu dans la saison fleurie,"] Poésie de G. de Larenaudière. Paroles allemandes de W. Langhans. Mélodie pour une voix avec accomp^t. de piano. Op. 18. *Paris*, [1885.] fol. **H. 2836. h. (45.)**

— Sonate pour Piano et Violon. Op. 4. *Hamburg*, [1874.] fol.
h. 1728. d. (6.)

— Sonate pour Piano et Violoncelle. Op. 6. *Hamburg*, [1875.] fol. **h. 1487. p. (48.)**

— Suite de Valses Sérieuses. Op. 42. [P. F.] *J. Williams: London*, [1896.] fol. **h. 3282. f. (26.)**

LENOX

— Lenox Avenue. Choreographic Street Scenes. *See* STILL (W. G.)

LENOX (F.)

— "I arise from dreams of thee;" song, the poetry by P. B. Shelley. *London*, [1844.] fol. **H. 1695. (11.)**

LENSCHOW (CARL C. H.)

— Potpourri on favorite airs from Donizetti's "La fille du régiment" ... arranged for the Piano Forte ... by ... C. C. H. Lenschow. *R. Cocks & Co.: London*, [1848.] fol.
h. 708. (19.)

LENSELINK (W. A.)

— Twelve Studies for Cornet. pp. 19. *Hawkes & Son: London*, [1957.] 4°. **g. 1105. b. (10.)**

LENSEN (JEAN)

— Deux Pièces. No. 1. Epitaphe. (Op. 8.) No. 2. Sérénade. (Op. 9.) Pour violoncelle et piano. 2 no. *Schott & Co.: London*, 1923. fol. **h. 1851. k. (14.)**

LENSKI (KARL)

— 18 Cells for Flute. A technical analysis on works by Bach, Mozart, Schubert, Debussy. pp. 50. *Musica rara: London*, [1976.] 4°. **g. 761. pp. (3.)**

— *See* CIMAROSA (Domenico) [6 quartetti. No. 1.] Quartet No. 1 in D. For flute, violin, viola and cello. ⟨Ed. K. Lenski.⟩ [1975.] 4°. **g. 410. mm. (1.)**

— *See* CIMAROSA (Domenico) [6 quartetti. No. 4.] Quartet No. 2 in F. For flute, violin, viola and cello. ⟨Ed. K. Lenski.⟩ [1975.] 4°. **g. 410. mm. (2.)**

— *See* CIMAROSA (Domenico) [6 quartetti. No. 6.] Quartet No. 3. in a minor. For flute, violin, viola and cello. ⟨Ed. K. Lenski.⟩ [1975.] 4°. **g. 1796. (21.)**

LENSKY (ALEKSANDR STEPANOVICH)

— *See* ZUBKOV (N. M.) and LENSKY (A. S.) Мелодии Памира. Составители: Н. М. Зубков и А. С. Ленский. 1941. 4°.
G. 936. ww.

LENSKY (BORIS)

— Sérénade, for violin and piano. *Ascherberg, Hopwood & Crew: London*, [1925.] 4°. **g. 505. kk. (36.)**

LENSKY (BORIS)

— Sérénade espagnole, pour Violon avec accompagnement de Piano. *Ascherberg, Hopwood & Crew: London*, [1911.] fol.
h. 1612. aa. (15.)

LENT

— Lent Lilies. [Anthem.] *See* WOODGATE (L.)

— The Lent Lily. Song. *See* IRELAND (J. N.) [The Land of Lost Content. No. 1.]

— The Lent Lily. Song. *See* MARILLIER (C.)

LENT (CARRIE B.)

— He that dwelleth. Unison Anthem, *etc. J. Curwen & Sons: London*, 1932. 8°.
[*Choruses for Equal Voices. No.* 1842.] **E. 861.**

LENT (ERNEST)

— The Border Land. Sacred Song for Soprano or Tenor, words by W. F. Johnson. (With Violin obligato.) *Columbia Music Pub. Co.: Washington*, (1908.) fol. **G. 517. v. (31.)**

— Two Compositions for Piano. [No. 1.] A Persian Pearl. [No. 2.] Spring Melody. *Washington Music Co.: Washington*, (1909.) fol. **g. 606. f. (25.)**

— Cradle Song, for the Pianoforte. *T. Presser: Philadelphia*, (1906.) fol. **h. 3283. p. (23.)**

— En avant! March and Two-Step for the Pianoforte. *T. Presser Co.: Philadelphia*, (1910.) fol. **h. 3286. uu. (49.)**

— Georgetown University March. March and Song. (Words by Rev. D. H. Buel.) [P. F.] *Washington Music Co.: Washington*, (1909.) fol. **h. 3286. uu. (48.)**

— Heart of the Rose, for the Pianoforte. *T. Presser Co.: Philadelphia*, (1910.) fol. **h. 3283. jj. (45.)**

— Mélodie amoureuse, for the Pianoforte. *T. Presser: Philadelphia*, (1906.) fol. **h. 3283. p. (24.)**

— Nymph of the Woods. Air de Ballet for Piano, *etc. E. Schuberth & Co.: New York, London*, (1909.) fol.
h. 3283. jj. (46.)

— Old Amos, the Taverner. Song for Bass voice, text by F. Huff, *etc. O. Ditson Co.: Boston*, (1910.) fol.
H. 1792. s. (10.)

— Passing Birds. Oiseaux passants. Tarantelle for Pianoforte. *Church, Paxson and Co.: New York*, (1912.) fol.
h. 3284. g. (18.)

— Pastoral Minuet, for the Pianoforte. *T. Presser: Philadelphia*, (1906.) fol. **h. 3283. p. (25.)**

— Scherzino, for the Pianoforte. *Church, Paxson and Co.: New York*, (1912.) fol. **h. 3284. g. (19.)**

— Sweetheart be mine. [Song.] Words and music by E. Lent, *etc. Washington Music Co.: Washington*, (1909.) fol.
H. 1794. vv. (42.)

— When the Twilight softly falls. [Song.] Words and music by E. Lent, *etc. Washington Music Co.: Washington*, (1910.) fol.
H. 1792. s. (11.)

LENT (Mrs ERNEST)

— *See* DEBUSSY (C. A.) Rêverie du Soir. Edited by Mrs. E. Lent. (1911.) fol. **h. 3283. xx. (11.)**

LENTELIED

— Lentelied. [Song.] *See* BECK (J. H. M.)

LENTELIED
— Lentelied. Walslied. *See* RICHFIELD (Sydney)

LENTEN
— Lenten Cantata. *See* HAENDEL (G. F.) [*Collected Works.—c.*]

— A Lenten Carol. Anthem. *See* DARST (William G.)

— Lenten is come. [Part-song.] *See* VOYNICH (E. L.)

— The Lenten Lily. Song. *See* MILVAIN (H.)

LENTO
— Lento il piè. Aria. *See* MOZART (W. A.) [Dans un bois solitaire. K. 308.]

LENTON (JOHN)
— [The Ambitious Stepmother.] Mʳ Lenton's Ayres in the Tragedy [by N. Rowe] of the Ambitious Stepmother. 1st Treble. *See* HARMONIA. Harmonia Anglicana, *etc.* [1701.] *obl.* fol. **b. 29.**

— [The Ambitious Stepmother.] [Another edition.] Mʳ Lenton's Ayres in the Tragedy [by N. Rowe] of the Ambitious Stepmother. ⟨1ˢᵗ treble.—Bass.⟩ [Parts.] 2 pt. [*J. Walsh and J. Hare: London*, 1702?] *obl.* fol.
Printed on one side of the leaf only. Imperfect; wanting the other parts. **d. 24. (4.)**

— [The Fair Penitent.] Mʳ Lentons Musick in the Tragedy [by N. Rowe] call'd the Fair Penitent. First Treble. (Second Treble.—Tenor.—Bass.) [Parts.] [*J. Walsh and J. Hare: London*, 1703.] *obl.* fol. **d. 24. a. (2.)**

— [The Gamester.] Mr. Lentons Musick in the Comedy call'd yᵉ Gamester. First Treble. (Second Treble.) (Tenor.) (Bass.) 4 pt. [*J. Walsh and J. Hart: London*, 1705.] fol. **g. 15. (1.)**

— [Liberty Asserted.] Mʳ Lentons Musick in the Play call'd Liberty Asserted. ⟨First treble.—Bass.⟩ [Parts.] 2 pt. [*J. Walsh and J. Hare: London*, 1704?] *obl.* fol.
Printed on one side of the leaf only. Imperfect; wanting the other parts. **d. 24. (19.)**

— [The Royal Captive.] Aires in the play called the Royall Captive, *etc.* ⟨First treble.—Bass.⟩ [Parts.] 2 pt. [*J. Walsh and J. Hare: London*, 1702.] *obl.* fol.
Printed on one side of the leaf only. Imperfect; wanting the other parts. **d. 24. (10.)**

— [Tamberlain.] Mʳ Lentons Aires in the Tragedy called Tamberlain. First Treble. *See* HARMONIA. Harmonia Anglicana, *etc.* [1702.] *obl.* fol. **b. 29. a.**

— *See* P., H. Wit and Mirth: or, Pills to Purge Melancholy, *etc.* (Wit and Mirth ... The Second Edition ... Corrected by J. Lenton. Vol. IV.) 1707 (1709). 12°. **1346. a. 28–31.**

— *See* SONGS. A Third Collection of New Songs ... by ... J. Lenton, *etc.* 1685. fol. **G. 152. (2.)**

LENTON (JOHN) and TOLLET (THOMAS)
— A Consort of Musick of Three Parts, *etc.* R. Brett: [*London,*] 1692. *obl.* 4°.
The bass viol part only. Imperfect; wanting all after p. 5. **K. 2. c. 14.**

LENTON (SYDNEY)
— The Char's Lament. Novelty Monologue, written by H. Simpson. *Reynolds & Co.: London*, 1944. 4°. [*Musical Monologues. No. 469.*] **H. 2087.**

LENTZ
— [For the German word of this form:] *See* LENZ.

LENTZ (CHARLES)
— Amusette, valse pour Piano. *Paris*, [1882.] fol. **h. 3276. g. (18.)**

— Caille et Coucou, valse pour Piano. *Paris*, [1882.] fol. **h. 3276. g. (17.)**

— Les Classiques de la Jeunesse. Transcriptions faciles des œuvres des Maîtres. 1ʳᵉ Cahier. *Lemoine et Fils: Paris, Bruxelles*, [1887.] 4°. **g. 543. k. (6.)**

— Fantaisie pastorale sur un thême favori de Bohême pour Piano. Op. 10. *Paris*, [1855.] fol. **h. 724. e. (21.)**

— Fantaisie pastorale sur un thême favori de Bohême pour piano. Op. 10. *London*, [1855.] fol. **h. 724. e. (22.)**

— Fleurette polka-mazurka pour Piano. *Paris*, [1879.] fol. **h. 1493. o. (17.)**

— Menuet du 11ᵉᵐᵉ Quintette de Boccherini, transcrit pour Piano. *Paris*, [1872.] fol. **h. 1487. p. (49.)**

— Raindrops. Valse for the Pianoforte. *London*, [1859.] fol. **h. 977. f. (32.)**

— Rondo brillant sur le Billet de Marguérite de Gevaert pour piano. Op. 8. *Paris*, [1855.] fol. **h. 724. e. (19.)**

— Rondo brillant sur le Billet de Marguérite de Gevaert pour piano. Op. 8. *London*, [1855.] fol. **h. 724. e. (20.)**

— Le Tambourin ... J. P. Rameau. Transcription de C. Lentz. *See* ALBUM. Album Lyrique ... No. 27. [1883.] fol. **h. 1481. p. (1.)**

— *See* BOSCH (J.) Passacaille. Sérénade pour guitare avec violon ad libitum par C. Gounod ... 10. Valse sérénade. Arrangement facile par C. Lentz. 1885. fol. **h. 80. e. (3.)**

— *See* LEMOINE (Achille P.) Air de Ballet pour deux pianos (arrangé ... par C. Lentz). 1885. fol. **h. 3291. (11.)**

— *See* THOMÉ (F. L. J.) [La Folie Parisienne.] Clic-Clac, Galop ... arrangé pour piano par C. Lentz. 1886. fol. **h. 3227. a. (9.)**

LENTZ (GERHARD)
— Choral-Schlag-Buch, in welchem der General-Bass mit dem Unterschied sine mensura zu dem Choral-Gesang ist componiret ... Vorhero ist eine Kurtze Unterrichtung von dem General-Bass ... beygefüget, *etc. Apud Hæredes Hæffner: per Ioann. Benjam. Waylandt: Moguntiæ*, 1761. *obl.* fol. **C. 834.**

LENTZ (HEINRICH GERHARD)
— Airs connûs variés pour le forte-piano ou le Clavecin. pp. 15. *Chez Mʳ Boyer; chez Madᵉ Le Menu: Paris*, [1790?] fol. [*Journal de pièces de clavecin. no. 70.*] **g. 996. b. (13.)**

— Ouverture del Fanatico burlato [by D. Cimarosa]. Arrangée pour le clavecin ou forte piano avec accompagnement d'un violon ad libitum par M. Lentz. *Chez H. Naderman: Paris*, [c. 1790.] fol.
Imperfect; wanting the violin part. **g. 996. b. (6.)**

— Six Preludes for the Pedal Harp or Piano Forte. pp. 5. *The Author; Longman and Broderip: London*, [c. 1795.] fol. **g. 1098. r. (6.)**

LENTZ (MICHAEL)
— Spâss an Iérscht. Liddercher ä Gedichten, *etc. Letzeburég*, 1873. 8°. **11528. bbb. 1.**

LENTZ (NICOLA)

— [2 concerti a sei stromenti.] Concerto I ... Cembalo obligato, tre violini, alto viola & violoncello ... Uitgave verzorgd door ... Willem Noske ... Basso continuo uitgewerkt door ... Hans Schouwman. [With a facsimile. Score.] pp. 31. *Edition Heuwekemeijer, etc.: Amsterdam, etc.,* [1961.] 4°. [*Heuwekemeijer Orkest-Bibliotheek. no.* 1.] **g. 1067. q.**

LENVEC ( )

— Amis chantons. Chansonette avec choeur. *Paris,* [1835?] fol. **G. 540. (70.)**

— Au pied de cette tour. Romance. *Paris,* [1835?] fol. **G. 541. (26.)**

— Les Gueux. [Song, begins: "Des gueux chantons la louange".] Paroles de P. J. de Béranger. *Paris,* [1835?] fol. **G. 540. (59.)**

— Le Pauvre Enfant. Romance [begins: "Près d'une église"] de Mr. E. M. ** de L**. *Paris,* [1835?] fol. **G. 552. (20.)**

LENZ

— Lenz. [Song.] *See* FRANZ (R.) 6 Gesänge ... Op. 14. No. 2.

— Lenz. [Song.] *See* HASSE (G.) Fünf Gesänge. Op. 23. No. 3.

— Lenz! [Song.] *See* KIENZL (W.) Fruehlingslieder ... Op. 33. No. 1.

— Der Lenz. [Song.] *See* LASSEN (E.) Sechs Lieder ... Op. 45. No. 6.

— Der Lentz belebet die Natur. Duetto. *See* MUELLER (W.) [Die Zauberzitter.]

— Der Lenz geht um. [Part-song.] *See* WEISS (G. O. T.)

— Der Lenz ist angekommen. Song. *See* DUERRNER (J.) Three Songs. Op. 23. No. 1.

— Der Lenz ist gekommen. Männerchor. *See* HOFMANN (F. H.) Drei Männerchöre. Op. 1. No. 1.

— Der Lenz ist gekommen. [Song.] *See* JACOBY (W.) Ein- und zweistimmige Lieder. No. 3.

— Der Lenz ist gekommen. [Song.] *See* KAUFFMANN (F.) Vier Lieder. No. 2.

— Der Lenz ist gekommen. [Song.] *See* SCHMIDT (O.) Fünf Gesänge. No. 5.

— Lenz, komm herbei. [Part-song.] *See* BRUCH (M. C. F.) Sieben Lieder ... Op. 71. No. 6.

— Lenz und Liebe. Lied. *See* ABT (F. W.) Drei Lieder ... Op. 289. No. 3.

— Lenz und Liebe. Liederspiel. *See* HOFMANN (H. K. J.)

— Lenz und Liebe. Eine Liederreihe. *See* KLEFFEL (A.)

— Lenz und Liebe. [Song.] *See* SCHLOTTMANN (L.) Lieder ... Op. 15. No. 2.

— Lenz und Liebe. Sechs Gesänge. *See* SCHMIDT (B.)

LENZ (CARL)

— *See* LENTZ (Charles)

LENZ (HEINRICH)

— Der Soldat. Gedicht von Hoffmann von Fallersleben [begins: "Bei Aspern"] für eine Barytonstimme mit Begleitung des Pianoforte. *Leipzig,* [1881.] fol. **H. 1786. e. (43.)**

LENZ (HENRY M.)

— The Bride. Part song [begins: "We'll miss her"]. *London,* [1877.] 8°. **F. 321. d. (39.)**

— The Mona schottische ... for the Pianoforte. *Manchester,* [1876.] fol. **h. 1482. z. (35.)**

— Peer of the Realm galop. [P. F.] *London,* [1873.] fol. **h. 1487. p. (50.)**

— Peer of the Realm galop. [P. F.] *London,* [1878.] 8°. No. 419 *of the "Alliance Musicale. Album Bijou".* **f. 406.**

— The Siona Waltzes. [P. F.] *Hopwood & Crew: London,* [1882.] fol. **h. 975. v. (11.)**

LENZ (J.)

Drei Clavierstücke. Op. 11

— Drei Clavierstücke. 3 no. *Dresden,* [1880.] fol. **h. 3272. j. (23.)**

— [Am Feierabend.] Evening Time (Op. 11, No. 1), for the pianoforte. *Hutchings & Romer: London,* [1882.] fol. **g. 543. j. (27.)**

— Rondo Militaire (Op. 11, No. 2), for the pianoforte. *Hutchings & Romer: London,* [1882.] fol. **g. 543. j. (28.)**

— [Silberquell.] The Silver Stream (Op. 11, No. 3), for the pianoforte. *Hutchings & Romer: London,* [1882.] fol. **g. 543. j. (29.)**

LENZ (LEOPOLD)

— An den Abendstern. *See* infra: [6 deutsche Lieder. Op. 20. No. 3.]

— Dein ist mein Herz. [Song, begins: "Ich schnitt' es gern".] *See* CONCERTS. Les Concerts de Société. No. 12. [1845, *etc.*] fol. **H. 2085. a.**

— VI. Deutsche Lieder für eine Singstimme mit Begleitung des Pianoforte. *Augsburg,* [1820?] obl. fol. **E. 253. b. (19.)**

— [6 deutsche Lieder. Op. 20. No. 3. An den Abendstern.] "Lamp of the Night,"—An den Abendstern ... [words] translated by F. W. Rosier. [For voice, violin and piano. Score and part.] *Eng. & Ger.* 2 pt. *Wessel & Co.: London,* [c. 1850.] fol. [*Les Concerts de Société. no.* 11.] *The score is for violoncello and piano.* **H. 2085. a.**

— [6 deutsche Lieder. Op. 20. No. 3. An den Abendstern.] "Lamp of the Night," *etc.* (Translated by F. W. Rosier. For voice, piano & violoncello.) [Score.] *Eng. & Ger. Wessel & Cᵒ: London,* [c. 1850.] fol. [*Les Concerts de société. no.* 11.] **H. 2085. g.**

— [6 deutsche Lieder. Op. 20. No. 3.] "Lamp of the night." An den Abendstern. *See* CONCERTS. Les concerts de société ... for voice and concertina. No. 11. [1854, *etc.*] fol. **H. 2085. d.**

— Gesaenge und Lieder aus der Tragödie Faust von Goethe, in Musick gesetzt für eine Singstimme mit Begleitung des Pianoforte. 14ᵗᵉˢ Werk. *Mainz,* [1840?] obl. fol. **E. 712.**

— Lamp of the Night. *See* supra: [6 deutsche Lieder. Op. 20. No. 3. An den Abendstern.]

— Der Landsknecht unter Georg von Frondsberg. Ein Cyklus von 12 Liedern und Gesängen gedichtet von Hofmann von Fallersleben, im Musik gesetzt für eine Bassstimme mit Begleitung des Pianoforte ... 38ᵗᵉˢ Werk. pp. 41. *Bei B. Schott's Söhnen: Mainz,* [1845.] fol. **H. 2134. n. (1.)**

LENZ (LEOPOLD)

— Mignon der Harfner und Philine, ein Cyclus von acht Gesaengen aus "Wilhelm Meisters Lehrjahre" in Musik gesetzt für eine tiefe Sopran- oder Barytonstimme mit Begleitung des Pianoforte ... Op: 12. pp. 29. *Falter u. Sohn: München*, 1832. *obl.* fol.   **Hirsch IV. 1691.**

— [Another copy.]   **R. M. 25. d. 9. (3.)**

— Minnefahrt, in neun Gesängen gedichtet von Ludwig Uhland, in Musik gesetzt für eine Singstimme mit Begleitung des Piano-Forte ... Opus [14]. pp. 21. *Falter und Sohn: München*, [c. 1830.] *obl.* fol.   **E. 712. a.**

LENZ (MAX VON)

— The Hero of Manila. March ... Op. 50. ⟨Solo B♭ cornet (conductor) [and wind band parts].⟩ 20 pt. *Oliver Ditson Co.: Boston, London*, [1899.] 8°.   **f. 800. (812.)**

— *See* CLOSE (E. F.) Twilight Shadows. Waltzes. Arranged by M. von Lenz. 1902. fol.   **h. 3286. w. (16.)**

— *See* LANE (O. W.) College Boys ... Arr. [for wind band] by M. von Lenz. [1901.] 8°.   **f. 800. (780.)**

LENZ (W.)

— Air de Danse. [Violin and P. F.] *See infra*: Les Duos de la Jeunesse ... No. 12.

— Album de Chants Nationaux transcrits pour Piano par W. Lenz. *Henry Litolff: Braunschweig*, [1881.] 4°. [*Collection Litolff, no.* 1280.]   **g. 375.**

— Le Baptême d'une Cloche. Fantaisie caracteristique pour Piano. *Paris*, [1876.] fol.   **h. 1487. p. (55.)**

— Le Briska. Mazurka Russe pour Piano. *Paris*, [1876.] fol.   **h. 1487. p. (53.)**

— Chacone. [Violin and P. F.] *See infra*: Les Duos de la Jeunesse ... No. 8.

— Chanson Basque pour Piano. *Paris*, [1877.] fol.   **h. 1493. o. (21.)**

— Les Classiques de l'Enfance. (Classics for the young.) Transcriptions très faciles ... des Œuvres des Grands Maîtres. Piano seul. 10 vol. *H. Litolff: Braunschweig*, [1881, *etc.*] 4°. [*Collection Litolff, no.* 1257–1264, 1277, 1699.]   **g. 375.**

— Les Classiques de l'Enfance ... Piano à Quatre Mains. 6 vol. *H. Litolff: Braunschweig*, [1881, *etc.*] 4°. [*Collection Litolff, no.* 1265, 1266, 1337–1339, 1700.]   **g. 375.**

— Les Classiques de l'Enfance ... Piano et Violon. 10 vol. *H. Litolff: Braunschweig*, [1881, *etc.*] 4°. [*Collection Litolff, no.* 1267–1274, 1278, 1721.]   **g. 375.**

— Classisches Jugendalbum ... 50 berühmte Stücke für das Pianoforte, bearbeitet von W. Lenz. *H. Litolff: Braunschweig*, [1885?] 4°. [*Collection Litolff, no.* 1492.]   **g. 375.**

— Danse Rustique. [Violin and P. F.] *See infra*: Les Duos de la Jeunesse ... No. 2.

— Les Duos de la Jeunesse pour Piano et Violon. 12 no. *Paris*, [1882.] fol.   **h. 1608. l. (12.)**

— L'Hippogriffe, galop brillant pour Piano. *Paris*, [1876.] fol.   **h. 1487. p. (52.)**

— Mazarinade. [Violin and P. F.] *See supra*: Les Duos de la Jeunesse ... No. 11.

— Mazurka Sentimentale. [Violin and P. F.] *See supra*: Les Duos de la Jeunesse ... No. 5.

LENZ (W.)

— Mélodie Suédoise. [Violin and P. F.] *See supra*: Les Duos de la Jeunesse ... No. 1.

— Mélodie Valse. [Violin and P. F.] *See supra*: Les Duos de la Jeunesse ... No. 3.

— Midi, caprice pour Piano. *Paris*, [1877.] fol.   **h. 1493. o. (19.)**

— Minuit, nocturne pour Piano. *Paris*, [1877.] fol.   **h. 1493. o. (20.)**

— Le Moulin Mignon. [Violin and P. F.] *See supra*: Les Duos de la Jeunesse ... No. 6.

— Le Nouveau-Né. Berceuse pour Piano. *Paris*, [1876.] fol.   **h. 1487. p. (56.)**

— Les Pages du Dauphin. [Violin and P. F.] *See supra*: Les Duos de la Jeunesse ... No. 7.

— La Petite Patrouille. Morceau caractéristique. [P. F.] *Paris*, [1884.] fol.   **h. 3280. k. (46.)**

— Le Picador, chanson Andalouse pour Piano. *Paris*, [1877.] fol.   **h. 1493. o. (18.)**

— Le Porte-Étendard, marche brillante pour Piano. *Paris*, [1876.] fol.   **h. 1487. p. (54.)**

— Près d'un Berceau. [Violin and P. F.] *See supra*: Les Duos de la Jeunesse ... No. 9.

— Le Retour à la Ferme. Pastorale pour piano. *Paris*, [1876.] fol.   **h. 1487. p. (5.)**

— Romanzetta. [Violin and P. F.] *See supra*: Les Duos de la Jeunesse ... No. 10.

— Les Veneurs du Roi. [Violin and P. F.] *See supra*: Les Duos de la Jeunesse ... No. 4.

— Ventre-Saint-Gris, galop brillant pour Piano. *Paris*, [1878.] fol.   **h. 1493. o. (22.)**

— *See* VOGEL (A.) and LEFORT (A.) Le Concert au Salon, *etc.* [Vol. 7 and 8. Transcribed by A. Vogel and W. Lenz.] [1881, *etc.*] 4°. [*Collection Litolff. no.* 1723, 1724.]   **g. 375.**

LENZBERG (JULIUS)

— "I'll be happy when I'm thinking of you." Song and chorus. Words by C. E. Smith. pp. 5. *Theatrical Music Supply Co.: New York*, [1904.] fol.   **H. 3985. t. (3.)**

LENZBUSCH

— Der Lenzbusch hat Triebe. [Song.] *See* HAMMA (B.) Acht Lieder, *etc.* Op. 48. No. 1.

LENZESTRAUM

— Lenzestraum. [Duet.] *See* ABT (F. W.) Vier zweistimmige Lieder, *etc.* Op. 461. No. 3.

LENZESTREIBE

— Lenzestreibe. [Part-song.] *See* BUELOW (H. G. von) Fünf Gesänge, *etc.* No. 4.

LENZESWONNE

— Lenzes-Wonne. [Chorus.] *See* PACHE (J.)

LENZEWSKI (GUSTAV) *the Elder*

— *See* ANNE AMELIA, *Princess of Prussia.* Vier Regimentsmärsche ... herausgegeben und für Streichorchester eingerichtet von G. Lenzewski sen. [c. 1930.] 4°.   **h. 2785. y. (7.)**

— *See* ANNE AMELIA, *Princess of Prussia.* Sonate für Flöte F-Dur ... Herausgegeben von ... G. Lenzewski sen., *etc.* [1975.] 4°.   **g. 280. kk. (6.)**

— *See* FREDERICK II., called *the Great, King of Prussia.* [Il Re pastore.] Rezitativ und Arie "Nota v'è questa dea" ... Herausgegeben von G. Lenzewski sen. [c. 1930.] 4°.   **G. 424. qq. (5.)**

— *See* FREDERICK II., called *the Great, King of Prussia.* [Il Re pastore.] Arie (Sulle più belle piante) ... Herausgegeben von G. Lenzewski sen. [1925.] 4°.   **G. 424. qq. (4.)**

— *See* FREDERICK II., called *the Great, King of Prussia.* Erste Sinfonie G-dur für Streichorchester mit Cembalo. Herausgegeben von G. Lenzewski sen. [1925.] 4°.   **g. 934. e. (1.)**

— *See* FREDERICK II., called *the Great, King of Prussia.* Zweite Sinfonie G-Dur, *etc.* ⟨Herausgegeben von G. Lenzewski sen.⟩ [1976.] 4°.   **g. 1067. xx. (4.)**

— *See* FREDERICK II., called *the Great, King of Prussia.* Dritte Sinfonie D-Dur, *etc.* ⟨Herausgegeben von G. Lenzewski sen.⟩ [1976.] 4°.   **g. 1067. xx. (5.)**

— *See* FREDERICK II., called *the Great, King of Prussia.* Vierte Sinfonie A-Dur, *etc.* ⟨Herausgegeben von G. Lenzewski sen.⟩ [1976.] 4°.   **g. 1067. xx. (6.)**

— *See* SCARLATTI (A.) [6 Concertos in seven parts. No. 3.] Sechs Concerti grossi. Drittes Konzert in F-dur ... Herausgegeben von ... G. Lenzewski sen., *etc.* [c. 1960.] 4°.   **g. 1052. c. (5.)**

— *See* STAMITZ (Carl) Sonate in B-dur. Für Viola und Klavier ... Herausgegeben von G. Lenzewski sen. [c. 1960.] 4°.   **g. 1065. g. (4.)**

— *See* STAMITZ (J. W. A.) [3 Symphonies. Op. 11. No. 3.] Sinfonie Es-dur ... Herausgegeben von G. Lenzewski, *etc.* [1929.] 4°.   **g. 1620. c. (6.)**

LENZEWSKI (GUSTAV) *the Younger*

— Divertimento. Acht kleine Stücke für Streicher. [Score.] pp. 11. *B. Schott's Söhne: Mainz,* [1966.] 4°.   **g. 934. f. (7.)**

— Musik für Violine. pp. 7. *B. Schott's Söhne: Mainz,* [1964.] 4°.   **g. 422. n. (7.)**

— Sonate für Violine und Klavier (1950). [Score and part.] 2 pt. *B. Schott's Söhne: Mainz,* [1969.] 4°.   **g. 500. tt. (2.)**

— *See* BACH (J. S.) [*Collected Works.—h.*] Kleine Stücke für zwei Geigen zusammengestellt von G. Lenzewski. [1950.] *obl.* 8°.   **b. 121. c. (6.)**

— *See* BEETHOVEN (L. van) Sechs Deutsche. Six Allemandes. [K.–H. 42.] Bearbeitet von G. Lenzewski. [1938.] fol.   **h. 400. o. (9.)**

— *See* MOZART (W. A.) [*Collected Works.—c.*] Musik für drei Violinen ... Herausgegeben von G. Lenzewski. [1949.] 4°.   **g. 1018. t. (3.)**

— *See* TELEMANN (G. P.) Sechs Sonatinen ... Aussetzung des bezifferten Basses und Bezeichnung der Violinstimme von G. Lenzewski. 1938. 4°.   **g. 500. s. (22.)**

— *See* VERACINI (F. M.) [Sonate Accademiche. Op. 2. No. 8.] Konzert-Sonate für Violine und Klavier. Durchgesehen ... von G. Lenzewski. [1949.] 4°.   **g. 505. vv. (19.)**

— *See* VIVALDI (A.) [L'Estro Armonico. Op. 3. No. 6.] Concerto in A. Herausgegeben ... von G. Lenzewski. 1939. 4°.   **g. 500. s. (25.)**

LENZFRAGE

— Lenzfrage. [Part-song.] *See* ISENMANN (C.) [Five Part Songs. Op. 96. No. 27.]

LENZKNOSPEN

— Lenzknospen. [Song.] *See* HUMPERDINCK (E.)

LEO

— Ka Leo hoomana. pp. 27. [c. 1875.] *obl.* 8°. *Without titlepage. The title is taken from the cover.*   **A. 1237. u.**

LEO ( )

— *See* OVERTURES. Sei ouverture a più stromenti composte da varri autorri ... VI. del Sig^r Leo, *etc.* [1755?] fol.   **g. 271. m. (8.)**

LEO ( ) *pseud.*

— Leo's farm yard, or farmers medley ... [for] the violin. *London,* [1858.] fol.   **h. 1613. (6.)**

LEO (ERNEST A.)

— In heav'nly Love abiding. [Sacred song.] *C. F. Summy Co.: Chicago,* (1910.) fol.   **H. 1187. rr. (10.)**

— The Mercy Seat. Sacred Recitation and Aria, *etc. C. F. Summy Co.: Chicago,* 1897. fol.   **H. 1187. u. (9.)**

LEO (FLORENCE N.)

— Reverie. Song for a high voice with Piano accompaniment, words and music by F. N. Leo. Italian version by G. Viafora. *G. Schirmer: New York,* (1911.) fol.   **H. 1792. s. (12.)**

LEO (FRANK)

— "A.B.C." ⟨Song.⟩ Written and composed by F. Leo. [Staff and tonic sol-fa notation. Voice part.] *Francis, Day & Hunter: London,* [1905.] *s. sh.* fol.   **H. 3985. t. (4.)**

— "A.B.C.," *etc.* ⟨Song.⟩ [With separate voice part.] 2 pt. *Francis, Day & Hunter: London,* [1905.] fol.   **H. 3985. t. (5.)**

— All becos 'e's minding a 'Ouse. Written and composed by F. Leo, *etc.* [Song. Staff and tonic sol-fa notation. Voice part.] *Francis, Day & Hunter: London,* [1897.] *s. sh.* fol.   **H. 3980. qq. (31.)**

— All Day. ⟨Song.⟩ Written and composed by F. Leo, *etc.* [Staff and tonic sol-fa notation. Voice part.] *Francis, Day & Hunter: London,* [1908.] *s. sh.* fol.   **H. 3985. t. (6.)**

— All Day, *etc.* ⟨Song.⟩ [With separate voice part.] 2 pt. *Francis, Day & Hunter: London,* [1908.] fol.   **H. 3985. t. (7.)**

— "Always give and take a little Bit." ⟨Song.⟩ Written and composed by F. Leo, *etc.* [Staff and tonic sol-fa notation. Voice part.] *Francis, Day & Hunter: London,* [1906.] *s. sh.* fol.   **H. 3985. t. (8.)**

— "Always give and take a little Bit," *etc.* ⟨Song.⟩ [With separate voice part.] 2 pt. *Francis, Day & Hunter: London,* [1906.] fol.   **H. 3985. t. (9.)**

— Am I in the Way? ⟨Song.⟩ Written and composed by F. Leo, *etc.* [Staff and tonic sol-fa notation. Voice part.] *Francis, Day & Hunter: London,* [1900.] *s. sh.* fol.   **H. 3985. t. (10.)**

— Am I in the Way? *etc.* ⟨Song.⟩ [With separate voice part.] 2 pt. *Francis, Day & Hunter: London,* [1900.] fol.   **H. 3985. t. (11.)**

LEO (FRANK)

— And so the poor Dog had none. ⟨Song.⟩ Written and composed by F. Leo, *etc.* [Staff and tonic sol-fa notation. Voice part.] *Francis, Day & Hunter: London*, [1903.] *s. sh.* fol.
H. 3985. t. (12.)

— And so the poor Dog had none, *etc.* ⟨Song.⟩ [With separate voice part.] 2 pt. *Francis, Day & Hunter: London*, [1903.] fol.
H. 3985. t. (13.)

— Anything for Peace and Quietness. Written and composed by F. Leo, *etc.* [Song. Staff and tonic sol-fa notation. Voice part.] *Francis, Day & Hunter: London*, [1898.] *s. sh.* fol.
H. 3980. qq. (32.)

— The Barman. [Song.] Written and composed by F. Leo, *etc.* ⟨Arranged by John S. Baker.⟩ pp. 5. *Howard & Co.: London*, [1898.] fol.
H. 3980. qq. (33.)

— Because I'm a Family Man. ⟨Song.⟩ Written and composed by F. Leo. [Staff and tonic sol-fa notation. Voice part.] *Francis, Day & Hunter: London*, [1903.] *s. sh.* fol.
H. 3985. t. (14.)

— Because I'm a Family Man, *etc.* ⟨Song.⟩ [With separate voice part.] 2 pt. *Francis, Day & Hunter: London*, [1903.] fol.
H. 3985. t. (15.)

— The Boy Scout ... ⟨Song.⟩ Written and composed by F. Leo, *etc.* [Staff and tonic sol-fa notation. Voice part.] *Francis, Day & Hunter: London*, [1909.] *s. sh.* fol.
H. 3985. t. (16.)

— The Boy Scout, *etc.* ⟨Song.⟩ pp. 5. *Francis, Day & Hunter: London*, [1909.] fol.
H. 3985. t. (17.)

— Boys of the Empire. Written and composed by F. Leo, *etc.* [Song. Staff and tonic sol-fa notation. Voice part.] *Francis, Day & Hunter: London*, [1897.] *s. sh.* fol.
H. 3980. qq. (34.)

— Bruvver Jim the Horfis Boy. Written by Harry Castling and F. Leo, *etc.* [Song. With separate voice part.] ⟨Arranged by John S. Baker⟩ 2 pt. *Howard & Co.: London*, [1898.] fol.
H. 3980. qq. (35.)

— Call again. Written and composed by F. Leo, *etc.* [Song. Staff and tonic sol-fa notation. Voice part.] *Francis, Day & Hunter: London*, [1898.] *s. sh.* fol.
H. 3980. qq. (36.)

— "Can't you see I want you to be my Girl?" ... ⟨Song.⟩ Written and composed by F. Leo. [Staff and tonic sol-fa notation. Voice part.] *Francis, Day & Hunter: London*, [1905.] *s. sh.* fol.
H. 3985. t. (18.)

— "Can't you see I want you to be my Girl?" *etc.* ⟨Song.⟩ [With separate voice part.] 2 pt. *Francis, Day & Hunter: London*, [1905.] fol.
H. 3985. t. (19.)

— The Cockney in France. Written and composed by F. Leo, *etc.* [Song. Staff and tonic sol-fa notation. Voice part.] *Francis, Day & Hunter: London*, [1897.] *s. sh.* fol.
H. 3980. qq. (37.)

— A Cold and frosty Morning. Written and composed by F. Leo, *etc.* [Song. Staff and tonic sol-fa notation. Voice part.] *Francis, Day & Hunter: London*, [1899.] *s. sh.* fol.
H. 3980. qq. (38.)

— Come up in my Balloon ... ⟨Song.⟩ Written and composed by F. Leo. [Staff and tonic sol-fa notation. Voice part.] *Francis, Day & Hunter: London*, [1909.] *s. sh.* fol. **H. 3985. t. (20.)**

— Come up in my Balloon, *etc.* ⟨Song.⟩ [With separate voice part.] 2 pt. *Francis, Day & Hunter: London*, [1909.] fol.
H. 3985. t. (21.)

— The Cowslip and the Cow. [Song.] Words and music by Frank Leo. [c. 1900.] fol.
A pirated edition. **H. 1848. b. (21.)**

— Ding dong. Written and composed by F. Leo, *etc.* [Song. Staff and tonic sol-fa notation. Voice part.] *Francis, Day & Hunter: London*, [1899.] *s. sh.* fol.
H. 3980. qq. (39.)

LEO (FRANK)

— Do you know any more funny Stories? ⟨Song.⟩ Written and composed by F. Leo, *etc.* [Staff and tonic sol-fa notation. Voice part.] *Francis, Day & Hunter: London*, [1901.] *s. sh.* fol.
H. 3985. t. (22.)

— Do you know any more funny Stories, *etc.* ⟨Song.⟩ [With separate voice part.] 2 pt. *Francis, Day & Hunter: London*, [1901.] fol.
H. 3985. t. (23.)

— Doctor Nevill. Written and composed by F. Leo, *etc.* [Song. Staff and tonic sol-fa notation. Voice part.] *Francis, Day & Hunter: London*, [1897.] *s. sh.* fol.
H. 3980. qq. (40.)

— Does it matter? ⟨Song.⟩ Written and composed by F. Leo, *etc.* [Staff and tonic sol-fa notation. Voice part.] *Francis, Day & Hunter: London*, [1902.] *s. sh.* fol.
H. 3985. t. (24.)

— Does it matter? *etc.* ⟨Song.⟩ [With separate voice part.] 2 pt. *Francis, Day & Hunter: London*, [1902.] fol.
H. 3985. t. (25.)

— "Don't go out without your Sunshade" ... ⟨Song.⟩ Written and composed by F. Leo. [Staff and tonic sol-fa notation. Voice part.] *Francis, Day & Hunter: London*, [1909.] *s. sh.* fol.
H. 3985. t. (26.)

— "Don't go out without your Sunshade" *etc.* ⟨Song.⟩ [With separate voice part.] 2 pt. *Francis, Day & Hunter: London*, [1909.] fol. **H. 3985. t. (27.)**

— "Don't hang your Trouble on me" ... ⟨Song.⟩ Written and composed by F. Leo. [Staff and tonic sol-fa notation. Voice part.] *Francis, Day & Hunter: London*, [1909.] *s. sh.* fol.
H. 3985. t. (28.)

— "Don't hang your Trouble on me," *etc.* ⟨Song.⟩ [With separate voice part.] 2 pt. *Francis, Day & Hunter: London*, [1909.] fol.
H. 3985. t. (29.)

— Don't run away, Sir! ⟨Song.⟩ Written and composed by F. Leo, *etc.* [Staff and tonic sol-fa notation. Voice part.] *Francis, Day & Hunter: London*, [1900.] *s. sh.* fol.
H. 3985. t. (30.)

— Don't run away, Sir! *etc.* ⟨Song.⟩ [With separate voice part.] 2 pt. *Francis, Day & Hunter: London*, [1900.] fol.
H. 3985. t. (31.)

— 'E's making a great Mistake. Written and composed by F. Leo, *etc.* [Song. Staff and tonic sol-fa notation. Voice part.] *Francis, Day & Hunter: London*, [1898.] *s. sh.* fol.
H. 3980. qq. (41.)

— The Eagle. Written and composed by F. Leo, *etc.* [Song. Staff and tonic sol-fa notation. Voice part.] *Francis, Day & Hunter: London*, [1897.] *s. sh.* fol. **H. 3980. qq. (42.)**

— The Echo of an old, old Tale. ⟨Song.⟩ Written and composed by F. Leo, *etc.* [Staff and tonic sol-fa notation. Voice part.] *Francis, Day & Hunter: London*, [1907.] *s. sh.* fol.
H. 3985. t. (32.)

— The Echo of an old, old Tale, *etc.* ⟨Song.⟩ [With separate voice part.] 2 pt. *Francis, Day & Hunter: London*, [1907.] fol.
H. 3985. t. (33.)

— "Everyone has a Love Affair." ⟨Song.⟩ Words and music by F. Leo. Arranged by Fred Eplett. *B. Feldman & Co.: London*, [1904.] 4°.
H. 3988. t. (34.)

— The Fish 'e 'asn't caught. ⟨Song.⟩ Written and composed by F. Leo, *etc.* [With separate voice part.] 2 pt. *Hopwood & Crew: London*, [1900.] fol. **H. 3985. t. (35.)**

— Francis & Day's Album of Wilkie Bard's popular Songs. (Written and composed [with an introduction] by F. Leo.) *Francis, Day & Hunter: London*, [1908.] 4°. **G. 385. ff. (9.)**

LEO (FRANK)

— Get on my Back! I'll carry you about! ⟨Song.⟩ Written and composed by F. Leo, *etc.* [Staff and tonic sol-fa notation. Voice part.] *Francis, Day & Hunter: London*, [1900.] *s. sh.* fol.
H. 3985. t. (36.)

— "Has anyone been asking for me?" ⟨Song.⟩ Written and composed by F. Leo, *etc.* [Staff and tonic sol-fa notation. Voice part.] *Francis, Day & Hunter: London*, [1902.] *s. sh.* fol.
H. 3985. t. (37.)

— Has anyone been asking for me? *etc.* ⟨Song.⟩ [With separate voice part.] 2 pt. *Francis, Day & Hunter: London*, [1902.] fol.
H. 3985. t. (38.)

— Has anyone seen our Cat? Written and composed by F. Leo, *etc.* [Song. Staff and tonic sol-fa notation. Voice part.] *Francis, Day & Hunter: London*, [1899.] *s. sh.* fol.
H. 3980. qq. (43.)

— Have a Game. ⟨Song.⟩ Written and composed by F. Leo, *etc.* [Staff and tonic sol-fa notation. Voice part.] *Francis, Day & Hunter: London*, [1900.] *s. sh.* fol.
H. 3985. t. (39.)

— Have a Game, *etc.* ⟨Song.⟩ [With separate voice part.] 2 pt. *Francis, Day & Hunter: London*, [1900.] fol.
H. 3985. t. (40.)

— "Have you ever looked in the Glass?" ⟨Song.⟩ Written and composed by F. Leo. [Staff and tonic sol-fa notation. Voice part.] *Francis, Day & Hunter: London*, [1907.] *s. sh.* fol.
H. 3985. t. (41.)

— "Have you ever looked in the Glass?" *etc.* ⟨Song.⟩ [With separate voice part.] 2 pt. *Francis, Day & Hunter: London*, [1907.] fol.
H. 3985. t. (42.)

— He lives in a World of his own. ⟨Song.⟩ Written and composed by F. Leo, *etc.* [Staff and tonic sol-fa notation. Voice part.] *Francis, Day & Hunter: London*, [1900.] *s. sh.* fol.
H. 3985. t. (43.)

— He lives in a World of his own, *etc.* ⟨Song.⟩ [With separate voice part.] 2 pt. *Francis, Day & Hunter: London*, [1900.] fol.
H. 3985. t. (44.)

— He's a very nice Man to know. Written and composed by F. Leo, *etc.* [Song. Staff and tonic sol-fa notation. Voice part.] *Francis, Day & Hunter: London*, [1899.] *s. sh.* fol.
H. 3980. qq. (44.)

— Her Beauty defies my Skill. ⟨Song.⟩ Words and music by F. Leo. pp. 9. *Francis, Day & Hunter: London*, [1905.] fol.
H. 3985. t. (45.)

— [Another issue.] Her Beauty defies my Skill, *etc. London*, [1905.] fol.
H. 3985. t. (46.)

— Her Smiles are for me. *See infra:* [The Lady Killer.]

— Hey!! Are you coming back? [Song.] Words & music by F. Leo, *etc.* pp. 4. *Frank Dean & Co.: London*, [1899.] fol.
H. 3980. qq. (45.)

— Hurrah for the Sea! ⟨Song.⟩ Written and composed by F. Leo, *etc.* [Staff and tonic sol-fa notation. Voice part.] *Francis, Day & Hunter: London*, [1901.] *s. sh.* fol. **H. 3985. t. (47.)**

— Hurrah! for the Sea, *etc.* ⟨Song.⟩ pp. 8. *Francis, Day & Hunter: London*, [1901.] fol. **H. 3985. t. (48.)**

— "I'd like to go halves in that!" [Song.] Written by F. Leo and Harry Castling, *etc.* pp. 4. *Frank Dean & Co.: London*, [1899.] fol.
H. 3980. qq. (46.)

— I don't know where he gets his Ideas. ⟨Song.⟩ Written and composed by F. Leo, *etc.* [Staff and tonic sol-fa notation. Voice part.] *Francis, Day & Hunter: London*, [1908.] *s. sh.* fol.
H. 3985. u. (1.)

LEO (FRANK)

— I don't know where he gets his Ideas, *etc.* ⟨Song.⟩ [With separate voice part.] 2 pt. *Francis, Day & Hunter: London*, [1908.] fol.
H. 3985. u. (2.)

— I don't think I'll bother you now. ⟨Song.⟩ Written and composed by F. Leo. [Staff and tonic sol-fa notation. Voice part.] *Francis, Day & Hunter: London*, [1903.] *s. sh.* fol.
H. 3985. u. (3.)

— I don't think I'll bother you now, *etc.* ⟨Song.⟩ [With separate voice part.] 2 pt. *Francis, Day & Hunter: London*, [1903.] fol.
H. 3985. u. (4.)

— I don't want to cause any Trouble. ⟨Song.⟩ Written and composed by F. Leo, *etc.* [Staff and tonic sol-fa notation. Voice part.] *Francis, Day & Hunter: London*, [1902.] *s. sh.* fol.
H. 3985. u. (5.)

— I don't want to cause any Trouble, *etc.* ⟨Song.⟩ [With separate voice part.] 2 pt. *Francis, Day & Hunter: London*, [1902.] fol.
H. 3985. u. (6.)

— I felt quite sorry for the Feller. ⟨Song.⟩ Written and composed by F. Leo, *etc.* [Staff and tonic sol-fa notation. Voice part.] *Francis, Day & Hunter: London*, [1900.] *s. sh.* fol.
H. 3985. u. (7.)

— I felt quite sorry for the Feller, *etc.* ⟨Song.⟩ [With separate voice part.] 2 pt. *Francis, Day & Hunter: London*, [1900.] fol.
H. 3985. u. (8.)

— I forgive you, but I can't forget. ⟨Song.⟩ Words and music by F. Leo. [Staff and tonic sol-fa notation. Voice part.] *Francis, Day & Hunter: London*, [1909.] *s. sh.* fol. **H. 3985. u. (9.)**

— I forgive you, but I can't forget. ⟨Song.⟩ [With separate voice part.] 2 pt. *Francis, Day & Hunter: London*, [1909.] fol.
H. 3985. u. (10.)

— I knocked at the Door with a Rat-a-tat-tat ... [Song.] Words & music by F. Leo. pp. 4. *Frank Dean & Co.: London*, [1900.] fol. **H. 3985. u. (11.)**

— "I'll call when you're not so busy." ⟨Song.⟩ Written and composed by F. Leo. [Staff and tonic sol-fa notation. Voice part.] *Francis, Day & Hunter: London*, [1904.] *s. sh.* fol.
H. 3985. u. (12.)

— I'll call when you're not so busy, *etc.* ⟨Song.⟩ [With separate voice part.] 2 pt. *Francis, Day & Hunter: London*, [1904.] fol.
H. 3985. u. (13.)

— I'll give him writing to Mignonette. Written and composed by F. Leo, *etc.* [Song. Staff and tonic sol-fa notation. Voice part.] *Francis, Day & Hunter: London*, [1898.] *s. sh.* fol.
H. 3980. qq. (47.)

— "I'm always doing something silly" ... ⟨Song.⟩ Written and composed by F. Leo. [Staff and tonic sol-fa notation. Voice part.] *Francis, Day & Hunter: London*, [1908.] *s. sh.* fol.
H. 3985. u. (14.)

— "I'm always doing something silly," *etc.* ⟨Song.⟩ [With separate voice part.] 2 pt. *Francis, Day & Hunter: London*, [1908.] fol.
H. 3985. u. (15.)

— I'm glad I went up in the Bar. ⟨Song.⟩ Written & composed by F. Leo, *etc.* pp. 6. *Empire Music Publishing Co.: London*, [1907.] fol.
H. 3985. u. (16.)

— I'm here, if I'm wanted. ⟨Song.⟩ Written and composed by F. Leo, *etc.* [Staff and tonic sol-fa notation. Voice part.] *Francis, Day & Hunter: London*, [1908.] *s. sh.* fol.
H. 3985. u. (17.)

— I'm here, if I'm wanted, *etc.* ⟨Song.⟩ [With separate voice part.] 2 pt. *Francis, Day & Hunter: London*, [1908.] fol.
H. 3985. u. (18.)

LEO (FRANK)

— I'm much better off where I am. Written by A. J. Mills, *etc.* [Song. Staff and tonic sol-fa notation. Voice part.] *Francis, Day & Hunter: London,* [1898.] *s. sh.* fol. **H. 3980. qq. (48.)**

— I'm not such a Goose as I look, *etc.* ⟨Song.⟩ [With separate voice part.] 2 pt. *Francis, Day & Hunter: London,* [1905.] fol. **H. 3985. u. (20.)**

— I'm not such a Goose as I look ... ⟨Song.⟩ Written and composed by F. Leo. [Staff and tonic sol-fa notation. Voice part.] *Francis, Day & Hunter: London,* [1906.] *s. sh.* fol. **H. 3985. u. (19.)**

— I think I'd better shift this Scene. ⟨Song.⟩ Written and composed by F. Leo, *etc.* [Staff and tonic sol-fa notation. Voice part.] *Francis, Day & Hunter: London,* [1905.] *s. sh.* fol. **H. 3985. u. (21.)**

— I think I'd better shift this Scene, *etc.* ⟨Song.⟩ [With separate voice part.] 2 pt. *Francis, Day & Hunter: London,* [1905.] fol. **H. 3985. u. (22.)**

— I think I shall stop here a bit. ⟨Song.⟩ Written and composed by F. Leo, *etc.* [Staff and tonic sol-fa notation. Voice part.] *Francis, Day & Hunter: London,* [1901.] *s. sh.* fol. **H. 3985. u. (23.)**

— I think I shall stop here a bit, *etc.* ⟨Song.⟩ [With separate voice part.] 2 pt. *Francis, Day & Hunter: London,* [1901.] fol. **H. 3985. u. (24.)**

— I thought there was something the matter. ⟨Song.⟩ Written and composed by F. Leo, *etc.* [Staff and tonic sol-fa notation. Voice part.] *Francis, Day & Hunter: London,* [1901.] *s. sh.* fol. **H. 3985. u. (25.)**

— I thought there was something the matter, *etc.* ⟨Song.⟩ [With separate voice part.] 2 pt. *Francis, Day & Hunter: London,* [1901.] fol. **H. 3985. u. (26.)**

— I've got a Beau! ⟨Song.⟩ Written and composed by F. Leo, *etc.* [Staff and tonic sol-fa notation. Voice part.] *Francis, Day & Hunter: London,* [1901.] *s. sh.* fol. **H. 3985. u. (27.)**

— I've got a Beau! *etc.* ⟨Song.⟩ [With separate voice part.] 2 pt. *Francis, Day & Hunter: London,* [1901.] fol. **H. 3985. u. (28.)**

— I've got to get back to Work. ⟨Song.⟩ Written and composed by F. Leo, *etc.* [Staff and tonic sol-fa notation. Voice part.] *Francis, Day & Hunter: London,* [1903.] *s. sh.* fol. **H. 3985. u. (29.)**

— I've got to get back to Work, *etc.* ⟨Song.⟩ [With separate voice part.] 2 pt. *Francis, Day & Hunter: London,* [1903.] fol. **H. 3985. u. (30.)**

— "I've just had a Couple of Ices." [Song.] Written and Composed by F. Leo. pp. 4. *B. Feldman & Co.: London,* [1909.] 4°. **H. 3985. u. (31.)**

— I've struck a Chorus. ⟨Song.⟩ Written and composed by F. Leo, *etc.* [With separate voice part.] 2 pt. *Shapiro, von Tilzer Music Co.: London,* [1908.] fol. *Popular 6ᵈ Edition. no.* 118. **H. 3985. u. (32.)**

— I want you to notice my Leggings ... ⟨Song.⟩ Written and composed by F. Leo. [Staff and tonic sol-fa notation. Voice part.] *Francis, Day & Hunter: London,* [1906.] *s. sh.* fol. **H. 3985. u. (33.)**

— I want you to notice my Leggings, *etc.* ⟨Song.⟩ [With separate voice part.] 2 pt. *Francis, Day & Hunter: London,* [1906.] fol. **H. 3985. u. (34.)**

— "I wish I'd bought Ducks." ⟨Song.⟩ Written and composed by F. Leo, *etc.* [Staff and tonic sol-fa notation. Voice part.] *Francis, Day & Hunter: London,* [1900.] *s. sh.* fol. **H. 3985. u. (35.)**

LEO (FRANK)

— "I wish I'd bought Ducks," *etc.* ⟨Song.⟩ [With separate voice part.] 2 pt. *Francis, Day & Hunter: London,* [1900.] fol. **H. 3985. u. (36.)**

— I wish they'd let me wear my Macintosh! *etc.* ⟨Song.⟩ [Staff and tonic sol-fa notation. Voice part.] *Francis, Day & Hunter: London,* [1906.] *s. sh.* fol. **H. 3985. u. (37.)**

— I wish they'd let me wear my Mackintosh! ... Song. Written and composed by F. Leo. [With separate voice part.] 2 pt. *Francis, Day & Hunter: London,* [1906.] fol. **H. 3985. u. (38.)**

— I wonder what he's going to do next. ⟨Song.⟩ Written and composed by F. Leo, *etc.* [Staff and tonic sol-fa notation. Voice part.] *Francis, Day & Hunter: London,* [1900.] *s. sh. fol.* **H. 3985. u. (39.)**

— I wouldn't lend you much on that. ⟨Song.⟩ Written by F. Leo & Edgar Bateman, *etc.* [Staff and tonic sol-fa notation. Voice part.] *Francis, Day & Hunter: London,* [1900.] *s. sh.* fol. **H. 3985. u. (40.)**

— If I'd only got the Impudence. ⟨Song.⟩ Written and composed by F. Leo, *etc.* [Staff and tonic sol-fa notation. Voice part.] *Francis, Day & Hunter: London,* [1902.] *s. sh.* fol. **H. 3985. u. (41.)**

— If I'd only got the Impudence, *etc.* ⟨Song.⟩ [With separate voice part.] 2 pt. *Francis, Day & Hunter: London,* [1902.] fol. **H. 3985. u. (42.)**

— "If you're doing that for me, you can stop." ⟨Song.⟩ Written and composed by F. Leo, *etc.* [Staff and tonic sol-fa notation. Voice part.] *Francis, Day & Hunter: London,* [1902.] *s. sh.* fol. **H. 3985. u. (43.)**

— If you're doing that for me, you can stop, *etc.* ⟨Song.⟩ [With separate voice part.] 2 pt. *Francis, Day & Hunter: London,* [1902.] fol. **H. 3985. u. (44.)**

— Iona of Arizona. ⟨Song.⟩ Written by Harry Castling, *etc.* [Staff and tonic sol-fa notation. Voice part.] *Francis, Day & Hunter: London,* [1906.] *s. sh.* fol. **H. 3985. u. (45.)**

— Iona of Arizona, *etc.* ⟨Song.⟩ [With separate voice part.] 2 pt. *Francis, Day & Hunter: London,* [1906.] fol. **H. 3985. u. (46.)**

— Is there anything else you'd like? Written and composed by F. Leo, *etc.* [Song. Staff and tonic sol-fa notation. Voice part.] *Francis, Day & Hunter: London,* [1899.] *s. sh.* fol. **H. 3980. qq. (49.)**

— It doesn't belong to me. Written and composed by F. Leo, *etc.* [Song. Staff and tonic sol-fa notation. Voice part.] *Francis, Day & Hunter: London,* [1898.] *s. sh.* fol. **H. 3980. qq. (50.)**

— It quite upset oi for the Day, *etc.* ⟨Song.⟩ [Staff and tonic sol-fa notation. Voice part.] *Francis, Day & Hunter: London,* [1909.] *s. sh.* fol. **H. 3985. u. (47.)**

— It quite upset oi for the Day, *etc.* ⟨Song.⟩ [With separate voice part.] 2 pt. *Francis, Day & Hunter: London,* [1909.] fol. **H. 3985. u. (48.)**

— It's been a nice Day. ⟨Song.⟩ Written and composed by F. Leo, *etc.* [Staff and tonic sol-fa notation. Voice part.] *Francis, Day & Hunter: London,* [1903.] *s. sh.* fol. **H. 3985. u. (49.)**

— It's been a nice Day, *etc.* ⟨Song.⟩ [With separate voice part.] 2 pt. *Francis, Day & Hunter: London,* [1903.] fol. **H. 3985. u. (50.)**

— It's lovely to be known. ⟨Song.⟩ Written and composed by F. Leo. [Staff and tonic sol-fa notation. Voice part.] *Francis, Day & Hunter: London,* [1903.] *s. sh.* fol. **H. 3985. u. (51.)**

LEO (FRANK)

— It's lovely to be known, *etc.* ⟨Song.⟩ [With separate voice part.] 2 pt. *Francis, Day & Hunter: London*, [1903.] fol.
H. 3985. u. (52.)

— It's not the Cage I'm after, it's the Bird. ⟨Song.⟩ Written and composed by F. Leo, *etc.* [Staff and tonic sol-fa notation. Voice part.] *Francis, Day & Hunter: London*, [1902.] *s. sh.* fol.
H. 3985. u. (53.)

— It's not the Cage I'm after, it's the Bird, *etc.* ⟨Song.⟩ [With separate voice part.] 2 pt. *Francis, Day & Hunter: London*, [1902.] fol.
H. 3985. u. (54.)

— It takes a dirty Hand to make a clean Hearth-Stone. [Song.] Words & music by F. Leo, *etc.* pp. 4. *Frank Dean & Co.: London*, [1899.] fol.
H. 3980. qq. (51.)

— It was a sad, sad Day for me. ⟨Song.⟩ Written and composed by F. Leo, *etc.* [Staff and tonic sol-fa notation. Voice part.] *Francis, Day & Hunter: London*, [1901.] *s. sh.* fol.
H. 3985. u. (55.)

— It was a sad sad Day for me, *etc.* ⟨Song.⟩ [With separate voice part.] 2 pt. *Francis, Day & Hunter: London*, [1901.] fol.
H. 3985. u. (56.)

— Jack Jones ... ⟨Song.⟩ Written and composed by F. Leo. [Staff and tonic sol-fa notation. Voice part.] *Francis, Day & Hunter: London, New York*, [1909.] *s. sh.* fol.
H. 3985. u. (57.)

— Jack Jones, *etc.* ⟨Song.⟩ [With separate voice part.] 2 pt. *Francis, Day & Hunter: London*, [1909.] fol.
H. 3985. u. (58.)

— Jenny Wren ... ⟨Song.⟩ Words and music by F. Leo. pp. 4. *Frank Dean & Co.: London*, [1900.] fol. **H. 3985. u. (59.)**

— "L" stands for Lovers. ⟨Song.⟩ Written and composed by F. Leo. [Staff and tonic sol-fa notation. Voice part.] *Francis, Day & Hunter: London*, [1902.] *s. sh.* fol. **H. 3985. v. (1.)**

— "L" stands for Lovers, *etc.* ⟨Song.⟩ [With separate voice part.] 2 pt. *Francis, Day & Hunter: London*, [1902.] fol.
H. 3985. v. (2.)

— A Labour of Love. ⟨Song.⟩ Words & music by F. Leo, *etc.* pp. 4. *Frank Dean & Co.: London*, [1901.] fol.
H. 3985. v. (3.)

— The Lady Killer. A Musical Comedy, written by J. H. Wood ... Arranged by F. Eplett. *Francis, Day & Hunter: London*, 1903. 4°.
F. 690. k. (4.)

— [The Lady Killer.] Her Smiles are for me. ⟨Song.⟩ Written and composed by F. Leo. [Staff and tonic sol-fa notation. Voice part.] *Francis, Day & Hunter: London*, [1903.] *s. sh.* fol.
H. 3985. v. (4.)

— [The Lady Killer.] Her Smiles are for me, *etc.* ⟨Song.⟩ [With separate voice part.] 2 pt. *Francis, Day & Hunter: London*, [1903.] fol.
H. 3985. v. (5.)

— The Language of Love. ⟨Song.⟩ Written and composed by F. Leo, *etc.* [Staff and tonic sol-fa notation. Voice part.] *Francis, Day & Hunter: London*, [1902.] *s. sh.* fol.
H. 3985. v. (6.)

— The Language of Love, *etc.* ⟨Song. Arranged by John S. Baker.⟩ [With separate voice part.] 2 pt. *Francis, Day & Hunter: London*, [1902.] fol. **H. 3985. v. (7.)**

— Leave them alone, Boys. Written and composed by F. Leo, *etc.* [Song. Staff and tonic sol-fa notation. Voice part.] *Francis, Day & Hunter: London*, [1897.] *s. sh.* fol.
H. 3980. qq. (52.)

— Let me sing! ... ⟨Song.⟩ Written and composed by F Leo. [Staff and tonic sol-fa notation. Voice part.] *Francis, Day & Hunter: London*, [1906.] *s. sh.* fol. **H. 3985. v. (8.)**

LEO (FRANK)

— Let me sing! *etc.* ⟨Song.⟩ [With separate voice part.] 2 pt. *Francis, Day & Hunter: London*, [1906.] fol. **H. 3985. v. (9.)**

— Let us pause. ⟨Song.⟩ Written and composed by F. Leo, *etc.* [Staff and tonic sol-fa notation. Voice part.] *Francis, Day & Hunter: London*, [1900.] *s. sh.* fol. **H. 3985. v. (10.)**

— "Limerick mad." ⟨Song.⟩ Written and composed by F. Leo, *etc.* [Staff and tonic sol-fa notation. Voice part.] *Francis, Day & Hunter: London*, [1907.] *s. sh.* fol. **H. 3985. v. (11.)**

— "Limerick mad," *etc.* ⟨Song.⟩ [With separate voice part.] 2 pt. *Francis, Day & Hunter: London*, [1907.] fol.
H. 3985. v. (12.)

— Looking at the Pictures. ⟨Song.⟩ Written and composed by F. Leo, *etc.* [Staff and tonic sol-fa notation. Voice part.] *Francis, Day & Hunter: London*, [1900.] *s. sh.* fol.
H. 3985. v. (13.)

— Ma Coon's got Lots o' Money. ⟨Song.⟩ Written and composed by F. Leo. [Staff and tonic sol-fa notation. Voice part.] *Francis, Day & Hunter: London*, [1902.] *s. sh.* fol.
H. 3985. v. (14.)

— Ma Coon's got Lots o' Money, *etc.* ⟨Song.⟩ [With separate voice part.] 2 pt. *Francis, Day & Hunter: London*, [1902.] fol.
H. 3985. v. (15.)

— Maisie mine. ⟨Song.⟩ Written and composed by F. Leo. [Staff and tonic sol-fa notation. Voice part.] *Francis, Day & Hunter: London*, [1908.] *s. sh.* fol. **H. 3985. v. (16.)**

— Maisie mine, *etc.* ⟨Song.⟩ [With separate voice part.] 2 pt. *Francis, Day & Hunter: London*, [1908.] fol.
H. 3985. v. (17.)

— Make yourself at Home. ⟨Song.⟩ Words & music by F. Leo, *etc.* pp. 3. *Frank Dean & Co.: London*, [1901.] fol.
H. 3985. v. (18.)

— May, my May. ⟨Song.⟩ Written and composed by F. Leo. [Staff and tonic sol-fa notation. Voice part.] *Francis, Day & Hunter: London*, [1902.] *s. sh.* fol. **H. 3985. v. (19.)**

— May, my May, *etc.* ⟨Song.⟩ [With separate voice part.] 2 pt. *Francis, Day & Hunter: London*, [1902.] fol.
H. 3985. v. (20.)

— Mister Watson. Song. Written and composed by F. Leo. pp. 5. *Hopwood & Crew: London*, [1905.] fol. **H. 3985. v. (21.)**

— Mother's Washing Day. Written, composed ... by F. Leo, *etc.* [Song. Staff and tonic sol-fa notation. Voice part.] *Francis, Day & Hunter: London*, [1898.] *s. sh.* fol. **H. 3980. qq. (53.)**

— The Moucher. Written and composed by F. Leo, *etc.* [Song. Staff and tonic sol-fa notation. Voice part.] *Francis, Day & Hunter: London*, [1896.] *s. sh.* fol. **H. 3980. qq. (54.)**

— My Cricket Girl. ⟨Song.⟩ Written and composed by F. Leo, *etc.* [Staff and tonic sol-fa notation. Voice part.] *Francis, Day & Hunter: London*, [1903.] *s. sh.* fol. **H. 3985. v. (22.)**

— "My Cricket Girl," *etc.* ⟨Song.⟩ [With separate voice part.] 2 pt. *Francis, Day & Hunter: London*, [1903.] fol.
H. 3985. v. (23.)

— My Girl is an Angel. ⟨Song.⟩ Words & music by F. Leo. pp. 4. *Frank Dean & Co.: London*, [1901.] fol. **H. 3985. v. (24.)**

— My Heart is your Heart. [Song.] Words and music by F. Leo. pp. 4. *Frank Dean & Co.: London*, [1899.] fol.
H. 3980. qq. (55.)

— My Heart is your Heart! [Song.] Words and music by Frank Leo. [c. 1900.] fol.
A pirated edition.
H. 1848. b. (22.)

LEO (FRANK)

— My inventive Pal. Written and composed by F. Leo, *etc.*
[Song. Staff and tonic sol-fa notation. Voice part.] *Francis,
Day & Hunter: London*, [1897.] *s. sh.* fol.　　**H. 3980. qq. (56.)**

— My Lily of the Valley. ⟨Song.⟩ Written and composed by
F. Leo. [Staff and tonic sol-fa notation. Voice part.] *Francis,
Day & Hunter: London*, [1903.] *s. sh.* fol.　　**H. 3985. v. (25.)**

— My Lily of the Valley, *etc.* ⟨Song.⟩ [With separate voice part.]
2 pt. *Francis, Day & Hunter: London*, [1903.] fol.
H. 3985. v. (26.)

— My Lily of the Valley. [Song.] Written and composed by
Frank Leo. pp. 4. [c. 1905.] fol.
A pirated edition.　　**H. 1848. b. (23.)**

— My little Deitcher Girl ... ⟨Song.⟩ Written and composed by
F. Leo. *B. Feldman & Co.: London*, [1907.] 4°.
H. 3985. v. (27.)

— My one and only Girl. ⟨Song.⟩ Written and composed by
F. Leo. [Staff and tonic sol-fa notation. Voice part.] *Francis,
Day & Hunter: London*, [1903.] *s. sh.* fol.　　**H. 3985. v. (28.)**

— My one and only Girl, *etc.* ⟨Song.⟩ pp. 7. *Francis, Day &
Hunter: London*, [1903.] fol.　　**H. 3985. v. (29.)**

— My Terpsichorean Gal. ⟨Song.⟩ Written and composed by
F. Leo. [Staff and tonic sol-fa notation. Voice part.] *Francis,
Day & Hunter: London*, [1903.] *s. sh.* fol.　　**H. 3985. v. (30.)**

— My Terpsichorean Gal, *etc.* ⟨Song.⟩ [With separate voice part.]
2 pt. *Francis, Day & Hunter: London*, [1903.] fol.
H. 3985. v. (31.)

— Nancy is my Fancy. ⟨Song.⟩ Words & music by F. Leo, *etc.*
pp. 4. *Frank Dean & Co.: London*, [1900.] fol.
H. 3985. v. (32.)

— Nice Thing for a Man like me! Written and composed by
F. Leo, *etc.* [Song. Staff and tonic sol-fa notation. Voice part.]
Francis, Day & Hunter: London, [1899.] *s. sh.* fol.
H. 3980. qq. (57.)

— No Coon am pining for me. ⟨Song.⟩ Written and composed
by F. Leo. [Staff and tonic sol-fa notation. Voice part.]
Francis, Day & Hunter: London, [1903.] *s. sh.* fol.
H. 3985. v. (33.)

— No Coon am pining for me, *etc.* ⟨Song.⟩ pp. 7. *Francis, Day
& Hunter: London*, [1903.] fol.　　**H. 3985. v. (34.)**

— No Show to-night. Written and composed by F. Leo, *etc.*
[Song. Staff and tonic sol-fa notation. Voice part.] *Francis,
Day & Hunter: London*, [1899.] *s. sh.* fol.　　**H. 3980. qq. (58.)**

— "Nothing shall part us now!" Written and composed by
F. Leo, *etc.* [Song. Staff and tonic sol-fa notation. Voice part.]
Francis, Day & Hunter: London, [1899.] *s. sh.* fol.
H. 3980. qq. (59.)

— Oh, be careful, my Friends. ⟨Song.⟩ Written and composed by
F. Leo, *etc.* [Staff and tonic sol-fa notation. Voice part.]
Francis, Day & Hunter: London, [1900.] fol.
H. 3985. v. (35.)

— Oh, be careful, my Friends, *etc.* ⟨Song.⟩ [With separate voice
part.] 2 pt. *Francis, Day & Hunter: London*, [1900.] fol.
H. 3985. v. (36.)

— Oh, Mister Noah! ... Written and composed by F. Leo, *etc.*
[Song. Staff and tonic sol-fa notation. Voice part.] *Francis,
Day & Hunter: London*, [1898.] *s. sh.* fol.　**H. 3980. qq. (60.)**

— Oh! Mother Eve. ⟨Song.⟩ Written and composed by F. Leo,
etc. [Staff and tonic sol-fa notation. Voice part.] *Francis,
Day & Hunter: London*, [1908.] *s. sh.* fol.　　**H. 3985. v. (37.)**

— Oh! Mother Eve, *etc.* ⟨Song.⟩ [With separate voice part.] 3 pt.
Francis, Day & Hunter: London, [1908.] fol.
H. 3985. v. (38.)

LEO (FRANK)

— An Old Oak Tree. [Song.] Written & composed by F. Leo.
pp. 5. *Howard & Co.: London*, [1896.] fol.
H. 3980. qq. (61.)

— Our Dramatic Club. Written and composed by F. Leo, *etc.*
[Song. Staff and tonic sol-fa notation. Voice part.] *Francis,
Day & Hunter: London*, [1896.] *s. sh.* fol.　　**H. 3980. qq. (62.)**

— "Our Empire."—March.—Arranged by J. Neat. [P. F.]
B. Feldman & Co.: London, [1904.] 4°.　　**g. 603. p. (6.)**

— Out all Night. Written by A. J. Mills, *etc.* [Song. Staff and
tonic sol-fa notation. Voice part.] *Francis, Day & Hunter:
London*, [1897.] *s. sh.* fol.　　**H. 3980. qq. (63.)**

— The Panama Hat. ⟨Song.⟩ Words & music by F. Leo. pp. 4.
Frank Dean & Co.: London, [1902.] fol.　　**H. 3985. v. (39.)**

— The Pet of the Crew. [Song.] Written & composed by F. Leo.
pp. 5. *Howard & Co.: London*, [1896.] fol.
H. 3980. qq. (64.)

— The Piccadilly Crawl. ⟨Song.⟩ Written & composed by F. Leo.
[With separate voice part.] 2 pt. *Francis, Day & Hunter:
London*, [1901.] fol.　　**H. 3985. v. (40.)**

— Polly ain't an Angel. Written and composed by F. Leo, *etc.*
[Song. Staff and tonic sol-fa notation. Voice part.] *Francis,
Day & Hunter: London*, [1897.] *s. sh.* fol.　　**H. 3980. qq. (65.)**

— "Put your Trust in me, little Girl" ... ⟨Song.⟩ Written and
composed by F. Leo. [Staff and tonic sol-fa notation. Voice
part.] *Francis, Day & Hunter: London*, [1909.] *s. sh.* fol.
H. 3985. v. (41.)

— "Put your Trust in me, little Girl," *etc.* ⟨Song.⟩ [With separate
voice part.] 2 pt. *Francis, Day & Hunter: London*, [1909.] fol.
H. 3985. v. (42.)

— Read between the Lines ... ⟨Song.⟩ Written and composed by
F. Leo. [Staff and tonic sol-fa notation. Voice part.] *Francis,
Day & Hunter: London*, [1907.] *s. sh.* fol.　　**H. 3985. v. (43.)**

— Read between the Lines, *etc.* ⟨Song.⟩ [With separate voice
part.] 2 pt. *Francis, Day & Hunter: London*, [1907.] fol.
H. 3985. v. (44.)

— The Rising Son. ⟨Song.⟩ Written and composed by F. Leo, *etc.*
[Staff and tonic sol-fa notation. Voice part.] *Francis, Day &
Hunter: London*, [1900.] *s. sh.* fol.　　**H. 3985. v. (45.)**

— Ruby. Written and composed by F. Leo, *etc.* [Song. With
separate voice part.] ⟨Arranged by John S. Baker.⟩ 2 pt.
Howard & Co.: London, [1898.] fol.　　**H. 3980. qq. (66.)**

— She ain't a Bit like the other Gals. ⟨Song.⟩ Written and
composed by F. Leo. [Staff and tonic sol-fa notation. Voice
part.] *Francis, Day & Hunter: London*, [1901.] *s. sh.* fol.
H. 3985. v. (46.)

— She ain't a Bit like the other Gals, *etc.* ⟨Song. Arranged by
Herbert Clark.⟩ [With separate voice part.] 2 pt. *Francis, Day
& Hunter: London*, [1901.] fol.　　**H. 3985. v. (47.)**

— She ain't a bit like the other Gals. [Song.] Written and
composed by Frank Leo. pp. 4. [c. 1905.] fol.
A pirated edition.　　**H. 1848. b. (24.)**

— She's just my plain Girl. ⟨Song.⟩ Written and Composed by
F. Leo. [With separate voice part.] 2 pt. *Francis, Day &
Hunter: London*, [1902.] fol.　　**H. 3985. v. (48.)**

— She's not everyone's Girl. ⟨Song.⟩ Words & music by F. Leo.
pp. 4. *Frank Dean & Co.: London*, [1901.] fol.
H. 3985. v. (49.)

— A Sixpenny-'a'Penny Tie. ⟨Song.⟩ Written and composed by
F. Leo, *etc.* [Staff and tonic sol-fa notation. Voice part.]
Francis, Day & Hunter: London, [1901.] *s. sh.* fol.
H. 3985. v. (50.)

LEO (FRANK)

— A Sixpenny-'a'Penny Tie, etc. ⟨Song.⟩ [With separate voice part.] 2 pt. *Francis, Day & Hunter: London*, [1901.] fol.
H. 3985. v. (51.)

— So long as I know what you're doing. ⟨Song.⟩ Written and composed by F. Leo, etc. [Staff and tonic sol-fa notation. Voice part.] *Francis, Day & Hunter: London*, [1903.] s. sh. fol.
H. 3985. v. (52.)

— So long as I know what you're doing, etc. ⟨Song.⟩ [With separate voice part.] 2 pt. *Francis, Day & Hunter: London*, [1903.] fol.
H. 3985. v. (53.)

— That's their Idea of a Lady. ⟨Song.⟩ Written and composed by F. Leo, etc. [Staff and tonic sol-fa notation. Voice part.] *Francis, Day & Hunter: London*, [1900.] s. sh. fol.
H. 3985. w. (1.)

— That's where she sits all Day. ⟨Song.⟩ Written and composed by F. Leo, etc. [Staff and tonic sol-fa notation. Voice part.] *Francis, Day & Hunter: London*, [1900.] s. sh. fol.
H. 3985. w. (2.)

— That's why I love her so. ⟨Song.⟩ Written and composed by F. Leo, etc. [Staff and tonic sol-fa notation. Voice part.] *Francis, Day & Hunter: London*, [1902.] s. sh. fol.
H. 3985. w. (3.)

— That's why I love her so, etc. ⟨Song.⟩ [With separate voice part.] 2 pt. *Francis, Day & Hunter: London*, [1902.] fol.
H. 3985. w. (4.)

— There are good Fish still in the Sea. ⟨Song.⟩ Written and composed by F. Leo, etc. [Staff and tonic sol-fa notation. Voice part.] *Francis, Day & Hunter: London*, [1904.] s. sh. fol.
H. 3985. w. (5.)

— There are good Fish still in the Sea, etc. ⟨Song.⟩ [With separate voice part.] 2 pt. *Francis, Day & Hunter: London*, [1904.] fol.
H. 3985. w. (6.)

— There can only be one Queen Bee in a Hive. ⟨Song.⟩ Written and composed by F. Leo, etc. [Staff and tonic sol-fa notation. Voice part.] *Francis, Day & Hunter: London*, [1905.] s. sh. fol.
H. 3985. w. (7.)

— There can only be one Queen Bee in a Hive, etc. ⟨Song.⟩ [With separate voice part.] 2 pt. *Francis, Day & Hunter: London*, [1905.] fol.
H. 3985. w. (8.)

— There is no one in the World like you. ⟨Song.⟩ Written and composed by F. Leo. [Staff and tonic sol-fa notation. Voice part.] *Francis, Day & Hunter: London*, [1901.] s. sh. fol.
H. 3985. w. (9.)

— There is no one in the World like you, etc. ⟨Song.⟩ [With separate voice part.] 2 pt. *Francis, Day & Hunter: London*, [1901.] fol.
H. 3985. w. (10.)

— There's a Home for you with me. Written and composed by F. Leo, etc. [Song. With separate voice part.] ⟨Arranged by John S. Baker.⟩ 2 pt. *Howard & Co.: London*, [1898.] fol.
H. 3980. qq. (67.)

— There's a peculiar Thing! Written and composed by F. Leo, etc. [Song. Staff and tonic sol-fa notation. Voice part.] *Francis, Day & Hunter: London*, [1898.] s. sh. fol.
H. 3980. qq. (68.)

— There's an Idea for a Song! ⟨Song.⟩ Written and composed by F. Leo, etc. [Staff and tonic sol-fa notation. Voice part.] *Francis, Day & Hunter: London*, [1901.] s. sh. fol.
H. 3985. w. (11.)

— There's an Idea for a Song, etc. ⟨Song.⟩ [With separate voice part.] 2 pt. *Francis, Day & Hunter: London*, [1901.] fol.
H. 3985. w. (12.)

— They're always taking me for someone else! Comic song. Written & composed by F. Leo, etc. pp. 5. *Jefferys: London*, [1898.] fol.
H. 3980. qq. (69.)

LEO (FRANK)

— Things that don't concern me. Written and composed by F. Leo, etc. [Song. Staff and tonic sol-fa notation. Voice part.] *Francis, Day & Hunter: London*, [1898.] s. sh. fol.
H. 3980. qq. (70.)

— Troubles. Written and composed by F. Leo, etc. [Song. Staff and tonic sol-fa notation. Voice part.] *Francis, Day & Hunter: London*, [1898.] s. sh. fol.
H. 3980. qq. (71.)

— Turn over Leaf ... Written and composed by F. Leo, etc. [Song. Staff and tonic sol-fa notation. Voice part.] *Francis, Day & Hunter: London*, [1898.] s. sh. fol.
H. 3980. qq. (72.)

— Victorious Troops. Polka March. [P. F.] *F. Dean & Co.: London*, 1900. fol.
h. 3286. r. (6.)

— Walking in my Sleep. Written and composed by F. Leo, etc. [Song. Staff and tonic sol-fa notation. Voice part.] *Francis, Day & Hunter: London*, [1899.] s. sh. fol.
H. 3980. qq. (73.)

— "Was that a Knock?" ⟨Song.⟩ Written and composed by F. Leo, etc. [Staff and tonic sol-fa notation. Voice part.] *Francis, Day & Hunter: London*, [1903.] s. sh. fol.
H. 3985. w. (13.)

— Was that a Knock? etc. ⟨Song.⟩ [With separate voice part.] 2 pt. *Francis, Day & Hunter: London*, [1903.] fol.
H. 3985. w. (14.)

— What a fine old Game you're having. ⟨Song.⟩ Written and composed by F. Leo, etc. [Staff and tonic sol-fa notation. Voice part.] *Francis, Day & Hunter: London*, [1900.] s. sh. fol.
H. 3985. w. (15.)

— What a fine old Game you're having, etc. ⟨Song.⟩ [With separate voice part.] 2 pt. *Francis, Day & Hunter: London*, [1900.] fol.
H. 3985. w. (16.)

— What a Friend we have in Mother. Written and composed by F. Leo, etc. [Song. Staff and tonic sol-fa notation. Voice part.] *Francis, Day & Hunter: London*, [1899.] s. sh. fol.
H. 3980. qq. (74.)

— What a nice little Thing. ⟨Song.⟩ Written and composed by F. Leo, etc. [Staff and tonic sol-fa notation. Voice part.] *Francis, Day & Hunter: London*, [1900.] s. sh. fol.
H. 3985. w. (17.)

— What a nice little Thing, etc. ⟨Song.⟩ [With separate voice part.] 2 pt. *Francis, Day & Hunter: London*, [1900.] fol.
H. 3985. w. (18.)

— What are we here for? [Song.] Written & composed by F. Leo. pp. 4. *Frank Dean & Co.: London*, [1899.] fol.
H. 3980. qq. (75.)

— "What d'yer think of me now?" Written and composed by F. Leo, etc. [Song. Staff and tonic sol-fa notation. Voice part.] *Francis, Day & Hunter: London*, [1899.] s. sh. fol.
H. 3980. qq. (76.)

— What d'yer want to talk about it for? ⟨Song.⟩ Written and composed by F. Leo, etc. [Staff and tonic sol-fa notation. Voice part.] *Francis, Day & Hunter: London*, [1904.] s. sh. fol.
H. 3985. w. (19.)

— What d'yer want to talk about it for? etc. ⟨Song.⟩ [With separate voice part.] 2 pt. *Francis, Day & Hunter: London*, [1904.] fol.
H. 3985. w. (20.)

— What is the Use of loving a Girl? ... ⟨Song.⟩ Written and composed by F. Leo. [Staff and tonic sol-fa notation. Voice part.] *Francis, Day & Hunter: London*, [1902.] s. sh. fol.
H. 3985. w. (21.)

— What is the Use of loving a Girl? etc. ⟨Song.⟩ [With separate voice part.] 2 pt. *Francis, Day & Hunter: London*, [1902.] fol.
H. 3985. w. (22.)

LEO (Frank)

— What is the Use of loving a Girl, *etc.* [P. F.] 1902. *See* Francis and Day. Francis and Day's Musical Bon-Bons, *etc.* No. 25. 1902, *etc.* fol.　　　　　　　　　　**h. 3474.**

— "What's the Idea of that?" ... ⟨Song.⟩ Written & composed by F. Leo. [With separate voice part.] 2 pt. *Francis, Day & Hunter: London*, [1904.] fol.　　　**H. 3985. w. (23.)**

— When the Bugle calls. ⟨Song.⟩ Written and composed by F. Leo, *etc.* [Staff and tonic sol-fa notation. Voice part.] *Francis, Day & Hunter: London*, [1909.] *s. sh.* fol.　　　　　　　　　　**H. 3985. w. (24.)**

— When the Bugle calls, *etc.* ⟨Song.⟩ [With separate voice part.] 2 pt. *Francis, Day & Hunter: London*, [1909.] fol.　　　　　　　　　　**H. 3985. w. (25.)**

— When the Day begins to dawn. Written and composed by F. Leo, *etc.* [Song. Staff and tonic sol-fa notation. Voice part.] *Francis, Day & Hunter: London*, [1899.] *s. sh.* fol.　　　**H. 3980. qq. (77.)**

— When we were twenty-one. ⟨Song.⟩ Written and composed by F. Leo, *etc.* [Staff and tonic sol-fa notation. Voice part.] *Francis, Day & Hunter: London*, [1901.] *s. sh.* fol.　　　　　　　　　　**H. 3985. w. (26.)**

— When we were twenty-one, *etc.* ⟨Song.⟩ [With separate voice part.] 2 pt. *Francis, Day & Hunter: London*, [1901.] fol.　　　　　　**H. 3985. w. (27.)**

— When you find 'em on the Pavement. Written and composed by F. Leo, *etc.* [Song. Staff and tonic sol-fa notation. Voice part.] *Francis, Day & Hunter: London*, [1898.] *s. sh.* fol.　　**H. 3980. qq. (78.)**

— Where is the Heart? ⟨Song.⟩ Words & music by F. Leo. pp. 4. *Frank Dean & Co.: London*, [1904.] fol.　　**H. 3985. w. (28.)**

— "Where's the Gold of London?" ⟨Song.⟩ Written and composed by F. Leo, *etc.* [Staff and tonic sol-fa notation. Voice part.] *Francis, Day & Hunter: London*, [1900.] *s. sh.* fol.　　**H. 3985. w. (29.)**

— "Where's the Gold of London?" *etc.* ⟨Song.⟩ [With separate voice part.] 2 pt. *Francis, Day & Hunter: London*, [1900.] fol.　　　**H. 3985. w. (30.)**

— "Why don't you tell your People?" ⟨Song.⟩ Written and composed by F. Leo. [Staff and tonic sol-fa notation. Voice part.] *Francis, Day & Hunter: London*, [1904.] *s. sh.* fol.　　　**H. 3985. w. (31.)**

— "Why don't you tell your People" *etc.* ⟨Song.⟩ [With separate voice part.] 2 pt. *Francis, Day & Hunter: London*, [1904.] fol.　　**H. 3985. w. (32.)**

— With "our" Money. Written and composed by F. Leo, *etc.* [Song. Staff and tonic sol-fa notation. Voice part.] *Francis, Day & Hunter: London*, [1899.] *s. sh.* fol.　　**H. 3980. qq. (79.)**

— "Wouldn't you be better in a Home?" ⟨Song.⟩ Written and composed by F. Leo, *etc.* [Staff and tonic sol-fa notation. Voice part.] *Francis, Day & Hunter: London*, [1904.] *s. sh.* fol.　　**H. 3985. w. (33.)**

— Wouldn't you be better in a Home? *etc.* ⟨Song.⟩ [With separate voice part.] 2 pt. *Francis, Day & Hunter: London*, [1904.] fol.　　**H. 3985. w. (34.)**

— You can get in a Row for that. ⟨Song.⟩ Written and composed by F. Leo, *etc.* [Staff and tonic sol-fa notation. Voice part.] *Francis, Day & Hunter: London*, [1901.] *s. sh.* fol.　　**H. 3985. w. (35.)**

— You can get in a Row for that, *etc.* ⟨Song.⟩ [With separate voice part.] 2 pt. *Francis, Day & Hunter: London*, [1901.] fol.　　**H. 3985. w. (36.)**

LEO (Frank)

— You can't get away,—there it is. ⟨Song.⟩ Written and composed by F. Leo, *etc.* [Staff and tonic sol-fa notation. Voice part.] *Francis, Day & Hunter: London*, [1903.] *s. sh.* fol.　　　　　　**H. 3985. w. (37.)**

— You can't get away,—there it is, *etc.* ⟨Song.⟩ [With separate voice part.] 2 pt. *Francis, Day & Hunter: London*, [1903.] fol.　　　**H. 3985. w. (38.)**

— You can't stop the Sun from shining. ⟨Song.⟩ Written and composed by F. Leo. [Staff and tonic sol-fa notation. Voice part.] *Francis, Day & Hunter: London*, [1904.] *s. sh.* fol.　　**H. 3985. w. (39.)**

— You can't stop the Sun from shining, *etc.* ⟨Song.⟩ [With separate voice part.] 2 pt. *Francis, Day & Hunter: London*, [1904.] fol.　　**H. 3985. w. (40.)**

— "You don't mind me asking you, do you?" ⟨Song.⟩ Written and composed by F. Leo. [Staff and tonic sol-fa notation. Voice part.] *Francis, Day & Hunter: London, New York*, [1907.] *s. sh.* fol.　　　**H. 3985. w. (41.)**

— "You don't mind me asking you, do you!" *etc.* ⟨Song.⟩ [With separate voice part.] 2 pt. *Francis, Day & Hunter: London*, [1907.] fol.　　　**H. 3985. w. (42.)**

— You don't mind me being here? ⟨Song.⟩ Words & music by F. Leo. pp. 4. *Frank Dean & Co.: London*, [1901.] fol.　　**H. 3985. w. (43.)**

— You'll have to pay. ⟨Song.⟩ Words and music by F. Leo. Arranged by J. Neat, *etc.* pp. 5. *Moon & Co.: London; Leipzig* [printed, 1900.] fol.　　**H. 3985. w. (44.)**

— "You'll hear from my Solicitors." ⟨Song.⟩ Written and composed by F. Leo. [Staff and tonic sol-fa notation. Voice part.] *Francis, Day & Hunter: London; T. B. Harms: New York*, [1909.] *s. sh.* fol.　　**H. 3985. w. (45.)**

— "You'll hear from my Solicitors," *etc.* ⟨Song.⟩ [With separate voice part.] 2 pt. *Francis, Day & Hunter: London*, [1909.] fol.　　**H. 3985. w. (46.)**

— You mustn't do a Thing like that. ⟨Song.⟩ Written and composed by F. Leo, *etc.* [Staff and tonic sol-fa notation. Voice part.] *Francis, Day & Hunter: London*, [1901.] *s. sh.* fol.　　**H. 3985. w. (47.)**

— You mustn't do a Thing like that, *etc.* ⟨Song. Arranged by Ernest Bostock.⟩ [With separate voice part.] 2 pt. *Francis, Day & Hunter: London*, [1901.] fol.　　**H. 3985. w. (48.)**

— "You mustn't take any away!" ⟨Song.⟩ Written and composed by F. Leo, *etc.* [Staff and tonic sol-fa notation. Voice part.] *Francis, Day & Hunter: London*, [1903.] *s. sh.* fol.　　　**H. 3985. w. (49.)**

— You mustn't take any away, *etc.* ⟨Song.⟩ [With separate voice part.] 2 pt. *Francis, Day & Hunter: London*, [1903.] fol.　　**H. 3985. w. (50.)**

— You, you, you! ... ⟨Song.⟩ Written and composed by F. Leo. [Staff and tonic sol-fa notation. Voice part.] *Francis, Day & Hunter: London*, [1907.] *s. sh.* fol.　　**H. 3985. w. (51.)**

— You, you, you! *etc.* ⟨Song.⟩ [With separate voice part.] 2 pt. *Francis, Day & Hunter: London*, [1907.] fol.　　　**H. 3985. w. (52.)**

— Zulu. ⟨Song.⟩ Words & music by F. Leo. pp. 4. *Frank Dean & Co.: London*, [1902.] fol.　　**H. 3985. w. (53.)**

— *See* Mills (Arthur J.) and Leo (F.) Farewell, pretty Selina. [Song.] Written and composed by A. J. Mills and F. Leo, *etc.* [1898.] *s. sh.* fol.　　**H. 3980. yy. (68.)**

— *See* Mills (Arthur J.) and Leo (F.) I'm not a-going to move, *etc.* [Song.] [1899.] *s. sh.* fol.　　**H. 3980. yy. (69.)**

LEO (J. B.)

— See LEO (Leonardo)

LÉO (JULIUSZ)

— Cztery inscenizacje utworów Mickiewicza. Opracowała Regina Kowalewska ... Muzyka: J. Léo. pp. 44.
Stowarzyszenie polskich kombatantów; Związek harcerstwa polskiego: Londyn, 1956. 8°. **X. 909/5657.**

LEO (LEONARDO)

— [Ahi che la pena mia.] Siciliana, *etc. See* GEVAERT (F. A.) Les Gloires de l'Italie, *etc.* No. 35. [1868.] fol. **H. 566. g.**

— [Alessandro in Persia.] Dirti ben mio vorrei. Aria. *See* GEMME. Gemme d'Antichità. No. 20. [1864, *etc.*] fol. **H. 2293.**

— Amor vuol sofferenza. ⟨Commedia per musica. Versi di Gennaro Antonio Federico.⟩ A cura di Giuseppe A. Pastore. [With facsimiles. Score.] pp. xxxiv. 59. 441. *Società di storia patria per la Puglia: Bari, 1962. 4°.*
Musiche e musicisti pugliesi. 2. **G. 1268. q.**

— [Amor vuol sofferenze.] Sinfonie, D-dur ... Herausgegeben und bearbeitet von Robert Sondheimer. [Score.] pp. 7.
Edition Bernoulli: Vienna, [1937.] fol.
[*Werke aus dem 18. Jahrhundert. no.* 46.] **Hirsch IV. 1020.**

— Andromaca ... Introduction by Howard Mayer Brown. ⟨Libretto by Antonio Salvi. Score reproduced from Mus. MS 3860 of the Musikbibliothek der Stadt Leipzig.⟩ *Garland Publishing: New York, London, 1979. obl. 4°.*
[*Italian Opera 1640–1770.* 39.] **F. 1899.**

— Arietta. ([Edited by] C. Palumbo.) [P. F.] *Augener & Co.: London,* [1893.] fol.
No. 79 of the Anthologie Classique et Moderne. **h. 1424.**

— Arietta for the Pianoforte. *Chappell & Co.: London,* [1901.] fol. **h. 3282. w. (40.)**

— Arietta ... Arranged for piano by C. Palumbo, and fingered by A. Roloff. *Augener: London, 1921. 4°.* **g. 1127. h. (4.)**

— Ave maris stella. Hymne à deux voix avec accompagnement de deux violons, alto et basse par J. B. Leo [or rather, L. Leo]. [Score.] pp. 21. *Chez P. Porro: Paris,* [c. 1815.] fol.
Musique sacrée. no. 8. **H. 1186. k. (4.)**

— [Another copy.] **G. 503. s. (18.)**

— [Cantata Spirituale.—Di contento.] Song of Joy. From "Cantata Spirituale" ... [sacred song.] Arranged from the Figured Bass with a free English translation by P. James. *Augener: London, 1927. 4°.* **G. 519. n. (18.)**

— [Cantata Spirituale.—Sciolto morte.] Hymn to the Holy Child. From "Cantata Spirituale" ... [sacred song.] Arranged from the Figured Bass with a free English translation by P. James. *Augener: London, 1927. 4°.* **G. 519. n. (17.)**

— Aria: Care luci, che regnate. *See* ZANON (M.) 30 Arie antiche, *etc.* [No. 11.] 1922. 4°. **G. 171.**

— Christus factus est pro nobis. Aria. *See* GEMME. Gemme d'Antichità. No. 126. [1864, *etc.*] fol. **H. 2293.**

— [La Clemenza di Tito.—Se mai senti.] Aria ... 1735. *See* GEVAERT (F. A.) Les Gloires de l'Italie, *etc.* No. 11. [1868.] fol. **H. 566. g.**

— Concerto a quattro violini obligati ... für 4 Violinen mit Klavier Begleitung bearbeitet ... von G. Jensen. [Score and parts.] *Augener & Co.: London,* [1895.] 4°. **g. 474. f. (6.)**

— Three Concertos for Violoncello solo, Strings and Harpsichord (1737–38). Edited by Douglass Green. [With facsimiles. Score.] pp. 79. *Theodore Presser Co.: Bryn Mawr,* [1973.] 4°.
[*Series of early Music. vol.* 7.] **G. 926.**

LEO (LEONARDO)

— Concerto in La per violoncello, archi e cembalo di ripieno. Revisione di Renato Fasano. [Score.] pp. 49. *G. Ricordi & c.: Milano,* [1967.] 8°.
Part of "Antica musica strumentale italiana". **e. 670. (2.)**

— Konzert in A dur für Violoncello und Streichorchester bearbeitet und bezeichnet von E. Rapp ... Ausgabe für Violoncello und Klavier. *B. Schott's Söhne: Mainz und Leipzig, 1938. 4°.* **g. 514. t. (6.)**

— Concerto D major. For violoncello and string orchestra ... Edited by Felix Schroeder. [Score.] pp. iv. 39. *Ernst Eulenburg: London,* [1959.] 8°.
[*Edition Eulenburg. no.* 1218.] **b. 212.**

— Concerto in re minore per violoncello e archi (1738). Edizione a cura di Giuseppe Pastore ... ⟨Revisione violoncellistica di Giorgio Sassi.⟩ Partitura, *etc.* pp. 24. *Guglielmo Zanibon: Padova,* [1970.] fol. **h. 2785. y. (2.)**

— Konzert für Violoncello, Streicher und Basso continuo F-moll. Zum ersten Mal herausgegeben von Felix Schroeder. Ausgabe für Violoncello und Klavier von Hans Feldigl. [Score and part.] 2 pt. *Henry Litolff's Verlag; C. F. Peters: Frankfurt, etc.,* [1969.] 4°. **g. 512. k. (1.)**

— Cosi con questo pianto. Aria. *See* GEMME. Gemme d'Antichità. No. 52. [1864, *etc.*] fol. **H. 2293.**

— [Demofoonte.—La destra ti chiedo.] Duetto ... 1740. *See* GEVAERT (F. A.) Les Gloires de l'Italie, *etc.* No. 34. [1868.] fol. **H. 566. g.**

— La destra ti chiedo. *See* supra: [Demofoonte.]

— Dirti ben mio vorrei. *See* supra: [Alessandro in Persia.]

— [Dixit Dominus for 5 voices, in A major.] Psalm 110. Clavierauszug ... Chorstimmen. *A. Kümmel: Halle,* [1850?] fol.
Lief. III. of "Sammlung von Musikwerken der vorzüglichsten Kirchencomponisten früherer Zeit, etc". **H. 1187. l. (8.)**

— Dixit Dominus ... in C major ... Edited ... by C. V. Stanford. *London,* [1879.] 8°. **E. 1423.**

— Dixit Dominus. [In C major.] Chorus for Double Choir. (With a separate accompaniment for the Organ or Pianoforte by V. Novello.) *Novello, Ewer & Co.: London,* [1885?] 8°.
No. 347 of Novello's Octavo Choruses. **E. 44. a.**

— [Dixit Dominus ... in C major.—Tecum principium.] Glorious, exalted and mighty ... Edited and arranged by E. Masson. *Leader & Cock: London,* [1852.] fol.
[*Songs for the Classical Vocalist. No.* 16.] **H. 1355. a.**

— [Dixit Dominus ... in C major.] Virgam virtutis tuæ. (Solo and Chorus.) [1902.] *See* OULD (S. G.) Cantiones Sacræ, *etc.* No. 37. 1899, *etc.* 8°. **F. 1108.**

— [Dixit Dominus in D.] The Grand Chorus "Sicut erat" ... from the Dixit Dominus in D ... Score ... and ... accompaniment adapted for the Organ or Piano Forte ... by V. Novello. *Published for the Editor: London,* [1840?] fol.
With V. Novello's autograph initials on the titlepage. **H. 879. k. (1.)**

— Dunque si sforza. [Song.] *See* ECHI. Echi d'Italia. Raccolta prima, *etc.* No. 85. [1880? *etc.*] fol. **H. 2397.**

— Emira ... Sinfonia dell'opera. Realizzazione e revisione di G. A. Pastore. Partitura. pp. 8. *Carisch: Milano,* [1957.] 4°. **g. 727. xx. (6.)**

— Glorious, exalted and mighty. *See* supra: [Dixit Dominus ... in C major.—Tecum principium.]

— Hymn to the Holy Child. *See* supra: [Cantata Spirituale.—Sciolto di morte.]

LEO (Leonardo)

— Miserere a due cori obligati col basso continuo ... Publicato ... da Aless. Steff. Choron, *etc.* pp. 26. *Presso Auguste le Duc e compagnia: Parigi,* [c. 1810.] fol.
Raccolta generale delle opere classiche musicali. no. 1.
H. 1186. k. (3.)

— [A reissue.] Miserere a due Cori obligati col Basso Continuo. *Parigi,* [c. 1815.] fol. **H. 1027.**

— Miserere concertato a due chori, con una ideale cantilena gregoriana riportata al comodo del tuono del salmo, *etc.* ⟨Psalm 50, Vulgate. Edited by H. Wiley Hitchcock.⟩ pp. 35. *Concordia Publishing House: St. Louis, Mo.,* [1961.] 8°.
F. 1176. qq. (1.)

— La Morte di Abel. Sinfonia dell'oratorio per archi, corni e clavicembalo. Realizzazione e revisione de G. A. Pastore. Partitura. pp. 12. *Carisch: Milano,* [1957.] 4°.
g. 727. xx. (7.)

— Le Nozze di Psiche con Amore. Introduzione all'opera per archi, 2 oboi, 2 trombe in do e cembalo. Trascrizione e realizzazione a cura di Giuseppe A. Pastore ... Partitura, *etc.* pp. 8. *Guglielmo Zanibon: Padova,* [1960.] fol.
h. 1567. u. (7.)

— O Jesu Salvator. Aria from a Salve. *See* GEMME. Gemme d'Antichità. No. 113. [1864, *etc.*] fol. **H. 2293.**

— L'Olimpiade ... Introduction by Howard Mayer Brown. ⟨Opera. Libretto by P. Metastasio. Score, reproduced from Milan Conservatorio di Musica Giuseppe Verdi, MS Noseda F94.⟩ pp. 413. *Garland Publishing: New York, London,* 1978. *obl.* 4°.
[*Italian Opera* 1640–1770. 36.] **F. 1899.**

— Olimpiade. Sinfonia dell'opera per archi, 2 oboi, 2 corni in fa e cembalo. Trascrizione e realizzazione a cura di Giuseppe A. Pastore ... Partitura, *etc.* pp. 8. *Guglielmo Zanibon: Padova,* [1960.] fol. **h. 1567. u. (8.)**

— Praebe, virgo, benignas aures. Motetto a canto solo con organo obligato. ⟨Herausgegeben von Rudolf Ewerhart.⟩ pp. 21. *Edmund Bieler: Köln,* [1957.] 8°.
[*Cantio sacra.* 15.] **G. 5. a.**

— Psalm 110. *See* supra: [Dixit Dominus for 5 voices, in A major.]

— Salve regina. Für Sopran, 2 Violinen und Basso continuo. Herausgegeben von Rudolf Ewerhart. [Score and parts.] 4 pt. *Edmund Bieler: Köln,* [1960.] 4°.
[*Die Kantate.* 4.] **G. 5.**

— [Sant' Elena al Calvario.] Sinfonie zum Oratorium Sant' Elena al Calvario ... eingerichtet von H. Kretzschmar. Partitur. *Breitkopf & Härtel: Leipzig, etc.,* 1896. fol.
h. 1509. q. (6.)

— [Sant' Elena al Calvario.] Sinfonie, G moll (1732) ... Herausgegeben und bearbeitet von Robert Sondheimer. [Score.] pp. 11. *Edition Bernoulli:* [*Vienna,* 1937.] fol.
[*Werke aus dem* 18. *Jahrhundert. no.* 47.] **Hirsch** IV. **1020.**

— [Sant' Elena al Calvario.] Sinfonia, G Minor ... Edited for the first time and with foreword by Richard Engländer. [Score.] pp. 14. *Ernst Eulenburg: London,* [1956.] 8°.
[*Edition Eulenburg. no.* 538.] **b. 212.**

— S. Elena al Calvario. Sinfonia dell'oratorio. Realizzazione e revisione di G. A. Pastore. Partitura. pp. 10. *Carisch: Milano,* [1957.] 4°. **g. 727. xx. (8.)**

— [Sant' Elena al Calvario.] Dal nuvoloso monte. Aria. *See* GEMME. Gemme d'Antichità. No. 114. [1864, *etc.*] fol.
H. 2293.

LEO (Leonardo)

— Santa Genoviefa. Melodramma sacro. Sinfonia. Realizzazione e revisione di G. A. Pastore. Partitura d'orchestra. pp. 16. *Carisch: Milano,* [1957.] 4°.
g. 727. xx. (9.)

— Se mai senti. *See* supra: [La Clemenza di Tito.]

— [La Sofronia.] Coro della Sofronia. *F. Mosca: Napoli,* 1729. 4°.
Part of the appendix to the Duca Annibale Marchese's 'Tragedie Cristiane'. **84. e. 24.**

— Solfeggien für eine tiefe Stimme ... mit Begleitung des Pianoforte herausgegeben von J. Sturm. 3 Hft. *Leipzig,* [1879.] fol. **H. 1781. i. (15.)**

— Song of Joy. *See* supra: [Cantata Spirituale.—Di contento.]

— Tenebrae. (1st Nocturne.) Edited by Denys Darlow. S.A.T.B. voices and organ. pp. 19. *Oxford University Press: London,* [1964.] 8°. **F. 1176. qq. (5.)**

— [Toccate.] Composizioni per clavicembalo ordinate in forma di suites ... Rivedute, diteggiate e pubblicate per la prima volta. A cura di Alessandro Longo. pp. 32. *Edizioni Mario Aromando: Milano,* [c. 1925.] 4°. **h. 3865. t. (3.)**

— Sei toccate per cembalo ... [no. 2–4, 6, 13, 10.] Rivedute da Maria Maffioletti-Visca, *etc.* pp. 13. *Carisch: Milano,* [1960.] 4°. **h. 3870. ii. (6.)**

— Virgam virtutis tuæ. *See* supra: [Dixit Dominus ... in C major.]

— La Voce del Cuore. Aria [begins: "Non so con dolce moto"]. *See* CARMUSCI (D.) Due Perle, *etc.* No. 2. [1871.] fol.
H. 2502. (9.)

— *See* LEVESQUE (P. C.) and BÊCHE (L.) Solfèges d'Italie ... composés par Leo, Durante, Scarlatti [and others], *etc.* [c. 1790.] *obl.* fol. **E. 601. ff.**

— *See* NOVELLO (V.) Select Organ pieces from the ... sacred works of ... Leo and other ... composers. [1830?] fol.
h. 137. c.

— *See* PIRANI (M.) Andantino, after L. Leo. 1918. fol.
h. 1612. ii. (21.)

— *See* SOLFÈGES. Nouvelle édition de Solfèges d'Italie, composés par Leo, *etc.* [1810?] *obl.* fol. **E. 746.**

LEO (Louis)

— A charm hangs o'er thee maiden fair. *See* MELODIST. The melodist, *etc.* No. 3. [1854.] fol. **H. 1254. (29.)**

— Come o'er the moonlit Sea. Duett. Written by C. Jefferys. Arranged [from the chorus, "Amis, Amis, le Soleil" in D. F. E. Auber's La Muette de Portici] with an accompaniment for the Guitar by L. Leo. *See* LAYS. Lays of Harmony, *etc.* No. 10. [1894.] fol. **H. 2086.**

— The Corsair, [song] ... by L. Devereaux. With an accompaniment for the Guitar arranged by L. Leo. *See* LAYS. Lays of Harmony, *etc.* No. 12. [1894.] fol. **H. 2086.**

— The Gondolier's Good Night. Duett. Written by C. Jefferys. Arranged with an accompaniment for the Guitar by L. Leo. *See* LAYS. Lays of Harmony, *etc.* No. 11. [1894.] fol.
H. 2086.

— Hebrew Melodies ... the poetry by F. Lawrence ... The Symphonies & Accompaniments arranged by L. Leo. 4 no. *Mori, Lavenu & Co.: London,* [1844.] fol. **H. 1698. (5.)**

— Maria. Ballad. *H. May: London,* [1855?] fol.
H. 2815. k. (26.)

LEO (LOUIS)

— Mountain Bells. [Song.] Composed by J. Barnett. Arranged with an accompaniment for the Guitar by L. Leo. *See* LAYS. Lays of Harmony, *etc.* No. 32. [1894.] fol.   **H. 2086.**

— My Home shall be the waves, a barcarole [begins: "Speed on my barque"] ... written by C. Jefferys. *London,* [1840?] fol.   **H. 2815. f. (16.)**

— Thou, my first love and my last! canzonette. [Begins: "Tell me not that vows once spoken".] *London,* [1855.] fol.   **H. 1758. (31.)**

— The Voices of my early home. Song, adapted to the Duc de Reichstadt's ... waltz. *London,* [1840?] fol.   **G. 806. c. (22.)**

— When will you meet me Love? The celebrated ballad ... Written by Chaˢ Jefferys. pp. 5. *Dale, Cockerill & Cᵒ: London,* [c. 1835.] fol.   **H. 1601. jj. (10.)**

— The Young Coquette ... Ballad [begins: "When first I heard"]. (Written by C. Jefferys.) *London,* [1840?] fol.   **H. 2815. f. (17.)**

— Zilla or the May Queen, serenade written by G. Kitchin. [Begins: "Softly slumber".] *London,* [1856.] fol.   **H. 1758. (30.)**

— Zilla, or the May Queen. Serenade, *etc. London,* [1861.] fol.   **H. 1772. r. (35.)**

— *See* AUBER (D. F. E.) [Lestocq.—My lov'd and native Home.] The Shepherd's Bride. Air [by J. A. Wade] introduced into the [English version of Auber's] opera "Lestocq". Arranged for the Guitar by L. Leo. [1894.] fol.   **H. 2086.**

— *See* BARNETT (J.) Mountain Bells ... arranged ... for the Guitar by L. Leo. [1840?] fol.   **H. 2830. (9.)**

LEO (MORRIS)

— Six Waltzes for the Pianoforte with an accompaniment for the Violin. *Liverpool,* [1805?] fol.   **g. 443. b. (18.)**

LÉOCADIE

— Léocadie. Drame lyrique. *See* AUBER (D. F. E.)

LEOD (P. MC.)

— *See* MACLEOD.

LEOITHIN

— Leoithin an Earraigh. Amhrán, *etc. See* Ó HAODHA (S.)

LEOLIN

— Dreaming ever of thee, my love. Serenade [begins: "When in the deep'ning twilight"]. Poetry by W. Norwood ... composed ... by Leolin. *London,* [1869.] fol.   **H. 1775. u. (21.)**

— What saith the river? [Song.] Written by Allingham, composed by Leolin. *London,* [1866.] fol.   **H. 1775. u. (20.)**

LEOLINE

— Leoline. Song. *See* FINDON (J.)

— Leoline. Opera. *See* FLOTOW (F. F. A. von) *Baron.*

— Leoline. Song. *See* LARA (I. de) *pseud.*

— Leoline. Song. *See* PETRIE (Henry W.)

LÉON (A. SAINT)

— *See* SAINT LÉON.

LEÓN (ARGELIERS)

— Akorín. Cantos negros para piano. pp. 16. *Ediciones del Departamento de música de la Biblioteca nacional: La Habana,* 1962. 4°.   **g. 1138. d. (1.)**

— 4 invenciones para piano. 4 no. *Ediciones del Departamento de música de la Biblioteca nacional "José Marti": La Habana,* 1964. 8°.   **d. 240. i. (2.)**

— *See* ORTEGA (J.) Música para guitarra de autores cubanos, N. Galán, A. Léon, *etc.* 1964. 4°.   **g. 660. v. (4.)**

LEON (FRED.) and MINTURN (MARIE)

— Queenie Claire. Ballad. Written & composed by F. Leon & M. Minturn. pp. 3–5. *Hurtig & Seamon:* [*New York,* 1900.] fol.   **H. 3985. x. (1.)**

LÉON (H. MISCHA)

— *See* MISCHA-LÉON.

LEON (J.)

— Six favorite Minuets for two Violins and a Violoncello, Harpsichord or Piano Forte. [Score.] pp. 8. *Printed for the Author: London,* [c. 1785.] *obl.* 8°.   **b. 53. m. (2.)**

LÉON (LAURENT)

— La Chanson du Saule. [Song.] Poésie de J. Aicard, chantée ... au 5ᵉ Acte d'Othello. [*Paris,*] 1899. 8°. *Supplement to "L'Illustration," No.* 2922.   **P. P. 4283. m. (3.)**

— Douceur de croire. [Play.] Paroles de J. Normand. I. Chœur à quatre voix. (II. Entrée des Étudiants hongrois. [P. F.]) [*Paris,*] 1899. 8°. *Supplement to "L'Illustration," No.* 2942.   **P. P. 4283. m. (3.)**

— Le Sphinx suite de valses ... pour le Piano. *Paris,* [1874.] fol.   **h. 1487. q. (1.)**

— Le Sphinx waltzes. [P. F.] *London,* [1876.] fol.   **h. 1482. z. (36.)**

— Tristan de Léonois. Drame en vers d'A. Silvestre. Chanson bretonne, *etc.* [Begins: "Couvrez de fleurs".] [*Paris,*] 1897. 8°. *Supplement to "L'Illustration," No.* 2853.   **P. P. 4283. m. (3.)**

LEON (LEO)

— Sacri Flores Binis, Ternis, et Quaternis Vocibus. Cum sua Partitura Organis accommoda, *etc.* Bassus. (Partitura.) 2 pt. *Apud Petrum Phalesium: Antuerpiæ,* 1619. 4°. *On p. 17 of both part books the bass and alto of a 'Sub tuum præsidium' are inserted in manuscript.*   **C. 263.**

LEON (S. PONCE DE)

— *See* PONCE DE LEON.

LÉON (VINCENT)

— Guardinier. March. [P. F.] *Brooks & Denton Co.: New York,* 1896. fol.   **h. 3282. f. (27.)**

— *See* NEVIN (E. W.) [Water Scenes. Op. 13. No. 4.] Narcissus ... Mandolin and Piano. (Arr. by V. Leon.) 1899. fol.   **h. 3619. (13.)**

LEÓN (W.)

— Dance of the Dwarfs, for the pianoforte. *J. R. Lafleur & Son: London,* 1918. fol.   **h. 3284. nn. (43.)**

— Harvest Moon. Intermezzo for piano. *L. Wright Music Co.: London,* 1915. fol.   **h. 3284. nn. (44.)**

LEON (W. Francis)

— A Girl of the 20th Century. [Song.] Words and music by
W. F. Leon. pp. 5. *Oliver Ditson Co.: Boston*, [1895.] fol.
H. 3980. rr. (1.)

LEON (Walter de)

— *See* De Leon.

LEONARD AND CO

— Leonard's Scales and Arpeggios for violin, *etc. Leonard &
Co.: London*, 1914. fol. **g. 505. ii. (22**.)**

LEONARD, GOULD AND BOLTTLER

— Leonard, Gould & Bolttler's Library of Unison and Part
Songs for Schools. *See* Gould and Boltler.

— Leonard, Gould & Bolttler Part Songs, *etc. See* Gould and
Co.

LÉONARD (   )

— Entends ma voix gémissante. *Romance, etc.* [*Paris*, 1790?] 8°.
B. 362. e. (14.)

LEONARD (   )

— *See* Whittey (   ) and Leonard (   ) As long as
the Sun will shine. [Song.] 1892. fol. **H. 1797. y. (33.)**

LEONARD (A. B.)

— Virginius. Quick march. [Parts for fife and drum band.] 32 pt.
J. R. Lafleur & Son: London, [1898.] 8°.
*Part of "J. R. Lafleur & Son's Fife & Drum Journal". Including
several copies of various parts.* **f. 800. (813.)**

LEONARD (A. E. B.)

— Colonial Dames. Waltzes. [P. F.] *M. Witmark & Sons: New
York & Chicago*, 1897. fol. **h. 3286. g. (32.)**

— La Coronation. Gavotte Royal. [P. F.] *M. Witmark & Sons:
New York, etc.*, 1896. fol. **h. 3282. f. (28.)**

— I's nevah gwine to lub yo' any moah. Song and chorus.
Words by Will Waters. pp. 5. *M. Witmark & Sons: New
York, Chicago*, [1897.] fol. **H. 3980. rr. (2.)**

— The Katy-Did's Wooing. [P. F.] *M. Witmark & Sons: New
York*, 1896. fol. **h. 3282. f. (29.)**

— Mushroom Dance. Dance Characteristic. [P. F.] *Howley,
Haviland & Co.: New York*, 1896. fol. **h. 3282. f. (30.)**

— My Dream came true. Song & chorus. Words by John
H. Devlin. pp. 5. *Howley, Haviland & Co.: New York*, [1896.]
fol. **H. 3980. rr. (3.)**

— Rosemary. Polka. [P. F.] *M. Witmark & Sons: New York &
Chicago*, 1898. fol. **h. 3286. g. (33.)**

— The Royal March. Two-Step for Pianoforte. *O. Ditson Co.:
Boston, etc.*, 1895. fol. **h. 3286. g. (34.)**

— The Spray. Characteristic Piece for Piano. *M. Witmark &
Sons: New York, etc.*, 1899. fol. **h. 3282. f. (31.)**

— Sweetheart. [Song. Words by] W. Gilder. *M. Witmark &
Sons: New York, etc.*, 1899. fol. **H. 1799. h. (37.)**

— Viola. March. [P. F.] *K. Dehnhof: New York*, [1895.] fol.
h. 1489. s. (42.)

— Wigwam Dance. [P. F.] *Howley, Haviland & Co.: New York*,
1896. fol. **h. 3282. f. (32.)**

LEONARD (Art)

— Meet me at our Trysting Place. [Song.] Words by Carl
Leonard. pp. 5. *Leonard Publish. Co.: Chicago*, [1908.] fol.
H. 3985. x. (2.)

LEONARD (Arthur)

— Impulse. Morceau pour violon et piano. *West & Co.:
London*, 1914. fol. **h. 1612. hh. (10.)**

LEONARD (Clair)

— If I speak with the Tongues of Men. Anthem for Mixed
Choir a cappella. *Composers Press: New York*, 1943. 8°.
E. 335. l. (1.)

— One Evening. For Unison Chorus. [Words by] G. Thurber.
H. W. Gray Co.: New York, 1943. 8°. **E. 1830. d. (43.)**

LEONARD (Eddie)

— Big brown booloo Eyes. [Song.] Arranged by Wᵐ
M. Redfield. pp. 5. *Cohan & Harris Publishing Co.:* [*New
York*, 1908.] fol. **H. 3985. x. (3.)**

— I want to go back to the Land of Cotton. ⟨Song.⟩ Words and
music by E. Leonard. *Jos. W. Stern & Co.: New York*, [1908.]
fol. **H. 3985. x. (4.)**

— "Louisiana Coon and the Moon." [Song.] Words and music
by E. Leonard. pp. 5. *Jos. W. Stern & Co.: New York*, [1909.]
fol. **H. 3985. x. (5.)**

— Lyna. [Song.] Words by Rogers and Frantzen. pp. 5.
F. B. Haviland Publishing Co.: New York, [1904.] fol.
H. 3985. x. (6.)

— Oh, oh, Sallie! ... [Song.] Words by Rogers & Frantzen. pp. 5.
F. B. Haviland Publishing Co.: New York, [1904.] fol.
H. 3985. x. (7.)

LEONARD (Eddie) and **CUPERO** (Edward V.)

— Sugar mine. [Song.] pp. 5. *Lew Dockstader:* [*New York*, 1906.]
fol. **H. 3985. x. (8.)**

LEONARD (Harold)

— The Road of Life. Song, words by F. Hoare. *Mathias &
Strickland: London*, [1895.] fol. **G. 805. aa. (20.)**

LEONARD (Harry)

— The Power and the Glory. Words by Paul Hollingdale & Bob
Halfin ... Arranged for SATB by Desmond Ratcliffe.
Orchestration by Ted Brenann, *etc.* [Score.] pp. 12. *Fairfield
Music Co.: Borough Green*, [1970.] 4°. **G. 814. c. (4.)**

— The Power and the Glory. Words by Paul Hollingdale and
Bob Halfin ... Arranged for SATB and piano by Desmond
Ratcliffe. pp. 7. *Fairfield Music Co.:* [*London*, 1969.] 8°.
[*Fairfield choral Series.* 2.] **E. 1746. b.**

LÉONARD (Hubert)

— À une étoile. [Violin and P. F.] *See infra*: 12 petites pièces ...
Op. 57. No. 11.

— Airs Bohémiens et Styriens, fantaisie de salon pour le Violon
avec accompagnement de Piano. *Mayence*, [1869.] fol.
h. 1609. c. (13.)

— Alla Stiriana. Andante pour violon avec accompagnement de
piano. *B. Schott's Söhne: Mayence*, [1888.] fol.
h. 1608. q. (42.)

— Angelus du Soir. [Violin and P. F.] *See infra*: 12 petites pièces
... Op. 57. No. 5.

LÉONARD (Hubert)

— Cadenza pour le Concerto de Violon de Beethoven.
Mayence, [1883.] fol.   **g. 505. w. (30.)**

— Cadenzas to Beethoven's Violin Concerto by H. Leonard.
Schott & Co.: London, [1919.] fol.   **h. 1613. e. (11*.)**

— Capricho español pour le violon avec accompagnement de
piano. Op. 58.   *B. Schott's Söhne: Mayence*, [1888.] fol.
h. 1608. q. (41.)

— La Captive. [Violin and P. F.] *See* infra: 12 petites pièces ...
Op. 57. No. 1.

— Cavatine pour le Violon avec accompagnement de Piano.
Mayence, [1880.] fol.   **h. 1609. q. (10.)**

— [2ᵉ Concerto. Op. 14.] Andante con Recit, *etc.* [Violin and
P. F.] *See* Kross (E.) Sammlung characteristischer Stellen aus
Violin-Concerten, *etc.* No. 5. [1890.] fol.   **h. 1732. (3.)**

— [3ᵉ Concerto. Op. 16.] Allegro moderato, *etc.* [Violin and P. F.]
See Kross (E.) Sammlung characteristischer Stellen aus
Violin-Concerten, *etc.* No. 6. [1890.] fol.   **h. 1732. (3.)**

— [5ᵉ Concerto. Op. 28.] Allegro. [Violin and P. F.] *See*
Kross (E.) Sammlung characteristischer Stellen aus
Violin-Concerten, *etc.* No. 7. [1890.] fol.   **h. 1732. (3.)**

— Dans un Songe. [Violin and P. F.] *See* infra: 12 petites pièces
... Op. 57. No. 8.

— Les Deux Tourterelles. [Violin and P. F.] *See* infra: 12 petites
pièces ... Op. 57. No. 7.

— Dove sono, air ... de l'opéra le Nozze di Figaro, de Mozart,
transcrit pour Violon avec accᵗ. de Piano. *Mayence*, [1863.]
fol.   **h. 1609. c. (6.)**

— Duo de Concert pour deux Violons. *Mayence*, [1864.] fol.
h. 1609. c. (8.)

— École Léonard pour le Violon. No. 1, 6, 7. *Paris*, [1877.] fol.
Imperfect; wanting no. 2–5.   **h. 1631. a.**

— Elégie pour le violon avec accompᵗ. de piano. Op. 20.
London, [1854.] fol.   **h. 1610. (21.)**

— Ernani (de Verdi), fantaisie de salon pour Violon avec
accompagnement de Piano. *Bruxelles*, [1869.] fol.
h. 1609. c. (11.)

— Gigue. [Violin and P. F.] *See* infra: 12 petites pièces ...
Op. 57. No. 2.

— La Gymnastique du violoniste ou Résumé des éléments les
plus utiles à travailler journellement, et offrant de nouvelles
ressources pour le doigter des gammes, *etc.* pp. 48.   *Chez les
fils de B. Schott: Mayence*, [1863.] fol.   **h. 1753. l. (4.)**

— [La Gymnastique du violiniste.] Gymnastische Übungen auf
der Violine. La Gymnastique du Violiniste ... Neue Ausgabe
revidiert von E. Kross. *Ger., Fr., & Eng. B. Schott's Söhne:
Mainz, etc.*, (1911.) 4°.   **g. 776.**

— [Another copy, issued in separate parts.]   **g. 498. o. (2.)**

— Martha, de Flotow, transcription-caprice pour le Violon avec
accompagnement de Piano. *Mayence*, [1867.] fol.
h. 1609. c. (10.)

— Mélancolie. [Violin and P. F.] *See* infra: 12 petites pièces ...
Op. 57. No. 3.

— Mouvement perpétuel. [Violin and P. F.] *See* infra: 12 petites
pièces ... Op. 57. No. 12.

— Pastorale. [Violin and P. F.] *See* infra: 12 petites pièces ...
Op. 57. No. 9.

— 12 petites pièces intimes pour Violon avec Accompagnement
de Piano. Op. 57, *etc.* 12 no. *Les Fils de B. Schott: Mayence*,
[1885.] fol.   **h. 1612. p. (29.)**

LÉONARD (Hubert)

— Pietà Signore, air d'eglise d'A. Stradella, transcrit pour le
Violon avec accompagnement de Piano.   *Paris*, [1866.] fol.
h. 1609. c. (9.)

— Prière à la Madone, de Gordigiani, transcrite pour le Violon
avec accᵗ. de Piano.   *Mayence*, [1863.] fol.   **h. 1609. e. (7.)**

— Le Retour du Paladin, polonaise pour le Violon avec
accompagnement de Piano.   *Paris*, [1877.] fol.
h. 1609. m. (12.)

— Scherzino. [Violin and P. F.] *See* supra: 12 petites pièces ...
Op. 57. No. 10.

— Sérénade humoristique à l'Espagnole pour trois Violons avec
accompagnement de Piano.   *Mayence*, [1877.] fol.
h. 1609. h. (7.)

— Six Solos for the Violin with Piano accompaniment. ⟨Op. 41.⟩
Edited and fingered by Otto. K. Schill, *etc.* [Score and part.]
2 pt.   *G. Schirmer: New York; Chappell & Co.: London;*
[*London* printed, 1951.] 4°.
Schirmer's Library of musical Classics. vol. 912.
g. 500. z. (2.)

— Souvenirs de Blankenberghe. 4 morceaux caractéristiques
pour le Violon, avec accompagnement de Piano. Op. 27.
Mayence, [1867.] fol.   **h. 1631.**

— Suite pour Violon avec Accompagnement ... de Piano.
Op. 53. 1. Pensée intime. 2. Gavotte. 3. Conte de la
Grand'mère. 4. Aveu. 5. La Rondo qui passe.   *Les Fils de
B. Schott: Mayence*, [1883.] fol.   **h. 1612. p. (28.)**

— Summer flowers, shedding fragrance, song, the poetry by
B. S. Turner.   *London*, [1857.] fol.   **H. 1771. l. (18.)**

— Il Trovatore [by F. G. F. Verdi], fantaisie de salon pour le
Violon, avec accompagnement de Piano.   *Bruxelles*, [1869.]
fol.   **h. 1609. c. (12.)**

— Valse. [Violin and P. F.] *See* supra: 12 petites pièces ...
Op. 57. No. 6.

— Valse-Caprice pour le Violon avec accomp. de Piano.
Mayence, [1878.] fol.   **h. 1609. m. (13.)**

— Variations sur une gavotte de Corelli pour le Violon avec
accompagnement ... de Piano.   *Mayence*, [1880.] fol.
h. 1609. q. (11.)

— Un Vieil Amateur. [Violin and P. F.] *See* supra: 12 petites
pièces ... Op. 57. No. 4.

— *See* Arditi (Luigi) Il Bacio ... Walzer ... Bearbeitet von
H. Léonard. [Violin or violoncello and P. F.] [c. 1920.] fol.
h. 4090. s. (1.)

— *See* Berlioz (L. H.) La Damnation de Faust ... Transcription
pour le Violon avec accompagᵉⁿᵗ de Piano par H. Léonard,
etc. [1882.] fol.   **h. 3250. d. (4.)**

— *See* Corelli (A.) [Sonatas. Op. 5. No. 12.] La Folia. Variations
sérieuses pour le violon ... Accompagnement ... et cadenza
par H. Léonard ... Orchestré par M. Reger, *etc.* [1914.] 8°.
f. 244. vv. (4.)

— *See* Corelli (A.) [Sonatas. Op. 5. No. 12.] La Folia ...
l'accompagnement de piano et cadence par H. Léonard, *etc.*
1916. fol.   **g. 505. hh. (31.)**

— *See* Corelli (A.) [Sonatas. Op. 5. No. 12.] La Folia. Variations
for violin. With accompaniment of piano, and cadenza by
H. Léonard, *etc.* [1950.] 4°.   **g. 500. v. (9.)**

— *See* Grégoir (J.) and Léonard (H.) Airs styriens. 3ᵐᵉ duo
pour piano et violon. [1854.] fol.   **h. 1610. (12.)**

— *See* Grégoir (J.) and Léonard (H.) Don Juan ... Duo pour
Piano et Violon, *etc.* [1870.] fol.   **h. 1638. (5.)**

LÉONARD (HUBERT)

— *See* GRÉGOIR (J.) and LÉONARD (H.) Lohengrin … Duo pour Piano et Violon. [1870.] fol.   **h. 1638. (2.)**

— *See* GRÉGOIR (J.) and LÉONARD (H.) Les Noces de Figaro … Duo, *etc.* [1877.] fol.   **h. 1638. (6.)**

— *See* GRÉGOIR (J.) and LÉONARD (H.) Norma … Duo, *etc.* [1877.] fol.   **h. 1638. (7.)**

— *See* GRÉGOIR (J.) and LÉONARD (H.) Oberon … Duo pour Piano et Violon, *etc.* [1870.] fol.   **h. 1638. (3.)**

— *See* GRÉGOIR (J.) and LÉONARD (H.) Das Rheingold … Duo pour Piano et Violon, *etc.* [1870.] fol.   **h. 1628. (4.)**

— *See* GRÉGOIR (J.) and LÉONARD (H.) Rienzi … Duo pour Piano et Violon. [1870.] fol.   **h. 1638. (1.)**

— *See* PAGANINI (N.) La Bataille, thême et variations … arrangés … par H. Léonard. [1877.] fol.   **h. 2849. (5.)**

— *See* PORPORA (N.) Sonate en ré mineur … pour violon avec accompagnement de piano … par H. Léonard. [1886.] fol.   **h. 1728. c. (10.)**

— *See* TARTINI (G.) [Sonatas. Op. 1. No. 8.] Cantabile … pour violon avec accompagnement de piano … par H. Léonard. [1886.] fol.   **h. 1608. r. (37.)**

— *See* TARTINI (G.) Variations … on a Gavotte by A. Corelli. Piano accompaniment by H. Léonard, *etc.* 1927. 4°.   **g. 500. n. (3.)**

LEONARD (J. J.)

— Courting where the sweet Magnolia blooms. Song & Dance. Words and music by J. J. Leonard. *C. Sheard: London,* [1889.] fol.
No. 7808 of the Musical Bouquet.   **H. 2345.**

LEONARD (JOHN F.)

— Darling Mazie. [Song.] Words & music by Gilmore & Leonard. pp. 5. *M. Witmark & Sons: New York, Chicago,* [1899.] fol.   **H. 3980. y. (57.)**

— Down to Coney Isle. ⟨Song and chorus.⟩ Words by B. F. Gilmore. pp. 5. *M. Witmark & Sons: New York, Chicago,* [1896.] fol.   **H. 3980. rr. (4.)**

— He looks just like you. [Song.] Words & music by J. F. Leonard. pp. 5. *T. B. Harms & Co.:* [*New York,* 1904.] fol.   **H. 3985. x. (9.)**

— Hogan's home again. [Song.] Words and music by Gilmore and Leonard. pp. 5. *M. Witmark & Sons: New York, Chicago,* [1896.] fol.   **H. 3980. y. (58.)**

— My Pale white Rose. ⟨Song.⟩ Written and composed by J. F. Leonard, *etc.* [Staff and tonic sol-fa notation. Voice part.] *Francis, Day & Hunter: London,* [1901.] *s. sh.* fol.   **H. 3985. x. (10.)**

— My pale white Rose, *etc.* ⟨Song.⟩ [With separate voice part.] 2 pt. *Francis, Day & Hunter: London,* [1901.] fol.   **H. 3985. x. (11.)**

— New York Town. ⟨Song and chorus.⟩ Written by B. F. Gilmore, *etc.* pp. 5. *M. Witmark & Sons: New York, Chicago,* [1896.] fol.   **H. 3980. rr. (5.)**

— One Love, the only one. [Song.] Words and Music by J. F. Leonard. *Weber, Fields and Stromberg: New York,* 1899. fol.   **H. 1799. h. (38.)**

— The Prettiest Girl in Town. [Song.] Words and music by Gilmore and Leonard. pp. 5. *M. Witmark & Sons: New York, Chicago,* [1899.] fol.   **H. 3980. y. (59.)**

LEONARD (JOHN F.)

— Rally round. March Song, words and music by J. F. Leonard, *etc. Leonard-Ingles Pub. Co.: Salmon Arm, B. C.,* (1914.) fol.   **G. 806. mm. (21.)**

— [Another copy.]   **G. 806. mm. (22.)**

— She's not like other Girls. [Song.] (Words and music by Gilmore and Leonard. Arranged by G. W. Hetzel.) *Broder & Schlam: San Francisco,* 1896. fol.   **H. 1798. m. (47.)**

— Take me to your Heart Love, once again. Ballad. Words by B. F. Gilmore. pp. 5. *M. Witmark & Sons: New York, Chicago,* [1899.] fol.   **H. 3980. rr. (6.)**

— A Wilson High Ball. A musical drink. [Song.] pp. 3–5. *Harry von Tilzer Music Pub. Co.:* [*New York,* 1904.] fol.   **H. 3985. x. (12.)**

LEONARD (LAWRENCE)

— Break for Orchestra, *etc.* ⟨Full score.⟩ pp. 16. *British & Continental Music Agencies: London,* [1966.] 4°.   **g. 836. c. (2.)**

— Processional, *etc.* ⟨Full score.⟩ pp. 8. *British & Continental Music Agencies: London,* [1966.] 4°.   **g. 836. c. (5.)**

— A Short Overture, *etc.* ⟨Full score.⟩ pp. 20. *British & Continental Music Agencies: London,* [1966.] 4°.   **g. 836. c. (4.)**

— A Swaying Tune, *etc.* ⟨Full score.⟩ pp. 8. *British & Continental Music Agencies: London,* [1966.] 4°.   **g. 836. c. (3.)**

— *See* MacCABE (John) Burlesque … [For orchestra.] Edited by L. Leonard. [1968.] 4°.   **g. 836. c. (6.)**

— *See* MUSORGSKY (Modest P.) [Tableaux d'une exposition.] Pictures at an Exhibition. Arranged for piano and orchestra by L. Leonard. Reduction for two pianos. [1980.] fol.   **h. 3617. a. (1.)**

LEONARD (LEONARD B.)

— The Cape Marching Song. Written and composed by L. B. Leonard. *Hawkes & Son: London,* 1899. fol.   **H. 1799. h. (39.)**

LEONARD (LOIS M.)

— Meerschaum Pipe. American college song for four-part chorus or quartet of male voices unaccompanied, arranged by Lois M. Leonard. ⟨Words adapted by L. M. L.⟩ pp. 7. *Roberton Publications: Wendover,* [1977.] 8°. *Part of "Lawson-Gould choral Series".*   **E. 352. a. (9.)**

LEONARD (PERCI)

— *See* DENNER (Osland) Hail! King George! [Song.] Written and composed by O. Denner, P. Leonard, *etc.* [1910.] fol.   **H. 3991. f. (22.)**

LÉONARD (RAFAEL)

— Album for the Cabinet-Organ or Harmonium. New edition by J. V. Müller. *Offenbach a. M.,* [1881.] 8°.   **f. 78. b. (6.)**

— Danse des Grâces, gavotte de salon pour le Piano. *Offenbach s. M.,* [1879.] fol.   **h. 1493. o. (24.)**

— Königs-Husaren, marche brillante. [P. F.] *Offenbach s. M.,* [1879.] fol.   **h. 1493. o. (23.)**

— Königs-Husaren. Marche brillante pour Piano. *London,* [1880.] fol.   **h. 1494. q. (28.)**

— Königs-Husaren, marche brillante pour Piano. *London,* [1881.] fol.   **h. 3273. a. (59.)**

LÉONARD (Rafael)

— Königs-Husaren. Marche brillante pour Piano. [Duet.]
London, [1880.] fol.   **h. 1484. c. (33.)**

— Méditation, thème varié pour le Piano. *Offenbach s. M.*,
[1879.] fol.   **h. 1493. o. (25.)**

— Les Poésies de la Tyrolienne, morceau de salon pour Piano.
Offenbach s. M., [1879.] fol.   **h. 1493. o. (29.)**

— Rêve des Fleurs. Der Blumen Traum. Mélodie pour le Piano.
Offenbach s. M., [1879.] fol.   **h. 1493. o. (27.)**

— Le Reveil des Roses, valse brillante ... pour le Piano.
Offenbach s. M., [1879.] fol.   **h. 1493. o. (28.)**

— Rêves du Coeur. Herzenswünsche. Mélodie pour Piano.
Offenbach s. M., [1879.] fol.   **h. 1493. o. (26.)**

— Souvenir du Valais ... Morceau pour le Piano. *Offenbach
s. M.*, [1879.] fol.   **h. 1493. o. (30.)**

— The Tenth Hussars' March. Pianoforte Solo in D major (in D♭
major). 2 no. *Augener & Co.: London*, [1882.] fol.
                                                          g. 543. j. (30.)

LEONARD (Silas W.) and FILLMORE (A. D.)

— The Christian Psalmist, a collection of tunes and hymns,
original and selected ... Compiled from many authors, by
S. W. Leonard and A. D. Fillmore. Revised and greatly
enlarged by S. W. Leonard. pp. vii. 480. *S. W. Leonard:
Louisville*, [1854.] 8°.   **A. 1236. y.**

LEONARD (Spencer)

— Three Contrasts for the pianoforte. *Weekes & Co.: London*,
1916. 4°.   **g. 272. gg. (12.)**

LEONARD (Stanley)

— Bachiana for ... Percussion. [Four pieces from the
"Notenbuch der Anna Magdalena Bach", 1725, arranged by
Stanley Leonard.] 6 players ... Score [and parts], *etc.* 5 pt.
N. Simrock: London, Hamburg, [1974.] 4°.   **g. 270. ll. (12.)**

— Fanfare & Allegro. For trumpet and solo timpani, *etc.* [Score
and parts.] 3 pt. *N. Simrock: London, Hamburg*, [1974.] 4°.
                                                          g. 270. ll. (13.)

— *See* Mozart (Wolfgang A.) [*Doubtful and Supposititious
Works.*] [4 Scherzduette. K. Anh. 284dd. No. 4.] Mirror Canon
... Arranged for mallet quartet by ... S. Leonard. [1976.] 4°.
                                                          g. 382. nn. (4.)

LEONARD (Stuart B.)

— Hush-a-ba, Birdie, croon, croon. Unison Song, *etc.*
J. Curwen & Sons: London, 1929. 8°.
[*Choruses for equal voices, No.* 1785.]   **E. 861.**

— Magnificat & Nunc dimittis. Unison. *The Faith Press:
London*, 1932. 8°.   **F. 1158. f. (11.)**

— You spotted Snakes with double Tongue. For Soprano Solo
and S. T. B. Chorus, unaccompanied, poem by Shakespeare,
etc. J. Curwen & Sons: London, 1925. 8°.
[*Choral Handbook. No.* 1191.]   **E. 862.**

LÉONARD (W.)

— The Kentish belle's waltz for the Piano Forte. *London*,
[1816.] fol.   **h. 117. (20.)**

— "Roy's wife of Aldivalloch;" a Scotch ballad [written by Mrs
Grant of Carron], as sung by Mr. Léonard and arranged by
him. *London*, [1826.] fol.   **H. 1675. (25.)**

LÉONARD (W.)

— The sensitive plant; a ballad [begins: "As animation's glow"],
written by Sir D. Ogilby. *London*, [1826.] fol.
                                                          H. 1675. (26.)

LEONARDA (Isabella)

— *See* Isabella Leonarda.

LEONARDI (A.)

— Quatre morceaux pour mandoline avec accompagnement de
piano (ou guitare) (avec iie mandoline et mandole ad lib.) ...
N° 1. Berceuse des fleurs. 2. Chant des naïades. Mélodie.
3. Danse de libellules. Barcarolle. 4. Poème d'amour. Mélodie,
etc. ⟨Per mandolino e pianoforte.⟩ no. 4. [Score and part.] 2 pt.
Carisch & Jänichen: Leipsic, Milan, [1903.] fol.
Part of "Il Mandolinista italiano". ser. 4. *Imperfect; wanting
no.* 1–3.   **h. 188. n. (4.)**

LEONARDI (Antonio)

— La Peri. Poema lirico in un prologo e due parti. Poesia e
musica di A. Leonardi ... Riduzione per canto e pianoforte.
Milano, [1886.] 8°.   **F. 1453.**

LEONARDI (Emil)

— Blumengruss. Gavotte für Pianoforte. Op. 51. *Hamburg*,
[1883.] fol.   **h. 3280. k. (47.)**

— Dank- und Jubel-Marsch zur glücklichen Errettung ... des
deutschen Kaisers ... Wilhelm I, *etc.* L. P. [P. F.] *Ill.
Patent-Blatt: Berlin*, [1875?] fol.   **R. M. 11. h. 8.**

— Militaria. Fantasia for the pianoforte, *etc. E. Ascherberg &
Co.: London*, [1885.] fol.   **h. 1484. t. (1.)**

— La Plainte d'Amour. Romance pour le pianoforte. Op. 53.
Boosey & Co.: London, [1884.] fol.
No. 5 of Spare Moments at the Pianoforte.   **h. 3278. d. (25.)**

LEONARDUS NERVIUS, *a Capuchin*

— Fasciculus Cantionum Sacrarum Quatuor, Quinque, et Sex
Vocum. Additis Litaniis Lauretanis Quatuor & Sex Vocum.
Cum Basso Generali ad Organum. Cantus. (Altus.) (Tenor.)
(Sextus.) 4 pt. *Ex Officina Petri Phalesii: Antuerpiæ*, 1628. 4°.
                                                          C. 89. a.

— R. P. Leonardi Neruii Ord. Cappuc, S. Francisci, Missæ
Decem Quatuor Quinque, Sex et Septem Vocum, cum Basso
pro Organo. Cantus. (Altus.) (Tenor.) (Sextus.) 4 pt. *Apud
Petrum Phalesium: Antuerpiæ*, 1618. 4°.   **C. 89.**

LEONCAVALLO (Ruggiero)

— Due liriche per canto e pianoforte. ⟨Déclaration (Armand
Silvestre). La Chanson des jeux (Andrea Chénier).⟩ A cura di
Pietro Spada. pp. 7. *Edizioni musicali Bèrben: Ancona,
Milano*, 1976. fol.   **G. 1271. jj. (15.)**

— A Ninon. Canzonetta. Paroles de A. de Musset. (Deutsche
Uebersetzung von Fr. Raimund.) Fr. & Ger. pp. 10. *Bartholf
Senff: Leipzig*, [1896.] fol.   **H. 1850. j. (11.)**

— Album Stecchetti, 4 poesie della "Postuma" musicate per
Canto e Piano. *Milan*, [1880.] fol.   **H. 1782. c. (17.)**

— [Are you there?] Rose-way. Song (Duet) from "Are you
there?" the words by E. Wallace, *etc.* 2 no. *Enoch & Sons:
London*, 1913. fol.   **G. 806. mm. (23.)**

— [Are you there?] Rose-way. Transcription ... for piano solo
by G. H. Clutsam. *Enoch & Sons: London*, 1914. fol.
                                                          h. 3284. nn. (46.)

LEONCAVALLO (Ruggiero)

— [Are you there?] Rose-way. Transcription ... for violin, or flute, and piano by G. H. Clutsam. *Enoch & Sons: London,* 1914. fol. **h. 1612. hh. (12.)**

— At peace. Song, written by Mrs. A. Roberts. *Hutchings & Romer: London,* [1884.] fol. **G. 806. k. (64.)**

— Ave Maria. Preghiera per voce di tenore con accompagnamento di arpa ed harmonium ad lib. [Score.] pp. 11. *R. Leoncavallo: Brissago,* [1905.] fol. *P. 2 bears the composer's dated autograph signature.* **G. 518. s. (6.)**

— Ave Maria. [Solo, with harp and ad libitum harmonium accompaniment.] *C. K. Harris: Chicago, etc.,* (1906.) fol. **G. 517. v. (32.)**

— Barcarola Veneziana. In forma di canzone. Venetian Barcarolle. Song with Italian and English words. Versi di Arlès, English version by R. Newmarch. *J. B. Cramer & Co.: London,* 1925. 4°. **G. 1270. m. (4.)**

— The Bell Chorus. *See* infra: [Pagliacci.—Din, don.]

— La Bohème. Commedia lirica in quattro atti, parole e musica di R. Leoncavallo, tratta dal Romanzo: Scènes de la Vie de Bohème di H. Murger. Riduzione per canto e pianoforte. pp. 417. *Edoardo Sonzogno: Milano,* 1897. 4°. **G. 704. d.**

— [Another copy.] *Autograph inscription to Queen Victoria by the composer, dated 18 July 1899.* **R. M. 9. d. 16.**

— La Bohème ... [Da quel suon soavamente.] Valse de Musette. [Begins: "Aux accords de la valse entrainante".] [*Paris,*] 1899. 8°. *Supplement to "L'Illustration," No.* 2958. **P. P. 4283. m. (3.)**

— C'est l'heure mystérieuse. *See* infra: The Dreamy Twilight is falling.

— Chanson d'Amour, pour piano. *Schott & Co.: London,* 1920. fol. **h. 3870. a. (29.)**

— Chatterton. Dramma lirico in tre atti, parole e musica di R. Leoncavallo ... per canto e pianoforte. pp. 194. *Achille Tedeschi: Bologna,* 1896. 4°. **G. 704. c.**

— [Another copy.] *Autograph inscription to Queen Victoria by the composer, dated 18 July 1899.* **R. M. 9. d. 17.**

— Chatterton. Drame lyrique en 3 actes et 4 tableaux. Paroles et musique de R. Leoncavallo. Adaptation française de Maurice Vaucaire. Traduction de E. Crosti. Partition piano et chant. pp. 154. *A. Joanin & cⁱᵉ. Paris,* [1906.] 4°. **G. 704. k.**

— The Clown. *See* infra: [Pagliacci.—Vesti la giubba.]

— Cortège de Pulcinella. Petite marche humoristique pour le piano. pp. 7. *Gebrüder Reinecke: Leipzig,* [1903.] fol. **h. 61. g. (6.)**

— Crepusculum. Poema epico in forma di Trilogia storica ... Parte Prima. I Medici. Azione storica in quattro atti, parole e musica di R. Leoncavallo. Riduzione per canto e pianoforte. *E. Sonzogno: Milano,* 1893. 4°. **G. 704. b.**

— Déclaration. Mélodie, paroles de A. Silvestre. *E. Ascherberg & Co.: London,* 1893. fol. **H. 1798. u. (52.)**

— Délivrance!—Deliverance!—Hymn to France. French lyric by G. Rivet. English translation by M. Goldsmith. *J. W. Stern & Co.: New York, etc.,* 1915. fol. **H. 1846. x. (48.)**

— The Dreamy Twilight is falling.—C'est l'heure mystérieuse.— ⟨Serenade.⟩ [Song.] Words & music by R. Leoncavallo, English version by P. Pinkerton. 2 no. [In E and G.] *Ascherberg, Hopwood & Crew: London,* 1912. fol. **H. 1792. s. (14.)**

LEONCAVALLO (Ruggiero)

— For I do love you so. Song, the words by A. de Courville, *etc. Enoch & Sons: London,* 1911. fol. **H. 1792. s. (13.)**

— Gavotte pour piano. *Cary & Co.: London,* 1897. fol. **h. 3282. f. (33.)**

— La Joyeuse. Valse. [P. F.] *J. Williams: London,* [1898.] fol. **h. 3282. f. (34.)**

— La Joyeuse. Valse. [P. F. duet.] *J. Williams: London,* [1901.] 4°. **g. 545. g. (2.)**

— [Lasciati amar.] Yearning for you! Song. Words by Sam Heppner. pp. 5. *Athenæum Music Publishing Co.: London,* [1946.] 4°. **F. 607. yy. (18.)**

— Lied des Bajazzo. *See* infra: [Pagliacci.—Vesti la giubba.]

— Lost Love. Song, written by Mrs. A. Roberts. *Hutchings & Romer: London,* [1884.] fol. **G. 806. k. (65.)**

— Maià. Dramma lirico in tre atti di Paolo de Choudens. (Paul Bérel.) ... Versione ritmica italiana di Angelo Nessi. Canto e piano trascritto dall'autore. pp. 224. *Edoardo Sonzogno: Milano; Choudens: Paris;* [*Paris* printed, 1910.] 4°. **G. 704. i.**

— Malbruk. Fantasia comica medioevale in tre atti di Angelo Nessi. [Vocal score.] pp. 169. *Carisch & Jänichen: Milano,* [1910.] 4°. **G. 704. g.**

Mattinata

— 'Tis the Day ... Song, words adapted from the Italian by E. Teschemacher, *etc. The Gramophone & Typewriter: London,* 1904. fol. **H. 1794. l. (9.)**

— Mattinata. (Frühlingserwachen.) [Song.] Deutscher Text von Max Reichardt. Parole e musica di Ruggiero Leoncavallo. *Ger. & Ital.* pp. 5. *J. D'Andria: Constantinople,* [c. 1910.] fol. **H. 2134. m. (25.)**

— Mattinata (Frühlingserwachen) ... Gesang u. Piano, *etc.* ⟨Deutscher Text von Max Reichardt. Parole e musica di Ruggiero Leoncavallo.⟩ *Ger. & Ital.* pp. 5. *C. M. Roehr: Berlin,* [1912?] fol. **H. 2134. n. (5.)**

— 'Tis the Day ... English words by E. Teschemacher ... Arranged for male voices by H. Johnson. *G. Ricordi & Co.: London,* 1926. 8°. **F. 163. x. (11.)**

— Mattinata. 'Tis the Day. Arranged for Male Voices by H. T. Burleigh, *etc. G. Ricordi & Co.: New York,* 1932. 8°. **F. 163. cc. (45.)**

— Mattinata. 'Tis the Day. For violin and piano ... Arranged by F. R. Barenblatt. *G. Ricordi & Co.: New York, etc.,* 1913. fol. **h. 1612. hh. (11.)**

— I Medici. *See* supra: Crepusculum ... Parte Prima.

— Nights of Italy. Intermezzo for the pianoforte. *Enoch & Sons: London,* 1914. fol. **h. 3284. nn. (45.)**

— No! Pagliaccio non son! *See* infra: [Pagliacci.]

— Nostalgia d'Amore. Love's Longings ... Scored by M. Baron. [P. F. conductor and orchestral parts.] *I. Berlin: N[ew] Y[ork] City,* 1927. 4°. **h. 3210. h. (240.)**

— Nuit de décembre. [Song.] Fragment de Alfred de Musset ... N°. 1. Baryton ou mezzo-soprano. pp. 5. *Choudens: Paris,* [1900?] fol. **H. 2004. f. (16.)**

— On with the Motley. *See* infra: [Pagliacci.—Vesti la giubba.]

LEONCAVALLO (Ruggiero)

Pagliacci

— Pagliacci. ⟨Dramma in due atti.⟩ [Score, with Intermezzo.] pp. 299. x. 128. [*Edoardo Sonzogno: Milano*, 1892.] fol. *The words, in French only, have been added in MS. throughout.* **Hirsch** ii. **513.**

— Pagliacci. Drama in two acts. [Score.] pp. 298. *Broude Bros.: New York*, [c. 1950.] 8°. **F. 1841.**

— Pagliacci. Komödianten (Der Bajazzo). Drama in zwei Akten und einem Prolog. Text vom Komponisten. Deutsche Übertragung von Ernst Märzendorfer. Partitur mit deutschem und italienischem Text herausgegeben von Joachim-Dietrich Link und Ernst Märzendorfer unter Mitarbeit von Reiner Zimmermann. pp. x. 371. *Edition Peters: Leipzig*, [1971.] 4°. **G. 704. l.**

— Pagliacci. Dramma in due atti, parole e musica di R. Leoncavallo. Riduzione per canto e pianoforte. pp. 204. *Edoardo Sonzogno: Milano*, 1892. 4°. **G. 704.**

— [Another copy.] **R. M. 9. d. 18.**

— Pagliacci.—Punchinello ... English adaptation by F. E. Weatherly. Vocal score. pp. 206. *E. Ascherberg & Co.: London*, 1893. 4°. **G. 704. a.**

— Pagliacci ... Piano Score. *E. Ascherberg & Co.: London*, [1893.] 4°. **g. 361. b. (2.)**

— Pagliacci ... Pianoforte Fantasia ... Vocal [selections], *etc.* *G. Newnes: London*, [1913.] fol. *No. 51 of "The Music-Lovers' Library".* **H. 3928.**

— Melodies from Pagliacci ... Arranged by C. Woodhouse. Piano-Conductor [and orchestral parts]. *Hawkes & Son: London*, 1935. 4°. *Hawkes School Series, No. 45.* **h. 3210. h. (514.)**

— Selection ... Arranged by J. Wright. [Military band parts.] *Hawkes & Son: London*, 1909. fol. *Part of "Hawkes & Son's Military Band Edition".* **h. 3211. a. (67.)**

— Selection ... for Violin, Violoncello and Piano. [Arranged by] L. Hintze. *E. Ascherberg & Co.: London*, [1906.] fol. **h. 2852. c. (2.)**

— Selection ... Arranged (for Piano-Accordion Orchestra) by G. S. Mathis. [Parts.] *Ascherberg, Hopwood & Crew: London*, 1937. 8°. **h. 3210. h. (629.)**

— Piano Selection from the ... Film Pagliacci, based on Leoncavallo's ... Opera, *etc.* (Arranged for the Piano by C. Lucas.) *Ascherberg, Hopwood & Crew: London*, 1937. 4°. **g. 1425. (9.)**

— Selection of airs from R. Leoncavallo's opera "Pagliacci". For violin and piano. [Score and part.] 2 pt. *Ascherberg, Hopwood & Crew: London*, [1920?] fol. **h. 1622. a. (8.)**

— [Di fare il segno convenuto.] Ah, yes! 'tis now the Hour entrancing! *etc.* [Scene.] *E. Ascherberg & Co.: London*, 1893. fol. **H. 1798. u. (56.)**

— [Din, don.] The Bell Chorus ... Arranged for Female Voices (Mixed Voices, S.A.T.B.) by P. J. Mansfield. 2 no. *Ascherberg, Hopwood & Crew: London*, 1944. 8°. [*Ascherberg Series of Part Songs. no.* 152, 153.] **F. 1659. a.**

— [E allor perchè.] The Sleep Song ... [Song] in the ... Film Pagliacci, based on the ... Opera ... Words by John Drinkwater. *Ascherberg, Hopwood & Crew: London*, 1937. 4°. **G. 1270. nn. (26.)**

— Pagliacci. Intermezzo. [P. F.] *E. Ascherberg & Co.: London*, 1893. fol. **h. 3282. f. (35.)**

— The Celebrated Minuet, *etc.* [P. F.] pp. 4. *E. Ascherberg & C[o]: London*, [1893.] fol. **h. 1226. a. (7.)**

LEONCAVALLO (Ruggiero)

— No! Pagliaccio non son, *etc.* [Song.] (No Punchinello no more. English words by F. E. Weatherly.) *Ascherberg, Hopwood & Crew: London*, 1928. 4°. **G. 1275. cc. (32.)**

— [O Colombina.] Serenade, *etc.* *E. Ascherberg & Co.: London*, 1893. fol. **H. 1798. u. (55.)**

— [O Colombina.] Paillasse ... Version française de E. Crosti. Sérénade d'Arlequin. [*Paris*,] 1894. 8°. *Supplement to "L'Illustration," No. 2698.* **P. P. 4283. m. (3.)**

— Prologue, *etc.* *E. Ascherberg & Co.: London*, 1893. fol. **H. 1798. u. (53.)**

— Paillasse ... Prologue, *etc.* [*Paris*,] 1902. 8°. *Supplement to "L'Illustration," No. 3121.* **P. P. 4283. m. (3.)**

— Prologue ... in the ... Film Pagliacci, based on Leoncavallo's ... Opera, *etc.* (English adaptation by F. E. Weatherly.) *Ascherberg, Hopwood & Crew: London*, [1937.] 4°. **G. 1270. nn. (24.)**

— The Prologue, *etc.* ⟨Words and music by R. Leoncavallo. English adaptation by Frederic E. Weatherly.⟩ *Eng. & Ital.* pp. 16. *Ascherberg, Hopwood & Crew; Chappell: London*, [1979.] 4°. *Part of "Operatic Elite Series".* **G. 206. m. (17.)**

— Prologue ... Arr. by P. Deiro. (Piano Accordion.) *Accordion Music Publishing Co.: New York*, 1938. 4°. **g. 657. b. (13.)**

— Prologue ... Arranged for the Piano-Accordion by P. Deiro. *Ascherberg, Hopwood & Crew: London*, [1939.] 4°. **g. 657. c. (8.)**

— Prolog. Bearbeitung von Hans Sitt. [Violoncello and P. F. Score and part.] 2 pt. *Adolph Fürstner: Berlin*, [1922.] fol. **h. 4090. r. (6.)**

— [Sei la?] Scena and Duet, "What! thou?" *etc.* *E. Ascherberg & Co.: London*, 1893. fol. **H. 1798. u. (54.)**

— [Stridono lassù.] Ballatella, *etc.* *E. Ascherberg & Co.: London*, 1893. fol. **H. 1798. u. (58.)**

Pagliacci.—Vesti la giubba

— Arioso ... "On with the Motley," *etc.* *E. Ascherberg & Co.: London*, 1893. fol. **H. 1798. u. (57.)**

— On with the Motley ... (Arioso) in the ... Film Pagliacci, based on ... Opera, *etc.* (English words by F. E. Weatherly.) *Ascherberg, Hopwood & Crew: London*, [1937?] 4°. **G. 1270. nn. (25.)**

— Lied des Bajazzo. Mittlere Stimme und Klavier. ⟨Tenor und Klavier. Deutscher Text von Ludwig Hartmann.⟩ *Ger. & Ital.* 2 no. *B. Schott's Söhne: Mainz*, [1977.] 4°. **G. 383. tt. (8.)**

— Arioso. On with the Motley. [Song.] ⟨English words by F. E. Weatherly.⟩ *Eng. & Ital.* pp. 6. *Ascherberg, Hopwood & Crew; Chappell: London*, [1979.] 4°. **G. 206. m. (10.)**

— The Clown ... Chorus for mixed voices. [Words by] G. Purcell ... Leoncavallo-[arranged by R.] Kountz. *M. Witmark & Sons: New York*, 1928. 8°. **F. 585. rr. (26.)**

— On with the Motley ... Arranged for men's voices (T.T.B.B.) by Denis Wright. English words by F. E. Weatherly. [Staff and tonic sol-fa notation.] pp. 6. *Ascherberg, Hopwood & Crew: London*, [1960.] 8°. [*Mortimer Series of modern Part-songs. no.* 519.] **F. 1659. a.**

— Vesti la giubba ... for Violin and Piano. Arranged by R. Halle. Edited by H. Dubin. *G. Lipkin & Son: New York*, 1927. 4°. **g. 505. oo. (12.)**

— [Pagliacci.] *See* Kuhe (W.) Fantasia on Airs from R. Leoncavallo's opera, *etc.* 1893. fol. **h. 755. d. (35*.)**

LEONCAVALLO (Ruggiero)

— Paillasse. *See* supra: [Pagliacci.]

— Pantins Vivants ... Danse de Caractère. [P. F.] *Ries & Erler: Berlin*, [1898.] fol. **g. 605. p. (25.)**

— Pantins vivants ... pour piano. *Schott & Co.: London*, [1924.] fol. **h. 3865. f. (5.)**

— "Pantins vivants." ⟨Minuetto. Conductor [and parts].⟩ 25 pt. *In:* BARWOOD (A. V.) "Canada", *etc.* 1898. fol. [*Boosey's supplemental military Journal. no.* 411.] **h. 1544.**

— "La Reginetta delle rose." Operetta in 3 atti di Forzano ... Spartito per canto e piano. pp. 128. *Casa musicale Lorenzo Sonzogno: Milano*, 1912. 4°. **G. 704. h.**

— Roland. Historisches Drama in vier Akten ... Deutsche Uebersetzung von G. Droescher ... Klavierauszug. *E. Sonzogno: Mailand*, 1904. 4°. **G. 704. f.**

— Rose-way. *See* supra: [Are you there?]

— Sérénade. Transcription pour piano par A. Ruthardt. *Cary & Co.: London*, 1898. fol. **h. 3282. f. (36.)**

— Serenade. (Arr. G. Jones.) Piano Conductor (Harp) [and orchestral parts]. *Cary & Co.: London*, 1935. 4°. **h. 3210. h. (515.)**

— Sérénade française. Mon gentil Pierrot. [Song.] Paroles de E. Collet, *etc.* [*Paris*,] 1906. 8°. *Supplement to "L'Illustration," No.* 3321. **P. P. 4283. m. (3.)**

— The Sleep Song. *See* supra: [Pagliacci.—E allor perchè.]

— Spanish Album. Airs de Ballets espagnols. Suite de Concert pour Pianoforte ... 1. Sevillana. 2. Gitano-Tango. 3. Playeras ancienne. 4. Granadinas. *Ascherberg, Hopwood & Crew: London*, 1911. 4°. **g. 543. xx. (8.)**

— A Summer Idyll. [Song.] Words by C. L. H. *Hutchings & Romer: London*, 1895. fol. **H. 1798. u. (59.)**

— 'Tis the Day. *See* supra: [Mattinata.]

— To-night and Tomorrow. Song, words by F. E. Weatherly. *E. Ascherberg & Co.: London*, 1893. fol. **H. 1798. u. (60.)**

— Valse à la lune. ⟨Sérénade française.⟩ Pour piano. pp. 7. *Choudens: Paris*, [c. 1900.] fol. **h. 61. g. (7.)**

— Valse mélancolique. [P. F.] *J. Williams: London*, 1901. 4°. **g. 603. m. (15.)**

— Vesti la giubba. *See* supra: [Pagliacci.]

— Viva L'America. March. [P. F.] *C. K. Harris: New York, Chicago*, (1906.) fol. **h. 3283. p. (26.)**

— Yearning for you! *See* supra: [Lasciati amar.]

— Zazà. [Opera. Score.] pp. 438. *Casa musicale Sonzogno di Piero Ostali: Milano*, [c. 1920.] fol. *Without titlepage.* **G. 704. j.**

— Zazà. Commedia lirica in quattro atti, parole e musica di R. Leoncavallo, tratta dalla commedia di P. Berton e C. Simon ... Riduzione per Canto e Pianoforte. *E. Sonzogno: Milano*, 1900. 4°. **G. 704. e.**

— Zingari. Dramma lirico in due episodi di E. Cavacchioli e G. Emanuel. Riduzione per canto e pianoforte dell'autore. *Ital. & Ger.* pp. 145. *Edoardo Sonzogno: Milano, etc.*, [1912.] 4°. **F. 1841. a.**

LEONCE

— Léonce, ou le Fils adoptif. Opéra. *See* ISOUARD (N.)

— Leonce und Lena. Lustspiel mit Musik. *See* ZEISL (Erich)

LEONE

— Leone. Drame lyrique. *See* SAMUEL-ROUSSEAU (M.)

— Il Leone. Episodio storico-lirico-drammatico. *See* SOFFREDINI (A.)

LEONE (Francesco B. de)

— Alglala. A Romance of the Mega. An Indian Opera in a prologue and two scenes, text by C. Fanning. Vocal Score. *G. Schirmer: New York*, 1924. 4°. **G. 782. rr. (8.)**

— Cave-Man Stuff. A Prehistoric Operetta in two acts, book and lyrics by F. H. Martens. *G. Schirmer: New York*, 1928. 8°. **E. 1592. cc. (3.)**

— Two Characteristic Pieces for the pianoforte. Opus 27. (No. 1.) Spring dance. (No. 2.) Scotch lullaby. 2 no. *G. Schirmer: New York, Boston*, 1920. 4°. **g. 1127. h. (5.)**

— Compositions for the pianoforte. Op. 26. No. 1. A message from the past. No. 2. Fairies dance. No. 3. Morning breezes. No. 4. Old Dutch dance. 4 no. *A. P. Schmidt Co.: Boston, New York*, 1922. 4°. **g. 1127. h. (6.)**

— Give ear to my Words, O Lord ... [Anthem.] Op. 32. No. 2. *T. Presser Co.: Philadelphia*, 1923. 8°. **F. 281. ww. (33.)**

— In the Days of the Iroquois. An Indian Love Song, words by F. H. Martens. *White-Smith Music Publishing Co.: Boston, etc.*, 1928. 4°. **G. 1270. x. (33.)**

— An Irish Love Song without Words. Op. 33. No. 2. (Pianoforte.) *T. Presser Co.: Philadelphia*, 1922. 4°. **g. 1127. h. (7.)**

— Little Tunes for little People. Twelve recreations ... for the pianoforte. *T. Presser Co.: Philadelphia*, 1919. 4°. **g. 1129. h. (31.)**

— Two Love-Songs ... Words by F. H. Martens. I. Sometime. A song of pensiveness. II. Shadow and gloaming. A song of longing. 2 no. *G. Schirmer: New York*, 1927. 4°. **G. 1275. aa. (7.)**

— Melody of Hope, for the pianoforte. *T. Presser Co.: Philadelphia*, 1919. 4°. **g. 1127. h. (8.)**

— Melody of Hope ... Arr. [for organ] by O. A. Mansfield. *T. Presser Co.: Philadelphia*, 1920. 4°. **g. 1380. h. (5.)**

— Polonaise in B flat minor, for the pianoforte. (Op. 7.) *T. Presser Co.: Philadelphia*, 1922. 4°. **g. 1127. h. (9.)**

— Scherzino for the Piano. (Op. 36.) *G. Schirmer: New York*, 1925. 4°. **g. 1127. dd. (10.)**

— Snowflakes at play. Op. 31. No. 1. (Pianoforte.) *T. Presser Co.: Philadelphia*, 1921. 4°. **g. 1127. h. (10.)**

— Song of May. Chanson du mai. For the pianoforte. (Op. 31. No. 3.) *T. Presser Co.: Philadelphia*, 1920. 4°. **g. 1127. h. (11.)**

— Two Songs of Eventide ... Op. 16. (No. 1.) Twilight. (No. 2.) Lullaby. [Words by L. Harpster.] 2 no. *G. Schirmer: New York*, 1923. 4°. **G. 1275. i. (16.)**

— A Southern Lullaby. Op. 31. No. 2. (Pianoforte.) *T. Presser & Co.: Philadelphia*, 1921. 4°. **g. 1127. h. (12.)**

— Turquoise River. A Song ... Words by F. H. Martens. *G. Schirmer: New York*, 1927. 4°. **G. 1275. aa. (8.)**

LEONE (G.)

— *See* CHAPMAN (A.) England! our England ... Arranged by G. Leone. [1911.] *s. sh.* 8°. **I. 600. d. (205.)**

LEONE (GABRIELE)

— Cantate à voix seule et Symphonie dans le Genre Italien ...
Avec les paroles Italiennes et les parties detachées. [Full score
with French words only.]   *L'Auteur:* [*Paris*, 1750?] fol.
H. 1648. b. (3.)

— A Complete Introduction to the Art of playing the
Mandoline. Containing the most essential Rules ... To which
are added ... Air, Lessons, Duets & Sonatas. Composed and
... arranged ... by Sigʳ Leoni of Naples, Master of the
Mandoline to the Duke de Chartres. pp. 64.   *Longman and
Broderip: London*, [1789.] obl. 4°.
b. 123.

— Methode raisonée pour passer du violon à la mandoline ...
Contenant XXIV. airs dansants à deux mandolines, VI.
menuets avec accompagnement, II. duo, I. sonate avec la
basse, *etc.* [With a frontispiece.] pp. 67.   *Mᵣ Bailleux: Paris*,
[c. 1780.] fol.
g. 1103. c.

— Six sonates pour la mandoline, avec la basse ... Œuvre IIᵉ.
Mis au jour par Mᵣ Bailleux. Gravées par Mᵐᵉ Lobry. [Score.]
pp. 31.   *Chez Mᵣ Bailleux, etc.: Paris, etc.*, [c. 1775.] fol.
g. 1780. yy. (1.)

LEONE (GIUSEPPE)

— Inno Popolare Nazionale di Gloria e di Pace. Omaggio dell'
autore Prof. P. Frese ... col Dies illa a Guglielmo.
A. Caldarola: Napoli, 1918. fol.
R. M. 26. g. 13. (8.)

LEONELLUS

— *See* POWER (Lionel)

LEONESI (UGO)

— Karina. Chanson dansée ... Violon, 'cello et piano, *etc.*
Schott & Co.: London, 1916. fol.
h. 2850. u. (18.)

— Karina. Chanson dansée ... Piano seul.   *Schott & Co.:
London*, 1916. fol.
g. 606. bb. (28.)

— Karina ... Violon et piano.   *Schott & Co.: London*, 1916. fol.
g. 505. ii. (23.)

LEONHARD (JULIUS EMIL)

— Johannes der Täufer. Oratorium in zwei Theilen nach Worten
der heiligen Schrift. Klavierauszug vom Componisten.
Leipzig, [1870?] fol.
G. 482.

— The Stars. *See infra:* [4 Trios for female Voices. No. 3.]

— Zweites Trio, G moll, für Pianoforte, Violine und Violoncell.
Op. 18.   *Leipzig*, [1857.] fol.
h. 2852. e. (1.)

— Four trios for female voices.   *London*, [1846.] fol.
H. 2138. (23.)

— [4 Trios for female Voices. No. 3.] The Stars. [For S.S.A.]
pp. 7.   *J. Curwen & Sons: London*, [1887.] 8°.
[*Choruses for equal Voices. no.* 22.]
E. 861.

— Sieben zweistimmige Volkslieder mit Begleitung des
Pianoforte. Op. 15. (No. 1. Lass rauschen. No. 2.
Frühlingsliebe. No. 3. Wanderlied. No. 4. Sehnsucht. No. 5.
Es weiss und räth es doch keiner. No. 6. Ach in Trauern.
No. 7. Sind wir geschieden.)   *Schubert & Co.: Hamburg &
Leipzig*, [1855?] fol.
H. 2262. b. (4.)

LEONHARDI (EMILE)

— *See* LEONARDI (Emil)

LEONHARDT (   )

— "Manoverian" Quick March. [Military band parts.] 20 pt.
S. A. Chappell: London, [1858.] obl. 8°.
[*Army Journal. no.* 6.]
h. 1562.

LEONHARDT (ANDREAS)   .

— Waffenfreude. Drey original Märsche für das Piano-Forte zu
4 Hände, *etc.* pp. 13.   *Lithographische Anstalt des J. F. Kaiser:
[Graz*, 1820?] obl. fol.
Lithographed throughout.
Hirsch III. 359.

LEONHARDT (GUSTAV)

— *See* FRESCOBALDI (G.) [Primo libro delle canzoni a 1, 2, 3 e 4
voci.] 6 canzoni ... herausgegeben von G. Leonhardt, *etc.*
[1959.] 4°.
g. 409. jj. (7.)

— *See* HACQUART (C.) [Harmonium Parnassia.—Sonata ottava.]
Sonata (1686), für 2 Violinen. Altgambe (Bratsche),
Tenorgambe (Bassgambe oder Cello) und Orgel (Cembalo).
〈Herausgegeben von G. Leonhard,〉 *etc.* [1959.] 4°.
g. 52. a. (1.)

— *See* SCHMELZER (J. H.) [Sacro-profanus concentus musicus
fidium aliorumque instrumentorum.] Zwei Sonaten für
Violine, 2 Altgamben (2 Bratschen), Tenorgambe (Cello) und
Orgel (Cembalo), *etc.* 〈Herausgegeben von G. Leonhardt.〉
[1959.] 4°.
g. 420. jj. (9.)

— *See* SWEELINCK (J. P.) Opera omnia, *etc.* 〈vol. 1. fasc. 1. Edited
by G. Leonhardt.〉 1968, 1957, *etc.* fol.
H. 920. b.

— *See* TURINI (F.) [Madrigali ... con alcune sonate. Libro
primo.] 6 sonate per 2 violini, violoncello e continuo.
〈Herausgegeben von G. Leonhardt.〉 [1957.] 4°.
g. 420. t. (2.)

— *See* YOUNG (William) *Violinist.* [Sonate à 3, 4 e 5, con alcune
allemand, *etc.*] 19 Tanzsätze für 2 Violinen, Gambe (Cello)
und Basso continuo. 〈Herausgegeben von G. Leonhardt.〉
[1962.] 4°.
g. 230. vv. (3.)

LEONI (   ) and **EVERETT** (   )

— Scenes in a Police Court. [Song.] pp. 4.   *M. Witmark & Sons:
New York*, [1893.] fol.
H. 3980. rr. (7.)

LEONI (   ) *of Naples*

— *See* LEONE (Gabriele)

LEONI (A.)

— Il Marinaio. Ballata per canto con accompᵒ. di pianoforte
[begins: "Di lontano riedendo il marinar"], parole di
P. Rotondi.   *Milano*, [1883.] fol.
H. 2836. h. (47.)

LEONI (BENEDETTO)

— Six Lessons for the Harpsichord, *etc.*   *H. Fougt: London*,
[1768?] fol.
h. 528.

LEONI (FRANCO)

— Franco Leoni Album. [Songs.]   *Chappell & Co.: London, etc.*,
[1910.] 4°.
Part of "The Portrait Series".
G. 1121. a. (2.)

— All for the best. Song. The words by C. Bingham.   *Boosey &
Co.: London and New York*, 1893. fol.
H. 3604. (9.)

— At Love's Close. Song, words by F. Hoare. 2 no. [In C and E.]
Chappell & Co.: London and Melbourne, 1905. fol.
H. 3604. a. (18.)

— Autumn Love. Song, words by G. A. Greenland. 2 no. [In B
flat and C.]   *Chappell & Co.: London, etc.*, 1907. fol.
H. 3604. b. (1.)

— Be good. Song, the words by W. Sawyer, *etc.   Boosey & Co.:
London and New York*, 1912. fol.   **H. 3604. b. (8.)**

— The Bells. Vocal Scena for Baritone or Contralto with
Orchestra, words by E. A. Poe.   *Chappell & Co.: London, etc.*,
1908. fol.
H. 3604. b. (2.)

LEONI (Franco)

— Beware of Love. Song, the words by F. E. Weatherly. *Boosey & Co.: London and New York*, 1892. fol. **H. 3604. (1.)**

— The Birth of Morn. Song, words by P. L. Dunbar. 3 no. [E flat, F and G.] *See* infra: Little Songs. No. 1.

— A Birthday Greeting. Song. Words by R. H. U. Bloor. *Chappell & Co.: London*, 1898. fol. **H. 3604. a. (1.)**

— Blue and Gold. Song, words by M. Earle, *etc.* 2 no. [In C and E flat.] *Chappell & Co.: London, etc.*, 1908. fol. **H. 3604. b. (3.)**

— The Brownies. Song, the words by F. E. Weatherly. *Boosey & Co.: London and New York*, 1912. fol. **H. 3604. b. (9.)**

— The Brownies. Part Song for Two Voices ... Arr. by A. Samuelson. *Boosey, Hawkes, Belwin: New York*, [1936.] 8°. **E. 263. j. (15.)**

— A Butterfly.—Papillon.—Song, French words by F. Rizzelli, English translation by M. P. 2 no. [In F and G.] *Chappell & Co.: London, etc.*, 1906. fol. **H. 3604. a. (19.)**

— The Clock. [Part-song.] For Women's Voices 4 Parts, words and music by F. Leoni. *Stainer & Bell: London*, 1938. 8°. *Part Songs, No.* 288. **F. 1137. a.**

— Coolan Dhu. Song, words by F. E. Weatherly. 3 no. [In D minor, E minor, and F minor.] *Chappell & Co.: London and Melbourne*, 1906. fol. **H. 3604. a. (20.)**

— Coolan Dhu. Three part Chorus or Trio, S.S.A. Arranged by W. Stickles, *etc. Chappell & Co.: New York*, 1937. 8°. **F. 217. h. (45.)**

— Cupid, the vagabond Boy. Song. Words by M. Ambient. 3 no. [In F, G and A.] *Chappell & Co.: London*, 1895. fol. **H. 3604. (10.)**

— Dame Nature. [Song.] Verse by E. Kook. *J. Church Co.: Cincinnati, etc.*, 1920. 4°. **H. 3604. b. (10.)**

— The Days gone by. Song. Words by J. W. Riley. *Chappell & Co.: London*, [1897.] fol. **H. 3604. (11.)**

— Dear is my little native Vale. Vocal Duet. Words by S. Rogers. *Chappell & Co.: London*, 1899. fol. **H. 3604. a. (2.)**

— The Drummer Boy. Song, the words by W. B. Rands. *Boosey & Co.: London and New York*, 1922. 4°. **G. 1270. f. (16.)**

— Earth's Wedding Ring. Song, words by B. Taylor. *Chappell & Co.: London*, 1901. fol. **H. 3604. a. (10.)**

— The Enchanted Hour. *See* infra: [Fairy Dreams.]

— The Eve of Angels' Day. Song, the words by F. E. Weatherly. *Boosey & Co.: London and New York*, 1892. fol. **H. 3604. (2.)**

— Fairy Dreams. Song Cycle for four voices, words by E. Teschemacher. *Chappell & Co.: London and Melbourne*, 1904. 4°. **G. 383. l. (7.)**

— [Fairy Dreams.] The Enchanted Hour. Duet, *etc. Chappell & Co.: London and Melbourne*, 1905. fol. **H. 3604. a. (21.)**

— [Fairy Dreams.] The Rose-Fairies. Song, *etc. Chappell & Co.: London and Melbourne*, (1905.) fol. **H. 3604. a. (22.)**

— Fall in! Song, words by F. E. Weatherly. *Chappell & Co.: London*, 1942. 4°. **F. 607. w. (20.)**

— A Farewell. Vocal Duet. Words by Lord Tennyson. *Chappell & Co.: London*, 1899. fol. **H. 3604. a. (3.)**

— The Gate of Life. Dramatic Cantata for Soprano, Tenor or Bass Soli, Chorus and orchestra, the verse ... by S. Wensley. *Novello, Ewer and Co.: London & New York*, 1898. 8°. **F. 1274. m. (4.)**

LEONI (Franco)

— The Gate of Life ... Translated into Tonic Sol-fa Notation by W. G. McNaught. *Novello & Co.: London*, 1897. 4°. **B. 415. (1.)**

— The Gate of Life, *etc.* [String parts.] *Novello & Co.: London*, 1898. fol. **h. 1508. e. (15.)**

— [The Gate of Life.] Weary Pilgrims, know no Fear ... Anthem for All Saints' Day or general use. The Words ... by S. Wensley. 1898. *See* NOVELLO AND CO. Novello's Collection of Anthems, *etc.* No. 610. [1876, *etc.*] 8°. **E. 618. a.**

— [The Gate of Life.] Weary Pilgrims know no Fear ... Anthem, *etc.* 1898. *See* NOVELLO AND CO. Novello's Tonic Sol-fa Series. No. 1072. [1876, *etc.*] 4°. **B. 885.**

— The Gates of Gladness. Song, words by J. A. McDonald. *Leonard & Co.: London*, 1922. fol. **H. 1860. e. (1.)**

— Golden Lilies. Song. Words by M. Ambient. 3 no. [In B flat, C, and D.] *Chappell & Co.: London*, 1894. fol. **H. 3604. (12.)**

— Golgotha. Words from the text of the New Testament narrated in music. (For soli, chorus and orchestra.) [Vocal score.] pp. xi. 123. *Chappell & Co.: London*, [1910.] 4°. **F. 1257. mm. (2.)**

— Haymaking. *See* infra: Four Vocal Duets. No. 4.

— Hey nonny no! Song. Words by G. Hubi-Hewcombe. 2 no. [In D minor and F minor.] *Chappell & Co.: London*, 1898. fol. **H. 3604. a. (4.)**

— Home of my Heart. Song. Words by A. Valdemar. 2 no. [In E flat and F.] *Chappell and Co.: London*, 1894. fol. **H. 3604. (13.)**

— The Home-Coming of the Unknown Warrior ... [song, words by] J. Kendall, *etc. J. H. Larway: London*, 1921. fol. **H. 1846. jj. (7.)**

— Hop-i-ty hop! For Men's Voices, words and music by F. Leoni. *Stainer & Bell: London*, 1938. 8°. *Male Voice Choir Library, No.* 209. **F. 1137. c.**

— Ib and Little Christina. A Picture in three Panels, written by B. Hood. Vocal Score. *Chappell & Co.: London*, 1901. 4°. **F. 690. j. (3.)**

— In Sympathy. Song, words by H. Blinn. 3 no. [In C, D and E.] *Chappell & Co.: London*, [1902.] fol. **H. 3604. a. (12.)**

— Jeune Fillette. Love while you may.—Chanson du XVIIIᵉ siècle.—English words by P. Pinkerton. 2 no. [In G and A.] *See* infra: Little Songs. No. 3.

— The Lark. Song, the words by G. H. Newcombe. *Boosey & Co.: London and New York*, 1892. fol. **H. 3604. (3.)**

— The Leaves and the Wind. [Song.] Words by G. Cooper. *See* infra: F. Leoni's Series of Recital Songs. No. 2.

— Leaves on the River. Song, words by H. Simpson. 2 no. [In A and C.] *Chappell & Co.: London, etc.*, 1907. fol. **H. 3604. b. (4.)**

— Little Barefoot. Song, words by C. Bingham, *etc.* 2 no. [In C and D.] *Chappell & Co.: London, etc.*, 1907. fol. **H. 3604. b. (5.)**

— Little Bo-Peep. Song. Words by E. Teschemacher. 2 no. [In D minor and E minor.] *Chappell & Co.: London*, 1900. fol. **H. 3604. a. (5.)**

— A Little China Figure. Song, *etc.* [Words by] (E. Lindsay.) *G. Schirmer: New York*, 1935. 4°. **G. 1275. pp. (10.)**

LEONI (FRANCO)

— A Little China Figure. For Three-Part Chorus of Women's Voices with Piano Accompaniment ... Arranged by Jeffrey Marlowe. pp. 12. *G. Schirmer: New York*, 1945. 8°.
F. 217. k. (34.)

— A Little Garden of Melodies for two little people, *etc.* [P. F. duets.] 5 no. *G. Schirmer: New York, Boston*, 1918. 4°.
g. 1129. k. (15.)

— A Little Prayer. Song, words by E. Teschemacher. 2 no. [In E and G.] *Chappell & Co.: London and Melbourne*, 1904. fol.
H. 3604. a. (13.)

— Little Songs ... 1. The Birth of Morn ... 2. The Wedding Day ... 3. Jeune fillette. (Love while you may.) ⟨4. The Passing Cloud. 5. The Retort.⟩ no. 1–4. *Chappell & Co.: London*, 1902, 03. fol.
Imperfect; wanting no. 5. **H. 3504. a. (16.)**

— [Little Songs. No. 1.] The Birth of the Morn ... Arr. for female Quartett by C. Lucas. *See* LUCAS (C.) Gray Days ... The Birth of the Morn, *etc.* (1914.) 8°. **F. 328. v. (24.)**

— [Little Songs. No. 1.] The Birth of Morn. Arr for Male Quartett by C. Lucas, *etc. See* LUCAS (C.) Gray Days ... The Birth of Morn, *etc.* (1914.) 8°. **F. 163. r. (20.)**

— Two Little Thoughts for violin and piano. 1. Moonbeam. 2. Sunbeam. 2 no. *G. Schirmer: New York, Boston*, 1918. 4°.
g. 500. a. (25.)

— Long Time ago. Songs. No. 1. Poor robin ... 2. The little bird. Walter de la Mare. 3. Long time ago. E. Prentiss. 4. Wishing. W. Allingham. *J. H. Larway: London*, 1922. 4°.
G. 1270. f. (17.)

— Love's Awakening. Song, words by E. Teschemacher. *Chappell & Co.: London*, 1903. fol. **H. 3604. a. (14.)**

— Love's Despair. Song, the words by J. S. Binnie, *etc. Boosey & Co.: London and New York*, 1892. fol. **H. 3604. (5.)**

— Love's Pathway. Song. Words by F. E. Weatherly. *Chappell & Co.: London*, 1895. fol. **H. 3604. (14.)**

— Love's Silent Song. Words by M. Ambient. *Chappell & Co.: London*, 1897. fol. **H. 3604. (15.)**

— The Lovers' Lullaby. Song, the words by M. Ambient. *Boosey & Co.: London and New York*, 1892. fol.
H. 3604. (4.)

— The May Queen's Requiem. *See infra:* Four Vocal Duets. No. 3.

— Memory. Song ... words by B. C. Stephenson. *Chappell & Co.: London*, [1891.] fol. **H. 3604. (6.)**

— Mirage. [Song.] Words by P. Pinkerton. *See infra:* F. Leoni's Series of Recital Songs. No. 3.

— My Shadow. Song, words by R. L. Stevenson. 3 no. [In E, F and G.] *Chappell & Co.: London, etc.*, 1908. fol.
H. 3604. b. (6.)

— Nursery Rhymes without words. Ten little pieces for piano. *G. Schirmer: New York, Boston*, 1918. 4°. **g. 1129. k. (16.)**

— L'Oracolo. Un Atto in prosa musicale dal "The Cat and the Cherub" di C. B. Fernald, di C. Zanoni. *Chappell & Co.: London and Melbourne*, 1905. fol. **G. 1062.**

— L'Oracolo. The Oracle. The Cat and the Cherub. A Music Drama in one act by C. B. Fernald, by C. Zanoni. English translation by C. Lucas. New edition. *Chappell & Co.: London, etc.*, 1919. 4°. **G. 1062. a.**

— L'Oracolo. Suite. Arranged for piano by Ward-Stephens. *Chappell & Co.: London, etc.*, 1918. fol. **h. 3284. nn. (47.)**

LEONI (FRANCO)

— The Passing Cloud. Song, words by P. L. Dunbar. 3 no. [In C, D and E.] *See supra:* Little Songs. No. 4.

— Pastorella. [Unison song.] Words and music by F. Leoni. *Stainer & Bell: London*, 1938. 8°.
Unison Songs, No. 183. **F. 1137. e.**

— Two Poems ... for ... voice. [Words by E. Lockton. No. 1.] The vesper bells. [No. 2.] The secret of the stars. 2 no. *G. Schirmer: New York*, 1925. 4°. **G. 1275. s. (2.)**

— [The Prayer of the Sword.] Reminiscences of the Music from J. B. Fagan's Play, The Prayer of the Sword. [P. F.] *Chappell & Co.: London and Melbourne*, 1905. 4°. **g. 603. o. (6.)**

— [The Prayer of the Sword.] Reminiscences of the Music from James Bernard Fagan's Play The Prayer of the Sword. ⟨Full orchestra.—Small orchestra.⟩ [Parts.] 2 no. *Chappell & Co.: London*, [1906.] 4°.
[*Chappell & Co.'s Operatic and popular Selections for Orchestra by various Composers. no.* 73.] **f. 424.**

— [The Prayer of the Sword.] Serenade from J. B. Fagan's Play, "The Prayer of the Sword". *Chappell & Co.: London and Melbourne*, 1904. fol. **H. 3604. a. (23.)**

— Prière d'Amour for Violin with Pianoforte accompaniment. *Chappell & Co.: London*, [1896.] fol. **h. 1612. c. (33.)**

— Princess of the sunny Smile. Song, words by H. Simpson, *etc.* 2 no. [In E minor and G minor.] *Chappell & Co.: London, etc.*, 1907. fol. **H. 3604. b. (7.)**

— Rip van Winkle. A romantic opera in three acts. (Founded upon Washington Irving's romance.) Written by William Akerman ... Vocal score. pp. 259. *G. Ricordi & Co.: Milan, etc.*, [1897.] 4°. **F. 1257. mm. (1.)**

— The Roman Sentinel. Song. Words by G. A. Binnie. 3 no. [In C minor, D minor and F minor.] *R. Cocks and Co.: London*, 1894. fol. **H. 3604. (16.)**

— The Rose-Fairies. *See supra:* [Fairy Dreams.]

— Roses of Dawn. Song, the words by H. Brasted. *Boosey & Co.: London and New York*, 1922. 4°. **G. 1270. f. (18.)**

— Sadness and Passion. Song. The words by M. Ambient. *Boosey & Co.: London & New York*, 1896. fol.
H. 3604. (17.)

— Sand Castles ... [Song, words by] W. Graham Robertson. *J. H. Larway: London*, 1922. fol. **H. 1846. jj. (8.)**

— Sea Breezes. Song. Words by E. Teschemacher. 2 no. [In B♭ and C.] *Chappell & Co.: London*, 1898. fol. **H. 3604. a. (6.)**

— The Seagulls' Lullaby. Duet, words from "The Story of an Excursion" by F. A. Minnitt. *A. Weekes & Co.: London*, 1922. fol. **H. 1846. jj. (9.)**

— F. Leoni's Series of Recital Songs. 1. Tranquil Night. Author Paul Laurence Dunbar ... 2. The Leaves and the Wind. George Cooper ... 3. Mirage. Percy Pinkerton. 3 no. *Boosey & Co.: London, New York*, [1903.] fol. **H. 3604. a. (17.)**

— [F. Leoni's Series of Recital Songs. No. 2.] The Leaves and the Wind. Unison Song, *etc. Boosey & Co.: London*, 1938. 8°.
Songs for Schools, No. 52. **F. 197. h.**

— Six Short Dances of medium difficulty. I. Pavane. II. A goblin's antics. III. In the shade. IV. Impish frolic. V. Eastern flower dance. VI. A savage dance. 6 no. *G. Schirmer: New York, Boston*, 1918. 4°. **g. 1129. k. (17.)**

— The Skylark ... [Song, words by] J. Hogg. *J. H. Larway: London*, 1922. fol. **H. 1846. jj. (10.)**

— The Song of my Life. Words by E. Teschemacher. 3 no. [In F, G and A.] *Chappell & Co.: London*, 1897. fol.
H. 3604. (18.)

LEONI (Franco)

— The Song of Saba. A Syrian Love Song. The Words by M. Ambient. *Boosey & Co.: London and New York*, 1894. fol.
H. 3604. (19.)

— A Song of the Cruise. [Song.] Words by J. W. Riley. 3 no. [In C, D and F.] *Chappell & Co.: London*, 1900. fol.
H. 3604. a. (7.)

— Three Songs ... [No. 1.] Orange blossoms. [Words by W. W. Duncan.] [No. 2.] The Roses of dawn. [Words by J. F. Powell.] [No. 3.] Tally-ho! [Words by C. P. Raydon.] 3 no. *G. Schirmer: New York, Boston*, 1919. 4°.
G. 390. u. (4.)

— Songs of the happy Piper. Five little Songs. No. 1. The happy piper. Words, W. Blake. 2. The pobble who has no toes. E. Lear. 3. Jenny Wren ... 4. Tricks of fortune. C. E. Benham. 5. Twinkle, twinkle, little star. A. J. Taylor. *J. H. Larway: London*, 1923. 4°.
G. 1270. f. (19.)

— 'Specially Jim. Song, words by B. Morgan. 2 no. [In D and E.] *Chappell & Co.: London*, 1903. fol.
H. 3604. a. (15.)

— A Spring Song. Words by W. Akerman. 3 no. [In D, F and G.] *Chappell and Co.: London*, 1894. fol.
H. 3604. (21.)

— Spring's Awakening. [Song.] Words by M. Ambient. *Houghton & Co.: London*, 1897. fol.
H. 3604. (20.)

— Stars. Song. Words by M. Nepean. 3 no. [In C, D and F.] *R. Cocks & Co.: London*, 1894. fol.
H. 3604. (22.)

— Sunbeam. [Song.] Verse by F. Ellis. *J. Church Co.: Cincinnati, etc.*, 1920. 4°.
H. 3604. b. (11.)

— Sweet Hour of Love. Song. Words by M. Ambient. *Chappell & Co.: London*, 1897. fol.
H. 3604. (23.)

— Sweet Vision of Delight. Song, words by S. J. Reilly. 2 no. [In E flat and G.] *Chappell & Co.: London*, [1891.] fol.
H. 3604. (7.)

— Tittle Tattle. *See* infra: Four Vocal Duets. No. 2.

— Too Late. Rondeau, the words by A. Wilkins. *Boosey & Co.: London and New York*, 1892. fol.
H. 3604. (8.)

— Tranquil Night. [Song.] Words by P. L. Dunbar. *See* supra: F. Leoni's Series of Recital Songs. No. 1.

— The Two Poets. Song, with Organ Accompaniment ad lib. Words by W. Akerman. 2 no. [In D and F.] *Chappell & Co.: London*, (1895.) fol.
H. 3604. (24.)

— Vanity Fair. *See* infra: Four Vocal Duets. No. 1.

— Vespers. Song ... (Words and music) by F. Leoni. *G. Schirmer: New York*, 1935. 4°.
G. 1275. pp. (11.)

— Vesuvius. Song, *etc.* (Words and music by F. Leoni.) *H. Flammer: New York*, 1937. 4°.
G. 1275. ss. (41.)

— Vesuvius. For Four-part Chorus of Men's Voices ... Arranged by W. Riegger. *H. Flammer: New York*, 1937. 8°.
F. 163. gg. (39.)

— Four vocal Duets, words by M. Ambient, illustrations by C. Hammond. *R. Cocks & Co.: London*, 1894. 4°.
G. 805. v. (16.)

— Four Vocal Duets. Words by M. Ambient. 4 no. *R. Cocks & Co.: London*, 1894. fol.
H. 3604. (25.)

— The Waggoner's Wedding. Song. Words by F. E. Weatherly. *Chappell & Co.: London*, 1900. fol.
H. 3604. a. (8.)

— Water Colours. Lyric pieces for pianoforte, *etc. Schott & Co.: London*, 1922. 4°.
g. 1127. h. (13.)

— Weary Pilgrims, know no Fear. *See* supra: [The Gate of Life.]

— The Wedding Day. Song, words by E. C. Stedman. 2 no. [In F and A flat.] *See* supra: Little Songs. No. 2.

LEONI (Franco)

— When he comes Home. Song, words from the French by M. Maeterlinck, English version by F. G. Bowles. *Chappell & Co.: London and Melbourne*, 1906. fol.
H. 3604. a. (24.)

— Whence? Song, words by D. L. A. Jephson. *Chappell & Co.: London*, 1902. fol.
H. 3604. a. (11.)

— Where Leaf-land lies. [Song.] Words by W. Akerman. *Chappell & Co.: London*, [1896.] fol.
H. 3604. (26.)

— The Whirligig of Time. Song. Words by M. Ambient. 3 no. [In E, G and A.] *Chappell & Co.: London*, 1895. fol.
H. 3604. (27.)

— The Wildflower. Song. The Words by C. Bingham. *Boosey & Co.: London*, 1893. fol.
H. 3604. (28.)

— The Wind, ho! Song. Words by F. E. Weatherly. 3 no. [In C, D and E.] *Chappell & Co.: London*, 1894. fol.
H. 3604. (29.)

— The Young Green. Song. Words by W. Akerman. *Chappell & Co.: London*, 1898. fol.
H. 3604. a. (9.)

LÉONI (Henri)

— *See* SQUIRE (W. H.) [Sérénade pour le Violoncelle.] Thine Eyes. Song, adapted ... by H. Léoni, *etc.* 1901. fol.
G. 807. u. (26.)

— *See* SQUIRE (W. H.) [Sérénade pour le Violoncelle.] Votre regard ... Adaptation et paroles de H. Léoni. 1901. fol.
G. 807. u. (27.)

LEONI (Leon)

— Il Primo Libro de Madrigali a Cinque Voci, *etc.* Canto. (Alto.) (Tenore.) (Basso.) 4 pt. *Appresso Angelo Gardano: Venetia*, 1588. obl. 4°.
A. 250.

— Il Terzo Libro de Madrigali a Cinque Voci, *etc.* Tenore. *Appresso Ricciardo Amadino: Venetia*, 1595. obl. 4°.
A. 250. a.

LÉONI (Léon) *Dance composer*

— L'Avalanche galop. [P. F.] *London*, [1864.] fol.
h. 1460. v. (27.)

— La Belle Italienne polka. [P. F.] *London*, [1864.] fol.
h. 1460. v. (28.)

— La Créole, polka. [P. F.] *London*, [1859.] fol. **h. 914. (1.)**

— Douce Alice valses sur des motifs de Zampa d'Hérold. [P. F.] *London*, [1864.] fol. **h. 1460. v. (29.)**

— Les Enfans de Paris quadrille pour le Piano. *London*, [1864.] fol. **h. 1460. v. (32.)**

— La Finlandaise valses. [P. F.] *London*, [1864.] fol.
h. 1460. v. (31.)

— La malle poste galop. [P. F.] *London*, [1859.] fol.
h. 914.(2.)

— Pluie de Mai, valse. [P. F.] *London*, [1859.] fol. **h. 914. (3.)**

— Léoni's Pluie de Mai valses, arranged as a pianoforte duet by E. F. Rimbault. *London*, [1860.] fol. **h. 486. (19.)**

— Polka de Berlin, pour le piano. *London*, [1859.] fol.
h. 914. (4.)

— Les premières roses, suite de valses. [P. F.] *London*, [1859.] fol. **h. 914. (5.)**

— Quadrille Napolitain, *etc.* [P. F.] *London*, [1859.] fol.
h. 914. (6.)

LÉONI (LÉON) *Dance composer*

— Léoni's Quadrille Napolitain ... arranged as a pianoforte duet by E. F. Rimbault. *London*, [1860.] fol. **h. 486. (20.)**

— St. Anthony polka pour le Piano. *London*, [1864.] fol. **h. 1460. v. (31.)**

LEONIDAS

— Leonidas. [Cantata.] *See* BRUCH (M. C. F.)

— Leonidas. Two-part Song. *See* SHAW (M. F.)

LÉONIE

— Léonie. Mélodie. *See* RADOUX (J. T.) Vingt Mélodies, *etc.* No. 7.

LÉONIN

— Magnus liber organi de gradali et antiphonario. Wolfenbüttel 677, olim Helmstadt 628. [Transcribed by William G. Waite.] pp. 254. *In:* WAITE (William G.) The Rhythm of Twelfth-Century Polyphony, *etc.* 1954. 8°. [*Yale Studies in the History of Music.* vol. 2.] **Ac. 2692. ma/20.**

— *See* WOLFENBÜTTEL. — *Biblioteca Augusta.* An Old St. Andrews Music Book (Cod. Helmst. 628). Published in facsimile, *etc.* [Including music by Léonin and Pérotin.] 1931. 8°. [*St. Andrews University Publications. no.* 30.] **Ac. 1489.**

LÉONNEC (JANIK)

— Sept vieilles chansons recueillies et chantées par Mademoiselle Janik Léonnec. Harmonisées par Jean Messager. Bois gravés par Maurice Savin. *Éditions Girard et Bunino: Paris*, [1926.] 4°. **F. 1199. tt. (4.)**

LEONOR

— Leonor. [Part-song.] *See* STEVENSON (F.)

LEONOR (V.)

— The Village Maidens Dance. Waltz Song. *W. Czerny: London*, [1882.] fol. **H. 1788. v. (42.)**

LEONORA

— Leonora. Song. *See* FISCHER (Fred)

— Leonora. [Cantata.] *See* MACFARREN (*Sir* G. A.)

— Leonora. Song. *See* MAYNARD (W.) *pseud.*

— Leonora. Melodramma. *See* MERCADANTE (S.)

— Leonora. Ballad. *See* NUNAN (Michael J.)

— Leonora. Oper. *See* PAER (F.)

— Leonora. Ballad. *See* REICHARDT (J. F.)

— Leonora. Song. *See* STANHAMMER (S.)

— Leonora. Song. *See* STIRLING (E.)

— Leonora. Serenade. *See* SYKES (C. T.)

— Leonora 40/45. Opera. *See* LIEBERMANN (R.)

— Leonora, the Miller's Daughter. [Song.] *See* MAYWOOD (George)

LEONORE

— Leonore. Opera. *See* BEETHOVEN (L. van)

— Léonore, ou l'Amour conjugal. [Opera.] *See* GAVEAUX (P.)

LEONORE

— Leonore. Ballad. *See* MILLARD (H.)

— Léonore. Song. *See* TROTÈRE (H.)

— Leonore. Ballad. *See* WEIGL (J.)

— Léonore d'Urgel. Romance. *See* P., D. L.

— Léonore et Félix, ou C'est la même. Opéra comique. *See* BENOIST (F.)

LEONOVA (MARIA FEDOROVNA)

— Симфонические произведения Р. М. Глиэра (симфонии, одночастные сочинения, коицерты). Справочник-путеводитель. pp. 114. *Советский композитор: Москва*, 1962. 8°. **e. 1. vv.**

LEONT'EV (N.) and DUBUC (ALEKSANDR IVANOVICH)

— Dreigespann. Moskowisches Zigeunerlied, *etc. See* SAMMLUNG. Sammlung Russischer Romanzen, *etc.* No. 67. [1860?–80?] fol. **H. 2171.**

LEONTIEFF (N.)

— *See* LEONT'EV.

LEONTOVICH (MIKOLA DMITROVICH)

— Хорові твори. Упорядкував М. Вериківський. [With a portrait.] pp. 232. *Державне видаиництво Образотворчого мистецтва і музичної літератури УРСР: Київ*, 1961. 4°. **G. 560. nn.**

— Two Ukrainian Songs. ⟨[No. 1.] Beyond the rocky Hills. [No. 2.] Folk Tune. Edited by Michael Fredericks. Arr. for piano by I. Berkovich.⟩ *Leeds Music Corporation: New York*, [1955.] 4°. **g. 1128. v. (17.)**

LÉONY (ROSA)

— Ah! si vous saviez comme on pleure. [Song.] Poésie de Sully-Prudhomme. *Novello, Ewer & Co.: London & New York*, [1895.] fol. **G. 805. aa. (21.)**

LEOPARDI

— Leopardi Fragments. Cantata. *See* DAVIES (Peter M.)

— Leopardi morente. Canto. *See* GAMMIERI (E.)

LEOPARDI (VENANTIO)

— Disperato amante. Cantata, *etc.* [*H. Champion: Paris*, 1913.] 8°.
Pp. 7–12 of the Musical Appendix to H. Prunières' "L'Opéra italien en France avant Lulli". **Ac. 338.**

LEOPOLD I., *Emperor of Germany*

— Suite. For alto-recorder and piano accompaniment ... Edited by Franz Wasner. [Score and part.] 2 pt. *G. Schirmer: New York*, [1956.] 4°. **g. 109. n. (7.)**

— Suite. For treble-recorder with piano accompaniment ... Edited by Franz Wasner. [Score and part.] 2 pt. *Chappell & Co.: London*, [1956.] 4°. **g. 109. k. (2.)**

— *See* FERDINAND III., *Emperor of Germany.* Musikalische Werke der Kaiser Ferdinand III., Leopold I. und Joseph I., *etc.* [1892, *etc.*] fol. **I. 160.**

LEOPOLD I., *King of the Belgians*

— Andenken. [Song.] Paroles de Matthisson ... Composée en 1811. [*Brussels?* 1840?] fol. **R. M. 14. b. 6. (16.)**

LEOPOLD GEORGE DUNCAN ALBERT, *Duke of Albany*

— Dir allein. Song [begins: "I sat upon the purple hill"]. Words by H. Gardner. *London,* [1879.] fol. **H. 1783. o. (47.)**

— [A reissue.] Dir allein. Song, words by Herbert Gardner. *Lamborn Cock: London,* [c. 1880.] fol. **R. M. 14. b. 10. (14.)**

— Fontainebleau. Valse. [P. F.] *Chappell and Co.: London,* [1883.] fol. **R. M. 25. i. 1. (5.)**

— Fontainebleau. Waltz. (Fontainebleau. . . . Arranged as a duet by H. Tinney.) 2 no. *Chappell & Co.: London,* [1883.] fol. **h. 975. v. (12.)**

— Fontainebleau Waltz. [Orchestral parts.] *See* CHAPPELL AND CO. Popular Quadrilles, *etc.* No. 146. [1883.] 8°. **e. 249.**

— Valse.—"Fontainebleau" . . . Arranged [for military band] by W. Winterbottom. [Parts.] 26 pt. *S. A. Chappell: London,* [1883.] fol. [*Army Journal. no.* 155.] **h. 1562.**

LEOPOLD (BERNARDO)

— La Belle Fleur mazurka pour Piano. pp. 5. *Swan & Pentland: London,* [1874.] fol. **h. 3110. (8.)**

— Home Recreations, a collection of popular melodies . . . arranged for the Pianoforte. 25 no. pp. 5. *Swan & Pentland: Glasgow,* [1869.] fol. **h. 3110. (1.)**

— The Irresistible quadrille. [P. F.] pp. 8. *Hutchings & Romer, etc.: London, etc.,* [1869.] fol. **h. 3110. (2.)**

— The Operatic Gem quadrilles. [P. F.] pp. 7. *Swan & Pentland: Glasgow,* [1869.] fol. **h. 3110. (3.)**

— Popular Germany melody, known as "The Mill," arranged with variations. [P. F.] pp. 4. *Swan & Pentland: Glasgow,* [1869.] fol. **h. 3110. (4.)**

— The Teviotdale quadrilles. [P. F.] pp. 5. *Swan & Pentland: Glasgow,* [1869.] fol. **h. 3110. (5.)**

— The Tourist's galop. [P. F.] pp. 5. *Swan & Pentland, etc.: Glasgow, etc.,* [1869.] fol. **h. 3110. (6.)**

— The Tweedale quadrilles. [P. F.] pp. 5. *Swan & Pentland: Glasgow,* [1869.] fol. **h. 3110. (7.)**

— Waltzes by classical Composers . . . Edited by B. Leopold. no. 3, 4, 7. *Swan & Pentland: London,* [c. 1875, 80.] fol. *Imperfect; wanting no.* 1, 2, 5, 6. *No.* 4, 7 *bear the imprint of Swan & C*ⁱ. **h. 3110. a.**

— *See* CHOPIN (F. F.) Nocturnes. Op. 9, N° 2 . . . and Op. 32, ⟨No. 1,⟩ *etc.* ⟨Edited by B. Leopold.⟩ [c. 1875.] fol. **h. 471. bb. (2.)**

— *See* DUSSEK (Jan L.) Sonata in B flat. Op. 24. ⟨Edited by B. Leopold.⟩ [c. 1885.] fol. **h. 751. m. (6.)**

— *See* SCHUBERT (Franz P.) Impromptu in B flat. Op. 142. ⟨N° 3. Edited by B. Leopold.⟩ [1877?] fol. **h. 3183. q. (2.)**

LEOPOLD (BOHUSLAV)

— *See* DVOŘÁK (A.) [Collections.] Op. 55. No. 4. & Op. 82. No. 1. Zwei Lieder. Als die alte Mutter. Lasst mich allein . . . Arr: B. Leopold. [1940.] 4°. **h. 3210. h. (765.)**

— *See* DVOŘÁK (A.) Polonaise Es dur, *etc.* ⟨Bearbeitet von B. Leopold.⟩ [P. F.] [1956.] 4°. **g. 1160. c. (17.)**

— *See* DVOŘÁK (A.) Polonaise in E flat. ⟨Violin & piano. Bearbeitet von B. Leopold.⟩ [1949.] 4°. **g. 1160. b. (10.)**

— *See* DVOŘÁK (A.) [Slavische Tänze. Op. 46. No. 8.] Slovanský tanec č. 8. Slavonic Dance No. 8 . . . New arrangement by B. Leopold based on the original score, *etc.* [1955.] 4°. **g. 1160. e. (1.)**

LEOPOLD (BOHUSLAV)

— *See* DVOŘÁK (A.) [Slavische Tänze. Op. 72. No. 1.] Slovanzký tanec č. 9. Slavonic Dance No. 9, *etc.* ⟨New arrangement by B. Leopold based on the original score.⟩ [1955.] 4°. **g. 1160. e. (2.)**

— *See* DVOŘÁK (A.) [Slavische Tänze. Op. 72. No. 3.] Slovanský tanec č. 11. Slavonic Dance No. 11, *etc.* ⟨New arrangement by B. Leopold based on the original score.⟩ [1955.] 4°. **g. 1160. e. (3.)**

— *See* DVOŘÁK (A.) [Slavische Tänze. Op. 72. No. 4.] Slovanský tanec č. 12. Slavonic Dance No. 12, *etc.* ⟨New arrangement by B. Leopold based on the original score.⟩ [1955.] 4°. **g. 1160. e. (4.)**

— *See* DVOŘÁK (A.) [Slavische Tänze. Op. 72. No. 5.] Slovanský tanec č. 13. Slavonic Dance No. 13, *etc.* ⟨New arrangement by B. Leopold based on the original score.⟩ [1955.] 4°. **g. 1160. e. (5.)**

— *See* DVOŘÁK (A.) [Slavische Tänze. Op. 72. No. 6.] Slovanský tanec č. 14. Slavonic Dance No. 14, *etc.* ⟨New arrangement by B. Leopold based on the original score.⟩ [1955.] 4°. **g. 1160. e. (6.)**

— *See* DVOŘÁK (A.) [Slavische Tänze. Op. 72. No. 7.] Slovanský tanec č. 15. Slavonic Dance No. 15 . . . New arrangement by B. Leopold based on the original score, *etc.* [1955.] 4°. **g. 1160. e. (7.)**

— *See* DVOŘÁK (A.) [Slavische Tänze. Op. 72. No. 8.] Slovanský tanec č. 16. Slavonic Dance No. 16 . . . Arrangement by B. Leopold. [Orchestra.] [1955.] 4°. **g. 1160. e. (8.)**

LEOPOLD (EDWARD A.)

— Could'st thou but know. Song, poem by I. V. H. Townsend, *etc.* *E. J. Hogben and Co.: New Haven, Conn.,* (1910.) fol. **H. 1792. s. (15.)**

— If. [Song, words by] W. W. Whitelock. *J. Church Co.: Cincinnati,* 1903. fol. **H. 1799. vv. (39.)**

— Little Flower. [Song.] *J. Church Co.: Cincinnati,* 1903. fol. **H. 1799. vv. (40.)**

— When Memory wakes, Sweetheart. Song for medium voice, words by L. Bosworth, *etc.* *E. J. Hogben and Co.: New Haven, Conn.,* (1910.) fol. **H. 1792. s. (16.)**

LEOPOLITA (MARCIN)

— Missa paschalis na 5-głosowy chór mieszany a cappella, *etc.* ⟨Według fragmentów rękopisu z XVII w. oraz wydania z roku 1889 przygotował Hieronim Feicht. Znakami wykonawczymi opatrzył Stanisław Wiechowicz.⟩ [With facsimiles.] pp. 80. *Polskie wydawnictwo muzyczne: Kraków,* [1957.] fol. [*Wydawnictwo dawnej muzyki polskiej.* 35.] **H. 17.**

LEPAGE (ADHÉMAR)

— *See* VANKENHOVE (Richard) and LEPAGE (A.) Het Volksleven in het straatlied, *etc.* 1932. 4°. **G. 935. i.**

LE PAGE (CHARLES)

— Oom Paul's Doom. Song. Words by A. M. Day. [*J. & W. Chester: Brighton,* 1900.] fol. *Lithographed throughout.* **H. 1799. h. (40.)**

LEPAGE (L.)

— Offertoire funèbre pour orgue ou harmonium. *See* RÉPERTOIRE. Répertoire moderne de Musique . . . d'Orgue, *etc.* No. 10. [1896, *etc.*] fol. **H. 1048.**

LEPAGE (L.)

— Traité de l'Accompagnement du Plain-Chant, *etc.* 1ere (2me) Partie. *Bossard-Bonnel: Rennes,* [1895?] 8°.
Part I is of the second edition. **f. 747.**

LE PAIGE (CHARLES E.)

— In ye olden Times. A Suite of Characteristic Dances. [P. F.] *M. Witmark & Sons: New York, etc.,* [1907.] 4°.
g. 543. kk. (13.)

— Mon cher Trésor. (My Treasure.) Waltz. [P. F.] pp. 9. *M. Witmark & Sons: New York, etc.,* [1909.] fol.
h. 4120. pp. (1.)

— Not for mine. [Song.] pp. 5. *M. Witmark & Sons: New York, etc.,* [1906.] fol. **H. 3985. x. (13.)**

— Run along. [Song.] pp. 5. *M. Witmark & Sons: New York, etc.,* [1906.] fol. **H. 3985. x. (14.)**

— What's all the Worry? Descriptive ballad and refrain. Words and music by C. E. LePaige. pp. 5. *M. Witmark & Sons: New York,* [1906.] fol. **H. 3985. x. (15.)**

LEPAK (ALEXANDER)

— *See* FRIESE (A.) and LEPAK (A.) The Alfred Friese Timpani Method. [1954.] 4°. **g. 761. gg. (6.)**

LE PATOUREL (HENRY)

— Harmonia Sacra, a Collection of Sacred Music adapted to the English Church Service, the words from Bishop Heber's Hymns and the Book of Common Prayer ... Harmonized and arranged for four voices with an accompaniment for the Organ or Piano-Forte by H. Le Patourel. *Pub. for the Author: Paris,* [1835?] 4°. **E. 1639.**

— Magnificat. Chant ... Arranged by J. T. Field. [1900.] *See* NOVELLO AND CO. Novello's Parish Choir Book, *etc.* No. 518. [1866, *etc.*] 8°. **E. 618.**

— *See* BLACKWOOD (H. S.) *Baroness Dufferin, afterwards* HAY (Helen Selina) *Countess of Gifford.* Terence's Farewell ... Arrangd by H. Le Patourel. [1850?] fol. **H. 2826. b. (23.)**

LE PEINTRE ( )

— Rien icy bas n'est ferme ny durable. *Air a Boire, etc.* [*Paris,*] 1735. *s. sh.* 4°.
Mercure de France, Feb., 1735. **297. b. 7.**

LE PELETIER ( )

— If my sad State. *See infra:* [Si mon malheur.]

— [Si mon malheur.] If my sad State ... For four-part chorus of mixed voices ... English words by A. S. ... Attaingnant, second livre, 1535. Edited by Albert Seay. *Eng. & Fr.* pp. 4. *G. Schirmer: New York,* [1960.] 8°. **F. 1744. ff. (10.)**

— [A reissue.] [Si mon malheur.] If my sad State ... For four-part chorus of mixed voices a cappella ... Edited by Albert Seay. *Chappell & Co.: London,* [1962.] 8°.
F. 1744. ii. (12.)

LEPER

— The Leper King. [Cantata.] *See* HOVHANESS (Alan)

— The Leper's Flute. Opera. *See* BRYSON (R. E.)

LE PERRIER (E. F.)

— Hunsdon valse for the Pianoforte. *London,* [1879.] fol.
h. 1494. q. (29.)

LE PETIT (JOHANNES)

— Opera omnia. Edidit Barton Hudson. pp. xxviii. 141. *American Institute of Musicology:* [*Dallas, Tex.?*] *Hänssler-Verlag: Neuhausen,* 1979. fol. [*Corpus mensurabilis musicae.* 87.] **H. 3.**

LE PETIT (NINOT)

— *See* LE PETIT (Johannes)

LE PIN ( )

— Six sonates pour le violoncelle ... Second œuvre. [Violoncello and bass. Score.] pp. 25. *Chez l'auteur: Paris,* [c. 1770.] fol. *The titlepage and pp.* 11, 12 *are mutilated.* **g. 511. u. (3.)**

LEPIN (ANATOLY YAKOVLEVICH)

— [Есть на Волге городок.] [3 numbers in vocal score.] *In:* IZBRANNUIE. Избранные отрывки из оперетт советских композиторов, *etc.* вып. 6. pp. 3–19. 1950. 4°.
G. 936. a. (2.)

LE PIN (H.)

— Variations sur l'air russe (Взвѣйся выше понесися) pour le piano forte. pp. 12. *Chez Paez: St Petersbourg,* [c. 1815.] fol.
h. 1426. ff. (3.)

LE PIN (H. N.)

— Premier concerto pour le clavecin ou piano forté avec accompagnement de deux violons alto et basse ... Gravé par Melle Michaud. [P. F. part.] pp. 9. *Chez l'auteur: Paris,* [c. 1780.] fol.
Without the string parts. **g. 271. x. (2.)**

— Second concerto pour le clavecin ou le forte-piano avec accompagnement de deux violons, alto et basse ... Gravé par Melle Michaud. [P. F. part.] pp. 10. *Chez l'auteur: Paris,* [c. 1780.] fol.
Without the string parts. **g. 271. x. (3.)**

L'EPINE (ERNEST)

— Croquignole XXXVI. Opérette bouffe en un acte. Paroles de MM. de Forges et Gastineau. Partition Chant et Piano avec texte. *Paris,* [1860.] 8°. **F. 37. a.**

— Ici-bas. Poésie de Sully-Prudhomme. [Song. With a portrait and a facsimile.] pp. 3. *In:* Album du Gaulois. [1869.] fol.
H. 2398. a.

— N'oubliez pas ma fenêtre. Chansonnette. Paroles de Mme E. Fleury, *etc. Chabal: Paris,* [c. 1845.] fol.
H. 1650. oo. (19.)

— Nous voyagions en Diligence. [Song, begins: "Je glissai".] Poésie de J. Alcard. *Paris,* [1874.] fol. **H. 1777. h. (46.)**

— Scènes et Chansons. *Paris,* [1868.] 8°. **F. 37.**

— Soleil couchant. [Song, begins: "Elle disait".] Poésie de J. Alcard. *Paris,* [1874.] fol. **H. 1777. h. (47.)**

LÉPINE (MAURICE) *pseud.* [i. e. FREDERIC MULLEN.]

— Intermezzo-Lyrique, pour Piano. *E. Ashdown: London, etc.,* 1910. fol. **h. 3284. g. (20.)**

LEPKE (CHARMA DAVIES)

— Call to Remembrance. For mixed chorus (SATB) with optional accompaniment. Text from English Hymnal. pp. 7. *Mercury Music Corp.: New York,* [1967.] 8°. **F. 1106. b. (40.)**

LE PLONGEON (ALICE DIXON)

— The Lover's Song ... Words and music by A. Le Plongeon.
Accompaniment by I. Simmons. (Invocation to the Sun, *etc.*)
Kegan Paul & Co.: London, 1902. 8°.
Appendix to 'Queen Moo's Talisman,' etc.   **11686. cc. 34.**

LEPNURM (HUGO)

— Трио. Trio. Для скрипки, виолончели и фортепиано. Viiulile,
cellole ja klaverile. [Score.] pp. 96. *Издательство
"Музыка": Москва, Ленинград*, 1965. 8°.   **d. 240. ee. (1.)**

LEPONT (   )

— Louise, polka pour le piano forte.   *London*, [1854.] fol.
h. 975. e. (34.)

LEPOT (LÉON)

— *See* FRELON (L. F. A.) L'Orgue, journal des dimanches et des
fêtes, publié sous la direction de L. F. A. Frelon, avec le
concours de M. M. ... L. Lepot, *etc.* 1858. fol.   **h. 1004.**

LEPPARD (RAYMOND)

— Angelus ad virginem. 14th century carol for unaccompanied
male voices. Arranged by R. Leppard. pp. 7. *Faber Music:
London*, 1966. 8°.   **F. 260. pp. (11.)**

— The National Anthem. In the version used by the Royal
Shakespeare Company. ⟨God save our noble King. Arranged
by R. Leppard from the earliest known source of the melody
c. 1740.⟩ [Score.]   *Gamut Publications: Cambridge*, [1962.] 4°.
g. 1780. z. (7.)

— *See* CAVALLI (P. F.) Five operatic Arias. For high voice (with
keyboard accompaniment). ⟨Realized by R. Leppard.⟩ 1966.
4°.   **G. 809. z. (2.)**

— *See* CAVALLI (P. F.) La Calisto ... Performing edition realised
by R. Leppard, *etc.* [1975.] 4°.   **G. 1273. yy. (2.)**

— *See* CAVALLI (P. F.) L'Egisto ... Performing edition realized
by R. Leppard. 1977. 4°.   **F. 1257. zz.**

— *See* CAVALLI (P. F.) [Musiche sacre.] Dixit Dominus ... Edited
and realised by R. Leppard. [1974.] fol.   **I. 605. b. (1.)**

— *See* CAVALLI (P. F.) [Musiche sacre.] Laetatus sum. For ATB,
strings, with keyboard continuo, *etc.* ⟨Edited by R. Leppard.⟩
1969. 8°. [*Faber Baroque choral Series. no. 8.*]   **F. 1175. uu.**

— *See* CAVALLI (P. F.) [Musiche sacre.] Laudate Dominum ...
For double chorus, cornetti, trombones, strings, with
keyboard continuo. ⟨Edited by R. Leppard.⟩ 1969. 8°. [*Faber
Baroque choral Series. no. 9.*]   **F. 1175. uu.**

— *See* CAVALLI (P. F.) [Musiche sacre.] Magnificat ... Realized
R. Leppard. [1974.] fol.   **I. 605. b. (2.)**

— *See* CAVALLI (P. F.) [Musiche sacre.] Magnificat. For double
chorus, cornetti (trumpets), trombones, strings and keyboard
continuo. ⟨Realized by R. Leppard.⟩ 1973. 8°.
E. 271. w. (14.)

— *See* CAVALLI (P. F.) [Musiche sacre.] Messa concertata ...
Realized by R. Leppard. [1966.] 4°.   **G. 503. p. (1.)**

— *See* CAVALLI (P. F.) [Musiche sacre.] Salve regina. For ATTB,
with keyboard continuo. ⟨Edited by R. Leppard.⟩ 1969. 8°.
[*Faber Baroque choral Series. no. 7.*]   **F. 1175. uu.**

— *See* CAVALLI (P. F.) L'Ormindo. Opera ... Realized by
R. Leppard, *etc.* 1969. 4°.   **G. 1273. x. (2.)**

— *See* CAVALLI (P. F.) [Ormindo.—Conosco gl'apparati.] Prison
scene ... For soprano and tenor with keyboard
accompaniment. ⟨Relized by R. Leppard.⟩ 1966. 4°.
G. 809. z. (3.)

LEPPARD (RAYMOND)

— *See* HAENDEL (G. F.) [Lucretia.] Cantata: Lucrezia ... Ed.
R. Leppard. [1974.] fol.   **I. 49. a.**

— *See* HAENDEL (G. F.) Lucrezia. O Numi eterni. Cantata ...
Performing edition by R. Leppard. 1980. 4°.
G. 170. dd. (1.)

— *See* MONTEVERDI (C.) [Il Ballo delle ingrate.] Ballo from "Il
Ballo delle ingrate". Realized by R. Leppard. 1967. 4°.
h. 3210. j. (97.)

— *See* MONTEVERDI (C.) L'Incoronazione di Poppea ... Opera in
two acts. Realized by R. Leppard, *etc.* 1966. 4°.   **G. 58. o.**

— *See* MONTEVERDI (C.) L'Incoronazione di Poppea ... Realized
by R. Leppard, *etc.* 1977. 4°.   **G. 58. s.**

— *See* MONTEVERDI (C.) L'Incoronazione di Poppea. Realized
by R. Leppard. Chorus part. 1978. 8°.   **F. 8. f. (3.)**

— *See* MONTEVERDI (C.) [L'Incoronazione di Poppea.—A Dio
Roma.] Ottavia's Farewell ... For soprano with keyboard
accompaniment. ⟨Realized by R. Leppard.⟩ 1967. 4°.
G. 58. p. (5.)

— *See* MONTEVERDI (C.) [L'Incoronazione di Poppea.— Adagiati
Poppea.] Arnalta's Lullaby ... For contralto with keyboard
accompaniment. ⟨Realized by R. Leppard.⟩ 1967. 4°.
G. 58. p. (2.)

— *See* MONTEVERDI (C.) [L'Incoronazione di Poppea.]
Coronation March ... Edited by R. Leppard, *etc.* [1968.] 4°.
g. 1378. dd. (2.)

— *See* MONTEVERDI (C.) [L'Incoronazione di Poppea.—
Disprezzata regina.] Ottavia's Lament ... For soprano with
keyboard accompaniment. ⟨Realized by R. Leppard.⟩ 1967. 4°.
G. 58. p. (6.)

— *See* MONTEVERDI (C.) [L'Incoronazione di Poppea.—Hor che
Seneca e morte.] Drinking Song ... Duet for two tenors with
keyboard accompaniment. ⟨Realized by R. Leppard.⟩ 1967. 4°.
G. 58. p. (3.)

— *See* MONTEVERDI (C.) [L'Incoronazione di Poppea.—Pur ti
miro.] Love Duet ... Duet for soprano and tenor with
keyboard accompaniment. ⟨Realized by R. Leppard.⟩ 1967. 4°.
G. 58. p. (4.)

— *See* MONTEVERDI (C.) [L'Incoronazione di Poppea.—Sento un
certo non so che.] Scena buffa ... Duet for soprano and tenor
with keyboard accompaniment. ⟨Realized by R. Leppard.⟩
1967. 4°.   **G. 58. p. (7.)**

— *See* MONTEVERDI (C.) [Scherzi musicali a 1 & 2 voci.] 5 scherzi
musicali ... For medium voice and keyboard. Realized by
R. Leppard. 1980. 4°.   **G. 58. p. (8.)**

— *See* SCARLATTI (Domenico) Salve regina ... for soprano and
keyboard. Edited by R. Leppard. 1979. 4°.   **H. 315. c. (1.)**

LEPPARD (SYDNEY)

— The First Prayer. Song, words by A. Fiske.   *Lyon & Hall:
Hove*, [1902.] fol.   **H. 1799. vv. (41.)**

— Warp and Woof. [Song.] Written by G. C. Bingham.
J. Parker & Co.: London, [1886.] fol.   **H. 1788. v. (43.)**

LEPPER (CHARLES)

— The Battenberg Polka. [P. F.]   *Finlayson Brothers: Glasgow*,
[1886.] fol.   **h. 975. v. (13.)**

LEPRACHAUN

— *See* LEPRECHAUN.

LEPRECHAUN

— The Leprehaun. Part-Song. *See* BANTOCK (*Sir* G.)

— The Leprechaun. [Song.] *See* EUSTIS (Frederick J.)

— The Leprechaun. [Song.] *See* GRAHAM (A. C.)

— Leprachaun. Two part song. *See* GWYNNE (Una)

— The Leprehaun. Part Song. *See* KEIGHLEY (T.)

— The Leprechaun. Part Song. *See* TREHARNE (B.)

LEPREHAUN

— *See* LEPRECHAUN.

LÉPREUSE

— La Lépreuse. Tragédie légendaire. *See* LAZZARI (J. L. S.)

LEPRÉVOST (ALEXANDRE)

— *See* LEPRÉVOST (Étienne A.)

LEPRÉVOST (ÉTIENNE ALEXANDRE)

— Communion. *See* BROWN (A. H.) Select Compositions ...
arranged for the Organ, No. 91. [1886.] fol. **h. 2686.**

— Larghetto in A. *See* BROWN (A. H.) Select Compositions ...
arranged for the Organ, No. 90. [1886.] fol. **h. 2686.**

— Messe des Solennels-mineurs, arrangée à 3 voix pour Dessus,
Tenors et Basses, avec accompagnement et interludes
d'Orgue. *Paris*, [1866.] 8°. **F. 352.**

— Messe en plain-chant musical dite de Bordeaux arrangée à
trois voix égales avec accompagnement d'Orgue. *Paris*,
[1877.] fol. **H. 1029. e. (6.)**

— 4ᵉ. Messe solennelle à trois voix, *etc. Paris*, [1850?] 8°.
F. 352. a.

— Messe Solennelle en Ré, à 4 voix, *etc. Paris*, [1869.] fol.
No. 18 of "Messes solennelles," *etc.* **H. 2827. a. (16.)**

— 5 Morceaux pour Orgue et Orgue expressif, *etc. Paris*,
[1862.] obl. fol. **e. 174. b. (8.)**

— Offertoire in C. *See* BROWN (A. H.) Select Compositions ...
arranged for the Organ, No. 89. [1886.] fol. **h. 2686.**

— Offertoire, or Sortie, E♭. *See* BROWN (A. H.) Select
Compositions ... arranged for the Organ, No. 92. [1886.] fol.
h. 2686.

— Rentreé de la Procession. *See* BROWN (A. H.) Select
Compositions ... arranged for the Organ, No. 88. [1886.] fol.
h. 2686.

— *See* HYMNS. [*French.*] 80 Cantiques ... avec accompagnement
d'orgue ... par ... A. Leprévost, *etc.* [1886.] 8°.
F. 322. a. (2.)

LEPRINCE (CHARLES)

— Faut-il céder. [Song.] Paroles de Mr. de Villegarde. *Paris*,
[1815?] fol. **G. 547. (58.)**

LEPS (WASSILI)

— Goldenrod. Three-part Song for women's voices ... text by
E. M. Dunn. *C. Fischer: New York*, 1923. 8°.
F. 328. y. (45.)

— The Miracle of Gar-Anlaf. A Cantata for Chorus of Men's
voices and Orchestra, poem by J. L. Long. Op. 15. Vocal
Score. *G. Schirmer: New York*, (1907.) 8°. **F. 1270. r. (4.)**

LEPS (WASSILI)

— Yo-nennen. A Japanese Cicada Drama set to music in the
form of a Cantata for Four-Part Chorus of women's voices,
with Accompaniment of Small Orchestra or Piano, poem by
J. L. Long. Vocal Score. Op. 11. *G. Schirmer: New York*,
(1905.) 8°. **E. 100. c. (3.)**

LE QUESNE (F. A.)

— Klondyke. ⟨Song. Words & music by F. A. Le Quesne.⟩ pp. 4.
Weekes & Co.: London; W. H. Milne: Jersey, [1897.] fol.
H. 3980. rr. (8.)

LE QUESNE (FLORENCE)

— The Golden Gorse. Ballad.—The Blackbird's Song.—Words
and Music by F. Le Quesne. *Moore, Smith & Co.: London*,
[1899.] fol. **H. 1799. h. (41.)**

LE R*** (   ) Mˡˡᵉ

— Cessez, charmante Iris. *Air, etc. Récoquilliée:* [*Paris,*] 1770.
s. sh. 8°.
Mercure de France, Dec., 1770. **298. e. 1.**

LERAY (C.)

— Album of Christy's Minstrels, for the Pianoforte. 24 no.
London, [1864.] fol. **h. 3111. (1.)**

— Album of Dance Music for the Pianoforte. no. 1–9, 11, 12,
14, 16, 17, 21, 22. *London*, [1860.] fol.
Imperfect; wanting no. 10, 13, 15, 18–20, 23, 24.
h. 3111. (2.)

— Colleen Bawn, two melodies for the Pianoforte. 2 no.
London, [1861.] fol. **h. 3111. (3.)**

— Juvenile Library, a selection of popular airs for the
Pianoforte. 24 no. *London*, [1861.] fol. **h. 3111. (4.)**

LERCHE

— Die Lerche. Song. *See* ABT (F. W.) [Zwei Lieder für Sopran
... Op. 501. No. 2.]

— Die Lerche. [Song.] *See* DVOŘÁK (A.) Vier Lieder ... Op. 7.
No. 4.

— Die Lerche. Romanze. *See* GLINKA (M. I.)

— Die Lerche. [Song.] *See* TAUBERT (C. G. W.)

— Die Lerche. [Song.] *See* VARLAMOV (A. E.)

— Die Lerche gleicht. [Song.] *See* SCHMIDT (B.) Drei Lieder ...
Op. 16. No. 2.

— Der Lerche Morgenlied. [Chorus.] *See* ZENGER (M.) Fünf
Chorlieder ... Op. 52. No. 3.

— Lerche und Nachtigall. [Duet.] *See* SCHNAUBELT (H.) Vier
zweistimmige Gesänge. Op. 23. No. 2.

LERCHE (C. A.) *Lehnsgreve*

— Sex Sange efter A. Munchs Texter til A. Tidemands
"Bondeliv i Norge," *etc.* 1899. *See* COPENHAGEN.—
Samfundet til Udgivelse af dansk Musik. Bilag II. for 1899.
1872, *etc.* fol. **G. 728.**

LERCHE (JULIANE)

— Neues Kompendium der Klaviertechnik. New Compendium
of Piano Technique. Heft II. Repetition mit und ohne
Fingerwechsel, *etc.* ⟨Heft III. Abwechseln der Hände.⟩ Hft. 2,
3. 2 vol. *Edition Peters: Leipzig*, [1969.] 4°.
Imperfect; wanting Hft. 1. **g. 353. p. (1.)**

LERCHEN

— Die Lerchen. [Song.] See DEPROSSE (A.) Vier Lieder. Op. 39. No. 3.

— Die Lerchen. [Song.] See HORNEMAN (C. F. E.) Fünf Gedichte, etc. No. 1.

— Die Lerchen. [Song.] See LASSEN (E.) Sechs Lieder. Op. 59. No. 4.

— Die Lerchen. [Song.] See NAUMANN (E.) 6 Lieder, etc. Op. 2. No. 4.

— Die Lerchen. [Song.] See PHILIPP (R.) Sechs Lieder, etc. No. 4.

— Lerchen in heitrer Luft. [Song.] See RHEINBERGER (J.) [Wache Träume. Op. 57. No. 3.]

— Lerchen und Blumen. [Chorus.] See MOHR (H.) Zwei Weinphantasien ... Op. 32. No. 2.

LERCHENSANG

— Lerchensang. [Duet.] See LASSEN (E.) Sechs Duette, etc. Op. 55. No. 6.

LERCHLE

— 's Lerchle. [Song.] See TAUBERT (W. C. G.)

LERCHUNDI (GABRIEL)

— Kantikak. Cantiques basques, anciens et modernes. [Edited by G. Lerchundi.] pp. xxxvi. 629. *Abbaye N.-D. de Belloc: Urt; Librairie "Le Livre": Bayonne*, 1948. 8°.　**D. 622. pp.**

LERDO (A. DE)

— Bi-ba-bo. Two Step ... Pour Piano, etc. *Schott & Co.: London*, 1908. fol.　**h. 3286. uu. (50.)**

LE REDDE (   )

— Ah, que l'Hyver est ennuyeux. *Air Nouveau.* (Les Paroles sont de Mʳ Noel, etc.) [Paris, 1679.] s. sh. obl. 4°. *Nouveau Mercure Galant, March*, 1679, p. 22.　**P. P. 4482.**

LE REY (FRÉDÉRIC)

— Don Cesar de Bazan. Drame de MM. Dumanoir et d'Ennery. Chanson, chantée au 3ᵉ acte, etc. [Begins: "Amis, le bonheur sur terre".] [Paris,] 1896. 8°. *Supplement to "L'Illustration," No.* 2804.　**P. P. 4283. m. (3.)**

— La Mégère apprivoisée. Comédie-Lyrique en trois actes et quatre tableaux, d'après Shakespeare, par E. Deshays, etc. *P. Dupont: Paris*, 1895. 8°.　**F. 1454.**

— Pavane de "Jacques Callot," Drame de MM. H. Cain et E. Adenis, etc. [P. F.] [Paris,] 1896. 8°. *Supplement to "L'Illustration," No.* 2796.　**P. P. 4283. m. (3.)**

— Thi-Teu. Opéra en 3 actes et 4 tableaux. Poème de Édouard Noël et Lucien d'Hève. [Vocal score.] pp. 321. *Léon Grus: Paris*, [c. 1900.] 8°. *Imperfect; wanting the titlepage. The title is taken from the head of p.* 1.　**F. 1454. a.**

LERICH (RUDOLF)

— Im Hagedorn. Spielstücke für Sopranblockflöte c" und Altblockflöte f'. [Score.] pp. 8. *B. Schott's Söhne: Mainz*, [1952.] 8°.　**e. 340. e. (2.)**

— Melodische Duette. Tuneful Duos. Spielstücke für Sopran-und Alt-Blockflöte oder andere Melodieinstrumente. Easy pieces for descant and treble recorder or other melody instruments. [Score.] pp. 16. *Musikverlag zum Pelikan: Zürich*, [1957.] obl. 8°.　**a. 40. k. (12.)**

LERICH (RUDOLF)

— Sonatine in F-dur für C-Sopranblockflöte oder Oboe und Klavier. Sonatine in F major. For descant recorder or oboe and piano. [Score and part.] 2 pt. *Bärenreiter: Kassel, etc.*, [1971.] 8°.　**g. 109. ll. (4.)**

LERICHE (CHARLES)

— *See* DESORMES (L. C.) Popular Compositions. No. 4. Sous les Branches. Valse. [Edited by] C. Leriche. [1883.] fol.　**h. 3405. (34.)**

— *See* DESORMES (L. C.) Sous les Branches valse sur les motifs de C. Leriche. [1877.] *obl.* fol.　**e. 272. d. (46.)**

— *See* DESORMES (L. C.) Sous les Branches, valse sur les motifs de C. Leriche, etc. [1878.] *obl.* fol.　**e. 272. h. (21.)**

LE RICHE (J. L.)

— La Ulisse. [Contre danse. For two violins.] *Chez Frère: [Paris*, 1805?] 8°.　**b. 40. (26.)**

LE RICHEUX (CHARLES E.)

— Three merry Dentists. An Action Song and Dialogue. Words by A. B. Cooper. *J. Curwen & Sons: London*, 1900. fol.　**H. 1984. c. (14.)**

LE RISCH (GODFREY)

— The Hamburgh quadrille, for the piano forte. *London*, [1858.] fol.　**h. 977. f. (33.)**

LERMAN (JOSEPH W.)

— Across the hot Sands. Intermezzo and two step. [P. F.] pp. 5. *Continental Music Co.: [New York*, 1903.] fol.　**h. 4120. pp. (2.)**

— And one cried unto another. Quartet. *G. Molineux: New York*, (1907.) 8°.　**F. 281. h. (24.)**

— At the Manger. A Christmas Solo ... Words by B. Bell. *Fillmore Music House: Cincinnati*, 1916. fol.　**H. 1186. c. (38.)**

— At the Play. Five pianoforte pieces ... [1.] Drum and Bugle. Fanfare. [2.] The Comedians. Scherzo. [3.] The Magic Wand. Polka Caprice. [4.] A Love Scene. Nocturne. [5.] Parade of the Amazons. March. 5 no. *Theodore Presser: Philadelphia*, [1907.] fol.　**h. 4120. pp. (3.)**

— Awake, and sing the Song. [Anthem, words by] W. Hammond. *Tullar-Meredith Co.: New York, Chicago*, (1912.) 8°.　**F. 281. ff. (22.)**

— Belfry Echoes. [P. F.] pp. 5. *Theodore Presser: Philadelphia*, [1906.] fol.　**h. 4120. pp. (4.)**

— Blessed, Holy Bible. [Hymn, words by] L. De Armond. [Staff and tonic sol-fa notations.] *Bayley & Ferguson: London, Glasgow*, [1913.] s. sh. 8°. *Anniversary Hymns, No.* 55.　**F. 272. c.**

— Blossom Time. Two Part Song for women's voices. *T. Presser Co.: Philadelphia*, (1913.) 8°.　**F. 328. q. (27.)**

— Bright and joyful is the Morn. Hymn Anthem for Christmas, etc. *Tullar-Meredith Co.: New York, Chicago*, (1913.) 8°.　**F. 281. kk. (11.)**

— Bugle Song. Chorus ... [Words by] Lord Tennyson. *Tullar-Meredith Co.: New York, Chicago*, (1913.) 8°.　**F. 1744. a. (19.)**

— Cajolery. Scherzo valse. [P. F.] pp. 5. *Theodore Presser: Philadelphia*, [1906.] fol.　**h. 4120. pp. (5.)**

LERMAN (Joseph W.)

— Christ is risen. An Easter Song, words by A. T. Gurney. *Tullar-Meredith Co.: New York, Chicago*, (1910.) fol.
H. 1187. rr. (11.)

— Clarissa. Military Schottische. [P. F.] *K. Dehnkoff: New York*, 1895. fol.
h. 3286. g. (35.)

— The Comedians. Scherzo. *See* supra: At the Play ... [2.]

— The Coming of the King ... Christmas Cantata-Service for ... Choir and Sunday School. Text by E. S. Tillotson. Anthems by J. W. Lerman. Carols by I. H. Meredith. *Tullar-Meredith Co.: New York, etc.*, 1911. 8°.
D. 675. w. (14.)

— Dance of the Automatons. [P. F.] pp. 7. *Theodore Presser: Philadelphia*, [1904.] fol.
h. 4120. pp. (6.)

— Daphne. [P. F.] pp. 5. *Oliver Ditson Co.: Boston*, [1904.] fol.
h. 4120. pp. (7.)

— The Darktown Shuffle. Danse characteristique. [P. F.] *F. W. Helmick: New York*, 1893. fol.
h. 1489. s. (43.)

— "Depth of Mercy." Solo.—Bass.—Words by C. Wesley. *G. Molineux: New York, etc.*, (1907.) fol.
G. 517. v. (33.)

— Doth God pervert Judgment? Ten. Solo and Cho. *G. Molineux: New York*, (1907.) 8°.
F. 281. h. (25.)

— Drum and Bugle. Fanfare. *See* supra: At the Play ... [1.]

— The Earth is the Lord's. Anthem. *T. Presser: Philadelphia*, (1910.) 8°.
F. 281. u. (26.)

— An Easter Emblem. [P. F.] pp. 5. *Armstrong Music Pub. Co.: [New York, 1903.] fol.
h. 4120. pp. (8.)

— The Easter Story. A Service, *etc.* [Words by G. Humphris.] *Tullar-Meredith Co.: New York, Chicago*, 1913. 8°.
D. 675. v. (4.)

— Ecstasy-Waltzes for Piano. *O. Ditson Co.: Boston, etc.*, 1897. fol.
h. 3286. g. (36.)

— The Eyes of the Lord. Quartette and Chorus. *G. Molineux: New York*, (1907.) 8°.
F. 281. h. (26.)

— Flowers of Memory. [Words by] E. S. Tillotson. [Music by] J. W. Lerman. (Unfurl the Flag. [Words by] E. S. Tillotson. [Music by] Mendelssohn-Snelling. O Skies of Springtime. [Words by] E. S. Tillotson. [Music by] T. Moore, arr. by E. G. Snelling.) [Three part-songs for male voices.] *Tullar-Meredith Co.: New York, Chicago*, (1914.) 8°.
F. 163. o. (54.)

— For my Thoughts are not your Thoughts. Sop. Solo and Cho. *G. Molineux: New York*, (1907.) 8°.
F. 281. h. (34.)

— Four Hand Piano Arrangements of fifty Selections from Sunday School Melodies. [Edited by I. H. Meredith and G. C. Tullar.] Arranged by J. W. Lerman. *Tullar-Meredith Co.: New York, Chicago*, 1915. 4°.
g. 1191.

— God is everywhere. [Hymn, words by] C. I. Ford. [Staff and tonic sol-fa notations.] *Bayley & Ferguson: London, Glasgow*, 1915. s. sh. 8°.
Anniversary Hymns, No. 75.
F. 272. c.

— God is not a Man. Chorus. *G. Molineux: New York*, (1907.) 8°.
F. 281. h. (27.)

— Grace and Beauty. Mazurka. [P. F.] pp. 5. *Theodore Presser: Philadelphia*, [1909.] fol.
h. 4120. pp. (9.)

— Great is the Lord. Chorus. *G. Molineux: New York*, (1907.) 8°.
F. 281. h. (28.)

— Guide me, O Thou great Jehovah. Sacred Song. *T. Presser Co.: Philadelphia*, (1910.) fol.
H. 1187. rr. (12.)

— The Guiding Star. A Christmas Duet, *etc. Fillmore Music House: Cincinnati*, 1915. fol.
H. 1186. c. (39.)

LERMAN (Joseph W.)

— Hail Emmanuel! A Christmas Solo ... Words by E.E. Hewitt. *Fillmore Music House: Cincinnati*, 1916. fol.
H. 1186. c. (40.)

— Happy Days. Duet and Chorus. [Words by] A. S. Garbett. *Bayley & Ferguson: London, Glasgow*, [1914.] s. sh. 8°.
Anniversary Hymns, No. 60.
F. 272. c.

— Hazel Blossoms. Reverie. [P. F.] pp. 5. *Armstrong Music Pub. Co.: [New York, 1903.] fol.
h. 4120. pp. (10.)

— "He is wise in Heart." Solo.—Tenor.— *G. Molineux: New York*, (1907.) 8°.
F. 281. n. (21.)

— Hear, O Israel. Chorus. *G. Molineux: New York*, (1907.) 8°.
F. 281. h. (29.)

— Holy, Lord God Almighty. Chorus. *G. Molineux: New York*, (1907.) 8°.
F. 281. h. (30.)

— The Hope of Heaven. A Sacred Cantata, poem by Bernard of Cluny, tr. J. M. Neale. *Tullar-Meredith Co.: New York, Chicago*, 1909. 8°.
E. 541. w. (2.)

— How great are His Signs. Chorus. *G. Molineux: New York*, (1907.) 8°.
F. 281. h. (31.)

— I will lift up mine Eyes. Anthem, *etc. T. Presser: Philadelphia*, (1909.) 8°.
F. 281. u. (27.)

— I will praise Thee, O Lord. Anthem, *etc. T. Presser Co.: Philadelphia*, (1914.) 8°.
F. 281. oo. (27.)

— If a Man die. [Anthem.] Introducing Themes from Händel's Messiah, *etc. Tullar-Meredith Co.: New York, Chicago*, (1913.) 8°.
F. 281. gg. (50.)

— In Thee, O Lord, do I put my Trust, *etc.* [Anthem.] *Tullar-Meredith Co.: New York, Chicago*, (1913.) 8°.
F. 281. gg. (51.)

— Jehovah. A Sacred Cantata setting forth the Attributes of God. *G. Molineux: New York*, 1907. 8°.
E. 541. t. (4.)

— Jesus victorious. Duet ... words by Rev. I. O. Rankin. *Fillmore Music House: Cincinnati*, (1915.) fol.
H. 1187. xx. (16.)

— The Junior Illustrated Violin Method. Part One ... by J. W. Lerman, G. and J. Molineux. pp. 47. *G. Molineux: New York*, 1917. fol.
h. 1753. f. (4.)

— The Land of Liberty. An Operetta for Young Folks, book and lyrics by A. S. Garbett. *Tullar-Meredith Co.: New York, etc.*, 1911. 8°.
D. 834. d. (4.)

— Lo, a risen Lord we sing. Quartet for women's voices. [Words by] R. M. Offord. *Fillmore Music House: Cincinnati*, (1915.) 8°.
E. 602. ee. (41.)

— The Lord, He is risen. A Baritone Solo, *etc. Fillmore Music House: Cincinnati*, (1915.) fol.
H. 1187. xx. (11.)

— The Lord is good to all. Chorus. *G. Molineux: New York*, (1907.) 8°.
F. 281. h. (32.)

— The Lord is Risen. Easter Trio for women's voices. Words by (C. E. Burke). *Fillmore Music House: Cincinnati*, (1915.) fol.
H. 1187. xx. (12.)

— "Lord, Thy Glory fills the Heaven." Solo.—Soprano. *G. Molineux: New York*, (1907.) 8°.
F. 281. n. (22.)

— Love one Another. Solo ... words by E. K. Behrman. *Fillmore Music House: Cincinnati*, (1915.) fol.
H. 1187. xx. (13.)

— A Love Scene. Nocturne. *See* supra: At the Play ... [4.]

— Love's Quest. [P. F.] pp. 6. *Theodore Presser: Philadelphia*, [1904.] fol.
h. 4120. pp. (11.)

LERMAN (Joseph W.)

— The Magic Wand. Polka Caprice. *See* supra: At the Play ... [3.]

— Mary's Lullaby. A Christmas Song, words by A. S. Garbett. *Tullar-Meredith Co.: New York, etc.,* (1910.) fol.
H. 1187. rr. (13.)

— Merry Manikins (Dance alla Tarantella). [P. F.] pp. 7. *Oliver Ditson Co.: Boston,* [1906.] fol. **h. 4120. pp. (12.)**

— Mighty God, while Angels bless Thee. [Anthem, words by] R. Robinson. *Tullar-Meredith Co.: New York, Chicago,* 1914. 8°. **F. 281. oo. (28.)**

— The Morning of Life. A Sacred Juvenile Cantata for Children's Day, text by L. De Armond. *Tullar-Meredith Co.: New York, Chicago,* 1909. 8°. **E. 496. i. (4.)**

— Now may the God of Grace and Power. *See* infra: [Our Country.]

— O for a thousand Tongues. Hymn Anthem. [Words by] C. Wesley. *T. Presser Co.: Philadelphia,* (1911.) 8°.
F. 281. cc. (24.)

— O Lord, our Fathers oft have told. *See* infra: [Our Country.]

— Old Aunt Chloe. Ethiopian ditty. [Song.] Words and music by J. W. Lerman. pp. 5. *F. W. Helmick: New York,* [1893.] fol.
H. 3980. rr. (9.)

— The Old Farm-House on the Hill. Song and refrain. Words and music by J. W. Lerman. pp. 3. *Union Mutual Music & Novelty Co.: New York,* [1899.] fol. **H. 3980. rr. (10.)**

— Old Folks at Home, with brilliant variations. [P. F.] *Union Mutual Music Co.: New York,* 1899. fol. **h. 3282. f. (37.)**

— On Earth, Goodwill and Peace. Solo ... Words by Archdeacon Farrar. *Fillmore Music House: Cincinnati,* 1915. fol. **H. 1186. c. (41.)**

— On Wings of living Light ... Duet for Easter. [Words by] W. W. How. *Fillmore Music House: Cincinnati,* 1916. fol.
H. 1186. c. (42.)

— Our Country. A Sacred Cantata for national occasions ... Text from Hymnology. *Tullar-Meredith Co.: New York, Chicago,* 1913. 8°. **F. 1269. l. (5.)**

— [Our Country.] Now may the God of Grace and Power, *etc.* [Anthem.] *Tullar-Meredith Co.: New York, Chicago,* (1913.) 8°. **F. 281. kk. (13.)**

— [Our Country.] O Lord, our Fathers oft have told, *etc.* [Anthem.] *Tullar-Meredith Co.: New York, Chicago,* (1913.) 8°. **F. 281. kk. (12.)**

— Our Lord Emmanuel. A Christmas Cantata. *Fillmore Music House: Cincinnati,* 1915. 8°. **F. 1269. s. (4.)**

— Parade of the Amazons. March. *See* supra: At the Play ... [5.]

— Paradise. A Cantata for Choirs, *etc. Fillmore Music House: Cincinnati, New York,* 1913. 8°. **F. 1269. m. (4.)**

— Praise to God, immortal Praise. Sacred Solo, *etc.* (Mrs. A. L. Barbauld.) *T. Presser Co.: Philadelphia,* 1917. 4°.
G. 519. h. (28.)

— The Prince of Peace. A Sacred Cantata for Christmas. *Tullar-Meredith Co.: New York, Chicago,* (1915.) 8°.
E. 541. bb. (5.)

— "Rejoice in the Lord." Duett.—Soprano and Contralto. *G. Molineux: New York,* (1907.) 8°. **F. 281. n. (23.)**

— Revels in Dixie Land. Characteristic Dance. [P. F.] *O. Ditson Co.: Boston, etc.,* 1896. fol. **h. 3282. f. (38.)**

— Rise crowned with Light. Anthem, *etc. T. Presser Co.: Philadelphia,* (1912.) 8°. **F. 281. ff. (23.)**

LERMAN (Joseph W.)

— The Risen Redeemer. A Sacred two-part Cantata for Easter. *Tullar-Meredith Co.: New York, Chicago,* 1914. 8°.
F. 1269. n. (5.)

— Rustic Joys. Five characteristic pieces for the pianoforte. 5 no. *T. Presser Co.: Philadelphia,* 1917. 4°.
g. 603. mm. (34.)

— Sing and be glad. [Hymn, words by] L. De Armond. [Staff and tonic sol-fa notations.] *Bayley & Ferguson: London, Glasgow,* [1913.] *s. sh.* 8°. *Anniversary Hymns, No.* 56. **F. 272. c.**

— Sing with Hearts and Voices. [Hymn, words by] L. De Armond. [Staff and tonic sol-fa notations.] *Bayley & Ferguson: London, Glasgow,* [1913.] *s. sh.* 8°. *Anniversary Hymns, No.* 53. **F. 272. c.**

— The Song of the Morning. An Easter Solo, words by H. Butterworth. 2 no. [In G and E flat.] *Fillmore Music House: Cincinnati,* (1915.) fol. **H. 1187. xx. (14.)**

— Sound over all Waters. Bass Solo for Christmas ... [Words by] J. G. Whittier. *Fillmore Music House: Cincinnati,* 1915. fol. **H. 1186. c. (43.)**

— The Spanish Coquette. Bolero for the pianoforte. pp. 7. *Theodore Presser: Philadelphia,* [1905.] fol. **h. 4120. pp. (13.)**

— Spook Dance, *etc.* [P. F.] *Howley, Haviland & Co.: New York,* 1896. fol. **h. 3282. f. (39.)**

— The Star of Bethlehem. Christmas Song. [Words by] H. K. White. *T. Presser Co.: Philadelphia,* (1912.) fol.
H. 1187. xx. (15.)

— The Strife is o'er. Anthem for Easter, *etc. Tullar-Meredith Co.: New York, Chicago,* (1911.) 8°. **F. 281. y. (32.)**

— Superior Anthems for Quartette & Chorus Choirs. Volume two. Edited by J. W. Lerman. *Tullar-Meredith Co.: New York, Chicago,* 1915. 8°. **F. 281. rr. (2.)**

— "There is no Darkness." Solo.—Contralto. *G. Molineux: New York,* (1907.) fol. **G. 517. v. (34.)**

— "Thus saith the Lord." Recitative and Air.—Bass. *G. Molineux: New York,* (1907.) fol. **G. 517. v. (35.)**

— 'Tis Night. Christmas Solo, *etc. Fillmore Music House: Cincinnati,* 1915. fol. **H. 1186. c. (44.)**

— Treasured Love-Tokens. [Song.] Written and composed by J. W. Lerman. *O. Ditson Company: Boston, etc.* 1896. fol.
H. 1798. v. (1.)

— We have been Friends together. Two-Part Chorus. [Words by] C. E. Morton. *Tullar-Meredith Co.: New York, Chicago,* (1913.) 8°. **F. 328. p. (24.)**

— We'll learn to say no. [Hymn, words by] L. De Armond. [Staff and tonic sol-fa notations.] *Bayley & Ferguson: London, Glasgow,* [1913.] *s. sh.* 8°. *Anniversary Hymns, No.* 54. **F. 272. c.**

— The Welcome. Two-part Chorus. [Words by] T. Davis. *Tullar-Meredith Co.: New York, Chicago,* (1915.) 8°.
F. 328. v. (27.)

— When the Whistle blows at six o'clock. Song and chorus. ⟨Words and music by J. W. Lerman.⟩ pp. 5. *F. W. Helmick: New York,* [1893.] fol. **H. 3980. rr. (11.)**

— While Shepherds watched. Christmas Anthem. [Words by] N. Tate. *Tullar-Meredith Co.: New York, Chicago,* (1909.) 8°. **F. 281. t. (17.)**

— "Whither shall I go?" Solo.—Soprano.— *G. Molineux: New York,* (1907.) 8°. **F. 281. n. (24.)**

LERMAN (JOSEPH W.)

— Why do the Heathen rage, *etc.* [Anthem.] *Tullar-Meredith Co.: New York, Chicago,* (1912.) 8°.   **F. 281. ff. (24.)**

— With Banners bright. [Hymn, words by] L. De Armond. [Staff and tonic sol-fa notations.] *Bayley & Ferguson: London, Glasgow,* [1913.] *s. sh.* 8°.
Anniversary Hymns, No. 57.   **F. 272. c.**

— With deepest Reverence. Double Quartet, *etc.* *G. Molineux: New York,* (1907.) 8°.   **F. 281. h. (33.)**

— Wondrous Love. Hymn Anthem founded on the old English tune Calcutta. [By T. Clark.] *Tullar-Meredith Co.: New York, Chicago,* (1913.) 8°.   **F. 281. gg. (52.)**

— You never can tell beforehand. ⟨Comic song.⟩ Words and music by J. W. Lerman. pp. 6. *Himan & Reichenbach: New York,* [1894.] fol.   **H. 3980. rr. (12.)**

— Zoula Voula. An Oriental Two-Step & Polka. [P. F.] *M. Muetzler: New York,* 1900. fol.   **h. 3286. r. (7.)**

— *See* DONIZETTI (Domenico G. M.) [Lucia di Lammermoor.— Spargi d'amaro pianto.] This is the happy Morning. [Sacred two-part chorus.] Arr. from "Donizetti" by J. W. Lerman, *etc.* [1915.] 8°.   **F. 1893. x. (10.)**

— *See* MEREDITH (I. H.) The American Songster No. 2 ... Edited by ... J. W. Lerman. (1914.) 8°.   **C. 756. d. (2.)**

— *See* MEREDITH (I. H.) Christmas Classics, *etc.* (No. 2 ... selected and arranged by J. W. Lerman.) 1909, 13. 8°.   **D. 619. gg. (23.)**

— *See* MEREDITH (I. H.) and LERMAN (J. W.) Morn of Hope, *etc.* 1913. 8°.   **D. 675. v. (11.)**

— *See* MEREDITH (I. H.) and LERMAN (J. W.) Uncle Sam's Celebration, *etc.* 1910. 8°.   **E. 1594. x. (4.)**

— *See* PERIODICAL PUBLICATIONS.— *New York.* The Standard Choir Monthly. J. W. Lerman, editor. 1909, *etc.* 8°.   **F. 1750.**

LERNER (EDWARD R.)

— *See* AGRICOLA (A.) Opera omnia. Edidit E. R. Lerner. 1961, *etc.* fol. [*Corpus mensurabilis musicae.* 22.]   **H. 3.**

— *See* ISAAC (H.) Henrici Isaac ... opera omnia. Edidit E. R. Lerner. 1974, *etc.* fol. [*Corpus mensurabilis musicae.* 65.]   **H. 3.**

LERNER (SAMUEL M.)

— I'm Popeye the Sailor Man. *See infra:* [Popeye the Sailor.]

Popeye the Sailor

— I'm Popeye the Sailor Man. For two-part chorus and piano. Words and music by Sammy Lerner. Arranged by Andrew Balent. pp. 6. *Warner Bros. Publications: New York,* [1978.] 8°.
Part of "Supersounds Series for young Chorus".   **F. 1656. m. (2.)**

— I'm Popeye the Sailor Man ... Arranged by Kelly Love. ⟨Score [and military band parts].⟩ 73 pt. *Warner Bros. Publications: New York,* [1978.] 8° & obl. 8°.
Part of "WB easy Marching Bands Series". With several copies of various parts.   **e. 1330. (3.)**

— I'm Popeye the Sailor Man ... Arranged by John Stuart. [For wind band, percussion and chorus. Score and parts.] 50 pt. *Warner Bros. Publications: New York,* [1978.] 4°.
Part of "Supersound Series for young Bands". With several copies of various parts.   **h. 3210. j. (964.)**

LERNER (SAMUEL M.)

— I'm Popeye the Sailor Man ... Arranged by Bill Holcombe & Paul A. Nagle, *etc.* [Wind band.] ⟨Score [and parts].⟩ 44 pt. *Musicians Publications:* [*New York?* 1980.] 4°.
Part of "Instant Band Series".   **h. 3810. j. (671.)**

LERNT

— Lernt Bescheidenheit! Kantate. *See* ZUMSTEEG (J. R.) Kantate ... No. 10.

LE ROC (ANDREW)

— College Chums forever. [Song.] Words by Dan Packard, *etc.* pp. 5. *Myll Bros.: New York,* [1898.] fol.   **H. 3980. rr. (13.)**

— Gracie Lee. [Song.] Words by Al. Trahern. pp. 5. *A. W. Tams: New York,* [1898.] fol.   **H. 3980. rr. (14.)**

— The Price of a Kiss. Ballad. Poem by Genevieve McCloud. pp. 5. *Hamilton S. Gordon: New York,* [1896.] fol.   **H. 3980. rr. (15.)**

— Silver March, for piano. *H. S. Gordon: New York,* 1896. fol.   **g. 605. p. (26.)**

— Tell me Honey, do. [Song.] Words by Dan Packard. pp. 5. *A. W. Tams: New York,* [1898.] fol.   **H. 3980. rr. (16.)**

— Vaudeville. Schottische. [P. F.] *H. S. Gordon: New York,* 1897. fol.   **h. 3286. g. (37.)**

LEROI (JEAN)

— *See* VENEUX (T.) and LEROI (J.) Clair de lune ... Transcription pour "orchestre à plectre" par S. Dagosto. [1971.] 4°.   **h. 1568. nn. (3.)**

LEROI (JEAN) and BONNEAU (PAUL)

— Gamineries. Conducteur réduit en C (ut) ... Arrangement pour harmonie et fanfare de Désiré Dondeyne. pp. 6. *Chappell: Paris,* [1970.] 4°.   **h. 1568. v. (11.)**

LE'ROSE (EDW.)

— Valse poétique. [P. F.] pp. 7. *M. Witmark & Sons: New York,* [1909.] fol.   **h. 4120. pp. (14.)**

LE ROUGE (GUILLAUME)

— Missa super "Soyez aprantiz". ⟨Anhang. Missa super "Soyez aprantiz". Fassung Rom.⟩ *In:* FLOTZINGER (R.) Trienter Codices. Siebente Auswahl, *etc.* pp. 47–61, 95–108. 1970. fol. [*Denkmäler der Tonkunst in Österreich Bd.* 120.]   **H. 988.**

LE ROUSSAU (F.)

— A Chacoon for a Harlequin. With all the Postures, Attitudes, Motions of the Head and Arms, and other Gestures proper to this Character ... Compos'd writt in Characters and engraved by F. Le Roussau, Dancing-master. *Sold by yͤ Author ... and at Mͬ Barrett's musik-shop: London,* [1725?] fol.   **K. 1. i. 13.**

— A New Collection of Dances, containing a great number of the beast and stage dances ... Recollected, put in characters, and engraved, by Monsieur Roussau. ff. 96. [c. 1725.] 4°. *See* L'ABBÉ (Anthony)   **K. 11. c. 5.**

LEROUX (ALBERT)

— *See* LITOLFF (H. C.) [Concert symphonique pour piano et orchestre. Op. 102.] Scherzo ... Arranged ... by A. Leroux. 1946. 4°.   **f. 133. ii. (40.)**

LEROUX (FÉLIX)

— Le Lorrain. Pas redoublé pour piano. *Paris*, [1885.] fol.
h. 3280. k. (48.)

— La Lusinga, polka-mazurka. [P. F.] *Paris*, [1882.] fol.
h. 3276. g. (19.)

— Une Soirée près du Lac, mazurka pour Piano. *Paris*, [1880.] fol.
h. 3272. j. (24.)

— *See* HÉROLD (L. J. F.) Gloire à notre France éternelle ... instrumentée par Mr. Leroux. [1882.] fol.
H. 1793. c.

LE ROUX (GASPARD)

— Pièces de Clavecin suivies d'un Air sérieux ... mises au-jour par Paul Brunold. *Paris*, 1924. 8°.
La Revue musicale. 5ᵉ année. No. 5. Supplément musical.
P. P. 1948. tda.

— [Pièces de clavecin.] Pieces for Harpsichord. Edited with a preface by Albert Fuller. [With facsimiles.] pp. xxxiv. 77.
C. F. Peters Corporation: New York, etc., [1959.] obl. 4°.
e. 5. v.

— [Pièces de clavecin.] Quatre pièces ... ⟨Prélude—Menuet—La Pièce sans titre—La Favoritte.⟩ Mise au jour par Paul Brunold. [P. F.] pp. 5. *Éditions Maurice Senart: Paris*, [1922.] fol.
Part of "Les Maîtres français du clavecin des XVIIᵐᵉ et XVIIIᵐᵉ siècles".
h. 722. ww. (9.)

— [Pièces de clavecin. Suite 7.] Sarabande. Diversifiée en douze couplets. Mise au jour par Paul Brunold. [P. F.] pp. 12.
Éditons Maurice Senart: Paris, [1922.] fol.
Part of "Les Maîtres français du clavecin des XVIIᵐᵉ et XVIIIᵐᵉ siècles".
h. 722. ww. (8.)

— Sarabande. *See* supra: [Pièces de clavecin. Suite 7.]

LEROUX (J.)

— Amadise. Bolero [begins: "N'entends tu pas"]. Paroles de D. Thiebaux. *Paris*, [1835?] fol.
G. 556. (66.)

— Le Départ. Romance [begins: "O mon ami"]. Paroles de Mᵐᵉ Gabriel de Plancy. *Paris*, [1835?] fol.
G. 545. (29.)

— Le Seigneur du Quartier. Chansonnette [begins: "C'est moi"]. Paroles de D. Thiebaux. *Paris*, [1835?] fol.
G. 553. (25.)

LEROUX (XAVIER HENRI NAPOLÉON)

— Astarté. Opéra en quatre actes et cinq tableaux. Poème de Louis de Gramont ... Partition chant et piano. pp. 449.
Alphonse Leduc: Paris, [1901.] 8°.
G. 1268. ss.

— Astarté. Opéra en quatre actes et cinq tableaux, poème de L. de Gramont ... Invocation de Iole à Vesta, *etc.* [Begins: "Toi qui te réjouis".] [*Paris*,] 1901. 8°.
Supplement to "L'Illustration," No. 3030.
P. P. 4283. m. (3.)

— Les Cadeaux de Noël. Conte héroïque en un acte de Émile Fabre ... Partition chant et piano. pp. 125. *Choudens: Paris*, [1915.] 8°.
F. 1257. cc.

— Le Carillonneur. Pièce lyrique en trois actes et sept tableaux d'après le roman de G. Rodenbach. Poème de Jean Richepin ... Partition, chant et piano. pp. 286. *Choudens: Paris*, [1913.] 4°.
F. 1257. g.

— [Another copy.]
G. 190. s.

— Chanson de Praga [begins: "Il faut que ce peuple périsse," words from] La Guerre, drame de MM. Erckmann-Chatrian. *G. Hartmann: Paris*, [1886.] 8°.
F. 321. c. (20.)

— Le Chemineau. Drame lyrique. Poème de Jean Richepin. [Score.] pp. 408. *Choudens: Paris*, [1907?] fol.
Imperfect; wanting the titlepage.
I. 503.

LEROUX (XAVIER HENRI NAPOLÉON)

— Le Chemineau. Drame lyrique en quatre actes, de J. Richepin ... Partition chant et piano. *Choudens: Paris*, 1907. 8°.
H. 610. a.

— Le Chemineau ... Duetto du 2ᵉ acte, *etc.* [Begins: "Hélas! nos pauvres amours".] [*Paris*,] 1907. 8°.
Supplement to "L'Illustration," No. 3382.
P. P. 4283. m. (3.)

— Musique de Scène pour Cléopâtre. Drame en 5 actes et 6 tableaux de M. M. V. Sardou et E. Moreau. Partition réduite pour piano. *G. Hartmann & Cie.: Paris*, [1890?] 8°.
F. 158. t. (5.)

— Endymion. Scène lyrique de Auger de Lassus. [Vocal score.] pp. 55. *G. Hartmann: Paris*, [1885.] 8°.
Without titlepage. The title is taken from the cover.
F. 1257. ff. (5.)

— Évangéline. Légende arcadienne en quatre actes avec prologue et épilogue. Tirée du poëme de Longfellow ... Partition chant et piano réduite par l'auteur. pp. 259. *Choudens: Paris*, [1895.] 8°.
F. 1256. pp.

— L'Ingénu. Opéra-bouffe en trois actes d'après Voltaire. Livret de Charles Méré et Régis Gignoux ... Partition chant et piano. pp. 423. *Choudens: Paris*, [1931.] 8°.
G. 1268. tt.

— L'oublier! ... Poésie de P. Gille. *G. Hartmann & Cie.: Paris*, [1887.] fol.
H. 2836. v. (26.)

— [Le Nil.] The Nile. For three-part Chorus with Soprano Solo, Violin obligato and Piano or Orchestra. (Arr. by L. V. Saar.) *C. Fischer: New York, etc.*, (1914.) 8°.
F. 328. w. (20.)

— Les Perses. Tragédie antique. Suite d'orchestre.
I. Invocation— II. Air de ballet—III. Choral et marche funèbre ... Partition, *etc.* pp. 47. *Alphonse Leduc: Paris*, [1897.] 8°.
f. 244. y. (6.)

— La Plus forte. Drame lyrique en 4 actes de Jean Richepin et P. de Choudens ... Partition d'orchestre. pp. 403. *Choudens: Paris*, [1924.] fol.
H. 610. c.

— La Plus forte. Drame lyrique en 4 actes de Jean Richepin et P. de Choudens ... Partition chant et piano. pp. 249. *Choudens: Paris*, [1924.] 8°.
H. 610. d.

— La Reine Fiammette. Conte dramatique en quatre actes et six tableaux de Catulle Mendès ... Partition orchestre. pp. 486. *Choudens: Paris*, [c. 1910.] fol.
Imperfect; wanting pp. 377–396, supplied in photographic facsimile. With a photographic facsimile of the corresponding pages of another version.
I. 503. a.

— La Reine Fiammette. Conte Dramatique en quatre actes et six tableaux, de C. Mendès ... Partition chant et piano. *Choudens: Paris*, 1903. fol.
H. 610.

— La Reine Fiammette ... Sonnet de Pétrarque, *etc.* [Begins: "C'est un sonnet de Pétrarque". [*Paris*,] 1904. 8°.
Supplement to "L'Illustration," No. 3175.
P. P. 4283. m. (3.)

— Scherzo Fantastique pour piano. *Paris*, [1884.] fol.
h. 3280. k. (49.)

— Théodora. Drame musical en trois actes et six tableaux de Victorien Sardon et Paul Ferrier ... Partition chant et piano. pp. 429. *Choudens: Paris*, [1907.] fol.
H. 610. b.

— Vénus et Adonis. Scène lyrique. Poème de L. de Gramont. [Vocal score.] pp. 75. *Alphonse Leduc: Paris*, [1897.] 8°.
F. 1196. yy. (3.)

— William Ratcliff. Tragédie musicale en quatre actes "d'après Henri Heine". Poème de Louis de Gramont ... Partition chant et piano. pp. 255. *Choudens: Paris*, [1906.] 8°.
The fly-leaf bears a MS. dedication in the composer's autograph.
F. 1256. z.

— *See* LALO (É. V. A.) Symphonie en sol mineur. Réduction pour piano ... par X. Leroux. [1887.] fol.
h. 3290. h. (17.)

LEROUX (Xavier Henri Napoléon)

— *See* Massenet (J. É. F.) [Le Crocodile.] Musique de scène … partition transcrite pour piano par X. Leroux. [1887.] 8°.
f. 133. g. (6.)

— *See* Massenet (J. É. F.) Scènes dramatiques. 3ème suite d'orchestre, *etc.* ⟨Réduction pour piano par X. Leroux.⟩ [c. 1890.] fol.
g. 1675. c. (2.)

— *See* Messager (A. C. P.) and Leroux (X. H. N.) La Montagne enchantée. Pièce fantastique en 5 actes et 12 tableaux, *etc.* [1897.] 8°.
F. 1471. v.

— *See* Messager (A. C. P.) and Leroux (X. H. N.) La Montagne enchantée, *etc.* 1897. 8°. *Supplement to "L'Illustration," No.* 2823.
P. P. 4283. m. (3.)

LE ROY (Adrian)

— Psaumes. Tiers livre de tabulature de luth. 1552. Instruction. 1574. Édition et transcription par Richard de Morcourt. [Staff notation and lute tablature.] pp. xx. 61. *Éditions du centre national de la recherche scientifique: Paris,* [1962.] 4°.
Part of "Les Luthistes".
h. 1759. g. (2.)

— A Briefe and easye instrution to learne the tableture to conducte and dispose thy hande vnto the Lute [by A. Le Roy], *etc.* 1568. *obl.* 4°. *See* Instructions.
K. 1. c. 25.

— [A Brief and easy Instruction.] Fantaisies et danses … Édition et transcription par Pierre Jansen. Étude des concordances par Daniel Heartz. [Staff notation and lute tablature.] pp. xiii. 30. *Éditions du centre national de la recherche scientifique: Paris,* 1962. 4°.
Part of "Les Luthistes".
h. 1759. f. (1.)

— [Another copy.]
h. 1759. g. (1.)

— A briefe and plaine Instruction to set all Musicke of eight diuers tunes in Tableture for the Lute. With a briefe Instruction how to play on the Lute by Tablature, to conduct and dispose thy hand vnto the Lute, with certaine easie lessons for that purpose. And also a third Booke containing diuers new excellent tunes. All first written in French by Adrian Le Roy, and now translated into English by F. Ke. Gentelman. *Ihon Kyngeston for Iames Rowbothame: London,* 1574. *obl.* 4°.
Leaves 1, 2, 3, 77 and 78 are mutilated. The pagination (1–78) is continuous, but each book has a separate titlepage.
K. 1. c. 19.

— [A briefe and plaine Instruction.] Les Instructions pour le luth (1574). Édition et étude critique par Jean Jacquot, Pierre-Yves Sordes et Jean-Michel Vaccaro. Transcriptions par Jean-Michel Vaccaro. Volume I. Introduction et texte des instructions. ⟨Volume II. Textes musicaux.⟩ [With facsimiles.] 2 vol. *Éditions du Centre national de la recherche scientifique: Paris,* 1977. fol.
Part of "Corpus des luthistes français".
h. 1759. z.

— Fantaisies et danses. *See supra*: [A Brief and easy Instruction.]

— Les Instructions pour le luth (1574). *See supra*: [A Briefe and plaine Instruction.]

— [Livres de Tabulature de Guiterre.] Adrian Le Roy & Robert Ballard. Five Guitar Books (1551–1555). Complete facsimiles edition with an introduction by James Tyler, *etc.* [Originally published by A. Le Roy and R. Ballard. Bk. 1–3, 5 composed or arranged by A. Le Roy. Bk. 4 composed by G. Brayssing. Guitar tablature.] *Éditions Chanterelle: Monte Carlo; printed in the United Kingdom,* [1979.] *obl.* 8°.
a. 76. r.

— 10 Compositions selected from Premier livre de tabulature de guiterre, et Tiers livre de tabulature de guiterre. ⟨Transcribed and edited by Alexander Bellow.⟩ pp. 11. *Franco Colⁱombo: New York,* [1967.] 4°.
[Renaissance and Baroque. vol. 1.]
g. 660. dd.

LE ROY (Adrian)

— Premier Liure de Tabulature de Guiterre, Contenant plusieurs Chansons, Fantasies, Pauanes, Gaillardes, Almandes, Branles, tant simples qu'autres, *etc. Adrian le Roy & Robert Ballard: Paris,* 1551. *obl.* 4°.
The following names of composers appear in this collection: Maillard and Boyvin.
K. 2. h. 12. (1.)

— Second Liure de Guiterre, contenant Plusieurs Chansons en forme de voix de ville: nouuellement remises en tabulature, *etc. Adrian le Roy, & Robert Balard: Paris,* 1555. *obl.* 4°.
K. 2. h. 12. (2.)

— Tiers Liure de Tabulature de Guiterre, contenant plusieurs Préludes, Chansons, Basse-dances, Tourdions, Pauanes, Gaillardes, Almandes, Bransles, tant doubles que simples, *etc. Adrian le Roy, & Robert Ballard: Paris,* 1552. *obl.* 4°.
K. 2. h. 12. (3.)

— Quart Liure de Tabulature de Guiterre, contenant plusieurs Fantasies, Pseaulmes, & Chansons: auec L'alouette, & la Guerre, Composées par M. Gregoire Brayssing deaugusta. *Adrian le Roy, & Robert Balard: Paris,* 1553. *obl.* 4°.
K. 2. h. 12. (4.)

— Cinqiesme Liure de Guiterre, contenant Plusieurs Chansons à Trois & quatre parties, par bons & excelens Musiciens: Reduites en Tabulature par A. le Roy. *Adrian le Roy, & Robert Balard: Paris,* 1554. *obl.* 4°.
The following composers' names occur in this collection: Bonard, Arcadet, De Bussy, Certon and A. Le Roy.
K. 2. h. 12. (5.)

— Premier livre de tabulature de luth (1551). Édition et transcription par André Souris et Richard de Morcourt. Introduction historique par Jean Jacquot. Étude des concordances par Daniel Heartz. [Staff notation and lute tablature.] pp. xxvi. 77. *Éditions du centre national de la recherche scientifique: Paris,* [1960.] 4°.
Part of "Les Luthistes".
h. 1759. f. (2.)

— Sixiesme livre de luth (1559). Édition et transcription par Jean-Michel Vaccaro. [Staff notation and lute tablature.] pp. 73. *Éditions du centre national de la recherche scientifique: Paris,* 1978. fol.
Part of "Corpus des luthistes français".
h. 1759. w. (2.)

LEROY (Adrian) and **BALLARD** (Robert)

— Premier livre de chansons à deux parties. 1578. ⟨[Edited by] Bernard Thomas.⟩ *London Pro Musica Edition: London,* [1977, *etc.*] 4°.
[Renaissance Music Prints. 1, etc.]
g. 1784. n.

LE ROY (Bartholomeo)

— Messa a quattro sopra Panis quem ego dabo tibi, de Lupo. [Parts.] *In:* Masses. Di M. Giovanni Pierluigi da Palestina una Messa a otto voci, *etc.* 1585. 4°.
R. M. 15. e. 1. (1.)

LEROY (Édouard)

— Galop de Chasse pour piano. *Paris,* [1883.] fol.
h. 3285. b. (60.)

— Galop de Chasse pour piano. (Arrangement à 4 mains par L. Lemoine.) *Lemoine & Fils: Paris, Bruxelles,* [1886.] fol.
h. 3290. h. (21.)

LE ROY (Felix)

— Melody of Peace. Tone poem for piano. With separate violin & cello parts—ad lib. *Beal, Stuttard & Co.: London,* 1917. fol.
h. 3284. nn. (48.)

LEROY (G.)

— L'Eucharistie et Marie. Cantique [begins: "Quand mon Jésus m'appelant"], solo ou duo ad libitum. Poésie et musique de l'Abbé G. Leroy. *Paris*, 1885. fol. **H. 1187. i. (28.)**

LEROY (HENRI)

— Evening Star.—L'Etoile du Soir.—Polka Caprice. [P. F.] *O. Ditson Co.: Boston*, 1899. fol. **h. 3282. w. (41.)**

— Happy Memories.—Souvenirs heureux.—Morceau de Salon. [P. F.] *O. Ditson Co.: Boston*, 1900. fol. **h. 3282. w. (42.)**

LEROY (JULES)

— La Légende du Léopard, quadrille sur les motifs connus de F. Boissière. [P. F.] *Paris*, [1872.] *obl.* fol. **e. 272. b. (22.)**

LE ROY (M.)

— An Aspiration operatic. [Song.] Words and music by M. Le Roy. pp. 6. *S. Brainard's Sons Co.: Chicago*, [1893.] fol. **H. 3980. rr. (17.)**

— La Belle Carmen. Grande Valse pour piano. *M. Le Roy: Paris*, [1895.] fol. **h. 3285. q. (27.)**

— Call me Colonel. Comic song and refrain. 〈Words and music by M. Le Roy.〉 pp. 5. *S. Brainard's Sons Co.: Chicago*, [1893.] fol. **H. 3980. rr. (18.)**

— The Captive Dove, *etc.* [P. F.] *S. Brainard's Sons Co.: Chicago*, 1893. fol. **h. 1489. s. (44.)**

— Come back, Sweetheart. Waltz song and refrain. 〈Words and music by M. Le Roy.〉 Soprano in B♭. 〈Contralto in A♭.〉 2 no. *S. Brainard's Sons Co.: Chicago*, [1893.] fol. **H. 3980. rr. (19, 19*.)**

— Free Lunch March. [P. F.] *S. Brainard's Sons Co.: Chicago*, 1893. fol. **h. 1489. s. (45.)**

— I know not why. Song ... Words by J. June. *Magazine of Music: London*, [1888.] fol. **H. 1788. v. (44.)**

— Love's Guiding Star. Waltz Song, words by W. Lowell. *Metzler & Co.: London*, [1889.] fol. **H. 1788. uu. (39.)**

— Memories. Ballad, words and music by M. Le Roy. *M. Le Roy: Paris, etc.* 1895. fol. **G. 805. aa. (22.)**

— My first Cigar. [Song.] Words and music by M. le Roy. pp. 5. *S. Brainard's Sons Co.: Chicago*, [1893.] fol. **H. 3980. rr. (20.)**

— Nikita. Waltz for the pianoforte. (Op. 180.) Song ad libitum. Words by H. R. Watson, *etc.* *Magazine of Music Office: London*, [1888.] fol. **h. 975. v. (14.)**

— Nikita Waltzes. [P. F.] *S. Brainard's Sons Co.: Chicago*, 1893. fol. **h. 3285. q. (28.)**

— Supplication. A Sacred Song, *etc.* *S. Brainard's Sons Co.: Chicago*, 1893. fol. **H. 1187. u. (10.)**

— Sweetheart, I'll return to thee. Waltz song and refrain. 〈Words and music by M. Le Roy.〉 Soprano in F. 〈Contralto in D.〉 2 no. *S. Brainard's Sons Co.: Chicago*, [1893.] fol. **H. 3980. rr. (21, 21*.)**

— Venus. Pizzicato Polka. [P. F.] *S. Brainard's Sons Co.: Chicago*, 1893. fol. **h. 3285. q. (29.)**

— Waiting and longing for thee. Ballad. Words and music by M. Le Roy. 2 no. [In D flat and B flat.] *S. Brainard's Sons Co.: Chicago*, 1893. fol. **H. 1798. v. (2.)**

— A Whisper of Love. A Ballad. Words and music by M. Le Roy. 2 no. [In B flat and G.] *S. Brainard's Sons Co.: Chicago*, 1893. fol. **H. 1798. v. (3.)**

LE ROY (RENÉ)

— Die Flöte. Geschichte, Spieltechnik und Lehrweise. Unter Mitarbeit von Dr. Claude Dorgueille. pp. 86. *Bärenreiter: Kassel, etc.*, [1970.] 4°. **X. 435/160.**

— *See* ALBRECHT (G. von) Preludio e fuga per flauto traverso e pianoforte. 〈Op. 59. Revision et annotations de R. LeRoy.〉 [1959.] 4°. **g. 70. y. (1.)**

LERT (RICHARD)

— *See* FLOTOW (F. F. A. von) *Baron.* Martha ... Adaptation by R. Lert, *etc.* 1940. 8°. **F. 136. o.**

LERTES (LOUIS)

— "La Marquise." 〈Tango argentine. Conductor [and military band parts].〉 32 pt. *In:* DAVIES (Uriel) "La Conchita," *etc.* 1913. fol. [*Boosey's military Journal. ser.* 135. *no.* 5.] **h. 1549.**

— "Le Touquet." 〈Tango brésilien. Conductor [and military band parts].〉 32 pt. *In:* DAVIES (Uriel) "La Conchita," *etc.* 1913. fol. [*Boosey's military Journal. ser.* 135. *no.* 5.] **h. 1549.**

LESAGE (ALAIN RENÉ) and **ORNEVAL** (D')

— Le Théâtre de la Foire, ou l'Opéra Comique, contenant les meilleures Pièces qui ont été représentées aux Foires de S. Germain & de S. Laurent ... avec une Table de tous les Vaudevilles & autres Airs gravez notez à la fin de Chaque Volume. 10 Tom. *Chez Z. Chatelain: Amsterdam, Paris*, 1722(–34). 12°.
The composers mentioned in this collection are: de Grandval, Gillier, Mdlle. de Languerre, de la Croix, Aubert, Bernier, de la Coste and des Rochers. **241. l. 18–27.**

LESAGE (EMILE)

— The March of the Kitcheners. [Song.] The words arranged by ... M. Drake. Music (arranged) by E. Lesage, *etc.* *T. Werner Laurie: London*, [1915.] fol. **H. 1793. t. (10.)**

— The Mayfair Classics. Edited by E. Lesage. Pianoforte pieces, *etc.* 〈Annotated and fingered by F. Corder, F. Swinstead.〉 no. 1–56, 58–60, 62–65, 69 and 70. *Murdoch, Murdoch & Co.: London*, [1921.] fol. & 4°.
Imperfect; wanting no. 57, 61, 66–68. A reissue of no. 4, 5, 7–9, 11, 19, 20, 22, 23, 26–30, 36, 40, 45 and 48 in a series entitled "New Mayfair Piano Classics," without the name of Emile Lesage, is entered under "Mayfair Piano Classics". **h. 3576.**

— The Mayfair Classics. [P. F.] 〈Annotated by F. Corder.— Annotated and fingered by Felix Swinstead.〉 [A reissue of no. 8, 10, 12, 19, 34, 37, 41, 43 and 59 of the series originally edited by Emile Lesage.] 9 no. [1945–59.] 4°. *See* MAYFAIR. **h. 3576. a.**

— The New Mayfair Piano Classics. [P. F.] 〈Annotated by F. Corder.—Annotated and fingered by Felix Swinstead.〉 [A reissue of no. 4, 5, 7–9, 11, 19, 20, 26–30, 36, 40, 45, 48, 66–69 of "The Mayfair Classics" originally edited by E. Lesage.] 21 no. [1946.] 4°. *See* MAYFAIR. **h. 3576. b.**

— Nuit etoilée. Pour piano. *E. Ashdown: London, etc.*, 1923. 4°. **g. 1125. k. (14.)**

— Twilight Musings. Six illustrative pieces for pianoforte, *etc.* 2 bk. *A. Hammond & Co.: London*, [1924.] 4°.
The Academic Edition, No. 658, 659. **g. 1130. r. (5*.)**

— *See* HAENDEL (G. F.) [Serse.—Ombra mai fù.] Largo, *etc.* (Arranged by E. Lesage.) 1943. 4°. **g. 74. hh. (14.)**

LESAGE (J.)

— Les Étoiles Lyriques. Twelve operatic illustrations. [P. F.] 12 no. *London*, [1871.] fol. **h. 3109. (1.)**

LESAGE (J.)

— See RUMMEL (J.) Grand Operatic Duets for the Pianoforte. [No. 6–8 by J. Lesage.] [1874.] fol.   **h. 523. e. (23.)**

LE SAGE (J. MONIQUE)

— Daisies. Part Song for two voices, written and composed by J. M. Le Sage. *Swan & Co.: London*, 1913. 8°.   **F. 506. a. (10.)**

— England's Song. [Song.] Words by L. Foott. *West & Co.: London*, 1915. fol.   **H. 1793. t. (11.)**

— Good Night, Love. Song. Words by M. Pryon. *S. Rose & Co.: Bombay*, 1899. fol.   **H. 1799. h. (42.)**

— The Harebell. Part Song for two voices, written and composed by J. M. Le Sage. *Swan & Co.: London*, 1913. 8°.   **F. 506. a. (9.)**

— Life's fleeting Hour. Song, words by R. Lynn. *West & Co.: London*, 1915. fol.   **H. 1793. t. (12.)**

LE SAGE DE RICHÉE (PHILIPP FRANZ)

— Cabinet der Lauten, in welchem zu finden 12. neue Partien, aus unterschiedenen Tonen und neuesten Manier so aniezo gebräuchlich, welche bestehen in Præludien, Allemanden, Couranten, Sarabanden, Giquen, Gavotten, Menuetten, Boureen, Chagonen, Passacaglien, Ouverturen, Rondeau sambt Echo, *etc.* [With a frontispiece.] [1695.] ff. 37. [*The Composer: Breslau*,] 1735. obl. fol.
Printed on one side of the leaf only. The figures 6 and 9 of the original date have been erased and a 7 and 3 substituted with a stamp.   **Hirsch III. 360.**

LESBEA

— *See* LESBIA.

LESBIA

— Lesbia hath a beaming eye. [Song.] *London*, [1879.] fol. *No. 711 of C. Boosey's "Universal" music.*   **H. 2324.**

— Lesbia hath a beaming Eye. [Part-song.] *See* LAMBETH (H. A.)

— Lesbia hath a beaming Eye. [Song.] *See* MOORE (Thomas) *the Poet.* [A Selection of Irish Melodies. 4th Number.]

— Lesbia, live to Love and Pleasure! [Song.] *See* RIGHINI (V.) [Sechs Lieder. Op. 12. No. 1. Frühlingslied.]

— Lesbia's Cruelty. [Song.] *See* SHE. She whom above my self I prize, *etc.* [By G. Vanbrughe.] [1730?] *s. sh.* fol.   **G. 303. (85.)**

— Lesbea's smiles shall ne'er deceive me. *Love's Conquest over Reason.* [Song.] [*London*, 1715?] *s. sh.* fol.   **G. 316. g. (37.)**

— Lesbia's Sparrow. [Song.] *See* LLOYD (C. H.)

LESBIAN

— The Lesbian Maid. Song. *See* GLEDHILL (J.) Six songs. No. 4.

— The Lesbian Maid. Song. *See* SLINN (E. B.)

LESBOS

— Lesbos. [Song.] *See* SOUTHAM (T. W.)

LESCA ( )

— Les Thyoliers. (Louis Tilholès.) Chanson Bayonnaise [begins: "Voyez là bas"] ... arrangée à deux voix par Ad. Barthe. *Paris*, [1869.] fol.   **H. 1781. i. (16.)**

LESCAUT (PIERRE) *pseud.* [i. e. FREDERIC MULLEN.]

— The City of Dreams. Four tone pictures. 1. In the palace of happiness. 2. The princess. 3. The city of dreams. 4. Love's awakening. *E. Ashdown: London, etc.*, 1920. 4°.   **g. 1127. h. (14.)**

— A Dream Melody, for piano. *E. Ashdown: London, etc.*, 1922. 4°.   **g. 1127. h. (15.)**

— The Enchanted Isle. Four impressions. [P. F.] *E. Ashdown: London*, 1917. 4°.   **g. 603. nn. (1.)**

— In Arcady. Four Tone Pictures for Piano. 1. A Song of Twilight. 2. Dianeme. 3. Golden Youth. 4. Zephyr. *E. Ashdown: London*, 1912. 4°.   **g. 232. s. (4.)**

— In Arcady. Four tone pictures for piano ... duet. *E. Ashdown: London, etc.*, 1919. 4°.   **g. 603. ww. (18.)**

— Indian Scenes. Four Impressions (for Piano). 1. Snake-Charmer. 2. Siva. 3. By the Taj Mahal. 4. Nautch Dance. *E. Ashdown: London*, 1915. 4°.   **g. 442. u. (9.)**

— Invocation, pour le piano. *E. Ashdown: London, etc.*, 1920. 4°.   **g. 1125. c. (28.)**

— An Orchard in Spring. Suite for piano. I. The perfume of spring. II. The primrose path. III. Petals. IV. Rustling leaves. *E. Ashdown: London, etc.*, 1922. 4°.   **g. 1125. c. (29.)**

— Scènes Pittoresques. 1. 'Mid the Hush of the Corn. 2. By the murmuring Stream. 3. Where Fairies rove. 4. Into the crimson West. Pour Piano. *E. Ashdown: London, etc.*, 1913. 4°.   **g. 603. z. (8.)**

— Shadow Pictures. Six miniatures. [P. F.] *E. Ashdown: London*, 1916. 4°.   **g. 603. kk. (4.)**

— Solitude. Romance pour piano. *E. Ashdown: London*, 1915. fol.   **g. 606. bb. (29.)**

— The Valley of Repose. Four Impressions for piano. 1. Night thoughts. 2. The water nymph. 3. At twilight's magic hour. 4. The meeting of the waters. *E. Ashdown: London, etc.*, 1919. 4°.   **g. 1129. r. (17.)**

— Valse passionée, pour Piano. *E. Ashdown: London, etc.*, 1913. fol.   **g. 606. n. (41.)**

LESCHETIZKY (THEODOR) *Pianist*

— *See* LESZETYCKI.

LESCHETIZKY (THEODOR HERMANN)

— Filmszenen. Ein Satz für Orchester. Partitur. pp. 27. *Universal-Edition: Wien, Leipzig*, [1938.] 4°.   **g. 474. gg. (2.)**

— Variationen über ein Thema von Beethoven für Oboe und Klavier. *B. Schott's Söhne: Mainz und Leipzig*, 1937. 4°.   **h. 2665. c. (1.)**

— *See* FIELD (John) Nocturne in B dur. [No. 5.] ⟨Herausgegeben von T. Leschetizky.⟩ [1883.] fol.   **h. 3465. s. (6.)**

LESCOT (C. FRANÇOIS)

— La Négresse. [For songs, etc., published anonymously:] *See* NÉGRESSE.

— Ier recueil portatif de chansons, airs, ariettes, et duo, avec accompagnement, *etc.* ⟨2e recueil portatif, ou suite de chansons, airs, ariettes, duo et trio, avec accompagnement.⟩ 2 vol. pp. 123. *Chez Mlle Castagneri, etc.: Paris*, [1765.] 4°. *With a MS. copy of the words and melody of a chanson, "Sur la rose nouvellement éclose," inserted.*   **E. 1717. y.**

— Les Solitaires de Normandie. [For songs, etc., published anonymously:] *See* SOLITAIRES.

LESCOT (C. François)

— Les Solitaires de Normandie, opéra comique en un acte, en vaudeville, par M. de Piis ... Les airs arrangés par M. Lescot. [Vocal score.] pp. 46. *Chez Brunet: Paris*, [1788?] fol.
Hirsch III. 987.

L'ESCUREL (Jehannot de)

— Balades, rondeaux et diz entez sus refroiz de rondeaux. Herausgegeben von Friedrich Gennrich. pp. xiv. 82. *Langen bei Frankfurt*, 1964. 8°.
[*Summa musicae medii aevi.* Bd. 13.] **E. 1319.**

— The Works of Jehan de Lescurel. Edited from the manuscript Paris, B. N., f. fr. 146 by Nigel Wilkins. [With facsimiles.] pp. vii. 40. *American Institute of Musicology:* [*Dallas, Tex.?*,] 1966. fol.
[*Corpus mensurabilis musicæ.* 30.] **H. 3.**

LESEN (F. von)

— I look unto the golden west. Song, words by Mrs. E. C. Fleetwood. *London*, [1880.] fol. **H. 1787. j. (30.)**

— Love me little, love me long. Song. *London*, [1878.] fol.
H. 1783. o. (49.)

— Repentance. Song [begins: "She sits at morn"]. Words by E. B. Manning. *London*, [1878.] fol. **H. 1783. o. (48.)**

— We shall meet again. Song, words by Mrs. E. C. Fleetwood. *London*, [1881.] fol. **H. 1787. j. (31.)**

LEŠETÍNSKÝ

— Lešetínský kovář. Lidová opera. *See* Weis (K.)

L'ESGU (J.)

— Affreux Rochers, demeures sombres. *Air Nouveau.* [*Paris*, 1678.] *s. sh.* 4°.
Nouveau Mercure Galant, Oct., 1678, *p.* 171. **P. P. 4482.**

— Pendant que nos braves Guerriers. *Air Nouveau.* [*Paris*, 1678.] *s. sh. obl.* 4°.
Nouveau Mercure Galant, May, 1678, *p.* 109. **P. P. 4482.**

— Si vous voulez charmer. *Air Nouveau.* [*Paris*, 1678.] *s. sh. obl.* 4°.
Nouveau Mercure Galant, June, 1678, *p.* 37. **P. P. 4482.**

LESHURE (John)

— The Choral Host. Christmas Anthem ... [Words by] O. W. Holmes. *H. W. Gray Co.: New York*, 1926. 8°.
E. 335. d. (22.)

LE SIEUTRE (Maurice)

— Chansons et Cantilènes. Douze Chansons tant v[i]eilles que v[i]eillottes, réunies par M. Le Sieutre. Harmonisées par V. Trassard, *etc. Augener: London*, (1913.) 4°.
G. 390. f. (5.)

LESKÓ (Vilmos)

— *See* Donizetti (Domenico G. M.) Messa di requiem ... Canto e pianoforte, *etc.* ⟨Revisione e riduzione di V. Leskó.⟩ 1975. 4°. **E. 142. gg.**

— *See* Stamitz (A.) Konzert für zwei Flöten in G-Dur und Streichorchester ... Herausgegeben von W. Lebermann. Klavierauszug ⟨von V. Leskó⟩, *etc.* [1967.] 4°. **g. 70. ii. (1.)**

LESLIE

— Leslie Gray. Ballad. *See* Gabriel, afterwards March (M. A. V.)

LESLIE ( )

— Leslie's Cabinet Organ, containing full and complete instruction for learning the instrument, *etc. Boston* [*Mass.*], 1867. *obl.* 4°. **a. 71.**

LESLIE ( )

— Leslie's Premier Violin Tutor. *Moore, Smith & Co.: London*, [1907.] fol. **h. 1753. e. (6.)**

LESLIE (A. H.)

— The Hero of Mafeking ... Song ... Words and music by A. H. Leslie, *etc.* [*London*, 1900.] 8°. **F. 637. i. (3.)**

LESLIE (Alexander)

— The Auld Beech Tree, ballad [begins: "Oh! the sunny days," written by R. Crosbie]. With Pianoforte accompaniments by J. Justice. *Edinburgh*, [1867.] fol. **H. 1772. r. (36.)**

LESLIE (Alexander J.)

— The rainbow galop. [P. F.] *London*, [1854.] fol.
h. 975. e. (35.)

— The snow drop waltz. [P. F.] *London*, [1854.] fol.
h. 975. e. (36.)

LESLIE (Arthur)

— Song of the North Wind. [Song.] Words by O. Thorpe. *Vincent Music Co.: London*, 1904. fol. **H. 1799. vv. (42.)**

LESLIE (Arthur S.)

— The Loss of the Titanic. Song, words and music by A. S. Leslie. *A. S. Leslie: New Westminster, B. C.*, (1912.) fol.
G. 806. mm. (24.)

LESLIE (Birdie)

— Rose Petals. For the Pianoforte. 1. To a Butterfly. 2. To a pink Rose. 3. Mazurka, *etc. J. Williams: London*, (1911.) *obl.* fol. **f. 760. i. (4.)**

— [Another edition.] Rose Petals, *etc. J. Williams: London*, (1911.) *obl.* fol. **f. 760. i. (5.)**

LESLIE (C. E.)

— We all have a very bad Cold. [Part-song. Tonic sol-fa and staff notation.] [1899?] *See* Choral. Choral Leaflets. No. 207. [1882–1915.] *s. sh.* 4°. **F. 569.**

— We all have a very bad Cold. [Four-part song. Staff and tonic sol-fa notations.] *J. Curwen & Sons: London*, [1919.] 8°.
F. 590. a. (35.)

LESLIE (Charles) *Composer of Dance Music*

— First set of Reels and Strathspeys. [P. F.] *London*, [1838.] fol.
h. 117. (22.)

— The Victoria or Coronation set of Reels and Strathspeys. [P. F.] *London*, [1839.] fol. **h. 117. (21.)**

LESLIE (Charles) *of Boston, Massachusetts*

— *See* Paine (J. K.) O bless the Lord, my Soul ... Revised ... by C. Leslie. (1911.) 8°. **F. 281. y. (36.)**

LESLIE (Edgar)

— *See* Berlin (Irving) Let's all be Americans now. [Song.] By I. Berlin, E. Leslie, *etc.* [1917.] fol. **H. 3989. q. (8.)**

LESLIE (EDGAR)

— *See* BRYAN (Alfred) American Beauty. [Song.] By A. Bryan, E. Leslie, *etc*. [1918.] fol.　　　　　**H. 3989. uu. (23.)**

— *See* BRYAN (Alfred) Girls of France. [Song.] By A. Bryan, E. Leslie, *etc*. [1918.] fol.　　　　**H. 3989. uu. (24.)**

— *See* BRYAN (Alfred) If you're crazy about the Women, you're not crazy at all. [Song.] By A. Bryan, E. Leslie, *etc*. [1918.] fol.　　　　　　　　　**H. 3989. uu. (26.)**

— *See* BRYAN (Alfred) When Alexander takes his Ragtime Band to France. [Song.] By A. Bryan ... & E. Leslie, *etc*. [1918.] fol.　　　　　　　　　**H. 3989. uu. (29.)**

LESLIE (ERNEST)

— Angels, my loved one, will rock thee to sleep. [Song and chorus.] [1869.] *See* TONIC. The Tonic Sol-fa Times, *etc*. No. 60. [f.] [1864–73.] 4°.　　　**B. 559. f.**

— Faust de Gounod. Potpourri, *etc*. [P. F.] *Boston* [*Mass.*], 1864. fol.　　　　　　　　　**h. 1459. d. (17.)**

— The Meteor, a choice collection of popular melodies, *etc*. *Boston* [*Mass.*, 1867.] obl. 8°.　　　　**A. 784.**

— Our Boys afloat. Ballad [begins: "Cheers for our sailors"]. Words by W. D. Smith. *Boston* [*Mass.*], 1864. fol.　　　　　　　　　　**H. 1780. f. (15.)**

— Sweet Visions, or Rock me to sleep, mother. [Song, begins: "Backward, turn backward".] The poetry by F. Percy. *London*, [1865.] fol.　　　　　**H. 1772. r. (37.)**

— [Sweet Visions.] Rock me to sleep, mother ... pour le Piano. [1867.] fol. *See* MATTINI (F.)　　**h. 3002. (13.)**

— Uncle Sam is bound to win. [Song, begins: "Oh! General Lee".] Words by W. D. Smith. *Boston* [*Mass.*], 1864. fol.　　　　　　　　　　**H. 1780. f. (16.)**

— Year after Year. Love Song, words by the author of "John Halifax, Gentleman". *E. Ashdown: London*, [1883.] fol.　　　　　　　　　　　**G. 806. n. (7.)**

LESLIE (EVA)

— Love, you and I. Song, the words by N. Labertouche. *Boosey & Co.: London and New York*, 1892. fol.　　　　　　　　　　　**H. 1797. o. (36.)**

— Severed. Song, the words by E. Nesbitt. *Boosey & Co.: London*, [1891.] fol.　　　　**H. 1797. o. (37.)**

LESLIE (F.)

— The Nativity of Our Lady. [Hymn.] Words by ... Dr. Bagshawe, *etc*. *Burns & Oates: London*, [1887.] *a card*.　　　　　　　　　**I. 600. (37.)**

LESLIE (FRANCES M.)

— Johanna's "Lebewohl". [Song, begins: "Lebt wohl".] German words from Schillers Maid of Orleans. *London*, [1863.] fol.　　　　　**H. 1772. r. (40.)**

— Johanna's "Lebewohl," *etc*. *London*, [1867.] fol.　　　　　　　　　　　**H. 1772. r. (41.)**

LESLIE (FRANK)

— Leslie's Barn Dance. [P. F.] *Chappell & Co.: London*, [1894.] fol.　　　　　　　　**h. 3285. q. (30.)**

— Beauty's Eyes. Waltz on ... melodies by F. P. Tosti. [P. F.] *Chappell & Co.: London*, 1892. fol.　**h. 3285. q. (31.)**

LESLIE (FRANK)

— Utopia Limited. Quadrille on airs from ... A. Sullivan's opera. [P. F.] *Chappell & Co.: London*, [1893.] fol.　　　　　　　　　　　**h. 3285. q. (32.)**

LESLIE (FREDERICK)

— Arabella Stuart's Lament. Song [begins: "No more will I plead"]. *London*, [1865.] fol.　**H. 1772. r. (39.)**

— The Birthday Garland. [Song, begins: "With the flowers".] *London*, [1873.] fol.　　**H. 1778. y. (7.)**

— The Captive Bird. Song [begins: "O Lady I am pining"]. *London*, [1862.] fol.　　　**H. 1772. r. (38.)**

— The Cherry Time. Part song [begins: "On the whitest plumes". *See* HULLAH (J. P.) The Singer's Library of Concerted Music. Secular. No. 65. [1859, *etc*.] 8°.　**G. 435.**

— The Merry Spring Time. Part song [begins: "We greet thee"]. The words by S. R. Redman. *See* HULLAH (J. P.) The Singer's Library of Concerted Music. Secular. No. 54. [1859, *etc*.] 8°.　　　　　　　　　　　**G. 435.**

— Silent river, song, the poetry by Longfellow. [Begins: "River that in silence windest".] *London*, [1856.] fol.　　　　　　　　　　　**H. 1771. l. (19.)**

LESLIE (FREDERICK) *pseud*. [i. e. FREDERICK HOBSON.]

— Love in the Lowther. Humorous Song, written and composed by F. Leslie. *J. B. Cramer & Co.: London*, [1882.] fol.　　　　　　　　　**H. 1260. f. (49.)**

— Love in the Orchestra. [Song.] Written and composed by F. Leslie, *etc*. *C. Jeffreys: London*, [1888.] fol.　　　　　　　　　　　**H. 1260. f. (50.)**

LESLIE (GEORGE W.)

— La Marchioness. Gavotte ... pour le piano. *M. Witmark & Sons: New York, etc.*, 1896. fol.　　**h. 3282. f. (40.)**

LESLIE (GODFREY)

— I do not love thee. Song. Words by Caroline Norton. pp. 6. *G. Ricordi & Cᵒ: London*, [1918.] fol.　**H. 1654. qq. (31.)**

— Just a while ago. Song. Words and music by Godfrey Leslie. ⟨Nᵒ 1 in C. Nᵒ 2 in D.⟩ 2 no. *G. Ricordi & Cᵒ: London*, [1917.] fol.　　　　　　**H. 1650. rr. (19.)**

LESLIE (HENRY)

— *See* LESLIE (W. Henry)

LESLIE (HENRY DAVID)

— Henry Leslie's Part-Songs. Tonic Sol-fa. 14 no. *Tonic Sol-fa Agency: London*, [1882–3.] 4°.　**B. 559. p. (12.)**

— Air of Himmel, arranged for four voices by H. Leslie. *See* CHAPPELL AND CO. Chappell's Vocal Library, *etc*. No. 60. [1863–1962.] 8°.　　　　　**G. 440.**

— Always. Ballad [begins: "I think on thee"]. Words by T. K. Hervey. *London*, [1877.] fol.　**H. 1778. y. (12.)**

— The Angels' Visit. *See infra*: [Four Part-Songs for mixed voices. No. 3.]

— Arise, sweet Love. *See infra*: [Six Four-part Songs. Op. 25. No. 6.]

— Auld Lang Syne, arranged for four voices ... by H. Leslie. *See* CRAMER AND CO. J. B. Cramer's Select Library of Part Songs. No. 5. [1880? *etc*.] 4°.　　　**F. 157. a.**

LESLIE (Henry David)

— Awake, awake, the Flow'rs unfold. *See infra:* [Six Four-Part Songs. Op. 23. No. 3.]

— The Beautiful Death. Song [begins: "He died the beautiful death"]. The words by ... S. J. Stone. *London,* [1878.] fol. **H. 1783. o. (50.)**

— Believe me, if all those endearing young Charms. Irish melody [words by T. Moore] arranged for four voices ... by H. Leslie. *See* Cramer and Co. J. B. Cramer's Select Library of Part Songs. No. 7. [1880? *etc.*] 4°. **F. 157. a.**

— Believe me, if all those endearing young Charms. Irish Melody arranged [for S. C. T. B.] by H. Leslie. [1905.] *See* Choral. The Choral Handbook. No. 735. [1885, *etc.*] 8°. **E. 862.**

— Blow ye the Trumpet in Zion. Full Anthem, *etc. See* Novello and Co. Novello's Collection of Anthems, *etc.* Vol. IV. No. 97. [1876, *etc.*] 8°. **E. 618. a.**

— Blow ye the Trumpet in Zion. Full Anthem for Advent Sunday, *etc.* [1904.] *See* Church. The Church Choralist. No. 311. [1886, *etc.*] 8°. **E. 1330.**

— Blow ye the Trumpet in Zion, *etc.* [1908.] *See* Novello and Co. Novello's Tonic Sol-fa Series. No. 1615. [1876, *etc.*] 4°. **B. 885.**

— Boat Song [begins: "Hail to the chief"]. (The words by Sir W. Scott.) *London,* [1853.] fol. **H. 2832. o. (46.)**

— The Boatswain's Leap, song [begins: "The stately vessel"] ... The words by C. J. Rowe. *London,* [1871.] fol. **H. 1775. u. (23.)**

— Bridal March. *See infra:* [The Daughter of the Isles.]

— Bridal Song in honor of the marriage of ... the Princess Royal ... Words by H. F. Chorley. *See* Cramer and Co. J. B. Cramer's Select Library of Part Songs. No. 9. [1880? *etc.*] 4°. **F. 157. a.**

— Bridal Song. Four-Part Song, *etc.* [1902.] *See* Novello and Co. Novello's Part-Song Book. Second Series. No. 878. [1869, *etc.*] 8°. **F. 280. b.**

— The Brookside. Ballad [begins: "I wandered"]. Words by Lord Houghton. *London,* [1878.] fol. **H. 1783. o. (52.)**

— The Bushranger's Home ... Song [begins: "Leave behind"]. *London,* [1862.] fol. **H. 2622. (29.)**

— By the sunset glow, romance [begins: "Is aught on earth more pleasant"]. The words by J. P. Simpson. *London,* [1856.] fol. **H. 1758. (32.)**

— Calm & serene is the Night. Song, *etc. Jullien & Co.: London,* [1845?] fol. **H. 1650. n. (20.)**

— The Captain's Song [begins: "Blow, blow"]. Words by W. C. Bennett. *London,* [1874.] fol. **H. 1778. y. (8.)**

— Carmen Oswestriense. School Song, *etc. Weekes & Co.: London,* [1889.] 8°. **F. 585. u. (13.)**

— Cassell's Choral Music. Edited, with copyright marks of expression, by H. Leslie. 11 pt. 50 no. *Cassell, Petter and Galpin: London and New York,* [1867.] fol. **H. 1236.**

— [Cassell's Choral Music.] [A reissue.] Choral Music. *Novello, Ewer & Co.: London,* [c. 1880.] fol. **H. 1236. d.**

— Charm me asleep. A Madrigal for six Voices, the words by Herricks. Op. 24. No. 3. *See* Novello and Co. Novello's Part-Song Book. Second Series. Vol. II. No. 85. [1869, *etc.*] 8°. **F. 280. b.**

— Charm me asleep. A Madrigal ... No. 3. Op. 24. [1899.] *See* Novello and Co. Novello's Tonic Sol-fa Series. No. 1074. [1876, *etc.*] 4°. **B. 885.**

LESLIE (Henry David)

— Clarior ex obscuro, solo with chorus [begins: "Ingeri parvam tegat umbra lucem"]. The words by ... L. Sanderson. *London,* [1872.] fol. **H. 1775. u. (24.)**

— Come Hope, thy Ray. *See infra:* [Ida.]

— Come unto Him. *See* infra: [Immanuel.]

— The Daughter of the Isles. A cantata ... Words by A. Matthison. *London,* [1862.] fol. **H. 1094. a.**

— [The Daughter of the Isles.] Bridal March. [P. F.] *London,* [1862.] fol. **H. 2622. (15.)**

— [The Daughter of the Isles.] Bridal March for the Pianoforte. *London,* [1876.] fol. **h. 1482. z. (45.)**

— [The Daughter of the Isles.] The Fair Sun of my Heart. Serenade ... Words by A. Matthison. *London,* [1862.] fol. **H. 2622. (14.)**

— Daylight is fading. *See infra:* [Six Four-part Songs. Op. 25. No. 3.]

— Down in a pretty Valley. *See infra:* [Six Four-part Songs. Op. 25. No. 4.]

— A Dream of Calm [begins: "How calm, how beautiful"] the poetry by T. Moore, set to music for a choir of mixed voices. *London,* [1876.] fol. **H. 1778. y. (9.)**

— A Dream of Calm. Quartett ... Words by T. Moore. *See* Cramer and Co. J. B. Cramer's Select Library of Part Songs. No. 2. [1880? *etc.*] 4°. **F. 157. a.**

— A Dream of Calm. Part Song ... for ... S. A. A. T. B. B. *See* Cramer and Co. J. B. Cramer's Select Library of Part Songs. No. 3. [1880? *etc.*] 4°. **F. 157. a.**

— A Dream of Calm. For Tenor Solo and Four-Part Chorus, *etc.* [1902.] *See* Novello and Co. Novello's Part-Song Book. Second Series. No. 892. [1869, *etc.*] 8°. **F. 280. b.**

— Three Duetts for female voices. The words by H. F. Chorley. No. 2, 3. *London,* [1856.] fol.
Imperfect; wanting no. 1. **H. 2827. a. (17.)**

— Dunois the Brave.—Partant pour la Syrie.—French National Air arranged for S. A. T. B. by H. Leslie. The words from the French by Sir Walter Scott. *See* Cramer and Co. J. B. Cramer's Select Library of Part Songs. No. 15. [1880? *etc.*] 4°. **F. 157. a.**

— Evening. Four-part Song, the words by Lord Byron. *See* Novello and Co. Novello's Part-Song Book. Second Series. Vol. XIV. No. 397. [1869, *etc.*] 8°. **F. 280. b.**

— Evening. Part-Song for Alto, two Tenors and Bass, *etc.* [1879.] *See* Orpheus. The Orpheus, *etc.* New Series. Vol. II. No. 35. [1879, *etc.*] 8°. **E. 1748.**

— Evening, *etc.* [Part-song for A. T. T. B.] *J. Curwen & Sons: London,* [1904.] 8°.
The Apollo Club, No. 252. **F. 667.**

— Evening. Four-Part Song, *etc.* [1905.] *See* Choral. The Choral Handbook. No. 707. [1885, *etc.*] 8°. **E. 862.**

— Evening. Arranged for A. T. T. B. (S. A. T. B.) 2 no. [1903.] *See* Novello and Co. Novello's Tonic Sol-fa Series. No. 1326, 1328. [1876, *etc.*] 4°. **B. 885.**

— Fair Nell of Berrie Brae, romance, [begins: "The queen is fair,"] the words by J. P. Simpson. *London,* [1856.] fol. **H. 1758. (34.)**

— The Fair Sun of my heart. *See supra:* [The Daughter of the Isles.]

— The Fan Duett. *See supra:* Three Duetts, *etc.* No. 2.

LESLIE (HENRY DAVID)

—— The First Christmas Morn, a Biblical pastoral, the words ... written by ... Rev. S. J. Stone. [Vocal score.] pp. 49. *Novello, Ewer & Co.: London*, [1880.] 8°.　　　**F. 1285.**

—— [Another copy.]　　　**R. M. 8. h. 12.**

—— [Another copy.]　　　**R. M. 25. f. 6.**

—— Flora gave me fairest Flowers. Madrigal ... by J. Wilbye. Edited by H. Leslie. [1902.] *See* NOVELLO AND CO. Novello's Tonic Sol-fa Series. No. 1270. [1876, *etc.*] 4°.　　　**B. 885.**

—— The Flower Girl. Ballad [begins: "Buy my flowers"]. (Words by J. S. L.) *London*, [1860.] fol.　　　**H. 2622. (25.)**

—— The flower Girl. Ballad. (Words by J. S. L.) *London*, [1878.] fol.　　　**H. 1783. o. (53.)**

Six Four-part Songs. Op. 23

—— Six Four-part Songs. Op. 23. *London*, [1866.] fol. *Bk. 7 of "Novello's Part-Song Book. Second series".*　　　**F. 280. b.**

—— Choral Songs. (S. A. T. B.) Op. 23. No. 1–3. *London*, [1865.] fol.　　　**H. 2622. (1.)**

—— [No. 1.] The Pilgrims. A Four-part Song, *etc. See* NOVELLO AND CO. Novello's Part-Song Book. Second Series. Vol. II. No. 74. [1869, *etc.*] 8°.　　　**F. 280. b.**

—— [No. 1.] The Pilgrims, *etc.* [1909.] *See* CHORAL. The Choral Handbook. No. 806. [1885, *etc.*] 8°.　　　**E. 862.**

—— [No. 1.] The Pilgrims. A four-part Song. Words by A. A. Procter. [1881.] *See* NOVELLO AND CO. Novello's Tonic Sol-fa series. No. 114. [1876, *etc.*] 4°.　　　**B. 885.**

—— [No. 1. The Pilgrims.] Gweddi'r pererinion ... Rhangan gysegredig ... English words by Adelaide Anne Proctor. Geiriau Cymraeg gan G. M. Probert. [Tonic sol-fa notation.] *Hughes & Son: Wrexham*, [1918.] 8°. [*Y Cerddor. rhif* 349.]　　　**P. P. 1947. l.**

—— [No. 2.] My Soul to God, my Heart to thee. A Four-part Song, *etc. See* NOVELLO AND CO. Novello's Part-Song Book. Second Series. Vol. II. No. 75. [1869, *etc.*] 8°.　　　**F. 280. b.**

—— [No. 3.] Awake, awake, the Flow'rs unfold. A Four-part Song. *See* NOVELLO AND CO. Novello's Part-Song Book. Second Series. Vol. II. No. 76. [1869, *etc.*] 8°.　　　**F. 280. b.**

—— [No. 3.] Awake, awake, the Flower's unfold, *etc.* [1909.] *See* CHORAL. The Choral Handbook. No. 807. [1885, *etc.*] 8°.　　　**E. 862.**

—— [No. 3.] Awake, awake, the Flowers unfold. Four-part Song, *etc.* [1892.] *See* NOVELLO AND CO. Novello's Tonic Sol-fa Series. No. 752. [1876, *etc.*] 4°.　　　**B. 885.**

—— [No. 4.] How sweet the Moonlight sleeps. A Four-part Song, the words by Shakespeare. *See* NOVELLO AND CO. Novello's Part-Song Book. Second Series. Vol. II. No. 77. [1869, *etc.*] 8°.　　　**F. 280. b.**

—— [No. 4.] How sweet the Moonlight sleeps. A Four-Part Song. Words by Shakespeare. 1883. *See* PERIODICAL PUBLICATIONS. — *London*. The Musical Times, *etc.* No. 482. 1844, *etc.* 8°.　　　**P. P. 1945. aa.**

—— [No. 4.] How sweet the Moonlight sleeps, *etc.* [1909.] *See* CHORAL. The Choral Handbook. No. 813. [1885, *etc.*] 8°.　　　**E. 862.**

—— [No. 4.] How sweet the Moonlight sleeps. A four-part song, words by Shakespeare. [1886.] *See* NOVELLO AND CO. Novello's Tonic Sol-fa Series. No. 508. [1876, *etc.*] 4°.　　　**B. 885.**

LESLIE (HENRY DAVID)

—— [No. 5.] Land-ho. A Four-part Song, the words by H. Farnie. *See* NOVELLO AND CO. Novello's Part-Song Book. Second Series. Vol. II. No. 78. [1869, *etc.*] 8°.　　　**F. 280. b.**

—— [No. 5.] Land-ho, *etc.* [1909.] *See* CHORAL. The Choral Handbook. No. 820. [1885, *etc.*] 8°.　　　**E. 862.**

—— [No. 6.] Up, up, ye Dames. A Four-part Song, the words by Coleridge. *See* NOVELLO AND CO. Novello's Part-Song Book. Second Series. Vol. II. No. 79. [1869, *etc.*] 8°.　　　**F. 280. b.**

—— [No. 6.] Up, up, ye Dames, *etc.* [1909.] *See* CHORAL. The Choral Handbook. No. 821. [1885, *etc.*] 8°.　　　**E. 862.**

Six Four-part Songs. Op. 25

—— Six Four-part Songs. Op. 25. *London*, [1869.] 8°. *Bk. 16 of "Novello's Part-song Book. Second series".*　　　**F. 280. b.**

—— [No. 1.] The Violet. Words by Mrs. Freake. *See* NOVELLO AND CO. Novello's Part-Song Book. Second Series. Vol. IV. No. 132. [1869, *etc.*] 8°.　　　**F. 280. b.**

—— [No. 2.] One Morning Sweet in May. Words by J. Phillips. *See* NOVELLO AND CO. Novello's Part-Song Book. Second Series. Vol. IV. No. 133. [1869, *etc.*] 8°.　　　**F. 280. b.**

—— [No. 3.] Daylight is fading. Words by J. S. L. *See* NOVELLO AND CO. Novello's Part-Song Book. Second Series. Vol. IV. No. 134. [1869, *etc.*] 8°.　　　**F. 280. b.**

—— [No. 3.] Daylight is fading, *etc.* [1909.] *See* CHORAL. The Choral Handbook. [No. 904.] [1885, *etc.*] 8°.　　　**E. 862.**

—— [No. 3.] Daylight is fading. [Part-song.] Words by J. S. L. [1880.] *See* NOVELLO AND CO. Novello's Tonic Sol-fa Series. No. 34. [1876, *etc.*] 4°.　　　**B. 885.**

—— [No. 4.] Down in a pretty Valley. Words by J. Phillips. *See* NOVELLO AND CO. Novello's Part-Song Book. Second Series. Vol. IV. No. 135. [1869, *etc.*] 8°.　　　**F. 280. b.**

—— [No. 4.] Down in a pretty Valley, *etc.* [1909.] *See* CHORAL. The Choral Handbook. [No. 907.] [1885, *etc.*] 8°.　　　**E. 862.**

—— [No. 5.] The Primrose. Words by T. Carew. *See* NOVELLO AND CO. Novello's Part-Song Book. Second Series. Vol. IV. No. 136. [1869, *etc.*] 8°.　　　**F. 280. b.**

—— [No. 5.] The Primrose, *etc.* [1909.] *See* CHORAL. The Choral Handbook. [No. 905.] [1885, *etc.*] 8°.　　　**E. 862.**

—— [No. 6.] Arise, sweet Love. Words by J. Phillips. *See* NOVELLO AND CO. Novello's Part-Song Book. Second Series. Vol. IV. No. 137. [1869, *etc.*] 8°.　　　**F. 280. b.**

—— [No. 6.] Arise, sweet Love, *etc.* [1909.] *See* CHORAL. The Choral Handbook. [No. 906.] [1885, *etc.*] 8°.　　　**E. 862.**

—— From Greenland's icy Mountains. Unison Song. [1899.] *See* MACNAUGHT (W. G.) Novello's School Songs. [Book 19.] No. 436. 1892, *etc.* 8°.　　　**F. 280. d.**

—— The Gipsy Queen Polka, *etc.* [P. F.] pp. 5. *Jullien & Cº: London*, [1852.] fol.　　　**h. 723. ll. (17.)**

—— God save the King. Arranged [for S. C. T. B.] by H. Leslie. [1910.] *See* CHORAL. The Choral Handbook. [No. 952.] [1885, *etc.*] 8°.　　　**E. 862.**

—— God save the Queen, arranged as a Four-Part Song ... by H. Leslie. *See* CRAMER AND CO. J. B. Cramer's Select Library of Part Songs. No. 19. [1880? *etc.*] 4°.　　　**F. 157. a.**

—— Golden slumbers kiss your eyes. Serenade for a choir of mixed voices. *London*, [1885.] 4°.　　　**F. 585. p. (18.)**

LESLIE (Henry David)

—— The Golden Year. Choral four-part song [begins: "We sleep and wake"]. Poetry by A. Tennyson. *London*, [1880.] 4°.
F. 585. e. (31.)

—— The Golden Year. Choral Four Part Song, *etc.* [1909.] *See* Novello and Co. Novello's Part-Song Book. Second Series. No. 1137. [1869, *etc.*] 8°.
F. 280. b.

—— Gone are the days of chivalry. *See* infra: [Romance.]

—— Good Night. *See* infra: [Three Trios for Female Voices. No. 2.]

—— Gweddi'r pererinion. *See* supra: [Six Four-part Songs. Op. 23. No. 1. The Pilgrims.]

—— Hail! Smiling Morn. Glee ... composed by R. Spofforth, arranged by H. Leslie. [1886.] *See* Novello and Co. Novello's Tonic Sol-fa Series. No. 455 (a). [1876, *etc.*] 4°.
B. 885.

—— Hail to the Chief. [Part-song] ... The words taken from Sir W. Scott's "Lady of the Lake". *See* Novello and Co. Novello's Part-Song Book. Second Series. Vol. XIV. No. 399. [1869, *etc.*] 8°.
F. 280. b.

—— Hail to the Chief.—Boat Song [for S. C. T. B.].—, *etc.* [1905.] *See* Choral. The Choral Handbook. No. 708. [1885, *etc.*] 8°.
E. 862.

—— Hail to the Chief.—Boat Song.—, *etc.* [Four-part song.] [1903.] *See* Novello and Co. Novello's Tonic Sol-fa Series. No. 1331. [1876, *etc.*] 4°.
B. 885.

—— Hail to the Chief. (Boat song.) (Arranged for S. S. C.), *etc.* pp. 7. *J. Curwen & Sons: London*, [1904.] 8°.
[*Choruses for equal Voices. no.* 845.]
E. 861.

—— Hark! the Lark. Part-Song ... by Dr. Cooke. Arranged for female voices by H. Leslie. [1885.] *See* Novello and Co. Novello's Collection of Trios, *etc.* Vol. VII. No. 158. [1879, *etc.*] 8°.
E. 1746.

—— Hark! The Lark ... Arranged for S.S.A.A. by H. Leslie. [1883.] *See* Novello and Co. Novello's Tonic Sol-fa Series. No. 187. [1876, *etc.*] 4°.
B. 885.

—— Holiday Song [begins: "O come and play"], for even voices. *London*, [1860.] fol.
H. 2622. (4.)

—— Holy Mother. *See* infra: [Ida.]

—— Holyrood. A Cantata, the words by Henry F. Chorley. (Op. 17.) [Vocal score.] pp. 83. *Addison, Hollier & Lucas: London*, [1860.] fol.
H. 1099.

—— [Another copy.]
R. M. 11. d. 15.

—— Holyrood, a cantata, the words by Henry F. Chorley. no. 3. *Lamborn & Cock, Addison & Cº: London*, [1867?] fol. *Imperfect; wanting no.* 1, 2, 4–14.
H. 892. a.

—— Homeward. A Four-part Song, the poetry written by H. Macdowall, *etc.* [1884.] *See* Novello and Co. Novello's Part-Song Book. Second Series. Vol. XVI. No. 443. [1869, *etc.*] 8°.
F. 280. b.

—— Homeward! A four-part Song. Words by H. Macdowall. [1880.] *See* Novello and Co. Novello's Tonic Sol-fa series. No. 110. [1876, *etc.*] 4°.
B. 885.

—— [Homeward.] The Day dies slowly in the western Sky. Song, being a free transcription of his Part-Song "Homeward". *Novello, Ewer and Co.: London & New York*, [1883.] fol.
G. 806. n. (8.)

—— How sweet the Moonlight sleeps. *See* supra: [Six Four-part Songs. Op. 23. No. 4.]

—— Two Hymns ... Words by ... H. R. Haweis. *London*, [1882.] 8°.
E. 605. k. (43.)

LESLIE (Henry David)

—— I do not ask a brighter lot, ballad, the poetry by Lady F. Hastings. *London*, [1854.] fol.
H. 1758. (35.)

—— "I saw a golden sunbeam fall," sacred ballad. *London*, [1856.] fol.
H. 1758. (40.)

—— "I saw a golden sunbeam fall," sacred ballad. [Duet.] *London*, [1856.] fol.
H. 1758. (39.)

—— I saw a golden Sunbeam fall. Sacred duet. pp. 4. *J. Curwen & Sons: London*, [1905.] 8°.
[*Choruses for equal Voices. no.* 918.]
E. 861.

—— Motett, "I will extol thee, O God, my King," for soprano, contralto and chorus, with accompaniment of harp and organ ... Op. 15. *London*, [1859.] fol.
H. 1187. a. (17.)

Ida

—— Ida, a Legendary Opera in three Acts, by J. P. Simpson. Op. 22. *Addison & Co.: London*, [1864.] fol.
H. 1099. a.

—— Come Hope, thy ray. Song. *London*, [1866.] fol.
H. 2622. (21.)

—— Holy Mother. Air. *London*, [1866.] fol.
H. 2622. (20.)

—— Lord Rupert bold & wild. [Song.] ... Written by J. P. Simpson. *London*, [1866.] fol.
H. 2622. (16.)

—— Lord Rupert bold & wild. *See* Osborne (G. A.) Lord Rupert ... for the Pianoforte. [1866.] fol.
h. 644. b. (11.)

—— A Loving Heart. Ballad. *London*, [1866.] fol.
H. 2622. (18.)

—— My Liege Lord and Master. Air. *London*, [1866.] fol.
H. 2622. (23.)

—— 'Twas but a dream. Song. *London*, [1866.] fol.
H. 2622. (22.)

—— When first I saw his noble form. Ballad. *London*, [1866.] fol.
H. 2622. (19.)

—— While Life shall last. Romance. *London*, [1866.] fol.
H. 2622. (24.)

—— With heart confiding, duet. *London*, [1866.] fol.
H. 2622. (17.)

—— If we were king and queen. Song [begins: "When we were young"] written by G. Weatherly. *London*, [1882.] fol.
H. 1789. a. (35.)

—— Immanuel, an oratorio, in two parts, the words selected from the Holy Scriptures. Op. 8. [Vocal score.] pp. 177. *Chappell: London*, [1854.] fol.
H. 1094.

—— [Another copy.]
A word-book of the first performance (2 March, 1854) is inserted.
R. M. 14. e. 10.

—— [Immanuel.] Come unto Him. Anthem for Tenor Solo and Chorus ... Edited by H. E. Button. 1909. *See* Novello and Co. Novello's Collection of Anthems, *etc.* No. 946. [1876, *etc.*] 8°.
E. 618. a.

—— [Immanuel.] Come unto Him ... Edited by H. E. Button. [1912.] *See* Novello and Co. Novello's Tonic Sol-fa Series. No. 2021. [1876, *etc.*] 4°.
B. 885.

—— Important is my Mission. *See* infra: [Romance.]

—— In these delightful pleasant Groves. Chorus ... by H. Purcell. Edited by H. Leslie. [1889.] *See* Novello and Co. Novello's Tonic Sol-fa Series. No. 674. [1876, *etc.*] 4°.
B. 885.

—— The Ivy. Romance for the Piano Forte, *etc. Cramer, Beale & Co.: London*, [1850?] fol.
g. 232. d. (25.)

LESLIE (Henry David)

— Jephthah's daughter, scena [begins: "The altar is prepared"]. The words by J. P. Simpson. Op. 9. *London,* [1856.] fol. **H. 1758. (33.)**

— Judith, a biblical Cantata, in three scenes. The words selected from the Holy Scriptures by H. F. Chorley, *etc. London,* [1859.] fol. **I. 264.**

— Kind Words. Part song [begins: "There is a legend"]. *London,* [1883.] 4°. **F. 585. g. (24.)**

— Kind Words. Four-Part Song, *etc.* [1902.] *See* NOVELLO AND CO. Novello's Part-Song Book. Second Series. No. 883. [1869, *etc.*] 8°. **F. 280. b.**

— Ladye fair, thou hast my Life. A Choral Song for four voices, the words written by P. Latimer. The music ... edited by H. Leslie. [1892.] *See* NOVELLO AND CO. Novello's Part-Song Book. Second Series. No. 636. [1869, *etc.*] 8°. **F. 280. b.**

— Ladye fair, thou hast my Life. A choral Song for four voices ... edited by H. Leslie. [1892.] *See* NOVELLO AND CO. Novello's Tonic Sol-fa Series. No. 769. [1876, *etc.*] 4°. **B. 885.**

— Land-ho. *See supra:* [Six Four-part Songs. Op. 23. No. 5.]

— The Lass of Richmond Hill [by J. Hook] arranged for four voices. *London,* [1877.] 8°. *No. 51 of the "Choristers' Album".* **E. 1708.**

— The Lass of Richmond Hill. Old Ballad composed by J. Hook, arranged as a Four-part Song by H. Leslie. [1885.] *See* NOVELLO AND CO. Novello's Part-Song Book. Second Series. Vol. XVIII. No. 501. [1869, *etc.*] 8°. **F. 280. b.**

— The Lass of Richmond Hill. J. Hook. Arranged [for S. C. T. B.] by H. D. Leslie. [1905.] *See* CHORAL. The Choral Handbook. No. 736. [1885, *etc.*] 8°. **E. 862.**

— The Lass of Richmond Hill ... Four-part Song. By J. Hook, arranged by H. Leslie. [1889.] *See* NOVELLO AND CO. Novello's Tonic Sol-fa Series. No. 678. [1876, *etc.*] 4°. **B. 885.**

— "Let God arise," a festival anthem, the words selected from the 68th Psalm ... Op. 5. [Vocal score.] pp. 65. *J. Alfred Novello: London,* [1850.] fol. **H. 892.**

— [Another copy.] **R. M. 14. f. 7. (3.)**

— Little Songs for me to sing. The illustrations by J. E. Millais, *etc. Cassell, Petter & Galpin: London,* [1865.] 4°. **11648. bb. 53.**

— Look forth, look forth. *See infra:* [Romance.]

— Lord Rupert bold & wild. *See supra:* [Ida.]

— Love, the last, best Gift. Trio [begins: "There is a sweeter flower"] ... Words from Keble's Christian Year. *London,* [1866.] fol. **H. 2622. (31.)**

— Love, the last, best Gift. Trio for Soprano, Contralto and Tenor, *etc.* [1907.] *See* CHORAL. The Choral Handbook. No. 792. [1885, *etc.*] 8°. **E. 862.**

— "Love." The last, best Gift. Arranged for S. S. C., *etc.* pp. 7. *J. Curwen & Sons: London,* [1908.] 8°. [*Choruses for equal Voices. no.* 1020.] **E. 861.**

— A Loving Heart. *See supra:* [Ida.]

— Lullaby of Life. *See infra:* [Four Part-Songs for mixed voices. No. 1.]

Memory

— Memory, trio [begins: "O Memory"] ... The poetry by Miss L. Smith. *London,* [1866.] fol. **H. 2622. (32.)**

LESLIE (Henry David)

— O Memory! Trio for Soprano, Contralto, and Tenor. [Words by] L. Smith. [1905.] *See* CHORAL. The Choral Handbook. No. 720. [1885, *etc.*] 8°. **E. 862.**

— O Memory. Trio for Soprano, Contralto and Tenor, *etc.* [1908.] *See* NOVELLO AND CO. Novello's Part-Song Book. Second Series. No. 1046. [1869, *etc.*] 8°. **F. 280. b.**

— O Memory. Trio for Soprano, Contralto and Tenor, *etc.* [1908.] *See* NOVELLO AND CO. Novello's Tonic Sol-fa Series. No. 1673. [1876, *etc.*] 4°. **B. 885.**

— O Memory. Trio. Soprano, Mezzo Soprano and Contralto, *etc.* [1905.] *See* SAINT. St. Cecilia, *etc.* Eleventh Series. No. 13. [1890? *etc.*] 4°. **F. 1526.**

— "O Memory!" Trio. (Arranged for S. S. C.), *etc.* pp. 7. *J. Curwen & Sons: London,* [1907.] 8°. [*Choruses for equal Voices. no.* 1048.] **E. 861.**

— O Memory. Trio arranged by the Composer for Soprano, Mezzo-Soprano and Contralto, *etc.* [1908.] *See* NOVELLO AND CO. Novello's Collection of Trios, *etc.* No. 368. [1879, *etc.*] 8°. **E. 1746.**

— O Memory. Trio arranged by the Composer for Soprano, Mezzo-Soprano and Contralto, *etc.* [1909.] *See* NOVELLO AND CO. Novello's Tonic Sol-fa Series. No. 1742. [1876, *etc.*] 4°. **B. 885.**

— Memory, arranged as a song ... with additional verses by ... S. J. Stone. *London,* [1879.] fol. **H. 1783. o. (54.)**

— Merry May. Song [begins: "Up, up"]. *London,* [1860.] fol. **H. 2622. (26.)**

— The Moonbeam and the Dewdrop ... Scotch ballad [begins: "O cozie"]. *London,* [1862.] fol. **H. 2622. (28.)**

— The Mountain Maid. Song [begins: "Gaily on the mountain side"]. Words by E. Oxenford. *London,* [1877.] fol. **H. 1778. y. (11.)**

— H. Leslie's Musical Annual. 1871. *London,* [1871.] fol. **G. 438.**

— H. Leslie's Musical Annual, 1872. *London,* [1871.] fol. **G. 438. a.**

— My bonny Lass she smileth ... Composed by T. Morley ... Edited by H. Leslie. [1909.] *See* NOVELLO AND CO. Novello's Tonic Sol-fa Series. No. 1820. [1876, *etc.*] 4°. **B. 885.**

— My Darling, hush! A Mother's lullaby. [Song, begins: "Lullaby".] Written by F. J. B. ⟨In B flat.⟩ *London,* [1868.] fol. **H. 2622. (6.)**

— My darling, hush. ⟨In G.⟩ *London,* [1868.] fol. **H. 2622. (7.)**

— My Liege Lord and Master. *See supra:* [Ida.]

— My Love is fair. Madrigal for five Voices, the words by G. Peele. *See* NOVELLO AND CO. Novello's Part-Song Book. Second Series. Vol. II. No. 84. [1869, *etc.*] 8°. **F. 280. b.**

— My Love is fair. Madrigal for five voices, *etc.* [1899.] *See* NOVELLO AND CO. Novello's Tonic Sol-fa Series. No. 1082. [1876, *etc.*] 4°. **B. 885.**

— My Soul to God, my heart to thee. *See supra:* [Six Four-part Songs. Op. 23. No. 2.]

— The Nightingale, Madrigal for four [or rather, three] voices, composed by T. Weelkes ... Arranged for female voices by H. Leslie. [Two editions.] [1887, 1935.] *See* NOVELLO AND CO. Novello's Collection of Trios, *etc.* No. 200. [1879, *etc.*] 8°. **E. 1746.**

LESLIE (HENRY DAVID)

— The Nightingale. Madrigal ... Composed ... by T. Weelkes ... Arranged by H. Leslie. [1904.] *See* MACNAUGHT (W. G.) Novello's School Songs. No. 695. 1892, *etc.* 8°. **F. 280. d.**

— The Nightingale. Madrigal for four voices. Composed by T. Weelkes ... Arranged for three female voices by H. Leslie. [1886.] *See* NOVELLO AND CO. Novello's Tonic Sol-fa series. No. 428. [1876, *etc.*] 4°. **B. 885.**

— Now the bright Morning Star. Four-part Song, *etc. See* NOVELLO AND CO. Novello's Part-Song Book. Second Series. Vol. XIV. No. 398. [1869, *etc.*] 8°. **F. 280. b.**

— Now the bright Morning Star. A four-part Song, the words by Milton. [1887.] *See* NOVELLO AND CO. Novello's Tonic Sol-fa Series. No. 547. [1876, *etc.*] 4°. **B. 885.**

— O gentle Sleep. Choral Song for four voices ... words by Shakespeare. Op. 13. *See* CRAMER AND CO. J. B. Cramer's Select Library of Part Songs. No. 34. [1880? *etc.*] 4°. **F. 157. a.**

— O gentle Sleep. Choral Song for four voices, S. A. T. B., *etc.* [1903.] *See* NOVELLO AND CO. Novello's Part-Song Book. Second Series. No. 902. [1869, *etc.*] 8°. **F. 280. b.**

— O have mercy upon me. Full Anthem for Lent. 1883. *See* PERIODICAL PUBLICATIONS.— *London*. The Musical Times, *etc.* No. 480. 1844, *etc.* 8°. **P. P. 1945. aa.**

— O let me play the fool. Madrigal for six voices, S. S. A. T. B. B. Poetry by Shakespeare, from the Merchant of Venice. *London*, [1885.] 4°. **F. 585. p. (19.)**

— "Oh let me sing to thee," song [begins: "When tear drops"], words by J. P. Simpson. *London*, [1854.] fol. **H. 1758. (36.)**

— O Memory. *See* supra: [Memory.]

— Oh! slumber my darling. Part song, words by I. F. B. *London*, [1872.] 4°. **F. 585. b. (33.)**

— One Morning sweet in May. *See* supra: [Six Four-part Songs. Op. 25. No. 2.]

— Parting and Meeting. Volkslied of Mendelssohn. Arranged for a Choir by H. Leslie. Translated from the German by N. Macfarren. 1875. *See* PERIODICAL PUBLICATIONS.— *London*. The Musical Times, *etc.* No. 385. 1844, *etc.* 8°. **P. P. 1945. aa.**

— Parting and Meeting. Volkslied of Mendelssohn ... Arranged for a Choir by H. Leslie. [1886.] *See* NOVELLO AND CO. Novello's Tonic Sol-fa Series. No. 514. a. [1876, *etc.*] 4°. **B. 885.**

Two Part-Songs

— Two Part songs for mixed voices. Words by R. [or rather, A.] Matthison. *London*, [1861.] fol. **H. 2622. (2.)**

— [No. 1.] Song of the Flax Spinner. [Parts.] *London*, [1861.] fol. **H. 2622. (3.)**

— [No. 1.] Song of the Flax Spinner. No. 1 of Two Part Songs for Mixed Voices. Op. 18. Words by A. Matthison, *etc. See* CRAMER AND CO. J. B. Cramer's Select Library of Part Songs. No. 44. [1880? *etc.*] 4°. **F. 157. a.**

— [No. 1.] Song of the Flax Spinner. Four-Part Song, *etc.* [1902.] *See* NOVELLO AND CO. Novello's Part-Song Book. Second Series. No. 877. [1869, *etc.*] 8°. **F. 280. b.**

— [No. 1.] Song of the Flax Spinner. Four-Part Song, *etc.* [1905.] *See* CHORAL. The Choral Handbook. No. 709. [1885, *etc.*] 8°. **E. 862.**

— [No. 1.] Song of the Flax Spinner. Four-Part Song, *etc.* [1903.] *See* NOVELLO AND CO. Novello's Tonic Sol-fa Series. No. 1329. [1876, *etc.*] 4°. **B. 885.**

LESLIE (HENRY DAVID)

— [No. 2.] The Troubadour, four-part song [begins: "Glowing with love"]. London, [1877.] 8°. *No. 53 of the "Choristers' Album".* **E. 1708.**

— [No. 2.] The Troubadour. A Five part Song, the poetry translated by Sir W. Scott from the poems of the Duchesse de St. Leu. [1885.] *See* NOVELLO AND CO. Novello's Part-Song Book. Second Series. Vol. XVIII. No. 500. [1869, *etc.*] 8°. **F. 280. b.**

— [No. 2.] The Troubadour. (Arranged for S. S. C.), *etc.* pp. 6. *J. Curwen & Sons: London*, [1904.] 8°. *[Choruses for equal Voices. no. 846.]* **E. 861.**

— [No. 2.] The Troubadour. A Five-Part Song, *etc.* [1905.] *See* CHORAL. The Choral Handbook. No. 710. [1885, *etc.*] 8°. **E. 862.**

— [No. 2.] The Troubadour. A Five-Part song. Translated from the French by Sir W. Scott. [1886.] *See* NOVELLO AND CO. Novello's Tonic Sol-fa Series. No. 444. [1876, *etc.*.] 4°. **B. 885.**

Four Part-Songs for mixed voices

— [No. 1.] Lullaby of Life. No. 1 of a set of four-part songs ... Poetry by ... S. J. Stone [begins: "Sleep little flower"]. *London*, [1874.] 4°. **F. 321. a. (17.)**

— [No. 1.] Lullaby of Life. Four-Part Song, *etc.* [1902.] *See* NOVELLO AND CO. Novello's Part-Song Book. Second Series. No. 881. [1869, *etc.*] 8°. **F. 280. b.**

— [No. 1.] Lullaby of Life ... Adapted for ... school choruses by R. L. Baldwin. *G. Schirmer: New York*, 1927. 8°. **F. 585. qq. (14.)**

— [No. 1.] Lullaby of Life ... Edited by N. Cain. *H. Flammer: New York*, 1938. 8°. **F. 585. zz. (30.)**

— [No. 2.] The Rainbow. No. 2 of a set of four-part songs ... Poetry by ... J. S. Monsell [begins: "I am not one"]. *London*, [1874.] 4°. **F. 321. a. (18.)**

— [No. 2.] The Rainbow. Four-Part Song, *etc.* [1902.] *See* NOVELLO AND CO. Novello's Part-Song Book. Second Series. No. 882. [1869, *etc.*] 8°. **F. 280. b.**

— [No. 3.] The Angels' Visit. No. 3 of a set of four-part songs ... Poetry by H. Joyce [begins: "The pallid face"]. *London*, [1874.] 4°. **F. 321. a. (19.)**

— [No. 4.] We roam and rule the sea. No. 4 of a set of four-part songs ... The poetry ... by W. C. Bennett [begins: "The surge's salt"]. *London*, [1876.] 4°. **F. 321. a. (20.)**

— [No. 4.] We roam and rule the Sea. Four-Part Song, *etc.* [1902.] *See* NOVELLO AND CO. Novello's Part-Song Book. Second Series. No. 880. [1869, *etc.*] 8°. **F. 280. b.**

— Pibroch of Donuil Dhu. Part-Song for Alto, Tenor and two Basses, the words by Sir Walter Scott. [1879.] *See* ORPHEUS. The Orpheus, *etc.* New Series. Vol. II. No. 36. [1879, *etc.*] 8°. **E. 1748.**

— The Pilgrims. *See* supra: [Six Four-part Songs. Op. 23. No. 1.]

— Poor silly heart. Ballad. *See* infra: [Romance.]

— The Primrose. *See* supra: [Six Four-part Songs. Op. 25. No. 5.]

— The Rainbow. *See* supra: [Four Part-Songs for mixed voices. No. 2.]

— Raise again the bold Refrain. [Four-part song.] Adapted to a Russian melody by H. Leslie. Words by C. J. Rowe. 1872. *See* PERIODICAL PUBLICATIONS.— *London*. The Musical Times, *etc.* No. 351. 1844, *etc.* 8°. **P. P. 1945. aa.**

LESLIE (Henry David)

— The Red Sun is sinking. A lullaby for male voices. *London*, [1881.] 4°.   **F. 585. e. (33.)**

— The Red Sun is sinking. A lullaby for mixed voices. *London*, [1881.] 4°.   **F. 585. e. (34.)**

— The Red Sun is sinking ... Male voices, *etc.* [1916.] *See* Orpheus. The Orpheus, *etc.* New Series. No. 552. [1879, *etc.*] 8°.   **E. 1748.**

— The Red Sun is sinking, *etc.* [1908.] *See* Novello and Co. Novello's Tonic Sol-fa Series. No. 1730. [1876, *etc.*] 4°.   **B. 885.**

— The Rejected Lover. Four-Part Song for male voices. *See* Cramer and Co. J. B. Cramer's Select Library of Part Songs. No. 39. [1880? *etc.*] 4°.   **F. 157. a.**

— Resurgam. [Part-song, begins: "I watched the glorious sun".] The words by J. Enderssohn. *London*, [1877.] fol.   **H. 1778. y. (10.)**

— Resurgam. Choral Part Song, *etc. See* Cramer and Co. J. B. Cramer's Select Library of Part Songs. No. 40. [1880? *etc.*] 4°.   **F. 157. a.**

— Resurgam. Four-Part Song, *etc.* [1902.] *See* Novello and Co. Novello's Part-Song Book. Second Series. No. 879. [1869, *etc.*] 8°.   **F. 280. b.**

— Rise again, glad Summer Sun. *See* infra: [Three Trios for Female Voices. No. 1.]

Romance

— Overture ... for the Pianoforte. *London*, [1860.] fol.   **H. 2622. (8.)**

— Gone are the days of chivalry. Ballad ... The words by J. P. Simpson. *London*, [1860.] fol.   **H. 2622. (9.)**

— Important is my Mission. Buffo Air ... The words by J. P. Simpson. *London*, [1860.] fol.   **H. 1771. l. (20.)**

— Look forth, look forth. Serenade. *London*, [1860.] fol.   **H. 2622. (10.)**

— Poor silly heart. Ballad. *London*, [1860.] fol.   **H. 2622. (11.)**

— Welcome Spring. Part song. *London*, [1860.] fol.   **H. 2622. (12.)**

— Welcome Spring. Four-Part Song, *etc. See* Cramer and Co. J. B. Cramer's Select Library of Part Songs. No. 52. [1880? *etc.*] 4°.   **F. 157. a.**

— Welcome! Spring. Four-Part Song for S. A. T. B. [1903.] *See* Novello and Co. Novello's Part-Song Book. Second Series. No. 931. [1869, *etc.*] 8°.   **F. 280. b.**

— Welcome Spring. [Four-part song, words by] J. S. L. [1905.] *See* Choral. The Choral Handbook. No. 714. [1885, *etc.*] 8°.   **E. 862.**

— Welcome! Spring. Four-Part Song, *etc.* [1903.] *See* Novello and Co. Novello's Tonic Sol-fa Series. No. 1330. [1876, *etc.*] 4°.   **B. 885.**

— When firmly knit in friendship fond ... Duet. *London*, [1860.] fol.   **H. 2622. (13.)**

— The Rose. Romance for the Piano Forte, *etc. Cramer, Beale & Co.: London*, [1850?] fol.   **g. 232. d. (26.)**

— A Rose of the Garden ... Quartett [begins: "A beauteous rose"] ... Poetry by M. A. Baines. *London*, [1881.] 4°.   **F. 585. e. (32.)**

— A Rose of the Garden. Four-Part Song, *etc.* [1902.] *See* Novello and Co. Novello's Part-Song Book. Second Series. No. 876. [1869, *etc.*] 8°.   **F. 280. b.**

LESLIE (Henry David)

— Rule Britannia, arranged as a Four-Part Song for S. A. T. B. by H. Leslie. *See* Cramer and Co. J. B. Cramer's Select Library of Part Songs. No. 41. [1880? *etc.*] 4°.   **F. 157. a.**

— The Secret of Life. Part song for even voices. [Begins: "They say".] Words by C. Rawlings. *London*, [1860.] fol.   **H. 2622. (5.)**

— "Shall I be remembered," song. *London*, [1855.] fol.   **H. 1758. (37.)**

— Sing, O sing, this blessed Morn ... Anthem ... poetry by Wordsworth. [1886.] *See* Periodical Publications.— *London*. The Lute, *etc.* No. 48. 1883–99. 8°.   **P. P. 1945. hdc.**

— The Sirens. *See* supra: Three Duetts, *etc.* No. 3.

— Song of the Flax Spinner. *See* supra: Two Part Songs, *etc.* No. 1.

— Song of the Minnesingers, "Come fill your glasses high". Words by J. S. L., set to music for male voices. *London*, [1881.] 4°.   **F. 585. e. (35.)**

— Song of the Minnesingers. Four-Part Song for men's voices, *etc.* [1902.] *See* Orpheus. The Orpheus, *etc.* New Series. No. 350. [1879, *etc.*] 8°.   **E. 1748.**

— Leslie's Songs for Little Folks. *London*, [1873.] 8°.   **B. 407.**

— Leslie's Songs for Little Folks. *London*, [1883.] 8°.   **B. 407. a.**

— Songs of Praise. Choral song ... Words by Montgomery. *See* also supra: Cassell's Choral Music. No. 7.

— Songs of Praise. Choral Song ... Words by Montgomery. [1884.] *See* Novello and Co. Novello's Tonic Sol-fa Series. No. 194. [1876, *etc.*] 4°.   **B. 885.**

— Soul of the Age, Shakespeare rise. Madrigalian chorus. The poetry ... by B. Johnson. *London*, [1864.] fol.   **H. 2622. (30.)**

— Speed on my Bark. Ballad. (Words by M. Dee.) *London*, [1861.] fol.   **H. 2622. (27.)**

— Speed on my bark. Ballad. (Words by M. Dee.) *London*, [1870.] fol.   **H. 1775. u. (22.)**

— Speed on my Bark. Song, *etc. W. Paxton: London*, [1912.] fol.   **H. 1792. s. (17.)**

— The Swallow. *See* infra: [Three Trios for female voices. No. 3.]

— Sweet honey-sucking Bees [from J. Wilbye's "Second Set of Madrigales"] ... Edited by H. Leslie. [1910.] *See* Choral. The Choral Handbook. No. 968. [1885, *etc.*] 8°.   **E. 862.**

— Sweet honey-sucking Bees ... Composed by J. Wilbye. Edited by H. Leslie. [1907.] *See* Novello and Co. Novello's Tonic Sol-fa Series. No. 1611. [1876, *etc.*] 4°.   **B. 885.**

— Take thy banner! arranged from the Hymn of the Moravian Nuns. *London*, [1877.] fol.
No. 110 *of a set of Vocal Trios.*   **H. 1785. c. (33.)**

— The Tar's Dream. Sea song [begins: "Last night, my lads"]. Words by E. Oxenford. *London*, [1878.] fol.   **H. 1783. o. (51.)**

— Thine Eyes so bright. [Madrigal.] The words by T. Watson. *See* Novello and Co. Novello's Part-Song Book. Second Series. Vol. ii. No. 80. [1869, *etc.*] 8°.   **F. 280. b.**

— Thine Eyes so bright. Madrigal for six Voices, words by T. Watson. [1886.] *See* Novello and Co. Novello's Tonic Sol-fa Series. No. 525. [1876, *etc.*] 4°.   **B. 885.**

LESLIE (Henry David)

— This Morning, at the Dawn of Day. A Four-part Song, the words written by P. Latimer. The Music, from the French ... edited by H. Leslie. [1892.] *See* Novello and Co. Novello's Part-Song Book. Second Series. No. 656. [1869, *etc.*] 8°.
F. 280. b.

— This Morning, at the Dawn of Day. Four-part Song ... edited by H. Leslie. [1892.] *See* Novello and Co. Novello's Tonic Sol-fa Series. No. 770. [1876, *etc.*] 4°.
B. 885.

3 Trios for Female Voices

— [No. 1.] Rise again, glad Summer Sun ... Words by A. F. C. Knight. [1879.] *See* Novello and Co. Novello's Collection of Trios, *etc.* Vol. III. No. 43. [1879, *etc.*] 8°.
E. 1746.

— [No. 1.] Rise again, glad Summer Sun, *etc.* [1893.] *See* Novello and Co. Novello's Tonic Sol-fa Series. No. 795. [1876, *etc.*] 4°.
B. 885.

— [No. 2.] Good Night ... Words by D. Greenwell, *etc.* [1879.] *See* Novello and Co. Novello's Collection of Trios, *etc.* Vol. III. No. 44. [1879, *etc.*] 8°.
E. 1746.

— [No. 2.] Good Night ... Words by D. Greenwell. [1885.] *See* Novello and Co. Novello's Tonic Sol-fa Series. No. 270. [1876, *etc.*] 4°.
B. 885.

— [No. 3.] The Swallow, *etc.* [1879.] *See* Novello and Co. Novello's Collection of Trios, *etc.* Vol. III. No. 45. [1879, *etc.*] 8°.
E. 1746.

— [No. 3.] The Swallow. [1888.] *See* Novello and Co. Novello's Tonic Sol-fa Series. No. 581. [1876, *etc.*] 4°.
B. 885.

— Les Trois Grâces, valse. [P. F.] *London*, [1850?] fol.
h. 726. h. (22.)

— The Troubadour. *See* supra: Two Part-Songs, *etc.* No. 2.

— "True heart let your motto be," [song, begins: "Life is a troublesome fight,"] words by J. P. Simpson. *London*, [1855.] fol.
H. 1758. (38.)

— 'Twas but a dream. *See* supra: [Ida.]

— Up, up, ye Dames. *See* supra: [Six Four-part Songs. Op. 23. No. 6.]

— Victoria! Victoria! ... Jubilee Ode ... words by H. R. Haweis. *J. B. Cramer & Co.: London*, [1889.] 4°.
F. 585. r. (7.)

— The Violet. *See* supra: [Six Four-part Songs. Op. 25. No. 1.]

— We roam and rule the Sea. *See* supra: [Four Part-Songs for mixed voices. No. 4.]

— Welcome Spring. *See* supra: [Romance.]

— What ho! are all on board asleep. Four-part song, arranged from the Syrens' duet. *London*, [1877.] 8°. *No. 70 of the "Choristers' Album".*
E. 1708.

— What ho! are all on board asleep? Four-part song, arranged from a duet. *London*, [1877.] fol.
H. 1785. c. (34.)

— What ho! are all on board asleep? Four-Part-Song, *etc.* [1899.] *See* Novello and Co. Novello's Part-Song Book. Second Series. No. 826. [1869, *etc.*] 8°.
F. 280. b.

— When firmly knit in friendship fond. *See* supra: [Romance.]

— When first I saw his noble form. *See* supra: [Ida.]

— When the Shades of Eve descending. Four-Part Song ... words by W. U. Whitney. Op. 16. No. 3. *See* Cramer and Co. J. B. Cramer's Select Library of Part Songs. No. 54. [1880? *etc.*] 4°.
F. 157. a.

— While Life shall last. *See* supra: [Ida.]

LESLIE (Henry David)

— Windsor Castle. Mr. Henry Leslie's Choir. Monday, July 5th, 1880. [11 part-Songs, madrigals, *etc.*] [*London*, 1880.] 8°.
R. M. 25. e. 11.

— With heart confiding. *See* supra: [Ida.]

— Ye Mariners of England. Four-Part Song ... Words by T. Campbell. *See* Cramer and Co. J. B. Cramer's Select Library of Part Songs. No. 58. [1880? *etc.*] 4°.
F. 157. a.

— Ye Mariners of England. Four Part Song, *etc.* [1909.] *See* Novello and Co. Novello's Part-Song Book. Second Series. No. 1116. [1869, *etc.*] 8°.
F. 280. b.

— *See* Bouverie (B. P.) An Order of service for children ... Music by ... H. Leslie, *etc.* 1884. 8°.
E. 1326.

— *See* Carissimi (Giacomo) Jonah ... Adapted by H. Leslie. [1872.] 8°.
E. 501.

— *See* Carissimi (Giacomo) Jonah ... adapted ... by H. Leslie. [c. 1875.] 8°.
E. 541. nn. (5.)

— *See* Gibbons (O.) [First Set of Madrigals.] The Silver Swan ... Edited by H. Leslie. [1910.] 8°. [*Choral Handbook. No. 965.*]
E. 862.

— *See* Gounod (C. F.) [Ave Maria. No. 1.] Holy Lord Almighty ... The arrangement ... by H. Leslie. [1873.] fol.
H. 2550. d. (37.)

— *See* Horn (C. E.) Cherry Ripe ... arranged ... by H. Leslie. [1881.] 4°.
F. 585. e. (23.)

— *See* Mendelssohn-Bartholdy (J. L. F.) [*Doubtful and Supposititious Works.*] Breathe not of parting ... arranged as a four-part song by H. Leslie. [1874.] 8°.
F. 321. h. (1.)

— *See* Morley (T.) [The First Booke of Ballets.] Fire, fire, my Heart ... Edited by H. Leslie. [1910.] 8°. [*Choral Handbook. No. 966.*]
E. 862.

— *See* Morley (T.) [The First Booke of Ballets.] Fire, Fire! my Heart ... Edited by H. Leslie. [1884.] fol. [*Novello's Tonic Sol-fa Series. No. 195.*]
B. 885.

— *See* Shield (William) [The Loadstars.] O happy fair ... Trio ... Arranged for female voices by H. Leslie. [1885.] 8°. [*Novello's Collection of Trios, etc. vol. 7. no. 157.*]
E. 1746.

— *See* Shield (William) [The Loadstars.] O happy fair ... Arranged for S. S. A. by H. Leslie. [1904.] 8°. [*Novello's School Songs. no. 694.*]
F. 280. d.

— *See* Shield (William) [The Loadstars.] O happy Fair ... Arranged for S. S. A. by H. Leslie. [1883.] 4°. [*Novello's Tonic Sol-fa Series. No. 186.*]
B. 885.

LESLIE (Henry J.)

— April Weather. Song, words by H. Wynne. *Chappell & Co.: London*, [1887.] fol.
H. 1788. v. (45.)

— Girlie. [Song.] Written and composed by H. J. Leslie. *O. Ditson Company: Boston, etc.* 1894. fol.
H. 1798. v. (4.)

— Praise, my soul, the King of Heaven. Hymn. *London & New York*, [1885.] 8°.
B. 579. c. (12.)

— Watching all through the weary night. Hymn, written by the Rev. H. R. Haweis. *London & New York*, [1885.] 8°.
B. 579. c. (13.)

LESLIE (Henry J.) *Mus. Doc.*

— *See* Leslie (Henry T.)

LESLIE (Henry T.)

— Twenty-two Sacred Songs ... mostly composed by H. T. Leslie. *See* Pitman (F.) Pitman's Sixpenny Musical Library. No. 17. [1880, *etc.*] 4°. **F. 630. a.**

— Twenty-four Band of Hope pearls, music and words ... Edited and composed by Dr. Leslie. *London*, [1877.] 8°. **E. 1733.**

— Beautiful Snow. Sacred Part-Song, words by W. A. H. Sigourney. Arranged by T. Crampton. [1890.] *See* Crampton (T.) The Part-Singer, *etc.* No. 146, 147. [1868–98.] 8°. **E. 628.**

— Blessed be thy name for ever. Sacred song ... The poetry by the Ettrick Shepherd [J. Hogg]. *London*, [1863.] fol. **H. 1775. u. (26.)**

— The Christian Mariner.—Sacred-Part Song.— ... Words by Mrs. Southey. New ... Edition. [1872.] *See* Crampton (T.) The Part-Singer, *etc.* No. 98, 99. [1868–98.] 8°. **E. 628.**

— Clifton Conference Hymns. By the Rev. S. A. Walker ... with appropriate music for each hymn ... also an appendix, containing ... single and double chants, arranged to suit the Te Deum, canticles, or psalms. *F. Pitman: London*, 1872. 8°. **B. 1174. a.**

— The Drunkard's poor child. A ballad [Begins: "Oh! my clothes are all ragged"]. *Leeds*, [1874.] fol. **H. 1778. y. (13.)**

— The Four Jolly Smiths ... Song, written by J. L. Rockliffe. *London*, [1868.] fol. **H. 1775. u. (27.)**

— The Four jolly Smiths. A right jovial song, *etc.* pp. 5. *Hutchings & Romer: London*, [1883.] fol. **H. 1653. e. (39.)**

— The Four Jolly Smiths. Part-song. *London*, [1874.] 8°. *No. 44 of the "Choristers' Album"*. **E. 1708.**

— The Four Jolly Smiths. Four-part Song, *etc.* [1889.] *See* Novello and Co. Novello's Part-Song Book. Second Series. No. 571. [1869, *etc.*] 8°. **F. 280. b.**

— Four Jolly Smiths. Duett. *Mathias & Strickland: London*, [1893.] 8°. *No. 10 of "Mathias & Strickland's Vocal Duets," etc.* **E. 263. d. (16.)**

— The Four Jolly Smiths. [Part-song.] Words by L. L. Rockliffe. Arranged by C. Locknane. [1902.] *See* Grosvenor. The Grosvenor Series of Part Songs. No. 41. [1886, *etc.*] 8°. **F. 1601.**

— The Four jolly Smiths ... Arranged for male voices by E. Newton. *Leonard & Co.: London*, [1905.] 8°. *Leonard & Co.'s Part Songs, No. 111.* **F. 1658.**

— The Four jolly Smiths. Unison song, *etc.* pp. 4. *J. Curwen & Sons: London*, [1911.] 8°. [*Choruses for equal Voices. no.* 1269.] **E. 861.**

— The Four jolly Smiths ... Arranged for male voices. *J. Curwen & Sons: London*, 1912. 8°. *The Apollo Club, No.* 515. **F. 667.**

— The Four Jolly Smiths. Arranged by Clement Locknane, *etc.* [S. A. T. B.] pp. 6. *Edwin Ashdown: London*, [c. 1935.] 8°. [*Enoch choral Series. no.* 243.] *Issued as part of "Ashdown Four-part Songs".* **F. 1097.**

— The Four Jolly Smiths. Arranged by Harry Dexter. (For unison voices and piano, with optional melody instruments, tuned percussion and rhythm percussion.) [Words by] Louis Rockliffe. [Score.] pp. 7. *Collier/Dexter Music: London*, [1968.] 8°. *Part of "Choral plus".* **E. 812. j. (13.)**

— The Four jolly Smiths, *etc.* [1908.] *See* Novello and Co. Novello's Tonic Sol-fa Series. No. 1718. [1876, *etc.*] 4°. **B. 885.**

LESLIE (Henry T.)

— Four jolly Smiths. Vocal polka. [Parts for fife and drum band.] 32 pt. *J. R. Lafleur & Son: London*, [1898.] 8°. *Part of "J. R. Lafleur & Son's Fife & Drum Journal". Including several copies of various parts.* **f. 800. (814.)**

— The Four Jolly Smiths ... for the Pianoforte. [1873.] fol. *See* Layland (W.) **h. 3001. a. (4.)**

— The Four jolly Smiths ... Easily arranged for the Pianoforte, *etc. See* Gautier (L.) Golden Thoughts, *etc.* No. 11. [1905?] fol. **h. 3483. d. (13.)**

— Fragments from the Mountains. A garland of poetry & music, written by C. Watson. *London*, [1872.] fol. **H. 1775. u. (28.)**

— The Grass is green & bonnie. Song [begins: "O the grass"] written by J. P. Robson. *London*, [1863.] fol. **H. 1775. u. (25.)**

— The Hop Girls' Song. [Four-part song.] Words by E. Capern. [1868.] *See* Crampton (T.) The Part-Singer, *etc.* No. 45. [1868–98.] 8°. **E. 628.**

— The Lord is my Shepherd. Anthem. [1872.] *See* Tonic. The Tonic Sol-fa Times, *etc.* No. 97. [a.] [1864–73.] 4°. **B. 559. f.**

— The Minster Bell. Part-Song, words by J. Stammers. [1868.] *See* Crampton (T.) The Part-Singer, *etc.* No. 42. [1868–98.] 8°. **E. 628.**

— The Mountain Echo. [Four-part song.] Words translated from Heine. [1868.] *See* Crampton (T.) The Part-Singer, *etc.* No. 43. [1868–98.] 8°. **E. 628.**

— Odes and select pieces for festivals and demonstrations, *etc.* *London*, [1873.] 4°. **E. 605. r. (31.)**

— The Olive Branch. A Collection of original tunes ... adapted to ... psalms and hymns for congregational use. *London*, [1866.] 8°. **A. 618. g.**

— The Pupils' Desideratum, or brief outline of the One Line, and Letter Value system of musical notation; being a simplification and union of the Tonic Sol-Fa and the old notation. *Bristol*, 1871. 4°. **7897. bbb. 41.**

— Summer Woods. [Four-part song.] Words by M. Farningham. [1872.] *See* Crampton (T.) The Part-Singer, *etc.* No. 96. [1868–98.] 8°. **E. 628.**

— The Templar's book of harmony and song ... Edited by ... H. T. Leslie. *London*, [1875.] 8°. **E. 601. b. (4.)**

— Thou art with me O my Father, sacred song, composed & arranged with piano forte accompaniment by H. T. Leslie. pp. 4. *Hart & Cᵒ: London*, [c. 1890.] fol. **G. 295. mm. (4.)**

— A Winter's Evening, and Christmas Cantata, consisting of ... vocal and instrumental pieces by popular authors ... compiled ... by H. T. Leslie. *London*, [1872.] 4°. **E. 601. n. (6.)**

— *See* Bateman (C. H.) and Inglis (R.) Harmonized edition of the 200 Sacred Melodies ... Harmonized by H. T. Leslie. [1872.] 8°. **B. 377.**

LESLIE (Herbert)

— The Cows are in the Corn. Ballad. *C. Sheard: London*, [1883.] fol. *No. 6916 of the Musical Bouquet.* **H. 2345.**

LESLIE (Howard)

— As in Days of Yore. Ballad, written by J. P. McBride (& J. Archibald). *Howard & Co.: London*, [1897.] fol. **H. 1798. v. (5.)**

LESLIE (HOWARD)

—[Another edition.] As in Days of Yore. Ballad, written by
A. Horspool. *Howard & Co.: London*, [1897.] fol.
H. 1798. v. (6.)

—Gleanings of Summer. Ballad, words by H. Dare.
B. Williams: London, [1896.] fol. **H. 1798. v. (7.)**

—Old Chimes. Valse for the pianoforte. *C. Sheard & Co.:
London*, 1891. fol. **h. 3285. q. (33.)**

LESLIE (J. A.)

—Gaily beloved you're singing ... Song and Chorus. *London*,
[1879.] fol. **H. 1783. o. (55.)**

LESLIE (J. H.) and **OGDEN** (W. A.)

—Silver Carols, a collection of new music ... by J. H. Leslie
and W. A. Ogden. pp. 158. *W. Nicholson & Son: Wakefield*,
[1877.] *obl.* 8°.
Bound in orange cloth. **A. 793.**

—[Another copy.]
Bound in red cloth. **A. 1234. mm.**

—[Silver Carols.] [A reissue.] Silver Bells, a collection of new
music for board schools, high schools ... By J. H. Leslie and
W. A. Ogden. pp. 158. *W. Nicholson & Sons: Wakefield*,
[1877.] *obl.* 8°. **A. 793. a.**

LESLIE (J. S.)

—The Bells. Song, written and composed by J. S. Leslie.
A. Cary: London, [1892.] 8°.
No. 8 of A. Cary's Diamond Edition. **F. 637. c. (9.)**

—Clouds & Sunshine. Song, written & composed by J. S. Leslie.
A. Cary: London, [1892.] 8°.
No. 5 of A. Cary's Diamond Edition. **F. 637. c. (6.)**

—Farmer Mullins. Song, written and composed by J. S. Leslie.
A. Cary: London, [1892.] 8°.
No. 6 of A. Cary's Diamond Edition. **F. 637. c. (7.)**

—The Four Donkeys. Song, written and composed by J. S.
Leslie. *A. Cary: London*, [1892.] 8°.
No. 3 of A. Cary's Diamond Edition. **F. 637. c. (4.)**

—The Harvest Home. Song, written and composed by J. S.
Leslie. *A. Cary: London*, [1892.] 8°.
No. 4 of A. Cary's Diamond Edition. **F. 637. c. (5.)**

—Hunting. Song, written and composed by J. S. Leslie.
A. Cary: London, [1892.] 8°.
No. 2 of A. Cary's Diamond Edition. **F. 637. c. (3.)**

—The Merry Blacksmith. Song, written and composed by J. S.
Leslie. *A. Cary: London*, [1892.] 8°.
No. 7 of A. Cary's Diamond Edition. **F. 637. c. (8.)**

—The Musical King. Humorous Song, written and composed
by J. S. Leslie. *A. Cary: London*, [1892.] 8°.
No. 15 of Cary's Diamond Edition. **F. 637. c. (10.)**

—Springtime. Impromptu for piano. *A. Cary: London, etc.*,
[1892.] 8°.
No. 10 of A. Cary's Diamond Edition. **f. 133. m. (3.)**

—Sweet and bitter. Song, written and composed by J. S. Leslie.
A. Cary: London, [1892.] 8°.
No. 16 of A. Cary's Diamond Edition. **F. 637. c. (11.)**

LESLIE (JOHN) *Composer for the concertina*

—Le premier [*sic*] pensées musicales, comprising a collection of
original waltzes and polkas, composed for the concertina.
pp. 3. *Wheatstone & Cⁱ: London*, [c. 1850.] fol.
h. 2495. c. (21.)

LESLIE (JOHN) *Composer for the piano accordion*

—Tyrolean Carnival. (Accordion solo.) pp. 4. *Bosworth & Co.:
London*, [1970.] 4°.
Part of "The Piano Accordion Player". **g. 657. n. (9.)**

LESLIE (JOHN HENRY)

—A Carol with a tune, *etc. Hathersage*, 1900. *obl.* 4°.
B. 512. n. (2.)

—A Carrolle olde! A Carol new! [Christmas carol.] The words
... by A. R. Marshall, *etc.* [*Chesterfield*, 1905.] 4°.
E. 270. h. (7.)

—Christmas and Home. A Carol, verses by A. R. Marshall, *etc.*
[*Sheffield?* 1909.] 4°. **E. 270. h. (8.)**

—Christmas of Yore. A Carol, written by A. H. Webb. *Sir
W. C. Leng & Co.: Sheffield*, 1898. fol. **H. 1792. s. (18.)**

—A Christmas Song, with a Chorus. The words ... by A. R.
Marshall, *etc.* [*Sheffield?* 1907.] 4°. **E. 270. h. (9.)**

—Christmas—The Children's Time. A Carol. (Words by A. R.
Marshall.) *Pawson & Brailsford: Sheffield*, [1900?] 8°.
D. 836. (2.)

—From the Baby's Point of View. A Notion from the Nursery.
[Song.] Written by A. R. Marshall, *etc. J. Bath: London*,
1899. fol. **H. 1799. h. (43.)**

—God bless us everyone. A Carol, verses by A. R. Marshall,
etc. Sheffield, 1910. 4°. **E. 270. h. (10.)**

—Hail! Season of Christmas. A Carol ... [words] by A. R.
Marshall, *etc.* [*Sheffield?* 1911.] 4°. **E. 270. h. (11.)**

—Here's a good Wish! (Carolle.) The words ... by A. R.
Marshall, *etc. Chesterfield*, 1904. 4°. **E. 270. h. (12.)**

—If those we love be true. A Carol, *etc.* [Music by J. H. Leslie?]
See WHAT. What matter if the Days seem long, *etc.* [1905?]
obl. 8°. **C. 738. k. (3.)**

—"If you only tidy up the Part that shows!" ⟨Humorous song.⟩
Written by A. R. Marshall. pp. 5. *J. Bath: London*, [1901.]
fol. **H. 3985. x. (17.)**

—It's Christmas. A Carol, written by A. R. Marshall, *etc.* [With
separate chorus arrangement.] *Sir W. C. Leng & Co.:
Sheffield*, 1899. fol. **H. 1792. s. (19.)**

—Jones minor. Humorous song. Written by A. H. Webb. pp. 5.
J. Bath: London, [1899.] fol. **H. 3980. rr. (22.)**

—She didn't mean it. Humorous song. Written by W. J.
Featherstone. pp. 5. *J. Bath: London*, [1899.] fol.
H. 3980. rr. (23.)

—"They used to sue to Sue." Humorous song. Written by A. R.
Marshall. pp. 5. *J. Bath: London*, [1900.] fol.
H. 3985. x. (18.)

—Thinking of Home at Christmas. (Carolle.) The words ... by
A. R. Marshall, *etc. Eyre & Spottiswoode:* [*London*,] 1903.
fol. **H. 1792. s. (20.)**

—Where does Father Christmas live? (Christmas Carol.) The
lyrics ... by A. R. Marshall, *etc.* [*Sheffield?* 1906?] 4°.
E. 270. h. (13.)

LESLIE (JULIA)

—The Stag Hunt. Hunting song [begins: "First came the
harbouret"]. Words by W. Melville. *London*, [1873.] fol.
H. 1778. y. (14.)

LESLIE (MICHAEL)

—*See* PEREZ FREIRE (O.) Ay-ay-ay! (Spanish serenade), *etc.*
⟨Arranged by M. Leslie.⟩ [1927.] 4°. **G. 1276. nn. (4.)**

LESLIE (MICHAEL)

— *See* VERDI (F. G. F.) Aida ... Ballet Music and Grand March. (Arr. by M. Leslie.) 1929. 4°.   **g. 1125. cc. (28.)**

LESLIE (PAUL)

— "A Girl like you" ... Waltz song. ⟨Words and music by P. Leslie.⟩ pp. 3. *Windsor Music Co.: Chicago, New York,* [1900.] fol.   **H. 3985. x. (19.)**

— In the Shadow of the Church. [Song.] Words and music by P. Leslie. pp. 3. *Windsor Music Co.: Chicago, New York,* [1899.] fol.   **H. 3980. rr. (24.)**

— A Picture that deserves a better Frame. [Song.] Words and music by P. Leslie. pp. 5. *Sol Bloom: Chicago,* [1901.] fol.   **H. 3985. x. (20.)**

LESLIE (PEARL)

— A Dream at Sea, romance for the Pianoforte. *London,* [1862.] fol.   **h. 1460. v. (33.)**

LESLIE (R. J.)

— *See* LESLIE (Henry T.)

LESLIE (SCOTT)

— The Blue Bell. Schottische. [P. F.] *Phillips & Page: London,* [1888.] fol.   **h. 975. v. (15.)**

— The Horse Guards. Schottische. [P. F.] *Phillips & Page: London,* [1890.] fol.   **h. 3285. q. (34.)**

— The Old Mill. Waltz. [P. F.] *Phillips & Page: London,* [1887.] fol.   **h. 975. v. (16.)**

— The Old Mill. Waltz. [P. F.] *See* BAPTISTE (A.) Forest Echoes ... No. 8. [1891.] fol.   **h. 3329. (1.)**

— The Thistle. Lancers on ... Scotch airs. *Phillips & Page: London,* [1888.] fol.   **h. 975. v. (17.)**

LESLIE (STEWARD)

— Russian Dance. "Danse des Zauves" ... (Piccolo solo.) [Military band parts.] 26 pt. *In:* FETRÁS (Oscar) Polka. "Gruss aus Mürren," *etc.* 1899. fol. [*Boosey's military Journal. ser.* 107. *no.* 5.]   **h. 1549.**

LESLIE (VERA)

— In Memoriam. Song. Words by Lord Tennyson. *Weekes & Co.: London,* [1901.] fol.   **H. 1187. z. (16.)**

— On with you, Boys! [Song.] (Words and Music by V. Leslie.) *Weekes & Co.: London,* [1900.] fol.   **H. 1799. h. (44.)**

LESLIE (W. C.)

— A Bruised Reed shall he not break. Full anthem. *Worthing,* [1860?] fol.   **H. 2832. e. (21.)**

LESLIE (W. HENRY)

— The Blessing of the Children. Trio and Chorus. (Tonic Solfa translation by H. J. Timothy.) *Stainer & Bell: London,* 1926. 8°.   **E. 442. s. (12.)**

— The Montgomeryshire Song Book. *See infra:* Old National Airs.

— Old National Airs. Arranged by Nicholas Gatty and Alan Gray ... Compiled by W. H. Leslie. 4 vol. The Shropshire Song Book. Part. I. ⟨No. 1–12.⟩ pp. 55. The Shropshire Song Book. Part II. ⟨No. 13–25.⟩

LESLIE (W. HENRY)

pp. vi. 57–106. The Montgomeryshire Song Book. [Part I.] ⟨No. 26–37.⟩ pp. vi. 107–156. The Montgomeryshire Song Book. Part II. ⟨No. 38–48.⟩ pp. vi. 157–198. *Woodhall, Minshall, Thomas & Co.: Wrexham,* [1922, 23?] 8°.   **C. 889.**

— Old National Airs with Descants. Arranged by Nicholas Gatty and Alan Gray ... Compiled by W. H. Leslie ... Voice part. *Stainer & Bell: London,* [c. 1930.] 8°. *Imperfect; part 2 of the "Montgomeryshire Song Book" only.*   **C. 889. a. (1.)**

— [A reissue.] Old National Airs with Descants, Pianoforte Accompaniment (ad lib.), *etc.* no. 47. *Stainer & Bell: London,* [c. 1930.] 8°. *Imperfect; wanting the other no.*   **C. 889. a. (2.)**

— The Shropshire Song Book. *See* supra: Old National Airs.

LESLIE (WALTER)

— Romance.— Un Rêve.— Violin or Violoncello and Pianoforte. [*London?* 1907.] fol.   **h. 1612. p. (30.)**

LESLIE-SMITH (KENNETH)

— *See* SMITH.

LESNAYA

— Лесная сторона. Песни. *See* SVIRIDOV (Y. V.)

LESNE (HIRTRAM)

— So mote it be! A Masonic Melody ... Written & composed by H. Lesne, *etc. J. B. Cramer & Co.: London,* [1865?] fol.   **H. 1788. v. (46.)**

LESONNÉ (BERTRAND) *pseud.* [i. e. FREDERIC MULLEN.]

— La Fée d'Amour. The Love Fairy ... Suite de ballet pour pianoforte. *H. Sharples & Son: London,* 1919. 4°.   **g. 1129. o. (26.)**

— Fleur d'Amande. Almond blossom. Sérénade. [P. F.] *H. Sharples & Son: London,* 1919. 4°.   **g. 1129. n. (29.)**

LE SOUEF (J.)

— Longchamps. Valse brillante pour le Piano Forte. *London,* [1850.] fol.   **h. 947. (46.)**

LESPINASSE (L. PAULIN)

— Enseignement complet de l'art du chant ... Translated into English by Miss F. Burdett ... Les accompagnements de Piano par Renaud de Vilbac. *Paris,* [1866.] fol.   **H. 2899.**

L'ESPOIR, *pseud.*

— At Last. [Song.] Words by A. Trevelyan. *F. A. Mills: New York,* 1899. fol.   **H. 1799. h. (45.)**

— Dream on, Beloved. Song. Words by A. Trevelyan. *F. A. Mills: New York,* 1899. fol.   **H. 1799. h. (46.)**

— The New-born King. Sacred Song. Poem by W. C. Kreusch. *F. A. Mills: New York, Chicago,* 1900. fol.   **H. 1187. z. (17.)**

— The Toreador am I. [Song.] Words by A. Trevelyan. *F. A. Mills: New York, etc.,* 1899. fol.   **H. 1799. h. (48.)**

— Two Roses. [Song.] Words by A. Trevelyan. *F. A. Mills: New York,* 1899. fol.   **H. 1799. h. (47.)**

LESS

— The Less said about it the better. Song. *See* HUTCHISON (W. M.)

— Less than the Dust. [Song.] *See* WARD, afterwards FINDEN (A. W.) Four Indian Love Lyrics … No. 2.

LESSA (BARBOSA)

— Cancioneiro do Rio Grande, *etc.* pp. 95. *Seresta edições musicais: São Paulo,* [1963.] 8°. **D. 836. n. (4.)**

LESSARD (JOHN)

— Little Concert. Suite for piano. pp. 17. *Joshua Corp.: New York,* [1964.] 4°. **g. 1128. uu. (3.)**

— Toccata in four Movements. (For harpsichord or piano.) pp. 20. *Joshua Corp.: New York,* [c. 1960.] 4°. **g. 1129. gg. (9.)**

LESSEL (FRANCISZEK)

— Koncert na fortepian z orkiestrą. Fortepian solo z wyciągiem fortepianowym partii orkiestrowej. Oryginalny głos fortepianu solo opracował Z. Drzewiecki. Na podstawie partii orkiestrowej z instrumentowanej przez K. Sikorskiego wyciąg fortepianowy opracowała S. Lachowska. pp. 76. *Polskie wydawnictwo muzyczne: Cracow,* [1951.] fol. **h. 3700. (5.)**

— Three grand Duetts, for two German Flute [*sic*]. [Parts.] 2 pt. *J. Fentum: London,* [WM1806.] fol. **h. 2052. a. (1.)**

— Kwartet na flet, skrzypcę, altówkę i wiolonczelę. Opracował Stanisław Tauros. Partytura i głosy. 5 pt. *Polskie wydawnictwo muzyczne: Kraków,* 1954. fol. **h. 2784. u. (3.)**

— 3 sonaty op. 2 na fortepian. Three Sonatas op. 2 for Piano. ⟨Przygotowała do wydania Ludomira Stawowy.⟩ pp. 65. *Polskie wydawnictwo muzyczne: Kraków,* [1970.] 4°. **g. 442. rr. (10.)**

— Wariacje na flet i orkiestrę, *etc.* [Edited by Piotr Perkowski. Score, including P. F. reduction, and flute part.] 2 pt. *Polskie wydawnictwo muzyczne: Cracow,* [1953.] fol. **h. 1508. rr. (4.)**

LESSEL (MARC)

— Patrouille Algérienne—Algerian Patrol—pour Piano. *Turner & Phillips: Plymouth,* 1906. fol. **h. 3283. p. (27.)**

LESSELL (F.)

— *See* LESSEL.

LESSEN

— Lessen van den mechelschen catechismus op verscheide aengenaeme liedekens gesteld, en byzonderlyk ten voordeele der Christelyke jongheid uitgegeeven door eenen priester van 't bisdom van Ipre [i. e. Benoit de Paeuw]. 2 pt. *J. F. Moerman: Iper,* [c. 1795.] 8°. **3507. bb. 9.**

LESSEPS (LOUIS)

— Bonne Vie. Polka. [P. F.] *Francis Bros. and Day: London,* [1885.] fol. **h. 975. v. (18.)**

— Bonne Vie. Polka. [P. F. and orchestral parts.] *See* FRANCIS AND DAY. Francis & Day's String Band Journal … No. 64. [1886? *etc.*] 8°. **e. 1341.**

LESSER (ANTHONY)

— … Meet me by Moonlight … Play with music … Lyrics by David Dearlove, *etc.* ⟨Piano selection. Arranged by Felton Rapley.⟩ pp. 11. *Chappell & Co.: London,* [1957.] 4°. **f. 65. (8.)**

LESSER (BERTRAM C.)

— Aid[e] de Camp. March & Two Step. [P. F.] *T. B. Harms & Co.:* [*New York,*] 1901. fol. **h. 3286. r. (8.)**

— Gossip. March and Two-Step. [P. F.] *Howley, Haviland & Dresser: New York,* 1901. fol. **h. 3286. r. (9.)**

LESSER (EUGENE C.)

— An Autumn Bud. [P. F.] *T. B. Harms & Co.:* [*New York,*] 1900. fol. **h. 3282. w. (43.)**

— An Autumn Bud. Waltz song. Text by Jerome D. Kern. pp. 7. *T. B. Harms Co.:* [*New York,* 1905.] fol. **H. 3985. x. (21.)**

— Farewell to you dear Heart. Serenade. [Song.] Words by Percy Campbell Mason. pp. 5. *T. B. Harms Co.: New York,* [1905.] fol. **H. 3985. x. (22.)**

— The Girl that just suits me. [Song.] Words by Percy Campbell Mason. pp. 6. *T. B. Harms Co.: New York,* [1905.] fol. **H. 3985. x. (23.)**

— Heart-Throbs. Waltzes. [P. F.] *T. B. Harms Co.: New York,* [1904.] fol. **h. 4120. pp. (15.)**

LESSER (RENA SILVERMAN)

— God bless this Day. A wedding song. pp. 5. *G. Schirmer: New York,* [1957.] 4°. **G. 1276. r. (24.)**

LESSER (STANISLAS)

— Die Gemüthliche Polka. [P. F.] *Breslau,* [1872.] fol. **h. 1487. q. (6.)**

LESSER (WOLFGANG)

— Kleine Stücke für kleine Leute. Klavier. pp. 20. *Verlag Neue Musik: Berlin,* [1979?] 4°. **g. 652. b. (3.)**

LESSI (LEAH B.)

— Leatra. Schottische for Piano. *O. Ditson Co.: Boston, etc.,* 1898. fol. **h. 3286. g. (38.)**

LESSIG ( )

— Sechs Schottische 6-tourige Angloisen von G. L. Klemm, Tanzmeister, mit vollstimiger Musik vom Musicus Lessig. (Violino I.) (Violino II.) (Flauto I.) (Flauto II.) (Corno I.) (Corno II.) (Basso.) (Touren.) 8 pt. *Bey dem Autor: Leipzig,* [1750?] *obl.* 4°. **b. 62.**

LESSING (A.)

— Elizabethen [*sic*] Polka composed and arranged for the piano forte by A. Lessing. pp. 4. *Wood & Cᵒ: Edinburgh,* [c. 1845.] fol. **h. 721. uu. (4.)**

— Lilien Mazurka composed & arranged for the piano forte by A. Lessing. pp. 5. *Wood & Cᵒ: Edinburgh,* [c. 1845.] fol. **h. 721. uu. (5.)**

LESSMANN (OTTO)

— Du rothe Rose auf grüner Heid, aus J. Wolff's "Rattenfänger von Hameln," für eine Sopran- oder Tenorstimme mit Begleitung des Pianoforte. *Berlin,* [1879?] fol. **H. 1781. i. (17.)**

LESSMANN (Otto)

— Erinnerungen. Sechs Characterstücke für das Pianoforte. *Berlin & Posen*, [1874.] fol.   **h. 1487. q. (7.)**

— Es wartet ein bleiches Jungfräulein, aus J. Wolff's "Der wilde Jäger" für eine Singstimme mit Begleitung des Pianoforte. *Berlin*, [1880.] fol.   **H. 1786. e. (46.)**

— Vier Lieder für eine Singstimme mit Begleitung des Pianoforte. Op. 3. no. 1. *Berlin*, [1877.] fol.
Imperfect; wanting no. 2–4.   **G. 385. d. (10.)**

— Drei Lieder aus J. Wolff's Tannhäuser. *See* LISZT (F.) Drei Lieder ... für Pianoforte. [1883.] fol.   **h. 585. f. (11.)**

— Tarantella. Op. 25. *See* ALBUMBLAETTER. Albumblätter für das Klavier. No. 8. [1880.] fol.   **h. 1481. p. (7.)**

— Walzer, C dur, für das Pianoforte zu vier Händen mit Begleitung von Kinderinstrumenten. *Berlin*, [1876.] fol.   **h. 1487. q. (8.)**

— Wüchsen mir Flügel, aus J. Wolff's "Till Eulenspiegel redivivus," für eine Singstimme mit Begleitung des Pianoforte. *Berlin*, [1880.] fol.   **H. 1786. e. (45.)**

— *See* CHAIKOVSKY (P.) Jugend-Album ... mit Fingersatz von O. Lessmann. [1880.] fol.   **h. 2988. a. (7.)**

— *See* WAGNER (W. R.) [*Collected Works.—c.*] Richard Wagner-Album für Gesang mit Pianofortebegleitung ... Herausgegeben von O. Lessmann. [1877.] 8°.   **F. 530. e.**

LESSON

— The Lesson. [Sacred song.] *See* BARTLETT (J. C.)

— Lesson Books. Song. *See* BARRI (O.)

— A Lesson every Gentleman should know. Song. *See* HELF (J. F.)

— A Lesson for a Lover. [Song.] *See* PRELLEUR (P.)

— A Lesson from a Cloud. [Song.] *See* OLGA.

— A Lesson from Ecclesiastes. Anthem. *See* SHAW (Christopher G.)

— A Lesson from the Birds. [Song.] *See* BARTHOLOMEW (L. I.)

— The Lesson I've been taught. Song. *See* KRAUSE (C.)

— A Lesson in Flirting. Duet. *See* MONTAGUE (Harold)

— A Lesson in Kissing. Song. *See* ORME (Ilda M.)

— A Lesson in Love. Song. *See* PARKER (K.)

— The Lesson in the Polka. Song. *See* AÏDÉ (H.)

— The Lesson of Love. Song. *See* BARNBY (*Sir* J.)

— The Lesson of Love. Madrigal. *See* MEE (J. H.)

— The Lesson of Spring. Two-part Song. *See* LEE (E. M.)

— The Lesson of the Leaves. Part Song. *See* ALEXANDER (A.)

— The Lesson of the Lilies. [Anthem.] *See* DODDS (G. R.)

— The Lesson of the Water Mill. [Musical monologue.] *See* ANDREWS (J. C. B.)

— The Lesson of the Water Mill. Ballad. *See* BARKER (G. A.)

— The Lesson of Youth. Song. *See* RANDEGGER (A.) Songs of the Rhine-land. No. 8.

— A Lesson with the Fan. Song. *See* HARDELOT (G. d') *pseud.*

LESSON (George)

— *See* ŠEVČÍK (O.) 18 Trill Exercises for the violin ... edited by G. Lesson. 1917. fol.   **h. 1612. jj. (17*.)**

LESSONNÉ (Bertrand)

— *See* LESONNÉ.

LESSONS

— A Collection of favourite Lessons for the Harpsichord, in an easy pleasing taste, proper for young practitioners on that instrument, composed by different authors. pp. 24.
A. Hummel: London, [c. 1770.] *obl. fol.*   **d. 161. v. (1.)**

— A Collection of Lessons for the Harpsichord. Compos'd by Sig^r Jozzi, St Martini of Milan, Alberti, Agrell ... Book I $\binom{MS}{}$ [II, III.]) 3 bk. *Printed for I. Walsh: London*, [1761–63.] *obl.* fol.   **f. 20.**
& Hirsch IV. 3. (2.)

— A Collection of Lessons for the Harpsicord, compos'd by Sig^r Jozzi, St Martini of Milan, Alberti, Agrell. Never before printed. Book I(–III). 3 bk. *Printed for I. Walsh: London*, [1761–63.] *obl.* fol.   **R. M. 16. a. 6. (1.)**

— [Another copy. Book II.] [1762.] *obl.* fol.
R. M. 16. a. 14. (6.)

— A Collection of Lessons for the Harpsichord compos'd by Sig^r Kunzen, Kellery, Agrell & Hoppe. pp. 33. *Printed for Thompson and Sons: London*, [1762.] *obl.* fol.   **d. 160. (1.)**

— Six easy Lessons for the Harpsichord. Compos'd by Sig^r: Binder.—Mazzinghi.—Ritstchel. Sig^r: Legne.—Galluppi.—Zamperelli. ⟨James Turpin, sculp^t.⟩ Book I. pp. 25. *Joseph Hill: London*, [1765?] *obl.* fol.   **e. 5. k. (5.)**

— Six Instructive Lessons for the Piano Forte. Taken from familiar airs, with appropriate chords & preludes, *etc.* no. 4. *Printed by Clementi & Co: London*, [c. 1810.] fol.
Imperfect; wanting the other numbers.   **h. 3821. s. (1.)**

— Twelve Instructive Lessons for the Piano Forte, taken from familiar airs, with appropriate chords & preludes, *etc.* no. 3, 5, 7, 9, 10. *Printed by Clementi & Co: London*, [c. 1815.] fol.
No. 1–6 are a later edition of the preceding. Imperfect; wanting no. 1, 2, 4, 6, 8, 11, 12.   **h. 3821. s. (2.)**

— Six Lessons for the Harpsichord, by ... Bach ... Benda ... Graun ... Wagenseil ... Hasse ... Kernberger. *Welcker: London*, [1770?] *obl.* fol.   **e. 5. d.**

— Lessons for the Recorder. [*London?* 1680?] *s. sh.* fol.
K. 8. h. 25.

— Periodical Lessons. [P. F.] 4 no. *Bland: [London,* 1790?] fol.
g. 149. (7.)

— Progressive Lessons for the Piano Forte or Harpsichord, *etc.* 2 bk. *R. Birchall: London*, [1795?] *obl.* fol.   **e. 470.**

— Select Lessons, or a Choice Collection of Airs neatly contriv'd for Two German Flutes or Two Violins. And Extracted from the Works of ... Handel, Weideman, Turner, De Fesch, Peschetti, Festing. The Whole being never before Publish'd. [Parts.] *Danl Wright & D. Wright Junr: London*, [1735?] *obl.* 4°.
Imperfect; wanting pp. 23, 24 of the first flute part. This collection also contains compositions by Dubourg and Deperr.
b. 30. (2.)

APPENDIX

— Lessons from the Clock. [Action song.] *See* KIRKPATRICK (W. J.)

— Lessons of the Flowers. Service of Song. *See* CRIPPEN (T. G.)

— Lessons of the Harvest. Service of Song. *See* CRIPPEN (T. G.)

LESSOUR (A.)

— Guillerette. Valse. Pour le piano. pp. 5. *A. Lemoine: Paris; A. Roussel: Marseille*, [c. 1865.] fol.
Issued as music supplement to "La Musique populaire".
P. P. 1948. s/2. (147.)

LESSUR (R. J.)

— Sixty-seven Chants, a collection designed for all Protestant Churches. *Boston*, [1865.] *obl.* 4°.　　　　　**A. 841.**

LEST

— Lest I forget. Song. *See* ANDREWS (A. M.)

— Lest the lattice may be shaking. Part song. *See* BULLOCK (H. A.)

— Lest we forget. [Song.] *See* BALL (Ernest R.)

— Lest we forget. Anthem. *See* BOHANNAN (Jean)

— Lest we forget. [Anthem.] *See* BUNNING (H.)

— Lest we forget. [Hymn.] *See* CARTER (E. S.)

— Lest Winter come. Song. *See* GAYNOR (J. L.)

— Lest you forget. [Song.] *See* LORAINE (William)

LESTAN (THOMAS)

— Método elemental de Viola, y nociones generales de la Viola de Amor. *Madrid*, [1870?] 8°.　　　　**g. 342.**

LESTER (ALFRED)

— Jack's Philosophy. Song, the words by W. Pitt. *J. B. Cramer & Co.: London*, [1885.] fol.　　　　**H. 1788. v. (47.)**

— The Little Torment. Song [begins: "Were I to ask her"]. *London*, [1872.] fol.　　　　**H. 1775. u. (32.)**

— The Miner's Wife. Song [begins: "Dark night was falling"]. Words by J. A. Joseph. *London*, [1871.] fol.
　　　　H. 1775. u. (29.)

— Sing me the songs you used to sing. Song. *London*, [1871.] fol.　　　　**H. 1775. u. (31.)**

— The Three O'Clock polka. [P. F.] *London*, [1878.] fol.
　　　　h. 1494. q. (30.)

— When I sing my own song. Song [begins: "Oh! when I sing"]. *London*, [1871.] fol.　　　　**H. 1775. u. (30.)**

LESTER (BRYAN)

— Essential Guitar Skill, *etc.* ⟨[1.] The Tremolo. [2.] The Barre. [3.] The Arpeggio. [4.] The Scale.⟩ 4 no. *G. Ricordi & Co.: Chesham*, [1977–80.] 4°.　　　　**g. 1650. d. (1.)**

— Explorations in Guitar Playing for Beginners ... Vol. I. One guitar, *etc.* ⟨Vol. II. 2 and 3 guitars.⟩ 2 vol. *G. Ricordi & Co.: Chesham*, [1974.] 4°.　　　　**f. 530. c. (6.)**

— Ghost Story and other Pieces. Easy duos for descant recorder and guitar, *etc.* [Score.] pp. 13. *Ricordi: Chesham*, [1980.] 4°.
　　　　g. 109. yy. (9.)

— 10 little Canons. For descant recorder and guitar, *etc.* pp. 12. *Ricordi: Chesham*, [1980.] 4°.　　　　**g. 109. yy. (8.)**

LESTER (BRYAN) and **COLE** (KEITH R.)

— The Guitar in the Classroom. *Kitharicon Publications: [London*, 1970, *etc.*] 4°.　　　　**e. 138. u. (1.)**

LESTER (EDDIE)

— Cherry Blossom. A Caprice for the Piano. *J. Church Co.: Cincinnati, etc.*, 1902. fol.　　　　**h. 3282. kk. (29.)**

LESTER (ERNEST)

— *See* ROBSON (T. F.) Down by the River. ⟨Song.⟩ Written and composed by T. F. Robson ... & E. Lester. [1906.] *s. sh.* fol.
　　　　H. 3986. tt. (6.)

— *See* ROBSON (T. F.) Down by the River. ⟨Song.⟩ Written and composed by T. F. Robson ... and E. Lester, *etc.* [1906.] fol.
　　　　H. 3986. tt. (7.)

LESTER (GEORGE)

— Back again. [Song.] Written by Fred[k] Thomas, *etc.* pp. 4. *Francis, Day & Hunter: London*, [1890.] fol.
　　　　H. 3980. rr. (25.)

— Brothers. ⟨Song.⟩ Written and composed by G. Lester, *etc.* [Staff and tonic sol-fa notation. Voice part.] *Francis, Day & Hunter: London*, [1901.] *s. sh.* fol.　　　　**H. 3985. x. (24.)**

— Brothers, *etc.* ⟨Song.⟩ [With separate voice part.] 2 pt. *Francis, Day & Hunter: London*, [1901.] fol.　　　　**H. 3985. x. (25.)**

— "Couldn't make the old Girl hear." [Song.] Written and composed by G. Lester, *etc.* ⟨Arranged by John S. Baker.⟩ pp. 4. *Reeder & Walsh: London*, [1897.] fol.
　　　　H. 3980. rr. (26.)

— I had a good Home and I left. Written and composed by G. Lester, *etc.* [Song. Staff and tonic sol-fa notation. Voice part.] *Francis, Day & Hunter: London*, [1897.] *s. sh.* fol.
　　　　H. 3980. rr. (27.)

— I'm lonely. Song, written and composed by G. Lester. With Tonic Sol-fa, *etc.* *E. Marks & Son: London*, [1907.] fol.
　　　　H. 1794. vv. (43.)

— I was underneath. [Song.] Written, composed ... by G. Lester. ⟨Arranged by Henry E. Pether.⟩ pp. 5. *Francis, Day & Hunter: London*, [1891.] fol.　　　　**H. 3980. rr. (28.)**

— I wonder what the Time is now? ⟨Song.⟩ Written and composed by G. Lester. [Staff and tonic sol-fa notation. Voice part.] *Francis, Day & Hunter: London*, [1903.] *s. sh.* fol.
　　　　H. 3985. x. (26.)

— I wonder what the Time is now? *etc.* ⟨Song.⟩ [With separate voice part.] 2 pt. *Francis, Day & Hunter: London*, [1903.] fol.
　　　　H. 3985. x. (27.)

— It may look nothing to you. Song ... Written & composed by G. Lester. ⟨Arranged by Henri Prevost. With tonic sol-fa.⟩ pp. 3. *E. R. Smith & C[o]: London*, [c. 1890.] fol.
　　　　H. 1860. gg. (13.)

— Just as good as new. Written and composed by G. Lester, *etc.* [Song. Staff and tonic sol-fa notation. Voice part.] *Francis, Day & Hunter: London*, [1898.] *s. sh.* fol.　　　　**H. 3980. rr. (29.)**

— May, May, May. ⟨Song.⟩ Written by Maurice Crosby and F. J. Barnes. [Staff and tonic sol-fa notation. Voice part.] *Francis, Day & Hunter: London*, [1905.] *s. sh.* fol.　　　　**H. 3985. x. (28.)**

— May, May, May, *etc.* ⟨Song.⟩ [With separate voice part.] 2 pt. *Francis, Day & Hunter: London*, [1905.] fol.
　　　　H. 3985. x. (29.)

— Oh, that Box of Cigars! ⟨Song.⟩ Written and composed by G. Lester, *etc.* [Staff and tonic sol-fa notation. Voice part.] *Francis, Day & Hunter: London*, [1904.] *s. sh.* fol.
　　　　H. 3985. x. (30.)

— Oh! that Box of Cigars! *etc.* ⟨Song.⟩ [With separate voice part.] 2 pt. *Francis, Day & Hunter: London*, [1904.] fol.
　　　　H. 3985. x. (31.)

LESTER (GEORGE)

— Oh, to-night! Written and composed by G. Lester, *etc.* [Song. Staff and tonic sol-fa notation. Voice part.] *Francis, Day & Hunter: London*, [1898.] *s. sh.* fol.   **H. 3980. rr. (30.)**

— That's the Sort of Pal! ⟨Song.⟩ Written and composed by G. Lester, *etc.* [Staff and tonic sol-fa notation. Voice part.] *Francis, Day & Hunter: London*, [1903.] *s. sh.* fol.   **H. 3985. x. (32.)**

— That's the Sort of Pal. Comic song, *etc.* [With separate voice part.] 2 pt. *Francis, Day & Hunter: London*, [1903.] fol.   **H. 3985. x. (33.)**

— Ti ol the diddle ol the Day. [Song.] Written and composed by G. Lester, *etc.* ⟨Arranged by H. E. Pether.⟩ pp. 5. *Reeder & Walsh: London*, [1898.] fol.   **H. 3980. rr. (31.)**

— Whiskers round the Bottom of his Trousers. Written by A. J. Mills, *etc.* [Song. Staff and tonic sol-fa notation. Voice part.] *Francis, Day & Hunter: London*, [1898.] *s. sh.* fol.   **H. 3980. rr. (32.)**

— *See* LAWRENCE (Albert E.) Keep on the sunny Side. ⟨Song.⟩ Written & composed by A. E. Lawrence, G. Lester, *etc.* [1900.] *s. sh.* fol.   **H. 3985. k. (1.)**

— *See* LAWRENCE (Albert E.) Keep on the sunny Side ... ⟨Song.⟩ Written and composed by A. E. Lawrence, G. Lester, *etc.* [1900.] fol.   **H. 3985. k. (2.)**

— [For editions and arrangements of songs written and composed by G. Lester in sole collaboration with Albert E. Lawrence:] *See* LAWRENCE (Albert E.) and LESTER (G.)

— *See* WESTON (Robert P.) and LESTER (G.) I won't desert you, Captain. ⟨Song.⟩ Written and composed by R. P. Weston and G. Leigh, *etc.* [1899.] *s. sh.* fol.   **H. 3981. rr. (15.)**

LESTER (GEORGE) and **BARNES** (FRED. J.)

— The Boy that looks after his Mother. ⟨Song.⟩ Written and composed by G. Lester and F. J. Barnes, *etc.* [Staff and tonic sol-fa notation. Voice part.] *Francis, Day & Hunter: London*, [1904.] *s. sh.* fol.   **H. 3985. x. (34.)**

LESTER (GEORGE) and **LANGLEY** (PERCIVAL)

— It's a Wonder what Money will do ... ⟨Song.⟩ Written and composed by G. Lester and P. Langley. [Staff and tonic sol-fa notation. Voice part.] *Francis, Day & Hunter: London*, [1905.] *s. sh.* fol.   **H. 3985. x. (35.)**

— It's a Wonder what Money will do, *etc.* ⟨Song.⟩ [With separate voice part.] 2 pt. *Francis, Day & Hunter: London*, [1905.] fol.   **H. 3985. x. (36.)**

LESTER (IDA)

— Crimson Blushes. Op. 6. [P. F.] *Century Music Publishing Co.: New York*, 1902. fol.   **h. 3282. kk. (30.)**

— Crimson Blushes. Caprice ... Arr. by L. O. Smith. (Violin and Piano.) *Century Music Publishing Co.: New York*, (1906.) fol.   **h. 1612. p. (31.)**

LESTER (J. D.)

— You're more than seven. [Song, begins: "This is a very wicked world".] *London*, [1876.] fol.   **H. 1778. y. (15.)**

LESTER (JOHN HENRY)

— The Dear Old Stile. [Song.] Written & composed by J. H. Lester, *etc.* (Arranged by E. Forman.) *Francis Bros. & Day: London*, [1887.] fol.   **H. 1260. f. (51.)**

LESTER (JOHN HENRY)

— Forgive and forget. [Song.] Written & composed by J. H. Lester, *etc.* (Arranged by E. Forman.) *Francis Bros. & Day: London*, [1887.] fol.   **H. 1260. f. (52.)**

— How they nurse the Baby. Written and composed by J. H. Lester, *etc.* [Song. Staff and tonic sol-fa notation. Voice part.] *Francis, Day & Hunter: London*, [1897.] *s. sh.* fol.   **H. 3980. rr. (33.)**

— Justice in England. [Song, begins: "This is a free and happy land".] Written ... by W. Laburnum. *London*, [1877.] fol.   **H. 1783. o. (56.)**

— The Lichfield Mission Tune Book, containing hymn tunes, chants and litanies for "The Lichfield Mission Hymn Book" ... Compiled by J. H. Lester. ⟨New edition.⟩ pp. vii. 111. *Bemrose & Sons: London*, [c. 1905.] 8°.   **C. 19. pp.**

— The Lion's roused at last. [Song, begins: "We've calmy borne the insults".] Words by J. F. Mitchell. *London*, [1878.] fol.   **H. 1783. o. (57.)**

LESTER (KATE)

— A Spring Posy. Action Song, words by M. Farrell, *etc.* *J. Williams: London*, (1909.) 4°.   **F. 607. dd. (5.)**

— The Star of Spain. Lullaby, with Violin obbligato, words by C. Hurst, *etc.* *W. H. Broome: London*, 1907. fol.   **H. 1794. vv. (44.)**

— To April. Song, words by M. Doney. *Opus Music Co.: London*, 1914. fol.   **H. 1793. t. (13.)**

LESTER (L. M.)

— Swinging, swinging. [Song.] Words and music by L. M. Lester. pp. 5. *Hamilton S. Gordon: New York*, [1898.] fol.   **H. 3980. rr. (34.)**

LESTER (LEON)

— So easy Trios. For clarinets or trumpets. ⟨Flutes or oboes.⟩ 2 no. *Chappell & Co.: London; Boston Music Co.: Boston, Mass.*, [1964.] 4°.   **g. 409. xx. (3.)**

— *See* DOBRÉE (Georgina) and KING (Thea) Clarinet Duets, *etc.* ⟨Volume 3. Transcribed by L. Lester.⟩ [1979, *etc.*] 4°.   **g. 1635. f.**

LESTER (PERCY)

— Azalea. Schottische. [P. F.] *B. Williams: London*, [1884.] fol.   **h. 975. v. (19.)**

— The Azalea. Schottische. [Fife and drum band parts.] Arranged by R. Dyke. *J. R. Lafleur & Son: London*, [1887.] 8°.
Part of the "Alliance Musicale".   **f. 403. g. (32.)**

— Gardenia. Schottische. [P. F.] *B. Williams: London*, [1885.] fol.   **h. 975. v. (20.)**

— Gladiola. Schottische. [P. F.] *B. Williams: London*, [1887.] fol.   **h. 975. v. (21.)**

— Heather Bell. Waltz. [P. F.] *B. Williams: London*, [1888.] fol.   **h. 3285. q. (35.)**

— White Wings. Waltz. [P. F.] *B. Williams: London*, [1889.] fol.   **h. 3285. q. (36.)**

LESTER (SYDNEY)

— Ten little Motorists. Humorous song. Written by Archie Hesse and Oscar Parkes. pp. 5. *Reynolds & Co.: London*, [1908.] fol.   **H. 3985. x. (37.)**

LESTER (WILLIAM)

— Alla Toccata. Op. 93. No. 4. [Organ.] *H. W. Gray Co.: New York*, 1925. 4°.
St. Cecilia, no. 348, 349. Part of the "American Organ Quarterly". Vol. 6. No. 14. **g. 1380. b. (28.)**

— Alone with Night. Song, the poem by F. H. Martens. *G. Ricordi & Co.: New York, etc.*, 1916. fol. **H. 1846. y. (1.)**

— Along the Hwang-Ho. A Song Cycle ... Op. 79. The poems by F. H. Martens, *etc. C. Fischer: New York, etc.*, 1921. 4°. **G. 426. n. (28.)**

— Apple Blossoms. [Song, words by] S. M. Becker ... Op. 31. No. 3. *White-Smith Music Publishing Co.: Boston, etc.*, (1913.) fol. **G. 806. mm. (25.)**

— As a Perfume doth remain. [Song, words by] A. Symons, *etc. White-Smith Music Publishing Co.: Boston, etc.*, (1913.) fol. **G. 806. mm. (27.)**

— Ballad of the Golden Sun ... for chorus of men's voices with soprano solo, text by F. H. Martens. Op. 68. *O. Ditson Co.: Boston*, 1917. 8°. **F. 1268. u. (5.)**

— A Bearnais Lament. [Three-part song.] English version by M. Lester. Ancient Bearnais Folk Tune. Arr. by W. Lester. *Gamble Hinged Music Co.: Chicago*, 1934. 8°. **F. 1771. b. (11.)**

— The Birth of Love. A Cantata for Christmas or general use; for chorus ... and ... soli, with organ accompaniment. Libretto by M. L. Dawson ... Op. 63. *C. F. Summy Co.: Chicago*, 1917. 8°. **F. 1269. z. (3.)**

— Carols of the Christ-Child. VIII. Cradle Hymn. [Words by] M. Lester. Arranged and composed by W. Lester. Op. 78. No. 8. *H. W. Gray Co.: New York*, 1924. 8°. **E. 602. kk. (24.)**

— Christmas Lullaby. [Song, words by] F. L. Gratiot. Op. 39. No. 1. *White-Smith Music Publishing Co.: Boston, etc.*, (1914.) fol. **G. 806. mm. (26.)**

— The Christmas Rose. A Legend of the Birth of Christ, for mixed chorus and soli with organ ... accompaniment. Words by F. H. Martens. (Op. 66.) *H. W. Gray Co.: New York*, 1916. 8°. **F. 1268. s. (4.)**

— Come unto these yellow Sands. For Chorus of men's voices ... [Words] by W. Shakespeare. Op. 15. No. 3, *etc. G. Schirmer: New York*, (1914.) 8°. **F. 163. p. (26.)**

— Compensation. [Song, words by] J. J. Piatt, *etc. White-Smith Music Publishing Co.: Boston, etc.*, (1913.) fol. **G. 806. mm. (28.)**

— Cradle Hymn. *See* supra: Carols of the Christ-Child. VIII.

— A Dirge. Song with piano accompaniment ... poem by F. D. Hemans. *G. Schirmer: New York, Boston*, 1918. 4°. **G. 383. ff. (50.)**

— The Ebon Lute ... Op. 62. No. 1. (Organ.) *H. W. Gray Co.: New York*, 1918. 4°.
St. Cecilia Series of compositions for the organ, No. 104. **g. 1380. c. (31.)**

— Echo. [Song, words by] T. Moore, *etc. White-Smith Publishing Co.: Boston, etc.*, (1913.) fol. **G. 806. mm. (29.)**

— Epilogue. Op. 93. No. 6. [Organ.] *H. W. Gray Co.: New York*, 1925. 4°.
St. Cecilia, no. 348, 349. Part of the "Ameri-Organ Quarterly". Vol. 6. No. 14. **g. 1380. b. (26.)**

— Evening Hymn. [Sacred song.] Words and music by W. Lester, *etc. C. F. Summy Co.: Chicago*, (1914.) fol. **H. 1187. xx. (17.)**

— Everyman. A Morality Play or Choral Opera ... Op. 87. *J. Fischer & Bro.: New York, Birmingham*, 1927. 8°. **E. 1592. bb. (4.)**

LESTER (WILLIAM)

— Give Thanks unto God. Christmas Hymn-Anthem ... [Words by] M. L. Dawson. *White-Smith Music Publishing Co.: Boston, etc.*, (1913.) 8°. **F. 281. ll. (17.)**

— The Glory of the King. Hymn-Anthem for Christmas ... [Words by] M. L. Dawson. *White-Smith Music Publishing Co.: Boston, etc.*, (1913.) 8°. **F. 281. ll. (18.)**

— The Golden Syon. A Sacred Cantata for soli, chorus, organ or orchestra. The text adapted and written by F. H. Martens. Op. 75, *etc. H. W. Gray Co.: New York*, 1918. 8°. **F. 1269. bb. (2.)**

— Greater Love hath no Man. *See* infra: [The Triumph of the greater Love.]

— Heart o' me. A Song, poem by H. Vanderhoof. (Op. 71. No. 1.) *C. F. Summy Co.: Chicago*, 1917. fol. **H. 1846. y. (2.)**

— Home. Four-Part Song ... [Words by] D. Greenwell ... Op. 23. No. 2, *etc. White-Smith Music Publishing Co.: Boston, etc.*, 1913. 8°. **F. 1744. a. (45.)**

— Home on the Range. (Traditional Cowboy Song.) S. S. A.-T. B. Arr. W. Lester. *Gamble Hinged Music Co.: Chicago*, 1936. 8°. **F. 1771. c. (20.)**

— Hushabye my Baby. [Song.] Poem by M. L. Dawson, *etc. Studio Publishing Co.: Chicago*, (1913.) fol. **H. 1793. t. (15.)**

— I'll love you, Love, when Roses blow. Song, text by F. H. Martens. *O. Ditson Co.: Boston*, 1917. fol. **H. 1846. y. (3.)**

— If she be made of white and red. For chorus of men's voices ... [Words] by W. Shakespeare. Op. 15. No. 2, *etc. G. Schirmer: New York*, (1914.) 8°. **F. 163. p. (25.)**

— In a Cloister Garden. Idylle. Op. 97. (Organ.) *H. W. Gray Co.: New York*, 1921. 4°. **g. 1380. h. (6.)**

— In the quiet Hours with Jesus. [Duet.] Poem by M. L. Dawson, *etc. Studio Publishing Co.: Chicago*, (1913.) fol. **H. 1187. xx. (19.)**

— Jerusalem, thou City fair and high. Jerusalem, du hochgebaute Stadt. [Words by] J. M. Meyfart ... C. Winkworth, translator. Melody by M. Frank [or rather, Franck]. (Wake, awake, for Night is flying. Wachet auf, ruft uns die Stimme. [Words by] Dr. P. Nicolai. Melody by P. Nicolai.) Arr. for Chorus of Mixed Voices and Descant, with Organ, by W. Lester. *Gamble Hinged Music Co.: Chicago*, 1934. s. sh. 8°. **E. 602. rr. (27.)**

— Just as I am ... [Sacred song.] Poem by M. L. Dawson. *Studio Publishing Co.: Chicago*, (1913.) fol. **H. 1187. xx. (18.)**

— The Light of God. Anthem for Christmas ... Poem by S. M. Becker. Op. 39. No. 2. *White-Smith Music Publishing Co.: Boston, etc.*, (1914.) 8°. **F. 281. tt. (30.)**

— The Little Lord Jesus. Christmas Cantata based upon medieval French Noëls, for chorus of mixed voices with solos. Text compiled by F. H. Martens. Op. 77. Vocal Score. *C. Fischer: New York, etc.*, 1917. 8°. **F. 1269. z. (2.)**

— The Lord is in His Holy Temple. [Anthem.] For ... mixed voices ... with Organ accompaniment. [Words by M. L. Dawson.] *G. Schirmer: New York*, (1914.) 8°. **F. 281. nn. (24.)**

— Four Love Vignettes, poems by F. H. Martens. (Op. 64. No. 1.) Lace. (No. 2.) June. (No. 3.) Why. (No. 4.) To show that I was true. 4 no. *Huntzinger & Dilworth: New York*, 1916. fol. **H. 1846. y. (4.)**

— Maiden sweet, be more discreet. [Three-part song.] English version by M. Lester. Provencal Folk Tune. Arr. by W. Lester. *Gamble Hinged Music Co.: Chicago*, 1934. 8°. **F. 1771. b. (12.)**

LESTER (William)

— Manaboza. An Opera in three acts. The first part of a Trilogy entitled "The Wampum Belt," by F. Neilson. Op. 80. *J. & W. Chester: London*, 1929. fol. **H. 3618.**

— Mavourneen. My Darling. For voice & piano, the words by F. H. Martens. *C. Fischer: New York, etc.*, 1917. 4°. **G. 390. r. (4.)**

— May and Love. [Song, words by] S. A. Brooke. Op. 16. No. 2. *White-Smith Music Publishing Co.: Boston, etc.*, 1915. fol. **H. 1846. y. (5.)**

— Meditation—Carillon, for Organ. *G. Schirmer: New York*, 1929. 4°. **g. 1380. o. (8.)**

— My Prayer. [Sacred song.] Poem by H. K. Tootle, *etc. C. F. Summy Co.: Chicago*, (1913.) fol. **H. 1187. xx. (20.)**

— My Rose. [Song, words by] M. MacBurney ... Op. 31. No. 1. *White-Smith Music Publishing Co.: Boston, etc.*, (1913.) fol. **G. 806. mm. (30.)**

— O Mistress mine. For Chorus of men's voices ... [Words] by W. Shakespeare. Op. 15. No. 1, *etc. G. Schirmer: New York*, (1914.) 8°. **F. 163. p. (24.)**

— Out amang the Heather. For voice & piano, poem by F. H. Martens. (Op. 71. No. 2.) *C. Fischer: New York, etc.*, 1917. 4°. **G. 390. r. (5.)**

— Out of the East. Song Cycle, poems by F. H. Martens. Op. 57. *C. Fischer: New York*, 1916. 4°. **G. 295. n. (12.)**

— Phyllis and Damon. Three-part Chorus for women's voices, poem by N. Hopper. Op. 21. No. 1. *G. Schirmer: New York*, (1914.) 8°. **F. 328. v. (28.)**

— A Psalm of Thanksgiving. A Sacred Cantata for soli and chorus of mixed voices ... Op. 55. *White-Smith: Boston, etc.*, 1915. 8°. **F. 1269. aa. (8.)**

— Rejoice in the Lord. *See* infra: [The Triumph of the greater Love.]

— Remembrance. [Song, words by] W. E. Mayne ... Op. 31. No. 2. *White-Smith Music Publishing Co.: Boston, etc.*, (1913.) fol. **G. 806. mm. (31.)**

— Rockabye Town. [Song.] Poem by M. L. Dawson, *etc. Studio Publishing Co.: Chicago*, (1913.) fol. **H. 1793. t. (14.)**

— Two Short Songs. Poems by P. B. Shelley. [No. 1.] To Music. [No. 2.] Song of Proserpine. *Studio Publishing Co.: Chicago*, (1913.) fol. **G. 806. mm. (32.)**

— Sing the Resurrection Day! [Sacred song.] The text by F. H. Martens. *H. W. Gray Co.: New York*, 1917. 4°. **G. 519. d. (13.)**

— Sleep, Holy Babe. Trio for women's voices ... [Words by] E. Caswall. Op. 39. No. 3. *White-Smith Music Publishing Co.: Boston, etc.*, (1914.) 8°. **F. 328. w. (21.)**

— A Song of Triumph. Anthem based on Welsh Hymn Tune Llanfair. [By Robert Williams.] Text by J. Cennick ... Op. 37. No. 1. *Gamble Hinged Music Co.: Chicago*, 1934. 8°. **E. 335. h. (15.)**

— Soon I'm goin' Home. Negro Spiritual, text arranged by M. Lester. Op. 33. No. 2c. (Vocal Solo.) *J. Fischer & Bro.: New York, Birmingham*, 1926. 4°. **G. 815. b. (5.)**

— Soon I'm goin' Home. Negro Spiritual ... Op. 33. No. 2e. [Two-part chorus.] *J. Fischer & Bro.: New York, Birmingham*, 1926. 8°. **E. 602. ll. (41.)**

— A Southern Idyll. In Georgia. Op. 93. No. 2. [Organ.] *H. W. Gray Co.: New York*, 1925. 4°.
St. Cecilia, No. 343. **g. 1380. b. (34.)**

LESTER (William)

— A Southland Song. In Alabama. Op. 30. No. 1. [Organ.] *C. F. Summy Co.: Chicago*, 1927. obl. 4°. **e. 1093. r. (14.)**

— Souvenir rococo ... Op. 62. No. 2. (Organ.) *H. W. Gray Co.: New York*, 1918. 4°.
St. Cecilia Series of compositions for the organ, No. 103. **g. 1380. c. (32.)**

— The Spanish Gypsies. [Words by] M. Lester. A Choral Dance-Suite ... For women's voices, S. S. A. (Op. 101c.) *J. Fischer & Bro.: New York, Birmingham*, 1923. 8°. **F. 585. nn. (31.)**

— Spring Fever. Four-part Song for men's voices ... [Words by] S. M. Becker, *etc. White-Smith Music Publishing Co.: Boston, etc.*, (1914.) 8°. **F. 163. o. (55.)**

— That Song my Love once sang. Song. (Translated from Heine by F. H. Martens.) *O. Ditson Co.: Boston*, 1918. 4°. **G. 383. ff. (48.)**

— Threnody. In memoriam. Op. 93. No. 1. [Organ.] *H. W. Gray Co.: New York*, 1925. 4°.
St. Cecilia, No. 342. **g. 1380. k. (30.)**

— Thyre the Fair. Choral Ballad. [Baritone solo and chorus of female voices.] Poem by F. H. Martens. Op. 52. No. 2. *H. W. Gray Co.: [New York,]* 1916. 8°. **F. 1268. p. (6.)**

— Thyre the Fair. A Choral Ballad. Arranged for baritone solo and chorus of mixed voices, *etc. H. W. Gray Co.: New York*, 1918. 8°. **F. 158. r. (4.)**

— To Phillis. [Song, words by] Sir C. Sedley, *etc. White-Smith Music Publishing Co.: Boston, etc.*, (1913.) fol. **G. 806. mm. (33.)**

— The Trail to the Shadow-land. For voice & piano ... poem by F. H. Martens. *C. Fischer: New York*, 1918. 4°. **G. 383. ff. (49.)**

— The Triumph of the greater Love. An Easter Cantata for ... mixed voices with Organ accompaniment, text compiled by F. H. Martens. Op. 50, *etc. C. Fischer: New York, Boston*, (1915.) 8°. **F. 1269. r. (7.)**

— [The Triumph of the greater Love.] Greater Love hath no Man. Air, *etc. C. Fischer: New York, etc.*, 1918. 4°. **G. 519. e. (44.)**

— [The Triumph of the greater Love.] Rejoice in the Lord ... Duet for soprano and alto, *etc. C. Fischer: New York, etc.*, 1918. 4°. **G. 519. e. (45.)**

— The Tryst. For three-part Chorus of women's voices, poem by Lady Gilbert. Op. 21. No. 2. *G. Schirmer: New York*, (1914.) 8°. **F. 328. v. (29.)**

— Under the Rose. Four-Part Song ... [Words by] R. H. Stoddard ... Op. 23. No. 1, *etc. White-Smith Music Publishing Co.: Boston, etc.*, (1913.) 8°. **F. 1744. a. (44.)**

— Vagrant Sketches for piano solo. Op. 54. *C. Fischer: New York*, 1916. 4°. **g. 272. hh. (13.)**

— Wake, awake, for Night is flying. *See* supra: Jerusalem, thou City fair and high.

— The Way of Righteousness. Anthem ... with Piano or Organ accompaniment. *G. Schirmer: New York*, (1914.) 8°. **F. 281. nn. (25.)**

— When I am dead, my Dearest. [Song, words by] C. Rossetti. Op. 16. No. 1. *White-Smith Music Publishing Co.: Boston, etc.*, 1915. fol. **H. 1846. y. (6.)**

— The Words on the Cross. A Lenten Meditation ... Text from the Holy Scriptures and the Hymnal arranged by M. Lester. *H. W. Gray Co.: New York*, 1938. 8°. **F. 1269. vv. (5.)**

LESTER (WILLIAM)

— *See* BACH (J. S.) [*Doubtful and Supposititious Works.*] [Notenbuch der Anna Magdalena Bach ... 1725. no. 25. Bist du bei mir.] Arioso cantabile. Vocalise ... Transcribed ... by W. Lester. 1935. 8°.   **F. 956. x. (13.)**

— *See* BEETHOVEN (L. van) Sonata. Opus 49. No. 2 ... The Second Part added by W. Lester. 1935. 4°.   **g. 249. dd. (8.)**

— *See* BOHM (C.) [Lieder. Op. 326. No. 27. Still wie die Nacht.] Silent as Night. Father of Love ... Arr. for Chorus by W. Lester. 1935. 8°.   **E. 335. i. (31.)**

— *See* GRIEG (E. H.) [Lyrische Stücke. Op. 43. No. 6. An den Frühling.] To Spring ... Choral transcription by W. Lester. 1935. 8°.   **F. 217. f. (56.)**

— *See* RAKHMANINOV (S. V.) [Morceaux de Fantaisie. Op. 3. No. 2. Prélude.] Message of the Bells ... Arr. for Chorus by W. Lester. 1935. 8°.   **F. 585. ww. (36.)**

— *See* STRADELLA (A.) [*Doubtful and Supposititious Works.*] [Pietà Signore.] O Lord most Holy ... Arr. ... by W. Lester. 1935. 8°.   **E. 335. h. (23.)**

L'ESTOCART (PASCHAL DE)

— Premier Livre des Octonaires de la vanité du Monde. *Éditions Maurice Senart: Paris,* 1929. 4°. [*Monuments de la musique française au temps de la renaissance. liv.* 10.]   **G. 59. a.**

— Second livre des octonaires de la vanité du monde. Révision et introduction par J. Chailley et. M. Honegger, *etc.* pp. xiii. 110. *Éditions Salabert: Paris,* [1958.] 4°. [*Monuments de la musique française au temps de la renaissance. liv.* 11.]   **G. 59. a.**

— Cent Cinquante Pseaumes de Dauid, mis en Rime Francoise par Clement Marot et Théodore de Besze, et mis en Musique à Quatre, Cinq, Six, Sept et Huit Parties, par Paschal de L'Estocart, *etc.* [Superius.] Tenor. [Contratenor.] 3 pt. *Chez Barthelemi Vincent: Lyon,* 1583. obl. 4°. *Imperfect; the Superius wanting all but pp.* 161–164, *and the Contratenor all but pp.* 61–64, 153–156 *and* 169–176.   **A. 62.**

— Cent cinquante pseaumes de David mis en rime françoise par Clément Marot et Théodore de Bèsze, et mis en musique à quatre, cinq, six, sept et huit parties ... 1583. Faksimile-Nachdruck herausgegeben von Hans Holliger und Pierre Pidoux. [Parts.] ⟨Superius.—Tenor.—Quinta pars.— Contratenor.—Bassus.⟩ 5 pt. *Bärenreiter-Verlag: Kassel & Basel,* 1954. obl. 8°. [*Documenta musicologica. Reihe* 1. *no.* 7.]   **W. P. 11059 (a.) / 7.**

— [150 pseaumes de David.] Dix psaumes et un canon. Restitution: J. Feuillie. pp. 25. *Éditions musicales de la Schola Cantorum: Paris,* [1975.] 4°. *Part of "La Reverdie".*   **F. 1174. k. (2.)**

LESTOCQ

— Lestocq. Opéra-comique. *See* AUBER (D. F. E.)

LESTON (HAROLD)

— Bells at Eventide, for the pianoforte. (Op. 20. No. 2.) *O. Ditson Company: Boston, etc.,* 1894. fol.   **h. 3118. (4.)**

— Breaking Heart. Morceau de Salon for pianoforte. (Op. 42.) *White-Smith Music Pub. Co.: Boston, etc.,* 1896. fol.   **h. 3118. (7.)**

— Bring ye all the Tithes. Mixed Quartet ... Op. 52. *O. Ditson Co.: [Boston, etc.,]* 1896. 8°.   **F. 1529. b. (36.)**

— The Carol of the Shepherdess, for the pianoforte. (Op. 20. No. 1.) *O. Ditson Company: Boston, etc.,* 1894. fol.   **h. 3118. (3.)**

LESTON (HAROLD)

— Evening Twilight gathers. Duet for Soprano and Tenor. Op. 56. *O. Ditson Company: Boston, etc.,* 1896. fol.   **H. 1798. v. (8.)**

— Farewell, oh, beauteous Night. *See* infra: Three Songs ... No. 2.

— The Gipsy's Farewell, for piano. Op. 64. *O. Ditson Co.: Boston, etc.,* 1897. fol.   **h. 3118. (10.)**

— Give me thy Hand. *See* infra: Three Songs ... No. 3.

— Good-bye, my bonnie Lass. Song, words by C. Clifford. Op. 39. *O. Ditson Company: Boston, etc.,* 1895. fol.   **H. 1798. v. (9.)**

— Memories of Golden Days, for pianoforte. Op. 50. *White-Smith Music Pub. Co.: Boston, etc.,* 1896. fol.   **h. 3118. (8.)**

— Memories of Youthful Days, for pianoforte. Op. 13. 8 no. *O. Ditson Company: Boston, etc.,* 1894. fol.   **h. 3118. (1.)**

— My first five Pianoforte Pieces. (Op. 36.) 5 no. *O. Ditson Company: Boston, etc.,* 1894. fol.   **h. 3118. (5.)**

— An October Morning. Four-Part Song for mixed Voices. *White-Smith Music Pub. Co.: Boston, etc.,* 1896. 8°.   **F. 321. m. (18.)**

— Two Pianoforte Pieces. Op. 38. 2 no. *O. Ditson Company: Boston, etc.,* 1895. fol.   **h. 3118. (6.)**

— Two Pianoforte Pieces. Op. 65. No. 1. Parting. No. 2. Lullaby. 2 no. *O. Ditson Co.: Boston, etc.,* 1897. fol.   **h. 3118. (11.)**

— The Robin's Matinee. Caprice facile for piano. (Op. 61.) *White-Smith Music Publishing Co.: Boston, etc.,* 1896. fol.   **h. 3118. (9.)**

— Three Songs. 1. Sunset Hour. (Words by M. M. Bowen. Op. 32.) 2. Farewell, oh beauteous Night. (Words by O. L. C. Op. 31.) 3. Give me thy Hand. (Words by E. L. Martyn. Op. 33.) 3 no. *White-Smith Music Publishing Co.: Boston,* 1894. fol.   **H. 1798. v. (10.)**

— Songs of the Fairies. First teaching Pieces for the pianoforte. Op. 14, 15. 10 no. *O. Ditson Company: Boston, etc.,* 1894. fol.   **h. 3118. (2.)**

— Sunset Hour. *See* supra: Three Songs. No. 1.

— Thou art the Queen of the beauteous Night. Serenade. Words by O. L. C. *O. Ditson Company: Boston,* 1893. fol.   **H. 1798. v. (11.)**

L'ESTRANGE (ARTHUR)

— Chant des Matelots, caprice de concert pour le Piano. *London,* [1882.] fol.   **h. 3275. j. (33.)**

— Gavotte ... for the piano. *Patey & Willis: London,* [1886.] fol.   **h. 1484. t. (4.)**

— Under the Lindens. Song, words by F. Hoare. *Mathias & Strickland: London,* [1894.] fol.   **H. 1798. v. (12.)**

L'ESTRANGE (BERTRAM)

— "Beneath the Stars." ⟨Serenade Two-step.⟩ (Whistling Serenade.) [Military band parts.] 34 pt. *In:* JOYCE (Archibald) "Dreaming." ⟨Valse,⟩ *etc.* 1911. fol. [*Boosey's military Journal. ser.* 131. *no.* 4.]   **h. 1549.**

— Chanson Rivière. Valse for Piano. *Ascherberg, Hopwood & Crew: London,* 1909. fol.   **h. 3286. uu. (51.)**

— "Embers." ⟨Valse lente.⟩ B. Lestrange ... "Confidence." ⟨Valse miniature.⟩ Chater Robinson ... "As you pass by." ⟨Cornet solo.⟩ Kennedy Russell ... "Tip-toes." ⟨Intermezzo.⟩ Herbert L. Cooke ... "Tell her so." ⟨Song fox-trot.⟩ Kenneth

L'ESTRANGE (Bertram)

Park ... "Keep me going." ⟨Song fox-trot.⟩ Sydney Baynes ... "Oh you mystery Tune." ⟨Song fox-trot.⟩ Trevor and Ancliffe ... Arranged [for military band] by J. Ord Hume. ⟨Conductor [and parts].⟩ 30 pt. *Boosey & Co.: London*, [1921.] fol. [*Boosey's military Journal. ser.* 143. *no.* 3.]   **h. 1549.**

—— "The Hobble Skirt Walk." ⟨One-step.⟩ ... Arranged [for military band] by M. Retford. *In:* FLETCHER (Percy E.) Two characteristic Pieces, *etc.* 1912. fol. [*Boosey's military Journal. ser.* 132. *no.* 2.]   **h. 1549.**

—— The Land of Home, sweet Home. [Song.] Written by L. Cooke. *F. Howard: London*, (1914.) fol.   **H. 1793. t. (16.)**

—— Love's Song. Waltz. [P. F.] *Ascherberg, Hopwood & Crew: London*, 1910. fol.   **h. 3286. uu. (52.)**

—— Melodiana. Selection. Arranged by B. Lestrange. [P. F.] *Ascherberg, Hopwood & Crew: London*, 1915. fol.   **h. 3284. nn. (49.)**

—— Nevada. Scenes of the Prairie. Two Step. [P. F.] *Ascherberg, Hopwood & Crew: London*, 1910. fol.   **h. 3286. uu. (53.)**

—— Red Wing. Two Step. [P. F.] *Ascherberg, Hopwood & Crew: London*, 1909. fol.   **h. 3286. uu. (54.)**

—— Two-step "Red Wing". (A Prairie Romance) ... Arr. [for military band] by M. Retford. [Parts.] 33 pt. [1911.] fol. [*Boosey's military Journal. ser.* 129. *no.* 5.]   **h. 1549.**

—— Russian Patrol. [P. F.] *Ascherberg, Hopwood & Crew: London*, 1915. fol.   **h. 3284. nn. (50.)**

—— *See* GILBERT (Jean) *pseud.* [Autoliebchen.] "The Joyride Lady." ⟨Waltz. On melodies from the musical farce⟩ ... Arranged [for military band] by B. Lestrange. [1914.] fol. [*Boosey & Co.'s supplemental Journal for military Bands. no.* 124.]   **h. 1544. a.**

—— *See* GILBERT (Jean) *pseud.* [Die keusche Susanne.] "The Girl in the Taxi." ⟨Waltz.⟩ On melodies from the musical comedy composed by J. Gilbert. Arr. [for military band] by B. Lestrange. 1913. fol. [*Boosey & Co.'s supplemental Journal for military Bands. no.* 109.]   **h. 1544. a.**

L'ESTRANGE (George)

—— The Echo of thy Voice. Song, words by A. Skovgaard-Pedersen. *J. B. Cramer & Co.: London*, 1913. fol.   **H. 1793. t. (17.)**

—— The Exile's Grave. Song, words by A. Skovgaard-Pedersen. *J. B. Cramer & Co.: London*, 1913. fol.   **H. 1793. t. (18.)**

—— Just one more. Encore Song, words by F. G. Bowles, *etc.* *J. B. Cramer & Co.: London*, 1915. fol.   **H. 1793. t. (19.)**

—— Love's silent Song. [Song.] Words by E. Teschemacher. 2 no. [In E flat and F.] *J. B. Cramer & Co.: London*, 1915. fol.   **H. 1793. t. (20.)**

—— Pan the Piper. Song, words by A. Skovgaard-Pedersen, *etc.* 2 no. [In G and A.] *J. B. Cramer & Co.: London*, 1913. fol.   **H. 1793. t. (21.)**

—— This Rose.—Liebste Rose.—Song, words by O. Fricksen. 3 no. [In C, D flat and E flat.] *J. B. Cramer & Co.: London*, 1911. fol.   **H. 1792. s. (21.)**

—— When Eyes are sad. Song, words by F. G. Bowles. 4 no. [In B flat, C, D flat and E flat.] *J. B. Cramer & Co.: London*, 1913. fol.   **H. 1793. t. (22.)**

L'ESTRANGE (Julian)

—— Les Jolies Filles. Gavotte. [P. F.] *Francis Bros. & Day: London*, [1888.] fol.   **h. 1484. t. (5.)**

L'ESTRANGE (Moray)

—— The Holy Message. Sacred Song, words by K. M. Luck. *R. Maynard: London*, [1912.] fol.   **H. 1187. rr. (14.)**

L'ESTRANGE (Nellie)

—— Jack's the Lad. [Song.] Written by George Horncastle, *etc.* pp. 5. *Hopwood & Crew: London*, [1892.] fol.
   H. 3980. rr. (35.)

L'ESTRANGE (Victor)

—— Adelaïda, deux mazurkas pour Piano. *London*, [1859.] fol.
   h. 1460. v. (34.)

—— La Belle Chatelaine, quadrille brillante. [P. F.] *London*, [1862.] fol.   **h. 1460. v. (37.)**

—— Electra galop. [P. F.] *London*, [1862.] fol.   **h. 1460. v. (35.)**

—— Follow my leader. Galop. [P. F.] *Shepherd & Kilner: London*, [1882.] fol.   **h. 975. v. (22.)**

—— May Bud, valse à deux temps. [P. F.] *London*, [1862.] fol.
   h. 1460. v. (36.)

LESUEUR (Jean François)

—— Recueil de morceaux sacrés, avec accomp[t]. d'Orgue. *Paris*, [1830?] fol.   **H. 1032.**

—— Primo. Super Flumina, pseaume à grands choeurs et à grand orchestre. Secundo. Troisième Oratorio du Carême en morceaux d'ensemble. [Score.] *Paris*, [1833?] fol.
   H. 1032. a.

—— Ensemble. Primo. Messe basse et Domine salvum, soli et chœurs. Secundo. Motet. Joannes Baptizat et Domine salvum, soli et chœurs ... Avec accompagnement d'orgue. [Score.] 2 no. pp. 126. *Lemoine; Sieber: Paris*, [1840?] fol. *Oeuvres sacrées de Lesueur. livr.* 15, 16.   **Hirsch iv. 820.**

—— Adam. Tragédie lyrique religieuse en trois actes, suivie du ciel. Paroles de feu Guillard, imitée du célèbre Klopstock, *etc.* [Score.] pp. 512. *Chez J. Frey: Paris*, [1809?] fol.
   Hirsch ii. 514.

—— La Caverne. Drame lyrique en trois actes ... Paroles de Dercis ... Gravé par Huguet. [Score.] pp. 330. *Chez Naderman: Paris*, [1793.] fol.
Plate number 699.   **Hirsch ii. 515.**

—— [Another copy.] *Imperfect; wanting the titlepage.*   **G. 290. b.**

—— La Caverne. Drame lyrique en trois actes ... Paroles de Dercis, *etc.* [Score.] pp. 330. *J. H. Naderman: Paris*, [1793.] fol.   **R. M. 11. d. 16.**

—— [La Caverne.] Il y a cinquante ans et plus. *Air, etc.* [*Paris*, 1793.] 8°.   **B. 362. (110.)**

—— [La Caverne.] Le pauvre tems, le pauvre tems. *Air, etc.* [*Paris*, 1793.] 8°.   **B. 362. (109.)**

—— Oratorio de Debbora à grands chœurs et à grand orchestre ... avec accompagnement de piano ou orgue par Aléxandre Piccini. [Score, including P. F. reduction.] pp. 120. *J. Frey: Paris*, 1828. fol.   **H. 1032. e.**

—— Il y a cinquante ans et plus. *See supra:* [La Caverne.]

—— Laudate Pueri. Motet pour voix seule. [1857.] *See* NIEDERMEYER (L.) La Maîtrise, *etc.* 1re Année. No. 4. [1857–61.] fol.   **H. 1237.**

—— Levons nous, un Tribun perfide. *Chant du ix. Thermidor.* Paroles de T. Desorgues. *Du Magazin de Musique à l'usage des fêtes Nationales:* [*Paris*, 1794.] 8°.   **E. 1717. b. (15.)**

LESUEUR (Jean François)

— Menuet favori de Madame Récamier. (D'après) J. F. Lesueur, pour violon avec accomp. de piano par A. de Keyser. Revu et doigté par H. Wessely. *Schott & Co.: London*, 1916. fol.
g. 505. ii. (17.)

— Menuet favori de Madame Récamier. (D'après) J. F. Lesueur … par A. de Keyser. Revu … par H. Wessely … Piano seul. *Schott & Co.: London*, 1916. fol. **h. 3284. ll. (42*.)**

— Menuet favori de Madame Récamier, d'après J. F. Lesueur. [Transcribed for P. F. by] A. de Keyser. *Schott & Co.: London*, [1927.] fol.
[*Classical Transcriptions for Pianoforte. No.* 3.]
h. 3870. f. (25.)

— 1re. (2e., 3e.) Messe solennelle, avec accompagt. d'Orgue, *etc.* 3 no. *Paris*, [1860?] 8°. **F. 543.**

— Première messe solennelle à grand orchestre … Avec accompagnement d'orgue ou de piano par Ermel. [Score, with reduction for keyboard.] pp. 150. *J. Frey: Paris*, [c. 1830.] fol. **H. 1032. d.**

— Deuxième messe solennelle à grands chœurs et à grand orchestre … Avec accompagnement séparé de piano ou d'orgue par Cornette. [Score.] pp. 173. *J. Frey: Paris*, [1831.] fol.
Livr. 5 *of Lesueur's sacred works.* **Hirsch iv. 821.**

— Troisième Messe solennelle. [Score.] *Paris*, [1835?] fol
H. 1032. b.

— Oratorio de Debbora. *See* supra: Debbora.

— Oratorio de Noël, à grands chœurs, *etc.* [Score.] *A. Petit: Paris*, [1826.] fol.
Livr. 16 *of Lesueur's sacred works.* **H. 1032. c.**

— [Another copy.] **Hirsch iv. 825.**

— Oratorio ou Messe de Noël pour le chant avec accompagnement de Piano ou Orgue (ad libitum). Revu par C. Le Corbeiller. *Paris*, [1870?] 8°. **F. 543. b.**

— Premier ⟨deuxième, troisième⟩ oratorio pour le couronnement des princes souverains de toute la chretienté n'importe les communions. [Score.] 3 vol. *J. Frey: Paris*, [1825?] fol.
Livr. 9, 10, 11 *of Lesueur's sacred works.* **Hirsch iv. 822.**

— 1er. (2e., 3e.) Oratorio pour le Couronnement des Princes Souverains de la Chretienté … avec accompt. d'Orgue ou Harmonium. 3 no. *Paris*, [1860?] 8°. **F. 543. a.**

— Ossian, ou les Bardes. Opéra en cinq actes, paroles de feu Dercis et Mr Deschamps, *etc.* [Score.] pp. 546. *Chez Janet et Cotelle: Paris*, [1804?] fol. **Hirsch ii. 516.**

— Ossian, ou les Bardes. Opéra en cinq actes. Paroles de feu Dercis, & Mr Deschamps, *etc.* [Score.] pp. 540. *Paris*, [1810?] fol.
A slip bearing the imprint "A Paris chez Aug^{te} Le Duc" has been pasted beneath the word "Paris". **G. 290.**

— Ossian ou Les Bardes. Libretto by P. Dercy and Jean Marie Deschamps … A facsimile edition of the printed orchestral score [published by Imbault, Paris], with an introduction by Charles Rosen. pp. 546. *Garland Publishing: New York, London*, 1979. fol.
[*Early romantic Opera.* 37.] **G. 927.**

— Ossian, ou les Bardes. Opéra en 5 actes. Paroles de Dercy et J. N. Deschamps … Réduit pour Piano et Chant par T. Salomé. *Paris*, [1883.] 8°.
One of the "Chefs-d'œuvre de l'Opéra François". **F. 700. i.**

— Paul et Virginie. [For songs, etc., published anonymously:] *See* PAUL.

LESUEUR (Jean François)

— Paul et Virginie (ou le Triomphe de la Vertu). Drama Lyrique en Trois Actes … Paroles de l'Auteur d'Iphigénie en Tauride de Piccini [i.e. A. Du Congé Dubreuil] … Gravé par Huguet, *etc.* [Score.] *Chez H. Nadermann: Paris*, [1794.] fol.
G. 292. a.

— Paul et Virginie, ou le Triomphe de la vertu. Drame lyrique en trois actes … Paroles de l'auteur d'Iphigénie en Tauride de Piccini [i. e. A. Du Congé Dubreuil]. [Score.] pp. 346. *Chez Naderman: Paris*, [1815?] fol. **Hirsch ii. 517.**

— Le pauvre tems, le pauvre tems. *See* supra: [La Caverne.]

— Quand des montagnes de Pyrène. *Le Chant des Triomphes de la République Française.* Ode par La Harpe, *etc. Au Magazin de Musique à l'usage des Fêtes Nationales: Paris*, [1794.] fol. **Fren. 69*. (4.)**

— [Another edition.] Quand des montagnes de Pyrène. *Le Chant des Triomphes de la République Française.* Ode par Laharpe. *Du Magasin de musique, à l'usage des Fêtes Nationales:* [*Paris*, 1794.] 8°. **E. 1717. b. (9.)**

— Rachel. Oratorio historique et prophétique à grands chœurs & à g^{d} orchestre, avec soli. [Score.] *Lat.* pp. 156. *J. Frey: Paris*, [c. 1825.] fol.
Livr. 7 *of Lesueur's sacred works.* **H. 1032. g.**

— Ruth et Noëmi, oratorio historique à grands chœurs, suivi de Ruth et Booz, autre oratorio historique et prophétique à grands chœurs, tiré du livre de Ruth et qui est le complément du premier. [Score.] *Lat.* pp. 136. *J. Frey: Paris*, [c. 1830.] fol.
Livr. 8 *of Lesueur's sacred works.* **H. 1032. f.**

— Trois Te Deum à grand orchestre … avec accompagnement de piano ou orgue par MM^{rs} Ermel et Prévôt. [Score.] 3 vol. pp. 233. *J. Frey: Paris*, [1829.] fol.
Livr. 3 *of Lesueur's sacred works.* **Hirsch iv. 826.**

— Télémaque dans l'Isle de Calypso, ou le Triomphe de la Sagesse. Tragédie Lyrique en trois Actes … Paroles de P. Dercy … Gravé par Huguet, *etc.* [Score.] *Chez H. Naderman: Paris*, [1796.] fol.
G. 292.

— [Another copy.] **Hirsch ii. 518.**

— *See* AGUS (H.) Solféges pour servir à l'étude dans le Conservatoire de Musique à Paris par … Agus … Le Sueur, *etc.* [1795?] fol. **H. 2851.**

— *See* PIERRE (C.) Musique des Fêtes et Cérémonies de la Révolution Française. Œuvres de … Lesueur, *etc.* 1899. fol.
G. 1022. a.

LE SUEUR (Peter)

— Fivefold Amen. [S. A. T. B.] *B. F. Wood Music Co.: Boston, Mass.*, (1907.) 8°.
Choir Journal, No. 214 b. **F. 986.**

LESUR (Daniel)

— Messe du jubilé, *etc.* [S. A. T. B. with organ accompaniment.] ⟨Réduction effectuée par l'auteur.⟩ pp. 53. *Éditions Ricordi: Paris*, [1961.] 4°. **G. 886. a. (1.)**

— Sarabande et farandole. ⟨Partition d'orchestre.⟩ [A facsimile of the composer's autograph.] *In:* GUIRLANDE. La Guirlande de Campra, *etc.* pp. 5–20. [1954.] 4°. **g. 860. e. (1.)**

— Suite pour quatuor à cordes. [Score.] pp. 36. *Lucien de Lacour: Paris*, [c. 1940.] 8°. **c. 140. cc. (1.)**

— Suite pour hautbois, clarinette et basson. [Score.] pp. 24. *Éditions de l'Oiseau-lyre: Monaco*, [1953.] 8°. **c. 140. pp. (3.)**

LESURE (FRANÇOIS)

— Anthologie de la chanson parisienne au XVIᵉ siècle, réunie par François Lesure avec la collaboration de N. Bridgman, I. Cazeaux, M. Levin, K. J. Levy et D. P. Walker. *Éditions de l'Oiseau-lyre: Monaco*, [1953.] fol. **H. 4009.**

— Le Pupitre. Collection de musique ancienne publiée sous la direction de F. Lesure. *Heugel & cⁱᵉ: Paris*, [1967, *etc.*] 4°. **G. 51.**

— *See* BÉTHUNE ( ) Manuscrit Béthune ... ⟨Fac-similé.⟩ Introduction de F. Lesure, *etc.* 1978 [1979]. *obl.* 8°. **a. 173. f.**

— *See* DEBUSSY (Claude A.) [Pelléas et Mélisande.] Esquisses de Pelléas et Mélisande (1893–1895). Publiées en fac-similé avec une introduction par F. Lesure. 1977. 4°. **X. 0900/490 (2.)**

— *See* JANNEQUIN (C.) Chansons polyphoniques. Édition complète publiée ... par A. T. Merritt et F. Lesure. [1965, *etc.*] 4°. **G. 923.**

— *See* JANNEQUIN (C.) Congregati sunt ... Publié par F. Lesure. [1949.] 4°. **G. 519. u. (18.)**

— *See* MOUTON (Charles) Pièces de luth sur différents modes ... ⟨Réimpression de l'édition de c. 1698.⟩ Introduction de F. Lesure, *etc.* 1978. *obl.* 8°. **a. 173. e.**

— *See* PARIS.— *Bibliothèque Nationale.* Manuscrit Bauyn. Pièces de clavecin ... Introduction de F. Lesure, *etc.* 1977. 4°. **g. 1529. h.**

— *See* PARIS.— *Bibliothèque Nationale.* Manuscrit italien de frottole (1502). Facsimile ... Introduction de F. Lesure, *etc.* 1979. 8°. **E. 352. g.**

LESURE (LOUIS A.)

— I never have been false to thee. Song and chorus, words by C. O. Marsh. *Howley, Haviland & Co.: New York*, 1895. fol. **H. 1798. v. (13.)**

— If I'd only had my Razor in the War. [Song.] Words by P. C. Johnson. pp. 5. *W. B. Gray & Co.: New York*, [1898.] fol. *The date has been altered in MS to* 1899. **H. 3980. rr. (36.)**

LESWOOD (CHARL)

— Sun-Bonnet Dance for the pianoforte. *E. Ashdown: London*, [1898.] fol. **g. 605. p. (27.)**

LESZETYCKI (TEODOR)

— Deux Arabesques. 1. En forme d'étude ... Op. 45. No. 1. *Ed. Bote & G. Bock: Berlin*, [1943.] fol. *Printed in England by Novello & Co.* **h. 3870. k. (18.)**

— L'Aveu. (Das Geständniss.) Improvisation pour Piano. *Leipzig*, [1876.] fol. **h. 1487. q. (2.)**

— Le Bal d'Hier. Mazurka-rêverie pour Piano. *Leipzig*, [1876.] fol. **h. 1487. q. (4.)**

— Berceuse (Wiegenlied) for the Pianoforte. *London*, [1876.] fol. **h. 1482. z. (43.)**

— Berceuse. Wiegenlied. [P. F.] [1892.] *See* FLEURS. Fleurs et Diamants, *etc.* No. 4. [1882–93.] fol. **h. 3294.**

— Les Deux Alouettes, impromptu ... pour Piano. *London*, [1874.] fol. **h. 1482. z. (37.)**

— Les Deux Alouettes, impromptu pour Piano. *London*, [1875.] fol. **h. 1482. z. (39.)**

— Les Deux Alouettes, impromptu pour le Piano. *London*, [1876.] fol. **h. 1482. z. (44.)**

—[Les Deux Alouettes.] The Two Skylarks, impromptu for the Pianoforte. *London*, [1876.] fol. **h. 1482. z. (41.)**

LESZETYCKI (TEODOR)

— Les Deux Alouettes. [P. F.] *Augener & Co.: London*, [1887.] fol. **g. 543. j. (31.)**

— Sechs Gesänge für eine tiefe Stimme mit Begleitung des Pianoforte. Op. 26. 2 Hft. *Leipzig u. Berlin*, [1861.] fol. **H. 2139. b. (25.)**

— 2 Gesänge ... mit Begleitung des Pianoforte. Op. 28. *Leipzig u. Berlin*, [1861.] fol. **H. 2139. b. (23.)**

— Six improvisations pour le piano. Op. 11. ... No. 1. Le doux rêve. No. 2. Souvenir. No. 3. Le premier amour. No. 4. Barcarolle. No. 5. Chant du soir. No. 6. La petite coquette. no. 1. *Chez A. O. Witzendorf: Vienne*, [1855?] fol. *Imperfect; wanting no. 2–6.* **g. 443. q. (20.)**

— Little Coquette, scherzino in E♭ for the Pianoforte. *London*, [1874.] fol. **h. 1482. z. (38.)**

— Deux Mazurkas pour Piano. *Leipzig et Berlin*, [1861.] fol. **h. 1462. r. (42.)**

— Quatre Morceaux pour piano. Op. 36. No. 1. Aria ... No. 2. Gigue ... No. 3. Humoresque ... No. 4. La Source, *etc. D. Rahter: Hambourg*, [1887.] fol. **h. 3281. l. (24.)**

— Papillon. Intermezzo en forme d'étude pour Piano. *Leipzig*, [1876.] fol. **h. 1487. q. (3.)**

— Pastels ... Quatre morceaux pour piano ... Op. 44. 1. Prélude ... 2. Gigue all'antica ... 3. Humoresque ... 4. Intermezzo en octaves. *Ed. Bote & G. Bock: Berlin*, [1897.] fol. *Imperfect; no. 4 only.* **h. 722. cc. (6.)**

— Réjouissance, morceau de genre pour le Piano. *London*, [1875.] fol. **h. 1482. z. (40.)**

— Scherzino. Impromptu pour Piano. *Leipzig et Berlin*, [1861.] fol. **h. 1462. r. (43.)**

— Souvenir d'Ischl. Valse pour Piano. *Leipzig*, [1876.] fol. **h. 1487. q. (5.)**

— The Two Skylarks. *See* supra: [Les Deux Alouettes.]

— Valse-Caprice pour piano. Op. 37. *D. Rahter: Hambourg*, [1887.] fol. **h. 3281. l. (25.)**

— Valse chromatique pour Piano. *London*, [1876.] fol. **h. 1482. z. (42.)**

— Valse Chromatique pour piano. (Op. 22.) *R. Cocks & Co.: London*, [1886.] fol. **h. 1484. t. (3.)**

— Valse Chromatique. [P. F.] *Augener & Co.: London*, [1887.] fol. **g. 543. j. (32.)**

— 3 zweistimmige Gesänge mit Begleitung des Pianoforte. Op. 27. *Leipzig u. Berlin*, [1861.] fol. **H. 2139. b. (24.)**

DOUBTFUL AND SUPPOSITITIOUS WORKS

— [Cadenza to the Étude de concert No. 2 by Liszt.] *In:* DOSCHER (David) Franz Liszt: two Cadenzas. [1.] To the Étude de concert No. 2 ... [here attributed to] Leschetizky, *etc.* [1975.] fol. **h. 896. jj.**

APPENDIX

— *See* PRENTNER (M.) [The Modern Pianist.] The Leschetizky Method, *etc.* [1903.] 4°. **g. 337. i. (4.)**

— *See* PRENTNER (M.) The Modern Pianist ... according to the Principles of Prof. T. Leschetizky, *etc.* [1903.] 4°. **g. 337. i. (5.)**

LET

— Let a noble Courage incite thee. Air. *See* GLUCK (C. W. von) [Iphigénie en Aulide.—Armez-vous d'un noble courage.]

— Let all be friends together. [Part-song.] *See* SALISBURY (J.)

— Let all Creatures of God His Praises sing. [Motet.] *See* KALINNIKOV (V. S.)

— Let all Men everywhere rejoice. Anthem. *See* WILLS (Arthur W.)

— Let all Men hear. Anthem. *See* TUTTLE (Lloyd B.)

— Let all Men praise the Lord. Anthem. *See* BOCHAU (C. H.)

— Let all Men praise the Lord. [Anthem.] *See* MENDELSSOHN-BARTHOLDY (J. L. F.) [Lobgesang.—Nun danket alle Gott.]

— Let all mortal Flesh keep Silence. Introit. *See* BAIRSTOW (*Sir* E. C.)

— Let all mortal Flesh keep Silence. Anthem. *See* CANDLYN (T. F. H.)

— Let all mortal Flesh keep Silence. Anthem. *See* CASHMORE (Donald J.)

— Let all mortal Flesh keep Silence. Hymn-Anthem. *See* EMERY (Walter H. J.)

— Let all mortal Flesh keep Silence. [Anthem.] *See* GRIEB (Herbert C.)

— Let all mortal Flesh. [Anthem.] *See* HILTY (Everett J.)

— Let all mortal Flesh keep silence. [Chorus.] *See* HOLST (G. T. von)

— Let all mortal Flesh keep Silence. Anthem. *See* PASQUET (Jean)

— Let all my Life be Music. [Song.] *See* SPROSS (C. G.)

— Let all Nations lay down their Arms. [Song.] *See* DILLON (John)

— Let all of us stay at Home. Song. *See* DAVIS (G. L.)

— Let all on Earth their Voices raise. [Anthem.] *See* FORD (Virgil T.)

— Let all on Earth their Voices raise. [Anthem.] *See* KIRK (Theron)

— Let all on Earth their Voices raise. [Anthem.] *See* PENINGER (David)

— Let all our Brethren join in one. Hymn. *See* BARNBY (*Sir* J.)

— Let all rejoice. Carol anthem. *See* SOMERSET (Henry V. F.)

— Let all rejoice at Christmas Time. [Carol.] *See* EHRET (Walter)

— Let all the Just with fervent Joy. *Psalm XXXIII*. As sung at the Rev. M[r] Sellon's chapel, Portman Square. *In:* The New Christian's Magazine. vol. 3, no. 25. [1784.] 8°.
P. P. 324. na.

— Let all the Lands. Anthem. *See* NEWSOME (J.)

— Let all the nations of the earth rejoice. Duet. *See* PHILLIPS (H.)

— Let all the Nations praise the Lord. [Motet.] *See* LEISRING (V.) [O filii et filiae.]

— Let all the People praise Thee, O God. Anthem. *See* SHAW (Martin F.)

— Let all the People rejoice. Anthem. *See* HAENDEL (G. F.) [Coronation Anthems.—Zadok the Priest.—And all the People rejoic'd.]

— Let all the Sons of Temperance. *See* RICE (E. C.)

LET

— Let all the Strains of Joy. [Song.] *See* RONALD (*Sir* L.) [Song Offerings. 2nd Series. No. 4.]

— Let all the World. Anthem. *See* BAKER (Robert)

— Let all the World. Anthem. *See* BISHOP (F. G.)

— Let all the World in every Corner sing. [Hymn.] *See* BUTTON (H. E.)

— Let all the World in every Corner sing. [Unison and part-song.] *See* CHAPMAN (E. T.)

— Let all the World in every Corner sing. Anthem. *See* CHRISTOPHER (C. S.)

— Let all the World. Anthem. *See* GILBERT (N.)

— Let all the World. [Anthem.] *See* GREIG (W. S.)

— Let all the World. [Song.] *See* ILLING (Robert)

— Let all the World in every Corner sing. Anthem. *See* IVES (Grayston)

— Let all the World in every Corner sing. Anthem. *See* JORDAN (C. W.)

— Let all the World in every Corner sing. For Chorus and Orchestra. *See* LANG (C. S.)

— Let all the World in every Corner sing. Anthem. *See* LARBALESTIER (P. G.)

— Let all the World. Anthem. *See* LEDINGTON (Stanley)

— Let all the World in every Corner sing. Anthem. *See* LEIGHTON (Kenneth)

— Let all the World in every Corner sing. [Anthem.] *See* LEKBERG (Sven)

— Let all the World in every Corner sing. [Hymn.] *See* MACALISTER (R. A. S.)

— Let all the World. [Part-song.] *See* NICHOLAS (John M.) Two choral Songs. No. 1.

— Let all the world. [Anthem.] *See* NICHOLAS (John M.)

— Let all the World. [Anthem.] *See* NOBLE (T. T.) Six (Twelve) Unaccompanied Anthems, *etc.* [No. 11.]

— Let all the World in every Corner sing. Anthem. *See* OUSELEY (*Sir* Frederick A. G.) *Bart.*

— Let all the World in every Corner sing. [Anthem.] *See* RAPLEY (Edmund F.)

— Let all the World in every Corner sing. [Anthem.] *See* ROBERTON (*Sir* Hugh S.)

— Let all the World in every Corner sing. Anthem. *See* ROWLEY (Alec)

— Let all the World in every Corner sing. Unison Song. *See* SHAW (G. T.)

— Let all the World. [Part-song.] *See* SOMERVELL (*Sir* A.)

— Let all the World in every Corner sing. [Unison song.] *See* SPEDDING (Frank)

— Let all the World in every Corner sing. Anthem. *See* THIMAN (E. H.)

— Let all the World in every Corner sing. Anthem. *See* TOMLINS (Greta)

— Let all the World. Anthem. *See* TURNER (Charles K.)

— Let all the World in every Corner sing. Anthem. *See* WALKER (F. G.)

LET

— Let all the World in every Corner sing. Anthem. *See* WATERS (C. F.)

— Let all the World in every Corner sing. Hymn-anthem. *See* WILLAN (Healey)

— Let all the World. [Anthem.] *See* WILLIAMS (David H.)

— Let all the World in every Corner sing. [Anthem.] *See* WILLIAMS (Ralph V.) [Five Mystical Songs. No. 5. Antiphon.]

— Let all the World in every Corner sing. [Anthem.] *See* YOUNG (Gordon)

— Let all the World this Day rejoice. Carol. *See* MARSH (F. T.)

— Let all them that put their Trust in Thee rejoice. Anthem. *See* PEACE (F. W.)

— Let all those that seek thee. Anthem. *See* LODGE, afterwards LODGE ELLERTON (J.)

— Let all Together praise our God. Christmas cantata. *See* WILLIAMS (David H.)

— Let Ambition fire thy Mind. Song. *See* also WELDON (J.) [The Judgment of Paris.]

— Let Ambition fire thy Mind. *A Song for two Voices.* [From "The Judgment of Paris" by John Weldon.] ... Had she not care enough. *A Catch for three Voices.* Set by Mr. Henry Purcel. *R. Falkner: London,* [c. 1770.] *s. sh.* fol.
H. 1648. f. (26.)

— Let an empty flatt'ring Spirit. *Advice to the Ladies.* [Song.] The words by a Gent[n] of Exeter. *L[ongman] & B[roderip: London,* 1780?] fol.
G. 310. (49.)

— [Another setting.] Let an empty flattering spirit. Rondo. *See* SHIELD (W.)

— Let angry Ocean to the Sky. Song. *See* STORACE (Stephen)

— Let Bacchus's sons be not dismayed. *Garryowen.* [Song.] *London,* [1879.] fol.
No. 696 of C. Boosey's "Universal" music. **H. 2324.**

— Let Braves, who to the army go. *Beauty more powerfull than War.* [Song.] [*London,* 1715?] *s. sh.* fol. **H. 1601. (280.)**

— Let Britain be for British Men. Song. *See* GOODEVE (F. E.) *Mrs.*

— Let British Might uphold the Right. Song. *See* LE MAÎTRE (A.)

— Let Britons hold their landed Rights. Song. *See* ROLAND (G.)

— Let Britons in triumphant praise. Song. *See* AMATEUR.

— Let brotherly Love continue. Anthem. *See* ANDREWS (A. F.)

— Let Bucks a-hunting go. [Folk-song.] *See* GOULD (S. B.) and SHARP (C. J.) [English Folk Songs for Schools. No. 35.]

— Let Burgundy flow. *Joy after Sorrow* made to the Duke Aumond's Minuet by T. D[urfey]. [Song.] *Daniel Wright: [London,* 1715.] *s. sh.* fol. **H. 1601. (266.)**

— [Another edition.] Let Burgundy flow. *Joy after Sorrow.* A new Song. The words made to the D'Aumonds Minuet by T. D[urfey]. [*London,* 1715.] *s. sh.* fol. **G. 310. (30.)**

— Let but love and wine befriend me. Song. *See* BATES (W.)

— Let Bygones be Bygones. [Song.] *See* BARCLAY (Lawrence)

— Let Bygones be Bygones. [Song.] *See* SHACKFORD (Charles) and MILLS (K.)

— Let Caesar and Urania live. Two-part Song. *See* PURCELL (H.) [Ode for King James II's Birthday, 1687.]

LET

— Let Care be a Stranger. *May we live all the Days of our Lives.* [Song. By J. Hook.] Sung by M[r] Vernon at Vauxhall. pp. 3. [*S. A. & P. Thompson: London,* c. 1780.] fol.
Followed by an arrangement for the German flute. Reissued from Thompson's first collection of Hook's Vauxhall songs for 1780. **H. 1653. kk. (29.)**

— Let Carols ring. Christmas Carol. *See* BLACK (C.)

— Let charming Sounds our cares divert. Song. *See* LEVERIDGE (Richard)

— Let chearful Smiles in ev'ry Face. Hymn. *See* ALCOCK (John) *Doctor in Music.*

— Let Cherbourg with her bastions, *Cherbourg.* An English song ... (Written by C. Jefferys.) *London,* [1859.] fol.
H. 1255. (19.)

— Let Christ come in. Hymn. *See* HOWITZ (I.)

— Let Christian Men rejoice. Old German Carol, "In dulci jubilo". Words by J. Guard. *J. Curwen & Sons: London,* [1921.] 8°.
[*Anthems of Praise. No.* 184.] **E. 336.**

— Let Christians all. Carol. *See* HULL (M.)

— Let Christians all with joyful Mirth. [Christmas carol.] *See* CASHMORE (Donald J.)

— Let de Heb'n-light shine on me. Negro spiritual. *See* JOHNSON (Hall) [Thirty Negro Spirituals.]

— Let down the Bars, O Death. [Part-song.] *See* BARBER (Samuel)

— Let each Briton and Gaul. *General Suwarrow,* a favorite song, written by J. Nelson [to the tune called "The Rogues March"]. *Printed by Longman Clementi & C[o].: London,* [1799.] fol. **G. 376. (27.)**

— Let Earth rejoice. [Anthem.] *See* FORD (Virgil T.)

— Let Eastern Tribes. [Hymn.] *See* PASCOE (J. H.)

— Let Eloquence boast of her Pow'r. Song. *See* ARNE (M.) [Tristram Shandy.]

— Let 'em all come. [Song.] *See* CONNOR (T. W.)

— Let 'em all come—We're ready! Song. *See* VALENTINE, *pseud.*

— Let 'em all go. [Song.] *See* MILLS (Arthur J.) and CARTER (F. W.)

— Let 'em eat Cake. [Solo and chorus.] *See* GERSHWIN (George) [Let 'em eat Cake.]

— Let 'em go. Song. *See* WILSON (Mozart)

— Let England guard her laurels. National song. *See* ALLWOOD (F. W.)

— Let England mourn for Livingstone. Song. *See* GUEST (J.)

— Let English Song aloud ring out. [Part-song.] *See* FIBY (H.)

— Let Epicures boast of their delicate Feasts. *The Generous Soul.* A favorite new Song. *P. E[vans: London,* 1780?] *s. sh.* fol. **G. 310. (41.)**

— Let Erin remember. Unison Song. Old Irish Air—"The Little Red Fox." [1908.] *See* MACNAUGHT (W. G.) Novello's School Songs. No. 896[a]. 1892, *etc.* 8°. **F. 280. d.**

— Let Erin remember the Days of old. Part Song. *See* DIX (L.)

— Let Erin remember. Song with Descant. *See* DUNHILL (T. F.) Arnold's Descant Series. No. 50.

— Let Erin remember. Part-Song. *See* JOZÉ (T. R. G.) Irish Part-Songs *etc.* No. 14.

LET

— Let Erin remember the Days of old. [Part-song.] *See* MACFARREN (*Sir* G. A.) National Melodies. No. 6.

— Let Erin remember. [Part-song.] *See* MINNETT (J.)

— Let Erin remember the Days of old. [Song.] *See* MOORE (Thomas) *the Poet.* [A Selection of Irish Melodies. 2nd Number.]

— Let e'ery [*sic*] Face be fill'd wth Joy. *On the Prospect of Peace.* [Song, words and music by H. Carey.] *Cross:* [*London*, 1728?] *s. sh.* fol.　　　**G. 310. (65.)**

— Let ev'ry Heart be merry. [Part-song.] *See* VECCHI (H.) [Selva di varia Ricreatione.—So ben mi ch' a bon tempo.]

— Let every Heart rejoice and sing. [Anthem.] *See* BISSELL (A. H.)

— Let every Heart rejoice and sing. [Hymn.] *See* SCHUMANN (R. A.) [Der deutsche Rhein.]

— Let every Man be jolly. [Two-part song.] *See* GILBERT (Norman)

— Let every Martial Soul advance. Song. *See also* BRYAN (J.)

— Let ev'ry Martial Soul advance. *A New Song* in Honour of the King of Prussia. Sung by Mr. Kear. [Music by J. Bryan.] [*London*, 1758.] *s. sh.* 8°.
New Universal Magazine, Dec., 1758.　　**P. P. 5439. ab.**

— Let every Soul be subject unto the higher Powers. Anthem. *See* STAINER (*Sir* J.)

— Let ev'ry Voice raise. Ballett. *See* STEPHANI (J.) [Neue teutsche weltliche Madrigalia und Balletten.—Lasst uns zusammen.]

— Let everything praise the Lord. Anthem. *See* SIMPER (C.)

— Let Everything that hath Breath praise the Lord. [Anthem.] *See* TROWBRIDGE (J. E.)

— Let every Thing that hath Breath. Anthem. *See* WARNER (Richard)

— Let Fame sound the trumpet. Song. *See* SHIELD (W.)

— Let Folly praise what Fancy loves. [Unison song.] *See* LE FLEMING (Christopher)

— Let fools their fate deserving. Song. *See* COOKE (T. S.)

— Let Freedom ring. [Part-song.] *See* BORODIN (A. P.) [Песня темного леса.]

— Let fusty old Greybeards of Apathy boast. *The Nod Wink and Smile.* [Song.] Sung by Mr. Vernon. *S[amuel] A[nn and] P[eter] T[hompson: London, 1785?] s. sh.* fol.　**I. 530. (89.)**

— Let go, Eliza! Song. *See* LEIGH (Fred W.)

— Let go the Anchor, Boys. [Song.] *See* TABRAR (J.)

— Let God arise. *Exurgat Deus.* Set with fauxbourdons for use in procession, as sung in Westminster Abbey. *Faith Press:* [*London*, 1924.] 8°.　　**E. 602. kk. (53.)**

— Let God arise. [Anthem.] *See* BINGHAM (Seth)

— Let God arise. Anthem. *See* GREENE (M.) [Forty Select Anthems.]

— Let God arise. Anthem. *See* HAENDEL (G. F.) [Chandos Anthems. H. G. vol. 35. no. 11b.]

— Let God arise. Anthem. *See* HALL (T.)

— Let God arise. [Anthem.] *See* HOWELLS (H. N.) Four Anthems ... No. 4.

— Let God arise, a festival anthem. *See* LESLIE (Henry D.)

LET

— Let God arise. Anthem. *See* LINLEY (Thomas) *the Younger.*

— Let God arise. Anthem. *See* SIMPER (C.)

— Let God arise. Hymn. *See* STAINER (*Sir* J.)

— Let God arise. Anthem. *See* SURETTE (T. W.)

— Let God arise. Anthem. *See* TRIMNELL (T. T.)

— Let God arise. Psalm. *See* WILLIAMSON (*Sir* Malcolm B. G. C.) [Psalms of the Elements.—Fire Psalms. 5.]

— Let God arise. Anthem. *See* WILLS (Arthur W.)

— Let God arise. Anthem. *See* YOUNG (F. H.)

— Let God arise. [Anthem.] *See* YOUNG (Gordon)

— Let good enough alone. [Song.] *See* SUTTON (Harry O.)

— Let happy Lovers fly. [Glee.] *See* SMITH (John S.)

— Let her apply to me. [Song.] *See* WARE (G.)

— Let her drown. Song. *See* RAY (Phil)

— Let her in. [Song.] *See* WEIDIG (A.) Five Songs. Op. 21. No. 2.

— Let her own Works praise her. Anthem. *See* ELLSWORTH (A. E.)

— Let her rest. Duet. *See* GLOVER (C. W.)

— Let Heroes boast of Deeds of Arms. *Patt.* [Song.] Sung at Sadlers Wells.　[*London*, c. 1760.] *s. sh.* fol.
　　　　　　H. 1601. u. (113.)

— Let Heroes boast of Deeds of Arms. *Patt.* A New Song, sung at Saddlers-Wells.　[*London*,] 1761. 8°.
London Magazine, 1761, *p.* 45.　　**158. l. 6.**

— Let him go, let him tarry. [Part-song.] *See* DENNIS (Paul)

— Let him go, let him tarry. Song. *See* VINE (J.)

— Let him let him go. Ballad. *See* HOOK (J.)

— Let him lie! What do you care? [Song.] *See* BRATTON (John W.)

— Let him that is taught in the word. Anthem. *See* PRINGLE (R. W.)

— Let him that the cap fits wear it. Ballad. *See* NELSON (S.) [The Cadi's Daughter.]

— Let him that will be free. [Song.] *See* ROSSETER (P.) [Booke of Ayres.]

— Let him who is without Sin cast the first Stone. [Song.] *See* BROOKHOUSE (Winthrop)

— Let him who would not smart. Ballett. *See* STEPHANI (J.) [Neue teutsche weltliche Madrigalia und Balletten.—Wer leben will ohn' Schmerz.]

— Let His Tears o'erflow my Eyes. [Anthem.] *See* BORCH (G.)

— Let Hope be the watchword. [Song.] *See* WILLIAMS (W. L.)

— Let in dis little Coon. [Song.] *See* ELLIS (L. Bruininger)

— Let India boast her Plants. Glee. *See* WEBBE (Samuel) *the Younger.*

— Let it alone. [Song.] *See* WILLIAMS (Bert A.)

— Let it be forgotten. [Song.] *See* FARLEY (R.) Two Poems by Sara Teasdale, *etc.* [No. 2.]

— Let it be forgotten. [Part-song.] *See* MERRILL (Marlin)

LET

— Let it be forgotten. [Song.] *See* WATTS (W. H.) Two Songs by S. Teasdale. II.

— Let it be soon. Song. *See* TOSTI (*Sir* F. P.)

— Let it be you. Song. *See* BURHOLT (H. J.)

— Let it shine. [Part-song.] *See* STOCKTON (Robert)

— Let Jesus come into your Heart. Anthem. *See* HOWARD (F. M.)

— Let Joy alone be remembered now. Song. *See* BECHTEL (F.)

— Let joy alone be remembered now. Ballad. *See* MOORE (T.) *the Poet.*

— Let Joy your Carols fill. Christmas carol. *See* RUSSELL (Leslie)

— Let joyous Peace reign everywhere. Sacred Song. *See* ROBYN (A. G.) [Answer.]

— Let Justice roll down as the Waters. Anthem. *See* MABON (C. B.)

— Let kindest feelings reign. Ballad. *See* STEVENS (H. J.)

— Let life be bright. Ballad. *See* KNIGHT (J. P.)

— Let Love awake. Song. *See* OLIVER (H.)

— Let Love awake. Song. *See* SANDERSON (W. E.)

— Let Love awake. Song. *See* TOSTI (*Sir* F. P.)

— Let love by love be guarded. Cavatina. *See* LEE (G. A.)

— Let Love decide. [Song.] *See* JENEPPE (Bianca de)

— Let Love in one delightful Stream. Response. *See* GREENE (C. W.)

— Let lovers prize their maidens' eyes. Song. *See* ALLEN (G. B.) [Castle Grim.]

— Let maids be false so wine be true. Part song. *See* MARTIN (G. C.)

— Let Maloney near the Fire. Song. *See* NICHOLLS (Harry)

— Let Mary go 'round on the Merry-go-round. [Song.] *See* REED (David)

— Let me alone. [Song.] *See* AS. As I was a walking to Chelsea one Day. [c. 1760.] *s. sh.* fol.　　　**H. 1601. u. (93.)**

— Let me alone, I'm busy. Song. *See* LAWRENCE (Albert E.) and LESTER (G.)

— Let me approach my sleeping Love. [Song.] *Printed by W. Gibson: Dublin,* [c. 1770.] *s. sh.* fol. *Followed by an arrangement for the guitar.*　　**G. 426. kk. (79.)**

— Let me arise! Choral Hymn. *See* MONK (E. G.)

— Let me ask. Song. *See* GAMBOGI (F. E.) Two Songs. (a.)

— Let me be. Song. *See* HOWARD (R.)

— Let me be a Violet. [Song.] *See* RICH (M.)

— Let me be ever near thee. Song. *See* BARRY (E. de)

— Let me be free. [Song.] *See* HERBERT (V.) [The Duchess.]

— Let me be near thee. Song. *See* HEAD (W.)

— Let me be near thee. Ballad. *See* WEISS (W. H.)

— Let me be near to thee. Ballad. *See* GILBERT (E. B.)

— Let me be thine. Song. *See* WILSON (H. C.)

LET

— Let me be Thine forever. Anthem. *See* SELNECCERUS (N.) [Christliche Psalmen, Lieder, und Kirchengesänge.—Lass mich Dein sein und bleiben.]

— Let me be with Thee. Anthem. *See* PAGE (A. T.)

— Let me be your Honey Bee. [Song.] *See* LOWITZ (John B.)

— Let me be your last Love. [Song.] *See* O'CONNOR (C. W.)

— Let me bring my Clothes back home. [Song.] *See* JONES (Irving)

— Let me but call thee mine own. *See* HERE. Here, here, deep in my Bosom ... A celebrated German air [by C. E. Pax], *etc.* [c. 1840.] fol.　　　　　**H. 1980. r. (24.)**

— Let me but hope. Song. *See* PETHER (Henry E.)

— Let me but love. [Song.] *See* SCOTT (H.)

— Let me call you Daddy. Song. *See* ROGERS (E. W.)

— Let me call you "Dearie". [Song.] *See* STULTS (R. M.)

— Let me call you my Sweetheart again. Ballad. *See* THORNTON (James) *Songwriter.*

— Let me careless. Madrigal. *See* LINLEY (T.) *the Elder.*

— Let me confess. Song. *See* O'CONNOR (E.)

— Let me crown you Queen of May with Orange Blossoms. [Song.] *See* HELF (J. F.)

— Let me die. Ballad. *See* ATTWOOD (T.)

— Let me dye an old Maid, *etc.* [Song.] *See* SAID. Said my Mother O trust not dear Daughter to Men, *etc.* [1764?] *s. sh.* fol. [*Sadler's Wells Collection. Vol.* 8.]　　**Crach. 1. Tab. 4. b. 4/8. (94.)**

— Let me die on the Deep. Song. *See* DEWEY (James G.)

— Let me die with my face to the foe. Quartette. *See* CLARK (J. G.)

— Let me down easy. [Song.] *See* FARREL (Tom)

— Let me dream. Song. *See* MEHER (J. D.)

— Let me dream. Aria. *See* MERCADANTE (S.) Io credea.

— Let me Dream. Song. *See* OREFICE (L. dell')

— Let me dream again. [Song.] *See* NEWMAN (Joseph)

— Let me dream again. Song. *See* SULLIVAN (*Sir* Arthur S.)

— Let me dream o'er my Life's happy Spring. *Spring and Autumn.* Ballad. 2 no. [In D and E.] *See* FLOWERS. Flowers of Germany. No. 111. [1859–70?] fol.　　**H. 2133.**

— Let me dream o'er my life's happy Spring. *Spring & Autumn.* Swedish ballad. ⟨In D.⟩ *London,* [1870.] fol.　　　　　　　　　　**H. 1790. a. (62.)**

— Let me dream o'er my life's happy spring, *etc.* ⟨In E.⟩ *London,* [1870.] fol.　　　　**H. 1790. a. (63.)**

— Let me dream of happy days. Ballad. *See* AIDÉ (H.) [A Nine Day's Wonder.]

— Let me dream of those sweet hours. Ballad. *See* LODGE, afterwards LODGE-ELLERTON (J.)

— Let me dream on. Song. *See* BARRI (O.)

— Let me dream on. [Song.] *See* GLAZUNOV (A. K.) [Concerto in A minor. Op. 82.]

— Let me forget. Song. *See* FÉLISE, *pseud.*

— Let me forget. Song. *See* HOPE (Adrian)

— Let me forget! Song. *See* KING (C. H.)

— Let me forget. Song. *See* NEVIN (G. B.)

— Let me forget thee. Song. *See* HARRISON (A. F.) afterwards HILL (*Lady* A.)

— Let me gaze into your Eyes. Song. *See* JENNER (H.)

— Let me gaze on the Cross. [Song.] *See* MACCRAW (T. G.)

— Let me go back Chillun. [Song.] *See* HOWARD (Minnie F.)

— Let me have a little Chat with you, Pretty Poll. Song. *See* COLLINS (Charles) and RIDGWELL (C.)

— Let me hear that Obbligato. Song. *See* ARTHURS (George)

— Let me hear the Band play "The Girl I left behind". [Song.] *See* CASEY (Charles E.)

— Let me hear thy Voice. Song. *See* ALLNATT (M. M.)

— Let me hear your Voice again. Song. *See* TATE (A. F.)

— Let me help you over the Stile. [Song.] *See* COLLINS (Charles)

— Let me hold it till I die. Song. *See* LOVEGROVE (H.)

— Let me in, dat's all. Song. *See* BARRON (Ted S.)

— Let me in sorrow weep. Aria. *See* HAENDEL (G. F.) [Rinaldo.—Lascia ch'io pianga.]

— Let me keep the Picture you gave me. [Song.] *See* BRACKEN (Jess)

— Let me kiss him for his mother. Ballad with chorus ad lib. *London*, [1859.] fol.   **H. 1401. (17.)**

— Let me kiss him for his mother. Ballad with chorus. *London*, [1860.] fol.   **H. 1401. a. (22.)**

— Let me kiss him for his mother. Song and chorus. Words and music transcribed by Professor Clare. *London*, [1860.] fol.   **H. 1401. a. (23.)**

— Let me kiss him for his mother. (The Cottage by the Sea [by J. R. Thomas].) Popular American ballads. *Leeds*, [1869.] fol.   **H. 1790. a. (64.)**

— Let me kiss him for his mother. Song & chorus. *See* EMERSON (L. O.)

— Let me kiss him for his mother. Song and chorus. *See* ORDWAY (J. P.)

— Let me kiss my boy again. Song. *See* CORK (T.)

— Let me kiss your Tears away. [Song.] *See* COUCHOIS (G. J.)

— Let me kiss your Tears away. [Song.] *See* FRANCIS (W.)

— Let me kiss your Tears away Mama dear. [Song.] *See* ENGELKE (Sandy)

— Let me linger at the Gate. Song. *See* GILBERT (Ernest T. B.)

— Let me love her for you while you're away. Song. *See* DAREWSKI (Hermann E.)

— Let me love thee. [Song.] *See* ABT (F. W.)

— Let me love thee. Song. *See* ARDITI (L.)

— Let me love you as of old. [Song.] *See* MORELAND (Charles A.)

— Let me not wait. [Song.] *See* JOHNS (C.) Songs. No. 2.

— Let me not wait in vain. [Song.] *See* STARLING (F.)

— Let me rejoice. Anthem. *See* JOUBERT (John)

— Let me return to Dreamland. Song. *See* LIDDEN (Cecil)

— Let me say my little Prayer. Song. *See* MACY (J. C.)

— Let me see my home again. Romance. *See* HÉROLD (L. J. F.) [Le Pré aux Clercs.—Souvenirs de jeune âge.]

— Let me see your Rainbow Smile. [Song.] *See* BARRON (Ted S.)

— Let me sing! Song. *See* LEO (Frank)

— Let me sing, love! [Song.] *See* BLESSNER (G.)

— Let me sink to the regions of Shade. Elegy. *See* ALCOCK (J.) *the Younger.*

— Let me sit in your Garden. Song. *See* RUSSELL (R. C. K.)

— Let me sleep in the auld Kirkyard at Hame. [Song.] *See* GILBERT (J. L.)

— Let me sleep my last Sleep in the Land of my Birth. [Song.] *See* HEWITT (John H.)

— Let me spend my Vacation with you. [Song.] *See* BROWN (Albert W.)

— Let me stay and live in Dixieland. [Song.] *See* BRICE (Elizabeth) and KING (C.)

— Let me strike the first Blow in the Battle. [Song.] *See* DAVIES (E.)

— Let me take yer Home again. [Song.] *See* DACRE (H.) *pseud.*

— Let me take your Photograph. Duet. *See* PETHER (Henry E.)

— Let me teach thee how to pray. Sacred song. *See* WEST (W.)

— Let me the Canakin Clink. Part-Song. *See* MACEWEN (*Sir* J. B.)

— Let me think I'm someone. Song. *See* CALVERT (Frank) and POWELL (O.)

— Let me this Day. [Part-song.] *See* WARREN (Peter)

— Let me wait for Daddy. Song. *See* RIDGWELL (Charles)

— Let me wander. Part-Song. *See* SPOHR (L.)

— Let me wander far away. Ballad. *See* ROBINSON (J.)

— Let me wander, not unseen. [Song.] *See* HAENDEL (G. F.) [L'Allegro, Il Pensieroso, ed il Moderato.]

— Let me wander where I will. Ballad. *See* LINLEY (G.)

— Let me wander where I will. Song. *See* SMITH (W. S.)

— Let me whisper, I am thine. [Song.] *See* GREGORI (E.)

— Let me whisper in thine ear. Ballad. *See* BALFE (M. W.)

— Let me woo thee. Song. *See* CHASSAIGNE (F.) [Nadgy.]

— Let me worship at your Shrine. Song. *See* BALL (E. R.)

— Let me worship thee. Song. *See* COWEN (*Sir* F. H.)

— Let me write what I never dared to tell. [Song.] *See* CASEY (Charles E.) and ROSENFELD (M. H.)

— Let mine Eye the Farewell make thee. [Part-song.] *See* HERVEY (F. A. J.)

— Let mine Eyes run down. Anthem. *See* PURCELL (Henry)

— Let Miss Lindsay pass. Song. *See* ROGERS (W. L.)

— Let Mount Zion rejoice. [Anthem.] *See* HERBERT (J. B.)

— Let Music and Joy resound. Song. *See* LIEBICH (I.)

LET

— Let music and song be our pastime tonight. Duet. *See* GLOVER (S.)

— Let my care be no man's sorrow. Ballad. *See* WRIGHTON (W. T.)

— Let my Complaint come before Thee. Anthem. *See* BATTEN (A.)

— Let my Complaint come before Thee. Anthem. *See* GREENE (M.) [Forty Select Anthems.]

— Let my Complaint come before Thee. Anthem. *See* THORNE (E. H.)

— Let my Cry come before Thee. [Anthem.] *See* NEWBURY (Kent A.)

— Let my Cry come near before Thee. Anthem. *See* BARNES (E. S.)

— Let my Cry come near before Thee. Anthem. *See* SMITH (D. S.)

— Let my Dream come true! [Song.] *See* GIBILARO (A.)

— Let my fair one only be. *The General Lover.* [Song.] *I. R.* [*J. Rutherford: London*, 1775?] *s. sh. fol.*
Followed by accompaniments for German flute and guitar.
G. 316. l. (23.)

— Let my Harbour be your Arms. Song. *See* HOOK (James)

— Let my Mouth be filled with thy Praise. Anthem. *See* PASQUET (Jean)

— Let my Name be kindly spoken. Song. *See* DANKS (H. P.)

— Let my People go. Negro Spiritual. *See* SCOTT (T.)

— Let my Prayer. Anthem. *See* HARRIS (*Sir* William H.) *K. C. V. O.*

— Let my Prayer be set forth. [Anthem.] *See* MACPHERSON (C.)

— Let my Prayer be set forth. Anthem. *See* MARTIN (*Sir* G. C.)

— Let my Prayer be set forth. Motet. *See* MIDDLETON (H. S.)

— Let my Prayer be set forth. Anthem. *See* TORRANCE (G. W.)

— Let my Prayer come unto Thy Presence. Sacred Song. *See* BINDER (A. W.)

— Let my Prayer come up into Thy Presence. [Anthem.] *See* BAIRSTOW (*Sir* E. C.)

— Let my Prayer come up into Thy Presence. Offertorium. *See* PURCELL (H.) [Jehova, quam multi sunt hostes.—Ego cubui et dormivi.]

— Let my Song. Songs. *See* GIBB (Steve)

— Let my Song fill your Heart. Song. *See* CHARLES (E.)

— Let my Supplication come before Thee. [Anthem.] *See* PRICHARD (E. L. M.)

— Let my Voice ring out. Part-Song. *See* LLOYD (C. H.)

— Let my Voice ring out. [Song.] *See* TREHARNE (B.) Ten Dramatic and Descriptive Songs. [No. 6.]

— Let nature henceforward neglect. Song. *See* GALLIARD (J. E.) [Circe.]

— Let no earthly or sordid feeling. [Song.] *See* BELLINI (V.) [La Sonnambula.—Ah! non giunge.]

— Let no longer Winter reign. Duet. *See* BARNETT (J.)

— Let nobody know. Ballad. *See* MAYNARD (W.) *pseud.*

LET

— Let not a moonborn Elf. [Song.] *See* PURCELL (H.) [King Arthur.]

— Let not Age. Cantata. *See* GIORDANI (T.)

— Let not dull sluggish Sleep. Quartet. *See* MARTIN (George W.)

— Let not Love go, too. Song. *See* PRIDHAM (D.)

— Let not Love on me bestow. Song. *See* PURCELL (D.) [The Funeral.]

— Let not my harp. Canzonetta. *See* ASPULL (W.)

— Let not Rage. [Song.] *See* ARTAXERXES.

— Let not the sluggish Sleep. [Part-song.] *See* BYRD (W.) [Psalmes, Songs and Sonnets.]

— Let not the sun go down on your wrath. Sacred Song. *See* THOMAS (J. R.)

— Let not the sun go down upon your wrath. Sacred Song. *See* PARKER (J. R.)

— Let not thine Eye upon me rest. Chorus. *See* NEVIN (G. B.)

— Let not thine Hand. Anthem. *See* STAINER (*Sir* J.)

— Let not thy Tomb-stone. [Part-song.] *See* BINKERD (Gordon W.) To Electra. IX.

— Let not your heart be troubled. Sacred song. *See* ALLNATT (M. M.)

— Let not your heart be troubled. Sacred ballad. *See* AQUILA, *pseud.*

— Let not your Heart be troubled. Anthem. *See* BELSHAM (O. D.)

— Let not your Heart be troubled. [Anthem.] *See* BERWALD (W. H.)

— Let not your Heart be troubled. [Sacred song.] *See* BRACKETT (F. H.)

— Let not your heart be troubled. Sacred duet. *See* BRUNNEN (T.)

— Let not your Heart be troubled. Duet. *See* EYER (F. L.)

— Let not your Heart be troubled. Anthem. *See* FANING (J. E.)

— Let not your Heart be Troubled. Anthem. *See* FOSTER (M. B.)

— Let not your Heart be troubled. Anthem. *See* GARDNER (G. L. H.)

— Let not your Heart be troubled. Duet. *See* HARRIS (H. W.)

— Let not your heart be troubled. Recit & Air. *See* LODARE (H.)

— Let not your heart be troubled. Anthem. *See* LOTT (E. M.)

— Let not your Heart be troubled. Anthem. *See* LUCAS (B. S.)

— Let not your Heart be troubled. Motet. *See* MALONEY (C. E.)

— Let not your Heart be troubled. Sacred Song. *See* MARSCHAL-LOEPKE (G.)

— Let not your Heart be troubled. Anthem. *See* MILLER (E. W.)

— Let not your Heart be troubled. [Sacred song.] *See* NEIDLINGER (W. H.) Offertory Solos. [No. 4.]

— Let not your Heart be troubled. Anthem. *See* OSBORNE (M. G.)

— Let not your Heart be troubled. Anthem. *See* REES (Louis)

— Let not your Heart be troubled. [Sacred song.] *See* ROMA (C.)

— Let not your Heart be troubled. [Sacred song.] *See* RUTENBER (C. B.) Three Sacred Songs, *etc.* [No. 3.]

— Let not your Heart be troubled. Sacred Song. *See* SANDIFERE (C.)

— Let not your Heart be troubled. Anthem. *See* SIMPER (C.)

— Let not your Heart be troubled. Sacred Song. *See* SPEAKS (O.)

— Let not your Heart be troubled. Anthem. *See* STAPLES (H. J.)

— Let not your Heart be troubled. [Anthem.] *See* STILLMAN (G.)

— Let not your Heart be troubled. [Song.] *See* TORRANCE (G. W.) Songs of Faith and Hope ... No. 2.

— Let not your Heart be troubled. Anthem. *See* TREMBATH (H. G.)

— Let not your Heart be troubled. Solo. *See* WARD (F. E.) [The Saviour of the World.]

— Let not your Heart be troubled. Motet. *See* WOOD (F. H.) The Last Hours ... Op. 26. No. 7.

— Let nothing disturb thee. Song. *See* MELLIN (E. F.) Two Songs ... No. 1.

— Let nothing ever grieve thee. [Part-song.] *See* BRAHMS (J.) [Geistliches Lied. Op. 30.]

— Let Nothing make thee sad. Part-Song. *See* MOSS (A. M.)

— Let Nought that's earthly pain thee. [Song.] *See* MENDELSSOHN-BARTHOLDY (J. L. F.) [12 Gesänge. Op. 8. No. 5. Pilgerspruch.]

— Let now the heavenly Hosts. Anthem. *See* WEBBE (W. Y.)

— Let old Love awake. Song. *See* KELLIE (L.)

— Let old Time hammer away at the clock. Song. *See* MELLON (A.)

— Let other Bards in lofty Verse. *Polly Green.* [Song.] [*London?*, c. 1765.] *s. sh.* fol.　　　　　　　G. 310. (64.)

— [Another copy.]　　　　　　　　　　H. 1601. u. (112.)

— Let other Bards of Angels sing. Song. *See* KELLIE (L.)

— Let other bards of angels sing. [Song.] *See* SPARK (W.) The Wordsworth Lyrics. No. 3.

— Let other Beauties. [Song.] *See* CLOTILDA.

— Let other Men envy. *The Happy Fellow.* [Song.] [*London?*, c. 1765.] *s. sh.* fol.　　　　　　　H. 1601. u. (45.)

— Let other Men envy the Pomp of the Great. *The Happy Fellow.* A New Song. [*London,* 1765.] 8°.
Universal Magazine, Vol. XXXVII., p. 208.　　P. P. 5439.

— Let others boast of sunnier Climes. Song. *See* SPINNEY (T. E.)

— Let others depicture the mossy-green Mead. [Song.] *See* BACON (John)

— Let others for beauties the city explore. *Miss Snow:* a New Song. [*London,* 1765.] 8°.
Royal Magazine, Vol. XIII., p. 46.　　　　P. P. 5441.

— Let others quaff the racy wine. Glee. *See* O'NEILL (W.) *Baron.*

— Let others roam to foreign shores. Ballad. *See* PRATTEN (W. S.)

— Let others seek the peaceful Plain. Song. *See* SULLIVAN (*Sir* Arthur S.)

— Let others sing in loftier Lays. *Polly of the Plain.* A New Song [by W. Defesch]. Sung by Mrs. Chambers, at Mary-le-Bon Gardens. [*London,* 1754.] 8°.
Universal Magazine, Vol. XV., p. 125.　　　P. P. 5439.

— Let Others sing in Rustic Lays. *Fanny of the Hill.* [Song, by James Hook.] Sung by Mr. Vernon at Vauxhall. [*Printed for C. and S. Thompson: London,* 1768?] fol.
From Thompson's Second Book of Hook's Vauxhall and Marylebone Songs.　　　　　　　　G. 310. (50.)

— Let others sing in rustick Lays. *Fanny of the Hill.* [Song, by James Hook.] Sung by Mʳ Vernon at Vauxhall. [1770?] fol.
Followed by an accompaniment for German flute and guitar.　　　　　　　　　　　　　G. 316. l. (24.)

— Let others sing of purling streams. [Song.] *See* MONTGOMERY (W. H.)

— Let others sing of ruby wine. Song. *See* BARNETT (J.) [Blanche of Jersey.]

— Let others, Stella. Glee. *See* ADDISON (John) *Dramatic composer.*

— Let others to London go roam. [Song.] *See* ARNE (T. A.)

— Let our Gladness have no End. Carol. *See* RESKE (W.)

— Let our Gladness know no End. Carol. *See* HARRIS (Jerry W.)

— Let our Gladness know no End. Bohemian hymn. *See* SHEPPARD (J. S.)

— Let our great Song arise. [Part-song.] *See* WILSON (Harry R.)

— Let our Halls & Towers decay. [Song.] *See* MAZZINGHI (J.)

— Let our hearts be joyful. Anthem. *See* MENDELSSOHN-BARTHOLDY (J. L. F.)

— Let Parties and Rage awhile quit the Stage. *The British Hector, or the Taking of Pondichery.* [Song.] [*London,* 1779?] *s. sh.* fol.　　　　　　　　I. 530. (88.)

— Let pleasure be our goddess. *See* VERDI (F. G. F.) [La Traviata.—Libiamo ne' lieti calici.]

— Let Pleasure's gay Queen. *The Court of Vauxhall.* [Song.] Written for and Sung by Mr. Vernon, 1778 and 1779. Set to Musick by the Author. *S[amuel and] A[nn] T[hompson: London,* 1779.] fol.　　　　　　　　　G. 310. (54.)

— Let pleasure's magic power. *See* VERDI (F. G. F.) [La Traviata.—Libiamo ne' lieti calici.]

— Let Poets and Historians. *The Gregorian Constitution Song.* [Words and music by H. Carey.] [*London,* 1735?] *s. sh.* fol.　　　　　　　　　　　　　G. 316. e. (64.)

— Let Poets boast of Egypt's Queen. *The Toast.* A new Song. [*London,* 1756.] 8°.
London Magazine, 1756, p. 604.　　　　　158. l. 1.

— Let Poets of Learning. *The Lass of the Hatch.* [Song.] *L[ongman and] B[roderip: London,* 1785?] fol.　　G. 310. (48.)

— Let Poets praise the Pasture Mead. *Dear Delia.* A new song. Set to music by an eminent master. *In:* The New Lady's Magazine. vol. 5. pp. 616–618. 1790. 8°.　　P. P. 5141. b.

— Let Praise devote Thy Work. Unison Song. *See* BULLOCK (*Sir* E.)

— Let Praise devote thy Work. Unison song. *See* WHITFIELD (John B. R.)

— Let prentice Bards poetic scribble. *Buntinella.* [Song.] The words by G. A. Stevens. *Sk[illern: London,* 1780?] *s. sh.* fol.　　　　　　　　　　　　　G. 310. (43.)

— Let Rakes and Libertines. [Song.] *See* HAENDEL (George F.) [Susanna.—Ask if yon damask Rose be sweet.]

— Let Rubinelli charm the ear. Duet. Words by ... Dr. Wake. *London,* [1875.] fol.　　　　　　　H. 1791. b. (37.)

— Let's all be Americans now. [Song.] *See* BERLIN (Irving)

— Let's all be Kids again. [Song.] *See* CAREY (Thomas W.)

— Let's all get together and sing. [Song.] *See* BROWNE (Ted)

— Let's all go around to Mary Ann's. [Song.] *See* CARROLL (Harry)

— Let's all go down the Strand. Song. *See* CASTLING (Harry) and MURPHY (C. W.)

— Let's all go home. [Song.] *See* COCHRANE (P. D.)

— Let's all go into the Ballroom! Song. *See* ALLEN (Andrew N.) and MURPHY (C. W.)

— Let's all go up to Maud's. [Song.] *See* MILLS (Kerry)

— Let's all make Hay while the Sun shines. Song. *See* FURTH (Seymour J.)

— Let's all sing a happy Song. Songs. *See* DIAMOND (Eileen)

— Let's all stay until the Morning. Song. *See* COLLINS (Charles)

— Let's banish Strife and Sorrow. Round. *See* ATTERBURY (L.)

— Let's be a joyous band. Song. *See* ALLMAN (G. J. O.)

— Let's be Children once again. Song. *See* BUSKIRK (F.)

— Let's be Friends. [Song.] *See* STRAUSS (J.) *the Younger.* [Die Fledermaus.—Brüderlein, Brüderlein und Schwesterlein.]

— Let's be friends again. [Song.] *See* YOUNG (H. M.)

— Let's be Friends and love again. Song. *See* ZANKE (C.)

— Let's be gay, boys. Song. *See* RUSSELL (H.)

— Let's be Jolly, fill our Glasses. *The Charms of the Bottle,* [song] the words by Mr. Estcourt. [*London*, 1720?] *s. sh.* fol. **H. 1601. (281.)**

— Let's be jolly while we may. Song. *See* VICTOR (R.)

— Let's be jubilant! [Song.] *See* CONNOR (T. W.)

— Let's be lazy. Song. *See* LAVAL (L.)

— Let's be lively! Song. *See* MYDDLETON (William H.)

— Let's be lonesome together. [Song.] *See* GERSHWIN (George) [George White's Scandals of 1923.]

— Let's be merry. Chorus. *See* WEBER (C. M. F. E. von) [Oberon.]

— Let's be off to the diggins. Song. *See* BEULER (J.)

— Let's be Pals again. Song. *See* DONNELLY (Robert) and ALLEN (P.)

— Let's be prepared for Peace or War. [Song.] *See* BROWNE (Raymond A.)

— Let's be ready! That's the Spirit of '76. [Song.] *See* BAYHA (Charles A.) and COWAN (R.)

— Let's be the same old Sweethearts. Ballad. *See* BELLIN (Betty) and LIVERNASH (W. L.)

— Let's bow to Solomon. Glee. *See* NATHAN (I.)

— Let's build a Bridge from your Heart to mine. [Song.] *See* CUNNINGHAM (Paul F.)

— Let's build a City. [Two-part song.] *See* WINFREY (Robert)

— Let's build a Town. Play for Children. *See* HINDEMITH (P.) [Wir bauen eine Stadt.]

— Let's call all the Money in. Song. *See* CASTLING (Harry)

— Let's call the whole Thing off. [Song.] *See* GERSHWIN (George) [Shall we dance.]

— Lets cheerfully live till we dye. Song. *See* BRAVE. Brave Boys let us live. [c. 1790.] fol. **H. 1652. pp. (11.)**

— Let's drink a toast to liberty. Song. *See* JANSEN (L.)

— Let's drink and be merry. *The Good Fellow.* [Song, by G. Vanbrughe.] [*Walsh: London*, 1713?] fol. *Pp.* 26–27 *of Vanbrughe's "Mirth and Harmony".* **G. 303. (24.)**

— [Another edition.] Let's drink and be merry. *The Good Fellow.* [Song.] Set for the German Flute. [By G. Vanbrughe.] [*London*, 1720?] *s. sh.* fol. **G. 316. e. (75.)**

— Let's enjoy, while the Season invites us. Duet and Chorus. *See* MOZART (W. A.) [Don Giovanni.—Giovinette, che fate all' amore.]

— Let's fly to the sweet Bye and Bye. [Song.] *See* BLOOM (I. T.)

— Let's forget the Past and be Sweethearts again. [Song.] *See* CHURCH (Frank)

— Let's forget we ever met. Ballad. *See* ALLEN (Thomas S.)

— Let's get acquainted. [Song.] *See* KEITH (Lester W.)

— Let's get spooney awhile. [Song.] *See* BROWN (Albert W.)

— Let's get the Umpire's Goat. [Song.] *See* BAYES, afterwards BAYES-NORWORTH (Nora) and NORWORTH (J.)

— Let's give three Cheers. Two-part Song. *See* SULLIVAN (Sir A. S.) [H. M. S. Pinafore.]

— Let's go a-Maying. Cantata. *See* DYSON (Sir George)

— Let's go and sit on the Piazza. [Song.] *See* SPINK (George A.)

— Let's go back to Baby Days. [Song.] *See* MEYER (George W.)

— Let's go, Boys, let's go! Song. *See* ALSTON (Toussaint L.)

— Let's go for a Walk. [Song.] *See* HOLT (Stanley) *Songwriter.*

— Let's go home. [Song.] *See* BURT (Benjamin H.)

— Let's go in the Garden and play. Unison Song. *See* AUSTIN (E.)

— Let's go in the Garden, Mary. Song. *See* ALBERT (Fred E. d')

— Let's go into a Picture Show. [Song.] *See* TILZER (Albert von)

— Let's go on Holiday. [Song-cycle.] *See* DETWEILER (Alan)

— Let's go out on a Jamboree. [Song.] *See* DEELY (Ben)

— Let's go out to White City, Kitty. [Song.] *See* JEROME (Benjamin M.)

— Let's go the longest Way. Song. *See* COLLINS (Charles) and MURRAY (F.)

— Let's go to Sans Souci, Susie. [Song.] *See* BARRON (Ted S.)

— Let's have a Catch. [Catch.] *See* COOKE (Thomas S.)

— Let's have a Chorus we can all sing. Song. *See* DAVID (Worton) and CASTLING (H.)

— Let's have a dance upon the heath. [Song.] *See* LOCKE (M.) [*Doubtful and Supposititious Works.*] [Macbeth.]

— Let's have a Dance upon the Heath. Song. *See also* MACBETH.

— Let's have a Day with the Ladies. Song. *See* CARLTON (Harry) and SULLIVAN (T.)

— Let's have a Game at Soldiers. Song. *See* CLIFFORD (Nat)

LET

— Let's have a Ha'porth of England! Song. *See* ROGERS (E. W.)

— Let's have a jolly good Chorus. [Song.] *See* GODWIN (Will J.)

— Let's have a Peal for John Cooke's Soul. *Canon nine in one.* [By Benjamin Cooke.] pp. 3. *Printed by Clementi & C⁰: London,* [c. 1810.] *obl.* fol.　　**E. 205. a. (10.)**

— Let's have a Song about the Boys. Song. *See* ELLERTON (Alfred) *the Younger.*

— Let's have a Song with a Chorus. [Song.] *See* MATHEWS (E. N.)

— Let's have a Union. Negro spiritual. *See* JOHNSON (Hall)

— Let's have another. Song. *See* WEST (Arthur)

— Let's have Free Trade amongst the Girls! Song. *See* CASTLING (Harry) and KIND (J. A. G.)

— Let's help the Red Cross now. [Song.] *See* BARRON (Ted S.)

— Let's hold Hands in the Moonlight, Mary. Song. *See* WOOD (Leo)

— Let's hope for brighter days. Ballad. *See* MALCOLM (　　　)

— Let's hope for brighter days. Ballad. *See* MANSFIELD (A. J.)

— Let's imitate her Notes above. Two-part Song. *See* HAENDEL (G. F.) [Alexander's Feast.]

— Let's jog along. [Song.] *See* CADDIGAN (Jack J.) and STORY (C.)

— Let's join in. [Action songs.] *See* SMITH (Geoffrey E. R.)

— Let's jolly be, 'tis Christmas time. [Song.] *See* WILSON (W.)

— Let's joyful be to-day. [Song.] *See* EASTES, afterwards D'ESTÉ (John)

— Let's kiss and make up. Duet. *See* GERSHWIN (George) [Smarty.]

— Let's live and let's love. *A Glee.* For Three Voices. [*Dublin,* 1779.] *s. sh.* 4°.
Hibernian Magazine, Dec., 1779.　　**P. P. 6154. k.**

— Let's make a little Home for the old Folks. Song. *See* WHEELER (J. W.)

— Let's make it up again. Song. *See* SCOTT (Bennett)

— Let's make Love. [Song.] *See* BOWERS (Frederick V.)

— Let's make up with a Kiss. Song. *See* GEDULDIG (M. M.)

— Let's play a Game of Soldier. [Song.] *See* LEMONIER (Thomas)

— Let's play House. Song. *See* WESTON (Sam.)

— Let's play that you are Daddy. [Song.] *See* BALL (E. R.)

— Let's pretend. [Recitation with P. F. accompaniment.] *See* ADAMS (J. H.)

— Let's pretend. Unison Song. *See* BANTOCK (*Sir* G.)

— Let's pretend we're married. Song. *See* ARTHURS (George) and LEE (B.)

— Let's pretend we're Soldiers. Song. *See* DAREWSKI (Hermann E.)

— Let's put the best Foot forward. Song. *See* BRAHAM (Philip E.) Put the best Foot forward.

— Let's Range the Fields my Sally. Song. *See* LINLEY (Thomas) *the Elder.*

— Let's read the good Book. [Part-song.] *See* KLEIN (John)

LET

— Let's run away. [Song.] *See* SPERO (M. J.)

— Let's say goodbye. [Song.] *See* COWARD (*Sir* Noël P.) [Words and Music.]

— Let's sing. [Part-songs.] *See* SIMPSON (Kenneth)

— Let's sing a Song of America. [Part-song.] *See* ROFF (Joseph)

— Let's sing for Fun. Songs. *See* AGER (Laurence)

— Let's speak of all the good we can. Song. *See* DISTIN (T.) *the Elder.*

— Let's sport and play. [Part-song.] *See* HAENDEL (G. F.) [Parnasso in festa.]

— Let's start all over again. Song. *See* DENVER (Austen)

— Let's swop! Song. *See* CARPENTER (Alfred)

— Let's take this world as some wide scene. Song. *See* MOORE (T.) *the Poet.*

— Let's talk of Bow or Dart no more. Song. *See* FRANCK (J. W.)

— Let's tell you about it. Songs. *See* BROOM (P.)

— Let's tie the Knot, my Sally. Song. *See* HOOK (J.)

— Let's tope and be merry. *The Jolly Bacchanal.* [Song.] [*London,* 1740?] *s. sh.* fol.　　**G. 316. e. (60.)**

— Let's twine the three together. Song. *See* MACFARREN (J. H.)

— Let's wait and see the Pictures. Song. *See* CARTER (Frank W.) and KIND (J. A. G.)

— Let's walk in the Sunshine. Song. *See* BOEHR (F.)

— Let's welcome Father Christmas. [Song.] *See* ANDREWS (Richard H.) *the Elder.*

— Let Saints on Earth in concert sing. Anthem. *See* BUTCHER (F. C.)

— Let Saints on Earth in concert sing. Anthem. *See* THIMAN (E. H.)

— Let Shepherd Lads and Maids advance. [Part-song.] *See* PORTER (L. A.)

— Let Sinners saved give thanks and sing. Hymn. *See* DIBDIN (H. E.)

— Let soft desires your Heart engage. Song. *See* ISLAND. The Island Princess.

— Let Souldiers fight for Pay and Praise. *Bacchus turn'd Doctor.* [Song] written by Ben. Johnson. *Printed and Sold by Sutton Nicholls: London,* [c. 1710.] *s. sh.* fol.　　**Harl. 5931. (53.)**

— Let Soldiers fight for Prey or Praise. *A new Drinking Song.* Sung at Sadlers Wells. [1760?] *s. sh.* fol.
[*Sadler's Wells Collection. Vol.* 8.]
　　Crach. 1. Tab. 4. b. 4/8. (140.)

— Let Soldiers fight for Prey or Praise. *A new Drinking Song, etc.* [*London,* 1765?] *s. sh.* fol.　　**H. 1994. (40.)**

— Let some gentle word. Ballad. *See* LAVENU (L. H.)

— Let somebody else have a go. [Song.] *See* COBORN (C.) *pseud.*

— Let Songs of Rejoicing be raised. Cantata. *See* BACH (J. S.) [Man singet mit Freuden.]

— Let Sorrow come. Chorus. *See* VAN DER STUCKEN (Frank V.)

— Let Sorrow seek her native Night. Duett. *See* STEVENSON (*Sir* J. A.)

— Let Strife cease, welcome Peace. [Chorus.] *See* HAENDEL (G. F.) [Berenice.—Con verace dolce pace.]

LET

— Let Sunlight smile on him. Song. *See* CHAMBERLAYNE (A.)

— Let Temperance advance! Song and Chorus. *See* MILLARD (H.)

— Let the angels in. Song & chorus. *See* DANKS (H. P.)

— Let the Band play in Irish Tune. [Song.] *See* ACCOOE (William J.)

— Let the Bells ring. [Part-song.] *See* HATHAWAY (J. W. G.) [Two Part-songs. Op. 22. No. 2.]

— Let the Bells ring out. [Part-song.] *See* STEFFANI (Arturo) [The Story of Christmas.]

— Let the bright Seraphim. [Song.] *See* HAENDEL (G. F.) [Samson.]

— Let the Bullgine run. Part-song. *See* WILKINSON (Philip G.)

— Let the Children sing. Songs. *See* DALE (Mervyn)

— Let the Dance go on. Song. *See* DAREWSKI (Max)

— Let the daring Advent'rers be toss'd on the Main. *What will make every man rich.* [Song, words from Shadwell's play "The Woman-Captain".] fol. *Printed for J. Bland:* [*London*, 1780?] *s. sh.* fol.　　　**G. 310. (38.)**

— Let the dead and the beautiful rest. Song and chorus. *See* MARTIN (S. W.)

— Let the declining Damask Rose. Song. *See* HUDSON (R.)

— Let the dreadful engines. Song. *See* PURCELL (H.) [Don Quixote. Part I.]

— Let the Dream go! [Song.] *See* WEIL (O.) Three Songs. (Op. 34. No. 2.)

— Let the Earth be glad. [Anthem.] *See* GORDON (Philip)

— Let the Earth bring forth Grass. Anthem. *See* SHARROTT (W.)

— Let the Earth rejoice. Anthem. *See* WOODCOCK (E. W.)

— Let the earth resound. Song. *See* PURCELL (Henry) [*Doubtful and Supposititious Works*.] [Trumpet Voluntary.]

— Let the Epicure boast. Song. *See* WHITAKER (J.) [The Outside Passenger.]

— Let the farmer praise his grounds. The cruiskeen-lawn, an Irish song, the symphonies ... by W. M. Herbert. *London*, [1857.] fol.　　　**H. 1549. (2.)**

— Let the farmer praise his grounds. *The Cruiskeen Lawn* ... Song. *London*, [1876.] fol.　　　**H. 1791. b. (36.)**

— Let the farmer praise his grounds. *Cruiskeen Lawn.* Irish ... song. *London*, [1877.] fol.
No. 193 of C. Boosey's "Universal" music.　　　**H. 2324.**

— Let the Fields be joyful. Anthem. *See* WOODCOCK (E. W.)

— Let the Fifes and the Clarions. [Two-part song.] *See* PURCELL (H.) [The Fairy Queen.]

— Let the French hop and sing. *British Freedom.* A Favourite Song. Set by an Eminent Master. S[*traight*] & Sk[*illern:* *London*, 1775?] fol.
Imperfect; wanting the second leaf.　　　**G. 310. (72.)**

— Let the Frenchmen make a noise. *The Boys of Britain* ... Song, written ... by T. Dibdin. *London*, [1803.] fol.　　　**H. 2830. f. (92.)**

— Let the furious billows. [Song.] *See* HÉROLD (L. J. F.) [Zampa.— Que la vague écumante.]

— Let the Goblet sparkle high. Song. *See* DUNN (J.)

LET

— Let the great big World keep turning. Song. *See* AYER (Nat. D.)

— Let the heart be gay. Ballad. *See* BLEWITT (J.)

— Let the Heart of them rejoice that seek the Lord. Anthem. *See* DAVIS (A. J.)

— Let the Heavens be glad. Anthem. *See* HIGGS (H. M.)

— Let the Heav'ns be glad. Anthem. *See* KNIGHT (V.)

— Let the Heavens be glad. Offertory. *See* ROFF (Joseph)

— Let the Heavens be joyful. Anthem. *See* FLETCHER (P. E.)

— Let the Heavens rejoice. Anthem. *See* BINKERD (Gordon W.)

— Let the Heavens rejoice. Anthem. *See* EDGAR (C. B.)

— Let the Heavens rejoice. Anthem. *See* ERNEST (G.)

— Let the Heavens rejoice. Anthem. *See* JACKSON (B.)

— Let the Hills resound. Song. *See* RICHARDS (H. R.)

— Let the Ivy grow. Song. *See* HOPKINS (R. B.)

— Let the King reign. Choral March. *See* WHITEHEAD (P. A.)

— Let the Kingdom be united. Song. *See* CHRIMES (W.)

— Let the Lady do the Work. Song. *See* REID (John M.)

— Let the Lasses merry be. Song. *See* LEE (G. A.)

— Let the Light of thy Countenance. [Anthem.] *See* ROFF (Joseph)

— Let the Lion go, Boys. Song. *See* MENEAR (F.)

— Let the lower Lights be burning. [Part-song.] *See* BLISS (Philip P.) *the Elder.*

— Let the Lusty shout. [Part-song.] *See* ABT (F. W.)

— Let the lutes play their loudest. [Trio.] *See* BENEDICT (*Sir* J.)

— Let the merry Bells ring out. Chorus. *See* VINCENT (C. J.) Songs and Part Songs, *etc.* No. 70.

— Let the merry Church Bells ring. Carol. *See* MARSCHAL-LOEPKE (G.)

— Let the Most Blessed. Part-song. *See* FITZWILLIAM (E. F.) Four Part-songs. No. 4.

— Let the Mountains shout for Joy. [Anthem.] *See* STEPHENS (E.)

— Let the Music Flow. [Chorus.] *See* CLARK (T. M.)

— Let the mystic orange flowers. Duet. *See* BENEDICT (*Sir* J.) [The Lily of Killarney.]

— Let the night darken in. Song. *See* TOPLIFF (R.)

— Let the Nymph still avoid. [Song.] *See* REPRISAL.

— Let the Nymph, who designs. *Seasonable advice to Maidens.* [Song.] [*London*, 1720?] *s. sh.* fol.　　　**H. 1601. (285.)**

— Let the Past be dead. [Chorus.] *See* MACKENZIE (*Sir* A. C.) [Colomba.]

— Let the Peace of God rule in your Hearts. Anthem. *See* STAINER (*Sir* J.)

— Let the People give Thanks. [Anthem.] *See* SCHUETZ (H.) [Psalmen Davids nach Cornelius Beckers Dichtungen.— Danket dem Herren, unserm Gott.]

— Let the People praise Thee. Anthem. *See* BREWER (*Sir* A. H.)

— Let the People praise Thee. [Anthem.] *See* CLEMENS (M.)

LET

— Let the People praise Thee. [Anthem.] *See* DIETERICH (M.)

— Let the People praise Thee. Anthem. *See* FLETCHER (P. E.)

— Let the People praise Thee. Anthem. *See* GLOVER (R.)

— Let the People praise Thee. Anthem. *See* KEANE (D. M.)

— Let the People praise Thee. Anthem. *See* PALESTRINA (G. P. da) [Missa O sacrum convivium.—Gloria in excelsis Deo.]

— Let the People Praise Thee. Anthem. *See* PEARSON (A.)

— Let the People praise Thee. Anthem. *See* SILVER (A. J.)

— Let the People praise Thee, Lord. Anthem. *See* HAM (A.)

— Let the People praise Thee, O God. Anthem. *See* CHALLINOR (F. A.)

— Let the People praise Thee, O God. Anthem. *See* GAUL (A. R.)

— Let the People praise Thee, O God. Anthem. *See* HARWOOD (B.)

— Let the People praise Thee, O God. Anthem. *See* NUNN (E. C.)

— Let the Peoples praise thee. [Anthem.] *See* TUČAPSKÝ (Antonín)

— Let the Persian adoring the splendor of nature. Ballad. *See* STEVENSON (*Sir* J. A.)

— Let the Rafters ring. [Two-part song.] *See* SIDEBOTHAM (M. A.)

— Let the Rest of the World go by. [Song.] *See* BALL (Ernest R.)

— Let the Righteous be glad. Anthem. *See* LLOYD (R. F.)

— Let the Righteous be glad. [Anthem.] *See* WITTY (Robert)

— Let the River sing on. Song. *See* SANDERSON (H.)

— Let the Roses tell my Story. [Song.] *See* CHAPMAN (Olive) and STEVENSON (A.)

— Let the Schools about Happiness warmly dispute. *The Omnium of Life.* A new drinking song. Sung by Mr Lowe. [1770?] fol.
Followed by an accompaniment for German flute.
G. 316. l. (25.)

— Let the Sea roar. Canon. *See* BROWNSETT (J.)

— Let the shadows fall behind thee. Song. *See* RAIT (J. C.)

— Let the Silver come. [Song.] *See* JEWELL (E. B.)

— Let the slave of ambition and wealth. Song. *See* GIORDANI (T.)

— Let the Smiles of Youth. A favorite glee for three voices, the words by Mr Webbe. *J. Bland: London*, [1790?] fol.
H. 1652. z. (11.)

— Let the social Can go round. *An easy Duo for Two Voices.* *T. G. Williamson: London*, [1802.] fol. G. 354. (52.)

— Let the soft tear. Ballad. *See* GOLDSTONE (H.)

— Let the Souldiers rejoyce. Song. *See* PURCELL (H.) [Dioclesian.]

— Let the solemn organ blow. Anthem. *See* BACH (J. Christian)

— Let the Song be begun. Easter Carol. *See* MEDLEY (E. S.)

— Let the sparkling Wine go round. Glee. *See* ROCK (Michael)

— Let the tempest of war. *The Tempest of War.* A New Song. [*London*, 1761.] 8°.
Royal Magazine, Vol. IV., *p.* 195. P. P. 5441.

LET

— [Another edition.] Let the Tempest of War. A Song. [*London*, c. 1765.] *s. sh.* fol. H. 1994. b. (49.)

— Let the Tempest of War be heard from afar. *The Tempest of War.* [Song.] [*London*, c. 1765.] *s. sh.* fol. G. 425. aa. (18.)

— Let the Thrush awake my Love. [Song.] *See* ADAMS (James B.) Select Songs ... N°. 16.

— Let the Toast be dear Woman. Song. *See* RODWELL (G. H.)

— Let the Trumpet sound. [Song.] *See* VERDI (F. G. F.) [Il Trovatore.—Squilli e cheggi.]

— Let the Voice of Praise resound. [Christmas carol.] *See* HAENDL (J.) called *Gallus.* [Tomus primus operis musici.— Resonet in laudibus.]

— Let the voice of the people decide. Song and chorus. *See* HOGGETT (C.)

— Let the Waiter. [Song.] *See also* HAENDEL (G. F.) [Rinaldo.—Il Tricerbero humiliato.]

— Let the Waiter bring clean Glasses. [Song, adapted to "Il Tricerbero humiliato," by G. F. Haendel.] [*London*, 1790?] *s. sh.* fol. G. 805. i. (9.)

— Let the wearied taste in Sleep. Catch. *See* OVEREND (M.)

— Let the Welkin ring again. [Part-song.] *See* TRUTSCHEL (A.)

— Let the whole Creation cry. [Anthem.] *See* HANSON (Geoffrey)

— Let the whole World know the Secret. [Song.] *See* GRANADOS (E.)

— Let the Wicked forsake his Way. Anthem. *See* HARVEY (R. M.)

— Let the Word of Christ. Anthem. *See* NEWBURY (Kent A.)

— Let the words of my mouth. Anthem. *See* BARNBY (*Sir* Joseph)

— Let the Words of my Mouth. Response. *See* BARTLETT (H. N.)

— Let the Words of my Mouth. Anthem. *See* BEETHOVEN (L. van) [Sonatas for piano and violin. Op. 12. No. 1. Tema con Variazioni.]

— Let the Words of my Mouth. Anthem. *See* BLAIR (H.)

— Let the Words of my Mouth. Introit. *See* CROWE (R. W.)

— Let the Words of my Mouth. Anthem. *See* CULLEY (A. D.)

— Let the Words of my Mouth. Motet *See* DRESSLER (W.)

— Let the Words of my Mouth. Sentence. *See* EATON (A. L.)

— Let the Words of my Mouth. Response. *See* GOWEN (E. A.)

— Let the Words of my Mouth. Response. *See* GREENE (C. W.)

— Let the Words of my Mouth. [Anthem.] *See* HOLDEN (A. J.)

— Let the Words of my Mouth. Response. *See* JAMES (B. P.)

— Let the Words of my Mouth. Anthem. *See* LANG (Craig S.)

— Let the words of my mouth. Sacred song. *See* MACFARREN (W. C.)

— Let the words of my mouth. Sacred song. *See* MOZART (W. A.) [Requiem.—Tuba mirum.]

— Let the Words of my Mouth. Duet. *See* ROBYN (A. G.) Two Sacred Duets, *etc.* [No. 2.]

— Let the Words of my Mouth. Introit. *See* TITCOMB (Howard E.)

LET

— Let the Words of my Mouth. Anthem. *See* WARD (F. E.) Five Anthems. [No. 5.]

— Let the Words of my Mouth. [Anthem.] *See* ZUNDEL (J.)

— Let the Work of every Briton be protected. Song. *See* SOUSA (C. de)

— Let the World rejoice. Christmas Carol. *See* KOSHETZ (A.)

— Let them all come in. [Song.] *See* SILVER (Maxwell)

— Let them alone, they're married. [Song.] *See* CARROLL (Earl)

— Let them be ashamed. Air. *See* ROWLAND (A.)

— Let them be one, O Father. Hymn. *See* METCALFE (J. A.)

— Let them boast of the Land. *The Red blooming Heather & Thistle so green.* A favorite new song, arranged for the voice & piano forte. pp. 3. *Davie & Morris: Aberdeen,* [c. 1815.] fol.
G. 426. dd. (44.)

— Let them ever sing for Joy. [Anthem.] *See* NEWBURY (Kent A.)

— Let them for their reward. Quartet. *See* ROWLAND (W.)

— Let them give Thanks. Anthem. *See* FEDERLEIN (G. H.)

— Let them give Thanks. Anthem. *See* WESTBROOK (W. J.)

— Let them give Thanks. [Anthem.] *See* WILLIAMSON (*Sir* Malcolm B. G. C.)

— Let them not vanish. [Song.] *See* MALLINSON (J. A.) Two Songs from abroad. [No. 1.]

— Let there be light. Sacred Song. *See* DAVIS (Eliza)

— Let there be Light. Hymn. *See* HAVERGAL (William H.)

— Let there be Light. Sacred Song. *See* HEMERY (V.)

— Let there be Light. [Anthem.] *See* IVES (Charles E.) Processional.

— Let there be Light. Motet. *See* JOUBERT (John)

— Let there be light. Sacred song. *See* WILSON (W.)

— Let there be Music. [Part-song.] *See* WEIGL (Vally)

— Let there be Music. [Part-song.] *See* WILLIAMS (Frances)

— Let these but pass. Ballad. *See* GUERNSEY (W.)

— Let Thine Hand help me. [Anthem.] *See* HAENDEL (G. F.) [Rinaldo.—Lascia ch'io pianga.]

— Let this Mind be in you. Anthem. *See* ANDREWS (M.)

— Let this Mind be in you. Anthem. *See* BEACH (A. M. C.) *Mrs.*

— Let this Mind be in you. Anthem. *See* CADMAN (C. W.)

— Let this Mind be in you. Anthem. *See* HEWARD (L. H.)

— Let this Mind be in you. Anthem. *See* LITTLEJOHN (C. E. S.)

— Let this Mind be in you. Anthem. *See* WILLS (Arthur W.)

— Let those laugh that lose. Song. *See* LEE (Alfred)

— Let those who wou'd wish to hear reason. *To Day* a favourite Song. *W. R*[*andall: London,* 1770?] *s. sh.* fol. **G. 310. (57.)**

— Let thy care O Lord be around me. Prayer. *See* HAENDEL (G. F.)

— Let thy celestial light. [Sacred song.] *See* MEYERBEER (G.) [L'Étoile du Nord.—Veille sur eux toujours.]

— Let thy dear Eyes. [Song.] *See* CLUTSAM (G. H.)

LET

— Let thy Hand be strengthened. Anthem. *See* ATTWOOD (T.)

— Let Thy Hand be strengthened. Anthem. *See* BLOW (J.)

— Let thy Hand be strengthened. [Anthem.] *See* DEARNLEY (Christopher H.)

— Let thy Hand be strengthened. [Anthem.] *See* HAENDEL (G. F.) [Coronation Anthems.]

— Let Thy holy Presence. [Part-song.] *See* CHESNOKOV (P. G.)

— Let Thy holy Spirit come upon us. [Anthem.] *See* CHESNOKOV (P. G.)

— Let Thy loving Mercy. Anthem. *See* TYE (C.) [The Actes of the Apostles.]

— Let Thy merciful Ears. Anthem. *See* BELL (W. B.)

— Let Thy merciful Ears. Anthem. *See* GAUL (A. R.)

— Let Thy merciful Ears. [Anthem.] *See* GAUL (H. B.)

— Let Thy merciful Ears, O Lord, be open. [Anthem.] *See* HORSLEY (W.)

— Let Thy merciful Ears. [Anthem.] *See* LYON (J.)

— Let Thy merciful Ears, O Lord. [Motet.] *See* MUDD ( )

— Let Thy merciful Ears. Anthem. *See* NORTHCOTE (S.)

— Let Thy merciful Ears. [Anthem.] *See* O'HARE (W. C.)

— Let Thy merciful Ears. Anthem. *See* SHAW (J.)

— Let Thy merciful Ears, O Lord. [Anthem.] *See* THIMAN (E. H.)

— Let Thy merciful Ears. Anthem. *See* WEELKES (T.)

— Let Thy merciful Kindness. [Anthem.] *See* BARNBY (*Sir* J.)

— Let thy Mercy, O Lord, be upon us. [Anthem.] *See* ROFF (Joseph)

— Let thy Mind be upon the Ordinances of the Lord. Duet. *See* BENNETT (*Sir* W. S.) Six Sacred Duetts ... Op. 30. No. 2.

— Let Tomorrow take Care of Tomorrow. [Part-song.] *See* BAVICCHI (John) Five short Poems. No. 3.

— Let trusting Faith be ever thine. Sacred Song. *See* ANDREWS (Richard H.) *the Elder.*

— Let Truth and sportless [*sic*] Faith be thine. *Free Mason's Song.* ⟨Der alte Landmann an seinen Sohn.⟩ [Melody by W. A. Mozart, words] by Hölty. *C. Geisweiler:* [*London,*] 1800. *s. sh. obl.* 4°.
German Museum, Aug. 1800. **266. l. 25.**

— [Another setting.] Let Truth and spotless Faith be thine. [Glee.] *See* CALLCOTT (J. W.)

— Let us adore. Chorus. *See* MÉHUL (E. N.)

— Let us adore Thee, O Christ. [Motet.] *See* RUFFO (V.) [Adoramus te, Christe.]

— Let us advance the Good Old Cause. *An Excellent New Hymne To the Mobile,* exhorting them to Loyalty the Clean contrary Way. To the Tune or [*sic*] 41, Or Hey Boys up go We. *Nath. Thompson: London,* 1682. *s. sh.* fol.
Case 121. g.

— Let us all be friends together. Song and chorus. *See* TAYLOR (T. J.)

— Let us all be glad. [Anthem.] *See* RIDOUT (Alan J.)

— Let us all be ready. [Song.] *See* MONTROSE (Sidney)

LET

— Let us all be unhappy together. [Song.] *See* WE. We Bipeds made up of frail Clay, *etc.* [c. 1800.] *s. sh.* fol.

G. 809. xx. (5.)

— Let us all go Maying. Part-song. *See* GRANT (J. B.)

— Let us all go Maying. Madrigal. *See* MANSFIELD (P. J.)

— Let us all go Maying. Ballad madrigal. *See* PEARSALL (R. L.)

— Let us all help one another. Song. *See* NEW (S. W.)

— Let us all rejoice. Anthem. *See* HALAHAN (Guy)

— Let us all sing. [Songs.] *See* EAGLE (Doris)

— Let us all speak our minds if we die for it. [Song.] *See* REED (T. G.)

— Let us all take to Singing. [Part-song.] *See* DIAMOND (David L.)

— Let us all to the Fields repair. Trio. *See* FERRARI (G. G.) [Tirsi non mi seccar.]

— Let us all try to do a good turn when we can. Ballad. *See* MONTGOMERY (W. H.)

— Let us all with Voices sing. Part Song. *See* VEITCH (W.)

— Let us be Friends. Song. *See* SABEL (S. A.)

— Let us be Friends again. [Song.] *See* CUYAS ( ) and LACALLE (J.)

— Let us be Friends as of yore. [Song.] *See* HAMILTON (George)

— Let us be gay. Chanson. *See* LASSO (Orlando di) [Les Meslanges.—Soyons joyeux.]

— Let us be gay. Song. *See* LINLEY (G.) [The Queen and the Cardinal.]

— Let us be happy now. Ballad. *See* ALLMANN (G. J. O.)

— Let us be happy together. [Song.] *See* DONIZETTI (D. G. M.) [Lucrezia Borgia.—Il Segreto per esser felici.]

— Let us be joyful. Part-Song. *See* SCHNEIDER (J. C. F.)

— Let us be joyous. Ballad. *See* ASHMORE (John)

— Let us be merry. Part-Song. *See* DUNHILL (T. F.)

— Let us be merry and gay. Part Song. *See* SUMMERS (J.)

— Let us be merry in our old Cloaths. [Catch.] *See* GREGORY (E.)

— Let us be Sweethearts again. [Song.] *See* GODWIN (W.) and MAYNE (W.)

— Let us be true to each other. [Song.] *See* BAKER (W. C.)

— Let us be up and doing. [Hymn.] *See* MEREDITH (I. H.)

— Let us break Bread together. Spiritual. *See* CAIN (Noble)

— Let us break Bread together. Spiritual. *See* DE CORMIER (Robert)

— Let us break Bread together. Negro spiritual. *See* HEATH (Fenno)

— Let us break Bread together. Negro spiritual. *See* RYDER (Noah F.)

— Let us break Bread together. Negro spiritual. *See* WILSON (Harry R.)

— Let us break Bread together. Negro spiritual. *See* WILSON (Harry R.) and EHRET (W.)

LET

— Let us but rest awhile in quiet. *See* BACH (J. S.) [Wer nur den lieben Gott lässt walten.—Man halte nur ein wenig stille.]

— Let us call back the time. Duet. *See* GLOVER (S.)

— Let us carol a song. Carol. *See* KELLAM (Ian)

— Let us cheer the weary Traveller. Negro Spiritual. *See* BURLEIGH (H. T.) Negro Spirituals, *etc.* [No. 20.]

— Let us cheer the weary Traveller. Spiritual. *See* CLARK (Rogie)

— Let us cheer the weary Traveler. Negro Spiritual. *See* KEMMER (G. W.)

— Let us come boldly. Anthem. *See* LLOYD (C. H.)

— Let us dance. [Two-part song.] *See* HAENDEL (G. F.) [Ottone.—Overture.—Gavotte.]

— Let us dance and sing. [Unison song.] *See* ROWLEY (Alec)

— Let us dance, and sing in chorus. *St. David's Day.* Welch Air [for three voices]. *Skillern: London,* [1800?] fol.

G. 809. b. (16.)

— Let us dance, let us sing. [Song.] Sung by Mr. Shuter in the character of a Sailor. [*London,* 1760?] *s. sh.* fol.

G. 316. e. (61.)

— [Another setting.] Let us dance, let us sing. Song. *See* PURCELL (H.)

— Let us dance on the sands. Duet. *See* GLOVER (S.)

— Let us dream the old Dream out. [Song.] *See* WALSH (Austin)

— Let us drift and dream. [Song.] *See* FARLEY (R.) Three Songs of Skies and Waters, *etc.* [No. 1.]

— Let us drink and be merry. Part-song. *See* LANG (Craig S.)

— Let us drink and be merry. Part-song. *See* WILKINSON (Philip G.)

— Let us drop these Rose-Leaves. Duet. *See* NOUGUÈS (J.) [Quo vadis? Effeuillons les roses.]

— Let us fill the circling Glass. *Love and Opportunity.* [Song.] Sung by Mr. Vernon. *S[amuel and] A[nn] T[hompson: London,* 1779?] *s. sh.* fol. **G. 310. (39.)**

— Let us flee this wild Desire. Chanson. *See* LASSO (O. di) [Les Meslanges.—Fuyons tous d'amour le jeu.]

— Let us forget. [Song.] *See* CASEY (James W.)

— Let us forget. [Song.] *See* GEBHARDT (Reinhard W.)

— Let us forget. [Song.] *See* WHITE (M. V.) Three Little Songs. No. 3.

— Let us Garlands bring. Shakespeare Songs. *See* FINZI (G.)

— Let us gather bright flowers. Duet. *See* GLOVER (S.)

— Let us gather up the sunbeams. *Scatter the seeds of kindness* ... Song. *London,* [1873.] fol. **H. 1791. a. (1.)**

— Let us glide on the lake. Duet. *See* GLOVER (C. W.)

— Let us go a roaming. Song. *See* PHILLIPS (H.)

— Let us go forth therefore unto Him. [Anthem.] *See* ROBERTS (J. V.) [The Passion.]

— Let us go hence. Part Song. *See* BROWN (H. P.)

— Let us go, Lassie, go. The Braes o' Balquhither. A favorite new Scotch song written by R. Tannahill. ⟨Eng^d by Walker & Hutton.⟩ *J. McFadyen: Glasgow,* [c. 1810.] fol.

H. 1601. cc. (4.)

LET

— Let us go lassie, go. *The Braes o'Balquither.* Scotch Ballad. *London,* [1855.] fol.
No. 529 *of the "Musical Bouquet".* **H. 2345.**

— Let us go the long Way round. Song. *See* LYLE (Kenneth)

— Let us go to Bethlehem. Song. *See* PEILE (T. W.)

— Let us go to Bethlehem. [Carol.] *See* TUČAPSKÝ (Antonín) The Time of Christemas. No. 5.

— Let us guard our Native land. The celebrated Bohemian March, *etc. London,* [1825?] fol. **G. 424. a. (23.)**

— Let us haste to Bethlehem. Christmas Carol. *See* MORRIS (H. C.)

— Let us haste to Kelvin Grove. Ballad. *See* PRINA (J. F.)

— Let us haste to Kelvin Grove. [Song.] *See* SIM (John)

— Let us haste to Kelvin Grove, bonnie Lassie O. Song. *See* SMITH (Robert A.) [The Scotish Minstrel. Vol. 2.]

— Let us haste to Kelvin Grove. Ballad. *See* WARING (J.)

— Let us haste to the fields. Trio. *See* BISHOP (*Sir* H. R.)

— Let us haste to the river. Duet. *See* MACFARREN (*Sir* G. A.)

— Let us hasten o'er the meadows. Part Song. *See* DANCEY (H.)

— Let us hasten to the woodlands. [Song.] *See* GLOVER (S.)

— Let us have a Song we can all sing. Song. *See* LE BRUNN (George)

— Let us have Peace! [Sacred song.] *See* BALL (E. R.)

— Let us hence! Song. *See* LINWOOD (Mary)

— Let us Homage bring. Chorus. *See* ROBERTON (*Sir* H. S.)

— Let us hope for the best. [Song.] *See* HIME (Benjamin)

— Let us keep the Feast. Introit. *See* MEAD (George)

— Let us keep the Feast. Anthem. *See* SIMPER (C.)

— Let us laugh and sing. [Song.] *See* GLOVER (S.)

— Let us lift up our Heart. Anthem. *See* WESLEY (S. S.)

— Let us light a Candle. Carol. *See* CLARK (June)

— Let us live while we may. Air. *See* KING (Matthew P.)

— Let us make the best Use of our Leisure. Chorus. *See* MOZART (W. A.) [Don Giovanni.—Giovinette che fate all' amore.]

— Let us meet the spring. Trio. *See* SMART (H.)

— Let us mingle bright joys. Song. *See* KING (J. L.)

— Let us mingle together. Hymn. *See* MITCHELL (W. W.)

— Let us mount. Song. *See* COSTA (*Sir* M.) A Cavallo.

— Let us not be weary. Motet. *See* TOVEY (*Sir* D. F.)

— Let us now fear the Lord. Anthem. *See* COLBORN (A. G.)

— Let us now fear the Lord our God. Anthem. *See* GOODHART (A. M.)

— Let us now fear the Lord. Anthem. *See* GRIFFITH (W.)

— Let us now fear the Lord. Anthem. *See* STEANE (B. H. D.)

— Let us now fear the Lord our God. Anthem. *See* WEST (J. E.)

— Let us now go even unto Bethlehem. Anthem. *See* BRADFORD (J.)

LET

— Let us now go even unto Bethlehem. Christmas Anthem. *See* BROWN (J.) *Organist of S. Peter's, West Bromwich.*

— Let us now go even unto Bethlehem. Anthem. *See* FIELD (J. T.)

— Let us now go even unto Bethlehem. Full Anthem. *See* HATTON (J. L.)

— Let us now go even unto Bethlehem. Anthem. *See* HOPKINS (E. J.)

— Let us now go even unto Bethlehem. Anthem. *See* KEMPTON (A.)

— Let us now go even unto Bethlehem. Anthem. *See* PEACE (F. W.)

— Let us now go even unto Bethlehem. Anthem. *See* SIMPER (C.)

— Let us now go even unto Bethlehem. Anthem. *See* STEANE (B. H. D.)

— Let us now go even unto Bethlehem. Anthem. *See* WARREN (J. C.)

— Let us now go even unto Bethlehem. Anthem. *See* WINCHESTER (E. C.)

— Let us now go even unto Bethlehem. Anthem. *See* WOODCOCK (E. W.)

— Let us now go to Bethlehem. Christmas Carol. *See* DICKINSON (M. A.)

— Let us now go unto Bethlehem. Anthem. *See* BUCKLEY (H.)

— Let us now praise famous Men. [Anthem.] *See* ARMSTRONG (G. A.)

— Let us now praise famous Men. Unison Song. *See* BANTOCK (*Sir* G.)

— Let us now praise famous Men. For choir and organ. *See* BULLOCK (*Sir* Ernest)

— Let us now praise famous Men. Anthem. *See* DAVIES (*Sir* H. W.)

— Let us now praise famous Men. [Part-song.] *See* ENGEL (L.)

— Let us now praise famous Men. Two-part choral song. *See* FINZI (Gerald)

— Let us now praise famous Men. [Anthem.] *See* FRANCIS (G. T.)

— Let us now praise famous Men. [Unison song.] *See* GALWAY (V. E.)

— Let us now praise famous Men. [Part-song.] *See* KIRK (Theron)

— Let us now praise famous Men. Anthem. *See* LANG (C. S.)

— Let us now praise famous Men. [Anthem.] *See* LEY (H. G.)

— Let us now praise famous Men. [Anthem.] *See* LINK (C. W.)

— Let us now praise famous Men. Chorus. *See* MEYER (A. H.)

— Let us now praise famous Men. Anthem. *See* NICHOLSON (*Sir* S. H.)

— Let us now praise famous Men. Unison Song. *See* PETERS (J. V.)

— Let us now praise famous Men. Anthem. *See* SILVER (A. J.)

— Let us now praise famous Men. [Part-song.] *See* THOMAS (David V.)

— Let us now praise famous Men. Anthem. *See* THORNE (E. H.)

LET

— Let us now praise famous men. Anthem. *See* WESLEY (S. S.)

— Let us now praise famous Men. Unison Song. *See* WILLIAMS (R. V.)

— Let us now praise famous Men. Anthem. *See* WOOD (T.) *Mus. Doc.*

— Let us now take Time. Chorus. *See* AUSTIN (F.)

— Let us o'er the Waters go. Unison Song. *See* DUNCAN (W. E.)

— Let us offer the Sacrifice of Praise. Anthem. *See* YOUNG (F. H.)

— Let us onward steer our way. Boat song. *See* HENSLOWE (F. H.)

— Let us part. Ballad. *See* WRIGHTON (W. T.)

— Let us pause. Song. *See* LEO (Frank)

— Let us pause in life's pleasures. *Hard times come again no more.* Song with (ad lib.) chorus [by S. C. Foster]. Arranged by M. Neiss. *London*, [1858.] fol.   **H. 1401. (18.)**

— Let us pause in life's pleasures. *Hard Times come again no more* ... Song. *London*, [1872.] fol.   **H. 1791. a. (2.)**

— Let us pause in Life's Pleasures. *Hard Times come again no more.* Song, with chorus for four voices [by S. C. Foster]. pp. 4. *Hart & Cº: London*, [c. 1890.] fol.   **H. 1860. vv. (14.)**

— Let us play at Sweethearts. Song. *See* HALL (David)

— Let us praise the Lord. Anthem. *See* BORCH (G.)

— Let us Protect. Song. *See* GLOVER (James M.)

— Let us quaff the cup of joy. [Duet.] *See* LANCELOTT (F.)

— Let us rejoice. Anthem. *See* DARST (W. G.)

— Let us rejoice. [Two-part song.] *See* PEARSON (Edith)

— Let us rejoice, the Fight is won. Carol. *See* ALDRIDGE (Richard V.)

— Let us return. Anthem. *See* GALBRAITH (J. L.)

— Let us revel and roar. Two Part Song. *See* ECCLES (J.) [The Lover's Luck.]

— Let us roam. Chorus. *See* DONIZETTI (D. G. M.) [Lucia di Lammermoor.—Percorrete le spiagge vicine.]

— Let us roam. Duet. *See* GLOVER (S.)

— Let us roam. Cavatina. *See* ROMER (F.)

— Let us roam away. Duet. *See* CHERRY (J. W.)

— Let us rove. Duet. *See* LODER (E. J.)

— Let us search and try our Ways. Anthem. *See* FLORIO (C.)

— Let us seek the yellow shore. [Song.] *See* BISHOP (*Sir* H. R.) [Maid Marian.]

— Let us shout Victory. *The Parting Song.* (Le Chant du Départ [by E. H. Méhul]. English version by Speranza.) *London*, [1874.] fol. *No.* 4562 *of the "Musical Bouquet".*   **H. 2345.**

— Let us sing a Hymn to Jesus. [Hymn.] *See* CHALLINOR (F. A.)

— Let us sing His hallow'd Praises. [Anthem.] *See* MENDELSSOHN-BARTHOLDY (J. L. F.) [Anthem for a Mezzo-Soprano Solo with Chorus. No. 4.]

— Let us sing in praise of music. [Song.] *See* WEBER (C. M. F. E. von) [Singet dem Gesang zu Ehre.]

— Let us sing Noel. [Part-song.] *See* GOULD (Raymond)

LET

— Let us sing the Christmas Song. [Christmas carol.] *See* LLOYD (K.) *Composer of Christmas carols.*

— Let us sing to Him whose Wisdom. [Hymn.] *See* DARNTON (C.)

— Let us sing together. [Part-song.] *See* HAYDN (F. J.) [Divertimento, Feldpartita, für 8 stimmigen Bläserchor. Hob. II/46.—Chorale St. Antoni.]

— Let us sing unto the Lord. Anthem. *See* FREUDENTHAL (J.) Three Psalms of David 1.

— Let us speak of a Man as we find him. Song. *See* SPORLE (Nathan J.)

— Let us spend a Day together. [Song.] pp. 5. *J. Williams: London*, [c. 1850.] fol. *[Home Gift Songs. no.* 5.]   **H. 1653. k. (15.)**

— Let us swear it by the pale Moonlight. [Song.] *See* JEROME (Benjamin M.)

— Let us take the Road. Solo and chorus. *See* BEGGAR. The Beggar's Opera.

— Let us talk of the past. Ballad. *See* BAYLY (T. H.)

— Let us teach the Heart to love. Recit & polacca. *See* ROOKE (William M.)

— Let us thank the Lord our God. Anthem. *See* BERRIDGE (A.)

— Let us thank the Lord our God. Anthem. *See* SIMPER (C.)

— Let us, the sheep by Jesus nam'd. *Hymn.* [Words by J. Cennick.] [*London*, 1778.] 8°. *Gospel Magazine, Dec.,* 1778.   **P. P. 716. b.**

— Let us then cheerily wait for the Spring. Song. *See* LINDRIDGE (G.)

— Let us think of old times. [Song.] *See* HILL (James F.)

— Let us think of the days of our youth. [Song.] *See* TEMPLETON (H.)

— Let us to the Woods away. Trio. *See* KNIGHT (H.) *Composer of vocal music.*

— Let us twine a rosy garland. Duet. *See* SPOHR (L.) [Jessonda.—Lass für ihn den ich geliebet.]

— Let us twine the clust'ring roses. [Trio.] *See* BISHOP (*Sir* H. R.)

— Let us wake. Two-part Song. *See* PURCELL (H.) [King Arthur.—You say 'tis Love.]

— Let us wander. [Part-song.] *See* PURCELL (H.)

— Let us wander by the fountain. Ballad. *See* LODER (E. J.)

— Let us wander by the ocean. Duet. *See* LODER (E. J.)

— Let us wander by the sea. Duettino. *See* SMART (H.)

— Let us wander forth alone. Ballad. *See* WALLERSTEIN (F.)

— Let us wander on unseen. [Unison song.] *See* HAENDEL (G. F.) [L'Allegro, il Pensieroso, ed il Moderato.—Let me wander not unseen.]

— Let us, with a gladsome Mind. Anthem. *See* ARNATT (Ronald K.)

— Let us with a gladsome Mind. [Hymns.] *See* B., H. C.

— Let us with a gladsome Mind. [Anthem.] *See* BLAIR (H.)

— Let us with a gladsome Mind. Anthem. *See* CHAPMAN (E. T.)

— Let us with a gladsome Mind. Anthem. *See* COOKE (G. V. T.)

LET

— Let us with a gladsome Mind. Anthem. *See* CRONHAM (Charles R.)

— Let us with a gladsome Mind. [Anthem.] *See* DURRANT (Frederick T.)

— Let us, with a gladsome Mind. Anthem. *See* ELDRIDGE (Guy H.)

— Let us, with a gladsome Mind. Unison song. *See* GRIFFITHS (Thomas V.)

— Let us, with a gladsome Mind. Anthem. *See* NICHOLSON (*Sir* Sydney H.)

— Let us with a gladsome Mind. [Anthem.] *See* RIDOUT (Alan J.)

— Let us, with a gladsome Mind. Chorale. *See* STANFORD (*Sir* C. V.)

— Let us with a gladsome Mind. Anthem. *See* THOMAS (Christopher)

— Let us with a gladsome Mind. Hymn. *See* WILSON (F. E.)

— Let us worship and fall down. [Motet.] *See* WILLAN (H.) [Six Motets. No. 6.]

— Let us worship together. [Anthem.] *See* WILSON (Harry R.)

— Let voice and heart unite. *God safe the Czar.* Russian national anthem [by A. F. L'vov]. *London*, [1874.] fol.
H. 1791. b. (35.)

— Let well enough alone. Song. *See* PHELPS (E. S.)

— Let Wine to social Joys give Birth. Song. *See* HUDSON (R.)

— Let your blue Eyes look into mine. Ballad. *See* WILLIS (Edwin)

— Let your Heart decide. [Song.] *See* RUSSELL (R. C. K.)

— Let your Heart sing. Song. *See* POPE (G.)

— Let your Light shine. Anthem. *See* PARCELL (A. E.)

— Let your Light shine. Anthem. *See* WARD (F. M.)

— Let your Light so shine. Offertory sentence. *See* BARNBY (*Sir* Joseph)

— Let your Light so shine. Anthem. *See* CALKIN (J. B.)

— Let your light so shine. [Anthem.] *See* MOODIE (W.)

— Let your Light so shine. Offertory Sentence. *See* PAYNE (G.)

— Let your Light so shine before Men. [Anthem.] *See* WILVERLEY (A.)

— Let your Mind wander over America. [Part-song.] *See* EFFINGER (Cecil)

— Let your Moderation be known. Anthem. *See* WILLIAMS (C. L.)

— Let your Tears kiss the Flowers on my Grave. Song. *See* RUTLEDGE (J. T.)

— Let your tears kiss the flowers on my grave. [Song.] *See* SAWYER (J. J.)

— Let your Trouble end in Smoke. Song. *See* WARD (G.)

— Let your Troubles all go up in Smoke. [Song.] *See* CHAMBERLIN (Bob)

— Let youthful bards, in wanton verse. *Miranda.* A New Song [by J. Wogan]. [*London*, 1753.] 8°.
Universal Magazine, Vol. XIII., p. 134. **P. P. 5439.**

— Let Zion rejoice. Anthem. *See* WOODCOCK (E. W.)

LET

— Let Zion resound with Praise. Motet. *See* LASSO (O. di) [Cantiones aliquot quinque vocum.—Resonet in laudibus.]

LETANG (E.)

— Gavotte des Duchesses, pour Piano. [*Paris,*] 1903. 8°. *Supplement to "L'Illustration," No.* 3141. **P. P. 4283. m. (3.)**

LETANIE

— *See* LITANY.

LETELIER LLONA (ALFONSO)

— Canciones antiguas para voz y piano. Ancient Songs, *etc.* pp. 12. *Pan American Union: Washington, D. C.,* [1960.] 4°.
G. 980. a. (9.)

— Ocho canciones corales. (Para voces mixtas.) pp. 18. *Instituto interamericano de musicología: Montevideo,* [1941.] fol.
[*Editorial Cooperativa interamericana de compositores. Publicación. no.* 7.] **H. 3647.**

— Cuatro canciones de cuna. (Voz de mujer y orquesta de cámara.) Partitura. pp. 22. *Instituto interamericano de musicología: Montevideo,* [1943.] fol.
[*Editorial Cooperativa interamericana de compositores. Publicación. no.* 30.] **H. 3647.**

LE TELLIER (CHARLES)

— Une Histoire de chien, racontée par lui même. [Song.] Paroles et musique de C. Le Tellier. *Chez E. Challiot: Paris,* [1850?] fol. **G. 561. (15.)**

— La Servante du Docteur. Scène comique [begins: "Je suis la petite servante"]. *Paris,* [1881.] fol. **H. 1786. e. (44.)**

LETHBRIDGE (H. O.)

Australian Aboriginal Songs

— Australian Aboriginal Songs ... Collected and translated by Dr. H. O. Lethbridge. Accompaniments arranged by Arthur S. Loam, *etc. Allan & Co.: Melbourne, etc.,* 1937. 4°.
G. 981. t. (14.)

— Three Australian Aboriginal Songs. Collected and translated by Dr. H. O. Lethbridge. Accompaniments arranged by Arthur S. Loam. *Chappell & Co.: London,* 1937. 4°.
G. 981. q. (9.)

— Australian Aboriginal Songs for Medium or Low Voice. Collected and translated by H. O. Lethbridge. Accompaniments arranged by Arthur S. Loam. [No. 1.] Jabbin, Jabbin. [No. 2.] Maranoa Lullaby. 2 no. [*G. Schirmer: New York,* 1944. 4°. **G. 981. aa. (4.)**

— Two Australian Aboriginal Songs. Arranged for equal voices by A. S. Loam. 1. Maranoa Lullaby. 2. Jabbin Jabbin ... Collected by H. O. Lethbridge. [1963.] 8°. [*Choruses for equal Voices. no.* 2550.] *See* LOAM (Arthur S.) **E. 861.**

— Jabbin Jabbin ... Aboriginal Song for Mixed Voices. Collected and translated by Dr. H. O. Lethbridge. Arranged by A. S. Loam. *Allan & Co.: Melbourne,* 1937. 8°.
F. 1771. g. (48.)

— Jabbin Jabbin ... Arranged for mixed voices S. A. T. B. by A. S. Loam ... Collected by H. O. Lethbridge, *etc.* [1963.] 8°. [*Choral Handbook.* 1529.] *See* LOAM (Arthur S.) **E. 862.**

— Maranoa Lullaby. An Australian Aboriginal Song ... Collected and translated by Dr. H. O. Lethbridge. Arranged for mixed voices unaccompanied by A. S. Loam, *etc. Allan & Co.: Melbourne, etc.,* 1937. 8°. **F. 1771. g. (49.)**

LETHBRIDGE (H. O.)

— Maranoa Lullaby ... Collected by H. O. Lethbridge.
Arranged for mixed voices by A. S. Loam. [1963.] 8°. [*Choral Handbook.* 1528.] *See* LOAM (Arthur S.)   **E. 862.**

LETHBRIDGE (LIONEL)

— Baloo, my Boy. (Lady Ann Bothwell's Lament.) [Words]
anon. 17th century Scottish melody, arranged by
L. Lethbridge. ⟨S. A. T. B.⟩ pp. 6.   *Oxford University Press:
London*, [1960.] 8°.
[*Oxford choral Songs. X 54.*]   **F. 1777. m.**

— The Brass Quartet. Volume III. Eight pieces by romantic
composers. ⟨Volume IV. Five pieces by romantic composers.⟩
Arranged by L. Lethbridge. For two trumpets in B flat and
two trombones or two trumpets in B flat, horn in F, and
trombone (with optional piano), Piano score [and parts].
2 vol. 12 pt.   *Oxford University Press: London*, [1969.] 4°.
*Vol. I and II, edited by Sidney M. Lawton, are entered under
his name.*   **g. 1110. h. (8.)**

— Three Christmas Carols from Austria and Germany.
Arranged by Lionel Lethbridge. ⟨S. S. A. (unacc.)⟩ 1. Cradle
Song (from Salzburg). ⟨2. The Nightingale. 3. Cradle Song
(from the Tyrol).⟩ English version by Lionel Lethbridge, *etc.*
pp. 4.   *Banks Music Publications: York*, [1980.] 8°.
[*Eboracum choral Series.* 108.]   **F. 1874. x.**

— A First Organ Album. Edited by L. Lethbridge. Six short,
easy pieces by J. S. Bach, Buxtehude, Frescobaldi, and
Walther. pp. 7.   *Oxford University Press: London*, [1958.] fol.
          g. 1380. ff. (22.)

— Six French Carols (in two sets). Arranged [with English
words] by Lionel Lethbridge. ⟨S. S. A. (unacc.)⟩ 2 no.   *Banks
Music Publications: York*, [1976.] 8°.
[*Eboracum choral Series.* 57 a, b.]   **F. 1874. x.**

— Mélodies de France. Arranged ⟨from the music of
nineteenth-century composers⟩ by L. Lethbridge. ⟨For oboe
and piano.⟩ [Score and part.] 2 pt.   *Oxford University Press:
London*, [1966.] 4°.   **g. 1078. m. (2.)**

— Opera Song Book. Ten ⟨Eight⟩ operatic choruses for unison,
two-part, or SAB voices and piano. Arranged by Lionel
Lethbridge. 2 bk.   *Oxford University Press: London*, [1967.] 8°.
          **F. 1267. vv. (5.)
& F. 931. (2.)**

— Eight Solos for Horn in F. From Handel: Messiah and
Haydn: The Creation. Arranged and edited by L. Lethbridge.
pp. 8.   *Oxford University Press: London*, [1962.] 4°.
          g. 1094. g. (13.)

— Tell me where is Fancy bred. [Words by] Shakespeare, *etc.*
⟨Two-part.⟩ pp. 4.   *Oxford University Press: London*, [1963.]
8°.
[*Oxford Choral Songs. T 64.*]   **F. 1777. m.**

— *See* BACH (J. S.) [*Collected Works.—f.*] An Album for
Manuals only. Selected and edited by L. Lethbridge, *etc.*
[1959.] 4°.   **g. 699. u. (11.)**

— *See* BACH (J. S.) [Geistliche Lieder aus Schemelli's
Gesangbuch und aus dem Notenbuch der Anna Magdalena
Bach.] Communion Service. Adapted from the melodies of
J. S. Bach by L. Lethbridge. [1957.] 8°. [*Parish Choir Book.*
1342.]   **E. 618.**

— *See* BACH (J. S.) [Notenbuch der Anna Magdalena Bach ...
1725. No. 20b. So oft ich meine Tabakspfeife.] Open my
Heart ... Melody by J. S. Bach arranged by L. Lethbridge.
⟨S.A.T.B.⟩ [1961.] 8°. [*Oxford Anthems. A* 171.)   **F. 1776.**

— *See* BYRD (William) [La Volta. Fellowes No. 1.] This little
Babe. A Christmas song ... Arranged by L. Lethbridge.
[1962.] 8°. [*Oxford choral Songs from the old Masters. OM* 48.]
          F. 1777. n.

LETHBRIDGE (LIONEL)

— *See* DEBUSSY (C. A.) Mandoline ... Arranged by
L. Lethbridge. ⟨Two-part or unison.⟩ [1970.] 8°. [*Oxford choral
Songs. T* 101.]   **F. 1777. m.**

— *See* DELIBES (C. P. L.) [Lakmé.—Sous le ciel tout étoilé.]
Indian Song ... arrangement by L. Lethbridge. [1965.] 8°.
[*Oxford choral Songs. no. W.* 61.]   **F. 1777. m.**

— *See* DELIBES (C. P. L.) [Lakmé.—Sous le dôme épais.]
Barcarolle ... Arranged ... by L. Lethbridge, *etc.* [S. A.]
[1968.] 8°. [*Two-part Songs.* 384.]   **F. 280. e.**

— *See* FRANCK (C. A. J. G. H.) [6 duos. No. 1. L'Ange gardien.]
The Guardian Angel ... Arranged for four-part choir,
unaccompanied ... by L. Lethbridge. [1957.] 8°.
          E. 442. z. (14.)

— *See* FRANCK (C. A. J. G. H.) [6 duos. No. 2. Aux petits enfants.]
The Three Kings at Bethlehem. Carol ... Arranged by
L. Lethbridge. [1959.] 8°.   **F. 260. n. (16.)**

— *See* FRANCK (C. A. J. G. H.) [6 duos. No. 3. La Vierge à la
crèche.] Mary at the Crib ... Arranged for four-part choir
unaccompanied ... by L. Lethbridge. [1957.] 8°.
          F. 260. h. (20.)

— *See* GRIEG (E. H.) [2 elegische Melodien. Op. 34. No. 2.
Letzter Frühling.] The Last Springtime ... Arranged by
L. Lethbridge. ⟨S. S. A. T. B.⟩ [1961.] 8°.   **F. 647. f. (5.)**

— *See* HAENDEL (G. F.) [*Collected Works.—h.*] A Handel Solo
Album. For trumpet or trombone & piano (or bassoon &
piano). Arranged & edited by L. Lethbridge. [1971.] 4°.
          g. 1320. a. (5.)

— *See* HAENDEL (G. F.) [Rinaldo.—Lascia ch'io pianga.]
Evening Hymn ... Adapted by L. Lethbridge. ⟨S. A. T. B.⟩
[1973.] 8°. [*Oxford easy Anthems.* 134.]   **F. 1001.**

— *See* HAENDEL (G. F.) [Suites de pièces. 1st collection. No. 8.]
Prelude and Fugue in F minor ... Arranged by L. Lethbridge.
[Organ.] [1962.] 4°.   **g. 61. c. (8.)**

— *See* MAHLER (G.) [Des Knaben Wunderhorn.—Lob des
hohen Verstands.] The Cuckoo, the Nightingale, and the
Donkey ... Arranged ... by L. Lethbridge. ⟨Two-part.⟩
[*Oxford choral Songs. T* 75.]   **F. 1777. m.**

— *See* MAHLER (G.) [Des Knaben Wunderhorn.—
Rheinlegendchen.] Rhine Legend ... Arranged by
L. Lethbridge. ⟨Two-part (or unison).⟩ [1966.] 8°. [*Oxford
choral Songs. T* 84.]   **F. 1777. m.**

— *See* MAHLER (G.) [14 Lieder und Gesänge. Hft. 2. No. 1. Um
schlimme Kinder artig zu machen.] The Knight and the
hateful Children ... ⟨Two-part (or unison).⟩ Arranged, with
English words, by L. Lethbridge. [1966.] 8°. [*Oxford choral
Songs. T* 85.]   **F. 1777. m.**

— *See* MARCELLO (B.) [Estro poetico-armonico.—Psalm 45.]
Heart's Adoration ... ⟨Two-part⟩ ... Adapted by
L. Lethbridge. [1971.] 8°. [*Oxford easy Anthems. E* 122.]
          F. 1001.

— *See* MASSENET (J. É. F.) Madrigal ... Arranged by
L. Lethbridge. [Two-part song.] [1963.] 8°. [*Oxford choral
Songs. T* 60.]   **F. 1777. m.**

— *See* MASSENET (J. É. F.) [Werthur.—Du gai soleil plein de
flamme.] Arietta ... Arranged by L. Lethbridge. ⟨Two-part.⟩
[1963.] 8°. [*Oxford Choral Songs. T* 61.]   **F. 1777. m.**

— *See* MOSZKOWSKI (Moritz) [Spanische Tänze. Op. 12. No. 2,
5.] 2 Spanish Dances. Arranged for clarinet in B flat and
piano by L. Lethbridge. [1977.] 4°.   **f. 568. f. (3.)**

— *See* MOZART (W. A.) [*Collected Works.—c.*] A Mozart Solo
Album. For trumpet in B♭ (or trombone) and piano (or
bassoon and piano). Arranged and edited by L. Lethbridge,
etc. [1959.] 4°.   **g. 382. a. (4.)**

LETHBRIDGE (LIONEL)

— *See* MOZART (W. A.) [Vesperae solennes de confessore. K. 339. No. 5.] Laudate Dominum ... Arranged by L. Lethbridge. ⟨S. S. A.⟩ [1971.] 8°. [*Oxford choral Songs. W*90.]
F. 1777. m.

— *See* RAMEAU (Jean P.) [Les Indes galantes.] Four Oboe Melodies ... arranged for oboe and piano by L. Lethbridge. [1976.] 4°.
g. 82. c. (2.)

— *See* SAINT-SAËNS (C. C.) [Le Carnaval des animaux.] Two Pieces ... Arranged for bassoon and piano by L. Lethbridge, *etc.* [1974.] 4°.
g. 270. ll. (16.)

— *See* SAINT-SAËNS (C. C.) [Le Carnaval des animaux.] Two Pieces ... arranged for clarinet and piano by L. Lethbridge, *etc.* [1974.] 4°.
g. 1104. rr. (8.)

— *See* SCHUBERT (F. P.) [*Collected Works.—h.*] Nature's Harmony. A choral suite for soprano and alto voices (3-part) and piano ... Adapted by L. Lethbridge, *etc.* [1970.] 8°.
F. 409. pp. (17.)

— *See* SULLIVAN (*Sir* Arthur S.) Sigh no more Ladies ... Arranged by L. Lethbridge. [1961.] 8°. [*Oxford choral Songs. U*69.]
F. 1777. m.

— *See* VERDI (F. G. F.) [*Collections, Instrumental.*] A Verdi Solo Album. For trumpet or trombone and piano (or bassoon and piano). Arranged and edited by L. Lethbridge. [1977.] 4°.
h. 1492. r. (1.)

LETHE

Lethe

— The Card invites. [Song, by T. A. Arne.] Sung by Mrs. Clive in Lethe. [Words by D. Garrick.] [*London*, 1760?] *s. sh.* fol.
I. 530. (87.)

— Ye mortals whom fancies and troubles perplex. *A Song in Lethe.* [By William Boyce.] Sung by Mr. Beard, in the Character of Mercury. [Written by D. Garrick.] [*London*, 1749.] 8°.
Gentleman's Magazine, Vol. XIX., p. 323.
249. c. 19.

— Ye mortals whom fancies and troubles perplex. *Song in Mr. Garrick's Lethe.* [By William Boyce.] Sung by Mr. Beard. [*London*, 1749.] 8°.
London Magazine, 1749, *p.* 36.
157. l. 11.

— Ye Mortals whom Fancies and Troubles perplex. *A Song in Lethe.* [By William Boyce.] [Written by D. Garrick.] Sung by Mercury. [*London*, 1750?] *s. sh.* fol.
G. 295. (20.)

— [Another copy.]
H. 1994. a. (19.)

— [Another edition.] Ye Mortals whom Fancies and Troubles perplex. *A Song in Lethe.* [By William Boyce.] [*London*, 1755?] *s. sh.* fol.
H. 1994. b. (109.)

— [Another edition.] Ye Mortals whom Fancies and Troubles perplex. *A Song in Lethe.* [By William Boyce.] [Written by D. Garrick.] Sung by Mr. Beard in the Character of Mercury. Within Compass of German Flute. *See* CHLOE. Chloe, or the Musical Magazine, *etc.* No. 61. [1760?] fol.
G. 433.

— Ye Mortals whom Fancies and Troubles perplex. A favorite song in Lethe. [c. 1770.] *s. sh.* fol.
Followed by an accompaniment for guitar or German flute.
I. 596. (48.)

— The Lethe. Song. *See* BATSON (A. W.)

— Lethe. Song. *See* BOOTT (F.)

— Lethe. [Song.] *See* HERZOGENBERG (H. von) Vier Gesänge ... Op. 40. No. 3.

LETHE

— Lethe. Song. *See* KELLIE (L.) New Album of Ten ... Songs ... No. 5.

— Lethe. [Song.] *See* PALMER (C.) Two Songs, *etc.* [No. 2.]

— Lethe. [Song with orchestra.] *See* PFITZNER (H.)

— Lethe. Song. *See* PHILLIPS (M. F.)

— Lethe. [Song.] *See* ROBBINS (R. C.) Songs ... 149.

— Die Lethe des Lebens. Trinklied. *See* WEBER (C. M. F. E. von) [Lieder und Gesänge. Op. 66. No. 5.]

— Lethe's Stream. [Song.] *See* BRUCE (Michael)

LETHE

— Be thou that dove. Song [begins: "Oh! fairest, oh! purest"]. Words by T. Moore. Music by Lethe. *London*, [1874.] fol.
H. 1178. y. (16.)

LE THIERE (CHARLES)

— The Allies. Patriotic March. [Small orchestra. Parts.] *Cinema Music Co.: London & New York*, (1915.) 4°.
No. 2 of "The Cinema Music Journal".
g. 1434.

— L'Allouette des Champs. Polka for Piccolo. [Orchestral parts.] *London*, [1884.] 8°.
Part of the "Alliance Musicale".
f. 400. gg. (12.)

— Les Alsachiennes. Divertisment [*sic*] for clarinet in B♭. [Military band parts.] 26 pt. *S. A. Chappell: London*, [1885.] fol.
[*Army Journal. no.* 164.]
h. 1562.

— "Alvanian." ⟨Divertissement for B♭ clarinet.⟩ [Military band parts.] 22 pt. *In:* WALDTEUFEL (E.) "Etincelles," *etc.* 1896. fol.
[*Boosey's supplemental military Journal. no.* 399.]
h. 1544.

— Amourette. Polka. [Orchestral parts.] *See* FRANCIS AND DAY. Francis & Day's String Band Journal ... No. 21. [1886–8.] 8°.
e. 1341.

— Amourette. Polka. [Fife and drum band parts.] *London*, [1882.] 8°.
f. 414. a. (47.)

— Andalucia. Valse. [P. F.] *Francis Bros. & Day: London*, [1889.] fol.
h. 3285. q. (37.)

— Andante and Polonaise. *See infra:* [Californian.]

— Belgravia. Quick March. [Reed band parts.] *London*, [1883.] 8°.
f. 412. q. (14.)

— Belle Vue. Fantasia. Op. 110. [Reed band parts.] *Rivière & Hawkes: London*, [1887.] 8°.
e. 372. f. (1.)

— The Bohemian. Bolero. [Reed band parts.] *London*, [1885.] 8°.
Part of the "Alliance Musicale".
f. 401. aa. (15.)

— Bohemian Dance for flute and pianoforte. · *Rudall, Carte & Co.: London*, [1892.] fol.
h. 234. (26.)

— Bolero, for flute and pianoforte. *Rudall, Carte & Co.: London*, [1892.] fol.
h. 234. (27.)

— [Californian.] "Andante and Polonaise." ⟨Clarionet solo. Conductor [and military band parts].⟩ 29 pt. *In:* BOHM (C.) "Auf Schwingen der Liebe," *etc.* 1903. fol. [*Boosey's supplemental military Journal. no.* 444.]
h. 1544.

— Californian. Andante and Polonaise, *etc.* [Clarinet and P. F.] *Cundy-Bettoney Co.: Boston, Mass.*, (1912.) 4°.
g. 1104. (4.)

— Caracalla. Quick March. [Reed band parts.] *London*, [1884.] 8°.
Part of the "Alliance Musical".
f. 401. aa. (13.)

LE THIERE (CHARLES)

— Le Charme. Gavotte. [Orchestral parts.] *See* FRANCIS AND DAY. Francis & Day's String Band Journal ... No. 39. [1886–8.] 8°.   **e. 1341.**

— Le Charme. Gavotte. [P. F.] *Francis Bros. & Day: London,* [1884.] fol.   **h. 1484. t. (6.)**

— Chords of Memory. Ballad, words by N. Taillefer. *S. Lucas, Weber & Co.: London,* [1883.] fol.   **H. 1788. v. (48.)**

— Clarions. Slow March. [Reed band parts.] *Rivière & Hawkes: London,* [1887.] 8°.   **e. 372. f. (7.)**

— Clear the Road. Galop. Op. 91. [Orchestral parts.] *Rivière & Hawkes: London,* [1887.] 8°.   **e. 370. g. (8.)**

— Clear the Road. Galop. [Reed band parts.] *Rivière & Hawkes: London,* [1887.] 8°.   **e. 372. f. (5.)**

— Clear the road. Galop. (Op. 91.) [P. F.] *Rivière & Hawkes: London,* [1887.] fol.   **h. 975. v. (23.)**

— Les Cuirassiers. Galop. [Brass band parts.] *London,* [1883.] 8°.   **f. 402. e. (21.)**

— Danse de Satyrs. [Orchestral parts and P. F.] *See* FRANCIS AND DAY. Francis & Day's String Band Journal ... No. 27. [1886–8.] 8°.   **e. 1341.**

— Danse de Satyrs, arranged by R. Dyke. [Fife and drum band parts.] *London,* [1883.] 8°. Part of the "Alliance Musicale".   **f. 403. f. (37.)**

— Danse de Satyrs. Caprice pour piano. pp. 7. *Francis Broˢ & Day: London,* [c. 1885.] fol.   **h. 61. pp. (4.)**

— Danse des Aborigenes. [Orchestral parts.] *See* FRANCIS AND DAY. Francis & Day's String Band Journal ... No. 49. [1886–8.] 8°.   **e. 1341.**

— Danse des aborigènes. [Military band parts.] 26 pt. *In:* STRAUSS (J.) *the Younger.* "Wiener Bon-bons," *etc.* 1883. fol. [*Boosey's supplemental military Journal. no.* 323.]   **h. 1544.**

— Danse des Aborigènes. [Fife and drum band parts.] *London,* [1885.] 8°. Part of the "Alliance Musical".   **f. 403. f. (38.)**

— Danse des Aborigènes, pour piano. *Francis Bros. & Day: London,* [1884.] fol.   **h. 1484. t. (7.)**

— Danse des Maoris. Op. 45. Danse caractéristique. [P. F.] *J. B. Cramer & Co.: London,* [1887.] fol.   **h. 1484. t. (8.)**

— Danse Fantastique. [Orchestral parts.] *See* FRANCIS AND DAY. Francis & Day's String Band Journal ... No. 18. [1886–8.] 8°.   **e. 1341.**

— Danse fantastique pour Piano. *London,* [1882.] fol.   **h. 3275. j. (34.)**

— Danse Irlandaise.—Irish dance. [P. F. and orchestral parts.] *London,* [1883.] 8°.   **f. 410. k. (6.)**

— Dreams of Venice. Barcarolle. Mandoline Solo, with Pianoforte accompaniments and additional parts for 2nd Mandoline and Guitar. *W. J. Fletcher: London,* [1896.] fol.   **h. 188. e. (31.)**

— Eclat. Gavotte. [Reed band parts.] *Rivière & Hawkes: London,* [1887.] 8°.   **e. 372. f. (6.)**

— Egypt. March for the pianoforte. *Francis Bros. & Day: London,* [1884.] fol.   **h. 1484. t. (9.)**

— Elka. Quick March. [Reed band parts.] *Rivière & Hawkes: London,* [1887.] 8°.   **e. 372. f. (9.)**

— L'Encore. Polacca. Solo for Piccolo [with P. F. accompaniment], *etc. Cundy-Bettoney Co.: Boston, Mass.,* (1913.) 4°.   **g. 70. f. (1.)**

LE THIERE (CHARLES)

— L'Esprit Français ... Marche-Fantaisie. [P. F.] *Francis, Day & Hunter: London,* [1890.] fol.   **h. 1489. s. (46.)**

— Falling Stars. Polka. Op. 90. [Piccolo and P. F.] *Rivière & Hawkes: London,* [1887.] fol. No. 66 of The Concert Edition.   **g. 790. (22.)**

— Fantasia on Weber's last Valse. Op. 104. [Clarinet and P. F.] *Rivière & Hawkes: London,* [1887.] fol. No. 68 of The Concert Edition.   **g. 790. (40.)**

— Fantasia on Weber's last Valse. Op. 104. [Flute and P. F.] *Rivière & Hawkes: London,* [1887.] fol. No. 67 of The Concert Edition.   **g. 790. (28.)**

— Feu de Joie. Galop. [Orchestral parts and P. F.] *See* FRANCIS AND DAY. Francis & Day's String Band Journal ... No. 43. [1886–8.] 8°.   **e. 1341.**

— Feu de Joie. Galop. [Reed band parts.] *London,* [1883.] 8°.   **f. 412. r. (1.)**

— Feu de Joie. Galop. [P. F.] *Francis Bros. and Day: London,* [1884.] fol.   **h. 975. v. (24.)**

— Fleur d'Or. Gavotte. [P. F.] *J. & J. Hopkinson: London,* [1886.] fol.   **h. 1484. t. (10.)**

— Gipsy Life. Descriptive Fantasia. [Orchestral parts.] 18 pt. *Rivière & Hawkes: London; Leipzig* [printed, 1887.] 4°. *Compositions for Orchestra. no. 9.*   **g. 1800. (203.)**

— Gipsy Life. (Original fantasia.) [Military band parts.] 27 pt. *S. A. Chappell: London,* [1885.] fol. [*Army Journal. no.* 163.]   **h. 1562.**

— The Gipsy Queen. Bolero. [Reed band parts.] *London,* [1883.] 8°.   **f. 412. r. (2.)**

— Golden Ensign. Polka March. Mandoline Solo with Pianoforte accompaniment. Additional ad lib. parts for 2nd Mandoline and Guitar. *W. J. Fletcher: London,* [1895.] fol.   **h. 188. e. (32.)**

— The Grenade. Quick March. [Reed band parts.] *Rivière & Hawkes: London,* [1887.] 8°.   **e. 372. f. (8.)**

— Hecla. Polka. [Orchestral parts.] 17 pt. *Lafleur & Son: London,* [1892.] 8°. Part of the "Alliance Musicale".   **f. 800. (815.)**

— Home, sweet Home. Fantasia [for clarinet and P. F.]. Op. 94. *Rivière & Hawkes: London,* [1887.] fol. No. 45 of The Concert Edition.   **g. 790. (39.)**

— Honeymoon Polka. [Orchestral parts.] *Rivière & Hawkes: London,* [1887.] 8°.   **e. 370. g. (7.)**

— Honeymoon Polka. [Reed band parts.] *Rivière & Hawkes: London,* [1887.] 8°.   **e. 372. f. (3.)**

— Honeymoon Polka. Piano solo. *Rivière & Hawkes: London,* [1887.] fol.   **h. 975. v. (25.)**

— Inésilla. Quick March. [Reed band parts.] *Rivière & Hawkes: London,* [1887.] 8°.   **e. 372. f. (4.)**

— The Irish Guards Patrol. [P. F.] *W. Paxton: London,* [1901.] fol.   **h. 3282. w. (44.)**

— Jolly Boys at Sea. A nautical and vocal polka. [Song.] Words by C. Baron. pp. 3. *F. W. Hetherington: London,* [1902.] fol.   **H. 3985. x. (39.)**

— Libua March. [Reed band parts.] *Rivière & Hawkes: London,* [1887.] 8°.   **e. 667. c. (1.)**

— Libua March. [P. F.] *Rivière & Hawkes: London,* [1889.] 8°.   **f. 133. j. (7.)**

— Love's Adieu. Vocal Waltz. [Orchestral and vocal parts.] *Rivière & Hawkes: London,* [1887.] 8°.   **e. 370. g. (6.)**

LE THIERE (Charles)

— Love's Adieu. Valse. [Fife and drum band parts.] *Rivière & Hawkes: London*, [1887.] 8°.   **f. 414. b. (21.)**

— Love's Adieu. Vocal Waltz. Op. 79. [Reed band parts.] *Rivière & Hawkes: London*, [1887.] 8°.   **e. 372. f. (14.)**

— Love's Adieu! Vocal-Valse. (Op. 79.) Piano solo. *Rivière & Hawkes: London*, [1887.] fol.   **h. 975. v. (26.)**

— Lucerne. Quick March. [Reed band parts.] *London*, [1885.] 8°.
Part of the "Alliance Musicale".   **f. 401. aa. (14.)**

— Marche Indienne. Characteristic piece. Op. 160. [Orchestral parts.] *Rivière & Hawkes: London*, [1887.] 8°.   **e. 370. g. (9.)**

— Marche indienne. Characteristic piece. ⟨Op. 160.⟩ 1st B♭ clarinet conductor [and military band parts]. 21 pt. *Rivière & Hawkes: London*, [1887.] 4°.
Compositions for Military Bands. no. 91.   **g. 1800. (204.)**

— The Merry Prince. Polka. Op. 82. [Orchestral parts.] *Rivière & Hawkes: London*, [1887.] 8°.   **e. 370. g. (5.)**

— The Merry Prince. [Reed band parts.] *Rivière & Hawkes: London*, [1887.] 8°.   **e. 372. f. (11.)**

— Merry Prince. Polka. (Op. 82.) [P. F.] *Rivière & Hawkes: London*, [1887.] fol.   **h. 975. v. (27.)**

— Moonlight in the Forest and Dance of the Nymphs. Op. 140. [Orchestral parts.] *Rivière & Hawkes: London*, [1887.] 8°.   **e. 370. g. (11.)**

— Moonlight in the Forest and Dance of the Nymphs ... Op. 140. 1st B♭ clarinet conductor [and military band parts]. 20 pt. *Rivière & Hawkes: London*, [1887.] 4°.
Compositions for Military Band. no. 106. Various parts are in duplicate.   **g. 1800. (205.)**

— Moonlight in the Forest, and Dance of the Nymphs. Descriptive piece. (Op. 140.) [P. F.] *Rivière & Hawkes: London*, [1887.] fol.   **h. 1484. t. (11.)**

— Nabuco. Troop. [On Verdi's opera, 'Nabucodonosor'. Reed band parts.] *Rivière & Hawkes: London*, [1887.] 8°.   **e. 372. f. (15.)**

— Nocturne & Gavotte, for flute and pianoforte. *Rudall, Carte & Co.: London*, [1882.] fol.   **h. 234. (28.)**

— L'Oiseau du Bois. Polacca de Concert. [Orchestral parts and P. F.] *See* FRANCIS AND DAY. Francis & Day's String Band Journal ... No. 32. [1886–8.] 8°.   **e. 1341.**

— Six Original Solos (Turner's Second Album of Six Original Solos) for the Piccolo or Flute, with Pianoforte accompaniments & a separate Piccolo part, composed & arranged by C. Le Thiere. 2 no. *J. A. Turner: London*, [1898–1905.] 4°.   **f. 759. (3.)**

— Two Pieces. [Flute and P. F.] *Rudall, Carte & Co.: London*, [1896.] fol.
Part of "Leaflets, a Journal of Music for Flute and Pianoforte".   **h. 2103. (6.)**

— Polka de la Reine ... Piccolo Solo [with P. F. and orchestral accompaniment. Parts]. *Cundy Bettoney Co.: Boston, Mass.*, (1913.) 4° & 8°.   **g. 70. f. (6.)**

— Punjaub. March. Arranged by C. Le Thiere. [Orchestral parts.] *Rivière & Hawkes: London*, [1887.] 8°.   **e. 370. g. (3.)**

— Punjaub. Quick March, arr^d. by C. Le Thiere. [Fife and drum band parts.] *Rivière & Hawkes: London*, [1887.] 8°.   **f. 414. b. (22.)**

— Punjaub. Quick March. Arranged by C. Le Thiere. [Reed band parts.] *Rivière & Hawkes: London*, [1887.] 8°.   **e. 372. f. (10.)**

LE THIERE (Charles)

— Punjaub. March, arranged by C. Le Thière. [P. F.] *Rivière & Hawkes: London*, [1887.] fol.   **h. 1484. t. (12.)**

— Queen of Hearts. Gavotte. Op. 214. [Orchestral parts.] *Rivière & Hawkes: London*, [1887.] 8°.   **e. 370. g. (10.)**

— Queen of Hearts ... Gavotte. (Op. 214.) [P. F.] *Rivière & Hawkes: London*, [1887.] fol.   **h. 1484. t. (13.)**

— Ragtimemania. Cake Walk des Coons, words by N. Atkins. [P. F.] *F. W. Hetherington: London*, [1902.] fol.   **g. 605. ee. (36.)**

— Ramleh. Quick March. [Reed band parts.] *Rivière & Hawkes: London*, [1887.] 8°.   **e. 372. f. (2.)**

— The Return home. Quick March. [Reed band parts.] *London*, [1883.] 8°.   **f. 412. q. (15.)**

— The Rival Lovers. Characteristic serenade. [Orchestral parts.] 16 pt. *J. R. Lafleur & Son: London; Paris* [printed, 1892.] 8°.   **f. 800. (816.)**

— Descriptive Fantasia (original) "Roman Life". C. Le Thière. ⟨[Followed by] Song without Words. (Cornet solo.) G. P. Hans.—Polonaise de concert. For B♭ cornet. Warwick Williams.⟩ ⟨Conductor [and military band parts].⟩ 33 pt. *Boosey & Co.: London*, [1911.] fol.
[*Boosey's military Journal. ser. 129. no. 6.*]   **h. 1549.**

— Romance and Bolero. Solo for B♭ clarinet. Arranged for military band by W. J. Duthoit. ⟨Conductor [and parts].⟩ 32 pt. *In:* PURCELL (Henry) [*Doubtful and Suppositious Works.*] Trumpet Voluntary, *etc.* [1966?] fol. [*Chappell's Army Journal. no. 686.*]   **h. 1562.**

— Romance & Polacca. For B flat clarionet solo. [Military band parts.] 24 pt. *In:* PROUT (Edwin H.) Valse "The Cloister," *etc.* 1885. fol. [*Boosey's military Journal. ser. 78. no. 5.*]   **h. 1549.**

— Romance and Polacca for Clarionet and Pianoforte. *Boosey & Co.: London*, [1885.] fol.   **h. 2189. e. (7.)**

— Romance and Polonaise. [Flute and P. F.] *Rudall, Carte & Co.: London*, [1884.] fol.
Part of "The Flute Player's Journal. First Series".   **h. 232. a. (16.)**

— Roquefort. Quick march. Solo B♭ conductor & 1st cornet [and wind band parts]. 33 pt. *J. R. Lafleur & Son: London*, [1892.] 8°.
The conductor part is in duplicate.   **f. 800. (817.)**

— The Royal Guards. Quick March. Op. 132. [Orchestral parts.] *Rivière & Hawkes: London*, [1887.] 8°.   **e. 370. g. (12.)**

— The Royal Guards. Quick March. [Reed band parts.] *Rivière & Hawkes: London*, [1887.] 8°.   **e. 372. f. (13.)**

— The Royal Guards. (Pas redoublé. Op. 132.) [P. F.] *Rivière & Hawkes: London*, [1887.] fol.   **h. 1484. t. (14.)**

— Scherzo brillante. Solo for piccolo ... Arrd. by A. Morelli. F piccolo [and fife and drum band parts]. 8 pt. *J. R. Lafleur & Son: London*, [1892.] 8°.
Part of "Alliance Musicale".   **f. 800. (818.)**

— Serenade. Op. 55. [Bassoon and P. F.] *Rivière & Hawkes: London*, [1887.] fol.
No. 85 of The Concert Edition.   **g. 790. (46.)**

— Serenade. Op. 55. [Euphonium and P. F.] *Rivière & Hawkes: London*, [1887.] fol.
Part of The Concert Edition.   **g. 790. (56.)**

— Serenade. Op. 55. [For flute solo with pianoforte accompaniment.] *Rivière & Hawkes: London*, [1887.] fol.
No. 23 of The Concert Edition.   **g. 790. (24.)**

LE THIERE (Charles)

— Serenade. Op. 55. [Trombone and P. F.] *Rivière & Hawkes: London*, [1887.] fol.
No. 21 of The Concert Edition. **g. 790. (59.)**

— Serenade. Op. 55. [Violin and P. F.] *Rivière & Hawkes: London*, [1887.] fol.
No. 19 of The Concert Edition. **g. 790. (3.)**

— Serenade. Op. 55. [Violoncello and P. F.] *Rivière & Hawkes: London*, [1887.] fol.
No. 21 of The Concert Edition. **g. 790. (15.)**

— Silver Birds. [Orchestral and P. F. parts.] *J. R. Lafleur & Son: London*, [1887.] 8°.
Part of the "Alliance Musicale". **f. 400. ll. (3.)**

— Silver Birds. Valse. [Reed band parts.] *J. R. Lafleur & Son: London*, [1887.] 8°.
Part of the "Alliance Musicale". **f. 401. ff. (1.)**

— Solos [Mandoline] with Pianoforte accompaniment, *etc. See* TURNER (J. A.) Turner's Mandoline Journal, *etc.* No. 20. [1898, *etc.*] 4°. **f. 581.**

— Sylvia. Scherzo. Piccolo solo [and orchestral parts.] 17 pt. *Rivière & Hawkes: London*, [1887.] 4°.
Compositions for orchestra. no. 85. The 1ˢᵗ cornet part is in duplicate. **g. 1800. (206.)**

— Sylvia. Scherzo. Piccolo solo [and military band parts]. 21 pt. *Rivière & Hawkes: London*, [1887.] 4°.
Compositions for Military Bands. no. 90. Various parts are in duplicate. **g. 1800. (207.)**

— Sylvia. Scherzo. [P. F.] *Rivière & Hawkes: London*, [1887.] fol. **h. 1484. t. (15.)**

— Sylvia. Scherzo. [Piccolo and P. F.] *Rivière & Hawkes: London*, [1887.] fol.
No. 86 of the Concert Edition. **g. 790. (23.)**

— Syringa Waltz, for flute and pianoforte. *Rudall, Carte & Co.: London*, [1889.] fol. **h. 234. (31.)**

— Theodora. Gavotte. Op. 78. [Orchestral parts.] *Rivière & Hawkes: London*, [1887.] 8°. **e. 370. g. (4.)**

— Theodora. Gavotte. [Fife and drum band parts.] *Rivière & Hawkes: London*, [1887.] 8°. **f. 414. b. (23.)**

— Theodora. Gavotte. ⟨Op. 78.⟩ Solo clarinet B♭ [and military band parts]. 22 pt. *Rivière & Hawkes: London*, [1887.] 4°.
Military Band Music. New edition. no. 30. Various parts are in duplicate. **g. 1800. (208.)**

— Theodora. Gavotte. (Op. 78.) [P. F.] *Rivière & Hawkes: London*, [1887.] fol. **h. 1484. t. (16.)**

— Turner's Complete Tutor for the Coach Horn, Post or Tandem Horn, Bugle and Cavalry Trumpet, giving ... a great variety of Road & Military Calls, Arranged by C. Le Thiere. *J. A. Turner: London*, [1898.] 4°. **f. 581. c. (17.)**

— Turner's Universal Tutor for the Cornet ... Arranged by C. Le Thiere. *J. A. Turner: London*, [1898.] 4°. **f. 581. c. (19.)**

— Turner's Universal Tutor for the Musette ... Arranged by C. Le Thiere. *J. A. Turner: London*, [1898.] 4°. **f. 581. c. (18.)**

— Turner's Universal Tutor for the Piccolo, *etc. J. A. Turner: London*, [1898.] 4°. **f. 581. c. (16.)**

— Tyrolienne for flute and pianoforte. *Rudall, Carte & Co.: London*, [1892.] fol. **h. 234. (30.)**

— Union. Suite de Valses for the pianoforte. *F. W. Hetherington: London*, 1895. fol. **h. 3285. q. (38.)**

LE THIERE (Charles)

— Valse for flute and pianoforte. *Rudall, Carte & Co.: London*, [1892.] fol. **h. 234. (29.)**

— The Warrior. Quick March. [Fife and drum band parts.] *Rivière & Hawkes: London*, [1887.] fol. **f. 414. b. (24.)**

— The Warrior. Quick March. [Reed band parts.] *Rivière & Hawkes: London*, [1887.] 8°. **e. 372. f. (12.)**

— *See* BALFE (M. W.) [The Bohemian Girl. — Instrumental selections. — (c.)] Fantasia ... arr. by C. Le Thière. [1887.] fol. **g. 790. (41.)**

— *See* BALFE (M. W.) [The Bohemian Girl. — Instrumental selctions. — (c.)] Fantasia ... Arr. by C. Le Thière. [1887.] fol. **g. 790. (30.)**

— *See* BEETHOVEN (L. van) [Septet. Op. 20.] Beethoven's Minuet ... Transcribed by C. le Thière. ⟨Piano and violin.⟩ [c. 1890.] fol. **h. 1613. v. (2.)**

— *See* BUCK (Dudley) When the Heart is young. Song, *etc.* ⟨Arranged by C. le Thière.⟩ [c. 1900.] fol. **H. 1860. vv. (10.)**

— *See* BISHOP (*Sir* H. R.) [The Comedy of Errors.] Lo! here the gentle Lark ... arranged as a Duett for Flute and Clarinet by C. Le Thière. [1887.] fol. **g. 790. (38.)**

— *See* TURNER (J. A.) Turner's Ocarina Journal, *etc.* (No. 2. Containing six ... Solos ... by C. Le Thière.) [1898.] 4°. **f. 759. (5.)**

LETI

— Лети в Москву, соловушко. [Song.] *See* VASIL'EV-BUGLAI (D. S.)

LETNYAYA

— Лѣтняя ночь. [Song.] *See* ARENSKY (A. S.) [Шесть романсовъ. Op. 44. No. 2.]

LETO

— Leto, blessed Leto. [Song.] *See* KING (Godfré R.)

LETOCART (H.)

— Chant funèbre. *See* BELLAIRS (R. H.) The Enoch Organ Library, *etc.* No. 10. 1906. 4°. **g. 1283.**

— Pièce pour Harmonium. [*Paris*,] 1903. 8°.
Supplement to "L'Illustration", No. 3166. **P. P. 4283. m. (3.)**

LETOCART (Henry)

— *See* CHARPENTIER (M. A.) Messe de minuit sur des airs de Noël ... Restitution H. Letocart, *etc.* [1957.] 4°. **G. 519. kk. (2.)**

— *See* LULLI (G. B.) [*Complete Works.*] Œuvres complètes, *etc.* ⟨Les Motets. tom. 2. Réalisation de la basse-continue à l'orgue par H. Letocart et G. Sazerac de Forge.⟩ 1930–1939. fol. **Hirsch IV. 983.**

LETONDAL (Arthur)

— Sarabande. [P. F.] *O. Ditson Co.: Boston, etc.*, 1898. fol. **g. 605. p. (28.)**

LETOREY (Pierre)

— *See* ALBENIZ (I.) Pepita Jiménez ... 1ʳᵉ (2ᵉ) Fantaisie. Arrangement en Trio par P. Letorey. 1925. 4°. **h. 3307. b. (13.)**

LE TOUQUET
— Le Touquet. Song. *See* B., G. W.

LE TOUZEL (JAMES C.)
— My Canadian Home ... A Patriotic Air, with English and French words. Words & Melody by J. C. Le Touzel. (Accompaniment by S. Sauer.) *Whaley, Royce & Co.: Toronto*, 1897. fol. **H. 1798. v. (14.)**

LETT (HUGH)
— Romance in D minor, for Cello & Piano. *E. Ashdown: London*, 1928. 4°. **g. 514. r. (14.)**

LETTER
— A Letter. [Song.] *See* BLUMENTHAL (J.)

— The Letter. Song. *See* CRAWFORD (W.)

— The Letter. Song. *See* ESIPOFF (S.)

— The Letter. Song. *See* GAMBOGI (F. E.)

— A Letter. Song. *See* GEIBEL (A.)

— The Letter. Part Song. *See* HATTON (J. L.)

— The Letter. Ballad. *See* KNIGHT (J. P.)

— The Letter. [Song.] *See* LOVER (Samuel) [Songs of the Superstitions of Ireland. No. 12.]

— The Letter. [Song.] *See* ROBBINS (R. C.) Songs ... 130.

— The Letter. Song. *See* WALTHEW (R. H.) [An Album of Twelve Songs. No. 5.]

— The Letter came at last. [Song.] *See* PRATT (C. E.)

— A Letter from afar. Song. *See* LINCOLN (C.)

— A Letter from her Boy. [Song.] *See* NANKEVILLE (Will E.)

— A Letter from Home. Song. *See* FOSTER (H.)

— A Letter from Home. Song. *See* ROCKWELL (G. N.)

— A Letter from Ohio. [Song.] *See* BOCK (William E.)

— A Letter from Pete. Cantata. *See* ROGERS (Bernard)

— A Letter from the Front. [Song.] *See* MAXWELL (George S.)

— A Letter from the old Folks. Song. *See* WEGEFARTH (L. C.)

— The Letter in my Heart. Romanza. *See* FOX (W. H.)

— The Letter in the Candle. Ballad. *See* COOTE (R.)

— The Letter N. [Song.] *See* DIBDIN (Charles) [A Frisk.]

— The Letter Song. [Song.] *See* CHAIKOVSKY (P. I.) [Евгений Онегин.—Сцена письма.]

— The Letter Song. *See* LEHMANN, afterwards BEDFORD (L.) [The Eternal Feminine.]

— Letter Song. *See* NEWCOMB (E. A. P.)

— The Letter Song. [Song.] *See* OFFENBACH (J.) [La Périchole.—O mon cher amant.]

— The Letter Song. *See* PLANQUETTE (R.) [Rip van Winkle.]

— The Letter that never arrived. Song. *See* STURM (M.)

— A Letter to say "Good bye". Ballad. *See* SERPETTE (G.)

— The Letter was returned to her unread. [Song.] *See* KELLER (C. L.)

LETTERA
— La Lettera. Canto popolare. *See* BLUME (A.)

— La Lettera. [Song.] *See* VERA (E.) Sei Ariette. No. 4.

— La Lettera Anonima. Opera buffa. *See* DONIZETTI (D. G. M.)

— Lettera d'un figlio di Marte alla sua amante. [Song.] *See* CORRI (P. A.)

LETTERE
— Lettere. [Song.] *See* NASALLI (S.) Convolvoli ... No. 2.

— Lettere. [Song.] *See* PINSUTI (C. E.)

LETTERS
— Letters. [Duet.] *See* BOWERS (Robert H.) [The Maid and the Mummy.—Sisters are a Nuisense.]

— Letters. Ballad. *See* HARVEY (R. F.)

— Letters found near a Suicide. [Song.] *See* KIM (Earl)

— Letters from Composers. [Song-cycle.] *See* ARGENTO (D.)

— Letters from Paris. [Cantata.] *See* ROREM (Ned)

— Letters from those you love. [Song.] *See* EDWARDS (Robert W.)

— Letters in the Sand. [Part-song.] *See* HOVHANESS (Alan) [Symphony No. 24. Majnun.]

— Letters that I'm waiting for. [Song.] *See* DUBIN (Alfred) and CUNNINGHAM (P. A.)

LETTERS (WILL)
— All little Girls are pretty. [Song.] Words & music by W. Letters, Whit Cunliffe and J. A. Glover-Kind, *etc.* [With separate voice part.] 2 pt. *W. Paxton; Price & Reynolds: London*, [1907.] fol. *Price & Reynolds Sixpenny Series. no. 74.* **H. 3985. x. (40.)**

— Annabelle. [Song.] Written and composed by W. Letters, Chas. Collins & Fred Murray. pp. 4. *B. Feldman & Co.: London*, [1909.] 4°. **H. 3985. x. (41.)**

— The Dear little Girl in the Goal ... [Song.] Written and composed by W. Letters. pp. 4. *B. Feldman & Co.: London*, [1909.] 4°. **H. 3985. x. (42.)**

— Dolly Dimple. ⟨Song.⟩ Written and composed by W. Letters, *etc.* [Staff and tonic sol-fa notation. Voice part.] *Francis, Day & Hunter: London*, [1903.] s. sh. fol. **H. 3985. x. (43.)**

— Dolly Dimple, *etc.* ⟨Song.⟩ [With separate voice part.] 2 pt. *Francis, Day & Hunter: London*, [1903.] fol. **H. 3985. x. (44.)**

— Good bye little Humming Bird. Song. Words & music by W. Letters, *etc.* [With separate voice part.] 2 pt. *W. Paxton; Price & Reynolds: London*, [1907.] fol. *Price & Reynolds Sixpenny Series. no. 99.* **H. 3985. x. (45.)**

— I'm going away. ⟨Song.⟩ Written and composed by W. Letters. pp. 5. *Empire Music Publishing Co.: London*, [1907.] fol. **H. 3985. x. (46.)**

— If you hav'nt the Money to spend. [Song.] Written and composed by W. Letters, *etc.* ⟨With tonic sol-fa setting. Arranged by J. Chas. Moore.⟩ pp. 3. *National Music Publishing Co.: London*, [1909.] fol. *National 6ᵈ Edition. no. 46.* **H. 3985. x. (47.)**

— It's as easy as easy to roller skate. Written and composed by W. Letters, *etc.* ⟨Song. Arranged by J. Chas. Moore.⟩ pp. 3. *National Music Publishing Co.: London*, [1909.] fol. *National 6ᵈ Edition. no. 32.* **H. 3985. x. (48.)**

LETTERS (Will)

— The Lilac Girl ... ⟨Song.⟩ Written and composed by
W. Letters. [Staff and tonic sol-fa notation. Voice part.]
Francis, Day & Hunter: London, [1906.] *s. sh.* fol.
H. 3985. x. (49.)

— The Lilac Girl, *etc.* ⟨Song.⟩ [With separate voice part.] 2 pt.
Francis, Day & Hunter: London, [1906.] fol.
H. 3985. x. (50.)

— "Now I know that you love me still" ... [Song.] Written and
composed by W. Letters. pp. 4. *B. Feldman & Co.: London*,
[1909.] 4°. **H. 3985. x. (51.)**

— Poppies. ⟨Song.⟩ Written and composed by W. Letters ...
Arranged by J. A. Tunbridge. *Star Music Publishing Co.:
London*, [1909.] fol. **H. 3985. x. (52.)**

— Put me upon an Island where the Girls are few. Written and
composed by W. Letters, *etc.* ⟨Song. With tonic sol-fa setting.
Arranged by J. Chas. Moore.⟩ *National Music Publishing Co.:
London*, [1908.] fol.
National 6ᵈ Edition. no. 23. **H. 3985. x. (53.)**

— Ring up Lucky Boy, London. [Song.] Written and composed
by W. Letters, Alf. J. Lawrance and Harry Gifford. pp. 4.
B. Feldman & Co.: London, [1909.] 4°. **H. 3985. x. (54.)**

— Something seems to tell me you'll forget me. ⟨Song.⟩ Written,
composed ... by W. Letters. [Staff and tonic sol-fa notation.
Voice part.] *Francis, Day & Hunter: London*, [1902.] *s. sh.* fol.
H. 3985. x. (55.)

— Something seems to tell me you'll forget me, *etc.* ⟨Song.⟩
[With separate voice part.] 2 pt. *Francis, Day & Hunter:
London*, [1902.] fol. **H. 3985. x. (56.)**

— Two brown Eyes, *etc.* ⟨Song.⟩ [With separate voice part.] 2 pt.
Francis, Day & Hunter: London, [1901.] fol.
H. 3985. x. (58.)

— Two brown Eyes. ⟨Song.⟩ Written and composed by
W. Letters, *etc.* [Staff and tonic sol-fa notation. Voice part.]
Francis, Day & Hunter: London, [1905.] *s. sh.* fol.
H. 3985. x. (57.)

— You have a Friend in me. ⟨Song.⟩ Written, composed ... by
W. Letters. [Staff and tonic sol-fa notation. Voice part.]
Francis, Day & Hunter: London, [1901.] *s. sh.* fol.
H. 3985. x. (59.)

— You have a Friend in me, *etc.* ⟨Song.⟩ [With separate voice
part.] 2 pt. *Francis, Day & Hunter: London*, [1901.] fol.
H. 3985. x. (60.)

— *See* COLLINS (Charles) "She may be wealthy, she may be
poor." ⟨Song.⟩ Written and composed by C. Collins ... and
W. Letters, *etc.* [1911.] *s. sh.* fol. **H. 3990. x. (37.)**

— *See* COLLINS (Charles) "She may be wealthy, she may be
poor," *etc.* ⟨Song.⟩ [1911.] fol. **H. 3990. x. (38.)**

— *See* MURPHY (C. W.) and LETTERS (W.) "Has anybody here
seen Kelly?" ... ⟨Song.⟩ Written and composed by C. W.
Murphy and W. Letters. [1909.] fol. **H. 3986. i. (19.)**

— *See* MURPHY (C. W.) and LETTERS (W.) "Has anybody here
seen Kelly?" *etc.* ⟨Song.⟩ [1909.] fol. **H. 3986. i. (20.)**

— *See* MURPHY (C. W.) and LETTERS (W.) [Has anybody here
seen Kelly?] The "Kelly" Two-step. (Founded on W. Letters
& C. W. Murphy's song "Has anybody here seen Kelly?") By
C. W. Murphy. [1909.] fol. **h. 3286. vv. (52.)**

LETTERS (Will) and GODFREY (Fred)

— "Molly O'Morgan." (The Irish-Italian Girl.) [Song.] Written
and composed by W. Letters and F. Godfrey. pp. 4.
B. Feldman & Co.: London, [1909.] 4°. **H. 3985. x. (61.)**

LETTERS (Will) and KIND (John A. Glover)

— Peter Peacock Esq.! Written & composed by W. Letters and
J. A. G. Kind, *etc.* [Song. With separate voice part.] 2 pt.
W. Paxton; Price & Reynolds: London, [1906.] fol.
Price & Reynolds Sixpenny Series. no. 58. **H. 3985. x. (62.)**

— Take a cosy little Home for two. [Song.] Written and
composed by W. Letters & J. A. G. Kind. pp. 4. *B. Feldman &
Co.: London*, [1909.] 4°. **H. 3985. x. (63.)**

LETTICE

— Lettice White. Song. *See* LEE (Alfred)

LETTISCH

— Lettisch Vade mecum. Handbuch, darinnen folgende ...
Stücke begriffen ... 4. Geistliche Lieder vnd Psalmen,
Collecten vnd Gebehte, so das gantze Jahr ... gesungen
werden ... vbersehen, corrigiret vnd gemehret, durch
Georgium Mancelium, *etc.* pp. 196. *In Verlegung Gerhard
Schröders: Riga*, 1631 [–1636?] 4°. **3040. c. 23.**

LETTRE

— La Lettre, Comédie en un acte, en prose et Vaudevilles, par
C. J. Lœuillart-Davrigni ... Avec la Musique [of the
concluding vaudeville]. *Chez le Libraire, au Théâtre du
Vaudeville: Paris*, An Troisième [1795]. 8°.
11738. cc. 12. (2.)

— La Lettre. [Song.] *See* MASSENET (Jules E. F.)

— Lettre à Jeanne. Mélodie. *See* POISE (J. A. F.)

— Lettre à mon mari, réserviste. [Song.] *See* PLANQUETTE (R.)

— Lettre à mon Tailleur. Chanson. *See* DASSIER (A.)

— Lettre à Monsieur le Soleil. [Song.] *See* LEDUC (A.)

— Une Lettre au Bon Dieu. Recit de Village. *See* POTIER (H.)

— La Lettre d'Adieu. [Song.] *See* KRIENS (C. P. W.)

— Lettre d'amour. [Song.] *See* GUMBERT (F.)

— Lettre d'Enfant. [Song.] *See* GANNE (L. G.)

— Lettre d'un Collégien à sa Cousine. [Song.] *See* OFFENBACH
(A. J.)

— Lettre d'un pinson à sa bienfaitrice. Mélodie. *See* POURNY
(C.)

— Lettre d'une Cousine à son Cousin. [Song.] *See* LECOCQ
(A. C.)

— Lettre d'une Pensionnaire. [Song.] *See* GREGH (L.)

— La Lettre de Change. Opéra. *See* BOCHSA (R. N. C.)

— La Lettre de faire part. Romance. *See* LHUILLIER (E.)

— Lettre de Marianne à Nicolas. [Song.] *See* MARIETTI (G.)

— La Lettre de Tommy. [Song.] *See* BERETTA (R.)

— Lettre écrite d'Alger, par Dumanet. [Song.] *See* PLANTADE
(C. H.)

LETTS (Egerton)

— Take those Lips away. Song, words by Shakespeare. *Weekes
Co.: London*, [1915.] fol. **H. 1793. t. (23.)**

LETTS (Ralph)

— Can a Maiden sigh for ever. Song, the words by N. Barron.
Boosey & Co.: London, etc., 1919. fol. **H. 1846. y. (7.)**

LETTS (Ralph)

— The Flower's Kiss. Song, words by E. Oxenford. *H. Sharples & Son: London*, 1919. fol.   **H. 1860. b. (23.)**

— Her dear Words. Song, words by F. Clements. *H. Sharples & Son: Blackpool*, 1917. fol.   **H. 1846. y. (8.)**

— Magnificat and Nunc dimittis in A. *Stainer & Bell: London*, (1909.) 8°.
Stainer & Bell's Modern Church Services, No. 24.   **F. 1137.**

— Now you have gone! Song, words by F. C. Coulter. *H. Sharples & Son: Blackpool*, 1918. fol.   **H. 1846. y. (9.)**

— O Lord of Hosts, Whose sovereign Sway. (Coronation Hymn, words by H. D. Wright.) *Stainer & Bell: London*, [1911]. 8°.
Stainer & Bell's Church Choir Library, No. 107.   **F. 1137. b.**

— Roses white and red. Song, words by E. Oxenford. *H. Sharples & Son: Blackpool*, [1918.] fol.   **H. 1846. y. (10.)**

— Silver Jubilee March. (Here's a health unto their Majesties.) ⟨To commemorate the Silver Jubilee of their Majesties the King and Queen, 1935.⟩ [Orchestral parts.] 14 pt. *Chappell & Co.: London*, [1934.] 4°.
[*Chappell & Co.'s Popular Orchestral Works. no. 285.*]   **f. 424.**

— Silver Jubilee March. Arranged for military band by Denis Wright. ⟨Conductor [and parts].⟩ 31 pt. *In*: Somers (Debroy) Operas in Rhythm, *etc.* [1935.] fol. [*Chappell's Army Journal. no. 611.*]   **h. 1562.**

— Two Songs. No. 1. When thou art nigh. (Words by T. Moore.) No. 2. Three Shadows. (Words by D. G. Rossetti.) *Stainer & Bell: London*, [1909.] fol.
Stainer & Bell's Modern Songs, No. 13.   **H. 1794. vv. (45.)**

— Sweet little Child. Song, words by A. H. Hyatt. *Metzler & Co.: London*, 1911. fol.   **H. 1792. s. (22.)**

— Te Deum laudamus ... in ... B flat. *Novello and Co.: London*, 1908. 8°.   **F. 1169. h. (13.)**

— Two dear brown Eyes. Song, words by F. G. Bowles. *Metzler & Co.: London*, 1913. fol.   **H. 1793. t. (24.)**

— Willow, O Willow. Song, the words by F. C. Coulter. *Boosey & Co.: London, etc.*, 1919. fol.   **H. 1846. y. (11.)**

LETTURA

— Lettura di Michelangelo. [Cantata.] *See* Vlad (R.)

LETTY

— Letty the Basket Maker. Comic opera. *See* Balfe (M. W.)

LETZ (Hans)

— *See* Giannini (V.) Quartet, *etc.* (Edited by H. Letz.) 1931. fol.   **h. 2784. k. (7.)**

LETZN (Gieuspo)

— Leipsig, or the Allies grand march. And a favorite waltz ... for the piano forte. pp. 3. *Phipps & Cº: London*, [WM1811.] fol.   **h. 61. e. (25.)**

LETZTE

— Der letzte Abschied des Volkes. [Chorus.] *See* Bruch (M. C. F.)

— Letzte Bitte. [Song.] *See* Bronsart (J. von) Fünf Gedichte. No. 5.

— Letzte Bitte. [Song.] *See* Schillings (M. von)

LETZTE

— Letzte Bitte. [Part-song.] *See* Wolf (H.) Sechs geistliche Lieder nach Gedichten von Joseph v. Eichendorff. 4.

— Der letzte Blick. [Song.] *See* Ganz (R.) Lieder und Gesänge. Opus 2. No. 5.

— Der letzte Dienst. [Melodrama.] *See* Weninger (L.)

— Der letzte Gruss. [Song.] *See* Jansen (F. G.) Zwei Lieder. Op. 45. No. 2.

— Der letzte Gruss. Lied. *See* Levi (H.)

— Der letzte Heller. [Song.] *See* Mohr (H.)

— Letzte Hose. [Song.] *See* Hamma (F. B.) Zwei Lieder, *etc.* No. 1.

— Das letzte Kännchen. [Song.] *See* Kleffel (A.) Sechs Lieder ... Op. 42. No. 6.

— Das letzte Kännchen. [Song.] *See* Meyer-Helmund (E.) Spielmannslieder ... Op. 8. No. 5.

— Das letzte Kännchen. [Song.] *See* Schmidt (B.) Fünf Lieder ... Op. 24. No. 3.

— Das letzte Kännchen. [Chorus.] *See* Zerlett (J. B.)

— Letzte Liebe. [Song.] *See* Hernried (R. F. R.) Lieder ... Nr. 2.

— Die letzte Loge. [Song.] *See* Werkenthin (A.)

— Der letzte Ritter. [Song cycle.] *See* Loewe (J. C. G.)

— Letzte Rose. Romanza. *See* Flotow (F. F. A. von) *Baron.* [Martha.]

— Die letzte Rose. [Song.] *See* Franz (R.) Sechs Gesänge. Op. 20. No. 2.

— Letzte Rose. [Song.] *See* Hasse (G.)

— Letzte Rose. Volkslied. Doppelkanon. *See* Jadassohn (S.)

— Der letzte Skalde. [Chorus.] *See* Sturm (W.)

— Die letzte Sonne. [Song.] *See* Peterka (R.)

— Der letzte Traum. Quartett. *See* Kuecken (F. W.)

— Der letzte Versuch. Humoristisches Männerquartett. *See* Kuntze (C.)

— Der letzte Walzer. Operette. *See* Straus (O.)

— Der letzte Wunsch. Duett. *See* Dvořák (A.) Duette. Op. 20. No. 4.

— Der letzte Wunsch. [Song.] *See* Jensen (A.) Sechs Gesänge, *etc.* Op. 53. No. 6.

LETZTEN

— Die letzten Dinge. Oratorio. *See* Spohr (L.)

— Die letzten Mohikaner. Operette. *See* Genée (R.)

— Die letzten Sonnenstrahlen bleichen. Terzett. *See* Tappert (W.)

— Die letzten Zehn vom vierten Regiment. [Song.] *See* Berger (L.) *Berlin.* [Zehn Lieder. Op. 27. No. 10.]

— Die letzten Zehn vom vierten Regiment. [Song.] *See* Hesselbach (F.)

— Die letzten Zehn vom 4ten Regiment. [Song.] *See* Schnyder von Wartensee (X.)

LETZTER

— Letzter Frühling. [Song.] *See* GRIEG (E. H.) [2 elegische Melodien. Op. 34. No. 2.]

— Letzter Trost. [Song.] *See* GRUND (F. W.) Drei Kriegs-Lieder. No. 2.

— Letzter Wunsch. [Song.] *See* BRADSKÝ (T.)

— Letzter Wunsch. [Song.] *See* MEYER-HELMUND (E.) Zwei Lieder ... Op. 17. No. 1.

— Letzter Wunsch. [Song.] *See* ZARZYCKI (A.) Drei Lieder ... Op. 22. No. 2.

LETZTES

— Letztes Gebet. Part Song. *See* RHEINBERGER (J. G.) [Jahreszeiten. Op. 186. No. 8.]

— Letztes Glück. [Part-song.] *See* BRAHMS (J.) [Fünf Gesänge. Op. 104. No. 3.]

— Letztes Glück. [Song.] *See* HASSE (G.)

— Letztes Glück. [Song.] *See* HEIJDEN (F. J. van der) Fünf Lieder. No. 2.

LEU (FRANZ)

— Abendstimmung. Clavierstück. *Leipzig*, [1874.] fol.
$\qquad$ **h. 1487. q. (9.)**

— Barbarossa, Dichtung von F. Horrmann componirt für Männerchor und Solo mit grossem Orchester. Partitur. *Leipzig*, [1874.] fol. **G. 625.**

— Enzio der letzte Staufe. (Gedicht von W. Zimmermann.) Concertstück für eine Baritonstimme mit gemischtem oder Männerchor und Orchester ... Klavierauszug. *Leipzig*, [1874.] fol. **H. 1777. h. (49.)**

— Schilflied. Auf dem Teich dem regungslosen, von Lenau, für eine tiefere Stimme mit Begleitung des Pianoforte, *etc*. *Leipzig*, [1873.] fol. **H. 1777. h. (48.)**

— *See* BRUCH (M. C. F.) Carmosenella ... Arrangirt von F. Leu. [1890?] 8°. **F. 321. i. (1.)**

LEUCHT

— Leucht im dunkeln Erdenthale. Kantate. *See* ZUMSTEEG (J. R.) Kantate ... No. 17.

LEUCHTE

— Leuchte auf uns alle. Chor a cappella. *See* MEYER (Ernst H.)

— Leuchte meiner stillen Nächte. Romanze. *See* GURILEV (A.)

LEUCHTENDE

— Der Leuchtende Stern. [Song.] *See* VARLAMOV (A. E.)

— Leuchtende Tage. Kriegslieder. *See* KAHN (R.)

LEUCHTER (ERWIN)

— Florilegium musicum. History of music in 180 examples from antiquity to the eighteenth century ... Selection and notes by E. Leuchter. pp. xv. 359. *Ricordi americana: Buenos Aires*, [1964.] 4°.

$\qquad$ — Florilegium musicum, *etc*. (Supplement.) pp. 75. *Ricordi americana: Buenos Aires*, [1964.] 4°. **G. 1388. d.**

LEUCIPPO

— [Leucippo e Zenocrita.] The Favorite Songs in the Opera Leucippo and Zenocrita [a pasticcio], for the Voice and Harpsichord, *etc*. R. Bremner: *London*, [1764.] fol. *The composers named are Vento, Hasse and Giardini.*
$\qquad$ **G. 805. r. (5.)**

LEUCKART (F. E. C.)

— Leuckart's Hausmusik. Serie VIII. *F. E. C. Leuckart: Leipzig*, [1877.] *obl*. fol. **e. 455.**

LEUCOLIA

— Leucolia's Song. *See* BINFIELD (H. R.)

LEUCOSIA. — Σχολη ἐκκλησιαστικης Βυζαντιης Μουσικης

— Θεοδουλου Καλλινικου ... Ἐθνικη ψαλμωδια. Περιεχουσα τας φημας και πολυχρονισμους της ιερας Συνοδου Κυπρου, δοξολογιας, *etc*. pp. 85. ἐν Λευκοσεια, 1948. 8°.
$\qquad$ **B. 512. y. (1.)**

LEULIETTE (ÉDOUARD)

— L'Aïeule. Gavotte pour piano. Op. 6. *Paris*, [1885.] fol.
$\qquad$ **h. 3280. k. (54.)**

— Ave Maria pour voix de soprano avec accompagnement de piano. Op. 5. *Calais, etc.*, [1885.] fol. **H. 1187. i. (29.)**

— Fleurs de printemps. Mazurka élégante de salon pour piano. (Op. 3.) [*Paris*, 1885.] fol. **h. 3285. b. (61.)**

— La Gaieté. Grand galop brillant pour piano. Op. 2. [*Paris*, 1885.] fol. **h. 3280. k. (52.)**

— Prière de l'enfant à son réveil [begins: "O Père, qu'adore mon père"], avec accompagnement de piano. Paroles de Lamartine. *Paris*, [1885.] fol. **H. 2836. h. (52.)**

— 1re Rêverie. Morceau de salon pour piano. Op. 4. *Paris*, [1885.] fol. **h. 3280. k. (53.)**

— Romance sans paroles pour piano. Op. 1. [*Paris*, 1885.] fol.
$\qquad$ **h. 3280. k. (51.)**

LEULIETTE (JOSEPH)

— Les Charmes de Paris. Valse. [P. F.] *In:* The Musical Bijou ... for MDCCCXLVIII. pp. 66–68. [1848.] fol. **H. 2330.**

— La Cité quadrilles. [P. F.] *In:* The Musical Bijou ... for MDCCCXLVIII. pp. 62–64. [1848.] fol. **H. 2330.**

— L'Impromptu quadrille. [P. F.] *In:* The Musical Bijou for MDCCCXLVIII. pp. 85–87. [1848.] fol. **H. 2330.**

— Un Souvenir. Quadrille de Valses pour le Piano Forte. *London*, [1848.] fol. **h. 939. (37.)**

LEUMAS (SARA) *pseud.* [i. e. SARA SAMUEL.]

— Dolly Varden valse. [P. F.] *London*, [1871.] fol.
$\qquad$ **h. 1485. s. (49.)**

— The Sandringham galop. [P. F.] *London*, [1872.] fol.
$\qquad$ **h. 1482. z. (47.)**

LEUM'AS (TEBRO'C) *pseud.* [i. e. SAMUEL CORBETT.]

— Captain Webb, the champion swimmer. [Song, begins: "There is a name".] Written by W. R. Corbett. *Wellington*, [1876.] fol. **H. 1778. y. (19.)**

LEUNER (KARL)

— The Shepherds' Cradle Song. *See infra:* [Wiegenlied.]

LEUNER (KARL)

— [Wiegenlied.] The Shepherds' Cradle Song. Tr. A. Foxton Ferguson ... For SSA & organ (or piano) ... arr. Philip Lane. pp. 4. *Roberton Publications:* [*Wendover*, 1980.] 8°.
F. 1874. ff. (9.)

LEUNG (TOMMY)

— Sunflower. Guitar themes. ⟨Songs & music arr. Tommy Leung.⟩ [Tablature.] pp. 63. *Sunshine Service:* [*Hong Kong*, 1978?] 4°.
f. 760. z. (4.)

LEUPOLD (A. W.)

— Berceuse. (Op. 15.) [Organ.] 1914. *See* PERIODICAL PUBLICATIONS.—*London*. The Organ Loft, *etc.* Book 103. No. 309. 1901, *etc. obl.* 4°.
e. 1094.

— Ecce Homo. (Op. 15c.) [Organ.] 1914. *See* PERIODICAL PUBLICATIONS.—*London*. The Organ Loft, *etc.* Book 104. No. 312. 1901, *etc. obl.* 4°.
e. 1094.

— Passacaglia über ein eigenes Thema für Orgel. Op. 8, *etc. See* ALBUM. Album für Orgel-Spieler, *etc.* Lief. 133. [1880–1935.] *obl.* fol.
e. 119.

LEUPOLD (E.)

— Carmen. Schottische for the Piano. *O. Ditson Co.: Boston*, 1899. fol.
h. 3286. g. (43.)

— Esmeralda. Valse de Salon. [P. F.] *S. Brainard's Sons Co.: New York, Chicago*, 1902. fol.
h. 3282. kk. (32.)

— Forget-me-not. Romance. [P. F.] *S. Brainard's Sons Co.: New York, Chicago*, 1902. fol.
h. 3282. kk. (33.)

— Graziosa Mazurka for the Piano. *O. Ditson Co.: Boston*, [1899.] fol.
h. 3286. g. (44.)

— Impromptu. [P. F.] *S. Brainard's Sons Co.: New York, Chicago*, 1902. fol.
h. 3282. kk. (34.)

— Sapphire.—Zafiro.—Schottische de Salon. [P. F.] *O. Ditson Co.: Boston*, 1903. fol.
h. 3282. kk. (35.)

LEUPOLD (THÉRÈSE) *Madame*

— Brilliants, valse de salon for the Pianoforte. *London*, [1863.] fol.
h. 1460. v. (39.)

— My first polka, for the pianoforte. *London*, [1857.] fol.
h. 977. f. (34.)

— O may it still a Summer be. [Song, begins: "A Maiden knelt at eventide".] The words by M. Douglas. *London*, [1859.] fol.
H. 1771. l. (22.)

— Parting words, song. [Begins: "And must we then for ever part".] *London*, [1858.] fol.
H. 1771. l. (23.)

— The Queen Mab galop. [P. F.] *London*, [1863.] fol.
h. 1460. v. (38.)

— Soleil Couchant. Nocturne pour le Piano. *London*, [1864.] fol.
h. 1462. r. (45.)

— Whither I love to stray. Song, words by Bertha Leupold. The music composed ... by Madame Leupold. pp. 3. *G. Augener & Co.: London*, [1889.] fol. [*Germania. no.* 80.]
H. 2128.

LEUPOLD (U. S.)

— *See* MOZART (W. A.) God is our Refuge and Strength. ⟨Edited by U. S. Leupold.⟩ [1967.] 8°.
F. 307. k. (23.)

LEUR

— Leur chaumière. Mélodie. *See* VOGEL (A.)

LEURS

— Leurs petits sont pour les oiseaux. Air. *See* GEORGES. Georges et Gros Jean.

LEUTNER (ALBERT)

— Bajazzo-Polka für das Pianoforte. *Berlin & Posen*, [1869.] fol.
h. 1462. r. (52.)

— Beliebte Tänze für das Pianoforte. No. 24, 26, 34, 38. *Berlin*, [1855–59.] *obl.* fol.
Imperfect; wanting all the other no.
e. 272. o. (8.)

— Berliner Quadrille für das Pianoforte. *Berlin & Posen*, [1868.] fol.
h. 1462. r. (49.)

— Capriolen-Polka für das Pianoforte. *Berlin & Posen*, [1870.] fol.
h. 1462. r. (53.)

— Galop. "Carillon." [Op. 21. Arranged for military band. Parts.] 26 pt. *In:* LOWTHIAN, afterwards PRESCOTT (Caroline) Valse. "A Maid of Kent," *etc.* 1884. fol. [*Boosey's military Journal.* ser. 76. no. 3.]
h. 1549.

— Fest-Ouvertüre ... (Op. 42.) Arrangiert von L. Artok. [Parts.] *B. Schott's Söhne: Mainz*, 1928. 4°. [*Domesticum Salon-Orchester. No.* 290.]
g. 1053. a.

— Heimath-Gruss. Geschwind-Marsch. [P. F.] *Berlin & Posen*, [1868.] fol.
h. 1462. r. (50.)

— Hochzeits-Polonaise. [P. F.] *Berlin & Posen*, [1868.] *obl.* fol.
e. 217. b. (32.)

— Louisen-Polka-Mazurka für das Pianoforte. *Berlin & Posen*, [1868.] fol.
h. 1462. r. (48.)

— Opernball-Quadrille. [P. F.] *Berlin*, [1870.] fol.
h. 1462. r. (54.)

— Oreaden-Galopp für das Pianoforte. *Berlin & Posen*, [1870.] fol.
h. 1462. r. (55.)

— Pomona Galopp für das Pianoforte. *Berlin & Posen*, [1868.] fol.
h. 1462. r. (46.)

— "Pomona." ⟨Galop.⟩ [Military band parts.] 26 pt. *In:* AUBER (D. F. E.) [Le Serment.] Overture, *etc.* 1881. fol. [*C. Boosé's supplemental military Journal. no.* 307.]
h. 1544.

— Staberle-Polka für das Pianoforte. *Berlin & Posen*, [1868.] fol.
h. 1462. r. (47.)

— Vom Fels zum Meer. Hohenzollern-Marsch für das Pianoforte. *Berlin & Posen*, [1872.] fol. **h. 1487. q. (10.)**

LEUTNER (ALBERT) *Madame*

— Amazonen Marsch, für das Pianoforte. *Berlin & Posen*, [1868.] fol.
h. 1462. r. (51.)

LEUTO (ARCANGELO DEL)

— Cantata a voce sola [begins: "Dimmi Amor"] ... Verso il 1645. *See* GEVAERT (F. A.) Les Gloires de l'Italie, *etc.* No. 14. [1868.] fol.
H. 566. g.

LEUTRUM-ERTINGEN (A. von)

— Es will durch Land. *See* LIEDER-REPERTORIUM. Lieder Repertorium, *etc.* No. 86. [1847, *etc.*] fol.
H. 2274.

LEUTTNER (GEORG CHRISTOPH)

— Cithara Davidica, sive Psalmi per annum consueti, cum duabus lytaniis lauretanis. In I. parte. à 4. voc. ordinar. concertantibus; cum 5. instrum. ad lib. & ripienis. In secunda à 5. CC. A. T. B. cum totid. instrum. ad lib. & ripienis ... Cantus II. concert. ⟨Altus concert.—Tenor Concert.—Bassus

LEUTTNER (Georg Christoph)

concert.—Violino i.—Violino ii.⟩ *Sumptibus authoris, typis Lucæ Straub: Monarchij, 1682. 4°. Imperfect; wanting the other parts.* **K. 5. a. 21.**

LEUTWILER (Toni)

— Weekend en Suisse. Impressions pour orchestre, *etc.* [Score.] pp. 40. *Edition Cadenza: Genève; Sidernton Verlag: Köln; printed in Germany,* [1959.] 4°. **g. 474. qq. (5.)**

LEUVILLE (William Redivivus Oliver de Lorncourt de) *Marquis*

— *See* Oliver de Lorncourt (W. R.) *Marquis de Leuville.*

LEUX (Irmgard)

— Christian Gottlob Neefe, 1748—1798. Mit zwei Bildnissen, *etc.* *F. Kistner & C. F. W. Siegel: Leipzig,* 1925. 8°. [*Veröffentlichungen des Fürstlichen Institutes für musikwissenschaftliche Forschung zu Bückeburg. Reihe v. Bd. ii.*] **G. 1. 400.**

LEUX (Leo)

— Die erste Liebe warst du für mich. Lied aus dem Bavaria-Film "Der dunkle Tag". Mana pirmā mīla reiz biji tu ... Deutscher Text von Josef Petrak. Arvēda Andersona latv. teksts. *Ger. & Lett. Arwed Anderson Verlag: Riga,* [1943.] 4°. **G. 1443. c. (4.)**

LEV (Ray)

— *See* Bach (J. S.) [*Doubtful and Supposititious Works.*] [Notenbuch der Anna Magdalena Bach ... 1725.—No. 25.] Aria—Bist du bei mir ... Arranged by R. Lev. 1940. 4°. [*The Two-Piano Series. No. 24.*] **g. 1393.**

LEVA (Enrico de)

— Au Temps jadis. Past Memories. (Op. 150.) [P. F.] *Ascherberg, Hopwood & Crew: London,* 1910. fol. **h. 3283. kk. (1.)**

— Bon Soir Colombine, for Pianoforte. *Ascherberg, Hopwood & Crew: London,* 1911. fol. **h. 3284. g. (21.)**

— Canzone, pezzo caratteristico per Pianoforte. Op. 1. *Milano,* [1883.] fol. **h. 3280. k. (50.)**

— The Dream divine. Tes caresses! Valse chantée, English words by P. Pinkerton. In A♭ and B♭. 2 no. *Ascherberg, Hopwood & Crew: London,* (1913.) fol. **H. 1793. t. (25.)**

— Duo pastoral, pour Pianoforte. *Ascherberg, Hopwood & Crew: London,* 1913. fol. **h. 3284. g. (22.)**

— Fantasia di S. di Giacomo ... Spunti musicali di E. de Leva. *Tipa Bideri: Napoli,* [c. 1900.] 8°. **X. 900/1258.**

— Fantasia estiva. Cantilena per mezzo-soprano o baritono [begins: "In un paese lontano"], versi di E. Rosati. *Milano, etc.* [1886.] fol. **H. 2836. h. (50.)**

— Fleur-de-Lys.—Mouvement de Valse.—Pour Piano. *Enoch & Sons: London,* 1910. fol. **h. 3283. kk. (2.)**

— Idylle Pastoral. Morceau caractéristique pour Piano. *Ferrara,* 1908. fol. *Printed in facsimile. Pp. 102–105 of "Ferrara a Geolamo Frescobaldi," etc.* **7895. i. 4.**

— Nanniné ... Canzone popolare ... Versi di F. Russo. *Ricordi: Milano, etc.,* [1887.] fol.⟩ **H. 2836. v. (27.)**

— Non me guardà. Canzone napoletana, versi di Sciù-Sciù. *Milano, etc.,* [1885.] fol. **H. 2836. h. (48.)**

LEVA (Enrico de)

— Risoluzione. Melodia per Mezzo-Soprano o Tenore. Versi del Conte di Lara. *Ricordi: Milano, etc.,* [1887.] fol. **H. 2836. v. (28.)**

— Rosa, Rusè! Canzone popolare per la Festa di Piedigrotta. Versi di S. di Giacomo. *Milano, etc.,* [1886.] fol. **H. 2836. h. (49.)**

— S'era all' aperto! Melodia per mezzo-soprano o tenore. Versi di D. Milelli. *Ricordi: Milano, etc.,* [1887.] fol. **H. 2836. v. (29.)**

— Scusate si ve prego. Canzonetta napoletana, versi di R. Bracco. *Ascherberg, Hopwood & Crew: London,* 1913. fol. **H. 1793. t. (26.)**

— Souvenir d'une Valse. Rêverie pour Piano, *etc. Ascherberg, Hopwood & Crew: London,* (1913.) fol. **h. 3284. g. (23.)**

— Voi siete l'alba! Stornello per mezzo-soprano o tenore. Versi di F. Dall' Ongaro. *Ricordi: Milano, etc.,* [1887.] fol. **H. 2836. v. (30.)**

LEVACK (E. B. Noble)

— The Three Chimes. Song [begins: "The bells are ringing"]. Words by R. Atkinson. *London,* [1877.] fol. **H. 1778. y. (17.)**

LEVADÉ (Charles Gaston)

— Les Hérétiques. Opéra en trois actes. Poème de A.-Ferdinand Herold. Partition piano et chant réduite par l'auteur. pp. 271. *Enoch & cⁱᵉ, etc.: Paris, etc.,* [1905.] 4°. *With press cuttings inserted.* **F. 935. uu.**

— Les Hérétiques. Opéra en 3 actes, poème de F. Hérold ... Fragment, *etc.* [Begins: "Loin du monde impur".] [*Paris,*] 1905. 8°. *Supplement to "L'Illustration", No. 3262.* **P. P. 4283. m. (3.)**

— J'ai cueilli le lys. [Song.] Poésie de Maurice Boukay. pp. 3. *Henri Gregh: Paris,* [c. 1905.] fol. **H. 346. l. (7.)**

— Orientale. Pièce caractéristique pour le piano. *R. Cocks & Co.: London,* [1890.] fol. **h. 1484. t. (2.)**

— La Peau de chagrin. Comédie lyrique en 4 actes d'après H. de Balzac. Poème de Pierre Decourcelle et Michel Carré. [Score.] pp. 485. *Heugel: Paris,* [1929.] fol. *Without titlepage.* **H. 746. a.**

— La Rôtisserie de la Reine Pédauque. Comédie lyrique en 4 actes et 5 tableaux d'après le roman d'Anatole France par G. Docquois. Partition pour piano et chant, réduite par l'auteur. *Enoch & Co.: Paris,* 1919. fol. **H. 746.**

— *See* Béranger (P. J. de) 50 Chansons choisies ... Accompagnements ... de C. Levadé, *etc.* 1920. 4°. **G. 980. (1.)**

LÉVAI (Julia)

— Sej, a lészpedi erdőn ... Összeállítás népdalkörök és kisegyüttesek számára. ⟨Szerkesztette: Lévai Julia.⟩ pp. 49. *Népművelési propaganda iroda: Budapest,* [1976.] 8°. **D. 483. (4.)**

LEVALLEY (C. W.)

— Lullaby Baby Darling. Mother's Song and Waltz. Words and Music by C. W. Levalley. *C. W. Levalley: Milwaukee, Wis.,* 1901. fol. **H. 1799. h. (49.)**

— National Invocation. Hymn. *C. W. Levalley: Milwaukee, Wis.,* 1901. fol. **G. 517. k. (24.)**

LEVALLOIS (Marcel)

— Omnes gentes plaudite manibus. [Motet.] À 4 voix mixtes. *See*
Répertoire. Répertoire moderne de Musique vocale, *etc.*
No. 75. [1896, *etc.*] fol. **H. 1048.**

LEVANT (Oscar)

— Sonatina. [P. F.] *Robbins Music Corporation: New York*, 1934.
4°. **g. 1127. ss. (35.)**

— *See* Khachaturyan (A. I.) [Gayaneh.] Sabre Dance ...
Transcribed for piano by O. Levant. [1948.] 4°.
g. 1548. a. (1.)

LEVANTINE

— The Levantine Boatman. *See* Linley (G.)

LEVASHEV (E.)

— *See* Pashkevich (Vasily A.) "Как поживешь, так прослывешь,
или Санктпетербургский гостиный двор". Опера. Партитура.
Публикация, редакция текста, переложение для фортепиано,
исследование и комментарии Е. Левашева. 1980. 4°.
[*Памятники русского музыкального искусства. вып.* 8.]
F. 1594. cc.

— *See* Pashkevich (Vasily A.) "Скупой." Опера. Партитура.
Публикация, переложение для фортепиано и исследование
Е. Левашева. 1973. 4°. [*Памятники русского музыкального
искусства. вып.* 4.] **F. 1594. cc.**

LEVASHEVA (Ol'ga Evgen'evna)

— Русская вокальная лириыка XVIII века. Составление,
публикация, исследование и комментарии О. Левашевой.
⟨Eighteenth Century Russian lyrical Songs. Compiled,
prepared for publication, investigated and annotated by
O. Leevasheva.⟩ pp. 385. *Издателыство "Музыка":
Москва*, 1972. 4°.
[*Памятники русского музыкального искусства. вып.* 1.]
F. 1594. cc.

LE VASSEUR (   )

— Doux Messagers du jour. *Air, etc.* [Words by] Lombard.
[*Paris,*] 1729. *s. sh.* 4°.
Mercure de France, June, 1729. **298. a. 5.**

LEVASSEUR (Jean Henri)

— *See* Baillot (P. M. F. de S.) Méthode de Violoncelle ... par
... Levasseur, *etc.* [1805?] fol. **g. 347.**

— *See* Baillot (P. M. F. de S.) [Méthode de violoncelle.—
Supplément.] Exercises for the Violoncello, in all positions of
the thumb ... by Baillot, Levasseur, *etc.* [1832.] fol.
h. 1851. z. (2.)

— *See* Baillot (P. M. F. de S.) Method for the Violoncello by
Baillot, Levasseur, *etc.* [c. 1850.] fol. **h. 1870. m.**

LEVASSEUR (Louis)

— Le Lilliputien, a set of quadrilles for two performers on the
pianoforte. *Leader & Cock: London*, [1853.] fol.
h. 964. (31.)

— Nouvelles variations pour le Forte Piano sur une Tyrolienne,
etc. pp. 9. *Chez Viguerie: Paris*, [1825?] fol. **g. 272. z. (11*.)**

LEVATE

— Levate sta frangetta! Canzone. *See* Orefice (G. dell')

LEVATIER (Gustave)

— Valse sur des motifs de l'opéra La Croix d'Or ... de I. Brüll.
[P. F.] *Berlin & Posen*, [1879.] fol. **h. 1493. o. (31.)**

LEVAVI

— Levavi oculos. [Anthem.] *See* Harrison (H.)

— Levavi oculos meos. [Motet.] *See* Lasso (O. di) [Sacrae
Cantiones Sex et Octo Vocum. Liber quartus.]

LEVE (J. Frank)

— Estellita. A Love Song. [P. F.] *A. Himan: New York*, 1902.
fol. **h. 3282. kk. (31.)**

— *See* Loth (L. L.) An Autumn Idyl, *etc.* (Edited ... by J. F.
Leve.) 1917. fol. **h. 3588. (2.)**

— *See* Morris (J. R.) At Eventide ... Revised ... by J. F. Leve.
(1913.) fol. **g. 606. p. (35.)**

— *See* Morris (J. R.) Prelude ... Revised ... by J. F. Leve.
(1913.) fol. **g. 606. p. (34.)**

— *See* Morris (J. R.) Swing Song. Revised ... by J. F. Leve.
(1913.) fol. **g. 606. p. (33.)**

LEVEAUX (Edward Henry)

— Four Hebrew Melodies as sung in the Jewish Synagogues
[compiled] with a vocal introduction by Edward H. Leveaux,
the whole arranged for the piano forte by John Hopkinson,
etc. ⟨Part 1.⟩ *J. & J. Hopkinson: Leeds*, [c. 1840.] fol.
Pt. 1 *only.* **H. 1186. aa. (1.)**

— The King of Saxony's gallope ... for the Pianoforte.
London, [1840?] fol. **h. 1480. n. (30.)**

— "Oh weep, weep for those," [song,] the words by Lord Byron.
pp. 3. *Duncombe & Moon: London*, [c. 1850.] fol.
H. 1654. ee. (30.)

— The Scarborough promenade waltzes, arranged for the Piano
Forte by G. Leng. *London*, [1842.] fol. **h. 932. (33.)**

L'EVEILLÉ (Auguste)

— La Marigryska, nouvelle danse de salon ... pour Piano.
Paris, [1865.] fol. **h. 1462. r. (44.)**

LÉVEILLÉ-GROS (Auguste)

— Souvenir de Fontainebleau, morceau de salon pour Piano.
Paris, [1881.] fol. **h. 3272. j. (25.)**

LEVÉL

— Levél az otthoniakhoz. [Part-song.] *See* Bartók (B.)
[Kórusművek.]

LEVELLER

— The Leveller. Song. *See* Harvey (A.)

LEVENSON (Boris)

— The Arabian Nights. Four impressions of Eastern legends,
etc. [P. F.] *W. Paxton & Co.: London*, 1925. 4°.
g. 1125. k. (15.)

— Autumn Sorrow. Osseniaya petschal. Part-Song for Men's
Chorus, a cappella. [Words] Traditional, English version by
... W. E. Brown. Russian Folk-Song. Arranged by
B. Levenson. *H. W. Gray Co.: New York*, 1936. 8°.
F. 1771. c. (21.)

— Ten Bagatelles for piano. (Op. 27. Op. 38.) 2 bk. *Keith,
Prowse & Co.: London*, [1920.] 4°. **g. 1125. d. (1.)**

LEVENSON (Boris)

— The Bells toll. Les Cloques ... For Woman's [sic] Voices, a cappella. English version by M. H. Popkin. Belgian Folk Song. Transcribed by B. Levenson. *M. Baron Co.: New York*, 1943. 8°. **F. 1771. i. (36.)**

— Canzona for Violin and Piano. (Op. 65.) *G. Schirmer: New York*, 1926. 4°. **g. 500. m. (6.)**

— The Charming Songster. Bureano. For Chorus of Men's Voices unaccompanied, English version by M. H. Popkin. Bulgarian Folk Sing, harmonization and choral version by B. Levenson. *Galaxy Music Corporation: New York*, 1942. 8°. **F. 1771. i. (8.)**

— Come, Holy Spirit. Veni, sancte spiritus. For Chorus of Mixed Voices (Women's Voices). XI. century chant. Arranged and harmonized by B. Levenson. 2 no. *H. W. Gray Co.: New York*, 1944. 8°. **E. 335. m. (9.)**

— Danse orientale, for violin and piano. Op. 66. *G. Schirmer: New York*, 1924. 4°. **g. 500. l. (6.)**

— The Days of Sorrow. Paetschalneeye dnee. Russian Folk Song. Harmonized and arranged for Men's Voices, a cappella, by B. Levenson. (English version by M. H. Popkin.) *C. F. Summy Co.: Chicago, New York*, 1938. 8°. **F. 1771. g. (16.)**

— Dreams. A lyric poem for violin and piano. Op. 67. *G. Schirmer: New York*, 1924. 4°. **g. 500. l. (7.)**

— The Fickle Maid. Le Changement. French-Canadian Folk Song for 3 part Womens Voices, English version by M. H. Popkin. Harmonized and arranged by B. Levenson. *Axelrod-Music: Providence, R. I.*, 1938. 8°. **F. 1771. g. (17.)**

— The First Love. Lyric Poem. (For piano. Op. 58.) *Ascherberg, Hopwood & Crew: London*, 1922. 4°. *The International Series of Works for the Pianoforte, No. 1.* **g. 1125. d. (2.)**

— A Folk Song Lullaby. Cradle Song for Mixed Chorus, English version by ... W. E. Brown. Jewish Folk Song. Freely transcribed by B. Levenson. *H. W. Gray Co.: New York*, 1938. 8°. **F. 1771. g. (18.)**

— From the distant land of Volga. Eaz stranee dalyokoy. Part-Song for Men's Chorus, a cappella. [Words] Traditional, English version by M. H. Popkin. Russian Folk-Song. Arranged by B. Levenson. *H. W. Gray Co.: New York*, 1936. 8°. **F. 1771. c. (22.)**

— The Happy Vagabond. Der freilicher Kaptzen. For Men's Chorus a cappella. English version by E. Linden. Jewish Folk Song. Transcribed by B. Levenson. *H. W. Gray Co.: New York*, 1939. 8°. **F. 1771. g. (44.)**

— Heart's Ease. Old English. Harmonized and arranged for Men's Voices, a cappella, by B. Levenson. *C. F. Summy Co.: Chicago, New York*, 1939. 8°. **F. 1771. g. (45.)**

— Hebrew grand Fantasia on traditional Hebrew Melodies. Op. 54. (Piano Solo.) *Belwin: N[ew]. Y[ork]. C[ity]*, 1927. 4°. **g. 822. d. (10.)**

— Hopi Indian Lullaby. Puwuch tawis. For High or Medium Voice ... English text by Princess Neioma Whitecloud. Indian Folk Song. Harmonized and freely transcribed by B. Levenson. *H. W. Gray Co.: New York*, 1941. 4°. **G. 981. x. (1.)**

— King Vladimir's Feast. Peer oo Knyazia Vladimira. Part-Song for Men's Chorus, a cappella. [Words] Traditional, English version by M. H. Popkin. An old Russian Saga. Transcribed by B. Levenson, *etc. H. W. Gray Co.: New York*, 1936. 8°. **F. 1771. c. (23.)**

LEVENSON (Boris)

— The Legend of the wondrous Book. Steekh o goloobeenoy kneegae. For Men's Voices, a cappella. English version by W. E. Brown. Old Russian Saga. Arranged by B. Levenson. *G. F. Summy Co.: Chicago, New York*, 1938. 8°. **F. 1771. g. (19.)**

— The Little Bird. To Poolakee. For Two-part Treble Voices S. A. (Three-part Treble Voices S. S. A.) with Piano accompaniment. English version by V. Lakond. Greek Folk Song. Transcribed by B. Levenson. 2 no. *M. Baron Co.: New York*, 1943. 8°. **F. 1771. i. (37.)**

— The Lone Oak-Tree. Odeen-okey Doob. For Mixed Voices, a cappella ... English version by M. H. Popkin. Russian Folk-Song. Arranged by B. Levenson. *H. Flammer: New York*, 1937. 8°. **F. 1771. e. (15.)**

— The Lost Maiden. Iskhodila mladenka. Russian Folk Song. Arranged for Women's Voices ... S. S. A., a cap[p]ella by B. Levenson. English version by E. Linden. *Elkan-Vogel Co.: Philadelphia*, 1935. 8°. **F. 1771. c. (24.)**

— Four Lyric Pieces for violoncello ... with pianoforte accompaniment. Op. 45, *etc. Hawkes & Son: London, etc.*, 1920. 4°. **g. 510. g. (21.)**

— Minuet in G. Op. 43. No. 2. (For violin, 'cello and piano.) *A. P. Schmidt Co.: Boston, New York*, 1924. 4°. **g. 409. n. (13.)**

— Trois Morceaux lyrique [sic] pour violon et piano. 1. Canzonetta. (Op. 18. No. 1.) 2. Berceuse. (Op. 18. No. 2.) 3. Serenade. (Op. 51.) 3 no. *Keith, Prowse & Co.: London*, 1920. fol. **h. 1612. ll. (28.)**

— Nocturne in D, for ... Violoncello with Piano accompaniment. (Op. 46.) *G. Schirmer: New York*, 1925. 4°. **g. 514. q. (11*.)**

— Oh, mighty Sun. Soontsae Yarko. Mixed Voices. (Women's Voices.) English version by M. H. Popkin. Yugoslav Folk Song. Arranged by B. Levenson. 2 no. *Galaxy Music Corporation: New York* 1937. 8°. **F. 1771. f. (4.)**

— Oh, mighty Sun. Soontsae yarko ... Yugoslav Folksong. Arranged [for T. T. B. B.] by B. Levenson. *Galaxy Music Corporation: New York*, 1939. 8°. **F. 1771. g. (20.)**

— Oh, my Man is dull. Oo menia lee moosch vodopianitsa. Russian Folk Song. Arranged for Female Voices, S. S. A. A., a cap[p]ella by B. Levenson. English version by E. Linden. *Elkan-Vogel Co.: Philadelphia*, 1935. 8°. **F. 1771. c. (25.)**

— The Pavilion of Dreams. Four Songs of Old Japan. I. The pavilion. II. Oh! bring you golden vases. III. The room of dreams. IV. The silver river. Words by E. Lockton. *W. Paxton & Co.: London*, 1922. 4°. **G. 1275. i. (17.)**

— Pictures in the Fire. Six easy miniatures for the piano, *etc. W. Paxton & Co.: London*, 1921. 4°. **g. 1125. d. (3.)**

— Three Pieces. (Op. 14.) 1. Air du XVIII. siècle. 2. Minuet. 3. Chant sans paroles. Cello & piano. *J. R. Lafleur & Son: London*, 1921. 4°. **g. 510. g. (22.)**

— Six Pieces for the pianoforte. Op. 34. No. 1. Russian dance. No. 2. Chant sans paroles. No. 3. Tarantelle. No. 4. Menuetto. No. 5. La plainte ... No. 6. Dance of the marionettes. 6 no. *B. F. Wood Music Co.: Boston*, 1921. 4°. **g. 1127. h. (16.)**

— Prière. Op. 43. No. 1. (For violin, 'cello and piano.) *A. P. Schmidt: Boston, New York*, 1925. 4°. **g. 409. n. (14.)**

— Russian Collegiate Drinking Song. Zastolnaya Stoodentchaeskaya Paesnya. For Chorus of Men's Voices. English version by M. H. Popkin. Russian Folk Song arranged by B. Levenson. *Galaxy Music Corporation: New York*, 1936. 8°. **F. 1771. f. (5.)**

LEVENSON (BORIS)

— Shepherd's Song. For Chorus of Men's Voices. [Words] Traditional, English version by M. H. Popkin. Bosnian Folk Song. Harmonization and Choral version by B. Levenson. *Galaxy Music Corporation: New York*, 1938. 8°.

F. 1771. g. (21.)

— Five Short Pieces ... pour violon et piano. Op. 37. I. Gondolière ... II. Chanson militaire ... III. Chanson orientale ... IV. Berceuse ... V. Bagatelle, *etc. J. Williams: London*, 1920. 4°.

g. 505. jj. (16.)

— Slowly sinks the weary Sun. Kolybelnaia Pesnia ... Russian Lullaby. Song. Lyrics by E. Lockton. Russian words by N. Zscharintzeff. Op. 33. *E. B. Marks Music Co.: New York*, 1928. 4°.

G. 1275. aa. (9.)

— Sweet Agnes. For Chorus of Men's Voices unaccompanied, English version by M. H. Popkin. Dutch Folk Song. Harmonization and choral version by B. Levenson. *Galaxy Music Corporation: New York*, 1940. 8°.   **F. 1771. h. (16.)**

— Two Tone Poems. Op. 55. No. 1. Lyric poem. No. 2. Prelude. Piano Solo. *Keith Prowse & Co.: London*, 1921. fol.

h. 3865. c. (6.)

— La triste Lune. The mournful Moon, pour piano. Op. 59. No. 1. *Bosworth & Co.: London, etc.*, 1920. fol.

h. 3870. a. (30.)

— Twining Dance. Zaplyeteesya plyetyen. Part-Song for Women's Chorus, S. S. A., a cappella. [Words] Traditional. English version by ... W. E. Brown. Russian Folk-Song. Transcribed by B. Levenson. *H. W. Gray Co.: New York*, 1937. 8°.   **F. 1771. e. (16.)**

— The Village Gossip. Taranenta. For Chorus of Women's Voices. English version by M. H. Popkin. Roumanian Folk Song. Choral Version by B. Levenson. *Galaxy Music Corporation: New York*, 1939. 8°.   **F. 1771. g. (46.)**

— The Village Gossip. Tarenenta. For Chorus of Mixed Voices, with Soprano Solo ... Roumanian Folk Song. Harmonization and choral version by B. Levenson. *Galaxy Music Corporation: New York*, 1941. 8°.   **F. 1771. h. (17.)**

— *See* GAMBLE (J.) Heigh-ho! for a Husband ... Arranged ... by B. Levenson, *etc.* 1937. 8°.   **F. 1771. e. (8.)**

— *See* LOVER (S.) The Low-backed Car ... Arranged ... by B. Levenson. 1935. 8°.   **F. 1771. c. (26.)**

— *See* L'VOVSKY (S. V.) Hospodi pomilui. Mighty Lord, have Mercy ... Transcribed ... by B. Levenson, *etc.* 1938. 8°.

F. 1776. l. (38.)

LEVENSON (CHARLES)

— First Book in Violin Playing for Beginners. Compiled and arranged by C. Levenson. *Span., Eng. & Fr. G. Schirmer: New York*, 1921. 4°.   **g. 498. z. (10.)**

— First Exercises in bowing for the Violin. *G. Schirmer: New York, Boston*, 1917. 4°.   **g. 498. x. (4.)**

— The First Finger-Exercises. 25 studies for the Violin preparatory to Charles Dancla. Op. 74. Cjercicios primarios de digstación ... Traducido por M. P. Gainsborg. *G. Schirmer: New York*, 1923. 4°.   **g. 498. cc. (4.)**

— First Scale Studies for the Violin ... Las primeras prácticas de escalas para violín, *etc. G. Schirmer: New York*, 1922. 4°.

g. 498. z. (11.)

— Twelve Recreations by famous Masters for two violins, compiled and arranged by C. Levenson. Second violin part revised by D. Robinson. *G. Schirmer: New York, Boston*, 1918. 4°.   **g. 500. b. (12*.)**

LEVENTHAL (HAROLD)

— *See* GUTHRIE (Woodrow W.) The Woody Guthrie Song Book. Edited by H. Leventhal & M. Guthrie, *etc.* [1976.] 4°.

F. 1875. ff.

LEVENTHAL (SAMUEL)

— Serenade, for Violin and Piano. *J. Church Co.: Cincinnati, etc.*, (1907.) fol.   **h. 1612. p. (32.)**

LEVÈQUE (ÉMILE)

— Un Songe de Vestris. Morceau pour violon et piano. *J. Williams: London*, [1894.] fol.   **h. 1608. x. (41.)**

LEVER

— Le Lever. Mélodie. *See* CHESNEAU (C.) Les Soirées Parisiennes. No. 6.

— Lever. Mélodie. *See* GEORGES (A.)

— Le Lever. Chanson. *See* GOUNOD (C. F.) Vingt mélodies ... 1ᵉʳ. recueil. No. 8.

— Le Lever. [Song.] *See* LACOME D'ESTALENX (P. J. J.) Six nouvelles Mélodies ... No. 5.

— Le Lever. [Song.] *See* MONPOU (H.)

— Le Lever de l'Aurore. Cantatille. *See* LEFÉBURE (A.)

— Lever de Soleil sur le Nil. [Song.] *See* SAINT-SAËNS (C. C.)

— Le Lever des Etoiles. [Song.] *See* MASINI (F.)

LEVER (HAROLD)

— Children of the Empire. [Unison song.] Words by E. Shirley, *etc. Beal, Stuttard & Co.: London*, 1919. 8°. *Choral Miscellany, No. 91.*   **E. 1766. w. (10.)**

— Radcliffe. [Hymn. Begins: "Art thou weary".] *Beal, Stuttard & Co.: London*, [1912.] *a card.*   **I. 600. d. (227.)**

LEVER (SYDNEY) *pseud.* [i. e. *Mrs* CRAFTON E. SMITH.]

— All in all. Song, poetry by Tennyson. *W. D. Cubitt, Son & Co.: London*, [1883.] fol.   **H. 1788. v. (49.)**

— Ave Maria, religious melody for Soprano. *W. D. Cubitt, Son & Co.: London*, [1882.] fol.   **H. 879. e. (16.)**

— Drifting. A boat song in four parts. *London*, [1880.] fol.

H. 1783. o. (59.)

— Drifting. A four part song. Words and music by S. Lever. *London*, [1882.] 8°.   **F. 585. h. (34.)**

— E quando a udir la predica. Canzonetta, parole di T. Trollope. *W. D. Cubitt, Son & Co.: London*, [1882.] fol.

H. 1788. v. (50.)

— Giovanottino non mel dimandate. Stornello. *London*, [1880.] fol.   **H. 1783. o. (58.)**

— A Loveless Life. Song, poetry by Tennyson. *W. D. Cubitt, Son & Co.: London*, [1883.] fol.   **H. 1788. v. (51.)**

— Mother's Advice. Song, words and music by S. Lever. *R. Cocks & Co.: London*, [1884.] fol.   **H. 1788. v. (53.)**

— O Fair Dove, O fond dove. Song [begins: "Methought the stars"]. Words by J. Ingelow. *London*, [1870.] fol.

H. 1775. u. (33.)

— A Place in the Memory. Canzonet, words by G. Griffin, *etc. W. D. Cubitt, Son & Co.: London*, [1883.] fol.

H. 1788. v. (52.)

LEVER (SYDNEY) *pseud.* [i. e. *Mrs* CRAFTON E. SMITH.]

— Sailing beyond Seas. Song, words by J. Ingelow. *W. D. Cubitt & Co.: London*, [1882.] fol. **H. 1788. v. (54.)**

— Twilight. Part song for four voices [begins: "Mark the shades"]. Words and music by S. Lever. *London*, [1882.] 8°. **F. 585. h. (35.)**

— Volubilis, stornello [begins: "Dicon che son mobil"]. Parole di F. Sambuy. *London*, [1870.] fol. **H. 1775. u. (34.)**

LEVERET

— The Leveret. [Part-song.] *See* KODÁLY (Z.) [Nyulacska.]

LEVERIDGE (RICHARD)

— A New Book of Songs, with a through bass to each song. ff. 14. *Sould by I. Walsh ... & I. Hare: London*, 1697. fol. *Printed on one side of the leaf only.* **K. 2. g. 22. (1.)**

— A Second Book of Songs with a through Bass to each Song. pp. 2–4. ff. 5–12. *Sould by I. Walsh ... & I. Hare ... & I. Young: London*, [1699.] fol. *Ff. 5–12 are printed on one side of the leaf only.* **K. 2. g. 22. (2.)**

— A New Book of Songs, Engraven, Printed and Published for R. Leveridge. [*London*, 1711.] fol. **H. 41.**

— [Another copy.] **H. 82. (2.)**

— A Collection of Songs ... In Two Volumes. *Printed for the Author: London*, 1727. 8°. **C. 371.**

— [Another copy.] *Wanting the frontispiece.* **C. 371. a.**

— Advice. [Song.] [*London*, 1730?] *s. sh.* fol. **G. 310. (88.)**

— [Æsop.] Shou'd I once change my Heart. *A Song in the Comedy* [by Sir John Vanburgh] *call'd Æsop* ... Sung by Mrs. Cross and exactly engrav'd by T. Cross. [*London*, 1697.] fol. **K. 7. i. 2. (65.)**

— [Another edition.] Shou'd I once change my Heart. *A Song in ... Æsope, etc.* [*London*, 1700?] fol. **G. 304. (140.)**

— [Another copy.] **G. 311. (46.)**

— [Another copy.] **Hirsch M. 1475. (5.)**

— Ah Silvia, never baulk my Pleasure. [Song.] [c. 1715.] fol. *See* AH. **G. 151. (19.)**

— [Albacinda drew the Dart.] [For editions and arrangements of this song published anonymously:] *See* ALBACINDA.

— Awake, my Eyes, awake. A Song, *etc.* [*London*, 1700?] *s. sh.* fol. **G. 304. (16.)**

— Bacchus God of mortal Pleasure. *A two part Drinking Song* sett and sung by Mr Leveridge [or rather, the words by Leveridge, the music adapted to the gavotte in the overture to "Ottone" by Händel]. [*London*, c. 1730.] *s. sh.* fol. *Followed by an arrangement for the flute.* **H. 1653. uu. (17.)**

— [The Beau Demolish'd.] Whilst I'm carrouzing ... *Song* ... [composed] by Mr. Leveridge. [1715?] *s. sh.* fol. *See* BEAU. The Beau Demolish'd. **G. 313. (130.)**

— [The Beau Demolish'd.] Whilst I'm carrouzing. *A Song in the Beau Demolish'd;* sung by Mr Leveridge. [c. 1720.] fol. *Printed on one side of the leaf only. Followed by an accompaniment for flute.* **G. 316. o. (8.)**

— [The Beau Demolish'd.] Whilst I'm carousing. A Bacchanalian Song ... Edited and arranged by E. Newton. *Keith Prowse & Co.: London*, 1926. 4°. **G. 1270. cc. (11.)**

LEVERIDGE (RICHARD)

— [The Beau Demolish'd.] Whilst I'm carousing. Arrangement for Male Voices by F. Tapp. *Keith Prowse & Co.: London*, 1937. 8°. **F. 163. gg. (40.)**

— The Beggar's Song. Arranged by H. L. Wilson. *Boosey & Co.: London & New York*, 1899. fol. **H. 1799. h. (50.)**

— [The Beggar's Song.] How jolly are we Beggars ... Arranged for Chorus of Men's Voices by J. C. Fyfe ... Based on the Song as in the collection Old English Melodies, edited by H. Lane Wilson. *Boosey & Co.: London*, 1939. 8°. [*Boosey's Choral Miscellany. No.* 193.] **F. 160. e.**

— The Beggar's Song ... [Melody arranged by] H. Lane Wilson. Arr. (for Male Voices, T. T. B.) by Wayne Howorth. *Boosey Hawkes Belwin, Inc.: New York*, 1940. 8°. **F. 163. ii. (55.)**

— The Biter Bit. [Song.] [*London*, 1720?] *s. sh.* fol. **H. 1994. b. (97.)**

— Black and gloomy as ye Grave. [Song, words from T. D'Urfey's "Cinthia and Endimion".] [c. 1715.] fol. *See* BLACK. **G. 151. (25.)**

Black-ey'd Susan

— Black-Ey'd Susan to Mr. Leveridge's tune. For the Flute. [*London*, 1720?] *s. sh.* fol. **G. 305. (177.)**

— Sweet William's Farewell to Black ey'd Susan, *etc.* (Mr. Leveridge's Tune.) [1720?] *s. sh.* fol. *See* CAREY (H.) [Black-eyed Susan.] **H. 1601. (24.)**

— [Another edition.] Sweet William's Farewell, *etc.* (The Tune by Mr. Leveridge.) [1725?] *s. sh.* fol. *See* CAREY (H.) [Black-eyed Susan.] **G. 316. g. (2.)**

— All in the Downs, *etc.* (Mr. Leveridge's Tune.) [1750?] *s. sh.* fol. *See* CAREY (H.) [Black-eyed Susan.] **G. 806. r. (11.)**

— Sweet William's Farewell, *etc.* [Song.] ⟨Mr Leveridge Tune.⟩ [c. 1770.] *s. sh.* fol. *See* CAREY (H.) [Black-eyed Susan.] **G. 426. kk. (6.)**

— All in the Downs. [Song, melody only.] *In:* CEASE. Cease rude Boreas. *The Storm, etc.* p. 3. [^{WM}1799.] fol. **G. 426. pp. (19.)**

— Black ey'd Susan. [Song.] As sung by Mr. Incledon, *etc. See* ALL. All in the Downs the Fleet was moor'd, *etc.* [1800?] *s. sh.* fol. **H. 1601. f. (17.)**

— All in the Downs the Fleet was moor'd. *Black ey'd Susan, etc.* ⟨Mr Handel's [or rather, R. Leveridge's] tune.⟩ [c. 1800.] fol. *See* ALL. **H. 1860. ww. (21.)**

— All in the Downs. [Song.] ⟨Mr Leveridge's Tune.⟩ *In:* CEASE. Cease rude Boreas, *etc.* p. 3. [c. 1815.] fol. **G. 295. cc. (29.)**

— All in the Downs. *Black eyed Susan.* A popular ballad, sung by Mr Incledon. pp. 3. [c. 1815.] fol. *See* ALL. **G. 424. pp. (14.)**

— All in the Downs. *Black eyed Susan,* the favorite song sung by Mr Incledon. [c. 1815.] fol. *See* ALL. **G. 295. ss. (21.)**

— All in the Downs. *Black Eye'd Susan.* A favorite song, sung by Mr Incledon, *etc.* pp. 3. [^{WM}1816.] fol. *See* ALL. **H. 2401. f. (1.)**

— Black eyed Susan, celebrated nautical ballad written by John Gay, composed by Carey [or rather, R. Leveridge]. Newly arranged by Henri Schubert. pp. 3. [1854.] fol. *See* CAREY (H.) [*Doubtful and Supposititious Works.*] **H. 1749. (25.)**

— All in the Downs. *Black-eyed Susan, etc.* [Song.] pp. 4. [1855.] fol. [*Musical Bouquet. no.* 611.] *See* ALL. **H. 2345.**

— Black eyed Susan ... Ballad. ⟨[Words by] John Gay. [Music by] H. Carey [or rather, R. Leveridge].⟩ pp. 3. [1873.] fol. *See* CAREY (H.) [*Doubtful and Supposititious Works.*] **H. 1778. f. (19.)**

LEVERIDGE (Richard)

— Black-eyed Susan ... Ballad. ⟨In A minor. In C minor.⟩ 2 no. *London*, [1877.] fol. **H. 1778. y. (18.)**

— All in the Downs. *Black-eyed Susan* ... Ballad, with new symphony & accompaniment by George Fox. pp. 3. [1877.] fol. [*Cunningham Boosey's "Universal" Music. no.* 139.] *See* ALL. **H. 2324.**

— Black eyed Susan ... with new symphony & accompaniment by R. Gaythorne. *London*, [1879.] fol. **H. 1783. o. (61.)**

— *See* DREYSCHOCK (A.) Mazurka sur la mélodie "Black eyed Susan". Pour le piano forte ... Op. 65. [1849.] fol. **h. 651. (26.)**

— *See* HARVEY (R. F.) Black Eyed Susan ... for the Pianoforte. [1872.] fol. **h. 649. c. (19.)**

— *See* HOBBES (T. R.) Black ey'd Susan ... arranged by T. R. Hobbes. [1825?] fol. **H. 1650. uu. (14.)**

— Blythe Jockey, young and gay. [Song.] *Sung by the Boy.* [*London*, 1700?] *s. sh.* fol. **G. 306. (234.)**

— [Another copy.] **G. 304. (26.)**

— [Another edition.] Blythe Jockey, young and gay. *A Scotch Song, etc.* [*London*, 1710?] *s. sh.* fol. **H. 1601. (67.)**

— [Caligula.—Tho' over all Mankind.] A Song made for the Entertainment of Her Royal Highness ... Sung by Mrs. Lindsey, in Caligula [by J. Crowne]; and exactly engrav'd by T. Cross. [*London*, 1698.] fol. **K. 7. i. 2. (66.)**

— [Another edition.] [*London*, 1700?] fol. *Wanting pp.* 1–3. **G. 315. (50.)**

— [Caligula.] Tho over all Mankind. *This Song made for the Entertainment of her royall Highness the Princess, in the Tragedy of Calligula.* Sung by Mrs Lindsey. [Score.] pp. 4. [*London*, c. 1705.] fol. **G. 425. rr. (11.)**

— [Caligula.] Tho over all Mankind. *This Song* made for the Entertainment of her Royall Highness the Princess, in the Tragedy of Calligula, Sung by Mrs Lindsey. [*London*, 1715?] fol. [*A Collection of the Choicest Songs & Dialogues. No.* 153.] **G. 151.**

— Chloe brisk and gay appears. *A Song* ... exactly engrav'd by T. Cross. [*London*, 1698?] fol. **K. 7. i. 2. (68.)**

— [Another edition.] Cloe brisk and gay appears. [*London*, 1710?] *s. sh.* fol. **G. 305. (23.)**

— [Another edition.] Chloe brisk and gay appears. *A Song* ... exactly engrav'd by D. Wright. [*London*, 1715?] *s. sh.* fol. **H. 601. (105.)**

— The Cobler's End. [Song.] Sung by Mr Leveridge at the Theatre in Lincolns Inn Feilds. [c. 1765.] *s. sh.* fol. *See* COBBLER. A cobler there was. **H. 1601. c. (24.)**

— The Cobler's End. [Song.] *R. Falkener: London*, [c. 1770.] *s. sh.* fol. *Followed by an accompaniment for German flute.* **H. 1648. f. (10.)**

— Come fair one be kind. *See infra:* [The Recruiting Officer.]

— Come Neighbours now. *See infra:* [Jupiter and Europa.]

— The Contented Man. [Song.] [*London*, 1740?] *s. sh.* fol. **G. 308. (8.)**

— [Another copy.] **G. 315. (17.)**

— Cry'd Celia to a Reverend Dean. [Song.] [*London*, 1730?] *s. sh.* fol. **G. 307. (42.)**

LEVERIDGE (Richard)

— [Another edition.] Cry'd Celia to a Reverend Dean. [Song.] For the Germ^{an} Flute. ⟨Long by an idle Passion tost. *Set by Mr. Stanley.* [Song.]⟩ [*London?* 1730?] *s. sh.* fol. **G. 316. d. (95.)**

— The Cuckow. [Song, the words by W. Shakespeare.] [*London*, 1725?] *s. sh.* fol. **G. 313. (62.)**

— Cupid my Pleasure. *A two part Song.* The words & Music by Mr. Leveridge. [*London*, 1750?] *s. sh.* fol. **G. 316. (95.)**

— [Another copy.] **H. 1994. a. (23.)**

— The Cure of all Grief. [Song.] [*London*, 1730?] *s. sh.* fol. **G. 307. (199.)**

— The Cure of Care. *See infra:* [Jupiter and Europa.]

— Drinking Excus'd. [Song.] [*London*, 1725?] *s. sh.* fol. **G. 313. (5.)**

— [Another copy.] **G. 303. (87.)**

— Early in the Dawning. [Song.] *Sung by Mr. Penkethman.* [*London*, 1700?] *s. sh.* fol. **G. 304. (51.)**

— [Another copy.] **I. 530. (52.)**

— England's young riflemen, a song for the times by M. F. Tupper [begins: "In days long ago"], symphonies & accomp^{ts}. by J. Clarke. *London*, [1859.] fol. **H. 1771. l. (21.)**

— The fair Aurelia's gone astray. [Song.] *Words by a Person of Quality.* [*London*, 1720?] *s. sh.* fol. **G. 305. (25.)**

— [Another copy.] **G. 312. (43.)**

Farewell Folly

— The Mountebank Song [begins "Here are People and Sports"], Sung by Dr. Leverigo and his Merry Andrew Pinkanello, in Farewell to Folly [words by P. A. Motteux], *etc.* [*London*, 1707.] *s. sh.* fol. **G. 305. (24.)**

— [Another copy.] **G. 308. (60.)**

— The Mountebank, a Song [begins: "See Sirs, see here,"] in the Quacks or Farewell Folly. [Words by P. A. Motteux.] Set and sung by Mr. Leveridge. [*London*, 1707.] *s. sh.* fol. **G. 305. (20.)**

— [Another copy.] **G. 315. (137.)**

— [Another edition.] The Mountebank. A Song, *etc.* 1707. *s. sh.* fol. *See* FAREWELL. Farewell Folly. **H. 1601. (383.)**

— The Fickle Fair. [Song, Words by J. Smith.] [*London*, 1730?] *s. sh.* fol. **G. 308. (67.)**

— Fly from his charming Language. [Song.] *Sung by Mrs. Lindsey.* [*London*, 1710?] *s. sh.* fol. **G. 305. (209.)**

— [The Fool in Fashion.] When Lovesick Mars ŷ God of War. [Song.] *Sung by Mr Willis* in the Second part of ŷ Foole in fashion. [*London*, 1715?] *s. sh.* fol. [*A Collection of the Choicest Songs & Dialogues. No.* 173.] **G. 151. (173.)**

— Foolish Swain thy Sighs forbear. *A Song* set and sung by Mr. Leveridge at the Theatre Royall. [*London*, 1715?] *s. sh.* fol. **H. 1601. (160.)**

— [Another edition.] Foolish Swain thy Sighs forbear. *A Song, etc.* [*London*, 1720?] *s. sh.* fol. **G. 305. (22.)**

— [Another copy.] **G. 307. (191.)**

— From good Liquor ne'er shrink. *Chanson à Boire.* [*London*, 1720?] *s. sh.* fol. **G. 307. (181.)**

LEVERIDGE (RICHARD)

— Fye Damon leave this foolish Passion. [Song.] [c. 1715.] *s. sh.* fol. *See* FIE.
G. 151. (51.)

— Good Advice. A Song set and sung by Mr. Leveridge at the New Play-house. [*London*, 1700?] *s. sh.* fol.
H. 1601. (286.)

— [Another edition.] Good Advice, *etc.* [*London*, 1715?] *s. sh.* fol.
G. 310. (28.)

— [Another edition.] Good Advice, *etc. Cluer:* [*London*, 1720?] *s. sh.* fol.
G. 316. g. (36.)

— A Health to the best in Christendom. [Song.] *See* BOAST. Boast no more of nice Beautys, *etc.* [1710?] *s. sh.* fol.
H. 1601. (74.)

— Hold, John, e'er you leave me. *See* ISLAND. The Island Princess.

— How jolly are we Beggars. *See* supra: [The Beggar's Song.]

— Hunting Song. *See* infra: [The sweet rosy Morn.]

— If Celia you had Youth at will. [Song, words from C. Gildon's tragedy, "The Roman Bride's Revenge".] [c. 1705.] *s. sh.* fol. *See* IF.
G. 305. (200.)

— If to Love or good Wine. *A New Song, etc.* [*London*, 1715?] fol.
G. 309. (50.)

— Iris beware when Strephon pursue [*sic*] you. *A Song* Sett, and Sung by Mr. Leveridge at the Theatre. [*London*, c. 1710.] *s. sh.* fol.
Followed by an accompaniment for flute.   **G. 316. m. (19.)**

— Iris beware when Strephon pursues you. *A Song* sett and sung by Mr. Leveridge at the Theatre. [*London*, 1720?] *s. sh.* fol.
G. 309. (77.)

— [For songs in the Island Princess composed by R. Leveridge:] *See* ISLAND. The Island Princess.

— Jenny long resisted. [Song.] *Sung by Mrs. Campion. I. Walsh, I. Hare & I. Young: London*, [1700?] *s. sh.* fol.   **G. 304. (85.)**

— [Another copy.]   **G. 309. (62.)**

— Jogging on from yonder Green. [Song.] *Sung by Mrs. Lindsey.* [*London*, 1700?] *s. sh.* fol.
G. 304. (79.)

— [Another copy.]   **G. 309. (78.)**

Jupiter and Europa

— Jupiter and Europa, a Masque of Song's as they were perform'd at the Theatre in Lincolns Inn Fields, *etc.* [By J. E. Galliard, Cobston and R. Leveridge.] 1723. fol. *See* JUPITER. Jupiter and Europa.   **Add. MSS. 31588. fol. 3.**

— [Another copy.]   **H. 76.**

— Come Neighbours now. A Song Sung in ... Jupeter & Europia, *etc.* 1723. fol. *See* JUPITER. Jupiter and Europa.
G. 315. (165.)

Jupiter and Europa.—The Cure of Care

— This great World is a Trouble. [1723.] *s. sh.* fol. *See* JUPITER. Jupiter and Europa.   **G. 312. (47.)**

— This great World is a Trouble, *etc.* [c. 1725.] *s. sh.* fol. *See* JUPITER. Jupiter and Europa.   **H. 1601. i. (7.)**

— The Cure of Care. Song ... arranged by J. Greenhill. *Boosey & Co.: London and New York*, 1895. fol.   **H. 1798. v. (15.)**

— This great World is a Trouble. Unison Song, words of second verse by W. G. Rothery. *Novello and Co.: London*, [1933.] 8°. [*Novello's School Songs. No.* 1514.]   **F. 280. d.**

LEVERIDGE (RICHARD)

— When dull Care. Arranged for mixed voices ⟨male voices⟩ by Eric H. Thiman. [Staff and tonic sol-fa notation.] 2 no. *Ascherberg, Hopwood & Crew: London*, [1966.] 8°. [*Mortimer Series of choral Music. no.* 644, 645.]   **F. 1659. a.**

— [The Lady in Fashion.] Tell me, Bellinda, *etc.* [Song, words from C. Cibber's "Woman's Wit".] [1697?] fol. *See* TELL.
H. 1601. c. (5.)

— [The Lady in Fashion.] Tell me, Belinda, prithee do. *A Song* in [Woman's Wit or] the Lady in fashion ... Sung by Mrs. Cibber and exactly engrav'd by T. Cross. [Words by C. Cibber.] [*London*, 1698?] *s. sh.* fol.   **K. 7. i. 2. (67.)**

— Lay aside the reap-hook. *See* infra: [The Mountebank.]

— Lead on brave Nimphs. [Song.] [*London*, 1715?] *s. sh.* fol. [*A Collection of the Choicest Songs & Dialogues. No.* 95.]
G. 151.

— Let charming Sounds our Cares divert. *A Song* set and sung by Mr Leveridge. With violins or hoboys. [Score.] [*London?* c. 1710.] fol.
Printed on one side of the leaf only.   **G. 316. n. (6.)**

— Let soft desires your Heart engage. *See* ISLAND. The Island Princess.

— [Love and a bottle.] When Cupid from his Mother fled. *Songs* in the new Comedy [by G. Farquhar] call'd Love and a Bottle. Sung by Mrs. Allinson. [*London*, 1699.] *s. sh.* fol.
G. 304. (172.)

— [Another edition.] When Cupid from his Mother fled. *A Song* ... exactly engrav'd by T. Cross. [*London*, 1699?] *s. sh.* fol.
G. 315. (150.)

— Love is lost. [Song.] [*London*, c. 1715.] fol. *See* LOVE.
G. 310. (11.)

— Love is lost. A song set to musick by Mr. Tho. Brown ... [In fact by R. Leveridge.] Sung by Mr. Platt at Sadlers Wells. [c. 1720.] fol. *See* BROWN (Thomas) *Songwriter.* [*Doubtful and Supposititious Works.*]   **H. 1601. (295.)**

— The Lusty Young Blacksmith, *etc.* [Song.] [*London*, 1705?] *s. sh.* fol.   **Gren. 559. (22.)**

— [The Lusty Young Blacksmith.] A lusty young Smith at his Vice stood a filing. *A Song* ... exactly engrav'd by D. Wright. [*London*, 1705?] *s. sh.* fol.   **H. 1601. (45.)**

— [Another edition.] A lusty young Smith at his Vice stood a filing. *A Song, etc.* [*London*, 1705?] *s. sh.* fol.   **G. 304. (8.)**

— The Lusty Young Blacksmith, *etc.* [*London*, 1710?] *s. sh.* fol.
G. 316. d. (15.)

— [Macbeth. For editions and arrangements of the music for Macbeth attributed to M. Locke but probably by R. Leveridge:] *See* LOCKE (Matthew) [*Doubtful and Supposititious Works.*]

— [Macbeth.] The Musick in the Tragedy of Macbeth. In Score. Composed by H. Purcell. [By R. Leveridge?] [1786.] *obl.* fol. [*New Musical Magazine. no.* 142, 143.] *See* PURCELL (Henry) [*Doubtful and Supposititious Works.*]   **E. 105.**

— [Macbeth.] Let's have a Dance upon the Heath. *The Witches Song* in the Tragedy of Macbeth. [By R. Leveridge?] Sung by Mrs. Clive. [c. 1750.] *s. sh.* fol. *See* MACBETH.   **I. 595. (15.)**

— Marinda's face like Cupid's bow. *A new Song* ... Sung att the Theater in Dublin. [*London*, 1700?] fol.   **G. 304. (105.)**

LEVERIDGE (RICHARD)

Masaniello

— Of all the World's enjoyments. *The Fishermans Song* in the First Part of Massaniello [by T. D'Urfey], Set and Sung by Mr. Leveridge, and exactly engrav'd by T. Cross. [*London*,1700.] *s. sh.* fol.   **H. 1994. c. (54.)**

— [Another edition.] Of all the World's enjoyments. The Fishermans Song in Massaniello, *etc.* [*London*, 1700.] *s. sh.* fol.   **G. 304. (115.)**

— [Another copy.]   **G. 310. (173.)**

— [Another copy.]   **G. 305. (185.)**

— [Another edition.] Of all the World's enjoyments. *The Fishermans Song, etc.* [1700.] *s. sh.* fol. See OF.   **H. 1601. (353.)**

— The Miser's Pursuit, *etc.* [Song, words by the Rev. S. Wesley.] [*London*, 1725?] *s. sh.* fol.   **G. 313. (36.)**

The Mountebank

— Lay aside the reaphook. [Song.] *Sung by Mr. Randall, in the Farce call'd the Mountebank or the Country Lass.* [*London*, 1715.] *s. sh.* fol.   **G. 305. (133.)**

— [Another copy.]   **G. 310. (23.)**

— [Another edition.] Lay aside the reap-hook, *etc.* [*London*, 1715.] *s. sh.* fol.   **H. 1601. (273.)**

— Now Roger and Harry. [Song.] *Sung by Mr. Jones in the Farce call'd the Mountebank or the Country Lass, etc.* [*London*, 1715.] *s. sh.* fol.   **H. 1601. (314.)**

— [Another edition.] Now Roger and Harry, *etc.* [*London*, 1715.] *s. sh.* fol.   **G. 310. (136.)**

— [Another copy.]   **G. 305. (13.)**

— The Mountebank Song. *See* supra: [Farewell Folly.]

— Now Roger and Harry. *See* supra: [The Mountebank.]

— Observations on a Gentlewoman, working by an Hour-Glass. [Song.] The Words by Ben Johnson. [*London*, 1753.] 8°. *Universal Magazine, Vol. XIII., p.*271.   **P. P. 5439.**

— Of all the World's enjoyments. *See* supra: [Masaniello.]

— Of good English Beer our Song let's raise. *A Song* in Praise of Old English Beer. [*London*, 1740?] *s. sh.* fol.   **G. 310. (198.)**

— [Another copy.]   **G. 303. (70.)**

— [Another edition.] Of good English Beer our Song let's raise, *etc.* [*London*, 1745?] *s. sh.* fol.   **G. 316. e. (101.)**

— Oft I'm by the Women told. *An Ode in Anacreon.* [Translated by A. Cowley.] *Printed for J. Simpson:* [*London*, 1735?] *s. sh.* fol.   **G. 315. (3.)**

— [Another edition.] Oft I'm by the Women told. *An Ode in Anacreon.* [*London*, 1740?] *s. sh.* fol.   **G. 310. (179.)**

— Oh cease, urge no more. *See* ISLAND. The Island Princess.

— Oh Death think on the Words you gave. *A Dialogue between Death and a Dying Person ...* The Words by Mr. Parrat. [*London*, 1740.] 8°. *Gentleman's Magazine, Vol. X., p.*88.   **249. c. 10.**

— Old Poets have told us, when they were grown mellow. [Song.] [*London*, 1720?] *s. sh.* fol.   **I. 530. (90.)**

— On Sunday after Mass. [Song.] *Sung by Mrs. Mills.* [*London*, 1700?] *s. sh.* fol.   **G. 304. (113.)**

LEVERIDGE (RICHARD)

— [Another copy.]   **G. 310. (182.)**

— [Another copy.]   **I. 530. (92.)**

— [Another edition.] On Sunday after Mass. *A Song, etc.* [*London*, 1710?] *s. sh.* fol.   **H. 1601. (350.)**

— [Plot and no Plot.] When Chloe I your Charms survey. *A Song* in the Plot and no Plot [words by T. Cheek], Set and Sung by Mr. Leveridge and exactly engrav'd by T. Cross. [*London*, 1698.] *s. sh.* fol.   **K. 7. i. 2. (69.)**

— [Another edition.] When Chloe I your Charms survey. [*London*, 1705?] *s. sh.* fol.   **G. 304. (170.)**

— [Another edition.] When Chloe I your Charms survey, *etc.* [*London*, 1710?] *s. sh.* fol.   **H. 1601. (511.)**

— [The Quacks.] To gentle Strephon tell your grief. *A Song* in the Play call'd the Quacks, or Lov's the Physitian, [adapted by O. Mac Swiney from Molière's 'L'Amour Médecin,'] Sung by the Boy. [*London*, 1705.] fol.   **G. 315. (9.)**

— [The Recruiting Officer.] Come fair one be kind. *A Song ...* Sung by Mr. Wilks in the Comedy call'd the Recruiting Officer. [Words by G. Farquhar.] Within Compass of the Flute. [*London*, 1706.] *s. sh.* fol.   **G. 307. (1.)**

— [Another copy.]   **G. 305. (19.)**

— The Reproach. [Song, words by Dr. Donne.] *See* YOUNG (A.) The Reproach, *etc.* (Mr. Leveridge's Tune.) [1720?] *s. sh.* fol.   **G. 311. (76.)**

— [Another edition.] The Reproach. *See* YOUNG (A.) The Reproach, *etc.* (Mr. Leveridge's Tune.) [1720?] *s. sh.* fol.   **H. 1601. (405.)**

— Resolution. [Song.] [*London*, 1725?] *s. sh.* fol.   **G. 310. (15.)**

The Roast Beef Song

— The Roast Beef Song [begins: "When mighty Roast Beef was the Englishman's Food"] ... by a Lady of Quality. [*London*, 1735?] *s. sh.* fol.   **G. 313. (135.)**

— [Another copy.]   **I. 530. (177.)**

— By the blessing of God we have Conquer'd at last, *etc.* [To the tune of the Roast Beef of Old England, by R. Leveridge.] [1782.] *s. sh.* fol. *See* BY.   **G. 308. (190.)**

— The Roast Beef of Old England ... with new symphony & accompaniment by R. Gaythorne. *London*, [1879.] fol.   **H. 1783. o. (60.)**

— Puissant rosbif de la vieille Angleterre ... Chant populaire, *etc.* 1897. 8°. *See* PUISSANT.   **P. P. 9021. (2838.)**

— The Roast Beef of Old England. Unison Song. *See* WHEN. When mighty roast Beef was the Englishman's Food, *etc.* [1919.] 8°. [*Novello's School Songs. No.*1185*b.*]   **F. 280. d.**

— Oh! the Roast Beef of Old England. A Four-Part Song, arranged by J. Pittman. [1886.] *See* NOVELLO AND CO. Novello's Tonic Sol-fa Series. No. 497 [a]. [1876, *etc.*] 4°.   **B. 885.**

— *See* WALPOLE (F.) The Roast Beef of Old England for the Pianoforte. [1870.] fol.   **h. 1486. f. (25.)**

— Should I dye by yᵉ Force of Good Wine. *A Song* Sett and Sung by Mr. Leveridge at the Theatre. [*London*, 1720?] *s. sh.* fol.   **H. 1601. (395.)**

— [Another edition.] Should I dye by yᵉ force of good Wine. *A Song, etc.* *T. Cluer:* [*London*, 1720?] *s. sh.* fol.   **G. 316. g. (55.)**

— [Another edition.] Should I dye by yᵉ force of good Wine, *etc.* [*London*, 1720?] *s. sh.* fol.   **G. 311. (81.)**

LEVERIDGE (Richard)

— [Another edition.] Should I dye by the Force of good Wine, *etc.* [*London*, 1730?] *s. sh.* fol.   **G. 316. e. (134.)**

— Shou'd I once change my Heart. *See* supra: [Æsop.]

— The Sun was just setting. *A new Song, etc.* H. *Playford:* [*London*, 1700?] *s. sh.* fol.   **G. 312. (28.)**

— [Another copy.]   **G. 304. (149.)**

— [Another edition.] The Sun was just setting, *etc.* [*London*, 1710?] *s. sh.* fol.   **H. 1601. (429.)**

— Sure ne'er was a Dog so wretched. *A Song* ... Set for the German Flute. [*London*, 1735?] *s. sh.* fol.   **G. 316. e. (144.)**

Sweet are the Charms of her I love

— Sweet are the Charms of her I love. A New Ballad. The Words by Mr. Barton Booth, *etc.* [*London*, 1710?] *s. sh.* fol.   **H. 1601. (404.)**

— [Another edition.] Sweet are the Charms of her I love. *A new Ballad, etc.* I. *Jones:* [*London*, 1710?] *s. sh.* fol.   **I. 530. (91.)**

— [Another edition.] Sweet are the charms of her I love. *A New Song, etc.* [*London*, 1710?] *s. sh.* fol.   **G. 305. (217.)**

— [Another copy.]   **G. 311. (52.)**

— [Another copy.]   **G. 316. g. (61.)**

— Fair soft and easy Celia walks ... to the Tune of Sweet are the Charms, *etc.* [1720?] *s. sh.* fol. *See* Fair.   **H. 1601. (140.)**

— [The sweet rosy Morn. For anonymous editions and arrangements of this song in Apollo and Daphne:] *See* Apollo. Apollo and Daphne.

— [The sweet rosy Morn.] Hunting Song. Three-part song for S. A. B., arranged by H. Reuben Holmes. [Staff and tonic sol-fa notation.] pp. 5. J. B. *Cramer & Co.: London*, [1956.] 8°. [*Cramer's choral Library B.* 68.]   **F. 157. g.**

— [The sweet rosy Morn.] Hunting Song. Two-part song for S. S. Arr. by H. Reuben Holmes. pp. 5. J. B. *Cramer & Co.: London*, [1956.] 8°. [*Cramer's Library of unison and Part-songs. no.* 271.]   **E. 1678. a.**

— Talk no more of Whig or Tory. [Song, begins: "Leave off this foolish prating".] *London*, [1856.] fol. *No.* 428 *of the "Cyclopedia of Music. Miscellaneous Series of Songs".*   **H. 2342.**

— Tell me, Belinda, prithee do. *See* supra: [The Lady of Fashion.]

— Tell me ye softer Powers above. [Song.] *Sung by Mrs Campion.* [*London*, 1715?] fol. [*A Collection of the Choicest Songs & Dialogues. No.* 152.]   **G. 151.**

— This great World is a Trouble. *See* supra: [Jupiter and Europa.—The Cure of Care.]

— Thus Damon knock't at Celia's Door. *A Song* ... sung at the Theater. [Words from G. Farquhar's "Constant Couple".] [*London*, 1700?] *s. sh.* fol.   **H. 1601. (448.)**

— [Another edition.] Thus Damon knock't at Celia's door. *A new Song* ... Sung at ye Theater in Dublin. [*London*, 1710?] *s. sh.* fol.   **G. 304. (155.)**

— Time Anticipated. [Song.] [*London*, 1725?] *s. sh.* fol.   **G. 303. (5.)**

LEVERIDGE (Richard)

— The Tippling Philosophers. [Song, words by E. Ward.] Set and Sung by Mr. Leveridge at the Theatre in Lincoln's Inn Fields. I. *Jones:* [*London*, 1710?] *s. sh.* fol.   **Gren. 559. (17.)**

— [Another edition.] The tippling Philosophers, *etc.* [*London*, 1715?] *s. sh.* fol.   **H. 1601. (136.)**

— To gentle Strephon tell your Grief. *See* supra: [The Quacks.]

— Truth. A song. D. *Wright jun':* [*London*, c. 1730.] *s. sh.* fol. *Followed by an arrangement for flute.*   **G. 425. aa. (8.)**

— The Wheel of Fortune. *See* Wheel. The Wheel of Life is turning quickly round ... A Song [composed and] Sung by Mr. Leveridge, *etc.* [1725?] *s. sh.* fol.   **G. 312. (21.)**

— When Chloe I your Charms survey. *See* supra: [Plot and no Plot.]

— When Cupid from his Mother fled. *See* supra: [Love and a Bottle.]

— When dull Care. *See* supra: [Jupiter and Europa.—The Cure of Care.]

— When lovesick Mars. *See* supra: [The Fool in Fashion.]

— When Sawney first did woe me. *A new Song* ... Sung at ye Theater in Dublin. [*London*, 1710?] *s. sh.* fol.   **G. 304. (173.)**

— [Another edition.] When Sawny first did woe me. *A Scotch Song, etc.* [*London*, 1710?] *s. sh.* fol.   **H. 1601. (503.)**

— [Another edition.] When Sawny first did woe me, *A Scotch Song, etc.* [*London*, 1715?] *s. sh.* fol.   **G. 313. (64.)**

— [Another copy.]   **G. 304. (6.)**

— Whilst I'm carrouzing. *See* supra: [The Beau Demolish'd.]

— Who is Silvia. Song. *See* Shakespeare. The Shakspeare Vocal Magazine. No. 23. [1864.] fol.   **H. 2389.**

— Who is Sylvia? [Song and chorus.] *See* Two. [Two Gentlemen of Verona.] The Vocal Music to ... Two Gentlemen of Verona. (By R. Leveridge.) 1925. 4°. [*The Vocal Music to Shakespeare's Plays. No.* 18.]   **G. 1243.**

— Why do you with disdain refuse. *A Song*, the Words by a Person of Quality ... exactly engrav'd by T. Cross. [*London*, 1700?] *s. sh.* fol.   **I. 530. (93.)**

— Why de' you with disdain refuse. *A Song* the Words by a Person of Quality. [*London*, 1715?] *s. sh.* fol. [*A Collection of the Choicest Songs & Dialogues. No.* 177.]   **G. 151.**

— A Yorkshire Tale. [Song.] [*London*, 1720?] *s. sh.* fol.   **G. 307. (6.)**

— [Another edition.] A Yorkshire Tale, *etc.* [*London?* 1720?] *s. sh.* fol.   **G. 316. d. (93.)**

— A Yorkshire Tale. [Song.] [*London*, c. 1730.] *s. sh.* fol.   **H. 1601. r. (44.)**

— You've been with dull Prologues. *See* Island. The Island Princess.

— Young Cupid I find. *A Song.* Set and Sung by Mr. Leveridge at the Theatre. [*London*, 1720?] *s. sh.* fol.   **G. 305. (152.)**

— *See* Harmonia. Harmonia Anglicana ... A Collection of ... Songs ... by ... Leveridge, *etc.* [c. 1745.] fol.   **G. 103. b.**

— *See* Shield (W.) [The Crusade.] The Songs ... in the ... Crusade, [a pasticcio,] composed by ... Carolan, Leveridge, *etc.* [1790.] *obl.* fol.   **D. 293. b.**

LEVERIDGE (RICHARD)

— *See* THESAURUS. Thesaurus Musicus. A Collection of ... Part Songs ... by ... Leveridge, *etc.* [1744.] fol.　　　**H. 73.**

— *See* THESAURUS. Thesaurus Musicus, *etc.* [1745.] fol.
　　　H. 73. a.

LEVERMORE (CHARLES HERBERT)

— The Abridged Academy Song-Book, for use in schools and colleges. Revised edition. *Ginn and Co.: Boston, etc.*, 1918. 4°.　　　**E. 1815. a.**

— The American Song Book; a collection of songs & hymns, *etc. Ginn & Co.: Boston, etc.*, 1917. 8°.　　　**E. 1815.**

LEVERNO (ALBERT)

— Come to me, Darling. Song, written & composed by A. Leverno, arranged by L. Gautier. *W. H. Broome: London,* [1895.] fol.　　　**H. 1798. v. (16.)**

LE VERRIER DE LA CONTERIE (JEAN BAPTISTE JACQUES) *Seigneur d'Amigny, etc.*

— L'École de la chasse aux chiens courants, *etc.* (Tons de chasse et fanfares.) 2 vol. *Nicolas et Richard Lallemant: Rouen,* 1763. 8°.　　　**451. g. 6, 7.**

—[L'École de la chasse aux chiens courants.] Venerie normande, ou l'école de la chasse au chiens courants ... Avec les tons de chasse, *etc.* pp. xv. 526. *Chez Laurent Dumesnil: Rouen,* 1778. 8°.　　　**453. c. 2.**

— L'École de la chasse aux chiens courants ... nouvelle édition ... avec ... les tons de chasse, *etc.* pp. lx. 496. *Mme v^e Bouchard-Huzard: Paris,* 1845. 8°.　　　**7905. d. 20.**

— Vénerie normande. *See supra:* [L'École de la chasse aux chiens courants.]

LEVERSON (ALBERT J.)

— Yamora. Tarantella in A minor. [P. F.] *W. Paxton & Co.: London,* 1916. fol.　　　**h. 3284. oo. (1.)**

LEVESON (ALBERT J.)

— Brighton Gavotte. [P. F.] *J. Green: Colne,* [1892.] fol.
　　　h. 1489. s. (48.)

— Geneva. Imitation of a Musical Box for the piano. *J. Green & Co.: Colne,* [1899.] fol.　　　**g. 605. p. (29.)**

— Summer Holidays. A Series of Pieces for the Pianoforte. No. 1. *J. Green: Colne,* [1889.] fol.　　　**h. 1489. s. (47.)**

— The Troubadour's Song. Serenade for the pianoforte. *J. Green: Colne,* [1895.] fol.　　　**h. 1489. s. (49.)**

L'EVESQUE (BESSIE)

— Far away. Ballad [begins: "Where the waves"]. *London,* [1870.] fol.　　　**H. 2619. (9.)**

— How beautiful is sunshine. Serenade. *London,* [1867.] fol.
　　　H. 2619. (3.)

— How beautiful is the sunshine. Serenade. *London,* [1870.] fol.
　　　H. 2619. (4.)

— The Moon and the Children. Ballad [begins: "Oh! moon"]. Words by Enoînein. *London,* [1870.] fol.　　　**H. 2619. (10.)**

— O'er the blue ocean gleaming. The Sailor's Wife. [Song.] Words by Dr. C. Mackay. *London,* [1867.] fol.
　　　H. 2619. (5.)

— O'er the blue ocean gleaming. *London,* [1870.] fol.
　　　H. 2619. (6.)

L'EVESQUE (BESSIE)

— O'er the wild ocean. Ballad. *London,* [1860.] fol.
　　　H. 2619. (1.)

— St. Katherine borne by angels. Song [begins: "Slow through the solemn air"]. *London,* [1864.] fol.　　　**H. 2619. (2.)**

— Where the Sun shines brightest. (The Birds' Song.) Written by R. A. Gunn. *London,* [1867.] fol.　　　**H. 2619. (7.)**

— Where the sun shines brightest. *London,* [1870.] fol.
　　　H. 2619. (8.)

LEVESQUE (PETER)

— XII. Canzonetts for One, Two and Three Voices, Adapted for the Harpsichord and Piano Forte, with Accompanyments. Opera Secunda. *Printed for the Author by Thos. Straight: London,* [1790?] *obl.* fol.　　　**F. 607. z. (2.)**

— Sacred Harmony. A new collecton of psalmody. In three parts including three anthems. For the organ or piano forte. Selected composed and adapted ... by P. Levesque. pp. 43. *Printed for the Author and sold at Longman* [sic], *etc.: London,* [^{WM} 1801.] fol.　　　**H. 3164. a.**

— Sacred Harmony. A new collection of Psalmody in three parts, *etc. London,* [1810?] fol.　　　**H. 3164.**

LEVESQUE (PIERRE CHARLES) and **BÊCHE** (L.)

— Solfèges d'Italie avec la basse chiffrée, composés par Leo, Durante, Scarlatti [and others] ... recueillis par les Srs Levesque & Beche ... Gravés par S^r Le Roy. (Troisième édition.) 4 pt. pp. vi. 218. 68. *Chés le Sr Cousineau: Paris; chés les éditeurs: Versailles,* [c. 1790.] *obl.* fol. *The pagination of pt. 1–3 is continuous.*　　　**E. 601. ff.**

LEVETT (D. M.)

— Berceuse. [Violin and P. F.] Op. 21. *O. Ditson Co.: Boston, etc.*, 1898. fol.　　　**h. 1612. c. (34.)**

— Capriccio. Op. 54. [P. F.] *C. Fischer: New York, etc.*, (1909.) fol.　　　**h. 3283. kk. (4.)**

— A Forest Idyl, for Piano. Op. 60. *C. Fischer: New York,* (1910.) fol.　　　**h. 3283. kk. (6.)**

— "Priscilla Valse." Grand Valse brillante. Op. 40. [P. F.] *C. Fischer: New York, etc.*, (1909.) fol.　　　**h. 3283. kk. (3.)**

— Romance. Op. 43. (Violin and Piano.) *C. Fischer: New York, etc.*, (1906.) fol.　　　**h. 1612. p. (33.)**

— Serenade in Italian Style. Op. 44. (Violin and Piano.) *C. Fischer: New York, etc.*, (1906.) fol.　　　**h. 1612. p. (34.)**

— Souvenir. Nocturne. Op. 55. [P. F.] *C. Fischer: New York, etc.*, (1909.) fol.　　　**h. 3283. kk. (5.)**

— That sacred Name. [Sacred song.] Words by I. J. Levy. Op. 32. *Levy & Levett: New York,* 1894. fol.　　　**H. 1187. z. (18.)**

— *See* PAULL MUSIC CO. Edition Paull ... revised ... by ... D. M. Levett, *etc.* (1905.) fol.　　　**h. 3822.**

LEVETZOW (ULLA VON)

— Blumen-Lieb. Song. *London,* [1882.] fol.　　　**H. 1787. j. (32.)**

LEVEY (ANDREW)

— *See* LEVEY (Andrew J.)

LEVEY (ANDREW JAMES)

— Clarice. Waltz. [P. F.] *Metzler & Co.: London,* [1884.] fol.
　　　h. 975. t. (28.)

LEVEY (Andrew James)

— The Court. Waltz. [P. F.] *J. B. Cramer and Co.: London,* 1891. fol.   **h. 3285. q. (39.)**

— Fidelité. Waltz. [P. F.] *E. Ascherberg & Co.: London,* 1893. fol.   **h. 3285. q. (40.)**

— Italia. A Dance. [P. F.] *Metzler & Co.: London,* [1885.] fol.   **h. 1484. t. (17.)**

— The King's March, *etc.* [P. F.] *Hopwood & Crew: London,* [1901.] fol.   **h. 3282. w. (45.)**

— Little Goody Two Shoes. Waltz. [P. F.] *Metzler & Co.: London,* [1889.] fol.   **h. 3285. q. (41.)**

— Little Miss Flimsy. Gavotte. [P. F.] *Metzler & Co.: London,* [1890.] fol.   **h. 3285. q. (42.)**

— Love and Beauty, [song,] *etc. Metzler & Co.: London,* [1883.] fol.   **H. 1788. v. (55.)**

— Love Thoughts. Waltz. [P. F.] *Boosey & Co.: London,* [1887.] fol.   **h. 975. v. (29.)**

— Mary Anderson. Waltz. [P. F.] *Metzler & Co.: London,* [1887.] fol.   **h. 975. v. (30.)**

— Parthenia. Waltz. [P. F. solo and duet.] 2 no. *Metzler & Co.: London,* [1883.] fol.   **h. 975. v. (31.)**

— Shepherds Dance. [P. F.] *Metzler & Co.: London,* [1887.] fol.   **h. 1484. t. (18.)**

— Two Songs. 1. O Mistress mine. 2. A Little tiny Boy. Words from Shakespeare's ... Twelfth Night. *Hopwood & Crew: London,* [1901.] fol.   **H. 1799. cc. (59.)**

— There let us dream. Song, written by C. Scott. *Metzler & Co.: London,* [1883.] fol.   **H. 1788. v. (56.)**

— La Veronese. Waltz. [P. F. solo and duet.] 2 no. *Metzler & Co.: London,* [1885.] fol.   **h. 975. v. (32.)**

— The Winter's Tale. A Comedy ... by W. Shakespeare ... with ... selections from the Incidental Music by A. Levey. *Field & Tuer: London,* [1888.] *obl.* 8°.   **11766. c. 25.**

LEVEY (F.)

— Sechs deutsche Gedichte, *etc. Hannover,* [1810?] fol.   **G. 806. g. (14.)**

LEVEY (Henry)

— The Chopin Technic. A Series of Daily Studies based on difficult passages taken from the Preludes and Études of F. Chopin. [P. F.] *G. Schirmer: New York,* (1908.) 4°.   **g. 337. o. (4.)**

— Lullaby. Song with Piano accompaniment, poem by Tennyson. *G. Schirmer: New York,* (1912.) fol.   **H. 1792. s. (23.)**

LEVEY (Nellie) *Miss*

— *See* LENNEP (H. M. van) In Seville's Groves ... (arranged for voice and guitar by N. Levey.) 1890. fol.   **H. 1568. (17.)**

— *See* LOGÉ (H.) Across the still Lagoon ... (arranged for voice & guitar by N. Levey.) [1890–1.] fol.   **H. 3611. (19.)**

LEVEY (Richard Michael)

— The Aladdin Quadrilles. [P. F.] *London,* [1862.] fol.   **h. 909. (3.)**

— Ali Baba or the Forty Thieves galop. [P. F.] *London,* [1873.] fol.   **h. 909. (7.)**

LEVEY (Richard Michael)

— The Banjo Quadrilles, for the piano forte, selected from the most celebrated negro melodies, by R. M. Levey. ⟨5ᵗʰ edition.⟩ pp. 5. *Cramer, Beale & Cⁱ: London; M'Cullagh & M'Cullagh: Dublin,* [c. 1845.] fol.   **h. 61. qq. (8.)**

— The Celebrated Banjo Quadrilles for the Piano Forte, selected from the most popular Negro melodies by R. M. Levey. ⟨7th edition.⟩ pp. 5. *McCullagh & McCullagh: Dublin,* [c. 1850.] fol.   **h. 722. s. (1.)**

— Second Set of Banjo Quadrilles, selected from the most favorite negro melodies, and arranged for the piano forte, by R. M. Levey. pp. 5. *Robinson & Bussell: Dublin,* [c. 1845.] fol.   **h. 61. oo. (9.)**

— Carnival de Venise arranged for Banjo and Piano. *London,* [1874.] fol.   **h. 909. (8.)**

— A Collection of the Dance Music of Ireland, consisting of upwards of one hundred National Jigs, Reels, Hornpipes, &c. Arranged with easy Basses, for the Piano Forte, the Treble line to suit Violin or Flute, by R. M. Levey. *C. Jefferys: London,* [1858.] fol.   **h. 909. (1.)**

— R. M. Levey's First Collection of the Dance Music of Ireland. (The Second Collection of the Dance Music of Ireland ... Arranged ... for the Piano Forte, *etc.*) *Frederick Harris Co.: London,* [1905?] fol.
The second collection is a reprint of the original edition published by C. Jefferys & Son.   **g. 1187.**

— Cracovienne arranged for Banjo and Piano. *London,* [1874.] fol.   **h. 909. (9.)**

— The Great Ka-foozle-um galop. [P. F. with cornet accompaniment.] *London,* [1866.] fol.   **h. 909. (4.)**

— [Harlequin Hurlothrumbo.] The Favorite Medley Overture (containing melodies of all nations) ... Selected, composed, arranged ... by R. M. Levey. [P. F.] pp. 13. *C. Jefferys: London,* [1849.] fol.   **h. 711. (14.)**

— Kathleen's Farewell. Irish ballad [begins: "Dear Erin"]. The words by J. Duggan. *London,* [1845?] fol.   **H. 2832. k. (18.)**

— Kerry. Quadrille on Irish airs, *etc.* [P. F.] pp. 9. *Pigott & Cⁱ: Dublin,* [c. 1880.] fol.   **h. 60. bb. (19.)**

— Limerick is beautiful. Song. The words by D. Boucicault. *London,* [1866.] fol.   **H. 1772. r. (42.)**

— [O'Donohue of the Lakes.] The Celebrated National Medley Overture, to the pantomime of O'Donohue of the Lakes ... selected, composed, arranged, for the piano forte ... by R. M. Levey. ⟨Eighth edition.⟩ pp. 15. *Cramer, Addisson [sic] & Beale: London,* [c. 1840.] fol.   **h. 61. oo. (10.)**

— Oh! I love him dearly. (Drimmin Dhu.) Song. *London,* [1866.] fol.   **H. 1772. r. (43.)**

— Phoul a Phuca quadrilles. [P. F. with cornet accompaniment.] *London,* [1866.] fol.   **h. 909. (5.)**

— The Robinson Crusoe Galop. Introducing the popular air "O'Donnell a-boo". [P. F.] pp. 5. *M. Gunn & Sons: Dublin, Cork,* [c. 1870.] fol.   **h. 725. m. (12.)**

— Robinson Crusoe quadrilles. [P. F.] *Dublin,* [1870.] fol.   **h. 909. (6.)**

— The White Cat quadrilles. [P. F.] *Dublin,* [1871.] fol.   **h. 1485. s. (48.)**

— The Yankee gal, or My Mary Anne quadrilles. [P. F.] *Dublin,* [1857.] fol.   **h. 909. (2.)**

LEVEY (Sivori)

— The Bell-ario ... A Series of Shakespeare's most beautiful Songs, arranged by S. Levey. *S. Levey (The Ludo Press): London,* 1922. 4°.   **F. 1725. (1.)**

LEVEY (Sivori)

— Daddy and Babsy. Song, words and music by S. Levey. *Chappell & Co.: London, etc.*, 1913. fol.   **H. 1793. t. (27.)**

— He met her on the Stairs. Song, words & music by S. Levey. 2 no. [In D and F.] *Chappell & Co.: London, etc.*, 1913. fol.   **H. 1793. t. (28.)**

— His little Teddy Bear. Song, words & music by S. Levey. *Chappell & Co.: London, etc.*, 1913. fol.   **H. 1793. t. (29.)**

— Melody-Harmony. A re-study of the Shakespeare Play Songs. no. 1. [*S. Levey: London,*] 1924. 4°. *Imperfect; wanting no. 2.*   **F. 1725. (2.)**

— Old Pierrot. [Musical monologue.] Written, composed ... by S. Levey. *Reynolds & Co.: London*, 1922. fol. [*Musical Monologues. No. 259.*]   **H. 2087.**

— Popular Recitations with Musical Accompaniment [for P. F.]. 1. The Brook.—Tennyson.—2. All the World's a Stage.— Shakespeare.—3. Sweet Music.—Shakespeare.—4. Le Corbeau et le Renard.—La Fontaine. *Metzler & Co.: London*, [1908.] 4°.   **g. 603. x. (10.)**

LEVEY (William)

— The Alliance polka. [P. F.] *Dublin*, [1857.] fol.   **h. 1314. (2.)**

— Aux pieds de la madone, invocation pour le piano. Op. 30. *Paris*, [1857.] fol.   **h. 1314. (11.)**

— Brises Vénitiennes, nouvelle mélodie-mazurke, pour piano. Op. 26. *Paris*, [1857.] fol.   **h. 1314. (7.)**

— The campaign waltzes. [P. F.] *Dublin*, [1857.] fol.   **h. 1314. (4.)**

— The Carton galop. [P. F.] *Dublin*, [1857.] fol.   **h. 1314. (3.)**

— L'électrique, nouvelle polka, sans octaves, pour le piano. Op. 29. *Paris*, [1857.] fol.   **h. 1314. (10.)**

— L'Esprit de Bal galop for the Pianoforte. *London*, [1873.] fol.   **h. 1482. z. (46.)**

— La fauvette du moulin à vent, nouvelle polka élégante, sur la chansonnette de A. Vialon et L. de Rillé, pour le piano sans octaves. Op. 37. *Paris*, [1857.] fol.   **h. 1314. (16.)**

— L'incomparable Mirobolanpouff, Nouvelle Schottische populaire, arrangée pour Piano ... sur la mélodie de A. Vialon. *Paris*, [1857.] fol.   **h. 1314. (14.)**

— Morto insecto! Chansonnette de A. Vialon et L. de Rillé, nouvelle polka ... pour piano. Op. 35. *Paris*, [1857.] fol.   **h. 1314. (15.)**

— Un nid de Bengalis, nouvelle polka originale, sans octaves, pour piano. Op. 31. *Paris*, [1857.] fol.   **h. 1314. (12.)**

— Nouvelle polka brillante: l'entrainante ... pour piano. Op. 27. *Paris*, [1857.] fol.   **h. 1314. (8.)**

— Nouvelle polka-mazurka de salon: Pepita, pour piano. Op. 22. *Paris*, [1857.] fol.   **h. 1314. (5.)**

— Le père sabremische, nouvelle polka militaire, sur la mélodie de V. Parizot, pour le piano, sans octaves. Op. 33. *Paris*, [1857.] fol.   **h. 1314. (13.)**

— Les perles de l'Aurore, nouvelles valses originales, pour piano. Op. 23. *Paris*, [1857.] fol.   **h. 1314. (6.)**

— La sémillante, nouvelle valse élégante, sans octaves, pour le piano. Op. 28. *Paris*, [1857.] fol.   **h. 1314. (9.)**

— "Souvenir de Paris," trois pièces caractéristiques pour piano. 3 no. *London*, [1857.] fol.   **h. 1314. (1.)**

LEVEY (William Charles)

— Amy. Ballad [begins: "My heart is rent"] written by W. F. N. Ellis. *London*, [1877.] fol.   **H. 2621. a. (29.)**

— Amy. Ballad written by W. F. Ellis. *London*, [1878.] fol.   **H. 2621. b. (6.)**

— Au Revoir! not Adieu! Song [begins: " 'Twas evening"], written by J. C. Levey. *London*, [1866.] fol.   **H. 2621. (15.)**

— Away, song [begins: "Sad is the cottage"], written by H. S. Clarke. *London*, [1869.] fol.   **H. 2621. (30.)**

— The Babes. Quadrille. Arr^d. by A. Morelli. [Reed band parts.] *J. R. Lafleur & Son: London*, [1887.] 8°. *Part of the "Alliance Musicale".*   **f. 401. ff. (2.)**

— Baby Mine. Cradle song [begins: "Sleep and rest thee"] ... written by L. H. F. Du Terreaux. *London*, [1876.] fol.   **H. 2621. a. (19.)**

— A Bad Boy's Diary. [Song.] Written by W. Shepherd. *Shepherd & Kilner: London*, [1884.] fol.   **H. 2621. b. (27.)**

— Beauties of Lohengrin. Fantasia. [P. F.] *C. Sheard: London*, [1876.] fol. *No. 5551, 52 of the Musical Bouquet.*   **H. 2345.**

— Beautiful Dreams, song, written by E. L. Blanchard. pp. 9. *Duff & Stewart: London*, [1873?] fol.   **H. 1654. tt. (9.)**

— Beautiful Dreams. [P. F. solo and duet.] 2 no. [1879.] *See* ROCHARD (J.) Popular Melodies, *etc.* No. 5. [1878, *etc.*] fol.   **h. 3032. b.**

— Behind the Curtain valses. [P. F.] *London*, [1870.] fol.   **h. 3112. (15.)**

— The Better land. Song [begins: "I hear them speak"]. Poetry by Mrs. Hemans. *London*, [1878.] fol.   **H. 2621. b. (5.)**

— The Breadwinner. [Song.] Words by F. W. Green. *Hopwood & Crew: London*, [1882.] fol.   **H. 2621. b. (28.)**

— A Bride among the Valleys. Ballad [begins: "While roving through"], written by L. H. F. Du Terreaux. *London*, [1866.] fol.   **H. 2621. (16.)**

— The Brigand Chief. Song, the words by M. F. Levey. *Boosey & Co.: London*, [1889.] fol.   **H. 1788. uu. (40.)**

— The Broken Rose. Song [begins: "She gave him when they parted"]. Words by C. W. Scott. *London*, [1878.] fol.   **H. 2621. b. (13.)**

— The Broken Rose waltz. [P. F.] *London*, [1879.] fol.   **h. 1494. q. (33.)**

— A Broken Tryst. Song, words by P. Vere. *J. F. Pettit: London*, [1882.] fol.   **H. 2621. b. (29.)**

— Brown eyes. Polka. [P. F.] *Shepherd & Kilner: London*, [1882.] fol.   **h. 975. v. (33.)**

— La Brunette valses. [P. F.] *London*, [1872.] fol.   **h. 3112. (19.)**

— Caught napping. Song, written by H. L. D'A. Jaxone. *J. Bath: London*, [1883.] fol.   **H. 2621. b. (30.)**

— The Charm. Song, words by S. Lover. *J. B. Cramer & Co.: London*, 1892. fol.   **H. 2621. c. (1.)**

— Children. Song [begins: "Come to me"]. Words by Longfellow. *London*, [1878.] fol.   **H. 2621. b. (3.)**

— Chinese Dance for the Pianoforte. *London*, [1866.] fol.   **h. 3112. (6.)**

— Christmas Time lancers on old English tunes. [P. F.] *London*, [1877.] fol.   **h. 3112. (21.)**

— Come home, my sailor boy. Song [begins: "Old Albion sat"]. Poetry by J. Ingelow. *London*, [1873.] fol.   **H. 2621. a. (2.)**

LEVEY (William Charles)

— Come Home soon, Acushla. Song, words by E. Falconer. *D. Davison & Co.: London*, [1884.] fol. **H. 2621. b. (31.)**

— Come to the Land ... Song, words by E. Falconer, *etc. Paterson & Sons: Edinburgh, etc.*, [1885.] fol. **H. 2621. b. (32.)**

— Coo! says the gentle dove. *See* infra: [Punchinello.]

— Cradle Song [begins: "Little babe"]. Poetry by J. Ingelow. *London*, [1873.] fol. **H. 2621. a. (3.)**

— Cumnor Hall. *See* infra: [Kenilworth.]

— The Damask Rose. Ballad, *etc. C. Sheard: London*, [1875.] fol. *No.* 5520, 21 *of the Musical Bouquet.* **H. 2345.**

— The Dear Emerald Isle. Song [begins: "Erin, dear Erin"] ... written by E. L. Blanchard. *London*, [1875.] fol. **H. 2621. a. (16.)**

— Dear Home again. Song [begins: "Oh! when we leave"] written by E. L. Blanchard. *London*, [1876.] fol. **H. 2621. a. (20.)**

— Dolores. Spanish Love Song, word by E. Oxenford, introducing the ... Valse by E. Waldteufel, *etc. Hopwood & Crew: London*, [1887.] fol. **H. 2621. b. (33.)**

— Don't run old England down ... Song, written by F. W. Green. *Hopwood & Crew: London*, [1882.] fol. **H. 2621. b. (34.)**

— Echoes of the Theatres ... Fantasia for the pianoforte. *C. Sheard: London*, [1877.] fol. *No.* 5744, 45 *of the Musical Bouquet.* **H. 2345.**

— [Eileen Oge.] Love in the Hay, Irish song [begins: "Oh! the pleasantest time"]. (Written by E. Falconer.) *London*, [1872.] fol. **H. 1775. u. (37.)**

— The Elm Tree near the Stile. Ballad, poetry by C. J. Rowe. *C. Sheard: London*, [1879.] fol. *No.* 6083, 84 *of the Musical Bouquet.* **H. 2345.**

— Empress and Queen ... Song [begins: "Where'er the sun"] written by W. H. Thomson. *London*, [1877.] fol. **H. 2621. a. (25.)**

— Empress and Queen ... Song written by W. H. Thomson. *London*, [1878.] fol. **H. 2621. b. (1.)**

— "Empress and Queen." (National song.) [Military band parts.] 25 pt. *In:* FAUST (C.) [Chaine de fleurs. Op. 229.] Quadrille, *etc.* [1878.] fol. [*Boosé's military Journal. ser.* 61. *no.* 3.] **h. 1549.**

— England ... Song, written by J. Orton. *C. Sheard: London*, [1879.] fol. *No.* 6081, 82 *of the Musical Bouquet.* **H. 2345.**

— England has stood to her guns. Song [begins: "We have furled up the banner"] written by C. W. Scott. *London*, [1878.] fol. **H. 2621. b. (10.)**

— Erin, song [begins: "Dear Erin"]. Written by G. Linley. *London*, [1870.] fol. **H. 2621. (34.)**

— Esmeralda. [Song, begins: "Where is the little gipsy's home".] Written by A. Halliday. *London*, [1876.] fol. **H. 2621. a. (14.)**

— Esmeralda, Bolero ... Arranged for the piano, by Brinley Richards. pp. 9. *Duff & Stewart: London*, [c. 1880.] fol. **h. 721. vv. (10.)**

— Esmeralda. [P. F. solo and duet.] 2 no. [1881.] *See* ROCHARD (J.) Popular Melodies, *etc.* No. 15. [1878, *etc.*] fol. **h. 3032. b.**

LEVEY (William Charles)

— L'Espagnolita. Waltz. [P. F.] *J. B. Cramer & Co.: London*, 1891. fol. **h. 3285. q. (43.)**

— Eventide. Ballad [begins: "When softly gleams"] written by L. H. F. Du Terreaux. *London*, [1875.] fol. **H. 2621. a. (9.)**

— Fairies of the Bell. Song, written by O. Brand. *Shepherd & Kilner: London*, [1884.] fol. **H. 2621. b. (35.)**

— Fairy Bells. *See* infra: [Metamorphoses.]

— The Fairy Glen. Duet [begins: "Whither, oh! whither"]. Words by W. H. Thomson. *London*, [1877.] fol. **H. 2621. a. (28.)**

— The Fairy's Dream. Song [begins: "They say that in the moonlit dell"]. The verse by F. Enoch. *London*, [1877.] fol. **H. 2621. a. (30.)**

Fanchette

— Fanchette. Operetta. The words by M. Morton. [Vocal score] *London*, [1864.] 4°. **F. 580.**

— Airs ... arranged for the Pianoforte, by F. Gautier. 2 bk. *London*, [1864.] fol. **h. 3015. (9.)**

— The Good Old Time. Duet. *London*, [1864.] fol. **H. 2621. (1.)**

— Home of our youth. Duet. *London*, [1864.] fol. **H. 2621. (2.)**

— How sad all Nature seems to be. [Song.] *London*, [1864.] fol. **H. 2621. (3.)**

— How sad all Nature seems to be ... with Flute obligato. *London*, [1864.] fol. **H. 2621. (4.)**

— How sad all nature seems to be ... for the Pianoforte. [1864.] fol. *See* RICHARDS (H. B.) **h. 760. d. (30.)**

— Look! this is joy, how gaily bright. [Song.] *London*, [1864.] fol. **H. 2621. (5.)**

— Look! this is joy ... for the Pianoforte. [1864.] fol. *See* RICHARDS (H. B.) **h. 760. d. (31.)**

— *See* VILLIERS (H. de) Fanchette galop, *etc.* [1864.] fol. **h. 3235. (2.)**

— *See* VILLIERS (H. de) Fanchette quadrilles, *etc.* [1864.] fol. **h. 3235. (1.)**

— Fashion, operetta in one act, for ladies, written by L. H. F. du Terreaux. [Vocal score.] *London*, [1870.] 8°. **E. 185.**

— The Fat Boys' Song ... sung ... in the Pantomime of Little Red Riding Hood, the words by F. W. Green. *C. Jefferys: London*, [1884.] fol. **H. 2621. b. (36.)**

— The Fat Boys' Polka, *etc.* [P. F.] *C. Jefferys: London*, [1884.] fol. **h. 975. v. (34.)**

— Ferryman. Dan. Song [begins: "Old Dan's afloat"]. Words by F. E. Weatherly. *London*, [1879.] fol. **H. 2621. b. (18.)**

— Fiorella. Polka from Offenbach's opera 'Les Brigands'. [P. F.] *Boosey & Co.: London*, [1890.] fol. **h. 3285. q. (44.)**

— Polka. "Fiorella" ... (On airs from Offenbachs "The Brigands".) [Military band parts.] 26 pt. *In:* FAHRBACH (P.) *the Younger.* Valse. "Au pays des chansons," *etc.* 1890. fol. [*Boosey's military Journal. ser.* 88. *no.* 3.] **h. 1549.**

— Fleur de Chypre ... Etude à la schottische. [P. F.] *London*, [1880.] fol. **h. 1494. q. (36.)**

— Florence suite de valses. *London*, [1880.] fol. **h. 1494. q. (35.)**

LEVEY (William Charles)

— "Forget-me-not" Eyes. [Song.] Written by H. Hunter. *Francis Bros. & Day: London*, [1884.] fol.   **H. 2621. b. (37.)**

— Formosa galop. [P. F.] *London*, [1869.] fol.   **h. 3112. (10.)**

— Formosa Quadrille. Pianoforte duet. *London*, [1864.] fol.   **h. 3112. (12.)**

— Formosa quadrille. [P. F.] *London*, [1869.] fol.   **h. 3112. (11.)**

— Friends only! Ballad, words by E. Oxenford. *Augener & Co.: London*, [1884.] fol.   **H. 2621. b. (38.)**

— From fair Auvergne I come. *See* infra: [Punchinello.]

— From far o'er the sea. Irish ballad [begins: "Three summers have come"]. (Written by J. Duggan.) *London*, [1866.] fol.   **H. 2621. (13.)**

— Gem of the soft purple even. [Song.] The poetry ... by P. Boyd. *London*, [1866.] fol.   **H. 2621. (17.)**

— Gentle Words. (A young rose in summer time.) Ballad. *London*, [1878.] fol.   **H. 2621. b. (4.)**

— Geraldine. Ballad, *etc.* (Written by H. Hunter.) *Francis Bros. & Day: London*, [1884.] fol.   **H. 2621. b. (39.)**

— The Gipsy Fortune Teller. Ballad [begins: "A Gipsy one day"] written by E. L. Blanchard. ⟨In C.⟩ *London*, [1875.] fol.   **H. 2621. a. (11.)**

— The Gipsy Fortune Teller. ⟨In D.⟩ *London*, [1875.] fol.   **H. 2621. a. (12.)**

— God preserve our Soldier Prince. Song and Chorus, written by W. Mitchell. *C. Sheard: London*, [1874.] fol. No. 5234, 35 *of the Musical Bouquet.*   **H. 2345.**

— Golden Corn. Song, written by C. W. Scott. *Hopwood & Crew: London*, [1882.] fol.   **H. 2621. b. (40.)**

— The Good Old Time. *See* supra: [Fanchette.]

— Grande Polka de Concert pour Piano. *London*, [1864.] fol.   **h. 3112. (2.)**

— Grande Valse, morceau de salon pour Piano. *London*, [1864.] fol.   **h. 3112. (3.)**

— Guessing. Song [begins: "It was a bright and sunny day"]. The poetry by J. Enderssohn. *London*, [1877.] fol.   **H. 2621. a. (27.)**

— Guinea Gold quadrille. [P. F.] *London*, [1878.] fol.   **h. 1494. q. (32.)**

— He does not love me now. Ballad [begins: "Ah! why does little Alice sit"]. Words by F. Langbridge. *London*, [1878.] fol.   **H. 2621. b. (8.)**

— Heart to Heart. Ballad, words by T. B. *E. Ascherberg & Co.: London*, 1892. fol.   **H. 2621. c. (2.)**

— Dance. Henry VIII. (Arranged by C. Tourville.) [P. F.] *J. Williams: London*, [1893.] fol.   **g. 605. f. (18.)**

— Here stands a post ... Song, written by C. W. Scott. *London*, [1878.] fol.   **H. 2621. b. (7.)**

— Home of our youth. *See* supra: [Fanchette.]

— How sad all Nature seems to be. *See* supra: [Fanchette.]

— Hurrah for the Bombadier! *See* infra: [Punchinello.]

— Hush! Our Birdie's gone to Sleep. Ballad, poetry by Nella. *C. Sheard: London*, [1874.] fol. No. 5357, 58 *of the Musical Bouquet.*   **H. 2345.**

LEVEY (William Charles)

— I'll be merry still. [Song, begins: "Care across my threshold".] Words by J. Enderssohn. *London*, [1878.] fol.   **H. 2621. b. (2.)**

— I've a Lover ... Ballad, poetry by W. S. Clarke. *C. Sheard: London*, [1874.] fol. No. 5351, 52 *of the Musical Bouquet.*   **H. 2345.**

— I've got a little Secret. Poetry by C. Searle. *Hopwood & Crew: London*, [1882.] fol.   **H. 2621. b. (41.)**

— Inesilla. Bolero, poetry by L. H. F. Du Terreaux. *London*, [1874.] fol.   **H. 1777. h. (50.)**

— It only seems the other day. [Song, begins: "Though swiftly time".] Written by E. L. Blanchard. *London*, [1875.] fol.   **H. 2621. a. (8.)**

— Jack's Adventures. Song, words by W. Maynard. *E. Donajowski: London*, [1885.] fol.   **H. 2621. b. (42.)**

— Jack's Vow. [Song, begins: "Said Jack to me".] The words by E. Oxenford. *London*, [1877.] fol.   **H. 2621. a. (26.)**

— Jack's Yarn quadrilles. [P. F.] *London*, [1878.] fol.   **h. 1494. q. (31.)**

— Katty Nolan, Irish ballad [begins: "Och! hark to my story"] written by Mrs. Groom. *London*, [1870.] fol.   **H. 1775. u. (35.)**

— [Kenilworth.] Cumnor Hall. Amy Robsart's song [begins: "The dews of summer night"]. *London*, [1871.] fol.   **H. 1775. u. (36.)**

— Kenilworth Castle quadrilles. [P. F.] *London*, [1870.] fol.   **h. 3112. (17.)**

— Kind Lady, let me go. Song, the words ... by Mrs. Hemans. *Novello, Ewer & Co.: London & New York*, 1892. fol.   **H. 2621. c. (3.)**

— King o' Scots. Quadrille. [P. F.] pp. 11. [*Cramer & Co.: London*, c. 1870.] fol. *The imprint is cropped.*   **h. 722. yy. (10.)**

— King of the Castle. Song, words by E. Oxenford, introducing Waldteufel's ... Valse, 'Toujours Fidéle,' *etc. Hopwood & Crew: London*, [1887.] fol.   **H. 2621. b. (43.)**

— Kingston Town. [Song.] Words by J. Runciman. *London Music Publishing Stores: London*, [1891.] fol.   **H. 2621. c. (4.)**

— Kingston Town. [Song.] Words by J. Runciman. New Edition with Tonic Sol-fa. 2 no. [In E flat and F.] *London Music Publishing Stores: London*, [1898.] fol.   **H. 2621. c. (14.)**

— Kitty Clare ... Song, *etc.* [Words by R. Morton.] *C. Sheard & Co.: London*, 1892. fol.   **H. 2621. c. (5.)**

— Laugh with a hearty good will. Song [begins: "Old Winter I ween"], written by J. Enderssohn. *London*, [1876.] fol.   **H. 2621. a. (23.)**

— The Legend of the Rose. Song [begins: "The Summer night"], written by L. H. F. Du Terreaux. *London*, [1868.] fol.   **H. 2621. (27.)**

— The Legend of the Rose. Song [begins: "The night and all around"]. (Written by J. F. Finlayson.) *London*, [1877.] fol.   **H. 2621. a. (31.)**

— The Lily of the Vale. Song, written by J. C. Levey. *London*, [1866.] fol.   **H. 2621. (18.)**

— Look! this is joy, how gaily bright. *See* supra: [Fanchette.]

— The Lord's Prayer. Solo and Quartett. *C. Sheard & Co.: London*, 1892. fol.   **H. 2621. c. (6.)**

— Love in the Hay. *See* supra: [Eileen Oge.]

LEVEY (WILLIAM CHARLES)

— Love's Arrows and Bow. Song [begins: "In the sweet spring time"]. The words by P. Vere. *London*, [1882.] fol.
    H. 2621. b. (26.)

— Love's Arrows and Bow. [Part-song.] Words by P. Vere. [1886.] *See* MARSHALL AND CO. Marshall's Series of Part Songs. No. 253. [1885–7.] 4°.
    F. 329.

— Love's Eventide. Ballad, words by W. Holland. New Edition with Tonic Sol-fa. *London Music Publishing Stores: London*, [1899.] fol.
    H. 2621. c. (15.)

— Love's Garden. Song, written by C. W. Scott. *Hopwood & Crew: London*, [1882.] fol.
    H. 2621. b. (45.)

— The Lover's Return. Song, written by E. M. Stevens. *J. B. Cramer & Co.: London*, [1885.] fol.
    H. 2621. b. (44.)

— The Magic Mirror. Song, the words by H. L. D'A. Jaxone. *C. Jefferys: London*, [1890.] fol.
    H. 2621. c. (7.)

— The Magic of Music. [P. F. solo and duet.] 2 no. [1881.] *See* ROCHARD (J.) Popular Melodies, *etc.* No. 60. [1878, *etc.*] fol.
    h. 3032. b.

— Many a year ago. Song [begins: "It was many"], written by E. A. Poe. ⟨In E flat.⟩ *London*, [1866.] fol.
    H. 2621. (23.)

— Many a year ago. ⟨In D.⟩ *London*, [1869.] fol.
    H. 2621. (24.)

— March in the drama Arrah-na-Pogue. [P. F.] *London*, [1866.] fol.
    h. 3112. (5.)

— Marche Turque, burlesque de diabolique, pour le Piano. *London*, [1864.] fol.
    h. 3112. (1.)

— Marguerite mazurka de salon. [P. F.] *London*, [1879.] fol.
    h. 1494. q. (34.)

— Maritana, gay Gitana ... for the Pianoforte. [1876.] fol. *See* RICHARDS (H. B.)
    h. 760. h. (33.)

— May and December. Song, words by E. Oxenford. *Augener & Co.: London*, [1884.] fol.
    H. 2621. b. (46.)

— Mercy! Song [begins: "A woman's life"]. Words by C. W. Scott. *London*, [1878.] fol.
    H. 2621. b. (15.)

— [Metamorphoses.] Fairy Bells. Song [begins: "In the silence"]. Words by H. S. Clarke. *London*, [1867.] fol.
    H. 2621. (25.)

— [Metamorphoses.] The Song of the Rose [begins: "I rested in peace"] ... Words by H. S. Clarke. *London*, [1867.] fol.
    H. 2621. (26.)

— The Miller's Legacy. Comic song & chorus [begins: "Come miller's men"] ... Written by E. L. Blanchard. *London*, [1870.] fol.
    H. 2621. (32.)

— The Minstrel Maiden. [Song, begins: "Soon as the blush of daylight".] Words by H. Hersee. *London*, [1879.] fol.
    H. 2621. b. (19.)

— Minuet, played ... in the School for Scandal, *etc.* [P. F.] *Hopwood & Crew: London*, [1882.] fol.
    h. 1484. t. (19.)

— The Month of May. Part-Song for T. T. B. B. Words by F. Enoch. *See* WATSON (W. M.) The Choral Society ... No. 53. [1884.] 4°.
    F. 589.

— My Darlings three. Song [begins: "What shall I bring thee"]. The words by C. W. Scott. *London*, [1879.] fol.
    H. 1785. c. (37.)

— My little Maid. [Song.] Poetry by F. E. Weatherly. *Hopwood & Crew: London*, [1882.] fol.
    H. 2621. b. (47.)

— My Mountain Lay, Tyrolienne song [begins: "High the Alpen summers"], written by L. H. F. Du Terreaux. ⟨In D.⟩ *London*, [1866.] fol.
    H. 2621. (20.)

LEVEY (WILLIAM CHARLES)

— My Mountain Lay. ⟨In D.⟩ *London*, [1867.] fol.
    H. 2621. (21.)

— The Nearest Way in summer time. Ballad [begins: "Where the willows spread their branches"] written by F. Wood. *London*, [1881.] fol.
    H. 2621. b. (25.)

— The New quadrille (with instructions for dancing). [P. F.] *London*, [1871.] fol.
    h. 3112. (18.)

— The Night Sortie. Song [begins: "Give me one kiss"] written by L. W. F. Du Terreaux. *London*, [1880.] fol.
    H. 2621. b. (23.)

— No Cross, no Crown. Song ... written by F. W. Green. *C. Sheard: London*, [1874.] fol. No. 5208, 09 *of the Musical Bouquet.*
    H. 2345.

— Noble Hearts. [Song, begins: "When seated by our own fireside"] written by E. Powell. *London*, [1880.] fol.
    H. 2621. b. (20.)

— Norah's First Letter. Irish Ballad, written by Nella. *C. Sheard: London*, [1874.] fol. No. 5355, 56 *of the Musical Bouquet.*
    H. 2345.

— Oh, give me back my Heart again. Ballad, written by F. W. Green. *C. Sheard: London*, [1874.] fol. No. 5397, 98 *of the Musical Bouquet.*
    H. 2345.

— Oh! leave me not alone, Ballad, written by L. Devereux. *London*, [1869.] fol.
    H. 2621. (28.)

— O merry Zingarella. Song. *London*, [1876.] fol.
    H. 2621. a. (21.)

— The Old School Time. Ballad [begins: "Year after year"] written by H. Ffrench. *London*, [1872.] fol.
    H. 2621. a. (1.)

— The Omen. Song [begins: "I launch on the water"], words by H. S. Clarke. *London*, [1869.] fol.
    H. 2621. (29.)

— On the wilds of bleak Dartmoor. National song [begins: "Oh! Englishmen"]. The words by W. F. N. Ellis. *London*, [1876.] fol.
    H. 2621. a. (22.)

— One by one. Ballad, poetry by Nella. *C. Sheard: London*, [1874.] fol. No. 5353, 54 *of the Musical Bouquet.*
    H. 2345.

— One little word. Song [begins: "I have told thee"] written by L. Novra. *London*, [1878.] fol.
    H. 1785. c. (35.)

— One morning, oh! so early. Song, words by J. Ingelow. *London*, [1874.] fol.
    H. 2621. a. (4.)

— Only a Dream. Reverie Song, written by F. W. Green. *C. Sheard: London*, [1874.] fol. No. 5279, 80 *of the Musical Bouquet.*
    H. 2345.

— Only this. Song, words by H. L. D'A. Jaxone. *Smith & Co.: London*, [1884.] fol.
    H. 2621. b. (48.)

— The Outward and the homeward bound. Song [begins: "Here's a health"]. Written by J. Enderssohn. *London*, [1878.] fol.
    H. 2621. b. (14.)

— Pat and the Widdy. Humourous song [begins: "In Ballinaha"], written by C. O'Neill. *London*, [1870.] fol.
    H. 2621. (31.)

Punchinello

— Punchinello. A comic opera in one act, written by H. Farnie. [Vocal score.] *London*, [1865.] 4°.
    G. 574.

— Punchinello: A comic opera in one act. The libretto by H. Farnie. [With the music of some of the songs.] *Cramer & Co.: London*, [1864.] 8°.
    11781. e. 39. (11.)

— Coo! says the gentle dove ... Ballad. ⟨In G.⟩ *London*, [1865.] fol.
    H. 2621. (9.)

LEVEY (WILLIAM CHARLES)

— Coo! says the gentle dove. ⟨In F.⟩ *London*, [1865.] fol.
H. 2621. (10.)

— From fair Auvergne I come … Song. *London*, [1865.] fol.
H. 2621. (6.)

— Hurrah for the Bombardier! [Song.] ⟨In A.⟩ *London*, [1865.]
fol. **H. 2621. (7.)**

— Hurrah for the Bombardier! ⟨In F.⟩ *London*, [1865.] fol.
H. 2621. (8.)

— The Showman's Ditty. [Song.] *London*, [1865.] fol.
H. 2621. (11.)

— Sixty's Serenade. [Song.] *London*, [1865.] fol.
H. 2621. (12.)

— *See* WARREN ( ) Fête Champêtre quadrille (on airs
from Levey's opera). [1865.] fol. **h. 1461. m. (23.)**

———

— Puss in Boots quadrille. [P. F.] *London*, [1870.] fol.
h. 3112. (13.)

— Queenstown, first galop de concert, for the Pianoforte.
London, [1865.] fol. **h. 3112. (4.)**

— Queenstown. Galop de Concert. [P. F.] *See* SAINT. The Saint
James's Album, 1865. No. 17. 1865. fol. **H. 1241.**

— Ramsgate Sands. Galop. [P. F.] *Hopwood & Crew: London*,
[1882.] fol. **h. 975. v. (35.)**

— The Raven. Song [begins: "Once upon a midnight dreary"].
The words by E. A. Poe. *London*, [1876.] fol.
H. 2621. a. (24.)

— The Return. Vocal Waltz, the words by M. B. *Boosey & Co.:
London*, [1890.] fol. **H. 2621. c. (8.)**

— The Ride to Ware. A humorous cantata for … soli & chorus
with pianoforte accompaniment, the words—founded on
Cowper's poem—arranged & written by E. Oxenford.
London, [1887.] 8°.
Augener & Co.'s edition, No. 9097. **F. 580. b.**

— Rip van Winkle's drinking song [begins: "Ho! comrades"].
(The words … by W. Maynard.) *London*, [1875.] fol.
H. 2621. (17.)

— The Rising Moon has hid the Stars. Duet … words by
Longfellow. Sixth Edition. *Doremi & Co.: London*, [1891.]
fol. **H. 2621. c. (9.)**

— Robin Hood. Cantata for Boys' Voices. Written by
E. Oxenford. *London*, [1884.] 8°. **F. 1273. a. (4.)**

— The Robin Redbreast. Song [begins: "He sailed away"]
written by J. Thomson. *London*, [1875.] fol.
H. 2621. a. (18.)

— Roman slow march. [Reed band parts.] *London*, [1877.] 8°.
f. 412. c. (33.)

— Romance and Reality. Song [begins: "In childhood oft"].
Words by M. A. B. *Brighton*, [1878.] fol. **H. 2621. b. (9.)**

— Rory of the Glen, Irish ballad [begins: "My heart"]. (Written
by J. Duggan.) *London*, [1866.] fol. **H. 2621. (14.)**

— Rosabelle, valse [begins: "Tis a rose"], written by
G. Caravoglia. English version by L. H. F. Du Terreaux.
London, [1867.] fol. **H. 2621. (22.)**

— Rosabelle waltz. [P. F.] *London*, [1867.] fol. **h. 3112. (8.)**

— La Rose Blanche, waltz. [P. F.] *London*, [1867.] fol.
h. 3112. (9.)

LEVEY (WILLIAM CHARLES)

— The Rose's Wooing. Ballad, written by L. H. F. Du Terreaux.
C. Sheard: London, [1879.] fol.
No. 6085, 86 *of the Musical Bouquet.* **H. 2345.**

— The Rosebud's Message. [Song, begins: "She left the town".]
Words by F. E. Weatherly. *London*, [1879.] fol.
H. 2621. b. (16.)

— The Sabbath Bell. Song [begins: "Yes hearken"]. Words by
E. Falconer. *London*, [1880.] fol. **H. 2621. b. (24.)**

— The Sailor Boy's Dream. [Song.] Written by A. Stanley.
London, [1866.] fol. **H. 2621. (19.)**

— A Sailor's Life. Song, words by A. Henry. *J. B. Cramer &
Co.: London*, [1884.] fol. **H. 2621. b. (49.)**

— A Sailor's Life. [P. F.] *See* SMALLWOOD (W.) Choice Melodies,
etc. No. 20. [1885, *etc.*] fol. **h. 1412. r. (2.)**

— Saraband (the motif by Henry VIII.) … arranged for Piano.
London, [1876.] fol. **h. 3112. (20.)**

— The Sea King. Baritone Song, words by F. W. Green.
C. Sheard & Co.: London, 1892. fol. **H. 2621. c. (10.)**

— The Ship's Cook. Song. The words by E. Marlowe.
C. Jefferys & Son: London, [1894.] fol. **H. 2621. c. (12.)**

— Showers of Rice. Morceau de Salon. [P. F.] *Metzler & Co.:
London*, [1891.] fol. **h. 1489. s. (50.)**

— The Showman's Ditty. *See* supra: [Punchinello.]

— Sixty's Serenade. *See* supra: [Punchinello.]

— The Skylark. [Song, begins: "Sing sweet Minstrel".] Words by
St. Germaine. *London*, [1878.] fol. **H. 2621. b. (12.)**

— The Slashing Carbineers. Song and chorus, words by
F. Bowyer. *Boosey & Co.: London*, [1890.] fol.
H. 2621. c. (11.)

— The Snow is on the hills. Ballad, written by F. W. Green.
London, [1874.] fol.
No. 5039, 40 *of the Musical Bouquet.* **H. 2345.**

— So the World goes. Song, poetry by B. Cornwall. *C. Sheard:
London*, [1875.] fol.
No. 5523, 24 *of the Musical Bouquet.* **H. 2345.**

— The Song of the Rose. *See* supra: [Metamorphoses.]

— The Song that Mary sang. Ballad [begins: "Come let us
drift"]. Words by J. Reid. *London*, [1878.] fol.
H. 2621. b. (11.)

— The Songs of Olden Days. [Song.] Written by H. S. Clarke. ⟨In
D.⟩ *London*, [1874.] fol. **H. 2621. a. (6.)**

— The Songs of Olden Days. ⟨In E.⟩ *London*, [1874.] fol.
H. 2621. a. (7.)

— Special edition galop. [P. F.] *London*, [1877.] fol.
h. 3112. (23.)

— Stars of the Season, waltzes. [P. F.] *London*, [1870.] fol.
h. 3112. (16.)

— Sweet Dangle, pride of Erin. Song, written by E. Ransford.
London, [1870.] fol. **H. 2621. (35.)**

— Sweethearts long ago. [Song.] Words by W. Shepherd.
Shepherd & Kilner: London, [1882.] fol. **H. 2621. b. (50.)**

— Thoughts of other Days. Ballad, words by Longfellow.
D. Davison & Co.: London, [1884.] fol. **H. 2621. b. (51.)**

— Three Days … Ballad, written by O. Allan. *C. Sheard:
London*, [1874.] fol.
No. 5236, 37 *of the Musical Bouquet.* **H. 2345.**

LEVEY (William Charles)

—— Three in One. National Song, words by C. Scott. *Francis Bros. & Day: London*, [1886.] fol. **H. 2621. b. (52.)**

—— The Tinkling of the Bell. Song [begins: "At early morn"] ... Written by E. L. Blanchard. *London*, [1870.] fol. **H. 2621. (33.)**

—— 'Tis Time to rest my weary Head. Child's Even Song, written by F. W. Green. *C. Sheard: London*, [1874.] fol. *No. 5288, 89 of the Musical Bouquet.* **H. 2345.**

—— Triumphal March. [P. F.] *London*, [1866.] fol. **h. 3112. (7.)**

—— Twilight Fancies. Ballad, words by Mrs. M. A. Baines. *D. Davison & Co.: London*, [1884.] fol. **H. 2621. b. (53.)**

—— The Ungovernable Governess. Operetta in two acts ... written by L. H. F. Du Terreaux. *London*, [1881.] 4°. **F. 580. a.**

—— Velocipede galop. [P. F.] *London*, [1870.] fol. **h. 3112. (14.)**

—— Violets, sweet violets. Song [begins: "Through the crowded city"], written by W. J. Stewart. *London*, [1880.] fol. **H. 2621. b. (22.)**

—— Voices of the Sky. [Song.] Words by Mrs. Hemans. *London Music Publishing Stores: London*, 1898. fol. **H. 2621. c. (13.)**

—— "Wanted a Parlour Maid," drawing room operetta for ladies written by H. Ffrench. *London*, [1872.] 8°. **E. 185. a.**

—— Westward. Song [begins: "Away to the west"] written by W. J. Stewart. *London*, [1880.] fol. **H. 2621. b. (21.)**

—— What are the joy bells ringing. Song, the poetry by A. Trevor. *London*, [1875.] fol. **H. 2621. a. (10.)**

—— When sparrows build. Ballad, the words by J. Ingelow. *London*, [1879.] fol. **H. 2621. b. (17.)**

—— When the leaves fall down. Song [begins: "In the mellow misty time"] written by E. L. *London*, [1875.] fol. **H. 2621. a. (13.)**

—— White Blossoms, transcribed for the Pianoforte. *London*, [1877.] fol. **h. 3112. (22.)**

—— Whittington and his Cat. Extravaganza, written by A. Henry. The music selected from Offenbach, with original numbers composed by Mrs. Henry and W. C. Levey. *London*, [1883.] 8°. **E. 1594. c. (7.)**

—— Why do I love thee. Ballad, the poetry by J. Enderson. *London*, [1874.] fol. **H. 2621. a. (5.)**

—— The Willow and the Brook. Song [begins: "O'er a brook"] written by C. Ascroft. *London*, [1878.] fol. **H. 1785. c. (36.)**

—— A Young Maiden's Thoughts. Song [begins: "I thought that he loved me"]. *London*, [1876.] fol. **H. 2621. a. (15.)**

—— *See* DUNWORTH (W.) Treasured Memories ... Arranged by W. C. Levey. 1893. fol. **H. 1798. i. (57.)**

—— *See* KING (J. C.) Time flies fast ... Harmonized ... by W. C. Levey. [1890.] fol. **H. 1799. cc. (17.)**

—— *See* KING (J. C.) Wave the Flag ... Harmonized ... by W. C. Levey. [1890.] fol. **H. 1799. cc. (15.)**

—— *See* MORTON (Richard) and PLEON (H.) The Professional Reunion ... [Song.] Arranged by W. C. Levey, *etc.* [1892.] fol. **H. 3981. (6.)**

—— *See* STRAUSS (J.) *the Younger.* [Annen Polka.] Gipsey Anna ... arranged ... [by W. C. Levey.] [1867.] fol. **H. 1773. e. (53.)**

LEVEZ

—— Levez vous, O ma bien aimée. Villanelle. *See* THEVENET (A.)

LEVEZ

—— Levez vous, paresseuse. [Song.] *See* BRUGUIÈRE (E.)

LÈVI (Edgardo)

—— Beauty and Time. Song. Poetry by Austin Dobson. pp. 4. *Willcocks & Cº.: London*, [1903.] fol. *The cover bears a MS. dedication in the composer's autograph.* **H. 1660. r. (2.)**

—— A Garden Serenade. [Song.] Words by P. Pinkerton. 3 no. [In F minor, G minor, and A minor.] *Chappell & Co.: London*, 1899. fol. **H. 1799. h. (51.)**

—— I loved a Rose. Song, words by E. Teschemacher. 3 no. [In F, G and A.] *E. Ashdown: London, etc.*, 1906. fol. **G. 807. kk. (6.)**

—— Last Night I dreamt. Song, the words by H. Simpson. *Enoch & Sons: London*, 1903. fol. **H. 1799. vv. (43.)**

—— Spring once more. Song, words by E. Teschemacher. *E. Ascherberg & Co.: London*, 1903. fol. **H. 1799. vv. (44.)**

—— Standard Duets, Trios ... Edited by E. Lèvi. No. 1–16. *Ascherberg, Hopwood & Crew: London*, 1909–14. fol. *With two editions, in different keys, of No. 1, 2, 4, 8.* **H. 3620. c.**

—— Standard Operatic Songs and Arias.—Original and English words.—Edited by E. Lèvi. Soprano. No. 1 (–20, 81–94). [Mezzo-soprano and contralto. No. 21–32.] (Tenor. No. 41–60.) [Bass and baritone. No. 61–74.] (No. 75. Soprano. Edited by Mrs. E. Lèvi.) *Ascherberg, Hopwood & Crew (International Music Co.): London*, (1908–26.) fol. *Two different works are numbered 94.* **H. 3620. b.**

—— Standard Songs by Old Masters for Students ... Edited by E. Lèvi. English words by M. F. Lloyd. 18 no. *Ascherberg, Hopwood & Crew: London*, (1906.) fol. **H. 3620.**

—— Standard Songs by Old Masters for Students. Edited by E. Lèvi. English words by M. F. Lloyd ... L. Hanray (A. Kalisch), *etc. Ascherberg, Hopwood & Crew: London*, (1907, *etc.*) fol. *An augmented edition of the previous series, with earlier and later issues of No. 21–25.* **H. 3620. a.**

—— When thou art sad. Song, words by E. Teschemacher. *E. Ascherberg & Co.: London*, 1903. fol. **H. 1799. vv. (45.)**

—— The World's Desire! Song, written by M. E. Rourke. *E. Ascherberg & Co.: London*, 1900. fol. **H. 1799. cc. (60.)**

—— *See* DONIZETTI (Domenico G. M.) [L'Elisir d'amore.] Una furtiva lagrima, *etc.* ⟨Edited by E. Lèvi.⟩ [1980.] 4°. **G. 206. m. (13.)**

—— *See* DONIZETTI (Domenico G. M.) [Lucia di Lammermoor.— Alfin son tua.] The Mad Scene, *etc.* ⟨Edited by E. Lèvi.⟩ [1980.] 4°. **G. 206. m. (14.)**

—— *See* GIORDANI ( ) Caro mio ben. (Heart of my Heart.) ⟨Edited by E. Lèvi.⟩ [1979.] 4°. **G. 206. m. (2.)**

—— *See* GLUCK (Christoph W. von) [Alceste.] Divinités du Styx! ... Edited by E. Lèvi, *etc.* [1980.] 4°. **G. 206. m. (15.)**

—— *See* GLUCK (Christoph W. von) [Orfeo.—Che farò.] Recit: Sposa! Euridice! ... Aria: Che farò senza Euridice? ... Edited by E. Lèvi. [1979.] 4°. **G. 206. m. (5.)**

—— *See* HAENDEL (Georg F.) [Rinaldo.] Lascia ch'io pianga ... Aria ... Edited by E. Lèvi, *etc.* [1980.] 4°. **G. 206. m. (16.)**

—— *See* HAENDEL (Georg F.) [Semele.—Where'er you walk.] Recit: "See, she appears." Aria: "Where-e'er you walk" ... Edited by E. Lèvi. [1979.] 4°. **G. 206. m. (7.)**

—— *See* HAENDEL (Georg F.) [Serse.] Ombra mai fù. (The Plane Tree.), *etc.* ⟨Recit. and aria. Edited by E. Lèvi.⟩ [1979.] 4°. **G. 206. m. (6.)**

LÈVI (EDGARDO)

— *See* MOZART (Wolfgang A.) [Don Giovanni.] "Batti, batti, o bel Masetto" … ⟨Aria.⟩ Edited by E. Lèvi. [1979.] 4°.
G. 206. m. (8.)

— *See* MOZART (Wolfgang A.) [Le Nozze di Figaro.] Deh vieni, non tardar, *etc.* ⟨Edited by E. Lèvi.⟩ [1980.] 4°.
G. 206. m. (20.)

— *See* MOZART (Wolfgang A.) [Le Nozze di Figaro.] Non più andrai, *etc.* ⟨Edited by E. Lèvi.⟩ [1979.] 4°.　**G. 206. m. (22.)**

— *See* MOZART (Wolfgang A.) [Le Nozze di Figaro.] Non so più cosa son, *etc.* ⟨Edited by E. Lèvi.⟩ [1979.] 4°.
G. 206. m. (23.)

— *See* MOZART (Wolfgang A.) [Le Nozze di Figaro.] Porgi amor … Edited by E. Lèvi, *etc.* [1979.] 4°.　**G. 206. m. (24.)**

— *See* MOZART (Wolfgang A.) [Le Nozze di Figaro.] Voi che sapete … [Song.] Edited by E. Lèvi. [1979.] 4°.
G. 206. m. (21.)

— *See* PERGOLESI (Giovanni B.) [*Doubtful and Supposititious Works.*] Se tu m'ami … Edited by E. Lèvi, *etc.* [1980.] 4°.
G. 206. m. (25.)

— *See* PURCELL (Henry) [The Indian Queen.] I attempt from Love's Sickness to fly, *etc.* [Song. Edited by E. Lèvi.] [1979.] 4°.　**G. 206. m. (9.)**

— *See* ROSSINI (Gioacchino A.) [Il Barbiere di Siviglia.] Una Voce poco fà … Edited by E. Lèvi. [1979.] 4°.
G. 206. m. (27.)

— *See* SPINELLI (N.) [A Basso Porto.] Intermezzo … arranged by E. Levi. 1894. fol.　**h. 1612. h. (47.)**

— *See* VERDI (Fortunino G. F.) [Rigoletto.] Caro nome, *etc.* ⟨Edited by E. Lèvi.⟩ [1980.] 4°.　**G. 206. m. (28.)**

— *See* VERDI (Fortunino G. F.) [Rigoletto.] La Donna è mobile … Edited by E. Lèvi. [1979.] 4°.　**G. 206. m. (29.)**

LEVI (*Mrs* EDGARDO)

— *See* LÈVI (E.) Standard Operatic Songs and Arias, *etc.* (No. 75. Soprano. Edited by Mrs. E. Levi.) 1908–26. fol.
H. 3620. b.

LEVI (ELMORE D.) and **DAVIS** (ED.)

— My Fiji Babe. [Song.] Words & music by E. D. Levi and E. Davis. pp. 4.　*Will Rossiter: Chicago*, [1906.] fol.
H. 3985. y. (1.)

LEVI (EUGENIA)

— Fiorita di Canti Tradizionali del Popolo Italiano, scelti nei vari dialetti e annotati da E. Levi. Con cinquanta melodie popolari tradizionali.　*R. Bemporad & Figlio: Firenze*, 1895. 8°.　**11429. bbb. 13.**

— Sei Pezzi Caratteristici per pianoforte.　*Novello, Ewer & Co.: London & New York*, [1888.] fol.　**g. 543. j. (33.)**

LEVI (HERMANN)

— Eight German Songs … translated by Mrs. V. Ashton. *London*, [1862.] fol.　**H. 1772. r. (44.)**

— [Der letzte Gruss.] The Last Meeting. Der letzte Gruss,— J. von Eichendorff. English version by B. F. Wyatt Smith. Song with pianoforte accompaniment [begins: "Ich kam vom Walde hernieder"]. Op. 2. No. 6.　*Leipzig*, 1885. fol.
H. 2836. h. (51.)

— Der letzte Gruss. The last Meeting … Op. 2. No. 6. Für vierstimmigen Männerchor gesetzt von A. Riedel. Partitur. *Leipzig*, 1886. 8°.　**E. 308. q. (23.)**

LEVI (HERMANN)

— Der letzte Kuss. *See* KELLER (R.) Zwei Paraphrasen, *etc.* No. 2. 1879. fol.　**h. 1493. m. (5.)**

LEVI (MAURICE)

— Airy Fairy Lillian. Song and chorus, words by T. Raymond. *M. Witmark & Sons: New York*, 1894. fol.　**H. 1798. v. (17.)**

— Armenonville. Valse lento. [P. F.] pp. 5.　*Chas. K. Harris: New York*, [1905.] fol.　**h. 4120. pp. (16.)**

— The Boulevard. March and Two-Step. [P. F.]　*M. Witmark & Sons: New York & Chicago*, 1896. fol.　**h. 3286. g. (39.)**

— Boys, she's a Dream! Song and chorus. Words by Harry Dillon. pp. 5.　*M. Witmark & Sons: New York, Chicago*, [1896.] fol.　**H. 3980. rr. (37.)**

— The Bridal Path. Polka brillanto. [P. F.] pp. 9.　*M. Witmark & Sons: New York, etc.*, [1908.] fol.　**h. 4120. pp. (17.)**

— The Brinkley bathing Girl. [Song.] Lyric by Harry B. Smith. pp. 5.　*Jerome H. Remick & Co.: New York, Detroit*, [1909.] fol.　**H. 3985. y. (2.)**

— The Duchess of the Table d'hote. ⟨Song.⟩ Lyric by Harry B. Smith. pp. 5.　*Cohan & Harris Publishing Co.: [New York*, 1908.] fol.　**H. 3985. y. (3.)**

— The Flowers' Serenade. Song … words by H. Anderson. *M. Witmark & Sons: New York*, 1893. fol.　**H. 1798. v. (18.)**

— Gay Coney Island. March and Two-Step. [P. F.]　*Whaley, Royce & Co.: Toronto*, 1897. fol.　**h. 3286. g. (40.)**

— The Graduates. March and Two-Step. [P. F.]　*M. Witmark & Sons: New York & Chicago*, 1897. fol.　**h. 3286. g. (41.)**

— Happy Days. March-two-step. [P. F.] pp. 5.　*M. Witmark & Sons: New York, etc.*, [1907.] fol.　**h. 4120. pp. (18.)**

— Hat Song. Lyric by Harry B. Smith. pp. 5.　*Cohan & Harris Publishing Co.: [New York*, 1908.] fol.　**H. 3985. y. (4.)**

— Higgledy-piggledy. ⟨Musical mélange.⟩ Book & lyrics by Edgar Smith. [Separate songs.] 11 no.　*Chas. K. Harris: New York*, [1904, 05.] fol.　**H. 3985. y. (5.)**

— Hush yo' Business, oh, go on! … [Song.] Words by Sager Midgley. pp. 5.　*M. Witmark & Sons: New York*, [1895.] fol.
H. 3980. rr. (38.)

— I'm a respectable working Girl. [Song.] Words by Edgar Smith. pp. 5.　*M. Witmark & Sons: New York, etc.*, [1909.] fol.
H. 3985. y. (6.)

— Little Bonnie Dean. Song and chorus. Words by Hattie Anderson.　*M. Witmark & Sons: New York*, [1893.] fol.
H. 3980. rr. (39.)

— Little Mary waited for the Pie. [Song.] Words by Arthur J. Lamb. pp. 5.　*M. Witmark & Sons: New York, etc.*, [1908.] fol.
H. 3985. y. (7.)

— Merry Widows of all Nations. ⟨Song.⟩ Lyric by Harry B. Smith. pp. 5.　*Cohan & Harris Publishing Co.: New York*, [1908.] fol.　**H. 3985. y. (8.)**

— M'lle New York. March and Two-Step. [P. F.]　*M. Witmark & Sons: New York & Chicago*, 1897. fol.　**h. 3286. g. (42.)**

— Moonlight Dance … for the piano.　*M. Witmark & Sons: New York*, 1893. fol.　**h. 1489. s. (51.)**

— Mosquito Song. Lyric by Harry B. Smith. pp. 5.　*Cohan & Harris Publishing Co.: New York*, [1908.] fol.
H. 3985. y. (9.)

— My Love's a gamblin' Man … song and chorus with dance ad lib. Words by Mathews and Bulger. pp. 5.　*M. Witmark & Sons: New York, Chicago*, [1897.] fol.　**H. 3980. rr. (40.)**

LEVI (MAURICE)

— The Napoleon March and Two-Step ... for the piano.
M. Witmark & Sons: New York, 1895. fol.　　**h. 1489. s. (52.)**

— Napoleon March. [P. F.]　*Whaley, Royce & Co.: Toronto*,
1895. fol.　　**g. 605. p. (30.)**

— Napoleon. Quick march. [Parts for fife and drum band.]
32 pt.　*J. R. Lafleur & Son: London*, [1898.] 8°.
*Part of "J. R. Lafleur & Son's Fife & Drum Journal". Including
several copies of various parts.*　　**f. 800. (819.)**

— The Nell Brinkley Girl. ⟨Song.⟩ Words by Harry B. Smith.
pp. 5.　*Cohan & Harris Publishing Co.: New York*, [1908.] fol.
　　H. 3985. y. (10.)

— Now will you be good? Comic song & refrain. Words by
William Jerome. pp. 5.　*M. Witmark & Sons: New York*,
[1893.] fol.　　**H. 3980. rr. (41.)**

— Peggy Cline. [Song.] Written by J. T. Kelly and C. W. Murphy,
etc. pp. 4.　*Francis, Day & Hunter: London*, [1892.] fol.
　　H. 3980. rr. (42.)

— Poor little Mary. Novelty song and refrain. Words by Walter
H. Ford. pp. 5.　*M. Witmark & Sons: New York*, [1894.] fol.
　　H. 3980. rr. (43.)

— The Rajah of Broadway. ⟨Song.⟩ Lyrics by Harry B. Smith.
pp. 5.　*Cohan & Harris Publishing Co.: New York*, [1908.] fol.
　　H. 3985. y. (11.)

— The Rolling Chair. March & two-step. [P. F.] pp. 5.　*Chas.
K. Harris: New York*, [1907.] fol.　　**h. 4120. pp. (19.)**

— "Sally." [Song.] Words by Richard Carle. pp. 3–5.　*Rogers
Bros. Music Publishing Co.:* [*New York*, 1900.] fol.
　　H. 3985. y. (12.)

— Sextette ... ⟨Song.⟩ Lyric by Harry B. Smith. pp. 11.　*Cohan &
Harris Publishing Co.:* [*New York*, 1908.] fol.
　　H. 3985. y. (13.)

— She's Grace and Grace itself. [Song.] Words by Hal
Homiston. pp. 5.　*M. Witmark & Sons: New York, Chicago*,
[1897.] fol.　　**H. 3980. rr. (44.)**

— Society. ⟨Song.⟩ Words by Harry B. Smith. pp. 5.　*Cohan &
Harris Publishing Co.: New York*, [1908.] fol.
　　H. 3985. y. (14.)

— A Song of the Navy. Lyric by Harry B. Smith. pp. 5.　*Cohan
& Harris Publishing Co.:* [*New York*, 1908.] fol.
　　H. 3985. y. (15.)

— The Soul Kiss. [Musical play. Separate songs.] Books by
Harry B. Smith. 10 no.　*M. Witmark & Sons: New York, etc.*,
[1908.] fol.　　**H. 3985. y. (16.)**

— Take a Tip from Venus. [Song.] Lyric by Henry B. Smith.
pp. 5.　*Jerome H. Remick & Co.: New York, Detroit*, [1909.]
fol.　　**H. 3985. y. (17.)**

— Twiddle twaddle. [Musical play. Separate songs.] Book &
lyrics by Edgar Smith. 9 no.　*Chas. K. Harris: New York*,
[1905, 06.] fol.　　**H. 3985. y. (18.)**

— Waxworks. ⟨Song.⟩ Lyric by Harry B. Smith. pp. 5.　*Cohan &
Harris Publishing Co.:* [*New York*, 1908.] fol.
　　H. 3985. y. (19.)

— What would your Answer be? Song and chorus. Words by
Raymond A. Browne, *etc.* pp. 5.　*M. Witmark & Sons: New
York, Chicago*, [1896.] fol.　　**H. 3980. rr. (45.)**

— When Reuben comes to Town. [Song.] Words by J. Cheever
Godwin. pp. 2–5.　*Rogers Bros. Music Pub. Co.:* [*New York*,
1900.] fol.　　**H. 3985. y. (20.)**

— *See* CARLE (Richard) and LEVI (M.) An Innocent young Maid
[Song], *etc.* [1899.] fol.　　**H. 3980. g. (34.)**

LEVI (NATALIYA)

— Шесть карельских песен. В обработке для голоса и
фортепиано Н. Леви. pp. 27.　*Музгиз: Ленинград, Москва*,
1939. 4°.　　**H. 2170. e. (1.)**

LEVI (SAMUEL)

— Iginia d'Asti. Melodramma in due atti del Sig. Rossi. [Vocal
score.]　*Milano*, [1837.] *obl.* fol.　　**E. 1100.**

LEVI (THOMAS)

— Undeb Ysgolion Sabbothol y Methodistiaid Calfinaidd. Dan
nawdd y Gymanfa Gyffredinol. Hymnau a Thonau ar gyfer
yr Ysgol Sabbothol a Chyfarfodydd Dirwestol. Wedi eu
dwyn allan ar gais y Gymanfa Gyffredinol. Dan olygiad
T. Levi. [Tonic sol-fa notation.]　*D. O'Brien Owen:
Caernarfon*, [1904.] 8°.　　**B. 1108.**

LEVIATHAN

— Leviathan. [Motet.] *See* KRENEK (E.) Three Motets. 3.

LEVIEN (ELLEN)

— April weeps. Part song, the words by W. Stigand. *See* HULLAH
(J. P.) The Singer's Library of Concerted Music. Secular.
No. 78. [1859, *etc.*] 8°.　　**G. 435.**

— The Song of Love & Death [begins: "Sweet is true love"].
Poetry by A. Tennyson.　*London*, [1863.] fol.
　　H. 1772. r. (45.)

LEVIEN (J. J. MEWBURN)

— Heart to Heart. Waltz. [P. F.]　*Moutrie & Son: London*, [1887.]
fol.　　**h. 975. v. (36.)**

— The Lotus Flower. Song, for Soprano or Tenor ... Poetry
translated by A. L. from the German of Heine.　*Moutrie &
Son: London*, [1888.] 8°.　　**H. 1788. v. (51.)**

— Parted Playmates. [Song.] Words by Longfellow.　*Rossini &
Co.: London*, [1900.] fol.　　**H. 1799. h. (52.)**

LEVIEN (MORDAUNT)

— A Collection of popular Songs, composed by Mess[rs]
Whitaker, Reeve, &c. &c. Arranged with an accompaniment
for the guitar, harp, lute, or lyre. pp. 25.　*Printed by Button &
Whitaker: London*, [[WM] 1813.] fol.　　**h. 255. a. (5.)**

— Divertimento for the guitar. No. 10.　*London*, [1844.] fol.
　　h. 140. (12.)

— Lieber Augustine, with variations for the Guitar.　*London*,
[1845?] fol.　　**h. 3213. f. (6.)**

LEVIN (JOSEPH A.)

— Montage. Composed and arranged by J. A. Levin, *etc.*
⟨Conductor [and military band parts].⟩ 73 pt.　*Robbins Music
Corp.: New York*, [1968.] 4°.
*Part of "Modern Concert Series for Band". With several copies
of various parts.*　　**h. 3210. j. (188.)**

LEVIN (MONROË)

— *See* LESURE (F.) Anthologie de la chanson parisienne au XVI[e]
siècle, réunie par F. Lesure avec la collaboration de ...
M. Levin, *etc.* [1953.] fol.　　**H. 4009.**

LEVIN (ROBERT D.)

— *See* MOZART (W. A.) [Quintets. K. 516[c].] Allegro in B zu einem
Quintett für Klarinette, zwei Violinen, Viola und Violoncello
... Fragment, ergänzt von ... R. D. Levin. [1970.] 4°.
　　g. 382. o. (4.)

LEVIN (S.)

— *See* GLAZUNOV (A. K.) [2 morceaux. Op. 14. No. 1.] Идиллия
... Редакция С. Левина, *etc.* 1960. 4°.　　　**g. 724. p. (6.)**

— *See* GLAZUNOV (A. K.) Серенада N° 2 ... Редакция С. Левина,
etc. 1961. 4°.　　　**g. 724. p. (7.)**

LEVIN (Yu.)

— *See* GEDIKE (A. Th.) Избранные сочинения для фортепиано
... Составление и педагогическая редакция Ю. Левина. 1970.
4°.　　　**g. 1594. i. (1.)**

LEVINA (ZARA ALEKSANDROVNA)

— Избранные романсы для голоса с фортепиано. pp. 76.
Советский композитор: Москва, 1963. 4°.　　　**F. 1594. n. (4.)**

— Лирические романсы. pp. 28. *Мосвка*, 1956. *obl.* 8°.
Нотное приложение к журналу "Советская музыка". 1956.
no. 6.　　　**P. P. 1933. c. (2.)**

LEVINE (DAVID)

— Nocturne. Der Traum. (For the Pianoforte.) *Hutchings &*
Romer: London, [1907.] fol.　　　**h. 3283. p. (28.)**

LEVINE (HANK)

— Sing along with J F K, *etc.* [Six excerpts from the inaugural
speech of President Kennedy.] ⟨Piano arr. by Lou Halmy.⟩
pp. 24. *Holly-Vine Music Co.: New York*, [1963.] 4°.
　　　G. 1276. aa. (15.)

LEVINE (HENRY)

— *See* ARENSKY (A. S.) [Suite für 2 Pianoforte. Op. 15. No. 2.]
Valse ... Arranged for piano solo by H. Levine. [1955.] 4°.
　　　g. 1128. u. (2.)

— *See* DEBUSSY (C. A.) [Petite suite. No. 1.] En bateau ...
Transcribed for piano solo by H. Levine. [1969.] 4°.
　　　f. 391. a. (16.)

— *See* FIBICH (Z.) [Nálady, dojmy a upomínky. Series I. Op. 41.
Book 4. No. 14.] Poem ... Arranged for the piano by
H. Levine. [1954.] 4°.　　　**g. 1128. r. (16.)**

— *See* HERBERT (Victor) [Natoma.] Dagger Dance ... Simplified
version, arranged for the piano by H. Levine. [1955.] 4°.
　　　g. 1128. v. (6.)

— *See* KHACHATURYAN (A. I.) [Gayaneh.] Sabre Dance ...
Arranged for the piano by H. Levine. [1954.] 4°.
　　　g. 1548. a. (15.)

— *See* LEVITZKI (M.) Valse. Op. 2 ... Arranged for one piano,
four hands by H. Levine. [1959.] 4°.　　　**g. 230. nn. (4.)**

— *See* MARTINI (G.) *il Tedesco, pseud.* Plaisir d'amour ...
Arranged for the piano by H. Levine. [1955.] 4°.
　　　g. 1128. v. (18.)

— *See* MENDELSSOHN-BARTHOLDY (J. L. F.) [Ein
Sommernachtstraum.] Scherzo ... Arranged for the piano by
H. Levine. [1954.] 4°.　　　**g. 635. x. (2.)**

— *See* SCHUBERT (F. P.) Schubert Waltzes. Selected and edited
by H. Levine. [1954.] 4°.　　　**g. 567. o. (17.)**

— *See* SCOTT (Cyril M.) Lotus Land ... ⟨Op. 47, No. 1.⟩ For
piano solo. Simplified arrangement by H. Levine. [1955.] 4°.
　　　g. 1128. w. (8.)

LEVINE (ISAAC)

— Bourrée. Composition for the Piano. *Gamble Hinged Music*
Co.: Chicago, (1912.) fol.　　　**g. 606. n. (42.)**

LEVINGSTON (　　　)

— Delia. [Song.] [*London?*, c. 1760.] *s. sh.* fol.
Followed by an arrangement for the German flute.
　　　H. 1601. u. (109.)

LEVINSKAYA (MARIA)

— Russian Folk-Songs. Arranged and revised by M. Levinskaya
for the Russian Folk-Song Choir. pp. 12. *M. Levinskaya:*
London, [1930?] 4°.　　　**G. 981. z. (18.)**

LEVINSOHN (ALBERT)

— Abendständchen. *See* infra: Vier Lieder ... Op. 7. No. 4.

— An einem Grabe. *See* infra: Drei Lieder ... Op. 6. No. 1.

— An Mignon. *See* infra: Drei Lieder ... Op. 1. No. 3.

— Frühlingsanfang. *See* infra: Vier Lieder. Op. 7. No. 1.

— Gefunden. *See* infra: Drei Lieder. Op. 2. No. 1.

— Ghasele. *See* infra: Drei Lieder. Op. 6. No. 2.

— Heimkehr. *See* infra: Vier Lieder ... Op. 5. No. 1.

— Ich hab' die Nacht geträumet. *See* infra: Fünf Lieder. Op. 8.
No. 1.

— Ich lieb' eine Blume. *See* infra: Drei Lieder. Op. 2 ... No. 2.

— In dem Walde spriesst und grünt es. *See* infra: Drei Lieder
... Op. 2 ... No. 3.

— Kein Feuer, keine Kohle. *See* infra: Fünf Lieder. Op. 8.
No. 2.

— Des Kukuks froher Ruf. *See* infra: Vier Lieder ... Op. 5.
No. 2.

— Liebster Schatz, halte fest. *See* infra: Fünf Lieder. Op. 8.
No. 5.

— Drei Lieder. Op. 1. 1. Schäfers Klagelied [begins: "Da droben
auf jenem Berge"],—Goethe. 2. Der Strauss, den ich
gepflücket,—Goethe. 3. An Mignon [begins: "Über Thal und
Fluss getragen"],—Goethe. *Berlin*, [1886.] fol.
　　　H. 2611. (1.)

— Drei Lieder. Op. 2. 1. Gefunden [begins: "Ich ging im Walde
so für mich hin"],—Goethe. 2. Ich lieb' eine Blume,—Heine.
3. In dem Walde spriesst und grünt es,—Heine. *Berlin*,
[1866.] fol.　　　**H. 2611. (2.)**

— Vier Lieder, für eine mittlere Stimme mit Begleitung des
Pianoforte ... Op. 5. No. 1. Heimkehr [begins: "Leiser
schwanken die Äste"] (Gedicht von F. A. von Schack). No. 2.
"Des Kukuks froher Ruf" (Ungarisches Volkslied). No. 3.
"Der Wald hat seine Vögelein" (Gedicht von A. Petöfi—
Übersetzung von J. Goldschmidt). No. 4. "Stand ein
Bettlerpärlein" (Gedicht von P. Heyse). *Berlin*, [1886.] fol.
　　　H. 2611. (3.)

— Drei Lieder für eine tiefe Stimme mit Begleitung des
Pianoforte. Op. 6. No. 1. An einem Grabe [begins: "Dem
Armen, der gebeugt von Jammer"] (Gedicht von
H. Leuthold). No. 2. Ghasele [begins: "Lieblich weht die Luft
uns zu"] (Gedicht von H. Leuthold). No. 3. Nachtgesang
[begins: "O gib vom weichen Pfühle"] (Gedicht von Goethe).
Berlin, [1886.] fol.　　　**H. 2611. (4.)**

— Vier Lieder. Op. 7. No. 1. Frühlingsanfang [begins: "Es
kommt so still der Frühlingstag"],—H. Lingg. No. 2. "Singet
leiser, o Cicaden,"—R. Kralik. No. 3. "Nun die Schatten
dunklen,"—E. Geibel. No. 4. Abendständchen [begins:
"Schlafe Liebchen"],—nach J. von Eichendorff. *Berlin*,
[1886.] fol.　　　**H. 2611. (5.)**

— Fünf Lieder. Op. 8. 1. Ich hab' die Nacht geträumet.
Deutsches Volkslied. 2. Kein Feuer, keine Kohle. Deutsches
Volkslied. 3. Wenn ich ein Vöglein wär'. Deutsches Volkslied.

LEVINSOHN (ALBERT)

4. Wenn du zu mein'm Schätzchen kommst. Deutsches Volkslied. 5. Liebster Schatz, halte fest. Deutsches Volkslied. *Berlin*, [1886.] fol. **H. 2611. (6.)**

— Nachtgesang. *See* supra: Drei Lieder ... Op. 6. No. 3.

— Nun die Schatten dunkeln. *See* supra: Vier Lieder ... Op. 7. No. 3.

— Schäfers Klagelied. *See* supra: Drei Lieder ... Op. 1. No. 1.

— Singet leiser, o Cicaden. *See* supra: Vier Lieder. Op. 7. No. 2.

— Stand ein Bettlerpärlein. *See* supra: Vier Lieder ... Op. 5. No. 4.

— Der Strauss, den ich gepflücket. *See* supra: Drei Lieder. Op. 1 ... No. 2.

— Der Wald hat seine Vögelein. *See* supra: Vier Lieder ... Op. 5. No. 3.

— Wenn du zu mein'm Schätzchen kommst. *See* supra: Fünf Lieder. Op. 8. No. 4.

— Wenn ich ein Vöglein wär'. *See* supra: Fünf Lieder. Op. 8. No. 3.

LEVINSON (JAY)

— *See* CHAIKOVSKY (P. I.) [Quartet No. 1. Op. 11. Andante cantabile.] Shadows of Midnight blue. Adapted ... by J. Levinson, *etc.* 1940. 4°. **G. 1275. xx. (29.)**

LEVIS (CARROLL)

— The Miners' Song. Arranged for Male Voices (T. T. B. B.) with Piano accompaniment, words and music by C. Levis. pp. 7. *Chappell & Co.: London, etc.*, 1947. 8°. [*Chappell's Vocal Library of Part-Songs, etc. No. 221.*] **G. 440.**

LEVIS (JOHN HAZEDEL)

— Foundations of Chinese Musical Art ... Illustrated with Musical Compositions. *Henri Vetch: Peiping*, 1936. 8°. **07899. i. 60.**

LEVISEUR (ELSA)

— Baker's Dozen. Little Songs for people of all ages. *J. Curwen & Sons: London*, 1924. 4°. **G. 1275. s. (3.)**

— The Faun. In the Forest. Song, words by O. Wilde. *Elkin & Co.: London*, 1917. fol. **H. 1846. y. (12.)**

— Federation. Barn Dance, *etc.* [P. F.] *Hawkes & Son: London*, 1908. fol. **h. 3286. vv. (1.)**

— Red Skies. Song, words by S. Phillips. *Elkin & Co.: London*, 1917. fol. **H. 1846. y. (13.)**

— The Throstle. [Song.] Words by Alfred, Lord Tennyson. *I. H. Haarburger: Bloemfontein*, [1903.] fol. **G. 807. z. (36.)**

— To Marietje. A Rocking-chair Song, words ... by Alfred, Lord Tennyson. *I. H. Haarburger: Bloemfontein*, [1903.] fol. **G. 807. z. (37.)**

— Twilight. Song, words by W. S. Walker, *etc. Elkin & Co.: London*, 1917. fol. **H. 1846. y. (14.)**

LEVISTER (ALONZO)

— The Prince of Peace. (A Child was born.) Words and music by A. Levister. Arranged by Elliot Gilman. ⟨SATB.⟩ pp. 11. *Hastings Music Corp.: New York*, [1971.] 8°. **F. 1892. d. (1.)**

LEVITIN (YURY ABRAMOVICH)

— Концертино. Concertino. Для виолончели с оркестром. For violoncello and orchestra. ⟨Op. 54.⟩ Партитура. Score. pp. 81. *Советский композитор: Москва*, 1970. 4°. **g. 1593. zz. (4.)**

— Концерт для кларнета и фагота с оркестром. Переложение для кларнета и фагота с фортепиано. [Score and parts.] 3 pt. *Советский котпозитор: Москва*, 1963. **g. 1590. rr. (1.)**

— Дни войны. Инструментальная-хоровая симфония. Days of war. Instrumental-choral symphony. ⟨Op. 82.⟩ Для большого симфонического оркестра и смешанного хора. For full symphony orchestra and mixed chorus. Стихи Л. Первомайского и А. Твардовского. Verses by L. Pervomaisky and A. Tvardovsky. Партитура. Score. pp. 116. *Советский композитор: Москва*, 1977. 4°. **F. 1594. rr. (1.)**

— Хиросима не должна повториться. Ораторио для большого симфонического оркестра, чтеца, сопрано соло, детского и смешанного хоров. ⟨Соч. 63.⟩ Стихи М. Матусовского. Партитура. ⟨Hiroshima must not be repeated. Oratorio for full symphony orchestra, reciter, soprano solo, children's and mixed choruses. Verses by M. Matussovsky. Score.⟩ *Russ.* pp. 95. *Советский композитор: Москва*, 1972. fol. **H. 2170. ii.**

— Огни над Волгой. ⟨Соч. 39.⟩ Оратория для чтеца, меццо-сопрано, смешанного хора и симфонического оркестра. Слова Д. Седых. Партитура. pp. 155. *Государственное музыкальное издательство: Москва*, 1952. fol. **H. 2170. z.**

— [Огни над Волгой.] Народам мир. Из оратории "Огни над Волгой". *In:* Вечер в доме культуры ... 1951 год. pp. 232–240. 1953. 8°. **W. P. c. 47.**

— Квартет № 6 для двух скрипок, альта и виолончели. ⟨Соч. 37.⟩ Партитура. pp. 56. *Государственное музыкальное издательство: Москва*, 1952. 8°. **b. 346. o. (3.)**

— Восьмой квартет для двух скрипок, альта и виолончели. ⟨Соч. 48.⟩ Партитура. pp. 47. *Издательство "Музыка": Москва*, 1964. 8°. **c. 139. e. (2.)**

— Девятый и десятый квартеты. Ninth and tenth quartets. ⟨Op. 66, 73.⟩ Для двух скрипок, альта и виолончели. For two violins, viola and cello. Партитура. Score. pp. 72. *Советский композитор: Москва*, 1974. 4°. **g. 1593. b. (3.)**

— Одиннадцатый и двенадцатый квартеты. Eleventh and twelfth Quartets. ⟨Op. 80, 86.⟩ Для двух скрипок, альта и виолончели. For two violins, viola and violoncello. Партитура. Score. pp. 60. *Советский композитор: Москва*, 1980. 4°. **g. 1594. y. (6.)**

— Сюита для квартета деревянных духовых инструментов ... Партитура. pp. 24. *Советский композитор: Москва*, 1959. 4°. **g. 420. ll. (4.)**

— Симфония. Symphony. Для камерного оркестра и меццо-сопрано. For chamber orchestra and mezzo-soprano. ⟨Op. 55.⟩ Партитура. Score. pp. 80. *Советский композитор: Москва*, 1969. 8°. **C. 374. dd. (1.)**

— Веселые нищие. The jolly beggars. Кантата для солистов и камерного оркестра. Cantata for singers and chamber orchestra. ⟨Op. 56.⟩ Стихи Р. Бернса. Перевод С. Маршака. Verses by R. Burns. Партитура. Score. *Russ.* pp. 136. *Советский композитор: Москва*, 1974. 4°. **F. 1594. ff. (2.)**

LEVITSKAYA (VIKTORIYA SERGEEVNA)

— *See* PROKOF'EV (S. S.) Симфония № 7 ... Редактор В. Левитская, *etc.* 1959. 4°. **h. 3573. ee.**

— *See* PROKOF'EV (S. S.) Sinfonie Nr. 7. Opus 131. Herausgegeben von W. Lewitskaja. [1970.] 8°. **c. 109. h. (1.)**

LEVITS'KY (B.)

— See ULITS'KY (S.) and LEVITS'KY (B.) Український народній співаник, *etc.* (Муз. ред.: С. Улицький, Б. Левицький.) 1946. 8°.   **D. 399. b.**

LEVITS'KY (M.)

— Наука. [Song.] Слова С. Руданьскьаго. *у Київі*, 1908. 8°.
Part of B. D. Hrinchenko's "Досвітні Огні".   **011586. c. 15.**

— Смутни Картыны. [Song.] Слова Б. Гринченко. *у Київі*, 1908. 8°.
Part of B. D. Hrinchenko's "Досвітні Огні".   **011586. c. 15.**

LEVITT (RICHARD)

— Gerippentanz. [Song.] Heine, with an English version by E. Lazarus. *Stainer & Bell: London*, (1914.) fol.
Stainer & Bell's Modern Songs, No. 89.   **H. 1793. t. (30.)**

— The Listener. Song, words by F. W. Home. *Elkin & Co.: London*, 1914. fol.   **H. 1793. t. (31.)**

LEVITT (ROD)

— Babylon. For stage band. [Score.] pp. 8. *Associated Music Publishers: New York, London*, [1978.] 4°.   **g. 1071. c. (5.)**

— Mamma's Eyes. For stage band. [Score.] pp. 7. *Associated Music Publishers: New York, London*, [1978.] 4°.
                                                           g. 1071. c. (6.)

— Mon Plaisir. For stage band. [Score.] pp. 8. *Associated Music Publishers: New York, London*, [1978.] 4°.   **g. 1071. c. (7.)**

— Woodmen of the World. Jazz fantasy on a rock theme. For woodwind quintet (with finger cymbals and tambourine), *etc.* [Score.] pp. 21. *Associated Music Publishers: New York, London*, [1973.] 4°.   **g. 270. gg. (9.)**

LEVITZKI (MISCHA)

— Ah, thou beloved one. A Song, *etc.* [Words by] (B. Galland. Op. 4.) *G. Schirmer: New York*, 1929. 4°.   **G. 1275. ff. (28.)**

— Cadenza ... to Concerto No. 3 in C minor, Opus 37, first movement by Ludwig van Beethoven. [P. F.] *G. Schirmer: New York*, 1924. 4°.   **g. 1127. w. (4.)**

— The Enchanted Nymph. A Poem for Piano. *G. Schirmer: New York*, 1928. 4°.   **g. 1127. kk. (5.)**

— Gavotte, for pianoforte. (Op. 3.) *G. Schirmer: New York*, 1923. 4°.   **g. 1127. w. (5.)**

— Valse, A major, for the pianoforte. *Nicholson & Co.: Sydney*, 1921. 4°.   **g. 1127. h. (17.)**

— Valse de Concert, for pianoforte. Op. 1. *G. Schirmer: New York*, 1924. 4°.   **g. 1127. w. (6.)**

— Valse, for pianoforte. Op. 2. *G. Schirmer: New York*, 1922. 4°.   **g. 1127. h. (18.)**

— Valse ... Op. 2 ... For two pianos, four hands. Transcribed by Ralph Berkowitz, *etc.* pp. 7. *G. Schirmer: New York*, [1951.] 4°.
Two copies.   **g. 1122. u. (7.)**

— Valse. Op. 2 ... Arranged for one piano, four hands by Henry Levine. pp. 7. *G. Schirmer: New York*, [1959.] 4°.
                                                           g. 230. nn. (4.)

— Valse ... Op. 20 [or rather, Op. 2]. Transcribed (for E flat Alto Saxophone and Piano) by J. Gurewich. *G. Schirmer: New York*, 1927. 4°.   **g. 1112. (11.)**

— Valse ... Op. 2 ... For violin and piano, transcription by S. Jacobsen. *G. Schirmer: New York*, 1924. 4°.
                                                           g. 500. l. (8.)

LEVOMMI

— Levommi il mio pensier in parte ov'era. [Song.] *See* PIZZETTI (I.) Tre Sonetti del Petrarca ... III.

LEVONS

— Levons nous, un Tribun perfide. Chant. *See* LESUEUR (J. F.)

LEVVY (A.)

— Had you but known that I loved you. Song and Chorus. *Lyceum Pub. Co.: New York*, 1900. fol.   **H. 1799. h. (53.)**

LÉVY (   )

— Bacchus, dans ce repas tu vas perdre ta gloire. *Recit de Basse.* Les parolles sont de M^r le Chevalier de Lauret, *etc.* [*Paris*,] 1751. *s. sh.* 4°.
Mercure de France, May, 1751.   **298. c. 3.**

— La Bagatelle. Vaudeville. Les paroles sont de Mr Meslé, *etc.* [*Paris*,] 1751. *s. sh.* 4°.
Mercure de France, Sept., 1751.   **298. c. 5.**

LEVY (A.)

— See KING (J. C.) Wave the Flag ... Harmony by A. Levy. [1912.] fol.   **H. 1793. r. (13.)**

LEVY (ALEXANDRE)

— Fantasia brillante sull' opera Il Guarany, di C. Gomes, composta per due Pianoforti. Op. 2. *Milano*, [1882.] fol.
                                                           h. 3291. (12.)

— Trois Improvisations pour piano. Op. 4. No. 1. Romance sans paroles. No. 2. À la Hongroise. No. 3. Pensée fugitive. *Mayence*, [1884.] fol.   **h. 3280. k. (55.)**

— Mazurka pour piano. Op. 6. No. 1. *Mayence*, [1884.] fol.
                                                           h. 3280. k. (56.)

— Deuxième Mazurka pour piano. Op. 6. No. 2. *Mayence*, [1884.] fol.   **h. 3280. k. (57.)**

— Valse Caprice pour Piano. *Mayence*, [1883.] fol.
                                                           h. 3276. g. (20.)

LEVY, afterwards GOETZ (ANGELINA)

— *See* ANGELINA.

LEVY (BERT)

— Artist Dreams. Valse artistique. [P. F.] pp. 7. *Theo. Bendix Music Pub.: New York*, [1908.] fol.   **h. 4120. pp. (20.)**

LEVY (BURT)

— Orbs with Flute. ff. 3. *Apogee Press: Cincinnati*, [1966.] fol. [*Apogee Series* 1. *no.* 4.]   **i. 38. g.**

LEVY (CHARLES S. H.)

— Ben-my-chree. Ballad, words by G. F. Howley. *Klene & Co.: London*, [1898.] fol.   **G. 807. o. (44.)**

— Forward. Polka. [P. F.] *Klene & Co.: London*, [1898.] fol.
                                                           h. 3286. g. (45.)

— The White Falcon. Quick March. [P. F.] *Klene & Co.: London*, [1898.] fol.   **g. 605. p. (31.)**

LEVY (DUDLEY)

— Blondinetta. Waltz. [P. F.] *Ascherberg, Hopwood & Crew: London*, 1909. fol.   **h. 3286. vv. (2.)**

LEVY (DUDLEY)

— Royal Edward Gavotte, for Pianoforte Solo. *Keith Prowse &
Co.: London*, 1909. fol.   **h. 3286. vv. (3.)**

LEVY (E.)

— They met but once ... Ballad, words by T. Moore.
Philadelphia, (1867.) fol.   **H. 1780. p. (35.)**

LEVY (ELLIS)

— Perpetuo Mobile, for Violin and Piano ... Op. 10. No. 6.
C. Fischer: New York, Boston, (1911.) fol.   **h. 1612. aa. (16.)**

LÉVY (ERNEST)

— Deux Airs italiens du XVIIᵉ siècle, publiés pour la première
fois ... Réalisation de la Basse continue par E. Lévy. ([No. 1.]
Canzone. Auteur inconnu. [No. 2.] Berceuse tragique. Totila.
1677. Legrenzi.) *Paris*, 1923. 8°.
La Revue musicale. 4ᵉ année. No. 9. Supplément musical.
                                                  P. P. 1948. tda.

— Seven Piano Pieces. pp. 28. *Boosey & Hawkes: [New York*,
1954.] 4°.
Fromm Music Foundation Series. 7.   **g. 1128. t. (2.)**

LEVY (ESTHER A.)

— Memories of Friendship. Ballad [begins: "How much are
changed"]. *London*, [1871.] fol.   **H. 1775. u. (38.)**

— Think of me, forget me not. Ballad. *London*, [1871.] fol.
                                                  H. 1775. u. (39.)

LÉVY (HENIOT)

— Two Compositions for Piano. Op. 9. 1. Barcarolle in F min. 2.
Menuet in E♭, *etc.* 2 no. *G. Schirmer: New York*, (1908.) fol.
                                                  g. 606. f. (26.)

— Love repentant. A Song, words by J. Stanford. *C. F. Summy
Co.: Chicago*, 1916. fol.   **H. 1860. b. (24.)**

— Mazourka. [P. F.] *C. Fischer: New York, etc.*, 1917. 4°.
                                                  g. 1129. g. (11.)

— Menuet. [P. F.] *C. Fischer: New York, etc.*, 1917. 4°.
                                                  g. 1129. g. (9.)

— Passacaglia, for violin and piano. (Violin part edited by
L. Sametini.) *C. Fischer: New York*, 1920. 4°.
                                                  g. 500. e. (18.)

— Pièce romantique. (Violin and Piano.) *C. F. Summy Co.:
Chicago*, (1908.) fol.   **h. 1612. p. (35.)**

— Poème de Mai. [P. F.] *C. Fischer: New York, etc.*, 1917. 4°.
                                                  g. 1129. g. (10.)

LEVY (HENRY)

— Minuet for pianoforte. Op. 1. No. 3. *O. Ditson Company:
Boston, etc.*, 1895. fol.   **h. 1489. s. (54.)**

LEVY (HUBERT)

— Shine! Shine! Shine! (The proverb song.) pp. 3–7.
M. Witmark & Sons: [New York, 1904.] fol.   **H. 3985. y. (21.)**

LEVY (ISAAC)

— Chants judéo-espagnols. Recueillis et notés par I. Levy.
Introduction de O. Camhy. 3 tom. *World Sephardi
Federation: London*, [1959–71.] 4°.
*Tom. 1 is part of "Publications de la fédération Séphardite
mondiale, Département culturel". Tom. 2, 3 bear the imprint
"Édition de l'auteur, Jerusalem".*   **E. 1499. i.**

LEVY (J.)

— A tanto amor ... [from La Favorite by D. G. M. Donizetti,
arranged] for Cornet & Piano by J. Levy. *A. Hammond &
Co.: London*, [1876.] fol.   **h. 2245. (32.)**

— Andante for Cornet & Piano. *London*, [1875.] fol.
                                                  h. 2245. (13.)

— The Army valse. [P. F. duet.] *London*, [1865.] fol.
                                                  h. 2245. (5.)

— The Best Shot polka, arranged by J. Hecker. [Reed band
parts.] *London*, [1879.] 8°.
Part of the "Alliance Musicale".   **f. 401. m. (13.)**

— The Best Shot polka arranged for the Cornet & Piano.
London, [1878.] fol.   **h. 2245. (35.)**

— Blue Bells of Scotland [by Mrs D. Jordan] for Cornet &
Piano. *London*, [1878.] fol.   **h. 2245. (39.)**

— The Carnival of Venice, for Cornet & Piano. *London*, [1864.]
fol.   **h. 2245. (2.)**

— Cruda funesta [from D. G. M. Donizetti's opera Lucia di
Lammermoor] arranged for Cornet & Piano by J. Levy.
A. Hammond & Co.: London, [1876.] fol.   **h. 2245. (27.)**

— Cujus animam [from G. A. Rossini's Stabat Mater] arranged
for Cornet & Piano. *London*, [1876.] fol.   **h. 2245. (30.)**

— Du du liegst ... arranged for the Cornet & Piano by J. Levy.
London, [1878.] fol.   **h. 2245. (50.)**

— Emily polka. [Reed band parts.] *London*, [1878.] 8°.
Part of the "Alliance Musicale".   **f. 401. k. (4.)**

— Emily Polka for the Pianoforte (with Cornet ad lib.).
London, [1862.] fol.   **h. 1462. r. (56.)**

— Fairy Palace Waltzes. Orchestré par E. Frewin. [Orchestral
parts.] *See* CHAPPELL AND CO. Popular Quadrilles, *etc.* No. 52.
[1868.] 8°.   **e. 249.**

— "Fairy Palace" Waltz ... Arrᵈ [for military band] by Fred
Godfrey. [Parts.] 23 pt. *S. A. Chappell: London*, [1868.] fol.
[*Army Journal.* no. 66.]   **h. 1562.**

— Fairy Palace waltz. [P. F.] *London*, [1868.] fol.   **h. 2245. (4.)**

— Fra poco. [From D. G. M. Donizetti's opera] Lucia di
Lammermoor. For Cornet & Pianoforte by J. Levy. *London*,
[1876.] fol.   **h. 2245. (26.)**

— God save the Queen, for Cornet & Piano. *London*, [1878.]
fol.   **h. 2245. (46.)**

— Grand Russian fantasia for Cornet & Piano. *London*, [1875.]
fol.   **h. 2245. (12.)**

— The Harp that once thro' Tara's halls, for Cornet & Piano.
London, [1878.] fol.   **h. 2245. (43.)**

— The Last Rose of Summer, arranged for the Cornet & Piano.
London, [1878.] fol.   **h. 2245. (37.)**

— Levy-athen polka. [Brass band parts.] *London*, [1877.] 8°.
                                                  f. 413. b. (31.)

— Levy-athen polka for Cornet & Piano. *London*, [1878.] fol.
                                                  h. 2245. (45.)

— Lizzie waltzes. [P. F. and cornet.] *London*, [1875.] fol.
                                                  h. 2245. (18.)

— Lydia polka for Cornet in B♭ and Piano. *London*, [1875.] 8°.
No. 262 of the "Alliance Musicale. Album Bijou".   **f. 406.**

— Il Mio Tesoro [from Don Giovanni by W. A. Mozart]
arranged for Cornet & Piano. *London*, [1876.] fol.
                                                  h. 2245. (29.)

— Nilsson valse. [P. F.] *London*, [1878.] fol.   **h. 2245. (48.)**

LEVY (J.)

— Original & operatic melodies ... arranged for the Cornet & Piano. 6 no. *London,* [1863.] fol.   **h. 2245. (1.)**

— Original & operatic melodies composed & arranged for the Cornet & Piano. 6 no. *London,* [1878.] fol.   **h. 2245. (47.)**

— The Promenade. Polka. [Brass band parts.] *London,* [1878.] 8°.
Part of the "Alliance Musicale".   **f. 402. f. (16.)**

— Promenade polka for Cornet & Piano. *London,* [1874.] fol.   **h. 2245. (7.)**

— Russian melody with variations for Cornet & Piano. *London,* [1875.] fol.   **h. 2245. (16.)**

— The Russian waltz. [P. F.] *London,* [1873.] fol.   **h. 2245. (6.)**

— The Salute polka for Cornet & Piano. *London,* [1875.] fol.   **h. 2245. (15.)**

— Six Studies for the Cornet à Piston. *London,* [1864.] fol.   **h. 2245. (3.)**

— [Tutto è sciolto.] All is lost [from La Sonnambula by V. Bellini] arranged for Cornet & Piano. *London,* [1876.] fol.   **h. 2245. (33.)**

— Vi ravviso [from La Sonnambula by V. Bellini] for Cornet & Pianoforte. *London,* [1876.] fol.   **h. 2245. (28.)**

— The Whirlwind polka. [P. F. and cornet.] *London,* [1862.] fol.   **h. 1462. r. (57.)**

— The White Rose valse. [P. F.] *London,* [1878.] fol.   **h. 2245. (36.)**

— Yankee Doodle, arranged for the Cornet & Piano. *London,* [1878.] fol.   **h. 2245. (38.)**

— *See* ABT (F. W.) [7 Lieder. Op. 39. No. 1. Agathe.] When the swallows ... for Cornet & Piano by J. Levy. [1875.] fol.   **h. 2245. (19.)**

— *See* BEETHOVEN (L. van) Adelaide ... for Cornet & Piano by J. Levy. [1875.] fol.   **h. 2245. (14.)**

— *See* BELLINI (V.) [Norma.] Casta Diva, for Cornet & Piano by J. Levy. [1875.] fol.   **h. 2245. (17.)**

— *See* BELLINI (V.) [I Puritani.] A te O cara, for Cornet & Piano by J. Levy. [1875.] fol.   **h. 2245. (24.)**

— *See* CAUSSINUS (V.) [Solfège-Méthode de Cornet à Pistons.] Progressive Method for the Cornet ... to which has been added ... Studies by Levy, *etc.* 1910. fol.   **h. 2225. a.**

— *See* DONIZETTI (D. G. M.) [Don Pasquale.] Bella siccome, [arranged] for Cornet & Pianoforte by J. Levy. [1876.] fol.   **h. 2245. (34.)**

— *See* GLUCK (C. W. von) [Orfeo.] Che farò senza Euridice, arranged for Cornet & Piano by J. Levy. [1876.] fol.   **h. 2245. (31.)**

— *See* HALÉVY (J. F. F. É.) L'Éclair, arranged for Cornet & Piano by J. Levy. [1875.] fol.   **h. 2245. (10.)**

— *See* MENDELSSOHN-BARTHOLDY (J. L. F.) [6 Gesänge. Op. 34. No. 2. Auf Flügeln des Gesanges.] On Music's softest pinions ... for Cornet & Piano by J. Levy. [1875.] fol.   **h. 2245. (25.)**

— *See* MENDELSSOHN-BARTHOLDY (J. L. F.) [Sechs Lieder. Op. 47. No. 6. Bei der Wiege.] Cradle Song ... for Cornet & Piano by J. Levy. [1875.] fol.   **h. 2245. (23.)**

— *See* MEYERBEER (G.) [Robert le Diable.] Robert toi que j'aime, for Cornet and Piano by J. Levy. [1874.] fol.   **h. 2245. (8.)**

— *See* MOZART (W. A.) [Le Nozze di Figaro.] Voi che sapete, for Cornet & Piano by J. Levy. [1875.] fol.   **h. 2245. (20.)**

LEVY (J.)

— *See* RODE (P.) Rode's Air for Cornet & Piano by J. Levy. [1878.] fol.   **h. 2245. (49.)**

— *See* ROSSINI (G. A.) [Semiramide.] Bel raggio, arranged ... by J. Levy. [1878.] fol.   **h. 2245. (44.)**

— *See* SCHUBERT (F. P.) [7 Gesänge. Op. 52. No. 6.] Ave Maria ... for Cornet & Piano by J. Levy. [1878.] fol.   **h. 2245. (42.)**

— *See* SCHUBERT (F. P.) [Schwanengesang. No. 4. Ständchen.] Serenade [arranged for cornet and P. F.] by J. Levy. [1878.] fol.   **h. 2245. (40.)**

— *See* SCHUBERT (F. P.) [*Doubtful and Supposititious Works.*] The Adieu ... for Cornet & Piano by J. Levy. [1878.] fol.   **h. 2245. (41.)**

— *See* VENZANO (L.) Ah che assorta, arranged for Cornet & Piano by J. Levy. [1875.] fol.   **h. 2245. (21.)**

— *See* VERDI (F. G. F.) [Ernani.] Ernani, Ernani involami, for Cornet & Piano by J. Levy. [1874.] fol.   **h. 2245. (9.)**

— *See* VERDI (F. G. F.) [I Lombardi.] La mia letizia, arranged for Cornet & Piano by J. Levy. [1875.] fol.   **h. 2245. (22.)**

— *See* VERDI (F. G. F.) [Il Trovatore.—Miserere Scene.] Ah! che la morte, for Cornet & Piano by J. Levy. [1875.] fol.   **h. 2245. (11.)**

LEVY (KENNETH JAY)

— *See* LA GROTTE (N. de) Quand je te veux raconter, *etc.* [Edited by K. J. Levy.] [1953.] fol.   **H. 1860. n. (2.)**

— *See* LESURE (F.) Anthologie de la chanson parisienne au XVIᵉ siècle, réunie par F. Lesure avec la collaboration de ... K. J. Levy, *etc.* [1953.] fol.   **H. 4009.**

LEVY (LEON THEODORE)

— A Feather in the Wind. A Song ... words by N. R. Eberhart. (Op. 27.) *G. Schirmer: New York,* 1929. 4°.   **G. 1275. ff. (29.)**

— Francesca's Song. For High Voice and Piano, poem by N. R. Eberhart. (Op. 24.) *G. Schirmer: New York,* 1928. 4°.   **G. 1275. aa. (10.)**

— Mignonette. A caprice for piano. *G. Schirmer: New York,* 1925. 4°.   **g. 1127. dd. (11.)**

— O World be gay with me. A Song, *etc.* [Words by] (N. R. Eberhart. Op. 29.) *G. Schirmer: New York,* 1929. 4°.   **G. 1275. ff. (30.)**

— Deux Petites Danseuses. A descriptive piece for the piano. *G. Schirmer: New York,* 1925. 4°.   **g. 1127. w. (7.)**

— Rondel ... For High Voice and Piano, poem by A. C. Swinburne. *G. Schirmer: New York,* 1927. 4°.   **G. 1275. aa. (11.)**

— Seven old Women sit for Tea. Song, *etc.* (Poem by W. Saunders.) *G. Schirmer: New York,* 1930. 4°.   **G. 1275. ff. (31.)**

— The Sound of Flutes. Orientale for ... Voice and Piano, words by N. R. Eberhart. (Op. 30.) *G. Schirmer: New York,* 1929. 4°.   **G. 1275. ff. (32.)**

LEVY (LESTER S.)

— *See* SOUSA (John P.) Sousa's great Marches. In piano transcription ... Selected, with an introduction, by L. S. Levy. 1975. 4°.   **h. 3662. b. (1.)**

LEVY (LEWIS)

— Wife and Child. A realistic song from life. Words and music by L. Levy. pp. 5. *Sherman, Clay & Co.: Seattle, San Francisco,* [1898.] fol. **H. 3980. rr. (46.)**

LEVY (LIONEL E.)

— Nocturne pour le Piano. *Paris,* [1870.] fol. **h. 1462. r. (58.)**

LEVY (LOUIS)

— *See* CHOPIN (F. F.) [*Collected Works.—f.*] [A Song to remember.] Selection of Melodies by Chopin from the Columbia Picture "A Song to remember" ... Arranged and adapted for Piano Solo by L. Levy. 1945. 4°.
g. 553. w. (17.)

— *See* STRAUSS (J.) *the Younger.* [Die Fledermaus.—Selections.] Gaumont-British Picture Corporation ... Waltz Time ... Adapted by L. Levy. 1933. 4°. **H. 1964. b. (9.)**

LEVY (MARTIN)

— Bagatellen für das Pianoforte. *Berlin & Posen,* [1885.] fol.
h. 3280. k. (58.)

LEVY (MARVIN DAVID)

— Alice in Wonderland. Four choruses for women's voices and bassoon or violoncello or piano. Texts by Lewis Carroll. 1. Turtle Soup. 2. The Little Crocodile. 3. The Little Fishes. 4. The Lobster Quadrille. pp. 18. *Boosey & Hawkes:* [*New York,* 1966.] 8°. **F. 217. s. (19.)**

— During Wind and Rain. 〈S. A. T. B. [Words by] Thomas Hardy.〉 pp. 22. *Boosey & Hawkes:* [*New York,* 1965.] 8°. *Brown University choral Series.* 5536. **F. 1744. tt. (7.)**

— Escorial. Lyric drama in one act ... Libretto adapted by the composer from Lionel Abel's English version of the play "Escurial" by Michel de Ghelderode. German translation by Susanne Szekely. Vocal score by the composer. *Eng. & Ger.* pp. 63. *Boosey & Hawkes: New York,* [1966.] 4°.
G. 1268. rr. (2.)

— For the Time being. Christmas oratorio from the poem of W. H. Auden. For soloists, narrator, mixed chorus and orchestra ... Piano-vocal score. pp. 205. *G. Ricordi & Co.: New York,* [1959.] 8°. **E. 460. k.**

— For the Time being. Christmas oratorio for soloists, narrator, mixed chorus and orchestra ... Vocal score. 〈Revised.〉 *Eng. & Ger.* pp. 216. *Boosey & Hawkes: New York,* [1967.] 4°.
G. 517. pp.

— Kyros. Dance-poem for orchestra. Full score. pp. 56. *Boosey & Hawkes: New York,* [1966.] 4°. **g. 1620. vv. (4.)**

— One Person. 〈Der Eine.〉 For alto and orchestra. Poem by Elinor Wylie. 〈German translation by Susanne Szekely.〉 [Voice and P. F.] *Eng. & Ger.* pp. 28. *Boosey & Hawkes: New York,* [1967.] 4°. **G. 1273. i. (4.)**

— Prayer. (May the Words of my Mouth) ... Psalm XIX: 15. 〈Mixed chorus.〉 pp. 4. *Boosey & Hawkes:* [*New York,* 1966.] 8°. **E. 1499. r. (5.)**

LEVY (MAY)

— A Cradle Song, words anon. *E. Ashdown: London, etc.,* 1906. fol. **G. 807. kk. (7.)**

LEVY (SOL.)

— *See* LEVY (Sol Paul)

LEVY (SOL P.)

— *See* LEVY (Sol Paul)

LEVY (SOL PAUL)

— Memories. Song. "Just let me see again that Smile" ... words by H. Dozier. *American Song Publishing Co.: New York City,* (1911.) fol. **H. 1792. s. (24.)**

— "That naughty Valse" ... Arranged by J. Ord Hume. 〈Solo clarinet in B♭ [and military parts].〉 30 pt. *In:* TATE (James W.) "Love's Lullabye," *etc.* [1920.] fol. [*Boosey's military Journal.* ser. 140. no. 5.] **h. 1549.**

LEVY (THEODORE)

— "Electra." Intermezzo caprice. 〈Solo & 1st B♭ cornet [and wind band parts].〉 34 pt. *Carl Fischer: New York,* [1906.] 8°. *Various parts are in duplicate.* **f. 800. (820.)**

— The Ganges River. Hindu Love Song, lyric by J. Villars. *M. Witmark & Sons: New York, etc.,* (1914.) fol.
G. 806. mm. (34.)

— "A Maid of Mexico." Mexican novelette. 〈Solo or 1st B♭ cornet (conductor) [and wind band parts].〉 33 pt. *Carl Fischer: New York,* [1906.] 8°. *Various parts are in duplicate.* **f. 800. (821.)**

— The World's Way, *etc.* [Song.] *M. Witmark & Sons: New York, etc.,* (1914.) fol. **G. 806. mm. (35.)**

LEWALD (AUGUST)

— *See* PERIODICAL PUBLICATIONS.— *Leipzig.* Europa 〈Das neue Europa〉, Chronik der gebildeten Welt ... Herausgegeben von A. Lewald. 1835–46. 8°. **P. P. 4793. c.**

LEWANDOWSKI (LAZARUS)

— An den Krug. *See infra:* Zwei Trinklieder ... (Op. 32.) No. 1.

— Bonbons de Paris polka. [P. F.] *Paris,* [1874.] fol.
h. 1487. q. (11.)

— A Chafer's Wedding. *See infra:* [Ein Käfer-Hochzeit.]

— Deutsches Landwehrlied von D. Hirschfeld [begins: "Norden, Süden, Westen, Osten"], Lied für eine Singstimme mit Pianoforte-Begleitung. Op. 17. *Berlin,* [1870?] fol.
H. 2836. h. (54.)

— Die Excellenz Gedicht von G. Jacobsohn. Komisches Duett für zwei Frauenstimmen mit Begleitung des Pianoforte. *Berlin,* [1882.] fol. **H. 1793. d. (12.)**

— Halalujoh, halalu el b'kod'sho. *See infra:* [Psalm 150.]

— Hebräische Melodien. Duo für Pianoforte und Violine. Op. 32. *Berlin & Posen,* [1882.] fol. **h. 1608. l. (13.)**

— Hurrah! die deutsche Fahne [begins: "Sie wird bald wieder aufersteh'n"] ... von D. Hirschfeld für eine Singstimme mit Begleitung des Piano ... Op. 16. *Berlin,* [1870?] fol.
H. 2836. h. (53.)

— Ein Käfer-Hochzeit. Gedicht von R. Loewenstein [begins: "Ich will das Eisenhütlein fragen"] für gemischten Chor ... componirt. *Berlin,* [1880.] 8°. **E. 308. k. (14.)**

— [Ein Käfer-Hochzeit.] A Chafer's Wedding. A Four-part Song, the words translated ... by ... J. Troutbeck. Op. 30. [1884.] *See* NOVELLO AND CO. Novello's Part-Song Book. Second Series. Vol. XVII. No. 482. [1869, *etc.*] 8°. **F. 280. b.**

— ... Kol Rinnah U' T' Fillah. Ein- und zweistimmige Gesänge für den israelitischen Gottesdienst ... Vierte vermehrte und verbesserte Auflage. *Berlin,* [1885?] fol. **H. 1839. (1.)**

— Lied vom Wasser. *See infra:* Zwei Trinklieder ... (Op. 32.) No. 2.

— Achtzehn liturgische Psalmen für Solo und Chor mit Begleitung der Orgel. *Leipzig,* [1879.] fol. **G. 912.**

LEWANDOWSKI (LAZARUS)

— [Achtzehn liturgische Psalmen. Psalm LXXXV.] Shew us Thy Mercy, O Lord . . . For mixed voices with Alto Solo and Organ Accompaniment, arranged . . . by M. Spicker. *G. Schirmer: New York*, (1905.) 8°.
G. Schirmer's . . . Octavo Church Music, No. 4617.
F. 281. b. (45.)

— Marrons Glacés polka. [P. F.] *Paris*, [1874.] fol.
h. 1487. q. (12.)

— Psalm 150. For Mixed Chorus. Arranged from the Hebrew by N. Lindsay Norden. *H. W. Gray Co.: New York*, 1938. 8°.
E. 335. i. (46.)

— Psalm 150. SATB with solo passages for soprano, contralto, tenor and baritone. Psalm 150 adapted by Willard Sniffin . . . Arr. by Wallingford Riegger. pp. 10. *Harold Flammer:* [*New York*, 1956.] 8°. **E. 460. c. (9.)**

— [Psalm 150.] Halalujoh, halalu el b'kod'sho. Hallelujah, praise ye the Lord. For three-part chorus of mixed voices. ⟨Three-part chorus of women's voices.⟩ Psalm CL . . . Arranged by William Stickles. *Heb. & Eng.* 2 no. *G. Schirmer: New York*, [1961.] 8°. **E. 335. ee. (1.)**

— Psalm 150. (S. A. B.) . . . [Words] adapted by the arranger . . . Arr. by Elwood Coggin. pp. 11. *J. Fischer & Bro.: Glen Rock, N. J.*, [1963.] 8°. **E. 335. pp. (1.)**

— Rhapsodie hébraïque pour le piano. Op. 34. *Berlin & Posen*, [1883.] fol. **h. 3280. k. (59.)**

— Shew us Thy Mercy, O Lord. *See supra:* [Achtzehn liturgische Psalmen.—Psalm LXXXV.]

—... Todah W'simrah. Vierstimmige Chöre und Soli für den israelitschen Gottesdienst mit und ohne Begleitung der Orgel, ad libitum . . . Erster Theil: Sabbath. (Zweiter Theil: Festgesänge.) 2 pt. *E. Bote & G. Bock: Berlin & Posen*, [1876, 82.] fol. **H. 1839. a.**

— Zwei Trinklieder aus alter Zeit für Bariton. (Op. 32.) I. An dem Krug, von Abul Hassan . . . "Begeistrung quillt mir aus den Kruge". II. Lied vom Wasser, von Gabriol . . . "Vertrunken ist der Wein". (Deutsch von S. Kristeller.) 2 no. *Berlin & Posen*, [1883.] fol. **H. 2836. h. (55.)**

LEWANDOWSKI (LOUIS)

— *See* LEWANDOWSKI (Lazarus)

LEWANDOWSKY (MAX)

— Sonate (G moll) für Pianoforte und Violine . . . Op. 8. [Score and part.] 2 pt. *C. F. Peters: Leipzig*, [1907.] 4°.
g. 619. m. (1.)

— [Sonate (G moll) für Pianoforte und Violine. Op. 8.] *See* RIEGER (O.) Sonate (F moll) für Bratsche und Klavier. [The first movement adapted from the Sonata for violin and P.F., Op. 8, by M. Lewandowsky.] [1924.] fol. **h. 1785. l.**

LEWELLIN (FLORENCE LLOYD)

— The Primrose League. Song & Chorus, words by a Dame. *Weekes & Co.: London*, [1887.] fol. **H. 1788. v. (58.)**

LEWELLYN

— Lewellyn's Bride. [Song.] *See* MACFARREN (*Sir* G. A.)

LEWENGLY (S.)

— Ungarn und Brandenburg. ⟨Quick March.⟩ [Military band parts.] 29 pt. *In:* PACINI (G.) [Bondelmonte.] Terzetto, *etc.* [1880.] *obl.* 8°. [*Boosé's military Journal. ser.* 68. *no.* 4.]
h. 1549.

LEWENTHAL (RAYMOND)

— *See* ALKAN (C. H. V.) *pseud.* [*Collections.*] The Piano Music of Alkan. Edited and annotated by R. Lewenthal. [1964.] 4°.
g. 1128. uu. (7.)

— *See* ALKAN (C. H. V.) *pseud.* [Marcia funebre sulla morte d'un pappagallo.] Funeral March on the Death of a Parrot . . . For four-part chorus of mixed voices with organ, or piano, or woodwind accompaniment. Edited . . . by R. Lewenthal. [1972.] 8°. **F. 321. ff. (24.)**

LEWERD (FRANK)

— At the Wheel. Song, words and music by F. Lewerd. *Beal & Co.: London*, [1896.] fol. **H. 1798. v. (19.)**

LEWES (SIDNEY)

— Beautiful Garden of Love. Song, words by R. A. Davis, *etc. E. Marks & Son: London*, (1914.) fol.
No. 219 *of the "Champion Edition," etc.* **H. 1793. t. (32.)**

— Come Love to me. Song, written & composed by E. Graham & S. Lewes, *etc. E. Marks & Son: London*, (1914.) fol.
No. 232 *of the "Champion Edition," etc.* **H. 1793. t. (33.)**

— Good-bye, Minnie. [Song.] Written by H. Rees, *etc. E. Marks & Son: London*, (1914.) fol.
No. 243 *of the "Champion Edition," etc.* **H. 1793. t. (34.)**

— Roses remind me of you. Song, written by E. Graham, *etc. E. Marks & Son: London*, (1914.) fol.
No. 229 *of the "Champion Edition," etc.* **H. 1793. t. (35.)**

— Song of Summer. Intermezzo for the piano. *E. Marks & Son: London*, 1915. fol.
Champion Edition, No. 256. **h. 3284. oo. (2.)**

— Woodland Scenes. Intermezzo. [P. F.] *E. Marks & Son: London*, 1918. fol.
Champion Edition, No. 313. **h. 3284. oo. (3.)**

LEWICKI (ERNST)

— *See* MOZART (W. A.) [*Collected Works.—c.*] 4 Sätze aus den 5 Divertimenti für 2 Klarinetten und Fagott [K. Anh. 229, 229a] . . . Herausgegeben . . . von E. Lewicki . . . für Klarinette (oder Violine) und Klavier, *etc.* [1906.] 4°. [*Die Musik. Jahrg.* 5. *Hft.* 7.] **P. P. 1946. ah.**

— *See* MOZART (W. A.) [*Collected Works.—e.*] Sonate und Fuge, *etc.* ⟨Adagio (Einleitung zur C moll Fuge), für 2 Klaviere zu 4 Händen gesetzt von E. Lewicki.⟩ [1933.] 4°. **g. 382. s. (4.)**

— *See* MOZART (W. A.) [*Collected Works.—e.*] Sonate (K. V. 448) and Fuge (K. V. 426) . . . Als Einlage: Adagio zur Fuge für 2 Klaviere zu 4 Händen gesetzt von E. Lewicki. [1943.] 4°.
g. 1018. s. (2.)

— *See* MOZART (W. A.) [Cosi dunque tradisci. K. 432.—Aspri rimorsi atroce.] Zu "Idomeneus" . . . Recitativ und Ersatz-Arie (Bass) des Arbaces. (III. Akt, Scene 5.) Klavier-Auszug mit Text, *etc.* [Edited by E. Lewicki.] [1905.] 4°. [*Die Musik. Jahrg.* 4. *Hft.* 11.] **P. P. 1946. ah.**

LEWIE

— Lewie Gordon. [Song.] *See* O. Oh send Lewie Gordon hame. [1815?] fol. [*AND. And are ye sure the News is true.*]
H. 1652. n. (15.)

— Lewie Gordon. Song. *See* O. O send Lewie Gordon hame, *etc.* [WM 1815.] fol. **G. 425. ss. (26.)**

— Lewie Gordon. Song. *See* O. Oh! send Lewie Gordon hame, *etc.* [1825?] fol. **G. 807. d. (60.)**

— Lewie Gordon. Song. *See* O. Oh send Lewie Gordon hame. [c. 1825.] fol. **H. 1654. v. (6.)**

LEWIE

— Lewie Gordon. Arranged as a rondo for the piano forte [by Thomas H. Butler]. pp. 3. *Printed by G. Walker: London,* [^{WM} 1802.] fol.   **g. 271. e. (2.)**

— Lewie Gordon, arranged as a Rondo for the Pianoforte. *London,* [1805?] fol.   **g. 271. e. (2.)**

— Lewie Gordon. A favorite rondo for the piano forte [by Thomas H. Butler]. pp. 2. *J. McFadyen: Glasgow,* [c. 1810.] fol.   **g. 1529. g. (17.)**

— Lewie Gordon. *See* BUTLER (T. H.) A new ... Sonata ... in which is introduced ... Lewie Gordon, *etc.* 1807. fol.   **h. 280. (14.)**

— Lewie Gordon. *See* DUSSEK, afterwards DUSSEK-MORALT (S.) Two favorite airs, *etc.* [1812.] fol.   **h. 307. (46.)**

— Lewie Gordon. *See* NEATE (C.) Fantasia ... on Lewie Gordon. [1848.] fol.   **h. 709. (1.)**

— Lewie Gordon. [Part-song.] *See* PRENDERGAST (A. H. D.) Two Scotch ... Airs. (a).

LEWIN (C. M.)

— Quartet in C, for 2 violins, viola & violoncello. Op. 1. [Parts.] *International Independent Music Club: London,* 1916. 4°.   **g. 417. j. (3.)**

LEWIN (CHARLOTTE)

— Roland the Brave, a ballad of the Rhine. (The poetry by T. Campbell.) *London,* [1867.] fol.   **H. 1772. r. (46.)**

LEWIN (GORDON)

— Caribbean Sketches. For flute and B♭ clarinet. [Score and parts.] 3 pt. *Boosey & Hawkes: New York,* [1962.] 4°.   **g. 421. z. (6.)**

— Three Latin-American Impressions. For flute and B♭ clarinet. [Score.] pp. 8. *Boosey & Hawkes: London,* [1955.] 4°.   **g. 421. w. (10.)**

— Nostalgia d'España. For flute and B♭ clarinet. [Score.] pp. 10. *Boosey & Hawkes: London,* [1960.] 4°.   **g. 421. y. (4.)**

— Scherzola. Oboe, B♭ clarinet, bassoon. [Parts.] 3 pt. *New Wind Music Co.: London,* [1959.] 4°.   **g. 409. mm. (6.)**

— *See* BACH (J. S.) [Suites for Violoncello. No. 3.] Bourrée ... Arranged by G. Lewin, *etc.* [1960.] 4°.   **g. 699. w. (6.)**

— *See* CORELLI (A.) [Sonatas. Op. 5. No. 7.] Preludio and Giga ... Arranged by G. Lewin, *etc.* [1960.] 4°.   **g. 45. cc. (1.)**

— *See* SCARLATTI (D.) [Sonata. K. 30.] Cat's Fugue. Arranged by G. Lewin, *etc.* [1960.] 4°.   **g. 47. i. (4.)**

— *See* SCHUBERT (F. P.) [Fantasie. Op. 78.] Menuetto from Piano Sonata in G ... Arranged by G. Lewin, *etc.* [1960.] 4°.   **g. 567. z. (3.)**

— *See* TSCHAIKOV (Basil) Play the Clarinet. [With exercises and ensemble pieces composed or arranged by G. Lewin.] [1970.] 4°.   **f. 759. gg. (9.)**

— *See* TSCHAIKOV (Basil) Play the Clarinet. [With exercises and ensemble pieces arranged by G. Lewin.] 1976. 4°.   **g. 1104. xx. (10.)**

LEWIN (GUSTAV)

— Night, softly falling. *See* infra: [Die Weihe der Nacht.]

— [Die Weihe der Nacht.] Night, softly falling. Four-Part Song, the English words ... by W. G. Rothery. [1909.] *See* NOVELLO AND CO. Novello's Part-Song Book. Second Series. No. 1158. [1869, *etc.*] 8°.   **F. 280. b.**

LEWIN (MARCUS)

— Sweet Sophie So-so. [Song.] Words by Horace B. Liveright. pp. 2–5. *M. Witmark & Sons:* [New York, 1904.] fol.   **H. 3985. z. (1.)**

LEWIN (MAURICE)

— Mammy's gwine to buy the Moon. [Song.] Words by Horace Liveright. pp. 3–5. *M. Witmark & Sons:* [New York, 1903.] fol.   **H. 3985. z. (2.)**

LEWIN (OLIVE)

— Alle, alle, alle. 12 Jamaican folk-songs. Collected & arranged for schools by Olive Lewin. pp. 19. *Oxford University Press: London,* [1977.] obl. 8°.   **A. 700. c. (8.)**

— Beeny Bud. 12 Jamaican folk-songs for children. Collected & arranged for schools by Olive Lewin. pp. 24. *Oxford University Press: London,* [1975.] obl. 8°.   **A. 700. c. (5.)**

— Brown Gal in de Ring. ⟨12 Jamaican folk-songs.⟩ Collected & arranged for schools by Olive Lewin. pp. 16. *Oxford University Press: London,* [1974.] obl. 8°.   **A. 700. c. (3.)**

— Dandy Shandy. 12 Jamaican folk-songs for children. Collected & arranged for schools by Olive Lewin. pp. 20. *Oxford University Press: London,* [1975.] 4°.   **A. 700. c. (4.)**

— Forty Folk Songs of Jamaica. Collected and transcribed by Olive Lewin. pp. 107. *General Secretariat of the Organization of American States: Washington,* 1973. 4°.   **F. 1771. xx. (3.)**

LEWING (ADÈLE)

— Berceuse for piano. (Op. 14.) *White-Smith Music Pub. Co.: Boston, etc.,* 1897. fol.   **h. 3282. f. (41.)**

— Fair Rohtraut.—Schön Rohtraut.—A Ballad with English and German Text. [Words by] (Mörike. English Version by Mrs. J. P. Morgan. Op. 18.) *O. Ditson Co.: Boston,* 1899. fol.   **H. 1799. h. (54.)**

— Two Piano Pieces. Song without Words. Op. 16. Romance. Op. 17. 2 no. *O. Ditson Co.: Boston, etc.,* 1898. fol.   **h. 3282. f. (42.)**

LEWINSON (LEONARD J.)

— On the Speedway. March and Two-Step. [P. F.] *J. A. Miller: New York,* 1900. fol.   **h. 3286. r. (10.)**

LEWIS

— Lewis Boat Song. [Song.] *See* ROBERTON (*Sir* Hugh S.) Songs of the Isles. [No. 23.]

— Lewis Bridal Song. Mairi's Wedding. [Song.] *See* ROBERTON (*Sir* Hugh S.) Songs of the Isles. [No. 3.]

— Lewis's beautiful Tea. Vocal waltz. *See* FROST (William L.)

LEWIS (   )

— *See* KIMBALL ( ) and LEWIS ( ) My Kerry Colleen. [Song.] Words and music by Kimball & Lewis. [1909.] fol.   **H. 3985. a. (25.)**

LEWIS (A. E.)

— *See* DAVID (Worton) Khaki Boy! ⟨Song.⟩ Written and composed by W. David, A. E. Lewis, *etc.* [1914.] fol.   **H. 3990. yy. (19.)**

LEWIS (A. G.) *Mrs* and LEWIS (LEO R.)

— The Dairymaids' Supper. A Cantata ... Both notations. *J. Curwen & Sons: London,* [1890.] 8°.   **D. 832. b. (5.)**

LEWIS (ADEN G.)

— *See* RODNEY (Don) Give a Faith to your Child. For SATB chorus and soloist ... Arranged by A. G. Lewis. [1979.] 8°.

E. 1857. d. (11.)

LEWIS (AL.)

— I want you to know I love you. Song, words and music by A. Lewis. *Cary & Co.: London*, [1914.] fol. **H. 1793. t. (36.)**

LEWIS (ALFRED)

— Summer Evening. Song [begins: "Sweetly blend the evening shadows"]. *London*, [1879.] fol. **H. 1783. o. (62.)**

LEWIS (ANDY)

— "Baby Lize." [Song.] Words and music by A. Lewis. pp. 2–5. *F. A. Mills:* [*New York*, 1897.] 4°. **H. 3980. ss. (1.)**

— The Bohemians. Two-Step. [P. F.] *F. A. Mills: New York*, 1897. fol. **h. 3286. g. (46.)**

— The Bohemians. Quick march. [Parts for fife and drum band.] 30 pt. *J. R. Lafleur & Son: London*, [1898.] 8°.
Part of "J. R. Lafleur & Son's Fife & Drum Journal". Including several copies of various parts. **f. 800. (822.)**

— Helen Gonne. [Song.] Words by Aaron S. Hoffman. *Harry von Tilzer Music Pub. Co.:* [*New York*, 1902.] 4°.
H. 3985. z. (3.)

— I'm satisfied. [Song.] Words by Aaron S. Hoffman. *Harry von Tilzer Music Pub. Co.:* [*New York*, 1902.] 4°.
H. 3985. z. (4.)

— Just as two Children will do. [Song.] Words by Aaron S. Hoffman. pp. 3–5. *Harry von Tilzer Music Pub. Co.:* [*New York*, 1903.] fol. **H. 3985. z. (5.)**

— [Just as two Children will do.] Just as two Children would do. [Song.] Words by Aaron S. Hoffman. *Harry von Tilzer Music Pub. Co.:* [*New York*, 1903.] 4°. **H. 3985. z. (6.)**

— "My California Poppy." [Song.] Words by Aaron S. Hoffman. *Harry von Tilzer Music Pub. Co.:* [*New York*, 1902.] fol. **H. 3985. z. (7.)**

— Pinky Panky Poo. Chinese love song. Written by Aaron S. Hoffman. pp. 7. *Francis, Day & Hunter: London*, [1902.] fol. **H. 3985. z. (8.)**

— "Roly Poly San." [Song.] Words by Aaron S. Hoffman. *Harry von Tilzer Music Pub. Co.:* [*New York*, 1903.] 4°. **H. 3985. z. (9.)**

— Roly Poly San. [Song.] Written by Aaron S. Hoffman. [Staff and tonic sol-fa notation. Voice part.] *Shapiro, von Tilzer Music Co.: London*, [1903.] *s. sh.* fol.
With partly different words from the preceding. **H. 3985. z. (10.)**

— "The Swell Miss Fitzwell." [Song.] Words and music by A. Lewis. pp. 2–5. *F. A. Mills:* [*New York*, 1898.] 4°. **H. 3980. ss. (2.)**

LEWIS (Sir ANTHONY CAREY)

— Concerto for Horn & String Orchestra. Version for horn & piano. [Score and part.] 2 pt. *Alfred Lengnick & Co.: London*, [1959.] 4°. **g. 1094. c. (7.)**

— Concerto for Trumpet & Orchestra. Version for trumpet & piano. [Parts.] 2 pt. *Alfred Lengnick & Co.: London*, [1950.] 4°. **g. 1110. b. (9.)**

— The Cuckoo. Partsong ... based on the folksong. [S. A. T. B.] pp. 7. *Stainer & Bell: London*, [1956.] 8°.
[*Choral Library. no.* 349.] **F. 1137. d.**

LEWIS (Sir ANTHONY CAREY)

— The Heavens proclaim the Glory of God. Anthem for SATB and organ. Psalm 18. pp. 16. *Novello & Co.: London*, [1965.] 8°.
[*Octavo Anthems.* 1459.] **E. 618. a.**

— A Restoration Suite. Airs and Dances by Purcell and his contemporaries for String Orchestra or String Quartet. Arranged and edited by A. Lewis. Full Score, *etc. Universal Edition: London*, 1937. 4°. **g. 417. x. (6.)**

— Rorate coeli. Carol for voices in unison. Words by William Dunbar. pp. 7. *Stainer & Bell: London*, [1951.] 8°.
[*Church Choir Library. no.* 564.] **F. 1137. b.**

— Te Deum [in C. S. A. T. B.]. ⟨Congregation part.⟩ 2 pt. *Stainer & Bell: London*, [1958.] 8°.
[*Modern Church Services. no.* 321, 321a.] **F. 1137.**

— A Tribute of Praise. For soprano & baritone soli and chorus (organ ad lib.). 1. A Song of Thanksgiving. 2. A Song of Love. 3. A Prayer. 4. A Blessing. 5. A Psalm of Honour, *etc.* pp. 64. *Alfred Lengnick & Co.: London*, [1953.] 8°. **E. 1598. (7.)**

— *See* ARNE (Thomas A.) Libera me. Motet for soli, choir and organ ... Edited by A. Lewis. [1950.] 8°. **F. 1. c. (1.)**

— *See* BACH (J. S.) [Die Kunst der Fuge.] Suite from the Art of Fugue. For chamber orchestra. Arranged by A. Lewis, *etc.* [1968.] 4°. **g. 699. tt. (1.)**

— *See* BLOW (John) [Amphion Anglicus.] Three Songs ... Edited by A. Lewis. [1938.] 16°. [*Lyrebird Books. no.* 6.] **A. 1170.**

— *See* BLOW (John) Coronation Anthems, *etc.* ⟨Edited by A. Lewis.⟩ 1953. fol. [*Musica Britannica.* 7.] **N. 10.**

— *See* BLOW (John) Coronation Anthems and three Anthems for Strings. Edited by A. Lewis & Watkins Shaw. Second, revised edition. 1969. fol. [*Musica Britannica.* 7.] **N. 10. b.**

— *See* BLOW (John) God spake sometime in Visions ... Edited by A. Lewis. [1953.] 8°. **E. 442. x. (2.)**

— *See* BLOW (John) Venus and Adonis. Edited by A. Lewis. [1939.] 4°. **Hirsch M. 792.**

— *See* BLOW (John) Venus and Adonis. First suite for strings. ⟨Second suite for strings.⟩ Edited by A. Lewis. [1950.] 8°. **C. 121. hh. (3.)**

— *See* HAENDEL (G. F.) Apollo and Daphne ... Edited ... by A. Lewis. [1956.] 8°. **F. 249. aa. (2.)**

— *See* HAENDEL (G. F.) Athalia ... Edited by A. Lewis. [1967.] 8°. **F. 249. dd. (11.)**

— *See* HAENDEL (G. F.) Imeneo. Hymenaeus. An opera ... 1740. Edited by A. Lewis, *etc.* [1980.] 8°. **F. 249. pp.**

— *See* HAENDEL (G. F.) [Rodrigo.] Overture & Dances ... Edited and arranged by A. Lewis and P. Cranmer, *etc.* [1956.] 4°.
[*Oxford Orchestral Series. ser.* 2. *no.* 159.] **g. 1263.**

— *See* HENRY VIII., *King of England.* Henry VIII. Three songs ... Edited and arranged by A. Lewis. [1936.] 16°. [*Lyrebird Books. no.* 3.] **A. 1170.**

— *See* JOHNSON (Robert) William Shakespeare. Two songs from The Tempest ... Edited by A. Lewis. [1936.] 16°. [*Lyrebird Books. no.* 2.] **A. 1170.**

— *See* LAWES (Henry) [The Treasury of Musick.] Three Songs ... Edited by A. Lewis. [1938.] 16°. [*Lyrebird Books. no.* 7.] **A. 1170.**

— *See* LOCKE (Matthew) [*Collections.*] Three Songs. Edited by A. Lewis. [1938.] 16°. [*Lyrebird Books. no.* 8.] **A. 1170.**

LEWIS (*Sir* ANTHONY CAREY)

— *See* LONDON.— *Royal Musical Association.* Musica Britannica, *etc.* ⟨Professor A. Lewis general editor.⟩ 1951, *etc.* fol.
N. 10.

— *See* PEPYS (Samuel) Samuel Pepys. Three songs of his choice. ⟨Edited by A. Lewis.⟩ [1936.] 16°. [*Lyrebird Books. no.* 4.]
A. 1170.

— *See* PURCELL (Henry) [*Collected Works.—a.*] The Works of Henry Purcell. ⟨Volume XXVIII. Miscellaneous Odes and Cantatas. Edited ... by ... A. Goldsbrough ... A. Lewis.⟩ [1957.] fol.
I. 466.

— *See* PURCELL (Henry) [*Collected Works.—a.*] The Works of Henry Purcell. ⟨Vol. XXIX. Sacred Music. Part V. Anthems. Edited ... by A. Lewis and N. Fortune.⟩ [1960.] fol.
I. 466.

— *See* PURCELL (Henry) [*Collected Works.—a.*] The Works of Henry Purcell. ⟨Vol. XXXII. Sacred Music. Part VII. Anthems and miscellaneous Church Music. Edited ... by A. Lewis and N. Fortune.⟩ [1962.] fol.
I. 466.

— *See* PURCELL (Henry) [*Collected Works.—a.*] The Works of Henry Purcell. Volume XXX. Sacred Music. Part VI. Songs and vocal ensemble music. Edited ... by A. Lewis and Nigel Fortune. [1965.] fol.
I. 466.

— *See* PURCELL (Henry) [*Collected Works.—a.*] The Works of Henry Purcell. ⟨Volume XII. The Fairy Queen. Revised edition by A. Lewis.⟩ [1968.] 8°.
F. 937.

— *See* PURCELL (Henry) [*Collected Works.—b.*] Six sacred Songs. For (mezzo-) soprano, tenor or baritone with accompaniment for organ, harpsichord or piano. Edited by A. Lewis and Nigel Fortune. [1966.] 4°.
G. 103. p. (1.)

— *See* PURCELL (Henry) Blow up the Trumpet in Sion. For S. S. S. A. A. T. T. T. B. B. and organ. Edited by A. Lewis and Nigel Fortune, *etc.* [1968.] 8°. [*Purcell Society Reprints.* 17.]
G. 98. a.

— *See* PURCELL (Henry) Early, O Lord, my fainting Soul ... Edited by A. Lewis and N. Fortune. [1966.] 8°. [*Purcell Society. Reprints.* 8.]
G. 98. a.

— *See* PURCELL (Henry) [The Fairy Queen.] The Music in The Fairy Queen ... Edited by A. Lewis, *etc.* [1966.] 8°.
F. 659. i. (5.)

— *See* PURCELL (Henry) Hear me, O Lord, the great Support ... Edited by A. Lewis and N. Fortune. [1966.] 8°. [*Purcell Society Reprints.* 9.]
G. 98. a.

— *See* PURCELL (Henry) Jehova, quam multi sunt hostes ... Edited by A. Lewis and N. Fortune, *etc.* [1978.] 8°. [*Purcell Society Reprints.* 19.]
G. 98. a.

— *See* PURCELL (Henry) Let mine Eyes run down. Anthem ... Edited by A. Lewis and Nigel Fortune. [1959.] 8°. [*Purcell Society Reprints.* 3.]
G. 98. a.

— *See* PURCELL (Henry) Lord, I can suffer ... Edited by A. Lewis and N. Fortune. [1966.] 8°. [*Purcell Society Reprints.* 10.]
G. 98. a.

— *See* PURCELL (Henry) [Man that is born of a Woman.] Funeral Sentences ... Edited by A. Lewis and N. Fortune, *etc.* [1960.] 8°. [*Purcell Society Reprints.* 6.]
G. 98. a.

— *See* PURCELL (Henry) The Meditation ... Transcribed and edited by A. Lewis. 1951. 8°. [*The Score. no.* 4. pp. 3–10.]
P. P. 1945. abe.

— *See* PURCELL (Henry) O all ye People, clap your Hands ... Edited by A. Lewis and N. Fortune. [1966.] 8°. [*Purcell Society Reprints.* 11.]
G. 98. a.

— *See* PURCELL (Henry) O give Thanks. For S. A. T. B. (verse and chorus) (strings) and organ. Edited by A. Lewis and N. Fortune, *etc.* [1970.] 8°. [*Purcell Society Reprints.* 18.]
G. 98. a.

LEWIS (*Sir* ANTHONY CAREY)

— *See* PURCELL (Henry) O God, the King of Glory. For chorus (S. A. T. B.) and organ continuo ... Edited by A. Lewis and Nigel Fortune, *etc.* [1961.] 8°. [*Purcell Society Reprints.* 7.]
G. 98. a.

— *See* PURCELL (Henry) O God, Thou art my God. Anthem ... Edited by A. Lewis and Nigel Fortune, *etc.* [1959.] 8°. [*Purcell Society Reprints.* 5.]
G. 98. a.

— *See* PURCELL (Henry) O God, Thou hast cast us out. Anthem for S. S. A. A. T. B. continuo and organ. Edited by A. Lewis and Nigel Fortune. [1957.] 8°. [*Purcell Society Reprints.* 1.]
G. 98. a.

— *See* PURCELL (Henry) O happy Man ... Edited by A. Lewis and N. Fortune, *etc.* [1966.] 8°. [*Purcell Society Reprints.* 12.]
G. 98. a.

— *See* PURCELL (Henry) O, I'm sick of Life ... Transcribed by A. Lewis and N. Fortune, *etc.* [1966.] 8°. [*Purcell Society Reprints.* 13.]
G. 98. a.

— *See* PURCELL (Henry) O Lord God of Hosts. Anthem ... Edited by A. Lewis and Nigel Fortune. [1958.] 8°. [*Purcell Society Reprints.* 2.]
G. 98. a.

— *See* PURCELL (Henry) O Lord our Governor ... Transcribed by A. Lewis and N. Fortune, *etc.* [1966.] 8°. [*Purcell Society Reprints.* 14.]
G. 98. a.

— *See* PURCELL (Henry) Plung'd in the Confines of Despair ... Edited by A. Lewis and Nigel Fortune, *etc.* [1966.] 8°. [*Purcell Society Reprints.* 15.]
G. 98. a.

— *See* PURCELL (Henry) When on my Sick Bed I languish ... Edited by A. Lewis and N. Fortune. [1966.] 8°. [*Purcell Society Reprints.* 16.]
G. 98. a.

LEWIS (C. L.)

— "Whisper the Story." [Song.] Words by Richard Henry Buck. pp. 5. *F. A. Mills: New York, Chicago,* [1901.] 4°.
H. 3985. z. (11.)

LEWIS (C. S.)

— Somehow. [Song.] Words by Richard Henry Buck. pp. 3–5. *M. Witmark & Sons:* [*New York,* 1903.] fol.
H. 3985. z. (12.)

LEWIS (C. T.)

— My Watermelon Coon. [Song.] Words by Richard Henry Buck. pp. 5. *Aldrich Linton & Hylands: New York,* [1901.] fol.
H. 3985. z. (13.)

— When the crimson Sun is setting in the West. [Song.] Words by Richard Henry Buck. pp. 3. *F. A. Mills: New York, Chicago,* [1900.] fol.
H. 3985. z. (14.)

LEWIS (CARLTON)

— Pebbles on the Beach. Song, words by A. Eliot. *E. D. Lloyds: London,* 1897. fol.
H. 1798. v. (20.)

LEWIS (CHARLES)

— Cantica Mariana; a collection of canticles and antiphons of Our Lady ... compiled and edited by C. Lewis. *Boston* [*Mass.*], 1879. 8°.
E. 1436.

LEWIS (CHARLES HUTCHINS)

— A was an Archer. Action Song ... words by W. H. Parker. *J. Curwen & Sons: London,* [1892.] fol.
H. 1984. (25.)

— Afternoon Tea and other Action Songs for Schools. The words and actions by M. Farrah. *J. Curwen & Sons: London,* 1907. 4°.
G. 383. p. (7.)

LEWIS (CHARLES HUTCHINS)

— Alice in Dreamland. Operetta for Girls' voices, words by J. Watson. *J. Curwen & Sons: London*, 1898. 8°.

F. 1271. c. (3.)

— Alice in Dreamland … Operetta for girls' voices, *etc.* (Tonic sol-fa edition.) pp. 20. *J. Curwen & Sons: London*, [1898.] 8°.

B. 418. xx. (1.)

— Alice in Wonderland. An Operetta for Children, written and adapted from Lewis Carroll's Story by M. C. Gillington. *J. Curwen & Sons: London*, 1907. 8°.

F. 1271. i. (3.)

— Alice in Wonderland, *etc.* [Tonic sol-fa edition.] *J. Curwen & Sons: London*, 1907. 4°.

B. 382. j. (1.)

— The Ambulance Maids. An Action Song for School Concerts. Words by K. F. Tutt. *J. Curwen & Sons: London*, 1898. fol.

H. 1984. b. (1.)

— The Angels of the Harvest. A short Harvest Cantata … the words by K. T. Sizer. *J. Curwen & Sons: London*, 1905. 4°.

E. 541. p. (1.)

— The Angels of the Harvest, *etc.* [Tonic sol-fa notation.] *J. Curwen & Sons: London*, 1905. 4°.

B. 415. b. (5.)

— The Anglers. Action Song … words by A. J. Foxwell. *J. Curwen & Sons: London*, [1893.] fol.

H. 1984. (24.)

— Beneath the golden Orange Grove. Tambourine Song, words by A. J. Foxwell. *J. Curwen & Sons: London*, [1891.] fol.

H. 1984. (26.)

— The Bona Fide Traveller. An Action Song for Temperance Societies and Concerts. Words by A. J. Foxwell. *J. Curwen & Sons: London*, 1897. fol.

H. 1984. b. (2.)

— The Boy and the Girl. Action Song … words by A. J. Foxwell. *J. Curwen & Sons: London*, [1893.] fol.

H. 1984. (27.)

— The Boy Scout. A Concert Action Song, words by M. Byron. *J. Curwen & Sons: London*, 1909. fol. H. 1984. e. (20.)

— Boys will be Boys. Action Song … words by A. J. Foxwell. *J. Curwen & Sons: London*, [1893.] fol. H. 1984. (28.)

— Britannia's Sons. [Song. Words by] M. C. Gillington. pp. 11. *J. Curwen & Sons: London*, [1903.] 8°. [*Choruses for equal Voices. no.* 714.] E. 861.

— Carolina Coon Songs. Words by F. Hoare. *J. Curwen & Sons: London*, 1904. 4°. G. 385. aa. (5.)

— Charge of the Bargain Brigade. Part-Song for male voices. *J. Curwen & Sons: London*, 1911. 8°. *The Apollo Club, No.* 493. F. 667.

— The Children of Jerusalem, and other Sacred Action Songs, words by M. Gillington. *J. Curwen & Sons: London*, 1908. 4°. G. 295. l. (8.)

— The Chinee Boy. An Action Song … Words by M. C. Gillington. *J. Curwen & Sons: London*, 1902. fol.

H. 1984. d. (14.)

— A Chinese Fair. An Action Song … words by F. Hoare. *J. Curwen & Sons: London*, 1902. fol. H. 1984. d. (15.)

— The Chinese Umbrella … Action Song … words by A. J. Foxwell. *J. Curwen & Sons: London*, [1890.] fol.

H. 1984. (29.)

— Choral Fantasia on English Airs. [1894.] *See* CHORAL. The Choral Handbook. No. 327. [1885, *etc.*] 8°. E. 862.

— Choral Fantasia on [C. F. Gounod's] Faust. [Words by] M. C. Gillington. [Arranged by] C. H. Lewis. [1905.] *See* CHORAL. The Choral Handbook. No. 717. [1885, *etc.*] 8°.

E. 862.

LEWIS (CHARLES HUTCHINS)

— Choral Fantasia on Nautical Airs. [1895.] *See* CHORAL. The Choral Handbook. No. 369. [1885, *etc.*] 8°. E. 862.

— Chrysanthemum Land … Action Song … words by M. C. Gillington. *J. Curwen & Sons: London*, 1904. fol.

H. 1984. d. (37.)

— Come ye thankful People, come! Song for Harvest Festivals, for Soprano or Tenor, words by Dean Alford. *J. Curwen & Sons: London*, 1905. fol. H. 1187. ff. (53.)

— The Cross Triumphant. A Sacred Cantata … the Dialogue and Lyrics by F. Hoare. *J. Curwen & Sons: London*, [1904.] 8°. E. 541. m. (2.)

— The Cross triumphant. A sacred cantata, *etc.* [Tonic sol-fa notation.] pp. 39. *J. Curwen & Sons: London*, [1904.] 8°.

B. 418. xx. (2.)

— [The Cross Triumphant.] Y Groes orchfygol. Cantawd gysegredig … Yr aralleiriad i'r Gymraeg o dan olygiaeth D. E. Evans. [Tonic sol-fa notation.] *J. Curwen a'i Feib: Llundain*, [1904.] 4°. B. 415. a. (4.)

— The Crown of Harvest. Action scene. [For S. S. Words by] May Gillington. pp. 15. *J. Curwen & Sons: London*, [1908.] 8°. [*Choruses for equal Voices. no.* 1144.] E. 861.

— A Crown of Thorns. A Passion Cantata, the libretto compiled and written by F. Hoare. *J. Curwen & Sons: London*, 1907. 8°. E. 541. q. (2.)

— A Crown of Thorns … A Passion cantata, *etc.* [Tonic sol-fa.] pp. 29. *J. Curwen & Sons: London*, [1907.] 8°.

B. 418. xx. (3.)

— [A Crown of Thorns.] Y Goron Ddrain … Cantawd y dioddefaint … Y trefniad i'r gymraeg gan D. E. Evans. [Tonic sol-fa notation.] *J. Curwen a'i Feibion: Llundain*, 1907. 4°. B. 415. d. (1.)

— Daisy. Temperance Song, the words by A. J. Foxwell. [Tonic sol-fa and staff notation.] *J. Curwen & Sons: London*, [1887.] fol. *No.* 95, 96 *of The Temperance Vocalist.* H. 3852.

— The Dentist's Den … Song and scena for school concerts. Words by A. J. Foxwell. [Staff and tonic sol-fa notation.] pp. 8. *J. Curwen & Sons: London; G. Schirmer: New York*, [c. 1935.] fol. H. 1984. m. (2.)

— Down by the Sea. A Humorous Cantata for Schools, words by A. B. C. *J. Curwen & Sons: London*, [1904.] 8°.

F. 1271. g. (2.)

— Down by the Sea, *etc.* [Tonic sol-fa edition.] *J. Curwen & Sons: London*, [1905.] 4°. B. 1024. d. (4.)

— The Dunces … Action Song … words by A. J. Foxwell. *J. Curwen & Sons: London*, [1891.] fol. H. 1984. (30.)

— A Dutch Fair. An Action Song for School Concerts, written by M. C. Gillington. *J. Curwen & Sons: London*, 1908. fol.

H. 1984. e. (21.)

— Erin. Fantasia on Irish Airs. [1896.] *See* CHORAL. The Choral Handbook. No. 407. [1885, *etc.*] 8°. E. 862.

— The Family Coach … Action Song … written by H. Blakeston. *J. Curwen & Sons: London*, 1905. fol.

H. 1984. d. (38.)

— The Family Linen … Action Song … words by A. J. Foxwell. *J. Curwen & Sons: London*, [1891.] fol. H. 1984. (31.)

— The Farmer's Boy … Action Song … words by A. J. Foxwell. *J. Curwen & Sons: London*, [1891.] fol. H. 1984. (32.)

LEWIS (CHARLES HUTCHINS)

— Father is drinking again. Temperance Song. [Tonic sol-fa and staff notation.] *J. Curwen & Sons: London*, [1887.] fol.
No. 115 of The Temperance Vocalist. **H. 3852.**

— Father, Wife and Child. Temperance Trio for S., C., B., the words by A. J. Foxwell. [Tonic sol-fa and staff notation.] *J. Curwen & Sons: London*, [1887.] fol.
No. 130, 131 of The Temperance Vocalist. **H. 3852.**

— The Fire-Brigade. An Action Song for School Concerts. Words by A. J. Foxwell. *J. Curwen & Sons: London*, 1898. fol. **H. 1984. b. (3.)**

— The Fisher Girls ... An action song for school concerts. Words by A. J. Foxwell. [Staff and tonic sol-fa notation.] pp. 5. *J. Curwen & Sons: London; Curwen: Germantown*, [c. 1930.] fol. **H. 1984. m. (3.)**

— The Floral Chain. A Short Operetta for young Children, words by E. A. Andrews. *J. Curwen & Sons: London*, 1905. 4°. **G. 770. d. (4.)**

— Flowers, beautiful Flowers! ... An action song for school concerts. Words by Edward Parkinson. [Staff and tonic sol-fa notation.] pp. 7. *J. Curwen & Sons: London; G. Schirmer: New York*, [c. 1935.] fol. **H. 1984. m. (4.)**

— Flowery Garlands. An Action Song for School Concerts. The Words by A. J. Foxwell. *J. Curwen & Sons: London*, 1894. fol. **H. 1984. b. (4.)**

— The Fly Catchers. An Action Song for School Concerts. The Words by A. J. Foxwell. *J. Curwen & Sons: London*, 1894. fol. **H. 1984. b. (5.)**

— Forward, Soldiers! Storm the Ramparts. Temperance Song and Chorus. [Tonic sol-fa and staff notation.] *J. Curwen & Sons: London*, [1887.] fol.
No. 117 of The Temperance Vocalist. **H. 3852.**

— The Gipsy Polka. [P. F.] *Mathias & Strickland: London*, 1892. fol. **h. 3285. q. (45.)**

— Glory's Dream. Duet for Contralto and Baritone, the words by W. R. Glanvill. [Tonic sol-fa and staff notation.] *J. Curwen & Sons: London*, [1889.] fol.
No. 144, 145 of The Temperance Vocalist. **H. 3852.**

— Good Night! [For S. C. Words by] Sheila E. Braine. pp. 4. *J. Curwen & Sons: London*, [1906.] 8°.
[*Choruses for equal Voices. no. 990.*] **E. 861.**

— A Good Umbrella. An Action Song for School Concerts. Words by A. J. Foxwell. *J. Curwen & Sons: London*, 1895. fol. **H. 1984. b. (6.)**

— Goosey, Goosey, Gander. [Two-part song.] pp. 8. *J. Curwen & Sons: London; Leipzig* [printed, 1894.] 8°.
[*Choruses for equal Voices. no. 214.*] **E. 861.**

— Y Goron Ddrain. *See* supra: [A Crown of Thorns.]

— Grace Darling. An Action Scene for School Concerts, verses by F. Hoare ... Arranged by H. Faulkner & S. E. Thornhill. *J. Curwen & Sons: London*, 1907. fol. **H. 1984. e. (22.)**

— Grecian Girls. Action Song for School Concerts. Words by A. J. Foxwell. *J. Curwen & Sons: London*, 1893. fol. **H. 1984. b. (7.)**

— Y Groes orchfygol. *See* supra: [The Cross Triumphant.]

— Hard Times come again no more. [By S. C. Foster.] Arranged by C. H. Lewis [for T. T. B. B.]. *J. Curwen & Sons: London*, [1905.] 8°.
The Apollo Club, No. 266. **F. 667.**

— Hats. An Action Song ... words by F. Hoare. *J. Curwen & Sons: London*, 1905. fol. **H. 1984. d. (39.)**

LEWIS (CHARLES HUTCHINS)

— Home sweet Home. [By Sir H. R. Bishop.] Arranged by C. H. Lewis [for T. T. B. B.]. *J. Curwen & Sons: London*, [1905.] 8°.
The Apollo Club, No. 265. **F. 667.**

— The Horsemen. Action Song ... words by A. J. Foxwell. *J. Curwen & Sons: London*, [1893.] fol. **H. 1984. (33.)**

— House-Work. Action Song for School Concerts. Words by A. J. Foxwell. *J. Curwen & Sons: London*, 1893. fol. **H. 1984. b. (8.)**

— Hush-a-by Baby. [S. A.] pp. 7. *J. Curwen & Sons: London; Leipzig* [printed, 1894.] 8°.
[*Choruses for equal Voices. no. 212.*] **E. 861.**

— In hot Hindustan. An Action Song ... words by M. C. Gillington. *J. Curwen & Sons: London*, 1902. fol. **H. 1984. d. (17.)**

— Inquest on Cock Robin. Action Song and Scena. Words by A. J. Foxwell. *J. Curwen & Sons: London*, 1897. fol. **H. 1984. b. (10.)**

— Ivanhoe. A Romantic Opera, adapted from Sir Walter Scott's Novel by M. Byron. *J. Curwen & Sons: London*, 1907. 8°. **F. 1271. i. (4.)**

— Ivanhoe, *etc.* [Tonic sol-fa edition.] *J. Curwen & Sons: London*, 1907. 4°. **B. 382. j. (2.)**

— The Japanese Doll Feast. An Action Song ... words by M. C. Gillington. *J. Curwen & Sons: London*, 1902. fol. **H. 1984. d. (16.)**

— The Japanese Tea-House. An Action Song for School Concerts. Words by A. J. Foxwell. *J. Curwen & Sons: London*, 1893. fol. **H. 1984. b. (9.)**

— Jerusalem the golden. [Anthem.] [1908.] *See* CHURCH. The Church Choralist. No. 401. [1886, *etc.*] 8°. **E. 1330.**

— The Jolly Eskimo. An Action Song ... words by M. C. Gillington. *J. Curwen & Sons: London*, 1902. fol. **H. 1984. d. (18.)**

— The Jolly Jack Tar. Action Song ... words by A. J. Foxwell. *J. Curwen & Sons: London*, [1890.] fol. **H. 1984. (34.)**

— Jolly little Geishas. An Action Song ... words by M. C. Gillington. *J. Curwen and Sons: London*, 1904. fol. **H. 1984. d. (40.)**

— Little Housemaids. An Action Song ... words by F. Hoare. *J. Curwen & Sons: London*, 1905. fol. **H. 1984. d. (41.)**

— Little Maids of long ago. (Action Song.) Words by E. A. Andrews. *J. Curwen & Sons: London*, 1904. fol. **H. 1984. d. (19.)**

— A Little Ricksha' Boy. An Action Song ... words by M. Farrah. *J. Curwen & Sons: London*, 1906. fol. **H. 1984. d. (42.)**

— The Maids of Sevilla. An Action Song ... words by M. C. Gillington. *J. Curwen & Sons: London*, 1902. fol. **H. 1984. d. (20.)**

— The Melancholy Man ... Temperance Song & Chorus, the words by A. J. Foxwell. [Tonic sol-fa and staff notation.] *J. Curwen & Sons: London*, [1887.] fol.
No. 127 of The Temperance Vocalist. **H. 3852.**

— The Merry Shoeblack. Action Song ... words by A. J. Foxwell. *J. Curwen & Sons: London*, [1891.] fol. **H. 1984. (35.)**

— Miss Milligan's Girls. (Action Song.) Words by S. E. Braine. *J. Curwen & Sons: London*, 1905. fol. **H. 1984. d. (43.)**

LEWIS (CHARLES HUTCHINS)

— A Musical Muddle. [Part-song for T. T. B. B.] *J. Curwen & Sons: London,* [1907.] 8°.
The Apollo Club, No. 345. **F. 667.**

— My good old Golliwog ... Action Song for Schools, words by M. Byron. *J. Curwen & Sons: London,* 1909. fol.
H. 1984. f. (18.)

— My Love and my Heart. [Part-song for A. T. B. B., words by] H. S. Leigh. *J. Curwen & Sons: London,* [1904.] 8°.
The Apollo Club, No. 241. **F. 667.**

— My old Kentucky Home. [By S. C. Foster.] Arranged by C. H. Lewis [for T. T. B. B.]. *J. Curwen & Sons: London,* [1905.] 8°.
The Apollo Club, No. 267. **F. 667.**

— My precious Teddy Bear. Action Song for Children, words by M. Byron. *J. Curwen & Sons: London,* 1909. fol.
H. 1984. e. (23.)

— Nature Songs ... Thirty-six Songs for unison singing with Pianoforte accompaniment, words by F. Hoare ... With ... Designs ... by M. Emra. *J. Curwen & Sons: London,* 1903. 4°. **G. 383. d. (5.)**

— O merry is the Meeting. A song to be sung at the close of a concert. [For S. C. and chorus. Words by] A. J. Foxwell. pp. 7. *J. Curwen & Sons: London; Leipzig* [printed, 1894.] 8°.
[*Choruses for equal Voices. no.* 207.] **E. 861.**

— O Strength and Stay. Hymn Anthem, from the Latin by Ellerton and Hort. *J. Curwen & Sons: London,* 1912. 8°.
[*Church Choralist. no.* 522.] **E. 1330.**

— "O that my Ways were made so direct." Psalm CXIX verses 5. 6. 7. 8. [Anthem.] pp. 8. *J. Curwen & Sons: London,* [1907.] 8°.
[*Church Choralist. no.* 379.] **E. 1330.**

— Off to Klondyke. A Musical Sketch for School Concerts. Words by M. C. Gillington. *J. Curwen & Sons: London,* [1898.] fol. **H. 1984. b. (11.)**

— Old Dog Tray. [By S. C. Foster.] Arranged by C. H. Lewis [for T. T. B. B.]. *J. Curwen & Sons: London,* [1905.] 8°.
The Apollo Club, No. 269. **F. 667.**

— Old King Cole. [Two-part song.] [Vocal score and part for two violins.] 2 pt. *J. Curwen & Sons: London; Leipzig* [printed, 1894.] 8°.
[*Choruses for equal Voices. no.* 215.] *The parts for violins are printed in score.* **E. 861.**

— Only seven. Humorous Part Song. [Words by] H. S. Leigh. *J. Curwen & Sons: London,* 1901. 8°.
The Apollo Club, No. 222. **F. 667.**

— Our little serving Maids. A School Action Song. Words by K. F. Tutt. *J. Curwen & Sons: London,* 1897. fol.
H. 1984. b. (12.)

— Our merry See-Saw. An Action Song for School Concerts. Words by E. Parkinson. *J. Curwen & Sons: London,* 1895. fol. **H. 1984. b. (13.)**

— Oxenford's Action Songs, set to music by C. H. Lewis. Both Notations. *J. Curwen & Sons: London,* 1897. 8°.
E. 1781. b. (3.)

— [Another copy.] **E. 1766. g. (4.)**

— The Pedlar. Action Song for School Concerts. Words by A. J. Foxwell. *J. Curwen & Sons: London,* 1893. fol.
H. 1984. b. (14.)

— The Perfect Life. Sacred Cantata, the words selected and lyrics written by F. Hoare. *J. Curwen & Sons: London,* 1906. 4°. **E. 541. p. (2.)**

LEWIS (CHARLES HUTCHINS)

— The Perfect Life, *etc.* [Tonic sol-fa notation.] *J. Curwen & Sons: London,* 1906. 4°. **B. 415. d. (2.)**

— Peter Piper. Quartet for male voices. *J. Curwen & Sons: London,* [1907.] 8°.
The Apollo Club, No. 344. **F. 667.**

— The Pilgrim's Progress. A Sacred Cantata—founded on the Allegory of J. Bunyan—, words by F. Hoare. *J. Curwen & Sons: London,* [1905.] 8°. **F. 1274. jj. (3.)**

— The Pilgrim's Progress, *etc.* [Tonic sol-fa notation.] *J. Curwen & Sons: London,* [1906.] 4°. **B. 415. b. (6.)**

— [The Pilgrim's Progress.] Taith y Pererin ... Cantawd gysegredig ... y geiriau Saesneg gan F. Hoare, wedi eu Cymreigio gan D. E. Evans. [Tonic sol-fa notation.] *J. Curwen a'i Feib.: Llundain,* [1906.] 4°. **B. 415. b. (7.)**

— The Premier Song Book. A Collection of the most popular Songs, with Accompaniments arranged by C. H. Lewis. *J. Curwen & Sons: London,* [1905.] 8°. **F. 637. y. (4.)**

— The Premier Song Book. Standard songs for schools. Arranged by C. H. Lewis. [String parts.] 4 pt. *J. Curwen & Sons: London,* [1905?] 8°.
The parts for cello and bass are printed in score.
E. 1501. s. (10.)

— The Publican's Song. Temperance Song, the words by A. J. Foxwell. [Tonic sol-fa and staff notation.] *J. Curwen & Sons: London,* [1889.] fol.
No. 135, 136 *of The Temperance Vocalist.* **H. 3852.**

— Queen Anne Fan Song ... Action Song ... words by A. J. Foxwell. *J. Curwen & Sons: London,* [1891.] fol.
H. 1984. (36.)

— The Queen of Hearts. [Two-part song.] pp. 6. *J. Curwen & Sons: London; Leipzig* [printed, 1894.] 8°.
[*Choruses for equal Voices. no.* 213.] **E. 861.**

— The Red Indians. An Action Song ... Words by M. C. Gillington. *J. Curwen & Sons: London,* 1899. fol.
H. 1984. c. (15.)

— Red, White and Blue. Action Song ... words by M. Gillington. *J. Curwen & Sons: London,* [1905.] fol.
H. 1984. d. (44.)

— Riding in the Tram. An Action Song for School Concerts. Words by A. J. Foxwell. *J. Curwen & Sons: London,* 1897. fol. **H. 1984. b. (15.)**

— Robin Adair. Arranged by C. H. Lewis [for T. T. B. B.]. *J. Curwen & Sons: London,* [1905.] 8°.
The Apollo Club, No. 268. **F. 667.**

— The Sandow Girls and Boys and other Action Songs for Schools. The words and actions by M. Farrah. *J. Curwen & Sons: London,* 1907. 4°. **G. 383. p. (8.)**

— Scarf-Drill. Action Song ... words by A. J. Foxwell. *J. Curwen & Sons: London,* [1893.] fol. **H. 1984. (37.)**

— Scène de Ballet pour piano. *E. Ashdown: London,* [1897.] fol.
g. 605. p. (32.)

— Scotia. Choral Fantasia. [1896.] *See* CHORAL. The Choral Handbook. No. 393. [1885, *etc.*] 8°. **E. 862.**

— Signals. An Action Song for School Concerts. The words by A. J. Foxwell. *J. Curwen & Sons: London,* 1893. fol.
H. 1984. b. (16.)

— Sing, Brothers, Sing. Temperance Song. [Tonic sol-fa and staff notation.] *J. Curwen & Sons: London,* [1887.] fol.
No. 105 *of The Temperance Vocalist.* **H. 3852.**

— A Song of Greeting. [For S. C. Words by] Sheila E. Braine. pp. 4. *J. Curwen & Sons: London,* [1906.] 8°. **E. 861.**

LEWIS (CHARLES HUTCHINS)

— A Song of Slumber. An Action Song ... words by M. C. Gillington. *J. Curwen & Sons: London*, 1902. fol.
H. 1984. d. (21.)

— A Song, please. Songs for children, the words by various authors. *J. Curwen & Sons: London*, [1890.] 4°.
G. 385. h. (6.)

— Songs of the Eighteenth Century, the words mostly by F. Hoare. Arranged for Two-Part singing with Accompaniments by C. H. Lewis. *J. Curwen & Sons: London*, [1903.] 8°.
F. 637. y. (3.)

— Sparrow talk. Song, words by G. Weatherly. *Hutchings & Romer: London*, [1892.] fol.
H. 1797. o. (37*.)

— The Stilts. An Action Song for School Concerts. Words by A. J. Foxwell. *J. Curwen & Sons: London*, 1893. fol.
H. 1984. b. (17.)

— Storming the Fort ... Action Song, words by A. J. Foxwell. *J. Curwen & Sons: London*, 1902. fol.
G. 781. a. (3.)

— The Sweeping Brush Brigade ... Action Song ... words by A. J. Foxwell. *J. Curwen & Sons: London*, [1891.] fol.
H. 1984. (38.)

— The Sweeps. An Action Song ... words by F. B. Smith. *J. Curwen & Sons: London*, [1903.] fol.
H. 1984. d. (22.)

— Taith y Pererin. *See* supra: [The Pilgrim's Progress.]

— Tales of Childhood. A Series of Tableaux with Music for Performance at School Festivals. The words by A. J. Foxwell. *J. Curwen & Sons: London*, 1893. fol.
H. 1984. b. (18.)

— Tattlebury Market. [Part-song for T. T. B. B.] *J. Curwen & Sons: London*, [1905.] 8°.
The Apollo Club, No. 293.
F. 667.

— This World of Ours. A Spectacular Action Song. Words by A. J. Foxwell. *J. Curwen & Sons: London*, [1896.] fol.
H. 1984. b. (19.)

— The Tin Whistle ... An action song for boys. Words by J. J. Taylor. [Staff and tonic sol-fa notation.] pp. 7. *J. Curwen & Sons: London; Curwen: Germantown*, [c. 1925.] fol.
H. 1984. m. (5.)

— The Toyshop. A Musical Play for elder Children, words by A. Ingham. *J. Curwen & Sons: London*, [1904.] 4°.
G. 782. d. (2.)

— Triangle Song ... words by A. J. Foxwell. *J. Curwen & Sons: London*, [1893.] fol.
H. 1984. (39.)

— The Verdict of the Flowers. Cantata for female Voices, Soli & Chorus ... with Pianoforte Accompaniment. The Words by J. Watson. *Augener & Co.: London*, [1900.] 8°.
F. 1270. f. (5.)

— Village Minstrels are we. Humorous Song ... with refrain to be sung through combs covered with paper, the words by A. J. Foxwell. *J. Curwen & Sons: London*, [1890.] fol.
H. 1984. (40.)

— Vivat Regina. Choral Fantasia on Victorian Airs. [1899.] *See* CHORAL. The Choral Handbook. No. 533. [1885, *etc.*] 8°.
E. 862.

— The Wagoners' Chorus ... Action Song ... words by A. J. Foxwell. *J. Curwen & Sons: London*, [1891.] fol.
H. 1984. (41.)

— We resolute stand. [Four-part song.] Music by G. F. Root. Accompaniment by C. H. Lewis, *etc.* [1894.] *See* CHORAL. The Choral Handbook. No. 325. [1885, *etc.*] 8°.
E. 862.

— Welsh Girls. Action Song for School Concerts. Words by A. J. Foxwell. *J. Curwen & Sons: London*, 1893. fol.
H. 1984. b. (20.)

LEWIS (CHARLES HUTCHINS)

— Where are you going to, my pretty Maid? An Action Song, *etc.* *J. Curwen & Sons: London*, [1902.] fol.
H. 1984. d. (23.)

— Whosoever would be happy. Temperance Song. [Tonic sol-fa and staff notation.] *J. Curwen & Sons: London*, [1887.] fol. *No.* 113, 114 *of The Temperance Vocalist.*
H. 3852.

— Witches Three. A Children's Fairy Play. Both notations. *J. Curwen & Sons: London*, 1902. 8°.
F. 1271. f. (2.)

— Witches Three, *etc.* [Tonic sol-fa edition.] *J. Curwen & Sons: London*, [1905.] 4°.
B. 1024. d. (5.)

— The Wonderful Hat. An Action Song ... Words by M. Gillington. *J. Curwen & Sons: London*, 1900. fol.
H. 1984. c. (16.)

— The Wreck of the Hesperus. Cantata for treble voices, words by Longfellow. *Hutchings & Co.: London*, [1886.] 8°.
E. 1594. g. (7.)

— *See* BALFE (Michael W.) The Bohemian Girl. Choral Fantasia. [Arranged by] C. H. Lewis. [1899.] 8°. [*Choral Handbook. no.* 536.]
E. 862.

— *See* BALFE (Michael W.) [The Bohemian Girl.] Choral Fantasia on The Bohemian Girl ... Arranged by C. H. Lewis. [1906?–1913?] 8°.
f. 246. jj. (1.)

— *See* FOXWELL (A. J.) Donald's Hamper ... The Symphonies ... by C. H. Lewis. [1888.] 8°.
D. 832. (7.)

— *See* FOXWELL (A. J.) German Trios. Set to English words by A. J. Foxwell. ⟨Pianoforte edition. With symphonies and accompaniments by C. H. Lewis. Second series.⟩ [c. 1885.] 8°.
F. 1196. k. (10.)

— *See* FOXWELL (A. J.) Winter ... Service of Song ... with ... music ... by ... C. H. Lewis, *etc.* [1887.] 8°.
D. 675. k. (7.)

— *See* LILLIE (L. C.) and LEWIS (C. H.) The Battle of the Books ... Operetta, *etc.* [1889.] 8°.
D. 832. a. (7.)

— *See* STALLYBRASS (J. S.) The Fire Brigade ... Arr. by C. H. Lewis. 1902. fol.
H. 1984. d. (25.)

— *See* TOWNE (T. M.) We are jolly Blacksmiths. Action Song ... Arranged ... by C. H. Lewis. [1889.] fol.
H. 1795. e. (42.)

— *See* VEAZIE (George A.) Skies bright and clear ... [For S. S. A.] The accompaniment by C. H. Lewis. [1894.] 8°. [*Choruses for equal Voices. no.* 187.]
E. 861.

— *See* WALLACE (William V.) Maritana. Choral Fantasia arranged by C. H. Lewis. [1902.] 8°. [*Choral Handbook. no.* 555.]
E. 862.

— *See* WALLACE (William V.) [Maritana.] Choral Fantasia on Maritana ... Arranged by C. H. Lewis. [1906?–1912?] 8°.
f. 246. kk. (2.)

LEWIS (D. A.)

— Missus Johnson's Rent Rag Ball. [Song.] Words by Fred. "Statia" Hamill. pp. 4. *National Music Co.: Chicago, New York*, [1897.] fol.
H. 3980. ss. (3.)

— *See* WILLIAMS (Bert A.) "Oh! I don't know," you're not so warm! Comic song, *etc.* ⟨Refrain with rag-time accompaniment. Arr. by D. A. Lewis.⟩ [1897.] fol.
H. 3981. ss. (12.)

LEWIS (DAFYDD) *of Llanrhystud*

— Detholiad o donau, anthemau a rhanganau y diweddar Dafydd Lewis ... Dan olygiaeth J. T. Rees ... Ynghyd a byr-gofiant o'r awdur gan D. Wyre Lewis. [Tonic sol-fa notation.] pp. 128. *Argraffwyd gan Wm. Jones a'i Feibion: Abermaw*, [c. 1910.] 8°.
B. 7. g.

LEWIS (DAFYDD) *of Llanrhystud*

— Canig ddirwestol. [Part-song.] *In:* Greal y corau. suppl.
pp. 105–108. 1863. 8°.   **1601/349.**

— Glan Wyre ... [Hymn.] Cyng. gan W. Ellis. *In:* Greal y corau.
suppl. p. 84. 1862. 8°. *Without the words.*   **1601/349.**

— Gwalia ... ⟨Glee.⟩ Y geiriau gan Eos Glyn Wyre. *In:* Greal y
corau. suppl. pp. 97–100. 1863. 8°.   **1601/349.**

— "Hwn fydd mawr." Anthem. [Tonic sol-fa notation.] pp. 4.
Hughes & Son: Wrexham, [1889.] 8°.
[*Y Cerddor. rhif* 12.]   **P. P. 1947. l.**

— Trewch, trewch y tant. Canig. [Words by] J. Ceiriog Hughes.
[Tonic sol-fa notation.] *In:* WILLIAMS (William A.) called
Gwilym Gwent. Yr Haf, *etc.* pp. 5–8. [c. 1950.] 8°.
                              B. 8. h. (18.)

LEWIS (DANIEL)

— Eighteen Pence ... Comic Song, words by B. Mortimer.
Howard & Co.: London, [1884.] fol.   **H. 1260. f. (53.)**

LEWIS (DAVE)

— The Geezer of Geck. By D. Lewis, Paul Schindler & Bob
Adams. [Musical play. Separate songs.] 11 no.   *Chas. K.
Harris: New York*, [1905.] fol.   **H. 3985. z. (15.)**

— "My Alabama Lady Love." ⟨Ballad.⟩ Words and music by
D. Lewis. pp. 5.   *Jos. W. Stern & Co.: New York*, [1899.] fol.
                              H. 3980. ss. (4.)

— "Nannette." [Song.] Words and music by D. Lewis. Arr. by
Jac. L. Schetter. pp. 3.   *Chas. K. Harris: [Milwaukee*, 1902.] 4°.
                              H. 3985. z. (16.)

— [A reissue.] Nannette, *etc.*   [*Milwaukee*, 1902.] fol.
                              H. 3985. z. (17.)

— They're waiting there for me. ⟨Song.⟩ Words and music by
D. Lewis. pp. 5.   *Chas. K. Harris: New York*, [1905.] fol.
                              H. 3985. z. (18.)

LEWIS (DAVID) *of Llanrhystud*
— *See* LEWIS (Dafydd) *of Llanrhystud.*

LEWIS (DAVID WILLIAM)

— Adlau mawl. ⟨Rhanau 1, 2, 3 a 4. Yn cynwys tonau ac
anthemau byrion a syml, er gwasanaeth cyfarfodydd y plant
a chymanfaoedd canu.⟩ [Tonic sol-fa notation.] pp. 64.
D. W. Lewis: Brynamman, [c. 1895.] 8°.   **B. 8. u. (2.)**

— Adlau mawl. ⟨Rhanau 1, 2, 3, 4, 5 a 6. Yn cynwys tonau ac
anthemau byrion a syml, er gwasanaeth cyfarfodydd y plant
a chymanfaoedd canu.⟩ [Tonic sol-fa notation.] pp. 96.
D. W. Lewis & Son: Brynamman, [1896?] 8°.   **B. 8. u. (3.)**

— "Can y bugeiliaid." Rhan-gan. [T. T. B. B.] Geiriau gan
Watcyn Wyn. [Staff and tonic sol-fa notation.] pp. 4.
D. Williams & Son: Llanelly, [1885.] 8°.
[*Cerddor y Cymry. cyf.* 2. *rhif* 23. *Cerddoriaeth. rhif* 23.]
                              P.P. 1947. m.

— Caneuon y Plant. The Children's Songbook. Words by L. D.
Jones ... Old Notation edition. English and Welsh words.
Educational Publishing Co.: Cardiff & Wrexham, [1929.] 8°.
                              D. 814.

— Caneuon y plant ... The children's songbook ... [Words by]
Llew Tegid. [Tonic sol-fa notation.] *Welsh & Eng.* rhan 1, 2.
The Educational Publishing Co.: Cardiff, [c. 1920.] 8°.
Imperfect; wanting rhan 3.   **C. 273. m. (23.)**
                              & C. 273. vv. (1.)

LEWIS (DAVID WILLIAM)

— [Cwsg, f'anwylyd, cwsg.] ("Sleep, my Darling, sleep.")
("Cwsg, f'anwylyd, cwsg.") Part-song—S. S. A. ... English
words by Llew Tegid. Welsh words by Wnion. [Tonic sol-fa
notation.] pp. 3.   *D. W. Lewis & Son: Brynamman*, [c. 1895.]
8°.   **C. 273. j. (37.)**

— "Cwsg, f'anwylyd, cwsg." ("Sleep, my darling, sleep.")
Rhangan. S. S. A. ... Geiriau Cymraeg gan Wnion. English
words by Llew Tegid. [Tonic sol-fa notation.] pp. 4.   *Hughes
& Son: Wrexham*, [1916.] 8°.
[*Y Cerddor. rhif* 336.]   **P. P. 1947. l.**

— 'Cwsg fy Noli.' ('Sleep my Dolly.') Rhangan i blant ... [S. A.]
Geiriau gan ... L. D. Jones ... Solfa. *Welsh & Eng. Hughes
& Son: Cardiff*, [c. 1940.] 8°.   **B. 7. a. (16.)**

— Deuwch ataf Fi. Anthem. Yr wythfed fil. [Tonic sol-fa
notation.] pp. 3.   *D. W. Lewis: Brynamman*, [c. 1895.] 8°.
                              C. 273. h. (3.)

— Diliau'r dolydd. (Woodland and meadow.) Cymwys i gorau
plant [S. A.], neu ddawns at wasanaeth ysgolion. Geiriau gan
... Llew Tegid. [Tonic sol-fa notation.] *Welsh & Eng.* pp. 4.
Hughes & Son: Wrexham, [1917.] 8°.
[*Y Cerddor. rhif* 342.]   **P. P. 1947. l.**

— "Dysg i mi Dy lwybrau." Anthem. [Tonic sol-fa notation.]
D. W. Lewis & Son: Brynamman, [c. 1890.] 8°.
                              C. 273. k. (14.)

— Pedair o hen alawon Cymreig ... Wedi eu cynganeddu gan
D. W. Lewis. ⟨Pumed argraffiad.⟩ [Tonic sol-fa notation.] pp. 3.
D. W. Lewis: Brynamman, [c. 1890.] 8°.   **C. 273. j. (36.)**

— Llanon ... [Hymn.] Geiriau gan J. Rees Jones. [Tonic sol-fa
notation.] *In:* Y Lladmerydd. cyf. 16. p. 320. 1900. 8°.
                              P. 101/472.

— Odlau mawl. ⟨Yn cynwys tonau ac anthemau byrion a syml.⟩
[Tonic sol-fa notation.] rhan 1–5.   *D. W. Lewis: Brynamman*,
[c. 1895–99.] 8°.
Imperfect; wanting rhan 6. *Rhan* 1 *is of the sixth edition; rhan* 2
is of the third edition.   **B. 7. e. (9.)**

— [Another copy of rhan 1, 2.]
Imperfect; wanting pp. 5–12 *of rhan* 1.   **C. 531. kk. (3.)**

— Y Pererin. Rhangan gysegredig. Y geiriau gan Gwydderig.
[Tonic sol-fa notation.] pp. 4.   *Hughes & Son: Wrexham*,
[1896.] 8°. [*Y Cerddor. rhif* 96.]   **P. P. 1947. l.**

— *See* WALES.— *Undeb yr Annibynwyr Cymreig.— Pwyllgor y
Caniedydd Cynulleidfaol.* Y Caniedydd cynulleidfaol ... Y
tônau, &c., o dan olygiaeth y Parch. W. Emlyn Jones ...
D. W. Lewis, etc. 1895. 8°.   **C. 531. n.**

— *See* WALES.— *Undeb yr Annibynwyr Cymreig.— Pwyllgor y
Caniedydd Cynulleidfaol.* Y Caniedydd cynulleidfaol ... Y
tônau, &c., o dan olygiaeth y Parch. W. Emlyn Jones ...
D. W. Lewis, etc. 1895. 8°.   **C. 531. o.**

— *See* WALES.— *Undeb yr Annibynwyr Cymreig.— Pwyllgor y
Caniedydd Cynulleidfaol.* Y Caniedydd cynulleidfaol ... Y
tônau, &c., o dan olygiaeth y Parch W. Emlyn Jones ...
D. W. Lewis, etc. 1906. 8°.   **C. 531. e.**

— *See* WALES.— *Undeb yr Annibynwyr Cymreig.— Pwyllgor y
Caniedydd Cynulleidfaol.* [Y Caniedydd cynulleidfaol.] Y
Caniedydd cynulleidfaol newydd ... Yr emynau dan
olygiaeth ... H. E. Lewis ... A'r gerddoriaeth dan olygiaeth
Dr. C. Roberts ... D. W. Lewis, *etc.* 1921. 8°.   **B. 7. pp.**

— *See* WALES.— *Undeb yr Annibynwyr Cymreig.— Pwyllgor y
Caniedydd Cynulleidfaol.* [Y Caniedydd cynulleidfaol.] Y
Caniedydd cynulleidfaol newydd ... Yr emynau dan
olygiaeth ... H. E. Lewis ... A'r gerddoriaeth dan olygiaeth
Dr. C. Roberts ... D. W. Lewis, *etc.* 1921. 8°.   **C. 531. r.**

LEWIS (David William)

— *See* Wales.— *Undeb yr Annibynwyr Cymreig.— Pwyllgor y Caniedydd Cynulleidfaol.* Caniedydd yr Ysgol Sul. Casgliad o dônau ac emynau, corganau, ac anthemau ... Y tônau, &c., o dan olygiaeth ... W. E. Jones ... D. Lewis, *etc.* 1899. 8°.
C. 141. q.

LEWIS (E.)

— The Merry Maids quadrille. [P. F.] *London*, [1866.] fol.
h. 1460. v. (40.)

LEWIS (Edward) *L. T. S. C.*

— Mi garwn fod yn angel. (I'd like to be an angel.) Cân gysegredig i blant. Welsh words by Sidney P. Gill ... English words by Rev. William Walters, *etc.* [Staff and tonic sol-fa notation.] pp. 3. *Snell & Sons: Swansea*, [c. 1930.] fol.
H. 1634. n. (18.)

LEWIS (Edward) *of the U. S. A.*

— Arioso. For piano solo. pp. 5. *Mercury Music Corporation: New York*, [1952.] 4°.
g. 1128. n. (3.)

— Two Lyric Pieces for Clarinet and Piano. [Score and part.] 2 pt. *Mercury Music Corporation: New York*, [1953.] 4°. *Part of "The Mercury Wind Instrument Library".*
g. 1104. h. (3.)

LEWIS (Edward J.)

— Hosanna: sef Casgliad o donau ac emynau at wasanaeth y cysegr, *etc.* pp. 341. *Argraffwyd gan Evan E. Roberts: Utica, N. Y.*, 1864. 8°.
1550/4.

— *See* Mills (Richard) *of Llanidloes.* Caniadau Seion ... Yr ail argraffiad Americanaidd ... dan olygiad J. Mills ... E. J. Lewis, ac ereill. 1853. *obl.* 8°.
C. 531. z.

LEWIS (Edward Norman)

— Indolence v. Perseverance.—A Cure for Laziness.—[Song.] Words and Music by E. N. Lewis. *J. Curwen & Sons: London*, [1903.] 8°.
Unison Songs, No. 61.
E. 812.

— A Joyous Song in Music's Praise. (Vocal gavotte.) [For S. S.] Words and music by E. N. Lewis. pp. 7. *J. Curwen & Sons: London*, [1903.] 8°.
[Choruses for equal Voices. no. 720.]
E. 861.

— The Merry Maids' Protest. An Action Trio or Chorus Song ... Words and music by E. N. Lewis. *J. Curwen & Sons: London*, 1899. fol.
H. 1984. c. (17.)

— An "Odd" Ditty. [Unison song.] Words and music by E. N. Lewis. *J. Curwen & Sons: London*, [1903.] 8°.
Unison Songs, No. 62.
E. 812.

— Past and Present. [Song, begins: "I remember".] Words by ... T. Hood. *London*, [1880.] fol.
H. 1785. c. (38.)

— The School Brigade March.— Prize Vocal March. *J. Curwen & Sons: London*, [1895.] 8°.
Unison Songs, No. 7.
E. 812.

— Sneezers, Yawners, and Laughers. [Action song for S. S. C.] Words and music by E. N. Lewis. pp. 7. *J. Curwen & Sons: London*, [1901.] 8°.
[Choruses for equal Voices. no. 480.]
E. 861.

— The Woes of three Duffers ... A humorous song for school concerts. Words and music by E. N. Lewis. [Staff and tonic sol-fa notation.] pp. 5. *J. Curwen & Sons: London; G. Schirmer: New York*, [c. 1935.] fol.
H. 1984. m. (6.)

LEWIS (Edwin)

— ... [Tatrīb al-ādān, a musical primer.] ... [*Beirut*, 1873.] 8°.
14546. d. 2.

— *See* Jessop (Samuel) and Ford (G.) [Kitāb mazamir wa tasābīh wa aghānī ruhiyyah, *etc.*] [A book of hymns and psalms compiled by S. Jessop and G. Ford, based on an earlier work by E. Lewis.] [1885.] 8°.
C. 17. cc.

LEWIS (Eric) *Composer of pianoforte music*

— 20 very easy Carols. Arranged by E. Lewis, *etc.* [P. F.] pp. 20. *Forsyth Bros.: London, Manchester*, [1968.] 4°.
F. 260. zz. (2.)

— 20 more easy Carols. Book II. Arranged by E. Lewis, *etc.* pp. 22. *Forsyth Bros.: London, Manchester*, [1970.] 4°.
F. 260. zz. (5.)

— 20 easy Folk Songs. Arranged by E. Lewis, *etc.* ⟨[Songs.] With guitar chords.⟩ pp. 21. *Forsyth Bros.: London, Manchester*, [1969.] 4°.
F. 1199. q. (13.)

— Metropolis. Etude. [P. F.] pp. 7. *Forsyth Bros.: London, Manchester*, [1960.] fol.
g. 1128. hh. (10.)

— *See* Bach (J. S.) [Drei Toccaten für Orgel. No. 2.] Organ Toccata and Fugue in D minor ... Transcribed for piano solo by E. Lewis. [1947.] 4°.
g. 548. ww. (11.)

— *See* Liszt (F.) [Fantasie über ungarische Volksmelodien.] Liszt's Hungarian Fantasie. Concert arrangement for solo piano by E. Lewis. [1965.] 4°.
g. 547. s. (4.)

LEWIS (Eric) *Songwriter*

— The Intellectual Youth ... Song. *London*, [1882.] fol.
H. 1787. j. (33.)

LEWIS (Eric D. Mansel)

— Air marziale ... for the Pianoforte. *Chappell & Co.: London and Melbourne*, 1906. fol.
h. 3283. p. (29.)

LEWIS (Esme)

— Deg o ganeuon gwerin i blant. Wedi'u trefnu ar gyfer lleisiau ac offerynnau syml gan Esme Lewis. [Score.] pp. 17. *Gwasg prifysgol cymru: Caerdydd*, 1973. 4°.
G. 1310. n. (3.)

— [Deg o ganeuon gwerin i blant.] Ten Welsh Folk Songs for Juniors. Arranged for voices with easy instrumental accompaniment by Esme Lewis. English translations by Ifor Rees. [Score.] pp. 17. *University of Wales Press: Cardiff*, 1973. 4°.
G. 1310. n. (2.)

LEWIS (Esther)

— The grove where thou didst stray; ballad, written and composed by E. Lewis. *London*, [1824.] fol.
H. 1691. (7.)

— The Grove where thou didst stray. Ballad. *London*, [1868.] fol.
H. 1775. u. (40.)

LEWIS (Evan)

— *See* Hyfforddwr. Hyfforddwr ar y gân eglwysig ... Rhan I. ... gan E. Lewis, *etc.* 1884. 8°.
B. 370. j.

LEWIS (F. A.)

— Six Voluntaries for American Organ or Harmonium. *Weekes & Co.: London*, [1918.] 4°.
g. 575. bb. (12.)

LEWIS (Flora Landsberg)

— The Grasshopper, morceau de salon pour Piano. *London*, [1870.] fol.
h. 1485. s. (50.)

LEWIS (Flora Landsberg)

— Hopeless. Song [begins: "There is a love"]. The poetry by
E. Schiff. *London*, [1874.] fol.   H. 1778. y. (20.)

LEWIS (Frances Owen)

— O let me hear that song again. Song. *London*, [1877.] fol.
H. 1778. y. (2.)

— The Stars are with the voyager. Song, words by T. Hood.
London, [1877.] fol.   H. 1778. y. (21.)

LEWIS (Frank W.)

— Gaelic Folk Songs of the Isles of the West, (Traditional
melody and Gaelic words preserved) by ... J. MacMillan ...
Translations by ... P. McGlynn. Music arranged by
F. W. Lewis. 11 no. *Boosey & Co.: London and New York*,
1930 [–31]. 8°.   F. 585. ss. (20.)

— Gaelic Folk Songs of the Isles of the West. Six Songs,
traditional and original, [collected] by Father J. MacMillan,
with legends and translations, by Dr. P. McGlynn ... Music
arranged by F. W. Lewis. 2 vol. *Boosey & Co.: London and
New York*, 1930. 4°.   G. 1189.

— Iona Bells. Cluig-ghliongaich na H-ì. For Solo Voice and
Mixed Choir with accompaniment for Clarsach or two
Harps, muted Trumpet and muffled Timpani. Poem by
H. Boulton, Gaelic translation by I. M. Ghille-Mhaoil. [Vocal
score.] *Bosworth & Co.: London, etc.*, 1934. 8°.
F. 1267. k. (1.)

— The Princess of Lochlann. A Legend for Mixed Choir,
Baritone and Soprano Soli and Orchestra, words by
H. Boulton. [Vocal score.] *Bosworth & Co.: London, etc.*,
1933. 8°.   F. 1267. k. (2.)

— Shadowy Isles. Three-part Song for Ladies' Voices, words by
H. Boulton. Music arranged from the Gaelic by F. W. Lewis.
Boosey & Co.: London and New York, 1931. 8°.
[*Boosey's Modern Festival Series, No. 213.*]   F. 160. f.

— Introit: "Thou wilt keep him in perfect Peace" and Vesper,
etc. *Weekes & Co.: London*, 1910. 8°.   F. 231. aa. (9.)

LEWIS (Fred)

— *See* Strauss (J.) *the Younger.* [Die Fledermaus.] Oh,
Rosalinda!! Piano selection ... Arranged by F. Lewis. [1956.]
4°.   g. 1413. c. (8.)

LEWIS (G. H.)

— "Anthem gwynfyd." Rhangan. Geiriau gan Isgaer. [Tonic
sol-fa notation.] *In:* Y Cerddor. rhif 324. suppl. pp. 1–3.
[1915.] 8°.   P. P. 1947. l.

LEWIS (G. H. Sunderland)

— The Boys will soon be back. Patriotic Song. Words and
Music by G. H. S. Lewis. *E. Donajowski: London*, [1900.] fol.
H. 1799. h. (55.)

— Six Christmas Carols ... 1. Christian Men in Christian
Dwelling. 2. By Angels, bright Angels. 3. Of the Father's
Love begotten. 4. It came upon the Midnight clear. 5. Angels
from the Realms of Glory. 6. What means this Glory round
our Feet? *Weekes & Co.: London*, [1903.] 8°.
D. 619. v. (13.)

— Close the Book. Song, the words by F. M. Hueffer. *Boosey &
Co.: London and New York*, 1903. fol.   H. 1799. vv. (46.)

— Fighting for England. Song. Words and Music by G. H. S.
Lewis. *E. Donajowski: London*, [1898.] fol.
H. 1799. h. (56.)

LEWIS (G. H. Sunderland)

— Give a Man a Horse. Song, the words by J. Thomson.
Boosey & Co.: London and New York, 1903. fol.
H. 1799. vv. (47.)

— In the old Plantation. Song, words and music by G. H. S.
Lewis. *Weekes & Co.: London*, [1905.] fol.   H. 1794. l. (10.)

— Songs without Sense ... written and composed by G. H. S.
Lewis. 2 no. *Novello, Ewer and Co.: London & New York*,
[1888.] 8°.   E. 1761. e. (8.)

— Take a cheerful View. Song from "Prince Eucalyptus,"
written and composed by G. H. S. Lewis. *Weekes & Co.:
London*, [1903.] fol.   H. 1799. vv. (48.)

— To-Night the Stars are shining. A Christmas Part-Song,
words and music by G. H. S. Lewis. *Weekes & Co.: London*,
[1903.] 8°.   F. 1171. ee. (33.)

LEWIS (G. P.)

— A grand sonata for the harp, with a favorite rondo. Op. 1.
Dublin, [1814.] fol.   h. 117. (23.)

LEWIS (George)

— Checkers. March & two step. [P. F.] pp. 5. *Whaley, Royce &
Co.: [Toronto*, 1906.] fol.   h. 4120. pp. (21.)

LEWIS (George E.)

— Hymn Tune and Double Chant. *Novello and Co.: London*,
etc., 1901. *a card.*   I. 600. a. (195.)

LEWIS (George F.)

— I sing you Songs of Love. Song, written & composed by
G. F. Lewis. *Parker-Charles Music Publishing Co.: London*,
1919. 4°.
The Parker-Charles Series of popular publications, etc. No. 5.
G. 426. i. (10.)

— A Last Request. Song, written by L. Webb, *etc. Clifford &
Co.: London*, [1915.] fol.   H. 1793. t. (37.)

— The Prince of Peace. A Christmas Carol, words by T. H.
Lewis. *Whitehall Music Co.: London*, 1925. 8°.
E. 1498. t. (27.)

— When Britannia calls to Arms. Song, written by F. Foster.
Clifford & Co.: London, (1914.) fol.   H. 1793. t. (38.)

— *See* Briggs (A. C.) and Lewis (G. F.) Dear Love o' mine, *etc.*
1919. fol.   H. 1846. h. (27.)

— *See* Miller (B.) and Lewis (G. F.) Homeland, *etc.* [1915.] fol.
H. 1793. x. (32.)

LEWIS (George G.)

— The E. C. S. Song Book for Singing Classes in connection
with Evening Continuation ... Schools. Edited by G. G.
Lewis. Both Notations. *J. Curwen & Sons: London*, [1899.]
8°.   E. 1766. i. (3.)

— *See* Longhurst (H.) and Lewis (G. G.) Caractacus ... A
juvenile operetta, *etc.* (Staff notation edition.) [1924?] 8°.
E. 100. j. (7.)

— *See* Longhurst (H.) and Lewis (G. G.) Caractacus ... A
juvenile operetta, *etc.* [Tonic sol-fa.] [1932?] 8°.
B. 418. xx. (8.)

— *See* Longhurst (H.) and Lewis (G. G.) The Dance of the
Vampires, *etc.* 1897. fol.   h. 3286. g. (56.)

— *See* Longhurst (H.) and Lewis (G. G.) The Graphic Trios,
etc. [1898.] 8°.   B. 570. g. (3.)

LEWIS (George G.)

— *See* Longhurst (H.) and Lewis (G. G.) Hindoo Maidens, *etc.* [1900.] fol.　　　　　　　　　**H. 1984. c. (19.)**

— *See* Longhurst (H.) and Lewis (G. G.) King Arthur. A Juvenile Operetta, *etc.* 1896. 8°.　　　　**F. 1271. a. (4.)**

— *See* Longhurst (H.) and Lewis (G. G.) A Night in a Dormitory, *etc.* 1898. fol.　　　　　**H. 1984. c. (20.)**

— *See* Longhurst (H.) and Lewis (G. G.) Onward March, *etc.* 1900. fol.　　　　　　　　　**H. 1984. c. (21.)**

— *See* Longhurst (H.) and Lewis (G. G.) Pink-a-Pong, *etc.* 1898. fol.　　　　　　　　　**H. 1984. c. (22.)**

LEWIS (Gwen)

— The Foe is "Made in Germany". Song ... words by E. L. Shute, *etc.* *Kibble & Co.: London*, 1914. fol.
　　　　　　　　　　　　　　　H. 1793. t. (39.)

— If only —. [Musical monologue.] Written, composed ... by G. Lewis. *Reynolds & Co.: London*, 1931. fol.
[*Musical Monologues. No. 360.*]　　　　**H. 2087.**

— My Love is dead. Song, with violin or violoncello obbligato, words by A. I. M. S. *Stanley Lucas & Co.: London & Leipzig*, [1893.] fol.　　　　　　**G. 805. aa. (23.)**

— Sunshine Album. Words by M. Elliott, *etc.* *Reynolds & Co.: London*, 1936. 4°.
[*Reynolds & Co.'s 2/6 Series of Concert Party Albums. No. 14.*]
　　　　　　　　　　　　　　　G. 821. a.

— Well, I didn't. [Musical monologue.] Words by M. Constanduros, *etc.* *Reynolds & Co.: London*, 1941. 4°.
[*Musical Monologues. No. 450.*]　　　　**H. 2087.**

LEWIS (H. A.)

— How beautiful upon the Mountains. [Anthem.] [1892.] *See* Choral. The Choral Handbook. No. 282. [1885, *etc.*] 8°.
　　　　　　　　　　　　　　　E. 862.

— How beautiful upon the Mountains. [Anthem. Tonic sol-fa and staff notation.] 2 no. [1895.] *See* Anthems. Anthems of Praise. No. 43. [1892, *etc.*] 8°.　　　**E. 336.**

LEWIS (H. Merrills)

— They led my Lord away. For Chorus of Men's Voices. Adapted from a Negro Spiritual and arranged by H. M. Lewis. *Galaxy Music Corporation: New York*, 1937. 8°.
　　　　　　　　　　　　　　　E. 602. vv. (29.)

— *See* Bach (J. S.) [Jesu, nun sei gepreiset.—Woferne du den edlen Frieden.] As Thou hast bestowed Thy heavenly Peace ... [Organ.] Arranged by H. M. Lewis. [1952.] 4°.
　　　　　　　　　　　　　　　g. 699. d. (10.)

LEWIS (H. R.)

— U. C. S. Football Song, words by J. Russell. *Games Club, University College School: London*, [1907.] 4°.
U. C. S. School Songs, No. 4.　　　**F. 607. ee. (12.)**

LEWIS (Harold)

— *See* Lieurance (T.) From an Indian Village, *etc.* (Transcribed by H. Lewis.) 1921. 4°.　　　**g. 1127. h. (21.)**

LEWIS (Harold Clare)

— The Sailor's Grave. Song, words by the Rev. H. F. Lyte. *Harrison & Harrison: Birmingham*, [1888.] fol.
　　　　　　　　　　　　　　　H. 1788. v. (59.)

LEWIS (Henry)

— Musica. B. M. Additional MS. 14905. [A facsimile with a preface by H. Lewis.] 1936. 8°. *See* England.— *British Library Reference Division.*　　　　　　　**g. 2.**

LEWIS (Henry) *Songwriter*

— *See* Creamer (Henry) The Bombo-shay. Song. ⟨By⟩ H. Creamer, H. Lewis, *etc.* [1917.] fol.　**H. 3990. kk. (1.)**

— *See* Creamer (Henry) Follow me around. Song. ⟨By⟩ H. Creamer, H. Lewis, *etc.* [1917.] fol.　**H. 3990. kk. (3.)**

LEWIS (Henry A.)

— *See* Beaumont (　　　) Sweet the Moments ... Quartette ... arranged ... by H. A. Lewis. (1914.) 8°.　**E. 602. dd. (1.)**

LEWIS (Henry King)

— Praise Notes. Song. The Words ... by C. E. Mudie. *Novello, Ewer & Co.: London & New York*, [1897.] fol.
　　　　　　　　　　　　　　　G. 517. j. (19.)

— Songs for little Singers in the Sunday School and Home. Second edition. *London*, 1881. 8°.　　**F. 636. b.**

— Songs for Little Singers in the Sunday School and Home. Fourth Edition. *Simpkin, Marshall & Co.: London*, 1896. 8°.
　　　　　　　　　　　　　　　F. 1581.

LEWIS (Henry Vincent)

— A happy new year, song. [Begins: "The new year's come on charger bold".] *Liverpool*, [1858.] fol.　**H. 1771. l. (24.)**

— The Ocean Queen waltz. [P. F.] *London*, [1882.] fol.
　　　　　　　　　　　　　　　h. 3275. j. (35.)

— Seven Sacred Songs. Words by ... Mrs. J. Gray. *London*, [1865?] fol.　　　　　　　　　　　**H. 2043.**

— They may talk of their flowers, ballad ... the words by M^rs. Gray. *Liverpool*, [1858.] fol.　　**H. 1771. l. (25.)**

— *See* Field (R.) The Labour Marseillaise ... Arranged by H. V. Lewis. [1896.] fol.　　　　**H. 1798. k. (13.)**

LEWIS (*Lady* Herbert)

— *See* Lewis (Ruth) *Lady.*

LEWIS (Howell Elvet)

— Songs of Victory: for mission, anniversary, and other special services ... Edited by Rev. H. E. Lewis. *Hughes & Son: Wrexham*, [1908.] 8°.　　　　　　**D. 619. cc. (9.)**

— Songs of Victory ... Edited by Rev. H. E. Lewis. Sol-fa. *Hughes and Son: Wrexham*, [1908.] 8°.　**B. 591. c. (3.)**

LEWIS (Howell Elvet) and **ROBERTS** (Caradog)

— Rhaglen cymanfa ganu ganmlwyddiant y Parch. E. Stephen a'i gydweithwyr yng nghaniadaeth y cysegr Ieuan Gwyllt a J. Ambrose Lloyd: gydag emynau Cymraeg a Seisneg. Dan olygiaeth y Parch. H. Elvet Lewis ... a Caradog Roberts, *etc.* [With a portrait of E. Stephen. Tonic sol-fa notation.] pp. 48. *Lyfrfa yr Annibynwyr: Abertawe*, 1922. 8°.　**C. 531. ll. (1.)**

LEWIS (Idris)

— Alawon Cymru. Wedi eu trefnu i S. A. T. B. gan Idris Lewis. Ynghyd â geiriau newydd gan Wil Ifan. ⟨Solffa.⟩ pp. 16. *Cerdd y Castell: Caerdydd*, [1948.] 8°.　**C. 273. gg. (3.)**

— Blue Nile. Words by Dion Titheradge ... Song fox-trot featured in 'Fires of Fate', *etc.* pp. 5. *Hawkes & Son: London*, [1932.] fol.　　　　　　　**G. 1415. (36.)**

LEWIS (Idris)

— Brethyn cartref. S. A. T. B. Geiriau gan Crwys. Hen alaw Gymreig. O drefniant Idris Lewis. pp. 4. *Joseph Williams: London,* [c. 1945.] 8°.   **F. 1974. i. (14.)**

— Bugail Aberdyfi. (Sweet Gwen of Aberdovey.) Can i soprano neu denor. Geiriau (o "Alun Mabon") gan Geiriog. English words by Wil Ifan. [Staff and tonic sol-fa notation.] *Welsh & Eng.* pp. 5. *Snell & Sons: Swansea,* [1943.] 4°.
G. 1311. d. (23.)

— Bugail Aberdyfi. Arranged for S. A. T. B. Y geiriau gan Ceiriog. [Tonic sol-fa notation.] pp. 4. *Snell & Sons: Swansea,* [1948.] 8°.   **C. 273. mm. (39.)**

— Cân yr arad goch. The song of the plough. [Song.] Y geiriau Cymraeg gan Ceiriog. English translation by Gwili. [Staff and tonic sol-fa notation.] *Hughes & Son: Wrexham,* [1922.] fol.   **H. 1634. f. (31.)**

— Clychau Cantre'r Gwaelod. Song. I soprano neu denor. Geiriau gan J. J. Williams. [Staff and tonic sol-fa notation.] pp. 7. *Snell & Sons: Swansea,* [1941.] 4°.   **G. 1311. c. (18.)**

— Cymru'n un. Welsh air. [Part-song.] Arranged for male chorus, tenor solo and piano ... Words by D. Lloyd George. pp. 7. *Snell & Sons: Swansea,* [1934.] 8°.   **E. 626. j. (22.)**

— Dyddiau ysgol. School-days. Cân unsain neu rhan-gan i. S. A. Unison song or part-song for S. A. [Words by] Wil Ifan. [Staff and tonic sol-fa notation.] *Welsh & Eng.* pp. 4. *Gwynn Publishing Co.: Llangollen,* [1939.] 8°.   **F. 217. aa. (6.)**

— Ein dyled i'r Nadolig. [Carol.] For unaccompanied voices. Geiriau gan W. D. Williams. *Snell & Sons: Swansea,* [1943.] 8°.   **F. 1974. i. (1.)**

— Ein dyled i'r Nadolig. [Carol.] For unaccompanied voices, *etc.* [Tonic sol-fa notation.] *Snell & Sons: Swansea,* [1943.] *s. sh.* 8°.   **C. 273. mm. (18.)**

— Fy nghariad mwyn. Love's Poem. Welsh words by Ceiriog, English words by H. Ege. Arranged for Male Voices, by M. Williams. *J. B. Cramer & Co.: London,* 1938. 4°. [*Cramer's Choral Library. No.* 40.]   **F. 157. d.**

— Geneth y fro. Cân, geiriau gan Ceiriog, *etc. D. J. Snell: Swansea,* [1914.] fol.   **H. 1793. t. (40.)**

— Gogoniant i Gymru. Alaw Gyrmeig tref. i S. S. A. ... Geiriau gan "Talhaearn". pp. 7. *Snell & Sons: Swansea,* [1937.] 8°.
E. 626. j. (23.)

— Gogoniant i Gymru. Alaw Gymreig tref i S. S. A., *etc.* [Tonic sol-fa notation.] pp. 3. *Snell & Sons: Swansea,* [1937.] 8°.
C. 273. mm. (40.)

— Green Lawns. Round Dance. Welsh Folk-Song arranged for Piano [by] I. Lewis. *Keith Prowse & Co.: London,* 1935. 4°.
g. 823. c. (3.)

— Home again. Song. The lyric by Helen Taylor. pp. 7. *Boosey & Co.: Paris, etc.; printed in England,* [1934.] fol.
G. 425. jj. (14.)

— Hwyrnos. (Evening.) An old Welsh air. Arranged by Idris Lewis. Words by T. Rowland Hughes. [Staff and tonic sol-fa notation.] *Welsh & Eng.* pp. 5. *Hughes & Son: Cardiff,* [1944.] 4°.   **G. 1311. d. (21.)**

— Llanstephan. (Over the sea to white Llanstephan.) Trefniant o hen alaw Gymreig gan Idris Lewis. Geiriau Wil Ifan. [Staff and tonic sol-fa notation.] *Welsh & Eng.* pp. 7. *Hughes & Son: Wrexham,* [1947.] 4°.   **G. 1311. a. (9.)**

— Love's Poem. [Song.] Words by Henrik Ege. Welsh words by Ceiriog. *Eng. & Welsh.* pp. 7. *J. B. Cramer & Cᵒ.: London,* [1934.] fol.
With a separate leaf, containing the words in English and Welsh, inserted.   **G. 425. jj. (15.)**

LEWIS (Idris)

— Mab y mynydd. Can i mezzo-soprano neu baritone. Y geiriau gan Eifion Wyn. [Staff and tonic sol-fa notation.] pp. 5. *Snell & Sons: Swansea,* [1934.] 4°.   **G. 1311. c. (19.)**

— Meadow Flowers. Blodau'r maes. Song, Welsh words by Prof. T. J. Williams, English words by B. Morgan. *Joseph Williams: London,* 1937. 4°.   **G. 1270. nn. (27.)**

— Morning Song. (Plygeingan.) [Song.] Words by Osyth Cay. Welsh words by Talhaearn. [Staff and tonic sol-fa notation.] *Eng. & Welsh.* pp. 5. *Chappell & Cᵒ.: London,* [1936.] fol.
G. 425. jj. (16.)

— My Heart's in the Homeland. Adgofion. Song, Welsh words by Ceiriog, English words by G. H. Clutsam. Music arr. from an old Welsh Air by I. Lewis. *Keith Prowse & Co.: London,* 1935. 4°.   **G. 981. o. (2.)**

— Roundabouts and Swings. Song. Words by Patrick Chalmers. pp. 7. *Keith Prowse & Cᵒ.: London,* [1934.] fol.
G. 425. jj. (17.)

— A Song of Exile. Mynyddoedd hen fy ngwlad. Song, Welsh lyric by Alafon, English lyric by L. Griffiths. *Keith Prowse & Co.: London,* 1937. 4°.   **G. 1270. nn. (28.)**

— Song of the Exile. (Cân yr alltud.) [Song.] English and Welsh words by A. G. Prys-Jones. [Staff and tonic sol-fa notation.] pp. 6. *Ascherberg, Hopwood & Crew: London,* [1943.] 4°.
G. 1311. d. (22.)

— Y Wennol gyntaf. Can i soprano neu denor. Geiriau gan Hiraethog. [Staff and tonic sol-fa notation.] pp. 5. *Snell & Sons: Swansea,* [1934.] 4°.   **G. 1311. c. (20.)**

— Ystrad Fflur. "Strata Florida." (A part-song for S. A. T. B.) Words by T. Gwynn Jones ... English translation by the author. pp. 4. *University Council of Music and the University of Wales Press Board: Cardiff,* 1944. 8°. *Y Cerddor N. S.* 120.   **P.P. 1947. l.**

— *See* Hughes (Richard S.) Elen fwyn ... Arranged for T. T. B. B. by I. Lewis. [1952.] 8°.   **F. 1965. (16.)**

— *See* Hughes (Richard S.) Elen fwyn ... Arranged for male voices by I. Lewis. [Tonic sol-fa notation.] [1952.] 8°.
C. 273. mm. (27.)

— *See* Roberts (John) *of Aberdare.* Alexander ... Arranged by I. Lewis. 1938. 8°.   **F. 1176. k. (52.)**

LEWIS (J.)

— *See* Strauss (J.) *the Younger.* [An der schönen blauen Donau.] Beautiful Danube galop. (Arranged by J. Lewis.) [1874.] fol.   **h. 3193. a. (13.)**

LEWIS (J. Edward)

— The Reaper and the Flowers. Song ... the poetry by Longfellow. *Novello, Ewer & Co.: London & New York,* 1893. fol.   **G. 805. aa. (24.)**

LEWIS (J. Kinnersley)

— Britannia Series. Two-Part Songs, edited by K. Lewis. Tonic Sol-fa edition. Part 1. No. 1. Silvery Sea. No. 2. Men of Harlech. No. 3. Calm is the Hero's Breast. No. 4. The Merry Men of Sherwood. No. 5. Peace; good night. No. 6. Song to my Steed. *J. K. Lewis: London,* 1893. 8°.
A later edition is entered under Lewis (*J. Kinnersley*) *and* Donald (*H. A.*).   **D. 1080. a. (10.)**

— Sons of Erin. Song ... words & music by K. Lewis. *Cramer, Wood & Co.: Dublin,* [1892.] fol.   **H. 1797. o. (38.)**

— Star Series. Two Part Songs, edited by K. Lewis. Complete Series. Tonic Sol-fa edition. *J. K. Lewis: London,* 1892. 8°.
C. 756. (7.)

LEWIS (J. Kinnersley)

— Star Series. Two Part Songs ... New Edition. Tonic Sol-fa. *J. K. Lewis: London*, 1893. 8°.   **C. 756. (8.)**

LEWIS (J. Kinnersley) and **DONALD** (H. A.)

— Britannia Series. Two-Part Songs, edited by K. Lewis and H. A. Donald. Tonic Sol-fa edition. *J. K. Lewis: London*, [1897.] 8°.
An earlier edition, edited by J. Kinnersley Lewis only, is entered under his name.   **D. 1080. a. (11.)**

LEWIS (James Henry)

— Allegro Pomposo, for the Amercian Organ. *London Music Press: London*, 1912. fol.   **h. 2731. t. (29.)**

— Benedicite, omnia opera ... in chant form. *Novello, Ewer and Co.: London and New York*, [1891.] 8°.   **F. 1170. g. (25.)**

— Benedictus and Agnus Dei. *London*, [1885.] *s. sh.* 8°.   **E. 597. i. (16.)**

— Kyries with Gloria Tibi and Gratias by eminent composers ... Edited by J. H. Lewis. [*London*, 1883.] 8°.   **E. 1451.**

— Love's Message. Song, words by W. Whitacre. *Novello, Ewer & Co.: London & New York*, [1897.] fol.   **G. 805. aa. (25.)**

— Magnificat and Nunc Dimittis ... in ... B♭. *Novello, Ewer & Co.: London & New York*, [1887.] 8°.   **F. 1170. d. (17.)**

— Magnificat and Nunc Dimittis ... in ... F. *Novello, Ewer and Co.: London & New York*, [1891.] 8°.   **E. 597. n. (22.)**

— The Maiden's Bower. Serenade for four voices, words by E. Holmes. [1897.] *See* UNION. The Union Choralist, *etc.* No. 45. [1882, *etc.*] 8°.   **F. 687.**

— March Royal for the Organ. *Novello, Ewer & Co.: London & New York*, 1897. obl. fol.   **f. 314. f. (18.)**

— The Marionettes. Sketch for the pianoforte. pp. 5. *London Music Press: London*, [c. 1900.] fol.   **h. 3865. xx. (5.)**

— A Memory of Home. Sketch for the Pianoforte. *B. Williams: London*, 1912. fol.   **h. 3284. g. (24.)**

— Te Deum laudamus, chantwise. *Novello and Co.: London*, [1899.] 8°.   **C. 799. e. (14.)**

LEWIS (John)

— Jazz Ostinato. [For orchestra.] Score. pp. 32. *MJQ Music: New York*, [1969.] 8°.   **f. 641. n. (3.)**

— Little David's Fugue. [For S. S. A. A. T. T. B. B. with vibraphone, piano, bass and drums. Score.] pp. 16. *MJQ Music: New York*, [1969.] fol.   **G. 1271. ee. (5.)**

— The Spiritual. [For orchestra.] Score. pp. 32. *MJQ Music: New York*, [1969.] 8°.   **f. 641. n. (2.)**

LEWIS (*Sir* John Herbert)

— Emyn-donau: sef casgliad o donau ac emynau at wasanaeth cynnulleidfaoedd Cymreig. Yn y ddau nodiant. [Tunes by Sir John H. Lewis, harmonized by David Evans.] pp. 24. [1919.] 8°. *See* HYMNS. [*Welsh.*]   **D. 619. qq. (26.)**

LEWIS (John Leo)

— Come, Thou long-expected Jesus. For four-part chorus of mixed voices. [Words by] Charles Wesley, *etc.* pp. 7. *G. Schirmer: New York*, [1962.] 8°.   **E. 335. jj. (17.)**

— For ever, O Lord. For four-part chorus of mixed voices with organ or piano accompaniment. From Psalm 119. pp. 7. *G. Schirmer: New York*, [1959.] 8°.   **E. 335. y. (8.)**

LEWIS (John Leo)

— God who made the Earth. For unison or two-part chorus with organ or piano accompaniment ... [Words by] Sarah Betts Rhodes. pp. 3. *G. Schirmer: New York*, [1958.] 8°.   **E. 335. u. (20.)**

— Lamb of God, I look to Thee. For two-part chorus of treble voices with organ or piano accompaniment. [Words by] Charles Wesley, *etc.* pp. 6. *G. Schirmer: New York*, [1962.] 8°.   **E. 335. jj. (18.)**

— Lead on, O King eternal. Anthem for S. A. T. B. [Words by] E. W. Shurtleff. pp. 6. *H. W. Gray Co.: New York*, [1962.] 8°.   **E. 335. dd. (35.)**

— Lord Jesus, think on me. [Anthem.] For four-part chorus of mixed voices a cappella. [Words from] Synesius, c. 375–430. pp. 4. *G. Schirmer:* [*New York*, 1960.] 8°.   **E. 335. z. (13.)**

— Mister Jones. For four-part mixed voices S. A. T. B. Words by Marion James. pp. 7. *Remick Music Corporation: New York*, [1960.] 8°.   **F. 1744. cc. (18.)**

— O God, the Protector. For S. A. T. B. mixed chorus. Words from the Book of Common Prayer. pp. 7. *Walton Music Corporation: North Hollywood*, [1962.] 8°.   **E. 335. ee. (26.)**

— O Lord, the Hope of Israel. For four-part chorus of mixed voices. Jeramiah [*sic*] 17 : 13, 14. pp. 4. *G. Schirmer: New York*, [1961.] 8°.   **E. 335. bb. (39.)**

— O Thou, from whom all Goodness flows. For four-part chorus of mixed voices. [Words by] Marion James, based on Thomas à Kempis, *etc.* pp. 8. *G. Schirmer: New York*, [1960.] 8°.   **E. 335. z. (14.)**

— Save me, O God, by Thy Name. (Psalm 54.) For four-part chorus of mixed voices, *etc.* pp. 8. *G. Schirmer: New York*, [1962.] 8°.   **E. 335. ii. (13.)**

— Soldiers of Christ, arise. For four-part chorus of mixed voices. [Words by] Charles Wesley, *etc.* pp. 8. *G. Schirmer: New York*, [1961.] 8°.   **E. 497. dd. (3.)**

— There is a Land. For four-part chorus of mixed voices a cappella. [Words by] Isaac Watts. pp. 7. *G. Schirmer: New York*, [1963.] 8°.   **E. 335. ll. (20.)**

— There's a Wideness in God's Mercy. Anthem for S. A. T. B. [Words by] F. W. Faber, *etc.* pp. 8. *H. W. Gray Co.: New York*, [1965.] 8°.   **E. 335. ww. (17.)**

— To Bethlem Shepherd-Brethren ran. Christmas carol for S. A. T. B. Words of a Greek sticheron, translated by G. R. W. pp. 4. *H. W. Gray Co.: New York*, [1959.] 8°.   **F. 260. o. (25.)**

— Verdant Pastures. For organ ... based on John Stainer's "God so loved the World". pp. 5. *G. Schirmer: New York*, [1959.] 4°.   **g. 1380. nn. (13.)**

— We sing of God. Anthem for mixed voices. [Words by] Christopher Smart, 1765. pp. 11. *H. W. Gray Co.: New York*, [1954.] 8°.   **E. 335. q. (17.)**

— A Wonder. For junior choir, unison, with optional descant and keyboard accompaniment. pp. 4. *Galaxy Music Corp.: New York; Galliard: London*, [1966.] 8°.   **E. 353. g. (4.)**

LEWIS (Joker)

— Lady Windermere. Waltzes. [P. F.] *M. Witmark & Sons: New York*, 1893. fol.   **h. 3285. q. (46.)**

— Mother's Eventide. Song, words by J. Arthur. *A. & S. Nordheimer: Montreal, etc.*, 1896. fol.   **G. 805. aa. (26.)**

LEWIS (JOSEPH)

— Comfortable Words. An Oratorio from the Oratorios. Music from Handel and Mendelssohn. Compiled and edited by J. Lewis. Staff and Sol-fa. *Paterson's Publications: London, Edinburgh*, 1934. 8°. **F. 1269. tt. (5.)**

— Old Favourites. Arranged for Mixed (Female) Voices ... Compiled by J. Lewis. 2 no. *Ascherberg, Hopwood & Crew: London*, 1939. 8°.
[*Ascherberg's Series of Part Songs. No.* 67, 70.] **F. 1659. a.**

— *See* SUNDAY. Sunday at Home. (Songs and Piano Pieces.) [With an introduction by J. Lewis.] [1943.] 4°.
F. 1176. q. (2.)

LEWIS (JOSEPH RHYS) called ALAW RHONDDA

— Y Carwr siomedig: (cân i denor) ... Y geiriau gan Mynyddog. Yn y ddau nodiant. pp. 5. *Hughes & Son: Wrexham*, [c. 1880.] fol. **H. 1634. o. (31.)**

— Cymru rydd. A song. The poetry by the late Mynyddog. [Staff and tonic sol-fa notation.] pp. 5. *Hughes & Son: Wrexham*, [c. 1880.] fol. **H. 1634. f. (32.)**

— Y Ferch a'r lloer. [Song.] Y geiriau gan Mynyddog. [Staff and tonic sol-fa notation.] pp. 3. *Hughes & Son:* [*Wrexham*, c. 1890.] 4°. **G. 1311. a. (7.)**

— Hen alawon gwlad y gan. Cân i denor. Y geiriau gan Mynyddog ... Yn y ddau nodiant. pp. 7. *Hughes & Son: Wrexham*, [c. 1900.] fol. **H. 1634. f. (33.)**

— Murmur Rhondda, *etc.* [Tonic sol-fa notation.] rhan 3. *Yr Awdwr: Ferndale*, [c. 1900.] 8°.
Imperfect; rhan 3 only. **B. 7. k. (9.)**

— [Murmur Rhondda.] Nazareth ... [Hymn.] English words translated from Pantycelyn's hymn, "Dros bechadur," by Silurian. ⟨72nd thousand.⟩ *Welsh & Eng. The Composer: Ferndale*, [c. 1905.] *s. sh.* 8°. **I. 601. (41.)**

— [Murmur Rhondda.] Nazareth, *etc.* [Hymn.] *Welsh & Eng. Snell & Sons: Swansea*, [1941.] *s. sh.* 8°. **E. 626. ff. (7.)**

— Nazareth. *See supra*: [Murmur Rhondda.]

— The Saviour's Voice. (Llais yr Iesu), *etc.* ⟨English words translated by Alaw Rhondda.⟩ [Song. Staff and tonic sol-fa notation.] *Eng. & Welsh. The Composer: Ferndale*, [c. 1920.] 4°. **H. 1634. d. (1.)**

LEWIS (L. L.)

— Alice. Waltz. [P. F.] *Weekes & Co.: London*, [1884.] fol.
h. 975. v. (37.)

— Flirtation. Waltz. [P. F.] *Weekes & Co.: London*, [1885.] fol.
h. 975. v. (38.)

— Gliding. Waltz. [P. F.] *Enoch & Sons: London*, [1887.] fol.
h. 975. v. (39.)

— Une Pensée, pour le Violon avec accompagnement de Piano. *Wickins & Co.: London*, [1892?] fol.
No. 35 of "Wickins' Violin Literature". **h. 1743. (6.)**

— The Primrose & Blue. Waltz. *Weekes & Co.: London*, [1884.] fol. **h. 975. v. (40.)**

LEWIS (L. W.)

— The Old Log Cabin Home. [Song.] Words & music by L. W. Lewis. pp. 5. *Hamilton S. Gordon: New York*, [1900.] fol. **H. 3985. z. (19.)**

LEWIS (L. WILLIAM)

— A Little Rosebud, for the Pianoforte. *London*, [1860.] fol.
h. 1460. v. (41.)

LEWIS (L. WILLIAM)

— Melodia. Six easily arranged pieces for the Pianoforte. No. 1, 2, 6. *London*, [1860.] fol.
Imperfect; wanting no. 3–5. **h. 1481. c. (13.)**

— The Victoria Regis Polka. [P. F.] *Brighton*, [1860.] fol.
h. 977. f. (35.)

— The Wild Rose. Polka brilliant ... Op. 2. ⟨2nd edition.⟩ [P. F.] pp. 7. *T. Harrison: Birmingham; Metzler & Co.: London*, [1860?] fol. **h. 721. n. (25.)**

— The wild Rose. Polka Brilliant, *etc.* ⟨Op. 2. 4th edition.⟩ [P. F.] pp. 7. *Metzler & Co.: London*, [c. 1860.] fol. **h. 725. q. (14.)**

LEWIS (LEO RICH)

— Caught napping ... Operetta ... words by A. G. Lewis. Old Notation (Tonic Sol-fa) edition. 2 no. *J. Curwen & Sons: London*, [1892.] 8°. **D. 832. c. (5.)**

— For all Thy Saints. Memorial Hymn, men's voices. [Words by] Bishop W. W. How. *O. Ditson Co.:* [*Boston*,] 1906. 8°.
F. 1529. e. (24.)

— Hunt the Thimble; or Little Nell's Surprise Party. A School operetta. Words by A. G. Lewis. *London*, [1886.] 8°.
F. 1272. a. (2.)

— School Songs with College Flavor for high schools and upper-grammar grades, compiled and edited by L. R. Lewis. *Hinds, Noble & Eldredge: New York*, (1904.) 8°. **E. 887.**

— When for me the silent Oar. [Part-song for] Men's voices. Arr. by F. F. B. *O. Ditson Co.: Boston, etc.*, 1897. 8°.
F. 1528. a. (8.)

— When the Mourner, weeping. [Quartet for male voices.] Arr. by F. F. B. *O. Ditson Co.:* [*Boston, etc.*,] 1897. 8°.
F. 1529. b. (37.)

— *See* COLE (S. W.) Melodia ... Course in Singing ... Exercises written and selected by L. R. Lewis. 1910. 8°.
F. 1650. v. (1.)

— *See* LEWIS (A. G.) *Mrs.* and LEWIS (L. R.) The Dairymaids' Supper. A Cantata, *etc.* [1890.] 8°. **D. 832. b. (5.)**

LEWIS (LEONARD)

— Buxton slow Drag. [P. F.] pp. 5. *Leo Feist: New York*, [1905.] fol. **h. 4120. pp. (22.)**

— [A reissue.] Buxton slow Drag. *New York*, [1907.] fol.
h. 4120. pp. (23.)

LEWIS (LEWIS ELWYN)

— Echo, far away. [Part-song, begins: "Within a bow'r a lady gay".] *London*, [1885.] 8°. **F. 585. i. (33.)**

— Magnificat and Nunc dimittis ... in ... A. *Novello and Co.: London*, [1904.] 8°. **E. 597. r. (25.)**

— The Magnificat & Nunc Dimittis ... in ... E flat, for voices chiefly in unison, with organ accompaniment. *Novello, Ewer & Co.: London & New York*, [1889.] 8°. **F. 1170. e. (16.)**

— Magnificat and Nunc dimittis ... in ... E flat, *etc. Novello and Co.: London*, [1923.] 8°. **F. 1158. b. (10.)**

— Magnificat and Nunc dimittis ... in ... F, *etc. Novello and Co.: London*, [1924.] 8°. **E. 597. z. (19.)**

— Magnificat and Nunc Dimittis ... in ... G. *Weekes & Co.: London*, [1899.] 8°. **F. 1170. s. (15.)**

— O let your Songs ... Anthem ... Words taken from the Psalms and a Hymn by the ... Bishop of Wakefield. *Weekes & Co.: London*, [1895.] 8°. **F. 231. f. (16.)**

LEWIS (LEWIS WILLIAM) called LLEW LLWYFO

— Y Bugail dedwydd. (Chorus—The mountaineer.) Trefnedig ... gan Llew Llwyvo. *In:* Greal y corau. suppl. pp. 57–60. 1862. 8°. **1601/349.**

— Can cartref. [Part-song.] Trefnedig ... gan Llew Llwyvo. *In:* Greal y corau. suppl. pp. 79, 80. 1862. 8°. **1601/349.**

— Y Dymuniad ... (Can bedwar llais.) Y geiriau gan Talhaiarn. *In:* Greal y corau. suppl. pp. 101–103. 1863. 8°. **1601/349.**

— Llongau Madog. [Song.] Written by John Ceiriog Hughes ... Melody composed by Llew Llwyfo. Arrangements & accompaniments by W. Jarrett Roberts, *etc.* [Staff and tonic sol-fa notation.] pp. 5. *W. Jarrett Roberts: Carnarvon, Bangor,* [c. 1880.] fol. **H. 1634. f. (49.)**

— Llongau Madog. [Song.] Y geiriau gan John Ceiriog Hughes. Yr alaw gan Llew Llwyfo. Wedi ei threfnu i'r piano gan E. D. Williams. (Argraphiad newydd.) [Staff and tonic sol-fa notation.] pp. 3. *D. J. Snell: Swansea,* [c. 1920.] fol. **H. 1634. k. (27.)**

LEWIS (LIZZIE)

— He doeth all things well. Song [begins: "I hoped that with the brave"]. Words by A. Bronti. *London,* [1876.] fol. **H. 1778. y. (24.)**

— The Streamlet's Song [begins: "A little brook went singing"]. Words by L. R. *London,* [1876.] fol. **H. 1778. y. (23.)**

LEWIS (LORENZO)

— *See* LOCKYEAR (F. W.) The F. O. S. Waltz ... arranged ... by L. Lewis. [1888.] fol. **h. 975. v. (44.)**

LEWIS (M. D.)

— Love Birds. [P. F.] *E. Ascherberg & Co.: London,* 1905. fol. **h. 3282. ww. (40.)**

— Sea Swallows. Waltz. [P. F.] *E. Ascherberg & Co.: London,* (1904.) fol. **h. 3286. dd. (61.)**

LEWIS (M. M.)

— A Dedication. Song ... Music by M. M. L[ewis]. 1915. fol. *See* L., M. M. **H. 1846. x. (5.)**

LEWIS (MARION BEACH)

— Dress Rehearsal. Two-step. [P. F.] pp. 2–5. *Jos. W. Stern & Co.:* [New York, 1903.] fol. **h. 4120. pp. (24.)**

LEWIS (MARY LUCILLE)

— Four Words, I love thee Dear. Song. *J. H. Remick & Co.: New York, Detroit,* (1915.) fol. **H. 1793. t. (41.)**

LEWIS (MATTHEW GREGORY)

— Twelve Ballads. The words and music by M. G. Lewis, with an accompaniment for the harp or piano forte, *etc.* pp. 35. *R[t] Birchall: London,* [1808.] fol. **H. 1416. (3.)**

— [Another copy.] **G. 295. p. (2.)**

— [12 Ballads. No. 5.] The Silly blind Harper, [song] the words and melody by M. G. Lewis ... Arranged with an accompaniment for the harp or piano forte by M[r] Biggs. *R[t] Birchall: London,* [WM1817.] fol. **G. 1277. a. (5.)**

— [12 Ballads. No. 5.] The Silly Blind Harper. [Song.] *See* NATIONAL. National & popular Ballads, *etc.* No. 38. [1863, *etc.*] fol. **H. 1248. a.**

— A Collection of Melodies, chiefly Russian, harmonized, & arranged for the voice, with an accompaniment for the piano

LEWIS (MATTHEW GREGORY)

forte or harp, the words written to them by M[rs] Opie, to which is added, The Cossack, a favourite ballad from the Ukrainian. *R[t] Birchall: London,* [WM1806.] fol. **H. 1652. t. (22.)**

— Evelina's Lullaby, a favorite Ballad. Sung ... at the Theatre Royal Drury Lane by M[rs] Bland. The poetry and music by M. G. Lewis. pp. 4. *Printed for M[rs] Bland & to be had of Mess[rs] Monzani & Cimador: London,* [WM1801.] fol. **H. 2831. a. (14.)**

— He loves and he rides away. A Favorite Ballad, the words and music by M. G. Lewis, Esqr., with an accompaniment for the Harp or Piano Forte. *R. Birchall: London,* [WM 1822.] fol. **H. 1797. pp. (12.)**

— Ply the Oar Brother, the celebrated boat glee ... written & the melody composed by M. G. Lewis ... Harmonized & arranged by Mich[l] Kelly. pp. 6. *At Falkner's Opera Music Warehouse: London,* [c. 1830.] fol. **H. 1601. ii. (8.)**

— Ply the Oar Brother, a celebrated boat glee, written & composed by M. G. Lewis ... Newly arranged with an accompaniment for the piano forte by Ja[s] M[c]Ewen. pp. 4. *Duncombe: London,* [c. 1845.] fol. **H. 1653. v. (12.)**

— The Silly blind Harper. *See* supra: [12 Ballads. No. 5.]

LEWIS (MAY)

— "Our next." Barn Dance. [P. F.] *Weekes & Co.: London,* 1895. fol. **h. 3285. q. (47.)**

LEWIS (MERRILLS)

— A Hymn of Praise. (SATB, organ or wind instruments.) [Words from the Psalms.] pp. 16. *J. Fischer & Bro.: Glen Rock, N. J.,* [1968.] 8°. **F. 1106. b. (46.)**

LEWIS (MICHAEL)

— The Kennington Mass. (Series 2.) [S. A. T. B. and organ.] pp. 8. *Thames Publishing: London,* [1977.] 8°. **D. 835. kk. (3.)**

LEWIS (MICHAEL J.)

— Before we say Goodbye. *See* infra: [The Madwoman of Chaillot.]

— The Lonely Ones. *See* infra: [The Madwoman of Chaillot.]

— The Madwoman of Chaillot ... Motion picture, *etc.* (Souvenir song book.) pp. 32. *Warner Bros.—Seven Arts Music: New York,* [1969.] 4°. **G. 1271. qq. (18.)**

— [The Madwoman of Chaillot.] Before we say Goodbye. [Song.] (Based on the theme from the ... motion picture "The Madwoman of Chaillot".) Words by Al Stillman. pp. 3. *Warner Bros.—Seven Arts Music: New York,* [1969.] 4°. **G. 1271. qq. (16.)**

— [The Madwoman of Chaillot.] The Lonely Ones. [Song] ... Words by Gil King. pp. 3. *Warner Bros.—Seven Arts Music: New York,* [1969.] 4°. **G. 1271. qq. (17.)**

LEWIS (MILTON) and **WEIL** (SANDY)

— Ada. Characteristic song & refrain. Words & music by M. Lewis & S. Weil. pp. 5. *M. Witmark & Sons: New York,* [1905.] fol. **H. 3985. z. (20.)**

LEWIS (MORGAN)

— *See* LEWIS (William M.)

LEWIS (PAUL)

— De New brack Coon. [Song.] Words by Andrew Romeyn, *etc.*
pp. 6.   *Howley, Haviland & Co.: New York*, [1898.] fol.
H. 3980. ss. (5.)

LEWIS (PETE)

— Sing Life sing Love ... [Songs. Edited by] P. Lewis, Roy
Lawrence, Gordon Simpson. Arranged for schools by
William M. Mc Intyre, *etc.* ⟨Pianoforte edition. [Melody
edition.]⟩ 2 no.   *Holmes McDougall: Edinburgh*, [1971.] 8°.
D. 789. m.

LEWIS (PETER)

— Evolution. For chamber orchestra. Full score, *etc.* pp. 48.
Mercury Music Corp.: New York, [1967.] 4°.   **g. 934. c. (9.)**

— Septet. Flute/clarinet/bassoon/piano/violin/viola/cello.
Score, *etc.* pp. 27.   *Merrymount Music: New York*, [1967.] 8°.
e. 668. vv. (5.)

— Septet. Flute/clarinet/bassoon/piano/viola/cello ... Parts.
7 pt.   *Merrymount Music: New York*, [1967.] 4°.
g. 934. j. (1.)

LEWIS (PETER HUGH)

— Y Bugeiliaid a'r Doethion. Cantawd i S. A. T. B. Y geiriau
gan ... E. G. Davies. Y gerddoriaeth gan ... P. H. Lewis.
Sol-fa.   *Telynor Mawddwy: Barmouth*, [1916?] 8°.
C. 799. x. (9.)

— Cân y cwch. [Song.] Y geiriau gan J. J. Williams. [Tonic sol-fa
notation.]   *P. H. Lewis: Barmouth*, [c. 1915.] *s. sh.* 8°.
I. 601. (43.)

— "Dowch ataf Fi." [Hymn.] (S. S. A. B.) Y geiriau gan "L".
[Tonic sol-fa notation.] *In:* Y Lladmerydd. cyf. 12. pp. 29, 30.
1896. 8°.   **P. 101/472.**

— Hosanna'r plant. Cantawd syml i blant. Y geiriau gan y
Parch. D. Adams. pp. 43.   *Yr Awdwr: Pencader*, 1904. 8°.
E. 626. k. (17.)

— Hosanna'r plant, *etc.* [Tonic sol-fa notation.] pp. 28.   *Hughes
a'i Fab: Gwrecsam*, 1910. 8°.   **B. 7. c. (33.)**

— [A reissue.] Hosanna'r plant, *etc.   Gwrecsam*, 1933. 8°.
B. 7. h. (2.)

— O! tyr'd yn ol. Rhangan i S. A. T. B., y geiriau gan R. E. Rees,
etc. [Tonic sol-fa notation.]   [*The Composer:*]
Llanfihangel-ar-Arth, Carm., [1916.] 4°.   **C. 745. f. (16.)**

— "Rwy'n sefyll ar dymhestlog Lan." Rhangan gysegredig i
S. A. T. B. [Words by Ieuan Glan Geirionydd, i. e. Evan
Evans.] Sol-fa.   *Yr Awdwr: Carmarthen*, [1916?] 8°.
B. 559. x. (14.)

— Seren Bethlehem. Rhangan i S. A. T. B. Y geiriau wedi eu
cyfieithu gan Alun. [Tonic sol-fa notation.] pp. 3.   *Yr Awdwr:
Pencader*, [1902.] 8°.   **B. 7. d. (1.)**

— Seren Bethlehem. Rhangan i S. A. T. B., *etc.* ⟨Ail argraffiad.⟩
[Tonic sol-fa notation.] pp. 3.   *P. H. Lewis: Pencader*, [c. 1910.]
8°.   **C. 273. l. (2.)**

— "Seren Bethlehem." "The star of Bethlehem." Rhangan
gysegredig ... Geiriau Cymraeg gan Alun (o H. K. White).
English words by Llew Tegid. [Tonic sol-fa notation.] pp. 4.
Snell & Sons: Swansea, [c. 1935.] 8°.   **C. 273. k. (15.)**

— *See* ROBERTS (David) called TELYNOR MAWDDWY, and LEWIS
(P. H.) Y Tant Aur. Gwers-lyfr, *etc.* [1916?] 8°.
B. 675. j. (3.)

— *See* WALES.— *Undeb yr Annibynwyr Cymreig.— Pwyllgor y
Caniedydd Cynulleidfaol.* [Caniedydd yr Ysgol Sul.]
Caniedydd newydd yr Ysgol Sul ... Y gerddoriaeth o dan
olygiaeth Dr. C. Roberts ... P. H. Lewis. 1930. 8°.   **B. 7. bb.**

LEWIS (PETER HUGH)

— *See* WALES.— *Undeb yr Annibynwyr Cymreig.— Pwyllgor y
Caniedydd Cynulleidfaol.* [Caniedydd yr Ysgol Sul.]
Caniedydd newydd yr Ysgol Sul ... Y gerddoriaeth o dan
olygiaeth Dr. C. Roberts ... P. H. Lewis. 1959. 8°.   **B. 7. aa.**

LEWIS (PETER HUGH) and **ROBERTS** (DAVID) called
TELYNOR MAWDDWY

— Cainc y delyn. ⟨Rhan I.⟩ Deuddeg o hen alawon Cymreig
wedi eu trefnu at wasanaeth chwareuwyr a datganwyr
penillion (yn y ddau nodiant) gan P. H. Lewis ... a
D. Roberts. ⟨Rhan II. Deuddeg o alawon wedi eu casglu gan
Dafydd Roberts a'u trefnu at wasanaeth cyfeilyddion a
gosodwyr gan J. Rhyddid Williams.⟩ 2 rhan.   *Telynor
Mawddwy: Barmouth*, [1915, 60.] 8°.
Rhan 2 bears the imprint of Snell & Sons, Swansea.
F. 636. mm. (9.)
& E. 626. dd. (1.)

LEWIS (R. W.)

— Adieux. Melodie pour le piano.   *C. Herzog & Co.: London*,
[1883.] fol.   **h. 1484. t. (20.)**

— Not alone. Song, words by E. M. A. F. S., *etc.   Weekes & Co.:
London*, [1885.] fol.   **H. 879. e. (17.)**

— Not alone. Song, *etc.   Novello and Co.: London*, [1927.] 4°.
G. 519. m. (33.)

— Primrose. Gavotte for the pianoforte.   *Weekes & Co.:
London*, [1885.] fol.   **h. 1484. t. (21.)**

LEWIS (RALPH C.)

— *See* CHAIKOVSKY (P. I.) [12 Morceaux. Op. 40. No. 2.] Chanson
triste ... (arr.) by ... R. C. Lewis. 1937. 4°.   **g. 557. f. (7.)**

— *See* GOLTERMANN (G. E.) [Concerto in A minor. Op. 14.
Cantilena.] Andante ... (arr.) by ... R. C. Lewis. 1937. 4°.
g. 762. e. (16.)

— *See* SCHUMANN (R. A.) [Kinderscenen. Op. 15. No. 7.]
Träumerei ... (arranged) by ... R. C. Lewis. 1937. 4°.
g. 715. l. (9.)

— *See* WAGNER (W. R.) [Tannhäuser.—O! du mein holder
Abendstern.] Song to the Evening Star ... (Arranged) by
R. C. Lewis. 1938. 4°.   **g. 379. v. (8.)**

LEWIS (RUSSELL)

— The Exile's Song. Words by F. G. Halliwell, *etc.   J. A. Mills:
London*, [1889.] fol.   **H. 1788. uu. (41.)**

— Remember Trafalgar Square! [Song.] Words by
F. G. Halliwell, *etc.   J. A. Mills: London*, [1889.] fol.
H. 1788. uu. (42.)

LEWIS (RUTH) *Lady*

— Folk-Songs collected in Flintshire and the Vale of Clwyd by
Mrs. Herbert Lewis ... Accompaniments by Miss M. Owen,
etc. (Second Collection of Welsh Folk-Songs. Collected by
Lady Herbert Lewis. Accompaniments by M. Owen and
G. G. Davies.) 2 no.   *Hughes and Son: Wrexham*, 1914 [1934].
4°.   **F. 636. jj. (4.)**

LEWIS (S. A.)

— Benedicite, omnia opera ... in ... F.   *Novello, Ewer and Co.:
London & New York*, [1887.] 8°.   **E. 597. k. (18.)**

— Benedicite, omnia opera, No. 2 ... in E.   *Novello, Ewer and
Co.: London & New York*, [1892.] 8°.   **F. 1170. g. (26.)**

LEWIS (S. A. STEELE)

— The Lady-Bird. Waltz for the Pianoforte, *etc. Holloway Music Publishing Stores: London*, [1909.] fol.

h. 3286. vv. (4.)

— Una. Waltz for the Pianoforte. *F. Pitman Hart & Co.: London*, [1907.] fol. **h. 3283. p. (30.)**

LEWIS (S. R.)

— A Hot Rag. Two Step. [P. F.] *S. Brainard's Sons Co.: New York, Chicago*, 1900. fol. **h. 3286. r. (11.)**

LEWIS (SAMUEL)

— S. Lewis's Hallelujah Chorus, for four voices, with an accompaniment for the Organ or Piano Forte. *London*, [1853.] fol. **H. 1183. (14.)**

LEWIS (SAMUEL M.)

— *See* ROSENFELD (Monroe H.) and LEWIS (S. M.) I'm Head and Heels in Love with you. [Song.] Words & music by M. H. Rosenfeld and S. M. Lewis. [1907.] fol.

H. 3986. zz. (49.)

LEWIS (SAMUEL M.) and **ROSENFELD** (MONROE H.)

— 'Tis not the Uniform that makes the Soldier, *etc.* [Song.] ⟨Words and music by S. M. Lewis and M. H. Rosenfeld.⟩ pp. 5. *Jos. W. Stern & Co.: New York, etc.*, [1905.] fol.

H. 3985. z. (21.)

LEWIS (SAMUEL R.)

— Beauty. [Song.] Poem by J. Masefield. *C. C. Birchard & Co.: Boston, New York*, 1927. 4°. **G. 1275. y. (10.)**

— Cape Horn Gospel. [Song.] Poem by J. Masefield. *C. C. Birchard & Co.: Boston, New York*, 1927. 4°.

G. 1275. y. (11.)

— Cargoes. [Song.] Poem by J. Masefield. *C. C. Birchard & Co.: Boston, New York*, 1927. 4°. **G. 1275. y. (12.)**

— Cavalier. A Song ... Poem by J. Masefield. *G. Schirmer: New York*, 1927. 4°. **G. 1275. aa. (12.)**

— I am a Lute. [Song.] Lyrics by J. W. Haywood. *C. C. Birchard & Co.: Boston, New York*, 1928. 4°. **G. 1275. aa. (13.)**

— Memory. [Song.] Poem by A. Symons, *etc. C. C. Birchard & Co.: Boston, New York*, 1921. 4°. **G. 1275. y. (13.)**

— A Night at Dago Tom's. [Song.] Poem by J. Masefield. *C. C. Birchard & Co.: Boston, New York*, 1927. 4°.

G. 1275. y. (14.)

— Roadways. [Song.] Poem by J. Masefield. *C. C. Birchard & Co.: Boston, New York*, 1927. 4°. **G. 1275. y. (15.)**

— Two Songs of the Sea ... 1. On Dover Pier. (J. A. Sterry.) 2. Trade winds. (J. Masefield.) 2 no. *G. Schirmer: New York*, 1928. 4°. **G. 1275. aa. (14.)**

LEWIS (SENECA G.)

— The Colored Cadets. Two-Step. [P. F.] *M. Witmark & Sons: New York & Chicago*, 1899. fol. **h. 3286. g. (47.)**

— Down in Arkansaw. Two-step. [P. F.] pp. 6. *Shapiro, Remick & Co.: Detroit, New York*, [1904.] fol. **h. 4120. pp. (25.)**

LEWIS (SIDNEY)

— *See* LEWES.

LEWIS (SILBY)

— Praise Jesus, Lord and King. A Christmas Carol, words and music by S. Lewis. *Stainer & Bell: London*, 1931. 8°. *Carols, No. 56.* **C. 624. d.**

LEWIS (STEELE)

— *See* LEWIS (S. A. Steele)

LEWIS (THOMAS C.)

— Come buy my images, comic song, words by G. E. C. *London*, [1854.] fol. **H. 1758. (41.)**

— The Cornopeanist, being a selection of airs from operas; also a variety of popular songs, quadrilles ... intended expressly for amateur cornopeanists, selected and arranged by T. C. Lewis. No. 1–6. *London*, [1854.] fol. **h. 2285. (3.)**

— The Flautist, being a selection of airs from ... operas ... for ... amateur flautists, selected and arranged by T. C. Lewis. 6 no. *London*, [1854.] fol. **h. 252. (4.)**

— "Just starve us," comic song, words by W. H. Freeman, music by Auber, adapted by T. C. L[ewis]. [1843.] fol. *See* AUBER (D. F. E.) [Gustave III.—Vive, vive à jamais.] **H. 1260. (1.)**

— Just starve us, a parochial comic song, [begins: "Hear! oh hear us,"] words by Freeman, arranged and adapted [to Vive, vive à jamais from D. F. E. Auber's opera Gustave III] for the piano forte by T. C. Lewis. *London*, [1854.] fol.

H. 1758. (42.)

— Lewis's Times. (Musical Periodical.) Edited by T. C. Lewis. No. 1–20. *Lewis's Times Office: London*, [1854.] fol.

H. 2343.

— The Violinist, being a selection of airs from operas, popular songs, quadrilles ... for amateur violinists. No. 1–6. *London*, [1854.] fol. **h. 217. (6.)**

LEWIS (THOMAS CURLING)

— Advent Litany. *London*, [1878.] 8°. **B. 579. d. (34.)**

— Art thou weary, *etc.* [Hymn.] *Novello and Co.: London*, [1907.] *s. sh.* 8°. **D. 619. aa. (12.)**

— By and By. Song, the words by F. E. Weatherly. *London*, [1880.] fol. **H. 1783. a. (63.)**

— Magnificat and Nunc Dimittis, *etc. London*, [1879.] 8°.

E. 597. a. (12.)

— O God, the Floods are risen ... Anthem for Soprano and Tenor soli and chorus. *Novello, Ewer and Co.: London & New York*, [1894.] 8°. **F. 1171. p. (42.)**

— Our blest Redeemer. Anthem for Whitsuntide, *etc. Novello, Ewer and Co.: London & New York*, [1887.] 8°.

E. 442. j. (39.)

— The Reproaches. Anthem for Good Friday [begins: "O my people"] by ... G. Moultrie. Also Processional hymn for Easter [begins: "Eastward, ever eastward"] by ... S. J. Stone. *London*, [1878.] 8°. **B. 579. d. (35.)**

— The Story of the Cross. [Hymn, begins: "In his own raiment clad".] The verses by ... E. Monro. *London*, [1878.] 8°.

B. 579. d. (36.)

— When my feet have wandered. A Litany of the Passion. The verses by ... Dr. Monsell. *London*, [1884.] 8°.

B. 835. b. (11.)

— Ye men of Galilee. Anthem for Ascensiontide. *London*, [1881.] 8°. **E. 442. d. (26.)**

— *See* HYMNS. [*English.*] Ten Hymn Tunes by ... T. C. Lewis, *etc.* [1894.] 8°. **D. 619. h. (13.)**

LEWIS (TOM)

— "Bugail Israel." ⟨Anthem i blant.⟩ [Tonic sol-fa notation.] pp. 4. *Y Cyfansoddwr: Hendy*, [c. 1950.] 8°. **I. 601. (79.)**

LEWIS (W.)

— Deerfoot Galop ... [P. F.] Arranged by W. Lewis. pp. 5. *Hopwood & Crew: London*, [c. 1870.] fol. **h. 60. j. (6.)**

— *See* PIERNÉ (H. C. G.) "Marche des petits soldats de plomb" ... Arr. [for orchestra] by W. Lewis. [1909.] 8°. [*SMITH* (*Lee O.*) *"Bohemiana."*] **f. 800. a. (345.)**

LEWIS (W. H.)

— Nyniaw. ⟨[Hymn. Words by] E. J.⟩ [Tonic sol-fa notation.] *J. Henry Jones: Port Dinorwic*, [c. 1940.] *s. sh.* 8°. **C. 797. (3.)**

LEWIS (WALTER)

— Dear Heart of mine. Song, words and music by W. Lewis. *Collard Moutrie: London*, 1915. fol. **H. 1793. t. (42.)**

— Dear Heart of mine ... Vocal Duet. *Collard Moutrie: London*, 1916. fol. **H. 1846. y. (15.)**

— Dear Land by the Sea. Song, words & music by W. Lewis. *Collard Moutrie: London*, 1917. fol. **H. 1846. y. (16.)**

— Homeland of mine. Song, words and music by W. Lewis. *Collard Moutrie: London*, 1919. fol. **H. 1846. y. (17.)**

— Little Baby mine. Song, words and music by W. Lewis, *etc.* *Collard Moutrie: London*, 1914. fol. **H. 1793. t. (43.)**

— The Lotus Flower. Song, words & music by W. Lewis. *Collard Moutrie: London*, 1920. fol. **H. 1846. y. (18.)**

— Love's Charm. Song, words and music by W. Lewis. *Collard Moutrie: London*, 1915. fol. **H. 1793. t. (44.)**

— Love's wondrous Garden. Song, words and music by W. Lewis. *Collard Moutrie: London*, 1918. fol. **H. 1846. y. (19.)**

— Songs of Remembrance. 1. Solitude. 2. Do you remember? 3. Laughing eyes. (Words and music) By W. Lewis. *Collard Moutrie: London*, 1924. 4°. **G. 1270. f. (20.)**

— Songs of Sincerity. 1. A world of song. 2. Life's perfect day. 3. Love's eventide. (Words and music) By W. Lewis, *etc.* *C. Moutrie: London*, 1919. 4°. **G. 426. d. (49.)**

— The Verifirst Band Book for Beginners ... Complete System of Instruction, arranged in progressive manner ... Written and compiled by W. Lewis ... Solo B♭ Cornet, *etc.* *J. Church Co.: Cincinnati, etc.*, (1907.) *obl.* 8°. **a. 301. b. (1.)**

LEWIS (WALTER FAY)

— The Cambridge Patrol. Arr. for two Banjos by W. F. Lewis. *O. Ditson Company: Boston, etc.*, 1893. fol. **h. 1971. (42.)**

— Easy Encore Jig, for two Banjos. Arr. by W. F. Lewis. *O. Ditson Company: Boston, etc.*, [1893.] fol. **h. 1971. (41.)**

— Fantaisie Espagnole. (For two Mandolins and Guitar.) *Oliver Ditson Co.: Boston* [*Mass.*], 1893. fol. **h. 188. a. (32.)**

— Harvard Banjo Club Schottische, for two Banjos. Arr. by W. F. Lewis. *O. Ditson Company: Boston, etc.*, 1893. fol. **h. 1971. (39.)**

— Nigger on a Fence. Jig. Arr. for 2 Banjos by W. F. Lewis. *O. Ditson Company: Boston, etc.*, (1893.) fol. **h. 1971. (40.)**

LEWIS (WALTER H.)

— Come, little Bee. [Song.] Words by O. A. Court. *M. Witmark & Sons: New York, etc.*, (1905.) fol. **H. 1937. (4.)**

LEWIS (WALTER H.)

— Down the Garden Alley. [Song.] Words by O. A. Court. *M. Witmark & Sons: New York, etc.*, (1907.) fol. **H. 1937. (6.)**

— The Explorers. A Musical Comedy in Two Acts. Lyrics by B. L. Taylor. [20 detached vocal and instrumental no.] *M. Witmark & Sons:* [*New York, etc.*,] 1901–2. fol. **H. 1937. (1.)**

— [The Explorers.] Selection ... arranged by H. Anderson. [P. F.] *M. Witmark & Sons:* [*New York, etc.*], 1901. fol. **h. 3282. ee. (5.)**

— Had she been kissed before? [Song.] *M. Witmark & Sons: New York, etc.*, (1906.) fol. **H. 1937. (9.)**

— Mammy's little yaller Rose.—A Plantation Lullaby.— [Song.] Words by N. W. Houk. *M. Witmark & Sons: New York, etc.*, (1907.) fol. **H. 1937. (7.)**

— My Lassie. Ballad, words & music by W. H. Lewis. *M. Witmark & Sons: New York, etc.*, (1907.) fol. **H. 1937. (10.)**

— Paquita. Waltz. [P. F.] pp. 7. *M. Witmark & Sons: New York, etc.*, [1905.] fol. **h. 4120. pp. (26.)**

— Pensacola Sue. [Song.] Words by O. A. Court. *M. Witmark & Sons: New York, etc.*, (1907.) fol. **H. 1937. (8.)**

— The Rose that she wore. Ballad & Refrain. *M. Witmark & Sons: New York, etc.*, (1906.) fol. **H. 1937. (5.)**

— The Summer Coquette. March and Two Step. [P. F.] *M. Witmark & Sons:* [*New York, etc.*,] 1902. fol. **h. 3286. y. (31.)**

— Teddy. March Song, words by O. A. Court. *M. Witmark & Sons:* [*New York, etc.*,] 1904. fol. **H. 1937. (2.)**

— Twin Hearts. Intermezzo and two step. [P. F.] pp. 5. *M. Witmark & Sons: New York, etc.*, [1908.] fol. **h. 4120. pp. (27.)**

— When Father rode the Goat. Male Quartet, *etc.* *M. Witmark & Sons: New York, etc.*, (1906.) 8°. **F. 163. e. (20.)**

— Where the Jasmine twines. For Baritone and Male Quartet, words by O. A. Court. *M. Witmark & Sons: New York, etc.*, (1907.) fol. **H. 1937. (11.)**

— Yallelly. [Song.] Words by O. A. Court. *M. Witmark & Sons:* [*New York, etc.*,] 1903. fol. **H. 1937. (3.)**

— *See* LIEURANCE (T.) Maleana ... Arranged ... by W. H. Lewis. 1924. 8°. **F. 163. v. (24.)**

LEWIS (WILLIAM) *Composer of "March on"*

— March on! march on! ... Glee. Words by ... S. B. Raymond. *Chicago*, [1864.] fol. *No. 2 of "Root & Cady's Vocal Quartetts".* **H. 1780. l. (25.)**

LEWIS (WILLIAM) *of Llangyfelach*

— "Bethlehem." Rhangan i blant. (S. S. A. neu S. A. B.) Y geiriau a'r gerddoriaeth gan William Lewis. [Tonic sol-fa notation.] pp. 3. *In:* Y Cerddor. rhif 191. suppl. pp. 1–3. [1904.] 8°. **P. P. 1947. l.**

— Bugail Israel. (Ton i blant.) [Tonic sol-fa notation.] *In:* Y Lladmerydd. cyf. 11. p. 348. 1895. 8°. **P. 101/472.**

— Calfaria. [Hymn.] Geiriau gan Tegfelyn. [Tonic sol-fa notation.] *In:* Y Lladmerydd. cyf. 22. p. 96. 1906. 8°. **P. 101/472.**

— "Canu'r ochr draw." [Hymn.] Geiriau gan W. Jones. [Tonic sol-fa notation.] *In:* Y Lladmerydd. cyf. 9. pp. 285, 286. 1893. 8°. **P. 101/472.**

LEWIS (WILLIAM) *of Llangyfelach*

— Gorphwys yn y bedd. [Hymn. Tonic sol-fa notation.] *In:* Y Lladmerydd. cyf. 19. p. 32. 1903. 8°. **P. 101/472.**

— Llangyfelach. [Hymn.] Geiriau gan y Parch. Hugh Edwards. [Tonic sol-fa notation.] *In:* Y Lladmerydd. cyf. 32. p. 280. 1916. 8°. **P. 101/472.**

— "Y Messiah addawedig." Ton i blant. Y geiriau gan D. Jones. [Tonic sol-fa notation.] *In:* Y Cerddor. rhif 173. suppl. pp. 1–3. [1903.] 8°. **P. P. 1947. l.**

LEWIS (WILLIAM H.)

— Odlau Seion. (Rhan I.) Sef cyfres o donau ac anthemau. [Tonic sol-fa notation.] pp. 20. *W. Gwenlyn Evans: Caernarfon*, [1901.] 8°. **B. 7. k. (4.)**

LEWIS (WILLIAM M.)

— The Inchcape Rock. Ballad by R. Southey ... for Male Voices ... with pianoforte accompaniment, *etc. Linwood Music Publishing Co.: Eastwood, Nottingham*, 1925. 8°. **E. 1592. kk. (3.)**

LEWIS (WILLIAM MORGAN)

— How high the Moon. [Song.] *See infra:* [Two for the Show.]

— [Two for the Show.] How high the Moon. [Song.] Words by Nancy Hamilton. pp. 6. *Chappell: London*, [1979.] 4°. *Part of "Elite Series".* **F. 1680. q. (5.)**

— [Two for the Show.] How high the Moon. S. S. A. T. B., with piano, optional guitar, string bass and drum set. Words by Nancy Hamilton ... Arranged by Chuck Cassey. [Score.] pp. 12. *Chappell & Co.:* [*New York*, 1980.] 8°. **E. 1501. zz. (2.)**

LEWIS-BARNED (HARRY B.)

— *See* BARNED.

LEWITSKAJA (W.)

— *See* LEVITSKAYA (V. S.)

LEWITUS (HANS)

— *See* BACH (J. S.) [Geistliche Lieder aus Schemelli's Gesangbuch und dem Notenbuch der Anna Magdalena Bach.] Geistliche Lieder für Blockflöten-Quartett ... bearbeitet von ... H. Lewitus, *etc.* [1974.] *obl.* 8°. **B. 368. f. (1.)**

LEWKOVITCH (BERNHARD)

— Twelve Motets of the Spanish golden Age. Edited by B. Lewkovitch. pp. 22. *J. & W. Chester: London*, [1971.] 8°. **E. 1439. ee. (2.)**

LEWY (CARL)

— Bud brightly blooming. *See infra:* Three Songs with Pianoforte Accompaniment ... 3.

— For ever thine. (À toi toujours.) Song [begins: "Twas in the dreaming age". "C'était je crois"]. (Paroles françaises du Comte Fredro.) English words by J. Goddard. *London*, [1878.] fol. **H. 1783. o. (64.)**

— Go to Rest. *See infra:* Three Songs with Pianoforte Accompaniment ... 2.

— Impromptu pour Piano. *Leipzig*, [1880.] fol. **h. 3272. j. (27.)**

— Polonaise pour Piano. *Leipzig*, [1877.] fol. **h. 1493. o. (33.)**

LEWY (CARL)

— Song of Spring. *See infra:* Three Songs with Pianoforte Accompaniment ... No. 1.

— Three Songs with Pianoforte Accompaniment ... No. 1. Song of Spring. Frühlingslied. 2. Go to Rest. Geh' zur Ruh! 3. Bud brightly blooming. Neig' schöne Knospe. *Eng. & Ger.* 3 no. *Augener & Co.: London*, [1889.] fol. [*Germania. no.* 430, 429, 428.] **H. 2128.**

— Toccata für Pianoforte. *Leipzig*, [1877.] fol. **h. 1493. o. (32.)**

— Ville Giulia, morceau pour Piano. *Leipzig*, [1880.] fol. **h. 3272. j. (26.)**

— *See* ALVARS (ÉLIE P.) [The Legend of Teignmouth.] Ouverture ... Arrangée pour le piano à quatre mains par C. Lewy. [1842?] fol. **h. 60. v. (6.)**

LEWY (J.)

— Freundschaft oder Liebe. [Song, begins: "Welch ein nie empfund'nes Sehnen".] *See* CONCERTS. Les Concerts de Société. No. 6. [1845, *etc.*] fol. **H. 2085. a.**

LEWY (JOSEPH RUDOLPH)

— [Freundschaft oder Liebe.] "Magic power my soul enthralling." Freundschaft oder Liebe. Op. 7. No. 1. *See* CONCERTS. Les concerts de société for voice and concertina. No. 6. [1854, *etc.*] fol. **H. 2085. d.**

— Das Körbchen [song, begins: "Lieblich fand ich hier"], von Herzenskron. *See* CONCERTS. Les Concerts de Société. No. 7. [1845, *etc.*] fol. **H. 2085. a.**

LEWYN (HELENA)

— To the beloved one. [Song.] Poem by Shell[e]y, *etc. I. Lewyn: Houston, Texas*, (1910.) fol. **H. 1792. s. (25.)**

LEWYS (DYVED)

— Bedd y dyn tylawd. (Rhangan i T. T. B. B.) ⟨Y geiriau gan Ioan Emlyn.⟩ [Staff and tonic sol-fa notation.] pp. 3. *J. R. Lewis: Carmarthen*, [c. 1900.] 8°. **E. 626. k. (16.)**

— "Meibion y bryniau." Gorymdeithgan eisteddfodol i T. T. B. B. Y geiriau a'r gerddoriaeth gan Dyved Lewys. [Tonic sol-fa notation.] pp. 3. *J. R. Lewis: Caerfyrddin*, [c. 1900.] 8°. **C. 273. j. (1.)**

— Pussy and the Mice. [Part-song.] *J. Curwen & Sons: London*, [1899.] 8°. *The Apollo Club. No.* 131. **F. 667.**

LEX, *pseud.*

— The Drowned at Sea. Song [begins: "Never bronze"]. The words by E. H. O. ... Composed by Lex. *London*, [1861.] fol. **H. 1772. r. (47.)**

LEXHIME (J. F.)

— Affection. Adagio pour le violon avec accompt. de piano. *H. Pollack: Barrow in Furness*, [1891.] fol. **h. 1608. x. (42.)**

— Diamond Jubilee. Song, words by T. H. Stephenson. *St. Cecilia Music Publishing Co.: London*, [1897.] fol. **H. 1798. v. (21.)**

— Duet for one violin. *E. Donajowski: London*, [1894.] fol. **h. 1608. x. (43.)**

— God save the King. [Anthem.] *St. Cecilia Music Publishing Co.: London*, [1901.] 8°. **E. 602. u. (30.)**

LEY

— Ley de raza. Canción. *See* FONT Y DE ANTA (Manuel)

LEY (HENRY GEORGE)

— First Album of Songs. Op. 6. (I. Music when soft Voices die. Shelley. II. Christ in a Garden, buried by C. Wordsworth. III. A Cradle Song. J. Hogg. IV. As the Moon's soft Splendour. Shelley. V. A Litany. P. Fletcher. VI. The Call. G. Herbert.) *S. Acott & Co.: Oxford*, [1913.] 8°.   **F. 636. hh. (14.)**

— [First Album of Songs. Op. 6. No. 1.] Music when soft Voices die. Song, *etc.* (Revised edition.) *J. Williams: London*, 1932. 4°.   **G. 1270. dd. (47.)**

— [First Album of Songs. Op. 6. No. 2.] Christ in a Garden buried lay, *etc.* (Revised edition.) *J. Williams: London*, 1932. 4°.   **G. 519. p. (7.)**

— Second Album of Songs ... Op. 8. pp. 29. *Sydney Acott & Co.: Oxford*, [1915.] 8°.
The wrapper bears a MS. dedication to W. H. Hadow in the composer's autograph.   **F. 1965. q. (1.)**

— Third Album of Songs. Poems by Mary Coleridge ... Op. 10. pp. 27. *Sydney Acott & Co.: Oxford*, [1915.] 8°.
The wrapper bears a MS. dedication to W. H. Hadow in the composer's autograph.   **F. 1965. q. (2.)**

— Fourth Album of Songs. Words by R. L. Stevenson & Henry Newbolt. pp. 29. *Sydney Acott & Co.: Oxford*, [1917.] 8°.
The wrapper bears a MS. dedication to W. H. Hadow in the composer's autograph.   **F. 1965. q. (3.)**

— Anthem for a Harvest Festival. [Anthem.] Words: 1928. Prayer Book (Modified). pp. 5. *Oxford University Press: London*, [1947.] 8°.
[*Oxford Series of easy Anthems. no.* 46.]   **F. 1001.**

— Benedicite. *The Faith Press: London*, [1922.] 8°.
    F. 1158. b. (12.)

— A Carol for Christmas. Mixed Voices. [Words by] E. Ley. *Oxford University Press: London*, 1943. 8°.
[*The Oxford Choral Songs. No.* 851.]   **F. 1777. a.**

— Chanticleer. A short choral hymn for Christmas. [Words by] William Austin (1587–1634). ⟨S. A. T. B.⟩ pp. 6. *Oxford University Press: London*, [1951.] 8°.
[*Oxford Series of easy Anthems. no.* 58.]   **F. 1001.**

— A Choral Hymn for Advent or Ascensiontide. Based on the Scottish melody 'Montrose' (1855). Arranged for S. A. T. B. choir and organ by H. G. Ley, *etc.* ⟨Advent words by John Milton (1608–74). Ascensiontide words by Edward Perronet (1726–92) & John Rippon (1751–1836).⟩ pp. 6. *Oxford University Press: London, etc.*, [1952.] 8°.   **F. 1176. f. (15.)**

— Christ in a Garden buried lay. *See* supra: [First Album of Songs. Op. 6. No. 2.]

— Come gentle Shepherds. *See* infra: [Quittez pasteurs.]

— Come, Thou Holy Spirit come. *See* infra: Six Short Anthems for the Seasons of the Church. No. 3.

— Come, Thou long expected Jesus. Anthem for Advent ... [Words by] Charles Wesley, *etc. Oxford University Press: London*, 1937. 8°.
[*The Oxford Series of Easy Anthems. No.* 24.]   **F. 1001.**

— Communion Service in A minor. pp. 12. *Oxford University Press: London*, [1948.] 8°.
[*Oxford Church Music. no.* 515.]   **F. 1777. c.**

— Ninefold Kyrie for Communion Service in A minor. ⟨S. A. T. B.⟩ *Lat. & Eng. Oxford University Press: London*, [1956.] *s. sh.* 8°.
[*Oxford Church Services. S.* 515 *a.*]   **F. 1777. c.**

LEY (HENRY GEORGE)

— [Communion Service in B flat.] (1913.) *See* MARTIN (*Sir* G. C.) Short Settings of the Office for the Holy Communion, *etc.* No. 51. [1883, *etc.*] 8°.   **E. 1433. a.**

— A Short Communion Service for unaccompanied voices. *The Faith Press: London*, [1920.] 8°.   **F. 1158. (20.)**

— The Office of the Holy Communion ... for choir & congregation. *The Faith Press: London and Leighton Buzzard*, [1923.] 8°.   **F. 1158. b. (11.)**

— A Short Communion Service. *Novello & Co.: London*, 1938. 8°.
[*Novello's Parish Choir Book. No.* 1223.]   **E. 618.**

— Cradle Song for Organ. Based on the Christmas carol "Come rock the cradle for Him". pp. 4. *Oxford University Press: London*, [1949.] 4°.   **g. 575. rr. (4.)**

— Credo. For the Communion Service in E minor. *Faith Press: London*, 1927. 8°.   **F. 1158. d. (29.)**

— The Dandelion. Two-part Song ... words by F. Cornford. 1919. *See* AKERMAN (R. F. M.) The Year Book Press Series of Unison and Part-Songs, *etc.* No. 154. 1908, *etc.* 8°.   **F. 223.**

— The Dandelion. Unison Song for treble voices, *etc. H. F. W. Deane & Sons: London*, 1929. 8°.
[*The Year Book Press Series of Unison and Part-Songs. No.* 322.]   **F. 223.**

— Dirge. Words by Shelley ... for S. A. T. B. ... Op. 1. No. 2, *etc. Novello & Co.: London*, [1913.] 8°.   **F. 321. z. (30.)**

— Eternal Ruler. *See* infra: Six Short Anthems for the Seasons of the Church No. 4.

— The Evening Hymn, of King Charles 1. *See* infra: Six Short Anthems for the Seasons of the Church. No. 6.

— Six Evening Hymns. Edited and arranged as short anthems by H. G. Ley. To which is added, Come, Holy Ghost, Tallis, arranged as an Anthem ... by W. H. Harris. *S. P. C. K.: London*, 1924. 8°.
S. P. C. K. Church Music, No. 21–27.   **E. 602. jj. (6.)**

— Fairy Spring. [Two-part.] [Words by] E. Ley. *Oxford University Press:* [*London*, 1923.] 8°.
[*The Oxford Choral Songs. No.* 112.]   **F. 1777. a.**

— Fantasia on the Welsh Hymn Tune Aberystwyth, (Joseph Parry) for Organ. *Oxford University Press: London*, 1928. 4°.   **g. 575. hh. (23.)**

— Far in a Western Brookland. Song, words by A. E. Housman. *Stainer & Bell: London*, 1921. fol.   **H. 1846. jj. (11.)**

— Faster than Fairies! Faster than Witches! Unison Song, words by R. L. Stevenson, *etc.* 1919. *See* AKERMAN (R. F. M.) The Year Book Press Series of Unison and Part-Songs, *etc.* No. 158. 1908, *etc.* 8°.   **F. 223.**

— Fight the good Fight. Hymn ... Words by J. N. Monsell. *H. F. W. Deane and Sons: London*, 1919. 8°. [*The Year Book Press Series of Anthems and Church Music. No. A* 16.]   **H. 802.**

— German Songs. Arranged by H. G. Ley ... Selected by Hugh Haworth. pp. 71. *Macmillan and Co.: London*, 1949. 4°.   **F. 1844.**

— The Gipsies' Call. A Song for children, words by E. M. Ley. *J. Williams: London*, 1922. 8°.
Unison School Songs. Series II, No. 23.   **F. 197. g.**

— The Glow-Worm ... Set as a Unison Song. [Words by] E. Ley. *Oxford University Press: London*, 1925. 8°.
[*The Oxford Choral Songs. No.* 40.]   **F. 1777. a.**

LEY (Henry George)

— God so loved the World, *etc.* [Anthem for A. T. T. B.] *Stainer & Bell: London*, (1910.) 8°.
Stainer & Bell's Church Choir Library, No. 80.　　**F. 1137. b.**

— God so loved the World, *etc.* [Anthem for S. A. T. B.] *Stainer & Bell: London*, (1911.) 8°.
Stainer & Bell's Church Choir Library, No. 93.　　**F. 1137. b.**

— The Heavens declare the Glory of God ... [Hymn, words by] MacNeece Foster. *Novello and Co.: London*, [1941.] *s. sh.* 8°.
　　D. 835. e. (3.)

— Hymn for Airmen. [Hymn.] Words by E. H. Blakeney.
S. P. C. K.: London, [1941.] 8°.
S. P. C. K. Church Music, No. 81.　　**B. 512. s. (20.)**

— Introits. For the seasons of the Church and special occasions.
Oxford University Press: London, 1944. 8°.　　**E. 602. xx. (4.)**

— Jubilate Deo for Organ. pp. 7. *Oxford University Press: London*, [1950.] 4°.　　**g. 575. rr. (5.)**

— The Lake Isle of Innisfree. [Song.] Words by W. B. Yeats. pp. 6. *Oxford University Press: London*, [1950.] 4°.
　　G. 1270. zz. (2.)

— Lead, kindly Light. [Anthem.] Words by J. H. Newman, *etc. H. F. W. Deane & Sons: London*, 1919. 8°.
[*The Year Book Press Series of Anthems and Church Music. No. A* 15.]　　**H. 802.**

— Leaves a-dancing. Unison Song, words by Lady Strachey. 1921. *See* Dunhill (T. F.) Singing Class Music, *etc.* No. 40. 1918, *etc.* 8°.　　**E. 802.**

— Let us now praise famous Men, *etc.* [Anthem.] *Oxford University Press: London*, 1938. 8°.
[*The Oxford Series of Modern Anthems. No.* 87.]　　**F. 1776.**

— "Llawenhewch yn yr Arglwydd Iôr. *See infra:* [Six Short Anthems for the Seasons of the Church. No. 5.]

— Lo, round the Throne a glorious Band. *See infra:* [Six Short Anthems for the Seasons of the Church. No. 2.]

— The Lord is my Shepherd, *etc.* [Anthem.] *Stainer & Bell: London*, 1912. 8°.
Church Choir Library, No. 144.　　**F. 1137. b.**

— Lord, though we perish, Thou art strong. Hymn for use in time of war, words by ... H. Scott Holland. *Novello and Co.: London*, [1914.] 8°.　　**C. 799. u. (21.)**

— The Lord's Prayer ... for unison singing or for S. A. T. B. *Oxford University Press: London*, 1925. 8°.
[*Oxford Church Music. No.* 418.]　　**F. 1777. c.**

— Magnificat and Nunc dimittis in A minor, *etc. Oxford University Press: London*, 1931. 8°.
[*Oxford Church Music. No.* 446.]　　**F. 1777. c.**

— Magnificat and Nunc dimittis in C minor. T. T. B. B. (S. A. T. B.) 2 no. *Stainer & Bell: London*, (1912.) 8°.
Stainer & Bell's Modern Church Services, No. 136, 137.
　　F. 1137.

— Magnificat and Nunc dimittis [in E minor]. (S. A. T. B.) pp. 14. *J. Curwen & Sons: London; G. Schirmer: New York*, [1956.] 8°.
[*Church Choralist. no.* 820.]　　**E. 1330.**

— Magnificat and Nunc dimittis. Modal. Arranged by H. G. Ley. *Oxford University Press: London*, 1937. 8°.
[*Oxford Church Music. No.* 480.]　　**F. 1777. c.**

— Magnificat and Nunc dimittis. Modal. Arranged for Men's Voices ... by H. G. Ley. *Oxford University Press: London*, 1941. 8°.
[*Oxford Church Music. No.* 503.]　　**F. 1777. c.**

LEY (Henry George)

— Magnificat and Nunc dimittis. (S. S. S.) pp. 10. *Oxford University Press: London*, [1949.] 8°.
[*Oxford Church Music. no.* 516.]　　**F. 1777. c.**

— Music when soft Voices die. *See supra:* [First Album of Songs. Op. 6. No. 1.]

— Four Nine-fold Kyries. Adapted by H. G. Ley. [S. A. T. B.] pp. 4. *Novello & Co.: London*, [1954.] 8°.
[*Parish Choir Book.* 1326.]　　**E. 618.**

— O be joyful in the Lord. Anthem for boys' or women's voices (S. S. S.). Ps. 100. pp. 8. *Oxford University Press: London*, [1951.] 8°.　　**E. 442. w. (24.)**

— O come this Day and praise Him. Christmas Carol, words by E. M. L. *Novello and Co.: London*, 1925. 8°.
Novello's Christmas Carols, No. 427.　　**C. 754.**

— Organ Solos, edited and arranged by H. G. Ley. *Stainer & Bell: London*, 1922, *etc.* 4°.　　**g. 1305.**

— Pasture. A Short Anthem for S. A. T. B. [Words by] E. Ley. *Oxford University Press: London*, 1944. 8°.
[*The Oxford Series of Easy Anthems. No.* 38.]　　**F. 1001.**

— Peterkin, the black Cat. [Unison song.] Words by E. Ley. *Elkin & Co.: London*, 1942. 8°.
The Elkin New Choral Series, No. 2061.　　**E. 1830. e. (48.)**

— Postlude, for Organ. *Oxford University Press: London*, 1931. 4°.　　**g. 575. jj. (3.)**

— A Prayer for Peace. [Anthem.] Words attributed to Francis Paget. *Oxford University Press: London*, 1938. 8°.
[*The Oxford Series of Easy Anthems. No.* 32.]　　**F. 1001.**

— A Prayer of King Henry VI. (Introit), *etc.* (Composed for the Royal Foundations of King Henry VI at Eton College and King's Collge, Cambridge, (1928). S. A. T. B.) *Eng. & Lat. Oxford University Press: London*, [1962.] *s. sh.* 8°.
[*Oxford easy Anthems. E* 98.]　　**F. 1001.**

— Prelude on 'Down Ampney' [by Ralph Vaughan Williams]. [Organ.] pp. 4. *Oxford University Press: London*, [1959.] 4°.
　　g. 1380. ff. (23.)

— Quittez pasteurs. Unison. Air and words from "Noels anciens". French Carol. Arranged by H. G. Ley. *Oxford University Press: London*, 1931. 8°.
[*The Oxford Choral Songs. No.* 1070.]　　**F. 1777. a.**

— [Quittez pasteurs.] Come, gentle Shepherds. [Unison song] ... English words by K. Fortescue. Arranged by H. G. Ley. pp. 3. *Oxford University Press: London*, [1952.] 8°.
[*Oxford choral Songs. no.* 1241.]　　**F. 1777. a.**

— Rejoice in the Lord alway. *See infra:* Six Short Anthems, *etc.* No. 5.

— Remember, O Lord. Short Anthem or Introit, words 7th century. pp. 4. *Novello and Co.: London*, 1946. 8°.
[*The Musical Times. No.* 1235.]　　**P. P. 1945. aa.**

— Requiescat in Pace. [Organ.] *In:* Album. An Album of memorial and funeral Music. pp. 12–14. [1960.] 4°.
　　g. 1380. nn. (8.)

— The Rose. Song, words by E. M. Ley. *Stainer & Bell: London*, 1920. fol.　　**H. 1846. y. (20.)**

— Savernake; or, the Professor's Dilemma. A Fairy Play, words by E. Ley, *etc. Oxford University Press: London*, 1930. 8°.
　　E. 890. h. (1.)

— The Saylor's Song. Unison. [Words] From "Wit and Drollery," 1682. *Oxford University Press:* [*London*, 1923.] 8°.
[*The Oxford Choral Songs. No.* 18.]　　**F. 1777. a.**

LEY (HENRY GEORGE)

— [Service in B flat.] Te Deum. (Benedictus.) (Magnificat.) 3 no. *Stainer & Bell: London,* 1920. 8°.
Modern Church Services, No. 217–219.   **F. 1137.**

— [Service in C minor.] A Morning Service.—Te Deum and Jubilate Deo—for unison voices ... in ... C minor, *etc.*
Novello & Co.: London, [1909.] 8°.   **F. 1169. n. (18.)**

— The Sheep under the Snow. A Manx Folk Song. Freely arranged for S. A. T. B., unaccompanied, by H. G. Ley.
Stainer & Bell: London, 1923. 8°.
Choral Library, No. 181.   **F. 1137. d.**

— The Sheep under the Snow. A Manx Folk Song ... [Unison song.] Arranged by H. G. Ley. *Stainer & Bell: London,* [1927.] 8°.
Unison Songs, No. 53.   **F. 1137. e.**

Six Short Anthems for the Seasons of the Church

— Six Short Anthems for the Seasons of the Church. [Arranged and composed] By H. G. Ley. 6 no. *Oxford University Press: London,* 1925–37. 8°.   **E. 442. s. (20.)**

— [No. 2.] Lo, round the Throne a glorious Band ... Set in an extended version ... Melody, N. Herman ... Arranged by H. G. Ley. *Oxford University Press: London,* 1929. 8°.   **E. 442. t. (11.)**

— [No. 2.] Lo, round the Throne a glorious Band. Anthem for Saints Days ... Melody (N. Herman, 1560) arranged for boys and women's voices by H. G. Ley. pp. 7. *Oxford University Press: London,* [1951.] 8°.   **E. 442. w. (23.)**

— [No. 5.] "Llawenhewch yn yr Arglwydd Iôr" ... Geiriau Cymraeg gan Enid Parry. Dan olygiaeth John Hughes. [Tonic sol-fa notation.] *In:* HOLST (Gustavus T. von) [All People that on Earth do dwell.] "Wrth orsedd y Jehofa mawr," *etc.* pp. 5, 6. 1951. 8°.   **C. 273. h. (20.)**

— Six Short Anthems for the Seasons of the Church ... No. 5a ... Rejoice in the Lord alway. ⟨S. A. T. B.⟩ pp. 7. *Oxford University Press: London,* [1952.] 8°.   **E. 442. w. (33.)**

— The Soldier. [Four-part song.] Words by Rupert Brooke. *Novello & Co.: London,* [1941.] 8°.
[*Novello's Part-Song Book. No.* 1521.]   **F. 280. b.**

— The Soldier, *etc. Novello and Co.: London,* [1941.] 8°.
[*Novello's Tonic Sol-fa Series. No.* 2738.]   **B. 885.**

— Song of the Cyclops. Unison. [Words by] T. Dekker. *Oxford University Press: London,* [1923.] 8°.
[*The Oxford Choral Songs. No.* 19.]   **F. 1777. a.**

— Song of the West Wind. Unison. [Words by] E. Ley. *Oxford University Press: London,* 1930. *s. sh.* 8°.
[*The Oxford Choral Songs. No.* 1029.]   **F. 1777. a.**

— A Study in Phrasing. [P. F.] *J. Williams: London,* 1930. 4°.
Public School Series, No. 1.   **g. 1400.**

— Te Deum and Jubilate in C minor. For A. T. B. B. or T. T. B. B. *Oxford University Press: London,* 1944. 8°.
[*Oxford Church Music. No.* 508.]   **F. 1777. c.**

— Te Deum, for unison singing, *etc.* [Vocal score and voice part.] 2 no. *Oxford University Press: London,* [1924.] 8°.
[*Oxford Church Music. No.* 409, 409 *a.*]   **F. 1777. c.**

— That Easter-tide with Joy was bright. Choral hymn for Easter. Words 4th cent. (tr. J. M. Neale). Grenoble melody (17th cent.) arr. H. G. Ley. ⟨S. A. T. B.⟩ pp. 5. *Oxford University Press: London,* [1954.] 8°.
[*Oxford easy Anthems. no.* 67.]   **F. 1001.**

LEY (HENRY GEORGE)

— That Eastertide with Joy was bright. [Anthem.] Words 4th century (trans: J. M. Neale). Grenoble melody (17th cent.) arranged by H. G. Ley. ⟨S. A. T. B. (unaccompanied).⟩ pp. 4. *Oxford University Press: London,* [1956.] 8°.
[*Oxford Anthems. A* 145.]   **F. 1776.**

— There's a clean Wind blowing. Unison Song, words by W. H. Ogilvie. 1919. *See* AKERMAN (R. F. M.) The Year Book Press Series of Unison and Part-Songs, *etc.* No. 159. 1908, *etc.* 8°.   **F. 223.**

— Turmut-hoeing ... for Treble, Alto, Tenor and Bass. An Oxfordshire Folk Song. Arranged by H. G. Ley. *J. Williams: London,* 1931. 8°.
Public School Series, No. 2.   **F. 163. cc. (46.)**

— Up the Hillside. Two-part Song, words by E. Ley, *etc. E. Arnold & Co.: London,* 1923. 8°.
[*Singing Class Music. No.* 158.]   **E. 802.**

— Where go the Boats. Two-part Song ... words by R. L. Stevenson, *etc.* 1919. *See* AKERMAN (R. F. M.) The Year Book Press Series of Unison and Part Songs, *etc.* No. 160. 1908, *etc.* 8°.   **F. 223.**

— White in the Moon the long Road lies. Song, words by A. E. Housman. *Stainer & Bell: London,* 1921. fol.   **H. 1846. jj. (12.)**

— Ye Watchers and ye holy Ones ... Anthem arranged for boys' or women's voices by H. G. Ley. [Words by] Athelstan Riley. Melody from "Geistliche Kirchengesäng". (Coln, 1623.) pp. 8. *Oxford University Press: London,* [1949.] 8°.   **E. 442. w. (14.)**

— Zion's Children. Jubilee Tune, 1887 ... Arranged for S. A. T. B. by H. G. Ley. *Oxford University Press: London,* 1934. 8°.
[*The Oxford Choral Songs. No.* 765.]   **F. 1777. a.**

— Zion's Children. Jubilee tune (1887). Arranged by H. G. Ley. ⟨Two-part.⟩ pp. 4. *Oxford University Press: London,* [1959.] 8°.
[*The Oxford choral Songs. T* 32.]   **F. 1777. m.**

— *See* ARNOLD (Samuel) [Service in A.] Magnificat and Nunc dimittis ... in ... A ... Edited by H. G. Ley. [1952.] 8°. [*Parish Choir Book.* 1316.]   **E. 618.**

— *See* BACH (J. S.) [*Collected Works.—f.*] Two Choral Preludes for Organ ... Edited by H. G. Ley, *etc.* 1935. 4°.   **g. 548. bb. (13.)**

— *See* BACH (J. S.) [*Collected Works.—h.*] Blessed Jesu, we are here. (Liebster Jesu, wir sind hier.) Choral prelude. [S. 731.] ⟨Alternative version. [S. 706.]⟩ Edited and arranged by H. G. Ley. ⟨String orchestra.⟩ [1953.] 4°.   **g. 699. e. (17.)**

— *See* BACH (J. S.) [Sechs Choräle von verschiedener Art. No. 1. Wachet auf.] Sleepers wake! A Voice is calling ... Edited by H. G. Ley. 1927. 4°. [*The Year Book Press Series of Instrumental Music. No.* 19.]   **g. 1383.**

— *See* BACH (J. S.) [18 Choräle von verschiedener Art. No. 18. Vor deinen Thron tret' ich.] When in my deepest Hour of Need ... Edited and arranged by H. G. Ley. ⟨String orchestra.⟩ [1953.] 4°.   **g. 699. e. (19.)**

— *See* BACH (J. S.) [Weihnachts-Oratorium.—Sinfonia.] Pastoral Symphony ... Arranged as an organ solo by H. G. Ley. [1954.] *obl.* 4°.   **e. 113. n. (3.)**

— *See* BEALE (W.) This pleasant Month of May ... Arranged for S. A. T. B. ... by H. G. Ley. 1933. 8°. [*The Musical Times. No.* 1082.]   **P. P. 1945. aa.**

— *See* BEALE (W.) This pleasant Month of May ... Arranged for S. A. T. B. ... by H. G. Ley. [1937.] 8°. [*Novello's Tonic Sol-fa Series. No.* 2702.]   **B. 885.**

LEY (Henry George)

— *See* Brahms (J.) [Fugue for Organ. A flat minor.] Organ Fugue in A minor. Arranged for strings (with optional wind parts) by H. G. Ley. [1953.] 4°.   **g. 609. m. (24.)**

— *See* Brahms (J.) [3 Gesänge für sechsstimmigen Chor. Op. 42. No. 2.] Vineta ... Arranged for S. A. T. B. by H. G. Ley. 1944. 8°. [*Part-Song Book. No.* 1530.]   **F. 280. b.**

— *See* Buxtehude (D.) [*Smaller Instrumental Collections.*] Six Organ Preludes on Chorales ... Edited by H. G. Ley. [1947.] 4°.   **g. 575. pp. (29.)**

— *See* Buxtehude (D.) Prelude & Fugue, No. VI, [in E minor] for Organ ... Edited by H. G. Ley. 1933. 4°.   **g. 575. kk. (11.)**

— *See* Buxtehude (D.) Prelude & Fugue, No. XIV, [in G minor] for Organ ... Edited by H. G. Ley. 1933. 4°.   **g. 575. kk. (12.)**

— *See* Child (W.) O bone Jesu. O blessed Jesu ... Edited by H. G. Ley. [1924.] 8°. [*Novello's Octavo Anthems. No.* 1132.]   **E. 618. a.**

— *See* Child (W.) Sing we merrily ... Transposed ... and edited by H. G. Ley. 1933. 8°. [*Novello's Octavo Anthems. No.* 1190.]   **E. 618. a.**

— *See* Crotch (William) [Palestine.] Be Peace on Earth. (Arranged for the Lower Chapel Choir, Eton College.) By H. G. Ley, *etc.* [1949.] 8°.   **F. 231. mm. (33.)**

— *See* Davies (*Sir* Henry W.) and Ley (H. G.) The Church Anthem Book, *etc.* 1933. 8°.   **F. 983. k.**

— *See* Davies (*Sir* Henry W.) and Ley (H. G.) The Church Anthem Book. One hundred anthems edited by Sir Walford Davies and H. G. Ley, *etc.* [1959.] 8°.   **F. 983. r.**

— *See* Eperson (D. B.) The Charminster Chant Book. Compiled by ... D. B. Eperson with the assistance of ... H. G. Ley [and others], *etc.* [1952.] *obl.* 8°.   **A. 628. a.**

— *See* Gastoldi (G. G.) [Balletti a cinque voci. — A lieta vita.] In Thee is Gladness, *etc.* ⟨Melody arranged by H. G. Ley.⟩ [1956.] 8°.   **E. 442. aa. (6.)**

— *See* Gastoldi (G. G.) [Balletti a cinque voci. — A lieta vita.] In Thee is Gladness ... Arranged by H. G. Ley. [1957.] 8°. [*Oxford easy Anthems. E.* 80.]   **F. 1001.**

— *See* Gibbons (O.) [Hymnes and Songs of the Church. Song 31. Lord, Thy Answer I did hear.] Ye that do your Master's Will ... Edited by H. G. Ley. 1927. *a card.*   **I. 600. f. (26.)**

— *See* Greene (M.) [Forty Select Anthems. Vol. 2. Thou O God art praised in Sion.] Thou visitest the Earth ... Arr. ... by H. G. Ley. 1945. 8°. [*The Oxford Series of easy Anthems. No.* 41.]   **F. 1001.**

— *See* Guidetti (G.) [Aeterna Christi munera.] The Eternal Gifts of Christ the King ... Arranged by H. G. Ley. [1951.] 8°. [*Oxford Series of easy Anthems. no.* 57.]   **F. 1001.**

— *See* Haendel (G. F.) [*Collected Works. — h.*] Six Movements from the Overtures ... Arranged for 1. Violin & piano, or 2. Flute & piano, or 3. Organ by H. G. Ley. [1947.] 4°.   **g. 74. ii. (15.)**

— *See* Haendel (G. F.) [*Collected Works. — h.*] Minuets from the Overtures. Arranged for violin or flute and pianoforte by H. G. Ley. [1948.] 4°.   **g. 74. oo. (3.)**

— *See* Haendel (G. F.) [*Collected Works. — h.*] Six Short Movements from the Overtures ... Arranged for organ by H. G. Ley. [1948.] 4°.   **g. 74. i. (14.)**

— *See* Haendel (G. F.) [Esther. — Overture.] Finale ... Arranged for organ by H. G. Ley. [1952.] 4°.   **g. 74. oo. (13.)**

LEY (Henry George)

— *See* Haendel (G. F.) [Messiah. — And lo, the Angel of the Lord.] Aria ... Edited by H. G. Ley, *etc.* [1947.] 8°. [*Year Book Press Series of Anthems and Church Music. no.* 96.]   **H. 802.**

— *See* Herzogenberg (H. von) [Orgel-Phantasie über die Melodie "Nun danket alle Gott". Op. 46. — Pastorale.] Pastorale for Organ on the Chorale "Now thank we all our God" ... Edited by H. G. Ley. [1948.] 4°.   **g. 575. rr. (1.)**

— *See* Holst (G. T. von) [First Suite in E flat for Military Band.] Chaconne ... Arranged for the Organ by H. G. Ley. 1933. 4°.   **g. 1206. (17.)**

— *See* Krebs (S. L.) Prelude in A minor for Organ ... Edited by H. G. Ley. [1949.] 4°.   **g. 575. rr. (2.)**

— *See* Mozart (W. A.) [Adagio and Allegro. K. 594.] Fantasia in F minor & major for a mechanical Organ ... Edited and arranged for organ by H. G. Ley. [1954.] 4°.   **g. 1018. qq. (1.)**

— *See* Mozart (W. A.) Ave verum ... Arranged by H. G. Ley. ⟨Two-part.⟩ [1958.] 8°. [*Oxford easy Anthems. E* 82.]   **F. 1001.**

— *See* Nares (J.) [These Lessons for the Harpsicord. Op. 2. No. 3.] Sonata, *etc.* (Edited for Piano by H. G. Ley.) 1926. 4°. [*The Year Book Press Series of Instrumental Music. No.* 7.]   **g. 1383.**

— *See* Ouseley (*Sir* F. A. G.) *Bart.* O Saviour of the World ... Edited by H. G. Ley. 1933. 8°. [*Novello's Octavo Anthems. No.* 1185.]   **E. 618. a.**

— *See* Palestrina (G. P. da) [Motettorum ... partim Quinis ... Vocibus ... Liber Primus.] Alleluia! Tulerant Dominum meum. Alleluia! They have taken my Lord away ... Edited ... by H. G. Ley. [1937.] 8°. [*Novello's Octavo Anthems. No.* 1222.]   **E. 618. a.**

— *See* Palestrina (G. P. da) [Motettorum ... partim Quinis ... Vocibus ... Liber Primus.] Dum complerentur dies Pentecostes ... Edited ... by H. G. Ley. 1936. 8°. [*Novello's Octavo Anthems. No.* 1206.]   **E. 618. a.**

— *See* Palestrina (G. P. da) [Motettorum ... partim Quinis ... Vocibus ... Liber Primus.] Hodie beata virgo Maria. On this Day, the blessed Virgin Mary ... Edited ... by H. G. Ley. [1937.] 8°. [*Novello's Octavo Anthems. No.* 1217.]   **E. 618. a.**

— *See* Palestrina (G. P. da) [Motettorum ... partim Quinis ... Vocibus ... Liber Primus.] Stella quam viderant Magi. The Star which the Wise Men had seen ... Edited ... by H. G. Ley. 1937. 8°. [*Novello's Octavo Anthems. No.* 1216.]   **E. 618. a.**

— *See* Palestrina (G. P. da) [Motettorum ... partim Quinis ... Vocibus ... Liber Primus.] Venit Michael archangelus. Then came Michael the Archangel ... Edited ... by H. G. Ley. [1936.] 8°. [*Novello's Octavo Anthems. No.* 1211.]   **E. 618. a.**

— *See* Palestrina (G. P. da) [Motettorum ... partim Quinis ... Vocibus ... Liber Primus.] Vidi turbam magnam. I behold and lo! a great Multitude ... Edited ... by H. G. Ley. [1936.] 8°. [*Novello's Octavo Anthems. No.* 1215.]   **E. 618. a.**

— *See* Purcell (H.) [*Collected Works. — c.*] Two Trumpet Tunes and Air ... Arranged for Strings ... adapted from H. Ley's Organ arrangement, *etc.* 1937. 4°.   **g. 25. d. (9.)**

— *See* Russell (William) *Organist.* [Twelve Voluntaries for the Organ. No. 9.] Largo and Fugue in A minor. Edited by H. G. Ley. [1927.] 4°. [*The Year Book Press Series of Instrumental Music. No.* 18.]   **g. 1383.**

— *See* Saboly (N.) [Recueil des Noels. — Venès lèu veire la pièucello.] A Christmas Carol ... Arranged by H. G. Ley. 1931. 8°. [*The Oxford Choral Songs. No.* 1069.]   **F. 1777. a.**

LEY (Henry George)

— *See* SCHICHT (J. G.) The Lord ascendeth up on high. *Ascension Hymn.* Arranged ... by H. G. Ley. 1923. 8°. [*Novello's Parish Choir Book. No.* 1077.]   **E. 618.**

— *See* SCHUBERT (F. P.) [An die Musik. Op. 88. No. 4.] To Music ... Arranged for organ by H. G. Ley. [1949.] 4°.   **g. 567. r. (4.)**

— *See* SCHUBERT (F. P.) Fugue ... (Op. 152.) Arranged for the organ by H. G. Ley. [1948.] 4°.   **g. 567. r. (5.)**

— *See* SCHUMANN (R. A.) [6 Fugen über den Namen "Bach". Op. 60.] Fugue No. 5 on the name "Bach" ... Arranged and edited by H. G. Ley. [1953.] 4°.   **g. 715. t. (10.)**

— *See* SCHUMANN (R. A.) [6 Fugen über den Namen "Bach". Op. 60.] Fugue No. 5, *etc.* ⟨Arranged for two pianos by H. G. Ley.⟩ [1955.] 4°.   **g. 715. y. (1.)**

— *See* SCHUMANN (R. A.) [Skizzen für den Pedal-Flügel. Op. 58.] Four sketches for pedal piano. Transcribed for organ by W. A. Wightman. Edited by H. G. Ley. 1925. 4°.   **g. 715. i. (9.)**

— *See* SCHUMANN (R. A.) [Studien für den Pedalflügel. Op. 56. No. 5.] Study for Organ ... Edited by H. G. Ley. 1925. 4°.   **g. 715. y. (7.)**

— *See* SCHUMANN (R. A.) [Studien für den Pedalflügel. Op. 56.] Study No. 5, *etc.* ⟨Arranged for two pianos by H. G. Ley.⟩ [1955.] 4°.   **g. 715. y. (2.)**

— *See* SMITH (Isaac) [A Collection of Psalm Tunes.—Abridge.] Be Thou my Guardian and my Guide. Hymn anthem ... arranged by H. G. Ley. [1961.] 8°. [*Year Book Press Music Series. A* 142.]   **H. 802.**

— *See* STANFORD (*Sir* Charles V.) [The Morning, Communion and Evening Service in C. Op. 115.] Ninefold Kyrie for Stanford in C ... Adapted by H. G. Ley. [1953.] *s. sh.* 8°.   **F. 1158. m. (26.)**

— *See* STANFORD (*Sir* Charles V.) [Morning, Communion and Evening Service in F. Op. 36.] Kyrie eleison, Benedictus qui venit, and Agnus Dei ... Music adapted by H. G. Ley. [1954.] 8°. [*Parish Choir Book.* 1325.]   **E. 618.**

— *See* TALLIS (Thomas) [Nine Psalm Tunes. no. 1.] Choral Hymn for Sundays, Lent, or Passiontide. My Lord, my Love, was crucified ... Arranged by H. G. Ley. [1953.] 8°. [*Year Book Press Series of Anthems and Church Music. no.* 127.]   **H. 802.**

— *See* VULPIUS (M.) [Ein schön geistlich Gesangbuch. No. 44. Gelobt sei Gott in höchsten Thron.] The Strife is o'er. Arranged for boys' or women's voices (S. S. A.) by H. G. Ley, *etc.* [1948.] 8°.   **E. 442. w. (19.)**

— *See* WALTON (*Sir* William T.) [Henry v.] Passacaglia "Death of Falstaff" ... Arranged for organ by H. G. Ley. [1949.] 4°.   **h. 4005. d. (8.)**

— *See* WELDON (John) Hear my Crying ... Edited by H. G. Ley. 1931. 8°.   **E. 442. t. (40.)**

— *See* WELDON (John) Hear my crying. Anthem ... Edited by H. G. Ley, *etc.* [1960.] 8°. [*Church Music Society Reprints. no.* 39.]   **E. 1617.**

— *See* WESLEY (S. S.) The Face of the Lord. Edited by H. G. Ley. 1934. 8°.   **E. 442. u. (63.)**

— *See* WESLEY (S. S.) [Service in E.] Completion of S. S. Wesley's Communion Service in E, comprising Benedictus qui venit, Agnus Dei, adapted ... by H. G. Ley, *etc.* [1933.] 8°.   **F. 1158. g. (16.)**

— *See* WESLEY (S. S.) [Service in E.] Magnificat and Nunc dimittis ... in E ... Edited by H. G. Ley. [1952.] 8°. [*Parish Choir Book.* 1297.]   **E. 618.**

LEY (Henry George)

— *See* WESLEY (S. S.) [Chant Service in F.] Magnificat ... (Nunc dimittis.) Arranged for two Voices by H. G. Ley. 1932. 8°.   **F. 1158. f. (20.)**

— *See* WESLEY (S. S.) [Studio for the organ. No. 1.] Introduction and Fugue in C sharp minor. For organ. Edited by H. G. Ley. [1952.] 4°. [*Original Compositions. new ser. no.* 231.]   **g. 1270.**

— *See* WILLIAMS (Ralph V.) [English Hymnal. No. 641.] For all the Saints ... Arranged by H. G. Ley. [1948.] 8°.   **F. 928. b. (12.)**

— *See* WILLIAMS (Ralph V.) [English Hymnal. No. 641.] For all the Saints ... Arranged by H. G. Ley. [1949.] 8°.   **F. 928. b. (13.)**

— *See* WOOD (C.) *Mus. Doc.* [Suite in ancient style.] Allemande and Courante for Organ ... Edited by H. G. Ley. 1928. 4°. [*The Year Book Press Series of Instrumental Music. No.* 23.]   **g. 1383.**

— *See* WOOD (C.) *Mus. Doc.* [Suite in ancient style.] Sarabande for Organ ... Edited by H. G. Ley. 1928. 4°. [*The Year Book Press Series of Instrumental Music. No.* 22.]   **g. 1383.**

LEY (Henry George) and **ROPER** (Edgar Stanley)

— The Oxford Chant Book No. 2. A Collection of Chants compiled for use with the Oxford Psalter and edited by H. G. Ley ... and S. Roper, *etc. Oxford University Press: London*, 1934. *obl.* 8°.
No. 1 *is catalogued under E. S. Roper and A. E. Walker.*   **B. 515. a.**

LEY (Luis)

— Quo vadis? Valse. [P. F.] *Monte Carlo Publishing Co.: London*, [1905.] fol.   **h. 3286. dd. (62.)**

LEY (Salvador)

— Copla triste (Elegy) for Voice and Piano. pp. 3. *Edward B. Marks Music Corporation: New York*, [1948.] 4°.   **G. 1276. d. (17.)**

— Danza exotica ... For piano. pp. 11. *Peer International Corporation: New York; Peer Musikverlag: Hamburg*, [1964.] 4°.   **g. 352. h. (6.)**

LEYBACH (Ignace)

— Six celebrated Fantasias and original pieces. [P. F.] *See* BOOSEY AND CO. Boosey's Musical Cabinet. No. 87. [1861–81.] 4°.   **F. 160.**

— Les Abeilles, caprice brillant pour Piano. *Mayence*, [1880.] fol.   **h. 1299. g. (12.)**

— L'Acanthe, valse brillante pour Piano. Op. 103. *Paris*, [1868.] fol.   **h. 1299. d. (2.)**

— Les Adieux, caprice pour Piano. Op. 123. *Paris*, [1869.] fol.   **h. 1299. d. (19.)**

— Aida de Verdi, fantaisie brillante pour Piano. *Milano*, [1873.] fol.   **h. 1489. a. (26.)**

— Aida, opéra de Verdi. Fantaisie brillante pour Piano. *Paris*, [1873.] fol.   **h. 1299. f. (23.)**

— Aïda ... opéra de G. Verdi. Fantaisie ... pour piano. Op. 158. Nouvelle édition. *Paris*, [1886.] fol.   **h. 1299. g. (45.)**

— Airs Alsaciens. Souvenir d'Enfance. Fantaisie brillante pour Piano. *Paris*, [1873.] fol.   **h. 1299. f. (20.)**

LEYBACH (IGNACE)

— Alla Stella Confidente, romanza de V. Robaudi. Fantaisie-nocturne pour Piano. *Paris*, [1874.] fol.
h. 1299. f. (45.)

— Alleluia du Printemps, caprice brillant pour Piano. *Paris*, [1883.] fol. **h. 1299. g. (35.)**

— Alleluia du Printemps. Caprice ... pour piano. Op. 247. *Hutchings & Romer: London*, [1883.] fol. **h. 1299. h. (2.)**

— L'Alsacienne, fantaisie-valse pour Piano. *London*, [1876.] fol.
h. 1299. b. (30.)

— Les Amarantes, caprice mazurke pour Piano. Op. 74. *Paris*, [1866.] fol. **h. 1299. c. (8.)**

— Andante con espressione. [Organ.] *See* WESTBROOK (W. J.) New Organ Arrangements. No. 19. [1886, *etc.*] fol.
h. 2750. b.

— L'Ange du Souvenir, caprice brillant pour Piano. *Paris*, [1883.] fol. **h. 1299. g. (39.)**

— Anna Bolena. Fantaisie brillante [on D. G. M. Donizetti's opera]. Op. 100, *etc.* [P. F.] *Colombier: Paris*, [1868.] fol.
h. 1299. c. (35.)

— Arioso du Roi de Lahore, de J. Massenet. Transcription brillante pour Piano. *London*, [1879.] fol. **h. 1494. q. (39.)**

— Le Astuzie Femminili, opéra de Cimarosa. Fantaisie brillante pour Piano. *Paris*, [1874.] fol. **h. 1299. f. (40.)**

— Au bord du Lac. Rêverie pour Piano. *Paris*, [1879.] fol.
h. 1299. g. (6.)

— Au Printemps, mélodie de C. Gounod. Fantaisie-caprice brillante pour Piano. *Mayence*, [1875.] fol. **h. 1299. f. (44.)**

— Au Printemps, mélodie de C. Gounod. Fantaisie-caprice brillante pour Piano. *Paris*, [1875.] fol. **h. 1299. f. (46.)**

— Aubade. *See* infra: Récréations caractéristiques. No. 2.

— The Autumn Wind. *See* infra: [Deuxième Nocturne.]

— Aux bords du Danube. Caprice Mazurke pour le Piano. *Mayence*, [1861.] fol. **h. 1299. a. (7.)**

— Aux bords du Gange ... de Mendelssohn-Bartholdy. Caprice ... pour piano. Op. 24. [Duet.] *Mayence*, [1884.] fol.
h. 1299. g. (44.)

— Ay Chiquita. Chanson Espagnole de Yradier. Fantaisie brillante pour Piano ... Op. 182. pp. 11. *Heugel & c^(ie).: Paris*, [1875.] fol. **h. 1299. f. (50.)**

— Ballade pour piano ... Op. 19. pp. 9. *Chez les fils de B. Schott: Mayence*, [1858.] fol. **h. 1203. ss. (12.)**

— Ballade composée pour le Piano. ⟨Op. 19. Edited ... by B. Richards.⟩ pp. 9. *Robert Cocks & Co.: London*, [1870.] fol.
h. 1299. b. (16.)

— Ballade pour Piano. ⟨Op. 19.⟩ pp. 9. *Chappell & Co.: London*, [1870.] fol. **h. 1299. b. (17.)**

— Deuxième Ballade. Caprice pour Piano ... Op. 136. pp. 8. *Cartereau: Paris*, [1870.] fol. **h. 1299. f. (3.)**

— Balladine, souvenir d'enfance pour Piano. Op. 106. *Paris*, [1868.] fol. **h. 1299. d. (7.)**

— Balladine pour Harmonium ou Orgue Expressif. *Paris*, [1870.] fol. **h. 2575. b. (21.)**

— Un ballo in maschera. Opéra de Verdi. Fantaisie brillante pour Piano. *Paris*, [1862.] fol. **h. 1299. a. (20.)**

— Le Barbier de Seville, fantaisie brillante sur l'opéra de G. Rossini, pour le Piano. Op. 70. *Paris*, [1865.] fol.
h. 1299. c. (5.)

LEYBACH (IGNACE)

— Barcarolle pour Piano & Harmonium, *etc. Paris*, [1874.] fol.
h. 2510. a. (14.)

— Les Batelières. Idylle rustique pour Piano. *Paris*, [1873.] fol.
h. 1299. f. (19.)

— Les Batelières de Naples; canzonetta pour Piano. Op. 92. *Paris*, [1867.] fol. **h. 1299. c. (33.)**

— Les Bateliers de Venise, caprice brillant pour Harmonium. *London*, [1876.] fol. **h. 2575. e. (14.)**

— Les Bateliers de Venise, caprice brillant pour Harmonium. *Paris*, [1876.] fol. **h. 2510. a. (17.)**

— Beatrice di Tenda. (Bellini.) Fantaisie brillante. [P. F.] *Paris*, [1872.] fol.
One of "Souvenirs des Grands Maîtres". **h. 1299. f. (8.)**

— La Bohémienne. Mazurka brillante pour Piano. *Paris*, [1863.] fol. **h. 1299. a. (26.)**

— Premier boléro brillant pour Piano. *Paris*, [1863.] fol.
h. 1299. a. (30.)

— Premier Bolero brillant pour Piano à quatre mains. Op. 64 bis. *Paris*, [1865.] fol. **h. 1299. c. (6.)**

— 1er Boléro brillant. Op. 64. [Violin and P. F.] *See* RITTER (E. W.) Les Succès du Salon, *etc.* No. 32. [1891, *etc.*] fol.
h. 3665. a.

— 2^(me) Bolero brillant. Op. 90. *Paris*, [1867.] fol.
h. 1299. c. (25.)

— 2me. Bolero brillant pour Piano. *Mayence*, [1880.] fol.
h. 1299. g. (9.)

— 2^(me) Boléro brillant pour Piano. (Arrangé à 4 mains par G. Micheuz.) *Paris*, [1876.] fol. **h. 1299. f. (58.)**

— Bolero Concertant pour Piano et Harmonium ou Orgue Expressif. *Paris*, [1870.] fol. **h. 2575. b. (22.)**

— La Branche Cassée, opéra de G. Serpette, fantaisie brillante pour Piano. *Paris*, [1879.] fol. **h. 1299. g. (7.)**

— Calme et Solitude, caprice pour le Piano. *London*, [1876.] fol. **h. 1299. b. (27.)**

— Calme et Solitude. Caprice pour le Piano. *Paris*, [1876.] fol.
h. 1299. f. (54.)

— Cantilena pour le Piano. Op. 73. *Paris*, [1866.] fol.
h. 1299. c. (9.)

— Canzonetta Napolitana pour Harmonium ou Orgue Expressif. *Paris*, [1870.] fol. **h. 2575. b. (23.)**

— Caprice-Nocturne pour Piano. Op. 111. *Paris*, [1868.] fol.
h. 1299. c. (36.)

— I Capuletti ed i Montecchi, de Bellini. Fantaisie pour Piano. *Paris*, [1871.] fol. **h. 1299. f. (6.)**

— Carmen, opéra de G. Bizet, fantaisie brillante. [P. F.] *London*, [1878.] fol. **h. 1299. g. (10.)**

— Il Carnevale di Venezia, opéra de E. Petrella. Fantaisie brillante pour Piano. *Paris*, [1870.] fol. **h. 1299. f. (1.)**

— La Cenerentola [by G. A. Rossini], fantaisie brillante. [P. F.] Op. 107. *Paris*, [1868.] fol. **h. 1299. c. (37.)**

— Chanson à boire pour Piano. *Paris*, [1862.] fol.
h. 1299. a. (11.)

— 2e Chanson à Boire pour le Piano. Op. 110. *Paris*, [1868.] fol.
h. 1299. d. (4.)

— Chanson Allemande pour piano, *etc.* Op. 30. *Londres*, [1859.] fol. **h. 1299. (12.)**

LEYBACH (Ignace)

— Chanson Slave pour Piano. *Mayence*, [1880.] fol.
h. 1299. g. (19.)

— Chanson Slave pour Piano. *Paris*, [1880.] fol.
h. 1299. g. (20.)

— Chant du Dimanche, mélodie de F. Mendelssohn Bartholdy, transcription brillante pour Piano. *Mayence*, [1880.] fol.
h. 1299. g. (17.)

— Chant du Dimanche. Mélodie de Mendelssohn. [Fantasia for the P. F.] Op. 225. *Paris*, [1880.] fol.
One of the "Souvenirs des Grands Maîtres". **h. 1299. g. (48.)**

— Le Chant du Nautonnier, caprice brillant pour Piano. *Mayence*, [1882.] fol. **h. 1299. g. (28.)**

— Chant du Printemps. Caprice brillant pour Piano. *Paris*, [1870.] fol. **h. 1299. f. (2.)**

— Chant du Proscrit, rêverie pour Piano. Op. 75. *Paris*, [1866.] fol. **h. 1299. c. (10.)**

— Charles II. (Halévy.) Fantaisie brillante pour Piano. *Paris*, [1872.] fol. **h. 1299. f. (14.)**

— Charme du Salon. Caprice. *See* ALBUM. Album des Pianistes contemporains. No. 7. [1861.] fol. **h. 3213. (3.)**

— Charme du Souvenir. Caprice brillant pour Piano. *Paris*, [1875.] fol. **h. 1299. f. (59.)**

— Le Conservatoire des Pianistes. Collection classique, progressive et choisie, *etc. Paris*, [1869.] fol. **h. 1299. e.**

— La Dame Blanche, opera de Boieldieu, fantaisie brillante pour Piano. Op. 105. *Paris*, [1868.] fol. **h. 1299. d. (5.)**

— Dans les Montagnes, ydylle [*sic*] pour l'Harmonium. *Paris*, [1867.] fol. **h. 2510. a. (6.)**

— La Danse des Elfes. Caprice brillante pour Piano. *Paris*, [1862.] fol. **h. 1299. a. (21.)**

— Danse des Naïades. *See* infra: Recréations caractéristiques. No. 5.

— La Danse des Sylphes. Caprice brillant pour Piano. *Paris*, [1874.] fol. **h. 1299. f. (37.)**

— Danse Napolitaine pour Piano. *Paris*, [1882.] fol.
h. 1299. g. (30.)

— La Dernière Rose d'Été. Air Irlandais, transcription brillante pour le Piano. *Paris*, [1874.] fol. **h. 1299. f. (30.)**

— La Diabolique. 2ᵉ Grande étude caractéristique pour Piano. *Londres*, [1861.] fol. **h. 1299. a. (8.)**

— [La Diabolique.] 2ᵐᵉ Grande Étude caractéristique pour Piano. Op. 47. *B. Schott's Söhne: Mayence*, [1865?] fol.
g. 232. d. (27.)

— La Diabolique ... Op. 47. Edited and fingered by P. Gallico. [P. F.] *J. W. Stern & Co.: New York*, (1912.) fol.
g. 606. n. (44.)

— [La Diabolique.] 2ᵐᵉ Grande Étude ... pour Piano, *etc. W. Paxton: London*, [1912.] fol. **h. 3284. g. (26.)**

— Don Juan de W. Mozart, fantaisie brillante pour le Piano. Op. 81. *Paris*, [1866.] fol. **h. 1299. c. (18.)**

— Don Juan de W. Mozart. Fantaisie brillante pour le piano ... Op. 81. *Chez les fils de B. Schott: Mayence*, [1866?] fol.
h. 721. s. (5.)

— Don Pasquale [by D. G. M. Donizetti], fantaisie pour Piano. Op. 93. *L. Grus: Paris*, [1867.] fol. **h. 1299. c. (31.)**

— Echo de Venise, 2ᵐᵉ sérénade pour Piano. Op. 98. *Paris*, [1867.] fol. **h. 1299. c. (32.)**

LEYBACH (Ignace)

— Echo des Muses, caprice brillant pour Piano. *Paris*, [1882.] fol. **h. 1292. g. (33.)**

— L'Écho du lac. Nocturne. Op. 262. [P. F.] *Offenbach a. Main*, [1885.] fol. **h. 1299. g. (60.)**

— Écossaise, caprice brillant pour Piano. Op. 121. *Paris*, [1869.] fol. **h. 1299. d. (15.)**

— Première Élégie, caprice pour le Piano. Op. 88. *Paris*, [1866.] fol. **h. 1299. c. (22.)**

— 2ᵐᵉ Élégie. Op. 207. [P. F.] *See* BELLINI (V.) [*Appendix.*] Alla memoria di V. Bellini ... No. 21. [1885.] fol. **h. 3312.**

— L'Elisire d'Amore, Caprice pour Piano sur l'Opéra de Donizetti ... Op. 114, *etc. Schott: Paris*, [1868.] fol.
h. 1299. d. (9.)

— Ernani, opéra de Verdi, fantaisie brillante pour Piano. *Paris*, [1875.] fol. **h. 1299. f. (42.)**

— L'Etudiant Pauvre. Opéra Comique de C. Millœcker. Fantaisie brillante pour piano. Op. 269. *A. Cranz: Hambourg*, 1886. fol. **h. 1299. h. (4.)**

— Evening Prayer. Andante religioso. [Organ.] *See* WESTBROOK (W. J.) New Organ Arrangements. No. 18. [1886, *etc.*] fol.
h. 2750. b.

— Excelsior, musique de R. Marenco, fantaisie brillante pour Piano. Op. 241. *Milano*, [1882.] fol. **h. 1299. g. (52.)**

— L'Extase, valse de L. Arditi, transcription de salon pour Piano. Op. 99. *London*, [1867.] fol. **h. 1299. b. (8.)**

— La Fanchonnette [by A. L. Clapisson], fantaisie brillante pour Piano. Op. 115. *Paris*, [1868.] fol. **h. 1299. d. (8.)**

— Les Faneuses, caprice brillant. [P. F.] *Paris*, [1881.] fol.
h. 1299. g. (26.)

— Fantaisie brillante. Solo pour la Flûte avec accompt. de Piano. *Paris*, [1875.] fol. **h. 2510. a. (16.)**

Fantaisie sur un Thême Allemand

— Fantaisie pour le Piano, sur un Thême Allemand. pp. 13. *R. Mills: London*, [1853.] fol. **h. 723. m. (6.)**

— Fantaisie sur un thème allemand, pour piano. ⟨Op. 5.⟩ pp. 11. *D'Almaine & Co.: London*, [c. 1855.] fol. **h. 726. s. (6.)**

— Fantaisie sur un thème Allemand pour piano. Op. 5. pp. 11. *D'Almaine & Co.: London*, [1857.] fol. **h. 1299. (3.)**

— Fantaisie pour le piano, sur un thème Allemand, *etc.* (Op. 5.) pp. 13. *Robert Cocks & Co.: London*, [1859.] fol.
h. 1299. (4.)

— Fantaisie sur un thème allemand. [P. F.] pp. 11. *Brewer & Co.: London*, [1859.] fol. **h. 1299. a. (1.)**

— Fantaisie, sur un thème allemand. [P. F.] pp. 13. *Cramer, Beale & Cᵒ.: London*, [c. 1860.] fol. **g. 232. dd. (3.)**

— Fantaisie sur un thème Allemand pour piano. Op. 5, *etc.* pp. 13. *Chez Jean André: Offenbach s/M.*, [c. 1860.] fol.
h. 721. s. (6.)

— Fantasia on a German air. [P. F.] *London*, [1860.] fol.
No. 1655, 56 of the "Musical Bouquet". **H. 2345.**

— Fantaisie sur un thème Allemand. [P. F.] pp. 13. *W. Williams & Co.: London*, [1861.] fol. **h. 1299. a. (4.)**

— Fantaisie sur un thème Allemand. [P. F.] pp. 13. *Leader & Cock: London*, [1861.] fol. **h. 1299. a. (6.)**

— Fantasia sur un thème Allemand pour le Piano. Op. 3. pp. 13. *B. Williams: London*, [1862.] fol. **h. 1299. a. (10.)**

LEYBACH (Ignace)

— Fantaisie sur un thème Allemand. pp. 11. *L'Enfant & Hodgkins: London*, [1863.] fol.   **h. 1299. a. (19.)**

— Fantaisie sur un thème Allemand. [P. F.] pp. 13. *Cramer, Wood & Co.: London*, [1864.] fol.   **h. 1299. b. (12.)**

— Fantaisie, sur un thème allemand. [P. F.] pp. 11. *Brewer & Cᵒ: London*, [c. 1870.] fol.   **h. 722. v. (1.)**

— Fantasie sur un thème allemand. ⟨Edited & revised by Wilhelm Kuhe.⟩ [P. F.] pp. 13. *Wood & Cᵒ: London*, [c. 1875.] fol.   **h. 3870. vv. (8.)**

— Fantaisie sur un thème Allemand pour Piano. pp. 11. *G. W. Gunston: London*, [1877.] fol.   **h. 1299. b. (33.)**

— Fantaisie sur un thème allemand. [P. F.] pp. 11. *Moutrie & Son: London*, [1879.] fol.   **h. 1494. q. (37.)**

— Fantaisie sur un thème allemand pour piano. Op. 5. Édition simplifiée par L. Streabbog. pp. 7. *Les fils de B. Schott: Mayence*, [1883.] fol.   **h. 1299. g. (43.)**

— Fantaisie sur un Thème Allemand pour piano. Revised ... by L. Schumann. *Ransford & Sons: London*, [1884.] fol.   **h. 1299. h. (3.)**

— Fantaisie sur un Thème allemand ... Op. 5. Edited and fingered by P. Gallico. (Piano.) *J. W. Stern & Co.: New York*, (1913.) fol.   **g. 606. n. (43.)**

— Fantaisie sur un thème allemand. Op. 5. [Violin and P. F.] *See* RITTER (E. W.) Les Succès du Salon, *etc.* No. 24. [1891, *etc.*] fol.   **h. 3665. a.**

— Fantaisie brillante pour Piano sur l'Africaine de G. Meyerbeer. *Paris*, [1875.] fol.   **h. 1299. f. (48.)**

— L'Africaine, musique de G. Meyerbeer, fantaisie brillante pour le Piano. *London*, [1875.] fol.   **h. 1299. b. (25.)**

— Fantaisie brillante sur Astorga, opéra de J. J. Albert, pour Piano. Op. 116 [or rather, Op. 124]. *Paris*, [1869.] fol.   **h. 1299. d. (23.)**

— Fantaisie à quatre mains pour le Piano, sur l'opéra Le Barbier de Séville (de G. Rossini). Op. 78. *Paris*, [1866.] fol.   **h. 1299. c. (11.)**

— Fantaisie brillante sur Boccace. Opéra ... de F. de Suppé pour piano. Op. 270. *Hambourg*, [1885.] fol.   **h. 1299. g. (63.)**

— Fantaisie sur le Capitaine Fracasse, opéra ... d'E. Pessard, pour Piano. *Paris*, [1880.] fol.   **h. 1299. g. (13.)**

— Fantaisie brillante pour Harmonium ... sur les motifs de I Capuleti e i Montecchi (de Bellini). *Paris*, [1865.] fol.   **h. 2510. a. (5.)**

— Fantaisie brillante pour Piano à quatre mains sur les motifs de l'opéra Euriante de C. M. de Weber. Op. 66. *Paris*, [1864.] fol.   **h. 1299. c. (1.)**

— Fantaisie élégante sur Faust de C. Gounod pour Piano. *London*, [1862.] fol.   **h. 1299. a. (18.)**

— Fantaisie élégante sur Faust de C. Gounod pour Piano. Op. 35. *Paris*, [1868.] fol.   **h. 1299. d. (11.)**

— Faust, opéra ... de C. Gounod. Deuxième fantaisie brillante pour Piano. *Berlin & Posen*, [1876.] fol.   **h. 1299. f. (52.)**

— Fantaisie brillante sur La Fiancée d'Abydos, opéra de A. Barthe. Op. 84. *Paris*, [1866.] fol.   **h. 1299. c. (17.)**

— Fantaisie brillante pour le Piano sur des motifs de l'opéra Ione, dal maëstro E. Petrella. *Paris*, [1863.] fol.   **h. 1299. a. (27.)**

LEYBACH (Ignace)

— Fantaisie brillante pour Piano sur Le Jour & la Nuit, opéra bouffe de C. Lecocq. *Paris*, [1882.] fol.   **h. 1299. g. (31.)**

— Fantaisie brillante pour le piano sur La Muette de Portici d'Auber. Op. 268. *Paris*, 1885. fol.   **h. 1299. g. (62.)**

— Fantaisie brillante pour Piano sur les motifs de l'opéra Norma ... de Bellini. Op. 67. *Paris*, [1864.] fol.   **h. 1299. c. (2.)**

— Fantaisie brillante pour Piano à quatre mains sur des motifs de l'opéra Oberon de C. M. de Weber. Op. 65. *Paris*, [1864.] fol.   **h. 1299. c. (3.)**

— I Puritani. Fantaisie brillante [on V. Bellini's opera] composée pour le Piano. pp. 13. *Schott & Cᵉ: Londres*, [1862.] fol.   **h. 1299. a. (14.)**

— I Puritani [by V. Bellini], fantaisie brillante pour Piano. Op. 48. pp. 13. *Schott et Cᵉ.: London*, [1865.] fol.   **h. 1299. b. (1.)**

— Fantasia brilliant on airs from Bellini's opera I Puritani. [P. F.] pp. 13. *B. Williams: London*, [1866.] fol.   **h. 1299. b. (6.)**

— I Puritani, fantaisie brillante pour Piano. pp. 13. *Metzler & Cᵒ.: London*, [1866.] fol.   **h. 1299. b. (4.)**

— I Puritani, fantaisie brillante pour Piano. Op. 48. pp. 13. *Chappell & Cᵒ.: London*, [1867.] fol.   **h. 1299. b. (9.)**

— I Puritani, fantaisie brillante pour Piano. Op. 48. pp. 13. *Robert Cocks & Cᵒ.: London*, [1869.] fol.   **h. 1299. b. (13.)**

— I Puritani. Fantasia de salon pour piano [on V. Bellini's opera] ... Op. 48. pp. 13. *Augener & Cᵒ: London*, [c. 1870.] fol.   **h. 61. cc. (23.)**

— I Puritani (de Bellini). Fantaisie brillante pour le Piano. pp. 13. *J. B. Cramer & Cᵒ.: London*, [1874.] fol.   **h. 1299. b. (22.)**

— I Puritani, (Bellini) fantaisie brillante, pour piano ... Op. 48. Revised and fingered by J. T. Trekell. pp. 12. *Alfred Phillips: London*, [c. 1880.] fol. *Part of "The Hanover Edition".*   **h. 61. pp. (5.)**

— Fantaisie brillante à quatre mains pour le Piano sur l'opéra de Bellini, I Puritani. Op. 79. *Paris*, [1866.] fol.   **h. 1299. e. (12.)**

— Fantaisie sur Roland à Roncevaux, de A. Mermet. Op. 71. [P. F.] *Paris*, [1865.] fol.   **h. 1299. c. (7.)**

— Fantaisie brillante sur la Sonnambula, opéra de Bellini pour piano, *etc. London*, [1859.] fol.   **h. 1299. (9.)**

— Fantaisie brillante sur la Sonnambula, opéra de Bellini. [P. F.] *London*, [1865.] fol.   **h. 1299. b. (2.)**

— La Sonnambula, opéra de Bellini, fantaisie brillante pour Piano. Op. 27. *London*, [1866.] fol.   **h. 1299. b. (3.)**

— [Another edition.] La Sonnambula, fantaisie brillante ... pour Piano. *London*, [1866.] fol.   **h. 1299. b. (5.)**

— Fantaisie brillante sur la Sonnambula ... pour Piano. Op. 27. *London*, [1867.] fol.   **h. 1299. b. (10.)**

— [Another edition.] Fantaisie brillante sur la Sonnambula, *etc. London*, [1867.] fol.   **h. 1299. b. (11.)**

— Fantaisie brillante sur la Sonnambula, *etc. London*, [1869.] fol.   **h. 1299. b. (15.)**

— La Sonnambula, fantaisie brillante sur l'opéra de Bellini pour le Piano. *London*, [1876.] fol.   **h. 1299. b. (26.)**

— Festa Romana, fantaisie brillante pour Piano sur la melodie de E. Paladilhe. *London*, [1874.] fol.   **h. 1299. b. (23.)**

LEYBACH (IGNACE)

— Fête des moissonneurs. 2me Galop pastoral composé pour le Piano. *Mayence*, [1863.] fol. **h. 1299. a. (22.)**

— Fête des Naïades. Caprice brillant pour piano. Op. 275. *Vernède: Versailles*, [1888.] fol. **h. 1299. h. (7.)**

— Fête Hongroise, caprice brillante pour piano. Op. 26. *London*, [1859.] fol. **h. 1299. (8.)**

— Fête Villageoise. Caprice pour Piano. Op. 44. *London, Mayence* [printed], [1862.] fol. **h. 1299. a. (12.)**

— Fête Villageoise. Idylle rustique pour Harmonium, *etc. Paris*, [1877.] fol. **h. 2510. a. (20.)**

— Les Feuilles d'Automne. Rêverie pour Piano. *Paris*, [1873.] fol. **h. 1299. f. (18.)**

— La Fille de Mme Angot [by C. A. Lecocq] fantaisie brillante pour Piano. *London*, [1874.] fol. **h. 1299. b. (21.)**

— La Fille de Mme. Angot [by C. A. Lecocq]. Fantaisie brillante pour Piano. *Paris*, [1874.] fol. **h. 1299. f. (39.)**

— La Fille du Tambour Major. Opéra-comique ... de J. Offenbach. Fantaisie Brillante. Op. 228. [P. F.] *Paris*, [1881.] fol. **h. 1299. g. (50.)**

— Il Fiore di Harlem, de F. Flotow. Fantaisie brillante pour Piano. *Turin*, [1877.] fol. **h. 1299. f. (57.)**

— Fleur de Salon, deuxième nocturne pour le piano. *London*, [1853.] fol. **h. 723. m. (7.)**

— Fleur de Salon. Deuxième Nocturne pour le Piano. *London*, [1864.] fol. **h. 1299. b. (14.)**

— Fleur de Salon, deuxième nocturne pour le Piano. *London*, [1874.] fol.
No. 4038, 39 of the "Musical Bouquet". **H. 2345.**

— Fleur du souvenir, rêverie pour piano. Op. 29. *London*, [1859.] fol. **h. 1299. (11.)**

— Fleur Printanière, caprice brillant pour Piano. *Paris*, [1882.] fol. **h. 1299. g. (32.)**

— Fleurs Azurées caprice-mazurke pour Piano. Op. 102. *Paris*, [1868.] fol. **h. 1299. d. (1.)**

— La Flûte Enchantée, opéra de Mozart, fantaisie élégante pour le Piano. Op. 77. *Paris*, [1866.] fol. **h. 1299. c. (13.)**

— La Flûte Enchantée, opéra de Mozart, fantaisie élégante pour le Piano. *Mayence*, [1880.] fol. **h. 1299. g. (8.)**

— La Forza del Destino, opéra de G. Verdi. Fantaisie brillante pour Piano. *Paris*, [1875.] fol. **h. 1299. f. (43.)**

— Freyschütz de C. M. de Weber, fantaisie brillante pour l'Harmonium, *etc. Paris*, [1867.] fol. **h. 2510. a. (7.)**

— Freyschütz de C. M. de Weber, fantaisie brillante pour le Piano. Op. 96. *Paris*, [1867.] fol. **h. 1299. c. (26.)**

— Gabrielle, simple mélodie pour Piano. *Paris*, [1873.] fol. **h. 977. l. (11.)**

— Galathée, caprice brillant pour le Piano. Op. 109. *Paris*, [1868.] fol. **h. 1299. d. (6.)**

— Galop de Concert pour Piano. *Londres*, [1873.] fol. **h. 1299. f. (26.)**

— Gasparone, Opéra Comique de C. Millœcker. Fantaisie brillante pour piano. Op. 272. *A. Cranz: Hambourg*, 1885. fol. **h. 1299. h. (5.)**

— La Gazza Ladra de Rossini, fantaisie brillante pour le Piano. Op. 80. *Paris*, [1866.] fol. **h. 1299. c. (16.)**

LEYBACH (IGNACE)

— Gille et Gillotin (opéra de A. Thomas), Fantaisie brillante. [P. F.] *Paris*, [1875.] fol.
One of the "Souvenirs des Grands Maîtres". **h. 1299. f. (12.)**

— Les Glaneuses, caprice brillant pour Piano. *Paris*, [1875.] fol. **h. 1299. f. (49.)**

— Grande valse brillante pour piano ... Op. 14. pp. 9. *Robert Cocks & Co.: London*, [1859.] fol. **h. 726. s. (5.)**

— [Another copy.] **h. 1299. (6.)**

— Grande Valse de Concert. Caprice pour Piano. *London*, [1862.] fol. **h. 1299. a. (13.)**

— Il Guarany (A. C. Gomes). Fantaisie brillante pour Piano. Op. 147. *London*, [1872.] fol. **h. 1299. b. (18.)**

— Il Guarany, opéra de A. C. Gomes. Fantaisie brillante. [P. F.] *Paris*, [1872.] fol.
One of "Souvenirs des Grands Maîtres". **h. 1299. f. (10.)**

— La Guerre Joyeuse. Opéra ... de J. Strauss. Fantaisie brillante pour piano. Op. 271. *Hambourg*, [1885.] fol. **h. 1299. g. (64.)**

— Guillaume Tell, fantaisie brillante sur l'opéra de Rossini, pour Piano. Op. 82. *Paris*, [1866.] fol. **h. 1299. c. (19.)**

— Harmonie du Soir. 4e. Rêverie pour le Piano. *Londres*, [1860.] fol. **h. 1299. a. (2.)**

— Harmonie du Soir. Caprice pour Harmonium, *etc. Paris*, [1874.] fol. **h. 2510. a. (12.)**

— L'Harmonium ou l'Orgue expressif. Méthode complète théorique et pratique. *Paris*, [1864.] fol. **h. 2510.**

— Henry VIII. opéra de C. Saint-Saëns. Fantaisie brillante pour piano. Op. 254. *Paris*, [1883.] fol. **h. 1299. g. (55.)**

— Herculaneum de F. David, fantaisie brillante. [P. F.] Op. 112. *Paris*, [1868.] fol. **h. 1299. d. (12.)**

— Heureux Présage pour Piano et Harmonium. *Paris*, [1876.] fol. **h. 2510. a. (18.)**

— L'Hortensia. Caprice brillant pour Piano. *Paris*, [1863.] fol. **h. 1299. a. (28.)**

— Idylle pastorale pour Piano. *Londres*, [1873.] fol. **h. 1299. f. (28.)**

— Idylle pastorale pour Harmonium. *Mayence*, [1881.] fol. **h. 2575. h. (10.)**

— 1re. Idylle rustique, pour le piano, *etc.* (Op. 10.) *London*, [1859.] fol. **h. 1299. (5.)**

— 2^e. idylle rustique pour le piano. Op. 28. *London*, [1859.] fol. **h. 1299. (10.)**

— Les Illustrations musicales pour Piano. [Fantasias on operas.] no. 4. *L. Grus: Paris*, [1875.] fol.
Wanting no. 1–3, 5, 6. **h. 1299. h. (8.)**

— L'Isolement, rêverie pour Piano. Op. 94. *Paris*, [1867.] fol. **h. 1299. c. (27.)**

— Joseph de Méhul. Op. 233. [Fantasia for P. F.] *Paris*, [1881.] fol.
One of the "Souvenirs des Grands Maîtres". **h. 1299. g. (51.)**

— Joyeux Réveil, caprice brillant pour Piano. *Paris*, [1883.] fol. **h. 1299. g. (41.)**

— La Juive, fantaisie brillante [on J. F. F. É. Halévy's opera] pour Piano. Op. 129. *Paris*, [1869.] fol. **h. 1299. d. (20.)**

— Land of Enchantment. Song, words by H. S. Leigh. *London*, [1880.] fol. **H. 1783. o. (66.)**

LEYBACH (IGNACE)

— Land of Enchantment. Song, words by H. S. Leigh. *London,* [1881.] fol.   **H. 1787. j. (34.)**

— Lohengrin, opéra de R. Wagner, fantaisie brillante pour Piano. Op. 125. *Paris,* [1869.] fol.   **h. 1299. d. (16.)**

— I Lombardi ... opéra de Verdi, Fantaisie brillante pour Piano. *Paris,* [1876.] fol.   **h. 1299. f. (56.)**

— I Lombardi, fantaisie brillante sur l'opéra de Verdi. [P. F.] *London,* [1876.] fol.   **h. 1299. b. (29.)**

— Lucie de Lammermoor [by D. G. M. Donizetti]. Fantaisie brillante pour Piano [duet]. Op. 183. (Arr. par H. Rupp.) *Les Fils de B. Schott: Mayence,* [1877.] fol.   **h. 1299. g. (3.)**

— Luisa Miller, opéra de G. Verdi, fantaisie brillante pour Piano. *Paris,* [1877.] fol.   **h. 1299. g. (1.)**

— Macbeth, fantaisie brillante sur l'opéra de Verdi. [P. F.] *London,* [1876.] fol.   **h. 1299. b. (28.)**

— Macbeth, opéra de Verdi, Fantaisie brillante pour Piano. *Paris,* [1876.] fol.   **h. 1299. f. (55.)**

— Les Maccabées, opéra de A. Rubinstein. Fantaisie brillante pour Piano. *Berlin & Posen,* [1876.] fol.   **h. 1299. f. (53.)**

— Magali, grande valse brillante pour Piano. Op. 83. *Paris,* [1867.] fol.   **h. 1299. c. (24.)**

— Le Maître de Chapelle. Fantaisie brillante [on F. Paer's opera]. Op. 218. [P. F.] *Paris,* [1879.] fol. *One of the "Souvenirs des Grands Maîtres".*   **h. 1299. g. (47.)**

— Mandolinata (souvenir de Rome), fantaisie brillante sur le motif de E. Paladilhe. [P. F.] Op. 130. *Paris,* [1869.] fol.   **h. 1299. d. (24.)**

— Mandolinata, fantaisie brillante pour Piano. [Duet.] *London,* [1873.] fol.   **h. 1299. b. (20.)**

— Marche brillante, caprice pour Piano. Op. 113. *Paris,* [1868.] fol.   **h. 1299. d. (13.)**

— Marche brillante pour Piano. *Paris,* [1883.] fol.   **h. 1299. g. (40.)**

— La Marseillaise, chant national [by C. J. Rouget de Lisle] transcrit pour Piano. *Paris,* [1879.] fol.   **h. 1494. q. (40.)**

— Marta, opéra comique de F. de Flotow. Fantaisie brillante pour le Piano. *Paris,* [1874.] fol.   **h. 1299. f. (33.)**

— I Masnadieri ... opéra de G. Verdi, fantaisie pour Piano. *Paris,* [1877.] fol.   **h. 1299. g. (2.)**

— 2ᵉ. mazurka, caprice brillant pour piano. Op. 31. *London,* [1859.] fol.   **h. 1299. (13.)**

— Mazurke Hongroise. Caprice pour Piano. *Paris,* [1874.] fol.   **h. 1299. f. (32.)**

— Méditation et Prière, deux morceaux religieuse [*sic*] pour Harmonium. *London,* [1864.] fol.   **h. 2510. a. (1.)**

— Meditation and Prayer. [Organ.] *See* WESTBROOK (W. J.) New Organ Arrangements. No. 16. [1886, *etc.*] fol.   **h. 2750. b.**

— 20 Mélodies pour Chant avec accompagnement de Piano. Poésie de M. Paland. *Paris,* [1876.] 8°.   **F. 595.**

— Mes Souvenirs. Valse brillante pour Piano. *Paris,* [1873.] fol.   **h. 1299. f. (22.)**

— Mignon regrettant sa Patrie. Transcription brillante. [P. F.] *Paris,* [1883.] fol.   **h. 1299. g. (37.)**

— Mignonette, caprice-valse pour Piano. *Paris,* [1883.] fol.   **h. 1299. g. (42.)**

LEYBACH (IGNACE)

— Moïse, de Rossini, fantaisie brillante. [P. F.] Op. 117. *Paris,* [1869.] fol.   **h. 1299. d. (14.)**

— Myosotis, grande valse brillante pour Piano. *Paris,* [1870.] fol.   **h. 1299. f. (4.)**

— Les Noces de Figaro de W. A. Mozart, fantaisie brillante pour le Piano. Op. 101. *Paris,* [1867.] fol.   **h. 1299. c. (30.)**

— Les Noces de Jeannette [by F. M. V. Massé] fantaisie brillante pour Piano. *London,* [1873.] fol.   **h. 1299. b. (19.)**

— Les Noces de Jeannette [by F. M. V. Massé]. Fantaisie brillante pour Piano. *Paris,* [1873.] fol.   **h. 1299. f. (17.)**

— Première (deuxième) Nocturne pour Piano. Edited by G. Rolande. 2 no. *London,* [1881.] fol.   **h. 3275. j. (36.)**

— 1ᵉʳ nocturne pour piano ... Op. 3. 2ᵉ édition. pp. 9. *Henry Lemoine: Paris,* [1855?] fol.   **h. 3870. v. (11.)**

— 1ᵉʳ. Nocturne, pour le piano, *etc.* (Op. 3.) *London,* [1859.] fol.   **h. 1299. (1.)**

— 1ᵉʳ. Nocturne pour le Piano. *London,* [1860.] fol.   **h. 1299. a. (3.)**

— [1ᵉʳ.] Nocturne pour Piano. *London,* [1880.] fol.   **h. 1494. q. (41.)**

— 2ᵈ Nocturne pour piano ... Op. 4. *Chez les fils de B. Schott: Mayence,* [1835?] fol.   **h. 721. i. (5.)**

— 2ᵉ nocturne pour piano ... Op. 4 ... 2ᵉ édition. pp. 7. *Henry Lemoine: Paris,* [1855?] fol.   **h. 3870. v. (12.)**

— 2ᵉᵐᵉ. Nocturne pour piano, *etc.* (Op. 4.) *London,* [1859.] fol.   **h. 1299. (2.)**

— Deuxième Nocturne. [P. F.] *London,* [1861.] fol.   **h. 1299. a. (5.)**

— Deuxième Nocturne pour Piano. *London,* [1867.] fol.   **h. 1299. b. (7.)**

— 2ᵈ. Nocturne pour Piano à 4 mains. *Mayence,* [1876.] fol.   **h. 1299. f. (60.)**

— [2ᵈ Nocturne. Op. 4.] The Autumn Wind. [Two-part song.] *See* CHRISTIE (N.) Six Two Part Songs, *etc.* 1. [1902.] 8°.   **F. 1530. i. (2.)**

— 3ᵉᵐᵉ Nocturne pour le piano. Op. 25. *London,* [1859.] fol.   **h. 1299. (7.)**

— 5ᵉ. Nocturne pour Piano. *Mayence,* [1862.] fol.   **h. 1299. a. (16.)**

— 5ᵐᵉ Nocturne pour Piano. Op. 52. *W. Paxton: London,* [1912.] fol.   **h. 3284. g. (25.)**

— 5me Nocturne ... Op. 52. Arrang. par G. Popp. [Violin and P. F.] *See* RITTER (E. W.) Les Succès du Salon, *etc.* No. 25. [1891, *etc.*] fol.   **h. 3665. a.**

— Fifth Nocturne. [Violin and P. F.] *W. Paxton & Co.: London,* [1922.] fol. *Part of the "Anthology of Violin Music".*   **h. 1612. ll. (29.)**

— [5ᵉ nocturne. Op. 52.] Soft sighs the Night ... [Part-song for S. A. T. B.] Vocal score and words by Louis Lavater. pp. 8. *Leonard, Gould & Bolttler: London,* [1947.] 8°. [*L. G. B. choral Repertoire. no.* 58.]   **F. 1843. a.**

— 6ᵐᵉ. Nocturne pour Piano. Op. 91. *Paris,* [1867.] fol.   **h. 1299. c. (28.)**

— Norma. (Divertimento.) *See* infra: Recréations caractéristiques. No. 7.

LEYBACH (IGNACE)

— Le Nouvel Organiste. Cent morceaux pour orgue-harmonium, divisés en dix offices, dont deux offices funèbres. 2 pt. *Paris*, [1883–4.] 8°.
No. 52, 53 *of the Bibliothèque-Leduc.* **f. 140. b.**

— Les Nymphes, caprice brillant pour Piano. *Paris*, [1883.] fol. **h. 1299. g. (36.)**

— Les Nymphes du Ruisseau. Impromptu-Mazurka. [P. F.] *See* infra: Récréations caractéristiques. 2ᵐᵉ série. Op. 197. No. 5.

— O Salutaris pour Baryton ou Mezzo-Soprano. *See* LYRA. Lyra Sacra, *etc.* [1879.] 4°. **G. 990.**

— O Salutaris, pour Tenor ou Soprano avec accompagnement d'Orgue. [Words by St. Thomas Aquinas.] *Paris*, [1868.] fol. **H. 1028. d. (6.)**

— Oberon de C. M. de Weber, fantaisie brillante pour le Piano. Op. 86. *Paris*, [1866.] fol. **h. 1299. c. (20.)**

— L'Ombre, musique de F. de Flotow, Fantaisie brillante pour Piano. *Paris*, [1873.] fol. **h. 1299. f. (21.)**

— L'Ombre, musique de F. de Flotow, fantaisie brillante pour Piano. *London*, [1874.] fol. **h. 1299. b. (24.)**

— Opéras de Ambroise Thomas. Dix fantaisies brillantes pour piano. Op. 246. *Paris*, [1883.] fol.
Imperfect; no. 4 (*Le Caïd*) *only.* **h. 1299. g. (54.)**

— L'Organiste pratique. Cent-vingt morceaux faciles composés pour Harmonium ou Orgue, *etc. Paris*, [1866.] 8°. **f. 140.**

— L'Organiste Pratique. Cent-vingt morceaux faciles composés pour Harmonium ou Orgue. *Toulouse, Paris*, [1875.] 8°. **f. 140. a.**

— L'Organiste Pratique. 120 morceaux faciles pour Harmonium ou Orgue. 2 vol. *London*, [1878.] 8°. **e. 1153.**

— Otello de Rossini, fantaisie brillante pour le Piano. Op. 85. *Paris*, [1866.] fol. **h. 1299. c. (21.)**

— Parfum des Roses. Valse élégante pour piano. Op. 259. *Berlin*, [1884.] fol. **h. 1299. g. (58.)**

— Parfum des Roses. Valse élégante pour piano. Op. 259. *E. Ashdown: London*, [1889.] fol. **h. 1299. h. (9.)**

— Parfums d'Italie, mélodie de F. Mendelssohn Bartholdy, transcription brillante pour Piano. *Mayence*, [1880.] fol. **h. 1299. g. (18.)**

— Parfums d'Italie. Mélodie de Mendelssohn. Op. 226. [Fantasia for P. F.] *Paris*, [1880.] fol.
One of the "Souvenirs des Grands Maîtres". **h. 1299. g. (49.)**

— Pastorale et Idylle, deux morceaux caractéristiques pour Harmonium, *etc. Paris*, [1864.] fol. **h. 2510. a. (2.)**

— Pastorale and Idylle. [Organ.] *See* WESTBROOK (W. J.) New Organ Arrangements. No. 17. [1886, *etc.*] fol. **h. 2750. b.**

— Pastorella, idylle rustique pour Piano. *Paris*, [1882.] fol. **h. 1299. g. (29.)**

— Pégase, galop de concert pour Piano. *London*, [1876.] fol. **h. 1299. b. (31.)**

— Pensée de Jeune Fille. Mazurka brillante pour Piano. *Londres*, [1873.] fol. **h. 1299. f. (29.)**

— Pensée intime pour Piano. *Paris*, [1881.] fol. **h. 1299. g. (24.)**

— Pensée Mystérieuse, Mélodie [begins: "Parfois comme une fraiche aurore"]. Poésie de T. Tuffier. *Paris*, [1864.] fol. **H. 1774. c. (28.)**

— Pensée Romantique. Nocturne pour piano. Op. 258. *Offenbach a. M.*, [1885.] fol. **h. 1299. g. (57.)**

LEYBACH (IGNACE)

— Pie Jesu, pour Tenor ou Soprano avec accompagnement d'Orgue. *Paris*, [1868.] fol. **H. 1028. a. (5.)**

— Il Pirata [by V. Bellini]. Fantaisie brillante. [P. F.] *Paris*, [1872.] fol.
One of "Souvenirs des Grands Maîtres". **h. 1299. f. (9.)**

— Plainte d'une Captive, prière du soir pour Piano. *Paris*, [1881.] fol. **h. 1299. g. (25.)**

— La plainte de l'exilé. Romance sans paroles pour Piano. *Paris*, [1863.] fol. **h. 1299. a. (29.)**

— Polonaise. Duo concertant pour Piano et Harmonium. *Paris*, [1877.] fol. **h. 2510. a. (19.)**

— Polonaise, F min. Op. 51. (Edited and fingered by A. Fraemcke.) [P. F.] *G. Schirmer: New York*, 1915. fol. **h. 3284. oo. (4.)**

— Polonaise pour le Piano. *Mayence*, [1863.] fol. **h. 1299. a. (23.)**

— Polyeucte, opéra ... de C. Gounod, fantaisie pour Piano. *Paris*, [1880.] fol. **h. 1299. g. (11.)**

— Pourquoi garder ton coeur. (Giulia gentil.) Transcription pour le Piano. Op. 68. *Paris*, [1864.] fol. **h. 1299. c. (4.)**

— Le Pré aux Clercs, fantaisie brillante [on L. J. F. Hérold's opera] pour Piano. Op. 122. *Paris*, [1869.] fol. **h. 1299. d. (21.)**

— Prière. 1ᵉʳ Caprice-Etude pour piano. Op. 11. *London*, [1854.] fol. **h. 723. m. (4.)**

— Prière du Soir, andante religioso pour Harmonium ou Orgue Expressif. *Paris*, [1870.] fol. **h. 2575. b. (24.)**

— The Progressive Music School. A selected collection of ... Sonatinas, &c. ... edited ... by I. Leybach. 1st Series. 15 no. *J. Williams: London*, [1881.] fol. **h. 1299. h. (1.)**

— I Puritani (Divertimento). *See* infra: Récréations caractéristiques. No. 6.

— Quatuor pour instruments à Cordes de G. Verdi. Illustrations pour Piano. *Milano*, [1877.] fol. **h. 1489. a. (27.)**

— Rafaëla. Echos de Venise pour Piano. *Paris*, [1873.] fol. **h. 977. l. (19.)**

— Les Rameaux, J. Faure. Fantaisie pour Piano. *Paris*, [1875.] fol.
One of the "Souvenirs des Grands Maîtres". **h. 1299. f. (13.)**

— Rappelle-toi. (Mélodie de G. Rupès.) Transcription brillante pour Piano. *Paris*, [1874.] fol. **h. 1299. f. (35.)**

— Récréations Caractéristiques pour le Piano. Op. 118. 7 no. *Paris*, [1869.] fol. **h. 1299. d. (10.)**

— Récréations Caractéristiques pour le Piano. No. 8–11. *Paris*, [1870.] fol.
Imperfect; wanting all the other no. **h. 3213. c. (18.)**

— Récréations caractéristiques, *etc.* No. 12. 16–21. *Paris*, [1872–75.] fol.
Imperfect; wanting no. 13–15. **h. 1481. l. (9.)**

— Récréations caractéristiques. 2ᵐᵉ série. Op. 197. No. 5. *Paris*, [1879.] fol.
Imperfect; wanting the other numbers. **h. 1299. g. (46.)**

— Reflets du printemps. Caprice pour le piano, *etc.* Op. 32. *Londres*, [1859.] fol. **h. 1299. (14.)**

— Reflets du printemps. Caprice pour le piano ... Op. 32. pp. 11. *Chez les fils de B. Schott: Mayence*, [c. 1860.] fol. **h. 721. ss. (19.)**

LEYBACH (IGNACE)

— La Régente. 4ᵉ. grande Valse pour Piano. *Paris*, [1863.] fol.
h. 1299. a. (25.)

— Regrets, barcarolle pour Piano. *Paris*, [1880.] fol.
h. 1299. g. (15.)

— Regrets, barcarolle pour Piano. *Mayence*, [1880.] fol.
h. 1299. g. (16.)

— Retour au Village, caprice brillant pour Piano. *Paris*, [1881.] fol.
h. 1299. g. (22.)

— Le Reveil des Chasseurs. Duo concertant pour Piano et Harmonium. *Mayence*, [1881.] fol.
h. 2575. h. (9.)

— Le Réveil des Elfes, caprice brillant pour Piano. *Paris*, [1870.] fol.
h. 1299. f. (5.)

— Le Réveil des Fées pour Piano. *Paris*, [1881.] fol.
h. 1299. g. (27.)

— Le Réveil des Naïades, caprice pour Piano. Op. 76. *Paris*, [1866.] fol.
h. 1299. c. (14.)

— 1ʳᵉ. rêverie pour piano. Op. 12. *London*, [1854.] fol.
h. 723. m. (5.)

— 2ᵐᵉ. Rêverie pour le Piano ... Op. 13. pp. 11. *Schott & Cᵒ.:* *London*, [1873.] fol.
h. 1299. f. (27.)

— Rêverie [No. 2. Op. 13.] ... Transcribed by J. A. Kappey. ⟨Conductor [and military band parts].⟩ 29 pt. *In:* MATTEI (T.) Grande valse de concert, *etc.* 1904. fol. [*Boosey's military Journal. ser.* 117. *no.* 2.]
h. 1549.

— Rêveries du soir, caprice pour le piano forte. *London*, [1859.] fol.
h. 1299. (15.)

— Richard Coeur de Lion (de Gretry), fantaisie brillante. [P. F.] Op. 119. *Paris*, [1869.] fol.
h. 1299. d. (17.)

— Rigoletto, opéra de Verdi. Fantaisie brillante pour Piano. *Paris*, [1874.] fol.
h. 1299. f. (34.)

— Le Roi de Lahore, fantasia on airs from Massenet's opera. [P. F.] *London*, [1879.] fol.
h. 1494. q. (38.)

— Ronde Villageoise, fantaisie pastorale pour Harmonium, *etc.* *Paris*, [1864.] fol.
h. 2510. a. (3.)

— Rondino. *See* supra: Recréations caractéristiques. No. 1.

— Rondo polka pour Piano. *Londres*, [1873.] fol.
h. 1299. f. (24.)

— Ruy Blas, opéra de F. Marchetti. Fantaisie brillante pour Piano. *Paris*, [1875.] fol.
h. 1299. f. (47.)

— Première Saltarella pour le Piano. *Paris*, [1863.] fol.
h. 1290. a. (24.)

— Salvia, valse brillante pour Piano. Op. 116. *Paris*, [1869.] fol.
h. 1299. d. (18.)

— Semiramide de G. Rossini, fantaisie brillante pour l'Harmonium, *etc.* *Paris*, [1867.] fol.
h. 2510. a. (8.)

— Sémiramide [by G. A. Rossini], fantaisie brillante. Op. 95. *Paris*, [1867.] fol.
h. 1299. c. (29.)

— Sérénade, caprice pour le Piano. Op. 87. *Paris*, [1866.] fol.
h. 1299. c. (23.)

— Si j'étais Roi (opéra d'A. Adam). Fantaisie brillante pour Piano. *Paris*, [1874.] fol.
h. 1299. f. (36.)

— Siciliano pour Piano et Harmonium. *London*, [1868.] fol.
h. 2510. a. (11.)

— Simple Mélodie, romance sans paroles. [P. F.] Op. 97. *Paris*, [1867.] fol.
h. 1299. c. (34.)

— Soft sighs the Night. *See* supra: [5ᵉ nocturne. Op. 52.]

LEYBACH (IGNACE)

— Le Soir. Mélodie [begins: "En vain l'aurore"]. Poésie de Madame Desbordes-Valmore. *Paris*, [1882.] fol.
H. 1793. d. (13.)

— Le Soir. Mélodie ... Transcription pour Piano. *Paris*, [1882.] fol.
h. 1299. g. (34.)

— Le Soir ... Op. 244. Transcription brillante pour harmonium. *Mayence*, [1883.] fol.
h. 1299. g. (53.)

— Un soir d'automne. Grande étude caractéristique ... pour le Piano. *Londres*, [1861.] fol.
h. 1299. a. (9.)

— La Solitude, élégie pour Piano. *Mayence*, [1881.] fol.
h. 1299. g. (21.)

— Song of the Muleteer. Bolero [begins: "Brightly the morning beams"]. Words by H. S. Leigh. *London*, [1880.] fol.
H. 1783. o. (65.)

— Song of the Muleteer. Bolero. Words by H. S. Leigh. *London*, [1881.] fol.
H. 1787. j. (35.)

— Sous la Roche. *See* supra: Recréations caractéristiques. No. 3.

— Souvenance. Caprice brillant pour Piano. *Paris*, [1872.] fol.
h. 1299. f. (16.)

— Souvenance. Caprice pour piano. Op. 255. *Mayence*, [1885.] fol.
h. 1299. g. (56.)

— Souvenir, caprice pour Piano. Op. 120. *Paris*, [1869.] fol.
h. 1299. d. (22.)

— Souvenir de Castelnau. Rêverie pour Harmonium, *etc. Paris*, [1875.] fol.
h. 2510. a. (13.)

— Souvenir de Marie Stuart ... Transcription brillante ... pour Piano. *Paris*, [1883.] fol.
h. 1299. g. (38.)

— Souvenir de Venise. Sérénade pour piano. Op. 273. *Vernède: Versailles*, 1888. fol.
h. 1299. h. (6.)

— Souvenir du Lac de Côme. Idylle pour Piano. *Paris*, [1874.] fol.
h. 1299. f. (38.)

— Souvenirs de Wiesbaden. Fantaisie en forme de valse pour Piano. *Londres*, [1873.] fol.
h. 1299. f. (25.)

— Souvenirs & Regrets. Marche funèbre pour Piano & Harmonium. *Paris*, [1875.] fol.
h. 2510. a. (15.)

— La Straniera, de Bellini. Fantaisie pour Piano. *Paris*, [1870.] fol.
h. 1299. f. (7.)

— Suisse et Tyrol, fantaisie pour Piano. *Paris*, [1880.] fol.
h. 1299. g. (14.)

— Sweet Babe. Song, words by H. S. Leigh. *London*, [1880.] fol.
H. 1783. o. (67.)

— Sweet Babe. Song, words by H. S. Leigh. *London*, [1881.] fol.
H. 1787. j. (36.)

— Les Sylphes, caprice brillant pour Piano. *Paris*, [1881.] fol.
h. 1299. g. (23.)

— Sylvana. (Weber.) Fantaisie brillante. [P. F.] *Paris*, [1874.] fol. One of "*Souvenirs des Grands Maîtres*".
h. 1299. f. (11.)

— Tabarin. Opéra d'E. Pessard. Transcription brillante pour piano. Op. 267. *Paris*, [1885.] fol.
h. 1299. g. (61.)

— Tancredi (de Rossini) transcription brillante pour Piano. *London*, [1876.] fol.
h. 1299. b. (32.)

— Tarantella pour le Piano. Op. 72. *London*, [1866.] fol.
h. 1299. c. (15.)

— Le Temple. Méditation religieuse pour Piano. *Paris*, [1872.] fol.
h. 1299. f. (15.)

LEYBACH (IGNACE)

— Thème Allemande. [P. F.] *See* SMALLWOOD (W.) Little
Footprints, *etc.* No. 17. [1900–2.] fol.   **h. 1412. w. (1.)**

— Thème Italien, fantaisie brillante sur La Sonnambula [by
V. Bellini. P. F.]. *London*, [1874.] fol.
No. 4036, 4037 *of the "Musical Bouquet".*   **H. 2345.**

— La Traviata, opéra de Verdi. Fantaisie brillante pour Piano.
Paris, [1873.] fol.   **h. 1299. f. (31.)**

— Tristesse, élégie pour le Piano. Op. 108. *Paris*, [1868.] fol.
     h. 1299. d. (3.)

— Il Trovatore, opéra de Verdi. Fantaisie brillante pour Piano.
Paris, [1875.] fol.   **h. 1299. f. (41.)**

— Il Trovatore, opera de G. Verdi, fantaisie brillante pour
Piano. [Duet.] *Mayence*, [1877.] fol.   **h. 1299. g. (4.)**

— Tyrolienne pour piano ... Op. 54. pp. 9. *Chez les fils de
B. Schott: Mayence*, [1862?] fol.   **h. 722. bb. (5.)**

— Tyrolienne pour Piano. [Op. 54.] *London*, [1862.] fol.
     h. 1299. a. (17.)

— Tyrolienne. Caprice brillant pour le pianoforte. Op. 260.
Berlin, [1884.] fol.   **h. 1299. g. (59.)**

— Tyrolienne. Caprice brillant pour piano. Op. 260.
E. Ashdown: London, [1889.] fol.   **h. 1299. h. (10.)**

— Tyrolienne. *See* supra: Recréations caractéristiques. No. 4.

— Tyrolienne & Valse brillante, deux morceaux caractéristiques
pour Harmonium, *etc. Paris*, [1864.] fol.   **h. 2510. a. (4.)**

— Valse poétique pour Piano. *Paris*, [1879.] fol.
     h. 1299. g. (5.)

— Les Vendangeurs. Caprice pour Piano. *Londres*, [1862.] fol.
     h. 1299. a. (15.)

— Les Vendangeurs. Caprice pour piano ... Op. 55. pp. 9. *Chez
les fils de B. Schott: Mayence*, [1863?] fol.   **h. 61. pp. (6.)**

— Les Vendangeurs. Caprice. [Violin and P. F.] *See* RITTER
(E. W.) Les Succès du Salon, *etc.* No. 33. [1891, *etc.*] fol.
     h. 3665. a.

— Verdi's Requiem. Illustrations pour Piano. *Milan*, [1875.] fol.
     h. 1492. h. (8.)

— [Verdi's Requiem.] Messe de Requiem de G. Verdi.
Illustrations pour Piano. *Paris*, [1875.] fol.   **h. 1299. f. (51.)**

— *See* BEETHOVEN (L. van) [Sonata. Op. 53.] Adagio ... arrangé
... par L. Leybach. [1868.] fol.   **h. 2510. a. (9.)**

— *See* MOZART (W. A.) [Sonatas. P. F. K. 330.] Andante de la
Sonate en Ut majeur ... arrangé ... par J. Leybach. [1868.]
fol.   **h. 2510. a. (10.)**

— *See* RUMMEL (J.) Fantaisie sur un thème Allemand par
J. Leybach, *etc.* [1861.] fol.   **h. 523. b. (2.)**

LEYBACH (J.)

— *See* LEYBACH (Ignace)

LEYBOURNE (GEORGE)

— Twelve of George Leybourne's new and popular Comic
Songs, *etc.* pp. 24. *H. D'Alcorn: London*, [1878.] 4°.
[*"D'Alcorn's Musical Miracles." no. 14.*]   **E. 1711.**

— The Barber's Apprentice Boy. [Song, begins: "Of William
Brown".] *London*, [1868.] fol.   **H. 1775. u. (41.)**

— If ever I cease to love. [Comic song.] Written, composed and
sung by G. Leybourne. *Hopwood & Crew: London*, [1871.]
fol.   **H. 1650. e. (10.)**

LEYDEN.— *Gemeente Archief*

— De Leidse koorboeken. The Leyden Choir Books. Codex A
... Ediderunt K. Ph. Bernet Kempers et Chris Maas. 2 tom.
Vereniging voor nederlandse muziekgeschiedenis: Amsterdam,
1970–73. fol.
[*Monumenta musica neerlandica. 9.*]   **G. 12. b.**

LEYDEN (DENIS)

— Red Riding Hood. A musical fairy tale for young children,
etc. pp. 16. *W. Paxton & Co.: London*, [1967.] 8°.
     F. 1656. l. (3.)

LEYDEN (NORMAN)

— *See* BOCK (Jerry) [Fiddler on the Roof.] Matchmaker ...
(S. S. A.) ... Arranged by N. Leyden. [1967.] 8°.
     F. 217. dd. (5.)

— *See* BOCK (Jerry) [Fiddler on the Roof.] Sabbath Prayer ...
Arranged for mixed voices (S. A. T. B.) by N. Leydon [*sic*], *etc.*
[1967.] 8°.   **F. 1874. e. (12.)**

— *See* BOCK (Jerry) [Fiddler on the Roof.] Sunrise, Sunset ...
(S. A. T. B.) ... Arranged by N. Leyden. [1967.] 8°.
     F. 1874. e. (11.)

— *See* GOEHRING (George) Hootenanny. Words and music by
G. Goehring. E. V. Deane, P. Horther. Arranged by
N. Leyden. ⟨S. A. T. B.⟩ [1963.] 8°.   **F. 1744. nn. (32.)**

— *See* KANDER (John) Cabaret. Selection ... [Military] band
arrangement by N. Leyden. [1968.] 4°. [*Chappell Band
Journal. no.* 866.]   **h. 1562.**

— *See* WRUBEL (Allie) [Song of the South.] Zip-a-dee doo-dah
... Arranged by N. Leyden. ⟨S. A. T. B.⟩ [1963.] 8°.
     F. 1744. nn. (33.)

LEYDEN (ROLF VAN)

— *See* BACH (C. P. E.) Sonate für Viola da Gamba und Bass ...
Herausgegeben von R. van Leyden. [Wq. 137.] 1933. 4°.
     g. 48. h. (3.)

— *See* BACH (J. S.) Drei Sonaten für Viola di Gamba und
Cembalo (Klavier) ... [B. G. Jahrg. 9. p. 175.] Herausgegeben
von R. van Leyden. [1933.] 4°.   **g. 548. ee. (17.)**

LEYDI (ROBERTO)

— Canti sociali italiani, *etc.* [With melodies.] *Edizioni Avanti!:
Milano*, 1963, *etc.* 8°.   **X. 0909/25.**

LEYDING (GEORG DIETRICH)

— *See* LEIDING.

LEYDING (JOHANN DIETRICH)

— Zwölf italiænische Arietten aus den dramatischen Wercken
des Herrn Abts Metastasio ... in Music gesetzt von
J. D. Leyding. Erster Theil. *Bey G. C. Grund: Hamburg*,
[1765?] obl. fol.   **D. 357.**

— Oden und Lieder mit ihren eigenen Melodien. *Bey
D. Iversen: Altona*, 1757. 8°.   **D. 357. a.**

LEYE (L.)

— Quintetto für zwei Horne ... Floete, Bassetthorn oder
Clarinette und Fagott, mit Begleitung des Piano-Forte, *etc.*
[Parts.] *Sinner: Coburg*, [1850?] fol.   **R. M. 17. f. 15. (2.)**

LEYER

— Leyer und Schwerdt. [Cantata.] *See* WEBER (C. M. F. E. von)

LEYERMANN
— Der Leyermann. [Song.] *See* HIMMEL (F. H.)

LEYLAND (CLAUDE FENN)
— Ah me! when shall I marry me? Song ... Words by Oliver Goldsmith. [*F. Harrison: London*, 1909.] fol.
   H. 1794. vv. (46.)

— Anguish. A tone poem for the pianoforte. *May Walter Publishing Co.: London*, 1918. fol.
   h. 3284. oo. (5.)

— Apple Blossoms. Song, words by ... D. James. *May Walter Publishing Co.: London*, 1918. fol.
   H. 1846. y. (21.)

— Dreamily drifting. Song, words by R. C. Tharp. *Orpheus Music Publishing Co.: London*, 1909. fol.
   H. 1794. vv. (47.)

— Had I your Heart. [Song.] Words by R. C. Tharp, *etc. Philharmonic Publishing Co.: London*, 1913. fol.
   H. 1793. t. (45.)

— I stood in a lovely Garden. Song, words by R. C. Tharp. *Orpheus Music Publishing Co.: London*, 1909. fol.
   H. 1794. vv. (48.)

— If Hearts grow sad. [Song.] Words by R. C. Tharp, *etc. Philharmonic Publishing Co.: London*, 1912. fol.
   H. 1793. t. (46.)

— Jimmy. Whistling Song, words by R. C. Tharp. *Philharmonic Publishing Co.: London*, 1912. fol.
   H. 1793. t. (47.)

— King and Country. Military March Song, words by W. H. C. Baddeley. *Orpheus Music Publishing Co.: London*, 1909. fol.
   H. 1794. vv. (49.)

— Knight of the Road. Song, words by Captain James. *May Walter Publishing Co.: London*, 1918. fol.
   H. 1846. y. (22.)

— Love of the starry Night. Song, the words by R. C. Tharp, *etc. Philharmonic Publishing Co.: London*, 1911. fol.
   H. 1792. s. (26.)

— Method for Violin. pp. xi. 51. *B. Feldman & Co.: London*, [1905.] fol.
   h. 1753. aa. (3.)

— Peter, Henry, Timothy and Toddlekins. Humorous Song, words by R. C. Tharp. *Orpheus Music Publishing Co.: London*, 1909. fol.
   H. 1794. vv. (50.)

— Red Rose. Song, words by W. H. C. Baddeley. *Orpheus Music Publishing Co.: London*, 1909. fol.
   H. 1794. vv. (51.)

— The Secret of Violin Playing. *Philharmonic Publishing Co.: London*, 1910. 4°.
   g. 498. m. (4.)

— The Secret of Violin Playing. (3rd edition.) *Philharmonic Publishing Co.: London*, 1911. 4°.
   g. 498. o. (3.)

— The Song of Love. [Song.] Words by R. C. Tharp. *Philharmonic Publishing Co.: London*, 1912. fol.
   H. 1792. s. (27.)

— Sweetheart of mine. Song, words by Captain James. *May Walter Publishing Co.: London*, 1918. fol.
   H. 1846. y. (23.)

— The White Ensign. Song, words by W. H. C. Baddeley. *Orpheus Music Publishing Co.: London*, 1909. fol.
   H. 1794. vv. (52.)

— The White Ensign. Song, words by W. H. C. Baddeley, *etc. West & Co.: London*, 1914. fol.
   H. 1793. t. (48.)

— Willy Willy Wiltshire. Humorous Song, words by R. C. Tharp, *etc. Philharmonic Publishing Co.: London*, 1911. fol.
   H. 1792. s. (28.)

— A World of Dreams. Song, words by R. C. Tharp. *May Walter Publishing Co.: London*, 1918. fol.
   H. 1846. y. (24.)

— Zara. An Eastern Chant. Foxtrot, words by M. Richards, *etc. Wilford: London*, 1921. 4°.
   G. 426. u. (21.)

LEYLAND (REGINALD) *pseud.* [i. e. R. W. HENEY.]
— Our Tommies on the march. Military march for pianoforte. *Cary & Co.: London*, 1919. 4°.
   g. 603. xx. (9.)

LEYS (W. H.)
— Has Sorrow thy young days shaded. Arranged by W. H. Leys. *London*, [1879.] 8°.
No. 20 *of "Swan and Pentland's Part Music".*
   E. 1770.

LEYSTAN (H.)
— *See* RESCH (J.) Secret Love ... Arranged ... by H. Leystan. [1894.] fol.
   h. 3290. m. (4.)

LEYTON (BLAIR)
— Meet me in Dreamland. Song. Words and music by B. Leyton. pp. 5. *Sydney P. Harris Co.: Detroit, New York*, [1909.] fol.
   H. 3985. z. (22.)

LEZARD (STANLEY C.)
— The Valda Waltz. [P. F.] *Jackson Bros.: London, etc.*, [1904.] fol.
   h. 3286. dd. (63.)

L'HÉRITIER (JEAN)
— Johannis Lhéritier opera omnia. Edidit Leeman L. Perkins. 2 vol. pp. lxvi. 349. *American Institute of Musicology:* [*Dallas, Tex.?,*] 1969. fol.
[*Corpus mensurabilis musicae.* 48.]
   H. 3.

L'HERMINÉ (J.)
— [3ᵉ] Recueil de nouvelles contre-danses walzes et anglaises. pp. 45. *Chez Frère: Paris*, [1800?] 8°.
   b. 55. i. (1.)

L'HERVILLIERS (E. DE)
— Valse de salon pour le Piano. *Paris*, [1883.] fol.
   h. 3276. g. (21.)

LH'ING-YÜN
— *See* CH'ING-YUN.

L'HIVER (G.)
— *See* GOLDMARK (C.) [Ländliche Hochzeit. Op. 26. Im Garten.] Au Jardin. Andante de la Symphonie ... arrangé pour harmonium et piano par G. L'Hiver. [1885.] fol.
   h. 2576. a. (5.)

— *See* SCHULHOFF (J.) Chant du berger ... arrangé pour piano et harmonium par G. L'Hiver. [1884.] fol.   **h. 2576. a. (18.)**

L'HOSTE (SPIRITO)
— De l'Hoste da Reggio il Primo Libro de Madrigali a Tre Voci ... Nouamente da lui fatti, corretti, & posti in luce. Alto. *Appresso di Francesco et Simone Moscheni: Milano*, 1554. obl. 4°.
   A. 262.

— De l'Hoste da Reggio il Primo Libro de Madregali a Tre Voci Nouamente per Antonio Gardano Ristampati, *etc.* Canto. (Tenore.) 2 pt. *Appresso di Antonio Gardano: Venetia*, 1562. obl. 4°.
   A. 262. a.

L'HÔTE (ALBERT)
— La Chanson du Printemps. [Song, begins: "Ah! voici le renouveau".] Paroles de Brizeux. *Paris*, [1863.] fol.
   H. 1774. c. (29.)

L'HÔTE (ALBERT)

— Matelots au Départ, choeur à 4 voix d'hommes [begins: "Nous quittons la Bretagne"]. Paroles d'A. Catelin. *Paris*, [1862.] 8°. **E. 600. a. (29.)**

— Soir d'Été. Mélodie [begins: "Au milieu du ciel"]. Paroles de A. de Montaiglon. *Paris*, [1863.] fol. **H. 1774. e. (30.)**

LHOTKA (FRAN)

— [Ðavo u selu.] Der Teufel im Dorf. The Devil in the Village. Ðavo u selu. Ballett in acht Bildern von … Pia-Pino Mlakar … Klavierauszug, *etc.* pp. 8. 227. *Zagreb*, 1935. fol.
With an English libretto comprising 6 pages inserted.
H. 1653. gg.

— [Ðavo u selu.] Der Teufel im Dorf … The Devil in the Village. Ballett in drei Akten … Szenarium: Pia und Pino Mlakar. Revidierte Fassung von … Ivo Lhotka-Kalinski. Klavierauszug, *etc.* pp. 192. *B. Schott's Söhne: Mainz*, [1964.] 4°.
With a synopsis in English inserted. **g. 230. vv. (4.)**

— Elegija i scherzo. Za gudački kvartet ili gudački orkestar. Partitura. pp. 16. *Savez kompozitora Jugoslavije; Udruženje kompozitora Hrvatske: [Zagreb*, 1931?] 4°. **g. 410. v. (7.)**

— Dvije hrvatske rapsodije. Žetelačke. Za violinu i klavir. II. izdanje. Deux rhapsodies croates. Chant des moissonneurs. Pour violon et piano, *etc.* [Score and part.] 2 pt. *Izdanja Hrvatskog glazbenog zavoda: Zagreb*, 1956. fol.
h. 1438. a. (4.)

— Kakva j' to ptica. [Part-song. S. A. T. B.] *Izdanje Muzičkog nakladno-prodajnog Saveza muzičkih udruženja Hrvatske: Zagreb*, 1952. fol. **H. 2175. a. (4.)**

— Koncert za gudače. Concerto for Strings. Partitura, *etc.* pp. 48. *Udruženje kompozitora Hrvatske: Zagreb*, 1957. 4°.
g. 1655. (1.)

— Šest narododnih pjesama, op. 21, za sitno grlo uz pratnju glasovira. 3 no. *Slavenski izdavački zavod: Beč*, [c. 1920.] fol.
H. 1653. p. (5.)

— Oj Ilija. Obradio: F. Lhotka. *See* HERCIGONJA (N.) Padaj silo, *etc.* 1946. 4°. **G. 615. (8.)**

— Ples paževa. *See* infra: [Srednje vjekovna ljubav.]

— Polet mladosti. Dvoglasno uz klavir. ⟨Tekst: Slobodan Manojlović.⟩ *Nakladni zavod Hrvatske: Zagreb*, 1947. 4°.
G. 615. (12.)

— [Srednje vjekovna ljubav.] Ples paževa … Dance of the Pages. Iz baleta "Srednje vjekova ljubav" … Za violinu i klavir, *etc.* [Score and part.] 2 pt. *Tisak Nakladnog zavoda Hrvatske: Zagreb*, 1950. fol. **g. 1591. a. (3.)**

— Der Teufel im Dorf … Ballett. *See* supra: [Ðavo u selu.]

— Zemlja slobode. Masovni zbor i klavir. Tekst: Ivan Kocijan. *Glas Rada: Zagreb*, [1950?] fol. **H. 1860. j. (32.)**

— *See* DEVČIĆ (N.) Mitraljeza … Obradio F. Lhotka, *etc.* 1946. fol. **H. 2175. (4.)**

— *See* LISINSKI (V.) [Ljubav i zloba.] Blago onom … Muzička obradba: F. Lhotka, *etc.* [1946.] fol. **H. 2175. (9.)**

— *See* LISINSKI (V.) Porin … Potpuni izvadak za klavir i pjevanje udesio F. Lhotka. 1919. fol. **G. 1371.**

— *See* LISINSKI (V.) Porin. Viteška opera u 5 činova. Glasovirski izvadak F. Lhotka, *etc.* 1969. 4°. **G. 1371. b.**

LHOTKA-KALINSKI (IVO)

— Analfabeta. Der Analphabet. The Analphabete. Muzička burleska u jednom činu. Libreto prema istoimenoj aktovki

LHOTKA-KALINSKI (IVO)

Branislava Nušića sastavio I. Lhotka-Kalinski … Übertragung ins Deutsche von B. Begović … Translated into English by M. Matišić and M. Zorčić. Klavirski Izvadak, *etc.* Serbocr., Ger. & Eng. pp. 73. *Izdanje Udruženja kompozitora Hrvatske: Zagreb*, 1957. fol. **H. 2175. d. (2.)**

— Bugarštice iz "Ribanja" Petra Hektorovića. ⟨Kada mi se Radoseve. I kliče devojka.⟩ Za glas i klavir. *Vlastita naklada: Zagreb*, 1955. fol. **H. 2175. c. (8.)**

— Dugme … Muzička groteska u jednom činu … Libreto prema istoimenoj aktovki Branislava Nušića … ⟨Der Knopf. Musikalische Groteske in einem Aufzug. Libretto nach dem gleichnamigen Einakter von Branislav Nušić. Übertragung ins Deutsche von Theo Tabaka.⟩ Klavirski izvadak, *etc.* Serbocr. & Ger. pp. 40. *Naklada Saveza kompozitora Jugoslavije: Zagreb*, 1961. fol. **H. 1847. i. (5.)**

— Kerempuhova pesem. Kantata za sole, zbor i orkestar. Stihovi iz "Balada Petrice Kerempuha" Miroslava Krleže. Partitura. pp. 125. *Naklada Saveza kompozitora Jugoslavije: Zagreb*, 1962. fol. **I. 525. f.**

— Lepo moje Zagorje. Suita za djecu, prema motivima iz Hrvatskog Zagorja, za klavir. [*Zagreb?*, c. 1950.] 4°.
g. 1591. b. (2.)

— Međimurje malo. Suita za djecu. Redigirao Prof. Evgenij Vaulin … Za klavir. pp. 12. *Nakladni zavod Hrvatske: Zagreb*, 1947. fol. **H. 2175. (8.)**

— Međimurje malo. Suita za djecu, za klavir. pp. 7. *Štamparski zavod "Ognjen Prica": Zagreb*, [c. 1950.] fol. **h. 1438. a. (2.)**

— Mikroformen. Mikroforme, *etc.* [P. F.] *In:* LUECK (Rudolf) Neue jugoslawische Klaviermusik, *etc.* Hft. 1. pp. 22, 23. [1966.] 4°. **g. 1529. bb. (2.)**

— Pet monologa za violoncello solo. pp. 8. *Udruženje kompozitora Hrvatske: Zagreb*, 1970. 4°. **g. 511. l. (4.)**

— Putovanje. Die Reise. Muzička satira u jednom činu … Libreto prema aktovki "Kirija" Branislava Nušića sastavio I. Lhotka-Kalinska … Übertragung ins Deutsche von Theo Tabaka. Klavirski izvadak, *etc.* Serbocr. & Ger. pp. 74. *Alkor-Edition: Kassel*, [1958.] 4°. **G. 762. g. (2.)**

— 2 sonatine, za klavir. pp. 16. *Zagreb*, 1952. fol.
h. 3865. p. (15.)

— Stari dalmatinski plesovi. Za klavir. pp. 8. *Vlastita naklada: [Zagreb?*, c. 1950.] fol. **g. 1591. a. (2.)**

— Vesele pjesme. Riječi Gvido Tartalja, *etc.* pp. 23. *Mladost: Zagreb*, 1955. 8°. **G. 615. j. (1.)**

— Vlast. Die Macht. Muzički portret u jednom činu … Libreto prema istoimenoj aktovki Branislava Nušića sastavio I. Lhotka-Kalinski … Klavirski izvadak, *etc.* Serbocr. & Ger. pp. 69. *Alkor-Edition: Kassel*, [1961.] 4°. **G. 762. g. (1.)**

— *See* LHOTKA (F.) [Ðavo u selu.] Der Teufel im Dorf … Revidierte Fassung von … I. Lhotka-Kalinski. [1964.] 4°.
g. 230. vv. (4.)

LHOUMEAU (   )

— *See* MÉLODIES. Mélodies de Chant Gregorian, *etc.* (4ᵉ Livraison … avec accompagnement … par … R. P. Lhoumeau, *etc.*) [1892.] 4°. **G. 867.**

L'HOYER (ANTOINE)

— Ouverture pour Guitarre et Violon. Oeuvre 18. *J. A. Böhme: Hambourg*, [1805?] fol. **h. 259. d. (11.)**

— Trois Sonates pour la Guitare avec une [*sic*] Violon obligé … Oeuv. 17. *J. A. Böhme: Hambourg*, [1810?] fol.
h. 259. d. (10.)

LHUILIER (CONRAD)

— Méthode complète de Trompe de Chasse, avec les airs, fanfares &c. usités dans les chasses royales. *Paris*, [1845?] *obl.* 4°. **b. 182.**

L'HUILLER (EDMOND)

— *See* LHUILLIER.

LHUILLIER (EDMOND)

— Agnès. Chansonnette [begins: "Je suis déjà"]. *Paris*, [1876.] fol. **H. 2624. (42.)**

— Aimable en Société — Chansonnette [begins: "Dans un salon"]. *Paris*, [1870.] fol. **H. 2624. (16.)**

— L'Anglais d'aujourd'hui. Chanson [begins: "J'étais moi"]. *Paris*, [1876.] fol. **H. 2624. (39.)**

— L'Anglais en traversée. Oppression de voyage. [Song.] ... Paroles de E. Bourget. *J. Meissonnier et fils: Paris*, [1850?] fol. **Hirsch M. 1296. (13.)**

— Bijou. Chansonnette-Portrait [begins: "On l'avait arraché"]. *Paris*, [1870.] fol. **H. 2624. (17.)**

— Le Bon Docteur. Chansonnette [begins: "Ah l'excellent cœur"]. *Paris*, [1869.] fol. **H. 2624. (12.)**

— La Carrière amoureuse de chauvin, Chanson ... Arrangée pour la guitare par Meissonnier jeune. pp. 3. *Chez J. Frey: Paris*, [1825?] 8°. **Hirsch M. 1293. (19.)**

— Ce cher Docteur. Grande scène [begins: "Je suis le médecin"]. *Paris*, [1875.] fol. **H. 2624. (36.)**

— Le Chant du Soldat. [Song, begins: "Marche au combat".] *Paris*, [1830?] fol. **G. 553. (42.)**

— Le Cotillon. Grand scène [begins: "Il est tard"]. *Paris*, [1869.] fol. **H. 2624. (9.)**

— La Croix du village, romance. Paroles de Mʳ Emile Barateau. *Chez Maurice Schlesinger: Paris*, [c. 1830.] fol. **G. 559. a. (31.)**

— De ta promesse qu'as tu fait. Romance. Paroles de M. Polak. *Paris*, [1830?] fol. **G. 390. (9.)**

— Devant Paris. Jérémiade Tudesque [begins: "Ma Gretchen adorée"]. Paroles de F. Berthel. *Paris*, [1872.] fol. **H. 2624. (24.)**

— Le Discret. Chansonnette [begins: "On m'accuse"]. *Paris*, [1875.] fol. **H. 2624. (38.)**

— L'Editeur de Musique. Chansonnette [begins: "Vous qui possédez"]. Paroles d'E. Bourget. *Paris*, [1866.] fol. **H. 2624. (2.)**

— En avant, chant national, paroles de Méry. *Londres*, [1854.] fol. **H. 1758. (43.)**

— Le Farceur. Chansonnette [begins: "Mon cousin est un grand farceur"]. Paroles de Mr. Jaime. *Paris*, [1835?] fol. **G. 552. (39.)**

— La Fleur d'Interlaken. Pastorale [begins: "Je suis né"]. *Paris*, [1870.] fol. **H. 2624. (18.)**

— La Grand mère et la petite fille. Chansonette dialoguée, paroles de Mʳ Gabriel de L**, *etc.* pp. 3. *Chez Ph. Petit: Paris*, [c. 1830.] fol. **G. 561. b. (15.)**

— L'Ingénu. Romance chansonnette [begins: "Lorsque l'on est jeune"]. *Paris*, [1873.] fol. **H. 2624. (32.)**

— J'ai dix huit ans. Romance, paroles de Mr. E. Souvestre. *Paris*, [1830?] fol. **G. 551. (2.)**

LHUILLIER (EDMOND)

— J'aime la valse. Fantaisie ... Paroles et musique de E. Lhuillier. *J. Meissonnier fils: Paris*, [1840?] fol. **Hirsch M. 1298. (17.)**

— "Je suis la Bayadère." Chansonette de Mr. Betourné. *Paris*, [1830?] fol. **G. 390. (10.)**

— Le Jeune homme charmant. Chansonette de Mʳ Boucher de Perthes, *etc.* pp. 3. *Chez J. Frey: Paris*, [1830?] fol. **Hirsch M. 1298. (18.)**

— Un Jeune Homme timide. Chansonnette [begins: "Je suis l'être"]. *Paris*, [1876.] fol. **H. 2624. (41.)**

— Les Jeunes valent bien les Vieux. Chanson [begins: "Le Grandpère"]. *Paris*, [1870.] fol. **H. 2624. (21.)**

— Les Jolies Petites Songes d'un Anglais ... Romance [begins: "Goddam! Goddam!"]. *Paris*, [1830?] fol. **G. 553. (13.)**

— La Lettre de faire part, ou la Mort du Conscrit. Romance sentimentale et militaire. pp. 3. *Chez S. Richault: Paris*, [1840?] fol. **G. 543. (42.)**

— Loijs, ou le Couvre-feu. Romance du 15ᵐᵉ siècle, mise en musique par E. L'Huillier. *Paris*, [1830?] fol. **G. 390. (5.)**

— Le Loup et l'Agneau. Grande scène comique [begins: "Allons petits enfants"]. *Paris*, [1870.] fol. **H. 2624. (23.)**

— M'direz vous qu' j'en ai menti? Chansonette. Paroles de Mʳ Jaime ... Arrangée pour la guitare par Meissonnier jeune. *Chez J. Meissonnier:* [*Paris*, 1825?] 8°. **Hirsch M. 1293. (15.)**

— Ma Denise. Scène populaire [begins: "Chut! silence!"]. *Paris*, [1873.] fol. **H. 2624. (29.)**

— Le Mari de la Chanteuse. Chansonnette [begins: "Avez vous entendu"]. *Paris*, [1876.] fol. **H. 2624. (40.)**

— Les Maris ont bon dos! Chansonnette. *Paris*, [1869.] fol. **H. 2624. (10.)**

— Le Meilleur ne vaut rien. Chansonnette [begins: "Grand Dieu"]. *Paris*, [1866.] fol. **H. 2624. (3.)**

— La Ménagerie. Chanson parade. Paroles de Mʳ Théodore P ... K. ... Arrangée pour guitare par Meissonnier jeune. *Chez Ph. Petit:* [*Paris*, 1825?] 8°. **Hirsch M. 1293. (17.)**

— Miss Sensitive. Chansonnette [begins: "On nommait moi"]. Paroles de E. Bourget. *Paris*, [1866.] fol. **H. 2624. (4.)**

— Monsieur et Madame Jean. Saynète pastorale en un acte ... Partition Chant et Piano. *Paris*, [1873.] 8°. **F. 441.**

— Monsieur fait ses visites. Scène de genre [begins: "J'ai trois visites"]. *Paris*, [1873.] fol. **H. 2624. (31.)**

— Un Monsieur très pressé. [Song, begins: "Hein! quoi".] *Paris*, [1877.] fol. **H. 2624. (43.)**

— La Mort du Contrebandier. [Song, begins: "A toi, mon brave".] (Paroles de A. Bétourné.) *Paris*, [1830?] fol. **G. 545. (20.)**

— Né pour être avocat. Grande scène [begins: "Ah! quel plaisir"]. *Paris*, [1878.] fol. **H. 2624. (45.)**

— Noël de ma nourrice. [Song.] *Paris*, [1830?] fol. **G. 390. (8.)**

— Nos Amateurs. Grande scène bouffe [begins: "D'où vient que toujours"]. *Paris*, [1875.] fol. **H. 2624. (35.)**

— Nos Danseuses. Chansonnette [begins: "Dans tous les salons"]. *Paris*, [1866.] fol. **H. 2624. (5.)**

— Nos Jolies Baigneuses. [Song.] *Paris*, [1882.] fol. **H. 1793. d. (14.)**

LHUILLIER (Edmond)

— Notre Dame de Bon Secours. Chansonnette [begins: "On dit que les femmes"]. *London*, [1870.] fol.   **H. 2624. (19.)**

— Ou!!! Chanson de tous les pays [begins: "Il est un être affreux"]. *Paris*, [1869.] fol.   **H. 2624. (13.)**

— Pamela; oder, Das ist meine Tochter! [Musical sketch for voice and P. F.] Von E. Bourget. *R. Schlingmann: Berlin*, 1869. 8°.
Pp. 84–99 of "Humoristisch-dramatische Hausblüetten," part of "Der Gesellschafts-Salon," etc.   **11746. k. 33.**

— Les Parisiens à Londres … ⟨Rondo.⟩ Paroles de M. Clairville. [Song.] pp. 3. *H. L. d'Aubel: Paris*, [c. 1865.] fol.
Issued as music supplement to "La Musique populaire," année 4. no. 23.   **P. P. 1948. s/2. (90.)**

— Une Partie de Dominos. Chansonnette [begins: "Un soir"]. *Paris*, [1873.] fol.   **H. 2624. (30.)**

— Pas de Fête. Chansonnette [begins: "N'auriez vous pas trouvé"]. *Paris*, [1877.] fol.   **H. 2624. (44.)**

— Pauv' Jérôm'Pointu! Lamentation comique. *Paris*, [1866.] fol.   **H. 2624. (6.)**

— Les Petits Jeux de Société. Scène comique [begins: "Vous êtes le soir"]. *Paris*, [1872.] fol.   **H. 2624. (27.)**

— Le Pigeon Blessé. Romance [begins: "Gentil messager"]. *Paris*, [1872.] fol.   **H. 2624. (26.)**

— La Portière romanique [*sic*] ou La lecture dans la loge. Épisode en quatre couplets. Paroles de T. Polak. *Paris*, [1830?] fol.   **G. 390. (7.)**

— Une Première Représentation. Grande scène [begins: "Du fin fond de la Normandie"]. *Paris*, [1873.] fol.   **H. 2624. (33.)**

— La Province a du bon. Chansonnette [begins: "Enfants, embrassez moi"]. *Paris*, [1866.] fol.   **H. 2624. (7.)**

— Le P'tit Cousin. Chansonnette [begins: "Tel que vous m'voyez"]. *Paris*, [1869.] fol.   **H. 2624. (14.)**

— Quatre Bêtes dans une Scène … comique [begins: "Je suis un vivant phénomène"]. *Paris*, [1873.] fol.   **H. 2624. (28.)**

— Les Rats de l'opéra. Cri de guerre. [Song.] Paroles de E. Bourget. *J. Meissonnier fils: Paris*, [1850?] fol.   **Hirsch M. 1296. (8.)**

— La Reine du Bal. Valse chantée [begins: "Valse enchanteresse"]. *Paris*, [1875.] fol.   **H. 2624. (37.)**

— Reproches à Ste. Catherine. Chansonnette [begins: "Jeune fille"]. *Paris*, [1870.] fol.   **H. 2624. (20.)**

— Le Rêve d'un Aspirant. [Song, begins: "Un jeune aspirant"]. *Paris*, [1869.] fol.   **H. 2624. (22.)**

— Le Roi des Tenors. Grand scène en trois langues [begins: "Je suis tenor"]. *Paris*, [1869.] fol.   **H. 2624. (15.)**

— Rosinette. [Song, begins: "Il était un beau jeune homme".] *Paris*, [1878.] fol.   **H. 2624. (47.)**

— La Sentinelle perdue. Chansonnette [begins: "Le peut-il"]. Paroles de T. Polak. *Paris*, [1830?] fol.   **G. 390. (6.)**

— La Sérénade. Nocturne [begins: "Nuit calme et sombre"]. Paroles de Mr. E. Deschamps. *Paris*, [1830?] 8°.   **E. 1717. (88.)**

— Il Signor Fugantini. Grande scène [begins: "Fanatique de mousique"]. *Paris*, [1878.] fol.   **H. 2624. (46.)**

— Le Supplice d'un Maître de Maison. Scène de Mœurs [begins: "Avez vous vu"]. *Paris*, [1866.] fol.   **H. 2624. (8.)**

— Suzette, chansonnette [begins: "Je suis muette"]. *Paris*, [1864.] fol.   **H. 2624. (1.)**

LHUILLIER (Edmond)

— Une Tapisserie. Romance. *Paris*, [1855?] fol.   **H. 2827. d. (6.)**

— Trois Lettres d'un Soldat. [Song, begins: "Quand je partis".] *Paris*, [1872.] fol.   **H. 2624. (25.)**

— La Trompette. Chanson militaire [begins: "Je suis troupier"] de Mr. Jaime. *Paris*, [1830?] fol.   **G. 553. (19.)**

— Vers le Printemps. Mélodie-tyrolienne. *Paris*, [1875.] fol.   **H. 2624. (34.)**

— Voilà l'plaisir, Messieurs! Chansonnette. *Paris*, [1869.] fol.   **H. 2624. (11.)**

LI

— Li Choi. [Song.] *See* Barten (G.) *of Blackburn.*

LI (Bao-lian)

— Sonata for Piano. pp. 10. *Lee Bo Luen: Hong Kong*, [1978.] 4°.   **g. 354. y. (4.)**

— … Suite for Horn & Piano No. 1. [Score and part.] 2 pt. *Lee Bo Luen: Hong Kong*, [1978.] 4°.   **g. 1094. cc. (4.)**

LI (Huan-chih)

— Ch'un-chieh hsü-ch'ü. [For orchestra of traditional Chinese instruments. Score, in numerical notation.] pp. 33. *Yin-yüeh Ch'u-pan-she: Peking*, 1960. 4°.   **G. 1363. jj. (1.)**

LI (Kuang-yeh)

— *See* Osgood (Howard C.) and Li (Kuang-yeh) Salvation Songs, *etc.* 1951. 8°.   **G. 1363. g.**

LI (Kuo-ch'üan)

— Ch'ing-nien yüan-wu ch'ü. [Young people's round dance. Orchestral score.] pp. 19. *Yin-yüeh Ch'u-pan-she: Peking*, 1958. 8°.   **G. 1363. l. (5.)**

LI (Po)

— Hsiao-hsiao ko-sheng hsiang ting-ting. [Children's songs. Melodies only. Staff and numerical notation.] pp. 24. *Ai-hua Yin-yüeh-she: Singapore*, 1949. obl. 8°.   **G. 1363. hh. (1.)**

LI (Yen-sung)

— Ch'ing-lien yüeh-fu. [Four traditional p'i-pa themes.] pp. 16. *Yin-yüeh Ch'u-pan-she: Peking*, 1956. 8°.   **G. 1363. l. (6.)**

LIADOFF (A.)

— *See* Lyadov (Aleksandr N.)

LIADOV (Anatoly Konstantinovich)

— *See* Lyadov.

LIADOW (Anatole)

— *See* Lyadov (Anatoly K.)

LIANG (Chen-Kuang)

— Sheng-sung. Sacred hymns. ⟨Compiled, edited and translated by Leung Chan Kwong.⟩ *South China Peniel Press: Hong Kong*, 1950. 8°.   **G. 1363. bb. (1.)**

— [Another issue.] Sheng-sung. Sacred hymns. *Hong Kong*, 1950. 8°.   **G. 1363. bb. (2.)**

LIANG (CHEN-KUANG)

— Sheng sung. Sacred hymns. [Compiled and translated by Liang Chen-kuang. Third edition.] *South China Peniel Press: Hong Kong*, [1951.] 8°.　　　　　**G. 1363. p. (5.)**

— Songs of Praise. Sheng tsan. [no.] 1. *Pien-i-li Shu-chü: Hong Kong*, 1950. 8°.　　　　　**G. 1363. p. (3.)**

LIANG (FU-CH'ÜAN)

— *See* HONGKONG.— *Salesian Orphanage School*. Tzŭ-yu ko-p'u. [School song book, compiled by Liang Fu-ch'üan.] [1949.] 8°.　　　　　**G. 1363. q. (2.)**

LIANG (JING YOU)

— Zhong wen ge jié ta shou zhi pu. [Chinese songs with guitar. Editor Liang Jing you. Tablature.] pp. 106. *Xiang gang jié ta yin yue she:* [*Hong Kong*, 1978.] 8°.　　　**E. 1771. c. (1.)**

LIANG (SHAN-PO)

— Liang Shan-po yü Chu Ying-t'ai. [Songs from the film. Numerical notation.] pp. 83. *Yu-lien T'u-shu Kung-ssu: Singapore*, 1956. 8°.　　　　　**G. 1363. ee. (1.)**

LIANI (DAVIDE)

— Cjantis. Sette canzoni friulane per canto e pianoforte su testi originali di L. Cjanton, E. Bortolussi, A. Negro, D. Virgili del gruppo letterario "risultive" ... Parte di canto-piano, *etc.* *Friulian & Ital.* pp. 19. *Edizioni G. Zanibon: Padova*, [1972.] fol.　　　　　**G. 1310. q. (1.)**

LIANOWSKI (TRISTAN)

— Dookhee. Moods—Ghosts. For pianoforte. *J. P. Hull: London*, 1926. 4°.　　　　　**g. 1125. q. (24.)**

— Impromptu for Pianoforte. *J. P. Hull: London*, 1927. 4°.　　　　　**g. 1125. w. (24.)**

— Intermezzo in G♭ for Pianoforte. *J. P. Hull: London*, 1925. 4°.　　　　　**g. 1125. q. (25.)**

LIAPOUNOW (SERGE)

— *See* LYAPUNOV (Sergyei Mikhailovich)

LIARS

— Liars all. Song. *See* NORMAN (Jules)

LIATOSCHINSKY (BORIS)

— *See* LYATOSHINS'KY (B.)

LIBANI (GIUSEPPE)

— Il Conte Verde. Dramma lirico in 4 atti di C. d'Ormeville. Riduzione per Canto e Pianoforte di G. Foschini. *Torino*, [1875.] 4°.　　　　　**G. 671.**

LIBARDI (M.)

— *See* NICOLÓ (M.) Fantasia ... [Song.] Music arr. by A. Libardi. [1965.] 4°.　　　　　**F. 1196. ff. (1.)**

LIBBERT (JUERGEN)

— *See* CORRETTE (Michel) Les Dons d'Apollon (Paris 1762). 16 Lieder und Tänze für Gitarre herausgegeben von J. Libbert. [1979.] 4°.　　　　　**g. 1650. oo. (6.)**

— *See* HUMMEL (Bertold) Metamorphosen für Gitarre, *etc.* ⟨Eingerichtet von J. Libbert.⟩ [1976.] 4°.　　**g. 1650. b. (1.)**

LIBBERT (JUERGEN)

— *See* SOR (Fernando) Fantasie Nr. 2 für Gitarre ⟨op. 4⟩ ... (⟨Bearb. von⟩ J. Libbert.) [1976.] 4°.　　**g. 1650. b. (4.)**

— *See* SOR (Fernando) Fantasie Nr. 3 für Gitarre ... (⟨Bearb. von⟩ J. Libbert.) [1976.] 4°.　　　　**g. 1650. b. (5.)**

— *See* SOR (Fernando) Fantasie Nr. 4 für Gitarre ... ⟨Op. 12.⟩ (⟨Bearb. von⟩ J. Libbert). [1978.] 4°.　　**h. 804. b. (1.)**

— *See* SOR (Fernando) Fantasie Nr. 5 ... für Gitarre ... ⟨Op. 16.⟩ Bearb. von ... J. Libbert. [1978.] 4°.　**g. 1650. r. (10.)**

— *See* SOR (Fernando) [Introduction et variations. Op. 26.] Introduktion, Thema und Variationen über das Lied "Que ne suis-je la fougère?" für Gitarre ... (⟨Bearb. von⟩ J. Libbert.) [1979.] 4°.　　　　　**g. 1650. r. (11.)**

— *See* WHITE (Robert) [Fantasias. 4 part. No. 1–3.] Drei Fantasien ... Bearbeitet und herausgegeben von J. Libbert. [1979.] 4°.　　　　　**g. 128. e. (5.)**

LIBBEY (JAMES ALDRICH)

— In the Blossom Time. [Song.] Words by W. A. Cook and J. A. Libbey. pp. 5. *Barron & Thompson: New York*, [1907.] fol.　　　　　**H. 3985. z. (23.)**

— Nora. Arr. by Everett J. Evans. [Orchestral parts.] 10 pt. *Hamilton S. Gordon: New York*, [1904.] 8°.　**f. 800. (823.)**

— Only a Summer Girl. [Song.] Words by Will A. Cook. pp. 3. *Chas. K. Harris: [Milwaukee*, 1902.] 4°.　**H. 3985. z. (24.)**

— [Another issue.] Only a Summer Girl, *etc.* *Milwaukee*, [1902.] fol.　　　　　**H. 3985. z. (25.)**

— The Sweetest Melody, Song, *etc.* *G. T. Worth & Co.: New York*, 1893. fol.　　　　　**H. 1798. v. (22.)**

LIBBEY (JAMES ALDRICH) and **HAYES** (WILLIAM) *Songwriter*

— You'll want some one to love you when you're old. [Song.] Words by W. A. Cook. pp. 5. *Windsor Music Co.: Chicago, New York*, [1905.] fol.　　　　　**H. 3985. z. (26.)**

LIBBY (JAMES ALDRICH)

— *See* LIBBEY.

LIBBY (JOHN)

— The Australasian Flag. The Ensign of the Southern Cross. Song, written and composed by J. Libby. *Astriter Agency: Melbourne*, [1917.] 4°.　　　　**G. 383. cc. (20.)**

LIBELLA

— Libella. Grosse Oper. *See* REISSIGER (C. G.)

LIBELLEN

— Die Libellen. [Three-part song.] *See* BARGIEL (W.) Drei Frühlingslieder, *etc.* No. 2.

— Die Libellen. Walzerreigen. *See* GRABEN-HOFFMANN (G.)

— Die Libellen. [Duet.] *See* REISSMANN (A.) Sechs zweistimmige Lieder. No. 2.

LIBELLENTANZ

— Libellentanz. [Song.] *See* LACHNER (Franz) 4 Lieder, *etc.* Op. 116. No. 3.

— Libellentanz. Operette. *See* LEHÁR (F.)

LIBELLULE
— La Libellule. Valse. *See* SAINT-SAËNS (C. C.)

LIBER
— Liber Canticorum, quae uulgo Responsoria uocantur, secundum anni ordinem, Dominicis & Festis diebus Lactenus seruatum. [Apparently for use in Nuremberg. With prefatory verses by S.H., i.e. Sebaldus Heyden?] *Impressum . . . in officina Ioannis Montani, & Ulrici Neuberi: Norimbergæ*, 1550. 8°.   **K. 8. b. 3.**

— Liber fratrum cruciferorum Leodiensium. *See* LIÈGE.— *Academia Leodiensis.— Bibliothèque.*

— Liber Musicus: a Collection of Voluntaries for the organ, harmonium, and pianoforte. [Tonic sol-fa notation.] 4 pt. *J. Curwen & Sons: London*, [1888.] *obl.* 4°.   **b. 241.**

— Liber organi. [Edited by E. Kaller and others.] *B. Schott's Söhne: Mainz*, [1931, *etc.*] *obl.* 4°.   **e. 1147.**

— Liber scriptus. [Aria.] *See* VERDI (F. G. F.)

LIBER (ANTON JOSEPH)
— Six Sonates en Trio pour le Clavecin avec Accompagnement de Violon et Basse. [Parts.] *Chez Sᵣ Götz: Mannheim*, [1775?] fol.   **g. 79. a. (3.)**

LIBERA
— Libera. [Motet.] *See* BRAND (M. G.) afterwards MOSONYI (M.)

— Libera. Responsorium. *See* HAYDN (F. J.)

— Le Libéra de la Bourbonnoise. [Song.] *See* DANS. Dans Paris grande ville. [1785?] 8°.   **B. 362. i. (40.)**

— Libera me. Motet. *See* ARNE (Thomas A.)

— Libera me. Arie for Sopran und Orchester. *See* DONIZETTI (Domenico G.M.) [Miserere. D minor.]

— Libera me, Domine. [Motet.] *See* BRUCKNER (A.)

— Libera me, Domine. Motet. *See* LIONCOURT (G. de)

— Libera me, Domine. [Motet.] *See* MAWBY (Colin)

— Libera me Domine. [Motet.] *See* PERRUCHOT (L.)

— Libera me Domine. [Motet.] *See* SEYFRIED (I. X. von)

— Libera me, Domine. [Motet.] *See* WHITE (R.)

— Libera me Domine et pone me. [Anthem.] *See* BYRD (W.) [Cantiones. 1575.]

— Libera nos. [Motet.] *See* HUNKINS (Arthur B.)

— Libera nos. [Cantata.] *See* KUBELÍK (R.)

— Libera nos, salva nos. [Motets.] *See* SHEPHERD (John) *Organist of Magdalen College, Oxford.*

— Libera plebem. Motet. *See* JOUBERT (John)

LIBERA (SANDRO DALLA)
— Antologia organistica italiana. (Sec. XVI–XVII.) pp. 75. *G. Ricordi & c.: Milano*, [1957.] *obl.* 4°.   **e. 1093. ff. (4.)**

— *See* BACH (J. S.) Passacaglia per organo. Revisione di S. D. Libera, *etc.* [1958.] *obl.* fol.   **e. 113. s. (1.)**

— *See* FRESCOBALDI (G.) Nove toccate inedite a cura di S. D. Libera. [Organ.] 1962. *obl.* fol. [*Monumenti di musica italiana. ser.* 1. *vol.* 2.]   **H. 1356.**

— *See* GABRIELI (A.) 3 messe per organo, a cura di S. D. Libera. [1959.] *obl.* 4°.   **e. 1093. qq. (8.)**

LIBERA (SANDRO DALLA)
— *See* GABRIELI (G.) Composizioni per organo. ([Edited by] Dalla Libera.) [1957,59.] *obl.* 4°.   **e. 1093. uu.**

— *See* MERULO (C.) Toccate per organo . . . ([Edited by] Dalla Libera), *etc.* [1959,60?] *obl.* fol.   **f. 314. uu. (1.)**

— *See* RAVANELLO (O.) Cento studi ed esercizi per organo. ⟨Opera 94.⟩ Nuova edizione a cura di S. Dalla Libera. [1961.] fol.   **h. 2732. s. (3.)**

LIBERATED
— Liberated Woman. [Part-song.] *See* DANOFF (Bill)

LIBERATI (A.)
— Heim. March and two-step. [P.F.] pp. 3. [*A. Liberati: New York?* 1905.] fol.   **h. 4120. pp. (28.)**

— The Military Hop. Waltz. [P.F.] pp. 9. *A. Liberati: New York*, [1904.] fol.   **h. 4120. pp. (29.)**

— Our Hero in Command. ⟨Arr. by August Damm.⟩ [P.F.] pp. 5. *A. Liberati: New York*, [1903.] fol.   **h. 4120. pp. (30.)**

— Our Iowa. ⟨March. Arr. for piano by Speranza Liberati.⟩ pp. 3. *A. Liberati: New York*, [1908.] fol.   **h. 4120. pp. (31.)**

LIBERATI (ALESSANDRO)
— Alessandro Liberati's Method for Cornet, *etc. A. Liberati: New York*, [1925, *etc.*] 4°.   **g. 761. aa. (1.)**

LIBERATI (SPERANZA)
— My Dad's Birthday. March and two-step. [P.F.] pp. 3. *A. Liberati: New York*, [1904.] fol.   **h. 4120. pp. (32.)**

— *See* LIBERATI (A.) Our Iowa . . . Arr. for piano by S. Liberati. [1908.] fol.   **h. 4120. pp. (31.)**

LIBERATION
— Liberation. Song. *See* ARNOLD (W.) *Songwriter.*

— La Liberation des Antilles. Two songs. *See* MILHAUD (D.)

LIBERAZIONE
— La Liberazione di Ruggiero dall'Isola d'Alcina. Balletto. *See* CACCINI (F.)

LIBERIA
— Liberia's all my Thought and Dream. Song. *See* BARRETT (J.) *Organist.*

LIBERIAN
— Liberian National Anthem. [Part-song.] *See* LUCA (O.)

LIBERT (RAYNALDUS)
— *See* LIEBERT (Reginald)

LIBERTÀ
— La Libertà. Canzonetta. *See* GIARDINI (F.)

— La Libertà. Canzonetta. *See* HERBAIN (d') *Chevalier.*

— La Liberta. [Song.] *See* PAULET (J.)

— La Libertà a Nice. [Duet.] *See* CHERUBINI (M. L. C. Z. S.)

— La Liberta a Nice. Canzonetta. *See* GOMIS (J. M.)

LIBERTY

— Liberty. Song. *See* SINCE. Since ev'ry Charm on Earth combines, *etc.* [By R. Hudson.] [1766.] 8°.   **P. P. 5439.**

— Liberty. Song. *See* ADAMS (E. P.)

— L-i-b-e-r-t-y. Song. *See* BARRON (Ted S.)

— Liberty. Song. *See* BENDALL (W. E.)

— Liberty. Song. *See* BROWN (Harold) *of Middlesbrough.*

— Liberty. Hymn. *See* CHALMERS (M. H.)

— Liberty. [Song.] *See* CORRI (M. P.) [The Flag of the Lake.]

— Liberty. Dramatic Chorus. *See* FANING (E.)

— Liberty. Cantata. *See* HARGREAVES (G.)

— Liberty. [Song, begins: "Since ev'ry Charm on Earth combines".] *See* HUDSON (R.)

— Liberty. [Song.] *See* LOWE (Augustus)

— Liberty. Song. *See* MELLOR (Grace E.)

— Liberty! [Part-song.] *See* PALIARD (L.)

— Liberty. Two-Part Song. [Begins: "Happy Britain!"] *See* R., J.

— Liberty. Temperance Song. *See* SMITH (G. E.)

— Liberty. Song [begins: "In vain I wish'd for Liberty"]. *See* SWIFT (W.)

— Liberty. [Part-song.] *See* WALKER (E.)

— Liberty & Life. Song. *See* THOMAS (J. R.)

— Liberty and Union. [Song.] *See* WARNELINK (J. T.)

— Liberty Bell. [Song.] *See* CARTER (Cal)

— The Liberty Bell. Cantata. *See* HAMMOND (W. G.)

— Liberty Bell. Part-Song. *See* MATTHEWS (J. S.)

— The Liberty Bell. Vocal march. *See* SOUSA (John P.)

— Liberty Bell, ring on! Song. *See* BROWN (Albert W.)

— Liberty, dear Liberty. [Song.] *See* ANDERSEN (A. O.)

— Liberty for ever. Song. *See* CARUSO (E.) and BELLEZZA (V.)

— Liberty forever in the U.S.A. [Song.] *See* CHAMBERLAIN (S. J.)

— Liberty for me. Song. *See* ADAM (A.C.) [Le Chalet.—Dans ce modeste et simple asile.]

— Liberty-Hall. [Song.] *See* OLD. Old Homer, but what have we with him to do? [1775?] *s. sh.* fol.   **H. 1994. a. (76.)**

— Liberty Hall. Comic Opera. *See* DIBDIN (C.)

— Liberty Hall. [Song.] *See* GILBERT (Frederick)

— Liberty March. Song. *See* NETTLEFOLD (F. J.)

— Liberty regain'd. Ode. *See* BASILI (A.)

— Liberty shall not die. [Song.] *See* LUCKSTONE (I.)

— Liberty's Call. [Song.] *See* STARKWEATHER (L. B.)

LIBIAMO

— Libiamo ne' lieti calici. Brindisi. *See* VERDI (F. G. F.) [La Traviata.]

LIBIEZ (ALBERT)

— Chansons populaires de l'Ancien Hainault. Recueillies par A. Libiez (et Roger Pinon). *Schott frères: Bruxelles,* 1939, *etc.* 8°.
Publication of "Ministère de l'instruction publique. Commission de la vieille chanson populaire".   **E. 1878.**

LIBONATI (ERNESTO)

— Absent from thee Waltz. [Mandoline and P. F.] *Lyon & Healy: Chicago,* 1902. fol.   **h. 188. i. (7.)**

— Balance all Quadrille. [Mandoline and P. F.] *Lyon & Healy: Chicago,* 1902. fol.   **h. 188. i. (8.)**

— Because it's you Polka. [Mandoline and P. F.] *Lyon & Healy: Chicago,* 1902. fol.   **h. 188. i. (9.)**

— Climax Quadrille. [Mandoline and P. F.] *Lyon & Healy: Chicago,* 1902. fol.   **h. 188. i. (10.)**

— Could I forget Waltz. [Mandoline and P. F.] *Lyon & Healy: Chicago,* 1902. fol.   **h. 188. i. (11.)**

— Echo of the Past Gavotte. [Mandoline and guitar.] *Lyon & Healy: Chicago,* 1902. fol.   **h. 188. i. (12.)**

— Heart's Delight Schottische. [Mandoline and P. F.] *Lyon & Healy: Chicago,* 1902. fol.   **h. 188. i. (13.)**

— Jewels of Joy Polka. [Mandoline and P. F.] *Lyon & Healy: Chicago,* 1902. fol.   **h. 188. i. (14.)**

— Kiss in a Letter Schottische. [Mandoline and P. F.] *Lyon & Healy: Chicago,* 1902. fol.   **h. 188. i. (15.)**

— Love and Duty March. Two-Step. [Mandoline and P. F.] *Lyon & Healy: Chicago,* 1902. fol.   **h. 188. i. (16.)**

— Love in the Heart Waltz. [2 mandolines and P. F.] *Lyon & Healy: Chicago,* 1902. fol.   **h. 188. i. (17.)**

— Mazurka di Concert. [Mandoline and P. F.] *Lyon & Healy: Chicago,* 1902. fol.   **h. 188. i. (18.)**

— Our Country's Call March. [Mandoline and P. F.] *Lyon & Healy: Chicago,* 1902. fol.   **h. 188. i. (19.)**

— Passion's Dream Waltz. [Mandoline and P. F.] *Lyon & Healy: Chicago,* 1902. fol.   **h. 188. i. (20.)**

— Round of Pleasure Schottische. [Mandoline and P. F.] *Lyon & Healy: Chicago,* 1902. fol.   **h. 188. i. (21.)**

— Seaside Galop. [Mandoline and P. F.] *Lyon & Healy: Chicago,* 1902. fol.   **h. 188. i. (22.)**

— Smiles and Tears Mazurka. [Mandoline and P. F.] *Lyon & Healy: Chicago,* 1902. fol.   **h. 188. i. (23.)**

— String of Pearls Waltz. [Mandoline and P. F.] *Lyon & Healy: Chicago,* 1902. fol.   **h. 188. i. (24.)**

— Sunshine in Looks Schottische. [Mandoline and P. F.] *Lyon & Healy: Chicago,* 1902. fol.   **h. 188. i. (26.)**

— Sweet Emotions March. [Mandoline and P. F.] *Lyon & Healy: Chicago,* 1902. fol.   **h. 188. i. (25.)**

— Thou art welcome Galop. [Mandoline and P. F.] *Lyon & Healy: Chicago,* 1902. fol.   **h. 188. i. (27.)**

LIBOTTON (G.)

— Six Pieces for the Violoncello, with pianoforte accompaniment, composed and arranged by G. Libotton. 6 no. *Novello, Ewer & Co.: London & New York,* [1893.] fol.   **h. 1851. c. (24.)**

— *See* ALBUM. Album célèbre. 10 morceaux ... transcrits pour violoncelle et piano par G. Libotton. Vol. II. [1880.] 4°. [*Format Litolff. vol.*461.]   **g. 375.**

LIBRARY

— Library of Congress. *See* UNITED STATES OF AMERICA.— *Congress.— Library.*

LIBRO

— Il Primo Libro delle Muse, a tre voci. Madrigali de diuersi autori di nuouo raccolti, & datti in luce, *etc. Appresso Girolamo Scotto: Vinegia,* 1562. 8°.
Imperfect; the basso part only. The composers named are: A. Festa, H. Rampolino, G. Nasco, O. di Lassus, V. Ferro, Lerma, F. Rosello, A. Barre, G. Fiesco, V. Lusitano, Perissone, G. Matelart, G. B. Montanaro, L. Courtoys. **A. 277. h. (1.)**

— Il Libro santo. [Song.] *See* PINSUTI (C. E.)

LIBUŠA

— Libuša. Slavnostní zpěvohra. *See* SMETANA (B.)

LIBUSSA

— Libussa. Romantische Oper. *See* KREUTZER (C.)

LI CALSI (GIUSEPPE)

— Addio a Venezia, canzone, parole del Sig.A. Montuora. *London,* [1853.] fol. **H. 1735. (36.)**

— Angeline, Nocturne mélodique pour piano. *London,* [1853.] fol. **h. 723. m. (8.)**

— Arianna, impromptu pour le piano. Op. 23. *London,* [1855.] fol. **h. 724. e. (23.)**

— A Canadian Serenade. [Song, begins: "The red sun is setting".] Written by B. Barrie. *London,* [1871.] fol. **H. 1775. u. (42.)**

— A Canadian Serenade. [Song.] Written by B. Barrie. *London,* [1873.] fol. **H. 1778. y. (25.)**

— La forosetta. Romanza [begins: "Su scoscesa alpina"]. *London,* [1853.] fol. **H. 1735. (35.)**

— Galop de concert. [P.F.] *London,* [1868.] fol. **h. 1485. t. (1.)**

— The Hermit and the Birdies ... [Song, begins: "The winged tribes".] Words by J. F. Stanford. *Milano,* [1879.] fol. **H. 1782. a. (12.)**

— L'Infedelta, aria [begins: "Quando in me rapita"]. Parole del Sigʳ. T.Rossetti. *London,* [1853.] fol. **H. 1735. (34.)**

— The Last Dream. Song by F. H. Cowen. Transcription for the pianoforte by G. Li Calsi. *Milan, etc.,* [1883.] fol. **h. 3280. l. (1.)**

— Léonie, Schottische pour le piano. *London,* [1854.] fol. **h. 975. e. (37.)**

— Léonie schottische. [P.F.] *London,* [1873.] fol. **h. 1482. z. (48.)**

— L'oblio. Canzone. [Begins: "Perche fuggir crudele?"] *London,* [1853.] fol. **H. 1735. (37.)**

— Il Segreto. Stornello [begins: "Passando un di"]. Parole di G. Zaffira. *London,* [1880.] fol. **H. 1783. o. (68.)**

— Separation. (Separazione.) Song [begins: "Come at last."—"Vien ah vien"]. (Words by E. Oxenford. Italian translation by Signor Caravoglia.) *London,* [1881.] fol. **H. 1787. j. (37.)**

LI CALSI (J.)

— *See* LI CALSI (G.)

LICAS

— Licas. Romance. *See* CARDON (L.)

— Licas adorait Oriane. Romance. *See* PHILIDOR (F. A. Danican)

— Licas Amant d'Aminte. *Ah! s'ils s'éveilloient.* [Song.] Air, Tandis que tout someille [by A. E. M. Grétry]. *Chez Camand: [Paris,* 1789?] 8°. **B. 362. a. (192.)**

— Licas auprès de ma Bergère. *Musette.* [*Paris,*] 1751. *s. sh.* 4°. *Mercure de France, Dec.,* 1751. **298. c. 6.**

LICENCE (W. J.)

— Vesper Hymn. [Begins: "Meekly kneeling".] *Novello and Co.: London,* [1907.] *a card.* **I. 600. c. (165.)**

LICHARD (MILAN)

— Slovak Popular Melodies ... (ɪ.) By M. Lichard. (ɪɪ. By Rev. A. Kolísek.) [Chapter on Slovak music, with examples.] [*A. Constable & Co.: London,* 1908.] 8°.
Pp. 372–391 *of "Racial Problems in Hungary," by R. W. S. Watson.* **08072. bb. 14.**

— Slovak Popular Melodies. *See* WATSON (R. W. S.) Slovak Peasant Art, *etc.* 1911. 8°. **07805. b. 6. (5.)**

LICHARZ (JOSEF)

— *See* BRAHMS (J.) [Walzer. Op. 39. No. 15.] Walzer As-dur. "Horch der erste Laut." Bearbeitung für vierstimmigen Männerchor mit Klavierbegleitung ad lib ... Chorsatz: J. Licharz. [1957.] 8°. **F. 359. l. (28.)**

LICHFIELD

— Lichfield Diocesan Choral Association. *See* LICHFIELD, *Diocese of.*

LICHFIELD, *Diocese of.— Lichfield Diocesan Choral Association*

— The Order of Service appointed for the thirteenth Diocesan Festival of Parish Choirs, to be held in Lichfield Cathedral on Thursday, July 1, 1886. pp. 47. *Printed by Novello, Ewer and Co.: London,* [1886?] 8°. **E. 597. aa. (1.)**

LICHFIELD (HENRY)

— *See* LICHFILD.

LICHFILD (HENRY)

— Alas my Daphne, stay. *See* infra: [The First Set of Madrigals of 5 Parts.]

— All yee that sleepe in Pleasure. *See* infra: [The First Set of Madrigals of 5 Parts.]

— I always loved to call my Lady Rose. *See* infra: [The First Set of Madrigals of 5 Parts.]

— Injurious Hours. *See* infra: [The First Set of Madrigals of 5 Parts.]

The First Set of Madrigals of 5 Parts

— The First Set of Madrigals of 5. Parts: apt both for Viols and Voyces. (Cantus.— Altus. — Tenor.— Bassus.— Quintus.) 5 pt. *Printed for M[atthew] L[ownes], I[ohn] B[rowne] and T[homas] S[nodham] the Assignes of W. Barley: London,* 1613. 4°. **K. 8. f. 5.**

— [Another copy of the altus part.]
Imperfect; wanting the last two leaves of the altus part which have been supplied in facsimile, and the other parts. **K. 8. f. 5*.**

LICHFILD (Henry)

— The First Set of Madrigals of 5 Parts, *etc.* [A facsimile of the edition of 1613.] 5 pt. *Theatrum orbis terrarum: Amsterdam; Da Capo Press: New York*, 1972. 8°.
[*The English Experience. no. 472A.*] **1653/472A.**

— First Set of Madrigals of Five Parts, *etc. Stainer and Bell: London*, 1922. 8°.
[*The English Madrigal School. Edited by E. H. Fellowes. Vol. XVII.*] **F. 1709.**

— Madrigals of five Parts (1613). ⟨Edited by Edmund H. Fellowes. Revised by Thurston Dart.⟩ Associate reviser ... David Scott. pp. xiv. 135. *Stainer & Bell:* [*London,* 1970.] 8°.
[*English Madrigalists.* 17.] **F. 1709. g.**

— Alas my Daphne, stay, *etc. Oxford University Press: London,* 1936. 8°.
[*Euterpe. No. 70.*] **F. 1684. a.**

— All yee that sleepe in Pleasure. Madrigal for five voices. Edited by W. B. Squire. *Laudy & Co.: London,* [1892.] 8°.
F. 585. u. (14.)

— All yee that sleepe in Pleasure. Madrigal for five voices ... Edited by W. B. Squire. *See* ARION. Arion, *etc.* [Vol. I. No. 13.] [1899.] 8°.
G. 771.

— All ye that sleep in pleasure, *etc. Oxford University Press: London,* 1936. 8°.
[*Euterpe. No. 69.*] **F. 1684. a.**

— I always lov'd to call my Lady 'Rose'. Madrigal, *etc.* 1906. *See* SCOTT (C. K.) Euterpe, *etc.* Vol. 3. 1905, *etc.* 8°.
F. 1684.

— "I always loved to call my Lady Rose." "Herzliebchen ist ein Röslein rot, fürwahr!" Fünfstimmiges Madrigal ... Deutscher Text von J. Bernhoff, *etc.* [1906.] *See* SQUIRE (W. B.) Ausgewählte Madrigale, *etc.* No. 29. [1895, *etc.*] 8°.
F. 1604.

— I always lov'd to call my Lady "Rose," *etc. Oxford University Press: London,* 1929. 8°.
[*Euterpe. No. 27.*] **F. 1684. a.**

— "Injurious Hours." "Stunden, ihr trügt." Fünfstimmiges Madrigal ... Deutscher Text von J. Bernhoff, *etc.* [1906.] *See* SQUIRE (W. B.) Ausgewählte Madrigale, *etc.* No. 30. [1895, *etc.*] 8°.
F. 1604.

LICHNER (Heinrich)

— Compositions pour Piano. 33 no. *Berlin,* [1883.] fol.
h. 3103. b. (11.)

— A l'Attaque. Galop militaire pour le piano. *E. Donajowski: London,* [1884.] fol.
h. 3103. d. (1.)

— Album für die Jugend ... Sechs ... nicht schwere Salonstücke ... für Pianoforte. Op. 261. 6 no. *Leipzig,* [1885.] fol.
h. 3103. c. (20.)

— Alice und Gertrud. Zwei Salon-Mazurkas. Op. 253. [P. F.] *Leipzig,* [1884.] fol.
h. 3103. c. (14.)

— Am Congo. Sechs ... leicht spielbare Bilder in Tönen für Pianoforte. Op. 275, *etc.* 6 no. *C. F. W. Siegel: Leipzig,* [1887.] fol.
h. 3103. e. (9.)

— Amoretten. Tanzweisen ... for the Pianoforte. Op. 31. 6 no. *E. Ashdown: London,* [1889.] fol.
h. 3103. f. (3.)

— Aquarellen. 12 leichte ... Uebungsstücke zur Ermunterung für die Klavier spielende Jugend. 2 Hft. *Leipzig,* [1882.] fol.
h. 3103. b. (7.)

— At Home. Six characteristic Pieces for the pianoforte. Op. 112. 6 no. *E. Ashdown: London,* [1891.] fol.
h. 3103. f. (4.)

LICHNER (Heinrich)

— Aurore. Valse de Salon pour le piano. *E. Donajowski: London,* [1884.] fol.
h. 3103. d. (2.)

— Aus der Jugendzeit. Zwölf leichte und melodische Tonstücke ... für Pianoforte zu vier Händen. 3 Hft. *Berlin,* [1877.] fol.
h. 3103. (2.)

— Aus der Jugendzeit ... Twelve ... pianoforte duets. Op. 85. 12 no. *E. Ashdown: London,* [1886.] fol.
h. 3103. d. (23.)

— Aus der Kinderzeit ... Vier ... Tonstücke für Klavier. Op. 249. 4 no. *Leipzig,* [1884.] fol.
h. 3103. c. (10.)

— Aus der Liedertafelrunde. Potpourri über beliebte Männerchöre für Pianoforte. Op. 276. *C. F. W. Siegel: Leipzig,* [1887.] fol.
h. 3103. e. (10.)

— La Belle Anglaise. Morceau de Salon pour le piano. *E. Donajowski: London,* [1885.] fol.
h. 3103. d. (3.)

— La Belle Polonaise. Mazourka pour le piano. *E. Donajowski: London,* [1885.] fol.
h. 3103. d. (4.)

— Bilder aus der Vergangenheit ... Sechs leichte ... Tonstücke ... für Pianoforte. Op. 283, *etc.* 6 no. *C. F. W. Siegel: Leipzig,* [1888.] fol.
h. 3103. e. (17.)

— Sechs Bilder aus Kamerun für Pianoforte. Op. 264. 6 no. *Leipzig,* [1886.] fol.
h. 3103. c. (21.)

— Blätterrauschen. Impromptu. *See infra:* Vier ... Klavierstücke. Op. 247. No. 2.

— Blättlein im Winde ... Leichte ... Tänze ... für Pianoforte. 6 no. *Leipzig,* [1883.] fol.
h. 3103. b. (13.)

— Blau Veilchen ... Leichte Quadrille ... Op. 281. [P. F. duet.] *C. F. W. Siegel: Leipzig,* [1888.] fol.
h. 3103. e. (15.)

— Brieftauben ... Grosser Walzer. Op. 282. [P. F. duet.] *C. F. W. Siegel: Leipzig,* [1888.] fol.
h. 3103. e. (16.)

— Vier brillante Klavierstücke. Op. 247. 4 no. *Leipzig,* [1884.] fol.
h. 3103. c. (8.)

— Le Carnaval de Cracovie. Mazurka de Salon pour le piano. *E. Donajowski: London,* [1884.] fol.
h. 3103. d. (5.)

— Chant du Printemps. Morceau joyeux pour le piano. *E. Donajowski: London,* [1884.] fol.
h. 3103. d. (6.)

— Le Chant du Rossignol. Idylle pour le piano. *E. Donajowski: London,* [1885.] fol.
h. 3103. d. (7.)

— Das Christfest ... Zwölf Weihnachtsbilder für Klavier. 4 Hft. *Leipzig,* [1883.] fol.
h. 3103. b. (10.)

— 4 Clavierstücke. 4 no. *Leipzig,* [1878.] fol.
h. 3103. (7.)

— Dans la forêt. Capriccio pour le piano. *E. Donajowski: London,* [1884.] fol.
h. 3103. d. (8.)

— Danse gracieuse pour piano. 2 no. [Solo and duet.] *E. Ashdown: London,* [1890.] fol.
h. 3103. f. (6.)

— Deutsche Mörchen und Sagen. Fünfzehn kleine ... Uebungsstücke für Pianoforte. 5 Hft. *Leipzig,* [1880.] fol.
h. 3103. a. (7.)

— Die Dorfschwalben. [P. F.] *See infra:* Vier ... Salon-Kompositionen ... Op. 260. No. 3.

— Doux espoir. Bluette pour le piano. *E. Donajowski: London,* [1884.] fol.
h. 3103. d. (9.)

— Du hast mir viel gegeben. Lied von M. von Lüttwitz. Transcription für Pianoforte. *Berlin & Posen,* [1877.] fol.
h. 3103. (5.)

— Ducca's Polka, pour le piano. *E. Donajowski: London,* [1884.] fol.
h. 3103. d. (10.)

LICHNER (HEINRICH)

— Durch die Lüfte. Galopp. [P. F.] *See* infra: Salon-Perlen ...
Op. 258. No. 1.

— Easy Classical Movements for the Pianoforte ... —Edited by
Dr. C. Vincent.—No. 1. Allegro moderato in C. No. 2.
Andante in F. No. 3. Allegretto in G. No. 4. Andante con
expressione in C. No. 5. Rondo in G. No. 6. Moderato in F.
No. 7. Minuetto in F. *Vincent Music Co.: London*, (1911.) 4°.
g. 543. zz. (9.)

— Erinnerungs-Blätter ... Zwölf leichte ... Tonbilder ... für
Pianoforte. Op. 268, *etc.* 12 no. *C. F. W. Siegel: Leipzig*,
[1886.] fol. **h. 3103. e. (3.)**

— Evening Bells ... Nocturne for the pianoforte. *E. Ashdown:
London*, [1890.] fol. **h. 3103. f. (2.)**

— Familien-Kränzchen ... Sieben kleine ... Tänze für
Pianoforte ... Op. 270, *etc.* 7 no. *C. F. W. Siegel: Leipzig*,
[1886.] fol. **h. 3103. e. (4.)**

— Zwölf Fantasien über beliebter Volkslieder für Piano in
leichtester Spielart ... Op. 256. 4 Hft. *Offenbach a. M.*, [1885.]
fol. **h. 3103. c. (15.)**

— Ferienfreuden. Sechs leichte ... Tänze ... für das Pianoforte.
Op. 280, *etc.* 6 no. *C. F. W. Siegel: Leipzig*, [1887.] fol.
h. 3103. e. (14.)

— Flick und Flock. Zwei Walzer-Rondos für Pianoforte. 2 no.
Leipzig, [1883.] fol. **h. 3103. b. (12.)**

— Flitterwochen ... Salonstück für Pianoforte. *Leipzig*, [1880.]
fol. **h. 3103. a. (4.)**

— Freudvoll, leidvoll ... Nocturno. [P. F.] *See* infra: Vier
Salon-Kompositionen. ... Op. 260. No. 2.

— Frühling. *See* infra: [Die vier Jahreszeiten. Op. 169. No. 1.]

— Frühlingsbilder. Leichte Salonstücke für Pianoforte. Op. 248.
4 no. *Leipzig*, [1884.] fol. **h. 3103. c. (9.)**

— Frühlings Blüthen ... Drei Idyllen für Pianoforte. 3 no.
Leipzig, [1881.] fol. **h. 3103. a. (17.)**

— Gabrielle. Idylle pour le piano. *E. Donajowski: London*,
[1884.] fol. **h. 3103. d. (11.)**

— The Gondolier.—Gondellied.—Song without words for the
pianoforte. *E. Ashdown: London*, [1889.] fol.
h. 3103. f. (7.)

— Hangen und Bangen ... Salon-Walzer für Pianoforte.
Leipzig, [1880.] fol. **h. 3103. a. (5.)**

— Harfenklänge ... Salon-Etude für Pianoforte. *Leipzig*, [1880.]
fol. **h. 3103. a. (2.)**

— Heimat und Fremde ... Sechs Klavierstücke ... Op. 244. 6 no.
Leipzig, [1883.] fol. **h. 3103. c. (5.)**

— Heimliche Liebe. Nocturno. *See* infra: Vier ... Klavierstücke.
Op. 247. No. 3.

— Im Blumenhain. Flowery Grove. Lyrisches Tonbild für
Piano. *Leipzig*, [1879.] fol. **h. 3103. (16.)**

— Im Fliederbusch. Charakterstück. *See* infra: Vier ...
Klavierstücke. Op. 247. No. 4.

— Im frohen Kreise ... Zwei characteristische Tonstücke für
Pianoforte. *Leipzig*, [1882.] fol. **h. 3103. b. (2.)**

— Im Kinder-Garten ... Zwölf ... Klavierstücke für die ...
Jugend ... Op. 240. 4 Hft. *Leipzig*, [1883.] fol.
h. 3103. c. (3.)

— Im Sommersalon. Schnell-Polka. [P. F.] *See* infra:
Salon-Perlen ... Op. 258. No. 5.

LICHNER (HEINRICH)

— Drei Improvisationen für Pianoforte. *Leipzig*, [1882.] fol.
h. 3103. b. (1.)

— In der Heimath. Home. Sechs ... Lieder ohne Worte für das
Pianoforte. 2 Hft. *Leipzig*, [1878.] fol. **h. 3103. (11.)**

— In der Tanzstunde. Sechs ... Tänze für Pianoforte. 6 no.
Leipzig, [1880.] fol. **h. 3103. a. (14.)**

— In Elb-Florenz. Walzer. [P. F.] *See* infra: Salon-Perlen ...
Op. 258. No. 2.

— Invitation à la mazurka pour Piano. *London*, [1877.] fol.
h. 3103. (3.)

— Johannis-Triebe. Zwei Klavierstücke. Op. 328. *Leipzig*,
[1883.] fol. **h. 3103. c. (1.)**

— Jorinde und Joringel ... Zwei ... Rondo für Pianoforte. 2 no.
Leipzig, [1880.] fol. **h. 3103. a. (6.)**

— Jours heureux. Morceau elegant pour piano. *R. Cocks & Co.:
London*, [1885.] fol. **h. 3103. d. (12.)**

— Jugendleben. 12 leichte und melodische Tonstücke. [P.F.]
2 Hft. *Berlin*, [1877.] fol. **h. 3103. (1.)**

— [Jugendleben.] Pictures of Youth. Twelve ... pieces for the
pianoforte. Op. 84. 12 no. *E. Ashdown: London*, [1883.] fol.
h. 3103. d. (19.)

— Jugendlust ... Sechs leichte ... Tonbilder für Pianoforte ...
Op. 273, *etc.* 6 no. *C. F. W. Siegel: Leipzig*, [1886.] fol.
h. 3103. e. (7.)

— Kastor und Pollux. Zwei Walzer für Pianoforte. 2 no.
Leipzig, [1880.] fol. **h. 3103. a. (11.)**

— Kinderleben. 12 kleine und instructive Tonbilder in den
leichtesten Dur- und Molltonarten fortschreitend für
Pianoforte. Op. 144. Heft 1. Daheim. Vier Mährchen. No. 1.
Schneewittchen, *etc. C. F. W. Siegel: Leipzig*, [1875?] fol.
Wanting the other no. **g. 232. d. (28.)**

— Des Kindes Lust und Freude ... Zwölf ... Klavierstücke in
Liedform ... Op. 243. 2 Hft. *Leipzig*, [1883.] fol.
h. 3103. c. (4.)

— Klänge aus der sächsischen Schweiz. Walzer. Op. 271. [P. F.
duet.] *C. F. W. Siegel: Leipzig*, [1886.] fol. **h. 3103. e. (5.)**

— Zwei Klavierstücke. Op. 225. 2 no. *Leipzig*, [1882.] fol.
h. 3103. b. (6.)

— Kleine Blumen, kleine Blätter. Sechs leichte melodische
Tonstücke für Pianoforte. *Berlin*, [1870.] fol.
h. 1462. s. (3.)

— Ländliche Abendruhe. [Nocturno. P. F.] *See* infra: Zwei
Nocturnos. Op. 252. No. 2.

— Das Leben ein Traum. Life a Dream. Sechs Bilder in Tönen
für Pianoforte. 6 no. *Leipzig*, [1878.] fol. **h. 3103. (12.)**

— Leben und Lieben ... Mazurka für Pianoforte. *Leipzig*,
[1880.] fol. **h. 3103. a. (9.)**

— Die Lehre von den musikalischen Verzierungen oder
Manieren. Zehn leichte ... Tonbilder für Pianoforte. 3 Hft.
Leipzig, [1879.] fol. **h. 3103. (18.)**

— 24 leichte und instructive vierhändige Klavierstücke. 4 Hft.
Leipzig, [1879.] fol. **h. 3103. (17.)**

— Liebes-Botschaft ... Valse Brillante. [P. F.] *See* infra: Vier
Salon-Kompositionen ... Op. 260. No. 1.

— Liebesklänge ... Drei Idyllen für Pianoforte. 3 no. *Leipzig*,
[1880.] fol. **h. 3103. a. (15.)**

— Sechs Lieder ohne Worte für Pianoforte. III. Folge. *Leipzig*,
[1880.] fol. **h. 3103. a. (1.)**

LICHNER (HEINRICH)

— Sechs Lieder ohne Worte, für Pianoforte. IV. Folge. Op. 278, *etc.* 6 no. *C. F. W. Siegel: Leipzig*, [1887.] fol.
h. 3103. e. (12.)

— Le Lion du Jour. Morceau de Salon pour piano. Op. 10. *Augener & Co.: London*, [1887.] fol. **h. 3103. d. (13.)**

— Le Lion du Jour. Op. 10. [1907.] *See* MORCEAUX. Morceaux favoris pour piano à quatre mains. No. 84. [1886–1907.] *obl.* fol.
e. 379. c.

— Vier Märsche für Pianoforte zu vier Händen. 4 no. *Leipzig*, [1878.] fol. **h. 3103. (10.)**

— Fünf Märsche für Pianoforte zu vier Händen. 5 no. *Leipzig*, [1879.] fol. **h. 3103. (13.)**

— Maienblüten. Sechs melodiöse ... Tonstücke für Klavier. *Leipzig*, [1882.] fol. **h. 3103. b. (4.)**

— Maienlust ... Tonbild für das Pianoforte. *E. Ashdown: London*, [1884.] fol. **h. 3103. d. (14.)**

— Mailied ... for the pianoforte. *E. Ashdown: London*, [1889.] fol. **h. 3103. f. (8.)**

— Maria und Anna. Zwei characteristische Tonstücke für das Pianoforte. 2 no. *Leipzig*, [1880.] fol. **h. 3103. a. (10.)**

— Three Melodies for the Piano. Op. 13. 3 no. *E. Ashdown: London*, [1890.] fol. **h. 3103. f. (1.)**

— Zwei melodiöse Salonstücke für Pianoforte. 2 no. *Leipzig*, [1880.] fol. **h. 3103. a. (13.)**

— Mignonette. Petit morceau pour piano. *E. Ashdown: London*, [1884.] fol. **h. 3103. d. (15.)**

— 6 Morceaux caractéristiques pour piano. 6 no. *Augener & Co.: London*, [1887.] fol. **h. 3103. d. (34.)**

— 6 Morceaux caractéristiques pour Piano ... Op. 14. 1. Contentement. 2. Scène de Bal. 3. Souvenir. 4. Resolution. 5. Mal du Pays. 6. Revoir. Revised by O. Thümer. *Augener: London*, [1909.] 4°. **g. 543. oo. (13.)**

— Musikalische Rückblicke ... Sammlung leichter und eleganter Klavierstücke zu vier Händen. Op. 250. 10 no. *Leipzig*, [1884.] fol. **h. 3103. c. (11.)**

— Musikalische Unterhaltung am häuslichen Herd. Eine Sammlung ... Tanzweisen für Pianoforte zu vier Händen. 6 no. *Leipzig*, [1881.] fol. **h. 3103. a. (18.)**

— Die musikalischen Geschwister ... Sechs ... leicht spielbare Bilder in Tönen ... für Pianoforte. Op. 277, *etc.* 6 no. *C. F. W. Siegel: Leipzig*, [1887.] fol. **h. 3103. e. (11.)**

— Nacht und Morgen. Characteristisches Tonstück für Pianoforte. *Leipzig*, [1880.] fol. **h. 3103. a. (3.)**

— Zwei Nocturnos. Op. 252. 2 no. [P. F.] *Leipzig*, [1884.] fol.
h. 3103. c. (13.)

— Une Nuit étoilée. Rêverie pour le piano. *E. Donajowski: London*, [1884.] fol. **h. 3103. d. (16.)**

— Op. 70. *See* LEIPZIG. Leipzig Album. A collection of two-part Songs. [1887.] 8°. **C. 738. b. (4.)**

— Pensée fugitive. Morceau de Salon pour le piano. *E. Donajowski: London*, [1884.] fol. **h. 3103. d. (17.)**

— La Perle du Bal, pour le piano. [Solo and duet.] 2 no. *E. Donajowski: London*, [1886.] fol. **h. 3103. d. (18.)**

— Réminiscences du Tyrol. Mélodies pour le piano. *E. Donajowski: London*, [1885.] fol. **h. 3103. d. (20.)**

— Drei Romanzen für Pianoforte. 3 no. *Leipzig*, [1879.] fol.
h. 3103. (15.)

LICHNER (HEINRICH)

— Drei Romanzen für die linke Hand allein für Pianoforte. Op. 267. 3 no. *C. F. W. Siegel: Leipzig*, [1886.] fol.
h. 3103. e. (2.)

— Drei Rondinos für Pianoforte. 3 no. *Leipzig*, [1881.] fol.
h. 3103. a. (16.)

— Deux Rondinos faciles pour le piano. *E. Donajowski: London*, [1885.] fol. **h. 3103. d. (21.)**

— Vier Rondos ... für Pianoforte zu vier Händen. 4 no. *Leipzig*, [1879.] fol. **h. 3103. (14.)**

— Zwei Rondos. Op. 272. 2 no. [P. F. duet.] *C. F. W. Siegel: Leipzig*, [1886.] fol. **h. 3103. e. (6.)**

— Rosamunde. Salonwalzer. *See supra*: Vier ... Klavierstücke. Op. 247. No. 1.

— Le Rouet. Etude de salon pour le piano. *E. Donajowski: London*, [1884.] fol. **h. 3103. d. (22.)**

— Vier Salon-Kompositionen für Klavier. Op. 260. 4 no. *Leipzig*, [1885.] fol. **h. 3103. c. (19.)**

— Salon-Perlen. Fünf Klavierstücke. Op. 258. 5 no. *Leipzig*, [1885.] fol. **h. 3103. c. (18.)**

— Zwei Salonstücke. Op. 251. 2 no. [P. F.] *Leipzig*, [1884.] fol.
h. 3103. c. (12.)

— Sang und Klang. Ein Blütenkranz von Original-Melodien. Op. 279. [P. F. duet.] *C. F. W. Siegel: Leipzig*, [1887.] fol.
h. 3103. e. (13.)

— Scheiden und Meiden ... zwei Idyllen für Pianoforte. 2 no. *Leipzig*, [1880.] fol. **h. 3103. a. (8.)**

— Schlafe süss! Sweet Sleep. Nocturne for the pianoforte. Op. 113. *E. Ashdown: London, etc.,* [1892.] fol.
h. 3103. f. (5.)

— Die schöne Polin ... Mazurka. [P. F.] *See supra*: Vier Salon-Kompositionen. ... Op. 260. No. 4.

— Silhouetten. Zwölf leichte und melodiöse Klavierstücke. 12 no. *Leipzig*, [1879.] fol. **h. 3103. (19.)**

— Sinnen und Träumen. [Nocturne. P. F.] *See supra*: Zwei Nocturnos. Op. 252. No. 1.

— Sommer. *See infra*: [Die vier Jahreszeiten. Op. 169. No. 2.]

— Der Sommernachts-Ball ... Sechs leichte Tänze für Pianoforte zu 4 Händen. 6 no. *Leipzig*, [1882.] fol.
h. 3103. b. (9.)

— Nine Sonatinas for the Piano. ⟨Op. 4, 49, and 66.⟩ pp. 59. *G. Schirmer: New York; Chappell & Co.: London;* [*London* printed, 1950.] 4°.
Schirmer's Library of musical Classics. vol. 989.
g. 1128. i. (8.)

— Trois Sonatines faciles, instructives et progressives pour Piano ... Oeuvre 49. No. 1. (No. 2.) 2 no. *Julius Hainauer: London*, [1940?] 4°. **g. 1125. uu. (14.)**

— 3 Sonatinen für das Pianoforte. Op. 66. 3 no. *Berlin*, [1870.] fol. **h. 1462. s. (4.)**

— Sechs Sonatinen im leichten Styl ... für Pianoforte zu vier Händen. Op. 153. 6 no. *Leipzig*, [1876.] fol. **h. 1487. q. (13.)**

— Drei Sonatinen für Klavier ... Op. 202. 3 no. *Leipzig*, [1880.] fol. **h. 3103. a. (12.)**

— Sechs Sonatinen im leichten Styl ... für Pianoforte zu vier Händen. Op. 153. 6 no. *Leipzig*, [1876.] fol. **h. 1487. q. (13.)**

— Drei Sonatinen zu 4 Händen. Op. 245. 3 no. *Leipzig*, [1884.] fol. **h. 3103. c. (6.)**

LICHNER (Heinrich)

— Drei Sonatinen in erweiterter Form. Op. 266. 3 no. [P. F.]
C. F. W. Siegel: Leipzig, [1886.] fol.   **h. 3103. e. (1.)**

— Sonatine No. 1 ... pour le piano. *E. Donajowski: London*,
[1884.] fol.   **h. 3103. d. (25.)**

— Sonatine No. 2 ... pour le piano. *E. Donajowski: London*,
[1884.] fol.   **h. 3103. d. (26.)**

— Sonatine No. 3 ... pour le piano. *E. Donajowski: London*,
[1884.] fol.   **h. 3103. d. (27.)**

— Sonatina for four hands, pour le piano. *E. Donajowski:
London*, [1886.] fol.   **h. 3103. d. (24.)**

— Souvenir de Varsovie ... Polonaise pour le piano.
E. Donajowski: London, [1885.] fol.   **h. 3103. d. (28.)**

— Die Spieluhr. Im langsamen Polka-Tempo. [P. F.] *See* supra:
Salon-Perlen. ... Op. 258. No. 3.

— Spring Festival. Frühlingsfest. Op. 320. No. 1. [P. F. duet.]
A. P. Schmidt: Boston, etc., (1906.) fol.
Part of "Twin Flowers".   **h. 3103. f. (9.)**

— Still-Leben. Vier ... Rondos für Pianoforte. Op. 239. 4 no.
Leipzig, [1883.] fol.   **h. 3103. c. (2.)**

— Stimmungsbilder. Scenes from Life. Zwölf Klavierstücke.
12 no. *Leipzig*, [1877.] fol.   **h. 3103. (6.)**

— Tanz-Suite für Haus und Familie ... Acht leichte ... Stücke
für Klavier zu 4 Händen. Op. 257. 8 no. *Leipzig*, [1885.] fol.
    h. 3103. c. (16.)

— Traumgestalten. Mazurka. [P. F.] *See* supra: Salon-Perlen ...
Op. 258. No. 4.

— The Tulip. Melody for the pianoforte. *E. Ashdown: London*,
[1884.] fol.   **h. 3103. d. (29.)**

— Valse Etude No. 1 ... pour le piano. *E. Donajowski: London*,
[1886.] fol.   **h. 3103. d. (30.)**

— Valse Etude No. 2 ... pour le piano. *E. Donajowski: London*,
[1886.] fol.   **h. 3103. d. (31.)**

— Vergangenheit und Gegenwart. 24 leichte ... Uebungsstücke
für Pianoforte zum Gebrauch beim Unterricht ... Op. 259.
6 Hft. *Leipzig*, [1885.] fol.   **h. 3103. c. (17.)**

— Die vier Jahreszeiten. The four Seasons. 4 kleine ...
Tonbilder für Pianoforte. 4 no. *Leipzig*, [1878.] fol.
    h. 3103. (8.)

— [Die vier Jahreszeiten. Op. 169. No. 1.] Frühling. Spring.
Edited and fingered by P. Gallico. [P. F.] *J. W. Stern & Co.:
New York*, (1912.) fol.   **g. 606. o. (1.)**

— [Die vier Jahreszeiten. Op. 169. No. 2.] Sommer. Summer.
Edited and fingered by P. Gallico. [P. F.] *J. W. Stern & Co.:
New York*, (1912.) fol.   **g. 606. o. (2.)**

— 18 vierhändige Clavierstücke, *etc.* 4 Hft. *Leipzig*, [1877.] fol.
    h. 3103. (4.)

— La Violette. Idylle pour le piano. *E. Donajowski: London*,
[1884.] fol.   **h. 3103. d. (32.)**

— Von dir geliebt. [P. F.] *See* supra: Zwei Salonstücke. Op. 251.
No. 2.

— Was sich der Wald erzählt ... Vier instructive Tonbilder für
Pianoforte. 4 no. *Leipzig*, [1881.] fol.   **h. 3103. a. (19.)**

— Weihnachtsjubel ... Sechs leichte Tänze für Pianoforte.
Op. 246. 6 no. *Leipzig*, [1883.] fol.   **h. 3103. c. (7.)**

— Zwei Weihnachtsstücke ... für Pianoforte. Op. 265. *Leipzig*,
[1886.] fol.   **h. 3103. c. (22.)**

LICHNER (Heinrich)

— Die Welt ist so schön ... Sechs melodiöse ... Tonbilder für
Pianoforte. 6 no. *Leipzig*, [1882.] fol.   **h. 3103. b. (8.)**

— Wintermärchen ... Caprice à la polka pour piano. *Augener
& Co.: London*, [1884.] fol.   **h. 3103. d. (33.)**

— Wonnige Maienzeit. [P. F.] *See* supra: Zwei Salonstücke.
Op. 251. No. 1.

— Zeitbilder ... Acht leichte ... Tanzweisen für Pianoforte ...
Op. 274, *etc.* 8 no. *C. F. W. Siegel: Leipzig*, [1887.] fol.
    h. 3103. e. (8.)

— Zephiretten. Fünf leichte und melodiöse Tanzweisen für
Pianoforte. 5 no. *Leipzig*, [1878.] fol.   **h. 3103. (9.)**

— Zu Herzensfreude und Seelenfrieden ... 18 kleine ...
Fantasien für Klavier zu 4 Händen. 3 Hft. *Leipzig*, [1882.]
fol.   **h. 3103. b. (5.)**

LICHNER (P.)

— Arrival of the Friends. Polka. *See* infra: My Birthday Party
... 3.

— As the Dance goes on. Waltz. *See* infra: My Birthday Party
... 4.

— Dreaming. Meditation. *See* infra: My Birthday Party ... 6.

— A Letter from Auntie. Reverie. *See* infra: My Birthday Party
... 2.

— My Birthday Party. A set of six easy piano pieces ...
1. Waiting for the Mail. March. 2. A Letter from Auntie.
Reverie. 3. Arrival of the Friends. Polka. 4. As the Dance goes
on: Waltz. 5. Telling Stories. Mazurka. 6. Dreaming.
Meditation. 6 no. *Century Music Publishing Co.: New York*,
[1909.] fol.   **h. 4120. pp. (33.)**

— Telling Stories. Mazurka. *See* supra: My Birthday Party ... 5.

— Waiting for the Mail. March. *See* supra: My Birthday Party
... 1.

LICHNER (R.)

— Day Dreams. Reverie. [P.F.] pp. 3. *Century Music Publishing
Co.: New York*, [1909.] fol.   **h. 4120. pp. (34.)**

— Dreaming. Nocturne. [P.F.] pp. 3. *Century Music Publishing
Co.: New York*, [1909.] fol.   **h. 4120. pp. (35.)**

— Idle Moments. Waltz. [P.F.] pp. 3. *Century Music Publishing
Co.: New York*, [1909.] fol.   **h. 4120. pp. (36.)**

LICHNOWSKY (Moritz) *Count*

— 7 variations pour le clavecin ou piano-forte sur l'air Nel cor
più non mi sento de l'opéra la Molinara [by G. Paisiello].
pp. 11. *Chez Jean Traeg:* [*Vienna*, 1805?] *obl.*   **Hirsch III. 361.**

LICHNOWSKY (Wilhelm von)

— 12 Ländlerische Tänze ... für das Pianoforte. *Wien*, [1815?]
obl. fol.   **e. 284. b. (15.)**

LICHT

— Licht. [Chorus.] *See* BARTH (R.) Vier Frauenchöre ... Op. 10.
No. 3.

— The Licht Heart. Song. *See* HINTON (J. H.)

— Licht, mehr Licht! [Part-song.] *See* LISZT (F.) [Fest-Album zur
Säcular-Feier von Goethe's Geburtstag.]

— Licht sei dein Traum. [Song.] *See* JENSEN (A.) 7 Lieder, *etc.*
Op. 50. No. 1.

LICHT

— Licht Sonnenwenden ist da. [Part-song.] *See* HEUBERGER (R.)

LICHT (CARL)

— Descants ... On ten famous hymns. For S.A.T.B. or unison, *etc.* pp. 16. *Harold Flammer: New York,* [1953.] 8°.
F. 1176. w. (33.)

LICHT (MYRTHA BIEHUSEN)

— 10 Anthems. For S.A.B. choir. A collection of ... anthems arranged by M. B. Licht. pp. 31. *G. Schirmer: New York,* [1962.] 8°. **E. 335. ee. (40.)**

— Twelve Anthems. For two-part chorus (S.A.) with organ accompaniment. Arranged by M. B. Licht. pp. 38. *G. Schirmer: New York,* [1965.] 8°. **F. 1106. a. (8.)**

— The Children's Church Choir Book. A collection of hymn-anthems arranged for 2-part junior choir by M. B. Licht. pp. 15. *G. Schirmer: New York,* [1959.] 8°.
E. 497. z. (2.)

— [A reissue.] The Children's Church Choir Book, *etc.* *Chappell: London; G. Schirmer: New York,* [1964.] 8°.
E. 353. (27.)

— The Dove. A Christmas miniature for two-part chorus. [Words by] Mary Dellena White. pp. 4. *G. Schirmer: New York,* [1962.] 8°. **E. 263. n. (47.)**

— The Dove. A Christmas miniature. For two-part chorus. [Words by] Mary Dellena White. [Staff and tonic sol-fa notation.] pp. 4. *Chappell & Co.: London,* [1962.] 8°.
E. 263. n. (42.)

— Fair Easter. For three-part chorus of mixed voices with organ or piano accompaniment. [Words by] St. John of Damascus (8th century), tr: J. M. Neale (1863). pp. 7. *G. Schirmer: New York,* [1961.] 8°. **E. 335. cc. (3.)**

— The Halo. For two-part chorus with piano accompaniment and chimes. [Words by] Mary Dellena White. pp. 4. *G. Schirmer: New York,* [1962.] 8°. **E. 263. p. (22.)**

— Thanksgiving. Carol for S.A. German 15th century, tr. by Eleanor Farjeon. pp. 7. *H. W. Gray Co.: New York,* [1960.] 8°. **F. 260. o. (52.)**

— Thanksgiving. Carol for S.A.T.B., *etc.* pp. 7. *H. W. Gray Co.: New York,* [1963.] 8°. **F. 260. w. (31.)**

— *See* BACH (J. S.) [*Collected Works.—c.*] Two Choruses, *etc.* ⟨[2.] Chorale from the St. Matthew Passion. For three-part chorus of mixed voices with piano or organ accompaniment. Arranged by M. B. Licht.⟩ [1964.] 8°. **F. 956. oo. (6.)**

LICHTE

— Eine lichte Mitternacht. [Part-song.] *See* HINDEMITH (P.) Zwei Männerchöre ... Nr. 2.

LICHTENBERG (LEOPOLD)

— Scale Studies for the Violin. *G. Schirmer: New York,* 1902. fol. **h. 1753. c. (2.)**

— *See* ALARD (J. D.) Twenty-Four Études-Caprices for the Violin. ⟨Op. 41.⟩ Edited by L. Lichtenberg. [1950.] 4°.
g. 498. d. (1.)

— *See* CORELLI (A.) [Sonata. Op. 5. No. 12.] La Folia. Variations for violin ... Edited ... by L. Lichtenberg. [1950.] 4°.
g. 500. v. (9.)

— *See* FRANCK (C. A. J. G. H.) Sonata for Violin and Piano. Edited ... by L. Lichtenberg, *etc.* [1950.] 4°. **h. 2693. e. (9.)**

LICHTENBERG (LEOPOLD)

— *See* GAVINIÉS (P.) Twenty-Four Studies (Matinées) for the Violin. Edited ... by L. Lichtenberg. [1950.] 4°.
g. 498. d. (8.)

— *See* GRIEG (E. H.) Sonata No. 1 for Piano and Violin, *etc.* ⟨Edited and fingered by L. Lichtenberg.⟩ [1958.] 4°.
g. 705. m. (3.)

— *See* GRIEG (E. H.) Sonata No. II. ⟨Op. 13.⟩ For violin and piano, *etc.* ⟨Edited ... by L. Lichtenberg.⟩ [1950.] 4°.
g. 705. h. (15.)

— *See* GRIEG (E. H.) Sonata No. III. ⟨Op. 45.⟩ For violin and piano, *etc.* ⟨Edited and fingered by L. Lichtenberg.⟩ [1958.] 4°.
g. 705. m. (4.)

— *See* LALO (E. V. A.) Symphonie espagnole. For violin and piano. Edited by L. Lichtenberg. [1950.] 4°. **g. 500. w. (4.)**

— *See* LECLAIR (J. M.) [Sonatas. Bk. 4. Op. 9. No. 3.] Sonata III. in D ... Edited ... by L. Lichtenberg, *etc.* 1903. 4°.
g. 223. k. (18.)

— *See* LECLAIR (J. M.) [Sonatas. Bk. 4. Op. 9. No. 3.] Sonata III in D for the Violin with Piano accompaniment. Edited and fingered by L. Lichtenberg, *etc.* [1952.] 4°. **g. 500. z. (1.)**

— *See* PAGANINI (N.) Moto perpetuo ... ⟨Op. 11.⟩ For the violin with piano accompaniment. Edited and fingered by L. Lichtenberg. [1951.] 4°. **g. 500. z. (6.)**

— *See* PAGANINI (N.) Le Streghe ... (Edition for Violin and Piano.) The Violin part edited ... by L. Lichtenberg, *etc.* 1903. 4°. **g. 223. k. (24.)**

— *See* RODE (J. P. J.) Concerto No. VIII in E minor for Violin and Piano. (Op. 13.) Edited ... by L. Lichtenberg. [1950.] 4°.
g. 500. w. (18.)

— *See* RODE (J. P. J.) Twelve Études for the Violin. Edited by L. Lichtenberg. [1951.] 4°. **g. 498. oo. (6.)**

— *See* TARTINI (G.) [L'Arte dell'arco.] The Art of Bowing, for the Violin ... Edited ... by L. Lichtenberg. [1950.] 4°.
g. 498. mm. (2.)

— *See* TARTINI (G.) Two Sonatas. [Op. 1. No. 5. Op. 3. No. 12.] For violin and piano. Edited and fingered by L. Lichtenberg. [1955.] 4°. **g. 500. cc. (13.)**

— *See* TARTINI (G.) Le Trille du diable. For violin and piano. Edited ... by L. Lichtenberg, *etc.* [1950.] 4°. **g. 500. w. (19.)**

— *See* VIEUXTEMPS (H.) Fantasia appassionata for the Violin. ⟨Op. 35.⟩ With piano accompaniment. Edited ... by L. Lichtenberg. [1950.] 4°. **g. 500. x. (7.)**

— *See* VIOTTI (G. B.) [Concerto No. 17.] First Movement of Concerto No. 17 in D minor for the Violin. With piano accompaniment ... Edited ... by L. Lichtenberg. [1950.] 4°.
g. 500. x. (8.)

— *See* VIOTTI (G. B.) [Concerto No. 22 in A minor.] First Movement of Concerto No. 22 ... For the violin with piano accompaniment ... Edited and fingered by L. Lichtenberg. [1951.] 4°. **g. 500. z. (14.)**

— *See* VIOTTI (G. B.) Six Duets for two Violins. Edited by L. Lichtenberg ... Op. 29 ... Op. 20 ... Op. 9. [1951, 53.] 4°.
g. 218. j. (1.)

— *See* WIENIAWSKI (H.) Capriccio-Valse for the Violin with Piano Accompaniment. ⟨Op. 7.⟩ Edited by ... L. Lichtenberg. [1950.] 4°. **g. 500. x. (13.)**

— *See* WIENIAWSKI (H.) Second Concerto in D minor ... ⟨Op. 22.⟩ For violin and piano. Edited ... by L. Lichtenberg. [1950.] 4°. **g. 500. x. (14.)**

LICHTENBERG (LEOPOLD)

— *See* WIENIAWSKI (H.) Polonaise brillante in D major for Violin and Orchestra. ⟨Op. 4.⟩ The orchestra accompaniment arranged for the piano. Edited ... by L. Lichtenberg. [1950.] 4°.
    g. 500. x. (16.)

— *See* WIENIAWSKI (H.) Second Polonaise brillante for Violin and Piano. ⟨Op. 21.⟩ Edited ... by L. Lichtenberg. [1950.] 4°.
    g. 500. x. (17.)

— *See* WIENIAWSKI (H.) Romance sans paroles et rondo élégant. ⟨Op. 9.⟩ Pour le violon avec accompagnement de piano. Edited and fingered by L. Lichtenberg. [1951.] 4°.
    g. 500. z. (16.)

— *See* WIENIAWSKI (H.) Scherzo-Tarentelle for Violin with Accompaniment of Piano. ⟨Op. 16.⟩ Edited ... by L. Lichtenberg. [1950.] 4°.
    g. 500. x. (18.)

LICHTENBERG (THEODORE)

— Der Abendfalter Walzer für das Piano Forte. *London,* [1843.] fol.
    h. 932. (34.)

— Krieger Lust, fünf Walzer und eine Polka für das Piano Forte (für zwei Clavier Spieler). *Liverpool,* [1844.] fol.
    h. 932. (35.)

LICHTENBERGER (FRANCIS)

— Three Drawing-Room Pieces for the Pianoforte. Second series. N° 1. March des Gnomes. N° 2. Advent of Spring ... N° 3. Spielzeit, *etc.* no. 1. *Forsyth Brothers: London, Manchester,* [c. 1880.] fol.
Imperfect; wanting no. 2, 3.
    h. 61. u. (3.)

— Three Drawing Room pieces. [P. F.] 3 no. *London,* [1881.] fol.
    h. 3275. j. (37.)

LICHTENSTEIN

— Lichtenstein. Grosse Oper. *See* LINDPAINTNER (P. J. von)

LICHTENSTEIN (BESSIE FLORENCE)

— La Coterie Waltzes for pianoforte. *O. Ditson Company: Boston, etc.,* 1894. fol.
    h. 3285. q. (48.)

— Heart's Devotion. [Song.] Words and music by B. F. Lichtenstein. *O. Ditson Company: Boston, etc.,* 1895. fol.
    H. 1798. v. (23.)

— The New Arverne Waltzes for Pianoforte. *O. Ditson Company: Boston, etc.,* 1895. fol.
    h. 3285. q. (49.)

— Reverie de l'Ange, for pianoforte. *O. Ditson Company: Boston, etc.,* 1895. fol.
    h. 1489. t. (1.)

— Triumphal America. March militaire, *etc.* [P. F.] *O. Ditson Company: Boston, etc.,* 1894. fol.
    h. 1489. t. (2.)

— Visions of Love. Waltzes. [P. F.] *O. Ditson Company: Boston, etc.,* 1895. fol.
    h. 3285. q. (50.)

LICHTENSTEIN (F.)

— Zwei Clavierstücke, *etc.* *S. Lucas, Weber & Co.: London,* [1884.] fol.
    h. 1484. t. (22.)

— O Salutaris Hostia, *etc.* [In D. Solo.] *R. Butler: London,* [1884.] fol.
    H. 879. e. (19.)

— O Salutaris Hostia, *etc.* [In F. Solo.] *R. Butler: London,* [1885.] fol.
    H. 879. e. (18.)

LICHTENSTEIN (GASTON)

— Edgecombe Cake Walk. For piano. pp. 5. *Geo. Jaberg Music Co.: Cincinnati,* [1900.] fol.
    h. 4120. pp. (37.)

LICHTENSTEIN (GEORGE)

— Hungarian fantasia for the pianoforte. *London,* [1854.] fol.
    h. 723. m. (9.)

— "My dream" waltz for the pianoforte (with cornet ad lib.). *London,* [1854.] fol.
    h. 975. e. (41.)

— Pensées patriotiques, mélodies originales pour piano. *London,* [1855.] fol.
    h. 724. e. (24.)

— Tempi futuri, polka. [P.F. with accompaniment for the cornet.] *London,* [1854.] fol.
    h. 975. e. (40.)

— Tempi passati, galopade brillante for the piano [with accompaniment for cornet]. *London,* [1854.] fol.
    h. 975. e. (39.)

— War march for the pianoforte. *London,* [1855.] fol.
    h. 724. e. (25.)

— Wedding quadrille. [P.F. with accompaniment for cornet à pistons.] *London,* [1854.] fol.
    h. 975. e. (38.)

LICHTENSTEIN (KARL AUGUST LUDWIG VON) *Baron*

— [Bathmendi.—Lasse die Blüthe des Lebens.] Aus der Oper: Bathmendi. [Duet.] [*Breitkopf und Haertel: Leipzig,* 1799.] 4°. [*Beilage zur Allgemeinen musikalischen Zeitung. Jahrg. 1. no. 10.*]
    P. P. 1945.

— *See* AUBER (D. F. E.) Gustave ... nach dem Französischen ... bearbeitet von dem Freiherrn von Lichtenstein, *etc.* [1840?] fol.
    H. 590. y.

LICHTENSTEIN (LEOPOLD)

— *See* HAGADAH. Hagada ... nebst drei Musikblätter: 1. Ein Tischgesang, componirt v. L. Lichtenstein, *etc.* 1841. 8°.
    1974. d. 61.

LICHTENSTEIN (LOUIS)

— Equitable Jubilee. March two-step. ⟨Op. 29.⟩ [P.F.] pp. 5. *Lyric Music Publishing Co.: New York,* [1909.] fol.
    h. 4120. pp. (38.)

— Her Poke Bonnet. [Song.] Verse by M. G. Hays. *J. Church Co.: Cincinnati, etc.,* 1910. fol.
    H. 1792. s. (29.)

— Through the Woods. A Melody for Piano. *J. Church Co.: Cincinnati, etc.,* (1912.) fol.
    g. 606. o. (3.)

— Tired. [Song.] Words by E. W. Wilcox. (Op. 18.) *J. Church Co.: Cincinnati, etc.,* 1910. fol.
    H. 1792. s. (30.)

LICHTENSTEIN (SAMUEL A.)

— Prince of India. An Oriental intermezzo and two step. [P.F.] pp. 2–5. [1906.] fol.
    h. 4120. pp. (39.)

LICHTENTHAL (PETER)

— Album musicale sacro. *Milano,* [1850?] fol.
    H. 3165.

— Orpheik, oder Anweisung die Regeln der Composition auf eine leicht fassliche Art grundlich zu erlernen. *Wien,* [1813.] *obl.* fol.
    E. 778.

— Quatuor pour le piano-forte avec violon, alto, et violoncelle concertantes ... Oeuv. 2ᵐᵃ [Parts.] 4 pt. *Au magasin de l'imprimerie chymique: Vienne,* [1805?] *obl.* fol. & fol.
Lithographed throughout.
    Hirsch III. 362.

— VII variations pour le clavecin ou pianoforte ... Œuvre III. pp. 9. *Au magasin de l'imprimerie chymique: Vienne,* [1805?] *obl.* fol.
Lithographed throughout.
    Hirsch III. 363.

LICHTENTHAL (PETER)

— *See* MOZART (W. A.) [Symphonies. K. 504.] Grande sonate ... arrangée pour le piano à quatre mains ... par ... P. Lichtenthal. [c. 1820.] *obl. fol.*　　　**f. 67. j. (4.)**

LICHTER (CHARLES)

— Vermont Summer. For orchestra. [Score.] pp. 29. *Galaxy Music Corporation: New York,* [1963.] 4°. *Kinhaven Series. no.* 1.　　　**g. 860. i. (6.)**

LICHTER (HANS)

— April Weather. *See* infra: Three second grade Pieces for the Piano ... Op. 1. No. 2.

— June Days. *See* infra: Three second grade Pieces for the Piano ... Op. 1. No. 3.

— May Time Waltz. *See* infra: Three second grade Pieces for the Piano ... Op. 1. No. 1.

— Three second grade Pieces for the Piano ... Op. 1. No. 1. May Time Waltz. No. 2. April Weather. No. 3. June Days. 3 no. *Oliver Ditson Co.: New York, etc.,* [1904.] fol.　　　**h. 4120. pp. (40.)**

— *See* BARTLETT (J. C.) A Dream ... Arranged by H. Lichter. 1902. 8°.　　　**F. 163. b. (1.)**

LICHTHYMNE

— Lichthymne. Männerchor. *See* KOELLNER (E.)

LICHTLEIN (WILHELM)

— Capriccio für 6 Melodie-Instrumente ... (Bläser oder Streicher/Wind instruments or strings.) Praktische Erstausgabe von ... Paul Winter. Partitur, *etc.* pp. 7. *Musikverlag Hans Gerig: Köln,* [1966.] 4°.　　**g. 1067. o. (1.)**

LICHTWARK (K.)

— Konzertfuge in G moll für die Orgel. Op. 2. *See* ALBUM. Album für Orgel-Spieler, *etc.* Lief. 111. [1880, *etc.*] *obl.* fol.　　　**e. 119.**

— Praeludium und Fugato für Orgel. *See* ALBUM. Album für Orgel-Spieler, *etc.* Lief. 108. [1880, *etc.*] *obl.* fol.　　　**e. 119.**

— Toccata und Fuge für Orgel. Op. 5. [1903.] *See* ALBUM. Album für Orgel-Spieler, *etc.* Lief. 112. [1880? *etc.*] *obl.* fol.　　**e. 119.**

LĪCĪTE (PAULA)

— Latviešu tautasdziesmas solo balsij un ansambļiem. Sastādījusi P. Līcīte. pp. 99. *Latvijas valsts izdevniecība: Rīgā,* 1960. 4°.　　　**G. 1310. b.**

LICKL (CARL GEORG)

— Élégie. *See* ALBUM. [Ewer's] Album de Piano, 1858. No. 12. 1858. fol.　　　**h. 1211.**

— Evening Bells ... Idylle pour piano. *Augener & Co.: London,* [1884.] fol.　　　**g. 543. j. (34.)**

— Grande march allemand [*sic*]. [P.F.] *In:* The Musical Bijou ... for MDCCCXLVIII. p. 58. [1848.] fol.　　　**H. 2330.**

— Ischler-Bilder. Am Wolfgang-See. Idylle für das Piano-Forte ... 57tes. Werk. No. 1. *Bei A. Diabelli u. Comp.: Wien,* [1842?] 4°.　　　**g. 543. ll. (5.)**

— Ischler-Bilder. Am Hallstädter-See. Idylle für das Piano-Forte ... 57tes. Werk. No. 2. *Bei A. Diabelli u. Comp.: Wien,* [1842?] 4°.　　　**g. 543. ll. (6.)**

LICKL (CARL GEORG)

— Ischler-Bilder. Im Ischler-Thale. Idylle für das Piano-Forte ... 57tes Werk. No. 3. *Bei A. Diabelli: Wien,* [1842?] 4°.　　　**g. 543. ll. (7.)**

— Ischler-Bilder. In der Gosau. Idylle für das Piano-Forte ... 57tes. Werk. No. 4. *Bei A. Diabelli u. Comp.: Wien,* [1842?] 4°.　　　**g. 543. ll. (8.)**

— Ischler-Bilder. Am Kalvarien-Berge. Idylle für das Piano-Forte ... 57tes. Werk. No. 6. *Bei A. Diabelli und Comp.: Wien,* [1842?] 4°.　　　**g. 543. ll. (9.)**

— Reminiscenzen aus der Oper: Die Hugenotten, von G. Meyerbeer. Vier Potpourris in 2 Abtheilungen für die Physharmonica mit Begleitung des Pianoforte, *etc.* 2 pt. *A. Diabelli et Comp.: Wien,* [1840?] fol. 14*th Heft of "Wiener-Salon Musik". Imperfect; wanting the* 2*nd Part.*　　　**h. 1568. a. (3.)**

— Rondino, à la Paganini, sur les motifs de son second concert, pour le piano ... Op. 34. *In:* The Harmonicon. vol. 9, pt. 2. pp. 201–203. 1831. 4°.　　　**P. P. 1947.**

— Theoretisch-Practische Anleitung zur Kenntnis und Behandlung der Phys-Harmonica; mit erläuternden Beispielen und fortschreitenden Übungen ... 50ᵗᵉˢ Werk. [With a frontispiece.] pp. 40. *Bei Ant. Diabelli & Comp.: Wien,* [1835?] 8°.　　　**e. 138. a.**

— Theoretisch-Practische Anleitung zur Kenntniss und Behandlung der Physharmonica ... 50ᵗᵉˢ Werk. Neue vermehrte Ausgabe. Instruction théorique et pratique sur la connaissance et l'emploi de la physharmonica, *etc.* Ger. & Fr. pp. 43. *Bei A. Diabelli et comp.: Wien,* [1848?] fol.　　**g. 343.**

— Theoretisch-Practische Anleitung zur Kenntniss und Behandlung der Physharmonika ... 50ᵗᵉˢ Werk. Neue ... Ausgabe.—Instruction ... sur ... l'emploi de la Physharmonica, *etc.* (Anhang ... Praktisch fortschreitende Übungen für die Physharmonika ... 77ᵗᵉˢ Werk.) 2 pt. *A. Diabelli et Comp.: Wien,* [1848.] fol.　　**R. M. 17. f. 15. (3.)**

— *See* BEETHOVEN (L. van) Grosses Septett (in Es) ... Op. 20. Übertragen für Physharmonica und Pianoforte ... von C. G. Lickl. [1843.] fol.　　　**h. 2782. y. (3.)**

— *See* FRELON (L. F. A.) L'Orgue, journal des dimanches et des fêtes, publié sous la direction de L. F. A. Frelon, avec le concours de MM ... E. [*sic*] G. Lickl, *etc.* 1858. fol.　　　**h. 1004.**

— *See* THALBERG (S.) Fantaisie sur des motifs de l'opera: La Straniera de Bellini pour la piano forte ... Ouvre [*sic*] 9, *etc.* ⟨Arrangée à 4 m. par C. G. Lickl.⟩ [1838.] fol.　　**g. 443. n. (13.)**

LICKL (GEORG)

— III. Grands Quatuors concertans pour deux Violons, Alto et Violoncelle. Oeuvre 1. [Parts.] *Chez J. André: Offenbach s. M.,* [1800?] fol.　　　**g. 410. a. (9.)**

LICKL (JOHANN GEORG)

— Three Duets for two German Flutes. *London,* [1810?] fol.　　　**g. 71. e. (8.)**

LICORIS

— Licoris Bouquetière. [Song.] *See* JE. Je suis jeune bouquetière. [1780?] 8°.　　　**B. 362. b. (145.)**

LIDA

— Лида. [Song.] *See* BLEIKHMAN (Yu. I.) [Cinq romances. Op. 19. No. 3.]

LIDARTI (Cristiano Giuseppe)

— Six Duetts for a Violin and Violoncello. [Parts.] *Welcker: London*, [1775?] fol.   **g. 421. d. (9.)**

— Six Sonatas for two German flutes or Violins with a Thorough Bass for the Harpsichord. [Parts.] *Welcker: London*, [1770?] fol.   **g. 242. (4.)**

— [Another copy.]   **h. 2852. a. (12.)**

— Sei Trii per Due Violini con Basso ... Opera III. [Parts.] *Au Bureau d'Abonnement Musical: Paris*, [1770?] fol.   **g. 1003.**

— *See* ADLER (I.) Oeuvres du répertoire de la communauté portugaise d'Amsterdam ... [By C. G. Lidarti and others.] (Ed. I. Adler), *etc.* [1966.] 8°. [*Early Hebrew Art Music. no.* 4–6.]   **E. 1499. t. (1.)**

— *See* GALEOTTI (S.) Six Sonatas for Two Violins, with a Thorough Bass ... one by Sig.ʳ C. G. Lidardi. [1762.] fol.   **g. 516. a.**

LIDARTI (Giovanni Battista)

— Sei Trii per due Violine e Basso, *etc.* [Parts.] *Stampati a spese di G. Soderini:* [*London*, 1780?] fol.   **g. 409. c. (2.)**

— [Another issue.] Sei Trii per due Violini e Basso ... dedicati all illᵐᵒ Sig.ʳ Watkin Williams Wynne Bart. [Parts.] *Stampati a spese di Giuseppe Soderini:* [*London*, 1780?] fol. *The title-page of this copy gives the author's names as Cri.ⁿᵒ Giuseppe. In the preface he is called Giovanni Battista.*   **R. M. 17. a. 2. (1.)**

LIDDELL (Charles)

— Meadow-Sweet. Melody. [P. F.] *C. Vincent: London*, [1899.] 4°. *No.* 3 *of the "New Century Series," etc.*   **g. 1132.**

— Melodious Recreations for Young Pianists. 6 no. *C. Vincent: London*, 1900–6. 4°.   **g. 543. ee. (6.)**

— [Melody in A minor.] *See* HUENTEN (F.) [Allegro moderato in C.] Two little Pieces ... Melody in A minor, C. Liddell. 1903. 4°. *No.* 6 *of the "New Century Series," etc.*   **g. 1132.**

— Rondoletto in C. [P. F.] *C. Vincent: London*, [1901.] 4°. *No.* 5 *of the "New Century Series," etc.*   **g. 1132.**

LIDDELL (Claire)

— Ae fond Kiss. Old Highland melody arranged for unaccompanied mixed voice choir with soprano and tenor soli by Claire Liddell. ⟨Words by Robert Burns.⟩ [Staff and tonic sol-fa notation.] pp. 8. *Roberton Publications: Wendover*, [1976.] 8°.   **F. 1744. kk. (22.)**

— Fine Flowers in the Valley. Scottish folk ballad arranged for unaccompanied mixed choir with female solo. ⟨Words: anon.⟩ [Staff and tonic sol-fa notation.] pp. 8. *Roberton Publications: Wendover*, [1976.] 8°.   **E. 1885. ee. (4.)**

— I'll ay ca' in by yon Toon. Old Scottish air arranged for 3-part male voice choir unaccompanied by Claire Liddell. ⟨Words by Robert Burns.⟩ [Staff and tonic sol-fa notation.] pp. 4. *Roberton Publications: Wendover*, [1976.] 8°.   **F. 163. rr. (17.)**

— The Kindling Fire. Twelve Burns songs arranged for high voice using the airs to which Burns set his verses. Piano accompaniments and notes by Claire Liddell. pp. 31. *Roberton Publications: Wendover*, [1974.] 4°. *With a correction slip inserted on p.* 30.   **G. 1415. d. (9.)**

— Five Orkney Scenes. A song cycle for female voice and piano. Words by George Mackay Brown. pp. 16. *Roberton Publications, etc.: Wendover, etc.*, [1975.] 4°.   **G. 1277. n. (10.)**

LIDDELL (Claire)

— Three Pieces for Piano. 1. Minuet. 2. Spanish Dance. 3. Humoresque. pp. 7. *Ascherberg, Hopwood & Crew: London*, [1960.] 4°.   **g. 1128. mm. (3.)**

— A Scottish Carol. For 3-part treble voices with optional solo. Words by JCM. pp. 4. *Roberton Publications: Wendover*, [1975.] 8°.   **E. 460. pp. (14.)**

— So you want to play by Ear? A practical guide to improvisation. pp. 95. *Stainer and Bell: London*, 1980. 8°.   **e. 138. c. (4.)**

— Some may doubt. Carol for S.S.A. unaccompanied. Words by J. C. Mathieson. *Oecumuse: Ryde*, [1979.] *s. sh.* 8°. *Part of "Canticum novum choral Series".*   **C. 950. a. (37.)**

— Where are the Joys? Traditional Scottish air arranged for unaccompanied mixed voice choir with tenor solo by Claire Liddell. ⟨Words by Robert Burns.⟩ [Staff and tonic sol-fa notation.] pp. 7. *Roberton Publications: Wendover*, [1976.] 8°.   **E. 1885. ee. (5.)**

— Ye Banks and Braes, for unaccompanied mixed voice chorus. Words by Robert Burns. Air: Caledonian Hunt's Delight arranged by Claire Liddell. [Staff and tonic sol-fa notation.] pp. 4. *Roberton Publications: Wendover*, [1976.] 8°.   **F. 321. hh. (8.)**

LIDDELL (Dickson)

— Merry Douglas. Schottische or Barn Dance. [P. F.] *J. H. Larway: London*, 1908. fol.   **h. 3286. ll. (26.)**

LIDDELL (E. M. G.)

— Shepherds' Pipes and Tunes for them. A collection of well-known Airs arranged for Bamboo Pipes. Compiled by E. M. G. Liddell. *H. F. W. Deane and Sons: London*, 1932. *obl.* 8°.   **b. 99.**

— Shepherds' Pipes and Tunes for them, *etc.* (Revised edition.) *H. F. W. Deane and Sons: London*, 1934. *obl.* 8°.   **b. 99. a.**

LIDDELL (Edward Thomas)

— Baby Seed Song. [Song.] Words by E. Nesbit, *etc. Year Book Press: London*, 1912. 8°.   **E. 1766. t. (10.)**

LIDDELL (Guy)

— For Hearth and Home. Patriotic Song, words by A. Ross. *West & Co.: London*, 1914. fol.   **H. 1793. t. (49.)**

— Gather round for England ... Song ... Words by A. Wilkin. *J. B. Cramer & Co.: London*, 1902. fol.   **H. 1799. cc. (61.)**

— Say that you love me truly. Waltz Song, words by E. Austen. *West & Co.: London*, 1914. fol.   **H. 1793. t. (50.)**

— We Two. Waltz. [P. F.] *Ransford & Son: London*, [1892.] fol.   **h. 3285. q. (51.)**

LIDDELL (John)

— Indiana. Lancers (Waltz) on Audran's ... Opera. [P. F.] 2 no. *Boosey & Co.: London*, [1886.] fol.   **h. 3580. (2.)**

— Lancers "Indiana" ... (On Audran's new opera.) [Military band parts.] 26 pt. *In:* OSTLERE (May) Valse "Only once more," *etc.* 1886. fol. [*Boosey's military Journal. ser.* 81. *no.* 6.]   **h. 1549.**

— The Maid of the Mill. Waltz, on S. Adams' ... Song. [P. F.] *Boosey & Co.: London*, [1885.] fol.   **h. 3580. (3.)**

LIDDELL (John)

— Valse. "The Maid of the Mill." Liddell. On Stephen Adams' popular song.—Quadrille. "Pantomime." C. Coote ... Galop. "Wonnetrunken." C. Faust. [Op. 358.] [Military band parts.] 26 pt. *Boosey & Co.: London,* 1886. fol. [*Boosey's military Journal. ser.* 80. *no.* 4.]　　　　**h. 1549.**

— The May Flower. Lancers on ... American Airs. [P. F.] *Boosey & Co.: London,* [1886.] fol.　　　　**h. 3580. (4.)**

— "The Mayflower." ⟨Lancers.⟩ On popular American airs. [Military band parts.] 26 pt. *In:* WALDTEUFEL (E.) "Tendresse," *etc.* 1887. fol. [*Boosey's supplemental military Journal. no.* 347.]　　　　**h. 1544.**

— Mona. Waltz on S. Adam's ... Songs. [P. F.] *Boosey & Co.: London,* [1891.] fol.　　　　**h. 3580. (8.)**

— Morning on the Moor. Ballad [begins: "Where the flow'rets"] ... The words by A. Davis. *London,* [1861.] fol.　　　　**H. 1772. s. (1.)**

— Nell Gwynne. Galop (Lancers) (Waltz) on R. Planquette's Opera. [Solos and duets.] 6 no. *Metzler & Co.: London,* [1884.] fol.　　　　**h. 3580. (5.)**

— Nell Gwynne. Galop. [Brass band parts.] *London,* [1885.] 8°.　　　　**f. 402. e. (22.)**

— Nell Gwynne. Lancers on Planquette's Opera, arranged by Liddell. [Reed band parts.] *London,* [1885.] 8°.　　　　**f. 412. r. (3.)**

— Our Diva. Waltz (Lancers) (Quadrille) on Airs from the ... Opera by ... V. Roger. [P. F.] 3 no. *Metzler & Co.: London,* [1886.] fol.　　　　**h. 3580. (6.)**

— The River of Years. Waltz on Marzials' ... Song. *Boosey & Co.: London,* [1886.] fol.　　　　**h. 3580. (1.)**

— The River of Years. On Marzials' popular song. ⟨Conductor [and military band parts].⟩ 26 pt. *In:* FLOTOW (F. F. A. von) *Baron.* [Alessandro Stradella.—Oh! come bello e il giorno.] Finale, *etc.* 1886. fol. [*Boosey's military Journal. ser.* 81. *no.* 3.]　　　　**h. 1549.**

— They all love Jack. Lancers (Waltz) on S. Adams' Sea Songs. [P. F.] 2 no. *Boosey & Co.: London,* [1887.] fol.　　　　**h. 3580. (7.)**

— *See* FAHRBACH (P.) *the Younger.* Go as you please. Polka, arranged by Liddell. [1886.] fol.　　　**h. 3452. b. (19.)**

— *See* KOENIG (H.) Valse d'Amour. New edition by J. Liddell. [1884.] fol.　　　**h. 975. u. (12.)**

LIDDELL (Kate Georgina)

— Recollections of the Philharmonic Concerts. National Airs ... arranged for the pianoforte. *J. M. West & Co.: Glasgow,* [1885.] fol.　　　　**h. 1484. t. (23.)**

LIDDELL (Rosa Lyne)

— No Tidings. Song, the words by J. C. Simpson. *London,* [1876.] fol.　　　　**H. 1778. y. (26.)**

LIDDELL (Rosa P.)

— Hidden Joys. Song, words by C. L. Pirkis. *R. Cocks & Co.: London,* [1896.] fol.　　　　**H. 1798. v. (24.)**

— Love it was not I. Song, the words from 'Di Fawcett'. *Moutrie & Son: London,* [1886.] fol.　　　**H. 1788. w. (1.)**

LIDDELL (William M.)

— Mary had a Baby. Traditional Christmas spiritual arranged for two-part or unison voices with piano by William M. Liddell. pp. 4. *Roberton Publications: Wendover,* [1977.] 8°.　　　　**E. 352. a. (10.)**

LIDDEN (Cecil)

— Baby Pearl. ⟨Song.⟩ Written and composed by C. Lidden. Arranged by J. Chas. Moore. pp. 3. *Shapiro, von Tilzer Music Co.: London,* [1907.] 4°.　　　**H. 3985. z. (27.)**

— Boys will be Boys. ⟨Song.⟩ Written and composed by C. Lidden. pp. 4. *Shapiro, von Tilzer Music Co.: London,* [1907.] 4°.　　　**H. 3985. z. (28.)**

— Brave Boys of the D. L. I. ... [Song] Written and composed by C. Lidden, *etc. M. D. Elliott & Sons: Esh Winning, Co. Durham,* [1915.] fol.　　　**H. 1793. t. (51.)**

— Buttercups and Daisies. Song, words and music by C. Lidden. *Elkin & Co.: London,* 1905. fol.　　　**H. 1794. l. (11.)**

— Daisy. ⟨Song.⟩ Written and composed by C. Lidden. [Staff and tonic sol-fa notation. Voice part.] *Francis, Day & Hunter: London,* [1904.] *s. sh.* fol.　　　**H. 3985. z. (29.)**

— Daisy. ⟨Song.⟩ Written and composed by C. Lidden. [Staff and tonic sol-fa notation. Voice part.] *Francis, Day & Hunter: London,* [1904.] *s. sh.* fol. *With different words from the preceding.*　　　**H. 3985. z. (30.)**

— Daisy, *etc.* ⟨Song.⟩ [With separate voice part.] 2 pt. *Francis, Day & Hunter: London,* [1904.] fol.　　　**H. 3985. z. (31.)**

— D-i-a-b-olo ... ⟨Song.⟩ Written and composed by C. Lidden, *etc.* [With separate voice part.] 2 pt. *Empire Music Publishing Co.: London,* [1908.] fol.　　　**H. 3985. z. (32.)**

— Don't take "No" for an Answer. ⟨Song.⟩ Written and composed by C. Lidden. pp. 3. *Shapiro, von Tilzer Music Co.: London,* [1908.] 4°.　　　**H. 3985. z. (33.)**

— Good old Saturday Afternoon. ⟨Song.⟩ Written and composed by C. Lidden. Arranged by J. Chas. Moore. pp. 4. *Shapiro, von Tilzer Music Co.: London,* [1907.] 4°.　　**H. 3985. z. (34.)**

— "I've something to say to you!" Written and composed by C. Lidden. [Song. With separate voice part.] 2 pt. *Hopwood & Crew: London,* [1905.] fol.　　　**H. 3985. z. (35.)**

— Let me return to Dreamland. ⟨Song.⟩ Written by Percy Edgar. pp. 3. *Shapiro, von Tilzer Music Co.: London,* [1907.] 4°.　　　**H. 3985. z. (36.)**

— My English Sailor Man. [Song.] Written and composed by C. Lidden. [With separate voice part.] 2 pt. *Hopwood & Crew: London,* [1904.] fol.　　　**H. 3985. z. (37.)**

— My Star of Hope. ⟨Song.⟩ Written and composed by C. Lidden. [Staff and tonic sol-fa notation. Voice part.] *Francis, Day & Hunter: London,* [1904.] *s. sh.* fol.　　　**H. 3985. z. (38.)**

— My Star of Hope, *etc.* ⟨Song.⟩ [With separate voice part.] 2 pt. *Francis, Day & Hunter: London,* [1904.] fol.　　　**H. 3985. z. (39.)**

— Queen of my English Home. Written & composed by C. Lidden, *etc.* ⟨Song. Arranged by J. Chas. Moore.⟩ pp. 4. *Shapiro, von Tilzer Music Co.: London,* [1906.] fol. *Popular 6ᵈ Edition. no.* 73.　　　**H. 3985. z. (40.)**

— *See* DEWSON (Conan) and LIDDEN (C.) The Mountaineer, *etc.* ⟨Song.⟩ [1908.] *s. sh.* fol.　　　**H. 3983. t. (50.)**

— *See* DEWSON (Conan) and LIDDEN (C.) The Mountaineer, *etc.* ⟨Song.⟩ [1908.] fol.　　　**H. 3983. t. (51.)**

LIDDICOAT (J. G.)

— *See* FOX (Sam) Fox Mandolin and Guitar Folio. ⟨no. 2, 3.⟩ Arranged [for first mandoline or violin] by J. G. Liddicoat. [1909, *etc.*] 4°.   **g. 1800. (92.)**

LIDDLE (F. J.)

— The Troubadour. Song [begins: "Glowing with love"]. Words by Sir W. Scott. *London,* [1879.] fol.   **H. 1783. p. (1.)**

LIDDLE (JOHN SHEPHERD)

— Idle Days. [Part-song.] Words by F. W. Bourdillon. [1887.] *See* CHORAL. Choral Gems, *etc.* No. 2. [1887–9.] 4°.   **F. 585. t. (3.)**

— A Lay of June. [Four-part song.] Words by M. M. P. *A. Cary: Newbury,* [1896.] 4°.
No. 12 *and* 13 *of "A. Cary's Musical Treasury".*   **F. 585. r. (37.)**

— The Modern Violin Method. *A. Cary: Newbury; London,* [1889.] fol.   **h. 1753. (17.)**

— Six [or rather, five] Original Pieces for Violin and Piano. No. 1–5. *A. Cary: Newbury,* [1889.] fol.
No. 26–30 *of "Original Violin Solos".*   **h. 1701. (6.)**

— Serenade. ⟨Septett.⟩ [Parts.] 7 pt. *Alphonse Cary: Newbury, London,* [1889.] 8°.
Alphonse Cary's Orchestral Journal. no. 5.   **f. 800. (824.)**

— *See* BACH (J. S.) [Overture for Orchestra in D major. No. 1.] Aria & Gavotte ... arranged ... by J. S. Liddle. [1877.] fol.   **h. 1608. d. (8.)**

— *See* HAENDEL (G. F.) [15 Solos. Op. 1. No. 14.] Sonata in A ... arranged ... by J. S. Liddle. [1875.] fol.   **h. 435. a. (7.)**

— *See* HAENDEL (G. F.) [15 Solos. Op. 1. No. 15.] Sonata in E ... arranged ... by J. S. Liddle. [1875.] fol.   **h. 435. a. (8.)**

— *See* HIME (E. L.) Victory ... March ... Arranged for the Organ by J. S. Liddle. [1889.] *obl.* fol.   **e. 174. i. (5.)**

LIDDLE (ROBERT W.)

— O send out Thy Light. Short Full Anthem for four voices, *etc. City Music Publishing Co.: Lichfield,* [1909.] 8°.   **F. 231. aa. (25.)**

LIDDLE (SAMUEL)

— Album of nine Songs with Pianoforte accompaniment. (1. A Country Cradle Song ... N. C. Sutton. 2. Oh doubting Heart! ... A. Procter. 3. If I were a Rose ... C. Runcie. 4. A Love Song ... E. Crawford. 5. My true Love hath my Heart ... Sir Philip Sidney. 6. He and She ... E. Bisland. 7. At Parting ... P. B. Martin. 8. A Day of Sunshine ... Longfellow. 9. King Charles ... R. Browning.) *Boosey & Co.: London and New York,* 1897. 4°.   **F. 637. d. (5.)**

— Two Sacred Songs. [No. 1.] Like as the Hart ... [No. 2.] The Lord is my Shepherd ... 2nd setting. *Boosey & Co.: London and New York,* 1909. fol.   **H. 3606. a. (29.)**

— Abide with me. Sacred Song. The words by H. F. Lyte. With Organ Accompaniment. *Boosey & Co.: London and New York,* 1896. fol.   **H. 3606. (10.)**

— Abide with me. Sacred song, *etc.* [c. 1900.] fol.
A pirated edition.   **H. 1653. u. (6.)**

— Abide with me. Sacred song. The words by Henry Francis Lyte. pp. 7. *Boosey & Co.: London, etc.,* [1924?] 8°.   **F. 1893. a. (9.)**

— Abide with me. Arranged for Male Voice Chorus by Doris Arnold, *etc. Boosey & Co.: London,* 1938. 8°.
[*Boosey's Choral Miscellany, No.* 183.]   **F. 160. e.**

LIDDLE (SAMUEL)

— Abide with me. Arranged for female voices (S.S.A.) by Ronald V. Cawthorne, *etc. Boosey & Co.: London,* [1951.] 8°. [*Boosey's choral Miscellany. no.* 259.]   **F. 160. e.**

— Abide with me. Transcribed for the pianoforte by the composer. *Boosey & Co.: London and New York,* 1899. fol.   **h. 3282. f. (43.)**

— "Abide with me." ⟨Song. Cornet solo. Conductor [and military band parts].⟩ 26 pt. *In:* WILLIAMS (A.) "Sancho Panza," *etc.* 1899. fol. [*Boosey's supplemental military Journal. no.* 417.]   **h. 1544.**

— Abide with me. ⟨Song.⟩ [Accompaniment for strings with optional cornet solo.] Orchestrated by Sydney Baynes. [Parts.] 4 pt. *Boosey & Co.: London,* [c. 1925.] 4°.
The parts for 1*st violin and solo cornet are printed in score.*   **g. 1067. zz. (3.)**

— Abide with me ... Arranged for the Organ by B. Mason. *Boosey & Co.: London and New York,* 1926. 4°.   **g. 575. gg. (27.)**

— Abide with me ... Arranged for the violin with pianoforte accompaniment by B. Robinson. *Boosey & Co.: London and New York,* 1926. 4°.   **g. 505. mm. (13.)**

— Abide with me ... Arranged for the violoncello with pianoforte accompaniment by B. Robinson. *Boosey & Co.: London and New York,* 1926. 4°.   **g. 514. q. (12.)**

— Arabic Love Song. [Song.] Words by Shelley. *Forsyth Brothers: London, Manchester,* 1899. fol.   **H. 1846. nn. (33.)**

— Art Thou not from Everlasting ... Introit. *Stainer & Bell: London,* (1909.) 8°.
Stainer & Bell's Church Choir Library, No. 17.   **F. 1137. b.**

— At last. Sacred Song, the poem by J. G. Whittier ... organ accompaniment ad lib. *Boosey & Co.: London and New York,* 1900. fol.   **H. 3606. (11.)**

— At Parting. Song, the words by P. B. Marston, *etc. Boosey & Co.: London and New York,* 1897. fol.   **H. 3606. (12.)**

— Be ye kind one to another. Anthem, *etc. J. Curwen & Sons: London,* 1934. 8°.
[*Church Choralist. No.* 698.]   **E. 1330.**

— Because of you. Song, words by N. B. Marsland. *Chappell & Co.: London, etc.,* 1917. fol.   **H. 3606. b. (6.)**

— Begone! Carking Care! Song. The Words translated from the French of Charles, Duke of Orleans ... by H. W. Longfellow. *Boosey & Co.: London and New York,* 1897. fol.   **H. 3606. (1.)**

— The Bells of Spring, and The Challenge of Spring. Two Songs, the words by C. G. Mortimer. *Boosey & Co.: London and New York,* 1924. 4°.   **H. 3606. b. (22.)**

— A Birthday. *See* infra: [Eight Christina Rossetti Poems. No. 3.]

— Blackbird's Pool. Two-part Song ... Poem by F. C. Liddle, *etc. J. Curwen & Sons: London,* 1941. 8°.
[*Choruses for Equal Voices. No.* 2038.]   **E. 861.**

— Bright is the Ring of Words. Song, words by R. L. Stevenson, *etc.* 4 no. [In C, D flat, E flat and F.] *Chappell & Co.: London, etc.,* 1907. fol.   **H. 3606. a. (20.)**

— Calling me. *See* infra: [Eight Christina Rossetti Poems. No. 8.]

— Castles in the Air. Two-part Song for Equal Voices ... Poem by J. Ballantine ... Old Scottish Melody. Arr.: by S. Liddle. *J. Curwen & Sons: London,* 1936. 8°.
[*Choruses for Equal Voices. No.* 1904.]   **E. 861.**

LIDDLE (Samuel)

— The Child Musician. Song, the words by A. Dobson, *etc. Boosey & Co.: London and New York*, 1898. fol.
H. 3606. (13.)

— A Child's Song. Little Lamb, who made thee? [Song.] Words by W. Blake. 2 no. [In C and E flat.] *Chappell & Co.: London, etc.*, 1914. fol.
H. 3606. b. (2.)

— Eight Christina Rossetti Poems set to Music. *Boosey & Co.: London and New York*, 1900. 4°.
G. 424. h. (4.)

— [Eight Christina Rossetti Poems. No. 3.] A Birthday. Song, *etc. Boosey & Co.: London and New York*, [1902.] fol.
H. 3606. a. (1.)

— [Eight Christina Rossetti Poems. No. 8.] Calling me. Song, *etc. Boosey & Co.: London and New York*, [1906.] fol.
H. 3606. a. (14.)

— Christmas Bells. Song, words ... by Longfellow, *etc.* 4 no. [In C, D flat, E flat and F.] *Chappell & Co.: London, etc.*, 1907. fol.
H. 3606. a. (21.)

— Christmas Bells. Arranged for Female Trio ... by W. Stickles, *etc. Chappell-Harms: New York*, 1930. 8°.
F. 217. d. (39.)

— Come to Me! Sacred Song, *etc.* [Words by] (C. Elliott.) *G. Schirmer: New York*, 1931. 4°.
G. 519. o. (22.)

— Come unto Me ... Introit. *Stainer & Bell: London*, (1909.) 8°.
Stainer & Bell's Church Choir Library, No. 16. **F. 1137. b.**

— Come unto Me. Short Anthem in four parts, S. A. T. B., to be sung without accompaniment. *Stainer & Bell: London*, (1910.) 8°.
Stainer & Bell's Church Choir Library, No. 73. **F. 1137. b.**

— Come, walk with Love. Sacred Song, the words by M. M. H. Ayers. *Boosey, Hawkes, Belwin: New York*, 1937. 4°.
G. 519. q. (47.)

— A Country Cradle Song. The Words by N. C. Sutton, *etc. Boosey & Co.: London and New York*, 1897. fol.
H. 3606. (2.)

— Dirge for Phillida. Old Melody arranged for Chorus of Men's Voices by S. Liddle, poem from Percy's Reliques. *J. Curwen & Sons: London*, 1936. 8°.
[*The Apollo Club. No.* 729.] **F. 667.**

— The Dove said 'Give us Peace'. Song, the Poem by J. Ingelow. *Boosey & Co.: London and New York*, 1900. fol.
H. 3606. (14.)

— Four Duets for Soprano and Contralto with Pianoforte accompaniment. No. 1. There be none of Beauty's Daughters. Byron. No. 2. The Sea hath its Pearls. Heine.—Translation by Longfellow.— No. 3. To Blossoms. Herrick. No. 4. Spring. Nash. *Stainer & Bell: London*, 1907. 8°. **F. 1530. k. (10.)**

— Easter-Tide. Sacred Song, the words by Mrs. L. B. Walford. *Boosey & Co.: London and New York*, 1906. fol.
H. 3606. a. (15.)

— Easter-Tide. Sacred Song ... Edition with Organ accompaniment only, in C. *Boosey & Co.: London and New York*, 1906. fol. **H. 3606. a. (16.)**

— Elegy, for Violoncello with Pianoforte Accompaniment, *etc. Boosey & Co.: London and New York*, 1900. fol.
h. 204. g. (8.)

— Elegy ... Adapted for Violin [and P. F.] by T. Nachèz. *Boosey & Co.: London and New York*, 1900. fol.
h. 1612. h. (4.)

— The Evening Sea. Song, the words by E. Daplyn. *Boosey & Co.: London and New York*, 1902. fol. **H. 3606. a. (2.)**

LIDDLE (Samuel)

— Fall, Snowflakes. Song, words by F. Liddle. *Chappell & Co.: London, etc.*, 1920. fol. **H. 3606. b. (12.)**

— A Farewell. Song, the poem by C. Kingsley, *etc. Boosey & Co.: London and New York*, 1907. fol. **H. 3606. a. (22.)**

— Song (Cornet Solo), "A Farewell". ⟨Arr. by M. Retford. Conductor [and military band parts].⟩ 33 pt. *In:* DVOŘÁK (A.) [Slavische Tänze. Op. 46. No. 3.] Slavonic Dance, No. 3, *etc.* 1908. fol. [*Boosey's military Journal. ser.* 125. *no.* 4.]
h. 1549.

— Fierce raged the Tempest. Sacred Song, the words by G. Thring. [With organ accompaniment.] *Boosey & Co.: London and New York*, 1897. fol. **H. 3606. (15.)**

— Friar John. Old Flemish Air, with English words by P. England, arranged by S. Liddle. *Boosey & Co.: London and New York*, 1901. fol. **H. 3606. a. (3.)**

— Fulfilment. Song, words by Sir E. Arnold. *Chappell & Co.: London, etc.*, 1920. fol. **H. 3606. b. (13.)**

— A Garden Love Song. [Song.] The words by G. Hadath. *Boosey & Co.: London and New York*, 1909. fol.
H. 3606. a. (23.)

— The Garden where the Praties grow. Song. Old Irish Melody arranged by S. Liddle. *Stainer & Bell: London*, 1929. 4°.
H. 3606. b. (24.)

— The Gay Gordons. Song.—Second Setting.—The Words by H. Newbolt. *Boosey & Co.: London and New York*, 1899. fol.
H. 3606. (16.)

— "The Gay Gordons." ⟨Song. Euphonion solo.⟩ [Military band parts.] 26 pt. *In:* ANDRÉ ( ) "Endoria," *etc.* 1899. fol. [*Boosey's supplemental military Journal. no.* 419.] **h. 1544.**

— Give a Man a Horse he can ride. Song, words by J. Thomson. *Chappell & Co.: London, etc.*, 1921. 4°. **H. 3606. b. (15.)**

— God is our Refuge and Strength. Sacred Song, *etc. Boosey & Co.: London*, 1932. 4°. **G. 519. p. (19.)**

— He and She. Song, the words by E. Bisland, *etc. Boosey & Co.: London and New York*, 1897. fol. **H. 3606. (17.)**

— Home Song. The Words by Longfellow. *Boosey & Co.: London and New York*, 1896. fol. **H. 3606. (3.)**

— Hope of the Ages. Sacred Song, the poem by J. G. Whittier. Organ accompaniment ad lib. *Boosey & Co.: London and New York*, 1900. fol. **H. 3606. (18.)**

— How lovely are Thy Dwellings. Sacred Song ... Organ accompaniment, ad lib. *Boosey & Co.: London and New York*, 1908. fol. **H. 3606. a. (24.)**

— How lovely are Thy Dwellings ... Anthem for Soprano and mixed Chorus, arranged ... by A. Fagge. *Boosey & Co.: London, etc.*, (1915.) 8°.
[*Boosey's Choral Miscellany. no.* 47.] **F. 160. e.**

— How lovely are Thy Dwellings. Part Song for Female Voices ... Arr. by A. Samuelson. *Boosey, Hawkes, Belwin: New York*, 1936. 8°. **E. 602. uu. (33.)**

— How lovely are Thy Dwellings. Part Song for Two Voices ... Arr. by A. Samuelson. *Boosey, Hawkes, Belwin: New York*, 1936. 8°. **E. 602. tt. (73.)**

— How lovely are Thy Dwellings. Part Song for S.A.B. ... Arr. by W. Howorth. *Boosey Hawkes Belwin, Inc.: New York*, 1940. 8°. **F. 1176. o. (17.)**

— How lovely are Thy Dwellings. For Mixed Voices— S.A.T.B.— ... arr. by A. Rowley. *Boosey & Hawkes: London, etc.*, 1941. 8°.
[*Choral Miscellany. No.* 198.] **F. 160. e.**

LIDDLE (Samuel)

— How lovely are Thy Dwellings ... S.S.A. Arr. by Noble Cain. pp. 7. *Boosey & Hawkes: New York, etc.*, 1946. 8°.
F. 1176. r. (39.)

— How lovely are Thy Dwellings ... Anthem ... arranged ... by A. Fagge. (Tonic Sol-fa edition.) *Boosey & Co.: London, etc.*, 1915. 4°.
Boosey's Choral Miscellany, No. 47. **C. 745. f. (17.)**

— How sleep the Brave. Ode [song], words by W. Collins, *etc. Chappell & Co.: London, etc.*, 1918. fol. **H. 3606. b. (7.)**

— I love thee, Life! Song, the words Anon. *Boosey & Co.: London and New York*, 1898. fol. **H. 3606. (20.)**

— I will extol Thee, O Lord. *See* infra: Sacred Songs. Two Psalms. No. 1.

— I will sing unto the Lord. *See* infra: Sacred Songs. Two Psalms. No. 2.

— If Love might keep thee young. Song, words by Lady Lindsay. 3 no. [In D, E flat and F.] *Chappell & Co.: London*, 1898. fol. **H. 3606. (19.)**

— In a little Wrath I hid my Face from thee ... Introit. *Stainer & Bell: London*, (1909.) 8°.
Stainer & Bell's Church Choir Library, No. 18. **F. 1137. b.**

— In dulci Jubilo, German Carol ... with English Translation by P. England. The Music arranged by S. Liddle. *Boosey & Co.: London and New York*, 1900. fol. **H. 3606. (21.)**

— In dulci jubilo. xivth century German Carol ... Unison Song. Music arranged by S. Liddle. *Boosey & Co.:* [*London*, 1935.] 8°.
[*Boosey's Choral Miscellany. No. 162.*] **F. 160. e.**

— "In my Garden." *See* infra: "To tell thee how I love," *etc.*

— It is His Will. Sacred Song, the words by I. Williams. *Boosey & Co.: London and New York*, 1929. 4°. **H. 3606. b. (25.)**

— The Kerry Recruit. An Irish recruiting Song at the time of the Crimean War. Arranged by S. Liddle. *Stainer & Bell: London*, 1938. 4°. **G. 1270. pp. (2.)**

— Lead, kindly Light. Sacred Song, words by Cardinal Newman. 3 no. [In C, D and E.] *Chappell & Co.: London, etc.*, 1912. fol. **H. 3606. b. (3.)**

— Like as the Hart desireth the Waterbrooks, *etc.* [Anthem.] *Stainer & Bell: London*, (1910.) 8°.
Stainer & Bell's Church Choir Library, No. 85. **F. 1137. b.**

— Little Boy Blue. Song. The Words by E. Field. *Boosey & Co.: London and New York*, 1897. fol. **H. 3606. (4.)**

— The Little Dancers. Two-part Song ... Poem by L. Binyon, *etc. J. Curwen & Sons: London*, 1940. 8°.
[*Choruses for Equal Voices. No. 2042.*] **E. 861.**

— A Little Longer. Song, words by A. Procter. 2 no. [In E flat and F.] *Chappell & Co.: London*, 1898. fol. **H. 3606. (22.)**

— Little Love. Song, the words by B. M. Ramsay. *Boosey & Co.: London and New York*, 1905. fol. **H. 3606. a. (17.)**

— Little white Snowflakes. Song, the words by E. Teschemacher. *Boosey & Co.: London and New York*, 1903. fol. **H. 3606. a. (4.)**

— The Lord is my Shepherd. A setting of the xxiiird Psalm for a Solo Voice with accompaniment for Piano. *Boosey & Co.: London and New York*, 1902. fol. **H. 3606. a. (5.)**

— The Lord is my Shepherd. Anthem ... Arr. by S. Salter. *Boosey & Co.: New York, London*, 1930. 8°. **E. 335. e. (58.)**

— The Lord's Prayer ... for four voices in unison, with Organ accompaniment. *Boosey & Co.: London and New York*, 1906. 8°. **F. 538. c. (29.)**

LIDDLE (Samuel)

— The Lord's Prayer ... for four voices—S. A. T. B.—without accompaniment, also Psalm xix., verse 14. *Boosey & Co.: London and New York*, 1907. 8°. **F. 231. v. (27.)**

— A Love Melody. Song, the poem by A. O'Shaughnessy. *Boosey & Co.: London and New York*, 1902. fol. **H. 3606. a. (6.)**

— The Love of a Friend. Vocal Duet. The Words by J. Canning, *etc. Boosey & Co.: London and New York*, 1896. fol. **H. 3606. (5.)**

— Two Love Songs. (1. Love hath Echoes. Words by T. Moore.) (2. Love's Philosophy. Words by Shelley.) *Boosey & Co.: London and New York*, 1902. fol. **H. 3606. a. (7.)**

— [Two Love Songs. No. 2.] Love's Philosophy. Song, *etc. Boosey & Co.: London and New York*, 1902. fol. **H. 3606. a. (8.)**

— Love's Captive. Song, words by F. Liddle. *Chappell & Co.: London, etc.*, 1923. 4°. **H. 3606. b. (16.)**

— Love's Evensong. Song, the words by F. Crawford. *Boosey & Co.: London and New York*, 1897. fol. **H. 3606. (23.)**

— Love's Mastery. Song, the words by G. Hadath. *Boosey & Co.: London and New York*, 1908. fol. **H. 3606. a. (25.)**

— Love's Philosophy. *See* supra: [Two Love Songs. No. 2.]

— Lovely kind and kindly loving. Song, words by N. Breton, *etc. Murdoch, Murdoch & Co.: London*, 1930. 4°. **G. 1275. ff. (33.)**

— The Mermaid. Short Cantata for female voices and Orchestra. The Poem by Tennyson ... Vocal Score with Pianoforte Accompaniment. *Boosey & Co.: London and New York*, 1899. 8°. **F. 1270. g. (4.)**

— The Moth and the Maiden. Song, the words imitated from the German of Wegener by E. Grey. *Boosey & Co.: London and New York*, 1899. fol. **H. 3606. (24.)**

— Mother o' Mine. Song, the words by Rudyard Kipling, *etc. Boosey & Co.: London and New York*, 1908. fol. **H. 3606. a. (26.)**

— My Beloved is mine. Song, *etc.* 2 no. [In F and A flat.] *Chappell & Co.: London, etc.*, 1912. fol. **H. 3606. b. (4.)**

— My Lady Love. Waltz. [P. F.] *Boosey & Co.: London and New York*, 1907. fol. **h. 3286. ll. (27.)**

— "My Lady Love." ⟨Waltz.⟩ Arr. by W. H. Myddleton. [Military band parts.] 33 pt. *In:* Bilton (Manuel) "Hungarian," *etc.* 1908. fol. [*Boosey & Co.'s new supplemental Journal for military Bands. no.* 51.] **h. 1544.**

— My Lute. Song, words by C. Urmy, *etc.* 3 no. [In E flat, F and G flat.] *Chappell & Co.: London, etc.*, 1908. fol. **H. 3606. a. (27.)**

— My Voice shalt Thou hear in the Morning. O Lord. Introit for Solo Tenor & Chorus.—S. A. T. B. *Stainer & Bell: London*, (1910.) 8°.
Stainer & Bell's Church Choir Library, No. 82. **F. 1137. b.**

— Night and Dreams, words by F. Liddle. I am thine, words by A. Akerman. Two Songs. *Chappell & Co.: London, etc.*, 1924. 4°. **H. 3606. b. (19.)**

— Nocturne, pour Violon avec Accomp. de Piano. *Schott & Co.: London*, [1904.] fol. **g. 505. t. (32.)**

— Now. Song, the words by E. W. Wilcox. *Boosey & Co.: London and New York*, 1907. fol. **H. 3606. a. (28.)**

— Oh, doubting Heart! Song. The Words by A. Procter. *Boosey & Co.: London and New York*, 1897. fol. **H. 3606. (6.)**

LIDDLE (SAMUEL)

— O Good beyond compare. Sacred Song, the words by Bishop R. Heber. *Boosey & Co.: London and New York*, 1929. 4°.   **H. 3606. b. (26.)**

— O how amiable are Thy Dwellings ... Anthem for 4 voices.—S. A. T. B. *Stainer & Bell: London*, (1910.) 8°. *Stainer & Bell's Church Choir Library, No.* 81.   **F. 1137. b.**

— Oh, like a Queen. Song, words by Sir W. Watson. *Chappell & Co.: London, etc.*, 1922. 4°.   **H. 3606. b. (17.)**

— O my Love's like a red, red Rose. Song, the poem by Burns. *Boosey & Co.: London & New York*, 1913. fol.
     H. 3606. b. (5.)

— Seven Old English Lyrics set to music. *Boosey & Co.: London and New York*, 1898. 4°.   **H. 1650. h. (5.)**

— [Seven Old English Lyrics. No. 3.] What care I how fair she be? Song ... the words by G. Wither. *Boosey & Co.: London and New York*, 1898. fol.   **H. 3606. (29.)**

— [Seven Old English Lyrics. No. 4.] Thou art my Life. Song, the words by the Earl of Rochester, *etc. Boosey & Co.: London and New York*, 1898. fol.   **H. 3606. (28.)**

— An Old French Carol. *See* infra: Quelle est cette odeur agréable?

— On Earth, Peace. Sacred Song, with Organ obbligato, words by E. H. Sears. *Chappell & Co.: London, etc.*, 1928. 4°.
     H. 3606. b. (27.)

— Onward!—Thick is the Darkness.—Song, words by W. E. Henley. *Chappell & Co.: London, etc.*, 1918. fol.
     H. 3606. b. (8.)

— Out of the Deep. Sacred Song, *etc. Boosey & Co.: London and New York*, 1931. 4°.   **G. 519. o. (23.)**

— Over the Moor. For voice and piano, words by M. W. Were. Par monts et vaux ... Traduction libre française par ***. *J. & W. Chester: London, Brighton*, 1916. fol.
     H. 3606. b. (14.)

— The Pilgrims of the Night. Sacred Song, the words by F. W. Faber. [With organ accompaniment.] *Boosey & Co.: London and New York*, 1899. fol.   **H. 3606. (25.)**

— Song. "Pilgrims of the Night" ... Arranged as a cornet solo by Kappey. ⟨Conductor [and military band parts].⟩ 26 pt. *In:* SUPPÉ (F. von) [Isabella.] Overture, *etc.* 1899. fol. [*Boosey's military Journal. ser.* 107. *no.* 6.]   **h. 1549.**

— Pilgrims of the Night. Sacred Song. Transcribed for the Pianoforte by the Composer. *Boosey & Co.: London & New York*, 1900. fol.   **h. 3282. w. (46.)**

— A Piper. Two-part Song ... Poem by S. O'Sullivan, *etc. J. Curwen & Sons: London*, 1939. 8°. [*Choruses for Equal Voices. No.* 2016.]   **E. 861.**

— Prevent us, O Lord, in all our Doings. Introit. *Stainer & Bell: London*, (1909.) 8°. *Stainer & Bell's Church Choir Library, No.* 19.   **F. 1137. b.**

— Quelle est cette odeur agréable? (An Old French Carol.) The English version by F. Liddle. The Music arranged by S. Liddle. *Boosey & Co.: London and New York*, 1923. 4°.
     H. 3606. b. (18.)

— [Quelle est cette odeur agréable?] What Perfume this? O Shepherds say! Old French Carol for chorus, S. A. T. B., unaccompanied, English version by F. Liddle. Arranged by S. Liddle. *Boosey & Co.: London and New York*, 1923. 8°. [*Boosey's Choral Miscellany. No.* 84.]   **F. 160. e.**

— Romance for Violin with Pianoforte Accompaniment. *Boosey & Co.: London and New York*, 1900. fol.
     h. 1612. h. (5.)

LIDDLE (SAMUEL)

— The Rowan Tree. Old Scottish Melody. [Words by] Lady Nairne. Arranged as a Duet with Pianoforte accompaniment by S. Liddle. *Stainer & Bell: London*, 1934. 8°. *Part Songs, No.* 239.   **F. 1137. a.**

— Three Sacred Songs. [No. 1.] I will praise Thee, O Lord. [No. 2.] O send out Thy Light. [No. 3.] Sorrow and Sighing shall flee away, *etc. Boosey & Co.: London*, 1933. 4°.
     G. 519. p. (41.)

— Sacred Songs. Two Psalms. No. 1. I will extol Thee, O Lord. No. 2. I will sing unto the Lord. 2 no. *A. P. Schmidt: Boston, New York*, 1934. 4°.   **G. 519. q. (14.)**

— Salome. Song. The Words ... by A. O'Shaughnessy. *Boosey & Co.: London and New York*, 1900. fol.   **H. 3606. (26.)**

— The Morning, Communion and Evening Service ... in ... F. *Stainer & Bell: London*, (1913.) 8°. *Stainer & Bell's Modern Church Services, No.* 156.   **F. 1137.**

— [Service in F.] Te Deum laudamus. (Benedictus.) (Jubilate.) [Communion Service.] (Magnificat. Nunc dimittis.) (Kyrie. Credo.) 6 no. *Stainer & Bell: London*, (1913.) 8°. *Stainer & Bell's Modern Church Services, No.* 157–161.
     F. 1137.

— Two Short Songs. I. Open my Window to the Stars. II. Love, pluck your Flowers. Words by E. Clifford. 4 no. [Low, medium, high no. 1, 2.] *Chappell & Co.: London, etc.*, 1911. fol.   **H. 3606. b. (1.)**

— Since thou, O fondest. Song, the words by R. Bridges. *Boosey & Co.: London and New York*, 1901. fol.
     H. 3606. a. (9.)

— Three Sketches for Pianoforte. 1. Impromptu ... 2. Intermezzo ... 3. Capriccio, *etc. Boosey & Co.: London & New York*, 1900. fol.   **h. 3282. w. (47.)**

— A Song of Consolation. [Song.] The words by H. Simpson. *Boosey & Co.: London and New York*, 1904. fol.
     H. 3606. a. (18.)

— A Song of good Courage. [Song.] The words by G. Hadath, Organ accompaniment ad lib. *Boosey & Co.: London and New York*, 1901. fol.   **H. 3606. a. (10.)**

— Song of the River. The Words by C. Kingsley. *Boosey & Co.: London and New York*, 1897. fol.   **H. 3606. (7.)**

— Song of the Sons oversea. [Song.] The words by B. M. Ramsay. *Boosey & Co.: London and New York*, 1904. fol.
     H. 3606. a. (11.)

— Song of the Sons oversea ... New edition. *Boosey & Co.: London and New York*, 1908. fol.   **H. 3606. a. (30.)**

— A Song of Trust. [Song.] The words by I. Williams. *Boosey & Co.: London and New York*, 1924. 4°.   **H. 3606. b. (23.)**

— Song without Words, for the Violoncello with Pianoforte Accompaniment. *Augener & Co.: London*, 1901. fol.
     h. 204. g. (7.)

— Three Songs, the words by Walter de la Mare. 1. The song of shadows. 2. Melmillo. 3. The bees' song. *Boosey & Co.: London and New York*, 1923. 4°.   **H. 3606. b. (20.)**

— The Still Voices. Song, the words by G. Hadath. *Boosey & Co.: London and New York*, 1909. fol.   **H. 3606. a. (31.)**

— Sylvia May. Song, the poem by G. Massey, *etc. Boosey & Co.: London and New York*, 1899. fol.   **H. 3606. (27.)**

— Teach me to live. Sacred Song, the words by R. Harte. *Boosey & Co.: London and New York*, 1923. 4°.
     H. 3606. b. (21.)

— They that wait upon the Lord. [Sacred song.] *J. Curwen & Sons: London*, 1934. 4°.   **G. 519. q. (15.)**

LIDDLE (SAMUEL)

— This, then, is Love. Song, the words by B. M. Ramsay. *Boosey & Co.: London and New York*, 1904. fol.
H. 3606. a. (12.)

— Thou art my Life. *See* supra: [Seven Old English Lyrics. No. 4.]

— Through the Palm Trees. Song, words by G. Emanuel, *etc.* 3 no. [In D, F and G flat.] *Chappell & Co.: London, etc.*, 1909. fol.
H. 3606. a. (32.)

— Thy Faith hath saved thee. Song, *etc. Boosey & Co.: London*, 1934. 4°.
G. 519. p. (42.)

— Thy Will be done. Sacred Song, words by C. Elliott. *S. Lucas & Son: London*, 1901. fol.
G. 517. m. (30.)

— "To tell thee how I love" and "In my Garden". Two Short Love Songs, written by G. Hadath. *Boosey & Co.: London and New York*, 1904. fol.
H. 3606. a. (19.)

— The Two Princesses. Song, the words by E. Clifford. *Boosey & Co.: London and New York*, 1904. fol.
H. 3606. a. (13.)

— The Way Home. A Miniature Cycle of three short Love Songs. 1. Sing, happy Birds! 2. A Pearl for every Tear. 3. The Way Home. Words by G. Hadath, *etc.* 2 no. [Low and high.] *Chappell & Co.: London, etc.*, 1908. fol.
H. 3606. a. (33.)

— Were my Hart. Song. Ye Wordes by T. Campion, *etc. Boosey & Co.: London and New York*, 1897. fol.
H. 3606. (8.)

— What care I how fair she be? *See* supra: [Seven Old English Lyrics. No. 3.]

— What Perfume this? O Shepherds say! *See* supra: [Quelle est cette odeur agréable?]

— When first you came. Song, words by E. Lockton. *Chappell & Co.: London, etc.*, 1916. fol.
H. 3606. b. (9.)

— When Rest is mine. Song. Words by R. V. C. Myers. [2 no. In E flat and F.] *Chappell & Co.: London*, 1897. fol.
H. 3606. (9 & 30.)

— When Snowdrops ring. Song, words by E. Lockton. *Chappell & Co.: London, etc.*, 1917. fol.
H. 3606. b. (10.)

— White Bear. Two-part Song ... Words by F. C. Liddle. *J. Curwen & Sons: London*, 1940. 8°.
[*Choruses for Equal Voices. No.* 2037.]
E. 861.

— A Woodland Bouquet. Song, words by W. H. Ogilvie. *Chappell & Co.: London, etc.*, 1920. fol.
H. 3606. b. (11.)

— Ye shall be comforted. Sacred Song, *etc. Boosey & Co.: London*, 1934. 4°.
G. 519. p. (43.)

— *See* BACH (J. S.) [Geistliche Lieder aus Schemelli's Gesangbuch. No. 37. Jesu, meines Herzens Freud'.] At Thy Feet ... Anthem ... Adapted ... by S. Liddle. (1912.) 8°.
F. 1137. b. (142.)

— *See* BLOW (J.) [Amphion Anglicus.] The Self-banished ... Arranged for S.A.T.B. by S. Liddle. 1939. 8°.
F. 1137. d.

— *See* CORNER (D.) [Ein neues andächtiges Kindelwiegen.] An Old sacred Lullaby ... The Accompaniment arranged by S. Liddle. 1900. fol.
H. 1187. x. (24.)

— *See* LOVER (S.) [Il Paddy Whack in Italia.] Molly Bawn ... Pianoforte accompaniment by S. Liddle. 1934. 4°.
G. 1275. nn. (19.)

— *See* MORLEY (T.) [The First Booke of Ballets.] Now is the Month of Maying ... Arranged by S. Liddle. [1934.] 8°.
[*Boosey's modern Festival Series. no.* 138.]
F. 160. f.

— *See* NACHÈZ (T.) Concert für Violine mit Begleitung des Orchesters ... Op. 30. Clavierauszug von S. Liddle, *etc.* [1895.] fol.
h. 1729. y. (1.)

LIDDLE (SAMUEL)

— *See* TALLIS (T.) [Cantiones 1575.] In manus tuas ... Motet by T. Tallis ... Edited by S. Liddle. 1912. 8°.
F. 1137. b. (139.)

— *See* TALLIS (T.) [Cantiones 1575.] O sacrum convivium ... Motet by T. Tallis ... Edited by S. Liddle. 1912. 8°.
F. 1137. b. (140.)

LIDDLE (WILLIAM HENRY)

— Song of Queen Mary's School, Basingstoke. [Words by] Mrs. S. W. Long. *Novello and Co.: London*, [1903.] *a card.*
I. 600. b. (123.)

LIDDY (W. H.)

— *See* HARRINGTON (John P.) and LIDDY (W. H.) "Where are you going to, my pretty Maid?"⟨Song.⟩ Written by J. P. Harrington & W. H. Liddy. [1905.] *s. sh.* fol.
H. 3984. l. (32.)

— *See* HARRINGTON (John P.) and LIDDY (W. H.) "Where are you going to, my pretty Maid?" ⟨Song.⟩ Written by J. P. Harrington and W. H. Liddy, *etc.* [1905.] fol.
H. 3984. l. (33.)

LIDEL (ANDREAS)

— Ah what racking Thoughts he proves. A favorite song. The words by Prior. [Score.] pp. 4. *Printed for the Author: London*, [c. 1780.] fol.
P. 4 contains arrangements for the guitar and for the German flute.
H. 1601. x. (3.)

— Six Duettos, for the Violin and Tenor, with a separate part for the Violoncello ... Opera 3ᵈ. *Printed by the Author: London*, [1778.] fol.
g. 421. (13.)

— [Another copy.]
Hirsch M. 1470. (3.)

— [Another edition.] Six Duettos ... Opera 3ᵈ. [Parts.] *W. Forster: London*, [1780?] fol.
h. 219. (5.)

— A Second Sett of Six Duettos, three for Violin and Tenor, and three for Violin and Violoncello ... Op. VI. [Parts.] *Printed by the Author: London*, [1785?] fol.
g. 421. (12.)

— A Third Sett of Six Duettos for Two Violins or Violin and Violoncello ... Opera VIII. [Parts.] *Printed by the Author: London*, [1781.] fol.
g. 426. b.

— In vain you tell your parting Lover. A Favorite Song. The Words by Prior. *Printed for the Author: London*, [1780.] fol.
G. 309. (101.)

— Six Quartettos, Three for two Violins, Tenor & Violoncello, and three for Flute, Violin, Tenor & Violoncello Obligato ... Opera 2ᵈ. [Parts.] *Printed for the Author: London*, [1777.] fol.
g. 426.

— [Another copy.] (Violino Primo.) **L. P.**
Wanting the other parts.
R. M. 26. a. 13. (1.)

— A Second Sett of Six Quartetto's, five for two Violins, Tenor and Violoncello, and one for a Flute or Oboe, Violin, Tenor and Violoncello ... Op. VII. [Parts.] 4 pt. *William Forster: London*, [1785?] fol.
Hirsch III. 364.

— [Another copy.]
R. M. 17. f. 8. (4.)

— Three Quintettos for a Flute, Violin, two Tenors and Violoncello obligato ... Opera V. [Parts.] 5 pt. *The Author: London*, [c. 1780.] fol.
g. 398. k. (2.)

— Three Quintettos for a Flute, Violin, two Tenors and Violoncello Obligato ... Opera V. [Parts.] *W. Forster: London*, [1784?] fol.
g. 426. a.

— Six Solos for a Violin and Bass ... Op: 9. [Score.] pp. 37. *Printed for W. Forster: London*, [c. 1780.] fol.
g. 1780. aa. (1.)

LIDEL (ANDREAS)

— Six Sonatas for Violin, Tenor & Violoncello ... Opera 4to. [Parts.] *Printed by the Author: London,* [1778.] fol.
g. 416. (1.)

— [Another edition.] Six Sonatas for Violin, Tenor & Violoncello ... Opera 4to. [Parts.] *Printed for W. Forster: London,* [1780?] fol.
g. 420. c. (7.)

— Six Trios for a Violin or Flauto, Violino Secondo, and Violoncello Obligato ... Opera 1mo. [Parts.] *Longman, Lukey and Broderip: London,* [1776.] fol.
g. 409. (8.)

— [Another copy.]
Wanting the violoncello part.
R. M. 26. c. 1. (6.)

LIDEL (BLANCHE)

— Eveline waltz ... for the Pianoforte. *London,* [1865.] fol.
h. 1460. w. (4.)

— Nocturne pour Violoncelle ou Violon avec accompagnement de Piano. *London,* [1866.] fol.
h. 1849. (21.)

— Podoliana mazurka ... for the Pianoforte. *London,* [1864.] fol.
h. 1460. w. (3.)

— Valse de Salon, for the Pianoforte. *London,* [1860.] fol.
h. 1460. w. (1.)

— Waltz, Mayblümchen. (Lilly [*sic*] of the Valley.) [P.F.] *London,* [1862.] fol.
h. 1460. w. (2.)

LIDEL (FRANCIS)

— Music the fiercest Grief can charm. *A favorite Glee, etc.,* I[ohn] F[entu]m: [London, 1784?] fol.
G. 310. (109.)

LIDEL (JOSEPH)

— À Leonora, nocturne de J. Ascher arrangé pour Violoncelle avec acc. de Piano par J. Lidel. *London,* [1870.] fol.
h. 1851. b.

— À Léonora. Nocturne de J. Ascher. Arrangé par J. Lidel. [Violin and P. F.] *See* RITTER (E. W.) Les Succés du Salon, *etc.* No. 37. [1891, *etc.*] fol.
h. 3665. a.

— Air d'Église de Stradella transcrit pour Violoncelle avec accomp. de Piano. *Londres,* [1873.] fol.
h. 1849. c. (5.)

— Chant du Berger. Idylle de J. Schulhoff arrangée par J. Lidel. [Violin and P. F.] *See* RITTER (E. W.) Les Succès du Salon, *etc.* No. 38. [1891, *etc.*] fol.
h. 3665. a.

— La Charité, chœur de G. Rossini, transcription pour Violoncello, ou Violon, ou Concertina, avec accompagnement de Piano. *Londres,* [1867.] fol.
h. 1849. (22.)

— Major and minor scales for the Violoncello. *London,* [1860.] fol.
h. 1851. b. (6.)

— 9 Mélodies favorites arrangées pour Violoncelle avec accomp. de Piano. No. 4 – 9. *Londres,* [1860.] fol.
Imperfect; wanting all the other no.
h. 3213. d. (1.)

— Two melodies of Henselt, transcribed for Violin with Pianoforte accompaniment ... by J. Lidel. 2 no. *London,* [1861.] fol.
h. 1608. a. (16.)

— Two melodies of Henselt, transcribed for Violoncello with Pianoforte accompaniment ... by J. Lidel. *London,* [1861.] fol.
h. 1851. b. (7.)

— Six sacred pieces for violoncello & piano ... transcribed by J. Lidel. 6 no. *London,* [1858.] fol.
h. 1855. (3.)

— Santa Lucia ... Neapolitan air [by T. Cottrau] ... arranged for Violin and Piano by J. Lidel. *London,* [1861.] fol.
h. 1608. a. (17.)

LIDEL (JOSEPH)

— Santa Lucia ... Neapolitan air ... arranged for Violoncello & Piano by J. Lidel. *London,* [1861.] fol.
h. 1851. b. (8.)

— *See* DONIZETTI (D. G. M.) [Parisina.] Les Bluettes de Parisina ... Melodies ... pour Violoncello & Piano ... par J. Lidel. [1850.] fol.
h. 667. (5.)

— *See* FRANCHOMME (A.) A. Franchomme's works, edited by J. Lidel, *etc.* [1845, *etc.*] fol.
h. 1895.

— *See* LEE (S.) Méthode pour le Violoncelle ... revised and translated ... by J. Lidel. [1882.] fol.
h. 1875. a.

— *See* REGONDI (G.) and LIDEL (J.) Santa Lucia, *etc.* [1861.] fol.
h. 2455. a. (4.)

— *See* VERDI (F. G. F.) "La Traviata," six favorite pieces from Verdi's opera ... transcribed for violin & piano ... by J. Lidel. [1857.] fol.
h. 1627. (1.)

— *See* VERDI (F. G. F.) "La Traviata," six favorite pieces from Verdi's opera ... transcribed for Violoncello & piano ... by J. Lidel. [1857.] fol.
h. 1855. (1.)

— *See* VERDI (F. G. F.) Il Trovatore, eight favorite pieces from Verdi's opera ... transcribed for violin and piano ... by J. Lidel. [1858.] fol.
h. 1627. (2.)

— *See* VERDI (F. G. F.) Il Trovatore, eight favorite pieces from Verdi's opera ... transcribed for Violoncello and piano ... by J. Lidel. [1858.] fol.
h. 1855. (2.)

— *See* WALLACE (W. V.) Premier nocturne, pour violoncelle & piano, arrangé par J. Lidel. [1857.] fol.
h. 1850. a. (9.)

LIDELLE (CH.)

— Couronne de Bluets. Valse pour piano. *R. Bertam: Bruxelles,* 1886. fol.
h. 3281. l. (26.)

LIDEN

— Liden Kirsten. Opera. *See* HARTMANN (J. P. E.)

LIDGEY (C. A.)

— Two German Folk Songs, with the original German words, and English translations by P. England. The music arranged for four voices—S. A. T. B.—by C. A. Lidgey. ([No. 1.] An Old Sacred Cradle Song. Ein neues andächtiges Kindelwiegen. [No. 2.] Swedish Cradle Song. Wiegenlied.) *Boosey & Co.: London and New York,* 1910. 8°.
F. 321. w. (15.)

— "Earl Bristol's Farewell." 〈Song.〉 (Cornet solo) ... "A Roundelay". 〈Song.〉 ... Arranged for military band by A. H. Behrend. 〈Conductor [and parts].〉 32 pt. *In:* MACKENZIE (Gordon) "The Kiltie's Kourtship," *etc.* [1914.] fol. [*Boosey & Co.'s supplemental Journal for military Bands. no.* 127.]
h. 1544. a.

— All in a Garden green. *See infra:* [A Song of Life.]

— Archy's Song, from King Charles I ... Song, words by Shelley. *Pitt & Hatzfeld: London,* [1888.] fol.
H. 1788. w. (2.)

— As I love thee. Song, the words by A. C. Swinburne. *Boosey & Co.: London and New York,* 1903. fol.
H. 1799. vv. (49.)

— Birdlip. Song, the words by N. Gale. *Boosey & Co.: London and New York,* 1902. fol.
H. 1799. vv. (50.)

— The Call! March ... arranged for the pianoforte by the composer. *Boosey & Co.: London, etc.,* 1915. fol.
h. 3284. oo. (8.)

— The Cheery Philosopher. Song, the words by A. P. Herbert. *Boosey & Co.: London, etc.,* 1921. 4°.
G. 426. u. (22.)

LIDGEY (C. A.)

— Dream Fancies. Song, words by D. Beck. *Pitt & Hatzfeld: London*, [1888.] fol. **H. 1788. w. (3.)**

— A Health to the nut-brown Lass. Song. Words by Sir John Suckling. *Pitt & Hatzfeld: London*, [1888.] fol. **H. 1788. w. (4.)**

— In Absence. Song, words from the German of Goethe, by R. Garnett. *Pitt & Hatzfeld: London*, [1888.] fol. **H. 1788. w. (5.)**

— 4 Lieder by Heine for voice with pianoforte accompaniment. Op. 6. *Augener & Co.: London*, [1892.] 4°. **G. 385. i. (9.)**

— The Likes of they. Song, words by A. P. Herbert. *Chappell & Co.: London, etc.*, 1918. fol. **H. 1846. y. (25.)**

— Two little Songs. [No. 1.] Earl Bristol's Farewell. . . . [No. 2.] See where my Love a-maying goes. *Boosey & Co.: London and New York*, 1902. fol. **H. 1799. vv. (51.)**

— A Lover's Moods. A Song Cycle, the words by Herrick, Sir T. Wyatt, F. Davison and others. *Boosey & Co.: London*, 1903. 4°. **G. 424. n. (3.)**

— The Mummers' Carol. Old Sussex Folk-Song with a Pianoforte accompaniment by C. A. Lidgey. *Boosey & Co.: London and New York*, 1906. fol. **H. 1187. ff. (54.)**

— My only Jo and dearie O! Song, words by R. Gall. *Pitt & Hatzfeld: London*, [1888.] fol. **H. 1788. w. (6.)**

— Three Norwegian Folk-Songs. The English words adapted from the Norwegian by V. MacClure. Arranged as duets for soprano, or mezzo-soprano, & baritone by C. A. Lidgey. *Boosey & Co.: London, etc.*, 1921. 4°. **G. 426. u. (23.)**

— An Old Sacred Cradle Song . . . A Babe lies in the Cradle. English words by P. England. Arranged as a Four-part Song by C. A. Lidgey. *Boosey & Co.: London & New York*, (1910.) 8°.
[*Boosey's Choral Miscellany.* no. 34.] **F. 160. e.**

— An Old sacred Cradle Song. Christmas Carol . . . Arranged by C. A. Lidgey. (Tonic Sol-fa edition.) *Boosey & Co.: London and New York*, [1914.] 4°.
No. 34 of "Boosey's Choral Miscellany". **C. 745. f. (18.)**

— One Word is too often profaned. Song, words by Shelley. *Pitt & Hatfeld: London*, [1888.] fol. **H. 1788. w. (7.)**

— Out of the Night. *See* infra: [A Song of Life.]

— A Roundelay—Now is the Month of Maying, *etc. Boosey & Co.: London and New York*, 1901. fol. **H. 1799. cc. (62.)**

— The Sea-Dogs of England. Song. *Chappell & Co.: London, etc.*, 1919. fol. **H. 1846. y. (26.)**

— Since all my Hopes, dear Maid. Song, *etc. Boosey & Co.: London and New York*, 1901. fol. **H. 1799. cc. (63.)**

— A Song of Life. Cycle of seven Songs, the words by W. E. Henley, *etc.* ([No. 1.] A Sigh sent wrong. [No. 2.] The Wind on the Wold. [No. 3.] All in a Garden green. [No. 4.] Sing to me. [No. 5.] Gray Hills. [No. 6.] Out of the Night. [No. 7.] Dearest, when I am dead.) *Boosey & Co.: London and New York*, 1909. 4°. **G. 385. jj. (6.)**

— [A Song of Life.] All in a Garden green. Song, *etc. Boosey & Co.: London and New York*, [1911.] fol. **H. 1792. s. (31.)**

— [A Song of Life.] Out of the Night. Song, *etc. Boosey & Co.: London & New York*, [1912.] fol. **H. 1793. t. (52.)**

— Two Songs. No. 1. Lullaby. No. 2. The Starlings. Words by C. Kingsley, *etc. Pitt & Hatzfeld: London*, [1888.] fol. **H. 1788. w. (9.)**

— Sunny March. Song, the words by N. Gale. *Boosey & Co.: London and New York*, 1903. fol. **H. 1799. vv. (52.)**

LIDGEY (C. A.)

— To Constance. Song, words by R. Garnett. *Pitt & Hatzfeld: London*, [1888.] fol. **H. 1788. w. (8.)**

— When all the World is young, Lad. Song, words by C. Kingsley. *Chappell & Co.: London*, [1902.] fol. **H. 1799. cc. (64.)**

— A Widow Bird sate mourning.—Archy's Song.— [Song.] Words by Shelley, *etc.* 2 no. [In E minor and F minor.] *Chappell & Co.: London, etc.*, 1908. fol. **H. 1794. vv. (53.)**

— The Wounded Robin. Song, the words by N. Gale. *Boosey & Co.: London and New York*, 1903. fol. **H. 1799. vv. (53.)**

LIDGLEY (WILLIAM)

— The Viennese College of Music for the Mandoline. Mandoline Tutor . . . Arranged and composed by W. Lidgley. *E. Donajowski: London*, [1905.] 4°. **f. 759. a. (3.)**

LIDHOLM (INGVAR)

— Mutanza per orchestra. Partitura. (Riproduzione fotografica del manoscritto originale.) pp. 45. *Universal Edition: London; printed in Austria*, [1961.] 8°. **e. 669. b. (2.)**

— Quattro pezzi per violoncello e pianoforte. [Score and part.] 2 pt. *Universal Edition: London; printed in Austria*, [1972.] 4°. **g. 511. p. (10.)**

— Poesies per orchestra. 1963. Partitur. ⟨Reproduktion nach der Handschrift des Autors.⟩ pp. 31. *Universal Edition: London; printed in Austria*, [1966.] 8°.
The leaf bearing pp. 19–20 is a cancel. **e. 669. jj. (2.)**

— Riter. Ballett und Konzertsuite. Partitur. pp. 108. *Universal Edition: London; printed in Austria*, [1970.] fol. **h. 1564. i. (1.)**

— Riter. Ein Ballett. Klavierauszug. pp. 34. *Universal Edition: London; printed in Austria*, [1970.] 4°. **g. 1129. xx. (9.)**

— Ritornello per orchestra. Partitura. (Riproduzione fotografica del manuscritto originale.) pp. 87. *Universal Edition: Wien, etc.*, [1958.] 8°. **e. 666. bb. (5.)**

— Sonatin (1950). [With a portrait and facsimile.] *In*: NY. Ny Nordisk klavermusik, *etc.* pp. 131–137. [1951.] 4°. **g. 606. mm. (3.)**

LIDI

— Lidi amati. Romanza. *See* SCHIMON (A.)

LIDIA

— Lidia. Ballata. *See* GORDIGIANI (L.)

LIDIČE

— Lidiče. [Part-song.] *See* BUSH (Alan D.)

LIDL (ANDREAS)

— *See* LIDEL.

LIDON (JOSÉ)

— Ave maris stella, à 4 y 8 voces, con accompañamiento de cuarteto de cuerda. *See* ESLAVA (M. H.) Lira Sacro-Hispana, *etc.* Sigl. XVIII. Ser. 2ª. Tom. 1°. [1869.] fol. **H. 4.**

LIDZKI-ŚLEDZIŃSKI (Stefan)

— See Moniuszko (S.) Muzyka baletowa to opery "Kumoszki windsorskie" ... Na wielką koncertową orkiestrę dętą zinstrumentował S. Lidzki-Śledziński, etc. [1952.] fol.
h. 1508. rr. (5.)

LIE

— The Lie. Part-Song. See Edmonds (P. N.)

— A Lie-awake Song. [Song.] See Whitfield (K. T.)

— Lie, Britannia! See When. When Britain first at Hell's Command ... Rule Britannia, etc. [With the melody by T. A. Arne.] [1915?] fol.
I. 600. e. (159.)

— Lie down, poor Heart. Madrigal. See Woods (F. C.)

— Lie down, sad soul. Song. See Horsley (C.E.) Three Songs. No. 2.

— Lie low. Unison Song. See Sumsion (C.C.)

— Lye on, while my revenge shall be. Glee. See Bates (W.)

— Lie quiet, Soul. [Part-song.] See Hastings (Ross)

— Lie still, beloved, lie still. Hymn. See Lloyd (C. H.)

— Lie still, little Robin. Song. See Johnson (W. N.)

— Lie still, my heart. [Song.] See Panormo (F.)

— Lie still my little Heart. Song. See Willson (J.)

— Lie still, my little one. Part-Song. See Harris (C. A. E.)

— Lie still my trembling Heart. Duetto. See Reeve (W.) [Joan of Arc.]

— Lie still, sleep becalmed. [Part-song.] See Roy (Klaus G.)

— Lie strewn the white Flocks. Pastoral for Chorus, etc. See Bliss (Sir A. E. D.)

— Lie there, my Lute. Song. See MacCunn (H.)

LIE (Sigurd)

— Aarstidsbilleder. (Jahrzeitsbilder.) Klaverstykker. I. Sommerminder ... II. Høststemning ... III. Julemorgen. IV. Vaarjubel, etc. pp. 23. Wilhelm Hansen: Kjøbenhavn, Leipzig, [1905.] fol.
h. 722. cc. (11.)

— The Call of the Sun. Song ... (English) words by E. M. Lockwood. J. & W. Chester: London, Brighton, [1917?] fol.
G. 806. ww. (16.)

— No Day was e'er so bright. Song ... (English) words by E. M. Lockwood. J. & W. Chester: London, [1917?] fol.
G. 806. ww. (17.)

— Shut your little drowsy Eye. Song ... (English) words by E. M. Lockwood. J. & W. Chester: London, Brighton, [1917?] fol.
G. 806. ww. (19.)

— A Song of Midsummer. Song ... (English) words by E. M. Lockwood. J. & W. Chester: London, Brighton, [1917?] fol.
G. 806. ww. (18.)

LIEB (F.X.)

— 3 zweistimmige Lieder mit Begleitung des Pianoforte. Op. 5. Offenbach a. M., [1862.] fol.
H. 2139. b. (26.)

LIEB (Richard)

— See Henderson (Skitch) Curacao ... For concert band. Arranged by R. Lieb, etc. [1966.] 4°.
g. 1072. c. (6.)

— See Henderson (Skitch) Curacao ... Arranged by R. Lieb, etc. [Military band.] [1966.] 8°.
h. 3210. j. (50.)

LIEB (Richard)

— See Hunter (Ralph) Ein' feste Burg. Antiphonal setting for band, orchestra and chorus ... Orchestration by R. Lieb. [1966.] 8°.
E. 902. b. (10.)

LIEBAU (Friedrich Wilhelm)

— Die Reue des Petrus. Oratorium in zwei Abtheilungen (von H. Bode). [Score.] Quedlinburg & Leipzig, [1837.] fol.
H. 1840.

LIEBCHEN

— Liebchen. [Song.] See Kummer (Clare)

— Liebchen ade! [Chorus.] See Hess (L.)

— Liebchen am Rhein. [Song.] See Weiprecht (W.)

— Liebchen heut' in Gesellschaft geht. [Song.] See Goldschmidt (A. von)

— Liebchen ist da. [Song.] See Franz (R.) Zwölf Gesänge. Op. 5. No. 2.

— Das Liebchen von der Ruhe. [Song.] See Beethoven (L. van) VIII. Lieder. Op. 52. No. 3.

— Liebchen, wo bist du? [Song.] See Marschner (H. A.) Fünf Lieder ... 101tes Werk. No. 2.

LIEBCHENS

— Liebchens Äugelein. [Song.] See Sieber (F.) Fünf heitere Lieder. Op. 124. No. 2.

— Liebchens Bote. [Part-song.] See Reger (M.) Fünf ausgewählte Volkslieder für Männerchor ... No. 2.

— Liebchen's Erinnerung. [Song.] See Reissiger (C.G.) Deutsche Lieder. Op. 23. No. 3.

— Liebchen's Kuss. [Song.] See Reissiger (C.G.) Sechs Gesaenge, etc. 3te. Samml. No. 6.

— Liebchen's Schätze. [Song.] See Winkelmann (C.) Drei Lieder. No. 3.

— Liebchen's Ungewissheit. [Song.] See Reissiger (C. G.) Deutsche Lieder. No. 7.

LIEBE

— Liebe. [Song.] See Bleikhman (Yu. I.) 11 Lieder ... Op. 35. No. 8.

— Liebe. Ein Cyklus von drei Chorliedern. See Cornelius (C.A.P.)

— Liebe. [Song.] See Déprosse (A.) Vier Lieder. Op. 37. No. 3.

— Liebe. [Song.] See Duerrner (J.) Six Songs. Op. 18. No. 1.

— Liebe. Für gemischten Chor. See Glazunov (A. K.)

— Liebe. [Song.] See Graener (P.) Lieder ... Op. 21. No. 1.

— Die Liebe. [Part-song.] See Meyer-Helmund (E.)

— Die Liebe. [Song.] See Meyer-Helmund (E.) Drei Lieder ... Op. 22. No. 3.

— Liebe. [Part-song.] See Strauss (R. G.)

— Liebe. [Song.] See Voříšek (J. H.)

— Liebe. [Song.] See White (M. V.) Sixteen German Songs. No. 1.

— Die Liebe. [Duet.] See Winterberger (A.) Fünf Slavische Volks-Poesien. No. 4.

LIEBE

— Die Liebe als Nachtigall. [Song.] *See* MUELLER (M.)

— Die Liebe als Staatsverbrecherin. Solo-Scene. *See* KIPPER (H.)

— Lieb am Rhein. [Part-song.] *See* DRUMM (R.) Drei Lieder, *etc.* No. 1.

— Liebe auch du! [Song.] *See* CHOPIN (F. F.) [Nocturne. Op. 9. No. 2.]

— Die Liebe auf dem Lande. Comische Oper. *See* HILLER (J. A.)

— Der liebe Augustin. [Musical play.] *See* BITTNER (J.)

— Der Liebe Augustin. Operette. *See* FALL (L.)

— Liebe bis in den Tod. [Duet.] *See* WINTERBERGER (A.) Sechs slavische volkspoesien. No. 6.

— Der liebe Dauer. Volkslied. *See* MOHR (H.)

— Die Liebe der Danae. [Opera.] *See* STRAUSS (R. G.)

— Die Liebe der Zigeunerin. [Song.] *See* DUBUC (A. I.)

— Die Liebe des Nächsten. [Song.] *See* BEETHOVEN (L. van) VI Lieder. Op. 48. No. 3.

— Liebe dir ergeb' ich mich. [Chorus.] *See* CORNELIUS (C. A. P.) Liebe ... Op. 18. Heft I.

— Der Liebe Erwachen. Lied. *See* GURILEV (A.)

— Liebe Glühen. [Song.] *See* WEBER (C. M. F. E. von) [5 deutsche Lieder. Op. 25. No. 1.]

— Der Liebe Gott hat's treu gemeint. [Four-part song.] *See* ABT (F. W.) Fünf Lieder, *etc.* Op. 389. No. 1.

— Die Liebe Gottes ist ausgegossen. Kantate. *See* BACH (Johann E.)

— Die Liebe hat gelogen. [Song.] *See* FRANZ (R.) Sechs Gesänge ... Op. 6. No. 4.

— Die Liebe hat gelogen. [Song.] *See* MACLEANE (C.) Three Songs. No. 2.

— Die Liebe hat gelogen. [Song.] *See* NAUBERT (A.) Sechs Lieder, *etc.* No. 5.

— Die Liebe hat gelogen. [Song.] *See* SCHUBERT (F. P.)

— Liebe hat uns nun vereint. Duet. *See* ALBERT, *Prince Consort of Victoria, Queen of Great Britain and Ireland.*

— Der liebe Hergott hält die Wacht. [Part-song.] *See* ABT (F. W.)

— Der Liebe himmlisches Gefühl. Arie. *See* MOZART (W. A.)

— Die Liebe im Narrenhaus, eine comische Oper. *See* WALTER (I.)

— Liebe im Schnee. [Song.] *See* JENSEN (A.)

— Liebe in der Fremde. [Song.] *See* SAHR (H. von) Sechs Lieder, Op. 14. No. 6.

— Liebe ist die zarte Blume. [Song.] *See* SPOHR (L.) [Faust.]

— Die Liebe ist ein Rosenstrauch. [Part-song.] *See* RHEINBERGER (J. G.) Liebesgarten. Op. 80. No. 3.

— Die Lieb' ist erwacht. [Song.] *See* ABT (F. W.) Drei Lieder, *etc.* Op. 388. No. 3.

— Die Liebe ist's. Lied. *See* ABT (F. W.) Drei Lieder ... Op. 311. No. 2.

LIEBE

— Die Lieb' ist über mich gekommen. [Song.] *See* RAIDA (C. A.) Repertoir Lieder. Op. 109. No. 1.

— Die Lieb ist wie ein Vögelein. [Duet.] *See* REICHEL (A.) Drei Duette ... Op. 73. No. 2.

— Die Liebe kann nicht enden. [Song.] *See* BEHR (F.)

— Der Liebe Kommen. [Song.] *See* HOPFFER (B.) Zwölf Lieder, *etc.* Op. 6. No. 4.

— Der Liebe Leichenbegängniss. [Song.] *See* HORN (A.)

— Liebe, Liebe, ach die Liebe. [Song.] *See* WHITE (M. V.)

— Liebe macht Diebe. [Song.] *See* REINICK (R.) Vier Lieder, *etc.* Op. 52. No. 1.

— Liebe macht kurzen process, oder die Heyrath auf gewisse Art. Komische Oper. *See* HOFFMEISTER (F. A.)

— Liebe mich. Zigeunerlied. *See* STUTZMAN (S. J. von)

— Die Liebe nur. [Song.] *See* WALLNOEFER (A.) Drei Lieder. Op. 14. No. 2.

— Liebe ohne Ende. [Song.] *See* WALLNOEFER (A.) 4 Gesänge. Op. 4. No. 1.

— Die Liebe sass als Nachtigall. [Four-part song.] *See* BLUMMER (N.) Sechs Lieder. Op. 10. No. 2.

— Die Liebe sass als Nachtigall. [Song.] *See* HARTOG (E. de) Zwei Lieder ... No. 2.

— Die Liebe sass als Nachtigall. [Chorus.] *See* RUDORFF (E.) Zwei Gesänge ... Op. 19. No. 1.

— Das liebe Schmeichelkätzchen ... Polka für 4 Männerstimmen, *etc. See* VOIGT (H.)

— Liebe und Freundschaft. Duetto. *See* LIEBE (L.)

— Liebe und Frühling. [Song.] *See* BRAHMS (J.) [Sechs Gesänge. Op. 3. No. 2, 3.]

— Liebe und Frühling. 4 Lieder. *See* SCHWALM (R.)

— Lieb und stirb. Männerchor. *See* BAUER (H.)

— Lieb' und stirb. [Song.] *See* BOLCK (O.) Vier Lieder. Op. 52. No. 2.

— [Lieb' und Versöhnen.] Compositionen ... zu dem Festspiel: "Lieb' und Versöhnen". *See* WEBER (C. M. F. E. von)

— Lieb' und Wein. [Part-song.] *See* HAESER (C.)

— Liebe, Unschuld, Hoffnung. [Song.] *See* REISSIGER (C.G.) Gesänge, *etc.* 42s. Werk. No. 4.

— Der Liebe Weh und Lust. [Song.] *See* REISSIGER (C.G.) Deutsche Lieder. No. 6.

— Der Liebe will ich singen. Minnelieder. *See* REUTTER (Hermann)

— Liebe wohl ist ein besondrer Saft. [Song.] *See* BARTH (R.) Lieder, *etc.* Op. 5. No. 5.

— The Battle of Waterloo, or La Belle Alliance, a grand descriptive musical piece ... for the Pianoforte. *London,* [1820.] fol.   **g. 271. a. (49.)**

— "Madame Taillien;" a French air, with six variations for the Piano Forte by H. Liebe. *London,* [1815?] fol.   **h. 117. (24.)**

LIEBE (H.)

— Liebe's [MS Second] Collection of Quadrilles ... Arranged for the piano forte. pp. 7. *Preston: London*, [WM 1815.] fol.
g. 1529. g. (18.)

— Russian Marches ... arranged for the Piano Forte. *London*, [1815?] fol.
h. 1458. j. (10.)

LIEBE (LOUIS)

— *See* LIEBE (Ludwig)

LIEBE (LUDWIG)

— Agnes of the Sea. Cantata ... The poetry by G. E. Johnstone. *London*, [1883.] 4°.
F. 607. q. (5.)

— [Agnes of the Sea.] Farewell. Duet, *etc.* *S. Lucas, Weber & Co.: London*, [1883.] fol.
H. 2620. (17.)

— The Angels descended. A Christmas two-part song for female voices. German words by A. von Einsiedel, English version by L. N. Parker. *London*, [1874.] fol.
H. 2620. (10.)

— Arène des organistes, No. 10. 25 morceaux faciles pour orgue ou harmonium ... propres au service divin. Op. 27. *Paris*, [1855.] fol.
f. 78. c. (6.)

— [Auf Wiedersehn.] Hope in Parting ... [Song, begins: "Sunny light, sunny showers".—"Sonnenlicht, Sonnenschein".] German words by A. Becker, English version by G. E. Johnstone. ⟨In C.⟩ *London*, [1873.] fol.
H. 2620. (2.)

— [Auf Wiedersehn.] We'll meet above, *etc.* [Song.] *London*, [1874.] fol.
H. 2620. (5.)

— [Auf Wiedersehn.] Hope in Parting. ⟨In A.⟩ *London*, [1876.] fol.
H. 2620. (13.)

— Auf wiedersehn! *See* LANGE (G.) Lieder-Blüthen. Fantasien ... für das Pianoforte. Op. 171. No. 12. [1873, *etc.*] fol.
h. 3101. f.

— Christmas Roses. [Part-song.] *See* infra: [Die weisse Weihnachtsrose.]

— Come, charm of night. [Part-song.] *See* infra: [Die Nachtigall.]

— Day dreams. Six melodies for the pianoforte. Op. 38. 2 bk. *London*, [1857.] fol.
h. 1489. t. (3.)

— [Es muss das Herz an Etwas hangen.] The Heart's Rest. Es muss das Herz an Etwas hangen. Part song [begins: "Each heart must clasp".—"Wohl muss das Herz"] ... German words by A. Grün. English version by G. E. Johnstone. *London*, [1883.] 4°.
F. 585. g. (30.)

— Zwei Fantasiestücke für Pianoforte. 2 no. *Leipzig*, [1873.] fol.
h. 1487. q. (14.)

— Farewell. *See* supra: [Agnes of the Sea.]

— La gaité, rondo-polka, étude de salon pour piano. Op. 26. *Paris*, [1855.] fol.
g. 543. f. (5.)

— Glory to God in the highest. A Christmas three-part song for female voices. German words by A. H. Niemeyer. English version by L. N. Parker. *London*, [1874.] fol.
H. 2620. (12.)

— [Gottvertrauen.] The Soul's Repose. Gottvertrauen. Part song [begins: "In God's decrees repose thy trust."—"Vertrau' auf Gottes weisen Plan"] ... German words by F. Weber. English version by G. E. Johnstone. *London*, [1883.] 4°.
F. 585. g. (31.)

— The Heart's Rest. [Part-song.] *See* supra: [Es muss das Herz an Etwas hangen.]

LIEBE (LUDWIG)

— Hope in Parting. [Song.] *See* supra: [Auf Wiedersehn.]

— Hymn of Consolation. Duetto. *See* infra: [Trostlied.]

— Hymn of the Goths ... for four male voices ... Translated from the German (E. Ziehen) by G. E. Johnstone. *London*, [1884.] 4°.
F. 585. g. (32.)

— [Im Frühling.] Spring-Tide ... Duetto [begins: "The sun his cloudy tent".—"Die Sonn' hebt an"]. German words by E. Geibel. English version by G.E. Johnstone. *London*, [1876.] fol.
H. 1777. h. (51.)

— [Im Maien.] In May Time ... Duetto [begins: "Nun bricht aus".—"From every branch"]. German words by J. Rodenberg. English version by G. E. Johnstone. *London*, [1876.] fol.
H. 1777. h. (53.)

— In May Time. Duetto. *See* supra: [Im Maien.]

— [In milder Lenznacht.] The Soft Spring Night ... Part song for three female voices [begins: "Sweet lilies white". "Die Lilien glühn"]. German words by E. Geibel, English version by G. E. Johnstone. *London*, [1874.] fol.
H. 2620. (7.)

— Komm, Trost der Nacht. *See* infra: [Die Nachtigall.]

— [Liebe und Freundschaft.] Love and Friendship ... Duetto [begins: "O kennst du Herz".—"Dost know, my heart"]. German words by E. Geibel. English version by G. E. Johnstone. *London*, [1876.] fol.
H. 1777. h. (54.)

— [Lobgesang.] Song of Praise. Lobgesang. Part song [begins: "Who bears the world."—"Wer trägt die Welt"] ... German words by J. Altmann. English version by G. E. Johnstone. *London*, [1883.] 4°.
F. 585. g. (26.)

— Love and Friendship. Duetto. *See* supra: [Liebe und Freundschaft.]

— [Mein Heimathsthal.] My Home of yore. Mein Heimathsthal. [Song, begins: "Gently falls from heaven's arch".—"Hoch vom Himmel droben fällt".] German words by A. Becker, English version by G. E. Johnstone. *London*, [1874.] fol.
H. 2620. (9.)

— [Mein Heimathsthal.] My Home of Yore ... Op. 34. No. 3. *S. Lucas, Weber & Co.: London*, [1883.] 8°.
No. 92 of a Collection of Part-Songs for Female Voices.
F. 1623. a. (5.)

— [Mein Heimathsthal. Op. 34. No. 3.] My Home of Yore. [Three-part song.] Words translated from the German by G. E. Johnstone. *S. Lucas, Weber & Co.: London*, [1903.] 8°.
Leonard & Co.'s Part-Songs. No. 38.
F. 1658.

— Mein Heimathsthal. Lied. *See* LANGE (G.) Lieder-Blüthen. Fantasien ... für das Pianoforte. Op. 171. No. 36. [1873, *etc.*] fol.
h. 3101. f.

— [Muss Einer von dem Andern.] We Two. Muss Einer von dem Andern. Part song ... German words by F. Oser. English version by G. E. Johnstone. *London*, [1883.] 4°.
F. 585. g. (28.)

— My Home of Yore. *See* supra: [Mein Heimathsthal. Op. 34. No. 3.]

— My native Vale. *See* QUARTETS. Strollers' Society ... Quartets, *etc.* No. 6. [1886, *etc.*] 8°.
F. 298.

— My Woodland Home. Song [begins: "How blest was I"]. Words by M. X. Hayes. *London*, [1880.] fol.   **H. 2620. (14.)**

— [Die Nachtigall.] The Nightingale ... Part song for three, female voices [begins: "Come charm of night". "Komm' Trost der Nacht"]. German words from the Simplicissimus (1713), English version by G. E. Johnstone. *London*, [1874.] fol.
H. 2620. (8.)

LIEBE (Ludwig)

— [Die Nachtigall.] Come, charm of night. Komm, Trost der Nacht. Part song ... Aus dem "Simplicissimus" von Grimmelshausen ... The English version by G. E. Johnstone. *London*, [1882.] 4°. **F. 585. g. (25.)**

— The Nightingale. [Part-song.] *See supra:* [Die Nachtigall.]

— One only prayer—Forget-me-not. Song, poetry by G. E. Johnstone. Op. 92. No. 1. *S. Lucas, Weber & Co.: London*, [1882.] fol. **H. 2620. (18.)**

— [Five part-songs, by] C. Isenmann ... Für Männerchor arr. von L. Liebe. 5 no. 1889. *See* Neue. Neue ausgewählte Chöre für Männerstimmen. No. 82–86. 1886, *etc.* 8°. **E. 866.**

— Pearl of the Seasons. Perle des Jahres. Part song [begins: "Blue is the heaven".—"Blau ist der Himmel"] ... German words by J. Altmann. English version by G. E. Johnstone. *London*, [1883.] 4°. **F. 585. g. (27.)**

— Regensburger Liederkranz. Sammlung ausgewählte vierstimmiger Lieder. Partitur. Zwölfte Auflage. Auf's neue sorgfältig durchgesehen. pp. 6. 241. *Alfred Coppenrath: Regensburg*, 1887. *obl.* 4°.

   — [Parts. T.T.B.B.] 4 pt. *Alfred Coppenrath: Regensburg*, 1886. *obl.* 8°.
   The tenor parts are of the 29th edition, the first and second bass are of the 31st and 30th edition respectively. **D. 367.**

— Romanze für die Violine mit Begleitung des Pianoforte. Op. 103. *F. Luckhardt: Berlin*, 1886. fol. **h. 1608. q. (43.)**

— Scherzo pour piano. Op. 39. *London*, [1857.] fol. **h. 1489. t. (4.)**

— [Schlaflied.] Slumber Song ... Part song for three female voices [begins: "The darkened heaven". "Am dunkeln Himmel"]. German words by V. F. Strauss, English version by G. F. Johnstone. *London*, [1874.] fol. **H. 2620. (6.)**

— Serenade [begins: "Come while the fragrant breezes"]. Words by G. E. Johnstone. *London*, [1881.] fol. **H. 2620. (16.)**

— Slumber Song. *See supra:* [Schlaflied.]

— The Soft Spring Night. [Part-song.] *See supra:* [In milder Lenznacht.]

— Song of Praise. *See supra:* [Lobgesang.]

— The Soul's Repose. [Part-song.] *See supra:* [Gottvertrauen.]

— Three Spring Songs for three female voices. The German words by H. Rollet, the English words by A. Karstens. 3 no. *London*, [1873.] fol. **H. 2620. (1.)**

— Spring-Tide. Duetto. *See supra:* [Im Frühling.]

— Das stille Thal ... Volksweise für Männerchor arr. von L. Liebe. Edited ... by G. Luckhardt. 1890. *See* Neue. Neue ausgewählte Chöre für Männerstimmen. No. 98. 1886, *etc.* 8°. **E. 866.**

— The Stripling's Armour. Ballad [begins: "The mother looked"]. Words by G. E. Johnstone. *London*, [1880.] fol. **H. 2620. (15.)**

— [Trostlied.] Hymn of Consolation ... Duetto [begins: "When grief awakes".—"Wie gross dein Leid"]. German words by F. Oser. English version by G. E. Johnstone. *London*, [1876.] fol. **H. 1777. h. (52.)**

— Valse mélancolique. [P.F.] *London*, [1875.] fol. **h. 1482. z. (49.)**

LIEBE (Ludwig)

— 13 Voluntaries and other Pieces for the Organ or Harmonium. Op. 40. *London*, [1857.] *obl.* fol. **e. 174. (6.)**

— Die Wacht auf den Vogesen, Gedicht von G. Mühl [begins: "Hoch durch's Gebirg"] ... für Männerchor ... arrangirt von C. Scherling. Partitur. *Leipzig*, [1874.] 8°. **E. 600. p. (3.)**

— [Waldesruf.] Woodland Voices ... [Duet, begins: "From the forest". "Aus den Bergen".] German words by E. Brämer, English version by G. E. Johnstone. *London*, [1873.] fol. **H. 2620. (3.)**

— [Waldwünsche.] Woodland Dreams ... Duet [begins: "In the woodland".—"In dem Walde"]. German words by E. Brämer, English version by G. E. Johnstone. *London*, [1873.] fol. **H. 2620. (4.)**

— We'll meet above, *etc.* [Song.] *See supra:* [Auf Wiedersehn.]

— We Two. [Part-song.] *See supra:* [Muss Einer von dem Andern.]

— [Die weisse Weihnachtsrose.] Christmas Roses. Die weisse Weihnachtsrose. Part song [begins: "When o'er the deep snow covered ways".—"Wenn über Wege."] ... German words by H. Lingg. English version by J. E. Johnstone. *London*, [1883.] 4°. **F. 585. g. (29.)**

— When Matadors are fighting. Bolero ... arranged for two equal voices by L. Liebe. *Stanley Lucas, Weber & Co.: London*, [1890.] fol. **H. 2620. (19.)**

— Woodland Dreams. *See supra:* [Waldwünsche.]

— Woodland Voices. *See supra:* [Waldesruf.]

— Your truest friend is here. A Christmas three-part song for female voices [begins: "Oh! Lord my soul aspiring".—"Wie soll ich dich empfangen"]. German words by P. Gerhard ... English version by L. N. Parker. *London*, [1874.] fol. **H. 2620. (11.)**

— *See* Cramer (J. B.) [Studio. Op. 39, 40.—Selections.] Celebrated Studies ... revised by L. Liebe. [1880.] fol. **h. 3821. a. (5.)**

— *See* Glinka (M. I.) [Жизнь за царя.] Ballet music ... Transcribed for the pianoforte by L. Liebe. [1874.] fol. **h. 1494. j. (27.)**

— *See* Macfarren (*Sir* G.A.) [St. John the Baptist.] Blessed are they ... arranged ... by L. Liebe. [1876.] fol. **H. 1227. a. (12.)**

— *See* Macfarren (*Sir* G. A.) [St. John the Baptist.] Blessed are they ... arranged ... by L. Liebe. [1876.] 4°. **F. 321. a. (22.)**

— *See* Mendelssohn-Bartholdy (J. L. F.) [6 Gesänge. Op. 34. No. 2. Auf Flügeln des Gesanges.] On Music's Wing. Arr. [for three voices] by L. Liebe, *etc.* [1882.] 8°. **F. 1623. a. (3.)**

— *See* Mendelssohn-Bartholdy (J. L. F.) [6 Gesänge. Op. 34. No. 2. Auf Flügeln des Gesanges.] On Music's Wing ... Arr. by L. Liebe. [1903.] 8°. **F. 1658.**

— *See* Mendelssohn-Bartholdy (J. L. F.) [6 Gesänge. Op. 34. No. 3. Frühlingslied.] The Parable of the Seasons. Arr. [for three voices] by L. Liebe. [1882.] 8°. **F. 1623. a. (2.)**

— *See* Mendelssohn-Bartholdy (J. L. F.) [6 Gesänge. Op. 34. No. 3. Frühlingslied.] The Parable of the Seasons ... Arr. by L. Liebe. [1903.] 8°. **F. 1658.**

— *See* Moniuszko (S.) Polonaise ... arranged ... by L. Liebe. [1880.] fol. **h. 1608. f. (14.)**

LIEBE (Ludwig)

— *See* Naumann (J.G.) Chaconne ... arranged ... by L. Liebe. [1879.] fol.   **h. 1494. w. (4.)**

— *See* Naumann (J.G.) Chaconne ... arranged ... by L. Liebe. [1879.] 8°.   **e. 370. b. (13.)**

— *See* Naumann (J.G.) The Lord's Prayer ... with Pianoforte accompaniment by L. Liebe. [1881.] 8°.   **E. 235. a.**

— *See* Raff (J.J.) [Suite de Morceaux. Op. 75. No. 1.] Fleurette ... Arranged ... by L. Liebe. [1901.] fol.   **h. 1297. b. (8*.)**

— *See* Schumann (R.A.) [Kinderscenen. Op. 15.] Scenes of Childhood (Kinder Scenen) ... Op. 15. Revised and fingered by L. Liebe. [1882.] fol.   **h. 88. e. (23.)**

— *See* Taubert (C. G. W.) [12 Gesänge. Op. 27. No. 5. Schlaf in guter Ruh.] Cradle Song ... Arranged by L. Liebe. [1882.] 4°.   **F. 585. g. (46.)**

LIEBE (Ludwig) and SCHILLING (Frederick)

— Nearer my God to Thee. [Anthem.] Music by Liebe-Schilling. *E. Ashdown: London, etc.,* [1885?] 8°. *Select Sacred Harmony, No.* 54.   **F. 1146.**

— Nearer my God to Thee. Music by Liebe-Schilling. (S. A. T. B.) *E. Ashdown: London,* [1937.] 8°.   **E. 602. vv. (30.)**

LIEBELEERES

— Ein Liebeleeres Menschenleben. Männerchor. *See* Grill (L.) Zwei Männerchöre. No. 1.

LIEBELEI

— Liebelei. Lied. *See* Neumann (F.)

LIEBEN

— Die lieben Blätter. [Song.] *See* Arensky (A. S.) Пять романсовъ. Op. 60. Тетрадь II. No. 3.

— Lieben bringt Freud. [Part-song.] *See* Boehme (F. M.)

— Das Lieben bringt gross Freud. Volkslied. *See* Fischer (T.)

— Das Lieben bringt gross Freud'. [Part-song.] *See* Franz (R.) Sechs Lieder ... Op. 32. No. 5.

— Das Lieben bringt gross' Freud'. [Part-song.] *See* Reger (M.) Neun ausgewählte Volkslieder für Männerchor. No. 4.

— Das Lieben bringt gross Freud. Folk-song. *See* Smith (Gregg)

— Das Lieben bringt gross Freud. [Part-song.] *See* Track (G.)

— Lieben bringt Leid. [Part-song.] *See* Piutti (C.) Acht Lieder. No. 2.

— Den Lieben langen Tag. Volkslied. *See* Silcher (F.)

— Den Lieben langen Tag. [Song.] *See* Wetmore (W.T.)

— Das Lieben war leicht. [Part-song.] *See* Gauby (J.)

LIEBENAMM (Oscar)

— All for the Sake of Love. [Song.] Words by Harry Dillon. pp. 3–5. *M. Witmark & Sons:* [*New York,* 1901.] fol.   **H. 3985. z. (41.)**

— Fair Lillian. Schottische. [P. F.] *Howley, Haviland & Co.: New York,* 1896. fol.   **h. 3286. g. (48.)**

LIEBENAMM (Oscar)

— Zephyrette. Entr'acte. [P.F.] pp. 7. *F. B. Haviland Publishing Co.: New York,* [1905.] fol.   **h. 4120. qq. (1.)**

LIEBEND

— Liebend gedenk' ich dein. [Song.] *See* Krebs (C. A.) [An Adelheid.]

— Liebend gedenk' ich Dein. [Song.] *See* Lund (E.) Fünf Gedichte, *etc.* No. 5.

LIEBENDE

— Der Liebende. [Song.] *See* Beethoven (L. van)

— Die Liebende. [Song.] *See* Rottenberg (L.)

— Die Liebende schreibt. [Song.] *See* Bungert (A.) Junge Lieder. Op. 2. No. 6.

LIEBENDEN

— Die Liebenden. [Part-song.] *See* Zillig (W.)

LIEBENWEIN (Caspar)

— Theoretisch-Practische Anleitung zum Choral Gesange. pp. 42. *Bei J. F. Kaiser:* [*Graz,* 1831?] obl. 4°.   **B. 218.**

LIEBER

Lieber Augustin

— Leiber [*sic*] Augustine. A favorite Suabian air with variations for the piano forte or harp. (Second edition.) pp. 3. *Rob' Purdie: Edin',* [c. 1815.] fol.   **h. 723. ee. (28.)**

— *See* Bochsa (R. N. C.) Lieber Augustine, with ... variations for the Harp. [1822.] fol.   **h. 163. (30.)**

— *See* Butler (Neville C.) Lieber Augustine, a favorite German Air, with new variations ... for the harp ... by N. B. Challoner. [c. 1820.] fol.   **g. 661. b. (22.)**

— *See* Davies (O.) Lieber Augustine ... with variations for the Harp, *etc.* [1824.] fol.   **h. 107. (16.)**

— *See* Ferrari (G. G.) 48 Preludes for the Piano Forte ... and 12 Variations on ... Oh mein lieber Augustin, *etc.* [c. 1805.] fol.   **e. 5. t. (5.)**

— *See* Jamson (J.) Lieber Augustine ... arranged as a duett for ... the Pianoforte, *etc.* [1844.] fol.   **h. 702. (37.)**

— *See* Kirmair (F. J.) Airs for the Pianoforte. No. 22. Lieber Augustine. [P. F.] [1815?] fol.   **h. 2994.**

— *See* Latour (T.) Lieber Augustine, with variations for the Pianoforte, *etc.* [1810.] fol.   **h. 315. (24.)**

— *See* Spindler (L.) Augustine ... arranged with variations for the Pianoforte, *etc.* [1815?] fol.   **h. 123. (31.)**

— Lieber Casper lehr' michs doch. Duetto. *See* Mueller (W.) [Die Zauberzitter.]

— Lieber guter Weihnachtsmann. [Song.] *See* Graben-Hoffmann (G.) Drei Weihnachtslieder. No. 2.

— Lieber Herr Gott, wecke uns auf. [Motet.] *See* Bach (Johann Christoph)

— Lieber Herre Gott. Kantate. *See* Rosenmueller (J.) [Kern-Sprüche. No. 9.]

— Lieber Hirte, zarter Jüngling. [Song.] *See* Schnett (E.) Vier Lieder ... Op. 23. No. 2.

258

LIEBER

— Lieber kleiner Gott der Liebe. Aria. *See* MUELLER (W.) [Das neu Sonntagskind.]

— Lieber Schatz, sei wieder gut. [Song.] *See* FRANZ (R.) Sechs Gesänge. Op. 26. No. 2.

— Lieber Schatz, sei wieder gut. [Part-song.] *See* HUBER (H.) Sechs Lieder, *etc.* No. 2.

— Lieber Schatz sei wieder gut mir. [Part-song.] *See* KAESLIN (E.) Sechs Lieder. No. 6.

— Lieber Schatz, sei wieder gut mir. [Song.] *See* PAULS (J.) Lieder ... Op. 12. No. 7.

— Lieber Schatz, sei wieder gut mir. [Part-song.] *See* REITER (E.) Zwei Lieder. Op. 17. No. 1.

LIEBER (ARTHUR)

— The Foaming Stein. [Song, words by] C. Loeb. *O. Ditson Co.: Boston*, 1904. fol. **H. 1799. vv. (54.)**

— Mother's Song. Song for medium voice with Piano accompaniment. *G. Schirmer: New York*, (1905.) fol. **G. 807. kk. (8.)**

— When Gloamin' falls. [Song, words by] A. Bullion. *O. Ditson Co.: Boston*, (1907.) fol. **H. 1794. vv. (54.)**

LIEBER (L.)

— Bavarian waltz. [P.F.] *London*, [1873.] fol. *No. 18 of "Popular German Dance Music".* **h. 1481. j. (10.)**

LIEBERMANN (F.)

— Maiden Fair. Waltzes. [P. F.] *W. Marshall & Co.: London*, [1882.] fol. **h. 975. v. (41.)**

LIEBERMANN (M.)

— ... [Rannᵉ nū ṣaddīkīm.] Tunes and Songs of the Rabbis. Collected and arranged by M. Liebermann. pp. 20. ... [*London*,] 1948. 8°. **01979. d. 11.**

LIEBERMANN (ROLF)

— Capriccio per soprano, violino ed orchestra. Partitura. pp. 76. *Universal Edition: Zürich; Wien* [printed, 1960.] 8°. **c. 121. yy. (3.)**

— Chinesische Liebeslieder. Chinese Love-Songs. Nach Übersetzungen von ... Klabund. English version by Eric Smith. Gesang und Klavier, *etc. Ger. & Eng.* pp. 6. *Universal Edition: Wien, etc.*, [1956.] 4°. **G. 1331. b. (1.)**

— Concerto for Jazz Band and Symphony Orchestra. Score. pp. 127. *Universal Edition: Wien, etc.*, [1954.] 8°. **c. 121. dd. (3.)**

— Furioso für Orchester. Partitur. pp. 56. *Universal-Edition: Wien*, [1948.] 4°. **g. 727. nn. (2.)**

— Geigy Festival Concerto. For snare drum and orchestra. (A phantasy on Basle folk-tunes.) Partitura. pp. 74. *Universal Edition: Wien*, [1958.] 4°. **g. 1620. aa. (1.)**

— Giraudoux-Kantate. (Une des fins du monde.) D'après les paroles tirées de "Sodome et Gomorrhe". Für mittlere Singstimme und Orchester. Deutsche Übertragung von Albin Kaiser. Klavierauszug (Karlheinz Füssl). *Fr. & Ger.* pp. 18. *Universal Edition: Wien, etc.*, [1958.] 4°. **G. 1331. b. (2.)**

— "Leonore 40/45". Opera semiseria in einem Vorspiel und sieben Bildern (zwei Akte) von Heinrich Strobel ... Partitur. pp. 333. *Universal-Edition: Wien*, [1952.] 4°. **G. 1331.**

LIEBERMANN (ROLF)

— Penelope. Opera semiseria in 2 Teilen von Heinrich Strobel. Partitur. pp. 354. *Universal Edition: Wien, etc.*, [1955.] 4°. **G. 1331. f.**

— Penelope. Opera semiseria in 2 Teilen von Heinrich Strobel. Klavierauszug mit Singstimmen von H. E. Apostel. pp. 142. *Universal Edition: Wien, etc.*, [1954.] 4°. **G. 1331. a.**

— School for Wives. Rondo buffo after Molières comedy L'école des femmes. Libretto by Heinrich Strobel. English adaptation by Elizabeth Montagu. pp. 190. *Universal Edition: Wien, etc.*, [1955.] fol. **G. 1331. d.**

— [School for Wives.] Die Schule der Frauen. Opera buffa in drei Akten. Libretto nach Molières Komödie "L'école des femmes" von Heinrich Strobel. Englische Version: Elisabeth Montagu. Deutsche Übersetzung: Hans Weigel. Erweiterte Neufassung: Heinrich Strobel. Klavierauszug (Karlheinz Füssl). *Ger.* pp. 234. *Universal Edition: Wien, etc.*, [1957.] fol. **G. 1331. e.**

— Die Schule der Frauen. *See* supra: [School for Wives.]

— Sonate für Klavier. pp. 19. *Universal Edition: Wien*, [1951.] 4°. **g. 1128. p. (9.)**

— Streitlied. Kantate ... Partitur. pp. 95. *Ars viva: Wien, etc.*, [1951.] fol. **G. 1331. c.**

— Streitlied zwischen Leben und Tod. The Song of Life and Death. Dramatische Kantate nach einem Text von Robert Kothe. Für Sopran- Mezzosopran-, Tenor- und Bass-Solo, gemischten Chor und Orchester. Studien-Partitur. *Ger. & Eng.* pp. 73. *Ars Viva Verlag: Mainz*, [1959.] 8°. **D. 834. i. (2.)**

— Suite über sechs schweizerische Volkslieder. Partitur. pp. 26. *Universal-Edition: Wien*, [1947.] 4°. **g. 727. nn. (3.)**

— Sinfonie Nr. 1 für Orchester. [Score. With a portrait.] pp. 79. *Ars Viva-Verlag: Zürich, Brüssel*, [c. 1950.] 4°. **g. 727. ss. (4.)**

— Sinfonie 1949 für Orchester. Studien-Partitur. pp. 59. *Ars Viva Verlag: Mainz*, [1957.] 8°. **d. 134. tt. (4.)**

— Symphonie ... Les Échanges. Für Percussions-Ensemble (7 Spieler) bearbeitet von ... Siegfried Fink ... Score [and parts], *etc.* 8 pt. *N. Simrock: Hamburg, London*, [1971.] 4°. **g. 1780. mm. (3.)**

LIEBERSON (GODDARD)

— String Quartet. ⟨Score.⟩ pp. 16. *Oxford University Press: New York*, [1965.] 4°. **g. 410. aa. (6.)**

LIEBERSON (S. A.)

— In a Winter Garden. Suite for Grand Orchestra. [Score.] *C. C. Birchard & Co.: Boston*, 1936. fol. **i. 109.**

LIEBERT (JOHANNA)

— When on my bed the moonlight falls. [Song.] Verses by A. Tennyson. *London*, [1860.] fol. **H. 1771. l. (26.)**

LIEBERT (REGINALD)

— Messe mit allen Gesängen des Ordinarium und Proprium. *See* FICKER (R.) and OREL (A.) Sechs Trienter Codices ... Vierte Auswahl: I, *etc.* 1920. fol. [*Publikationen der Gesellschaft zur Herausgabe der Denkmäler der Tonkunst in Österreich. XXVII. Jahrgang. 1. Teil. Band* 53.] **H. 988.**

LIEBERT (SAMUEL)

— Everything is Sunshine when you're close to my Heart. [Song.] Words and music by S. Liebert. pp. 5. *M. Witmark & Sons: New York, etc.*, [1908.] fol. **H. 3985. z. (42.)**

LIEBERT (SAMUEL)

— You'll come back Sweetheart to me. [Song.] Words and music by S. Liebert. pp. 5. *M. Witmark & Sons: New York, etc.,* [1908.] fol. **H. 3985. z. (43.)**

LIEBES

— Lieb' Aennelein! Lied. *See* ABT (F. W.)

— Lieb' Kindlein, gute Nacht. [Song.] *See* TAUBERT (C. G. W.) Fünf Gesänge. Op. 99. No. 5.

— Liebes Lection. Humoristisches Lied. *See* HOELZEL (G.)

— Lieb' Liebchen. Lied. *See* ECKERT (C.A.F.) Sechs Lieder, *etc.* Op. 28. No. 5.

— Lieb' Liebchen. [Song.] *See* FRANZ (R.) Sechs Gesänge ... Op. 17. No. 3.

— Lieb' Liebchen leg's Händchen auf's Herze mein. [Song.] *See* GAUBY (J.) Zwei Lieder. Op. 14. No. 2.

— Liebes Mädchen. Zigeunerlied. *See* BAKHMETEV (N.)

— Liebes Mädchen, hör' mir zu. Terzett. *See* MOZART (W. A.) [*Doubtful and Supposititious Works.*]

— Lieb' Röschen. [Song.] *See* ERNST (H.) Fünf Lieder. No. 3.

— Liebes Schmerzen. [Song.] *See* BROWN (M. H.)

— Lieb' Seelchen lass' das Fragen sein. [Song.] *See* FISCHHOF (R.) Three Songs ... No. 2.

— Lieb' Seelchen, lass das Fragen. [Song.] *See* WALLNOEFER (A.) Lieder, *etc.* Op. 32. No. 1.

— Der Liebes Stern. [Song.] *See* SCHULHOFF (J.)

— Liebes Thal, warum so stille! Wanderlied. *See* ŠKROUP (F. J.)

LIEBES (JOHANNES)

— Two Songs. 1. Rise, for the Day is passing. 2. We ask for Peace, O Lord. Words by A. A. Procter, *etc. Whaley, Royce & Co., for the Composer: Winnipeg, Toronto,* (1914.) fol. **G. 806. mm. (36.)**

LIEBESAHNUNG

— Liebesahnung. [Song.] *See* BEHM (E.) Fünf Lieder. Op. 2. No. 5.

— Liebesahnung. [Song.] *See* KLEFFEL (A.) Lenz und Liebe. No. 4.

— Liebesahnung. Quartett. *See* KRUG (A.) Aus verwehten Blättern ... Op. 32. No. 2.

LIEBESANDACHT

— Liebesandacht. [Song.] *See* KLEFFEL (A.) Lenz und Liebe. No. 7.

LIEBES-AUFGANG

— Liebes-Aufgang. [Part-song.] *See* EBERHARDT (A.)

LIEBESAUFRUF

— Liebesaufruf. [Song.] *See* ECKERT (C. A. F.) Sechs Lieder, *etc.* Op. 28. No. 6.

LIEBESBEGEGNUNG

— Liebesbegegnung. [Song.] *See* BRADSKY (T.) Zwei Lieder, *etc.* No. 2.

LIEBESBEKENNTNISS

— Liebesbekenntniss. [Song.] *See* HERVEY (A.) Sechs Liebeslieder. No. 4.

LIEBESBITTE

— Liebesbitte. Minnelied. *See* REINECKE (C. H. C.)

LIEBESBOTE

— Liebesbote. [Part-song.] *See* ISENMANN (C.) [Five Part Songs. Op. 96. No. 5.]

— Liebesbote. [Song.] *See* KUECKEN (F. W.)

LIEBESBOTSCHAFT

— Liebesbotschaft. [Song.] *See* FESCA (A. E.)

— Liebesbotschaft. [Three-part song.] *See* HERING (C.) Vier Lieder. Op. 116. No. 1.

— Liebesbotschaft. [Song.] *See* KLEFFEL (A.) Lenz und Liebe. No. 10.

— Liebesbotschaft. [Part-song.] *See* MOEHRING (F.) Drei Gesänge. Op. 112. No. 1.

— Liebesbotschaft. [Song.] *See* SCHLOTTMANN (L.)

— Liebesbotschaft. [Song.] *See* SCHUMANN (R. A.) 6 Gedichte. Op. 36. No. 6.

LIEBESBRIEFCHEN

— Liebesbriefchen. [Song.] *See* KORNGOLD (E. W.) Einfache Lieder. Op. 9. No. 4.

LIEBESCHMIED

— Der Liebeschmied. [Chorus.] *See* MEYER-OLBERSLEBEN (M.) Drei dreistimmige Frauenchöre ... Op. 80. No. 3.

LIEBES-EPISTEL

— Liebes-Epistel. [Song.] *See* REINTHALER (C. M.)

LIEBESERFUELLUNG

— Liebeserfüllung. [Song.] *See* SONNECK (O. G. T.) Six Songs, *etc.* [No. 1.]

LIEBESERWACHEN

— Liebeserwachen. [Song.] *See* KIRCHNER (T.)

LIEBESFEIER

— Liebesfeier. [Four-part song.] *See* BLUMMER (M.) Sechs Lieder. Op. 10. No. 3.

— Liebesfeier. [Song.] *See* FRANZ (R.) Sechs Gesänge. Op. 21. No. 4.

— Liebesfeier. [Song.] *See* HARTMANN (L.) Sechs Lieder. Op. 22. No. 1.

— Liebesfeier. [Part-song.] *See* HERMAN (R. L.)

LIEBESFRAGEN

— Liebesfragen. [Part-song.] *See* DEBOIS (F.)

LIEBESFRIEDE

— Liebesfriede. [Song.] *See* GLUECK (A.) Sechs Lieder. No. 6.

LIEBESFRIEDEN

— Liebesfrieden. [Song.] *See* MANGOLD (C. A.) Liebensfrühling, *etc.* No. 3.

LIEBESFRUEHLING

— Liebesfrühling. Song. *See* ABT (F.W.)

— Liebesfrühling. [Song.] *See* BEER (M.) Sechs Lieder, *etc.* No. 1.

LIEBESFRUEHLING

— Liebes-Frühling. [Song.] *See* FRANKE (H.) Drei Lieder ... Op. 11. No. 3.

— Liebesfrühling. [Song.] *See* FRANZ (R.) 6 Gesänge ... Op. 14. No. 5.

— Liebesfrühling. [Song.] *See* FRANZ (R.) 6 Gesänge. Op. 50. No. 6.

— Liebesfrühling. [Song.] *See* GOLTERMANN (G. E.) Ausgewählte Lieder ... No. 2.

— Liebesfrühling. [Song.] *See* NAUMANN (E.) Loschwitzer Liederbuch. No. 5.

— Liebesfrühling. [Song.] *See* RIEMANN (H.) Vier Minnelieder. No. 1.

LIEBESGARTEN

— Liebesgarten. [Song.] *See* MARSCHNER (H. A.) Fünf Lieder ... 101tes Werk. No. 1.

LIEBESGEDANKEN

— Liebesgedanken. Song. *See* KUECKEN (F.W.) Five Songs. Op. 53. No. 4.

— Liebesgedanken. [Song.] *See* TIEHSEN (O.) Sieben Gedichte, *etc.* Op. 6. No. 7.

LIEBESGEFANGENSCHAFT

— Liebesgefangenschaft. Männerquartett. *See* FITTIG (C.)

LIEBESGESCHENKE

— Liebesgeschenke. [Song.] *See* STRAUSS (R. G.) Gesänge des Orients ... Opus 77. 3.

LIEBESGESTAENDNISS

— Liebesgeständniss. [Part-song.] *See* FITTIG (C.) 2 Männerquartette ... Op. 141.

LIEBESGLAUBE

— Liebesglaube. [Song.] *See* MICHAELIS (J.)

LIEBESGLOCKEN

— Liebesglocken. Duett. *See* MUEHLDORFER (W. C.) [Der Kaufmann von Venedig.]

LIEBESGLUECK

— Liebesglück. [Song.] *See* BECKER (A.) Fünf Lieder. Op. 7. No. 1.

— Liebesglück. Walzer-Arie. *See* BOHM (C.)

— Liebesglück. [Song.] *See* FOERSTER (A.) Vier Lieder. Op. 74. No. 4.

— Liebesglück. [Song.] *See* FOERSTER (A.) Zwei Lieder. Op. 81. No. 2.

— Liebesglück. [Song.] *See* GLINKA (M. I.) [Какъ сладко съ тобою мнѣ быть.]

— Liebesglück. [Song.] *See* RHEINBERGER (J.G.) Wache Träume. Op. 57. No. 6.

— Liebesglück. Ein Cyclus von sechs Liedern. *See* RIEDEL (H.)

— Liebesglück. [Part-song.] *See* STEINER (H.) Fünf Gesänge ... Op. 1. No. 3.

LIEBESGOETTER

— Liebesgötter. [Song.] *See* REINTHALER (C. M.) Acht ... Liebes-Lieder ... Op. 37. No. 5.

LIEBESGRUESSE

— Liebesgrüsse. Walzer für Chor. *See* PACHE (J.)

LIEBESGRUSS

— Liebesgruss. Moskauisches Ziegeunerlied, *etc. See* SAMMLUNG. Sammlung Russischer Romanzen, *etc.* No. 206. [1860?–80?] fol. **H. 2171.**

— Liebesgruss. [Song.] *See* ABT (F. W.) 3 Lieder, *etc.* Op. 527. No. 2.

— Liebesgruss. [Song.] *See* HETZEL (M.) Drei Lieder. Op. 8. No. 3.

— Liebesgruss. [Song.] *See* HOFMANN (H. K. J.) [Liebes-Leid und Lust. No. 1.]

— Liebesgruss. [Song.] *See* KLEFFEL (A.) Sechs Lieder. Op. 23. No. 2.

— Liebesgruss. [Duet.] *See* REICHEL (A.) Drei Duette ... Op. 73. No. 1.

— Liebesgruss. [Part-song.] *See* STANGE (M.) Sechs Lieder. Op. 7. No. 4.

— Liebesgruss aus der Ferne. Volkslied. *See* WEBER (C.M.F.E. von)

LIEBESHAENDEL

— Liebeshändel. [Song.] *See* SIEBER (F.) Fünf heitere Lieder. Op. 124. No. 5.

LIEBESHOFFEN

— Liebeshoffen. [Duet.] *See* SOKOLOV (V. T.)

LIEBES-HOFFNUNG

— Liebes-Hoffnung. [Song.] *See* BISCHOFF (K. J.) Vier Lieder. No. 3.

— Liebeshoffnung. [Song.] *See* ESSER (H.) 6 Lieder, *etc.* Op. 68. No. 1.

— Liebes-Hoffnung. [Song.] *See* SCHARWENKA (X.) Vier Lieder, *etc.* No. 3.

LIEBESHYMNUS

— Liebeshymnus. [Song.] *See* STRAUSS (R.) Fünf Lieder ... Op. 32. No. 3.

LIEBES-JUBEL

— Liebes-Jubel. [Song.] *See* RITTER (A.) Drei Lieder. No. 1.

LIEBESKALENDER

— Liebeskalender. Chor. *See* LACHNER (F.) Drei Chöre, *etc.* Op. 167. No. 1.

LIEBESKAMPF

— Liebeskampf. [Song.] *See* NOVÁČEK (O.) Ten Songs, *etc.* [No. 2.]

— Liebeskampf. [Song.] *See* SPEYER (W.)

LIEBESKETTEN

— Liebesketten. Oper. *See* ALBERT (E. F. C. d')

LIEBESKIND (Josef)

— Zwei Fugen für die Orgel. Op. 6. *Reinecke: Leipzig,* [1894.]
fol.   **h. 2731. j. (23.)**

— "Lobe den Herrn." Motette für gemischten Chor ... Op. 1.
Partitur. *Breitkopf & Härtel: Leipzig und Brüssel,* [1894.] fol.
H. 879. l. (4.)

— Symphonie No. 1, A moll, für Orchester. Op. 4. Partitur. *Jost
& Sander: Leipzig,* [1894.] fol.   **f. 660.**

— *See* Ditters von Dittersdorf (Carl) Ausgewählte
Orchesterwerke ... herausgegeben von J. Liebeskind.
[1899–1904.] fol.   **h. 3889.**

— *See* Gluck (C. W. von) Thematisches Verzeichnis der Werke
von C. W. v. Gluck, *etc.* (Ergänzungen und Nachträge ...
Herausgegeben von J. Liebeskind, *etc.*) 1904 (1911). 8°.
e. 1. v.

— *See* Gluck (C. W. von) I Lamenti d'Amore ... herausgegeben
von J. Liebeskind. [1908.] fol.   **G. 1111. a. (4.)**

— *See* Haydn (F. J.) [Nor can I think. Hob. xxiva/9.]
Unvollendetes Oratorium ... Bearbeitung ... von
J. Liebeskind. (1894.) fol.   **H. 1050. g. (1.)**

LIEBESKIND (Otto)

— La Coquette. Tyrolienne. Op. 19. [P. F.] *R. Salzer: Leipzig,*
[1884.] fol.
*No. 35 of 'Sammlung ... neuer Vortragsstücke für
Pianofortespielen'.*   **h. 3281. l. (27.)**

LIEBES-KLAGE

— Liebes-Klage. [Song.] *See* Beethoven (L. van) [Vier Arietten,
etc. Op. 82. No. 2.]

— Liebesklage. [Song.] *See* Hermann (R.) Drei Gesänge. No. 3.

— Liebesklage des Mädchens. [Song.] *See* Mayer (M.) Sechs
Lieder. Op. 18. No. 1.

LIEBESKLANG

— Liebesklang. [Song.] *See* Abt (F. W.) Drei Lieder. Op. 344.
No. 1.

LIEBESKRANK

— Liebeskrank. [Song.] *See* Sekles (B.)

LIEBESKRIEG

— Der Liebeskrieg. Komische Oper. *See* Várady (L.)

LIEBESLAUSCHEN

— Liebeslauschen. [Song.] *See* Schubert (F. P.) Widerschein,
etc.

LIEBESLEBEN

— Liebesleben. Lied. *See* Abt (F. W.) Vier Lieder ... Op. 269.

— Liebesleben. Liederspiel. *See* Beer (M. J.)

— Liebesleben. [Song.] *See* Dessau (B.) Sechs Lieder. Op. 2.
No. 4.

LIEBESLIED

— Liebeslied. [Part-song.] *See* Binkerd (Gordon W.)

— Liebeslied. [Song.] *See* Cruickshank (W. A. C.) Love Song.

— Liebeslied. [Part-song.] *See* Eberhardt (A.)

LIEBESLIED

— Liebeslied. [Song.] *See* Fesca (A.E.) Drei Lieder, *etc.* Op. 45.
No. 3.

— Liebeslied. [Part-song.] *See* Gastoldi (G. G.) [Balletti a
Cinque Voci.—A lieta vita.]

— Liebeslied. Song. *See* Hadley (H. K.)

— Liebeslied. [Duet.] *See* Hofmann (H. K. J.) Vier zweistimmige
Lieder. Op. 4. No. 3.

— Liebeslied. [Song.] *See* Kienzl (W.) Fruehlingslieder ...
Op. 33. No. 2.

— Liebeslied. [Song.] *See* Klughardt (A.) Drei Lieder, *etc.*
No. 2.

— Liebeslied. Gesang. *See* Křenek (E.) [Gesänge des späten
Jahres. Op. 71. No. 3.]

— Liebeslied. [Cantata.] *See* Nono (L.)

— Liebeslied. [Song.] *See* Rottenberg (L.)

— Liebeslied. [Part-song.] *See* Schwalm (R.) Drei Lieder, *etc.*
Op. 33. No. 1.

— Liebeslied. [Song.] *See* Strachwitz (T. von) 4 Lieder, *etc.*
No. 2.

— Liebeslied. Volkslied. *See* Weber (C. M. F. E. von)
Volkslieder. Op. 54. No. 3.

— Liebeslied eines Handwerksgesellen. [Part-song.] *See* Meyer
(C.)

LIEBESLOOS

— Liebesloos. [Part-song.] *See* Bohn (E.) Drei Lieder, *etc.* Op. 2.
No. 3.

LIEBESLUST

— Liebeslust. [Song.] *See* Bungert (A.) Junge Lieder. Op. 6.
No. 6.

— Liebeslust. [Song.] *See* Kiel (F.) Liederkreis. No. 4.

— Liebeslust. Bravour-Walzer. *See* Mulder (R.)

— Liebes-Lust und -Leid. Liedercyclus. *See* Zopff (H.)

LIEBESMAHL

— Das Liebesmahl der Apostel. Eine biblische Scene. *See*
Wagner (W. R.)

LIEBESMARSCH

— Liebesmarsch, für Männerchor. *See* Blasser (G.)

LIEBESMESSE

— Die Liebesmesse. Chorwerk. *See* Zilcher (H. K. J.)

LIEBESNAEHE

— Liebesnähe. [Song.] *See* Bohn (E.) Vier Lieder. No. 2.

LIEBES-ODE

— Liebes-Ode. [Song.] *See* Saar (L. V. F.) Three Songs ...
Op. 54. No. 3.

LIEBESPEIN

— Liebespein. Romanze. *See* Glinka (M. I.) [Слышу ли голосъ
твой.]

LIEBESPREDIGT

— Liebespredigt. [Song.] *See* KLEFFEL (A.) Sechs Gesänge, *etc.* No. 3.

— Liebespredigt. [Song.] *See* ZOELLNER (H.) Drei Lieder, *etc.* No. 3.

LIEBESPROBE

— Die Liebesprobe. Komische Oper. *See* ROSSINI (G. A.) [La Pietra del paragone.]

LIEBESQUAL

— Liebesqual. Romanze. *See* DARGOMUIZHSKY (A. S.)

— Liebesqual. Song. *See* KUECKEN (F. W.) Five Songs. Op. 53. No. 1.

LIEBESRACHE

— Liebesrache. [Song.] *See* GUMBERT (F.)

LIEBESRAUCH

— Liebesrauch. Song. *See* SCHUBERT (F. P.)

LIEBESREIM

— Ein Liebesreim. [Song.] *See* HEISER (W.)

LIEBESROSE

— Die Liebesrose. [Song.] *See* GUMBERT (F.)

LIEBESSCHMERZ

— Liebesschmerz. [Part-song.] *See* REINECKE (C. H. C.) Sechs altfranzösische Volkslieder. No. 4.

— Liebesschmerz. [Song.] *See* REINECKE (C. H. C.)

LIEBESSCHWUR

— Liebesschwur. [Song.] *See* DAVID (Ferdinand)

LIEBESSEHNEN

— Liebessehnen. Lied. *See* HOELZEL (G. von)

LIEBESSEHNSUCHT

— Liebessehnsucht. [Song.] *See* ROEDER (M.) Zwei Lieder ... No. 1.

LIEBESSELIGKEIT

— Liebesseligkeit. Lied. *See* FRITZE (A.)

— Liebesseligkeit. Lied. *See* HEINS (C.)

LIEBESSORGEN

— Liebessorgen. [Song.] *See* SMITH (G. N.) Six Songs ... No. 3.

LIEBESSPIEL

— Liebesspiel. Duett. *See* DARGOMUIZHSKY (A. S.)

LIEBESSPRACHE

— Liebessprache. [Song.] *See* ABT (F. W.) [Drei Lieder, *etc.* Op. 534. No. 3.]

LIEBESSTATIONEN

— Liebesstationen. [Duet.] *See* LASSEN (E.) Sechs Duette, *etc.*, Op. 55. No. 3.

LIEBESSTICKEREI

— Liebesstickerei. [Song.] *See* PROHASKA (C.) Lieder ... Op. 24 ... Nr. 3.

LIEBESTAENDELEI

— Liebeständelei. [Song.] *See* FEIST (O.) 3 Lieder. No. 2.

— Liebeständelei. [Part-song.] *See* HANDWERG (W.) Drei ... Männerchöre. Op. 23 ... No. 2.

LIEBESTOD

— Liebestod. [Song.] *See* BUNGERT (A.) Der Rhapsode der Dimbowitza. Op. 50. No. 6.

LIEBESTODT

— Liebestodt. [Part-song.] *See* KRETSCHMER (E.) Vier Männerchöre. Op. 38. No. 2.

LIEBESTRANK

— Liebestrank. [Song.] *See* REINTHALER (C. M.) Acht ... Liebes-Lieder ... Op. 37. No. 4.

LIEBESTRAUM

— Liebestraum. Romanze. *See* FESSLER (E.)

— Liebestraum. Ein Cyclus von sechs Gesängen. *See* KLUGHARDT (A.)

— Ein Liebestraum. Operette. *See* LINCKE (Paul)

— Liebestraum. [Song.] *See* LISZT (F.) [Drei Lieder für eine Sopran- oder Tenor-Stimme.]

— Liebestraum. [Song.] *See* MAHLENDORFF (P.)

— Liebestraum. Song. *See* MORLEY (C.)

— Liebes-Traum. Lied. *See* PROCH (H.)

— Liebestraum. Lied. *See* ROEDER (M.)

— Liebestraum und Erwachen. Duett. *See* FUCHS (O.)

LIEBESTREU

— Liebestreu. [Song.] *See* BRAHMS (J.) [Sechs Gesänge. Op. 3. No. 1.]

LIEBES-UNGEDULD

— Liebes-Ungeduld. [Song.] *See* BEETHOVEN (L. van) [Vier Arien, *etc.* No. 4.]

LIEBESVERBOT

— Das Liebesverbot. Oper. *See* WAGNER (W. R.)

LIEBESWALZER

— Der Liebeswalzer. Operette. *See* ZIEHRER (C. M.)

LIEBESWEIHE

— Liebesweihe. [Song.] *See* GAST (P.)

LIEBESWONNE

— Liebeswonne. [Song.] *See* ABT (F. W.)

LIEBESWONNE

— Liebeswonne. Vocalquartett. *See* SCHNEIDER (Johann C. F.)

— Liebes-Wonne und -Weh. Sechs Gesänge. *See* DRAESEKE (F.)

LIEBESWUENSCHE

— Liebeswünsche. [Song.] *See* HILLER (F.)

— Liebeswünsche. [Song.] *See* LILIENCRON (F. von) Sechs Lieder, *etc.* No. 4.

— Liebeswünsche. [Song.] *See* MICHAELIS (J.)

— Liebeswünsche. Volkslied. *See* SCHMIDT (G.)

— Liebeswünsche. [Part-song.] *See* STURM (W.) Vier Gesänge. Op. 31. No. 1.

LIEBESZAUBER

— Liebeszauber. [Song.] *See* CURSCHMANN (C. F.) [6 Gesänge. Op. 3. No. 2.]

— Liebeszauber. Für Bariton und Orchester. *See* STEPHAN (R.)

— Liebeszauber. Operette. *See* STRAUS (Oscar)

— Liebeszauber. [Song.] *See* WEBER (C.M. F.E. von) [5 Gesänge und 1 Canon. Op. 13. No. 3.]

— Liebeszauber. [Song.] *See* WIECK, afterwards SCHUMANN (C. J.) [6 Lieder. Op. 13. No. 3.]

LIEBESZEICHEN

— Liebeszeichen. [Song.] *See* ABT (F. W.) [Drei Lieder. Op. 376. No. 2.]

LIEBET

— Liebet eure Feinde! Kantate. *See* ZUMSTEEG (J. R.) Kantate ... No. 9.

LIEBHABER

— Der Liebhaber als Arzt. Musicalisches Lustspiel. *See* WOLF-FERRARI (E.) [L'Amore Medico.]

LIEBHART

— Liebhart polka for voice and Piano. *See* MULDER (R.)

LIEBHOLD (   )

— Lo! To us is born an Infant. For Four-part Chorus ... English version by A. C. Giffen ... Edited by J. F. Williamson. *G. Schirmer: New York*, 1931. 8°.
E. 335. f. (16.)

LIEBICH (AGNES)

— All in white as the angels are. Song, written by C. Robertson. *London*, [1881.] fol. **H. 1787. j. (38.)**

— Easter hymn [begins: "Halleluja"]. *Brighton*, [1881.] *s. sh.* 8°.
E. 605. n. (23.)

— Gruss.—Greeting.—Song. German Words by J. Kerner. Translated by R. Liebich. *Lyon & Hall: Brighton*, [1899.] fol.
H. 1799. h. (57.)

— A Psalm of Life. Duet for Mezzo Soprano and Contralto, words by Longfellow. *Lyon & Hall: Brighton*, [1896.] fol.
H. 1798. v. (25.)

— Stille Thränen ... Musical Reflection, the words by Kerner, the English version by F. B. *Cramer Watts & Co.: London*, [1887.] fol. **H. 1788. w. (10.)**

LIEBICH (AGNES)

— *See* BEETHOVEN (L. van) [Sonata. Op. 13.] Evening Devotion. [Song.] ... Adapted by A. Liebich to melody of Beethoven. [1883.] fol. **H. 2430. c. (21.)**

— *See* WEBER (C. M. F. E. von) [Gesänge und Lieder. Op. 71. No. 5. Lied der Hirtin.] Christmas hymn ... arranged by A. Liebich. [1882.] *s. sh.* 8°. **E. 605. n. (57.)**

LIEBICH (CARL)

— Beaming Eyes. Song [begins: "Little maiden"]. Words by W. Czerny. *London*, [1876.] fol. **H. 1778. y. (29.)**

— Dear Ireland. Song and chorus [begins: "Let others sing"]. *London*, [1876.] 8°. **E. 308. c. (31.)**

— Figaro, scherzo for the Pianoforte. *London*, [1876.] fol.
h. 1482. z. (53.)

— Haunting Eyes. Song [begins: "In the hour I first beheld thee"]. Words by C. Norton. *London*, [1876.] fol.
H. 1778. y. (28.)

— Short and Sweet, serenade for the Pianoforte. *London*, [1876.] fol. **h. 1482. z. (52.)**

LIEBICH (IMMANUEL)

— Adieu, romance for Piano. *London*, [1876.] fol.
h. 3020. b. (12.)

— Amaranth, morceau pour le Piano. *London*, [1865.] fol.
h. 3020. (9.)

— Anglo-Russian wedding march for Piano. *London*, [1876.] fol. **h. 3020. b. (19.)**

— Anna of Tharau, transcribed for the Pianoforte. *London*, [1868.] fol. **h. 3020. a. (17.)**

— Annie Lisle, melody [by W. H. Thompson] transcribed for the Pianoforte. *London*, [1865.] fol. **h. 3020. (13.)**

— Au Revoir, rêverie pour Piano. *London*, [1877.] fol.
h. 3020. b. (27.)

— Aubade pour Piano. *London*, [1876.] fol. **h. 3020. b. (18.)**

— Auf Wiedersehen: the theme improvised upon ... by J. Hofmann. [P. F.] *E. Ascherberg & Co.: London*, [1887.] fol.
h. 1484. t. (24.)

— Auf Wiedersehen. The Theme improvised upon by J. Hofmann ... Easily arranged and fingered (by S. Shaw). [P. F. duet, and violin and P. F.] 2 no. *E. Ascherberg & Co.: London*, (1901.) fol.
Gems of Melody, No. 11. **h. 3487. (11.)**

— Ballade ... for the Pianoforte. *London*, [1866.] fol.
h. 3020. (25.)

— La Belle Sabine, polka de salon pour Piano. *London*, [1876.] fol. **h. 3020. b. (17.)**

— Bianca, morceau élégante [*sic*] pour piano. pp. 5. *Brewer & Cᵒ: London*, [c. 1870.] fol. **h. 61. pp. (7.)**

— The Bird Organ, scherzo-extravaganza [for the] Pianoforte. *London*, [1867.] fol. **h. 3020. a. (6.)**

Birthday Album

— Birthday Album. Twenty ... Pieces for the Pianoforte. *E. Ascherberg & Co.: London*, [1889.] 4°. **g. 543. a. (8.)**

—[No. 4, 5.] Minuet and Frühlingslied. [P. F.] (1913.) *See* DUNHILL (T. F.) and VOLK (W. A.) Recreative Pieces, *etc.* Series II. No. 10a. (1912, *etc.*) fol. **h. 2912. a.**

LIEBICH (IMMANUEL)

— [No. 6, 7.] The Harpist and Tarantelle. [P. F.] (1913.) *See* DUNHILL (T. F.) and VOLK (W. A.) Recreative Pieces, *etc.* Series II. No. 12a. (1912, *etc.*) fol.   **h. 2912. a.**

— [No. 11, 14.] Two Moorland Scenes. [P. F.] (1913.) *See* DUNHILL (T. F.) and VOLK (W. A.) Recreative Pieces, *etc.* Series II. No. 14c. (1912, *etc.*) fol.   **h. 2912. a.**

— [No. 15, 2.] Canzonetta and Scherzino. [P. F.] (1913.) *See* DUNHILL (T. F.) and VOLK (W. A.) Recreative Pieces, *etc.* Series II. No. 8c. (1912, *etc.*) fol.   **h. 2912. a.**

— [No. 18, 16.] Zwei Fantasiestücke. (No. 1. Schlummerlied. No. 2. Erntliedchen.) [P. F.] (1913.) *See* DUNHILL (T. F.) and VOLK (W. A.) Recreative Pieces, *etc.* Series II. No. 9b. (1912, *etc.*) fol.   **h. 2912. a.**

— [No. 13.] Valse-Mignonne. [P. F.] (1913.) *See* DUNHILL (T. F.) and VOLK (W. A.) Recreative Pieces, *etc.* Series II. No. 13b. (1912, *etc.*) fol.   **h. 2912. a.**

———————————

— [Die Botschaft.] Message, for the Pianoforte. *London,* [1870.] fol.   **h. 3020. b. (8.)**

— La Brabançonne, air nationale [by F. van Campenhout] transcrit pour le Piano. *London,* [1866.] fol.   **h. 3020. (33.)**

— The Brighton quadrille. [P.F.] *London,* [1868.] fol.   **h. 3020. a. (10.)**

— The Brighton quadrilles ... as a Pianoforte duet. *London,* [1868.] fol.   **h. 3020. a. (13.)**

— Catch me if you can! Scherzo ... for the Pianoforte. *London,* [1866.] fol.   **h. 3020. (29.)**

— Cheerfulness. (Allegria.) [P.F.] *London,* [1869.] fol.   **h. 3030. a. (23.)**

— Les Cloches du Tyrol. Morceau élégant pour Piano. *London,* [1867.] fol.   **h. 3020. a. (1.)**

— Come Home, Father, melody [by H. C. Work] transcribed for the Piano. *London,* [1868.] fol.   **h. 3020. a. (11.)**

— La Coquette, mazurka de salon pour Piano. *London,* [1873.] fol.   **h. 1482. z. (50.)**

— The Cuckoo. (F. Abt.) Melody transcribed for the Pianoforte. *London,* [1866.] fol.   **h. 3020. (23.)**

— Dahlia. Divertissement pour le piano. *Agate & Co.: London,* [1889.] fol.   **h. 1489. t. (5.)**

— Don Juan [by W. A. Mozart]. Recital pour Piano. *London,* [1862.] fol.   **h. 3020. (2.)**

— Doux Yeux, petit morceau de salon pour Piano. *London,* [1877.] fol.   **h. 3020. b. (25.)**

— Drink to me only with thine eyes, transcribed for the Pianoforte. *London,* [1866.] fol.   **h. 3020. (31.)**

— L'Élégante, nocturne pour le Piano. *London,* [1865.] fol.   **h. 3020. (11.)**

— En beaux Esprits, valse impromptu pour Piano. *London,* [1877.] fol.   **h. 1494. q. (42.)**

— Les Étincelles, caprice pour Piano. *London,* [1870.] fol.   **h. 3020. b. (2.)**

— Evening Chimes ... for the Pianoforte. *London,* [1865.] fol.   **h. 3020. (14.)**

— Fairy Bells, for the Pianoforte. *London,* [1870.] fol.   **h. 2020. b. (5.)**

— Fairy Song [begins: "In a mossy dell"]. Words by Miss King. *London,* [1876.] fol.   **H. 1778. y. (27.)**

LIEBICH (IMMANUEL)

— Falka. Pianoforte duet [on F. Chassaigne's opera]. *A. Hays: London,* [1884.] fol.   **h. 3290. f. (39.)**

— Zwei Fantasiestücke. *See* supra: [Birthday Album. No. 18, 16.]

— La Félicité, thème original et variations pour Piano. *London,* [1876.] fol.   **h. 3020. b. (13.)**

— Fête des Sirènes pour Piano. *London,* [1870.] fol.   **h. 3020. b. (6.)**

— Feuille d'Album pour piano. *Agate & Co.: London,* [1889.] fol.   **h. 1489. t. (6.)**

— The Gallant Tars of England, (J. L. Hatton,) transcribed for the Pianoforte. *London,* [1868.] fol.   **h. 3020. a. (20.)**

— La Gazelle, impromptu pour Piano. *London,* [1865.] fol.   **h. 3020. (17.)**

— Gipsy Revels, morceau characteristique, for the Pianoforte. *London,* [1870.] fol.   **h. 3020. b. (7.)**

— The Good Old Times. *See* infra: [Die guten alten Zeiten.]

— Grand March, for the Pianoforte. *London,* [1864.] fol.   **h. 3020. (6.)**

— Graziletta. [P.F.] *London,* [1869.] fol.   **h. 3020. a. (25.)**

— Greeting, for the pianoforte. *Chappell & Co: London,* [1882.] fol.   **h. 1484. t. (25.)**

— [Die guten alten Zeiten.] To Thee alone, sacred song [begins: "When sorrow's clouds"] written and adapted to ["The Good Old Times"] ... by A. Fricker. *London,* [1866.] fol.   **H. 1524. a. (9.)**

— Die guten alten Zeiten. (The Good Old Times.) Andante con variazioni pour le Piano. *London,* [1865.] fol.   **h. 3020. (15.)**

— Her Bright Smile haunts me still, (W. T. Wrighton,) arranged as a Pianoforte duet. *London,* [1867.] fol.   **h. 3020. a. (2.)**

— Imperial Funeral March, for the Piano Forte, *etc. Chappell & Co.: London,* [1888.] fol.   **h. 1484. t. (26.)**

— Je vous écoute ... pour Piano. *London,* [1862.] fol.   **h. 3020. (3.)**

— Je vous écoute ... pour Piano. *London,* [1876.] fol.   **h. 3020. b. (20.)**

— Kasimir, alla Polacca pour Piano. *London,* [1865.] fol.   **h. 3020. (18.)**

— [Kleiner Schalk.] La Petite Espiègle pour Piano. *London,* [1877.] fol.   **h. 3020. b. (23.)**

— [Künstlers Klage.] Plainte d'Artiste, morceau characteristic [*sic*] pour Piano. *London,* [1867.] fol.   **h. 3020. a. (4.)**

— Let Music and Joy resound. Jubilee Song with chorus ... [Words] by M. J. Reilly. *E. Donajowski: London,* [1887.] fol.   **H. 1788. w. (11.)**

— The Liquid Gem, (W. T. Wrighton,) arranged as a Pianoforte duet. *London,* [1867.] fol.   **h. 3020. a. (3.)**

— Lusigna, morceau de salon pour Piano. *London,* [1870.] fol.   **h. 3020. b. (3.)**

— Madelon, mazurka de salon, pour Piano. *London,* [1865.] fol.   **h. 3020. (19.)**

— Mazurka, Souvenir de Moscow. [P.F.] *London,* [1874.] fol.   **h. 3020. b. (10.)**

— Mendelssohn's part song "The Huntsman's Farewell" (Jäger's Abschied) arranged for the Piano. *London,* [1876.] fol.   **h. 3020. b. (11.)**

LIEBICH (IMMANUEL)

— Mignonette, petit morceau élégant pour Piano. *London,* [1877.] fol.   **h. 3020. b. (26.)**

— Mill May; melody, transcribed for the Pianoforte. *London,* [1868.] fol.   **h. 3020. a. (18.)**

— Moonlight Rambles, nocturne ... for the Pianoforte. *London,* [1866.] fol.   **h. 3020. (30.)**

— Two Moorland Scenes. *See* supra: [Birthday Album. No. 11, 14.]

— The most important Cadences & Modulations through the major & minor keys, with harmonised scales, *etc. London,* [1861.] 8°.   **E. 600. (21.)**

— Muleteers' march for Piano. *London,* [1876.] fol.
                                  h. 3020. b. (14.)

— The Musical Birthday Book. Words selected ... by M. Liebich. *London,* [1883.] *obl.* 16°.   **A. 941.**

— The Musical Box, a caprice ... for the Pianoforte. *London,* [1866.] fol.   **h. 3020. (21.)**

— The Musical Box. [P. F. solo and duet.] *See* SMALLWOOD (W.) Home Treasures, *etc.* No. 14. [1872, *etc.*] fol.   **h. 1412. o.**

— The Musical Box. [P. F. solo and duet.] *See* SMALLWOOD (W.) Little Buds, *etc.* No. 53. [1874, *etc.*] fol.   **h. 1412. p.**

— Immanuel Liebich's second Musical Box, for the Pianoforte. *London,* [1870.] fol.   **h. 3020. b. (1.)**

— Musical Box Gavotte for the pianoforte. *E. Ascherberg & Co.: London,* [1889.] fol.   **h. 1489. t. (7.)**

— The Nest Birds' Call. Caprice for the Pianoforte. *London,* [1868.] fol.   **h. 3020. a. (22.)**

— A new School of Velocity & Expression, for the Pianoforte, *etc. London,* [1867.] fol.   **h. 3020. a. (7.)**

— Nocturne pour Piano. *London,* [1877.] fol.   **h. 3020. b. (22.)**

— Novellette for the pianoforte. *Chappell & Co.: London,* [1887.] fol.   **h. 1484. t. (27.)**

— The Opera Bouquet. Twelve operatic fantasias arranged for two performers on one Piano by I. Liebich. 12 no.   *R. Cocks & Co.: London,* [1868, 69.] fol.   **h. 3020. a. (15.)**

— Six Operatic Recitals for the Pianoforte. 6 no. *London,* [1864.] fol.   **h. 3020. (7.)**

— Orphée aux Enfers, fantasia [on J. Offenbach's] opera ... for the Pianoforte. *London,* [1866.] fol.   **h. 3020. (28.)**

— Peaceful Slumber, morceau de salon ... for the Pianoforte. *London,* [1866.] fol.   **h. 3020. (24.)**

— Persian Diamonds, brilliant fantasia for the Pianoforte. *London,* [1876.] fol.   **h. 3020. b. (16.)**

— Petites Pièces mélodiques ... pour Quatuor à Cordes ... Les mêmes pour piano seul, pouvant servir comme accompagnement aux instruments. [Parts.]   *Schott & Co.: Londres,* [1891.] fol.   **h. 2830. h. (8.)**

— Pianoforte Trios, for three performers on one Pianoforte. 3 no. *London,* [1867.] fol.   **h. 3020. (35.)**

— The Pilgrims of the Night, transcribed for the Pianoforte. *London,* [1868.] fol.   **h. 3020. a. (14.)**

— Pilgrims' Chorus (Wagner) transcription. [P.F.] *London,* [1877.] fol.   **h. 3020. b. (24.)**

— Poor Bessy was a Sailors' Wife [by E. J. Loder] transcribed for the Piano. *London,* [1867.] fol.   **h. 3020. a. (8.)**

— Two Popular German Melodies, transcribed for the Pianoforte. 2 no. *London,* [1864.] fol.   **h. 3020. (8.)**

LIEBICH (IMMANUEL)

— Two Popular Melodies, for the Pianoforte. 2 no. *London,* [1860.] fol.   **h. 3020. (1.)**

— Quatre Préludes faciles pour deux violons, alto & violoncelle. [Score and parts.]   *F. W. Chanot: London,* [1890.] fol.
                                  h. 1681. c. (9.)

— Deux Récitations Operatiques sur [G. Meyerbeer's opera] Les Huguenots. [P.F.] 2 no. *London,* [1863.] fol.   **h. 3020. (5.)**

— Reminiscences of Beethoven, set of waltzes. [P. F.] *London,* [1881.] fol.   **h. 3275. j. (38.)**

— Robin Adair, transcribed for the Pianoforte. *London,* [1866.] fol.   **h. 3020. (34.)**

— Rosalinde. Paraphrase on an original Air by Sir Julius Benedict for the pianoforte.   *R. Cocks & Co.: London,* [1898.] fol.   **h. 3282. f. (44.)**

— Russian airs transcribed for the Pianoforte. *London,* [1874.] fol.   **h. 3020. b. (9.)**

— A Rustic Rondo ... for the Pianoforte. *London,* [1866.] fol.
                                  h. 3020. (26.)

—— S. Glover's Scotch Ballad, Oh! for the bloom of my own native heather, arranged for the Pianoforte. *London,* [1869.] fol.   **h. 3020. a. (26.)**

— She Smiles. Impromptu ... for the Pianoforte. *London,* [1866.] fol.   **h. 3020. (27.)**

— Shylie Bawn, melody by W. T. Wrighton, transcribed for the Pianoforte. *London,* [1865.] fol.   **h. 3020. (16.)**

— Sing me that song again, (Guglielmo,) arranged as a Pianoforte duet. *London,* [1867.] fol.   **h. 3020. a. (9.)**

— The Snuff Box extravaganza, for the Pianoforte. [*London,* 1867.] fol.   **h. 3020. a. (5.)**

— Softly sighs the voice of evening, air from [C. M. F. E. von Weber's opera] Der Freyschütz, transcribed for the Pianoforte. *London,* [1868.] fol.   **h. 3020. a. (16.)**

— Une Soirée de Famille. Morceaux mélodieux pour trois violons et piano.   *B. Schott's Söhne: Mayence,* [1891.] fol.
                                  h. 2831. c. (6.)

— The Soldiers of our Land, (J. L. Hatton,) transcribed for the Pianoforte. *London,* [1869.] fol.   **h. 3020. a. (21.)**

— Souvenir de Sᵗ. Petersburgh mazurka. [P.F.] *London,* [1874.] fol.   **h. 1482. z. (51.)**

— Speciosa, valse impromptu for Piano. *Brighton,* [1870.] fol.
                                  h. 3020. b. (4.)

— Still mein süsses Kind. (Old German Cradle Song.) Transcribed [P.F.], *etc. London,* [1869.] fol.
                                  h. 3020. a. (24.)

— Tarantelle pour Piano. *London,* [1865.] fol.   **h. 3020. (12.)**

— To Thee alone, *etc. See* supra: [Die guten alten Zeiten.]

— Toujours de bonne humeur, pour Piano. *London,* [1862.] fol.
                                  h. 3020. (4.)

— Toujours de bonne humeur, pour Piano. *London,* [1876.] fol.
                                  h. 3020. b. (21.)

— 'Twas within a mile of Edinbro' Town [by J. Hook], transcribed for the Piano. *London,* [1868.] fol.
                                  h. 3020. a. (12.)

— Valse-Mignonne. *See* supra: [Birthday Album. No. 13.]

— Welcome Home, galop de concert, pour Piano. *London,* [1865.] fol.   **h. 3020. (20.)**

LIEBICH (IMMANUEL)

— Woodland Trillings, morceau de salon ... for the Pianoforte. *London*, [1866.] fol. **h. 3020. (32.)**

— Woodland Trillings, as a Pianoforte duet. *London*, [1868.] fol. **h. 3020. a. (19.)**

— The Wood-Pecker, (M. Kelly,) transcribed for the Pianoforte. *London*, [1866.] fol. **h. 3020. (22.)**

— *See* BACH (J. S.) [Sei solo ... No. 2. Bourrée.] Gavotte in B minor ... arranged ... by I. Liebich. [1878.] fol. **h. 3007. b. (5.)**

— *See* CLIFTON. The Clifton Tune Book, *etc.* [Harmonized by I. Liebich.] [1871.] 12°. **A. 618. j.**

— *See* HAY (G. R.) *Viscount Dupplin.* Gavotte, arranged ... by I. Liebich. [1882.] fol. **h. 3275. h. (14.)**

— *See* KUHE (W.) Chevalier Kuhe's Marche de la Victoire, arranged ... by I. Liebich. [1865.] fol. **h. 3020. (10.)**

— *See* PLANQUETTE (R.) [Rip van Winkle.] The most Favorite Airs from Rip van Winkle, *etc.* [1883.] fol. **h. 3290. k. (6.)**

— *See* SCHUMANN (R. A.) Nachtstuck [Op. 23, No. 4], easy arrangement by I. Liebich. [1878.] fol. **h. 88. e. (4.)**

— *See* STERN (Leopold) [Yellow Dwarf.] L. Stern's ... children's song ... easily arranged for the Piano. [1876.] fol. **h. 3020. b. (15.)**

LIEBICH (RUDOLPH)

— [Norwegian Suite.] A Farewell. Intermezzo. [P. F.] *O. Ditson Co.: Boston*, 1900. fol. **h. 3282. w. (48.)**

— Sonnet without Words, for the Piano. *O. Ditson Co.: Boston*, 1900. fol. **h. 3282. w. (49.)**

LIEBIG (JULIUS)

— Grüss an Ems. Quick march. ("Aus Freundschaft." Polka.) [Military band parts.] 59 pt. *In:* LANNER (J. F. C.) [Die Osmanen. Op. 146.] Valse, *etc.* [1880.] *obl.* 8° & fol. [*Boosé's military Journal. ser.* 64. *no.* 4.] **h. 1549.**

— Abschied von Riga. Walzer für Pianoforte. *Berlin & Posen*, [1879.] fol. **h. 1493. o. (36.)**

— Aus Freundschaft. Polka für das Pianoforte. *Berlin & Posen*, [1875.] fol. **h. 1487. q. (21.)**

— Aus Freundschaft (Friendship) polka. [P.F.] *London*, [1880.] fol. **h. 1484. c. (34.)**

— Berlin Stadtbahn-Galopp für das Pianoforte. *Berlin & Posen*, [1882.] fol. **h. 3276. g. (25.)**

— Cavalierball-Quadrille für das Pianoforte. *Berlin & Posen*, [1881.] fol. **h. 3272. j. (33.)**

— Die Colonnaden Walzer. [P.F.] *Berlin & Posen*, [1868.] *obl.* fol. **e. 217. b. (33.)**

— Die Colonnaden waltzes. [P.F.] *London*, [1877.] fol. **h. 1482. z. (57.)**

— Concert-Haus Quadrille. [P.F.] *Berlin & Posen*, [1873.] fol. **h. 1487. q. (18.)**

— La Coquette Polka-Mazurka für Pianoforte. *Berlin & Posen*, [1873.] fol. **h. 1487. q. (15.)**

— Emser Kränchen. Polka für Pianoforte. *Berlin & Posen*, [1879.] fol. **h. 1493. o. (38.)**

— Erinnerung an London waltz. [P.F.] *London*, [1876.] fol. **h. 1482. z. (54.)**

LIEBIG (JULIUS)

— Fest-Polonaise für das Pianoforte und Männerquartett (ad libitum). *Berlin & Posen*, [1881.] fol. **h. 3272. j. (29.)**

— Feurig Blut. Galopp für das Pianoforte. *Berlin & Posen*, [1881.] fol. **h. 3272. j. (32.)**

— Freie Geister. Walzer für das Pianoforte. *Berlin & Posen*, [1875.] fol. **h. 1487. q. (19.)**

— Freie Geister waltzes. [P.F.] *London*, [1877.] fol. **h. 1482. z. (56.)**

— Friendship polka. *See* supra: Aus Freundschaft.

— Gedenkblätter. Walzer für das Pianoforte. *Berlin & Posen*, [1883.] fol. **h. 3276. g. (26.)**

— Gruss an Ems. Marsch für das Pianoforte. *Berlin & Posen*, [1877.] fol. **h. 1493. o. (35.)**

— Kaiserhof-Polka für das Pianoforte. *Berlin & Posen*, [1881.] fol. **h. 3272. j. (31.)**

— Ketty-Polka für das Pianoforte. *Berlin*, [1879.] fol. **h. 1493. o. (34.)**

— Künstler-Tänze. Walzer für das Pianoforte. *Berlin & Posen*, [1881.] fol. **h. 3272. j. (28.)**

— Kutschke-Polka. [P.F.] *Berlin & Posen*, [1873.] fol. **h. 1487. q. (16.)**

— Myrthentänze Walzer. [P.F.] *Berlin & Posen*, [1873.] fol. **h. 1487. q. (17.)**

— Myrthentänze waltzes. [P.F.] *London*, [1877.] fol. **h. 1482. z. (55.)**

— Novelle. Polka für das Pianoforte. *Berlin & Posen*, [1882.] fol. **h. 3276. g. (24.)**

— Salon Royal Polka ... für Pianoforte. *Berlin & Posen*, [1868.] fol. **h. 1462. s. (1.)**

— Serben-Marsch für das Pianoforte. *Berlin & Posen*, [1882.] fol. **h. 3276. g. (23.)**

— Treue Liebe Polonaise für das Pianoforte. *Berlin & Posen*, [1875.] fol. **h. 1487. q. (20.)**

— Wo ist die Katz? Polka für Pianoforte. *Berlin*, [1878.] fol. **h. 1493. o. (37.)**

— Zum Geburtstag. Polka-Mazurka für das Pianoforte. *Berlin & Posen*, [1881.] fol. **h. 3272. j. (30.)**

LIEBIG (RUDOLPH)

— Two Songs of Robert Browning. 1. That was thy Face! 2. Fairest of all. *J. & J. Hopkinson: London*, 1892. fol. **H. 1797. o. (39.)**

LIEBITZ (CHRISTIAN)

— Star of my future life. Ballad, written by A. Hartz. *Cincinnati*, 1864. fol. **H. 1780. f. (17.)**

LIEBKOSUNG

— Liebkosung. Lied. *See* ABT (F.W.) Zwei Lieder ... Op. 188. No. 1.

LIEBLICH

— Lieblich erscheint am Waldessaume. *Der Trauernde Postillon, etc.* Zigeunerlied, *etc. See* SAMMLUNG. Sammlung Russischer Romanzen, *etc.* No. 153. [1860?–80?] fol. **H. 2171.**

— Lieblich hat sich gesellet. [Part-song.] *See* REGER (M.) Acht Gesänge für Männerchor. Opus 83. No. 2.

LIEBLICH

— Lieblich ist's, dem Ew'gen danken. Chorus. *See* SCHUBERT (F. P.) [Psalm xcii.]

— Lieblich wie der goldne Morgen. Duet. *See* KELLER (C.)

LIEBLICHE

— Liebliche Blumen. *Die Sprache der Blumen.* [Song.] [*Breitkopf und Haertel: Leipzig,* 1804.] 4°. [*Beilage zur Allgemeinen musikalischen Zeitung. Jahrg.* 6. *no.* 7.]   **P. P. 1945.**

— Liebliche Maid. Song. *See* GOLDBERG (J. P.)

— Liebliche Rose. [Song.] *See* GLINKA (M. I.) [Люблю тебя.]

— Der liebliche Stern. [Song.] *See* SCHUBERT (F. P.)

— Liebliche Töne. [Duet.] *See* KELLER (C.)

LIEBLING (EMIL)

— Albumblatt.—Album-Leaf.—For the Pianoforte. Op. 18. Newly revised by the Author. *G. Schirmer: New York,* (1909.) fol.   **h. 3283. kk. (9.)**

— The Complete Scales for the Piano, with explanatory notes ... Op. 13. Newly revised by the Author. *G. Schirmer: New York,* (1908.) fol.   **h. 3820. t. (8.)**

— Compositions for Pianoforte. Op. 34 ... Op. 35 ... Op. 36 ... Op. 38. 5 no. *G. Schirmer: New York,* 1899. fol.
g. 605. p. (33.)

— Concert Polonaise in G minor. Op. 41. [P. F.] *G. Schirmer: New York,* (1907.) fol.   **g. 605. vv. (40.)**

— Feu Follet.—Will-o'-the-Wisp.—Scherzo for the Piano. Op. 17. Newly revised by the Author. *G. Schirmer: New York,* (1909.) fol.   **h. 3283. kk. (8.)**

— Florence. Grande Valse de Concert pour le Piano. Op. 12. Nouvelle édition, revue par l'Auteur. *G. Schirmer: New York,* (1908.) fol.   **g. 605. vv. (37.)**

— Instructive Pieces for the Piano ... Opus 32 (37). 6 no. *C. F. Summy Co.: Chicago,* 1896–9. fol.   **h. 3282. f. (45.)**

— Lolita. Souvenir for the Piano. Op. 39. *G. Schirmer: New York,* (1907.) fol.   **g. 605. vv. (38.)**

— Le Météore.—The Meteor.—Grand Galop brillant pour le Piano. Op. 10 ... Nouvelle édition revue par l'auteur. *G. Schirmer: New York,* (1909.) fol.   **h. 3283. kk. (7.)**

— The Princess Waltz, for Piano. (Op. 42.) *J. Church Co.: Cincinnati, etc.,* (1907.) fol.   **h. 3286. ll. (28.)**

— Scherzo in B♭. Op. 40. [P. F.] *G. Schirmer: New York,* (1907.) fol.   **g. 605. vv. (39.)**

— A United Commonwealth. Two-step march. [P.F.] pp. 7. *John Church Co.: Cincinnati, etc.,* [1908.] fol.
h. 4120. qq. (2.)

— *See* CHOPIN (F. F.) [12 Etuden. Op. 25. No. 9.] Salon Étude ... Transcription ... by E. Liebling. (1905.) fol.   **h. 471. f. (4.)**

— *See* PAULL MUSIC CO. Edition Paull ... revised ... by ... E. Liebling, *etc.* (1905.) fol.   **h. 3822.**

LIEBLING (ESTELLE)

— Diva bravura. Coloratura and operatic airs for soprano. Edited and provided with cadenzas by E. Liebling and others. 2 vol. *G. Schirmer: New York; Chappell & Co.: London; London printed,* [1963.] 8°. *With separate flute parts to Adam's "Bravura Variations" and to Mozart's "L'amerò, sarò costante" inserted in vol.* 1 *and* 2 *respectively.*   **G. 206. l.**

LIEBLING (ESTELLE)

— Hast thou, O night? A nocturne. [Words by] Eugene Field. pp. 5. *Galaxy Music Corporation: New York,* [1952.] 4°.
G. 1276. m. (27.)

— Indian Love Song. [Song.] Words by Mrs. J. P. Sousa. *J. Church Co.: Cincinnati, etc.,* (1904.) fol.   **H. 1794. l. (12.)**

— Mother dear. [Words by] Y. Ravell. Polish Folk-Song. Arranged by E. Liebling. *G. Schirmer: New York,* 1939. 4°.
G. 981. w. (6.)

— [A reissue.] Mother dear ... Polish folk-song, *etc. Chappell & Co.: London,* [1948.] 4°.   **G. 981. jj. (2.)**

— No quiero casarme. No, I'd rather be single. English version by Willis Wager. Spanish folk-song. Arranged by E. Liebling. *Span. & Eng.* pp. 5. *Chappell & Co.: London,* [1958.] 4°.
G. 981. jj. (11.)

— Five (Four) Old Melodies. Arranged by E. Liebling for Voice and Piano. 5 no. *Galaxy Music Corporation: New York,* 1939, 40. 4°.   **G. 981. t. (13.)**

— Pastourelles, pastoureaux. Shepherds, Shepherdesses. [Song.] French Noël, from the province of Anjou. Arranged by E. Liebling ... English version by E. Liebling, *etc. Galaxy Music Corporation: New York,* 1944. 4°.   **G. 981. y. (11.)**

— [A reissue.] Pastourelles, pastoureaux. Shepherds, Shepherdesses. French noël ... Arranged by E. Liebling, *etc. Augener: London,* [1961.] 4°.   **G. 950. (7.)**

— Philomel. [Song, words by] William Shakespeare. pp. 5. *Galaxy Music Corporation: New York,* [1950.] 4°.
G. 1276. m. (28.)

— A Shepherd to his Love. ([Song.] Based on "A la bienaimée" by Edouard Schütt.) [Words by] Christopher Marlowe, adapted by E. Liebling, *etc.* pp. 7. *Galaxy Music Corporation: New York,* [1953.] 4°.   **G. 1276. m. (29.)**

— Straussiana, for voice and piano. Arranged by E. Liebling on themes by J. Strauss. English text by K. Bellaman, Italian text by P. Gallico. *C. Fischer: New York, etc.,* 1925. 4°.
G. 1275. s. (4.)

— The Estelle Liebling Vocal Course. For coloratura soprano, lyric soprano and dramatic soprano. ⟨Lyric tenor and dramatic tenor. Mezzo-soprano and contralto. Baritone, bass baritone and bass.⟩ Edited by Bernard Whitefield. 4 bk. *Chappell & Co.: New York,* [1956.] 4°.   **H. 2245. o.**

— *See* ALYAB'EV (A. A.) [Соловей.] The Russian Nightingale ... New concert version ... by E. Liebling. 1928. 4°.
G. 1275. z. (2.)

— *See* ALYAB'EV (A. A.) [Соловей.] The Russian Nightingale ... Alabieff—[Arranged by E.] Liebling. [1948.] 4°.
F. 607. xx. (7.)

— *See* ARDITI (L.) [Il Gitano.] The Gypsy ... Revised by E. Liebling. 1946. 4°.   **G. 1276. a. (2.)**

— *See* BELLINI (V.) [I Puritani.] Qui la voce ... Edited and supplied with cadenzas by E. Liebling. 1944. 4°.
G. 1276. a. (5.)

— *See* BELLINI (V.) [I Puritani.] Son vergin vezzosa ... Edited and arranged with traditional cadenzas by E. Liebling. 1946. 4°.   **G. 1276. a. (6.)**

— *See* BENEDICT (*Sir* J.) Carnival of Venice ... Revised by E. Liebling, *etc.* 1939. 4°.   **G. 1275. w. (6.)**

— *See* BENEDICT (*Sir* J.) The Gipsy and the Bird ... Edited and supplied with additional cadenzas by E. Liebling. 1944. 4°.
G. 1276. (2.)

— *See* BISHOP (*Sir* Henry R.) [The Two Gentlemen of Verona.] Should he upbraid ... Edited, abridged and supplied with cadenzas by E. Liebling. 1944. 4°.   **G. 1276. a. (7.)**

LIEBLING (ESTELLE)

— *See* BOCCHERINI (L.) [Quintets. Op. 13. No. 5.] Minuet ... [Song.] Boccherini-[Arranged by E.] Liebling. 1939. 4°.

G. 1275. ww. (4.)

— *See* BRAHMS (J.) [Ungarische Tänze.] The Legend of the Violin ... Adapted ... by E. Liebling. [1958.] 4°.

G. 473. h. (16.)

— *See* CHAIKOVSKY (P. I.) [Casse-Noisette.—Valse des Fleurs.] Waltz of the Flowers. Love and the Time of Flowers ... Arranged ... by E. Liebling. 1942. 4°. **G. 1275. yy. (21.)**

— *See* CHOPIN (F. F.) [3 Mazurkas. Op. 50. No. 2.] The Violet loves a grassy Bank ... Arranged by E. Liebling. 1945. 4°.

G. 1148. (2.)

— *See* COOKE (Thomas S.) [A Midsummer Night's Dream.] Over Hill, over Dale ... Edited and revised by E. Liebling. 1946. 4°. **G. 1276. a. (12.)**

— *See* DEFESCH (W.) Tu fai la superbetta ... Edited by E. Liebling. 1945. 4°. **G. 1276. a. (14.)**

— *See* DONIZETTI (D. G. M.) [La Favorite.—O mon Fernand.] O mio Fernando ... Edited by E. Liebling. 1944. 4°.

G. 1276. (6.)

— *See* DONIZETTI (D. G. M.) [Lucia di Lammermoor.—Alfin son tua.] Ardon gl' incensi. The Mad Scene ... Edited by E. Liebling. 1938. 4°. **G. 1275. tt. (17.)**

— *See* DONIZETTI (D. G. M.) [Lucia di Lammermoor.] Regnava nel silenzio ... Revised and supplied with cadenzas by E. Liebling. 1944. 4°. **G. 1276. (7.)**

— *See* ECKERT (C. A. F.) [Er liebt nur mich.] None he loves but me ... Edited with an added original Cadenza by E. Liebling. 1938. 4°. **G. 1275. tt. (18.)**

— *See* GELLI (E.) [La Farfalla.] The Butterfly ... Revised and re-arranged by E. Liebling. 1943. 4°. **G. 1275. zz. (11.)**

— *See* GOUNOD (C. F.) [Faust.—Ballet.] "Faustiana." A vocal fantasy for coloratura soprano by E. Liebling, *etc.* [1950.] 4°.

H. 2550. m. (25.)

— *See* GOUNOD (C. F.) [Mireille.] O légère hirondelle ... Edited by E. Liebling. [1947.] 4°. **H. 2550. m. (21.)**

— *See* GOUNOD (C. F.) [Philémon et Baucis.] Ô riante nature ... Edited by E. Liebling, *etc.* [1955.] 4°. **G. 190. g. (3.)**

— *See* HALÉVY (J. F. F. É.) [La Juive.] Il va venir ... Edited by E. Liebling. 1946. 4°. **G. 1276. a. (25.)**

— *See* LAMPERTI (F.) [Studi di bravura.] Vocal Studies in Bravura, *etc.* ⟨Revised and edited by E. Liebling.⟩ [1951.] 8°.

F. 1692. e. (6.)

— *See* LITERES (A.) [Accis y Galatea.] Confiado gilguerillo ... Arranged by E. Liebling. [1955.] 4°. **G. 1271. c. (18.)**

— *See* MASSÉ (F. M.) [Les Noces de Jeannette.] Air du rossignol ... Revised and provided with cadenzas by E. Liebling. 1944. 8°. **G. 1276. (18.)**

— *See* MEYERBEER (G.) [L'Étoile du nord.] C'est bien l'air. That's the Tune ... Revised with special cadenza by E. Liebling. [1948.] 4°. **G. 1276. d. (23.)**

— *See* MEYERBEER (G.) [Les Huguenots.] Nobles seigneurs, salut ... Edited by E. Liebling. 1938. 4°. **G. 1275. uu. (13.)**

— *See* MEYERBEER (G.) [Les Huguenots.] O beau pays ... Revised and supplied with cadenzas by E. Liebling. 1944. 4°.

G. 1276. b. (4.)

— *See* PINSUTI (C. E.) [Welcome pretty Primrose.] Pretty Primrose ... Revised by E. Liebling. [1952.] 4°.

G. 1276. i. (20.)

LIEBLING (ESTELLE)

— *See* PROCH (H.) Theme and Variations. Op. 164 ... Edited by E. Liebling. 1940. 4°. **G. 1275. xx. (24.)**

— *See* ROSSINI (G. A.) [Il Barbiere di Siviglia.] Una voce poco fà ... Edited by E. Liebling. 1938. 4°. **G. 1275. uu. (25.)**

— *See* ROSSINI (G. A.) [Il Barbiere di Siviglia.] Una Voce poco fà ... Cavatina ... Edited by E. Liebling. [1965.] 4°.

G. 1276. rr. (3.)

— *See* STRAUSS (J.) *the Younger.* [Frühlingsstimmen. Op. 410.] Voci di primavera ... Edited and supplied with cadenzas by E. Liebling. 1944. 4°. **H. 1964. j. (1.)**

— *See* THOMAS (C. L. A.) [Hamlet.] Mad Scene ... Abridged, edited, and supplied with cadenzas by E. Liebling. 1943. 4°.

G. 1276. b. (27.)

— *See* VERDI (F. G. F.) [Ernani.] Ernani, involami. Ernani, fly with me ... Edited by E. Liebling. 1943. 4°.

G. 1275. zz. (31.)

— *See* WADE (J. A.) [The Two Houses of Grenada.] Love was once a little Boy ... Arranged by E. Liebling. 1943. 4°.

G. 1275. zz. (32.)

— *See* WEBER (C. M. F. E. von) [Aufforderung zum Tanz.] Invitation to the Dance ... Arranged by E. Liebling. 1933. 4°.

G. 1275. nn. (48.)

LIEBLING (GEORG)

— A la Watteau. Quatre Pièces caractéristiques pour piano ... Op. 15. *A. Hammond & Co.: London,* [1899.] 4°. *The Academic Edition, No.* 162. **g. 1130. d. (13.)**

— Bridal Song. *See infra:* [Six Romances sans Paroles. Op. 24. No. 3. Chanson nuptiale.]

— By-By Time. [Song.] Words by E. Oxenford. *Elkin & Co.: London,* 1905. fol. **H. 1794. l. (13.)**

— Concert-Menuett für das Pianoforte. Op. 17. *Augener & Co.: London,* 1898. fol. **g. 605. p. (34.)**

— Concerto in D, for Violin and Piano. (Op. 86.) *G. Schirmer: New York,* 1929. 4°. **g. 500. o. (10.)**

— Cradle Song.—Wiegenlied.—Op. 39. Words by A. Rose. German version by G. Liebling. 2 no. [In E flat and C.] *Novello and Co.: London, etc.,* 1899. fol. **G. 807. o. (49.)**

— The Dawn of Light. Sacred Song.—Es wohnt ein Gott. Geistliches Lied.—Op. 20. Words by E. Schulze, English version by A. Rose. *Novello and Co.: London,* 1899. fol.

G. 517. k. (25.)

— England will ne'er forget ... Song. The words ... by M. C. de Gomez-Farias. Op. 48. *Novello and Co.: London,* [1900.] fol.

G. 807. o. (52.)

— The Faded Garland.—Der welke Kranz.—[Song.] Op. 40. Words by W. Hertz. English version by A. Rose. *Novello and Co.: London, etc.,* 1899. fol. **G. 807. o. (50.)**

— The Great glorious Spirit. Song, the words ... by M. C. de Gomez-Farias. Op. 51. No. 1. *Novello and Co.: London, etc.,* 1900. fol. **G. 807. o. (53.)**

— Humoresque pour piano. Op. 43. *E. Ashdown: London,* 1899. fol. **g. 605. p. (37.)**

— The Indian Serenade. Song, words by Shelley.—Abends. Lied. Gedicht von G. Kinkel.—Op. 37. *Novello and Co.: London, etc.,* 1899. fol. **G. 807. o. (47.)**

— Lord, teach us to pray. Anthem—for Soli, Chorus and Organ— ... Op. 30. *C. Vincent: London,* 1900. 8°.

F. 231. l. (48.)

LIEBLING (GEORG)

— Love Song. *See* infra: [Six Romances sans Paroles. Op. 24. No. 6. Chant d'Amour.]

— Marquise—Op. 15. No. 2.—Pièce caractéristique pour Piano. *A. Hammond & Co.: London*, [1900.] fol.   **g. 605. x. (12.)**

— The Mill in the Woods. *See* infra: [Six Romances sans Paroles. Op. 24. No. 2. Au Moulin.]

— Miniature Polonaise. Op. 47, No. 1. [P.F.] *J. Church Co.: [Cincinnati,]* 1900. fol.   **h. 3282. w. (51.)**

— Miniature Russe. Op. 47. No. 2. [P. F.] *J. Church Co.: [Cincinnati,]* 1900. fol.   **h. 3282. w. (52.)**

— Noces de Village—Op. 15. No. 4—Pièce caractéristique pour Piano. *A. Hammond & Co.: London*, [1900.] fol.   **g. 605. x. (13.)**

— The Open Window. Song. Words by Longfellow—Wie flüchtig rinnt die Stunde. Lied. Gedicht von Geibel. Op. 36. *Novello and Co.: London, etc.,* 1899. fol.   **G. 807. o. (46.)**

— River Song. *See* infra: [Six Romances sans Paroles. Op. 24. No. 4. Chant de Batelier.]

Six Romances sans Paroles. Op. 24

— [No. 1. Larmes.] Tears. Thränen, *etc.* [P. F.] *E. Ascherberg & Co.: London*, 1901. fol.   **h. 3282. kk. (36.)**

— [No. 2. Au Moulin.] The Mill in the Woods. Müllerliedchen, *etc.* [P. F.] *E. Ascherberg & Co.: London*, 1901. fol.   **h. 3282. kk. (37.)**

— [No. 3. Chanson nuptiale.] Bridal Song. Brautlied, *etc.* [P.F.] *E. Ascherberg & Co.: London*, 1901. fol.   **h. 3282. kk. (38.)**

— [No. 4. Chant de Batelier.] River Song. Schifflied, *etc.* [P. F.] *E. Ascherberg & Co.: London*, 1901. fol.   **h. 3282. kk. (39.)**

— [No. 5. Crépuscule.] Twilight. Dämmerstunde, *etc.* [P. F.] *E. Ascherberg & Co.: London*, 1901. fol.   **h. 3282. kk. (40.)**

— [No. 6. Chant d'Amour.] Love Song. Liebeslied, *etc.* [P. F.] *E. Ascherberg & Co.: London*, 1901. fol.   **h. 3282. kk. (41.)**

— Sacred Fire. Song, the words ... by M. C. de Gomez-Farias. Op. 51. No. 2. *Novello and Co.: London, etc.,* 1900. fol.   **G. 807. o. (54.)**

— Sonatine for the Piano. Op. 21. *Rossini & Co.: London*, 1900. fol.   **g. 605. x. (14.)**

— Sorrow and Joy.—Stummer Schmerz, lautes Glück.—[Song.] Words by M. Falter. English Translation by A. Rose. Op. 34. *Boosey & Co.: London & New York*, 1899. fol.   **H. 1799. h. (59.)**

— Suite Italienne pour piano. Op. 42. 1. Serenata ... 2. Romanza ... 3. Tarantella ... 4. Barcarola ... 5. Marcia di Carnovale. 5 no. *Novello & Co.: London*, 1899. 4°.   **g. 442. l. (16.)**

— Tarantella für des Pianoforte. Op. 25. *Augener & Co.: London*, 1898. fol.   **g. 605. p. (35.)**

— Tears. *See* supra: [Six Romances sans Paroles. Op. 24. No. 1. Larmes.]

— Tema con Variazioni for Piano. Op. 23. *E. Ascherberg & Co.: London*, 1900. fol.   **h. 3282. w. (50.)**

— Thee.—Du.—[Song.] Op. 35. Words by J. Ambrosius. English version by A. Rose. *Novello and Co.: London, etc.,* 1899. fol.   **G. 807. o. (45.)**

— Thine Eyes, Love. Song. Words by J. A. McDonald.—Dein Auge. Lied. German version by G. Liebling.—Op. 44. *Novello and Co.: London, etc.,* 1899. fol.   **G. 807. o. (51.)**

LIEBLING (GEORG)

— Time long past. Song. Words by Shelley.—Mein Herz ist am Rhein. Lied. Gedicht von W. Muller.—Op. 38. *Novello and Co.: London, etc.,* 1899. fol.   **G. 807. o. (48.)**

— Toccata de Concert in E minor. Op. 41. *Novello and Co.: London*, 1899. fol.   **g. 605. p. (36.)**

— Twilight. *See* supra: [Six Romances sans Paroles. Op. 24. No. 5. Crépuscule.]

— The Voices of the Wind. Song or melodrama. Words by Sir Edwin Arnold ... Op. 50. pp. 11. *Oppenheimer Bros: London; Leipzig printed*, [1900.] fol.   **H. 1654. q. (11.)**

— Wanderer's Song.—Wanderlied.—Words by R. Hamerling. English Translation by A. Rose. Op. 33. *Boosey & Co.: London & New York*, 1899. fol.   **H. 1799. h. (58.)**

LIEBLING (MAX)

— Berceuse. [Violoncello and P. F.] *G. Schirmer: New York*, 1898. fol.   **h. 204. e. (24.)**

— I am thine.—Nimm mich hin!—Song for high voice. (Reinhard, translated by L. Liebling.) *O. Ditson Co.: Boston*, (1910.) fol.   **H. 1792. s. (32.)**

— Isola. Song, words by B. Cornwall, *etc. L. Feist: New York*, (1910.) fol.   **H. 1792. s. (33.)**

— Love came in at the Door. *See* infra: Four Songs ... 1.

— My Wife. Song, words by R. L. Stevenson, *etc. L. Feist: New York*, (1910.) fol.   **H. 1792. s. (34.)**

— Four Songs with Piano accompaniment. 1. Love came in at the Door ... 2. Spring Magic ... Words by R. Baughman. 3. To a Swallow ... Words by V. Thompson. 4. Träumerei.—Revery— ... Words by E. Staus. (English version by H. G. Chapman.) 4 no. *G. Schirmer: New York*, (1912.) fol.   **H. 1792. s. (35.)**

— Spring Magic. *See* supra: Four Songs ... 2.

— To a Swallow. *See* supra: Four Songs ... 3.

— Three Tone-Pictures. [P. F.] 1. Rainy Day. 2. On the Lake. 3. In the Woods. 3 no. *G. Schirmer: New York*, 1899. fol.   **g. 605. p. (38.)**

— Träumerei. *See* supra: Four Songs ... 4.

LIEBLINGSTAEUBCHEN

— Das Lieblingstäubchen. [Song.] *See* KLUGHARDT (A.) Drei Lieder. Op. 39. No. 3.

LIEBMANN (AXEL)

— *See* HARTMANN (Johann P. E.) Foraarssang ... Claverudtog af A. Liebmann. 1975. 8°.   **E. 889. m. (2.)**

— *See* WEYSE (C. E. F.) Festen paa Kenilworth ... Klaver-Udtog af A. Liebmann, *etc.* 1877. fol. [*Samfundet til Udgivelse af dansk Musik. VII.*]   **G. 728.**

LIEBNER (ADOLPH)

— Christ or Artemis. Song and chorus, words by D. A. Grant. *C. Sheard & Co.: London*, 1895. fol.   **H. 1798. v. (26.)**

LIEBNER (JÁNOS)

— *See* BARTÓK (B.) [Gyermekeknek. füz. 1. No. 13, 14, 6, 16, 17, 21, 18, 11, 19, 8, 3, 10.] For Children. For violoncello with piano accompaniment ... Arranged by ... J. Liebner. [1966?] 4°.   **h. 3377. k. (3.)**

LIEBNIG (F. L.)

— I care for nobody Dear, but you. [Song.] Words by
L. McEvoy. *M. Witmark & Sons:* [*New York, etc.,*] 1904. fol.
H. 1799. vv. (55.)

LIEBREICH (　　　) *Mrs*

— 24 Songs for Children for one or two voices, *etc.* 2 ser.
C. Woolhouse: London, [1891.] 4°. **G. 385. h. (7.)**

LIEBST

— Liebst du um Schönheit. [Song.] *See* BEER (M. J.) Sturm und
Stille. No. 4.

— Liebst du um Schönheit. [Song.] *See* MAHLER (G.)

— Liebst du um Schönheit. [Song.] *See* STERN (J.) *of the Berlin
Conservatorium.*

LIEBSTE

— Die Liebste. [Song.] *See* BUNGERT (A.) Junge Lieder. Op. 2.
No. 4.

— Der Liebste. [Song.] *See* WEYRAUCH (A. H.)

— Die liebste Buhle. [Song.] *See* BERGMANN (G.) Drei Lieder,
etc. No. 3.

— Die Liebste fragt warum ich liebe. [Song.] *See* KLEFFEL (A.)
Sechs Gesänge, *etc.* No. 2.

— Die Liebste harrend. [Song.] *See* BUNGERT (A.) Junge Lieder.
Op. 6. No. 3.

— Der liebste Lied. [Song.] *See* DEPROSSE (A.) Sechs Gedichte,
etc. Op. 42. No. 5.

— Der Liebste schläft. [Song.] *See* SCHMIDT (H.) Liebeslieder.
No. 6.

LIEBSTEN

— Der Liebsten Haus. [Song.] *See* SEKLES (B.)

— Des Liebsten Schwur. [Song.] *See* BRAHMS (J.) Neun Gesänge.
Op. 69. No. 4.

LIEBSTER

— Liebster deine Worte stehlen. [Song.] *See* RUEFER (P.) Vier
Gedichte, *etc.* Op. 12. No. 2.

— Liebster gieb Acht. [Song.] *See* KLEFFEL (A.) Spanische
Lieder, *etc.* No. 6.

— Liebster Gott, wann werd' ich sterben. Cantata. *See* BACH
(J. S.)

— Liebster Immanuel, Herzog der Frommen. Cantata. *See* BACH
(J. S.)

— Liebster nur dich seh'n, dich hören. [Song.] *See* GLUECK (A.)
Sechs Lieder. No. 6.

— Liebster O Liebster. [Song.] *See* FLUEGEL (E.) Sieben Lieder
No. 6.

LIEBT

— Liebt er mich nicht? [Song.] *See* MOHR (H.)

LIEBTEST

— Liebtest du mich. Melodie. *See* DENZA (L.) [Si tu m'aimais.]

LIEBWOHL (FELIX)

— Repose, romance for the Pianoforte. *London,* [1862.] fol.
h. 1460. w. (5.)

LIECHANOWIECKA (AMÉLIE)

— Nadzieja (l'Espérance) pour Piano. *Paris,* [1864.] fol.
h. 1462. s. (2.)

LIECHTENSTEIN (RUDOLPH VON) *Prince*

— *See* VERDI (F. G. F.) Messa da Requiem ... Riduzione ... del
Principe R. de Liechtenstein. [1877.] fol. **h. 1492. f.**

LIECK (FREDERICK J.)

— Mazurka Russe pour piano. *Orpheus Music Publishing Co.:
London,* [1899.] 4°.
The Guildhall Edition, No. 4. **g. 1440.**

— Two Polish Dances, for Piano. *Orpheus Music Publishing
Co.: London,* [1909.] 4°.
The Guildhall Edition, No. 36. **g. 1440.**

LIED

— Lied an den Maj. [Duet.] *See* ZUMSTEEG (J. R.)

— Lied an der Toilette der Geliebten. [Song.] *See* FOERSTER
(E. A.) Zwölf neue deutsche Lieder, *etc.* No. 7.

— Schillers Lied an die Freude. [Song with orchestra.] *See*
SATZENHOVEN (F.)

— Lied an meinen Sohn. [Song.] *See* STRAUSS (R. G.) Fünf
Lieder ... Op. 59. No. 4.

— Lied aus der Ferne. [Song.] *See* BEETHOVEN (L. van)

— Lied aus Dixieland. [Song.] *See* REINITZ (B.) Schatten über
Harlem ... Einzelausgaben, *etc.* [No. 1.]

— Lied bij de bevrijding van Nederland. [Song.] *See*
DIEPENBROCK (A. J. M.)

— Das Lied das meine Mutter sang. [Song.] *See* HERRMANN (A.)

— Lied der Anna Lyle. [Song.] *See* SCHUBERT (F. P.) Sieben
Gesänge. Op. 52. No. 7.

— Lied der Baumwollpflücker. [Song.] *See* EISLER (H.)

— Das Lied der Begeisterung. [Part-song.] *See* LISZT (F.)

— Lied der Bergarbeiter. [Song.] *See* EISLER (H.)

— Lied der Christen. [Song.] *See* EBERWEIN (T. M.) [Das befreite
Jerusalem.]

— Lied der Desdemona. [Song.] *See* JENSEN (A.) 4 Gesänge, *etc.*
Op. 58. No. 4.

— Das Lied der Deutschen. *See* HAYDN (F. J.) [Gott erhalte
Franz den Kaiser.]

— Lied der Erinnerung. Kantate. *See* MUELLER-HERMANN (J. F.)

— Lied der Frauen. [Song.] *See* STRAUSS (R. G.) Sechs Lieder ...
Op. 68. Nr. 6.

— Lied der Freiheit. [K. 506.] [Song.] *See* MOZART (W. A.)

— Lied der Freude. [Song.] *See* SPOHR (L.)

— Lied der Freundschaft. [Song.] *See* BORNHARDT (J. H. C.)

— Lied der Gertrud. [Song.] *See* GOETZ (H.) Sechs Lieder.
Op. 12. No. 4.

— Lied der Grete. [Song.] *See* CONRADI (A.) [Das Wunderhorn.]

LIED

— Lied der Hirtin. [Song.] *See* WEBER (C. M. F. E. von) Gesänge und Lieder. Op. 71. No. 5.

— Lied der Königin Elisabeth. [Song.] *See* LOEWE (J. C. G.)

— Lied der Kreuzfahrer. [Part-song.] *See* KLEFFEL (A.) Sechs Gesänge, *etc.* Op. 22. No. 1.

— Das Lied der Lerche. [Song.] *See* LALO (É. V. A.) Cinq Lieder. No. 5.

— Lied der Liebe. [Song.] *See* ANDRÉ (J. A.)

— Lied der Liebe. [Song.] *See* PREYER (G.)

— Das Lied der Liebe. Operette. *See* STRAUSS (J.) *the Younger.* [*Composite Works.*]

— Lied der Mignon. [Song.] *See* HOLTER (I.) Vier Gesänge. No. 2.

— Das Lied der Nacht. Dramatische Ballade. *See* GÁL (H.)

— Lied der Nacht. [Song.] *See* HASSE (G.) Fünf Lieder. Op. 22. No. 1.

— Lied der Sänftenträger. [Song.] *See* SHAW (Martin F.) [The Song of the Palanquin Bearers.]

— Lied der Schmiedegesellen. [Part-song.] *See* RHEINBERGER (J. G.)

— Lied der Sehnsucht. Duett. *See* BECKER (J.) 3 Duetten. No. 1.

— Lied der Städte. [Part-song.] *See* GERNSHEIM (F.)

— Lied der Vöglein. [Duet.] *See* HOLSTEIN (F. von)

— Lied der Vöglein. [Part-song.] *See* KLEINMICHEL (R.) Acht Lieder. Op. 32. No. 7.

— Lied der Vöglein. [Trio.] *See* RADECKE (R.) Vier Terzette. Op. 27. No. 4.

— Lied der Waldtraut. [Song.] *See* ECKBERG (C.)

— Lied der Wasser Fee. [Song.] *See* HAMMOND (W. G.) Heine Songs. [No. 9.]

— Lied der Wolga-Schiffer. [Song.] *See* KENEMAN (F.) [Эй укнемъ!]

— Lied des abgebrochenen Zweiges. [Song.] *See* WÜERST (R.) Vier Lieder, *etc.* No. 1.

— Lied des gefangenen Jägers. [Song.] *See* SCHUBERT (F. P.) [Sieben Gesänge. Op. 52. No. 7.]

— Lied des Genius. [Song.] *See* KALINNIKOV (V. S.) [Въ 1812 году.] Романсъ Генія.

— Lied des Harfners. [Song.] *See* MUSORGSKY (M. P.) [*Collections, Vocal.*] Oeuvres vocales. No. 25.

— Lied des kleinen Vöglein. Quartett. *See* SCHULTZ (E.) Zwei Männerquartette. No. 2.

— Das Lied des Lammes. [Oratorio.] *See* MATTHESON (J.)

— Lied des Ludolf. [Song.] *See* KAUFFMANN (F.) Vier Lieder. No. 1.

— Lied des Mädchens. [Song.] *See* JENSEN (A.) Sechs Lieder, *etc.* Op. 57. No. 1.

— Lied des Mädchens. [Song.] *See* RIES (A.) Vier Lieder, *etc.* Op. 2. No. 1.

— Lied des Mädchens. [Duet.] *See* RIES (F.)

— Lied des Mähers. Zigeunerlied, *etc. See* SAMMLUNG. Sammlung Russischer Romanzen, *etc.* No. 154. [1860?–80?] fol. **H. 2171.**

LIED

— Lied des Mainzer Landsturms. [Song.] *See* STERKEL (J. F. X.)

— Lied des Mephistopheles. [Song.] *See* BUSONI (F. B.)

— Lied des Nassauer. [Song.] *See* FEST. Das Fest der Handwerker.

— Lied des Schmieds. [Chorus.] *See* ZOELLNER (H.)

— Das Lied des Steinklopfers. [Song.] *See* STRAUSS (R. G.) Acht Lieder ... Op. 49. No. 4.

— Lied des Unmuts. [Song.] *See* BUSONI (F. B.) Zwei Gedichte von Goethe ... 1.

— Lied des Verfolgten im Thurme. [Song.] *See* MAHLER (G.) Des Knaben Wunderhorn. No. 8.

— Lied des Vogelstellers. [Part-song.] *See* GENZMER (Harald) Drei leichte Chorlieder. No. 1.

— Das Lied des Zwergen. [Song.] *See* NATROWSKI (M.)

— Lied eines Alpenmädchens. [Song.] *See* TOMÁŠEK (V. J.)

— Lied eines deutschen Knaben. [Song.] *See* SPAZIER (J. C. G.)

— Lied eines fahrenden Schülers. [Song.] *See* KAUFFMANN (F.) Fünf Gesänge. Op. 3. No. 1

— Lied eines Gefangenen. [Song.] *See* KAMINSKI (Heinrich)

— Lied eines Mädchens. [Song.] *See* REGER (M.) Sechs Lieder ... Op. 104. No. 4.

— Lied eines Mädchens auf den Tod ihrer Gespielin. [Song.] *See* GUERRLICH (J. A.)

— Lied eines Räubers. [Song.] *See* VARLAMOV (A. E.)

— Lied eines Schmiedes. [Song.] *See* BOHLMANN (T. F.) Five Songs for Alto or Baritone. [No. 4.]

— Lied eines Vögleins in der Oasis. [Song.] *See* SHAPLEIGH (B.) Fünf Lieder ... Op. 19. No. 2.

— Lied eines wahnsinnigen Mädchens. [Song.] *See* SCHULTZ (J. P. C.) Sechs Volkslieder. No. 4.

— Lied für deutsche Landwehrmänner. Männerchor. *See* REICHEL (F.) Vier Männerchöre. Op. 7. No. 2.

— Lied für Deutschland. [Part-song.] *See* SMITH (Waldemar)

— Ein Lied für ihn. Ode. *See* MEYER (E. H.)

— Lied für Preussische Patrioten. [Song.] *See* ZELTER (C. F.)

— Lied im Freien. [Part-song.] *See* SCHUBERT (F. P.)

— Das Lied im Grünen. [Song.] *See* SCHUBERT (F. P.)

— Lied in der Abwesenheit. Song. *See* SCHUBERT (F. P.)

— Lied in der Fremde. [Song.] *See* KUECKEN (F. W.)

— Lied in der Nacht. [Song.] *See* SMITH (G. N.) Four Songs, *etc.* [No. 2.]

— Ein Lied in die Haushaltung. [Part-song.] *See* MARX (K.)

— Lied in drei Noten, B. C. D. *See* DUSSEK (J. L.)

— Lied Margaretha's. [Song.] *See* HETZEL (M.) Drei Lieder. Op. 8. No. 2.

— Lied maritime. [Song.] *See* INDY (P. M. T. V. d')

— Lied nach Heinrich von der Vogelweide. [Song.] *See* MARSCHNER (H. A.) Sechs Lieder ... 92${}^{\text{tes}}$ Werk. No. 5.

— Lied nach Reimar der Alte. [Song.] *See* MARSCHNER (H. A.) Sechs Lieder ... 92${}^{\text{tes}}$ Werk. No. 4.

LIED

— Lied op den verrader Frans Vergonet, *etc.* [Words by Fedde Schurer, music by Margit Leiker.] *See* HOORT. Hoort het lied van een verrader. 1944. *s. sh.* fol.   **P. 1504. (2.)**

— Lied über den Frieden. [Song.] *See* EISLER (Hans)

— Ein Lied um Regen. [Part-song.] *See* MARX (K.)

— Lied und Leben. Ein Hymnus. *See* WUELLNER (F.)

— Lied und Liebe. [Part-song.] *See* BLUMNER (M.)

— Lied unter der Veste Wyschegrad. [Song.] *See* BRADSKÝ (T.)

— Het Lied van't maagdelijn. [Song.] *See* TINEL (E.) Drie Liederen. No. 1.

— Das Lied vom blinden Hessen. *See* MEYERBEER (G.)

— Das Lied vom Blucher. *See* CALLCOTT (W. H.) Was blasen die Trompeten.

— Das Lied vom Deutschen Kaiser. [Chorus.] *See* BRUCH (M. C. F.)

— Das Lied vom gefeiten Oleg. [Chorus.] *See* RIMSKY-KORSAKOV (N. A.)

— Ein Lied vom grünen Kranze. [Song.] *See* MEYER (C.) Sechs Lieder. No. 5.

— Das Lied vom Heidelberger Fass. [Song.] *See* HETSCH (C. L. F.)

— Lied vom Herzen. [Song.] *See* SAUER (E. von)

— Das Lied vom Mantel, aus Leonore von C. v. Holtei, *etc. See* SCHIER. Schier dreissig Jahre bist du alt. [Song.] [c. 1830.] 8°.   **D. 836. oo. (1.)**

— Das Lied vom Rauch. [Part-song.] *See* ZILLIG (W.)

— Lied vom Rhein. [Song.] *See* HILLER (F.) [7 Gesänge. Op. 185. No. 7.]

— Das Lied vom Scheiden. Volkslied. [Part-song.] *See* ISENMANN (C.)

— Das Lied vom Wasserrad. [Part-song.] *See* ZILLIG (W.)

— Ein Lied vom Wein. [Song.] *See* SIXT (J. A.) Sechs Lieder, *etc.* No. 4.

— Lied vom Winde. [Trio.] *See* BECKER (R.)

— Das Lied von den Bergen. Symphonische Dichtung. *See* BITTNER (J.)

— Das Lied von den Wäldern. Oratorium. *See* SHOSTAKOVICH (D. D.) [Песнь о лесах.]

— Lied von der blauen Fahne. [Song.] *See* EISLER (H.)

— Lied von der Einheit. [Song.] *See* WAGNER-RÉGENY (R.)

— Das Lied von der Erde. Symphonie. *See* MAHLER (G.)

— Das Lied von der Glocke. [Cantata.] *See* BRUCH (M. C. F.)

— Das Lied von der Glocke. [Cantata.] *See* HURKA (F. F.)

— Das Lied von der Glocke. [Cantata.] *See* NICOLAI (W. F. G.)

— Das Lied von der Glocke. [Cantata.] *See* ROMBERG (A. J.)

— Das Lied von der Lanze. Song. *See* HOELZEL (G.) Six Songs, *etc.* No. 2.

— Das Lied von der Liebsten rothem Mund. [Duet.] *See* WÜERST (R.) Vier zweistimmige Lieder. No. 1.

— Lied von der Mühle. [Song.] *See* RAIDA (C. A.) Gesänge, *etc.* No. 1.

LIED

— Lied von der Musik. [Part-song.] *See* HINDEMITH (P.)

— Das Lied von der Mutter. Oratorium. *See* HAAS (Joseph)

— Das Lied von der Nachtigall. [Part-song.] *See* HANDWERG (W.) Drei Gesänge. Op. 17. No. 3.

— Lied von der neuen Erde. [Unison song.] *See* DESSAU (P.)

— Das Lied von Treue. Ballade. *See* ZUMSTEEG (J. R.)

— Lied voor de Koninklijke Jagers. *See* OP. Op Jagers! op, *etc.* [1830.] 8°.   **11556. f. 33. (5.)**

— Das Lied wird That. [Part-song.] *See* BILLETER (A.)

— Ein Lied zu deinem Ruhme. [Part-song.] *See* GAUBY (J.)

— Lied zum Einschlummern. [Song.] *See* HERMANN (H.) Lieder ... 1.

— Lied zum Tanz unter der Linde. [Song.] *See* SCHLOTTMANN (L.) 10 Goethe'sche Dichtungen. No. 10.

LIEDCHEN

— Liedchen! habe dich auf Schwingen. [Song.] *See* KALLIWODA (J. W.)

— Das Liedchen von der Ruhe. [Part-song.] *See* HILLER (F.) [8 Gesänge ... Op. 165. No. 2.]

LIEDECK (WALTHER)

— *See* GOTOVAC (J.) Ero s onoga svijeta ... ⟨Op. 17.⟩ Klavirski izvadak izradio ... W. Liedeck. [1955.] 4°.   **G. 1269. v.**

LIEDEL

— Das Liedel vom Glück. [Part-song.] *See* SCHULTZ (C. A.)

— S'Liedel vom Glück. [Song.] *See* WOETHER (Charles W.)

LIEDER

— Die Lieder. [Part-song.] *See* HAESER (C.)

— Lieder auf der Flucht. [Cantata.] *See* REIMANN (A.)

— Lieder aus dem fahrenden Zug. [Songs.] *See* ANDERT (Reinhold)

— Drey Lieder aus den Blüthen und Früchten, herausgegeben von Joseph Wismayr. ⟨Rundgesang für eine Gesellschaft Studierender, in Musik gesetzt von J. Michael Haydn. Gute Nacht, mit Musik von A. Jos. Emmert. Der Lebensmüde an den Tod, mit Musik von Philipp Schmelz.⟩ *In der Mayrischen Buchhandlung: Salzburg,* 1797. *obl.* fol.   **B. 925. j.**

— Lieder aus der Fremde. Songs. *See* WELLESZ (E. J.)

— Lieder der Deutschen mit Melodien. Erstes(–Viertes) Buch. 4 pt. *Bey G. L. Winter: Berlin,* 1767–8. 4°.   **85. g. 13.**

— Die Lieder der Verliebten. Cyclus. *See* SCHERFF (L.)

— Die Lieder des Anglers. [Songs.] *See* WAGNER-RÉGENY (R.)

— Lieder des Herbstes. [Song-cycle.] *See* ZILLIG (W.)

— Die Lieder des Mirza Schaffy. Operette. *See* ROTH (L.)

— Die Lieder, die Leiden, die oft ich besang. *See* SAKHNOVSKY (Yu. S.) Семь романсовъ ... Op. 5. No. 7.

— Lieder eines Mägdchens, beym Singen und Claviere. *Bey P. H. Perrenon: Münster,* 1774. *obl.* fol.   **C. 750.**

—[Another copy.]   **Hirsch III. 1149.**

LIEDER

— Lieder für die Weltkonferenzen der Evangelischen Jünglingsvereine und Christlichen Vereine Junger Männer. Hymns. For world's conferences of Young Men's Christian Associations. Cantiques, *etc. Ger., Eng. & Fr.* pp. iv. 96. *Genf.*, 1909. 8°.　　　　　　**C. 20. uu. (2.)**

— Lieder für gemischten Chor. Die Einheitsfront ... (Hanns Eisler, Satz: Paul Kurzbach.) Im schönsten Wiesengrunde ... (Deutsches Volkslied, Satz: Fritz Höft.) Ging auf den Jahrmarkt ... (Tschechisches Volkslied, Satz: Otto Hilliger.) Im Walde ... (Robert Schumann.) pp. 11. *Friedrich Hofmeister: Leipzig*, [1968.] 8°. *FDGB-Liedblätter. no. 39.*　　　　　**C. 374. i. (4.)**

— Lieder mit Melodien. *Bey Posch: Anspach*, 1758. 8°.　　　　　　**Hirsch III. 899.**

— Zwölf Lieder mit Melodien und eben so viel untermischte Galanteriestücke für das Clavier. pp. 55. *Bey George Jacob Decker: Berlin*, 1775. 8°.　　**Hirsch III. 900.**

— Lieder und Bilder aus der Schweiz. *I. I. Burgdorfer: Bern*, 1837. 4°.　　　　　　**11527. g. 27.**

— Drei Lieder von Meyerbeer, Spohr und Lachner. Autographa. Zum deutschen Stammbuche auss Jahr 1838. *Im Verlage des oberrheinischen Comptoirs: Kandern*, [1838.] *obl.* 8°.　　　　　　**D. 729.**

— Lieder, von Stilling. [Four songs, "Es leuchten drei Sterne über ein Königes Haus," "Zu Kindelsberg auf dem hohen Schloss," "Hört ihr lieben Vögelein," "Noch einmal blickt mein mattes Auge".] *Bei Julius Eduard Hitzig: Berlin*, 1811. *obl.* 8°. *Issued as a supplement to "Die Jahreszeiten. Eine Vierteljahrschrift für romantische Dichtungen ... Frühlingsheft".*　　　　　　**Hirsch III. 852.**

— Lieder zur Ehre des Erretters. Vereinslieder des Blauen Kreuzes. (Schweizerausgabe.) Achte, vermehrte Auflage. pp. xvi. 384. *Agentur des Blauen Kreuzes: Bern; Elim, Buchhandlung des Blauen Kreuzes: Barmen*, 1904. 8°.　　　　　　**B. 1179. cc.**

— Lieder zur öffentlichen und häuslichen Andacht [by Ferdinand Kindermann], mit Melodien grösstenteils von den besten vaterländischen Meistern. Herausgegeben auf Veranlassung der k. k. Normalschuldirektion. pp. xiv. 241. pl. v. *In der k. k. Normalschulbuchdruckerey: Prag*, 1783. 8°.　　　　　　**Case. 109. ff. 29.**

LIEDER-ALBUM

— Lieder-Album. A Collection of German Songs—with English and German words—for a medium voice with pianoforte accompaniment. 5 pt. *London*, [1882–6.] 8°. *Augener & Co.'s edition, No. 8854ᵃ⁻ᵈ. There are two editions of Book I.: the second edition contains an additional song.*　　　　　　**F. 636. c. (4.)**

— Lieder-Album. A Collection of German Songs, with English and German words, for a medium voice with Pianoforte accompaniment. 8 bk. *Augener & Co.: London*, [1887.] 8°.　　　　　　**F. 1567.**

— Lieder-Album aus Tyrol, Kärnten und Steiermark. 30 beliebte Volks- und Nationallieder für Pianoforte mit unterlegtem Text. Hft. 2. *Gebrüder Hug: Leipzig*, [c. 1895.] 4°. *Imperfect; wanting Hft. 1.*　　　　　　**G. 981. ww. (2.)**

— Lieder-Album für eine Singstimme mit Pianoforte und Violin-Begleitung. [Score.] *Ger. & Eng.* pp. 29. *C. F. Peters: Leipzig, Berlin*, [1876.] 4°.　　　**G. 295. z. (3.)**

LIEDERBUCH

— Liederbuch der Anna von Köln (um 1500). *See* ANNA, *von Koeln.*

LIEDERBUCH

— Liederbuch der Christlichen Wissenschaft. (Christian Science Hymnal) ... German edition. *Ger. & Eng.* pp. v. 682. *Christian Science Publishing Society: Boston, Mass.*, [1955.] 8°.　　　　　　**D. 622. kk.**

— Das Liederbuch des Arnt von Aich, Köln um 1510. *See* AICH (A. von)

— Liederbuch für Bürger- und Landschulen. Auswahl beliebter Lieder und Gesänge aus alter und neuer Zeit. Herausgegeben von Lehrern des Fürstenthums Lüneburg. Erstes Heft, *etc. Herold & Mahlstab: Lüneburg*, [1845?] 8°.　　**D. 856. b. (8.)**

— Liederbuch für deutsche Künstler. *Berlin*, 1833. 8°.　　　　　　**B. 700.**

— Liederbuch für Deutsche Studenten. Mit grösstentheils mehrstimmigen Sangweisen. Zweite Auflage. *H. W. Schmidt: Halle*, 1852. 16°.　　　　　　**A. 1168.**

— Liederbuch für Turner. *Thorn*, 1846. *obl.* 8°.　　**A. 718.**

— Peter Schöffers Liederbuch. Mainz 1513. [For a modern facsimile:] *See* DEUTSCHE. [Fünff und sechzig teutscher Lieder, vormals iñ truck nie ussgangen.]

— [Peter Schöffers Liederbuch. For the edition of 1536:] *See* TEUTSCHE. [Fünff und sechzig teütscher Lieder, *etc.*]

LIEDEREN

— Liederen van Groot-Nederland. *See* COERS (F. R.)

LIEDEREN-ALBUM

— Liederen-Album. 24 der meest geliefkoosde Coupletten en Comique Scènes voorgedragen en gezogen in de Salons des Variétés te Amsterdam. *Amsterdam*, 1859. 8°.　　**B. 730.**

— Liederen-Album. 48 ... Coupletten en Comique Scènes, gezongen en voorgedragen in de Salons des Variétés te Amsterdam. *Leiden*, [1870.] 8°.　　　　　　**B. 703.**

LIEDERFRUEHLING

— Liederfrühling. [Part-song.] *See* HEGAR (F.)

LIEDERGARTEN

— Liedergarten für Höhere Töchterschulen. *See* ABT (F. W.)

LIEDERHAIN

— Liederhain für Kinder. 25 Lieder. *See* GRAMM (C.)

LIEDERHEFT

— Liederheft für Margot und ... [H. H. S., i.e. H. H. Stuckenschmidt.] Sieben Lieder nach Gedichten von Carl Sandburg. pp. 16. *Ed. Bote & G. Bock: Berlin, Wiesbaden*, [1952.] 4°. *On the titlepage the initials H. H. S. are represented by a musical cipher.*　　　　　　**G. 1276. o. (24.)**

LIEDERHORT

— Der Liederhort Dichtungen von Müller von der Werra, mit Originalcompositionen von L. Spohr, P. v. Lindpaintner, Schnyder v. Wartensee, F. Lachner, und H. Sczadrowsky. 2 pt. *St. Gallen*, 1855. 8°.　　　　**11525. bb. 42.**

LIEDERKRAENZCHEN

— Liederkränzchen. I. Serenade. [Words by] Isidorus. ⟨II. Vergiss mein nicht. [Words by] Koch. Sternfeld. III. Das Herz. [Words by] Aloys Schreiber. IV. An's ferne Liebchen. [Words by] Lotte. V. Auf der Reise. [Words by] Theodor Hell.

LIEDERKRAENZCHEN

— VI. Schlummerlied. [Words by] Fouqué.⟩ [*Breitkopf und Haertel: Leipzig,* 1817.] 4°.
[*Beilage zur Allgemeinen musikalischen Zeitung. Jahrg.* 19. *no.* 8.] **P. P. 1945.**

— Liederkränzchen. 1. Das Herz. ⟨2. An's ferne Liebchen. 3. Schlummerlied. 4. Vergissmeinnicht.⟩ [*Breitkopf und Haertel: Leipzig,* 1818.] *obl.* 4°.
[*Beilage zur Allgemeinen musikalischen Zeitung. Jahrg.* 20. *no.* 2.] **P. P. 1945.**

LIEDERKREISS

— Liederkreiss. 100 vorzügliche Lieder und Gesänge für eine Stimme mit Begleitung des Pianoforte. *Leipzig,* [1877.] 8°.
F. 596.

LIEDERLUST

— Liederlust. [Part-song.] *See* LACHNER (F.) Neun Gesänge. Op. 169. No. 1.

LIEDERQUELL

— Liederquell. [Song.] *See* WALLNOEFER (A.) Drei Lieder. Op. 3. No. 2.

— Liederquell. [Songs.] *See* WOLFF (B.)

LIEDER-REPERTORIUM

— Lieder-Repertorium. Songs of Germany, with the original words and English, French or Italian versions, adapted & edited by Eminent masters. [The English versions by W. Ball, J. E. E., G. Edwards, H. J. Gauntlett, E. J. Gill, J. Hine, J. J. and E. M. S.] *London,* [1847, *etc.*] fol.
Imperfect; wanting no. 3, 5–9, 11–30, 40–45, 47, 49–68, 70–72, 105, 106, 110–151. **H. 2274.**

LIEDERSAMMLUNG

— Liedersammlung für den schweizerischen Turnverein. Dritte Auflage. pp. 238. *Verlag der Brodtmann'schen Buchhandlung: Schaffhausen,* 1852. 8°. **Hirsch M. 220.**

LIEDERSCHATZ

— Liederschatz. 200 der beliebtesten Volks- Vaterlands- Soldaten- Jäger- Studenten und Liebes-Lieder für eine Singstimme mit Pianofortebegleitung. pp. 216. *C. F. Peters: Leipzig,* [1870.] 8°. **R. M. 25. e. 12.**

— Lieder-Schatz. Eine Auswahl der beliebtesten Volks-, Vaterlands-, Soldaten-, Jäger-, Studenten-, und Liebes-Lieder für eine Singstimme mit Pianoforte-Begleitung. 2 Bd. *C. F. Peters: Leipzig & Berlin,* [1875?] 8°. **F. 612.**

LIEDERSPENDE

— Liederspende aus dem Verlage von Trautwein und Cº ... Sammlung ausgewählter Gesänge für eine Singstimme mit Pianoforte Begleitung, *etc.* 24 no. *Trautwein und Co.: Berlin,* [1840?] *obl.* fol.
No. 5, 7, 9, 11, 13, 15, 17, 32, 33, 34, 36, 43, 47, 53–7, 59, 61, 67, 70, 71 *and* 76 *only.* **R. M. 25. d. 9. (1.)**

LIEDERTAFEL

— Der Liedertafel im Grünen. [Part-song.] *See* ABT (F. W.) Frühlingsfeier. No. 8.

— Liedertafel-Polka. Quartet. *See* SCHAEFFER (H.)

LIEDERTAUFE

— Liedertaufe. Männerchor. *See* REICHEL (F.) Vier Männerchöre. Op. 7. No. 4.

LIEDER-WALZER

— Lieder-Walzer für vierstimmigen Männerchor. *See* LOHR (F.)

LIEDES

— Des Liedes Gruss. [Part-song.] *See* PHILLIPS (L. B.)

LIEDESBOTSCHAFT

— Liedesbotschaft. [Song.] *See* GOLTERMANN (G. E.) Ausgewählte Lieder ... No. 4.

LIEDLER

— Der Liedler. Ballade. *See* SCHUBERT (F. P.)

LIEFDE (JAN DE)

— Liefdeklanken. Nagelaten Liederen van J. de Liefde. Verzameld door C. R. Frowein, *etc.* I. *Höveker & Zoon: Amsterdam,* [1888.] 8°. **C. 577.**

LIEFELD (ALBERT D.)

— Rockaway Waltzes. [P. F.] *Haydn Music Pub. Co.: Pittsburgh, Pa.,* 1899. fol. **h. 3286. g. (27.)**

LIEGE

— Liege Lady of the Millions. Chorus. *See* VINCENT (C. J.) Songs and Part-Songs, *etc.* No. 55.

LIÈGE. — *Academia Leodiensis.* — *Bibliothèque*

— Liber fratrum cruciferorum Leodiensium. ⟨Manuscrit 888 de la Bibl. de l'Université de Liège. Pièces diverses de A. Gabrieli, P. Phillips, J.P. Sweelinck, Cl. Merulo, G. Scronx, Brown. [Edited by] Alexandre Guilmant, avec la collaboration de André Pirro.⟩ *In:* GUILMANT (Alexandre) Archives des maîtres de l'orgue. vol. 10. pp. 1–165. [1909–11.] fol. **h. 2699.**

LIEGL (LEOPOLD)

— *See* CHOPIN (F. F.) Prelude ... Op. 28. No. 7 ... Transcribed by L. Liegl. 1940. 8°. **e. 668. i. (11.)**

— *See* GLUCK (C. W. von) [Orfeo. Act II.—Ballet.] Dance of the happy Spirits ... Transcribed by L. Liegl. 1940. 8°
e. 668. i. (12.)

— *See* HAENDEL (G. F.) [Suite de Pièces. 2nd Collection. No. 4.] Sarabande ... Transcribed by L. Liegl. 1940. 8°.
e. 668. l. (1.)

— *See* MOZART (W. A.) [Don Giovanni.] Menuet [Finale, Act I] ... Quartet for B♭ Clarinets ... Transcribed by L. Liegl. 1940. 8°. **e. 668. i. (16.)**

— *See* SCHARWENKA (F. X.) [Album für die Jugend. Op. 62. No. 11.] Andante. Quartet for B♭ Clarinets ... Transcribed by L. Liegl. 1940. 8°. **e. 668. i. (14.)**

LIEHMANN (Jos.)

— Alboni Polka, für das Piano Forte. *London,* [1845.] fol. **h. 935. (28.)**

— Banquet-walzer, für das Piano Forte. *London,* [1845.] fol. **h. 935. (29.)**

LIEMANN (OSCAR)

— Oscar Liemann's Miniature Overtures for the Piano. Op. 85
... No. 1. The Poet and the Bird. No. 2. The Caliph's
Daughter. No. 3. The Soldiers of the Crown. No. 4. The
Masked Ball. No. 5. A Midsummer Day Dream. No. 6. A
Night in Naples. No. 7. The Magic Magpie. No. 8. The Bridal
of the Queen. No. 9. The Diamonds of Bagdad. No. 10. The
Miller and the Maid. No. 11. The Lady of the Isle. No. 12. A
Fête in Seville. 12 no. *Beal, Stuttard & Co.: London*, [1912.]
fol.   **h. 3284. g. (27.)**

LIEMOHN (EDWIN)

— His Strength is in the Hills. O Vermeland. For Chorus of
Mixed Voices unaccompanied. Swedish Folk Melody. Choral
arrangement and harmonization by E. Liemohn. *Galaxy
Music Corporation: New York*, 1941. 8°.   **F. 1771. h. (18.)**

— In the midst of Christmas Night. For chorus of mixed voices
unaccompanied. [Words by] Nicolai Grundtvig. English
version by I. Dorrum. Danish carol, arranged by E. Liemohn.
pp. 6. *Galaxy Music Corporation: New York*, [1954.] 8°.
F. 260. f. (28.)

LIEPE (EMIL)

— *See* WAGNER (W. R.) Der fliegende Holländer. Album für
eine Singstimme mit Pianoforte. Herausgegeben ... von
E. Liepe, *etc.* 1913. 8°.   **E. 1683. c. (1.)**

— *See* WAGNER (W. R.) Der fliegende Holländer. Album für
Pianoforte ... Herausgegeben ... von E. Liepe, *etc.* (1911.) 4°.
g. 379. m. (1.)

— *See* WAGNER (W. R.) Die Meistersinger von Nürnberg. Album
für eine Singstimme mit Pianoforte, herausgegeben ... von
E. Liepe, *etc.* (1912.) 8°.   **E. 1683. a. (2.)**

— *See* WAGNER (W. R.) Die Meistersinger von Nürnberg. Album
für Pianoforte ... Herausgegeben ... von E. Liepe, *etc.* (1912.)
4°.   **g. 379. m. (3.)**

— *See* WAGNER (W. R.) Die Meistersinger von Nürnberg.
Walters Preislied. Herausgegeben ... von E. Liepe, *etc.* (1912.)
8°.   **F. 637. qq. (6.)**

— *See* WAGNER (W. R.) [Der Ring des Nibelungen.] Das
Rheingold. Album für eine Singstimme mit Pianoforte,
herausgegeben ... von E. Liepe, *etc.* (1912.) 8°.
E. 1683. b. (1.)

— *See* WAGNER (W. R.) [Der Ring des Nibelungen.] Das
Rheingold. Album für Pianoforte ... Herausgegeben ... von
E. Liepe, *etc.* (1912.) 4°.   **g. 379. m. (5.)**

— *See* WAGNER (W. R.) [Der Ring des Nibelungen.] Die
Walküre. Album für eine Singstimme mit Pianoforte,
herausgegeben ... von E. Liepe, *etc.* (1912.) 8°.
E. 1683. b. (2.)

— *See* WAGNER (W. R.) [Der Ring des Nibelungen.] Die
Walküre. Album für Pianoforte ... Herausgegeben ... von
E. Liepe, *etc.* (1912.) 4°.   **g. 379. m. (10.)**

— *See* WAGNER (W. R.) Tannhäuser. Album für eine Singstimme
mit Pianoforte herausgegeben ... von E. Liepe, *etc.* (1912.) 8°.
E. 1683. a. (1.)

— *See* WAGNER (W. R.) Tannhäuser. Album für Pianoforte ...
Herausgegeben ... von E. Liepe, *etc.* (1912.) 4°.
g. 379. m. (7.)

LIEPMANN (KLAUS)

— *See* BACH (J. S.) [Collected Works.—h.] Bach for Beginners.
Nine easy pieces for violin in the first position. Transcribed
and edited by K. Liepmann. [1952.] 4°.   **g. 699. i. (2.)**

LIER (JACQUES VAN)

— Arrangements for Classical Manuscripts for the Violoncello
and Piano. 6 no. *The Strad Edition: London*, 1925. 4°.
g. 510. i. (34.)

— *See* BURMESTER (Willy) Stücke alter Meister ... für
Violoncello und Klavier ... bearbeitet von W. Burmester, *etc.*
⟨Bearbeitung f. Violoncello v. J. van Lier.⟩ [c. 1910.] 4°.
h. 4090. f. (2.)

— *See* MAJOR (Jacob G.) Concerto en la mineur ... pour le
violoncelle avec accompagnement d'orchestre ... Op. 44.
⟨Piano et violoncelle. Revidiert von J. van Lier.⟩ [1904.] fol.
h. 1851. aa. (3.)

— *See* WAGNER (W. R.) [Collected Works.—d.] New
Arrang[e]ments ... by ... J. van Lier, *etc.* [1922.] 4°.
g. 379. q. (3.)

LIES

— Lies. [Song.] *See* ZUCCA (M.) *pseud.*

LIESENBORGHS (FRANZ)

— Rêverie, pour Violon et Piano. Op. 14. No. 1.   *B. Schott's
Söhne: Mayence*, [1907.] fol.   **g. 505. w. (31.)**

LIESS (ANDREAS)

— *See* FUX (J. J.) Zwei Triosonaten ... A-moll ... G-moll ... für
zwei Violinen, Violoncello ... und Continuo, *etc.*
⟨Herausgegeben von A. Lies.⟩ [1941.] 4°.   **g. 409. ll. (5.)**

LIETA

— Lieta al pudico talamo. Aria. *See* CRIVELLI (G.) Due Arie.
No. 1.

LIETH (LEONORE)

— *See* LEITH.

LIETI

— I Lieti amanti. Primo libro de madrigali a cinque voci, di
diversi eccellentissimi musici nouamente composti, & dati in
luce. ⟨Canto.⟩ [The dedication signed by Hippolito Zanluca.]
*Presso Giacomo Vincenzi, & Ricciardo Amadino, compagni:
Venetia*, 1586. 4°.
*The composers named are: H. Fiorino, A. Striggio, O. Vecchi,
R. del Mel, I. Alberti, A. Rota, A. Milleuille, L. Marenzio,
M. Tosoni, A. Ganassi, D. L. Agostini, C. Porta, A. l'hocca,
R. Giouanelli, P. Virchi, G. Vuert, P. Isnardi, A. Gabrielli,
L. Luzzaschi, L. Bertani. Imperfect; wanting the other parts.*
C. 123. s.

— Lieti fiori. Air & Glee. *See* WINTER (P. von) [Il Ratto di
Proserpina.]

LIETO

— Lieto e placido ritorni. Duetto. *See* CARAFA DI COLOBRANO
(M. E. F. V. A. P.) *Prince.* [Elisabetta in Derbyshire.]

— Lieto fra voi ritorno. Quartetto. *See* DONIZETTI (D. G. M.)
[Maria Padilla.]

— Lieto godea sedendo. Madrigal. *See* GABRIELI (A.)
[Concerti.—Libro primo et secondo.]

— Lieto respira omai. Finale. *See* GUGLIELMI (P. C.) [Atalida.]

LIEURANCE (THURLOW)

— From the Yellowstone. A Musical Drama introducing ...
"Four Songs from the Yellowstone" also ... "The bird and
the babe" ... "By weeping waters" and "Where cedars rise"

LIEURANCE (Thurlow)

for mixed quartette and chorus. Drama by C. O. Roos and J. E. Roos. *T. Presser Co.: Philadelphia*, 1921. 8°.
F. 690. gg. (3.)

— All Smiles. Caprice. [P. F.] *T. Presser Co.: Philadelphia*, 1915. fol. **h. 3284. oo. (9.)**

— [American Indian Rhapsody.] Sioux Scalp Dance for the pianoforte for four hands. Arranged ... by P. W. Orem. *T. Presser Co.: Philadelphia*, 1920. 4°. **g. 1127. h. (22.)**

— And I aint got weary yet. [Four-part song for] Men's voices. Arr. by T. Lieurance. *T. Presser Co.: Philadelphia*, 1921. 8°.
F. 163. t. (28.)

— And I aint got weary yet. Mixed voices. Arr. by T. Lieurance. *T. Presser Co.: Philadelphia*, 1921. 8°. **F. 585. gg. (26.)**

— The Angelus. Creole Legend No. 1. Song, words by J. F. Cooke. *T. Presser Co.: Philadelphia*, 1924. 4°.
H. 3622. a. (21.)

— Antonine. [Song, words by] C. O. Roos. *T. Presser Co.: Philadelphia*, 1922. 4°. **H. 3622. a. (22.)**

— April first. *See infra*: Encore Songs. [No. 4.]

— At Parting. Song. [Words by W. Felter.] *T. Presser Co.: Philadelphia*, (1911.) fol. **H. 1792. s. (36.)**

— At the Foot of the Mound. Scene characteristic from the American Indian, for soprano with flute ad libitum. [Words by A. Fletcher.] No. 1. The red birds sing o'er the crystal spring. No. 2. The owl's bleak call. 2 no. *T. Presser Co.: Philadelphia*, 1917. 4°. **G. 426. l. (29.)**

— Autumn Tints. Waltz caprice. [P. F.] *T. Presser Co.: Philadelphia*, 1914. fol. **h. 3284. oo. (10.)**

— Away in a Manger. Lullaby, solo or duet. [Words by] M. Luther. *T. Presser Co.: Philadelphia*, 1919. 4°.
G. 519. g. (35.)

— Beautiful Catalina. Barcarolle. Piano solo. *T. Presser Co.: Philadelphia*, 1916. fol. **h. 3284. oo. (11.)**

— The Bird and the Babe. Lullaby, words and music by T. Lieurance, *etc. T. Presser Co.: Philadelphia*, 1921. 4°.
H. 3622. a. (23.)

— Blossom Dear. [Song, words by] L. Landis. *T. Presser Co.: Philadelphia*, (1911.) fol. **H. 1792. s. (37.)**

— A Blush Rose. Flower song for the piano. *O. Ditson Co.: Boston*, 1916. fol. **h. 3284. oo. (12.)**

— But the Lord is mindful of His own. Sacred Song. *T. Presser Co.: Philadelphia*, (1910.) fol. **H. 1187. rr. (15.)**

— By the Waters of Minnetonka. *See infra*: [Indian Songs. No. 9.]

— By the weeping Waters. [P. F.] *T. Presser Co.: Philadelphia*, 1916. 4°. **g. 442. v. (5.)**

— By the weeping Waters. (Arranged for mixed voices.) *T. Presser Co.: Philadelphia*, 1921. 8°. **F. 585. ll. (30.)**

— By the Wishing Well. An April reverie. [P. F.] *T. Presser Co.: Philadelphia*, 1914. fol. **h. 3284. oo. (14.)**

— Canoe Song. Indian Love. With flute ad lib. *T. Presser Co.: Philadelphia*, 1920. 4°. **H. 3622. a. (17.)**

— Come Holy Ghost, *etc.* [Sacred song.] *T. Presser Co.: Philadelphia*, (1910.) fol. **H. 1187. rr. (16.)**

— Coral Isle. Idyl for the pianoforte. *T. Presser Co.: Philadelphia*, 1919. 4°. **g. 1127. h. (20.)**

— The Dachshund. *See infra*: Encore Songs. [No. 2.]

LIEURANCE (Thurlow)

— The Deserted Lodge. [Song, words by C. O. Roos.] *T. Presser Co.: Philadelphia*, 1922. 4°. **H. 3622. a. (24.)**

— The Donkey Trail, from "Breckinridge Park," for the pianoforte. *T. Presser Co.: Philadelphia*, 1924. 4°.
g. 1127. w. (7*.)

— Down the Stream. Idyl for the pianoforte. *T. Presser Co.: Philadelphia*, 1914. fol. **h. 3284. oo. (15.)**

— Dying Moon Flower. Indian Song. *T. Presser Co.: Philadelphia*, 1919. 4°. **G. 426. l. (30.)**

— The Eagle and the Lark. *See infra*: Songs from the Yellowstone. [No. 2.]

— Encore Songs, *etc. T. Presser Co.: Philadelphia*, 1915, *etc.* fol. & 4°. **H. 3622. (1.)**

— Ever near. [Sacred song, words by] W. Felter. *T. Presser Co.: Philadelphia*, 1915. fol. **H. 3622. (2.)**

— Fantasia on American Indian Themes. For violin and piano. [Score and part.] 2 pt. *G. Schirmer: New York*, [1955.] 4°.
g. 822. m. (16.)

— Farewell! Cabin mine. *See infra*: Songs from the Yellowstone. [No. 4.]

— Felice. Waltz Song, words by L. Landis. *T. Presser Co.: Philadelphia*, (1910.) fol. **H. 1792. s. (38.)**

— Forgotten Trails. Four Songs, words by C. O. Roos ... [No. 1.] In my bark canoe ... [No. 2.] Far off I see a paddle flash ... [No. 3.] A gray wood dove is calling ... [No. 4.] On Cherry Hill. 4 no. *T. Presser Co.: Philadelphia*, 1923. 4°.
H. 3622. a. (25.)

— From a Spanish Garden. Caprice for the pianoforte. *T. Presser Co.: Philadelphia*, 1914. fol. **h. 3284. oo. (16.)**

— From an Indian Village. Song. (Flute and chorus ad lib.) *T. Presser Co.: Philadelphia*, 1919. 4°. **G. 426. l. (31.)**

— From an Indian Village, for the pianoforte. (Transcribed by H. Lewis.) *T. Presser Co.: Philadelphia*, 1921. 4°.
g. 1127. h. (21.)

— From Ghost Dance Canyon. Indian Song. *T. Presser Co.: Philadelphia*, 1920. 4°. **H. 3622. a. (18.)**

— From the Santa Fe Trail. Songs. [No. 1.] Two hundred years ago in Santa Fe ... [No. 2.] Wild bird ... With flute obbligato. 2 no. *T. Presser Co.: Philadelphia*, 1921. 4°.
H. 3622. a. (19.)

— A Garden Coronation. Song. *T. Presser: Philadelphia*, (1909.) fol. **H. 1794. vv. (55.)**

— George and his Father. *See supra*: Encore Songs. [No. 5.]

— Ghost Pipes. Song, words by C. O. Roos. *T. Presser Co.: Philadelphia*, 1923. 4°. **H. 3622. a. (26.)**

— Ghost Pipes. Indian idyl for violin and piano, with 'cello ad lib. by Lieurance-Cardin. *T. Presser Co.: Philadelphia*, 1924. 4°. **g. 409. n. (15.)**

— The Good Rain. Song, words by C. O. Ross [or rather, Roos]. *T. Presser Co.: Philadelphia*, 1921. 4°. **H. 3622. a. (8.)**

— Holiday Pleasures. Valse caprice for the pianoforte. *T. Presser Co.: Philadelphia*, 1916. fol. **h. 3284. oo. (17.)**

— Hymn to the Sun God. Indian Song. ([Words by] A. Fletcher.) *T. Presser Co.: Philadelphia*, 1917. 4°. **G. 425. x. (26.)**

— I wonder why? *See supra*: Encore Songs. [No. 1.]

— If I hadn't had you, my dear. [Song, words by] E. M. Clark. *T. Presser Co.: Philadelphia*, (1911.) fol. **H. 1792. s. (39.)**

LIEURANCE (THURLOW)

— In a Jinrikisha. Song. *T. Presser Co.: Philadelphia*, 1914. fol.
H. 3622. (3.)

— Indian Flute Call and Love Song. Recorded and harmonized by T. Lieurance. [P. F.] *T. Presser Co.: Philadelphia*, 1914. fol.
h. 3284. oo. (19.)

— Indian Melodies, for violin and piano. *T. Presser Co.: Philadelphia*, 1917. 4°.
g. 223. dd. (19.)

— Indian Songs. [Composed on native melodies] By T. Lieurance, *etc.* [With English words by E. D. Proctor and others.] 11 no. *T. Presser Co.: Philadelphia*, 1913–15. fol.
H. 3622. (4.)

— Nine Indian Songs with descriptive Notes, [collected and arranged] by T. Lieurance. *T. Presser Co.: Philadelphia*, (1913.) 4°.
G. 385. tt. (9.)

— Nine Indian Songs with descriptive notes, [collected and arranged] by T. Lieurance. *Chappell & Co.: London and Sydney*, [1925.] 4°.
G. 981. d. (1.)

Indian Songs. No. 9

— By the Waters of Minnetonka. An Indian Love Song, with violin or flute accompaniment ad lib., words by J. M. Cavanass. *Chappell & Co.: London*, 1917. fol.
H. 3622. (12.)

— By the Waters of Minnetonka ... Recital edition. High voice. *T. Presser Co.: Philadelphia*, 1921. 4°.
H. 3622. (13.)

— By the Waters of Minnetonka ... Vocal Duet. *T. Presser Co.: Philadelphia*, 1919. 4°.
G. 390. u. (5.)

— By the Waters of Minnetonka, *etc.* [P. F.] *T. Presser Co.: Philadelphia*, 1915. fol.
h. 3284. oo. (13.)

— By the Waters of Minnetonka. Arranged for violin & pianoforte by T. Lieurance. *Chappell & Co.: London and Sydney*, [1924.] 4°.
g. 505. kk. (37.)

— By the Waters of Minnetonka. An Indian love song. Cornet solo. Arranged for military band by W. J. Duthoit. ⟨Conductor [and parts].⟩ 32 pt. *In:* CHURCHILL (Frank E.) Snow White and the seven Dwarfs, *etc.* [1938.] fol. [*Chappell's Army Journal. no.* 647.]
h. 1562.

— Indian Spring Bird. Ski-bi-bi-la. Indian Song. [Words by A. Fletcher.] *T. Presser Co.: Philadelphia*, 1919. 4°.
G. 426. f. (17.)

— Indian Suite. Harmonized by T. Lieurance. [P. F.] *T. Presser Co.: Philadelphia*, 1914. fol.
h. 3284. oo. (18.)

— Irish Spring Song. *See supra:* Encore Songs. [No. 3.]

— The Lily Pond, for the pianoforte. *T. Presser Co.: Philadelphia*, 1914. fol.
h. 3284. oo. (20.)

— Lola. [Song.] *T. Presser Co.: Philadelphia*, (1911.) fol.
H. 1792. s. (40.)

— The Lone Loon's Cry. *See infra:* Under Northern Skies, *etc.* [No. 1.]

— A Lone Owl is calling. *See infra:* Under Northern Skies, *etc.* [No. 3.]

— Long will be the Years of Parting. [Song. Words by] C. O. Roos. *T. Presser Co.: Philadelphia*, 1924. 4°. One of *"Songs from the White Dawn"*.
H. 3622. a. (4.)

— Lullaby. Wiegenlied. Berceuse. [Song, words by] C. F. Horner. *T. Presser Co.: Philadelphia*, 1915. fol.
H. 3622. (5.)

LIEURANCE (THURLOW)

— Maleana. A Love Song from the Hawaiian. [Words by] C. F. Horner. *T. Presser Co.: Philadelphia*, 1915. fol.
H. 3622. (6.)

— Maleana ... Arranged for male voices by W. H. Lewis. *T. Presser Co.: Philadelphia*, 1924. 8°.
F. 163. v. (24.)

— Maytime. [Song.] *T. Presser Co.: Philadelphia*, (1912.) fol.
H. 1792. s. (41.)

— Medicine Dance.—Menominee Indians.—Three or Five-part Mixed Chorus with Tom-Toms—Indian Drums—Bass Drum, Gong—or Cymbals—with Piano accompaniment. Based on traditional Indian Melodies. Adapted and arranged by T. Lieurance. *C. Fischer: New York, etc.*, 1939. 8°.
F. 1771. g. (47.)

— Moonlit Lake of the Isles. Legend and Barcarolle. [Three-part song.] *C. C. Birchard & Co.: Boston*, [1925.] 8°.
F. 371. (28.)

— A Mountain Madrigal. *See infra:* Songs from the Yellowstone. [No. 1.]

— My Collie Dog. *See infra:* Songs from the Yellowstone. [No. 3.]

— My Flute Call haunts the wild Wood. Song, words by C. O. Roos. *T. Presser Co.: Philadelphia*, 1924. 4°.
H. 3622. a. (1.)

— My Spanish Rosa. Song. [Words by W. Felter.] *T. Presser Co.: Philadelphia*, 1913. fol.
H. 3622. (7.)

— The Nightingale and the Rose. Waltz ... Vocal solo. [Words by W. Felter.] *T. Presser Co.: Philadelphia*, 1914. fol.
H. 3622. (8.)

— The Owl's bleak Call. *See supra:* At the Foot of the Mound ... No. 2.

— Paying more for it. *See supra:* Encore Songs. [No. 8.]

— A Prayer. Sacred Song, words by W. Felter. *T. Presser: Philadelphia*, (1909.) fol.
H. 1187. ll. (7.)

— Proposal. Waltz Song. [Words by] B. Taylor. *T. Presser Co.: Philadelphia*, 1912. fol.
H. 3622. (9.)

— Rainbow Land. [Song.] With violin and 'cello ad lib. *T. Presser Co.: Philadelphia*, 1916. fol.
H. 3622. (14.)

— The Red Birds sing o'er the crystal Spring. *See supra:* At the Foot of the Mound ... No. 1.

— Romance in A. Piano solo. *T. Presser Co.: Philadelphia*, 1915. fol.
h. 3284. oo. (21.)

— A Rose on an Indian Grave. Indian Song. *T. Presser Co.: Philadelphia*, 1919. 4°.
G. 426. l. (32.)

— Rue. [Song, words by A. Fletcher.] Violin or flute obbligato. *T. Presser Co.: Philadelphia*, 1916. fol.
H. 3622. (16.)

— Sad Moon of Falling Leaf. [Song, words by] C. O. Roos. *T. Presser Co.: Philadelphia*, 1922. 4°.
H. 3622. a. (9.)

— Sa-ma-wee-no. Menominee Love Song. Dearest sweetheart. Song with violin obbligato. *T. Presser Co.: Philadelphia*, 1924. 4°.
H. 3622. a. (2.)

— The Sand Man. [Song, words by] P. H. Miles, *etc. T. Presser Co.: Philadelphia*, (1910.) fol.
G. 807. yy. (37.)

— Sioux Indian Fantasie, for flute and piano. *T. Presser Co.: Philadelphia*, 1921. 4°.
g. 70. g. (5.)

— A Sioux Maiden's Dream. Sioux Indian Song. (Text in Sioux.) *T. Presser Co.: Philadelphia*, 1924. 4°.
H. 3622. a. (3.)

— Sioux Scalp Dance. *See supra:* [American Indian Rhapsody.]

LIEURANCE (THURLOW)

— A Sioux Serenade. [Song, words by A. Fletcher.] With flute ad lib. *T. Presser Co.: Philadelphia*, 1916. fol.   **H. 3622. (15.)**

— Sketches in Miniature. 5 piano compositions, *etc. T. Presser Co.: Philadelphia*, 1924. 4°.   **g. 1127. w. (8.)**

— Smile. [Song, words by] C. F. Horner, *etc. T. Presser Co.: Philadelphia*, 1915. fol.   **H. 3622. (10.)**

— Snapshots. *See* supra: Encore Songs. [No. 7.]

— Sometime. [Song.] Words by W. Felter. *Windsor Music Co.: Chicago, New York*, 1903. fol.   **G. 807. z. (38.)**

— Songs from the Yellowstone. [No. 1.] A mountain madrigal. [No. 2.] The eagle and the lark. [No. 3.] My collie dog. [No. 4.] Farewell! Cabin mine. 4 no. *T. Presser Co.: Philadelphia*, 1920, 21. 4°.   **H. 3622. a. (20.)**

— The Spirit of Wanna. Indian Song. (Translation by Medicine Moon.) *T. Presser Co.: Philadelphia*, 1919. 4°.   **G. 426. f. (18.)**

— The Spirit of Wanna. Indian Song ... Violin and piano. *T. Presser Co.: Philadelphia*, 1919. 4°.   **g. 500. d. (9.)**

— The Swallows. *See* infra: Under Northern Skies, *etc.* [No. 2.]

— Tender Musings. For the pianoforte. pp. 5. *Theodore Presser: Philadelphia*, [1909.] fol.   **h. 4120. qq. (3.)**

— To Celia. Song, words by J. C. Lindberg. *T. Presser Co.: Philadelphia*, 1924. 4°.   **H. 3622. a. (5.)**

— Towona. Descriptive two-step. [P.F.] pp. 4. *Windsor Music Co.: Chicago, New York*, [1904.] fol.   **h. 4120. qq. (4.)**

— The Tulip. [Song, words by] C. F. Horner. *T. Presser Co.: Philadelphia*, 1915. fol.   **H. 3622. (11.)**

— Two Hundred Years ago in Santa Fe. *See* supra: From the Santa Fe Trail, *etc.* [No. 1.]

— 'Um, not me. *See* supra: Encore Songs. [No. 10.]

— Under Northern Skies. Three Songs, words by J. E. Roos. [No. 1.] The lone loon's cry. [No. 2.] The swallows. [No. 3.] A lone owl is calling. 3 no. *T. Presser Co.: Philadelphia*, 1924. 4°.   **H. 3622. a. (6.)**

— Valse Impromptu. For the pianoforte. pp. 7. *Theodore Presser: Philadelphia*, [1909.] fol.   **h. 4120. qq. (5.)**

— Wasté wala ka kelo. I love you so. Song, words by A. Fletcher. *T. Presser Co.: Philadelphia*, 1923. 4°.   **H. 3622. a. (10.)**

— Where Cedars rise. [Song, words by] C. O. Roos. *T. Presser Co.: Philadelphia*, 1921. 4°.   **H. 3622. a. (11.)**

— Where Dawn and Sunset meet. Song, words by C. O. Roos. *T. Presser Co.: Philadelphia*, 1923. 4°.   **H. 3622. a. (12.)**

— Where drowsy Waters steal. Song, words by C. O. Roos. *T. Presser Co.: Philadelphia*, 1924. 4°.   **H. 3622. a. (13.)**

— Where the Papoose swings. Two Songs. [No. 1.] My love, my lark ... [No. 2.] O'er the Indian cradle. 2 no. *T. Presser Co.: Philadelphia*, 1918. 4°.   **G. 390. u. (6.)**

— Where the sad Waters flow. [Song, words by] C. O. Roos. *T. Presser Co.: Philadelphia*, 1922. 4°.   **H. 3622. a. (14.)**

— The Whistling Mallards fly. [Song, words by] C. O. Roos. *T. Presser Co.: Philadelphia*, 1922. 4°.   **H. 3622. a. (15.)**

— Wild Bird. *See* supra: From the Santa Fe Trail, *etc.* [No. 2.]

— Winnebago Lament. Indian Song, words and music by T. Lieurance. *T. Presser Co.: Philadelphia*, 1924. 4°.   **H. 3622. a. (7.)**

— A Wise Bird. *See* supra: Encore Songs. [No. 9.]

LIEURANCE (THURLOW)

— With Spanish Grace. Entr'acte. [P. F.] *T. Presser Co.: Philadelphia*, 1914. fol.   **h. 3284. oo. (22.)**

— Wounded Fawn. Song. *T. Presser Co.: Philadelphia*, 1919. 4°.   **G. 390. u. (7.)**

— The Year of dry Leaves. [Song, words by] C. O. Roos. *T. Presser Co.: Philadelphia*, 1922. 4°.   **H. 3622. a. (16.)**

— *See* CARDIN (F.) Cree War Dance. On an Indian melody, recorded by T. Lieurance, *etc.* 1924. 4°.   **g. 822. (6.)**

— *See* CHOPIN (F. F.) Prelude. Op. 28. No. 7. Arr. by T. Lieurance. 1916. fol.   **h. 471. f. (19.)**

— *See* SYKES (P.) I want to go to Heaven like a Feather in the Air ... Adapted by T. Lieurance. 1918. 4°.   **G. 519. f. (35.)**

LIEUTENANT

— Lieutenant Luff. Comic ballad. *See* BLEWITT (J.)

— Lieutenant Luff. Part Song. *See* WAIT (W. M.)

LIEUX

— Lieux fortunés où Gabrielle. Duo. *See* MÉHUL (É. N.) [Gabrielle d'Estrées.]

LIEVEN (NILS V.)

— *See* MOZART (W. A.) [*Collected Works.—b.*] Hausmusik von Mozart und Weber. Kanons, Duette, Lieder. Klavierbegleitung zu den Kanons von N. V. Lieven. [1936.] *obl.* 8°. [*Völkische Musikerziehung. Jahrg. 2. Hft. 11. Notenbeilage* 19.]   **07903. d. 33.**

LIEW (MARY B. VAN)

— *See* VAN LIEW.

LIFAR (SERGE)

— *See* HONEGGER (A.) Le Cantique des Cantiques ... Musique ... sur les rythmes de S. Lifar. 1938. 8°.   **f. 541. d. (1.)**

LIFE

— Life. [Song.] *See* AUSTIN (E.) [Songs. Op. 10. No. 3.]

— Life. [Part-song.] *See* BATSON (A. W.)

— Life. [Song.] *See* BLUMENTHAL (Jacob)

— Life. [Song.] *See* BROAKER (Ethel)

— A Life. [Song.] *See* BROCKWAY (H.)

— Life. [Song.] *See* BURLEIGH (H. T.)

— Life. Cantata. *See* BURTON (L. L.)

— Life! [Part-song.] *See* CASEY (S. W.)

— Life. Part-Song. *See* CUMMINGS (W. H.)

— Life. Song. *See* DUMBRECK (E. K.)

— Life. [Song.] *See* GOATLEY (A.)

— Life. Duet. *See* HECHT (E.)

— Life. [Song.] *See* KAVANAGH (I.) Six Songs for high voice. No. 1.

— Life. Song. *See* KNIGHT (J. P.)

— Life! Part Song. *See* KNIGHT (R.)

— Life. Song. *See* KRENKEL (G.)

LIFE

— Life. Cantata. *See* MacCalla (J.)

— Life. [Service of song.] *See* Meredith (I. H.)

— Life. Song. *See* O'Hara (G. de V.)

— Life. [Song.] *See* Riker (F. W.) Two Songs, *etc.* [No. 2.]

— Life. [Song.] *See* Salter (M. T.) Five Songs, *etc.* [No. 5.]

— Life. Song. *See* Sharpe (E.) A Short Series of Encore Songs. No. 7.

— Life! [Song.] *See* Sherwood (P.) Songs from the "Golden Treasury". Op. 16. No. 3.

— Life. [Musical play.] *See* Skillings (Otis)

— Life. Song. *See* Smyth (C. F.)

— Life. Song. *See* Sparrowe (J. E.)

— Life. [Song.] *See* Speaks (O.)

— Life. [Song.] *See* Thomas (Mansel)

— Life again to-day! Song. *See* Neidlinger (W. H.)

— Life and Blossom. Song. *See* Quayle (E.)

— Life and Death. [Song.] *See* Neidlinger (W. H.)

— Life and Death. Song. *See* Taylor (S. C.)

— Life and Death. Song. *See* Wood (*Sir* H. J.)

— Yᵉ. Life and Death of bad Macbethe. [Song.] *See* Locke (M.) [*Doubtful and Supposititious Works.*] [Macbeth.]

— Life and I. Song. *See* Solomon (E.) [The Red Hussar.]

— Life and its Follies. Part Song. *See* Wood (C.) *Mus.Doc.*

— Life and Liberty. Song. *See* Guise (H. J. W.)

— Life and Light. Song. *See* Edwards (H. J.)

— Life and Light. [Sacred song.] *See* Hawley (C. B.)

— Life and Light and Joy. [Unison song.] *See* Palmer (Florence M. S.)

— Life and Love. Song. *See* Ajello (G.)

— Life and Love. Song. *See* Baker (H. S.)

— Life and Love. Songs. *See* Bruce (E.)

— Life and Love. [Song.] *See* Guion (D. W.) Three Songs ... II.

— Life and Love. Sacred Song. *See* Haddock (G. P.)

— Life and Love. [Song.] *See* Herbert (V.)

— Life and Love. Song. *See* Hill (D.)

— Life and Love. Song. *See* Izett (D.)

— Life and Love. Song. *See* Marlois (E.) [The Crimean Cross.]

— Life and Love. Song. *See* Thomson (B.)

— Life and the Day. Song. *See* Carnell (F. D.)

— Life and the Flower. Song. *See* Lee (A.)

— Life and the Flower. [Song.] *See* Louis (E.)

— Life and the Rose. Song. *See* Johnson (H.)

— Life and the Rose. [Song.] *See* Needham (E. E.)

— Life at Sea. Operetta. *See* Pattison (T. M.)

— Life, be kind. Song. *See* Purcell (Daniel) [Wanton Cupids cease to hover.]

LIFE

— A Life beyond. Song. *See* Appleton (N.)

— The Life beyond. Song. *See* Aylward (F.)

— The Life beyond. Solo and Chorus. *See* Jamouneau (A. J.)

— The Life beyond. Song. *See* Rodney (P.) *pseud.*

— The Life Brigade. Song. *See* Haswell (T.)

— A Life Builder. Part-Song. *See* Geibel (A.)

— A Life by de Galley Fire. Song. *See* Keller (Albert)

— Life calls to me. [Song.] *See* Zádor (E.)

— The Life Chase. Song. *See* Silas (E.)

— The Life-Clock. Song. *See* Barnett (J.)

— Life Cycle. Cantata. *See* Mellers (Wilfrid H.) The Resources of Music.

— The Life, Death and Burial of Cock Robin. *See* Little. Little Robin Red Breast sat upon a Pole. [Cantata. By Elizabeth, Princess of England?] [1797?] fol.   **K. 9. c. 13.**

— The Life Divine. Sacred Cantata. *See* Elliott (J.)

— Life eternal. Anthem. *See* Fox (O. J.)

— Life Eternal. [Anthem.] *See* Jordan (J.)

— Life eternal. Processional. *See* Leighter (H. C.)

— The Life Everlasting. Cantata. *See* Matthews (H. A.)

— The Life everlasting. [Song.] *See* Mayo (J.)

— The Life everlasting. Sacred Song. *See* Pearce (C. W.)

— Life Everlasting. Cantata. *See* Petrie (H. W.)

— Life, fair Moments is bringing. Song. *See* Gounod (C. F.) [Roméo et Juliette.—Je veux vivre.]

— Life for Life. [Song.] *See* Hely (A. A.)

— Life for the Boys. Song-Cycle. *See* Moffat (A. E.)

— Life for the King. [Part-song.] *See* Glinka (M. I.) [Жизнь за царя.]

— Life for thee is brightly smiling. [Song.] *See* Verdi (F. G. F.) [Un Ballo in Maschera.—Alla vita che t'arride.]

— Life for To-day. Song. *See* Fisher (A. W.)

— Life forevermore! Anthem. *See* Bergé (I.)

— Life has sent me many Roses. Song. *See* Loehr (H.) [Songs of Roumania. No. 2.]

— Life hath many joys. Ballad. *See* Morden (P. E. van)

— Life hath Nothing that's eternal. Song. *See* Brentnall (E.)

— Life! I know not what thou art. Part Song. *See* Wadely (F. W.)

— The Life I owe. Song service. *See* Witty (Robert)

— Life in a day. [Song.] *See* MacHardy (J. M. P.)

— Life in a Love. [Song.] *See* Bantock (*Sir* G.)

— Life in a love. [Song.] *See* MacHardy (J. M. P.)

— Life in Christ. Sacred Song. *See* Tiller (J. G.)

— Life in Death. [Song.] *See* Laurens (H. A.)

— Life in London. Song. *See* Voigt (A.)

— Life in Love. Song. *See* Le Jeune (A.)

LIFE

— Life in Quashibungo. [Comic song.] *See* WALKER (H.)

— Life in the East of London. Song. *See* WEST (Arthur)

— A Life in the Fields. [Song.] *See* WILSON (W.)

— Life in the Loom. [Hymn.] *See* STEBBINS (G. C.)

— Life in the old Girl yet. [Song.] *See* COWARD (*Sir* Noël P.) [London Calling.]

— A Life in the West. [Song.] *See* RUSSELL (H.)

— Life in the West End of London. Song. *See* WEST (Arthur)

— A Life in the woods for me. Song. *See* HODSON (G. A.)

— Life is a Caravan. Song. *See* RIEGO (T. del)

— Life is a Chase. Unison song. *See* AGER (Laurence)

— Life is a child. Ballad. *See* KNIGHT (J. P.)

— Life is a Garden. Song. *See* ABT (F. W.)

— Life is a Merry-go-round. [Song.] *See* BURT (Benjamin H.)

— Life is a Nightingale. Song. *See* BORTON (A.)

— Life is a River. [Hymn.] *See* CHALLINOR (F. A.)

— Life is a river. Song. *See* NELSON (S.)

— Life is a river. Part song. *See* WRIGLEY (F.)

— Life is a Song. Song. *See* MEALE (A.)

— Life is a Sonnet. Song. *See* BARTLETT (H. N.)

— Life is bright. Duet. *See* HONIG (L.) [The King's Command.]

— Life is but a Dream. [Song.] *See* OLCOTT (Grace)

— Life is but a dream. Song. *See* PECKET (A. J.)

— Life is but a little Moment. Song. *See* CHAPPELL (Harold)

— Life is but a melancholy Flower. [Part-song.] *See* ROMA (C.)

— Life is but a Song. [Song.] *See* PETRIE (Henry W.)

— Life is but a Summer Day. Duetto. *See* BALFE (Michael W.) [Diadeste.]

— Life is chequered. [Song.] *See* GREENE (M.) [The Chaplet.]

— Life is darkened o'er with Woe. Song. *See* WEBER (Carl M. F. E. von) [Der Freischütz.—Hier im ird'schen Jammerthal.]

— Life is empty. [Song.] *See* DARÈME (George)

— Life is fleet, my darling. [Song.] *See* TENNANT (C. R.)

— Life is floating o'er me! [Song.] *In:* The Musical Bijou ... for MDCCCXLII. p. 55. [1842.] fol. **H. 2330.**

— Life is full of happy Hours. Duet. *See* MAYNARD (W.) *pseud.*

— Life is full of pearls. Song. *See* MOUNSEY, afterwards BARTHOLOMEW (A. S.)

— Life is just what you make it. Song. *See* HILLIER (L. H.)

— Life is like a game of cricket. Song. *See* HALL (F.)

— Life is like a Game of Football. [Musical monologue.] *See* PARRY (A. W.)

— Life is like a game of See Saw. [Song.] *See* HUNT (G.W.)

— Life is like a Song. Song. *See* TURNER (Olive M.)

— Life is like a summer morning. Song. *See* GLOVER (S.)

LIFE

— Life is like an evening shadow. Sacred song. *See* WEBER (C. M. F. E. von) [Der Freischütz.—Leise, leise.]

— Life is Nothing without Money. Aria. *See* BEETHOVEN (L. van) [Leonore.—Hat man nicht auch Gold beneben.]

— Life is passing. [Song.] *See* BEETHOVEN (L. van) [6 Lieder. Op. 48. No. 3. Vom Tode.]

— Life is passing away. Two-part song. *See* PINSUTI (C. E.)

— Life is passing like a Dream. Song. *See* FERNER (A.)

— Life is quite endurable. [Song.] *See* CORLISS (Edward W.) What happened then? [4.]

— Life is short. *See* FLOTOW (F. F. A. von) *Baron.* [Martha.—Jägerinn schlau in Sinn.]

— Life is so short. Song. *See* LANZEROTTI (A.)

— Life is so sweet. Song. *See* QUAYLE (E.)

— Life is such a Bore. [Song.] *See* AARONS (Alfred E.)

— Life is such a little Thing. Song. *See* DREVOR (O.)

— Life is sweet, Brother. [Song.] *See* HARRIS (G.) *Songwriter.* Three Songs, *etc.* [No. 3.]

— Life is sweet, the world is fair. Song. *See* BOSCHER (E.)

— Life is too short to be sad. [Song.] *See* STANISLAUS (H.)

— Life is too short to be wasting your Time. [Song.] *See* BRATTON (John W.) [The Man from China.—What's the Use.]

— Life is what you make it. [Song.] *See* ARNOLD (B.)

— Life Leaves. Song. *See* REUTER (G. J. de)

— A Life Lesson. [Song.] *See* HOLLINS (A.)

— A Life-Lesson. Song. *See* MAUD (C.)

— A Life Lesson. [Song.] *See* NEVIN (E. W.)

— Life let us cherish. [First edited by H. G. Nägeli.] Harmonized for the Musical Magazine & Review. [S.S.B.] *In:* The New Musical Magazine. vol. 1, no. 3. pp. 29–31. 1809. 4°. **R. M. 8. a. 2.**

— Life let us cherish. With variations for the piano forte. pp. 3. *Printed for G. Walker: London,* [WM1815.] fol. **h. 723. ee. (22.)**

— Life let us cherish. Ballad. *See* MOZART (W. A.) [*Doubtful and Supposititious Works.*]

— Life let us cherish. [Song.] *See* NAEGELI (H. G.) [Freut euch des Lebens.]

— Life, Life, Life. Song. *See* HELLMAN (C. A.)

— Life, Love and Death. Song. *See* POWELL (Orlando)

— Life, Love and you. Song. *See* WILSON (H. J. L.)

— Life nor death shall us dissever. Trio. *See* SMART (H.)

— Life, not Death. [Hymn.] *See* LOTT (J. B.)

— The Life of a Beau. [Song.] *See* CAREY (H.) [The Coffee House.]

— The Life of a Belle. [Song.] *See* CAREY (H.)

— The Life of a Man. Folk songs. *See* STUBBS (Ken)

— The Life of a Rose. [Song.] *See* GERSHWIN (George) [George White's Scandals of 1923.]

— The Life of a Rose. Songs. *See* LEHMANN, afterwards BEDFORD (L.)

LIFE

— The Life of a Sailor free. Song. *See* WARREN (A. E.)

— The Life of a Soldier. Song. *See* LANE (G. M.)

— The Life of a Soldier. [Song.] *See* MILLS (Arthur J.)

— Life of Ages. [Anthem.] *See* BRANDON (George)

— Life of Ages, richly poured. Anthem. *See* DAVIES (Gwynfor)

— The Life of King William. [Song.] *See* MONCRIEFF (W.T.) *pseud.*

— Life of Life. [Sacred song.] *See* PONTIUS (W. H.)

— The Life of Love. Song. *See* OSTLERE (M.)

— A Life of Love. Song. *See* PARTRIDGE (C.)

— The Life of Love is but a Day. Song. *See* KOMZAK (K.)

— A Life of Love with thee. Song. *See* BARNETT (J.)

— Life of my Heart. Song. *See* BARRETT (O.)

— Life of my Life. Song. *See* GATTY, afterwards SCOTT-GATTY (*Sir* A. S.)

— The Life of Samuel. Cantata. *See* SHINN (G.)

— The Life of the Zephyr. Song. *See* CAMPANA (F.)

— The Life of William the Fourth. Ballad. *See* BALL (W.)

— Life of Youth. Valse de Concert. *See* GEIBEL (A.)

— Life on a Man-o-war. [Song.] *See* STARR (Hattie)

— A Life on the ocean wave. Song. *See* RUSSELL (H.)

— A Life on the Sea. Song. *See* WILSON (W.)

— A Life-Picture. [Song.] *See* BUCK (D.) Seven Songs, *etc.* [No. 6.]

— Life's a Bumper. Glee. *See* WAINWRIGHT (R.)

— Life's a Dance. Song. *See* BRADLEY (O.)

— Life's a Dream worth dreaming. Part Song. *See* HOLLINS (A.)

— Life's a Dream worth dreaming. Song. *See* SCHMIDT (L.)

— Life's a Pilgrimage. Part Song. *See* GOUNOD (C. F.) [Quatorze grands Chœurs. No. 4. L'Éternité.]

— Life's a Pun. [Song.] *See* DIBDIN (C.) [Private Theatricals.]

— Life's a scene of ups and downs. Song. *See* WEST (W.)

— Life's a Song. [Song.] *See* BRAUN (C.)

— Life's a Song. [Song.] *See* GALLIARD (J. E.)

— Life's a Song. Vocal Waltz. *See* TALBOT (H.) [The Three Kisses.]

— Life's like a ship. Song. *See also* DIBDIN (C.)

— Life's like a Ship. A much admir'd new song. *Edmund Lee: Dublin,* [c. 1800.] *s. sh.* fol.　　　G. 426. kk. (16.)

— Life's like a Ship. [Song, by Charles Dibdin.] Nº. 41. ⟨There lives a sweet lovely dear Girl. Lango Lee. [Song.] Nº. 48.⟩ pp. 3. *Printed by the Polyhymnian Company, & sold by G. Walker: London,* [WM 1822.] fol.　　　G. 425. ss. (20.)

— Life's like a ship. Song. *See* STANISLAUS (F.)

— Life's like an April Day. Air. *See* HÉROLD (Louis J. F.) [Le Pré aux clercs.—Nargue de la folie.]

— Life's the Candy. [Song.] *See* BALL (E. R.)

— Life's too short to quarrel. Song. *See* MACGLENNON (F.)

LIFE

— A Life Scroll. Song. *See* GABRIEL, afterwards MARCH (M. A. V.)

— A Life Song. [Song.] *See* ROBINSON (P.)

— A Life-Story. Song. *See* HUTCHISON (W. M.)

— The Life that lasts for aye. [Song.] *See* TREVELYAN (A.)

— A Life that lives for you. Song. *See* SULLIVAN (*Sir* Arthur S.)

— The Life that might have been. Song. *See* DOLBY, afterwards SAINTON (C.H.)

— Life, the Organist. Song. *See* GRAY (H.) *pseud.*

— The Life, the Truth, the Way. Hymn. *See* FOULDS (R.)

— Life Time and Love Time. Song. *See* WAKEFIELD (A. M.)

— Life to Care is still the Prey. Song. *See* WEBER (C. M. F. E. von) [Der Freischütz.—Hier im ird'schen Jammerthal.]

— The Life to come. Sacred Song. *See* EDWARDES (L.)

— Life to me is no longer dear. *See* MACFARREN (*Sir* G. A.) [Robin Hood.]

— Life to the Life Boat. Song. *See* SELBY (B. L.)

— Life was a Maid. [Song.] *See* FERRARI (G.) Three Little Poems. No. 3.

— Life was made for Love and Cheer. Song. *See* ZARDO (N.)

— Life we've been long together. Ballad. *See* HELMER (E.)

— Life with you. Song. *See* BINGHAM (H.)

— Life without thee, Euridice. Aria. *See* GLUCK (C. W. von) [Orfeo.—Che farò.]

— Life would be sweet with thee. Song. *See* SPINNEY (W.)

— Life's All in All! Song. *See* LANE (G. M.)

— Life's Autumn. Song. *See* MEREWETHER (M. R.)

— Life's Balcony. Song. *See* BRAHE (M. H.)

— Life's beautiful Dreams. [Song.] *See* ARNOLD (Malcolm)

— Life's bleak winter day. Ballad. *See* PHILIPPS (T.)

— Life's Blessing. Song. *See* FLETCHER (P. E.)

— Life's Bouquet. [Song.] *See* KEATES (James E.)

— Life's Bowling Alley. Service of song. *See* LARBALESTIER (Philip G.)

— Life's chequer'd scene of light and shade. *Glee* [for three voices]. As Perform'd at the Pantheon Masquerade, *etc. P. H[odgson: London,* 1780?] *s. sh.* fol.　　　G. 310. (56.)

— Life's Consolation. Song. *See* BARNARD (D'A.)

— Life's Crossway. Song. *See* MACMURROUGH (D.)

— Life's Crown is Love. Part-Song. *See* SCHUMANN (R. A.) [Sechs Lieder für vierstimmigen Männergesang. Op. 33. No. 4. Rastlose Liebe.]

— Life's Curfew Bell. [Song.] *See* ARDITI (L.)

— Life's Day. Song. *See* MACALASTER (M.)

— Life's Devotion. [Song.] *See* CALDICOTT (A. J.)

— Life's Dream. Song. *See* DENHAM (Reginald)

— Life's Dream. Song. *See* WAYLAND (E.)

— Life's Dream is o'er. [Duet.] *See* ASCHER (J.) [Alice, where art thou?]

LIFE

— Life's Dreams, or What the Cuckoo said. Song. *See* LENNOX (Lindsay)

— Life's Dreams. Canon. *See* SCHUMANN (R. A.) [Ritornelle. Op. 65. No. 3.]

— Life's early friends. [Song.] *See* LINLEY (G.)

— Life's Early Morn. Song. *See* ALQUEN (F. C. d')

— Life's Echo. [Song.] *See* WOOLER (A.)

— Life's Eden Rose. [Song.] *See* LEE (L. S.) *Mrs.*

— Life's Elixir. Song. *See* WEISS (W. H.)

— Life's Epitome. Song. *See* RAE (K.) *pseud.*

— Life's Even Song. [Anthem.] *See* FREY (J. F.)

— Life's Evening. [Part-song.] *See* ASHFORD (E. L.)

— Life's Eventide. Song. *See* BARRENGER (P.)

— Life's Eventide. Song. *See* BUTTON (H. E.)

— Life's Eventide. Song. *See* DAVIDSON (Herbert W.)

— Life's Excelsior. Song. *See* MARKS (G.) *pseud.*

— Life's fair Morning. [Hymn.] *See* DENNIS (H.) School Anniversary Music ... Part II. No. 43.

— Life's first wreath. Ballad. *See* WRIGHTON (W. T.)

— Life's fleeting Hour. Song. *See* LE SAGE (J. M.)

— Life's Fragrance. Song. *See* GALBRAITH (J. L.)

— Life's Game of See-Saw. Song. *See* WEGEFARTH (L. C.)

— Life's Garden. [Song.] *See* BOND (C. J.)

— Life's Garden. Song. *See* CARTER (E. S.)

— Life's Garden. Song. *See* COWDELL (E.)

— Life's Garden. Sacred Song. *See* ELLIS (S.) *pseud.*

— Life's Garden. [Two-part song.] *See* MOZART (W. A.) [Sonata in D. K. 311. Andante.]

— Life's Gift. [Song.] *See* BARNARD (D'A.)

— Life's Gifts. Song. *See* CLUTSAM (G. H.)

— Life's glorious Anthem. [Song.] *See* RAE (K.) *pseud.*

— Life's Glory. Song. *See* O'KEEFE (John A.)

— Life's golden Morn. Song. *See* JONES (W. P. H.)

— Life's golden Rule. Song. *See* WATSON (E.)

— Life's grand sweet Song. [Song.] *See* ROSE (L.)

— Life's great Sunset. Song. *See* ADAMS (A. E.)

— Life's happy Day. Song. *See* IDLE (F.)

— Life's happy sunshine. Cavatina. *See* WILLIAMS (W. L.) [The Miller's Daughter.]

— Life's Heritage. Song. *See* ARMSTRONG (A. E.)

— Life's Hey-Day. Song. *See* DENZA (L.)

— Life's Highway. Song. *See* EYRE (L.)

— Life's Highway. [Song.] *See* MACGLENNON (F.)

— Life's Honeymoon. Song. *See* VERNON (W. C.)

— Life's Hope. Song. *See* CHARTERIS (G.)

— Life's Hope. Song. *See* KING (W.)

LIFE

— Life's Hostel. Song. *See* ROECKEL (J. L.)

— Life's Husbandman. [Song.] *See* MACFADYEN (A.)

— Life's Illusions. [Song.] *See* HOLDER (E. G. B.)

— Life's Journey. Song. *See* CARNELL (F. D.)

— Life's Journey. Song. *See* CLARKSON (J.)

— Life's Journey. Ballad. *See* COOPER (G.)

— Life's Journey. Song. *See* DAVIS (D. M.)

— Life's Joyful Moments. Song. *See* SHRIVALL (F. R.)

— Life's Joys. Song. *See* SPEAKS (O.)

— Life's lang Journey. Song. *See* DRUMMOND, afterwards SCOTT (Clementina)

— Life's last Moment. Aria. *See* BACH (J. S.) [Der Himmel lacht, die Erde jubiliret.—Letzte Stunde, brich herein.]

— Life's Lessons. Song. *See* WOOD (W. M.)

— Life's little Round. [Song.] *See* PRUTTING (R. H.) Four Songs ... Op. 9. No. 1.

— A Life's Love. [Song.] *See* WALDECK (J. B.)

— Life's Lucky Bag. Song. *See* LEIGHTON (D. M.)

— Life's Lullaby. Song. *See* LANE (G. M.)

— Life's Lute. Song. *See* TEMPLE (R. B.)

— Life's Maytime. Song. *See* LOUIS (E.)

— Life's Maytime. Song. *See* NEWTON (E. R.)

— Life's Melody. [Song.] *See* TOURJÉE (H.)

— Life's Memories. Song. *See* WOOD (C.) *Mus. Doc.*

— Life's Miniature. Song. *See* QUAYLE (E.)

— Life's Morning. Song. *See* CHAIKOVSKY (P. I.) [6 Romanzen. Op. 6. No. 3.]

— Life's Morning. [Service of song.] *See* WILSON (I. B.)

— Life's Morning Star. Song. *See* SIMSON (H. F.)

— Life's Mystery. Song. *See* HOORN (A. van)

— Life's Mystery. Song. *See* ROECKEL (J. L.)

— Life's Noontide. [Song.] *See* KODÁLY (Z.) [Megkésett melódiak. Op. 6.] Seven Songs ... No. 3.

— Life's Olympics. Demonstration service. *See* LARBALESTIER (Philip G.)

— Life's Paradise. [Song.] *See* BROWN (M. H.)

— Life's passing clouds. Song. *See* GOTTHEIMER (M. B.)

— Life's Pathway. [Musical monologue.] *See* ROUSE (W.)

— Life's Pathway. Song. *See* WHITE (E. G.)

— Life's perfect Promise. Song. *See* STICKLES (W.)

— Life's Philosophy. Song. *See* KAHN (P. B.)

— Life's Philosophy. Song. *See* WALTON (L.)

— Life's Pilgrim. Song. *See* MARKS (G.) *pseud.*

— Life's Pilgrimage. Song. *See* DANA (G.)

— Life's Pilgrimage. [Song.] *See* PETTIT (J. F.)

LIFE

— Life's Privilege. [Sacred song.] *See* SHELLEY (H. R.) Two Sacred Songs, *etc.* [No. 2.]

— Life's Question. [Song.] *See* CALLCOTT (W. H.)

— Life's radiant Star. [Song.] *See* MacKINSTRY (Floyd)

— Life's Recompense. Song. *See* RIEGO (T. del)

— Life's Refrain. Song. *See* TURNER (V. M.)

— A Life's Regret. [Song.] *See* LAMSON (G.)

— A Life's Regret. Song. *See* WAINWRIGHT (B.)

— Life's Requiem. Song. *See* WELLS (G. W.)

— Life's Rest. Song. *See* BARRY (K. E.)

— Life's Roadway. Song. *See* ADAMS (A. E.)

— Life's Roll-Call. Song. *See* LOUIS (E.)

— Life's romance. Song. *See* WELLINGS (M.)

— Life's Rose. [Song.] *See* MALLINSON (J. A.)

— Life's Roses. Song. *See* HEMERY (V.)

— Life's rosy Hours. Recitative. *See* BALFE (Michael W.) [The Maid of Artois.—Then silly is the Heart.]

— Life's rosy Morn. Duet. *See* EVANS (D. O.)

— Life's Rosy Morning. Sacred song. *See* PERRING (J. E.)

— Life's Seasons. Song. *See* MACFARREN (W. C.)

— Life's Seasons. Song. *See* MORI (F.)

— Life's Seasons. [Song.] *See* RÔZE (R.)

— Life's Secret. Song. *See* BARNES (L.)

— Life's Secret. Song. *See* SCHENSTRÖM (W. L.)

— Life's Shadows. Song. *See* HOPE (Herbert A.)

— Life's short Span. Song. *See* PAULTON (Dan)

— Life's short Tale. Song. *See* LEMARE (E. H.)

— Life's Shuttle. [Song.] *See* MERTON (C. D.)

— Life's silver Thread. Song. *See* DRUMMOND, afterwards SCOTT (Clementina)

— Life's Sorrows. Song. *See* HODGSON (R.)

— Life's Springtime. [Hymn.] *See* CHALLINOR (F. A.)

— Life's Springtime. [Song.] *See* HAWLEY (C. B.) Two Songs. [No. 1.]

— Life's Springtime. Song. *See* MOTTRAM (C. H. G.)

— Life's Story. Song. *See* PEASE (F. H.)

— Life's Stream. Song. *See* BLACKITH (H. D.)

— Life's Sun with Vigour glows. *Friendship.* A new song or duett ... German music. [First edited by H. G. Nägeli.] The words translated from the German language. *Cooke's Music Warehouse: Dublin,* [WM 1798.] *s. sh.* fol. **H. 1654. n. (55.)**

— Life's Sunny Hours. Ballad. *See* CALKIN (J.)

— Life's Sunset Bar. Song. *See* RUSSELL (R. C. K.)

— Life's Sunshine. Song. *See* CLARKE (E. A.)

— Life's sweet Day is gently closing. Song. *See* BIRD (P. D.)

— Life's sweetest Song. *See* MARKS (C. M.)

LIFE

— Life's tangled Garden. [Song.] *See* NOSIVAD (W. R.) *pseud.*

— Life's Tempest. Song. *See* BARRONS (M. J.) Songs. No. 1.

— Life's Thanksgiving. Song. *See* HEMERY (V.)

— Life's Thorns. Sacred song. *See* RONGET (H.)

— Life's Thorny Cross. Song. *See* LOCKNANE (C.)

— Life's Three Chapters. [Song.] *See* REEVE (W.) [The White Plume.]

— Life's transient Dream. [Song.] *See* DONIZETTI (D. G. M.) [La Fille du Régiment.—Qui tratto son da lieta speme.]

— Life's Treasure. Song. *See* YOUNGER (W.)

— Life's troubled sea. Sacred song. *See* RAMSEY (B. M.)

— Life's true Motto. Song. *See* FARMAR (F.)

— Life's Twilight. Song. *See* CUMMINGS (W. H.)

— Life's Twilight. [Song.] *See* DOWNING (L. J.) Three Songs. [No. 2.]

— Life's Twilight. Song. *See* DYER (H.)

— Life's Twilight. Song. *See* SPEAKS (O.)

— Life's Twilight. Song. *See* TANNENBAUM (J.)

— Life's Uphill. Song. *See* GATTY, afterwards SCOTT-GATTY (Sir A. S.)

— [Life's Vagaries.] I can dance and sing ... A Favorite Song sung by Mrs. Lee, in the new Comedy of Life's Vagaries ... The Words by J. O'Keefe. *Preston & Son: London,* [1795.] fol. **G. 249. (38.)**

— Life's Vision. Song. *See* GRANT (C.)

— Life's Vision. Quartet. *See* JOHNSON (H.)

— Life's Voyage. Song. *See* DUSS (J. S.)

— Life's Voyage. Duet. *See* MOUNSEY, afterwards BARTHOLOMEW (A. S.)

— Life's Way. Sacred Song. *See* WOLCOTT (J. T.)

— Life's Work. Part Song. *See* FRIEDLAENDER (A. M.)

— Life's Yesterday. Song. *See* FORD (E. C.)

— Life's young dawn of love. *See* BELLINI (V.) [La Straniera.—Meco tu vieni.]

— Life's young Day. Ballad. *See* GUERNSEY (W.)

LIFE-BELT

— The Life-Belt. [Song.] *See* MacGLENNON (F.)

LIFEBOAT

— The Lifeboat. Duet. *See* WHEN. When skies are all beauty. [1862.] fol. **H. 1790. c. (52.)**

— The Lifeboat. [Service of song.] *See* BARSTOW (C. A.)

— The Life Boat. Song. *See* CLARIBEL, *pseud.*

— The Life-Boat. Part song. *See* CROSS (C. J.)

— The Life Boat. Part-Song. *See* HATTON (J. L.)

— The Life-Boat. Action Song. *See* JACKMAN (P.)

— The Lifeboat. Song. *See* LIMPUS (H. F.)

— The Life Boat. Song. *See* NEUKOMM (S. von)

LIFEBOAT

— The Lifeboat. Chorus. *See* PEARSON (W. W.)

— The Life-Boat. Song. *See* PESKETT (Frank)

— The Life-Boat. Song. *See* PINSUTI (C. E.)

— The Lifeboat. [Song.] *See* SMART (G.)

— The Lifeboat. Song. *See* STARK (H. J.)

— The Lifeboat Crew. [Song.] *See* BRADFORD (J.)

— The Life-Boat Crew. [Song.] *See* COBORN (Charles) *pseud.*

— The Lifeboat Crew. Song. *See* DAVIES (A. W.)

— The Lifeboat Crew. [Song.] *See* DAVIES (T. V.)

— The Lifeboat Crew. [Song.] *See* DRYDEN (Leo)

— The Lifeboat Crew. Two-Part Song. *See* FACER (T.)

— The Lifeboat Crew. [Song.] *See* JONES (David T.) called TAWE BENCERDD.

— The Lifeboat Crew. Song. *See* SAINT MAUR (E.)

— The Life Boat Crew. [Song.] *See* STAMFORD (J.)

— The Life-Boat was there. Song. *See* MAY (A.)

LIFEBOATMAN

— The Lifeboatman. Choral Scena. *See* PEARCE (C. W.)

— The Lifeboatman. Song. *See* TROTÈRE (H.)

— The Lifeboatman's Story. Song. *See* LEAMORE (Tom E.)

LIFEBOATMEN

— The Lifeboat Men. Song. *See* ADAMS (S.) *pseud.*

— The Lifeboatmen. [Song.] *See* PIETRONI (J.)

LIFEGUARDSMAN

— The Lifeguardsman. [Song.] *See* ASHER (Angelo A.)

LIFERMAN (GEORGES)

— Sicilienne pour flûte et piano. [Score and part.] 2 pt. *Chappell: Paris*, [1975.] 4°.   **g. 280. bb. (7.)**

LIFERMAN (GEORGES) and BONNEAU (PAUL)

— Nymphes et driades. [For orchestra. Compressed score.] pp. 11. *Éditions Chappell: Paris*, [1972.] fol. *Série Télécinéradio. no.* 132.   **h. 1568. nn. (13.)**

LIFFEY

— The Liffey Waltz. [Song.] *See* BLITZSTEIN (Marc) [Juno.]

LIFKA (CHARLES)

— *See* STOJOWSKI (Z.) Mélodie ... Arr. par C. Lifka. [1905.] fol.   **h. 3029. (7.)**

LIFSCHEY (SAMUEL)

— Daily Technical Studies for the Viola. *G. Schirmer: New York*, 1929. 4°.   **g. 762. e. (2.)**

— Double-Stop Studies for the Viola. *G. Schirmer: New York*, 1943. 4°.   **g. 762. g. (1.)**

— Twelve Modulatory Studies for the Viola. *G. Schirmer: New York*, 1936. 4°.   **g. 762. e. (17.)**

LIFSCHEY (SAMUEL)

— *See* BACH (J. S.) [Suites for Violoncello.] Six Suites for Viola ... Adapted ... by S. Lifschey. 1936. 4°.   **g. 548. ee. (24.)**

— *See* BACH (J. S.) [Suites for Violoncello.] Six Suites. For the viola ... Adapted and edited by S. Lifschey. [1950.] 4°.   **g. 699. a. (9.)**

— *See* CAMPAGNOLI (B.) Forty-One Caprices for the Viola ... Study-version prepared by S. Lifschey. 1944. 4°.   **g. 762. g. (2.)**

— *See* RAMEAU (J. P.) [Platée.] Minuet ... Transcribed ... by S. Lifschey. 1929. 4°.   **g. 500. o. (13.)**

LIFT

— Lift a Glass to Friendship. [Part-song.] *See* LUBOFF (Norman)

— Lift Boy. Part-Song. *See* BRITTEN (Edward B.) *Baron Britten of Aldeburgh.*

— Lift every Voice and sing. Hymn. *See* JOHNSON (J. R.)

— Lift high the Cross. Prose. *See* BENNETT (J. L.)

— Lift high the Cross. A Prose. *See* POWELL (J. B.)

— Lift high your Hearts. Easter Song. *See* BURDETT (G. A.)

— Lift my Spirit up to thee. Song. *See* MACKENZIE (*Sir* A. C.) [Songs. Op. 31. No. 9.]

— A Lift on the Way. Song. *See* GALLIE (J.)

— Lift the Gospel Banner. Choral March. *See* FROST (W. L.)

— Lift the latch, come in! Song. *See* OFFENBACH (J.)

— Lift the Strain of high Thanksgiving. [Anthem.] *See* WATKINSON (J. R.)

— Lift the Trumpet, up and tell. [Part-song.] *See* SMART (H.)

— Lift thine Eyes. Song. *See* BENNETT (M. E.)

— Lift thine Eyes. [Anthem.] *See* DEMAREST (C.)

— Lift thine Eyes. Sacred Song. *See* LELAND (H. G.)

— Lift thine Eyes. Song. *See* LOGAN (F. K.) [Song Miniatures. No. 3.]

— Lift thine Eyes to the Mountains. Trio. *See* MENDELSSOHN-BARTHOLDY (J. L. F.) [Elijah.—Hebe deine Augen auf zu den Bergen.]

— Lift thy Heart. Sacred Song. *See* ALLITSEN (F.) *pseud.*

— Lift up, lift up your Voices now. Anthem. *See* BERWALD (W. H.)

— Lift up our Hearts. [Anthem.] *See* BUTLER (Eugene S.)

— Lift up the everlasting Gates. Anthem. *See* TYE (C.) [The Actes of the Apostles. Chap. VIII.]

— Lift up thine Eyes. Hymn. *See* BICKFORD (W. P.)

— Lift up thine eyes. Anthem. *See* GOSS (*Sir* J.)

— Lift up thine Eyes, O Mother! Hymn. *See* FETHERSTON (*Sir* G. R.) *Bart.*

— Lift up thy drooping head, sweet rose. Trio. *See* GLUCK (C. W. von) [Iphigénie en Tauride.—Overture.]

— Lift up thy Heart to Him. Solo and Chorus. *See* PARCELL (A. E.)

— Lift up thy Voice with Strength. Anthem. *See* SMIETON (J. M.)

— Lift up your Eyes. Anthem. *See* HAYDEN (J. A.)

— Lift up your Eyes. Anthem. *See* ROBINS (A.)

LIFT

— Lift up your Eyes. Anthem. *See* WARD (F. E.)

— Lift up your Eyes to the Hills. [Hymn.] *See* CHALLINOR (F. A.)

— Lift up your Heads. [Anthem with figured bass.] [1815?] fol. *Pp.* 12–14 *of an unidentified collection from G. F. Haendel's "Messiah".*　　　　　**H. 1652. n. (18.)**

— Lift up your Heads. [Anthem.] *See* ADAMS (C. B.)

— Lift up your Heads. [Anthem.] *See* AMNER (John)

— Lift up your Heads. Anthem. *See* BENNETT (W. H.)

— Lift up your Heads. Anthem. *See* BLOW (J.)

— Lift up your Heads. Anthem. *See* COERNE (Louis A.)

— Lift up your Heads. Motet. *See* DARKE (Harold E.)

— Lift up your Heads. Easter Anthem. *See* FAWCETT (J.) *the Elder.*

— Lift up your Heads. Anthem. *See* GIBBONS (O.)

— Lift up your Heads. Anthem. *See* GOLDMAN (Maurice)

— Lift up your Heads. [Chorus.] *See* HAENDEL (G. F.) [Messiah.]

— Lift up your Heads. Hymn. *See* HELMER (F. F.)

— Lift up your Heads. Anthem. *See* HOPKINS (J. L.)

— Lift up your Heads. [Anthem.] *See* JACKSON (Francis A.)

— Lift up your Heads. Anthem. *See* KEY (J.)

— Lift up your Heads. Introit. *See* KITSON (C. H.)

— Lift up your Heads. Anthem. *See* LEHMANN (R. F.)

— Lift up your Heads. [Anthem.] *See* LYNES (F.)

— Lift up your Heads. [Anthem.] *See* LYNN (George)

— Lift up your Heads. Anthem. *See* MINSHALL (E.)

— Lift up your Heads. [Anthem.] *See* MOLITOR (J. B.)

— Lift up your heads. Anthem. *See* PRINGLE (R.)

— Lift up your Heads. Anthem. *See* ROGERS (J. H.)

— Lift up your Heads. [Anthem.] *See* ROREM (Ned)

— Lift up your heads. Anthem. *See* SMITH (T.)

— Lift up your Heads. Anthem. *See* STORER (H. J.)

— Lift up your Heads. Anthem. *See* STOUGHTON (R. S.)

— Lift up your Heads. Anthem. *See* TAYLOR (S. C.)

— Lift up your Heads. [Anthem.] *See* TENNY (J. H.)

— Lift up your Heads. Anthem. *See* TURNER (W.) *Mus. Doc.*

— Lift up your Heads. Anthem. *See* VALENTINE (C. W.)

— Lift up your Heads. Anthem. *See* WATSON (E.)

— Lift up your Heads. Anthem. *See* WITTY (Robert)

— Lift up your Heads, great Gates, and sing. Anthem. *See* BULLOCK (*Sir* Ernest)

— Lift up your Heads, o ye Gates. [Anthem.] *See* DAVIDSON (Charles S.)

— Lift up your Heads, O ye Gates. Anthem. *See* GREENE (C. W.)

— Lift up your Heads, O ye Gates. Anthem. *See* LEIGHTON (Kenneth)

LIFT

— Lift up your Heads, O ye Gates. [Anthem.] *See* MATHIAS (William)

— Lift up your Heads, O ye Gates. Anthem. *See* PALESTRINA (G. P. da) [Motecta Festorum Totius Anni … Quaternis Vocibus … Liber Primus.—Loquebantur variis linguis.]

— Lift up your Heads, O ye Gates. [Anthem.] *See* SMALLWOOD (W.)

— Lift up your Heads on high. Air. *See* BACH (J. S.) [Wachet, betet.—Hebt euer Haupt empor.]

— Lift up your Heads, ye Gates. [Anthem.] *See* ADAMS (T.) *Organist of St. Alban's, Holborn.* [The Story of Calvary.]

— Lift up your Heads ye Gates of Brass. Hymn. *See* WARREN (Gladstone)

— Lift up your Heads ye Gates of Brass. [Anthem.] *See* WILLIAMS (Patrick)

— Lift up your Heads, ye mighty Gates. Motet. *See* LEISRING (V.)

— Lift up your Heads, ye mighty Gates. Solo and Quartet. *See* TROWBRIDGE (J. E.)

— Lift up your Heads, ye mighty Gates. Anthem. *See* WARNER (Richard)

— Lift up your Heads, ye People. [Anthem.] *See* DARST (William G.)

— Lift up your Heart. [Anthem.] *See* BAMPTON (Ruth)

— Lift up your Hearts. Anthem. *See* BARNBY (*Sir* J.)

— Lift up your Hearts. [Anthem.] *See* BORLAND (J. E.)

— Lift up your Hearts. Hymn-Anthem. *See* CHAMBERS (H. A.)

— Lift up your Hearts. Song. *See* KAHN, afterwards CARNE (Gerald F.)

— Lift up your Hearts. Sacred Symphony. *See* DAVIES (*Sir* H. W.)

— Lift up your Hearts. [Hymn tune.] *See* MATTHEWS (A. P.)

— Lift up your Hearts. Anthem. *See* MERRITT (G.)

— Lift up your Hearts. Song. *See* MORGAN (Reginald)

— Lift up your Hearts. Unison song. *See* NOBLE (Harold)

— Lift up your Hearts. Choral Song. *See* THIMAN (E. H.)

— Lift up your Hearts. [Hymn.] *See* WYATT (Edward)

— Lift up your Voices now! Anthem. *See* REDHEAD (A.) [Behold! I shew you a Mystery.]

— Lift your Eyes. [Song.] *See* SELLARS (S. G.)

— Lift your glad Voices. Anthem. *See* BERWALD (W. H.)

— Lift your glad Voices. Anthem. *See* FLETCHER (J.)

— Lift your glad Voices. [Sacred song.] *See* HAWLEY (C. B.)

— Lift your glad Voices. Anthem. *See* LAER (C. E. van)

— Lift your glad Voices. Carol. *See* MACY (J. C.)

— Lift your glad Voices. [Anthem.] *See* STEANE (B. H. D.)

— Lift your glad Voices. [Anthem.] *See* WISEMAN (F. L.)

— Lift your Heads. Anthem. *See* BACH (J. S.) [Geistliche Lieder aus Schemelli's Gesangbuch und dem Notenbuch der Anna Magdalena Bach. No. 15. Eins ist Noth.]

— Lift your Heads, ye Gates of God. Hymn. *See* WESLEY (S. S.)

LIFTED

— The Lifted Burden. Song. *See* Mascheroni (A.)

— The Lifted Veil. Song. *See* Barnby (*Sir* J.)

LIFTER (M.)

— By the Cottage where I was born. [Song.] pp. 5. *Lyon & Healy: Chicago*, [1898.] fol. **H. 3980. ss. (6.)**

LIFTL (Franz J.)

— *See* Wagner (W. R.) Die Meistersinger von Nürnberg. Drei Stücke … bearbeitet von F. J. Liftl, *etc.* (1910, *etc.*) fol. **h. 356. q. (7.)**

LIFTMAN (Baruch)

— Concert hora. For violin and piano. [Score and part.] 2 pt. *Novello and Co.: London*, [1957.] 4°. **g. 500. ee. (5.)**

LIGARIUS (Johannes)

— *See* Psalms. [*Dutch.*] Dat Woerdische Sangboeck, *etc.* [With a preface by J. Ligarius.] 1647. 12°. **3433. de. 33. (1.)**

LÎGEOIS

— Li Lîgeois ĕgagî. Opéra. *See* Hamal (Jean N.)

LIGETI (György)

— György Ligeti. From sketches and unpublished scores 1938–56. From the collection of Ove Nordwall. Excerpted from Artes, 1976: 3, Stockholm. ⟨Sonatina (p. quatuor), mi-minore. Kalmár jött nagy madarakkal. Ricercare (Omaggio a G. Frescobaldi.) Sötét és világos.⟩ [Facsimiles.] *Norstedts Tryckerei: Stockholm*, 1976. 8°.
Publications issued by the Royal Swedish Academy of Music. 16. **c. 160. i. (4.)**

— Apparitions. 1958/59. Für Orchester. Partitur, *etc.* ⟨Reproduktion der Originalhandschrift des Komponisten.⟩ pp. 27. *Universal Edition: Wien*, [1964.] fol. **P. 1803.**

— Apparitions. 1958/59. Für Orchester. Studienpartitur, *etc.* ⟨2. verbesserte Auflage. Reproduktion der Originalhandschrift des Komponisten.⟩ pp. 26. *Universal Edition: Wien*, 1971. fol. **e. 667. k. (2.)**

— Artikulation. Elektronische Musik. Eine Hörpartitur von Rainer Wehinger, *etc.* ⟨Electronic music. An aural score by Rainer Wehinger.⟩ [With facsimiles.] pp. 55. *B. Schott's Söhne: Mainz*, [1970.] obl. fol. **P. 48.**

— Atmosphères. Für grosses Orchester ohne Schlagzeug. ⟨Reproduktion der Originalhandschrift des Komponisten.⟩ [Score.] ff. 24. *Universal Edition: Wien*, [1963.] obl. fol. **f. 641. e.**

— Atmosphères. Für grosses Orchester ohne Schlagzeug. Studienpartitur, *etc.* ⟨3. verbesserte Auflage. Reproduktion der Originalhandschrift des Komponisten.⟩ pp. 23. *Universal Edition: Wien*, 1971. fol. **e. 667. k. (1.)**

— Aventures. Für drei Sänger und sieben Instrumentalisten. For three singers and seven instrumentalists. Studienpartitur, *etc.* ⟨Reproduktion der Originalhandschrift des Komponisten.⟩ pp. 29. *Henry Litolff's Verlag; C. F. Peters: Frankfurt, etc.*, [1964.] 4°.
Inserted are three booklets, entitled "Anmerkungen," "Comments" and "Transcript of handwritten annotations in score. Translation of footnotes in score." **G. 809. y. (5.)**

— Nouvelles aventures. Für drei Sänger und sieben Instrumentalisten. For three singers and seven instrumentalists. Studienpartitur, *etc.* ⟨Reproduction of the original manuscript of the composer.⟩ ⟨Transcript of handwritten annotations in score/translation of footnotes in

LIGETI (György)

score.—Anmerkungen.—Comments.⟩ 4 pt. *Henry Litolff's Verlag; C. F. Peters: Frankfurt, etc.*, [1966.] 4°. **g. 1620. vv. (5.)**

— Sechs Bagatellen für Bläserquintett (1953). Six Bagatelles for Wind Quintet … Studien-Partitur. pp. 35. *B. Schott's Söhne, etc.: Mainz, etc.*, [1973.] 8°. **e. 501. c. (5.)**

— Ballade und Tanz nach rumänischen Volksliedern für Schulorchester. Ballad and Dance after Roumanian Folksongs. For school orchestra. (1949–50.) Partitur. pp. 20. *B. Schott's Söhne: Mainz*, [1974.] 4°. *Concertino.* 177. **g. 934. oo. (6.)**

— Konzert für Violoncello und Orchester. 1966. Studienpartitur, *etc.* pp. 48. *Henry Litolff's Verlag; C. F. Peters: Frankfurt, etc.*, [1969.] 4°. **g. 511. s. (4.)**

— Konzert für Violoncello und Orchester 1966. Solo-Violoncello. pp. 10. *Henry Litolff's Verlag; C. F. Peters: Frankfurt, etc.*, [1969.] 4°. **g. 510. cc. (6.)**

— Doppelkonzert für Flöte, Oboe und Orchester. Double Concerto for Flute, Oboe and Orchestra (1972). Studien-Partitur. pp. 72. *B. Schott's Söhne, etc.: Mainz, etc.*, [1974.] 4°. **g. 860. oo. (3.)**

— Continuum für Cembalo. pp. 11. *B. Schott's Söhne: Mainz*, [1970.] 4°. **g. 1138. z. (10.)**

— Dereng már a hajnal. [Words by] Fodor Balázs. Vegyeskar. pp. 5. *Cserépfalvi: Budapest*, [1946.] 8°. **D. 840. m. (29.)**

— [Dereng már a hajnal.] Early comes the Summer. English text by John Manifold, *etc.* [Staff and tonic sol-fa notation.] pp. 4. *Workers' Music Association: London*, [1947.] 8°. **D. 840. m. (30.)**

— Early comes the Summer. *See* supra: [Dereng már a hajnal.]

— Éjszaka/Night/Nacht. Reggel/Morning/Morgen. Zwei A-cappella-Chöre (1955) nach Texten von Sándor Weöres für gemischten Chor (ungarisch/englisch/deutsch). Partitur. pp. 15. *B. Schott's Söhne: Mainz*, [1973.] 8°. **F. 1874. l. (7.)**

— Zwei Etüden für Orgel … 1. Harmonies. 2. Coulée. pp. 11. *B. Schott's Söhne: Mainz*, [1971?] obl. fol. **f. 337. k.**

— Fragment. ⟨Für Kammerorchester.⟩ Partitur. pp. 6. *Universal Edition: Wien*, [1974.] 4°. **g. 1067. l. (4.)**

— Hortobágy. Három nepdal, vegyeskarra. pp. 16. *Zeneműkiadó vállalat: Budapest*, [1953.] 8°. **B. 418. v. (7.)**

— Kállai kettős. (Magyar népdalok után.) [Part-song.] pp. 11. *Zeneműkiadó vállalat: Budapest*, [1952.] 8°. **D. 840. m. (28.)**

— Kammerkonzert für 13 Instrumentalisten … Studien-Partitur, *etc.* pp. 106. *B. Schott's Söhne, etc.: Mainz, etc.*, [1974.] 4°. **g. 934. oo. (7.)**

— Négy lakodalmi tánc. ⟨Három női hangra (v. háromszólamú nőikarra) zongorakísérettel.⟩ Ligety György feldolgozása (1950). pp. 6. *Zeneműkiadó vállalat: Budapest*, [1952.] 8°. **C. 374. i. (6.)**

— Lontano. Für grosses Orchestra … Studien-Partitur. pp. 40. *B. Schott's Söhne: Mainz, etc.*, [1969.] 4°. **g. 1620. xx. (2.)**

— Lux aeterna. Für sechzehnstimmigen gemischten Chor a cappella, *etc.* pp. 15. *Henry Litolff's Verlag, C. F. Peters: Frankfurt, etc.*, [1967.] obl. 4°. **D. 836. r. (4.)**

— Melodien für Orchester (1971). ⟨Faksimileausgabe nach dem Manuskript des Komponisten.⟩ Studien-Partitur, *etc.* pp. 39. *B. Schott's Söhne, etc.: Mainz, etc.*, [c. 1975.] 4°. **g. 860. xx. (1.)**

— Monument, Selbstportrait, Bewegung. Drei Stücke für zwei Klaviere … (1976). Faksimileausgabe, *etc.* [Score.] ff. 20. *B. Schott's Söhne: Mainz*, [1976.] fol. **i. 37.**

LIGETI (György)

— Passacaglia ungherese für Cembalo, *etc.* pp. 7. *Schott:*
Mainz, etc., [1979.] 4°.　　　　　　　　**g. 338. vv. (9.)**

— Streichquartett No. 2 ... (1968). Studien-Partitur. pp. 31.
B. Schott's Söhne, etc.: Mainz, etc., [1976.] 4°.
　　　　　　　　g. 410. nn. (1.)

— Streichquartett No. 2 ... (1968). Stimmen, *etc.* 4 pt. *Schott:*
Mainz, etc., [1979.] fol.　　　　　　　　**i. 37. g.**

— Ramifications. For string orchestra or 12 solo strings.
Studien-Partitur. pp. 62. *B. Schott's Söhne: Mainz, etc.,*
[1970.] 8°.　　　　　　　　**f. 390. ii. (8.)**

— Requiem für Sopran- und Mezzosopran-Solo, zwei gemischte
Chöre und Orchester. For soprano and mezzo soprano solo,
two mixed choruses and orchestra, 1963/65, *etc.*
⟨Reproduktion der Originalhandschrift des Komponisten.
Studienpartitur.⟩ pp. 49. *Henry Litolff's Verlag; C. F. Peters:*
Frankfurt, etc., [1965.] fol.　　　　　　　　**I. 583.**

— Requiem für Sopran, Mezzosopran, zwei gemischte Chöre
und Orchester ... Klavierauszug von ... Zsigmond
Szathmáry. pp. 84. *Henry Litolff's Verlag; C. F. Peters:*
Frankfurt, etc., [1975.] fol.　　　　　　　　**G. 976. j. (4.)**

— Zehn Stücke für Bläserquintett ... Ten Pieces for Wind
Quintet. (1968.) Studien-Partitur. pp. 35. *B. Schott's Söhne,*
etc.: Mainz, etc., [1969.] 8°.
Part of "Musik des 20. Jahrhunderts".　　　**f. 390. mm. (5.)**

— Volumina. Für Orgel. ⟨Reproduktion der Originalhandschrift
des Komponisten. Revidiert 1966.⟩ pp. 24. *Henry Litolff's*
Verlag; C. F. Peters: Frankfurt, etc., [1967.] *obl.* fol.
With a separate folded leaf inserted, bearing directions for
performance.　　　　　　　　**f. 314. ss. (7.)**

LIGĘZA (Józef)

— Pieśni ludowe ze Śląska. Wydanie przygotował: J. Ligęza.
Część muzyczną opracował: Franciszek Ryling. Tom III.
Zeszyt 2. Pieśni rodzinne. pp. 224. *Wydawnictwo "Śląsk":*
Katowice, 1961. 8°.
The titlepage headed "Śląski instytut naukowy w Katowicach".
　　　　　　　　E. 1881. c.

— *See* DYGACZ (A.) and LIGĘZA (J.) Pieśni ludowe Śląska
Opolskiego, *etc.* 1954. 8°.　　　　　　　　**D. 836. p. (1.)**

LIGGINS (Ethel)

— *See* LEGINSKA (E.) *pseud.*

LIGHT

— Light. Song. *See* ADLER (F.)

— Light. Song. *See* AYLWARD (F.) [Album of Six Songs. No. 2.]

— Light. Song. *See* BARNBY (*Sir* J.)

— Light. Song. *See* BAUER (M. E.)

— Light. Sacred Song. *See* BEHNKE (K.)

— Light. Canon. *See* BUSCH (C.)

— The Light. Motet. *See* CASTELNUOVO-TEDESCO (M.)

— Light. Cantata. *See* KOUNTZ (R.)

— Light. Song. *See* LOCKNANE (C.)

— Light. Song. *See* MACFARREN (*Sir* G. A.)

— Light. Song. *See* MASSON (R.)

— Light. Mélodie. *See* ROUSSEL (A.)

— Light. Sacred Song. *See* SCOTT (J. P.)

LIGHT

— Light. Sacred Song. *See* STEVENSON (F.)

— Light. [Song.] *See* STULTS (R. M.)

— Light. Song. *See* ZARDO (N.)

— Light after Darkness. Song. *See* BARNES (Edward S.)

— Light after Darkness. Sacred Song. *See* PUNTER (W. H.)

— Light after Darkness. [Part-song.] *See* ROBERTSON (G. E.)
Four-part Songs. No. 2.

— Light after Darkness. Sacred Song. *See* SIMPER (C.)

— Light and Darkness. [Duet.] *See* HAENDEL (G. F.) [Chamber
Duets. No. 12. Tanti strali.]

— Light and free. [Song.] *See* EGENER (C. A.)

— Light and laughing summer sky. Trio. *See* MACFARREN (*Sir*
G. A.)

— Light and Shade. [Song.] *See* BAUMER (C.)

— Light and Shade. Song. *See* GRANT (L. H.)

— Light and shadow. Song. *See* GLOVER (S.)

— Light and Shadow. Song. *See* GREENHILL (J.)

— Light and Shadow. Sacred Song. *See* SCOVILLE (J. G.)

— Light and Truth. Cantata. *See* CROSSLEY (W. T.)

— Light and Truth. Song. *See* REY (V.) *pseud.*

— Light as Air. Chorus. *See* GOUNOD (C. F.) [Faust.—Ainsi que
la brise.]

— Light as Fairy Foot can fall. Chorus. *See* WEBER (C. M. F. E.
von) [Oberon.]

— Light as falling snow. Ballad. *See* LINLEY (G.)

— Light as falling snow. Ballad. *See* MASSÉ (F. M. V.) [*Doubtful*
and Supposititious Works.]

— Light as Foot of Fay can fall. Chorus. *See* WEBER (C. M. F. E.
von) [Oberon.]

— Light as the shadows. [Song.] *See* STEVENSON (*Sir* J. A.)

— Light as thistle down. Song. *See* SHIELD (W.) [Rosina.]

— Light as Zephyrs. Duet. *See* MACGHIE (W.)

— Light at Evening-tide. Song. *See* DRUMMOND, afterwards
SCOTT (Clementina)

— Light at Evening Time. [Sacred song.] *See* CANDLYN (T. F. H.)

— Light at Evening-Time. Anthem. *See* DALTON (S. C.)

— Light at Evening Time. Hymn. *See* MILLER (E. W.)

— Light at Eveningtime. [Anthem.] *See* PROTHEROE (Daniel)

— Light at Evening-Time. [Sacred song.] *See* SPEAKS (O.) Two
Vesper Song. [No. 2.]

— Light at Evening Time. Anthem. *See* STULTS (R. M.)

— Light at Eventide. [Sacred song.] *See* EDWARDS (P.)

— Light at Eventide. Sacred Duet. *See* GAINES (S. R.)

— Light at Eventide. Song. *See* GALLICO (R. C.)

— Light at Eventide. Song. *See* MILLER (G. C.)

— Light at Eventide. Song. *See* REYNOLDS (W. J.)

— Light at Eventide. Song. *See* RONALD (*Sir* L.)

LIGHT

— Light at Eventide. [Anthem.] *See* THOMPSON (R. G.)

— Light, at last! Song. *See* BARRI (O.)

— Light at last. Ballad. *See* PETTIT (J. F.)

— The Light Bark. [Song.] *See* CRAVEN (John T.)

— The Light Barque. Song. *See* TRAVIS (E.)

— Light be around thee. Song. *See* PHILLIPS (W. L.)

— Light be the Earth on Billy's Breast. *Mad Song,* [words] from the Man of Feeling. [*Edinburgh,* 1785.] *s. sh.* 4°. *Edinburgh Magazine, Nov.,* 1785.   **257. b. 15.**

— The Light beyond. Sacred Song. *See* HUTCHINSON (T.)

— The Light beyond. Song. *See* JONES (W. P. H.)

— Light beyond. Ode. *See* PEARCE (C. W.)

— The Light beyond. Sacred Solo. *See* TOURJÉE (H.)

— Light beyond the Cloud. Song. *See* WEISS (Willoughby H.)

— Light Blue and Dark Blue. Song. *See* CAREY (C.)

— Light bounding bark. *See* SEE. See now the light bark bounding. [1855.] fol.   **h. 1254. (47.)**

— The Light Castanet. Andalusian Duet. *See* PARKER (Henry T.)

— The Light Cause. Song. *See* DAVISON (J. W.)

— The Light Cigar. Song and trio. *See* DEVEREAUX (L.)

— The Light Divine. Song. *See* BONHEUR (T.) *pseud.*

— The Light divine. Sacred Song. *See* ROBARTS (A. M.)

— The Light eternal. [Sacred song.] *See* ALFORD (H. L.)

— Light eternal. Cantata. *See* COOMBS (C. W.)

— Light eternal. Song. *See* NASH (W. M.)

— Light eternal. Solo and Duet. *See* PARCELL (A. E.)

— The Light eternal. Sacred Song. *See* PARKER (L.)

— The Light eternal. Cantata. *See* PETRIE (H. W.)

— Light eternal Light is streaming. Song. *See* BATCHELOR (H.)

— The Light Everlasting. Cantata. *See* GILLETTE (J. R.)

— Light everlasting. [Anthem.] *See* YOUNG (Gordon)

— A Light fantastic Tour. Song. *See* HAINES (Herbert E.)

— Light from a Sunken Sun. Song. *See* VINCENT (C.)

— The light from loving eyes. Song. *See* BALFE (M. W.)

— A Light from St. Agnes. Lyric Tragedy. *See* HARLING (W. F.)

— Light! glorious Light. [Quartet.] *See* DOW (H. M.) Four Masonic Quartets, *etc.* [No. 4.]

— The Light Guitar. Duet. *See* BARNETT (J.)

— The Light hath shined. Anthem. *See* SIMPER (C.)

— The Light hath shined upon us. Anthem. *See* SILAS (E.)

— The Light hath shined upon us. [Anthem.] *See* VERRINDER (C. G.)

— The Light Heart. Unison song. *See* BLOWER (Maurice)

— Light Hearts. Song. *See* DRAPER (A. M.)

— The Light Horse Volunteers. Song. *See* SCHROEDER (H. B.)

— Light in darkness. Sacred Song. *See* COWEN (*Sir* F. H.)

LIGHT

— Light in Darkness. Song. *See* CROSSLEY (H.)

— Light in Darkness. [Part-song.] *See* HATHAWAY (J. W. G.)

— Light in Darkness. Anthem. *See* JENKINS (D. C.)

— Light in Darkness. Anthem. *See* PEARSON (A.)

— The Light in girlish Eyes. [Song.] *See* BOWERS (Robert H.)

— Light in Spring Poplars. [Part-song.] *See* WILSON (Richard)

— The Light in the Cradle. [Song.] *See* PLUMSTEAD (Mary)

— Light in the Darkness. [Song.] *See* SCHOENBACH (J.)

— Light in the East is glowing. Duett. *See* GLOVER (Stephen)

— The Light in the Quay. Song. *See* SWIFT (F. W.)

— Light in the West. Ballad. *See* LOTT (E. M.)

— A Light in the Window. Sacred Song. *See* BRADBURY (W. B.)

— The light in the window. Ballad. *See* GABRIEL, afterwards MARCH (M. A. V.)

— The Light in the Window. Ballad. *See* PEREIRA (L.)

— The Light in your Eyes. Song. *See* FERRARI (G.) [The Rainbow of Love.]

— The Light invisible. Sinfonia sacra. *See* LEIGHTON (Kenneth)

— The Light invisible. [Anthem.] *See* WILLS (Arthur W.)

— The Light is fading in the valley. Ballad. *See* GOODBAN (H. W.)

— Light is my Heart. Song. *See* MONCKTON (L.) and TALBOT (H.) [The Arcadians.]

— Light is the Heart. [Song.] *See* COWARD (*Sir* Noël P.) [After the Ball.]

— Light Leaves whisper. [Part-song.] *See* HOLST (G. T. von)

— Light 'mid the Shadows. Christmas Carol. *See* HAVERGAL, afterwards GRANT (C.)

— Light, more Light. Song. *See* HUMPHREYS (J. W.)

— Light more Light. [Song.] *See* PONTET (Henry T.)

— Light Mountain Fay. Song. *See* LUTZ (W. M.)

— Light my Life with Love. [Song.] *See* ARNSTEIN (Ira B.)

— Light O'Love. Ancient melody [begins: "How can I learn"]. The words by W. Ball. *See* SHAKESPEARE. The Shakspeare Vocal Magazine. No. 26. [1864.] fol.   **H. 2389.**

— The Light o' your Eye. Song. *See* NICHOLLS (E.)

— The Light of a Love more pure. [Song.] *See* JEWITT (J. M.)

— The Light of Ages. Cantata. *See* PEACE (F. W.)

— Light of all space. Morning hymn. *See* PHILLIPS (H.)

— The Light of Asia. Cantata. *See* BUCK (D.)

— The Light of Asia. Sacred Legend. *See* LARA (I. de) *pseud.*

— The Light of Bethlehem. Carol. *See* LYNAS (Frank)

— The Lights of boyhood's years. Ballad. *See* ROLT (E.)

— The Light of Christmas. Carol. *See* THORPE (Frank)

— The Light of Christmas Morning. Carol. *See* AINGER (J. H.)

— The Light of Dawning. Chorus. *See* CHAIKOVSKY (P. L.) [Symphony No. 5. Op. 64.—Andante cantabile.]

LIGHT

— The Light of Day. Song. *See* MARTIN (George)

— The Light of Early Hope. Ballad. *See* ROEFS (B.)

— The Light of Earth. Anthem. *See* COOMBS (C. W.)

— The Light of Earth. [Sacred song.] *See* COOMBS (C. W.)

— The Light of eternal Day. Song. *See* GOODACRE (E. R.)

— Light of Eternity. Sacred Song. *See* PARKER (W. C.)

— The Light of Eventide. Song. *See* FULCHER (H. M.)

— Light of Eventide. Hymn. *See* HEPBURN (J.)

— Light of Foot, but heavy hearted. Chorus. *See* BRAHMS (J.) [Ungarische Tänze. No. 6.]

— Light of Gladness, Beam divine. Hymn. *See* GIBBONS (O.) [Hymnes and Songs of the Church. Song 13. Oh, my Love how comely now.]

— The Light of God. [Cantata.] *See* JAMES (P.)

— The Light of God. Anthem. *See* LESTER (W.)

— The Light of God. Anthem. *See* WORK (John W.)

— The Light of golden Summer. [Song.] *See* RUMBOLD (*Sir* H.) Six German Songs ... No. 2.

— The Light of Heart. Song. *See* ADDINSELL (Richard S.)

— Light of Heart. Ballad. *See* PETTIT (J. F.)

— Light of heart am I. Cavatina. *See* BARNETT (J.)

— Light of Heart one early Morning. Song. *See* ASTLE (A. M.)

— The Light of Heaven's own Day. [Sacred song.] *See* BRIGGS (C. S.)

— The Light of His Love. Sacred Song. *See* WEBB (R.)

— The Light of Home. Song. *See* AMES (*Mrs* L.)

—– The Light of Home. Song. *See* MOIR (F. L.)

— The Light of Home. Cavatina. *See* VERDI (F. G. F.)

— The Light of Hope. Song. *See* BELTON (*Mrs* W. H.)

— The Light of Hursley. Song. *See* BANTON (C. E.)

— The Light of Life. Sacred Cantata. *See* ASHFORD (E. L.)

— The Light of Life. Song. *See* CARSE (A. von Ahn)

— The Light of Life. [Hymn.] *See* CHALLINOR (F. A.)

— Light of Life. Sacred Song. *See* COOMBS (C. W.)

— The Light of Life. Oratorio. *See* ELGAR (*Sir* E. W.) *Bart.*

— The Light of Life. Sacred Song. *See* EVILLE (V. M.)

— The Light of Life. Cantata. *See* GEIBEL (A.)

— Light of Life. Hymn-Anthem. *See* GREENE (C. W.)

— Light of Life. Anthem. *See* HOSMER (E. S.)

— The Light of Life. Part-Song. *See* LEMMENS (J. N.)

— Light of Life that shineth. Anthem. *See* BRACKETT (F. H.)

— Light of Light. Hymn anthem. *See* BERWALD (William H.)

— Light of Light. Hymn. *See* HAGUE (A.)

— Light of Light. Choral Processional March. *See* LE JEUNE (G. F.)

— Light of Light. Cantata. *See* RHEINBERGER (J. G.)

LIGHT

— Light of Light. [Song.] *See* SEALY (F. L.)

— Light of Light. Anthem. *See* WEISEL (J. H.)

— Light of Light. [Sacred song.] *See* WOOLER (A.)

— Light of Light, celestial Brightness. Carol. *See* NEVIN (G. B.)

— A Light of Light uprises. [Anthem.] *See* HALL (W. H.)

— Light of Lights. Anthem. *See* STEBBINS (G. W.)

— The Light of Love. Part-Song. *See* BATSON (A. W.)

— The Light of Love. Lullaby. *See* DOBSON (A. M. R.)

— The Light of Love. Song. *See* HENRI (J.)

— The Light of Love. [Song.] *See* OFFENBACH (J.) [Les Bavards.—C'est l'Espagne.]

— The Light of Love. Song. *See* O'NEILL (N.)

— The Light of Love. Song. *See* PINSUTI (C. E.)

— The light of lovers' eyes. [Song.] *See* BISHOP (*Sir* H. R.)

— The Light of Man. Carol. *See* OLDEN (G. R. C.)

— The Light of Memory. Canzone Pisana. *See* ROTOLI (A.)

— Light of Memory. Song. *See* SAINT QUENTIN (E.) *pseud.*

— The Light of Memory. Song. *See* SCUDERI (S.)

— The Light of Midnight Stars. Cavatina. *See* ROSSINI (Gioacchino A.) [La Donna del lago.—Elena! Oh tu ch'io chiamo.—Oh quante lagrime.]

— Light of mine Eyes. Song. *See* WARD, afterwards FINDEN (A. W.)

— Light of my Heart. Song. *See* LARA (A. de) *pseud.*

— Light of my Heart, goodbye. Ballad. *See* WILSON (Charles J.)

— Light of my life. Duet. *See* BISHOP (*Sir* H. R.)

— Light of my Life. Song. *See* CROOK (J. S.)

— The Light of my Life. [Part-song.] *See* DANOFF (Bill)

— Light of my Life. Song. *See* GOOLD (W.)

— Light of my Life, forever. Song. *See* WILSON (I. B.)

— Light of my Soul. Serenade. *See* ASPULL (W.)

— Light of my Soul. Song. *See* BESSEY (E. B. E.)

— Light of my Soul. [Song.] *See* BLOCKLEY (John J.) Songs of Grenada. 2.

— Light of my soul. Ballad. *See* HILL (James F.)

— Light of my Soul. Madrigal. *See* PEARSALL (R. L.)

— Light of my Soul. Song. *See* SOLLA (I. de)

— Light of my Soul. Song. *See* STRATFORD (R. H.)

— Light of my soul, arise. Canzonet. *See* PRATTEN (W. S.)

— Light of my soul, good night. Song. *See* SMITH (W. S.)

— The Light of other days. Ballad. *See* BALFE (M. W.)

— The Light of other Days. Song. *See* BRENTNALL (E.)

— The Light of other Days. Part Song. *See* EDWARDS (A. H.)

— The Light of other Days. Part Song. *See* GIBBS (C. A.)

— The Light of other Days. Folk Song. *See* ROBINSON (Stanford F. H.)

LIGHT

— The Light of other Days. Song. *See* ROLT (B.)

— The Light of other Days. Song-romance. *See* SAFRONI (Arnold) *pseud.*

— Light of our Life. Song. *See* LOUGHBOROUGH (R.)

— Light of our Love. [Song.] *See* SONGS. English Songs, *etc.* No. 7. [1857.] fol.   **H. 1235.**

— Light of our Nation. Song. *See* GIBBS (F. G.)

— The Light of Stars. [Song.] *See* ANDERSON (C. A.)

— The Light of Stars. Song. *See* COWEN (*Sir* F. H.)

— The Light of Stars. Song. *See* HOLMES (W. H.)

— The Light of the Ages. Cantata. *See* DARNTON (C.)

— The Light of the Christmas Star. Part Song. *See* KNIGHT (R.)

— Light of the Church. [Anthem.] *See* ILLING (Robert)

— Light of the eyes. [Song.] *See* SUMMERS (J. L.)

— The Light of the Gentiles. Sacred Cantata. *See* GUEST (J.)

— The Light of the Gospel. Anthem. *See* PHILLPOT (J. H.)

— The Light of the Lamp. [Play with music.] *See* OGLE (C.)

— Light of the lonely Pilgrim's Heart. Anthem. *See* MEALE (J. A.)

— The Light of the Lord. Chorus. *See* MOZART (W. A.) [3 teutsche Lieder. No. 2. Im Frühlingsanfang. K. 597.]

— Light of the Moon. [Song.] *See* REEDE (G.)

— The Light of the Morning. Duet. *See* STULTS (R. M.)

— The Light of the Soul. [Sacred song.] *See* WILKES (R. W.) Two Songs, *etc.* [No. 2.]

— The Light of the Stars abide. Song. *See* ARUNDALE (C.)

— The Light of the Sunset Glow. Song. *See* MARTIN (E.) [Evensong.]

— The Light of the Valley: or, The Maid of Kilkenny. [Song.] *See* LINLEY (G.)

— The Light of the World. Song. *See* ADAMS (S.) *pseud.*

— The Light of the World. Sacred Song. *See* BARRI (O.)

— Light of the World. [Anthem.] *See* BRACKETT (F. H.)

— The Light of the World. Cantata. *See* CANDLYN (T. F. H.)

— The Light of the World. Sacred Song. *See* COLEMAN (J.)

— The Light of the World. Anthem. *See* ELGAR (*Sir* E. W.) *Bart.* [The Light of Life.]

— Light of the World. Hymn. *See* ELLIOTT (P.)

— Light of the World. [Anthem.] *See* HAENDEL (G. F.) [Serse.— Ombra mai fù.]

— The Light of the World. Sacred Song. *See* HALL (F.)

— The Light of the World. Cantata. *See* HOLTON (F. B.)

— The Light of the World. Sacred Song. *See* KOVEN (H. L. R. de)

— Light of the World. Service of song. *See* LARBALESTIER (Philip G.)

— Light of the World. Duet. *See* MACY (J. C.)

— Light of the World. [Sacred song.] *See* MURRAY (J. H.)

LIGHT

— Light of the World. Sacred Song. *See* NEIDLINGER (W. H.)

— Light of the World. Hymn. *See* PURDAY (C. H.) [Lead, kindly Light.]

— Light of the World. Sacred Song. *See* SAINT QUENTIN (E.) *pseud.*

— The Light of the World. Anthem. *See* SJOLUND (Paul T.)

— Light of the World. Motet. *See* STARNES (P.)

— The Light of the World. Oratorio. *See* SULLIVAN (*Sir* Arthur S.)

— The Light of these days ne'er forget. Song. *See* MARSH (J. B.)

— The Light of thy Love. Song. *See* PFEIFFER (G. J.)

— Light of Verity. [Canticle.] *See* SWAN (Alfred J.) Liturgical Canticles of the Eastern Church. No. 2.

— The Light of Woman's Eyes. Ballad. *See* HERVÉ DE LA MORINIÈRE (C. S.) [Inez de Castro.]

— The Light of your Eyes. Song. *See* RAY (H.)

— Light of Youth. March-Song. *See* MACY (J. C.)

— Light out of Darkness. Chorus. *See* ELGAR (*Sir* E. W.) *Bart.* [The Light of Life.]

— Light out of Darkness. Cantata. *See* GEIBEL (A.)

— The Light Quadrille. Quadrille Song. *See* BALL (W.)

— Light so tender. [Anthem.] *See* CHEREPNIN (A. N.) Six liturgical Chants ... Opus 103. No. 3.

— The Light still shines beyond. [Song.] *See* WATSON (W. M.)

— A Light streams downward. Duet. *See* SHELLEY (H. R.)

— The Light that guides. Song. *See* THOMPSON (J.)

— The Light that is felt. [Song.] *See* IVES (Charles E.)

— The Light that lies. [Song.] *See* HUHN (B. S.) Three Songs. [No. 2.]

— The Light that lies in my Sweetheart's Eyes. Ballad. *See* SMITH (E.)

— The Light that lies in Woman's Eyes. [Song.] *See* PENN (William H.)

— "Light!"—the Christmas Octave. Cantata. *See* HUNTER (Florence M. L.)

— Light the Lamps up, Lamplighter. [Unison song.] *See* FARJEON (H.)

— The Light to-day is sevenfold. Hymn. *See* BROWN (Arthur H.)

— The Light upon the river. Song. *See* BEHREND (J. A. H.)

— A Light upon the Shore. Sacred Song. *See* LAMARQUÉ (H.)

— A Light upon the shore. [Hymn.] *See* MACGRANAHAN (J.)

— Light upon the twilight Hour. Anthem. *See* CUSTANCE (A. F. M.)

— Light, wandering, murmuring wind. Part Song. *See* PRENDERGAST (A. H. D.)

— The Light within the Window. [Song.] *See* TREVELYAN (A.)

— Light's Abode, celestial Salem. Hymn. *See* FETHERSTON (*Sir* G. R.) *Bart.*

— Light's Abode, celestial Salem. [Anthem.] *See* STANTON (Walter K.)

LIGHT

— Light's glittering Morn. Hymn. *See* RATCLIFFE (W.)

— Light's glittering Morn. Anthem. *See* SANDERS (H.)

— Light's glittering Morn. Easter Solo. *See* SCOTT (J. P.)

— Light's glittering Morn. Anthem. *See* THIMAN (Eric H.)

— Light's glittering Morn. Anthem. *See* WADELY (F. W.)

— Light's glittering Morn. Anthem. *See* WEST (J. E.)

— Light's Morning. [Part-song.] *See* WARRELL (A. S.)

LIGHT (EDWARD)

— The Art of Playing the Guitar ... To which is added a variety of ... Lessons, Airs, Divertimentos, Songs &c. ... adapted for that Instrument. *J. Preston: London*, [1785?] 8°. **e. 321.**

— A Collection of Italian Canzonets &c. for the piano forte or harp, with an accompaniment adapted for the harp-lute. 〈N° 2. Vol. 2.〉 *Printed for the Author: London*, [c. 1810.] 8°. **b. 400. aa. (1.)**

— A Collection of Psalms Hymns, &c. adapted for the Harp-Lute and Lyre. pp. 32. *Printed for the Author: London*, [WM 1814.] 8°.
Engraved by T. C. Bates. **e. 321. b. (7.)**

— [A Collection of Songs and instrumental Pieces for Harp-Lute and P. F., compiled and arranged by E. Light.] pp. 41. *Engrav'd by J. Balls:* [*London*, c. 1805.] 8°.
Imperfect; wanting the titlepage. **e. 138. j. (2.)**

— [A Collection of Songs and instrumental Pieces for Harp-Lute and P. F., probably compiled and arranged by E. Light.] [*London*, c. 1810.] 8°.
Imperfect; pp. 1–32 only. **e. 138. j. (3.)**

— [A Collection of Songs, probably for Harp-Lute, and probably compiled and arranged by E. Light.] pp. 28. [*London*, c. 1810.] 8°.
"No. 1" occurs at the foot of each page. Imperfect; wanting the titlepage. **e. 138. j. (4.)**

— A Collection of Songs properly adapted for the Harplute, Lyre and Guitar. 〈N°[MS 4].〉 pp. 28. *Printed for the Editor: London*, [c. 1810.] fol. **e. 138. j. (5.)**

— Divertimentos, for the Harp-Lute, composed and arranged by E. Light ... Book the First. *Printed for the Author: London*, [1817?] 8°. **e. 321. a.**

— [Another copy.] **e. 321. b. (6.)**

— A First Book, or Master and Scholar's Assistant, being a Treatise on, and an Instructor for Learning Music ... with ... Practical Lessons in progressive order ... in Three Numbers. Composed & arranged by E. Light, *etc.* [No. 1.] *Printed for the Author: London*, [1794.] fol. **h. 3213. g. (6.)**

— The Ladies' Amusement, being a Collection of Favourite Songs and Lessons within Compass of the Guitar, *etc.* No. 1. *Printed for the Author: London*, [1783.] obl. 4°. **a. 76. (3.)**

— Low in a Vale young Willy sat. *A Favourite Scotch Song.* The Words by a young Gentⁿ. *Str[aight] & Sk[illern: London*, 1775?] *s. sh.* fol. **I. 530. (95.)**

— National Airs, Songs, Waltzes, &c. Arranged for the Harp-Lute, *etc.* (Vol. 3. No. 3.) *Printed for the Editor: London*, [1810?] 8°. **E. 1766. f. (3.)**

— [Another copy.] **e. 321. b. (4.)**

— A New and Complete Directory to the Art of playing on the Patent British Lute-harp, with suitable lessons, &c. Composed, arranged and fingered by E. Light. [With a plate.] pp. 26. *Printed for the Author: London*, [1819?] fol. **h. 998.**

LIGHT (EDWARD)

— New and Compleat Instructions for playing on the Harp-Lute. pp. 40. *Printed for the Author: London*, [WM 1812.] 8°. **e. 321. b. (1.)**

— Preludes, Exercises, and Recreations for the Harp-Lute. pp. 44. [*The Author.*] *London*, [1810?] 8°. **e. 321. b. (2.)**

— To please me the more. A favorite song. *Str: & Sk:* [*Straight and Skillern: London*, 1775?] *s. sh.* fol.
Followed by an accompaniment for German flute or guitar. **G. 316. k. (41.)**

— [A Tutor, with a Tablature, for the Harp-Lute-Guitar.] pp. 40. *Engrav'd by J. Balls:* [*London*, c. 1810.] 8°.
Imperfect; wanting the titlepage. Pp. 25–28 are in duplicate. **e. 138. j. (1.)**

— Ye gentle Nymphs. A ballad, *etc. Printed for T. Skillern: London*, [1785?] fol. **G. 316. k. (42.)**

— *See* MOZART (W. A.) [Die Zauberflöte.] Duets for the Harp-Lute, & Piano Forte or Pedal Harp, selected ... from Mozart's favorite opera of the Zauberflotte [*sic*], arranged ... by E. Light. [1814?] 8°. **e. 321. b. (3.)**

LIGHT (FREDERICK PARSONS)

— Diamond Jubilee Song for Ringers. Words by Canon C. Deedes. *J. & W. Chester: Brighton*, [1897.] 8°. **F. 321. n. (24.)**

— Te Deum Laudamus ... in ... D. *Patey & Willis: London*, [1888.] 8°. **E. 579. l. (21.)**

LIGHT (HAROLD E.)

— Love's Awakening. Song, the words by Avatar. *Novello and Co.: London*, [1907.] fol. **G. 805. nn. (11.)**

— Maitai. Waltz for the Pianoforte. *Leonard & Co.: London*, [1901.] fol. **h. 3286. r. (12.)**

— Romance in B flat, for Violin & Piano. *A. Eady & Co.: Auckland*, [1906.] fol. **h. 1612. p. (36.)**

LIGHT (RICHARD)

— An Athenian melody, with variations for the Piano Forte. *London*, [1820.] fol. **h. 117. (27.)**

— Dear is the blush of early light. A canzonet ... from Lord Strangford's translation of Camoens. *London*, [1820?] fol. **G. 860. c. (23.)**

— Loch Errock Side, an admired Scotch Air with Variations for the Piano Forte, *etc. R. Birchall, for the Author: London*, [1820?] fol. **h. 721. c. (3.)**

— Twenty six miscellaneous Little Pieces, for the Piano Forte, *etc.* pp. 12. *Printed for the Author: London*, [c. 1810.] fol. **h. 60. i. (11.)**

— Il Ritorno dal campo, a favorite divertimento, for the piano forte, *etc.* pp. 5. *Bland & Wellers: London*, [WM 1807.] fol. **g. 352. s. (6.)**

— The Salamanca, new waltz, for the piano forte, *etc.* pp. 3. *Goulding, D'Almaine, Potter & Cᵒ: London, Dublin*, [1812.] fol. **h. 1226. d. (8.)**

— [Another copy.] **h. 1480. w. (18.)**

— The Favorite Sicilian Air, "Se tu sarai costante," with Twelve Variations and an Introductory Movement for the Piano Forte, *etc. Printed for the Author: London*, [1823?] fol. **g. 232. d. (29.)**

— Soft as the falling dews of night ... Ballad. *London*, [1820?] fol. **G. 809. b. (17.)**

LIGHT (RICHARD)

— "Softly blow ye breezes." [A ballad, the poetry by H. K. White.] *London*, [1827.] fol.   **H. 1675. (27.)**

— The Admired Swedish Air, "Goda gosse glaset töm" with ten variations for the piano forte. pp. 7. *Printed for the Author: London*, [WM 1813.] fol.   **h. 60. f. (22.)**

— Twelve waltzes in the German style for the Pianoforte. *London*, [1829.] fol.   **h. 117. (26.)**

— The Woodlark. A ballad, *etc.* pp. 5. *J. Balls: London*, [c. 1830.] fol.   **H. 1652. mm. (19.)**

LIGHT (ROBERT)

— An Air with Variations and Accompaniments for Flute and Violin obligati, *etc.* [Parts.] *T. Williamson, for the Author: London*, [1802.] fol.   **h. 117. (25.)**

LIGHT (THOMAS)

— A Selection of Favorite Airs with Var^ns Rondos, Waltzes, Marches &c. Composed & adapted for the Harp-Lute, to which is added a Divertimento, as a Duetto, for Two Harp-Lutes, by T. Light. pp. 28. *Printed for the Editor: London*, [WM 1814.] 8°.   **e. 321. b. (5.)**

LIGHTBOWN (BERTRAM)

— Songs of Innocence. 1. Two little Flowers. 2. Sleep little Daisy. Words by B. Southworth, *etc.* *Weekes & Co.: London*, [1908.] fol.   **H. 1794. vv. (56.)**

LIGHTED

— The Lighted Cross. Cantata. *See* WILSON (I. B.)

— Lighted Home. Song. *See* LARA (I. de)

— The Lighted Hour. [Part-song.] *See* LOHR (Al.)

LIGHTEN

— Lighten our Darkness. Sacred song. *See* BERGER (F.)

— Lighten our Darkness. [Anthem.] *See* BOOTH (J.)

— Lighten our Darkness. [Anthem.] *See* CUSTANCE (A. F. M.)

— Lighten our Darkness. Anthem. *See* DRIVER (N. E.)

— Lighten our Darkness. [Anthem.] *See* GILL (W. H.)

— Lighten our Darkness. Collect. *See* LE FLEMING (C.)

— Lighten our Darkness. [Song.] *See* MERCADANTE (S.)

— Lighten our Darkness. Anthem. *See* PULLEIN (J.)

— Lighten our Darkness. Song. *See* SAINT QUENTIN (E.) *pseud.*

— Lighten our Darkness. Anthem. *See* STORER (H. J.)

— Lighten our Darkness. Anthem. *See* VICARS (G. R.)

— Lighten our Darkness, gracious Lord. Choral. *See* CRESER (W.)

— Lighten our Darkness, we beseech thee, the evening prayer, arranged for one or two voices, with an accompaniment for the piano forte. pp. 3. *J. Duncombe: London*, [c. 1840.] fol.   **G. 517. gg. (21.)**

— Lighten our Darkness, we beseech thee O Lord. [Anthem.] *See* JANSEN (L.)

LIGHTENER

— The Light'ner of the Stars. [Hymn.] *See* BOYLE (I.) Gaelic Hymns. 3.

LIGHTERMAN

— Lighterman Tom. Song. *See* SQUIRE (William H.)

LIGHTEST

— The Lightest, brightest Time. [Two-part song.] *See* LEE (E. M.) [A Poppyland Lullaby, and other Part-Songs.]

LIGHTFOOT (ETHEL M.)

— Three Songs. No. 1. Cradle song. No. 2. Hearts and dreams. No. 3. How will the night take flight. *Weekes & Co.: London*, [1917.] 4°.   **G. 425. v. (16.)**

LIGHTFOOT (FRANCES HARRIET)

— And art thou, love, come back; a ballad, the words by Miss Mitford. *London*, [1829.] fol.   **H. 1675. (29.)**

— "Ben my chree." Song written on the occasion of the royal visit to the Isle of Man ... The words by Miss Musket, adapted to a Manx melody by Miss Lightfoot. pp. 5. *John Mylrea: Douglas*, [c. 1855.] fol.   **H. 1601. jj. (11.)**

— Duettino for two performers on the Pianoforte. *London*, [1828.] fol.   **h. 117. (28.)**

— The Fisherman's Song [begins: "These pearls"]. The words ... from Miss L. S. Costello's "Specimens of the early poetry of France". *London*, [1835.] fol.   **H. 2832. i. (54.)**

— Moonbeams are glancing, duet, *etc.* pp. 7. *Duff & Hodgson: London*, [1839.] fol.   **H. 1601. jj. (12.)**

— [The Nautilus Bark.] "Make ready! make ready! my nautilus Bark;" or, "The Fairy's Voyage" [song] ... The words by a Lady. *Duff & Co.: London*, [1835?] fol.   **G. 385. dd. (4.)**

— The Nautilus Bark. [Song, begins: "Make ready".] Arranged ... by T. J. Dipple. *London*, [1858.] fol. *No. 7 of "Guitar Melodies".*   **H. 2348.**

— Now I come to my peaceful home ... [Song.] Written by Miss Haworth. *London*, [1845?] fol.   **H. 2830. a. (51.)**

— The Saxe Weimar Quadrilles (the subjects taken from various composers). Arranged for two performers on the piano forte by F. H. Lightfoot. pp. 11. *J. Dean: London*, [1836?] fol.   **h. 3290. z. (12.)**

— "See! who is she, with Eyes of Brightness," a ballad, *etc.* *J. Dean: London*, [1835.] fol.   **H. 1650. zz. (13.)**

— A song for the Christmas time, the words by A. Moline. *London*, [1845.] fol.   **H. 1695. (12.)**

— Spirit voices; a song. *London*, [1839.] fol.   **H. 1675. (28.)**

— Turn me to the setting sun, the words by Miss James. [*London*, 1854.] fol.   **H. 1758. (44.)**

LIGHTFOOT (G.)

— The Volunteers of England. Song, the words ... by J. Askham. *Novello and Co.: London*, [1900.] fol.   **G. 807. o. (55.)**

LIGHTFOOT (GORDON)

— The Pony Man. Two part treble voices—S. A. Words and music by Gordon Lightfoot. Arr. by Joe Fortune pp. 5. *Warner Bros.-Seven Arts Music: New York*, [1969.] 8°.   **E. 293. u. (10.)**

LIGHTFOOT (JOHN)

— The "John George Gibson" Royal Arch Chapter, No. 2929. Chapter Hymns, Royal Arch Degree, *etc.* ... by ... J. G. Gibson ... Arranged to music by ... Dr. Lightfoot, *etc.* [*J. G. Gibson: Ebchester*,] 1908. 8°.   **F. 1176. b. (30.)**

LIGHTFOOT (John)

— Winter. [Part-song.] Words from Montgomery. *See* Glee. The Glee Garland, No. 16. [1884.] 8°.　　　　　　**E. 1333.**

LIGHT-FOOTED

— The Light-Footed Fairy. Three-part song. *See* Blower (Maurice)

LIGHTHEART

— Lightheart Lane. Song. *See* Bowie (P. A.)

LIGHT-HEARTED

— Light-hearted are we and free from care. Chorus. *See* Root (G. F.) [The Haymakers.]

— The Light-hearted Fairy. Part-Song. *See* Hyatt (N. I.)

— The Light-hearted Fairy. Two-part song. *See* Silver (Alfred J.)

— The Light-hearted Fairy. [Song.] *See* White (F. H.)

LIGHTHILL (A. P.)

— Why art thou far away. [Song, begins: "Warum sind denn die Rosen so blass". "Why are the roses all so pale."] Words by H. Heine. (Trans. by C. Sprague.) *Boston* [*Mass.*], 1864. fol.　　　**H. 1780. f. (18.)**

LIGHTHOUSE

— The Lighthouse. [Song.] *See* Burleigh (C.) Songs ... Op. 32. No. 5.

— The Lighthouse. Song. *See* Cherry (J. W.)

— The Lighthouse. Song. *See* Croxall (J. F.)

— The Lighthouse. Song. *See* Deane (H. C.) *Mrs.*

— The Lighthouse. [Song.] *See* Dye (A. J.)

— The Light-House. [Recitation.] *See* Gest (E.)

— The Lighthouse. Song. *See* Horner (B. W.)

— The Lighthouse. Song. *See* Klitz (P.) Songs of the Mid-Watch. No. 6.

— The Light-House. Part-Song. *See* Linders (K.)

— The Lighthouse. Song. *See* Moir (F. L.)

— The Lighthouse. Song. *See* Nelson (H. H.)

— The Lighthouse. Part-Song. *See* Young (G.)

— The Lighthouse at the Bar. [Sacred song.] *See* Hart (M. R.)

— The Lighthouse by the Sea. Vocal Waltz. *See* Davis (G. L.)

— The Lighthouse Keeper. Song. *See* Devers (W. J.)

— The Lighthouse Keeper. Song. *See* Molloy (J. L.)

— The Lighthouse Keeper. Song. *See* Mountfort (J.)

— The Lighthouse Keeper. [Two-part song.] *See* Moy (E.)

— The Lighthouse Keeper. [Song.] *See* Silvani (L.)

— The Lighthouse Keeper's Story. [Musical monologue.] *See* Clarke (C.)

— The Lighthouse Keepers. Song. *See* Hime (E. L.)

— The Lighthouse Light. Song. *See* Mount (J.)

— The Lighthouse Song. [Song.] *See* Dennée (C. F.) [The Defender.]

LIGHTHOUSE

— The Lighthouse Tower. Song. *See* Clemens (T. L.)

— The Lighthouse Tower. Song. *See* Loewe (G.) *pseud.*

LIGHTLY

— Lightly bounding o'er the green. Ballad. *See* Craven (J. T.)

— Lightly, brightly, cheerily go. Part-Song. *See* Troup (E. J.)

— Lightly foot it. [Part-song.] *See* Richter (R.)

— Lightly leaping o'er the mountains. Song. *See* Hewke (C. M.)

— Lightly, lightly. Song & Chorus. *See* Chassaigne (F.) [Nadgy.]

— Lightly, lightly swiftly follow. [Song.] *See* Lee (George A.)

— Lightly o'er the dewy way. Song. *See* Hook (J.)

— Lightly o'er the rapid Rhine. [Two-part song.] *See* Bishop (*Sir* Henry R.)

— Lightly o'er the Village Green. Glee. *See* Spofforth (R.)

— Lightly o'er the Wave. Glee. *See* Smith (John) *Mus. Doc.* [The Minstrel.]

— Lightly she tripped o'er the Dales. Madrigal. *See* Mundy (J.)

— Lightly, softly. Trio. *See* Flotow (F. F. A. von) *Baron.*

— Lightly tread, 'tis hallow'd Ground. A celebrated glee for three voices. [By George Berg.] *John Lee: Dublin,* [c. 1795.] *s. sh.* fol.　　　　　　**H. 1653. j. (44.)**

— Lightly tread. A favorite glee for three voices. [By George Berg.] *In:* Wine. Wine does wonders, *etc.* [c. 1800.] fol.　　　　　　**H. 1653. j. (49.)**

— Lightly tread. Glee. *See* Purcell (H.) [*Doubtful and Supposititious Works.*]

— Lightly tread, 'tis hallowed Ground. Trio. *See* Scotland (John) *pseud.*

— Lightly treading, onward creeping. Trio. *See* Rossini (G. A.) [Il Barbiere di Siviglia.—Zitti, zitti.]

— Lightly tripping. Choral Dance. *See* Pearson (A.)

— Lightly tripping o'er the mountain. Cavatina. *See* Lee (George A.)

— Lightly we met. Song. *See* Claudette (E.)

— Lightly won is lightly held. Duet. *See* A'Beckett (Mary A.) [The Young Pretender.]

— Lightly wreathe the mazy dances. Song. *See* Clifford (W.)

LIGHTNING

— The Lightning King. [Song.] *See* Ervini (J. C.)

— Lightning Results. Song. *See* Randall (Harry) *Comedian.*

LIGHTOLLERS (C. W.)

— Three Hymn Tunes. *Novello, Ewer & Co.: London & New York,* [1888.] 8°.　　　　　　**B. 579. d. (37.)**

LIGHTON (William)

— Woodland nymphs. Mazurka. [P. F.] *New York,* 1863. fol.　　　　　　**h. 1459. p. (7.)**

LIGHTS

— Lights and Shadows. Song. *See* Gottheimer (M. B.)

LIGHTS

— The Lights are fair in my father's hall. Ballad. *See* HOGARTH (G.)

— The Lights far out at sea. Song. *See* GATTY, afterwards SCOTT-GATTY (*Sir* A. S.)

— Lights in Fishing Boats at Sea. Song. *See* FERRARI (G.) Three Songs. [No. 3.]

— The Lights o' Cowtown. [Part-song.] *See* RUFFNER (H. W.) Frontier Scenes ... 2.

— The Lights o' Home. Song. *See* TEMPLE (H.) *pseud.*

— The Lights of Bantry Bay. [Song.] *See* SANDERSON (W. E.)

— The Lights of Easter. Chorus. *See* GAUL (H. B.)

— The Lights of Home. Song. *See* ALLON (O.)

— The Lights of Home. [Part-song.] *See* BARTHOLOMEW (Marshall)

— The Lights of Home. Song. *See* EDEN (R.)

— The Lights of Home. [Song.] *See* GILL (Mason)

— The Lights of Home. [Song.] *See* GODWIN (Will J.)

— The Lights of Home. Song. *See* GRAY (H.)

— The Lights of Home. Song. *See* HUBBARD (S. W.)

— The Lights of Home. Two-part Song. *See* RATHBONE (G.)

— The Lights of Home. Song. *See* SEILER (C. L.)

— Lights of Home. [Song.] *See* TRAHERN (Al.)

— The Lights of London Town. Song. *See* DIEHL (L.)

— The Lights of Venice. Song. *See* MOIR (F. L.)

— Lights out! Song. *See* BATH (H. C.)

— Lights out. [Songs.] *See* GURNEY (I.)

LIGHTSOME

— Lightsome I wander. Ballad. *See* MACFARREN (W. C.)

LIGHTWOOD (JAMES THOMAS)

— Choosing the Right. Temperance Song, with Chorus, words by A. Wallington. *C. H. Kelly:* [*London*, 1911.] 8°.
The "Choir" Series of Music Leaflets, No. 4. **D. 619. kk. (7.)**

— "Head of Thy Church triumphant." Anthem, words by C. Wesley. *R. Culley: London*, [1907.] 8°.
No. 11 of the "Choir" Series of copyright Anthems.
F. 987. a.

— Head of Thy Church triumphant, *etc.* [Tonic sol-fa notation.] *R. Culley: London*, [1910.] 4°.
No. 11a of the "Choir" Series of Tonic Sol-fa Anthems.
B. 1097.

— Methodist Church Music. First series—eighteenth century. [Hymns.] pp. 23. *Robert Culley: London*, [1908?] 8°.
"Choir" Series Services of Song. no. 3. **C. 812. a. (1.)**

— The Music of the Methodist Hymn-Book, being the story of each tune with biographical notices of the composers. [With facsimiles.] pp. xxiii. 549. *Epworth Press: London*, 1935. 8°.
B. 1179. kk.

— The Radiant Sun. Anthem for S. A. T. B., words by R. C. Trampleasure. *C. H. Kelly: London*, [1907.] 8°.
No. 10 of the "Choir" series of copyright Anthems. **F. 987. a.**

LIGHTWOOD (JAMES THOMAS)

— The Radiant Sun, *etc.* [Tonic sol-fa notation.] *R. Culley: London*, [1910.] 4°.
No. 10a of the "Choir" Series of Tonic Sol-fa Anthems.
B. 1097.

— Two Sketches for Violin & Piano. 2 no. *J. Williams: London*, [1896.] fol. **h. 1612. c. (34*.)**

— Thou didst leave Thy Throne. Sacred Song, words by ... E. E. S. Elliott. *R. Culley: London*, [1908.] fol.
H. 1187. ll. (8.)

— Thou didst leave Thy Throne ... (Anthem.) Arranged by Dr. R. Dunstan from the Song, *etc.* *"The Choir" Office: London*, [1922.] 8°.
"Choir" Series of Anthems, No. 153. **F. 987. a.**

— 12 Tunes to popular hymns. *London*, [1883.] 8°.
E. 605. n. (24.)

— *See* HYMNS. [*English.*] The "New Series" of Hymns and Tunes for Anniversary Services. (Joint Editors ... J. T. Lightwood.) [1915, *etc.*] 8°. **E. 497. r.**

LIGNER (F.)

— Ah! vous dirai-je maman, thème varié pour harmonie ou fanfare. [Conductor's part.] *Paris*, [1883.] 8°.
f. 419. (19.)

— Lune de Miel polka. [P. F.] *London*, [1877.] 8°.
No. 386 of the "Alliance Musicale ... Album Bijou". **f. 406.**

— Thème Suisse varié pour Fanfare avec Clarinettes, Hautbois et Flûtes ad lib. [Conductor's part.] *Paris*, [1883.] 8°.
f. 419. (20.)

— *See* ADAM (A. C.) [La Poupée de Nuremberg.] Ouverture ... orchestration militaire par F. Ligner. [1884.] 8°.
e. 666. g. (19.)

— *See* MÉHUL (E. H.) [La Chasse du Jeune Henri.] Ouverture ... arrangée ... par F. Ligner. [1883.] 8°. **f. 419. (21.)**

LIGNIVILLE (EUGÈNE DE) *Marquis*

— Stabat Mater à tre voci in canone, *etc.* [*Bologna*, 1767.] obl. fol. **C. 839.**

LIGTELIJN (JOHAN)

— *See* DUSSEK (J. L.) Sonate posthume à quatre mains. Pour le pianoforte. ⟨Revision: J. Ligtelijn.⟩ [1957.] *obl.* 4°.
e. 379. m. (1.)

— *See* ECKARD (J. G.) Œuvres complètes pour le clavecin ou le pianoforte. Publiées avec une introduction par Eduard Reeser, annotées par J. Ligtelijn. [1956.] 4°. **g. 1126. i. (5.)**

LIGUORI, JADVIGA, *Princess*

— *See* CHLUDZINSKA (Jadviga) *Princess Liguori.*

LIGUORI (ALPHONSO MARIA DE')

— *See* ALPHONSO MARIA [de' Liguori], *Saint.*

LIGUORO (FEDERICO GUGLIELMO DE)

— La Fioraja. Arietta [begins: "Chi vuole"]. *London*, [1867.] fol. **H. 1772. s. (2.)**

— Il gondoliere [begins: "Del meriggio al sole ardente"] ... parole di M. Maggioni. *London*, [1859.] fol.
H. 1788. w. (13.)

— Le illusioni d'amore, [begins: "Del mar, del mar gl'irati flutti"] ricercata su parole di M. Maggioni. *London*, [1859.] fol. **H. 1788. w. (14.)**

LIGUORO (Federico Guglielmo de)

— La maschera [begins: "Dell'invocato giorno"] ... parole di M. Maggioni. *London*, [1859.] fol.   **H. 1788. w. (15.)**

— Pelican Polka. [P. F.] *London*, [1866.] fol.   **h. 1460. w. (6.)**

— Serenata, "Bogli astri che largite" ... parole di M. Maggioni. *London*, [1859.] fol.   **H. 1788. w. (12.)**

— *See* Alphonso Maria [de' Liguori], *Saint*. Cantata on the Passion of our Lord Jesus Christ ... arranged ... by the Chevalier F. W. de Liguoro. 1860. fol.   **H. 1187. q. (1.)**

LIGURISCHES

— Ligurisches Lied. [Song.] *See* Kahn (R.) Fünf Gesänge ... Op. 12. No. 3.

— Ligurisches Volkslied. [Song.] *See* Zizold (W.) Sechs Lieder, *etc.* No. 3.

LIHU (Annette de)

— Maman c'est bien dommage. Romance. *London*, [1815?] fol.   **G. 806. c. (24.)**

— L'Orphéline; Romance [for two voices]. *London*, [1817?] fol.   **H. 1675. (30.)**

LIHU (Annette de) and LIHU (Victorine de)

— French Song ⟨Filles du hameau⟩, arranged for two voices, by Mesd^lles de Lihu, *etc.* pp. 3. *Printed for the Mesd^lles de Lihu: London*, [1812.] fol.   **G. 809. n. (6.)**

LIHU (Victorine de)

— *See* Gilles (H. N.) "Le troubadour," ... arrangée par V. de Lihu. [1817?] fol.   **H. 1670. (15.)**

— *See* Lihu (A. de) and Lihu (V. de) French Song ⟨Filles du hameau⟩, arranged for two voices, by Mesd^lles de Lihu, *etc.* [1812.] fol.   **G. 809. n. (6.)**

LIKE

— Like a cloudless summer morning. Grand scena. *See* Marschner (H.) [Der Vampyr.]

— Like a Cradle rocking. [Song.] *See* Scott (C. P.) Two Songs. [No. 1.]

— Like a Diamond from the Sky. [Song.] *See* Bennett (Leo)

— Like a dream, bright and fair. *See* Flotow (F. F. A. von) *Baron*. [Martha.—Ach! so fromm.]

— Like a dream of my childhood. Ballad. *See* Linley (G.)

— Like a dream that fleeteth. Sicilienne. *See* Balfe (M. W.) [Sicilian Bride.]

— Like a dream the Past forgetting. Cavatina. *See* Donizetti (D. G. M.)

— Like a Flower. Song for Christmas. *See* Stanton (W. K.)

— Like a Flower. Ballad. *See* Wrighton (W. T.)

— Like a Garden after Rain. Song. *See* Allitsen (F.) *pseud.*

— Like a Girl. Song. *See* Tabrar (Joseph)

— Like a good little Girl should do. Song and chorus. *See* Bratton (John W.)

— Like a good little Wife should do. Song. *See* Leigh (Fred W.) and Keen (W. P.)

— Like a kindly Spider. Song. *See* Thomas (A. G.) [The Golden Web.]

LIKE

— Like a Lady. [Song.] *See* Le Brunn (G.)

— Like a Lilac. [Song.] *See* Sveinbjørnsson (S.)

— Like a red, red Rose. Song. *See* Thorne (C.)

— Like a River gently gliding. [Hymn.] *See* Challinor (F. A.)

— Like a sad Song. [Part-song.] *See* Denver (John)

— Like a Sailor of the King. Song. *See* Mellor (Tom)

— Like a Ship adrift at Sea. [Song.] *See* Ellis (Harry A.)

— Like a Ship that drifted away. [Song.] *See* Bowers (Frederick V.)

— Like a snow flake on the stream. Song. *See* Kuecken (F. W.) [Lieder nach Volksmelodien. Op. 74a. No. 2. Als ein Kind ich noch war.]

— Like a Star that falls from Heaven. [Song.] *See* Mills (Kerry)

— Like a summer shower. Ballad. *See* Plumpton (A.)

— Like a tale that is told. Song. *See* Barri (O.)

— Like a tree beside the river. Song. *See* Aïdé (H.)

— Like a Turk. Comic Song. *See* Corri (W.)

— Like a virgin Heart. Song. *See* Clayton (I. M.)

— Like a virgin Heart. [Song.] *See* Parker (G.) *of London.*

— Like a Vision. Song. *See* Collard (W. F.)

— Like a Voice from afar. [Chorus.] *See* Bauer (O.)

— Like a Well-spring in the Desert. Song. *See* Abt (F. W.) [Drei Lieder. Op. 213. No. 1. Ich denke dein.]

— Like an Island in a River. [Song.] *See* Norcott (S. L.)

— Like an island in a river. [Song.] *See* Rudall (H. A.)

— Like angel bright. Song. *See* Linwood (E.)

— Like Angel Voices. Song. *See* Wyse (E.)

— Like Angel's Eyes they gleam. *Gentle Smiles.* [Part-song.] *See* Songs. Short Songs, No. 14. [1882.] *s. sh.* 8°.   **D. 856. e. (10.)**

— Like Apple-Blossom. Part Song. *See* Lloyd (C. H.)

— Like Apple Blossom. Song. *See* Wellings (J. M.)

— Like April's kissing May. [Song.] *See* Crist (L. B.)

— Like as a damask rose. Four-part song. *See* Mounsey, afterwards Bartholomew (A. S.)

— Like as a Father. Anthem. *See* Bennett (*Sir* W. S.)

— Like as a Father. Anthem. *See* Berridge (Arthur)

— Like as a Father. [Anthem.] *See* Candlyn (T. F. H.)

— Like as a Father. Anthem. *See* Challinor (F. A.)

— Like as a Father. [Sacred song.] *See* Chase (C. C.)

— Like as a Father. Sacred song. *See* Davis (Eliza)

— Like as a Father. Anthem. *See* Dodds (G. R.)

— Like as a Father. Anthem. *See* Field (J. T.)

— Like as a Father. Anthem. *See* Hatton (J. L.)

— Like as a Father. [Anthem.] *See* Kay (Ulysses) A new Song ii.

— Like as a Father. Sacred Song. *See* MacAlpin (C.)

— Like as a father. Duet. *See* Macfarren (*Sir* G. A.)

LIKE

— Like as a Father. Anthem. *See* MARTIN (*Sir* G. C.) [O come before His Presence with Singing.]

— Like as a Father. Anthem. *See* PALMER (Peggy S.)

— Like as a Father. Anthem. *See* PULL (R.)

— Like as a Father. Anthem. *See* RICKMAN (F. R.)

— Like as a Father. Sacred Song. *See* SCOTT (J. P.)

— Like as a Father. Anthem. *See* SHENTON (A. E.)

— Like as a Father. Anthem. *See* STAPLES (H. J.)

— Like as a Father. [Anthem.] *See* STARR (T. B.)

— Like as a Father doth pity his Children. [Anthem.] *See* GEISLER (J. C.) [Wie sich ein Vater über Kinder erbarmet.]

— Like as a Father pitieth his Children. Anthem. *See* ELLIS (W.)

— Like as a Hart. Anthem. *See* WOLSTENHOLME (W.)

— Lyke as a ship. [Song.] *See* CUNYNGHAME (L.)

— Like as Christ was raised. Anthem. *See* HARRIS (C.)

— Like as the damask rose you see. Glee. *See* CROTCH (W.)

— Like as the doleful Dove. [Part-song.] *See* TALLIS (Thomas)

— Like as the Hart. Anthem. *See* ADAMS (T.)

— Like as the Hart desireth. Sacred Song. *See* ALLITSEN (F.) *pseud.*

— Like as the Hart desireth the Water Brooks. Aria. *See* ALWYN (William C.)

— Like as the Hart. Anthem. *See* BARRENGER (P.)

— Like as the Hart. Anthem. *See* CLARKE (J. H. S.)

— Like as the Hart. Anthem. *See* GILL (W. H.) Easy Anthems ... No. 4.

— Like as the Hart. [Anthem.] *See* GREENE (Maurice)

— Like as the Hart desireth the Water-brooks. [Sacred song.] *See* HARKER (F. F.)

— Like as the Hart. Anthem. *See* HEWLETT (W. H.)

— Like as the Hart desireth the Waterbrooks. [Anthem.] *See* HOWELLS (H. N.) Four Anthems ... No. 3.

— Like as the Hart. Introit. *See* HOYTE (W. S.)

— Like as the Hart. [Anthem.] *See* KING (O. A.)

— Like as the Hart. Anthem. *See* LACY (F. St. J.)

— Like as the Hart. Motet. *See* LASSO (O. di) [Cantiones Aliquot Quinque Vocum.—Quem ad modum.]

— Like as the Hart. Motett. *See* LE JEUNE (Charles A.)

— Like as the Hart. [Anthem.] *See* LIDDLE (S.)

— Like as the Hart. Anthem. *See* LOCKNANE (C.)

— Like as the Hart. Anthem. *See* MARKS (J. C.) *the Younger.*

— Like as the Hart. [Anthem.] *See* NOVELLO (V.) [In manus tuos.]

— Like as the hart. Anthem. *See* PACEY (F. W.)

— Like as the Hart. [Anthem.] *See* REDHEAD (A.) Three Short Anthems ... No. 1.

— Like as the Hart. [Anthem.] *See* RICHARDSON (A. M.)

— Like as the hart. Introit. *See* ROBERTS (G. B.)

LIKE

— Like as the Hart. Anthem. *See* ROBERTS (J. E.)

— Like as the Hart. [Anthem.] *See* ROE (Betty E.)

— Like as the Hart. [Anthem.] *See* SCOTT (S.)

— Like as the hart. Anthem. *See* SMITH (T.)

— Like as the Hart. Anthem. *See* SPENCE (W. R.)

— Like as the Hart desireth. Anthem. *See* STORER (H. J.)

— Like as the Hart desireth. Solo. *See* STUTFIELD (G. L.)

— Like as the Hart. Anthem. *See* TALINTYRE (R. J.)

— Like as the Hart. [Anthem.] *See* WARE (H.)

— Like as the Hart. [Anthem.] *See* WEST (J. A.) *Composer.*

— Like as the Hart. Anthem. *See* WHELPLEY (B. L.)

— Like as the Hart. Psalm. *See* WILLIAMSON (*Sir* Malcolm B. G. C.) [Psalms of the Elements.—Water Psalms. 3.]

— Like as the Hart. Sentence. *See* YOUNG (F. H.)

— Like as the Waves. [Song.] *See* AMES (J. C.)

— Like as we do put our Trust in Thee. Anthem. *See* WESLEY (Charles)

— Like as we lie. Golf Song. *See* MOLLOY (J. L.)

— Like desert Woods. [Part-song.] *See* STANFORD (*Sir* C. V.) Six Elizabethan Pastorals. Second Set. Op. 53. No. 2.

— Like Fairy Elves. Vocal Polka. *See* LAURENT DE RILLÉ (F. A.)

— Like gentle Turtles cooing. *The Happy Swain.* The Words by Mr. A. Bradley, a New Song. [*London*, 1720?] fol.
H. 1601. (293.)

— [Another edition.] Like gentle Turtles cooing. *The Happy Swain.* The Words by Mr. A. Bradley, *etc.* [*London*, 1725?] *s. sh.* fol.
G. 316. g. (40.)

— [Another copy.]
G. 305. (295.)

— Like Him. Song. *See* GEORGE (R. S.)

— Like his Father. Song. *See* WINCOTT (Harry)

— Like leaves in the autumn. Ballad. *See* LINLEY (G.)

— Like Love for thee. Ballad. *See* DE BEAUVOIR (*Sir* J. E.) *Bart.*

— Like Mistress, like Maid. Ballad. *See* SANDERSON (J.) [The London Apprentice.]

— Like Morning Dew. Song. *See* CHIGNELL (R.)

— Like morning in beauty shining. *See* VERDI (F. G. F.) [I Masnadieri.—Di ladroni.]

— Like Music on the Waters. [Song.] *See* WATTS (W. H.) Two Songs, *etc.* No. 1.

— Like my own Mother dear. [Song.] *See* O'HARA (Fiske)

— Like Pearls the Dewdrops rest. Part-Song. *See* SCHUMANN (R. A.) [Ritornelle. Op. 65. No. 1.]

— Like Rivers Flowing. [Part-song.] *See* BUSH (Alan D.)

— Like silver Lamps. Anthem. *See* BARNBY (*Sir* J.)

— Like Soldiers do. Part-Song. *See* VINCENT (C. J.) Songs and Part-Songs, *etc.* No. 30.

— Like some bright Bird. Song. *See* DONIZETTI (D. G. M.) [Linda di Chamounix.—O luce di quest' anima.]

— Like some bright bird. [Song.] *See* VENZANO (L.)

LIKE

— Like some frail Bark I wander. Aria. *See* ARIOSTI (A.) [Artaserse.—Son come navicella.]

— Like some pure angel. Song. *See* ROMER (F.)

— Like some young Troubadour. Song. *See* CADMAN (C. W.)

— Like sparkling Champaigne. [Song.] *See* BATTISHILL (J.) [The Foundling.]

— Like Stars above. Song. *See* SQUIRE (W. H.)

— Like Stars in Heav'n. Song. *See* BROWN (M. H.) Two Songs, *etc.* [No. 1.]

— Like Swallows in Air. [Song.] *See* ESSEX (George)

— Like the Birds on yonder Tree. Chorus. *See* VINCENT (C. J.) [The Persian Princess.]

— Like the dawn, soft and calm. *See* FLOTOW (F. F. A. von) *Baron.* [Martha.—Ach! so fromm.]

— Like the dew in the heart of a blossom. [Song.] *See* BARKER (G. A.)

— Like the driven Cloud. [Song.] *See* BRAHMS (J.) [6 Gesänge. Op. 6 No. 5. Wie die Wolke nach der Sonne.]

— Like the evergreen so shall our friendship be. [Song.] *See* LODER (E. J.)

— Like the flowing Tide, I'll come back to you. Ballad. *See* CASTLING (Harry) and MILLS (A. J.)

— Like the Grass are all Man's Days. [Anthem.] *See* DAVIES (Thomas) *of Ebbw Vale.* [Dyddiau dyn sydd fel glaswelltyn.]

— Like the Hues of Morning. [Song.] *See* SCHUBERT (F. P.) [Ganymed. Op. 19. No. 3.]

— Like the Lark. [Song.] *See* ABT (F. W.) [Zwei Lieder für Sopran ... Op. 501. No. 2. Die Lerche.]

— Like the lily in the valley. Song. *See* TULLY (J. H.)

— Like the low murmur of the secret stream. Sacred song. *See* DAVIS (Eliza)

— Like the moon fair and bright. [Song.] *See* FLOTOW (F. F. A. von) *Baron.* [Martha.—Ach! so fromm.]

— Like the Nestling's Note. Song. *See* MOORE (I. M.)

— Like the Pear-Tree. [Part-song.] *See* IL'YASHENKO (A.)

— Like the Rose he wears To-Day. [Song.] *See* BALL (E. R.)

— Like the Rose, you're the fairest Flower. Ballad. *See* NEWMAN (Harry L.)

— Like the Rosebud. Song. *See* LA FORGE (F.)

— Like the Roses bloom and wither. Song. *See* DANDAR (John)

— Like the Sea in full Flood. Song. *See* REICHENBACH (M. von)

— Like the Sunshine. [Hymn.] *See* CHALLINOR (F. A.)

— Like the swell of Summer's ocean. Ballad. *See* WRIGHT (T. H.)

— Like the Woodlark. Part Song. *See* MUNRO (D. R.)

— Like the young God of Wine. Song. *See* GREENE (M.) [Phœbe.]

— Like Thee. Ballad. *See* BISHOP (*Sir* H. R.)

— Like this. [Action song.] *See* FRISE (J.) Frise's Songs. No. 10.

— Like this Flower, my Love is fading. [Song.] *See* PYNE (Will)

— Like to a Rosebud in my Fair. [Song.] *See* SPENCE (W. R.)

LIKE

— Like to a water lily. Song. *See* ZOELLER (C.)

— Like to Like. Song. *See* DENZA (L.)

— Like to like. Song. *See* FARRELL (R.)

— Like to the Damask Rose. Song. *See* ELGAR (*Sir* E. W.) *Bart.*

— Like to the Damask Rose. [Song.] *See* LAWES (Henry)

— Like to the falling of a star. Song. *See* MACMURDIE (J.)

— Like two proud armies. Madrigal. *See* WEELKES (T.)

— Like Violets pale. Song. *See* ALLITSEN (F.) *pseud.*

— Like Waves which o'er the Ocean. Barcarole. *See* WALLACE (William V.)

— Like yer Mammy did. [Song.] *See* WALSH (Austin)

— Like yon bright bird. Song. *See* KELLER (Matthias)

— Like yon Mountain Eagle. [Song.] *See* NEULAND (Wilhelm) [Hätt' ich Flügel.]

— Like you. Song. *See* MARIANI (M.)

— Like you clear and tranquil River. Ballad. *See* LINLEY (George)

— Like your Apron and your Bonnet (and your little Quaker Gown). [Song.] *See* LAWRANCE (Alfred J.)

LIKELYKE-MUNELY ( )

— Kuu ipo. (Hawaiian song.) For four-part chorus of men's voices a cappella ... Arranged by Elliot Forbes. *Hawaiian & Eng.* pp. 6. *G. Schirmer: New York*, [1965.] 8°. *Part of "Harvard-Radcliffe choral Music".* **F. 163. xx. (5.)**

LIKENESS

— Likeness without Flattery. [Song.] *See* HOOK (J.)

LIKES

— The Likes of her. Song. *See* GAINES (S. R.)

— The Likes of they. Song. *See* LIDGEY (C. A.)

LIKHODY (A.)

— *See* LUFER (A.) and LIKHODY (A.) Збірник українських пожовтневих народних пісень, *etc.* 1936. 8°. **F. 1771. d.**

LIKING

— Likin' ain't like Lovin'. [Song.] *See* EUROPE (James R.)

— Liking's not a Bit like Loving. [Song.] *See* LEBOY (Grace)

LI'L'

— *See* LITTLE.

LILA

— Lila. [Hymn.] *See* JONES (I. I.)

LILAC

— The Lilac. Song. *See* DERANSART (E.)

— Lilac. Song. *See* WELLER (W. H.)

— Lilac and Apple-Spray. Song. *See* ROECKEL (J. L.)

— Lilac and Laburnum. Song. *See* PARKER (C. J. S.)

LILAC

— Lilac and Laburnam. Song. *See* READ (J. C.)

— Lilac and Lilies. Song. *See* STUBBS (A. M.)

— Lilac and Star and Bird. [Song.] *See* ROGERS (W. L.)

— Lilac Bloom. Song. *See* BENEDICT (*Sir* J.)

— The Lilac Bloom. Song. *See* SOLLA (I. de)

— Lilac Blossoms. Song. *See* THOMÉ (F. L. J.)

— Lilac Blossoms. Song. *See* WENRICH (Percy)

— The Lilac Cotton Gown. Song. *See* HILL (D.)

— The Lilac Domino. Operetta. *See* CUVILLIER (C.) [Der lila Domino.]

— The Lilac-Flower. Song. *See* LEATH (V. de)

— The Lilac Girl. Song. *See* LETTERS (Will)

— The Lilac Hour. [Song.] *See* WACHTMEISTER (A. R.) Three Songs, *etc.* [No. 2.]

— The Lilac is out. [Part-song.] *See* GRIFFITH (W.)

— The Lilac-spotted Gown. Two-part song. *See* WREFORD (Reynell)

— Lilac Time. Song. *See* FOOTE (A. W.)

— Lilac-Time. Play with Music. *See* SCHUBERT (F. P.) [*Collected Works.—h.*] [Das Dreimäderlhaus.]

— Lilac-Time. [Song.] *See* SCOTT (C. M.)

— Lilac Time. Song. *See* WILLEBY (C.)

— The Lilac Tree. Song. *See* MOIR (F. L.)

— The Lilac Tree. Song. *See* YOUNG (H. M.)

LILACS

— Lilacs. [Song.] *See* CADMAN (C. W.)

— Lilacs. [Song.] *See* CALDWELL (Anna P.)

— Lilacs. [Song.] *See* COLE (R. G.) Songs ... Op. 37. No. 1.

— Lilacs. [Song.] *See* KERNOCHAN (M.) Two Short Songs, *etc.* [No. 1.]

— The Lilacs. [Song.] *See* PFEFFERKORN (Otto)

— Lilacs. [Song.] *See* RAKHMANINOV (S. V.) [Romanzen. Op. 21. No. 5. Flieder.]

— Lilacs. [Part-song.] *See* SHALLENBERG (Robert)

— Lilacs. Song. *See* SPEYER (C. A.)

— The Lilacs. Song. *See* TOURS (F. E.)

— Lilacs. [Song.] *See* WOLPE (Stefan) Six Songs from the Hebrew. 1.

— Lilacs. Song. *See* WRIGHT (E.)

— Lilacs are blooming in Maytime. [Song.] *See* ELLIOTT (Dorothy)

— The Lilacs are in bloom. Song. *See* MANN (A.)

LILAS

— Les Lilas. Valse chantée. *See* DERANSART (E.)

— Les Lilas. [Song.] *See* LAMOUREUX (A.) Fleurs de mon Pays ... Op. 1. No. 1.

— Les Lilas. Mélodie. *See* POISOT (C.)

LILAS

— Les Lilas Blancs. Valse chantée. *See* GOUNOD (C. F.)

— Lilas blancs. [Song.] *See* LACOME D'ESTALENX (P. J. J.)

— Les Lilas ont fleuri. [Song.] *See* MARTI (E.)

LILBURN (CHARLES)

— All the Days of the Week. ⟨Song.⟩ Written, composed ... by C. Lilburn. [Staff and tonic sol-fa notation. Voice part.] *Francis, Day & Hunter: London,* [1905.] *s. sh.* fol.
H. 3985. aa. (1.)

— All the Days of the Week, *etc.* ⟨Song.⟩ [With separate voice part.] 2 pt. *Francis, Day & Hunter: London,* [1905.] fol.
H. 3985. aa. (2.)

— "I will love you just the same." ⟨Song.⟩ Written and composed by C. Lilburn, *etc.* [Staff and tonic sol-fa notation. Voice part.] *Francis, Day & Hunter: London,* [1906.] *s. sh.* fol.
H. 3985. aa. (3.)

— "I will love you just the same," *etc.* ⟨Song.⟩ [With separate voice part.] 2 pt. *Francis, Day & Hunter: London,* [1906.] fol.
H. 3985. aa. (4.)

— What will become of England? ⟨Song.⟩ Written, composed ... by C. Lilburn. [Staff and tonic sol-fa notation. Voice part.] *Francis, Day & Hunter: London,* [1909.] *s. sh.* fol.
H. 3985. aa. (5.)

— What will become of England? ⟨Song.⟩ [With separate voice part.] 2 pt. *Francis, Day & Hunter: London,* [1909.] fol.
H. 3985. aa. (6.)

— You're the Girl I've been waiting for. ⟨Song.⟩ Written, composed ... by C. Lilburn. [Staff and tonic sol-fa notation. Voice part.] *Francis, Day & Hunter: London, New York,* [1907.] *s. sh.* fol. **H. 3985. aa. (7.)**

— You're the Girl I've been waiting for, *etc.* ⟨Song.⟩ [With separate voice part.] 2 pt. *Francis, Day & Hunter: London,* [1907.] fol. **H. 3985. aa. (8.)**

LILBURN (DOUGLAS)

— Allegro for Strings. [Score.] pp. 31. *Price Milburn Music: Wellington, N. Z.,* [1975.] 8°. **b. 346. n. (6.)**

— Chaconne for Piano. [A facsimile of the composer's autograph.] pp. 23. *University of Otago Press: Dunedin,* 1972. 8°. **f. 770. r. (5.)**

— Diversions for string Orchestra. ⟨Score.⟩ pp. 34. *Oxford University Press: London,* [1963.] 8°. **e. 669. q. (1.)**

— Elegy. Poems by Alistair Campbell ... Song cycle for baritone voice and piano. Study score, *etc.* [A facsimile of the composer's autograph.] pp. 16. *Wai-te-ata Press: Wellington, N. Z.,* [1967.] 4°.
Music Editions. 1967. *no.* 6. **G. 1271. zz. (9.)**

— Occasional Pieces for Piano. pp. 27. *Price Milburn Music: Wellington, N. Z.,* [1975.] 4°. **g. 606. vv. (4.)**

— Seventeen Pieces for Guitar. Edited by Milton Parker. pp. 19. *Price Milburn Music: Wellington, N. Z.,* [1975.] 4°.
g. 1650. a. (9.)

— Sings Harry. For tenor voice and piano. Poems by Denis Glover, *etc.* pp. 15. *Otago University Press:* [*Otago,*] 1966. 8°.
F. 1196. kk. (2.)

— Sonata for Violin and Piano. [Score and part.] 2 pt. *Price Milburn & Company: Wellington, N. Z.; Amersham* printed, [1973.] 4°. **g. 762. ll. (6.)**

— Two Sonatinas for Piano. pp. 24. *Price Milburn & Company: Wellington, N. Z.; Amersham* printed, [1973.] 4°.
g. 606. vv. (5.)

LILBURN (Douglas)

— Sonatina No. 2. For piano, *etc.* [A facsimile of the composer's autograph.] pp. 12. *Wai-te-ata Press: Wellington, N. Z.,* [1967.] 4°.
Music Editions. 1967. *no.* 9.   **g. 1129. II. (10.)**

— Three Songs for Baritone and Viola, *etc.* pp. 9. *Wai Te Ata Press: Wellington, N. Z.,* [1972.] 4°.
Music Editions. 1972. *no.* 4.   **g. 1795. e. (4.)**

— Symphony No. 2. [Score.] pp. 116. *Price Milburn Music: Wellington, N. Z.,* 1979. 8°.   **b. 276. y. (2.)**

— Symphony No. 3. [Score.] pp. 65. *Faber Music: London, etc.,* 1968. 8°.   **e. 669. rr. (1.)**

— String Trio. [Parts.] 3 pt. *Hinrichsen Edition: London,* [1953.] 4°.   **g. 409. x. (9.)**

LILEYA

— Лилея. [Song.] *See* POGOZHEV (V. P.) Четыре романса. Сочинение 9. No. 3.

LILGE (Hermann)

— Sonate für Flöte und Klavier. Op. 57. *Henry Litolff's Verlag: Braunschweig,* 1937. 4°.
Collection Litolff, No. 2856.   **g. 70. k. (5.)**

LILI

— Lili. [Song.] *See* GUETARY (G.)

— Lili. Comédie-opérette. *See* HERVÉ (F.) *pseud.*

— Y Lili. Serch-gan. *See* MENDELSSOHN-BARTHOLDY (Jacob L. F.) [Vier Lieder für vierstimmigen Männerchor. Op. 75. No. 2. Abendständchen.]

— Y Lili. [Song.] *See* POWELL (Tom T.) called PENCERDD DWYFOR.

— Y Lili a'r rhosyn. Deuawd. *See* WILLIAMS (John) *of Blaenau Ffestiniog.*

— Lili Marlene. Song. *See* SCHULTZE (N.)

LILIA

— Lilia. Song. *See* BERROW (I.)

— Lilia. Mélodie. *See* CHOUDENS (A.)

— Lilia. Cantilène. *See* WECKERLIN (J. B. T.) Mélodies. No. 55.

LILIAN

— Lilian. [Song.] *See* DANCE (C. A.)

— Lilian. [Song.] *See* HILL (C. S.) Four Songs by Tennyson. No. 2.

— Lilian or the Rose of Haysted. Ballad. *See* MONTGOMERY (W. H.)

— Lilian. [Song.] PARES (A. M.)

— Lilian. Song. *See* PHILLIPS (*Mrs* A.)

— Lilian. Part-Song. *See* PULLEIN (J.)

— Lilian. Part-Song. *See* WADDINGTON (S. P.)

— Lilian. Cantilena. *See* WECKERLIN (J. B. T.)

— Lilian May. Ballad. *See* BALL (W.)

— Lilian of the Dale. [Song.] *See* IGNOTUS, *pseud.* Melodies of England. No. 2.

LILIAN

— Lilian's Love. Ballad. *See* BOUCHER (J. B.)

LILIANA

— Liliana. Song. *See* BISHOP (T. B.)

LILIE

— Lilie du im Rosengarten. *See* KRILL (C.) Fünf Lieder, *etc.* No. 3.

— Lilie, sieh' mich. Lied aus Ariels Offenbarungen. Von F. A. v. Arnim. [Song.] *See* REICHARDT (L.)

LILIEN

— Lilien und Rosen. Duett. *See* GLUECK (A.) Sechs Duette. No. 5.

— Lilien und Rosen. [Song.] *See* HARTMANN (E.) Lieder ... Op. 35 A. No. 5.

LILIEN (Ignacy)

— Die grosse Katharina. Great Catherine. Komische Oper in 3 Akten, 4 Szenen. Text von G. B. Shaw. Deutscher Text mit Zustimmung des Übersetzers Siegfried Trebitsch von Konrad Maril. Klavierauszug mit Text. *Universal-Edition A. G.: Wien, Leipzig,* 1932. 4°.   **G. 1338.**

LILIENCRON (Ferdinand von)

— Sechs Lieder für eine Singstimme mit Begleitung des Pianoforte. *Leipzig,* [1876.] fol.   **H. 1777. h. (55.)**

LILIENCRON (Rochus von) *Baron*

— Deutsches Leben im Volkslied um 1530. Herausgegeben von Rochus Freiherrn von Liliencron. pp. lxx. 436. *W. Spemann: Berlin, Stuttgart,* [1884.] 8°.
Deutsche National-Literatur. Bd. 13.   **Hirsch 1952.**

— Deutsches Leben im Volkslied um 1530. Herausgegeben von Rochus Freiherrn von Liliencron. *Union Deutsche Verlagsgesellschaft: Stuttgart, etc.,* [1926.] 8°.   **11528. cc. 49.**

— Die historischen Volkslieder der Deutschen vom 13. bis 16. Jahrhundert, gesammelt und erläutert von R. v. Liliencron, *etc.* 1865–69. 8°. *See* MUNICH.—*Königliche Akademie der Wissenschaften.*   **Ac. 714/2.**

— [Another copy.]   **Hirsch 1967.**

— Die horazischen Metren in deutschen Kompositionen des XVI. Jahrhunderts. Herausgegeben von R. von Liliencron. Mit Notenbeilagen. (Originalpartitur nebst Uebertragung in moderne Notenschrift.) 2 pt. *Breitkopf & Härtel: Leipzig,* 1887. 8°.   **Hirsch 1953.**

— *See* LEIPZIG.— *Musikgeschichtlicher Kommission.* Denkmäler deutscher Tonkunst. Erste Folge. Herausgegeben ⟨Bd. 4–42⟩ ... unter Leitung des ... Freiherrn von Liliencron. 1892–1931. fol.   **H. 993.**

LILIENCRON (Rochus von) *Baron* and STADE (Friedrich Wilhelm)

— Lieder und Sprüche aus der letzten Zeit des Minnesanges übersetzt für gemischten und Männerchor vierstimmig bearbeitet von R. von Liliencron und W. Stade. *H. Böhlau: Weimar,* [1854.] 4°.   **11511. e. 31. (3.)**

LILIENTHAL (Abraham Wolf)

— Sonata for violoncello and piano. Op. 40. *C. Fischer: New York,* 1921. 4°.   **g. 510. g. (23.)**

LILIENTHAL (ABRAHAM WOLF)

— *See* DAMROSCH (W. J.) The Dove of Peace ... Vocal Score
arranged by A. W. Lilienthal. 1912. 4°.   **G. 1047.**

LILIES

— Lilies. Two-Part Song. *See* BEHREND (J. A. H.) [Through the
Year.]

— Lilies. Ballad. *See* LOCKITT (W. J.)

— Lilies. Song. *See* RICHFIELD (S.)

— Lilies. Song. *See* SANDERSON (W. E.)

— Lilies. [Song.] *See* TAYLOR (L.)

— Lilies. Part-Song. *See* WOOD (C.) *Mus. Doc.*

— Lilies—and you. [Song.] *See* EWING (M.)

— Lilies are white. Unison Song. *See* SHARMAN (C.)

— Lilies fair. [Song.] *See* HORN (Charles E.)

— Lilies in my Garden. Song. *See* JOHNSON (W. N.)

— Lilies in the Pond. [Song.] *See* FERNALD (Albert H.)

— The Lillies in the Pond are not for me. [Song.] *See* JEROME
(Benjamin M.)

— The lillies of France and the fair English rose. *The Soldier's
Song.* [*London*, 1756.] 8°.
Universal Magazine, Vol. XIX., p. 183.   **P. P. 5439.**

— The Lillies of France and the fair English Rose. *The Soldier's
Song.* [Song.] [*London*, 1756.] 8°.
London Magazine, 1756, *p.* 500.   **158. l. 1.**

— The Lillies of France & the fair English Rose. *Soldier's Song.*
[*London*, 1756.] *s. sh.* fol.   **G. 315. (76.)**

— [Another edition.] The Lillies of France and the fair English
Rose. *Soldier's Song.* [*London*, 1756.] *s. sh.* fol.
   G. 312. (77.)

— The Lillies of France and the fair English Rose. *The Lillies of
France. A Favorite Soldier's Song. Printed for H. Andrews:
London*, [1793.] *s. sh.* fol.   **G. 360. (50.)**

— The Lilies of France and the fair English Rose. [Song.]
London, [1856.] fol.
No. 214 *of the "Cyclopedia of Music. Miscellaneous Series of
Songs".*   **H. 2342.**

— Lilies of Paradise. Song. *See* WEAVER (F. M.)

— The Lilies of the Field. Three-part song. *See* SILCHER (F.)

— Lilies of the Valley. Duettino. *See* AMES (*Mrs* H.)

— Lillies of the Valley. Song. *See* HOOK (James) [Sweet Lillies
of the Valley.]

— Lilies of the Valley. [Songs.] *See* LEHMANN, afterwards
BEDFORD (L.)

— Lilies! sweet Lilies, buy! Ballad. *See* DENMAN (H.)

— Lilies white, crimson Roses. Madrigal. *See* MARENZIO (L.) [Il
Terzo Libro de Madrigali a Cinque Voci.—Rose bianche e
vermiglie.]

LILINE

— Liline et Valentin. Opérette. *See* LECOCQ (A. C.)

LILI-TSÉ

— Lili-Tsé. [Operetta.] *See* CURTI (Franz)

LILIUM

— Lilium regis. [Part-song.] *See* CRESTON (Paul)

LILIUOKALANI, *Queen of Hawaii*

— He pule. (A Prayer.) And a Chant. [Song.] 2 no. *Pacific
Music Co.: San Francisco*, [1897.] fol.   **H. 1943. (12.)**

— [Another copy.]   **R. M. 13. f. 11. (5.)**

— Ahe lau makuni. Waltz song no. 3. pp. 3. *Pacific Music Co.:
San Francisco*, [1897.] fol.   **H. 1943. (11.)**

— [Another copy.]   **R. M. 13. f. 11. (11.)**

   Aloha oe

— Aloha oe. Farewell to thee. Words and music by Her Majesty
Liliuokalani of Hawaii. [Song, with four-part chorus. With a
portrait.] pp. 5. *John Wortley Co.: Boston*, [1884?] fol.
   H. 1943. (3.)

— Aloha oe. Song and chorus. [1884?] fol.
A proof sheet of the music, without titlepage.   **H. 1943. (2.)**

— Aloha oe. Farewell to thee. [Song.] Words and music by Her
Majesty Liliuokalani of Hawaii. *C. M. Clark Publishing Co.:
Boston*, 1906. 8°.
Pp. 28, 29 *of F. Chamberlin's 'Around the World in ninety
Days'.*   **10024. g. 23.**

— Aloha oe. Farewell to thee. [Song.] Arr. by J. B. Lampe. *J. H.
Remick & Co.: New York, Detroit*, (1912.) fol.
   G. 806. mm. (37.)

— [Another copy, without the illustrated titlepage.]
   H. 1793. t. (53.)

— Aloha oe.—Farewell to thee.—[Song.] Written by C. Wilmott,
etc. Francis, Day & Hunter: London, 1915. fol.
   H. 1846. y. (27.)

— Aloha oe. Farewell to thee. Song ... Arranged by L. S.
Roberts. *A. H. Goetting: Chicago, New York*, 1915. fol.
   H. 1846. y. (28.)

— Aloha oe ... Song. *H. Darewski Music Publishing Co.:
London*, 1919. fol.   **H. 1846. y. (29.)**

— Aloha oe. Farewell to thee ... As Song Waltz & Pianoforte
Solo (Arranged by E. Montelle), *etc. W. H. Paling & Co.:
Sydney, etc.*, 1927. 4°.   **G. 1270. t. (31.)**

— Auf Wiedersehn, Marie-Madlen! Hawaisches Lied ...
Bearbeitet von R. Bender. Text von L. Andersen. *B. Schott's
Söhne: Mainz*, 1933. 4°.   **G. 1270. ff. (29.)**

— Aloha. Aloha oe—Hawaiian Song of Farewell. Words by
J. Kennedy. Ukulele arranged by R. S. Stoddon. *B. Feldman
& Co.: London*, 1933. 4°.   **G. 1270. ii. (3.)**

— Farewell to thee ... Arranged for two or three part school
chorus. *P. A. Schmidt: Minneapolis*, 1916. 8°.
   F. 506. a. (11.)

— Aloha oe. Farewell to thee ... Free Choral transcription by
A. W. Kramer. (S. S. A.) *Galaxy Music Corporation: New
York*, 1935. 8°.   **F. 217. g. (36.)**

— Aloha oe. Farewell to thee. Choral transcription for S. A. by
A. W. Kramer. *Galaxy Music Corporation: New York*, 1935.
8°.   **E. 263. j. (23.)**

— Aloha oe. Farewell to thee. For four-part chorus of mixed
voices a cappella. English text by F. W. ... Arranged by
Franz Wasner. pp. 4. *G. Schirmer: New York*, [1959.] 8°.
   F. 1771. rr. (12.)

— Aloha oe ... Bearbeitet von F. Kreisler. (Violin and Piano.)
Schott & Co.: London, 1931. 4°.
Fritz Kreisler, Transcriptions, No. 25.   **g. 505. qq. (33.)**

LILIUOKALANI, *Queen of Hawaii*

— Aloha oe! Hawaisches Lied und Tango ... Bearb. von
H. Krome. (Auf Wiedersehn, Marie-Madlen!) [Parts.]
B. Schott's Söhne: Mainz, 1933. 8°.
[*Schott & Co.'s Domesticum-Salon-Orchestra. No.* 353.]
g. 1053. a.

— Auf Wiedersehn, Marie-Madlen! *See* supra: [Aloha oe.]

— A Chant. *Pacific Music Co.: San Francisco*, [1897.] fol.
R. M. 13. f. 11. (13.)

— He mele lahui Hawaii. (The Hawaiian National Anthem.)
[Song.] pp. 3. *Pacific Music Co.: San Francisco*, [1897.] fol.
H. 1943. (1.)

— He mele lahui Hawaii. The Hawaiian National Anthem.
Pacific Music Co.: San Francisco, [1897.] fol.
R. M. 13. f. 11. (2.)

— Hooheno. Song and chorus. pp. 3. *Pacific Music Co.: San
Francisco*, [1897.] fol. **H. 1943. (4.)**

— [Another copy.] **R. M. 13. f. 11. (7.)**

— Ka oiwi nani. (Beautiful one.) Song and chorus. pp. 3.
Pacific Music Co.: San Francisco, [1897.] fol. **H. 1943. (6.)**

— [Another copy.] **R. M. 13. f. 11. (6.)**

— Ka wai mapuna. The Water Spring. Song and chorus. pp. 3.
Pacific Music Co.: San Francisco, [1897.] fol. **H. 1943. (7.)**

— [Another copy.] **R. M. 13. f. 11. (8.)**

— [Ko'u pua o Hawaii.] My Flower of Hawaii, *etc.* [Song.]
C. S. De Lano: Los Angeles, 1915. fol. **H. 1846. y. (30.)**

— Ko'u pua o Hawaii. (My Flower of Hawaii.) Arranged by
Alfred Akamai ... Hawaiian guitar solo ... (with guitar
accompaniment). [Score.] *Clifford Essex Music Co.: London*,
[1967.] *s. sh.* 4°. **h. 259. y. (6.)**

— Kuu pua i Paoakalani. My Flower at Paoakalani, *etc.* [Song.]
J. H. Wilson: Honolulu, [1895.] fol. **R. M. 13. f. 11. (4.)**

— My Flower of Hawaii. *See* supra: [Ko'u pua o Hawaii.]

— Nani na pua. (The Flower of Koolau.) Song. ⟨Words adopted
[*sic*] by J. C. J. Arranged by L. K. Paki.⟩ pp. 5. *Pacific Music
Co.: San Francisco*, [1897.] fol. **H. 1943. (8.)**

— [Another copy.] **R. M. 13. f. 11. (12.)**

— Liliuokalani's Prayer and Serenade, *etc. Sanders and
Stayman: Washington*, [1895.] fol. **R. M. 13. f. 11. (3.)**

— Puia ka nahele. (The Fragrant Woods.) Waltz song no. 1.
pp. 3. *Pacific Music Co.: San Francisco*, [1897.] fol.
H. 1943. (9.)

— [Another copy.] **R. M. 13. f. 11. (9.)**

— Puna paia aala. (Puna's Bowery Walls.) Waltz song no. 2.
pp. 3. *Pacific Music Co.: San Francisco*, [1897.] fol.
H. 1943. (10.)

— [Another copy.] **R. M. 13. f. 11. (10.)**

— The Queen's Jubilee. Song and chorus. pp. 3. *Pacific Music
Co.: San Francisco*, [1897.] fol. **H. 1943. (5.)**

— [Another copy.]
An autograph letter, dated 24 *April* 1897, *from the composer to
Queen Victoria is inserted.* **R. M. 13. f. 11. (1.)**

LILIUS (FRANCISZEK)

— Iubilate Deo omnis terra. Motetto a 11. Due canti, alto,
tenore, basso, due violini, viola alta, due tromboni, fagotto
con basso continuo. ⟨Przygotował do wydania Zygmunt
M. Szweykowski. Bas cyfrowany zrealizował Jan Jargoń.⟩
[Score.] pp. 25. *Polskie wydawnictwo muzyczne: Kraków*,
[1959.] fol.
[*Wydawnictwo dawnej muzyki polskiej.* 40.] **H. 17.**

— Nabożne pieśni, które przy gromadnym odprawowaniu
różańców tak błogosławionej Panny Maryjej, jak też
Najświętszego Imienia Jezus śpiewane być mogą. ⟨[Music by]
Franciszek Lilius. Wydanie fototypiczne druku z 1645 roku.
Błażej Deney.⟩ *Instytut wydawniczy Pax: W Warzawie*, 1977.
8°. **X. 439/10328.**

— Tua Jesu dilectio, a canto e basso con basso continuo.
⟨Przygotował do wydania Zygmunt M. Szweykowski. Bas
cyfrowany zrealizował Kazimierz Sikorski.⟩ pp. 14. *Polskie
wydawnictwo muzyczne: Kraków*, [1965.] fol.
[*Wydawnictwo dawnej muzyki polskiej.* 56.] **H. 17.**

LILJA (BERNHARD)

— Andante religioso för orgel. *Stockholm*, 1940. *obl.* 4°.
[*Musikaliska Konstföreningen. Årg.* 1940.] **H. 700/126.**

LILJESTRAND (PAUL F.)

— If ye be merry. [Anthem.] For four-part chorus of mixed
voices a cappella. [Words by] Christopher Smart. pp. 7.
G. Schirmer: New York, [1970.] 8°. **F. 1106. f. (16.)**

LILLA

— Lilla bella dove sei. Cavatina. *See* MARTIN Y SOLAR (V.) [La
Cosa Rara.]

— Lilla come down to me. Serenade. *See* COOKE (T. S.) [The
Siege of Belgrade.]

— Lilla Maylie. Song. *See* GILL (J. B.)

— Lilla mia. Air. *See* MARTIN Y SOLAR (V.) [Una Cosa Rara.]

— Lilla's a lady. [Song.] *See* BAYLY (T. H.)

— Lilla's a Lady. Song. *See* DICK (C. G. C.)

— Lilla's a Lady! Air. *See* RAWLINGS (Thomas A.) [Songs to
Rosa.]

— Lilla Slafvinnan. Opera. *See* CRUSELL (B. H.)

— Lilla, then I'll come to thee. Ballad. *See* WHITAKER (John)

— Lilla's Vows. Song. *See* ROECKEL (J. L.)

LILLE (GASTON DE)

— Abergeldie valse. [P. F.] *London*, [1866.] fol. **h. 908. (13.)**

— Avec Entrain. Polka pour piano. (Op. 155.) *A. Leduc: Paris*,
[1888.] fol. **h. 3281. l. (29.)**

— Biarritz, polka-mazurka pour le Piano. *Paris*, [1868.] fol.
h. 908. a. (8.)

— The Boulevards quadrille. [P. F.] *London*, [1866.] fol.
h. 908. (14.)

— Bright Eyes valses. [P. F.] *London*, [1866.] fol. **h. 908. (15.)**

— Chants d'oiseaux, polka-mazurka. [P. F.] Op. 45. *London*,
[1858.] fol. **h. 908. (4.)**

— Clorinda valses, *etc.* [P. F.] *London*, [1859.] fol. **h. 908. (6.)**

— Columbini polka-mazurka. [P. F.] Op. 41. *Paris*, [1858.] fol.
h. 908. (2.)

LILLE (GASTON DE)

— Constantinople, suite de valses pour le Piano. *Paris*, [1870.] *obl*. fol.   **e. 217. b. (34.)**

— Dans les Bois. Valse pour Piano. *Paris*, [1860.] fol.   **h. 908. a. (1.)**

— De Paris à Berlin, marche militaire pour Piano. *Paris*, [1870.] fol.   **h. 908. a. (11.)**

— Défile de la garde. Polka-mazurka pour Piano. *Paris*, [1864.] fol.   **h. 908. a. (5.)**

— En Avant! polka pour le Piano. *Paris*, [1868.] fol.   **h. 908. a. (9.)**

— Feu et flammes, 2ème. polka-mazurka. [P. F.] *London*, [1855.] fol.   **h. 976. d. (26.)**

— Feuilles d'Automne, polka brillante pour le Piano. *Paris*, [1870.] fol.   **h. 908. a. (12.)**

— Frou-Frou, polka-mazurka pour Piano. *Paris*, [1870.] fol.   **h. 908. a. (13.)**

— High Pressure galop. [P. F.] *London*, [1866.] fol.   **h. 908. (16.)**

— Iris. Polka pour piano. Op. 152. *Colombier: Paris*, [1886.] fol.   **h. 3285. b. (62.)**

— [Another copy.]   **h. 3281. l. (28.)**

— The Japanese polka, *etc.* [P. F.] *London*, [1859.] fol.   **h. 908. (7.)**

— Jersey. Suite de Valses pour piano. Op. 151. *Paris*, [1886.] *obl*. fol.   **e. 272. n. (25.)**

— London-polka pour Piano. *Paris*, [1860.] fol.   **h. 908. a. (2.)**

— Madrid, polka-mazurka. [P. F.] *Paris*, [1864.] fol.   **h. 908. a. (6.)**

— Minuit, polka-mazurka pour Piano. *Paris*, [1860.] fol.   **h. 908. a. (3.)**

— The Moselle valses. [P. F.] Op. 70. *London*, [1859.] fol.   **h. 908. (8.)**

— Paillasse, polka de carnaval, *etc.* Op. 44. [P. F.] *London*, [1858.] fol.   **h. 908. (3.)**

— Polka Chinoise … pour piano. Op. 48. *Paris*, [1858.] fol.   **h. 908. (5.)**

— Polka des postillons. [P. F.] *London*, [1860.] fol.   **h. 908. (10.)**

— Polka des Roses. [P. F.] *Paris*, [1864.] fol.   **h. 908. a. (7.)**

— Polka des singes, pour piano. [Op. 46.] pp. 6. *Colombier: Paris*, [1860?] fol.   **Hirsch M. 1298. (20.)**

— Polka des singes. Op. 46. [P. F.] pp. 4. *Schott & Co.:* [*London*, c. 1880.] fol.   **h. 721. vv. (8.)**

— Polka des Singes. Op. 46. Arrangée [for small orchestra] par F. A. Geverding. [Parts.] *Schott & Co.: Londres*, [1878.] 8°.   **f. 245. i. (2.)**

— Le rappel, polka militaire. [P. F.] Op. 40. *Paris*, [1858.] fol.   **h. 908. (1.)**

— Rayons de soleil … suite de valses. [P. F.] Op. 42. *London*, [1858.] *obl*. fol.   **e. 40. (12.)**

— La retraite, polka militaire. [P. F.] *Londres*, [1855.] fol.   **h. 976. d. (27.)**

— Rêve Charmant, berceuse pour Piano. *London*, [1866.] fol.   **h. 908. (17.)**

LILLE (GASTON DE)

— Rêve Charmant, berceuse pour Piano. *London*, [1880.] fol.   **h. 1494. q. (43.)**

— Rêve Charmant (berceuse) … transcribed for Violin and Piano by B. Tours. *London*, [1881.] fol.   **g. 505. m. (13.)**

— Rosina valse. [P. F.] *London*, [1866.] fol.   **h. 908. (18.)**

— Rouge et noire, suite de valses. Op. 29. *Londres*, [1855.] *obl*. fol.   **e. 38. (30.)**

— The Snow drift galop. [P. F.] Op. 69. *London*, [1859.] fol.   **h. 908. (11.)**

— Sous la Feuillée, valse brillante pour le Piano. *Paris*, [1868.] fol.   **h. 908. a. (10.)**

— Sous les Tilleuls polka pour Piano. *Paris*, [1872.] fol.   **h. 908. a. (14.)**

— Summer quadrille. [P. F.] *London*, [1859.] fol.   **h. 908. (9.)**

— A Summer's Night, Polka Mazurka. [P. F.] pp. 7. *Metzler & Cᵒ: London*, [1860?] fol.   **Hirsch M. 1316. (8.)**

— Tintamarre polka pour Piano. *Paris*, [1860.] fol.   **h. 908. a. (4.)**

— Tonnerre galop. [P. F.] *London*, [1866.] fol.   **h. 908. (19.)**

— Venus, suite de valses … pour piano. Op. 47. *Paris*, [1858.] *obl*. fol.   **e. 40. (13.)**

— Vestri valse pour Piano. *Paris*, [1872.] *obl*. fol.   **e. 217. b. (35.)**

— The Winter's Night polka. [P. F.] Op. 66. *London*, [1859.] fol.   **h. 908. (12.)**

LILLENAS (HALDOR)

— Hymns of Conquest … H. Lillenas, Editor. Compiled by J. E. Moore [and others], *etc. Lillenas Publishing Co.: Kansas City*, 1940. 8°.   **B. 512. t. (3.)**

— *See* SCOVILLE (C. R.) Scoville's Sacred Solos. [Music by H. Lillenas and others.] 1913. 8°.   **E. 602. cc. (6.)**

LILLEY (E. A. MULHEARIN)

— Springtide Waltz. [P. F.] *J. Walch & Sons: Hobart*, [1906.] fol.   **h. 3286. ll. (29.)**

LILLEY (GEORGE HERBERT)

— Hymn [begins: "Let saints on earth"]. The words … by … C. Wesley. *London*, [1878.] 8°.   **E. 1498. b. (18.)**

— Unto us a Child is born. A Christmas Carol, written by E. M. Lilley. *Novello, Ewer & Co.: London and New York*, [1896.] *s. sh.* 8°.   **D. 619. l. (10.)**

LILLEY (JAMES HENRY)

— Benedicite omnia Opera.—In chant form. *Vincent Music Co.: London*, [1901.] 8°.   **F. 1170. y. (16.)**

— Gavotte moderne in G. [P. F.] *C. Vincent: London*, [1900.] fol.   **h. 3282. w. (53.)**

— Kyrie, Vesper Hymn, and Final Amen—four-fold. *Novello and Co.: London*, 1904. *a card*.   **I. 600. b. (208.)**

LILLEY (JOSEPH J.)

— *See* LOESSER (Frank) and LILLEY (J. J.) [The Forest Rangers.] Jingle, jangle, jingle … Arranged by B. Chase, *etc.* [1974.] 4°.   **h. 3210. j. (731.)**

LILLIAN

— Lillian. Ballad. *See* HIME (E. L.)

— Lillian. Ballad. *See* MOORAT (S.)

— Lillian's Bye, Bye. [Song.] *See* CLARKE (J. H.)

— Lillian's Fan. Song. *See* LEHMANN, afterwards BEDFORD (L.)

LILLIBULERO

— *See* LILLIBURLERO.

LILLIBURLERO

— Lillibulero. [Song.] *See* ALFORD (K. J.) *pseud.*

— Lilliburlero. Book of Songs. *See* BELL (F. E. E.) *Lady.*

— Lilliburlero. [Song with descant.] *See* CHATER (M. C.)

— Lilliburlero. Folk song. *See* EDMUNDS (John) Irish Folk Songs. [No. 1.]

— Lilliburlero. Song. *See* PURCELL (Henry) [*Doubtful and Supposititious Works.*]

— Lilliburlero. [Part-song.] *See* TIPPETT (*Sir* Michael K.) Four Songs from the British Isles. 2.

LILLIE

— *See* LILY.

LILLIE (H. W. R.)

— *See* L., H. W. R.

LILLIE (JOHN)

— The Waefu' Heart. Scottish Air, arranged [for four voices] by J. Lillie. [Tonic sol-fa and staff notation.] [1885?] *See* CHORAL. Choral Leaflets. No. 43. [1882–1915.] *s. sh.* 4°.　　**F. 569.**

LILLIE (LUCY C.) and LEWIS (CHARLES HUTCHINS)

— The Battle of the Books. A Juvenile Operetta, words and music by L. C. Lillie and C. H. Lewis. Old notation (Tonic Sol fa) edition. 2 no.　*J. Curwen & Sons: London,* [1889.] 8°.　　**D. 832. a. (7.)**

LILLIE (VINNIE)

— Venetian Evening Song.　*Boston* [*Mass.*], 1867. fol.　　**H. 1780. p. (36.)**

LILLIES (MABEL)

— Midnight. Waltz. [P. F.]　*Reid Bros.: London,* [1886.] fol.　　**h. 975. v. (42.)**

LILLINGSTON (SEPTIMUS ERNEST LUKE SPOONER)

— Ave verum corpus, for Tenor Solo & Chorus.　*Novello & Co.: London,* [1899.] 8°.　　**F. 1171. aa. (16.)**

— Ave verum. [Tenor solo and chorus, with English words.] *G. Schirmer: London,* [1915.] 8°.　　**F. 231. ff. (14.)**

— Two Christmas hymns.　*London,* [1880.] 8°.　　**E. 605. i. (29.)**

— The Clouds that wrap the setting Sun. Vocal Quartette, A. T. B. B., words by Rev. J. Keble, *etc. Vincent Music Co.: London,* [1912.] 8°.　　**F. 163. q. (19.)**

— The Office for the Holy Communion, *etc. Weekes & Co.: London,* 1918. 8°.
No. 161 of "Weekes & Co.'s Series of Services".　　**F. 334. f. (36.)**

LILLINGSTON (SEPTIMUS ERNEST LUKE SPOONER)

— Hail! true Body. Anthem for Tenor Solo and Chorus. *Novello, Ewer & Co.: London & New York,* [1896.] 8°.　　**F. 1171. u. (16.)**

— Three Hymn Tunes. The words ... by ... T. H. Passmore. (No. 1. Final Processional Hymn. No. 2. Hymn of St. Thomas Aquinas. No. 3. After Holy Communion.)　*Vincent Music Co.: London,* 1904. 8°.　　**C. 799. k. (15.)**

— Hymn Tunes.　*Vincent Music Co.: London,* [1908.] 8°.　　**C. 799. p. (21.)**

— Lo the Angels' Food is given. Anthem for Tenor solo and Chorus, *etc. Novello, Ewer & Co.: London & New York,* [1897.] 8°.　　**F. 1171. aa. (17.)**

— Mass in C.　*J. Williams: London,* 1909. 8°.　　**E. 597. u. (17.)**

— O saving Victim. Short Anthem.　*Novello, Ewer & Co.: London & New York,* [1895.] 8°.　　**F. 1171. u. (17.)**

— Oh saving Victim. Anthem for Communion.　*Vincent Music Co.: London,* [1906.] 8°.　　**F. 231. w. (15.)**

— Four original tunes set to popular hymns.　*London,* [1879.] 8°.　　**E. 605. i. (31.)**

— Six Trios for the organ.　[*Winthrop Rogers: London,*] 1921. *obl.* 4°.　　**e. 1093. k. (13.)**

— Urbs coelestis. Anthem, *etc. G. Schirmer: London,* [1915.] 8°.　　**E. 442. q. (22.)**

LILLIPUT

— Lilliput. A dramatic romance. *See* CORRI (D.)

— Lilliput Lane. Song. *See* STRELEZKI (A.) *pseud.*

LILLIPUTIAN

— The Lilliputian. [Song.] *See* SNIBSON (J.)

— The Lilliputian Police. [Action song.] *See* HOSCHNA (K. L.)

LILLIPUTION

— *See* LILLIPUTIAN.

LILLO

— Lillo Lee. [Song.] *See* MAZZINGHI (Joseph)

LILLO (GIUSEPPE)

— A me ritorna sogna d'amore, Melodia.　*London,* [1853.] fol.　　**H. 1735. (39.)**

— Al chiaror d'amica luna. *See infra:* [L'Osteria d'Andujar.]

— L'abbandonato, romanza. [Begins: "Qui sopra questo lido".] *London,* [1854.] fol.　　**H. 1758. (47.)**

— Un angiolo reggera il mio destin, stornello.　*London,* [1854.] fol.　　**H. 1758. (46.)**

La Desolazione

— La desolazione, melodia. [Begins: "Ritorna ch'io t'amo".] *London,* [1854.] fol.　　**H. 1758. (48.)**

— Watching for thee. Melody [begins: "I weary"] ... written and adapted by G. Linley.　*London,* [1860.] fol.　　**H. 1298. (32.)**

— La Desolazione. Melodia.　*London,* [1875.] fol.　　**H. 1778. y. (30.)**

— Watching for thee. Melody written and adapted by G. Linley. *London,* [1876.] fol.　　**H. 1778. y. (31.)**

LILLO (Giuseppe)

—— *See* Devrient (F.) La Desolazione ... fantaisie, *etc.* [1881.] fol.   **h. 3272. d. (25.)**

—— *See* Devrient (F.) La Desolazione ... pour Piano. [1882.] fol.   **h. 3273. a. (12.)**

—— "Flow gentle River." Duet. The Words written by H. Russell. *London*, [1860.] fol.   **H. 1563. (6.)**

—— La Giovinezza, duettino. [Begins: "Poichè a goder c'invita di giovinezza il fior"]. *London*, [1854.] fol.   **H. 1758. (45.)**

—— Good Morning. [Trio.] *London*, [1871.] fol.
No. 26 of a set of Vocal Trios.   **H. 2368.**

—— Io pur sento ... Romanza for flute and pianoforte, arranged by R. Carte. *Rudall, Carte & Co.: London*, [1883.] fol.   **h. 234. (15.)**

—— Mia vezzosa. Brindisi. *London*, [1853.] fol. **H. 1735. (41.)**

—— [L'Osteria d'Andujar.] 'Quando d'eterea luce.'—Romanza.— 'Vieni o cara.'—Variazioni finali. *See* Carte (R.) Italian Operatic Airs, *etc.* Second Series. No. 6. [1883.] fol.   **h. 232. d. (8.)**

—— [L'Osteria d'Andujar.] Al chiaror d'amica luna. Duettino. *London*, [1843.] fol.   **H. 2831. g. (34.)**

—— I Paesani, terzetto [begins: "Guarda come striscia il lampo"], poesia di M. Maggioni. *London*, [1857.] fol. **H. 1563. (2.)**

—— Il pensiero, canzone [begins: "Due lumi languenti"], poesia di M. Maggioni. *London*, [1857.] fol.   **H. 1563. (5.)**

—— Per ottener colei. *See* infra: [Rosmunda di Ravenna.]

—— La preghiera di' Pellegrini, terzettino [begins: "Per le selve"], poesia di Conte C. Pepoli. *London*, [1857.] fol.   **H. 1563. (4.)**

—— La Preghiera de Pellegrini, terzettino. Poesia di ... C. Pepoli. *London*, [1864.] fol.   **H. 1772. s. (4.)**

—— Qual cura, mai, melodia, poesia di M. Maggioni. *London*, [1864.] fol.   **H. 1772. s. (3.)**

—— Romance for the Piano Forte. *London*, [1853.] fol.   **h. 723. m. (10.)**

—— [Rosmunda di Ravenna.] Per ottener colei. Aria, in the Opera of Rosmunda di Ravenna. *Cramer, Addison & Beale: London*, [1840?] fol.   **H. 1652. b. (27.)**

—— Il ruscello ed il canto, duettino. [Begins: "Di quel ruscello che al mar dechina".] *London*, [1854.] fol.   **H. 1758. (50.)**

—— Il Saluto, duetto [begins: "Buon giorno, mia vita"], poesia di M. Maggioni. *London*, [1857.] fol.   **H. 1563. (1.)**

—— Una sera a Sorrento, duettino [begins: "In Sorrento a Primavera"], poesia di Conte C. Pepoli. *London*, [1857.] fol.   **H. 1563. (3.)**

—— [Una sera a Sorrento.] Sorrento, vocal duet. English version by Mrs. H. Ames. *London*, [1866.] fol. **H. 1772. s. (6.)**

—— Il sogno d'amore, melodia [begins: "Oh bella in velo candido"], poesia di Conte Pepoli. *London*, [1857.] fol.   **H. 1563. (8.)**

—— Sorrento. *See* supra: [Una sera a Sorrento.]

—— Un sorriso tu mi chiedi. Canzone. *London*, [1853.] fol.   **H. 1735. (40.)**

—— Il Traverso, barcarola [begins: "La bruna tua barchetta"], poesia di M. Maggioni. *London*, [1857.] fol. **H. 1563. (7.)**

—— La tua diletta immagine. Romanza. *London*, [1853.] fol.   **H. 1735. (38.)**

LILLO (Giuseppe)

—— La tua diletta immagine. Romanza. *London*, [1864.] fol.   **H. 1772. s. (5.)**

—— L'ultimo addio, canzone. [Begins: "Per tu me struggo".] *London*, [1854.] fol.   **H. 1758. (49.)**

—— Where Wild-Flowers bloom. Duet. The Words written by H. Russell. *London*, [1860.] fol.   **H. 1563. (9.)**

—— Where Wild Flowers bloom. Duet, *etc. Hutchings & Romer: London*, [1910.] 8°.
Two-Part Choruses for treble voices, No. 28. **F. 1623. d. (25.)**

—— *See* Arte. L'Arte antica e moderna. Scelta di composizioni [by G. Lillo], *etc.* Vol. 14. [1875.] 8°.   **f. 127.**

—— *See* Mercadante (Saverio) Gran sinfonia sopra motivi dello Stabat mater del celebre Rossini ... Ridotta per pianoforte de maes°: G. Lillo. [1843.] fol.   **g. 232. ee. (3.)**

LILLY
—— *See* Lily.

LILLY (Arthur)
—— Songs from the Psalms. Op. 1. No. 1. God is our Hope. *Whitcombe & Tombs: Christchurch* [*N.Z.*], 1914. fol.   **H. 1187. xx. (21.)**

LILLY (Richard P.)
—— I'll take your Place, Jack. [Song.] Words by Frank Dumont. pp. 2–5. *M. Witmark & Sons:* [*New York*, 1901.] fol.   **H. 3985. aa. (9.)**

—— The Sweetest Words, "All for you". Ballad. Words by Frank Dumont. pp. 3–5. *M. Witmark & Sons:* [*New York*, 1901.] fol.   **H. 3985. aa. (10.)**

—— Unlucky Lew. ⟨Song and monologue.⟩ Words by John H. Braceland, *etc.* pp. 5. *Herman & Co.: Philadelphia*, [1905.] fol.   **H. 3985. aa. (11.)**

—— *See* Dumont (Frank) and Lilly (R. P.) Plant a Watermelon on my Grave and let the Juice soak through, *etc.* [Song.] [1910.] fol.   **H. 3991. o. (39.)**

LILLYA (Clifford P.)
—— *See* Isaac (M. J.) and Lillya (C. P.) Deep South, *etc.* 1941. 4°.   **g. 727. l. (9.)**

—— *See* Purcell (Henry) [Sonata for trumpet and strings.] Sonata for Trumpet. For B♭ trumpet (cornet) ⟨C trumpet⟩ and piano ... Arranged by C. Lillya and M. Isaac. [1961.] 4°.   **g. 1105. g. (5.)**

LILLYCROP (S.)
—— A Celebrated Swiss Melody, arranged with an introduction & variations, for the piano forte ... by S. Lillycrop. pp. 7. *Preston: London*, [WM 1828.] fol.   **h. 61. oo. (11.)**

—— *See* Rossini (G. A.) [La Donna del Lago.] Grand March ... arranged ... by S. Lillycrop. [1820?] fol. **h. 184. c. (18.)**

LILLYGAY
—— Lillygay. [Songs.] *See* Warlock (P.) *pseud.*

LILO
—— Lilo Herrmann. Melodram. *See* Dessau (P.)

LILT
—— The Lilt of a Laugh. [Recitation with music.] *See* Dale (F.)

LILTING

— Lilting Fancy. [Part-song.] *See* COWELL (Henry D.)

— A Lilting Song. *See* THOMSON (S.)

LILWALL (NORMAN S.)

— Benedicite, omnia opera.—Easy setting in … C. *Vincent Music Co.: London*, [1905.] 8°.   **E. 597. s. (16.)**

LILY

— The Lily, Polka brilliante [*sic*]. [P. F.] *London*, [1860.] fol.   **h. 977. e. (21.)**

— The Lily. Song. *See* BOEHR (F.)

— Lily. Song. *See* DENZA (L.)

— The Lily. Song. *See* EIGHER (A. L.) Six Songs. No. 1.

— The Lily. *See* ESSEX (T.)

— The Lily. Sacred Song. *See* HOBERG (B. M.)

— The Lily. [Song, begins: "In vale retir'd".] *See* HUDSON (R.)

— The Lily. Song. *See* KING (G. M.)

— The Lilly. [Song.] *See* LANIER (N.)

— Lilly. [Song.] *See* LINLEY (G.)

— Lilly. Ballad. *See* MONTGOMERY (W. H.)

— The Lily. Part song. *See* PRICE (Thomas) *of Merthyr*.

— The Lilly. Song. [Begins: "Shelter'd from the blythe ambition".] *See* PRING (J. C.)

— The Lily. Trio. *See* WASA (F. von)

— The Lily. [Song.] *See* WRIGHTON (W. T.)

— The Lily and the Bird. Song. *See* HARVEY (R. F.)

— The Lily and the Bluebell. Song. *See* SMITH (H. W.)

— The Lily and the blushing Rose. Song. *See also* CORRESPONDENT.

— The Lily and the blushing Rose. *Song in Praise of Women.* Set to Music by a Correspondent [of the Lady's Magazine]. [*London*, 1776.] *s. sh.* 4°.
Lady's Magazine, Sept., 1776.   **P. P. 5141.**

— The Lily and the Butterfly. Chansonnette. *See* NOEL (J.)

— The Lily and the Leaf. Song. *See* PHILP (E.)

— The Lily and the Rose. [Song.] *See* FISHER (B. W.)

— The Lily and the Rose. Song. *See* GREENHILL (J.) A set of easy songs.

— The Lily and the Rose. Duett. *See* HAVERGAL (William H.)

— The Lily and the Rose. Ballad. *See* LECOCQ (A. C.) [Les Prés St. Gervais.—Je vais vous débrouiller la chose.]

— The Lily and the Rose. Song & chorus. *See* MARTYN (H.)

— The Lily and the Rose. [Song.] *See* RYDER (F. L.)

— The Lily and the Rose. [Song.] *See* SUTTON (Harry O.)

— The Lily and the stream. Ballad. *See* MACFARREN (*Sir* G. A.)

— The Lily and the Sun. [Song.] *See* CHAIKOVSKY (P. I.) [*Collected Works.—f.*] [Catherine.]

— The Lily and the Sunbeam. [Song.] *See* TREVELYAN (A.)

— The Lily and the Violet. Song. *See* MORI (F.)

LILY

— Lilly Baker. Negro Ballad. *See* VERE (P.)

— Lilly Bell. *See* O. Oh Lilly Bell. [1854.] fol.   **H. 1254. (39.)**

— Lily Bell. Song. *See* MUELLER (C.)

— Lilly Bell. Song and chorus. *See* PITTS (W. S.)

— Lily-Bell. A Cantata. *See* SARONI (H. S.)

— Lily-Bell, the Culprit Fay. Operetta. *See* SARONI (H. S.)

— The Lily Bells. Song. *See* DYMOND (J. J.)

— Lily Bells. Ballad and chorus. *See* PARKER (Henry T.)

— Lily Bells. Song. *See* SMITH (G. T.)

— The Lily-Bells. [Song.] *See* SOUSA (J. P.)

— Lilly Bliss. Solo and chorus. *See* MONTGOMERY (W. H.)

— The Lily Bride. Song. *See* DIEHL (L.)

— Lilly bright and shine-a. Two-part song. *See* COPLEY (I. A.)

— Lily bright and shine-a. Unison song. *See* JACOB (Gordon P. S.)

— Lily Brook. [Song and chorus.] *See* ROOT (G. F.)

— Lillie Dale. Song. *See* CRAVEN (J. T.)

— Lilly Dale. Ballad. *See* THOMPSON (H. S.)

— Lily Dear, don't you remember. Ballad. *See* WEST (W.)

— The Lily Flower. Song. *See* PETERSEN (A.)

— Lily, Germander and Sops-in-Wine. [Part-song.] *See* CRUFT (Adrian F.)

— Lily Graeme. Scottish Song. *See* GABRIEL, afterwards MARCH (M. A. V.)

— Lily Gray. Song. *See* SAINT JULIANS (F.)

— The Lily has a smooth Stalk. Unison song. *See* FINZI (Gerald) [School Songs. No. 3.]

— Lily, I am longing, Love, for you. Song. *See* MACEY (Alan)

— The Lily in a Vase of gold. Song. *See* DAREWSKI (Hermann E.)

— A Lily in God's Garden. Song. *See* BREARLEY (H.)

— Lily is a Lady. Song. *See* BAYNES (Eustace) and ARTHUR (G. W.)

— Lily is an angel now. Song. *See* RICHARDSON (G.)

— Lillie Lee. Ballad. *See* GLOVER (S.)

— Lily Lee. Song. *See* HOPE (S.)

— Lily Lee. Ballad. *See* SIMMONS (Julia)

— Lilly Lee. Song and chorus. *See* WOOD (T.)

— The Lily lies drooping. [Song.] *See* MORRIS (V.)

— Lily Lye. Song. *See* MACFARREN (*Sir* G. A.)

— The Lily Maid. Cycle of Songs. *See* FIELITZ (A. von)

— Lil', my Easter Lily. [Song.] *See* RAYNES (J. A.)

— The Lily of Boulter's Lock. Song and Chorus. *See* ROLT (B.)

— The Lily of Killarney. Opera. *See* BENEDICT (*Sir* J.)

— The Lily of Laguna. [Song.] *See* STUART (L.) *pseud.*

— The Lily of Léoville. Comic opera. *See* CARYLL (I.) *pseud.*

LILY

— The Lily of Loch Lomond. Song. *See* MACKINNON (A. U.)

— The Lily of Lorraine. [Song.] *See* LINTER (R.)

— Lily of Love's Lake. Ballad. *See* LOVER (S.)

— Lily of my Heart. Song. *See* GEEHL (H. E.)

— The Lily of my Life. Song. *See* DANVERS (Johnny)

— The Lily of St. Goar. Romance. *See* CLARIBEL, *pseud.*

— Lily of Snow. Song. *See* BARNETT (J. F.)

— The Lily of the Ganges. [Song.] *See* MORGAN (R. O.) Songs of the Ganges.—Op. 36.—No. 2.

— The Lily of the Lake. Song. *See* DUGGAN (J. F.)

— Lily of the Prairie. [Song.] *See* MILLS (Kerry)

— Lillie of the snowstorm. Song and chorus. *See* WORK (H. C.)

— The Lily of the Vale. [Song.] *See* FRAGRANT. The Fragrant Lily of the Vale. [c. 1765.] *s. sh.* fol. **H. 1601. u. (4.)**

— Lily of the Vale. Song. *See* GEAR (H. H.)

— Lily of the vale. (Ballad.) *See* HATTERSLEY (W. F.)

— The Lily of the Vale. [Song.] *See* HUDSON (R.)

— The Lily of the Vale. Duet. *See* KOCH (C.) Das Maiblümchen.

— The Lily of the Vale. Song. *See* LEVEY (W. C.)

— The Lily of the Vale. [Song.] *See* MOUNSEY, afterwards BARTHOLOMEW (Ann S.)

— The Lily of the Valley. Song. *See* BISHOP (A. E.)

— The Lily of the Valley. [Song.] *See* BRILL (Edwin S.)

— The Lily of the Valley. *See* CAHUSAC (W.)

— Lily of the Valley. Song. *See* DELEHANTY (W. H.)

— The Lily of the Valley. Song. *See* JOLLY (J. M.) A set of six Songs, *etc.* No. 3.

— The Lily of the Valley. [Song.] *See* KEELER (H.)

— A Lily of the Valley. [Song.] *See* MILLER (R.)

— Lily of the Valley. [Song.] *See* OLIVER (H.)

— The Lily of the Valley. Vocal Mazurka. *See* PUZZI (F.)

— Lily of the Valley. Song. *See* SMITH (B.)

— The Lily of the Valley. Song. *See* TRACY (G. L.)

— The Lily of the Valley. Song. *See* VERDI (F. G. F.) [I Lombardi.—La Mia letizia infondere, *etc.*]

— The Lily of the Wear. Ballad. *See* ROCHE (A. D.)

— The Lily of the West. Song & chorus. *See* MARRIOTT (C. H. R.)

— The Lily Pond. Song. *See* CLEMENTS (C. E.)

— The Lily-Pool. Two-part Canon. *See* HOWELL (D.)

— A Lily pure. Song. *See* WYATT (E. W.)

— The Lily, Rose and Vine. [Song.] *See* LEMONIER (Thomas)

— A Lily Song. Two-part Song. *See* JOHNSON (W. N.)

— Lily, sweet Lily. [Song.] *See* HARRISON (E. D.)

— Lily, sweet Lily. Part-Song. *See* MONK (E. G.)

— The Lily that blooms in the vale. Song. *See* WHITAKER (J.)

— The lily that grew in the vale. Ballad. *See* SMITH (C.)

LILY

— The Lily, the Butterfly and the Bee. Trio. *See* HORNE (M.)

— Lily, the Llandudno Lady. Song. *See* PARRY (Arthur W.)

— A Lily thou wast. Song. *See* HECHT (E.)

— The Lily too is fair. Ballad. *See* OFT. Oft when the moon is beaming. [1830?] fol. **H. 2835. b. (24.)**

— The Lily was the only flower. [Song.] *See* BUCKLEY (F.)

— Lily White. [Song.] *See* BRATTON (John W.) [The Pearl and the Pumpkin.—In a Field of Lillies.]

— Lilly Willy Woken. Song and chorus. *See* WORK (H. C.)

— Lily's Ball. Two-Part Song. *See* MARCHANT (A. W.)

— Lilly's Fortune. [Song.] *See* ADOWN. Adown where the lindens blossom. [1869.] fol. **H. 1790. (1.)**

— The Lily's Lament. [Part-song.] *See* COWELL (Henry D.)

— Lillie's Picture Music. 2 bk. *Boosey & Co.: London & New York,* [1874–8.] fol. **h. 3278. (3.)**

— Lily's Prayer. [Song.] *See* MOZART (W. A.) [*Doubtful and Supposititious Works.*] [Mass No. 12.]

— The Lily's Promenade. [Song.] *See* LEDERER (George W.)

— Lily's Quarrel. Ballad. *See* ARNOLD (G.)

— Lillie's Second Music Book, containing Instructions and Exercises for … the pianoforte, *etc. Boosey & Co.: London,* [1880.] fol. **h. 3278. (4.)**

— Lily's Shadow. Song. *See* COLLETT (J.)

LILYBOURNE

— Lilybourne Lock. Ballad. *See* HUDSON (J. W.)

LILYCROFT

— Lilycroft. [Anthem.] *See* WITTY (John S.)

LIMA (CORINA H. DE)

— Andando. No. 3. Op. 18. Para piano. *Ricordi americana: Buenos Aires,* [1958.] fol. **g. 1129. z. (16.)**

LIMA (D. A. DE)

— The Kentucky Camp-Fire. Two Step and Cake Walk. [P. F.] *Perry & De Lima: New York,* 1901. fol. **h. 3286. r. (13.)**

LIMA (JERÓNIMO FRANCISCO)

— Le Nozze d'Ercole ed Ebe. Abertura. Revisão e realização de Luís Pereira Leal. [Score and parts.] 26 pt. *Fundação Calouste Gulbenkian: Lisboa,* 1973. 4°. [*Portugaliæ musica.* 23.] **G. 27.**

LIMA (JOÃO DE SOUZA)

— Valsa amorosa … Piano. pp. 4. *Editôra Arthur Napoleão: Rio de Janeiro,* [1973.] 4°. **g. 1128. rr. (11.)**

— Valsa chorosa … Piano. pp. 5. *Editôra Arthur Napoleão: Rio de Janeiro,* [1973.] 4°. **g. 1128. rr. (12.)**

LIMA FRAGOSO (ANTÓNIO DE)

— Obras póstumas, *etc. Valentin de Carvalho: Lisboa,* 1971, *etc.* 4°. **H. 2435.**

LIMA FRAGOSO (António de)

— Nocturno. [For orchestra.] Revisão e estudo de Jorge Croner de Vasconcellos. [Score.] pp. 30. *Fundação Calouste Gulbenkian: Lisboa*, 1968. 4°.
[*Portugaliæ musica. no.* 18.] **G. 27.**

LIMAGNE (A.)

— Solfége-Manuel composé spécialement pour les cours Solfége. 3 pt. *Paris*, 1864. 8°. **D. 767.**

LIMBERT (Frank Leland)

— Es hat die Rose sich beklagt. *See* infra: Drei Gesänge. Op. 2. No. 1.

— Drei Gesänge. Op. 2. No. 1. Es hat die Rose sich beklagt. Gedicht von M. Schaffy. Für 2 Singstimmen mit Begleitung des Pianoforte. No. 2. Schlaf ruhig süsser Knabe. Aus Sintram. Für Sopran mit Begleitung des Pianoforte. No. 3. In Memory of Sir Grey Morville's Death ... Für Alt mit Begleitung des Pianoforte. 3 no. *R. Forberg: Leipzig*, [1887.] fol. **H. 2836. v. (31.)**

— In Memory of Sir Grey Morville's Death. *See* supra: Drei Gesänge. Op. 2. No. 3.

— Drei Präludien und Fugen für das Pianoforte. Op. 1. *R. Forberg: Leipzig*, [1887.] fol. **h. 3281. l. (30.)**

— Quartett für 2 Violinen, Bratsche und Violoncell (F moll) ... Op. 15. Partitur. pp. 51. *N. Simrock: Berlin*, 1898. 8°. **e. 668. x. (6.)**

— Schlaf ruhig süsser Knabe. *See* supra: Drei Gesänge. Op. 2. No. 2.

LIME

— The Lime-Blossoms. [Song.] *See* BARKER (G. A.)

— The Lime Kiln Masquerade. Song. *See* CAREY (M. F.)

— The Lime Tree. Song. *See* BUNNING (H.)

— The Lime Tree. [Song.] *See* SCHUBERT (F. P.) [Winterreise. Op. 89. No. 5. Der Lindenbaum.]

— The Lime Trees by the River. Ballad. *See* MACFARREN (*Sir* G. A.)

LIMEHOUSE

— Limehouse. Song. *See* HYDEN (C. W.)

— Limehouse Nights. [Song.] *See* GERSHWIN (George) [Morris Gest Midnight Whirl.]

— Limehouse Reach. Song. *See* GREGG (H. P.)

— Limehouse Reach. [Song.] *See* HEAD (Michael) Six Sea Songs ... 2.

— Limehouse Wharf. [Song.] *See* READ (H. V. J.)

LIMÈNIENNE

— La Limènienne. [Song.] *See* COHEN (J.)

LIMENTA (Fernando)

— Serenata Zingara ... Riduzione dell' Autore per Orchestrina con Pianoforte Conduttore. [Parts.] *G. Ricordi e C.: Milano, etc.*, 1929. 8°. **h. 3210. h. (341.)**

LIMERICK

— Limerick Bells. [Song.] *See* CROUCH (Frederick N.) [Irish Songs. No. 11.]

LIMERICK

— Limerick Fair. Song. *See* MILTON (F.)

— The Limerick Girls. [Song.] *See* OLCOTT (C.)

— Limerick is beautiful. Song. *See* LEVEY (Richard M.)

— Limerick mad. Song. *See* LEO (Frank)

— The Limerick Point to Point Race. [Song.] *See* STANFORD (*Sir* C. V.)

— Limerick Races. Comic Irish song. *See* I. I'm a simple country lad. [1858.] fol. **H. 1771. g. (49.)**

— Limerick Races. Comic Irish song. *See* GRANTHAM (W.)

— Limerick's running yet. [Song.] *See* BRAHAM (George)

LIMERICK, May Imelda, *Countess of*

— *See* PERY (M. I.) *Countess of Limerick.*

LIMERICKITIS

— Limerickitis. Song. *See* SCOTT (Bennett)

LIMITED

— The Limited. [Part-song.] *See* KRATZ (L. G.)

LIMMER (Franz)

— Quatuor pour quatre violoncelles ... Oeuvre 11. [Parts.] 4 pt. *Chez Pietro Mechetti: Vienne*, [1830.] fol. **h. 1871. d. (2.)**

LIMNANDER DE NIEUWENHOVE (Armand Marie Ghislain)

— Les Chants du Sacré Coeur ... Choix de morceaux à 2 ou 3 voix ... Paroles françaises de Mr. de Charlemagne. *Paris*, [1850?] fol. **H. 1028. f. (27.)**

— Le Château de la Barbe-Bleue, opéra comique en trois actes. Paroles de M. de Saint Georges ... Partition pour Chant et Piano arrangée par A. Garaudé. [*Paris*, 1852.] 8°. **F. 810.**

— Le Château de la Barbe-Bleue. Opéra comique en 3 actes. Paroles de M^r de St Georges. [Vocal score by A. A. G. de Garaudé.] no. 6, 7, 13. *Heugel et Cie: Paris*, [1852?] fol. *Imperfect; wanting no.* 1–5, 8–12, 14–17. **H. 1652. q. (13.)**

— [Le Château de la Barbe-Bleue.] *See* LE CARPENTIER (A.) Trois petites fantaisies dansantes sur l'opéra ... Le Chateau de la Barbe-Bleue, *etc.* [1854.] fol. **h. 637. (3.)**

— Maximilien à Francfort. Opéra en trois actes de H. Trianon et H. Leroy. Partition Chant et Piano réduite par L. Bärwolf. *Paris*, [1870?] 8°. **F. 810. a.**

Les Monténégrins

— Les Monténégrins. Opéra-comique en 3 actes. Paroles de MM. Alboize et Gerard ... Partition piano et chant. pp. 232. *Heugel & cie.: Paris*, [1849?] 8°. **F. 810. c.**

— Les Monténégrins. Opéra comique en 3 actes. Paroles de MM. Gérard et Alboize. [Vocal score, by A. A. G. de Garaudé.] no. 7. *J. Meissonier fils: Paris*, [1850?] fol. *Imperfect; wanting no.* 1–6, 8–17. **H. 1652. q. (14.)**

— *See* GORIA (A.) Fantaisie sur les Monténégrins. [1850.] fol. **h. 781. (17.)**

— *See* HUENTEN (F.) Fantaisie sur des thèmes ... de l'opéra, *etc.* [1849.] fol. **h. 676. (5.)**

— *See* HUENTEN (F.) Three Rondos. No. 2. [1849.] fol. **h. 676. (6.)**

LIMNANDER DE NIEUWENHOVE (Armand Marie Ghislain)

— Pensée du Soir. [Song, begins: "Penche ton front".] Paroles de V. Corbisier. *Paris*, [1845.] *s. sh.* fol.　　**G. 808. a. (18.)**

— Safe in Port. [Solo and chorus.] Words by A. J. Foxwell. *J. Curwen & Sons: London*, [1895.] 8°. *The Apollo Club, No.* 96.　　**F. 667.**

— Salve Regina à une voix. [1859.] *See* Niedermeyer (L.) La Maîtrise, *etc.* 3ᵉ Année. Grande Maîtrise. No. 10. [1857–61.] fol.　　**H. 1237.**

— The Smugglers. [Part-song.] Words by A. J. Foxwell. *J. Curwen & Sons: London*, [1899.] 8°. *The Apollo Club. No.* 121.　　**F. 667.**

— Vénus de Milo. Scene [begins: "Marbre sacré"]. Poésie de Mr. Leconte de l'Isle. *Paris*, [1870.] fol.　　**H. 1774. e. (31.)**

— Yvonne. Drame lyrique en trois actes. Poème de Mr. E. Scribe. Partition Piano et Chant. *Paris*, [1859.] 8°.　　**F. 810. b.**

LIMOSNA

— La Limosna de Amor. Melodia. *See* Winter (J. C.)

LIMPING

— The Limping Man. Unison song. *See* Gwynne (Una)

LIMPUS (Henry Francis)

— Bold as a lion. Song, written by A. M. Limpus. *London*, [1878.] fol.　　**H. 1783. p. (5.)**

— Characteristic Pieces for the Pianoforte ... Book I. *Weekes & Co.: London*, [1886.] fol. *No more published.*　　**h. 1489. t. (8.)**

— The Departure of the Swallows, a musical sketch for the Pianoforte. *London*, [1860.] fol.　　**h. 1460. w. (7.)**

— Evangeline, valse brillante pour piano. *London*, [1856.] fol.　　**h. 977. f. (36.)**

— Evermore. Ballad [begins: "In the happy hours"], written by A. M. Limpus. *London*, [1877.] fol.　　**H. 1778. y. (34.)**

— Horae apud Musas. Clio, a first Series of Short Pieces for Violin and Piano. 6 no. *E. Ashdown: London*, [1889.] fol.　　**g. 505. m. (14.)**

— Impromptu à la Mazourka, for the piano forte. *London*, [1856.] fol.　　**h. 976. d. (28.)**

— Joy Bells. Song, written by A. M. Limpus. *London*, [1878.] fol.　　**H. 1783. p. (4.)**

— The Life Boat. Song [begins: "Man the life boat"] written by A. M. Limpus. *London*, [1878.] fol.　　**H. 1783. p. (3.)**

— Mazourka brillante, for the pianoforte. *London*, [1855.] fol.　　**h. 976. d. (29.)**

— Our Blue Jackets. Song [begins: "Dear to fame"] written by A. M. Limpus. *London*, [1881.] fol.　　**H. 1787. j. (39.)**

— The Prodigal's Return. An oratorio. [Vocal score.] *London*, [1871.] fol.　　**H. 1064.**

— Recollections of Scotland 3 fantasias. [P. F.] No. 1. Charlie is my darling. *London*, [1856.] fol. *Imperfect; wanting no.* 2, 3.　　**h. 1458. d. (10.)**

— La Rose de Provence, étude de salon pour le Piano. *London*, [1873.] fol.　　**h. 1482. z. (58.)**

— The Skylark. Song [begins: "Birds of the wilderness"] written by J. Hogg. *London*, [1877.] fol.　　**H. 1778. y. (32.)**

— Slumber Song [begins: "Sweet and low"] ... Words by A. Tennyson. *London*, [1877.] fol.　　**H. 1778. y. (33.)**

LIMPUS (Henry Francis)

— To Inez. Song [begins: "There be none of beauty's daughters"]. Poetry by Lord Byron. *London*, [1880.] fol.　　**H. 1783. p. (6.)**

— Wayside Flowers. Song [begins: "As I roamed"] written by A. B. Limpus. *London*, [1878.] fol.　　**H. 1783. p. (2.)**

LIMPUS (Richard)

— La Belle Eliphalette, mazourka pour le Piano. *London*, [1860?] fol.　　**h. 726. h. (21.)**

— "The Bride is away." Ballad, the Poetry by R. Story. *London*, [1860.] fol.　　**H. 1564. (3.)**

— The British Court Quadrilles ... for the Piano Forte. *London*, [1842.] fol.　　**h. 932. (36.)**

— "The Christmas holly;" song. *London*, [1843.] fol.　　**H. 1691. (8.)**

— The Falling Dew-drop. Ballad, written by H. W. Godfrey, *etc. J. & J. Hopkinson: London*, [1855?] fol.　　**H. 2815. m. (2.)**

— Her cheek was pale. Ballad, poetry by J. W. Lake. *London*, [1850.] fol.　　**H. 1717. (16.)**

— The Nicene Creed set to music in the key of G major, *etc. London*, [1871.] fol.　　**H. 1775. u. (44.)**

— Oh! Lady, strike the Harp once more. Ballad written by A. W. Cole. *London*, [1860.] fol.　　**H. 1564. (2.)**

— The Rosa Polka ... for the Pianoforte. *London*, [1860.] fol.　　**h. 1460. w. (8.)**

— Speak gently; song. *London*, [1849.] fol.　　**H. 1708. (26.)**

— Sweet Evening Breeze, *etc.* [Four-part song.] [1873.] *See* Crampton (T.) The Part-Singer, *etc.* No. 118. [1868–98.] 8°.　　**E. 628.**

— To ev'ry lovely Lady bright. [Four-part song.] [1868.] *See* Crampton (T.) The Part-Singer, *etc.* No. 34. [1868–98.] 8°.　　**E. 628.**

— Violet Time. Ballad [begins: "I saw her"]. The words by R. Story. *London*, [1869.] fol.　　**H. 1775. u. (43.)**

— A Welcome to the Ivy, [song] written by L. E. L. *London*, [1860.] fol.　　**H. 1564. (1.)**

LIN

— Lin was a mighty great Mandarin. *Love in Canton.* [Song.] pp. 5. *A. Hammond & Cᵒ: London*, [1875?] fol.　　**H. 1653. d. (36.)**

LIN (Shih-ch'eng)

— P'i-pa ch'ü-p'u. [35 exercises for the piba. A companion volume to P'i-pa yen-tsou fa.] pp. 65. *Yin-yüeh Ch'u-pan-she: Peking*, 1959. 8°.　　**G. 1363. kk. (2.)**

LINA

— Lina. [Song.] *See* Clark (Maurice W.)

— Lina. Ballade. *See* Filliette (C. B.)

— Lina! Song. *See* Godfrey (P.)

— Lina. [Song.] *See* Järnefelt (A.)

— Lina. Song. *See* Orsini (A.)

— Lina. Dramma lirico. *See* Ponchielli (A.)

— Lina. Pensai che un angelo. Aria. *See* Verdi (F. G. F.) [Stiffelio.]

LINA

— Lina Lee. Song. *See* O'DEA (James) and NORTHRUP (T. H.)

— Lina mia. Serenade. *See* VALMENCY (R.)

— Lina, ou le Mystère. Opéra. *See* DALAYRAC (N.)

LINA

— The Extra Galop ... for the piano forte. pp. 5. *Edward Hale & Cº: Cheltenham*, [c. 1865.] fol.　　　**h. 61. pp. (8.)**

LINCKE (ANDREAS FREDERIK)

— *See* PONTEMOLLE. Pontemolle. Ballet af A. Bournonville. Charakteerstykker og Dandse for Piano, *etc.* [By A. F. Lincke and others.] [1866.] fol.　　　**g. 1529. ff. (2.)**

LINCKE (JOSEPH)

— Air varié sur un Thème russe pour le Violoncelle avec l'Accompagnement du Clavecin, *etc.* [Parts.] *Magasin de l'imprimerie chimique: Vienne*, [1820?] fol.
　　　R. M. 17. e. 8. (28.)

LINCKE (PAUL)

— Amina. Egyptian Serenade, and Siamese Patrol. [Military band parts.] *Hawkes & Son: London*, 1908. fol.
Part of "Hawkes & Son's Military Band Edition".
　　　h. 3211. a. (84.)

— Coon's Birthday. (Negers Geburtstag.) Cake walk—two step. ⟨Kwang Hsü. (Kwang See.) Chinese march.⟩ [Orchestral parts.] 24 pt. *Jos. W. Stern & Co.: [New York*, 1909.] 8°.
　　　f. 800. (825.)

— Die Afrikareise ... A Trip to Africa. Ouvertüre nach Melodien der Operette von Franz v. Suppé ... Salon-Orchester. [Parts.] *B. Schott's Söhne: Mainz*, 1939. 4°. [*Schott & Co.'s Domesticum Salon Orchestra. No.* 516.]
　　　g. 1053. a.

— [Amina.] Queen of the Night Amina mine. Arr. by Robert Recker. [Orchestral parts.] 11 pt. *Jos. W. Stern & Co.: [New York*, 1909.] 8°.　　　**f. 800. (827.)**

— Amina. Sérénade Égyptienne ... Piano. Simplified edition, *etc. J. W. Stern & Co.: New York, etc.*, (1909.) fol.
　　　h. 3753. a. (1.)

— Amina ... for Piano. *J. W. Stern & Co.: New York, etc.*, [1913.] fol.　　　**h. 3753. a. (6.)**

— Amina ... Arr. by P. Eno. [2 banjos.] *J. W. Stern & Co.: New York, etc.*, (1909.) fol.　　　**h. 3753. a. (3.)**

— Amina ... Arr. by L. Tozetti [or rather Tozzeti. 2 mandolins, guitar and P. F. Parts]. *J. W. Stern & Co.: New York*, (1909.) fol.　　　**h. 3753. a. (2.)**

— Amina, Queen of the Night. Song (words) by B. Macdonald. Arranged to the Melody of Amina, Sérénade Égyptienne. *J. W. Stern & Co.: New York, etc.*, (1909.) fol.　　**H. 1939. (9.)**

— [Amina.] Queen of the Night. Amina mine. Quartette for male voices ... words by B. Macdonald ... Arr. by C. F. Williams. *J. W. Stern & Co.: New York*, (1910.) 8°.　　**F. 163. k. (24.)**

— Artist's Love. Aus Liebe zur Kunst. Waltzes. [P. F.] *J. W. Stern & Co.: New York, etc.*, (1912.) fol.
　　　h. 3753. a. (7.)

— Die Bajadere! [Song.] Text von R. Steidl, *etc. Apollo-Verlag: Berlin*, (1909.) fol.　　　**H. 1939. (14.)**

— Beautiful Spring. Valse (Arr. for Military Band by T. C. Brown.) [Parts.] *Boosey & Hawkes: London*, 1938. 4°. [*Boosey & Hawkes Military Band Edition. No.* 79.]
　　　h. 3211. b.

LINCKE (PAUL)

— Berlin Echoes. March and Two Step ... Arr. by L. Tozzeti. [2 mandolins, guitar and P. F. Parts.] *J. W. Stern & Co.: New York*, (1908.) 4°.　　　**g. 1102. b. (13.)**

Berlin so siehste aus

— "Berlin so siehste aus." (Donnerwetter-tadellos!) Grosse Ausstattungs-Revu in 11 Bildern von J. Freund ... Für Gesang und Klavier, *etc.* 16 no. *Apollo-Verlag: Berlin*, (1908.) fol.　　　**H. 1939. (1.)**

— "Berlin so siehste aus." (Donnerwetter-tadellos!) Grosse Ausstattungs-Revu in 11 Bildern von J. Freund. Musik von P. Lincke ... Für Piano Solo ... Potpourri I ... II ... Lieder der Liebesnacht. Walzer ... Die fixe Donaunixe. Rheinländer ... Donnerwetter-tadellos! Marsch ... Sappermentnochmal. Polka ... Auf nach Spree-Athen. Marsch, *etc.* 7 no. *Apollo-Verlag: Berlin*, (1908.) fol.　　　**h. 3753. (10.)**

— "Die fixe Donaunixe." Rheinländer aus der Revue "Donnerwetter—tadellos!" Klarinette I in B (Direktion) [and wind band parts]. 26 pt. *Apollo-Verlag: Berlin*, [1909.] 8°. *The 1ˢᵗ clarinet part is in duplicate.*　　**f. 800. (828.)**

— [Lieder der Liebesnacht.] Songs of the sweet Love-Night, *etc.* [Song.] *J. W. Stern & Co.: New York, etc.*, (1909.) fol.
　　　H. 1939. (7.)

— Lieder der Liebesnacht! Lied aus der Revue "Donnerwetter—tadellos!" ⟨Orchesterstimmen.⟩ 21 pt. *Apollo-Verlag: Berlin*, [1909.] 8°.　　　**f. 800. (829.)**

— Lieder der Liebesnacht! Lied a.d. Revue: Donnerwetter—tadellos. Harmoniemusik. Clarinetto 1 in B (direction) [and parts]. 24 pt. *Apollo-Verlag: Berlin*, [1909.] 8°. *The 1ˢᵗ clarinet part is in duplicate.*　　**f. 800. (830.)**

— "Lieder der Liebesnacht." Walzer nach Motiwen der Revue: Donnerwetter, tadellos! ... Arr. v. J. P. Ehmig. ⟨Klarinette 1 in B (Direktion) [and wind band parts].⟩ 27 pt. *Apollo-Verlag: Berlin*, [1909.] 8°. *The 1ˢᵗ clarinet part is in duplicate.*　　**f. 800. (831.)**

— [Berliner Luft.] The Gay Hussar. Song ... words by A. Ross, *etc. Hawkes & Son: London*, 1907. fol.　**H. 1939. (12.)**

— Berliner Luft. (The Gay Hussar.) March. [Orchestral parts.] 17 pt. *Hawkes & Son: London*, [1907.] 8°.　**f. 800. (832.)**

— Berliner Luft.—The Gay Hussar.—March. [P. F.] *Hawkes & Son: London*, 1907. fol.　　　**h. 3753. (1.)**

— [Berliner Luft.] Ninetta Waltzes, *etc.* [P. F.] *J. W. Stern & Co.: New York, etc.*, (1912.) fol.　**h. 3753. a. (12.)**

— Birthday Serenade ... Risette. Waltz ... By L. Fall. (Arranged for Military Band by F. Winterbottom.) [Parts.] *Hawkes & Son: London*, 1913. fol
No. 391 of "Hawkes & Son's Military Band Edition".
　　　h. 3211. a. (107.)

— Casanova. Operette in drei Akten von Jaques Glück und Will Steinberg ... Klavierauszug mit Text, *etc.* pp. 178. *Apollo-Verlag: Berlin*, [1914.] fol.
A typed slip bearing the words "Nach einer Text-Idee von Lebrun" has been pasted over the words "Von Jaques Glück und Will Steinberg".　　　**H. 1939. a. (1.)**

— Castles in the Air. Ballad with Waltz Refrain, words by J. Herbert, *etc. J. W. Stern & Co.: New York, etc.*, (1907.) fol.
　　　H. 1939. (10.)

— Castles in the Air ... Arr. by L. Tozzeti. [2 mandolins, guitar and P. F. Parts.] *J. W. Stern & Co.: New York*, (1908.) 4°.
　　　g. 1102. b. (14.)

— The Cherry in the Glass. [Song.] Lyric by W. D. Cobb, *etc. J. W. Stern & Co.: New York*, (1907.) fol.　**H. 1939. (11.)**

LINCKE (PAUL)

— The Cherry in the Glass. Introduced in "The Girl behind the Counter". [Orchestral parts.] 11 pt. *Jos. W. Stern & Co.: [New York, 1907.]* 8°.   **f. 800. (833.)**

— The Cherry in the Glass. (Es war einmal.) Song. ⟨Solo B♭ cornet (conductor) [and wind band parts].⟩ 35 pt. *Jos. W. Stern & Co.: [New York, 1909.]* 8°. *Various parts are in duplicate.*   **f. 800. (834.)**

— Do you reverse? Waltz. [P. F.] *F. Harris Co.: London,* (1908.) fol.   **h. 3753. (2.)**

— Donnerwetter—tadellos! *See supra:* "Berlin so siehste aus."

— Fireflies. Idyl, *etc.* [P. F.] *J. W. Stern & Co.: New York, etc.,* (1910.) fol.   **h. 3753. a. (4.)**

— Die fixe Donaunixe. *See supra:* [Berlin so siehste aus.]

— Folies Bergère. March and Two-Step. Arr. by G. Rosey. *J. W. Stern & Co.: New York,* 1899. fol.   **h. 3286. g. (49.)**

— Paul Lincke. Folio for Violin, Cornet and Piano. No. 1. *J. W. Stern & Co.: New York City,* 1910. 8°.   **f. 760. h. (6.)**

— Fräulein Loreley. Operette. pp. 61. *Apollo-Verlag: Berlin,* [1901?] fol. *Imperfect; wanting the titlepage. The title is taken from p. 2.*   **H. 1939. b. (2.)**

— [Frau Luna.] Overture from the Operetta, Frau Luna. [Military band parts.] *Hawkes & Son: London,* 1907. fol. *Part of "Hawkes & Son's Military Band Edition".*   **h. 3211. a. (50.)**

— [Frau Luna.] Luna-Walzer aus der Operette Frau Luna ... Piano solo. pp. 11. *Hawkes & Son: London; Leipzig printed,* [c. 1910.] fol.   **h. 3866. e. (10.)**

— Fresh Flowers. (Frische Blumen.) Intermezzo. [Orchestral parts.] 12 pt. *Jos. W. Stern & Co.: [New York,* 1908.] 8°.   **f. 800. (835.)**

— Fresh Flowers. Frische Blumen ... Intermezzo, *etc.* [P. F.] *J. W. Stern & Co.: New York,* (1909.) fol.   **h. 3753. (11.)**

— Fun of the Fair. Written by Malcolm Arnold. [Song. Staff and tonic sol-fa notation. Voice part.] *Francis, Day & Hunter: London,* [1896.] *s. sh.* fol.   **H. 3980. ss. (7.)**

— Fun of the Fair ... March. [P. F.] *Francis, Day & Hunter: [London,]* 1897. fol.   **h. 3282. f. (46.)**

— The Gay Hussar. *See supra:* [Berliner Luft.]

— The Glow-worm. *See infra:* [Lysistrata.—Glühwürmchen.]

— Grigri. Operette in drei Akten von Bolten-Baeckers und Jules Chancel ... Klavierauszug, *etc.* pp. 116. *Apollo-Verlag: Berlin,* [1913.] fol.   **H. 1939. a. (2.)**

— Hanako. Japanisches Intermezzo, *etc.* [Parts.] *B. Schott's Söhne: Mainz,* 1939. 8°. *[Schott & Co.'s Domesticum Salon Orchestra. No. 494.]*   **g. 1053. a.**

— Im Reiche des Indra. Operette von Leopold Ely und Bolten Bäckers. [Vocal score.] pp. x. 63. *Apolloverlag: Berlin,* [1900.] fol. *Imperfect; wanting all before p. v.*   **H. 1939. b. (3.)**

— [Im Reiche des Indra.—Es war einmal.] Once upon a Time ... Song, English (by L. C. Robinson) & German text by P. Lincke, from the Opera "Im Reiche des Indra". *J. W. Stern & Co.: New York, etc.,* (1909.) fol.   **H. 1939. (15.)**

— [Im Walzerrausch.] That fascinating Waltz, *etc.* [P. F.] *J. W. Stern & Co.: New York, etc.,* (1910.) fol.   **h. 3753. a. (5.)**

— Kwang Hsü. Chinese March, *etc.* [P. F.] *J. W. Stern & Co.: New York, etc.,* (1909.) fol.   **h. 3753. (13.)**

LINCKE (PAUL)

— Kwang Hsü. Chinese March. ⟨Piano solo.⟩ pp. 3. *Hawkes & Son: London,* [c. 1910.] fol.   **h. 725. m. (13.)**

— Kwang Hsü. Chinese March for Piano. *J. W. Stern & Co.: New York, etc.,* (1912.) fol.   **h. 3753. a. (8.)**

— The Laughing Cavalier. Wenn die Bombe platzt! March, *etc.* [P. F.] *J. W. Stern & Co.: New York, etc.,* (1911.) fol.   **h. 3753. a. (9.)**

— Ein Liebestraum. Operette in 3 Akten von Alexander Oskar Erler und Max Neumann. Gesangstexte von Paul Lincke ... Vollständiger Klavierauszug mit Text. pp. 132. *Apollo-Verlag: Berlin,* [1940.] fol.   **H. 1939. b. (1.)**

— Lieder der Liebesnacht. *See supra:* [Berlin so siehste aus.]

— Love's Fancies.—Sinnbild.—Symbole Waltzes. [P. F.] *J. W. Stern & Co.: New York, etc.,* (1909.) fol.   **h. 3753. (14.)**

— Love's Island. Die Liebesinsel. March-Polka. [P. F.] *J. W. Stern & Co.: New York, etc.,* (1912.) fol.   **h. 3753. a. (10.)**

— Luna-Walzer. *See supra:* [Frau Luna.]

— [Eine lustige Doppelehe.] Onkel Fichte. Intermezzo. [Orchestral parts.] 17 pt. *Hawkes & Son: London,* [1908.] 8°.   **f. 800. (837.)**

— [Eine lustige Doppelehe.] Wenn der Mondschein scheint! Marsch ... Blechmusik. Kornett 1 in B (direction) [and parts]. 24 pt. *Apollo-Verlag: Berlin,* [1909.] 8°. *The 1ˢᵗ cornet part is in duplicate.*   **f. 800. (838.)**

— Eine lustige Spreewaldfahrt. Burleske mit Gesang in 2 Bildern von A. Schmasow ... Für Piano: Potpourri ... Spreewald-Marsch ... Die lustige Spreewälderin ... Für Gesang mit Piano ... "Mein Schätzchen braucht nicht reich zu sein," Lied; Spreewald-Marschlied; Duett—Wenn du willst dass du stillst. 6 no. *Apollo-Verlag: Berlin,* (1908.) fol.   **H. 1939. (4.)**

— [Eine lustige Spreewaldfahrt.] Mein Schätzchen braucht nicht reich zu sein. Lied ... (Blechmusik.) Cornett 1 in B (direction) [and parts]. ⟨[With] Wein-Walzer. Sam. Gross. Cornet 1 in B [and wind band parts].⟩ 38 pt. *Apollo-Verlag: Berlin,* [1909.] 8°. *The 1ˢᵗ cornet part is in duplicate.*   **f. 800. (839.)**

— [Eine lustige Spreewaldfahrt.] Spreewald-Marsch, *etc.* ⟨Orchesterstimmen.⟩ 21 pt. *Apollo-Verlag: Berlin,* [1909.] 8°. *The 1ˢᵗ violin part is in duplicate.*   **f. 800. (840.)**

— [Eine lustige Spreewaldfahrt.] Spreewald Marsch ... Cornett 1 in B (Direktions-Stimme) [and wind band parts]. 20 pt. *Apollo-Verlag: Berlin,* [1909.] 8°. *The 1ˢᵗ cornet part is in duplicate.*   **f. 800. (841.)**

Lysistrata. — Glühwürmchen

— Le Ver luisant ... [Song.] Paroles française[s] de A. Arimini. [Voice part and words only.] *J. W. Stern & Co.: New York, etc.,* (1909.) 8°.   **F. 637. ii. (3.)**

— The Glow-worm. Song. English words by Lilla Cayley Robinson. pp. 7. *Jos. W. Stern & Co.: New York,* [c. 1910.] fol.   **H. 1980. zz. (11.)**

— The Glow-Worm. Quartette for male voices. *J. W. Stern & Co.: New York,* (1908.) 8°.   **F. 163. f. (27.)**

— Glow-Worm. Ver luisant. Glühwürmchen. Idyl. [Orchestral parts.] 17 pt. *Hawkes & Son: London,* [1906.] 8°.   **f. 800. (836.)**

— The Glow-Worm. Glühwürmchen. Idyl. [Orchestral parts.] *J. W. Stern & Co.: [New York,]* 1908. fol.   **h. 3753. (4.)**

— The Glow-Worm. Glühwürmchen. Idyl. [P. F. solo and duet.] 2 no. *J. W. Stern & Co.: New York, etc.,* (1907, 08.) fol.   **h. 3753. (3.)**

LINCKE (PAUL)

—— The Glow-worm. Idyl … Piano solo, *etc.* pp. 7. *Hawkes & Son: London*, [1916?] fol. **h. 62. x. (15.)**

—— The Glow-Worm … Arr. by L. Tozzeti. [2 mandolins, guitar and P. F. Parts.] *J. W. Stern & Co.: New York*, (1908.) 4°. **g. 1102. b. (15.)**

—— The Glow-Worm … Arr. by P. Eno. [2 banjos.] *J. W. Stern & Co.: New York, etc.*, (1909.) fol. **h. 3753. (12.)**

Lysistrata.—Walzer

—— Lysistrata. Walzer. [Orchestral parts.] 16 pt. *Hawkes & Son: London*, [1905.] 8°. **f. 800. (842.)**

—— Lysistrata-Waltz. (From the Operette "Lysistrata".) [Orchestral parts.] 15 pt. *Jos. W. Stern & Co.: [New York,* 1907.] 8°. *The 1st violin part is in duplicate.* **f. 800. (843.)**

—— Lysistrata Valse. [Military band parts.] *Hawkes & Son: London*, 1906. fol. *Part of "Hawkes & Son's Military Band Edition".* **h. 3211. a. (32.)**

—— Lysistrata Waltz, *etc.* [P. F.] *J. W. Stern & Co.: New York, etc.*, (1909.) fol. **h. 3753. (15.)**

—— Lysistrata. Valse. [P. F.] pp. 11. *Hawkes & Son: London*, [c. 1920.] fol. **h. 725. m. (14.)**

————

—— Many happy Returns. *See infra*: [O, ihr Weiber!]

—— "May I have the Pleasure?" ⟨Waltz.⟩ [Military band parts.] 33 pt. *Boosey & Co.: London*, 1908. fol. [*Boosey & Co.'s new supplemental Journal for military Bands. no.* 56.] **h. 1544. a.**

—— May I have the Pleasure? Waltz. [P. F.] *F. Harris Co.: London*, (1908.) fol. **h. 3753. (5.)**

—— "Meet me at the Masquerade."—The Tabarin.—[Song.] Lyric by H. B. Smith. *J. W. Stern & Co.: New York, etc.*, 1908. fol. **H. 1939. (2.)**

—— Mein Schätzchen braucht nicht reich zu sein. *See supra*: [Eine lustige Spreewaldfahrt.]

—— Melanie: Gavotte. [P. F.] *Chappell & Co.: London*, [1899.] fol. **h. 3282. f. (47.)**

—— "Nachfalter." (Moths.) ⟨Valse. Conductor [and military band parts].⟩ 26 pt. *In:* COULDERY (C. H.) Fantasia for Trumpet, *etc.* 1899. fol. [*Boosey's supplemental Journal. no.* 418.] **h. 1544.**

—— Neptune. *See infra*: [Die Spree Amazone.]

—— The Nigger's Birthday. (Negers Geburstsag [*sic*].) Two-step. [Orchestral parts.] 17 pt. *Hawkes & Son: London*, [1906.] 8°. **f. 800. (826.)**

—— The Nigger's Birthday. Two-Step … and Echo des Bastions. Caprice. By H. Kling. [Military band parts.] *Hawkes & Son: London*, 1907. fol. *Part of "Hawkes & Son's Military Band Edition".* **h. 3211. a. (44.)**

—— Nimm mich mit! (Take me too.) Polka. [Orchestral parts.] 17 pt. *Hawkes & Son: London*, [1907.] 8°. **f. 800. (844.)**

—— O, ihr Weiber!—Oh, you Women.—Humorous March for the Pianoforte.—With Vocal part, ad lib. *Chappell & Co.: London and Melbourne*, [1906.] fol. **h. 3753. (6.)**

—— [O, ihr Weiber!] Many happy Returns. March Two-Step. [P. F.] *J. W. Stern & Co.: New York, etc.*, (1911.) fol. **h. 3753. a. (11.)**

—— [Ob du mich liebst?] Within your Eyes, Love … Song, with English and German text, *etc.* (English version by L. C. Robinson.) 3 no. [In F, E flat and C.] *J. W. Stern & Co.: New York*, (1908, 09.) fol. **H. 1939. (8.)**

LINCKE (PAUL)

—— [Ob du mich liebst.] Within your Eyes Love … Cornet or bariton solo. ⟨Solo B♭ cornet (conductor) [and wind band parts].⟩ 35 pt. *Jos. W. Stern & Co.: [New York*, 1909.] 8°. *Various parts are in duplicate.* **f. 800. (854.)**

—— On the Bosporus.—Am Bosporus.—Turkish Intermezzo. [P. F.] *J. W. Stern & Co.: New York, etc.*, (1910.) fol. **h. 3753. (16.)**

—— Once upon a Time. *See supra*: [Im Reiche des Indra.—Es war einmal.]

—— Onkel Fichte. *See supra*: [Eine lustige Doppelehe.]

—— The Outside Inn. Gehn wir noch in's Café! March Two-Step. [P. F.] *J. W. Stern & Co.: New York, etc.*, (1912.) fol. **h. 3753. a. (13.)**

—— Pomponette. *See infra*: [Tears of Joy.]

—— Prinzess Rosine. Operette in zwei Akten. [Libretto by H. Bolten-Baeckers and Friedendorf.] ⟨Klavier-Auszug mit Text.⟩ pp. v. 2–98. *Apollo Verlag: Berlin*, [1907.] fol. **H. 1939. b. (4.)**

—— Queen of the Night. *See supra*: [Amina.]

—— Remember, to err is human, to forgive, divine. A Song, *etc.* *J. W. Stern & Co.: New York, etc.*, (1909.) fol. **H. 1939. (5.)**

—— Remember "To err is human, to forgive divine!" … Arr. by Robert Recker. [Orchestral parts.] 11 pt. *Jos. W. Stern & Co.: [New York*, 1909.] 8°. **f. 800. (845.)**

—— [Rosen, Tulpen, Nelken.] Roses, Tulips, Pansies … Song, *etc.* *J. W. Stern & Co.: New York*, (1908.) fol. **H. 1939. (3.)**

—— [Rosen, Tulpen, Nelken.] Roses, Tulips, Pansies. (Rosen, Tulpen, Nelken.) Song. Cornet or Baritone Solo. ⟨Solo B♭ cornet (conductor) [and wind band parts].⟩ 35 pt. *Jos. W. Stern & Co.: [New York*, 1909.] 8°. *Various parts are in duplicate.* **f. 800. (846.)**

—— Schlager auf Schlager. Fröhlicher Rundgesang in Form eines Potpourris. ⟨Orchesterstimmen.⟩ 21 pt. *Apollo-Verlag: Berlin*, [1909.] 8°. *The 1st violin part is in duplicate.* **f. 800. (847.)**

—— Schlager auf Schlager! Fröhlicher Rundgesang in Form eines Potpourris. Clarinette 1 in B (direktion) [and wind band parts]. 27 pt. *Apollo-Verlag: Berlin*, [1909.] 8°. *The 1st clarinet part is in duplicate.* **f. 800. (848.)**

—— Schlager auf Schlager. Ein fröhlicher Rundgesang in Form eines Potpourris—mit unterlegtem Text—. Für Piano, *etc.* *Apollo-Verlag: Berlin*, (1909.) fol. **H. 1939. (6.)**

—— Siamese Patrol. (Siamesische Wachtparade.) Characteristic. [Orchestral parts.] 15 pt. *Jos. W. Stern & Co.: [New York*, 1907.] 8°. *The 1st violin part is in duplicate.* **f. 800. (849.)**

—— Siamese Patrol. Siamesische Wachtparade. Characteristic. [P. F.] *J. W. Stern & Co.: New York, etc.*, (1908.) fol. **h. 3753. (7.)**

—— Songs of the sweet Love-Night. *See supra*: [Berlin so siehste aus.—Lieder der Liebesnacht.]

—— [Die Spree Amazone.] "Neptune." ⟨Waltz.⟩ Paul Lincke. ⟨Arr. by M. Retford⟩ … "King's Men". ⟨Military march. For band and chorus.⟩ Words by Owen Seaman. Music by Paul Durban. ⟨Arranged by J. Mackenzie Rogan.⟩ ⟨Conductor [and military band parts].⟩ 33 pt. *Boosey & Co.: London*, 1910. fol. [*Boosey & Co.'s new supplemental Journal for military Bands. no.* 75.] **h. 1544. a.**

—— Spreewald-March. *See supra*: [Eine lustige Spreewaldfahrt.]

—— Sternlein am Himmelszelt. Salonstück für das Pianoforte. Op. 121. *Augener & Co.: London*, [1894.] fol. **g. 605. f. (22.)**

LINCKE (PAUL)

— Tanzfreuden. Taschen-Tanz-Album. 5ᵗᵉʳ Band ...
herausgegeben von P. Lincke. Für Pianoforte. *Apollo-Verlag:*
Berlin, [1909.] *obl.* 8°. **a. 170.**

— [Tears of Joy.] Pomponette. March Intermezzo on the ...
Valse ... Arranged by R. Bernard. Piano solo. *Whitehall*
Music Co.: London, 1916. fol. **h. 3753. a. (14.)**

— That fascinating Waltz. *See supra:* [Im Walzerrausch.]

— Träume vom Lido ... Lido Dreams. [Parts.] *B. Schott's*
Söhne: Mainz, 1939. 8°.
[*Schott & Co.'s Domesticum Salon Orchestra. No.* 493.]
g. 1053. a.

— Umti-umti-um! Song. From the comedy An Artist's Model.
Words by Harry Greenbank. pp. 5. *Hopwood & Crew:*
London, [1895.] fol. **H. 3980. ss. (8.)**

— Under Love's Window.—Unter Liebchen's Fenster.—Waltzes.
[P. F.] *J. W. Stern & Co.: New York, etc.*, (1909.) fol.
h. 3753. (17.)

— Venus on Earth. (Venus steig hernieder.) Valse. [Orchestral
parts.] 17 pt. *Hawkes & Son: London*, [1907.] 8°.
f. 800. (50.)

— Venus on Earth. Valse. [Military band parts.] *Hawkes &*
Son: London, 1908. fol.
Part of "Hawkes & Son's Military Band Edition".
h. 3211. a. (52.)

— Venus on Earth.—Venus steig hernieder.—Valse, from the
Operetta. [P. F.] *Hawkes & Son: London*, 1907. fol.
h. 3753. (8.)

— Le Ver luisant. *See supra:* [Lysistrata.—Glühwürmchen.]

— Verschmähte Liebe. (Unrequited Love.) Valse. [Orchestral
parts.] 17 pt. *Hawkes & Son: London*, [1906.] 8°.
f. 800. (851.)

— Verschmähte Liebe. (Unrequited Love.) Walzer. [P. F.] pp. 9.
Hawkes & Son: London; Leipzig printed, [c. 1910.] fol.
h. 725. m. (15.)

— The Way to the Heart. *See infra:* [Der Weg zum Herzen.]

— Wedding-Dance. (Hochzeitsreigen.) Waltz. [Orchestral parts.]
14 pt. *Jos. W. Stern & Co.:* [*New York*, 1907.] 8°.
The 1ˢᵗ *violin part is in duplicate.* **f. 800. (852.)**

— Wedding Dance.—Hochzeitsreigen.—Waltzes. [P. F.]
J. W. Stern & Co.: New York, etc., (1908.) fol. **h. 3753. (9.)**

— Wedding Dance. Waltz ... Arr. by L. Tozzeti. [2 mandolins,
guitar and P. F. Parts.] *J. W. Stern & Co.: New York*, (1908.)
4°. **g. 1102. b. (16.)**

— Der Weg zum Herzen. (The Way to the Heart.) Gavotte.
[Orchestral parts.] 19 pt. *Hawkes & Son: London*, [1907.] 8°.
f. 800. (853.)

— [Der Weg zum Herzen.] The Way to the Heart. Gavotte ...
Darby and Joan.—Brüderlein Fein.—Valse. By L. Fall, *etc.*
(Arranged for Military Band by F. Winterbottom.) [Parts.]
Hawkes & Son: London, 1912. fol.
No. 372 *of "Hawkes & Son's Military Band Edition".*
h. 3211. a. (93.)

— [Der Weg zum Herzen.] The Way to the Heart ... Gavotte,
etc. [P. F.] *J. W. Stern & Co.: New York, etc.*, (1909.) fol.
h. 3753. (18.)

— Wenn der Mondschein scheint! *See supra:* [Eine lustige
Doppelehe.]

— Where the Oak and Ivy twine. Written by Edgar Bateman.
[Song. Staff and tonic sol-fa notation. Voice part.] *Francis,*
Day & Hunter: London, [1898.] *s. sh.* fol. **H. 3980. ss. (9.)**

— Within your Eyes, Love. *See supra:* [Ob du mich liebst?]

LINCKE (PAUL)

— You are the Star that guides my Way. [Song.] Words by
M. H. Rosenfeld. *J. W. Stern & Co.: New York, etc.*, (1909.)
fol. **H. 1939. (13.)**

LINCO

— Linco found Damon lying. *Linco's Advice to Damon.* [Song.]
[*London*, 1730?] *s. sh.* fol. **G. 316. e. (72.)**

— [Another edition.] Linco found Damon lying. *Linco's Advice*
to Damon. [1740?] *s. sh.* fol. **G. 310. (22.)**

— Linco's Travels. [Songs.] *See also* ARNE (M.) and VERNON (J.)

— [Linco's Travels.] I'll never go abroad again. *Favourite Song*
in Linco's Travels. [By J. Vernon.] [*Dublin*, 1770?] *s. sh.* fol.
G. 808. f. (35. b.)

— [Linco's Travels.] I saw sprightly France. *Linco's Travels.*
[Song, by M. Arne.] Taken from a Favourite Interlude of that
name, *etc.* [*Dublin*, 1770?] *s. sh.* fol. **G. 808. f. (35. a.)**

— [Linco's Travels.] Welcome Linco, welcome home. [Song and
chorus by J. Vernon.] *Linco's Travels*, as Sung by Mr. King.
S. Lee: [*Dublin*, 1770?] *s. sh.* fol. **G. 808. f. (35. c.)**

LINCOLN

— Lincoln. [Song.] *See* BRAINE (R.)

— Lincoln. [Part-song.] *See* CLOKEY (J. W.)

— Lincoln. [Cantata.] *See* ELWELL (George H.)

— Lincoln, Grant and Lee. [Song.] *See* DRESSER (Paul)

— Lincoln Green. Unison Song. *See* DEMUTH (N. F.)

— A Lincoln Letter. [Part-song.] *See* KAY (Ulysses)

— Lincoln Monument. [Song.] *See* RAPHLING (Sam)

— Lincoln, oh! Lincoln, we honor you to-day. [Action song.]
See HOSCHNA (K. L.)

— Lincoln Portrait for Speaker and Orchestra. *See*
COPLAND (A.)

— From "Lincoln, the great Commoner". [Song.] *See* IVES
(Charles E.)

— Lincoln's Gettysburg Address. [For a solo voice.] *See*
TINTURIN (P.)

— Lincoln's Gettysburg Address. Song. *See* WAYNE (Bernie)

— Lincoln's Second Inaugural. Anthem. *See* GAUL (Harvey B.)

LINCOLN (C.)

— A Letter from afar. Song, words by G. Weatherly. *Weekes &*
Co.: London, [1891.] fol. **H. 1797. o. (40.)**

LINCOLN (ED.)

— Smokin' Charley. Two Step or Cake Walk. [P. F.] *Brooks &*
Denton: New York, 1901. fol. **g. 543. gg. (12.)**

LINCOLN (FRED)

— After many Years. [Song.] Written by A. E. Lawrence, *etc.*
⟨Arranged by John S. Baker.⟩ pp. 4. *R. Maynard: London*,
[1895.] fol. **H. 3980. ss. (10.)**

— The Boy and the Telescope. ⟨Song.⟩ Written by E. J. Hilliary.
etc. [Staff and tonic sol-fa notation. Voice part.] *Francis,*
Day & Hunter: London, [1903.] *s. sh.* fol. **H. 3985. aa. (12.)**

— The Boy and the Telescope, *etc.* ⟨Song.⟩ Written by
E. J. Hilliary. [With separate voice part.] 2 pt. *Francis, Day &*
Hunter: London, [1903.] fol. **H. 3985. aa. (13.)**

LINCOLN (FRED)

— That's the Job for me. Written by A. E. Lawrence, *etc.* [Song. Staff and tonic sol-fa notation. Voice part.] *Francis, Day & Hunter: London*, [1898.] *s. sh.* fol.　　　**H. 3980. ss. (11.)**

— *See* LAWRENCE (Albert E.) and LINCOLN (F.) That little Home of mine. ⟨Song.⟩ Written and composed by A. E. Lawrence and F. Lincoln, *etc.* [1903.] *s. sh.* fol.　　**H. 3985. k. (60.)**

— *See* LAWRENCE (Albert E.) and LINCOLN (F.) That little Home of mine, *etc.* ⟨Song.⟩ [1903.] fol.　　**H. 3985. k. (61.)**

LINCOLN (HARRY B.)

— Seventeenth-century Keyboard Music in the Chigi Manuscripts of the Vatican Library ... Edited by H. B. Lincoln. [With facsimiles.] 3 vol. *American Institute of Musicology: [Dallas, Tex.,]* 1968. 4°. [*Corpus of early Keyboard Music.* 32.]　　**g. 1750.**

— *See* AMOROSA. [L'Amorosa Ero.] The Madrigal Collection L'Amorosa Ero. (Brescia, 1588.) Transcribed and edited with introduction by H. B. Lincoln. [1968.] 8°.　**E. 270. pp.**

LINCOLN (HARRY J.)

— Alameda. Waltzes. [P. F.] pp. 5. *Vandersloot Music Pub. Co.: Williamsport*, [1908.] fol.　　**h. 4120. qq. (6.)**

— Alpine Rose. A flower song. [P. F.] pp. 5. *Vandersloot Music Pub. Co.: Williamsport*, [1909.] fol.　　**h. 4120. qq. (7.)**

— Angels of Night. Reverie-transcription. [P. F.] pp. 7. *Vandersloot Music Pub. Co.: Williamsport*, [1909.] fol.　　**h. 4120. qq. (8.)**

— Babbling Brook. Reverie, caprice. [P. F.] pp. 7. *Vandersloot Music Pub. Co.: Williamsport*, [1908.] fol.　　**h. 4120. qq. (9.)**

— Baldwin Commandery. March and two step. [P. F.] pp. 5. *Vandersloot Music Pub. Co.: Williamsport*, [1906.] fol.　　**h. 4120. qq. (10.)**

— "The Buffalo Flyer." March & two step. [P. F.] pp. 5. *Vandersloot Music Co.: Williamsport*, [1904.] fol.　　**h. 4120. qq. (11.)**

— The Circuit. March and two step. [P. F.] pp. 5. *Vandersloot Music Pub. Co.: Williamsport*, [1908.] fol.　　**h. 4120. qq. (12.)**

— The Crater. March and two step. [P. F.] pp. 5. *Vandersloot Music Pub. Co.: Williamsport*, [1907.] fol.　　**h. 4120. qq. (13.)**

— A Dream of the South. Waltzes. [P. F.] pp. 7. *Vandersloot Music Pub. Co.: Williamsport*, [1909.] fol.　　**h. 4120. qq. (14.)**

— Empire Express. March and two step. [P. F.] pp. 5. *Vandersloot Music Pub. Co.: Williamsport*, [1908.] fol.　　**h. 4120. qq. (15.)**

— Evening Thoughts. Waltzes. [P. F.] pp. 5. *Vandersloot Music Pub. Co.: Williamsport*, [1907.] fol.　　**h. 4120. qq. (16.)**

— Excuse me, but isn't your Name Johnson? [Song.] Words by Wm Hauser. pp. 5. *Vandersloot Music Pub. Co.: Williamsport*, [1907.] fol.　　**H. 3985. aa. (14.)**

— The False Alarm. March and two-step. [P. F.] *Vandersloot Music Co.: Williamsport*, [1905.] fol.　　**h. 4120. qq. (17.)**

— Fire Drill. March-two step. [P. F.] pp. 5. *Vandersloot Music Pub. Co.: Williamsport*, [1909.] fol.　　**h. 4120. qq. (18.)**

— The Fire Master. March and two step. [P. F.] pp. 5. *Vandersloot Music Co.: Williamsport*, [1904.] fol.　　**h. 4120. qq. (19.)**

— Fire Worshippers. March and two step. [P. F.] pp. 5. *Vandersloot Music Pub. Co.: Williamsport*, [1904.] fol.　　**h. 4120. qq. (20.)**

LINCOLN (HARRY J.)

— The Flash Light. March two step. [P. F.] pp. 5. *Vandersloot Music Pub. Co.: Williamsport*, [1908.] fol.　　**h. 4120. qq. (21.)**

— The Focus. March—two step. [P. F.] pp. 5. *Vandersloot Music Pub. Co.: Williamsport*, [1908.] fol.　　**h. 4120. qq. (22.)**

— Garden of Dreams. Reverie, serenade. [P. F.] pp. 5. *Vandersloot Music Pub. Co.: Williamsport*, [1909.] fol.　　**h. 4120. qq. (23.)**

— "Heaven's Artillery March." Two step. [P. F.] pp. 5. *Vandersloot Music Co.: Williamsport*, [1904.] fol.　　**h. 4120. qq. (24.)**

— Honest Confession. Morceau characteristic. [P. F.] pp. 5. *Vandersloot Music Pub. Co.: Williamsport*, [1909.] fol.　　**h. 4120. qq. (25.)**

— A Jolly Sailor. March—two-step. [P. F.] pp. 5. *Vandersloot Music Pub. Co.: Williamsport*, [1908.] fol.　　**h. 4120. qq. (26.)**

— Just at the Break of Day. [Song.] Words & music by H. J. Lincoln. pp. 5. *Vandersloot Music Co.: Williamsport*, [1905.] fol.　　**H. 3985. aa. (15.)**

— The Lost Phase. Waltzes. [P. F.] pp. 5. *Vandersloot Music Pub. Co.: Willlamsport*, [1907.] fol.　　**h. 4120. qq. (27.)**

— The Merry Makers. March and two step. [P. F.] pp. 5. *Vandersloot Music Pub. Co.: Williamsport*, [1906.] fol.　　**h. 4120. qq. (28.)**

— The Midnight Fire Alarm. March and Two Step ... Arranged by E. T. Paull. [P. F.] *E. T. Paull Music Co.: New York*, 1900. fol.　　**h. 3286. r. (14.)**

— Moss Rose. Morceau characteristic. [P. F.] pp. 5. *Vandersloot Music Pub. Co.: Williamsport*, [1909.] fol.　**h. 4120. qq. (29.)**

— My southern Home. [Song.] Words by Rev. J. A. Patton. pp. 5. *Vandersloot Music Pub. Co.: Williamsport*, [1907.] fol.　　**H. 3985. aa. (16.)**

— Nippono. Intermezzo. (March two step.) [P. F.] pp. 5. *Vandersloot Music Pub. Co.: Williamsport*, [1907.] fol.　　**h. 4120. qq. (30.)**

— Nuptial Waltzes. [P. F.] pp. 7. *Vandersloot Music Pub. Co.: Williamsport*, [1906.] fol.　　**h. 4120. qq. (31.)**

— Observatory. March & two step. [P. F.] pp. 5. *Vandersloot Music Pub. Co.: Williamsport*, [1906.] fol.　　**h. 4120. qq. (32.)**

— Only a Dream of you. [Song.] From the melody "Garden of Dreams" reverie. Words by Carl Loveland. pp. 5. *Vandersloot Music Pub. Co.: Williamsport*, [1909.] fol.　　**H. 3985. aa. (17.)**

— Orpheus. Waltzes. [P. F.] pp. 5. *Vandersloot Music Pub. Co.: Williamsport*, [1907.] fol.　　**h. 4120. qq. (33.)**

— Our victorious Nation. March, galop, or two step. [P. F.] pp. 5. *Vandersloot Music Pub. Co.: Williamsport*, [1908.] fol.　　**h. 4120. qq. (34.)**

— The Pacifier. March and two-step. [P. F.] pp. 5. *Vandersloot Music Pub. Co.: Williamsport*, [1908.] fol.　　**h. 4120.qq. (35.)**

— The Palm Limited. March and two-step. [P. F.] pp. 5. *Vandersloot Music Co.: Williamsport*, [1905.] fol.　　**h. 4120. qq. (36.)**

— Peace Conference. March and two step. [P. F.] pp. 5. *Vandersloot Music Co.: Williamsport*, [1905.] fol.　　**h. 4120. qq. (37.)**

— "Playmates." March—two step. [P. F.] pp. 5. *Vandersloot Music Pub. Co.: Williamsport*, [1909.] fol.　**h. 4120. qq. (38.)**

— Rag-bag. Rag. (A rag-time galop.) [P. F.] pp. 5. *Vandersloot Music Pub. Co.: Williamsport*, [1909.] fol.　**h. 4120. qq. (39.)**

LINCOLN (HARRY J.)

— The Rifle Range. March and two step. [P. F.] pp. 5. *Vandersloot Music Co.: Williamsport,* [1905.] fol.
h. 4120. qq. (40.)

— Salute to America. March and two step. [P. F.] pp. 5. *Vandersloot Music Co.: Williamsport,* [1904.] fol.
h. 4120. qq. (41.)

— Sounds from the Orient. March and two step. [P. F.] pp. 5. *Vandersloot Music Co.: Williamsport,* [1906.] fol.
h. 4120. qq. (42.)

— A Southern Dream. Waltzes. [P. F.] pp. 7. *Vandersloot Music Co.: Williamsport,* [1905.] fol.
h. 4120. qq. (43.)

— Susquehanna. March & two step. [P. F.] pp. 5. *Vandersloot Music Pub. Co.: Williamsport,* [1906.] fol.
h. 4120. qq. (44.)

— The Tournament. March and two step. [P. F.] pp. 5. *Vandersloot Music Pub. Co.: Williamsport,* [1906.] fol.
h. 4120. qq. (45.)

— Tri State. March and two step. [P. F.] pp. 5. *Vandersloot Music Pub. Co.: Williamsport,* [1906.] fol.
h. 4120. qq. (46.)

— The Twelfth Regiment. March and two step. *Vandersloot Music Pub. Co.: Williamsport,* [1908.] fol.
h. 4120. qq. (47.)

— Vallamont. (Valley and mountain.) Reverie. [P. F.] pp. 5. *Vandersloot Music Co.: Williamsport,* [1903.] fol.
h. 4120. qq. (48.)

— Vesuvius. March and two step. [P. F.] pp. 5. *Vandersloot Music Pub. Co.: Williamsport,* [1907.] fol.
h. 4120. qq. (49.)

— Which Way did my Mamma go? ... Song ... Words and music by H. J. Lincoln. pp. 5. *Vandersloot Music Pub. Co.: Willlamsport,* [1908.] fol.
H. 3985. aa. (18.)

— Whispering Waves. Waltzes. [P. F.] pp. 5. *Vandersloot Music Pub. Co.: Williamsport,* [1906.] fol.
h. 4120. qq. (50.)

— "Zenith." Intermezzo. March and two step. [P. F.] pp. 5. *Vandersloot Music Co.: Williamsport,* [1905.] fol.
h. 4120. qq. (51.)

— *See* CHAMPLIN (Charles K.) The Flag of Uncle Sam. March song, *etc.* [Followed by an arrangement of the chorus for male or mixed voice quartet by H. J. Lincoln.] [1910.] fol.
H. 3990. m. (20.)

— *See* CHAMPLIN (Charles K.) Love me Dearie, *etc.* [Song. Followed by an arrangement of the chorus for male or mixed voice quartet by H. J. Lincoln.] [1910.] fol.
H. 3990. m. (21.)

— *See* COHEN (Charles) Baby Lou, *etc.* [Song. Followed by an arrangement of the chorus for male or mixed voice quartet by H. J. Lincoln.] [1911.] fol.
H. 3990. w. (19.)

— *See* COHEN (Charles) I love you still, *etc.* [Song. Followed by an arrangement of the chorus for male or mixed voice quartet by H. J. Lincoln.] [1911.] fol.
H. 3990. w. (20.)

— *See* DEMPSEY (James L.) Beautiful Girl, *etc.* [Song.] ⟨Arr. by H. J. Lincoln.⟩ [1919.] 4°.
H. 3991. f. (15.)

— *See* DUSENBERRY (E. F.) Darby and Joan, *etc.* [Song. Followed by an arrangement of the chorus for male or mixed voice quartet by H. J. Lincoln.] [1912.] fol.
H. 3991. p. (10.)

— *See* DUSENBERRY (E. F.) "Good-bye Dad," *etc.* [Song. Followed by an arrangement of the chorus for male or mixed voixe quartet by H. J. Lincoln.] [1912.] fol.
H. 3991. p. (13.)

— *See* DUSENBERRY (E. F.) Molly Brown, *etc.* [Song. Followed by an arrangement of the chorus for male or mixed voice quartet by H. J. Lincoln.] [1912.] fol.
H. 3991. p. (23.)

— *See* DUSENBERRY (E. F.) My Dreamland Girl, *etc.* [Song. Followed by an arrangement of the chorus for male or mixed voice quartet by H. J. Lincoln.] [1913.] fol.
H. 3991. p. (24.)

LINCOLN (HARRY J.)

— *See* SCHMID (J. C.) When they gather in the Sheaves, *etc.* [With four-part arrangement of the chorus by H. J. Lincoln.] 1911. fol.
H. 1792. bb. (46.)

LINCOLN (HENRY JOHN)

— The Organist's Anthology, a series of classical compositions ... arranged ... for the organ by H. J. Lincoln. no. 11, 12. *London,* [1845.] fol.
Imperfect; wanting no. 1–10.
h. 3212. (10.)

— Wessel & C⁰'s Series of modern Symphonies and Overtures, as Septetts, for flute, two violins, two tenors, violoncello & contra basso, or two violoncellos ... Arranged by H. J. Lincoln. [Parts.] no. 1. *Wessel & Cⁱ.: London,* [1839.] fol.
Imperfect; wanting the other numbers.
h. 2782. qq.

— *See* HESSE (A.) The practical organist; compositions by A. Hesse, for the organ. Edited by H. J. Lincoln. [1854.] fol.
h. 3212. (9.)

LINCOLN (STODDARD)

— Five eighteenth Century Piano Sonatas. Edited, with introductory notes, by Stoddard Lincoln. pp. 52. *Oxford University Press: London,* [1975.] 4°.
g. 270. nn. (4.)

— *See* JONES (Richard) Suits or Setts of Lessons for the Harpsichord or Spinnet ... Édition par S. Lincoln. [1974.] 4°. [*Le Pupitre.* 49.]
G. 51.

— *See* MOZART (W. A.) *the Younger.* [4 Polonaises mélancoliques. Op. 22.] Four Polonaises for Piano ... A facsimile of the first edition with an introduction by S. Lincoln. [1975.] *obl.* 4°.
e. 282. ee. (11.)

LINCOLN (W. B.)

— Abide with me. [Anthem.] Alto Solo, Soprano solo and Quartet or Chorus. *B. F. Wood Music Co.: Boston, Mass.,* (1900.) 8°.
Choir Journal, No. 42a.
F. 986.

— Jubilate Deo. Sop. and Alto Solos and Md. Qt. *O. Ditson Co.: [Boston, etc.,]* 1896. 8°.
F. 1529. b. (38.)

LINCOLNENSIS, *pseud.*

— Lincoln. Polka. [P. F.] pp. 4. *Hopwood & Crew: London,* [1880?] fol.
h. 721. n. (26.)

LINCOLNSHIRE

— A Lincolnshire Love Song. [Song.] *See* O'NEILL (F.)

— The Lincolnshire Poacher. [Song.] *See* WHEN. When I was bound apprentice. [1856.] fol.
H. 2342.

— The Lincolnshire Poacher. Chorus. *See* BANTOCK (*Sir* G.)

— The Lincolnshire Poacher. Folk-Song. *See* DUNHILL (T. F.)

— The Lincolnshire Poacher. Chorus. *See* HUFSTADER (R.)

— The Lincolnshire Poacher. Unison Song. *See* LAPORTE (B.)

— The Lincolnshire Poacher. Two-part song. *See* PITFIELD (Thomas B.)

— The Lincolnshire Poacher. Song. *See* REEVES (E.)

— The Lincolnshire Poacher. [Part-song.] *See* WHITTAKER (W. G.)

— The Lincolnshire Poacher's Song. Part-Song. *See* MOFFAT (A. E.)

LINCOURT (OLIVIER)

— Tintamarre-Polka pour Piano. *Paris*, [1878.] fol.
          h. 1493. o. (39.)

LIND

— Lind duftig hält die Maiennacht. [Song.] *See* BRUCH (M. C. F.)
[Vier Lieder ... Op. 33. No. 4.]

LIND (ED. ALBERT)

— Valse Idéale pour piano. *Hambourg*, [1884?] fol.
          h. 3280. l. (2.)

LIND (GUSTAVE) *pseud.* [i.e. FREDERIC MULLEN.]

— Piano Album, *etc. Augener: London*, [1929.] 4°.   **g. 1448.**

— Gustave Lind Selection. Arranged by the Composer for
Piano. *Augener: London*, 1931. 4°.   **g. 1127. oo. (6.)**

— Andalusian Serenade, for piano. *Augener: London*, 1913. fol.
          g. 606. bb. (30.)

— At Teddington Lock, for pianoforte. *Augener: London*, 1922.
4°.   **g. 1127. h. (23.)**

— At the Castle. 1. Dames & knights. 2. On the moonlit terrace.
For pianoforte. *Augener: London*, 1918. 4°.   **g. 1129. i. (1.)**

— [At the Castle. No. 1.] Dames & Knights, for violin,
violoncello & piano. Arranged by A. Carse. *Augener:
London*, 1921. 4°.   **g. 419. m. (7.)**

— [At the Castle. No. 1.] Dames & Knights, for violin & piano.
Arranged by A. Carse. *Augener: London*, 1921. 4°.
          g. 500. h. (5.)

— At the Window. Serenade for piano. *Augener: London*, 1925.
4°.   **g. 1127. dd. (12.)**

— Barcarolle, for pianoforte. *Augener: London*, 1925. 4°.
          g. 1127. w. (9.)

— Berceuse for Piano. *Augener: London*, 1925. 4°.
          g. 1127. dd. (13.)

— The Black Iris. Suite for piano. *Augener: London*, 1917. 4°.
          g. 603. nn. (2.)

— Bygone Days. A Lyric Suite for Pianoforte. (1. An Old Song.
2. Ophelia. 3. 'Twas Springtime. 4. Under the Orange
Blossoms. 5. Cypress Trees.) *Augener: London*, (1914.) 4°.
Album Series, No. 2.   **g. 603. aa. (4.)**

— Cossacks' Dance. Piano solo. *Augener: London*, 1914. fol.
          g. 606. bb. (31.)

— Dames and Knights. *See* supra: [At the Castle. No. 1.]

— Edda. Northern suite for piano. 1. Frigga and the shepherd.
2. The magic mead. 3. In flower land. 4. The new world.
Augener: London, 1921. 4°.   **g. 1127. h. (24.)**

— Eventide, for Piano, *etc. Augener: London*, 1930. 4°.
          g. 1127. oo. (7.)

— Fireside Dreams, for the piano. *Augener: London*, 1916. 4°.
          g. 442. v. (6.)

— For the Young. Album for piano, *etc. Augener: London*,
1924. 4°.   **g. 1127. w. (10.)**

— Forest Magic. Fairy suite for piano, *etc. Augener: London*,
1923. 4°.   **g. 1127. w. (11.)**

— In an old world City. A suite for pianoforte. *Augener:
London*, 1915. 4°.   **g. 603. dd. (13.)**

— Mazurek, for Piano. *Augener: London*, 1929. 4°.
          g. 1127. mm. (3.)

LIND (GUSTAVE) *pseud.* [i.e. FREDERIC MULLEN.]

— An Old Italian Garden, for the Piano, *etc. Augener: London*,
(1904.) 4°.
Album Series, No. 4.   **g. 1129. a. (7.)**

— Quick Step, for piano. *Augener: London*, 1925. 4°.
          g. 1127. w. (12.)

— Rubáiyát. Suite for piano, *etc. Augener: London*, 1924. 4°.
          g. 1127. w. (13.)

— Saga, for Piano. *Augener: London*, (1912.) fol.
          g. 606. o. (4.)

— The Silent Mere. 3 Impressions for Piano. 1. Once upon a
Time. 2. The Woodnymph. 3. Moonrise. *Augener: London*,
(1912.) 4°.   **g. 232. s. (5.)**

— The Silent Mere. Three Impressions for piano duet, *etc.*
Augener: London, 1923. 4°.   **g. 1123. (5.)**

— [The Silent Mere. No. 1.] Once upon a Time. Arranged [for
violin, violoncello and P. F.] by Adam Carse. *In:* Monthly
Musical Record. vol. 50. pp. 227–229. 1920. 4°.
          P. P. 1945. hd.

— The Silent Mere. Song ... Words by P. J. O'Reilly. *Augener:
London*, 1922. 4°.   **G. 1275. i. (18.)**

— Spanish Love Song. Song, with Pianoforte accompaniment.
(Words by W. Carpenter.) *Augener: London*, (1914.) fol.
          G. 806. mm. (38.)

— Two Spring Songs, for piano. No. 1. A bird Song. 2. Melody
in G. 2 no. *Augener: London*, 1919. 4°.   **g. 1129. q. (13.)**

— Spring Tales. Suite for piano. *Augener: London*, 1918. 4°.
          g. 1129. g. (12.)

— Tonbilder für Klavier. 1. Fairy Tale. 2. Spring's Awakening.
3. Mazurka. 4. Water Wagtail. 5. Saltarello. 6. Evening Song.
6 no. *Augener: London*, (1912.) fol.   **g. 606. o. (5.)**

— Valse-Impromptu, for piano. *Augener: London*, 1925. 4°.
          g. 1127. w. (14.)

— Visions of an unknown Land, for the Piano. [No. 1.] The
Golden Dawn. [No. 2.] Silvery Clouds. [No. 3.] Whisper of the
Moonflowers. 3 no. *Augener: London*, (1913.) 4°.
Album Series, No. 3.   **g. 232. y. (5.)**

— Western Dances for pianoforte (pianoforte duet). 1. Merry
England. 2. Modern French dance. 3. In sunny Spain. 6 no.
Augener: London, 1921. 4°.   **g. 1127. h. (25.)**

— Winter. Suite for piano. 1. A winter landscape. 2. At the inn.
3. In the spinnery. 4. The little stranger's lullaby. *Augener:
London*, 1919. 4°.   **g. 1129. q. (14.)**

LIND (JANET)

— *See* WEBER (C. M. F. E. von) [Aufforderung zum Tanz.]
Invitation to the Waltz ... Arranged by J. Lind, *etc.* 1933. 4°.
          G. 1275. ll. (27.)

LIND (JENNY)

— Jenny Lind's favorites for the Piano forte. Composed in
honor of the celebrated Cantatrice Jenny Lind. No. 42.
London, [1846.] fol.   **h. 952. (16.)**

— Jenny Lind's Note Book; a bouquet of songs, illustrative of
the leading incidents in the life of this distinguished
songstress. *London*, [1848.] fol.   **H. 1409.**

— La Pensée, melodie de Mlle Jenny Lind transcrite pour le
piano par J. Schad. *See* MACCALLA (J.) Morceaux d'élite, *etc.*
No. 13. [1845, *etc.*]   **h. 359.**

LIND (JENNY)

— See ROCKSTRO (William S.) Jenny Lind. A record and analysis of the "method" of the late Madame Jenny Lind-Goldschmidt … Together with a selection of cadenze, solfeggi, abbellimenti, etc. in illustration of her vocal art, edited by Otto Goldschmidt. 1894. 8°.　　**7896. aaa. 46.**

LIND (JON)

— See WILLIS (Allee) and LIND (J.) Boogie Wonderland. Words and music by A. Willis and J. Lind, *etc.* [1979.] 4°.　　**F. 1966. v. (3.)**

LIND (LETTY)

— [The Lady Slavey.] Dorothy Flop. Song, *etc. Hopwood & Crew: London*, 1894. fol.　　**H. 1798. v. (27.)**

LIND (W. MURDOCK)

— Lal-la-pa-loo-zer … [Song.] Words & music by W. M. Lind. pp. 5.　*T. B. Harms & Co.:* [*New York*, 1895.] fol.　　**H. 3980. ss. (12.)**

LINDA

— Linda. Cantata. *See* PRENTICE (T. R.)

— Linda di Chamounix. Opera. *See* DONIZETTI (D. G. M.)

— Linda è povera, ma onesta. Terzettino. *See* DONIZETTI (D. G. M.) [Linda di Chamounix.]

— Linda Lady Love. [Song.] *See* TILZER (Albert von)

— Linda Lee. [Song.] *See* HOFFMANN (Max)

— Linda Lou. [Song.] *See* BLACK (Ben) *Musical Director, California Theater, San Francisco.*

— 'Linda Lucy Jane. Song. *See* NORRIS (Harry B.)

— Linda, ma Lady Love. Song. *See* STEVENS (Samuel H.)

LINDA

— Love, what wilt thou? Song, words by Longfellow, music by Linda. *London*, [1873.] fol.　　**H. 1778. y. (35.)**

— My Bonnie Love and me. Song [begins: "Oh! speed thee on"] … by Linda. *London*, [1873.] fol.　　**H. 1778. y. (36.)**

LINDA, pseud.

— Willie, Scotch ballad [begins: "Oh! where art thou"]. Words and music by Linda. *London*, [1855.] fol.　　**H. 1759. (1.)**

LINDAHL (ALBERT)

— Nine Pianoforte Pieces by G. A. Osborne and A. Lindahl. *See* CHAPPELL & CO. Chappell's Musical Magazine, No. 17. [1861, *etc.*] 4°.　　**F. 161.**

— A te o cara … air in [V. Bellini's opera] I Puritani, arranged for the pianoforte by A. Lindahl. *London*, [1854.] fol.　　**h. 1350. (15.)**

— Absence (Die Abwesenheit), Lied ohne Wörte for the pianoforte. *London*, [1854.] fol.　　**h. 1350. (2.)**

— Alma, a battle piece for the piano forte. *London*, [1854.] fol.　　**h. 1350. (1.)**

— Au revoir. Pastorelle Suisse arranged for the Pianoforte. *London*, [1860.] fol.　　**h. 1350. a. (7.)**

— Cathedral Chimes, rêverie for the pianoforte. *London*, [1855.] fol.　　**h. 1350. (24.)**

LINDAHL (ALBERT)

— Cathedral Chimes. Song. *London*, [1874.] fol.　　**H. 1778. y. (37.)**

— Le chant des religieuses, pour piano. *London*, [1855.] fol.　　**h. 1350. (27.)**

— Le chant du captif, nocturne, pour piano. *London*, [1857.] fol.　　**h. 1350. a. (2.)**

— The Convent Hymn, for the Pianoforte. *London*, [1860.] fol.　　**h. 1350. a. (8.)**

— La Donna è mobile … air in [F. G. F. Verdi's opera] Rigoletto, arranged for the piano forte by A. Lindahl. *London*, [1854.] fol.　　**h. 1350. (16.)**

— Evangeline's lament, romance pour le pianoforte. *London*, [1854.] fol.　　**h. 1350. (3.)**

— La Fête des Rosières, morceau de salon, pour piano. *London*, [1857.] fol.　　**h. 1350. a. (3.)**

— Fête des Vignerons, Mazurka brillante pour piano. *London*, [1860.] fol.　　**h. 1350. a. (9.)**

— Germany, morceau de salon pour piano forte. *London*, [1856.] fol.
No. 3 of A. Lindahl's favorite melodies.　　**h. 1458. d. (12.)**

— The girl I left behind me, national air … arranged for the pianoforte by A. Lindahl. *London*, [1854.] fol.　　**h. 1350. (4.)**

— The gondola, morceau de salon for the pianoforte. *London*, [1855.] fol.　　**h. 1350. (25.)**

— The Gondola, for the Pianoforte. *London*, [1874.] fol.　　**h. 1482. z. (59.)**

— Heimweh, for the piano forte. *London*, [1853.] fol.　　**h. 1350. (5.)**

— Home Favorites, a selection of favorite airs, arranged for the Pianoforte. 12 no. *London*, [1867.] fol.　　**h. 1350. a. (14.)**

— India, a lament, for the pianoforte. *London*, [1857.] fol.　　**h. 1350. a. (4.)**

— An Irish melody (the bard's legacy, Moore) pour piano. *London*, [1857.] fol.　　**h. 1350. a. (1.)**

— Italy. (Serenade.) Morceau de salon pour piano. pp. 5. *Chappell: London*, [c. 1855.] fol.　　**h. 3870. zz. (18.)**

— Johanna's Lebewohl, for the pianoforte. *London*, [1853.] fol.　　**h. 1350. (6.)**

— Lieblings polka. [P. F.] *London*, [1854.] fol.　　**h. 1350. (19.)**

— La lune des fleurs, nocturne for the piano forte. *London*, [1853.] fol.　　**h. 1350. (7.)**

— Midnight chimes. *See* RICHARDS (H. B.) The Pianist's Album. [1853, *etc.*] fol.　　**h. 1390.**

— Midnight chimes, for the piano forte. *London*, [1854.] fol.　　**h. 1350. (8.)**

— Midnight Song. Pensée fugitive for the Pianoforte. *London*, [1863.] fol.　　**h. 1350. a. (11.)**

— The mountain stream, for the piano forte. *London*, [1854.] fol.　　**h. 1350. (9.)**

— Music on the waters, morceau de salon, for the piano forte. *London*, [1854.] fol.　　**h. 1350. (10.)**

— Ocean Waves. Rêverie pour le Piano. *London*, [1861.] fol.　　**h. 1350. a. (10.)**

— Ondine. Rêverie for the Piano Forte. *London*, [1853.] fol.　　**h. 1350. (11.)**

LINDAHL (ALBERT)

— Ondine. *See* RICHARDS (H. B.) The Pianist's Album. [1853, *etc.*] fol.   **h. 1390.**

— Ondine, rêverie, for the Piano Forte. ⟨New edition.⟩ pp. 5. *Chappell: London*, [c. 1855.] fol.   **h. 722. bb. (1.)**

— Lindahl's [or rather Queen Hortense's air] Partant pour la Syrie, arranged as a pianoforte duet. *London*, [1854.] fol.   **h. 1350. (12.)**

— Partant pour la Syrie [melody by Hortense, Queen Consort of Louis, King of Holland] ... arranged for the piano forte by A. Lindahl. *London*, [1854.] fol.   **h. 1350. (13.)**

— La plainte des ondes, nocturne for the piano forte. *London*, [1853.] fol.   **h. 1350. (14.)**

— La Prise du voile, choral et romance, pour piano. *London*, [1857.] fol.   **h. 1350. a. (5.)**

— The Russian retreat. [P. F.] *London*, [1854.] fol.   **h. 1350. (17.)**

— The Russian retreat. [P. F.] *London*, [1856.] fol.   **h. 1350. (28.)**

— Sebastopol. A hymn of praise for the pianoforte. *London*, [1855.] fol.   **h. 1350. (29.)**

— The Siren's song. *See* RICHARDS (H. B.) The Pianist's Album. [1853, *etc.*] fol.   **h. 1390.**

— The Siren's song, nocturne, for the pianoforte, *etc. London*, [1859.] fol.   **h. 1350. a. (6.)**

— The Siren's Song. [P. F.] *W. Paxton & Co.: London*, [1913.] fol.   **h. 3284. g. (28.)**

— The Skating waltz from [G. Meyerbeer's opera] Le Prophète, arranged for the Pianoforte. *London*, [1867.] fol.   **h. 1350. a. (15.)**

— The soldier's adieu. *See* RICHARDS (H. B.) The Pianist's Album. [1853, *etc.*] fol.   **h. 1390.**

— The soldier's adieu, for the pianoforte. pp. 4. *Chappell & Cⁱⁱ.: London*, [1855.] fol.   **h. 1350. (21.)**

— The soldier's prayer, for the piano forte. *London*, [1855.] fol.   **h. 1350. (23.)**

— Switzerland, morceau de salon pour piano forte. *London*, [1856.] fol.
No. 2 of A. Lindahl's favorite melodies.   **h. 1458. d. (11.)**

— The sylph, valse brillante. [P. F.] *London*, [1853.] fol.   **h. 1350. (20.)**

— The Wedding Waltzes. [P. F.] *London*, [1863.] fol.   **h. 1350. a. (12.)**

— The Wedding Waltzes as [P. F.] Duets. *London*, [1863.] fol.   **h. 1350. a. (13.)**

— The Wedding Waltzes. [Orchestral parts.] *See* CHAPPELL AND Co. Popular Quadrilles, *etc.* No. 7. [1862, *etc.*] 8°.   **e. 249.**

— What will they say in England? for the piano forte. *London*, [1855.] fol.   **h. 1350. (22.)**

— Der Wiederhall, or the echo, for the piano forte. *London*, [1853.] fol.   **h. 1350. (18.)**

— *See* VERDI (F. G. F.) [Il Trovatore.] Lindahl's Trovatore ... Verdi's Il Trovatore arranged for the piano forte by A. Lindahl. [1855.] fol.   **h. 1350. (26.)**

LINDAHL (OSCAR)

— Gloriana. Danse fantastique. [P. F.] *Mathias & Strickland: London*, [1892.] fol.   **h. 1489. t. (9.)**

LINDANE

— Lindane. Feen-Oper. *See* KANNE (F. A.)

LINDAUER

— Lindauer Lied'l. [Part-song.] *See* NESSLER (V. E.) Drei Lieder, *etc.* Op. 60. No. 3.

LINDBERG (ALBERT)

— Le Carnaval de Venise, morceau fantastique pour le Pianoforte. *London*, [1870.] fol.   **h. 1301. (10.)**

— The Day of Rest. Transcription pour Piano. *London*, [1865.] fol.   **h. 1301. (9.)**

— My Lord Chamberlain's Reel, and the "Clever Fellows" Double-Shuffle, for the Piano. *London*, [1876.] fol.   **h. 1482. z. (60.)**

LINDBERG (CARL)

— Alpenlied, Transcription. [P. F.] *London*, [1860.] fol.   **h. 1301. (6.)**

— Bouquet Irlandais, Fantaisie sur un thème favori de [Flotow's opera] Martha, avec variations par Oesten, Herz, et Czerny, transcrites par Lindberg. *London*, [1858.] fol.   **h. 1301. (1.)**

— Cujus animam (de Rossini). Transcription pour Piano. *London*, [1861.] fol.   **h. 1301. (8.)**

— Enid, Idylle musicale pour Piano. *London*, [1860.] fol.   **h. 1301. (7.)**

— Fantasie, für das Piano, über Amerikanische Lieder. *London*, [1857.] fol.   **h. 1301. (2.)**

— Luisa Miller, fantasia [on Verdi's opera]. [P. F.] *London*, [1858.] fol.   **h. 1301. (3.)**

— [Another edition.] Luisa Miller, fantasia [on Verdi's opera]. [P. F.] *London*, [1858.] fol.   **h. 1301. (4.)**

— The Star Shower waltzes. [P. F.] *London*, [1867.] fol.   **h. 1460. w. (9.)**

— Il Trovatore, fantasia [on Verdi's opera]. [P. F.] *London*, [1858.] fol.   **h. 1301. (5.)**

LINDBERG (ERIK)

— Sweden in Springtime ... Arr. Fred Hartley, *etc.* ⟨Piano conductor [and orchestral parts].⟩ 22 pt. *F. H. P. (Fred Hartley Publications): London*, [1958.] 4°.   **h. 3210. i. (723.)**

LINDBERG (OSKAR)

— Från de stora skogarna. Aus den grossen Wäldern. Symfonisk dikt ... Partitur. pp. 58. *Edition suecia: Stockholm; Leipzig* printed, [1934.] fol.
The titlepage headed: Föreningen svenska tonsättare.   **h. 1564. yy. (3.)**

— Jungfru Maria [song], klaverutdrag, dikt af E. A. Karlfeldt. *Stockholm*, 1934. fol.
[*Musikaliska Konstföreningen. Årg. 1934.*]   **H. 700/114.**

— Rapsodi över svenska folkmelodier, Per spelman, han spelte. Rhapsodie über schwedische Volksmelodien. Partitur. *Föreningen Svenska Tonsättare: Stockholm*, 1932. fol.   **h. 1509. tt. (4.)**

— Requiem för soli, kör, orkester och orgel ... Klaverutdrag. *Stockholm*, 1929. fol.
[*Musikaliska Konstföreningen. Årg. 1929.*]   **H. 700/104.**

LINDBERG (THEODORE)

— T. Lindberg's Modern Violin School. bk. I. *Philharmony Publishing Co.: Wichita, Kansas, 1912. 4°.*　　　**g. 498. o. (4.)**

LINDBERGHFLUG

— Der Lindberghflug. Für Soli, Chor und Orchester. *See* WEILL (K.)

LINDBLAD (ADOLPH FREDRIK)

— Lieder mit Begleitung des Pianoforte ... aus dem Schwedischen übertragen von A. Dohrn, *etc.* Hft. 1. *Bei N. Simrock: Bonn, [c. 1840.] obl. fol.*
Imperfect; wanting Hft. 2.　　　**F. 1196. jj. (1.)**

— Lieder mit Begleitung des Pianoforte ... aus dem Schwedischen übertragen von A. Dohrn. no. 9. *Bei N. Simrock: Bonn, [1840?] obl. fol.*
Imperfect; wanting no. 1–8, 10–25.　　**Hirsch M. 1278. (6.)**

— A. F. Lindblad's schwedische Lieder mit Begleitung des Pianoforte. Lieblings-Gesänge der gefeierten Sängerin Jenny Lind. In deutsche Uebertragung mit Beibehaltung des Originaltextes von D'. A. E. Wollheim. *Swed. & Ger.* 10 Hft. *Schuberth & C'.: Hamburg, Leipzig, [1842–50.] fol.*
　　　H. 2406. c.

— A. F. Lindblads Sänger och Visor för en röst med accompagnement af piano. Ny upplaga. 16 Hft. *A. Hirsch: Stockholm, [1870?] fol.*　　**H. 2406. a.**

— A. F. Lindblad's Schwedische Lieder in deutscher Uebertragung mit Pianoforte-Begleitung ... Vollständige Ausgabe. 14 Cah. *Schuberth & Co.: Hamburg, [1870?] fol.*
　　　H. 2406.

— Aftonstunder i hemmet. Nya sånger och visor vid piano. Hft. 1. *A. Lundquist: Stockholm, [1875?] fol.*　　**h. 2815. r. (9.)**

— Ah! no, thou know'st it not. *See* SONGS. Gems of German song. Book 18. No. 7. [1843, *etc.*] fol.　　**H. 2123.**

— Allegro, andante, scherzo för piano och violin. *Stockholm, 1892. fol.*
[Musikaliska Konstföreningen. Årg. 1892.]　　**H. 700/47.**

— Auf dem Berge. *See also supra:* Lieder. no. 9.

— Auf dem Berge, *etc. See* LIEDER-REPERTORIUM. Lieder Repertorium, *etc.* No. 107. [1847, *etc.*] fol.　　**H. 2274.**

— Auf dem Berge. *See* OESTEN (T.) Das Füllhorn, *etc.* No. 6. [1857.] fol.　　**h. 699. p. (6.)**

— Birds blithely singing. *See infra:* [Nära.]

— Birds gaily singing. *See infra:* [Nära.]

— Birds in the branches. *See infra:* [Nära.]

— Birds on the Branches. *See infra:* [Nära.]

— Birds swiftly flying. *See infra:* [Nära.]

— Duo pour piano et violon ... Op. 9. [Score and part.] 2 pt. *Chez les fils de B. Schott: Mayence, [1843?] fol.*
　　　h. 1613. w. (5.)

— Duo pour piano et violon ... Op. 11. [Score and part.] 2 pt. *Chez les fils de B. Schott: Mayence, [1843.] fol.*
　　　h. 1613. w. (6.)

— Fänrik Ståls sägner ... För sång vid pianoforte. pp. 50. *Abr. Hirsch: Stockholm, [1856?] fol.*　　**H. 2406. b.**

— For Ever! [Song, begins: "Over seas".] The words translated from the Swedish by J. E. L. *London, [1863.] fol.*
　　　H. 1772. s. (8.)

LINDBLAD (ADOLPH FREDRIK)

— [Frieriet.] My pretty bird, sing on ... [Song.] English words by W. Guernsey. *London, [1870.] fol.*
No. 2 of "Mlle. Christine Nillson's Vocal Repertoire".
　　　H. 2184. a. (12.)

— [Hier auf dieser Höhe.] Midst mountain streams ... transcribed for the pianoforte by T. Oesten. *London, [1857.] fol.*　　**h. 699. q. (23.)**

— [Eines jungen Mädchens Morgen Betrachtung.] What joys around me play ... Swedish Song ... [begins: "Wie mich's im Herzen freut"], translated into German by A. Dohrn, the English Version by J. Hine. *London, [1847.] fol.*
　　　H. 2167. (5.)

— Midst mountain streams. *See supra:* [Hier auf dieser Höhe.]

— My pretty bird, sing on. *See supra:* [Frieriet.]

Nära

— Birds swiftly flying. *See* SONGS. Gems of German Song. Book 20. No. 5. [1843, *etc.*] fol.　　**H. 2123.**

— Nahe, (Nära) Schwedische Lied von Lindblad. *See* LIEDER-REPERTORIUM. Lieder-Repertorium, *etc.* No. 69. [1847, *etc.*] fol.　　**H. 2274.**

— Birds on the Branches. (Nahe.) *See* LIEDER-REPERTORIUM. Lieder-Repertorium, *etc.* No. 177. [1847, *etc.*] fol.　**H. 2274.**

— Birds on the Branches. (Nahe or Nara.) *See* GESAENGE. Zweistimmige Gesänge, *etc.* No. 22. [1848, *etc.*] fol.
　　　H. 2271.

— Birds blithely singing. "Nahe" or "Nära". Swedish song. The English verson by J. J. *London, [1852.] fol.*　**H. 1735. (43.)**

— Song birds are winging. Swedish Melody. *London, [1852.] fol.*　　**H. 1735. (42.)**

— Birds on the branches, Nahe or Nära, Swedish song. English words by T. A. [No. 1 as a song, No. 2 as a duet.] 2 no. *London, [1854.] fol.*　　**H. 1759. (2.)**

— Song-Birds are warbling. (Nara.) *See* FLOWERS. Flowers of Germany. No. 77. [1859, *etc.*] fol.　　**H. 2133.**

— Birds gaily singing. (Nara.) *See* WILLIAMS (W. L.) The Beauties of German Song. No. 6. [1860, *etc.*] fol.
　　　H. 2771. a. (58.)

— Notes of the Song Birds. ("Nahe" or "Nara".) Swedish melody. (Words by A. G. Howard.) *London, [1861.] fol.*
　　　H. 1772. s. (7.)

— Birds in the Branches. (Nara.) *London, [1872.] fol.*
　　　H. 1775. u. (45.)

— Birds in the Branches, *etc.* [Song.] *Cramer & Co.: London, [1875?] fol.*　　**H. 2134. a. (18.)**

— Near. [Song.] pp. 3. *Augener & Co.: London, [1889.] fol.*
[Germania. no. 174.]　　**H. 2128.**

— Notes of the Song Birds. *See supra:* [Nära.]

— Qvintett for 2 violiner, 2 altar och violoncell ... Stämmor. *Stockholm, 1885. fol.*
[Musikaliska Konstföreningen. Årg. 1885.]　　**H. 700/32.**

— Qvintett for två violiner, två altar och violoncell ... Arrangement för piano fyra händer. *Stockholm, 1885. fol.*
[Musikaliska Konstföreningen. Årg. 1885.]　　**H. 700/33.**

— Sju sångstycken vid forte-piano. pp. 12. *Hos J. C. Hedbom: Stockholm, [1827.] obl.*　　**E. 600. hh. (2.)**

— Song-Birds are warbling. *See supra:* [Nära.]

LINDBLAD (ADOLPH FREDRIK)

— Trio pour piano, violon et viola ... Op. 10. [Score and parts.] 3 pt. *Chez les fils de B. Schott: Mayence,* [1842? c. 1885.] fol. *The viola part is of a later issue.* **h. 5. q. (2.)**

— *See* JUNGMANN (A.) Voglein in Lüften. Auf dem Berge. Zwei Fantasien über Schwedische Lieder von A. F. Lindblad. [1853.] fol. **h. 723. k. (10.)**

LINDBLAD (CARL)

— *See* LINDBLAD (Adolph F.)

LINDBLAD (OTTO JONAS)

— Naturen och Hjertat.—Natur und Herz.—[Part-song.] *See* LUTTEMAN (H.) Nordiske Sanger ... No. 8. [1879?] 8°. **F. 1571.**

— Neckens Polska. Altschwedische Melodie. [Part-song, words by] A. A. Afzelius. *See* LUTTEMANN (H.) Nordiske Sanger ... No. 2. [1878.] 8°. **F. 1571.**

— Necken's Polska. *See* QUARTETS. Stroller's Society ... Quartets, *etc.* No. 18. [1886, *etc.*] 8°. **F. 298.**

— [Ur svenska hjärtans djup.] *See* SJOGREN (J. G. E.) Sju variationer för piano över den svenska kungssången (... af O. Lindblad), *etc.* [1915.] fol. **h. 3865. uu. (1.)**

— Valda Mansqvartetter ... utgifna af Henrik Möller. pp. 53. *Wilhelm Hansen, Musik-Förlag: Köpenhamn,* [c. 1890.] 8°. **F. 1542. a. (2.)**

LINDDUFTIG

— Lindduftig hält die Maiennacht. [Part-song.] *See* KREMSER (E.)

LINDE

— Die Linde. [Song.] *See* MAYER (M.) Vier kleine Lieder. No. 3.

— Die Linde. [Song.] *See* MEYER-HELMUND (E.) Zwei Lieder ... Op. 37. No. 1.

— Die Linde. [Song.] *See* NESSLER (V. E.)

— Die Linde. Duett. *See* SCHMIDT (H.) Vier Duette. No. 2.

— Die Linde. [Part-song.] *See* SPICKER (M.)

LINDE (ANNA)

— *See* COUPERIN (F.) *the Younger.* L'Art de toucher le clavecin ... Herausgegeben und ins Deutsche übersetzt von A. Linde, *etc.* [1933.] 4°. **Hirsch M. 118.**

LINDE (AUGUST)

— 4 Charakter-Stücke für das Pianoforte. 2 no. *Weekes & Co.: London,* [1881.] fol. **h. 1484. t. (28.)**

LINDE (BERNARD VAN DER)

— *See* BEETHOVEN (Ludwig van) Sonaten für Klavier und Violoncello ... herausgegeben von B. van der Linde, *etc.* [1971.] 4°. **g. 700. ll. (3.)**

LINDE (DORIS) and **LINDE** (HANS PETER)

— Leichte Stücke und Lieder russische und sowjetischer Komponisten. Für Violoncello und Klavier. Ausgewählt, methodisch geordnet und bezeichnet von D. und H.-P. Linde. [Score and part.] 24pt. *Edition Peters: Leipzig,* [1969.] 4°. **g. 512. i. (9.)**

LINDÉ (ERNST)

— Bright Star of Victory. Solo with Chorus, arranged by E. Linde. *Weekes & Co.: London,* [1881.] 8°. *No.* 100 *of the Collegiate Series.* **E. 758.**

— The Echo Chorus. Words by E. Oxenford, arranged by E. Linde. *Patey & Willis: London,* [1889.] 8°. *No.* 96 *of the Collegiate Series.* **E. 758.**

— The Last Rose of Summer. Part-Song for two tenors and two basses, arranged by E. Lindé. [1897.] *See* UNION. The Union Choralist, *etc.* No. 54. [1882, *etc.*] 8°. **F. 687.**

— "Where the lordly stag o'er the heather bounds." (Scotland.) Solo & chorus written by R. H. Fraser. *London,* [1867.] fol. **H. 1772. s. (9.)**

— "Where the lordly stag." Solo and chorus. (Words by R. H. Fraser.) *London,* [1874.] 8°. *No.* 9 *of the "Collegiate Series".* **E. 758.**

— *See* AUBER (D. F. E.) [La Muette de Portici.] The Market Chorus ... arranged ... by E. Linde, *etc.* [1881.] 8°. **E. 758.**

— *See* BACH (J. S.) [Suites for Violoncello. No. 3.] Bourrée ... transcribed ... by E. Lindé. [1886.] fol. **h. 3007. b. (21.)**

— *See* BACH (J. S.) [Suites for Violoncello. No. 6.] Two Gavottes ... Transcribed ... by E. Lindé. [1886.] fol. **h. 3007. b. (20.)**

— *See* CORELLI (A.) [Concerto. Op. 6. No. 9.] Adagio and Gavotte ... transcribed ... by E. Lindé. [1881.] fol. **h. 3275. d. (13.)**

— *See* HAENDEL (G. F.) [Water Music.—Bourrée.] Gavotte ... transcribed ... by E. Lindé. [1881.] fol. **h. 435. b. (31.)**

LINDE (HANS MARTIN)

— Amarilli mia bella. Hommage à Johann Jacob van Eyck. Für Blockflöte solo. (Sopran-, Alt- und Bassblockflöte wechselnd.) For recorder solo. (Descant-, treble- and bass-recorder.) [Theme by Giulio Caccini, with variations by J. J. van Eyk and H. M. Linde.] pp. 11. *B. Schott's Söhne: Mainz,* [1973.] 4°. *Originalmusik für Blockflöte.* 133. **g. 109. qq. (5.)**

— Capriccio für drei Blockflöten (Alt-Alt-Tenor) oder drei Querflöten und drei Gamben (Diskant-Alt oder Diskant-Bass) oder Violine, Viola und Violoncello mit Handtrommel. [Score and parts.] 7 pt. *B. Schott's Söhne: Mainz,* [1965.] 4°. **g. 1067. f. (10.)**

— Four Caprices. For unaccompanied alto recorder or flute. pp. 5. *Galaxy Music Corp.: New York,* [1967.] 4°. *American Recorder Society Editions.* no. 59. **g. 109. bb. (6.)**

— Fantasien und Scherzi für Altblockflöte solo. pp. 6. *B. Schott's Söhne: Mainz,* [1965.] 4°. **g. 109. x. (4.)**

— Inventionen für Alt-Blockflöte, *etc.* pp. 7. *Otto Heinrich Noetzel Verlag: Wilhelmshaven,* [1959.] obl. 8°. **a. 40. m. (9.)**

— Kinder-Suite für Sopran-, Alt- und Tenorblockflöte. Suite for Children. For descant, treble and tenor recorder. [Score.] pp. 8. *Otto Heinrich Noetzel Verlag: Wilhelmshaven,* [1959.] obl. 8°. **a. 40. m. (10.)**

— Kleine Anleitung zum Verzieren alter Musik. pp. 47. *B. Schott's Söhne: Mainz,* [1958.] 4°. **g. 759. c. (1.)**

— Die kleine Übung. Tägliche Studien für die Sopranblockflöte. pp. 31. *B. Schott's Söhne: Mainz,* [1960.] obl. 8°. **a. 40. w. (5.)**

— Die Kunst des Blockflötenspiels. Eine Anleitung zum Erlernen der Soloblockflöte f'. pp. 63. *B. Schott's Söhne: Mainz,* [1958.] 4°. *With two leaves containing "Trillertabelle" and "Grifftabelle" inserted.* **g. 109. i. (5.)**

LINDE (Hans Martin)

— Music for a Bird. Für Altblockflöte solo. pp. 7. *B. Schott's Söhne: Mainz*, [1971.] 4°.　　　　　**g. 109. hh. (16.)**

— Musica da camera (1972). Für Blockflöte (Altblockflöte und Bassblockflöte) und Gitarre ... Partitur, *etc.* pp. 19. *B. Schott's Söhne: Mainz*, [1974.] 4°. *Originalmusik für Blockflöte.* 135.　　　　**g. 109. xx. (9.)**

— Neuzeitliche Übungsstücke für die Altblockflöte. Modern exercises for treble recorder. pp. 19. *B. Schott's Söhne: Mainz*, [1958.] 4°.　　　　**g. 109. n. (1.)**

— Quartett-Übung für Blockflöten. pp. 27. *B. Schott's Söhne: Mainz*, [1963.] 4°.　　　　**g. 109. r. (13.)**

— Serenata a tre for Blockflöte (Sopran, Alt, Bass), Gitarre und Violoncello oder Viola da gamba. [Score and parts.] 4 pt. *B. Schott's Söhne: Mainz*, [1966.] 4°.　　　**g. 934. f. (8.)**

— Sonate in d für Altblockflöte und Klavier. [Score and part.] 2 pt. *B. Schott's Söhne: Mainz*, [1961.] 4°.　　**g. 109. r. (2.)**

— Sopranblockflöten—Schule für Fortgeschrittene. pp. 35. *B. Schott's Söhne: Mainz*, [1960.] 8°. *With a leaf containing "Trillertabelle" and "Grifftabelle" inserted.*　　　　　**e. 184. b. (2.)**

— Trio für Altblockflöte, Querflöte und Cembalo (Klavier). [Score and parts.] 3 pt. *B. Schott's Söhne: Mainz*, [1963.] 4°.　　　　**g. 409. ss. (11.)**

— Venezianische Musik um 1600. Stücke von Frescobaldi, Castello und Fontana für Sopran- oder Tenorblockflöte (oder andere Melodieinstrumente) und Basso continuo. Herausgegeben von H. M. Linde. Partitur mit zwei Stimmen. 3 pt. *B. Schott's Söhne: Mainz*, [1972.] 4°. *Originalmusik für Blockflöte* 122.　　**g. 112. o. (4.)**

— *See* CARR (Robert) [The Delightful Companion.] Divisions upon an Italian Ground ... Für Altblockflöte (oder Sopranblockflöte) und Basso continuo ... Herausgegeben von H.-M. Linde. [1965.] 4°.　　**g. 109. u. (9.)**

— *See* CORELLI (A.) [Sonatas. Op. 5. No. 12.] La Follia. Für Altblockflöte und Basso continuo. Herausgegeben von H. M. Linde. [1972.] 4°.　　　**g. 109. oo. (5.)**

— *See* DIVISION. The Division Flute ... Divisions für Altblockflöte und Basso continuo. Herausgegeben von H.-M. Linde. [1968.] 4°.　　**g. 109. bb. (10.)**

— *See* MIGOT (G.) Sonatine Nr. 2. Für Blockflöte und Klavier. Spieleinrichtung von H. M. Linde. [1964.] 4°.　**g. 109. u. (1.)**

— *See* TELEMANN (G. P.) [Zwölf Fantasien für Querflöte ohne Bass. No. 1, 3, 7, 8, 10, 11.] Sechs Fantasien für Altblockflöte Solo. Herausgegeben von H.-M. Linde. [1962.] 4°.　　　　　**g. 401. j. (11.)**

— *See* VIVALDI (A.) Konzert C-Dur [Rinaldi Op. 44. No. 11. Ryom 443] ... für Piccoloblockflöte (Altblockflöte), zwei Violinen, Viola und Basso continuo ... Herausgegeben von H.-M. Linde. Partitur, *etc.* [1968.] 4°.　　**g. 33. o. (3.)**

— *See* VIVALDI (A.) Konzert C-Dur [Rinaldi Op. 44. No. 11. Ryom 443] ... für Piccoloblockflöte (Altblockflöte), zwei Violinen, Viola und Basso continuo ... Herausgegeben von H.-M. Linde. Klavierauszug, *etc.* [1968.] 4°.　　**g. 33. o. (4.)**

LINDE (Hans Peter)

— Duo concertante. Für Viola und Violoncello. [Score.] pp. 12. *Edition Peters: Leipzig*, [1972.] 4°. *Two copies.*　　　　**g. 1067. kk. (4.)**

— Erstes Zusammenspiel. Zwölf sehr leichte Duette in der engen ersten Lage für Violoncelli. [Score.] pp. 10. *Edition Peters, Collection Litolff: Leipzig*, [1965.] 4°. *Collection Litolff. no.* 5401. *Two copies.*　　**g. 510. w. (4.)**

LINDE (Hans Peter)

— Ein kleines Trio für zwei Violinen und Violoncello. [Score and parts.] 5 pt. *Edition Peters, Collection Litolff: Leipzig*, [1967.] 4°. *Collection Litolff.* 5419. *The first violin part is in duplicate.*　　　　**g. 1000. b. (5.)**

— Leichte Cellomusik. Zwanzig Stücke mit Klavier für den Anfang in Violoncellospiel ... Im Anhang: zwei Stücke in der engen vierten Lage. [Score and part.] 2 pt. *Edition Peters, Collection Litolff: Leipzig*, [1967?] 4°.　　**g. 512. i. (10.)**

— Sonatine in C für Violoncello und Klavier. [Score and part.] 2 pt. *Edition Peters, Collection Litolff: Leipzig*, [1966.] 4°. *Collection Litolff. no.* 5410.　　**g. 510. w. (7.)**

— *See* LINDE (D.) and LINDE (H. P.) Leichte Stücke und Lieder russischer und sowjetischer Komponisten. Für Violoncello und Klavier. Ausgewählt, methodisch geordnet und bezeichnet von D. und H.-P. Linde. [1969.] 4°.　**g. 512. i. (9.)**

LINDEGREN (Johan)

— Fuga uti fri stil för piano. *Abr. Hirsch: Stockholm*, [1866?] fol. [*Musikaliska Konstföreningen. Årg.* 1866.]　**H. 700/11.**

— Kvintett för 2 violiner, 2 altvioliner och violoncell ... Partitur. (Stämmor.) *Stockholm*, 1909. fol. [*Musikaliska Konstföreningen. Årg.* 1908.]　　**H. 700/74.**

— Stor sonat, canon, för piano ... Op. 2. *Abr. Hirsch: Stockholm*, [1869.] fol. [*Musikaliska Konstföreningen. Årg.* 1867.]　　**H. 700/13.**

LINDELL (Johan)

— Cantilenarum selectiorum editio nova, in gratiam Scholarium Notis Musicis, Distinctis Strophis aliaque adhibita emendatione evulgata a Joh: Lindell, *etc.* [*Abo*,] 1776. 8°. *Engraved throughout.*　　　**B. 438. a.**

— Mässan kortelgen. Åbo 1784. Utgiven i faksimil med inledning av Folke Bohlin. pp. 20. 8. *Tord Wetterquist: Uppsala*, 1968. 8°. [*Laurentius Petri sällskapets urkundserie. no.* 9.]　　　　**WP. 16306/9.**

LINDEMAN (J.)

— It Heitelân. Frysk Folksliet. Ien—en fjouwerstimmich mei Piano—en Oargellieding ... wirden fen J. L. van der Burg. *R. van der Velde: Ljouwert*, [1903.] 4°.　　**G. 225. h. (14.)**

LINDEMAN (J. R.)

— *See* STEENBERG (J.) Steenbergs menuett arrangerad för pianoforte af J. R. Lindeman. [1863.] fol.　　**h. 726. r. (14.)**

LINDEMAN (Ludvig Matthias)

— Ældre og nyere Norske Fjeldmelodier. Samlede og bearbeidede for Pianoforte af L. M. Lindeman. 3 Bd. *P. T. Mallings Folagshandel: Christiania*, [1853–67.] fol. *Imperfect; wanting Bd.* 3. *Hft.* 2.　　**H. 1399.**

— Ældre og nyere norske fjeldmelodier. Samlede og bearbeidede for pianoforte af L. M. Lindeman. 〈Faksimileutgave.〉 3 Bd. *Univesitetsforlaget: Oslo*, [1963.] 4°. [*Norsk Musikksamling. Publikasjon no.* 3.]　　**G. 35.**

— Built on the Rock. *See infra:* [Melodien til Landstads Salmebog.—Kirken den er et.]

— Gjæternes Vexelsang. Redigeret og harmoniseret af L. M. Lindeman. [*J. W. Cappelen: Christiania*, 1868.] 8°. *Appendix to P. M. Söegaard's "I Fjeldbygderne".*　　　　**12581. dd. 22.**

LINDEMAN (Ludvig Matthias)

— Kroningsmarsch ved D.D.M.M. Kong Oscar II^s og Dronning Sofies Kroning i Trondhjems Domkirke den 18de Juli 1873 ... Piano 2/h, *etc.* pp. 5. *Carl Warmuths Musikforlag: Christiania; Leipzig* printed, [1897.] fol.   **g. 352. zz. (17.)**

— Melodier til Landstads Salmebog, ordnede og harmoniserede af L. M. Lindeman. Tredie oplag, *etc.* 2 pt. *J. W. Cappelens Forlag: Christiania*, 1873. obl. fol. *Each part has a separate titlepage (dated 1872) and pagination.*   **F. 1574. a.**

— [Melodier til Landstads Salmebog.—Kirken den er et.] Built on the Rock. Anthem for unison choir or solo voice and organ ... [Words by] N. F. S. Grundtvig. Translated by Carl Döving ... Arranged by Everett Jay Hilty. pp. 4. *Oxford University Press: New York*, [1971.] 8°.   **F. 1106. g. (18.)**

— Halvhundrede Norske Fjeldmelodier harmoniserede for Mandstemmer af L. M. Lindeman. Udgivne af det Norske Selskab. *W. C. Fabritius: Kristiania*, 1862. 4°.   **F. 440.**

— Norske Folkeviser udsatte for fire Mandsstemmer. [Scores and parts.] 3 no. 15 pt. *A. Th. Nissen: Christiania*, [1850?] 8°. *Each no. contains four songs. The wrapper of no. 1 bears a MS. dedication in the arranger's autograph.*   **F. 1574. b.**

— Norske Kjæmpevise-Melodier, harmoniserede for blandede Stemmer, enkelt og kanonisk. 6 Hft. *C. Warmuth: Christiania*, [1885?] 8°.   **F. 1574. (1.)**

— Samlarferd 1851. Oppskrifter og ei dagbok. Merknader ved Åse Røynstrand. [The melodies reproduced in a facsimile of the collector's autograph. With illustrations and a portrait.] pp. 167. *Universitetsbiblioteket: Oslo*, [1980?] 4°. [*Norsk Musikksamling: Publiskasjon no.* 11.]   **G. 35.**

LINDEMAN (Ole Andreas)

— Choral-Bog, indeholdende de i Kingos, Guldbergs og den evangelisk-christelige Psalmebog forekommende Melodier. Paa ny gjennemseede og rettede efter Originalmelodierne og fürstemmigt udsatte ved O. A. Lindeman, *etc.* *W. C. Fabritius: Christiania*, 1874. obl. fol.   **E. 1642.**

— Pièces pour le clavecin. 1861. See FARRENC (J. H. A.) Le Trésor du Pianiste, *etc.* Livr. II. 1861–72. fol.   **h. 26.**

LINDEMANN (Fritz)

— See MOZART (W. A.) [Exsultate jubilate. K. 165.] Alleluja ... Klaviersatz von F. Lindemann. [1943.] 4°.   **G. 519. t. (27.)**

LINDEMANN (Otto)

— See ALBERT (E. F. C. d') Scirocco ... Klavierauszug mit Text von O. Lindemann. 1919. fol.   **G. 682. j. (2.)**

— See BITTNER (J.) Der Bergsee ... Klavierauszug ... von O. Lindemann. (1911.) fol.   **H. 741.**

— See BRUCH (Max C. F.) Doppelkonzert für Klarinette (oder Violine) und Viola mit Orchester. 〈Op. 88.〉 Klavierauszug und Solostimmen vom Komponisten ... Arr. O. Lindemann. [1977.] 4°.   **g. 1655. d. (1.)**

— See DELIUS (F.) Fennimore and Gerda ... Vocal Score by O. Lindemann, *etc.* 1919. 4°.   **G. 1044. (3.)**

— See DELIUS (F.) Romeo und Julia auf dem Dorfe ... Vocal Score by O. Lindemann. [1920?] fol.   **H. 600. b. (2.)**

— See FALL (L.) Der heilige Ambrosius. Musikalisches Lustspiel ... Klavierauszug ... von O. Lindemann. [1922.] 4°.   **H. 3492. e. (1.)**

— See FALL (L.) Die spanische Nachtigall. Operette ... Klavierauszug ... von O. Lindemann, *etc.* [1921.] fol.   **H. 3492. h.**

LINDEMANN (Otto)

— See GILBERT (J.) *pseud.* Jung muss man sein! Operette ... Klavier-Partitur eingerichtet von O. Lindemann. [1915.] fol.   **G. 1273. nn. (1.)**

— See HUBAY (J.) Hejre Kati ... Oeuvre 32, *etc.* (Für Violine-Solo mit Salon-Orchester von O. Lindemann.) [1940?] fol.   **h. 3210. h. (881.)**

— See REEVES (Ernest) Hobomoko ... Blasmusik v. O. Lindemann. [1909.] 8°.   **f. 800. a. (176.)**

— See SCHULTZE (N.) Lili Marleen, *etc.* 〈Klaviersatz von O. Lindemann.〉 [1940.] 4°.   **G. 1276. h. (14.)**

— See SINDING (C.) [Sechs Stücke. Op. 32. No. 1.] Marche grotesque ... Instr. von O. Lindemann. 1929. 8°.   **h. 3210. h. (308.)**

— See STOLZ (R.) Der Hampelmann ... Klavierauszug mit Singstimmen ... eingerichtet von O. Lindemann. 1924. fol.   **G. 782. oo. (3.)**

— See STOLZ (R.) Der Hampelmann ... Klavierauszug zu zwei Händen ... arrangiert von O. Lindemann. 1923. fol.   **h. 3870. e. (36.)**

— See STOLZ (R.) Mädi. Operette ... Klavierauszug mit Singstimmen ... eingerichtet von O. Lindemann. [1923.] fol.   **G. 1274. e. (1.)**

— See STOLZ (R.) Ein Rivieratraum ... Klavierauszug mit Singstimmen ... eingerichtet v. O. Lindemann. 1925. fol.   **G. 782. w. (1.)**

— See STOLZ (R.) Die Tanzgräfin. Operette, *etc.* 〈Klavierauszug. Zum Dirigieren eingerichtet von O. Lindemann.〉 [1921.] fol.   **H. 232. w. (1.)**

— See STRAUS (O.) Die törichte Jungfrau. Operette ... Klavierauszug ... eingerichtet von O. Lindemann. [1923.] fol.   **H. 3847. j.**

LINDEMANN (W. C.)

— Roger Williams. March and two step. Intermezzo. [Orchestral parts.] 10 pt. *Lindemann Music Co.: Providence, R. I.*, [1907.] 8°.   **f. 800. (855.)**

— "Roger Williams" Two Step—Intermezzo. Solo B♭ cornet [and wind band parts]. 36 pt. *Lindemann Music Co.: [Providence, R.I.,* 1907.] 8°. *Various parts are in duplicate.*   **f. 800. (856.)**

— Roger Williams. March two step. [P. F.] pp. 5. *Lindemann Music Co.: [Providence, R.I.,* 1907.] fol.   **h. 4120. rr. (1.)**

— See GERSHWIN (George) [The Goldwyn Follies.] Love walked in. Arranged by W. C. Lindemann, *etc.* [Orchestral parts.] [1938.] 8°.   **f. 801. (1.)**

— See GERSHWIN (George) [Shall we dance.] Let's call the whole Thing off ... Arr. by W. C. Lindemann. [Orchestral parts.] [1937.] 8°.   **f. 801. (3.)**

— See GERSHWIN (George) [Shall we dance.] They can't take that away from me ... Arr. by W. C. Lindemann. [Orchestral parts.] [1937.] 8°.   **f. 801. (4.)**

— See KENNEDY (T.) Radio Rube's Collection of Hill Country Ballads and Comic Songs ... Arranged by W. C. Lindemann. 1933. 4°.   **G. 981. l. (9.)**

LINDEMANN (Wilhelm)

— [Eine Muh, eine Mäh.] Santa Claus is here ... [Part-song.] English text by Peter Carroll ... Arrangement by Frank Naylor. [Staff and tonic sol-fa notation.] pp. 8. *Bosworth & Co.: London*, [1964.] 8°.   **F. 217. y. (8.)**

— Santa Claus is here. *See* supra: [Eine Muh, eine Mäh.]

LINDEMANN-RABE (   )

— Schöne Welt. *See infra:* [Unter dem Grillenbanner.]

— [Unter dem Grillenbanner.] Schöne Welt. Marsch-Lied nach dem Marsch "Unter dem Grillenbanner" für Männerchor mit Klavier ... Text: Max Barthel. pp. 8. *Bosworth & Co.: Köln, Wien,* [1961.] 8°.   **F. 163. ss. (7.)**

LINDEN

— The Linden Blossom. Part-Song. *See* MOELLENDORF (W. VON) [Drei Lieder für Männerchor. Op. 24. No. 3. Die Lindenbäume duften.]

— Linden Blossoms. Song. *See* HALLEY (T. G. B.)

— Linden Lea. Song. *See* WILLIAMS (R. V.)

— The Linden Tree. Part song. *See* BUCKNALL (C.)

— The Linden tree. Song. *See* HATTON (J. L.)

— The Linden Tree. Song. *See* MANN (W.)

— The Linden Tree. [Part-song.] *See* SCHUBERT (F. P.) [Winterreise. Op. 89. No. 5. Der Lindenbaum.]

— The Linden Tree Carol. [Part-song.] *See* BEECHEY (Gwilym E.)

— The Linden Tree Carol. Carol. *See* COPLEY (Ian A.)

— The Linden Tree Carol. [Carol.] *See* HINTON (James)

— Linden Tree Carol. [Carol.] *See* SUMSION (Herbert W.)

— The Linden Trees. Song. *See* ALTHAUS (B.)

— The Linden Waltz. Song. *See* AÏDÉ (H.)

LINDEN (ADRIEN)

— Je t'attends! Nocturne. [Song.] Paroles et musique de A. Linden. pp. 3. *Lebeau aîné: Paris,* [c. 1865.] fol.
P. P. 1948. s/2. (145.)

LINDEN (ALBERT VANDER)

— Thesaurus musicus. Sub directione Albert Vander Linden. *Office international de librairie: Bruxelles,* [1973?, *etc.*] fol.
H. 997.

LINDEN (LEOPOLD)

— Fantaisie, pour le piano, sur les motifs de l'Opéra, Il Trovatore, de Verdi. *London,* [1857.] fol.   **h. 725. f. (27.)**

LINDEN (LILLA)

— Linden Harp: a rare collection of popular melodies, *etc. New York,* 1856. 16°.   **A. 942.**

LINDEN (PAUL)

— Ma belle Barque.— My beautiful Boat.— Pour Piano. *C. Woolhouse: London,* 1906. fol.   **h. 3283. kk. (10.)**

— Trois Morceaux pour Pianoforte. (Op. 20.) No. 1. Beauty. No. 2. Grace. No. 3. Elegance. 3 no. *C. Woolhouse: London,* 1906. fol.   **h. 3283. kk. (11.)**

LINDENBAUM

— Der Lindenbaum. [Song.] *See* SCHUBERT (F. P.) [Winterreise. Op. 89. No. 5.]

LINDENBLAUER (CARL) *pseud.* [i.e. GEORGE HILLS.]

— Mazurka brillante pour Piano. *London,* [1866.] fol.
h. 1485. t. (2.)

LINDENBLAUER (CARL) *pseud.* [i.e. GEORGE HILLS.]

— Moonlight. Ballad [begins: "Calm evening comes"]. (Written by A. Fricker.) *London,* [1869.] fol.   **H. 1775. u. (46.)**

— On a lake in Summer by moonlight, rêverie for the piano forte. *London,* [1854.] fol.   **h. 723. m. (11.)**

LINDENBLUETE

— Lindenblüte. [Chorus.] *See* SUESS (O.)

LINDENBORN (HEINRICH)

— Neues Gott und dem Lamm geheiligtes Kirchen- und Hauss-Gesang der auf dem dreyfachen Wege der Volkommenheit nach dem himmlischen Jerusalem wandernden Tochter Sion ... Mit jedem Lied beygetruckten, von bewehrten Music-Verstãndigen neu-gefertigten Sing-Weisen, samt Bass-General, *etc.* ⟨Zum Erstenmal in Truck verlegt.⟩ [The music compiled and the texts written by Heinrich Lindenborn.] pp. 15. 615. 1741. 12°. *See* HYMNS. [German.]   **A. 499. dd.**

— Neues Gott und dem Lamm geheiligte[s] Kirchen- und Haus-Gesan[g] der auf dem dreyfachen Wege d[er] Vollkommenheit nach dem himmlischen Jerusalem wandernden Tochter Sion, *etc.* [The music compiled and the texts written by Heinrich Lindenborn.] pp. 656. 1790. 12°. *See* HYMNS. [German.]   **A. 499. g.**

— *See* REGIS (J.) Opera omnia. Edidit Cornelius Lindenburg. 1956. fol. [*Corpus mensurabilis musicæ.* 9.]   **H. 3.**

LINDENERUS (FRIDERICUS)

— *See* LINDNER.

LINDENTHAL (AUGUST)

— "Essayez moi," romance sans paroles. [P. F.] pp. 3. *Evans & Co.: London,* [1866?] fol.   **h. 61. pp. (9.)**

— "Flora," 10 sketches for the piano forte. Op. 12. 10 no. *London,* [1856.] fol.   **h. 1260. (5.)**

— "Melodie mazurque" d'après C. Oberthür, transcrite pour le piano forte par A. Linderthal. Op. 18. *London,* [1855.] fol.
h. 1260. (4.)

— Three melodies for the Piano forte. Op. 6. 3 no. *London,* [1852.] fol.   **h. 1260. (1.)**

— Voyage lyrique, 24 politico-national airs for the pianoforte. 24 no. *London,* [1852–56.] fol.   **h. 1261.**

— *See* OBERTHUER (C.) Three characteristic melodies for the Piano Forte ... Transcribed by A. Lindenthal. [1853.] fol.
h. 1260. (2.)

— *See* OBERTHUER (C.) Pensées musicales, trois pièces de salon de C. Oberthür. Op. 110, transcrites pour le Piano Forte, par A. Lindenthal. Op. 14. [1853.] fol.   **h. 1260. (3.)**

— *See* OBERTHUER (C.) and LINDENTHAL (A.) Agréments de société, collection de trios brillants & concertants sur des motifs d'opéras populaires, pour flute, violon & piano. Arrangés par C. Oberthür & A. Lindenthal. [1855, *etc.*] fol.
h. 2855.

— *See* OBERTHUER (C.) and LINDENTHAL (A.) "Portefeuille d'amateurs" collection de trios brillants & concertants sur des motifs d'opéras populaires, pour piano, flute & violoncelle. Arrangés par C. Oberthür & A. Lindenthal. [1855, *etc.*] fol.
h. 2856.

— *See* OBERTHUER (C.) and LINDENTHAL (A.) "Reminiscences d'opéras," collection de trios ... Arrangés par C. Oberthür & A. Lindenthal. [1855, *etc.*] fol.   **h. 2854.**

LINDENTHAL (August)

— See OBERTHUER (C.) and LINDENTHAL (A.) "Réunions d'amateurs," collection de quatuors brillants sur des motifs d'opéras populaires, arrangés pour piano, flute, violon et violoncelle par C. Oberthuer et A. Lindenthal. [1855, *etc.*] fol.
h. 2802.

— See OBERTHUER (C.) and LINDENTHAL (A.) "Soirées d'amateurs," collection de quatuors ... arrangés ... par C. Oberthür & A. Lindenthal. [1855, *etc.*] fol. **h. 2803.**

— See OBERTHUER (C.) and LINDENTHAL (A.) "Souvenirs d'opéras," collection de trios brillants & concertants, sur des motifs populaires, pour deux violons et piano. Arrangés par C. Oberthür & A. Lindenthal. [1855, *etc.*] fol. **h. 2853.**

LINDENTHAL (Caspar)

— Love's Whisperings. [P. F.] *London*, [1861.] fol.
h. 1460. w. (10.)

— The Scarborough galop for the Pianoforte. *London*, [1874.] fol. **h. 1482. z. (62.)**

— We're a noddin', arranged for the Pianoforte. *London*, [1874.] fol. **h. 1482. z. (61.)**

LINDENTHAL (Conrad)

— The Caesarewitch galop for the piano forte with acc¹. for cornet à pistons. *London*, [1851.] fol. **h. 964. (33.)**

— Die Edelstein Walzer pour piano forte, avec accomp¹. de cornet à pistons. *London*, [1852.] fol. **h. 964. (32.)**

— "Our youthful thoughts." Duet for Soprano and Contralto, with Pianoforte. [Begins: "In youth we never pause to think".] *London*, [1850.] fol. **H. 1735. (44.)**

LINDENWALD (A.)

— Abschied, Characterstück für das Pianoforte. *London*, [1864.] fol. **h. 1485. t. (5.)**

— A First Dream, rêverie for the Pianoforte. *London*, [1862.] fol. **h. 1485. t. (3.)**

— Glittering Spray, characteristic piece for the Pianoforte. *London*, [1868.] fol. **h. 1485. t. (7.)**

— Ocean Spray, characteristic piece for the Pianoforte. *London*, [1862.] fol. **h. 1485. t. (4.)**

— Das Rieseln Waltz für das Pianoforte. *London*, [1864.] fol. **h. 1485. t. (6.)**

— Sunbeam, sketch for the Pianoforte. *London*, [1868.] fol. **h. 1485. t. (8.)**

LINDENWIRTHIN

— Die Lindenwirthin. [Song.] *See* SCHARWENKA (P.)

LINDER (August)

— Deutsche Weisen. Die beliebtesten Volks- und geistlichen Lieder für Klavier mit Text. Herausgegeben von A. Linder. pp. 240. *Lausch & Zweigle Musikverlag: Stuttgart*, [1957.] 8°.
F. 1771. ee.

LINDER (Gottfried)

— Allegro alla Tarantella für Pianoforte. *Leipzig*, [1879.] fol.
h. 1493. o. (41.)

— [Roswitha.] Vorspiel zu der Oper. Partitur. *Stuttgart*, [1875?] fol. **h. 1509. d. (12.)**

— Waldidyll. Tonbild für Pianoforte. *Leipzig*, [1879.] fol.
h. 1493. o. (40.)

LINDER (J. S.)

— See BACH (J. S.) [Clavierübung. Tl. 2.] Italian Concerto. For the keyboard. W. A. Palmer and J. S. Linder, editors. [1972.] 4°. **g. 699. ss. (6.)**

LINDER (Joe)

— "I'll love you Honey all the Time." [Song.] Words by Frank Fogarty. *Howley, Dresser Co.: New York*, [1904.] fol.
H. 3985. aa. (19.)

LINDER (Oscar)

— My little Wife and I. [Song, begins: "How happily".] The poetry by W. D. Smith. *London*, [1867.] fol.
H. 1772. s. (10.)

— [Another edition.] My little Wife, *etc. London*, [1867.] fol.
H. 1772. s. (11.)

LINDERS (Karl)

— Alpine Love-Song. Part-Song for Male Voices. Words by R. H. Buck. *White-Smith Music Pub. Co.: Boston, etc.*, 1899. 8°. **F. 163. a. (28.)**

— Blow, gentle Breezes. Part-Song for Mixed Voices. Words by R. H. Buck. *White-Smith Music Pub. Co.: Boston, etc.*, 1899. 8°. **F. 321. p. (24.)**

— Bright is the Summer's Morn. Four-Part Song for women's voices, words by Mrs. J. M. Hunter. *White-Smith Music Pub. Co.: Boston, etc.*, (1908.) 8°. **F. 328. g. (29.)**

— Come, laughing Spring. Three-Part Song for women's voices. [Words by] A. J. Cleator. *White-Smith Music Publishing Co.: Boston, etc.*, 1909. 8°. **F. 328. k. (30.)**

— Come, to my Mountain Home. Four-Part Song for women's voices, words by M. M. Leighton. *White-Smith Music Pub. Co.: Boston, etc.*, (1908.) 8°. **F. 328. i. (10.)**

— Courage, Boys, Courage! Part-Song for Male Voices. Words by R. H. Buck. *White-Smith Music Pub. Co.: Boston, etc.*, 1899. 8°. **F. 163. a. (29.)**

— Emulation. Part Song for men's voices. [Words by] M. E. Hicks. *White-Smith Music Pub. Co.: Boston, etc.*, (1908.) 8°. **F. 163. f. (28.)**

— First Lady-Slippers. Three-part Song for women's voices. [Words by] E. R. Worrell. *White-Smith Music Publishing Co.: Boston, etc.*, (1914.) 8°. **F. 328. t. (12.)**

— Fisher Folk-Song. Part-Song for men's voices. [Words by] W. H. Gardner. *White-Smith Music Pub. Co.: Boston, etc.*, (1909.) 8°. **F. 163. k. (25.)**

— Four little Country Maids. Four-Part Song for Ladies' Voices. Words by G. D. Pennington. *White-Smith Music Pub. Co.: Boston, etc.*, 1899. 8°. **F. 328. b. (13.)**

— Good-bye. Part-Song for Ladies' Voices. Words by A. Sanford. *White-Smith Music Pub. Co.: Boston, etc.*, 1897. 8°. **F. 328. b. (14.)**

— Haste to greet the Morn. Part-Song for Mixed Voices. Words by A. J. Cleator. *White-Smith Music Pub. Co.: Boston, etc.*, 1899. 8°. **F. 321. p. (23.)**

— I wait for thee! Part-Song for Ladies' Voices. *White-Smith Music Pub. Co.: Boston, etc.*, 1899. 8°. **F. 328. b. (16.)**

— In the Time of May. Three-Part Song for Ladies' Voices. Words by A. J. Cleator. *White-Smith Music Pub. Co.: Boston, etc.*, 1898. 8°. **F. 328. b. (15.)**

— Keep-a-goin'! — Part-Song for Male Voices. — Words by T. Mac Kellar. *White-Smith Music Pub. Co.: Boston, etc.*, 1899. 8°. **F. 163. a. (30.)**

LINDERS (KARL)

— The Light-House. Part-Song for Mixed Voices. Words by A. J. Cleator. *White-Smith Music Pub. Co.: Boston, etc.,* 1901. 8°.   **F. 321. p. (22.)**

— Lullaby Baby. Part Song for Ladies' Voices. Words by A. J. Cleator. *White-Smith Music Pub. Co.: Boston, etc.,* 1897. 8°.
                                          F. 328. b. (17.)

— A Merry Heart. The Voyagers. Part-Song for mixed voices. [Words by] M. E. Hicks. *White-Smith Music Publishing Co.: Boston, etc.,* 1908. 8°.   **F. 585. y. (13.)**

— The Merry Shepherd. Four-Part Song for Ladies' Voices. Words by A. Sanford. *White-Smith Music Pub. Co.: Boston, etc.,* 1898. 8°.   **F. 328. b. (18.)**

— The Old Home. Part-Song for Mixed Voices. Words by G. D. Pennington. *White-Smith Music Pub. Co.: Boston, etc.,* 1898. 8°.   **F. 321. p. (21.)**

— Red Rose. Four-part Song for Ladies' Voices. Words by A. J. Cleator. *White-Smith Music Pub. Co.: Boston, etc.,* 1899. 8°.   **F. 328. b. (19.)**

— Skating Glee. Four-Part Song for men's voices. [Words by] H. C. Sheffer. *White-Smith Music Pub. Co.: Boston, etc.,* (1908.) 8°.   **F. 163. f. (29.)**

— Sleep, weary World. Part-Song for Mixed Voices. Words by A. J. Cleator. *White-Smith Music Pub. Co.: Boston, etc.,* 1898. 8°.   **F. 321. p. (20.)**

— Softly sleep. Serenade. For Male Voices. Words by A. J. Cleator. *White-Smith Music Pub. Co.: Boston, etc.,* 1898. 8°.
                                          F. 163. a. (31.)

— The Song and the Star. Christmas Quartette for women's voices. [Words by] J. G. Holland. *White-Smith Music Pub. Co.: Boston, etc.,* (1908.) 8°.   **F. 328. g. (30.)**

— Song of Freedom. Part-Song for Male Voices. Words by A. J. Cleator. *White-Smith Music Pub. Co.: Boston, etc.,* 1898. 8°.   **F. 163. a. (32.)**

— The Storm-Wind. Part-Song for Mixed Voices. Words by A. J. Cleator. *White-Smith Music Pub. Co.: Boston, etc.,* 1899. 8°.   **F. 321. p. (19.)**

— The Strong-minded Maid … Four-part Song for women's voices. [Words by] E. R. Worrell. *White-Smith Music Publishing Co.: Boston, etc.,* (1914.) 8°.   **F. 328. t. (13.)**

— Sweet Maiden, rest. Serenade for men's voices. [Words by] H. C. Sheffer. *White-Smith Music Pub. Co.: Boston, etc.,* (1908.) 8°.   **F. 163. f. (30.)**

— Unrest. Part-Song for Male Voices. Words by A. J. Cleator. *White-Smith Music Pub. Co.: Boston, etc.,* 1900. 8°.
                                          F. 163. a. (33.)

— Water-Lilies. Gavotte for Mixed Voices. Words by R. H. Buck. *White-Smith Music Pub. Co.: Boston, etc.,* 1898. 8°.
                                          F. 321. p. (18.)

— When Eventide is near. Part-Song for Mixed Voices. Words by R. H. Buck. *White-Smith Music Pub. Co.: Boston, etc.,* 1898. 8°.   **F. 321. p. (17.)**

— When Summer smiles. Four-Part Song for Ladies' Voices. Words by A. J. Cleator. *White-Smith Music Pub. Co.: Boston, etc.,* 1898. 8°.   **F. 328. b. (20.)**

— When the Starlight gilds the Stream. Part-Song for Mixed Voices. Words by R. H. Buck. *White-Smith Music Pub. Co.: Boston, etc.,* 1898. 8°.   **F. 321. p. (16.)**

— Winter. Part-Song for men's voices, words by W. H. Gardner. *White-Smith Music Pub. Co.: Boston, etc.,* (1908.) 8°.
                                          F. 163. f. (31.)

LINDERS (KARL)

— With a fresh Breeze. Glee for mixed voices, words and music by K. Linders. *White-Smith Music Pub. Co.: Boston, etc.,* (1908.) 8°.   **F. 585. y. (14.)**

LINDESRAUSCHEN

— Lindes Rauschen in den Wipfeln. [Song.] *See* BRAHMS (J.) Sechs Gesänge. Op. 3. No. 6.

— Lindes Rauschen in den Wipfeln. [Song.] *See* HASSE (G.) Funf Lieder. Op. 31. No. 3.

LINDFELDT (CARL)

— La Belle Marie. Sérénade pour Piano. *London,* [1861.] fol.
                                          h. 1485. t. (12.)

— La Belle Marie. Sérénade. *See* PIANIST. The Pianist's Portfolio. No. 20. [1870, *etc.*] fol.   **h. 1446.**

— La Belle Marie serenade for the Pianoforte. *London,* [1872.] fol.   **h. 1482. z. (63.)**

— Colpevol sono, de l'opéra [by F. G. F. Verdi] La Traviata, transcrit pour Piano. *London,* [1859.] fol.   **h. 1485. t. (10.)**

— La Coquette, polka de bravoura, pour le piano. *London,* [1857.] fol.   **h. 1485. t. (11.)**

— Meine erste Liebe (My first love). Romance Nocturne für das Pianoforte. *London,* [1859.] fol.   **h. 1485. t. (9.)**

— L'Ondée de Roses. Mazurka brillante pour le Piano. *London,* [1861.] fol.   **h. 1485. t. (13.)**

LINDHAL (OSCAR)

— Asphodel. Sketch for the pianoforte. *Bowerman & Co.: London,* [1894.] fol.   **g. 605. f. (24.)**

— Le Songe d'Amour. Mazurka de Salon. [P. F.] *Bowerman & Co.: London,* [1894.] fol.   **g. 605. f. (23.)**

LINDHEIM (ADOLPHE)

— À Venise quadrille. [P. F.] *London,* [1875.] 8°. *No. 300 of the "Alliance Musicale. Album Bijou".*   **f. 406.**

— All Together. Quadrille. [Orchestral parts.] *London,* [1884.] 8°. *Part of the "Alliance Musicale".*   **f. 400. gg. (13.)**

— Beautiful Fairy valse. [P. F.] *London,* [1873.] fol.
                                          h. 1482. z. (64.)

— Bilbao, bolero for Cornet. [Orchestral parts.] *London,* [1875.] 8°. *Part of the "Alliance Musicale".*   **f. 400. d. (2.)**

— Bilbao, bolero. [P. F.] *London,* [1880.] 8°. *No. 168 of the "Alliance Musicale. Album Bijou".*   **f. 406.**

— Clic Clac galop. [P. F.] *London,* [1876.] fol.   **h. 1482. z. (67.)**

— Don't make me laugh … Song [begins: "I'm ticklish by birth"] written by H. B. Farnie. *London,* [1873.] fol.
                                          H. 1778. y. (38.)

— Fleur de Lys polka. [P. F.] *London,* [1873.] fol.
                                          h. 1482. z. (65.)

— Les Folies du Carnival quadrille. [P. F.] *London,* [1872.] fol.   **h. 1485. t. (14.)**

— Les Folies du Carnival quadrille. [P. F.] *London,* [1873.] fol.   **h. 1482. z. (66.)**

— Julia, valse pour Piano. *Paris,* [1872.] fol.   **h. 977. l. (5.)**

LINDHEIM (Adolphe)

— The London March. [P. F.] *Francis, Day & Hunter: London, etc.*, 1893. fol.   **h. 1489. t. (10.)**

— Melo-drama-serio-comic Music. 8th (–13th) part. [Conductor's P. F. part.] 6 pt. *London*, [1881.] 8°. *No. 682–7 of the "Alliance Musicale, Album Bijou".*   **f. 406.**

— Un Quiproquo. Saynète [*sic*]. Paroles de A. Ameline. Musique de A. Lindheim. *Paris*, [1863.] 8°.   **11739. g. 32.**

— Royal Philharmonic galop. [Orchestral parts.] *London*, [1875.] 8°. *Part of the "Alliance Musicale".*   **f. 400. g. (11.)**

— Royal Philharmonic galop. [P. F.] *London*, [1875.] 8°. *No. 273 of the "Alliance Musicale. Album Bijou".*   **f. 406.**

— Le Royaume des Femmes marche. [Orchestral parts.] *London*, [1873.] 8°. *Part of the "Alliance Muiscale".*   **f. 400. d. (1.)**

— Le Royaume des Femmes, marche. [P. F.] *London*, [1873.] 8°. *No. 133 of the "Alliance Musicale. Album Bijou".*   **f. 406.**

— Le 16 Mars (1874) marche pour le Piano. *London*, [1876.] fol.   **h. 1482. z. (68.)**

— Women's Kingdom quick step, arranged by Hare. [Reed band parts.] *London*, [1879.] 8°. *Part of the "Alliance Musicale".*   **f. 401. o. (29.)**

— *See* AUDIBERT (E.) The Musical Director's Vade Mecum ... by ... Lindheim, *etc.* [1873, *etc.*] 8°.   **f. 405.**

LINDHEIM (Paul)

— The Chase. Polka. [Orchestral parts.] *J. R. Lafleur & Son: London*, [1887.] 8°. *Part of the "Alliance Musicale".*   **f. 400. ll. (4.)**

— The Chase. Polka. [P. F.] *J. R. Lafleur & Son: London*, [1887.] 8°. *Part of the "Alliance Musicale. Album Bijou".*   **f. 406. a. (13.)**

— Drum Polka, with special Drum Solo. Arr^d. by A. Morelli. [Reed band parts.] *J. R. Lafleur & Son: London*, [1887.] 8°. *Part of the "Alliance Musicale".*   **f. 401. ff. (3.)**

— Drum Polka. [Parts for fife and drum band.] 8 pt. *Lafleur & Son: London*, [1892.] 8°. *Part of "Alliance Musicale".*   **f. 800. (857.)**

— Fest Glocken Galop. [Parts for fife and drum band.] 8 pt. *Lafleur & Son: London*, [1892.] 8°.   **f. 800. (858.)**

— Golden Bird. Waltz for Piccolo Solo. [Orchestral and P. F. parts.] *J. R. Lafleur & Son: London*, [1887.] 8°. *Part of the "Alliance Musicale".*   **f. 400. ll. 5.**

— Herzblatt. Schottische. [P. F.] *Lafleur & Son: London*, [1892.] fol.   **h. 3285. q. (52.)**

— Regina. Mazurka. [P. F.] *Lafleur & Son: London*, [1892.] fol.   **h. 3285. q. (53.)**

— Thalgeläute. (Bells of the Valley.) Waltz. [Orchestral parts.] 17 pt. *J. R. Lafleur & Son: London*, [1892.] 8°. *Part of "Alliance Musicale".*   **f. 800. (859.)**

— Thalgeläute. (Bells of the Valley.) Valse. [Parts for fife and drum band.] 8 pt. *J. R. Lafleur & Son: London*, [1892.] 8°. *Part of "Alliance Musicale".*   **f. 800. (860.)**

— Thalgeläute ... Waltz. [P. F.] *Lafleur & Son: London*, [1892.] fol.   **h. 3285. q. (54.)**

LINDHOLM (Steen)

— *See* GADE (Niels V.) Orgelkompositioner. Udgivet af S. Lindholm. [1969.] *obl.* 4°.   **e. 1093. mm. (3.)**

LINDLEY ( )

— *See* LINLEY (Thomas)

LINDLEY (Francis) and HARTLEY (James)

— Fourteen Country Dances, two Cotillons & two Minuets, with their proper figures, adapted for the harpsichord, piano forte, *etc.* pp. 24. [c. 1790.] *obl.* 4°.   **a. 9. dd. (3.)**

LINDLEY (Gerald)

— Love's Sacrifice. Song, words & music by G. Lindley. *Collard Moutrie: London*, 1914. fol.   **H. 1793. u. (1.)**

LINDLEY (Lucy)

— At the Eleventh Hour, Sacred song. The poetry by M. W. A. S. Gibson. *London*, [1862.] fol.   **H. 1772. s. (12.)**

— Nae Peer (Napier) a historical song. [Begins: "To the chieftains around him spake Scotland's braw king".] *London*, [1854.] fol.   **H. 1759. (3.)**

LINDLEY (Robert)

— Capriccios & Exercises, for the Violoncello ... Op. 15. pp. 27. *J. B. Cramer, Addison & Beale: London*, [c. 1825.] fol.   **h. 1870. h.**

— Caprice Bohème, pour le piano-forte, *etc. London*, [1858.] fol.   **h. 725. f. (28.)**

— Three Duetts for a violin & violoncello. Op. 2. *London*, [1802.] fol.   **g. 225. (17.)**

— Three duettos for a violin and violoncello. Op. 12. *London*, [1812.] fol.   **h. 201. (3.)**

— A Duett, for Violin and Violoncello, *etc.* [Parts.] 2 pt. *A. Betts: London*, [1810.] fol.   **g. 890. i. (3.)**

— Three Duets, for Two Violoncellos ... Op. 1ma. [Parts.] *Printed for Monzani & Cimador: London*, [1800.] fol.   **h. 219. (9.)**

— [Another copy.]   **g. 421. k. (5.)**

— Three duetts for two violoncellos. Op. 3. *London*, [1802.] fol.   **h. 201. (1.)**

— Three easy duetts for two violoncellos. Op. 4. *London*, [1803.] fol.   **h. 201. (2.)**

— Six Duets for two Violoncellos. Op. 8. 2 bk. *London*, [1810?] fol.   **g. 421. e. (7.)**

— Three Duetts for two Violoncellos ... Op. XI. *L. Lavenu: London*, [1805?] fol.   **h. 1849. m. (2.)**

— Three Duets, for two Violoncellos ... Opera 14. *Royal Harmonic Institution: London*, [^WM 1820.] fol. *The violoncello secondo part only.*   **h. 1870. e. (2.)**

— Three duets for two violoncellos. Op. 14. *London*, [1821.] fol.   **h. 201. (4.)**

— Fantasia for the violoncello obligato to be performed on the first string only, with an accompaniment for the Piano Forte. Op. 18. *London*, [1849.] fol.   **h. 1851. (1.)**

— Hand-book for the violoncello, *etc. London*, [1855.] fol.   **b. 160. (1.)**

— A Solo for the Violoncello. Op. 13. *London*, [1811.] fol.   **g. 24. c. (11.)**

— Six easy Solos for a Violoncello & Bass. Op. 9. *London*, [1810?] fol.   **h. 201. a. (1.)**

LINDLEY (ROBERT)

— Six easy Solos, in which are introduced popular airs, composed for the violoncello, with a bass accompaniment ... (Op. 9). [Score.] bk. 1. *Printed by Messʳˢ R. Cocks & Cᵒ.: London*, [c. 1840.] fol.
Imperfect; wanting bk. 2. **h. 204. k. (1.)**

— Three Solos for the Violoncello with an accompaniment for the Bass. Op. 16. 2 no. *London*, [1830?] fol. **h. 201. a. (2.)**

— A Trio for Bassoon, Tenor & Violoncello, or two Violoncellos & Tenor. Op. 7. *London*, [1810?] fol.
g. 409. a. (6.)

— Trio pour violon, viola & violoncelle ... Op. 13. [Parts.] *N. Simrock: Bonn et Cologne*, [1820?] fol. **h. 2851. h. (2.)**

LINDLEY (SIMON GEOFFREY)

— Come sing and dance. ⟨S.A.T.B.⟩ Words adapted from an ancient carol. pp. 3. *Banks Music Publications: York*, [1978.] 8°.
[*Eboracum choral series.* 87.] **F. 1874. x.**

— *See* BACH (Johann S.) [Also hat Gott die Welt geliebt.—Mein gläubiges Herz.] My Heart ever faithful ... Edited by S. Lindley. [1979.] 8°. **F. 1143. n. (1.)**

— *See* LALLOUETTE (Jean F.) [Motets à 1, 2, et 3 voix. Lib. 1.] O mysterium ineffabile ... Edited by S. Lindley. [1979.] 8°.
F. 1143. n. (9.)

— *See* WESLEY (Samuel S.) [O give Thanks unto the Lord.] Who can express? ... Edited by S. Lindley. [1979.] 8°.
F. 1143. n. (7.)

LINDLY (C.)

— The Chapter of Life. Song [begins: "Let the epicure boast"] written by W. L. B. *Leeds*, [1868.] fol. **H. 1775. u. (47.)**

— Teddy O'Neale. Irish ballad [begins: "I've seen the mud cabin"]. *Leeds*, [1868.] fol. **H. 1775. u. (48.)**

LINDNER (AUGUST)

— *See* LINDNER (Roderich August)

LINDNER (E.)

— Adeline valse. [P. F.] *London*, [1856.] fol. **h. 976. d. (30.)**

LINDNER (EMIL)

— Andante grazioso for Violin and Piano. *E. Ashdown: London*, [1897.] fol. **h. 1612. c. (35.)**

LINDNER (ERNST OTTO TIMOTHEUS)

— Geschichte des deutschen Liedes im XVIII. Jahrhundert ... Nachgelassenes Werk. Herausgegeben von L. Erk. Mit LXXXIII. musikalischen Beilagen. *Breitkopf und Härtel: Leipzig*, 1871. 8°. **11850. i. 18.**

— [Another copy.] **Hirsch 1954.**

LINDNER (FRIEDERICH)

— The Rose. *See* SONGS. Gems of German Song. Bk. 8. [1843, *etc.*] fol. **H. 2123.**

LINDNER (FRIEDRICH)

— Bicinia Sacra, ex Variis Autoribus in Usum Iuventutis Scholasticæ ... collecta: Quibus adjuncta est compendiaria in artem canendi Introductio ... Zweystimmige Gesänglein, sampt einen kurtzen vnterricht, wie man soll lernen singen, für die jungen Schuler neulich im druck aussgegangen. Vox Inferior. *In officina typographica Catharinæ Gerlachiæ: Noribergae*, 1591. obl. 4°.
The composers named are: O. di Lassus, Lupi, A. Scandellus, J. Reinerus, Jachet Berchem, Finot, Certon, V. Ruffi, T. Massaino, Gomperth, J. Handl, A. Goswinus, Josquin, Jovan Nasco, R. di Lasso, M. Schram, J. Guami, G. de Antiquis, G. B. Pace, Tarquinio Papa, G. F. Palumbo, F. Facciola, S. Felis, C. M. Pizziolis, G. F. Capoani and C. V. Fanelli.
K. 2. b. 13.

— Corollarium Cantionum Sacrarum Quinque, Sex, Septem, Octo, et Plurium Vocum de Festis Præcipuis Anni. Quarum quædam anteà, a præstantissimis nostræ ætatis Musicis, in Italia separatim editæ sunt, quædam vero nuperrimè concinnatæ ... at nunc in unum quasi corpus redactæ studio ... Friderici Lindneri, *etc.* Cantus. (Altus.) (Tenor.) (Bassus.) (Quinta Vox.) (Sexta Vox) 6 pt. *In officina typographica Catharinæ Gerlachiæ: Noribergae*, 1590. obl. 4°.
The composers named are: G. Aichinger, J. Cartarius, O. Columbanus, J. Corfinus, J. Florius, A. and G. Gabrieli, M. A. Ingignerius, B. Klingenstein, D. Laurus, O. di Lasso, R. del Mel, C. Merulus, P. de Monte, Sylla Petraloysius, J. P. A. Praenestinus (J. P. Aloisius), A. Scandellus, A. Stabile and A. Trombetti. **A. 251. b.**

— [Another copy. Altus. (Bassus.) (Sexta Vox.)] 3 pt. **A. 251. f.**

— Gemma Musicalis: Selectissimas varii stili Cantiones (vulgo Italis Madrigali et Napolitane dicuntur) Quatuor, Quinque, Sex et Plurium Vocum Continens: Quæ ex diversis ... Musicorum libellis ... uni quasi corpori insertae & in lucem editæ sunt, studio ... Friderici Lindneri ... Liber Primus. Canto. (Quinto.) 2 pt. *In officina typographica Catharinæ Gerlachiæ: Noribergae*, 1588. obl. 4°.
The composers named are: L. Bertani, B. Donato, A. Ferabosco, A. Gabrieli, G. Gabrieli, O. di Lasso, J. de Macque, L. Marenzio, C. Merulo, G. B. Moscaglia, G. M. Nanino, B. Palavicino, Gioanetto da Palestrina, C. de Rore, F. Soriano, A. Striggio, H. Vecchi, H. Waelrant, J. Werth and A. Zoilo. **A. 251. d.**

— Liber Secundus Gemmae Musicalis: Selectissimas varii stili Cantiones, quae Madrigali et Napolitane Italis dicuntur, Quatuor, Quinque, Sex & plurium vocum, continens ... Editæ studio ... Friderici Lindneri, *etc.* Canto. *Ex Typographia Musica Catharinae Gerlachiae: Noribergae*, 1589. obl. 4°.
The composers named are: G. Gabrieli, A. Gabrieli, G. Croce, L. Marenzio, O. Vecchi, G. de Werth, Cav. Antinori, H. Sabino, G. Ferretti, P. de Monte, G. Biffi, C. da Correggio, G. Conversi, G. Pallavicino, C. Antegnati, N. Faignient and F. Anerio.
A. 251. g.

— Tertius Gemmae Musicalis Liber: Selectissimas diversorum Autorum cantiones, Italis Madrigali & Napolitane dictas, Octo, Septem, Sex, Quinque & Quatuor vocum continens. Nunc primum in lucem editus studio ... Friderici Lindneri. Canto. *In officina typographica Catharinæ Gerlachiæ: Noribergae*, 1590. obl. 4°.
The composers named are: G. Werth, G. Eremita, P. Duc, B. Spontoni, O. Vecchi, B. Pallavicino, G. G. Gastoldi, G. Renaldi, Sessa d'Aranda, P. de Monte, A. Coma, P. Marni and F. Cedraro. **A. 251. h.**

— Magnificat, Beatissimæ Deiparæque Virginis Mariæ Canticum, Quinque et Quatuor vocibus,—secundum octo vulgares musicæ modos, a diversis nostræ ætatis musicis compositum ... in lucem editum opera ... Friderici Lindneri. Cantus. (Altus.) (Tenor.) (Bassus.) (Quinta Vox.) 5 pt. *In officina Musica Catharinæ Gerlachiæ: Noribergæ*, 1591. fol.
The composers named are: J. M. Asula, H. Faa, T. Riccius, M. Varotto, V. Ruffius and F. Guerrero. **K. 4. h. 5.**

LINDNER (Friedrich)

— Missæ Quinque, Quinis Vocibus, a diuersis et ætatis nostræ
praestantissimis musicis compositae: Ac in usum Ecclesiæ Dei
nuperrimè editæ, studio & opera Friderici Lindeneri. Cantus.
(Altus.) (Tenor.) (Bassus.) (Quinta Vox.) 5 pt. *In officina
typographica Catharinæ Gerlachiæ: Noribergae,* 1590. *obl.* 4°.
*The Masses are by Palestrina, P. de Monte, G. Guami,
R. di Lasso and G. Florius.* **A. 251. e.**

— Sacræ Cantiones, Cum Quinque, Sex et Pluribus Vocibus, de
Festis Praecipuis Totius Anni, a praestantissimis Italiae
Musicis nuperrime concinnatae ... in unum Corpus redactæ,
studio ... Friderici Lindneri, *etc.* Discantus. (Altus.) (Tenor.)
(Bassus.) (Quinta Vox.) (Sexta Vox.) 6 pt. *In officina
typographica Catharinæ Gerlachiæ: Noribergæ,* 1585. *obl.* 4°.
*The composers named are: J. A. Cardillo, J. Corfinus,
S. Cornettus, N. Doratus, N. Faignient, A. Ferabosco,
J. Guamus, Don Ferdinando de Las Infantas, S. Marazzius,
T. Massainus, C. Merulus, Gioannetto da Palestrina,
J. Pennequinus, J. P. A. Praenestinus and P. Zallamella.*
A. 251.

— Continuatio Cantionum Sacrarum Quatuor, Quinque, Sex,
Septem, Octo et Plurium Vocum, de Festis Præcipuis Anni, a
præstantissimis Italiæ Musicis nuperrimè concinnatarum ...
in unum corpus redactæ, studio ... Friderici Lindneri, *etc.*
Cantus. (Altus.) (Tenor.) (Bassus.) (Quinta Vox.) (Sexta Vox.)
6 pt. *In officina typographica Catharinæ Gerlachiæ:
Noribergae,* 1588. *obl.* 4°.
*The composers named are: F. Anerius, J. A. Cardillus, A. and
G. Gabrieli, J. C. Gabutius, J. L. Hasler, Don F. de las Infantas,
L. Marenzio, R. del Mel, N. Parma, C. Porta, V. Ruffus, J. de la
Sala and A. Stabile.* **A. 251. a.**

LINDNER (Friedrich Wilhelm)

— Musikalischer Jugendfreund oder instructive Sammlung von
Gesängen für die Jugend gebildeter Stände ... geordnet von
M. Friedrich Wilhelm Lindner. Hft. 1–3. *Auf Kosten des
Herausgebers: Leipzig,* [c. 1815, 1812?] *obl.* 4°.
Hft. 1, 2 *are of the "zweite Ausgabe" and "zweite Auflage"
respectively. Imperfect; wanting Hft.* 4. **C. 738. kk.**

LINDNER (George F.)

— Suite pour deux Mandolines. Op. 3. *Lyon & Healy: Chicago,*
1902. fol. **h. 188. i. (28.)**

LINDNER (Gussie C.)

— How 'bout your Baby, Honey. Coon song and chorus. Words
by Todd. pp. 5. *Howley, Haviland & Co.: New York,* [1898.]
fol. **H. 3980. ss. (13.)**

— If we should never meet again. [Song.] Words by M. H.
Rosenfeld. *T. B. Harms & Co.: [New York],* 1897. fol.
H. 1798. v. (28.)

— Vesta. March. [P. F.] *Howley, Haviland & Co.: New York,*
1897. fol. **h. 3282. f. (48.)**

LINDNER (Gustav)

— Maskerade. Symphon. Intermezzo. [Parts.] *B. Schott's Söhne:
Mainz und Leipzig,* [1935.] 8°.
[*Schott & Co.'s Domesticum-Salon-Orchester. No.* 384.]
g. 1053. a.

LINDNER (Mary Murray)

— The Reverse waltz. [P. F.] *London,* [1879.] fol.
h. 1484. c. (35.)

— Traumbild. Song [begins: "Ich stand in dunkeln Träumen"]
... written by H. Heine. *London,* [1878.] fol.
H. 1785. c. (39.)

LINDNER (P. E.)

— Valse charmante. [P. F.] *E. Donajowski: London,* [1907.] fol.
h. 3283. ll. (30.)

LINDNER (Paul)

— Airs Styriens pour piano. 4 no. *E. Ashdown: London,* [1897.]
fol. **g. 605. p. (39.)**

— Burleske für das Pianoforte. *E. Ashdown: London,* [1904.]
fol. **g. 605. ll. (19.)**

— Two characteristic Pieces for the Pianoforte. No. 1. Spring's
Message.—Frühlings-Boten.— No. 2. Spring Revels.—
Frühlings-Reigen. 2 no. *E. Ashdown: London,* [1902.] fol.
g. 605. ee. (37.)

— Home Greetings—Heimathsgruss—Sketch for the Pianoforte.
E. Ashdown: London, [1900.] fol. **g. 605. x. (15.)**

— Ländler für das Piano. 2 no. *E. Ashdown: London,* [1897.] fol.
g. 605. p. (40.)

— Madrigal pour Piano. *E. Ashdown: London,* [1901.] fol.
g. 605. x. (16.)

— Mélodie pastorale pour Piano. *E. Ashdown: London,* [1901.]
fol. **g. 605. x. (17.)**

— Sans Souci. Morceau pour Piano. *E. Ashdown: London,*
[1900.] fol. **g. 605. x. (18.)**

— Souvenirs de Voyage—Reise-Bilder.— ... pour piano. 5 no.
E. Ashdown: London, [1899.] fol. **g. 605. p. (41.)**

— Tantivy—Jagd-Fanfaren.—Characteristic Piece for the
pianoforte. *E. Ashdown: London,* [1897.] fol.
g. 605. p. (42.)

— The Trooper's Song.—Reiterlied.—Sketch for the Piano.
E. Ashdown: London, [1900.] fol. **g. 605. x. (19.)**

— La Zingara. Mazurka pour Piano. *E. Ashdown: London,*
[1900.] fol. **g. 605. x. (20.)**

LINDNER (Roderich August)

— 6 airs favoris, transcriptions ... pour Violoncelle avec
accompagnement de Piano. *Offenbach s. M.,* [1864.] fol.
h. 1849. (23.)

— Alte Weisen für Violoncell und Pianoforte bearbeitet, *etc.*
2 Hft. *Offenbach a. M.,* [1872.] fol. **h. 1849. c. (6.)**

— Altitalienische Canzonetten und Arien für Gesang mit
Pianoforte eingerichtet von A. Lindner. 2 Hft. *Offenbach
a. M.,* [1877.] fol.
Imperfect; wanting Hft. 1. **H. 2836. h. (56.)**

— [Altitalienische Canzonetten. Op. 40. No. 1–6.] Old Italian
Canzonettas and Arias of unknown masters ... between
1625–1750, edited by A. Lindner ... revised and edited by
E. T. Evetts. English version by C. Aveling. Book I. High
(Low) Voice. (Book II.) 3 bk. *Augener: London,* 1915–17. 4°.
G. 425. x. (27.)

— Bagatelles pour le piano à quatre mains. Op. 24. 3 no.
London, [1854.] fol. **h. 723. m. (12.)**

— Bagatellen für das Pianoforte zu vier Händen. 24ᵗᵉˢ Werk.
no. 2, 5, 6. *C. Bachmann: Hannover,* [1855?] fol.
Wanting no. 1, 3, 4. Autograph of Queen Alexandra.
R.M. 26. d. 9. (8.)

— Caprice pour le violoncelle avec accompagnement de piano.
Oeuv. 22. *London,* [1852.] fol. **h. 1851. (2.)**

— Chant d'Amour. Morceau de Salon pour le Piano. Oeuv. 21.
London, [1852.] fol. **h. 723. m. (13.)**

LINDNER (RODERICH AUGUST)

— [Concerto. Violoncello. Op. 34.] Concert, *etc.* [Orchestral parts.] 20 pt. [*C. F. W. Siegel: Leipzig*, 1860?] fol.
h. 4090. l. (7.)

— Concert E. moll für Violoncell mit Begleitung des Orchesters oder des Pianoforte ... Op. 34. Mit Pianoforte. [Score and part.] 2 pt. *Bei C. F. W. Siegel: Leipzig*, [1860.] 4°.
h. 4090. w. (5.)

— Fantasia on themes from [V. Bellini's opera] Norma, for violoncelle & piano forte. Op. 25. *London*, [1854.] fol.
h. 1851. (3.)

— Sechs Fantasiestücke für Pianoforte und Violoncell. *Offenbach a. M.*, [1872.] fol.
h. 1847. (41.)

— Morceaux de salon sur des thêmes favoris pour Violoncelle avec accompagnement de Piano. no. 8. *Offenbach s. M.*, [1877.] fol.
Imperfect; wanting no. 1–7, 9.
h. 3213. s. (2.)

— Six morceaux de salon sur des thêmes favoris pour violon avec acc¹. de piano. Op. 18. New edition by R. Hoffmann. 2 no. *Offenbach a. M.*, [1881.] 4°.
g. 505. c. (10.)

— [6 Morceaux de Salon. Op. 18. No. 1.] Serenade, by F. Schubert. [Arranged for violoncello and P. F. by] A. Lindner. [1904.] *See* TRANSCRIPTIONS. Transcriptions of Standard Vocal Works, *etc.* No. 23. [1904, *etc.*] fol. **h. 1868.**

— [6 Morceaux de Salon. Op. 18. No. 5.] Adelaide, by L. van Beethoven. [Arranged for violoncello and P. F. by] A. Lindner. [1904.] *See* TRANSCRIPTIONS. Transcriptions of Standard Vocal Works, *etc.* [No. 2.] [1904, *etc.*] fol. **h. 1868.**

— [6 Morceaux de Salon. Op. 18. No. 6.] Ave Maria from Flotow's Stradella ... [Arranged for violoncello and P. F. by] A. Lindner. [1904.] *See* TRANSCRIPTIONS. Transcriptions of Standard Vocal Works, *etc.* No. 5. [1904, *etc.*] fol. **h. 1868.**

— Transcriptionen berühmter Musikstücke für Violoncell mit Pianoforte. no. 6. *Offenbach a. M.*, [1877.] fol.
Imperfect; wanting no. 1–5, 7, 8.
h. 3213. s. (3.)

— Unterhaltungen für junge Cellisten. Leichte Stücke für das Violoncell mit Begleitung des Pianoforte komponirt ... eingerichtet von August Lindner. Op. 32. [Score and parts.] 2 Hft. 4 pt. *Bei Joh. André: Offenbach a. M.*, [c. 1880.] fol.
h. 4090. r. (7.)

— *See* FLEURS. Les Fleurs des opéras. Potpourris pour piano & violoncello, *etc.* ⟨Les transcriptions pour violoncelle par A. Lindner.⟩ [c. 1880.] fol.
h. 4090.

LINDO (ALGERNON H.)

— Love's Choice. Song, words by K. H. Green. *E. Ascherberg & Co.: London*, 1901. fol.
H. 1799. cc. (65.)

— Morris Dance, for the Pianoforte. Arranged by A. H. Lindo, *etc. Elkin & Co.: London*, 1913. fol.
h. 3284. g. (29.)

— The Song of Hope. Song, words by R. Henry. pp. 7. *Marriott & Williams: London*, [1881?] fol.
h. 1654. uu. (3.)

— Sweet & low. Song, words by Tennyson. 2 no. [In C and E flat.] *Chappell & Co.: London*, [1888.] fol.
H. 1788. w. (16.)

— There is no one like Phillis. Duet for Men's Voices. Words and Music by A. H. Lindo. *E. Ascherberg & Co.: London*, 1899. fol.
H. 1799. h. (60.)

— A Treatise on Modulation, with typical Examples from well-known Works, *etc. Bosworth & Co.: London*, 1913. 4°.
g. 759. (3.)

— Were I a Lady fair. Song, the words by E. Dietz. *Boosey & Co.: London*, [1889.] fol.
H. 1788. w. (17.)

LINDO (SYLVIA)

— Easy Solo for Piano, *etc.* pp. 22. *Oxford University Press: London*, [1968.] *obl.* 4°.
d. 161. x. (3.)

— Folks-songs for Piano, *etc.* 2 bk. *Oxford University Press: London*, [1968, 69.] *obl.* 4°.
d. 161. x. (2.)

LINDOFF (KUHE)

— *See* KUHE LINDOFF.

LINDON (LILY)

— Heaven guard thee in thy rest, darling. [Song, begins: "The night is coming".] Words by J. B. Murphy. *Saint Louis*, [1864.] fol.
H. 1780. f. (19.)

LINDON (ROBERT)

— Wild grows the Heather. Selection. Arranged for orchestra by Felton Rapley. [Parts.] 20 pt. *Chappell & Co.: London*, [1956.] 4°.
[*Chappell & Co.'s Orchestral Works. no.* 511.] *The 1ˢᵗ violin part is in duplicate.*
f. 424.

— Wild grows the Heather. ⟨Musical play founded on J. M. Barrie's "The Little Minister". Adaptation by Hugh Ross Williamson. Lyric by William Henry.⟩ Selection, arranged by Felton Rapley. [P. F.] pp. 11. *Chappell & Co.: London*, [1956.] 4°.
f. 133. uu. (28.)

LINDOO

— Lindoo, my Hindoo Queen. [Song.] *See* HENRY (S. R.)

LINDOR

— Lindor's Sonnet on the Departure of Rosalie. [Song.] *See* CARNABY (W.)

LINDORF (A.)

— "The Rose and the Stars." Song written by L. Dornberg. [Begins: "Tell me ye brilliant stars".] *London*, [1853.] fol.
H. 1735. (45.)

LINDORFF (ERNST)

— *See* MENDELSSOHN-BARTHOLDY (J. L. F.) [*Collected Works.—j.*] Andante con Moto ... transcrit par E. Lindorff. [Based on the coda of Op. 15, and Op. 41, No. 1.] [1885.] fol.
h. 575. m. (37.)

LINDOS

— Lindos olhos. Modinha. *See* SOLA (Carlo M. A.)

LINDPAINTNER (F.)

— *See* LINDPAINTNER (P. J.)

LINDPAINTNER (PETER JOSEPH)

— Wessel & Co.'s editions of the works of P. Lindpaintner. no. 12–15. *London*, [1846.] fol.
Imperfect; wanting all the other no.
h. 252. (5.)

— Abend am Meere. *See infra*: Six Lieder ... Op. 164. No. 4.

— [Ach! mein Herz ist stets bei dir.] "Ever is my heart with thee." Romance; the English version by T. Oliphant. *London*, [1845.] fol.
H. 2136. (25.)

— [Ach! mein Herz ist stets bei dir.] The Brighter Day. *London*, [1858.] fol.
No. 58 of "Beauties of German Song".
H. 2071. (58.)

LINDPAINTNER (Peter Joseph)

— An die Welle. [Song.] Gedicht von Franz Dingelstedt. *In:* Album für Gesang, *etc.* Jahrg. 2. pp. 23–25. [1843.] 4°.
F. 1199. dd.

— Are we then parted. (Auf Wiederseh'n, Lied von A. Meissner.) [Begins: "Sind wir geschieden".] ... The English version by D. Ryan. *See* infra: Six Lieder ... Op. 164. No. 5.

— [Der arme Knabe.] Why weep'st thou? Ballad, *etc. London,* [1848.] fol.
No. 400 *of Wessel's series of German Songs.* **H. 2079.**

— Auf Wiederseh'n. *See* infra: Six Lieder ... Op. 164. No. 5.

— Ave Maria. Solo for soprano or tenor. *R. Butler: London,* [1887.] fol. **H. 879. e. (20.)**

— Ave Maria. [Organ.] [1892.] *See* LOTT (E. M.) Popular Pieces, *etc.* No. 23. [1880, *etc.*] fol. **h. 2716. a. (1.)**

— Bärbele's Lied. ("My native land.") Swabian song for voice and Piano. The English version by P. Inchbald [begins: "I praise mine own my native land"]. *London,* [1853.] fol.
No. 542 *of Wessel's series of German songs.* **H. 2082.**

— [Bärbele's Lied.] My Swabian Land. *See* SONGS. Select German Songs ... No. 12. [1869, *etc.*] fol. **H. 2134.**

— Der Bergkönig, romantische Oper in 5 Aufzügen ... Vollständiger vom Componisten verfertigter Clavier-Auszug. *Mannheim,* [1830.] *obl.* fol. **E. 236.**

— Der blinde Gärtner, oder die blühende Aloe. Liederspiel von A. v. Kotzebue. 18tes. Werk. Klavierauszug. *Leipzig,* [1820?] *obl.* fol. **E. 236. c.**

— Blumenlieder von J. N. Vogel, for voice and pianoforte ... The English version by D. Ryan. Op. 150. 6 no. *London,* [1853.] fol.
No. 550 *to* 555 *of Wessel's series of German Songs.*
H. 2083.

— Cologne "Liedertafel" a series of German quartetts (Männerchor) for two tenor & two bass voices, selected by P. von Lindpaintner. no. 1–4. *London,* [1854.] 8°.
E. 236. b.

— Concertino pour le Violon [with orchestral accompaniment]. Oeuv. 35. *Mayence,* [1825?] fol. **h. 1729. b. (4.)**

Danina oder Joko

— Danina oder Joko, der Brasilianische Affe, idealisches Ballet in 4. Acten von Ph. Taglioni ... Vollständiger von ... Ludwig Schunke verfertigter Clavier Auszug. pp. 95. *Bei Ferd. Heckel: Mannheim,* [1830?] *obl.* fol. **Hirsch IV. 1172.**

— [Another copy.]
The imprint has been erased. **e. 910.**

— Selection. [Military band parts.] 21 pt. *Jullien & C°: London,* [1856.] fol.
[*Jullien's military Journal. no.* 153.] *Without titlepage. The title is taken from the head of the clarinet solo part.* **h. 1543.**

— Ouverture ... pour le Pianoforte. *Leipzig,* [1830?] *obl.* fol.
e. 368. (12.)

— [Act 2. No. 5. Allegro molto.] The Danina Galop. [P. F.] *In:* The Musical Bijou ... for MDCCCXLVIII. p. 59. [1848.] fol.
H. 2330.

— [Drohung.] Ida's lament (Drohung. Gedicht von Klesheim) for voice and piano. (The English version by D. Ryan.) [Begins: "My mother will not have that I think of my lad".] Op. 159. *London,* [1853.] fol.
No. 567 *of Wessel's series of German songs.* **H. 2083.**

LINDPAINTNER (Peter Joseph)

— Early snow lies on the forest. (Erster Schnee, von M. Hartmann.) ... The English version by D. Ryan. *See* infra: Six Lieder ... Op. 164. No. 3.

— [Electra.] Overture ... For the piano forte. pp. 10. *Wessel & C°.: London,* [1853.] fol.
[*Wessel & C°'s Series of Overtures. no.* 31.] **h. 1321. a.**

— Erinnerungen. [Song.] Gedicht von J. N. Vogl. pp. 5. *In:* Orpheus, musikalisches Taschenbuch für das Jahr 1840, *etc.* Between pp. 82, 83. [1840.] *obl.* 8°. **Hirsch 5759.**

— Erster Schnee. *See* infra: Six Lieder ... Op. 164. No. 3.

— [Es war eine Ratt.] The Rat, [song] from Göthe's Faust [begins: "A rat in a cellar"] translated by W. Mc. Gregor Logan. *See* MOMENTS. Moments recréatifs. No. 89. [1840?] 4°.
F. 299.

— 50 Études pour la flute. *London,* [1847.] fol. **h. 250. (8.)**

— Vingt Études ... pour la Flûte (extraites de l'Œuvre 126) avec accompagnement d'une 2de. Flûte ... par H. Altès. *Paris,* [1880.] fol. **h. 2143. (7.)**

Die Fahnenwacht. Op. 114

— Die Fahnenwacht. [Song.] Gedicht von F. Löwe, für eine Singstimme mit Clavierbegleitung ... Op. 114. 3te Auflage. *Allgemeine Musikhandlung: Stuttgart,* [1845?] fol.
H. 2156. a. (18.)

— The Standard Watch. (Die Fahnenwacht.) Ballad, with German and English words. *London,* [1845.] fol.
H. 2136. (22.)

— With sword at rest. Die Fahnenwacht, or standard watch ... The English version by C. J. Riethmüller. *London,* [1845.] fol.
No. 309 *of Wessel's series of German songs.* **H. 2078.**

— The Standard Bearer. (Die Fahnenwacht.) The English translation by G. F. Willis. *London,* [1845.] fol.
H. 2136. (23.)

— Where floats the standard. (The Standard Bearer. Die Fahnenwacht.) The English version by T. Oliphant. *London,* [1845.] fol. **H. 2136. (21.)**

— To watch the banner (The Standard Bearer); song, translated by E. Fitzball. *London,* [1846.] fol. **H. 2136. (24.)**

— The Standard-bearer. [Song. Words by] E. FitzBall. *In:* The Musical Bijou ... for MDCCCXLVII. p. 13. [1847.] fol.
H. 2330.

— The Standard Bearer. (Die Fahnenwacht.) *See* LIEDER-REPERTORIUM. Lieder-Repertorium, *etc.* No. 165. [1847, *etc.*] fol. **H. 2274.**

— The Standard Bearer ... [Song.] Poetry by J. W. Mould. *Eng. & Ger.* pp. 12–17. [*Jullien & C°: London,* c. 1850.] fol.
[*Deutsche Lyra. no.* 3.] *Cropped.* **G. 1443. p.**

— The Standard Bearer ... [Song.] The English version by Tyrrell West, *etc. Eng. & Ger.* pp. 7. *J. Williams: London,* [c. 1850.] fol. **H. 1980. oo. (9.)**

— The standard bearer. (Die Fahnenwacht.) *See* ROCKSTRO (W. S.) Lyra Anglo-Germanica, *etc.* No. 13. [1853, *etc.*] fol.
H. 2265.

— The standard bearer, [song] written by E. M. Spencer. [Begins: "The night watch guards the tented battle field".] *London,* [1854.] fol. **H. 1759. (5.)**

— The Standard Bearer. (With German & English words.) *London,* [1855.] fol.
No. 110 *of the "Musical Bouquet".* **H. 2345.**

— The Standard-Bearer. (Die Fahnenwacht.) *London,* [1858.] fol.
No. 18 *of "Beauties of German Song".* **H. 2071. (18.)**

LINDPAINTNER (Peter Joseph)

— The Standard Bearer. (Die Fahnenwacht.) See FLOWERS. Flowers of Germany. No. 50. [1859, *etc.*] fol.   **H. 2133.**

— Der Sänger hält im Feld die Fahnenwacht ... Cancion [by Lindpaintner], *etc.* [1859.] fol. *See* SAENGER.   **H. 1771. s. (7.)**

— The Minstrel Holds the Standard Bearer's watch. [1873.] fol. *See* MINSTREL.   **H. 1791. a. (8.)**

— The Standard Bearer ... ballad ... the words from the original German by Charles Arnold, *etc.* Eng. & Ger. pp. 5. *Augener & Co.: London,* [1889.] fol. [*Germania.* no. 269.]   **H. 2128.**

— The Standard Bearer ... Arranged for the piano forte by Ferd. Beyer, *etc.* pp. 9. *Robert Cocks & C°: London,* [1850.] fol.   **h. 1203. dd. (13.)**

— Lindpaintner's standard bearer, arranged for the piano forte, by W. H. Palmer. *London,* [1853.] fol.   **h. 723. q. (6.)**

— The Standard Bearer. *See* GOODBAN (H. W.) H. W. Goodban's edition of popular piano forte duetts. No. 3. [1851, *etc.*] fol.   **h. 971. (14.)**

— The Standard Bearer, arranged for the flute, *etc. See* DIPPLE (T. J.) [1849.] fol.   **h. 139. (21.)**

— *See* BEYER (Ferdinand) [6 Morceaux élégants. Op. 90. No. 5.] The Standard Bearer, pour le Piano. [1850.] fol.   **h. 793. (3.)**

— *See* BEYER (Ferdinand) [6 Morceaux élégants. Op. 90. No. 5.] The Standard-bearer ... A favorite air by Lindpainter, *etc.* [c. 1855.] fol.   **h. 723. bb. (31.)**

— *See* BEYER (Ferdinand) [6 Morceaux élégants. Op. 90. No. 5.] The Standard Bearer ... pour le Piano. [1862.] fol.   **h. 814. a. (14.)**

— *See* BEYER (Ferdinand) Répertoire des Jeunes pianistes, *etc.* No. 2. Standard bearer. [1853.] fol.   **h. 814. e. (7.)**

— *See* BOCHSA (R. N. C.) La Mode. Two favorite melodies ... arranged for the harp, *etc.* [1846.] fol.   **h. 169. (15.)**

— *See* CHATTERTON (J. B.) Souvenir de Pischek ... caprice for the harp, *etc.* [1845.] fol.   **h. 180. (12.)**

— *See* GOODBAN (H. W.) Souvenir à la Pischek ... The Standard Bearer ... arranged as a Divertimento for the Pianoforte. [1847.] fol.   **h. 789. (17.)**

— *See* KULLAK (T.) "Marziale" on Lindpaintner's song "With sword at rest". [1852.] fol.   **h. 797. (1.)**

— *See* KULLAK (T.) "Marziale" on Lindpaintner's song ... for the Pianoforte. [1860.] fol.   **h. 799. c. (5.)**

— *See* LINTER (R.) Fantaisie militaire sur Die Fahnenwacht. [1847.] fol.   **h. 906. (23.)**

— *See* SAINTON (P.) Die Fahnenwacht mélodie de Lindpaintner, fantaisie pour le violon, *etc.* [1854.] fol.   **h. 1611. (14.)**

— Fair and soft the winds are blowing. (Der Schalck, von H. Eichendorf.) [Begins: "Läuten kaum die Maienglocken".] The English version by D. Ryan. *See infra:* Six Lieder ... Op. 164. No. 2.

— Fantaisie, variations et rondeau pour deux cors de chasse et pianoforte ... Oeuv. 49. [Parts.] 3 pt. *Chez Breitkopf & Härtel: Leipsic,* [1824.] fol.   **g. 1094. ff. (1.)**

— The Free Lance. [Song, begins: "As off he rode".] Written by H. B. Farnie. *London,* [1866.] fol.   **H. 1772. s. (14.)**

— [Frühlingslied.] Arise, sweet Spring. *London,* [1858.] fol. *No.* 21 *of "Beauties of German Song".*   **H. 2071. (21.)**

LINDPAINTNER (Peter Joseph)

— Die Genueserin. Grosse romantische Oper in zwey Aufzügen. Gedicht von C. P. Berger. 106tes. Werk. Vollständiger Klavierauszug. *Wien,* [1838.] fol.   **H. 760. a.**

— [Die Genueserin.] Ouverture ... für das Piano-Forte ... 106tes Werk. pp. 13. *Bei Tobias Haslinger: Wien,* [1838?] fol.   **Hirsch M. 1304. (11.)**

— [Giulia.] Overture ... For the piano forte, *etc.* pp. 9. *Wessel & Co.: London,* [1854.] fol. [*Wessel & C°'s Series of Overtures. no.* 30.]   **h. 1321. a.**

— The Gondolier. (Gondolier, Lied von E. Geibel.) [Begins: "O come to me".—"O komm zu mir"] ... The English version by D. Ryan. *See infra:* Six Lieder ... Op. 164. No. 6.

— Herr Gott, dich loben wir, nach Klopstock in Musik gesetzt. 27stes. Werk. [Score.] *Leipzig,* [1825?] *obl.* fol.   **E. 1420.**

Der Hirte und das Meerweib

— The Mermaid. (Der Hirte und das Meerweib.) Ballade von Klesheim [begins: "Schöner Hirte".—"Lovely Shepherd"] ... The English version by D. Ryan. Op. 186. *London,* [1858.] fol. *No.* 569 *of "Wessel & Co.'s Series of German songs".*   **H. 2083.**

— The Mermaid. (Der Hirte und das Meerweib.) Op. 156. *See* CONCERTS. Les Concerts de Société ... for Voice ... & Clarionet. No. 57. [1857, *etc.*] fol.   **H. 2085. b.**

— The Mermaid. (Der Hirte und das Meerweib.) *See* CONCERTS. Les Concerts de Société ... for Voice ... and Flute. No. 57. [1852, *etc.*] fol.   **H. 2085. e.**

— The Mermaid. (Der Hirte und das Meerweib.) *See* CONCERTS. Les Concerts de Société ... for Voice ... and Violin. No. 57. [1845, *etc.*] fol.   **H. 2085. a.**

— The Mermaid. (Der Hirte und das Meerweib.) *See* CONCERTS. Les Concerts de Société ... for Voice ... and Violoncello. No. 57. [1846, *etc.*] fol.   **H. 2085. g.**

— Hirten-Messe. *See infra:* Missa Pastoralis.

— "In these shades." Canzonetta, adapted to original words. *London,* [1823.] fol.   **H. 1675. (31.)**

— Irene. Gedicht von C. Herlosssohn. *In:* Album für Gesang, *etc.* Jahrg. 1. pp. 25–27. 1842. 4°.   **F. 1199. dd.**

— Joko. *See supra:* Danina oder Joko.

— [Der Jüngling von Nain.] The widow of Nain. (Der Jüngling von Nain. Gedicht von C. Grüneisen.) Oratorio. The English version by D. Ryan. Op. 155. [Orchestral parts and choruses.] *London,* [1853.] fol.   **H. 1092. a.**

— [Der Jüngling von Nain.] The widow of Nain. (Der Jüngling von Nain. Gedicht von C. Grüneisen.) Oratorio for voices and Piano. The English version by D. Ryan. Op. 155. *London,* [1853.] fol.   **H. 1092.**

— [Der Jüngling von Nain.] The Widow of Nain, oratorio ... arranged ... for the Organ by W. T. Best. 6 no. *London,* [1854.] fol.   **h. 2731. c. (1.)**

— [Der König und der Sänger.] The King and his bard. Ballad [begins: "A northern king"] the English words by W. Bartholomew. *London,* [1849.] fol.   **H. 1717. (18.)**

— Lichtenstein, grosse Oper in 5 Acten. Text nach W. Hauff von F. Dingelstedt ... Vollständiger Clavierauszug vom Componisten. *Hamburg & Leipzig,* [1845?] fol.   **H. 760.**

— Drei Lieder ... für eine Singstimme. Op. 139. *Braunschweig,* [1851.] fol.   **H. 1717. (17.)**

— Six German songs (Lieder) for voice and piano. [The English version by D. Ryan.] Op. 154. 6 no. *London,* [1853.] fol. *No.* 556–561 *of Wessel's series of German Songs.*   **H. 2083.**

LINDPAINTNER (PETER JOSEPH)

—— Six Lieder for Voice and Piano. Op. 164. *London*, [1857.] fol.
No. 591–596 *of "Wessel & Co.'s Series of German Songs".*
H. 2083.

—— Die Macht des Liedes. Komische Oper in drei Acten mit
Tanz von J. F. Castelli ... Klavierauszug. *Leipzig*, [1840?]
obl. fol. **F. 31.**

—— Grosse Messe (in B) für 4 Singstimmen und Orchester.
[Parts.] *Wien*, [1845?] fol. **H. 816. c.**

—— [Missa pastoralis.] Hirten-Messe in G dur. No. 5. [Parts.]
Wien, [1855?] fol. **H. 816. b.**

—— Missa solemnis, C moll, für vier Solo- und Chor-Stimmen
mit Orchester-Begleitung. Op. 110. Score. *Stuttgart*, [1850?]
fol. **H. 816. a.**

—— [Mönch und Rose.] The Monk and rose, (Mönch und Rose,
Gedicht von J. N. Vogel) for voice and piano ... The English
version by D. Ryan. [Begins: "By a rose tree".] Op. 158.
London, [1853.] fol.
No. 562 *of Wessel's Series of German Songs.* **H. 2083.**

—— Non mi lagno di morir. Preghiera per voce di
Basso.—Unrepining I will die, translated by J. Rhing.
London, [1861.] fol.
No. 2 *of Wessels & Co.'s series of modern Bass songs.*
H. 1772. s. (13.)

—— Oh Sea, when evening shines. (Abend am Meere von
A. Meissner.) [Begins: "O Meer im Abendstrahl".] ... The
English version by D. Ryan. *See* supra: Six Lieder ...
Op. 164. No. 4.

—— Jubel Overture. ⟨Camp Overture.⟩ [Military band parts.] 24 pt.
Boosey & Co.: London, [1880.] fol.
[*Boosé's military Journal. ser.* 18. *no.* 2.] **h. 1549.**

—— Ouverture zu Faust von Göthe für grosses Orchester. Op. 80.
Partitur. *Leipzig*, [1858.] 8°. **e. 61. (2.)**

—— Ouverture à grand orchestre de la tragédie Faust de Goethe
... Oeuv. 80. [Parts.] 23 pt. *C. F. Peters: Leipzig*, [1832.] fol.
Hirsch IV. 1629.

—— Ouverture guerrière pour le grand orchestre ... Kriegerische
Jubel-Ouverture zur Feier 25jähriger Regierung König's
Wilhelm von Württemberg. Op. 109. Partitur, *etc.* pp. 75.
A^d Mt Schlesinger: Berlin, [1842.] fol. **h. 1140.**

—— Die Pflegekinder. Operette in einem Act von K. Thienemann.
Leipzig, [1820?] *obl.* fol. **E. 236. d.**

—— [Die Pflegekinder.] Overture, *etc.* ⟨[Followed by] Grand Storm
Galop. Kéler Béla.⟩ [Military band parts.] 25 pt. *Boosey &
Co.: London*, [1875.] fol.
[*Boosé's military Journal. ser.* 52. *no.* 1.] **h. 1549.**

—— 24 Psalmen nach verschiedenen Dichtungen in Solo- und
Chor-Gesängen, mit Orchester oder Pianoforte Begleitung.
Op. 145. No. 1–6. *Braunschweig*, [1853.] fol. **H. 816.**

—— Premier quatuor pour 2 violons, viola et violoncelle ...
Oeuv. 30. [Parts.] 4 pt. *Au magasin de musique de C. F.
Peters: Leipzig*, [1820?] fol.
*A label bearing the imprint of C. C. Lose, Copenhague, has
been pasted over the original imprint.* **g. 410. d. (2.)**

—— Roland the Brave ... Song [begins: "The pennons flutter".
"O Morgenluft"]. *London*, [1855.] fol.
No. 254 *of the "Musical Bouquet".* **H. 2345.**

—— Der Schalck. *See* supra: Six Lieder ... Op. 164. No. 2.

—— Des Schweitzers Knaben Weh, Gedicht von K. Hemm, for
voice and piano. ⟨The Swiss boy's lament.⟩ (The English
version by D. Ryan.) Op. 157. *London*, [1853.] fol.
No. 568 *of Wessel's series of German Songs.* **H. 2083.**

LINDPAINTNER (PETER JOSEPH)

—— Die Sicilianische Vesper. Grosse heroische Oper in 4 Acten
von Heribert Rau ... 113tes Werk. Vollständiger
Clavier-Auszug vom Componisten. Mit unterlegtem
italienischem Text v. Wilhelm Häser. *Ger. & Ital.* pp. 211.
Bei B. Schott's Söhnen: Mainz, [c. 1845.] fol. **H. 1092. b.**

—— The Standard Bearer. *See* supra: [Die Fahnenwacht. Op. 114.]

—— [Der standhafte Prinz.] Overture ... For the piano forte.
pp. 13. *Wessel & Co: London*, [1854.] fol.
[*Wessel & Co's Series of Overtures. no.* 32.] **h. 1321. a.**

—— Stars of night, canon for soprano, tenor and bass with piano
forte accompaniment. [Begins: "Hope and faith, bright stars
of night".] *London*, [1854.] fol. **H. 1759. (4.)**

—— The Steadfast Prince. *See* supra: [Der standhafte Prinz.]

—— Stech-Palmen. Satyrisches und Lyrisches aus
Süd-Deutschland von H. Wagner. Mit Lieder-Compositionen
von Lindpaintner, Müller, Kocher, Silcher, Frech, *etc.* 6 Bd.
P. Neff: Stuttgart, 1833, 34. 12°. **11525. ccc. 1.**

—— [Süsser Glaube, Stern der Nacht.] "Sweet the Thought, thou
Star of Night." Canon ⟨for soprano, tenor & bass. Translated
and adapted by Jn°. Rhing⟩. *Eng. & Ger.* pp. 6. *Wessel & Co.:
London*, [1836.] fol.
Wessel & Co's Series of Vocal Trios. no. 8. **G. 804. i. (1.)**

—— [Sulmona.—Ach wie ängstlich wird er spähen.] Romanze aus
der neuen Oper Sulmona. [Song.] [*Breitkopf und Haertel:
Leipzig*, 1823.] 4°.
[*Beilage zur Allgemeinen musikalischen Zeitung. Jahrg.* 25.
no. 4.] **P. P. 1945.**

—— [Sulmona.—Ach, wie ängstlich wird er spähen.] Romance,
etc. In: The Harmonicon. vol. 1, pt. 2. no. 73. 1823. 4°.
P. P. 1947.

—— Sweet the Thought, thou Star of Night. *See* supra: [Süsser
Glaube, Stern der Nacht.]

—— [Die Trauernde.] "The despairing lover." Swabian national
Song for voice & Piano. The English version by P. Inchbald.
[Begins: "My mother likes me not".] *London*, [1853.] fol.
No. 534 *of Wessel's series of German Songs.* **H. 2082.**

—— [Die Trauernde.] The Despairing Lover. Song [begins: "My
mother loves me not"] written by Speranza. *London*, [1874.]
fol.
No. 4543 *of the "Musical Bouquet".* **H. 2345.**

—— Treuer Tod, von Scheuerlen, for voice and piano. ⟨The dying
soldier. Ballad.⟩ [Begins: "We marched right on together".]
London, [1853.] fol.
No. 549 *of Wessel's series of German Songs.* **H. 2082.**

—— Trois grands trios pour violon, alto et violoncelle ... Oeuvre
52, *etc.* [Parts.] 3 no. 9 pt. *Chez H. A. Probst: Leipzig*, [1825?]
fol. **h. 5. n.**

—— Der Vampyr, romantische Oper von C. Heigel ...
Vollständiger Klavierauszug. *Leipzig*, [1830?] *obl.* fol.
E. 236. a.

—— Ouverture zur Oper. Der Vampyr, für grosses Orchester.
Op. 70. Partitur. *Leipzig*, [1858.] 8°. **e. 61. (1.)**

—— [Vater unser.] The Lord's Prayer for voice and piano ... The
English words adapted by D. Ryan. Op. 163. *London*, [1854.]
fol. **H. 1185. (5.)**

—— [Another issue.] The Lord's Prayer, Vater unser, for Voice
and Piano, with Responses in Chorus ... The English words
adapted by Desmond Ryan. Op. 163. pp. 31. *Wessel and Co.:
London*, [1854.] fol. **R. M. 14. e. 11.**

—— [Vater unser.] The Lord's Prayer. [Separate chorus parts.]
London, [1856.] fol. **H. 1185. (6.)**

—— [Was winkt dort.] The Gnome king, a romance. *See*
LIEDER-REPERTORIUM. Lieder Repertorium, *etc.* No. 48.
[1847, *etc.*] fol. **H. 2274.**

LINDPAINTNER (Peter Joseph)

— Was zagst du holdes Mädchen? *Lied, von Fues.* [1839.]
s. sh. 4°.
Contained between p. 520 *and p.* 521 *of "Europa. Chronik der
gebildeten Welt," Bd.* 4. **Hirsch M. 659.**

— Wilt thou then with me come. *See* Songs. Gems of German
Song. Book 15. No. 5. [1843, *etc.*] fol. **H. 2123.**

— [Zeila.] Contredanse, *etc.* [P. F.] *In:* The Harmonicon. vol. 10.
pt. 2. pp. 204–207. 1832. 4°. **P. P. 1947.**

— [Zeila.] March, *etc.* [P. F.] *In:* The Harmonicon. vol. 9, pt. 2.
p. 236. 1831. 4°. **P. P. 1947.**

— [Zéphir et Rose.] Six pièces favorites du ballet Zéphir et
Rose, pour le piano-forte à quatre mains ... Op. 75, *etc.*
pp. 29. *Au Bureau de Musique de C. F. Peters: Leipzig,*
[1829?] *obl.* fol. **f. 770. cc. (7.)**

— [Zéphir et Rose.] Andante and Rondoletto, *etc.* [P. F.] *In:* The
Harmonicon. vol. 10. pt. 2. pp. 10–13. 1832. 4°. **P. P. 1947.**

— *See* Haendel (G. F.) Israel in Egypten ... Nach
Lindpaintner's Bearbeitung, *etc.* [1860.] 8°. **E. 146. ee.**

— *See* Liederhort. Der Liederhort. Dichtungen ... mit
Originalcompositionen von ... P. von Lindpaintner, *etc.*
1855. 8°. **11525. bb. 42.**

— *See* Marcello (B.) [Estro poetico-armonico.] Solo- und
Chor-Gesänge aus "Marcello's" Psalmen ... bearbeitet und
instrumentirt von P. Lindpaintner, *etc.* [1840?] fol.
Hirsch IV. 845.

LINDQUIST (Orvil A.)

— One hundred Exercises for the weak Fingers. [P. F.]
O. Ditson Co.: Boston, (1914.) 4°. **g. 337. ee. (4.)**

— Whole-Tone Scale Finger Technics. Twenty-five exercises on
the pianoforte. Técnica para los dedos en escala de tonos
enteros ... Traducido por M. P. Gainsborg. *G. Schirmer:
New York,* 1924. 4°. **g. 338. a. (13.)**

— *See* Grieg (E. H.) [Lyrische Stücke. Op. 54. No. 1. Gjaetergut.]
Shepherd Boy ... Transcribed [for organ] by O. A. Lindquist.
1922. 4°. **g. 1380. g. (26.)**

LINDRIDGE (George)

— A Collection of Psalm and Hymn Tunes, with Chants and
Services, arranged for the Organ or Pianoforte, *etc.*
pp. xvi. 104. *J. Alfred Novello: London,* [c. 1850.] 8°.
Imperfect; wanting pp. 19, 20. *With an additional titlepage,
printed in colour, and with a hymn tune in MS. inserted.*
B. 1174. d.

— Flowers, beautiful flowers. Duet, words by ... M. Wilkinson.
London, [1868.] fol. **H. 1775. u. (49.)**

— Jubilate, in score, with an accompaniment for the Organ.
London, [1847.] fol. **H. 1181. (21.)**

— Let us then cheerily wait for the spring, a winter's song
[begins: "Come love, let us chat"], the words by A. Ransom.
Hastings & London, [1855.] fol. **H. 1759. (6.)**

— Let us then cheerily wait for the spring, song, the words by
A. Ransom. *Hastings,* [1857.] fol. **H. 1771. l. (27.)**

LINDROTH (Adolf Fredrik)

— Andante och bolero för violin med ackompagnement af
piano. *Stockholm,* 1884. fol.
[*Musikaliska Konstföreningen. Årg.* 1884.] **H. 700/29.**

— Fem studier för violin-solo, *etc. Abr. Hirsch: Stockholm,*
[1865?] fol.
[*Musikaliska Konstföreningen. Årg.* 1865.] **H. 700/9.**

LINDSAY (   ) Mrs

— Songs, Movement Plays and Recitations, adapted for little
children. *O. Newmann & Co.: London,* 1895. 8°.
B. 675. b. (2.)

LINDSAY, afterwards BARNARD (*Lady* Anne)

— *See* Marches. A Collection of celebrated Marches & Quick
Steps ... Composed by the Right Honble Countess of
Balcarras, *etc.* [c. 1795.] fol. **g. 1780. q. (12.)**

LINDSAY (Caroline Blanche Elizabeth) *Lady*

— At her wheel. Song [begins: "Sitting and spinning"].
London, [1879.] fol. **H. 1783. p. (8.)**

— Boat Song, for Violin—or Violoncello—and Pianoforte.
Chappell & Co.: London, [1882.] fol. **h. 210. e. (28.)**

— By the Shore. Song. *London,* [1878.] fol. **H. 1778. y. (43.)**

— A Farewell, song ... Words and music by Lady Lindsay.
pp. 5. *Chappell & C⁰: London,* [c. 1880.] fol.
H. 1860. y. (15.)

— The Fisherman of Sᵗ Monan's, song, *etc.* pp. 4. *Wood & C⁰:
Edinburgh,* [c. 1875.] fol. **H. 1860. y. (16.)**

— The Fishermen of Sᵗ. Monan's. Song. *London,* [1876.] fol.
H. 1778. y. (40.)

— Honest Heart. [Song, begins: "Weeping eyes".] Words by Sir
C. Lindsay. *London,* [1879.] fol. **H. 1783. p. (9.)**

— Love at the gate. Song [begins: "In the summer"]. *London,*
[1878.] fol. **H. 1778. y. (45.)**

— [A reissue.] Love at the Gate. Song, *etc. London,* [c. 1880.]
fol. **H. 1652. jj. (16.)**

— Musical Miniatures. Twelve songs in three books. *London,*
[1878.] fol. **H. 1778. y. (46.)**

— The Prodigal. Sacred song [begins: "The scath of sin"].
Words by the Hon. J. L. Warren. *London,* [1877.] fol.
H. 1778. y. (42.)

— Raindrops. Song [begins: "Listen to the raindrops"].
London, [1880.] fol. **H. 1783. p. (10.)**

— A Sister's Lullaby for Violin (or Violoncello) and Pianoforte.
London, [1881.] fol. **g. 505. m. (15.)**

— Three songs for children. *London,* [1876.] fol.
H. 1778. y. (41.)

— The Sweetest Smile for me. Song [begins: "My love hath
eyes"]. *London,* [1878.] fol. **H. 1778. y. (44.)**

— Waft me on a wandering dream. Song ... Words by Sir
C. Lindsay. *London,* [1881.] fol. **H. 1787. j. (40.)**

— A Wintry Evening. Song [begins: "It was a wintry evening"].
London, [1879.] fol. **H. 1783. p. (7.)**

LINDSAY (Charles)

— All is rosy. Polka. [P. F.] *T. Presser Co.: Philadelphia,* (1913.)
fol. **h. 3123. a. (6.)**

— Approach of Spring, for the pianoforte. *T. Presser Co.:
Philadelphia,* 1916. fol. **h. 3123. a. (23.)**

— Autumn Days. March for the Pianoforte. Piano Solo (Duet).
2 no. *T. Presser Co.: Philadelphia,* (1906.) fol. **h. 3123. (1.)**

— Bold Robin Hood. In Sherwood Forest. Five Dances for the
Pianoforte. 1. Bold Robin Hood ... 2. Maid Marion [*sic*] ...
3. Alan-a-Dale ... 4. Little John ... 5. Friar Tuck, *etc.* 5 no.
T. Presser Co.: Philadelphia, (1912.) fol. **h. 3123. a. (7.)**

LINDSAY (Charles)

— The Bumble Bee. [P. F.] *T. Presser Co.: Philadelphia*, (1910.) fol.   **h. 3123. a. (1.)**

— Two Characteristic Marches for the Pianoforte. [No. 1.] The Betrothal March. Introducing "Annie Laurie". [By Lady John Scott.] [No. 2.] Homeward March. Introducing "My old Kentucky Home". [By S. C. Foster.] 2 no. *T. Presser: Philadelphia*, (1908.) fol.   **h. 3123. (2.)**

— Chimes at Twilight. Reverie. [P. F.] *T. Presser Co.: Philadelphia*, 1916. fol.   **h. 3123. a. (24.)**

— Church Bells ringing. Idyl for the pianoforte. *T. Presser Co.: Philadelphia*, 1914. fol.   **h. 3123. a. (25.)**

— Dance of the Village Maidens, for the Pianoforte. *T. Presser Co.: Philadelphia*, (1912.) fol.   **h. 3123. a. (8.)**

— 3 Dances. [No. 1.] The War Game. March. [No. 2.] Grace and Beauty. Waltz. [No. 3.] Arms entwined. Schottische. [P. F.] 3 no. *T. Presser: Philadelphia*, (1908.) fol.   **h. 3123. (3.)**

— Danses mignonnes for the Piano. [No. 1.] On the Promenade. March. [No. 2.] Shining Stars. Waltz. [No. 3.] Merry Trifles. Polka. 3 no. *T. Presser: Philadelphia*, (1907.) fol.   **h. 3123. (4.)**

— Dewdrops. [P. F.] *T. Presser: Philadelphia*, (1907.) fol.   **h. 3123. (5.)**

— Early Morn. [P. F.] *T. Presser: Philadelphia*, (1907.) fol.   **h. 3123. (6.)**

— A Foreign Tour. Four characteristic Pieces for the Pianoforte. 1. Holiday Scene ... 2. Venetian Days ... 3. Brave Hearts ... 4. Sunny Days, *etc.* 4 no. *T. Presser Co.: Philadelphia*, (1913.) fol.   **h. 3123. a. (9.)**

— Fraternal March, for the Pianoforte. *T. Presser Co.: Philadelphia*, (1910.) fol.   **h. 3123. a. (2.)**

— From the Orient. [P. F.] *T. Presser Co.: Philadelphia*, 1914. fol.   **h. 3123. a. (26.)**

— Garden Scenes. Four Dances for the Pianoforte. 1. On the Terrace ... 2. Fountain Spray ... 3. Lovers' Nook ... 4. Gathering Nosegays, *etc.* 4 no. *T. Presser Co.: Philadelphia*, (1912.) fol.   **h. 3123. a. (10.)**

— Gay and Graceful. Three Step. [P. F.] *T. Presser Co.: Philadelphia*, (1913.) fol.   **h. 3123. a. (11.)**

— Good Cheer. March. [P. F.] *T. Presser: Philadelphia*, (1908.) fol.   **h. 3123. (7.)**

— Halcyon Days. Waltz. [P. F.] *T. Presser Co.: Philadelphia*, (1912.) fol.   **h. 3123. a. (12.)**

— Happy Inspirations. Four Piano Pieces. 1. Oriental Patrol. 2. In Sevilla ... 3. In leafy Bower ... 4. Flight of the Fairies, *etc.* 4 no. *T. Presser Co.: Philadelphia*, (1911.) fol.   **h. 3123. a. (13.)**

— Harvest Days. Three Pieces for the Pianoforte. 1. In the Barn ... 2. Love Story. 3. On the Hayrack, *etc.* 3 no. *T. Presser: Philadelphia*, (1909.) fol.   **h. 3123. a. (3.)**

— Heart's Appeal. Reverie. [P. F.] *T. Presser: Philadelphia*, (1906.) fol.   **h. 3123. (8.)**

— Hopes and Fears. Reverie for the pianoforte. *T. Presser Co.: Philadelphia*, 1914. fol.   **h. 3123. a. (27.)**

— In an old Garden. Meditation for the Pianoforte. *T. Presser Co.: Philadelphia*, (1912.) fol.   **h. 3123. a. (14.)**

— In full Sail. Galop. [P. F.] *T. Presser: Philadelphia*, (1908.) fol.   **h. 3123. (9.)**

— In Romany. [P. F.] *T. Presser Co.: Philadelphia*, 1915. fol.   **h. 3123. a. (28.)**

LINDSAY (Charles)

— In the Hills. Rondo-Scherzo. [P. F.] *T. Presser: Philadelphia*, (1907.) fol.   **h. 3123. (10.)**

— In the Open Air. Four little Dances for the Pianoforte. [No. 1.] Military Drill. March. [No. 2.] Flower Carnival. Polka. [No. 3.] Dance of the Pansies. Waltz. [No. 4.] Helter Skelter. Galop. 4 no. *T. Presser: Philadelphia*, (1907.) fol.   **h. 3123. (11.)**

— In the Pasture. Rondo. [P. F.] *T. Presser: Philadelphia*, (1907.) fol.   **h. 3123. (12.)**

— In the treble Clef and on the white Keys. Five characteristic Piano Pieces. 1. Attention ... 2. Away we go ... 3. On Tiptoe ... 4. Come, Pussy ... 5. On the Dot, *etc.* 5 no. *T. Presser Co.: Philadelphia*, (1912.) fol.   **h. 3123. a. (15.)**

— In Tone Colour. Four characteristic pieces for the pianoforte. [No. 1.] In war time ... [No. 2.] Sweet secrets ... [No. 3.] Merry plowman ... [No. 4.] Alpine idyl, *etc.* 4 no. *T. Presser Co.: Philadelphia*, 1914. fol.   **h. 3123. a. (29.)**

— Italy and Spain. Valse mignonne. [P. F.] *T. Presser: Philadelphia*, (1907.) fol.   **h. 3123. (13.)**

— Jolly Sleigh Ride. [P. F.] *T. Presser Co.: Philadelphia*, (1911.) fol.   **h. 3123. a. (16.)**

— Joyous Days. Three step. [P. F.] *T. Presser Co.: Philadelphia*, 1914. fol.   **h. 3123. a. (30.)**

— Left! Right! Parade March for the Pianoforte. *T. Presser Co.: Philadelphia*, (1912.) fol.   **h. 3123. a. (17.)**

— Four Little Songs without Words for the Pianoforte. [No. 1.] Lullaby of the Flowers. [No. 2.] Spinning a Yarn. [No. 3.] Noontide Reverie. [No. 4.] At the Races. 4 no. *T. Presser: Philadelphia*, (1907.) fol.   **h. 3123. (14.)**

— Love of Pleasure. Graceful dance. [P. F.] *T. Presser Co.: Philadelphia*, 1916. fol.   **h. 3123. a. (31.)**

— Love's Magic. Idyl for the Pianoforte. *T. Presser: Philadelphia*, (1906.) fol.   **h. 3123. (15.)**

— The Maid of Honor. Stately Dance for the Pianoforte. *T. Presser: Philadelphia*, (1906.) fol.   **h. 3123. (16.)**

— Melodic Fancies. Six little Songs without Words for the Pianoforte. 1. Choral Melody. 2. An Autumn Afternoon. Reverie. 3. Sweet Phyllis. Gavotte. 4. Hop o' my Thumb. Scherzo. 5. By the Meadow Brook. Rondo. 6. In Vintage Time. Tarantella. 6 no. *T. Presser: Philadelphia*, (1906.) fol.   **h. 3123. (17.)**

— Military Escort. March. [P. F.] *T. Presser Co.: Philadelphia*, (1911.) fol.   **h. 3123. a. (18.)**

— Mistress mine. Old English dance. [P. F.] *T. Presser Co.: Philadelphia*, 1916. fol.   **h. 3123. a. (32.)**

— Mountain and Shore. Four Dances for the Pianoforte. [No. 1.] On the Trail ... [No. 2.] By the rolling Surf ... [No. 3.] Picnic Pranks ... [No. 4.] Summer Night Ramble, *etc.* 4 no. *T. Presser Co.: Philadelphia*, (1912.) fol.   **h. 3123. a. (19.)**

— Three Old English Dances for the Pianoforte. [No. 1.] Lady Beatrice ... [No. 2.] Powder & Patches ... [No. 3.] Maid Marian, *etc.* 3 no. *T. Presser: Philadelphia*, (1906.) fol.   **h. 3123. (18.)**

— Opening of the Ball. Waltz. [P. F.] *T. Presser: Philadelphia*, (1907.) fol.   **h. 3123. (19.)**

— The Palm Dance. Air de Ballet for the Pianoforte. *T. Presser: Philadelphia*, (1906.) fol.   **h. 3123. (20.)**

— Paola. Spanish dance. [P. F.] *T. Presser Co.: Philadelphia*, 1915. fol.   **h. 3123. a. (33.)**

LINDSAY (Charles)

— Picnic for two. Waltz. [P. F.] *T. Presser: Philadelphia*, (1909.) fol. **h. 3286. vv. (5.)**

— Five Picturesque Pieces in dance form. [No. 1.] Class Reception. March. [No. 2.] Lilies and Violets. Waltz. [No. 3.] Evening Stroll. Polka. [No. 4.] Dance of the Jugglers. Schottische. [No. 5.] Day in the Woods. Galop. [P. F.] 5 no. *T. Presser: Philadelphia*, (1906.) fol. **h. 3123. (21.)**

— Picturesque Scenes. Four pianoforte pieces. [No. 1.] Battalion drill ... [No. 2.] In green fields ... [No. 3.] In Switzerland ... [No. 4.] Lords and ladies, *etc.* 4 no. *T. Presser Co.: Philadelphia*, 1914. fol. **h. 3123. a. (34.)**

— Four Pieces in lighter vein, for the Piano. [No. 1.] In swift Flight. [No. 2.] Dance of the Jesters. [No. 3.] Military Dance. [No. 4.] Sylvan Revels. 4 no. *T. Presser: Philadelphia*, (1906.) fol. **h. 3123. (22.)**

— Pleasant Thoughts. [P. F.] *T. Presser: Philadelphia*, (1907.) fol. **h. 3123. (23.)**

— Pomp and Panoply. March. [P. F.] *T. Presser Co.: Philadelphia*, (1910.) fol. **h. 3123. a. (4.)**

— Priscilla. Three-Step for the Pianoforte. *T. Presser Co.: Philadelphia*, (1912.) fol. **h. 3123. a. (20.)**

— Reminiscences in Tone. Four pianoforte pieces. [No. 1.] Evening chimes ... [No. 2.] Call to worship ... [No. 3.] In the Alps ... [No. 4.] Round the capstan, *etc.* 4 no. *T. Presser Co.: Philadelphia*, 1913. fol. **h. 3123. a. (35.)**

— Shadow Pictures. Six little Dances for the Pianoforte. 1. Soldier Boys. March. 2. Little Sisters. Waltz. 3. The Toy House. Polka. 4. Young Farmers. Schottische. 5. Playful Pussy. Mazurka. 6. Jolly Rover. Galop. 6 no. *T. Presser: Philadelphia*, (1906.) fol. **h. 3123. (24.)**

— Shepherd's Pipes. [P. F.] *T. Presser Co.: Philadelphia*, 1915. fol. **h. 3123. a. (36.)**

— Snowflakes. Four Piano Pieces. [No. 1.] In the Nick of Time ... [No. 2.] Just in Play ... [No. 3.] Hither and thither ... [No. 4.] The Vesper Hour, *etc.* 4 no. *T. Presser Co.: Philadelphia*, (1910.) fol. **h. 3123. a. (21.)**

— Song of the Road. March. [P. F.] *T. Presser: Philadelphia*, (1908.) fol. **h. 3123. (25.)**

— Spring Time Joys. [P. F.] *T. Presser: Philadelphia*, (1907.) fol. **h. 3123. (26.)**

— Stray Musical Thoughts. Five Pianoforte Pieces. 1. After the Opera. March. 2. Gently gliding. Waltz. 3. Autumn Canter. Petite Polka. 4. In the Flower Shop. Mazurka. 5. Jolly Partners. Schottische. 5 no. *T. Presser Co.: Philadelphia*, (1910.) fol. **h. 3123. a. (5.)**

— The Summer Girl. Waltz. [P. F.] *T. Presser: Philadelphia*, (1907.) fol. **h. 3123. (27.)**

— Sweethearts. Reverie. [P. F.] *T. Presser: Philadelphia*, (1907.) fol. **h. 3123. (28.)**

— Under the Crescent. Turkish march. [P. F.] *T. Presser Co.: Philadelphia*, 1916. fol. **h. 3123. a. (37.)**

— Under the Willows. Reverie. [P. F.] *T. Presser: Philadelphia*, (1906.) fol. **h. 3123. (31.)**

— Vacation Sketches. Five little Dances for the Pianoforte. 1. Holyday Pranks. March. 2. Among the Lilies. Waltz. 3. Through the Cornfield. Polka. 4. Croquet Party. Schottische. 5. Welcome Home. Galop. 5 no. *T. Presser: Philadelphia*, (1906.) fol. **h. 3123. (29.)**

— Visions celestial. Meditation for the Pianoforte. *T. Presser: Philadelphia*, (1906.) fol. **h. 3123. (30.)**

LINDSAY (Charles)

— Whispered Secrets. Song without Words for the Pianoforte. *T. Presser Co.: Philadelphia*, (1911.) fol. **h. 3123. a. (22.)**

LINDSAY (Charles) Junior

— Folk Song Sing along. Words and music to the great folk songs of America and other countries. Features a set of eight separate lyric sheets, *etc.* ⟨Piano arrangements by C. Lindsay Jr.⟩ 9 pt. *Amsco Music Publishing Co.: New York*, [1962.] 4°. *Everybody's favourite Series. no.* 116. *The "lyric sheets," each containing the words only, are identical.* **H. 1248. k.**

— The Golden Harvest. World famous themes from opera, symphony and song. Arranged for piano by C. Lindsay, Jr. pp. 126. *Amsco Music Publishing Co.: New York*, [1961.] 4°. *Everybody's favorite Series. no.* 100. **g. 272. nn.**

— *See* ARANY (Cornel) Have Fun. ⟨Piano pieces.⟩ Compiled and arranged by C. Arany in association with C. Lindsay Jr. [1960.] 4°. **g. 272. xx. (1.)**

— *See* ARNOLD (Jay) A Collection of easy Viola Solos. Compiled and edited by J. Arnold in association with C. Lindsay, Jr. [1960.] 4°. **g. 762. r. (6.)**

— *See* ARNOLD (Jay) A Collection of easy Violin Solos. Compiled and edited by J. Arnold in association with C. Lindsay, Jr. [1960.] 4°. **g. 500. ll. (9.)**

— *See* ARNOLD (Jay) A Collection of easy Cello Solos. Compiled and edited by J. Arnold in association with C. Lindsay, Jr. [1960.] 4°. **g. 510. s. (3.)**

— *See* ARNOLD (Jay) More easy Clarinet Solos. Compiled and edited by J. Arnold in association with C. Lindsay, Jr. [1960.] 4°. **g. 1104. y. (6.)**

— *See* ARNOLD (Jay) More easy Flute Solos. Compiled and edited by J. Arnold in association with C. Lindsay, Jr. [1961.] 4°. **g. 280. o. (6.)**

— *See* ARNOLD (Jay) More easy Saxophone Solos. Compiled and edited by J. Arnold in association with C. Lindsay Jr. [1960.] 4°. **g. 1112. f. (7.)**

— *See* ARNOLD (Jay) More easy Trombone Solos. Compiled and edited by J. Arnold in association with C. Lindsay, Jr. [1960.] 4°. **g. 1117. e. (2.)**

— *See* ARNOLD (Jay) More easy Trumpet Solos. Compiled and edited by J. Arnold in association with C. Lindsay, Jr. [1960.] 4°. **g. 1105. f. (15.)**

— *See* ARNOLD (Jay) Quartet Score ... Arranged and edited by J. Arnold in association with C. Lindsay, Jr., *etc.* [1964.] 4°. **g. 271. y. (10.)**

LINDSAY (Hon. Charles Hugh)

— Die alte Zeit, a set of waltzes for the Pianoforte. *London*, [1860?] fol. **g. 443. e. (15.)**

— The Geraldine waltzes for the Pianoforte with accompaniment (ad lib.) for Cornet à pistons. *London*, [1860?] fol. **h. 1480. l. (2.)**

— Providenza. [Duet, begins: "Qual madre".] The words by Signor Filicaza. *London*, [1870.] fol. **H. 1775. u. (50.)**

— The St. George Rifle Galop. [P. F.] *London*, [1860.] fol. **h. 1460. w. (11.)**

LINDSAY (Charles M.)

— Hero's March. [P. F.] *Chicago*, 1864. fol. **h. 1459. g. (12.)**

— The Idaho schottisch. [P. F.] *Chicago*, 1864. fol. **h. 1459. g. (11.)**

LINDSAY (George L.)

— See LINDSAY (George Le Roy)

LINDSAY (George Le Roy)

— See MacCONATHY (O.) Music. The Universal Language. Edited by O. McConathy ... G. L. Lindsay, *etc.* 1941. 8°.
    F. 1848.

— See MAUNDER (J. H.) America, to thee ... Arr. by G. Le R. Lindsay. 1943. 8°.
    F. 1744. e. (14.)

LINDSAY (*Lady* JANE)

— The Grosvenor march. [P. F.] *London,* [1873.] fol.
    h. 1482. z. (69.)

— The Silent Land. [Song, begins: "Into the silent land".] Words by Longfellow. *London,* [1873.] fol.
    H. 1778. y. (39.)

LINDSAY (JEAN)

— Rosemary Ann. [Play.] By Rosalind Vallance. Music by J. Lindsay. *Thomas Nelson and Sons: London,* 1940. 8°. *Part of "The Nelson Theatre".*
    WP. 6834/30.

LINDSAY (JENNIE)

— Listen to Mother's Words they're always true. [Song.] pp. 3–5. *M. Witmark & Sons:* [*New York,* 1902.] fol.
    H. 3985. aa. (20.)

LINDSAY, afterwards **BLISS** (M.)

— Wickins' Album of Miss M. Lindsay's Songs. [1900.] *See* WICKINS AND CO. Grosvenor College Albums. No. 85. [1891, *etc.*] fol.
    h. 3803. a.

— Absolom, sacred song [begins: "And behold"]. *London,* [1868.] fol.
    H. 1565. (31.)

— Airy fairy Lilian. Song, words by A. Tennyson. *London,* [1857.] fol.
    H. 1565. (1.)

— Alice. A Lament. Words [beginning: "I weep beside the well"] by E. H. W. *London,* [1865.] fol.
    H. 1565. (25.)

— All, all around is still. Serenade. Written by W. P. L. *London,* [1865.] fol.
    H. 1565. (21.)

— Alone. Song, written by Mrs. R. B. Tritton. *London,* [1871.] fol.
    H. 1565. (43.)

— Always take Mother's Advice. [P. F.] *See* WARREN (W. A.) Always take Mother's Advice. Waltz, arranged on Miss Lindsay's ... Song. [1889.] fol.
    H. 2345.

— The Arrow and the Song. Words [beginning: "I shot an arrow"] by Longfellow. *London,* [1861.] fol.
    H. 1565. (9.)

— The Border lands, sacred song [begins: "Father into thy loving hands"], the words by J. E. B[rown] from the "Dove on the Cross," *etc. London,* [1859.] fol.
    H. 1186. (35.)

— The bridge, [begins: "I stood on the bridge at midnight,"] words by H. W. Longfellow. *London,* [1856.] fol.
    H. 1759. (13.)

— The Bridge, *etc.* [Song.] pp. 5. *Robert Cocks & Cᵒ: London,* [1863.] fol.
    H. 1653. d. (11.)

— [A reissue.] The Bridge, *etc. London,* [c. 1865.] fol.
    H. 1860. aa. (12.)

— The Bridge. [Song.] Words by Longfellow, *etc.* pp. 5. *Robert Cocks & Co.: London,* [c. 1870.] fol. **H. 1652. v. (11.)**

— The melody of the bridge ... transcribed for the piano forte ... by B. Richards. *London,* [1858.] fol.
    h. 762. b. (9.)

LINDSAY, afterwards **BLISS** (M.)

— The Bridge, arranged as a ... duet. *London,* [1871.] fol.
    H. 1565. (38.)

— The Bridge. [P. F. solo and duet.] *See* SMALLWOOD (W.) Home Treasures, *etc.* No. 7. [1872, *etc.*] fol. **h. 1412. o.**

— The Bridge. [P. F. solo and duet.] *See* SMALLWOOD (W.) Little Buds, *etc.* No. 11. [1874, *etc.*] fol. **h. 1412. p.**

— The Brook. Song. Poetry [begins: "With many a curse"] by A. Tennyson. *London,* [1861.] fol. **H. 1565. (11.)**

— Bury thy sorrow. Sacred song. *London,* [1874.] fol.
    H. 1565. a. (5.)

— Carol, carol, Christians. [Song.] Words by ... A. C. Coxe. *London,* [1865.] 8°. **H. 1980. (122.)**

— [Carol, carol, Christians.] Christmas Carol. For four voices, *etc.* pp. 3. *Novello, Ewer & Co.: London, New York,* [c. 1880.] 8°. **F. 260. r. (6.)**

— Carol, carol, Christians. ⟨Christmas carol. [S. A. T. B.] Words by A. Cleveland Coxe.⟩ pp. 3. *Novello & Co.: London,* [c. 1910.] 8°. [*Novello's Christmas Carols. no.* 228.] **C. 754.**

— Christian submission, [Song, begins: "O Lord my God," words] from "Wednesday before Easter" in the Christian Year, by the Rev. J. Keble. *London,* [1858.] fol.
    H. 1187. a. (19.)

— The Christian's "Good Night". Song [begins: "Good night beloved"]. Poetry by Miss S. Doudney. *London,* [1876.] fol.
    H. 1565. a. (8.)

— Christmas Carol. *See supra:* [Carol, carol, Christians.]

— Come unto me. Sacred song. Words by J. W. Bellamy. *London,* [1863.] fol. **H. 1565. (15.)**

— [A reissue.] Come unto me. Sacred song, *etc. London,* [c. 1870.] fol. **H. 1860. tt. (7.)**

— Come unto Me, *etc. W. Paxton: London,* [1912.] fol.
    H. 1187. rr. (17.)

— The Cuckoo. Song. (Words by Mrs. R. B. Tritton.) *See infra:* Songs for Children. No. 3.

— The Danish Maid. Poetry [begins: "She may be fair"] by Sir W. Scott. *London,* [1865.] fol. **H. 1565. (26.)**

— The day its last good night hath said. Words ... by Lady C. Pepys. *London,* [1865.] fol. **H. 1565. (22.)**

— Daybreak. [Song, begins: "A wind came up out of the sea".] The words by H. W. Longfellow. *London,* [1859.] fol.
    H. 1565. (2.)

— The Dog & the Cow. (Words by Mrs. R. B. Tritton.) *See infra:* Songs for Children. No. 8.

— The Duck. Song [begins: "My Duckling, come near"]. *See infra:* Songs for Children. No. 2.

— The Duck and the Kangaroo. [Song.] (Words by E. Lear.) *See infra:* Songs for Children. No. 7.

— Echoes. Song. Poetry [begins: "Still the angel stars"] by Miss Procter. *London,* [1861.] fol. **H. 1565. (10.)**

— England and England's queen, words by W. P. Lindsay. *London,* [1855.] fol. **H. 1759. (11.)**

— An Evening Prayer. *London,* [1865.] fol. **H. 1565. (24.)**

— Excelsior, [begins: "The shades of night"] words by H. W. Longfellow. *London,* [1854.] fol. **H. 1759. (7.)**

LINDSAY, afterwards BLISS (M.)

— Excelsior. ⟨[Song.] Poem by Henry Wadsworth Longfellow. New edition.⟩ pp. 5. *Robert Cocks & Cº: London*, [c. 1855.] fol. **H. 1980. hh. (12.)**

— Excelsior. Solo, *etc.* pp. 5. *Robert Cocks & Cº: London*, [1860?] fol. **H. 1653. d. (12.)**

— Excelsior. *See* WHITTINGHAM (A.) School Songs ... No. 6. [1886.] 8°. **E. 1761. a. (7.)**

— Excelsior! Unison Song, *etc.* [1901.] *See* MACNAUGHT (W. G.) Novello's School Songs. No. 636. 1892, *etc.* 8°. **F. 280. d.**

— Excelsior. Quartett. *London*, [1879.] 8°. *No. 55 of R. Cocks & Co.'s Vocal Quartetts.* **F. 156. a.**

— Excelsior ... for the Pianoforte. [1872.] fol. *See* RICHARDS (H. B.) **h. 760. g. (38.)**

— Excelsior. [P. F. solo and duet.] *See* SMALLWOOD (W.) Home Treasures, *etc.* No. 8. [1872, *etc.*] fol. **h. 1412. o.**

— Excelsior. [P. F. solo and duet.] *See* SMALLWOOD (W.) Little Buds, *etc.* No. 17. [1874, *etc.*] fol. **h. 1412. p.**

— Fair Inez. Song [begins: "O saw ye not"]. The words by T. Hood. *London*, [1879.] fol. **H. 1565. a. (16.)**

— Far Away. Song [begins: "Where is now"]. *London*, [1868.] fol. **H. 1565. (29.)**

— Far away. *See* WHITTINGHAM (A.) School Songs ... Second Series. No. 2. [1895.] 8°. **E. 1761. f. (1.)**

— Far Away. Song, *etc. Gould & Co.: London*, [1904.] fol. **H. 1799. vv. (56.)**

— Far away, *etc.* [Song.] *Gould & Co.: London*, [1916.] 4°. *No. 9 of 'The Royal 6d. edition'.* **G. 805. zz. (16.)**

— Far Away ... duet. *London*, [1870.] fol. **H. 1565. (35.)**

— Far away. [Four-part song.] *London*, [1874.] 8°. **E. 600. q. (20.)**

— Far away. Quartett. *London*, [1877.] 8°. *No. 6 of R. Cocks & Co.'s Vocal Quartetts.* **F. 156. a.**

— Far away. Two-part song. pp. 6. *J. Curwen & Sons: London*, [1911.] 8°. *[Choruses for equal Voices. no. 1309.]* **E. 861.**

— Far Away, *etc.* [Part-song. Tonic sol-fa.] [1893.] *See* COCKS AND CO. R. Cocks & Co.'s Part Songs ... No. 1. [1865–97.] 4°. **D. 774.**

— Far Away ... for the Piano. [1868.] fol. *See* LUINI (C.) **h. 3120. (3.)**

— Far Away ... for the Pianoforte. [1871.] fol. *See* RICHARDS (H. B.) **h. 760. g. (31.)**

— Far Away. [P. F. solo and duet.] *See* SMALLWOOD (W.) Home Treasures, *etc.* No. 1. [1872, *etc.*] fol. **h. 1412. o.**

— Far Away. [P. F. solo and duet.] *See* SMALLWOOD (W.) Little Buds, *etc.* No. 1. [1874, *etc.*] fol. **h. 1412. p.**

— Far Away ... for the Pianoforte. [1877.] fol. *See* LEMOINE (Frederic) *pseud.* **h. 1482. z. (33.)**

— Far Away. [P. F.] [1899.] *See* WEST (S.) and SMALLWOOD (W.) Echoes of Home. No. 1. [1899, *etc.*] fol. **h. 3808.**

— Far Away. [P. F.] [1901.] *See* GREVILLE (M.) Sunbeams, *etc.* No. 1. [1900–1.] fol. **h. 3507. a.**

— Far away. [Violin and P. F.] *See* BANTI (G.) Twelve Favourite Melodies, *etc.* No. 5. [1883–96.] fol. **h. 1612. a. (12.)**

— The Fox and the Hen Song. (Words by Mrs. R. B. Tritton.) *See* infra: Songs for Children. No. 4.

LINDSAY, afterwards BLISS (M.)

— Give us thy rest. Sacred song [begins: "The day's long trial"]. Poetry by H. Burnside. *London*, [1871.] fol. **H. 1565. (37.)**

— Good Night, good night beloved. Part song, the poetry by Longfellow. *London*, [1872.] 4°. **F. 585. b. (39.)**

— Home they brought her warrior dead. Song, words by A. Tennyson. *London*, [1858.] fol. **H. 1565. (3.)**

— Home they brought her warrior dead ... for the Pianoforte. [1868.] fol. *See* KUHE (W.) **h. 755. e. (20.)**

— Home they brought her Warrior dead. [P. F. solo and duet.] *See* SMALLWOOD (W.) Home Treasures, *etc.* No. 4. [1872, *etc.*] fol. **h. 1412. o.**

— Home they brought her Warrior dead. [P. F. solo and duet.] *See* SMALLWOOD (W.) Little Buds, *etc.* No. 18. [1874, *etc.*] fol. **h. 1412. p.**

Hymn of the Moravian Nuns

— Hymn of the Moravian nuns at the consecration of the banner of Pulaski, [begins: "When the dying flame of day"] words by H. W. Longfellow. *London*, [1854.] fol. **H. 1759. (10.)**

— Hymn of the Moravian Nuns at the Consecration of the Banner of Pulaski. ⟨Duet for soprano and contr'alto.⟩ Words by H. W. Longfellow, *etc.* pp. 9. *Robert Cocks & Cº: London*, [c. 1855.] fol. **H. 1653. qq. (27.)**

— Pulaski. Song. The poetry by H. W. Longfellow. *London*, [1872.] fol. **H. 1565. (46.)**

— Pulaski ... Duet for ladies' voices, *etc. Gould & Co.: London*, [1909.] 8°. *[Gould & Co.'s Part Songs, No. 20.]* **F. 1843. a.**

— Pulaski's Banner. [P. F. solo and duet.] *See* SMALLWOOD (W.) Home Treasures, *etc.* No. 9. [1872, *etc.*] fol. **h. 1412. o.**

— Pulaski's Banner. [P. F. solo and duet.] *See* SMALLWOOD (W.) Little Buds, *etc.* No. 24. [1874, *etc.*] fol. **h. 1412. p.**

— I do confess thou'rt smooth and fair. Song, written by Sir R. Ayton. *R. Cocks & Co.: London*, [1860?] fol. **H. 2815. k. (27.)**

— I do confess thou'rt smooth and fair. Song, written by Sir R. Ayton. *See* BURLINGTON. The Burlington Album, 1863. No. 8. [1862.] fol. **h. 1240.**

— In this I hope. Sacred song [begins: "Hold it up"], written by Miss H. M. Burnside. *London*, [1872.] fol. **H. 1565. (45.)**

— Sacred Song, Jacob. [Begins: "Me have ye bereaved".] *London*, [1858.] fol. **H. 1187. a. (18.)**

— "Lady Clara Vere de Vere." Song, written by A. Tennyson. *London*, [1860.] fol. **H. 1771. b. (13.)**

— The Lord will provide. Sacred song, *etc.* ⟨Gen: xxii. v. 7–8.⟩ pp. 5. *Robert Cocks & Cº: London*, [1855.] fol. **H. 1601. jj. (13.)**

— Low at thy Feet. Sacred song [begins: "I have so slighted thee"]. Words by Rea. *London*, [1871.] fol. **H. 1565. (39.)**

— Low at thy feet ... Duet. *London*, [1871.] fol. **H. 1565. (44.)**

— Low at thy feet ... for the Pianoforte. [1871.] fol. *See* RICHARDS (H. B.) **h. 760. g. (32.)**

— The Mariner's Song. *London*, [1862.] fol. **H. 1565. (12.)**

— Miserere Domine. [Song, begins: "Through the crashing storm".] The words by W. P. Lindsay. *London*, [1872.] fol. **H. 1565. a. (1.)**

LINDSAY, afterwards BLISS (M.)

— A Morning Prayer. *London*, [1865.] fol.　　**H. 1565. (23.)**

— Mr. Gorilla at home. [Song.] *See* infra: Songs for Children. No. 9.

— Mrs. Bluebottle fly. [Song.] *See* infra: Songs for Children. No. 6.

— My Laddie far away. Song [begins: "Ye'll know him"] written by Miss Saxby. *London*, [1876.] fol.
　　H. 1565. a. (9.)

— My old Mate and me. Song [begins: "The night is creeping"]. Poetry by Miss Saxby. *London*, [1874.] fol.　　**H. 1565. a. (6.)**

— O love my Willie. Poetry [begins: "Like me, love me"] by J. Ingelow. *London*, [1864.] fol.　　**H. 1565. (19.)**

— Oh! when wilt thou come to me. Sacred song [begins: "Come to me"]. *London*, [1869.] fol.　　**H. 1565. (33.)**

— The Old Clock on the Stairs. Song. Words [beginning: "Somewhat back,"] by H. W. Longfellow. *London*, [1860.] fol.　　**H. 1565. (7.)**

— The Old sweet story. Song [begins: "Ah! me"]. Poetry by Rea. *London*, [1872.] fol.　　**H. 1565. (47.)**

— The Old Sweet Story. Song. Poetry by Rea. New Edition with Tonic Sol-fa. *London Music Pub. Co.: London*, [1900.] fol.
　　H. 1799. h. (61.)

— The Open Window. Song. Poetry [begins: "The old house by the Lindens"] by W. H. [or rather, H. W.] Longfellow. *London*, [1867.] fol.　　**H. 1565. (27.)**

— Out in the Morning early ... Song, written and composed by Miss Lindsay, *etc. R. Cocks & Co.: London*, [1885.] fol.
　　H. 1788. w. (18.)

— Out in the Morning early. [P. F.] *See* WEST (G. F.) Easy Lessons, *etc.* No. 10. [1886.] fol.　　**h. 1395. f. (12.)**

— The Owl & The Cockatoo. [Song.] (Words by T. G. G. Faussett.) *See* infra: Songs for Children. No. 10.

— The Owl & the Pussy Cat. Song. (Words by E. Lear.) *See* infra: Songs for Children. No. 5.

— Peace be still. Sacred song. *London*, [1861.] fol.
　　H. 1565. (8.)

— The pilgrim's rest, ballad [begins: "Oh whither is the old man gone,"] words by H. Lindsay. *London*, [1855.] fol.
　　H. 1759. (8.)

— A psalm of life, [begins: "Tell me not in mournful numbers,"] words by H. W. Longfellow. *London*, [1855.] fol.
　　H. 1759. (12.)

— Pulaski. *See* supra: [Hymn of the Moravian Nuns.]

— Sacred song. Resignation. [Begins: "And he said 'While the child was yet alive I fasted and wept' ".] *London*, [1856.] fol.
　　H. 1187. a. (20.)

— Resignation. Vocal Duet. *R. Cocks & Co.: London*, [1883.] fol.　　**H. 879. e. (21.)**

— Resignation ... for the Pianoforte. [1869.] fol. *See* LUINI (C.)
　　h. 3120. (4.)

— Resignation. [Violin and P. F.] *See* BANTI (G.) Twelve Favourite Melodies, *etc.* No. 8. [1883–96.] fol.
　　h. 1612. a. (12.)

— Rest. Sacred Song. *London*, [1867.] fol.　　**H. 1565. (28.)**

— The Robin. Song [begins: "Hopity, hopity"]. *See* infra: Songs for Children. No. 1.

LINDSAY, afterwards BLISS (M.)

— A serenade from Maud, by A. Tennyson. [Begins: "Come into the garden Maud".] *London*, [1856.] fol.
　　H. 1759. (14.)

— A Serenade from Maud by A. Tennyson. *London*, [1857.] fol.　　**h. 725. f. (29.)**

— She reigns alone. Ballad [begins: "O'er all the kingdom"]. Words by E. Oxenford. *London*, [1877.] fol.
　　H. 1565. a. (10.)

— The Snow lies white. (An Old Wife's song.) The poetry by J. Ingelow. *London*, [1869.] fol.　　**H. 1565. (32.)**

— The Song of Love and Death. Poetry [begins: "Sweet is true love"] by A. Tennyson. *London*, [1864.] fol.　　**H. 1565. (18.)**

Songs for Children

— Songs for Children. Nº 1. The Robin. ⟨2. The Duck. 3. The Cuckoo. 4. The Fox & the Hen. 5. The Owl & the Pussy-Cat.⟩ 5 no. *Lamborn Cock & Co.: London*, [1871, 72.] fol.
　　H. 1565. (36.)

— [A reissue.] Songs for Children, *etc.* no. 3. *J. B. Cramer & Cº: London*, [c. 1880.] fol.
Imperfect; wanting no. 1, 2, 4–10.　　**H. 1660. d. (1.)**

— Songs for Children. Nº 6. Mʳˢ Bluebottle Fly. pp. 7. *Lamborn Cock: London*, [1873?] fol.　　**H. 1660. d. (2.)**

— [No. 6.] Mrs. Bluebottle Fly. [Song, begins: "I am Mrs. Bluebottle".] *London*, [1873.] fol.　　**H. 1565. a. (2.)**

— [No. 7.] The Duck and the Kangaroo. [Song, begins: "Said the duck".] Words by E. Lear. *London*, [1874.] fol.
　　H. 1565. a. (3.)

— [No. 8.] The Dog & the Cow. Song, words by Mrs. R. B. Tritton. *London*, [1875.] fol.　　**H. 1565. a. (12.)**

— [No. 9.] Mr. Gorilla at home. [Song.] *London*, [1876.] fol.
　　H. 1565. a. (13.)

— [No. 10.] The Owl & the Cockatoo. [Song.] (Words by T. G. G. Fausset.) *London*, [1877.] fol.　　**H. 1565. a. (14.)**

———————

— Speak gently, ballad, *etc.* pp. 7. *Robert Cocks & Cº: London*, [1855.] fol.　　**H. 1654. zz. (19.)**

— Speak gently, *etc.* [Song.] ⟨Second edition.⟩ pp. 7. *Robert Cocks & Cº: London*, [1855?] fol.　　**H. 1980. mm. (43.)**

— Speak gently, vocal duett. *London*, [1855.] fol.
　　H. 1759. (9.)

— Speak gently. *See* WHITTINGHAM (A.) School Songs ... Second Series. No. 7. [1895.] 8°.　　**E. 1761. f. (1.)**

— Speak gently ... transcribed for the Pianoforte. [1861.] fol. *See* BELLAK (J.)　　**h. 1242. (9.)**

— Stars of the summer night, serenade (words by Longfellow). *London*, [1857.] fol.　　**H. 1565. (4.)**

— Thalassa. A yachting song. The poetry [begins: "Who cares on the land to stay"] by E. Arnold. *London*, [1862.] fol.
　　H. 1565. (14.)

— There's no dearth of kindness [song], words by G. Massey. *London*, [1857.] fol.　　**H. 1565. (5.)**

— They shall hunger no more. Sacred song. *London*, [1863.] fol.
　　H. 1565. (16.)

— Thou, O Lord God. Sacred Song. *London*, [1864.] fol.
　　H. 1565. (20.)

— Thou wert the first of all I knew. Sacred song. Words ... by T. Whytehead. *London*, [1864.] fol.　　**H. 1565. (17.)**

LINDSAY, afterwards **BLISS** (M.)

—— Tired. Sacred song. Poetry by Miss H. Burnside. *London,*
[1870.] fol.   **H. 1565. (34.)**

—— Tired ... duet, *etc. London,* [1871.] fol.   **H. 1565. (41.)**

—— Tired ... for the Pianoforte. [1870.] fol. *See* RICHARDS (H. B.)
                                                h. 760. g. (24.)

—— Tired. [P. F.] [1901.] *See* GREVILLE (M.) Sunbeams, *etc.* No. 15.
[1900–1.] fol.   **h. 3507. a.**

—— Tired ... Transcribed for the Piano Forte by B. Richards, *etc.*
[1903.] fol. *See* RICHARDS (H. B.)   **h. 3283. (23.)**

—— Tired. [Violin and P. F.] *See* BANTI (G.) Twelve Favourite
Melodies, *etc.* No. 9. [1883–96.] fol.   **h. 1612. a. (12.)**

—— La toilette de Constance. [Begins: "Vite, Anna, vite, au
miroir".] Words by C. Delavigne. *London,* [1858.] fol.
                                                H. 1565. (6.)

—— Too late, too late! Sacred Song, [begins: "Late, late,"] poetry
by A. Tennyson, *etc. London,* [1860.] fol.   **H. 1186. (36.)**

—— Too late ... Duet, *etc. London,* [1871.] fol.   **H. 1565. (42.)**

—— Too late, too late, ye cannot enter now, *etc.* [Song.] pp. 4.
J. Curwen & Sons: London, [1905.] 8°.
[*Choruses for equal Voices.* no. 904.]   **E. 861.**

—— Too Late ... for the Pianoforte. [1869.] fol. *See* LUINI (C.)
                                                h. 3120. (5.)

—— What makes the World so bright To-Day? Song, written and
composed by Miss M. Lindsay, *etc. Hopwood & Crew:
London,* [1882.] fol.   **H. 1788. w. (20.)**

—— When Sparrows build. Song. The poetry by Miss J. Ingelow.
London, [1868.] fol.   **H. 1565. (30.)**

—— When Sparrows build. Song, *etc. Leonard & Co.: London,*
[1903.] fol.   **H. 1799. vv. (57.)**

—— When Sparrows build. [P. F. solo and duet.] *See* SMALLWOOD
(W.) Home Treasures, *etc.* No. 33. [1872, *etc.*] fol.
                                                h. 1412. o.

—— When Sparrows build. [P. F. solo and duet.] *See* SMALLWOOD
(W.) Little Buds, *etc.* No. 33. [1874, *etc.*] fol. **h. 1412. p.**

—— When Sparrows build ... for the Pianoforte. [1874.] fol. *See*
RICHARDS (H. B.)   **h. 760. h. (14.)**

—— When Summer dies. Song [begins: "I watch the russet leaflets
fade"] written by E. Oxenford. ⟨In C. In D.⟩ 2 no. *London,*
[1878.] fol.   **H. 1565. a. (15.)**

—— When the Ship comes home. Song. *London,* [1871.] fol.
                                                H. 1565. (40.)

—— When the ship comes home. Song. *London,* [1874.] fol.
                                                H. 1565. a. (11.)

—— When the Ship comes Home. [P. F. solo and duet.] *See*
SMALLWOOD (W.) Home Treasures, *etc.* No. 31. [1872, *etc.*]
fol.   **h. 1412. o.**

—— When the Ship comes Home. [P. F. solo and duet.] *See*
SMALLWOOD (W.) Little Buds, *etc.* No. 31. [1874, *etc.*] fol.
                                                h. 1412. p.

—— When the Ship comes home ... for the Pianoforte. [1874.]
fol. *See* RICHARDS (H. B.)   **h. 760. h. (13.)**

—— Where I would be. Song. (Duet.) 2 no. *London,* [1874.] fol.
                                                H. 1565. a. (7.)

—— Why sit'st thou by that ruined hall. Song. The words by Sir
W. Scott. *London,* [1862.] fol.   **H. 1565. (13.)**

—— Ye have done it unto me. Sacred song, the poetry by "Rea".
London, [1875.] fol.   **H. 1565. a. (4.)**

LINDSAY (MARGARET)

—— Loch Tay. Barn Dance, *etc.* [P. F.] *Lyon & Hall: Brighton,*
1910. fol.   **h. 3286. vv. (6.)**

LINDSAY (MARTIN)

—— Two Songs. [No. 1.] Weep you no more, sad Fountains.
[No. 2.] See where my Love a-maying goes. The words ...
16th century. *Oxford University Press: London,* 1938. 4°.
                                                G. 1270. pp. (3.)

LINDSAY (R. H.)

—— The Office of the Holy Communion including Benedictus,
Agnus Dei and Post Communion in ... F. *Weekes & Co.:
London,* [1913.] 8°.   **F. 1169. v. (19.)**

LINDSAY (SHIRLEY)

—— *See* HOVEY (Judy) and LINDSAY (S.) A Salute to America. For
mixed chorus and narrator. [1969.] 8°.   **F. 1874. j. (13.)**

LINDSAY (THOMAS)

—— The Elements of Flute-Playing ... In two parts. pp. 150.
T. Lindsay: London, [1828, 30.] fol.
*Pt. 2 was published by the author. The cover bears the imprint
of Cramer, Addison and Beale.*   **h. 2104.**

—— Introduction and three favorite airs, arranged as a mélange
for the flute, with an accompaniment for the Piano Forte.
London, [1821?] fol.   **h. 117. (29.)**

—— A second mélange for the flute and piano forte ... arranged
from Der Freischütz. *London,* [1825?] fol.   **g. 70. b. (9.)**

LINDSAY (W.)

—— Danse des Zéphyrs pour Piano. *London,* [1879.] fol.
                                                h. 1484. c. (36.)

—— Twilight, easy lesson for the Piano. *London,* [1876.] fol.
                                                h. 1482. z. (70.)

LINDSLEY (CHARLES EDWARD)

—— Five early American Hymn Tunes. For men's or mixed
voices unaccompanied, *etc.* pp. 11. *Oxford University Press:
New York,* [1975.] 8°.   **E. 497. dd. (20.)**

LINDSTEDT (ADOLPH)

—— Papoose Dance. Danse des enfants. Marche indienne.
Arranged by Hugo O. Marks. [P. F.] pp. 5. *Windsor Music
Co.: Chicago, New York,* [1904.] fol.   **h. 4120. rr. (2.)**

LINDSTRÖM (ALBERT)

—— Svenska psalmboken jemte de af J. C. F. Hæffner utgifne
koralerna till alla den svenska kyrkans psalmer samt messan
... för sång, äfven i stämmor, och orgel eller piano.
Genomsedde af ... Albert Lindström. Porträtt af framstående
psalmförfattare med biografier af ... Fredrik Sandberg, *etc.*
pp. 601, 384, 120. *Fröléen & comp.: Stockholm,* 1899. 4°.
                                                3425. n. 10.

LINDUSKY (EUGENE)

—— The Propers of Christmas, Circumcision, Easter, Pentecost.
In falso-bordone settings for three equal voices (S. S. A. or
T. T. B.) or three mixed voices (S. A. B.) bk 1. pp. 12.
Gregorian Institute of America: Toledo, Ohio, [1952.] 8°.
                                                F. 1175. dd. (37.)

LINDY

— Lindy. [Song.] *See* COLE (Robert A.) and JOHNSON (J. R.) Sounds of the Times. No. 6.

— Lindy. [Song.] *See* NEIDLINGER (W. H.)

— Lindy. [Song.] *See* OLIVER (James B.)

— Lindy. Song. *See* SPROSS (C. G.)

— Lindy does you love me? Song. *See* SILBERBERG (J. A.)

— Lindy! is yo' true to me? Song. *See* STAUFFER (Aubrey)

— Lindy Lee. [Song.] *See* HOWARD (Stephen)

— Lindy Lu. Song. *See* WEEKS (Seth)

— Lindy, what you're gwine to do? [Song.] *See* BRYMN (James T.)

— Lindy's Wedding. Song. *See* GORDON (J. S.)

LINE

— Line blocked. [Song.] *See* CARDEN (W. B.)

— Line it out M'Ginnity. [Song.] *See* SCHWARTZ (Jean)

— Line up. Song. *See* SEISMIT-DONA (Albano)

— Line up Boys! Song. *See* FARRINGTON (A. C.)

— Line up, Lads! Song. *See* WEST (A. H.)

— The Line was form'd. [Song.] *See* GLORIOUS. The Glorious First of June.

LINE (GEORGE)

— Songs by the Way, for Praise and Proclamation. *Morgan & Scott: London*, [1899.] 8°. **D. 913.**

LINÉ (HANS S.)

— Afar from thee, my Love. [Song, words by] L. N. Curtis. *T. Presser: Philadelphia*, (1904.) fol. **G. 807. kk. (9.)**

— Are you a single Man or are you married? [Song.] Words by James M. Reilly & Henry A. Gillespie. ⟨[From] The Burlesque of the Music Master.⟩ *M. Witmark & Sons: New York, etc.*, [1905.] fol. **H. 3985. aa. (21.)**

— At Coontown's Picnic. A characteristic march & two-step in "real" cakewalk time. [Song.] Words by Arthur J. Lamb. pp. 3. *Windsor Music Co.: Chicago, New York*, [1899.] fol. **H. 3980. ss. (14.)**

— At Coontown's Picnic. Characteristic March and Two-Step. Piano Solo. *Windsor Music Co.: Chicago & New York*, 1899. fol. **h. 3286. g. (50.)**

— L'Azora. March and Two Step. [P. F.] *Windsor Music Co.: Chicago, New York*, 1901. fol. **h. 3286. r. (15.)**

— Bacchus true blue. Drinking song. Words by Joseph Herbert. pp. 5. *M. Witmark & Sons: New York, etc.*, [1905.] fol. **H. 3985. aa. (22.)**

— Belle of Richmond. March. [P. F.] *J. W. Stern & Co.: New York*, 1902. fol. **h. 3286. y. (32.)**

— Consolation Waltzes. [P. F.] *Windsor Music Co.: Chicago, New York*, 1899. fol. **h. 3286. r. (16.)**

— Consolation Waltzes. Mandolin and Guitar (2 Mandolins and Guitar). 2 no. *Windsor Music Co.: Chicago, New York*, 1900. fol. **h. 188. h. (3.)**

— Cunning Coons. Characteristic March and Two-Step. [P. F.] *Windsor Music Co.: Chicago, New York*, 1900. fol. **h. 3286. r. (17.)**

LINÉ (HANS S.)

— Cunning Coons ... Mandolin and Guitar (2 Mandolins and Guitar). 2 no. *Windsor Music Co.: Chicago, New York*, 1900. fol. **h. 188. h. (4.)**

— Forgotten days. [Song.] Words by E. Gross. 2 no. [In F and E flat.] *National Music Co.: Chicago*, 1895. fol. **H. 1798. v. (29.)**

— The Futurity March. For the pianoforte. pp. 5. *Theodore Presser: Philadelphia*, [1904.] fol. **h. 4120. rr. (3.)**

— In the Shadow of the Cross. Sacred Song, with Organ Accompaniment. The words by A. J. Lamb. *Windsor Music Co.: Chicago, New York*, 1901. fol. **H. 1187. z. (19.)**

— Little Houston Street. [Song.] Words by Joseph Herbert. ⟨[From] The Burlesque of the Music Master.⟩ *M. Witmark & Sons: New York*, [1905.] fol. **H. 3985. aa. (23.)**

— Une Pensée. A Thought. (Violin and Piano.) *O. Ditson Co.: Boston*, (1911.) fol. **h. 1612. aa. (17.)**

— Scarf Dance. (Piano.) *Boosey & Co.: New York and London*, 1927. 4°. *Boosey's Artistic Series for Piano, No. 17.* **g. 1127. gg. (21.)**

— Simplicity. Intermezzo. [P. F.] *M. Witmark & Sons: New York, etc.*, 1900. fol. **h. 3282. w. (54.)**

— Sweethearts in the Park. [Song.] Words by Arthur J. Lamb. pp. 3. *National Music Co.: Chicago, New York*, [1896.] fol. **H. 3980. ss. (15.)**

— You say you were dreaming. [Song.] Written by C. Bronson. *F. A. Mills: New York, Chicago*, 1901. fol. **H. 1799. cc. (66.)**

— *See* FALL (L.) [Die geschiedene Frau.] The Girl in the Train ... Waltzes ... Arr. by H. S. Linné. (1910.) fol. **h. 3454. (16.)**

— *See* FALL (L.) [Die geschiedene Frau.] Gonda Waltzes ... Arr. by H. S. Linné. (1910.) fol. **h. 3454. (17.)**

— *See* HAMILL (F. J.) Adrift. [Song] ... Arrangement by H. S. Liné. 1899. fol. **H. 1799. c. (53.)**

LINED

— Lined with Gold. Part-Song. *See* FOSTER (M. B.)

LINEFF (EUGENIE)

— *See* LINEVA (Evgeniya E.)

LINEGER (M.)

— Fleurs d'Espagne ... Waltz for Piano. *R. C. W. Left: Ottawa, Can.*, 1898. fol. **h. 3286. g. (51.)**

— Nadia Waltz. [P. F.] *Orme and Son: Ottawa*, (1906.) fol. **h. 3286. ll. (31.)**

LINEK (JIŘÍ IGNÁC)

— Sinfonia pastoralis ex C. Partitura ... Editor Vít Chlup. pp. x. 21. *Editio Supraphon: Praha*, 1976. 4°. [*Musica viva historica.* 36.] **g. 818.**

— [Symphonia pastoralis. D major.] Weihnachtssinfonie ... Für Streichorchester, Orgel oder Cembalo (Klavier) und 2 Hörner (ad lib.) ... Christmas Symphony ... Herausgegeben von ... Felix Schroeder. Partitur, *etc.* pp. 19. *Chr. Friedrich Vieweg: Berlin*, [1963.] 4°. **g. 1780. v. (3.)**

— Weihnachtssinfonie. *See* supra: [Symphonia pastoralis. D major.]

LINEKAR (T. J.)

— Chant du Moine. The Monk's Prayer. Larghetto pour Violoncelle et Piano. *B. Schott's Söhne: Mainz, Leipzig,* (1912.) fol.   **g. 510. e. (10.)**

— Entreat me not to leave thee. Ruth's Song. *Vincent Music Co.: London,* [1903.] fol.   **H. 1187. cc. (40.)**

— God be with you till we meet again [hymn], *etc. Novello and Co.: London,* [1905.] *a card.*   **I. 600. c. (34.)**

— God bless our King. (Duw bendithia'n teyrn.) [Hymn.] Words by Rev. W. E. Jones, *etc.* [Staff and tonic sol-fa notations.] *A. J. Fleet: Colwyn Bay,* (1911.) 8°.   **C. 799. s. (7.)**

— The Iron Bar. Song, the words by F. Hill. *Weekes & Co.: London,* [1888.] fol.   **H. 1788. w. (20.)**

— It came upon the Midnight clear. Christmas Carol, words by E. H. Sears. *A. J. Fleet: Colwyn Bay,* 1911. 8°.   **C. 799. s. (8.)**

— Ar haner nos yn glir y daeth. It came upon the midnight clear. [Christmas carol.] Welsh words by Rev. W. Evans Jones. [Tonic sol-fa notation.] *A. J. Fleet: Colwyn Bay,* 1911. *s. sh.* 8°.   **E. 602. aa. (10.)**

— Jesu, Lover of my Soul. Sacred Song, the words ... by C. Wesley. *Novello and Co.: London,* [1906.] fol.   **H. 1187. ff. (55.)**

— The King of Love. Sacred Song, the words by Rev. Sir H. W. Baker. *Novello and Co.: London,* (1913.) fol.   **G. 517. dd. (5.)**

— Lord, keep us safe this Night. [Vesper hymn.] *Novello and Co.: London,* 1913. *a card.*   **I. 600. e. (65.)**

— A Masonic Musical Service Book for the three Degrees of Craft Freemasonry. Being a selection of appropriate Psalms, newly pointed; Hymns; Kyries, etc.; with settings of the E. A.'s Song; the Masonic Honours, Prosper the Art; Worthy Mason he; and a new setting of Burns' Song of "Farewell to Tarbolton Lodge" by Bro. E. Farnall ... With new Chants and Hymn Tunes ... The whole compiled and edited ... by Bro. T. J. Linekar, *etc. W. Reeves: London,* [1911.] 8°.   **F. 1176. e. (10.)**

— A Masonic Musical Service Book ... Second edition, revised. *W. Reeves: London,* [1912.] 8°.   **F. 1091. b.**

— The Young Organ Student. A Series of Studies on Hymn Tunes, for the development of independence of movement between hands and feet, and of reading from alto and tenor clefs. *J. H. Larway: London,* [1910.] *obl.* fol.   **f. 314. aa. (18.)**

LINES

— Lines. [Song.] *See* LANDSBERG (S.)

— Lines forming a Musical Stave, placed in their due relation to the Major Diatonic Scale of "Natural" notes. [By G. Mackenzie.] [*London,* 1873.] *s. sh.* fol.   **1811. a. 1. (13.)**

— Lines from "A Song for Occupations". [Part-song.] *See* LUENING (Otto)

— Lines from Milton. [Part-song.] *See* BRANDON (George)

— Lines from the Prophet Micah. [Song.] *See* WOLPE (Stefan) Six Songs from the Hebrew. 4.

— Lines of Flame. [Song.] *See* KUERSTEINER (J. P.) Three Love-Songs ... Op. 12. No. 3.

— Lines on the Pleasures of Music. [Part-song.] *See* STOKES (C.)

— Lines to a Beauty. [Song.] *See* CIANCHETTINI (P.)

— Lines to his Ladye. Song. *See* PITT (P.)

— Lines written in March. Part-song. *See* JACOB (Gordon P. S.)

LINES (RUTH W.)

— Sanctus. For S. A. T. B. unaccompanied. [Words from the] Book of Common Prayer. pp. 3. *H. W. Gray Co.: New York,* [1969.] 8°.   **F. 1176. ss. (27.)**

LINET (HANK)

— "Hank's" Book of Eukadidles for the Ukulele No. 2. A collection of ditties, camp songs and jingles arranged for the ukulele by "Hank" Linet, *etc. J. Mills, Inc.: New York,* 1924. 8°.   **f. 759. m. (2.)**

— Hank's "Ten Lesson Course" in Ukulele Playing, *etc. J. Mills, Inc.: New York,* 1924. 8°.   **f. 759. m. (1.)**

LINETTE

— Linette. Chansonette. *See* CANTOR (O.)

LINEVA (EVGENIYA EDUARDOVNA)

— Великорусскія пѣсни въ народной гармонизаціи. Записаны Е. Линевой ... Текстъ подъ редакціей академика Ѳ. Е. Корша. вып. 1, 2. *Императорская Академія Наукъ: С.-Петербургъ,* 1904, 09. 8°.   **Ac. 1124/39.**

— The Peasant Songs of Great Russia as they are in the Folk's Harmonization. Collected and transcribed from Phonograms by E. Lineff. Ser. 1, 2. *St. Petersburg,* [1905–11.] 8°.   **Ac. 1124/41.**

— [Twelve folk-songs, collected by E. E. Lineva.] *In:* KANN-NOVIKOVA (E.) Собирательница русских народных песен Евгения Линева. pp. 157–183. 1952. 8°.   **7889. a. 59.**

LINFIELD (ARTHUR F.)

— The Sacrifice. [Sacred] Song, words and music by A. F. Linfield. *West & Co.: London,* 1914. fol.   **H. 1187. xx. (22.)**

LINFOOT (G. E.)

— *See* WALL (David) Five Country Dances ... Circa A. D. 1764, *etc.* (Arranged by G. E. Linfoot.) [P. F.] 1934. 4°.   **f. 760. bb.**

— *See* WHITTAKER (William G.) The Sheffield Song Book ... Selection of songs ... from various books in the Clarendon Song Book Series, by G. E. Linfoot. [1934.] 8°.   **F. 1777. u.**

LING (GERTRUDE)

— The Call from Yonder. Song, words and music by G. Ling. *West & Co.: London,* 1915. fol.   **H. 1793. u. (2.)**

LING (J. R.)

— Ballad recreations. Fantasia for the Piano Forte. Op. 56. *London,* [1844.] fol.   **h. 374. (2.)**

— "Be not afraid 'tis I." [Sacred song.] ⟨Written by W. M. Tolkien.⟩ pp. 5. *H. Tolkien: London,* [1845?] fol. *Sacred Gems. no.* 10.   **H. 1186. f. (28.)**

— The Bijou Quadrilles. [P. F.] *In:* The Musical Bijou ... for MDCCCXLVII. pp. 88–90. [1847.] fol.   **H. 2330.**

— Blest Saviour from thy throne on high. A prayer. (The words by W. M. Tolkien.) *London,* [1845?] fol.   **H. 2832. n. (6.)**

— "Bright scenes of early days;" ballad, written and composed by J. R. Ling. *London,* [1845.] fol.   **H. 1333. (9.)**

— Brilliant capriccio, on favorite airs from Donizetti's opera "Parisina" ... for the Pianoforte. *Monro and May: London,* [1844.] fol.   **h. 374. (3.)**

— Christmas Carol Quadrilles ... arranged for the Piano Forte. *London,* [1844.] fol.   **h. 374. (5.)**

LING (J. R.)

— The Crystal Palace polka. [P. F.] *London*, [1851.] fol.
h. 964. (34.)

— The Crystal Palace polka. [P. F.] *See* CRYSTAL. The Crystal Promenade Music. No. 2. [1859.] fol. **h. 727. (10.)**

— "Dreams, dreams;" ballad, written by J. J. Reynolds. *London*, [1846.] fol. **H. 1333. (13.)**

— Fantasia for the Piano Forte, introducing Polish melodies. *See* VOYAGEUR. Le Voyageur. No. 14. [1842.] fol. **h. 445.**

— Fantasia for the Piano Forte, introducing the airs "Va pensiero" and "Anch'io dischiuso" from Verdi's opera "Nino". *London*, [1847.] fol. **h. 374. (9.)**

— "Farewell to thee;" ballad, written and composed by J. R. Ling. *London*, [1844.] fol. **H. 1333. (2.)**

— Gems à la Donizetti. Fantasia for the Piano Forte, on celebrated Italian airs, *etc. Duff & Hodson: London*, [1846.] fol. **h. 374. (8.)**

— The Holyrood palace polka, for the piano forte. *London*, [1851.] fol. **h. 964. (35.)**

— I'll ne'er forget thee. Ballad [begins: "Alien from my native land"]. *London*, [1840?] fol. **H. 2832. k. (19.)**

— I'll think of thee when evening closes. [Song.] Written by Miss H. Sheargold. *London*, [1861.] fol. **H. 1772. s. (15.)**

— I'll think of thee when evening closes. [Song.] Written by Miss H. Sheargold. *London*, [1868.] fol. **H. 1775. u. (51.)**

— The Liliputian Polka for the Pianoforte. *London*, [1850.] fol. **h. 947. (47.)**

— The Lilliputian Quadrilles, for the Piano Forte. *London*, [1844.] fol. **h. 374. (6.)**

— Mary Blane Quadrille, for the piano forte, introducing the popular airs, as sung by the Ethiopian Serenaders. Arranged by J. R. Ling. Solo, *etc.* pp. 5. *J. Williams: London*, [c. 1850.] fol. **h. 3870. oo. (4.)**

— Mary Blane. Quadrille, for the pianoforte, introducing the popular airs, as sung by the Ethiopian Serenaders, arranged by J. R. Ling ... Duet. pp. 11. *J. Williams: London*, [1850?] fol. **Hirsch M. 1314. (17.)**

— The Miser guards his Treasure. [Song. Words and music by] J. R. Ling. *In:* The Musical Bijou ... for MDCCCXLV. p. 21. [1845.] fol. **H. 2330.**

— "My well loved home;" ballad, written by T. Duncan. *London*, [1846.] fol. **H. 1333. (12.)**

— Oh! do not think of me. [Song. Words and music by] J. R. Ling. *In:* The Musical Bijou ... for MDCCCXLVII. p. 34. [1847.] fol. **H. 2330.**

— "Oh! farewell then;" ballad, written and composed by J. R. Ling. *London*, [1845.] fol. **H. 1333. (8.)**

— Oh! forget not the time;" ballad, the words by H. Sheargold. *London*, [1844.] fol. **H. 1333. (5.)**

— "Oh! think not that absence;" ballad, written and composed by J. R. Ling. *London*, [1846.] fol. **H. 1333. (11.)**

— Oh! where's the chain I treasured so. Ballad, written by H. Tolkien. *London*, [1845?] fol. **H. 2832. n. (5.)**

— "Oh! yes, I love thee;" ballad, the poetry by S. Fearon. *London*, [1844.] fol. **H. 1333. (6.)**

— Old English Quadrilles ... arranged for the Piano Forte. *London*, [1844.] fol. **h. 374. (4.)**

— The Overland galop. [P. F.] *London*, [1855?] fol. **h. 1480. e. (16.)**

LING (J. R.)

— "The parting smile;" ballad, written and composed by J. R. Ling. *London*, [1844.] fol. **H. 1333. (1.)**

— Petite Fantasia for the Piano Forte, on the Rataplan and march from [D. G. M. Donizetti's opera] La Figlia del Reggimento. *T. E. Purday: London*, [1849.] fol. **H. 1333. (14.)**

— Seconde petite fanta[i]sie pour Piano, sur les motifs favoris de La Fille du Régiment [by D. G. M. Donizetti]. *Duff & Hodgson: London*, [1849.] fol. **h. 716. (1.)**

— Les petits enfans quadrilles, for the Piano Forte. *London*, [1845.] fol. **h. 374. (7.)**

— Pretty little changes for pretty little fingers, a collection of popular airs for juvenile performers on the Piano Forte. No. 1–6. *London*, [1843.] fol. **h. 374. (1.)**

— "Return Naomi to thy Land." [Song.] ⟨Written by Johanna Chandler.⟩ pp. 5. *H. Tolkien: London*, [c. 1845.] fol. *Sacred Gems.* no. 9. **H. 1028. v. (23.)**

— Rondo à la Polka for the Pianoforte. *London*, [1845?] fol. **h. 1480. o. (17.)**

— "Il segreto per esser felice." Ballata: Lucrezia Borgia [by D. G. M. Donizetti], arranged for the Piano Forte by J. R. Ling. *T. E. Purday: London*, [1849.] fol. **H. 1333. (15.)**

— The popular Styrian melody sung ... in the Spirit of the Rhine, arranged with variations for the Pianoforte. *London*, [1840?] fol. **h. 1485. t. (15.)**

— "That loved familiar face;" ballad, written and composed by J. R. Ling. *London*, [1844.] fol. **H. 1333. (4.)**

— Then danced the Young. A song ... written ... by W. M. Tolkien. pp. 5. *H. Tolkien: London*, [1845?] fol. **H. 1653. f. (1.)**

— [Another copy.] *Cropped.* **H. 2832. n. (7.)**

— "Think not of me when fortune smiles;" ballad, written and composed by J. R. Ling. *London*, [1844.] fol. **H. 1333. (3.)**

— Tiny tunes for tiny tryers; or, Recollections of the Nursery. No. 1–3. *London*, [1847.] fol. **h. 374. (10.)**

— "'Tis sad to part;" ballad, written and composed by J. R. Ling. *London*, [1844.] fol. **H. 1333. (7.)**

— "Valse élégant" [*sic*] for the piano forte, arranged ... by I. R. Ling. pp. 5. *George & Manby: London*, [c. 1840.] fol. **h. 61. qq. (9.)**

— The Voice of those we love. [Song. Words and music by] I. R. Ling. *In:* The Musical Bijou ... for MDCCCXLV. p. 36. [1845.] fol. **H. 2330.**

— When first we met she knelt in Prayer. [Song.] ⟨Written by Louisa Chandler.⟩ pp. 5. *H. Tolkien: London*, [c. 1845.] fol. *Sacred Gems.* no. 5. **H. 1601. jj. (14.)**

— "Yes! we shall meet again;" ballad, written by E. G. Wilson. *London*, [1845.] fol. **H. 1333. (10.)**

— *See* AUBER (D. F. E.) [Zerline.] Alboni's favorite Canzonetta ... arranged for the Pianoforte by J. R. Ling. [1852.] fol. **h. 723. m. (14.)**

— *See* PESTAL ( ) *Count*. Pestal. [Song.] ⟨Arranged by J. R. Ling.⟩ [1848?] fol. **H. 1654. vv. (30.)**

— *See* STRAUSS (Johann) *the Elder*. Come sing and be happy, *etc.* ⟨The symphonies and accompaniments by I. R. Ling.⟩ [1845?] fol. **H. 1653. f. (37.)**

LING (J. R.)

— *See* Strauss (Johann) *the Elder*. [Pfennig-Walzer. Op. 70.]
The Happy Meeting, *etc.* ⟨The symphonies &
accompaniments by J. R. Ling.⟩ [1845?] fol.

H. 1653. f. (38.)

LING (James)

— I drink to thee. [Song.] Written by W. M. Cowell. *London*,
[1840?] fol. **H. 2832. e. (22.)**

LING (Vivian)

— Brighton. Waltz. [P. F.] *R. Cocks & Co.: London*, [1897.] fol.
h. 3286. g. (52.)

LING (William)

— L'Allegro Rondo for the Piano Forte, with an
accompaniment for the flute or violin ad libitum. *London*,
[1822.] fol. **h. 325. (1.)**

— The Dettingen Waltz, Rondo for the Piano Forte, with an
accompaniment for the flute or violin ad libitum. *London*,
[1822.] fol. **h. 325. (2.)**

— Eliza, a Canzonetta, with an accompaniment for the
Pianoforte ... The Words by N. Rolfe. pp. 8. *W. Rolfe:
London*, [WM1803.] fol. **H. 1652. p. (15.)**

— Euterpe. Theme and variations for the Piano Forte, with an
accompaniment for the flute or violin ad libitum. Op. 22.
London, [1822.] fol. **h. 325. (3.)**

— Introduction and air of Robin Adair, arranged for the
Pianoforte. *London*, [1810?] fol. **g. 270. d. (29.)**

— Light as Thistle Down & When the rosy Morn. Arranged by
Mr Ling. pp. 336–343. *Printed by Clementi, Banger, Collard,
Davis & Collard: London*, [c. 1810.] fol.
[*Clementi & Compys Collection of Rondos, etc. no.* 60.]
g. 1129. nn.

— The Loyal Briton, a much admired Song, *etc. Longman and
Broderip: London*, [1798.] fol. **G. 376. (24.)**

— The Rising of the Lark. A Favorite Welsh Song with an
Accompaniment for the Piano Forte or Harp, also Arranged
with Variations for the Piano Forte by W. Ling. *W. Rolfe:
London*, [1800?] fol. **G. 805. k. (7.)**

— [Another copy.] **G. 796. (13.)**

— The Rising of the Lark. A favorite Welsh song with an
accompaniment for the piano forte or harp also arranged
with variations for the piano forte. pp. 4. *Printed by
C. Wheatstone: London*, [WM1817.] fol. **G. 809. p. (6.)**

— A Rondo for the Pianoforte. No. 1. *London*, [1825?] fol.
h. 1480. m. (14.)

— A Second Sett of Three Duetts for Two German Flutes, in
which are introduced Favorite National Airs ... Op. 3d.
[Parts.] *W. Rolfe: London*, [1799.] fol. **g. 225. (5.)**

— Three Setts of progressive Preludes for the Piano Forte, in
major and minor keys ... Op. 9. pp. 15. *The Author:*
[*London*, WM1810.] fol. **g. 443. aa. (24.)**

— Three Sonates for the Harpsichord or Piano Forte one with
an Accompaniment for a Flute Obligato and two with an
Accompaniment for a Violin ... Opera 1mo. [Parts.] *Printed
by the Author: London*, [1792.] fol. **g. 161. e. (8.)**

LING (William Thomas)

— L'Alexandre. Thème alla Russe, with variations ... for the
Piano Forte. Op. 6. *London*, [1823.] fol. **h. 325. (5.)**

LING (William Thomas)

— Ceres, introduction and pastorale rondo for the Pianoforte.
London, [1825?] fol. **g. 443. e. (16.)**

— L'Eloise, introduction and rondo for the Pianoforte.
London, [1825?] fol **g. 443. e. (17.)**

— Fantaisie Anacréontique for the Pianoforte. *London*, [1830?]
fol. **h. 1480. m. (18.)**

— Fantasia Scozzese for the Pianoforte. *London*, [1830?] fol.
g. 443. e. (18.)

— A favorite air of Rossini's, arranged as a rondo for the
Pianoforte. *London*, [1825?] fol. **g. 443. e. (19.)**

— Germanicus, rondo alla waltz ... for the Pianoforte.
London, [1825?] fol. **h. 1480. m. (16.)**

— Les Graces, three waltzes ... for the Pianoforte. *London*,
[1830?] fol. **g. 443. e. (20.)**

— Grand Rondo alla Polonoise ... for the Pianoforte. *London*,
[1825?] fol. **h. 1480. m. (15.)**

— Une Offrande aux Sœurs, rondo ... for the Pianoforte.
London, [1825?] fol. **g. 443. e. (21.)**

— The Peasants' Dance in the opera "Der Freyschütz"
[composed by C. M. F. E. von Weber], with variations for the
Piano Forte, and an accompaniment for the flute (Air from
the opera "Der Freyschütz," with an introduction and
variations for the Piano Forte) by W. T. Ling. Op. 11. No.
1, 2. *London*, [1822.] fol. **h. 325. (4.)**

— Rondo brillant on an admired Air of Rossini's ["Il mio
piano" from "La Gazza ladra"], arranged for the piano forte
... by W. T. Ling. No 2. pp. 11. *John Gow & Son: London*,
[1823?] fol. **g. 1529. j. (5.)**

— Rondo, the theme an admired air of Rossini's ... for the
Pianoforte. *John Gow & Son: London*, [1825?] fol.
g. 443. e. (22.)

— A Rondoletto, with an introduction for the Pianoforte. Op. 4.
London, [1825?] fol. **h. 1485. t. (16.)**

— Theme alla Caccia ["Was gleicht wohl" from "Der
Freischütz" by C. M. F. E. von Weber], with variations by
W. T. Ling. Op. 8. *London*, [1825.] fol. **h. 325. (6.)**

— Theme alla caccia [Was gleicht wohl] from Weber's ... opera
of Der Freischütz ... for the Pianoforte. *London*, [1825?] fol.
g. 443. e. (23.)

— Le Zéphire, divertimento for the Pianoforte with an
accompaniment (ad lib.) for the Flute. *London*, [1830?] fol.
h. 1480. m. (17.)

LINGALING

— Lingaling! Chansonette. *See* Dédé (E.)

LINGARD (Frederick)

— Antiphonal Chants for the Psalter, as ordered at Morning
and Evening Prayer and for the proper psalms, hymns and
anthems, appointed to be used in the ... liturgy of the United
Church of England and Ireland; composed and arranged in
score with an organ accompaniment by F. Lingard. pp. 47.
J. Alfred Novello: London, [1842.] fol. **H. 1186. t. (5.)**

LINGARD (George W.)

— Transcriptions from the Works of Mendelssohn, arranged by
G. W. Lingard. [Harmonium.] [1897.] *See* Holyrood. The
Holyrood Series of Albums, *etc.* Book 8. [1897, *etc.*] 4°.
f. 329.

LINGARD (George W.)

— *See* MacPherson (J. G.) Bride of my Heart. [Song] ...
Pianoforte accompaniment ... by G. W. Lingard. [1897.] fol.
H. 1798. x. (23.)

LINGARD (William)

— Italian Guinea Pig Boy. [Song, begins: "I'm poor Italian".]
London, [1866.] fol. **H. 1772. s. (16.)**

— *See* Cull (A.) Captain Jinks Quadrilles, introducing
Lingard's popular airs. 1868. fol. **h. 1459. n. (56.)**

LINGENFELTER (Richard E.)

— Songs of the American West. Compiled and edited by
Richard E. Lingenfelter, Richard A. Dwyer, & David Cohen,
etc. [Music edited by David Cohen.] pp. xii. 595. *University
of California Press: Berkeley, Los Angeles*, 1968. 4°.
G. 935. u.

LINGER

— Linger awhile. Duett. *See* Thomson (H. T.)

— Linger awhile my dearest. Cavatina. *See* Donizetti (D. G. M.)
[Lucia di Lammermoor.—Alfin son tua.]

— Linger by the Fountain. [Song.] *See* Chauvenet (Jules)

— Linger, linger. Song. *See* Oliver (C. M. E.)

— Linger, linger Gentle Maiden. Ballad. *See* Morley (H. K.)

— Linger long sweet dream. Song. *See* Wright (M.)

— The Linger longer Girl. [Song.] *See* Solman (Alfred)

— Linger, longer, Loo. Song. *See* Jones (Sidney)

— Linger near me. Song. *See* Stevens (A. S.)

— Linger not long. Song. *See* Croxall (J. H.)

— Linger not long. Canzonet. *See* Salaman (C.)

— Linger oh gentle Time. [Two-part song.] *See* Atkins (F.)

— Linger, oh gentle Time. [Duet.] *See* Cowen (*Sir* F. H.) [Six
Duets. No. 6.]

— Linger, Twilight, linger. Glee. *See* Roeckel (J. L.)

LINGER (Carl)

— The Song of Australia. Song. Words by Mrs. C. J. Carleton.
Wickins & Co.: London, [1894.] fol. **H. 1798. v. (30.)**

LINGERING

— Ling'ring Days. Song. *See* Allbut (R. H.)

— Lingering Fancies. Song. *See* Rivenhall (F.)

— Lingering, lonely Rose. Song. *See* Sibella (G.)

— Lingering Love. [Song.] *See* Armstrong (Henry W.)

— Lingering o'er the past. Song. *See* Abt (F. W.) [Three Songs.
Op. 463. No. 2.]

— The Lingering Spark. [Song.] *See* Alexander (J. R.)

— Lingering thoughts. Song. *See* Cowen (*Sir* F. H.)

LINGO

— Lingo's Triumph. [Song.] *See* Once. Once more good Friends
with Latin grac'd, *etc.* [1785?] fol. **G. 316. l. (43.)**

LING TI LO

— Ling Ti Lo. Song. *See* Lyle (Kenneth)

LINGUA

— La Lingua batte dove il dente duole. Stornello-proverbio. *See*
Michelis (V. de)

— Lingua di musica, Lingua d'amore. Melodia. *See* Bucalossi
(P.)

LINICKE (Johann Georg)

— Concerto G-dur. Altblockflöte (Querflöte), Violinen, Viola
und B. c. ... [Edited by] Felix Schroeder. Partitur, *etc.* pp. 16.
Otto Heinrich Noetzel Verlag: Wilhelmshaven, [1962.] 4°.
g. 420. mm. (6.)

— [Mortorium à 5.] Sonata (Mortorium) à 5 (1737). For trumpet,
oboe, flute, violin & basso continuo. ⟨Edited by Robert
Minter [assisted by] Michael Turnbull.⟩ [Score and parts.] 6 pt.
Musica rara: London, [1974.] 4°.
[*17th and 18th Century Sonatas, Concerti and Overtures for
Trumpets & Orchestra*. 54.] **g. 1613.**

— Sonata (Mortorium) à 5 (1737). *See supra:* [Mortorium à 5.]

LINIKE (Johann Georg)

— *See* Linicke.

LINK

— The Link. Song. *See* Simpson (G.)

— Link by Link. Song. *See* Millard (H.)

— A Link of the Past. Song. *See* Foster (M. B.)

LINK (Charles W.)

— Let us now praise famous Men. [Hymn.] Words by Rev.
W. G. Tarrant. [In B flat and C.] 2 no. *Weekes & Co.:
London*, [1917, 23.] 8°. **D. 619. rr. (27.)**

— Reedham. *See infra:* The Wise may bring their Learning.

— School Song for Reedham Orphanage. Words by H. E.
Clarke. *Weekes & Co.: London*, [1911.] 8°. **F. 197. i. (11.)**

— Toddle up the Brae. Baby Song. Words by G. Paulin.
Weekes & Co.: London, [1901.] fol. **H. 1799. h. (62.)**

— The Wise may bring their Learning. *Reedham.* [Hymn.]
A. Weekes & Co.: London, [1923.] *s. sh.* 8°. **B. 507. (10.)**

LINK (Emil)

— Sechs Charakterstücke für Pianoforte. 2 Hft. *Berlin*, [1880.]
fol. **h. 3272. j. (34.)**

— Acht Lieder für eine Singstimme mit Begleitung des
Pianoforte. 8 no. *Berlin*, [1880.] fol. **H. 1786. e. (47.)**

— Tarantella für Pianoforte zu vier Händen. *Berlin*, [1880.] fol.
h. 3272. j. (35.)

LINK (Fr.)

— Drei Fugen für die Orgel. Op. 14. *Offenbach a. M.*, [1877.]
obl. fol. **e. 174. e. (5.)**

LINK (Joachim Dietrich)

— *See* Leoncavallo (Ruggiero) Pagliacci ... Drama in zwei
Akten und einem Prolog ... Partitur ... herausgegeben von
J.-D. Link und E. Märzendorfer, *etc.* [1971.] 4°. **G. 704. l.**

LINK (JOACHIM DIETRICH)

—— *See* MATTHUS (Siegfried) Omphale. Oper in drei Akten ... Klavierauszug von J.-D. Link. 1977. 4°.　　**F. 1373. kk.**

—— *See* VERDI (F. G. F.) [La Forza del destino.] Die Macht des Schicksals ... Oper ... Klavierauszug ... von J.-D. Link. 1972. 4°.　　**G. 344. f.**

LINK (PETER) and **COURTNEY** (C. C.)

—— Salvation ... Vocal selection. Book, music and lyrics by P. Link and C. C. Courtney, *etc.* pp. 36.　*Chappell & Co.: New York*, [1969.] 4°.　　**G. 1271. qq. (15.)**

LINK-BOY

—— The Link-Boy. Song. *See* MOULDS (J.)

LINKED

—— Linked for ever. Ballad. *See* GUGLIELMO (P. D.)

—— Linked to the Past. Song. *See* BARRI (O.)

—— Linked together. Song. *See* TOURS (B.)

—— Linked with many bitter tears. Ballad. *See* ALICE, *pseud.*

LINKLATER (R. JAMES)

—— Wenonah Waltz. [P. F.]　*M. M. Leidt: Buffalo*, (1903.) fol.
　　h. 3286. dd. (64.)

LINKS

—— The Links o' Love. [Song.] *See* CATHCART (I.) Two Songs. No. 1.

—— The Links o' Love. Song. *See* LOCKHART (G.)

—— The Links o' Love. Part-Song. *See* MACEWEN (*Sir* J. B.)

—— The Links o' Love. Song. *See* TAYLOR (S. C.)

—— Links of Friendship. Song. *See* MOZART (W. A.) [Don Giovanni.—Dalla sua pace.]

—— The Links of Life. Monologue. *See* ARTHURS (George)

LINLEY (FRANCIS)

—— Linley's Continuation of Bland's Collection divine Music. N° [MS 17–20]. [1797?] fol. *See* BLAND (John) Bland's collection of divine Music, *etc.*　　**H. 817.**

—— Bland's Collection, continued by F. Linley, of duetts for two performers on one harpsichord or piano-forte, *etc.* [c. 1795.] fol. *See* BLAND (John)　　**g. 12. d.**

—— A Christmas Box, containing Six Canzonettino's for One, Two or Three Voices, with an Accompaniment for the Piano Forte. Composed by the late F. Linley. Bk. 1.　*E. Riley: London*, [1800?] fol.　　**H. 1650. j. (5.)**

—— Thirty Familiar Airs for Two German Flutes ... To which are added Remarks on the utility of this Work, *etc. Messrs. Hamilton, for the Editor: London*, [1791.] obl. 4°.　　**b. 60. (4.)**

—— A Practical Introduction to the Organ in five Parts, vizt. necessary observations, preludes, voluntarys, fugees [*sic*], & full pieces, and a selection of ... psalms ... with interludes ... Op. 6 ... 9th edition corrected and enlarged. pp. 119. *Printed for A. Hamilton: [London*, c. 1805.] obl. 4°.　**b. 330. a.**

—— A Practical Introduction to the Organ, in five Parts ... Op. 6. Twelfth edition corrected and enlarged. pp. 119.　*Wheatstone & C°.: London*, [c. 1810.] obl. 4°.　　**b. 330.**

LINLEY (FRANCIS)

—— Three Solos, for the German Flute, in which is introduced three Scotch Airs, with an Accompaniment for the Violoncello ad libitum ... by the late F. Linley. 2 pt. *G. Walker: London*, [^WM1811.] fol.　　**g. 280. g. (17.)**

—— Three Sonatas for the Harpsichord or Piano Forte ... Op. 3. pp. 27.　*Fentum's: [London*, c. 1795.] fol.
The titlepage and pp. 17, 18 are mutilated.　　**g. 443. ll. (22.)**

—— Through Groves and Flow'ry Fields. A Favorite Song, the Words by T. Dutton.　*Lewis, Houston & Hyde: London*, [1796?] fol.　　**G. 808. e. (32.)**

—— When Angry Nations. A Favorite Song ... Written by T. Dutton.　*Printed for Lewis, Houston & Hyde: London*, [1796?] fol.　　**G. 808. e. (33.)**

LINLEY (GEORGE)

—— *See* also BURTON (B.) *pseud.*

—— Twelve popular Songs, composed by ... Linley, *etc. See* BOOSEY AND CO. Boosey's Musical Cabinet. No. 13. [1861, *etc.*] 4°.　　**F. 160.**

—— Thirteen ... Songs and Ballads ... by ... G. Linley, *etc. See* CHAPPELL AND CO. Chappell's Musical Magazine. No. 24. [1861, *etc.*] 4°.　　**F. 161.**

—— Thirteen Songs and Ballads by G. Linley. *See* CHAPPELL AND CO. Chappell's Musical Magazine. No. 79. [1861, *etc.*] 4°.　　**F. 161.**

—— Eight Celebrated Songs. *See* ALEXANDRA. The Alexandra Music Books. No. 11. [1893, *etc.*] fol.　　**H. 2328.**

—— The Absent One, ballad, written by J. E'Astes, *etc.* pp. 5. *B. W. Barwick: Keighley; Chappell & C°: London*, [1859.] fol.
　　H. 1601. kk. (6.)

—— Ada, written by W. H. Bellamy.　*London*, [1854.] fol.
　　H. 1297. (1.)

—— A'e fareweel; for ever, two part song, the poetry by Burns. [Begins: "Ae fond kiss and then we sever".]　*London*, [1854.] fol.　　**H. 1297. (3.)**

—— Alice, sequel to the May Queen [song, begins: "I thought to pass away before"], the words by A. Tennyson.　*London*, [1857.] fol.　　**H. 1298. (29.)**

—— Alice Lyle [song], written by S. Clifton.　*London*, [1859.] fol.
　　H. 1298. (1.)

—— Amplius lava me. O Lord be merciful. The English words taken from the Psalms.　*London*, [1853.] fol.　**H. 1295. (35.)**

—— The Angel's in the House. [Song.]　*London*, [1864.] fol.
　　H. 1299. a. (7.)

—— [Annie Laurie.] The admired Scotch melody. Annie Laurie, arranged as a vocal duet. [Begins: "Maxwelton banks are bonnie".]　*London*, [1853.] fol.　　**H. 1295. (37.)**

—— Are you coming? bonnie Annie! [Song, begins: "Oh! hear you not the linnet?"]　*London*, [1858.] fol.　**H. 1298. (42.)**

—— Art thou not mine own one. Ballad.　*London*, [1840?] fol.
　　H. 2831. b. (45.)

—— Astarte! Romanza, written & composed by George Linley. pp. 4.　*Cramer, Beale & C°: London*, [1851?] fol.
　　H. 1601. kk. (7.)

—— "Autumn is near." Duettino.　*London*, [1844.] fol.
　　H. 1292. (5.)

—— "Autumn winds are sighing;" ballad, the music and words by G. Linley. pp. 5.　*Chappell: London*, [1841.] fol.
　　H. 1288. (25.)

LINLEY (George)

— Away to the forest green. Song [begins: "Softly o'er mount"].
London, [1840?] fol.   **G. 807. (18.)**

— Away, ye gay landscapes, poetry by Lord Byron. *London*,
[1854.] fol.   **H. 1297. (24.)**

— The ballad singer. [Begins: "Waking at early day".] *London*,
[1854.] fol.   **H. 1296. (1.)**

— [Another edition.] The Ballad-Singer, *etc. C. Sheard & Co.:
London*, [1889.] fol.
No. 7916 of the Musical Bouquet.   **H. 2345.**

— [The Ballad Singer.] Waking at early Day, *etc.* [Song. Written
and composed by] G. Linley. pp. 3. *J. Curwen & Sons:
London; Leipzig* [printed, 1894.] 8°.
[*Choruses for equal Voices. no. 147.*]   **E. 861.**

— The Ballad Singer, *etc. J. Curwen & Sons: London*, [1906.]
8°.
Unison Songs. No. 91.   **E. 812.**

— The Ballad Singer. *See* RUMMEL (J.) Linley's Ballad Singer …
for the Pianoforte. [1862.] fol.   **h. 523. b. (13.)**

— The banks of the Tay, ballad. [Begins: "I saw my true love
first".] *London*, [1854.] fol.   **H. 1296. (2.)**

— The Banks of the Tay. Ballad. *London*, [1868.] fol.
H. 1299. a. (28.)

— Be but the same, ballad. pp. 4. *S. Chappell: London*, [1835?]
fol.   **H. 1291. b. (1.)**

— Bear me back to my native shore. [Song, begins: "Oh! bear
me".] Written by R. C. Welsh. *London*, [1855?] fol.
G. 805. p. (3.)

— Bear me back to my native shore. [Song.] Written by R. C.
Welsh. *London*, [1861.] fol.   **H. 1299. (13.)**

— The Beauties of Song. (First series.) The most admired airs
selected from the works of Beethoven, Mozart [and others] …
Newly adapted to English words by G. Linley. no. 1–8.
Addison & Hollier: London, [1855, 56.] fol.   **H. 1299. a. (34.)**

— Bessie, ballad [begins: "Life would indeed be dark without
thee"], written and composed by G. Linley. *London*, [1855.]
fol.   **H. 1296. (3.)**

— The Black Friar. Ballad [begins: "Beware"]. (Words by Lord
Byron.) *London*, [1866.] fol.   **H. 1299. a. (25.)**

— The blind man's lament, ballad. [Begins: "O where are the
visions".] *London*, [1855.] fol.   **H. 1296. (4.)**

— Blue ey'd Nell, ballad, written and composed by G. Linley.
[Begins: "When at blush of day".] *London*, [1856.] fol.
H. 1297. (42.)

— Blushing spring time. Ballad [begins: "Now spring is
smiling"], written and arranged from D'Albert's Adeline
Waltz. *London*, [1857.] fol.   **H. 1298. (38.)**

— The bonnie blooming heather, vocal duet, written by
Tannahill arranged and partly composed by G. Linley.
[Begins: "Will you go Lassie?"] *London*, [1859.] fol.
H. 1297. (47.)

— Bonny Jean. [Song.] As sung by Mʳ Sims Reeves. *Chappell &
Cᵒ.: London*, [1856.] fol.
*The titlepage bears a MS. dedication in the composer's
autograph.*   **H. 1291. b. (2.)**

— Bonny Jean. [Song.] ⟨New edition.⟩ pp. 5. *Chappell: London*,
[1856.] fol.   **H. 2835. b. (4.)**

— Bonny Ladye Moon. Song. *London*, [1862.] fol.
H. 1299. (40.)

— Breathe not her name to me. Ballad. *London*, [1835?] fol.
H. 2832. b. (2.)

LINLEY (George)

— "The Bright Stars are met," a song … Written and composed
by George Linley. pp. 5. *Paine & Hopkins: London*, [c. 1835.]
fol.   **H. 1291. b. (3.)**

— The British grenadier [song, begins: "The trumpet note hath
sounded"]. *London*, [1854.] fol.   **H. 1296. (5.)**

— Brothers in Arms, duet, written & composed by George
Linley. pp. 5. *John Alvey Turner: London*, [1855?] fol.
H. 1291. b. (4.)

— By the fading hues of twilight [song], to the air of Tic e Toc,
adapted to English words by J. Linley. *London*, [1856?] fol.
H. 1288. a. (23.)

— By the spangled Starlight, Fairy Song, written & composed
by G. Linley. pp. 5. *Wood & Co.: Edinburgh; Cramer,
Addison & Beale: London*, [c. 1840.] fol.   **H. 1980. aa. (14.)**

— The Calabrian Brigand Song. *London*, [1851.] fol.
H. 1294. (3.)

— Calm in beauty lies the valley. Song, written by E. Ellison.
London, [1861.] fol.   **H. 1299. (3.)**

— Charlie. [Song.] ⟨Written and composed by G. Linley.⟩ pp. 5.
Jullien & Cᵒ.: London, [1854.] fol.   **H. 1291. b. (24.)**

— Charlie, sequel to Minnie [song, begins: "Oh, my heart is
gay"]. *London*, [1855.] fol.   **H. 1296. (29.)**

— Charming Sorrentina [song, begins: "As the chamois o'er the
mountain"], arranged and adapted to English words by
G. Linley. *London*, [1859.] fol.   **H. 1298. (4.)**

— Charming Vision. *See* infra: [The Toy-Maker.]

— The Chieftain's Daughter; a duet, written and composed by
G. Linley. pp. 7. *S. Chappell: London*, [1832.] fol.
H. 1288. (37.)

— The Child's Wish in June, song. pp. 5. *Chappell: London*,
[1842.] fol.   **H. 1650. qq. (21.)**

— Children [song, begins: "Come to me"], words by
Longfellow. *London*, [1859.] fol.   **H. 1298. (9.)**

— [Another edition.] Children, *etc. F. Brooks & Co.: London*,
[1889.] fol.   **H. 1788. w. (21.)**

— Christine. [Song, begins: "All that recalls one trace of thee".]
London, [1856.] fol.   **H. 1298. (6.)**

— Claire, ballad, written & composed by George Linley. pp. 5.
A. W. Hammond: London, [1855?] fol.   **H. 1291. b. (18.)**

— Come away to the Masquerade. A ballad, written &
composed by G. Linley. pp. 7. *Goulding & D'Almaine:
London*, [c. 1830.] fol.   **H. 1653. s. (16.)**

— Come away to the Masquerade. [Song. Words and music by
G. Linley.] *In:* The Musical Bijou … for MDCCCXXXII.
pp. 16–24. [1832.] 4°.   **F. 149.**

— Come! banish care away. A ballad. *London*, [1835?] fol.
H. 2832. b. (3.)

— Come beloved one. *See* infra: [The Toy-Maker.]

— Come hither, pretty Fairy! Song … written, and composed
by G. Linley. pp. 7. *Cramer, Beale & Cᵒ: London*, [c. 1855.]
fol.   **H. 1650. qq. (22.)**

— Constance; a ballad [begins: "I do not ask"]. *London*,
[1847.] fol.   **H. 1293. (13.)**

— Constance, *etc.* [Song.] ⟨Written by L. E. L.⟩ pp. 5. *Chappell:
London*, [c. 1850.] fol.   **H. 1860. w. (12.)**

— [A reissue.] Constance, *etc.* [Song.] *London*, [c. 1860.] fol.
H. 1650. ii. (13.)

LINKEY (George)

— [Constance.] See RICHARDS (Henry B.) Constance, arranged for the piano forte ... by B. Richards. [1851?] fol.
h. 60. vv. (10.)

— The Contrabandista. [Song, begins: "Worn with speed".] *London*, [1858.] fol. **H. 1295. (1.)**

— Corinne. Ballad. *London*, [1850.] fol. **H. 1294. (28.)**

— Corinne, ballad, words by Lady Granard's nieces. *London*, [1854.] fol. **H. 1296. (6.)**

— The Corsair's Farewell. Song, written and composed by G. Linley. pp. 5. *D'Almaine & Co.: London*, [1840?] fol. *Illustrated Songs, Ballads & Duets. no. 4.*
Hirsch M. 1272. (2.)

— A country girl's account of the Exhibition. [Song.] *London*, [1851.] fol. **H. 1294. (1.)**

— A country girl's petition to see the Exhibition. [Song.] *London*, [1851.] fol. **H. 1294. (4.)**

— "Dance with me;" a song, written and composed by G. Linley. pp. 5. *S. Chappell: London*, [1832.] fol.
H. 1288. (34.)

— Dark eyed rover. [Song, begins: "When the may was blooming".] *London*, [1858.] fol. **H. 1297. (38.)**

— David's lament for Jonathan. The words from Scripture [beginning: "How are the mighty fallen"]. *London*, [1859.] fol. **H. 1298. (17.)**

— The day will dawn again. Song [begins: "Tho' dark awhile"], the words and music by G. Linley. *London*, [1857.] fol.
H. 1297. (34.)

— Daybreak [song, begins: "A wind came up out of the sea"], words by Longfellow. *London*, [1859.] fol. **H. 1298. (7.)**

— "A dear English Girl;" [song, begins: "I've wander'd the world"] written and composed by G. Linley. *London*, [1845.] fol. **H. 1292. (6.)**

— "Dear land that gave me birth;" ballad, written and composed by G. Linley. *London*, [1845.] fol. **H. 1292. (9.)**

— Dear Native Home. Ballad. *London*, [1850?] fol.
H. 1772. s. (17.)

— "Dear native land;" duet, adapted to [Berat's] popular air "Ma Normandie," written and arranged by G. Linley. *London*, [1845.] fol. **H. 1292. (16.)**

— Dearer still. Ballad, written by S. Clifton [begins: "I've loved thee in thy sunny hour"]. *London*, [1860.] fol.
H. 1298. (31.)

— Dennis and Nora. Irish ballad, written and composed by G. Linley. *London*, [1849.] fol. **H. 1294. (17.)**

— Dinah, ballad from the novel Adam Bede [begins: "Like the dawn of morning"], written [and] composed ... by G. Linley. *London*, [1859.] fol. **H. 1298. (24.)**

— Do what is right, ballad, written and composed by G. Linley. *London*, [1855.] fol. **H. 1296. (7.)**

— Do what is right. Ballad. *London*, 1873. fol.
H. 1299. b. (10.)

— "Dream no more of that sweet time;" ballad, written by L. E. L[andon]. *London*, [1848.] fol. **H. 1293. (22.)**

— The dream of early years "Ah never another dream". Ballad. The words by L. E. L[andon]. *London*, [1849.] fol.
H. 1294. (16.)

— The dreams of the heart. Ballad by Christabel. *London*, [1850.] fol. **H. 1294. (27.)**

LINKEY (George)

— The Dying Child. Ballad, written, composed ... by G. Linley. pp. 4. *Cramer, Addison & Beale: London*, [1839.] fol.
H. 2831. g. (35.)

— The Dying Child. Sacred song. *London*, [1873.] fol.
H. 1299. b. (8.)

— The Edinburgh Musical Album, edited by George Linley ... ⟨No 1.⟩ With an engraving of Miss Eliza Paton. pp. 2, 77. *John Lothian, etc.: Edinburgh, etc.*, 1829. fol. **H. 1291. a.**

— Edith. Ballad [begins: "The golden dreams of bliss"] ... by E. H. Reed. *London*, [1851.] fol. **H. 1294. (7.)**

— Elise. Ballad [begins: "Make my grave"] written and composed by G. Linley. *London*, [1846.] fol. **H. 1293. (6.)**

— Ellen Tree, a ballad, written and composed by George Linley. pp. 5. *S. Chappell: London*, [1832?] fol.
H. 1291. b. (5.)

— Ellenore, Ballad [begins: "Vainly I weep for thee, Ellenore"]. *London*, [1857.] fol. **H. 1297. (39.)**

— Elves of the Waters! Song. Written by Edward Gill. pp. 5. *S. Nelson: London*, [c. 1845.] fol. **H. 1601. mm. (18.)**

— England the home of the free. *London*, [1851.] fol.
H. 1294. (14.)

— Estelle. Ballad [begins: "By him forsaken"]. *London*, [1845?] fol. **G. 805. g. (19.)**

— Estelle. Ballad. *London*, [1873.] fol. **H. 1299. b.(14.)**

— Evening thoughts. Ballad [begins: "An old man sat at a cottage door"], the words by W. H. Bellamy. *London*, [1852.] fol. **H. 1295. (20.)**

— The exile of Erin, Irish ballad (written by W. Kennedy). [Begins: "Oh while I live, I'll ne'er forget".] *London*, [1854.] fol. **H. 1297. (14.)**

— The fading of the flowers, duettino, written by W. C. Bryant. [Begins: "The melancholy days are come".] *London*, [1856.] fol. **H. 1297. (2.)**

— Fair dream of youth; ballad, written and composed by G. Linley. *London*, [1847.] fol. **H. 1293. (17.)**

— Fair star of beauty. Serenata, written and composed by G. Linley. *London*, [1850.] fol. **H. 1294. (20.)**

— The Fairy Gondolet. Song [begins: "In the sky"]. *London*, [1862.] fol. **H. 1299. (28.)**

— Far, far, away; ballad, written by J. E. Carpenter. pp. 5. *Chappell: London*, [1842.] fol. **H. 1288. (38.)**

— Far over land! Far over sea. Ballad, written and composed by G. Linley. *London*, [1857.] fol. **H. 1298. (12.)**

— Far up the mountain. A Lay of the Alps. *London*, [1849.] fol.
H. 1293. (24.)

— Fare thee well my ancient Home, ballad ... The music & words by George Linley. pp. 5. *Coventry & Hollier: London*, [c. 1840.] fol. **H. 1654. cc. (5.)**

— Fare thee well my own true love. Ballad, words and music by G. Linley. *London*, [1865?] fol. **H. 1288. a. (12.)**

— Farewell, if ever fondest prayer. The poetry by Lord Byron. *London*, [1854.] fol. **H. 1297. (25.)**

— "Farewell my lute;" ballad, written and composed by G. Linley. pp. 5. *S. Chappell: London*, [1834.] fol.
H. 1288. (29.)

— Farewell ye tranquil days. Ballad. *London*, [1861.] fol.
H. 1299. (15.)

LINLEY (George)

— Fill, soldiers! fill ... Song. *London*, [1835?] fol.
H. 2832. b. (5.)

— "The first green leaf;" [song,] written and composed by G. Linley. pp. 4. *Goulding & D'Almaine: London*, [1830?] fol.
H. 1288. (36.)

— The Fisher-Girl. [Song, begins: "With a light net".] *London*, [1865.] fol.
H. 1299. a. (14.)

— The flower girl ... written and arranged by G. Linley. *London*, [1848.] fol.
H. 1293. (18.)

— Fondly of Thee. Song, the words by Litchfield Moseley, *etc.* pp. 5. *Metzler & C°: London*, [c. 1870.] fol.
H. 1860. aa. (13.)

— For love of thee. Ballad. *London*, [1850.] fol.
H. 1294. (26.)

— For thee! for thee. ⟨[Song. Words and music] by G. Linley.⟩ *In:* The Musical Bijou ... for MDCCCXXXIII. pp. 44–48. [1833.] 4°.
F. 149.

— Forget that I have loved you. Ballad. *London*, [1853.] fol.
H. 1295. (23.)

— The fox and the crow, written and adapted by G. Linley. [Begins: "Once, master crow".] *London*, [1855.] fol.
H. 1296. (8.)

— [Francesca Doria.] Ring no more (Naples is the place. What soft emotion. Fair one, good night. Oh! for the olden glories. Far do I roam. Now my home's deserted. 'Neath your roof. Moor'd is my boat. O! gentle lady, hear me), sung in the opera of "Francesca Doria," written and composed by G. Linley. *London*, [1849.] fol.
H. 216.

— [Francesca Doria.] Select airs from ... Francesca Doria arranged for the Piano Forte, with an accompaniment for the flute by J. F. Burrowes. *London*, [1849.] fol.
h. 716. (2.)

— [Francesca Doria.] *See* MORRIS (V.) Francesca Polka, *etc.* [1849.] fol.
h. 948. (45.)

— Freedom now her banner's waving ... Chant national des Croates, adapted to English words. *London*, [1873.] fol.
H. 1299. b. (12.)

— The Friends of early Years, ballad, the poetry written by Mrs Abdy, *etc.* pp. 5. *Chappell: London*, [1840.] fol.
H. 1291. b. (6.)

— Gabrielle; romance, written and composed by G. Linley. *London*, [1847.] fol.
H. 1293. (16.)

— Gaston de Foix, romance. [Begins: "Evening's faint shadows".] *London*, [1854.] fol.
H. 1296. (9.)

— Gay summer bee. Cavatina. *London*, [1873.] fol.
H. 1299. b. (13.)

— Gentle mother; ballad, written and composed by G. Linley. *London*, [1845.] fol.
H. 1292. (17.)

— Gerald, ballad, written and composed by G. Linley. [Begins: "Your love hath passed away".] *London*, [1855.] fol.
H. 1296. (10.)

— Gertrude [a song, begins: "When first I fell"] written by C. Young. *London*, [1850.] fol.
H. 1294. (19.)

— The Gipsy Mother [song, begins: "Night her mantle dark hath spread"], written and composed by G. Linley. *London*, [1850?] fol.
H. 1288. a. (13.)

— Gisella, ballad [begins: "Ere Night Orbs paling"]. *London*, [1864.] fol.
H. 1299. a. (9.)

— "Go, beautiful and gentle dove;" song, written by the Rev^d. W. L. Bowles. *London*, [1844.] fol.
H. 1292. (7.)

LINLEY (George)

— Go, lov'd one. [Song.] *In:* The Musical Bijou ... for MDCCCXXXV. pp. 58–62. [1835.] 4°.
F. 149.

— Go whispering wind. Romance. (Words by G. Linley the Younger.) *London*, [1862.] fol.
H. 1299. (29.)

— God defend the right [song, begins: "Our country's standard floats above"]. *London*, [1854.] fol.
H. 1296. (11.)

— The Golden Chain is broken. Ballad, the words by Lady H. d'Orsay. *London*, [1870.] fol.
H. 1299. b. (1.)

— The golden ring, Scotch ballad. [Begins: "O Jamie where's the golden ring?"] *London*, [1855.] fol.
H. 1296. (12.)

— "Good night, sweet mother;" the sister's evening song, arranged as a duet for two voices, the poetry and music by G. Linley. *London*, [1847.] fol.
H. 1293. (12.)

— Grace Darling. Ballad, written and composed by George Linley. ⟨Third edition.⟩ pp. 5. *Cramer, Addison & Beale: London*, [c. 1840.] fol.
H. 1650. qq. (23.)

— "Guide our bark, Gondolier;" duet, written and composed by G. Linley. *London*, [1846.] fol.
H. 1293. (10.)

— Happy Childhood. Song [begins: "O'er the path"], written by C. Jefferys. *London*, [1861.] fol.
H. 1299. (2.)

— "Happy hours I've passed with thee;" duet, written and composed by G. Linley. *London*, [1846.] fol.
H. 1293. (8.)

— Happy Hours I've pass'd with thee. Duet. Written and composed by G. Linley. *See* DUETS. Vocal Duets, *etc.* No. 41. [1865? *etc.*] fol.
H. 2259.

— He comes no more. Ballad. *London*, [1860.] fol.
H. 1298. (15.)

— He is gone! Ballad, *etc.* ⟨The words by W. Motherwell.⟩ pp. 5. *C. Lonsdale: London*, [1854.] fol.
The titlepage bears a MS. dedication in the composer's autograph.
H. 1291. b. (21.)

— The Heart of thy Norah is breaking for thee. Ballad [begins: "The world is at rest"], written, composed ... by G. Linley. pp. 5. *Chappell's Musical Circulating Library: London*, [1845?] fol.
Hirsch M. 1272. (3.)

— The Heart of thy Norah is breaking for thee. Ballad, written ... by G. Linley. Second edition. *London*, [1845?] fol.
H. 1288. a. (15.)

— Here it was we met. Song, written by W. H. Bellamy. *London*, [1860.] fol.
H. 1298. (16.)

— Here it was we met. Song, written by W. H. Bellamy. *London*, [1866.] fol.
H. 1299. a. (21.)

— Hetty, ballad, from Adam Bede [begins: "Ill-gifted tokens"], written [and] composed ... by G. Linley. *London*, [1859.] fol.
H. 1298. (23.)

— A Highland Lad my love was born. *See* infra: [The Jolly Beggars.]

— The Hindoo Wife. Ballad [begins: "Do not, do not leave me"] written ... by Violet Linley. pp. 5. *George & Manby: London*, [1840?] fol.
H. 1653. f. (2.)

— The Hindoo Wife. [Song.] (Poetry by V. Linley.) *London*, [1861.] fol.
H. 1299. (16.)

— Hither come. Ballad, written by T. Blake. *London*, [1855?] fol.
H. 1288. a. (17.)

— Holy father hear my prayer, the hymn of Mary Stuart, written [and] composed ... by G. Linley. *London*, [1854.] fol.
H. 1296. (13.)

— Home of Childhood. Song. *London*, [1845?] fol.
G. 805. p. (4.)

LINKEY (George)

— Home of Childhood. Ballad. *London*, [1862.] fol.
H. 1299. (1.)

— Hope's like a minstrel bird, a song written by J. Grant. *London*, [1854.] fol. H. 1297. (9.)

— Hour of Twilight. Duettino. (Words by S. Clifton.) *London*, [1864.] fol. H. 1299. a. (16.)

— How idly goes the Mill, Mother. *London*, [1850.] fol.
H. 1294. (24.)

— The Hunter's Song ... [Song. Words and music by] G. Linley. *In:* The Musical Bijou ... for MDCCCXLIX. pp. 27–31. [1849.] fol. H. 2330.

— "Hurrah! for the guards." [Song, begins: "For us, beneath the sword they fell".] Written and arranged by G. Linley. *London*, [1857.] fol. H. 1298. (13.)

— The hymn of the allied armies [begins: "God of battle"], written and composed by G. Linley. *London*, [1855.] fol.
H. 1296. (14.)

— I am a Son of Mars. *See* infra: [The Jolly Beggars.]

— I am blamed because I love thee, ballad. *London*, [1854.] fol.
H. 1296. (15.)

— I am blest in loving thee. Ballad [begins: "Not for wealth"]. *London*, [1872.] fol. H. 1299. b. (5.)

— I am happy, I am happy, in my lowly Cottage Home, ballad, written by Thomas Blake, *etc*. pp. 5. *J. Keegan: London*, [1842?] fol. H. 1291. b. (26.)

— I am never alone. Ballad ... by Lady Jarvis. *London*, [1851.] fol. H. 1294. (9.)

— I can but breathe thy name. *See* infra: Six Venetian Melodies, No. 3.

— I can know thee no more. Ballad, words by E. Ellison. *London*, [1853.] fol. H. 1295. (33.)

— I cannot deem thee lost to me, ballad (written by E. Ellison). *London*, [1853.] fol. H. 1295. (34.)

— I cannot deem thee lost to me. Ballad. (Written ... by E. Ellison.) *London*, [1866.] fol. H. 1299. a. (22.)

— I cannot gaze upon my child. [Song.] *See* SONGS. Songs ... from the White Slave. No. 4. [1853.] fol. H. 2184. (18.)

— I cannot mind my wheel, mother. *See* SWAIN (C.) Swain's English melodies, *etc*. No. 5. [1851, *etc*.] fol. H. 2184. (31.)

— I cannot mind my Wheel, Mother. Song, *etc*. *R. Cocks & Co.: London*, [1894.] fol. H. 1798. v. (31.)

— G. Linley's popular song, "I cannot mind my wheel," arranged for the piano forte by T. Chantrey. *London*, [1854.] fol. h. 1248. (13.)

— I cannot mind my Wheel. [P. F.] *See* SMALLWOOD (W.) Sunny Hopes, *etc*. No. 4. [1894.] fol. h. 1412. u.

— I don't forget. Ballad. *London*, [1860.] fol. H. 1298. (18.)

— I know a pair of bright eyes [song], written and composed by G. Linley. *London*, [1858.] fol. H. 1298. (19.)

— I'll build me a bower, song (words by E. Ellison). *London*, [1854.] fol. H. 1297. (5.)

— I'll sing a song to thee, the poetry by H. Ainslie. *London*, [1858.] fol. H. 1298. (25.)

— I love thee, ballad, written and composed by G. Linley. *London*, [1854.] fol. H. 1296. (17.)

LINKEY (George)

— I love thee the more. [Song, begins: "Though the laurels of fame are entwining"], words by T. D. Jones. *London*, [1860?] fol. H. 1288. a. (11.)

— I'm a gipsy maid. *London*, [1852.] fol. H. 1295. (15.)

— I'm leaving old Ireland. *London*, [1853.] fol.
H. 1295. (25.)

— I'm the little flower girl, ballad. *London*, [1854.] fol.
H. 1296. (19.)

— I mark from my cell. A song, the poetry by Miss Pardoe. *London*, [1830?] fol. H. 2832. (29.)

— I mourn thee in silence, ballad ... written and composed by G. Linley. *London*, [1854.] fol. H. 1296. (18.)

— I mourn thine absence. Ballad. (Words by G. Linley the Younger.) ⟨In A flat.⟩ *London*, [1861.] fol. H. 1299. (7.)

— I mourn thine absence. ⟨In C.⟩ *London*, [1861.] fol.
H. 1299. (6.)

— I resign thee ev'ry Token ... [Song.] Written & composed ... by George Linley. pp. 5. *Chappell: London*, [1840?] fol. *The English Ballad Singer. no. 2.* H. 1291. b. (7.)

— "I roam through the Valley," ballad, written & composed by George Linley. pp. 5. *At Chappell's Musical Circulating Library: London*, [1836.] fol. *The titlepage bears a MS. dedication in the composer's autograph.* H. 1291. b. (8.)

— I saw thee when summer was smiling, ballad, written and composed by G. Linley. *London*, [1858.] fol.
H. 1298. (27.)

— "I turn my steps to home" ballad written and composed by G. Linley. pp. 5. *T. Swain: London*, [1837.] fol.
H. 1288. (31.)

— "I turn my steps to home;" ballad, written and composed by G. Linley, with an accompaniment for the Guitar by C. M. Sola. pp. 3. *T. Swain: London*, [1838.] fol. H. 1288. (30.)

— "I've given to him my heart;" ballad, written and composed by G. Linley. *London*, [1845.] fol. H. 1292. (22.)

— I wander alone. Song. [Begins: "They are no longer around me".] (Words by C. Churchill.) *London*, [1853.] fol.
H. 1295. (3.)

— "I was happy ere I loved you;" ballad, written and composed by G. Linley. *London*, [1849.] fol.
H. 1293. (23.)

— I was happy ere I lov'd you. Ballad. *London*, [1865.] fol.
H. 1299. a. (13.)

— I will come. A ballad [begins: "When the sun has sunk to rest"]. The poetry by Miss Pardoe. *London*, [1830?] fol.
H. 2835. b. (5.)

— I wish myself back in Old England, song [begins: "They talk'd of the birds and the spring time"], words founded on the poem "Miles Standish" by Longfellow. *London*, [1859.] fol. H. 1297. (32.)

— I wish myself back in Old England. [Song.] *London*, [1867.] fol. H. 1299. a. (27.)

— Ianthe, ballad, written by C. Jordan. [Begins: "And is it not enough".] *London*, [1856.] fol. H. 1297. (11.)

— Ida. (The words by J. Moultrie.) [Begins: "Forget thee".] *London*, [1852.] fol. H. 1295. (10.)

— Ida May, Ballad. [Begins: " 'Mid the rose-vines".] *London*, [1857.] fol. H. 1298. (35.)

LINLEY (GEORGE)

— In a soft summer twilight, ballad, written by W. Motherwell. *London*, [1856.] fol. **H. 1297. (19.)**

— In childhood's fair morning, ballad, poetry and music by G. Linley. *London*, [1856.] fol. **H. 1296. (20.)**

— In forest glade. Song ... music and words by G. Linley. New edition in a lower key. *London*, [1850?] fol. **H. 1288. a. (14.)**

— In vain, from Justice. *See infra*: [The Toy-Maker.]

— It is not so, ballad. *London*, [1854.] fol. **H. 1296. (21.)**

— It is not that I love thee. Ballad. *London*, [1851.] fol. **H. 1295. (9.)**

— "It is the song she used to sing," ballad, written and composed by G. Linley. *London*, [1858.] fol. **H. 1298. (30.)**

— It seemed to me a happy dream. [Song.] *See* SONGS. Songs ... from the White Slave. No. 2. [1853.] fol. **H. 2184. (18.)**

— It seemed to me a happy dream. [Song.] Words by J. E. Carpenter. *London*, [1858.] fol. *No. 2 of "Songs ... from the White Slave".* **H. 2828. b. (7.)**

— Jamie, ballad. [Begins: "Your love hath past away".] *London*, [1859.] fol. **H. 1297. (48.)**

— Janet. Ballad [begins: "Dear Janet"]. (Words by G. Linley Jun.) *London*, [1880.] fol. **H. 1783. p. (11.)**

— Jeanie Morrison. Ballad [begins: "I've wander'd east"] written by W. Motherwell. *London*, [1850.] fol. **H. 1294. (18.)**

— Jeanie Morrison. Ballad. (Words by W. Motherwell.) *London*, [1861.] fol. **H. 1299. (17.)**

— Jeannie, ballad, written and composed by G. Linley. [Begins: "You're not merry, now, Jeannie".] *London*, [1854.] fol. **H. 1296. (16.)**

— Jessie, [song,] written and composed by G. Linley. *London*, [1846.] fol. **H. 1293. (2.)**

— Jessie. Ballad. 〈Written and composed by G. Linley. New edition.〉 pp. 5. *Chappell: London*, [1855.] fol. **H. 1291. b. (23.)**

— Jessie Mowbray. Scotch Ballad. [Begins: "Gentle Jessie Mowbray".] *London*, [1853.] fol. **H. 1295. (2.)**

The Jolly Beggars

— Burns' celebrated poem, The Jolly Beggars, set to music. *London*, 1862. fol. **G. 399. a.**

— A Highland Lad my love was born. Song ... The words by Burns. *London*, [1862.] fol. **H. 1299. (32.)**

— I am a Son of Mars. Song. *London*, [1862.] fol. **H. 1299. (33.)**

— My Bonny Lass. Song. *London*, [1862.] fol. **H. 1299. (34.)**

— O! once I was young. Song. *London*, [1862.] fol. **H. 1299. (35.)**

— Sir Wisdom's a fool. Song. *London*, [1862.] fol. **H. 1299. (36.)**

— When I bade good bye to Phoebe. Song. *London*, [1862.] fol. **H. 1299. (37.)**

— Whistle o'er the lave o't. Song. *London*, [1862.] fol. **H. 1299. (38.)**

— With quaffing and laughing. Introducing chorus. *London*, [1862.] fol. **H. 1299. (39.)**

LINLEY (GEORGE)

— *See* COOTE (C.) *the Elder*. The Jolly Beggars Quadrille. [1862.] fol. **h. 2947. a. (20.)**

————————

— Karin, ballad. [Begins: "Karin is the flower of the young King's hall".] *London*, [1856.] fol. **H. 1298. (34.)**

— Kate O'Shane. Ballad ... written [and] composed ... by G. Linley. pp. 5. *F. C. Leader: London*, [1842.] fol. **H. 1288. (40.)**

— Kate O'Shane. Ballad, 〈music & words〉 by G. Linley. pp. 5. *Jefferys & Nelson: London*, [1843.] fol. **H. 1288. (39.)**

— [Another edition.] Kate O'Shane, *etc*. *C. Sheard & Co.: London*, [1889.] fol. *No. 7875 of the Musical Bouquet.* **H. 2345.**

— Kathleen is breathing a pray'r for thee. Ballad [begins: "Round my lone dwelling"], written and composed by G. Linley. *London*, [1850?] fol. **H. 1288. a. (20.)**

— Kathleen's reply to Terence's farewell [begins: "Now don't ye, because I am going"], poetry by Miss F. Lacy, arranged by G. Linley. *London*, [1849.] fol. **H. 1294. (15.)**

— Lady de Mey, ballad [written by E. H. Reed, begins: "In the old baron's hall"]. *London*, [1854.] fol. **H. 1297. (23.)**

— Ladye Jane. Ballad [begins: "The language of her dark blue eye"]. *London*, [1863.] fol. **H. 1299. a. (3.)**

— Lassie, ballad [begins: "Blithe is my heart"]. *London*, [1855.] fol. **H. 1296. (22.)**

— Lassie, are you waking. [Song, begins: "O Lassie".] *London*, [1860.] fol. **H. 1298. (48.)**

— The last of the fairies. Ballad (written by C. Churchill). *London*, [1851.] fol. **H. 1294. (10.)**

— Laugh and be glad, song ... The music & words by George Linley. pp. 6. *Cramer, Addison & Beale: London*, [1837.] fol. *The titlepage bears a MS. dedication in the composer's autograph.* **H. 1291. b. (9.)**

— Laurette, ballad, [begins: "The sweet spring time is coming,"] music and words by G. Linley. *London*, [1855.] fol. **H. 1296. (23.)**

— Laurette. [Song.] *London*, [1855.] fol. *No. 1 of "G. Linley's Book of Ballads".* **H. 1299. a. (35.)**

— Leila; or, The Bridal Dance. Duetto for two sopranos [begins: "Crown'd with white roses"], music and words by G. Linley. *London*, [1845.] fol. **H. 1292. (13.)**

— Let me wander where I will. Ballad. (Written by G. Turnbull.) *London*, [1876.] fol. **H. 1299. b. (19.)**

— Let us be gay. *See infra*: [The Queen and the Cardinal.]

— The levantine Boatman, by Sir E. B. Lytton. *London*, [1851.] fol. **H. 1294. (3.)**

— Life's early friends [song, begins: "No more in hall or bower"]. *London*, [1855.] fol. **H. 1296. (24.)**

— Light as falling snow. Ballad. *London*, [1861.] fol. **H. 1299. (11.)**

— Light as falling Snow, ballad ... in the opera Queen Topaze ... the words by G. Linley. Composed by Victor Massé [or rather, by George Linley]. pp. 5. [1861?] fol. *See* MASSÉ (Félix M.) [*Doubtful and Supposititious Works.*] **H. 1650. ii. (4.)**

— Light as falling snow ... for the Pianoforte. [1861.] fol. *See* RICHARDS (H. B.) **h. 760. f. (9.)**

LINLEY (George)

— The light of the valley, or The Maid of Kilkenny [song, begins: "Down by the waters"] written by E. A. Reed. *London*, [1850.] fol. **H. 1294. (21.)**

— Like a dream of my childhood. Ballad ... arranged with an accompaniment for the Guitar ... by T. J. Dipple. *London*, [1840?] fol. **H. 2830. a. (52.)**

— Like leaves in the autumn. Ballad. *London*, [1840?] fol. **H. 2835. c. (36.)**

— Like yon clear and tranquil River, ballad, *etc.* ⟨Music and words by G. Linley.⟩ pp. 4. *T. Prowse, at C. Nicholson's Flute Manufactory: London*, [c. 1840.] fol. **H. 1291. b. (10.)**

— Lilly. [Song, begins: "Bird of the Mountain".] *London*, [1863.] fol **H. 1299. a. (6.)**

— Liska, ballad ... Written & composed by G. Linley. pp. 5. *Duff & Hodgson: London*, [1846.] fol. **H. 1660. n. (3.)**

— Little Dorrit's Vigil. [Song.] Written by John Barnes. [In G.] [*Cramer, Beale & Chappell: London*, 1855?] fol. *Imperfect; wanting the titlepage.* **H. 1652. k. (11.)**

— Little Dorrit's Vigil, *etc.* [Song. In E flat.] *Cramer, Beale & Chappell: London*, [1856.] fol. **H. 1298. (8.)**

— Little Nell, Ballad, the words by Miss Charlotte Young, *etc. Cramer, Beale & Co.: London*, [1857?] fol. **H. 1652. k. (12.)**

— Little Nell. *See* ZOTTI (C.) Six favorite melodies, *etc.* No. 2. [1865.] fol. **h. 3031. a. (4.)**

— Little Nell. Waltz.—On Linley's song.—[By] D. Godfrey. [Orchestral parts.] *See* CHAPPELL AND Co. Popular Quadrilles, *etc.* No. 68. [1872.] 8°. **e. 249.**

— Little Sophy, ballad from the novel "What will he do with it" [begins: "Oh! darling let me see thee smile"], written [and] composed by G. Linley. *London*, [1859.] fol. **H. 1298. (41.)**

— The London Orpheonist. A collection of part songs ... edited by G. Linley. No. 1. *London*, 1861. 8°. *Imperfect; wanting all the other no.* **E. 600. h. (27.)**

— The Lone Hills of Arvon. [Song, begins: "The feuds are at rest"], written by Mrs. Crawford. *London*, [1850?] fol. **H. 1288. a. (16.)**

— "Lord Albert to the tournay's gone;" ballad, written and composed by G. Linley. pp. 6. *S. Chappell: London*, [1834.] fol. **H. 1288. (24.)**

— Lorelei, Romance [begins: "A maiden sits on the beetling rock"] written by G. Linley. *London*, [1857.] fol. **H. 1298. (2.)**

— "Love, art thou waking." Linley's ... serenade, arranged for the guitar by T. J. Dipple. *London*, [1848.] fol. **H. 1293. (20.)**

— Love! art thou waking, or dreaming of me? Song, *etc.* ⟨Written & composed by G. Linley. Second edition.⟩ pp. 5. *John Alvey Turner: London*, [c. 1855.] fol. **H. 1980. tt. (36.)**

— Love dwells in sunshine. [Song.] *London*, [1855.] fol. **H. 1296. (25.)**

— Lute of the greenwood bower ... written by Christabel. *London*, [1851.] fol. **H. 1294. (8.)**

— Maid of Athens. [Song.] The poetry by Lord Byron. *London*, [1854.] fol. **H. 1297. (26.)**

— Maiden of the Rhine. Song [begins: "Where the ripe"]. *London*, [1876.] fol. **H. 1299. b. (18.)**

— Maidens young and tender, ballad ... Written and arranged by G. Linley. pp. 5. *Goulding & D'Almaine, etc.: London*, [c. 1830.] fol. **H. 1980. o. (14.)**

LINLEY (George)

— Marion ... [Song, begins: "My own, my true-lov'd Marion".] (Written by R. Gilfillan.) *London*, [1851.] fol. **H. 1294. (12.)**

— Marion Lee. Ballad [begins: "The snow-white plume"]. *London*, [1862.] fol. **H. 1299. a. (1.)**

— Marion May. (Song. Words by H. H. Paul.) *London*, [1853.] fol. **H. 1295. (29.)**

— Mary Dunbar, Song. [Begins: "O! see yon green mountain".] *London*, [1858.] fol. **H. 1298. (50.)**

— "Mary, fairest queen of beauty." Chatelar's song; the words and music by G. Linley. *London*, [1844.] fol. **H. 1292. (2.)**

— "Mary, fairest queen of beauty" ... arranged for the guitar by T. J. Dipple. *London*, [1848.] fol. **H. 1293. (21.)**

— The matin call. [Song, begins: "Ah! is it not the matin bell".] *London*, [1854.] fol. **H. 1296. (26.)**

— The May-blossom trees, Ballad. [Begins: "Oh! those May-blossom trees".] *London*, [1858.] fol. **H. 1298. (46.)**

— Meet me in the Piazetta. *See* infra: Six Venetian Melodies. No. 5.

— The merry castanet. Song written by Miss Pardoe [begins: "At twilight's shade"]. *London*, [1860.] fol. **H. 1298. (5.)**

— The Merry Days of England, a Conservative Song ... written by Thomas Blake, *etc.* pp. 7. *Cramer, Addison & Beale: London*, [1855?] fol. **H. 1653. f. (3.)**

— The Merry rolling Drum ... [Song.] Music & words by George Linley, *etc.* pp. 5. *George & Manby: London*, [c. 1835.] fol. **H. 1660. m. (22.)**

— The merry woodland Maid. [Song, begins: "I'm the merry woodland Maid.] *London*, [1851.] fol. **H. 1294. (11.)**

— Metrical annals of the Kings and Queens of England, from the time of the Conquest to the reign of Victoria. The words written and the music arranged and composed by George Linley. *Addison, Hollier and Lucas: London*, 1860. fol. **G. 399.**

— [Another copy.] **R. M. 13. f. 12.**

— A Midsummer Day's Ramble. Duet [begins: "Forth let us stray"]. (Words by G. Linley Junᵣ.) *London*, [1861.] fol. **H. 1299. (10.)**

— Mine. Ballad [begins: "O how my heart is beating"]. *London*, [1860.] fol. **H. 1298. (22.)**

— Minnie [song, begins: "When the sun is high"]. *London*, [1854.] fol. **H. 1296. (28.)**

— Minnie. [Song.] *London*, [1855.] fol. **H. 1296. (27.)**

— Minnie. *See* JULLIEN (L. A.) AND Co. Jullien & Co.'s collection of English ballads. No. 4. [1855.] fol. **H. 2828. b. (3.)**

— [Minnie.] *See* BOURNE (J. H.) Grand Fantasia ... sur la mélodie "Minnie". [1876.] fol. **h. 1482. d. (47.)**

— The Minstrel Knight. Ballad [begins: " 'Neath a Moorish tower"]. *London*, [1840?] fol. **H. 2815. f. (18.)**

— Mirth. Song. [Begins: "Thro' the maze of life".] *London*, [1850.] fol. **H. 1295. (8.)**

— Mona Macree; [song,] written and composed by G. Linley. *London*, [1847.] fol. **H. 1293. (14.)**

— The monarch of the main, the song of the British sailor [begins: "A ship, a ship"], words by E. Pinkerton. *London*, [1854.] fol. **H. 1297. (22.)**

LINKEY (George)

— Moonlight, Duet. Soprano and Tenor, written and composed by G. Linley. *London*, [1857.] fol. **H. 1298. (37.)**

— "Moonlight is sleeping o'er tree and tower;" [song,] written and composed by G. Linley. pp. 5. *S. Chappell: London*, [1834.] fol. **H. 1288. (32.)**

— "Morning! breathe thy balm around me." Ballad (written and composed by G. Linley). *London*, [1847.] fol. **H. 1293. (15.)**

— Mother dear. [Song.] *London*, [1873.] fol. *Another edition of "The Dying Child".* **H. 1299. b. (7.)**

— The Mountain Daisy ... [Song.] Written & composed by G. Linley. ⟨Third edition.⟩ pp. 5. *Jullien & C⁰: London*, [c. 1855.] fol. **H. 1650. qq. (24.)**

— [The Mountain Daisy.] *See* WALLACE (William V.) Souvenir de Jetty Treffz. The Mountain Daisy, ballad ... arranged for the piano forte, by W. V. Wallace. [1851.] fol. **h. 62. a. (17.)**

— The Mountain Wanderer. Song [begins: "I wander"]. *London*, [1865.] fol. **H. 1299. a. (17.)**

— Muriel, ballad from "John Halifax, gentleman," *etc.* [Begins: "By the green and waving elm tree".] *London*, [1859.] fol. **H. 1298. (20.)**

— My bonny lass. *See* supra: [The Jolly Beggars.]

— My gentle bride. Ballad. *London*, [1835?] fol. **H. 2831. j. (3.)**

— My hunter love! [Song, begins: "Oh! who is so bold".] *London*, [1855.] fol. **H. 1296. (30.)**

— My love for thee, ballad, written and composed by G. Linley. *London*, [1854.] fol. **H. 1296. (31.)**

— My Love lies slain on yonder Plain. Song. [Words and music by G. Linley.] *In:* The Musical Bijou ... for MDCCCXLVII. p. 23. [1847.] fol. **H. 2330.**

— My Mary's no more, ballad, the poetry by Burns. pp. 5. *Cramer, Beale & C⁰: London*, [1850.] fol. **H. 1654. qq. (32.)**

— My Mary's no more. Ballad. The poetry by Burns. *London*, [1873.] fol. **H. 1299. b. (11.)**

— My own happy home. Ballad [begins: "I have roamed"] ... The words by T. Blake. *London*, [1868.] fol. **H. 1299. a. (29.)**

— [A reissue.] My own happy Home, Ballad, *etc. Ashdown & Parry: London*, [c. 1870.] fol. **H. 1980. gg. (21.)**

— My Spirit pines for thee, romanza, written and composed by George Linley. pp. 5. *C. Lonsdale: London*, [1854?] fol. **H. 1291. b. (22.)**

— My sweetest of dreams, ballad [begins: "The last hope is shaken"]. *London*, [1855.] fol. **H. 1296. (32.)**

— My sweetest of dreams, Ballad. *London*, [1857.] fol. **H. 1298. (60.)**

— "Night around our steps is falling." Duettino for two voices, written and composed by G. Linley. pp. 7. *T. Swain: London*, [1838.] fol. **H. 1288. (23.)**

— The Night before the Bridal, ballad, written by J. E. Carpenter. pp. 5. *Jefferys & C⁰: London*, [c. 1845.] fol. **H. 1980. nn. (8.)**

— Night is closing, ballad ... written and composed by G. Linley. *London*, [1854.] fol. **H. 1296. (33.)**

— Night on the Waters. Barcarolle [begins: "Placid and calmly"]. *London*, [1860.] fol. **H. 1298. (53.)**

LINKEY (George)

— None other love than thine. Romance [begins: "Thou art wand'ring with me still"] written and composed by G. Linley. *London*, [1859.] fol. **H. 1297. (35.)**

— A Noonday Dream. Song [begins: "Winds that murmur"]. *London*, [1864.] fol. **H. 1299. a. (11.)**

— "Not in thy Sunshine;" ballad, the poetry and music by G. Linley. *London*, [1846.] fol. **H. 1293. (5.)**

— "Now at moonlight's fairy hour;" duet, the poetry by Mrs. Radcliffe. *London*, [1844.] fol. **H. 1292. (8.)**

— Now at Moonlight's Fairy Hour. Duet. The Poetry by Mrs. Radcliffe, *etc. See* DUETS. Vocal Duets, *etc.* No. 119. [1865? *etc.*] fol. **H. 2259.**

— Nursery Rhymes of England. Adapted to familiar tunes. pp. 52. *Brewer & Co.: London*, [1860.] 8°. **E. 373. a.**

— Nursery Rhymes of England. Selected and adapted to familiar tunes by George Linley. pp. 51. *F. Pitman Hart & C⁰: London*, [c. 1920.] 8°. **E. 373. d. (4.)**

— Nursery Rhymes of England. Selected and adapted to familiar tunes by George Linley. pp. 51. *F. Pitman Hart & Co.: London*, [c. 1925.] 8°. **E. 373. d. (3.)**

— Fifty Nursery Songs and Rhymes. Adapted to familiar Tunes by G. Linley. Second Series. *Metzler & Co.: London*, [1864.] 8°. **E. 373.**

— O! Days of summer bloom. Ballad. *London*, [1863.] fol. **H. 1299. a. (4.)**

— Oh! dont tease me Donald now. Ballad written by W. H. Bellamy. *London*, [1853.] fol. **H. 1295. (4.)**

— Oh! don't tease me, Donald, now. Ballad. *London*, [1866.] fol. **H. 1299. a. (23.)**

— O Fair and glowing Star! (Ach wie wärs möglich dann.) Volkslied. The English words & adaption by G. Linley. *London*, [1865.] fol. **H. 1299. a. (19.)**

— Oh! follow me. Garibaldi's song [begins: "The night's still hours are wearing fast away"]. Written and composed by G. Linley. *London*, [1860.] fol. **H. 1298. (61.)**

— "Oh! for the days of Chivalry;" romance, written and composed by G. Linley. *London*, [1845.] fol. **H. 1292. (20.)**

— Oh! for the gay & joyous dance. *See* infra: Six Venetian Melodies. No. 4.

— Oh! gay joyous dance. *See* infra: [The Toy-Maker.]

— Oh! had my fate been joined with thine. The poetry by Lord Byron. *London*, [1854.] fol. **H. 1297. (27.)**

— Oh! how sweet through woods to rove ... written and adapted by G. Linley. *London*, [1857.] fol. **H. 1298. (43.)**

— Oh if she had never known him, ballad, written & composed by George Linley. pp. 5. *Wood & Com⁰: Edinburgh; Cramer, Addison & Beale: London*, [c. 1835.] fol. **H. 1291. b. (11.)**

— Oh! is it thus we part, ballad. *London*, [1858.] fol. **H. 1298. (45.)**

— O! lone and languid Flow'r, ballad, the poetry written by Mʳˢ Abdy. pp. 4. *Chappell: London*, [1840.] fol. **H. 1291. b. (12.)**

— O Love. *See* infra: [The Toy-Maker.]

— O lov'd Italia. Duet ... from Verdi's Opera 'La Traviata', written and arranged by G. Linley. *See* DUETS. Vocal Duets, *etc.* No. 87. [1865?] fol. **H. 2259.**

— O! once I was young. *See* supra: [The Jolly Beggars.]

LINLEY (GEORGE)

— O say you love me truly. Ballad. *London*, [1873.] fol.
H. 1299. b. (9.)

— Oh! short and few those sunny hours. Song. *London*, [1862.] fol.
H. 1299. (27.)

— "Oh! thou fair and verdant meadow;" ballad, the poetry and music by G. Linley. pp. 5. *C. Lonsdale: London*, [1843.] fol.
H. 1288. (45.)

— Oh! where are they, the kind and true? ... Written & composed ... by George Linley. pp. 5. *Chappell: London*, [c. 1840.] fol.
The English Ballad Singer. no. 1. **H. 2401. c. (1.)**

— Oh! why should we think of the future. Ballad ... by E. H. Reed. *London*, [1850.] fol. **H. 1294. (25.)**

— Oh! why should we think of the future ... written by E. H. Reed. *London*, [1851.] fol. **H. 1294. (13.)**

— Oh! yes, thy love is dead ... Song. *Edinburgh*, [1835?] fol.
H. 2830. a. (53.)

— O'Connor's fair child. Irish ballad, [written and composed] by G. Linley. pp. 7. *Fred. C. Leader: London*, [1843.] fol.
H. 1288. (41.)

— O'er the mountains. Duet. (Words by E. Ellison.) *London*, [1853.] fol. **H. 1295. (24.)**

— O'er the sparkling snow (sledge song) written and composed by G. Linley. [Begins: "Swiftly now we speed along".] *London*, [1859.] fol. **H. 1298. (58.)**

— Old Friends at Home ... [Song.] Written by George Linley. [In fact an arrangement of "The Old Folks at Home" by Stephen C. Foster.] pp. 5. *Jullien & Cº: London*, [1854.] fol.
H. 1296. (34.)

— Old Friends at home. *See* JULLIEN (L. A.) AND CO. Jullien & Co's collection of English ballads. No. 29. [1855.] fol.
H. 2828. b. (3.)

— The old guard, (la vieille garde,) music and English words [beginning: "The eagle soars above"] by G. Linley. The French words [beginning: "Voyez notre bannière"] by H. Drayton. *London*, [1855.] fol. **H. 1296. (35.)**

— "The old man's dream;" a ballad, ⟨poetry and music⟩ by G. Linley. pp. 5. *F. C. Leader: London*, [1842.] fol.
H. 1288. (42.)

— On the past look not with sorrow, ballad. *London*, [1855.] fol.
H. 1296. (36.)

— On the past look not with sorrow. Ballad, written and composed by G. Linley. *London*, [1857.] fol.
H. 1298. (49.)

— Once I lov'd thee, ballad. *London*, [1855.] fol.
H. 1296. (37.)

— One of those dear dreams. Song. *London*, [1871.] fol.
H. 1299. b. (2.)

— One who loved but thee, the poetry and music by G. Linley. *London*, [1856.] fol. **H. 1297. (46.)**

— Only for thee. Romance. (Words by G. Linley the Younger.) *London*, [1861.] fol. **H. 1299. (4.)**

— Only for thee. Romance. (Written by G. Linley the younger.) *London*, [1872.] fol. **H. 1299. b. (6.)**

— Only thee. Ballad [begins: "As fades the dew"]. *London*, [1865.] fol. **H. 1299. a. (20.)**

— The open window, the poetry by Longfellow. [Begins: "The old house by the lindens".] *London*, [1855.] fol.
H. 1297. (17.)

LINLEY (GEORGE)

— [Opposite Neighbours.] Pit-pat, [song] in H. Paul's Vaudeville "Opposite neighbours" [begins: "A beau I had"]. *London*, [1855.] fol. **H. 1297. (21.)**

— The orphan wanderer, song, written and composed by G. Linley. [Begins: "O'er moorland and mountain".] *London*, [1856.] fol. **H. 1296. (39.)**

— The orphan's prayer. [Duet, begins: "Let our grateful pray'rs ascend".] *London*, [1855.] fol. **H. 1296. (38.)**

— Our ain burn side, Scotch song (written by R. Gilfillan). [Begins: "Well I mind the days".] *London*, [1854.] fol.
H. 1297. (8.)

— The Over crafty Fox. Junior Unison Song, adapted by G. Linley from "Old Pictures in New Frames". [1894.] *See* MacNaught (W. G.) Novello's School Songs. Book XXVIII. 1892, *etc.* 8°. **F. 280. d.**

— Over the blue lagoon, duet, written and composed by G. Linley. *London*, [1858.] fol. **H. 1298. (51.)**

— Over the Wave. *See infra*: Six Venetian Melodies. No. 6.

— Past ten o'clock. *See infra*: [The Toy-Maker.]

— [Une Pastorale.] *See* SMALLWOOD (W.) Une Pastorale ... for the Pianoforte. [1880.] fol. **h. 1412. k. (25.)**

— Patrick, Irish ballad. *London*, [1854.] fol. **H. 1296. (40.)**

— "Patrick has left me;" ballad, written and composed by G. Linley. *London*, [1844.] fol. **H. 1292. (11.)**

— Pauline. Ballad (written by E. H. Reed). [Begins: "I press thy gentle hand in mine".] *London*, [1852.] fol. **H. 1295. (12.)**

— The peasant of Granada [song, begins: "By the flow'ry mountain"]. *London*, [1854.] fol. **H. 1296. (41.)**

— Poor Nelly. Ballad written by E. H. Reed. [Begins: "She stood upon the mountain's brow".] *London*, [1852.] fol.
H. 1295. (11.)

— The Prince of our brave land. The new national hymn [begins: "Heaven crown his path"]. *London*, [1863.] fol.
H. 1299. a. (5.)

— [The Queen and the Cardinal.] Let us be gay. A favorite Song in the Musical Drama of The Queen and the Cardinal, written and composed by G. Linley. *Chappell: London*, [1835?] fol. **H. 1650. p. (2.)**

— The Reaper, written and composed by G. Linley. *London*, [1848.] fol. **H. 1293. (19.)**

— The Red Rover. [Song, begins: "Our sails are set"] ... written & composed by G. Linley. *London*, [1850?] fol.
H. 1288. a. (19.)

— The Red Rover, *etc.* [Song.] pp. 5. *Cramer, Beale & Cº: London*, [1855?] fol. **H. 1653. f. (4.)**

— Regret [song, begins: "I think of thee with pain"], written and composed by G. Linley. *London*, [1858.] fol.
H. 1298. (28.)

— Regret ... melody ... arranged for the piano forte by B. Richards. *London*, [1859.] fol. **h. 762. b. (41.)**

— Riflemen form. [Song, begins: "There is a sound of thunder afar".] *London*, [1859.] fol. **H. 1298. (62.)**

— The ring and the maiden, legendary ballad. [Begins: "There sits a lovely maiden".] *London*, [1854.] fol. **H. 1296. (42.)**

— The River ran between them. Ballad. (Words by J. S. Le Fanu.) *London*, [1868.] fol. **H. 1299. a. (32.)**

— "River, so bright and flowing;" ballad, written and arranged by G. Linley. *London*, [1845.] fol. **H. 1292. (21.)**

LINLEY (George)

— Rixa ... Song. [Begins: "The harp and gay tambour".] *London*, [1857.] fol.   **H. 1298. (59.)**

— Rixa. [Song.] pp. 4. *J. Curwen & Sons: London*, [1902.] 8°. [*Choruses for equal Voices. no.* 795.]   **E. 861.**

— The Rolling Drum. *See* infra: [The Toy-Maker.]

— The rose of the Alps [song, begins: " 'Mong the beauteous flow'rs I love"], arranged and adapted to English words by G. Linley. *London*, [1859.] fol.   **H. 1298. (36.)**

— The Rose of the Alps. [Song.] *J. Curwen & Sons: London*, [1903.] 8°. *Unison Songs, No.* 80.   **E. 812.**

— Round our own Fireside. [Song. Words and music by G. Linley.] *In:* The Musical Bijou ... for MDCCCXXXIII. pp. 22–26. [1833.] 4°.   **F. 149.**

— Row me o'er the bonnie stream [duet], written and arranged by G. Linley. *London*, [1860.] fol.   **H. 1298. (54.)**

— Sacred songs and hymns, selected ... adapted and arranged with accompaniment for Piano Forte or Harmonium. 6 no. *London*, 1859. fol.   **H. 1187. a. (21.)**

— "Sad solitary star;" ballad, written and composed by G. Linley. *London*, [1846.] fol.   **H. 1293. (7.)**

— The Saucy Milkmaid. Song [begins: "The morn was glowing"]. *London*, [1866.] fol.   **H. 1299. a. (26.)**

— Say farewell and go. [Song, begins: "Look into my face, dear".] *London*, [1859.] fol.   **H. 1298. (21.)**

— The Scotch Emigrant. [Begins: "Oh fare thee well, my bonnie Jean".] *London*, [1853.] fol.   **H. 1295. (30.)**

— The sea spirit. Cavatina written by W. H. Bellamy. [Begins: "From the depths of the ocean".] *London*, [1853.] fol.   **H. 1295. (26.)**

— The seasons of love. Song [begins: "I will love thee in the spring time"], written by J. E. Carpenter, *etc. London*, [1859.] fol.   **H. 1298. (33.)**

— She dreams of the past, [song] written by E. Ellison. *London*, [1854.] fol.   **H. 1297. (4.)**

— She dwells among the mountains, ballad, the words by F. Enoch. *London*, [1853.] fol.   **H. 1295. (36.)**

— She is lost to us now. Ballad. *London*, [1853.] fol.   **H. 1295. (27.)**

— She is lost to us now, ballad. *London*, [1854.] fol.   **H. 1296. (43.)**

— She told him when they parted. Ballad ... the music and words by George Linley. *London*, [1850?] fol.   **H. 2818. e. (12.)**

— Shepherd boy, ballad. (Written by F. Enoch.) *London*, [1855.] fol.   **H. 1297. (7.)**

— G. Linley's first Singing book. *London*, [1852.] fol.   **F. 182.**

— Sir Wisdom's a fool. *See* supra: [The Jolly Beggars.]

— Sister lov'd, song, written & composed by George Linley. pp. 5. *At Chappell's Musical Circulating Library: London*, [1839.] fol.   **H. 1291. b. (13.)**

— The Slave's Appeal. [Song, begins: "From my home".] *See* SONGS. Songs ... from the White Slave. No. 3. [1853.] fol.   **H. 2184. (18.)**

— The Slave's Appeal. Words by J. E. Carpenter. *London*, [1858.] fol. *No.* 3 *of "Songs, &c. from the White Slave".*   **H. 2828. b. (8.)**

LINLEY (George)

— The Snow is falling fast, Jamie. Ballad. *London*, 1850. fol.   **H. 1294. (23.)**

— The Snow is falling fast, Jamie. Ballad. *London*, [1866.] fol.   **H. 1299. a. (24.)**

— The soft and gentle twilight, ballad [begins: "I love the gentle twilight"]. The words by C. Jordan. *London*, [1856.] fol.   **H. 1297. (12.)**

— Soft winds are breathing. [Song.] *London*, [1857.] fol.   **H. 1298. (55.)**

— The soldier's widow, written by J. S. B. Monsell. [Begins: "She is crush'd and broken hearted".] *London*, [1855.] fol.   **H. 1297. (18.)**

— Some one to love; a song, written and composed by G. Linley. pp. 5. *Fred. C. Leader: London*, [1843.] fol.   **H. 1288. (44.)**

— Song of the roving gypsey. *London*, [1830?] fol.   **G. 809. b. (18.)**

— Song of the wood nymph [begins: "Where the crystal waters flow"], written and composed by G. Linley. *London*, [1844.] fol.   **H. 1292. (10.)**

— Songs of Fashionable Life, the words by T. H. Baily. No. 1–6. *London*, [1831–4.] fol.   **H. 1291. (2.)**

— Songs of the camp. *London*, 1831. fol.   **I. 277.**

— Songs of the Trobadore; words and music by G. Linley. *London*, [1828?] fol.   **H. 1291. (1.)**

— The soul of music's gone [song, begins: "Oh 'tis not joy now to remember"], written and adapted by G. Linley. *London*, [1859.] fol.   **H. 1298. (47.)**

— "Spirit of Air." Cavatina; the poetry by W. H. Bellamy. *London*, [1844.] fol.   **H. 1292. (4.)**

— Spirit of Air, cavatina, the poetry written by W. H. Bellamy. pp. 7. *Leader & Cock: London*, [c. 1855.] fol.   **H. 1650. ii. (2.)**

— Spirit of my dream! written and composed by G. Linley. [Begins: "Ever thine".] *London*, [1859.] fol.   **H. 1298. (10.)**

— The Spirit of the Lake. [Song.] pp. 7. *Addison & Hollier: London*, [1854.] fol.   **H. 1291. b. (20.)**

— Spring time returning. Ballad, written and composed by G. Linley. *London*, [1882.] fol.   **H. 1288. a. (27.)**

— The Star and the Water-Lily, ballad [begins: "The Sun stepped down"]. (Words by O. W. Holmes.) *London*, [1861.] fol.   **H. 1299. (12.)**

— Star of my life, aria with English and German words [begins: "Fast from my sight" and "Hin schwindet Englands weiser Felsen Strand"]. German words by A. Marschan. *London*, [1855.] fol.   **H. 1296. (44.)**

— Starlight is glowing. [Song, begins: "Inez dearest".] *London*, [1858.] fol.   **H. 1298. (26.)**

— Stars of the Summer Night, [song,] written by H. W. Longfellow. pp. 5. *Brewer & Cº: London*, [c. 1860.] fol.   **H. 1980. oo. (10.)**

— The Stranger's Bride, ballad ... Written & composed by George Linley, *etc.* (Second edition.) pp. 5. *J. Duff: London*, [c. 1835.] fol.   **H. 1601. kk. (8.)**

— The stranger's bride, ballad, written and composed by G. Linley [begins: "They plac'd her hand in his"], arranged for the ... Guitar ... by F. Pelzer. *London*, [1858.] fol.   **H. 1771. o. (20.)**

LINLEY (George)

— Such an Outrage n'er was heard of, song ... in the opera Queen Topaze ... the words by George Linley, the music by Victor Massé [probably composed or arranged by George Linley]. pp. 8. [1861.] fol. *See* MASSÉ (Félix M.) [*Doubtful and Supposititious Works.*]   **H. 620. a. (10.)**

— A summer revel [song, begins: "Thro' the trembling aspens"], written & composed by G. Linley. *London,* [1858.] fol.   **H. 1297. (36.)**

— Summer Time is pleasant. *See* infra: Six Venetian Melodies. No. 1.

— The Sunbeam, the Dewdrop, and the Rose. Ballad [begins: "Trembling on a rose's bosom"]. (Words by G. Linley Junᵣ.) *London,* [1861.] fol.   **H. 1299. (14.)**

— The sunshine will return, ballad, [begins: "The light of hope"] words by H. Nokes. *London,* [1856.] fol.   **H. 1297. (20.)**

— The Sunshine will return. (The words by H. Nokes.) *London,* [1864.] fol.   **H. 1299. a. (12.)**

— The Swede's return. Duettino [begins: "Now the daylight fast is fading"]. *London,* [1853.] fol.   **H. 1295. (7.)**

— Sweet bird of the South. Ballad (written by E. H. Reed). *London,* [1853.] fol.   **H. 1295. (5.)**

— "Sweet haunt of youth;" song, written and composed by G. Linley. pp. 6. *Chappell: London,* [1837.] fol.   **H. 1288. (26.)**

— "Sweet Hawthorn Den;" ballad, written and composed by G. Linley. *London,* [1845.] fol.   **H. 1292. (18.)**

— "Sweet hope, like a bird;" ballad, written and composed by G. Linley. *London,* [1846.] fol.   **H. 1293. (11.)**

— Sweet rose bud of Glennarra! ballad, written and composed by G. Linley. *London,* [1859.] fol.   **H. 1298. (57.)**

— "Sweet vale of Chamouni;" song, written and composed by G. Linley. *London,* [1846.] fol.   **H. 1293. (3.)**

— Sweet was the Dream. [Song.] Written and adapted by G. Linley. pp. 5. *R. Mills: London,* [1864.] fol.   **H. 1299. a. (8.)**

— Sweet was the Dream. Written and adapted by George Linley. ⟨The symphonies & accompaniment by Sigᵣ Muratori.⟩ *London,* [c. 1865.] fol. *Imperfect; wanting page* 5.   **H. 1650. qq. (26.)**

— Swifter far than Summer's flight. (Poetry by P. B. Shelley.) *London,* [1852.] fol.   **H. 1295. (17.)**

— The Swiss Girl. [Song.] *London,* [1845?] fol.   **H. 2831. j. (4.)**

— The Swiss Girl. [P. F. solo and duet.] *See* SMALLWOOD (W.) Home Treasures, *etc.* No. 70. [1872, *etc.*] fol.   **h. 1412. o.**

— The Swiss Girl. [P. F. solo and duet.] *See* SMALLWOOD (W.) Little Buds, *etc.* No. 54. [1874, *etc.*] fol.   **h. 1412. p.**

— [The Swiss Girl.] *See* OSBORNE (George A.) The Swiss Girl [by G. Linley], arranged as a fantasia for the piano forte. [1852.] fol.   **h. 62. s. (18.)**

— The Swiss peasant [song], written by Mrs. Jennings. [Begins: "Go, revel ye gay ones".] *London,* [1854.] fol.   **H. 1297. (10.)**

— "Take a hint from me;" ballad, written and arranged [from F. A. Boieldieu's air "Au clair de la lune"] by G. Linley. *Leeds,* [1845.] fol.   **H. 1292. (15.)**

— Take back the gems you gave me ... Ballad by the author of "We've lived & loved together". (Music by G. Linley.) *London,* [1845?] fol.   **H. 1288. a. (26.)**

LINLEY (George)

— Take back the Gems you gave me, *etc. C. Sheard & Co.: London,* [1889.] fol. *No.* 7895 *of the Musical Bouquet.*   **H. 2345.**

— That sweet song, ballad. [Begins: "Yes in days of happy childhood".] *London,* [1854.] fol.   **H. 1296. (45.)**

— There are dreams that cannot die, [song, begins: "Often I think of the beautiful town"] words by Longfellow. *London,* [1859.] fol.   **H. 1298. (39.)**

— "There is a charm in sadness; [song,] written by J. W. Lake. *London,* [1845.] fol.   **H. 1293. (1.)**

— There's a fairy abroad. Ballad (the words by E. Ellison). *London,* [1855?] fol.   **H. 1288. a. (24.)**

— There's Sunshine yet for Charlie, Jacobite song, written and composed by George Linley. pp. 5. *A. W. Hammond: London,* [c. 1855.] fol. *The titlepage bears a MS. dedication in the composer's autograph.*   **H. 1291. b. (14.)**

— Thérèse. [Begins: "When to grief they left me".] *London,* [1852.] fol.   **H. 1295. (16.)**

— They are not all Joy's Roses, Ballad, written, composed ... by ... G. Linley. pp. 5. *Chappell: London,* [1840.] fol.   **H. 1980. bb. (16.)**

— "They are weeping, they are weeping," duet, the poetry by J. E. Carpenter. pp. 5. *C. Lonsdale: London,* [1843.] fol.   **H. 1288. (46.)**

— "They have given thee to another;" a ballad, written and composed by G. Linley. pp. 5. *J. B. Cramer, Addison & Beale: London,* [1830.] fol.   **H. 1288. (21.)**

— They have given thee to another, *etc. C. Sheard & Co.: London,* [1889.] fol. *No.* 7867 *of the Musical Bouquet.*   **H. 2345.**

— "They parted;" a ballad, the words by Lady H. D'Orsay. pp. 5. *R. Mills: London,* [1840.] fol.   **H. 1288. (28.)**

— Think of me. Ballad. Poetry and Music by G. Linley. *London,* [1860.] fol.   **H. 1297. (33.)**

— Think of me never more. Ballad. *London,* [1853.] fol.   **H. 1295. (28.)**

— "Think on me," written by T. Blake. *London,* [1853.] fol.   **H. 1295. (31.)**

— "Thou art dear as my fancy can make thee;" ballad, written and composed by G. Linley. pp. 5. *Dufour: London,* [1843.] fol.   **H. 1288. (47.)**

— Thou art gone from my gaze. *See* infra: [Thy spirit of love keeps a watch over me.]

— Thou art near me again! Ballad. *London,* [1852.] fol.   **H. 1295. (13.)**

— Thou com'st in the visions of the night. Ballad (words & music) by G. Linley. *London,* [1845?] fol.   **H. 1288. a. (22.)**

— Thou wilt remember me. Ballad. *London,* [1853.] fol.   **H. 1295. (6.)**

— Tho' lost to sight to mem'ry dear, words and music by G. Linley. *London,* [1855.] fol.   **H. 1296. (46.)**

— Though the day of my destiny's over. Poetry by Lord Byron. *London,* [1854.] fol.   **H. 1297. (28.)**

— The Three Callers, [song] written ... by Charles Swain. pp. 7. *Addison & Hollier: London,* [1851?] fol. [*Swain's English Melodies. no.* 4.]   **H. 2184. i.**

LINLEY (George)

— "Through the emerald woods;" a song, written and partly composed by G. Linley. pp. 6. *S. Chappell: London*, [1833.] fol.   **H. 1288. (20.)**

— Thy mem'ry comes like some sweet dream, ballad ... written and composed by G. Linley. *London*, [1859.] fol.   **H. 1297. (37.)**

— Thy Mem'ry comes like some sweet dream. *See* FAVARGER (R.) Thy Mem'ry ... morceau de salon, *etc.* [1861.] fol.   **h. 1282. b. (17.)**

— Thy name is ever on my lips, ballad, written and composed by G. Linley. [Begins: "Ask of the breeze".] *London*, [1858.] fol.   **H. 1298. (3.)**

Thy spirit of love keeps a watch over me

— Thou art gone from my gaze. Ballad. *London*, [1840?] fol.   **H. 2826. b. (36.)**

— Thy Spirit of Love keeps watch over me; ballad [begins: "Thou art gone from my gaze"], written and composed by G. Linley. *London*, [1844.] fol.   **H. 1292. (1.)**

— "Thy Spirit of Love keeps a Watch over me." Ballad, written, composed ... by George Linley. pp. 5. *Addison & Hodson: London*, [c. 1845.] fol.   **H. 1654. ff. (9.)**

— Thou art gone from my gaze. Ballad. *London*, [1845?] fol.   **G. 805. a. (9.)**

— Thou art gone from my Gaze, or The Spirit of Love keeps a Watch over me, ballad ... Poetry and music by G. Linley. ⟨New edition in a lower key.⟩ pp. 5. *Addison & Hodson: London*, [c. 1845.] fol.   **G. 425. ss. (22.)**

— Thou art gone from my Gaze. ... Song. *C. Sheard: London*, [1889.] fol.
No. 7642 of the Musical Bouquet.   **H. 2345.**

— Thou art gone from my Gaze. [Four-part song.] Words and melody by G. Linley. Arr. by D. Baptie. *See* PATERSON, SONS AND CO. Paterson's Part Music, *etc.* No. 57. [1890? *etc.*] 8°.   **F. 1686.**

— Thou art gone ... for the concertina. [1872.] fol. *See* REGONDI (G.)   **h. 2455. a. (20.)**

— Thy Spirit of Love, *etc. See* HOLMES (W. H.) Fantasia, *etc.* [1846.] fol.   **h. 646. (5.)**

———

— To be belov'd again. Ballad [begins: "His smile was cold at parting"] ... (written and composed) by G. Linley. *London*, [1850?] fol.   **H. 1288. a. (18.)**

— To horse, to horse. The poetry by Lord Byron. *London*, [1854.] fol.   **H. 1297. (29.)**

— To meet again with thee. Ballad [begins: "Years have roll'd"]. *London*, [1861.] fol.   **H. 1299. (9.)**

— To muse upon thee. *See* infra: Six Venetian Melodies. No. 2.

— "To the woods away;" a song, written and composed by G. Linley. pp. 7. *T. Swain: London*, [1838.] fol.   **H. 1288. (22.)**

— To the Woods away. Song. *London*, [1861.] fol.   **H. 1299. (8.)**

— Topsy. Song from Uncle Tom's Cabin. *London*, [1852.] fol.   **H. 1366. (4.)**

— Topsy. Song. *London*, [1873.] fol.   **H. 1299. b. (15.)**

— The torreador. Romance. *London*, [1851.] fol.   **H. 1294. (2.)**

LINLEY (George)

The Toy-Maker

— Charming Vision. Cavatina. *London*, [1861.] fol.   **H. 1299. (18.)**

— Come, beloved one. Ballad. *London*, [1861.] fol.   **H. 1299. (19.)**

— In vain, from Justice. Trio. *London*, [1861.] fol.   **H. 1299. (20.)**

— Oh! gay joyous dance. Duet. *London*, [1861.] fol.   **H. 1299. (21.)**

— Oh! gay joyous Dance. Two part song. With castanet obbligato. Words and music by G. Linley. [Score.] pp. 8. *J. Curwen & Sons: London*, [1905.] 8°.
[*Choruses for equal Voices. no.* 952.]   **E. 861.**

— O Love! Air. *London*, [1861.] fol.   **H. 1299. (22.)**

— Past ten o'clock. Chorus. *London*, [1861.] fol.   **H. 1299. (23.)**

— The Rolling Drum. Air. *London*, [1861.] fol.   **H. 1299. (24.)**

— The Rolling Drum. Unison song. With side drum obbligato. Words and music by G. Linley. [Score.] pp. 7. *J. Curwen & Sons: London*, [1905.] 8°.
[*Choruses for equal Voices. no.* 951.]   **E. 861.**

— We'll forget all sorrow. Quartette finale. *London*, [1861.] fol.   **H. 1299. (25.)**

— Yes, 'twas the dream of my life. Air. *London*, [1861.] fol.   **H. 1299. (26.)**

———

— The trees are in blossom, song, written and composed by G. Linley. *London*, [1859.] fol.   **H. 1297. (31.)**

— The Trysting Place. Song [begins: "They would not let us"] written by J. V. Bridgeman. *London*, [1873.] fol.   **H. 1299. b. (17.)**

— 'Twas my Fault for loving so, ballad ... Written and composed by George Linley. pp. 5. *At Chappell's Musical Circulating Library: London*, [1836.] fol.
The titlepage bears a MS. dedication in the composer's autograph.   **H. 1291. b. (15.)**

— 'Twas you [song, begins: "When summer days were glowing"], written and composed by G. Linley. *London*, [1858.] fol.   **H. 1297. (45.)**

— Uncle Tom's Cabin. [Ballads, *etc.*] No. 1–6. *London*, [1852.] fol.   **H. 1366. (8.)**

— G. Linley's songs from Uncle Tom's Cabin. No. 1, Eva, arranged with an accompaniment for the guitar by L. Sagrini. *London*, [1852.] fol.   **H. 1366. (9.)**

— Under the Linden. Ballad. (Words and music by G. Linley.) *Addison, Hollier & Lucas: London*, [1857.] fol.   **H. 1297. (40.)**

— Under the sea. Song by C. Churchill. *London*, [1850.] fol.   **H. 1294. (22.)**

— Under the Vine Tree. Song. *London*, [1871.] fol.   **H. 1299. b. (3.)**

— Under the Violets. Ballad [begins: "When yonder tow'ring forest trees"]. *London*, [1861.] fol.   **H. 1299. (5.)**

— "Under the walnut tree;" ballad, the words and music by G. Linley. pp. 5. *S. Chappell: London*, [1832.] fol.   **H. 1288. (35.)**

— Under the Walnut Tree, *etc. C. Sheard & Co.: London*, [1889.] fol.
No. 7944 of the Musical Bouquet.   **H. 2345.**

LINLEY (George)

— [Under the walnut tree.] *See* RAWLINGS (T. A.) Introduction
... on "Under the walnut tree". [1833.] fol.   **h. 273. (3.)**

— Up, merry fay; Cavatina, words and music by G. Linley.
London, [1845.] fol.   **H. 1292. (14.)**

— "Up to the hills with me;" ballad, written by W. Ball. pp. 5.
T. Swain: London, [1837.] fol.   **H. 1288. (27.)**

— Venetia. Ballad [begins: "No sigh"]. *London*, [1865.] fol.
   H. 1299. a. (18.)

— Six Venetian Melodies, written and arranged by G. Linley.
6 no. *London*, [1862.] fol.   **H. 1299. a. (2.)**

— Vesper Chime. Ballad. *Boston*, [*Mass.*, 1855?] fol.
   H. 1780. p. (37.)

— The Vesper Chime. Arranged [for four voices] by
T. Crampton, *etc.* [1890.] *See* CRAMPTON (T.) The Part-Singer,
etc. No. 132. [1868–98.] 8°.   **E. 628.**

— Victor Galbraith [song, begins: "Under the walls of
Monterey"], words by Longfellow. *London*, [1859.] fol.
   H. 1297. (41.)

— The visions of night, arranged for the pianoforte by
I. Gibsone. *London*, [1856.] fol.   **h. 1304. (33.)**

— Wake up, my own sweet Rose. Song, written by C. Churchill.
Cramer, Beale & Co.: London, [1850?] fol.   **H. 1652. f. (11.)**

— Waking at early Day. *See* supra: [The Ballad Singer.]

— The warning voice. Song [begins: "Thou art free"], words by
W. H. Bellamy. *London*, [1852.] fol.   **H. 1295. (21.)**

— The warrior sleeps. A tribute to Wellington (written by
S. Fearon). *London*, [1852.] fol.   **H. 1295. (19.)**

— The Warrior's Bride. A ballad [begins: "He leaves the
home"]. *London*, [1835?] fol.   **H. 2832. b. (4.)**

— The Warriors Bride, *etc.* [Song.] *In:* The Musical Bijou ... for
MDCCCXLVI. pp. 28. [1846.] fol.   **H. 2330.**

— The warriors of our day. [Song, begins: "Oh! brave were
England's mailed Knights".] *London*, [1857.] fol.
   H. 1298. (40.)

— We'll forget all sorrow. *See* supra: [The Toy-Maker.]

— "We loved not wisely;" ballad, the poetry and music by
G. Linley. *London*, [1846.] fol.   **H. 1293. (4.)**

— The Wedding Ring ... Jutland Peasant song ... Written and
arranged by G. Linley. *London*, [1865.] fol.
   H. 1299. a. (15.)

— Weep for the love, sequel to Constance, the poetry by
L. E. L[andon]. *London*, [1854.] fol.   **H. 1297. (15.)**

— Welcome as the Sunlight. Ballad. *London*, [1852.] fol.
   H. 1295. (14.)

— Welcome my bonnie lad. Scotch song. *London*, [1852.] fol.
   H. 1295. (18.)

— Welcome, my bonnie lad. Scotch ballad. *London*, [1877.] fol.
   H. 1299. b. (20.)

— "Welcome, rosy May;" song, written and composed by
G. Linley, with flute accompaniment by S. T. Saynor.
London, [1844.] fol.   **H. 1292. (12.)**

— "Well-a-day." Duet. (Words by W. H. Bellamy.) *London*,
[1845.] fol.   **H. 1292. (19.)**

— Twenty Welsh Melodies. The Words written, and the
Symphonies and Accompaniments composed, and arranged
by G. Linley, *etc.* *Boosey & Sons: London*, [1861.] 4°.
[*Boosey's Musical Cabinet. No.* 42.]   **F. 160.**

LINLEY (George)

— What is Prayer. Sacred song. [Words by J. Montgomery.] The
symphonies & accompaniments by G. Linley. *London*,
[1861.] fol.   **H. 1299. (31.)**

— When beams the star of morning. Ballad. *London*, [1858.]
fol.   **H. 1297. (43.)**

— When beneath the cold Earth I am sleeping, canzonet, the
words by W. Motherwell. pp. 5. *C. Lonsdale: London*, [1854?]
fol.   **H. 1291. b. (25.)**

— When I bade good bye to Phoebe. *See* supra: [The Jolly
Beggars.]

— When the daylight fades away. Ballad [begins: "In the
valley"]. *London*, [1872.] fol.   **H. 1299. b. (4.)**

— "When the first star;" a serenade, written and composed by
G. Linley. pp. 5. *S. Chappell: London*, [1832.] fol.
   H. 1288. (33.)

— When the Flow'rs of Hope are fading, ballad ... written,
composed ... by George Linley. pp. 5. *T. E. Purday: London*,
[c. 1850.] fol.   **H. 1650. qq. (27.)**

— When we two parted, poetry by Lord Byron. *London*, [1854.]
fol.   **H. 1297. (30.)**

— Where are now those happy days, duet, written by E. Ellison.
London, [1856.] fol.   **H. 1297. (6.)**

— Where is she now? Ballad ... written and composed by
G. Linley ... arranged for the Guitar by F. Pelzer. *London*,
[1858.] fol.   **H. 1771. o. (19.)**

— While my Lady sleepeth. Song. The words from the Spanish.
pp. 5. *Cramer, Beale & C°.: London*, [1856.] fol.
*The titlepage bears a MS. dedication in the composer's
autograph.*   **H. 1291. b. (16.)**

— Whisper not, how much I love thee. Ballad, *etc.* (Poetry &
Music by G. Linley.) *W. Allcroft: London*, [1830?] fol.
   H. 2815. p. (8.)

— Whistle and I'll come to you, my lad. Ballad. *London*,
[1858.] fol.   **H. 1298. (52.)**

— Whistle o'er the lave o't. *See* supra: [The Jolly Beggars.]

— Who'll fight for the Queen? [Song.] *London*, [1855.] fol.
   H. 1296. (48.)

— Who'll share in my sadness. Ballad, words by E. Ellison.
London, [1853.] fol.   **H. 1295. (32.)**

— Who loves thee not? Agnes! [song,] the words by W. Jones.
pp. 4. *Ransford: London*, [1843.] fol.   **H. 1288. (43.)**

— Why do I love thee yet? *London*, [1853.] fol.
   H. 1295. (22.)

— Why seek I, now, the bow'r? [Song.] (Words and music) by
G. Linley. *London*, [1850?] fol.   **H. 1288. a. (21.)**

— Why watch I by the lonely sea, ballad, words by
W. Kennedy. *London*, [1855.] fol.   **H. 1297. (13.)**

— Why watch I by the lonely sea. Ballad. (Words by
W. Kennedy.) *London*, [1866.] fol.   **H. 1299. a. (31.)**

— The Wide Wide Sea. Air and chorus [begins: "Oh! the briny
deep"]. *London*, [1873.] fol.   **H. 1299. b. (16.)**

— Will she speak to me no more, ballad written and composed
by G. Linley. *London*, [1855.] fol.   **H. 1296. (47.)**

— Will you come. A ballad. *London*, [1835?] fol.
   H. 2831. j. (5.)

— With quaffing and laughing. *See* supra: [The Jolly Beggars.]

LINLEY (George)

— With the first Blush of Morn, song, founded on Strauss' … Rosa Waltz. pp. 3. *Cramer, Addison & Beale: London*, [1838?] fol.   **G. 295. ll. (19.)**

— The Wood-Nymph. [Song, begins: "Where the crystal waters".] *London*, [1868.] fol.   **H. 1299. a. (30.)**

— Woods of green Erin. Irish Ballad. *London*, [1851.] fol.   **H. 1294. (6.)**

— Yes, 'twas the dream of my life. *See* supra: [The Toy-Maker.]

— You cannot forget, ballad, [begins: "I say not regret me,"] the words from L. E.L[andon]'s popular novel "Ethel Churchill". *London*, [1854.] fol.   **H. 1297. (16.)**

— Youthful Isabel, ballad … The poetry & music … by George Linley. pp. 5. *Cramer, Addison & Beale: London*, [1832.] fol.   **H. 1291. b. (17.)**

— The Zephyr and the streamlet, song [begins: "Thou Zephyr"]. *London*, [1854.] fol.   **H. 1296. (49.)**

— The Zingarina [song, begins: "Far over mountains"], written and composed by G. Linley. *London*, [1857.] fol.   **H. 1298. (11.)**

— Zorayda; ballad [begins: "Dost thou remember"], written by W. H. Bellamy. *London*, [1846.] fol.   **H. 1293. (9.)**

— *See* ADAM (A. C.) Cantique de Noël. Star of the sea [song, written and adapted by G. Linley]. [1858.] fol.   **H. 1297. (44.)**

— *See* AUBER (D. F. E.) [Les Diamants de la Couronne.] Daughter of the mountain, canzonetta, written and adapted by G. Linley. [1855.] fol.   **H. 590. (3.)**

— *See* AUBER (D. F. E.) [Emma.] The young mountaineer. English adaptation [by G. Linley] of the air Une rose bien fleurie. [1866.] fol.   **H. 590. a. (6.)**

— *See* DONIZETTI (D. G. M.) [La Favorite.—Viens, je cède.] Come where the Fountains play … arranged by G. Linley. [1876.] fol.   **H. 1778. k. (55.)**

— *See* DONIZETTI (D. G. M.) [Lucrezia Borgia.—Di pescatore ignobile.] Visions of Youth … adapted by G. Linley. [1857.] fol. [*Italian Minstrelsy. Vol.* 1. *No.* 3.]   **H. 2400.**

— *See* DONIZETTI (D. G. M.) [Lucrezia Borgia.—M' odi, ah m'odi.] Peace be with thee … adapted by G. Linley. [1857.] fol. [*Italian Minstrelsy. Vol.* 1. *No.* 10.]   **H. 2400.**

— *See* DONIZETTI (D. G. M.) [Lucrezia Borgia.—Maffio Orsini, signora, son' io.] Venice … adapted by G. Linley. [1857.] fol. [*Italian Minstrelsy. Vol.* 1. *No.* 4.]   **H. 2400.**

— *See* DONIZETTI (D. G. M.) [Lucrezia Borgia.—Maffio Orsini, signora, son' io.] Venice … Duet … adapted by G. Linley. [1876.] fol.   **H. 379. a. (46.)**

— *See* DONIZETTI (D. G. M.) [Matinées musicales. No. 1. Vieni la barca è pronta.] Come, Love! my Bark is waiting … adapted by G. Linley. [1857.] fol. [*Italian Minstrelsy. Vol.* 1. *No.* 11.]   **H. 2400.**

— *See* FLOTOW (F. F. A. von) *Baron.* [Martha.—Ach! so fromm!] Fair as the rose. (Written and arranged by G. Linley.) [1858.] fol.   **H. 750. (3.)**

— *See* FLOTOW (F. F. A. von) *Baron.* [Martha.—Ja, seit früher Kindheit Tagen.] Native valley. (Written and arranged by G. Linley.) [1858.] fol.   **H. 750. (16.)**

— *See* FLOTOW (F. F. A. von) *Baron.* [Martha.—Jägerinn schlau in Sinn.] Thro' the wood (Il tuo stral nel lanciar) … written & arranged by G. Linley. [1859.] fol.   **H. 750. (25.)**

LINLEY (George)

— *See* FLOTOW (F. F. A. von) *Baron.* [Martha.—Schlafe wohl.] Pleasant dreams. (Written and arranged by G. Linley.) [1858.] fol.   **H. 750. (18.)**

— *See* GARDINER (*Lady* M.) Blighted rose, arranged by G. Linley. [1844.] fol.   **H. 1292. (3.)**

— *See* GLOVER (S.) Little Boy Blue Quadrille on melodies from G. Linley's Nursery Rhymes. [1861.] fol.   **h. 744. (35.)**

— *See* GODFREY (D.) The Little Nell waltz. (On melodies by … G. Linley.) [1871.] fol.   **h. 2932. b. (18.)**

— *See* GUNG'L (J.) Speed bark! on thy light way, song, melody by Gung'l, written and arranged by G. Linley. [1854.] fol.   **H. 1754. (32.)**

— *See* HENRION (P.) Virginie, written and adapted by G. Linley. [1855?] fol.   **H. 1653. d. (2.)**

— *See* KUECKEN (F. W.) 6 Motetts … adapted … by G. Linley. [1858.] fol.   **H. 2828. b. (5.)**

— *See* LAMPLIGHTER. Songs from the Lamplighter … the music by G. Linley, *etc.* [1854.] fol.   **H. 1467. (4.)**

— *See* OSBORNE (*Lady* E.) Thy will be done … The symphonies & accompaniments by G. Linley. [1861.] fol.   **H. 1299. (30.)**

— *See* REED (J. H.) I do not ask. Piano Forte accompaniment by G. Linley. [1849.] fol.   **H. 1721. (17.)**

— *See* SONGS. Songs … from the White slave, words by J. E. Carpenter. Music by J. L. Hatton (and G. Linley). [1853.] fol.   **H. 2184. (18.)**

— *See* VENZANO (L.) [Ah! che assorta.] The Gipsy, ballad, written and arranged by G. Linley. [1855.] fol.   **H. 1769. (13.)**

— *See* VENZANO (L.) The Zingarella, written and arranged by G. Linley. [1856.] fol.   **H. 1298. (14.)**

— *See* VERDI (F. G. F.) [Luisa Miller.—Sacra la scelta.] Sweet tie of friendship, *etc.* (Written and arranged by G. Linley.) [1858.] fol.   **H. 476. a. (17.)**

— *See* VERDI (F. G. F.) [Luisa Miller.—Tu puniscime.] Leave me not, *etc.* (Written and arranged by G. Linley.) [1858.] fol.   **H. 476. a. (13.)**

— *See* VERDI (F. G. F.) [Il Trovatore.—Il balen.] Brighter than the stars of summer, air … in Il Trovatore, written and adapted by G. Linley. [1855.] fol.   **H. 470. f. (33.)**

— *See* VERDI (F. G. F.) [Il Trovatore.—Miserere Scene.] Fair, life's morning dawn'd … written and adapted by G. Linley. [1855.] fol.   **H. 470. f. (26.)**

— *See* VERDI (F. G. F.) [Il Trovatore.—Si, la stanchezza.] Oh that I could sweetly slumber, duet written and arranged by G. Linley. [1855.] fol.   **H. 470. f. (42.)**

LINLEY (Herbert)

— The Old Folks at Home. Ballad, with chorus composed and adapted by Herbert Linley. [In fact by Stephen C. Foster.] pp. 4. *Jewell and Letchford: London*, [1852.] fol.   **H. 1654. zz. (20.)**

— The Old Folks at Home. Ballad with Chorus, composed [by S. C. Foster] and adapted by H. Linley. *Jewell & Letchford: London*, [1852.] fol. *Uncle Tom's Cabin Songs, No.* 1.   **H. 1366. (10.)**

LINLEY (James)

— O lead me to the meadow fair, or the last wish, for two voices. Written by G. Linley. *London*, [1856.] fol.   **H. 1297. (49.)**

LINLEY (JAMES)

—— O lead me to the Meadow fair, *etc. See* DUETS. Vocal Duets, *etc.* No. 78. [1865–1901.] fol.   **H. 2259.**

LINLEY (THOMAS) *the Elder*

—— A Collection of Twenty four Songs by English Composers ... From Lawes to Linley, *etc.* 1908. 4°. *See* ARKWRIGHT (G. E. P.)   **G. 295. k. (1.)**

—— And has she then fail'd in her Faith. *See* infra: [Selima and Azor.]

—— Twelve Ballads, *etc. Printed for A. Portal: London,* (1780.) *obl.* fol.   **E. 271. (10.)**

—— [Twelve Ballads. No. 8.] The Lark sings high in the Cornfield. Song. ... Arranged by J. A. Fuller Maitland. [1895.] *See* BROADWOOD (L. E.) and MAITLAND (J. A. F.) Old World Songs, *etc.* No. 3. [1895.] fol.   **H. 3439. (8.)**

The Camp

—— [The Camp. For songs, etc. published anonymously:] *See* also CAMP.

—— The Camp, an Entertainment, *etc.* [Words partly by R. Tickell.] *Printed for S. & A. Thompson: London,* [1778.] *obl.* fol.   **E. 82. b. (2.)**

—— The Camp. A Musical Entertainment, *etc.* [1800.] *See* PERIODICAL PUBLICATIONS.— *London.* The Piano-Forte Magazine. Vol. IX. [No. 7.] [1797–1802.] 8° *Imperfect, wanting all after p.* 22.   **D. 854.**

—— Nancy of the Dale. [Song.] Sung by Mr Webster, *etc. S. A. P. T.* [*Samuel, Ann and Peter Thompson: London,* c. 1780.] fol. *Followed by an accompaniment for German flute.*   **H. 1653. j. (4.)**

—— When war's alarms entic'd my Willy from me. *Wars alarms entic'd my Willy, etc.* [Song, music by T. Linley the Elder.] [1770?] *s. sh.* fol. *See* WHEN.   **I. 530. (179.)**

—— When Wars Alarms. Sung by Miss Walpole, *etc. S. A. P. T.* [*S. A. & P. Thompson: London,* c. 1780.] fol. *Followed by an arrangement for the guitar.*   **H. 1653. uu. (16.)**

—— When War's Alarms, a Favorite Song ... for the Piano Forte or Flute. *R. Major: London,* [1820?] fol.   **G. 424. a. (24.)**

—— [When War's Alarms.] *See* SMART (T.) When War's Alarms. With Variations, *etc.* [1790?] fol.   **h. 141. a. (17.)**

The Carnival of Venice

—— [For songs, etc., published anonymously:] *See* CARNIVAL.

—— The Carnival of Venice, a Comic Opera ... for the Voice and Harpsichord. [Words by R. Tickell.] *Printed for S. A. & P. Thompson: London,* [1781.] *obl.* fol.   **E. 82. e.**

—— In my pleasant Native Plains. The Favourite Roundelay, *etc. Printed for S. A. & P. Thompson: London,* [1781.] fol.   **G. 309. (98.)**

—— [Another copy.]   **G. 296. (6.)**

—— [Another copy.]   **G. 297. (11.)**

—— In my pleasant native Plains. A favourite song sung by Mrs Cargill, *etc. S. A. & P. Thompson: London,* [c. 1785.] fol. *The last page contains accompaniments for German flute and guitar.*   **Mad. Soc. 21. (12.)**

—— Young Lubin was a Shepherd Boy ... Song, *etc. Printed for S. A. & P. Thompson: London,* [1781.] fol.   **G. 297. (14.)**

—— [Another copy.]   **Mad. Soc. 21. (40.)**

LINLEY (THOMAS) *the Elder*

—— Cheerly my Hearts of Courage true, [song,] ... Written by R. B. Sheridan, *etc. Preston: London,* [1797?] fol.   **H. 2830. f. (93.)**

—— Cheerly my Hearts of Courage true. *Sung by Mr Vernon.* [Song, by T. Linley the Elder.] pp. [4.] [c. 1800.] fol. *See* CHEERLY.   **H. 1980. r. (16.)**

—— Cheerly my Hearts of Courage true. *Britons to Arms!* [Song, by T. Linley the Elder.] 1803. *s. sh.* fol. *See* CHEERLY.   **I. 600. (132.)**

—— Cheerly my hearts of courage true. [Song.] *London,* [1856.] fol. *No.* 433 *of the "Cyclopedia of Music. Miscellaneous Series of Songs".*   **H. 2342.**

—— Come my Jolly Lads. *See* infra: [Robinson Crusoe.]

—— The Departure of Robinson Crusoe. *See* infra: [Robinson Crusoe.—Come, come my jolly Lads.]

—— [Dissipation.] Smiling Love, to thee belong. *Roundelay in the Comedy of Dissipation.* [Written by M. P. Andrews.] Sung by Miss Field and Miss Wright. [*Dublin,* 1781.] *s. sh.* 4°. *Hibernian Magazine, October,* 1781.   **P. P. 6154. k.**

—— [Dissipation.] Smiling Love to thee belong. *Roundelay in the Comedy of Dissipation.* Sung by Miss Field and Miss Wright. *S. A. P. T.* [*S., A. and P. Thompson: London,* 1781?] fol.   **H. 1653. a. (24.)**

—— Drink to me only. Glee. Words by B. Jonson. *London,* [1858.] fol. *No.* 15 *of the "Cyclopedia of Music. Select Glees, etc."*   **H. 2342. c.**

—— [The Duenna. For editions of the vocal score of, and separate numbers from, "The Duenna," a comic opera with music partly composed and partly compiled by T. Linley the Elder and T. Linley the Younger:] *See* DUENNA.

—— The Duenna, a Comick Opera ... Composed by Mr. Linley [and T. Linley the Younger]. [1798.] *See* PERDIODICAL PUBLICATIONS.— *London.* The Piano-Forte Magazine. Vol. V. No. 1. [1797–1802.] 8°.   **D. 854.**

—— Elegies for three Voices with an Accompanyment for a Harpsichord and Violoncello. *P. Welcker, for the Author: London,* [1770.] fol.   **H. 1192. a.**

—— [Another copy.]   **G. 385. (2.)**

—— [Fortunatus.] The Favorite Song [by T. Linley the Elder] sung ... in the revived Pantomime of Fortunatus, *etc.* [1780?] fol. *See* FORTUNATUS.   **H. 1648. a. (2.)**

—— From the Light down. *The Favourite Song in the Comedy of the New Peerage,* sung by Mrs Crouch. pp. 4. *Printed for S. A. & P. Thompson: London,* [1787?] fol. *P.* 4 *contains accompaniments for German flute and guitar.*   **H. 1653. j. (58.)**

—— [The Generous Impostor.] A Pastoral Interlude ... perform'd in the Comedy [by T. L. Obeirne] of the Generous Impostor, *etc. S. A. & P. Thompson: London,* [1780.] *obl.* fol.   **E. 601. a. (9.)**

—— [The Gentle Shepherd.] The Overture, Songs & Duetts in the Pastoral Opera of the Gentle Shepherd, *etc.* [Words adapted from A. Ramsay by R. Tickell. Music, composed and arranged by T. Linley the Elder.] [1781.] *obl.* fol. *See* GENTLE.   **E. 82.**

—— The Gentle Shepherd. A Pastoral Opera, *etc.* [1800.] *See* PERIODICAL PUBLICATIONS.— *London.* The Piano-Forte Magazine. Vol. X. No. 1. [1797–1802.] 8°. *Imperfect, wanting pp.* 19, 20.   **D. 854.**

—— The God of Love a Bandeau wears. *The favorite Duett* sung by Mrs Jordan & Mrs Crouch in Richard Cœur de Lion [by

LINLEY (THOMAS) *the Elder*

A. E. M. Grétry], at the Theatre Royal in Drury Lane. Adopted to the English words by Mr Linley. pp. 4. *Printed for S. A. & P. Thompson: London*, [1786?] fol.
Pp. 3 and 4 contain accompaniments for German flute and guitar.   **H. 1652. u. (27.)**

— The God of Love a Bandeau wears. *The Favorite Duett.* Sung by Mrs Jordan & Mrs Crouch in Richard Cœur de Lion [by A. E. M. Grétry] at the Theatre Royal in Drury Lane. Adapted to the English words by Mr Linley. pp. 4. *Printed for S. A. & P. Thompson: London*, [1786?] fol.
Pp. 3 and 4 contain accompaniments for German flute and guitar.   **H. 1653. j. (59.)**

— Here's to the maiden of bashful fifteen. *See* infra: [The School for Scandal.]

— In my pleasant Native Plains. *See* supra: [The Carnival of Venice.]

— The Lark sings high in the Cornfield. *See* supra: [Twelve Ballads. No. 8.]

— Let me careless … Madrigal for five voices. *London*, [1810?] fol.   **G. 805. p. (5.)**

— "Let me careless," *etc.* [Madrigal for Tr. A. T. B. B.] *Printed by Clementi and Comp^y: [London*, c. 1830.] fol.
Pp. 86–95 of an unidentified collection.   **H. 1202. u. (26.)**

— Let's Range the Fields my Sally. A favorite song sung by Mr Dignum. pp. 4. *Printed for Messrs Thompson: London*, [c. 1790.] fol.
P. 4 contains an accompaniment for flute.   **H. 1653. a. (9.)**

— Love in the East, or Adventures of Twelve Hours, a Comic Opera [written by J. Cobb] … The Music composed & compiled by Mr. Linley, for the Harpsichord and Voice. *Printed for S. A. & P. Thompson: London*, [1788.] *obl.* fol.   **E. 82. d.**

— The Merry Dance I dearly love. *Antonio's favorite Song.* Sung by Miss Romanzini in Richard Cœur de Lion [by A. E. M. Grétry], at the Theatre Royal Drury Lane. Adapted to the English words by Mr Linley. pp. 3. *Printed for S. A. & P. Thompson: London*, [1786?] fol.
P. 3 contains an accompaniment for guitar.   **H. 1652. u. (28.)**

The Mid-watch

— The Glorious First of June. [For editions of this song published anonymously:] *See* GLORIOUS. [The Glorious First of June.]

— When 'tis Night and the Mid-Watch is come. [For editions of this song published anonymously:] *See* WHEN.

— When 'tis Night, and the Mid Watch is come. A favorite song, sung by Mr Bannister. [Followed by an accompaniment for the guitar.] [*London?* ^WM 1795.] fol.   **H. 1652. hh. (27.)**

— The Mid-Watch. A sea-song, written by … R. B. Sheridan. *In:* The Harmonicon. vol. 3, pt. 2. pp. 272, 273. 1825. 4°.   **P. P. 1947.**

— When 'tis Night and the Mid-Watch is come, a celebrated national sea song, in The Glorious First of June (1794). The words by R. B. Sheridan … Newly arranged by H. J. Gauntlett. pp. 3. *C. Lonsdale: London*, [1850.] fol.   **H. 1735. (46.)**

— The Mid-Watch, popular song written by R. B. Sheridan. pp. 4. *C. Sheard: London*, [1874.] fol.
[*Musical Bouquet. no.* 5122.]   **H. 2345.**

— Nancy of the Dale. *See* supra: [The Camp.]

— Ne'er ah ne'er let sorrow's sting. *See* infra: [Selima and Azor.]

LINLEY (THOMAS) *the Elder*

— No Flow'r that blows. *See* infra: [Selima and Azor.]

— O bid your faithful Ariel fly. *See* infra: [The Tempest.]

— Oh! Richard Oh! my Love. A favourite song, sung by Mrs Jordan in Richard, Cœur de Lion [by A. E. M. Grétry], at the Theatre Royal in Drury Lane, adapted to the English words by Mr Linley. pp. 3. *Printed for S. A. & P. Thompson: London*, [1786?] fol.
P. 3 contains an accompaniment for German flute.
                                                       H. 1652. u. (29.)

— Primroses deck the bank's green side. *See* infra: [Sally.]

— Richard Cœur de Lion, an Historical Romance … Music by Monsieur Gretry, adapted … by Mr. Linley. [1801.] *See* PERIODICAL PUBLICATIONS.— *London.* The Piano-Forte Magazine. Vol. XIV. [No. 9.] [1797–1802.] 8°.   **D. 854.**

— The Songs, Duets, Trios & Chorusses of … Richard Cœur de Lion … Adapted … by Mr. Linley. [1786?] *obl.* fol. *See* GRÉTRY (A. E. M.) [Richard Cœur de Lion.]   **E. 135.**

Robinson Crusoe

— [For excerpts published anonymously:] *See* ROBINSON.

— Come my Jolly Lads. *The Song Sung by Mr. Gaudry* in the New Pantomime of Robinson Crusoe, *etc.* [Words ascribed to R. B. Sheridan.] [*London*, 1781.] fol.   **G. 307. (62.)**

— [Come come my jolly Lads.] The Song sung by Mr Guadry [*sic*], in the new pantomime of Robinson Crusoe. *S. A. P. T.* [*S. A. & P. Thompson: London*, c. 1785.] fol.
Followed by an arrangement for the German flute.
                                                       H. 1601. t. (10.)

— [Come, come my jolly Lads.] The Departure of Robinson Crusoe … (Unison) … Arranged by Richard Graves. [Staff and tonic sol-fa notation.] pp. 3. *J. Curwen & Sons: London; G. Schirmer: New York*, [1967.] 8°.
[*Choruses for equal Voices.* 2659.]   **E. 861.**

— [Come, come my jolly Lads.] While the foaming Billows roll … [Melody arranged by] H. Lane Wilson. Arr. (for Male Voices, T. B. B.) by W. Howorth. *Boosey Hawkes Belwin, Inc.: New York*, 1940. 8°.   **F. 163. jj. (56.)**

——————

— The Royal Merchant. A Comic Opera … The Words by Mr. Hull. *Welcker: London*, [1768.] *obl.* fol.   **E. 82. c.**

Sally

— Sally. A favorite Song. [Begins: "Primroses deck the bank's green side".] *E. Rhames: Dublin*, [1780?] *s. sh.* fol.
                                                       H. 1601. b. (95.)

— Primroses deck the bank's green side. [Song.] *London*, [1854.] fol.   **H. 1759. (16.)**

— Primroses deck the bank's green side, ballad. *London*, [1855.] fol.   **H. 1759. (15.)**

— Primroses deck the bank's green side. [Song.] *London*, [1858.] fol.
No. 10 of the "Cyclopedia of Music. Select Songs, Gentlemen's Series".   **H. 2342. b.**

— Primroses deck the bank's green side. Ballad. *London*, [1872.] fol.   **H. 1778. y. (47.)**

— Primroses deck the bank's green side. Ballad. *London*, [1874.] fol.   **H. 1778. y. (48.)**

— Primroses deck the bank's green side. Ballad. *London*, [1878.] fol.   **H. 1783. p. (12.)**

— Primroses deck the bank's green side. Song. *London*, [1879.] fol.
No. 721 of C. Boosey's "Universal" music.   **H. 2324.**

LINLEY (THOMAS) the Elder

— Primroses deck the Bank's green Side. An admired Ballad ... Arranged by A[melia] L[ehmann]. *Boosey & Co.: London & New York*, 1899. fol.   **H. 3599. (39.)**

— Primroses deck the Bank's green Side. [Two-part song.] Edited by F[lorian] P[ascal, i. e. Joseph Williams]. [1905.] *See* REDHEAD (A.) The Vocal Garland, *etc.* Series II. No. 4. [1905, *etc.*] 8°.   **E. 263. f. (4.)**

— Primroses deck the Bank's green Side. Song ... Arranged and the accompaniment composed by E. Ivimey. *Augener: London*, 1938. 4°.   **G. 1275. uu. (10.)**

— [A School for Grey Beards.] Sweet rosy Sleep oh do not fly. *The favourite Song* sung by Mrs Crouch, *etc.* pp. 4. *Printed for S. A. & P. Thompson: London*, [1786?] fol.
P. 4 *contains an accompaniment for the German flute.*
                    H. 1652. nn. (8.)

— [The School for Scandal.] Here's to the maiden of bashful fifteen. Song ... Words by Sheridan. *See* NATIONAL. National & popular Ballads, *etc.* No. 75. [1863, *etc.*] fol.   **H. 1248. a.**

Selima and Azor

— [For songs, etc. published anonymously:] *See* SELIMA.

— Selima and Azor, a Persian Tale, *etc.* [Opera, the words imitated from the French of Marmontel by Sir G. Collier.] *Printed for C. and S. Thompson: London*, [1776.] obl. fol.
                    E. 82. b. (1.)

— Overture, *etc.* [P. F.] pp. 4. *G. Walker: London*, [^WM 1808.] fol.
                    g. 272. b. (44.)

— And has she then failed in her Faith, a favorite ballad, *etc.* pp. 3. *Polyhymnian Co.: London*, [^WM 1819.] fol.
Followed by an arrangement for flute.   **H. 1654. ff. (24.)**

— [And has she then fail'd.] The Original Song of And has she then fail'd in her Faith, a favorite ballad ... for the piano forte. pp. 3. *W. & S. Wybrow:* [*London*, c. 1825.] fol.
Followed by an arrangement for the flute.   **G. 1277. a. (6.)**

— Ne'er ah ne'er let sorrow's sting. *An Additional Favourite Song* sung by Miss Romanzini, *etc. Printed for S. A. & P. Thompson: London*, [1788.] fol.   **G. 806. c. (25.)**

— No Flow'r that blows, *etc.* [Song.] S[amuel] A[nn and] P[eter] T[hompson: London*, 1780?] fol.   **G. 310. (152.)**

— [Another copy.]   **Mad. Soc. 21. (39.)**

— No Flow'r that blows is like the Rose. [Song. By T. Linley the Elder.] [^WM 1802.] fol. *See* No.   **G. 383. kk. (37.)**

— No Flower that blows, a favorite song, *etc.* pp. 3. *Shade:* [*London*, ^WM 1822.] fol.   **H. 3690. ww. (26.)**

— No Flow'r that blows ... Song ... Arranged by J. B. Sale. pp. 4. *Printed by the Royal Harmonic Institution: London*, [^WM 1822.] fol.   **H. 3691. d. (13.)**

— [No Flow'r that blows.] *See* CARTER (C. T.) The celebrated song of the Rose with Variations, *etc.* [1780?] fol.
                    g. 271. (18.)

— [No Flow'r that blows.] *See* HAIGH (Thomas) *of Manchester.* A Divertimento, for the piano forte, in which is introduced ... "No Flower that blows" [by T. Linley, the Elder] *etc.* [^WM 1810.] fol.   **g. 606. ii. (23.)**

— Smiling Love to thee belong. *See* supra: [Dissipation.]

— [The Spanish Rivals.] The Overture, Songs, Duetts, &c., in the Spanish Rivals, a Musical Farce, *etc.* [Written by M. Lonsdale.] *Printed for S. A. & P. Thompson: London*, [1784.] obl. fol.   **E. 100. a. (5.)**

LINLEY (THOMAS) the Elder

— [The Spanish Rivals.] Still the Lark finds Repose. The favourite Rondo sung by Miss Phillips, *etc. Printed for S. A. & P. Thompson: London*, [1784.] fol.   **H. 1797. pp. (13.)**

— [The Spanish Rivals.] Still the Lark finds Repose. Song ... Arranged and the accompaniment composed by E. Ivimey. *Augener: London*, 1934. 4°.   **G. 1275. pp. (12.)**

— Still the Lark finds Repose. *See* supra: [The Spanish Rivals.]

— The Strangers at Home, a Comic Opera [written by J. Cobb] ... Selected & Composed by T. Linley. *Printed for Longman & Broderip: London*, [1786.] *obl.* fol.   **E. 100. a. (6.)**

— Sweet rosy Sleep oh do not fly. *See* supra: [A School for Grey Beards.]

The Tempest

— The original musick in the Tempest, *etc.* [1821.] fol. *See* DAVY (J.)   **H. 127.**

— The Music in Shakespeare's Tempest, by ... Linley, *etc.* [1865.] fol. *See* PURCELL (H.) [*Doubtful and Supposititious Works.*] [The Tempest.]   **H. 101. g.**

— The Vocal Music to ... the Tempest. [By T. Linley, the Elder, and others.] 1924. 4°. [*The Vocal Music to Shakespeare's Plays. No.* 8.] *See* TEMPEST.   **G. 1243.**

— Arise ye spirits of the storm. Chorus. *See* SHAKESPEARE. The Shakspeare Vocal Magazine. No. 76. [1864, *etc.*] fol.
                    H. 2389.

— O bid your faithful Ariel fly ... Song ... Arranged by J. Davy. *R. Birchall: London*, [1820?] fol.   **H. 1650. f. (17.)**

— [Another edition.] O bid your faithful Ariel fly, *etc. Birchall & Co.: London*, [1825?] fol.   **H. 1650. n. (21.)**

— O bid your faithful Ariel fly. Song, *etc. Mori & Lavenu: London*, [1830?] fol.   **H. 1652. e. (2.)**

— "O! bid your faithful Ariel fly" ... [Song.] Arranged by S. Nelson. pp. 7. *Jefferys & Co: London*, [c. 1840.] fol.
Standard Songs. (*England.*) no. 3.   **H. 1860. oo. (2.)**

— O bid your faithful Ariel fly ... [Song.] Arranged from the author's score ... by Wm Horsley. *Cramer, Beale & Co: London*, [c. 1840.] fol.
Cramer & Co.'s Selection of vocal Music. no. 7.
                    H. 1860. oo. (6.)

— O bid your faithful Ariel fly. Song, *etc. R. Mills: London*, [1845?] fol.   **H. 1652. f. (12.)**

— O bid your faithful Ariel fly. [Song.] *London*, [1856.] fol.
No. 423 *of the "Cyclopedia of Music. Miscellaneous Series of Songs".*   **H. 2342.**

— O bid your faithful Ariel fly. Song. *See* SHAKESPEARE. The Shakspeare Vocal Magazine. No. 32. [1864.] fol.   **H. 2389.**

— O bid your faithful Ariel fly ... Song. *London*, [1874.] fol.
No. 3278, 3279 *of the "Musical Bouquet".*   **H. 2345.**

— O bid your faithful Ariel fly. Song. *London*, [1877.] fol.
No. 202–3 *of C. Boosey's "Universal" music.*   **H. 2324.**

— O bid your faithful Ariel fly. Song, *etc.* (1907.) *See* LÉVI (E.) Standard songs, *etc.* No. 2. (1907, *etc.*) fol.   **H. 3620. a.**

— [The Tempest.] O bid your faithful Ariel fly. Unison song, *etc.* pp. 6. *J. Curwen & Sons: London*, [1913.] 8°.
[*Choruses for equal Voices.* no. 1374.]   **E. 861.**

— O bid your faithful Ariel fly, *etc.* [P. F.] [1892?] *See* STEPHANO (C.) Wickins' Gems for little Players, *etc.* No. 93. [1890?–96.] fol.   **h. 2832. b.**

— *See* CALLCOTT (W. H.) Favorite airs sung in ... the Tempest ... for the Pianoforte. [1850?] fol.   **g. 272. m. (27.)**

LINLEY (Thomas) *the Elder*

— *See* ROCHARD (J.) Operatic Echoes. No. 14. The Tempest. [Fantasia. P. F. solo and duet.] 2 no. [1887–92.] fol.
h. 3032. c. (1.)

— To the woods away. *See* ROEFS (B.) The Woodland March. [1866.] fol.
h. 1355. a. (31.)

— [The Triumph of Mirth.] The Tunes, Songs, Glee, &c., in the Pantomime of The Triumph of Mirth, or Harlequin's Wedding … Composed and Selected by Mr. Linley. *Printed for S. A. & P. Thompson: London*, [1782.] obl. fol.
The Overture is by T. Linley the Younger. **E. 82. a.**

— When 'tis Night, and the Mid Watch is come. *See* supra: [The Mid-watch.]

— When War's Alarms. *See* supra: [The Camp.]

— While the foaming Billows roll. *See* supra: [Robinson Crusoe.—Come, come my jolly Lads.]

— The Woodman. [Song.] Written by W. Pearce, *etc. Preston & Son: London*, [1795?] fol.
H. 2821. (19.)

— The Woodman. [Song.] *H. Andrews: Lambeth*, [1805?] fol.
H. 1652. p. (16.)

— The Woodman. A Favorite Song. [*Dean and Munday: London*, 1827.] 8°.
Ladies' Monthly Museum, etc. Vol. XXV., XXVI. Musical Appendix, pp. 293–297. **P. P. 5153. i.**

— The Woodman, *etc. London*, [1856.] fol.
No. 363 *of the "Cyclopedia of Music. Miscellaneous Series of Songs".* **H. 2342.**

— Young Lubin was a Shepherd Boy. *See* supra: [The Carnival of Venice.]

— *See* PAISIELLO (G.) [Il Barbiere di Siviglia.—Saper bramate.] For tenderness form'd. *A Favourite Song* in … the Heiress … Adapted … by Mr. Linley. [1786.] fol. **H. 131. (40.)**

LINLEY (Thomas) *the Elder* and **LINLEY** (Thomas) *the Younger*

— The Posthumous Vocal Works of Mr. Linley and Mr. T. Linley, Consisting of Songs, Duetts, Cantatas, Madrigals and Glees. In two Volumes. [Published by Mrs Linley.] *Preston, for the Proprietor: London*, [1800?] fol. **H. 1192.**

— [Another copy.] **R. M. 13. f. 13.**

— Songs of the Linleys. ⟨By Thomas Linley senior, Thomas Linley junior.⟩ For high voice. Edited by Michael Pilkington, *etc.* pp. 32. *Stainer & Bell: London*, [1979.] 8°.
E. 1766. ll. (5.)

— [The Duenna. For editions of the vocal score of, and separate numbers from, "The Duenna," a comic opera with music partly composed and partly compiled by T. Linley the Elder and T. Linley the Younger:] *See* DUENNA.

LINLEY (Thomas) *the Younger*

— Two Madrigals … Edited by Gwilym Beechey. For (1) SSAB, (2) SSATB (unaccompanied). ⟨1. Alinda's Form. 2. Hark! the Birds.⟩ pp. 14. *Novello: Borough Green*, [1978.] 8°.
[*Musical Times.* 1627.] **F. 280. n.**

— [The Duenna. For editions of the vocal score of, and separate numbers from, "The Duenna," a comic opera with music partly composed and partly compiled by T. Linley the Elder and T. Linley the Younger:] *See* DUENNA.

— Ere you can say come and go. *See* infra: [The Tempest.]

LINLEY (Thomas) *the Younger*

— Hark! the birds melodious sing. Madrigal. *See* HULLAH (J. P.) The Singer's Library of Concerted Music. Secular. No. 86. [1859, *etc.*] 8°.
G. 435.

— Master Linley's Hornpipe. As perform'd at the Theatre Royal in Covent Garden in the new masque call'd the Fairy Favour. [P. F.] [*London*, 1767?] *s. sh.* fol.
Followed by separate accompaniments for German flute and for guitar. **i. 260. (2.)**

— Anthem: Let God arise. Edited by Gwilym Beechey. [Score. With facsimiles.] pp. ix. 100. *A-R Editions: Madison, Wisc.*, [1977.] 4°.
[*Recent Researches in the Music of the Classical Era. vol.* 7.]
G. 1490. c.

— O bid your faithful Ariel fly. [For editions of this song attributed to T. Linley the Younger:] *See* LINLEY (Thomas) *the Elder*. [The Tempest.]

— Shakespeare Ode. Transcribed and edited by Gwilym Beechey. [With facsimiles.] pp. xxiv. 182. *Stainer & Bell: London*, 1970. fol.
[*Musica Britannica.* 30.] **N. 10.**

— [The Tempest.] Ere you can say come and go. Song. *See* SHAKESPEARE. The Shakspeare Vocal Magazine. No. 62. [1864, *etc.*] fol. **H. 2389.**

— [The Tempest.] While you here do snoring lie. Song. *See* SHAKESPEARE. The Shakspeare Vocal Magazine. No. 63. [1864, *etc.*] fol. **H. 2389.**

— While you here do snoring lie. *See* supra: [The Tempest.]

— *See* LINLEY (T.) *the Elder* and LINLEY (T.) *the Younger*. The Posthumous Vocal Works of Mr. Linley and Mr. T. Linley, *etc.* [1800?] fol. **H. 1192.**

— *See* LINLEY (T.) *the Elder* and LINLEY (T.) *the Younger*. Songs of the Linleys, *etc.* ⟨By T. Linley senior, T. Linley junior.⟩ [1979.] 8°. **E. 1766. ll. (5.)**

LINLEY (William)

— The Bacchanalian. *See* infra: Eight Glees. No. 1.

— Six Canzonetts, with an Accompaniment for the Piano Forte or Harp. *Broderip & Wilkinson: London*, [1800?] obl. fol.
E. 600. n. (6.)

— Ere Sin could blight. Glee. *See* GLEES. A selection of Glees, *etc.* No. 9. [1805?] obl. fol. **E. 207. a. (1.)**

— Faith. *See* infra: Eight Glees. No. 2.

— Fill all the Air with Music's Flame. *See* infra: [Fill high the Cup.]

— "Fill high the Cup," Glee, for three voices, *etc.* ⟨The poetry is a translation from the Greek of Meleager by T. Moore.⟩ pp. 7. *W. Hawes: London*, [1832.] fol. **H. 2788. d. (11.)**

— [Another copy.] **H. 1202. m. (21.)**

— [Fill high the Cup.] Fill all the Air with Music's Flame. (Arranged for S. S. C.) pp. 7. *J. Curwen & Sons: London*, [1905.] 8°.
[*Choruses for equal Voices. no.* 913.] **E. 861.**

— Flights of Fancy, in Six new Glees for four Voices, *etc. Thompson: London*, [1799.] obl. fol. **D. 401. (7.)**

— Eight Glees, *etc.* pp. 81. *W. Hawes: London*, [1832?] fol.
The titlepage bears a MS. dedication in the composer's autograph. **H. 1271. b.**

— [Another copy.] **H. 1271. a.**

LINLEY (WILLIAM)

— [Eight Glees. No. 5.] Queen Mab. (Arranged for S. S. C.), *etc.*
pp. 8. *J. Curwen & Sons: London*, [1904.] 8°.
[*Choruses for equal Voices. no. 854.*] **E. 861.**

— [Eight Glees. No. 8.] Oberon's Festival. (Arranged for S. S. C.
by Geo. Oakey.) Words from "Fairy Fantasies" by Leftly.
pp. 11. *J. Curwen & Sons: London; Leipzig* [printed, 1901.]
8°.
[*Choruses for equal Voices. no. 438.*] **E. 861.**

— Go, musing traveller. Elegy, the poetry by C. Marsh. *See*
supra: Eight Glees. No. 2.

— [The Honey Moon.] The Favorite Dance in the Honey Moon.
[Music by W. Linley?] Arranged as a rondo for the
piano-forte ... by J. Monro. pp. 4. [1805?] fol. *See* MONRO
(John) **g. 443. t. (16.)**

— Honour, Riches, Marriage Blessing. *See* infra: [Shakspeare's
Dramatic Songs. Vol. 1.]

— I will not ask one Glance from thee. *Song* ... The poetry by
Miss Costello. *In:* The Harmonicon. vol. 1, pt. 2. no. 27. 1823.
4°. **P. P. 1947.**

— The Invocation. *See* supra: Eight Glees No. 4.

— It was a Lover and his Lass. *See* infra: [Shakspeare's
Dramatic Songs. Vol. II.]

— Last Whitsunday they brought me. *See* infra: [Vortigern.]

— Lawn, as white as driven Snow. *See* infra: [Shakspeare's
Dramatic Songs. Vol. II.]

— The Lullaby. *See* supra: Eight Glees. No. 6.

— "Mourn we his Loss," Elegy ... The words and music by
W. Linley. [A. T. T. B.] pp. 4. *Royal Harmonic Institution:
London*, [1823.] fol. **H. 2788. c. (16.)**

— The Night was dark. *See* infra: [A Trip to the Nore.]

— Now the hungry Lion roars. *See* infra: [Shakspeare's
Dramatic Songs. Vol. I.]

— Oberon's Festival. *See* supra: Eight Glees. No. 8.

— The Opening Glee & Chorus, as sung by Messrs Smith, Pyne,
Clarke, & I. Smith &c., with the greatest Applause in the
revived Play of the Merchant of Bruges, *etc.* pp. 8. *Preston:
London*, [1815.] fol. **H. 2788. f. (6.)**

— Orpheus with his Lute. *See* infra: [Shakspeare's Dramatic
Songs. Vol. II.]

— Queen Mab. *See* supra: Eight Glees. No. 5.

— A Requiem to the memory of ... S. Webbe. *See* FANE (J.) *Earl
of Westmorland*. A Requiem, *etc.* [1820?] *obl.* fol. **E. 180. d.**

— Shakspeare's Dramatic Songs the music partly new and
partly selected, with new symphonies ... to which are
prefixed a general introduction and explanatory remarks.
[With an appendix of the music in Macbeth, attributed to
M. Locke, arranged by S. Wesley.] 2 vol. *London*, [1816.] fol.
 H. 1271.

— [Shakspeare's Dramatic Songs.] The Vocal Music to ... King
Lear. [By W. Linley and others.] 1925. 4°. [*The Vocal Music to
Shakespeare's Plays. No. 13.*] *See* KING. **G. 1243.**

Shakspeare's Dramatic Songs. Vol. I

— Honour, riches, marriage blessing. Duet. *See* SHAKESPEARE.
The Shakspeare Vocal Magazine. No. 64. [1864, *etc.*] fol.
 H. 2389.

— Honour, Riches, Marriage—Blessing. Duet, *etc. See* DUETS.
Vocal Duets, *etc.* No. 179. [1865? *etc.*] fol. **H. 2259.**

LINLEY (WILLIAM)

— Now the hungry lion roars. [Song.] *See* SHAKESPEARE. The
Shakspeare Vocal Magazine. No. 28. [1864.] fol. **H. 2389.**

— Now the hungry Lion roars. [Song, words by] W. Shakespeare
... Edited by Dr. C. Vincent. *O. Ditson Co.: Boston*, (1906.)
fol. **H. 1794. l. (14.)**

— Pardon, Goddess of the Night. *Duet and Chorus* ... the
poetry from "Much Ado about Nothing". *In:* The
Harmonicon. vol. 5, pt. 2. pp. 72–75. 1827. 4°. **P. P. 1947.**

— Tell me where is fancy bred. [Trio.] *See* MERCHANT. The
Merchant of Venice. [1856.] fol. **H. 2342.**

— [Who is Sylvia?] Song, in The Two Gentlemen of Verona,
Act IV, Sc. 2, *etc. In:* The Harmonicon. vol. 4, pt. 2. pp. 44–46.
1826. 4°. **P. P. 1947.**

Shakspeare's Dramatic Songs. Vol. II

— It was a lover and his lass. [Duet.] *See* As. As you like it.
[1856.] fol. **H. 2342.**

— [Lawn as white as driven Snow.] The Song of Autolycus, in
the Winter's Tale, Act IV. Sc. 3. *In:* The Harmonicon. vol. 1,
pt. 2. no. 54. 1823. 4°. **P. P. 1947.**

— Lawn as white as driven snow. [Song.] *See* WINTER. A
Winter's Tale. [1856.] fol. **H. 2342.**

— Lawn as white as driven snow. Song. *See* SHAKESPEARE. The
Shakspeare Vocal Magazine. No. 14. [1864.] fol. **H. 2389.**

— Lawn, as white as driven Snow ... Song ... Edited by
J. Coates. *Novello and Co.: London*, 1929. 4°.
[*Old English Songs. 1a. John Coates Edition.*]
 G. 1275. bb. (24.)

— Orpheus with his Lute ... Arranged and edited by
D. Arundell. *Oxford University Press: London*, 1928. 4°.
 G. 1275. cc. (33.)

— [Was this fair Face.] Song of the Clown, in All's well that
ends well, Act I. Sc. 3, *etc. In:* The Harmonicon. vol. 3, pt. 2.
pp. 274, 275. 1825. 4°. **P. P. 1947.**

— Was this fair face the cause. [Song.] *See* ALL. All's well that
ends well. [1856.] fol. **H. 2342.**

— Wedding is great Juno's crown. [Song.] *See* As. As you like it.
[1856.] fol. **H. 2342.**

——————

— She sung whilst from her Eye ran down. *See* infra:
[Vortigern.]

— Song of the Clown. *See* supra: [Shakspeare's Dramatic Songs.
Vol. II. — Was this fair Face.]

— Eight songs for a Tenor, or Soprano voice, with an
accompaniment for the Piano Forte. *London*, [1810.] fol.
 H. 1416. (4.)

— Tell me where is Fancy bred. *See* supra: [Shakspeare's
Dramatic Songs. Vol. I.]

— To Fear. [Glee, begins: "Thou to whom the world
unknown".] The words from Collins' Ode on the Passions.
See supra: Eight Glees. No. 7.

— Tom Clewline. A much admired song sung by Mr Dignum ...
Written and composed by William Linley. pp. 4. *At
Thompson's Warehouse: London*, [c. 1800.] fol.
Followed by an arrangement for the guitar. **G. 426. ww. (22.)**

— [A Trip to the Nore.] The Night was dark. A much admired
Song sung by Mrs. Bland in A Trip to the Nore [words by
A. Franklin], *etc. Longman and Broderip:* [*London*, 1797.] fol.
 G. 250. (24.)

LINLEY (WILLIAM)

— [Vortigern.] Last Whitsunday they brought me. *Miss Leake's Favorite Song* in Vortigern [word by W. H. Ireland], *etc. Longman & Broderip: London*, [1796.] fol. **G. 250. (27.)**

— [Vortigern.] She sung whilst from her Eye ran down. *Mrs. Jordan's Favorite Song* in Vortigern [words by W. H. Ireland], *etc. Longman & Broderip: London*, [1796.] fol. **G. 250. (26.)**

— Was this fair Face the Cause. *See* supra: [Shakspeare's Dramatic Songs. Vol. II.]

— Wedding is great Juno's Crown. *See* supra: [Shakspeare's Dramatic Songs. Vol. II.]

— Ye sportive Loves. [Glee for three voices.] pp. 6. *W. Hawes: London*, [1831.] fol. **H. 2788. f. (7.)**

— *See* GLEES. A Selection of Glees from the MSS. of the Concentores, being the Compositions of ... W. Linley, *etc.* [1800?] *obl.* fol. **E. 207. a. (1.)**

— *See* SALE (J.) A Collection of New Glees ... To which are added Four Others ... by Dr. Arnold, Messr. Webb[e], Callcott and Lindley, *etc.* [1800?] *obl.* fol. **E. 600. r. (6.)**

LINN (CARGILL)

— Arm! Arm! Arm! [Song.] Words by W. S. Reid, *etc. Paterson, Sons & Co.: Glasgow, etc.*, [1909.] fol. **H. 1794. vv. (57.)**

— Heroes of Scotia. Song, words by J. Macaulay. *M. Allan: Glasgow*, [1910.] fol. **H. 1792. s. (42.)**

— Jack and the Mermaid ... Song for Bass or Baritone, words by W. Park. *Paterson, Sons & Co.: Glasgow, etc.*, [1909.] fol. **H. 1794. vv. (58.)**

— The Maid that makes the Hay. Song, words by J. W. Lyall. [Staff and tonic sol-fa notation.] *M. Allan: Glasgow*, [1912.] fol. **H. 1793. u. (3.)**

— The Stand of the Belgians. Song, words by J. Crosthwaite, *etc.* 2 no. [In F and A.] *Paterson, Sons & Co.: Glasgow, etc.*, 1915. fol. **H. 1793. u. (4.)**

LINN (HARRY)

— Get a little Table ... [Song.] Written & composed by H. Linn, *etc.* (Arranged by W. Sim.) *Hopwood & Crew: London*, [1882.] fol. **H. 1260. f. (54.)**

— John Macraw ... Scotch humorous song. Written and composed by H. Linn. Music arranged by Charles W. Curtiss. [With separate voice part in tonic sol-fa.] 2 pt. *Frank Simpson: Glasgow*, [1908.] fol. **H. 3985. aa. (24.)**

— Known to the Police ... Comic Song, written & composed by H. Linn. *C. Sheard: London*, [1877.] fol. *No. 5705–6 of the Musical Bouquet.* **H. 2345.**

— "Never push a Man when he's going down the Hill." Or "Help one another, Boys". [Song.] Written & composed by H. Linn. ⟨Arranged by M. Hobson.⟩ pp. 5. *Hopwood & Crew: London*, [1869.] fol. **H. 1601. mm. (19.)**

LINN (ROBERT)

— Holla hiaho. T. T. B. B. accompanied. English version by Basil Swift. German folk song, arr. R. Linn. [Staff and tonic sol-fa notation.] pp. 7. *Lawson-Gould Music Publishers: New York; J. Curwen & Sons: London; London* [printed, 1962.] 8°. [*Apollo Club. no.* 858.] **F. 667.**

LINN (ROBERT) Composer of "The Jester's Rondo"

— The Jester's Rondo. Piano solo. *Phillips & Page: London*, [1895.] fol. **h. 1489. t. (11.)**

LINNARZ (ROBERT)

— 2 Festvorspiele für Orgel. Op. 23. No. 1. Vorspiel über: "Nun danket alle Gott". No. 2. Vorspiel über: "Ein' feste Burg ist unser Gott". *J. Rieter-Biedermann: Leipzig*, 1887. fol. **h. 2731. i. (7.)**

— Drei patriotische Lieder f. gemischten Chor. Part. (1. Deutsches Weihelied.—O. Rocca.—2. Mein Vaterland.— G. Müller.—Heil dem Vaterlande.—O. Rocca.) *H. Weinholtz: Berlin*, [1887?] 8°. *No. 13 of "Sammlung mehrstimmiger Gesänge".* **F. 585. q. (31.)**

— Praktische Violinschule ... Zweite ... Auflage. *Berlin*, [1886.] fol. **h. 1112. a. (4.)**

LINNÉ (HANS S.)

— *See* LINÉ.

LINNELL, afterwards GOSLING, afterwards HERBERT (OLIVE)

— Autumn Songs with Music from "Flower Fairies of the Autumn". Words and pictures by C. M. Barker. *Blackie & Son: London and Glasgow*, [1927.] 8°. **E. 1548. b.**

— Clouds. Song, words and music by O. Linnell, *etc. Orpheus Music Publishing Co.: London*, 1910. fol. **H. 1792. s. (43.)**

— Flower Songs of the Seasons. Words and pictures by C. M. Barker. *Blackie & Son: London and Glasgow*, [1928.] 8°. **E. 1548. c.**

— The Glorious Reign. March, *etc.* [P. F.] *R. Cocks & Co.: London*, [1897.] fol. **h. 3282. f. (49.)**

— Hope. Song, words and music by O. Linnell. *Bunz & Co.: London*, 1907. fol. **H. 1794. vv. (59.)**

— Three Little Love Songs. [No. 1.] Affection's Gift. [No. 2.] A Parting Plea. [No. 3.] Love's Parting. Words and music by O. Linnell, *etc. Orpheus Music Publishing Co.: London*, 1913. 4°. **G. 385. vv. (7.)**

— Nature's Voice, and Roses of Summer. Songs, written & composed by O. Linnell. *Orpheus Music Publishing Co.: London*, 1910. fol. **H. 1792. s. (44.)**

— Poppy Faces. Song, words by M. L. Worsfold, *etc. Bunz & Co.: London*, 1907. fol. **H. 1794. vv. (60.)**

— Songs of the Wind and the Sun. Words and music by O. Linnell. *Orpheus Music Publishing Co.: London*, 1909. fol. **H. 1792. s. (45.)**

— Spring Songs with music from "Flower Fairies of the Spring". Words and pictures by C. M. Barker. *Blackie and Son: London, etc.*, [1924.] 8°. **E. 1548.**

— Summer Dawn. Song, words and music by O. Linnell. *G. Whithers & Sons: London*, (1909.) fol. **H. 1794. vv. (61.)**

— Summer Songs with Music from "Flower Fairies of the Summer". Words and pictures by C. M. Barker. *Blackie and Son: London*, [1926.] 8°. **E. 1548. a.**

— The Sweet Path. Song, words by C. Becker. *Bunz & Co.: London*, 1907. fol. **H. 1794. vv. (62.)**

— A Thought Harvest. Song, words and music by O. Linnell. *Bunz & Co.: London*, 1909. fol. **H. 1794. vv. (63.)**

— When Spring came in at the Window. A One-act Play. With songs from Flower Fairies of the Spring by C. M. Barker. Music by O. Linnell. *Blackie & Son: London & Glasgow*, 1942. 8°. **11783. aaa. 4.**

— When Winter is asleep. Song, words and music by O. Linnell. *Bunz & Co.: London*, 1907. fol. **H. 1794. vv. (64.)**

LINNET

— The Linnet, a choice collection of ... popular songs ... arranged for the Violin, Flute and Voice. *London*, [1830?] 8°. **B. 644.**

— The Linnet. [Song.] *See* WARBLING. The warbling Linnet from his Mate. [1740.] *s. sh.* fol. **G. 312. (130.)**

— The Linnett. Song. *See* ARNE (Michael) [Cymon.—You gave me last week a young Linnet.]

— The Linnet. Song. *See* BAILEY (L.)

— The Linnet. Song. *See* CLARKE (R. C.)

— The Linnet. [Song.] *See* COOPER (J. W.)

— The Linnet. Song. *See* FREMANTLE (H.)

— The Linnet. [Song.] *See* HERBERT (Ivy)

— The Linnet. Unison song. *See* LEIGH (Eric)

— The Linnet. [Song, begins: "As passing by a shady Grove".] *See* REEVE (W.)

— The Linnet. [Song.] *See* STANFORD (*Sir* C. V.)

— The Linnet. [Song.] *See* STONE (David)

— The Linnet. Part Song. *See* TURNER (James O.)

— The Linnet and the River. Ballad. *See* HALLEY (T. G. B.)

— A Linnet in a gilded Cage. Two-part Song. *See* FINZI (G.)

— The Linnet is tuning her Flute. Song. *See* BAUER (M. E.)

— A Linnet, just fledg'd. [Song] *See* DALL (   ) *Miss.*

— The Linnet Song. *See* MACFARREN (W. C.)

— The Linnet's Answer. [Song.] *See* PINSUTI (C. E.)

— The Linnet's Nest. Ballad. *See* MONRO (John)

— A Linnet's nest with anxious care. Ballad. *See* DIBDIN (C.)

— The Linnet's Secret. Song. *See* ROWLEY (A.)

LINNET

— Ever there. Song [begins: "Amid life's cares"] ... by Linnet. *London*, [1872.] fol. **H. 1775. u. (52.)**

LINNETS

— The Linnets. [For anonymous editions of this song, beginning: "As bringing home the other Day":] *See* As.

— The Linnets. [Song.] *See* AT. At setting Sun, tho' half afraid. [1780?] *s. sh.* fol. **G. 306. (101.)**

— The Linnets of Coleraine. Two-part song. *See* THIMAN (Eric H.)

— The Linnets' Lament. Part-Song. *See* FORSYTH (C.)

LINSCOTT (ELOISE HUBBARD)

— Folk Songs of old New England. Collected and edited by E. H. Linscott. With an introduction by James M. Carpenter. pp. xxi. 337. *Macmillan Co.: New York*, 1939. 8°. **11689. dd. 1.**

— Folk Songs of old New England. Collected and edited by E. H. Linscott. With an introduction by James M. Carpenter. Second edition. pp. xxiii. 344. *Archon Books: Hamden, London*, 1962. 8°. **07902. bbb. 39.**

LINSELL (EMILY)

— The Wild White Rose. Song [begins: "When the summer sun is sinking"]. Words by A. Wyatt. *London*, [1882.] fol. **H. 1787. j. (41.)**

LINSELL (W. J.)

— Sunlight to the Mind. Ballad [begins: "Come sit, old friend"] written by Mrs. V. Roberts. *London*, [1862.] fol. **H. 1772. s. (18.)**

— The Winter Eve polka. [P. F.] *London*, [1861.] fol. **h. 1460. w. (12.)**

LINSÉN (G.)

— Suomalaisia Kansan-Lauluja. Koonnut A. A. Borenius. Pianon myötäilykselle sovittanut G. Linsén. 1 Vihko. *K. E. Holm: Helsingissä*, 1880. 8°. **E. 1766. a. (4.)**

LINSTEAD

— Linstead Market. Folk-song. *See* BENJAMIN (Arthur L.)

— Linstead Market. Folk-song. *See* GREEN (A. H.)

— Linstead Market. [Two-part song.] *See* HUDSON (Hazel)

LINSTEAD (GEORGE FREDERICK)

— Le Babil. Chatter. For pianoforte. *Graham Gill: London*, [1960.] 4°. **g. 1128. hh. (8.)**

— Begone dull Care. T. T. B. B. Arranged for male voice choir by G. Linstead. [Staff and tonic sol-fa notation.] pp. 8. *Francis, Day & Hunter: London*, [1951.] 8°. [*F. D. H. choral Library.* no. 19.] **F. 672. l.**

— I mun be married a Sunday. For Chorus, or Quartet, of Men's Voices ... unaccompanied. Poem from Ralph Roister Doister, N. Udall, 1550. *J. Curwen & Sons: London*, 1934. 8°. [*The Apollo Club.* No. 714.] **F. 667.**

— Two Irish Tunes. [No. 1.] I'm a poor Stranger. [No. 2.] Kilkenny Races. For Pianoforte. *Graham Gill: [Beckenham, Kent*, 1938.] fol. **g. 823. b. (14.)**

— Four Moods. [No. 1.] Aubade. [No. 2.] Night Piece. [No. 3.] Pas de chien. [No. 4.] Blue Willow. For Piano. *Augener: London*, 1938. 4°. **g. 1127. xx. (2.)**

— O Bethlehem. S. A. T. B. ⟨T. T. B. B.⟩ Basque carol. English version by G. F. L. Arranged by G. Linstead. 2 no. *Francis, Day & Hunter: London*, [1955.] 8°. [*F. D. H. choral Library.* no. 113, 114.] **F. 672. l.**

— *See* DIBDIN (Charles) [The Oddities.] Tom Bowling. T. T. B. B. ... Arranged by G. Linstead. [1954.] 8°. [*F. D. H. choral Library.* no. 73.] **F. 672. l.**

— *See* FOSTER (Stephen C.) Camptown Races. T. T. B. B. ... Arr. by G. Linstead. [1954.] 8°. [*F. D. H. choral Library.* no. 80.] **F. 672. l.**

— *See* PURCELL (H.) [King Arthur.] Fairest Isle ... Arr. by G. Linstead. [1953.] 8°. [*F. D. H. choral Library.* no. 53.] **F. 672. l.**

LINTANT (C.)

— *See* AUVRAY (J. B.) Rose ... Arrangée pour la guitare ou lyre par Lintant, *etc.* [c. 1815.] 8°. **E. 1717. o. (3.)**

— *See* BERTON (H. M.) [Le Concert interrompu.—Oui fuyez loin.] Air ajouté dans l'opéra du Concert interrompu ... Arrangé pour lyre ou guitare par Lintant. [1805?] 8°. **E. 1717. g. (31.)**

LINTANT (C.)

— See BOIELDIEU (F. A.) On tente peu quand l'amour est extrême. *Romance* ... Arrangée pour la guitare ou lyre par Lintant. [1805?] 8°.   **Hirsch M. 660. (5.)**

— See CARBONEL (J. F. N.) Le Mariage de l'amour ... Arrangée pour guitarre par Lintant, *etc.* [c. 1810.] 8°.   **E. 1717. p. (10.)**

— See DELLA MARIA (D.) [L'Opera comique.—Ah pour l'amant le plus discret.] Romance ... Avec accomp^t de guittare par Lintant. [c. 1800.] 8°.   **E. 1717. p. (25.)**

— See FAY (É.) Amour et rose, c'est même chose ... Arrangé pour lyre ou guitare par Lintant. [1805?] 8°.   **E. 1717. g. (32.)**

— See GARAT (P. J.) Les Miracles de la beauté ... Arrangée pour guitare ou lyre par Lintant, *etc.* [1805?] 8°.   **E. 1717. g. (1.)**

— See GAVEAUX (P.) [Le Locataire.—J'offre donc encor un tuteur.] Vaudeville ... Accompagnement de guitare ou lyre par Lintant. [1805?] 8°.   **E. 1717. g. (36.)**

— See GAVEAUX (P.) [Le Locataire.—Le point d'honneur.] Couplets ... Accompagnement de guitare ou lyre par Lintant. [1805?] 8°.   **E. 1717. g. (35.)**

— See GAVEAUX (P.) [Ovinska.—Heureux qui dans sa maisonnette.] Couplets de la veillée d'Ovinska ... Arrangé pour la guitare, ou lyre, par Lintant. [c. 1810.] 8°.   **E. 1717. o. (43.)**

— See GAVEAUX (P.) La Patrie absente ... Arrangée pour la guitare par Lintant. [c. 1810.] 8°.   **E. 1717. o. (42.)**

— See GAVEAUX (P.) [Le Trompeur trompé.—Vous qui souffrés du mal d'amour.] Romance ... Accompagnement de guitare ou lire [*sic*] par Lintant. [1805?] 8°.   **E. 1717. g. (23.)**

— See LEBRUN (L. S.) [Marcelin.—Auprès de ce qu'on aime.] Couplets ... Arrangé [*sic*] pour guitarre par Lintant. [1805?] 8°.   **E. 1717. g. (30.)**

— See LEBRUN (L. S.) [Marcelin.—Ce jeune homme depuis huit jours.] Romance ... Arrangée pour la guitare ou lyre par Lintant. [1805?] 8°.   **E. 1717. g. (29.)**

— See MARTIN Y SOLAR (V.) [La Scuola dei maritati.— Guardami un poco.] Ma Zétulbé ... Avec accompagnement de lyre ou guitar, par Lintant. [c. 1820.] 8°.   **E. 1717. p. (50.)**

— See PLANTADE (C. H.) Le Jour se lève ... Arrangée pour guitare ou lyre par Lintant. [c. 1810.] 8°.   **E. 1717. p. (58.)**

— See PLANTADE (C. H.) [Palma.—Les amoureux me font pitié.] Rondeau ... Arrangé pour la guitare par Lintant. [1800?] 8°.   **E. 1717. g. (16.)**

— See PLANTADE (C. H.) [Palma.—Caché sous les habits.] Romance de Palma ... Arrangée pour la guitarre par Lintant. [c. 1800.] 8°.   **E. 1717. p. (59.)**

— See PLANTADE (C. H.) [Palma.—Petits chagrins de tems en tems.] Air ... Arrangé pour la guitarre par Lintant. [1800?] 8°.   **E. 1717. g. (17.)**

— See PLANTADE (C. H.) [Palma.—Petits chagrins de tems en tems.] Air ... Arrangé pour la guitarre par Lintant. [c. 1800.] 8°.   **E. 1717. o. (66.)**

— See PLANTADE (C. H.) [Palma.—Pour une femme à caractère.] Air de Palma ... Arrangé pour la guitarre par Lintant. [c. 1800.] 8°.   **E. 1717. p. (60.)**

— See PLANTADE (C. H.) [Romagnesi.—Ce n'est qu'auprès des femmes.] Rondeau ... Arrangé pour guitare ou lyre par Lintant. [1800?] 8°.   **E. 1717. g. (18.)**

— See PLANTADE (C. H.) [Romagnesi.—Je sens mon cœur tresaillir.] Duo ... Accomp^t de guitare ou lyre par Lintant. [1800?] 8°.   **E. 1717. g. (19.)**

LINTANT (C.)

— See PLANTADE (C. H.) [Romagnesi.—Si par le milan poursuivi.] Romance ... Arrangée pour guitare ou la lyre par Lintant. [1800?] 8°.   **E. 1717. g. (20.)**

— See PLANTADE (C. H.) [Le Roman.—Aux plaisirs vrais de la nature.] Romance ... Arrangée pour guitare ou cistre par Lintant. [1800?] 8°.   **E. 1717. g. (24.)**

LINTER (EDWIN)

— Adieu ruisseaux au doux murmure, nocturne, pour le piano. Op. 9. *London*, [1857.] fol.   **h. 1489. t. (13.)**

— Archer's quadrilles, *etc.* [P. F.] *London*, [1853.] fol.   **h. 975. e. (42.)**

— I cannot sing to-night, song, written by T. Loker. [Begins: "Oh, press me not".] *London*, [1855.] fol.   **H. 1759. (17.)**

—— "Moonlit streams," nocturne, for the piano forte. Op. 6. *London*, [1857.] fol.   **h. 1489. t. (12.)**

— La promenade du soir, capriccio élégant, pour le piano. *London*, [1858.] fol.   **h. 1489. t. (14.)**

— S. Michael's Hymns. No. 1. *London*, [1866.] 8°.   **E. 605. (48.)**

LINTER (G.)

— Lord Raglan polka. [P. F.] *London*, [1855.] fol.   **h. 976. d. (31.)**

LINTER (HENRI P.)

— The Alexandrina quadrilles for the Piano Forte. *London*, [1838.] fol.   **h. 117. (30.)**

— The magnet polka, for the pianoforte. *London*, [1852.] fol.   **h. 964. (42.)**

— The star polka for the pianoforte. *London*, [1851.] fol.   **h. 964. (50.)**

LINTER (RICARDO)

— Linter's Polkas, Quadrilles, and Waltzes for a full orchestra. No. 1. *London*, [1844.] fol.   **h. 905. (21.)**

— 100 Polkas [P. F.] composed and edited by R. Linter. No. 2, 4–31, 33–35. *London*, [1853.] fol.
Imperfect; wanting no. 1 *and* 3, *and all after* 35.   **h. 964. (51.)**   **& H. 1289.**

— Les adieu, or the parting of summer, romance, for the piano forte. *London*, [1857.] fol.   **h. 907. a. (1.)**

— The Aeolian Harp. Ballad [begins: "Sounds of sweet music"], the poetry by Miss G. Bennet. *London*, [1846.] fol.   **H. 1454. (8.)**

— The Alberta Polka. [P. F.] *London*, [1848.] fol.   **h. 906. (18.)**

— All Nations Polkas. [P. F.] *In:* The Musical Bijou ... for MDCCCLI. pp. 134–139. [1851.] fol.   **H. 2330.**

— The Amaranthine Quadrilles. [P. F.] *London*, [1847.] fol.   **h. 906. (10.)**

— The Amaranthine Quadrilles for the Pianoforte. [Duet.] *London*, [1848.] fol.   **h. 906. (11.)**

— Les amours des oiseaux, quadrilles. [P. F. solo and duet.] 2 no. *London*, [1854.] fol.   **h. 1288. (8.)**

— Andante Cantabile for the Piano Forte. *London*, [1846.] fol.   **h. 906. (30.)**

LINTER (RICARDO)

— The Angel of Light [song, begins: "She comes like an Angel of Light"] written by R. Brown. *London*, [1859.] fol.
H. 1455. (4.)

— Annie Laurie. A Scotch Air, with variations for the Piano Forte by R. Linter. *London*, [1847.] fol.　　h. 906. (24.)

— Ask not why the Tear-drop glistens, *etc.* [Song.] *In:* The Musical Bijou ... for MDCCCXLVII. p. 14. [1847.] fol.
H. 2330.

— Ask not why the tear drop glistens. Ballad, written by Mrs. Alexander. *London*, [1848.] fol.　　H. 1454. (14.)

— Auld Robin Gray ... Scotch Air [by W. Leeves] with variations for the Pianoforte. *London*, [1850.] fol.
h. 716. (4.)

— Balmoral, fantasia on national Scottish melodies for the pianoforte. *London*, [1856.] fol.　　h. 907. a. (2.)

— The Bay of Biscay [by J. Davy], fantasia for the Pianoforte. *London*, [1861.] fol.　　h. 907. b. (22.)

— Beautiful Waves. Duet [begins: "O sweet are the spells"], written by R. Brown. *London*, [1859.] fol.　　H. 1455. (3.)

— The Bell Galop. [P. F.] *In:* The Musical Bijou ... for MDCCCXLVII. pp. 51, 52. [1847.] fol.　　H. 2330.

— The Bell Galop for the Pianoforte. *London*, [1850.] fol.
h. 907. (12.)

— The Bella Donna Quadrilles for the Pianoforte. *London*, [1848.] fol.　　h. 906. (14.)

— La belle Fleuriste. Quadrille. *London*, [1859.] fol.
h. 907. a. (32.)

— La Belle Fleuriste, quadrille. [P. F.] *London*, [1861.] fol.
h. 907. b. (15.)

— La Belle Fleuriste, quadrille. [P. F. duet.] *London*, [1861.] fol.
h. 907. b. (16.)

— The Birds of Paradise Quadrille. [P. F.] *In:* The Musical Bijou ... for MDCCCLII. pp. 158–162. [1852.] fol.　　H. 2330.

— The Birthday Waltz. [P. F.] *In:* The Musical Bijou ... for MDCCCXLVII. p. 91. [1847.] fol.　　H. 2330.

— Blighted Rose, fantasia & variations for the piano forte on the favorite melody sung by Madame Gassier. *London*, [1856.] fol.　　h. 1288. (15.)

— The blind lover. Ballad [begins: "Deep, deep in my heart"], the poetry by D. Ryan. *London*, [1847.] fol.　　H. 1454. (9.)

— The Blue Bells of Scotland ... Scotch air [by Mrs. Jordan] with variations for the Pianoforte. *London*, [1850.] fol.
h. 716. (3.)

— A Bohemian Melody with variations for the Piano Forte. *London*, [1848.] fol.　　h. 906. (37.)

— Bonnie wee flowers. Song. *London*, [1878.] fol.
H. 1783. p. (13.)

— The Bullfinch quadrilles. [P. F.] *London*, [1856.] fol. *No.* 16 *of "R. Cocks & Co.'s Illustrated Dances".*
h. 1481. c. (18.)

— The Cameo Quadrilles. [P. F.] Solo. Duetts. *London*, [1848.] fol.　　h. 906. (15.)

The Canary Bird

— The Canary Bird, Quadrilles for the Piano Forte, *etc.* ⟨Duetts.⟩ pp. 11. *Robert Cocks & Cᵒ: London*, [c. 1880.] fol.
h. 1203. h. (5.)

LINTER (RICARDO)

— The Canary Bird quadrilles. [P. F.] *London*, [1881.] fol.
h. 3275. j. (39.)

— Extract from the Canary Quadrille. [P. F. solo and duet.] *See* SMALLWOOD (W.) Little Buds, *etc.* No. 55. [1874, *etc.*] fol.
h. 1412. p.

— Rondo on the Canary Bird Quadrilles. [P. F. solo and duet.] *See* SMALLWOOD (W.) Home Treasures, *etc.* No. 24. [1872, *etc.*] fol.　　h. 1412. o.

— Rondo on the Canary Bird Quadrilles. [P. F.] [1900.] *See* WEST (S.) and SMALLWOOD (W.) Echoes of Home. No. 17. [1899, *etc.*] fol.　　h. 3808.

— Carlotta Grisi. [Polka. P. F.] ⟨Les Trois grâces. No. 2.⟩ *In:* The Musical Bijou ... for MDCCCXLVI. p. 65. [1846.] fol.
H. 2330.

— Carnaval de Venice for the Piano Forte, arranged by R. Linter. *London*, [1846.] fol.　　h. 906. (31.)

— Carnaval de Venise, fantaisie pour le Piano. *London*, [1861.] fol.　　h. 907. b. (23.)

— The Cellarius Waltz for the Piano Forte. *London*, [1845.] fol.
h. 905. (17.)

— Les Chants du rossignol. Quadrille. [P. F.] *In:* The Musical Bijou ... for MDCCCXLV. pp. 54–56. [1845.] fol.　　H. 2330.

— Les Chants du Rossignol, or, Nightingale Quadrilles. For the Piano Forte. *London*, [1846.] fol.　　h. 906. (2.)

— Chime again Sweet Bells. Song [begins: "Welcome Preludes"], written by R. Brown. *London*, [1859.] fol.
H. 1455. (6.)

— Clara. Polka Caprice for the Piano forte, *etc. London*, [1858.] fol.　　h. 907. a. (18.)

— The Cleopatra galop. [P. F.] *London*, [1878.] fol.
h. 1494. q. (45.)

— Come to my home. Ballad, written by D. Ryan. *London*, [1846.] fol.　　H. 1454. (5.)

— Come unto me all ye that labour. *See* infra: [Pearls from Holy Writ. No. 1.]

— Consolation, impromptu gavotte for the Pianoforte. *London*, [1878.] fol.　　h. 1494. q. (47.)

— La Coquetterie. Morceaux de salon, for the piano, *etc. London*, [1858.] fol.　　h. 907. a. (3.)

— Coronella waltzes, for the pianoforte. *London*, [1852.] fol.
h. 964. (49.)

— Le Corsaire Quadrilles. [P. F.] *In:* The Musical Bijou ... for MDCCCXLVII. pp. 98–100. [1847.] fol.　　H. 2330.

— The Corsair Quadrilles. [P. F.] *London*, [1850.] fol.
h. 907. (16.)

— The dearest Voice to me. Song [begins: "There breaks a glad exultant Tide"], written by R. Brown. *London*, [1859.] fol.
H. 1455. (5.)

— Don Pasquale, brilliant duet for two performers on one piano forte introducing ... Com'è gentil [from D. G. M. Donizetti's opera], *etc. Duncan Davison & Co.: London*, [1858.] fol.　　h. 907. a. (5.)

— The Dream of the dying Maiden. [Song. Words by] I. H. Jewell. *In:* The Musical Bijou ... for MDCCCXLVI. p. 32. [1846.] fol.　　H. 2330.

— Duncan Gray, a Scotch air, with variations for the Piano Forte by R. Linter. *London*, [1847.] fol.　　h. 906. (28.)

LINTER (Ricardo)

— Echoes of Switzerland, for the Piano Forte. *London*, [1845.] fol. **h. 905. (31.)**

— The emerald waltzes. [P. F.] *London*, [1848.] fol. **h. 906. (16.)**

— The Enchanted Grotto, a ... nocturne for the Pianoforte. *London*, [1859.] fol. **h. 907. b. (4.)**

— L'Enfant de France, quadrille. [P. F.] *London*, [1856.] fol. **h. 1288. (14.)**

— "Les étoiles." Trois morceaux de concert, pour le piano-forte. *London*, [1854.] fol. **h. 1288. (5.)**

— The Exhibition waltzes. [P. F.] *London*, [1851.] fol. **h. 964. (36.)**

— Grand Exhibition Waltzes 1851. [P. F.] *In:* The Musical Bijou ... for MDCCCLI. pp. 151–155. [1851.] fol. **H. 2330.**

— The Fairy Boat, *etc.* [Song.] *In:* The Musical Bijou ... for MDCCCXLVII. p. 28. [1847.] fol. **H. 2330.**

— The fairy boat. Song written by M^rs. Alexander. *London*, [1848.] fol. **h. 1454. (15.)**

— The fairy land, quadrilles ... for the pianoforte. *London*, [1857.] fol. **h. 907. a. (23.)**

— The Falcon quadrilles. [P. F.] *London*, [1856.] fol. *No.* 14 *of "R. Cocks & Co.'s Illustrated Dances".* **h. 1481. c. (16.)**

— The Falconer quadrilles. [P. F.] *London*, [1850.] fol. **h. 964. (40.)**

— Grande Fantaisie de Concert pour le Piano Forte. *London*, [1848.] fol. **h. 906. (35.)**

— Fantaisie for the pianoforte on Auber's opera of Le Domino noir. *London*, [1859.] fol. **h. 907. a. (4.)**

— Fantaisie militaire sur [Lindpaintner's song] "Die Fahnenwacht" (the Standard Bearer) for the Piano Forte. *London*, [1847.] fol. **h. 906. (23.)**

— Grand Fantasia with Variations on God save the Queen, for the Piano Forte. *London*, [1852.] fol. **h. 907. (2.)**

— Grand fantaisie di bravura from Lucrezia Borgia [by D. G. M. Donizetti] for the Pianoforte, *etc.* *D. Davison & Co.: London*, [1878.] fol. **h. 1494. q. (48.)**

— Fantasie de concert, on the favorite melody, My lodging is on the cold ground. [P. F.] *London*, [1857.] fol. **h. 907. a. (8.)**

— Grand fantasia on national airs for the Piano Forte. *London*, [1848.] fol. **h. 906. (20.)**

— Grande Fantaisie de concert on [Bellini's opera] Norma, for the Pianoforte. *London*, [1859.] fol. **h. 907. b. (5.)**

— Grande fantaisie on Norma, for the Pianoforte. *London*, [1869.] fol. **h. 907. b. (33.)**

— Fantasia [P. F.] on the national song "The queen and the navy for ever". *London*, [1855.] fol. **h. 1288. (17.)**

— Fantasia on Beethoven's march in the Ruin of Athens. [P. F.] *London*, [1858.] fol. **h. 907. a. (13.)**

— Three favorite Waltzes for the Piano Forte. *London*, [1844.] fol. **h. 905. (4.)**

— Fern Leaves quadrille. [P. F.] *London*, [1873.] fol. **h. 1482. z. (72.)**

— Les fleurs, polka. [P. F.] [*London*, 1852.] fol. **h. 964. (41.)**

— Fleurs champêtres, waltz. [P. F.] *London*, [1856.] fol. **h. 1288. (13.)**

LINTER (Ricardo)

— Les fleurs de noblesse, quadrille à quatre mains. [P. F.] *London*, [1852.] fol. **h. 964. (48.)**

— Flowers of the Ocean. Quadrilles. *London*, [1859.] fol. **h. 907. a. (24.)**

— Flowers of the Ocean quadrilles. [P. F. duet.] *London*, [1859.] fol. **h. 907. b. (8.)**

— Fly o'er the deep blue sea. Duet, written by M^rs. Alexander. *London*, [1848.] fol. **H. 1454. (16.)**

— The Fontainbleau Quadrilles. [P. F. duet.] *London*, [1846.] fol. **h. 906. (4.)**

— The Forget Me Not quadrilles. [P. F.] *London*, [1859.] fol. **h. 907. b. (6.)**

— The Full Cry Quadrilles. [P. F.] pp. 6. *D'Almaine & Co.: London*, [1850.] fol. **h. 721. q. (3.)**

— The Garland Quadrilles. [P. F.] *London*, [1847.] fol. **h. 906. (9.)**

— [The Garland Quadrilles.] La guirlande, quadrille for two performers on the Piano Forte. *London*, [1846.] fol. **h. 906. (3.)**

— Golden Dreams, berceuse for the Pianoforte. *London*, [1877.] fol. **h. 1494. q. (44.)**

— The Golden Fountain quadrille. [P. F.] *London*, [1866.] fol. **h. 907. b. (27.)**

— The Gondola Waltzes for the Pianoforte. *London*, [1850.] fol. **h. 907. (8.)**

— The Gondolier quadrilles ... for the pianoforte. *London*, [1857.] fol. **h. 907. a. (22.)**

— Grand March from Bellini's Norma with brilliant variations, for the piano forte, *etc.* pp. 7. *D'Almaine & Co: London*, [1847.] fol. **h. 723. cc. (11.)**

— Grande galop pour le Piano Forte. *London*, [1844.] fol. **h. 905. (2.)**

— Grande Marche historique for the Piano forte. Op. 15. *London*, [1852.] fol. **h. 907. (3.)**

— Grande Valse. [P. F.] *In:* The Musical Bijou ... for MDCCCXLVIII. pp. 83, 84. [1848.] fol. **H. 2330.**

— Grande valse caracteristique pour le Piano Forte. *London*, [1845.] fol. **h. 905. (26.)**

— Grand [*sic*] valse, caractéristique. [P. F.] *In:* The Musical Bijou ... for MDCCCXLVI. pp. 72–74. [1846.] fol. **H. 2330.**

— The Grasshopper Polka. [P. F.] *London*, [1849.] fol. **h. 907. (20.)**

— The Grenadier's March. [P. F.] *In:* The Musical Bijou ... for MDCCCLII. pp. 151–153. [1852.] fol. **H. 2330.**

— The Hail Storm, grand rondo bravura for the Pianoforte. *London*, [1878.] fol. **h. 1494. q. (46.)**

— Have I not loved thee. Ballad, written by M^rs. Crawford. *London*, [1848.] fol. **H. 1454. (12.)**

— Heart Whispers. Song [begins: "I love the gems in the crown of night"], written by R. Brown. *London*, [1859.] fol. **H. 1455. (1.)**

— The heiress Quadrilles for the Pianoforte. No. 1. Solos. *London*, [1850.] fol. **h. 907. (7.)**

— The Helena Mazurka. [P. F.] *In:* The Musical Bijou ... for MDCCCXLIX. pp. 111, 112. [1849.] fol. **H. 2330.**

— L'Heliotrope. Valse. [P. F.] *In:* The Musical Bijou ... for MDCCCXLV. p. 57. [1845.] fol. **H. 2330.**

LINTER (RICARDO)

— Her Majesty's Court Polkas. [P. F.] *In:* The Musical Bijou ... for MDCCCXLV. pp. 74–76. [1845.] fol.   **H. 2330.**

— Her Majesty's Court Polkas ... arranged for two performers on the Piano Forte ... by E. Flood. *London*, [1848.] fol.   **h. 906. (12.)**

— Homage to Great Britain, grand paraphrase de concert on national airs. *London*, [1865.] fol.   **h. 907. b. (26.)**

— Homage to the ladies of Sherborne, a grand fantasia for the Piano Forte. *London*, [1843.] fol.   **h. 905. (7.)**

— Homage to Wellington, military fantasia for the Pianoforte. *London*, [1845.] fol.   **h. 1460. w. (13.)**

— The Hunter's Quadrilles. [P. F.] *In:* The Musical Bijou ... for MDCCCXLIX. pp. 106–110. [1849.] fol.   **H. 2330.**

— "I'm afloat, I'm afloat," [composed by H. Russell,] with introduction and variations for the Piano Forte by R. Linter. *London*, [1846.] fol.   **h. 906. (32.)**

— "If I were a fairy;" ballad, the words by E. H. Newson. *London*, [1846.] fol.   **H. 1454. (4.)**

— If I were a Fairy. *See* HILES (J.) Six Rondinos, *etc.* No. 2. [1869.] fol.   **h. 1485. p. (2.)**

— Illustrations of the Opera. Drawing Room Pianoforte pieces. No. 1. *London*, [1859.] fol.   **h. 907. b. (3.)**

— Impromptu, for the piano forte, the subject from the (old) 100th psalm. *London*, [1857.] fol.   **h. 907. a. (6.)**

— Innocence, valse sentimentale for the pianoforte. *London*, [1858.] fol.   **h. 907. a. (29.)**

— Introduction and familiar variations on [H. Russell's song] "The Ivy green," for the Piano Forte. *London*, [1844.] fol.   **h. 905. (5.)**

— [A reissue.] Introduction and familiar Variations on The Ivy Green, *etc. London*, [1850?] fol.   **h. 721. n. (27.)**

— Introduction and variations for the Piano forte on the air "Maiden I will ne'er deceive thee". *London*, [1844.] fol.   **h. 905. (10.)**

— "Isabel and Rupert," Serenade nocturne for the Piano Forte. Op. 20. *London*, 1852. fol.   **h. 907. (4.)**

— Jenny Lind Polka, for the Piano Forte. *London*, [1847.] fol.   **h. 906. (5.)**

— Jock o'Hazeldean ... Scotch Air with variations for the Pianoforte. *London*, [1850.] fol.   **h. 716. (7.)**

— Les Jolis Oiseaux, quadrille brillant for the Pianoforte. *London*, [1867.] fol.   **h. 907. b. (28.)**

— Les jolis oiseaux; quadrille brillant for two performers on the Piano Forte. *London*, [1844.] fol.   **h. 905. (6.)**

— Les Jolis Oiseaux, quadrille brillant for two performers on the Pianoforte. *London*, [1867.] fol.   **h. 907. b. (29.)**

— Les jolis oiseaux; a set of quadrilles, arranged as a trio for three performers on the Piano Forte by E. Flood. *London*, [1848.] fol.   **h. 906. (13.)**

— Les Jolis Oiseaux ... quadrilles ... arranged as a trio for ... Pianoforte by E. Flood. *London*, [1867.] fol.   **h. 1485. t. (17.)**

— Les jolis papillons, quadrilles. [P. F. solos and duets.] 2 no. *London*, [1854.] fol.   **h. 1288. (9.)**

— The Kingfisher quadrilles. [P. F.] *London*, [1856.] fol. *No. 15 of "R. Cocks & Co.'s Illustrated Dances".*   **h. 1481. c. (17.)**

LINTER (RICARDO)

— Kossuth galop. [P. F.] *London*, [1852.] fol.   **h. 964. (45.)**

— Kossuth quadrilles. [P. F.] *London*, [1852.] fol.   **h. 964. (44.)**

— Lady, take this little Wreath, *etc.* [Song.] *In:* The Musical Bijou ... for MDCCCXLVII. p. 1. [1847.] fol.   **H. 2330.**

— "Lady, take this little wreath;" ballad, written by Mrs. Delhost. *London*, [1848.] fol.   **H. 1454. (10.)**

— The Lady-bird quadrilles, for the pianoforte. *London*, [1856.] fol.   **h. 907. a. (25.)**

— The Land of our Loved. [Song. Words by] Mrs Abdy. *In:* The Musical Bijou ... for MDCCCXLVI. p. 2. [1846.] fol.   **H. 2330.**

— The lost meeting. *See infra:* [Meet me tonight.]

— Lavinia, mazurka elegant for the piano forte. *London*, [1850.] fol.   **h. 964. (38.)**

— Lavinia mazurka. [P. F.] *London*, [1873.] fol.   **h. 1482. z. (71.)**

— Libiamo ... air from Verdi's opera La Traviata, arranged as a waltz for the piano by R. Linter. *London*, [1858.] fol.   **h. 907. a. (30.)**

— Lilla's a Lady, arranged as a rondino for the Pianoforte. *London*, [1869.] fol.   **h. 907. b. (31.)**

— The Lily of Lorraine; [song, begins: "Thou tellest me,"] written by Mrs. Crawford. *London*, [1846.] fol.   **H. 1454. (7.)**

— [The Lily of Lorraine.] Linter's Ballad "Sweet Lily of Loraine," arranged as a brilliant rondo for the Piano Forte, by G. P. Cittadini. *London*, [1848.] fol.   **h. 707. (8.)**

— The Lily Quadrille. [P. F.] pp. 5. *Brewer & Cᵒ: London*, [c. 1860.] fol.   **h. 61. pp. (10.)**

— The Lisette quadrille. [P. F.] *London*, [1854.] fol.   **h. 1288. (7.)**

— Louisa. Romanza per il Pianoforte. *London*, [1859.] fol.   **h. 907. a. (7.)**

— "Lucinda," grande valse capriccioso, for the piano forte. *London*, [1857.] fol.   **h. 907. a. (31.)**

— Lucy, mazurka elegant. [P. F.] *London*, [1852.] fol.   **h. 964. (47.)**

— Lucy Neale ... with brilliant variations for the Piano Forte by R. Linter. *London*, [1846.] fol.   **h. 906. (29.)**

— Lydia, mazurka elegant, for the piano forte. *London*, [1850.] fol.   **h. 964. (39.)**

— La Margheritina, romance for the Pianoforte. *London*, [1871.] fol.   **h. 1485. t. (18.)**

— Marie Louise. Mazurka for the piano forte, *etc. London*, [1858.] fol.   **h. 907. a. (19.)**

— Maritana Polka. [P. F.] *In:* The Musical Bijou ... for MDCCCLII. pp. 107, 108. [1852.] fol.   **H. 2330.**

— Mazeppa. Polka. [P. F.] *London*, [1850.] fol.   **h. 907. (13.)**

— Trois Mazurkas élégans for the Piano forte. *London*, [1848.] fol.   **h. 906. (17.)**

— Meet me tonight. [Song. Words by] Mrs Crawford. *In:* The Musical Bijou ... for MDCCCXLVII. p. 39. [1847.] fol.   **H. 2330.**

— [Meet me tonight.] "The last meeting;" or "meet me tonight;" a pathetic ballad, written by Mrs Crawford. *London*, [1848.] fol.   **H. 1454. (11.)**

LINTER (Ricardo)

— [Meet me tonight.] The last meeting, ballad, arranged for the guitar by N. W. Gould. *London*, [1852.] fol. **H. 1735. (47.)**

— Merry old Christmas Quadrilles. [P. F.] *London*, [1850.] fol. **h. 907. (15.)**

— Military Quadrille. [P. F.] *In:* The Musical Bijou ... for MDCCCLI. pp. 140–145. [1851.] fol. **H. 2330.**

— Le Mimique, grand galop di Bravura for the Piano Forte. *London*, [1853.] fol. **h. 1288. (2.)**

— Le Mimique, grand galop de bravura for the Pianoforte. *London*, [1864.] fol. **h. 907. b. (25.)**

— The Minuet Quadrilles. [P. F.] *London*, [1845.] fol. **h. 905. (30.)**

— Miriam's song "Sound the loud Timbrel," [the melody by Avison,] arranged for two performers on the Piano Forte by R. Linter. *London*, [1846.] fol. **h. 906. (33.)**

— The misseltoe quadrilles, for two performers on the Piano Forte. *London*, [1846.] fol. **h. 906. (1.)**

— Moonlight on the Ocean. Nocturne for the Pianoforte. Op. 21. *London*, [1852.] fol. **h. 1288. (3.)**

— Morceaux de salon, on favorite airs from the Trovatore, for the piano forte. *London*, [1857.] fol. **h. 907. a. (16.)**

— Moselle quadrille, *etc.* [P. F.] *London*, [1861.] fol. **h. 907. b. (19.)**

— "My God, and do I live to see." A hymn [for three voices] written by the Rev. J. Lakes. *London*, [1840.] fol. **H. 1675. (32.)**

— My lodging is on the cold ground ... Scotch Air with variations for the Pianoforte. *London*, [1850.] fol. **h. 716. (5.)**

— Nankin quadrille. [P. F.] *London*, [1861.] fol. **h. 907. b. (9.)**

— The National Russian Hymn, with variations for the Piano Forte by R. Linter. *London*, [1848.] fol. **h. 906. (36.)**

— Nelly Gray [by B. R. Hanby], fantasia ... for Pianoforte. *London*, [1861.] fol. **h. 907. b. (20.)**

— New morning, evening, and other hymns and sanctus, *etc.* *London*, [1859.] fol. **H. 1187. a. (22.)**

— The new Post Horn Polka. [P. F.] *In:* The Musical Bijou ... for MDCCCXLVIII. p. 53. [1848.] fol. **H. 2330.**

— A new schottische Polka. [P. F.] *In:* The Musical Bijou ... for MDCCCLII. pp. 163, 164. [1852.] fol. **H. 2330.**

— New year's bells. Song, [begins: "Hark how the chime"] written by Mrs. Crawford. *London*, [1845.] fol. **H. 1454. (3.)**

— New Years Bells. [Song,] *etc. In:* The Musical Bijou ... for MDCCCXLV. p. 43. [1845.] fol. **H. 2330.**

— New Year's Bells. Song. *London*, [1868.] fol. **H. 1455. (8.)**

— The novel bloomer galop. [P. F.] *London*, [1852.] fol. **h. 964. (43.)**

— Oh breathe once more that dulcet Strain. [Song. Words by] Mrs Delhoste. *In:* The Musical Bijou ... for MDCCCXLVIII. p. 9. [1848.] fol. **H. 2330.**

— Oh! Logie o Buchan ... Scotch air with variations for the Pianoforte. *London*, [1850.] fol. **h. 716. (6.)**

— Oh! merrie row the bonnie bark ... Scotch air, with variations for the Pianoforte. *London*, [1850.] fol. **h. 716. (9.)**

LINTER (Ricardo)

— Oh sing me any song but this. Ballad, the poetry by M^{rs}. Abdy. *London*, [1845.] fol. **H. 1454. (1.)**

— Oh! sing me any Song but this. [Song,] *etc. In:* The Musical Bijou ... for MDCCCXLV. p. 25. [1845.] fol. **H. 2330.**

— Oh! we never mention her (English Air), arranged for the Pianoforte. *London*, [1862.] fol. **h. 907. b. (21.)**

— Les oiseaux orientales quadrille. [P. F.] *London*, [1849.] fol. **h. 907. (18.)**

— The old arm chair [by H. Russell], arranged as a Divertisement for the Piano Forte. *London*, [1846.] fol. **h. 906. (34.)**

— The Old Ivy Tower, *etc.* [Song.] *In:* The Musical Bijou ... for MDCCCXLVII. p. 5. [1847.] fol. **H. 2330.**

— The old ivy tower. Song written by M^{rs}. Alexander. *London*, [1848.] fol. **H. 1454. (17.)**

— Olden Time, gavotte in E flat, for the Pianoforte. *London*, [1877.] fol. **h. 1482. z. (73.)**

— The Owl Quadrilles for the Pianoforte. *London*, [1848.] fol. **h. 906. (19.)**

— The Palace Polka. [P. F.] *In:* The Musical Bijou ... for MDCCCXLIX. pp. 81, 82. [1849.] fol. **H. 2330.**

— Le Palais royale, valse. [P. F.] *In:* The Musical Bijou ... for MDCCCXLVII. pp. 66–70. [1847.] fol. **H. 2330.**

— The palpitation, Il tremolo, nocturne dramatique, for the piano forte. *London*, [1858.] fol. **h. 907. a. (9.)**

— The Parting waltz. [P. F.] *London*, [1868.] fol. **h. 907. b. (30.)**

— The peace march. [P. F.] *London*, [1856.] fol. **h. 1288. (12.)**

— The peacock quadrilles. [P. F.] *London*, [1854.] fol. **h. 1288. (10.)**

— Pearl drops. Mazurka for the piano forte. *London*, [1858.] fol. **h. 907. a. (20.)**

— The Pearl Waltzes for the Pianoforte. *London*, [1850.] fol. **h. 907. (14.)**

— Pearls from Holy Writ [six sacred songs] ... for soprano & contralto or tenor & contralto. 6 no. *London*, [1860.] fol. **H. 1187. a. (1.)**

— [Pearls from Holy Writ. No. 1.] (Come unto me all ye that labour. Sacred song ... St Matthew, Ch. XI. Ver. 28. pp. 4. *John Blockley: London*, [c. 1870.] fol. **H. 1028. v. (24.)**

— Pearls of Morning Dew, caprice brillante for the Pianoforte. *London*, [1879.] fol. **h. 1494. q. (49.)**

— Pekin quadrille. [P. F.] *London*, [1861.] fol. **h. 907. b. (10.)**

— Pestal, with introduction and variations for the Piano Forte. *London*, [1846.] fol. **h. 343. (4.)**

— Pestal, with introduction and ... variations for the Pianoforte. *London*, [1870.] fol. **h. 907. b. (34.)**

— Pestal waltz for the Piano Forte [on the melody composed by Pestal]. *London*, [1846.] fol. **h. 343. (5.)**

— La Petite coquette Polka. [P. F.] *In:* The Musical Bijou ... for MDCCCLII. pp. 132, 133. [1852.] fol. **H. 2330.**

— Poetical studies for the Pianoforte. No. 2, 5. *London*, [1857.] fol. *Imperfect; wanting all other no.* **h. 907. b. (1.)**

— The polkas of all nations. [P. F.] *London*, [1850.] fol. **h. 964. (37.)**

LINTER (RICARDO)

— The postillion polka, for the pianoforte. *London*, 1851. fol.
h. 964. (46.)

— Princess of Wales quadrille. [P. F.] *London*, [1863.] fol.
h. 907. b. (24.)

— Promenade waltz. *See* HILES (J.) Six Rondinos, *etc.* No. 6.
[1869.] fol. **h. 1485. p. (2.)**

— Queen Mab Polka. [P. F.] *In:* The Musical Bijou ... for
MDCCCXLVIII. p. 54. [1848.] fol. **H. 2330.**

— Queen of the Stars. Valse à deux temps for the Pianoforte.
London, [1850.] fol. **h. 907. (23.)**

— La Rafale de Neige. Nocturne pour le Pianoforte. *London*,
[1850.] fol. **h. 907. (11.)**

— The Rainbow Quadrilles for the Pianoforte. *London*, [1850.]
fol. **h. 907. (6.)**

— The real Irish Polkas ... arranged for the Piano Forte.
London, [1844.] fol. **h. 905. (13.)**

— The real Polkas ... arranged for the Piano Forte. 2 set.
London, [1844.] fol. **h. 905. (12.)**

— The real polkas, [no. 4–6,] composed by R. Linter, arranged
for two performers on the Piano Forte, by W. H. Holmes.
London, [1844.] fol. **h. 905. (22.)**

— The real Polkas [no. 1, 2, 4, 6,] arranged for the harp and
Piano Forte by N. C. Bochsa. *London*, [1845.] fol.
h. 905. (23.)

— [The Real Polkas. No. 1, 2.] Real Polka, arranged for the
Harp, *etc.* [1846.] fol. *See* BOCHSA (R. N. C.) **h. 169. (29.)**

— The real Scotch and Irish Polkas ... arranged for the harp
and Piano Forte, by N. C. Bochsa. *London*, [1845.] fol.
h. 905. (24.)

— The real Scotch Polkas ... arranged for the Piano Forte.
London, [1844.] fol. **h. 905. (14.)**

— La Redowa Polka ... for the Piano Forte. *London*, [1845.]
fol. **h. 905. (25.)**

— La Redowa Polka. [P. F.] *In:* The Musical Bijou ... for
MDCCCXLVI. pp. 51–53. [1846.] fol. **H. 2330.**

— Reminiscences of Burns, Fantasia for the Piano Forte in
honour of the Burns Festival. *London*, [1844.] fol.
h. 905. (11.)

— Reminiscences of Moore. Fantasia on Irish Melodies, for the
Pianoforte. *London*, [1852.] fol. **h. 907. (1.)**

— Reminiscences of Sontag, fantasia for the Pianoforte.
London, [1869.] fol. **h. 907. b. (32.)**

— Rhoda and Minna, romance for the Pianoforte. *London*,
[1858.] fol. **h. 907. a. (11.)**

— The rippling brook, capriccio, for the pianoforte. *London*,
[1857.] fol. **h. 907. a. (10.)**

— Robin Goodfellow quadrilles for the Piano Forte [arranged
from E. J. Loder's opera]. *London*, [1849.] fol. **h. 907. (21.)**

— Rondeau militaire for the Piano Forte, introducing the air
"Ciàscun [*sic*] lo dice" ... in [D. G. M. Donizetti's opera] La
Figlia del Reggimento, *etc.* *D'Almaine & Co.: London*,
[1848.] fol. **h. 906. (21.)**

— La rose mazurka; or, Cellarius valse ... for the Piano Forte.
London, [1845.] fol. **h. 905. (28.)**

— Rosina, nocturne in D♭, for the piano forte. *London*, [1858.]
fol. **h. 907. a. (12.)**

LINTER (RICARDO)

— The Royal Alice Polka for the Piano Forte. pp. 3. *D'Almaine
& Cº: London*, [1845.] fol.
With the titlepage printed in green. **h. 905. (18.)**

— [Another issue.] The Royal Alice Polka, *etc.* *D'Almaine & Cº:
London*, [1845.] fol.
With a plain titlepage. **h. 721. q. (4.)**

— The Royal Horse Guards quadrilles for the Piano Forte.
London, [1848.] fol. **h. 906. (8.)**

— The Royal Mazurka. *See* supra: La rose mazurka.

— The Royal Mazurka, for the Piano Forte. *London*, [1845.]
fol. **h. 905. (19.)**

— The Royal Mazurka or Cellarius Valse. [P. F.] *In:* The
Musical Bijou ... for MDCCCXLVI. pp. 62, 63. [1846.] fol.
H. 2330.

— The Royal Military quadrille. [P. F.] *London*, [1861.] fol.
h. 907. b. (12.)

— The Royal Military quadrille. [P. F. duet.] *London*, [1861.]
fol. **h. 907. b. (13.)**

— The Royal Portrait Quadrilles. [P. F. solo and duet.] *London*,
[1845.] fol. **h. 905. (29.)**

— The Royal Welsh Quadrilles, for the Piano Forte. *London*,
[1845.] fol. **h. 905. (16.)**

— Sacred Melodies, adapted to Hymns of peculiar metre,
composed and arranged for the organ or pianoforte by
R. Linter. [*London?* 1860?] *obl.* 4°. **B. 512. c. (3.)**

— Sacred Songs without Words ... Easy rondos [for the]
Pianoforte. no. 2, 3. *London*, [1858.] fol.
Imperfect; wanting no. 1. **h. 907. b. (2.)**

— La Salterelle pour le Pianoforte. *London*, [1850.] fol.
h. 907. (9.)

— The Sea Serpent Polka. [P. F.] *London*, [1849.] fol.
h. 907. (19.)

— Season Quadrilles, *etc.* [P. F.] *In:* The Musical Bijou ... for
MDCCCLI. pp. 120–124. [1851.] fol. **H. 2330.**

— The Seasons, a set of quadrilles on old English airs. [P. F.]
London, [1859.] fol. **h. 907. a. (26.)**

— The Seasons, a set of Quadrilles on old English airs. Duet.
London, [1859.] fol. **h. 907. a. (27.)**

— Serenade Waltzes. [P. F.] *In:* The Musical Bijou ... for
MDCCCXLVI. pp. 90–94. [1846.] fol. **H. 2330.**

— The Serenade waltzes for the piano forte. *London*, [1854.]
fol.
A different work from the preceding. **h. 1288. (11.)**

— Shadows of the past, nocturne poetical, for the piano forte.
London, [1858.] fol. **h. 907. a. (14.)**

— The shower of diamonds, valse brillante for the pianoforte.
London, [1855.] fol. **h. 1288. (18.)**

— The Singing Birds. Morceaux brillantes [*sic*] de salon ... for
the piano. ⟨Duet.⟩ no. 1, 2. 6. *J. Blockley: London*, [c. 1860.]
fol.
Imperfect; wanting no. 3–5. **H. 1454. a.**

— Sister Spirit come away, [song, begins: "Mother, Mother",]
written by R. Brown. *London*, [1859.] fol. **H. 1455. (2.)**

— The Sisters, a set of quadrilles. [P. F.] *London*, [1849.] fol.
h. 907. (17.)

— The skylark, quadrilles for two performers on the piano forte.
London, [1855.] fol. **h. 1288. (16.)**

LINTER (Ricardo)

— The Snow-drop, *etc.* [Song.] *In:* The Musical Bijou ... for MDCCCXLVII. p. 49. [1847.] fol.   **H. 2330.**

— The Snowdrop; song, written by Mrs. Alexander. *London*, [1848.] fol.   **H. 1454. (13.)**

— Sound the loud Timbrel. *See* supra: Miriam's song.

— Un Souvenir des Alpes. Fantasia and variations for the Piano Forte. *London*, [1847.] fol.   **h. 906. (22.)**

— "Sunrise on the mountain," romance for the Piano Forte. *London*, [1853.] fol.   **h. 1288. (6.)**

— Sunset on the lake, nocturne pastorale for the piano-forte. Op. 25. *London*, [1854.] fol.   **h. 1288. (4.)**

— The Surprise or Game of Romps galop ... for the Pianoforte. *London*, [1861.] fol.   **h. 907. b. (14.)**

— The Swallow quadrilles. [P. F. duet.] *London*, [1855.] fol. *No. 9 of "R. Cocks & Co.'s Illustrated Dances".*   **h. 1481. c. (14.)**

— The Swan quadrilles. [P. F.] *London*, [1856.] fol. *No. 13 of "R. Cocks & Co.'s Illustrated Dances".*   **h. 1481. c. (15.)**

— The Swedish Nightingale Quadrilles, for the Piano Forte. *London*, [1847.] fol.   **h. 906. (6.)**

— Sweet Years of Youth, *etc.* [Song.] *In:* The Musical Bijou ... for MDCCCXLV. p. 7. [1845.] fol.   **H. 2330.**

— "Sweet Years of Youth;" ballad, the poetry by Mrs. Crawford. *London*, [1845.] fol.   **H. 1454. (2.)**

— Tally-Ho! brilliant fantasia (à la chasse) for the Pianoforte. *London*, [1861.] fol.   **h. 907. b. (17.)**

— The Tambourine Polka. [P. F.] *In:* The Musical Bijou ... for MDCCCLI. pp. 156, 157. [1851.] fol.   **H. 2330.**

— "There's nae luck about the house;" a Scotch air, with variations for the Piano Forte by R. Linter. *London*, [1847.] fol.   **h. 906. (26.)**

— Thy Mother is near. [Song. Words by] Mrs Abdy. *In:* The Musical Bijou ... for MDCCCXLVI. p. 16. [1846.] fol.   **H. 2330.**

— 'Tis for me to remember; song. *London*, [1846.] fol.   **H. 1454. (6.)**

— Le Tourbillon [solo], pour le Pianoforte. *London*, [1850.] fol.   **h. 907. (10.)**

— La Tourterelle, quadrille ... for the piano forte. *London*, [1857.] fol.   **h. 907. a. (28.)**

— Trab! Trab! Trab! [by F. W. Kuecken,] with Variations for the Pianoforte. *London*, [1850.] fol.   **h. 716. (8.)**

— Twilight stars, caprice, pour le piano. *London*, [1858.] fol.   **h. 907. a. (15.)**

— The United Service. Song, words by the son of an old naval officer. *London*, [1849.] fol.   **H. 1454. (18.)**

— Valse buffa for the Pianoforte. *London*, [1850.] fol.   **h. 907. (5.)**

— Valse di bravura. [P. F.] *In:* The Musical Bijou ... for MDCCCXLVII. pp. 94–97. [1847.] fol.   **H. 2330.**

— The Venetian Quadrilles. [P. F. duet.] *London*, [1845.] fol.   **h. 905. (27.)**

— The Verbena Quadrilles for the Pianoforte. No. 1. Solos. *London*, [1850.] fol.   **h. 907. (22.)**

— Vesper Dew Drops, caprice for the Pianoforte. *London*, [1859.] fol.   **h. 907. b. (7.)**

LINTER (Ricardo)

— Vesperus, morceau religioso for the Pianoforte. *London*, [1879.] fol.   **h. 1494. q. (50.)**

— The Villa polka. [P. F.] *London*, [1872.] fol.   **h. 1485. t. (19.)**

— Violante Polka. [P. F.] *In:* The Musical Bijou ... for MDCCCLII. pp. 115, 116. [1852.] fol.   **H. 2330.**

— La visite heureuse. A set of quadrilles for the Piano Forte. *London*, [1844.] fol.   **h. 905. (8.)**

— "La Vistule," mazurka élégante pour le piano. *London*, [1857.] fol.   **h. 907. a. (21.)**

— Voice of the waves, étude de concert. [P. F.] *London*, [1858.] fol.   **h. 907. a. (17.)**

— Warblings at eve, Vocal duet [begins: "O beautiful melody"] written by J. E. Carpenter. *London*, [1860.] fol.   **H. 1455. (7.)**

— The Water Nymph quadrille. [P. F.] *London*, [1861.] fol.   **h. 907. b. (11.)**

— The Waterfall, caprice, for the piano forte. pp. 9. *Brewer & Cᵒ: London*, [1858.] fol.   **h. 61. pp. (11.)**

— What is Love? pretty Maiden say. [Song. Words by] Mrs Alexander. *In:* The Musical Bijou ... for MDCCCXLVIII. p. 25. [1848.] fol.   **H. 2330.**

— The Winter Garden quadrille. [P. F.] *London*, [1861.] fol.   **h. 907. b. (18.)**

— Within a mile of Edinburgh. Scotch air [by J. Hook], with variations for the Piano Forte by R. Linter. *London*, [1847.] fol.   **h. 906. (25.)**

— Woodman spare that tree. The popular ballad [composed by H. Russell] arranged with an introduction and variations for the Piano Forte by R. Linter. *London*, [1844.] fol.   **h. 905. (9.)**

— The Wreath Waltzes. [P. F.] *In:* The Musical Bijou ... for MDCCCXLIX. pp. 88–93. [1849.] fol.   **H. 2330.**

— The yellow haired laddie. A Scotch air, with variations for the Piano Forte by R. Linter. *London*, [1847.] fol.   **h. 906. (27.)**

— The Zephyrs; a brilliant set of quadrilles, for the Piano Forte. *London*, [1844.] fol.   **h. 905. (1.)**

— The Zephyrs quadrilles brillantes, and a galop, as duets for two performers on the Piano Forte. *London*, [1843.] fol.   **h. 905. (3.)**

— *See* BEETHOVEN (L. van) [*Doubtful and Supposititious Works.*] [Waltz. K.-H. Anhang 14. No. 1.] Le Désir valse de Beethoven, for the Piano Forte [arranged] by R. Linter. [1853.] fol.   **h. 1288. (1.)**

— *See* BELLINI (V.) [*Norma.—Ah! bello a me ritorna.*] The Cavatina ... with variations by R. Linter. [1845.] fol.   **h. 905. (20.)**

— *See* BOCHSA (R. N. C.) The Pas de fascination ... arranged by R. Linter. [1845.] fol.   **h. 905. (15.)**

— *See* VENZANO (L.) The Gassier Valse ... arranged with variations for the piano forte by R. Linter. [1856.] fol.   **h. 1288. (19.)**

LINTER (T. H.)

— The Lucknow Polka, *etc.* [P. F.] pp. 5. *H. D'Alcorn: London*, [1858?] fol.   **h. 721. j. (17.)**

LINTER (W. Brine)

— A favorite German air with variations for the Harp. *London,* [1850?] fol.   **h. 3213. j. (9.)**

LINTER (William)

— The Favorite German Hymn ⟨by I. J. Pleyel⟩, arranged with variations, for the piano forte ... by Wm Linter. pp. 6. *B^w Harris, for the author: London,* [^WM 1828.] fol.
     h. 61. oo. (12.)

LINTHORN (E. A.)

— Hawthorn Berries. [P. F.] *Orpheus Music Publishing Co.: London,* 1916. fol.   **h. 3284. oo. (23.)**

LINTHORST (Frans)

— Classical Ballet Music. [P. F.] pp. 13. *Royal Academy of Dancing: London,* [1977.] 4°.   **f. 541. p. (5.)**

— *See* London.— *Royal Academy of Dancing.* Intermediate Examination. Girls' syllabus. Book 2. ⟨[Composed by] N. Higgins, F. Linthorst.⟩ [1977.] 4°.   **f. 541. o. (9.)**

LINTON

— Linton Lowrie. Ballad. *See* Mackenzie (A.)

LINTON (Arthur Henry)

— Gather ye Rose-buds. Two-Part Song, words by R. Herrick. *Novello and Co.: London,* [1911.] 8°.   **F. 328. m. (15.)**

— In the Spring Time. Two-Part Song, words by Shakespeare. *Novello and Co.: London,* [1911.] 8°.   **F. 328. m. (16.)**

— In the Spring Time, *etc.* [Tonic sol-fa notation.] *Novello and Co.: London,* [1913.] 4°.   **B. 559. w. (21.)**

— The Lady Night. "Night coming into a Garden." Song, words by Lord A. Douglas, *etc. Vincent Music Co.: London,* [1911.] fol.   **H. 1792. s. (46.)**

— Love is a Torment. Two-Part Song, words by S. Daniel, *etc. Novello and Co.: London,* [1913.] 8°.   **F. 328. r. (16.)**

— Molly McGee. Written and composed by A. Linton, *etc.* [Song. Staff and tonic sol-fa notation. Voice part.] *Francis, Day & Hunter: London,* [1899.] *s. sh.* fol.   **H. 3980. ss. (16.)**

— My True-Love hath my Heart. Part-Song for two equal voices, words by Sir P. Sidney. *Novello & Co.: London,* [1917.] 8°.   **F. 506. a. (14.)**

— A Red, red Rose. Two-Part Song for female or boys' voices, poem by R. Burns. *Novello and Co.: London,* [1912.] 8°.   **F. 328. r. (17.)**

— Silvia. Two-part Song, words by Shakespeare. *Novello & Co.: London,* [1917.] 8°.   **F. 506. a. (13.)**

— Sweet and twenty. Two-part Song, words by Shakespeare. *Novello & Co.: London,* [1917.] 8°.   **F. 506. a. (12.)**

— Sweet and Twenty, *etc.* [Tonic sol-fa.] *Novello and Co.: London,* [1922.] 4°.   **B. 559. y. (7.)**

— "The Sweetest little Flow'r in all the Garden." ⟨Song.⟩ Written and composed by A. Linton. [Staff and tonic sol-fa notation. Voice part.] *Francis, Day & Hunter: London,* [1908.] *s. sh.* fol.   **H. 3985. aa. (25.)**

— "The Sweetest little Flow'r in all the Garden," *etc.* ⟨Song.⟩ [With separate voice part.] 2 pt. *Francis, Day & Hunter: London,* [1908.] fol.   **H. 3985. aa. (26.)**

— To give my Love Good-morrow. Two-Part Song, words by T. Heywood. *Novello and Co.: London,* [1911.] 8°.   **F. 328. m. (17.)**

LINTON (Arthur Henry)

— Under the Greenwood Tree. Part-Song for two equal voices, words by Shakespeare. *Novello and Co.: London,* [1911.] 8°.   **F. 328. n. (17.)**

— Under the Greenwood Tree, *etc.* [Tonic sol-fa notation.] *Novello and Co.: London,* [1913.] 4°.   **B. 559. w. (22.)**

LINTON (Harry)

— Ching-a-ling Fong. [Song.] Words by Bert St. John. Arr. by Alexander Spencer. pp. 6. *Jerome H. Remick & Co.: Detroit, New York,* [1905.] fol.   **H. 3985. aa. (27.)**

— Down where the Ocean Breezes blow. [Song.] Words by J. Gilroy. *Aldrich, Linton & Hylands: New York,* 1901. fol.   **H. 1799. cc. (67.)**

— I'll be busy all next Week. [Song.] Written by John Gilroy. pp. 7. *Francis, Day & Hunter: London,* [1902.] fol.   **H. 3985. aa. (28.)**

— Lucy Dale. ⟨Song and chorus.⟩ Written and composed by H. Linton. pp. 5. *Feist & Frankenthaler: New York,* [1899.] fol.   **H. 3980. ss. (17.)**

— Mama, will you stay at Home to-night? [Song.] Words by John Gilroy. *F. A. Mills: New York, Chicago,* [1901.] 4°.   **. H. 3985. aa. (29.)**

— Mary Lee. *See infra:* The Time will pass merrily, Mary Lee.

— My Whitewash Man. [Song.] Words by Bert St. John. Arr. by Alexander Spencer. *Jerome H. Remick & Co.: Detroit, New York,* [1905.] fol.   **H. 3985. aa. (30.)**

— Ruby. [Song.] Words by Leila McIntyre. pp. 5. *Feist & Frankenthaler: New York,* [1900.] fol.   **H. 3985. aa. (31.)**

— The Time will pass merrily Mary Lee. [Song.] Words by John Gilroy. pp. 5. *Aldrich, Linton & Hylands: New York,* [1901.] fol.   **H. 3985. aa. (32.)**

— You're going to be a long Time dead. [Song.] Words by Anita Lawrence. pp. 5. *Theo. Bendix Music Pub.: New York,* [1908.] fol.   **H. 3985. aa. (33.)**

LINTON (Harry) and **GILROY** (John)

— Abel and Mabel. [Song.] pp. 3. *Howley, Haviland & Dresser: New York,* [1902.] fol.   **H. 3985. aa. (34.)**

— I sing a little tenor. [Song.] pp. 3. *Howley, Haviland & Dresser: New York,* [1902.] fol.   **H. 3985. aa. (35.)**

LINTON (Harvey)

— Marjorie, Jean, and Kathleen. Song Cyclette, written ... by L. Johnston. *Ascherberg, Hopwood & Crew: London,* 1913. fol.   **H. 1793. u. (5.)**

— Old Skipper Bob. Musical Monologue, written by L. Johnston, *etc. Reynolds & Co.: London,* (1912.) fol. *Musical Monologues, No. 72.*   **H. 2087.**

— The Prayer of Empire. Song, words by C. Bingham. 2 no. [In E flat and F.] *J. B. Cramer & Co.: London,* 1911. fol.   **H. 1792. s. (47.)**

— Shy? Song, words by L. Johnston. *J. B. Cramer & Co.: London,* 1911. fol.   **H. 1792. s. (48.)**

— Three short Years. [Song.] Words by L. Johnston. (In G and B♭.) 2 no. *Ascherberg, Hopwood & Crew: London,* (1913.) fol.   **H. 1793. u. (6.)**

— *See* Johnston (L.) and Linton (H.) King Hilarity, *etc.* 1911. fol.   **H. 1792. p. (25.)**

— *See* Thomas (J. R.) Eileen Alannah ... Arranged by H. Linton. [1911.] 8°.   **F. 321. z. (49.)**

LINTON (Thomas Alexander)
— Memories of Erin. March. [P. F.] *F. Pitman, Hart & Co.:
London*, [1904.] fol.   **h. 3282. ww. (41.)**

LINTUR (P. V.)
— *See* Krechko (M. M.) and Lintur (P. V.) Закарпатські пісні
та коломийки. 1965. 8°.   **X. 439/896.**

LINTWHITE
— The Lintwhite. Scotch ballad. *See* Naumann (T. W.)

LINVAL
— Linval, no more. Duetto. *See* Kelly (M.) [Youth, Love and
Folly.]

LINWOOD (Arthur)
— The Beatitudes. A Dialogue for Four Girls and Four Boys
interspersed with music. Written by W. E. Hopkin, the music
... by Linwood and others, *etc.* *A. Linwood: Eastwood,
Notts.*, [1903.] 4°.   **E. 496. c. (8.)**

— Caleb Fulham's Harvest-Time. A Sacred Song Service,
written by L. Slade. Illustrated with new and original music
by A. Linwood, G. Booth, J. Barker, T. Merritt and others.
A. Linwood: Eastwood, Notts., [1902.] 8°.   **E. 496. b. (10.)**

— The Colliers' Spurgeon; or, The Life of Matthew Hayes. A
Sacred Song Service, written by M. Wheeler. Illustrated with
new and original music by A. Linwood, T. Brookfield,
W. H. Bennett and others. *A. Linwood: Eastwood, Notts.*,
[1902.] 8°.   **E. 496. b. (9.)**

— Gideon. A Dialogue ... interspersed with Music. Written by
W. E. Hopkin. *A. Linwood: Eastwood, Notts.*, [1900.] 8°.
                                                E. 496. b. (8.)

— Hawthorn Meadow. A Sacred Song Service. Written by Mrs.
Haycraft ... With ... music by A. Linwood, G. Booth,
W. H. Bennett, J. France, and others, *etc.* *A. Linwood:
Eastwood, Notts.*, [1901.] 4°.   **E. 496. a. (17.)**

— His Time of Reaping. A Sacred Song Service, written by
B. E. Slade ... music by A. Linwood and others. *A. Linwood:
Eastwood, Notts.*, [1903.] 4°.   **E. 496. c. (9.)**

— Invitation. [Prize hymn tune. Tonic sol-fa and staff notation.]
[1892.] *See* Festive. The Festive Choralist, *etc.* No. 11.
[1889–1952.] 8°.   **F. 989.**

— Marching Song. [Hymn.] Words by W. A. Eaton. [1899.] *See*
Sheffield. The Sheffield Voice of Praise, *etc.* No. 46. [1891,
etc.] 4°.   **E. 1483.**

— The Saviour's Love. [Hymn.] [1899.] *See* Sheffield. The
Sheffield Voice of Praise, *etc.* No. 39. [1891, *etc.*] 4°.
                                                E. 1483.

LINWOOD (Arthur) and **BROOKFIELD** (Thomas)
— The Harvest of Pity ... Sacred Song Service. Written by Mrs.
Haycraft, *etc.* *A. Linwood: Eastwood, Notts.*, [1899.] 4°.
                                                E. 496. a. (18.)

LINWOOD (E.)
— Like angel bright. Song & chorus. *Troy, N. Y.*, 1868. fol.
                                                H. 1780. p. (38.)

LINWOOD (Mary)
— David's First Victory, a sacred oratorio ... with an
accompaniment for the Organ or Pianoforte. *London*, [1840.]
fol.   **H. 1069.**

LINWOOD (Mary)
— [The Kellerin.] I ponder on those happy hours. Ballad from
an unpublished Opera, *etc. London*, [1853.] fol.
No. 1 *of "Operatic Fragments".*   **H. 2828. b. (9.)**

— Let us hence! *Canzonet* ... the subject from a rondo by
W. Plachy, *etc. In:* The Harmonicon. vol. 6, pt. 2.
pp. [101]–105. 1828. 4°.   **P. P. 1947.**

— Pretty Fairy! *Canzonet. In:* The Harmonicon. vol. 6, pt. 2.
pp. 45–49. 1828. 4°.   **P. P. 1947.**

— The Sabbath Bridal. A dialogue. [Song.] *In:* The Harmonicon.
vol. 10, pt. 2. pp. 38–40. 1832. 4°.   **P. P. 1947.**

— [The White Wreath.] Leave me to sorrow awhile. Ballad from
an unpublished opera, *etc. London*, [1853.] fol.
No. 2 *of "Operatic Fragments".*   **H. 2828. b. (10.)**

LINZ (   )
— Don Quixote Polka for the Pianoforte. *London*, [1850.] fol.
                                                h. 947. (48.)

— The Restless Polka. [P. F.] *See* Linter (R.) 100 Polkas, *etc.*
No. 20. [1853.] fol.   **h. 1289.**

LINZ (Marta)
— *See* Dvořák (A.) Humoreske. Op. 101. No. 7. Violin and
piano. Arranged by M. Linz, *etc.* [1954.] 4°. **g. 1160. c. (15.)**

— *See* Dvořák (A.) [Slavische Tänze. Op. 72. No. 2.] Slavonic
Dance in E minor ... Violin and piano. Arranged by
M. Linz, *etc.* [1954.] 4°.   **g. 1160. c. (16.)**

LINZZ (   )
— Der Schottische [arranged by Linzz] for two performers on
the Piano Forte and Der Rahelose, a new Schottischer
composed by Linzz. *London*, [1848.] fol.   **h. 952. (7.)**

LION
— The Lion. Song. *See* Pitfield (T. B.)

— The Lion and Flag of Old. Song. *See* Clark (H.)

— The Lion and four Bulls. [Song.] *See* Erle (T.) The Sunny
Side ... No. 6.

— The Lion and Fox. Cantata. *See* Lambourn (   ) *Mr.*

— The Lion and his Cubs. Song. *See* Campbell (A. W.)

— The Lion and its Cubs. Song. *See* Nicholls (E.)

— The Lion and the Bear. [Song.] *See* Carlton (G.)

— The Lion and the Bear. Song. *See* Johnson (W.)

— The Lion and the Bird. [Song.] *See* Weslyn (Louis)

— The Lion and the Lamb. [Song.] *See* Bowers (Robert H.)
[The Maid and the Mummy.—A Lion enraged.]

— The Lion and the Unicorn. Unison song. *See* Rendall
(Honor)

— Le Lion de Belfort. [Song.] *See* Darcier (J.)

— Le Lion de St. Marc. Opéra-bouffe. *See* Legouix (I. E.)

— Le Lion de Waterloo. Chant patriotique. *See* Gobbaerts (L.)

— Le Lion et le Rat. Duo. *See* Magner (C.)

— The Lion Guard. Song. *See* Hiller (H. C.)

— The Lion Hearts of England. Song. *See* Lee (A.)

LION

— The Lion in his Den. Song. *See* DIBDIN (C.) British War-Songs. No. 7.

— The Lion of England. [Song.] *See* SMYTH (C.)

— The Lion of Judah. *See* DAWRE (R.)

— The Lion's on guard. Song. *See* CARR (F. O.)

— The Lion's roused at last. Song. *See* LESTER (John H.)

— The Lion Tamer. Unison Song. *See* ROWLEY (A.)

— The Lion Tamer. Comic Opera. *See* STAHL (R.)

— The Lion, the Witch and the Wardrobe. Opera. *See* MACCABE (John)

— The Lion's Bride. Ballad. *See* SCHUMANN (R. A.) [Drei Gesänge. Op. 31. No. 1. Die Löwenbraut.]

— The Lion's Sons. Song. *See* TAYLOR (W. A.)

LIONCOURT (GUY DE)

— Libera me, Domine. Motet à 4 voix mixtes. *See* RÉPERTOIRE. Répertoire moderne de musique vocale, *etc.* No. 60. [1896, *etc.*] fol. **H. 1048.**

LIONEL

Lionel and Clarissa

— A School for Fathers; a Comic Opera: as performed at the Theatre-Royal, in Drury-Lane. The Words and music by the Author [I. Bickerstaffe] and Composer [C. Dibdin] of the Padlock. [A pasticcio, arranged by C. Dibdin.] *Printed for J. Johnston: London,* [1768.] *obl.* fol.
The composers named in this work are: Dibdin, Scolari, Galuppi, Vento, Dr. Arne, Vinci and Potenza. **D. 279. a.**

— Lionel and Clarissa, or A School for Fathers, a Comic Opera as perform'd at the Theatre-Royal. [Words] By the Author of Love in a Village [I. Bickerstaffe]. The Music composed by Eminent Masters. [Arranged by C. Dibdin.] *J. Johnston, for the Author: London,* [1770?] *obl.* fol.
This edition is the same as that issued as "A School for Fathers," with the exception of the title-page. **D. 279. (2.)**

— Lionel & Clarissa, or a School for Fathers, a comic opera ... By the author of Love in a Village [i. e. Isaac Bickerstaffe]. The music composed by eminent masters. [Edited by Charles Dibdin.] pp. 77. *Printed by Longman & Broderip: London,* [c. 1790.] *obl.* fol. **E. 91. f. (2.)**

— Lionel and Clarissa; or a School for Fathers. A Comic Opera, *etc.* [1799.] *See* PERIODICAL PUBLICATIONS.— *London.* The Piano-Forte Magazine. Vol. VI. No. 6. [1797–1802.] 8°. **D. 854.**

— Lionel and Clarissa. By Isaac Bickerstaff. As performed at the Lyric Theatre, Hammersmith. Music by Charles Dibdin and others. Arranged by Alfred Reynolds. (Vocal Score.) *Elkin & Co.: London,* 1926. 4°. **F. 690. rr. (3.)**

— Lionel and Clarissa, a comic opera [arranged by Charles Dibdin], adapted for the German-flute, violin, hautboy and guittar. pp. 32. *Iohn Iohnston, for the Author: London,* [1768.] *obl.* 4°. **c. 105. s. (4.)**

— [Another copy.]
Partly cropped. **a. 19. (3.)**

— Songs from the eighteenth-century Opera Lionel and Clarissa. [1] Ah! How delightful the morning ... Alfred Reynolds. [2] Ye gloomy thoughts ... Dibdin. [3] Come then, pining, peevish lover ... Vinci. no. 1. *Elkin & Co.: London,* [1926.] fol.
Imperfect; wanting no. 2, 3. **G. 425. jj. (18.)**

LIONEL

— Go and on my Truth relying ... Air ... in ... Lionel & Clarissa ... Arranged by J. Addison. *Fentum: London,* [1807.] fol. **G. 578. c. (29.)**

— Hope and fear alternate rising. ⟨Rondeau. [By Charles Dibdin.]⟩ *Sung by Miss Macklin in the comic Opera of Lionel and Clarissa.* [Followed by an arrangement for the German flute.] *In:* The Court Miscellany. vol. 4 between pp. 216, 217. 1768. 8°. **P. P. 5457.**

— Hope and Fear. [Song, by Charles Dibdin.] Sung by Miss Macklin in ... Lionel and Clarissa. [*London,* 1773.] *s. sh.* 4°. *London Magazine, Oct.,* 1773. **159. n. 5.**

— Hope and Fear. [Song, by Charles Dibdin.] Sung by Miss Ashmore, in Lionel & Clarissa. *S. Lee:* [*Dublin,* 1775?] *s. sh.* fol. **G. 316. (96.)**

— Immortal Powers. [Song. By Charles Dibdin.] Sung by Miss Ashmore in Lionel and Clarissa. *Printed by John Rice: Dublin,* [c. 1780.] *s. sh.* fol. **G. 426. kk. (17.)**

— Oh dry those Tears. A Favorite Song in Lionel and Clarissa ... by Galuppi. *J. Lee:* [*Dublin,* 1780?] fol. **G. 383. j. (19.)**

— The Pilgrim of Love ... [song,] in the opera of Lionel & Clarissa, written by H. Siddons. The accompaniments & arrangement by J. Addison. *Kelly: London,* [1807.] fol. **G. 578. c. (27.)**

— When Love gets in to the youthful Brain, a favorite song, in Lionel & Clarissa. pp. 4. *Printed by Goulding & C°.: London, Dublin,* [WM 1822.] fol. **H. 3400. c. (18.)**

— Ye Banks on which we oft have strayed ... Duet ... in the opera of Lionel & Clarissa, written by H. Siddons. The accompaniments & arranged by J. Addison. *Kelly: London,* [1807.] fol. **G. 578. c. (28.)**

LIONEL (A.)

— À mon ami, pour le Piano. *London,* [1877.] fol. **h. 1494. r. (1.)**

LIONEL (F.)

— The Brook ... 2nd edition. [P. F.] *C. C. Publishing Co.: Syracuse, New York,* (1907.) fol. **g. 605. vv. (41.)**

— Two Idyls, *etc.* [P. F.] *C. C. Publishing Co.: Syracuse, N. Y.,* (1908.) fol. **g. 605. vv. (42.)**

LION-HEARTED

— The Lion-Hearted Bishop. Service of Song. *See* COLE (J. P.)

— A Lion-hearted Soldier was Colonel Burnaby. Song. *See* READ (J.) *Composer of comic songs.*

LIONNE

— La Lionne au Cage. Duo comique. *See* VILLEBICHOT (A. de)

LIONNET (ANATOLE)

— À Trianon. [Song, begins: "Marquise, vous souvenez vous".] Poésie de F. Coppée. *Paris,* [1880.] fol. **H. 1786. e. (51.)**

— C'est mon ami, rendez-le moi! [Song, begins: "Ah! s'il est dans votre village"] poésie de Florian. *Paris,* [1884.] fol. **H. 2836. h. (59.)**

— Chanson d'Avril. Duetto. Paroles & Musique de A. Lionnet. *Lemoine & Fils: Paris; Bruxelles,* [1887.] fol. **H. 2836. v. (32.)**

— La Chanson de l'amour. Psyche! [Begins: "Tout l'univers obéit à l'amour"] poésie de La Fontaine. *Paris,* [1884.] fol. **H. 2836. h. (60.)**

LIONNET (ANATOLE)

— La Charité. [Song, begins: "Voici l'hiver".] *Paris*, [1880.] fol.
H. 1786. e. (52.)

— Hymne à la Nuit [begins: "C'est l'heure du repos"], paroles et musique de A. Lionnet. *Paris*, [1884.] fol.
H. 2836. h. (57.)

— Hymne d'Amour. [Song, begins: "Avril est de retour".] *Paris*, [1880.] fol.
H. 1786. e. (50.)

— John Anderson.—Traduit de R. Burns.—Poésie de A. Barbier. *Lemoine & Fils: Paris; Bruxelles*, 1887. fol.
H. 2836. v. (33.)

— Nanon. Pastorale [begins: "Filant ma quenouillette"], paroles et musique de A. Lionnet. *Paris*, 1885. fol.
H. 2836. h. (61.)

— Nous étions trois filles. Ronde à dancer. Paroles de ***. *Lemoine & Fils: Paris, Bruxelles*, 1887. fol. **H. 2836. v. (34.)**

— Pendant qu'elle dort. Sérénade [begins: "Astres des nuits d'été"]. Paroles de C. Chincholle. *Paris*, [1880.] fol.
H. 1786. e. (48.)

— La Petite Fée. Chanson de Béranger [begins: "Enfants il était autrefois"]. *Paris*, [1877.] fol. **H. 1781. i. (18.)**

— Le Premier Mai. Mélodie [begins: "Chantez oiseaux"]. Poésie de G. Mathieu. [Solo and duet.] 2 no. *Paris*, [1882.] fol.
H. 1793. d. (15.)

— Primavera [song, begins: "Couronné de frais lilas"], poésie de G. Mathieu. *Paris*, 1885. fol. **H. 2836. h. (62.)**

— La Recette pour faire un nid. [Song, begins: "Pour faire un nid".] Paroles de C. M. Lefébure. *Paris*, [1881.] fol.
H. 1786. e. (53.)

— Ronde de Mai. Chœur à 4 voix [begins: "Plantons le mai"], paroles et musique de A. Lionnet. *Paris*, [1884.] fol.
H. 1795. a. (9.)

— Sérénade ... poésie de F. Coppée. *Lemoine & Fils: Paris: Bruxelles*, 1887. fol. **H. 2836. v. (35.)**

— Sérénade du Passant. Poésie de F. Coppée. *Lemoine & Fils: Paris; Bruxelles*, 1887. fol. **H. 2836. v. (36.)**

— Le Songe d'un fils. Mélodie [begins: "Dans mon sommeil parfois je vois ma mère"], paroles de H. Boutet. *Paris*, 1886. fol. **H. 2836. h. (58.)**

— Sous les grands marronniers. Mélodie. Paroles et musique de A. Lionnet. *Lemoine & Fils: Paris; Bruxelles*, 1887. fol.
H. 2836. v. (37.)

— Le Tambour. [Song, begins: "Vive le tambour".] Paroles de C. Vincent. *Paris*, [1881.] fol. **H. 1786. e. (54.)**

— Les Trois Angelus. [Song, begins: "Le jour est né".] Paroles de M. Rude. *Paris*, [1880.] fol. **H. 1786. e. (49.)**

LIONS

— Lions and Crocodiles. Songs. *See* ROBERTON (*Sir* H. S.)

LÍONTAR

— Líontar dúinn an crúisgín. [Part-song.] *See* Ó FRIGHILL (R.)

LIOUVILLE (FRANTZ)

— C'est l'amour. Mélodie valse [begins: "Je me disais"]. Paroles de P. Théolier. *Paris*, [1881.] fol. **H. 1786. e. (55.)**

— Les Rendez-vous. Chansonnette [begins: "Mon cousin sortait du collège"]. Paroles de L. Delormel. *Paris*, [1882.] fol.
H. 1793. d. (16.)

LIOUVILLE (FRANTZ)

— Le Voyage à Deux. Chansonnette [begins: "Après notre dîner"]. Paroles de Péricaud & Delormel. *Paris*, [1882.] fol.
H. 1793. d. (17.)

LIP

— The Lip of her I love. Ballad. *See* HODSON (G. A.) Six Ballads, *etc.* No. 6.

LIPATTI (DINU)

— Aubade. For woodwind quartet. [Score.] pp. 30. *Rongwen Music: New York*, [1958.] 4°.
Contemporary Composers—Study Score Series. no. 17.
f. 390. k. (1.)

— Cadenţe pentru concertul în do major K. V. 467 de W. A. Mozart. [P. F.] pp. 11. *In:* TĂNĂSESCU (D.) and BĂRGĂUANU (G.) Dinu Lipatti. ⟨Anexa.⟩ 1971. 8°.
X. 439/2759.

— Concertino im klassischen Stil für Klavier und kleines Orchester ... Op. 3. Partitur, *etc.* pp. 62. *Universal-Edition: Wien*, [1941.] fol. **h. 2782. ii. (3.)**

— Concertino im klassischen Stil für Klavier und kleines Orchester ... Op. 3. Für 2 Klaviere zu 4 Händen übertragen vom Komponisten, *etc.* pp. 46. *Universal-Edition: Wien*, [1951.] 4°. **h. 4015. l. (2.)**

— Danses roumaines. Pour deux pianos ou piano et orchestre. Version pour deux pianos. pp. 44. *Éditions Salabert: Paris*, [1954.] 4°.
Two copies. **h. 4015. m. (3.)**

— Nocturne en fa♯ mineur pour piano. pp. 4. *Éditions Salabert: Paris*, [1961.] 4°. **h. 3865. dd. (2.)**

— Sonatine pour piano (main gauche seule). pp. 11. *Éditions Salabert: Paris, New York*, [1953.] 4°. **g. 1126. f. (15.)**

— Sonatina pentru violină şi pian. [Score and part.] 2 pt. *Editura muzicală a Uniunii compozitorilor: Bucureşti*, 1970. fol. **h. 1729. mm. (1.)**

— *See* BACH (J. S.) Pastorale in F. [B. G. Jahrg. 38. No. 22.] Transcribed for piano by D. Lipatti. [1953.] 4°.
g. 699. j. (7.)

— *See* BACH (J. S.) [Was mir behagt, ist nur die muntre Jagd.] Two Bach Transcriptions ... 1. Weil die wollenreichen Herden. 2. Schafe koennen sicher weiden ... Piano solo. [Arranged by D. Lipatti.] [1953.] 4°. **g. 699. j. (9.)**

LIPAVSKY (JOSEPH)

— Six Fugues pour les Orgues ou le Piano Forte ... Œuvre 29. *Vienne*, [1808?] *obl.* fol. **e. 1090. (4.)**

— [Another copy.] **e. 174. m. (5.)**

— Grande sonate pathétique pour le piano-forte ... Oeuv. 27. pp. 21. *Chez Breitkopf & Härtel: Leipsic*, [1806?] *obl.* fol.
e. 282. w. (5.)

— VIII variations pour le piano-forte sur la romance: In des Tirannes Eisenmacht ... tirée de l'opéra de Mʳ Méhul Die beiden Füchse. pp. 11. *Au magasin de l'imprimerie chymique: Vienne*, [1805?] *obl.* fol.
Lithographed throughout. **Hirsch III. 366.**

LIPAVSKY (STANISLAW)

— March of the Polish Scythe bearers ... arranged for the Pianoforte by H. F. Hassé. *London*, [1851.] fol.
h. 723. h. (6.)

LIPINSKI (Carl)
— *See* Lipiński (K. J.)

LIPIŃSKI (Charles)
— *See* Lipiński (K. J.)

LIPIŃSKI (Karol Józef)
— Deux caprices pour le violon ... Oeuv. 3. pp. 24. *Au bureau de musique de C. F. Peters: Leipzig*, [1817?] fol.
h. 210. ff. (1.)

— Tre capricci per il violino ... Op. 10. pp. 25. *Presso E. A. Probst: Lipsia*, [1827?] fol.
h. 210. ff. (14.)

— Concert. Op. 21. *See* David (F.) Violin-Concerte, *etc.* No. 4. [1875.] fol.
g. 319. a.

— Concerto militaire (ii koncert skrzypcowy D op. 21). Wyciąg fortepianowy, opracował Edward Statkiewicz. [Score and part.] 2 pt. *Polskie wydawnictwo muzyczne: Kraków*, 1951. fol.
h. 1729. o. (1.)

— [Concerto. Op. 21.] Allegro ... für Violine mit ... Pianoforte-Begleitung frei bearbeitet von A. Wilhelmj. *Leipzig und Brüssel*, [1884.] fol.
h. 1608. m. (41.)

— Troisième concerto pour le violon avec accompagnement d'orchestre ... Oeuvre 24. [Parts.] 18 pt. *Chez Fr. Hofmeister: Leipzig*, [1836.] fol.
g. 478. b.

— Quatrième concerto de violon avec accompagnement d'orchestre ... Oeuvre 32. [Parts.] 23 pt. *Fréderic Hofmeister: Leipzig*, [c. 1850.] fol.
Imperfect; wanting the second bassoon part, for which a duplicate copy of the first bassoon part has been substituted in error.
g. 478. a.

— Quatrième Concerto pour le violon avec accompagnement ... de Pianoforte. Œuvre 32. *Leipzig*, [c. 1850.] fol.
h. 1729. d. (4*.)

— Fantaisie pour violon sur l'opéra Ernani de Verdi, avec accompagnement de piano. Op. 30. *Leipzig*, [1851.] fol.
h. 1611. (1.)

— Fantaisie sur des airs Napolitains nationaux pour le violon avec accompagnement de Piano ... Op. 31. *C. F. Peters: Leipzig*, [1851.] fol.
h. 1611. (2.)

— Muzyka do Pieśni polskich i ruskich ludu galicyjskiego zebranych i wydanych przez Wacława z Oleska do śpiewu i na fortepian ułożył K. Lipiński. *F. Piller: we Lwowie*, 1833. 8°.
1462. g. 14.

— Trois polonoises pour le pianoforte ... Oeuv. 5. pp. 9. *Chez Breitkopf & Härtel: Leipsic*, [1815.] obl. fol.
e. 5. aa. (5.)

— Rondo alla Polacca pour le Violon avec accompagnement d'Orchestre. Op. 13. *Leipzig*, [1825?] fol.
g. 478. (1.)

— Siciliano varié pour le violon avec accompagnement d'un second violon, alto et basso ... Oeuv. 2. [Parts.] 4 pt. *Chez C. F. Peters: Leipzig*, [1817?] fol.
h. 141. h. (7.)

— Trio pour deux violons & violoncelle ... Oeuvre 8. [Parts.] 3 pt. *Chez Breitkopf & Härtel: Leipsic*, [1824?] fol.
h. 409. kk.

— Trio pour deux violons et violoncelle ... Op. 12. [Parts.] 3 pt. *Au bureau de musique de C. F. Peters: Leipsic*, [1830?] fol.
g. 478. c.

— Variationi per il violino principale coll accomp[to] di violino secondo, alto et basso ... Oeuv. 4. [Parts.] 4 pt. *Presso C. F. Peters: Lipsia*, [1820.] fol.
h. 2801. u. (4.)

— Variations de Bravoure sur une romance militaire pour le Violon avec accompagnement d'Orchestre, *etc.* Op. 22. *Leipzig*, [1825?] fol.
g. 478. (2.)

LIPIŃSKI (Karol Józef)
— Variations pour le Violon avec accompagn[l]. de grand orchestre sur la cavatine "Ecco ridente il cielo" ... de Rossini. *Leipsic*, [1835?] fol.
h. 1613. b. (6.)

— *See* Donizetti (D. G. M.) [Parisina.] Les Bluettes de Parisina ... Mélodies (pour Violon & Piano (Flute & Piano) ... par C. Lipinski), *etc.* [1850.] fol.
h. 667. (5.)

— *See* Haydn (F. J.) [Quartets.—Collections.] Vollständige Sammlung der Quartetten für zwei Violinen, Viola u. Violoncello ... Neue Ausgabe. Revidirt ... von C. Lipinski. [1848–52.] fol.
Hirsch iii. 266.

LIPINSKI (P.)
— *See* Mayseder (J.) J. Mayseder's 3 grand duets for violin and tenor ... the violin part fingered by P. Lipinski, *etc.* [1852.] fol.
h. 1613. (8.)

LIPKA (Alfred)
— Viola ... Stücke für Viola und Klavier. Herausgegeben von Alfred Lipka. [Score and part.] 2 pt. *Verlag Neue Musik: Berlin*, [1976, *etc.*] 4°.
f. 810. a.

LIPKE (Felix)
— König Wilhelm i. Vierzehn patriotische Lieder zur Benutzung bei der Geburtstagsfeier ... des Königs. *Grünberg*, 1869. 8°.
11528. g. 2.

LIPKIN (Malcolm)
— Concerto No. 2. For violin and orchestra. [Violin and P. F. Score and part.] 2 pt. *J. & W. Chester: London*, [1965.] 4°.
g. 223. uu. (1.)

— [Another copy.]
A dedication has been stamped on the first page of the music of both score and part.
g. 223. uu. (2.)

— Mosaics. For chamber orchestra. [Score.] pp. 28. *J. & W. Chester: London*, [1971.] 8°.
c. 156. dd. (1.)

— O praise the Lord, all ye Nations. Anthem for SATB (unaccompanied). Psalm 117. pp. 3. *Novello & Co.: [London*, 1969.] 8°.
[*Musical Times.* 1522.]
P. P. 1945. aa.

— Sonata. For violin and piano. [Score and part.] 2 pt. *J. & W. Chester: London*, [1961.] fol.
g. 500. hh. (12.)

— Suite. For flute and violoncello, *etc.* [Score.] pp. 11. *J. & W. Chester: London*, [1964.] 4°.
Two copies.
g. 1780. x. (3.)

— String Trio. [Score.] pp. 24. *J. & W. Chester: London*, [1967.] 8°.
e. 668. zz. (5.)

— The White Crane ... Words by M. K. Richardson, *etc.* [For voices, descant recorders, percussion and piano, violins and guitar ad lib. Score.] pp. 20. *J. & W. Chester: London*, [1974.] 4°.
[*Junior Music. Stage 1. Series A.*] *With a separate leaf bearing a narrator's part inserted.*
G. 1487. g.

— *See* Eccles (Henry) [Premier livre de sonates. No. 11.] Sonata in G minor. Arranged by M. Lipkin for solo violoncello, *etc.* [1957.] 4°.
g. 511. b. (2.)

LIPOVŠEK (Marijan)
— Jugoslawisches-Jugendalbum für Klavier. Yugoslav Youth Album for Piano ... Herausgegeben ... von ... Marijan Lipovšek. pp. 53. *Edition Peters: Leipzig*, [1975.] 4°.
g. 1529. f. (5.)

LIPPA (Arthur)

— Canterette. [P. F. duet.] *O. Ditson Co.: Boston*, (1907.) fol.
h. 3290. r. (15.)

LIPPA (Kate Ockleston)

— *See* Ockleston, afterwards Lippa.

LIPPACHER (A.)

— Airs de ballet à quatre mains pour piano. 2 Suites. *Paris*, [1884.] fol.
h. 3290. c. (6.)

LIPPACHER (Clément)

— Le Christ. Drame sacré ... C. Grandmougin. Avec un mélodie originale de C. Lippacher. *J. Rouam & Cie: Paris*, 1892. 8°.
11739. d. 28.

— Mazurka. [In B flat, P. F. With a portrait.] *In:* La Danse. pp. 271–275. [1888.] fol.
H. 2349. b.

— *See* Pugno (R.) and Lippacher (C.) Les Papillons, *etc.* [1884.] 4°.
f. 281. a.

— *See* Pugno (R.) and Lippacher (C.) Viviane. Ballet ... musique de R. Pugno & C. Lippacher, *etc.* 1886. 8°.
f. 281.

LIPPAI

— Lippai, wake up! Carol. *See* Warner (Richard)

LIPPARINO (Guglielmo)

— Sacri Concerti a Cinque Voci con il suo Basso per l'Organo ... Libro Primo. Opera Undecima, *etc.* Canto. (Alto.) (Tenore.) (Basso.) (Quinto.) (Basso per l'Organo.) 6 pt. *Appresso Alessandro Vincenti: Venetia*, 1629. 4°.
D. 1000.

LIPPHARD (William Benjamin)

— Art thou weary. [Anthem.] The poem by H. F. Lyte. *W. Maxwell Music Co.: New York City*, (1911.) 8°.
F. 281. y. (33.)

LIPPHARDT (Walther)

— Gesellige Zeit. Liederbuch für gemischten Chor. Herausgegeben von Walther Lipphardt. pp. 132. *Bärenreiter-Verlag: Kassel, Basel*, [1965.] 8°.
D. 420. i.

— Das Männerlied. Liederbuch für Männerchöre. Herausgegeben von W. Lipphardt, *etc.* pp. 136. *Bärenreiter-Verlag: Kassel*, [1934.] 8°.
Hirsch M. 221.

— *See* Beuttner (N.) Catholisch Gesang-Buch. Faksimile-Ausgabe der 1. Auflage, Graz 1602. Herausgegeben ... von W. Lipphardt. 1968. 8°.
C. 549. jj.

— *See* Lasso (O. di) and Lasso (R. di) Geistliche Psalmen mit dreyen stimmen ... Neu herausgegeben von W. Lipphardt. [1951.] 8°.
F. 1176. v. (14.)

— *See* Lechner (L.) Deutsche Sprüche von Leben und Tod ... Für vierstimmigen gemischten Chor ... Herausgegeben von ... W. Lipphardt. [1971.] 8°.
F. 1199. qq. (2.)

— *See* Lechner (L.) Das Hohelied Salomonis ... Für vierstimmigen gemischten Chor ... Herausgegeben von ... W. Lipphardt. [1971.] 8°.
F. 1199. qq. (1.)

— *See* Lechner (L.) [Liber missarum, *etc.*] Missa prima Domine Dominus noster ... Herausgegeben von W. Lipphardt. [1964.] 8°.
F. 274. rr. (1.)

— *See* Lechner (L.) [Sanctissimae Virginis Marie canticum.] Magnificat primi toni ... Herausgegeben von W. Lipphardt. [1960.] 8°.
F. 1176. jj. (8.)

LIPPHARDT (Walther)

— *See* Leisentrit (J.) Geistliche Lieder und Psalmen, *etc.* ⟨Das ander Theil Geistlicher lieder. Gesangbuch von 1567. Faksimileausgabe mit einem Nachwort von W. Lipphardt.⟩ 1966. 8°.
B. 740. bb.

LIPPITT (F. J.)

— The Lily Bolero for Piano and Violin or Flute. *O. Ditson Co.: Boston*, 1893. fol.
h. 1612. c. (35*.)

LIPPMAN (Sidney)

— I'm thrilled. Words by Sylvia Dee. [Orchestral score.] pp. 9. obl. 4°. *In:* Miller (Glen) Method for Orchestral Arranging. [1956.] 8°.
7902. l. 10.

— *See* Nohavec (H. B.) Dusky Clouds ... By H. B. Nohavec in collaboration with S. Lippman, *etc.* 1938. 8°.
E. 1562.

LIPPMANN (Friedrich)

— *See* Haydn (F. J.) [Mass. Hob. xxii/14.] "Harmoniemesse." 1802. Herausgegeben von F. Lippmann. [1967.] 8°.
D. 781. d. (3.)

LIPPMANN, afterwards DAGMAR (Hetta)

— Caprice Hongrois pour Piano. *Novello & Co.: London*, 1904. 4°.
g. 442. n. (22.)

— Fleurs de Mai. Waltz. [P. F.] *R. Cocks & Co.: London*, [1893.] fol.
h. 3285. q. (55.)

LIPPOLD (Max)

— *See* Chaikovsky (P. I.) Serenade für Streichorchester ... Op. 48 ... Für Pianoforte zu 2 Händen von M. Lippold, *etc.* [1895.] fol.
h. 2988. q. (3.)

— *See* Chaikovsky (P. I.) Suite n° 3 pour orchestre ... Op. 55, *etc.* ⟨Réduction pour piano à 2 mains par M. Lippold.⟩ [1902?] fol.
h. 2988. s. (1.)

LIPPSTADT (Sig.)

— *See* Buerger (L.) and Lippstadt (S.) A Ragged Proposition. [P. F.] 1901. 4°.
g. 442. m. (2.)

LIPS

— Lips and eyes. Canzonet. *See* W., G.

— Lips o' Poppy. Ballad. *See* Mitchell (A. H. C.)

— Lips so sweet and tender. [Part-song.] *See* Tosti (Sir Francesco P.)

— The Lips that sang me that strain. Song. *See* Parkes (M. H.)

— The Lips we love the best. [Song.] *See* MacGregor (D. C.)

LIPSCOMB (Helen)

— Alleluia! Let us sing! 14 hymns for children with introits and amens. Composed and arranged by H. Lipscomb for unison or two-part singing. pp. 47. *G. Schirmer: New York*, [1961.] 8°.
E. 353. b. (2.)

— Ancient Prayer. For three-part chorus of mixed voices with organ or piano accompaniment. [Words] from the Breastplate of Saint Patrick, *etc.* pp. 4. *G. Schirmer: [New York*, 1962.] 8°.
F. 1744. ll. (31.)

— Aura Lee. For four-part chorus of men's voices with piano accompaniment ... Traditional. Arranged by H. Lipscomb. pp. 8. *G. Schirmer: New York*, [1958.] 8°.
F. 163. oo. (14.)

LIPSCOMB (Helen)

— Bethelehem Town. For two-part chorus of treble voices with organ or piano accompaniment. [Words by] Edna Lipscomb. pp. 4.   *G. Schirmer:* [*New York*, 1963.] 8°.   **F. 260. u. (19.)**

— Brightest and best. Christmas anthem arranged for voices in unison by H. Lipscomb. [Words by] Reginald Heber, *etc.* pp. 4.   *H. W. Gray Co.: New York*, [1959.] 8°.   **E. 335. w. (33.)**

— Brightest and best. Christmas song for high or medium voice. Kentucky folk hymn. Arranged by H. Lipscomb. pp. 3. *H. W. Gray Co.: New York*, [1959.] fol.   **G. 519. dd. (18.)**

— 18 Hymn Duets. For piano, four hands, with words. Eleven of the hymns have descants for flute, recorder or violin. Arranged by H. Lipscomb, *etc.* pp. 47.   *G. Schirmer: New York*, [1963.] *obl.* 4°.   **e. 379. n. (9.)**

— Hymns to remember. 44 easy piano arrangements by H. Lipscomb. (With words.) pp. 48.   *G. Schirmer: New York*, [1963.] 4°.   **G. 519. bb. (18.)**

— I sing the mighty Power of God. For three-part chorus of mixed chorus [*sic*] with organ or piano accompaniment ... [Words by] Rev. Isaac Watts. pp. 7.   *G. Schirmer: New York*, [1959.] 8°.   **E. 335. x. (30.)**

— Jesu, Jesu, why did you die? For three-part chorus of mixed voices with organ or piano accompaniment. [Words by] Edna Lipscomb. pp. 7.   *G. Schirmer: New York*, [1962.] 8°.   **F. 1744. gg. (15.)**

— O Holy Spirit sent from Heaven. For two-part chorus of treble voices or junior choir, [words by] Edna Lipscomb. pp. 4.   *G. Schirmer: New York*, [1962.] 8°.   **E. 263. p. (21.)**

— A Pastoral Prayer. For three-part chorus of mixed voices with organ or piano accompaniment, [words] adapted from the Psalms by Edna Lipscomb. pp. 7.   *G. Schirmer: New York*, [1964.] 8°.   **E. 335. tt. (13.)**

— Sleep, gentle Jesus. Christmas anthem arranged for S. S. A. H. Lipscomb. [Words by] Edna Lipscomb. Bohemian folk song. pp. 4.   *H. W. Gray Co.: New York*, [1962.] 8°.   **F. 217. t. (15.)**

— Song of Praise. For two-part chorus with organ or piano accompaniment ... [Words by] Rev. Isaac Watts. pp. 4. *G. Schirmer:* [*New York*, 1959.] 8°.   **E. 335. x. (31.)**

— We have seen His Star in the East. For three-part chorus of mixed voices with organ or piano accompaniment. [Words by] Molly Anderson Haley. pp. 6.   *G. Schirmer: New York*, [1963.] 8°.   **E. 335. ll. (19.)**

— We praise Thee, O God. For two-part chorus ... [Words by] Edna Lipscomb. pp. 4.   *G. Schirmer: New York*, [1960.] 8°.   **E. 335. z. (15.)**

— *See* BACH (J. S.) [Herz und Mund und That und Leben. —Wohl mir, dass ich Jesum habe.] Jesu, Joy of Man's Desiring ... Simplified arrangement for piano solo by H. Lipscomb. [1964.] 4°.   **g. 699. mm. (2.)**

— *See* MOZART (W. A.) [*Doubtful and Supposititious Works.*] [Wiegenlied. K. Anh. 284. f.] The First Christmas Morn. For two-part chorus of treble voices with organ or piano accompaniment ... Arranged ... by H. Lipscomb. [1963.] 8°.   **F. 307. n. (5.)**

LIPSCOMBE (Edith F.)

— The Fairy's Reverie. [Song.] The words and music by E. F. Lipscombe, *etc.   Lyon & Hall: Brighton*, 1907. fol.   **H. 1794. vv. (65.)**

LIPTING

— Lipting Pingewing. Chinese Serenade. *See* STEELE (C. T.)

LIPTON (Dan)

— The Music of the Band. [Song.] Words by Raymond A. Browne. Original lyrics by C. W. Murphy. pp. 5.   *Sol Bloom: New York*, [1906.] fol.
The cover bears the words "Music by E. [sic] *W. Murphy. Original lyrics by Dan Lipton".*   **H. 3985. aa. (36.)**

— *See* CASTLING (Harry) and LIPTON (D.) Money and Misery ... ⟨Song.⟩ Written and composed by H. Castling and D. Lipton. [1914.] fol.   **H. 3990. k. (56.)**

— *See* MURPHY (Clarence W.) "I've a Garden in Sweden." ⟨Song.⟩ Written and composed by C. W. Murphy ... and D. Lipton. [1907.] *s. sh.* fol.   **H. 3986. g. (14.)**

— *See* MURPHY (Clarence W.) "I've a Garden in Sweden." ⟨Song.⟩ Written and composed by C. W. Murphy ... and D. Lipton. [1907.] fol.   **H. 3986. g. (15.)**

— *See* MURPHY (Clarence W.) I wonder what it feels like to be poor! Written and composed by C. W. Murphy, D. Lipton and Magini. [1920.] fol.   **H. 1660. d. (3.)**

— *See* MURPHY (Clarence W.) She's a Lassie from Lancashire. ⟨Song.⟩ Written and composed by C. W. Murphy, D. Lipton, *etc.* [1907.] 4°.   **H. 3986. h. (13.)**

— [For editions and arrangements of songs written and composed by D. Lipton in collaboration with Clarence W. Murphy:] *See* MURPHY (Clarence W.) and LIPTON (D.)

LIPTON (Dan) and HARGREAVES (James)

— Napoleon's white Horse. ⟨Song.⟩ Written and composed by D. Lipton and J. Hargreaves, *etc.* [Staff and tonic sol-fa notation. Voice part.]   *Francis, Day & Hunter: London*, [1903.] *s. sh.* fol.   **H. 3985. aa. (37.)**

— Napoleon's white Horse, *etc.* ⟨Song.⟩ [With separate voice part.] 2 pt.   *Francis, Day & Hunter: London*, [1903.] fol.   **H. 3985. aa. (38.)**

LIPTON (Dan) and HARGREAVES (William)

— The Dark Clouds will turn to blue. ⟨Song.⟩ Written and composed by D. Lipton and W. Hargreaves, *etc.* [Staff and tonic sol-fa notation. Voice part.]   *Francis, Day & Hunter: London*, [1903.] *s. sh.* fol.   **H. 3985. aa. (39.)**

— The Dark Clouds will turn to blue, *etc.* ⟨Song.⟩ [With separate voice part.] 2 pt.   *Francis, Day & Hunter: London*, [1903.] fol.   **H. 3985. aa. (40.)**

LIPTON (Dan) and MURPHY (Clarence Wainwright)

— "We don't want more Daylight" ... ⟨Song.⟩ Written and composed by D. Lipton and C. W. Murphy. [Staff and tonic sol-fa notation. Voice part.]   *Francis, Day & Hunter: London*, [1908.] *s. sh.* fol.   **H. 3985. aa. (41.)**

— "We don't want more Daylight," *etc.* ⟨Song.⟩ [With separate voice part.] 2 pt.   *Francis, Day & Hunter: London*, [1908.] fol.   **H. 3985. aa. (42.)**

LIQUID

— Liquid and wat'ry Pearls. Madrigal. *See* MARENZIO (L.) [Il primo libro de madrigali a cinque voci.—Liquide perle.]

— The Liquid Gem. Song. *See* WRIGHTON (W. T.)

— Liquid Jim. [Song.] *See* VONDERFINCK (L.)

— Liquid were those bright Pearls. [Madrigal.] *See* MARENZIO (L.) [Il primo libro de madrigali a cinque voci.—Liquide perle.]

LIQUOR

— The Liquor Traffic. Song. *See* PHILLIPS (D. E.)

LIQUORISH (WILLIAM)

— The first Regiment of Royal Tower Hamlets Militia, March and Quick Step ... [Full score] and Adapted for the Piano Forte, *etc. W. Hodsoll: London*, [1796?] fol.　　**g. 133. (36.)**

— The Loyal Hampstead Association March and Quick Step ... [Full score] and Adapted for the Piano Forte, *etc. W. Hodsoll: London*, [1801.] fol.　　**g. 133. (37.)**

LIRA

— La Lira. [Song.] *See* MARIANI (A.)

— La Lira. Canzonetta. *See* PANOFKA (H.)

— Lira d'Italia. Classe 1ª. fas^lo 5°. [Airs, Duets, *etc.*, by Meyerbeer, Rossini, and Vaccai.] *Grua, Ricordi and Co.: London*, [1825?] fol.　　**R. M. 14. b. 12.**

— La Lira d'Italia. Collection d'Ariettes, Romances et petits Duis Italiens, *etc.* 5 collections. 150 no. *Bernard Latte: Paris*, [1840?] fol.　　**R. M. 14. b. 13.**

— Ka Lira Hawaii. He mau mele hirneni a me na mele oli halelu, na na ekalesia o Hawaii nei, *etc. Honolulu*, 1855. *obl.* 8°.　　**A. 618. p.**

— [Another copy.]　　**A. 842.**

— Lira Kamalii. Oia na himem harpule me na himeni walea pai pu ia me na mele, no na kamalii Hawaii. [The Children's Lyre. A book of hymns and songs with music, for Hawaian children.] *Paiia e Ka Ahahni taraka Amerika: Nu Ioka*, [i. e. New York, 1860?] 8°.　　**3436. g. (52.)**

— Lira lira. Song. *See* ARNOLD (Samuel) [The Surrender of Calais.]

LIRA (JORGE A.)

— Himnos sagrados de los Andes. Recopilados, ordenados y anotados por Jorge A. Lira. 2 tom. *Jorge A. Lira: Cusco; Buenos Aires* printed, 1960. 8°.　　**F. 272. gg. (4.)**

LIRE

— La Lire Maçonne. Recueil de Chansons. *See* VIGNOLES (　　　) and DU BOIS (　　　)

LIROUX (JEAN FRANÇOIS ESPIC DE)

— Alise et Arsème. Romance. (Paroles de M. de la Place, *etc.*) [*Paris*,] 1782. 8°. *Mercure de France, June*, 1781, *p.* 101.　　**298. f. 16.**

LIRUM

— Lirum lirum. [Ballett.] *See* MORLEY (Thomas) [First Booke of Balletts.—You that wont to my Pipe's Sound.]

LIS

— Lis épouse l'beau Gernance. Air. *See* DOCHE (J. D.) [Fanchon la Vielleuse.]

LIS (CHARLES AUGUSTE)

— Album musical composé de six mélodies, et orné de vignettes, dessinées par P. Lauters, *etc. Société des beaux-arts: Bruxelles*, [c. 1840.] fol.　　**H. 346. f.**

— [Another issue.] [Album musical composé de six mélodies, *etc.*] pp. 17. [*Brussels*, 1840?] fol. *Wanting the titlepage.*　　**R. M. 13. f. 14.**

— Le Pêcheur. Romance. *Paris*, [1825?] fol.　　**G. 809. b. (19.)**

LIS (GUSTAVE DE)

— Fiancée. Valse. [P. F.] *Phillips & Page: London*, [1891.] fol.　　**h. 3285. q. (56.)**

LISA

— Lisa, Canzone Napolitana. *London*, [1858.] fol.　　**H. 1255. (20.)**

— Lisa. Operetta. *See* KREISLER (F.) [Sissy.]

— Lisa. Canzonetta. *See* REISSIGER (C. G.)

— Lisa e Gianetto. Duettino. *See* BADIA (L.)

— Lisa gentil di questo cuor. *La Bella Lisa.* Canto Pisano. *London*, [1865.] fol.　　**H. 1790. a. (65.)**

— Lisa lân. Part-song. *See* DAVIES (Jayne)

— Lisa lan. Folk Song. *See* HOLST (G. T. von)

LISA

— Guarda che bianca luna. Melodia. Parole da Vittorelli. Posta in musica ... da Lisa. *London*, [1859.] fol.　　**H. 1772. s. (19.)**

LÍSA (VALEŠ)

— Slovácké a lidové písně z Uher. Hradišt'ska. Upravil Valeš Lísa. II. vydání. [Melodies only.] pp. 212. *Nákladem Prvního českého knihkupectví; nakladatelství Josefa Pitharta: v Kroměříži*, 1919. 8°.　　**C. 860. l.**

LISBETH

— Lisbeth. Opéra comique. *See* GRÉTRY (A. E. M.)

LISBIA

— Lisbia. Canzonet. *See* GRAEFF (J. G.)

LISBON

— The Lisbon Story. [Play with music.] *See* DAVIES (H. P.)

LISBON.— *Fundação Calouste Gulbenkian*

— Portugaliæ musica. *Lisboa*, 1959, *etc.* fol.　　**G. 27.**

Sociedade de Geographia de Lisboa

— Musicas populares de Cabo Verde.—Musique populaires des Iles du Cap-Vert, *etc.* [P. F.] *Lisboa*, [1895.] fol.　　**g. 605. j. (2.)**

LISBONIAN, *pseud*

— Devotional Hymn Tunes for congregational use. *Cary & Co.: London*, [1908.] 8°.　　**F. 1176. b. (31.)**

LISCHEN

— Lischen and Fritzchen. Operetta. *See* OFFENBACH (J.)

LISCHKA (RAINER)

— Quartetto curioso. Zwei Violinen, Violoncello und Klavier. Partitur und Stimmen. 5 pt. *Verlag Neue Musik: Berlin*, [1976.] 4°. *Part of "Reihe Kammermusik".*　　**g. 411. n. (1.)**

LISCO

— Lisco und Salding. Zaubermärchen. *See* DRECHSLER (J.)

LISE

— Lise. [Song.] *See* GODARD (B.) 12 Morceaux, *etc.* 2me série. No. 5.

— Lise. [Song.] *See* MOREAU (L.)

— Lise chantoit dans la prairie. Ariette. *See* DEZÈDE (N.) [Blaise et Babet.]

— Lise d'une main alerte. *Le Verrou, ou la Sage précaution.* [Song.] Air: [Coeurs sensibles] du Mariage de Figaro. *Chez Camand:* [Paris, 1790?] 8°.　　　　　**B. 362. e. (93.)**

— Lise, entends tu l'orage. Ariette. *See* ALBANESE (É. J. I. A.)

— Lise et Colin. Romance. *See* CHARLES (　　　　)

— Lise et Colin. Opéra. *See* GAVEAUX (P.)

— Lise fut voir un Médecin. *Le Mal d'Avanture.* [Song.] Air: du Confiteor, *etc.* [*Paris*, 1785?] 8°.　　**B. 362. (228.)**

— Lise la Chanteuse. Romance. *See* MOLINOS (A.)

— Lise m'aimoit. Chanson. *See* DUGUÉ (P.)

— Lise par fantaisie un jour. *L'Arithmétique.* Air Anglais, adressé à M. de B ... (Par D. G. J.) [*Paris*, 1790?] 8°.
　　　　　B. 362. a. (135.)

— Lise penitente. Song. *See* MON. Mon pere je viens devant vous, *etc.* [c. 1785.] fol.　　　　**H. 1653. b. (17.)**

— Lise Penitente. Romance. *See* MON. Mon père je viens devant vous, *etc.* [1785?] 8°.　　　　**B. 362. e. (70.)**

— Lise voyoit deux pigeons se caresser. Ariette. *See* ALBANESE (É. J. I. A.)

LISELOTT

— Liselott. Singspiel. *See* KUENNEKE (E.)

LISELOTTE

— Liselotte. Song. *See* ADAM (L.)

LIS'EN

— *See* LISTEN.

LISENKA (N. V.)

— *See* LISENKO (M. V.)

LISENKO (MIKOLA VITALIEVICH)

— Зібрання творів, *etc.* [With portraits and facsimiles.] том 2–6, 8–20. *Мистецтво: Київ*, 1950–59. 4°.
Imperfect; wanting том 1, 7.　　　　**H. 3617.**

— Збірник Музею Діячів Науки та Мистецтва України. Том 1. присвячений Миколі Лисенкові. [With portraits and musical notes.] *Київ*, 1930. 8°.
Всеукраїнська Академія Наук. Збірник Іст.—Філолог. Відділу, No. 94.　　　　**Ac. 1101. e.**

— Dunya. A Danube Song of Bessarabia, for mixed chorus and alto ... solo. After the notation of Lissenko. Setting by K. Schindler. Op. 17, *etc. See* SCHINDLER (K.) Folk Songs of Russia, *etc.* [No. 9.] 1917. 8°.　　**F. 1748. a. (9.)**

— Різдвяна ніч. Коміко-лірична опера в чотирьох діях (тема по Гоголю) М. Старицького. [Vocal score.] pp. 349. *Українська Накладня: Київ, Ляйпціг; printed in Germany,* [c. 1885.] 8°.
　　　　　F. 1903. a.

— Драматычни сцены "Сапфо". Мельодеклямація. Слова Л. Старицькои-Черняхівскои. Музыку складъ М. Лисенко. *у Кціві*, 1908. 8°.
Part of B. D. Hrinchenko's "Досвітні Огни".　　**011586. c. 15.**

LISENKO (MIKOLA VITALIEVICH)

— Тарас Бульба. Історична опера на 5 дій, 7 одслон. Лібрето М. Старицького, *etc.* [Vocal score.] *Ukr. & Russ.* pp. 379. *Українська Накладня: Київ, Ляйпціг; printed in Germany,* [c. 1890.] 4°.　　　　**H. 1404. a.**

— [Тарас Бульба.] Увертюра ... [Revised version by L. M. Revuts'ky.] Для большого симфонического оркестра. Инструментовка Б. Лятошинского. Партитура. pp. 44. *Государственное музыкальное издательство: Москва*, 1952. fol.　　　　**h. 1426. x. (4.)**

— Українська сюіта для фортепіано. ⟨тв. 2. У формі старовинних танців на основі народних пісень.⟩ pp. 38 *Державне видавництво образотворчого мистецтва і музичної літератури УССР: Київ*, 1961. 4°.
　　　　　g. 1590. cc. (1.)

— Українські народні пісні в музичній обробці М. В. Лисенка. Малюнки А. Базилевича. [A series of 16 postcards.] *Мистецтво: Київ*, 1963. 8°.　　　　**D. 398. p.**

— Утоплена. Майська ніч. Лірично-фантастична опера у трьох діях, чотирьох одмінах. Текст по Гоголю склав Мих. Старицький. [Vocal score.] pp. 208. *Українська Накладня: Київ, Ляйпціг: printed in Germany,* [c. 1885.] 8°.　　**F. 1903.**

— Юнацька симфонія. Редакція М. Скорика. Партитура ... Юношеская симфония, *etc.* pp. 63. *"Музична Україна": Київ*, 1973. 4°.　　　　**g. 1593. b. (2.)**

— Збірникъ українськихъ пісенъ. Зібравъ и у ноти завівъ М. Лисенко. *Липський; Петербурхъ*, [1868.] fol.　　**H. 1404.**

— Збірникъ українськихъ пісень. Зібравъ и у ноти завівъ М. Лисенко ... Трете виданне. вип. 1–4. *у Болеслава Корейко: Кіевъ, Одесса; Leipsic* [printed c. 1890.] fol. *Bun.* 1 *only is of the third edition. Bun.* 2 *is of the second edition. Bun.* 3, 4 *bear the imprint Kiev without publisher's name. Imperfect; wanting вип.* 5, 6.　　　　**H. 1404. b.**

— *See* VERESAI (O.) Кобзарь О. Вересай, *etc.* [With biographical sketches of O. Veresai by A. A. Rusov and N. V. Lisenka.] 1874. 8°.　　　　**E. 858.**

LISENKO (NIKOLAI VITAL'EVICH)

— *See* LISENKO (Mikola Vitalievich)

LISETTA

— Lisetta. Canzonetta. *See* MORGANTI (G.)

LISETTE

— Lisette. Ballad. *See* BALL (W.)

— Lisette. Romance. *See* GABRIEL, afterwards MARCH (M. A. V.)

— Lisette. Song. *See* LAMBELET (N.)

— Lisette. Song. *See* MALLANDAINE (J. E.) [The Two Orphans.]

— Lisette a un joli rosier. *Les Abricots, ou le Rosier défleuri.* [Song.] Air, Phillis demande son portrait. *Chez Camand: Paris*, [1785?] 8°.　　　　**B. 362. f. (25.)**

— Lisette, belle Lisette. Air. *See* CROISÉE.

— Lisette est faites pour Colin. *Colin et Lisette.* Vaudeville. [*Paris*, 1790?] 8°.　　　　**B. 362. e. (72.)**

— [Another copy.]　　　　**B. 362. b. (112.)**

— Lisette et Lublin. [Song.] *See* PETIT. Le petit Dieu charmant, *etc.* [1780?] 8°.　　　　**B. 362. e. (88.)**

— Lisette ne possedait rien. [Song.] *Le Cupidon de Lisette,* [words] par M. Déduit. Air: du Tonnelier. [By N. M. Audinot.] *Chez Rayer: Paris,* [1775?] 8°.　　　　**B. 362. j. (1.)**

LISETTE

— Lisette, vous n'en saurez rien. Mélodie. *See* COEDÈS (A.)

LISHIN (G. A.)

— Her Laughter. Ballad for Baritone or Bass. English version by R. Newmarch. *J. & W. Chester: London*, 1933. 4°.
H. 1860. h. (11.)

LISHMAN (GEORGE)

— Beneath the Flag. Vocal March, words by … C. Parkinson. *Novello and Co.: London*, 1908. 8°. *The "Chester" Series of Unison Songs, No. 2.*
F. 637. cc. (14.)

— Benedicite, omnia opera. *C. Vincent: London*, [1897.] 8°.
F. 1171. v. (11.)

— A Cricket Song. Vocal March with Chorus, words by A. A. Purry. *Novello and Co.: London*, 1908. 8°. *The "Chester" Series of Unison Songs, No. 4.*
F. 637. cc. (16.)

— Hymn for beginning and end of term, for school and college use. *Novello and Co.: London*, [1907.] *a card.*
I. 600. c. (181.)

— Our dear old England. Vocal March, words by A. Thompson. *Novello and Co.: London*, 1908. 8°. *The "Chester" Series of Unison Songs, No. 1.*
F. 636. ff. (11.)

— Three Quadruple Chants. *C. Vincent: London*, [1900.] *a card.*
I. 600. a. (153.)

— A Song of Britain. Vocal March, words by E. Oxenford. *Novello and Co.: London*, 1908. 8°. *The "Chester" Series of Unison Songs, No. 3.*
F. 637. cc. (15.)

— Vesper Hymn for S. A. T. *C. Vincent: London*, [1897.] *a card.*
I. 600. a. (29.)

LISI (ERNEST)

— Won't you be sorry. [Song.] Written by Will W. Harris. pp. 5. *American Music Pub. Co.: New York*, [1905.] fol.
H. 3985. aa. (43.)

LISIA

— Un Espagnol qui voit venir. *Air de Lisia* [words by Monnet, music by E. Scio] avec Accompagnement de Guitarre. [*Paris*, 1793.] 8°.
B. 362. g. (87.)

LISINSKI (VATROSLAV)

— Blago onom … *See* infra: [Ljubav i zloba.]

— Dika plava. More diko. Dvije obradbe momačkih narodnih pjesama iz Bačke. [T. T. B. B.] *Nakladno poduzeće "Glas rada": Zagreb*, 1950. fol.
G. 615. c. (5.)

— Ljubav i zloba. Opera u 2 čina. Glasovirski izvadak skladateljev. Priredio Lovro Županović. pp. v.15.127.152. *Udruženje kompozitora Hrvatske: Zagreb*, 1969. fol. *Vatroslav Lisinski: Izabrana djela. 6.*
G. 1371. a.

— [Ljubav i zloba.] Blago onom … Arija obrena iz opere "Ljubav i zloba". Riječi: Dimitrije Demetar. Obradba teksta: Tito Strozzi. Muzička obradba: Fran Lhotka. Za koncertnu upotrebu priredio: Lav Vrbanič. pp. 7. *Nakladni zavod Hrvatske: Zagreb*, [1946.] fol.
H. 2175. (9.)

— Mazurka za glasovir. Priredio Ladislav Šaban. pp. 7. *Udruženje kompozitora Hrvatske: [Zabreb,]* 1972. fol. *Vatroslav Lisinski: Izabrana djela. 3, no. 6.*
g. 1591. i. (2.)

LISINSKI (VATROSLAV)

— [Ouvertura.] Uvertira za violinu i klavir. Priredili Miroslav Miletić, Lovro Županović. [Score and part.] 2 pt. *Udruženje kompozitora Hrvatske: [Zagreb,]* 1969 [1972]. fol. *Vatroslav Lisinski: Izabrana djela. 3, no. 3.*
g. 1591. i. (1.)

— Porin. Vitežka opera u 5 čina … Slova od Dra. Dimitrije Demetra. Potpuni izvadak za klavir i pjevanje udesio Fran Lhotka. [With a portrait.] pp. 292. *Izdanje Hrvatske Filharmonije: u Zagrebu*, 1919. fol.
G. 1371.

— Porin. Viteška opera u 5 činova. Glasovirski izradak Fran Lhotka. Priredio Lovro Županović. [Vocal score.] pp. vii. 292. *Udruženje kompozitora Hrvatske: Zagreb*, 1969. 4°. *Vatroslav Lisinski: Izabrana djela. 7.*
G. 1371. b.

— Prosto zrakom ptica leti. [T. T. B. B.] *Izdanje Muzičke naklade Saveza muzičkih udruženja Hrvatske: Zagreb*, [c. 1955.] *s. sh.* fol.
G. 615. d. (5.)

LISIO (GIUSEPPE)

— *See* DUFAY (G.) [Vergene bella.] Una Stanza del Petrarca … tratta da due codici antichi, e le poesie volgari contenute in essi pubblicate per cura di G. Lisio. 1893. fol.
H. 2815. q. (2.)

LISIS

— Lisis avait de la jeunesse. [Song.] *See* CANDEILLE, afterwards SIMON, afterwards PÉRIÉ (A. J.)

LISITSA

— Лисица и виноградъ. Дѣтская опера. *See* ORLOV (V. M.)

LISITSIAN (SRBUI)

— Старинные пляски и театральные представления армянского нарада. [With melodies.] *Издательство Академии наук артянской ССР: Ереван*, 1958, *etc.* 8°.
W. P. 17049.

LISITSUIN (M.)

— Quatre Préludes pour Piano. Op. 4. *P. Jurgenson: Moscou, Leipzig*, [1909.] fol.
h. 1426. m. (23.)

LISKA

— Liska. Ballad. *See* LINLEY (George)

— Liska oder die Hexe von Gyllensteen. Oper. *See* RIES (F.) [The Sorceress.]

LISKARD (   )

— It's enough to make a girl go mad. [Song, begins: "Young Cupid".] Written by C. Merion. *London*, [1867.] fol.
H. 1772. s. (20.)

LISKEN (GERD)

— Vibration. Modell für eine Gruppenimprovisation auf Orff-Instrumentarium oder anderen Instrumenten … Partitur. pp. 15. *B. Schott's Söhne: Mainz*, [1971.] obl. 4°. *Part of "Workshop".*
d. 240. w. (1.)

LISLE (DE)

— *See* DELISLE.

LISLE (ANTOINE DE)

— Les Bavards waltzes upon airs from Offenbach's operetta. [P. F.] *London*, [1877.] fol.
h. 1483. (2.)

LISLE (ANTOINE DE)

— La Créole (de J. Offenbach). Select airs for Pianoforte. *London*, [1877.] fol.   **h. 1494. r. (2.)**

— Tarantella from La Fille du Tambour Major (Offenbach). [P. F.] *London*, [1880.] fol.   **h. 1494. r. (4.)**

— Valse Arietta on an air from Offenbach's ... opera Madame Favart ... for the Piano. *London*, [1879.] fol.   **h. 1494. r. (3.)**

— Le Voyage dans la Lune (opéra d'Offenbach) suite de valses (galop). [P. F.] 2 no. *London*, [1876.] fol.   **h. 1483. (1.)**

— *See* VARNEY (L.) Les Mousquetaires ... arranged by A. de Lisle. [1880.] 4°.   **f. 299.**

LISLE (BERNARD DE)

— *See* DE LISLE (B. C. M. P.)

LISLE (BERTRAM)

— The Darkest Hour. A War Lullaby. [Song.] Words by W. R. Lisle. *West & Co.: London*, 1915. fol.   **H. 1793. u. (7.)**

— Never forgotten. Song, words by W. R. Lisle, *etc. West & Co.: London*, 1914. fol.   **H. 1793. u. (8.)**

LISLE (D. S. DE)

— *See* BRANEN (Jeffrey T.) Call again, *etc.* [Song.] ⟨Arranged by D. S. de Lisle.⟩ [1897.] fol.   **H. 3980. e. (23.)**

— *See* FURCHGOTT (Mortimer) My Indiana Hannah. [Song.] Arranged by D. S. DeLisle, *etc.* [1901.] 4°.   **H. 3983. mm. (39.)**

— *See* FURCHGOTT (Mortimer) The Sand Man's Song. A plantation lullaby. Arranged by D. S. DeLisle. [1900.] 4°.   **H. 3983. mm. (40.)**

— *See* JOPLIN (Scott) The Entertainer. A ragtime two-step ... Arr. [for orchestra] by D. S. de Lisle, *etc.* [1974.] 4°.   **g. 1755. a. (3.)**

— *See* JOPLIN (Scott) and HAYDEN (S.) Sun Flower Slow Drag ... Arranged [for orchestra] by D. S. de Lisle, *etc.* [1974.] 4°.   **g. 1755. (7.)**

— *See* TURPIN (T.) Bowery Buck ... Arranged by D. S. DeLisle. 1899. fol.   **h. 3286. u. (36.)**

LISLE (E. I. DE)

— Magnificat and Nunc Dimittis ... in ... C. *Novello, Ewer & Co.: London & New York*, [1894.] 8°.   **F. 1170. k. (21.)**

— Vesper Hymn. *Novello, Ewer and Co.: London and New York*, [1893.] a card.   **I. 600. (97.)**

LISLE (EUGÈNE DE)

N'effeuillez-pas les roses

— N'effeuillez pas les roses. Romance [P. F.]. *See* SOIRÉES. Les Soirées de Salon. No. 22. [1847–55.] fol.   **h. 525. (7.)**

— N'effeuillez-pas les roses. Transcription ... pour piano sur la romance, *etc.* [1884.] fol. *See* DEVRIENT (F.)   **h. 3280. e. (7.)**

— *See* SCHUBERT (C.) Fantaisie élégante sur la romance ... de E. Delisle, *etc.* [1854.] fol.   **h. 893. (5.)**

— *See* STREICH (H.) N'effeuillez pas les roses, romance d'E. Delisle avec variations brillantes pour le piano forte par H. Streich. [1852.] fol.   **h. 723. t. (31.)**

LISLE (EUGÈNE DE)

— *See* STREICH (H.) Streich's Romance "N'effeuillez pas les roses," *etc.* [1853.] fol.   **h. 723. t. (30.)**

— Zampa. Petite fantaisie pour piano. [On Hérold's opera.] *Paris*, [1884.] fol.   **h. 3280. d. (43.)**

LISLE (FRANK DE)

— For love and fame. Song. *London*, [1881.] fol.   **H. 1783. p. (15.)**

— Jersey ... Ballad [begins: "When she had shaped"]. *London*, [1880.] fol.   **H. 1783. p. (14.)**

LISLE (JOSEPH ROUGET DE)

— *See* ROUGET DE LISLE.

LISLE (KINGSTON)

— Down the Old Lane. [Song.] Words by G. C. Bingham. *B. Williams: London*, [1888.] fol.   **H. 1788. w. (22.)**

— On the broad Atlantic. [Song.] Words by G. H. Newcombe. *B. Williams: London*, [1889.] fol.   **H. 1788. uu. (43.)**

— To meet again! Song, words by G. C. Bingham. *B. Williams: London*, [1888.] fol.   **H. 1788. w. (23.)**

LISLEY (JOHN)

— Fair Citharea. Madrigal for S. S. A. T. T. B. ... No. 23 of "The Triumphs of Oriana". Edited by L. Benson. [1908.] *See* ORIANA. The Oriana, *etc.* No. 23. [1905, *etc.*] 8°.   **F. 1685.**

LISMOR

— Lismor. [Hymn.] *See* JONES (John) *of Llanddulas.*

LISMORE (   )

— Le Maître d'École. Opéra-Comique meslé d'Ariettes, *etc.* [Words by Anseaume, music by Lismore.] 1760. 8°.   **11738. b. 15. (4.)**

LISON

— Lison avec son cher Colin. *Deuxieme Faux-Pas; ou les Amans satisfaits.* Parodie de "Colin disoit à Lise un jour". [Song.] [*Paris*, 1780?] 8°.   **B. 362. b. (109.)**

— Lison dormait. Chanson. *See* WECKERLIN (J. B. T.)

— Lison dormoit dans un bocage. Ariette. *See* JULIE.

— Lison guettoit une fauvette. Le Trébuchet. [Song.] [*Paris*, 1780?] 8°.   **B. 362. b. (118.)**

— Lison, jeune et timide. Air. *See* DALAYRAC (N.) [L'Éclipse Totale.]

— Lison revenant seulette. *L'Heureuse Rencontre.* Ronde a danser. [*Paris*, 1780?] 8°.   **B. 362. g. (84.)**

— Lison revenoit au Village. *Le Soir.* Ariette Nouvelle. [*Paris*, 1780?] 8°.   **B. 362. b. (102.)**

LISOWSKA (H.) and SUZIN (A.)

— Śpiewnik dla klasy I i II szkoły podstawowej. pp. 35. *Państwowe Zakłady Wydawnictw Szkolnych: Warszawa*, 1951. 8°.   **D. 836. k. (1.)**

LISP

— Lisp in sweetest Numbers. Part Song. *See* WHITING (C. E.)

LISSA (ARTHUR DE)

— Emilie. Morceau de salon for the pianoforte. *Ambrose & Co.: London*, [1884.] fol. **h. 1484. t. (29.)**

LISSA (GEORGES)

— Chimères. Suite de valses [for P. F.]. *Paris*, [1884.] *obl.* fol. **e. 283. c. (12.)**

— Qui vivra verra! Suite de Valses pour piano. *Lissarague: Paris*, [1887.] *obl.* fol. **e. 272. o. (9.)**

— Tête folle. Mazurka pour piano. *Lissarague: Paris*, [1887.] fol. **h. 3281. l. (31.)**

LISSA (ZOFIA)

— *See* CHOMIŃSKI (J. M.) and LISSA (Z.) Muzyka polskiego odrodzenia, *etc.* 1953. fol. **H. 2214.**

— *See* CHOMIŃSKI (J. M.) and LISSA (Z.) Music of the Polish Renaissance, *etc.* 1955. fol. **H. 2214. a.**

LISSA (ZOFIA) and **ŁADA** (OLGA)

— Adam Mickiewicz. Glos z fortepianem. Redakcja Zofia Lissa, Olga Łada. pp. 225. *Polskie wydawnictwo muzyczne: Cracow*, [1955.] 4°. *Part of "Wielcy poeci w pieśni polskiej i obcej".* **G. 762. b.**

LISSANT (GEORGE B.)

— Hymn to be used at the dedication of a stained glass window. Words by J. Bownes. *Novello, Ewer and Co.: London*, [1892.] *s. sh.* 8°. **C. 566. p. (10.)**

— Idle Dreams. Song, words by L. Garston. *E. Ashdown: London*, [1883.] fol. **G. 806. n. (9.)**

— India, fantasia for the Pianoforte, *etc.* *London*, [1876.] fol. **h. 1483. (3.)**

— Love's Choice. Song, the words by H. Ancketill. *Enoch & Sons: London*, [1882.] fol. **H. 1788. w. (24.)**

— The Musical Bee, valse de salon. [P. F.] *London*, [1876.] fol. **h. 1483. (4.)**

— The Soldiers of the Cross. Song, written by H. L. D'A. Jaxone. *J. B. Cramer & Co.: London*, [1889.] fol. **H. 879. c. (22.)**

— Songs for children. *London*, [1878.] 8°. **B. 699. g. (4.)**

— Songs for children. *London*, [1878.] 4°. **G. 805. u. (8.)**

— Songs for children. Tonic Sol-Fa notation. *London*, [1878.] 8°. **B. 699. g. (3.)**

— The Spirit of the Gulf. Song, words by C. Bellamy. *J. B. Cramer & Co.: London*, [1883.] fol. **H. 1788. w. (25.)**

— *See* DUSSEK (J. L.) [Collections.] Three movements ... arranged ... by G. B. Lissant. [1880.] fol. **h. 2732. d. (6.)**

LISSANT (HERBERT OTHO)

— Zephyrs d'Amour.—Whispers of Love.—Valse. [P. F.] *W. Dunkley: London*, [1901.] fol. **h. 3286. r. (18.)**

LISSEN

— *See* LISTEN.

LISSENDEN (JENNIE E.)

— Go 'long, go 'long! [Song.] Words by Ella M. Burke. pp. 5. *T. B. Harms & Co.: New York*, [1894.] fol. **H. 3980. ss. (18.)**

— Going Home to Mother. Ballad, words by E. M. Burke. *K. Dehnhoff: N[ew] Y[ork]*, 1894. fol. **H. 1798. v. (33.)**

LISSENDEN (JENNIE E.)

— Golden Starlight. Schottische. [P. F.] *K. Dehnhof: New York*, 1894. fol. **h. 3285. q. (57.)**

— "Hustle Children" ... Plantation song. Words by George Cooper. pp. 5. *K. Dehnhoff: [New York*, 1894.] fol. **H. 3980. ss. (19.)**

— I'se gwine back. [Song.] Words & music by J. E. Lissenden. pp. 5. *T. B. Harms & Co.: New York*, [1894.] fol. **H. 3980. ss. (20.)**

— A Single Spray of Mignonette. Romance, words and music by J. E. Lissenden. *K. Dehnhoff: New York*, 1894. fol. **H. 1798. v. (34.)**

— Why he never married. Song. Words by Joseph P. Skelly. pp. 5. *K. Dehnhoff: New York*, [1896.] fol. **H. 3980. ss. (21.)**

LISSENDEN (W. COOPER)

— "The Gallant Greys." Song. Words and music by W. C. Lissenden. pp. 7. *Francis, Day & Hunter: London*, [1907.] fol. *Without a colophon.* **H. 3985. aa. (44.)**

— [Another copy, with a colophon.] **H. 3985. aa. (45.)**

LISSENKO (NIKOLAI VITAL'EVICH)

— *See* LISENKO.

LISSER (HENRY)

— Follow the Drum. Quick march. [P. F.] *West & Co.: London*, 1916. fol. **h. 3284. oo. (24.)**

LISSITZIN (M.)

— *See* LISITSUIN.

LIST

— List and learn. [Two-part song.] *See* SULLIVAN (*Sir* Arthur S.) [The Gondoliers.]

— List! for the Breeze. Glee. *See* GOSS (*Sir* J.)

— List gegen List. Eine Operette. *See* BERGT (C. G. A.)

— List! How still. [Song.] *See* FRANZ (R.) [6 Gesänge. Op. 10. No. 2. Stille Sicherheit.]

— List, I hear the Sabbath bell. Ballad. *See* WILLIAMS ( ) *Mrs.*

— List! in Song of rapturous Glory. Carol. *See* LOUD (Annie F.)

— List! Lady, be not coy. Madrigal. *See* PEARSALL (R. L.)

— List lady list. *See* FLOTOW (F. F. A. von) *Baron.* [Alessandro Stradella.]

— List, Love, to me. Part-song. *See* HAYDN (F. J.) [Drey- und vierstimmige Gesänge.—An den Vetter.]

— List, Love, while I sing. Serenade. *See* ERNEST (G.)

— List Maiden list. Song. *See* R-FFE (J.)

— List! the Cherubic Host. Anthem. *See* HARRIS (Cuthbert)

— List thy troubadour. Serenade. *See* BALFE (M. W.)

— List 'tis music stealing. [Song.] *See* BLOCKLEY (J. J.)

— List 'tis Music stealing. Duet. *See* PANSERON (A. M.)

— List, 'tis music stealing. Song. *See* SPENCER (J.)

— List! 'tis the lay of the gondolier. Ballad. *See* SPORLE (N. J.)

LIST

— List 'tis the parting hour. Duet. *See* AMATEURIA (C.) *pseud.*

— List to me. Romance. *See* AUDRAN (E.) [La Cigale et la Fourmi.—Oui, la raison guidant son cœur.]

— List to my prophetic muse! Song. *See* VOX (V.) *pseud.*

— List to my song, O lady mine. Serenade. *See* PHILLIPS (A.) *of Bristol.*

— List to old Bacchus, counsel divine. Song. *See* KUEFFNER (J.)

— List to the Children's Singing. [Hymn.] *See* DENNIS (H.) School Anniversary Music ... Part II. No. 29.

— List to the chime of the distant bell. Ballad. *See* NICHOLS (W. H.)

— List! to the church bells. Round. *See* VINCENT (C.)

— List to the Convent Bells. Notturno. *See* BLOCKLEY (J. J.)

— List to the gay castanet. Solo. *See* BALFE (M. W.) [Rose of Castille.]

— List to the Lark. [Part-song.] *See* DICKINSON (Clarence)

— List to the lively guitar. Serenade. *See* BLEWITT (J.)

— List to the Message. [Song.] *See* KETÈLBEY (A. W.) [Twelve Lyrics. No. 7.]

— List to the minstrel's lay. Romance. *See* MEYERBEER (G.) [Les Huguenots.—Une Dance noble et sage.]

— List to the Music stealing. Duetto. *See* MOZART (W. A.) [Die Zauberflöte.—Wir wandelten durch Feuergluten.]

— List to the Nightingale. Serenade. *See* ELWIN (J.)

— List to the Storm. Song. *See* GOSS (E. I.)

— List to the Voice divine. Sacred Song. *See* JEWITT (J. M.)

— List und Liebe. Komische Oper. *See* HAYDN (F. J.) [La Vera costanza.]

— List while the Sabbath bells. Sacred song. *See* JARVIS (F. A.)

— List ye now, sister, listen! Waltz song. *See* NEULAND (W.)

LIST (ERICH)

— *See* DEBUSSY (C. A.) [6 sonates. No. 2.] Sonate pour flûte, alto et harpe ... (1915.) Herausgegeben von ... E. List, *etc.* [1970.] 4°.　　　**g. 1159. g. (1.)**

— *See* MOZART (W. A.) [Concertos. Flute. K. 313.] Konzert Nr. 1. G dur für Flöte und Orchester ... Ausgabe für Flöte und Klavier von E. List, *etc.* [1966.] 4°.　　　**g. 382. ff. (1.)**

— *See* MOZART (W. A.) [Concertos. Flute. K. 314.] Konzert Nr. 2 D dur für Flöte und Orchester ... Ausgabe für Flöte und Klavier (mit Kadenzen) von E. List, *etc.* [1972.] 4°.　　　**g. 382. o. (6.)**

LIST (EUGENE)

— *See* GOTTSCHALK (L. M.) [Tarentella. Op. 67.] Grand Tarentelle. Piano and orchestra ... Solo piano edited by E. List, *etc.* [1963.] 4°.　　　**h. 4015. q. (4.)**

— *See* GOTTSCHALK (L. M.) L'Union. Paraphrase de concert sur les airs nationaux. [Op. 48.] Arranged for piano and orchestra by S. Adler. Two-piano score. Edited by E. List. [1972.] 4°.　　　**g. 338. pp. (3.)**

LISTE (ANTOINE)

— Sehnsucht nach dem Righi [song, begins: "Was schlägt mir wohl"] von M. Hirzel, *etc.* [*Zurich?* 1830?] *obl.* fol.　　　**E. 600. t. (7.)**

— Deux sonates pour le piano forte. pp. 48. *Chez Jean George Naigueli: Zuric,* [1804.] *obl.* fol. [*Répertoire des clavecinistes. suite* 9.]　　　**Hirsch IV. 1012.**

— Grande sonate pour le piano-forté. pp. 45. *Chez J. George Naigueli & comp.: Zuric,* [1805?] *obl.* fol. [*Répertoire des clavecinistes. suite* 17.]　　　**Hirsch IV. 1012.**

— Grande sonate pour le piano forte avec accompagnement de basson ou violoncelle obligé ... Op. 3. [Parts.] 2 pt. *Chez Jean George Naigueli et comp^e: Zuric,* [c. 1805.] fol.　　　**h. 2010. b.**

— *See* KOESTLICHSTEN. Die köstlichsten Blumen und Früchte ... Mit Musik von J. F. Reichardt ... u. a. [1811.] 8°.　　　**Hirsch III. 658.**

LISTE (ANTON)

— *See* LISTE (Antoine)

LISTEMANN (FRITZ)

— Berceuse ... for Violin and Piano. Op. 3. *Boston Music Co.: Boston, Mass.,* 1904. fol.　　　**g. 505. t. (33.)**

— Valse-Mazurka for Violin and Piano. Op. 10. *Boston Music Co.: Boston, Mass.,* 1904. fol.　　　**g. 505. t. (34.)**

LISTEN

— Listen. Song. *See* BEHREND (J. A. H.)

— Listen! Song. *See* CLAY (F.)

— Listen. [Song.] *See* JEFFERSON (W. T.)

— Listen! Song. *See* LANE (G. M.)

— Listen! Song. *See* LOVER (Samuel)

— Listen. Song. *See* MOIR (F. L.)

— Listen! Song. *See* ROBSON (R. W.)

— Listen. Song. *See* TAYLOR (W. F.)

— Listen a Minute. Song. *See* HERITTE-VIARDOT (L. P. M.)

— Listen all. *Useful knowledge* ... Comic song, written by J. Labern. *London,* [1873.] fol.　　　**H. 1791. a. (3.)**

— Listen all who enter these Portals. [Anthem.] *See* HERBST (J.) [Höret alle die ihr von Hause.]

— Listen and come to me. Serenade. *See* MARRIOTT (M.)

— Listen dear Fanny. [Song.] *See* NELSON (S.)

— Listen Dinah. Song. *See* VERDEN (H.)

— Listen! he must be near. Glee. *See* BISHOP (*Sir* Henry R.)

— Listen here, Laddie Boy. *Garry Owen.* [Song.] Lyric by H. Pease. *Robbins Music Corporation: New York,* 1943. 4°.　　　**G. 981. x. (13.)**

— Listen, ladies, listen. Ballad. *See* OLLIVE (T. H.)

— Listen Lester. Musical Comedy. *See* ORLOB (H.)

— Listen, listen how those bells. [Song.] *See* HINE (J.)

— Listen, listen, to the Voice of Love. Song. *See* HOOK (J.)

— Listen, Lord. [Anthem.] *See* WARD (William R.)

— Listen, Lordlings, unto me. Carol. *See* NEEDHAM (A. A.)

LISTEN

— Listen lovely lady. Serenade. *See* WILLIAMS (T. R.) *Composer of "Listen lovely lady"*

— Listen, maiden fair. [Song.] *See* THOMAS (C. L. A.)

— Listen, Mary. Song. *See* BRAHE (M. H.)

— Listen Mary! Song. *See* MOLLOY (J. L.)

— Listen, O Isles. Anthem. *See* ALLEN (G. B.)

— Listen, O Isles, unto me. [Anthem.] *See* FOOTE (A. W.)

— Listen, O Isles unto me. Anthem. *See* STEVENSON (F.)

— Listen sweet Dove. Anthem. *See* IVES (Grayston)

— Listen, sweet lady love, listen. Serenade. *See* BIRD (J.)

— Lissen ter dis Story. Song. *See* PEASE (J. L.)

— Listen! the Wind. [Song.] *See* DOUGHERTY (Celius)

— Listen! tis the Nightingale. *See* LEE (G. A.)

— Listen to me and I'll prove that I'm right. Song. *See* EARLE (Frederick)

— Listen to Mother's Words they're always true. [Song.] *See* LINDSAY (Jennie)

— Listen to my Tale of Woe. Male Quartette. *See* SMITH (Hubbard T.) and WYE (D. A.) [A Little Peach in an Orchard grew.]

— Listen to my wild Guitar. [Song.] *See* BARNETT (John)

— Listen to that Dixie Band. [Song.] *See* COBB (George L.)

— Listen to the Air that I love best. [Song.] *See* SPORLE (Nathan J.)

— Listen to the Angel's Song. [Song.] *See* VALMORE (G.)

— Listen to the big Brass Band. Song. *See* REED (David)

— Listen to the Bugle calling. Song. *See* HAWLING (G. D.)

— Listen to the buzzing of the Bees. [Song.] *See* THIELE (H. H.)

— Listen to the carol'd ditty. [Song.] *See* SPENCER (J.)

— Listen to the Children. Song. *See* COWEN (*Sir* F. H.)

— Listen to the Christmas bells! Carol. *See* HALLETT (D. H.)

— Listen to the Curfew bell. Part-song. *See* DISTIN (J.)

— Listen to the golden Horn. Spiritual. *See* SIBLEY (Ben)

— Listen to the Knocking Bird. [Song.] *See* INGRAHAM (Herbert)

— Listen to the Lambs. Anthem. *See* DETT (R. N.)

— Listen to the Lambs. Negro spiritual. *See* DEXTER (Harry)

— Listen to the Lambs. Negro Spiritual. *See* ROBERTON (*Sir* H. S.)

— Lis'en to de Lam's. Negro Spiritual. *See* SARGENT (*Sir* M.)

— Listen to the Mocking Bird. Song. *See* HAWTHORNE (A.) *pseud.*

— Listen to the Night. [Song.] *See* BRUGUIERE (Emile A.) [Baroness Fiddlesticks.—Oh Honey, ma Honey.]

— Listen to the silv'ry Bells. *The Bells of Aberdovey.* Unison Song, words by W. G. Rothery. Welsh Air. [1908.] *See* MACNAUGHT (W. G.) Novello's School Songs. No. 820. 1892, *etc.* 8°. **F. 280. d.**

LISTEN

— Listen to the silv'ry Bells. *The Bells of Aberdovey.* Arranged as a Two-part Song, *etc.* Novello and Co.: London, [1933.] 8°.
[*Novello's School Songs. No.* 1354.] **F. 280. d.**

— Listen to the Singing of the Mocking Bird. [Song.] *See* COLMAN (Amos L.)

— Listen to the village chime. [Song.] *See* SPENCER (J.)

— Listen to the Voice of Love. Song. *See* O. O listen to the Voice of Love, *etc.* [By James Hook.] [c. 1795.] *s. sh.* fol. **H. 1653. j. (47.)**

— Listen to the Voice of Love. A favorite new song as sung by Master Welsh at Vauxhall. [By James Hook.] *See* O. O listen listen to the Voice of Love, *etc.* [c. 1795.] *s. sh.* fol. **G. 426. kk. (27.)**

— Listen to the Voice of Love. Glee. *See* GEARY (T. A.)

— Listen to the Wind. [Musical play.] *See* ELLIS (Vivian)

— Listen to the wondrous Story. Hymn Anthem. *See* DANKS (H. P.)

–– Listen to the wondrous Story. Anthem. *See* HAWLEY (C. B.)

— Listen to yo' Gyarden Angel. Song. *See* BURLEIGH (H. T.)

— Listen while I tell you, dear. Ballad. *See* STULTS (Robert M.)

— Listen while the bluebells ring. Duettino. *See* KALLIWODA (J. W.)

LISTENER

— The Listener. Song. *See* LEVITT (R.)

LISTENERS

— The Listeners. [Part-song.] *See* GIBBS (Cecil A.)

— The Listeners. [Cantata.] *See* STEPHENSON (Robin)

— The Listeners. [Part-song.] *See* WHITE (L. J.)

— The Listeners. Cantata. *See* YOUNG (Douglas)

LISTENGART (BENJAMIN)

— *See* BRAHMS (J.) [Ungarische Tänze. No. 5.] Hungarian Dance No. 5 ... Edited by B. Listengart. 1926. 4°. **g. 609. g. (11.)**

— *See* DRIGO (R.) [Les Millions d'Arlequin.] Serenade ... Edited by B. Listengart. 1926. 4°. **g. 500. m. (21.)**

— *See* SCHUBERT (F. P.) [Schwanengesang. No. 4. Ständchen.] Serenade ... Edited by B. Listengart. 1926. 4°. **g. 567. e. (19.)**

LISTENING

— Listening. Part-Song. *See* BAIRSTOW (*Sir* E. C.) Three Part-Songs ... 2.

— Listening. [Song.] *See* BENDL (Karl)

— Listening. [Song.] *See* BESLY (E. M.)

— Listening. Ballad. *See* LASCELLES (A. B.)

— Listening. Song. *See* O'LEARY (A.)

— Listening. Three-part song. *See* THIMAN (Eric H.)

— Listenin'. Song. *See* WOOD (H.)

— Listening Angels. Song. *See* BARRI (O.)

— Listening angels. Song. *See* BLOCKLEY (John J.)

LISTENING

— Listening Angels. Song. *See* COWEN (*Sir* F. H.)

— Listening Angels. Song. *See* KING (O. A.)

— Listening Angels. [Song.] *See* WEST (W.)

— Listening for you! Song. *See* KAHN, afterwards CARNE (Gerald F.)

— Listening in a waking dream. Song. *See* SALA (C. K.)

— Listening in darkness speaking in light. [Song.] *See* WINTER (M.)

— The listening mother. Song. *See* GABRIEL, afterwards MARCH (M. A. V.)

— The Listening Oak. Song. *See* TENNANT (C. R.)

— Listning she turns. Song. *See* ISAAC ( ) *Dancing Master*

— Listening to the nightingales. Arietta. *See* SMART (H.) [King René's Daughter.]

— Listening to the Singer. Ballad. *See* PINSUTI (C. E.)

— Listening to the Thrush. Song. *See* PLUMPTON (A.)

— List'ning to the Vesper Bell. Song. *See* SWEENEY (Ada)

LISTENIUS (NICOLAUS)

— Musica Nicolai Listenii ab authore denuo recognita multisque novis regulis et exemplis adaucta ... Anno MDXLIX. Im Faksimile herausgegeben mit einer Einführung von G. Schünemann. *M. Breslauer: Berlin*, 1927. 8°.
[*Veröffentlichungen der Musik-Bibliothek Paul Hirsch.* 8.]
G. 1401.

LISTER ( ) *Miss*

— Six Songs. First series of three. *London*, [1865.] fol.
Imperfect; wanting the second series. **H. 2828. b. (11.)**

LISTER (DOUGLAS)

— Hymn to Jesus [begins: "King of kings"] ... Words by Sir G. R. Fetherston. *London*, [1878.] 8°. **E. 1498. b. (19.)**

— Patti quadrilles. [P. F.] *London*, [1873.] fol. **h. 1483. (6.)**

— The Scarborough Belle galop. [P. F.] *London*, [1873.] fol.
h. 1483. (5.)

— Take up thy cross. Hymn. *London*, [1876.] 8°.
H. 1980. (180.)

— The Yorkshire Belle Galop. [P. F.] *E. Donajowski: London*, [1898.] fol.
Popular Dance Music, etc. No. 50. **h. 3299. a.**

LISTER (FREDERICK)

— Nocturno—Eventide—for Pianoforte. *Oppenheimer Bros.: London*, 1901. fol. **h. 3282. w. (55.)**

LISTER (GEORGE)

— The Lancashire and Yorkshire Harmonist; being a selection of Anthems and Tunes with choruses ... by G. Lister, J. Newsome, G. Kingham, W. Muff, and other ... composers. 100 no. *J. Broadbent: Leeds*, [1892.] 4°. **E. 1643.**

— My God look upon me. Anthem. [1896.] *See* WOOD AND SONS. Wood's Collection of Glees, *etc.* No. 5. [1896, *etc.*] 8°.
E. 1689.

LISTER (HAYDN)

— A Lover gay. Song, written and composed by H. Lister. *West's: London*, 1919. 4°. **G. 426. d. (50.)**

LISTER (MADELINE)

— Springtide. Song, written and composed by M. Lister. 2 no. [In G and A flat.] *Ransford & Son: London*, [1892.] fol.
H. 1797. o. (41.)

— Through the Hawthorn Glade. Song, written & composed by M. Lister. *Ransford & Son: London*, [1892.] fol.
H. 1797. o. (42.)

LISTER (RICHARD)

— A favorite lesson for the Piano Forte. *Leeds*, [1811.] fol.
h. 117. (31.)

LISTER (*Mrs* ROBERT N.)

— In the bleak Mid-Winter. (Sacred Song.) Christmas ... [Words by] C. Rossetti, [altered by] R. N. Lister. *White-Smith Music Publishing Co.: Boston, etc.*, (1911.) fol.
H. 1187. rr. (18.)

LISTMAN (FRED)

— Chicago Hustle. March two-step. [P. F.] pp. 5. *Music Co.: Chicago*, [1907.] fol. **h. 4120. rr. (4.)**

LISTNING

— *See* LISTENING.

LISTON (HARRY)

— The Baronet. [Song, begins: "I knew an opera singer".] *London*, [1867.] fol. **H. 1772. s. (22.)**

— The Days to come. Humorous song. Written, composed ... by H. Liston. pp. 5. *Reynolds & Co.: London*, [1898.] fol.
H. 3980. ss. (22.)

— Faithless Rose, or I shall never more be jolly. Comic song [begins: "Once I was"]. Arranged by R. Coote. *London*, [1866.] fol. **H. 1772. s. (21.)**

Merry Moments

— Do you know Smit. [Song, begins: "I nevare in my life".] *London*, [1876.] fol. **H. 1778. y. (57.)**

— Don't quit the land of the shamrock. [Song, begins: "Oh! it's jokin'".] *London*, [1876.] fol. **H. 1778. y. (56.)**

— Fancy goes a very long way. [Song, begins: "Some folks are so romantic".] (Words by T. Dodsworth.) *London*, [1876.] fol. **H. 1778. y. (55.)**

— The Fruits of living too well. [Song, begins: "To be born".] Arranged by Miss F. Moss. *Leeds*, [1873.] fol.
H. 1778. y. (49.)

— I hope I don't intrude. [Song, begins: "I've just popped in".] *Leeds*, [1875.] fol. **H. 1778. y. (52.)**

— I'll tell my ma. Comic song [begins: "I'm what they call a nice spoiled boy"]. Words by W. Greenaway. *Leeds*, [1873.] fol. **H. 1778. y. (51.)**

— I love the verdant fields ... Song. *London*, [1876.] fol.
H. 1778. y. (53.)

— I love the verdant fields ... Song. *London*, [1881.] fol.
H. 1787. j. (42.)

— Isn't it provoking. [Song, begins: "I'm told by my friends".] (Words by T. Dodsworth.) *London*, [1876.] fol.
H. 1778. y. (58.)

LISTON (Harry)

— It's easy if you only know the way. [Song, begins: "I've heard some people say".] Written by J. H. Stringer. *London*, [1873.] fol.   **H. 1778. y. (50.)**

— A Novel Idea. Song [begins: "Ah! gentlemen"]. Words by J. B. Geoghegan ... Arranged by F. Moss. *Leeds*, [1873.] fol.
H. 1783. p. (16.)

— Peter Simple. [Song, begins: "If you please".] (Words by W. Greenaway.) *London*, [1876.] fol.   **H. 1778. y. (54.)**

— Peter Simple, *etc.* [Song.] (Words by W. Greenaway.) *J. B. Cramer & Co.: London*, [1889.] fol.   **H. 1260. f. (55.)**

— *See* Dodsworth (T.) and Liston (H.) A Fwightful Dilemma, *etc.* [1873.] fol.   **H. 1778. k. (48.)**

LISTOPADOV (Aleksandr Mikhailovich)

— Песни донских казаков. Под общей редакцией ... Г. Сердюченко. *Музгиз: Москва*, 1949, *etc.* 4°.   **G. 560. b.**

LISTZ (Franz)

— *See* Liszt.

LISUART

— Lisuart und Dariolette, oder die Frage und die Antwort. Romantisch-comische Oper. *See* Hiller (J. A.)

LISUORI (Emerik)

— Annie, polka mazurka. [P. F.] *London*, [1861.] fol.
h. 1460. w. (14.)

LISZNIEWSKI (Karol)

— Amid the Silence of the starlit Night. Old Polish Christmas Carol for four-part Chorus of Mixed Voices ... English version by K. Liszniewski. Arranged by K. Liszniewski. *Boston Music Co.: Boston*, 1935. 8°.   **E. 602. tt. (75.)**

— Lullaby Carol. Old Polish Christmas Carol. Chorus of Women's Voices ... English version by K. Liszniewski. Arranged by K. Liszniewski. *Boston Music Co.: Boston*, 1935. 8°.   **E. 602. tt. (76.)**

LISZT

— Liszt Society. *See* London.

LISZT (Franz)

1. Thematic Catalogues.
2. Collected Works:—
   a. Complete Works.
   b. Pianoforte and Organ Works and Arrangements.
   c. Vocal and Instrumental Selections, combined.
   d. Songs.
   e. Instrumental Selections and Arrangements.
   f. Composite Works.
3. Main alphabetical sequence.
4. Appendix.

THEMATIC CATALOGUES

— Thematisches Verzeichniss der Werke von F. Liszt. Von dem Autor verfasst. pp. 97. *Breitkopf & Härtel: Leipzig*, 1855. 8°.
e. 1. b.

— Thematisches Verzeichniss der Werke, Bearbeitungen und Transcriptionen von F. Liszt. Neue vervollständigte Ausgabe. pp. iv. 162. *Breitkopf & Härtel: Leipzig*, [1877.] 8°.   **e. 1. e.**

LISZT (Franz)

— [Another copy.]   **Hirsch 172.**

— [A reissue.] Thematisches Verzeichniss der Werke ... Neue vervollständigte Ausgabe. *Reprinted for H. Baron: London*, 1965. 8°.   **Music Reading Area 789.**

COLLECTED WORKS.—a. Complete Works

— Franz Liszt's musikalische Werke. Herausgegeben von der Franz Liszt-Stiftung. [With portraits and a facsimile.]
   I.   Für Orchester. Bd. 1–13. [1907–17?]
   II. Pianoforte Werke. Bd. 1–10, 12. [1910–26.]
   V.   Kirchliche und geistliche Gesangswerke. Bd. 3, 5, 6, 7. [1918]–36.
   VII. Einstimmige Lieder und Gesänge. Bd. 1–3. [1919–22.]
        Freie Bearbeitungen. Bd. 1–3. [1910–22.]
Breitkopf & Härtel: Leipzig, [1907]–36. fol. *Section II, Bd. 11 was never published.*   **Hirsch IV. 979.**

— Franz Liszt's musikalische Werke. Herausgegeben von der Franz Liszt-Stiftung. [With portraits.]
   I.   Für Orchester. Bd. 1–13.
   II. Pianoforte Werke. Bd. 1–10, 12.
   V.   Kirchliche und geistliche Gesangswerke. Bd. 3, 5, 6.
   VII. Einstimmige Lieder und Gesänge. Bd. 1–3.
        Freie Bearbeitungen. Bd. 1–3.
Breitkopf & Härtel: Leipzig, [1907]–36. fol.
Imperfect; wanting Bd. 7 of section V. Section II, Bd. 11 was never published.   **N. 2.**

— Liszt Society Publications, *etc.*
   vol. 1. Late Piano Works. pp. 62. [1951.]
   vol. 2. Early and Late Piano Works. pp. 58. [1952.]
   vol. 3. Hungarian and Late Piano Works. pp. 62. [1954.]
   vol. 4. Dances for Piano. pp. 61. [1957.]
   vol. 5. Various Piano Pieces. pp. 114. [1968.]
   vol. 6. Selected Songs. pp. 73. [1975.]
   vol. 7. Unfamiliar Piano Pieces. pp. 74. [1978.]
[1951, *etc.*] 4°. *See* London.— *Liszt Society.*   **G. 461. d.**

— Franz Liszts musikalische Werke. Herausgegeben von der Franz Liszt-Stiftung, *etc.* 33 vol. *Gregg Press: Farnborough, Hants; printed in Western Germany*, 1966. 4° & 8°. *A reissue of the edition of* 1907–36.   **H. 1878. j.**

— Neue Ausgabe sämtlicher Werke. [With facsimiles.]
   ser. 1.   Werke für Klavier zu zwei Händen.
Bärenreiter: Kassel, etc.; Editio musica: Budapest, 1970, *etc.* 4°.   **H. 4027.**

— [Another copy.]   **H. 4027. a.**

COLLECTED WORKS.—b. Pianoforte and Organ Works and Arrangements

— Réveries religieuses de Schubert et Beethoven. 10 sacred melodies ... transcribed for the piano forte by François Liszt ... Followed by two additional numbers ... transcribed by Rudolf Willmers. 12 no. *Wessel & Cᵒ: London*, [1846, 45.] fol.   **h. 584. (3.)**

— 6 Märsche für Pianoforte zu 2 & 4 Händen ... Nᵒ 1. Fest-Marsch. 2. Göthe-Fest-Marsch. 3. Marsch: Die heiligen drei Könige ... 4. Rakoczy-Marsch. 5. Tscherkessen-Marsch. 6. Ungarischer Marsch. Zu 2 Händen, *etc.* pp. 74. *J. Schuberth & Cᵒ: Leipzig*, [1876.] fol.   **g. 547. cc. (4.)**

— Liszt-Album ... Selected Pianoforte pieces, edited by A. Schloesser. *London*, [1880.] 4°.
[*Format Litolff.* vol. 457.]   **g. 375.**

— 22 Songs by F. Schubert transcribed for the Pianoforte ... Revised by E. Pauer. *London*, [1880.] 8°.   **f. 470.**

— Transcriptions for the Pianoforte by F. Liszt. Revised by E. Pauer, *etc.* no. 6. *Augener & Cᵒ: London*, [c. 1880.] fol. *Imperfect; wanting no. 1–5, and 7–11.*   **h. 896. hh.**

LISZT (Franz)

— Popular pieces for the pianoforte. Selected, partly simplified and revised by E. Pauer. *London*, [1886.] 4°.
Augener & Co.'s edition, No. 8221.   **g. 547. (1.)**

— Three Songs by F. Mendelssohn Bartholdy, transcribed for the pianoforte ... Revised by E. Pauer. *London*, [1887.] 4°.
No. 6230 of Augener & Co.'s edition.   **g. 547. a. (5.)**

— Two Favourite Pieces for Piano. 1. La Campanella. 2. Rhapsodie hongroise. *A. Hammond & Co.: London*, [1900.] 4°.
The Academic Edition, No. 131.   **g. 1130. d. (4.)**

— Selected Compositions for the Pianoforte, edited by R. Joseffy. *G. Schirmer: New York*, 1902, *etc.* fol.
    h. 896. c. (10.)

— Album of original Pieces for the Pianoforte. *Augener & Co.: London*, [1903.] 4°.   **g. 547. c. (2.)**

— A Collection of selected original Pianoforte Compositions. Compiled, edited and fingered by P. Gallico. *J. W. Stern & Co.: New York*, 1907. 4°.
Part of "Half-Hours with the Favorite Composers".
    g. 719. a. (2.)

— 12 Klavierstücke. Neue, revidierte Ausgabe von E. d'Albert. *C. F. Kahnt Nachfolger: Leipzig*, 1908. 4°.   **g. 232. n. (9.)**

— Original Works and Transcriptions for the Piano. Edited and fingered by R. Joseffy, *etc.* 14 no. *G. Schirmer: New York*, (1909.) fol. & 4°.   **h. 896. f.**

— Liszt-Pädagogium. Klavier-kompositionen Franz Liszt's, nebst noch unedirten Veränderungen, Zusätzen und Kadenzen nach des Meisters Lehren pädagogisch glossirt von L. Ramann, *etc.*
   ser. 1.   Stücke religiöser Richtung. pp. 22.
   ser. 2.   Grössere und kleinere Formen. pp. 12.
   ser. 3.   Ungarisch. pp. 17.
   ser. 4.   Grössere und kleinere Formen verschiedener Richtung. pp. 15.
   ser. 5.   Anhang.
Breitkopf & Härtel: Leipzig, [c. 1910.] fol.
Part of "Breitkopf & Härtel's Klavierbibliothek". Imperfect; ser. 1–4 only.   **h. 896. l. (6.)**
    & h. 896. aa. (1.)

— Celebrated Piano Solos ... No. 1. Waldesrauschen ... No. 2. Gnomenreigen ... No. 3. J. S. Bach's Organ Fantasia and Fugue in G minor, arranged by F. Liszt. Arranged and revised by A. O'Leary. 3 no. *Duff, Stewart & Co.: London*, [1912.] fol.   **h. 896. g. (6.)**

— Lieder für Harmonium übertragen von Sigfrid Karg-Elert, *etc.* no. 1, 3, 6, 14, 18, 20, 24, 37, 39, 46, 53, 55. *C. F. Kahnt Nachfolger: Leipzig*, [1913.] fol.
The numeration is that of Liszt's "Gesammelte Lieder" in the Kahnt edition. Imperfect; wanting no. 7, 10, 28, 29.
    h. 2739. h. (11.)

— Selected Pianoforte Works, *etc.* *G. Newnes: London*, [1913.] fol.
No. 63 of "The Music-Lovers' Library".   **H. 3928.**

— Favourite Pianoforte Pieces. *A. Lengnick & Co.: London*, [1919.] 4°.
The Eclipse Series of artistic Albums, No. 12.   **g. 547. e. (3.)**

— Bildern aus Ungarn. Scènes hongroises. Scenes from Hungary ... Piano solo. pp. 25. *Josef Weinberger: Wien, etc.*, [1920?] 4°.
In die "Universal-Edition" aufgenommen.   **g. 547. g. (16.)**

— Orgelcompositionen ... Herausgegeben von Karl Straube. 2 Bd. *C. F. Peters: Leipzig*, [1921?] *obl.* fol.   **e. 58. i.**

LISZT (Franz)

— A Selection of eight favourite Pieces ... easily arranged & fingered by J. E. Newell. Piano solo. *Gould & Bolttler: London*, [1922.] 4°.
The Royal College Edition, No. 151.   **g. 547. e. (4.)**

— Lieder für Harmonium übertragen von Sigfrid Karg-Elert. Für Normal-Harmonium, *etc.* pp. 30. *C. F. Kahnt Nachfolger: Leipzig*, [c. 1930.] 4°.   **h. 896. s. (2.)**

— Liszt. (Popular & well known works for Piano.) *Keith Prowse & Co.: London*, 1932. 4°.
[*The Home Series of the Great Masters. Book* 8.]   **f. 461.**

— Gems of Liszt. Easily arranged for the Pianoforte. Edited & fingered by G. H. Farnell, *etc.* *Banks Music House: Leeds*, 1934. 4°.
Gem Series, Book 14.   **g. 547. f. (14.)**

— Popular Pieces for Piano ... Selected, edited and revised by A. M. Henderson. *Bayley & Ferguson: London, Glasgow*, 1937. 4°.   **g. 547. f. (26.)**

— Compositions for the Organ. Selected and edited by A. M. Henderson. *Bayley & Ferguson: London, Glasgow*, 1940. *obl.* 4°.   **e. 1093. v. (1.)**

— Favourite Compositions ... Arranged for the Pianoforte edited by O. A. Mansfield, *etc.* *W. Paxton & Co.: London*, 1940. 4°.
One of "The Great Composers Series".   **f. 470. a. (6.)**

— Liszt. Excerpts from his greatest works. ⟨Arranged by Victor Ambroise.⟩ [P. F.] pp. 22. *Lawrence Wright Music Co.: London*, [1947.] 4°.   **f. 470. a. (1.)**

— Consolations (Nos. 1–6). Liebesträume, three nocturnes. For the piano. Edited and fingered by Rafael Joseffy. pp. 39. *G. Schirmer: New York; Chappell & Co.: London;* [*London printed*, 1950.] 4°.
Schirmer's Library of musical Classics, vol. 341.
    g. 547. h. (1.)

— Liszt Album. Herausgegeben und bezeichnet von ... Percival Garratt. pp. 24. *Hinrichsen Edition: London*, [1953.] 4°.
    g. 547. l. (1.)

— Two Concert Etudes. 1. Waldesrauschen ... 2. Gnomenreigen ... Edited and fingered by Rafael Joseffy. Two Legends. 1. St. François d'Assise. La prédication aux oiseaux ... 2. St. François de Paule marchant sur les flotes [*sic*] ... Edited and fingered by Louis Oesterle ... For the piano. pp. 48. *G. Schirmer: New York; Chappell & Co.: London;* [*London printed*, 1953.] 4°.
Schirmer's Library of musical Classics. vol. 1753.
    g. 547. j. (10.)

— Eine Sammlung wenig bekannter Klavierstücke (leicht bis mittelschwer). Ausgewählt und herausgegeben von Bruno Hinze-Reinhold. ⟨Neue Ausgabe.⟩ pp. 55. *Edition Peters: Leipzig*, [1956.] 4°.   **g. 547. l. (8.)**

— Five Liszt Discoveries. For piano solos ... Edited by Jack Werner. [1.] Ländler in A♭ ... [2.] Wiegenlied. (Chant du berceau) ... [3.] Ave Maria ... [4.] Tyrolean Melody ... [5.] La Cloche sonne. pp. 12. *J. Curwen & Sons: London; G. Schirmer: New York*, [1958.] 4°.
[*Autograph Series of unknown Classics. no.* 3.]   **g. 1600.**

— Оперные транскрипции для фортепьяно, *etc.* ⟨Редакция и примечания В. С. Белова и К. С. Сорокина.⟩ [With a portrait.] 4 том. 9 част. *Государственное музыкальное издательство: Москва*, 1958–68. fol.   **h. 896. x.**

— Сочинения для фортепьяно. ⟨Редакция и комментарии Я. И. Мильштейна.⟩ *Государственное музыкальное издательство: Москва*, 1960, *etc.* fol.   **h. 896. w.**

LISZT (FRANZ)

— Négy orgonamű. 〈Four Compositions for Organ.〉 "Ad nos, ad salutarem undam." B-A-C-H. A halottak. "Weinen, klagen, sorgen, zagen." Az összövegek alapján sajtó alá rendezte Pécsi Sebestyén. pp. 142. *Zeneműkiadó Vállalat: Budapest*, 1961. *obl.* 4°.　　　　　　　**e. 1093. z. (8.)**

— Fourteen original Piano Pieces. Edited and fingered by Frances Dillon, *etc.* pp. 32. *Augener: London*, [1961.] fol. *The cover bears the title "The Easier Liszt".*　**g. 547. r. (1.)**

— Famous Pieces. Arranged by Geoffry Russell-Smith. Piano solo. pp. 22. *Boosey & Hawkes: London, etc.*, [1962.] 4°. [*Everbody's Music Library. vol.* 25.]　　　**g. 1502.**

— Tizenhárom orgonamű … Thirteen compositions for organ. Az első kiadások alapján közreadja … Gergely Ferenc. pp. 88. *Zeneműkiadó vállalat: Budapest*, 1963. *obl.* 4°. 　　　　　　　　　　　　　　　**e. 1096. t. (1.)**

— Four shorter Organ Pieces. Ora pro nobis—Ave Maria by Arcadelt—Angelus— Introitus, *etc.* 〈Edited by William L. Sumner.〉 pp. 24. *Hinrichsen Edition: London*, [1963.] *obl.* 4°.　　　　　　　　　**e. 1093. tt. (3.)**

— Easy Liszt. 12 famous concert pieces for piano. Arranged … by William Scher. pp. 20. *G. Schirmer: New York*, [1965.] 4°.　　　　　　　　　　　　　**g. 547. r. (3.)**

— Trois œuvres pour orgue … Revues, annotées et doigtées par Marcel Dupré, *etc.* pp. ix. 90. *S. Bornemann: Paris*, [c. 1965.] *obl.* fol.　　　　　　　　　　　　**f. 470. j.**

— The Final Years. (Piano compositions of the late period.) For piano. Selected and edited by Joseph Prostakoff. pp. 159. *G. Schirmer: New York*, [1968.] 4°. *Schirmer's Library of musical Classics. vol.* 1845.　　　　　　　　　　　　　　**g. 547. r. (6.)**

— Miniatures. For piano. Selected and edited by Joseph Prostakoff. pp. 21. *G. Schirmer: New York, London*, [1968.] 4°. *Schirmer's Library of Musical Classics. vol.* 1899.　　　　　　　　　　　　　　**g. 547. z. (4.)**

— Drei späte Klavierstücke … Erstausgabe … Herausgegeben von … Robert Charles Lee. pp. 15. *Bärenreiter: Kassel, etc.*, [1969.] 4°. *Part of "The 19th Century".*　　　**g. 547. x. (1.)**

— Complete Organ Works … Edited by Sándor Margittay. 4 vol. *Boosey & Hawkes: London, etc.; Editio musica: Budapest*, 1970–73. *obl.* fol.　　　**f. 470. h.**

— Транскрипции сочинений разных композиторов для фортепиано. 〈Составление, редакция и примечания К. С. Сорокина и Ю. К. Комалькова.〉 *Издательство "Музыка": Москва*, 1970, *etc.* 4°.　　　　**g. 547. y.**

— Werke für Klavier zu 2 Händen. [With facsimiles.] *Bärenreiter: Kassel, etc.; Editio musica: Budapest; printed in Hungary*, 1970, *etc.* 4°. *Another issue of ser.* 1 *of the "Neue Ausgabe sämtlicher Werke".*　　　　　　　　　**H. 4027. b.**

— Ab irato. Zwei Konzertetüden. Two Concert Studies. Für Klavier … Herausgegeben von … Zoltán Gárdonyi, István Szelényi. pp. 28. *Bärenreiter: Kassel, etc.; Editio musica: Budapest; printed in Hungary*, 1971. 4°.　　　**g. 547. aa. (9.)**

— Franz Liszt. His greatest piano solos … Compiled by Alexander Shealy. pp. 191. *Copa Publishing Co.: Carlstadt*, [1972.] 4°.　　　　　　　**g. 1138. jj. (1.)**

— Liszt. A selection. Edited and annotated by Gordon Green. [With a facsimile. P. F.] pp. 63. *Oxford University Press: London, New York*, [1973.] 4°. [*Oxford Keyboard Classics. no.* 3.]　　**g. 1231. a.**

LISZT (FRANZ)

— Liszt … Transcribed and simplified by Cyril C. Dalmaine. [P. F.] pp. 30. *Warren & Phillips: Manchester*, [1976.] 4°. 　　　　　　　　　　　　　　**g. 547. x. (5.)**

— Selected Works for Piano Solo. Compiled by Margaret Gresh. pp. 159. *G. Schirmer: New York, London*, [1977.] 4°. 　　　　　　　　　　　　　　**g. 547. ee. (1.)**

— Consolations. Liebesträume. Für Klavier zu zwei Händen. Herausgegeben von Emil von Sauer. pp. 35. *Edition Peters: London, etc.*, [1978.] 4°.　　　**g. 547. ee. (2.)**

— Einzelne Charakterstücke II. 〈Für Klavier zu 2 Händen.〉 Herausgegeben von Imre Sulyok, Imre Mező. Fingersatz revidiert von Kornél Zempléni, *etc.* 〈Simultaneous publication with: Franz Liszt, Neue Ausgabe sämtlicher Werke, Serie I, Band 12.〉 [With facsimiles.] pp. xviii. 101. *Bärenreiter: Kassel, etc.; Editio musica: Budapest; printed in Hungary*, 1978. 4°.　　　　　**g. 547. ee. (3.)**

— Ave Maria (No. 4). O sacrum convivium. Per organo ossia armonio solo. Közreadja … Sulyok Imre. pp. 6. *Editio Musica: Budapest*, [1980.] 4°.　　**g. 547. ii. (2.)**

COLLECTED WORKS.—c. Vocal and Instrumental Selections, combined

— Liszt. By Sir A. C. Mackenzie. [With P. F. selections and songs.] [1913.] *See* HATZFELD (E.) Masterpieces of Music, *etc.* 1912, *etc.* 4°.　　　　　　　**G. 1180.**

— László Teleki (1885) … Unstern (zwischen 1880–1886) … Trübe Wolken (1881) … Csárdás obstiné (1884) … Abschied (1885) … Ossa arida (1879), *etc. In:* SZABOLCSI (B.) Franz Liszt an seinem Lebensabend. pp. 91–142. 1959. 8°. 　　　　　　　　　　　　　　**7903. ccc. 14.**

COLLECTED WORKS.—d. Songs

— F. Liszt's Songs. English version by C. Bache. 17 no. *Stanley Lucas, Weber & Co.: London*, [1874–87.] fol. *No.* 1 *is in two keys.*　　　　　　**H. 1878. b.**

— Franz Liszt's gesammelte Lieder mit Begleitung des Pianoforte. 57 no. *C. F. Kahnt Nachfolger: Leipzig*, [c. 1880.] fol.　　　　　　　　　　　　**H. 1878. e.**

— Songs with pianoforte accompaniment. 5 no. *London*, [1883–6.] fol.　　　　　　　**H. 1878. c. (5.)**

— Twenty songs with pianoforte accompaniment. *See* HUEFFER (F.) Albums of German Song … No. II. [1884.] fol.　**F. 637.**

— Gesammelte Lieder für eine Singstimme mit Pianofortebegleitung. pp. 228. *C. F. Kahnt Nachfolger: Leipzig*, [1885?] fol.　　　　　　**R. M. 13. f. 15.**

— Songs with Pianoforte Accompaniment … No. 1. Mignon. (Kennst du das Land.) … 2. Thou who from thy heavenly Home. (Der du von dem Himmel bist.) … 3. It is a wondrous Sympathy. (Es muss ein Wunderbares sein.) … 4. Thou art like a Flower. (Du bist wie eine Blume.) … 5. Loreley. (Die Loreley.) Eng. & Ger. 5 no. *Augener & Co.: London*, [1889.] [*Germania. no.* 340, 341, 529–531.]　**H. 2128.**

— Two Songs, with German and English Words. 1. Thou bloomest like a Flow'ret. 2. It must a wondrous Rapture be. *Stanley Lucas & Co.: London, etc.*, [1898.] fol. 　　　　　　　　　　　　　**H. 1878. c. (1.)**

— Lieder … Neue Ausgabe, rev. von W. Höhne. no. 9, 19, 52. *C. F. Kahnt: Leipzig*, [c. 1900.] 4°. *Imperfect; wanting the other numbers.*　**H. 1648. k. (5.)**

— F. Liszt's Songs, *etc.* (Songs by F. Liszt.) (Lieder mit deutschem & englischem Text.) 26 no. *Schott & Co.: London*, [1904, *etc.*] fol.

LISZT (Franz)

*A made-up edition. No. 1–4, 7, 8, 15–17 consist of Stanley
Lucas & Co.'s edition, English words by C. Bache; no. 1a, 5, 6,
9–14, 22, 24 and 25 are Schott's edition with English title page;
no. 18–21, 23 and 26 have the German title page.*
          H. 1878. f.

— Lieder ... Revidiert von Eugen d'Albert. ⟨English words by
John Bernhoff.⟩ *Ger., Eng. & Fr. no. 6, 17, 18. C. F. Kahnt:
Leipzig,* [1908.] 4°.
Imperfect; wanting the other numbers.   **H. 1648. k. (6.)**

— 5 Selected Songs, with English text by Mrs. G. F. Byron.
J. Williams: London, (1910.) 4°.
No. 408 of J. Williams' Albums.   **G. 785. (408.)**

— Thirty Songs ... Edited by C. Armbruster. For high voice.
O. Ditson Co.: Boston, (1911.) 4°.
Part of "The Musicians Library".   **G. 461. c.**

— Twelve Songs. For voice and piano. With a critical note by
Richard Aldrich. The English translations by Dr. Theodore
Baker. For low voice ... high voice, *etc.* 2 vol. *G. Schirmer:
New York,* [1951.] 4°.
Schirmer's Library of musical Classics. vol. 1613, 1614.
    G. 1276. g. (20.)

— Thirty Songs. Edited by Carl Armbruster. For high voice.
[With a portrait.] *Eng. & Ger.* pp. xii. 144. *Dover Publications:
New York,* 1975. 4°.   **G. 461. h. (2.)**

COLLECTED WORKS.—e. Instrumental Selections and Arrangements

— Gems of Melody, No. 1. Fantasia. Extracts adapted from the
works of Liszt. Brass Band Score. *R. Smith & Co.: London,*
[1933.] obl. 8°.   **e. 503. b. (6.)**

— Liszt. Fantasie. [Excerpts arranged for orchestra.] By
Frederick G. Charrosin. Piano conductor [and orchestral
parts]. 23 pt. *Bosworth & Co.: London,* [1949.] 4°.
The part for B♭ tenor saxophone is in duplicate.
    h. 3210. i. (35.)

— The Christmas Tree. Suite for string orchestra (with
glockenspiel or celesta ad lib.). Arranged from the piano
works of Liszt by Anthony Collins. 1. Lighting the Candles.
2. In olden Times. 3. Games. 4. Bedtime. (Dreaming.) Full
score, *etc.* pp. 21. *Francis, Day & Hunter: London,* [1952.] 4°.
[*Francis, Day and Hunter's Series of Works of string Orchestra
& small Orchestra.* 5.] *No. 1–3 are transcriptions of
"Weihnachtsbaum," no. 5, 10, 6; no. 4 of "En rêve".*
    g. 1396. a.

— Grand duo concertant (R.-V. 462). ⟨Based on the romance
"Le Marin" by Philippe Lafont.⟩ Epithalam (R.-V. 466).
(Hochzeitsmusik. Wedding music) ... Für Klavier und
Violine ... Herausgegeben von ... Zoltán Gárdonyi. [Score
and part.] 2 pt. *Bärenreiter: Kassel, etc.,* [1971.] 4°.
Part of "The 19th Century".   **g. 547. x. (2.)**

COLLECTED WORKS.—f. Composite Works

— [Song without End.] Music from the Film Song without End.
Arranged by Harry Sukman, *etc.* (P. F.) pp. 28. *Robbins
Music Corporation: London,* [1960.] 4°.   **f. 470. a. (13.)**

— A la Chapelle Sixtine. Miserere d'Allegri et Ave verum
corpus de Mozart pour piano. ⟨A deux mains.⟩ pp. 19.
C. F. Peters: Leipzig, Berlin, [1865.] fol. **h. 896. cc. (2.)**

— A la Chapelle Sixtine. Miserere d'Allegri et Ave verum
corpus de Mozart pour piano ⟨à 2 mains⟩ par François Liszt.
pp. 19. *C. F. Peters: Leipzig & Berlin,* [1875?] 4°.
    g. 547. g. (17.)

LISZT (Franz)

— [A la Chapelle Sixtine.] Ave Verum von W. A. Mozart, für
Orgel oder harmonium gesetzt von F. Liszt. *See* ALBUM.
Album für Orgel-Spieler, *etc.* Lief. 82 [a]. [1880? *etc.*] obl. fol.
    e. 119.

— Ab-irato. *See infra:* [Morceau de salon.]

— Ad nos, ad salutarem undam. *See infra:* [Fantasie und Fuge.]

— Adagio. [Organ.] *See infra:* [Consolations. No. 4.]

— Les Adieux, rêverie sur un motif de l'opéra de C. Gounod
Roméo et Juliette. [P. F.] *Berlin & Posen,* [1868.] fol.
    h. 585. b. (5.)

— Agnus Dei della Missa da Requiem di G. Verdi. Trascrizione
per Organo ossia Harmonium o Pianoforte. *Milano,* [1879.]
fol.   **h. 3213. n. (13.)**

— Agnus Deï de la Messe de Requiem de G. Verdi.
Transcription pour Orgue ou Harmonium ou Piano, *etc.
Milan,* [1883.] fol.   **h. 2732. f. (24.)**

— Aida di G. Verdi ... Trascrizione per Pianoforte. *Milano,*
[1879.] fol.   **h. 1489. a. (28.)**

— Trois airs suisses. *See infra:* [Album d'un voyageur.
No. 10–12.]

Album d'un voyageur

— [Album d'un voyageur. Compositions pour le piano, *etc.*]
[No. 1–12.] pp. 200. [*Tobias Haslinger: Wien,* 1842.] fol.
Imperfect; wanting the titlepage.   **h. 896. o.**

— [No. 1–7.] 1ʳᵉ année de pélerinage. Suisse. Compositions pour
piano, *etc. Chez S. Richault: Paris,* [c. 1840.] fol.
    h. 896. dd.

— Album d'un voyageur. [No. 7–9.] 2ᵉ année. Compositions
pour le piano ... Suisse. ⟨Fleurs mélodiques des Alpes.⟩
pp. 1–13. 2–19. 2–15. *Chez Bernard Latte: Paris,* [c. 1840.] fol.
    h. 896. q. (6.)

— [Album d'un voyageur. 1ʳᵉ année. Suisse.] [No. 7–9.] pp. 1–13.
2–21. 2–15. [*L. Lavenu: London,* 1840.] fol.
The titlepage is in MS.   **h. 583. (8.)**

— [No. 10–12.] Trois airs suisses pour le piano ... Op. 10, *etc.*
3 no. *Chez Bernard Latte: Paris,* [1836?] fol.
*The fly-leaf bears a MS. dedication in the autograph of
Bernard Latte.*   **h. 896. bb.**

— [No. 10–12.] Trois airs suisses pour le piano. ⟨Schweizerische
Alpenklänge ... L'Echo des alpes suisses.⟩ No. 1. Improvisata
sur le ranz des vaches: "Depart pour les alpes" ... de Ferd.
Huber. No. 2. Nocturne sur le "Chant montagnard" ...
d'Ernest Knop. No. 3. Rondeau sur le "Ranz de chèvres" ...
de Ferd. Huber. Op. 10. 3 no. *Chez Erneste Knop: Basle,*
[1836.] fol.   **Hirsch M. 952. (1.)**

— [No. 10–12.] Trois airs suisses, pour le piano forte ... N° 1.
Improvvisata sur les Ranz des vaches. N° 2. Un soir dans les
montagnes. Nocturne pastoral. N° 3. Allegro finale sur un
Ranz des chèvres. Op. 10. no. 1, 2. *R. Mills: London,* [1838.]
fol.
Imperfect; wanting no. 3.   **h. 585. m. (9.)**

— [No. 10–12.] Trois morceaux suisses. 1. Ranz de vaches ... 2.
Un soir dans la montagne ... 3. Ranz de chèvres ... Pour
piano. 3 no. *Chez C. F. Kahnt: Leipzig,* [1877.] fol.
    h. 896. aa. (6.)

— [No. 7.—Mélodie 3.] La Fête villageoise pour piano. pp. 5.
Heugel & cⁱᵉ.: Paris, [1840.] fol. **g. 547. cc. (10.)**

— Album d'un voyageur. Mélodies hongroises. *See infra:*
[Magyar dallok. No. 1–7.]

LISZT (Franz)

— Albumblatt, für Pianoforte. [1841.] *See* Periodical Publications.— *Leipzig.* [Neue Zeitschrift für Musik.] [Sammlung von Musik-Stücken, *etc.*] Hft. 15. [1838, *etc.*] fol.
Hirsch M. 1134.

2 allegri di bravura. Op. 4

— Deux allegri di bravura pour le piano-forte ... Œuvre 4. ⟨N° 2. Rondo di bravura.⟩ *Chez Mlles Erard: Paris,* [1825.] fol. *The titlepage bears a MS. dedication to Mademoiselle S. Müller in the composer's autograph. Imperfect; wanting no.* 1.
K. 5. c. 27. (2.)

— Deux allegri di bravura pour le pianoforte ... Œuvre 4. 2 livr. *Chez Thadé Weigl: Vienne,* [1826.] fol.
h. 585. m. (5.)

— [No. 1.] Allegro di bravura pour le piano-forte ... Œuvre 4. pp. 15. *Chez H. A. Probst: Leipzig,* [1825.] fol.
f. 65. l. (10.)

— [No. 1.] Allegro di bravura, pour le piano-forte ... Œuvre 4. pp. 15. *Chez Fr. Kistner: Leipzig,* [c. 1840.] *obl.* fol.
Hirsch M. 222.

— [No. 1.] Allegro di bravura pour le piano, arrangé pour le pianoforte à quatre mains par F. L. Schubert ... Oeuv. 4. pp. 15. *Chez Fr. Kistner: Leipsic,* [1842.] *obl.* fol.
f. 134. h. (3.)

— Der Alpenjäger. [Words by Schiller.] *See* supra: [*Collected Works.— d.*] F. Liszt's gesammelte Lieder, *etc.* No. 9.

— Die alten Sagen Kunden. *See* infra: Für Männergesang. No. 8.

— Am Rhein im schönen Strome. *See* infra: [Buch der Lieder. Bd. 1. No. 2.]

— Am stillen Herd, Lied aus R. Wagner's Meistersinger. Transcription für Pianoforte. *Berlin,* [1872.] fol.
h. 585. b. (7.)

— An den heiligen Franziskus (von Paula). Gebet für Männer-Stimmen ... mit Begleitung des Harmonium (oder Orgel), drei Posaunen und Pauken (ad libitum). Partitur und Stimmen. *Budapest,* [1875.] 8°.
E. 1644. a. (3.)

— An die Künstler. Gedicht von Schiller componirt für Männergesang (Soli und Chor) und Orchester ... Partitur und Clavierauszug. pp. 40. *Weimar,* 1854. fol.
Hirsch iv. 830.

— An die Künstler. Gedicht von Schiller componirt für Männergesang, Soli und Chor, und Orchester ... Partitur und Clavierauszug. pp. 41. *T. F. A. Kühn: Weimar,* [1856.] fol.
H. 1878. h. (4.)

— An die Künstler. Gedicht von Schiller componirt für Männergesang—Soli und Chor—und Orchester ... Partitur und Clavierauszug. *C. F. Kahnt: Leipzig,* [1865?] 4°.
G. 461. b. (5.)

— An Edlitam von Bodenstedt. *See* supra: [*Collected Works.— d.*] F.Liszt's gesammelte Lieder, *etc.* No. 50.

— Andante amoroso. *See* infra: [L'Idée fixe.]

— Andante final de Lucie de Lamermoor [*sic*], 2e acte. *See* infra: [Réminiscences de Lucia di Lammermoor.]

— Andante Finale und Marsch aus der Oper: "König Alfred" von Joachim Raff, für das Pianoforte übertragen. 2 no. *Verlag der Heinrichshofen'schen Musikalien-Handlung: Magdeburg,* [1853.] fol.
g. 547. o. (11.)

— Dem Andenken Petöfi's. Melodie ... für Pianoforte (zweihändig). pp. 5. *Táborszky & Parsch: Budapest,* [1877.] fol. *Later published as no. 6 of "Magyar történelmi arcképek," entered below.*
h. 585. b. (23.)

LISZT (Franz)

— Anfangs wollt' ich fast verzagen, von Heine. *See* supra: [*Collected Works.— d.*] F. Liszt's gesammelte Lieder, *etc.* No. 14.

— An Angel spake unto the Shepherds. *See* infra: [Christus.— Pastorale.]

— Angelus. Prière aux anges gardiens. *See* infra: [*Années de pèlerinage. Troisième année. No.* 1.]

Années de pèlerinage

— Années de pèlerinage. Suite de compositions. [P. F.] Première année. Suisse. ⟨Deuxième année. Italie.⟩ année 1. no. 1–3, 5–9. année 2. no. 1–7. *Chez les fils de B. Schott: Mayence,* [1855, 58.] fol. *Imperfect; wanting année* 1. *no.* 4.
Hirsch M. 942.

— [Suite de compositions.] [*Chez les fils de B. Schott: Mayence,* 1855.] fol. *Imperfect; année* 1. *no.* 4 *only, wanting the wrapper.*
g. 547. q. (4.)

— Années de Pèlerinage. Compositions pour piano. Première (—Troisième) Année. 3 pt. *B. Schott's Söhne: Mayence,* [1885?] fol.
h. 895. a.

— Années de Pèlerinage. Suite pour Piano. Edited and fingered by R. Joseffy. 1re Année. Suisse ... 2me Année. Italie ... Supplément à l'Italie, *etc. G. Schirmer: New York,* (1909, *etc.*) fol.
h. 896. e. (1.)

— Années de Pèlerinage pour Piano. Nouvelle édition revue par K. Klindworth. Première (Deuxième) Année, *etc.* 4 no. *B. Schott's Söhne: Mainz, Leipzig,* (1912.) fol. *Wanting all except no.* 1 *and* 2 *of each Année.*
h. 896. g. (4.)

— [Another copy of "Deuxième Année," no. 1, 2.]
Hirsch M. 948. (3.)

— Années de Pèlerinage. 1re année, "Suisse". ⟨2me année, "Italie".⟩ Suite for the piano. Edited and revised by Rafael Joseffy. 2 bk. *G. Schirmer: New York; Chappell & Co.: London;* [*London* printed, 1950, 51.] 4°. *Schirmer's Library of musical Classics. vol.* 910, 911.
g. 547. h. (2.)

— [Année 1–3.] Годы странствий. Для пьяно. ⟨Редакция и комментарии Я. И. Мильштейна.⟩ [With a portrait and facsimiles.] pp. 319. *Музгиз:* [*Moscow,*] 1959. fol.
h. 896. t.

Années de pèlerinage. Première année. Suisse

— Années de pèlerinage. Première année. Suisse. Nach der Erstausgabe herausgegeben von Ernst Herttrich. Fingersatz von Hans-Martin Theopold. pp. 91. *G. Henle Verlag: München, Duisburg,* [1972.] 4°.
g. 547. bb. (1.)

— Années de pèlerinage. Première année—Suisse. Herausgegeben von Imre Sulyok, Imre Mező. Fingersatz revidiert von Kornél Zempléni, *etc.* [P. F. With facsimiles.] pp. xiv. 129. *Bärenreiter: Kassel, etc.; Editio Musica: Budapest; printed in Hungary,* 1976. 4°.
g. 547. x. (6.)

— Années de pèlerinage. Première année. Suisse. Nach der Eigenschrift und der Originalausgabe herausgegeben von Ernst Herttrich. Fingersatz von Hans-Martin Theopold. Neuausgabe. [P. F.] pp. viii. 85. *G. Henle Verlag: München,* [1978.] fol.
g. 547. ff. (1.)

— [No. 3, 8, 7.] Pastorale, Le mal du pays et Eglogue. (For Flute, Oboe, Clarinet, Horn and Bassoon.) [Parts.] *See* Quintets. Quintets for Wind Instruments, *etc.* [No. 4.] 1937. 4°.
g. 417. z. (1.)

— [No. 2.] Au Lac de Wallenstadt ... Edited and fingered by T. F. Dunhill. (Piano.) *Augener: London,* 1917. fol.
h. 896. g. (9.)

LISZT (FRANZ)

— [No. 2.] Barcarolle. (Au lac de Wallenstadt.) Arranged for two pianos by Colin Taylor. pp. 11. *Augener: London*, [1949.] 4°. *Two copies.* **g. 547. g. (6.)**

— [No. 4.] Au bord d'une source . . . Revised . . . by O. Thümer. (Piano.) *Augener: London*, [1917.] fol. **h. 896. g. (10.)**

— [No. 4.] Au bord d'une source. *See* ZILOTI (A. I.) Alexander Siloti Concert Repertoire. Piano transcriptions, *etc.* [No. 7.] 1923. 4°. **g. 1267.**

— [No. 8.] Le Mal du Pays, arrangé pour piano et harmonium par A. Sokol. *B. Schott's Söhne: Mayence*, [1887.] fol. **h. 585. g. (8.)**

Années de pèlerinage. Deuxième année. Italie

— Années de pèlerinage. Deuxième année. Italie. Nach Autographen, Abschriften und der Originalausgabe herausgegeben von Ernst Herttrich. Fingersatz von Hans-Martin Theopold. [P. F.] pp. viii. 55. *G. Henle Verlag: München*, [1978.] fol. **g. 547. ff. (2.)**

— [No. 4, 5, 6.] Sonetto di Petrarca, No. 47 (104) (123). [P. F.] 3 no. 1910. *See* HAWLEY (S.) Hawley Edition. No. 5–7. 1909, *etc.* fol. **h. 3527. b.**

— [No. 1.] Sposalizio . . . Revised . . . by O. Thümer. (Piano.) *Augener: London*, [1917.] fol. **h. 896. g. (11.)**

— [No. 1.] Sposalizio . . . Revised by A. Siloti. [P. F.] *C. Fischer: New York, etc.*, 1924. 4°. *[Alexander Siloti Concert Repertoire. No. 13.]* **g. 1267.**

— [No. 1.] Sposalizio. Transcribed for the Organ, *etc.* 1899. *See* LEMARE (E. H.) Transcriptions for the Organ. No. 7. 1899, *etc.* fol. **h. 2710.**

— [No. 2.] Il Penseroso. *See* ZILOTI (A. I.) Alexander Siloti Concert Repertoire. Piano transcriptions, *etc.* [No. 6.] 1923. 4°. **g. 1267.**

— [No. 3.] Canzonetta del Salvator Rosa . . . Edited . . . by T. F. Dunhill. (Piano.) *Augener: London*, 1917. fol. **h. 896. g. (12.)**

— [No. 3.] Canzonetta del Salvator Rosa. [Organ.] *See* WESTBROOK (W. J.) Transcriptions, *etc.* No. 13. [1870–85.] fol. **h. 2750. a. (4.)**

— [No. 3.] Canzonetta. By S. Rosa and F. Liszt, *etc. See* ROSA (S.) Vado ben spesso, *etc.* 1939. 4°. **G. 1275. vv. (36.)**

— [No. 6.] Sonetto 123 del Petrarca . . . Edited . . . by T. F. Dunhill. (Piano.) *Augener: London*, 1917. fol. **h. 896. g. (13.)**

Années de pèlerinage. Deuxième année. Italie. Supplément

— Venezia e Napoli. Gondoliera, Canzone e Tarantella pour piano. Supplément aux Années de Pelerinage . . . 2ᵈᵉ Volume, Italie. *Schott & Co.: Londres*, [c. 1880.] fol. **h. 896. a. (15.)**

— Venezia e Napoli . . . Nouvelle édition revue par K. Klindworth. [P. F.] 3 no. *B. Schott's Söhne: Mainz, Leipzig*, (1912.) fol. **h. 896. g. (5.)**

— Venezia e Napoli. (Revised, phrased and fingered by O. Thümer.) [P. F.] *Augener: London*, [1919.] 4°. **g. 547. e. (2.)**

— Années de pèlerinage. "Venezia e Napoli." Supplement to "Italie". For the piano. Edited and revised by Rafael Joseffy. pp. 31. *G. Schirmer: New York; Chappell & Co.: London*; [*London* printed, 1951.] 4°. *Schirmer's Library of musical Classics. vol. 917.* **g. 547. i. (2.)**

— [No. 1.] Gondoliera . . . Revised, phrased and fingered by O. Thümer. [P. F.] *Augener: London*, [1910.] 4°. **g. 547. d. (2.)**

LISZT (FRANZ)

— [No. 3.] Tarantelle . . . für Orchester bearbeitet von Karl Müller-Berghaus. Partitur. *Mainz*, [1883.] fol. **h. 896. b. (2.)**

— [No. 3.] Venezia e Napoli. No. 3. Tarantella . . . Edited . . . by T. F. Dunhill. (Piano.) *Augener: London*, 1917. fol. **h. 896. g. (17.)**

Années de pèlerinage. Troisième année

— Années de Pélerinagé [*sic*]. Compositions pour Piano. Troisième Année. *Mayence*, [1883.] fol. **h. 585. f. (10.)**

— Années de pèlerinage. Compositions pour piano . . . Troisième année. no. 1. *Schott & Co.: London; B. Schott's Söhne: Mayence*, [1885.] fol. *Imperfect; wanting no. 2–7.* **Hirsch M. 948. (2.)**

— Années de pèlerinage. Troisième année. Nach Autographen, Abschriften und der Originalausgabe herausgegeben von Ernst Herttrich. Fingersatz von Hans-Martin Theopold. pp. viii. 49. *G. Henle Verlag: München*, [1980.] fol. **h. 585. r. (1.)**

— [No. 1.] Angelus. Prière aux anges gardiens pour quatuor d'instruments à cordes. Edition pour piano. *Mayence*, [1883.] fol. **h. 585. f. (14.)**

— [No. 1.] Angelus. Prière aux anges gardiens, pour quatuor ou quintuor d'instruments à cordes . . . Édition pour quintuor (partie de contrebasse ajoutée). Partition, *etc.* [Edited by Walter Bache.] pp. 11. *B. Schott's Söhne: Mayence*, [1887.] 8°. **e. 58. h. (3.)**

— [No. 1.] Angelus. Prière aux anges gardiens pour quatuor ou quintuor d'instruments à cordes . . . Édition pour quatuor. Partition, *etc.* pp. 9. *B. Schott's Söhne: Mainz, Leipzig*, [c. 1890.] 8°. **f. 470. b. (1.)**

— [No. 4.] Les Jeux d'eaux à la Villa d'Este . . . Revised by A. Siloti. [P. F.] *C. Fischer: New York*, 1924. 4°. *[Alexander Siloti Concert Repertoire. No. 12.]* **g. 1267.**

— [No. 7.] Sursum corda. Lift up your Hearts . . . Revised by A. Siloti. [P. F.] *C. Fischer: New York, etc.*, 1924. 4°. *[Alexander Siloti Concert Repertoire. No. 14.]* **g. 1267.**

— Apparitions pour piano seul. 2 pt. *Chez Frédéric Hofmeister: Leipzig*, [1835.] fol. **Hirsch M. 950. (1.)**

— [Apparitions. No. 1, 2.] First and Second Apparitions in E♯ [or rather, C♯] major & A minor. pp. 11. *Ashdown & Parry: London*, [1865?] fol. *Le Pianiste moderne. no. 6.* **h. 896. h. (14.)**

— Apparitions. 2 Liv. *F. Hofmeister: Leipzig*, [1880?] fol. **h. 896. d. (2.)**

— Deux arabesques. *See infra:* [Deux mélodies russes.]

— [Arbeiter-Chor.] A Munka himnusza . . . Férfikarra, basszuszszólóra és zenekarra Weiner Leó hangszerelésében. Für Männerchor, Bass-Solo und Orchester instrumentiert von Leo Weiner . . . Zongorakivonat. Klavierauszug. Férfikarra és basszusszólóra. (Eredeti letét.) Für Männerchor und Bass-Solo. (Original), *etc. Hung. & Ger.* pp. 30. *Zeneműkiadó Vállalat: Budapest*, 1954. 4°. **H. 1403. b. (4.)**

— [Arbeiter-Chor.] A Munka himnusza . . . Férfikarra, basszuszszólóra és zenekarra Weiner Leó hangszerelésében. Für Männerchor, Bass-Solo und Orchester instrumentiert von Leo Weiner . . . Zongorakivonat . . . Vegyeskarra Bárdos Lajos átirata. Für gemischten Chor, Bearbeitung: Lajos Bárdos, *etc. Hung. & Ger.* pp. 30. *Zeneműkiadó Vállalat: Budapest*, 1954. 4°. **H. 1403. b. (3.)**

— Der Asra. Lied von A. Rubinstein. Transcription für Pianoforte. *Leipzig*, [1884.] fol. **g. 271. h. (24.)**

LISZT (FRANZ)

— Au bord d'une source. *See* supra: [Années de pèlerinage. Première année. Suisse. No. 4.]

— Au Lac de Wallenstadt. *See* supra: [Années de pèlerinage. Première année. Suisse. No. 2.]

— Aus der Musik von Eduard Lassen zu Hebbel's Nibelungen und Goethe's Faust. Pianofortestücke zum Concertvortrag. Nibelungen. 1. Hagen und Kriemhild. 2. Bechlarn ... Faust. 3. Osterhymne ... 4. 5. Hoffest: Marsch und Polonaise. 3 no. *Julius Hainauer: Breslau*, [1879.] fol.   **h. 585. e. (6.)**

— Aus R. Wagner's Der Ring des Nibelungen. Walhall. Transcription für Pianoforte. pp. 10. *Bei B. Schott's Söhnen: Mainz*, [1876.] fol.   **h. 585. b. (15.)**

— [A reissue.] Aus R. Wagner's Der Ring des Nibelungen, *etc. Mainz*, [c. 1890.] fol.   **h. 896. a. (18.)**

— Ave Maria. [Raabe No. 67.] Für die grosse Clavierschule von Lebert u. Stark. pp. 5. *J. G. Cotta'sche Buchhandl.: Stuttgart*, [c. 1870.] fol.
A label bearing the imprint of T. Trautwein, Berlin, has been pasted over the original imprint.   **g. 547. p. (1.)**

— [Ave Maria. Raabe No. 67.] In Rome. (Tone picture.) ... Orchestrated by Anthony Collins. [P. F. conductor and parts.] 21 pt. *Bosworth & Co.: London*, [1957.] 4°.   **h. 3210. o. (352.)**

— Ave Maria. *See* infra: [Kirchen-Chor-Gesänge. No. 2.]

— Ave Maria. *See* infra: [Pater noster. Ave Maria.]

— Ave maris stella. *See* infra: [Neun Kirchen-Chor-Gesänge. No. 7.]

— Ave verum. *See* infra: [Zwölf Kirchen-Chor-Gesänge. No. 5.]

— [Bagatelle ohne Tonart.] Hangnemnélküli bagatell ... Auf Grund der originalen Handschrift ... zusammengestellt und redigiert von ... Szélényi István. [P. F.] pp. 12. *Zeneműkiadó Vállalat: Budapest*, 1956. 4°.   **f. 470. f. (1.)**

— La Bal de Berne. *See* infra: [Grande valse di bravura.]

— Two Ballades. [P. F.] I. D flat major ... II. B minor ... [Edited by] Emil von Sauer. pp. 33. *Edition Peters: London, etc.*, [1970?] 4°.   **g. 547. z. (1.)**

— Ballade [no. 1.] für Pianoforte. pp. 11. *Bei Fr. Kistner: Leipzig*, [1849.] fol.   **Hirsch M. 950. (2.)**

— [Ballade. No. 1.] Le Chant du croisé. Ballade pour piano. pp. 11. *J. Meissonnier fils: Paris*, [1849.] fol.   **h. 585. l. (7.)**

— 2ᵐᵉ Ballade pour piano. *F. Kistner: Leipzig*, [1854.] fol.   **h. 896. d. (3.)**

— [Another copy.]   **Hirsch M. 950. (3.)**

— [Ballade. No. 2.] Der ursprüngliche, bisher unveröffentlichte Schluss der zweiten Ballade (h moll) für Pianoforte. pp. 6. *In:* Die Musik. Jahrg. 5. Hft. 13. Musikbeilage. [1906.] 4°.   **P. P. 1946. ah.**

— Barcarolle. *See* supra: [Années de pèlerinage. Première année. No. 2.]

— A Beautiful Flower. *See* infra: [Du bist wie eine Blume.]

— Beethoven-Cantate. *See* infra: Zur Säcular-Feier Beethovens.

— Bénédiction de Dieu dans la Solitude. *See* infra: [Harmonies poétiques et religieuses. No. 3.]

— Benedictus. *See* infra: [Koronázási Mise.]

— Benedictus. *See* infra: [Missa choralis.]

LISZT (FRANZ)

— Berceuse. ⟨Wiegenlied.⟩ [P. F.] *In:* HASLINGER (C.) Elisabeth-Fest-Album für Pianoforte-Spieler, *etc.* pp. 21–25. 1854. fol.   **h. 1203. ee. (7.)**

— Berceuse für das Pianoforte. pp. 13. *Gustav Heinze: Leipzig*, [1865.] fol.   **Hirsch M. 950. (4.)**

— Bijou de Preciosa. *See* infra: [Einsam bin ich, nicht allein.]

— Bildern aus Ungarn. *See* supra: [Collected Works.—b.]

— Bist du! von E. Metschersky. *See* supra: [Collected Works.—d.] F. Liszt's gesammelte Lieder, *etc.* No. 47.

— Der blinde Sänger. *See* infra: Слѣпой.

— Blume und Duft, von Hebbel. *See* supra: [Collected Works.—d.] F. Liszt's gesammelte Lieder, *etc.* No. 38.

— Two Browning Choruses. *See* infra: [4 kleine Klavierstücke. No. 3, 4.]

— Buch der Lieder. Gedichte von Goethe, Heine, Victor Hugo etc. mit Begleitung des Pianoforte. Bd. 2. *In der Schlesinger'chen Buch- und Musikhandlung: Berlin*, [1844.] fol.
Imperfect; wanting Bd. 1. The wrapper bears the title "Poésies lyriques". Bd. 2 has French and German words.   **H. 1878. l. (1.)**

— Buch der Lieder. Gedichte von Goethe, Heine, Victor Hugo etc. mit Begleitung des Pianoforte. Bd. 1, no. 3–5. *In der Schlesinger'chen Buch- und Musikhandlung: Berlin*, [c. 1860.] fol.
Imperfect; wanting Bd. 1, no. 1, 2, 6 and Bd. 2.   **H. 2827. a. (18.)**

— Buch der Lieder für Piano allein. Poésies pour piano seul. 1. Loreley. 2. Au Rhin. 3. Mignon. 4. Le Roi de Thule. 5. Invocation. 6. Angiolin. 6 no. *Chez Aᵈ Mᵗ Schlesinger: Berlin*, [1844.] fol.   **Hirsch M. 951. (9.)**

Buch der Lieder. Bd. 1. No. 1. Die Loreley

— Die Lorelei. (Poésie de H. Heine. Paroles françaises de G. Lagye.) *See also* supra: [Collected Works.—d.] F. Liszt's gesammelte Lieder, *etc.* No. 10.

— Die Lore Ley, für Mezzo-Sopran ... Neue umgearbeitete Ausgabe. pp. 9. *Aᵈ Mᵗ Schlesinger: Berlin*, [1856.] fol.   **G. 461. i. (1.)**

— The Loreley, *etc.* 1899. *See* ENGLAND (P.) Classical Songs, *etc.* No. 28. 1899, *etc.* 4°.   **G. 1003.**

— The Loreley. [Song.] English words by Ed. Teschemacher. *Murdoch, Murdoch & Co.: London*, [1935?] 4°.
Part of "The Mayfair Classics".   **G. 1270. uu. (22.)**

— Loreley ... [Song.] (Mezzo Sopran oder Tenor.) English words by Edward Oxenford. *Eng. & Ger.* pp. 9. *Augener: London*, [1937?] 4°.   **G. 809. q. (11.)**

— The Loreley. (Die Loreley.) [Song.] English words by Ed. Teschemacher. *Eng. & Ger.* pp. 11. *Chappell & Co.: London*, [1947.] 4°.
Part of "The New Mayfair Vocal Classics".   **F. 607. xx. (30.)**

— Die Loreley. ⟨Heine. Für eine Singstimme, mit Begleitung des Orchesters. Partitur.⟩ pp. 35. *C. F. Kahnt: Leipzig*, [c. 1875.] 8°.
The titlepage reads "Mignon. Göthe. Die Loreley, Heine. Die drei Zigeuner. Lenau".   **E. 1644. g.**

— Die Loreley, für das Pianoforte. pp. 11. *Bei C. F. Kahnt: Leipzig*, [1862.] fol.   **g. 547. t. (2.)**

— Die Loreley. Für das Pianoforte. ⟨Neue Ausgabe.⟩ pp. 11. *Bei C. F. Kahnt: Leipzig*, [1877.] fol.   **h. 585. j. (9.)**

LISZT (Franz)

Buch der Lieder. Bd. 1. Other numbers

— [No. 2.] Am Rhein im schönen Strome. (Poésie de H. Heine. Paroles françaises de G. Lagye.) *See* also supra: [*Collected Works.—d.*] F. Liszt's gesammelte Lieder, *etc.* No. 11.

— [No. 2.] Poésie N° 2. Am Rhein. Au Rhin. [P. F.] pp. 8. *A^d Mt Schlesinger: Berlin,* [1844.] fol. **g. 547. u. (9.)**

— [No. 3.] Kennst du das Land. Mignon's Lied (La Chanson de Mignon. Poésie de Goethe. Paroles française de G. Lagye). *See* also supra: [*Collected Works.—d.*] F. Liszt's gesammelte Lieder, *etc.* No. 1.

— [No. 3.] Mignon. [Song.] English words by E. Oxenford. *Eng. & Ger.* pp. 9. *Augener: London,* [1928?] 4°. **G. 809. q. (10.)**

— [No. 3.] Mignon. Goethe. ⟨Für eine Singstimme, mit Begleitung des Orchesters. Partitur.⟩ pp. 39. *C. F. Kahnt: Leipzig,* [c. 1880.] 8°.
The titlepage reads "Mignon, Göthe. Die Loreley, Heine. Die drei Zigeuner, Lenau". **E. 1644. k.**

— [No. 3.] Mignon's Song. For Three-part Chorus of Women's Voices, and optional Second Alto ... Translation by Dr. T. Baker ... Arranged by V. Harris. *G. Schirmer: New York,* 1937. 8°. **F. 217. h. (13.)**

— [No. 4.] Es war ein König in Thule. (Paroles françaises de G. Lagye. Poésie de Goethe.) *See* also supra: [*Collected Works.—d.*] F. Liszt's gesammelte Lieder ... No. 2.

— [No. 4.] Der König von Thule. Für Mezzo-Sopran oder Tenor-Baryton. pp. 9. *A^d Mt Schlesinger: Berlin,* [1843?] fol. **H. 1878. h. (6.)**

— [No. 5.] Der Du von dem Himmel bist. (Poésie de Goethe. Paroles françaises de G. Lagye.) *See* also supra: [*Collected Works.—d.*] F. Liszt's gesammelte Lieder, *etc.* No. 3.

— [No. 5. Der Du von dem Himmel bist.] Thou who from Thy Realms, *etc.* [P. F.] *See* PAUER (E.) Vocal Works by Great Masters, *etc.* [No. 5.] [1887–97.] fol. **h. 3649. (2.)**

— [No. 6.] Angiolin dal biondo crin. Marchese Cesare Bocella. Deutsche Uebersetzung von P. Cornelius. *See* supra: [*Collected Works.—d.*] F. Liszt's gesammelte Lieder, *etc.* No. 26.

Buch der Lieder. Bd. 2. No. 1. Oh! quand je dors

— Oh! quand je dors. V. Hugo, traduit par P. Cornelius. *See* also supra: [*Collected Works.—d.*] F. Liszt's gesammelte Lieder, *etc.* No. 18.

— When dreamy Sleep ... Song with Pianoforte accompaniment ... English version by C. Aveling. *Augener: London,* [1906.] fol. **G. 807. kk. (10.)**

— When dreamy Sleep ... [Song.] English version by Claude Aveling. *Eng. & Fr.* pp. 7. *Augener: London,* [1928?] 4°. **G. 809. q. (12.)**

— Oh, quand je dors. Poésie de Victor Hugo. O komm im Traum. Deutsche Worte von P. Cornelius. O come to me in Dreams. English words by John Bernhoff ... Rev. v. Eugen d'Albert. Instr. v. Felix Mottl. [Score.] *Fr., Ger. & Eng.* pp. 28. *C. F. Kahnt Nachfolger: Leipzig,* [1908.] 8°. **E. 1500. c. (10.)**

— Oh, quand je dors. O komm in Traum ... Arranged (for violin with pianoforte accompaniment) by F. Drdla. Op. 162. *Hawkes & Son: London, etc.,* 1923. fol. **h. 896. h. (8.)**

Buch der Lieder. Bd. 2. Other numbers

— [No. 2.] Comment, disaient-ils. V. Hugo. *See* supra: [*Collected Works.—d.*] F. Liszt's gesammelte Lieder, *etc.* No. 17.

— [No. 3.] Enfant, si j'étais roi. V. Hugo, traduit par P. Cornelius. *See* supra: [*Collected Works.—d.*] F. Liszt's gesammelte Lieder, *etc.* No. 20.

LISZT (Franz)

— [No. 4.] S'il est un charmant gazon. V. Hugo, traduit par P. Cornélius. *See* supra: [*Collected Works.—d.*] F. Liszt's gesammelte Lieder, *etc.* No. 19.

— Bülow-Marsch für ... Piano 2 händig und für Piano 4 händig. 2 no. *Berlin,* [1884.] fol. **h. 585. g. (3.)**

— But I have trusted in thy Mercy. *See* infra: [Der 13. Psalm.—Ich aber hoffe.]

— By the Waters of Babylon. *See* infra: [Psalm 137.]

— C. M. Weber's Schlummerlied. Mit Araresken [*sic*] für das Pianoforte übertragen ... von F. Liszt. pp. 11. *Fr. Kistner: Leipzig,* [1849?] fol.
Transcriptionen für das Pianoforte von F. Liszt. no. 2. **h. 896. i. (16.)**

— [C. M. von Weber's Schlummerlied mit Arabesken.] Chanson au berceau de Ch. M. de Weber. Transcrite pour piano seul par Fr. Liszt. pp. 10. *S. Richault: Paris,* [1849?] fol.
Mélodies favorites. no. 2. **h. 585. m. (11.)**

— La Campanella. *See* infra: [Grandes Études de Paganini. No. 3.]

— Cantantibus organis. Antifona per la festa di Sta Cecilia per voce di contralto e coro con accompagnamento d'orchestra. [Score, including P. F. reduction.] pp. 20. *Autografia di P. Manganelli: Roma,* [1880.] fol. **H. 1860. kk. (2.)**

— Cantantibus organis. Antiphona in Festo St. Caeciliae. Chorgesang ... und Alt-Solo mit Begleitung des Orchesters oder des Pianoforte ... Klavierauszug. *C. F. Kahnt: Leipzig,* [1881.] 4°. **G. 461. b. (3.)**

— Cantico del sol di San Francesco d'Assisi, composto per voce di barytono (solo), coro d'homini, organo ed orchestre [*sic*] ... Der Sonnen Hymnus ... [The German translation by P. Cornelius.] Partitur, *etc.* Ital. & Ger. pp. 51. *C. F. Kahnt: Leipzig,* [1883.] fol.
The fly-leaf bears a MS. dedication in the composer's autograph. With a programme inserted. **H. 1878. k.**

— Cantico del Sol di San Francesco d'Assisi composto per Voce di Barytono (Solo), Coro d'uomini, Organo ed Orchestra. Der Sonnen Hymnus, *etc.* Klavierauszug. *Leipzig,* [1885.] 8°. **E. 1644. b.**

— [Cantico del sol.] San Francesco. Preludio per il Cantico del sol per pianoforte. A cura di Pietro Spada. Prima edizione. pp. 11. *Boccaccini & Spada: Roma,* 1979. fol. **g. 547. ii. (1.)**

— Canzone napolitana pour piano. pp. 7. *Chez Maurice Schlesinger: Paris,* [1843.] fol. **g. 547. cc. (8.)**

— Canzone napolitana. Notturno pour piano, *etc.* ⟨Édition nouvelle. Arrangement élégant.⟩ pp. 10. *C. F. Meser: Dresde,* [1848.] 8°. **e. 58. k. (3.)**

— Canzonetta del Salvator Rosa. *See* supra: [Années de pèlerinage. Seconde année. No. 3.]

— Capriccio alla turca sur des motifs de Beethoven (Ruines d'Athènes) pour piano. pp. 23. *Chez Pietro Mechetti q^m Carlo: Vienne,* [1847.] fol. **h. 896. j. (3.)**

— 3 caprices-valses pour le piano. *See* infra: [Valses.]

— Ce qu'on entend sur la montagne. *See* infra: Symphonische Dichtungen. no. 1.

— Célèbre mélodie hongroise (en si♭). *See* infra: [Magyar dallok. No. 11.]

— Chanson au berceau de Ch. M. de Weber. *See* supra: [C. M. von Weber's Schlummerlied mit Arabesken.]

LISZT (FRANZ)

— Chanson Bohémienne. *See* infra: [Deux Mélodies russes. No. 2.]

— Chanson du Béarn. *See* infra: Faribolo Pastour, *etc.*

— Trois chansons. *See* infra: [Geharnischte Lieder.]

— Le Chant du croisé. *See* supra: [Ballade. No. 1.]

— 6 Chants polonais de Chopin, transcrits pour le Piano par F. Liszt. Revus par O. Thümer. *Augener & Co.: London,* [1903.] 4°. **g. 547. c. (3.)**

— [6 Chants polonais de Chopin. No. 1. Mädchens Wunsch.] The Maiden's Wish. F. Chopin—Liszt, *etc.* [P. F.] *See* PAULL MUSIC CO. Edition Paull, *etc.* [No. 23.] (1905.) fol. **h. 3822. (23.)**

— [6 Chants polonais de Chopin. No. 1. Mädchens Wunsch.] Chant polonais, Chopin, No. 1. (Edited by M. Esposito.) [P. F.] *C. E. Music Publishers Co.: Dublin,* [1920.] 4°. **g. 547. f. (24.)**

— La Chasse. *See* infra: [Grandes études de Paganini. No. 5.]

Chöre zu Herder's "Entfesseltem Prometheus"

— Chöre zu Herder's "Entfesseltem Prometheus" ... Verbindender Text von Richard Pohl. Partitur. pp. 186. *Bei C. F. Kahnt: Leipzig,* [1861.] 4°. **G. 461. e.**

— Chöre zu Herder's "Entfesseltem Prometheus" ... Partitur. pp. 173. *Bei C. F. Kahnt: Leipzig,* [c. 1885.] fol. **H. 1878. i.**

— Chöre zu Herder's "Entfesseltem Prometheus" ... Verbindender Text von Richard Pohl. Klavierauszug. pp. 71. *C. F. Kahnt Nachfolger: Leipzig,* [c. 1890.] 8°. **E. 1644. l.**

— [Another issue.] Chöre zu Herder's "Entfesseltem Prometheus" ... Verbindender Text von Richard Pohl. Klavierauszug. pp. 71. *C. F. Kahnt Nachfolger: Leipzig,* [c. 1890.] 8°. **E. 270. vv. (3.)**

— [Chor der Schnitter.] Chorus of Reapers, *etc.* [Vocal score.] pp. 15. *Stanley Lucas, Weber & Cº: London,* [1876.] 4°. **F. 321. a. (21.)**

— [Chor der Schnitter.] Pastorale. Schnitter-Chor ... Für das Pianoforte übertragen vom Componisten. Ausgabe für 2 Hände, *etc.* pp. 11. *Bei C. F. Kahnt: Leipzig,* [c. 1880.] fol. **g. 547. o. (2.)**

— [Chor der Schnitter.] Pastorale. Schnitter-Chor ... Für das Pianoforte übertragen vom Componisten ... Ausgabe für 4 Hände. pp. 17. *Bei C. F. Kahnt: Leipzig,* [c. 1890.] fol. **h. 896. q. (3.)**

— Chor der Engel aus Göthe's Faust. *See* infra: [Fest-Album zur Säcular-Feier von Goethe's Geburtstag.]

— Chorus of Reapers. *See* supra: [Chöre zu Herder's "Entfesseltem Prometheus".—Chor der Schnitter.]

— The Christmas Tree. Suite for string orchestra. *See* supra: [Collected Works.—e.]

— The Christmas Tree. 12 piano pieces. *See* infra: [Weihnachtsbaum.]

Christus

— Christus. Oratorium, nach Texten aus der heiligen Schrift und der katholischen Liturgie, für Soli, Chor, Orgel und grosses Orchester ... Partitur, *etc.* pp. 332. *J. Schuberth & Co.: Leipzig, New York,* [1872.] fol.
The list of contents is preceded by 3 pages, issued in 1874 with a special titlepage, containing abridgments sanctioned by the composer at the first performance in 1873. Both titlepages bear the autograph signature of A. W. Gottschalg. **Hirsch IV. 829.**

LISZT (FRANZ)

— Christus. Oratorium nach Texten aus der heiligen Schrift und der katholischen Liturgie, für Soli, Chor, Orgel und grosses Orchester ... Partitur, *etc.* pp. 332. *J. Schubert & Co.: Leipzig,* [1875.] fol. **H. 1878.**

— Christus. Oratorium szólóhangokra, kórusra, orgonára es nagyzenekarra ... Partitúra ... Közreadja ... Darvas Gábor. pp. 412. *Editio Musica: Budapest,* [1973.] 8°. **F. 566. f. (2.)**

— Christus. Oratorio for soli, chorus, organ and orchestra ... Edited by Gábor Darvas. Foreword by Klára Hamburger. [Score.] *Lat.* pp. 412. *Ernst Eulenburg, etc.: London, etc.,* [1976.] 8°. [*Edition Eulenburg. no. 948.*] **b. 212.**

— Christus. Oratorium nach Texten aus der heiligen Schrift und der katholischen Liturgie, für Soli, Chor, Orgel und grosses Orchester ... Clavierauszug. *Lat.* pp. viii. 276. *J. Schuberth & Cº: Leipzig, New-York,* [1872.] 8°. **E. 1644. n.**

— [Hirtengesang an der Krippe.] Shepherds' Song at the Manger. Arranged for organ by Philip James. pp. 12. *H. W. Gray Co.: New York,* [1948.] 4°. **g. 547. g. (9.)**

— O filii et filiæ. Easter Hymn, *etc.* (Soprano and Alto.) *G. Schirmer: New York,* [1904.] 8°. **F. 1179. (56.)**

— [Pastorale.] An Angel spake unto the Shepherds ... Christmas Anthem for Mixed Voices with Children's Choir ad lib., the English text adapted by H. A. Dickinson. Arranged by C. Dickinson. *H. W. Gray Co.: New York,* 1941. 8°. **E. 335. k. (33.)**

— Christus ist geboren. Nato è Cristo Redentor. Weihnachtslied von T. Landmesser ... für mehrstimmigen Chor mit Orgelbegleitung ... [Two settings.] Die Uebertragung in das Italienische von P. Barghilioni ... Part. & Stimmen für Männer-Chor, *etc.* 5 pt. *Ed. Bote & G. Bock: Berlin, Posen,* [1866.] 8°.
The score contains an alternative version of the second setting for women's voices. **E. 600. c. (16.)**

— Christus ist geboren. Nato è Christo Redentor. [No. 2.] Weihnachtslied ... für Pianoforte, *etc.* pp. 3. *Ed. Bote & G. Bock: Berlin, Posen,* [1865.] fol. **g. 547. p. (2.)**

— Comment, disaient-ils. *See* supra: [Buch der Lieder. Bd. 2. No. 2.]

— "Comorn," Marche de Rakoczy. *See* infra: [Rhapsodie hongroise. No. 15.]

2 Concertetuden

— Zwei Concertetuden. 1. Waldesrauschen. 2. Gnomenreigen. Für die grosse Clavierschule von Lebert u. Stark. no. 2. *I. G. Cotta'sche Buchhandlung: Stuttgart,* [1863.] fol. *Imperfect; wanting no. 1.* **Hirsch M. 950. (5.)**

— Zwei Concertetuden für die grosse Clavierschule von Lebert u. Stark. 2 no. *Berlin,* [1874.] fol. **h. 585. b. (10.)**

— 2 Concert Studies.—Waldesrauschen & Gnomenreigen.— (Revised, phrased and fingered by O. Thümer.) [P. F.] *Augener: London,* [1911.] 4°. **g. 547. d. (3.)**

— Two Concert Studies, for the pianoforte, *etc.* (Edited by E. Cundell.) *W. Paxton & Co.: London,* [1921.] fol. **h. 896. h. (1.)**

— [No. 1.] Waldesrauschen ... for the pianoforte. (Edited by E. Cundell.) *W. Paxton & Co.: London,* [1920.] fol. **h. 896. h. (3.)**

— [No. 2.] Gnomenreigen ... for the pianoforte. (Edited by E. Cundell.) *W. Paxton & Co.: London,* [1920.] fol. **h. 896. h. (2.)**

LISZT (Franz)

— Grosse Concert-Fantasie über Spanische Weisen für das Pianoforte. *H. Licht: Leipzig,* [1888.] fol.   **h. 585. g. (11.)**

Grosses Concert-Solo für das Pianoforte

— Grosses Concert-Solo für das Pianoforte, *etc.* pp. 31. *Bei Breitkopf & Härtel: Leipzig,* [1851.] fol.   **Hirsch M. 954. (1.)**

— Concerto pathétique pour deux pianos. pp. 35. *Breitkopf & Härtel: Leipzig,* [1866.] fol.   **h. 896. y. (4.)**

— Concerto pathétique für zwei Pianoforte. Neue Ausgabe mit Zusätzen von Hans von Bülow, *etc. Leipzig und Brüssel,* [1885.] fol.   **h. 585. g. (2.)**

— Concerto pathétique in E minor. Edited by E. Hughes. (For two Pianos, four-hands.) *G. Schirmer: New York,* 1929. 4°.   **g. 547. f. (7.)**

— Concerto Pathétique ... Für Pianoforte mit Begleitung des Orchesters eingerichtet von E. Reuss ... Partitur. *Breitkopf & Härtel: Leipzig und Brüssel,* [1887.] fol.   **h. 896. b. (4.)**

— Concerto pathétique. Nach dem Original für 2 Pianoforte für ein Pianoforte und Orchester bearbeitet ... von Richard Burmeister. Partitur. pp. 65. *Breitkopf & Härtel: Leipzig,* [c. 1925.] fol.   **h. 896. aa. (2.)**

— Concerto pathétique. Zongorára és zenekarra átdolgozta Darvas Gábor. ⟨Arranged for piano and orchestra by G. Darvas.⟩ [Score.] pp. 109. *Zeneműkiadó Vállalat: Budapest,* 1962. 8°. *Kispartiturák* 102.   **c. 156. m. (3.)**

Piano Concerto No. 1 in E flat

— Erstes Concert für Pianoforte und Orchester ... Pianoforte mit Orchester, Partitur, *etc.* pp. 82. *Carl Haslinger: Wien,* [1865?] fol.   **h. 585. d.**

— [A reissue.] Erstes Concert für Pianoforte und Orchester ... Pianoforte mit Orchester Partitur, *etc. Carl Haslinger: Wien,* [1885?] fol.   **Hirsch M. 943.**

— Konzert No. 1, Es dur, für Pianoforte mit Orchester. *E. Eulenburg: Leipzig,* [1903.] 8°. *[Eulenburg's kleine Orchester-Partitur-Ausgabe. Konzerte. No. 10.]*   **b. 208.**

— Romantic and modern Piano Concertos. (Schumann ... Liszt, *etc.*) Edited ... by A. E. Wier. [Score.] *Longmans, Green and Co.: New York,* 1940. 4°. *[Longmans Miniature Arrow Score Series. Vol. 9.]*   **g. 1075.**

— Piano Concerto 1. E♭ major, *etc.* [Score, with analysis.] *Boosey & Hawkes: London, etc.,* [1946.] 8°. *[Hawkes Pocket Scores. No. 209.]*   **b. 211.**

— Concerto No. 1, E♭ major, for Pianoforte and Orchestra ... Foreword by Max Alberti. [Score.] pp. 110. *Ernst Eulenburg: London,* [1949.] 8°. *[Edition Eulenburg. no. 710.]*   **b. 212.**

— Erstes Concert für Pianoforte und Orchester ... Solopartie m. Begltg eines zweiten Pianoforte, *etc.* pp. 47. *Carl Haslinger: Wien,* [c. 1870.] fol.   **h. 896. q. (1.)**

— First Concerto in E flat.—With 2nd Piano. [Revised by C.] Klindworth. *Augener: London,* [1912.] 4°.   **g. 547. d. (4.)**

— Klavier-Konzert Nr. 1 ... Neue, kritisch bearbeitete Ausgabe von Eugen d'Albert. [The orchestral part arranged for a second P. F. Score.] pp. 46. *Alfred Lengnick & Cⁱᵉ: London; Schlesinger'sche Buch & Musikhandlung: Berlin; Leipzig* printed, [c. 1915.] fol.   **h. 896. ii. (6.)**

— Concerto No. 1 in E♭ major. For the piano. [The orchestral part arranged for a second P. F.] Edited and revised by

LISZT (Franz)

Rafael Joseffy. pp. 55. *G. Schirmer: New York; Chappell & Co.: London;* [London printed, 1952.] 4°. *Schirmer's Library of musical Classics. vol.* 1057.]   **g. 547. i. (3.)**

— Concerto No. 1 in E flat ... ⟨Themes from 1st & 2nd movements.⟩ Arranged by Victor Ambroise. [P. F.] pp. 6. *Lawrence Wright Music Co.: London,* [1947.] 4°.   **f. 470. a. (3.)**

— The Theme from Liszt Concerto No. 1 as featured in Metro Goldwyn Mayer's "The Secret Heart," *etc.* ⟨Arranged by Jack E. Bolesworth.⟩ [P. F.] pp. 6. *Cinephonic Music Co.: London,* 1947. 4°.   **f. 470. a. (10.)**

— Theme ... Arranged for piano solo by Walter Collins. pp. 5. *W. Paxton & Co.: London,* [1948.] 4°.   **f. 470. a. (4.)**

— Concerto Nᵒ 1 in E flat ... Adapted and arranged for piano solo by Albert Marland. pp. 11. *Chappell & Co.: London,* [1949.] 4°.   **f. 470. a. (2.)**

Piano Concerto No. 2 in A

— 2ᵗᵉˢ Concert. Pianoforte und Orchester, *etc.* ⟨A-dur. Partitur.⟩ pp. 84. *Bei B. Schott's Söhnen: Mainz,* [c. 1880.] fol.   **Hirsch M. 944.**

— [A reissue.] 2ᵗᵉˢ Concert. Pianoforte und Orchester, *etc.* ⟨A-dur. Partitur.⟩ pp. 84. *Mainz,* [c. 1890.] fol.   **h. 896. b. (5.)**

— Zweites Konzert, A dur, für Pianoforte mit Orchester. *E. Eulenburg: Leipzig,* [1906.] 8°. *[Eulenburg's kleine Orchester-Partitur-Ausgabe. Konzerte. No. 20.]*   **b. 208.**

— Romantic and modern Piano Concertos. (Schumann ... Liszt, *etc.*) Edited ... by A. E. Wier. [Score.] *Longmans, Green and Co.: New York,* 1940. 4°. *[Longmans Miniature Arrow Score Series. Vol. 9.]*   **g. 1075.**

— Concerto No. 2, A major, for Pianoforte and Orchestra ... Foreword by Max Alberti, *etc.* [Score.] pp. 108. *Ernst Eulenburg: London,* [1949.] 8°. *[Edition Eulenburg. no. 720.]*   **b. 212.**

— 2ᵗᵉˢ. Concert, Pianoforte und Orchester ... Die Orchester-Begleitung für ein 2ᵗᵉˢ. Pianoforte gesetzt vom Componisten. *Mainz,* [1863.] fol.   **h. 585. b. (1.)**

— 2ᵗᵉˢ. Concert ... für Pianoforte. [2 P. F.] (Eingerichtet von R. Kleinmichel.) *Mainz,* [1878.] fol.   **h. 585. e. (2.)**

— Concerto No. 2 in A major, for Pianoforte. Two pianos, four hands (in score). Edited and revised by Rafael Joseffy. pp. 67. *G. Schirmer: New York; Chappell & Co.: London;* [London printed, 1951.] 4°. *Schirmer's Library of musical Classics. vol.* 1058.   **g. 547. i. (4.)**

— Concerto pathétique. *See* supra: [Grosses Concert-Solo für das Pianoforte.]

Consolations

— Consolations. Six pensées pöetiques pour le piano. pp. 13. *Bureau central de musique: Paris,* [1850?] fol.   **h. 896. gg. (3.)**

— Consolations. Pour piano. pp. 15. *Léon Escudier: Paris,* [c. 1860.] fol.   **h. 585. m. (2.)**

— Consolations pour le piano. pp. 23. *Chez Breitkopf & Härtel: Leipzig,* [c. 1880.] fol.   **g. 547. p. (3.)**

— 6 Consolations for Piano. *A. Hammond & Co.: London,* [1910.] 4°. *The Academic Edition, No.* 438.   **g. 1130. u. (3.)**

LISZT (FRANZ)

— Consolations. [P. F.] *Chappell & Co.: London, etc.*, (1911.)
fol.
Chappell Edition of Popular Pianoforte Works, No. 45.
h. 3369.

— Consolations ... for the pianoforte ... Edited ... by
G. Farlane, with prefatory remarks by S. Macpherson.
J. Williams: London, [1922.] 4°. **g. 547. e. (5.)**

— Consolations. Revised by David Wilde. ⟨Piano.⟩ pp. 23.
Stainer & Bell: London, [1979.] 4°. **g. 547. ee. (4.)**

— Consolations ... transcrites pour Orgue-Melodium ... par
J. Skiva. *Leipzig,* [1875.] fol. **h. 2575. d. (10.)**

— Consolations ... Transcriptions by F. Hermann ... Tenor &
Piano. *Augener & Co.: London,* [1903.] 4°. **g. 762. b. (2.)**

— Consolations ... Transcriptions by F. Hermann. Violin and
Piano. *Augener & Co.: London,* [1903.] 4°. **g. 223. j. (13.)**

— Consolations ... Transcriptions by F. Hermann ...
Violoncello and Piano. *Augener & Co.: London,* [1903.] 4°.
g. 514. e. (14.)

— Consolations pour le piano. 3 no. *London,* [1883.] fol.
Imperfect; wanting no. 1. **h. 585. f. (20.)**

— Consolations. no. 1–3. 2 no. [P. F.] *Augener & Co: London,*
[1886–93.] fol.
Part of a Collection entitled "The Romantic School".
h. 3298. (20.)

— Consolation No. 3 (No. 6) for the Pianoforte. 2 no. *R. Cocks
& Co.: London,* [1896.] fol. **h. 896. c. (4.)**

— Consolation. No. 1. [For violoncello and piano.] *In:* COLE
(Hugo) Two Romantic Pieces, *etc.* [1.] [1968.] 4°.
g. 510. y. (7.)

— Consolation No. 2. Arranged (for Violoncello and Piano) by
C. Sharpe. *J. B. Cramer & Co.: London,* 1927. 4°.
[*Cramer's Library of Music for Violoncello and Piano. No. 2.*]
g. 804.

— [No. 3.] Consolation for the piano, *etc. London,* [1858.] fol.
h. 585. (7.)

— [No. 3.] Consolation. See ALBUM. [Ewer's] Album de Piano,
1858. No. 15. 1858. fol. **h. 1211.**

— [No. 3.] Consolation for the Piano. *London,* [1861.] fol.
h. 585. a. (3.)

— Consolation No. 3 in D flat. [P. F.] [1884.] *See* FLEURS. Fleurs
et Diamants, *etc.* No. 50. [1882–93.] fol. **h. 3294.**

— [No. 3.] Consolation. [P. F.] *See* SLOPER (E. H. L.) Repertory of
select Pianoforte Works, *etc.* Third Series. No. 7. [1892, *etc.*]
fol. **h. 736. c.**

— Consolation, in D flat, No. 3 ... Edited by M. Esposito. [P. F.]
C. E. Music Publishers Co.: Dublin, [1920.] 4°.
g. 547. f. (22.)

— [No. 3.] Consolation in D flat, *etc.* ⟨Annotated and fingered
by F. Corder.⟩ [P. F.] pp. 7. *Murdoch, Murdoch & Co.:
London,* [c. 1920.] fol.
[*Mayfair Classics. no. 21.*] **h. 3576.**

— Consolation N° 3. Arr. King Palmer. [P. F.] pp. 7. *W. Paxton
& Co.: London,* [1961.] 4°. **f. 470. a. (14.)**

— Consolation No. 3 in D♭. ⟨Edited by Henry Duke.⟩ [P. F.]
pp. 7. *H. Freeman & Co.: Brighton,* [1961.] 4°.
Grafton Classics. no. 162. **g. 547. s. (3.)**

— [No. 3.] Consolation. See GARIBOLDI (E.) Morceaux Favoris
pour Flute & Piano, No. 16. [1886.] fol. **h. 2096. e.**

— [No. 3.] Consolation. See HERMANN (F.) Morceaux Favoris
pour Violon & Piano, No. 16. [1886.] fol. **h. 1621. b.**

LISZT (FRANZ)

— [No. 4.] Adagio. [Organ.] *In:* GOTTSCHALG (A. W.) and
MUELLER-HARTUNG (K.) Album für Orgelspieler, *etc.* p. 69.
[1867.] fol. **h. 2733. i. (4.)**

— [No. 5.] Eugénie. Andantino. [P. F.] *Robt W. Ollivier: London,*
[1860.] fol.
Pp. 29–31 of an unidentified collection, with a special titlepage.
h. 585. (9.)

— Consolation in E. No. 5. [P. F.] [1883.] *See* FLEURS. Fleurs et
Diamants, *etc.* No. 44. [1882–93.] fol. **h. 3294.**

— Consolation, No. 5. [P. F.] [1907.] *See* ZILCHER (P.) Favourite
Pieces, *etc.* No. 2. [1907, *etc.*] fol. **g. 1269. a. (9.)**

— [No. 5.] Consolation. [Viola and P. F.] *See* STEHLING (K. A.)
Morceaux favoris, *etc.* No. 2. [1886.] fol. **h. 1785. b. (8.)**

— Consolations. No. 6. [P. F.] 1913. *See* HAWLEY (S.) Hawley
Edition. No. 57. 1909, *etc.* fol. **h. 3527. b.**

— Le Crucifix. Poésie de V. Hugo, composée pour une voix de
femme Contre Alto avec accompagnement de Piano ou
Harmonium. Trois versions musicales. *C. F. Kahnt: Leipzig,*
[1884.] 4°. **F. 607. w. (6.)**

— Crucifixus. *See infra:* [Variationen über das Motiv von Bach:
Weinen, Klagen, Sorgen, Zagen.]

— Crux. Hymne des marins, avec antienne approbative de
N. T. S. P. Pie IX, paroles de M. Guichon de Grandpont.
Imp. Anner.: Brest, 1865. 8°. **D. 835. u. (2.)**

— Cujus animam, air du Stabat mater de Rossini, transcrit pour
le piano. *See infra:* [2 transcriptions d'après Rossini. No. 1.]

— 2 Csárdás pour piano. 2 no. *F. Hofmeister: Leipzig,* [1886.]
fol. **h. 585. g. (10.)**

— Two Csárdás. For piano. Edited by Joseph Prostakoff. pp. 34.
G. Schirmer: New York, London, [1968.] 4°.
Schirmer's Library of Musical Classics. vol. 1900.
g. 547. z. (5.)

— Czardás macabre. Arranged and edited by J. Werner. ⟨Piano.⟩
J. B. Cramer & Co.: London, 1942. 4°.
[*Newly discovered Classics for Piano. No. 1.*]
g. 1125. uu. (25.)

— Csárdás macabre. [P. F.] Liszt kéziratai alapján összeállította
Szelényi István, *etc.* pp. 16. *In:* Új zenei szemle. évf. 6. sz. 1.
1955. 8°. **P. P. 1945. efa.**

— Csárdás macabre. Darvas Gábor hangszerelése.
⟨Orchestration par G. Darvas.⟩ [Score.] pp. 56. *Zeneműkiadó
vállalat: Budapest,* 1959. 8°.
Kispartitúrák. 60. **b. 276. j. (2.)**

— Danse Macabre, Pöeme Symphonique de C. Saint-Saëns.
Transcription pour Piano par F. Liszt. *Paris,* [1877.] fol.
h. 585. b. (19.)

— La Danza. *See infra:* Soirées musicales de Rossini. No. 9.

— A Death-Summons. *See infra:* [Die Vätergruft.]

— Der du von dem Himmel bist. *See supra:* [Buch der Lieder.
Bd. 1. No. 5.]

— Divertissement pour piano sur le cavatine de Pacini. *See
infra:* [Trois morceaux de salon. Op. 5. No. 1.]

— Don Carlos de Verdi, Coro di Festa e Marcia funebre.
Transcription. [P. F.] *B. Schott's Söhne: Mayence,* [c. 1880.]
fol. **h. 896. a. (17.)**

— Don Giovanni de Mozart. Grande fantaisie. *See infra:*
[Reminiscences de Don Juan.]

LISZT (FRANZ)

—[Don Sanche.] Ouverture und Arie des Don Sanche aus der einactigen Operette "Don Sanche" … für Klavier zu zwei Händen übertragen von Jean Chantavoine. pp. 16. *In:* Die Musik. Jahrg. 3. Hft. 16. Musikbeilage. [1904.] 4°.

P. P. 1946. ah.

— The Dream of Love. *See* infra: [Drei Lieder für eine Sopran- oder Tenor-Stimme. No. 3.]

— Die drei Zigeuner, von Lenau. (Les trois tziganes. Paroles françaises de G. Lagye.) *See also* supra: [*Collected Works.—d.*] F. Liszt's gesammelte Lieder, *etc.* No. 43.

— Die drei Zigeuner. [Song with orchestra. Score.] pp. 31. *C. F. Kahnt Nachfolger: Leipzig,* [c. 1910.] 8°. *Franz Liszt. Lieder mit Orchester. no. 43.* **E. 1644. i.**

— Die drei Zigeuner. Dichtung von N. Lenau. Paraphrase für Violine und Pianoforte, *etc.* [Score and part.] 2 pt. *C. F. Kahnt: Leipzig,* [1896.] fol. **h. 896. n. (4.)**

—[Die drei Zigeuner.] Ungarische Rhapsodie für die Violine nach der Paraphrase über "Die drei Zigeuner" … für den Konzertgebrauch eingerichtet von Jenő Hubay. Partitur. pp. 63. *Universal Edition: Wien, Leipzig,* [1931.] fol. **g. 547. k. (7.)**

— Du bist wie eine Blume, von Heine. *See also* supra: [*Collected Works.—d.*] F. Liszt's gesammelte Lieder, *etc.* No. 13.

—[Du bist wie eine Blume.] A Beautiful Flower. English words by E. Teschemacher. *Murdoch, Murdoch & Co.: London,* [1921.] fol. *Part of "The Mayfair Classics".* **H. 1846. jj. (13.)**

— Duo (Sonate) … For violin and piano. ⟨Based on the theme of Chopin's Mazurka in C sharp minor, Op. 6, No. 2. Prepared for publication by Tibor Serly.⟩ [Score and part.] 2 pt. *Southern Music Publishing Co.: New York; Peer Musikverlag: Hamburg,* [1964.] 4°. **g. 547. r. (5.)**

—[Another copy.] **g. 547. x. (3.)**

— Grand duo concertant pour piano et violon sur la romance de M. Lafont le Marin. 2 pt. *Chez les fils de B. Schott: Mayence,* [1852.] fol. **h. 1611. (3.)**

—[Another copy.] **Hirsch M. 952. (4.)**

—[Einsam bin ich, nicht allein.] "Bijou de Preciosa," Volkslied, de l'opéra de C. M. von Weber transcrit pour le piano forte par F. Liszt. pp. 5. *Wessel & Cᵒ: London,* [1852.] fol. **h. 895. (3.)**

— Einsam bin ich, nicht allein. Volkslied von Weber [from "Preciosa"]. Für das Pianoforte übertragen. pp. 6. *Schuberth & Cᵒ: Hamburg, New York,* [c. 1855.] fol. **g. 547. v. (3.)**

—[Einsam bin ich, nicht allein.] "Bijou de Preciosa," *etc. Edwin Ashdown: London,* [1870?] fol. *A reissue of the edition of 1852, entered above.* **h. 896. k. (10.)**

— Einst wollt' ich einen Kranz, von J. Bodenstedt. *See* supra: [*Collected Works.—d.*] F. Liszt's gesammelte Lieder, *etc.* No. 49.

— Élégie … Violoncelle, piano, harpe et harmonium. [Score, and parts for violoncello, harp and harmonium.] 4 pt. *Chez C. F. Kahnt: Leipzig,* [1875?] fol. **h. 896. r. (3.)**

— Élégie … Violoncelle et piano, *etc.* [Score and part.] 2 pt. *C. F. Kahnt Nachfolger: Leipzig,* [c. 1890.] fol. **h. 896. r. (4.)**

— Élégie … Piano (à deux mains), *etc.* pp. 7. *Chez C. F. Kahnt: Leipzig,* [1875.] fol. **h. 896. n. (5.)**

— Élégie pour piano seul. *See also* infra: [Die Zelle in Nonnenwerth.]

LISZT (FRANZ)

— Élégie sur des motifs du Prince Louis de Prusse, pour le Piano. *Berlin,* [1847.] fol. **h. 706. (15.)**

— Negyedik elfelejtett keringó. *See* infra: [Valse oubliée. No. 4.]

— En rêve. Nocturne pour piano. pp. 3. *Ludwig Doblinger: Wien,* [c. 1900.] fol. **h. 896. z. (3.)**

— Enfant, si j'étais roi. *See* supra: [Buch der Lieder. Bd. 2. No. 3.]

2 Episoden aus Lenau's Faust

— Zwei Episoden aus Lenau's Faust, für grosses Orchester. No. 1. Der nächtliche Zug. No. 2. Der Tanz in der Dorfschenke. (Mephisto Walzer.) Partitur, *etc.* 2 no. *J. Schuberth & Co.: Leipzig & New York,* [1866, 70?] fol. *No. 2 is of a later issue.* **h. 896. b. (6.)**

—[A reissue.] Zwei Episoden aus Lenau's Faust für grosses Orchester. No. 1. Der nächtliche Zug. No. 2. Der Tanz in der Dorfschenke. (Mephisto-Walzer.) Orchester-Partitur, *etc.* no. 2. *Leipzig,* [1875?] fol. *Imperfect; wanting no. 1.* **Hirsch M. 945.**

— Procession by Night and Mephisto Waltz … Foreword by Robert Collet. [Score.] pp. xvii. 102. *Ernst Eulenburg, etc.: London, etc.,* [1976.] 8°. [*Edition Eulenburg. no.* 1361.] **b. 212.**

— Zwei Episoden aus Lenau's Faust für grosses Orchester … Für das Pianoforte übertragen vom Componisten … Zu zwei Händen, *etc.* [No. 1 arranged by R. Freund, no. 2 by the composer.] 2 no. *J. Schuberth & Cᵒ: Leipzig, New York,* [1873?] fol. **h. 585. b. (12.)**

— Zwei Episoden aus Lenau's Faust für grosses Orchester … Für das Pianoforte übertragen vom Componisten, *etc.* ⟨Zu vier Händen.⟩ no. 1. *J. Schuberth & Cᵒ: Leipzig, New York,* [c. 1880.] fol. *Imperfect; wanting no. 2.* **h. 585. j. (3.)**

—[No. 2. Der Tanz in der Dorfschenke.] Mephisto Walzer … Bearbeitet für Pianoforte und Orchester … Von Richard Burmeister. ⟨Partitur.⟩ pp. 60. *J. Schuberth & Cᵒ: Leipzig,* [1907.] fol. **h. 896. ff. (1.)**

—[No. 2.] Episode aus Lenau's Faust. Der Tanz in der Dorfschenke—Mephisto Walzer— … Mit Anlehnung an die Orchesterpartitur für das Pianoforte neu bearbeitet … von F. Busoni. *G. Schirmer: New York,* (1904.) fol. **h. 896. c. (5.)**

—[No. 2. Der Tanz in der Dorfschenke.] Mephisto Walzer … for the Pianoforte … Revised by O. Thümer. *Augener: London,* [1907.] 4°. **g. 543. kk. (14.)**

—[No. 2. Der Tanz in der Dorfschenke.] Mephisto Waltz … Based on the orchestra score and newly arranged for the piano by Ferruccio Busoni. pp. 33. *G. Schirmer: New York; Chappell & Co.: London;* [*London* printed, 1954.] 4°. *Schirmer's Library of musical Classics. vol.* 1649. **g. 547. j. (11.)**

—[No. 2. Der Tanz in der Dorfschenke.] Mephisto Waltz No. 1 … [P. F. Edited by] Emil von Sauer. pp. 25. *Edition Peters: London, etc.,* [1971.] 4°. **g. 547. z. (3.)**

—[No. 2. Der Tanz in der Dorfschenke.] Love Theme from "The Mephisto Waltz" … Adapted by Jerry Goldsmith. [P. F.] pp. 3. *Fox Fanfare Music: New York; Twentieth Century Music Corp.: London,* [1971.] 4°. **f. 470. a. (15.)**

— Epithalam, Reményi Ede … esküvőjére, hededüre és zongorára. [Score and part.] 2 pt. *Táborszky és Parsch: Pest,* [1872?] fol. **h. 585. o. (5.)**

LISZT (FRANZ)

— [Epithalam zu E. Reményi's Vermählungsfeier.] Эпиталама, для скрипки и фортепиано. Редакция скрипичной партии И. Ямпольского. [Score and part.] 2 pt. *Государственное Музыкальное Издательство: Москва*, 1955. 4°.
g. 547. l. (7.)

— Epithalam, Reményi Ede ... esküvőjére, zongorára. pp. 9. *Táborszky és Parsch: Pest*, [1872?] fol. **h. 896. aa. (4.)**

— Eroica. *See* infra: [Études d'exécution transcendante. No. 7.]

— Des erwachenden Kindes Lobgesang. *See* infra: [Hymne de l'enfant à son réveil.]

Es muss ein Wunderbares sein

— Es muss ein Wunderbares sein. Redwitz. *See* also supra: [*Collected Works.—d.*] F. Liszt's gesammelte Lieder, *etc.* No. 28.

— How wonderful for Hearts ... [Song.] English words by Ed. Teschemacher. *Murdoch, Murdoch & Co.: London*, [1925?] fol.
Part of "The Mayfair Classics". **H. 1846. qq. (17.)**

— What heav'nly Wonder springs to sight ... [Song.] English text written by Mrs. G. F. Byron. Edited by D. Freer, *etc.* *J. Williams: London*, [1929.] 4°.
[*Classical and Standard Songs. No. XXV.*] **G. 1173.**

— Es muss ein Wunderbares sein. (Redwitz) ... Rev. v. Eugen d'Albert. Instrumentiert v. Felix Mottl. [Score.] pp. 7. *C. F. Kahnt: Leipzig*, [c. 1920.] 8°. **E. 1500. c. (9.)**

— O loving God. Mixed voices and organ. Words by Jean Phillips. Arranged by P. J. Mansfield. [Staff and tonic sol-fa notation.] pp. 6. *Aschberg, Hopwood & Crew: London*, [1964.] 8°.
[*Mortimer Series of choral Music. no.* 616.] **F. 1659. a.**

— Sympathy, *etc.* [P. F.] *See* PAUER (E.) Vocal Works by Great Masters, *etc.* [No. 4.] [1887–97.] fol. **h. 3649. (2.)**

— Es rauschen die Winde, von Rellstab. *See* supra: [*Collected Works.—d.*] F. Liszt's gesammelte Lieder, *etc.* No. 21.

— Es rufet Gott. [Words by] C. Götze. *See* infra: Für Männergesang. No. 6.

— Es war ein König in Thule. *See* supra: [Buch der Lieder. Bd. 1. No. 4.]

— [Étude. E minor.] Presto impetuoso. *In:* FÉTIS (François J.) and MOSCHELES (I.) [Méthode des méthodes de piano.] Complete System of Instruction for the Piano Forte, *etc.* bk. 3. pp. 45–47. [1841.] fol. **R. M. 16. e. 5.**

— Étude. [E minor.] *In:* FÉTIS (François J.) and MOSCHELES (I.) Méthode des méthodes de piano, *etc.* Abt. 3. pp. 25–27. [c. 1850.] fol. **g. 327.**

— Études pour le piano en douze exercices ... Oeuvre I. 2 livr. *Chez Fr. Hofmeister: Leipzig*, [1840.] fol.
Hirsch M. 950. (6.)

— [Études pour le piano en douze exercices.] Douze études, *etc.* ⟨Edited by Robert Howat.⟩ [P. F.] 2 bk. *Edition Peters: New York, etc.; printed in England*, [1961.] 4°. **g. 547. r. (2.)**

— Études pour le piano en douze exercices ... Oeuvre I. ... No. 9 in As, *etc. Chez Fr. Hofmeister: Leipzig*, [1840.] fol.
Hirsch M. 950. (7.)

— 24 grandes études pour le piano, *etc.* 2 liv. pp. 137. *Chez Tob. Haslinger: Vienne*, [1839.] fol.
Without titlepage to liv. 2. Etudes 1–12 only. No more composed. **h. 585. i.**

LISZT (FRANZ)

— [24 grandes études. No. 1–8.] [Huit premières études.] [P. F.] pp. 70. [*Mori and Lavenu: London*, 1839.] fol.
Without titlepage. The title and imprint have been supplied in MS. on p. 1. **h. 583. (9.)**

Études d'exécution transcendante

— Études d'exécution transcendente pour le piano ... Seule édition authentique revue par l'auteur. 2 cah. *Chez Breitkopf & Härtel: Leipzig*, [c. 1860.] fol. **g. 547. n. (1.)**

— Études d'exécution transcendante pour le piano ... Seule édition authentique revue par l'auteur. pp. 108. *Breitkopf & Härtel: Leipzig*, [1873?] 8°. **e. 58. b.**

— Twelve grand Studies for the Pianoforte. 2 bk. *Brewer & Co.: London*, [1873.] fol. **h. 585. c.**

— Études d'Éxécution transcendante. Edited by E. Dannreuther. In two Books. *Augener & Co.: London*, [1899.] 4°.
g. 547. a. (11.)

— Douze études d'exécution transcendante. For the piano. Instructive edition with fingering, phrasing, marks of expression and suggestions for practising by Paolo Gallico. pp. 142. *G. Schirmer: New York; Chappell & Co.: London; [London* printed, 1951.] 4°.
Schirmer's Library of musical Classics. vol. 788.
g. 547. i. (5.)

— Études d'exécution transcendante, *etc.* [Edited by Alfred Cortot. P. F.] 3 vol. *Éditions Salabert: Paris, New York*, [1951.] fol.
Part of "Édition de travail des œuvres de Liszt".
g. 547. m. (1.)

— Études d'exécution transcendante. No. 4. Mazeppa. (No. 5. Feux Follets.) (No. 9. Recordanza.) (No. 11. Harmonies du Soir.) Edited by E. Dannreuther. [P. F.] 4 no. *Augener & Co.: London*, [1903.] 4°. **g. 547. c. (4.)**

— [No. 4.] Mazeppa. Für Klavier ... Herausgegeben von ... Zoltán Gárdonyi, István Szelényi. pp. 16. *Bärenreiter: Kassel, etc.; Editio musica: Budapest; printed in Hungary*, 1971. 4°. **g. 547. aa. (1.)**

— [No. 5.] Feux follets. Für Klavier ... Herausgegeben von ... Zoltán Gárdonyi, István Szelényi. pp. 12. *Bärenreiter: Kassel, etc.; Editio musica: Budapest; printed in Hungary*, 1971. 4°. **g. 547. aa. (2.)**

— [No. 5.] Feux follets (Irrlichter), für Orchester bearbeitet von Leo Weiner. Partitur. pp. 43. *Rózsavölgyi & Cᵒ: Budapest*, [1934.] fol. **h. 896. r. (5.)**

— [No. 7.] Eroica. Für Klavier ... Herausgegeben von ... Zoltán Gárdonyi, István Szelényi. pp. 11. *Bärenreiter: Kassel, etc.; Editio musica: Budapest; printed in Hungary*, 1971. 4°.
g. 547. aa. (3.)

— [No. 8.] Wilde Jagd. Für Klavier ... Herausgegeben von ... Zoltán Gárdonyi, István Szelényi. pp. 14. *Bärenreiter: Kassel, etc.; Editio musica: Budapest; printed in Hungary*, 1971. 4°. **g. 547. aa. (4.)**

— [No. 9.] Ricordanza. Für Klavier ... Herausgegeben von ... Zoltán Gárdonyi. István Szelényi. pp. 15. *Bärenreiter: Kassel, etc.; Editio musica: Budapest; printed in Hungary*, 1971. 4°. **g. 547. aa. (5.)**

— [No. 10.] Etüde F-moll. Study in F minor. Für Klavier ... Herausgegeben von ... Zoltán Gárdonyi, István Szelényi. pp. 14. *Bärenreiter: Kassel, etc.; Editio musica: Budapest; printed in Hungary*, 1971. 4°. **g. 547. aa. (6.)**

— [No. 11.] Harmonies du soir. Für Klavier ... Herausgegeben von ... Zoltán Gárdonyi, István Szelényi. pp. 11. *Bärenreiter: Kassel, etc.; Editio musica: Budapest; printed in Hungary*, 1971. 4°. **g. 547. aa. (7.)**

LISZT (Franz)

— 3 études de concert pour piano, *etc.* 3 no. *Chez Fr. Kistner: Leipsic,* [1849.] fol. **g. 547. cc. (11.)**

— [Another copy.] *Imperfect; wanting no.* 2, 3. **Hirsch M. 950. (8.)**

— [3 études de concert.] Three Concert Studies. Edited by E. Dannreuther. *Augener & Co.: London,* 1898. 4°. **g. 547. a. (9.)**

— Trois études de concert. Trois caprices poétiques. Für Klavier ... Herausgegeben von ... Zoltán Gárdonyi, István Szelényi. pp. 40. *Bärenreiter: Kassel, etc.: Editio musica: Budapest; printed in Hungary,* 1971. 4°. **g. 547. aa. (8.)**

3 études de concert. No. 3

— Study in D flat. [P. F.] *See* WESTLAKE (F.) Lyra Studentium, *etc.* No. 38. [1874–98.] fol. **h. 3249.**

— Étude de Concert. [P. F.] *See* PAUER (E.) Études de Concert ... No. 39. [1887.] 4°. **g. 564. s.**

— Étude in D♭. [P. F.] [1898.] *See* SCHLOESSER (A.) Classical Music, *etc.* No. 81. [1888, *etc.*] fol. **h. 1396. b.**

— Étude in D flat. [P. F.] *Chappell & Co.: London, etc.,* (1910.) fol. *Chappell Edition of Popular Pianoforte Works, No.* 1. **h. 3369.**

— Study in D flat ... Edited by E. Kiver. [P. F.] *G. Ricordi & Co.: London,* [1920.] fol. **h. 896. h. (4.)**

— Étude de concert in D flat, *etc.* ⟨Annotated and fingered by F. Corder.⟩ [P. F.] pp. 11. *Murdoch, Murdoch & Co.: London,* [c. 1920.] fol. [*Mayfair Classics. no.* 22.] **h. 3576.**

— Concert Etude, D flat major ... Arranged ... by A. Siloti. [P. F.] *C. Fischer: New York,* 1931. 4°. [*Alexander Siloti Concert Repertoire. No.* 18.] **g. 1267.**

— Um sospiro ... Letra, arranjo e adaptação de Fred Jorge. [P. F.] *Fermata do Brasil: São Paulo,* [1961.] 4°. **g. 547. s. (1.)**

— Concert Study in D flat ... Arranged for Two Pianofortes, 4 hands, by B. Kirkby-Mason. *Bosworth & Co.: London,* 1940. 4°. **g. 547. g. (7.)**

— *See* STOLOFF (Morris) and DUNING (G. W.) Song without End. Based on "Un sospiro" by F. Liszt, *etc.* [1960.] 4°. **h. 3210. i. (679.)**

Grandes études de Paganini

— Études d'exécution transcendante d'après Paganini. Bravour-Studien nach Paganini's Capricen für das Piano-Forte bearbeitet, *etc.* 2 Abt. *Bei Tobias Haslinger: Wien,* [1840.] fol. **h. 896. n. (6.)**

— Études d'exécution transcendante d'après Paganini pour le forte piano. pp. 79. *R. Cocks & Co.: London,* [1840.] fol. **h. 583. (5.)**

— Grandes études de Paganini transcrites pour le piano ... par F. Liszt. Seule édition authentique, entièrement revue et corrigée par l'auteur. 2 cah. *Chez Breitkopf & Härtel: Leipzig,* [c. 1860.] fol. **g. 547. n. (2.)**

— Paganini Studies. Edited by E. Dannreuther. 2 bk. *Augener & Co.: London,* [1899.] 4°. **g. 547. a. (8.)**

— Études d'exécution transcendante d'après Paganini pour le piano. pp. 79. *Chez Schonenberger: Paris,* [c. 1900.] fol. **h. 896. y. (3.)**

— Nicolò Paganini. Six grand Etudes. Arranged for the piano by Liszt. Critically revised, with fingering, pedalling and marks of expression by Paolo Gallico. pp. 53. *G. Schirmer:*

LISZT (Franz)

New York; Chappell & Co.: London; [*London* printed, 1950.] 4°. *Schirmer's Library of musical Classics. vol.* 835. **g. 338. o. (8.)**

— Grandes études de Paganini. Für Klavier ... Herausgegeben von ... Zoltán Gárdonyi, István Szelényi. pp. 55. *Bärenreiter: Kassel, etc.; Editio musica: Budapest; printed in Hungary,* 1971. 4°. **g. 547. aa. (10.)**

Grandes études de Paganini. No. 3. La Campanella

— La Campanella. [Transcription of the Rondo from Paganini's Concerto, Op. 7. P. F.] *See* PAUER (E.) Études de Concert ... No. 12. [1887.] 4°. **g. 564. s.**

— La Campanella, *etc.* [P. F.] *See* PAULL MUSIC CO. Edition Paull, *etc.* [No. 48.] (1905.) fol. **h. 3822. (48.)**

— La Campanella. [P. F.] *Chappell & Co.: London, etc.,* (1910.) fol. *Chappell Edition of Popular Pianoforte Works, No.* 13. **h. 3369.**

— La Campanella ... for the pianoforte. *W. Paxton & Co.: London,* [1920.] fol. **h. 896. h. (5.)**

— La Campanella, *etc.* ⟨Annotated and fingered by F. Corder.⟩ [P. F.] pp. 15. *Murdoch, Murdoch & Co.: London,* [c. 1920.] fol. [*Mayfair Classics. no.* 20.] **h. 3576.**

— La Campanella. Transposed from G♯ minor ... Edited by H. E. Button. [P. F.] *J. H. Larway: London,* 1922. fol. [*Masterpieces. Simplified transcriptions. No.* 9.] **h. 3301.**

— La Campanella ... Arr. (for Two Pianos by) C. Taylor. *Oxford University Press: London, etc.,* 1939. 4°. [*The Two-Piano Series. No.* 21.] **g. 1393.**

— La Campanella. For viola and piano ... Arr. William Primrose. [Score and part.] 2 pt. *Schott & Co.: London,* [1952.] 4°. [*Transcriptions for Viola and Piano.* 1.] **g. 1031. (2.)**

Grandes études de Paganini. Other numbers

— [No. 4.] Arpeggio ... ⟨Paganini-Liszt.⟩ Eine Transkription-Studie von Ferruccio Busoni. pp. 9. *Breitkopf & Härtel: Leipzig, Berlin,* [1923.] 4°. **g. 547. x. (4.)**

— [No. 5.] La Chasse ... ⟨Paganini-Liszt.⟩ Eine Transcription-Studie von Ferruccio Busoni. [P. F.] pp. 7. *Breitkopf & Härtel: Leipzig, Berlin,* [1924.] 4°. **h. 3927. k. (2.)**

— [No. 6.] Paganini-Liszt Thema mit Variationen ... Eine Transkription-Studie von Ferruccio Busoni. pp. 30. [1914.] 4°. *See* PAGANINI (N.) [24 Capricci. Op. 1. No. 24.] **g. 1126. e. (5.)**

— Eugénie. Andantino. *See* supra: [Consolations. No. 5.]

— Grande fantaisie di bravura sur la Clochette de Paganini pour le piano ... Opera: 2. pp. 40. *Chez Maurice Schlesinger: Paris,* [1834.] fol. **g. 547. t. (9.)**

— Grande fantaisie de bravoure sur la clochette de Paganini, pour le piano-forte ... Oeuvre 2. pp. 39. *Chez Pietro Mechetti: Vienne,* [1840.] fol. **Hirsch M. 952. (5.)**

— Fantaisie romantique sur deux mélodies suisses. *See* infra: [Trois morceaux de salon. Op. 5. No. 2.]

— Grande fantaisie (réminiscences) de Don Juan. *See* infra: [Réminiscences de Don Juan.]

— Grande fantaisie pour le piano-forte sur la tirolienne de l'opéra: La Fiancée d'Auber. ⟨Oeuvre 1.⟩ pp. 23. *Chez Pietro Mechetti: Vienne,* [1839.] fol. **Hirch M. 952. (6.)**

LISZT (FRANZ)

— Fantasie über zwei Motive aus W. A. Mozarts Die Hochzeit des Figaro. Nach dem fast vollendeten Originalmanuskript ergänzt ... von Ferruccio Busoni. pp. 31. *Breitkopf & Härtel: Leipzig*, [1912.] 4°.
g. 547. g. (18.)

— [Grande fantaisie sur des thèmes de l'opéra Les Huguenots.] Réminiscences des Huguenots de Meyerbeer. Grande fantaisie dramatique pour le piano ... Op. 11. pp. 25. *Chez Maurice Schlesinger: Paris*, [1837.] fol.
h. 585. l. (2.)

— [Grande fantaisie sur des thèmes de l'opéra Les Huguenots.] Reminiscences des Huguenots [by Meyerbeer]. Grande fantaisie dramatique pour le pianoforte ... Op. 11. pp. 31. *Frédéric Hofmeister: Leipzig*, [1838.] fol.   **Hirsch M. 954. (7.)**

— [Grande fantaisie sur des thèmes de l'opéra Les Huguenots.] Fantaisie dramatique sur les Huguenots de Meyerbeer. Op. 11. ⟨2ᵗᵉ veränderte einzig rechtmässige Ausgabe.⟩ pp. 23. *Chez Aᵈ Mᵗ Schlesinger: Berlin*, [c. 1850.] fol.
The title is taken from the head of p. 3. The titlepage reads: "4 fantaisies. Nᵒ 1. Les Huguenots. 2ᵉ édition. Nᵒ 2. La Juive. Nᵒ 3. Robert le diable. Nᵒ 4. Don Juan".
g. 547. p. (5.)

— Fantaisie pour le piano sur des motifs favoris de l'opéra Lucrezia Borgia de C. [*sic*] Donizetti. pp. 27. *Chez Pietro Mechetti: Vienne*, [1841.] fol.
Later editions, forming the second part of "Réminiscences de Lucrezia Borgia," are entered below.   **h. 896. s. (13.)**

— Grande fantaisie sur la Niobe de Pacini. *See* infra: [Trois morceaux de salon. Op. 5. No. 1.]

— Grande fantaisie sur des motifs de Robert de Diable. *See* infra: [Réminiscences de Robert le Diable.]

— Fantasie über Motive aus Beethoven's Ruinen von Athen für Piano mit Orchesterbegleitung ... Partitur, *etc.* pp. 57. *C. F. W. Siegel: Leipzig*, [c. 1890.] fol.   **h. 896. l. (10.)**

— Fantasie über Motive aus Beethoven's Ruinen von Athen für Piano mit Orchesterbegleitung ... Arrangement für zwei Pianos ⟨vom Komponisten⟩, *etc.* pp. 33. *C. F. W. Siegel: Leipzig*, [c. 1870.] fol.
Two copies.   **g. 547. v. (2.)**

— Fantasie über Motive aus Beethoven's Ruinen von Athen für Piano mit Orchesterbegleitung ... Arrangement für Piano allein. pp. 21. *C. F. W. Siegel: Leipzig*, [c. 1880.] fol.
h. 896. l. (3.)

2 grandes fantaisies sur des motifs des Soirées musicales de Rossini

— La Sérenata, e l'Orgia, grande fantaisie ⟨La Pastorella dell'alpi, e li Marinari, 2ᵐᵉ fantaisie⟩ pour le piano sur des motifs des Soirées musicales de Rossini ... Op. 8. 2 no. *Willis & Cᵒ: London*, [1837.] fol.   **h. 583. (3.)**

— [No. 1.] La Sérenata e l'orgia. Grande fantaisie pour le piano sur des motifs des Soirées musicales de Rossini ... Nouvelle édition, revue et corrigée par l'auteur. Op. 8. Nᵒ 1. pp. 17. *Chez les fils de B. Schott: Mayence, Anvers*, [c. 1850.] fol.
g. 547. v. (1.)

— [No. 1.] [A reissue.] La Serenata et l'orgia. *Mayence*, [c. 1890.] fol.   **h. 896. a. (2.)**

— [No. 2.] La Pastorella dell'alpi e li marinari. 2ᵐᵉ fantaisie pour le piano sur des motifs des Soirées musicales de Rossini ... Op. 8. Nᵒ 2. pp. 17. *Chez les fils de B. Schott: Mayence, Anvers*, [1837?] fol.
h. 896. a. (2*.)

— [No. 2.] La Pastorella dell'alpi e li marinari ... Pour le piano, *etc.* pp. 17. *Chez E. Troupenas & Cᵒ: Paris*, [1837.] fol.
g. 547. cc. (2.)

— Fantaisie sur des motifs favoris de l'opéra Sonnambula de Bellini ... Pour le piano. pp. 24. *Chez Mᵐᵉ Vᵛᵉ Launer: Paris*, [1842?] fol.   **h. 585. l. (6.)**

LISZT (FRANZ)

— Fantaisie sur des motifs favoris de l'opéra Somnambula de Bellini ... pour le piano ... Seconde édition nouvelle et corrigée. pp. 26. *Schuberth & comp.: Hambourg, Leipsic*, [c. 1850.] fol.
h. 896. n. (1.)

— [Fantaisie sur des motifs favoris de l'opéra Sonnambula de Bellini.] Sonnambula (de Bellini). Grosse Concert-Fantasie für Piano-Forte ... 2ᵗᵉ veränderte Ausgabe, nach deren Vortrag im Concert zu Pest (März 1874) notiert von demselben. Vollständige Edition mit den Varianten, *etc.* pp. 25. *Jul. Schuberth & Cᵒ: Leipzig*, [1875.] fol.
h. 585. b. (14.)

— Fantaisie sur l'opéra hongroise. "Szép Ilonka" de Mosonyi M. pour piano. pp. 11. *Rózsavölgyi & cᵒ: Pest*, [1868.] fol.
g. 547. o. (3.)

Fantasie über ungarische Volksmelodien

— Fantasie über ungarische Volksmelodieen für Pianoforte und Orchester ... Partitur, *etc.* pp. 40. *Gustav Heinze: Leipzig*, [1864.] 4°.   **f. 470. l. (1.)**

— Fantasie über ungarische Volksmelodieen für Pianoforte und Orchester ... Partitur, *etc.* pp. 40. *C. F. Peters: Leipzig*, [c. 1880.] 4°.
A corrected issue.   **g. 547. k. (4.)**

— Fantasie über ungarische Volksmelodien für Pianoforte und Orchester, *etc.* ⟨Partitur.⟩ pp. 43. *C. F. Peters: Leipzig*, [1895?] fol.   **h. 896. j. (4.)**

— Phantasie über ungarische Volksmelodien. (Fantasia on Hungarian Folk Themes.) Foreword by Robert Collet. [Score.] pp. 44. *Ernst Eulenburg, etc.: London, etc.*, [1978.] 8°. [*Edition Eulenburg. no.* 1298.]   **b. 212.**

— Fantasie über ungarische Volksmelodieen für Pianoforte und Orchester ... Klavierstimme, *etc.* pp. 25. *Gustav Heinze: Leipzig*, [c. 1870.] fol.   **g. 547. p. (4.)**

— Ungarische Fantasie für Pianoforte u. Orchester ... Arrangement des Orchesters (zweites Pianoforte) von Hans von Bülow. [2 P. F. Score.] pp. 39. *C. F. Peters: Leipzig*, [1874.] fol.   **h. 585. q. (1.)**

— Fantasie über ungarische Volks Melodien für Pianoforte und Orchester. [P. F. solo.] pp. 23. *Stanley Lucas, Weber & Cᵒ: London*, [1876.] fol.   **h. 148. (37.)**

— Fantasie über ungarische Volksmelodien für Pianoforte und Orchester. ⟨Arrangement der Orchesterpartie von Hans von Bülow.⟩ [2 P. F. Score.] pp. 39. *C. F. Peters: Leipzig*, [1895?] fol.   **h. 585. q. (2.)**

— Fantasia on Hungarian Folk-Melodies ... [P. F. duet.] (Piano II. Arr. from the Orchestral Score by Hans von Bülow.) Edited and revised by R. Joseffy. *G. Schirmer: New York*, (1909.) fol.   **h. 896. e. (3.)**

— Hungarian Fantasia. (With second piano in score arranged by Bülow.) Edited and fingered by T. F. Dunhill. *Augener: London*, 1925. 4°.   **g. 547. e. (10.)**

— Phantasie über Ungarische Volksmelodien für Klavier und Orchester ... [The orchestral part arranged for second P. F.] Herausgegeben von Emil von Sauer. pp. 39. *C. F. Peters: New York, etc.*, [*London* printed, c. 1950.] 4°.   **g. 547. l. (3.)**

— Fantasia on Hungarian Folk-Melodies ... Edited and revised by R. Joseffy. *G. Schirmer: New York; Chappell & Co.: London;* [*London* printed, 1951.] 4°.
A reissue of the edition of 1909.   **g. 547. j. (1.)**

— Phantasie über Ungarische Volksmelodien. Hungarian Fantasia ... ⟨Abridged version for piano solo arranged by Noel Fisher.⟩ Moderately difficult, *etc.* pp. 8. *Hinrichsen Edition: London*, [1951.] 4°.   **g. 547. j. (2.)**

LISZT (FRANZ)

— Liszt's Hungarian Fantasie. Concert arrangement for solo piano by Eric Lewis. pp. 19. *Forsyth Bros.: Manchester, London*, [1965.] 4°. **g. 547. s. (4.)**

— Fantasie und Fuge über den Choral "Ad nos, ad salutarem undam," für Orgel oder Pedalflügel, *etc.* pp. 51. *Bei Breitkopf & Härtel: Leipzig*, [1852?] fol. **h. 896. s. (7.)**

— [Fantasie und Fuge.] Ad nos, ad salutarem undam. (Fantasy and fugue.) For organ. Edited by Anthony Newman. Foreword by Anthony Newman and Gary Schultz. pp. iv. 50. *G. Schirmer: New York, London*, [1974.] *obl.* 4°. *Part of "Great Performers' Edition".* **e. 58. m. (1.)**

— Phantasie und Fuge über den Choral Ad nos, ad salutarem undam aus G. Meyerbeers Oper Der Prophet. Für Pianoforte ⟨zu 4 Händen⟩ oder Pedalflügel oder Orgel, *etc.* pp. 51. *Breitkopf & Härtel: Leipzig*, [c. 1920.] 4°. **g. 547. j. (8.)**

— Fantasie und Fuge über den Choral Ad nos, ad salutarem undam. Von der Orgel auf das Pianoforte frei übertragen ... von Ferruccio B. Busoni. pp. 43. *Breitkopf & Härtel: Leipzig*, [c. 1925.] 4°. **g. 547. r. (4.)**

— Fantasie und Fuge über das Thema BACH. *See infra:* [Praeludium und Fuge.]

— Faribolo Pastour. Chanson tirée du poème de Françonnetto de Jasmin et la Chanson du Béarn, transcrite pour piano. [no. 1.] *Chez les fils de B. Schott: Mayence*, [1845.] fol. *Imperfect; wanting no. 2, entitled "Pastorale du Béarn".* **Hirsch M. 950. (11.)**

— Faribolo Pastour. Chanson tirée du Poëme de Françonnetto de Jasmin et la Chanson du Béarn, transcrite pour piano, *etc.* 2 no. *Chez les fils de B. Schott: Mayence, etc.*, [c. 1880.] fol. **h. 896. a. (11.)**

Eine Faust-Symphonie

— Eine Faust-Symphonie in drei Charakterbildern ... für grosses Orchester und Männer-Chor. Orchester Partitur ... Neue Auflage. pp. 328. *J. Schuberth & Co.: Leipzig, New York*, [1870?] 8°. **e. 58. e.**

— Eine Faust-Symphonie in drei Charakterbildern (nach Goethe). I. Faust. II. Gretchen. III. Mephistopheles und Schluss Chor: "Alles Vergängliche ist nur ein Gleichniss," für grosses Orchester und Männer-Chor. Orchester Partitur, *etc.* pp. 328. *J. Schuberth & Co.: Leipzig*, [1880?] 8°. **Hirsch M. 223.**

— [Another copy.] **R. M. 15. i. 4.**

— Eine Faust-Symphonie ... Mit Einführung von Dr. Georg Göhler. *E. Eulenburg: Leipzig*, [1917.] 8°. [*Eulenburg's kleine Orchester-Partitur-Ausgabe. Symphonien. No. 77.*] **b. 208. b.**

— Eine Faust-Symphonie (nach Goethe) in drei Characterbildern für grosses Orchester, Tenor-Solo und Männerchor ... Vorwort von Otto Peter Schneider. [Score.] pp. vi. 304. *Ernst Eulenburg: London; printed in Switzerland*, [1965?] 8°. [*Edition Eulenburg. no. 477.*] **b. 212.**

— Eine Faust-Symphonie in drei Charakterbildern (nach Goethe) ... Arrangement für 2 Pianofortes vom Componisten ... Neue revidirte Auflage. [Score.] pp. 77. *J. Schuberth & C⁰.: Leipzig, New York*, [1870.] fol. **h. 896. ff. (5.)**

— [A corrected issue.] Eine Faust-Symphonie in drei Charakterbildern (nach Goethe) ... Ausgabe für 2 Pianoforte vom Componisten, *etc.* pp. 77. *J. Schuberth & C⁰: Leipzig*, [c. 1890.] fol. **h. 896. q. (2.)**

— [Faust.—Lento assai.] *See* MacCabe (John) Fantasy on a Theme of Liszt (1967). [P. F.] [1969.] 4°. **g. 1128. yy. (8.)**

LISZT (FRANZ)

— [Faust.—Lento assai.] *See* Stevenson (Ronald) Prelude and Fugue on a Theme by Liszt. [Organ.] [1971.] 4°. **g. 1378. tt. (3.)**

— Gretchen ... Transcription für Pianoforte vom Componisten. pp. 17. *J. Schuberth & C⁰: Leipzig*, [1876.] fol. **h. 896. aa. (3.)**

— Feierlicher Marsch zum heiligen Gral. Aus dem Bühnenweihfestspiel Parsifal von R. Wagner. Für Pianoforte. pp. 11. *B. Schott's Söhne: Mainz*, [1883.] fol. **h. 896. gg. (6.)**

— [Another issue.] Marche solennelle vers le Saint Graal. Fragment du drame mystère Parsifal de R. Wagner pour piano. *Mayence*, [1883.] fol. **h. 356. f. (22.)**

— [Feierlicher Marsch zum heiligen Gral.] Marcia solenne al San Graal. Frammento del dramma mistico ... di Riccardo Wagner. Trascrizione per pianoforte di F. Liszt. pp. 9. *F. Lucca: Milano*, [c. 1885.] fol. **h. 356. cc. (2.)**

— Férfikari mise. *See infra:* [Missa quattuor vocum.]

Fest-Album zur Säcular-Feier von Goethe's Geburtstag

— Fest-Album zur Säcular-Feier von Goethe's Geburtstag am 28ᵗᵉⁿ August 1849 in Weimar ... I. Introduction. Fest Marsch. II. "Licht mehr Licht." (Goethes' letzte Worte.) Chorgesang. III. Weimars Todten! Gedicht von F. v. Schober, für Bariton oder Bass mit Orchester oder Piano. IV. Ueber allen Gipfeln is Ruh! (Solo Quartett.) V. Chor der Engel, aus Göthe's Faust. (2ᵗᵉʳ Theil.) Für Sopran und Altstimme mit Piano oder Harfe. Vollständiger Clavier-Auszug. pp. 42. *Schuberth & C⁰: Hamburg, New York*, [1849?] fol. *The later version of the "Fest Marsch," published separately, is entered below.* **H. 1878. h. (5.)**

— [No. 1.] Fest-Marsch zur Säcular-Feier von Goethe's Geburtstag am 28ᵗ August 1849 in Weimar ... Vollständiger Clavier-Auszug. pp. 8. *Schuberth & C⁰: Hamburg, New York*, [1849.] fol. *The wrapper bears the title "Goethe-Marsch".* **h. 585. j. (10.)**

— [No. 1.] (Göthe) Fest Marsch zur Göthe Jubiläum Feier für grosses Orchester ... Partitur. ⟨Neue revidirte Ausgabe.⟩ *J. Schubert & C⁰: Leipzig, New York*, [1870.] 8°. **e. 58. c.**

— [Another copy.] **R. M. 10. k. 5. (2.)**

— [No. 1.] Fest-Marsch zur Göthe Jubiläum-Feier für grosses Orchester ... Edit. für Piano à 2/ms ... Uebertragen für Pianoforte vom Componisten. pp. 15. *J. Schuberth & C⁰.: Hamburg, etc.*, [1859?] fol. **h. 896. ii. (8.)**

— [No. 1.] Fest-Marsch zur Göthe Jubiläum-Feier für grosses Orchester ... Edit. für Piano abgekürzte ... Uebertragen für Pianoforte vom Componisten. pp. 8. *J. Schuberth & C⁰: Hamburg, etc.*, [1859.] fol. **h. 585. j. (2.)**

— [No. 1.] Fest-Marsch zur Göthe Jubiläum-Feier für grosses Orchester ... Edit. für Piano à 4/ms ... Uebertragen für Pianoforte vom Componisten. pp. 23. *J. Schuberth & C⁰: Hamburg, etc.*, [1859?] fol. **h. 896. s. (5.)**

— [No. 1.] Göthe Fest Marsch zur Göthe Jubiläum Feier für grosses Orchester ... Edit. für Piano à 4 ms ... Uebertragen für Pianoforte vom Componisten. ⟨Neu revidirte Ausgabe.⟩ pp. 23. *J. Schuberth & C⁰: Leipzig, New-York*, [1870.] fol. **h. 585. m. (3.)**

— [No. 4.] Ueber allen Gipfeln ist Ruh. Solo Männer-Quartett mit Begleitung von 2 Hörnern.—Licht, mehr Licht! Männerchorgesang mit 2 Trompeten und 3 Posaunen, zur Göthe-Feier-Weimar componirt ... Partitur. *Schuberth & Co.: Hamburg, etc.*, [1860?] 8°. **E. 1644. d. (1.)**

LISZT (FRANZ)

— [No. 5.] Chor der Engel aus Göthe's Faust, II^{ter}. Theil., zur Säcular-Feier von Göthe's Geburtstag am 28ten August 1849 componirt ... für gemischten Chor. *J. Schuberth & Co.: Leipzig*, [1880?] 4°.　　　　　**G. 461. b. (4.)**

— Fest-Cantate componirt für die Inaugurations-Feier des Beethoven-Denkmales ... Text von V. L. B. Wolf ... Klavierauszug für 4 Hände. *Bei B. Schott's Söhnen: Mainz, etc.*, [1846.] fol.　　　　　**h. 896. a. (13.)**

— [Another copy.]　　　　　**Hirsch M. 949. (2.)**

— [Fest-Cantate.] *See* SAINT-SAËNS (C. C.) Improvisation sur la Beethoven-Cantate de F. Liszt, *etc.* [1870?] fol.
　　　　　h. 3181. j. (1.)

— Festgesang zur Eröffnung der zehnten Allgemeinen deutschen Lehrerversammlung, gedichtet von H. Hoffmann von Fallersleben, für vierstimmigen Männerchor mit beliebiger Begleitung der Orgel. Partitur. *T. F. A. Kühn: Weimar*, [1860?] 8°.　　　　　**E. 308. r. (22.)**

— Fest-Klänge. *See infra:* Symphonische Dichtungen. no. 7.

— Festlied [zu Schiller's Jubelfeier, 1859]. *See infra:* Für Männergesang. No. 11.

— Fest Marsch nach Motiven von E[rnst] H[erzog] z[u] S[achsen-Coburg-Gotha] für grosses Orchester. Partitur. *J. Schuberth & Co.: Leipzig*, [1865?] 8°.　　　　　**e. 58. g.**

— Festmarsch nach Motiven von E. H. Z. S. [i. e. from "Diana von Solange," an opera by Ernst, Herzog zu Sachsen-Coburg-Gotha] für grosses Orchester ... Edition für Piano a 2^m, *etc.* pp. 10. *J. Schuberth & Co.: Leipzig & New York*, [1860.] fol.　　　　　**Hirsch M. 952. (8.)**

— Fest Marsch nach Motiven von E. H. Z. S. [i. e. from "Diana von Solange," by Ernst, Herzog zu Sachsen-Coburg-Gotha] für grosses Orchester ... Edition für Piano à 4^m ... Die Pianoforte Uebertragung ist vom Componisten selbst. pp. 15. *J. Schuberth & Co: Leipzig, New York*, [1860.] fol.
　　　　　h. 896. v. (3.)

— Fest-Marsch zur Göthe Jubiläum-Feier. *See supra:* [Fest-Album zur Säcular-Feier von Goethe's Geburtstag. No. 1. Fest-Marsch.]

— [Fest-Polonaise.] Polonaise per pianoforte a 4 mani. ([Edited by] Piero Rattalino.) pp. 11. *G. Ricordi & c.: Milano*, [1972.] fol.　　　　　**g. 547. bb. (4.)**

— Fest-Vorspiel für grosses Orchester. Partitur, *etc.* pp. 23. *Eduard Hallberger: Stuttgart*, [1857.] 8°.　　　**f. 470. b. (2.)**

— Festvorspiel — Prélude. [P. F.] *See infra:* Das Pianoforte, *etc.* Jahrg. 1. Hft. 1. pp. 1–5. [1857.] fol.　　**h. 896. v. (6.)**

— La Fête villageoise. *See supra:* [Album d'un voyageur. No. 7.— Mélodie 3.]

— 2 feuilles d'album pour piano [in E major and A minor]. pp. 9. *Schuberth & Comp.: Leipzig & New York*, [1850?] fol. *Separate editions of these pieces are entered respectively under "Albumblatt" and "Die Zelle in Nonnenwerth".*
　　　　　Hirsch M. 951. (2.)

— Feuilles d'album. [A flat major. P. F.] pp. 3. *In:* PERIODICAL PUBLICATIONS.— *Paris.* [Le Monde musical.] Album de piano, *etc.* [1844?] fol.　　　　　**h. 62. n.**

— Feuilles d'album pour piano [in A flat]. pp. 3. *Chez les fils de B. Schott: Mayence*, [1844.] fol.　　**Hirsch M. 951. (1.)**

— Feuilles d'Album. [A flat major. P. F.] *B. Schott's Söhne: Mayence*, [c. 1890.] fol.　　　　　**h. 896. a. (6.)**

— Feux follets. *See supra:* [Études d'exécution transcendante. No. 5.]

LISZT (FRANZ)

— Ein Fichtenbaum steht einsam. (Poésie de H. Heine. Paroles françaises de G. Lagye.) [2 Settings.] *See supra:* [*Collected Works.— d.*] F. Liszt's gesammelte Lieder, *etc.* No. 16 bis.

— Der Fischerknabe. (Poésie de Schiller. Paroles françaises de G. Lagye.) *See supra:* [*Collected Works.— d.*] F. Liszt's gesammelte Lieder, *etc.* No. 7.

— Die Fischerstochter, von C. Coronini. *See supra:* [*Collected Works.— d.*] F. Liszt's gesammelte Lieder, *etc.* No. 52.

— "Der fliegende Holländer." Ballade von Richard Wagner. Transcription für Pianoforte. pp. 11. *C. F. Meser: Berlin, Dresden*, [1873.] fol.　　　　　**h. 585. b. (9.)**

— [Another copy.]　　　　　**h. 896. z. (8.)**

— [Le Forgeron.] A Kovács, férfikarra, tenor- és basszus szólóhangra, zongorakísérettel. F. Lamennais verse— Raics István fordítása ... Le Forgeron pour chœur d'hommes, deux voix seuls (ténor et basse), avec accompagnement de piano ... Rekonstruálta előadási jelekkel ellátta és elsőízben kiadta ... Szelényi István. *Hung. & Fr.* pp. 28. *Zeneműkiadó Vallalat: Budapest*, 1962. 8°.　　　　**F. 1196. aa. (2.)**

— Freudvoll und Leidvoll. (Poésie de Goethe. Paroles françaises de G. Lagye.) *See supra:* [*Collected Works.— d.*] F. Liszt's gesammelte Lieder, *etc.* No. 4.

— [Frühlingsnacht.] Spring Night. Nuit de printemps. Schumann— [Transcribed for P. F. by] Liszt. Edited ... by T. F. Dunhill. *Augener: London*, 1918. fol.　　**h. 896. g. (16.)**

— Für Männergesang. Partitur. 12 no. *C. F. Kahnt: Leipzig*, [1861.] 8°.　　　　　**E. 1644. d. (2.)**

— [Für Männergesang. No. 1. Vereinslied.] The Song of Brotherhood. [Part-song for male voices, words by] F. Hoare. *J. Curwen & Sons: London*, [1908.] 8°. *The Apollo Club, No. 417.*　　　　　**F. 667.**

— Grand galop chromatique, pour le piano forte. [Op. 12.] pp. 11. *Mori & Lavenu: London*, [1837.] fol.　　**h. 583. (4.)**

— Grand galop chromatique, pour le piano ... Op: [12]. pp. 11. *Chez Bernard Latte: Paris*, [1838?] fol.　　**h. 896. ii. (1.)**

— Grand galop chromatique ... pour le piano ... Oeuv. 12. pp. 15. *Chez Jean Ricordi: Milan*, [1838.] fol.　　**g. 547. w. (2.)**

— Grand galop chromatique pour le pianoforte ... Deuxième édition. Oeuv. 12. pp. 12. *Chez Fr. Hofmeister: Leipzig*, [c. 1840.] fol.　　　　　**h. 896. s. (10.)**

— Grand galop chromatique pour le pianoforte ... Deuxième édition. Oeuv. 12. pp. 13. *Chez Fr. Hofmeister: Leipzig*, [c. 1840.] fol.　　　　　**h. 896. n. (7.)**

— Grand galop chromatique pour pianoforte ... Op. 12. Troisième edition ... Édition facilitée. pp. 11. *Frédéric Hofmeister: Leipzig*, [1873.] fol.　　　**h. 585. b. (8.)**

— Grand galop chromatique pour pianoforte ... Op. 12. Troisième édition. Édition originale, *etc.* pp. 11. *Frédéric Hofmeister: Leipzig*, [c. 1880.] fol.　　**g. 547. u. (1.)**

— Grand Galop Chromatique. Op. 12. [P. F.] *See* SLOPER (E. H. L.) Repertory of select Pianoforte Works, *etc.* Third Series. No. 12. [1892, *etc.*] fol.　　　　　**h. 736. c.**

— Grand Galop chromatique ... (Op. 12. Piano.) Simplified edition. *Augener: London*, [1917.] fol.　　**h. 896. g. (15.)**

— Grand galop chromatique composé pour le piano à deux ou à quatre mains ... Oeuv. 12 ... à 4 mains. pp. 17. *Chez Fr. Hofmeister: Leipzig*, [1838.] fol.　**Hirsch M. 954. (2.)**

— Grand galop chromatique ... pour le piano à quatre mains ... Oeuv. 12. pp. 21. *Chez Jean Ricordi: Milan*, [1838.] fol.
　　　　　g. 547. w. (3.)

LISZT (Franz)

— Chromatischer Galopp orchestrirt von F. Doppler. [Orchestral parts.] *Leipzig*, [1880.] fol.   **h. 896. b. (3.)**

— [Grand galop chromatique.] *See* STRAUSS (J.) *the Elder.* Furioso-Galopp, nach Liszt's Motiven, für das Pianoforte ... Op. 114. [1840.] fol.   **h. 900. (20.)**

— Galop russe pour piano par F. Liszt. [Or rather, a transcription by him of a galop by Bulgakov.] pp. 7. *Chez M^{ce} Schlesinger: Paris*, [1844.] fol.   **h. 585. l. (1.)**

— Galop russe ... Composé par F. Liszt. [Or rather, a transcription by him of a galop by Bulgakov.] pp. 7. *C. Lonsdale: London*, [1847.] fol. [*Entretien chorégraphique. no. 5.*]   **h. 358.**

— Galop russe par Liszt. [Or rather, a transcription by him of a galop by Bulgakov.] pp. 5. *Campbell, Ransford & Co: London*, [1851.] fol.   **h. 895. (2.)**

— Der Gang um Mitternacht. [Words by] Herwegh. *See supra:* Für Männergesang. No. 10.

— Gaudeamus igitur. Humoreske für Orchester, Soli und Chor ... Partitur, *etc.* pp. 42. *J. Schuberth & Co.: Leipzig*, [1871.] fol.   **H. 1878. a. (3.)**

— Gaudeamus igitur. Humoreske für Orchester, Soli und Chor ... Für Pianoforte zu 2 Händen, *etc.* pp. 15. *J. Schuberth & Co.: Leipzig, New York*, [1871.] fol.   **h. 896. j. (5.)**

— Gaudeamus igitur. Paraphrase. [P. F.] pp. 17. *Bei Julius Hainauer: Breslau*, [1845?] fol.   **Hirsch M. 953. (1.)**

— Gaudeamus igitur—Humoreske. For four part chorus of men's voices with piano accompaniment ... Edited by Erich Kunzel. Lat. pp. 20. *Boosey & Hawkes: [New York*, 1961.] 8°. *Part of "Brown University choral Series".*   **F. 163. ss. (9.)**

— Gebet, von J. Bodenstedt. *See supra:* [*Collected Works.—d.*] F. Liszt's gesammelte Lieder, *etc.* No. 48.

— 3 Gedichte von Göthe. I. "Wer nie sein Brod mit Thränen ass." II. "Über allen Gipfeln ist Ruh." III. Lied aus Egmont. "Freudvoll, leidvoll" ... für eine Singstimme mit Begleitung des Pianoforte. pp. 39. *Bei Tobias Haslinger's Witwe und Sohn: Wien*, [1847.] fol.   **Hirsch M. 949. (1.)**

— [Geharnischte Lieder.] Trois chansons. No. I. Consolation. No. II. Avant la bataille. No. III. L'Espérance ... Transcription pour le piano. ⟨Transcr. fac. par Corno. [pseudonym of August Horn?]⟩ 3 no. *Chez C. F. Kahnt: Leipzig*, [1852.] fol.   **h. 896. j. (6.)**

— Geharnischte Lieder nach den Männer-Chorgesängen für das Pianoforte übertragen von Franz Liszt. pp. 11. *Bei C. F. Kahnt: Leipzig*, [1861.] fol.   **Hirsch M. 953. (2.)**

— La Gita in Gondola. *See infra:* Soirées musicales de Rossini. No. 4.

— Glanes de Woronince. 1. Ballade Ukraine ... 2. Mélodies polonaises. 3. Complainte, *etc.* [P. F.] pp. 19. *Chez Fr. Kistner: Leipsic*, [1849.] fol.   **h. 896. ii. (5.)**

— Glanes de Woronince pour piano. No. 1. Ballade ukraine ... No. 2. Mélodies polonaises. No. 3. Complainte, *etc.* *F. Kistner: Leipzig*, [1885?] fol.   **h. 896. d. (1.)**

— [Glanes de Woronince.] Mélodies polonaises. [1898.] *See* PERLES. Perles Musicales, *etc.* No. 87. [1890, *etc.*] fol.   **h. 3270.**

— Die Glocken des Strassburger Münsters. Gedicht von H. W. Longfellow [begins: "Hasten, hasten"] für Bariton-Solo, Chor und Orchester. Partitur. *Leipzig*, [1875.] fol.   **H. 1878. a. (1.)**

— Der Glückliche, von Wilbrand. *See supra:* [*Collected Works.—d.*] F. Liszt's gesammelte Lieder, *etc.* No. 54.

LISZT (Franz)

— Gnomenreigen. *See supra:* Zwei Concertetuden, *etc.* No. 2.

— Go not, happy day. Song. *London*, [1880.] fol. *No. 18 of "Tennyson's Songs".*   **H. 2107. (18.)**

— God save the Queen. Grande paraphrase de concert pour piano. *Hambourg, etc.*, [1850?] fol.   **g. 443. i. (5.)**

— God save the Queen. Vierte Paraphrase. Piano. ⟨Edited by Thomas A. Johnson.⟩ pp. 11. *Hinrichsen Edition: London*, [1953.] 4°.   **g. 547. l. (2.)**

— (Göthe) Fest Marsch, *etc. See supra:* [Fest-Album.— Fest-Marsch zur Säcular-Feier von Goethe's Geburtstag.]

— Goethe-Marsch. *See supra:* [Fest-Album.—Fest-Marsch zur Säcular-Feier von Goethe's Geburtstag.]

— Gondoliera. *See supra:* [Années de pèlerinage. Seconde année. Supplément No. 1.]

— Gottes ist der Orient. [Words by] Göthe. *See supra:* Für Männergesang ... No. 12.

— Great is Jehovah, the Lord ... Solo for a tenor voice ... by F. Schubert. Arranged with an accompaniment of men's voices ... by F. Liszt. *See* NOVELLO AND CO. Novello's Collection of Anthems, *etc.* Vol. XI. No. 223. [1876, *etc.*] 8°.   **E. 618. a.**

— Great is Jehovah the Lord ... F. Schubert ... Arrangement by F. Liszt adapted ... by J. E. West. 1911. *See* NOVELLO AND CO. Novello's Collection of Anthems, *etc.* No. 987. [1876, *etc.*] 8°.   **E. 618. a.**

— Great is Jehovah the Lord ... Composed by Schubert ... Arrangement by E. Liszt, *etc.* [1911.] *See* NOVELLO AND CO. Novello's Tonic Sol-fa Series. No. 1985. [1876, *etc.*] 4°.   **B. 885.**

— Gretchen. *See supra:* [Eine Faust-Symphonie.]

— Hallelujah (d'Arcadelt) pour piano par François Liszt. [In fact an original work by Liszt.] pp. 13. [1865.] fol. *See* ARCHADELT (J.) [*Doubtful and Supposititious Works.*]   **h. 896. k. (11.)**

— Halloh! Jagdchor und Steyrer aus der Oper Tony von E[rnst] H[erzog] zu S[achsen] C[oburg] G[otha] für das Pianoforte übertragen. *Leipzig*, [1855?] 4°.   **g. 547. (9.)**

— Hamlet. *See infra:* Symphonische Dichtungen. no. 10.

— Hangnemnélküli bagatell. *See supra:* [Bagatelle ohne Tonart.]

— Harmonies du soir. *See supra:* [Études d'exécution transcendante. No. 11.]

Harmonies poëtiques et religieuses

— Harmonies poëtiques et religieuses pour le pianoforte seul, *etc.* pp. 9. *Chez Frédéric Hofmeister: Leipzig*, [1835.] fol.   **Hirsch M. 951. (3.)**

— Harmonies poëtiques et religieuses. [P. F.] With Lamartin's [*sic*] advertisement. pp. 7. *Wessel & Co: London*, [c. 1840.] fol. *Wessel & C^{os} Collection of the Grand Solos for the Piano Forte composed by Fran^s Liszt. no. 3.*   **h. 896. r. (2.)**

— Harmonies poëtiques et religieuses pour le piano ... Liv. I. N° 1. Invocation. N° 2. Ave Maria, *etc.* ⟨Liv. III. N° 4. Pensée des morts.⟩ 2 no. *Fr. Kistner: Leipzig*, [1853.] fol. *Imperfect; wanting liv. II, IV–VII.*   **h. 896. i. (3.)**

— Harmonies poëtiques et religieuses pour piano. liv. 5, 6. *Fr. Kistner: Leipzig*, [c. 1900.] fol. *Imperfect; wanting liv. 1–4, 7.*   **h. 896. z. (5.)**

— [Harmonies poëtiques et religieuses. P. F.] no. 2–6, 10. *Fr. Kistner: Leipzig*, [1905?] fol. *Without titlepage. Imperfect; wanting no. 1, 7–9.*   **Hirsch M. 948. (1.)**

LISZT (Franz)

—— [No. 3.] Bénédiction de Dieu dans la Solitude, *etc.* [P. F.] *Augener & Co.: London*, [1900.] fol.   **h. 896. c. (7.)**

—— [No. 3.] Bénédiction de Dieu dans la Solitude. *See* Ziloti (A. I.) Alexander Siloti Concert Repertoire. Piano transcriptions, *etc.* [No. 5.] 1923. 4°.   **g. 1267.**

—— Die heilige Cäcilia. Legende, gedichtet von Madame Emile de Girardin. Für eine Mezzo-Sopran-Stimme mit Chor (ad libitum) und Orchester … Begleitung … Sainte Cécile. Légende … Partitur, *etc.* ⟨Anhang.⟩ pp. 57. iv.   *C. F. Kahnt: Leipzig*, [1876.] fol.
The titlepage bears the autograph signature of A. W. Gottschalg.   **Hirsch IV. 828.**

—— Die heilige Cäcilia. Legende, gedichtet von Mdme. E. de Girardin, für eine Mezzo-Sopran-Stimme mit Chor—ad libitum—und Orchester oder Pianoforte, Harmonium und Harfe … Klavier-Auszug.   *C. F. Kahnt: Leipzig*, [1876.] 8°.   **E. 1644. f.**

—— Der Heilige Franziskus von Paula auf den Wogen schreitend. *See infra:* [Légendes. No. 2.]

—— Heldenklage. *See infra:* [Symphonische Dichtungen. No. 8. Héroïde funèbre.]

—— Héroïde funèbre. *See infra:* Symphonische Dichtungen. no. 8.

—— Heroischer Marsch in ungarischem Styl für das Piano-Forte. pp. 13.   *In der Schlesinger'schen Buch- u. Musikhandlung: Berlin*, [1844?] fol.   **Hirsch M. 951. (4.)**

—— Heroischer Marsch in ungarischem Styl … Neu herausgegeben von Ferruccio Busoni. [P. F.] pp. 14. *Schlesinger'sche Buch & Musikhandlung: Berlin*, [1905.] fol.   **h. 896. n. (2.)**

Hexameron

—— Hexameron. Morceau de concert. Grandes variations de bravoure pour piano sur la marche des Puritains de Bellini. Composées … par MM. Liszt, Thalberg, Pixis, Henri Herz, Czerny et Chopin. [Edited, and with sections composed by F. Liszt.] pp. 31.   *Chez Tob. Haslinger: Vienne*, [1839.] fol.   **h. 896. l. (4.)**

—— Hexameron, morceau de concert … Grandes variations de bravoure, pour piano, sur la marche des Puritains de Bellini, composées par MM. Liszt, Thalberg, Pixis, Henri Herz, Czerny et Chopin, *etc.* [Edited, and with sections composed, by F. Liszt.] pp. 27.   *Cramer & Co.: London*, [1840?] fol.   **h. 896. h. (15.)**

—— Morceau de concert. Grandes variations de bravoure pour piano sur la marche des Puritains de Bellini, composées … par MM. Liszt, Thalberg, Pixis, Henri Herz, Czerny et Chopin. [Edited, and with sections composed, by F. Liszt.] pp. 27.   *Chez Jean Ricordi: Milan*, [c. 1840.] fol.   **h. 3865. ee. (16.)**

—— Hexaméron. Morceau de concert. Grandes variations de bravoure pour piano sur la marche des Puritains de Bellini composées … par MM. Liszt, Thalberg, Pixis, Henri Herz, Czerny et Chopin. pp. 27.   *Chez E. Troupenas & Cⁱᵉ.: [Paris, c. 1850.]* fol.   **h. 896. ii. (7.)**

—— Grandes variations de concert sur un thème des "Puritains" [by Bellini] tirée [sic] du "Hexameron" composé par Thalberg, Herz, Pixis, Czerny, Chopin et Liszt. Pour deux pianos, *etc.* [Score.] pp. 26.   *J. Schuberth & Cⁱᵉ: Leipsic, New-York*, [1870.] fol.
In this version the variations by Pixis, Czerny and Chopin are omitted. Two copies.   **h. 896. jj. (2.)**

—— Der Hirt. [Words by Schiller.] *See supra:* [*Collected Works.—d.*] F. Liszt's gesammelte Lieder, *etc.* No. 8.

LISZT (Franz)

—— [Hochzeitsmarsch und Elfenreigen aus der Musik zu Shakespeare's Sommernachtstraum.] Wedding March and Dance of the Fairies. From Mendelssohn's Music to Shakespeare's "Midsummer-Night's Dream". Transcribed for the Pianoforte by F. Liszt. *See* Paull Music Co. Edition Paull, *etc.* [No. 37.] (1905.) fol.   **h. 3822. (37.)**

—— Hohe Liebe. *See infra:* [Drei Lieder für eine Sopran- oder Tenorstimme. No. 1.]

—— A holt kötlő szerelme. Irta: Jókai Mór. Melodrámai zenéjét szerzé Liszt Ferenc. [P. F.] *In:* Kőrösi (H.) Jókai 1825–1925. emlékkönyv, *etc.* pp. 85–93. 1925. 8°.   **X. 900/3319.**

—— Homage to Mendelssohn. Seven Lieder ohne Worte. For the Piano Forte, transcribed by F. Liszt. *London*, [1845.] fol.   **h. 584. (4.)**

—— How wonderful for Hearts. *See supra:* [Es muss ein Wunderbares sein.]

—— Huldigungs-Marsch für das Piano-Forte. pp. 10.   *Bei Ed. Bote & G. Bock: Berlin und Posen*, [1858.] fol.   **h. 585. (8.)**

——[Another copy.]   **R. M. 25. i. 3. (5.)**

—— Huldigungs-Marsch für das Piano-Forte. pp. 10.   *Ed. Bote & G. Bock: Berlin & Posen*, [1865.] fol.   **Hirsch M. 951. (5.)**

—— Hungaria. *See infra:* Symphonische Dichtungen. no. 9.

—— Hungaria. 1848. Kantáta basszus-, tenor- és szoprán-szólóra, valamint férfikarra, zongorakísérettel … Német szöveg … Franz Schober. Magyar szöveg … László Zsigmond. Revideálta és első ízben kiadta … Szelényi István. *Hung. & Ger.* pp. 36.   *Zeneműkiadó Vállalat: Budapest*, 1961. 4°.   **F. 566. b. (2.)**

—— Hunnen-Schlacht. *See infra:* Symphonische Dichtungen. no. 11.

—— Hussiten-Lied aus dem 15ᵗᵉⁿ Jahrhunderte, für das Pianoforte gesetzt … von Fr. Liszt. pp. 13.   *Bei Joh. Hoffmann: Prag*, [1840.] fol.   **g. 547. p. (7.)**

—— Hussiten-Lied aus dem 15ᵗᵉⁿ Jahrhunderte, für das Pianoforte zu vier Händen. pp. 15.   *Bei Joh. Hoffmann: Prag*, [1840?] fol.   **Hirsch M. 953. (3.)**

—— Hymne de l'enfant à son reveil [begins: "O Père"]. Poésie de Lamartine, composée pour choeur de femmes avec accompagnement d'Harmonium, *etc.* *Budapest*, [1875.] 8°.   **E. 1644. a. (2.)**

—— [Hymne de l'enfant à son réveil.] Des erwachenden Kindes Lobgesang. Gedicht von Lamartine: deutsche Uebersetzung von Cornelius, für Chor von Frauenstimmen mit Harmonium- oder Pianoforte-Begleitung und Harfe (ad libitum) … Partitur & Stimmen, *etc. Fr., Ger. & Hung. Ferdinand Táborszky: Budapest*, [c. 1890.] 8°.
Imperfect; wanting the part for soprano 1 and alto. With two copies of the part for soprano 2, one of which bears the imprint of Josef Weinberger, Wien.   **E. 270. qq. (8.)**

—— L'Hymne du Pape. *See infra:* [Der Papst-Hymnus.]

—— Ich liebe dich, von Rückert. *See supra:* [*Collected Works.—d.*] F. Liszt's gesammelte Lieder, *etc.* No. 39.

—— Ich möchte hingehn, von Herwegh. *See supra:* [*Collected Works.—d.*] F. Liszt's gesammelte Lieder, *etc.* No. 34.

—— Ich scheide, von Hoffmann von Fallersleben. *See supra:* [*Collected Works.—d.*] F. Liszt's gesammelte Lieder, *etc.* No. 42.

—— Ich verlor die Kraft und das Leben. (A. Meissner.) *See supra:* [*Collected Works.—d.*] F. Liszt's gesammelte Lieder, *etc.* No. 57.

—— Die Ideale. *See infra:* Symphonische Dichtungen. no. 12.

LISZT (Franz)

— L'Idée fixe. Andante amoroso pour le piano d'après une mélodie de H. Berlioz. pp. 7. *Chez Pietro Mechetti: Vienne*, [1847.] fol.   **Hirsch M. 953. (4.)**

— [L'Idée fixe.] Andante amoroso. [P. F. On a theme from Berlioz's Épisode de la vie d'un artiste.] *In:* Album des pianistes, *etc.* pp. 16–21. 1847. fol.   **h. 3870. w.**

— Ihr Glocken von Marling. *See* supra: [*Collected Works.— d.*] F. Liszt's gesammelte Lieder, *etc.* No. 55.

— Il m'aimait tant (er liebte mich so sehr), mélodie, paroles de Mᵐᵉ Emile de Girardin, *etc.* pp. 5. *Chez les fils de B. Schott: Mayence*, [1843.] fol.
L'Aurore. no. 51.   **Hirsch M. 949. (3.)**

— Il m'aimait tant!! [Song.] Paroles de Mᵐᵉ Émile de Girardin. pp. 5. *Chez Bernard-Latte: Paris*, [1845?] fol.
                                                  Hirsch M. 1297. (35.)

— Il m'aimait tant!— Er liebte micht so sehr.— Mélodie. (Paroles de Mᵈᵐᵉ de Girardin … Uebersetzung von M. G. Friedrich.) *Les Fils de Schott: Mayence*, [c. 1880.] fol.
No. 51 of "L'Aurora. Collection de Morceaux de chant, etc".
                                                      H. 1878. c. (6.)

— Il m'aimait tant. Mélodie transcrite pour le piano, *etc. Les Fils de B. Schott: Mayence, etc.*, [c. 1880.] fol.   **h. 896. a. (10.)**

— Illustrations de l'opéra L'Africaine de G. Meyerbeer pour piano … N° 1. Prière des matelots. Oh! grand Saint Dominique. N° 2. Marche indienne. 2 no. *Ed. Bote & G. Bock: Berlin, Posen*, [1866.] fol.   **g. 547. p. (8.)**
                                                      & h. 585. k. (8.)

— Illustrations du Prophète de G. Meyerbeer. N° 1. Prière. Hymne triomphal. Marche du sacre. N° 2. Les Patineurs. N° 3. Pastorale. Appel aux armes. Pour le piano. no. 1, 3. *Breitkopf & Härtel: Leipzig*, [1849.] fol.
Imperfect; wanting no. 2.   **h. 896. i. (4.)**
                                                      & g. 547. o. (4.)

— Illustrations du Prophète de G. Meyerbeer. N° 1, Prière. Hymne triomphal. Marche du sacre. N° 2, Les Patineurs. N° 3. Pastorale. Appel aux armes. Pour le piano, *etc.* no. 2. *Chez Breitkopf & Härtel: Leipzig*, [c. 1870.] fol.
Imperfect; wanting no. 1, 3.   **g. 547. q. (1.)**

— [Illustrations du Prophète de G. Meyerbeer. No. 2.] Illustrations du Prophète, (Les Patineurs,) pour piano, par F. Liszt. pp. 23. *Chappell: London*, [1852.] fol.   **h. 895. (6.)**

— [Illustrations du Prophète de G. Meyerbeer. No. 2.] Le Prophète. Les Patineurs, pour piano. pp. 23. *Augener & Co.: London*, [1886.] 4°.   **g. 547. a. (1.)**

— L'Impatience. Air de F. Schubert, transcrit par F. Liszt. [P. F.] *M. Berwald: St. Petersbourg*, [1875?] fol.
No. 18, Année 8 of "Revue Musicale pour le Piano".
                                                      h. 896. d. (5.)

— Impromptu pour piano. pp. 5. *Breitkopf & Härtel: Leipzig*, [1877.] fol.
Der Improvisator. no. 14.   **h. 896. j. (7.)**

— Impromptu brillant pour le piano-forte, sur des thèmes de Rossini & Spontini … Opéra 3. pp. 12. *Chez Mᵉˡˡᵉˢ Erard: Paris*, [1825.] fol.   **h. 722. ll. (2.)**

— Impromptu brillant for the Piano Forte on Themes of Rossini and Spontini … Op. 3. pp. 12. *T. Boosey: London*, [1825.] fol.   **h. 583. (2.)**

— Impromptu pour le piano sur des thèmes de Rossini et Spontini … Oeuvre 3. pp. 11. *Chez Pietro Mechetti: Vienne*, [1841.] fol.   **Hirsch M. 953. (5.)**

— Improvisata sur le ranz des vaches da Ferd. Huber. *See* supra: [Album d'un voyageur. No. 10–12.] Trois airs suisses. no. 1.

LISZT (Franz)

— In Liebeslust, von Hoffmann v. Fallersleben. *See* supra: [*Collected Works.— d.*] F. Liszt's gesammelte Lieder, *etc.* No. 33.

— In Rome. *See* supra: [Ave Maria. Raabe No. 67.]

— L'Invito. *See* infra: Soirées musicales de Rossini. No. 3.

— Jeanne d'Arc au bucher (Johanna beim Scheiterhaufen), romance dramatique, paroles d'Alexandre Dumas, *etc.* pp. 9. *Chez les fils de B. Schott: Mayence*, [1846.] fol.
                                                      Hirsch M. 949. (4.)

— Jeanne d'Arc au bûcher. Scène dramatique. Paroles d'Alex. Dumas, composées pour mezzo-soprano avec accompagnement d'orchestre. Partition d'orchestre, *etc.* pp. 36. *Chez les fils de B. Schott: Mayence*, [1877.] 8°.
                                                      E. 1644. a. (4.)

— Jesu, give Thy Servants. *See* infra: [9 Kirchen-Chor-Gesänge. No. 7. Ave Maris Stella.]

— Jesu, Word of God incarnate. *See* infra: [12 Kirchen-Chor-Gesänge. No. 5. Ave verum.]

— Jesus, Loving Saviour. *See* infra: [9 Kirchen-Chor-Gesänge. No. 7. Ave Maris stella.]

— Les Jeux d'eaux à la Villa d'Este. *See* supra: [Années de pèlerinage. Troisième année. No. 4.]

— Jugendglück, von R. Pohl. *See* supra: [*Collected Works.— d.*] F. Liszt's gesammelte Lieder, *etc.* No. 36.

— Kennst du das Land. *See* supra: [Buch der Lieder. Bd. 1. No. 3.]

Kirchen-Chor-Gesänge

— Neun Kirchen-Chor-Gesänge mit Orgelbegleitung … Partitur, *etc.* pp. 45. *Bei C. F. Kahnt: Leipzig*, [1871.] 8°.
                                                      F. 566. c.

— Zwölf Kirchen-Chor-Gesänge mit Orgel-Begleitung … Partitur. *C. F. Kahnt: Leipzig*, [1882.] 8°.   **F. 566. a.**

— [No. 1, 2.] Pater Noster und Ave Maria für Chorgesang mit Orgel, *etc.* pp. 8. *Friedrich Pustet: Regensburg*, 1870. 8°.
                                                      E. 605. p. (8.)

— [No. 3, 4.] O Salutaris and Tantum ergo for four female voices. *See* Seymour (J.) Curwen's Latin Series, *etc.* No. 5. [1896.] 8°.   **F. 974.**

— [No. 2.] Ave Maria … Für das Pianoforte vom Komponisten. [D flat major.] pp. 9. *C. F. Kahnt: Leipzig*, [1873.] fol.
                                                      h. 896. z. (6.)

— [No. 5.] Ave verum. Arranged for Chorus of Mixed Voices by P. James. Alternative English text by R. Robinson, *etc. H. W. Gray Co.: New York*, 1943. 8°.   **E. 335. l. (2.)**

— [No. 5. Ave verum.] Jesu, Word of God incarnate … For SATB chorus. English text by Walter Ehret … Ed. by Walter Ehret. *Eng. & Lat.* pp. 5. *Chappell & Co.: New York*, [1967.] 8°.
Part of "Mastersinger Series for Choir".   **E. 335. ff. (31.)**

— [No. 7.] Ave maris stella. Hymnus ad quatuor voces inaequales et organum. *C. F. Kahnt: Lipsiae*, [1865.] 8°.
                                                      F. 1171. q. (3.)

— [No. 7. Ave Maris Stella.] Jesu, give Thy Servants … Anthem for four voices. English Words by W. C. Dix. 1886. *See* Periodical Publications.— *London*. The Musical Times, *etc.* No. 523. 1844, *etc.* 8°.   **P. P. 1945. aa.**

— [No. 7. Ave Maris Stella.] Jesus, loving Saviour. Anthem … English text by H. A. Dickinson … Edited by C. Dickinson. *H. W. Gray Co.: New York*, 1930. 8°.   **E. 335. f. (17.)**

LISZT (Franz)

— [No. 7. Ave Maris Stella.] Jesu give Thy Servants ... Full
Anthem ... the English words by W. C. Dix. *See* Novello
and Co. Novello's Tonic Sol-fa Series. No. 520. [1886.] 4°.
B. 885.

— [No. 8. O salutaris hostia.] O Lord above, whose Sacrifice ...
S. A. T. B., a cappella. English text by C. M. ... Edited by
Charles Marshall. *Eng. & Lat.* pp. 4. *Frank Music Corp.:
New York*, [1965.] 8°.
E. 1439. u. (4.)

— [4 kleine Klavierstücke. No. 3, 4.] Two Browning Choruses.
⟨S. A. T. B.⟩ Poems by Elizabeth Barrett Browning. ⟨Music
adapted by Gordon Binkerd.⟩ I. The Lost Bower. II. The Little
Friend. pp. 10. *Boosey & Hawkes:* [*New York*, 1976.] 8°.
F. 1874. bb. (24.)

— Kling leise mein Lied. Ständchen. Poésie de Nordmann.
Paroles françaises de G. Lagye. *See* supra: [*Collected
Works.—d.*] F. Liszt's gesammelte Lieder, *etc.* No. 27.

— Der König von Thule. *See* supra: [Buch der Lieder. Bd. 1.
No. 4.]

Koronázási mise

— Koronázási mise ⟨Missa coronationalis⟩ ... Partitura. pp. 100.
Schuberth J. & Farsa: Leipzig, [1870?] fol.
The cover bears the title "Ungarische Krönungs-Messe".
G. 461.

— Missa coronationalis. Krönungsmesse ... Edited by Imre
Sulyok. [Score.] pp. 110. *Ernst Eulenburg: London, etc.;
printed in Switzerland*, [1968.] 8°.
[*Edition Eulenburg. no.* 941.]
b. 212.

— Krönungs Messe ... Clavier Auszug, *etc.* pp. 76. *J. Schuberth
& Cᵒ: Leipzig, New York*, [1871?] 8°.
F. 1183. h. (1.)

— Missa coronationalis. Klavierauszug mit Singstimmen ...
Herausgegeben von ... Imre Sulyok. pp. 78. *Ernst
Eulenburg, etc.: London*, [1970.] 8°.
[*Eulenburg General Music Series.* 1.]
e. 526.

— Aus der Ungarischen Krönungs Messe. Benedictus.
Offertorium ... Orchester-Partitur, *etc.* 2 no. *J. Schuberth &
Co.: Leipzig, New York*, [1867.] fol.
Hirsch IV. 832.

— Aus der Ungarischen Krönungs Messe. Benedictus.
Offertorium ... für Pianoforte zu 2 Händen, *etc. J. Schuberth
& Cᵒ.: Leipzig, New-York*, [1871.] fol.
Imperfect; wanting the "Benedictus".
g. 547. kk. (1.)

— [Graduale.] Psalm 116 für Chor mit Piano-Forte. *J. Schuberth
& Co.: Leipzig, etc.*, [1871.] 8°.
E. 1644. d. (4.)

— A Kovács. *See* supra: [Le Forgeron.]

— Krönungs Messe. *See* supra: [Koronázási mise.]

— Künstler-Festzug. *See* infra: Zur Schiller-Feier—1859.

— The Land we love for ever! *See* infra: [Vierstimmige
Männergesänge. No. 1. Rheinweinlied.]

— Lasst mich ruhen, von Hoffmann von Fallersleben. *See*
supra: [*Collected Works.—d.*] F. Liszt's gesammelte Lieder,
etc. No. 31.

— Lebe wohl! von P. Horvath. *See also* supra: [*Collected
Works.—d.*] F. Liszt's gesammelte Lieder, *etc.* No. 44.

— Lebe Wohl! Isten veled ... Ungarische Romanze ... für eine
Violine mit Begleitung des Pianoforte gesetzt von E. Rentsch.
Leipzig, [1885.] fol.
h. 585. g. (4.)

LISZT (Franz)

Die Legende von der heiligen Elisabeth

— Die Legende von der heiligen Elisabeth. Oratorium nach
Worten von Otto Roquette ... Partitur. pp. iv. 313. *Bei
C. F. Kahnt: Leipzig*, [1869.] fol.
H. 1878. d.

— [Another copy.]
Hirsch IV. 831.

— Die Legende von der heiligen Elisabeth. Oratorium ... Kleine
Partitur. Text deutsch, englisch, französisch, *etc.* ⟨Dichtung
von O. Roquette. English words by John Bernhoff. Paroles
françaises de Gustave Lagye.⟩ pp. 313. *C. F. Kahnt
Nachfolger: Leipzig*, [c. 1890.] 8°.
F. 566. d.

— Die Legende von der heiligen Elisabeth. Oratorium nach
Worten von Otto Roquette ... Klavier-Auszug. pp. 195. *Bei
C. F. Kahnt: Leipzig*, [c. 1870.] 8°.
E. 1644.

— Die Legende von der heiligen Elisabeth. (The Legend of
Saint Elizabeth.) Oratorium ... ⟨Dichtung von O. Roquette.
English words by John Bernhoff.⟩ Klavierauszug mit Text,
etc. Ger. & Eng. pp. iii. 205. *C. F. Kahnt Nachfolger: Leipzig*,
[c. 1910.] 8°.
"In die Universal-Edition aufgenommen."
E. 1644. o.

— Drei Stücke aus der Legende der heiligen Elisabeth ... 1.
Orchester Einleitung. 2. Marsch der Kreuzritter. 3.
Interludium. Pianoforte-Arrangement vom Componisten.
3 no. *Bei C. F. Kahnt: Leipzig*, [1869.] 4°.
f. 470. e. (3.)

— [A reissue.] Drei Stücke aus der Legende der heiligen
Elisabeth ... 1. Orchester Einleitung. 2. Marsch der
Kreuzritter. 3. Interludium. Pianoforte-Arrangement vom
Componisten. no. 2. *Bei C. F. Kahnt: Leipzig*, [1875.] 8°.
Imperfect; wanting no. 1, 3.
f. 470. c.

— Gebet und Kirchenchor ... für die Orgel ... bearbeitet von
B. Sulze. *See* Album. Album für Orgel-Spieler, *etc.* Lief. 62.
[1880? *etc.*] *obl.* fol.
e. 119.

— Einleitung zur Legende von der heiligen Elisabeth für Orgel
übertragen von Müller-Hartung. *See* Album. Album für
Orgel-Spieler, *etc.* Lief. 14. [1880? *etc.*] *obl.* fol.
e. 119.

— March of the Crusaders ... arranged for the Piano by
W. Byrom. *London*, [1869.] fol.
h. 1485. d. (34.)

— March of the Crusaders ... arranged for the Organ by
W. Byrom. *London*, [1878.] fol.
h. 2731. f. (29.)

Légendes

— Légendes pour piano. 1. St. François d'Assise, "La
prédication aux oiseaux". 2. St. François de Paule marchant
sur les flots. no. 1. *Chez Rózsavölgyi & Co.: Pest*, [1866.] fol.
Imperfect; wanting no. 2.
Hirsch M. 951. (6.)

— Légendes pour piano. 1. St. François d'Assise, "La prédiction
aux oiseaux". 2. St. François de Paule marchant sur les flots.
no. 2. *Rozsavölgyi & cᵈᵉ: Budapest et Leipsic*, [1875?] fol.
Imperfect; wanting no. 1.
h. 896. i. (6.)

— Two Legends. 1. St. François d'Assise. "La Prédication aux
oiseaux". 2. St. François de Paule marchant sur les flots. [P. F.
Edited by] Emil von Sauer. pp. 30. *Edition Peters: London;
etc.*, [c. 1970.] 4°.
g. 547. z. (2.)

— [No. 1.] La Prédication aux Oiseaux.—The Sermon to the
Birds.— ... Revised and fingered by O. Thümer. [P. F.]
Augener: London, [1908.] 4°.
g. 719. a. (3.)

— [No. 1.] Die Vogelpredigt des heiligen Franz von Assisi ...
Für Orchester bearbeitet von Felix Mottl. Partitur, *etc.* pp. 37.
Rózsavölgyi & Co.: Budapest; Leipzig [printed, 1890.] 8°.
e. 58. k. (1.)

— [No. 2.] Légende. St. François de Paule marchant sur les flots.
Revised, phrased and fingered by O. Thümer. [P. F.]
Augener: London, (1914.) 4°.
g. 547. d. (6.)

LISZT (FRANZ)

— [No. 2.] St. Francois de Paule marchant sur les flots. *See* ZILOTI (A. I.) Alexander Siloti Concert Repertoire. Piano transcriptions, *etc.* [No. 8.] 1923. 4°.　　**g. 1267.**

— [No. 2.] Der Heilige Franziskus von Paula auf den Wogen schreitend. Übertragung der Klavierkomposition ... für die Orgel durch Max Reger (1901), herausgegeben von Gerd Sievers. pp. 19. *Breitkopf & Härtel: Wiesbaden*, [1978?] obl. 4°.　　**e. 58. m. (3.)**

— Lenore. Ballade von G. A. Bürger. Mit melodramatischer Pianoforte-Begleitung zur Declamation. pp. 19. *Bei C. F. Kahnt: Leipzig*, [1860.] fol.　　**H. 1878. h. (3.)**

— Leyer und Schwerdt nach Carl Maria von Weber und Körner, Heroide, für das Pianoforte ... Schwerdtlied. Lützow's wilde Jagd. Gebet. pp. 14. *In der Schlesinger'schen Buch u. Musikhandlung: Berlin*, [1848.] fol.　　**Hirsch M. 953. (6.)**

— Licht, mehr Licht! *See* supra: [Fest-Album zur Säcular-Feier von Goethe's Geburtstag.]

— Liebesszene und Fortuna's Kugel aus "Die sieben Todsünden" ... von A. von Goldschmidt. Phantasiestück für Pianoforte. *Hannover*, [1880.] fol.　　**h. 585. f. (4.)**

— Liebesträume. *See* infra: [Drei Lieder für eine Sopran- oder Tenor-Stimme.]

— Das Lied der Begeisterung [begins: "Was nützt mir"]. Text von C. Abrányi Jun. für vierstimmigen Männerchor. *Budapest*, [1875.] 8°.　　**E. 1644. a. (1.)**

— Drei Lieder aus J. Wolff's Tannhäuser componirt von O. Lessmann. Transcription für Pianoforte. 3 no. *Berlin*, [1883.] fol.　　**h. 585. f. (11.)**

— Lieder aus Schiller's "Wilhelm Tell". I. Der Fischerknabe. II. Der Hirt. III. Der Alpenjäger ... für eine Singstimme mit Begleitung des Pianoforte. pp. 24. *Bei Tobias Haslinger's Witwe und Sohn: Wien*, [1848.] fol.　　**Hirsch M. 949. (5.)**

— Drei Lieder aus Schillers "Wilhelm Tell" für eine Tenorstimme. Nº 1. Der Fischerknabe ... Nº 2. Der Hirt ... Nº 3. Der Alpenjäger, *etc.* ⟨Lieder mit Orchester.⟩ [Score.] pp. 40. *C. F. Kahnt Nachfolger: Leipzig*, [1871.] 8°.　　**E. 1644. h.**

Drei Lieder für eine Sopran- oder Tenor-Stimme

— Drei Lieder für eine Sopran- oder Tenor-Stimme, mit Begleitung des Pianoforte. pp. 13. *Bei Fr. Kistner: Leipzig*, [1850.] fol.　　**Hirsch M. 949. (6.)**

— Liebesträume.—Dreams of Love.— ... No. 1. ... Hohe Liebe. No. 2. ... Seliger Tod. No. 3. ... O Lieb' ... Songs ... with English and German words. *Augener & Co.: London*, [1904.] 4°.　　**G. 383. f. (6.)**

— Liebesträume. 3 Notturnos für das Pianoforte. pp. 22. *Bei Fr. Kistner: Leipzig*, [1850.] fol.　　**g. 547. t. (8.)**

— Liebestraum ... Notturno No. 1 (–3) for the Pianoforte. 3 no. *R. Cocks & Co.: London*, [1897.] fol.　　**h. 896. c. (3.)**

— Liebesträume. Revised, phrased and fingered by H. Germer. pp. 19. *Bosworth & Co.: London*, [1899.] 4°.　　**g. 547. t. (4.)**

— Liebesträume.—Dreams of Love.—Transcriptions for the Pianoforte ... No. 1, in A flat. Hohe Liebe. No. 2, in E. Seliger Tod. No. 3, in A flat. O Lieb'. *Augener & Co.: London*, [1904.] 4°.　　**g. 547. c. (5.)**

— Liebesträume.—Dreams of Love.—Three Nocturnes for Pianoforte. *Orpheus Music Publishing Co.: London*, [1909.] 4°. *The Guildhall Edition, No. 37.*　　**g. 1440.**

LISZT (FRANZ)

— Liebesträume. No. 1(–3). [P. F.] 3 no. 1911. *See* HAWLEY (S.) Hawley Edition. No. 23–25. 1909, *etc.* fol.　　**h. 3527. b.**

— Liebestraum ... Trois Nocturnes pour Piano. *W. Paxton: London*, [1912.] fol.　　**h. 896. g. (7.)**

— Liebesträume. Dreams of Love. Nos. 1, 2 & 3 for Pianoforte. Edition revised and fingered by E. Pozzoli. *G. Ricordi & Co.: London, etc.*, [1933.] 4°.　　**g. 547. f. (13.)**

Drei Lieder, für eine Sopran- oder Tenor-Stimme. No. 3. O lieb', o lieb'

— "O lieb'," Lied von F. Freiligrath für eine Singstimme mit Begleitung des Pianoforte. pp. 13. *Bei Fr. Kistner: Leipzig*, [1850.] fol.　　**Hirsch M. 949. (7.)**

— Liebestraum. Dream of Love. [Song.] English version by L. Lipton. Edited by M. Rosenfeld. Liszt-Schipa. *Forster Music Publisher: Chicago*, 1925. 4°.　　**G. 1275. s. (5.)**

— Liebestraum. Waltz Song ... Words by G. Hartel. Arr. by W. D. Moyer. *W. J. Smith Music Co.: New York*, 1937. 4°.　　**G. 1275. ss. (42.)**

— Dream of Love ... [Song.] Lyric by G. Kahn. *Robbins Music Corporation: New York*, 1938. 4°.　　**G. 1275. uu. (11.)**

— O lieb' so lang du lieben kannst. O love as long as e'er you can ... Edited by Carl Deis. pp. 10. *G. Schirmer: New York*, 1945. 4°.　　**G. 1276. a. (32.)**

— A Love Dream. [Words by] F. C. Bornschein ... Transcribed [for S. S. A.] by F. C. Bornschein. *J. Fischer & Bro.: New York, Birmingham*, 1926. 8°.　　**F. 217. b. (14.)**

— Love's Dream. [Duet.] Words by A. Dowdon. Arranged from Liszt's ... "Liebestraum" by M. Besly. *See* BESLY (E. M.) Three Duets, *etc.* [No. 2.] 1928. 8°.　　**F. 607. ll. (4.)**

— A Love-Dream. Part Song for S. A. T. B. [Words by] N. Weir. *W. Paxton & Co.: London*, 1929. 8°.　　**F. 585. ss. (17.)**

— A Love Dream. Liebestraum. Duet for Soprano & Contralto, words by N. Weir. *W. Paxton & Co.: London*, 1930. 4°.　　**G. 1275. ff. (34.)**

— My Dream of Love ... Chorus, or Quartet, for Male Voices, lyric by W. Preston. Arr ... by K. McLeod. *Chappell-Harms: New York*, 1931. 8°.　　**F. 163. cc. (11.)**

— My Dream of Love. Liebestraum ... for Mixed Voices ... Arr ... by K. McLeod. *Chappell-Harms: New York*, 1931. 8°.　　**F. 585. uu. (3.)**

— When through the Night. Part Song for two or three Baritone Voices, arranged ... [by] P. J. Clark. [Words by] E. M. Clark. *Gamble Hinged Music Co.: Chicago*, 1931. 8°.　　**F. 163. cc. (14.)**

— Liebestraume. The Theme of Love. For Ladies' Voices. Words and adaptation by D. R. Ford. *D. O. Evans: Cleveland*, 1932. 8°.　　**F. 217. e. (40.)**

— Liebestraum. Arranged as a Part-Song for Men's Voices ... with Pianoforte accompaniment by J. Bateson, poem by M. Lyell. *J. Curwen & Sons: London*, 1935. 8°. [*The Apollo Club. No. 715.*]　　**F. 667.**

— Liebestraum No. 3. Oh kindly Night ... (Words by J. Mathieson.) Arr. for S. A. T. B. by P. J. Mathieson. (Op. 84. No. 8.) *Bayley & Ferguson: London, Glasgow*, 1935. 8°. *The Choral Album, No. 1516.*　　**F. 946. f. (4.)**

— Liebestraum, No. 3. Words by J. Mathieson ... Arranged for Female Voices (S. S. C.) by P. J. Mansfield. Op. 97. No. 2. *Bayley & Ferguson: London, Glasgow*, 1935. 8°. *The Collegiate Choir, No. 456.*　　**F. 217. g. (1.)**

LISZT (Franz)

— Liebestraum. Dream of Love. English lyric by H. Johnson. Voice arrangement [for T. T. B. B.] by E. Smalle. *Robbins Music Corporation: New York*, 1936. 8°. **F. 163. ff. (31.)**

— Liebestraum. Love's Dream. For Piano Solo with Accompaniment of Mixed Voices, words by A. Marlhom ... Arranged by W. Riegger. *Harold Flammer: New York*, 1939. 8°. **F. 1744. c. (26.)**

— Woodland Dreaming ... Four-part Song, words by H. Taylor. Arr. by H. Geehl. *Edwin Ashdown: London*, 1940. 8°. [*Enoch Choral Series. No.* 125.] **F. 1097.**

— Dream of Love. Adapted from Liebestraum ... No. 3. ... Male Chorus ... Arranged by C. Henderson. Edited by R. Ringwald. Lyric by T. Waring. *Words and Music, Inc.: New York*, 1940. 8°. **F. 638. k. (2.)**

— Woodland Dreaming ... Two-part Song, words by H. Taylor ... Arr. by H. Geehl. *Edwin Ashdown: London*, 1940. 8°. [*Edwin Ashdown's Series of Vocal Duets, No.* 190.] **E. 1601.**

— Liebestraum. (Dream of Love.) Arranged for Mixed Voices by Hubert Bath. English version by Laurence Lipton. Music by Liszt-Schipa. pp. 12. *Keith Prowse & Co.: London*, 1946. 8°. **F. 1744. f. (32.)**

— The Dreams of Love. (Liebestraum.) Lyrics by Marilyn Keith and Alan Bergman. [S. A. T. B. Arranged by Norman Luboff.] pp. 12. *Walton Music: London*, [1961.] 8°. **F. 1744. dd. (7.)**

— Liebesträume ... Notturno No. 3 ... Arrangiert von L. Artok. [Parts.] *Schott & Co.: London*, 1931. 4°. [*Schott & Co.'s Domesticum-Salon-Orchestra. No.* 335.] **g. 1053. a.**

— Liebestraum. Arranged by T. Dorsey and C. Mastren ... for Orchestra. [Parts.] *L. Feist: New York*, 1937. 8°. **h. 3210. h. (565.)**

— Liebestraum ... Arr. by William Short. ⟨Conductor [and military band parts].⟩ 33 pt. *In:* WAGNER (W. R.) [Der Ring des Nibelungen.—Die Walküre.] "Wotan's Abschied" und "Feuerzauber," *etc.* 1909. fol. [*Boosey's military Journal. ser.* 127. *no.* 5.] **h. 1549.**

— Liebestraum. Arranged (for Military Band) by F. Winterbottom. [Parts.] *Hawkes & Son: London, etc.*, 1930. fol. *Hawkes & Son's Military Band Edition, No.* 504. **h. 3211. a. (193.)**

— Love's Dream ... Waltz ... Arr. by G. F. Briegel. [Brass band parts.] *G. F. Briegel: New York*, 1936. 8°. **h. 3210. h. (516.)**

— Liebesträume ... Arr. by F. Bradbury. [Banjo, guitar and mandoline orchestra. Parts.] *C. Essex & Son: London*, [1938.] fol. **h. 3210. h. (708.)**

— Liebestraum ... Orch. by Jay Arnold ... Piano Conductor & Accordeon Guide [and dance band parts]. *Campbell, Connelly & Co.: London*, [1946.] 8°. **h. 3210. h. (989.)**

— Liebestraum ... Piano Solo with Violin and Cello ad lib. Arranged by G. H. Farnell. *Banks' Music House: Leeds*, 1928. 4°. *Banks Sixpenny Edition, No.* 97. **g. 547. f. (10.)**

— Liebestraum. Transcription by C. Smith. Solo for Trombone, Baritone, Cornet, Cello, E♭ Alto, B♭ Tenor, or C Saxophone, also ... as a Duet for any combination of these instruments. [With P. F. accompaniment.] *C. L. Barnhouse: Oskaloosa, Iowa*, 1929. 4° & 8°. **g. 547. f. (6.)**

— F. Liszt's celebrated Liebestraume, Dream of Love, as Piano Solo with Violin and Violoncello parts. Simplified by W. Manhire. *London Music Publishing Stores: London*, 1930. 4°. **g. 547. f. (9.)**

LISZT (Franz)

— Dream of Love. Liebestraum ... Arr. by G. F. Briegel. [For B flat trumpets, trombone, baritone and P. F.] *G. F. Briegel: New York*, 1940. 8°. **h. 3210. h. (773.)**

— Liebestraum ... Nocturne for the pianoforte. Revised by E. Pauer. *Augener & Co.: London*, [1887.] fol. **h. 585. g. (7.)**

— Liebestraum, No. 3. [P. F.] *See* TRIPP (J. D. A.) The J. D. A. Tripp Teaching Edition, *etc.* No. 1. (1904.) fol. **h. 3283. w. (42.)**

— Liebestraum.—No. 3. [P. F.] *Chappell & Co.: London, etc.*, (1910.) fol. *Chappell Edition of Popular Pianoforte Works, No.* 2. **h. 3369.**

— Liebesträume. Edited by E. Haywood. [P. F.] *Keith, Prowse & Co.: London*, 1919. fol. **h. 896. h. (6.)**

— Love-Dream, *etc.* ⟨Annotated and fingered by F. Corder.⟩ [P. F.] pp. 7. *Murdoch, Murdoch & Co.: London*, [c. 1920.] fol. [*Mayfair Classics. no.* 19.] **h. 3576.**

— Liebestraume Valse. Founded on Liszt's ... "Liebestraume". Arranged by E[mile] J. B[ennet], *etc.* [P. F.] *C. Lennox & Co.: London*, 1923. fol. **h. 896. h. (9.)**

— Liebesträume. Nocturne No. 3 ... Edited by C. Woodhouse. [P. F.] *J. R. Lafleur & Son: London*, 1924. 4°. *Edition Lafleur, No.* 241. **g. 547. e. (11.)**

— Liebestraum. Dream of Love. Nocturne. [P. F.] *Reid Bros.: London*, 1927. 4°. *Classical Cameos, No.* 24. **g. 547. f. (4.)**

— The Dream of Love ... (Notturno No. 3.) Original (Simplified) edition. [P. F.] 2 no. *W. Paxton & Co.: London*, [1929.] fol. **h. 896. h. (12.)**

— Liebesträume. (Edited by A. W. Bunney.) [P. F.] *H. Freeman & Co.: London*, 1929. 4°. **g. 547. f. (3.)**

— Liebestraum. Dream of Love. [P. F.] *Rowland's: London*, [1929.] 4°. [*Rowland's Popular Series. No.* 39.] **g. 1258. c.**

— Liebesträume. Nocturne No. 3. (Arranged by R. Argentson.) [P. F.] *Leonard, Gould & Bolttler: London*, 1931. 4°. *The Portrait Gallery, No.* 24. **g. 547. f. (15.)**

— Liebestraum. Dream of Love. For the Piano ... Transcribed by H. Frey. *Robbins Music Corporation: New York*, 1935. 4°. **g. 547. f. (18.)**

— Liebestraum. A Fragment ... Easy arrangement by H. Geehl. [P. F.] *E. Ashdown: London*, [1936.] 4°. **g. 547. f. (21.)**

— Theme from Liebesträume No. 3 ... Adapted by John Thompson. (Piano.) *Willis Music Co.: Cincinnati*, 1937. 4°. **g. 547. f. (30.)**

— Liebestraum. Dream of Love ... Transcribed by W. Rolfe. (Piano.) *H. Flammer: New York*, 1938. 4°. **g. 547. f. (29.)**

— Notturno Nr. 3 aus "Liebesträume". Für Klavier zu 2 Händen. Revidiert von G. Groschwitz. pp. 7. *N. Simrock: Leipzig; Edmund Ullmann: Reichenberg*, [1944.] 4°. **g. 547. k. (9.)**

— Liebestraum ... as played in the Hunt Stromberg Film Production "Guest in the House," *etc.* [P. F.] *Chappell & Co.: London, etc.*, [1945.] 4°. **f. 470. a. (9.)**

— Liebesträume. [P. F.] pp. 7. *Cinephonic Music Co.: London*, [1946.] 4°. **f. 470. a. (11.)**

— Liebestraum No. 3. Simplified arrangement for the piano by Juan Jaume. pp. 5. *G. Schirmer: New York*, [1951.] 4°. **g. 547. h. (3.)**

LISZT (Franz)

— Sonho de amor … Arranjo e adaptação de Fred Jorge. [P. F.] *Fermata do Brasil: São Paulo*, [1961.] 4°.　　　**g. 547. s. (2.)**

— Liebestraum No. 3. [P. F.] pp. 4. *Chappell & Co.: London*, [1975.] 4°.
Part of "Magic Piano Silhouettes".　　　**f. 470. a. (16.)**

— Liebestraum. Dream of Love … for Two Pianos four hands, arranged by F. Guenther. *E. B. Marks Music Corporation: New York*, 1938. 4°.　　　**g. 547. f. (28.)**

— Liebesträume No. 3 … Arranged for Two Pianofortes, 4 hands, by B. Kirkby-Mason. *Bosworth & Co.: London*, 1939. 4°.　　　**g. 547. g. (1.)**

— Liebestraum, No. III. Arranged for Two Pianos by E. Bartlett and R. Robertson. *Oxford University Press: London, etc.*, 1944. 4°.
[*The Two-Piano Series. No. 28.*]　　　**g. 1393.**

— Liebesträume. Arranged by Fred. Pattison … For four hands. pp. 8. *Cinephonic Music Co.: London*, [1947.] 4°.　　　**f. 470. a. (5.)**

— Liebestraum (No. 3). Arranged for organ and piano by Donald A. Griscom. Hammond registration by Chester Kingsbury. pp. 16. *H. W. Gray Co.: New York*, [1955.] 4°.
Two copies.　　　**g. 547. k. (5.)**

— Liebestraum. Dream of Love … Arranged for the Piano Accordion by Al Richards. *W. Paxton & Co.: London*, 1942. 4°.
Paxton's Piano Accordion Solos, No. 86.　　　**g. 547. g. (8.)**

— Liebestraum. Dream of Love … Arr. by Lloyd Marvin. [Piano accordion.] *Chart Music Publishing House: Chicago*, 1945. 4°.　　　**g. 547. g. (10.)**

— Liebestraum … Arranged for Piano Accordion by Conway Graves. pp. 4. *Hohner Concessionaires:* [*London*,] 1946. 4°.　　　**g. 547. g. (14.)**

— Liebesträume … Arranged by E. Grimshaw. Plectrum Guitar Solo. *E. Grimshaw & Son: London*, [1934.] 4°.　　　**g. 547. f. (17.)**

— Dream of Love. Liebestraum … Plectrum Guitar Solo. Arranged by H. Volpe. *C. Fischer: New York, etc.*, 1936. 4°.　　　**g. 547. f. (20.)**

— Liebesträume. Nocturne. Adapted by Peter Sensier. Spanish guitar solo. *Clifford Essex Music Co.: London*, [1955.] *s. sh.* 4°.　　　**h. 896. n. (3.)**

— Liebestraum. Arranged for organ by L. Falk. *C. F. Summy Co.: Chicago*, 1899. fol.　　　**h. 896. c. (6.)**

— Liebestraum. Dream of Love … Organ Solo Transcription by Pattman. *De Wolfe: London*, 1927. 4°.　　　**h. 896. h. (11.)**

— Liebestraum. Nocturne, No. 3 … Arranged for Organ by J. S. Archer. *W. Paxton & Co.: London*, 1929. 4°.
Part of the "Anthology of Organ Music".　　　**g. 547. f. (5.)**

— Liebestraum. E♭ alto and B♭ tenor saxophone solos with piano accompaniment. Arrangement by Earl Bostic. [Score and parts.] 2 pt. *Peter Maurice Music Co.: London*, [1955.] 4°.　　　**f. 470. a. (12.)**

— Liebestraum … Arranged for viola & piano by Lionel Tertis. [Score and parts.] 2 pt. *Augener: London*, [1954.] 4°.　　　**g. 547. k. (2.)**

— Nocturne No. 3. [Violin and P. F.] *W. Paxton & Co.: London*, 1921. fol.
Part of the "Anthology of Violin Music".　　　**h. 896. h. (7.)**

— Liebestraum. Liszt—[arranged for violin and P. F. by] Such. *G. Schirmer: New York*, 1922. 4°.　　　**g. 547. e. (6.)**

LISZT (Franz)

— Liebestraum … Arranged (for violin & piano) by A. Mann. *Augener: London*, 1925. 4°.　　　**g. 547. f. (1.)**

— Liebestraum. Arranged by E. Reeves for Violin or Cello Solo with Piano accompaniment. *Walsh, Holmes & Co.: London*, 1926. fol.　　　**h. 896. h. (10.)**

— Liebesträume No. 3 … Arr. Louis Godowsky. (Violon et Piano.) *Bosworth & Co.: London, etc.*, 1926. 4°.
[*Transcriptions classiques. No. 6.*]　　　**g. 500. q. (15.)**

— Liebesträume. Notturno III. Transcription für Violine und Klavier von G. Larsen. *B. Schott's Söhne: Mainz und Leipzig*, 1934. 4°.　　　**g. 547. f. (16.)**

— Liebestraum, No. 3. For violoncello and piano. *See* DAMBOIS (M. F.) Arrangements by M. Dambois. I, *etc.* 1923. 4°.　　　**g. 510. i. (12.)**

— Love's Dream … Arranged for Violoncello Solo with Pianoforte accompaniment by W. H. Squire. *Boosey & Co.: London and New York*, 1926. 4°.　　　**g. 547. f. (2.)**

— Dreams of Love. Liebesträume … Transcribed by Mark Skalmer. ⟨For cello & piano.⟩ [Score and part.] 2 pt. *Carl Fischer: New York*, [c. 1930.] 4°.　　　**h. 4090. g. (5.)**

— *See* SCHWERTSIK (Kurt) Liebesträume. Op. 7. [Partly based on Liebesträume No. 3 by F. Liszt.] 1966. *obl.* 4°.　　　**c. 120. h. (1.)**

— Lieder von Robert und Clara Schumann für das Pianoforte übertragen von Franz Liszt. pp. 19. *Breitkopf & Härtel: Leipzig*, [1875.] fol.　　　**h. 585. b. (17.)**

— Die Lorelei. *See supra:* [Buch der Lieder. Bd. 1. No. 1.]

— A Love Dream. *See supra:* [Drei Lieder für eine Sopran- oder Tenor-Stimme. No. 3. O lieb', O lieb'.]

— Love Theme from the Film "So little Time". *See infra:* [Sonata in B minor.]

— Love Themes from "The Mephisto Waltz". *See supra:* [Zwei Episoden aus Lenau's Faust. No. 2. Der Tanz in der Dorfschenke.]

— Love's Dream. *See supra:* [Drei Lieder für eine Sopran- oder Tenor-Stimme. No. 3. O lieb', O lieb'.]

— Lucia. *See infra:* [Réminiscences de Lucia di Lammermoor.]

— Lucie de Lamermoor [by D. G. M. Donizetti]. Marche et cavatine pour le piano. pp. 13. *Chez les fils de B. Schott: Mayence*, [c. 1870.] fol.　　　**h. 896. s. (12.)**

— [A reissue.] Lucie de Lammermoor. Marche et cavatine. *Mayence*, [c. 1890.] fol.　　　**h. 896. a. (4.)**

— La lugubre gondola. Hegedűre (gordonkára) és zongorára. Für Violine (Violoncello) und Klavier. 1882 … Közreadja … Szelényi István. [Score and part.] 2 pt. *Editio Musica: Budapest*, [1974.] 4°.
The violoncello part is printed on the verso of the violin part.　　　**g. 547. s. (5.)**

— Die Macht der Musik. Gedicht von der Herzogin Helene von Orleans für eine Singstimme (Tenor, Soprano oder Mezzo-Sopran), mit Begleitung des Pianoforte. pp. 19. *Bei Fr. Kistner: Leipzig*, [1849.] fol.　　　**Hirsch M. 949. (8.)**

Magyar Dallok

— Magyar dallok zongorára … Ungarische National-Melodien für das Piano-Forte, *etc.* Hft. 1–4. *Bei Tobias Haslinger: Wien*, [1840.] fol.

[Continued as:]
Magyar rhapsodiák. Rapsodies hongroises pour piano seul, *etc.* Cah. 5–10. *Chez Veuve Haslinger et fils: Vienne*, [1846.] fol.　　　**K. 11. d. 9.**

LISZT (Franz)

— [No. 5, 4, 11.] Ungarische Melodien ... Im leichten Style bearbeitet. [P. F.] pp. 7. *Bei Tobias Haslinger's Witwe: Wien,* [1843.] fol.
Neuigkeiten für das Pianoforte im eleganten Style. Abt. 9. no. 86. **Hirsch M. 951. (11.)**

— [No. 5, 4, 11.] Ungarische National-Melodien für das Piano-Forte, *etc.* pp. 15. *Bei Tobias Haslinger's Witwe und Sohn: Wien,* [1845.] 4°. **g. 547. j. (7.)**

— [No. 5, 4, 11.] 3 mélodies hongroises. [P. F.] pp. 9. *Bernard Latte: Paris,* [c. 1845.] fol. **h. 722. ll. (1.)**

— [No. 1–7.] Album d'un voyageur. Mélodies hongroises. pp. 18. *Alphonse Leduc: Paris,* [c. 1890.] fol.
The sheets of an edition printed from the plates of Bernard Latte, in wrappers bearing the imprint of Alphonse Leduc. **h. 585. k. (7.)**

— [No. 6.] Nouvelle mélodie hongroise. [P. F.] *In:* PERIODICAL PUBLICATIONS.— *Paris.* [Le Monde musical.] Le Pianiste moderne, *etc.* pp. 7–9. [c. 1845.] fol. **h. 1203. r. (10.)**

— [No. 11.] Célèbre Mélodie Hongroise en Si♭ pour le piano ... Transcrite par F. Liszt. No. 1. Édition originale. No. 2. Édition facilitée. 2 no. *A. Leduc: Paris,* [1886.] fol. **h. 585. g. (9.)**

— [No. 20.] Rumänische Rhapsodie ... Op. posth. Erstveröffentlichung durch ... Octavian Beu. Piano solo. pp. 31. *Universal-Edition: Wien,* 1936. 4°. **g. 547. k. (8.)**

— Magyar Gyors induló ... Ungarischer Geschwind-Marsch für Pianoforte ... Herausgegeben von F. J. Schindler. pp. 7. *F. J. Schindler's Verlag: Pressburg, etc.;* [*Leipzig* printed, 1871.] fol. **h. 896. i. (7.)**

— Magyar rhapsodiák. *See supra:* Magyar dallok. cah. 5–10.

— Magyar történelmi arcképek. Historische ungarische Bildnisse. Portraits hongrois historiques. [P. F.] pp. 23. *In:* Új zenei szemle. évf. 7. sz. 1. 1956. 8°.
Editions of no. 6, 7, previously published under the titles "Dem Andenken Petőfi's" and "Mosonyi's Grab Geleit," are entered separately. **P. P. 1945. efa.**

— [Another issue.] Magyar történelmi arcképek, *etc.* [1956.] 8°. **e. 282. t. (1.)**

— Magyar történelmi arcképek zongorára. Historische ungarische Bildnisse für Klavier. Portraits hongrois historiques pour le piano. Átnézte ... Szelényi István. pp. 24. *Zeneműkiadó vállalat: Budapest,* 1959. 4°.
The titlepage bears the autograph signature of Humphrey Searle. **f. 470. f. (2.)**

— Marche de Rakoczy. *See infra:* [Rhapsodie hongroise. No. 15.]

— Marche funèbre de Dom Sébastien de C. [*sic*] Donizetti variée pour le piano. pp. 15. *Chez Pietro Mechetti: Vienne,* [1845.] fol. **Hirsch M. 953. (7.)**

— Marche hongroise. *See infra:* [Mélodies hongroises d'après Fr. Schubert. No. 2.]

Seconde Marche hongroise

— 2ᵉ marche hongroise pour piano, *etc.* pp. 11. *Chez Maurice Schlesinger: Paris,* [1843.] fol. **h. 585. l. (4.)**

— Seconde Marche hongroise, ungarische Sturm-Marsch, für das Piano-Forte. pp. 13. *Aᵈ Mᵗ Schlesinger: Berlin,* [1843?] fol. **Hirsch M. 954. (3.)**

— Seconde marche hongroise. Ungarischer Sturm-Marsch für das Pianoforte ... 2ᵗᵉ Auflage, *etc.* pp. 13. *Aᵈ Mᵗ Schlesinger: Berlin,* [1845?] fol. **h. 896. i. (8.)**

LISZT (Franz)

— Ungarischer Sturm-Marsch für grosses Orchester ... Neue Bearbeitung. Partitur, *etc.* pp. 50. *Verlag der Schlesinger'schen Buch & Musikhandlung: Berlin,* [1876.] 8°. **f. 245. a. (4.)**

— Ungarischer Sturm-Marsch für das Pianoforte ... Neue Bearbeitung 1876. Piano à 2 ms., *etc.* pp. 19. *Schlesinger'sche Buch- & Musikhandlung: Berlin; Carl Haslinger: Wien,* [1876.] fol. **h. 896. n. (8.)**

— Ungarischer Sturm-Marsch für das Pianoforte ... Neue Bearbeitung 1876. Piano ... à 4 ms., *etc.* pp. 23. *Schlesinger'sche Buch- & Musikhandlung: Berlin; Carl Haslinger: Wien,* [1876.] fol. **g. 547. q. (3.)**

— Marche solennelle vers le Saint Graal. *See supra:* [Feierlicher Marsch zum heiligen Gral.]

— Li Marinari. *See infra:* Soirées musicales de Rossini. No. 12.

— "La Marseillaise." [By C. J. Rouget de Lisle.] Transcription pour le pianoforte par F. Liszt. pp. 11. *J. Schubert & Cᵒ: Leipzig, New York,* [1872.] fol. **h. 896. n. (9.)**

— Missa choralis organo concinente. *C. F. Kahnt: Lipsiae,* [1869.] 4°. **G. 461. b. (1.)**

— [Missa choralis.] Benedictus. For Mixed Voices ... Edited and arranged by N. Cain. *H. Flammer: New York,* 1939. 8°. **F. 1158. i. (13.)**

— Missa coronationalis. *See supra:* Koronázási mise.

— [Missa pro organo.] Messe pour orgue, servant d'accompagnement à la célébration des messes basses, *etc. See* ALBUM. Album für Orgel-Spieler, *etc.* Lief. 54. [1880? *etc.*] *obl.* fol. **e. 119.**

— [Missa pro organo.] A short Organ Mass, *etc.* ⟨Edited by William L. Sumner.⟩ pp. 14. *Hinrichsen Edition: London,* [1963.] *obl.* 4°. **e. 1093. tt. (4.)**

— [Missa pro organo.] Messe in B-dur nach der 'Messe pour orgue' von Franz Liszt ... ⟨[With voice parts added by] Leoš Janáček.⟩ Coro misto e organo. Editor: Jarmil Burghauser. pp. 22. *Universal Edition: Wien,* [1978.] 8°. **F. 566. i. (1.)**

— [Missa quattuor vocum ad aequales (II TT. et II BB.) concinente organo. pp. 35. *Sumptibus et formis Breitkopfii et Härtelii: Lipsiae,* [1853.] fol. **G. 461. g.**

— [Missa quattuor vocum.] Messe pour quatre voix d'hommes (tenors et basses) avec accompagnement d'orgue. pp. 39. *Étienne Repos: Paris,* [1869.] 8°. **F. 1176. hh. (2.)**

— Missa quatuor vocum ad aequales—2 T. T. et 2 B. B.— concinente organo. Editio nova. *Sumptibus ... Breitkopfii et Härtelii: Lipsiae,* [1871.] 4°. **G. 461. b. (2.)**

— [Missa quattuor vocum.] Férifikari mise. Orgonakísérettel. Messe für Männerchor mit Orgelbegleitung. Közreadja ... Sulyok Imre. Partitúra, *etc.* pp. 33. *Editio Musica: Budapest,* 1972. 8°. **F. 566. f. (1.)**

— Missa solennis quam ad mandatum eminentissimi ac reverendissimi domini domini Johannis Scitovszky a Nagykér ... composuit Franciscus Liszt, *etc.* [Score.] pp. 130. *Typ. Caes. Reg. Status Officinae: Viennae Austriacorum,* 1859. fol. **I. 509.**

— Missa solennis quam ad mandatum eminentissimi ac reverendissimi domini domini Johannis Scitovszky a Nagykér ... composuit F. Liszt, *etc.* [Score.] pp. 130. *Typis Caes. Reg. Status Officinae: Viennae Austriacorum,* 1859. fol. **Hirsch IV. 833.**

LISZT (Franz)

— Missa solennis. ⟨Graner Festmesse.⟩ Edited by Imre Sulyok. [Score.] pp. 225. *Ernst Eulenburg: London, etc.; printed in Switzerland*, [1968.] 8°. [*Edition Eulenburg. no.* 942.] **b. 212.**

— Missa solennis zur Einweihung der Basilica in Gran ... Clavier Auszug m. Text, *etc.* pp. 104. *J. Schuberth & Co.: Leipzig*, [c. 1905.] 8°. **E. 1644. j.**

— Missa solennis zur Einweihung der Basilica in Gran ... Für Pianoforte zu 2 Händen von Aug. Stradal. pp. 55. *J. Schuberth & Co.: Leipzig*, [1901.] fol. **Hirsch M. 946.**

— Mazeppa. *See supra:* [Études d'exécution transcendante. No. 4.]

— Mazeppa. *See infra:* Symphonische Dichtungen. no. 6.

— Mazurka brillante pour le piano. pp. 13. *Chez Bartholf Senff: Leipzig*, [1850.] fol. **Hirsch M. 951. (7.)**

— Mazurka brillante. [P. F.] pp. 10. *Campbell, Ransford & Co.: London*, [1851.] fol. **h. 585. (5.)**

— Mazurka brillante. [P. F.] pp. 8. *Musical Bouquet Office; J. Allen: London*, [1855.] fol. [*Musical Bouquet. no.* 663, 664.] **H. 2345.**

— Mazurka brillante ... für grosses Orchester bearbeitet von Karl Müller-Berghaus. Partitur, *etc.* pp. 47. *Bartholf Senff: Leipzig*, [1878.] 8°. **e. 577. (1.)**

— Mazurka pour piano composée par un amateur de St. Pétersbourg paraphrasée, *etc. Berlin*, [1883.] fol. **h. 585. f. (21.)**

— IV. mefisztó-keringő. *See infra:* [Mephisto-Walzer. No. 4.]

— 3 mélodies hongroises. *See supra:* [Magyar Dallok. No. 5, 4, 11.]

Mélodies hongroises d'après Fr. Schubert

— Mélodies hongroises d'après Fr. Schubert, pour piano seul. [Based on Schubert's "Divertissement à la hongroise," Op. 54.] 3 cah. *Chez A. Diabelli et comp.: Vienne*, [1840.] fol. **Hirsch M. 955. (1.)**

— Schubert's ungarische Melodien aus dem ungarischen Divertissement zu 4 Händen, Op. 54. Zweihändig auf eine neue leichtere Art gesetzt. 3 no. *Bei A. Diabelli u. Comp.: Wien*, [1846.] fol. **Hirsch M. 955. (3.)**

— [No. 1.] Mélodie hongroise de François Schubert, transcrite pour piano seul. pp. 15. *Richault & cie: Paris*, [c. 1870.] fol. **h. 896. v. (4.)**

— [No. 2.] Marche hongroise. [P. F.] pp. 9. *L. Lavenu: London*, [1840.] fol. **g. 547. cc. (7.)**

— [A reissue.] [No. 2.] Marche hongroise. *Addison & Hodson: London*, [c. 1845.] fol. **h. 896. cc. (1.)**

— [No. 2.] Mélodies hongroises d'après Fr. Schubert. Marcia pour piano seul. pp. 9. *Stanley Lucas, Weber & Co: London*, [1876.] fol. **h. 1483. (8.)**

— [No. 2.] Marche hongroise (Fr. Schubert) transcrite ... par F. Liszt. [P. F.] Troisième édition revue et augmentée. pp. 15. *Aug. Cranz: Hambourg*, [1883.] fol. **h. 585. f. (12.)**

— [No. 3.] Schuberts 3. ungarische Melodie (aus dem ungarischen Divertissement zu vier Händen. Op. 54) zu zwei Händen gesetzt von F. Liszt. *In:* SCHUBERT (F. P.) Ungarische Melodie für Klavier, *etc.* pp. 7–12. [1928.] fol. **g. 567. r. (13.)**

LISZT (Franz)

Deux mélodies russes

— Deux arabesques pour le piano. No. 1. Le Rossignol. [A transcription of the song "Соловей" by A. N. Alyab'ev.] No. 2. Chanson Bohémienne. 2 no. *Ewer & Co.: London*, [1853.] fol. **h. 585. (4.)**

— Deux mélodies russes. Arabesques pour le piano ... N° 1. Le Rossignol. ⟨De A. Alabieff.⟩ Nouvelle édition révue par l'auteur. N° 2. Chanson bohémienne. 2 no. *Chez A. Cranz: Hambourg*, [c. 1860.] fol. **g. 547. u. (11.)**

— Deux arabesques pour le piano. No. 1. Le Rossignol. ⟨De A. Alabieff.⟩ No. 2. Chanson bohémienne. 2 no. *Augener & Co.: London*, [1861.] fol. **h. 585. a. (4.)**

— Deux mélodies russes. Arabesques pour le piano ... N° 1. Le Rossignol. Nouvelle édition revue par l'auteur. N° 2. Chanson bohémienne. no. 1. *Chez A. Cranz: Hambourg*, [c. 1880.] fol. *Imperfect; wanting no. 2.* **h. 896. z. (9.)**

— Deux Arabesques pour le Piano. No. 1. Le Rossignol (de A. Alabieff.) No. 2. Chanson Bohémienne. *London*, [1887.] 4°. *No. 8217 of Augener & Co.'s edition.* **g. 547. a. (3.)**

Deux mélodies russes. No. 1. Le Rossignol

— Соловей. (Le Rossignol.) Air russe de A. Alabieff transcrit pour le piano par F. Liszt. pp. 7. *Chez A. Cranz: Hambourg*, [1842.] fol. **g. 547. u. (8.)**

— Соловей. Air russe de A. Alabieff, transcrit pour le piano par F. Liszt. pp. 7. *Chez C. R. Klever: St. Pétersbourg*, [1845?] fol. **h. 896. h. (13.)**

— Соловей. Air russe de A. Alabieff transcrit pour le piano par Fr Liszt. pp. 147–151. *Chez M. Bernard: St Petersbourg; chez P. Lehnhold: Moscou*, [c. 1845.] fol. **g. 547. t. (7.)**

— Le Rossignol. Mélodie russe (d'Alabieff). Arabesque pour piano. pp. 6. *Ashdown & Parry: London*, [1880?] fol. **h. 896. j. (1.)**

— Le Rossignol. Air russe de A. Alabieff ... Transcrit pour le Piano par F. Liszt. [*Paris*,] 1895. 8°. *Supplement to "L'Illustration," No.* 2748. **P. P. 4283. m. (3.)**

— The Nightingale ... on a Theme by A. Alabieff. Edited by C. Deis. (Piano.) *G. Schirmer: New York*, 1937. 4°. **g. 547. f. (27.)**

— The Nightingale ... [Song.] French words by G. Le Maître Toupin, English translation by E. Zaugg. Alabieff-La Forge ... Arranged from the Piano transcription by Liszt. *C. Fischer: New York, etc.*, 1939. 4°. **G. 1275. vv. (27.)**

— Mephisto Polka ... für Klavier. *Berlin und Leipzig*, [1884.] fol. **h. 585. f. (15.)**

— Mephisto Walzer. *See supra:* [Zwei Episoden aus Lenau's Faust. No. 2. Der Tanz in der Dorfschenke.]

— 2ter Mephisto Walzer. Partitur. *Berlin*, [1882.] 8°. **e. 58. f.**

— 2ter Mephisto Walzer ... Für Pianoforte allein ... Arrangement vom Componisten. pp. 29. *Adolf Fürstner: Berlin*, [1881.] fol. **h. 585. f. (6.)**

— 2ter Mephisto Walzer ... Für Pianoforte zu 4 Händen ... Arrangement vom Componisten. pp. 35. *Adolf Fürstner: Berlin*, [1881.] fol. **h. 585. f. (6*.)**

— Dritter Mephisto Walzer ... für Clavier. *Berlin und Leipzig*, [1884.] fol. **h. 585. f. (7.)**

— [Mephisto-Walzer. No. 4.] IV. mefisztó-keringő. [P. F.] pp. 8. *In:* Új zenei szemle. évf. 7. sz. 4. 1956. 8°. **P. P. 1945. efa.**

LISZT (Franz)

— Mignon. *See* supra: [Buch der Lieder. Bd. 1. No. 3.]

— Le Moine, der Mönch, suivi de deux mélodies par Meyerbeer transcrits pour piano, *etc.* pp. 21. *Chez A^d Mt Schlesinger: Berlin,* [1842.] fol.   **Hirsch M. 953. (8.)**

— Morceau de concert. Grandes variations de bravoure, *etc. See* supra: [Hexameron.]

— Morceau de salon. Étude de perfectionnement de la méthode des méthodes pour le piano, *etc.* pp. 7. *Chez A^d Mt Schlesinger: Berlin,* [1840.] fol.   **Hirsch M. 951. (8.)**

— [Morceau de salon.] Ab-irato. Étude de perfectionnement de la Méthode des méthodes pour le piano ... Nouvelle édition entièrement revue et corrigée par l'auteur *etc.* pp. 7. *Chez Ad. Mt. Schlesinger: Berlin,* [1852.] fol.   **h. 585. j. (4.)**

— [Morceau de salon.] Ab Irato. Étude de Perfectionnement. Edited by E. Dannreuther. *Augener & Co.: London,* [1898.] 4°.   **g. 547. a. (10.)**

Trois morceaux de salon. Op. 5

— [No. 1.] Divertissement pour piano sur la cavatine de Pacini (I tuoi frequenti palpiti), *etc.* pp. 19. *Chez Fr. Hofmeister: Leipzig,* [1837.] fol.   **Hirsch M. 952. (3.)**

— [No. 1.] Divertissement pour piano, sur la cavatine de Pacini (I tuoi frequenti palpiti), *etc. Cramer, Addison & Beale: London,* [1840?] fol.   **h. 896. h. (16.)**

— [No. 1.] Grande fantaisie sur la Niobe de Pacini, pour le piano. pp. 23. *Chez A^d Mt Schlesinger: Berlin,* [1842.] fol.   **Hirsch M. 954. (6.)**

— [No. 1.] Souvenir à Pasta. Divertissement sur la cavatina "Il soave e bel contento" de Pacini. pp. 23. *Edwin Ashdown: London,* [c. 1890.] fol. *Wessel & C^os Collection of grand Solos for the Piano Forte composed by Fran^s Liszt. no. 7.*   **h. 896. z. (7.)**

— [No. 2.] Fantaisie romantique sur deux mélodies suisses ... pour le piano ... Op: 5. N°. 1. pp. 26. *Chez Bernard Latte: Paris,* [1836.] fol.   **g. 547. cc. (9.)**

— [No. 2.] Fantaisie romantique sur deux mélodies suisses, *etc.* [P. F.] pp. 23. *Chez Fr. Hofmeister: Leipzig,* [1837.] fol.   **Hirsch M. 950. (9.)**

— [No. 2.] Fantaisie romantique sur deux mélodies suisses pour le piano-forte ... Oeuvre 5. N° 1. Seule édition revue et augmentée par l'auteur. pp. 25. *Chez Tob. Haslinger: Vienne,* [1838.] fol.   **g. 547. t. (5.)**

— [No. 3.] Rondeau fantastique sur un thème espagnol (El Contrabandista) composé pour le piano. pp. 27. *Chez Fr. Hofmeister: Leipzig,* [1837.] fol.   **Hirsch M. 953. (11.)**

— [No. 3.] Rondeau fantastique sur un thème espagnol, El Contrabandista ... pour le piano, *etc. B. Latte: Paris,* [1837.] fol.   **h. 896. d. (4.)**

— [No. 3.] Rondeau fantastique sur un thème espagnol El Contrabandista pour piano. pp. 23. *Chez Schuberth & comp.: Hamburg, Leipsic,* [1843?] fol.   **h. 585. k. (2.)**

— Trois morceaux suisses. *See* supra: [Album d'un voyageur. No. 10–12.]

— Morgens steh' ich auf und frage, von Heine. *See* supra: [*Collected Works.—d.*] F. Liszt's gesammelte Lieder, *etc.* No. 15.

— Mosonyi's Grab Geleit' für Pianoforte. pp. 9. *Táborszky & Parsch: Pest,* [1871.] fol. *Later published as No. 7 of "Magyar történelmi arcképek", entered above.*   **h. 896. j. (8.)**

— A Munka himnusza. *See* supra: [Arbeiter-Chor.]

LISZT (Franz)

— Mutter-Gottes Sträusslein zum Maimonate. No. 1. Das Veilchen. Neue Ausgabe für eine tiefere Stimme. [Words by J. Müller.] *See* supra: [*Collected Works.—d.*] F. Liszt's gesammelte Lieder, *etc.* No. 29.

— Mutter-Gottes Sträusslein zum Maimonate. 2. Die Schlüsselblumen.—Les Primevères.—Poésie de J. Müller. Paroles françaises de G. Lagye. *See* supra: [*Collected Works.—d.*] F. Liszt's gesammelte Lieder, *etc.* No. 30.

— My Dream of Love. *See* supra: [Drei Lieder für eine Sopran-oder Tenor-Stimme. No. 3. O lieb', O lieb'.]

— Nicht gezagt. [Words by] C. Götze. *See* supra: Für Männergesang. No. 5.

— The Nightingale. *See* supra: [Deux mélodies russes. No. 1. Le Rossignol.]

— Nimm einen Strahl der Sonne, von Rellstab. *See* supra: [*Collected Works.—d.*] F. Liszt's gesammelte Lieder, *etc.* No. 23.

— Nocturne. No. 3. *See* supra: [Drei Lieder für eine Sopran-oder Tenor-Stimme. No. 3.]

— Nocturne sur le "Chant montagnard" de Ernest Knop. *See* supra: [Album d'un voyageur. No. 10–12.] Trois airs suisses. no. 2.

— Nonnenwerth. *See* infra: [Die Zelle in Nonnenwerth.]

— Nouvelle mélodie hongroise. *See* supra: [Magyar dallok. No. 6.]

— Nuits d'Été à Pausilippe. (No. 1. Il Barcajuolo (Barcarola) di Donizetti.—No. 2. L'Alito di Bice (Notturno) di Donizetti. —No. 3. La Torre di Biasone (Canzone Napoletana) di Donizetti). [P. F.] 3 no. *Les Fils de B. Schott: Mayence, etc.,* [1839.] 4°. *No. 7–9 of "Les Soirées Italiennes".*   **g. 547. a. (7.)**

— Nuits d'été à Pausilippe. Trois amusements pour le piano sur des motifs de l'album de Donizetti, *etc.* pp. 25. *Chez les fils de B. Schott: Mayence, Anvers,* [1839.] 4°.   **f. 470. k.**

— Nuits d'été à Pausilippe. [P. F.] 2 no. pp. 16. [no. 1.] Il Barcajuolo de Donizetti. [no. 2.] L'Alito di bice de Donizetti. *Chez les fils de B. Schott: Mayence,* [1840.] fol. *Imperfect; wanting no. 3 "La Torre de biasone de Donizetti". The numeration on the titlepages, no. 7[–9] is in continuation of that of "Soirées italiennes".*   **Hirsch M. 954. (4.)**

— Nuits d'été à Pausilippe. Trois amusements pour piano sur des motifs de l'album de Donizetti, *etc.* pp. 25. *Chez Jean Ricordi: Milan,* [c. 1840.] fol.   **g. 547. w. (1.)**

— Der Choral: "Nun danket Alle Gott," für die Orgel gesetzt ... Chor und Begleitung der Trompeten, Posaunen und Pauken ad lib. Partitur und Stimmen. *Leipzig und Brüssel,* [1884.] fol.   **H. 1878. c. (3.)**

— O filii et filiæ. *See* supra: [Christus.]

— O Lieb'. *See* supra: [Drei Lieder für eine Sopran- oder Tenor-Stimme. No. 3.]

— O Lord above, whose Sacrifice. *See* supra: [9 Kirchen-Chor-Gesänge. No. 8. O salutaris hostia.]

— O loving God. *See* supra: [Es muss ein Wunderbares sein.]

— O Meer im Abendstrahl. Duett für Sopran und Alt, mit Begleitung des Pianoforte oder Harmonium. [Words by] (A. Meissner). *Leipzig,* [1884.] fol.   **H. 1878. c. (2.)**

— [Oh pourquoi donc.] Romance ... Oeuvre posthume. ⟨Piano. Doigté par R. Strobl.⟩ pp. 6. *Friedrich Hofmeister: Leipzig; E. Wende & c^o: Varsovie,* [1909.] fol.   **h. 585. o. (3.)**

LISZT (Franz)

— Oh! quand je dors. *See* supra: [Buch der Lieder. Bd. 2. No. 1.]

— O Sorrow deep. [Anthem.] *See* infra: [Via crucis.—O Traurigkeit.]

— O wenn es doch immer so bliebe ... Lied ... von A. Rubinstein ... Transcription für Pianoforte (zum Concertvortrag). *Leipzig,* [1881.] fol.   **g. 549. (8.)**

— Offertorium. *See* supra: [Koronázási Mise.]

— "Ora pro nobis." Litanei für Harmonium oder Orgel. pp. 5. *Bei G. Wilh. Körner: Erfurt,* [1865.] *obl.* 4°. *The titlepage is mutilated.*   **d. 210. g.**

— L'Orgia. *See* infra: Soirées musicales de Rossini. no. 11.

— Orphée. *See* infra: Symphonische Dichtungen. no. 4.

— [Der Papst-Hymnus.] L'Hymne du Pape ... pour le piano. pp. 7. *Ed. Bote & G. Bock: Berlin, Posen,* [1865.] fol.   **h. 585. b. (4.)**

— Der Papst-Hymnus für Harmonium oder Orgel. pp. 5. *Bei G. Wilh. Körner: Erfurt,* [1865.] *obl.* 8°.   **e. 58. l. (1.)**

— Grande paraphrase de la marche de J. Donizetti composée pour Sa Majesté le Sultan Abdul Medjid-Khan, pour le pianoforte, *etc.* pp. 17. *Chez A^d Mr Schlesinger: Berlin,* [1848.] fol.   **g. 547. p. (6.)**

— Grande paraphrase de la marche de J. Donizetti composée pour Sa Majesté le Sultan Abdul Medjid-Khan, pour le pianoforte ... Version facilitée. pp. 12. *Chez A^d Mr Schlesinger: Berlin,* [1848.] fol.   **h. 896. l. (7.)**

Trois paraphrases de concert

— Trois paraphrases de concert pour piano ... N° 1. Trovatore ... N° 2. Ernani ... N° 3. Rigoletto. ⟨De Verdi.⟩ 3 no. *J. Schuberth & C°: Leipzig, New-York,* [1860.] fol. *Imperfect; wanting the titlepage to no. 3.*   **h. 896. ii. (3.)**

— [Another copy.] *Imperfect; wanting no. 1, 3.*   **h. 896. i. (17.)**

— Trois paraphrases de concert pour piano ... N° 1. Trovatore ... N° 2. Ernani ... N° 3. Rigoletto ⟨de Verdi⟩, *etc.* no. 1, 2. *Titus Ricordi: Milan,* [1860, c. 1870.] fol. *No. 2 is of a later issue. Imperfect; wanting no. 3.*   **h. 585. m. (12.)**

— Liszt-Verdi Album. Concert-Paraphrasen über Verdi's Rigoletto, Trovatore, Ernani, für Pianoforte. pp. 43. *J. Schuberth & Co.: Leipzig,* [1890?] fol. *The wrapper bears the title "Verdi Opern-Album".*   **h. 896. j. (9.)**

— [No. 3.] Rigoletto de Verdi. Fantaisie pour Piano. *Brewer & Co.: London,* [1872.] fol.   **h. 585. a. (8.)**

— [No. 3.] Rigoletto de Verdi. Paraphrase de Concert pour Piano ... Revised by E. Pauer. *Augener: London,* [1908.] fol.   **g. 719. b. (2.)**

— [No. 3.] Paraphrase on Themes from Verdi's Opera Rigoletto. Revised by C. Deis. (Piano.) *G. Schirmer: New York,* 1939. 4°.   **g. 547. g. (5.)**

— [Парафразы.] Paraphrases. 24 variations et 15 petites pièces pour piano ... par A. Borodine, César Cui, Anatole Liadow et Nicolas Rimsky-Korsakow. Nouvelle édition, augmentée d'une variation de François Liszt, d'une mazurka de Borodine et des "Bigarrures" de N. Stcherbatcheff, *etc.* pp. 47. [c. 1910.] fol. *See* BORODIN (A. P.)   **h. 1426. dd. (5.)**

— [Парафразы.] Tati-tati. Paraphrases sur un thème enfantin favori composées pour piano à quatre mains par A. Borodine, César Cui, Anatole Liadow, Nicolas

LISZT (Franz)

Rimsky-Korsakoff, François Liszt. Librement retravaillées et mises à l'orchestre par Nicolas Tcherepnine. [Score.] pp. 79. [1937.] *See* BORODIN (A. P.)   **i. 110. o. (6.)**

— La Partenza. *See* infra: Soirées musicales de Rossini. No. 7.

— Pastorale. *See* supra: [Chöre zu Herder's "Entfesseltem Prometheus".—Chor der Schnitter.]

— Pastorale. *See* infra: [Symphonische Dichtungen. No. 3. Les Préludes.—Allegretto pastorale.]

— La Pastorella dell'Alpi e li Marinari. Fantaisie. *See* supra: [2 grandes fantaisies sur des motifs des Soirées musicales de Rossini. No. 2.]

— La Pastorella dell' Alpi. *See* also infra: Soirées musicales de Rossini. No. 6.

— Pater noster quattuor vocum ad aequales (II TT. et II BB.) concinente organo secundum rituale SS. ecclesiae romanae. Ave Maria quattuor vocum concinente organo. pp. 11. *Sumptibus et formis Breitkopfii et Hartelii: Lipsiae,* [1853.] fol.   **h. 896. n. (10.)**

— Pater noster (Vater unser) für gemischten Chor (Sopran, Alt, Tenor und Bass) mit Begleitung der Orgel ... Partitur, *etc.* pp. 23. *Bei C. F. Kahnt: Leipzig,* [1864.] 8°.   **F. 1175. qq. (3.)**

— [Pater noster. Ave Maria.] Ave Maria.—S. A. T. B. and Organ. *G. Schirmer: New York,* [1903?] 8°.   **F. 1179. (55.)**

— Pater noster und Ave Maria. *See* supra: [Kirchen-Chor-Gesänge. No. 1, 2.]

— "Pax vobiscum." Mottet [sic] für 4 Männer Stimmen, Soli— oder für Männerchor, mit Orgel Begleitung, (ad libitum). [A facsimile of the composer's autograph. With a portrait.] *In:* STRASBURG.— *Strassburger Maenner-Gesangverein.* Strassburger Sängerhaus. pp. 64–68. 1886. fol.   **I. 526.**

— Il Penseroso. *See* supra: [Années de pèlerinage. Seconde année. No. 2.]

— La Pesca. *See* infra: Soirées musicales de Rossini. No. 8.

— Pester Carneval für das Piano-Forte. pp. 19. *Bei Tobias Haslinger's Witwe and Sohn: Wien,* [1847.] fol. *Editions of the second version of this work, published as no. 9 of the "Rhapsodies hongroises," are entered below.*   **h. 896. ff. (4.)**

— Petite valse favorite pour le piano. pp. 7. *Schuberth & Comp.: Hambourg, Leipsic,* [1843.] fol.   **g. 547. u. (4.)**

— Phantasiestück für das Pianoforte über Motive aus Rienzi von R. Wagner, *etc.* pp. 14. *Breitkopf & Härtel: Leipzig,* [1862.] fol.   **h. 896. i. (9.)**

— [Phantasiestück über Motive aus Rienzi.] Rienzi, opéra de R. Wagner. Morceau de fantaisie par F. Liszt. [P. F.] pp. 14. *G. Flaxland: Paris; Leipzig* [printed, 1865?] fol.   **h. 896. j. (10.)**

— Phantasiestück for the Pianoforte on airs from Wagner's Rienzi. *London,* [1880.] fol.   **h. 1494. r. (5.)**

— Das Pianoforte. Ausgewählte Sammlung älterer u. neuerer Original-Compositionen unter Redaction von Dr F. Liszt, und unter Mitwirkung von J. Abenheim, J. Abert [and others] ... Erstes (–Zwölftes) Heft, *etc.* Jahrg. 1. 11 no. *Eduard Hallberger: Stuttgart,* [1857.] fol. *Hft. 9, 10 form one number. Imperfect; wanting Jahrg. 2.*   **h. 896. v. (6.)**

— Polonaise pour le piano ... I ⟨I[I]⟩. 2 no. *Chez Bartholf Senff: Leipzig,* [1852.] fol.   **g. 547. p. (9.)**

— 1ère (2de) Polonaise pour le Piano ... Revue par X. Scharwenka. 2 no. *London,* [1882.] 4°.   **g. 547. (6.)**

LISZT (Franz)

— Zweite Polonaise ... für grosses Orchester bearbeitet von
C. Müller-Berghaus. *Leipzig,* [1878.] 8°. **e. 577. (3.)**

— Polonaise, No. 2 (in E♭), *etc.* [P. F.] *See* Paull Music Co.
Edition Paull, *etc.* [No. 46.] (1905.) fol. **h. 3822. (46.)**

— Polonaise No. 2. E dur. Nouvelle édition, augmentée d'une
cadence finale, par Ferruccio Busoni. pp. 21. *N. Simrock:
Berlin, Leipzig,* [1909.] fol. **h. 896. j. (11.)**

— Polonaise aus Jewgeny Onegin, Oper von P. Tschaikowsky,
für Piano. *Hamburg,* [1880.] fol. **h. 585. f. (2.)**

— Polonaise aus Tschaikowskys Oper Jewgeny Onegin für
Pianoforte. Zum Concertvortrag bearbeitet von F. Liszt.
pp. 18. *Bei P. Jurgenson: Moscau,* [1880.] fol. **h. 896. ii. (9.)**

— Polonaise per pianoforte a 4 mani. *See supra:*
[Fest-Polonaise.]

— La Prédication aux Oiseaux. *See supra:* [Légendes. No. 1.]

Praeludium und Fuge über das Thema B. A. C. H.

— Praeludium und Fuge über das Thema B. A. C. H. für Orgel,
etc. pp. 16. *Bei W. C. de Vletter: Rotterdam,* [1855.] obl. fol. **e. 58. j.**

— Fantasie und Fugue über das Thema ... BACH für das
Pianoforte. pp. 19. *C. F. W. Siegel's Musikalienhandlung:
Leipzig,* [1871.] fol.
*The verso of the titlepage bears a MS. dedication in the
composer's autograph to A. W. Gottschalg, relating to his
performance of the work.* **Hirsch M. 950. (10.)**

— Prelude & Fugue upon the name of B. A. C. H. for Organ.
Edited by H. F. Ellingford. *Augener: London,* [1935.] 4°. **g. 547. f. (23.)**

— Fantasia and Fugue on B. A. C. H. for the Organ ... Edited
by C. H. Trevor. *Novello & Co.: London,* [1942.] 4°.
Original Compositions, New Series, No. 180. **g. 1270.**

— Prelude and Fugue on the Theme BACH. For organ. Edited
by Anthony Newman. Foreword by Anthony Newman and
Gary Schultz. pp. iv. 20. *G. Schirmer: New York, London,*
[1974.] obl. 4°.
Part of "Great Performers' Edition". **e. 58. m. (2.)**

— Les Préludes. *See infra:* Symphonische Dichtungen. no. 3.

— Huit premières études. *See supra:* [24 grandes études.
No. 1–8.]

— Procession by Night and Mephisto Waltz. *See supra:* [Zwei
Episoden aus Lenau's Faust.]

— La Promessa. *See infra:* Soirées musicales de Rossini. No. 1.

— Prométhée. *See infra:* Symphonische Dichtungen. no. 5.

— Provenzalisches Minnelied (Chanson Provençale) von
R. Schumann, transcribirt für Pianoforte. *Berlin,* [1881.] 4°. **g. 547. (7.)**

Der 13. Psalm

— Der 13. Psalm. Le xiiime psaume. "Dieu sévère, ah! pourquoi
suis-je en ta disgrâce?" "Herr, wie lange willst du meiner
sogar vergessen?" ... Partitur. *C. F. Kahnt Nachfolger:
Leipzig,* [1900?] fol. **H. 1878. g.**

— Der 13. Psalm, für Tenor, gemischten Chor und Orchester.
Herausgegeben von Márta Papp. Partitur. pp. 96. *Henry
Litolff's Verlag/C. F. Peters: Frankfurt, etc.; Editio Musica:
Budapest; printed in Hungary,* [1975.] 4°. **G. 461. h. (1.)**

— The 13th Psalm, for Tenor solo & chorus. The English
adaptation by J. Goddard. [Vocal score.] *London,* [1876.] 4°. **F. 566.**

LISZT (Franz)

— Der 13. Psalm. "Herr, wie lange willst du meiner sogar
vergessen?" Für Tenor Solo, Chor und Orchester ...
Klavier-Auszug. pp. 46. *C. F. Kahnt: Leipzig,* [1878.] 8°. **E. 1644. m.**

— The Thirteenth Psalm ... for Tenor Solo Chorus and
Orchestra. The English adaptation by Dr. Troutbeck.
Novello, Ewer and Co.: London & New York, [1888.] 8°. **E. 1644. c.**

— Der 13. Psalm. Für Tenor, gemischten Chor und Orchester.
Herausgegeben von Márta Papp. Klavierauszug von Olivér
Nagy. pp. 52. *Henry Litolff's Verlag/C. F. Peters: Frankfurt,
etc.; Editio Musica: Budapest; printed in Hungary,* [1975.] 8°. **F. 566. h. (1.)**

— [Ich aber hoffe.] But I have trusted in thy Mercy. For
three-part chorus of mixed voices with piano accompaniment
... Arranged by Robert S. Hines. pp. 4. *G. Schirmer: New
York,* [1969.] 8°. **F. 1106. (25.)**

— Klänge aus dem 13. Psalm ... für Orgel übertragen von
B. Sulze, *etc. See* Album. Album für Orgel-Spieler, *etc.*
Lief. 31. [1880? *etc.*] obl. fol. **e. 119.**

— Der 18te Psalm ("Die Himmel erzählen die Ehre Gottes") für
Männerchor und Orchester ... Clavierauszug. pp. 12.
Autographirt von Carl Götze: Weimar, [1861?] 8°. **F. 1176. oo. (1.)**

— Der 18te. Psalm ... für Männer Chor mit deutschem und
lateinischem Text. Partitur. *Leipzig,* [1870?] fol. **H. 1878. a. (4.)**

— Der 18te. Psalm. "Coeli enarrant gloriam Dei." (Die Himmel
erzählen die Ehre Gottes.) Für Männer Chor mit deutschem
und lateinischem Text ... Clavier Auszug ... oder obligate
Orgel, *etc.* pp. 31. *J. Schuberth & c^ie: Leipzig,* [c. 1880.] 8°. **F. 566. e. (1.)**

— Der 23. Psalm: "Mein Gott der ist mein Hirt," nach Herder's
Uebersetzung, für eine Singstimme (Tenor oder Sopran) mit
Begleitung von Harfe (oder Pianoforte) und Orgel (oder
Harmonium). Der 137. Psalm: "An den Wassern zu
Babylon," für eine Singstimme mit Frauenchor mit
Begleitung der Violine, der Harfe, des Pianoforte und Orgel
(oder Harmoniums) ... Partitur, *etc.* 2 no. *C. F. Kahnt:
Leipzig,* [1864, c. 1880.] 8°.
No. 2 is of a later issue. **F. 1171. q. (5.)
& E. 1644. d. (3.)**

— Psalm 116. *See supra:* [Koronázási Mise. — Graduale.]

— Psalm 129. De Profundis ... für eine Bass- oder Altstimme
und Pianoforte oder Orgelbegleitung. Ausgabe für Bass.
Leipzig, [1884.] 8°. **F. 363. f. (12.)**

— Der 137. Psalm: "An den Wassern zu Babylon". *See also
supra:* Der 23. Psalm ... Der 137. Psalm.

— [Psalm 137.] By the Waters of Babylon, *etc.* [For voice, violin,
P. F., and optional organ or harmonium. Score.] pp. 14.
J. Curwen & Sons: London, [1907.] 8°.
[*Choruses for equal Voices. no.* 1052.] **E. 861.**

— Der 137. Psalm ... für die Orgel allein übertragen von
B. Sulze. *See* Album. Album für Orgel-Spieler, *etc.* Lief. 46.
[1880? *etc.*] obl. fol. **e. 119.**

— I Puritani. Introduction et polonaise pour le piano [on
Bellini's opera]. pp. 9. *Chez les fils de B. Schott: Mayence,*
[1841.] fol. **Hirsch M. 953. (9.)**

— I Puritani. Introduction et Polonaise pour le piano [on
Bellini's opera]. *Les Fils de B. Schott: Mayence,* [c. 1880.] fol. **h. 896. a. (7.)**

LISZT (Franz)

— Puszta-Wehmut. (Kleine ungarische Rhapsodie) ... Für das Pianoforte zu 2 Händen. [Based on a composition by Countess L. Gizyeka-Zamoyska.] Revision und Fingersatz von Alfred Kleinpaul. pp. 3. *Carl Rühle's Musik-Verlag: Leipzig*, [c. 1900.] fol. **h. 896. z. (1.)**

— Qui Mariam absolvisti, für Baryton-Solo, Gemischten Chor und Orgel oder Harmonium. Part. *Licht & Meyer: Leipzig*, 1885. 8°. **F. 231. f. (17.)**

— Rákóczy-Marsch. *See* infra: [Rhapsodie hongroise. No. 15.]

— Recueillement. [P. F.] *See* BELLINI (V.) [Appendix.] Alla memoria di V. Bellini ... No. 22. [1885.] fol. **h. 3312.**

— La Regata Veneziana. *See* infra: [Soirées musicales de Rossini. No. 2.]

— Reiterlied. *See* infra: Vierstimmige Männergesänge. No. 3 and 4.

— Réminiscences de Boccanegra de Verdi pour Piano. *Milan*, [1883.] fol. **h. 585. g. (5.)**

Réminiscences de Don Juan

— Grand fantaisie sur Don Juan de Mozart pour piano. pp. 33. *Chez M^ce Schlesinger: Paris*, [1843.] fol. **h. 585. l. (3.)**

— Réminiscences de Don Juan [by W. A. Mozart]. Grande fantaisie pour le piano, *etc.* pp. 35. *Chez A^d Mr Schlesinger: Berlin*, [1843.] fol. **g. 547. u. (10.)**

— [A reissue.] Grande fantaisie (réminiscences) de Don Juan [by W. A. Mozart]. ⟨Pour le piano.⟩ pp. 35. *Chez A^d Mr Schlesinger: Berlin*, [c. 1845.] fol.
The title is taken from the head of p. 3. The titlepage reads "4 fantaisies. N° 1. Les Huguenots. 2e édition. N° 2. La Juive. N° 3. Robert le diable. N° 4. Don Juan". **h. 896. s. (4.)**

— [A reissue.] Grande fantaisie (réminiscences) de Don Juan [by W. A. Mozart]. *Berlin*, [c. 1845.] fol.
With a dedicatory leaf. **h. 896. i. (2.)**

— Reminiscenses [*sic*] de Don Juan [by W. A. Mozart] pour piano ... Nouvelle édition revue par l'auteur, *etc.* pp. 35. *Verlag der Schlesinger'schen Buch- u. Musikhandlung: Berlin*, [c. 1875.] fol. **h. 896. l. (9.)**

— Don Giovanni de Mozart. Grande Fantaisie pour piano. Edition ... revue et doigtée par M. Pauer. *London*, [1887.] 4°.
No. 8216 of Augener & Co.'s edition. **g. 547. a. (2.)**

— Réminiscences de Don Juan. Konzert-Fantasie über Motive aus Mozarts "Don Giovanni" für das Pianoforte. Grosse kritisch-instruktive Ausgabe von Ferruccio Busoni. pp. 60. *Breitkopf & Härtel: Leipzig*, [1928?] 4°. **g. 547. j. (9.)**

— Réminiscences de Don Juan [by W. A. Mozart]. Fantaisie pour 2 pianos. pp. 29. *Schlesinger: Berlin*, [1877.] fol.
Two copies. **h. 585. b. (24.)**

— Réminiscences des Huguenots. *See* supra: [Grande fantaisie sur des thèmes de l'opéra Les Huguenots.]

— Réminiscences de La Juive [by J. F. F. É. Halévy]. Fantaisie brillante pour piano seul, *etc.* pp. 33. *Chez Maurice Schlesinger: Paris*, [1836.] fol. **g. 272. x. (20.)**

— Réminiscences de la Juive [by J. F. F. É. Halévy]. Fantaisie brillante pour piano seul, *etc.* pp. 25. *Chez Fréd. Hofmeister: Leipzig*, [1836.] fol. **g. 547. cc. (6.)**

— Réminiscences de La Juive—Die Judinn [by J. F. F. É. Halévy]. Op. . pp. 33. *Chez A^d Mr Schlesinger:* [c. 1850.] fol.
The title is taken from the head of p. 2. The titlepage reads: "4 fantaisies. N° 1. Les Huguenots. 2e édition. N° 2. La Juive. N° 3. Robert le diable. N° 4. Don Juan". **g. 547. p. (10.)**

LISZT (Franz)

— Réminiscences de Lucia de Lammermoor [by D. G. M. Donizetti]. Fantaisie dramatique pour le piano ... Oeuv. 13. 1re partie. pp. 10. *Chez Frédéric Hofmeister: Leipzig*, [1840?] fol. **h. 896. l. (8.)**

— Réminiscences de Lucia de Lammermoor [by D. G. M. Donizetti]. Fantaisie dramatique pour le piano ... Oeuv. 13. 1re partie. pp. 9. *Chez Frédéric Hofmeister: Leipzig*, [c. 1840.] fol. **h. 896. s. (11.)**

— [Réminiscences de Lucia di Lammermoor.] Andante final de Lucie de Lamermoor [*sic*] [by D. G. M. Donizetti], 2e acte, pour piano seul. pp. 9. *Chez Bernard Latte: Paris*, [c. 1845.] fol.
L'Année musicale. no. 337. **h. 585. j. (8.)**

— Réminiscences de Lucia di Lammermoor [by D. G. M. Donizetti]. No. 1. *Addison & Hodson: London*, [1850?] fol. **g. 443. i. (4.)**

— Réminiscences de Lucia de Lammermoor [by D. G. M. Donizetti]. Interprétation de A. Henselt. [P. F.] *F. Hofmeister: Leipzig*, [1879.] fol.
Cahier II. of Henselt's "Haute École du Piano". **h. 585. g. (12.)**

— [Réminiscences de Lucia di Lammermoor.] Lucia. ⟨Réminiscences de Lucia di Lammermoor [by D. G. M. Donizetti].⟩ pp. 10. *Ashdown & Parry: London*, [1880?] fol. **h. 896. k. (2.)**

— Réminiscences de Lucrezia Borgia [by D. G. M. Donizetti]. Grande fantaisie. 1^ière partie: Trio du seconde acte. 2de partie: Chanson à boire (Orgie)—Duo—Finale. ⟨Seconde édition de la fantaisie, entièrement revue, corrigée et augmentée par l'auteur.⟩ Pour piano. 2 no. *Chez Pietro Mechetti: Vienne*, [1853.] fol. **g. 547. p. (11.)**

— Réminiscences de Lucrezia Borgia de Donizetti ... Réduite, avec l'approbation de l'auteur, à un seul morceau de concert par G. Buonamici. pp. 19. *Aug. Cranz: Leipzig*, [c. 1880.] fol. **h. 896. z. (2.)**

— Réminiscences de Norma [by V. Bellini]. ⟨Grande fantaisie.⟩ [P. F.] pp. 24. *Chez les fils de B. Schott: Mayence*, [1844.] fol. **h. 585. l. (5.)**

— Réminiscences de Norma [by V. Bellini]. ⟨Grande fantaisie.⟩ [P. F.] pp. 23. *Chez les fils de B. Schott: Mayence*, [c. 1860.] fol. **Hirsch M. 953. (10.)**

— Réminiscences de Norma. Grande Fantaisie [on V. Bellini's opera. P. F]. *B. Schott's Söhne: Mayence*, [1880?] fol. **h. 896. a. (9.)**

— Réminiscences de l'opéra Norma. Grande fantaisie pour le piano ... Pour 2 pianos à 4 mains. [Parts.] 2 pt. *Chez les fils de B. Schott: Mayence*, [1846?] fol. **h. 585. k. (1.)**

— Reminiscences des Puritains [by V. Bellini]. Grande Fantasie pour le piano ... Op. 7. *B. Schott's Söhne: Mayence*, [c. 1880.] fol. **h. 896. a. (1.)**

— Reminiscences, des Puritains [by V. Bellini]. Grande fantaisie, pour le piano ... Op. 7. pp. 29. *Cramer, Addison & Beale: London*, [1840?] fol. **h. 896. h. (17.)**

— Reminiscences des Puritains [by V. Bellini]. Grande fantaisie pour le piano ... Op. 7. pp. 27. *Chez E. Troupenas: Paris*, [c. 1855.] fol. **h. 585. j. (6.)**

— Réminiscences de Robert le diable [by G. Meyerbeer]. Fantaisie pour piano, *etc.* pp. 24. *Chez A^d Mr Schlesinger: Berlin*, [1841.] fol. **h. 896. s. (1.)**

— Réminiscences de "Robert le diable" [by G. Meyerbeer], *etc.* [P. F.] pp. 21. *Chappell: London*, [1841.] fol. **h. 584. (1.)**

LISZT (Franz)

— [Réminiscences de Robert le Diable.] Grande fantaisie sur des motifs de Robert le Diable de Meyerbeer, pour piano. ⟨Valse infernale.⟩ pp. 22. *Maurice Schlesinger: Paris*, [1845?] fol.
h. 896. i. (10.)

— Fantaisie (reminiscences) sur des thèmes de l'opéra Robert le Diable de Meyerbeer, arrangée pour le piano à quatre mains. pp. 29. *Chez A^d Mr Schlesinger: Berlin*, [1843.] fol.
Hirsch M. 952. (7.)

— Requiem für Männerstimmen, Soli und Chor mit Begleitung der Orgel, 2 Trompeten, 2 Posaunen und Pauken ad libitum. Herausgegeben von Gábor Darvas. [Score.] pp. 66. *Ernst Eulenburg, etc.: London, etc.; printed in Switzerland*, [1970.] 8°.
[*Edition Eulenburg. no. 947.*] *A revised version of the English preface has been pasted over the original.* **b. 212.**

— Requiem für Männerstimmen (Soli und Chor) mit Orgelbegleitung *Leipzig*, [1860?] fol.
G. 461. a.

— Requiem für die Orgel. *See* Album. Album für Orgel-Spieler, *etc.* Lief. 81. [1880? *etc.*] obl. fol.
e. 119.

— Rhapsodie espagnole. (Folies d'Espagne et Jota arragonesa.) Pour piano. pp. 27. *C. F. W. Siegel: Leipzig*, [1867.] fol.
h. 896. k. (1.)

— Rhapsodie espagnole. [P. F.] *Augener: London*, [1920.] 4°.
g. 547. e. (7.)

— Rhapsodie espagnole. (Folies d'Espagne et Jota arragonesa.) Pour piano ... Ausgabe als Konzertstück mit Orchester, bearbeitet von Ferruccio B. Busoni, *etc.* [Score.] pp. 63. *C. F. W. Siegel's Musikalienhandlung (R. Linnemann): Leipzig*, [1902?] fol.
h. 896. i. (1.)

— Rhapsodie espagnole. (Folies d'Espagne de Jota arragonesa.) Pour piano. pp. 27. *C. F. W. Siegel: Leipzig*, [1867.] fol.
h. 896. k. (1.)

— Rhapsodie espagnole. (Folies d'Espagne et Jota arragonese.) Pour piano ... Ausgabe als Konzertstück mit Orchester, bearbeitet von Ferruccio B. Busoni ... Klavierauszug (Solostimme mit unterlegtem 2. Klavier als Begleitung), *etc.* pp. 51. *C. F. W. Siegel's Musikalienhandlung: Leipzig*, [c. 1910.] fol.
h. 585. o. (4.)

— [Rhapsodie espagnole.] Spanish Rhapsody (Folies d'Espagne and Jota aragonesa). For the pianoforte. Arranged as a concert piece for piano and orchestra by Ferruccio Busoni. [The orchestral part arranged for a second P. F.] pp. 51. *G. Schirmer: New York; Chappell & Co.: London;* [*London printed,* 1951.] 4°.
Schirmer's Library of musical Classics. vol. 1252.
g. 547. j. (6.)

Rhapsodies hongroises

— 1re (–15me) Rhapsodie hongroise pour Piano. Revue et doigtée par O. Thümer. 15 no. *Augener & Co.: London*, [1900–9.] 4°.
g. 547. c. (1.)

— Rhapsodies hongroises. Revues et doigtées par E. d'Albert, *etc.* [P. F.] 15 no. *A. Lengnick & Co.: London*, 1906. fol.
g. 719. b. (1.)

— Rhapsodies hongroises, for the Pianoforte. Edited and revised by R. Joseffy. no. 1–11, 13–15. *G. Schirmer: New York*, (1908–10.) fol.
Imperfect; wanting no. 12. **g. 719. c.**

— Rhapsodies hongroises pour Piano ... Revue[s] et doigtée[s] par O. Thümer. 2 vol. *Augener: London*, [1911.] 4°.
g. 719. d.

— Rhapsodies hongroises. For the piano. Edited by Rafael Joseffy ... Book I (Nos. 1–8) ... Book II (Nos. 9–15), *etc.* 2 bk.

G. Schirmer: New York; Chappell & Co.: London; [*London printed,* 1950.] 4°.
Schirmer's Library of musical Classics. vol. 1033, 1034.
g. 547. h. (4.)

— Венгерские рапсодии для фортепиано. ⟨Редакция и комментарии Я. И. Мильштейна.⟩ [With a portrait.] том. 1. *Музгиз:* [*Moscow,*] 1955. fol.
Imperfect; wanting том. 2. **h. 896. p.**

— Венгерские рапсодии для фортепьяно. ⟨Редакция и комментарии Я. И. Мильштейна.⟩ [With a portrait.] pp. 256. *Музгиз:* [*Moscow,*] 1960. fol.
h. 896. u.

— [No. 14, 12, 6, 2, 5, 9.] Franz Liszt's ungarische Rhapsodien für grosses Orchester bearbeitet vom Componisten und F. Doppler ... Partitur, *etc.* 6 no. *J. Schuberth & Co: Leipzig, New York*, [1875.] 8°.
f. 212.

— [Another copy.]
R. M. 15. i. 6.

— [No. 14, 12, 6, 2, 5, 9.] Franz Liszt's ungarische Rhapsodien für grosses Orchester bearbeitet vom Componisten und F. Doppler ... Frei bearbeitet für das Pianoforte zu vier Händen vom Componisten. 6 no. *J. Schuberth & Co: Leipzig, New York*, [1875.] fol.
h. 585. k. (9.)

— Rapsodies hongroises pour le piano. no. 3–7. *Chez Charles Haslinger: Vienne*, [1853.] fol.
h. 896. j. (12.)

— [A reissue.] Rapsodies hongroises pour le piano. no. 3–7. *Vienne*, [1878.] fol.
h. 585. h. (3.)

— Rhapsodies hongroises pour piano, *etc.* ⟨Arr. à 4 ms. par F. G. Jansen.⟩ no. 3–7. *Schlesinger'sche Buch- u. Musikhdlg.: Berlin; Carl Haslinger: Wien*, [1878.] fol.
h. 585. e. (4.)

— Rhapsodies hongroises pour le piano. no. 8–10. *B. Schott's Söhne: Mayence*, [c. 1885.] fol.
h. 585. h. (4.)

— Rhapsodies hongroises pour le piano. No. 8. Capriccio. No. 9. Le Carnaval de Pesth. No. 10. Preludio. *Schott & Co.: Londres*, [1891.] fol.
g. 547. a. (6.)

— 3me série des rhapsodies hongroises pour le piano. no. 11–15. *Chez Schlesinger: Berlin*, [1878.] fol.
h. 585. h. (5.)

— 3me série des rhapsodies hongroises pour le piano ... à 4 ms. ⟨Arr. par F. G. Jansen.⟩ no. 11–15. *Chez Schlesinger: Berlin*, [1875–78.] fol.
h. 585. c. (5.)

— Rhapsodies hongroises pour le piano. no. 17–19. *Chez Friedrich Hofmeister: Leipzig*, [1886.] fol.
h. 585. h. (7.)

— Rhapsodie hongroise pour le piano ... I. pp. 19. *Chez Bartholf Senff: Leipzig*, [c. 1880.]
h. 585. h. (1.)

— [No. 1.] Hungarian Rhapsody. (N° 1) ... Arranged for military band by Dan Godfrey. ⟨Conductor [and parts].⟩ 26 pt. *Chappell & Co: London*, [1961?] fol.
[*Chappell's Army Journal. no.* 284.] **h. 1562.**

Rhapsodies hongroises. No. 2

— Rhapsodies Hongroises. (No. 2.) [P. F.] *London*, [1878.] fol.
No more published of this edition. **h. 585. f. (17.)**

— Rhapsodie hongroise pour le piano ... II. pp. 19. *Chez Bartholf Senff: Leipzig*, [c. 1880.] fol.
h. 585. h. (2.)

— 2me rhapsodie hongroise pour piano ... à 2 mains, *etc.* pp. 17. *Éditions Ricordi: Milan*, [c. 1880.] fol.
h. 585. m. (1.)

— 2de Rhapsodie Hongroise pour piano. *London*, [1886.] 4°.
Augener & Co.'s edition, No. 8219. **g. 547. (2.)**

— Rhapsodie Hongroise. No. II. [P. F.] *See* Sloper (E. H. L.) Repertory of select Pianoforte Works, *etc.* Third Series. No. 8. [1892, *etc.*] fol.
h. 736. c.

— Rhapsodie hongroise. No. 2, *etc.* [P. F.] *See* Paull Music Co. Edition Paull, *etc.* [No. 44.] (1905.) fol.
h. 3822. (44.)

LISZT (FRANZ)

— Rhapsodie hongroise. No. 2. [P. F.] *Orpheus Music Publishing Co.: London*, [1909.] 4°.
The Guildhall Edition, No. 21.   **g. 1440.**

— Rhapsodie hongroise. No. 2. [P. F.] *Chappell & Co.: London*, (1910.) fol.
Chappell Edition of Popular Pianoforte Works, No. 19.
                                                    h. 3369.

— Rhapsodie hongroise No. 2. [P. F.] *E. Ashdown: London*, [1936.] 4°.
"Selected from the repertoire of Paderewski".   **g. 547. f. (25.)**

— Rhapsodie hongroise. No. 2. (Edited and fingered by J. Furze.) [P. F.] *H. Freeman & Co.: London*, 1938. 4°.
Grafton Classics, No. 106.   **g. 547. f. (31.)**

— Rhapsodie hongroise pour le piano ... II. ⟨Erleichterte Ausgabe von Franz Bendel.⟩ pp. 21. *Bartholf Senff: Leipzig*, [c. 1890.] fol.   **h. 585. m. (4.)**

— 2nd Hungarian Rhapsody. Transposed edition ... Edited by H. E. Button. [P. F.] *J. H. Larway: London*, 1915. 4°.
[*Masterpieces. Simplified transcriptions. No.* 5.] **h. 3301.**

— Hungarian Rhapsodie No. 2 ... Adapted for Piano Solo by J. Thompson. *Willis Music Co.: Cincinnati*, 1938. 4°.
                                                    g. 547. g. (2.)

— Rhapsodie hongroise. Last movement. [P. F.] pp. 6.
Cinephonic Music Co.: London, [1947.] 4°.   **f. 470. a. (7.)**

— Rhapsodie hongroise pour le piano ... II. ⟨Für zwei Pianoforte arrangirt von R. Kleinmichel⟩ pp. 27. *Chez Bartholf Senff: Leipzig*, [1877.] fol.   **h. 585. e. (3.)**

— Rhapsodie hongroise pour le piano ... II ... Arrangement für Pianoforte zu 4 Händen ⟨nach Franz Bendel⟩, *etc.* pp. 25.
Chez Bartholf Senff: Leipzig, [c. 1900.] fol.   **h. 896. z. (13.)**

— Rhapsodie hongroise, II. ... Arranged by F. Bendel. (Piano Duet.) *Augener: London*, [1915.] 4°.   **g. 547. d. (7.)**

— Hungarian rhapsody No. 2. For two pianos, four hands. Arranged by Richard Kleinmichel. pp. 27. *G. Schirmer: New York; Chappell & Co.: London;* [*London* printed, 1951.] 4°.
Schirmer's Library of musical Classics. vol. 1568.
Two copies.   **g. 547. j. (3.)**

— Hungarian Rhapsody No. 2. For two pianos, eight-hands. Arranged by Richard Kleinmichel. [Parts.] 2 pt. *G. Schirmer: New York, Chappell & Co.: London;* [*London* printed, 1951.] 4°.
Schirmer's Library of musical Classics. vol. 1570.
                                                    g. 547. j. (4.)

— Zweite ungarische Rhapsodie ... Für grosses Orchester bearbeitet von Karl Müller-Berghaus. [Score.] pp. 64.
N. Simrock: Berlin, Leipzig, [c. 1910.] 8°.   **e. 58. k. (2.)**

— Zweite ungarische Rhapsodie ... Für grosses Orchester bearbeitet von Karl Müller-Berghaus. [Conductor and parts.] 27 pt. *Bartholf Senff: Leipzig*, [1872.] fol.   **h. 1509. a. (9.)**

— Hungarian Rhapsody No. 2 in D & G (original key) ... Arranged by Adolf Lotter. [Orchestral parts.] 20 pt. *Hawkes & Son: London; Leipzig* [printed, 1907.] 4°.   **g. 1800. (209.)**

— 2. Ungarische Rhapsodie ... Bearb. von L. Windsperger. [Parts.] *Schott & Co.: London*, [1924.] 4°.
[*Schott & Co.'s Domesticum Salon Orchestra. No.* 64.]
                                                    g. 1053. a.

— A Paraphrase on 2nd Hungarian Rhapsody ... Arr. by L. Weninger. Piano-Direction [and orchestral parts]. *British Standard Music Co.: London*, [1942.] 4°.   **h. 3210. h. (840.)**

— Hungarian Rhapsody ... Arranged for Military Band by A. Seidel. [Parts.] *Hawkes & Son: London*, 1904. fol.
Part of "Hawkes & Son's Military Band Edition".
                                                    h. 3211. a. (20.)

LISZT (FRANZ)

— Hungarian Rhapsody No. 2. Liszt.—Morceau humoristique "En promenade". Ernest Gillet. ⟨Conductor [and military band parts].⟩ 28 pt. *Boosey & Co.: London*, 1905. fol.
[*Boosey's military Journal. ser.* 118. *no.* 3.]   **h. 1549.**

— Hungarian Rhapsody No. 2. (Arranged for Military Band by W. J. Duthoit.) [Parts.] *Boosey & Hawkes: London*, 1935. 4°.
[*Boosey & Hawkes Military Band Edition. No.* 44.]
                                                    h. 3211. b.

— Hungarian Rhapsody No. 2. Brass band score ... Arr. W. Rimmer. pp. 44. *Wright & Round: Liverpool*, [1951.] obl. 4°.   **e. 503. j. (3.)**

— 2de Rhapsodie hongroise ... Arr. by F. Hermann. (Piano & Violin.) (Piano, 3 Violins, Viola, Violoncello & Contrabasso.) [Parts.] 2 no. *Augener: London*, [1907.] 4°.   **g. 719. a. (1.)**

— Second ... Rhapsodie. Piano Solo with Violin & Cello ad lib. Arranged by G. H. Farnell. *Banks Music House: Leeds*, 1929. 4°.
Banks Sixpenny Edition, No. 105.   **g. 547. f. (11.)**

— Hungarian Rhapsody No. 2 ... Arranged by Bernard Sheaff. [Banjos, mandolins, guitar and P. F. Parts.] 9 pt. *John Alvey Turner: London*, [1952.] 4°.   **h. 3210. i. (112.)**

— Hungarian Rhapsody No. 2 ... Arr. by C. Nunzio. Accordion. *Alfred Music Co.: New York City*, 1939. 4°.   **g. 547. g. (3.)**

— See KROSS (G.) Cadence pour la rhapsodie hongroise n° II pour piano de F. Liszt. [c. 1890.] fol.   **h. 3870. m. (8.)**

— See LORENZO (L. de) Cadenza to Liszt's Second Hungarian Rhapsody ... for solo flute, two flutes, or flute and clarinet. 1917. 4°.   **g. 70. g. (6.)**

— See RAKHMANINOV (S. V.) Cadenza to the Liszt 2nd Hungarian Rhapsody. Edited by Jan Holcman. [1955.] 4°.
                                                    h. 3984. l. (1.)

— See REIBOLD (B.) Romany Life. Adapted from Second Hungarian Rhapsody—Liszt ... for Mixed Voices and Orchestra or Piano, *etc.* 1939. 4°.   **G. 770. u. (4.)**

— See SALZEDO (C.) Paraphrase (or Cadenza) on Liszt's "Second Rhapsody". For harp. [1961.] 4°.   **g. 1098. h. (1.)**

Rhapsodies hongroises. Other numbers

— [No. 3.] Hungarian Rhapsody No. 3 in D major. (Arranged by A. Winter.) [P. F. conductor and orchestral parts.] *Hawkes & Son: London*, 1934. 4°.   **h. 3210. h. (387.)**

— [No. 3.] Hungarian Rhapsody No. 3. (Arranged for Military Band by W. J. Duthoit.) [Parts.] *Boosey & Hawkes: London*, 1936. 4°.
[*Boosey & Hawkes Military Band Edition. No.* 53.]
                                                    h. 3211. b.

— 5. Rhapsodie ... Arrang. von H. Wolf. [Parts.] *Schott & Co.: London*, [1924.] 4°.
[*Schott & Co.'s Domesticum Salon Orchestra. No.* 134.]
                                                    g. 1053. a.

— [No. 6.] 6th Rhapsodie. Last movement. pp. 7. [P. F.]
Cinephonic Music Co.: London, [1947.] 4°.   **f. 470. a. (8.)**

— Rapsodies hongroises pour le piano. no. 8. *Chez les fils de B. Schott: Mayence*, [1853.] fol.   **g. 547. u. (7.)**

— Rapsodies hongroises pour le piano. ⟨IX. Pesther Carnevall.⟩ pp. 27. *Chez les fils de B. Schott: Mayence*, [1853.] fol.
An edition of the first version of this work published under the title "Pester Carneval" is entered above.   **h. 585. o. (6.)**

— Rapsodies hongroises pour le piano. ⟨IX. Rhapsodie hongroise. Pesther Carneval.⟩ pp. 27. *Chez les fils de B. Schott: Mayence*, [1870?] fol.   **h. 896. j. (13.)**

LISZT (Franz)

— Rhapsodie hongroise. IX. Le Carnaval de Pesth ... Arr. par E. Kronke. (2 Pianos à 4 mains.) *Schott & Co.: London,* [1909.] fol. **h. 896. e. (2.)**

— Rapsodies hongroises pour le piano. no. 10. *Chez les fils de B. Schott: Mayence,* [1853.] fol. **Hirsch M. 951. (10.)**

— 3ᵐᵉ Série des Rhapsodies Hongroises pour le Piano. No. 14. (Facilité par Eduard Schrader.) *Berlin,* [1885.] fol. **h. 585. f. (16.)**

— Rhapsodie hongroise No. 14 ... Piano Solo with Violin & Cello ad lib. Arr. by G. H. Farnell. *Banks Music House: Leeds,* 1932. 4°.
Banks Sixpenny Edition, No. 182. **g. 547. f. (12.)**

Rhapsodies hongroises. No. 15

— Rákóczy-Marsch für grosses Orchester symphonisch bearbeitet ... Orchester Partitur, *etc.* pp. 92. *J. Schuberth & Cⁱ: Leipzig, New York,* [1871.] 8°. **e. 58. d.**

— [A reissue.] Rákóczy Marsch für grosses Orchester, *etc. Leipzig, New York,* [c. 1875.] 8°. **f. 470. i.**

— Marche de Rakoczy. Édition populaire pour piano. pp. 11. *Chez Fr. Kistner: Leipzig,* [1851.] 4°. **f. 470. e. (4.)**

— "Comorn," Marche de Rakoczy, pour le piano-forte. pp. 9. *Wessel & Cⁱ: London,* [1852.] fol. **h. 895. (4.)**

— Marche de Rákóczy. Rákoczy induló. Liszt F. után zongorára négy kézre művészileg alkalmazá Réth N. Károly. pp. 11. *Rózsavölgyi és társa: Pesten,* [c. 1870.] fol. **g. 547. u. (6.)**

— Marche de Rakoczy pour piano ... Édition de salon, *etc.* pp. 9. *S. Richault: Paris,* [1877.] fol. **h. 585. b. (21.)**

— Marche de Rakoczy pour piano. *London,* [1886.] 4°. *Augener & Co.'s edition, No.* 8225. **g. 547. (3.)**

— Rakoczy March for the pianoforte. *Robert Cocks & Co.: London,* [1891.] fol. **h. 896. a. (7.)**

— Rakoczy March. (Arranged by J. E. Newell.) [P. F.] *Leonard, Gould & Bolttler: London,* [1929.] 4°. **g. 547. f. (8.)**

— Rákoczy March ... Arranged by Henry Geehl. [P. F.] pp. 5. *Edwin Ashdown: London,* [1948.] 4°. **g. 547. g. (12.)**

Rhapsodies hongroises. No. 16

— Ungarische Rhapsodie für Pianoforte ... Ausgabe zu zwei Händen. pp. 11. *Táborsky & Parsch: Budapest,* [1882.] fol. **h. 585. h. (6.)**

— [Another issue.] Ungarische Rhapsodie für Pianoforte, *etc. Friedrich Hofmeister: Leipzig,* [1882.] fol. **h. 585. f. (9.)**

— Rheinweinlied. *See infra:* Vierstimmige Männergesänge. No. 1.

— Ricordanza. *See supra:* [Études d'exécution transcendante. No. 9.]

— Rienzi ... Morceau de fantaisie. *See supra:* [Phantasiestück über Motive aus Rienzi.]

— Rigoletto de Verdi. Paraphrase de Concert. *See supra:* [Trois Paraphrases de Concert. No. 3.]

— Il Rimprovero. *See infra:* Soirées musicales de Rossini. No. 5.

— Romance. *See supra:* [Oh pourquoi donc.]

— Romance oubliée. (Vergessene Romanze) ... pour Piano seul. *Hanovre,* [1881.] fol. **h. 585. f. (5.)**

— Romance oubliée ... pour Viola & Piano. *Hanovre,* [1881.] fol. **h. 1609. q. (13.)**

LISZT (Franz)

— Romance oubliée ... pour Violon & Piano. *Hanovre,* [1881.] fol. **h. 1609. q. (12.)**

— Romance oubliée ... pour Violoncelle & Piano. *Hanovre,* [1881.] fol. **h. 1849. k. (17.)**

— La Romanesca. Mélodie du 16ᵉ siècle transcrite pour le piano. pp. 12. *Chez Tob. Haslinger: Vienna,* [1840.] fol. **h. 585. j. (1.)**

— La Romanesca. Mélodie (du 16ᵐᵉ siècle). Transcrite pour le piano. pp. 10. *Cramer, Addison & Beale: London,* [1842?] fol. **h. 896. i. (11.)**

— La Romanesca. Mélodie du 16ⁱᵉᵐᵉ siècle. Transcription pour le piano ... Nouvelle édition, entièrement revue et corrigée par l'auteur. pp. 11. *Chez Charles Haslinger: Vienne,* [c. 1870.] fol. **h. 896. z. (11.)**

— Rondeau fantastique sur un thème espagnol. *See supra:* [Trois Morceaux de Salon. Op. 5. No. 3.]

— Rondeau sur le "Ranz de chèvres" de Ferd. Huber. *See supra:* [Album d'un voyageur.] Trois airs suisses. no. 3.

— Le Rossignol. *See supra:* Deux Melodies russes. no. 1.

— Rumänische Rhapsodie. *See supra:* [Magyar Dallok. No. 20.]

— S'il est un charmant gazon. *See supra:* [Buch der Lieder. Bd. 2. No. 4.]

— Saatengrün. [Words by] Uhland. *See supra:* Für Männergesang. No. 9.

— St. Francois de Paule marchant sur les flots. *See supra:* [Légende.]

— Salve Maria, de Jérusalem (I Lombardi), opéra de G. Verdi, *etc.* [P. F.] pp. 7. *Chez les fils de B. Schott: Mayence,* [1848.] fol. **h. 585. o. (8.)**

— Salve Maria, de Jérusalem, opéra de G. Verdi. *Paris,* [1870.] fol. **h. 585. b. (16.)**

— Salve Maria de l'opéra de Verdi Jérusalem. Transcription pour Piano avec l'adaptation de la pédale-trémolo de l'Armonipiano, *etc. Milan,* [1883.] fol. **h. 585. g. (6.)**

— Salve regina. For 4-part chorus of mixed voices unaccompanied ... edited by Robert S. Hines. ⟨English text by R. S. H.⟩ *Lat. & Eng.* pp. 7. *Roberton Publications: Wendover,* [1976.] 8°.
Part of "Lawson-Gould sacred choral Series". **F. 566. g. (1.)**

— San Francesco. *See supra:* [Cantico del sol.]

— Sarabande und Chaconne aus dem Singspiel Almira von G. F. Händel für Pianoforte zum Concertvortrag bearbeitet. *Leipzig,* [1880.] fol. **h. 585. f. (3.)**

— Scherzo ... Herausgegeben von Ferruccio Busoni. Zum ersten Mal veröffentlicht. [A facsimile of the composer's autograph with a copy in Busoni's autograph.] [*Julius Bard: Berlin,* 1922.] 4°.
Issued as a supplement to "Faust. Eine Rundschau". Hft. 1. **g. 547. l. (5.)**

— Scherzo und Marsch für das Pianoforte. pp. 33. *Bei C. M. Meyer (Henry Litolff): Braunschweig,* [1854.] fol. **h. 585. (3.)**

— [Another copy.] **h. 896. i. (13.)**

— Schlüsselblümchen. *See supra:* Mutter-Gottes Sträusslein zum Maimonate. No. 2.

— Schlummerlied. Slumber Song. Oeuvre posthume for pianoforte. Edited by C. V. Lachmund, *etc. G. Schirmer: New York,* 1922. 4°. **g. 547. e. (8.)**

LISZT (Franz)

— Schubert's Märsche [Op. 40 and Op. 121] für das Pianoforte Solo. 3 no. *Bei A. Diabelli & Co.: Wien*, [1846.] fol.
Hirsch M. 955. (2.)

— [Schubert's Märsche für das Pianoforte Solo. No. 2.] Grande marche de Fr. Schubert, op. 40, transcrite pour piano seul. pp. 13. *Chez S. Richault: Paris*, [c. 1850.] fol.
h. 896. v. (5.)

— Schubert's ungarische Melodien. *See supra*: [Mélodies hongroises.]

— Schwebe blaues Auge, von Dingelstedt. *See supra*: [*Collected Works.—d.*] F. Liszt's gesammelte Lieder, *etc.* No. 24.

— Sei still, von H. v. Schorn. *See supra*: [*Collected Works.—d.*] F. Liszt's gesammelte Lieder, *etc.* No. 53.

— Seliger Tod. *See supra*: [Drei Lieder für eine Sopran- oder Tenor-Stimme. No. 2.]

— Die Seligkeiten ... für Chor-Gesang, Bariton-Solo und Orgelbegleitung ad libitum. Partitur. *C. F. Kahnt: Leipzig*, [1865?] 8°.
F. 1171. q. (4.)

— Septem sacramenta. Responsoriumok szólóhangokra, kórusra, organo- vagy harmóniumkísérettel ... Közreadja ... Sulyok Imre. Partitúra, *etc. Lat. & Ger.* pp. 41. *Editio Musica: Budapest*, 1972. 8°.
F. 566. f. (3.)

— La Serenata. *See infra*: Soirées musicales de Rossini. No. 10.

— La Sérenata e l'Orgia. Grande fantaisie. *See supra*: [2 grandes fantaisies sur des motifs des Soirées musicales de Rossini. No. 1.]

— Shepherd's Song at the Manger. *See supra*: [Christus.— Hirtengesang an der Krippe.]

— A short Organ Mass. *See supra*: [Missa pro organo.]

— Слѣпой. Галлада Графа Алексѣя Толстаго съ сопровожденіемъ мелодраматическай музыки ... Der blinde Sänger. Ballade vom Grafen Alexis Tolstoy mit melodramatischer Musikbegleitung ... Ausgabe für Pianoforte allein. pp. 9. *B.* [*sic*] *Bessel & Cᵒ: St. Petersbourg; C. F. Leede: Leipzig*, [1881.] fol.
h. 585. k. (5.)

— Soft as the Zephyr. Part Song for Female Voices, S. S. A. ... Arr. by A. Samuelson. *M. Keane: New York*, 1937. 8°.
F. 217. i. (5.)

— "Soirées de Vienne." Valses-Caprices d'après F. Schubert pour le Piano-Forte. 9 no. *Wessel & Co.: London*, [1852.] fol.
h. 895. (1.)

— Soirées de Vienne. Valses-caprices d'après Schubert ... En neuf livraisons. 9 livr. *Chez C. A. Spina: Vienne*, [1853.] fol.
h. 896. r. (6.)

— Soirées de Vienne, *etc.* no. 7. *Ashdown & Parry: London*, [c. 1870.] fol.
A reissue of the edition of 1852 *entered above. Imperfect; wanting the other no.*
g. 547. u. (3.)

— Soirées de Vienne. Valses-caprices d'après Franz Schubert pour piano, *etc.* pp. 90. *Edwin Ashdown: London*, [c. 1910.] 4°.
g. 547. k. (10.)

— Soirées de Vienne. Valses—Caprices—d'après F. Schubert—. Edited and fingered by T. F. Dunhill. [P. F.] *Augener: London*, 1917. 4°.
g. 547. e. (1.)

— Soirées de Vienne. Valses-caprices for the piano. D'après Franz Schubert. Edited by Arthur Friedheim, *etc.* 2 bk. *G. Schirmer: New York; Chappell & Co.: London; [London printed*, 1950, 51.] 4°.
Schirmer's Library of musical Classics. vol. 1369, 1370.
g. 547. i. (1.)

LISZT (Franz)

— Soirées de Vienne. (Valses-Caprices d'après F. Schubert.) No. 6. For Piano. *J. Williams: London*, (1910.) 4°.
No. 405 *of J. Williams' Albums.*
G. 785. (405.)

— Soirées de Vienne. No. 6 ... Schubert-Liszt. [P. F.] *Chappell & Co.: London, etc.*, (1911.) fol.
Chappell Edition of Popular Pianoforte Works, No. 44.
h. 3369.

— Soirées de Vienne. (Valses-Caprices d'après Schubert.) No. 6 ... Arranged for Piano Duet by E. Haywood. *Oxford University Press: London*, 1934. 4°.
g. 547. f. (19.)

— Soirées de Vienne [No. 6]. Schubert-Liszt. Arrangement for two pianos by Henry Geehl. pp. 19. *Edwin Ashdown: London*, [1948.] 4°.
g. 547. g. (15.)

— Soirées italiennes. [P. F.] 6 no. pp. 80.
    no. 1.   La Primavera de Mercadante.
    no. 2.   Jl Galop de Mercandante.
    no. 3.   Jl Pastore svizzero de Mercadante.
    no. 4.   La Serenata del Marinaro de Mercadante.
    no. 5.   Jl Brindisi de Mercadante.
    no. 6.   La Zingarella spagnola de Mercadante.
Ches les fils de B. Schott: Mayence, [1840.] fol.
No. 7–9 *of this work form no.* 1–3 *of "Nuits d'été à Pausilippe".*
Hirsch M. 954. (8.)

— Soirées Italiennes. Six Amusements pour le piano sur des motifs de Mercadante, *etc. Chez les fils de B. Schott: Mayence, etc.*, [1850?] 4°.
g. 603. e. (4.)

Soirées musicales de Rossini

— Soirées musicales de Rossini, transcrites pour le piano. no. 4. *Chez les fils de B. Schott: Mayence*, [1838.] fol.
Imperfect; wanting no. 1–3, 5–12.   **Hirsch M. 953. (12.)**

— Soirées musicales de Rossini transcrites pour le piano. 2 pt. pp. 59. *Chez les fils de B. Schott: Mayence*, [c. 1840.] fol.
h. 896. n. (11.)

— Soirées de Rossini. Piano forte solo, *etc.* [With a portrait.] pp. 72. *Willis & Cᵒ.: London*, [c. 1840.] fol.   **h. 896. m.**

— Liszt's Piano Forte, arrangement of the Airs in Rossini's Les Soirées musicales, *etc.* No. 10. *Willis & Co.: London*, [1845?] fol.
Imperfect; wanting no. 1–9, 11, 12.   **h. 721. i. (6.)**

— Soirées Musicales de Rossini transcrites pour le Piano par F. Liszt. 2 Suites. *B. Schott's Söhne: Mayence*, [c. 1880.] fol.
h. 896. a. (3.)

— Soirées musicales de Rossini. Pour Piano. [Transcribed by] F. Liszt. Nouvelle édition revue par K. Klindworth, *etc.* 12 no. *Schott & Co.: London*, (1910.) fol.   **h. 896. g. (1.)**

— [No. 2.] La Regata Veneziana. Notturno. *See* RICHARDS (H. B.) The Pianist's Library. No. 3. [1866, *etc.*] fol.
h. 1392. (1.)

— [No. 2.] La Regatta Veneziana. Notturno ... pour Piano. *C. Sheard: London*, [1874.] fol.
No. 5409, 10 *of the Musical Bouquet.*   **H. 2345.**

— [No. 2.] La Regata Veneziana. Notturno. Transcribed by F. Liszt. [P. F.] *Augener & Co.: London*, [1886.] fol.
Part of E. Pauer's "Pianoforte Library".   **h. 3649. (17.)**

— [No. 6.] La Pastorella dell'Alpi. Tyrolienne ... transcrite pour le piano par F. Listz [*sic*]. *G. Brandus, Dufour et cᵉ: [Paris,]* 1854. fol.
Supplement to "La Brodeuse," November 1854.
g. 547. cc. (1.)

— [No. 6.] La Pastorella dell'Alpi ... Arranged for military band by W. J. Duthoit. ⟨Conductor [and parts].⟩ 32 pt. *In:* GRIEG (E. H.) [*Composite Works.*] Song of Norway, *etc.* [1946.] fol. [*Chappell's Army Journal. no.* 727.]   **h. 1562.**

LISZT (Franz)

— [No. 9.] La Danza … [Transcribed for P. F. by] F. Liszt. Edited … by T. F. Dunhill. *Augener: London*, 1917. fol.
h. 896. g. (14.)

— Soldaten-Lied aus Faust von Göthe. *See* supra: Für Männergesang. No. 7.

— Соловей. *See* supra: [Deux Melodies russes. No. 1.]

Sonata in B minor

— Klaviersonate H-moll. Faksimile nach dem … Autograph. [With an afterword by Claudio Arrau.] *G. Henle Verlag: München*, 1973. fol.
h. 585. p.

— Sonate für das Pianoforte. pp. 35. *Bei Breitkopf & Härtel: Leipzig*, [1854.] fol.
g. 547. q. (2.)

— Sonate für das Pianoforte. *Breitkopf & Härtel: Leipzig*, [1880?] fol.
h. 896. a. (8.)

— Sonata in B minor for Piano. Edited and fingered by R. Joseffy. *G. Schirmer: New York*, 1909. 4°. *Schirmer's Library of Musical Classics. vol. 861.*
g. 547. d. (1.)

— Sonata (in B minor). Revised, phrased and fingered by O. Thümer. [P. F.] *Augener: London*, (1914.) 4°.
g. 547. d. (5.)

— Klavier-Sonate. H-moll. Herausgegeben von Moriz Rosenthal. pp. 44. *Verlag Ullstein: Berlin*, [1927.] 4°. *Tonmeister Ausgabe. no. 293.*
g. 547. g. (13.)

— [A reissue.] Sonata in B minor for the Piano. Edited and fingered by R. Joseffy. *G. Schirmer: New York; Chappell & Co.: London;* [*London* printed, 1950.] 4°.
g. 547. h. (5.)

— Sonate h-moll für Klavier zu 2 Händen … Herausgegeben von Emil von Sauer. pp. 35. *C. F. Peters: Frankfurt, etc.*, [1956.] 4°.
g. 547. l. (9.)

— Sonate h-moll … Nach dem Autograph und der Erstausgabe herausgegeben von Ernst Herttrich. Fingersatz von Hans-Martin Theopold. pp. 39. *G. Henle Verlag: München*, [1973.] 4°. *With a corrigenda slip inserted.*
g. 547. bb. (5.)

— Sonate h-moll für Klavier zu zwei Händen. Herausgegeben von Emil von Sauer. pp. 35. *Edition Peters: London, etc.*, [1978.] 4°.
g. 547. ee. (5.)

— Love Theme from the Film "So little Time". Freely adapted from Liszt's Piano Sonata … by Robert Gill, *etc.* [P. F. conductor and orchestral parts.] 219 pt. *Keith Prowse & Co.: London*, [1952.] 8°. *The first violin part is in triplicate.*
h. 3210. i. (113.)

— Love Theme from the Film "So little Time". Freely adapted from Liszt's Piano Sonata … by Robert Gill. [P. F.] pp. 4. *Keith Prowse & Co.: London*, [1952.] 4°.
g. 547. j. (5.)

— 3 sonetti di Petrarca, composti per il clavicembalo. 3 no. *Presso Haslinger vedova e figlio: Vienna*, [1846.] 4°.
f. 470. e. (5.)

— Tre sonetti de Petrarca. Posti in musica per la voce con accompagnamento di pianoforte. 3 no. *Presso Haslinger vedova e figlio: Vienna*, [1847.] fol. *A photographic copy made in 1960.*
G. 461. f. (1.)

— Tre Sonetti del Petrarca (Deutsche Uebersetzung von P. Cornelius) per voce con accompagnamento di Pianoforte. *Mayence*, [1883.] fol.
H. 1793. d. (18.)

LISZT (Franz)

— Sonetti 104 di Petrarca … per voce di tenore … L'accompagnamento originale per Pianoforte fu trascritto … per Orchestra, senza trombe, da F. Busoni … Traduzione inglese da H. G. Chapman. Partitura. *G. Schirmer: New York*, (1911.) fol.
h. 1567. (7.)

— Sonetto di Petrarca. No. 47 (104) (123). *See* supra: [Années de Pèlerinage. Année II. No. 4, 5, and 6.]

— The Song of Brotherhood. *See* supra: [Für Männergesang. No. 1. Vereinslied.]

— [Song without End.] Music from the Film, *etc. See* supra: [*Collected Works.—f.*]

— Sonho de amor. *See* supra: [Drei Lieder für eine Tenor- oder Sopranstimme. No. 3. O lieb', O lieb'.]

— Sonnambula (de Bellini). Grosse Concert-Fantasie für Piano-Forte. *See* supra: [Fantaisie sur des motifs favoris de l'opéra Sonnambula de Bellini.]

— Um sospiro. *See* supra: [3 études de concert. No. 3.]

— Souvenir de Russie. Feuillet d'album par Franz Liszt. [In fact, no. 22. from Liszt's P. F. arrangement of Ferdinand David's "Bunte Reihe".] *Chez M. Bernard: St Pétersbourg*, [c. 1870.] fol.
h. 585. k. (6.)

— Spanish Rhapsody. *See* supra: [Rhapsodie espagnole.]

— Spinnerlied aus "Der fliegende Holländer von Rich. Wagner" für das Pianoforte. pp. 15. *Breitkopf & Härtel: Leipzig*, [1862?] fol.
h. 896. s. (3.)

— Spinnerlied aus "Der fliegende Höllander von Rich. Wagner" für das Pianoforte … Neue revidirte Ausgabe. pp. 15. *Breitkopf & Härtel: Leipzig*, [c. 1880.] fol.
g. 547. u. (2.)

— Spinnerlied. From "Der fliegende Höllander" by R. Wagner. [Transcribed for P. F.] [1892.] *See* SLOPER (E. H. L.) Repertory of select Pianoforte Works, *etc.* Second Series. No. 10. [1892, *etc.*] fol.
h. 736. c.

— [Spinnerlied.] Spinning Song. Wagner-Liszt. [P. F.] [1910.] *See* HAWLEY (S.) Hawley Edition. No. 8. 1909, *etc.* fol.
h. 3527. b.

— Sposalizio. *See* supra: [Années de Pèlerinage. Seconde Année. No. 1.]

— Spring Night. *See* supra: [Frühlingsnacht.]

— Ständchen, von Rückert. *See* supra: Für Männergesang. No. 2.

— [Stanislaus.] Salve Polonia. Interludium aus dem Oratorium Stanislaus … Partitur. *Leipzig*, [1885.] fol.
g. 719.

— [Stanislaus.] Salve Polonia. Interludium … Für das Pianoforte. [I.] Ausgabe zu 2 Händen. [II.] Ausgabe zu 4 Händen. *Leipzig*, [1885.] fol.
h. 585. g. (1.)

— Die stille Wasserrose, von Geibel. *See* supra: [*Collected Works.—d.*] F. Liszt's gesammelte Lieder, *etc.* No. 40.

— Studentenlied aus Goethe's Faust. *See* supra: Vierstimmige Männergesänge. No. 2.

— The Liszt Studies. *See* infra: [Technische Studien.]

— Eine Symphonie zu Dante's Divina Commedia für grosses Orchester und Sopran- und Alt-Chor. Partitur. [With an introduction by Richard Pohl.] pp. 8. 216. *Breitkopf & Härtel: Leipzig*, [1859.] 8°.
e. 58. a.

— [Another copy.]
R. M. 15. i. 5.

LISZT (Franz)

— Symphonie zu Dante's Divina Commedia. [Score, with an introduction by Richard Pohl.] pp. 8. 216. *Breitkopf & Härtel: Leipzig*, [1893.] 8°.
Part of "Partitur-Bibliothek. Gruppe 1". **Hirsch M. 224.**

— Symphonie zu Dantes Divina commedia für Frauenchor und Orchester. Herausgegeben von Imre Sulyok. [Score.] pp. vii. 189. *Ernst Eulenburg, etc.: London, etc.; printed in Switzerland*, [1970.] 8°.
[*Edition Eulenburg, no. 590.*] **b. 212.**

— Eine Symphonie zu Dante's Divina commedia ...
Arrangement für zwei Pianofortes vom Componisten. pp. 75.
Breitkopf & Härtel: Leipzig, [c. 1885.] fol. **h. 896. y. (5.)**

Symphonische Dichtungen

— Symphonische Dichtungen für grosses Orchester. Partitur. 12 no.
   no. 1. Ce qu'on entend sur la montagne. (nach V. Hugo.)
   no. 2. Tasso. Lamento e trionfo.
   no. 3. Les Préludes. (nach Lamartine.)
   no. 4. Orphée.
   no. 5. Prométhée.
   no. 6. Mazeppa. (nach V. Hugo.)
   no. 7. Fest-Klänge.
   no. 8. Héroïde funèbre.
   no. 9. Hungaria.
   no. 10. Hamlet.
   no. 11. Hunnen-Schlacht. (nach Kaulbach.)
   no. 12. Die Ideale. (nach Schiller.)
   Anhang zu N° 7. Fest-Klänge. Kürzungen und Errata.
Breitkopf & Härtel: Leipzig, [1857, 1856–61.] 8°.
A made-up set of various issues. The title is taken from no. 2. **e. 58.**

— Symphonische Dichtungen für grosses Orchester. Partitur, *etc.* 12 no. *Breitkopf & Härtel: Leipzig*, [1857–95?] 8°.
A made-up set, of different issues. No. 3, 5, 6 form part of "Breitkopf & Härtel's Partitur-Bibliothek". **Hirsch M. 225.**

— Symphonische Dichtungen für grosses Orchester ...
Arrangement für zwei Pianofortes vom Componisten. 12 no.
Breitkopf & Härtel: Leipzig, [c. 1870, 1857–c. 1870.] fol.
A made-up set of various issues. **h. 896.**

— Symphonische Dichtungen für grosses Orchester ...
Arrangement für das Pianoforte zu vier Händen vom Componisten. *Breitkopf & Härtel: Leipzig*, [1875.] fol.
Imperfect; no. 6 only. **h. 896. ee.**

— Symphonische Dichtungen für grosses Orchester ...
Arrangement für das Pianoforte zu vier Händen vom Componisten. [In fact, only no. 1–7, 9, 10 arranged by the composer.] 2 Bd. *Breitkopf & Härtel: Leipzig*, [1884.] fol.
h. 585. n.

— [No. 1.] Ce qu'on entend sur la montagne. Was man auf dem Berge hört. Berg-Symphonie ... für grosses Orchester, nach Victor Hugo. *E. Eulenburg: Leipzig*, [1911.] 8°.
[*Eulenburg's kleine Orchester-Partitur-Ausgabe. Symphonien. No. 47.*] **b. 208. b.**

— [No. 1.] Ce qu'on entend sur la montagne. (Bergsymphonie), *etc.* [Score.] pp. vi. 166. *Ernst Eulenburg: London; printed in Switzerland*, [1967.] 8°.
[*Edition Eulenburg. no. 447.*] **b. 212.**

— [No. 1.] Ce qu'on entend sur la montagne ... Foreword by Humphrey Searle. ⟨Revised with corrections.⟩ pp. xviii. 166. *Ernst Eulenburg, etc.*, [1976.] 8°.
[*Edition Eulenburg. no. 447*.] **b. 212.**

— [No. 2.] Tasso. Lamento e Trionfo ... für grosses Orchester. *E. Eulenburg: Leipzig*, [1911.] 8°.
[*Eulenburg's kleine Orchester-Partitur-Ausgabe. Symphonien. No. 48.*] **b. 208. b.**

LISZT (Franz)

— [No. 2.] Tasso. Lamento e trionfo ... für grosses Orchester, *etc.* [Score.] pp. 92. *Ernst Eulenburg: London; printed in Switzerland*, [c. 1960.] 8°.
[*Edition Eulenburg. no. 448.*] **b. 212.**

— [No. 2.] Tasso, lamento e trionfo ... Foreword by Humphrey Searle. ⟨Revised with corrections. [Score.] pp. x. 92. *Ernst Eulenburg, etc.: London, etc.*, [1976.] 8°.
[*Edition Eulenburg. no. 448*.] **b. 212.**

— [No. 3.] Les Préludes ... für grosses Orchester nach Lamartine. *E. Eulenburg: Leipzig*, [1911.] 8°.
[*Eulenburg's kleine Orchester-Partitur-Ausgabe. Symphonien. No. 49.*] **b. 208. b.**

— [No. 3.] Les Préludes. Symphonic Poem, *etc.* [Score, with analysis.] *Boosey & Hawkes: London, etc.*, 1941. 8°.
[*Hawkes Pocket Scores. No. 159.*] **b. 211.**

— [No. 3.] Les Préludes. Symphonic Poem, No. 3 for Full Orchestra, *etc.* [Score.] *Ernst Eulenburg: London*, [1943.] 8°.
[*Edition Eulenburg. No. 449.*] **b. 212.**

— [No. 3.] Les Préludes ... ⟨[Revised by] Norman Del Mar.⟩ Foreword by Humphrey Searle. ⟨Score.⟩ pp. v. 86. *Ernst Eulenburg, etc.: London, etc.*, [1977.] 8°.
[*Edition Eulenburg. no. 449*.] **b. 212.**

— [No. 3.] Les Préludes. Symphonic Poem. (Arranged for Military Band by T. C. Brown.) [Parts.] *Boosey & Hawkes: London*, 1936. 4°.
[*Boosey & Hawkes Military Band Edition. No. 66.*]
h. 3211. b.

— [No. 3.] Symphonic Poem — "Les Preludes". Brass Band Score. pp. 36. *Wright & Round: Liverpool*, [1946.] obl. 4°.
e. 503. e. (6.)

— [No. 3.] Les Préludes. Poème symphonique pour grand orchestre ... Partition de piano par K. Klauser, avec des additions de F. Liszt. pp. 29. *Breitkopf & Härtel: Leipzig*, [1866?] fol. **h. 585. k. (4.)**

— [No. 3.] Les Préludes. Symphonic poem after Lamartine. Composer's arrangement for piano duet. pp. 35. *G. Schirmer: New York; Chappell & Co.: London;* [London printed, 1950.] 4°.
Schirmer's Library of musical Classics. vol. 783.
g. 547. h. (6.)

— [No. 3. Les Préludes. — Allegretto pastorale.] Pastorale ... For Woodwind Quintet, Flute, Oboe, Clarinet, Horn in F (or E♭ Alto Saxophone) and Bassoon ... Transcribed by A. Hamilton. [Score and parts.] *Galaxy Music Corporation: New York*, 1938. 4°. **g. 547. f. (32.)**

— [No. 4.] Orpheus ... für grosses Orchester. *E. Eulenburg: Leipzig*, [1911.] 8°.
[*Eulenburg's kleine Orchester-Partitur-Ausgabe. Symphonien. No. 50.*] **b. 208. b.**

— [No. 4.] Orpheus ... für grosses Orchester, *etc.* [Score.] pp. iv. 43. *Ernst Eulenburg: London; printed in Switzerland*, [c. 1960.] 8°.
[*Edition Eulenburg. no. 450.*] **b. 212.**

— [No. 4.] Symphonic Poem, No. 4. Orpheus ... Foreword by Humphrey Searle. [Score.] pp. ix. 43. *Ernst Eulenburg, etc.: London, etc.*, [1976.] 8°.
[*Edition Eulenburg. no. 450*.] **b. 212.**

— [No. 4.] Orpheus. Symphonic Poem No. 4. Full Orchestra. (Arranged by A. Winter.) [Piano conductor and parts.]
Hawkes & Son: London, 1940. 4°. **h. 3210. h. (774.)**

— [No. 4.] Orphée. Poème symphonique ... transcrit pour piano, violon et violoncelle par C. Saint-Saens. *Leipzig et Bruxelles*, [1885.] fol. **h. 2850. i. (4.)**

LISZT (FRANZ)

— [No. 5.] Prometheus ... für grosses Orchester. *E. Eulenburg: Leipzig*, [1911.] 8°.
[*Eulenburg's kleine Orchester-Partitur-Ausgabe. Symphonien. No. 51.*]   **b. 208. b.**

— [No. 5.] Prometheus ... for full orchestra, *etc.* [Score.] pp. iv. 76. *Ernst Eulenburg: London; printed in Switzerland*, [c. 1960.] 8°.
[*Edition Eulenburg. no. 451.*]   **b. 212.**

— [No. 5.] Prometheus ... Foreword by Humphrey Searle. [Score.] pp. ix. 76. *Ernst Eulenburg, etc.: London, etc.*, [1976.] 8°.
[*Edition Eulenburg. no. 451*.*]   **b. 212.**

— Symphonische Dichtungen für Orchester. No. 6. Mazeppa, nach V. Hugo. *E. Eulenburg: Leipzig*, [1911.] 8°.
[*Eulenburg's kleine Orchester-Partitur-Ausgabe. Symphonien. No. 52.*]   **b. 208. b.**

— [No. 6.] Mazeppa ... For full orchestra after Victor Hugo, *etc.* [Score.] pp. viii. 120. *Ernst Eulenburg: London; printed in Switzerland*, [c. 1960.] 8°.
[*Edition Eulenburg. no. 452.*]   **b. 212.**

— [No. 6.] Symphonic Poem, No. 6. Mazeppa ... Foreword by Humphrey Searle. ⟨Corrected edition 1976.⟩ [With facsimiles. Score.] pp. xix. 120. *Ernst Eulenburg, etc.: London, etc.*, [1977.] 8°.
[*Edition Eulenburg. no. 452*.*]   **b. 212.**

— [No. 7.] Festklänge ... for grosses Orchester. *E. Eulenburg: Leipzig*, [1911.] 8°.
[*Eulenburg's kleine Orchester-Partitur-Ausgabe. Symphonien. No. 53.*]   **b. 208. b.**

— [No. 7.] Festklänge ... für grosses Orchester, *etc.* [Score.] pp. 88. *Ernst Eulenburg: London; printed in Hungary*, [c. 1965.] 8°.
[*Edition Eulenburg. no. 453.*] *The wrapper bears the words "Printed in Switzerland".*   **b. 212.**

— [No. 7.] Symphonic Poem, No. 7. Festklänge ... Foreword by Humphrey Searle. ⟨Revised with corrections.⟩ [Score.] pp. vi. 126. *Ernst Eulenburg, etc.: London, etc.*, [1976.] 8°.
[*Edition Eulenburg. no. 453*.*]   **b. 212.**

— [No. 7.] Festklänge ... 2 Klaviere 4 händig. (Partitur.) pp. 43. *Breitkopf & Härtel: Leipzig*, [1905?] 4°.   **g. 547. g. (22.)**

— [No. 8. Héroïde funèbre.] Heldenklage. (Héroïde funèbre) ... für grosses Orchester, *etc.* [Score.] pp. iii. 56. *Ernst Eulenburg: London; printed in Hungary*, [c. 1965.] 8°.
[*Edition Eulenburg. no. 454.*] *The wrapper bears the words "Printed in Switzerland".*   **b. 212.**

— [No. 8.] Héroïde funèbre ... Foreword by Humphrey Searle. ⟨Revised with corrections.⟩ [Score.] pp. xii. 56. *Ernst Eulenburg, etc.: London, etc.*, [1976.] 8°.
[*Edition Eulenburg. no. 454*.*]   **b. 212.**

— [No. 9.] Hungaria ... für grosses Orchester. *E. Eulenburg: Leipzig*, [1911.] 8°.
[*Eulenburg's kleine Orchester-Partitur-Ausgabe. Symphonien. No. 55.*]   **b. 208. b.**

— [No. 9.] Hungaria ... for full orchestra, *etc.* [Score.] pp. 120. *Ernst Eulenburg: London; printed in Switzerland*, [c. 1960.] 8°.
[*Edition Eulenburg. no. 455.*]   **b. 212.**

— [No. 9.] Hungaria ... ⟨Revised with corrections.⟩ Foreword by Humphrey Searle. [Score.] pp. vi. 120. *Ernst Eulenburg, etc.: London, etc.*, [1976.] 8°.
[*Edition Eulenburg. no. 455*.*]   **b. 212.**

— [No. 10.] Hamlet ... für grosses Orchester. *E. Eulenburg: Leipzig*, [1911.] 8°.
[*Eulenburg's kleine Orchester-Partitur-Ausgabe. Symphonien. No. 56.*]   **b. 208. b.**

LISZT (FRANZ)

— [No. 10.] Hamlet ... For full orchestra, *etc.* [Score.] pp. 48. *Ernst Eulenburg: London; printed in Switzerland*, [c. 1960.] 8°.
[*Edition Eulenburg. no. 456.*]   **b. 212.**

— [No. 10.] Hamlet ... ⟨revised with corrections [and]⟩ foreword by Humphrey Searle. [Score.] pp. vi. 48. *Ernst Eulenburg, etc.: London, etc.*, [1976.] 8°.
[*Edition Eulenburg. no. 456*.*]   **b. 212.**

— [No. 11.] Hunnenschlacht ... For full orchestra, *etc.* [Score.] pp. ii. 96. *Ernst Eulenburg: London; printed in Switzerland*, [c. 1960.] 8°.
[*Edition Eulenburg. no. 457.*]   **b. 212.**

— [No. 11.] Hunnenschlacht. ⟨Für 2 Klaviere zu 4 Händen. Partitur.⟩ pp. 39. *Breitkopf & Härtel: Leipzig*, [1900?] fol. *With a preface in German, French and Italian inserted.*
                                                       h. 896. k. (5.)

— [No. 12.] Die Ideale ... für grosses Orchester, nach Schiller. *E. Eulenburg: Leipzig*, [1911.] 8°.
[*Eulenburg's kleine Orchester-Partitur-Ausgabe. Symphonien. No. 58.*]   **b. 208. b.**

— [No. 12.] Die Ideale ... für grosses Orchester nach Schiller, *etc.* [Score.] pp. 120. *Ernst Eulenburg: London; printed in Switzerland.* [c. 1965.] 8°.
[*Edition Eulenburg. no. 458.*]   **b. 212.**

— [No. 12.] Die Ideale ... ⟨Revised with corrections.⟩ Foreword by Humphrey Searle. [Score.] pp. ix. 119. *Ernst Eulenburg, etc.: London, etc.*, [1976.] 8°.
[*Edition Eulenburg. no. 458*.*]   **b. 212.**

— "Szózat" und "Hymnus". Zwei vaterländische Dichtungen von Vörösmarty und Kölcsey componirt von Egressi Béni und Franz Erkel. Orchestrirt von Franz Liszt. [Score.] pp. 48. *Rozsavölgyi & C^i: Budapest, Leipzig*, [c. 1905.] 8°.
                                                       e. 58. k. (4.)

— Szózat und Ungarischer Hymnus. Gedichte von Vörösmarty und Kölcsey, componirt von Egressy Béni und F. Erkel, für Clavier gesetzt von F. Liszt. pp. 15. *Rózsavölgyi & Co.: Budapest und Leipzig*, [1873.] fol.
The wrapper bears the title in Hungarian.   **h. 896. k. (6.)**

— Tarantella. *See* supra: [Années de pèlerinage. Seconde année. Supplement. No. 3.]

— Tarantelle (di bravura) d'après la tarantelle de la Muette de Portici d'Auber, pour piano, *etc.* pp. 23. *Chez Pietro Mechetti: Vienne*, [1847.] fol.   **Hirsch M. 954. (9.)**

— Tarantelle de [D. F. E. Auber's opera] La Muette de Portici. [P. F.] *London*, [1865.] fol.   **h. 585. a. (6.)**

— Tasso. Lamento e trionfo. *See* supra: [Symphonische Dichtungen. No. 2.]

— [Technische Studien.] The Liszt Studies. Essential selections from the ... technical studies for the piano, including the first English edition of the legendary Liszt Pedagogue, a lesson-diary of the master as teacher, as kept by Mme. Auguste Boissier, 1831–32. Selections, editions and English translation by Elyse Mach. "Reminiscences," (Memoirs by Liszt's great-granddaughter) by Mme. Blandine Ollivier de Prévaux. [With portraits and a facsimile.] pp. xxvi. 85. *Associated Music Publishers: New York, London*, [1973.] 4°.   **g. 547. z. (6.)**

— Die todte Nachtigall, von P. Kauffmann. *See* supra: [Collected Works.—d.] F. Liszt's gesammelte Lieder, *etc.* No. 46.

— Des todten Dichters Liebe. Gedicht von Moritz Jókai. Deutsch von Adolf Dux. Mit melodramatischer Musik. [P. F.]

LISZT (Franz)

pp. 17. *Táborszky & Parsch: Budapest; Lipcsében* [printed, 1874.] fol.
With a leaflet containing the words in Hungarian and German inserted.   **H. 1878. a. (2.)**

— Todtentanz. (Danse macabre.) Paraphrase über "Dies irae" für Piano und Orchester ... Partitur, *etc.* pp. 68. *C. F. W. Siegel: Leipzig,* [1865.] fol.   **h. 896. l. (1.)**

— Totentanz. Danse macabre. Paraphrase über: "Dies irae" für Piano und Orchester ... Neue, nach eignen Angaben des Komponisten revidierte Ausgabe, herausgegeben von A. Siloti. *E. Eulenburg: Leipzig,* [1912.] 8°.
[*Eulenburg's kleine Orchester-Partitur-Ausgabe. Konzerte. No. 22.*]   **b. 208.**

— Todtentanz. (Danse macabre.) Paraphrase über "Dies irae" für Piano und Orchester, *etc.* ⟨Arrangement für 2 Pianos vom Componisten.⟩ pp. 41. *C. F. W. Siegel's Musikalienhandlung: Leipzig,* [1910?] fol.   **h. 896. k. (7.)**

— Totentanz. (Danse macabre.) Paraphrase über "Dies irae" für Piano und Orchester ... Neue, nach eigenen Angaben des Komponisten revidierte Ausgabe, herausgegeben von A. Siloti ... Solostimme, zugleich Ausgabe für 2 Pianoforte, *etc.* pp. 45. *C. F. W. Siegel's Musikalienhandlung: Leipzig,* [1911.] fol.   **h. 585. o. (1.)**

— Todtentanz. (Danse macabre.) Paraphrase über "Dies irae" für Piano und Orchester ... Arrangement für Pianoforte allein, *etc.* pp. 31. *C. F. W. Siegel: Leipzig,* [1865.] fol.   **g. 547. cc. (5.)**

— [A reissue.] Todtentanz. (Danse macabre.) Paraphrase über "Dies irae" für Piano und Orchester, *etc.* ⟨Selbstständiges Arrangement für Piano allein vom Componisten.⟩ *C. F. W. Siegel: Leipzig,* [c. 1890.] fol.
Imperfect; wanting all after p. 30.   **h. 896. l. (2.)**

Deux Transcriptions d'après Rossini

— 2 transcriptions d'après Rossini pour piano ... N° 1. Air du Stabat Mater. N° 2. La Charité. no. 2. *Chez les fils de B. Schott: Mayence,* [1853.] fol.
Imperfect; wanting no. 1.   **h. 585. m. (6.)**

— 2 Transcriptions d'après Rossini pour piano. No. 1. Air du Stabat Mater. No. 2. La Charité. 2 no. *Schott & Co.: Londres,* [c. 1880.] fol.   **h. 896. a. (14.)**

— [No. 1.] Cujus animam, air du Stabat mater de Rossini, transcrit pour le piano par F. Liszt. pp. 7. *Brandus et cᵈᵉ: Paris,* [c. 1860.] fol.   **h. 585. j. (7.)**

— [No. 1. Air du Stabat Mater.] Cujus animam ... Transcribed for Piano by F. Liszt. *Augener: London,* [1908.] fol.   **g. 605. yy. (38.)**

— [No. 1. Air du Stabat Mater.] Cujus animam ... [P. F.] Neue sorgfältig durchgesehene Ausgabe (Erleichterte Ausgabe) von K. Klindworth. 2 no. *B. Schott's Söhne: Mainz,* (1911.) fol.   **h. 896. g. (2.)**

— [No. 1. Air du Stabat Mater.] Aria, "Cujus animam" für Posaune und Orgel von F. Liszt. *Schott & Co.: London,* [1874.] fol.   **h. 896. a. (16.)**

— [No. 2.] Rossini's La Charité arranged for the Pianoforte. *London,* [1860.] fol.
No. 1649, 50 of the "Musical Bouquet".   **H. 2345.**

— [No. 2.] La Charité ... [P. F.] Neue sorgfältig durchgesehene Ausgabe (Erleichterte Ausgabe) von K. Klindworth. 2 no. *B. Schotts Söhne: Mainz,* (1911.) fol.   **h. 896. g. (3.)**

————

— Die Trauer-Gondel (La lugubre gondola) für Pianoforte. pp. 11. *E. W. Fritzsch: Leipzig,* [c. 1895.] fol.   **h. 896. n. (12.)**

LISZT (Franz)

— Trauer-Vorspiel und Trauer-Marsch für Pianoforte. pp. 11. *Breitkopf & Härtel: Leipzig, Brüssel,* [1888.] fol.
                                                          h. 896. s. (9.)

— Der traurige Mönch. Ballade von N. Lenau. Mit melodramatischer Pianoforte-Begleitung zur Declamation. pp. 10. *Bei C. F. Kahnt: Leipzig,* [1872.] fol.
                                                    Hirsch M. 949. (9.)

— Le Triomphe funèbre des Tasse. Épilogue du poëme symphonique "Tasso," lamento e trionfo, pour grand orchestre. Partition. pp. 40. *Breitkopf & Härtel: Leipzig,* [1877.] 8°.   **e. 666. (4.)**

— Le Triomphe funèbre du Tasse. Epilogue du poëme symphonique "Tasso," lamento e trionfo, pour grand orchestre ... Transcription pour piano de l'auteur. pp. 13. *Breitkopf & Härtel: Leipzig,* [1877.] fol.   **h. 896. k. (8.)**

— Tscherkessen-Marsch für Pianoforte, componirt von F. Liszt [or rather, a transcription by him of the march from Glinka's "Ruslan and Ludmilla"]. 2ᵗᵉ revidirte und veränderte Ausgabe (vom Componisten), *etc.* pp. 13. *J. Schuberth & Co.: Leipzig,* [1875.] fol.   **h. 585. b. (13.)**

— Ueber allen Gipfeln ist Ruh'. Goethe. *See supra:* [*Collected Works.—d.*] F. Liszt's gesammelte Lieder, *etc.* No. 6.

— Ueber allen Gipfeln ist Ruh. *See also supra:* [*Fest-Album zur Säcular-Feier von Goethe's Geburtstag.*]

— Und sprich, von Rüdiger v. Bügeleben. *See supra:* [*Collected Works.—d.*] F. Liszt's gesammelte Lieder, *etc.* No. 51.

— Ungarische Fantasie. *See supra:* [Fantasie über ungarische Volksmelodien.]

— Ungarische Kronungs-Messe. *See supra:* Koronázási Mise.

— Ungarische Melodien. *See supra:* [Magyar Dallok. no. 5, 4, 11.]

— Ungarische National-Melodien für das Piano-Forte. *See supra:* [Magyar Dallok. no. 5, 4, 11.]

— Ungarische Rhapsodie für die Violine nach der Paraphrase über "Die drei Zigeuner". *See supra:* [Die drei Zigeuner.]

— 5 ungarische Volkslieder für das Pianoforte (in leichter Spielart) übertragen. pp. 9. *Táborszky & Parsch: Pest,* [1873.] 4°.   **h. 896. l. (5.)**

— Ungarischer Geschwind-Marsch. *See supra:* [Magyar Gyors induló.]

— Ungarischer Marsch zur Krönungs-Feier in Ofen-Pest am 8ᵗᵉⁿ Juni 1867 ... für Pianoforte zu 2 Händen. pp. 7. *J. Schuberth & C°: Leipzig,* [1871.] fol.   **h. 896. s. (6.)**

— Ungarischer Sturm-Marsch. *See supra:* Seconde marche hongroise.

— Ungarisches Königs-Lied ⟨Magyar király-dal⟩ (Gedicht von Cornél Abrányi jun.) nach einer alten ungarischen Weise ... Pianoforte zweihändig, *etc.* pp. 11. *Táborszky & Parsch: Budapest,* [1884.] fol.   **h. 896. z. (12.)**

— "Ungarn's Gott." ⟨A magyarok Istene.⟩ Gedicht von Alexander Petőfi ... Ausgabe für Pianoforte (zweihändig). pp. 7. *Táborszky & Parsch: Budapest,* [1881.] fol.
                                                          h. 896. gg. (1.)

— Ungarn's Gott. [T.T.B.B. Voice-parts.] 4 pt. *T. ès P.* [*Táborszky & Parsch: Budapest,* 1881.] obl. 8°.
                                                          B. 418. y. (3.)

— [Die Vätergruft.] A Death-Summons ... Song for baritone with orchestral accompaniment [begins: "Es schritt wohl über die Haide"], the English words translated from the German

LISZT (Franz)

of Uhland by W. Beatty Kingston. [With P. F. accompaniment.] *London & New York,* [1886.] fol.
H. 1878. c. (4.)

— Die Vätergruft, von Uhland. *See* supra: F. Liszt's gesammelte Lieder, *etc.* No. 25.

— [Valses.] 3 caprices-valses pour le piano. 1. Valse de bravoure. 2. Valse mélancolique. 3. Valse de concert sur deux motifs de Lucia et Parisina. Seconde édition, entièrement revue et corrigée par l'auteur. 3 no. *Chez Charles Haslinger: Vienne,* [1852.] fol.
g. 547. o. (1.)

— [Valse.] Waltz. [A major. P. F.] Composed by Master Listz [*sic*]. *In:* The Musical Gem ... for MDCCCXXXII. p. 92. [1832.] 4°.
G. 422.

— Valse a capriccio sur deux motifs de Lucia e Parisina [i.e. "Lucia di Lammermoor" and "Parisina" by D. G. M. Donizetti] pour le piano. pp. 23. *Chez Tobie Haslinger: Vienne,* [1842.] fol.
h. 896. k. (9.)

— Valse d'Adèle composée ... par le Comte Geza Zichy. Transcription brillante ... par F. Liszt. *Paris,* [1877.] fol.
h. 585. b. (20.)

— Valse de l'opéra Faust de Gounod pour le piano. pp. 23. *Ed. Bote & G. Bock: Berlin & Posen,* [1861.] fol.
h. 896. i. (15.)

— La Valse de [C. F. Gounod's opera] Faust, transcrite pour le Piano. *London,* [1863.] fol.
h. 585. a. (5.)

Grande valse di bravura

— Grande valse pour le piano. *In:* ALBUM. Album musical. Sammlung der neuesten original Compositionen für Piano und Gesang, *etc.* pp. 34–50. [1836.] 8°.
F. 1199. vv.

— Grande valse di bravura composé pour le piano ... Op. 6. pp. 13. *Chez Fr. Hofmeister: Leipzig,* [1836.] fol.
Hirsch M. 951. (12.)

— Grande valse di bravura pour le piano-forte ... Oeuvre 6. Seule édition revue par l'auteur. pp. 13. *Chez Tob. Haslinger: Vienne,* [1838.] fol.
g. 547. cc. (3.)

— Grande valse di bravura ... pour le piano ... Op. 6. pp. 17. *Bernard Latte: Paris,* [1840?] fol.
h. 896. i. (14.)

— Grande valse di bravura composée pour piano ... Op. 6. pp. 15. *Chez Aᵈ Mᵗ Schlesinger: Berlin,* [1840?] fol.
Hirsch M. 951. (13.)

— Grande valse di bravura pour le piano forte ... Seule édition revue par l'auteur ... Op. 6. pp. 13. *R. Cocks & Co.: London,* [1840?] fol.
g. 547. g. (19.)

— Le Bal de Berne. Grande valse di bravura pour le piano forte ... Op. 6. pp. 13. *Wessel & Co.: London,* [1845?] fol. *Le Pianiste moderne. no. 54.*
h. 896. h. (18.)

— Grande valse di bravura, pour le piano-forte à 4 mains ... Oeuvre 6. pp. 27. *Chez T. Haslinger: Vienne,* [1838.] fol.
Hirsch M. 954. (5.)

— Valse-Impromptu pour le piano ... Édition originale, *etc. Schuberth & Cᵛ: Hambourg, etc.,* [c. 1870.] fol. **h. 585. j. (5.)**

— Valse-Impromptu, for the Pianoforte. *J. Williams: London,* (1910.) 4°. *No. 387 of J. Williams' Albums.*
G. 785. (387.)

— Valse-Impromptu. (Piano.) *Augener: London,* [1921.] 4°.
g. 547. e. (9.)

— Valse mélancolique composée pour le piano. pp. 7. *Chez Tob. Haslinger: Vienne,* [1840.] fol. **Hirsch M. 951. (14.)**

LISZT (Franz)

3 Valses oubliées

— Valses oubliées (Vergessene Walzer) pour piano. 3 no. *Berlin & Posen,* [1882–1884.] fol.
h. 585. f. (13.)

— [No. 1.] Valse oubliée. Edited by C. Deis. (Piano.) *G. Schirmer: New York,* 1938. 4°.
g. 547. f. (33.)

— [No. 1.] Valse oubliée. Edited by H. Geehl. (Pianoforte.) *E. Ashdown: London,* 1939. 4°.
g. 547. g. (4.)

— [No. 1.] Valse oubliée. Freely arranged for two pianos by Colin Taylor. pp. 12. *Oxford University Press: London,* [1948.] 8°. [*Two-Piano Series. no. 33.*] *Two copies.*
g. 1393.

— [No. 1.] Vergessener Walzer ... Für Violoncell und Klavier. Übertragen von Ferruccio Busoni. [Score and part.] 2 pt. *Breitkopf & Härtel: Leipzig,* [1953.] 4°.
g. 547. k. (6.)

— Quatrième valse oubliée. (Forgotten Waltz) No. 4. Piano solo. ⟨[Edited by] George Rochberg, Walter Eckard.⟩ [With a portrait and a facsimile of the composer's autograph.] pp. 10. *Theodore Presser Co.: Bryn Mawr,* [1954.] 4°.
g. 547. l. (6.)

— [No. 4.] Negyedik elfelejtett keringő. Vierter vergessener Walzer. [P.F.] pp. 8. *In:* Új zenei szemle. évf. 6. sz. 7–8. 1955. 8°.
P. P. 1945. efa.

— Huit variations pour le piano forte ... Œuvre Iᵉʳ. pp. 11. *Chez Mᵉˡˡᵉˢ Erard: Paris,* [1825.] fol.
The titlepage bears a MS. dedication to Mademoiselle Müller in the composer's autograph.
K. 5. c. 27. (1.)

— Seven Brilliant Variations for the Piano Forte to a Theme of Rossini ... Op. 2. pp. 9. *T. Boosey & Cᵒ: London,* [1825.] fol.
h. 583. (1.)

— Grandes variations de concert sur un thêmes des "Puritains". *See* supra: [Hexameron.]

Variationen über das Motiv von Bach: Weinen, Klagen, Sorgen, Zagen

— Variations [for organ] on the Basso continuo of the first part of the Cantata "Weinen, Klagen" and of the Crucifixus of the B Minor Mass by J. S. Bach ... Arranged and edited [by J. Bonnet], *etc. J. Fischer & Bro.: New York,* 1942. 4°.
g. 1380. t. (2.)

— Variationen über das Motiv von Bach (Basso continuo des ersten Satzes seiner Cantata "Weinen, Klagen, Sorgen, Zagen" und des Crucifixus der H-moll-Messe) für das Pianoforte, *etc.* pp. 19. *Schlesinger: Berlin,* [c. 1910.] fol.
h. 896. s. (8.)

— Variations on the Theme by Bach ... Basso continuo of the first movement, of his Cantata "Weinen, Klagen" and the "Crucifixus" of the B-minor Mass. Edited by Isidor Philipp. [P.F.] *G. Schirmer: New York,* 1946. 4°. **g. 547. g. (11.)**

— Crucifixus. Passacaglia for piano and orchestra. ⟨[Arranged by] Anthony Collins. Pocket score.⟩ pp. 73. *Paterson's Publications: London,* [1955.] 8°.
c. 121. ee. (2.)

— "Weinen, Klagen." Változatok J. S. Bach egy motívuma fölött. Zenekarra átdolgozta Weiner Leó. (Variationen über ein Motiv von J. S. Bach. Für Orchester bearbeitet von Leo Weiner.) [Score.] pp. 53. *Zeneműkiadó vállalat: Budapest,* 1959. 8°.
Kispartiturák. 66.
c. 156. hh. (1.)

— Das Veilchen. *See* supra: Mutter-Gottes Sträusslein zum Maimonate. No. 1.

— Venezia e Napoli. [For editions and arrangements of this work:] *See* supra: [Années de pèlerinage. Seconde année. Supplément.]

LISZT (FRANZ)

— Венгерские рапсодии. *See* supra: [Rhapsodies hongroises.]

— Vereins-Lied. *See* supra: Für Männergesang. No. 1.

— Vergessener Walzer. *See* supra: [Trois valses oubliées. No. 1.]

— Vergiftet sind meine Lieder, von Heine. *See* supra: [*Collected Works.—d.*] F. Liszt's gesammelte Lieder, *etc.* No. 12.

— Verlassen! Lied aus dem Schauspiele "Irrwege," von G. Michell. *See* supra: [*Collected Works.—d.*] F. Liszt's gesammelte Lieder, *etc.* No. 56.

— Via crucis. The 14 stations of the Cross for mixed choir, vocal solos and organ or piano. Edited by Imre Sulyok. pp. 67. *Ernst Eulenburg: London, etc.; printed in Switzerland,* [1968.] 8°.
[*Edition Eulenburg. no.* 1082.] **b. 212.**

— [Via crucis.—O Traurigkeit.] O Sorrow deep ... For mixed voices (S.A.T.B.) and organ. [Words] Würzbrug 1628. English translation by Winfred Douglas ... Edited by Robert S. Hines. pp. 6. *Mills Music: New York,* [1969.] 8°.
F. 1106. e. (4.)

— Vierstimmige Männergesänge. No. 1. Rheinweinlied. Text von Herwegh. No. 2. Studentenlied aus Goethe's Faust. No. 3. Reiterlied. 1ᵗᵉ Version, Text von Herwegh. No. 4. Reiterlied. 2ᵗᵉ Version, *etc.* 4 no. *bei B. Schott's Söhnen: Mainz, etc.,* [1843.] 8°.
F. 163. (21.)

— [Vierstimmige Männergesänge. No. 1. Rheinweinlied.] "The Land we love for ever!" Patriotic Chorus for male voices. [Words by] F. Hoare. *J. Curwen & Sons: London,* [1907.] 8°. *The Apollo Club, No.* 381.
F. 667.

— Die Vogelpredigt des heiligen Franz von Assisi. *See* supra: [Légendes. No. 1.]

— Vom Fels zum Meer! Deutscher Sieges-Marsch ... Partitur, *etc.* pp. 23. *Verlag u. Eigenthum der Schlesinger'schen Buch-u. Musikhandlg.: Berlin,* [1865?] 8°. **e. 58. h. (1.)**

— Vom Fels zum Meer! Deutscher Sieges-Marsch ... für Piano. *Berlin,* [1865.] fol. **h. 585. b. (2.)**

— Vom Fels zum Meer! ... Arrangement für Piano zu vier Händen von H. v. Bülow. *Berlin,* [1865.] fol. **h. 585. b. (3.)**

— Vom Fels zum Meer. Triumphal march. *See* BEST (W. T.) Arrangements ... for the Organ. No. 91. [1862, *etc.*] obl. fol.
e. 300.

— Von der Wiege bis zum Grabe. Symphonische Dichtung nach einer Zeichnung von Michael Zichy ... Du berceau jusqu'à la tombe. Poème symphonique d'après un dessin de Michel Zichy ... Partitur, *etc.* pp. 29. *Ed. Bote & G. Bock: Berlin & Posen,* [1883.] fol. **h. 896. b. (1.)**

— [Another copy.] **Hirsch M. 947.**

— Von der Wiege bis zum Grabe. From the Cradle to the Grave ... ⟨Symphonic poem, No. 13.⟩ Foreword by Humphrey Searle. [Score. With a facsimile.] pp. vi. 24. *Ernst Eulenburg, etc.: London, etc.,* [1976.] 8°.
[*Edition Eulenburg. no.* 600.] **b. 212.**

— Vor der Schlacht. [Words by] C. Götze. *See* supra: Für Männergesang. No. 4.

— Waldesrauschen. *See* supra: 2 Concertetuden. No. 1.

— Wartburg-Lieder, aus dem lyrischen Festspiel: Der Braut Willkomm auf Wartburg, gedichtet von J. V. Scheffel. *C. F. Kahnt: Leipzig,* [1876.] 8°. **E. 1644. e. (2.)**

— Was Liebe sei? von C. v. Hagen. *See* supra: [*Collected Works.—d.*]F. Liszt's gesammelte Lieder, *etc.* No. 45.

— Weihnachtsbaum. 12 Clavierstücke. [Solo and duet.] 6 Hft. *Berlin,* [1882.] fol. **h. 585. f. (8.)**

LISZT (FRANZ)

— Weihnachtsbaum. Christmas Tree. Arbre de noël. I. Pianoforte. ⟨II. Pianoforte/Orgel. Herausgegeben Thomas A. Johnson.⟩ 2 vol. *Hinrichsen Edition: London,* [1953.] 4°.
g. 547. l. (4.)

— [Weihnachtsbaum. No. 1, 3.] The Christmas Tree. ⟨Two movements from the piano suite.⟩ Arranged for organ by E. Power Biggs. pp. 7. *H. W. Gray Co.: New York,* [1951.] 4°.
g. 547. k. (1.)

— Wei[h]nachtslied (Old Christmas song) [begins: "O heilige Nacht."—"O holy night"] für Tenor (solo), Sopran und Alt mit Orgel oder Harmonium. (English version by J. P. Morgan.) *Berlin,* [1882.] 8°. **E. 308. m. (21.)**

— Weimar's Volkslied. Zur Carl-August-Feier. (September 1857.) Gedichtet von Peter Cornelius ... Für Männerchor mit Orchester, *etc.* [Score, with P. F. reduction.] pp. 25. *T. F. A. Kühn: Weimar,* [1857.] 4°. **H. 1878. h. (1.)**

— Weimar's Volkslied. Zur Carl-August-Feier. (September 1857) Gedichtet von Peter Cornelius ... Für eine Singstimme mit Piano, *etc.* pp. 13. *T. F. A. Kühn: Weimar,* [1857.] fol.
Hirsch M. 949. (10.)

— Weimar's Volkslied. Zur Car-August-Feier. (September 1857) gedichtet von Peter Cornelius ... Pianoforte zu vier Händen. pp. 11. *T. F. A. Kühn: Weimar,* [1857.] fol. **h. 896. v. (2.)**

— Weimar's Volkslied ... Ausgabe für das Pianoforte allein, *etc.* pp. 3. *T. F. A. Kühn: Weimar,* [1873.] fol. **h. 585. m. (7.)**

— Weinen, Klagen. *See also* supra: [Variationen über das Motiv von Bach: Weinen, Klagen, Sorgen, Zagen.]

— "Weinen, Klagen, Sorgen, Zagen." Praeludium nach Joh. Seb. Bach für das Pianoforte. pp. 5. *Verlag der Schlesinger'schen Buch- und Musikhandlung: Berlin,* [1863.] fol. **Hirsch M. 953. (13.)**

— "Weinen, Klagen, Sorgen, Zagen." Praeludium nach Joh. Seb. Bach für das Pianoforte. pp. 5. *Schlesinger: Berlin,* [1910?] fol. **Hirsch M. 948. (4.)**

— [Weinen, Klagen, Sorgen, Zagen.] Prelude after J. S. Bach ... Edited ... by T. F. Dunhill. (Piano.) *Augener: London,* 1918. fol. **h. 896. g. (18.)**

— Wer nie sein Brot mit Thränen ass. Goethe. *See* supra: [*Collected Works.—d.*] F. Liszt's gesammelte Lieder, *etc.* No. 5.

— Wer nie sein Brod, von Goethe. *See* supra: [*Collected Works.—d.*] F. Liszt's gesammelte Lieder, *etc.* No. 41.

— What heav'nly Wonder springs to sight. *See* supra: [Es muss ein Wunderbares sein.]

— When dreamy Sleep. *See* supra: [Buch der Lieder. Bd. 2. No. 1. Oh! quand je dors.]

— When through the Night. *See* supra: [Drei Lieder für eine Sopran- oder Tenor-Stimme. No. 3. O lieb', O lieb'.]

— Wie singt die Lerche schön, von Hoffmann von Fallersleben. *See* supra: [*Collected Works.—d.*] F. Liszt's gesammelte Lieder, *etc.* No. 32.

— Wieder möcht' ich dir begegnen, von P. Cornelius. *See* supra: [*Collected Works.—d.*] F. Liszt's gesammelte Lieder, *etc.* No. 37.

— Wiegenlied. Chant du berceau. (1881.) Klavier. (⟨Hrsg. von⟩ László Szelényi.) pp. 7. *Verlag Doblinger: Wien, München,* [1979.] 4°. *Diletto musicale. no.* 820. **g. 547. s. (6.)**

— Wilde Jagd. *See* supra: [Études d'exécution transcendante. No. 8.]

LISZT (FRANZ)

— Wir sind nicht Mumien. [Words by] Hoffmann von Fallersleben. *See* supra: Für Männergesang. No. 3.

— Wo weilt er? von Rellstab. *See* supra: [*Collected Works.—d.*] F. Liszt's gesammelte Lieder, *etc.* No. 22.

— Woodland Dreaming. *See* supra: [Drei Lieder für eine Sopran- oder Tenor-Stimme. No. 3. O lieb', O lieb'.]

Die Zelle in Nonnenwerth

— Nonnenwerth. Lied für eine Singstimme und Klavier. Zweite, bisher unveröffentlichte Fassung, herausgegeben von den Nationalen Forschungs- und Gedenkstätten der klassischen deutschen Literatur in Weimar. [A facsimile of the autograph and transcription.] pp. 15. [*Weimar*,] 1961. 4°.
F. 566. b. (1.)

— Die Zelle in Nonnenwerth ... [Song.] Gedichtet von Fürst Felix Lichnowsky. pp. 9. *Bei Eck & Comp.: Cöln*, [1843.] fol.
H. 1878. h. (2.)

— Nonnenwerth. [Song, words by] F. Lichnowski. pp. 7. *C. F. Kahnt Nachfolger: Leipzig*, [c. 1880.] fol.
[*F. Liszt's Gesammelte Lieder. no. 35.*]
H. 1878. e.

— Élégie pour piano seul. pp. 3. *In*: PERIODICAL PUBLICATIONS. —*Paris*. [Le Monde musical.] Album de piano, *etc.* [1844?] fol.
h. 62. n.

— Die Zelle in Nonnenwerth. Élégie. ⟨Für Pianoforte.⟩ pp. 11. *Friedrich Hofmeister: Leipzig*, [c. 1910.] fol.
h. 896. q. (4.)

— Zur Säcular-Feier Beethovens. Cantate. Gedichtet von Adolf Stern ... Partitur. pp. 184. *Bei C. F. Kahnt: Leipzig*, [1870.] 8°.
The cover bears title "Beethoven-Cantate".
Hirsch IV. 827.

— Zur Säcular-Feier Beethovens. Cantate, gedichtet von A. Stern, componirt für Chor, Soli und Orchester ... Klavierauszug. *C. F. Kahnt: Leipzig*, [1870.] 8°.
E. 1644. e. (1.)

— Zur Säcular-Feier Beethovens. Cantate ... Instrumental-Einleitung. Partitur, *etc.* pp. 55. *Bei C. F. Kahnt: Leipzig*, [c. 1880.] 8°.
The cover reads "Beethoven's Andante cantabile aus dem Trio Op. 97. Für Orchester von Franz Liszt".
f. 470. g.

— Zur Schiller-Feier—1859.—Künstler-Festzug ... Partitur. pp. 58. *T. F. A. Kühn: Weimar*, [1859?] 8°.
e. 58. h. (2.)

— Zur Schillerfeier 1859 ... Künstler-Festzug. Für das Pianoforte zu zwei und vier Händen bearbeitet vom Componisten. Ausgabe für 2 Hände, *etc.* pp. 18. *T. F. A. Kühn: Weimar*, [1860.] 4°.
h. 896. cc. (3.)

— Zur Schillerfeier 1859 ... Künstler-Festzug. Für das Pianoforte zu zwei und vier Händen bearbeitet vom Componisten ... Ausgabe für 4 Hände. pp. 31. *T. F. A. Kühn: Leipzig*, [1860?] fol.
h. 896. i. (5.)

— Zur Trauung. Geistliche Vermählungsmusik für Orgel oder Harmonium, mit Gesang nach Belieben, *etc. Breitkopf & Härtel: Leipzig und Brüssel*, [1890.] fol.
h. 896. a. (5.)

APPENDIX

— *See* ANDREWS (Richard H.) *the Elder*. The Athenaeum musicale, containing songs and duet ... with a choice selection of foreign marches, waltzes, polonaises, quadrilles & polkas, Selected from the works of classical composers for the piano forte, including ... Liszt, *etc.* [1857–60.] fol.
H. 2344.

— *See* ARCHADELT (J.) [Nous voyons que les hommes.] Ave· Maria ... Pour piano par François Liszt. [1865.] fol.
h. 896. k. (12.)

LISZT (FRANZ)

— *See* ARCHADELT (J.) [Nous voyons que les hommes.] Ave Maria ... für Orgel oder Harmonium bearbeitet von Dr F. Liszt. [1865.] obl. 4°.
e. 1096. g. (2.)

— *See* ARTOK (Lothar) Rhaptofantasie über Themen von F. Liszt, *etc.* [1924.] 4°. [*Schott & Co.'s Domesticum Salon Orchestra. No. 83.*]
g. 1053. a.

— *See* BACH (J. S.) [Präludien und Fugen für Orgel.—Zweite Folge. No. 12.] J. Seb. Bachs Orgelfantasie u. Fuge in G moll, *etc.* ⟨Für Pianoforte gesetzt von F. v. Liszt.⟩ [1870.] fol.
h. 1626. e. (2.)

— *See* BACH (J. S.) [Präludien und Fugen für Orgel.—Zweite Folge. No. 12.] J. Seb. Bachs Orgelfantasie u. Fuge in G moll, *etc.* ⟨Für Pianoforte gesetzt von F. v. Liszt.⟩ [1877.] fol.
h. 585. b. (22.)

— *See* BACH (J. S.) [Präludien und Fugen für Orgel.—Zweite Folge. No. 12.] J. S. Bach's Organ Fantasia and Fugue in G minor. Arranged [for P. F.] by F. Liszt, *etc.* 1918. fol.
h. 896. g. (19.)

— *See* BACH (J. S.) [Präludien und Fugen für Orgel.—Zweite Folge. No. 12.] Fantasie and Fugue in G minor ... Transcribed for Piano by F. Liszt, *etc.* 1925. 4°.
g. 548. o. (6.)

— *See* BACH (J. S.) [Präludien und Fugen für Orgel.—Zweite Folge. No. 12.] Fantasie and Fugue. In G minor ... Transcribed for the piano by F. Liszt, *etc.* [1950.] 4°.
g. 699. a. (4.)

— *See* BACH (J. S.) [Präludien und Fugen für Orgel.—Dritte Folge. No. 13, 15, 16, 17, 18, 14.] 6 Praeludien und Fugen für die Orgel ... für das Pianoforte zu zwei Händen gesetzt von F. Liszt. [c. 1880.] 4°.
g. 547. bb. (3.)

— *See* BACH (J. S.) [Präludien und Fugen für Orgel.—Dritte Folge. No. 13, 15, 16, 17, 18, 14.] Orgel-Kompositionen für Klavier übertragen von F. Liszt, *etc.* [c. 1950.] 4°.
g. 699. k. (14.)

— *See* BACH (J. S.) [Präludien und Fugen für Orgel.—Dritte Folge. No. 13.] Prelude & Fugue in A minor ... Arranged for piano by F. Liszt. [1921.] 4°.
g. 548. j. (13.)

— *See* BACH (J. S.) [Präludien und Fugen für Orgel.—Dritte Folge. No. 13.] Organ Prelude & Fugue in A minor. Bach-[Transcribed by F.] Liszt. Arranged for Piano Duet, *etc.* 1934. 4°.
g. 548. bb. (12.)

— *See* BACH (J. S.) [Präludien und Fugen für Orgel.—Dritte Folge. No. 13.] Prelude und Fugue in A minor ... Transcribed for the piano by F. Liszt, *etc.* [1950.] 4°.
g. 699. a. (5.)

— *See* BEETHOVEN (L. van) [*Collected Works.—a.*] Ludwig van Beethoven's sämmtliche Compositionen. Erste vollständige Gesammtausgabe unter Revision von F. Liszt ⟨und G. Geissler⟩. [1857–69.] fol.
h. 216. b.

— *See* BEETHOVEN (L. van) [*Collected Works.—c.*] Beethoven's Lieder für das Pianoforte von F. Liszt. [1849.] fol.
g. 547. t. (3.)

— *See* BEETHOVEN (L. van) [*Collected Works.—c.*] Lieders de Beethoven transcrits pour piano par F. Liszt. [1863?] fol.
h. 585. b. (25.)

— *See* BEETHOVEN (L. van) [*Collected Works.—c.*] Sechs Lieder ... für Pianoforte zu 2 Händen, *etc.* ⟨Übertragen von F. Liszt.⟩ [1912?] 4°.
g. 547. k. (3.)

— *See* BEETHOVEN (L. van) Beethoven's Adelaide. Für das Pianoforte übertragen von F. Liszt. [1840.] fol. **g. 547. t. (1.)**

— *See* BEETHOVEN (L. van) Adélaïde ... Transcrite pour le piano par F. Liszt. Édition nouvelle et augmentée d'une grand cadence par Mr F. Liszt. [1840.] fol.
g. 547. t. (6.)

LISZT (Franz)

— *See* Beethoven (L. van) [Adelaide. Op. 46.] Beethoven's Celebrated Cantata, Adelaide, arranged for the piano forte ... by F. Liszt. [1840.] fol.　　　　　**g. 250. s. (4.)**

— *See* Beethoven (L. van) Adelaide. (Arranged by Liszt.) [1866.] fol.　　　　　**h. 216. (3.)**

— *See* Beethoven (L. van) Adélaïde ... [Op. 46.] Transcrite pour le piano par F. Liszt. Édition nouvelle et augmentée d'une grande cadence par M¹ F. Liszt. [c. 1870.] fol.　　**h. 585. l. (8.)**

— *See* Beethoven (L. van) Adelaide ... Pour piano par F. Liszt. [1887.] 4°.　　　　　**g. 547. a. (4.)**

— *See* Beethoven (L. van) An die ferne Geliebte ... Übertragen von F. Liszt. [1849.] 4°.　　　　　**g. 249. hh. (22.)**

— *See* Beethoven (L. van) [6 Lieder von Gellert. Op. 48.] Beethoven's geistliche Lieder von Gellert für das Pianoforte übertragen von F. Liszt. [1840.] fol.　　**h. 400. x. (7.)**

— *See* Beethoven (L. van) [6 Lieder von Gellert. Op. 48.] 6 Sacred Songs ... transcribed for the Pianoforte by F. Liszt. [1880.] 4°.　　　　　**g. 547. (4.)**

— *See* Beethoven (L. van) Grand septuor, Ov. 20 ... contenant: Adagio e Allegro con brio. Adagio cantabile. Menuetto e Scherzo. Andante con variazioni. Andante alla marcia e Presto. Transcrits pour le piano seul par Fr. Liszt. [1841?] fol.　　　　　**h. 383. p. (2.)**

— *See* Beethoven (L. van) Grand septuor ... Œuvre 20. Pour piano par F. Liszt, *etc.* [1842?] fol.　　**h. 585. m. (8.)**

— *See* Beethoven (L. van) [Septet. Op. 20.] Grand Septuor ... transcrit pour piano par F. Liszt, *etc.* [1886.] 8°.
　　　　　f. 133. e. (1.)

— *See* Beethoven (L. van) Sonatas ... Edited by F. Liszt, *etc.* 1915. 4°.　　　　　**g. 249. m.**

— *See* Beethoven (L. van) Sonatas. Piano solo. Edited by F. Liszt, *etc.* [1925?] 4°.　　　　　**g. 249. mm.**

— *See* Beethoven (L. van) Symphonies ... Partition de piano ... par F. Liszt. [1870.]　　　　　**h. 896. kk.**

— *See* Beethoven (L. van) Symphonien ... In leichtem Arrangement für das Pianoforte zu zwei Händen mit Benutzung der Bearbeitungen von ... Liszt und anderen, *etc.* [1879?] 8°.　　　　　**f. 200. t.**

— *See* Beethoven (L. van) Symphonien. Klavierauszug ... von F. Liszt, *etc.* [c. 1900.] 4°.　　　　　**h. 400. ee.**

— *See* Beethoven (L. van) Symphonien. Klavierauszug ... von F. Liszt. [1910?] fol.　　　　　**g. 249. ii. (10.)**

— *See* Beethoven (L. van) [Symphony No. 3. Op. 55.] Marche funèbre ... Partition de piano par F. Liszt. [1841.] 4°.
　　　　　g. 249. hh. (23.)

— *See* Beethoven (L. van) [Symphony. No. 3. Op. 55.] Marche funèbre ... Partition de piano par F. Liszt, *etc.* [1841.] fol. [*Mechetti* (*P.*) *Album-Beethoven, etc.*]　　**i. 143.**

— *See* Beethoven (L. van) [Symphony. No. 5. Op. 67.] Symphonies de Beethoven. Partition de piano par F. Liszt. N° v. [1839.] fol.　　　　　**h. 383. r. (2.)**

— *See* Beethoven (L. van) [Symphony. No. 7. Op. 92.] 7ᵗᵉ Sinfonie (A dur) ... Für das Piano-Forte übertragen von F. Liszt. [1842.] fol.　　　　　**h. 383. r. (1.)**

— *See* Beethoven (L. van) [Symphony No. 9. Op. 125.] Beethoven's 9ᵗᵉ Sinfonie ... für 2 Pianoforte gesetzt von F. Liszt. [c. 1870.] fol.　　　　　**h. 896. d. (6.)**

— *See* Berlioz (L.H.) [Benvenuto Cellini.] Bénédiction et serment, deux motifs de Benvenuto Cellini ... transcrits pour le piano par F. Liszt. [1854.] fol.　　**h. 585. (2.)**

LISZT (Franz)

— *See* Berlioz (L.H.) [Benvenuto Cellini.] Bénédiction et serment, deux motifs de Benvenuto Cellini ... transcrits pour le piano à quatre mains par F. Liszt. [1854.] fol.　**h. 585. (1.)**

— *See* Berlioz (L. H.) [La Dammation de Faust.—Ballet des Sylphes.] Danse des sylphes ... transcrite pour le piano par F. Liszt. [1866.] fol.　　　　　**Hirsch M. 775.**

— *See* Berlioz (L. H.) [La Damnation de Faust.—Ballet des Sylphes.] Danse des Sylphes ... Transcrite par F. Liszt. [1886.] fol.　　　　　**h. 3298. (1.)**

— *See* Berlioz (L. H.) [La Damnation de Faust.—Ballet des Sylphes.] Danse des Sylphes. Berlioz—[transcribed by F.] Liszt, *etc.* 1939. 4°.　　　　　**g. 1122. f. (1.)**

— *See* Berlioz (L. H.) Épisode de la vie d'un artiste ... Partition de piano par F. Liszt. [1850?] fol.　　**h. 456. a.**

— *See* Berlioz (L. H.) Épisode de la vie d'un artiste ... Partition de piano par F. Liszt. Seconde édition revue et corrigée par F. Liszt. [c. 1900.] fol.　　　　　**h. 896. r. (1.)**

— *See* Berlioz (L. H.) [Episode de la Vie d'un Artiste. Op. 14.] Symphonie fantastique, 2ᵐᵉ partie, ⟨un Bal⟩ ... pour piano seul par F. Liszt. [1842.] fol.　　　　　**Hirsch M. 778.**

— *See* Berlioz (L. H.) [Épisode de la Vie d'un Artiste. Op. 14.] Le Bal ... transcrite par F. Liszt. [1878.] fol.　**h. 1493. b. (5.)**

— *See* Berlioz (L. H.) [Épisode de la Vie d'un Artiste. Op. 14.] Marche au supplice ... transcrite pour le piano par F. Liszt. [1866.] fol.　　　　　**Hirsch M. 779.**

— *See* Berlioz (L. H.) [Épisode de la Vie d'un Artiste. Op. 14.] Marche au supplice ... transcrite par F. Liszt. [1878.] fol.
　　　　　h. 1493. b. (5*.)

— *See* Berlioz (L. H.) Harold en Italie ... Partition de Piano ... par F. Liszt. [1881.] fol.　　　　　**h. 3250. b. (10.)**

— *See* Berlioz (L. H.) [Harold en Italie.] Marche des pélerins ... transcrite pour le piano par F. Liszt. [1866.] fol.
　　　　　Hirsch M. 781.

— *See* Berlioz (L. H.) Ouverture des Francs juges ... Partition pour piano seul par F. Liszt. [1845.] fol.　　**h. 896. y. (1.)**

— *See* Berlioz (L. H.) Ouverture des Francs Juges ... Partition pour piano seul par F. Liszt. [c. 1880.] fol.　　**h. 896. a. (12.)**

— *See* Bertin (L. A.) Esméralda ... avec accompagnement de Piano par F. Liszt. [1836?] fol.　　　　　**H. 450. a.**

— *See* Braeunlich (A.) and Gottschalg (A. W.) Mädchenlieder. Unter Mitwirkung von Hoffmann von Fallersleben und F. Liszt herausgegeben von A. Bräunlich und W. Gottschalg, *etc.* 1861. 8°.　　**A. 833. (2.)**

— *See* Buelow (Hans G. von) Mazurka-Fantasie ... Op. 13. Für Orchester bearbeitet von F. Liszt, *etc.* [1868.] 8°.
　　　　　e. 58. n. (1.)

— *See* Bulgakov (　　　　) Bulhakow's russischer Galop für Piano Forte von F. Liszt. [1843.] fol.　　**h. 896. j. (2.)**

— *See* Bulgakov (　　　　) Galop Russe de Bulhakow, transcrit pour piano par F. Liszt. [1892.] fol. [*Repertory of select Pianoforte Works.* ser. 2. no. 7.]　　**h. 736. c.**

— *See* Chopin (F. F.) [*Collected Works.—a.*] F. Chopin's Werke. Herausgegeben von ... F. Liszt, *etc.* [1878–1902.] fol.
　　　　　g. 553. b.

— *See* Chopin (F. F.) [17 polnische Lieder. No. 1, 2, 14, 4, 12, 15.] 6 chants polonais, op. 74 ... transcrits pour le piano ... par F. Liszt, *etc.* [c. 1880.] fol.　　　　　**h. 471. i. (9.)**

— *See* Chopin (F. F.) [17 polnische Lieder. Op. 74. No. 1, 2, 14, 4, 12, 15.] 6 chants polonais, Op. 74 ... transcrits pour le piano ... par F. Liszt, *etc.* [c. 1890.] fol.　　**h. 896. z. (10.)**

LISZT (FRANZ)

— *See* CHOPIN (F. F.) [17 polnische Lieder.] Chants polonais. Op. 74. No. 1 ... [Transcribed for P. F. by F.] Liszt. 1914. fol. [*Hawley Edition. No. 96.*]   **h. 3527. b.**

— *See* CHOPIN (F. F.) [17 polnische Lieder. Op. 74. No. 1. Mädchens Wunsch.] Chant Polonaise ... Chopin-Liszt ... Arrangement for Two Pianos, *etc.* 1940. 4°. [*The Two-Piano Series. No. 25.*]   **g. 1393.**

— *See* CLEMENTI (Muzio) [Introduction to the Art of Playing on the Piano Forte.—Appendix. Op. 43.] Études et préludes gradués dans tous les tons majeurs et mineurs pour piano ... Édition corrigée ... par F. Liszt. [c. 1840.] fol.   **h. 319. q.**

— *See* CONRADI (A.) La Célèbre Zigeuner-Polka ... pour le piano par F. Liszt. [1849.] fol.   **Hirsch M. 836.**

— *See* DANIELE (G.) Polka hongroise ... d'après F. Listz [*sic*]. [P. F.] [c. 1845.] fol. [*Le Pianiste moderne.*]   **h. 1203. r. (10.)**

— *See* DARGOMUIZHSKY (A. S.) Tarantella ... transcrite pour le piano par F. Liszt. [1880.] fol.   **h. 585. f. (1.)**

— *See* DAVID (F.) Ferdinand David's Bunte Reihe ... für das Pianoforte übertragen von F. Liszt. [1851.] 4°.   **Hirsch M. 841.**

— *See* DAVID (F.) Bunte Reihe ... für das Pianoforte übertragen von F. Liszt. [1874.] fol.   **g. 554.**

— *See* DAVID (F.) [Bunte Reihe. Op. 30. No. 18.] Serenade ... Transcription by F. Liszt, *etc.* [1903.] fol.   **g. 605. tt. (5.)**

— *See* DAVID (F.) [Bunte Reihe. Op. 30. No. 19.] Ungarisch ... Arranged ... by F. Liszt. [1904.] 4°.   **g. 1132.**

— *See* DESSAUER (J.) Dessauer's Lieder ... für das Pianoforte übertragen von F. Liszt. [1847.] fol.   **Hirsch M. 855.**

— *See* DOSCHER (David) Franz Liszt: two Cadenzas. To the Étude de concert No. 2 ... [here attributed to] Leschetizky. To the Polonaise No. 2 in E major, by Busoni. Edited by D. Doscher. [1975.] fol.   **h. 896. jj.**

— *See* FIELD (John) 18 nocturnes ... ⟨Liszt's Edition.⟩ Nouvellement revue ... par K. Klauser, *etc.* [c. 1870.] 8°.   **f. 34. k.**

— *See* FIELD (John) 18 Nocturnes für Pianoforte ... Revidirt und mit Fingersatz versehen von F. Liszt. [c. 1880.] fol.   **h. 3465. s. (4.)**

— *See* FIELD (John) Eighteen Nocturnes. For the piano. Revised by F. Liszt, *etc.* [1950.] 4°.   **h. 3465. g. (2.)**

— *See* FIELD (John) [18 Nocturnes.] Six nocturnes pour le pianoforte, *etc.* [Edited by F. Liszt.] [1850?] fol.   **h. 3465. o. (11.)**

— *See* FIELD (John) [18 Nocturnes.] Huit nocturnes pour le pianoforte, *etc.* [Edited by F. Liszt.] [1852?] fol.   **h. 3465. o. (12.)**

— *See* FIELD (John) [18 Nocturnes.] N° [MS 1–6] of the Nocturnes ... Edited by F. Liszt. [1859, 60.] fol.   **h. 3465. (1.)**

— *See* FIELD (John) [18 Nocturnes.] Neuf nocturnes pour le pianoforte, *etc.* [Edited by F. Liszt.] [1863.] fol.   **h. 3465. o. (13.)**

— *See* FIELD (John) [18 Nocturnes.] Six Nocturnes for the Pianoforte, *etc.* ⟨Edited by F. Liszt.⟩ [c. 1895.] fol.   **h. 3465. u. (1.)**

— *See* FRANZ (R.) Lieder ... für das Pianoforte übertragen von F. Liszt. [1849.] fol.   **Hirsch M. 882.**

— *See* FRANZ (R.) [12 Gesänge. Op. 4. No. 7.] Er ist gekommen in Sturm und Regen ... für das Pianoforte übertragen von F. Liszt. [1849.] fol.   **Hirsch M. 881.**

LISZT (FRANZ)

— *See* FRANZ (R.) [12 Gesänge. Op. 4. No. 7.] Er ist gekommen ... Transcribed by F. Liszt, *etc.* [1903.] fol.   **h. 896. c. (9.)**

— *See* GLINKA (M. I.) [Русланъ и Людмила.—Маршъ.] Tscherkessen Marsch ... Für Piano-Forte, zu 2 Händen, *etc.* ⟨[Transcribed by] F. Liszt.⟩ [1843.] fol.   **h. 585. m. (10.)**

— *See* GOUNOD (C. F.) [La Reine de Saba.—Ballet.—Les Sabéennes.] Berceuse de l'opéra La Reine de Saba ... Pour piano par F. Liszt. [1865.] fol.   **g. 547. o. (6.)**

— *See* HERBECK (J. von) Tanz-Momente ... für Pianoforte von F. Liszt ... Für Clavier zu 2 Händen, *etc.* [c. 1890.] fol.   **h. 896. z. (4.)**

— *See* HERBECK (J. von) Tanz-Momente ⟨Op. 14⟩ ... für Pianoforte von F. Liszt ... Arrangement für Clavier zu 4 Händen. [c. 1890.] fol.   **g. 545. x. (1.)**

— *See* HUMMEL (J. N.) Grosses Septett in D-moll ... Op. 74. Neue revidirte Ausgabe von F. Liszt, *etc.* [c. 1890.] 8°.   **e. 96. j.**

— *See* HUMMEL (J. N.) Gr. Septett ⟨Op. 74.⟩ ... Pour piano seul par F. Liszt. [With violin, viola, violoncello and double bass parts for the P. F. quintet version of the work, edited by F. Liszt.] [c. 1890.] fol.   **h. 2785. u. (3.)**

— *See* KYUI (T. A.) Tarentelle. (Transcription de F. Liszt.) [1886.] fol.   **h. 3281. k. (42.)**

— *See* LASSEN (E.) 2 Lieder ... Für Pianoforte von F. Liszt, *etc.* [1872.] fol.   **g. 547. o. (8.)**

— *See* LASSEN (E.) [6 Lieder von Peter Cornelius. Op. 5. No. 3.] "Löse, Himmel, meine Seele!" ... Für das Pianoforte von F. Liszt. [1866.] fol.   **g. 547. o. (7.)**

— *See* LASSEN (E.) [6 Lieder von Peter Cornelius. Op. 5. No. 3.] "Löse, Himmel, meine Seele." "Sauve, ciel, mon âme" ... Für das Pianoforte von F. Liszt. [1900?] 4°.   **g. 547. g. (21.)**

— *See* LASSEN (E.) Symphonisches Zwischenspiel (Intermezzo) zu Calderon's Schauspiel "Ueber allen Zauber Liebe" ... Transcription für pianoforte von F. Liszt. [1883.] fol.   **h. 585. f. (19.)**

— *See* LEBERT (S.) Instructive Ausgabe Klassischer Klavierwerke. Unter Mitwirkung von ... F. Liszt ... herausgegeben von S. Lebert, *etc.* 1875, *etc.* fol.   **H. 1063. a.**

— *See* LYADOV (A. N.) Liszt. Réminiscences. Quadrille pour Piano, *etc.* [On melodies of Liszt.] [1840?] fol.   **h. 3571. (5.)**

— *See* MENDELSSOHN-BARTHOLDY (J. L. F.) [*Collected Works.—f.*] Mendelssohn's Lieder für das Pianoforte übertragen ... von F. Liszt. [1841.] fol.   **g. 547. o. (10.)**

— *See* MENDELSSOHN-BARTHOLDY (J. L. F.) [*Collected Works.—f.*] Mendelssohn's Lieder für das Pianoforte übertragen ... von F. Liszt, *etc.* [1876.] fol.   **h. 896. q. (7.)**

— *See* MENDELSSOHN-BARTHOLDY (J. L. F.) [6 Gesänge. Op. 34. No. 2.] Auf Flügeln des Gesanges ... transcribed by F. Liszt. [1882.] fol.   **h. 575. n. (18.)**

— *See* MENDELSSOHN-BARTHOLDY (J. L. F.) [6 Gesänge. Op. 34. No. 2.] Auf Flügeln des Gesanges ... [Transcribed for P. F. by F.] Liszt. 1914. fol. [*Hawley Edition. No. 95.*]   **h. 3527. b.**

— *See* MENDELSSOHN-BARTHOLDY (J. L. F.) [6 Gesänge. Op. 34. No. 2. Auf Flügeln des Gesanges.] The Maid of Ganges ... Mendelssohn- [arranged by F.] Liszt, *etc.* 1926. 4°.   **g. 635. o. (4.)**

— *See* MENDELSSOHN-BARTHOLDY (J. L. F.) [6 Gesänge. Op. 34. No. 6.] Mendelssohn's Lieder für das Pianoforte übertragen ... von F. Liszt, *etc.* ⟨No. 3. Reiselied.⟩ [1841.] fol.   **h. 1445. f. (12.)**

LISZT (Franz)

— *See* Mendelssohn-Bartholdy (J. L. F.) [6 Lieder. Op. 50. No. 4, 2.] Mendelssohn's Wasserfahrt u. Jäger-Abschied für das Pianoforte übertragen von F. Liszt. [1848.] fol.
g. 547. g. (20.)

— *See* Mendelssohn-Bartholdy (J. L. F.) [6 Lieder. Op. 50. No. 2. Der Jäger Abschied.] Hunter's Farewell ... Transcribed by F. Liszt. [1893.] fol.
h. 3271. (10.)

— *See* Mendelssohn-Bartholdy (J. L. F.) [Ein Sommernachtstraum.] Hochzeitsmarsch u. Elfenreigen aus der Musik zu Shakespeares Sommernachtstraum ... für das Pianoforte übertragen ... von F. Liszt. [1850.] fol.
h. 896. k. (13.)

— *See* Mendelssohn-Bartholdy (J. L. F.) [Ein Sommernachtstraum.] Wedding March and Fairies' Dance ... transcribed ... by F. Liszt. [1883.] fol.
h. 575. m. (31.)

— *See* Meyerbeer (G.) [Schiller-Marsch.] Fest-Marsch zu Schiller's 100 jähriger Geburtstagsfeier ... Zum Concertvortrag von F. Liszt, *etc.* [1860?] fol.
h. 1521. c. (1.)

— *See* Mozart (W. A.) [Requiem.—Confutatis. Lacrimosa.] Zwei Transcriptionen über Themen aus Mozart's Requiem für Piano von F. Liszt. [1865.] fol.
h. 896. k. (3.)

— *See* Musard (P.) Hommage à Liszt. Les Hongroises. Quadrille. [P. F.] [c. 1845.] fol. [*Le Pianiste moderne.*]
h. 1203. r. (10.)

— *See* Nicolai (C. O. E.) Kirchliche Eest-Ouvertüre [*sic*] üb. den Choral "Ein feste Burg ist unser Gott," f. Orgel (od. Pedalflügel) gesetzt von Fr. Liszt. [c. 1880.] fol.
h. 896. v. (1.)

— *See* Paganini (N.) Caprice xxiv. Variationen ... Nach der Klavierfassung von Franz Liszt, *etc.* 1935. 4°.
g. 70. i. (5.)

— *See* Rossini (G. A.) [Guillaume Tell.] Ouverture ... transcrite pour le piano par F. Liszt. [1842?] fol.
g. 547. o. (12.)

— *See* Rossini (G. A.) [Guillaume Tell.] Ouverture ... arrangée pour le piano par F. Liszt. [1843.] fol.
h. 584. (2.)

— *See* Rossini (G. A.) [Guillaume Tell.] Ouverture ... transcrite pour le piano par F. Liszt. [c. 1850.] fol.
h. 625. f. (5.)

— *See* Schubert (F. P.) [*Collected Works.—d.*] Vier Lieder ... für eine Singstimme mit kleinem Orchester. Instrumentirt von F. Liszt. [c. 1890.] 8°.
F. 409. oo. (1.)

— *See* Schubert (F. P.) [*Collected Works.—e.*] Hommage aux dames de Vienne. Lieder de Fr. Schubert. Transcrits pour piano par F. Liszt. [1838.] 8°.
E. 729. ll. (1.)

— *See* Schubert (F. P.) [*Collected Works.—e.*] Lieder ... für das Piano-forte übertragen von F. Liszt. [1838.] 4°.
g. 547. dd.

— *See* Schubert (F. P.) [*Collected Works.—e.*] Schubert's Admired German and French Melodies, arranged for the Piano Forte by F. Liszt. [1838.] fol.
h. 583. (6.)

— *See* Schubert (F. P.) [*Collected Works.—e.*] Schubert's Admired German and French Melodies, arranged ... for the Piano Forte by F. Liszt. [c. 1840.] fol.
i. 39. a. (1.)

— *See* Schubert (F. P.) [*Collected Works.—e.*] The Triumvirate or Homage to Schubert ... Transcribed for the piano forte ... by S. Heller, F. Liszt and C. Czerny, *etc.* [c. 1840.] fol.
h. 3183. m.

— *See* Schubert (F. P.) [*Collected Works.—e.*] F. Schubert's Geistliche Lieder für das Pianoforte übertragen von F. Liszt. [1841.] 4°.
f. 470. e. (1.)

— *See* Schubert (F. P.) [*Collected Works.—e.*] Two admired Melodies of Schubert, Serenade and Sois toujours mes seuls amours, arranged ... for the piano forte by F. Liszt. [c. 1845.] fol.
h. 3183. n. (1.)

LISZT (Franz)

— *See* Schubert (F. P.) [*Collected Works.—e.*] Lieder ohne Worte nach F. Schubert, für das Pianoforte componirt von F. Liszt. [c. 1845.] fol.
h. 896. y. (2.)

— *See* Schubert (F. P.) [*Collected Works.—e.*] Melodies of Franz Schubert. The Barcarole and The Wanderer. Arranged for the piano forte by F. Liszt, *etc.* [1852.] fol.
h. 895. (5.)

— *See* Schubert (F. P.) [*Collected Works.—e.*] Two songs ... transcribed by F. Liszt. [1855.] fol.
h. 585. (6.)

— *See* Schubert (F. P.) [*Collected Works.—e.*] 22 Songs ... Transcribed for the pianoforte by F. Liszt, *etc.* [1880.] 8°.
f. 470.

— *See* Schubert (F. P.) [*Collected Works.—e.*] Lieder, transcribed for the pianoforte by F. Liszt. [1886.] 4°.
g. 547. (5.)

— *See* Schubert (F. P.) [*Collected Works.—e.*] F. Schubert's Lieder, transcribed ... by F. Liszt. [1887.] fol.
g. 547. b.

— *See* Schubert (F. P.) [*Collected Works.—e.*] Lieder ... Transcribed ... by F. Liszt. [1904.] 4°.
g. 567. b. (4.)

— *See* Schubert (F. P.) [*Collected Works.—e.*] F. Liszt. Pianoforte Album. Schubert's Songs transcribed, *etc.* [1912.] fol.
h. 896. g. (8.)

— *See* Schubert (F. P.) [*Collected Works.—e.*] Twenty-four Songs. Transcribed for the piano by F. Liszt. [1951.] 4°.
g. 567. s. (1.)

— *See* Schubert (F. P.) [*Collected Works.—e.*] Шуберт—Лист. Песни, в переложении для фортепиано, *etc.* [With a portrait.] 1953, *etc.* fol.
h. 3040. k.

— *See* Schubert (F. P.) [*Collected Works.—g.*] Dances. (Edited by F.) Liszt, *etc.* [1921.] 4°.
g. 567. d. (13.)

— *See* Schubert (F. P.) Die Allmacht. [Op. 79. No. 2.] ... Für Männerchor und Orchester bearbeitet von F. Liszt, *etc.* [1872.] fol.
H. 2150. k. (1.)

— *See* Schubert (F. P.) [Die Allmacht. Op. 79. No. 2.] Great is Jehovah, the Lord ... Arranged ... by F. Liszt. [1914.] 4°. [*Novello's Tonic Sol-fa Series. No. 2161.*]
B. 885.

— *See* Schubert (F. P.) Auf dem Wasser zu singen ... [Transcribed for P. F. by F.] Liszt. 1914. fol. [*Hawley Edition. No. 98.*]
h. 3527. b.

— *See* Schubert (F. P.) [Auf dem Wasser zu singen. Op. 72.] To be sung on the Water ... Schubert-Liszt. Transcribed for two Pianos, four hands, *etc.* 1927. 4°.
g. 567. g. (8.)

— *See* Schubert (F. P.) Franz Schubert's Divertissement à la hongroise. Op. 54. Orchestrirt von M. Erdmannsdörfer und F. Liszt ... No. 2. Ungarischer Marsch (F. Liszt), *etc.* [1880.] 8°.
e. 288. b.

— *See* Schubert (F. P.) Erlkönig ... Für das Piano-Forte übertragen von F. Liszt. [c. 1850.] fol.
h. 896. q. (8.)

— *See* Schubert (F. P.) [Erlkönig.] Schubert's ... Melody ... Arranged ... by F. Liszt. [1860.] fol.
h. 726. n. (13.)

— *See* Schubert (F. P.) Erlkönig ... Transcription by F. Liszt. [1882.] fol.
h. 3183. b. (20.)

— *See* Schubert (F. P.) Erlkönig. [Transcribed by F. Liszt.] [1893.] fol.
h. 3298. (21.)

— *See* Schubert (F. P.) Grosse Fantasie Op. 15. Symphonisch bearbeitet für Piano und Orchester von F. Liszt. [1858.] fol.
g. 567. rr.

— *See* Schubert (F. P.) Grosse Fantasie. Op. 15. Symphonisch bearbeitet für Piano und Orchester von F. Liszt, *etc.* [1874?] fol.
Hirsch M. 1170.

LISZT (Franz)

— *See* Schubert (F. P.) Fantasia ... Opus 15. Symphonically transcribed for Piano and Orchestra [by] F. Liszt, *etc.* (1909.) fol.   **h. 3040. a. (1.)**

— *See* Schubert (F. P.) [Fantasia. Op. 15.] 'Wanderer' Fantasy for Piano and Orchestra, *etc.* ⟨F. Schubert/F. Liszt. Score.⟩ [1980.] 8°. *[Edition Eulenburg. no.* 1300.]   **b. 212.**

— *See* Schubert (F. P.) Grosse Fantasie. /Op. 15./ Symphonisch bearbeitet für Piano und Orchester von F. Liszt ... Arrangement für zwei Piano. [1862.] fol.   **h. 3183. i. (2.)**

— *See* Schubert (F. P.) Fantasia. The Wanderer. Op. 15. Edited by F. Liszt. [1921.] 4°.   **g. 567. d. (1.)**

— *See* Schubert (F. P.) Fantasia, or Sonata. Op. 78. Edited by F. Liszt. [1921.] 4°.   **g. 567. d. (2.)**

— *See* Schubert (F. P.) [Fantasia. Op. 78.] Menuetto ... Edited by F. Liszt. [1917.] fol.   **h. 3183. e. (5.)**

— *See* Schubert (F. P.) Die Forelle ... Für das Piano. Zweite Version von F. Liszt. [1846.] 4°. **Hirsch M. 1182. (4.)**

— *See* Schubert (F. P.) [Vier Gedichte. Op. 59. No. 3.] Du bist die Ruh ... [Transcribed for P. F. by F.] Liszt. 1914. fol. *[Hawley Edition. No.* 97.]   **h. 3527. b.**

— *See* Schubert (F. P.) [8 geistliche Lieder. No. 5. Litanei auf das Fest aller Seelen.] Schubert's Litany, transcribed ... by F. Liszt. [1886.] fol.   **h. 3183. b. (11.)**

— *See* Schubert (F. P.) [8 geistliche Lieder. No. 5. Litanei auf das Fest aller Seelen.] Litany ... [Arranged for P. F. by] F. Liszt. [1922.] 4°.   **g. 567. d. (4.)**

— *See* Schubert (F. P.) Der Gondelfahrer. Männer-Quartett für pianoforte transcribirt von F. Liszt. [1883.] fol.   **h. 585. f. (18.)**

— *See* Schubert (F. P.) [Horch, horch, die Lerch'.] Hark! Hark! the Lark ... [Transcribed for P.F. by F.] Liszt. 1914. fol. *[Hawley Edition. No.* 99.]   **h. 3527. b.**

— *See* Schubert (F. P.) [Horch, horch, die Lerch'.] Hark! Hark! the Lark. Schubert—Liszt, *etc.* 1933. 4°. **g. 567. i. (11.)**

— *See* Schubert (F. P.) [Horch, horch, die Lerch'.] Serenade. Hark, hark, the Lark. Schubert-Liszt. Arranged for Piano Duet, *etc.* 1934. 4°.   **g. 567. j. (22.)**

— *See* Schubert (F. P.) [Horch, horch die Lerch'.] Hark! Hark! The Lark. Schubert-Liszt. Arranged for Two Pianos, *etc.* [1945.] 4°.   **g. 567. l. (25.)**

— *See* Schubert (F. P.) Lob der Thränen [Op. 13. No. 2.] ... Lied ... Transcrit pour piano par F. Liszt. [1838?] 8°.   **f. 246. o. (5.)**

— *See* Schubert (F. P.) Lob der Thränen. [Op. 13. No. 2.] Lied ... für das Piano-Forte übertragen von F. Liszt. [c. 1845.] 8°.   **f. 31. e.**

— *See* Schubert (F. P.) Lob der Thränen. [Op. 13. No. 2.] Lied ... für das Piano-Forte übertragen von F. Liszt, *etc.* [c. 1850.] 8°.   **f. 470. d. (3.)**

— *See* Schubert (F. P.) F. Schubert's Märsche für das Orchester übertragen von F. Liszt. [1871.] 8°.   **e. 370. (8.)**

— *See* Schubert (F. P.) Vier Märsche ... Transcription ... von F. Liszt. [1880.] fol.   **h. 3183. c. (1.)**

— *See* Schubert (F. P.) [Die Rose. Op. 73.] La Rose. Poésie de Schlegel. Musique de Schubert. Arrangée pour le piano-forte ... par J. [or rather F.] Liszt. [1835?] 4°.   **h. 896. i. (12.)**

— *See* Schubert (F. P.) Die Rose. [Op. 73.] Lied ... für das Piano-Forte übertragen von F. Liszt, *etc.* [1840?] 8°.   **f. 470. d. (4.)**

LISZT (Franz)

— *See* Schubert (F. P.) [Die Rose. Op. 73.] La Rose, *etc.* ⟨Für Pianoforte von F. Liszt.⟩ [c. 1885.] fol.   **h. 896. ii. (4.)**

— *See* Schubert (F. P.) [Die schöne Müllerin.] Müller-Lieder ... Für das Pianoforte in leichteren Styl übertragen von F. Liszt, *etc.* [1847.] fol.   **Hirsch M. 1182. (2.)**

— *See* Schubert (F. P.) [Die schöne Müllerin. Op. 25. No. 2.] Wohin? ... Transcribed by Liszt, *etc.* [1900.] fol.   **h. 896. c. (8.)**

— *See* Schubert (F. P.) Schwanengesang ... Für das Pianoforte übertragen ... von Fr. Liszt. [1839.] fol. **h. 3183. h.**

— *See* Schubert (F. P.) Schwanengesang ... Für das Pianoforte übertragen ... von Fr. Liszt. [1840.] fol.   **g. 567. x.**

— *See* Schubert (F. P.) Schwanengesang ... Für das Piano Forte übertragen von F. Liszt. [1840.] fol.   **h. 583. (10.)**

— *See* Schubert (F. P.) [Schwanengesang.] Lied aus Fr. Schubert's Schwanengesang für das Piano-Forte übertragen von F. Liszt ... N° 1(–14). [1840?] fol.   **f. 470. d. (1.)**

— *See* Schubert (F. P.) [Schwanengesang. No. 4. Ständchen.] Serenade. Schubert-Liszt, *etc.* [1946.] 4°. **g. 567. n. (5.)**

— *See* Schubert (F. P.) [Schwanengesang. No. 4. Ständchen.] Serenade. Schubert-Liszt. Arranged for Two Pianos, *etc.* 1934. 4°.   **g. 567. j. (30.)**

— *See* Schubert (F. P.) [Die Winterreise ... für das Pianoforte übertragen von ... F. Liszt.] [1840.] fol. **h. 583. (7.)**

— *See* Schubert (F. P.) [Die Winterreise. No. 1, 4–6, 13, 17–19, 21–24.] Lied aus Fr. Schubert's Winterreise für das Piano-Forte übertragen von F. Liszt ... N° 15–24. [1840?] 8°.   **f. 470. d. (2.)**

— *See* Schubert (F. P.) [Die Winterreise. No. 1, 4–6, 13, 17–19, 21–24.] Schubert's Winter Rambles. Winterreise ... Für das Piano Forte, übertragen ... von Fr. Liszt. [1840.] fol.   **i. 39. a. (2.)**

— *See* Schumann (R. A.) [*Collected Works.—d.*] An den Sonnenschein [Op. 6. No. 4] und Rothes Röslein [Op. 27. No. 2]. Zwei Lieder ... für das Pianoforte übertragen von F. Liszt. [c. 1880.] fol.   **h. 88. m. (4.)**

— *See* Schumann (R. A.) [Liederkreis. Op. 39. No. 12.] Frühlingsnacht ... [Transcribed] für Pianoforte von F. Liszt. [1872.] fol.   **h. 585. b. (6.)**

— *See* Schumann (R. A.) [Liederkreis. Op. 39. No. 12.] Frühlingsnacht ... [Transcribed for P. F. by F.] Liszt. 1914. fol. *[Hawley Edition. No.* 78.]   **h. 3527. b.**

— *See* Schumann (R. A.) [Myrthen. Op. 25. No. 1. Widmung.] Liebeslied ... für das Pianoforte, übertragen von F. Liszt. [1845?] 4°.   **g. 543. ll. (15.)**

— *See* Schumann (R. A.) [Myrthen. Op. 25. No. 1. Widmung.] A ma fiancée ... Transcrite pour piano par F. Liszt. [c. 1880.] fol.   **h. 896. gg. (2.)**

— *See* Schumann (R. A.) [Myrthen. Op. 25. No. 1. Widmung.] Liebeslied ... (Transcribed) for the Pianoforte by F. Liszt. (1910.) 4°.   **G. 785. (388.)**

— *See* Schumann (R. A.) [Myrthen. Op. 25. No. 1.] Widmung ... [transcribed for the P. F. by] F. Liszt. (1911.) fol.   **h. 3369. (50.)**

— *See* Schumann (R. A.) [Myrthen. Op. 25. No. 1.] Widmung ... [transcribed for P. F. by F.] Liszt. 1914. fol. *[Hawley Edition. No.* 94.]   **h. 3527. b.**

— *See* Schumann (R. A.) [Myrthen. Op. 25. No. 1. Widmung.] Devotion, *etc.* ⟨Transcribed by F. Liszt.⟩ [P. F.] [c. 1920.] fol. *[Mayfair Classics. no.* 23.]   **h. 3576.**

LISZT (Franz)

— *See* SCHUMANN (R. A.) [Myrthen. Op. 25. No. 1. Widmung.] Dedication ... Schumann-Liszt. Transcribed for 2 Pianos 4 hands by E. Hesselberg. 1927. 4°.   **g. 715. h. (20.)**

— *See* SPOHR (L.) [Zemir and Azor.—Rose, wie bist du.] Die Rose ... für das Pianoforte übertragen von F. Liszt. [1876.] fol.   **h. 585. b. (18.)**

— *See* SPOHR (L.) [Zemir und Azor.—Rose, wie bist du.] Rose softly blooming. Romance ... transcribed for the pianoforte by F. Liszt. [1877.] fol.   **h. 585. e. (1.)**

— *See* SPOHR (L.) [Zemir und Azor.—Rose, wie bist du.] Rose, softly blooming, *etc.* ⟨Transcribed for pianoforte solo by F. Liszt.⟩ [c. 1940.] fol. [*Mayfair Classics. no.* 51.]   **h. 3576.**

— *See* SZABADY (F. I.) [Török magyar induló. Op. 116.] Marche hongroise ... Transcrite pour piano d'après l'orchestration de J. Massenet par F. Liszt. [1892.] fol.   **g. 547. o. (9.)**

— *See* SZÉCHÉNYI (I.) *Count.* Bevezetés és magyar induló ... Zongorára atirta Liszt F. [c. 1878.] fol.   **h. 896. aa. (5.)**

— *See* VIOLE (R.) Gartenlaube ... Etuden ... Herausgegeben ... von F. Liszt. [1870?] fol.   **h. 3821. e. (14.)**

— *See* WAGNER (W. R.) [*Collected Works.—d.*] Zwei Stücke aus R. Wagner's Tannhäuser und Lohengrin für das Pianoforte von F. Liszt. No. 1. Einzug der Gäste auf Wartburg, *etc.* [c. 1860.] fol.   **h. 585. k. (3.)** **& h. 356. s. (11.)**

— *See* WAGNER (W. R.) [*Collected Works.—d.*] Zwei Stücke aus R. Wagner's Tannhäuser und Lohengrin für das Pianoforte von F. Liszt ... Neu revidirte Ausgabe. [c. 1880.] fol.   **g. 547. u. (5.)** **& h. 896. gg. (4.)**

— *See* WAGNER (W. R.) [*Collected Works.—d.*] Franz Liszt. Transcriptionen über Richard Wagner's Opern. [1883–88.] fol.   **h. 896. c. (1.)**

— *See* WAGNER (W. R.) [*Collected Works.—d.*] Wagner. Pianoforte Album. Lohengrin. [Selections.] Transcribed by F. Liszt, *etc.* [1912.] fol.   **h. 356. r. (9.)**

— *See* WAGNER (W. R.) [*Collected Works.—d.*] Wagner. Second Pianoforte Album. Tannhäuser. [Selections.] Transcribed by F. Liszt, *etc.* [1912.] fol.   **h. 356. r. (10.)**

— *See* WAGNER (W. R.) [*Collected Works.—d.*] Wagner-Liszt Album. Transcriptions for the piano by F. Liszt, *etc.* [1951.] 4°.   **g. 379. w. (11.)**

— *See* WAGNER (W. R.) [Lohengrin.] Aus Richard Wagner's Lohengrin. I. Festspiel u. Brautlied. II. Elsa's Traum u. Lohengrin's Verweis an Elsa. Für das Pianoforte von F. Liszt. [1854.] fol.   **h. 896. ff. (3.)**

— *See* WAGNER (W. R.) [Lohengrin.] Aus Richard Wagner's Lohengrin ... Für das Pianoforte von F. Liszt, *etc.* [1862.] fol.   **h. 356. s. (10.)**

— *See* WAGNER (W. R.) [Lohengrin.] Aus Richard Wagner's Lohengrin. No. 1. Festspiel und Brautlied. No. II. Elsa's Traum und Lohengrin's Verweis an Elsa. Für das Pianoforte von F. Liszt. No. 1. Festspiel und Brautlied (Neue umgearbeitete Ausgabe), *etc.* [1870?] fol.   **h. 356. s. (12.)**

— *See* WAGNER (W. R.) [Lohengrin.] Aus Richard Wagner's Lohengrin. Nº I. Festspiel und Brautlied. ⟨Neue umgearbeitete Ausgabe.⟩ Nº II. Elsa's Traum und Lohengrin's Verweis an Elsa. Für das Pianoforte von F. Liszt ... Neue revidirte Ausgabe. [c. 1890.] fol.   **h. 896. gg. (5.)**

— *See* WAGNER (W. R.) [Lohengrin.] Elsa's Traum und Lohengrin's Verweis an Elsa ... Arranged for the Piano by F. Liszt. (1910.) 4°.   **G. 785. (413.)**

LISZT (Franz)

— *See* WAGNER (W. R.) [Lohengrin.—Gesegnet soll sie schreiten.] Marche religieuse, *etc.* [Arranged for P. F. by F. Liszt.] [c. 1860.] fol.   **h. 896. gg. (8.)**

— *See* WAGNER (W. R.) [Lohengrin.—Gesegnet soll sie schreiten.] Elsa's Bridal Procession. Transcription, *etc.* [P. F.] [1906.] fol. [*Edition Paull. No.* 22.]   **h. 3822. (22.)**

— *See* WAGNER (W. R.) [Lohengrin.—Gesegnet soll sie schreiten.] Elsa's Brautgang zum Münster ... Arranged for the Piano by F. Liszt. (1910.) 4°.   **G. 785. (412.)**

— *See* WAGNER (W. R.) [Tannhäuser.—Overture.] Ouverture zu Tannhäuser ... Concertparaphrase für Piano von F. Liszt. [1900?] fol.   **h. 356. s. (13.)**

— *See* WAGNER (W. R.) [Tannhäuser.—Beglückt darf nun.] Chœur des pélerins [*sic*]. Paraphrase par F. Liszt. [P. F.] [c. 1860.] fol.   **h. 896. gg. (9.)**

— *See* WAGNER (W. R.) [Tannhäuser.—Beglückt darf nun.] Pilgerchor aus R. Wagner's Tannhäuser. Paraphrase für Piano von F. Liszt. [1880?] fol.   **h. 356. s. (14.)**

— *See* WAGNER (W. R.) [Tannhäuser.—Beglückt darf nun.] Choeur des pélerins [*sic*] ... [Arranged by] F. Liszt. ⟨Für Klavier zu 2 Händen.⟩ [c. 1900.] fol.   **h. 356. cc. (1.)**

— *See* WAGNER (W. R.) [Tannhäuser.] Einzug der Gäste auf Wartburg. [Transcribed by] F. Liszt. [1893.] fol.   **h. 3271. (11.)**

— *See* WAGNER (W. R.) [Tannhäuser.] Einzug der Gäste auf Wartburg ... für Pianoforte zu zwei Händen. ⟨[Arranged by] F. Liszt.⟩ Neue Ausgabe mit bisher undruckten Zutaten und Varianten F. Liszts erstmalig herausgegeben von A. Stradal. [1917.] 4°.   **g. 547. bb. (2.)**

— *See* WAGNER (W. R.) [Tannhäuser.] March ... from R. Wagner's opera Tannhäuser, for the Pianoforte, by F. Liszt. [1861.] fol.   **h. 585. a. (1.)**

— *See* WAGNER (W. R.) [Tannhäuser.] "O du mein holder Abendstern." Recitativ u. Romanze aus der Oper: Tannhäuser ... für das Pianoforte übertragen von F. Liszt. [1849.] fol.   **h. 356. s. (15.)**

— *See* WAGNER (W. R.) [Tannhäuser.—O! du mein holder Abendstern.] L'Étoile du soir, romance pour le pianoforte, de l'opéra Tannhauser [*sic*], de R. Wagner, transcrite par F. Liszt. [1861.] fol.   **h. 585. a. (2.)**

— *See* WAGNER (W. R.) [Tannhäuser.—O! du mein holder Abendstern.] Wolfram's Invocation. Romance from Richard Wagner's opera Die [*sic*] Tannhäuser, arranged for the Piano by F. Liszt. [1868.] fol.   **h. 585. a. (7.)**

— *See* WAGNER (W. R.) [Tannhäuser.] O du mein holder Abendstern ... for the pianoforte by F. Liszt. [1883.] fol.   **h. 356. j. (12.)**

— *See* WAGNER (W. R.) [Tannhäuser.—O! du mein holder Abendstern.] Romance ... Transcribed by F. Liszt. [1886.] fol.   **h. 3298. (27.)**

— *See* WAGNER (W. R.) [Tannhäuser.] "O du mein holder Abendstern." Rezitativ und Romanze ... übertragen von F. Liszt. [P. F.] [c. 1890.] fol.   **h. 585. o. (7.)**

— *See* WAGNER (W. R.) [Tannhäuser.—O! du mein holder Abendstern.] Romance from ... Tannhäuser ... Transcribed for Piano by F. Liszt. (1910.) 4°.   **G. 785. (411.)**

— *See* WAGNER (W. R.) [Tannhäuser.—O! du mein holder Abendstern.] Star of Eve ... [transcribed for P. F. by F.] Liszt. 1914. fol. [*Hawley Edition. No.* 100.]   **h. 3527. b.**

— *See* WAGNER (W. R.) [Tannhäuser.—O! du mein holder Abendstern.] O Star of Eve ... Arranged [for P. F.] by F. Liszt, *etc.* [1919.] fol.   **h. 356. r. (15.)**

LISZT (Franz)

— *See* Wagner (W. R.) [Tannhäuser.—O! du mein holder Abendstern.] Evening Star, *etc.* ⟨Transcribed by F. Liszt.⟩ [P. F.] [c. 1920.] fol. [*Mayfair Classics. no.* 24.] **h. 3576.**

— *See* Wagner (W. R.) [Tristan und Isolde.] Isolden's Liebes-Tod ... für das Pianoforte bearbeitet von F. Liszt, *etc.* [1875.] fol. **h. 356. s. (16.)**

— *See* Wagner (W. R.) [Tristan und Isolde.] Isolden's Liebes-Tod ... Für das Pianoforte bearbeitet von F. Liszt. Arrangement für das Pianoforte zu vier Händen von A. Heintz. [1875.] fol. **h. 585. b. (11.)**

— *See* Wagner (W. R.) [Tristan und Isolde.] Isolden's Liebes-Tode ... for the Pianoforte by F. Liszt. [1886.] fol. **h. 356. j. (10.)**

— *See* Wagner (W. R.) [Tristan und Isolde.—Isolden's Liebes-Tod.] Isolde's Love Death. Scene from R. Wagner's Tristan und Isolde. [Transcribed for P. F. by] F. Liszt, *etc.* [1905.] fol. [*Edition Paull. no.* 49.] **h. 3822. (49.)**

— *See* Wagner (W. R.) [Tristan und Isolde.] Isolden's Liebes-Tod ... [Transcription] von F. Liszt, *etc.* [1911.] fol. **h. 356. q. (2.)**

— *See* Weber (C. M. F. E. von) [*Collected Works.—b.*] C. M. von Weber's Ouverturen ... Clavier Partitur von F. Liszt. [1847.] fol. **h. 706. (23.) & g. 547. jj. (1.)**

— *See* Weber (C. M. F. E. von) [*Collected Works.—b.*] Ouverturen, *etc.* ⟨Clavier-Partitur von F. Liszt.⟩ [c. 1910.] fol. **h. 5850. (2.)**

— *See* Weber (C. M. F. E. von) Polacca brillante ... instrumentirt ... von F. Liszt. [1880.] fol. **h. 1336. b. (9.)**

— *See* Weber (C. M. F. E. von) Polonaise brillante, Op. 72, für Pianoforte und Orchester instrumentirt ... von F. Liszt, *etc.* [1853.] 4°. **f. 130. (4.)**

— *See* Weber (C. M. F. E. von) Polonaise brillante, Op. 72, für Pianoforte und Orchester instrumentirt ... von F. Liszt ... Für Piano allein. [1853?] fol. **h. 1336. cc. (2.)**

— *See* Weber (C. M. F. E. von) Polonaise brillante. ⟨Op. 72.⟩ For two pianos. Orchestral accompaniment arranged for a second piano from the version for pianoforte and orchestra by F. Liszt, *etc.* [1948.] 4°. **h. 1336. j. (8.)**

— *See* Weber (C. M. F. E. von) Piano Sonatas. Edited by F. Liszt. [1917.] fol. **h. 1336. f. (5.)**

— *See* Weber (C. M. F. E. von) Piano Works. Sonatas, Op. 24, 39, 49 & 70. Edited by F. Liszt. [1933.] 4°. **g. 1127. qq. (30.)**

— *See* Whitehead (A. E.) O hearken Thou, O Lord ... Based on Liszt's transcription of the Ave Maria by Arcadelt, *etc.* 1940. 8°. **E. 335. k. (13.)**

— *See* Wielhorski (M.) *Count.* Любила я! "Autrefois." Romance ... Pour piano par F. Liszt. [c. 1870.] 4°. **f. 470. e. (2.)**

— *See* Wilhelmj (A. E. D. F. V.) All' Ungherese, nach F. Liszt. Concertstück für Violine mit ... Klavier. [1884.] fol. **h. 1608. m. (42.)**

LISZT (Franz) and GOTTSCHALG (A. W.)

— Transcriptionen für Harmonium, Pedalflügel oder Orgel von F. Liszt u. A. W. Gottschalg. 6 no. *Berlin,* [1879.] fol. *Imperfect; wanting no.* 1–5. **h. 3213. s. (4.)**

LISZT (J.)

— *See* Liszt (F.)

LIT

— Le Lit de Myrthe. Romance. *See* Goulé ( )

— The Lit de veille. [Song.] *See* Horn (Charles E.)

LI-TAI-PE

— Li-Tai-Pe. Oper. *See* Franckenstein (C. von)

LITAIZE (Gaston)

— Grand' messe pour tous les temps. *In:* Masses. Deux grand' messes. N. Le Bègue. G. Litaize. pp. 16–28. [1956.] 4°. **h. 2733. n. (1.)**

— Missa virgo gloriosa. Kyrie-Sanctus-Benedictus-Agnus Dei. ⟨Gloria-Credo.⟩ For soprano, tenor and bass voices and organ. 2 no. *Gregorian Institute of Music: Toledo, Ohio,* [1959.] 8°. *Part of "Connoisseur's Catalog. ser. 1".* **F. 1175. gg. (1.)**

LITAIZE (Gaston) and BONFILS (Jean Baptiste)

— Huit courantes extraites du Ms. Lynard A de Lübbenau. ⟨Les Pré-classiques français. La Barre—Gautier—Ballard et anonymes. [Organ. Edited by] G. Litaize, J. Bonfils.⟩ pp. 23. *Éditions musicales de la Schola cantorum et de la Procure générale de musique: Paris, Saint-Leu-la-Forêt,* [1967.] fol. *L'Organiste liturgique.* 58–59. **h. 2733. v. (13.)**

LITANEI

— Litanei. Für gemischten Chor. *See* Petirek (F.)

— Litanei. [Song.] *See* Schoenberg (A.) [String Quartet No. 2. Op. 10. 3rd movement.]

LITANIA

— Litania do Marii Panny. Na sopran solo, chór żeński i orkiestrę symfoniczną. *See* Szymanowski (K.)

LITANIAE

— Litaniæ Septem Deiparæ Virgini Musice decantandae. *Petrus Phalesius: Antuerpiæ,* 1598. 8°. **K. 8. c. 16.**

LITANIE

— *See* Litany.

LITANIES

— Six Litanies by the Daughters of the Cross. *Cary & Co.: London,* [1903.] 8°. **F. 1175. d. (4.)**

— Litanies de Mignon. [Song.] *See* Weckerlin (J. B. T.)

— Litanies des femmes. [Song cycle.] *See* Saminsky (L.)

— Three Litanies from Spirit World. Communicated through the mediumship of S. Harald. [1910?] 8°. **D. 835. (27.)**

— Easy Litanies, Hymns and Antiphons ... with an organ accompaniment, *etc. London,* [1853.] 8°. **E. 605. a. (7.)**

— Litanies with two trebles, with organ accompaniment. [*London,* 1856.] fol. **H. 1128. (24.)**

LITANY

— Litany. ⟨Salisbury Diocesan Choral Association.⟩ As sung in Salisbury Cathedral. *Novello and Co.: London,* 1903. a card. **I. 600. b. (122.)**

— Litany. [Song.] *See* Bache (Francis E.)

— Litany. Song. *See* Bell (G. F.)

LITANY

— A Litany. [Part-song.] *See* BLYTON (Carey)

— A Litany. [Part-song.] *See* BRIDGE (F.)

— A Litany. Chorus. *See* GIBBS (C. A.)

— A Litany. Song. *See* HAIGH (T.) *Mus. Doc.*

— A Litany. [Song.] *See* HURLSTONE (W. Y.)

— A Litany. Song. *See* LAMBELET (V.)

— Litany. [Song.] *See* MOLIQUE (W. B.) [6 sacred Songs. Op. 48. No. 4.]

— Litany. [Part-song.] *See* SCHUBERT (F. P.) [Acht geistliche Lieder. No. 5. Litanei auf das Fest aller Seelen.]

— A Litany. Song. *See* VIDAL (E.)

— A Litany. [Part-song.] *See* WALTON (*Sir* W. T.)

— For inserting Litany Chants. [Blank lines for music, etc.] *London*, [1854.] fol.   **H. 1128. (23.)**

— Nine Litany Chants. *London*, [1854.] fol.   **H. 1128. (17.)**

— Litany for All Souls' Day. [Sacred song.] *See* SCHUBERT (F. P.) [Acht geistliche Lieder. No. 5. Litanei auf das Fest aller Seelen.]

— A Litany for the War. *See* BRANSCOMBE (H. A.)

— Litany of Intercession. *See* ORMAN (C. E.)

— Litany of Jesus. Unison chorus. *See* CLOKEY (Joseph W.)

— Litany of Loretto and Litany No. 2, arranged for the Piano. *Chappell & Co.: London*, [1900.] fol.   **h. 727. a. (7.)**

— The litanie of our blessed Ladye Saint Marie commonly called of Loretto, with three chaunts, and organ accompaniment, *etc. Edinburgh*, [1855.] fol.   **H. 1128. (25.)**

— A Litany of Psalms. [Cantata.] *See* MUELLER (C. F.)

— The Litany of Solomon Ben Aaron. [Anthem.] *See* BERLINSKI (H.)

— Litany of Supplication. [Anthem.] *See* GRECHANINOV (A. T.) [Liturgia domestica. Op. 79.]

— Litany of the B. V. M. No. 1 in F for three treble voices with Organ or Pianoforte accompaniment. *London*, [1879.] fol.   **H. 1129. b. (15.)**

— Litany of the Incarnate Word. *See* POWELL (J. B.)

— Litany of the Sacred Heart of Jesus. [Hymn.] *See* HARDING (H. A.)

— The Litany set to the Chant of the Sarum Processional. *Oxford University Press: London*, 1935. 8°.   **D. 835. a. (4.)**

— Letanie to the Holy Spirite. [Song.] *See* HATTON (John L.)

— Litany to the Holy Spirit. [Unison song.] *See* HURFORD (Peter)

— A Litany to the Holy Spirit. Anthem. *See* MILFORD (Robin H.)

— Litany to the Holy Spirit. Song. *See* ROBERTON (*Sir* H. S.)

— Litany to the Holy Spirit. Duet. *See* THOMAS (V.)

— Litany to the Holy Spirit. [Song.] *See* VALE (Charles)

LITER (MONIA)

— Cossack Dance. Full score. pp. 25. *Hawkes & Son: London*, [1960.] fol.   **g. 1620. o. (4.)**

— The Gondola. *See* infra: [Mediterranean Suite. No. 3.]

LITER (MONIA)

— Jota and Rhumba. ⟨Piano-conductor [and orchestral parts].⟩ 24 pt. *Boosey & Hawkes: London*, [1956.] 4°. *The first violin part is in duplicate.*   **h. 3210. i. (389.)**

— [Mediterranean Suite.] Tango de Soller ... Piano conductor [and orchestral parts]. 22 pt. *Boosey & Hawkes: London*, [1957.] 4°. *The first violin part is in duplicate.*   **h. 3210. i. (436.)**

— [Mediterranean Suite. No. 2.] Tropical Moon ... Piano conductor [and orchestral parts]. 22 pt. *Hawkes & Son: London*, [1958.] 4°.   **h. 3210. i. (484.)**

— [Mediterranean Suite. No. 3.] The Gondola, *etc.* ⟨Piano conductor [and orchestral parts].⟩ 23 pt. *Boosey & Hawkes: London*, [1958.] 4°.   **h. 3210. i. (483.)**

— Prelude espagnole. For piano and orchestra. Reduction for two pianos. pp. 22. *Hawkes & Son: London*, [1955.] 4°.   **h. 4015. k. (6.)**

— Prelude to a Beguine. [For military band. Conductor's score and parts.] 32 pt. *Boosey & Hawkes: London*, [1955.] 4°. [*Q.M.B. Edition. no.* 197.] *With several copies of various parts.*   **h. 3211. b.**

— Scherzo transcendent. [For orchestra.] Full score. pp. 51. *Hawkes & Son: London*, [1957.] 4°.   **g. 727. ss. (12.)**

— Serenade for Strings and Harp. Full score. pp. 21. *Hawkes & Son: London*, [1955.] 4°.   **g. 727. kk. (5.)**

— Tango de Soller. *See* supra: [Mediterranean Suite.]

— Tropical Moon. *See* supra: [Mediterranean Suite. No. 2.]

— *See* ALBENIZ (I.) [Chants d'espagne. Op. 232. No. 4.] Córdoba. [Arranged by M. Liter.] [1960.] 4°.   **h. 3210. i. (657.)**

— *See* COATES (Eric) [Four Centuries.] Prelude ... Arranged for piano by M. Liter. [1955.] 4°.   **g. 1370. d. (5.)**

LITERARY

— Literary Transmigration. [Song.] *See* DIBDIN (Charles) [A Frisk.]

LITERAS (ANTONIO)

— *See* LITERES.

LITERES (ANTONIO)

— [Accis y Galatea.] Confiado gilguerillo. Little Linnet. [Song.] ... English version by Estelle Liebling ... Arranged by Estelle Liebling. *Span. & Eng.* pp. 9. *G. Schirmer: New York*, [1955.] 4°.   **G. 1271. c. (18.)**

— Confiado gilguerillo. *See* supra: [Accis y Galatea.]

— Dos Himnos à cuatro voces. *See* ESLAVA (M. H.) Lira Sacro-Hispana, *etc.* Sigl. XVIII. Ser. 1ª. Tom. 1°. [1869.] fol.   **H. 4.**

— *See* PEDRELL (F.) Teatro Lírico Español ... Vol. II. Varios.—Literes, *etc.* [1897, *etc.*] 8°.   **F. 68.**

— *See* PEDRELL (F.) Teatro Lírico Español, *etc.* Vol. IV. 1897, *etc.* 8°.   **F. 68.**

LITHANDER (C. L.)

— L'Allegrezza, rondino for the Pianoforte. *London*, [1818.] fol.   **g. 271. e. (3.)**

— L'amitié; a French quadrille, arranged as a rondo for the Piano Forte by C. L. Lithander. *London*, [1818.] fol.   **h. 117. (34.)**

LITHANDER (C. L.)

— Divertimento ⟨No. 1⟩, for the Flute and Piano Forte, in which is introduced an ancient Swedish national melody called Neck's Polonoise. [Score.] pp. 8. *Monzani & Hill: London,* [WM 1815.] fol. **g. 280. m. (8.)**

— Second divertimento; a Swedish air, with variations for the Piano Forte and Flute. *London,* [1816.] fol. **h. 117. (35.)**

— Donald, a favorite Scotch air with variations for the Pianoforte. *London,* [1820?] fol. **h. 1480. m. (19.)**

— Easy duet for the Piano Forte. Op. 7. No. 1, 2. *London,* [1818.] fol. **h. 117. (33.)**

— Fantasia, for the piano forte, in which are introduced several favourite airs ... Op. 12. pp. 17. *Robᵗ Purdie: Edinburgh,* [c. 1820.] fol. **h. 60. jj. (8.)**

— Introduction and rondo for the Piano Forte. Op. 6. *London,* [1818.] fol. **h. 117. (32.)**

— A first Set of twenty four favorite Melodies arranged as Trios for two Flutes and Pianoforte. [Parts.] *Monzani & Hill: London,* [c. 1820.] fol.
Imperfect; wanting the flauto secondo part. **h. 3213. j. (10.)**
& g. 280. gg. (7.)

— A First ⟨second, third⟩ Set of twenty four favorite Melodies, arranged as trios for two flutes and piano forte. [Parts.] 3 vol. 9 pt. *Monzani & Hill: London,* [c. 1825.] fol.
Sets 4–6, arranged by H. Hill, are entered under his name.
h. 2050. r. (1.)

LITHANDER (F.)

— Romance avec accompagnement de Pianoforte ... Paroles de Monsieur Yves de Guiraud. *St. Pétersbourg, chez J. Brieff:* [c. 1815.] fol. **g. 443. f. (10.)**

LITHANDER (FREDRIK)

— Sonate facile. Op. 8. No. 1. ⟨Pour le pianoforte.⟩ 2 ms. Facsimile. [Introduction by Alfhild Forslin.] pp. 12. *Edition Fazer: Helsinki,* [1980.] 4°.
[*Documenta musicae fennicae.* 14.] **G. 1495.**

LITHANDER (FREDRIK I.)

— Haydnin teema muunnelmineen ... Variations on a Theme [the Andante from Symphony Hob. I/53] by Haydn. [P. F.] 2 ms. ⟨Rev. Pentti Koskimies.⟩ pp. 12. *Edition Fazer: Helsinki,* 1978. 4°.
[*Documenta musicae fennicae.* 15.] **G. 1495.**

LITHGOW (ALEXANDER F.)

— March of the Anzacs. For piano solo. *C. Fischer: New York, etc.,* 1916. fol. **h. 3284. oo. (25.)**

— Pozieres. March for piano solo. *C. Fischer: New York, etc.,* 1918. 4°. **g. 272. kk. (19.)**

LITHGOW (W. H.)

— Old Scotland I love thee ... Song, written by A. Park. *London,* [1876.] fol. **H. 1778. y. (59.)**

LITHUANIAN

— Lithuanian National Anthem. [Melody by Vincas Kudirka. Military band parts.] 31 pt. *Boosey & Hawkes: London,* [1932.] *obl.* 8°.
With several copies of various parts. **h. 3210. i. (437.)**

— Lithuanian Song. Chorus. *See* CHOPIN (F. F.) [17 Polnische Lieder. Op. 74. No. 16.]

LITINSKY (G.)

— Второй квартет. Deuxième quatuor. Для 2 скрипок, альта и виолончели ... Партитура, *etc.* pp. 48. *Универсальное издательство: Вена, Leipzig; Музсектор Госиздата: Москва,* 1929. 8°. **c. 140. kk. (2.)**

— Квартет-сюита No. 4. Quatuor-suite No. 4. Для 2 скрипок, альта и виолончели. Pour 2 violons, viola et violoncelle. [Score.] pp. 14. *Государственное Музыкальное Издательство: Москва; Универсалное Издательсмво: Вена,* 1931. 8°. **c. 140. v. (3.)**

LI-TI-TI-TI

— Li-ti-ti-ti. Song. *See* PÉLISSIER (H. G.)

LITLER (JOSEPH BELLOT)

— Rêverie pour Piano. *London,* [1872.] fol. **h. 1485. t. (20.)**

— Songs of the Church, edited by J. B. Litler. *E. Stock: London,* 1891. 8°. **D. 1002.**

LITOLFF (A. A.)

— King William the fourth's quadrilles. Litolff's first set ... for the Piano Forte. [*London,* 1831.] fol. **h. 117. (36.)**

LITOLFF (CHARLES)

— The Alhambra polka. [P. F.] *London,* [1858.] fol.
h. 977. f. (37.)

— The Blue Eyed Beauty waltz. [P. F.] *London,* [1873.] fol.
h. 1483. (9.)

— The Manœuvre Polka. [P. F.] pp. 7. [*London,* c. 1865.] fol.
h. 61. pp. (12.)

— The Sandringham valses. [P. F.] *London,* [1863.] fol.
h. 1460. w. (16.)

— The Spirit of Love schottische. [P. F.] *London,* [1860.] fol.
h. 1460. w. (15.)

— The Wedding Ring Galop. [P. F.] pp. 7. *Hutchings & Romer: London,* [1866.] fol. **h. 722. vv. (20.)**

LITOLFF (HENRY CHARLES)

— Quatre morceaux faciles pour le piano. Nᵒ. 1. Premier divertissement. Nᵒ. 2. Rondo élégant. Nᵒ. 3. Variations sur un thême favori. Nᵒ. 4. Rêverie à la valse. 4 no. *Chez Ch. Bachmann: Hannovre,* [c. 1850.] fol. **h. 680. c. (12.)**

— Anna-mazourka. *See infra:* [3 mazurkas. Op. 17. No. 1.]

— Antolka-mazourka. *See infra:* [3 mazourkas. Op. 17. No. 3.]

— Ave Maria. [Solo.] *Paris,* [1869.] fol. **H. 1028. a. (7.)**

— Ballade pour Piano. Op. 73. *London,* [1860.] fol.
h. 1460. w. (17.)

— Ballade pour le Piano. ⟨Op. 73.⟩ *Paris,* [1861.] fol.
h. 680. a. (1.)

— Litolff's Bibliothek classischer Compositionen. ⟨Collection Litolff.⟩ vol. 163, *etc. Henry Litolff's Verlag: Braunschweig, New York,* [1865, *etc.*] 4° & 8°.
Imperfect; wanting many volumes. Vol. 451–499 bear the imprint "Enoch & Co.: London" and the series title "Format Litolff". The part of this series bearing the literal numeration G–Z is entered under FORMAT LITOLFF. **g. 375.**

— La Boîte de Pandore, opéra-bouffe en 3 actes. Paroles de T. Barriere. Partition Piano et Chant. *Paris,* [1872.] 8°.
F. 446. a.

— Bolero. *See infra:* Opuscules. Op. 25 ... 6.

LITOLFF (Henry Charles)

— Die Braut von Kynast. Grosse romantische Oper in drei Akten von F. Fischer ... Vollständiger Clavier-Auszug von L. Winkler. *Braunschweig,* [1847.] fol. **H. 676.**

— 3 caprices-valses pour le piano ... Op: 28. ⟨N°. 1 Légèreté. N°. 2 Grâce. N°. 3 Abandon.⟩ 3 no. *Heugel et c^{ie}.: Paris,* [c. 1850.] fol. **h. 680. c. (10.)**

— Chant de Mai, Rêverie sur les ondes, Inquietude. Trois esquisses musicales pour le piano, *etc.* Oeuvre 82. *Magdebourg,* [1854.] fol. **h. 680. (16.)**

— Chant des Belges, ouverture dramatique, *etc.* Partition. Op. 101. *Brunswick,* [1856.] 8°. **f. 130. (2.)**

— Sechs Characterstücke für das Pianoforte. Op. 65. *Braunschweig,* [1852.] fol. **h. 680. (8.)**

— Clair de Lune, impromptu pour Piano. *London,* [1861.] fol. **h. 1460. w. (22.)**

— Clair de Lune (Mondschein). Impromptu pour Piano. *Paris,* [1861.] fol. **h. 680. a. (2.)**

— Collection Litolff. *See* supra: Litolff's Bibliothek classischer Compositionen.

— Troisième concerto-symphonie national hollandois pour piano et orchestre ... Oeuv. 45. [P. F.] pp. 51. *Chez G. M. Meyer j^r: Brunswick,* [c. 1850.] fol. **h. 3865. mm. (6.)**

Concert symphonique pour piano et orchestre. Op. 102

— Concert symphonique pour piano et orchestre. Op. 102. *Brunswick,* [1856.] fol.
The P. F. part only. **h. 1458. d. (13.)**

— Scherzo from the fourth Concerto Symphonique ... Arranged for Piano Solo. *W. & G. Foyle: London,* [1944?] 4°. **g. 1125. uu. (15.)**

— Scherzo ... Arranged for Piano Solo by Albert Leroux. pp. 11. *Chappell & Co.: London, etc.,* 1946. 4°. **f. 133. ii. (40.)**

— Scherzo ... Transcribed for Piano by Henry Geehl. pp. 11. *Edwin Ashdown: London,* 1946. 4°. **g. 1125. ww. (23.)**

— Scherzo ... Arranged for piano solo by Philip Francis. pp. 11. *Classical Music Co.: London,* [1948.] 4°. **f. 770. kk. (5.)**

— Scherzo ... For piano. ⟨Transcription by Harry J. Stafford.⟩ pp. 5. *Campbell Connelly & Co.: London,* [1948.] 4°. **g. 352. gg. (6.)**

— Scherzo ... Transcribed for piano solo by Harry Dexter. pp. 12. *Keith Prowse & Co.: London,* [1948.] 4°. **f. 770. ff. (8.)**

— Scherzo ... Transcribed for piano by Henry Geehl ... Piano solo, simplified ... Piano duet, *etc.* 2 no. *Edwin Ashdown: London,* [1948.] 4°. **f. 770. ff. (9.)**

— Scherzo concerto ... Arranged for piano solo by Frederic Curzon. pp. 13. *Boosey & Hawkes: London,* [1948.] 4°. **g. 352. kk. (8.)**

— Scherzo from Concerto, No. 4, in D minor ... Arranged for piano solo by Walter Collins. pp. 11. *W. Paxton & Co.: London,* [1953.] 4°. **g. 1128. p. (10.)**

— Scherzo ... Arranged for piano solo by Henry Duke. pp. 6. *H. Freeman & Co.: Brighton,* [1961.] 4°. **g. 443. ii. (12.)**

— Scherzo. Arranged for piano solo by Thomas A. Johnson. pp. 12. *Hinrichsen Edition: London,* [1966.] 4°. **g. 1126. nn. (11.)**

— Scherzo concerto ... Arranged for B♭ clarinet and piano by Norman Richardson. [Score and part.] 2 pt. *Boosey & Hawkes: London,* [1948.] 4°. **h. 2189. t. (4.)**

LITOLFF (Henry Charles)

— [Scherzo.] Theme from the popular Scherzo ... Arranged for piano solo by Walter Collins. pp. 4. *W. Paxton & Co: London,* [1947.] 4°. **f. 770. kk. (7.)**

— [Scherzo.] Theme from the Scherzo ... Transcribed for piano solo by Harry Dexter. ⟨Simplified edition.⟩ pp. 5. *Keith Prowse & Co.: London,* [1948.] 4°. **f. 770. kk. (6.)**

— Dernière Aurore. Romance sans paroles pour Piano. *Paris,* [1873.] fol. **h. 680. a. (10.)**

— Élégie pour le Piano. Oeuv. 64. *Brunswick,* [1852.] fol. **h. 680. (7.)**

— Erinnerungen. *See* infra: Souvenance.

— Eroica. Erstes Concert für Violine u. Orchester ... Op. 42, *etc.* [Violin and P. F. Score and part.] 2 pt. *Henry Litolff's Verlag: Braunschweig,* [c. 1870.] fol. **h. 1729. i. (3.)**

— L'Escadron volant de la Reine. Opéra-comique en 3 actes. Paroles de M.M.Mrs A. d'Ennery & J. Brésil ... Partition piano & chant. pp. 317. *L. Bathlot & Vve Héraud: Paris,* [1888?] 8°. **F. 446. f.**

— L'Étoile du Soir, grande valse pour Piano. *Paris,* [1876.] fol. **h. 680. a. (13.)**

— Grande fantaisie pour le piano sur des motifs d'Otello, de Rossini ... Op. 6. pp. 17. *Chez les fils de B. Schott: Mayence, etc.,* [1846?] fol. **h. 680. c. (4.)**

— La Fiancée du Roi de Garbe, opéra comique en quatre actes. Paroles de MM. Dennery et Chabrillat ... Partition Piano et Chant réduite par C. Genet. *Paris,* [1875.] 8°. **F. 446. c.**

— Une fleur du Bal. Pensée musicale pour le piano. Oeuv. 77. *Brunswick,* [1853.] fol. **h. 680. (11.)**

— Frascati valse pour Piano. *Paris,* [1875.] fol. **h. 680. a. (11.)**

— Frascati valse, arrangée pour Piano à 4 mains par Renaud de Vilbac. *Paris,* [1875.] fol. **h. 680. a. (12.)**

— [Die Girondisten.] Les Girondins. Drame symphonique ... Op. 80. ⟨Partition d'orchestre.⟩ pp. 64. *Costallat & c^{ie}: Paris,* [c. 1910.] 8°.
Symphonies dramatiques. no. 2. **e. 669. n. (3.)**

— [Die Girondisten.] Les Girondins. 2ème Symphonie dramatique. [P. F.] Op. 80. *Paris,* [1877.] fol. **h. 680. a. (14.)**

— [Die Girondisten.] Ouverture. Op. 80. Partitur. *Braunschweig,* [1850?] 4°. **g. 706. (2.)**

— Ouvertur zu Die Girondisten. Trauerspiel von R. Griepenkerl. Op. 80. Für Pianoforte. *Braunschweig,* [1852.] fol. **h. 680. (14.)**

— La harpe d'Eole, morceau de salon pour le piano. Op. 72. *Brunswick,* [1853.] fol. **h. 680. (10.)**

— Hausmusik der Zeit. *See* supra: Litolff's Bibliothek classischer Compositionen. ⟨Collection Litolff.⟩ no. 2776–2780, 2782, 2808, 2807, 2818, 2850, 2867, 2849, 2868, 2875.

— Héloise et Abélard. Opéra comique en trois actes. Paroles de MM. Clairville et W. Busnach ... Partition Piano et Chant réduite par C. Genet. *Paris,* [1872.] 8°. **F. 446. b.**

— Impromptu pour Piano. *London,* [1860.] fol. **h. 1460. w. (18.)**

— Impromptu pour Piano. *Paris,* [1861.] fol. **h. 680. a. (3.)**

— Invitation to the Polka, for the Piano Forte. Op. 31. *London,* [1846.] fol. **h. 938. (27.)**

LITOLFF (Henry Charles)

— Julie. Chant d'amour. Etude de salon pour le Piano. Op. 78. *Brunswick*, [1853.] fol.   **h. 680. (12.)**

— Grande marche fantastique pour le piano ... Op. 3. pp. 12. *Chez A^d. M^r. Schlesinger: Berlin*, [c. 1840.] fol.   **h. 680. c. (2.)**

— [Maximilian Robespierre.] Ouverture. Op. 55. Partitur. *Braunschweig & New York*, [1870?] 4°.   **g. 706. (1.)**

— [Maximilian] Robespierre. Overture ... (Op. 55.) Arranged for Military Band by F. Winterbottom, *etc.* [Parts.] *Hawkes & Son: London*, 1914. fol.
No. 298 of "Hawkes & Son's Military Band Edition".   **h. 3211. a. (113.)**

— Ouverture zu Maximilian Robespierre. Trauerspiel von Griepenkerl. Op. 55. Für Pianoforte zu vier Händen. *Braunschweig*, [1852.] fol.   **h. 680. (1.)**

— La Mazourka. *See infra*: [Opuscules. Op. 25. No. 3.]

— [3 mazourkas. Op. 17. No. 1.] Anna-mazourka. Rêverie pour le piano, *etc.* pp. 8. *Chez A^d. M^r. Schlesinger: Berlin*, [1846?] fol.   **h. 680. c. (5.)**

— [3 mazourkas. Op. 17. No. 2.] Zofija-mazourka. Rêverie ... Op. 17. N°. 2. [P. F.] pp. 7. *A^d. M^r. Schlesinger: Berlin*, [1846?] fol.   **h. 680. c. (6.)**

— [3 mazourkas. Op. 17. No. 3.] Antolka-mazourka. Rêverie ... Op. 17. N°. 3. [P. F.] pp. 4. *A^d. M^r. Schlesinger: Berlin*, [1846?] fol.   **h. 680. c. (7.)**

— Mein Herz allein, Des Schäfers Sonntagslied. Zwei Lieder fur eine Singstimme mit Begleitung des Pianoforte [words by Uhland]. Op. 67. *Braunschweig*, [1852.] fol.   **H. 2156. (14.)**

— Mein Herz ist Krank, Gedicht von M. G. Saphir fur eine Singstimme. [Begins: "Das Kind ist krank".] Mit Begleitung des Pianoforte. Op. 76. *Braunschweig*, [1853.] fol.   **H. 2156. (15.)**

— Moments de tristesse. Deux nocturnes. N°. 1. Douleur. N°. 2. Consolation. Pour piano ... Oe. 30. 2 no. *Chez Ed. Bote & G. Bock: Berlin, Posen*, [1846?] fol.   **h. 680. c. (11.)**

— Mondschein. *See supra*: Clair de Lune.

— Nocturne pour le Piano. Oeuv. 62. *Brunswick*, [1852.] fol.   **h. 680. (5.)**

— Opuscules. Op. 25. 1. Tarantelle calabraise. 2. Vagabondes polka [*sic*]. 3. La mazourka. 4. Valse styrienne. 5. Polonaise brillante. 6. Bolero. Pour le piano. no. 2–6. *A^d. M^r. Schlesinger: Berlin*, [c. 1880, 1846–c. 1880.] fol.
A made-up set of various issues, Imperfect; wanting no. 1.   **h. 680. c. (9.)**

— [Opuscules. Op. 25. No. 1.] Tarentelle calabraise pour piano. pp. 9. *Ewer & Co.: London*, [c. 1850.] fol.   **h. 680. c. (8.)**

— [Opuscules. Op. 25. No. 3.] La Mazourka, pour le Piano. Op. 25. *London*, [1847.] fol.   **h. 938. (28.)**

— Où sont les Roses. Rêverie-valse chantée [begins: "Regardant naître le matin"]. Paroles de P. Maly & Delormel. *Paris*, [1875.] fol.   **H. 1777. h. (56.)**

— Perles harmoniques. Pensée musicale pour le piano. Oeuv. 95. *Brunswick*, [1853.] fol.   **h. 680. (19.)**

— Polka caractéristique pour Piano. Op. 108. *London*, [1860.] fol.   **h. 1460. w. (19.)**

— Polka caractéristique pour Piano. Op. 108. *Paris*, [1861.] fol.   **h. 680. a. (4.)**

— Polka caractéristique pour Piano. Op. 108. *Braunschweig*, [1861.] fol.   **h. 680. a. (7.)**

— Polonaise brillante. *See supra*: Opuscules. Op. 25 ... 5.

LITOLFF (Henry Charles)

— Le Retour. Pièce de Concert pour le Piano. Oeuv. 63. *Brunswick*, [1852.] fol.   **h. 680. (6.)**

— Rêverie à la valse. *See infra*: [Rêverie au bal. Op. 5.]

Rêverie au bal. Op. 5

— Rêverie au bal. Grande valse pour le piano ... Opera 5. pp. 9. *Chez les fils de B. Schott: Mayence, etc.*, [1840?] fol.   **h. 680. c. (3.)**

— Rêverie à la valse. Grand waltz, for the piano forte. pp. 7. *Charles Ollivier: London*, [1840.] fol.   **g. 352. jj. (17.)**

— [A reissue.] Rêverie à la valse, for the pianoforte. *Leader & Cock: London*, [1853.] fol.   **h. 975. e. (43.)**

— [A reissue.] Rêverie à la valse, *etc.* *Enoch & Sons: London*, [1873.] fol.   **h. 1483. (10.)**

— Rêverie à la valse. Grande valse pour piano ... Op. 3, *etc.* ⟨Arrangé à quatre mains par Ernest Cury.⟩ pp. 19. *Enoch père et fils: Paris; Enoch & Sons: London*, [1873.] fol.   **h. 1483. (10*.)**

— Rêveries. Op. 17. *See supra*: [3 mazourkas. Op. 17.]

— Robespierre. *See supra*: [Maximilian Robespierre.]

— Romance pour le Piano. Oeuv. 90. *Brunswick*, [1853.] fol.   **h. 680. (18.)**

— Rondo élégant pour piano ... Op: 2. pp. 9. *Chez Mme Lemoine et c^{ie}.: Paris*, [c. 1840.] fol.   **h. 680. c. (1.)**

— Ruth et Booz, scène biblique de H. Lefebvre. Partition Chant et Piano. *Paris*, [1869.] 8°.   **F. 446.**

— Scenen aus Goethe's Faust. Erste (Zweite) (Siebente) Scene. Partitur. (Op. 103.) 3 no. *H. Litolff: Braunschweig*, [1865?] 8°.   **F. 446. e.**

— Scherzo. *See supra*: [Concert symphonique pour piano et orchestre. Op. 102.]

— Sérénade pour le Piano. Op. 61. *Brunswick*, [1852.] fol.   **h. 680. (4.)**

— Sérénade pour piano et violon ou violoncelle. Op. 91. Avec violon. *Brunswick*, [1857.] fol.   **h. 1608. x. (44.)**

— Souvenance (Erinnerungen), impromptu pour Piano. *London*, [1860.] fol.   **h. 1460. w. (20.)**

— Souvenance (Erinnerungen). Impromptu pour Piano. *Paris*, [1861.] fol.   **h. 680. a. (5.)**

— Souvenir d'enfance. Pensée musicale pour le Piano. Oeuv. 59. *Brunswick*, [1851.] fol.   **h. 680. (3.)**

— Spinnlied für das Pianoforte. Op. 81. pp. 11. *Bei G. M. Meyer jr.: Braunschweig*, [1853.] fol.   **h. 680. (15.)**

— [A reissue.] Spinnlied für das Pianoforte ... Op. 81. *Henry Litolff's Verlag: Braunschweig*, [c. 1855.] fol.   **h. 1203. b. (4.)**

— Spinnlied. Op. 81. *See* BEAUTÉS. Beautés Allemands, *etc.* No. 2. [1858.] fol.   **h. 1448. (1.)**

— Spinnlied für das Pianoforte ... Op. 81. pp. 11. *Henry Litolff's Verlag: Braunschweig*, [1859.] fol.   **h. 3865. zz. (11.)**

— Spinnlied ... for the Pianoforte. Op. 81. Revised by O. Thümer. *Augener & Co.: London*, [1898.] 4°.   **g. 543. ff. (2.)**

— Spinnlied for the pianoforte. Op. 81. *E. Ashdown: London*, [1899.] fol.   **g. 605. p. (43.)**

— Spinnlied. ⟨Op. 81.⟩ Composed for the pianoforte. pp. 9. *Charles Sheard & Co: London*, [c. 1900.] fol.   **h. 3865. xx. (2.)**

LITOLFF (Henry Charles)

— Spinnlied. Op. 81. [1903.] *See* Holmes (G. A.) and Karn (F. G.) Contemporary Pianoforte Music, *etc.* No. 6. [1902, *etc.*] fol.   **h. 3545. a.**

— Litolff's Students' Edition—Akademische Ausgabe—of the Pianoforte Classics. Critically revised, annotated and edited by H. Germer, C. Kühner, W. Rehberg, C. Schultze, *etc.* 58 no. *Enoch & Sons: London,* [1907.] fol.   **h. 680. b.**

— Tarentelle calabraise. *See supra:* [Opuscules. Op. 25. No. 1.]

— Tarentelle infernale, grande étude de vélocité pour le piano. Oeuvre 79. *Magdebourg,* [1854.] fol.   **h. 680. (13.)**

— Les Templiers. Opéra en 5 actes. Poème de MM. J. Adenis, A. Silvestre, & L. Bonnemère. Partition piano & chant réduite par l'auteur. *Paris,* 1886. 8°.   **F. 446. d.**

— Terpsichore. Etude de Bravoure pour piano. Oeuv. 57. *Brunswick,* [1851.] fol.   **h. 680. (2.)**

— Trilby, impromptu pour Piano. *Paris,* [1873.] fol.
                                                          h. 680. a. (9.)

— Troisième grand trio pour piano, violon et violoncelle. Oeuvre 100. *Brunswick,* [1854.] fol.   **h. 2851. (8.)**

— 2 vagabondes polkas. *See supra:* Opuscules. Op. 25 ... 2.

— Grande valse brillante, pour le piano, *etc.* Oeuvre 89. *Magdebourg,* [1854.] fol.   **h. 680. (17.)**

— Valse de Bravoure pour le Piano. Oeuv. 66. *Brunswick,* [1852.] fol.   **h. 680. (9.)**

— Valse élégante pour Piano. Op. 107. *London,* [1860.] fol.
                                                          h. 1460. w. (21.)

— Valse élégante pour Piano. Op. 107. *Paris,* [1861.] fol.
                                                          h. 680. a. (6.)

— Valse élégante pour Piano. Op. 107. *Braunschweig,* [1861.] fol.   **h. 680. a. (8.)**

— Valse styrienne. *See supra:* Opuscules. Op. 25 ... 4.

— Grand Variations brilliant, for the piano forte, on the favorite air, Life's like an April Day, by Hérold ... Op. 10. pp. 16. *T. Welsh: London,* [c. 1835.] fol.   **g. 1259. g. (19.)**

— Das Welfenlied von G. von Meyern Musikalisch illustrirt, *etc.* Op. 99. Für Pianoforte, zu vier Händen. *Braunschweig,* [1857.] fol.   **h. 680. (19*.)**

— Zofija-mazurka. *See supra:* [3 mazurkas. Op. 17. No. 2.]

— *See* Fane (John) *Earl of Westmorland.* Prima sinfonia ... Ridotta per cembalo da H. Litolff. [1846?] *obl.* fol.
                                                          e. 80. (1.)

— *See* Mendelssohn-Bartholdy (J. L. F.) Symphonies arrangées pour piano à 2 mains par H. Litolff, *etc.* [1878.] 4°. [*Collection Litolff. no.* 907.]   **g. 375.**

LITOLFF (Louis)

— A Collection of quick and slow Waltzes, Allemands & Reels for the Pianoforte. *London,* [1810?] fol.   **g. 442. a. (9.)**

— Les Graces, a new set of French quadrilles ... for the Pianoforte. *London,* [1815.] fol.   **h. 1480. t. (27.)**

— New Dances, containing Cottillions, Waltzes, Reels and Jiggs, for the Pianoforte. *Printed by G. Walker: London,* [1810?] fol.   **g. 442. a. (10.)**

— Twelve new Waltzes and twelve Cotillons ... for the Pianoforte. *Printed by G. Walker: London,* [1810?] fol.
                                                          g. 272. u. (10.)

LITOLFF (Louis)

— A sett of fashionable Cotillions & Waltzes adapted to the Pianoforte or Harp. Op. 4. *London,* [1810?] fol.
                                                          g. 272. v. (11.)

— A set of fashionable Dances ... arranged for the Pianoforte. Op. 8. *Printed by G. Walker: London,* [1810?] fol.
                                                          g. 272. u. (9.)

— A Sett of fashionable new Dances. 〈Op. 3.〉 For the piano-forte. Containing waltzes, reels & jiggs, *etc.* pp. 19. *Printed by G. Walker: London,* [ᵂᴹ 1809.] fol.
                                                          h. 722. kk. (6.)

LITOLFF (Martin James)

— A Brilliant Set of Waltzes, for the piano forte, *etc.* pp. 6. *T. Welsh: London,* [c. 1835.] fol.   **h. 1226. e. (1.)**

LI-TSIN

— Li-Tsin. Choeur chinois. *See* Joncières (V.)

LITSKI (Casimir)

— A new Gavotte, with an introduction for the Piano Forte. *London,* [1810?] fol.   **h. 117. (37.)**

LITSTER (W.)

— Reading Practice. From the staff notation. pp. 16. *J. Curwen & Sons: London,* [c. 1935.] 8°.   **B. 418. xx. (6.)**

LITTA (Giulio)

— Il Viandante. Scena lirica. Parole di E. Praga. Canto e Pianoforte. *Milano,* [1875.] 8°.   **F. 811.**

LITTELL (Barbara)

— March for a Celebration. 〈Score [and military band parts].〉 49 pt. *Warner Bros. Publications: New York,* [1979.] 4°. *Part of "Supersound Series for young Bands". With several copies of various parts.*   **h. 3210. j. (994.)**

— March for a fat Cat. [Concert band.] 〈Score.〉 pp. 7. *Warner Bros. Publications: New York,* [1980.] 4°. *Part of "First Concert Series for beginning Band".*
                                                          f. 302. c. (3.)

— March for a free Spirit. [For wind band and percussion. Score and parts.] 51 pt. *Warner Bros. Publications: New York,* [1978.] 4°. *Part of "Supersound Series for young Bands". With several copies of various parts.*   **h. 3210. j. (925.)**

— Slightly lightly Latin. 〈Score [and military band parts].〉 50 pt. *Warner Bros. Publications: New York,* [1978.] 4°. *Part of "Supersound Series for young Bands". With several copies of various parts.*   **h. 3210. j. (924.)**

— Strawberry Rock. 〈Score [and military band parts].〉 49 pt. *Warner Bros. Publications: New York,* [1979.] 4°. *Part of "Supersound Series for young Bands". With several copies of various parts.*   **h. 3210. j. (995.)**

LITTELL (Joseph)

— The forest flower, valse. [P. F.] *London,* [1859.] fol.
                                                          h. 977. f. (38.)

LITTEN (William)

— William Litten's Fiddle Tunes 1800–1802. [Collected by W. Litten.] Transcribed by Gale Huntington. [With a facsimile.] pp. 63. *Hines Point Publishers: Vineyard Haven,* [1977.] 4°.   **f. 132. e. (8.)**